INDEX OF ECONOMIC ARTICLES
In Journals and Collective Volumes

Index of
Economic Articles

IN JOURNALS AND COLLECTIVE VOLUMES

Volume XXIX · 1987

Part One—Subject Index

Prepared under the auspices of

THE JOURNAL OF ECONOMIC LITERATURE

of the

AMERICAN ECONOMIC ASSOCIATION

JOHN PENCAVEL

Managing Editor

MOSES ABRAMOVITZ

Associate Editor

DRUCILLA EKWURZEL

Associate Editor

ASATOSHI MAESHIRO

Editorial Consultant

MARY KAY AKERMAN

Assistant Editor

NASHVILLE, TENNESSEE
AMERICAN ECONOMIC ASSOCIATION
1990

Student Classifiers: Ruben Berrios, Shailendra Gajanan, Nayyer Hussain, Chang-ky Lee, Simran Sahi, Robert Sinclair, and Walter Smith-Villavicencio.

Library of Congress Catalog Card Number: 61–8020
International Standard Book Number: 0–917290–18–6
International Standard Serial Number: 0536–647X
Printed in the United States of America

TABLE OF CONTENTS

Part One

Introduction.. vii

Introductory Discussion vii
List of Journals Indexed x
List of Collective Volumes Indexed xvi
Four-Digit Classification System xxxvi

Subject Index of Articles in Journals and Collective Volumes 1

000 General Economics; Theory; History; Systems 3
100 Economic Growth; Development; Planning; Fluctuations....................... 138
200 Quantitative Economic Methods and Data 211
300 Domestic Monetary and Fiscal Theory and Institutions 256
400 International Economics 364
500 Administration; Business Finance; Marketing; Accounting 472
600 Industrial Organization; Technological Change; Industry Studies 507
700 Agriculture; Natural Resources 613
800 Manpower; Labor; Population 691
900 Welfare Programs; Consumer Economics; Urban and Regional Economics 797

Topical Guide to Classification Schedule......................... liii

Part Two

Introduction.. vii

List of Journals Indexed vii
List of Collective Volumes Indexed xiii

Index of Authors of Articles in Journals and Collective Volumes.................. 879

INTRODUCTORY DISCUSSION

This volume of the *Index* lists, both by subject category and by author, articles in major economic journals and in collective volumes published during the year 1987. The articles listed include all articles published in English or with English summaries in the journals and books identified in the following sections. Part one includes the Subject Index of Articles in Journals and Collective Volumes, and Part Two consists of an alphabetical Author Index of all the articles indexed in Part One.

Relationship to JEL

This *Index* is prepared largely as an adjunct to the bibliographic activities of the *Journal of Economic Literature (JEL)*. Economies of joint production are pursued throughout the production process. Journals included are those indexed in the *JEL* quarterly; collective volumes are selected from the annotated 1987 books; the classification system is a more detailed version of the *JEL* system.

Journals Included

The 312 journals listed represent, in general, those journals that we believe will be most helpful to research workers and teachers of economics. These journals are listed below on page x.

Generally, articles, notes, communications, comments, replies, rejoinders, as well as papers and formal discussions in proceedings and review articles have been indexed. There are some exceptions; only articles in English or with English summaries are included—this practice results in a slightly reduced coverage compared with the *JEL* quarterly. Articles lacking author identification are omitted, as are articles without economic content. Identical articles appearing in two different journals in 1987 are listed from both sources. The journal issues included usually fall within a single volume. When a volume of a journal overlaps two calendar years, for example, Fall 1986 to Summer 1987, we include the issues from the two volumes relating to 1987 as best we can determine.

Collective Volumes

The collective volumes consist of the following:
1. *Festschriften*
2. Conference publications with individual papers
3. Collected essays, original, by one or more authors
4. Collected essays, reprinted, by one or more authors
5. Proceedings volumes
6. Books of readings

All original articles in English are indexed with the exception of unsigned articles or articles without economic content. Reprinted articles are included on the basis that a researcher would be interested in knowing about another source of the article. The original publication dates are shown in italics on the citations of reprinted articles. Excerpts are not included. The same article appearing for the first time in different collective volumes in the same year is cited from both publications.

In the article citation, reference to the book in which the article appears is by author or editor of the volume. If the same person or persons wrote or edited more than one book included in the 1987 *Index*, it is indicated by a I or II appearing in both the source given in the article citation and the bibliographic reference in the book listing. If the same person wrote one book and edited another in 1987, the specification of "ed" in the reference indicates which book is being cited.

The collective volumes are listed alphabetically by author or editor beginning on page xvi and include a full bibliographic reference. If there is more than one edition, the publisher cited is the one on the copy the *JEL* received, usually the American publisher.

Arrangement

The *Index* consists of two parts:
1. A Subject Index in which the articles are arranged by subject.
2. An Author Index.

Part One—Subject Index

In Part One, all articles are listed alphabetically by first author under each 4-digit subject category. Joint authors are listed up to three; beyond that, only the first author is listed, followed by *et al.*

There is one exception to the alphabetical author arrangement. In the 0322 category, a subdivision of **History of Thought** entitled **Individuals,** the arrangement is first alphabetical by the individual discussed in the article and then alphabetical by the article's author.

Articles with empirical content or discussing a particular geographic area carry a geographic descriptor (see discussion below).

Classification System

The classification system is an expansion of the 3-digit classification system used in the *Journal of Economic Literature* to a 4-digit system with slightly over 300 subcategories. The classification system, itself, is shown beginning on page xxxvi (Part One). In most cases the classification heading is self-explanatory; however, in some cases notes have been added to clarify the coverage or indicate alternative subject classifications. The basic approach in classification is from the point of view of the researcher rather than the teacher; course content does not necessarily coincide with subfields of our classification system. In all cases where there are two or more 4-digit classifications under a 3-digit category, there is a zero classification; in most instances this is labeled "General." The zero or general category has been used both as an inclusive and a residual category. For example, an article discussing *all* aspects of international trade theory appears in the general category. There are also some articles that do not fall in any of the individual subcategories, and these, too, are classified in the general or zero category.

The criterion used in the classifying process is whether persons interested in this topic would wish to have the article drawn to their attention. With the advent of the online ECONOMIC LITERATURE INDEX on DIALOG, the interpretation of "interest" has broadened slightly to include cross-classifications that indicate the subject matter, particularly in such categories as industry studies or occupational designations. Over half of the articles are classified in more than one subcategory. From time to time, we find it desirable to add subject classifications as particular topics become prominent or to change subject headings to make them more descriptive of the contents of the category.

Geographic Descriptors

Geographic descriptors appear in brackets at the end of any article entry in the Subject Index where the article cites data from or refers to a particular country or area. Research workers interested in these countries thus are made aware of the empirical content in the article. The descriptors used are countries or broader areas, such as Southeast Asia (S. E. Asia); articles referring to cities or regions within a country are classified under the country. In general, the country name is written out in full with some adaptations and abbreviations, *e.g.*, U.S. is used for United States, U.K. for United Kingdom, and U.S.S.R. for Union of Soviet Socialist Republics. Abbreviations include: W. for West, E. for East, S. for South, N. for North. A shortened name such as W. Germany is used rather than the correct, but longer, Federal Republic of Germany. When broader regions are used as descriptors, the article may or may not refer to the full unit. For example, OECD has been used at times when most, but not all, of the OECD member countries are referred to.

Index volumes prior to 1979 sometimes did not include geographic descriptors on articles listed under subject categories 1210, 1211, 1220, 1221, 1230, 1240, and 1241, involving general or comparative economic country studies. In the 1979 *Index* and later volumes, these articles carry geographic descriptors in order to facilitate online identification in the Economic Literature Index on DIALOG. Because the descriptor fields are limited to five, very general descriptors, such as LDCs (developing countries) and MDCs (developed countries), are often used on articles.

The fact that an article carries a geographic descriptor does not necessarily preclude its being primarily theoretical in nature. Any theoretical article drawing on empirical data to demonstrate its findings will carry a geographic descriptor.

Topical Guide to the Classification System

At the end of Part One there is an alphabetical listing of standard economic terms and concepts. References are to the appropriate 4-digit classification numbers, not to page numbers.

Part Two—Author Index

Part two consists of an alphabetical Author Index in which citations appear under each author (up to three) of an article. Wherever possible the full first name and middle initial or middle name(s) are used. Wherever it could be definitely ascertained, articles by the same person are grouped together with only one listing of the name. Authors' first names and initials are listed differently in various journals and books; for example, an individual may be identified as John L. Smith, J. L. Smith, or John Smith. Thus, despite our best efforts, we were left in doubt in several instances. Joint authors are listed up to three; beyond that, only the first author is listed, followed by *et al.* Under each author, articles are listed alphabetically. Names carrying prefixes are alphabetized according to the first *capitalized* letter, with occasional exceptions following national practices. Thus, van Arkadie would appear under A and D'Alabro under D.

LIST OF JOURNALS INDEXED 1987

Accounting Review, Vol. 62.

Acta Oeconomica, Vol. 38.

L'Actualité Economique, Vol. 63.

African Economic History, Issue no. 16.

Agricultural Economics Research, Vol. 39, Issue no. 1.
See **Journal of Agricultural Economics Research.**

American Economic Review, Vol. 77.

American Economist, Vol. 31.

American Historical Review, Vol. 92.

American Journal of Agricultural Economics, Vol. 69.
Title changed from **Journal of Farm Economics** in 1968.

American Journal of Economics and Sociology, Vol. 46.

American Political Science Review, Vol. 81, Issue no. 1.

American Real Estate and Urban Economics Association Journal, Vol. 15.

Annales d'Economie et de Statistique, Issues nos. 5–8, 1987.
Title changed from **Annales de l'INSEE** in 1986.

Annals of Public and Co-operative Economy, Vol. 58.

Annals of Regional Science, Vol. 21.

Antitrust Bulletin, Vol. 32.

Applied Economics, Vol. 19.

Asian-Pacific Economic Literature, Vol. 1.

Atlantic Economic Journal, Vol. 15.

Aussenwirtschaft, Vol. 42.

Australian Bulletin of Labour, Vol. 13, Issue nos. 2–4; Vol. 14, Issue no. 1.

Australian Economic History Review, Vol. 27.
Title changed from **Business Archives and History** in 1967; entitled **Bulletin of the Business Archives Council of Australia** prior to 1962.

Australian Economic Papers, Vol. 26.

Australian Economic Review, Issue nos. 77–80.

Australian Journal of Agricultural Economics, Vol. 31.

Australian Tax Forum, Vol. 4.

Banca Nazionale del Lavoro—Quarterly Review, Issue nos. 160–163.

Bangladesh Development Studies, Vol. 15.

British Journal of Industrial Relations, Vol. 25.

British Review of Economic Issues, Vol. 9

Brookings Papers on Economic Activity, Issue nos. 1–3, 1987.

Bulletin for International Fiscal Documentation, Vol. 41.

Bulletin of Economic Research, Vol. 39.
Title changed from **Yorkshire Bulletin of Economic and Social Research** in 1971.

Bulletin of Indonesian Economic Studies, Vol. 23.

Business Economics, Vol. 22.

Business History Review, Vol. 61.
Title changed from **Bulletin of the Business Historical Society** in 1954.

Cahiers Économiques de Bruxelles, Issue nos. 113–116.

Cambridge Journal of Economics, Vol. 11.

Canadian Journal of Agricultural Economics, Vol. 34, Annual Meeting Proceedings; Vol. 35.

Canadian Journal of Development Studies, Vol. 8.

Canadian Journal of Economics, Vol. 20.

Canadian Public Policy, Vol. 13.

Carnegie–Rochester Conference Series on Public Policy, Vols. 26–27.
Vols. 1–17 were listed as supplements to the **Journal of Monetary Economics.**

Cato Journal, Vol. 6, Issue no. 3; Vol. 7, Issue nos. 1–2.

Cepal Review, Issue nos. 31–33.

Challenge, Vol. 29, Issue no. 6; Vol. 30.

Chinese Economic Studies, Vol. 20, Issue nos. 2–4; Vol. 21, Issue no. 1.

Colección Estudios CIEPLAN, Issue nos, 21–22.

Comparative Economic Studies, Vol. 29.
Title changed from ACES Bulletin in 1985.

Contemporary Policy Issues, Vol. 5.

Cuadernos de Economia, Vol. 24.

Czechoslovak Economic Digest, Issue nos. 1–8, 1987.

Czechoslovak Economic Papers, Issue no. 24.

Demography, Vol. 24.

Desarrollo Económico, Vol. 26, Issue no. 104; Vol. 27, Issue nos. 105–107.

Developing Economies, Vol. 25.

Eastern Africa Economic Review, Vol. 3.

Eastern Economic Journal, Vol. 13.

Eastern European Economics, Vol. 25, Issue nos. 3–4; Vol. 26, Issue nos. 1–2.

Econometric Reviews, Vol. 6.

Econometrica, Vol. 55.

Economia (Pontifical Catholic University of Peru), Vol. 10.

Economia (Portuguese Catholic University), Vol. 11.

Economia Internazionale, Vol. 40.

Economia e Lavoro, Vol. 21.

Economía et Política, Vol. 4.

Economia delle Scelte Pubbliche/Journal of Public Finance and Public Choice, Vol. 5.

Economic Analysis and Workers' Management, Vol. 21.

Economic Computation and Economic Cybernetics Studies and Research, Vol. 22.
Title changed from Studii şi Cercetări Economicè in 1974. Changed from issue numbers to volume numbers in 1978.

Economic Development and Cultural Change, Vol. 35, Issue nos. 2–4; Vol. 36, Issue no. 1.

Economic Geography, Vol. 63.

Economic History Review, Vol. 40.

Economic Inquiry, Vol. 25.
Title changed from Western Economic Journal in 1974.

Economic Journal, Vol. 97; Supplement.

Economic Modelling, Vol. 4.

Economic Notes, Issue nos. 1–3, 1987.

Economic Record, Vol. 63.

Economic Review (Keizai Kenkyu), Vol. 38.

Economic and Social Review, Vol. 18, Issue nos. 2–4; Vol. 19, Issue no. 1.

Economic Studies Quarterly, Vol. 38.

Economica, Vol. 54.
Title changed from Economica, N.S. in 1974.

Económica, Vol. 33.

Economics of Education Review, Vol. 6.

Economics and Philosophy, Vol. 3.

Economics of Planning, Vol. 21.

Économie Appliquée, Vol. 40.

Économies et Sociétés, Vol. 21.

De Economist, Vol. 135.

Ekonomiska Samfundets Tidskrift, Vol. 40.

Empirica, Vol. 14.

Empirical Economics, Vol. 12, Issue nos. 1, 3–4.

Energy Economics, Vol. 9.

Energy Journal, Vol. 8.

Environment and Planning A, Vol. 19.

Estudios Económico, Vol. 2.

European Economic Review, Vol. 31.

European Review of Agricultural Economics, Vol. 14.

Explorations in Economic History, Vol. 24.
Title changed from Explorations in Entrepreneurial History in 1969–70.

Federal Reserve Bank of Dallas Economic Review, January, March, May, July, September, November, 1987.

Federal Reserve Bank of Minneapolis Quarterly Review, Vol. 11.

Federal Reserve Bank of New York Quarterly Review, Vol. 12.

Federal Reserve Bank of Richmond Economic Review, Vol. 73.

Federal Reserve Bank of San Francisco Economic Review, Issue nos. 1–4, 1987.

Federal Reserve Bank of St. Louis Review, Vol. 69.

Federal Reserve Bulletin, Vol. 73.

Finance, Vol. 8.

Finance and Development, Vol. 24.

Financial Review, Vol. 22.

Fiscal Studies, Vol. 8.

Food Research Institute Studies, Vol. 20, Issue nos. 2–3.

Foreign Affairs, Vol. 65, Issue nos. 2–5; Vol. 66, Issue nos. 1–2.

Giornale degli Economisti e Annali di Economia, Vol. 46.

Greek Economic Review, Vol. 9.

Growth and Change, Vol. 18.

History of Political Economy, Vol. 19.

Hitotsubashi Journal of Economics, Vol. 28.

Hong Kong Economic Papers, Issue no. 18.

Housing Finance Review, Vol. 6, Issue no. 1.

Ifo-Studien, Vol. 33.

Indian Economic Journal, Vol. 34, Issue nos. 3–4; Vol. 35, Issue nos. 1–2.

Indian Economic Review, Vol. 22.

Indian Economic and Social History Review, Vol. 24.

Indian Journal of Quantitative Economics, Vol. 3.

Industrial and Labor Relations Review, Vol. 40, Issue nos. 2–4; Vol. 41, Issue no. 1.

Industrial Relations, Vol. 26.

Industry and Development, Issue nos. 20–22.

Inquiry, Vol. 24.

International Economic Journal, Vol. 1.

International Economic Review, Vol. 28.

International Journal of Forecasting, Vol. 3, Issue no. 1.

International Journal of Game Theory, Vol. 16, Issue no. 4.

International Journal of Industrial Organization, Vol. 5.

International Journal of Social Economics, Vol. 14.

International Journal of Transport Economics, Vol. 14.

International Labour Review, Vol. 126.

International Monetary Fund Staff Papers, Vol. 34.

International Organization, Vol. 41.

International Regional Science Review, Vol. 11, Issue no. 1.

Investigaciones Economicas, Vol. 11.

Irish Journal of Agricultural Economics and Rural Sociology, Vol. 12.

Jahrbücher für Nationalökonomie und Statistik, Vol. 203.

Journal of Accounting and Economics, Vol. 9.

Journal of Accounting Research, Vol. 25; Supplement.

Journal of Agricultural Economics, Vol. 38.

Journal of Agricultural Economics Research, Vol. 39, Issue nos. 3–4.
   Title changed from Agricultural Economics Research in 1987.

Journal of the American Statistical Association, Vol. 82.

Journal of Applied Econometrics, Vol. 2.

Journal of Banking and Finance, Vol. 11.

Journal of Behavioral Economics, Vol. 16.

Journal of Business, Vol. 60.

Journal of Business and Economic Statistics, Vol. 5.

Journal of Common Market Studies, Vol. 25, Issue nos. 3–4; Vol. 26, Issue nos. 1–2.

Journal of Comparative Economics, Vol. 11.

Journal of Conflict Resolution, Vol. 31.

Journal of Consumer Affairs, Vol. 21.

Journal of Consumer Research, Vol. 13, Issue no. 4; Vol. 14, Issue nos. 1–3.

Journal of Cultural Economics, Vol. 11.

Journal of Developing Areas, Vol. 21, Issue nos. 2–4; Vol. 22, Issue no. 1.

Journal of Development Economics, Vols. 25–27.

Journal of Development Studies, Vol. 23, Issue nos. 2–4; Vol. 24, Issue no. 1.

Journal of Econometrics, Vols. 34–36.

Journal of Economic Behavior and Organization, Vol. 8.

Journal of Economic Development, Vol. 12.

Journal of Economic Dynamics and Control, Vol. 11.

Journal of Economic Education, Vol. 18.

Journal of Economic History, Vol. 47.

Journal of Economic Issues, Vol. 21.

Journal of Economic Literature, Vol. 25.

Journal of Economic Perspectives, Vol. 1

Journal of Economic and Social Measurement, Vol. 15.
   Title changed from **Review of Public Data Use** in 1985.

Journal of Economic Studies, Vol. 14.

Journal of Economic Surveys, Vol. 1

Journal of Economic Theory, Vols. 41–43.

Journal of Economics (Zeitschrift für Nationalökonomie), Vol. 47.
   Title changed from **Zeitschrift für Nationalokonomie** in 1986.

Journal of Economics and Business, Vol. 39.
   Title changed from **Economics and Business Bulletin** in 1972–73.

Journal of Energy and Development, Vol. 12, Issue no. 2; Vol. 13, Issue no. 1.

Journal of Environmental Economics and Management, Vol. 14.

Journal of European Economic History, Vol. 16.

Journal of Finance, Vol. 42.

Journal of Financial Economics, Vol. 18–19.

Journal of Financial and Quantitative Analysis, Vol. 22.

Journal of Financial Research, Vol. 10.

Journal of Financial Services Research, Vol. 1, no. 1.

Journal of Futures Markets, Vol. 7.

Journal of Health Economics, Vol. 6.

Journal of Human Resources, Vol. 22.

Journal of Industrial Economics, Vol. 35, Issue nos. 3–4; Vol. 36, Issue nos. 1–2.

Journal of International Economics, Vols. 22–23.

Journal of Institutional and Theoretical Economics, Vol. 143.
   Title changed from **Zeitschrift für die gesamte Staatswissenchaft** in 1986.

Journal of International Money and Finance, Vol. 6.

Journal of the Japanese and International Economies, Vol. 1.

Journal of Labor Economics, Vol. 5.

Journal of Labor Research, Vol. 8.

Journal of Law and Economics, Vol. 30.

Journal of Law, Economics, and Organization, Vol. 3.

Journal of Macroeconomics, Vol. 9.

Journal of Mathematical Economics, Vol. 16.

Journal of Monetary Economics, Vols. 19–20.

Journal of Money, Credit and Banking, Vol. 19.

Journal of Policy Analysis and Management, Vol. 6, Issue nos. 2–4; Vol. 7, Issue no. 1.

Journal of Policy Modeling, Vol. 9.

Journal of Political Economy, Vol. 95.

Journal of Portfolio Management, Vol. 13, Issue nos. 2–4; Vol. 14, Issue no. 1.

Journal of Post Keynesian Economics, Vol. 9, Issue nos. 2–4; Vol. 10, Issue no. 1.

Journal of Public Economics, Vols. 32–34.

Journal of Quantitative Economics, Vol. 3.

Journal of Regional Science, Vol. 27.

Journal of Risk and Insurance, Vol. 54.

Journal of the Royal Statistical Society, Series A, Vol. 150.

Journal for Studies in Economics and Econometrics, Vol. 11.

Journal of Transport Economics and Policy, Vol. 21.

Journal of Urban Economics, Vols. 21–22.

Journal of World Trade Law, Vol. 21.

Keio Economic Studies, Vol. 24.

Kobe University Economic Review, Issue no. 33.

Konjunkturpolitik, Vol. 33.

Kredit und Kapital, Vol. 20, Issue nos. 1–2, 4.

Kyklos, Vol. 40.

Labor History, Vol. 28.

Land Economics, Vol. 63.

Law and Contemporary Problems, Vol. 50.

Liiketaloudellinen Aikakauskirja, Vol. 36.

Lloyds Bank Review, Issue nos. 163–166.

Logistics and Transportation Review, Vol. 23.

Managerial and Decision Economics, Vol. 8.

Manchester School of Economics and Social Studies, Vol. 55.
Title changed from **The Manchester School** in 1939; entitled **The Manchester School of Economics, Commerce and Administration** prior to 1932.

Margin, Vol. 19, Issue nos. 2–4; Vol. 20, Issue no. 1.

Marine Resource Economics, Vol. 4.

Marketing Science, Vol. 6.

Matekon, Vol. 23, Issue nos. 3–4; Vol. 24, Issue nos. 1–2.
Title changed from **Mathematical Studies in Economics and Statistics in the USSR and Eastern Europe** in 1969.

Mathematical Social Sciences, Vols. 13–14.

METU—Studies in Development, Vol. 14.

Michigan Law Review, Vol. 85, Issue nos. 4–8; Vol. 86, Issue nos. 1–3.

Monthly Labor Review, Vol. 110.

National Institute Economic Review, Issue nos. 119–122.

National Tax Journal, Vol. 40.

National Westminster Bank Quarterly Review, February, May, August, November, 1987.

Nationaløkonomisk Tidsskrift, Vol. 125.

Natural Resources Journal, Vol. 27.

New England Economic Review, January/February, March/April, May/June, July/August, September/October, November/December, 1987.

New Zealand Economic Papers, Vol. 21.

OECD Economic Studies, Issue nos. 8–9, 1987.

Oxford Bulletin of Economics and Statistics, Vol. 49.
Title changed from **Bulletin Oxford University Institute of Economics and Statistics** in 1973; entitled **Bulletin of the Institute of Economics and Statistics** prior to 1972.

Oxford Economic Papers, Vol. 39.

Oxford Review of Economic Policy, Vol. 3.

Pakistan Development Review, Vol. 26.

Pakistan Economic and Social Review, Vol. 25.

Pakistan Journal of Applied Economics, Vol. 6.

Pesquisa e Planejamento Econômico, Vol. 17.

Policy Sciences, Vol. 20.

Politica Economica, Vol. 3, Issue no. 1.

Population and Development Review, Vol. 13.

Population Studies, Vol. 41.

Problems of Economics, Vol. 29, Issue nos. 9–12; Vol. 30, Issue nos. 1–8.

Public Budgeting and Finance, Vol. 7.

Public Choice, Vol. 52, Issue nos. 1–2; Vols. 53–55.

Public Finance, Vol. 42.

Public Finance Quarterly, Vol. 15.

Quarterly Journal of Business and Economics, Vol. 26.
Title changed from **Nebraska Journal of Economics and Business** in 1983.

Quarterly Journal of Economics, Vol. 102.

Quarterly Review of Economics and Business, Vol. 27.

Rand Journal of Economics, Vol. 18.
Title changed from **Bell Journal of Economics** in 1984.

Recherches Economiques de Louvain, Vol. 53.

Regional Science Perspectives, Vol. 17.

Regional Science and Urban Economics, Vol. 17.

Regional Studies, Vol. 21.

Review of Black Political Economy, Vol. 15, Issue nos. 3–4; Vol. 16, Issue nos. 1–2.

Review of Economic Conditions in Italy, Issue nos. 1–3, 1987.

Review of Economic Studies, Vol. 54.

Review of Economics and Statistics, Vol. 69.
Title changed from The Review of Economic Statistics in 1948.

Review of Income and Wealth, Vol. 33.

Review of Marketing and Agricultural Economics, Vol. 55.

Review of Radical Political Economics, Vol. 19.

Review of Regional Studies, Vol. 17.

Review of Social Economy, Vol. 45.

Revue d'Economie Politique, Vol. 97.

Revue Économique, Vol. 38.

Ricerche Economiche, Vol. 41.

Rivista Internazionale di Scienze Economiche e Commerciali, Vol. 34.

Rivista di Storia Economica, Vol. 4.

Scandinavian Economic History Review, Vol. 35.

Scandinavian Journal of Economics, Vol. 89.
Title changed from Swedish Journal of Economics in 1976; entitled Ekonomisk Tidskrift prior to 1965.

Schweizerische Zeitschrift für Volkswirtschaft und Statistik, Vol. 123.

Science and Society, Vol. 51.

Scottish Journal of Political Economy, Vol. 34.

Singapore Economic Review, Vol. 32.
Title changed from Malayan Economic Review in 1983.

Social Choice and Welfare, Vol. 4.

Social and Economic Studies, Vol. 36.

Social Science Quarterly, Vol. 68.

Social Security Bulletin, Vol. 50.

South African Journal of Economics, Vol. 55.

Southern Economic Journal, Vol. 53, Issue nos. 3–4; Vol. 54, Issue nos. 1–2.

Southern Journal of Agricultural Economics, Vol. 19.

Soviet and Eastern European Foreign Trade, Vol. 23.

Soviet Economy, Vol. 3.

Statistical Journal, Vol. 4, Issue nos. 3–4; Vol. 5, Issue no. 1.

Studi Economici, Vol. 42.

Survey of Current Business, Vol. 67.

Tijdschrift voor Economie en Management, Vol. 32.
Title changed from Tijdschrift voor Economie in 1975.

Urban Studies, Vol. 24.

Water Resources Research, Vol. 23.

Weltwirtschaftliches Archiv, Vol. 123.

Western Journal of Agricultural Economics, Vol. 12.

World Bank Economic Review, Vol. 1, Issue nos. 2–4.

World Bank Research Observer, Vol. 2.

World Development, Vol. 15; Supplement.

World Economy, Vol. 10.

Yale Journal on Regulation, Vol. 4, Issue no. 2.

Yale Law Journal, Vol. 96, Issue nos. 3–8; Vol. 97, Issue nos. 1–2.

Zeitschrift für Betriebswirtschaft, Vol. 57, Issue nos. 1–11.

Zeitschrift für Wirtschafts- und Socialwissenschaften, Vol. 107.

LIST OF COLLECTIVE VOLUMES INDEXED 1987

ADAM, JAN, ed. *Employment policies in the Soviet Union and Eastern Europe*. Second revised edition. New York: St. Martin's Press, [1982] 1987.

[ADELMAN, M. A.] *Energy: Markets and regulation. Essays in honor of M. A. Adelman*. Edited by RICHARD L. GORDON, HENRY D. JOCOBY, AND MARTIN B. ZIMMERMAN. Cambridge, Mass. and London: MIT Press, 1987.

AGRAWAL, GOVIND R., ET AL. *Low income countries: Problems and prospects*. New Delhi: Radiant; distributed by Advent Books, New York, 1987. (I)

AGRAWAL, GOVIND R., ET AL. *South–South economic cooperation: Problems and prospects*. New Delhi: Radiant; distributed by Advent Books, New York, 1987. (II)

AKEHURST, GARY AND GADREY, JEAN, eds. *The economics of services*. London: Cass, distributed in the U.S. by Biblio Distribution Center, Totowa, N.J., 1987.

AKINRINADE, OLUSOLA AND BARLING, J. KURT, eds. *Economic development in Arica: International efforts, issues and prospects*. London: Pinter; distributed by Columbia University Press, New York, 1987.

ALBELDA, RANDY; GUNN, CHRISTOPHER AND WALLER, WILLIAM, eds. *Alternatives to economic orthodoxy: A reader in political economy*. Armonk, N.Y. and London: Sharpe, 1987.

ALESSANDRINI, SERGIO AND DALLAGO, BRUNO, eds. *The unofficial economy: Consequences and perspectives in different economic systems*. Aldershot, U.K. and Brookfield, Vt.: Gower, 1987.

ALI, SHANTI SADIQ AND GUPTA, ANIRUDHA, eds. *Africa: Dimensions of the economic crisis. An analysis of the problems and constraints of development*. New Delhi: Sterling; disbributed by Apt Books, New York, 1987.

ALIBER, ROBERT Z., ed. *The reconstruction of international monetary arrangements*. New York: St. Martin's Press, 1987.

ALLEN, STEVEN G., ET AL. *Human resources and the performance of the firm*. Edited by MORRIS M. KLEINER ET AL. Industrial Relations Research Association series. Madison, Wis.: Industrial Relations Research Association, 1987.

ALONSO, WILLIAM, ed. *Population in an interacting world*. Cambridge, Mass. and London: Harvard University Press, 1987.

ALONSO, WILLIAM AND STARR, PAUL, eds. *The politics of numbers*. The Population of the United States in the 1980s: A Census Monograph Series. New York: Russell Sage Foundation for the National Committee for Research on the 1980 Census; distributed by Basic Books, 1987.

AMIN, SAMIR; CHITALA, DERRICK AND MANDAZA, IBBO, eds. *SADCC: Prospects for disengagement and development in Southern Africa*. United Nations University/Third World Forum Studies in African Political Economy series. London and Atlantic Highlands, N.J.: Zed Books; Tokyo: United Nations University in cooperation with the Third World Forum, 1987.

AMJAD, RASHID, ed. *Human resource planning: The Asian experience*. New Delhi: International Labour Organisation Asian Employment Programme, 1987.

ANDERSEN, RONALD M., ET AL. *Ambulatory care and insurance coverage in an era of constraint*. University of Chicago, Center for Health Administration Studies, Continuing Research Series, no. 35. Chicago: Pluribus Press, 1987.

ANDERSON, DAVID AND GROVE, RICHARD, eds. *Conservation in Africa: People, policies and practice*. Cambridge; New York and Melbourne: Cambridge University Press, 1987.

ANDERSSON, JAN OTTO, ed. *Nordic studies on intra-industry trade*. Åbo, Finland: Åbo Academy Press, 1987.

ARNDT, SVEN W. AND RICHARDSON, J. DAVID, eds. *Real–financial linkages among open economies*. Cambridge, Mass. and London: MIT Press, 1987.

ARNOTT, RICHARD J. AND MINTZ, JACK M., eds. *Rent control: The international experience. Proceedings of a conference held at Queen's University, 31 August–4 September 1987*. The Fifth John Deutsch Roundtable on Economic Policy. Kingston, Ont.: Queen's University, John Deutsch Institute for the Study of Economic Policy, 1987.

ARONSON, J. RICHARDS AND SCHWARTZ, ELI, eds. *Management policies in local government finance.* Third edition. Municipal Management Series. Washington, D.C.: International City Management Association for the ICMA Training Institute, [1975 . . . 1981] 1987.

ATACK, JEREMY, ed. *Business and economic history.* Second Series. Volume 16. Champaign: University of Illinois at Urbana–Champaign, College of Commerce and Business Administration, Bureau of Economic and Business Research, 1987.

AUSTIN, JAMES E. AND ESTEVA, GUSTAVO, eds. *Food policy in Mexico: The search for self-sufficiency.* Ithaca and London: Cornell University Press, 1987.

BAILEY, ELIZABETH E., ed. *Public regulation: New perspectives on institutions and policies.* MIT Press Series on the Regulation of Economic Activity, no. 14. Cambridge, Mass. and London: MIT Press, 1987.

BAMBERG, GÜNTER AND SPREMANN, K., eds. *Agency theory, information, and incentives.* New York; Berlin; London and Tokyo: Springer, 1987.

BAR-EL, RAPHAEL, ed. *Rural industrialization in Israel.* With the assistance of ARIELA NESHER. Westview Special Studies in Industrial Policy and Development series. Boulder, Colo. and London: Westview Press in cooperation with the Settlement Study Centre, 1987.

BARFIELD, CLAUDE E. AND MAKIN, JOHN H., eds. *Trade policy and U.S. competitiveness.* AEI Studies, no. 461. Washington, D.C.: American Enterprise Institute for Public Policy Research; distributed by University Press of America, Lanham, Md., 1987.

BARKER, P.; BODMAN, P. AND REMENYL, J., eds. *Small holders and export tree crops in Papua New Guinea: Data sources and collection methods. Papers presented at a workshop held at Goroka, Papua New Guinea, March 3–5, 1986.* IASER Special Publication series, no. 12. Port Moresby, Papua New Guinea: PNG Institute of Applied Social and Economic Research in collaboration with the PNG Department of Primary Industry and the Australian Centre for International Agricultural Research, 1987.

BARKER, TERRY AND PETERSON, WILLIAM, eds. *The Cambridge multisectoral dynamic model of the British economy.* Cambridge Studies in Applied Econometrics series, no. 5. Cambridge; New York and Sydney: Cambridge University Press, 1987.

BARNETT, WILLIAM A. AND SINGLETON, KENNETH J., eds. *New approaches to monetary economics: Proceedings of the Second International Symposium in Economic Theory and Econometrics.* International Symposia in Economic Theory and Econometrics series. Cambridge; New York and Melbourne: Cambridge University Press, 1987.

BARR, TREVOR, ed. *Challenges and change: Australia's information society.* Melbourne; Oxford; Auckland and New York: Oxford University Press in association with the Commission for the Future, 1987.

BATES, ROBERT H. *Essays on the political economy of rural Africa.* Paperback reprint. California Series on Social Choice and Political Economy, no. 8. Berkeley and London: University of California Press, [1983] 1987.

BATTEN, D.; CASTI, J. AND JOHANSSON, B., eds. *Economic evolution and structural adjustment: Proceedings of invited sessions on economic evolution and structural change held at the 5th International Conference on Mathematical Modelling at the University of California, Berkeley, California, U.S.A., July 29–31, 1985.* Lecture Notes in Economics and Mathematical Systems series, no. 293. Berlin; New York; London and Tokyo: Springer, 1987.

BAUMGARTNER, THOMAS AND MIDTTUN, ATLE, eds. *The politics of energy forecasting: A comparative study of energy forecasting in Western Europe and North America.* Oxford; New York; Toronto and Melbourne: Oxford University Press, Clarendon Press, 1987.

BECKER, DAVID G., ET AL. *Postimperialism: International capitalism and development in the late twentieth century.* Boulder and London: Lynne Rienner, 1987.

BECKER, WILLIAM E. AND WALSTAD, WILLIAM B., eds. *Econometric modeling in economic education research.* International Series in Economic Modeling. Norwell, Mass.; Dordrecht and Lancaster: Kluwer Academic, Kluwer-Nijhoff, 1987.

BEENSTOCK, MICHAEL, ET AL. *Work, welfare and taxation: A study of labour supply incentives in the UK.* Boston; London and Sydney: Allen and Unwin, 1987.

BEGG, DAVID K. H., ET AL. *Monetarism and macro-economics: Contributions on the current policy debate in the UK.* Edited and introduced by PATRICK MINFORD. With commentaries by ALAN BUDD ET AL. IEA Readings series, no. 26. London: Institute of Economic Affairs; distributed in N. America by Transatlantic Arts, Albuquerque, N.Mex., 1987.

BERKOWITZ, EDWARD D., ed. *Social Security after fifty: Successes and failures.* Studies in Social Welfare Policies and Programs series, no. 5. New York and London: Greenwood Press, 1987.

BEWLEY, TRUMAN F., ed. *Advances in economic theory: Fifth World Congress.* Econometric Society Monographs series, no. 12. Cambridge; New York and Melbourne: Cambridge University Press, 1987.

BHAGWATI, JAGDISH N., ed. *International trade: Selected readings.* Second edition. Cambridge, Mass. and London: MIT Press, [1981] 1987.

BINGHAM, RICHARD D.; GREEN, ROY E. AND WHITE, SAMMIS B., eds. *The homeless in contemporary society.* Sage Focus Editions series, no. 87. Newbury Park, Calif.; London and New Delhi: Sage in cooperation with the University of Wisconsin, Urban Research Center, 1987.

BLAUG, MARK. *The economics of education and the education of an economist.* New York: New York University Press; distributed by Columbia University Press, 1987.

BLOOM, PAUL N., ed. *Advances in marketing and public policy.* Volume 1. A Research Annual. Greenwich, Conn. and London: JAI Press, 1987.

BODIE, ZVI; SHOVEN, JOHN B. AND WISE, DAVID A., eds. *Issues in pension economics.* National Bureau of Economic Research Project Report series. Chicago and London: University of Chicago Press, 1987.

BOLLARD, ALAN AND BUCKLE, ROBERT, eds. *Economic liberalisation in New Zealand.* Wellington, New Zealand and Sydney: Allen and Unwin in association with Port Nicholson Press; distributed by Century Hutchinson New Zealand, Auckland, 1987.

BORNER, SILVIO AND TAYLOR, ALWYN, eds. *Structural change, economic interdependence and world development: Proceedings of the Seventh World Congress of the International Economic Association, Madrid, Spain.* Volume 2. *Natural and financial resources for development.* New York: St. Martin's Press, 1987.

BOSKIN, MICHAEL J.; FLEMING, JOHN S. AND GORINI, STEFANO, eds. *Private saving and public debt.* Oxford and New York: Blackwell, 1987.

BOSWORTH, BARRY P. AND RIVLIN, ALICE M., eds. *The Swedish economy.* Washington, D.C.: Brookings Institution, 1987.

BRAAT, LEON C. AND VAN LIEROP, WAL F. J., eds. *Economic–ecological modeling.* Studies in Regional Science and Urban Economics series, no. 16. Amsterdam; New York; Oxford and Tokyo: North-Holland, 1987.

BRADFORD, COLIN I., JR. AND BRANSON, WILLIAM H., eds. *Trade and structural change in Pacific Asia.* National Bureau of Economic Research Conference Report series. Chicago and London: University of Chicago Press, 1987.

BREMER, STUART A., ed. *The GLOBUS model: Computer simulation of worldwide political and economic developments.* With a foreword by KARL W. DEUTSCH. Boulder, Colo.: Westview Press; Frankfurt am Main: Campus, 1987.

BROWN, CLAIR AND PECHMAN, JOSEPH A., eds. *Gender in the workplace.* Washington, D.C.: Brookings Institution, 1987.

BROWN, LESTER R., ET AL. *State of the world 1987: A Worldwatch Institute report on progress toward a sustainable society.* Edited by LINDA STARKE. State of the World series. New York and London: Norton, 1987.

BROWNE, LYNN E. AND ROSENGREN, ERIC S., eds. *The merger boom: Proceedings of a conference held at Melvin Village, New Hampshire, October 1987.* Conference Series, no. 31. Boston: Federal Reserve Bank of Boston, 1987.

BRYANT, RALPH C. AND PORTES, RICHARD, eds. *Global macroeconomics: Policy conflict and cooperation.* New York: St. Martin's Press in association with the International Economic Association and the Centre for Economic Policy Research, 1987.

BUCHANAN, JAMES M. *Economia y politica: Escritos seleccionados.* Edicion a cargo de JOSE CASAS
PARDO Y SEGUNDO BRU PARRA. Valencia: University of Valencia, 1988. (I)

BUCHANAN, JAMES M. *Economics: Between predictive science and moral philosophy.* Compiled
and with a preface by ROBERT D. TOLLISON AND VIKTOR J. VANBERG. Texas A&M University
Economics Series, no. 7. College Station: Texas A&M University Press, 1987. (II)

BURTLESS, GARY, ed. *Work, health, and income among the elderly.* Studies in Social Economics
series. Washington, D.C.: Brookings Institution, 1987.

BUTLER, J. R. G. AND DOESSEL, D. P., eds. *Economics and health: 1986 proceedings of the
Eighth Australian Conference of Health Economics.* Australian Studies in Health Service Admin-
istration series, no. 59. Kensington, Australia: University of New South Wales, School of Health
Administration, 1987.

CAGAN, PHILLIP, ed. *Deficits, taxes, and economic adjustments.* SOMENSATTO, EDUARDO, associate
editor. AEI Contemporary Economic Problems series, no. 455. Washington, D.C.: American
Enterprise Institute for Public Policy Research, 1987.

CARRARO, CARLO AND SARTORE, DOMENICO, eds. *Developments of control theory for economic
analysis.* Advanced Studies in Theoretical and Applied Econometrics series, vol. 7. Hingham,
Mass.; Dordrecht; and Lancaster: Kluwer Academic, 1987.

CAVUSGIL, S. TAMER, ed. *Advances in international marketing.* Volume 2. A Research Annual.
Greenwich, Conn. and London: JAI Press, 1987.

DE CECCO, MARCELLO, ed. *Changing money: Financial innovation in developed countries.* New
York and Oxford: Blackwell in cooperation with the European University Institute, Florence,
1987.

DE CECCO, MARCELLO AND FITOUSSI, JEAN-PAUL, eds. *Monetary theory and economic institutions:
Proceedings of a conference held by the International Economic Association at Fiesole, Florence,
Italy.* New York: St. Martin's Press, 1987.

CHAN, JAMES L., ed. *Research in governmental and nonprofit accounting.* Volume 3, Part A. A
Research Annual. Greenwich, Conn. and London: JAI Press, 1987.

CHAN, JAMES L., ed. *Research in governmental and nonprofit accounting.* Volume 3, Part B. A
Research Annual. Greenwich, Conn. and London: JAI Press, 1987.

CHILD, JOHN AND BATE, PAUL, eds. *Organization of innovation: East–West perspectives.* De Gruyter
Studies in Organization series, vol. 11. Berlin and New York: de Gruyter, 1987.

CHISHOLM, ANTHONY AND DUMSDAY, ROBERT, eds. *Land degradation: Problems and policies.* CRES
Monograph series, no. 18. Cambridge; New York and Melbourne: Cambridge University Press
in association with the Centre for Resource and Environmental Studies, Australian National
University, 1987.

CHRYSTAL, K. A. AND SEDGWICK, ROBERT, eds. *Exchange rates and the open economy.* New York:
St. Martin's Press; Brighton, U.K.: Harvester Press, Wheatsheaf Books, 1987.

CIOCCA, PIERLUIGI, ed. *Money and the economy: Central bankers' views.* Translation. New York:
St. Martin's Press, [1983] 1987.

CNOSSEN, SIJBREN, ed. *Tax coordination in the European community.* Series on International Taxation, no. 7. London; Frankfurt; Boston and Deventer: Kluwer Law and Taxation,
1987.

[COCHRANE, DONALD] *Specification analysis in the linear model (In honour of Donald Cochrane).*
Edited by MAXWELL L. KING AND DAVID E. A. GILES. International Library of Economics
series. London and New York: Routledge and Kegan Paul, 1987.

COHEN, YOSEF, ed. *Applications of control theory in ecology: Proceedings of the Symposium on
Optimal Control Theory held at the State University of New York, Syracuse, New York, August
10–16, 1986.* Lecture Notes in Biomathematics series, no. 73. New York; Berlin; London and
Tokyo: Springer, 1987.

CONNOLLY, MICHAEL AND GONZÁLEZ-VEGA, CLAUDIO, eds. *Economic reform and stabilization in
Latin America.* New York and London: Greenwood Press, Praeger, 1987.

COOK, ROBERT F., ed. *Worker dislocation: Case studies of causes and cures.* Kalamazoo, Mich.:
W. E. Upjohn Institute for Employment Research, 1987.

COOPER, RICHARD N. *The international monetary system: Essays in world economics.* Cambridge, Mass. and London: MIT Press, 1987.

[CORDEN, W. M.] *Protection and competition in international trade: Essays in honor of W. M. Corden.* Edited by HENRYK KIERZKOWSKI. Oxford and New York: Blackwell, 1987.

CORDRAY, DAVID S. AND LIPSEY, MARK W., eds. *Evaluation studies: Review annual.* Volume 11. *1986.* Newbury Park, Calif.; London and New Delhi: Sage, 1987.

CORNFIELD, DANIEL B., ed. *Workers, managers, and technological change: Emerging patterns of labor relations.* With a foreword by RAY MARSHALL. Plenum Studies in Work and Industry series. New York and London: Plenum Press, 1987.

CORNIA, GIOVANNI ANDREA; JOLLY, RICHARD AND STEWART, FRANCES, eds. *Adjustment with a human face.* Volume 1. *Protecting the vulnerable and promoting growth.* Oxford; New York; Toronto and Melbourne: Oxford University Press, Clarendon Press, 1987.

CREW, MICHAEL A., ed. *Regulating utilities in an era of deregulation.* New York: St. Martin's Press, 1987.

DASGUPTA, PARTHA AND STONEMAN, PAUL, eds. *Economic policy and technological performance.* Centre for Economic Policy Research series. Cambridge; New York and Sydney: Cambridge University Press, 1987.

DAVIS, KINGSLEY; BERNSTAM, MIKHAIL S. AND RICARDO-CAMPBELL, RITA, eds. *Below-replacement fertility in industrial societies: Causes, consequences, policies.* Population and Development Review: A Supplement to Volume 12, 1986. Cambridge; New York and Melbourne: Cambridge University Press, 1987.

DAY, GRAHAM AND REES, GARETH, eds. *Contemporary Wales: An annual review of economic and social research.* Volume 1. Technical editor, MARTIN READ. Cardiff, U.K.: University of Wales Press; distributed by Humanities Press, Atlantic Highlands, N.J., 1987.

DAY, JOHN. *The medieval market economy.* Oxford and New York: Blackwell, 1987.

DEDIJER, STEVAN AND JÉQUIER, NICHOLAS, eds. *Intelligence for economic development: An inquiry into the role of the knowledge industry.* Oxford; Hamburg and New York: Berg; distributed in the U.S. and Canada by St. Martin's Press, New York, 1987.

DEERE, CARMEN DIANA AND LEÓN, MAGDALENA, eds. *Rural women and state policy: Feminist perspectives on Latin American agricultural development.* Series in Political Economy and Economic Development in Latin America. Boulder, Colo. and London: Westview Press, 1987.

DELL, SIDNEY, ed. *The international monetary system and its reform: Papers prepared for the Group of Twenty-four by a United Nations project directed by Sidney Dell, 1979–1986.* Part 1. Contributions to Economic Analysis series, no. 162. Amsterdam; New York; Oxford and Tokyo: North-Holland in cooperation with the United Nations; distributed in the U.S. and Canada by Elsevier Science, New York, 1987.

DELL, SIDNEY, ed. *The international monetary system and its reform: Papers prepared for the Group of Twenty-four by a United Nations project directed by Sidney Dell, 1979–1986.* Part 2. Contributions to Economic Analysis series, no. 162. Amsterdam; New York; Oxford and Tokyo: North-Holland in cooperation with the United Nations; distributed in the U.S. and Canada by Elsevier Science, New York, 1987.

DELL, SIDNEY, ed. *The international monetary system and its reform: Papers prepared for the Group of Twenty-four by a United Nations project directed by Sidney Dell, 1979–1986.* Part 3. Contributions to Economic Analysis series, no. 162. Amsterdam; New York; Oxford and Tokyo: North-Holland in cooperation with the United Nations; distributed in the U.S. and Canada by Elsevier Science, New York, 1987.

DE MENIL, GEORGES AND PORTES, RICHARD, eds. *Economic policy: The conservative revolution. A special report.* Cambridge and New York: Cambridge University Press; Paris: Editions de la Maison des Sciences de l'Homme for the Centre for Economic Policy Research and École des Hautes Études en Sciences Sociales, 1987.

DESAI, PADMA. *The Soviet economy: Problems and prospects.* Oxford: Blackwell, 1987.

DEWEY, CLIVE, ed. *The state and the market: Studies in the economic and social history of the third world.* Riverdale, Md.: Riverdale, 1987.

[DÍAZ-ALEJANDRO, CARLOS F.] *International trade, investment, macro policies and history: Essays in memory of Carlos F. Díaz-Alejandro.* Edited by P. BARDHAN, A. FISHLOW, AND J. BEHRMAN. New York; Amsterdam; Oxford and Tokyo: North-Holland; distributed in the U.S. and Canada by Elsevier Science, New York, 1987.

DICKE, DETLEV CHR., ed. *Foreign investment in the present and a new international economic order.* In cooperation with the INTERNATIONAL LAW ASSOCIATION'S COMMITTEE ON LEGAL ASPECTS OF A NEW INTERNATIONAL ECONOMIC ORDER. Progress and Undercurrents in Public International Law series, vol. 2. Fribourg, Switzerland: University Press; Boulder, Colo.: Westview Press, 1987.

DIETZ, JAMES L. AND STREET, JAMES H., eds. *Latin America's economic development: Institutionalist and structuralist perspectives.* Boulder, Colo. and London: Rienner, 1987.

DORN, JAMES A. AND SCHWARTZ, ANNA J., eds. *The search for stable money: Essays on monetary reform.* Chicago and London: University of Chicago Press; Washington, D.C.: Cato Institute, 1987.

DORNBUSCH, RUDIGER AND LAYARD, RICHARD, eds. *The performance of the British economy.* Oxford; New York; Toronto and Melbourne: Oxford University Press, Clarendon Press, 1987.

DRÈZE, JACQUES H. *Essays on economic decisions under uncertainty.* Cambridge; New York and Melbourne: Cambridge University Press, 1987.

DRUMMOND, IAN M. *Progress without planning: The economic history of Ontario from Confederation to the Second World War.* With contributions by PETER GEORGE ET AL. Ontario Historical Studies series. Toronto; Buffalo and London: University of Toronto Press, 1987.

DUCHÊNE, FRANÇOIS AND SHEPHERD, GEOFFREY, eds. *Managing industrial change in Europe.* London and New York: Pinter; distributed by Columbia University Press, New York, 1987.

DUNNING, JOHN H. AND USUI, MIKOTO, eds. *Structural change, economic interdependence and world development: Proceedings of the Seventh World Congress of the International Economic Association, Madrid, Spain.* Volume 4. *Economic interdependence.* Structural Change, Economic Interdependence and World Development series. New York: St. Martin's Press, 1987.

DUPRIEZ, LEÓN H., ed. *Economic progress: Proceedings of a conference held by the International Economic Association at Santa Margherita Ligure, Italy.* Second edition. With the assistance of DOUGLAS HAGUE. New York: St. Martin's Press, [1955] 1987.

DUTTA, M., ed. *Asia-Pacific economies: Promises and challenges.* Research in International Business and Finance series, vol. 6, part A. Greenwich, Conn. and London: JAI Press, 1987. (I)

DUTTA, M., ed. *Asia-Pacific economies: Promises and challenges.* Research in International Business and Finance series, vol. 6, part B. Greenwich, Conn. and London: JAI Press, 1987. (II)

[EBERL, WALTHER, SR.] *Contributions to stochastics: In honour of the 75th birthday of Walther Eberl, Sr.* Edited by WOLFGANG SENDLER. Heidelberg: Physica; New York: Springer, 1987.

ECONOMIC COUNCIL OF CANADA. *Aging with limited health resources: Proceedings of a colloquium on health care, May 1986.* Ottawa: Supply and Services Canada, Canadian Government Publishing Centre, 1987.

EDGREN, GUS, ed. *The growing sector.* New Delhi: International Labour Organization, Asian Employment Programme, 1987.

ELIASSON, GUNNAR. *Technological competition and trade in the experimentally organized economy.* Research Report series, no. 32. Stockholm: Industrial Institute for Economic and Social Research; distributed by Almqvist & Wiksell International, 1987.

ELIASSON, GUNNAR, ed. *The economics of institutions and markets: IUI Yearbook 1986–1987.* Stockholm: Industrial Institute for Economic and Social Research, Research Program, 1987.

EL-NAGGAR, SAID, ed. *Adjustment policies and development strategies in the Arab world: Papers presented at a seminar held in Abu Dhabi, United Arab Emirates, February 16–18, 1987.* Washington, D.C.: International Monetary Fund, 1987.

EMANUEL, HAN; DE GIER, ERIC H. AND KONIJN, PETER A. B. KALKER, eds. *Disability benifits: Factors determining application and awards.* Contemporary Studies in Economic and Financial Analysis series, vol. 59. Greenwich, Conn. and London: JAI Press, 1987.

ENGLAND, RICHARD W., ed. *Economic processes and political conflicts: Contributions to modern political economy.* New York and London: Praeger, 1987.

ESPENSHADE, THOMAS AND STOLNITZ, GEORGE J., eds. *Technological prospects and population trends.* AAAS Selected Symposia Series, no. 103. Boulder, Colo.: Westview Press for the American Association for the Advancement of Science, Washington, D.C., 1987.

EVANS, RICHARD J. AND GEARY, DICK, eds. *The German unemployed: Experiences and consequences of mass unemployment from the Weimar Republic to the Third Reich.* New York: St. Martin's Press, 1987.

FABOZZI, FRANK J., ed. *Advances in futures and options research.* Volume 2. A Research Annual. Greenwich, Conn. and London: JAI Press, 1987.

FARUQUI, AHMAD AND BROEHL, JOHN, eds. *The changing structure of American industry and energy use patterns: Issues, scenarios, and forecasting models.* EPRI Report series, no. EM-5075-SR. Columbus: Battelle Press; Palo Alto, Calif: Electric Power Research Institute; distributed by Westview Press, Boulder, Colo., 1987.

FEIWEL, GEORGE R., ed. *Arrow and the ascent of modern economic theory.* New York: New York University Press, 1987. (I)

FEIWEL, GEORGE R., ed. *Arrow and the foundations of the theory of economic policy.* New York: New York University Press, 1987. (II)

FELDMAN, ELLIOT J. AND GOLDBERG, MICHAEL A., eds. *Land rites and wrongs: The management, regulation and use of land in Canada and the United States.* Cambridge, Mass.: Lincoln Institute of Land Policy, 1987.

FELDSTEIN, MARTIN, ed. *The effects of taxation on capital accumulation.* A National Bureau of Economic Research Project Report. Chicago and London: University of Chicago Press, 1987. (I)

FELDSTEIN, MARTIN, ed. *Taxes and capital formation.* A National Bureau of Economic Research Project Report. Chicago and London: University of Chicago Press, 1987. (II)

FIELD, ALEXANDER J., ed. *The future of economic history.* Recent Economic Thought Series. Norwell, Mass.; Dordrecht and Lancaster: Kluwer Academic, Kluwer-Nijhoff, 1987.

FINK, RICHARD H. AND HIGH, JACK C., eds. *A nation in debt: Economists debate the federal budget deficit.* Frederick, Md.: University Publications of America, 1987.

FINN, RICHARD B., ed. *U.S.–Japan relations: A surprising partnership.* Harvard University Center for International Affairs, Program on U.S.–Japan Relations, Annual Review 1986. New Brunswick, N.J. and Oxford: Transaction Books, 1987.

FISCHER, MANFRED M. AND NIJKAMP, PETER, eds. *Regional labour markets: Analytical contributions and cross-national comparisons.* Contributions to Economic Analysis series, no. 168. Amsterdam and Oxford: North-Holland; distributed in the U.S. and Canada by Elsevier Science, New York, 1987.

FISCHER, STANLEY, ed. *NBER macroeconomics annual: 1987.* Cambridge, Mass. and London: MIT Press, 1987.

FOMBY, THOMAS B. AND RHODES, GEORGE F., JR., eds. *Advances in econometrics.* Volume 6. *Computation and simulation.* A Research Annual. Greenwich, Conn. and London: JAI Press, 1987.

FOX, KARL A. AND MILES, DON G., eds. *Systems economics: Concepts, models, and multidisciplinary perspectives.* Ames: Iowa State University Press, 1987.

FREDERICK, WILLIAM C., ed. *Empirical studies of business ethics and values.* Research in Corporate Social Performance and Policy series, vol. 9. Greenwich, Conn. and London: JAI Press, 1987.

FREEMAN, CHRISTOPHER AND SOETE, LUC, eds. *Technical change and full employment.* Oxford and New York: Blackwell, 1987.

GABEL, H. LANDIS, ed. *Product standardization and competitive strategy.* Advanced Series in Management, vol. 11. Amsterdam; Oxford and Tokyo: North-Holland; distributed in the U.S. and Canada by Elsevier Science, New York, 1987.

GANNON, THOMAS M., ed. *The Catholic challenge to the American economy: Reflections on the U.S. bishops' pastoral letter on Catholic social teaching and the U.S. economy.* New York: Macmillan; London: Collier Macmillan, 1987.

GARDENER, EDWARD P. M., ed. *Interest rate risk and banks.* Research Monographs in Banking and Finance series, no. 4. Bangor: University College of North Wales, Institute of European Finance, 1987.

GEMMELL, NORMAN, ed. *Surveys in development economics.* Oxford and New York: Blackwell, 1987.

GEMPER, BODO B., ed. *Structural dynamics of industrial policy.* New Brunswick, N.J. and Oxford: Transaction Books, 1987.

GEY, PETER; KOSTA, JIŘÍ AND QUAISSER, WOLFGANG, eds. *Crisis and reform in socialist economies.* Westview Special Studies in International Economics series. Boulder, Colo. and London: Westview Press, 1987.

GIARINI, ORIO, ed. *The emerging service economy.* Oxford; New York; Sydney and Toronto: Pergamon Press, 1987.

GIDADHUBLI, R. G., ed. *Socio-economic transformation of Soviet Central Asia.* New Delhi: Patriot; distributed by Advent Books, New York, 1987.

GIERSCH, HERBERT, ed. *Free trade in the world economy: Towards an opening of markets: Symposium 1986.* Tubingen, West Germany: Mohr (Siebeck), 1987.

GITTINGER, J. PRICE; LESLIE, JOANNE AND HOISINGTON, CAROLINE, eds. *Food policy: Integrating supply, distribution, and consumption.* Economic Development Institute Series in Economic Development. Baltimore and London: Johns Hopkins University Press for the World Bank, 1987.

GLYNN, SEAN AND BOOTH, ALAN, eds. *The road to full employment.* London; Winchester, Mass. and North Sydney: Allen and Unwin, 1987.

GOLDSTEIN, HARVEY A., ed. *The state and local industrial policy question.* Chicago: American Planning Association, Planners Press, 1987.

GOLOMBEK, ROLF; HOEL, MICHAEL AND VISLIE, JON, eds. *Natural gas markets and contracts.* Contributions to Economic Analysis series, no. 161. Amsterdam; New York; Oxford and Tokyo: Elsevier Science, North-Holland; distributed in N. America by Elsevier Science, New York, 1987.

GOODFRIEND, MARVIN. *Monetary policy in practice.* Richmond: Federal Reserve Bank of Richmond, 1987.

GOODHART, CHARLES; CURRIE, DAVID AND LLEWELLYN, DAVID T., eds. *The operation and regulation of financial markets.* Studies in Monetary Economics series. London: Macmillan Press in association with the Money Study Group; distributed by Sheridan House, Dobbs Ferry, N.Y., 1987.

GOODIN, ROBERT E. AND LE GRAND, JULIAN *Not only the poor: The middle classes and the welfare state.* With JOHN DRYZEK ET AL. London; Boston; Sydney and Wellington: Allen and Unwin, 1987.

GORDON, I., ed. *Unemployment, the regions and labour markets: Reactions to recession.* London Papers in Regional Science series, no. 17. London: Pion, distributed by Methuen, New York, 1987.

GRANDMONT, JEAN-MICHEL, ed. *Nonlinear economic dynamics.* Economic Theory, Econometrics, and Mathematical Economics series. Boston; London; Sydney and Toronto: Harcourt Brace Jovanovich, Academic Press, 1987.

GREEN, LEONARD AND KAGEL, JOHN H., eds. *Advances in behavioral economics.* Volume 1. Norwood, N.J.: Ablex, 1987.

GREILSAMMER, ILAN AND WEILER, JOSEPH H. H., eds. *Europe and Israel: Troubled neighbours.* European University Institute Series C, Political and Social Sciences, no. 9. Berlin and New York: de Gruyter, 1987.

GRIFFIN, KEITH. *World hunger and the world economy: And other essays in development economics.* New York: Holmes and Meier, 1987.

GUILE, BRUCE R. AND BROOKS, HARVEY, eds. *Technology and global industry: Companies and nations in the world economy.* Series on Technology and Social Priorities. Washington, D.C.: National Academy Press, 1987.

GULATI, I. S., ed. *Centre–state budgetary transfers.* Oxford; New York; Toronto and Bombay: Oxford University Press for Sameeksha Trust, 1987.

GUNDERSON, MORLEY; MELTZ, NOAH M. AND OSTRY, SYLVIA, eds. *Unemployment: International perspectives.* Toronto; Buffalo and London: University of Toronto Press for the Centre for Industrial Relations, 1987.

HAND, D. J. AND EVERITT, B. S., eds. *The statistical consultant in action.* Cambridge; New York and Melbourne: Cambridge University Press, 1987.

HANKE, STEVE H., ed. *Privatization and development.* San Francisco: ICS Press for the International Center for Economic Growth, 1987.

[HARBERGER, ARNOLD] *Modern developments in public finance: Essays in honor of Arnold Harberger.* Edited by MICHAEL J. BOSKIN. New York and Oxford: Blackwell, 1987.

HARTMANN, HEIDI I., ed. *Computer chips and paper clips: Technology and women's employment.* Volume 2. *Case studies and policy perspectives.* Washington, D.C.: National Academy Press, 1987.

HAUSNER, VICTOR A., ET AL. *Urban economic change: Five city studies.* Inner Cities Research Programme Series, no. 2. Oxford; New York; Toronto and Sydney: Oxford University Press, Clarendon Press, 1987.

HAVNEVIK, KJELL J., ed. *The IMF and the World Bank in Africa: Conditionality, impact and alternatives.* Seminar Proceedings series, no. 18. Uppsala: Scandinavian Institute of African Studies; distributed by Almqvist and Wiksell International, Stockholm, 1987.

HEIJMANS, RISTO AND NEUDECKER, HEINZ, eds. *The practices of econometrics: Studies on demand, forecasting, money and income.* International Studies in Economics and Econometrics series, vol. 15. Dordrecht; Boston and Lancaster: Kluwer Academic, 1987.

HEY, JOHN D. AND LAMBERT, PETER J., eds. *Surveys in the economics of uncertainty.* New York and Oxford: Blackwell, 1987.

HIBBS, DOUGLAS A., JR. *The political economy of industrial democracies.* Cambridge, Mass. and London: Harvard University Press, 1987.

HICKMAN, BERT G.; HUNTINGTON, HILLARD G. AND SWEENEY, JAMES L., eds. *Macroeconomic impacts of energy shocks.* Contributions to Economic Analysis series, no. 163. Amsterdam; Oxford and Tokyo: North-Holland; distributed in the U.S. and Canada by Elsevier Science, New York, 1987.

HIERONYMI, OTTO, ed. *Technology and international relations.* With contributions by MICHEL BARJON ET AL. New York: St. Martin's Press, 1987.

HILLS, PETER AND BOWIE, PADDY. *China and Malaysia: Social and economic effects of petroleum development.* Geneva: International Labour Office, 1987.

HIRSHLEIFER, JACK. *Economic behaviour in adversity.* Chicago: University of Chicago Press, 1987.

HODGMAN, DONALD R. AND WOOD, GEOFFREY E., eds. *Monetary and exchange rate policy.* New York: St. Martin's Press, 1987.

HOLMES, FRANK [SIR], ed. *Economic adjustment: Policies and problems.* Washington, D.C.: International Monetary Fund, 1987.

HOLZMAN, FRANKLYN D. *The economics of Soviet Bloc trade and finance.* Boulder, Colo.: Westview Press, 1987.

[HURWICZ, LEONID] *Information, incentives, and economic mechanisms: Essays in honor of Leonid Hurwicz.* Edited by THEODORE GROVES, ROY RADNER, AND STANLEY REITER. Minneapolis: University of Minnesota Press, 1987.

INTERNATIONAL FISCAL ASSOCIATION, ed. *The fiscal residence of companies.* Studies on International Fiscal Law, vol. 72a. Deventer, the Netherlands; Hingham, Mass.; London and Frankfurt: Kluwer Law and Taxation for the International Fiscal Association, 1987. (I)

INTERNATIONAL FISCAL ASSOCIATION, ed. *Tax problems of the liquidation of corporations.* Studies on International Fiscal Law, vol. 72b. Deventer, the Netherlands; Hingham, Mass.; London and Frankfurt: Kluwer Law and Taxation for the International Fiscal Association, 1987. (II)

INTERNATIONAL LABOUR OFFICE. *World recession and global interdependence: Effects on employment, poverty and policy formation in developing countries.* Geneva: Author, 1987.

INTERNATIONAL MONETARY FUND RESEARCH DEPARTMENT. *Staff studies for the world economic outlook, August 1987.* World Economic and Financial Surveys series. Washington, D.C.: International Monetary Fund, 1987.

ISLAM, RIZWANUL, ed. *Rural industrialisation and employment in Asia*. New Delhi: International Labour Organisation, Asian Employment Programme, 1987.

ISLAMOGLU-INAN, HURI, ed. *The Ottoman Empire and the world-economy*. Studies in Modern Capitalism series. Cambridge; New York and Sydney: Cambridge University Press; Paris: Éditions de la Maison des Sciences de l'Homme, 1987.

JAFFE, AUSTIN J., ed. *The economics of urban property rights*. Research in Law and Economics series, vol. 10. Greenwich, Conn. and London: JAI Press, 1987.

JAHN, J. AND KRABS, W., eds. *Recent advances and historical development of vector optimization: Proceedings of an international conference on vector optimization held at the Technical University of Darnstadt, FRG, August 4–7, 1986*. Lecture Notes in Economics and Mathematical Systems series, no. 294. Berlin; New York; London and Tokyo: Springer, 1987.

JEFFRIES, IAN AND MELZER, MANFRED, eds. *The East German economy*. Advisory editor, ELEONORE BREUNING. Translations by ELEONORE BREUNING AND IAN JEFFRIES. London; New York and Sydney: Croom Helm in association with Methuen, 1987.

JOHNSON, D. GALE, ed. *Agricultural reform efforts in the United States and Japan*. New York and London: New York University Press; distributed by Columbia University Press, New York, 1987.

JOHNSON, D. GALE AND LEE, RONALD D., eds. *Population growth and economic development: Issues and evidence*. Social Demography series. Madison: University of Wisconsin Press, 1987.

JONES, DEREK C. AND SVEJNAR, JAN, eds. *Advances in the economic analysis of participatory and labor-managed firms*. Volume 2. A Research Annual. Greenwich, Conn. and London: JAI Press, 1987.

JONES, SALLY M., ed. *Advances in taxation*. Volume 1. A Research Annual. Greenwich, Conn. and London: JAI Press, 1987.

JOSHI, P. C. *Institutional aspects of agricultural development: India from Asian perspective*. Foreword by M. L. DANTWALA. Perspectives on Asian and African Development series, no. 5. Riverdale, Md.: Riverdale, 1987.

JOYCE, PATRICK, ed. *The historical meanings of work*. Cambridge; New York and Melbourne: Cambridge University Press, 1987.

JUNANKAR, P. N., ed. *From school to unemployment? The labour market for young people*. London: Macmillan Press, 1987.

VAN DE KAR, HANS M. AND WOLFE, BARBARA L., eds. *The relevance of public finance for policy-making: Proceedings of the 41st Congress of the International Institute of Public Finance, Madrid, Spain, 1985*. Detroit: Wayne State University Press, 1987.

KATZ, JORGE M., ed. *Technology generation in Latin American manufacturing industries*. New York: St. Martin's Press, 1987.

KAUSHIK, S. K., ed. *International banking and world economic growth: The outlook for the late 1980s*. Westport, Conn. and London: Greenwood Press, Praeger, 1987.

KENT, CALVIN A., ed. *Entrepreneurship and the privatizing of government*. New York and London: Greenwood Press, Quorum Books, 1987.

KETTUNEN, LAURI, ed. *Supply management by government in agriculture: Proceedings of the 12th Symposium of the European Association of Agricultural Economists (EAAE) May 26th–29th, 1986, Espoo, Finland*. Kiel: Wissenschaftsverlag Vauk, 1987.

KHAN, MOHSIN S. AND MIRAKHOR, ABBAS, eds. *Theoretical studies in Islamic banking and finance*. Houston: Institute for Research and Islamic Studies, 1987.

KILBY, PETER, ed. *Quantity and quiddity: Essays in U.S. economic history*. Middletown, Conn.: Wesleyan University Press; distributed by Harper and Row, Scranton, Pa., 1987.

KILMER, RICHARD L. AND ARMBRUSTER, WALTER J., eds. *Economic efficiency in agricultural and food marketing*. Ames: Iowa State University Press for the Farm Foundation and the Institute of Food and Agricultural Sciences of the University of Florida, 1987.

KINDLEBERGER, CHARLES P. *Marshall plan days*. London; Winchester, Mass.; North Sydney and Wellington: Allen and Unwin, 1987.

KINGSTON, WILLIAM, ed. *Direct protection of innovation*. Norwell, Mass.; Lancaster and Dordrecht: Kluwer Academic for the Commission of the European Communities, 1987.

[KITAMURA, HIROSHI] *Protection, cooperation, integration and development: Essays in honour of Professor Hiroshi Kitamura.* Edited by ALI M. EL-AGRAA. Assisted by ICHIRO INUKAI AND SUMIMARU ODANO. Houndmills: Macmillan Press; distributed by Sheridan House, Dobbs Ferry, N.Y., 1987.

KLEINDORFER, PAUL R. AND KUNREUTHER, HOWARD C., ed. *Insuring and managing hazardous risks: From Seveso to Bhopal and beyond.* New York; Berlin; London and Tokyo: Springer, 1987.

KLINGAMAN, DAVID C. AND VEDDER, RICHARD K., eds. *Essays on the economy of the Old Northwest.* Athens: Ohio University Press, 1987.

KOZIARA, KAREN SHALLCROSS; MOSKOW, MICHAEL H. AND TANNER, LUCRETIA DEWEY, eds. *Working women: Past, present, future.* Industrial Relations Research Association Series. Washington, D.C.: Bureau of National Affairs, 1987.

KURZHANSKI, A. B. AND SIGMUND, K., eds. *Dynamical systems: Proceedings of an IIASA (International Institute for Applied Systems Analysis) workshop on mathematics of dynamic processes, held at Sopron, Hungary, September 9–13, 1985.* Lecture Notes in Economics and Mathematical Systems series, no. 287. New York; Berlin; London and Tokyo: Springer, 1987.

LANE, THEODORE, ed. *Developing America's northern frontier.* Lanham, Md. and London: University Press of America, 1987.

LANG, KEVIN AND LEONARD, JONATHAN S., eds. *Unemployment and the structure of labor markets.* New York and Oxford: Blackwell, 1987.

LAWLER, EDWARD J. AND MARKOVSKY, BARRY, eds. *Advances in group processes.* Volume 4. A Research Annual. Greenwich, Conn. and London: JAI Press, 1987.

LAWRENCE, ROBERT Z. AND SCHULTZE, CHARLES L., eds. *Barriers to European growth: A transatlantic view.* Washington, D.C.: Brookings Institution, 1987.

LAYARD, RICHARD AND CALMFORS, LARS, eds. *The fight against unemployment: Macroeconomic papers from the Centre for European Policy Studies.* Cambridge, Mass. and London: MIT Press, 1987.

LEE, CHENG F., ed. *Advances in financial planning and forecasting.* Volume 2. A Research Annual. Greenwich, Conn. and London: JAI Press, 1987.

LENEL, HANS OTTO, ET AL., eds. *ORDO: Jahrbuch für die Ordnung von Wirtschaft und Gesellschaft, Band 38.* Stuttgart and New York: Fischer, 1987.

LÉON, YVES AND MAHÉ, LOUIS, eds. *Income disparities among farm households and agricultural policy: Proceedings of the 14th Symposium of the European Association of Agricultural Economists (EAAE), September 3rd–5th, 1986, Rennes, France.* Kiel: Wissenschaftsverlag Vauk, 1987.

LEVICH, RICHARD M. AND SOMMARIVA, ANDREA, eds. *The ECU market: Current developments and future prospects of the European Currency Unit.* Lexington Books/Salomon Brothers Center Series on Financial Institutions and Markets. Lexington, Mass. and Toronto: Heath, Lexington Books, 1987.

LEVITT, M. S., ed. *New priorities in public spending.* Joint Studies in Public Policy series, no. 13. Aldershot, U.K. and Brookfield, Vt.: Gower, 1987.

LEWIN, DAVID; LIPSKY, DAVID B. AND SOCKELL, DONNA, eds. *Advances in industrial and labor relations.* Volume 4. A Research Annual. Greenwich, Conn. and London: JAI Press, 1987.

LEYTON-BROWN, DAVID, ed. *The utility of international economic sanctions.* New York: St. Martin's Press, 1987.

LIPSKY, DAVID B. AND DONN, CLIFFORD B., eds. *Collective bargaining in American industry: Contemporary perspectives and future directions.* Lexington, Mass. and Toronto: Heath, Lexington Books, 1987.

LOWE, ADOLPH. *Essays in political economics: Public control in a democratic society.* Edited and introduced by ALLEN OAKLEY. New York: New York University Press, 1987.

LOWRY, S. TODD, ed. *Pre-classical economic thought: From the Greeks to the Scottish enlightenment.* Recent Economic Thought Series. Norwell, Mass.; Dordrecht and Lancaster: Kluwer Academic, 1987.

LYNCH, JOHN E., ed. *Economic adjustment and conversion of defense industries.* Westview Special Studies in Public Policy and Public Systems Management series. Boulder and London: Westview Press, 1987.

MACKAY, ROBERT J.; MILLER, JAMES C., III AND YANDLE, BRUCE, eds. *Public choice and regulation: A view from inside the Federal Trade Commission.* Stanford, Calif.: Hoover Institution Press, 1987.

MACMILLEN, MALCOLM; MAYES, DAVID G. AND VAN VEEN, PIETER, eds. *European integration and industry.* Tilburg, the Netherlands: Tilburg University Press, 1987.

MADDOCK, RODNEY AND MCLEAN, IAN W., eds. *The Australian economy in the long run.* Cambridge; New York and Melbourne: Cambridge University Press, 1987.

MAIER, CHARLES S. *In search of stability: Explorations in historical political economy.* Cambridge Studies in Modern Political Economies. Cambridge; New York and Melbourne: Cambridge University Press, 1987.

MAILLET, PIERRE; HAGUE, DOUGLAS AND ROWLAND, CHRIS, eds. *The economics of choice between energy sources. Proceedings of a conference held by the International Economic Association in Tokyo, Japan.* New York: St. Martin's Press, 1987.

MARCUS, ALFRED A.; KAUFMAN, ALLEN M. AND BEAM, DAVID R., eds. *Business strategy and public policy: Perspectives from industry and academia.* Westport, Conn. and London: Greenwood Press, Quorum Books, 1987.

MARER, PAUL AND VAN VEEN, PIETER, eds. *East European economic trends and East–West trade: U.S., West and East European perspectives.* Advances in International Comparative Management series, supplement 2. Greenwich, Conn. and London: JAI Press, 1987.

[MARJOLIN, ROBERT] *Finance and the international economy: The AMEX Bank Review prize essays. In memory of Robert Marjolin.* Edited by JOHN CALVERLEY AND RICHARD O'BRIEN. With a preface by RAYMOND BARRE and a foreword by LORD ROLL. Oxford; New York; Toronto and Melbourne: Oxford University Press for the *AMEX Bank Review*, 1987.

[MARRAMA, VITTORIO] *Keynesian theory, planning models and quantitative economics: Essays in memory of Vittorio Marrama.* Volume 1. Edited by GIANCARLO GANDOLFO AND FERRUCCIO MARZANO. Università degli Studi di Roma "La Sapienza" series, no. 44, 1. Milan: Giuffrè, 1987.

[MARRAMA, VITTORIO] *Keynesian theory, planning models and quantitative economics: Essays in memory of Vittorio Marrama.* Volume 2. Edited by GIANCARLO GANDOLFO AND FERRUCCIO MARZANO. Università degli Studi di Roma "La Sapienza" series, no. 44, 2. Milan: Giuffrè, 1987.

MARSHALL, BURKE, ed. *A workable government? The constitution after 200 years.* American Assembly, Columbia University series. New York and London: Norton; Markham, Ont.: Penguin Books Canada, 1987.

MARTIN, LINDA G., ed. *The ASEAN success story: Social, economic, and political dimensions.* Honolulu: East–West Center; distributed by the University of Hawaii Press, 1987.

MARTIRENA-MANTEL, ANA MARÍA, ed. *External debt, savings, and growth in Latin America: Papers presented at a seminar sponsored by the International Monetary Fund and the Instituto Torcuato di Tella, held in Buenos Aires on October 13–16, 1986.* Washington, D.C.: International Monetary Fund; Buenos Aires: Instituto Torcuato di Tella, 1987.

MCCUBBINS, MATHEW D. AND SULLIVAN, TERRY, eds. *Congress: Structure and policy.* Political Economy of Institutions and Decisions series. Cambridge; New York and Melbourne: Cambridge University Press, 1987.

MCGUIRE, THOMAS G. AND SCHEFFLER, RICHARD M., eds. *The economics of mental health services.* Advances in Health Economics and Health Services Research series, vol. 8. Greenwich, Conn. and London: JAI Press, 1987.

MCKEE, DAVID L. AND BENNETT, RICHARD E., eds. *Structural change in an urban industrial region: The Northeastern Ohio case.* New York and London: Greenwood Press, Praeger, 1987.

MEIER, GERALD M., ed. *Pioneers in development.* Second Series. New York; Oxford; Toronto and Melbourne: Oxford University Press for the World Bank, 1987.

MELLOR, JOHN W.; DELGADO, CHRISTOPHER L. AND BLACKIE, MALCOLM J., eds. *Accelerating food production in Sub-Saharan Africa*. Baltimore and London: Johns Hopkins University Press for the International Food Policy Research Institute, 1987.

MENARD, SCOTT W. AND MOEN, ELIZABETH W., eds. *Perspectives on population: An introduction to concepts and issues*. New York; Oxford; Toronto and Melbourne: Oxford University Press, 1987.

MERLO, M., ET AL., eds. *Multipurpose agriculture and forestry: Proceedings of the 11th seminar of the European Association of Agricultural Economists (EAAE) 28 April–3 May, 1986*. Kiel: Wissenschaftsverlag Vauk, 1987.

MESA-LAGO, CARMELO, ed. *Cuban studies*. Volume 17. Pitt Latin American series. Pittsburgh: University of Pittsburgh Press, 1987.

MEYER, CHARLES W., ed. *Social security: A critique of radical reform proposals*. Lexington, Mass. and Toronto: Heath, Lexington Books, 1987.

MEYER, JACK A. AND LEWIN, MARION EIN, eds. *Charting the future of health care: Policy, politics and public health*. AEI Studies series, no. 449. Washington, D.C.: American Enterprise Institute for Public Policy Research; distributed by UPA, Lanham, Md., 1987.

MEYER, JOHN R. AND OSTER, CLINTON V., JR. *Deregulation and the future of intercity passenger travel*. With JOHN S. STRONG ET AL. MIT Press Series on the Regulation of Economic Activity. Cambridge, Mass. and London: MIT Press, 1987.

MILLAR, JAMES R., ed. *Politics, work, and daily life in the USSR: A survey of former Soviet citizens*. Cambridge; New York and Sydney: Cambridge University Press, 1987.

MINTZ, JACK M. AND PURVIS, DOUGLAS D., eds. *The impact of taxation on business activity: Proceedings of a conference held at the Conference Centre, Ottawa, 11–13 November 1985*. The Fourth John Deutsch Roundtable on Economic Policy. Kingston, Ont.: Queen's University, John Deutsch Institute for the Study of Economic Policy, 1987.

MIZRUCHI, MARK S. AND SCHWARTZ, MICHAEL, eds. *Intercorporate relations: The structural analysis of business*. Structural Analysis in the Social Sciences series, vol. 1. Cambridge; New York and Sydney: Cambridge University Press, 1987.

[MODIGLIANI, FRANCO] *Macroeconomics and finance: Essays in honor of Franco Modigliani*. Edited by RUDIGER DORNBUSCH, STANLEY FISCHER AND JOHN BOSSONS. Cambridge, Mass., and London: MIT Press, 1987.

MOST, KENNETH S., ed. *Advances in international accounting*. Volume 1. A Research Annual. Greenwich, Conn. and London: JAI Press, 1987.

MUNNELL, ALICIA H., ed. *Lessons from the income maintenance experiments: Proceedings of a conference held at Melvin Village, New Hampshire, September 1986*. Federal Reserve Bank of Boston Conference Series, no. 30. Boston: Federal Reserve Bank of Boston; Washington, D.C.: Brookings Institution, 1987.

MYERS, ROBERT J., ed. *The political morality of the International Monetary Fund: Ethics and foreign policy*. Volume 3. New Brunswick, N.J. and Oxford: Transaction Books for the Carnegie Council on Ethics and International Affairs, 1987.

NAGEL, STUART S., ed. *Research in public policy analysis and management*. Volume 4. A Research Annual. Greenwich, Conn. and London: JAI Press, 1987.

NALBANTIAN, HAIG R., ed. *Incentives, cooperation, and risk sharing: Economic and psychological perspectives on employment contracts*. Totowa, N.J.: Littlefield, Adams; Rowman and Littlefield, 1987.

NELSON, JOHN S.; MEGILL, ALLAN AND MCCLOSKEY, DONALD N., eds. *The rhetoric of the human sciences: Language and argument in scholarship and public affairs*. Rhetoric of the Human Sciences series. Madison and London: University of Wisconsin Press, 1987.

NOBEL, PETER, ed. *Refugees and development in Africa*. Seminar Proceedings series, no. 19. Uppsala: Scandinavian Institute of African Studies; distributed by Almqvist and Wiksell International, Stockholm, 1987.

OFFICER, LAWRENCE H., ed. *International economics*. Recent Economic Thought series. Norwell, Mass.; Dordrecht and Lancaster: Kluwer Academic, 1987.

OPPONG, CHRISTINE, ed. *Sex roles, population and development in West Africa: Policy-related studies on work and demographic issues.* Portsmouth, N.H.: Heinemann; London: Currey, 1987.

PACHAURI, R. K., ed. *Global energy interactions.* Riverdale, Md.: Riverdale, 1987.

PAPANICOLAOU, GEORGE, ed. *Random media.* IMA Volumes in Mathematics and Its Applications series, vol. 7. New York and Berlin: Springer, 1987.

PASINETTI, LUIGI AND LLOYD, PETER, eds. *Structural change, economic interdependence and world development: Proceedings of the Seventh World Congress of the Internatonal Economic Association, Madrid, Spain.* Volume 3. *Structural change and adjustment in the world economy.* New York: St. Martin's Press, 1987.

PATRICK, HUGH T. AND TACHI, RYUICHIRO, eds. *Japan and the United States today: Exchange rates, macroeconomic policies, and financial market innovations.* New York: Columbia University, Center on Japanese Economy and Business, 1987.

PEARSON, SCOTT R., ET AL. *Portuguese agriculture in transition.* Ithaca and London: Cornell University Press, 1987.

PECHMAN, JOSEPH A., ed. *Tax reform and the U.S. economy.* Brookings Dialogues on Public Policy series. Washington, D.C.: Brookings Institution, 1987.

PEDERSEN, PEDER J. AND LUND, REINHARD, eds. *Unemployment: Theory, policy and structure.* De Gruyter Studies in Organization series, no. 10. Berlin and New York: de Gruyter, 1987.

PEJOVICH, SVETOZAR, ed. *Socialism: Institutional, philosophical and economic issues.* International Studies in Economics and Econometrics series, vol. 14. Hingham, Mass.; Dordrecht and Lancaster: Kluwer Academic, 1987.

PENNINGS, JOHANNES M. AND BUITENDAM, AREND, eds. *New technology as organizational innovation: The development and diffusion of microelectronics.* Ballinger Series on The Management of Innovation and Change. Cambridge, Mass.: Harper and Row, Ballinger, 1987.

[PENROSE, ERNEST F.] *Japan and world depression: Then and now. Essays in memory of E. F. Penrose.* Edited by RONALD DORE AND RADHA SINHA. With assistance from MARI SAKO. New York: St. Martin's Press, 1987.

PERKINS, JOSEPH, ed. *A conservative agenda for black Americans.* Critical Issues series. Washington, D.C.: Heritage Foundation, 1987.

PETERS, H. J. M. AND VRIEZE, O. J., eds. *Surveys in game theory and related topics.* CWI Tract series, no. 39. Amsterdam: Centre for Mathematics and Computer Science, 1987.

PETHIG, RUDIGER AND SCHLIEPER, ULRICH, eds. *Efficiency, institutions, and economic policy: Proceedings of a workshop held by the Sonderforschungsbereich 5 at the University of Mannheim, June 1986.* New York; Berlin; London and Tokyo: Springer, 1987.

PICARD, LOUIS A. AND ZARISKI, RAPHAEL, eds. *Subnational politics in the 1980s: Organization, reorganization and economic development.* New York and London: Greenwood Press, Praeger, 1987.

PILLET, GONZAGUE AND MUROTA, TAKESHI, eds. *Environmental economics: The analysis of a major interface.* Geneva: Leimgruber, 1987.

POHL, HANS AND RUDOLPH, BERND, eds. *German yearbook on business history, 1986.* Berlin; New York; London and Tokyo: Springer, 1987.

PORTES, RICHARD AND SWOBODA, ALEXANDER K., eds. *Threats to international financial stability.* Cambridge; New York and Melbourne: Cambridge University Press, 1987.

POWELSON, JOHN P. AND STOCK, RICHARD. *The peasant betrayed: Agriculture and land reform in the third world.* With contributions by GRACE GOODELL ET AL. Lincoln Institute of Land Policy Book series. Boston: Oelgeschlager, Gunn and Hain in association with the Lincoln Institute of Land Policy, 1987.

PRESCOTT, EDWARD C. AND WALLACE, NEIL, eds. *Contractual arrangements for intertemporal trade.* Minnesota Studies in Macroeconomics series, vol. 1. Minneapolis: University of Minnesota Press, 1987.

QUIGLEY, JOHN M., ed. *Perspectives on local public finance and public policy.* Volume 3. A Research Annual. Greenwich, Conn. and London: JAI Press, 1987.

RADNITZKY, GERARD AND BERNHOLZ, PETER, eds. *Economic imperialism: The economic approach applied outside the field of economics*. Professors World Peace Academy Book series. New York: Paragon House, 1987.

RAUNIKAR, ROBERT AND HUANG, CHUNG-LIANG, eds. *Food demand analysis: Problems, issues, and empirical evidence*. Ames: Iowa State University Press, 1987.

RAZIN, ASSAF AND SADKA, EFRAIM, eds. *Economic policy in theory and practice*. New York: St. Martin's Press, 1987.

REES, JUDITH AND ODELL, PETER, eds. *The international oil industry: An interdisciplinary perspective*. New York: St. Martin's Press, 1987.

REIN, MARTIN; ESPING-ANDERSEN, GØSTA AND RAINWATER, LEE, eds. *Stagnation and renewal in social policy: The rise and fall of policy regimes*. Comparative Public Policy Analysis Series. Armonk, N.Y. and London: Sharpe, 1987.

RES, ZANNIS AND MOTAMEN, SIMA, eds. *International debt and central banking in the 1980s*. New York: St. Martin's Press, 1987.

REYNOLDS, BRUCE L. *Reform in China: Challenges and choices. A summary and analysis of the CESRRI Survey*. Armonk, N.Y. and London: Sharpe, East Gate, 1987.

RODRIGUEZ, RITA M., ed. *The Export–Import Bank at fifty: The international environment and the institution's role*. Lexington, Mass. and Toronto: Heath, Lexington Books, 1987.

ROSKAMP, KARL W., ed. *International Institute of Public Finance Semicentennial, 1937 to 1987*. Detroit: Wayne State University Press, 1987.

ROSS, GEORGE; HOFFMANN, STANLEY AND MALZACHER, SYLVIA, eds. *The Mitterrand experiment: Continuity and change in modern France*. Europe and the International Order series. New York: Oxford University Press, 1987.

ROSTOW, WALT WHITMAN. *Rich countries and poor countries: Reflections on the past, lessons for the future*. Boulder, Colo. and London: Westview Press, 1987.

ROTH, ALVIN E., ed. *Laboratory experimentation in economics: Six points of view*. Cambridge; New York and Sydney: Cambridge University Press, 1987.

ROTHBARD, MURRAY N., ed. *The review of Austrian economics*. Volume 1. Lexington, Mass., and Toronto: Heath, Lexington Books, 1987.

ROWLAND, KENDRITH M. AND FERRIS, GERALD R., eds. *Research in personnel and human resources management*. Volume 5. A Research Annual. Greenwich, Conn. and London: JAI Press, 1987.

RUBEL, MAXIMILIEN AND CRUMP, JOHN, eds. *Non-market socialism in the nineteenth and twentieth centuries*. New York: St. Martin's Press, 1987.

RUBINSTEIN, W. D. *Elites and the wealthy in modern British history: Essays in social and economic history*. New York: St. Martin's Press; Brighton, U.K.: Harvester Press, 1987.

RUTH, STEPHEN R. AND MANN, CHARLES K., eds. *Microcomputers in public policy: Applications for developing countries*. AAAS Selected Symposia Series, no. 102. Boulder, Colo.: Westview Press for the American Association for the Advancement of Science, Washington, D.C., 1987.

RUTTAN, VERNON W. AND PRAY, CARL E., eds. *Policy for agricultural research*. Boulder, Colo. and London: Westview Press, 1987.

SACHS, IGNACY. *Development and planning*. Translated by PETER FAWCETT. Cambridge; New York and Sydney: Cambridge University Press; Paris: Editions de la Maison des Sciences de l'Homme, 1987.

SAFARIAN, A. E. AND BERTIN, GILLES Y., eds. *Multinationals, governments and international technology transfer*. New York: St. Martin's Press, 1987.

SALAZAR-CARRILLO, JORGE AND TIRADO DE ALONZO, IRMA, eds. *Foreign investment and economic development in Latin America*. IESCARIBE Research Summaries series, no. 4. Miami: IESCARIBE, 1987.

SALVATORE, DOMINICK, ed. *The new protectionist threat to world welfare*. Amsterdam and London: North-Holland; distributed in N. America by Elsevier Science, New York, 1987.

SAMUELS, WARREN J., ed. *Research in the history of economic thought and methodology*. Volume 5. A Research Annual. Greenwich, Conn. and London: JAI Press, 1987.

SAMUELS, WARREN J. AND MILLER, ARTHUR S., eds. *Corporations and society: Power and responsi-*

bility. Contributions in American Studies series, no. 88. New York and London: Greenwood Press, 1987.

SANDELL, STEVEN H., ed. *The problem isn't age: Work and older Americans.* New York and London: Praeger, 1987.

SATO, RYUZO AND WACHTEL, PAUL, eds. *Trade friction and economic policy: Problems and prospects for Japan and the United States.* Cambridge; New York and Melbourne: Cambridge University Press, 1987.

SAUNDERS, CHRISTOPHER T., ed. *Industrial policies and structural change.* New York: St. Martin's Press, 1987.

SAWARAGI, Y.; INOUE, K. AND NAKAYAMA, H., eds. *Toward interactive and intelligent decision support systems.* Volume 1. *Proceedings of the Seventh International Conference on Multiple Criteria Decision Making, held at Kyoto, Japan, August 18–22, 1986.* Lecture Notes in Economics and Mathematical Systems series, no. 285. New York; Berlin; London and Tokyo: Springer, 1987.

SCHEFFLER, RICHARD M. AND ROSSITER, LOUIS F., eds. *Mergers in health care: The performance of multi-institutional organizations.* Advances in Health Economics and Health Services Research series, vol. 7. Greenwich, Conn. and London: JAI Press, 1987.

SCHICK, IRVIN CEMIL AND TONAK, ERTUGRUL AHMET, eds. *Turkey in transition: New perspectives.* With translations by REZAN BENATAR, IRVIN CEMIL SCHICK, AND RONNIE MARGULIES. New York; Oxford; Toronto and Melbourne: Oxford University Press, 1987.

SCHMANDT, JURGEN AND WILSON, ROBERT, eds. *Promoting high-technology industry: Initiatives and policies for state governments.* Boulder, Colo. and London: Westview Press in cooperation with the Houston Area Research Center, 1987.

SCHMIDT, CHRISTIAN, ed. *The economics of military expenditures: Military expenditures, economic growth and fluctuations. Proceedings of a conference held by the International Economic Association in Paris, France.* IEA Conference series. New York: St. Martin's Press, 1987.

SCHMIDT, CHRISTIAN AND BLACKABY, FRANK, eds. *Peace, defense and economic analysis: Proceedings of a conference held in Stockholm jointly by the International Economic Association and the Stockholm International Peace Research Institute.* New York: St. Martin's Press, 1987.

SCHRAMM, CARL J., ed. *Health care and its costs.* American Assembly, Columbia University series. New York and London: Norton, 1987.

SCHULTZ, RANDALL L., ed. *Applications of management science.* Volume 5. A Research Annual. Greenwich, Conn. and London: JAI Press, 1987.

SCHWARTZ, ANNA J. *Money in historical perspective.* With an Introduction by MICHAEL D. BORDO AND MILTON FRIEDMAN. National Bureau of Economic Research Monograph series. Chicago and London: University of Chicago Press, 1987.

SCHWARTZ, BILL N., ed. *Advances in accounting.* Volume 5. Associate editors are PHILIP M. J. RECKERS, JAMES C. STALLMAN, AND JAMES H. SCHEINER. A Research Annual. Greenwich, Conn. and London: JAI Press, 1987.

SEN, AMARTYA K., ET AL. *The standard of living: The Tanner Lectures, Clare Hall, Cambridge, 1985.* Edited by GEOFFREY HAWTHORN. Cambridge; New York and Melbourne: Cambridge University Press, 1987.

SETHI, S. PRAKASH, ed. *The South African quagmire: In search of a peaceful path to democratic pluralism.* Ballinger Series in Business in a Global Environment. Cambridge, Mass.: Harper and Row, Ballinger, 1987.

SHETH, JAGDISH N., ed. *Research in marketing.* A Research Annual, vol. 9. Greenwich, Conn. and London: JAI Press, 1987.

SHETH, JAGDISH N. AND HIRSCHMAN, ELIZABETH, eds. *Research in consumer behavior.* Volume 2. A Research Annual. Greenwich, Conn. and London: JAI Press, 1987.

SHETTY, Y. K. AND BUEHLER, VERNON M., eds. *Quality productivity and innovation: Strategies for gaining competitive advantage.* Foreword by ROGER SMITH. New York: Elsevier Science, 1987.

SINCLAIR, P. J. N., ed. *Prices, quantities and expectations: Keynes and macroeconomics in the fifty years since the publication of the* General Theory. Oxford; New York; Toronto and Melbourne: Oxford University Press, Clarendon Press, 1987.

SIVEN, CLAES-HENRIC, ed. *Unemployment in Europe: Analysis and policy issues.* Stockholm: Timbro, 1987.

SOLOMON, ELINOR HARRIS, ed. *Electronic funds transfers and payments: The public policy issues.* Norwell, Mass.; Dordrecht and Lancaster: Kluwer Academic, Kluwer-Nijhoff, 1987.

SOLOW, BARBARA L. AND ENGERMAN, STANLEY L., eds. *British capitalism and Caribbean slavery: The legacy of Eric Williams.* Studies in Interdisciplinary History series. Cambridge; New York and Sydney: Cambridge University Press, 1987.

SPENCER, SAMIA I., ed. *Foreign languages and international trade: A global perspective.* Athens and London: University of Georgia Press, 1987.

STAUDOHAR, PAUL D. AND BROWN, HOLLY E. *Deindustrialization and plant closure.* Lexington, Mass. and Toronto: Heath, Lexington Books, 1987.

STEGMAN, TREVOR, ET AL. *The future of income policies in Australia.* CAER Paper series, no. 24. Kensington: University of New South Wales, Centre for Applied Economic Research, 1987.

STEINHERR, ALFRED AND WEISERBS, DANIEL, eds. *Employment and growth: Issues for the 1980s.* International Studies in Economics and Econometrics series, vol. 16. Hingham, Mass.; Lancaster and Dordrecht: Kluwer Academic, 1987.

STERN, ROBERT M., ed. *U.S. trade policies in a changing world economy.* Cambridge, Mass. and London: MIT Press, 1987.

STEVENS, PAUL, ed. *Energy demand: Prospects and trends.* New York: St. Martin's Press, 1987.

STEWART, FRANCES, ed. *Macro-policies for appropriate technology in developing countries.* Boulder, Colo. and London: Westview Press in cooperation with Appropriate Technology International, Washington, D.C., 1987.

STEWART, MARION B., ed. *Energy deregulation and economic growth: Proceedings of the First Annual Conference on Energy Policy in the Middle Atlantic States, sponsored by Rutgers, the State University of New Jersey, and the New Jersey Department of Commerce and Economic Development.* New Brunswick, N.J.: Rutgers, Bureau of Economic Research, 1987.

SUMMERS, LAWRENCE H., ed. *Tax policy and the economy.* Volume 1. Chicago: National Bureau of Economic Research; Cambridge, Mass.: MIT Press, 1987.

TALMAN, DOLF AND VAN DER LAAN, GERARD, eds. *The computation and modelling of economic equilibria.* Contributions to Economic Analysis series, no. 167. Amsterdam; New York; Oxford and Tokyo: North-Holland; distributed in the U.S. and Canada by Elsevier Science, New York, 1987.

TARLING, ROGER, ed. *Flexibility in labour markets.* London; Orlando, Fla.; Sydney and Toronto: Harcourt Brace Jovanovich, Academic Press, 1987.

TCHIJOV, IOURI AND TOMASZEWICZ, LUCJA, eds. *Input–output modeling: Proceedings of the Sixth IIASA (International Institute for Applied Systems Analysis) Task Force Meeting on Input–Output Modeling held in Warsaw, Poland, December 16–18, 1985.* Lecture Notes in Economics and Mathematical Systems series, no. 292. New York; Berlin; London and Tokyo: Springer, 1987.

TECKENBERG, WOLFGANG, ed. *Comparative studies of social structure: Recent research on France, the United States, and the Federal Republic of Germany.* Armonk, N.Y.: Sharpe, 1987.

TEUBAL, MORRIS. *Innovation performance, learning, and government policy: Selected essays.* Madison and London: University of Wisconsin Press, 1987.

THAI, KHI V., ed. *Structural budget deficits in the federal government: Causes, consequences and remedies.* Lanham, Md. and London: University Press of America, 1987.

THIRLWALL, A. P., ed. *Keynes and economic development: The Seventh Keynes Seminar held at the University of Kent at Canterbury, 1985.* New York: St. Martin's Press, 1987.

THOMPSON, GRAHAME; BROWN, VIVIENNE AND LEVAĆIĆ, ROSALIND, eds. *Managing the UK economy: Current controversies.* Cambridge, U.K.: Polity Press in association with Blackwell, New York, 1987.

THORP, ROSEMARY AND WHITEHEAD, LAURENCE, eds. *Latin American debt and the adjustment crisis.* Pitt Latin American Series. Pittsburgh: University of Pittsburgh Press, 1987.

THORUP, CATHRYN L., ed. *The United States and Mexico: Face to face with new technology.* U.S.–Third World Policy Perspectives series, no. 8. New Brunswick, N.J. and Oxford: Transaction Books, 1987.

TIDRICK, GENE AND JIYUAN, CHEN, eds. *China's industrial reform.* Oxford; New York; Toronto and Melbourne: Oxford University Press for the World Bank, 1987.

TIMMER, C. PETER, ed. *The corn economy of Indonesia.* Ithaca, N.Y. and London: Cornell University Press, 1987.

TISMER, JOHANNES F.; AMBLER, JOHN AND SYMONS, LESLIE, eds. *Transport and economic development—Soviet Union and Eastern Europe.* Osteuropa-Institut an der Freien Universität Berlin, Wirtschaftswissenschaftliche Veröffentlichungen, band 42. Berlin: Duncker and Humblot, 1987.

TOBIN, JAMES. *Essays in economics.* Volume 1. *Macroeconomics.* Reprint. Cambridge, Mass. and London: MIT Press, [1971] 1987. (I)

TOBIN, JAMES. *Essays in economics.* Volume 2. *Consumption and econometrics.* Reprint. Cambridge, Mass. and London: MIT Press, [1975] 1987. (II)

TOBIN, JAMES. *Policies for prosperity: Essays in a Kenyesian mode.* Edited by P. M. JACKSON. Cambridge, Mass.: MIT Press, 1987. (III)

TOLLIDAY, STEVEN AND ZEITLIN, JONATHAN, eds. *The automobile industry and its workers: Between Fordism and flexibility.* New York: St. Martin's Press, 1987.

TREMBLAY, RODRIGUE, ed. *Issues in North American trade and finance: Fourth International Congress.* Papers and Proceedings, vol. 4, no. 1. Montreal: North American Economics and Finance Association, 1987.

TREVOR, MALCOLM, ed. *The internationalization of Japanese business: European and Japanese perspectives.* Boulder, Colo.: Westview Press; Frankfurt am Main: Campus, 1987.

[TULLOCK, GORDON] *Democracy and public choice: Essays in honor of Gordon Tullock.* Edited by and with contributions from CHARLES K. ROWLEY. Oxford and New York: Blackwell, 1987.

TURNER, BENGT; KEMENY, JIM AND LUNDQVIST, LENNART J., eds. *Between state and market: Housing in the post-industrial era.* Stockholm: Almqvist and Wiksell International, 1987.

UNITED NATIONS CONFERENCE ON TRADE AND DEVELOPMENT. *Compendium of selected studies on international monetary and financial issues for the developing countries.* U.N. Publication Sales No. E.87.II.D.3. New York: United Nations, 1987.

URQUIDI, VICTOR L., ed. *Structural change, economic interdependence and world development: Proceedings of the Seventh World Congress of the International Economic Association, Madrid, Spain.* Volume 1. *Basic issues.* New York: St. Martin's Press, 1987.

U.S. COMMITTEE FOR REFUGEES. *World refugee survey, 1986 in review.* Washington, D.C.: Author, 1987.

U.S. DEPARTMENT OF AGRICULTURE, ECONOMIC RESEARCH SERVICE, AGRICULTURE AND RURAL ECONOMY DIVISION. *Rural economic development in the 1980's: Preparing for the future.* ERS Staff Report series, no. AGES870724. Washington, D.C.: Author, 1987.

U.S. TREASURY, OFFICE OF TAX ANALYSIS. *Compendium of tax research, 1987.* No. 048-000-00395-8. Washington, D.C.: U.S.G.P.O., 1987.

VANE, HOWARD AND CASLIN, TERRY, eds. *Current controversies in economics.* Oxford and New York: Blackwell, 1987.

VARTIA, PENTTI, ET AL. *Growth policies in a Nordic perspective.* Helsinki: Research Institute of the Finnish Economy; Copenhagen: Institute for Future Studies; Stockholm: Industrial Institute for Economic and Social Research; Bergen, Norway: Institute of Industrial Economics, 1987.

VASKO, TIBOR, ed. *The long-wave debate: Selected papers from an IIASA (International Institute for Applied Systems Analysis) International Meeting on Long-term Fluctuations in Economic Growth: Their Causes and Consequences, held in Weimar, GDR, June 10–14, 1985.* New York; Berlin; London and Tokyo: Springer, 1987.

VINCENT, THOMAS L., ET AL., eds. *Modeling and management of resources under uncertainty: Proceedings of the Second U.S.–Australia Workshop on Renewable Resource Management held at the East–West Center, Honolulu, Hawaii, December 9–12, 1985.* Lecture Notes in Biomathematics series, vol. 72. New York; Berlin; London and Tokyo: Springer, 1987.

VISSER, HANS AND SCHOORL, EVERT, eds. *Trade in transit: World trade and world economy—Past, present and future.* Hingham, Mass., Dordrecht and Lancaster: Kluwer Academic, 1987.

VAN VLIET—, WILLEM, ET AL., eds. *Housing and neighborhoods: Theoretical and empirical contributions.* Contributions in Sociology series, no. 66. Westport, Conn. and London: Greenwood Press, 1987.

WALKER, CHARLS E. AND BLOOMFIELD, MARK A., eds. *The consumption tax: A better alternative?* Cambridge, Mass.: Harper and Row, Ballinger, 1987.

[WALLICH, HENRY C.] *International monetary cooperation: Essays in honor of Henry C. Wallich.* Essays in International Finance series, no. 169. Princeton, N.J.: Princeton University, Department of Economics, International Finance Section, 1987.

WALTMAN, JEROLD L. AND STUDLAR, DONLEY T., eds. *Political economy: Public policies in the United States and Britain.* Jackson and London: University Press of Mississippi, 1987.

WARNER, MALCOLM, ed. *Management reforms in China.* New York: St. Martin's Press, 1987.

WATANABE, SUSUMU, ed. *Microelectronics, automation and employment in the automobile industry.* Preface by AJIT S. BHALLA. Foreword by AUBREY SILBERSTON. An ILO–WEP Study. Chichester, U.K.; New York; Toronto and Singapore: Wiley, 1987.

WESTOBY, JACK. *The purpose of forests: Follies of development.* With a foreword by A. J. LESLIE. Oxford and New York: Blackwell, 1987.

WIENER, JOSHUA M., ed. *Swing beds: Assessing flexible health care in rural communities.* Brookings Dialogues on Public Policy series. Washington, D.C.: Brookings Institution, 1987.

WILCOX, JAMES A., ed. *Current readings on money, banking, and financial markets.* FREDERIC S. MISHKIN, Consulting Editor. Boston and Toronto: Little, Brown, 1987.

WILKS, STEPHEN AND WRIGHT, MAURICE, eds. *Comparative government–industry relations: Western Europe, the United States, and Japan.* Government–Industry Relations series, no. 1 Oxford; New York; Toronto and Melbourne: Oxford University Press, Clarendon Press, 1987.

WILLIAMSON, JOHN. *Political economy and international money: Selected essays of John Williamson.* Edited by CHRIS MILNER. New York: New York University Press; distributed by Columbia University Press, 1987.

WILLIAMSON, OLIVER. *Antitrust economics: Mergers, contracting, and strategic behavior.* Oxford and New York: Blackwell, 1987.

WILLS, ROBERT L.; CASWELL, JULIE A. AND CULBERTSON, JOHN D., eds. *Issues after a century of federal competition policy.* Lexington, Mass. and Toronto: Heath, Lexington Books, 1987.

WINSTON, CLIFFORD, ET AL. *Blind intersection? Policy and the automobile industry.* Washington, D.C.: Brookings Institution, 1987.

WISE, DAVID A., ed. *Public sector payrolls.* National Bureau of Economic Research Project Report series. Chicago and London: University of Chicago Press, 1987.

WITT, PETER-CHRISTIAN, ed. *Wealth and taxation in Central Europe: The history and sociology of public finance.* German Historical Perspectives series, vol. 2. Leamington Spa, U.K. and Hamburg: Berg; distributed in the U.S. and Canada by St. Martin's Press, New York, 1987.

WOLFF, EDWARD N., ed. *International comparisons of the distribution of household wealth.* Oxford; New York; Toronto and Melbourne: Oxford University Press, Clarendon Press, 1987.

WOODMAN, RICHARD W. AND PASMORE, WILLIAM A., eds. *Research in organizational change and development.* Volume 1. An Annual Series featuring Advances in Theory, Methodology and Research. Greenwich, Conn. and London: JAI Press, 1987.

WOODSIDE, ARCH G., ed. *Advances in business marketing.* Volume 2. A Research Annual. Greenwich, Conn. and London: JAI Press, 1987.

WORLD HEALTH ORGANIZATION. *Health care—Who pays?* Geneva: Author, 1987.

WRIGHT, GEORGE AND AYTON, PETER, eds. *Judgmental forecasting.* Chichester, U.K.; New York; Brisbane and Toronto: Wiley, 1987.

YAMAMURA, KOZO AND YASUBA, YASUKICHI, eds. *The political economy of Japan.* Volume 1. *The domestic transformation.* Stanford, Calif.: Stanford University Press, 1987.

YANARELLA, ERNEST J. AND GREEN, WILLIAM C., eds. *The unfulfilled promise of synthetic fuels:*

Technological failure, policy immobilism, or commercial illusion. Contributions in Political Science series, no. 179. Westport, Conn. and London: Greenwood Press, 1987.

YOUNG, R. H. AND MacCORMAC, C. W., eds. *Market research for food products and processes in developing countries: Proceedings of a workshop held in Singapore, 1–4 April 1986.* IDRC-249e. Ottawa: International Development Research Centre, 1987.

ZARTMAN, I. WILLIAM, ed. *The 50% solution: How to bargain successfully with hijackers, strikers, bosses, oil magnates, Arabs, Russians, and other worthy opponents in this modern world.* Paperback reprint. New Haven and London: Yale University Press, [1976] 1987. (I)

ZARTMAN, I. WILLIAM, ed. *Positive sum: Improving North–South negotiations.* New Brunswick, N.J. and Oxford: Transaction Books, 1987. (II)

ZIMBALIST, ANDREW, ed. *Cuba's socialist economy: Towards the 1990s.* Boulder, Colo. and London: Lynne Rienner, 1987.

CLASSIFICATION SYSTEM

Editor's note: Notes on the *Classification System* further clarify the subject matter covered under specific categories or point out specific topics included. They also may contain cross references to other categories. In addition, the *Topical Guide* at the end of this volume provides an index to classification numbers appropriate for specific topics. Please note that "General" categories may include *both* detailed articles covering all subcategories and very general articles falling into no subcategory.

000 General Economics; Theory; History; Systems
  010 General Economics   3
    011 General Economics   3
      0110 General   3
         Includes general bibliographies. For bibliographies relating to subfield, see general category in subfield.
      0112 Role of Economics; Role of Economists   5
      0113 Relation of Economics to Other Disciplines   6
      0114 Relation of Economics to Social Values   7
         Articles where the values discussed refer to the "economic system" may appear in subcategories 0510 or 0520.
      0115 Methods Used by Economists   9
         For methodology, see also 0360.
    012 Teaching of Economics   9
      0120 Teaching of Economics   9
         For teaching in specific subfields, see also general category in subfield.
  020 General Economic Theory   11
      0200 General Economic Theory   11
         Articles referring to entire field of economic theory.
    021 General Equilibrium and Disequilibrium Theory   12
      0210 General Equilibrium and Disequilibrium Theory   12
         For general equilibrium and disequilibrium in macroeconomic models, see 023 category. For computable general equilibrium models, see specific subject categories; for forecasting and policy simulations, see category 132; for discussions of solutions methods, see category 212 or 213.
    022 Microeconomic Theory   16
      0220 General   16
      0222 Theory of the Household (consumer demand)   18
         For empirical consumption function, see 921 category; for microfoundations of macroeconomic theory, see 0232. For consumer surplus, see also 0240.
      0223 Theory of Production   22
         Theory of the firm will generally appear here. For articles dealing with social objectives of the firm, see 5140. For theory of production functions for the economy as a whole, see 0234. For microtheory of investment, see also 5220. In general, empirical studies of production not used to illustrate theory will appear in industry studies, category 630.

0224 Theory of Factor Distribution and Distributive Shares 27
For macroeconomic factor (functional income) distribution, see 0235. For human capital theory, see 8510; for wage theory, see also 8210; for empirical wages, see 8242.

0225 Theory of Firm and Industry under Competitive Market Structures 27

0226 Theory of Firm and Industry under Imperfectly Competitive Market Structures 27
For studies of structure of industry, concentration ratios, see 6110; for policy toward monopoly, see 6120. For multimarket equilibrium, see 0210.

0227 Theory of Auction Markets 33
0228 Agent Theory 34
0229 Microeconomics of Intertemporal Choice 35

023 Macroeconomic Theory 36
0230 General 36
For business fluctuation theory, see also 1311; for stabilization theory and policies, see 1331; for inflation theory, see 1342; for fiscal theory, see also 3212.

0232 Theory of Aggregate Demand: Consumption 42
For empirical studies of the consumption and saving functions, see 9211.

0233 Theory of Aggregate Demand: Investment 44
For microtheory of investment, see 0223 and 5220.

0234 Theory of Aggregate Supply 45
0235 Theory of Aggregate Distribution 49
For microeconomic factor distribution, see 0224; for empirical studies of income distribution, see 2213; for labor market theories, see also 8210.

0239 Macroeconomics of Intertemporal Choice 50

024 Welfare Theory 51
0240 General 51
For theory of public goods and the public goods sector, see also 3212. For the social welfare function, see also 0251; for equity and justice, see also 0251.

0242 Allocative Efficiency Including Theory of Cost/Benefit 54
Articles in this section are concerned with theory rather than empirical application of cost/benefit studies to specific subfields. For empirical applications see the subfield involved. See also, 0226 for welfare distortions owing to monopoly. See the 411 category for welfare aspects of trade theory and policy.

0243 Redistribution Analyses 56
0244 Externalities 57
See 7220 for pollution.

025 Social Choice 58
Includes theory and studies of collective decision.
0250 General 58
0251 Social Choice Theory 59
0252 Social Choice Studies: Voting, Committees, etc. 65

026 Economics of Uncertainty and Information; Game Theory and Bargaining Theory 69
0260 General 69
0261 Theory of Uncertainty and Information 69

		0262	Game Theory and Bargaining Theory	77
			For applications see specific subfields.	
	027		Economics of Centrally Planned Economies	83
		0270	General	83
		0271	Microeconomic Theory	83
		0272	Macroeconomic Theory	85
030			History of Thought; Methodology	86
	031		History of Economic Thought	86
		0310	General	86
		0311	Ancient, Medieval	86
		0312	Preclassical	86
		0313	Mercantilist	86
		0314	Classical	87
		0315	Austrian, Marshallian, Neoclassical	87
		0316	General Equilibrium until 1945	88
		0317	Socialist and Marxian until 1945	88
			For current articles on figures such as Marx, see individuals, 0322; for articles on socialist systems in operation, see 0520.	
		0318	Historical and Institutional	89
	032		History of Economic Thought (continued)	91
		0321	Other Schools since 1800	91
		0322	Individuals	91
			Articles about individual figures in the history of thought are listed alphabetically by the person discussed.	
		0329	Other Special Topics	100
	036		Economic Methodology	103
		0360	Economic Methodology	103
040			Economic History	106
			Studies covering solely the period prior to 1946, the end of World War II, are designated as historical. In general, the articles are cross-classified in the relevant subject categories.	
	041		Economic History: General	106
		0410	General	106
		0411	Development of the Discipline	106
		0412	Comparative Intercountry or Intertemporal Economic History	106
	042		Economic History: United States and Canada	107
		0420	General	107
		0421	History of Product Prices and Markets	108
		0422	History of Factor Prices and Markets	109
		0423	History of Public Economic Policy (all levels)	112
	043		Economic History: Ancient and Medieval (until 1453)	114
			Articles, irrespective of the geographic area involved, dealing with this time period are all listed in this group.	
		0430	General	114
		0431	History of Product Prices and Markets	114
		0432	History of Factor Prices and Markets	114
		0433	History of Public Economic Policy (all levels)	114
	044		Economic History: Europe	114
		0440	General	114
		0441	History of Product Prices and Markets	116
		0442	History of Factor Prices and Markets	118
		0443	History of Public Economic Policy (all levels)	120

045   Economic History: Asia   122
        0450   General   122
        0451   History of Product Prices and Markets   123
        0452   History of Factor Prices and Markets   124
        0453   History of Public Economic Policy (all levels)   124
046   Economic History: Africa   124
        0460   General   124
        0461   History of Product Prices and Markets   124
        0462   History of Factor Prices and Markets   124
        0463   History of Public Economic Policy (all levels)   125
047   Economic History: Latin America and Caribbean   125
        0470   General   125
        0471   History of Product Prices and Markets   125
        0472   History of Factor Prices and Markets   125
        0473   History of Public Economic Policy (all levels)   126
048   Economic History: Oceania   126
        0480   General   126
        0481   History of Product Prices and Markets   126
        0482   History of Factor Prices and Markets   126
        0483   History of Public Economic Policy (all levels)   126
050   Economic Systems   126
    For studies of particular countries, as distinct from discussions of a
    system, see category 120.
        0500   General   126
051   Capitalist Economic Systems: Market Economies   127
        0510   Capitalist Economic Systems: Market Economies   127
               Includes articles discussing or critiquing capitalist sys-
               tems. Also includes articles on the cooperative as a system
               in predominantly market economies. Articles on mixed
               enterprise systems and nontheoretical articles on entre-
               preneurship also appear here (for theoretical articles on
               entrepreneurship and profits, see 0224).
052   Socialist and Communist Economic Systems   132
        0520   Socialist and Communist Economic Systems   132
               Articles discussing socialist or communist systems gener-
               ally or in a specific country are included here. For theory,
               see the 027 category and for planning, see the 113 category.
               Studies of particular communist or socialist countries or
               of particular sectors in the countries will be found in
               either the country division (124 subcategories) or the ap-
               propriate subject category for the article. For example,
               an article dealing with agriculture in the Soviet Union
               would be classified in one of the 710 subcategories.
053   Comparative Economic Systems   137
        0530   Comparative Economic Systems   137

100   Economic Growth; Development; Planning; Fluctuations
    110   Economic Growth; Development; Planning Theory and Policy   138
        For development theory, see 1120; for empirical studies of an individual
        country, see category 120, or for primarily historical studies, 040.
        111   Economic Growth Theory and Models   138
            Does not include theory and analyses of productivity, which
            appear in 2260.
            1110   Growth Theories   138

		1112	One and Two Sector Growth Models and Related Topics	139
		1113	Multisector Growth Models and Related Topics	139
		1114	Monetary Growth Models	140
	112	Economic Development Models and Theories		140
		1120	Economic Development Models and Theories	140

1120 *To be distinguished from individual country studies, although there will be some overlap and cross classification; for agriculture and development, see also 7100; for theory of export-led development and for import substitution and development, see also 4114.*

| | 113 | Economic Planning Theory and Policy | | 149 |

113 *For regional planning theory, see 9411; for regional planning models, see 9413.*

		1130	General	149
		1132	Economic Planning Theory	150
		1136	Economic Planning Policy	151
	114	Economics of War, Defense, and Disarmament		153
		1140	Economics of War, Defense, and Disarmament	153
120	Country Studies			158

120 *Country studies include complete country studies or broad studies involving several sectors of the economy, for centrally planned economies, see category 124. (The Index has adopted the breakdown used by the World Bank.)*

	121	Economic Studies of Developing Countries		158
		1210	General	158
		1211	Comparative Country Studies	159
		1213	European Countries	159
		1214	Asian Countries	160
		1215	African Countries	161
		1216	Latin American and Caribbean Countries	162
		1217	Oceanic Countries	164
	122	Economic Studies of Developed Countries		164
		1220	General	164
		1221	Comparative Country Studies	164
		1223	European Countries	165
		1224	Asian Countries	167
		1225	African Countries	
		1227	Oceanic Countries	167
		1228	North American Countries	167
	123	Comparative Studies of Developing, Developed, and/or Centrally Planned Economies	168
		1230	Comparative Studies of Developing, Developed, and/or Centrally Planned Economies	168

1230 *Includes comparisons of individual sectors.*

	124	Economic Studies of Centrally Planned Economies		169
		1240	General	169
		1241	Comparative Country Studies	169
		1243	European Countries	169

1243 *For Yugoslavia, see 1213.*

		1244	Asian Countries	171
		1246	Latin American and Caribbean Countries	171
130	Economic Fluctuations; Forecasting; Stabilization; Inflation			171
	131	Economic Fluctuations		171
		1310	General	171
		1312	Economic Fluctuations: Theory	171

| | | 1313 | Economic Fluctuations: Studies | 174 |

	132		Forecasting; Econometric Models	178
		1320	General	178
		1322	General Forecasts and Models	179
		1323	Specific Forecasts and Models	184
			For regional models see 9413.	
		1324	Forecasting and Econometric Models: Theory and Methodology	188
			See also 2120.	
	133		General Outlook and Stabilization Theories and Policies	190
		1330	General Outlook and General Economic Policy Discussions	190
		1331	Stabilization Theories and Policies	195
		1332	Wage and Price Controls	202
	134		Inflation and Deflation	203
		1340	General	203
			Nontheoretical articles (in general).	
		1342	Inflation Theories; Studies Illustrating Inflation Theories	205

200 Quantitative Economic Methods and Data
   210 Econometric, Statistical, and Mathematical Methods and Models   211

	211		Econometric and Statistical Methods and Models	211
		2110	General	211
			The general category includes many small statistical problems that are not classified into independent categories but are important for the general theory of statistical inference.	
		2112	Inferential Problems in Simultaneous Equation Systems	213
		2113	Distributed Lags and Serially Correlated Disturbance Terms; Inferential Problems in Single Equation Models	214
		2114	Multivariate Analysis, Statistical Information Theory, and Other Special Inferential Problems; Queuing Theory; Markov Chains	218
		2115	Bayesian Statistics and Bayesian Econometrics	218
		2116	Time Series and Spectral Analysis	220
		2117	Survey Methods; Sampling Methods	222
		2118	Theory of Index Numbers and Aggregation	222
		2119	Experimental Design; Social Experiments	223
			See 215 category for experimental economic methods.	
	212		Construction, Analysis, and Use of Econometric Models	223
		2120	Construction, Analysis, and Use of Econometric Models	223
			For actual models, see category 132. Includes control theory applications to econometric models. Also includes the analysis and comparison of different modeling strategies.	
	213		Mathematical Methods and Models	231
		2130	General	231
		2132	Optimization Techniques	231
		2133	Existence and Stability Conditions of Equilibrium	232
		2134	Computational Techniques	233
		2135	Construction, Analysis, and Use of Mathematical Programming Models	233
	214		Computer Programs	234
		2140	Computer Programs	234
	215		Experimental Economic Methods	234
		2150	Experimental Economic Methods	234

220   Economic and Social Statistical Data and Analysis   236
        2200   General   236
               For econometric and statistical methods, see categories
               211, 212, and 213.
   221   National Income Accounting   237
        2210   National Income Accounting Theory and Procedures   237
        2212   National Income Accounts   238
        2213   Income Distribution   241
               For theory of income distribution, see 0224 and 0235.
   222   Input–Output   244
        2220   Input–Output   244
               For regional input–output studies, see 9413; for theoretical
               general equilibrium models, see 0210.
   223   Financial Accounts   246
        2230   Financial Accounts; Financial Statistics; Empirical Analy-
               ses of Capital Adequacy   246
   224   National Wealth and Balance Sheets   247
        2240   National Wealth and Balance Sheets   247
               For consumer savings behavior, see 9211. For theories
               of bequests and intergenerational distribution of wealth,
               see 0243.
   225   Social Indicators: Data and Analysis   248
        2250   Social Indicators: Data and Analysis   248
   226   Productivity and Growth: Theory and Data   248
        2260   Productivity and Growth: Theory and Data   248
               For productivity studies, see also 8250.
   227   Prices   252
        2270   Prices   252
   228   Regional Statistics   255
        2280   Regional Statistics   255
               See also category 940.
   229   Microdata and Database Analysis   256
        2290   Microdata and Database Analysis   256

300   Domestic Monetary and Fiscal Theory and Institutions
   310   Domestic Monetary and Financial Theory and Institutions   256
        3100   General   256
   311   Domestic Monetary and Financial Theory and Policy   257
        3110   Domestic Monetary Theory and Policy   257
        3112   Monetary Theory; Empirical Studies Illustrating
               Theory   259
               Monetary theories of income determination are cross-ref-
               erenced to 0230.
        3116   Monetary Policy, Including All Central Banking Topics   274
               For relationship to commercial banks, see also 3120; for
               relationship to credit policies, see also category 315; for
               general policy discussions, see 1330.
   312   Commercial Banking   280
        3120   Commercial Banking   280
               Covers all aspects of commercial banks including regula-
               tion. For consumer credit, see 3151; for mortgages, see
               3152.
   313   Capital Markets   288
               For business finance and investment, see 520 categories; for inter-
               national finance, see 430 categories.

3130 General 288
3131 Capital Markets: Theory, Including Portfolio Selection, and Empirical Studies Illustrating Theory 289
For optimal bank portfolios, see also 3120; for valuation of the firm, see also 5220.
3132 Capital Markets: Empirical Studies, Including Regulation 296
Includes commodity markets. For foreign exchange markets see 4314.
314 Financial Intermediaries 309
3140 Financial Intermediaries 309
315 Credit to Business, Consumer, etc. (including mortgages) 311
3150 General 311
3151 Consumer Finance 312
3152 Mortgage Market 313
For effects on housing, see also 9320; for lending institutions, see 3120 and 3140.
3153 Business Credit 314
314 Fiscal Theory and Policy; Public Finance 314
3200 General 314
321 Fiscal Theory and Policy 315
3210 General 315
For relationship to business cycles, see also category 131; for stabilization, see 1331; for general macro, see also 0230.
3212 Fiscal Theory; Empirical Studies Illustrating Fiscal Theory 316
3216 Fiscal Policy 326
Includes only central government fiscal policy; for state and local fiscal policy, see 324 category.
322 National Government Expenditures and Budgeting 330
3220 General 330
3221 National Government Expenditures 331
For welfare expenditure, see 9110; for educational expenditure, see 9120; for health expenditure, see 9130.
3226 National Government Budgeting and Deficits 332
3228 National Government Debt Management 336
323 National Taxation, Revenue, and Subsidies 337
3230 National Taxation, Revenue, and Subsidies 337
For theory of taxation, see also 3212; for negative income taxes, see 9110; for social security taxes, see 9150; for local taxes, see 3242.
324 State and Local Government Finance 356
Includes theory of state and local public finance (see also 3212). For urban economics, see 930 category.
3240 General 356
3241 State and Local Government Expenditures and Budgeting 357
3242 State and Local Government Taxation, Subsidies, and Revenue 359
For national taxation, see 3230.
3243 State and Local Government Borrowing 362
325 Intergovernmental Financial Relationships 362
3250 Intergovernmental Financial Relationships 362

400 International Economics
4000 General 364
Most articles pertaining to the New International Economic Order are classified here.

410   International Trade Theory   366
      411   International Trade Theory   366
            4110   General   366
                   For theory of international investment, see 4410; for bal-
                   ance of payments theory, see 4312.
            4112   Theory of International Trade   366
            4113   Theory of Protection   370
                   For theory of protection in relation to development, see
                   also 4114; for commercial policy, see 4220.
            4114   Theory of International Trade and Economic Develop-
                   ment   374
                   For agriculture and development, see also 7100; for mul-
                   tinationals and development, see 4420; for inter-
                   national aid, see 4430; for international investment, see
                   4410.
420   Trade Relations; Commercial Policy; International Economic Integra-
      tion   377
            4200   General   377
      421   Trade Relations   377
            4210   Trade Relations   377
                   For trade policies designed to affect balance of payments,
                   see 4312 and 4313.
      422   Commercial Policy   396
            4220   Commercial Policy   396
                   For theoretical aspects of commercial policy, see
                   4113.
      423   Economic Integration   412
            4230   General   412
            4232   Theory of Economic Integration   412
            4233   Economic Integration: Policy and Empirical Studies   412
430   International Finance   417
            4300   General   417
      431   Open Economy Macroeconomics; Exchange Rates   417
                   Includes short-term capital movements. For International
                   Monetary Fund and other international monetary agencies
                   and groups, see 4320; for lending aspects of the IMF,
                   see 4430.
            4310   General   417
            4312   Open Economy Macroeconomic Theory: Balance of Pay-
                   ments and Adjustment Mechanisms   417
            4313   Open Economy Macroeconomic Studies: Balance of Pay-
                   ments and Adjustment Mechanisms   423
            4314   Exchange Rates and Markets: Theory and Studies   429
      432   International Monetary Arrangements   442
            4320   International Monetary Arrangements   442
      433   Private International Lending   448
            4330   Private International Lending   448
                   For aggregate debt service problem, see 4430.
440   International Investment and Foreign Aid   451
      441   International Investment and Long-term Capital Movements   451
            4410   General   451
            4411   International Investment and Long-term Capital Move-
                   ments: Theory   451
                   For theory of short-term capital movements and

flows related to balance of payments adjustments, see 4312.

4412   International Investment and Long-term Capital Movements: Studies   452
For empirical studies of short-term capital movements and flows related to balance of payments adjustments, see also 4313.

442   International Business and Multinational Enterprises   455
4420   International Business and Multinational Enterprises   455
Includes multinational firm management and policies and also host country policies.

443   International Lending and Aid (public)   462
4430   International Lending and Aid (public)   462
Includes technical assistance and debt services.

500   Administration; Business Finance; Marketing; Accounting
5000   General   472
510   Administration   472
511   Organization and Decision Theory   472
5110   Organization and Decision Theory   472
For collective decision-making, see 0250.
512   Managerial Economics   477
5120   Managerial Economics   477
513   Business and Public Administration   481
5130   General   481
For organization and decision theory, see 5110; for managerial economics, see 5120.
5131   Business Administration   482
5132   Public Administration   483
For administration of public enterprises, see 5131.
514   Goals and Objectives of Firms   484
5140   Goals and Objectives of Firms   484
See 0223 for theoretical discussions.
520   Business Finance and Investment   486
5200   Business Finance and Investment   486
521   Business Finance   486
5210   Business Finance   486
For multinational firm financing, see also 4420.
522   Business Investment   494
5220   Business Investment   494
For theory of investment by the firm, see also 0223; for macro investment theory, see also 0233; for capital markets and portfolio investment, see 313 categories.
530   Marketing and Advertising   497
531   Marketing and Advertising   497
5310   Marketing and Advertising   497
540   Accounting   503
541   Accounting   503
5410   Accounting   503

600   Industrial Organization; Technological Change; Industry Studies
6000   General
610   Industrial Organization and Public Policy   507
6100   General

611   Market Structure and Corporate Strategy   507
      6110   Market Structure and Corporate Strategy   507
             For microeconomic theory of monopoly, see also 0223,
             0225, and 0226; for antitrust policy, see 6120; for specific
             industry studies, see also the relevant industry study cate-
             gories.
612   Public Policy Toward Monopoly and Competition   524
      6120   Public Policy Toward Monopoly and Competition   524
             For public utility regulation, see 6130; for policy toward
             agriculture, see 7130; for policy toward transporta-
             tion, see 6150; for policy toward commercial banks, see
             3120.
613   Regulation of Public Utilities   530
      6130   Regulation of Public Utilities   530
             For supply, demand, and technology studies for individual
             firms or industries in electric and gas utilities, see 6352.
614   Public Enterprises   533
      6140   Public Enterprises   533
             For public utilities operated as a public enterprise, see
             also 6131.
615   Economics of Transportation   537
      6150   Economics of Transportation   537
             For urban transportation, see also 9330; for subsidies,
             see also 3230 and 3242; for location theory, see 9411.
616   Industrial Policy   542
      6160   Industrial Policy   542
619   Economics of Regulation   547
      6190   Economics of Regulation   547
620   Economics of Technological Change   552
      621   Technological Change; Innovation; Research and Development   552
             6210   General   552
             6211   Technological Change and Innovation   554
             6212   Research and Development   569
                    For effects of taxes and subsidies, see also 3230.
630   Industry Studies   573
             6300   General   573
                    Articles relating to all industrial sectors.
      631   Industry Studies: Manufacturing   575
             6310   General   575
             6312   Metals (iron, steel, and other)   583
             6313   Machinery (tools, electrical equipment, computers, com-
                    munication equipment, and appliances)   584
             6314   Transportation Equipment   585
             6315   Chemicals, Drugs, Plastics, Ceramics, Glass, Cement,
                    and Rubber   588
             6316   Textiles, Leather, and Clothing   590
             6317   Forest Products, Lumber, Paper, and Printing and Pub-
                    lishing   591
             6318   Food Processing, Tobacco, and Beverages   592
             6319   Other Industries
      632   Industry Studies: Extractive Industries   593
             6320   General   593
             6322   Mining (metal, coal, and other nonmetallic minerals)   593
                    For coal, see also 7230.

6323 Oil, Gas, and Other Fuels 594
See also 7230.
633 Industry Studies: Distributive Trades 599
6330 General 599
6332 Wholesale Trade
6333 Retail Trade 599
634 Industry Studies: Construction 600
6340 Construction 600
635 Industry Studies: Services and Related Industries 600
6350 General 600
6352 Electrical, Gas, Communication, and Information Services 602
For regulation of public utilities, see also 6130; for natural resource sources for the electrical and gas industries, see 7230; for conservation and pollution, see 7220.
6353 Personal Services 606
6354 Business and Legal Services 606
6355 Repair Services
6356 Insurance 606
6357 Real Estate 609
6358 Entertainment, Recreation, and Tourism 610
636 Nonprofit Industries: Theory and Studies 611
6360 Nonprofit Industries: Theory and Studies 611
For hospitals, see 9130; for education, see 9120; for entertainment, see 6358.
640 Economic Capacity 613
641 Economic Capacity 613
6410 Economic Capacity 613

700 Agriculture; Natural Resources
710 Agriculture 613
7100 General 613
For agriculture and development, see also 1120; for agricultural manpower, see also 8131; for agricultural migrant labor, see 8230.
711 Agricultural Supply and Demand Analysis 615
7110 Agricultural Supply and Demand Analysis 615
152 Agricultural Situation and Outlook 625
7120 Agricultural Situation and Outlook 625
713 Agricultural Policy, Domestic and International 627
7130 Agricultural Policy, Domestic and International 627
For farm subsidies, see also 3230; for agricultural commodity agreements, see also 4220.
714 Agricultural Finance 637
7140 Agricultural Finance 637
715 Agricultural Markets and Marketing; Cooperatives 638
7150 Agricultural Markets and Marketing; Cooperatives 638
For agricultural commodity agreements, see also 7130 and 4220; for futures markets, see 3132.
7151 Corporate Agriculture 642
716 Farm Management 642
7160 Farm Management 642
717 Land Reform and Land Use 649
7170 General 649
7171 Land Ownership and Tenure; Land Reform 650

7172   Land Development; Land Use; Irrigation Policy   651
*For urban and suburban land use, see category
930.*
718   Rural Economics   654
7180   Rural Economics   654
720   Natural Resources   660
7200   General
721   Natural Resources   660
7210   General   660
*For agricultural irrigation aspects, see 7172; for industrial
use of natural resources, see appropriate category 630
subdivision; for water and gas utilities, see also 6130;
for electricity, see also 6130 and 6352; for tax policies
and natural resources, see also 3230 and 3242.*
7211   Recreational Aspects of Natural Resources   668
722   Conservation and Pollution   669
7220   Conservation and Pollution   669
*For theoretical aspects of externalities and public goods,
see also 0240 and 0244; for tax policies and pollution,
see also 3230 and 3242; for energy, see 7230.*
723   Energy   678
7230   Energy   678
730   Economic Geography   690
731   Economic Geography   690
7310   Economic Geography   690
*For urban land, see 9310; for regional problems, see cate-
gory 940.*

800   Manpower; Labor; Population
8000   General   691
810   Manpower Training and Development; Labor Force and Supply   691
8100   General
811   Manpower Training and Development   691
8110   Manpower Training and Development   691
*Refers to government programs; for government spon-
sored programs for disadvantaged, see also 9110 and 9140;
for educational investment in human capital, see also 8510;
for executive training, see 5130.*
812   Occupation   693
8120   Occupation   693
*Includes supply and demand studies by occupation. For
employment studies, see 8243.*
813   Labor Force   696
Includes labor force studies by industry.
8130   General   696
8131   Agriculture   699
8132   Manufacturing   699
8133   Service   699
8134   Professional   700
8135   Government Employees   701
8136   Construction   702
8139   Other Sectors   702
820   Labor Markets; Public Policy   702
8200   General

821 Labor Economics 702
 8210 Labor Economics: Theory and Empirical Studies Illustrating Theory 702
  For empirical wage studies, see 8242; for empirical studies
  of employment, vacancies, and unemployment, see 8243.
  For distribution theory, see also 0224 and 0235. For dis-
  guised unemployment in agriculture, see 8131 and also
  8243.
822 Public Policy; Role of Government 713
 8220 General 713
 8221 Wages and Hours 714
 8222 Workmen's Compensation and Vocational Rehabilitation 715
  For other medical costs covered by employment, see 8242
  and 9130.
 8223 Factory Act and Safety Legislation 716
 8224 Unemployment Insurance 716
  For private pensions, see 8242.
 8225 Government Employment Policies (including employment services) 717
  For unemployment studies, see 8243.
 8226 Employment in the Public Sector 718
  See 8135 for statistical studies of government employees.
823 Labor Mobility; National and International Migration 719
 8230 Labor Mobility; National and International Migration 719
  For general migration, see 8410.
824 Labor Market Studies, Wages, Employment 723
 8240 General 723
 8241 Geographic Labor Market Studies 724
  Refers to labor market studies in specific geographical
  areas
 8242 Wage, Hours, and Fringe Benefit Studies 724
 8243 Employment Studies; Unemployment and Vacancies; Re-
  tirements and Quits 737
  For labor force shifts, see 8130; for labor market theory,
  see 8210.
825 Productivity Studies: Labor, Capital, and Total Factor 753
 8250 Productivity Studies: Labor, Capital, and Total Factor 753
826 Labor Markets: Demographic Characteristics 758
 8260 Labor Markets: Demographic Characteristics 758
  For economic effects of job discrimination involving minor-
  ities and women, see 9170.
830 Trade Unions; Collective Bargaining; Labor–Management Relations 764
 8300 General 764
831 Trade Unions 764
 8310 Trade Unions 764
832 Collective Bargaining 770
 8320 General 770
 8321 Collective Bargaining in the Private Sector 771
 8322 Collective Bargaining in the Public Sector 774
833 Labor–Management Relations 774
 8330 General 774
  For labor–management problems covered by collective
  bargaining agreements, see category 832; for theory of
  the labor-managed firm, see 0223 or 0271.

8331 Labor–Management Relations in the Private Sector 776
8332 Labor–Management Relations in the Public Sector 780
Includes labor–management relations in socialist countries.
840 Demographic Economics 781
  841 Demographic Economics 781
    8410 Demographic Economics 781
    For migration emphasizing labor market conditions, see 8230; for food supply, see also 7110; for nutrition, see also 9130.
850 Human Capital; Value of Human Life 793
  851 Human Capital; Value of Human Life 793
    8510 Human Capital; Value of Human Life 793
    For educational expenditures, financing, structure, and demand, see 9120; for manpower training, see 8110; for government sponsored employment policy, see 8225.

900 Welfare Programs; Consumer Economics; Urban and Regional Economics
  910 Welfare; Health; Education 797
    9100 General 797
  911 General Welfare Programs 798
    9110 General Welfare Programs 798
    For housing subsidies, see 9320.
  912 Economics of Education 800
    9120 Economics of Education 800
    For investment in human capital, see 8510.
  913 Economics of Health (including medical subsidy programs) 804
    9130 Economics of Health (including medical subsidy programs) 804
    For workmen's compensation, see 8222; for fringe benefits covering medical costs, see 8242; for general social security programs, see also 9150; for value of human life, see also 8510.
  914 Economics of Poverty 815
    9140 Economics of Poverty 815
    For negative income tax, see also 9110 and 3230; for rural poverty, see 7180.
  915 Social Security 818
    9150 Social Security 818
    For all pensions, see 8242; for medical subsidy programs, see 9130.
  916 Economics of Law; Economics of Crime 822
    9160 Economics of Law; Economics of Crime 822
    For antitrust law, see 6120.
  917 Economics of Minorities; Economics of Discrimination 829
    9170 Economics of Minorities; Economics of Discrimination 829
    For demographic characteristics in labor markets, see also 8260.
  918 Economics of Aging 838
    9180 Economics of Aging 838
  920 Consumer Economics 840
    921 Consumer Economics; Levels and Standards of Living 840
      9210 General 840
      For theory of the household, see 0222; for theory of con-

sumption function and saving, see also 0232; for consumers' cooperatives, see 0510; for consumer finance, see 3151.

9211 Living Standards, Composition of Overall Expenditures, and Empirical Consumption and Savings Studies 842
For consumer demand for or expenditures on specific commodities, see 9212; for distribution of wealth, see 2240.
9212 Expenditure Patterns and Consumption of Specific Items 848
For overall expenditure pattern, see 9211.
9213 Consumer Protection 853
930 Urban Economics 854
9300 General 854
931 Urban Economics and Public Policy 854
9310 Urban Economics and Public Policy 854
932 Housing Economics 860
9320 Housing Economics (including nonurban housing) 860
For construction industry studies, see 6340; for housing mortgages, see 3152.
933 Urban Transportation Economics 866
9330 Urban Transportation Economics 866
For other transportation studies, see 6150.
940 Regional Economics 866
941 Regional Economics 866
9410 General 866
For regional statistics, see 2280.
9411 Theory of Regional Economics 867
9412 Regional Economic Studies 869
9413 Regional Economic Models and Forecasts 877

Subject Index of Articles
in Current Periodicals and Collective Volumes

Abbreviated titles for journals are the same as those used in the *Journal of Economic Literature*. Full titles of journals may be found on pages x–xv.

Books have been identified by author or editor (noted *ed.*). In rare cases where two books by the same author appear, volumes are distinguished by I or II after the name. In some cases there appear two books by the same person, once as author, once as editor. These may be distinguished by *ed.* noted for the edited volume. Full titles and bibliographic references for books may be found on pages xvi–xxxv.

Geographic descriptors, when appropriate, appear in brackets at the end of the article citation.

000 General Economics; Theory; History; Systems

010 GENERAL ECONOMICS

011 General Economics

0110 General

Arrow, Kenneth J. Arrow and the Foundations of the Theory of Economic Policy: Reflections on the Essays. *Feiwel, G. R., ed. (II)*, 1987, pp. 727–34.

Barber, William J. Should the American Economic Association Have Toasted Simon Newcomb at Its 100th Birthday Party? *J. Econ. Perspectives*, Summer 1987, *1*(1), pp. 179–83.

Bauer, Peter. The Disregard of Reality. *Cato J.*, Spring/Summer 1987, *7*(1), pp. 29–42.

Baumann, Michael G.; Werden, Gregory J. and Williams, Michael A. Rankings of Economics Departments by Field. *Amer. Econ.*, Spring 1987, *31*(1), pp. 56–61.

Becker, William E. "Measurement" or Finding Things Out in Economics: A Comment. *J. Econ. Educ.*, Spring 1987, *18*(2), pp. 208–12. [G: U.S.]

Bergmann, Barbara R. "Measurement" or Finding Things Out in Economics. *J. Econ. Educ.*, Spring 1987, *18*(2), pp. 191–201.

Bliss, Christopher. Arrow's Vision of the Economic Process. *Feiwel, G. R., ed. (I)*, 1987, pp. 295–305.

Borcherding, Thomas E. Managing Editor's Comment [Economical Writing] [The Cost of Economical Writing]. *Econ. Inquiry*, October 1987, *25*(4), pp. 723–25.

Boulding, Kenneth E. The Economics of Pride and Shame. *Atlantic Econ. J.*, March 1987, *15*(1), pp. 10–19.

Brar, Jagjit S.; Nazemzadeh, Asghar and Chow, Peter C. Y. Ranking Top Economics Departments. *Atlantic Econ. J.*, March 1987, *15*(1), pp. 126. [G: U.S.]

Buchanan, James M. Bibliography of James M. Buchanan's Publications, 1949–1986. *Scand. J. Econ.*, 1987, *89*(1), pp. 17–37.

Buchanan, James M. Is Economics the Science of Choice? *Buchanan, J. M. (II)*, 1987, 1969, pp. 35–50.

Buchanan, James M. The Related but Distinct 'Sciences' of Economics and of Political Economy. *Buchanan, J. M. (I)*, 1987, 1982, pp. 87–97.

Colander, David and Klamer, Arjo. The Making of an Economist. *J. Econ. Perspectives*, Fall 1987, *1*(2), pp. 95–111. [G: U.S.]

DeLorme, Charles D., Jr. and Kamerschen, David R. What *Who's Who in Economics* Tells Us about the Economics Profession. *Quart. Rev. Econ. Bus.*, Winter 1987, *27*(4), pp. 65–79.

Dexter, Keith and Williams, Roland E. The Milk Marketing Board's Award Scheme for Study in Agricultural Economics. *J. Agr. Econ.*, January 1987, *38*(1), pp. 65–73. [G: U.K.]

Dugger, William M. Power: An Institutional Framework of Analysis. *Albelda, R.; Gunn, C. and Waller, W., eds.*, 1987, 1980, pp. 253–62.

da Empoli, Domenico. The 1987 Meeting of the European Public Choice Society. *Econ. Scelte Pubbliche/J. Public Finance Public Choice*, May-Aug. 1987, *5*(2), pp. 135–41. [G: Europe]

Fels, Rendigs. Fundamental Economic Concepts—Another Perspective: A Comment. *J. Econ. Educ.*, Spring 1987, *18*(2), pp. 121–26.

Gibbons, Jean D. and Fish, Mary. Football Rankings: A Forecast for Economists' Productivity. *Atlantic Econ. J.*, July 1987, *15*(2), pp. 92.

Goff, Brian L., et al. The Incentive to Cite. *J. Inst. Theoretical Econ.*, September 1987, *143*(3), pp. 467–76. [G: U.S.]

Golden, John M.; Carstensen, Fred and Weiner, Paul. An Evaluation of 50 "Ranked" Economics Departments: Comment. *Southern Econ. J.*, July 1987, *54*(1), pp. 212–15. [G: U.S.]

Gowdy, John M. Bio-economics: Social Economy versus the Chicago School. *Int. J. Soc. Econ.*, 1987, *14*(1), pp. 32–42.

Heilbroner, Robert L. Fundamental Economic Concepts—Another Perspective. *J. Econ. Educ.*, Spring 1987, *18*(2), pp. 111–20.

Henderson, Margaret. Thesis Titles for Degrees in the United Kingdom 1985/86 and 1986/87. *Econ. J.*, March 1987, *97*(385), pp. 219–26. [G: U.K.]

Henry, Jacques. The Economics of the Afterlife.

011 General Economics

Écon. Soc., September 1987, *21*(9), pp. 245–56.

High, Jack C. The Costs of Economical Writing. *Econ. Inquiry*, July 1987, *25*(3), pp. 543–45.

Highsmith, Robert J. and Kasper, Hirschel. Rethinking the Scope of Economics. *J. Econ. Educ.*, Spring 1987, *18*(2), pp. 101–05.

Hirshleifer, Jack. Natural Economy versus Political Economy. *Hirshleifer, J.*, 1987, *1978*, pp. 169–93.

Juster, F. Thomas. The Role of Microdata in the Production of Economic Knowledge. *Green, L. and Kagel, J. H., eds.*, 1987, pp. 67–90.

Klamer, Arjo. As if Economists and Their Subject Were Rational. *Nelson, J. S.; Megill, A. and McCloskey, D. N., eds.*, 1987, pp. 163–83.

Krislov, Joseph and Mead, John. Changes in IR Programs since the Mid-Sixties. *Ind. Relat.*, Spring 1987, *26*(2), pp. 208–12. [G: U.S.]

Kuttner, Robert. The Poverty of Economics. *Albelda, R.; Gunn, C. and Waller, W., eds.*, 1987, *1985*, pp. 18–34.

Laband, David N. A Qualitative Test of Journal Discrimination against Women. *Eastern Econ. J.*, Apr.-June 1987, *13*(2), pp. 149–53. [G: U.S.]

Laband, David N. An Evaluation of 50 "Ranked" Economics Departments: Reply. *Southern Econ. J.*, July 1987, *54*(1), pp. 216–18. [G: U.S.]

Lipscombe, Geoffrey. *Lloyds Bank Review* 1917–1987. *Lloyds Bank Rev.*, October 1987, (166), pp. 33–44. [G: U.K.]

Lowe, Adolph. What Is Evolutionary Economics? Remarks upon Receipt of the Veblen–Commons Award. *Lowe, A.*, 1987, *1980*, pp. 226–33.

Malouin, Jean-Louis and Outreville, J. François. The Relative Impact of Economics Journals: A Cross-Country Survey and Comparison. *J. Econ. Bus.*, August 1987, *39*(3), pp. 267–77. [G: U.S.; Canada; U.K.; France]

Marinović, Ljubica. Bibliografija ekonomske analize. (Bibliography of Economic Analysis and Workers' Management 1967–1986. With English summary.) *Econ. Anal. Workers' Manage.*, 1987, *21*(1), pp. 117–91.

Matthews, R. C. O. An Eclectic View from Cambridge: An Interview. *Feiwel, G. R., ed. (II)*, 1987, pp. 613–34.

McCloskey, Donald N. Reply [Economical Writing]. *Econ. Inquiry*, July 1987, *25*(3), pp. 547–48.

Meller, Patricio. Una Revisión de la Crisis de la Ciencia Económica. (A Review of the Crisis of the Economic Science. With English summary.) *Colección Estud. CIEPLAN*, December 1987, (22), pp. 153–72.

Nalebuff, Barry. Choose a Curtain, Duel-ity, Two Point Conversions, and More. *J. Econ. Perspectives*, Fall 1987, *1*(2), pp. 157–63.

Nalebuff, Barry. Noisy Prisoners, Manhattan Locations, and More. *J. Econ. Perspectives*, Summer 1987, *1*(1), pp. 185–91.

Nell, Edward J. Economics: The Revival of Political Economy. *Albelda, R.; Gunn, C. and Wal-*

ler, W., eds., 1987, *1972*, pp. 89–103.

Niemi, Albert W., Jr. Institutional Contributions to the Leading Finance Journals, 1975 through 1986: A Note. *J. Finance*, December 1987, *42*(5), pp. 1389–97.

Robinson, Joan. The Disintegration of Economics. *Albelda, R.; Gunn, C. and Waller, W., eds.*, 1987, *1980*, pp. 60–67.

Saffran, Bernard. Recommendations for Further Reading. *J. Econ. Perspectives*, Fall 1987, *1*(2), pp. 165–67.

Saffran, Bernard. Recommendations for Further Reading. *J. Econ. Perspectives*, Summer 1987, *1*(1), pp. 193–95.

Samuelson, Paul A. How Economics Has Changed. *J. Econ. Educ.*, Spring 1987, *18*(2), pp. 107–10.

Samuelson, Paul A. Joint Authorship in Science: Serendipity with Wolfgang Stolper. *J. Inst. Theoretical Econ.*, June 1987, *143*(2), pp. 235–43.

Saunders, Philip. Fundamental Economic Concepts—Another Perspective: A Comment. *J. Econ. Educ.*, Spring 1987, *18*(2), pp. 127–33.

Schmitz, Mark, et al. An Organizational Alternative for Academics: A Sporting Proposal. *Atlantic Econ. J.*, March 1987, *15*(1), pp. 63–66.

Schumpeter, Joseph A. Some Questions of Principle. *Samuels, W. J., ed.*, 1987, pp. 93–116.

Street, James H. The Reality of Power and the Poverty of Economic Doctrine. *Dietz, J. L. and Street, J. H., eds.*, 1987, *1983*, pp. 16–32. [G: Chile; Argentina; Paraguay; Uruguay]

Swanson, Dorothy. Annual Bibliography on American Labor History, 1986: Periodicals, Dissertations, and Research in Progress. *Labor Hist.*, Fall 1987, *28*(4), pp. 484–96. [G: U.S.]

Tool, Marc R. Evolutionary Economics I: Foundations of Institutional Thought: Introduction. *J. Econ. Issues*, September 1987, *21*(3), pp. 951–67.

Urquidi, Victor L. Structural Change, Economic Interdependence and World Development: Introduction. *Urquidi, V. L., ed.*, 1987, pp. 13–29.

Venkateswarlu, Tadiboyina. International Economics: Survey of Course Reading Materials in Universities in Canada and the United States of America. *Amer. Econ.*, Spring 1987, *31*(1), pp. 66–84. [G: U.S.; Canada]

Vredeveld, George M. Economics: Musing or Reality—Some Thoughts on Bergmann's Methodology. *J. Econ. Educ.*, Spring 1987, *18*(2), pp. 203–07.

Williams, William W. Institutional Propensities to Publish in Academic Journals of Business Administration: 1979–1984. *Quart. Rev. Econ. Bus.*, Spring 1987, *27*(1), pp. 77–94. [G: U.S.]

Zahid, Khan H. An Analysis of the Institutional Affiliation of Recent Ph.D.s in Economics in the Top 18 Graduate Programs, by Fields of Specialization. *Amer. Econ.*, Fall 1987, *31*(2), pp. 64–68. [G: U.S.]

0112 Role of Economics; Role of Economists

Aaron, Henry J. and Thompson, Lawrence H. Social Security and the Economists. *Berkowitz, E. D., ed.*, 1987, pp. 79–99.   [G: U.S.]

Åslund, Anders. Gorbachev's Economic Advisors. *Soviet Econ.*, July-Sept. 1987, *3*(3), pp. 246–69.   [G: U.S.S.R.]

Barre, Raymond. Finance and the International Economy: Preface. *[Marjolin, R.]*, 1987, pp. ix–xiv.

Bateman, Lanny. Agricultural Economics: A Fork in the Road or a Crooked Trail? *Southern J. Agr. Econ.*, July 1987, *19*(1), pp. 1–5.   [G: U.S.]

Beattie, Bruce R. and Watts, Myles J. The Proper Preeminent Role of Parent Disciplines and Learned Societies in Setting the Agenda at Land Grant Universities. *Western J. Agr. Econ.*, December 1987, *12*(2), pp. 95–103.   [G: U.S.]

Becker, Gary S. Economic Analysis and Human Behavior. *Green, L. and Kagel, J. H., eds.*, 1987, pp. 3–17.

Boynton, G. R. and Deissenberg, Christophe. Models of the Economy Implicit in Public Discourse. *Policy Sci.*, 1987, *20*(2), pp. 129–51.

Brunner, Karl. The Limits of Economic Policy. *Pejovich, S., ed.*, 1987, *1985*, pp. 33–52.

Buchanan, James M. Is Economics the Science of Choice? *Buchanan, J. M. (I)*, 1987, *1960*, pp. 63–77.

Buchanan, James M. What Should Economists Do? *Buchanan, J. M. (II)*, 1987, *1964*, pp. 21–33.

Butos, William N. Rhetoric and Rationality: A Review Essay. *Eastern Econ. J.*, July-Sept. 1987, *13*(3), pp. 295–304.

Clodius, Robert L. A Personal View of the Contributions of Willard F. Mueller. *Wills, R. L.; Caswell, J. A. and Culbertson, J. D., eds.*, 1987, pp. 12–17.   [G: U.S.]

Coats, A. W. and Pressman, Steven. The Rhetoric of Economics: Further Comments. *Eastern Econ. J.*, July-Sept. 1987, *13*(3), pp. 305–07.

Colander, David and Klamer, Arjo. The Making of an Economist. *J. Econ. Perspectives*, Fall 1987, *1*(2), pp. 95–111.   [G: U.S.]

Cookingham, Mary E. Social Economists and Reform: Berkeley, 1906–1961. *Hist. Polit. Econ.*, Spring 1987, *19*(1), pp. 47–65.

Culp, Jerome M. Economists on the Bench: Foreward. *Law Contemp. Probl.*, Autumn 1987, *50*(4), pp. 1–16.

Cummins, J. David. Revitalizing Risk and Insurance Education and Research. *J. Risk Ins.*, March 1987, *54*(1), pp. 9–20.

Dahlgran, Roger A. Agricultural Economists in the Information Age: Awareness, Usage, and Attitudes toward Electronic Bibliographic Databases. *Amer. J. Agr. Econ.*, February 1987, *69*(1), pp. 166–73.

Davis, Michael. The Use of Professions. *Bus. Econ.*, October 1987, *22*(4), pp. 5–10.

Deane, Phyllis. The Scope and Method of Economic Science. *Albelda, R.; Gunn, C. and Waller, W., eds.*, 1987, *1983*, pp. 35–47.

Debertin, David L. and Bradford, Garnett L. Agricultural Economics Research and the Experiment Station System. *Southern J. Agr. Econ.*, December 1987, *19*(2), pp. 195–201.

Dobbs, Thomas L. Toward More Effective Involvement of Agricultural Economists in Multidisciplinary Research and Extension Programs. *Western J. Agr. Econ.*, July 1987, *12*(1), pp. 8–16.   [G: U.S.]

Dow, Sheila C. The Scottish Political Economy Tradition. *Scot. J. Polit. Econ.*, November 1987, *34*(4), pp. 335–48.   [G: U.K.]

Duncan, Joseph W. Statistics Corner. *Bus. Econ.*, April 1987, *22*(2), pp. 57–58.   [G: U.S.]

Dunlop, John T. Economists in Labor–Management–Government Proceedings. *Bus. Econ.*, October 1987, *22*(4), pp. 21–26.

Eusepi, Giuseppe. The Third Revolution in Economic Thinking: Social Economy in a New Perspective. *Int. J. Soc. Econ.*, 1987, *14*(7/8/9), pp. 160–69.

Finn, Daniel Rush. When Are Economic Explanations Persuasive? A View from Social Economics. *Rev. Soc. Econ.*, April 1987, *45*(1), pp. 1–13.

Fullerton, Thomas M., Jr. The Business Economist at Work: Executive Office of the Governor of Idaho. *Bus. Econ.*, July 1987, *22*(3), pp. 43–45.   [G: U.S.]

Gottfries, Nils and Hylton, Keith. Are M.I.T. Students Rational? Report on a Survey. *J. Econ. Behav. Organ.*, March 1987, *8*(1), pp. 113–20.

Guthrie, William. The Roles of Intellectual Pedigrees in Economic Science. *Amer. J. Econ. Soc.*, January 1987, *46*(1), pp. 49–60.

Hoffman, A. C. Recollections of a Friend and Colleague. *Wills, R. L.; Caswell, J. A. and Culbertson, J. D., eds.*, 1987, pp. 18–22.   [G: U.S.]

James, George W. The Business Economist: Work in an Airline. *Bus. Econ.*, April 1987, *22*(2), pp. 54–56.   [G: U.S.]

Kerr, Roger. Ideas, Interests, Experience and the Economic Adviser. *World Econ.*, June 1987, *10*(2), pp. 131–53.   [G: New Zealand]

Lal, Deepak. Markets, Mandarins, and Mathematicians. *Cato J.*, Spring/Summer 1987, *7*(1), pp. 43–70.

Lawson, Tony. The Relative/Absolute Nature of Knowledge and Economic Analysis. *Econ. J.*, December 1987, *97*(388), pp. 951–70.

Lindner, Bob. Toward a Framework for Evaluating Agricultural Economics Research. *Australian J. Agr. Econ.*, August 1987, *31*(2), pp. 95–111.

Mangum, Garth L.; Mangum, Stephen L. and Phillips, Peter. The Three (at Least) Worlds of Economic Theory. *Challenge*, Mar./Apr. 1987, *30*(1), pp. 57–59.

Martin, James E. Land-Grant Organization to Meet the Future. *Southern J. Agr. Econ.*, July 1987, *19*(1), pp. 31–34.   [G: U.S.]

McCloskey, Donald N. The Rhetoric of Economics: Response to My Critics. *Eastern Econ. J.*,

July-Sept. 1987, *13*(3), pp. 308–11.

McKinney, George W. Ethics and the Business Economist. *Bus. Econ.*, October 1987, *22*(4), pp. 15–20.

Meier, Gerald M. Towards More Effective Development Policy-making. *[Kitamura, H.]*, 1987, pp. 204–11. **[G: LDCs]**

Moor, Roy E. Ethics for Businesses...and Their Economists. *Bus. Econ.*, October 1987, *22*(4), pp. 11–14.

Munroe, Tapan. The Business Economist at Work: The Pacific Gas & Electric Company. *Bus. Econ.*, January 1987, *22*(1), pp. 56–57. **[G: U.S.]**

Murray, Michael L. Pride in the Ties That Bind. *J. Risk Ins.*, December 1987, *54*(4), pp. 653–57. **[G: U.S.]**

Myrdal, Gunnar. Utilitarianism and Modern Economics. *Feiwel, G. R., ed. (II)*, 1987, pp. 273–78.

Naqvi, Syed Nawab Haider. The Anatomy of 'Failures'. *Pakistan Devel. Rev.*, Autumn 1987, *26*(3), pp. 257–72.

Nelson, Robert H. The Economics Profession and the Making of Public Policy. *J. Econ. Lit.*, March 1987, *25*(1), pp. 49–91. **[G: U.S.]**

O'Carroll, Lloyd T. The Business Economist at Work: Reynolds Metals Company. *Bus. Econ.*, October 1987, *22*(4), pp. 45–47.

Peden, G. C. The Policy Debate: Keynes. *Glynn, S. and Booth, A., eds.*, 1987, pp. 97–108. **[G: U.K.]**

Perlman, Mark. Concerning Winters of Discontent: Does Methodology or Rhetoric Contain the Answer to a Possible Malaise? *Int. J. Soc. Econ.*, 1987, *14*(7/8/9), pp. 9–18.

Portes, Richard. Economics in Europe. *Europ. Econ. Rev.*, August 1987, *31*(6), pp. 1329–40. **[G: E. Europe]**

Prawiranegara, Sjafruddin. Recollections of My Career. *Bull. Indonesian Econ. Stud.*, December 1987, *23*(3), pp. 100–108.

Rivlin, Alice M. Economics and the Political Process. *Amer. Econ. Rev.*, March 1987, *77*(1), pp. 1–10. **[G: U.S.]**

Roskamp, Karl W. History of the International Institute of Public Finance. *Roskamp, K. W., ed.*, 1987, pp. 1–17.

Ross, Jane L. Research and Social Security Policy in the United States. *Soc. Sec. Bull.*, October 1987, *50*(10), pp. 4–12. **[G: U.S.]**

Rostow, Walt W. Reflections on the Past and Future of Political Economy. *Rostow, W. W.*, 1987, pp. 1–18.

Sachs, Ignacy. The Logic of Development. *Sachs, I.*, 1987, pp. 12–18.

Solomon, David. What Boundaries for Business? Editorial. *Managerial Dec. Econ.*, March 1987, *8*(1), pp. 1–4.

Sprinkel, Beryl W. Confronting Monetary Policy Dilemmas: The Legacy of Homer Jones. *Fed. Res. Bank St. Louis Rev.*, March 1987, *69*(3), pp. 5–8. **[G: U.S.]**

Sun, Li-teh. Inner Equilibrium and Economic Equilibrium: A Confucian Complement to

Economic Man. *Int. J. Soc. Econ.*, 1987, *14*(10), pp. 40–55. **[G: U.S.]**

Truu, M. L. Confused Thinking, Intellectual Fashion and Received Knowledge in Economics Today. *S. Afr. J. Econ.*, December 1987, *55*(4), pp. 319–32.

Verdier, James M. Advising Congressional Decision-makers: Guidelines for Economists. *Cordray, D. S. and Lipsey, M. W., eds.*, 1987, *1984*, pp. 235–52. **[G: U.S.]**

Walters, Alan. Frameworks for Thinking about Reality [Markets, Mandarins, and Mathematicians]. *Cato J.*, Spring/Summer 1987, *7*(1), pp. 71–75.

Whalen, Charles J. A Reason to Look beyond Neoclassical Economics: Some Major Shortcomings of Orthodox Theory. *J. Econ. Issues*, March 1987, *21*(1), pp. 259–80.

Whitman, Marina von Neumann. New Directions for the Business Economist. *Bus. Econ.*, January 1987, *22*(1), pp. 51–55.

Williamson, John. Political Economy and International Money: Selected Essays of John Williamson: Autobiographical Introduction. *Williamson, J.*, 1987, pp. 1–12.

Williamson, Oliver E. Pretrial Uses of Economists: On the Use of 'Incentive Logic' to Screen Predation. *Williamson, O.*, 1987, *1984*, pp. 282–300. **[G: U.S.]**

Wing, Kennard T. What's an Economist to Do? *Bus. Econ.*, July 1987, *22*(3), pp. 34–37.

Yotopoulos, Pan A. The Anatomy of 'Failures': Comments. *Pakistan Devel. Rev.*, Autumn 1987, *26*(3), pp. 273–74.

Zellner, Arnold. Science, Economics and Public Policy. *Amer. Econ.*, Fall 1987, *31*(2), pp. 3–7.

0113 Relation of Economics to Other Disciplines

Ascher, William. Policy Sciences and the Economic Approach in a 'Post-positivist' Era: Editorial. *Policy Sci.*, April 1987, *20*(1), pp. 3–9.

Balabkins, Nicholas W. Value and Value-Judgements in Economics: Rugina's Contribution. *Int. J. Soc. Econ.*, 1987, *14*(3/4/5), pp. 50–62.

Bates, Robert H. Essays on the Political Economy of Rural Africa: Conclusion. *Bates, R. H.*, 1987, pp. 134–47.

Breyer, Stephen G. Economics and Judging: An Afterword on Cooter and Wald. *Law Contemp. Probl.*, Autumn 1987, *50*(4), pp. 245–52. **[G: U.S.]**

Brunner, Karl. The Perception of Man and the Conception of Society: Two Approaches to Understanding Society. *Econ. Inquiry*, July 1987, *25*(3), pp. 367–88.

Chanier, Paul. Les limites des postulats de symétrie et d'invariance dans les sciences et en économique. (On the Limits of Symmetry and Invariance Postulates in Science and Economics. With English summary.) *Écon. Soc.*, January 1987, *21*(1), pp. 5–84.

Cookingham, Mary E. Social Economists and Reform: Berkeley, 1906–1961. *Hist. Polit. Econ.*, Spring 1987, *19*(1), pp. 47–65.

Covich, Alan P. Optimal Use of Space by Neighboring Central Place Foragers: When and Where to Store Surplus Resources. *Green, L. and Kagel, J. H., eds.*, 1987, pp. 249–94.

Culp, Jerome M. Judex Economicus. *Law Contemp. Probl.*, Autumn 1987, *50*(4), pp. 95–140. **[G: U.S.]**

Fox, Eleanor M. Chairman Miller, the Federal Trade Commission, Economics, and *Rashomon. Law Contemp. Probl.*, Autumn 1987, *50*(4), pp. 33–55. **[G: U.S.]**

Ghiselin, Michael T. Principles and Prospects for General Economy. *Radnitzky, G. and Bernholz, P., eds.*, 1987, pp. 21–31.

Ghiselin, Michael T. The Economics of Scientific Discovery. *Radnitzky, G. and Bernholz, P., eds.*, 1987, pp. 271–82.

Hadari, Saguiv A. What Are Preference Explanations? The Interpretive Core of Economic Modeling. *Soc. Sci. Quart.*, June 1987, *68*(2), pp. 340–57.

Hirshleifer, Jack. Privacy: Its Origin, Function, and Future. *Hirshleifer, J.*, 1987, *1980*, pp. 194–210.

Hodgson, Geoffrey M. Economics and Systems Theory. *J. Econ. Stud.*, 1987, *14*(4), pp. 65–86.

Holbrook, Morris B. What Is Consumer Research? *J. Cons. Res.*, June 1987, *14*(1), pp. 128–32.

Hursh, Steven R. and Bauman, Richard A. The Behavioral Analysis of Demand. *Green, L. and Kagel, J. H., eds.*, 1987, pp. 117–65.

Kagel, John H. and Green, Leonard. Intertemporal Choice Behavior: Evaluation of Economic and Psychological Models. *Green, L. and Kagel, J. H., eds.*, 1987, pp. 166–84.

Latin, Howard. Legal and Economic Considerations in the Decisions of Judge Breyer. *Law Contemp. Probl.*, Autumn 1987, *50*(4), pp. 57–86. **[G: U.S.]**

Lea, S. E. G. Animal Experiments in Economic Psychology. *Green, L. and Kagel, J. H., eds.*, 1987, *1981*, pp. 95–116.

Lee, Li Way. Cognitive and Market Failures: Some Complex Policy Implications. *J. Behav. Econ.*, Fall 1987, *16*(3), pp. 51–57.

Liebhafsky, Herbert H. Law and Economics from Different Perspectives. *J. Econ. Issues*, December 1987, *21*(4), pp. 1809–36.

Lowe, Adolph. Is the Glass Half Full or Half Empty? A Self-critique. *Lowe, A.*, 1987, *1982*, pp. 234–50.

Magat, Wesley A. Howard Latin's Analysis of the Legal and Economic Considerations in the Decisions of Judge Breyer. *Law Contemp. Probl.*, Autumn 1987, *50*(4), pp. 87–93. **[G: U.S.]**

Mayhew, Anne. Culture: Core Concept under Attack. *J. Econ. Issues*, June 1987, *21*(2), pp. 587–603.

Montesano, Aldo. The Life and Works of Tullio Bagiotti (1921–1983). *Int. J. Soc. Econ.*, 1987, *14*(7/8/9), pp. 156–59.

Neale, Walter C. Institutions. *J. Econ. Issues*, September 1987, *21*(3), pp. 1177–1206.

Rachlin, Howard. Animal Choice and Human

Choice. *Green, L. and Kagel, J. H., eds.*, 1987, pp. 48–64.

Rizzo, Mario J. and Arnold, Frank S. An Economic Framework for Statutory Interpretation. *Law Contemp. Probl.*, Autumn 1987, *50*(4), pp. 165–80.

Sinder, Janet. Economists as Judges: A Selective, Annotated Bibliography. *Law Contemp. Probl.*, Autumn 1987, *50*(4), pp. 279–86.

Smith, T. Alexander. Policy Analysis, Policy Process Analysis, and the Murmurings of Ideology. *Nagel, S. S., ed.*, 1987, pp. 3–38.

Tobin, James and Dolbear, F. Trenery, Jr. On the Relevance of Psychology to Economic Theory and Research. *Tobin, J. (II)*, 1987, *1963*, pp. 291–98.

Vaughan, William, Jr. and Herrnstein, R. J. Stability, Melioration, and Natural Selection. *Green, L. and Kagel, J. H., eds.*, 1987, pp. 185–215.

Wald, Patricia M. Limits on the Use of Economic Analysis in Judicial Decisionmaking. *Law Contemp. Probl.*, Autumn 1987, *50*(4), pp. 225–44. **[G: U.S.]**

Whichard, Willis P. A Common Law Judge's View of the Appropriate Use of Economics in Common Law Adjudication. *Law Contemp. Probl.*, Autumn 1987, *50*(4), pp. 253–63.

Wilde, Louis L. Consumer Behavior under Imperfect Information: A Review of Psychological and Marketing Research as It Relates to Economic Theory. *Green, L. and Kagel, J. H., eds.*, 1987, pp. 219–48.

Wisman, Jon D. Human Interests, Modes of Rationality and the Social Foundations of Economic Science. *Int. J. Soc. Econ.*, 1987, *14*(7/8/9), pp. 88–98.

0114 Relation of Economics to Social Values

Atkinson, Glen W. Instrumentalism and Economic Policy: The Quest for Reasonable Value. *J. Econ. Issues*, March 1987, *21*(1), pp. 189–202.

Ault, Richard W.; Ekelund, Robert B., Jr. and Tollison, Robert D. The Pope and the Price of Meat: A Public Choice Perspective. *Kyklos*, 1987, *40*(3), pp. 399–413.

Balabkins, Nicholas W. Value and Value-Judgements in Economics: Rugina's Contribution. *Int. J. Soc. Econ.*, 1987, *14*(3/4/5), pp. 50–62.

Benne, Robert. The Bishops' Letter—A Protestant Reading. *Gannon, T. M., ed.*, 1987, pp. 76–85. **[G: U.S.]**

Biedenkopf, Kurt. The Catholic Challenge to the American Economy: A European Point of View. *Gannon, T. M., ed.*, 1987, pp. 207–17. **[G: U.S.]**

Birnbaum, Norman. The Bishops in the Iron Cage: The Dilemmas of Advanced Industrial Society. *Gannon, T. M., ed.*, 1987, pp. 153–78. **[G: U.S.]**

Brunner, Karl. The Perception of Man and the Conception of Society: Two Approaches to Understanding Society. *Econ. Inquiry*, July 1987, *25*(3), pp. 367–88.

Buchanan, James M. Markets, States, and the Extent of Morals. *Buchanan, J. M. (II)*, 1987, 1978, pp. 269–75.

Buchanan, James M. Moral Community, Moral Order, or Moral Anarchy. *Buchanan, J. M. (II)*, 1987, 1981, pp. 289–301.   [G: U.S.; Japan]

Buchanan, James M. The Moral Dimension of Debt Financing. *Fink, R. H. and High, J. C., eds.*, 1987, 1985, pp. 102–07.

Burke, James E. Reactions from Management: Manufacturing. *Gannon, T. M., ed.*, 1987, pp. 218–27.   [G: U.S.]

Burkett, Paul. Instrumental Justice and Social Economics: Some Comments from a Marxian Perspective. *Rev. Soc. Econ.*, December 1987, 45(3), pp. 313–24.

Byron, William J. The Bishops' Letter and Everyday Life. *Gannon, T. M., ed.*, 1987, pp. 246–55.   [G: U.S.]

Calvez, Jean-Yves. Economic Policy Issues in Roman Catholic Social Teaching: An International Perspective. *Gannon, T. M., ed.*, 1987, pp. 15–26.   [G: U.S.]

Choudhury, Masudul Alam. A Study of Ethico-Economics in the General Equilibrium Field. *Int. J. Soc. Econ.*, 1987, 14(3/4/5), pp. 207–18.

Christ, Carl. Unemployment and Macroeconomics. *Gannon, T. M., ed.*, 1987, pp. 116–27.   [G: U.S.]

Collazzo, Charles. The Need for Voluntary Consensus Systems in Setting Socio-economic Standards. *Int. J. Soc. Econ.*, 1987, 14(7/8/9), pp. 115–26.

Curran, Charles E. Relating Religious–Ethical Inquiry to Economic Policy. *Gannon, T. M., ed.*, 1987, pp. 42–54.   [G: U.S.]

Davis, John B. Marx's Conception of Ethics in Capitalist Society. *Samuels, W. J., ed.*, 1987, pp. 51–90.

Davis, John B. The Science of Happiness and the Marginalization of Ethics. *Rev. Soc. Econ.*, December 1987, 45(3), pp. 298–312.

Derry, Robbin. Moral Reasoning in Work-Related Conflicts. *Frederick, W. C., ed.*, 1987, pp. 25–49.   [G: U.S.]

Ditz, Gerhard W. Smith and Keynes: Religious Differences in Economic Philosophy. *Economia (Portugal)*, October 1987, 11(3), pp. 399–431.

Diwan, Romesh. Mahatma Gandhi and the Economics of Non-exploitation. *Int. J. Soc. Econ.*, 1987, 14(2), pp. 39–52.

Donahue, Thomas R. and Oswald, Rudolph A. Labor Views the Pastoral Letter on the Economy. *Gannon, T. M., ed.*, 1987, pp. 228–45.   [G: U.S.]

Elliott, John E. Moral and Ethical Considerations in Karl Marx's Robust Vision of the Future Society. *Int. J. Soc. Econ.*, 1987, 14(10), pp. 3–26.

Etzioni, Amitai. Toward a Kantian Socio-economics. *Rev. Soc. Econ.*, April 1987, 45(1), pp. 37–47.

Farrell, Kenneth R. Policy Issues and Options for Agriculture and Rural America. *Gannon,*

T. M., ed., 1987, pp. 128–37.   [G: U.S.]

Friedman, Milton. The Catholic Challenge to the American Economy: Good Ends, Bad Means. *Gannon, T. M., ed.*, 1987, pp. 99–106.   [G: U.S.]

Gannon, Thomas M. The Catholic Challenge to the American Economy: Introduction. *Gannon, T. M., ed.*, 1987, pp. 1–7.

Gore, Albert, Jr. The Shape of Our Destiny: America's Economic Choices. *Gannon, T. M., ed.*, 1987, pp. 179–86.   [G: U.S.]

Green, Ronald. The Bishops' Letter—A Jewish Reading. *Gannon, T. M., ed.*, 1987, pp. 86–96.   [G: U.S.]

Henley, Andrew. Economic Orthodoxy and the Free Market System: A Christian Critique. *Int. J. Soc. Econ.*, 1987, 14(10), pp. 56–66.

Hickerson, Steven R. Instrumental Valuation: The Normative Compass of Institutional Economics. *J. Econ. Issues*, September 1987, 21(3), pp. 1117–43.

Hill, Lewis E. A Pragmatic Methodology for Social Economics: A Preliminary Proposal. *Int. J. Soc. Econ.*, 1987, 14(3/4/5), pp. 140–45.

Johnson, Thomas S. An Agenda for Economic Growth and Social Justice. *Gannon, T. M., ed.*, 1987, pp. 187–206.   [G: U.S.]

Karsten, Siegfried G. Rugina's Contribution to Social Economics. *Int. J. Soc. Econ.*, 1987, 14(3/4/5), pp. 63–69.

Kent, Calvin A. Ethics and Economics: An Exploration of Christian Beliefs in Economic Relationships. *Int. J. Soc. Econ.*, 1987, 14(6), pp. 36–38.

Kleiman, Ephraim. Opportunity Cost, Human Capital, and Some Related Economic Concepts in Talmudic Literature. *Hist. Polit. Econ.*, Summer 1987, 19(2), pp. 261–87.

Kliemt, Hartmut. On Leland Yeager's Utilitarianism: A Comment [Rights, Contract, and Utility in Policy Espousal]. *Cato J.*, Spring/Summer 1987, 7(1), pp. 259–61.

LaBarbera, Priscilla A. Consumer Behavior and Born Again Christianity. *Sheth, J. N. and Hirschman, E., eds.*, 1987, pp. 193–222.   [G: U.S.]

Langan, John P. The Catholic Challenge to the American Economy: Afterword: A Direction for the Future. *Gannon, T. M., ed.*, 1987, pp. 256–67.   [G: U.S.]

Lawrence, John. Human Survival and Development: Our Urgent Need for a Reflective Universal Morality. *Int. J. Soc. Econ.*, 1987, 14(6), pp. 5–21.

Machan, Tibor R. Are Teleological Rights Theories Utilitarian? [Rights, Contracts, and Utility in Policy Espousal]. *Cato J.*, Spring/Summer 1987, 7(1), pp. 255–58.

Machan, Tibor R. A New Individualist Basis for the Free Market. *Int. J. Soc. Econ.*, 1987, 14(10), pp. 27–39.

Mayhew, Anne. Culture: Core Concept under Attack. *J. Econ. Issues*, June 1987, 21(2), pp. 587–603.

McKee, Arnold. Christian Economic Policy and the Role of Economic Science. *Rev. Soc. Econ.*, December 1987, 45(3), pp. 243–58.

McNelis, Paul D. The Preferential Option for the Poor and the Evolution of Latin American Macroeconomic Orthodoxies. *Gannon, T. M., ed.*, 1987, pp. 138–50.   **[G: U.S.; Latin America]**

van Meerhaeghe, Marcel, A. G. The Church and the Economy. *Econ. Scelte Pubbliche/J. Public Finance Public Choice*, May-Aug. 1987, *5*(2), pp. 97–104.

Neenan, William B. Poverty: Measurement, Trends and Causes. *Gannon, T. M., ed.*, 1987, pp. 107–15.   **[G: U.S.]**

de Neufville, Judith Innes and Barton, Stephen E. Myths and the Definition of Policy Problems: An Exploration of Home Ownership and Public–Private Partnerships. *Policy Sci.*, 1987, *20*(3), pp. 181–206.   **[G: U.S.]**

Nitsch, Thomas O. Social Economics: From Search for Identity to Quest for Roots; or, Social Economics: The First 100 Years (or So). *Int. J. Soc. Econ.*, 1987, *14*(3/4/5), pp. 70–90.

O'Brien, David J. The Economic Thought of the American Hierarchy. *Gannon, T. M., ed.*, 1987, pp. 27–41.   **[G: U.S.]**

O'Brien, John C. The Instauration of the New Man of Marxism: A Critique. *Int. J. Soc. Econ.*, 1987, *14*(3/4/5), pp. 22–32.

Pottenger, John R. Mormonism and the American Industrial State. *Int. J. Soc. Econ.*, 1987, *14*(2), pp. 25–38.   **[G: U.S.]**

Presser, Harriet B. Changing Values and Falling Birth Rates: Comment. *Davis, K.; Bernstam, M. S. and Ricardo-Campbell, R., eds.*, 1987, *1986*, pp. 196–200.   **[G: OECD]**

Preston, Samuel H. Changing Values and Falling Birth Rates. *Davis, K.; Bernstam, M. S. and Ricardo-Campbell, R., eds.*, 1987, *1986*, pp. 176–95.   **[G: OECD]**

Ravlin, Elizabeth C. and Meglino, Bruce M. Issues in Work Values Measurement. *Frederick, W. C., ed.*, 1987, pp. 153–83.

Rostow, Walt W. Reflections on the Past and Future of Political Economy. *Rostow, W. W.*, 1987, pp. 1–18.

Rowley, Charles K. The Economic Philosophy of James McGill Buchanan. *Econ. Scelte Pubbliche/J. Public Finance Public Choice*, Sept.-Dec. 1987, *5*(3), pp. 171–87.

Rugina, Anghel N. How a New Research Programme Was Born and Developed: A Long Journey to the Third Revolution in Social Economics. *Int. J. Soc. Econ.*, 1987, *14*(3/4/5), pp. 14–21.

Scaperlanda, Anthony. Institutionalist Methodology and Social Economics. *Int. J. Soc. Econ.*, 1987, *14*(3/4/5), pp. 146–53.

Skok, Charles D. Key Theological Positions Underlying the Bishops' Pastoral Letter on Catholic Social Teaching and the U.S. Economy. *Int. J. Soc. Econ.*, 1987, *14*(1), pp. 3–15.   **[G: U.S.]**

Sun, Li-teh. Inner Equilibrium and Economic Equilibrium: A Confucian Complement to Economic Man. *Int. J. Soc. Econ.*, 1987, *14*(10), pp. 40–55.   **[G: U.S.]**

Suttle, Bruce B. The Passion of Self-interest: The Development of the Idea and Its Changing Status. *Amer. J. Econ. Soc.*, October 1987, *46*(4), pp. 459–72.

Thanawala, Kishor. Nature and Scope of Rugina's Social Economics. *Int. J. Soc. Econ.*, 1987, *14*(3/4/5), pp. 91–96.

Unger, Laszlo. Changing Social Values and Lifestyles: From a Consumer towards a Conserver Society? *Hieronymi, O., ed.*, 1987, pp. 123–39.   **[G: U.S.]**

Velasquez, Manuel G. Ethics, Religion and the Modern Business Corporation. *Gannon, T. M., ed.*, 1987, pp. 55–75.   **[G: U.S.]**

Victor, Bart and Cullen, John B. A Theory and Measure of Ethical Climate in Organizations. *Frederick, W. C., ed.*, 1987, pp. 51–71.

Waterman, A. M. C. Economists on the Relation between Political Economy and Christian Theology: A Preliminary Survey. *Int. J. Soc. Econ.*, 1987, *14*(6), pp. 46–68.

Yeager, Leland B. Reply [Rights, Contracts, and Utility in Policy Espousal]. *Cato J.*, Spring/ Summer 1987, *7*(1), pp. 269–71.

0115 Methods Used by Economists

Balabkins, Nicholas W. Line by Line: Schmoller's *Grundriss:* Its Meaning for the 1980s. *Int. J. Soc. Econ.*, 1987, *14*(1), pp. 22–31.

Reid, Gavin C. Applying Field Research Techniques to the Business Enterprise. *Int. J. Soc. Econ.*, 1987, *14*(11), pp. 3–25.

012 Teaching of Economics

0120 Teaching of Economics

Barron, John M. and Lynch, Gerald J. The Aggregate Demand Curve: A Defense. *J. Econ. Educ.*, Winter 1987, *18*(1), pp. 41–46.

Baumol, William J. Microeconomics: A Comment on the Realism of Assumptions. *J. Econ. Educ.*, Spring 1987, *18*(2), pp. 155.

Becker, William E. Building Theoretical Models. *Becker, W. E. and Walstad, W. B., eds.*, 1987, pp. 19–26.

Becker, William E. Measuring Intervention, Interaction, and Distribution Effects with Dummy Variables. *Becker, W. E. and Walstad, W. B., eds.*, 1987, pp. 27–49. **[G: U.S.]**

Becker, William E. Teaching Statistical Methods to Undergraduate Economics Students. *Amer. Econ. Rev.*, May 1987, *77*(2), pp. 18–23.

Becker, William E. and Walstad, William B. Statistical Methods in Economic Education Research. *Becker, W. E. and Walstad, W. B., eds.*, 1987, pp. 1–17.   **[G: U.S.]**

Beckman, Steven. A Microcomputer Program That Simulates the Baumol–Tobin Transactions Demand for Money. *J. Econ. Educ.*, Summer 1987, *18*(3), pp. 309–17.

Bergmann, Barbara R. Women's Roles in the Economy: Teaching the Issues. *J. Econ. Educ.*, Fall 1987, *18*(4), pp. 393–407.

Buckles, Stephen. Microeconomics in the *Framework:* A Reconsideration. *J. Econ. Educ.*, Spring 1987, *18*(2), pp. 157–60.

Cain, Glen G. The Centrality of Economics in

Teaching Economic Statistics. *Amer. Econ. Rev.*, May 1987, 77(2), pp. 14–17.

Casarosa, Carlo. Economia e Commercio allo specchio: alcune considerazioni sul progetto di riforma. (The Faculty of "Economia e Commercio" Reconsidered: Some Considerations on the Reform Project. With English summary.) *Econ. Polít.*, August 1987, 4(2), pp. 181–87. **[G: Italy]**

Culbertson, John M. A Realistic International Economics. *J. Econ. Educ.*, Spring 1987, 18(2), pp. 161–75.

Day, Edward. A Note on Simulation Models in the Economics Classroom. *J. Econ. Educ.*, Summer 1987, 18(3), pp. 351–56.

DeBrock, Larry M. Selected Current Data Sources. *J. Econ. Educ.*, Summer 1987, 18(3), pp. 345–50.

Duggal, Vijaya G. Coping with the Diversity of Student Aptitudes and Interests. *Amer. Econ. Rev.*, May 1987, 77(2), pp. 24–28. **[G: U.S.]**

Ekwurzel, Drucilla and Saffran, Bernard. Low-Cost Online Searching Techniques. *J. Econ. Educ.*, Summer 1987, 18(3), pp. 287–307.

Feiner, Susan F. and Morgan, Barbara A. Women and Minorities in Introductory Economics Textbooks: 1974 to 1984. *J. Econ. Educ.*, Fall 1987, 18(4), pp. 376–92.

Fels, Rendigs. Fundamental Economic Concepts—Another Perspective: A Comment. *J. Econ. Educ.*, Spring 1987, 18(2), pp. 121–26.

Fleisher, Belton M. and Kopecky, Kenneth J. The Loanable-Funds Approach to Teaching Principles of Macroeconomics. *J. Econ. Educ.*, Winter 1987, 18(1), pp. 19–33.

Galbraith, James K. On Teaching a Fractured Macroeconomics. *J. Econ. Educ.*, Spring 1987, 18(2), pp. 213–26. **[G: U.S.]**

Grieves, Robin and Singleton, J. Clay. Analytic Methods of the All-America Research Team. *J. Portfol. Manage.*, Fall 1987, 14(1), pp. 4–8. **[G: U.S.]**

Hansen, Richard B.; McCormick, Ken and Rives, Janet M. The Aggregate Demand Curve: A Reply. *J. Econ. Educ.*, Winter 1987, 18(1), pp. 47–50.

Hansen, W. Lee. The Scope of Microeconomics: A Comment. *J. Econ. Educ.*, Spring 1987, 18(2), pp. 150–54.

Heilbroner, Robert L. Fundamental Economic Concepts—Another Perspective. *J. Econ. Educ.*, Spring 1987, 18(2), pp. 111–20.

Hemenway, David; Moore, Robert L. and Whitney, James. The Oligopoly Game. *Econ. Inquiry*, October 1987, 25(4), pp. 727–30.

Hewett, Roger S. Public Finance, Public Economics, and Public Choice: A Survey of Undergraduate Textbooks. *J. Econ. Educ.*, Fall 1987, 18(4), pp. 425–35. **[G: U.S.]**

Highsmith, Robert J. Professional Developments and Opportunities. *J. Econ. Educ.*, Spring 1987, 18(2), pp. 255–57. **[G: U.S.]**

Highsmith, Robert J. and Kasper, Hirschel. Rethinking the Scope of Economics. *J. Econ. Educ.*, Spring 1987, 18(2), pp. 101–05.

Hite, James C. Agricultural Economics Undergraduate and Graduate Curricula: Are We Competitive? Discussion. *Southern J. Agr. Econ.*, July 1987, 19(1), pp. 55–57. **[G: U.S.]**

Hu, Teh-wei. Research and Teaching of American Economy in the People's Republic of China. *Dutta, M., ed. (II)*, 1987, pp. 65–78. **[G: China; U.S.]**

Knechel, W. Robert and Snowball, Doug. Accounting Internships and Subsequent Academic Performance: An Empirical Study. *Accounting Rev.*, October 1987, 62(4), pp. 799–807. **[G: U.S.]**

Krynski, Kathy J. Women and Work: A Survey of Textbooks. *J. Econ. Educ.*, Fall 1987, 18(4), pp. 437–44. **[G: U.S.]**

Leuthold, Jane N. A Public Goods Experiment for the Classroom. *J. Econ. Educ.*, Winter 1987, 18(1), pp. 58–65. **[G: U.S.]**

Lovell, Michael C. CAI on PCs—Some Economic Applications. *J. Econ. Educ.*, Summer 1987, 18(3), pp. 319–29.

Lumsden, Keith G. and Scott, Alex. The Economics Student Reexamined: Male–Female Differences in Comprehension. *J. Econ. Educ.*, Fall 1987, 18(4), pp. 365–75. **[G: U.K.]**

Maasoumi, Esfandiar. Experimental and Nonexperimental Approaches to Statistical Research. *Becker, W. E. and Walstad, W. B., eds.*, 1987, pp. 51–72.

McNertney, Edward M. and Waits, C. Richard. The Role of Computer Software in the Teaching of Economics. *Amer. Econ.*, Spring 1987, 31(1), pp. 19–26.

Millerd, Frank W. and Robertson, Alastair R. Computer Simulations as an Integral Part of Intermediate Macroeconomics. *J. Econ. Educ.*, Summer 1987, 18(3), pp. 269–86. **[G: U.S.]**

O'Brien, Mary Utne and Ingels, Steven J. The Economics Values Inventory. *J. Econ. Educ.*, Winter 1987, 18(1), pp. 7–17. **[G: U.S.]**

Rangazas, Peter and Shapiro, Edward. Shifts in the Aggregate Demand Curve: Treatment and Mistreatment in Intermediate Textbooks. *J. Econ. Educ.*, Winter 1987, 18(1), pp. 35–39.

Rudd, Joel and Buttolph, Vicki L. Consumer Curriculum Materials: The First Content Analysis. *J. Cons. Aff.*, Summer 1987, 21(1), pp. 108–21. **[G: U.S.]**

Rushing, Francis W. In Defense of Realistic International Economics: Free Trade. *J. Econ. Educ.*, Spring 1987, 18(2), pp. 185–90.

Rycroft, Robert S. Econometric and Forecasting Software for the IBM PC and Compatibles. *J. Econ. Educ.*, Summer 1987, 18(3), pp. 331–44.

Salemi, Michael K. On Teaching a Fractured Macroeconomics: Thoughts. *J. Econ. Educ.*, Spring 1987, 18(2), pp. 227–31.

Salop, Steven C. Evaluating Uncertain Evidence with Sir Thomas Bayes: A Note for Teachers. *J. Econ. Perspectives*, Summer 1987, 1(1), pp. 155–59.

Samuelson, Paul A. How Economics Has Changed. *J. Econ. Educ.*, Spring 1987, 18(2), pp. 107–10.

Saunders, Philip. Fundamental Economic Concepts—Another Perspective: A Comment. *J.*

Econ. Educ., Spring 1987, *18*(2), pp. 127–33.

Schur, Leon M. Evaluating Economic Performance and Policies: A Comment. *J. Econ. Educ.*, Spring 1987, *18*(2), pp. 246–49.

Soper, John C. On Teaching a Fractured Macroeconomics: A Comment. *J. Econ. Educ.*, Spring 1987, *18*(2), pp. 232–36. **[G: U.S.]**

Soper, John C. and Brenneke, Judith Staley. A Note on Economic Content and Test Validity. *J. Econ. Educ.*, Fall 1987, *18*(4), pp. 421–24. **[G: U.S.]**

Strober, Myra H. The Scope of Microeconomics: Implications for Economic Education. *J. Econ. Educ.*, Spring 1987, *18*(2), pp. 135–49.

Swan, Craig. Simultaneous Equations Estimation. *Becker, W. E. and Walstad, W. B., eds.*, 1987, pp. 99–109.

Thurow, Lester C. Evaluating Economic Performance and Policies. *J. Econ. Educ.*, Spring 1987, *18*(2), pp. 237–46.

Vruwink, David R. and Otto, Janon R. Evaluation of Teaching Techniques for Introductory Accounting Courses. *Accounting Rev.*, April 1987, *62*(2), pp. 402–08.

Walker, Joe. Experimental Economics in the Classroom. *J. Econ. Educ.*, Winter 1987, *18*(1), pp. 51–57.

Walstad, William B. Applying Two-Stage Least Squares. *Becker, W. E. and Walstad, W. B., eds.*, 1987, pp. 111–34.

Walstad, William B. Evaluating Economic Performance and Policies: A Comment. *J. Econ. Educ.*, Spring 1987, *18*(2), pp. 250–54.

Walstad, William B. Measurement Instruments. *Becker, W. E. and Walstad, W. B., eds.*, 1987, pp. 73–98.

Watts, Michael. Survey Data on Precollege Scope-and-Sequence Issues in Economics. *J. Econ. Educ.*, Winter 1987, *18*(1), pp. 71–91. **[G: U.S.]**

Weidenaar, Dennis J. Teaching International Economics: A Response and Suggested Approach. *J. Econ. Educ.*, Spring 1987, *18*(2), pp. 177–84.

Weinstein, Michael M. Review of *Political Economy: An Introductory Text*, by Edmund S. Phelps. *J. Econ. Perspectives*, Fall 1987, *1*(2), pp. 179–82.

Williams, F. W. Agricultural Economics Undergraduate and Graduate Curricula: Are We Competitive? *Southern J. Agr. Econ.*, July 1987, *19*(1), pp. 49–54. **[G: U.S.]**

Zamagni, Stefano. Sull'insegnamento dell'economia politica. (On the Teaching of Economics. With English summary.) *Econ. Polít.*, April 1987, *4*(1), pp. 3–10.

020 General Economic Theory

0200 General Economic Theory

Albelda, Randy; Gunn, Christopher and Waller, William T., Jr. The Resurgence of Political Economy. *Albelda, R.; Gunn, C. and Waller, W., eds.*, 1987, pp. 3–17.

Allais, Maurice. The Equimarginal Principle: Meaning, Limits, and Generalization. *Rivista Int. Sci. Econ. Com.*, August 1987, *34*(8), pp. 689–750.

Arouh, Albert. The Mumpsimus of Economists and the Role of Time and Uncertainty in the Progress of Economic Knowledge. *J. Post Keynesian Econ.*, Spring 1987, *9*(3), pp. 395–423.

Arrow, Kenneth J. Arrow and the Ascent of Modern Economic Theory: Reflections on the Essays. *Feiwel, G. R., ed. (I)*, 1987, pp. 685–89.

Arrow, Kenneth J. Arrow and the Ascent of Modern Economic Theory: Oral History I: An Interview. *Feiwel, G. R., ed. (I)*, 1987, pp. 191–242.

Arrow, Kenneth J. Arrow and the Foundations of the Theory of Economic Policy: Reflections on the Essays. *Feiwel, G. R., ed. (II)*, 1987, pp. 727–34.

Arrow, Kenneth J. General Economic Theory and the Emergency of Theories of Economic Development. *Indian Econ. J.*, Apr.-June 1987, *34*(4), pp. 1–8.

Aumann, Robert J. Economic Theory and Mathematical Method: An Interview. *Feiwel, G. R., ed. (I)*, 1987, pp. 306–16.

Benetti, Carlo and Cartelier, Jean. Monnaie, valeur et propriété privée. (Money, Value and Private Ownership. With English summary.) *Revue Écon.*, November 1987, *38*(6), pp. 1157–70.

Berry, S. Keith. The Relevance of Quasi Rationality in Competitive Markets: Comment. *Amer. Econ. Rev.*, June 1987, *77*(3), pp. 496–98.

Brochier, Hubert. Les théories économiques sont-elles réfutables? (Are Economic Theories Falsifiable? With English summary.) *Écon. Soc.*, October 1987, *21*(10), pp. 107–18.

Buchanan, James M. What Should Economists Do? *Buchanan, J. M. (II)*, 1987, *1964*, pp. 21–33.

Caslin, Terry and Vane, Howard. Introductory Economics: An Overview. *Vane, H. and Caslin, T., eds.*, 1987, pp. 3–23.

Dandekar, Vinayak M. Economies as Differentiated Systems. *J. Econ. Issues*, June 1987, *21*(2), pp. 813–25. **[G: India]**

Day, Richard H. The General Theory of Disequilibrium Economics and of Economic Evolution. *Batten, D.; Casti, J. and Johansson, B., eds.*, 1987, pp. 46–63.

De Alessi, Louis. Nature and Methodological Foundations of Some Recent Extensions of Economic Theory. *Radnitzky, G. and Bernholz, P., eds.*, 1987, pp. 51–76.

Dow, Sheila C. The Scottish Political Economy Tradition. *Scot. J. Polit. Econ.*, November 1987, *34*(4), pp. 335–48. **[G: U.K.]**

Etzioni, Amitai. On Thoughtless Rationality (Rules-of-Thumb). *Kyklos*, 1987, *40*(4), pp. 496–514.

Fan, Liang-Shing. Institutional Design and Innovation: Discussion. *Amer. J. Agr. Econ.*, May

1987, *69*(2), pp. 418–19.

Feeny, David. Institutional Design and Innovation: Discussion. *Amer. J. Agr. Econ.*, May 1987, *69*(2), pp. 416–17.

Ghiselin, Michael T. Principles and Prospects for General Economy. *Radnitzky, G. and Bernholz, P., eds.*, 1987, pp. 21–31.

Gowdy, John M. Bio-economics: Social Economy versus the Chicago School. *Int. J. Soc. Econ.*, 1987, *14*(1), pp. 32–42.

Guitton, Henri. The Rational and the Non-rational in Economics. *Int. J. Soc. Econ.*, 1987, *14*(3/4/5), pp. 33–36.

Hahn, Frank H. Information, Dynamics and Equilibrium. *Scot. J. Polit. Econ.*, November 1987, *34*(4), pp. 321–34.

Hayden, F. Gregory. Evolution of Time Constructs and Their Impact on Socioeconomic Planning. *J. Econ. Issues*, September 1987, *21*(3), pp. 1281–1312.

Henry, Jacques. Equilibrium as a Process. *Écon. Appl.*, 1987, *40*(3), pp. 463–82.

Hodgson, Geoffrey M. Economics and Systems Theory. *J. Econ. Stud.*, 1987, *14*(4), pp. 65–86.

Hurwicz, Leonid. Inventing New Institutions: The Design Perspective. *Amer. J. Agr. Econ.*, May 1987, *69*(2), pp. 395–402.

Johansson, Börje; Batten, David F. and Casti, John. Economic Dynamics, Evolution and Structural Adjustment. *Batten, D.; Casti, J. and Johansson, B., eds.*, 1987, pp. 1–23.

Khalil, Elias L. The Process of Capitalist Accumulation: A Review Essay of David Levine's Contribution. *Rev. Radical Polit. Econ.*, Winter 1987, *19*(4), pp. 76–85.

Larson, Bruce. Edgeworth, Samuelson, and Operationally Meaningful Theorems. *Hist. Polit. Econ.*, Fall 1987, *19*(3), pp. 351–57.

Le Pen, Claude. "Falsifiabilite" et theorie economique ou comment rendre une theorie scientifique infalsifiable. ("Falsifiability" and Economic Theory or How to Make a Scientific Theory Unfalsifiable. With English summary.) *Écon. Soc.*, October 1987, *21*(10), pp. 119–28.

Lowe, Adolph. Economic Means and Social Ends: A Rejoinder. *Lowe, A.*, 1987, *1969*, pp. 193–225.

Lowe, Adolph. Toward a Science of Political Economics. *Lowe, A.*, 1987, *1969*, pp. 157–92.

Mangum, Garth L.; Mangum, Stephen L. and Phillips, Peter. The Three (at Least) Worlds of Economic Theory. *Challenge*, Mar./Apr. 1987, *30*(1), pp. 57–59.

Matthews, R. C. O. An Eclectic View from Cambridge: An Interview. *Feiwel, G. R., ed. (II)*, 1987, pp. 613–34.

McDonald, John. Muth's Concept of Rational Expectations. *Australian Econ. Pap.*, December 1987, *26*(49), pp. 265–74.

Mirowski, Philip. Shall I Compare Thee to a Minkowski–Ricardo–Leontief–Metzler Matrix of the Mosak–Hicks Type? Or, Rhetoric, Mathematics, and the Nature of Neoclassical Economic Theory. *Econ. Philos.*, April 1987, *3*(1), pp. 67–95.

Nell, Edward J. Economics: The Revival of Political Economy. *Albelda, R.; Gunn, C. and Waller, W., eds.*, 1987, *1972*, pp. 89–103.

Pelloni, Gianluigi. Atteggiamento neo-bayesiano e aspettative razionali: alcune considerazioni. (Rational Expectations and the Neo-Bayesian Approach. With English summary.) *Econ. Polit.*, December 1987, *4*(3), pp. 357–79.

Russell, Thomas and Thaler, Richard H. The Relevance of Quasi Rationality in Competitive Markets: Reply. *Amer. Econ. Rev.*, June 1987, *77*(3), pp. 499–501.

Sengupta, Jati K. The Concept of Variety in Systems Behavior: Applications to Behavior Settings, Product-Differentiation, and Representative Firms. *Fox, K. A. and Miles, D. G., eds.*, 1987, pp. 67–81.

Singh, Harinder. The Rationalist Conception of Action: Comment. *J. Econ. Issues*, March 1987, *21*(1), pp. 441–51.

Whalen, Charles J. A Reason to Look beyond Neoclassical Economics: Some Major Shortcomings of Orthodox Theory. *J. Econ. Issues*, March 1987, *21*(1), pp. 259–80.

Whitaker, John K. *The Limits of Organization* Revisited. *Feiwel, G. R., ed. (II)*, 1987, pp. 565–83.

021 General Equilibrium and Disequilibrium Theory

0210 General Equilibrium and Disequilibrium Theory

Aiyagari, S. Rao. Optimality and Monetary Equilibria in Stationary Overlapping Generations Models with Long-Lived Agents: Growth versus Discounting. *J. Econ. Theory*, December 1987, *43*(2), pp. 292–313.

Akin, Ethan. Competitive Growth of Firms in an Industry. *Batten, D.; Casti, J. and Johansson, B., eds.*, 1987, pp. 86–115.

Aliprantis, Charalambos D.; Brown, Donald J. and Burkinshaw, Owen. Edgeworth Equilibria. *Econometrica*, September 1987, *55*(5), pp. 1109–37.

Aliprantis, Charalambos D.; Brown, Donald J. and Burkinshaw, Owen. Edgeworth Equilibria in Production Economies. *J. Econ. Theory*, December 1987, *43*(2), pp. 252–91.

Anderson, Robert M. Gap-minimizing Prices and Quadratic Core Convergence. *J. Math. Econ.*, 1987, *16*(1), pp. 1–15.

Arrow, Kenneth J. Technical Information, Returns to Scale, and the Existence of Competitive Equilibrium. *[Hurwicz, L.]*, 1987, pp. 243–55.

Aumann, Robert J. Value, Symmetry, and Equal Treatment: A Comment [Non-symmetric Cardinal Value Allocations]. *Econometrica*, November 1987, *55*(6), pp. 1461–64.

Becker, Robert A. and Foias, Ciprian. A Characterization of Ramsey Equilibrium. *J. Econ. Theory*, February 1987, *41*(1), pp. 173–84.

Benhabib, J.; Majumdar, Mukul K. and Nishi-

mura, K. Global Equilibrium Dynamics with Stationary Recursive Preferences. *J. Econ. Behav. Organ.*, September 1987, *8*(3), pp. 429–52.

Bhagwati, Jagdish N.; Brecher, Richard A. and Hatta, Tatsuo. The Global Correspondence Principle: A Generalization. *Amer. Econ. Rev.*, March 1987, *77*(1), pp. 124–32.

Bhattacharya, Gautam. Notes on Optimality of Rational Expectations Equilibrium with Incomplete Markets. *J. Econ. Theory*, August 1987, *42*(2), pp. 191–208.

Bhattacharya, Sudipto and Hagerty, Kathleen M. Dealerships, Trading Externalities, and General Equilibrium. *Prescott, E. C. and Wallace, N., eds.*, 1987, pp. 81–104.

Bidard, Christian and Franke, Reiner. On the Existence of Long-term Equilibria in the Two-Class Pasinetti–Morishima Model. *Ricerche Econ.*, Jan.-Mar. 1987, *41*(1), pp. 3–21.

Bidard, Christian and Franke, Reiner. On Walras' Model of General Equilibrium: A Simpler Way to Demonstrate Existence. *J. Econ. (Z. Nationalökon.)*, 1987, *47*(3), pp. 315–19.

Brockway, George P. The Dilemma of General Equilibrium Analysis. *J. Post Keynesian Econ.*, Fall 1987, *10*(1), pp. 116–22.

Burke, Jonathan L. Inactive Transfer Policies and Efficiency in General Overlapping-Generations Economies. *J. Math. Econ.*, 1987, *16*(3), pp. 201–22.

Cavagnac, M.; Kephaliacos, C. and Marfaing, R. Efficience, rareté et domination dans une technologie de Von Neumann. (Efficiency, Scarcity and Domination in a Von Neumann Type Technology: A Twin Example. With English summary.) *Écon. Appl.*, 1987, *40*(1), pp. 35–47.

Chae, Suchan. Short Run Core Equivalence in an Overlapping Generations Model. *J. Econ. Theory*, October 1987, *43*(1), pp. 170–83.

Cheng, Harrison H. C. The Coalitional Approach to Core Theory. *J. Math. Econ.*, 1987, *16*(3), pp. 247–58.

van Damme, Eric. Equilibria in Noncooperative Games. *Peters, H. J. M. and Vrieze, O. J., eds.*, 1987, pp. 1–35.

Davidson, Carl; Martin, Lawrence W. and Matusz, Steven J. Search, Unemployment, and the Production of Jobs. *Econ. J.*, December 1987, *97*(388), pp. 857–76.

De Vroey, Michel. La possibilité d'une économie décentralisée. Esquisse d'une alternative à la théorie de l'équilibre général. (The Possibility of a Decentralized Economy. An Alternative to the General Equilibrium Framework. With English summary.) *Revue Écon.*, July 1987, *38*(4), pp. 773–805.

Debreu, Gerard. Arrow and the Ascent of Modern Economic Theory: Oral History II: An Interview. *Feiwel, G. R., ed. (I)*, 1987, pp. 243–57.

Deneckere, Raymond J. and Pelikan, Steve. Competitive Chaos. *Grandmont, J.-M., ed.*, 1987, *1986*, pp. 13–25.

Dewatripont, Mathias and Michel, Gilles. On

Closure Rules, Homogeneity and Dynamics in Applied General Equilibrium Models. *J. Devel. Econ.*, June 1987, *26*(1), pp. 65–76.

Doup, T. M.; van den Elzen, A. H. and Talman, A. J. J. Simplicial Algorithms for Solving the Nonlinear Complementarity Problem on the Simplotope. *Talman, D. and van der Laan, G., eds.*, 1987, pp. 125–53.

Drèze, Jacques H. (Uncertainty and) the Firm in General Equilibrium Theory. *Drèze, J. H.*, 1987, *1985*, pp. 321–43.

Drèze, Jacques H. Investment under Private Ownership: Optimality, Equilibrium and Stability. *Drèze, J. H.*, 1987, *1974*, pp. 261–97.

Driessen, Theo. The τ-Value: A Survey. *Peters, H. J. M. and Vrieze, O. J., eds.*, 1987, pp. 209–13.

Driessen, Theo. The Core of a Cooperative Game: Bounds and Characterizations. *Peters, H. J. M. and Vrieze, O. J., eds.*, 1987, pp. 181–208.

Dubey, Pradeep; Geanakoplos, John and Shubik, Martin. The Revelation of Information in Strategic Market Games: A Critique of Rational Expectations Equilibrium. *J. Math. Econ.*, 1987, *16*(2), pp. 105–37.

Duffie, Darrell. Stochastic Equilibria with Incomplete Financial Markets. *J. Econ. Theory*, April 1987, *41*(2), pp. 405–16.

Duménil, Gérard and Lévy, Dominique. The Dynamics of Competition: A Restoration of the Classical Analysis. *Cambridge J. Econ.*, June 1987, *11*(2), pp. 133–64.

Eaves, B. Curtis. Thoughts on Computing Market Equilibrium with SLCP. *Talman, D. and van der Laan, G., eds.*, 1987, pp. 1–17.

Epstein, Larry G. A Simple Dynamic General Equilibrium Model. *J. Econ. Theory*, February 1987, *41*(1), pp. 68–95.

Epstein, Larry C. The Global Stability of Efficient Intertemporal Allocations. *Econometrica*, March 1987, *55*(2), pp. 329–55.

Feiwel, George R. The Potentials and Limits of Economic Analysis: The Contributions of Kenneth J. Arrow. *Feiwel, G. R., ed. (I)*, 1987, pp. 1–187.

Feldman, Mark D. An Example of Convergence to Rational Expectations with Heterogeneous Beliefs. *Int. Econ. Rev.*, October 1987, *28*(3), pp. 635–50.

Forster, W. Computing "All" Solutions of Systems of Polynomial Equations by Simplicial Fixed Point Algorithms. *Talman, D. and van der Laan, G., eds.*, 1987, pp. 39–57.

Forsythe, Robert and Suchanek, Gerry L. Decentralizing Constrained Pareto Optimal Allocations in Stock Ownership Economies: An Impossibility Theorem. *Int. Econ. Rev.*, June 1987, *28*(2), pp. 299–313.

Froeschlé, Claude and Longhi, A. Connectance et stabilité locale d'un équilibre général. (Connectance and Local Stability of General Equilibrium. With English summary.) *Écon. Appl.*, 1987, *40*(1), pp. 49–78.

Fujimoto, Takao. A Simple Proof of the Nonsubstitution Theorem. *J. Quant. Econ.*, January 1987, *3*(1), pp. 35–38.

Gale, Douglas M. Limit Theorems for Markets with Sequential Bargaining. *J. Econ. Theory,* October 1987, *43*(1), pp. 20–54.

Gérard-Varet, Louis-André and Laffont, Jean-Jacques. Symétrie et équilibre concurrentiel. (Symmetry and Competitive Equilibrium. With English summary.) *Écon. Soc.,* January 1987, *21*(1), pp. 85–107.

Grandmont, Jean-Michel and Malgrange, Pierre. Nonlinear Economic Dynamics: Introduction. *Grandmont, J.-M., ed.,* 1987, *1986,* pp. 3–12.

Guesnerie, Roger. Stationary Sunspot Equilibria in an *N* Commodity World. *Grandmont, J.-M., ed.,* 1987, *1986,* pp. 103–27.

Hammond, Peter J. Markets as Constraints: Multilateral Incentive Compatibility in Continuum Economies. *Rev. Econ. Stud.,* July 1987, *54*(3), pp. 399–412.

Hellwig, Martin. Some Recent Developments in the Theory of Competition in Markets with Adverse Selection. *Europ. Econ. Rev.,* Feb./Mar. 1987, *31*(1/2), pp. 319–25.

Huang, Chi-fu. An Intertemporal General Equilibrium Asset Pricing Model: The Case of Diffusion Information. *Econometrica,* January 1987, *55*(1), pp. 117–42.

Hurwicz, Leonid. Arrow and the Ascent of Modern Economic Theory: Oral History III: An Interview. *Feiwel, G. R., ed. (I),* 1987, pp. 258–92.

Jacobsen, Hans Jørgen and Schultz, Christian. A General Equilibrium View of Unemployment. *Pedersen, P. J. and Lund, R., eds.,* 1987, pp. 17–46.

Jacobsen, Hans Jørgen and Schultz, Christian. On the Existence of Conjectural Equilibria with *a priori* Chosen Rationing Patterns. *Europ. Econ. Rev.,* December 1987, *31*(8), pp. 1561–80.

Jones, Larry E. Existence of Equilibria with Infinitely Many Commodities: Banach Lattices Reconsidered. *J. Math. Econ.,* 1987, *16*(2), pp. 89–104.

Jones, Larry E. The Efficiency of Monopolistically Competitive Equilibria in Large Economies: Commodity Differentiation with Gross Substitutes. *J. Econ. Theory,* April 1987, *41*(2), pp. 356–91.

Jordan, James S. The Informational Requirements of Local Stability in Decentralized Allocation Mechanisms. *[Hurwicz, L.],* 1987, pp. 183–212.

Khan, M. Ali and Vohra, Rajiv. On the Existence of Lindahl–Hotelling Equilibria. *J. Public Econ.,* November 1987, *34*(2), pp. 143–58.

Klein, Lawrence R. Interaction between General Equilibrium and Macroeconomics: An Interview. *Feiwel, G. R., ed. (I),* 1987, pp. 340–58.

Kolstad, Charles D. and Mathiesen, Lars. Necessary and Sufficient Conditions for Uniqueness of a Cournot Equilibrium. *Rev. Econ. Stud.,* October 1987, *54*(4), pp. 681–90.

van der Laan, Gerard and Talman, A. J. J. Adjustment Processes for Finding Economic Equilibria. *Talman, D. and van der Laan, G., eds.,* 1987, pp. 85–123.

Lawlor, Michael S. Is the Economy a Closed System? General Equilibrium and General Systems Theory. *Fox, K. A. and Miles, D. G., eds.,* 1987, pp. 19–49.

Le Breton, Michel. On the Generic Nonexistence of Pure Strategy Nash Equilibria in Continuous Games. *J. Econ. Theory,* December 1987, *43*(2), pp. 374–82.

Lippman, Steven A.; Mamer, John W. and McCardle, Kevin F. Comparative Statics in Non-cooperative Games via Transfinitely Iterated Play. *J. Econ. Theory,* April 1987, *41*(2), pp. 288–303.

van Maaren, Hans. Generalized Pivoting and Coalitions. *Talman, D. and van der Laan, G., eds.,* 1987, pp. 155–76.

Madrigal, Vicente; Tan, Tommy C. C. and da Costa Werlang, Sérgio Ribeiro. Support Restrictions and Sequential Equilibria. *J. Econ. Theory,* December 1987, *43*(2), pp. 329–34.

Mailath, George J. Incentive Compatibility in Signaling Games with a Continuum of Types. *Econometrica,* November 1987, *55*(6), pp. 1349–65.

Makowski, Louis and Ostroy, Joseph M. Vickrey–Clarke–Groves Mechanisms and Perfect Competition. *J. Econ. Theory,* August 1987, *42*(2), pp. 244–61.

Marschak, Thomas. Price versus Direct Revelation: Informational Judgments for Finite Mechanisms. *[Hurwicz, L.],* 1987, pp. 132–79.

Marshall, John M.; Sonstelie, Jon and Gilles, Christian. Money and Redistribution: Revisionist Notes on a Problem of Samuelson. *J. Monet. Econ.,* July 1987, *20*(1), pp. 3–23.

Mas-Colell, Andreu. On the Second Welfare Theorem for Anonymous Net Trades in Exchange Economies with Many Agents. *[Hurwicz, L.],* 1987, pp. 267–92.

Mas-Colell, Andreu. Transformation in General Equilibrium Theory and Methods: An Interview. *Feiwel, G. R., ed. (I),* 1987, pp. 317–24.

Maskin, Eric. On the Fair Allocation of Indivisible Goods. *Feiwel, G. R., ed. (II),* 1987, pp. 341–49.

Maskin, Eric and Tirole, Jean. Correlated Equilibria and Sunspots. *J. Econ. Theory,* December 1987, *43*(2), pp. 364–73.

Mehta, Ghanshyam and Tarafdar, Enayet. Infinite-Dimensional Gale–Nikaido–Debreu Theorem and a Fixed-Point Theorem of Tarafdar. *J. Econ. Theory,* April 1987, *41*(2), pp. 333–39.

Montesano, Aldo. Optimal Allocations and the Price System. *Rivista Int. Sci. Econ. Com.,* October 1987, *34*(10), pp. 913–36.

Morrison, Clarence C. A Note on Price Searching in General Equilibrium Models. *Atlantic Econ. J.,* March 1987, *15*(1), pp. 56–58.

Negishi, Takashi. On the Non-existence of Equilibrium: From Thornton to Arrow. *Feiwel, G. R., ed. (I),* 1987, pp. 361–74.

Norman, Alfred Lorn. A Theory of Monetary Exchange. *Rev. Econ. Stud.*, July 1987, *54*(3), pp. 499–517.

Novshek, William and Sonnenschein, Hugo. General Equilibrium with Free Entry: A Synthetic Approach to the Theory of Perfect Competition. *J. Econ. Lit.*, September 1987, *25*(3), pp. 1281–1306.

Osana, Hiroaki. Long-run Equilibria for Perfectly Competitive Markets. *Keio Econ. Stud.*, 1987, *24*(1), pp. 1–11.

Page, Frank H., Jr. On Equilibrium in Hart's Securities Exchange Model. *J. Econ. Theory*, April 1987, *41*(2), pp. 392–404.

Peck, James. Non-connectedness of the Set of Equilibrium Money Prices: The Static Economy. *J. Econ. Theory*, December 1987, *43*(2), pp. 348–54.

Peck, James. Non-connectedness of the Set of Equilibrium Money Prices: The Overlapping-Generations Economy. *J. Econ. Theory*, December 1987, *43*(2), pp. 355–63.

Perroni, Carlo. Valutazione degli effetti di politiche fiscali in presenza di razionamento. (Evaluation of the Effects of Fiscal Policies under a Rational Mechanism. With English summary.) *Giorn. Econ.*, Mar.-Apr. 1987, *46*(3–4), pp. 185–204.

Pietra, Tito and Siconolfi, Paolo. Sul ruolo della moneta interna e della moneta esterna. (On the Role of Inside Money and Outside Money. With English summary.) *Econ. Polit.*, April 1987, *4*(1), pp. 49–88.

Postlewaite, Andrew and Schmeidler, David. Differential Information and Strategic Behavior in Economic Environments: A General Equilibrium Approach. *[Hurwicz, L.]*, 1987, pp. 330–48.

Ray, Debraj. Nonpaternalistic Intergenerational Altruism. *J. Econ. Theory*, February 1987, *41*(1), pp. 112–32.

Repullo, Rafael. The Existence of Equilibrium without Free Disposal in Economies with Transaction Costs and Incomplete Markets. *Int. Econ. Rev.*, June 1987, *28*(2), pp. 275–90.

Roberts, John. An Equilibrium Model with Involuntary Unemployment at Flexible, Competitive Prices and Wages. *Amer. Econ. Rev.*, December 1987, *77*(5), pp. 856–74.

Roberts, John. General Equilibrium Analysis of Imperfect Competition: An Illustrative Example. *Feiwel, G. R., ed. (I)*, 1987, pp. 415–38.

Ruys, Pieter H. M. and van der Laan, Gerard. Computation of an Industrial Equilibrium. *Talman, D. and van der Laan, G., eds.*, 1987, pp. 205–29.

Scotchmer, Suzanne and Wooders, Myrna Holtz. Competitive Equilibrium and the Core in Club Economies with Anonymous Crowding. *J. Public Econ.*, November 1987, *34*(2), pp. 159–73.

Simon, Leo K. Bertrand Price Competition with Differentiated Commodities. *J. Econ. Theory*, April 1987, *41*(2), pp. 304–32.

Simon, Leo K. Games with Discontinuous Payoffs. *Rev. Econ. Stud.*, October 1987, *54*(4), pp. 569–97.

Simon, Leo K. Local Perfection. *J. Econ. Theory*, October 1987, *43*(1), pp. 134–56.

Sonnenschein, Hugo. Theory and Method—Second-Generation Perspective: An Interview. *Feiwel, G. R., ed. (I)*, 1987, pp. 325–39.

Stahl, Dale O., II. Queue-Rationing and Price Dynamics. *Scand. J. Econ.*, 1987, *89*(4), pp. 469–85.

Stahl, Dale O., II. Temporary Equilibrium with Storable Commodities. *J. Econ. Theory*, August 1987, *42*(2), pp. 262–74.

Svensson, Lars-Gunnar. Erratum [Large Indivisibles: An Analysis with Respect to Price Equilibrium and Fairness]. *Econometrica*, March 1987, *55*(2), pp. 489.

Tartarin, Robert. Efficacité et propriété. (Efficiency and Property. With English summary.) *Revue Écon.*, November 1987, *38*(6), pp. 1129–55.

Thomas, Mark. General Equilibrium Models and Research in Economic History. *Field, A. J., ed.*, 1987, pp. 121–83.

Tobin, Roger L. Sensitivity Analysis for General Spatial Price Equilibria. *J. Reg. Sci.*, February 1987, *27*(1), pp. 77–102.

Todd, Michael J. Reformulations of Economic Equilibrium Problems for Solution by Quasi-Newton and Simplicial Algorithms. *Talman, D. and van der Laan, G., eds.*, 1987, pp. 19–37.

Townsend, Robert M. Arrow–Debreu Programs as Microfoundations of Macroeconomics. *Bewley, T. F., ed.*, 1987, pp. 379–428.

Townsend, Robert M. Asset-Return Anomalies in a Monetary Economy. *J. Econ. Theory*, April 1987, *41*(2), pp. 219–47.

Townsend, Robert M. Taking Pure Theory to Data: Arrow's Seminal Contribution. *Feiwel, G. R., ed. (I)*, 1987, pp. 675–81.

Van der Heyden, Ludo. On a Theorem of Scarf. *Talman, D. and van der Laan, G., eds.*, 1987, pp. 177–92.

Vega-Redondo, Fernando. Efficiency and Nonlinear Pricing in Nonconvex Environments with Externalities: A Generalization of the Lindahl Equilibrium Concept. *J. Econ. Theory*, February 1987, *41*(1), pp. 54–67.

Weddepohl, Claus. Supply-Constrained Equilibria in Economies with Indexed Prices. *J. Econ. Theory*, December 1987, *43*(2), pp. 203–22.

Werner, Jan. Arbitrage and the Existence of Competitive Equilibrium. *Econometrica*, November 1987, *55*(6), pp. 1403–18.

Wilson, Robert B. On Equilibria of Bid–Ask Markets. *Feiwel, G. R., ed. (I)*, 1987, pp. 375–414.

Wooders, Myrna Holtz and Zame, William R. Large Games: Fair and Stable Outcomes. *J. Econ. Theory*, June 1987, *42*(1), pp. 59–93.

Woodford, Michael. Stationary Sunspot Equilibria in a Finance Constrained Economy. *Grandmont, J.-M., ed.*, 1987, *1986*, pp. 128–37.

Wright, Randall D. Market Structure and Competitive Equilibrium in Dynamic Economic

Models. *J. Econ. Theory*, February 1987, *41*(1), pp. 189–201.

Yamamoto, Yoshitsugu. Competitive Equilibria in the Market with Indivisibility. *Talman, D. and van der Laan, G., eds.*, 1987, pp. 193–204.

Yannelis, Nicholas C. Equilibria in Noncooperative Models of Competition. *J. Econ. Theory*, February 1987, *41*(1), pp. 96–111.

Zame, William R. Competitive Equilibria in Production Economies with an Infinite-Dimensional Commodity Space. *Econometrica*, September 1987, *55*(5), pp. 1075–1108.

022 Microeconomic Theory

0220 General

Albin, Peter S. Microeconomic Foundations of Cyclical Irregularities or 'Chaos.' *Math. Soc. Sci.*, June 1987, *13*(3), pp. 185–214.

Alger, Dan. Laboratory Tests of Equilibrium Predictions with Disequilibrium Data. *Rev. Econ. Stud.*, January 1987, *54*(1), pp. 105–45.

Arnott, Richard J. Essai sur le risque moral. (An Essay on Moral Hazard. With English summary.) *L'Actual. Econ.*, June-September 1987, *63*(2–3), pp. 74–97.

Ayres, Robert U. and Sandilya, Manalur S. Utility Maximization and Catastrophe Aversion: A Simulation Test. *J. Environ. Econ. Manage.*, December 1987, *14*(4), pp. 337–70.

Bagwell, Kyle. Introductory Price as a Signal of Cost in a Model of Repeat Business. *Rev. Econ. Stud.*, July 1987, *54*(3), pp. 365–84.

Barnett, William A. The Microeconomic Theory of Monetary Aggregation. *Barnett, W. A. and Singleton, K. J., eds.*, 1987, pp. 115–68.

Barro, Robert J. and Romer, Paul M. Ski-Lift Pricing, with Applications to Labor and Other Markets. *Amer. Econ. Rev.*, December 1987, *77*(5), pp. 875–90.

Baumol, William J. Microeconomics: A Comment on the Realism of Assumptions. *J. Econ. Educ.*, Spring 1987, *18*(2), pp. 155.

Beach, Lee Roy; Christensen-Szalanski, Jay and Barnes, Valerie. Assessing Human Judgment: Has It Been Done, Can It Be Done, Should It Be Done? *Wright, G. and Ayton, P., eds.*, 1987, pp. 49–62.

Becker, Gary S. Economic Analysis and Human Behavior. *Green, L. and Kagel, J. H., eds.*, 1987, pp. 3–17.

Besanko, David and Thakor, Anjan V. Competitive Equilibrium in the Credit Market under Asymmetric Information. *J. Econ. Theory*, June 1987, *42*(1), pp. 167–82.

Buchanan, James M. L.S.E. Cost Theory in Retrospect. *Buchanan, J. M. (II)*, 1987, *1973*, pp. 141–51.

Buckles, Stephen. Microeconomics in the *Framework:* A Reconsideration. *J. Econ. Educ.*, Spring 1987, *18*(2), pp. 157–60.

Bull, Clive; Schotter, Andrew and Weigelt, Keith. Tournaments and Piece Rates: An Experimental Study. *J. Polit. Econ.*, February 1987, *95*(1), pp. 1–33.   [G: U.S.]

Calsamiglia, Xavier. Informational Requirements of Parametric Resource Allocation Processes. *[Hurwicz, L.]*, 1987, pp. 115–31.

Camerer, Colin F. Do Biases in Probability Judgment Matter in Markets? Experimental Evidence. *Amer. Econ. Rev.*, December 1987, *77*(5), pp. 981–97.

Chateauneuf, Alain. Continuous Representation of a Preference Relation on a Connected Topological Space. *J. Math. Econ.*, 1987, *16*(2), pp. 139–46.

Chavas, Jean-Paul. Constrained Choices under Risk. *Southern Econ. J.*, January 1987, *53*(3), pp. 662–76.

Cheng, Hsueh-Cheng; Magill, Michael J. P. and Shafer, Wayne J. Some Results on Comparative Statics under Uncertainty. *Int. Econ. Rev.*, June 1987, *28*(2), pp. 493–507.

Chew, Soo Hong; Karni, Edi and Safra, Zvi. Risk Aversion in the Theory of Expected Utility with Rank Dependent Probabilities. *J. Econ. Theory*, August 1987, *42*(2), pp. 370–81.

Cressy, Robert C. Equilibrium Price Dispersion: An Extension of Reinganum's 'Simple Model.' *Bull. Econ. Res.*, July 1987, *39*(3), pp. 235–41.

De Vany, Arthur. Institutions for Stochastic Markets. *J. Inst. Theoretical Econ.*, March 1987, *143*(1), pp. 91–103.

Diamond, Peter. Equilibrium without an Auctioneer. *Bewley, T. F., ed.*, 1987, pp. 363–78.

Drèze, Jacques H. Axiomatic Theories of Choice, Cardinal Utility and Subjective Probability: A Review. *Drèze, J. H.*, 1987, *1974*, pp. 3–22.

Drèze, Jacques H. Decision Theory with Moral Hazard and State-Dependent Preferences. *Drèze, J. H.*, 1987, pp. 23–89.

Drèze, Jacques H. Demand Estimation, Risk Aversion and Sticky Prices. *Drèze, J. H.*, 1987, *1979*, pp. 144–49.

Drèze, Jacques H. Espérance morale avec risque moral. (Moral Expectation with Moral Hazard. With English summary.) *L'Actual. Econ.*, June-September 1987, *63*(2–3), pp. 40–57.

Drèze, Jacques H. Market Allocation under Uncertainty. *Drèze, J. H.*, 1987, *1971*, pp. 119–43.

Drynan, Ross G. Sufficient Conditions for Dominance of Simply Related Prospects. *Rev. Marketing Agr. Econ.*, April 1987, *55*(1), pp. 25–36.

Dyer, James S. and Ravinder, H. V. A Rationale for Additive Decomposition in Multiattribute Utility Assessment. *Sawaragi, Y.; Inoue, K. and Nakayama, H., eds.*, 1987, pp. 277–85.

Farrell, Joseph. Rigidity vs. License. *Amer. Econ. Rev.*, March 1987, *77*(1), pp. 195–97.

Feiwel, George R. The Many Dimensions of Kenneth J. Arrow. *Feiwel, G. R., ed. (II)*, 1987, pp. 1–115.

Feiwel, George R. The Potentials and Limits of Economic Analysis: The Contributions of Kenneth J. Arrow. *Feiwel, G. R., ed. (I)*, 1987, pp. 1–187.

Feldman, Mark D. An Example of Convergence to Rational Expectations with Heterogeneous

Beliefs. *Int. Econ. Rev.*, October 1987, *28*(3), pp. 635–50.

Fishburn, Peter C. Reconsiderations in the Foundations of Decision under Uncertainty. *Econ. J.*, December 1987, *97*(388), pp. 825–41.

Flaschel, Peter and Semmler, Willi. Classical and Neoclassical Competitive Adjustment Processes. *Manchester Sch. Econ. Soc. Stud.*, March 1987, *55*(1), pp. 13–37.

Galles, Gary M. Price Ceilings, Opportunity Costs, and the Demand for Related Goods. *Atlantic Econ. J.*, September 1987, *15*(3), pp. 74.

Gensemer, Susan H. Continuous Semiorder Representations. *J. Math. Econ.*, 1987, *16*(3), pp. 275–89.

Gensemer, Susan H. On Relationships between Numerical Representations of Interval Orders and Semiorders. *J. Econ. Theory*, October 1987, *43*(1), pp. 157–69.

Gilad, Benjamin; Kaish, Stanley and Loeb, Peter D. Cognitive Dissonance and Utility Maximization: A General Framework. *J. Econ. Behav. Organ.*, March 1987, *8*(1), pp. 61–73.

Gilboa, Itzhak. Expected Utility with Purely Subjective Non-additive Probabilities. *J. Math. Econ.*, 1987, *16*(1), pp. 65–88.

Gottinger, Hans W. Choice and Complexity. *Math. Soc. Sci.*, August 1987, *14*(1), pp. 1–17.

Hansen, W. Lee. The Scope of Microeconomics: A Comment. *J. Econ. Educ.*, Spring 1987, *18*(2), pp. 150–54.

Harris, Milton and Holmstrom, Bengt. On the Duration of Agreements. *Int. Econ. Rev.*, June 1987, *28*(2), pp. 389–406.

Harsanyi, John C. Von Neumann–Morgenstern Utilities, Risk Taking, and Welfare. *Feiwel, G. R., ed. (I)*, 1987, pp. 545–58.

Hart, Oliver and Holmstrom, Bengt. The Theory of Contracts. *Bewley, T. F., ed.*, 1987, pp. 71–155.

Hax, Herbert. Institutions for Stochastic Markets: Comment. *J. Inst. Theoretical Econ.*, March 1987, *143*(1), pp. 107–09.

Higgs, Robert. Identity and Cooperation: A Comment on Sen's Alternative Program [Goals, Commitment, and Identity]. *J. Law, Econ., Organ.*, Spring 1987, *3*(1), pp. 140–42.

Hodgson, Geoffrey M. Economic Pluralism and Self-management. *Jones, D. C. and Svejnar, J., eds.*, 1987, pp. 129–42.

Holcomb, James H. and Evans, Dorla A. The Effect of Sunk Costs on Uncertain Decisions in Experimental Markets. *J. Behav. Econ.*, Fall 1987, *16*(3), pp. 59–66.

Howe, Roger. Sections and Extensions of Concave Functions. *J. Math. Econ.*, 1987, *16*(1), pp. 53–64.

Inoue, K.; Moriyasu, T. and Masago, Y. Evaluation of Cardinal Utility Based on Weighted Paired-Comparisons. *Sawaragi, Y.; Inoue, K. and Nakayama, H., eds.*, 1987, pp. 257–66.

Islei, Gerd and Lockett, A. G. An Approach to Preference Vector Derivation Using Geometric Least Square. *Sawaragi, Y.; Inoue, K. and Na-*

kayama, H., eds., 1987, pp. 286–95.

Jordan, James S. The Informational Requirements of Local Stability in Decentralized Allocation Mechanisms. *[Hurwicz, L.]*, 1987, pp. 183–212.

Kagel, John H. Economics According to the Rats (and Pigeons Too): What Have We Learned and What Can We Hope to Learn? *Roth, A. E., ed.*, 1987, pp. 155–92.

Kmenta, Jan. Institutions for Stochastic Markets: Comment. *J. Inst. Theoretical Econ.*, March 1987, *143*(1), pp. 104–06.

Kodde, David A. and Palm, Franz C. A Parametric Test of the Negativity of the Substitution Matrix. *J. Appl. Econometrics*, July 1987, *2*(3), pp. 227–35. [G: W. Germany]

Lea, S. E. G. Animal Experiments in Economic Psychology. *Green, L. and Kagel, J. H., eds.*, 1987, *1981*, pp. 95–116.

Lippman, Steven A.; Mamer, John W. and McCardle, Kevin F. Comparative Statics in Non-cooperative Games via Transfinitely Iterated Play. *J. Econ. Theory*, April 1987, *41*(2), pp. 288–303.

Lowe, Adolph. Is Economic Value Still a Problem? *Lowe, A., 1987, 1981*, pp. 132–54.

Machina, Mark J. and Neilson, William S. The Ross Characterization of Risk Aversion: Strengthening and Extension. *Econometrica*, September 1987, *55*(5), pp. 1139–49.

Marschak, Thomas. Price versus Direct Revelation: Informational Judgments for Finite Mechanisms. *[Hurwicz, L.]*, 1987, pp. 132–79.

Meyer, Jack. Two-moment Decision Models and Expected Utility Maximization. *Amer. Econ. Rev.*, June 1987, *77*(3), pp. 421–30.

Nakamura, Yutaka. Expected Utility with a Threshold Function. *Sawaragi, Y.; Inoue, K. and Nakayama, H., eds.*, 1987, pp. 170–79.

Owen, P. Dorian. Aggregate Demand Curves in General-Equilibrium Macroeconomic Models: Comparisons with Partial-Equilibrium Microeconomic Demand Curves. *New Zealand Econ. Pap.*, 1987, *21*, pp. 97–104.

Peeters, Marcel. A Dismal Science; An Essay on New Classical Economics. *De Economist*, 1987, *135*(4), pp. 442–66.

Pratt, John W. Multiattribute Utility and Derived Utility. *Sawaragi, Y.; Inoue, K. and Nakayama, H., eds.*, 1987, pp. 149–54.

Rachlin, Howard. Animal Choice and Human Choice. *Green, L. and Kagel, J. H., eds.*, 1987, pp. 48–64.

Roberts, John. Incentives, Information, and Iterative Planning. *[Hurwicz, L.]*, 1987, pp. 349–74.

Rochet, Jean-Charles. A Necessary and Sufficient Condition for Rationalizability in a Quasi-linear Context. *J. Math. Econ.*, 1987, *16*(2), pp. 191–200.

Roy, B. and Vincke, Ph. Pseudo-orders: Definition, Properties and Numerical Representation. *Math. Soc. Sci.*, December 1987, *14*(3), pp. 263–74.

Saari, Donald G. and Williams, Steven R. On the Local Convergence of Economic Mechanisms. *Grandmont, J.-M., ed.*, 1987, *1986*, pp. 152–67.

Salazar-Carrillo, Jorge. Maximization and Rationality in Economics. *J. Behav. Econ.*, Summer 1987, *16*(2), pp. 65–66.

Samuelson, Larry. On the Restrictiveness of Monotonic Scalable Choice in Probabilistic Choice Models. *Math. Soc. Sci.*, August 1987, *14*(1), pp. 19–38.

Schick, Frederic. Rationality: A Third Dimension. *Econ. Philos.*, April 1987, *3*(1), pp. 49–66.

von der Schulenburg, J.-Matthias Graf. Marktgeschehen bei unvollständigen Nachfragerinformationen. Die Auswirkungen von Anbieterwechselkosten und Informationskosten in dynamischen Markprozessen. (With English summary.) *Z. Betriebswirtshaft*, July 1987, *57*(7), pp. 699–719. **[G: W. Germany]**

Serletis, Apostolos. Monetary Asset Separability Tests. *Barnett, W. A. and Singleton, K. J., eds.*, 1987, pp. 169–82.

Strober, Myra H. The Scope of Microeconomics: Implications for Economic Education. *J. Econ. Educ.*, Spring 1987, *18*(2), pp. 135–49.

Tamura, H.; Mori, Y. and Nakamura, Y. On a Measurable Value Function under Risk: A Descriptive Model of Preferences Resolving the Expected Utility Paradoxes. *Sawaragi, Y.; Inoue, K. and Nakayama, H., eds.*, 1987, pp. 210–19.

Thaler, Richard H. The Psychology of Choice and the Assumptions of Economics. *Roth, A. E., ed.*, 1987, pp. 99–130.

Vansnick, Jean-Claude. Intensity of Preference. *Sawaragi, Y.; Inoue, K. and Nakayama, H., eds.*, 1987, pp. 220–29.

Vaughan, William, Jr. and Herrnstein, R. J. Stability, Melioration, and Natural Selection. *Green, L. and Kagel, J. H., eds.*, 1987, pp. 185–215.

Wakker, Peter. Subjective Probabilities for State Dependent Continuous Utility. *Math. Soc. Sci.*, December 1987, *14*(3), pp. 289–98.

Wolinsky, Asher. Matching, Search, and Bargaining. *J. Econ. Theory*, August 1987, *42*(2), pp. 311–33.

Wriglesworth, John L. and Gravelle, Hugh S. E. The Three Consumer Surpluses as Individual Welfare Measures. *Scot. J. Polit. Econ.*, August 1987, *34*(3), pp. 230–48.

Yu, P. L. and Takeda, E. Verifying Preference Separability for Additive Value Functions. *Sawaragi, Y.; Inoue, K. and Nakayama, H., eds.*, 1987, pp. 230–38.

0222 Theory of the Household (consumer demand)

Alderman, Harold. Allocation of Goods through Non-price Mechanisms: Evidence on Distribution by Willingness to Wait. *J. Devel. Econ.*, February 1987, *25*(1), pp. 105–24.
[G: Egypt]

Allen, Beth. Smooth Preferences and the Approximate Expected Utility Hypothesis. *J. Econ. Theory*, April 1987, *41*(2), pp. 340–55.

Altonji, Joseph G. and Siow, Aloysius. Testing the Response of Consumption to Income Changes with (Noisy) Panel Data. *Quart. J. Econ.*, May 1987, *102*(2), pp. 293–328.
[G: U.S.]

Ando, Albert and Kennickell, Arthur B. How Much (or Little) Life Cycle Is There in Micro Data? The Cases of the United States and Japan. *[Modigliani, F.]*, 1987, pp. 159–223.
[G: U.S.; Japan]

Anglin, Paul M. and Baye, Michael R. Information, Multiprice Search, and Cost-of-Living Index Theory. *J. Polit. Econ.*, December 1987, *95*(6), pp. 1179–95.

Appleby, Lynda and Starmer, Chris. Individual Choice under Uncertainty: A Review of Experimental Evidence, Past and Present. *Hey, J. D. and Lambert, P. J., eds.*, 1987, pp. 25–45.

Archambault, Edith. The Family and the Dynamics of Personal Services. *Akehurst, G. and Gadrey, J., eds.*, 1987, pp. 46–55.

Basmann, Robert L.; Molina, David J. and Slottje, D. J. Price-Dependent Preferences and the Fechner–Thurstone Direct Utility Function: An Exposition. *J. Inst. Theoretical Econ.*, December 1987, *143*(4), pp. 568–94.

Battalio, Raymond C.; Dwyer, Gerald P., Jr. and Kagel, John H. Tests of Competing Theories of Consumer Choice and the Representative Consumer Hypothesis. *Econ. J.*, December 1987, *97*(388), pp. 842–56.

Battalio, Raymond C.; Kagel, John H. and Phillips, Owen R. Optimal Prices and Animal Consumers in Congested Markets: A Reply. *Econ. Inquiry*, October 1987, *25*(4), pp. 721–22.

Baumol, William J. Superfairness and Applied Microtheory. *Atlantic Econ. J.*, March 1987, *15*(1), pp. 1–9.

Becker, Gary S. and Barro, Robert J. Altruism and the Economic Theory of Fertility. *Davis, K.; Bernstam, M. S. and Ricardo-Campbell, R., eds.*, 1987, *1986*, pp. 69–76.

Beckmann, Martin J. Entscheidungsprozesse in kontinuierlicher Zeit: Optimale Konsumplanung oder vom Spartrieb zum Konsumrausch. (Decision Processes in Continuous Time: Optimal Consumption Plans or from Thrift to Splurge. With English summary.) *Jahr. Nationalökon. Statist.*, October 1987, *203*(5–6), pp. 476–84.

Berg, Morten. Giffen's Paradox Revisited. *Bull. Econ. Res.*, January 1987, *39*(1), pp. 79–89.
[G: Ireland]

Bezembinder, Th. and van Acker, P. Erratum [Factual versus Representational Utilities and Their Interdimensional Comparisons]. *Soc. Choice Welfare*, September 1987, *4*(3), pp. 240.

Bezembinder, Th. and van Acker, P. Factual versus Representational Utilities and Their Interdimensional Comparisons. *Soc. Choice Welfare*, June 1987, *4*(2), pp. 79–104.

Bockstael, Nancy E. and Strand, Ivar E., Jr. The Effect of Common Sources of Regression Error on Benefit Estimates. *Land Econ.*, February

1987, *63*(1), pp. 11–20.

Briys, Eric. Demande d'assurance, décisions de consommation et de portefeuille: Une analyse en temps continu. (Insurance Demand, Consumption and Portfolio Decisions. With English summary.) *L'Actual. Econ.*, June-September 1987, *63*(2–3), pp. 200–212.

Bronars, Stephen G. The Power of Nonparametric Tests of Preference Maximization [The Nonparametric Approach to Demand Analysis]. *Econometrica*, May 1987, *55*(3), pp. 693–98.

Brooks, Michael A. and Earl, Peter E. On the Implications of Jointness in a Normative Model of Behavior Based on an Activity Hierarchy. *J. Cons. Res.*, December 1987, *14*(3), pp. 445–48.

Browning, Martin. Eating, Drinking, Smoking, and Testing the Lifecycle Hypothesis. *Quart. J. Econ.*, May 1987, *102*(2), pp. 329–45.
[G: U.K.]

Campbell, D. E. Revealed Social Preference. *Soc. Choice Welfare*, September 1987, *4*(3), pp. 225–34.

Capps, Oral, Jr. and Havlicek, Joseph, Jr. Concepts of Consumer Demand Theory. *Raunikar, R. and Huang, C.-L., eds.*, 1987, pp. 3–32.

Caves, Douglas W.; Christensen, Laurits R. and Herriges, Joseph A. The Neoclassical Model of Consumer Demand with Identically Priced Commodities: An Application to Time-of-Use Electricity Pricing. *Rand J. Econ.*, Winter 1987, *18*(4), pp. 564–80.

Chiappori, Pierre-André and Rochet, Jean-Charles. Revealed Preferences and Differentiable Demand: Notes and Comments. *Econometrica*, May 1987, *55*(3), pp. 687–91.

Choi, Eun Kwan and Johnson, Stanley R. Consumer's Surplus and Price Uncertainty. *Int. Econ. Rev.*, June 1987, *28*(2), pp. 407–11.

Chu, C. Y. Cyrus. The Effect of Social Security on the Steady State Distribution of Consumption. *J. Public Econ.*, November 1987, *34*(2), pp. 189–210.

Clarida, Richard H. Consumption, Liquidity Constraints and Asset Accumulation in the Presence of Random Income Fluctuations. *Int. Econ. Rev.*, June 1987, *28*(2), pp. 339–51.

Corfman, Kim P. Group Decisionmaking and Relative Influence When Preferences Differ: A Conceptual Framework. *Sheth, J. N. and Hirschman, E., eds.*, 1987, pp. 223–57.

Cory, Dennis C. and Saliba, Bonnie Colby. Requiem for Option Value. *Land Econ.*, February 1987, *63*(1), pp. 1–10.

Coursey, Don L.; Hovis, John L. and Schulze, William D. The Disparity between Willingness to Accept and Willingness to Pay Measures of Value. *Quart. J. Econ.*, August 1987, *102*(3), pp. 679–90.

Coursey, Don L. and Mason, Charles. Investigations Concerning the Dynamics of Consumer Behavior in Uncertain Environments. *Econ. Inquiry*, October 1987, *25*(4), pp. 549–64.

Covich, Alan P. Optimal Use of Space by Neighboring Central Place Foragers: When and Where to Store Surplus Resources. *Green, L. and Kagel, J. H., eds.*, 1987, pp. 249–94.

Curien, Nicolas and Gensollen, Michel. Les théories de la demande de raccordement téléphonique. (The Theory of Demand for Telephone Access. With English summary.) *Revue Écon.*, March 1987, *38*(2), pp. 203–55.

Danilov, Vladimir I. Aggregation of Dichotomic Preferences. *Math. Soc. Sci.*, February 1987, *13*(1), pp. 49–58.

Darvish, Tikva and Kahana, Nava. Measuring Consumer's Surplus in the Factor Market. *Atlantic Econ. J.*, March 1987, *15*(1), pp. 59–62.

David, Paul A. Altruism and the Economic Theory of Fertility: Comment. *Davis, K.; Bernstam, M. S. and Ricardo-Campbell, R., eds.*, 1987, *1986*, pp. 77–86.

Dax, Peter. Estimation of Income Elasticities from Cross-Section Data. *Appl. Econ.*, November 1987, *19*(11), pp. 1471–82. [G: U.K.]

Delmas, Bernard and Gadrey, Jean. On the Substitution of Goods and Services. *Akehurst, G. and Gadrey, J., eds.*, 1987, pp. 12–25.

Diamond, Peter. Consumer Differences and Prices in a Search Model. *Quart. J. Econ.*, May 1987, *102*(2), pp. 429–36.

Doignon, Jean-Paul; Ducamp, André and Falmagne, Jean-Claude. On the Separation of Two Relations by a Biorder or a Semiorder. *Math. Soc. Sci.*, February 1987, *13*(1), pp. 1–18.

Downey, Ezekial H. The Futility of Marginal Utility. *Albelda, R.; Gunn, C. and Waller, W., eds.*, 1987, *1910*, pp. 48–59.

Drèze, Jacques H. Demand Estimation, Risk Aversion and Sticky Prices. *Drèze, J. H.*, 1987, *1979*, pp. 144–49.

Drèze, Jacques H. Logical Foundations of Cardinal Utility and Subjective Probability. *Drèze, J. H.*, 1987, pp. 90–104.

Drèze, Jacques H. and Dehez, Pierre. State-Dependent Utility, the Demand for Insurance and the Value of Safety. *Drèze, J. H.*, 1987, *1982*, pp. 153–81.

Drèze, Jacques H. and Modigliani, Franco. Consumption Decisions under Uncertainty. *Drèze, J. H.*, 1987, *1972*, pp. 182–212.

Drèze, Jacques H. and Modigliani, Franco. Earnings, Assets and Savings: A Model of Interdependent Choice. *Drèze, J. H.*, 1987, pp. 213–19.

Ebert, Udo. Axiomatic Foundations of Hicksian Measures of Welfare Change. *J. Public Econ.*, June 1987, *33*(1), pp. 115–24.

Eeckhoudt, Louis; Sneessens, Henri R. and Calcoen, Francis. L'épargne de précaution et les changements de risque. (Precautionary Saving and Changes in Risk. With English summary.) *L'Actual. Econ.*, June-September 1987, *63*(2–3), pp. 213–24.

Eichenbaum, Martin S. and Peled, Dan. Capital Accumulation and Annuities in an Adverse Selection Economy. *J. Polit. Econ.*, April 1987, *95*(2), pp. 334–54.

Encarnación, J. Preference Paradoxes and Lexicographic Choice. *J. Econ. Behav. Organ.*, June 1987, *8*(2), pp. 231–48.

Epstein, Larry G. The Unimportance of the Intransitivity of Separable Preferences. *Int. Econ. Rev.*, June 1987, *28*(2), pp. 315–22.

Falkinger, Josef. Lieber begehrt und im Überfluss als überflüssig und in Not: Ein Beispiel. (With English summary.) *Kyklos*, 1987, *40*(3), pp. 393–98.

Feichtinger, Gustav. Intertemporal Optimization of Wine Consumption at a Party: An Unusual Optimal Control Model. *[Marrama, V.]*, Vol. 2, 1987, pp. 777–97.

Feldstein, Martin S. The Welfare Cost of Social Security's Impact on Private Saving. *[Harberger, A.]*, 1987, pp. 1–13.

Fishburn, Peter C. and Gehrlein, William V. Aggregation Theory for SSB Utility Functionals. *J. Econ. Theory*, August 1987, *42*(2), pp. 352–69.

Frank, Robert H. If *Homo Economicus* Could Choose His Own Utility Function, Would He Want One with a Conscience? *Amer. Econ. Rev.*, September 1987, *77*(4), pp. 593–604.

Freixas, Xavier and Mas-Colell, Andreu. Engel Curves Leading to the Weak Axiom in the Aggregate. *Econometrica*, May 1987, *55*(3), pp. 515–31.

Friedman, David. Cold Houses in Warm Climates and Vice Versa: A Paradox of Rational Heating. *J. Polit. Econ.*, October 1987, *95*(5), pp. 1089–97.

Georgantelis, S.; Phillips, Garry D. A. and Zhang, W. Estimating and Testing an Almost Ideal Demand System. *Heijmans, R. and Neudecker, H., eds.*, 1987, pp. 15–29. [G: U.K.]

Gottinger, Hans W. Decision Costs and Microeconomic Demand for Money. *Z. Wirtschaft. Sozialwissen.*, 1987, *107*(3), pp. 361–78.

Grandmont, Jean-Michel. Distributions of Preferences and the "Law of Demand." *Econometrica*, January 1987, *55*(1), pp. 155–61.

Gray, John. The Economic Approach to Human Behavior: Its Prospects and Limitations. *Radnitzky, G. and Bernholz, P., eds.*, 1987, pp. 33–49.

Green, Jerry R. "Making Book against Oneself," the Independence Axiom, and Nonlinear Utility Theory. *Quart. J. Econ.*, November 1987, *102*(4), pp. 785–96.

Gross, Barbara L. Time Scarcity: Interdisciplinary Perspectives and Implications for Consumer Behavior. *Sheth, J. N. and Hirschman, E., eds.*, 1987, pp. 1–54.

Hartman, Richard and Plummer, Mark L. Option Value under Income and Price Uncertainty. *J. Environ. Econ. Manage.*, September 1987, *14*(3), pp. 212–25.

Haveman, Robert H.; Gabay, Mary and Andreoni, James R. Exact Consumer's Surplus and Deadweight Loss: A Correction. *Amer. Econ. Rev.*, June 1987, *77*(3), pp. 494–95.

Hennipman, Piet. A Tale of Two Schools: Comments on a New View of the Ordinalist Revolution. *De Economist*, 1987, *135*(2), pp. 141–62.

Hillier, Brian and Lunati, M. Teresa. On Nash versus Stackelberg Strategies and the Conditions for Operative Intergenerational Transfers. *Scot. J. Polit. Econ.*, February 1987, *34*(1), pp. 91–96.

Hirschman, Elizabeth C. Theoretical Perspectives of Time Use: Implications for Consumer Behavior Research. *Sheth, J. N. and Hirschman, E., eds.*, 1987, pp. 55–81.

Hirshleifer, Jack. Disaster Behavior: Altruism or Alliance? *Hirshleifer, J.*, 1987, pp. 134–41. [G: U.S.]

Hjorth-Andersen, Chr. Forbrugeroplysning spgsm om milliarder. (The Economic Importance of Imperfect Consumer Information. With English summary.) *Nationaløkon. Tidsskr.*, 1987, *125*(1), pp. 78–94. [G: Denmark]

Hoehn, John P. and Randall, Alan. A Satisfactory Benefit Cost Indicator from Contingent Valuation. *J. Environ. Econ. Manage.*, September 1987, *14*(3), pp. 226–47.

Honkapohja, Seppo. On Continuity of Compensated Demand. *Int. Econ. Rev.*, October 1987, *28*(3), pp. 545–57.

Houthakker, Hendrik S. and Tobin, James. Estimates of the Free Demand for Rationed Foodstuffs. *Tobin, J. (II)*, 1987, *1952*, pp. 379–96.

Hursh, Steven R. and Bauman, Richard A. The Behavioral Analysis of Demand. *Green, L. and Kagel, J. H., eds.*, 1987, pp. 117–65.

Hurwicz, Leonid; Jordan, James S. and Kannai, Yakar. On the Demand Generated by a Smooth and Concavifiable Preference Ordering. *J. Math. Econ.*, 1987, *16*(2), pp. 169–89.

Jasso, Guillermina. Choosing a Good: Models Based on the Theory of the Distributive-Justice Force. *Lawler, E. J. and Markovsky, B., eds.*, 1987, pp. 67–108.

Kagel, John H. and Green, Leonard. Intertemporal Choice Behavior: Evaluation of Economic and Psychological Models. *Green, L. and Kagel, J. H., eds.*, 1987, pp. 166–84.

Kanbur, S. M. Ravi. The Standard of Living: Uncertainty, Inequality and Opportunity. *Sen, A. K., et al.*, 1987, pp. 59–69.

Karni, Edi. Generalized Expected Utility Analysis of Risk Aversion with State-Dependent Preference. *Int. Econ. Rev.*, February 1987, *28*(1), pp. 229–40.

Karni, Edi and Safra, Zvi. "Preference Reversal" and the Observability of Preferences by Experimental Methods. *Econometrica*, May 1987, *55*(3), pp. 675–85.

Kim, Taesung. Intransitive Indifference and Revealed Preference. *Econometrica*, January 1987, *55*(1), pp. 163–67.

Kim, Young Chin and Yoon, Bong Joon. Risk Behavior under Linear Utility Function. *Int. Econ. J.*, Autumn 1987, *1*(3), pp. 49–56.

Knetsch, Jack L. and Sinden, J. A. The Persistence of Evaluation Disparities. *Quart. J. Econ.*, August 1987, *102*(3), pp. 691–95.

Knez, Marc and Smith, Vernon L. Hypothetical Valuations and Preference Reversals in the Context of Asset Trading. *Roth, A. E., ed.*, 1987, pp. 131–54.

Kooreman, Peter and Kapteyn, Arie. A Disaggregated Analysis of the Allocation of Time within the Household. *J. Polit. Econ.*, April 1987, 95(2), pp. 223–49. **[G: U.S.]**

Kosicki, George. A Test of the Relative Income Hypothesis. *Southern Econ. J.*, October 1987, 54(2), pp. 422–34. **[G: U.S.]**

Kotlikoff, Laurence J. Consumer Spending and the After-Tax Real Interest Rate: Comment. *Feldstein, M., ed. (I)*, 1987, pp. 67–68. **[G: U.S.]**

Krause, Ulrich. Hierarchical Structures in Multicriteria Decision Making. *Jahn, J. and Krabs, W., eds.*, 1987, pp. 183–93.

Kurz, Mordecai. The Life-Cycle Hypothesis as a Tool of Theory and Policy. *Feiwel, G. R., ed. (II)*, 1987, pp. 447–90. **[G: U.S.]**

Lee, Ronald D. The Value and Allocation of Time in High-Income Countries: Implications for Fertility: Comment. *Davis, K.; Bernstam, M. S. and Ricardo-Campbell, R., eds.*, 1987, 1986, pp. 108–10.

Lensberg, Terje. Stability and Collective Rationality. *Econometrica*, July 1987, 55(4), pp. 935–61.

Lentnek, Barry; Harwitz, Mitchell and Narula, Subhash C. A Contextual Theory of Demand: Beyond Spatial Analysis in Economic Geography. *Econ. Geogr.*, October 1987, 63(4), pp. 334–48.

Leroux, Alain. Preferences and Normal Goods: A Sufficient Condition. *J. Econ. Theory*, October 1987, 43(1), pp. 192–99.

Lewbel, Arthur. Bliss Levels That Aren't [Stochastic Implications of the Life Cycle–Permanent Income Hypothesis: Theory and Evidence]. *J. Polit. Econ.*, February 1987, 95(1), pp. 211–15. **[G: U.S.]**

Lewbel, Arthur. Characterizing Some Gorman Engel Curves. *Econometrica*, November 1987, 55(6), pp. 1451–59.

Loewenstein, George. Anticipation and the Valuation of Delayed Consumption. *Econ. J.*, September 1987, 97(387), pp. 666–84.

Loomes, Graham and Sugden, Robert. Some Implications of a More General Form of Regret Theory. *J. Econ. Theory*, April 1987, 41(2), pp. 270–87.

Loomes, Graham and Sugden, Robert. Testing for Regret and Disappointment in Choice under Uncertainty. *Econ. J.*, Supplement 1987, 97, pp. 118–29.

Machina, Mark J. Choice under Uncertainty: Problems Solved and Unsolved. *J. Econ. Perspectives*, Summer 1987, 1(1), pp. 121–54.

Mak, King-tim. Consistent Aggregation of Demand Functions over Restricted Income Distributions. *J. Econ. (Z. Nationalökon.)*, 1987, 47(2), pp. 195–206.

Maling, Charles. On the Consumers' Surplus of Money Holders and the Measuring of Money's Services. *J. Money, Credit, Banking*, November 1987, 19(4), pp. 469–83.

Mankiw, N. Gregory. Consumer Spending and the After-Tax Real Interest Rate. *Feldstein, M., ed. (I)*, 1987, pp. 53–67. **[G: U.S.]**

Mariger, Randall P. A Life-cycle Consumption Model with Liquidity Constraints: Theory and Empirical Results. *Econometrica*, May 1987, 55(3), pp. 533–57. **[G: U.S.]**

McConnell, Kenneth E. and Phipps, T. T. Identification of Preference Parameters in Hedonic Models: Consumer Demands with Nonlinear Budgets. *J. Urban Econ.*, July 1987, 22(1), pp. 35–52.

McKenna, Christopher J. Models of Search Market Equilibrium. *Hey, J. D. and Lambert, P. J., eds.*, 1987, pp. 110–23.

McKenna, Christopher J. Theories of Individual Search Behaviour. *Hey, J. D. and Lambert, P. J., eds.*, 1987, 1986, pp. 91–109.

Monteiro, Paulo Klinger. Some Results on the Existence of Utility Functions on Path Connected Spaces. *J. Math. Econ.*, 1987, 16(2), pp. 147–56.

Muellbauer, John. Estimating the Intertemporal Elasticity of Substitution for Consumption from Household Budget Data. *Heijmans, R. and Neudecker, H., eds.*, 1987, pp. 45–57. **[G: U.K.]**

Muellbauer, John. Professor Sen on the Standard of Living. *Sen, A. K., et al.*, 1987, pp. 39–58.

Nelson, Charles R. A Reappraisal of Recent Tests of the Permanent Income Hypothesis [Stochastic Implications of the Life Cycle–Permanent Income Hypothesis: Theory and Evidence]. *J. Polit. Econ.*, June 1987, 95(3), pp. 641–46. **[G: U.S.]**

Nielsen, Lars Tyge. Corrigenda [Unbounded Expected Utility and Continuity]. *Math. Soc. Sci.*, October 1987, 14(2), pp. 193–94.

Plummer, Mark L. Supply Uncertainty and Option Value: Reply. *Land Econ.*, November 1987, 63(4), pp. 408.

Pratt, John W. and Zeckhauser, Richard J. Proper Risk Aversion. *Econometrica*, January 1987, 55(1), pp. 143–54.

Quah, Euston. Household Production and the GNP: A Model for Use in Valuation. *Econ. Int.*, November 1987, 40(4), pp. 345–61.

Quiggin, John. Decision Weights in Anticipated Utility Theory: Response [A Theory of Anticipated Utility]. *J. Econ. Behav. Organ.*, December 1987, 8(4), pp. 641–45.

Reinhardt, Paul G. Demand Analysis and the Flow of Time in Consumption. *Int. J. Soc. Econ.*, 1987, 14(3/4/5), pp. 199–206.

Röell, Ailsa A. Risk Aversion in Quiggin and Yaari's Rank–Order Model of Choice under Uncertainty. *Econ. J.*, Supplement 1987, 97, pp. 143–59.

Sah, Raaj Kumar. Queues, Rations, and Market: Comparisons of Outcomes for the Poor and the Rich. *Amer. Econ. Rev.*, March 1987, 77(1), pp. 69–77.

Salamon, Peter, et al. A Geometric View of Welfare Gains with Non-instantaneous Adjustment. *Math. Soc. Sci.*, April 1987, 13(2), pp. 153–63.

Sandler, Todd. On Optimal Prices and Animal Consumers in Congested Markets. *Econ. Inquiry*, October 1987, 25(4), pp. 715–20.

Scapparone, Paolo. Una generalizzazione della teoria delle preferenze rivelate. (A Generalization of the Theory of Revealed Preferences. With English summary.) *Rivista Int. Sci. Econ. Com.*, Jan.-Feb. 1987, *34*(1–2), pp. 67–86.

Schimmelpfennig, Jörg. Das Gesetz des abnehmenden Grenznutzens in der ordinalen Nutzentheorie—eine neue alte Interpretation der Inferiorität. (The Law of Diminishing Marginal Utility in Ordinal Utility Theory—A New Old Interpretation of Inferiority. With English summary.) *Jahr. Nationalökon. Statist.*, January 1987, *203*(1), pp. 58–64.

Schultz, T. Paul. The Value and Allocation of Time in High-Income Countries: Implications for Fertility. *Davis, K.; Bernstam, M. S. and Ricardo-Campbell, R., eds.*, 1987, *1986*, pp. 87–108. [G: U.S.]

Scoggins, John Franklin. Welfare Evaluation and Household Production with Non-constant Returns to Scale. *Southern Econ. J.*, January 1987, *53*(3), pp. 643–49.

Segal, Uzi. Some Remarks on Quiggin's Anticipated Utility [A Theory of Anticipated Utility]. *J. Econ. Behav. Organ.*, March 1987, *8*(1), pp. 145–54.

Segal, Uzi. The Ellsberg Paradox and Risk Aversion: An Anticipated Utility Approach. *Int. Econ. Rev.*, February 1987, *28*(1), pp. 175–202.

Segerson, Kathleen. Supply Uncertainty and Option Value: Comment. *Land Econ.*, November 1987, *63*(4), pp. 406–07.

Sen, Amartya K. The Standard of Living: Lecture I, Concepts and Critiques. *Sen, A. K., et al.*, 1987, pp. 1–19.

Sen, Amartya K. The Standard of Living: Reply. *Sen, A. K., et al.*, 1987, pp. 103–12.

Slivinski, Alan D. The Normative Characterization of Aggregate Consumers' Surplus Measures. *Int. Econ. Rev.*, October 1987, *28*(3), pp. 559–81.

Smith, V. Kerry. Uncertainty, Benefit–Cost Analysis, and the Treatment of Option Value. *J. Environ. Econ. Manage.*, September 1987, *14*(3), pp. 283–92.

Solow, Robert M. How Much (or Little) Life Cycle Is There in Micro Data? The Cases of the United States and Japan: Comments. *[Modigliani, F.]*, 1987, pp. 224–28. [G: U.S.; Japan]

Stein, Jeremy C. Informational Externalities and Welfare-Reducing Speculation. *J. Polit. Econ.*, December 1987, *95*(6), pp. 1123–45.

Sugden, Robert. New Developments in the Theory of Choice under Uncertainty. *Hey, J. D. and Lambert, P. J., eds.*, 1987, pp. 1–24.

Swofford, James L. and Whitney, Gerald A. Nonparametric Tests of Utility Maximization and Weak Separability for Consumption, Leisure and Money. *Rev. Econ. Statist.*, August 1987, *69*(3), pp. 458–64. [G: U.S.]

Tellis, Gerard J. and Wernerfelt, Birger. Competitive Price and Quality under Asymmetric Information. *Marketing Sci.*, Summer 1987, *6*(3), pp. 240–53. [G: U.S.]

Timberlake, Richard H., Jr. A Critique of Monetarist and Austrian Doctrines on the Utility and Value of Money. *Rothbard, M. N., ed.*, 1987, pp. 81–96.

Tinbergen, Jan. Measuring Welfare of Productive Consumers. *De Economist*, 1987, *135*(2), pp. 231–36.

Tobin, James. A Survey of the Theory of Rationing. *Tobin, J. (II)*, 1987, *1952*, pp. 321–58.

Tobin, James. On the Predictive Value of Consumer Intentions and Attitudes. *Tobin, J. (II)*, 1987, *1959*, pp. 299–318.

Tobin, James and Dolbear, F. Trenery, Jr. On the Relevance of Psychology to Economic Theory and Research. *Tobin, J. (II)*, 1987, *1963*, pp. 291–98.

Tobin, James and Houthakker, Hendrik S. The Effects of Rationing on Demand Elasticities. *Tobin, J. (II)*, 1987, *1951*, pp. 359–77.

Uriarte, J. R. Topological Structure of a Space of Continuous Preferences as a Space of Retractions and the Aggregation Problem. *Math. Soc. Sci.*, June 1987, *13*(3), pp. 259–72.

Viscusi, W. Kip; Magat, Wesley A. and Huber, Joel C. An Investigation of the Rationality of Consumer Valuations of Multiple Health Risks. *Rand J. Econ.*, Winter 1987, *18*(4), pp. 465–79. [G: U.S.]

Vives, Xavier. Small Income Effects: A Marshallian Theory of Consumer Surplus and Downward Sloping Demand. *Rev. Econ. Stud.*, January 1987, *54*(1), pp. 87–103.

Vlačic, Lj.; Wierzbicki, A. and Matić, B. Aggregation Procedures for Hierarchically Grouped Decision Attributes with Application to Control System Performance Evaluation. *Jahn, J. and Krabs, W., eds.*, 1987, pp. 285–310.

Watts, Harold W. and Tobin, James. Consumer Expenditures and the Capital Account. *Tobin, J. (II)*, 1987, *1960*, pp. 247–90. [G: U.S.]

White, Michael. Porter's 'Hint'? A Note. *Australian Econ. Pap.*, December 1987, *26*(49), pp. 328–31.

Wieczorek, Andrzej. Pseudo-utilities. *Jahn, J. and Krabs, W., eds.*, 1987, pp. 241–53.

Wilde, Louis L. Consumer Behavior under Imperfect Information: A Review of Psychological and Marketing Research as It Relates to Economic Theory. *Green, L. and Kagel, J. H., eds.*, 1987, pp. 219–48.

Williams, Bernard. The Standard of Living: Interests and Capabilities. *Sen, A. K., et al.*, 1987, pp. 94–102.

Winston, Gordon C. Activity Choice: A New Approach to Economic Behavior. *J. Econ. Behav. Organ.*, December 1987, *8*(4), pp. 567–85.

Yaari, Menahem E. The Dual Theory of Choice under Risk. *Econometrica*, January 1987, *55*(1), pp. 95–115.

Zilcha, Itzhak. Characterizing the Efficient Set When Preferences Are State-Dependent. *J. Econ. Theory*, April 1987, *41*(2), pp. 417–23.

0223 Theory of Production

Akiba, Hiroya. Resource Allocation with Factor Price Differentials in a Simple Two-Sector

Model with Production Risk. *Ricerche Econ.*, Apr.-June 1987, *41*(2), pp. 174–89.

Alchian, Armen A. Some Perspectives on the Modern Theory of the Firm: A Conference in Honor of Armen A. Alchian: Concluding Remarks. *J. Inst. Theoretical Econ.*, March 1987, *143*(1), pp. 232–34.

Alchian, Armen A. and Woodward, Susan. Reflections on the Theory of the Firm. *J. Inst. Theoretical Econ.*, March 1987, *143*(1), pp. 110–36.

Altenburg, Lutz. Production Possibilities with a Public Intermediate Good. *Can. J. Econ.*, November 1987, *20*(4), pp. 715–34.

Anandalingam, G. and Kulatilaka, Nalin. Decomposing Production Efficiency into Technical, Allocative and Structural Components. *J. Roy. Statist. Soc.*, 1987, *150*(2), pp. 143–51.

Anderson, Curt L. The Production Process: Inputs and Wastes. *J. Environ. Econ. Manage.*, March 1987, *14*(1), pp. 1–12. **[G: U.S.]**

Baldone, Salvatore. Il capitale fisso come "specie" del "genere" produzione congiunta: un commento. (Fixed Capital as a "Species" of the "Genus" Joint Production: A Comment. With English summary.) *Econ. Polít.*, August 1987, *4*(2), pp. 247–58.

Bamberg, Günter. Risk Sharing and Subcontracting. *Bamberg, G. and Spremann, K., eds.*, 1987, pp. 61–79.

Baron, David P. and Besanko, David. Commitment and Fairness in a Dynamic Regulatory Relationship. *Rev. Econ. Stud.*, July 1987, *54*(3), pp. 413–36.

Bartlett, Will. Capital Accumulation and Employment in a Self-Financed Worker Cooperative. *Int. J. Ind. Organ.*, September 1987, *5*(3), pp. 277–87.

Bartlett, Will. Enterprise Investment and Public Consumption in a Self-managed Economy. *Jones, D. C. and Svejnar, J., eds.*, 1987, pp. 165–81. **[G: Yugoslavia]**

Barzel, Yoram. The Entrepreneur's Reward for Self-policing. *Econ. Inquiry*, January 1987, *25*(1), pp. 103–16.

Beckmann, Martin J. Managers as Principals and Agents. *Bamberg, G. and Spremann, K., eds.*, 1987, pp. 379–88.

Beladi, Hamid; Lee, Young-Kwang and Naqvi, Nadeem. The Long Run Behavior of the Firm under Uncertainty. *Atlantic Econ. J.*, December 1987, *15*(4), pp. 57–64.

Bernstein, Jeffrey I. and Nadiri, M. Ishaq. Corporate Taxes and Incentives and the Structure of Production: A Selected Survey. *Mintz, J. M. and Purvis, D. D., eds.*, 1987, pp. 178–208.

Berry, S. Keith. Rate-of-Return Regulation and Demand Uncertainty with a Symmetric Regulatory Constraint. *Amer. Econ.*, Fall 1987, *31*(2), pp. 8–12.

Bös, Dieter. On Supporting the Maximization Postulate. *J. Behav. Econ.*, Summer 1987, *16*(2), pp. 55–59.

Bradford, Garnett L. An Opportunity Cost View of Fixed Asset Theory and the Overproduction Trap: Comment. *Amer. J. Agr. Econ.*, May 1987, *69*(2), pp. 392–94.

Breyer, Friedrich. The "Homothetic" Firm in Illyria: Comment. *J. Compar. Econ.*, December 1987, *11*(4), pp. 603–05.

Bromiley, Philip. A Comparison of Behavioral and Conventional Conceptions of Investment. *J. Behav. Econ.*, Spring 1987, *16*(1), pp. 1–20.

Browning, Martin. Co-operatives, Closures, or Wage Cuts: The Choices Facing Workers in an Ailing Firm. *Can. J. Econ.*, February 1987, *20*(1), pp. 114–22.

Caravani, Paolo and De Luca, Alessandro. Aggregation in Sraffa's Simple Production Model. *J. Econ. (Z. Nationalökon.)*, 1987, *47*(2), pp. 167–93.

Chao, Hung-po and Wilson, Robert B. Priority Service: Pricing, Investment, and Market Organization. *Amer. Econ. Rev.*, December 1987, *77*(5), pp. 899–916.

Chen, Guo-quan and Yu, Eden S. H. Input Price, Isocost and Maximum Output under Fuzziness. *Math. Soc. Sci.*, June 1987, *13*(3), pp. 243–57.

Colangelo, Giuseppe. Il modello dell'acceleratore flessibile generalizzato come soluzione lineare globalmente ottimale. (The Generalized Flexible Accelerator as a Globally Optimal Linear Solution. With English summary.) *Econ. Polít.*, August 1987, *4*(2), pp. 189–211.

Curien, Nicolas. L'accès et l'usage téléphoniques: modélisation conjointe et tarification optimale. (Telephone Access and Usage: Joint Modelization and Optimal Pricing. With English summary.) *Revue Écon.*, March 1987, *38*(2), pp. 415–58.

Dasgupta, Partha and Maskin, Eric. The Simple Economics of Research Portfolios. *Econ. J.*, September 1987, *97*(387), pp. 581 95.

Dave, Upendra. On Two Deterministic Inventory Models for Items with Decreasing Demand. *Econ. Computat. Cybern. Stud. Res.*, 1987, *22*(2), pp. 45–50.

Davis, H. Craig. Alternative Approaches to the Estimation of Economic Impacts Resulting from Supply Constraints: Reply. *Ann. Reg. Sci.*, March 1987, *21*(1), pp. 83–84.

Demsetz, Harold. An Appreciation of Armen A. Alchian's Contribution to the Theory of the Firm. *J. Inst. Theoretical Econ.*, March 1987, *143*(1), pp. 3–6.

Diewert, Walter Erwin. Corporate Taxes and Incentives and the Structure of Production: A Selected Survey: Comment. *Mintz, J. M. and Purvis, D. D., eds.*, 1987, pp. 209–24.

Dionne, Georges and Pellerin, Marc. Investissement en incertitude: Extension du problème de la taille optimale d'une usine. (Investment under Uncertainty. With English summary.) *L'Actual. Econ.*, June-September 1987, *63*(2–3), pp. 256–81.

Dixon, Bruce L.; Garcia, Philip and Anderson, Margot. Usefulness of Pretests for Estimating Underlying Technologies Using Dual Profit Functions. *Int. Econ. Rev.*, October 1987, *28*(3), pp. 623–33.

Dixon, Huw. Approximate Bertrand Equilibria in a Replicated Industry. *Rev. Econ. Stud.*, January 1987, *54*(1), pp. 47–62.

Drèze, Jacques H. (Uncertainty and) the Firm in General Equilibrium Theory. *Drèze, J. H.*, 1987, *1985*, pp. 321–43.

Drèze, Jacques H. Decision Criteria for Business Firms. *Drèze, J. H.*, 1987, *1982*, pp. 298–320.

Drèze, Jacques H. Investment under Private Ownership: Optimality, Equilibrium and Stability. *Drèze, J. H.*, 1987, *1974*, pp. 261–97.

Drèze, Jacques H. Some Theory of Labour Management and Participation. *Drèze, J. H.*, 1987, *1976*, pp. 366–82.

Drèze, Jacques H. and Sheshinski, Eytan. Demand Fluctuations, Capacity Utilisation and Costs. *Drèze, J. H.*, 1987, *1976*, pp. 234–49.

Duda, Helga and Fehr, Ernst. Power, Efficiency and Profitability: A Radical Theory of the Firm. *Econ. Anal. Workers' Manage.*, 1987, *21*(1), pp. 1–26.

Edwards, Brian K. and Starr, Ross M. A Note on Indivisibilities, Specialization, and Economies of Scale. *Amer. Econ. Rev.*, March 1987, *77*(1), pp. 192–94.

Eichner, Alfred S. Prices and Pricing. *J. Econ. Issues*, December 1987, *21*(4), pp. 1555–84.

Eliasson, Gunnar. Information Technology, Capital Structure and the Nature of Technical Change in the Firm. *Eliasson, G.*, 1987, pp. 51–78.

Färe, Rolf; Grosskopf, Shawna and Lovell, C. A. Knox. Nonparametric Disposability Tests. *J. Econ. (Z. Nationalökon.)*, 1987, *47*(1), pp. 77–85.

Färe, Rolf and Lehmijoki, Ulla. On Quasi-convexity of the Cost Function. *Scand. J. Econ.*, 1987, *89*(1), pp. 115–18.

Färe, Rolf and Mitchell, Thomas M. On Shephard's Attainability Axiom. *J. Inst. Theoretical Econ.*, June 1987, *143*(2), pp. 343–50.

Folbre, Nancy R. A Patriarchal Mode of Production. *Albelda, R.; Gunn, C. and Waller, W.*, eds., 1987, pp. 323–38.

Franke, Günter. Reflections on the Theory of the Firm: Comment. *J. Inst. Theoretical Econ.*, March 1987, *143*(1), pp. 143–48.

Freeman, Christopher and Soete, Luc. Factor Substitution and Technical Change. *Freeman, C. and Soete, L.*, eds., 1987, pp. 36–48.

Fuss, Melvyn A. Corporate Taxes and Incentives and the Structure of Production: A Selected Survey: Comment. *Mintz, J. M. and Purvis, D. D.*, eds., 1987, pp. 225–27.

Galeotti, Marzio. On the Dual Relationship between Flexible Accelerator and *q* Theories of Investment. *Rivista Int. Sci. Econ. Com.*, August 1987, *34*(8), pp. 771–76.

Ghali, Moheb A. Seasonality, Aggregation and the Testing of the Production Smoothing Hypothesis. *Amer. Econ. Rev.*, June 1987, *77*(3), pp. 464–69. **[G: U.S.]**

Gintis, Herbert. The Nature of Labor Exchange and the Theory of Capitalist Production. *Albelda, R.; Gunn, C. and Waller, W.*, eds., 1987, *1976*, pp. 68–88.

Gordon, Daniel V. Modelling Multi-output Technologies: A Cobb–Douglas Approach. *Can. J. Agr. Econ.*, March 1987, *35*(1), pp. 221–27.

de la Grandville, Olivier. On Two-Regime Discrete-Time Models: A Methodological Note. *J. Econ. Behav. Organ.*, September 1987, *8*(3), pp. 513–30.

Griffin, Ronald C.; Montgomery, John M. and Rister, M. Edward. Selecting Functional Form in Production Function Analysis. *Western J. Agr. Econ.*, December 1987, *12*(2), pp. 216–27.

Grout, Paul A. and Laisney, François. The Effects of the Dispersion of Shareholdings on Performance of Owner Controlled Firms. *Ann. Écon. Statist.*, Jan./Mar. 1987, (5), pp. 77–87.

Gui, Benedetto. Internal Pay Schedules and Labour Mobility: The Problem of Firm Survival. *Econ. Notes*, 1987, (2), pp. 89–101.

Hadar, Josef and Seo, Tae Kun. Consistent Planning under Uncertain Lifetime. *Int. Econ. J.*, Summer 1987, *1*(2), pp. 95–108.

Hall, Christopher D. Heterogeneous Firms: A Consumer's Report [Heterogeneous Firms and the Organization of Production]. *Econ. Inquiry*, January 1987, *25*(1), pp. 175–80.

Harris, Frederick H. deB. Competing Theories of Firm Decision-Making under Risk. *Southern Econ. J.*, October 1987, *54*(2), pp. 271–86. **[G: U.S.]**

Haruna, Shoji. Random Input Price and the Theory of the Competitive Cooperative Firm. *J. Compar. Econ.*, March 1987, *11*(1), pp. 81–95.

Hertel, Thomas W. Inferring Long-run Elasticities from a Short-run Quadratic Profit Function. *Can. J. Agr. Econ.*, March 1987, *35*(1), pp. 169–80.

Hey, John D. The Dynamic Competitive Firm under Spot Price Uncertainty. *Manchester Sch. Econ. Soc. Stud.*, March 1987, *55*(1), pp. 1–12.

Hillman, Arye L.; Katz, Eliakim and Rosenberg, Jacob. Workers as Insurance: Anticipated Government Assistance and Factor Demand. *Oxford Econ. Pap.*, December 1987, *39*(4), pp. 813–20.

Hollander, Abraham; Huarie, Alain and L'Ecuyer, Pierre. Ratchet Effects and the Cost of Incremental Incentive Schemes. *J. Econ. Dynam. Control*, September 1987, *11*(3), pp. 373–89.

Horowitz, Ira. On the Price-Taking Labor-Managed Supplier of a Perishable Good of Uncertain Demand Quantity. *Atlantic Econ. J.*, July 1987, *15*(2), pp. 42–46.

Horstmann, Ignatius J. and Markusen, James R. Strategic Investments and the Development of Multinationals. *Int. Econ. Rev.*, February 1987, *28*(1), pp. 109–21.

Ireland, Norman J. The Economic Analysis of Labour-Managed Firms. *Bull. Econ. Res.*, October 1987, *39*(4), pp. 249–72.

Jensen, Keith Christian and Kamath, Shyam J. Liquidity in the Production Function: A Reexamination. *Indian Econ. J.*, Oct.-Dec. 1987, 35(2), pp. 91–114. **[G: U.S.]**

Johansson, Börje. Technological Vintages and Substitution Processes. *Batten, D.; Casti, J. and Johansson, B., eds.*, 1987, pp. 145–84.

Jose, Manuel L. and Stevens, Jerry L. Product Market Structure, Capital Intensity, and Systematic Risk: Empirical Results from the Theory of the Firm. *J. Finan. Res.*, Summer 1987, 10(2), pp. 161–75. **[G: U.S.]**

Jovanovic, Boyan and Rob, Rafael. Demand-Driven Innovation and Spatial Competition over Time. *Rev. Econ. Stud.*, January 1987, 54(1), pp. 63–72.

Kahana, Nava. The Multifactor Illyrian Firm Revisited: Comment. *J. Compar. Econ.*, December 1987, 11(4), pp. 611–12.

Kahana, Nava and Spiegel, Uriel. Do Egalitarian Labour-Managed Enterprises Respond Perversely? *Econ. Anal. Workers' Manage.*, 1987, 21(4), pp. 465–67.

Katz, Michael L. and Shapiro, Carl. R&D Rivalry with Licensing or Imitation. *Amer. Econ. Rev.*, June 1987, 77(3), pp. 402–20.

Kaulmann, Thomas. Managerialism versus the Property Rights Theory of the Firm. *Bamberg, G. and Spremann, K., eds.*, 1987, pp. 439–59. **[G: U.S.]**

Kim, H. Youn. Decomposition Analysis of Derived Demand for Factor Inputs with Biased Technical Change and Output Adjustment. *Bull. Econ. Res.*, April 1987, 39(2), pp. 179–83.

Kim, H. Youn. Economies of Scale in Multi-product Firms: An Empirical Analysis. *Economica*, May 1987, 54(214), pp. 185–206. **[G: U.S.]**

Kumbhakar, Subal C. The Specification of Technical and Allocative Inefficiency of Multi-product Firms in Stochastic Production and Profit Frontiers. *J. Quant. Econ.*, July 1987, 3(2), pp. 213–23.

La Manna, Manfredi M. A. The Simple Analytics of Agency Costs: A Pedagogical Comment. *Econ. Notes*, 1987, (2), pp. 145–56.

Laffont, Jean-Jacques and Tirole, Jean. Comparative Statics of the Optimal Dynamic Incentive Contract. *Europ. Econ. Rev.*, June 1987, 31(4), pp. 901–26.

Lambert, Jean-Paul. Conflicting Specifications for Investment Functions in Rationing Models: A Reconciliation. *Rech. Écon. Louvain*, 1987, 53(2), pp. 135–45.

Lee, Li Way. The Coasian Firm. *J. Behav. Econ.*, Summer 1987, 16(2), pp. 1–7.

Lee, Wayne Y. and Thakor, Anjan V. Regulatory Pricing and Capital Investment under Asymmetric Information about Cost. *Southern Econ. J.*, January 1987, 53(3), pp. 720–34.

Leech, Dennis. Ownership Concentration and the Theory of the Firm: A Simple-Game-Theoretic Approach. *J. Ind. Econ.*, March 1987, 35(3), pp. 225–40.

Löfgren, Karl-Gustaf and Ranneby, Bo. Behavioral Modes for a Firm Facing an Uncertain Supply or Demand Curve. *Scand. J. Econ.*, 1987, 89(1), pp. 39–54.

MacDonald, James M. Economies of Scope, Contestability Theory, and Economic Efficiency. *Kilmer, R. L. and Armbruster, W. J., eds.*, 1987, pp. 154–76.

MacLeod, W. Bentley. Behavior and the Organization of the Firm. *J. Compar. Econ.*, June 1987, 11(2), pp. 207–20.

MacMinn, Richard D. Forward Markets, Stock Markets, and the Theory of the Firm. *J. Finance*, December 1987, 42(5), pp. 1167–85.

Madan, Dilip B. Optimal Duration and Speed in the Long Run. *Rev. Econ. Stud.*, October 1987, 54(4), pp. 695–700.

Mahmud, S. F.; Robb, A. L. and Scarth, William M. On Estimating Dynamic Factor Demands. *J. Appl. Econometrics*, January 1987, 2(1), pp. 69–75. **[G: U.S.]**

Mai, Chao-Cheng. Demand Function and Location Theory of the Firm under Price Uncertainty: A Reply. *Urban Stud.*, April 1987, 24(2), pp. 162.

Malinvaud, Edmond. Capital productif, incertitudes et profitabilité. (Productive Capacity, Uncertainties and Profitability. With English summary.) *Ann. Écon. Statist.*, Jan./Mar. 1987, (5), pp. 1–36.

Marsden, James R.; Salas-Fumas, Vicente and Whinston, Andrew. Technology Transfer: Measuring the Impact of Organisational and Managerial Structures on Production Efficiency. *Pasinetti, L. and Lloyd, P., eds.*, 1987, pp. 47–73.

Maruyama, Shigeru. The Choice of Working Hours. *J. Econ. (Z. Nationalökon.)*, 1987, 47(1), pp. 1–14.

McElroy, Marjorie B. Additive General Error Models for Production, Cost, and Derived Demand or Share Systems. *J. Polit. Econ.*, August 1987, 95(4), pp. 737–57. **[G: U.S.]**

Meran, Georg and Wolfstetter, Elmar. Optimal Risk Shifting vs Efficient Employment in Illyria: The Labor-Managed Firm under Asymmetric Information. *J. Compar. Econ.*, June 1987, 11(2), pp. 163–79.

Miller, E. M. and Westmoreland, G. Limitations on the Interpretation of Frontier Efficiency with Fixed Inputs. *Atlantic Econ. J.*, September 1987, 15(3), pp. 77.

Miller, Edward M. A Graphical Analysis of Replacement. *Southern Econ. J.*, July 1987, 54(1), pp. 206–11.

Mino, Kazuo. A Model of Investment with External Adjustment Costs. *Econ. Stud. Quart.*, March 1987, 38(1), pp. 76–85.

Mongiovi, Gary. Returns to Scale, the Standard Commodity, and Sraffa's Production of Commodities by Means of Commodities: A Note. *Stud. Econ.*, 1987, 42(31), pp. 35–50.

Mossetti, Giovanna. Loanable Funds and Output in a Model of the Firm. *Giorn. Econ.*, Nov.-Dec. 1987, 46(11–12), pp. 617–38.

Murali, R. Demand Uncertainty and Input Constraints. *Quart. Rev. Econ. Bus.*, Summer 1987, 27(2), pp. 22–41.

Newman, Peter. Shephard's Lemma: A Small Gap

in the Literature. *[Marrama, V.]*, Vol. 2, 1987, pp. 849–56.

Oi, Walter Y. Heterogeneous Firms: Caveat Emptor [Heterogeneous Firms and the Organization of Production]. *Econ. Inquiry*, January 1987, 25(1), pp. 181–84.

Osterman, Paul. Choice of Employment Systems in Internal Labor Markets. *Ind. Relat.*, Winter 1987, 26(1), pp. 46–67.

Piacentini, Paolo. Costi ed efficienza in un modello di produzione a flusso lineare. (Costs and Efficiency in a Flow Production Process Model. With English summary.) *Econ. Polít.*, December 1987, 4(3), pp. 381–405.

van der Ploeg, Frederick. Trade Unions, Investment, and Employment: A Non-cooperative Approach. *Europ. Econ. Rev.*, October 1987, 31(7), pp. 1465–92.

Pollak, Robert A. and Wales, Terence J. Specification and Estimation of Nonseparable Two-Stage Technologies: The Leontief CES and the Cobb–Douglas CES. *J. Polit. Econ.*, April 1987, 95(2), pp. 311–33. [G: U.S.]

Pope, Rulon D. An Analogy between Risk Aversion and Homothetic Production under Certainty. *Amer. J. Agr. Econ.*, May 1987, 69(2), pp. 378–81.

Prescott, Edward C. and Boyd, John H. Dynamic Coalitions, Growth, and the Firm. *Prescott, E. C. and Wallace, N.*, eds., 1987, pp. 146–60.

Quadrio Curzio, Alberto; Manara, Carlo Felice and Faliva, Mario. Produzione ed efficienza con technologie globali. (Production and Efficiency with Global Technologies. With English summary.) *Econ. Polít.*, April 1987, 4(1), pp. 11–47.

Revier, Charles F. The Elasticity of Scale, the Shape of Average Costs, and the Envelope Theorem. *Amer. Econ. Rev.*, June 1987, 77(3), pp. 486–88.

Reynolds, Stanley S. Capacity Investment, Preemption and Commitment in an Infinite Horizon Model. *Int. Econ. Rev.*, February 1987, 28(1), pp. 69–88.

Rogerson, William P. The Dissipation of Profits by Brand Name Investment and Entry when Price Guarantees Quality. *J. Polit. Econ.*, August 1987, 95(4), pp. 797–809.

Rosefielde, Steven and Pfouts, Ralph W. The Effect of Radially Parallel Technologies on the Behavior of the Illyrian Firm: Reply. *J. Compar. Econ.*, December 1987, 11(4), pp. 606–10.

Salsecci, Gianluca. Determinazione delle misure di efficienza di Farrell in via duale. (Determination of the Farrell Measures of Efficiency Using a Dual Approach. With English summary.) *Econ. Polít.*, April 1987, 4(1), pp. 89–111.

Salvadori, Neri. Il capitale fisso come "specie" del "genere" produzione congiunta. Ulteriori precisazioni ed una risposta. (Fixed Capital as a "Species" of the "Genus" Joint Production: Further Remarks and a Reply. With English

summary.) *Econ. Polít.*, August 1987, 4(2), pp. 265–75.

Sato, Ryuzo and Ramachandran, Rama V. Factor Price Variation and the Hicksian Hypothesis: A Microeconomic Model. *Oxford Econ. Pap.*, June 1987, 39(2), pp. 343–56.

Scott, Kenneth E. Reflections on the Theory of the Firm: Comment. *J. Inst. Theoretical Econ.*, March 1987, 143(1), pp. 137–42.

Seidmann, Daniel J. Industry Factor Demand Curves Can Be Upward Sloping. *Econ. J.*, September 1987, 97(387), pp. 746–78.

Seidmann, Daniel J. The Impact of Interest Rates on Price and Supply. *Can. J. Econ.*, August 1987, 20(3), pp. 625–33.

Sertel, Murat R. Workers' Enterprises Are Not Perverse. *Europ. Econ. Rev.*, December 1987, 31(8), pp. 1619–25.

Shah, Salman and Thakor, Anjan V. Optimal Capital Structure and Project Financing. *J. Econ. Theory*, August 1987, 42(2), pp. 209–43.

Shieh, Yeung-Nan. Increasing Returns to Scale and Location Theory of the Firm under Price Uncertainty [Demand Function and Location Theory of the Firm under Price Uncertainty]. *Urban Stud.*, April 1987, 24(2), pp. 163–66.

Siebert, Horst. Risk Allocation in Large-scale Resource Ventures. *Kyklos*, 1987, 40(4), pp. 476–95.

Silverberg, Gerald. Technical Progress, Capital Accumulation, and Effective Demand: A Self-organization Model. *Batten, D.; Casti, J. and Johansson, B.*, eds., 1987, pp. 116–44.

Smith, Stephen C. and Ye, Meng-Hua. The Behavior of Labor-Managed Firms under Uncertainty: Product Diversification, Income Insurance and Layoff Policy. *Ann. Pub. Co-op. Econ.*, Jan.-Mar. 1987, 58(1), pp. 65–82.

Sproule, Robert A. The Owner-Managed Firm under Output-Price Uncertainty: A Model Based on a Synthesis of Sandmo (1971), Block and Heineke (1973), and Ishii (1977). *J. Econ. (Z. Nationalökon.)*, 1987, 47(2), pp. 125–41.

Stark, Oded. Cooperating Adversaries. *Kyklos*, 1987, 40(4), pp. 515–28.

Starrett, David A. *Production and Capital:* Kenneth Arrow's Contribution in Perspective—A Review Article. *J. Econ. Lit.*, March 1987, 25(1), pp. 92–102.

Steedman, Ian. Value, Price, and Profit. *Albelda, R.; Gunn, C. and Waller, W.*, eds., 1987, 1975, pp. 175–85.

Stefanou, Spiro E. Technical Change, Uncertainty, and Investment. *Amer. J. Agr. Econ.*, February 1987, 69(1), pp. 158–65.

Stevenson, Rodney E. Institutional Economics and the Theory of Production. *J. Econ. Issues*, December 1987, 21(4), pp. 1471–93.

Stiglitz, Joseph E. Learning to Learn, Localized Learning and Technological Progress. *Dasgupta, P. and Stoneman, P.*, eds., 1987, pp. 125–53.

Taylor, Timothy G. Economies of Scope, Contestability Theory, and Economic Efficiency: A Discussion. *Kilmer, R. L. and Armbruster, W.*

J., eds., 1987, pp. 177–80.

Vallée, Robert. About Harvey Leibenstein's Proposition of Relaxing the Maximization Postulate [On Relaxing the Maximization Postulate]. *J. Behav. Econ.*, Summer 1987, 16(2), pp. 61–63.

Van Cayseele, Patrick. Economies of Scope in Research and Development. *J. Econ. (Z. Nationalökon.)*, 1987, 47(3), pp. 273–85.

Varri, Paolo. Il capitale fisso come "specie" del "genere" produzione congiunta: alcune precisazioni. (Fixed Capital as a "Species" of the "Genus" Joint Production: Some Critical Remarks. With English summary.) *Econ. Polit.*, August 1987, 4(2), pp. 259–63.

Vroman, Susan B. Behavior of the Firm in a Market for Heterogeneous Labor. *J. Econ. Dynam. Control*, September 1987, 11(3), pp. 313–29.

Windsperger, Josef. Lohn- und Preisbildung der Firma. (With English summary.) *Z. Betriebswirtshaft*, April 1987, 57(4), pp. 410–25.

Ylönen, Sakari. Factor Demand and Substitution under Decreasing Returns to Scale. An Application to the Rybczynski Theorem. *Scand. J. Econ.*, 1987, 89(2), pp. 209–16.

Yordon, Wesley J. Evidence against Diminishing Returns in Manufacturing and Comments on Short-run Models of Price–Output Behavior. *J. Post Keynesian Econ.*, Summer 1987, 9(4), pp. 593–603. [G: U.S.]

Zeira, Joseph. Investment as a Process of Search. *J. Polit. Econ.*, February 1987, 95(1), pp. 204–10.

0224 Theory of Factor Distribution and Distributive Shares

Alcorn, John H. and Gleicher, David. Workers, Inputs and Exploitation: A Note on Roemer. *Rev. Radical Polit. Econ.*, Summer 1987, 19(2), pp. 77–82.

Bradley, Michael D. and Smith, Stephen C. Some Microeconomic Analysis of Income-Sharing Firms. *Jones, D. C. and Svejnar, J., eds.*, 1987, pp. 91–111.

Burgstaller, André. Demand and Relative Price in Ricardo: An Examination of Outstanding Issues. *Hist. Polit. Econ.*, Summer 1987, 19(2), pp. 207–15.

Handa, Jagdish. Labor Characteristics and the Return to General and Specific Skills. *Eastern Econ. J.*, Apr.-June 1987, 13(2), pp. 99–106.

Nell, Edward J. The Rate of Profit and the Choice of Technique in Competitive Conditions. *[Marrama, V.], Vol. 1*, 1987, pp. 449–55.

Petrović, Pavle. The Deviation of Production Prices from Labour Values: Some Methodology and Empirical Evidence. *Cambridge J. Econ.*, September 1987, 11(3), pp. 197–210. [G: Yugoslavia]

Schultz, Eric. Non-produced Inputs, Differential Profit Rates and the Okishio Theorem. *Rev. Radical Polit. Econ.*, Summer 1987, 19(2), pp. 43–60.

Taurand, Francis and Hung, Nguyen Manh. Pitfalls in a Received Idea: Ricardian Decreasing Returns at the Extensive Margin of a Natural Resource. *Can. J. Econ.*, February 1987, 20(1), pp. 61–73.

Woods, John E. A Note on Rent. *Oxford Econ. Pap.*, June 1987, 39(2), pp. 388–411.

0225 Theory of Firm and Industry under Competitive Market Structures

Appelbaum, Elie and Katz, Eliakim. Asymmetric Taxation and the Theory of the Competitive Firm under Uncertainty. *Can. J. Econ.*, May 1987, 20(2), pp. 357–69.

Belton, Terrence M. A Model of Duopoly and Meeting or Beating Competition. *Int. J. Ind. Organ.*, December 1987, 5(4), pp. 399–417.

Braulke, Michael. On the Comparative Statics of a Competitive Industry. *Amer. Econ. Rev.*, June 1987, 77(3), pp. 479–85.

Endres, Anthony M. The Origins of Böhm-Bawerk's 'Greatest Error': Theoretical Points of Separation from Menger. *J. Inst. Theoretical Econ.*, June 1987, 143(2), pp. 291–309.

MacDonald, Glenn M. and Slivinski, Alan D. The Simple Analytics of Competitive Equilibrium with Multiproduct Firms. *Amer. Econ. Rev.*, December 1987, 77(5), pp. 941–53.

MacDonald, James M. Economies of Scope, Contestability Theory, and Economic Efficiency. *Kilmer, R. L. and Armbruster, W. J., eds.*, 1987, pp. 154–76.

Novshek, William and Sonnenschein, Hugo. General Equilibrium with Free Entry: A Synthetic Approach to the Theory of Perfect Competition. *J. Econ. Lit.*, September 1987, 25(3), pp. 1281–1306.

Radner, Roy. Decentralization and Incentives. *[Hurwicz, L.]*, 1987, 1983, pp. 3–47.

Taylor, Timothy G. Economics of Scope, Contestability Theory, and Economic Efficiency: A Discussion. *Kilmer, R. L. and Armbruster, W. J., eds.*, 1987, pp. 177–80.

0226 Theory of Firm and Industry under Imperfectly Competitive Market Structures

Aghion, Philippe and Bolton, Patrick. Contracts as a Barrier to Entry. *Amer. Econ. Rev.*, June 1987, 77(3), pp. 388–401.

Agliardi, Elettra. Barriere all'entrata come beni pubblici in mercati oligopolistici. (Entry Barriers as Public Goods in Oligopolistic Markets. With English summary.) *Rivista Int. Sci. Econ. Com.*, June 1987, 34(6), pp. 523–46.

Akin, Ethan. Competitive Growth of Firms in an Industry. *Batten, D.; Casti, J. and Johansson, B., eds.*, 1987, pp. 86–115.

Andersen, Torben M. The Information Content of Quantity Signals and Downward Inflexible Prices. *Scand. J. Econ.*, 1987, 89(4), pp. 451–68.

Anderson, Richard K. and Enomoto, Carl E. Product Quality Regulation: A General Equilibrium Analysis. *Can. J. Econ.*, November 1987, 20(4), pp. 735–49.

Anderson, Simon. Spatial Competition and Price

Leadership. *Int. J. Ind. Organ.*, December 1987, *5*(4), pp. 369–98.

Antonelli, Cristiano and Ghezzii, Luca. Un'analisi teorica dei processi di diffusion e dell'innovazione tecnologica in regime di monopolio temporaneo. (A Theoretical Analysis of Diffusion Processees of Innovation under Temporary Monopoly. With English summary.) *Giorn. Econ.*, Mar.-Apr. 1987, *46*(3–4), pp. 125–48.

Ashton, R. K. X-inefficiency and Market Power. *Managerial Dec. Econ.*, December 1987, *8*(4), pp. 333–38.

d'Aspremont, Claude; Jacquemin, Alexis and Gabszewicz, Jean Jaskold. Imperfect Information and Market Organization. *Europ. Econ. Rev.*, June 1987, *31*(4), pp. 825–26.

Ausubel, Lawrence M. and Deneckere, Raymond J. One Is Almost Enough for Monopoly. *Rand J. Econ.*, Summer 1987, *18*(2), pp. 255–74.

Babilot, George; Frantz, Roger and Green, Louis. Natural Monopolies and Rent: A Georgist Remedy for X-Inefficiency among Publicly-Regulated Firms. *Amer. J. Econ. Soc.*, April 1987, *46*(2), pp. 205–17.

Badke, Michael. Corrigendum [Optimal Cartel Trigger Price Strategies]. *J. Econ. Theory*, February 1987, *41*(1), pp. 216–17.

Bae, Hyung. A Price-Setting Supergame between Two Heterogeneous Firms. *Europ. Econ. Rev.*, August 1987, *31*(6), pp. 1159–71.

Baron, David P. and Besanko, David. Monitoring, Moral Hazard, Asymmetric Information, and Risk Sharing in Procurement Contracting. *Rand J. Econ.*, Winter 1987, *18*(4), pp. 509–32.

Basu, Kaushik. Disneyland Monopoly, Interlinkage and Usurious Interest Rates. *J. Public Econ.*, October 1987, *34*(1), pp. 1–17.

Basu, Kaushik. Monopoly, Quality Uncertainty and 'Status' Goods. *Int. J. Ind. Organ.*, December 1987, *5*(4), pp. 435–46.

Belton, Terrence M. A Model of Duopoly and Meeting or Beating Competition. *Int. J. Ind. Organ.*, December 1987, *5*(4), pp. 399–417.

Benassy, Jean-Pascal. Imperfect Competition, Unemployment and Policy. *Europ. Econ. Rev.*, Feb./Mar. 1987, *31*(1/2), pp. 417–26.

Benoit, Jean-Pierre and Krishna, Vijay. Dynamic Duopoly: Prices and Quantities. *Rev. Econ. Stud.*, January 1987, *54*(1), pp. 23–35.

Benson, Bruce L. and Feinberg, Robert M. Chamberlin's Solution in a Spatial Model. *Rev. Reg. Stud.*, Spring 1987, *17*(2), pp. 47–52.

Berman, Lawrence E. and Dunn, Donald A. Service Bundling and Strategic Equilibrium in the Information Services Industry. *J. Econ. Bus.*, May 1987, *39*(2), pp. 115–29.

Besanko, David; Donnenfeld, Shabtai and White, Lawrence J. Monopoly and Quality Distortion: Effects and Remedies. *Quart. J. Econ.*, November 1987, *102*(4), pp. 743–67.

Bhatt, Swati. Strategic Product Choice in Differentiated Markets. *J. Ind. Econ.*, December 1987, *36*(2), pp. 207–16.

Bhattacharya, Sudipto and Hagerty, Kathleen M.

Dealerships, Trading Externalities, and General Equilibrium. *Prescott, E. C. and Wallace, N., eds.*, 1987, pp. 81–104.

Blair, Roger D. and Kaserman, David L. A Note on Bilateral Monopoly and Formula Price Contracts. *Amer. Econ. Rev.*, June 1987, *77*(3), pp. 460–63.

Blanchard, Olivier Jean and Kiyotaki, Nobuhiro. Monopolistic Competition and the Effects of Aggregate Demand. *Amer. Econ. Rev.*, September 1987, *77*(4), pp. 647–66.

Bonanno, Giacomo. Location Choice, Product Proliferation and Entry Deterrence. *Rev. Econ. Stud.*, January 1987, *54*(1), pp. 37–45.

Bonanno, Giacomo. Monopoly Equilibria and Catastrophe Theory. *Australian Econ. Pap.*, December 1987, *26*(49), pp. 197–215.

Bond, Eric W. and Samuelson, Larry. Durable Goods, Market Structure and the Incentives to Innovate. *Economica*, February 1987, *54*(213), pp. 57–67.

Boucher, Jacqueline; Hefting, Tom and Smeers, Yves. Economic Analysis of Natural Gas Contracts. *Golombek, R.; Hoel, M. and Vislie, J., eds.*, 1987, pp. 193–220.   [G: Norway]

Boyer, Marcel and Laffont, Jean-Jacques. Une analyse économique de l'usage de faux prix réguliers en publicité. (An Economic Analysis of the Use of False Regular Prices in Advertising. With English summary.) *L'Actual. Econ.*, June-September 1987, *63*(2–3), pp. 153–68.

Boyer, Marcel and Moreaux, Michel. Being a Leader or a Follower: Reflections on the Distribution of Roles in Duopoly. *Int. J. Ind. Organ.*, June 1987, *5*(2), pp. 175–92.

Boyer, Marcel and Moreaux, Michel. On Stackelberg Equilibria with Differentiated Products: The Critical Role of the Strategy Space. *J. Ind. Econ.*, December 1987, *36*(2), pp. 217–30.

Brack, John. Price Adjustment within a Framework of Symmetric Oligopoly: An Analysis of Pricing in 380 U.S. Manufacturing Industries, 1958–71. *Int. J. Ind. Organ.*, September 1987, *5*(3), pp. 289–301.   [G: U.S.]

Brander, James A. and Spencer, Barbara J. Tariffs and the Extraction of Foreign Monopoly Rents under Potential Entry. *Bhagwati, J. N., ed.*, 1987, *1981*, pp. 141–60.

Braverman, Avishay. Corporate Governance and Product Market Structure: Comments. *Razin, A. and Sadka, E., eds.*, 1987, pp. 495–99.

Browning, Edgar K. Comparing Monopoly and Competition: The Increasing-Cost Case. *Econ. Inquiry*, July 1987, *25*(3), pp. 535–42.

Caron-Salmona, Hélène and Lesourne, Jacques. Dynamics of a Retail Market with Search Processes. *Europ. Econ. Rev.*, July 1987, *31*(5), pp. 995–1021.

Cave, Jonathan and Salant, Stephen W. Cartels That Vote: Agricultural Marketing Boards and Induced Voting Behavior. *Bailey, E. E., ed.*, 1987, pp. 255–83.   [G: U.S.]

Colombo, Caterina. Exchange Rate and Prices: Firms' Behaviour in the Open Economy. *Giorn. Econ.*, Mar.-Apr. 1987, *46*(3–4), pp. 149–74.

Conrad, Klaus. Quality and Reputation Policies of Duopolists under Asymmetric Information. *Carraro, C. and Sartore, D., eds.*, 1987, pp. 261–76.

Cressy, Robert C. Equilibrium Costs and Prices in a Market with Imperfect Information and Technological Change. *Greek Econ. Rev.*, 1987, 9(2), pp. 162–82.

Curien, Nicolas and Gensollen, Michel. De la théorie des structures industrielles à l'économie des réseaux de télécommunication. (From the Theory of Industry Structure to the Economics of Telecommunication Networks. With English summary.) *Revue Écon.*, March 1987, 38(2), pp. 521–78.

Dafermos, Stella and Nagurney, Anna. Oligopolistic and Competitive Behavior of Spatially Separated Markets. *Reg. Sci. Urban Econ.*, May 1987, 17(2), pp. 245–54.

Dahlby, B. G. Monopoly versus Competition in an Insurance Market with Adverse Selection. *J. Risk Ins.*, June 1987, 54(2), pp. 325–31.

van Damme, Eric. Competition versus Monopoly in the Supply of Public Goods: Comment. *Pethig, R. and Schlieper, U., eds.*, 1987, pp. 219–25.

Dana, Rose-Anne and Montrucchio, Luigi. Dynamic Complexity in Duopoly Games. *Grandmont, J.-M., ed.*, 1987, 1986, pp. 40–56.

Dana, Rose-Anne and Montrucchio, Luigi. On Rational Dynamic Strategies in Infinite Horizon Models Where Agents Discount the Future. *J. Econ. Behav. Organ.*, September 1987, 8(3), pp. 497–511.

Danielsen, Albert L. and Cartwright, Phillip A. Inventory Theory in Cartelized Markets. *Energy Econ.*, July 1987, 9(3), pp. 167–75. [G: U.S.]

Daughety, Andrew F. and Forsythe, Robert. Industrywide Regulation and the Formation of Reputations: A Laboratory Analysis. *Bailey, E. E., ed.*, 1987, pp. 347–98.

De Fraja, Giovanni and Flavio, Delboni. Oligopoly, Public Firm and Welfare Maximization: A Game-Theoretic Analysis. *Giorn. Econ.*, July-August 1987, 46(7–8), pp. 416–35.

DeGraba, Patrick J. The Effects of Price Restrictions on Competition between National and Local Firms. *Rand J. Econ.*, Autumn 1987, 18(3), pp. 333–47.

Demski, Joel S.; Sappington, David E. M. and Spiller, Pablo T. Managing Supplier Switching. *Rand J. Econ.*, Spring 1987, 18(1), pp. 77–97.

Dewatripont, Mathias. Entry Deterrence under Trade Unions. *Europ. Econ. Rev.*, Feb./Mar. 1987, 31(1/2), pp. 149–56.

Dionne, Georges and Lasserre, Pierre. Adverse Selection and Finite-Horizon Insurance Contracts. *Europ. Econ. Rev.*, June 1987, 31(4), pp. 843–61.

Dixon, Huw. Approximate Bertrand Equilibria in a Replicated Industry. *Rev. Econ. Stud.*, January 1987, 54(1), pp. 47–62.

Dixon, Huw. The General Theory of Household and Market Contingent Demand. *Manchester Sch. Econ. Soc. Stud.*, September 1987, 55(3), pp. 287–304.

Doak, Ervin John. The Monopoly Supply Curve. *Atlantic Econ. J.*, September 1987, 15(3), pp. 75.

Drèze, Jacques H. and Sheshinski, Eytan. On Industry Equilibrium under Uncertainty. *Drèze, J. H.*, 1987, 1984, pp. 250–58.

Eaton, B. Curtis and Ware, Roger. A Theory of Market Structure with Sequential Entry. *Rand J. Econ.*, Spring 1987, 18(1), pp. 1–16.

Economides, Nicholas S. On Nash Equilibrium Existence and Optimality in Oligopolistic Competition in Prices and Varieties. *Greek Econ. Rev.*, 1987, 9(2), pp. 198–209.

Eldor, Rafael and Zilcha, Itzhak. Discriminating Monopoly, Forward Markets and International Trade. *Int. Econ. Rev.*, June 1987, 28(2), pp. 459–68.

Encaoua, David and Moreaux, Michel. Concurrence et monopole naturel: une approche par la théorie des jeux. (Competition and Natural Monopoly: A Game Theoretic Approach. With English summary.) *Ann. Écon. Statist.*, Oct./Dec. 1987, (8), pp. 89–116.

Epple, Dennis. Hedonic Prices and Implicit Markets: Estimating Demand and Supply Functions for Differentiated Products. *J. Polit. Econ.*, February 1987, 95(1), pp. 59–80.

Falvey, Rodney E. and Kierzkowski, Henryk. Product Quality, Intra-industry Trade and (Im)perfect Competition. *[Corden, W. M.]*, 1987, pp. 143–61.

Farm, Ante and Weibull, Jörgen W. Perfectly Flexible Pricing in a Homogeneous Market. *Scand. J. Econ.*, 1987, 89(4), pp. 487–95.

Farrell, Joseph. Cheap Talk, Coordination, and Entry. *Rand J. Econ.*, Spring 1987, 18(1), pp. 34–39.

Fehl, Ulrich and Güth, Werner. Internal and External Stability of Bidder Cartels in Auctions and Public Tenders: A Comparison of Pricing Rules. *Int. J. Ind. Organ.*, September 1987, 5(3), pp. 303–13.

Fershtman, Chaim and Judd, Kenneth L. Equilibrium Incentives in Oligopoly. *Amer. Econ. Rev.*, December 1987, 77(5), pp. 927–40.

Fershtman, Chaim and Kamien, Morton I. Dynamic Duopolistic Competition with Sticky Prices. *Econometrica*, September 1987, 55(5), pp. 1151–64.

Fluck, Zsuzsanna; Okuguchi, Koji and Szidarovszky, Ferenc. Contribution to Oligopoly Theory: The Case of Uncertain Collusions. *Keio Econ. Stud.*, 1987, 24(1), pp. 13–23.

Franchon, B.; Rifkin, E. and Sengupta, Jati K. A Dynamic and Stochastic Model of Price Leadership. *Carraro, C. and Sartore, D., eds.*, 1987, pp. 239–60.

Fudenberg, Drew and Kreps, David M. Reputation in the Simultaneous Play of Multiple Opponents. *Rev. Econ. Stud.*, October 1987, 54(4), pp. 541–68.

Fung, K. C. Industry Structure, Antitrust and Tariffs. *Int. J. Ind. Organ.*, December 1987, 5(4), pp. 447–56.

Gabszewicz, Jean Jaskold and Garella, Paolo G. Price Search and Spatial Competition. *Europ. Econ. Rev.*, June 1987, *31*(4), pp. 827–42.

Gal-Or, Esther. First Mover Disadvantages with Private Information. *Rev. Econ. Stud.*, April 1987, *54*(2), pp. 279–92.

Gal-Or, Esther. Strategic and Non-strategic Differentiation. *Can. J. Econ.*, May 1987, *20*(2), pp. 340–56.

Gale, Douglas M. Limit Theorems for Markets with Sequential Bargaining. *J. Econ. Theory*, October 1987, *43*(1), pp. 20–54.

Gelfand, Matthew D. and Spiller, Pablo T. Entry Barriers and Multiproduct Oligopolies: Do They Forebear or Spoil? *Int. J. Ind. Organ.*, March 1987, *5*(1), pp. 101–13. **[G: Uruguay]**

Golombek, Rolf and Hoel, Michael. The Relationship between the Price of Natural Gas and Crude Oil: Some Aspects of Efficient Contracts. *Golombek, R.; Hoel, M. and Vislie, J.*, eds., 1987, pp. 221–37.

Gul, Faruk. Noncooperative Collusion in Durable Goods Oligopoly. *Rand J. Econ.*, Summer 1987, *18*(2), pp. 248–54.

Güth, Werner and Hellwig, Martin. Competition versus Monopoly in the Supply of Public Goods. *Pethig, R. and Schlieper, U.*, eds., 1987, pp. 183–217.

Hagerty, Kathleen M. and Rogerson, William P. Robust Trading Mechanisms. *J. Econ. Theory*, June 1987, *42*(1), pp. 94–107.

Hamilton, James L. and Philippart, Nancy L. On the Nonequivalence of Maximum Resale Price Maintenance and Vertical Integration. *Eastern Econ. J.*, October-December 1987, *13*(4), pp. 411–19. **[G: U.S.]**

Harrington, Joseph E., Jr. Collusion in Multiproduct Oligopoly Games under a Finite Horizon. *Int. Econ. Rev.*, February 1987, *28*(1), pp. 1–14.

Harrington, Joseph E., Jr. Oligopolistic Entry Deterrence under Incomplete Information. *Rand J. Econ.*, Summer 1987, *18*(2), pp. 211–31.

Harrison, Glenn W. Experimental Evaluation of the Contestable Markets Hypothesis. *Bailey, E. E.*, ed., 1987, pp. 191–225.

Hart, Oliver. Corporate Governance and Product Market Structure: Comments. *Razin, A. and Sadka, E.*, eds., 1987, pp. 499–503.

Hayes, Beth. Competition and Two-Part Tariffs. *J. Bus.*, January 1987, *60*(1), pp. 41–54.

Hazlett, Thomas W. The Role of Property Rights in the Positive Theory of Monopoly. *Managerial Dec. Econ.*, September 1987, *8*(3), pp. 201–212.

Helpman, Elhanan. Imperfect Competition and International Trade: Evidence from Fourteen Industrial Countries. *J. Japanese Int. Economies*, March 1987, *1*(1), pp. 62–81.
[G: MDCs]

Henriet, Dominique, et al. Intérêt public, intérêt privé et discrimination. (Public Interest, Private Interest and Discrimination. With English summary.) *L'Actual. Econ.*, June-September 1987, *63*(2–3), pp. 98–117.

Hoel, Michael and Vislie, Jon. Bargaining, Bilateral Monopoly and Exhaustible Resources. *Golombek, R.; Hoel, M. and Vislie, J.*, eds., 1987, pp. 253–65.

Hollander, Abraham. On Price-Increasing Entry. *Economica*, August 1987, *54*(215), pp. 317–24.

Holt, Charles A. and Scheffman, David T. Facilitating Practices: The Effects of Advance Notice and Best-Price Policies. *Rand J. Econ.*, Summer 1987, *18*(2), pp. 187–97.

Horowitz, Ira. Regression-Estimated Market Demand and Quasi-Cournot Behavior. *Int. J. Ind. Organ.*, June 1987, *5*(2), pp. 247–53.

Hubbard, R. Glenn and Weiner, Robert J. Natural Gas Contracting in Practice: Evidence from the United States. *Golombek, R.; Hoel, M. and Vislie, J.*, eds., 1987, pp. 279–313. **[G: U.S.]**

Hwang, Hong; Liu, Jung-Chao and Mai, Chao-Cheng. Price, Profit and Market Share Effects of Tariffs, Volume Quotas and Ratio Quotas. *Manchester Sch. Econ. Soc. Stud.*, September 1987, *55*(3), pp. 274–86.

Hwang, Hong and Mai, Chao-Cheng. Industrial Location and Rising Energy Prices: A Case of Bilateral Monopoly. *Reg. Sci. Urban Econ.*, May 1987, *17*(2), pp. 255–64.

Jacquemin, Alexis. Comportements collusifs et accords en recherche-développement. (With English summary.) *Revue Écon. Polit.*, Jan.-Feb. 1987, *97*(1), pp. 1–23.

Jones, Larry E. Optimum Product Diversity and the Incentives for Entry in Natural Oligopolies. *Quart. J. Econ.*, August 1987, *102*(3), pp. 595–613.

Jones, Larry E. The Efficiency of Monopolistically Competitive Equilibria in Large Economies: Commodity Differentiation with Gross Substitutes. *J. Econ. Theory*, April 1987, *41*(2), pp. 356–91.

Jovanovic, Boyan and Rob, Rafael. Demand-Driven Innovation and Spatial Competition over Time. *Rev. Econ. Stud.*, January 1987, *54*(1), pp. 63–72.

Justman, Moshe. An Extension of Lerner's Monopoly Index for Markets with a Disparity between Long- and Short-run Demand Elasticities. *Econ. Inquiry*, October 1987, *25*(4), pp. 681–94.

Katz, Michael L. The Welfare Effects of Third-Degree Price Discrimination in Intermediate Good Markets. *Amer. Econ. Rev.*, March 1987, *77*(1), pp. 154–67.

Kilmer, Richard L. The Economic Efficiency of Alternative Exchange Mechanisms. *Kilmer, R. L. and Armbruster, W. J.*, eds., 1987, pp. 134–49.

Kim, Jong Seok. Optimal Price–Quality Schedules and Sustainability. *J. Ind. Econ.*, December 1987, *36*(2), pp. 231–44.

Klemperer, Paul. Entry Deterrence in Markets with Consumer Switching Costs. *Econ. J.*, Supplement 1987, 97, pp. 99–117.

Klemperer, Paul. Markets with Consumer Switching Costs. *Quart. J. Econ.*, May 1987, *102*(2), pp. 375–94.

Klemperer, Paul. The Competitiveness of Markets with Switching Costs. *Rand J. Econ.*, Spring 1987, *18*(1), pp. 137–50.

Kolstad, Charles D. and Mathiesen, Lars. Necessary and Sufficient Conditions for Uniqueness of a Cournot Equilibrium. *Rev. Econ. Stud.*, October 1987, *54*(4), pp. 681–90.

Krugman, Paul R. Increasing Returns, Monopolistic Competition, and International Trade. *Bhagwati, J. N., ed.*, 1987, *1979*, pp. 129–40.

Krugman, Paul R. Market Access and Competition in High Technology Industries: A Simulation Exercise. *[Corden, W. M.]*, 1987, pp. 128–42.

Kuenne, Robert E. Oligopolistic Uncertainty and Optimal Bidding in Government Procurement: A Subjective Probability Approach. *Feiwel, G. R., ed. (I)*, 1987, pp. 654–74.

La Manna, Manfredi M. A. A Note on Quality, Market Structure and the Importance of the 'Integer Constraint.' *Bull. Econ. Res.*, October 1987, *39*(4), pp. 303–07.

Laffont, Jean-Jacques. Optimal Taxation of a Nonlinear Pricing Monopolist. *J. Public Econ.*, July 1987, *33*(2), pp. 137–55.

Laffont, Jean-Jacques and Maskin, Eric. Monopoly with Asymmetric Information about Quality: Behavior and Regulation. *Europ. Econ. Rev.*, Feb./Mar. 1987, *31*(1/2), pp. 483–89.

Laffont, Jean-Jacques; Maskin, Eric and Rochet, Jean-Charles. Optimal Nonlinear Pricing with Two-Dimensional Characteristics. *[Hurwicz, L.]*, 1987, pp. 256–66.

Lambson, Val Eugene. Dynamic Behaviour in Large Markets for Differentiated Products. *Rev. Econ. Stud.*, April 1987, *54*(2), pp. 293–300.

Lambson, Val Eugene. Is the Concentration–Profit Correlation Partly an Artifact of Lumpy Technology? *Amer. Econ. Rev.*, September 1987, *77*(4), pp. 731–33.

Lambson, Val Eugene. Optimal Penal Codes in Price-Setting Supergames with Capacity Constraints. *Rev. Econ. Stud.*, July 1987, *54*(3), pp. 385–97.

Lanning, Steven G. Costs of Maintaining a Cartel. *J. Ind. Econ.*, December 1987, *36*(2), pp. 147–74.

Le Breton, Michel. On the Generic Nonexistence of Pure Strategy Nash Equilibria in Continuous Games. *J. Econ. Theory*, December 1987, *43*(2), pp. 374–82.

Legros, Patrick. Disadvantageous Syndicates and Stable Cartels: The Case of the Nucleolus. *J. Econ. Theory*, June 1987, *42*(1), pp. 30–49.

Li, Lode; McKelvey, Richard D. and Page, Talbot. Optimal Research for Cournot Oligopolists. *J. Econ. Theory*, June 1987, *42*(1), pp. 140–66.

Llerena, Patrick and Zuscovitch, Ehud. Valeur d'option et structure de marchés. Le cas du quasi-monopole. (Option Value and Market Structure: The Case of Quasi-monopoly. With English summary.) *Écon. Appl.*, 1987, *40*(1), pp. 97–113.

MacLeod, W. Bentley. Entry, Sunk Costs, and Market Structure. *Can. J. Econ.*, February 1987, *20*(1), pp. 140–51.

MacLeod, W. Bentley; Norman, G. and Thisse, Jacques-François. Competition, Tacit Collusion and Free Entry. *Econ. J.*, March 1987, *97*(385), pp. 189–98.

Makowski, Louis. Are 'Rational Conjectures' Rational? *J. Ind. Econ.*, September 1987, *36*(1), pp. 35–47.

Maskin, Eric and Tirole, Jean. A Theory of Dynamic Oligopoly, III: Cournot Competition. *Europ. Econ. Rev.*, June 1987, *31*(4), pp. 947–68.

Masson, Robert T. and Shaanan, Joseph. Optimal Oligopoly Pricing and the Threat of Entry: Canadian Evidence. *Int. J. Ind. Organ.*, September 1987, *5*(3), pp. 323–39. **[G: Canada]**

Matthews, Steven and Moore, John. Monopoly Provision of Quality and Warranties: An Exploration in the Theory of Multidimensional Screening. *Econometrica*, March 1987, *55*(2), pp. 441–67.

Matutes, Carmen and Regibeau, Pierre. Standardization in Multi-component Industries. *Gabel, H. L., ed.*, 1987, pp. 23–28.

McAfee, R. Preston and McMillan, John. Auctions and Bidding. *J. Econ. Lit.*, June 1987, *25*(2), pp. 699–738.

McDonald, Ian M. and Spindler, Karen J. An Empirical Investigation of Customer Market Analysis—A Microfoundation for Macroeconomics. *Appl. Econ.*, September 1987, *19*(9), pp. 1149–74. **[G: U.S.; U.K.; Australia]**

McFadden, Daniel L. Technological Change, Sunk Costs, and Competition: Comments and Discussion. *Brookings Pap. Econ. Act.*, 1987, (3), pp. 938–41.

Morrison, Clarence C. A Note on Price Searching in General Equilibrium Models. *Atlantic Econ. J.*, March 1987, *15*(1), pp. 56–58.

Moulin, Hervé J. A Core Selection for Regulating a Single-Output Monopoly. *Rand J. Econ.*, Autumn 1987, *18*(3), pp. 397–407.

Muto, Shigeo. Possibility of Relicensing and Patent Protection. *Europ. Econ. Rev.*, June 1987, *31*(4), pp. 927–45.

Myles, Gareth D. Tax Design in the Presence of Imperfect Competition: An Example. *J. Public Econ.*, December 1987, *34*(3), pp. 367–78.

Neven, Damien J. Endogenous Sequential Entry in a Spatial Model. *Int. J. Ind. Organ.*, December 1987, *5*(4), pp. 419–34.

Novshek, William and Sonnenschein, Hugo. General Equilibrium with Free Entry: A Synthetic Approach to the Theory of Perfect Competition. *J. Econ. Lit.*, September 1987, *25*(3), pp. 1281–1306.

Ochoa, Eduardo M. On Differing Views of the Long Run: Reflections on *Monopoly or Competition in the U.S. Economy? Rev. Radical Polit. Econ.*, Fall 1987, *19*(3), pp. 69–74. **[G: U.S.]**

Okuguchi, Koji. Equilibrium Prices in the Bertrand and Cournot Oligopolies. *J. Econ. Theory*, June 1987, *42*(1), pp. 128–39.

Okuguchi, Koji and Szidarovszky, Ferenc. Stability of the Linear Cournot Oligopoly with Multiproduct Firms. *Econ. Stud. Quart.*, June 1987, *38*(2), pp. 184–87.

Osborne, Martin J. and Pitchik, Carolyn. Cartels, Profits and Excess Capacity. *Int. Econ. Rev.*, June 1987, *28*(2), pp. 413–28.

Osborne, Martin J. and Pitchik, Carolyn. Equilibrium in Hotelling's Model of Spatial Competition. *Econometrica*, July 1987, *55*(4), pp. 911–22.

de Palma, André; Pontes, Jose Pedro and Thisse, Jacques-François. Spatial Competition under Uniform Delivered Pricing. *Reg. Sci. Urban Econ.*, August 1987, *17*(3), pp. 441–49.

Panzar, John C. and Rosse, James N. Testing for "Monopoly" Equilibrium. *J. Ind. Econ.*, June 1987, *35*(4), pp. 443–56.

Paulsen, Jim W. and Adams, Roy D. Optimal Taxation of a Monopoly. *Nat. Tax J.*, March 1987, *40*(1), pp. 121–25.

Peltzman, Sam. Technological Change, Sunk Costs, and Competition: Comments and Discussion. *Brookings Pap. Econ. Act.*, 1987, (3), pp. 941–46.

Pindyck, Robert S. On Monopoly Power in Extractive Resource Markets. *J. Environ. Econ. Manage.*, June 1987, *14*(2), pp. 128–42.

Png, Ivan Paak Liang and Hirshleifer, David. Price Discrimination through Offers to Match Price. *J. Bus.*, July 1987, *60*(3), pp. 365–83.

Raubitschek, Ruth S. A Model of Product Proliferation with Multiproduct Firms. *J. Ind. Econ.*, March 1987, *35*(3), pp. 269–79.

Reynolds, Stanley S. Capacity Investment, Preemption and Commitment in an Infinite Horizon Model. *Int. Econ. Rev.*, February 1987, *28*(1), pp. 69–88.

Rob, Rafael. Entry, Fixed Costs and the Aggregation of Private Information. *Rev. Econ. Stud.*, October 1987, *54*(4), pp. 619–30.

Roberts, John. Battles for Market Share: Incomplete Information, Aggressive Strategic Pricing, and Competitive Dynamics. *Bewley, T. F., ed.*, 1987, pp. 157–95.

Roberts, John. General Equilibrium Analysis of Imperfect Competition: An Illustrative Example. *Feiwel, G. R., ed. (I)*, 1987, pp. 415–38.

Rogerson, William P. A Note on the Existence of Single Price Equilibrium Price Distributions in Sequential Search Models. *Rev. Econ. Stud.*, April 1987, *54*(2), pp. 339–42.

Rogerson, William P. The Dissipation of Profits by Brand Name Investment and Entry when Price Guarantees Quality. *J. Polit. Econ.*, August 1987, *95*(4), pp. 797–809.

Ross, Howard N. Oligopoly Theory and Price Rigidity. *Antitrust Bull.*, Summer 1987, *32*(2), pp. 451–69.

Rotemberg, Julio J. and Saloner, Garth. The Relative Rigidity of Monopoly Pricing. *Amer. Econ. Rev.*, December 1987, *77*(5), pp. 917–26.

Rothschild, R. The Theory of Monopolistic Competition: E. H. Chamberlin's Influence on Industrial Organisation Theory over Sixty Years. *J. Econ. Stud.*, 1987, *14*(1), pp. 34–54.

Rothschild, R. Threats as Credible Deterrents to Cheating in Cartels: A Comparative Analysis in a Static Framework. *Australian Econ. Pap.*, December 1987, *26*(49), pp. 216–24.

Rubinstein, Ariel and Wolinsky, Asher. Middlemen. *Quart. J. Econ.*, August 1987, *102*(3), pp. 581–93.

Sadanand, Asha. Lost Profits, Market Damages, and Specific Performance: An Economic Analysis of Buyer's Breach. *Can. J. Econ.*, November 1987, *20*(4), pp. 750–73.

Saloner, Garth. Cournot Duopoly with Two Production Periods. *J. Econ. Theory*, June 1987, *42*(1), pp. 183–87.

Saloner, Garth. Predation, Mergers, and Incomplete Information. *Rand J. Econ.*, Summer 1987, *18*(2), pp. 165–86.

Salop, Steven C. and Scheffman, David T. Cost-Raising Strategies. *J. Ind. Econ.*, September 1987, *36*(1), pp. 19–34.

Salop, Steven C. and Stiglitz, Joseph E. Information, Welfare, and Product Diversity. *Feiwel, G. R., ed. (II)*, 1987, pp. 328–40.

Schmalensee, Richard. Competitive Advantage and Collusive Optima. *Int. J. Ind. Organ.*, December 1987, *5*(4), pp. 351–67.

Schwarz, Peter M. and Taylor, Thomas N. Public Utility Pricing under Risk; the Case of Self-Rationing: Comment and Extension. *Amer. Econ. Rev.*, September 1987, *77*(4), pp. 734–39.

Seidmann, Daniel J. Incentives for Information Production and Disclosure: Comment [The Strategic Role of Information on the Demand Function in an Oligopolistic Market]. *Quart. J. Econ.*, May 1987, *102*(2), pp. 445–52.

Shaffer, Sherrill. Myopic Monopoly. *Atlantic Econ. J.*, March 1987, *15*(1), pp. 118.

Shaffer, Sherrill. Two-Part Tariffs in a Contestable Natural Monopoly. *Economica*, August 1987, *54*(215), pp. 315–16.

Shaked, Avner and Sutton, John. Product Differentiation and Industrial Structure. *J. Ind. Econ.*, December 1987, *36*(2), pp. 131–46.

Shepard, Andrea. Licensing to Enhance Demand for New Technologies. *Rand J. Econ.*, Autumn 1987, *18*(3), pp. 360–68.

Sigurdsson, Brynjólfur. Prisdannelse og priskontrol. (Price Controls and Price Equilibrium. With English summary.) *Nationaløkon. Tidsskr.*, 1987, *125*(1), pp. 95–112.

Simon, Leo K. Bertrand Price Competition with Differentiated Commodities. *J. Econ. Theory*, April 1987, *41*(2), pp. 304–32.

Sklivas, Steven D. The Strategic Choice of Managerial Incentives. *Rand J. Econ.*, Autumn 1987, *18*(3), pp. 452–58.

Smith, Alasdair. Strategic Investment, Multinational Corporations and Trade Policy. *Europ. Econ. Rev.*, Feb./Mar. 1987, *31*(1/2), pp. 89–96.

Stern, Nicholas H. The Effects of Taxation, Price Control and Government Contracts in Oligopoly and Monopolistic Competition. *J. Public Econ.*, March 1987, *32*(2), pp. 133–58.

Stiglitz, Joseph E. Competition and the Number of Firms in a Market: Are Duopolies More

Competitive than Atomistic Markets? *J. Polit. Econ.*, October 1987, *95*(5), pp. 1041–61.

Stiglitz, Joseph E. Technological Change, Sunk Costs, and Competition. *Brookings Pap. Econ. Act.*, 1987, (3), pp. 883–937.

Stiglitz, Joseph E. The Causes and Consequences of the Dependence of Quality on Price. *J. Econ. Lit.*, March 1987, *25*(1), pp. 1–48.

Strand, Jon. Oligopolistic Fixed-Price Equilibria and the Number of Firms. *Scand. J. Econ.*, 1987, *89*(4), pp. 497–503.

Suzumura, Kotaro and Kiyono, Kazuharu. Entry Barriers and Economic Welfare. *Rev. Econ. Stud.*, January 1987, *54*(1), pp. 157–67.

Tapvong, Churai. A Note on the Effect of Changes in Demand upon Price: A Durable-Goods Monopoly. *Singapore Econ. Rev.*, April 1987, *32*(1), pp. 62–70.

Tisdell, Clem A. Profits and Technique Choice under Oligopoly/Monopoly Related to Fluctuations in Demand and Limit Price. *Rivista Int. Sci. Econ. Com.*, Jan.-Feb. 1987, *34*(1–2), pp. 51–66.

Tomek, William G. The Economic Efficiency of Alternative Exchange Mechanisms: A Discussion. *Kilmer, R. L. and Armbruster, W. J., eds.*, 1987, pp. 150–53.

Ulph, Alistair M. Recent Advances in Oligopoly Theory from a Game Theory Perspective. *J. Econ. Surveys*, 1987, *1*(2), pp. 149–72.

Veendorp, E. C. H. Oligoemporistic Competition and the Countervailing Power Hypothesis. *Can. J. Econ.*, August 1987, *20*(3), pp. 519–26.

Veugelers, Reinhilde. The Role of Information in a Duopoly Setting: Some Experimental Results. *Rech. Écon. Louvain*, 1987, *53*(4), pp. 357–77.

Vislie, Jon. Long-term Bilateral Contracts for Natural Gas. *Golombek, R.; Hoel, M. and Vislie, J., eds.*, 1987, pp. 267–77.

Waldman, Michael. Noncooperative Entry Deterrence, Uncertainty, and the Free Rider Problem. *Rev. Econ. Stud.*, April 1987, *54*(2), pp. 301–10.

Waterson, Michael. Recent Developments in the Theory of Natural Monopoly. *J. Econ. Surveys*, 1987, *1*(1), pp. 59–80.

Wenders, John T. On Perfect Rent Dissipation. *Amer. Econ. Rev.*, June 1987, *77*(3), pp. 456–59.

Williamson, Oliver E. Assessing Contract. *Williamson, O.*, 1987, *1985*, pp. 161–89.

Williamson, Oliver E. Economies as an Antitrust Defense: The Welfare Trade-Offs. *Williamson, O.*, 1987, *1968*, pp. 3–23. **[G: U.S.]**

Williamson, Oliver E. Predatory Pricing: A Strategic and Welfare Analysis. *Williamson, O.*, 1987, *1978*, pp. 225–81.

Williamson, Oliver E. The Economics of Antitrust: Transaction Cost Considerations. *Williamson, O.*, 1987, *1974*, pp. 71–122.

Williamson, Oliver E. The Vertical Integration of Production: Market Failure Considerations. *Williamson, O.*, 1987, *1971*, pp. 24–38.

Wilson, Robert B. Game-Theoretic Analyses of Trading Processes. *Bewley, T. F., ed.*, 1987, pp. 33–70.

Wirl, Franz. Joint Production of Substitutable, Exhaustible Resources, Or: Is Flaring Gas Rational? *J. Econ. Dynam. Control*, December 1987, *11*(4), pp. 499–511.

Wolinsky, Asher. Brand Names and Price Discrimination. *J. Ind. Econ.*, March 1987, *35*(3), pp. 255–68.

Wu, Shih-Yen and Rozek, Richard P. A Bidding Process for a Centralized Market with Trading Out of Equilibrium. *J. Econ. (Z. Nationalökon.)*, 1987, *47*(3), pp. 287–307.

0227 Theory of Auction Markets

Brannman, Lance; Klein, J. Douglass and Weiss, Leonard W. The Price Effects of Increased Competition in Auction Markets. *Rev. Econ. Statist.*, February 1987, *69*(1), pp. 24–32.
[G: U.S.]

Buccola, Steven T. and Smith, Vernon L. Uncertainty and Partial Adjustment in Double-Auction Markets. *J. Econ. Behav. Organ.*, December 1987, *8*(4), pp. 587–601.

Conroy, Robert M. and Hughes, John S. Delegated Information Gathering Decisions. *Accounting Rev.*, January 1987, *62*(1), pp. 50–66.

Crémer, Jacques. Auctions with Contingent Payments: Comment. *Amer. Econ. Rev.*, September 1987, *77*(4), pp. 746.

Fehl, Ulrich and Güth, Werner. Internal and External Stability of Bidder Cartels in Auctions and Public Tenders: A Comparison of Pricing Rules. *Int. J. Ind. Organ.*, September 1987, *5*(3), pp. 303–13.

Fishe, Raymond P. H. and McAfee, R. Preston. Nonlinear Contracts, Zero Profits and Moral Hazard. *Economica*, February 1987, *54*(213), pp. 97–101.

Graham, Daniel A. and Marshall, Robert C. Collusive Bidder Behavior at Single-Object Second-Price and English Auctions. *J. Polit. Econ.*, December 1987, *95*(6), pp. 1217–39.

Hausch, Donald B. An Asymmetric Common-Value Auction Model. *Rand J. Econ.*, Winter 1987, *18*(4), pp. 611–21.

Hendricks, Kenneth; Porter, Robert H. and Boudreau, Bryan. Information, Returns, and Bidding Behavior in OCS Auctions: 1954–1969. *J. Ind. Econ.*, June 1987, *35*(4), pp. 517–42.
[G: U.S.]

Kagel, John H.; Harstad, Ronald M. and Levin, Dan. Information Impact and Allocation Rules in Auctions with Affiliated Private Values: A Laboratory Study. *Econometrica*, November 1987, *55*(6), pp. 1275–1304.

Knez, Marc and Smith, Vernon L. Hypothetical Valuations and Preference Reversals in the Context of Asset Trading. *Roth, A. E., ed.*, 1987, pp. 131–54.

Kuenne, Robert E. Oligopolistic Uncertainty and Optimal Bidding in Government Procurement: A Subjective Probability Approach. *Feiwel, G. R., ed. (I)*, 1987, pp. 654–74.

Laffont, Jean-Jacques and Tirole, Jean. Auctioning Incentive Contracts. *J. Polit. Econ.*, October 1987, *95*(5), pp. 921–37.

Matthews, Steven. Comparing Auctions for Risk Averse Buyers: A Buyer's Point of View. *Econometrica*, May 1987, *55*(3), pp. 633–46.

McAfee, R. Preston and McMillan, John. Auctions and Bidding. *J. Econ. Lit.*, June 1987, *25*(2), pp. 699–738.

McAfee, R. Preston and McMillan, John. Auctions with a Stochastic Number of Bidders. *J. Econ. Theory*, October 1987, *43*(1), pp. 1–19.

Milgrom, Paul R. Auction Theory. *Bewley, T. F., ed.*, 1987, pp. 1–32.

Riordan, Michael H. and Sappington, David E. M. Awarding Monopoly Franchises. *Amer. Econ. Rev.*, June 1987, *77*(3), pp. 375–87.

Samuelson, William. Auctions with Contingent Payments: Comment. *Amer. Econ. Rev.*, September 1987, *77*(4), pp. 740–45.

Wilson, Robert B. Game-Theoretic Analyses of Trading Processes. *Bewley, T. F., ed.*, 1987, pp. 33–70.

Wu, Shih-Yen and Rozek, Richard P. A Bidding Process for a Centralized Market with Trading Out of Equilibrium. *J. Econ. (Z. Nationalökon.)*, 1987, *47*(3), pp. 287–307.

0228 Agent Theory

Ballwieser, Wolfgang. Auditing in an Agency Setting. *Bamberg, G. and Spremann, K., eds.*, 1987, pp. 327–46.

Bamberg, Günter. Risk Sharing and Subcontracting. *Bamberg, G. and Spremann, K., eds.*, 1987, pp. 61–79.

Banker, Rajiv D. and Patton, James M. Analytical Agency Theory and Municipal Accounting: An Introduction and an Application. *Chan, J. L., ed., Pt. B*, 1987, pp. 29–50.

Beckmann, Martin J. Managers as Principals and Agents. *Bamberg, G. and Spremann, K., eds.*, 1987, pp. 379–88.

Bester, Helmut and Hellwig, Martin. Moral Hazard and Equilibrium Credit Rationing: An Overview of the Issues. *Bamberg, G. and Spremann, K., eds.*, 1987, pp. 135–66.

Blickle, Marina. Information Systems and the Design of Optimal Contracts. *Bamberg, G. and Spremann, K., eds.*, 1987, pp. 93–103.

Bohn, Henning. Monitoring Multiple Agents: The Role of Hierarchies. *J. Econ. Behav. Organ.*, June 1987, *8*(2), pp. 279–305.

Border, Kim C. and Sobel, Joel. Samurai Accountant: A Theory of Auditing and Plunder. *Rev. Econ. Stud.*, October 1987, *54*(4), pp. 525–40.

Braverman, Avishay. Corporate Governance and Product Market Structure: Comments. *Razin, A. and Sadka, E., eds.*, 1987, pp. 495–99.

Brito, Dagobert L. and Intriligator, Michael D. Arms Races and the Outbreak of War: Application of Principal–Agent Relationships and Asymmetric Information. *Schmidt, C. and Blackaby, F., eds.*, 1987, pp. 104–20.

Cohen, Mark A. Optimal Enforcement Strategy to Prevent Oil Spills: An Application of a Principal–Agent Model with Moral Hazard. *J. Law Econ.*, April 1987, *30*(1), pp. 23–51.
[G: U.S.]

Demski, Joel S. and Sappington, David E. M. Delegated Expertise. *J. Acc. Res.*, Spring 1987, *25*(1), pp. 68–89.

Dimitri, Nicola. A Note on Risk Sharing in the Principal–Agent Relationship. *Econ. Notes*, 1987, (3), pp. 131–40.

Drèze, Jacques H. Decision Theory with Moral Hazard and State-Dependent Preferences. *Drèze, J. H.*, 1987, pp. 23–89.

Ewert, Ralf. The Financial Theory of Agency as a Tool for an Analysis of Problems in External Accounting. *Bamberg, G. and Spremann, K., eds.*, 1987, pp. 281–309.

Faith, Roger L. and Reid, Joseph D., Jr. An Agency Theory of Unionism. *J. Econ. Behav. Organ.*, March 1987, *8*(1), pp. 39–60.

Feichtinger, Gustav and Sorger, Gerhard. Intertemporal Sharecropping: A Differential Game Approach. *Bamberg, G. and Spremann, K., eds.*, 1987, pp. 415–38.

Firchau, Volker. Information Systems for Principal–Agent Problems. *Bamberg, G. and Spremann, K., eds.*, 1987, pp. 81–92.

Funke, Helmut. Incentive Compatible Mechanisms for the Allocation of Public Goods. *Bamberg, G. and Spremann, K., eds.*, 1987, pp. 105–16.

Gaynor, Martin and Kleindorfer, Paul R. Misperceptions, Equilibrium, and Incentives in Groups and Organizations. *Bamberg, G. and Spremann, K., eds.*, 1987, pp. 389–414.

Hart, Oliver. Corporate Governance and Product Market Structure: Comments. *Razin, A. and Sadka, E., eds.*, 1987, pp. 499–503.

Hart, Oliver and Holmstrom, Bengt. The Theory of Contracts. *Bewley, T. F., ed.*, 1987, pp. 71–155.

Holmstrom, Bengt and Milgrom, Paul R. Aggregation and Linearity in the Provision of Intertemporal Incentives. *Econometrica*, March 1987, *55*(2), pp. 303–28.

Ickes, Barry W. and Samuelson, Larry. Job Transfers and Incentives in Complex Organizations: Thwarting the Ratchet Effect. *Rand J. Econ.*, Summer 1987, *18*(2), pp. 275–86.

Kaulmann, Thomas. Managerialism versus the Property Rights Theory of the Firm. *Bamberg, G. and Spremann, K., eds.*, 1987, pp. 439–59.
[G: U.S.]

Kawasaki, Seiichi and McMillan, John. The Design of Contracts: Evidence from Japanese Subcontracting. *J. Japanese Int. Economies*, September 1987, *1*(3), pp. 327–49. [G: Japan]

La Manna, Manfredi M. A. The Simple Analytics of Agency Costs: A Pedagogical Comment. *Econ. Notes*, 1987, (2), pp. 145–56.

Laffont, Jean-Jacques. Le risque moral dans la relation de mandat. (Moral Hazard in the Principal–Agent Relationship. With English summary.) *Revue Écon.*, January 1987, *38*(1), pp. 5–23.

McAfee, R. Preston and McMillan, John. Competition for Agency Contracts. *Rand J. Econ.*,

Summer 1987, *18*(2), pp. 296–307.

McMillan, Henry. A Principal–Agent Analysis of Pension Policy. *Managerial Dec. Econ.*, December 1987, *8*(4), pp. 313–19.

Milde, Hellmuth. Managerial Contracting with Public and Private Information. *Bamberg, G. and Spremann, K., eds.*, 1987, pp. 39–59.

Nalbantian, Haig R. Incentive Compensation in Perspective. *Nalbantian, H. R., ed.*, 1987, pp. 3–43.

Page, Frank H., Jr. The Existence of Optimal Contracts in the Principal–Agent Model. *J. Math. Econ.*, 1987, *16*(2), pp. 157–67.

Pfingsten, Andreas. Incentives to Forecast Honestly. *Bamberg, G. and Spremann, K., eds.*, 1987, pp. 117–33.

Picard, Pierre. On the Design of Incentive Schemes under Moral Hazard and Adverse Selection. *J. Public Econ.*, August 1987, *33*(3), pp. 305–31.

Radner, Roy. Decentralization and Incentives. *[Hurwicz, L.]*, 1987, *1983*, pp. 3–47.

Rasmusen, Eric. Moral Hazard in Risk-Averse Teams. *Rand J. Econ.*, Autumn 1987, *18*(3), pp. 428–35.

Rees, Ray. The Theory of Principal and Agent: Part 2. *Hey, J. D. and Lambert, P. J., eds.*, 1987, *1985*, pp. 70–90.

Rees, Ray. The Theory of Principal and Agent: Part 1. *Hey, J. D. and Lambert, P. J., eds.*, 1987, *1985*, pp. 46–69.

Riordan, Michael H. and Sappington, David E. M. Information, Incentives, and Organizational Mode. *Quart. J. Econ.*, May 1987, *102*(2), pp. 243–63.

Sappington, David E. M. and Stiglitz, Joseph E. Information and Regulation. *Bailey, E. E., ed.*, 1987, pp. 3–43.

Schanze, Erich. Contract, Agency, and the Delegation of Decision Making. *Bamberg, G. and Spremann, K., eds.*, 1987, pp. 461–71.

Schmidt, Reinhard H. Agency Costs Are Not a "Flop"! *Bamberg, G. and Spremann, K., eds.*, 1987, pp. 495–509.

Schneider, Dieter. Agency Costs and Transaction Costs: Flops in the Principal-Agent–Theory of Financial Markets. *Bamberg, G. and Spremann, K., eds.*, 1987, pp. 481–94.

Sklivas, Steven D. The Strategic Choice of Managerial Incentives. *Rand J. Econ.*, Autumn 1987, *18*(3), pp. 452–58.

Spear, Stephen E. and Srivastava, Sanjay. On Repeated Moral Hazard with Discounting. *Rev. Econ. Stud.*, October 1987, *54*(4), pp. 599–617.

Spremann, Klaus. Agent and Principal. *Bamberg, G. and Spremann, K., eds.*, 1987, pp. 3–37.

Starks, Laura T. Performance Incentive Fees: An Agency Theoretic Approach. *J. Finan. Quant. Anal.*, March 1987, *22*(1), pp. 17–32.

Stiglitz, Joseph E. The Design of Labor Contracts: The Economics of Incentives and Risk Sharing. *Nalbantian, H. R., ed.*, 1987, pp. 47–68.

Swoboda, Peter. The Liquidation Decision as a Principal–Agent Problem. *Bamberg, G. and Spremann, K., eds.*, 1987, pp. 167–77.

Wagenhofer, Alfred. Investigation Strategies with Costly Perfect Information. *Bamberg, G. and Spremann, K., eds.*, 1987, pp. 347–77.

Wallace, Wanda A. Agency Theory and Governmental and Nonprofit Sector Research. *Chan, J. L., ed., Pt. B*, 1987, pp. 51–70.

Wilhelm, Jochen E. M. On Stakeholders' Unanimity. *Bamberg, G. and Spremann, K., eds.*, 1987, pp. 179–204.

0229 Microeconomics of Intertemporal Choice

Aiyagari, S. Rao. Optimality and Monetary Equilibria in Stationary Overlapping Generations Models with Long-Lived Agents: Growth versus Discounting. *J. Econ. Theory*, December 1987, *43*(2), pp. 292–313.

Becker, Robert A. and Foias, Ciprian. A Characterization of Ramsey Equilibrium. *J. Econ. Theory*, February 1987, *41*(1), pp. 173–84.

Beckmann, Martin J. Entscheidungsprozesse in kontinuierlicher Zeit: Optimale Konsumplanung oder vom Spartrieb zum Konsumrausch. (Decision Processes in Continuous Time: Optimal Consumption Plans or from Thrift to Splurge. With English summary.) *Jahr. Nationalökon. Statist.*, October 1987, *203*(5–6), pp. 476–84.

Bernheim, B. Douglas. Dissaving after Retirement: Testing the Pure Life Cycle Hypothesis. *Bodie, Z.; Shoven, J. B. and Wise, D. A., eds.*, 1987, pp. 237–74.   **[G: U.S.]**

Brown, Stephen P. A. The Fairness of Discounting: A Majority Rule Approach. *Public Choice*, October 1987, *55*(3), pp. 215–26.

Burke, Jonathan L. Inactive Transfer Policies and Efficiency in General Overlapping-Generations Economies. *J. Math. Econ.*, 1987, *16*(3), pp. 201–22.

Chae, Suchan. Short Run Core Equivalence in an Overlapping Generations Model. *J. Econ. Theory*, October 1987, *43*(1), pp. 170–83.

Chamley, Christophe and Wright, Brian D. Fiscal Incidence in an Overlapping Generations Model with a Fixed Asset. *J. Public Econ.*, February 1987, *32*(1), pp. 3–24.

Chang, Winston W. and Southwick, Lawrence, Jr. On the Pricing and Benefit Structure of a Private Club or Public Utility. *Public Choice*, October 1987, *55*(3), pp. 227–44.

Colangelo, Giuseppe. Il modello dell'acceleratore flessibile generalizzato come soluzione lineare globalmente ottimale. (The Generalized Flexible Accelerator as a Globally Optimal Linear Solution. With English summary.) *Econ. Polit.*, August 1987, *4*(2), pp. 189–211.

Dana, Rose-Anne and Montrucchio, Luigi. Dynamic Complexity in Duopoly Games. *Grandmont, J.-M., ed.*, 1987, *1986*, pp. 40–56.

Dana, Rose-Anne and Montrucchio, Luigi. On Rational Dynamic Strategies in Infinite Horizon Models Where Agents Discount the Future. *J. Econ. Behav. Organ.*, September 1987, *8*(3), pp. 497–511.

Epstein, Larry G. The Global Stability of Efficient Intertemporal Allocations. *Econometrica*,

March 1987, 55(2), pp. 329–55.

Flaschel, Peter and Semmler, Willi. Classical and Neoclassical Competitive Adjustment Processes. *Manchester Sch. Econ. Soc. Stud.*, March 1987, 55(1), pp. 13–37.

Guesnerie, Roger. Stationary Sunspot Equilibria in an *N* Commodity World. *Grandmont, J.-M., ed.*, 1987, *1986*, pp. 103–27.

Hillier, Brian and Lunati, M. Teresa. On Nash versus Stackelberg Strategies and the Conditions for Operative Intergenerational Transfers. *Scot. J. Polit. Econ.*, February 1987, 34(1), pp. 91–96.

Huang, Chi-fu. An Intertemporal General Equilibrium Asset Pricing Model: The Case of Diffusion Information. *Econometrica*, January 1987, 55(1), pp. 117–42.

Hurd, Michael D. Dissaving after Retirement: Testing the Pure Life Cycle Hypothesis: Comment. *Bodie, Z.; Shoven, J. B. and Wise, D. A., eds.*, 1987, pp. 275–79. **[G: U.S.]**

Ioannides, Yannis M. and Sato, Ryuzo. On the Distribution of Wealth and Intergenerational Transfers. *J. Lab. Econ.*, July 1987, 5(3), pp. 366–85.

Judd, Kenneth L. The Welfare Cost of Factor Taxation in a Perfect-Foresight Model. *J. Polit. Econ.*, August 1987, 95(4), pp. 675–709.

Kagel, John H. and Green, Leonard. Intertemporal Choice Behavior: Evaluation of Economic and Psychological Models. *Green, L. and Kagel, J. H., eds.*, 1987, pp. 166–84.

Kotlikoff, Laurence J.; Shoven, John B. and Spivak, Avia. Annuity Markets, Savings, and the Capital Stock. *Bodie, Z.; Shoven, J. B. and Wise, D. A., eds.*, 1987, pp. 211–34.

Kurz, Mordecai. The Life-Cycle Hypothesis as a Tool of Theory and Policy. *Feiwel, G. R., ed. (II)*, 1987, pp. 447–90. **[G: U.S.]**

Madrigal, Vicente; Tan, Tommy C. C. and da Costa Werlang, Sérgio Ribeiro. Support Restrictions and Sequential Equilibria. *J. Econ. Theory*, December 1987, 43(2), pp. 329–34.

Malinvaud, Edmond. The Overlapping Generations Model in 1947. *J. Econ. Lit.*, March 1987, 25(1), pp. 103–05.

Marimon, Ramon and Wallace, Neil. Trade Using Assets Divisible at a Cost. *J. Econ. Theory*, December 1987, 43(2), pp. 223–51.

Prescott, Edward C. and Boyd, John H. Dynamic Coalitions, Growth, and the Firm. *Prescott, E. C. and Wallace, N., eds.*, 1987, pp. 146–60.

Ray, Debraj. Nonpaternalistic Intergenerational Altruism. *J. Econ. Theory*, February 1987, 41(1), pp. 112–32.

Rothschild, Michael. Annuity Markets, Savings, and the Capital Stock: Comment. *Bodie, Z.; Shoven, J. B. and Wise, D. A., eds.*, 1987, pp. 234–36.

Scotchmer, Suzanne. Two-Tier Pricing of Shared Facilities in a Free-Entry Equilibrium: Erratum. *Rand J. Econ.*, Spring 1987, 18(1), pp. 164.

Shortle, James S. and Miranowski, John A. Intertemporal Soil Resource Use: Is It Socially Excessive? *J. Environ. Econ. Manage.*, June 1987, 14(2), pp. 99–111.

Stahl, Dale O., II. Temporary Equilibrium with Storable Commodities. *J. Econ. Theory*, August 1987, 42(2), pp. 262–74.

Wright, Randall D. Market Structure and Competitive Equilibrium in Dynamic Economic Models. *J. Econ. Theory*, February 1987, 41(1), pp. 189–201.

023 Macroeconomic Theory

0230 General

Ahtiala, K. Pekka. The Effects of Foreign Disturbances under Flexible Exchange Rates. *J. Int. Money Finance*, December 1987, 6(4), pp. 387–400. **[G: W. Europe]**

Akerlof, George A. and Yellen, Janet L. Rational Models of Irrational Behavior. *Amer. Econ. Rev.*, May 1987, 77(2), pp. 137–42.

Amadeo, Edward J. and Dutt, Amitava Krishna. Os keynesianos neo-ricardianos e os pós-keynesianos. (With English summary.) *Pesquisa Planejamento Econ.*, December 1987, 17(3), pp. 561–603.

Andersen, Torben M. Effective Demand, Differential Information and the Multiplier. *Econ. J.*, June 1987, 97(386), pp. 353–71.

Andersen, Torben M. Pre-set Prices, Differential Information and Monetary Policy. *Sinclair, P. J. N., ed.*, 1987, *1986*, pp. 283–307.

Arena, Richard. L'école internationale d'été de Trieste (1981–1985): vers une synthèse classico-keynesienne? (The Trieste International Summer School [1981–1985]: Towards a Ricardo-Keynesian Synthesis? With English summary.) *Écon. Soc.*, March 1987, 21(3), pp. 205–38.

Arida, Persio and Bacha, Edmar Lisboa. Balance of Payments: A Disequilibrium Analysis for Semi-industrialized Economies. *J. Devel. Econ.*, October 1987, 27(1–2), pp. 85–108. **[G: Latin America]**

Arida, Persio and Bacha, Edmar Lisboa. Balance of Payments: A Disequilibrium Analysis for Semi-industrialized Economies. *[Diaz-Alejandro, C. F.]*, 1987, pp. 85–108. **[G: Latin America]**

Asimakopulos, Athanasios. Approaches to Macroeconomics: Keynes and Others. *[Marrama, V.], Vol. 1*, 1987, pp. 3–21.

Azariadis, Costas. Les marchés imparfaits dans la théorie macroéconomique. (Imperfect Markets in Macroeconomics. With English summary.) *L'Actual. Econ.*, December 1987, 63(4), pp. 311–30.

Bailey, Ralph W.; Hall, V. B. and Phillips, Peter C. B. A Model of Output, Employment, Capital Formation and Inflation. *[Marrama, V.], Vol. 2*, 1987, pp. 703–67.

Baldani, Jeffrey P. and Michl, Thomas R. A Balanced Budget Multiplier for Interest Payments. *J. Post Keynesian Econ.*, Spring 1987, 9(3), pp. 424–39.

Barnett, William A. The Microeconomic Theory of Monetary Aggregation. *Barnett, W. A. and*

Singleton, K. J., eds., 1987, pp. 115–68.

Barro, Robert J. Government Spending, Interest Rates, Prices, and Budget Deficits in the United Kingdom, 1701–1918. *J. Monet. Econ.,* September 1987, *20*(2), pp. 221–47. **[G: U.K.]**

Bator, Francis M. The State of Macroeconomics. *Steinherr, A. and Weiserbs, D., eds.,* 1987, pp. 29–45.

Bernanke, Ben S. and Gertler, Mark. Banking and Macroeconomic Equilibrium. *Barnett, W. A. and Singleton, K. J., eds.,* 1987, pp. 89–111.

Berti, Lapo. Stoccolma e Cambridge: storia di una controversia. (With English summary.) *Stud. Econ.,* 1987, *42*(32), pp. 3–59.

Blackburn, Keith. Macroeconomic Policy Evaluation and Optimal Control Theory: A Critical Review of Some Recent Developments. *J. Econ. Surveys,* 1987, *1*(2), pp. 113–48.

Blackburn, Keith and Christensen, Michael. Macroeconomic Policy Games and Reputational Equilibria in a Contracting Model. *Ricerche Econ.,* Apr.-June 1987, *41*(2), pp. 190–209.

Bleaney, Michael F. Macroeconomic Theory and the Great Depression Revisited. *Scot. J. Polit. Econ.,* May 1987, *34*(2), pp. 105–19. **[G: U.S.]**

Blinder, Alan S. Keynes, Lucas, and Scientific Progress. *Amer. Econ. Rev.,* May 1987, *77*(2), pp. 130–36.

Bonnici, Josef. Imports in Keynesian Models. *Econ. Rec.,* December 1987, *63*(183), pp. 352–54.

Bronfenbrenner, Martin. Hoarding on the Wing. *Keio Econ. Stud.,* 1987, *24*(2), pp. 1–10.

Bronsard, Camille and Salvas-Bronsard, Lise. Growth, Desirability, Profitability and Unemployment. *Ann. Écon. Statist.,* Apr./Sept. 1987, (6/7), pp. 13–35.

Brown, Vivienne. Somme Reflections on the AD/AS Model. *Thompson, G.; Brown, V. and Levačić, R., eds.,* 1987, pp. 293–314. **[G: U.K.]**

Brunner, Karl. Has Monetarism Failed? *Dorn, J. A. and Schwartz, A. J., eds.,* 1987, pp. 163–99. **[G: U.S.]**

Bryant, John. The Paradox of Thrift, Liquidity Preference and Animal Spirits. *Econometrica,* September 1987, *55*(5), pp. 1231–35.

Buchanan, James M. and Wagner, Richard E. The Political Biases of Keynesian Economics. *Buchanan, J. M. (II),* 1987, *1978,* pp. 389–408.

Campbell, John Y. Macroeconomic Lessons from Britain: A Review Essay. *J. Monet. Econ.,* March 1987, *19*(2), pp. 315–24. **[G: U.K.]**

Cantor, Richard. Long-term Contracts, Consumption Smoothing and Wage–Profit Dynamics. *J. Macroecon.,* Winter 1987, *9*(1), pp. 59–70.

Caravale, Giovanni. The Neo-Keynesian School: Some Internal Controversies. *Atlantic Econ. J.,* December 1987, *15*(4), pp. 1–15.

Caravani, Paolo. Modeling Economic Policy with Non-symmetric Losses and Risk Aversion. *J.*

Econ. Behav. Organ., September 1987, *8*(3), pp. 453–67.

Carhill, M. Effective Demand Failure: Critique of an Anti-monetary Theory: A Note. *S. Afr. J. Econ.,* March 1987, *55*(1), pp. 86–89.

Carter, Michael G. and Maddock, Rodney. Inflation: The Invisible Foot of Macroeconomics. *Econ. Rec.,* June 1987, *63*(181), pp. 120–28.

Carvalho, Fernando. Alternative Analyses of Short and Long Run in Post-Keynesian Economics. *Albelda, R.; Gunn, C. and Waller, W., eds.,* 1987, *1984,* pp. 140–56.

Caskey, John and Fazzari, Steven M. Aggregate Demand Contractions with Nominal Debt Commitments: Is Wage Flexibility Stabilizing? *Econ. Inquiry,* October 1987, *25*(4), pp. 583–97.

Christiano, Lawrence J. and Eichenbaum, Martin S. Temporal Aggregation and Structural Inference in Macroeconomics. *Carnegie–Rochester Conf. Ser. Public Policy,* Spring 1987, *26,* pp. 63–130. **[G: U.S.]**

Christodoulakis, Nicos and Levine, Paul. The Trade-off between Simplicity and Optimality in Macroeconomic Policy Design. *J. Econ. Dynam. Control,* June 1987, *11*(2), pp. 173–78.

Cooper, Russell. Gale on Monetary Theory: A Review Essay. *J. Monet. Econ.,* March 1987, *19*(2), pp. 325–32.

Coppieters, Piet. Development of the Service Sector: A Critical Survey of Macro-economic Models. *Akehurst, G. and Gadrey, J., eds.,* 1987, pp. 89–98.

Corden, W. Max. The Relevance for Developing Countries of Recent Developments in Macroeconomic Theory. *World Bank Res. Observer,* July 1987, *2*(2), pp. 171–88. **[G: LDCs]**

Coulombe, Serge. A Note on the Pigou Effect and the Liquidity Trap: Comment. *J. Post Keynesian Econ.,* Fall 1987, *10*(1), pp. 163–65.

Croushore, Dean D. Government Financial Policy and Capital. *Southern Econ. J.,* October 1987, *54*(2), pp. 435–48.

Cunningham, Thomas J. Growing Out of Deficits: Debt Dynamics in a Disequilibrium Model. *J. Post Keynesian Econ.,* Winter 1986-87, *9*(2), pp. 297–306. **[G: U.S.]**

Currie, David and Levine, Paul. Credibility and Time Consistency in a Stochastic World. *J. Econ. (Z. Nationalökon.),* 1987, *47*(3), pp. 225–52.

Dalziel, Paul C. Aggregate Demand Curves in Macroeconomic Theory: Comment. *New Zealand Econ. Pap.,* 1987, *21,* pp. 105–11.

Danthine, Jean-Pierre; Donaldson, John B. and Smith, Lance. On the Superneutrality of Money in a Stochastic Dynamic Macroeconomic Model. *J. Monet. Econ.,* December 1987, *20*(3), pp. 475–99.

Darity, William A., Jr. and Cottrell, Allin F. Meade's *General Theory* Model: A Geometric Reprise. *J. Money, Credit, Banking,* May 1987, *19*(2), pp. 210–21.

Daub, M. An Institutional Approach to the Rationality of Expectations. *Appl. Econ.,* October

1987, *19*(10), pp. 1303–16.   [G: Canada]

Davidson, Paul. Sensible Expectations and the Long-run Non-neutrality of Money. *J. Post Keynesian Econ.*, Fall 1987, *10*(1), pp. 146–53.

Davis, John B. Three Principles of Post Keynesian Methodology. *J. Post Keynesian Econ.*, Summer 1987, *9*(4), pp. 552–64.

Day, Richard H. and Shafer, Wayne J. Ergodic Fluctuations in Deterministic Economic Models. *J. Econ. Behav. Organ.*, September 1987, *8*(3), pp. 339–61.

Deneckere, Raymond J. and Pelikan, Steve. Competitive Chaos. *Grandmont, J.-M., ed.*, 1987, *1986*, pp. 13–25.

Devereux, Michael. The Effect of Monetary Variability on Welfare in a Simple Macroeconomic Model. *J. Monet. Econ.*, May 1987, *19*(3), pp. 427–35.

Diamond, Peter. Equilibrium without an Auctioneer. *Bewley, T. F., ed.*, 1987, pp. 363–78.

Dixon, Huw. A Simple Model of Imperfect Competition with Walrasian Features. *Oxford Econ. Pap.*, March 1987, *39*(1), pp. 134–60.

Dixon, Huw. A Simple Model of Imperfect Competition with Walrasian Features. *Sinclair, P. J. N., ed.*, 1987, pp. 134–60.

Djajić, Slobodan. Government Spending and the Optimal Rates of Consumption and Capital Accumulation. *Can. J. Econ.*, August 1987, *20*(3), pp. 544–54.

Downe, Edward A. Minsky's Model of Financial Fragility: A Suggested Addition. *J. Post Keynesian Econ.*, Spring 1987, *9*(3), pp. 440–54.

Drèze, Jacques H. Underemployment Equilibrium: From Theory to Econometrics and Policy. *Europ. Econ. Rev.*, Feb./Mar. 1987, *31*(1/2), pp. 9–34.   [G: W. Europe]

Duca, John V. The Spillover Effects of Nominal Wage Rigidity in a Multisector Economy: A Note. *J. Money, Credit, Banking*, February 1987, *19*(1), pp. 117–21.

Duménil, Gérard and Lévy, Dominique. The Macroeconomics of Disequilibrium. *J. Econ. Behav. Organ.*, September 1987, *8*(3), pp. 377–95.

Dutt, Amitava Krishna. Alternative Closures Again: A Comment on 'Growth, Distribution and Inflation.' *Cambridge J. Econ.*, March 1987, *11*(1), pp. 75–82.

Dutt, Amitava Krishna. Keynes with a Perfectly Competitive Goods Market. *Australian Econ. Pap.*, December 1987, *26*(49), pp. 275–93.

Edwards, J. R. The Value of Money, Monetary Equilibrium and the Cambridge Effect: A Reply [Effective Demand Failure: Critique of an Anti-monetary Theory]. *S. Afr. J. Econ.*, September 1987, *55*(3), pp. 300–303.

Eichengreen, Barry. Macroeconomics and History. *Field, A. J., ed.*, 1987, pp. 43–90.

Elliott, John E. and Clark, Barry S. Keynes's *General Theory* and Social Justice. *J. Post Keynesian Econ.*, Spring 1987, *9*(3), pp. 381–94.

Fischer, Stanley. Macroeconomics and Finance:

1944, 1963, and 1985. *[Modigliani, F.]*, 1987, pp. 229–56.

Fleisher, Belton M. and Kopecky, Kenneth J. The Loanable-Funds Approach to Teaching Principles of Macroeconomics. *J. Econ. Educ.*, Winter 1987, *18*(1), pp. 19–33.

Foley, Duncan K. Liquidity–Profit Rate Cycles in a Capitalist Economy. *J. Econ. Behav. Organ.*, September 1987, *8*(3), pp. 363–76.

Fuhrer, Jeffrey C. Information Gathering and Expectation Formation under Model Uncertainty. *Southern Econ. J.*, January 1987, *53*(3), pp. 685–701.

Fujino, Shozaburo. The Present Position of Macroeconomics. *Econ. Stud. Quart.*, March 1987, *38*(1), pp. 1–14.

Garber, Peter M. Monetary History and Monetary Policy: A Review Essay. *J. Monet. Econ.*, July 1987, *20*(1), pp. 177–82.

Garrett, John R. Macroeconomic Policy and History. *Cambridge J. Econ.*, December 1987, *11*(4), pp. 375–92.   [G: U.S.; U.K.]

Girardin, E. and Marois, W. Déficit budgétaire et déficit externe: une analyse empirique. (With English summary.) *Revue Écon. Polit.*, Jan.-Feb. 1987, *97*(1), pp. 51–78.   [G: U.S.; U.K.; France]

Goodwin, Richard M. Competitive Capitalism as a System of Auto-control. *de Cecco, M. and Fitoussi, J.-P., eds.*, 1987, pp. 286–304.

Grandmont, Jean-Michel. Classical and Keynesian Unemployment in the IS–LM Model. *de Cecco, M. and Fitoussi, J.-P., eds.*, 1987, pp. 66–94.

Grandmont, Jean-Michel. Stabilizing Competitive Business Cycles. *Grandmont, J.-M., ed.*, 1987, *1986*, pp. 57–76.

Green, Steven L. Theories of Inflation: A Review Essay. *J. Monet. Econ.*, July 1987, *20*(1), pp. 169–75.

Greenwald, Bruce C. and Stiglitz, Joseph E. Keynesian, New Keynesian and New Classical Economics. *Oxford Econ. Pap.*, March 1987, *39*(1), pp. 119–33.

Greenwald, Bruce C. and Stiglitz, Joseph E. Keynesian, New Keynesian and New Classical Economics. *Sinclair, P. J. N., ed.*, 1987, pp. 119–33.

Greenwood, Jeremy and Huffman, Gregory W. A Dynamic Equilibrium Model of Inflation and Unemployment. *J. Monet. Econ.*, March 1987, *19*(2), pp. 203–28.

Guesnerie, Roger. Stationary Sunspot Equilibria in an *N* Commodity World. *Grandmont, J.-M., ed.*, 1987, *1986*, pp. 103–27.

Hahn, Sangmoon. Information Acquisition in an Incomplete Information Model of Business Cycle. *J. Monet. Econ.*, July 1987, *20*(1), pp. 123–40.

Hahn, Frank H. "Of Marx and Keynes and Many Things": A Review Article. *Sinclair, P. J. N., ed.*, 1987, *1986*, pp. 378–85.

Hahn, Frank H. The Foundations of Monetary Theory. *de Cecco, M. and Fitoussi, J.-P., eds.*, 1987, pp. 21–43.

Hargreaves Heap, Shaun P. Risk and Culture:

A Missing Link in the Post Keynesian Tradition. *J. Post Keynesian Econ.*, Winter 1986-87, *9*(2), pp. 267–78.

Hasan, M. Aynul. Rational Expectations Estimation of Macroeconomic Models: Some Monte Carlo Results. *J. Macroecon.*, Spring 1987, *9*(2), pp. 297–315.

Henry, Ken R. and Woodfield, Alan. Aggregate Demand Curves in Macroeconomic Theory: Reply. *New Zealand Econ. Pap.*, 1987, *21*, pp. 113–16.

Hong, Wontack. A Theory of Interest and the Steady-State Rate of Return on Capital. *Int. Econ. J.*, Autumn 1987, *1*(3), pp. 87–90.

Hoogduin, Lex and Snippe, J. Uncertainty in/of Macroeconomics: An Essay on Adequate Abstraction. *De Economist*, 1987, *135*(4), pp. 429–41.

Houmanidis, Lazaros. Keynesianism and Stagflation. *Int. J. Soc. Econ.*, 1987, *14*(7/8/9), pp. 211–20.

Jones, Stephen R. G. and Stock, James H. Demand Disturbances and Aggregate Fluctuations: The Implications of Near Rationality. *Econ. J.*, March 1987, *97*(385), pp. 49–64.

Joyeux, Roselyne. Misspecification Tests on Taylor's Version of a Keynesian Macromodel. *Southern Econ. J.*, July 1987, *54*(1), pp. 159–67. [G: U.S.]

Judd, Kenneth L. Debt and Distortionary Taxation in a Simple Perfect Foresight Model. *J. Monet. Econ.*, July 1987, *20*(1), pp. 51–72.

Kang, Myung Hun. Money, Income and Causality: Korea and Japan. *Int. Econ. J.*, Autumn 1987, *1*(3), pp. 57–70. [G: S. Korea; Japan]

Karacaoglu, Girol. Fitting Money into Conventional Macroeconomic Models. *Australian Econ. Pap.*, June 1987, *26*(48), pp. 83–100.

Keating, Giles. A Two-Good Model with Capital Accumulation and a Real Balance Effect. *Oxford Econ. Pap.*, September 1987, *39*(3), pp. 481–99.

King, Robert G. and Plosser, Charles I. Nominal Surprises, Real Factors, and Propagation Mechanisms. *Barnett, W. A. and Singleton, K. J., eds.*, 1987, pp. 273–92. [G: U.S.]

Klein, Lawrence R. Interaction between General Equilibrium and Macroeconomics: An Interview. *Feiwel, G. R., ed. (I)*, 1987, pp. 340–58.

van de Klundert, Theo C. M. J. Coordination Failure in an Industrial Society. *De Economist*, 1987, *135*(4), pp. 467–87.

Koenig, Evan F. The Short-run "Tobin Effect" in a Monetary Optimizing Model. *Econ. Inquiry*, January 1987, *25*(1), pp. 43–53.

Kofuji, Yasuo. Wealth Effects and Fiscal Policy in the Context of a Flexible Price Level—A Reply. *Public Finance*, 1987, *42*(1), pp. 160–63.

Kregel, Jan A. Markets and Institutions as Features of a Capitalistic Production System. *Albelda, R.; Gunn, C. and Waller, W., eds.*, 1987, *1980*, pp. 111–23.

Kregel, Jan A. Rational Spirits and the Post Keynesian Macrotheory of Microeconomics.

De Economist, 1987, *135*(4), pp. 520–32.

Kregel, Jan A. The Changing Place of Money in Keynes's Theory from the *Treatise* to the *General Theory*. *[Marrama, V.], Vol. 1*, 1987, pp. 97–114.

Larceneux, André. Previsions et rationnement dans une logique Keynésienne. (Expectations and Rationing Constraint in a Keynesian Logical Framework. With English summary.) *Écon. Soc.*, September 1987, *21*(9), pp. 121–47.

Lavoie, Marc. Monnaie et production: une synthèse de la théorie du circuit. (Money and Production: A Synthesis of the Circuit Theory. With English summary.) *Écon. Soc.*, September 1987, *21*(9), pp. 65–101.

Lavoie, Marc. Systemic Financial Fragility: A Simplified View. *J. Post Keynesian Econ.*, Winter 1986-87, *9*(2), pp. 258–66.

Leijonhufvud, Axel. Rational Expectations and Monetary Institutions. *de Cecco, M. and Fitoussi, J.-P., eds.*, 1987, pp. 44–65.

LeRoy, Stephen F. and Raymon, Neil. A Monetarist Model of Inflation. *J. Econ. Theory*, August 1987, *42*(2), pp. 275–310.

Levačic, Rosalind. The Analysis of Economic Management: The Aggregate Demand and Supply Model. *Thompson, G.; Brown, V. and Levačić, R., eds.*, 1987, pp. 38–76. [G: U.K.]

Levine, A. L. A Further Note on Prices Policy from a Sraffian Perspective. *Math. Soc. Sci.*, June 1987, *13*(3), pp. 283–88.

Lucas, Robert E., Jr. and Sargent, Thomas J. After Keynesian Macroeconomics. *Wilcox, J. A., ed.*, 1987, *1979*, pp. 252–67.

Lucas, Robert E., Jr. and Stokey, Nancy L. Money and Interest in a Cash-in-Advance Economy. *Econometrica*, May 1987, *55*(3), pp. 491–513.

MacKinnon, Keith T. More on the Inflation Tax and the Value of Equity. *Can. J. Econ.*, November 1987, *20*(4), pp. 823–31.

Madden, Paul John. A Diagrammatic Introduction to Disequilibrium Macroeconomics. *Bull. Econ. Res.*, April 1987, *39*(2), pp. 121–49.

Mankiw, N. Gregory. The New Keynesian Microfoundations: Comment. *Fischer, S., ed.*, 1987, pp. 105–10.

Marini, Giancarlo. Determinatezza dei prezzi ed effetti di stabilizzazione di manovre anticicliche del tasso d'interesse. (Interest Rate Rules, Price Level Determinancy and Stabilization Policy. With English summary.) *Econ. Polít.*, December 1987, *4*(3), pp. 343–55.

Marzano, Ferruccio. Keynesian Theory Planning Models and Quantitative Economics: An Overview of the Essays. *[Marrama, V.], Vol. 1*, 1987, pp. xxviii–liv.

McCallum, Bennett T. The Development of Keynesian Macroeconomics. *Amer. Econ. Rev.*, May 1987, *77*(2), pp. 125–29.

Meemken, Hermann. Keynes Entrepreneur or Money Wage Economy. *Stud. Econ.*, 1987, *42*(33), pp. 67–105.

Meller, Patricio and Solimano, Andrés. A Simple Macro Model for a Small Open Economy Facing a Binding External Constraint (Chile). *J.*

Devel. Econ., June 1987, *26*(1), pp. 25–35.
[G: Chile]

Millerd, Frank W. and Robertson, Alastair R. Computer Simulations as an Integral Part of Intermediate Macroeconomics. *J. Econ. Educ.*, Summer 1987, *18*(3), pp. 269–86.
[G: U.S.]

Mitchell, Douglas W. Implications of a Negatively Sloped LM Curve. *Atlantic Econ. J.*, July 1987, *15*(2), pp. 53–56.

Modigliani, Franco. Macroeconomics and Finance: 1944, 1963, and 1985: Comments. *[Modigliani, F.]*, 1987, pp. 257–64.

Morita, Masanori. A Post-Keynesian Model of Macrodynamics with an Expectations Hypothesis. *Australian Econ. Pap.*, June 1987, *26*(48), pp. 58–70.

Murat, Marina. Tra vecchia e nuova macroeconomia classica: una nota sul concetto di equilibrio di Leijonhufvud. (Between Old and New Classical Macroeconomics: A Note on Leijonhufvud's Concept of Equilibrium. With English summary.) *Econ. Polit.*, December 1987, *4*(3), pp. 407–20.

Niman, Neil B. Keynes and the Invisible Hand Theorem. *J. Post Keynesian Econ.*, Fall 1987, *10*(1), pp. 105–15.

Okishio, Nobuo. Theoretical Foundations of International Macro-economic Model. *Kobe Univ. Econ.*, 1987, *33*, pp. 1–16.

Owen, P. Dorian. Aggregate Demand Curves in General-Equilibrium Macroeconomic Models: Comparisons with Partial-Equilibrium Microeconomic Demand Curves. *New Zealand Econ. Pap.*, 1987, *21*, pp. 97–104.

Padoa Schioppa, Fiorella. Wealth Effects and Fiscal Policy in the Context of a Flexible Price Level—A Comment. *Public Finance*, 1987, *42*(1), pp. 156–59.

Parkin, Michael. The Quantity Theory of Money, Rational Expectations and the Relationship between Money, Income and Prices. *Greek Econ. Rev.*, 1987, *9*(1), pp. 57–87.

Patterson, Kerry David. The Development of Expectations Generating Schemes Which Are Asymptotically Rational. *Scot. J. Polit. Econ.*, February 1987, *34*(1), pp. 1–18. [G: U.S.; U.K.]

Peck, James. Non-connectedness of the Set of Equilibrium Money Prices: The Static Economy. *J. Econ. Theory*, December 1987, *43*(2), pp. 348–54.

Peck, James. Non-connectedness of the Set of Equilibrium Money Prices: The Overlapping-Generations Economy. *J. Econ. Theory*, December 1987, *43*(2), pp. 355–63.

Peeters, Marcel. A Dismal Science; An Essay on New Classical Economics. *De Economist*, 1987, *135*(4), pp. 442–66.

Penha Cysne, Rubens; Simonsen Leal, Carlos Ivan and da Costa Werlang, Sérgio Ribeiro. Macroeconomia com racionamento: um modelo simplificado para economia aberta. (With English summary.) *Pesquisa Planejamento Econ.*, August 1987, *17*(2), pp. 265–99.

Peterson, Wallace C. Macroeconomics: Where Are We? *Rev. Soc. Econ.*, April 1987, *45*(1), pp. 64–76.

Phaneuf, Louis. Propriétés dynamiques des modèles du cycle à contrats échelonnés. (The Dynamic Properties of Staggered Contracts Models. With English summary.) *Can. J. Econ.*, February 1987, *20*(1), pp. 123–39.

Pikoulakis, Emmanuel. The Cost of Disinflation Reexamined. *Economia (Portugal)*, May 1987, *11*(2), pp. 215–30.

Pizzutto, Giorgio. Un contronto tra modelli macroeconomici. (A Comparison between Macroeconomic Models. With English summary.) *Rivista Int. Sci. Econ. Com.*, May 1987, *34*(5), pp. 393–409.

van der Ploeg, Frederick. Benefits of Contingent Rules for Optimal Taxation of a Monetary Economy: A Note. *J. Money, Credit, Banking*, May 1987, *19*(2), pp. 252–59.

van der Ploeg, Frederick. Rationing in Open Economy and Dynamic Macroeconomics: A Survey. *De Economist*, 1987, *135*(4), pp. 488–519.

Poulon, F. Keynes et Robertson: naissance d'un désaccord sur la fonction de l'épargne dans la théorie monétaire. (Keynes and Robertson: The Beginning of a Disagreement about the Role of Saving in Monetary Theory. With English summary.) *Écon. Soc.*, September 1987, *21*(9), pp. 9–22.

Prachowny, Martin F. J. Macroeconomic Policy in a Conflict Environment. *J. Inst. Theoretical Econ.*, June 1987, *143*(2), pp. 244–60.

Prescott, Edward C. The New Keynesian Microfoundations: Comment. *Fischer, S., ed.*, 1987, pp. 110–14.

Pressman, Steven. The Policy Relevance of *The General Theory*. *J. Econ. Stud.*, 1987, *14*(4), pp. 13–23. [G: U.S.]

Rabin, Alan; Hutchinson, E. Bruce and Abraham, John. "The Neglected Market." *Eastern Econ. J.*, Apr.-June 1987, *13*(2), pp. 137–42.

Rabin, Alan and Keilany, Ziad. A Note on the Incompatibility of the Pigou Effect and a Liquidity Trap. *J. Post Keynesian Econ.*, Winter 1986-87, *9*(2), pp. 291–96.

Rabin, Alan and Keilany, Ziad. A Note on the Pigou Effect and Liquidity Trap: Reply. *J. Post Keynesian Econ.*, Fall 1987, *10*(1), pp. 166–67.

Rangazas, Peter and Shapiro, Edward. Shifts in the Aggregate Demand Curve: Treatment and Mistreatment in Intermediate Textbooks. *J. Econ. Educ.*, Winter 1987, *18*(1), pp. 35–39.

Rankin, Neil. Debt Policy under Fixed and Flexible Prices. *Sinclair, P. J. N., ed.*, 1987, *1986*, pp. 308–27.

Rankin, Neil. Disequilibrium and the Welfare-Maximising Levels of Government Spending, Taxation and Debt. *Econ. J.*, March 1987, *97*(385), pp. 65–85.

Riese, Hajo. Keynes als Kapitaltheoretiker. (Keynes as a Capital Theorist. With English summary.) *Kredit Kapital*, 1987, *20*(2), pp. 153–78.

Roberds, William. Models of Policy under Stochastic Replanning. *Int. Econ. Rev.*, October 1987, *28*(3), pp. 731–55.

Rogerson, Richard. The Economics of Worldwide Stagflation: A Review Essay. *J. Monet. Econ.*, January 1987, *19*(1), pp. 129–36.

Rojas-Suarez, Liliana. Devaluation and Monetary Policy in Developing Countries: A General Equilibrium Model for Economies Facing Financial Constraints. *Int. Monet. Fund Staff Pap.*, September 1987, *34*(3), pp. 439–70. **[G: LDCs]**

Rotemberg, Julio J. The New Keynesian Microfoundations. *Fischer, S., ed.*, 1987, pp. 69–104.

Rowe, Nicholas. A Simple Macroeconomic Model with Monopolistic Firms. *Econ. Inquiry*, January 1987, *25*(1), pp. 83–102.

Rowe, Nicholas. An Extreme Keynesian Macroeconomic Model with Formal Micro-economic Foundations. *Can. J. Econ.*, May 1987, *20*(2), pp. 306–20.

Rowley, Robin and Hamouda, Omar. Troublesome Probability and Economics. *J. Post Keynesian Econ.*, Fall 1987, *10*(1), pp. 44–64.

Roy, Raj and Rassuli, Ali. Transfer Models Using Mixed Keynesian-Classical Assumptions. *Rivista Int. Sci. Econ. Com.*, June 1987, *34*(6), pp. 513–22.

Roychowdhury, Krishna Ch. Keynes, Expectation and Employment. *Indian Econ. J.*, July-Sept. 1987, *35*(1), pp. 54–59.

Samuelson, Paul A. The 1985 Nobel Prize in Economics. *[Modigliani, F.]*, 1987, *1986*, pp. 29–35.

Scarth, William M. Can Economic Growth Make Monetarist Arithmetic Pleasant? *Southern Econ. J.*, April 1987, *53*(4), pp. 1028–36.

Schilirò, Daniele. Il modello IS–LM e la reinterpretazione di Hicks: una nota. (IS-LM Model and Its Reinterpretation by Hicks: A Note. With English summary.) *Econ. Polit.*, December 1987, *4*(3), pp. 421–35.

Schlesinger, Helmut and Jahnke, Wilfried. Geldmenge, Preise und Sozialprodukt: Interdependenzzusammenhänge im Lichte Ökonometrischer Forschungsergebnisse für die Bundesrepublik Deutschland. (Money, Prices, and Production: Interdependencies in the Light Econometric Results for the Federal Republic of Germany. With English summary.) *Jahr. Nationalökon. Statist.*, October 1987, *203*(5–6), pp. 576–90. **[G: W. Germany]**

Schwartz, Anna J. Why Money Matters. *Schwartz, A. J.*, 1987, pp. 167–82. **[G: U.K.; U.S.-X1 - 1969]**

Seidman, Laurence S. The Government Deficit in a Growth Model: Consequences and Trade-offs. *J. Macroecon.*, Fall 1987, *9*(4), pp. 593–611.

Shapiro, Nina. The Revolutionary Character of Post-Keynesian Economics. *Albelda, R.; Gunn, C. and Waller, W., eds.*, 1987, *1977*, pp. 124–39.

Shaw, Graham K. Macroeconomic Implications of Fiscal Deficits: An Expository Note. *Scot. J. Polit. Econ.*, May 1987, *34*(2), pp. 192–98.

Shaw, Graham K. Rational Expectations. *Bull.*

Econ. Res., July 1987, *39*(3), pp. 187–209.

Sheen, Jeffrey. Inflation Debt and Fiscal Policy Attitudes. *Oxford Econ. Pap.*, March 1987, *39*(1), pp. 90–110.

Sheen, Jeffrey. Inflation Debt and Fiscal Policy Attitudes. *Sinclair, P. J. N., ed.*, 1987, pp. 90–110.

Shiller, Robert J. Ultimate Sources of Aggregate Variability. *Amer. Econ. Rev.*, May 1987, *77*(2), pp. 87–92. **[G: U.S.]**

Shupp, Franklin R. Policy Effectiveness and the Divergence of Objectives of Private Agents and Public Authorities. *[Marrama, V.], Vol. 2*, 1987, pp. 899–917.

Sinclair, P. J. N. Prices, Quantities and Expectations: Keynes and Macroeconomics in the Fifty Years since the Publication of the *General Theory*: Preface. *Sinclair, P. J. N., ed.*, 1987, pp. vii–xxiv.

Singer, Hans W. What Keynes and Keynesianism Can Teach Us about Less Developed Countries. *[Kitamura, H.]*, 1987, pp. 229–45. **[G: LDCs]**

Smiley, Gene. Some Austrian Perspectives on Keynesian Fiscal Policy and the Recovery in the Thirties. *Rothbard, M. N., ed.*, 1987, pp. 145–79. **[G: U.S.]**

Smithin, John N. and Tu, Pierre N. V. Disequilibrium Adjustment in a "Classical" Macroeconomic Model: A Note. *J. Econ. (Z. Nationalökon.)*, 1987, *47*(2), pp. 207–13.

Snippe, J. Monetary Equilibrium versus the Wicksell Connection. *Banca Naz. Lavoro Quart. Rev.*, June 1987, (161), pp. 197–212.

Spaventa, Luigi. Public Debt and Rules of Monetary Growth: An Exercise in Monetarist Arithmetic. *de Cecco, M. and Fitoussi, J.-P., eds.*, 1987, pp. 269–85.

Stein, Jerome L. Short and Long-run Effects of Monetary and Fiscal Policy upon Real Output and Inflation. *[Marrama, V.], Vol. 1*, 1987, pp. 479–97.

Stemp, Peter J. and Turnovsky, Stephen J. Optimal Monetary Policy in an Open Economy. *Europ. Econ. Rev.*, July 1987, *31*(5), pp. 1113–35.

Sterman, John D. The Economic Long Wave: Theory and Evidence. *Vasko, T., ed.*, 1987, pp. 127–61.

Stock, James H. Temporal Aggregation and Structural Inference in Macroeconomics: A Comment. *Carnegie–Rochester Conf. Ser. Public Policy*, Spring 1987, *26*, pp. 131–39. **[G: U.S.]**

Subrahmanyam, Ganti. Wealth Effects, IS–LM Stability, and the Efficacy of Economic Policies: A Comment. *J. Macroecon.*, Spring 1987, *9*(2), pp. 293–96.

Sweeney, Richard J. Some Macro Implications of Risk. *J. Money, Credit, Banking*, May 1987, *19*(2), pp. 222–34.

Taylor, John B. Externalities Associated with Nominal Price and Wage Rigidities. *Barnett, W. A. and Singleton, K. J., eds.*, 1987, pp. 350–67.

Taylor, Mark P. On Long-run Solutions to Dynamic Econometric Equations under Rational Expectations [A Cautionary Note on the Interpretation of Long-run Equilibrium Solutions in Conventional Macro Models]. *Econ. J.*, March 1987, 97(385), pp. 215–18.

Thompson, Grahame. Objectives and Instruments of Economic Management. *Thompson, G.; Brown, V. and Levačić, R., eds.*, 1987, pp. 1–37. **[G: U.K.]**

Tobin, James. A Note on the Money Wage Problem. *Tobin, J. (I)*, 1987, *1941*, pp. 4–11.

Tobin, James. Asset Holdings and Spending Decisions. *Tobin, J. (I)*, 1987, *1952*, pp. 83–98.

Tobin, James. Comment from an Academic Scribbler (on *Democracy in Deficit*). *Tobin, J. (III)*, 1987, *1978*, pp. 226–36. **[G: U.S.]**

Tobin, James. Inflation and Unemployment. *Tobin, J. (II)*, 1987, *1972*, pp. 33–59.

Tobin, James. Keynesian Policies in Theory and Practice. *Tobin, J. (III)*, 1987, *1985*, pp. 4–14.

Tobin, James. Liquidity Preference and Monetary Policy. *Tobin, J. (I)*, 1987, *1947*, pp. 27–46. **[G: U.S.]**

Tobin, James. Macroeconomics. *Tobin, J. (I)*, 1987, *1970*, pp. vii–xiv.

Tobin, James. Money and Income: Post Hoc Ergo Propter Hoc? *Tobin, J. (I)*, 1987, *1970*, pp. 497–514.

Tobin, James. Money Wage Rates and Employment. *Tobin, J. (I)*, 1987, *1947*, pp. 12–26.

Tobin, James. Money, Capital, and Other Stores of Value. *Tobin, J. (I)*, 1987, *1961*, pp. 217–28.

Tobin, James. The Future of Keynesian Economics. *Tobin, J. (III)*, 1987, *1986*, pp. 14–23.

Tobin, James and Hall, Challis A. Income Taxation, Output and Prices. *Tobin, J. (I)*, 1987, *1955*, pp. 47–82.

Townsend, Robert M. Arrow–Debreu Programs as Microfoundations of Macroeconomics. *Bewley, T. F., ed.*, 1987, pp. 379–428.

Travaglini, Guido. Optimal Control and Differential Games. A Comparative Analysis of an Expectations-Augmented Phillips Curve Model. *Rivista Int. Sci. Econ. Com.*, September 1987, 34(9), pp. 801–21.

Turnovsky, Stephen J. Monetary Growth, Inflation, and Economic Activity in a Dynamic Macro Model. *Int. Econ. Rev.*, October 1987, 28(3), pp. 707–30.

Turnovsky, Stephen J. Optimal Monetary Policy and Wage Indexation under Alternative Disturbances and Information Structures. *J. Money, Credit, Banking*, May 1987, 19(2), pp. 157–80.

Turnovsky, Stephen J. and Scarth, William M. Non-uniqueness and Instability under Rational Expectations: The Case of a Bond-Financed Government Deficit. *[Marrama, V.], Vol. 2*, 1987, pp. 933–52.

Turnovsky, Stephen J. and Wohar, Mark E. Alternative Modes of Deficit Financing and Endogeneous Monetary and Fiscal Policy in the U.S.A. 1923–1982. *J. Appl. Econometrics*, January 1987, 2(1), pp. 1–25. **[G: U.S.]**

Ulmer, Melville J. Fifty Years of Keynes. *Atlantic Econ. J.*, September 1987, 15(3), pp. 3–8.

Vane, Howard. Supply-Side Economics. *Vane, H. and Caslin, T., eds.*, 1987, pp. 62–77. **[G: U.K.]**

Vane, Howard. The New Classical Macroeconomics. *Vane, H. and Caslin, T., eds.*, 1987, pp. 45–61.

Vanek, Jaroslav. Workers' Profit Participation, Unemployment, and the Keynesian Equilibrium. *Jones, D. C. and Svejnar, J., eds.*, 1987, pp. 5–11.

Vickers, Douglas. Aggregate Supply and the Producers' Expected Demand Curve: Performance and Change in the Macroeconomy. *J. Post Keynesian Econ.*, Fall 1987, 10(1), pp. 84–104.

Vinod, H. D. New Techniques for Estimation of Rational Expectation Models and Volcker Deflation. *Empirical Econ.*, 1987, 12(3), pp. 157–74. **[G: U.S.]**

Wadhwani, Sushil B. The Macroeconomic Implications of Profit Sharing: Some Empirical Evidence. *Econ. J.*, Supplement 1987, 97, pp. 171–83. **[G: OECD]**

Weinberg, David. Monetary Versions of the Balanced Budget Multiplier. *J. Macroecon.*, Summer 1987, 9(3), pp. 429–38.

van Wijnbergen, Sweder. Government Deficits, Private Investment and the Current Account: An Intertemporal Disequilibrium Analysis. *Econ. J.*, September 1987, 97(387), pp. 596–615.

Williams, Arlington W. The Formation of Price Forecasts in Experimental Markets. *J. Money, Credit, Banking*, February 1987, 19(1), pp. 1–18.

Woodford, Michael. Credit Policy and the Price Level in a Cash-in-Advance Economy. *Barnett, W. A. and Singleton, K. J., eds.*, 1987, pp. 52–66.

Woodford, Michael. Three Questions about Sunspot Equilibria as an Explanation of Economic Fluctuations. *Amer. Econ. Rev.*, May 1987, 77(2), pp. 93–98.

Yoshikawa, Hiroshi and Ohtake, Fumio. Postwar Business Cycles in Japan: A Quest for the Right Explanation. *J. Japanese Int. Economies*, December 1987, 1(4), pp. 373–407. **[G: Japan]**

Zimmermann, Klaus F. Transfers, Perfect Foresight and the Efficacy of Demand Policy. *J. Inst. Theoretical Econ.*, December 1987, 143(4), pp. 652–57.

0232 Theory of Aggregate Demand: Consumption

Abel, Andrew B. Aggregate Savings in the Presence of Private and Social Insurance. *[Modigliani, F.]*, 1987, pp. 131–57.

Anyadike-Danes, Michael and Godley, Wynne. A Stock Adjustment Model of Income Determination with Inside Money and Private Debt with Some Preliminary Empirical Results for the United States. *de Cecco, M. and Fitoussi, J.-P., eds.*, 1987, pp. 95–120. **[G: U.S.]**

Arnaudo, Aldo A. Trends and Prospects for Sav-

ings in Brazil: Comment. *Martirena-Mantel, A. M., ed.*, 1987, pp. 195–200.
[G: Latin America]

Barron, John M. and Lynch, Gerald J. The Aggregate Demand Curve: A Defense. *J. Econ. Educ.*, Winter 1987, *18*(1), pp. 41–46.

Bernheim, B. Douglas. Ricardian Equivalence: An Evaluation of Theory and Evidence. *Fischer, S., ed.*, 1987, pp. 263–304.

Blanchard, Olivier Jean and Kiyotaki, Nobuhiro. Monopolistic Competition and the Effects of Aggregate Demand. *Amer. Econ. Rev.*, September 1987, *77*(4), pp. 647–66.

Burkett, Paul and Vogel, Robert C. Microeconomic Foundations of Financial Liberalization: Interest Rates, Transactions Costs, and Financial Savings. *Connolly, M. and González-Vega, C., eds.*, 1987, pp. 305–21.

Campbell, John Y. Does Saving Anticipate Declining Labor Income? An Alternative Test of the Permanent Income Hypothesis. *Econometrica*, November 1987, *55*(6), pp. 1249–73.
[G: U.S.]

Christiano, Lawrence J. Is Consumption Insufficiently Sensitive to Innovations in Income? *Amer. Econ. Rev.*, May 1987, *77*(2), pp. 337–41.
[G: U.S.]

Christiano, Lawrence J. Why is Consumption Less Volatile than Income? *Fed. Res. Bank Minn. Rev.*, Fall 1987, *11*(4), pp. 2–20.
[G: U.S.]

Dixon, Huw. The General Theory of Household and Market Contingent Demand. *Manchester Sch. Econ. Soc. Stud.*, September 1987, *55*(3), pp. 287–304.

Djajić, Slobodan. Effects of Budgetary Policies in Open Economies: The Role of Intertemporal Consumption Substitution. *J. Int. Money Finance*, September 1987, *6*(3), pp. 373–83.

Dolde, Walter and Tobin, James. Monetary and Fiscal Effects on Consumption. *Tobin, J. (II)*, 1987, *1971*, pp. 175–215. [G: U.S.]

Dor, E.; Thurston, T. and Weiserbs, Daniel. On Testing the Permanent Income Hypothesis and Rational Expectations. *Empirical Econ.*, 1987, *12*(3), pp. 137–56. [G: U.S.]

Feiwel, George R. Intellectual Revolutions in Modern Economic Theory: Joan Robinson's Contributions and Challenges. *Keio Econ. Stud.*, 1987, *24*(2), pp. 47–86.

Flavin, Marjorie. Ricardian Equivalence: An Evaluation of Theory and Evidence: Comment. *Fischer, S., ed.*, 1987, pp. 304–09.

Freixas, Xavier and Mas-Colell, Andreu. Engel Curves Leading to the Weak Axiom in the Aggregate. *Econometrica*, May 1987, *55*(3), pp. 515–31.

Green, Edward J. Lending and the Smoothing of Uninsurable Income. *Prescott, E. C. and Wallace, N., eds.*, 1987, pp. 3–25.

Gupta, Kanhaya L. Aggregate Savings, Financial Intermediation, and Interest Rate. *Rev. Econ. Statist.*, May 1987, *69*(2), pp. 303–11.
[G: Latin America; Asia]

Hall, P. H. and Treadgold, M. L. Alternative Aggregate Demand Functions in Macroeconomics: Some Comments. *Australian Econ. Pap.*, December 1987, *26*(49), pp. 337–38.

Hamilton, David. Institutional Economics and Consumption. *J. Econ. Issues*, December 1987, *21*(4), pp. 1531–54.

Hansen, Richard B.; McCormick, Ken and Rives, Janet M. The Aggregate Demand Curve: A Reply. *J. Econ. Educ.*, Winter 1987, *18*(1), pp. 47–50.

Haque, Nadeem Ul and Mirakhor, Abbas. Saving Behavior in an Economy without Fixed Interest. *Khan, M. S. and Mirakhor, A., eds.*, 1987, pp. 125–39.

Hubbard, R. Glenn. Uncertain Lifetimes, Pensions, and Individual Saving. *Bodie, Z.; Shoven, J. B. and Wise, D. A., eds.*, 1987, pp. 175–206.
[G: U.S.]

Kotlikoff, Laurence J. Consumer Spending and the After-Tax Real Interest Rate: Comment. *Feldstein, M., ed. (I)*, 1987, pp. 67–68.
[G: U.S.]

Kotlikoff, Laurence J.; Shoven, John B. and Spivak, Avia. Annuity Markets, Savings, and the Capital Stock. *Bodie, Z.; Shoven, J. B. and Wise, D. A., eds.*, 1987, pp. 211–34.

Lewbel, Arthur. Bliss Levels That Aren't [Stochastic Implications of the Life Cycle–Permanent Income Hypothesis: Theory and Evidence]. *J. Polit. Econ.*, February 1987, *95*(1), pp. 211–15. [G: U.S.]

Littleboy, Bruce and Mehta, Ghanshyam. Patinkin on Keynes' Theory of Effective Demand. *Hist. Polit. Econ.*, Summer 1987, *19*(2), pp. 311–28.

Longo, Carlos A. Trends and Prospects for Savings in Brazil. *Martirena-Mantel, A. M., ed.*, 1987, pp. 180–95. [G: Brazil]

Mak, King-tim. Consistent Aggregation of Demand Functions over Restricted Income Distributions. *J. Econ. (Z. Nationalökon.)*, 1987, *47*(2), pp. 195–206.

Mankiw, N. Gregory. Consumer Spending and the After-Tax Real Interest Rate. *Feldstein, M., ed. (I)*, 1987, pp. 53–67. [G: U.S.]

Mason, Andrew. National Saving Rates and Population Growth: A New Model and New Evidence. *Johnson, D. G. and Lee, R. D., eds.*, 1987, pp. 523–60.

McMillin, W. Douglas and Laumas, G. S. Economic Policy and Consumption and Investment Expenditures: An Empirical Examination. *Appl. Econ.*, February 1987, *19*(2), pp. 167–77. [G: U.S.]

Mitchell, Olivia S. Uncertain Lifetimes, Pensions, and Individual Saving: Comment. *Bodie, Z.; Shoven, J. B. and Wise, D. A., eds.*, 1987, pp. 206–10. [G: U.S.]

Modigliani, Franco. Life Cycle, Individual Thrift, and the Wealth of Nations. *[Modigliani, F.]*, 1987, pp. 1–28.

Modigliani, Franco. The Key to Saving Is Growth, Not Thrift. *Challenge*, May/June 1987, *30*(2), pp. 24–29.

Nelson, Charles R. A Reappraisal of Recent Tests of the Permanent Income Hypothesis [Stochastic Implications of the Life Cycle–Permanent

Income Hypothesis: Theory and Evidence]. *J. Polit. Econ.*, June 1987, *95*(3), pp. 641–46. [G: U.S.]

Palma, Pedro A. Trends and Prospects for Savings in Brazil: Comment. *Martirena-Mantel, A. M., ed.*, 1987, pp. 200–207. [G: Latin America]

Patinkin, Don. Keynes' Theory of Effective Demand: A Reply. *Hist. Polit. Econ.*, Winter 1987, *19*(4), pp. 647–58.

Perasso, Giancarlo. The Ricardian Equivalence Theorem and the Consumption Function: A Survey of the Literature. *Rivista Int. Sci. Econ. Com.*, July 1987, *34*(7), pp. 649–74.

Plosser, Charles I. Ricardian Equivalence: An Evaluation of Theory and Evidence: Comment. *Fischer, S., ed.*, 1987, pp. 309–13.

Rothschild, Michael. Annuity Markets, Savings, and the Capital Stock: Comment. *Bodie, Z.; Shoven, J. B. and Wise, D. A., eds.*, 1987, pp. 234–36.

Sau, Ranjit. Household Debt and National Income: A Simple Short-run Model. *J. Macroecon.*, Winter 1987, *9*(1), pp. 127–37. [G: U.S.]

Summers, Lawrence H. The Impact of Tax Policy on Savings. *Walker, C. E. and Bloomfield, M. A., eds.*, 1987, pp. 172–77. [G: U.S.]

Theil, Henri. Associated with an Income Distribution and a Demand System Is a Multidimensional Expenditure Distribution. *Heijmans, R. and Neudecker, H., eds.*, 1987, pp. 59–63.

Tobin, James. A Statistical Demand Function for Food in the U.S.A. *Tobin, J. (II)*, 1987, *1950*, pp. 399–439. [G: U.S.]

Tobin, James. Consumer Debt and Spending: Some Evidence from Analysis of a Survey. *Tobin, J. (II)*, 1987, pp. 217–45. [G: U.S.]

Tobin, James. Life Cycle Saving and Balanced Growth. *Tobin, J. (II)*, 1987, *1967*, pp. 127–53.

Tobin, James. Milton Friedman's Theory of the Consumption Function. *Tobin, J. (II)*, 1987, *1958*, pp. 115–25.

Tobin, James. Relative Income, Absolute Income, and Saving. *Tobin, J. (II)*, 1987, *1951*, pp. 91–114. [G: U.S.]

Tobin, James. Taxes, Saving and Inflation. *Tobin, J. (I)*, 1987, *1949*, pp. 99–108.

Tobin, James. The Consumption Function. *Tobin, J. (II)*, 1987, *1968*, pp. 63–89.

Tobin, James. Wealth, Liquidity, and the Propensity to Consume. *Tobin, J. (II)*, 1987, *1972*, pp. 155–74.

Wu, Ho-mou. On the Theory of Effective Demand under Stochastic Rationing. *Econ. J.*, June 1987, *97*(386), pp. 487–92.

0233 Theory of Aggregate Demand: Investment

Abel, Andrew B. Anticipated Tax Changes and the Timing of Investment: Comment. *Feldstein, M., ed. (I)*, 1987, pp. 196–200. [G: U.S.]

Algahtani, Ibrahim M. and Alhiyari, Mohd. Real Balance Effect and the Consumption Function in LDC: A Comment [The Effect of Liquid Assets on the Consumption Function of a Less Developed Economy: A Note]. *Amer. Econ.*, Spring 1987, *31*(1), pp. 62–63. [G: Iran]

Auerbach, Alan J. and Hines, James R., Jr. Anticipated Tax Changes and the Timing of Investment. *Feldstein, M., ed. (I)*, 1987, pp. 163–96. [G: U.S.]

Bernheim, B. Douglas and Shoven, John B. Taxation and the Cost of Capital: An International Comparison. *Walker, C. E. and Bloomfield, M. A., eds.*, 1987, pp. 61–85. [G: Global]

Bruce, Neil. Will the Neoclassical Theory of Investment Please Rise? The General Structure of Investment Models and Their Implications for Tax Policy: Comment. *Mintz, J. M. and Purvis, D. D., eds.*, 1987, pp. 168–70.

Chirinko, Robert S. Will the Neoclassical Theory of Investment Please Rise? The General Structure of Investment Models and Their Implications for Tax Policy. *Mintz, J. M. and Purvis, D. D., eds.*, 1987, pp. 109–67.

Clark, John A. A Vintage–Capital Simulation Model. *Freeman, C. and Soete, L., eds.*, 1987, pp. 86–98.

Eastwood, Robert. Forecasting Investment in the Medium Term. *Freeman, C. and Soete, L., eds.*, 1987, pp. 73–85.

Fazzari, Steven M. and Mott, Tracy L. The Investment Theories of Kalecki and Keynes: An Empirical Study of Firm Data, 1970–1982. *J. Post Keynesian Econ.*, Winter 1986-87, *9*(2), pp. 171–87. [G: U.S.]

Feldstein, Martin S. and Jun, Joosung. The Effects of Tax Rules on Nonresidential Fixed Investment: Some Preliminary Evidence from the 1980s. *Feldstein, M., ed. (I)*, 1987, pp. 101–56. [G: U.S.]

Foster, Gladys Parker. Financing Investment. *J. Econ. Issues*, March 1987, *21*(1), pp. 101–12.

Galeotti, Marzio. On the Dual Relationship between Flexible Accelerator and *q* Theories of Investment. *Rivista Int. Sci. Econ. Com.*, August 1987, *34*(8), pp. 771–76.

Gordon, Roger H. The Effects of Tax Rules on Nonresidential Fixed Investment: Some Preliminary Evidence from the 1980s: Comment. *Feldstein, M., ed. (I)*, 1987, pp. 156–61. [G: U.S.]

de la Grandville, Olivier. On Two-Regime Discrete-Time Models: A Methodological Note. *J. Econ. Behav. Organ.*, September 1987, *8*(3), pp. 513–30.

Guth, Michael A. S. Functional Form in Finished Goods Inventory Investment: A Note. *J. Money, Credit, Banking*, August 1987, *19*(3), pp. 396–401. [G: U.S.]

Haag, Günter; Weidlich, Wolfgang and Mensch, Gerhard O. The Schumpeter Clock. *Batten, D.; Casti, J. and Johansson, B., eds.*, 1987, pp. 187–226. [G: W. Germany]

Hagemann, Harald and Rühl, Christof. Nicholas Johannsen's Early Analysis of the Saving–Investment Process and the Multiplier. *Stud. Econ.*, 1987, *42*(31), pp. 99–143.

Hartman, Richard. Monetary Uncertainty and Investment in an Optimizing, Rational Expectations Model with Income Taxes and Government Debt. *Econometrica*, January 1987, 55(1), pp. 169–76.

Helmedag, Fritz. Technikwahl, Profitstruktur und Arbeitsproduktivität. (Choice of Technique, Structure of Profits, and Labour Productivity. With English summary.) *Jahr. Nationalökon. Statist.*, July 1987, 203(4), pp. 408–21.

Hendershott, Patric H. Tax Changes and Capital Allocation in the 1980s. *Feldstein, M., ed. (I)*, 1987, pp. 259–90. **[G: U.S.]**

Jüttner, D. Johannes. The Wicksell–Tobin Investment Model. *J. Macroecon.*, Summer 1987, 9(3), pp. 457–62.

Kahn, James A. Inventories and the Volatility of Production. *Amer. Econ. Rev.*, September 1987, 77(4), pp. 667–79.

Lambert, Jean-Paul. Conflicting Specifications for Investment Functions in Rationing Models: A Reconciliation. *Rech. Écon. Louvain*, 1987, 53(2), pp. 135–45.

McMillin, W. Douglas and Laumas, G. S. Economic Policy and Consumption and Investment Expenditures: An Empirical Examination. *Appl. Econ.*, February 1987, 19(2), pp. 167–77. **[G: U.S.]**

Medio, Alfredo. A Multisector Model of the Trade Cycle. *Batten, D.; Casti, J. and Johansson, B., eds.*, 1987, pp. 291–312.

Mehdizadeh, Mostafa. Real Balance Effect and Consumption Function in Less Developed Countries: A Reply [The Effect of Liquid Assets on the Consumption Function of a Less Developed Economy: A Note]. *Amer. Econ.*, Spring 1987, 31(1), pp. 64–65. **[G: Iran]**

de Meza, David and Webb, David C. Too Much Investment: A Problem of Asymmetric Information. *Quart. J. Econ.*, May 1987, 102(2), pp. 281–92.

Mino, Kazuo. A Model of Investment with External Adjustment Costs. *Econ. Stud. Quart.*, March 1987, 38(1), pp. 76–85.

Mintz, Jack M. and Purvis, Douglas D. Taxation and Business Activity: Introduction. *Mintz, J. M. and Purvis, D. D., eds.*, 1987, pp. 2–57.

Pitelis, Christos N. Corporate Retained Earnings and the 'Kaldorian' Hypothesis of Saving. *Brit. Rev. Econ. Issues*, Spring 1987, 9(20), pp. 79–95. **[G: U.K.]**

Risager, Ole. The Effects of Currency Depreciation in a Model with Capital Formation. *Europ. Econ. Rev.*, Feb./Mar. 1987, 31(1/2), pp. 399–406. **[G: Denmark]**

Rock, James M. Book IV: The Inducement to Invest. *Amer. Econ.*, Spring 1987, 31(1), pp. 27–32.

Rosen, Harvey S. Tax Changes and Capital Allocation in the 1980s: Comment. *Feldstein, M., ed. (I)*, 1987, pp. 290–94. **[G: U.S.]**

Shapiro, Nina. The Revolutionary Character of Post-Keynesian Economics. *Albelda, R.; Gunn, C. and Waller, W., eds.*, 1987, 1977, pp. 124–39.

Singleton, Kenneth J. Asset Prices in a Time-Series Model with Disparately Informed, Com-

petitive Traders. *Barnett, W. A. and Singleton, K. J., eds.*, 1987, pp. 249–72.

Summers, Lawrence H. Will the Neoclassical Theory of Investment Please Rise? The General Structure of Investment Models and Their Implications for Tax Policy: Comment. *Mintz, J. M. and Purvis, D. D., eds.*, 1987, pp. 171–73.

Tobin, James. Liquidity Preference as Behavior towards Risk. *Tobin, J. (I)*, 1987, pp. 242–71.

Washida, Toyoaki and Okishio, Nobuo. Expectation of Money-Wage-Rates and Investment Decision—The Reconsideration of Keynes's Investment Models (In Japanese. With English summary.) *Econ. Stud. Quart.*, September 1987, 38(3), pp. 212–22.

0234 Theory of Aggregate Supply

Ahmed, Shaghil. Wage Stickiness and the Non-neutrality of Money: A Cross-Industry Analysis. *J. Monet. Econ.*, July 1987, 20(1), pp. 25–50. **[G: Canada]**

Akiba, Hiroya. Resource Allocation with Factor Price Differentials in a Simple Two-Sector Model with Production Risk. *Ricerche Econ.*, Apr.-June 1987, 41(2), pp. 174–89.

Alogoskoufis, George S. On Intertemporal Substitution and Aggregate Labor Supply. *J. Polit. Econ.*, October 1987, 95(5), pp. 938–60. **[G: U.S.]**

Aspromourgos, Tony. Unemployment, Economic Theory and Labour–Market Deregulation. *Australian Econ. Pap.*, June 1987, 26(48), pp. 130–44. **[G: Australia]**

Ball, Laurence Markham. Externalities from Contract Length. *Amer. Econ. Rev.*, September 1987, 77(4), pp. 615–29.

Barry, Frank G. A Note on the Employment Effects of Investment Subsidies. *Econ. Soc. Rev.*, July 1987, 18(4), pp. 307–14.

Baslé, Maurice. Les salaires et le cycle: fondements micro-économiques et analyse macro-économique des flexibilités. (Wages and the Cycle: Micro-economics' Foundations and Macro-economic Analysis of Flexibilities. With English summary.) *Écon. Soc.*, November 1987, 21(11), pp. 57–81. **[G: OECD]**

Beenstock, Michael and Minford, Patrick. Curing Unemployment through Labour-Market Competition. *Begg, D. K. H., et al.*, 1987, pp. 129–49. **[G: U.S.; U.K.]**

Benassy, Jean-Pascal. Imperfect Competition, Unemployment and Policy. *Europ. Econ. Rev.*, Feb./Mar. 1987, 31(1/2), pp. 417–26.

Bhattacharjea, Aditya. Keynes and the Long-Period Theory of Employment: A Note. *Cambridge J. Econ.*, September 1987, 11(3), pp. 275–84.

Blanchard, Olivier Jean and Summers, Lawrence H. Fiscal Increasing Returns, Hysteresis, Real Wages and Unemployment. *Europ. Econ. Rev.*, April 1987, 31(3), pp. 543–66. **[G: OECD]**

Blanchard, Olivier Jean and Summers, Lawrence H. Hysteresis in Unemployment. *Europ.*

Econ. Rev., Feb./Mar. 1987, *31*(1/2), pp. 288–95.

Booth, Laurence D.; Finkelstein, John M. and Lee, Wayne Y. A Note on the Demand for Labor by Firms and the Phillips Curve Phenomenon. *J. Econ. Bus.*, November 1987, *39*(4), pp. 349–56.

Brazelton, W. Robert. Aggregate Supply Once More: Two Further Replies in One. *Amer. Econ.*, Fall 1987, *31*(2), pp. 82–83.

Brothwell, John F. On the Nature and Use of the Concept of the Marginal Physical Product in Post Keynesian Economics: A Comment. *J. Post Keynesian Econ.*, Summer 1987, *9*(4), pp. 496–501.

Caravani, Paolo and De Luca, Alessandro. Aggregation in Sraffa's Simple Production Model. *J. Econ. (Z. Nationalökon.)*, 1987, *47*(2), pp. 167–93.

Carlberg, Michael. Makroökonomik der technologischen Arbeitslosigkeit. (Macroeconomics of Technological Unemployment. With English summary.) *Jahr. Nationalökon. Statist.*, March 1987, *203*(2), pp. 123–37.

Catz, F. L'étalon des prix: sens. et non-sens. (The Concept of Standard Commodity: Meaningful and Meaningless. With English summary.) *Écon. Appl.*, 1987, *40*(1), pp. 177–84.

Coen, Robert M. and Hickman, Bert G. Keynesian and Classical Unemployment in Four Countries. *Brookings Pap. Econ. Act.*, 1987, (1), pp. 123–93. [G: U.S.; U.K.; W. Germany; Austria]

Cross, Rod B. Hysteresis and Instability in the Natural Rate of Unemployment. *Scand. J. Econ.*, 1987, *89*(1), pp. 71–89.

Davidson, Paul. The Simple Macroeconomics of a Nonergodic Monetary Economy versus a Share Economy: Is Weitzman's Macroeconomics Too Simple? *J. Post Keynesian Econ.*, Winter 1986-87, *9*(2), pp. 212–25.

DeCoster, Gregory P. and Mitchell, Douglas W. Flexibility of the Capital Utilization Rate in a Rational Expectations Macro Model. *J. Macroecon.*, Winter 1987, *9*(1), pp. 139–49.

Devine, James N. Cyclical Over-Investment and Crisis in a Labor-Scarce Economy. *Eastern Econ. J.*, July-Sept. 1987, *13*(3), pp. 271–80. [G: U.S.]

Djajić, Slobodan and Purvis, Douglas D. Intersectoral Adjustment and the Dynamics of Wages and Employment Opportunities. *Weltwirtsch. Arch.*, 1987, *123*(2), pp. 216–31.

Drazen, Allan. Reciprocal Externality Models of Low Employment. *Europ. Econ. Rev.*, Feb./Mar. 1987, *31*(1/2), pp. 436–43.

Drèze, Jacques H. Underemployment Equilibrium: From Theory to Econometrics and Policy. *Europ. Econ. Rev.*, Feb./Mar. 1987, *31*(1/2), pp. 9–34. [G: W. Europe]

Dutt, Amitava Krishna. Wage Rigidity and Unemployment: The Simple Diagrammatics of Two Views. *J. Post Keynesian Econ.*, Winter 1986-87, *9*(2), pp. 279–90.

Eichner, Alfred S. McKenna and Zannoni on the Concept of Marginal Physical Product in Post-

Keynesian Economics. *J. Post Keynesian Econ.*, Summer 1987, *9*(4), pp. 502–06.

Ellis, Christopher J. and Fender, John. Bargaining and Wage Resistance in an Open Macroeconomic Model. *Econ. J.*, March 1987, *97*(385), pp. 106–20.

England, Richard W. Form vs. Content: A Critique of Morishima's Mathematical Marxism. *England, R. W., ed.*, 1987, pp. 20–34.

Erlich, S.; Ginsburgh, Victor and Van der Heyden, Ludo. Where Do Real Wage Policies Lead Belgium? A General Equilibrium Analysis. *Europ. Econ. Rev.*, October 1987, *31*(7), pp. 1369–83. [G: Belgium]

Falkinger, Josef. Technological Unemployment: A Note. *J. Post Keynesian Econ.*, Fall 1987, *10*(1), pp. 37–43.

Flemming, John S. Wage Flexibility and Employment Stability. *Oxford Econ. Pap.*, March 1987, *39*(1), pp. 161–74.

Flemming, John S. Wage Flexibility and Employment Stability. *Sinclair, P. J. N., ed.*, 1987, pp. 161–74.

Frydman, Roman and Rappoport, Peter. Is the Distinction between Anticipated and Unanticipated Money Growth Relevant in Explaining Aggregate Output? *Amer. Econ. Rev.*, September 1987, *77*(4), pp. 693–703. [G: U.S.]

Gapinski, James H. Capital Lessons in Leaning against the Wind. *J. Money, Credit, Banking*, May 1987, *19*(2), pp. 235–45.

Giorgi, Giorgio. On the Linearity of the Distribution Function and the Fundamental Marxian Theorem in Simple Sraffa's Models. *Econ. Notes*, 1987, (2), pp. 48–59.

Goldfeld, Stephen M. Keynesian and Classical Unemployment in Four Countries: Comments. *Brookings Pap. Econ. Act.*, 1987, (1), pp. 194–97. [G: U.S.; U.K.; W. Germany; Austria]

Greenwald, Bruce C. and Stiglitz, Joseph E. Imperfect Information, Credit Markets and Unemployment. *Europ. Econ. Rev.*, Feb./Mar. 1987, *31*(1/2), pp. 444–56.

Hahn, Frank H. On Involuntary Unemployment. *Econ. J.*, Supplement 1987, *97*, pp. 1–16.

Hall, Thomas E. and Fields, T. Windsor. Anticipated Nominal Demand Shocks and the Speed of Aggregate Price Adjustment. *Rev. Econ. Statist.*, February 1987, *69*(1), pp. 140–44. [G: U.S.]

Handler, Heinz. Short-run Relations between the Real Sector and Inflation. *Empirica*, 1987, *14*(2), pp. 187–212. [G: Austria]

Hart, Myra K. Specification Tests of the Lucas–Rapping Model. *Amer. Econ. Rev.*, June 1987, *77*(3), pp. 442–45. [G: U.S.]

Helliwell, John F., et al. Supply Oriented Macroeconomics: The MACE Model of Canada. *Econ. Modelling*, July 1987, *4*(3), pp. 318–40. [G: Canada]

Henry, Samuel G. Brian. Dynamic Modelling and Rational Expectations. *Ann. Écon. Statist.*, Apr./Sept. 1987, (6/7), pp. 183–206. [G: U.K.]

Hickman, Bert G. Real Wages, Aggregate Demand, and Unemployment. *Europ. Econ.*

Rev., December 1987, *31*(8), pp. 1531–60.
[G: U.S.]

Hof, Franz Xaver. The Lucas Supply Function and the Feasibility of Monetary Stabilization Policy with Rational Expectations. *Empirica*, 1987, *14*(2), pp. 227–48.

Howitt, Peter and McAfee, R. Preston. Costly Search and Recruiting. *Int. Econ. Rev.*, February 1987, *28*(1), pp. 89–107.

Jenkinson, Tim. The Natural Rate of Unemployment: Does It Exist? *Oxford Rev. Econ. Policy*, Autumn 1987, *3*(3), pp. 20–26. [G: U.K.]

Jensen, Keith Christian and Kamath, Shyam J. Liquidity in the Production Function: A Reexamination. *Indian Econ. J.*, Oct.-Dec. 1987, *35*(2), pp. 91–114. [G: U.S.]

Jensen, Keith Christian; Kamath, Shyam J. and Bennett, Robert E. Money in the Production Function: An Alternative Test Procedure. *Eastern Econ. J.*, July-Sept. 1987, *13*(3), pp. 259–69. [G: U.S.]

Jovanovic, Boyan. Work, Rest, and Search: Unemployment, Turnover, and the Cycle. *J. Lab. Econ.*, April 1987, *5*(2), pp. 131–48.

Kaufman, Roger T. and Woglom, Geoffrey. The Conformity of Wage Indexation Models with the "Stylized Facts": A Comment. *Amer. Econ. Rev.*, September 1987, *77*(4), pp. 747–49.
[G: Canada; W. Germany; Japan; U.S.; U.K.]

Kemp, Murray C.; Léonard, Daniel and Long, Ngo Van. Trades Unions, Seniority and Unemployment. *Europ. Econ. Rev.*, July 1987, *31*(5), pp. 1093–1112.

Kempf, Hubert. Irregular Staggered Contracts and Monetary Policy. *Europ. Econ. Rev.*, August 1987, *31*(6), pp. 1247–66.

Kniesner, Thomas J. and Goldsmith, Arthur H. A Survey of Alternative Models of the Aggregate U.S. Labor Market. *J. Econ. Lit.*, September 1987, *25*(3), pp. 1241–80. [G: U.S.]

Kregel, Jan A. Keynes's Given Degree of Competition: Comment. *J. Post Keynesian Econ.*, Summer 1987, *9*(4), pp. 490–95.

Kregel, Jan A. The Effective Demand Approach to Employment and Inflation Analysis. *J. Post Keynesian Econ.*, Fall 1987, *10*(1), pp. 133–45.

Landon, Stuart. Unanticipated Policy Shocks, Regime Changes and Unemployment in Canada, 1967–83. *Appl. Econ.*, August 1987, *19*(8), pp. 1065–81. [G: Canada]

Lawlor, Michael S.; Darity, William A., Jr. and Horn, Bobbie L. Was Keynes a Chapter Two Keynesian? *J. Post Keynesian Econ.*, Summer 1987, *9*(4), pp. 516–28.

Lindbeck, Assar and Snower, Dennis J. Efficiency Wages versus Insiders and Outsiders. *Europ. Econ. Rev.*, Feb./Mar. 1987, *31*(1/2), pp. 407–16.

Lowe, Adolph. A Structural Model of Production. *Lowe, A.*, 1987, *1952*, pp. 27–59.

MacLeod, W. Bentley and Malcomson, James M. Involuntary Unemployment in Dynamic Contract Equilibria. *Europ. Econ. Rev.*, Feb./Mar. 1987, *31*(1/2), pp. 427–35.

Malinvaud, Edmond. Investment and the Inflation–Unemployment Tradeoff in a Macroeconomic Rationing Model with Monopolistic Competition: Comments. *Europ. Econ. Rev.*, April 1987, *31*(3), pp. 808–11.

Malinvaud, Edmond. The Legacy of European Stagflation. *Europ. Econ. Rev.*, Feb./Mar. 1987, *31*(1/2), pp. 53–65. [G: W. Europe]

Marfán, Manuel. Reactivación y Restricción Externa: El Rol de la Política Fiscal. (Economic Recovery Under Payments Constraints: The Role of Short-run Fiscal Policy. With English summary.) *Colección Estud. CIEPLAN*, December 1987, (22), pp. 5–40.

Marini, Giancarlo. Price Variability, Supply-Side Policies and Monetary Rules. *Economica*, February 1987, *54*(213), pp. 109–11.

Martin, Robert E. Long-run Supply in Competitive Labor-Managed Industries. *Jones, D. C. and Svejnar, J., eds.*, 1987, pp. 113–28.

McAuliffe, Robert E. On the Keynesian Aggregate Supply Curve: A Note. *Amer. Econ.*, Fall 1987, *31*(2), pp. 76–77.

McCain, Roger A. Acceptable Contracts, Opportunism, and Rigid Hourly Wages. *Eastern Econ. J.*, July-Sept. 1987, *13*(3), pp. 205–13.

McCombie, John S. L. Does the Aggregate Production Function Imply Anything about the Laws of Production? A Note. *Appl. Econ.*, August 1987, *19*(8), pp. 1121–36. [G: Australia]

McDonald, Ian M. Customer Markets, Trade Unions and Stagflation. *Economica*, May 1987, *54*(214), pp. 139–53.

McDonald, Ian M. and Spindler, Karen J. An Empirical Investigation of Customer Market Analysis—A Microfoundation for Macroeconomics. *Appl. Econ.*, September 1987, *19*(9), pp. 1149–74. [G: U.S.; U.K.; Australia]

McKenna, Edward J. and Zannoni, Diane C. On the Nature and Use of the Concept of the Marginal Physical Product in Post Keynesian Economics. *J. Post Keynesian Econ.*, Summer 1987, *9*(4), pp. 483–89.

Melese, Francois and Transue, William. Unscrambling Chaos through Thick and Thin: An Explanation. *Quart. J. Econ.*, February 1987, *102*(1), pp. 171.

de Menil, Georges and Gordon, Robert J. 10th International Seminar on Macroeconomics: Introduction. *Europ. Econ. Rev.*, April 1987, *31*(3), pp. 537–42.

Mistri, Maurizio. Comportamenti innovativi di impresa con aspettative inflazionistiche dualistiche e struttura del mercato del lavoro. (Innovative Behaviours with Dualistic Inflationary Expectations and Labour Market Structure. With English summary.) *Rivista Int. Sci. Econ. Com.*, July 1987, *34*(7), pp. 609–21.

Mitchell, William F. The Nairu, Structural Imbalance and the Macroequilibrium Unemployment Rate. *Australian Econ. Pap.*, June 1987, *26*(48), pp. 101–18. [G: Australia]

Moene, Karl O. Keynesian Unemployment and Overmanning. *Econ. J.*, September 1987, *97*(387), pp. 740–45.

Mongiovi, Gary. Returns to Scale, the Standard

Commodity, and Sraffa's Production of Commodities by Means of Commodities: A Note. *Stud. Econ.*, 1987, *42*(31), pp. 35–50.

Montiel, Peter J. and Zaidi, Iqbal. Cross-Regime Tests of the Lucas Supply Function in Developing Countries. *Int. Monet. Fund Staff Pap.*, December 1987, *34*(4), pp. 760–69.
[G: LDCs]

Muysken, Joan. The Distribution Approach to the Aggregation of Production Functions. *Rech. Écon. Louvain*, 1987, *53*(3), pp. 269–82.

Myatt, Anthony E. and Scarth, William M. Fiscal Policy, Interest Sensitive Aggregate Supply and the Costs of Disinflation. *Manchester Sch. Econ. Soc. Stud.*, June 1987, *55*(2), pp. 144–57.

Newbery, David M. and Stiglitz, Joseph E. Wage Rigidity, Implicit Contracts, Unemployment and Economic Efficiency. *Econ. J.*, June 1987, *97*(386), pp. 416–30.

Newell, A. and Symons, J. S. V. Corporatism, Laissez-faire, and the Rise in Unemployment. *Europ. Econ. Rev.*, April 1987, *31*(3), pp. 567–601.
[G: OECD]

Ohyama, Michihiro. Unemployment and Inflation: Natural Wage Rate Hypothesis. *Keio Econ. Stud.*, 1987, *24*(2), pp. 11–26.

Ortona, Guido. Il lavoro superfluo può non essere superfluo. (Excess Employment May Be not in Excess. With English summary.) *Rivista Storia Econ.*, S.S., October 1987, *4*(3), pp. 887–96.
[G: LDCs]

Paldam, Martin. How Much Does One Percent of Growth Change the Unemployment Rate? A Study of 17 OECD Countries, 1948–1985. *Europ. Econ. Rev.*, Feb./Mar. 1987, *31*(1/2), pp. 306–13.
[G: OECD]

Phaneuf, Louis. Propriétés dynamiques des modèles du cycle à contrats échelonnés. (The Dynamic Properties of Staggered Contracts Models. With English summary.) *Can. J. Econ.*, February 1987, *20*(1), pp. 123–39.

Pissarides, Christopher A. Mass Unemployment: A Review Essay. *J. Monet. Econ.*, July 1987, *20*(1), pp. 183–88.
[G: E. Europe; U.S.]

Portes, Richard. Investment and the Inflation–Unemployment Tradeoff in a Macroeconomic Rationing Model with Monopolistic Competition: Comments. *Europ. Econ. Rev.*, April 1987, *31*(3), pp. 812–15.

Quadrio Curzio, Alberto; Manara, Carlo Felice and Faliva, Mario. Produzione ed efficienza con technologie globali. (Production and Efficiency with Global Technologies. With English summary.) *Econ. Polít.*, April 1987, *4*(1), pp. 11–47.

Reder, Melvin W. Specialization, Search Costs, and the Degree of Resource Utilization. *Feiwel, G. R., ed. (I)*, 1987, pp. 498–518.

Reinwald, Thomas P. Aggregate Supply and the Simple Keynesian Model: A Further Comment. *Amer. Econ.*, Fall 1987, *31*(2), pp. 84–86.

Roberts, John. An Equilibrium Model with Involuntary Unemployment at Flexible, Competitive Prices and Wages. *Amer. Econ. Rev.*, December 1987, *77*(5), pp. 856–74.

Rothschild, Kurt W. Is There a Weitzman Miracle? *J. Post Keynesian Econ.*, Winter 1986-87, *9*(2), pp. 198–211.

Sangha, Kehar S. Keynes and the Keynesians on Aggregate Supply: A Note. *Amer. Econ.*, Fall 1987, *31*(2), pp. 78–81.

Sauernheimer, K. Interest Rates, Exchange Rates, and Aggregate Supply. *J. Macroecon.*, Summer 1987, *9*(3), pp. 451–55.

Schittko, Ulrich K. Keynesian and Classical Unemployment in a Two-Country Model with Asset Markets. *[Marrama, V.], Vol. 2*, 1987, pp. 857–97.

Shields, Jon. Curing Unemployment through Labour-Market Competition: Commentary. *Begg, D. K. H., et al.*, 1987, pp. 150–54.
[G: U.K.]

Sneessens, Henri R. Investment and the Inflation–Unemployment Tradeoff in a Macroeconomic Rationing Model with Monopolistic Competition. *Europ. Econ. Rev.*, April 1987, *31*(3), pp. 781–808.

Solimano, Andrés. Emprego e salários reais: Uma análise macroeconômica de desequilíbrio para o Chile e o Brasil. (With English summary.) *Pesquisa Planejamento Econ.*, December 1987, *17*(3), pp. 605–31.
[G: Chile; Brazil]

Solow, John L. The Capital–Energy Complementarity Debate Revisited. *Amer. Econ. Rev.*, September 1987, *77*(4), pp. 605–14.

Summers, Lawrence H. Corporatism, Laissez-faire, and the Rise in Unemployment: Comments. *Europ. Econ. Rev.*, April 1987, *31*(3), pp. 606–14.
[G: OECD]

Sylos-Labini, Paolo. The Theory of Unemployment, Too, Is Historically Conditioned. *Banca Naz. Lavoro Quart. Rev.*, December 1987, (163), pp. 379–435.
[G: OECD]

Tobin, James. Keynesian and Classical Unemployment in Four Countries: Comments. *Brookings Pap. Econ. Act.*, 1987, (1), pp. 198–205.
[G: U.S.; U.K.; W. Germany; Austria]

Tucci, Marco P. Flexible Functional Forms and the Simultanaeous Estimation of Embodied and Disembodied Technical Progress. *Econ. Notes*, 1987, (2), pp. 102–20.

Vickers, Douglas. Aggregate Supply and the Producers' Expected Demand Curve: Performance and Change in the Macroeconomy. *J. Post Keynesian Econ.*, Fall 1987, *10*(1), pp. 84–104.

Waelbroeck, Jean. Corporatism, Laissez-faire, and the Rise in Unemployment: Comments. *Europ. Econ. Rev.*, April 1987, *31*(3), pp. 602–05.
[G: OECD]

Wagner, Helmut. Arbeitsangebot, Freizeitarbeit und Folgen einer Rationierung. Kritik und Erweiterung der traditionellen neoklassischen Arbeitsangebotstheorie. (Labor Supply and the Effects of Rationing. With English summary.) *Jahr. Nationalökon. Statist.*, March 1987, *203*(2), pp. 138–51.

Weitzman, Martin L. Steady State Unemployment under Profit Sharing. *Econ. J.*, March 1987, *97*(385), pp. 86–105.

Wells, Paul. Keynes's Employment Function and the Marginal Productivity of Labor. *J. Post Keynesian Econ.*, Summer 1987, *9*(4), pp. 507–15.

Woods, John E. Sraffa's Critical Proportion and the Standard Commodity. *Econ. Notes*, 1987, (2), pp. 60–66.

Wulwick, Nancy J. The Phillips Curve: Which? Whose? To Do What? How? *Southern Econ. J.*, April 1987, *53*(4), pp. 834–57.

0235 Theory of Aggregate Distribution

Alcorn, John H. and Gleicher, David. Workers, Inputs and Exploitation: A Note on Roemer. *Rev. Radical Polit. Econ.*, Summer 1987, *19*(2), pp. 77–82.

Bandyopadhyay, Pradeep. Value and Post-Sraffa Marxian Analysis. *Albelda, R.; Gunn, C. and Waller, W., eds.*, 1987, *1984*, pp. 186–94.

Brockway, George P. Normal Profits, Wages, and Prices. *J. Post Keynesian Econ.*, Winter 1986-87, *9*(2), pp. 307–08.

Brodbeck, Karl-Heinz. Two Class Economies with Overlapping Generations and Heritable Capital Stock. *J. Inst. Theoretical Econ.*, December 1987, *143*(4), pp. 643–51.

Brothwell, John F. On the Nature and Use of the Concept of the Marginal Physical Product in Post Keynesian Economics: A Comment. *J. Post Keynesian Econ.*, Summer 1987, *9*(4), pp. 496–501.

Catz, F. L'étalon des prix: sens. et non-sens. (The Concept of Standard Commodity: Meaningful and Meaningless. With English summary.) *Écon. Appl.*, 1987, *40*(1), pp. 177–84.

Davidson, Paul. The Simple Macroeconomics of a Nonergodic Monetary Economy versus a Share Economy: Is Weitzman's Macroeconomics Too Simple? *J. Post Keynesian Econ.*, Winter 1986-87, *9*(2), pp. 212–25.

Duménil, Gérard; Glick, Mark and Rangel, Jose. The Rate of Profit in the United States. *Cambridge J. Econ.*, December 1987, *11*(4), pp. 331–59. [G: U.S.]

Duménil, Gérard and Lévy, Dominique. Value and Natural Prices Trapped in Joint Production Pitfalls. *J. Econ. (Z. Nationalökon.)*, 1987, *47*(1), pp. 15–46.

Eichner, Alfred S. McKenna and Zannoni on the Concept of Marginal Physical Product in Post-Keynesian Economics. *J. Post Keynesian Econ.*, Summer 1987, *9*(4), pp. 502–06.

Eldred, Michael. The Unreflected Historicity of Historical Materialism. *Sci. Soc.*, Winter 1987-1988, *51*(4), pp. 475–77.

Englmann, Frank C. Structural Change, Heterogeneity of Capital over Time and the Non-uniqueness of "The" Uniform Rate of Profit. *Manchester Sch. Econ. Soc. Stud.*, June 1987, *55*(2), pp. 184–96.

Fleck, Florian H. and Domenghino, C.-M. Cambridge (U.K.) versus Cambridge (Mass.): A Keynesian Solution of "Pasinetti's Paradox." *J. Post Keynesian Econ.*, Fall 1987, *10*(1), pp. 22–36.

Glick, Mark and Ehrbar, Hans G. The Transformation Problem: An Obituary. *Australian Econ. Pap.*, December 1987, *26*(49), pp. 294–317.

Henley, Andrew. Labour's Shares and Profitability Crisis in the U.S.: Recent Experience and Post-war Trends. *Cambridge J. Econ.*, December 1987, *11*(4), pp. 315–30. [G: U.S.]

Horvat, Branko. Sraffa Systematized and Marx Vindicated. *Econ. Anal. Workers' Manage.*, 1987, *21*(3), pp. 289–97.

Kanth, Rajani. Against "Surplus" Theorizing: A Comment. *Rev. Radical Polit. Econ.*, Summer 1987, *19*(2), pp. 83–85. [G: LDCs]

Kregel, Jan A. Keynes's Given Degree of Competition: Comment. *J. Post Keynesian Econ.*, Summer 1987, *9*(4), pp. 490–95.

Kurz, Heinz D. and Salvadori, Neri. Burmeister on Sraffa and the Labor Theory of Value: A Comment [Sraffa, Labor Theories of Value, and the Economics of Real Wage Rate Determination]. *J. Polit. Econ.*, August 1987, *95*(4), pp. 870–81.

Larceneux, André. Previsions et rationnement dans une logique Keynésienne. (Expectations and Rationing Constraint in a Keynesian Logical Framework. With English summary.) *Écon. Soc.*, September 1987, *21*(9), pp. 121–47.

Lippit, Victor D. Surplus Theorizing Reaffirmed. *Rev. Radical Polit. Econ.*, Summer 1987, *19*(2), pp. 86–88. [G: LDCs]

Lowe, Adolph. Structural Analysis of Real-Capital Formation. *Lowe, A.*, 1987, *1955*, pp. 60–106.

Mair, Douglas. Prices and Income Distribution in Manufacturing Industry: Comment. *J. Post Keynesian Econ.*, Fall 1987, *10*(1), pp. 154–60. [G: Italy; U.S.]

Malinvaud, Edmond. Reflecting on the Theory of Capital and Growth. *Sinclair, P. J. N., ed.*, 1987, *1986*, pp. 395–413.

McKenna, Edward J. and Zannoni, Diane C. On the Nature and Use of the Concept of the Marginal Physical Product in Post Keynesian Economics. *J. Post Keynesian Econ.*, Summer 1987, *9*(4), pp. 483–89.

Moseley, Fred. The Profit Share and the Rate of Surplus Value in the U.S. Economy, 1975–85 [Marxian Crisis Theory and the Rate of Profit in the Postwar U.S. Economy]. *Cambridge J. Econ.*, December 1987, *11*(4), pp. 393–399. [G: U.S.]

O'Connell, Joan. Kaldor's Distribution Theory. *J. Post Keynesian Econ.*, Summer 1987, *9*(4), pp. 572–75.

Peach, James T. Distribution and Economic Progress. *J. Econ. Issues*, December 1987, *21*(4), pp. 1495–1529. [G: U.S.]

Pizzutto, Giorgio. Un contronto tra modelli macroeconomici. (A Comparison between Macroeconomic Models. With English summary.) *Rivista Int. Sci. Econ. Com.*, May 1987, *34*(5), pp. 393–409.

van der Ploeg, Frederick. Growth Cycles, Induced Technical Change, and Perpetual Conflict over the Distribution of Income. *J. Macroecon.*, Winter 1987, *9*(1), pp. 1–12.

023 Macroeconomic Theory

Reynolds, Peter J. Wage Rises and Income Distribution—A Note. *Manchester Sch. Econ. Soc. Stud.*, March 1987, *55*(1), pp. 77–87.
[G: U.K.]

Schultz, Eric. Non-produced Inputs, Differential Profit Rates and the Okishio Theorem. *Rev. Radical Polit. Econ.*, Summer 1987, *19*(2), pp. 43–60.

Shaikh, Anwar. The Poverty of Algebra. *Albelda, R.; Gunn, C. and Waller, W., eds.*, 1987, *1981*, pp. 297–322.

Steedman, Ian. Value, Price, and Profit. *Albelda, R.; Gunn, C. and Waller, W., eds.*, 1987, *1975*, pp. 175–85.

Steindl, Josef. The Rate of Interest and the Rate of Profit. *[Marrama, V.]*, Vol. 1, 1987, pp. 499–506.

Sylos-Labini, Paolo. Reply [Prices and Income Distribution in Manufacturing Industry]. *J. Post Keynesian Econ.*, Fall 1987, *10*(1), pp. 161–62. [G: U.S.; Italy]

Tobin, James. Toward a General Kaldorian Theory of Distribution: A Note. *Tobin, J. (1)*, 1987, *1960*, pp. 109–11.

Torii, Teruo. A Dynamic Analysis of the Macro Distribution Theory—In Connection with the Pasinetti Paradox (In Japanese. With English summary.) *Econ. Stud. Quart.*, September 1987, *38*(3), pp. 199–211.

Upadhyay, V. Tobin on Kaldor: A Comment. *Indian Econ. J.*, July-Sept. 1987, *35*(1), pp. 116–19.

Valdés, Benigno. Technical Change and Profitability: The "Law of the Tendency of the Rate of Profit to Fall" Reconsidered. *England, R. W., ed.*, 1987, pp. 107–17.

0239 Macroeconomics of Intertemporal Choice

Abel, Andrew B. Optimal Monetary Growth. *J. Monet. Econ.*, May 1987, *19*(3), pp. 437–50.

Aiyagari, S. Rao. Intergenerational Linkages and Government Budget Policies. *Fed. Res. Bank Minn. Rev.*, Spring 1987, *11*(2), pp. 14–23.

d'Autume, Antoine and Michel, Philippe. 'Transversality Conditions', Budget Constraints and the Determinancy of a Perfect Foresight Equilibrium in a Monetary Growth Model. *Europ. Econ. Rev.*, October 1987, *31*(7), pp. 1343–67.

Bernheim, B. Douglas and Ray, Debraj. Economic Growth with Intergenerational Altruism. *Rev. Econ. Stud.*, April 1987, *54*(2), pp. 227–41.

Bertocchi, Graziella. Il debito pubblico in un modello generazionale. (Government Debt in an Overlapping Generations Model. With English summary.) *Ricerche Econ.*, Jan.-Mar. 1987, *41*(1), pp. 22–40.

Brodbeck, Karl-Heinz. Two Class Economies with Overlapping Generations and Heritable Capital Stock. *J. Inst. Theoretical Econ.*, December 1987, *143*(4), pp. 643–51.

Constantinides, Marietta A. Optimum Population, Overlapping Generations and Social Security in a Model Mximizing $u(c^1, c^2, X)$. *J.*

Econ. (Z. Nationalökon.), 1987, *47*(1), pp. 69–75.

Croushore, Dean D. The Neutrality of Optimal Government Financial Policy: Supplying the Intergenerational Free Lunch. *Eastern Econ. J.*, Apr.-June 1987, *13*(2), pp. 123–36.

Farmer, Roger E. A. Deficits and Cycles. *Grandmont, J.-M., ed.*, 1987, *1986*, pp. 77–88.

Fender, John and Nandakumar, Parameswar. Oil in an Intertemporal Macroeconomic Model. *Greek Econ. Rev.*, 1987, *9*(1), pp. 38–56.

Grandmont, Jean-Michel. Stabilizing Competitive Business Cycles. *Grandmont, J.-M., ed.*, 1987, *1986*, pp. 57–76.

Grandmont, Jean-Michel and Laroque, Guy. Stability of Cycles and Expectations. *Grandmont, J.-M., ed.*, 1987, *1986*, pp. 138–51.

Henry, Samuel G. Brian. Dynamic Modelling and Rational Expectations. *Ann. Écon. Statist.*, Apr./Sept. 1987, (6/7), pp. 183–206.
[G: U.K.]

Kimball, Miles S. Making Sense of Two-Sided Altruism. *J. Monet. Econ.*, September 1987, *20*(2), pp. 301–26.

Kotlikoff, Laurence J.; Shoven, John B. and Spivak, Avia. Annuity Markets, Savings, and the Capital Stock. *Bodie, Z.; Shoven, J. B. and Wise, D. A., eds.*, 1987, pp. 211–34.

Kurz, Mordecai. The Life-Cycle Hypothesis as a Tool of Theory and Policy. *Feiwel, G. R., ed. (II)*, 1987, pp. 447–90. [G: U.S.]

Laitner, John. The Dynamic Analysis of Continuous-Time Life-Cycle Savings Growth Models. *J. Econ. Dynam. Control*, September 1987, *11*(3), pp. 331–57.

Leach, John E. Optimal Portfolio and Savings Decisions in an Intergenerational Economy. *Int. Econ. Rev.*, February 1987, *28*(1), pp. 123–34.

Malinvaud, Edmond. The Overlapping Generations Model in 1947. *J. Econ. Lit.*, March 1987, *25*(1), pp. 103–05.

McCallum, Bennett T. The Optimal Inflation Rate in an Overlapping-Generations Economy with Land. *Barnett, W. A. and Singleton, K. J., eds.*, 1987, pp. 325–39.

Modigliani, Franco. Life Cycle, Individual Thrift, and the Wealth of Nations. *[Modigliani, F.]*, 1987, pp. 1–28.

Peters, Wolfgang. Steady State Growth Paths in a Continuously Overlapping Generations Model. *Z. Wirtschaft. Sozialwissen.*, 1987, *107*(4), pp. 581–94.

Reichlin, Pietro. Equilibrium Cycles in an Overlapping Generations Economy with Production. *Grandmont, J.-M., ed.*, 1987, *1986*, pp. 89–102.

Rothschild, Michael. Annuity Markets, Savings, and the Capital Stock: Comment. *Bodie, Z.; Shoven, J. B. and Wise, D. A., eds.*, 1987, pp. 234–36.

Scarth, William M. Can Economic Growth Make Monetarist Arithmetic Pleasant? *Southern Econ. J.*, April 1987, *53*(4), pp. 1028–36.

Siebert, Horst. Foreign Debt and Capital Accumulation. *Weltwirtsch. Arch.*, 1987, *123*(4), pp. 618–30.

Tsukamoto, Jun. Bequest Behavior and the Steady-State Interest Rate. *Econ. Stud. Quart.*, September 1987, *38*(3), pp. 258–63.

Weil, Philippe. Confidence and the Real Value of Money in an Overlapping Generations Economy. *Quart. J. Econ.*, February 1987, *102*(1), pp. 1–22.

Weil, Philippe. Love Thy Children: Reflections on the Barro Debt Neutrality Theorem. *J. Monet. Econ.*, May 1987, *19*(3), pp. 377–91.

Weil, Philippe. Permanent Budget Deficits and Inflation. *J. Monet. Econ.*, September 1987, *20*(2), pp. 393–410.

Woodford, Michael. Stationary Sunspot Equilibria in a Finance Constrained Economy. *Grandmont, J.-M., ed.*, 1987, *1986*, pp. 128–37.

Zee, Howell H. Government Debt, Capital Accumulation, and the Terms of Trade in a Model of Interdependent Economies. *Econ. Inquiry*, October 1987, *25*(4), pp. 599–618.

024 Welfare Theory

0240 General

Abelson, Peter W. Fairness in the Real World: Rules, Choices, Expectations and Policies. *Australian Econ. Pap.*, June 1987, *26*(48), pp. 1–19.

Adams, Roy D. and McCormick, Ken. Private Goods, Club Goods, and Public Goods as a Continuum. *Rev. Soc. Econ.*, October 1987, *45*(2), pp. 192–99.

Atkinson, Anthony B. and Bourguignon, François. Income Distribution and Differences in Needs. *Feiwel, G. R., ed. (II)*, 1987, pp. 350–70.

Auerbach, Alan J. Weighted-Average Discount Rates in Public Expenditure Analysis: A Generalization. *[Harberger, A.]*, 1987, pp. 40–60.

Basu, Kaushik. Achievements, Capabilities and the Concept of Well-Being: A Review of *Commodities and Capabilities* by Amartya Sen. *Soc. Choice Welfare*, March 1987, *4*(1), pp. 69–76.

Basu, Kaushik. Axioms for a Fuzzy Measure of Inequality. *Math. Soc. Sci.*, December 1987, *14*(3), pp. 275–88.

Baumol, William J. Superfairness and Applied Microtheory. *Atlantic Econ. J.*, March 1987, *15*(1), pp. 1–9.

Bennett, Jeffrey W. Strategic Behaviour: Some Experimental Evidence. *J. Public Econ.*, April 1987, *32*(3), pp. 355–68.   [G: Australia]

Bergstrom, John C. and Stoll, John R. A Test of Contingent Market Bid Elicitation Procedures for Piecewise Valuation. *Western J. Agr. Econ.*, December 1987, *12*(2), pp. 104–08.
[G: U.S.]

Bernholz, Peter. A General Constitutional Possibility Theorem. *Radnitzky, G. and Bernholz, P., eds.*, 1987, pp. 383–400.

Berrebi, Zeev M. and Silber, Jacques G. Dispersion, Asymmetry and the Gini Index of Inequality. *Int. Econ. Rev.*, June 1987, *28*(2), pp. 331–38.

Biswas, Tapan. Distributive Justice and Allocation by the Market: On the Characterisation of a Fair Market Economy. *Math. Soc. Sci.*, December 1987, *14*(3), pp. 225–37.

Blackorby, Charles and Donaldson, David. Welfare Ratios and Distributionally Sensitive Cost–Benefit Analysis. *J. Public Econ.*, December 1987, *34*(3), pp. 265–90.

Bockstael, Nancy E. and Strand, Ivar E., Jr. The Effect of Common Sources of Regression Error on Benefit Estimates. *Land Econ.*, February 1987, *63*(1), pp. 11–20.

Brunner, Karl. Economic Inequality and the Quest for Social Justice. *Cato J.*, Spring/Summer 1987, *7*(1), pp. 153–58.

Buchanan, James M. Fiscal Institutions and Efficiency in Collective Outlay. *Buchanan, J. M. (II)*, 1987, *1964*, pp. 357–66.

Buchanan, James M. L.S.E. Cost Theory in Retrospect. *Buchanan, J. M. (II)*, 1987, *1973*, pp. 141–51.

Buchanan, James M. Notes for an Economic Theory of Socialism. *Buchanan, J. M. (II)*, 1987, *1970*, pp. 237–50.

Buchanan, James M. Positive Economics, Welfare Economics, and Political Economy. *Buchanan, J. M. (II)*, 1987, *1959*, pp. 3–19.

Buchanan, James M. Towards the Simple Economics of Natural Liberty: An Exploratory Analysis. *Kyklos*, 1987, *40*(1), pp. 3–20.

Burkett, Paul. Instrumental Justice and Social Economics: Some Comments from a Marxian Perspective. *Rev. Soc. Econ.*, December 1987, *45*(3), pp. 313–24.

Chakravarty, Satya Ranjan and Dutta, Bhaskar. A Note on Measures of Distance between Income Distributions. *J. Econ. Theory*, February 1987, *41*(1), pp. 185–88.

Choi, Eun Kwan and Johnson, Stanley R. Consumer's Surplus and Price Uncertainty. *Int. Econ. Rev.*, June 1987, *28*(2), pp. 407–11.

Choudhury, Masudul Alam. A Study of Ethico-Economics in the General Equilibrium Field. *Int. J. Soc. Econ.*, 1987, *14*(3/4/5), pp. 207–18.

Cohen, Yuval. Commuter Welfare under Peak-period Congestion Tolls: Who Gains and Who Loses? *Int. J. Transport Econ.*, October 1987, *14*(3), pp. 239–66.

Crenson, Matthew A. The Private Stake in Public Goods: Overcoming the Illogic of Collective Action. *Policy Sci.*, 1987, *20*(3), pp. 259–76.

Dalmulder, Jan J. J. The Relations between Expansion and the Progress of Economic Welfare. *Dupriez, L. H., ed.*, 1987, *1955*, pp. 43–56.

van Damme, Eric. Competition versus Monopoly in the Supply of Public Goods: Comment. *Pethig, R. and Schlieper, U., eds.*, 1987, pp. 219–25.

Darvish, Tikva and Kahana, Nava. Measuring Consumer's Surplus in the Factor Market. *Atlantic Econ. J.*, March 1987, *15*(1), pp. 59–62.

Dasgupta, Partha. Reflections on Social Project Evaluation: Comment. *Meier, G. M., ed.*, 1987, pp. 189–92.

De Borger, Bruno. Composite Commodities, Housing Characteristics and the Hicksian Surplus Measures of Welfare Change. *Reg. Sci. Urban Econ.*, November 1987, *17*(4), pp. 475–94.

Dierker, Egbert. Increasing Returns, Efficiency, and the Distribution of Wealth. *Europ. Econ. Rev.*, Feb./Mar. 1987, *31*(1/2), pp. 475–82.

Donaldson, David and Roemer, John E. Social Choice in Economic Environments with Dimensional Variation. *Soc. Choice Welfare*, December 1987, *4*(4), pp. 253–76.

Dupuy, Jean-Pierre. Le refus de l'arbitraire et ses limites dans l'œuvre de John Rawls. (Arbitrariness Denial and Its Limits in Rawls Theory. With English summary.) *Écon. Soc.*, March 1987, *21*(3), pp. 147–76.

Ebert, Udo. A Note on Social Welfare Orderings. *Europ. Econ. Rev.*, July 1987, *31*(5), pp. 1145–47.

Ebert, Udo. Axiomatic Foundations of Hicksian Measures of Welfare Change. *J. Public Econ.*, June 1987, *33*(1), pp. 115–24.

Ebert, Udo. Size and Distribution of Incomes as Determinants of Social Welfare. *J. Econ. Theory*, February 1987, *41*(1), pp. 23–33.

Elliott, John E. and Clark, Barry S. Keynes's *General Theory* and Social Justice. *J. Post Keynesian Econ.*, Spring 1987, *9*(3), pp. 381–94.

Fan, Liang-Shing and Fan, Chuen-Mei. On the Welfare Effects of Rent Seeking. *Indian Econ. J.*, July-Sept. 1987, *35*(1), pp. 136–39.

Feiwel, George R. Arrow's Weltanschauung. *Rivista Int. Sci. Econ. Com.*, Jan.-Feb. 1987, *34*(1–2), pp. 1–50.

Feiwel, George R. The Many Dimensions of Kenneth J. Arrow. *Feiwel, G. R., ed. (II)*, 1987, pp. 1–115.

Feiwel, George R. The Potentials and Limits of Economic Analysis: The Contributions of Kenneth J. Arrow. *Feiwel, G. R., ed. (I)*, 1987, pp. 1–187.

Fisher, Franklin M. Household Equivalence Scales and Interpersonal Comparisons. *Rev. Econ. Stud.*, July 1987, *54*(3), pp. 519–24.

French, Ben C. Comments on Economic Efficiency. *Kilmer, R. L. and Armbruster, W. J., eds.*, 1987, pp. 99–104.

Funke, Helmut. Incentive Compatible Mechanisms for the Allocation of Public Goods. *Bamberg, G. and Spremann, K., eds.*, 1987, pp. 105–16.

Gregory, Robin and McDaniels, Tim. Valuing Environmental Losses: What Promise Does the Right Measure Hold? *Policy Sci.*, April 1987, *20*(1), pp. 11–26.

Guitton, Henri. The Relation between Progress in Economic Welfare and Human Progress in a Broader Sense. *Dupriez, L. H., ed.*, 1987, *1955*, pp. 60–78.

Güth, Werner and Hellwig, Martin. Competition versus Monopoly in the Supply of Public Goods. *Pethig, R. and Schlieper, U., eds.*, 1987, pp. 183–217.

Guttman, Joel M. A Non-Cournot Model of Voluntary Collective Action. *Economica*, February 1987, *54*(213), pp. 1–19.

Hagenaars, Aldi J. M. A Class of Poverty Indices. *Int. Econ. Rev.*, October 1987, *28*(3), pp. 583–607.

Hampton, Jean. Free-Rider Problems in the Production of Collective Goods. *Econ. Philos.*, October 1987, *3*(2), pp. 245–73.

Harberger, Arnold C. Reflections on Social Project Evaluation. *Meier, G. M., ed.*, 1987, pp. 153–88.

Harel, Alon and Nitzan, Shmuel. The Libertarian Resolution of the Paretian Liberal Paradox. *J. Econ. (Z. Nationalökon.)*, 1987, *47*(4), pp. 337–52.

Harsanyi, John C. Von Neumann–Morgenstern Utilities, Risk Taking, and Welfare. *Feiwel, G. R., ed. (I)*, 1987, pp. 545–58.

Haveman, Robert H.; Gabay, Mary and Andreoni, James R. Exact Consumer's Surplus and Deadweight Loss: A Correction. *Amer. Econ. Rev.*, June 1987, *77*(3), pp. 494–95.

Hayes, Kathy J. and Porter-Hudak, Susan. Deadweight Loss: Theoretical Size Relationships and the Precision of Measurement. *J. Bus. Econ. Statist.*, January 1987, *5*(1), pp. 47–52. [G: U.S.]

Heertje, Arnold. Some Observations on the Welfare Economic Aspects of the Unofficial Economy. *Alessandrini, S. and Dallago, B., eds.*, 1987, pp. 303–10.

Hennipman, Piet. A Tale of Two Schools: Comments on a New View of the Ordinalist Revolution. *De Economist*, 1987, *135*(2), pp. 141–62.

Herrero, Carmen. Teorías alternativas de la utilidad esperada: Una interpretación en términos de bienestar social. (With English summary.) *Invest. Econ.*, September 1987, *11*(3), pp. 375–98.

Higgs, Robert. Identity and Cooperation: A Comment on Sen's Alternative Program [Goals, Commitment, and Identity]. *J. Law, Econ., Organ.*, Spring 1987, *3*(1), pp. 140–42.

Hirshleifer, Jack. From Weakest-Link to Best-Shot: The Voluntary Provision of Public Goods. *Hirshleifer, J.*, 1987, *1983*, pp. 145–63.

Jasso, Guillermina. Choosing a Good: Models Based on the Theory of the Distributive-Justice Force. *Lawler, E. J. and Markovsky, B., eds.*, 1987, pp. 67–108.

Jones-Lee, M. W. The Economic Value of Life: A Comment. *Economica*, August 1987, *54*(215), pp. 397–400.

Jorgenson, Dale W. and Slesnick, Daniel T. General Equilibrium Analysis of Natural Gas Price Regulation. *Bailey, E. E., ed.*, 1987, pp. 153–90. [G: U.S.]

Just, Richard E. Economic Efficiency and Welfare Measurement in a Dynamic, Uncertain, Multimarket World. *Kilmer, R. L. and Armbruster, W. J., eds.*, 1987, pp. 37–62.

Kadekodi, Gopal. A Welfare Approach to Energy Pricing: A Case Study from India. *Pachauri, R. K., ed.*, 1987, pp. 1035–47.

Kanemoto, Yoshitsugu. Asymmetric Information in the Credit Market and Discount Rates for

Public Investment. *J. Public Econ.*, December 1987, *34*(3), pp. 291–309.

Kendrick, John W. Happiness Is Personal Productivity Growth. *Challenge*, May/June 1987, *30*(2), pp. 37–44.

Khan, M. Ali and Vohra, Rajiv. On the Existence of Lindahl–Hotelling Equilibria. *J. Public Econ.*, November 1987, *34*(2), pp. 143–58.

Kokoski, Mary F. and Smith, V. Kerry. A General Equilibrium Analysis of Partial-Equilibrium Welfare Measures: The Case of Climate Change. *Amer. Econ. Rev.*, June 1987, *77*(3), pp. 331–41. **[G: U.S.]**

Lal, Deepak. Reflections on Social Project Evaluation: Comment. *Meier, G. M., ed.*, 1987, pp. 193–202.

Le Breton, Michel and Trannoy, Alain. Measures of Inequality as an Aggregation of Individual Preferences about Income Distribution: The Arrowian Case. *J. Econ. Theory*, April 1987, *41*(2), pp. 248–69.

Le Grand, Julian. Equity, Well-Being, and Economic Choice. *J. Human Res.*, Summer 1987, *22*(3), pp. 428–40.

Leibenstein, Harvey. On Some Economic Aspects of a Fragile Input: Trust. *Feiwel, G. R., ed. (II)*, 1987, pp. 600–612.

McNutt, Paddy. Ethical, Political and Economic Dimensions of an Ideal Society. *Int. J. Soc. Econ.*, 1987, *14*(2), pp. 53–60.

Melck, A. P. *Theoretical Welfare Economics* after Thirty Years. *S. Afr. J. Econ.*, September 1987, *55*(3), pp. 259–66. **[G: S. Africa]**

Meyer, Margaret A. and Mookherjee, Dilip. Incentives, Compensation, and Social Welfare. *Rev. Econ. Stud.*, April 1987, *54*(2), pp. 209–26.

Morton, R. B. A Group Majority Voting Model of Public Good Provision. *Soc. Choice Welfare*, June 1987, *4*(2), pp. 117–31.

Moulin, Hervé J. Egalitarian-Equivalent Cost Sharing of a Public Good. *Econometrica*, July 1987, *55*(4), pp. 963–76.

Mumy, Gene E. What Does Nozick's Minimal State Do? *Econ. Philos.*, October 1987, *3*(2), pp. 275–305.

Musgrave, Richard A. Equity Principles in Public Finance. *van de Kar, H. M. and Wolfe, B. L., eds.*, 1987, pp. 113–23.

Musgrave, Richard A. Fifty Years of Public Finance. *Roskamp, K. W., ed.*, 1987, pp. 19–50.

Ng, Yew-Kwang. "Political Distortions" and the Relevance of Second and Third-Best Theories. *Public Finance*, 1987, *42*(1), pp. 137–45.

Ng, Yew-Kwang. The Role of Economists and Third-Best Policies. *Public Finance*, 1987, *42*(1), pp. 152–55.

Palfrey, Thomas R. and Srivastava, Sanjay. On Bayesian Implementable Allocations. *Rev. Econ. Stud.*, April 1987, *54*(2), pp. 193–208.

Pope, Rulon D. Economic Efficiency and Welfare Measurement in a Dynamic, Uncertain, Multi-market World: A Discussion. *Kilmer, R. L. and Armbruster, W. J., eds.*, 1987, pp. 63–66.

Posner, Richard A. The Justice of Economics.

Econ. Scelte Pubbliche/J. Public Finance Public Choice, Jan.-Apr. 1987, *5*(1), pp. 15–25.

Pyatt, Graham. Measuring Welfare, Poverty and Inequality. *Econ. J.*, June 1987, *97*(386), pp. 459–67.

Ruiz-Castillo, Javier. Potential Welfare and the Sum of Individual Compensating or Equivalent Variations. *J. Econ. Theory*, February 1987, *41*(1), pp. 34–53.

Ruys, Pieter H. M. and van der Laan, Gerard. Computation of an Industrial Equilibrium. *Talman, D. and van der Laan, G., eds.*, 1987, pp. 205–29.

Salamon, Peter, et al. A Geometric View of Welfare Gains with Non-instantaneous Adjustment. *Math. Soc. Sci.*, April 1987, *13*(2), pp. 153–63.

Sandler, Todd; Sterbenz, Frederic P. and Posnett, John. Free Riding and Uncertainty. *Europ. Econ. Rev.*, December 1987, *31*(8), pp. 1605–17.

Satchell, Stephen E. Source and Subgroup Decomposition Inequalities for the Lorenz Curve. *Int. Econ. Rev.*, June 1987, *28*(2), pp. 323–29.

Sato, Toshihiro. Equity, Fairness and Lindahl Equilibria. *J. Public Econ.*, July 1987, *33*(2), pp. 261–71.

Schefter, John E. Increasing Block Rate Tariffs as Faulty Transmitters of Marginal Willingness to Pay. *Land Econ.*, February 1987, *63*(1), pp. 21–33. **[G: U.S.]**

Scoggins, John Franklin. Welfare Evaluation and Household Production with Non-constant Returns to Scale. *Southern Econ. J.*, January 1987, *53*(3), pp. 643–49.

Shibata, Hirofumi and Shibata, Aiko. Rent Redistribution through Provision of Public Goods. *[Kitamura, H.]*, 1987, pp. 268–84.

Slivinski, Alan D. Bergson Social Welfare Functions in Applied Welfare Analysis. *Soc. Choice Welfare*, December 1987, *4*(4), pp. 241–51.

Slivinski, Alan D. The Normative Characterization of Aggregate Consumers' Surplus Measures. *Int. Econ. Rev.*, October 1987, *28*(3), pp. 559–81.

Subramanian, S. Rights, Consensus and the Optimum Savings Problem. *J. Quant. Econ.*, January 1987, *3*(1), pp. 1–11.

Tartarin, Robert. Efficacité et propriété. (Efficiency and Property. With English summary.) *Revue Écon.*, November 1987, *38*(6), pp. 1129–55.

Tinari, Frank D. Reducing Income Inequality Is Not the Only "Equitable" Fairness Criterion. *Rev. Soc. Econ.*, April 1987, *45*(1), pp. 77–91.

Tinbergen, Jan. Measuring Welfare of Productive Consumers. *De Economist*, 1987, *135*(2), pp. 231–36.

Tinbergen, Jan. The Tension Theory of Welfare. *Feiwel, G. R., ed. (II)*, 1987, pp. 410–17.

Tsuneki, Atsushi. The Measurement of Waste in a Public Goods Economy. *J. Public Econ.*, June 1987, *33*(1), pp. 73–94.

Vaughan, R. N. Welfare Approaches to the Measurement of Poverty. *Econ. J.*, Supplement 1987, *97*, pp. 160–70.

Vives, Xavier. Small Income Effects: A Marshallian Theory of Consumer Surplus and Downward Sloping Demand. *Rev. Econ. Stud.*, January 1987, *54*(1), pp. 87–103.

Voeller, Joachim. A Note on Fair Equality of Rules. *Bamberg, G. and Spremann, K., eds.*, 1987, pp. 473–80.   [G: W. Germany]

Wriglesworth, John L. and Gravelle, Hugh S. E. The Three Consumer Surpluses as Individual Welfare Measures. *Scot. J. Polit. Econ.*, August 1987, *34*(3), pp. 230–48.

Yablon, Charles M. Arguing about Rights. *Mich. Law Rev.*, Apr.-May 1987, *85*(5–6), pp. 871–94.

0242 Allocative Efficiency Including Theory of Cost/Benefit

Aivazian, Varouj A.; Callen, Jeffrey L. and Lipnowski, Irwin. The Coase Theorem and Coalitional Stability. *Economica*, November 1987, *54*(216), pp. 517–20.

Anand, Sudhir and Nalebuff, Barry. Issues in the Application of Cost–Benefit Analysis to Energy Projects in Developing Countries. *Sinclair, P. J. N., ed.*, 1987, pp. 190–222.
                [G: LDCs]

Aoki, Masahiko. Incentive-Compatible Approximation of a Nashlike Solution under Nonconvex Technology. *[Hurwicz, L.]*, 1987, pp. 295–307.

Arnott, Richard J. Essai sur le risque moral. (An Essay on Moral Hazard. With English summary.) *L'Actual. Econ.*, June-September 1987, *63*(2–3), pp. 74–97.

Babb, Emerson M. The Science and Art of Efficiency Analysis: The Role of Other Performance Criteria: A Discussion. *Kilmer, R. L. and Armbruster, W. J., eds.*, 1987, pp. 88–90.

Baron, David P. and Besanko, David. Commitment and Fairness in a Dynamic Regulatory Relationship. *Rev. Econ. Stud.*, July 1987, *54*(3), pp. 413–36.

Baumol, William J. and Fischer, Dietrich. Peak Pricing, Congestion, and Fairness. *Feiwel, G. R., ed. (II)*, 1987, pp. 382–409.

Bernheim, B. Douglas and Ray, Debraj. Economic Growth with Intergenerational Altruism. *Rev. Econ. Stud.*, April 1987, *54*(2), pp. 227–41.

Besanko, David and Thakor, Anjan V. Competitive Equilibrium in the Credit Market under Asymmetric Information. *J. Econ. Theory*, June 1987, *42*(1), pp. 167–82.

Bhagwati, Jagdish N. The Generalized Theory of Distortions and Welfare. *Bhagwati, J. N., ed.*, 1987, *1971*, pp. 265–86.

Bhagwati, Jagdish N.; Brecher, Richard A. and Srinivasan, T. N. DUP Activities and Economic Theory. *Bhagwati, J. N., ed.*, 1987, *1984*, pp. 311–28.

Birch, Stephen and Donaldson, Cam. Applications of Cost–Benefit Analysis to Health Care: Departures from Welfare Economic Theory.

J. Health Econ., September 1987, *6*(3), pp. 211–25.

Blackorby, Charles and Donaldson, David. Welfare Ratios and Distributionally Sensitive Cost–Benefit Analysis. *J. Public Econ.*, December 1987, *34*(3), pp. 265–90.

Calsamiglia, Xavier. Informational Requirements of Parametric Resource Allocation Processes. *[Hurwicz, L.]*, 1987, pp. 115–31.

Chichilnisky, Graciela and Thomson, William. The Walrasian Mechanism from Equal Division Is Not Monotonic with Respect to Variations in the Number of Consumers. *J. Public Econ.*, February 1987, *32*(1), pp. 119–24.

Chipman, John S. When Is a Fixed Income Distribution Optimal? *Feiwel, G. R., ed. (II)*, 1987, pp. 371–81.

Cramton, Peter; Gibbons, Robert and Klemperer, Paul. Dissolving a Partnership Efficiently. *Econometrica*, May 1987, *55*(3), pp. 615–32.

Davidson, Carl; Martin, Lawrence W. and Matusz, Steven J. Search, Unemployment, and the Production of Jobs. *Econ. J.*, December 1987, *97*(388), pp. 857–76.

Desai, Padma and Martin, Ricardo. Measuring Resource-Allocational Efficiency in Centrally Planned Economies: A Theoretical Analysis. *Desai, P.*, 1987, *1983*, pp. 101–16.

Dinwiddy, Caroline L. and Teal, Francis J. Shadow Prices for Non-traded Goods in a Tax-Distorted Economy: Formulae and Values. *J. Public Econ.*, July 1987, *33*(2), pp. 207–21.

Dixit, Avinash K. On Pareto-Improving Redistributions of Aggregate Economic Gains. *J. Econ. Theory*, February 1987, *41*(1), pp. 133–53.

Drèze, Jacques H. and Sheshinski, Eytan. On Industry Equilibrium under Uncertainty. *Drèze, J. H.*, 1987, *1984*, pp. 250–58.

Eichenbaum, Martin S. and Peled, Dan. Capital Accumulation and Annuities in an Adverse Selection Economy. *J. Polit. Econ.*, April 1987, *95*(2), pp. 334–54.

Encaoua, David and Moreaux, Michel. L'analyse théorique des problèmes de tarification et d'allocation des coûts dans les télécommunications. (The Theoretical Approach to Pricing and Cost Allocation for Telecommunication Services. With English summary.) *Revue Écon.*, March 1987, *38*(2), pp. 375–413.

Endres, Alfred. On the Efficacy of Public Finance Instruments in Protecting the Environment. *van de Kar, H. M. and Wolfe, B. L., eds.*, 1987, pp. 181–92.

Farrell, Joseph. Information and the Coase Theorem. *J. Econ. Perspectives*, Fall 1987, *1*(2), pp. 113–29.

Forsythe, Robert and Suchanek, Gerry L. Decentralizing Constrained Pareto Optimal Allocations in Stock Ownership Economies: An Impossibility Theorem. *Int. Econ. Rev.*, June 1987, *28*(2), pp. 299–313.

French, Ben C. Comments on Economic Efficiency. *Kilmer, R. L. and Armbruster, W. J., eds.*, 1987, pp. 99–104.

Gibbard, Allan F. Ordinal Utilitarianism. *Feiwel,*

G. R., ed. *(II)*, 1987, pp. 135–53.

Graziani, Augusto. Efficiency Criteria at the Micro and Macro Levels. *Rivista Int. Sci. Econ. Com.*, October 1987, *34*(10), pp. 957–69.

Green, Jerry R. and Laffont, Jean-Jacques. Limited Communication and Incentive Compatibility. *[Hurwicz, L.]*, 1987, pp. 308–29.

Groves, Theodore and Ledyard, John O. Incentive Compatibility since 1972. *[Hurwicz, L.]*, 1987, pp. 48–111.

Guesnerie, Roger and Penz, Ph. L'évaluation des effets macroéconomiques des projets: une introduction critique. (Evaluating "Macroeconomic Effects" of Projects: A Critical Introduction. With English summary.) *Écon. Soc.*, April 1987, *21*(4), pp. 19–44.

Hammond, Peter J. Markets as Constraints: Multilateral Incentive Compatibility in Continuum Economies. *Rev. Econ. Stud.*, July 1987, *54*(3), pp. 399–412.

Haurie, Alain and Pohjola, Matti. Efficient Equilibria in a Differential Game of Capitalism. *J. Econ. Dynam. Control*, March 1987, *11*(1), pp. 65–78.

Hazlett, Thomas W. The Role of Property Rights in the Positive Theory of Monopoly. *Managerial Dec. Econ.*, September 1987, *8*(3), pp. 201–212.

Henriet, Dominique, et al. Intérêt public, intérêt privé et discrimination. (Public Interest, Private Interest and Discrimination. With English summary.) *L'Actual. Econ.*, June-September 1987, *63*(2–3), pp. 98–117.

Hirshleifer, Jack. Evolutionary Models in Economics and Law: Cooperation versus Conflict Strategies. *Hirshleifer, J.*, 1987, *1982*, pp. 211–72.

Hoehn, John P. and Randall, Alan. A Satisfactory Benefit Cost Indicator from Contingent Valuation. *J. Environ. Econ. Manage.*, September 1987, *14*(3), pp. 226–47.

Jones, Ronald W. The Population Monotonicity Property and the Transfer Paradox. *J. Public Econ.*, February 1987, *32*(1), pp. 125–32.

Jordan, James S. The Informational Requirements of Local Stability in Decentralized Allocation Mechanisms. *[Hurwicz, L.]*, 1987, pp. 183–212.

Katz, Michael L. The Welfare Effects of Third-Degree Price Discrimination in Intermediate Good Markets. *Amer. Econ. Rev.*, March 1987, *77*(1), pp. 154–67.

Khan, M. Ali and Vohra, Rajiv. An Extension of the Second Welfare Theorem to Economies with Nonconvexities and Public Goods. *Quart. J. Econ.*, May 1987, *102*(2), pp. 223–41.

Lee, Do Sung. An Incentive Compatible Price Mechanism for Attaining Lindahl Allocation. *Int. Econ. J.*, Summer 1987, *1*(2), pp. 47–59.

Lee, Dwight R. The Tradeoff between Equality and Efficiency: Short-run Politics and Long-run Realities. *Public Choice*, 1987, *53*(2), pp. 149–65.

Lee, Li Way. Cognitive and Market Failures: Some Complex Policy Implications. *J. Behav. Econ.*, Fall 1987, *16*(3), pp. 51–57.

Lensberg, Terje. Stability and Collective Rationality. *Econometrica*, July 1987, *55*(4), pp. 935–61.

Lucas, Robert E. B. On the Theory of DRC Criteria: Reply. *J. Devel. Econ.*, June 1987, *26*(1), pp. 169–71.

Lucas, Robert E. B.; Pursell, Garry G. and Tower, Edward. Ex Ante versus Ex Post DRC's and the Possibility of Negative Shadow Prices: Resolution. *J. Devel. Econ.*, June 1987, *26*(1), pp. 173–74.

Makowski, Louis and Ostroy, Joseph M. Vickrey–Clarke–Groves Mechanisms and Perfect Competition. *J. Econ. Theory*, August 1987, *42*(2), pp. 244–61.

Marshall, John M.; Sonstelie, Jon and Gilles, Christian. Money and Redistribution: Revisionist Notes on a Problem of Samuelson. *J. Monet. Econ.*, July 1987, *20*(1), pp. 3–23.

Mas-Colell, Andreu. On the Second Welfare Theorem for Anonymous Net Trades in Exchange Economies with Many Agents. *[Hurwicz, L.]*, 1987, pp. 267–92.

McKee, Michael and West, Edwin G. Further Perspectives on the Theory of Second-Best. *Public Finance*, 1987, *42*(1), pp. 146–51.

de Meza, David and Gould, J. R. Free Access versus Private Property in a Resource: Income Distributions Compared. *J. Polit. Econ.*, December 1987, *95*(6), pp. 1317–25.

Mezzetti, C. Paretian Efficiency, Rawlsian Justice and the Nozick Theory of Rights. *Soc. Choice Welfare*, March 1987, *4*(1), pp. 25–37.

Milne, Frank and Shefrin, H. M. Information and Securities: A Note on Pareto Dominance and the Second Best. *J. Econ. Theory*, December 1987, *43*(2), pp. 314–28.

Milon, J. Walter. The Science and Art of Efficiency Analysis: The Role of Other Performance Criteria. *Kilmer, R. L. and Armbruster, W. J.*, eds., 1987, pp. 67–87.

Mishan, Ezra J. Is Cost–Benefit Analysis a Bastard Science? *van de Kar, H. M. and Wolfe, B. L.*, eds., 1987, pp. 45–54.

Montesano, Aldo. Optimal Allocations and the Price System. *Rivista Int. Sci. Econ. Com.*, October 1987, *34*(10), pp. 913–36.

Moulin, Hervé J. Egalitarian-Equivalent Cost Sharing of a Public Good. *Econometrica*, July 1987, *55*(4), pp. 963–76.

Mount, Kenneth R. and Reiter, Stanley. On the Existence of a Locally Stable Dynamic Process with a Statically Minimal Message Space. *[Hurwicz, L.]*, 1987, pp. 213–40.

Nalebuff, Barry and Scharfstein, David. Testing in Models of Asymmetric Information. *Rev. Econ. Stud.*, April 1987, *54*(2), pp. 265–77.

Ng, Yew-Kwang. "Political Distortions" and the Relevance of Second and Third-Best Theories. *Public Finance*, 1987, *42*(1), pp. 137–45.

Ng, Yew-Kwang. Relative-Income Effects and the Appropriate Level of Public Expenditure. *Oxford Econ. Pap.*, June 1987, *39*(2), pp. 293–300.

Ng, Yew-Kwang. The Role of Economists and

Third-Best Policies. *Public Finance*, 1987, *42*(1), pp. 152–55.

Osana, Hiroaki. Long-run Equilibria for Perfectly Competitive Markets. *Keio Econ. Stud.*, 1987, *24*(1), pp. 1–11.

Papps, Ivy. Techniques of Project Appraisal. *Gemmell, N., ed.*, 1987, pp. 307–38.

Postlewaite, Andrew and Schmeidler, David. Differential Information and Strategic Behavior in Economic Environments: A General Equilibrium Approach. *[Hurwicz, L.]*, 1987, pp. 330–48.

Pratt, John W. and Zeckhauser, Richard J. Incentive-Based Decentralization: Expected-Externality Payments Induce Efficient Behaviour in Groups. *Feiwel, G. R., ed. (I)*, 1987, pp. 439–83.

Pursell, Garry G. and Tower, Edward. DRC Criteria: Comment. *J. Devel. Econ.*, June 1987, *26*(1), pp. 163–67.

Radner, Roy. Decentralization and Incentives. *[Hurwicz, L.]*, 1987, *1983*, pp. 3–47.

Radnitzky, Gerard. Cost–Benefit Thinking in the Methodology of Research: The "Economic Approach" Applied to Key Problems of the Philosophy of Science. *Radnitzky, G. and Bernholz, P., eds.*, 1987, pp. 283–331.

Robinson, Marc S. The Welfare Cost of Resource Taxation. *[Harberger, A.]*, 1987, pp. 95–108.

Roemer, John E. Egalitarianism, Responsibility, and Information. *Econ. Philos.*, October 1987, *3*(2), pp. 215–44.

Sah, Raaj Kumar. Queues, Rations, and Market: Comparisons of Outcomes for the Poor and the Rich. *Amer. Econ. Rev.*, March 1987, *77*(1), pp. 69–77.

Sah, Raaj Kumar and Stiglitz, Joseph E. Price Scissors and the Structure of the Economy. *Quart. J. Econ.*, February 1987, *102*(1), pp. 109–34.

Salop, Steven C. and Stiglitz, Joseph E. Information, Welfare, and Product Diversity. *Feiwel, G. R., ed. (II)*, 1987, pp. 328–40.

Samuelson, Paul A. Sparks from Arrow's Anvil. *Feiwel, G. R., ed. (II)*, 1987, pp. 154–78.

Sandmo, Agnar. A Reinterpretation of Elasticity Formulae in Optimum Tax Theory. *Economica*, February 1987, *54*(213), pp. 89–96.

Shaffer, James D. Does the Concept of Economic Efficiency Meet the Standards for Truth in Labeling When Used as a Norm in Policy Analysis? *Kilmer, R. L. and Armbruster, W. J., eds.*, 1987, pp. 91–98.

Shiozawa, Shuhei. Pareto Optimality, Core and Equilibria in a Cooperative Super Game without Side Payments. *Keio Econ. Stud.*, 1987, *24*(1), pp. 25–41.

Smith, V. Kerry. Nonuse Values in Benefit Cost Analysis. *Southern Econ. J.*, July 1987, *54*(1), pp. 19–26.

Smith, V. Kerry. Uncertainty, Benefit–Cost Analysis, and the Treatment of Option Value. *J. Environ. Econ. Manage.*, September 1987, *14*(3), pp. 283–92.

Spear, Stephen E. and Srivastava, Sanjay. On Repeated Moral Hazard with Discounting.

Rev. Econ. Stud., October 1987, *54*(4), pp. 599–617.

Stiglitz, Joseph E. The Wage–Productivity Hypothesis: Its Economic Consequences and Policy Implications. *[Harberger, A.]*, 1987, pp. 130–65.

Suzumura, Kotaro and Kiyono, Kazuharu. Entry Barriers and Economic Welfare. *Rev. Econ. Stud.*, January 1987, *54*(1), pp. 157–67.

Suzumura, Kotaro and Suga, Koichi. Arrow and the Problem of Social Choice. *Feiwel, G. R., ed. (II)*, 1987, pp. 255–71.

Svensson, Lars-Gunnar. Erratum [Large Indivisibles: An Analysis with Respect to Price Equilibrium and Fairness]. *Econometrica*, March 1987, *55*(2), pp. 489.

Thomson, William. The Vulnerability to Manipulative Behavior of Resource Allocation Mechanisms Designed to Select Equitable and Efficient Outcomes. *[Hurwicz, L.]*, 1987, pp. 375–96.

Usher, D. Theft as a Paradigm for Departures from Efficiency. *Oxford Econ. Pap.*, June 1987, *39*(2), pp. 235–52.

Vega-Redondo, Fernando. Efficiency and Nonlinear Pricing in Nonconvex Environments with Externalities: A Generalization of the Lindahl Equilibrium Concept. *J. Econ. Theory*, February 1987, *41*(1), pp. 54–67.

Wenders, John T. On Perfect Rent Dissipation. *Amer. Econ. Rev.*, June 1987, *77*(3), pp. 456–59.

Wooders, Myrna Holtz and Zame, William R. Large Games: Fair and Stable Outcomes. *J. Econ. Theory*, June 1987, *42*(1), pp. 59–93.

0243 Redistribution Analyses

Allen, Stephen P. Taxes, Redistribution, and the Minimum Wage: A Theoretical Analysis. *Quart. J. Econ.*, August 1987, *102*(3), pp. 477–89.

Ballard, Charles L. and Shoven, John B. The Value-Added Tax: The Efficiency Cost of Achieving Progressivity by Using Exemptions. *[Harberger, A.]*, 1987, pp. 109–29.

Breyer, Friedrich and von der Schulenburg, J.-Matthias Graf. Family Structure and Intergenerational Transfers in Social Health Insurance: A Public Choice Model. *Pethig, R. and Schlieper, U., eds.*, 1987, pp. 63–80.

Buchanan, James M. Fairness, Hope, and Justice. *Buchanan, J. M. (I)*, 1987, *1983*, pp. 223–52.

Buchanan, James M. The Justice of Natural Liberty. *Buchanan, J. M. (II)*, 1987, *1976*, pp. 253–68.

Christian, Ernest S., Jr. Consumption Taxes Are Not Regressive. *Walker, C. E. and Bloomfield, M. A., eds.*, 1987, pp. 329–32. **[G: U.S.]**

Cox, Donald. Motives for Private Income Transfers. *J. Polit. Econ.*, June 1987, *95*(3), pp. 508–46. **[G: U.S.]**

Das-Gupta, Arindam. A Note on the Effects of Tax-Subsidy Policies on the Personal Distribution of Income in Dual Economies. *Indian Econ. Rev.*, Jan.-June 1987, *22*(1), pp. 95–105. **[G: LDCs]**

Dasgupta, Partha. The Ethical Foundations of Population Policies. *Johnson, D. G. and Lee, R. D., eds.*, 1987, pp. 631–59.

Drèze, Jacques H. Investment under Private Ownership: Optimality, Equilibrium and Stability. *Drèze, J. H.*, 1987, *1974*, pp. 261–97.

Fallis, George. Rent Control: The Citizen, the Market and the State. *Arnott, R. J. and Mintz, J. M., eds.*, 1987, pp. 163–74.

Feldstein, Martin S. The Welfare Cost of Social Security's Impact on Private Saving. *[Harberger, A.]*, 1987, pp. 1–13.

Garcia Rocha, Adalberto. Inequality and Growth in Mexico. *Salazar-Carrillo, J. and Tirado de Alonzo, I., eds.*, 1987, pp. 1–6.   **[G: Mexico]**

Gevers, L. and Jacquemin, J. C. Redistributive Taxation, Majority Decisions and the Minmax Set. *Europ. Econ. Rev.*, Feb./Mar. 1987, *31*(1/2), pp. 202–11.

González-Vega, Claudio and Zinser, James E. Regulated and Nonregulated Financial and Foreign Exchange Markets and Income Inequality in the Dominican Republic. *Connolly, M. and González-Vega, C., eds.*, 1987, pp. 195–216.   **[G: Dominican Republic]**

Goodin, Robert E. and Dryzek, John. Risk-Sharing and Social Justice: The Motivational Foundations of the Post-war Welfare State. *Goodin, R. E. and Le Grand, J.*, 1987, pp. 37–73.   **[G: U.K.]**

Goodin, Robert E.; Le Grand, Julian and Gibson, D. M. Distributional Biases in Social Service Delivery Systems. *Goodin, R. E. and Le Grand, J.*, 1987, pp. 127–43.   **[G: Australia]**

Guesnerie, Roger and Roberts, Kevin. Minimum Wage Legislation as a Second Best Policy. *Europ. Econ. Rev.*, Feb./Mar. 1987, *31*(1/2), pp. 490–98.

Hammond, Claire Holton. Some Methodological Developments in the Measurement of the Benefit of an In-Kind Transfer. *Amer. Econ.*, Fall 1987, *31*(2), pp. 44–52.

Hansson, Ingemar. Optimal Income Taxation and the Untaxed Sector. *Alessandrini, S. and Dallago, B., eds.*, 1987, pp. 311–21.

Heuss, Ernst. Gerechtigkeit und Marktwirtschaft. (Justice in the Market Economy. With English summary.) *Lenel, H. O., et al., eds.*, 1987, pp. 3–19.

Hutter, Michael. Family Structure and Intergenerational Transfers in Social Health Insurance: A Public Choice Model: Comment. *Pethig, R. and Schlieper, U., eds.*, 1987, pp. 81–82.

Le Grand, Julian. Measuring the Distributional Impact of the Welfare State: Methodological Issues. *Goodin, R. E. and Le Grand, J.*, 1987, pp. 17–33.   **[G: U.K.]**

Matsui, Robert T. Issues of the Regressivity of a Consumption Tax: The Political Dynamics. *Walker, C. E. and Bloomfield, M. A., eds.*, 1987, pp. 333–36.   **[G: U.S.]**

Misiolek, Walter S. and Elder, Harold W. Cost-Effective Redistribution: Implications of a Basic Needs Approach to Public Assistance. *Public Finance Quart.*, January 1987, *15*(1), pp. 76–97.

Olson, Mancur. Why Some Welfare-State Redistribution to the Poor is a Great Idea. *[Tullock, G.]*, 1987, pp. 191–222.

Ray, Debraj. Nonpaternalistic Intergenerational Altruism. *J. Econ. Theory*, February 1987, *41*(1), pp. 112–32.

Rein, Martin and Rainwater, Lee. From Welfare State to Welfare Society. *Rein, M.; Esping-Andersen, G. and Rainwater, L., eds.*, 1987, pp. 143–59.   **[G: OECD]**

Schwartz, Pedro. The Market and the Metamarket: A Review of the Contributions of the Economic Theory of Property Rights. *Pejovich, S., ed.*, 1987, pp. 11–32.

Shibata, Hirofumi and Shibata, Aiko. Rent Redistribution through Provision of Public Goods. *[Kitamura, H.]*, 1987, pp. 268–84.

Shorrocks, Anthony F. and Foster, James E. Transfer Sensitive Inequality Measures. *Rev. Econ. Stud.*, July 1987, *54*(3), pp. 485–97.

Smolensky, Eugene; Hoyt, William and Danziger, Sheldon. A Critical Survey of Efforts to Measure Budget Incidence. *van de Kar, H. M. and Wolfe, B. L., eds.*, 1987, pp. 165–79.

Summers, Lawrence H. Taxation and the Size and Composition of the Capital Stock: An Asset Price Approach. *[Harberger, A.]*, 1987, pp. 61–94.

Tarditi, Secondo and Croci-Angelini, Elisabetta. Efficiency and Equity Components of Sector Policy Analysis and Evaluation. *Léon, Y. and Mahé, L., eds.*, 1987, pp. 43–80.   **[G: Italy]**

Tideman, T. Nicolaus and Coats, R. Morris. An Instrumental-Variables Approach to Income Redistribution. *Public Choice*, 1987, *52*(2), pp. 187–92.

Tobin, James. Considerations Regarding Taxation and Inequality. *Tobin, J. (III)*, 1987, *1977*, pp. 479–87.   **[G: U.S.]**

Turunen, Arja H. Economic Inequality and Public Policy in a Small Open Economy. *Scand. J. Econ.*, 1987, *89*(4), pp. 405–19.

Vasquez, Thomas E. Addressing Issues of the Regressivity of a Consumption Tax. *Walker, C. E. and Bloomfield, M. A., eds.*, 1987, pp. 311–28.   **[G: U.S.]**

Vaubel, Roland. The Philosophical Basis of the Free Society. *Lenel, H. O., et al., eds.*, 1987, pp. 21–29.

Zimmermann, Klaus F. Transfers, Perfect Foresight and the Efficacy of Demand Policy. *J. Inst. Theoretical Econ.*, December 1987, *143*(4), pp. 652–57.

0244 Externalities

Anderson, Terry L. and Hill, Peter J. Privatizing the Commons: Reply. *Southern Econ. J.*, July 1987, *54*(1), pp. 225–26.

Bird, Peter J. W. N. The Transferability and Depletability of Externalities. *J. Environ. Econ. Manage.*, March 1987, *14*(1), pp. 54–57.

Brito, Dagobert L. and Intriligator, Michael D. Stock Externalities, Pigovian Taxation and Dynamic Stability. *J. Public Econ.*, June 1987, *33*(1), pp. 59–72.

Buchanan, James M. Externality. *Buchanan, J. M. (I)*, 1987, *1962*, pp. 121–35.

Buchanan, James M. Rights, Efficiency, and Exchange: The Irrelevance of Transaction Cost. *Buchanan, J. M. (II)*, 1987, *1984*, pp. 153–68.

Buchanan, James M. and Stubblebine, William Craig. Externality. *Buchanan, J. M. (II)*, 1987, *1962*, pp. 97–111.

Buchanan, James M. and Tullock, Gordon. Public and Private Interaction under Reciprocal Externality. *Buchanan, J. M. (II)*, 1987, *1965*, pp. 113–39.

Coleman, James S. Norms as Social Capital. *Radnitzky, G. and Bernholz, P., eds.*, 1987, pp. 133–55.

Conrad, Klaus. An Incentive Scheme for Optimal Pricing and Environmental Protection. *J. Inst. Theoretical Econ.*, September 1987, *143*(3), pp. 402–21.

Furubotn, Eirik G. Privatizing the Commons: Comment. *Southern Econ. J.*, July 1987, *54*(1), pp. 219–24.

Grossman, Sanford J. and Hart, Oliver. Vertical Integration and the Distribution of Property Rights. *Razin, A. and Sadka, E., eds.*, 1987, pp. 504–46.

Harrison, Glenn W., et al. Coasian Solutions to the Externality Problem in Experimental Markets. *Econ. J.*, June 1987, *97*(386), pp. 388–402.

Ihlanfeldt, Keith R. and Boehm, Thomas P. Government Intervention in the Housing Market: An Empirical Test of the Externalities Rationale. *J. Urban Econ.*, November 1987, *22*(3), pp. 276–90. **[G: U.S.]**

Kolstad, Charles D. Uniformity versus Differentiation in Regulating Externalities. *J. Environ. Econ. Manage.*, December 1987, *14*(4), pp. 386–99.

Moulin, Hervé J. The Pure Compensation Problem: Egalitarianism versus Laissez-Fairism. *Quart. J. Econ.*, November 1987, *102*(4), pp. 769–83.

Segerson, Kathleen. Risk-Sharing and Liability in the Control of Stochastic Externalities. *Marine Resource Econ.*, 1987, *4*(3), pp. 175–92. **[G: U.S.]**

Tauman, Yair. Vertical Integration and the Distribution of Property Rights: Comments. *Razin, A. and Sadka, E., eds.*, 1987, pp. 547–48.

Taylor, John B. Externalities Associated with Nominal Price and Wage Rigidities. *Barnett, W. A. and Singleton, K. J., eds.*, 1987, pp. 350–67.

Teubal, Morris and Steinmueller, Edward. The Introduction of a Major New Technology: Externalities and Government Policy. *Teubal, M.*, 1987, pp. 259–79.

Veljanovski, Cento. The Demsetz-Hypothesis on the Emergence of Property Rights Reconsidered: Comment. *Pethig, R. and Schlieper, U., eds.*, 1987, pp. 95–101.

Willis, Robert J. Externalities and Population. *Johnson, D. G. and Lee, R. D., eds.*, 1987, pp. 661–702.

Witt, Ulrich. The Demsetz-Hypothesis on the Emergence of Property Rights Reconsidered. *Pethig, R. and Schlieper, U., eds.*, 1987, pp. 83–93.

025 Social Choice

0250 General

Aranson, Peter H.; Boyd, William A. and Lancaster, Thomas D. Political Science and Public Choice: A Quarter-Century Retrospective. *Nagel, S. S., ed.*, 1987, pp. 137–86.

Backhaus, Jürgen and Wagner, Richard E. The Cameralists: A Public Choice Perspective. *Public Choice*, 1987, *53*(1), pp. 3–20.

Bates, Robert H. Essays on the Political Economy of Rural Africa: Conclusion. *Bates, R. H.*, 1987, pp. 134–47.

Blankart, Charles B. Fourteen Years of European Public Choice Society Research. *Public Choice*, 1987, *52*(1), pp. 3–14. **[G: W. Europe]**

Blecha, Betty J. The Crowding Parameter and Samuelsonian Publicness [Micro Estimates of Public Spending Demand Functions and Tests of the Tiebout and Median-Voter Hypotheses]. *J. Polit. Econ.*, June 1987, *95*(3), pp. 622–31. **[G: U.S.]**

Buchanan, James M. Costituzione e politica economica. (The Constitution of Economic Policy. With English summary.) *Econ. Scelte Pubbliche/J. Public Finance Public Choice*, Jan.-Apr. 1987, *5*(1), pp. 3–14.

Buchanan, James M. The Public Choice Perspective. *Buchanan, J. M. (I)*, 1987, *1983*, pp. 253–60. **[G: U.S.]**

Buchanan, James M. and Brennan, Geoffrey. The Normative Purpose of Economic "Science": Rediscovery of an Eighteenth Century Method. *Buchanan, J. M. (II)*, 1987, *1981*, pp. 51–65.

Buchanan, James M. and Lee, Dwight R. Politics, Time, and the Laffer Curve. *Buchanan, J. M. (II)*, 1987, *1982*, pp. 409–13.

Caslin, Terry. The State and the Economy. *Vane, H. and Caslin, T., eds.*, 1987, pp. 24–42.

Faith, Roger L.; Leavens, Donald R. and Tollison, Robert D. Antitrust Pork Barrel. *MacKay, R. J.; Miller, J. C., III and Yandle, B., eds.*, 1987, *1982*, pp. 15–29. **[G: U.S.]**

Feiwel, George R. Arrow's Weltanschauung. *Rivista Int. Sci. Econ. Com.*, Jan.-Feb. 1987, *34*(1–2), pp. 1–50.

Feiwel, George R. The Many Dimensions of Kenneth J. Arrow. *Feiwel, G. R., ed. (II)*, 1987, pp. 1–115.

Feiwel, George R. The Potentials and Limits of Economic Analysis: The Contributions of Kenneth J. Arrow. *Feiwel, G. R., ed. (I)*, 1987, pp. 1–187.

Hewett, Roger S. Public Finance, Public Economics, and Public Choice: A Survey of Undergraduate Textbooks. *J. Econ. Educ.*, Fall 1987, *18*(4), pp. 425–35. **[G: U.S.]**

Hibbs, Douglas A., Jr. Economic Outcomes and Political Support for British Governments among the Occupational Classes: A Dynamic Analysis. *Hibbs, D. A., Jr.*, 1987, *1982*, pp. 258–89. **[G: U.K.]**

Hirshleifer, Jack. Toward a More General Theory of Regulation: Comment. *Hirshleifer, J.*, 1987, *1976*, pp. 164–68.

Hoppmann, Erich. Ökonomische Theorie der Verfassung. (Economic Theory of Constitutions. With English summary.) *Lenel, H. O., et al., eds.*, 1987, pp. 31–45.

Klein, Philip A. Power and Economic Performance: The Institutionalist View. *J. Econ. Issues*, September 1987, *21*(3), pp. 1341–77.

Lankford, R. Hamilton. A Note on Measuring Flypaper Effects [Income and Grant Effects on Local Expenditure: The Flypaper Effect and Other Difficulties]. *J. Urban Econ.*, July 1987, *22*(1), pp. 113–15. **[G: U.S.]**

Maier, Charles S. "Fictitious Bonds . . . of Wealth and law": On the Theory and Practice of Interest Representation. *Maier, C. S.*, 1987, *1981*, pp. 225–60. **[G: W. Europe]**

Mayer, Wolfgang. Endogenous Tariff Formation. *Bhagwati, J. N., ed.*, 1987, *1984*, pp. 329–52.

Naqvi, Syed Nawab Haider. The Anatomy of 'Failures'. *Pakistan Devel. Rev.*, Autumn 1987, *26*(3), pp. 257–72.

Ng, Yew-Kwang. "Political Distortions" and the Relevance of Second and Third-Best Theories. *Public Finance*, 1987, *42*(1), pp. 137–45.

Ng, Yew-Kwang. The Role of Economists and Third-Best Policies. *Public Finance*, 1987, *42*(1), pp. 152–55.

Orr, Daniel. Notes on the Mass Media as an Economic Institution. *Public Choice*, 1987, *53*(1), pp. 79–95.

Radnitzky, Gerard. An Economic Theory of the Rise of Civilization and Its Policy Implications: Hayek's Account Generalized. *Lenel, H. O., et al., eds.*, 1987, pp. 47–90.

Rowley, Charles K. Democracy and Public Choice: Introduction. *[Tullock, G.]*, 1987, pp. 1–5.

Sonnenschein, Hugo. Theory and Method—Second-Generation Perspective: An Interview. *Feiwel, G. R., ed. (I)*, 1987, pp. 325–39.

Weingast, Barry R. and Moran, Mark J. Bureaucratic Discretion or Congressional Control? Regulatory Policymaking by the Federal Trade Commission. *MacKay, R. J.; Miller, J. C., III and Yandle, B., eds.*, 1987, *1983*, pp. 30–62. **[G: U.S.]**

Yotopoulos, Pan A. The Anatomy of 'Failures': Comments. *Pakistan Devel. Rev.*, Autumn 1987, *26*(3), pp. 273–74.

0251 Social Choice Theory

Abdou, Joseph. Stability of Topological Effectivity Functions. *Soc. Choice Welfare*, September 1987, *4*(3), pp. 163–71.

Abdou, Joseph. Topological Veto Correspondences. *Écon. Appl.*, 1987, *40*(1), pp. 5–33.

Abrams, Burton A. and Lewis, Kenneth A. A Median-Voter Model of Economic Regulation. *Public Choice*, 1987, *52*(2), pp. 125–42.

Abrams, Burton A. and Lewis, Kenneth A. The Effect of Information Costs on Regulatory Outcomes. *J. Econ. Bus.*, May 1987, *39*(2), pp. 159–70.

Alesina, Alberto. Macroeconomic Policy in a Two-Party System as a Repeated Game. *Quart. J. Econ.*, August 1987, *102*(3), pp. 651–78.

Alesina, Alberto. Rules, Discretion and Reputation in a Two-Party System. *Giorn. Econ.*, Jan.-Feb. 1987, *46*(1–2), pp. 3–27.

Appelbaum, Elie and Katz, Eliakim. Seeking Rents by Setting Rents: The Political Economy of Rent Seeking. *Econ. J.*, September 1987, *97*(387), pp. 685–99.

Aranson, Peter H. Calculus and Consent. *[Tullock, G.]*, 1987, pp. 60–65.

Aranson, Peter H. Procedural and Substantive Constitutional Protection of Economic Liberties. *Cato J.*, Fall 1987, *7*(2), pp. 345–75. **[G: U.S.]**

Arnold, R. Douglas. Political Control of Administrative Officials. *J. Law, Econ., Organ.*, Fall 1987, *3*(2), pp. 279–86. **[G: U.S.]**

d'Aspremont, Claude; Jacquemin, Alexis and Mertens, J.-F. A Measure of Aggregate Power in Organizations. *J. Econ. Theory*, October 1987, *43*(1), pp. 184–91.

Atkinson, Anthony B. James M. Buchanan's Contributions to Economics. *Scand. J. Econ.*, 1987, *89*(1), pp. 5–15.

Aumann, Robert J.; Kurz, Mordecai and Neyman, Abraham. Power and Public Goods. *J. Econ. Theory*, June 1987, *42*(1), pp. 108–27.

Austen-Smith, David. Interest Groups, Campaign Contributions, and Probabilistic Voting. *Public Choice*, 1987, *54*(2), pp. 123–39.

Austen-Smith, David. Parties, Districts and the Spatial Theory of Elections. *Soc. Choice Welfare*, March 1987, *4*(1), pp. 9–23.

Baigent, Nick. Metric Rationalisation of Social Choice Functions According to Principles of Social Choice. *Math. Soc. Sci.*, February 1987, *13*(1), pp. 59–65.

Baigent, Nick. Preference Proximity and Anonymous Social Choice. *Quart. J. Econ.*, February 1987, *102*(1), pp. 161–69.

Baigent, Nick. Twitching Weak Dictators. *J. Econ. (Z. Nationalökon.)*, 1987, *47*(4), pp. 407–11.

Balisacan, Arsenio M. Political Investment in Economic Protection: A Note. *Philippine Rev. Econ. Bus.*, Mar.-June 1987, *24*(1–2), pp. 149–57.

Banks, Jeffrey S. and Gasmi, F. Endogenous Agenda Formation in Three-Person Committees. *Soc. Choice Welfare*, June 1987, *4*(2), pp. 133–52.

Barnett, Richard R. and Bone, John. A Note on Fiscal Preferences. *Scot. J. Polit. Econ.*, August 1987, *34*(3), pp. 285–90.

Baron, David P. and Ferejohn, John A. Bargaining and Agenda Formation in Legislatures. *Amer. Econ. Rev.*, May 1987, *77*(2), pp. 303–09.

Bendor, Jonathan and Mookherjee, Dilip. Institutional Structure and the Logic of Ongoing

Collective Action. *Amer. Polit. Sci. Rev.*, March 1987, *81*(1), pp. 129–54.

Bernheim, B. Douglas; Peleg, Bezalel and Whinston, Michael D. Coalition-Proof Nash Equilibria: Concepts. *J. Econ. Theory*, June 1987, *42*(1), pp. 1–12.

Bernheim, B. Douglas and Whinston, Michael D. Coalition-Proof Nash Equilibria: Applications. *J. Econ. Theory*, June 1987, *42*(1), pp. 13–29.

Bezembinder, Th. and van Acker, P. Erratum [Factual versus Representational Utilities and Their Interdimensional Comparisons]. *Soc. Choice Welfare*, September 1987, *4*(3), pp. 240.

Bezembinder, Th. and van Acker, P. Factual versus Representational Utilities and Their Interdimensional Comparisons. *Soc. Choice Welfare*, June 1987, *4*(2), pp. 79–104.

Bhagwati, Jagdish N.; Brecher, Richard A. and Srinivasan, T. N. DUP Activities and Economic Theory. *Bhagwati, J. N., ed.*, 1987, *1984*, pp. 311–28.

Bish, Robert L. Federalism: A Market Economics Perspective. *Cato J.*, Fall 1987, *7*(2), pp. 377–96.

Blankart, Charles B. Free Riders and Voluntary Contributions Reconsidered: Comment. *Pethig, R. and Schlieper, U., eds.*, 1987, pp. 179–81.

Brennan, Geoffrey and Lomasky, Loren E. The Logic of Electoral Preference: Response [The Impartial Spectator Goes to Washington: Toward a Smithian Theory of Electoral Behavior]. *Econ. Philos.*, April 1987, *3*(1), pp. 131–38.

Breyer, Friedrich and von der Schulenburg, J.-Matthias Graf. Family Structure and Intergenerational Transfers in Social Health Insurance: A Public Choice Model. *Pethig, R. and Schlieper, U., eds.*, 1987, pp. 63–80.

Brooks, Michael A. In Search of Optimum 'Relative Unanimity': A Comment. *Public Choice*, August 1987, *54*(3), pp. 283–88.

Brooks, Michael A. and Heijdra, Ben J. Rent-Seeking and Pollution Taxation: An Extension. *Southern Econ. J.*, October 1987, *54*(2), pp. 335–42.

Brown, Stephen P. A. The Fairness of Discounting: A Majority Rule Approach. *Public Choice*, October 1987, *55*(3), pp. 215–26.

Buchanan, James M. An Economic Theory of Clubs. *Buchanan, J. M. (II)*, 1987, *1965*, pp. 207–21.

Buchanan, James M. An Economic Theory of Clubs. *Buchanan, J. M. (I)*, 1987, *1965*, pp. 209–22.

Buchanan, James M. An Individualistic Theory of Political Process. *Buchanan, J. M. (II)*, 1987, *1966*, pp. 223–35.

Buchanan, James M. Can Policy Activism Succeed? A Public Choice Perspective. *Wilcox, J. A., ed.*, 1987, *1986*, pp. 268–79.

Buchanan, James M. Fairness, Hope, and Justice. *Buchanan, J. M. (I)*, 1987, *1983*, pp. 223–52.

Buchanan, James M. Foreword to *The Politics of Bureaucracy*. *Buchanan, J. M. (II)*, 1987, *1965*, pp. 199–206.

Buchanan, James M. Individual Choice in Voting and the Market. *Buchanan, J. M. (II)*, 1987, *1954*, pp. 185–97.

Buchanan, James M. Individual Choice in Voting and the Market. *Buchanan, J. M. (I)*, 1987, *1954*, pp. 197–208.

Buchanan, James M. Is Economics the Science of Choice? *Buchanan, J. M. (II)*, 1987, *1969*, pp. 35–50.

Buchanan, James M. Justification of the Compound Republic: The *Calculus* in Retrospect. *Cato J.*, Fall 1987, *7*(2), pp. 305–12.

Buchanan, James M. Moral Community, Moral Order, or Moral Anarchy. *Buchanan, J. M. (II)*, 1987, *1981*, pp. 289–301.   [G: U.S.; Japan]

Buchanan, James M. Politics, Policy, and the Pigovian Margins. *Buchanan, J. M. (II)*, 1987, *1962*, pp. 83–95.

Buchanan, James M. Positive Economics, Welfare Economics, and Political Economy. *Buchanan, J. M. (II)*, 1987, *1959*, pp. 3–19.

Buchanan, James M. Rights, Efficiency, and Exchange: The Irrelevance of Transaction Cost. *Buchanan, J. M. (II)*, 1987, *1984*, pp. 153–68.

Buchanan, James M. Social Choice, Democracy, and Free Markets. *Buchanan, J. M. (II)*, 1987, *1954*, pp. 171–83.

Buchanan, James M. The Constitution of Economic Policy. *Buchanan, J. M. (II)*, 1987, pp. 303–14.

Buchanan, James M. The Constitution of Economic Policy. *Amer. Econ. Rev.*, June 1987, *77*(3), pp. 243–50.

Buchanan, James M. The Relatively Absolute Absolutes. *Buchanan, J. M. (I)*, 1987, pp. 287–97.

Buchanan, James M. Towards a Theory of Rational Deference in Constitutional Construction. *Buchanan, J. M. (I)*, 1987, pp. 275–85.

Buchanan, James M. and Brennan, Geoffrey. The Normative Purpose of Economic "Science": Rediscovery of an Eighteenth Century Method. *Buchanan, J. M. (II)*, 1987, *1981*, pp. 51–65.

Buchanan, James M. and Tullock, Gordon. Public and Private Interaction under Reciprocal Externality. *Buchanan, J. M. (II)*, 1987, *1965*, pp. 113–39.

Buchanan, James M. and Wagner, Richard E. The Political Biases of Keynesian Economics. *Buchanan, J. M. (II)*, 1987, *1978*, pp. 389–408.

Cadot, Olivier. Corruption as a Gamble. *J. Public Econ.*, July 1987, *33*(2), pp. 223–44.

Calvert, Randall L. Reputation and Legislative Leadership. *Public Choice*, September 1987, *55*(1–2), pp. 81–119.

Campbell, D. E. Revealed Social Preference. *Soc. Choice Welfare*, September 1987, *4*(3), pp. 225–34.

Carson, Richard L. The Voting Paradox and the Possibility of a Social Welfare Function. *East-*

ern Econ. J., July-Sept. 1987, *13*(3), pp. 281–94.

Cave, Jonathan and Salant, Stephen W. Cartels That Vote: Agricultural Marketing Boards and Induced Voting Behavior. *Bailey, E. E., ed.*, 1987, pp. 255–83. [G: U.S.]

Cebula, Richard J. and Kafoglis, Milton Z. In Search of Optimum 'Relative Unanimity': Reply. *Public Choice*, August 1987, *54*(3), pp. 289–90.

Chan, James L. and Rubin, Marc A. The Role of Information in a Democracy and in Government Operations: The Public Choice Methodology. *Chan, J. L., ed., Pt. B*, 1987, pp. 3–27.

Chang, Winston W. and Southwick, Lawrence, Jr. On the Pricing and Benefit Structure of a Private Club or Public Utility. *Public Choice*, October 1987, *55*(3), pp. 227–44.

Chipman, John S. When Is a Fixed Income Distribution Optimal? *Feiwel, G. R., ed. (II)*, 1987, pp. 371–81.

Coleman, James S. Norms as Social Capital. *Radnitzky, G. and Bernholz, P., eds.*, 1987, pp. 133–55.

Collazzo, Charles. The Need for Voluntary Consensus Systems in Setting Socio-economic Standards. *Int. J. Soc. Econ.*, 1987, *14*(7/8/9), pp. 115–26.

Crenson, Matthew A. The Private Stake in Public Goods: Overcoming the Illogic of Collective Action. *Policy Sci.*, 1987, *20*(3), pp. 259–76.

Crew, Michael A. Rent-Seeking Is Here to Stay. *[Tullock, G.]*, 1987, pp. 158–62.

Cukierman, Alex and Meltzer, Allan H. Errata [A Positive Theory of Discretionary Policy, the Cost of Democratic Government and the Benefits of a Constitution]. *Econ. Inquiry*, April 1987, *25*(2), pp. 363–65.

Deb, Rajat and Kelsey, David. On Constructing a Generalized Ostrogorski Paradox: Necessary and Sufficient Conditions. *Math. Soc. Sci.*, October 1987, *14*(2), pp. 161–74.

Demange, Gabrielle. Nonmanipulable Cores. *Econometrica*, September 1987, *55*(5), pp. 1057–74.

Denicolò, V. Some Further Results on Nonbinary Social Choice. *Soc. Choice Welfare*, December 1987, *4*(4), pp. 277–85.

Deno, Kevin T. and Mehay, Stephen L. Municipal Management Structure and Fiscal Performance: Do City Managers Make a Difference? *Southern Econ. J.*, January 1987, *53*(3), pp. 627–42. [G: U.S.]

Donaldson, David and Roemer, John E. Social Choice in Economic Environments with Dimensional Variation. *Soc. Choice Welfare*, December 1987, *4*(4), pp. 253–76.

Dorn, James A. Government, the Economy, and the Constitution: Introduction. *Cato J.*, Fall 1987, *7*(2), pp. 283–303. [G: U.S.]

Dragun, A. K. Property Rights in Economic Theory. *J. Econ. Issues*, June 1987, *21*(2), pp. 859–68.

Dutta, Bhaskar. Fuzzy Preferences and Social Choice. *Math. Soc. Sci.*, June 1987, *13*(3), pp. 215–29.

Dye, Thomas R. The Politics of Constitutional Choice. *Cato J.*, Fall 1987, *7*(2), pp. 337–44. [G: U.S.]

Eavey, Cheryl L. Bureaucratic Competition and Agenda Control. *J. Conflict Resolution*, September 1987, *31*(3), pp. 503–24.

Ebert, Udo. A Note on Social Welfare Orderings. *Europ. Econ. Rev.*, July 1987, *31*(5), pp. 1145–47.

Enelow, J. M. and Hinich, Melvin J. Optimal Decision Making When the Shapes and Locations of Voter Preference Curves Are Unknown. *Econ. Scelte Pubbliche/J. Public Finance Public Choice*, Sept.-Dec. 1987, *5*(3), pp. 161–70.

Epple, Dennis and Riordan, Michael H. Cooperation and Punishment under Repeated Majority Voting. *Public Choice*, September 1987, *55*(1–2), pp. 41–73.

Eusepi, Giuseppe. General Implications of Subjectivism and Dynamics in Buchanan's Works. *Econ. Int.*, February 1987, *40*(1), pp. 55–66.

Findlay, Ronald and Wilson, John Douglas. The Political Economy of Leviathan. *Razin, A. and Sadka, E., eds.*, 1987, pp. 289–304.

Flanders, M. June. The Political Economy of Leviathan: Comments. *Razin, A. and Sadka, E., eds.*, 1987, pp. 305–06.

Flowers, Marilyn R. Rent Seeking and Rent Dissipation: A Critical View. *Cato J.*, Fall 1987, *7*(2), pp. 431–40.

Forte, Francesco. The Laffer Curve and the Theory of Fiscal Bureaucracy. *Public Choice*, 1987, *52*(2), pp. 101–24.

Garber, Steven. The Economics and Political Economy of Broadcasting: Challenges in Developing an Analytic Foundation: A Comment. *Public Finance Quart.*, July 1987, *15*(3), pp. 189–98.

Gardner, Roy J. A Theory of the Spoils System. *Public Choice*, 1987, *54*(2), pp. 171–85.

Gensemer, Susan H. and Kelly, Jerry S. An Efficient Algorithm for Voting Sequences. *Math. Soc. Sci.*, August 1987, *14*(1), pp. 59–75.

Gevers, L. and Jacquemin, J. C. Redistributive Taxation, Majority Decisions and the Minmax Set. *Europ. Econ. Rev.*, Feb./Mar. 1987, *31*(1/2), pp. 202–11.

Gibbard, Allan F. Ordinal Utilitarianism. *Feiwel, G. R., ed. (II)*, 1987, pp. 135–53.

Gibbard, Allan F.; Hylland, Aanund and Weymark, John A. Arrow's Theorem with a Fixed Feasible Alternative. *Soc. Choice Welfare*, June 1987, *4*(2), pp. 105–15.

Gifford, Adam, Jr. Rent Seeking and Nonprice Competition. *Quart. Rev. Econ. Bus.*, Summer 1987, *27*(2), pp. 63–70.

Gilligan, Thomas W. and Krehbiel, Keith. Collective Decisionmaking and Standing Committees: An Informational Rationale for Restrictive Amendment Procedures. *J. Law, Econ., Organ.*, Fall 1987, *3*(2), pp. 287–335.

Goetz, Charles J. Public Choice and the Law:

The Paradox of Tullock. *[Tullock, G.]*, 1987, pp. 171–80.

Goetze, David. Identifying Appropriate Institutions for Efficient Use of Common Pools. *Natural Res. J.*, Winter 1987, *27*(1), pp. 187–99.

Grafstein, Robert. Rational Choice and Social Theory. *Soc. Sci. Quart.*, June 1987, *68*(2), pp. 258–63.

Gray, John. The Economic Approach to Human Behavior: Its Prospects and Limitations. *Radnitzky, G. and Bernholz, P., eds.*, 1987, pp. 33–49.

Green, Edward J. Cooperation and Punishment under Repeated Majority Voting: A Comment. *Public Choice*, September 1987, *55*(1–2), pp. 75–79.

Groves, Theodore and Ledyard, John O. Incentive Compatibility since 1972. *[Hurwicz, L.]*, 1987, pp. 48–111.

Guttman, Joel M. A Non-Cournot Model of Voluntary Collective Action. *Economica*, February 1987, *54*(213), pp. 1–19.

Hadari, Saguiv A. Rational Choice in Social Theory. *Soc. Sci. Quart.*, June 1987, *68*(2), pp. 264–66.

Hammond, Peter J. On Reconciling Arrow's Theory of Social Choice with Harsanyi's Fundamental Utilitarianism. *Feiwel, G. R., ed. (II)*, 1987, pp. 179–221.

Hammond, Peter J. Social Choice: The Science of the Impossible? *Feiwel, G. R., ed. (II)*, 1987, pp. 116–31.

Hammond, Thomas H. and Miller, Gary J. Distant Friends and Nearby Enemies: The Politics of Legislative Coalition Formation. *Public Choice*, 1987, *53*(3), pp. 277–84.

Hansen, Stephen; Palfrey, Thomas R. and Rosenthal, Howard. The Downsian Model of Electoral Participation: Formal Theory and Empirical Analysis of the Constituency Size Effect. *Public Choice*, 1987, *52*(1), pp. 15–33. [G: U.S.]

Harel, Alon and Nitzan, Shmuel. The Libertarian Resolution of the Paretian Liberal Paradox. *J. Econ. (Z. Nationalökon.)*, 1987, *47*(4), pp. 337–52.

Hartley, Keith. Reducing Defence Expenditure: A Public Choice Analysis and a Case Study of the UK. *Schmidt, C. and Blackaby, F., eds.*, 1987, pp. 399–423. [G: U.K.]

Hartley, Richard and Kilgour, D. Marc. The Geometry of the Uncovered Set in the Three-Voter Spatial Model. *Math. Soc. Sci.*, October 1987, *14*(2), pp. 175–83.

Havrilesky, Thomas M. A Partisanship Theory of Fiscal and Monetary Regimes. *J. Money, Credit, Banking*, August 1987, *19*(3), pp. 308–25.

Hewitt, Daniel P. Market Vote Trading and Efficient Public Choice. *Public Finance*, 1987, *42*(1), pp. 85–104.

Hibbs, Douglas A., Jr. Economic Outcomes and Political Support for British Governments among the Occupational Classes: A Dynamic Analysis. *Hibbs, D. A., Jr.*, 1987, *1982*, pp. 258–89. [G: U.K.]

Hibbs, Douglas A., Jr. The Dynamics of Political Support for American Presidents among Occupational and Partisan Groups. *Hibbs, D. A., Jr.*, 1987, *1982*, pp. 143–63. [G: U.S.]

Hillman, Arye L. and Katz, Eliakim. Hierarchical Structure and the Social Costs of Bribes and Transfers. *J. Public Econ.*, November 1987, *34*(2), pp. 129–42.

Hillman, Arye L. and Samet, Dov. Characterizing Equilibrium Rent-Seeking Behavior: A Reply. *Public Choice*, 1987, *54*(1), pp. 85–87.

Hillman, Arye L. and Samet, Dov. Dissipation of Contestable Rents by Small Numbers of Contenders. *Public Choice*, 1987, *54*(1), pp. 63–82.

Holzman, R. Sub-core Solutions of the Problem of Strong Implementation. *Int. J. Game Theory*, 1987, *16*(4), pp. 263–89.

Hong, Yoo Soo. Power Structure and Rent Competition. *Int. Econ. J.*, Winter 1987, *1*(4), pp. 45–60.

Houston, Douglas A. The Mixed Interest in Regulation and Deregulation [Rent Seeking and Profit Seeking]. *Land Econ.*, November 1987, *63*(4), pp. 403–05.

Hudelson, Richard. A Note on the Empirical Adequacy of the Expressive Theory of Voting Behavior [The Impartial Spectator Goes to Washington: Toward a Smithian Theory of Electoral Behavior]. *Econ. Philos.*, April 1987, *3*(1), pp. 127–30.

Hutter, Michael. Family Structure and Intergenerational Transfers in Social Health Insurance: A Public Choice Model: Comment. *Pethig, R. and Schlieper, U., eds.*, 1987, pp. 81–82.

Ingberman, Daniel E. Reputation and Legislative Leadership: Comment. *Public Choice*, September 1987, *55*(1–2), pp. 121–26.

Jain, Satish K. Maximal Conditions for Transitivity and Monotonic Binary Social Decision Rules. *Econ. Stud. Quart.*, June 1987, *38*(2), pp. 124–30.

Jones, Philip R. and Cullis, John G. Fiscal Preferences and Tax-Prices: A Rejoinder. *Scot. J. Polit. Econ.*, August 1987, *34*(3), pp. 291–94.

Kelly, Jerry S. Conjectures and Unsolved Problems: Voting Sets. *Soc. Choice Welfare*, September 1987, *4*(3), pp. 235–39.

Kelly, Jerry S. Profile Restrictions and Strategy-Proofness. *Soc. Choice Welfare*, March 1987, *4*(1), pp. 63–67.

Kelsey, David. The Role of Information in Social Welfare Judgements. *Oxford Econ. Pap.*, June 1987, *39*(2), pp. 301–17.

Kemp, Murray C. and Ng, Yew-Kwang. Arrow's Independence Condition and the Bergson–Samuelson Tradition. *Feiwel, G. R., ed. (II)*, 1987, pp. 223–41.

Khalil, Elias L. Sir James Steuart vs. Professor James Buchanan: Critical Notes on Modern Public Choice. *Rev. Soc. Econ.*, October 1987, *45*(2), pp. 113–32.

Kirchgässner, Gebhard and Wolters, Jürgen. The Influence of Poll Results on Election Outcomes. *Math. Soc. Sci.*, April 1987, *13*(2), pp. 165–75. [G: W. Germany]

Koford, Kenneth J. Scale Economies and Rent-Seeking in Legislative Parties. *Public Choice*, 1987, *52*(1), pp. 35–55. [G: U.S.]

Krause, Ulrich. Hierarchical Structures in Multicriteria Decision Making. *Jahn, J. and Krabs, W., eds.*, 1987, pp. 183–93.

Krehbiel, Keith. Sophisticated Committees and Structure-Induced Equilibria in Congress. *McCubbins, M. D. and Sullivan, T., eds.*, 1987, pp. 376–402. [G: U.S.]

Krueger, Anne O. The Political Economy of the Rent-Seeking Society. *Bhagwati, J. N., ed.*, 1987, *1974*, pp. 291–309.

Kuran, Timur. Chameleon Voters and Public Choice. *Public Choice*, 1987, *53*(1), pp. 53–78.

Kuran, Timur. Preference Falsification, Policy Continuity and Collective Conservatism. *Econ. J.*, September 1987, *97*(387), pp. 642–65.

Laing, James D. and Slotznick, Benjamin. Viable Alternatives to the Status Quo: A Game-Theoretic and Laboratory Study of Four-Fifths Majority Rule. *J. Conflict Resolution*, March 1987, *31*(1), pp. 63–85.

Le Breton, Michel. On the Core of Voting Games. *Soc. Choice Welfare*, December 1987, *4*(4), pp. 295–305.

Le Breton, Michel and Salles, M. On the Generic Emptiness of the Local Core of Voting Games. *Soc. Choice Welfare*, December 1987, *4*(4), pp. 287–94.

Le Breton, Michel and Trannoy, Alain. Measures of Inequality as an Aggregation of Individual Preferences about Income Distribution: The Arrowian Case. *J. Econ. Theory*, April 1987, *41*(2), pp. 248–69.

Lee, Dwight R. The *Calculus of Consent* and the Constitution of Capitalism. *Cato J.*, Fall 1987, *7*(2), pp. 331–36. [G: U.S.]

Lee, Dwight R. The Tradeoff between Equality and Efficiency: Short-run Politics and Long-run Realities. *Public Choice*, 1987, *53*(2), pp. 149–65.

Lensberg, Terje. Stability and Collective Rationality. *Econometrica*, July 1987, *55*(4), pp. 935–61.

Lichbach, Mark Irving. Deterrence or Escalation? The Puzzle of Aggregate Studies of Repression and Dissent. *J. Conflict Resolution*, June 1987, *31*(2), pp. 266–97.

Long, Ngo Van and Vousden, Neil J. Risk-Averse Rent Seeking with Shared Rents. *Econ. J.*, December 1987, *97*(388), pp. 971–85.

Lott, John R., Jr. Externalities, Agency Structure, and the Level of Transfers. *Public Choice*, 1987, *53*(3), pp. 285–87.

MacIntyre, I. D. A. "The Liberal Paradox: A Generalisation" by D. Kelsey [Collective Choice and Social Welfare]. *Soc. Choice Welfare*, September 1987, *4*(3), pp. 219–23.

Marschak, Thomas. Price versus Direct Revelation: Informational Judgments for Finite Mechanisms. *[Hurwicz, L.]*, 1987, pp. 132–79.

Maussner, Alfred. Public Consumption, Optimal Capital Accumulation and the Social Rate of Time Preference. *J. Inst. Theoretical Econ.*,

June 1987, *143*(2), pp. 324–33.

McCubbins, Mathew D.; Noll, Roger G. and Weingast, Barry R. Administrative Procedures as Instruments of Political Control. *J. Law, Econ., Organ.*, Fall 1987, *3*(2), pp. 243–77. [G: U.S.]

McCubbins, Mathew D. and Schwartz, Thomas. Congressional Oversight Overlooked: Police Patrols versus Fire Alarms. *McCubbins, M. D. and Sullivan, T., eds.*, 1987, *1984*, pp. 426–40. [G: U.S.]

McEachern, William A. Federal Advisory Commissions in an Economic Model of Representative Democracy. *Public Choice*, 1987, *54*(1), pp. 41–62.

McGuire, Robert A.; Ohsfeldt, Robert L. and Van Cott, T. Norman. The Determinants of the Choice between Public and Private Production of a Publicly Funded Service. *Public Choice*, August 1987, *54*(3), pp. 211–30. [G: U.S.]

McKee, Michael and West, Edwin G. Further Perspectives on the Theory of Second-Best. *Public Finance*, 1987, *42*(1), pp. 146–51.

McKelvey, Richard D. and Ordeshook, Peter C. Elections with Limited Information: A Multidimensional Model. *Math. Soc. Sci.*, August 1987, *14*(1), pp. 77–99.

McKelvey, Richard D. and Schofield, Norman. Generalized Symmetry Conditions at a Core Point. *Econometrica*, July 1987, *55*(4), pp. 923–33.

Mezzetti, C. Paretian Efficiency, Rawlsian Justice and the Nozick Theory of Rights. *Soc. Choice Welfare*, March 1987, *4*(1), pp. 25–37.

Mitchell, Douglas W. Candidate Behavior under Mixed Motives. *Soc. Choice Welfare*, June 1987, *4*(2), pp. 153–60.

Mitchell, William C. The Calculus of Consent: Notes in Retrospection. *[Tullock, G.]*, 1987, pp. 66–73.

Monaco, Margaret A. and Rowley, Charles K. A Political Economy of Budget Deficits. *[Tullock, G.]*, 1987, pp. 223–42. [G: U.S.]

Moore, John and Repullo, Rafael. Implementation by Stage Mechanisms: An Introduction. *Europ. Econ. Rev.*, Feb./Mar. 1987, *31*(1/2), pp. 336–41.

Morton, R. B. A Group Majority Voting Model of Public Good Provision. *Soc. Choice Welfare*, June 1987, *4*(2), pp. 117–31.

Moulin, Hervé J. The Pure Compensation Problem: Egalitarianism versus Laissez-Fairism. *Quart. J. Econ.*, November 1987, *102*(4), pp. 769–83.

Mueller, Dennis C. Voting Paradox. *[Tullock, G.]*, 1987, pp. 77–99.

Ng, Yew-Kwang. "Political Distortions" and the Relevance of Second and Third-Best Theories. *Public Finance*, 1987, *42*(1), pp. 137–45.

Ng, Yew-Kwang. The Role of Economists and Third-Best Policies. *Public Finance*, 1987, *42*(1), pp. 152–55.

Niemi, Richard G. and Rasch, Bjørn Erik. An Extension of Black's Theorem on Voting Orders to the Successive Procedure. *Public Choice*,

1987, *54*(2), pp. 187–90.

Niou, Emerson M. S. A Note on Nanson's Rule. *Public Choice*, 1987, *54*(2), pp. 191–93.

Niskanen, William A. Bureaucracy. *[Tullock, G.]*, 1987, pp. 135–40.

Noam, Eli M. A Public and Private-Choice Model of Broadcasting. *Public Choice*, September 1987, *55*(1–2), pp. 163–87.

Noël, Alain. Accumulation, Regulation, and Social Change: An Essay on French Political Economy. *Int. Organ.*, Spring 1987, *41*(2), pp. 303–33. [G: France]

Noll, Roger G. The Political Foundations of Regulatory Policy. *McCubbins, M. D. and Sullivan, T., eds.*, 1987, *1983*, pp. 462–92.

North, Douglass C. Rent-Seeking and the New Institutional Economics. *[Tullock, G.]*, 1987, pp. 163–67.

Olson, Mancur. Why Some Welfare-State Redistribution to the Poor is a Great Idea. *[Tullock, G.]*, 1987, pp. 191–222.

Ordeshook, Peter C. and Schwartz, Thomas. Agendas and the Control of Political Outcomes. *Amer. Polit. Sci. Rev.*, March 1987, *81*(1), pp. 179–99.

Otway, Harry. Value Tree Analysis: An Introduction and an Application to Offshore Oil Drilling: Discussion. *Kleindorfer, P. R. and Kunreuther, H. C., ed.*, 1987, pp. 377–83.

Palfrey, Thomas R. and Srivastava, Sanjay. On Bayesian Implementable Allocations. *Rev. Econ. Stud.*, April 1987, *54*(2), pp. 193–208.

Pasour, E. C., Jr. Rent Seeking: Some Conceptual Problems and Implications. *Rothbard, M. N., ed.*, 1987, pp. 123–43.

Peleg, Bezalel. Cores and Capacities of Compound Simple Games. *Soc. Choice Welfare*, December 1987, *4*(4), pp. 307–16.

Pelikan, Pavel. Why Private Enterprise? Towards a Dynamic Analysis of Economic Institutions and Policies. *Eliasson, G., ed.*, 1987, pp. 133–46.

Pethig, Rüdiger. Free Riders and Voluntary Contributions Reconsidered. *Pethig, R. and Schlieper, U., eds.*, 1987, pp. 153–78.

Plott, Charles R. The Robustness of the Voting Paradox. *[Tullock, G.]*, 1987, pp. 100–102.

Pratt, John W. and Zeckhauser, Richard J. Incentive-Based Decentralization: Expected-Externality Payments Induce Efficient Behaviour in Groups. *Feiwel, G. R., ed. (I)*, 1987, pp. 439–83.

Pressler, Jonathan. Rights and Social Choice: Is There a Paretian Libertarian Paradox? *Econ. Philos.*, April 1987, *3*(1), pp. 1–21.

Ranade, R. R. On the Relative Strengths of Consistency Conditions on Choice Functions. *Soc. Choice Welfare*, September 1987, *4*(3), pp. 207–12.

Rasch, Bjørn Erik. Manipulation and Strategic Voting in the Norwegian Parliament. *Public Choice*, 1987, *52*(1), pp. 57–73. [G: Norway]

Rasmussen, David W. Federalism from a Market Perspective. *Cato J.*, Fall 1987, *7*(2), pp. 397–402.

Repullo, Rafael. A Simple Proof of Maskin's Theorem on Nash Implementation. *Soc. Choice Welfare*, March 1987, *4*(1), pp. 39–41.

Rosenthal, Isadore. Value Tree Analysis: An Introduction and an Application to Offshore Oil Drilling: Discussion. *Kleindorfer, P. R. and Kunreuther, H. C., ed.*, 1987, pp. 383–85.

Rowley, Charles K. The Calculus of Consent. *[Tullock, G.]*, 1987, pp. 41–59.

Russett, Bruce. Economic Change as a Cause of International Conflict. *Schmidt, C. and Blackaby, F., eds.*, 1987, pp. 185–205.

Saari, Donald G. Chaos and the Theory of Elections. *Kurzhanski, A. B. and Sigmund, K., eds.*, 1987, pp. 179–88.

Saari, Donald G. The Source of Some Paradoxes from Social Choice and Probability. *J. Econ. Theory*, February 1987, *41*(1), pp. 1–22.

Saijo, Tatsuyoshi. On Constant Maskin Monotonic Social Choice Functions. *J. Econ. Theory*, August 1987, *42*(2), pp. 382–86.

Samuelson, Paul A. Sparks from Arrow's Anvil. *Feiwel, G. R., ed. (II)*, 1987, pp. 154–78.

Saraydar, Edward. Preferences and Voting Behavior: Smith's Impartial Spectator Revisited [The Impartial Spectator Goes to Washington: Toward a Smithian Theory of Electoral Behavior]. *Econ. Philos.*, April 1987, *3*(1), pp. 121–25.

Schenk, Robert E. Altruism as a Source of Self-Interested Behavior. *Public Choice*, 1987, *53*(2), pp. 187–92.

Schlieper, Ulrich. Macroeconomic Policy, Rent Seeking and Economic Order. *Pethig, R. and Schlieper, U., eds.*, 1987, pp. 27–34.

von der Schulenburg, J.-Matthias Graf. The Growth of Government and the Rise of Pressure Groups: Comment. *Pethig, R. and Schlieper, U., eds.*, 1987, pp. 59–61.

Schwartz, Thomas. Votes, Strategies, and Institutions: An Introduction to the Theory of Collective Choice. *McCubbins, M. D. and Sullivan, T., eds.*, 1987, pp. 318–45.

Schwartz, Thomas. Your Vote Counts on Account of the Way It Is Counted: An Institutional Solution to the Paradox of Not Voting. *Public Choice*, 1987, *54*(2), pp. 101–21.

Scotchmer, Suzanne and Wooders, Myrna Holtz. Competitive Equilibrium and the Core in Club Economies with Anonymous Crowding. *J. Public Econ.*, November 1987, *34*(2), pp. 159–73.

Seldon, Arthur. Public Choice and the Choices of the Public. *[Tullock, G.]*, 1987, pp. 122–34.

Sertel, Murat R. Explorations in Aggregating Choices. *Math. Soc. Sci.*, December 1987, *14*(3), pp. 251–62.

Shapiro, Martin. The Concept of Information: A Comment on Gilligan and Krehbiel's "Collective Decisionmaking and Standing Committees." *J. Law, Econ., Organ.*, Fall 1987, *3*(2), pp. 345–50.

Shepsle, Kenneth A. Institutional Arrangements and Equilibrium in Multidimensional Voting Models. *McCubbins, M. D. and Sullivan, T., eds.*, 1987, *1979*, pp. 346–75.

Shepsle, Kenneth A. and Weingast, Barry R. The

Institutional Foundations of Committee Power. *Amer. Polit. Sci. Rev.*, March 1987, *81*(1), pp. 85–104.

Slivinski, Alan D. Bergson Social Welfare Functions in Applied Welfare Analysis. *Soc. Choice Welfare*, December 1987, *4*(4), pp. 241–51.

Storcken, Ton. Some Social Choice Problems. *Peters, H. J. M. and Vrieze, O. J., eds.*, 1987, pp. 307–30.

Streit, Manfred E. Economic Order and Public Policy—Market, Constitution and the Welfare State. *Pethig, R. and Schlieper, U., eds.*, 1987, pp. 1–21.

Strnad, Jeff. Full Nash Implementation of Neutral Social Functions. *J. Math. Econ.*, 1987, *16*(1), pp. 17–37.

Stroup, Richard L. Reflections on Freedom, Fairness, and the Constitution. *Cato J.*, Fall 1987, *7*(2), pp. 403–11.

Subramanian, S. Rights, Consensus and the Optimum Savings Problem. *J. Quant. Econ.*, January 1987, *3*(1), pp. 1–11.

Subramanian, S. The Liberal Paradox with Fuzzy Preferences [The Impossibility of a Paretian Liberal]. *Soc. Choice Welfare*, September 1987, *4*(3), pp. 213–18.

Suppes, Patrick. Maximizing Freedom of Decision: An Axiomatic Analysis. *Feiwel, G. R., ed. (II)*, 1987, pp. 243–54.

Suzumura, Kotaro and Suga, Koichi. Arrow and the Problem of Social Choice. *Feiwel, G. R., ed. (II)*, 1987, pp. 255–71.

Taylor, Dalmas A. and Moriarty, Beatrice F. Ingroup Bias as a Function of Competition and Race. *J. Conflict Resolution*, March 1987, *31*(1), pp. 192–99.

Thomson, William. Individual and Collective Opportunities. *Int. J. Game Theory*, 1987, *16*(4), pp. 245–52.

Tideman, T. Nicolaus. Independence of Clones as a Criterion for Voting Rules. *Soc. Choice Welfare*, September 1987, *4*(3), pp. 185–206.

Tideman, T. Nicolaus and Coats, R. Morris. An Instrumental-Variables Approach to Income Redistribution. *Public Choice*, 1987, *52*(2), pp. 187–92.

Tilman, Rick. The Neoinstrumental Theory of Democracy. *J. Econ. Issues*, September 1987, *21*(3), pp. 1379–1401.

Tollison, Robert D. Is the Theory of Rent-Seeking Here to Stay? *[Tullock, G.]*, 1987, pp. 143–57.

Tullock, Gordon. Another Part of the Swamp. *Public Choice*, 1987, *54*(1), pp. 83–84.

Tullock, Gordon. Autocracy. *Radnitzky, G. and Bernholz, P., eds.*, 1987, pp. 365–81.

Tullock, Gordon. The *Calculus*: Postscript after 25 Years. *Cato J.*, Fall 1987, *7*(2), pp. 313–21.

Uriarte, J. R. Topological Structure of a Space of Continuous Preferences as a Space of Retractions and the Aggregation Problem. *Math. Soc. Sci.*, June 1987, *13*(3), pp. 259–72.

Usher, D. and Engineer, M. The Distribution of Income in a Despotic Society. *Public Choice*, August 1987, *54*(3), pp. 261–76.

Vanek, Jaroslav. Toward a Just, Efficient, and Fully Democratic Society. *Jones, D. C. and Svejnar, J., eds.*, 1987, pp. 13–78.

Wade, Robert. The Management of Common Property Resources: Collective Action as an Alternative to Privatisation or State Regulation. *Cambridge J. Econ.*, June 1987, *11*(2), pp. 95–106.

Wagner, Richard E. Courts, Legislatures, and Constitutional Maintenance. *Cato J.*, Fall 1987, *7*(2), pp. 323–29.

Wagner, Richard E. Parchment, Guns, and the Maintenance of Constitutional Contract. *[Tullock, G.]*, 1987, pp. 105–21.

Weingast, Barry R. A Rational Choice Perspective on Congressional Norms. *McCubbins, M. D. and Sullivan, T., eds.*, 1987, *1979*, pp. 131–46. [G: U.S.]

Wenders, John T. On Perfect Rent Dissipation. *Amer. Econ. Rev.*, June 1987, *77*(3), pp. 456–59.

Whitaker, John K. *The Limits of Organization* Revisited. *Feiwel, G. R., ed. (II)*, 1987, pp. 565–83.

Wickström, Bengt-Arne. The Growth of Government and the Rise of Pressure Groups. *Pethig, R. and Schlieper, U., eds.*, 1987, pp. 39–57.

Wildavsky, Aaron. Choosing Preferences by Constructing Institutions: A Cultural Theory of Preference Formation. *Amer. Polit. Sci. Rev.*, March 1987, *81*(1), pp. 3–21. [G: U.S.]

van Winden, Frans A. A. M. Man in the Public Sector. *De Economist*, 1987, *135*(1), pp. 1–28.

Windisch, Rupert. Economic Order and Public Policy—Market, Constitution and the Welfare State: Comment. *Pethig, R. and Schlieper, U., eds.*, 1987, pp. 23–26.

von Winterfeldt, Detlof. Value Tree Analysis: An Introduction and an Application to Offshore Oil Drilling. *Kleindorfer, P. R. and Kunreuther, H. C., ed.*, 1987, pp. 349–77.

Ziemes, Georg. Macroeconomic Policy, Rent Seeking and Economic Order: Comment. *Pethig, R. and Schlieper, U., eds.*, 1987, pp. 35–37.

0252 Social Choice Studies: Voting, Committees, etc.

Anderson, Gary Michael. Welfare Programs in the Rent-Seeking Society. *Southern Econ. J.*, October 1987, *54*(2), pp. 377–86. [G: U.S.]

Arnold, R. Douglas. Legislators, Bureaucrats, and Locational Decisions. *McCubbins, M. D. and Sullivan, T., eds.*, 1987, *1981*, pp. 523–48. [G: U.S.]

Atkinson, Scott E.; Sandler, Todd and Tschirhart, John. Terrorism in a Bargaining Framework. *J. Law Econ.*, April 1987, *30*(1), pp. 1–21. [G: Global]

Ault, Richard W.; Ekelund, Robert B., Jr. and Tollison, Robert D. The Pope and the Price of Meat: A Public Choice Perspective. *Kyklos*, 1987, *40*(3), pp. 399–413.

Balisacan, Arsenio M. and Roumasset, James A. Public Choice of Economic Policy: The Growth of Agricultural Protection. *Weltwirtsch. Arch.*, 1987, *123*(2), pp. 232–48.   [G: Global]

Baysinger, Barry D.; Keim, Gerald D. and Zeithaml, Carl P. Constituency Building as a Political Strategy in the Petroleum Industry. *Marcus, A. A.; Kaufman, A. M. and Beam, D. R., eds.*, 1987, pp. 223–38.   [G: U.S.]

Bennett, James T. and Dilorenzo, Thomas J. How (and Why) Congress Twists Its Own Arm: The Political Economy of Tax-Funded Politics. *Public Choice*, October 1987, *55*(3), pp. 199–213.   [G: U.S.]

Bond, Ronald S. and Mitler, James C., Jr. Voting Patterns of FTC Commissioners. *MacKay, R. J.; Miller, J. C., III and Yandle, B., eds.*, 1987, pp. 322–30.   [G: U.S.]

Bordo, Michael D. and Landau, Daniel. The Growth of Government: A Protection Explanation. *Public Choice*, 1987, *53*(2), pp. 167–74.   [G: U.S.]

Boyne, George A. Median Voters, Political Systems and Public Policies: An Empirical Test. *Public Choice*, 1987, *53*(3), pp. 201–19.   [G: U.K.]

Brady, David; Cooper, Joseph and Hurley, Patricia A. The Decline of Party in the U.S. House of Representatives, 1887–1968. *McCubbins, M. D. and Sullivan, T., eds.*, 1987, *1979*, pp. 235–59.   [G: U.S.]

Brady, David and Morgan, Mark A. Reforming the Structure of the House Appropriations Process: The Effects of the 1885 and 1919–20 Reforms on Money Decisions. *McCubbins, M. D. and Sullivan, T., eds.*, 1987, pp. 207–34.   [G: U.S.]

Brann, Peter and Foddy, Margaret. Trust and the Consumption of a Deteriorating Common Resource. *J. Conflict Resolution*, December 1987, *31*(4), pp. 615–30.

Brennan, Geoffrey and Pincus, Jonathan J. Rational Actor Theory in Politics: A Critical Review of John Quiggin. *Econ. Rec.*, March 1987, *63*(180), pp. 22–32.

Buchanan, James M. Tax Reform as Political Choice. *J. Econ. Perspectives*, Summer 1987, *1*(1), pp. 29–35.   [G: U.S.]

Calvert, Randall L.; Moran, Mark J. and Weingast, Barry R. Congressional Influence over Policy Making: The Case of the FTC. *McCubbins, M. D. and Sullivan, T., eds.*, 1987, pp. 493–522.   [G: U.S.]

Capron, Henri. Cohérence et estimation des fonctions de popularite. Une application au cas français. (With English summary.) *Revue Écon.*, September 1987, *38*(5), pp. 1029–41.   [G: France]

Carpenter, Vivian L. The Effects of Interest Group Competition on Funding Government Management Information Systems. *Chan, J. L., ed., Pt. A*, 1987, pp. 67–105.   [G: U.S.]

Carter, Gregg Lee. Local Police Force Size and the Severity of the 1960s Black Rioting. *J. Conflict Resolution*, December 1987, *31*(4), pp. 601–14.   [G: U.S.]

Collier, Kenneth E., et al. Retrospective Voting: An Experimental Study. *Public Choice*, 1987, *53*(2), pp. 101–30.

Crain, W. Mark; Leavens, Donald R. and Abbot, Lynn. Voting and Not Voting at the Same Time. *Public Choice*, 1987, *53*(3), pp. 221–29.   [G: U.S.]

De Groot, Hans and Van der Sluis, Johan. Bureaucracy Response to Budget Cuts: An Economic Model. *Kyklos*, 1987, *40*(1), pp. 103–09.   [G: Netherlands]

Dollery, B. E. The Institutional Impetus to Social Waste in South Africa: A Note on Rent-Seeking and the Margo Commission. *S. Afr. J. Econ.*, December 1987, *55*(4), pp. 428–32.

Dudley, Leonard and Montmarquette, Claude. Bureaucratic Corruption as a Constraint on Voter Choice. *Public Choice*, September 1987, *55*(1–2), pp. 127–60. [G: Selected Countries]

Durden, Garey C. and Gaynor, Patricia. The Rational Behavior of Voting Participation: Evidence from the 1970 and 1982 Elections. *Public Choice*, 1987, *53*(3), pp. 231–42.   [G: U.S.]

Eismeier, Theodore J. and Pollock, Philip H., III. The Retreat from Partisanship: Why the Dog Didn't Bark in the 1984 Election. *Marcus, A. A.; Kaufman, A. M. and Beam, D. R., eds.*, 1987, pp. 137–47.   [G: U.S.]

Farnham, Paul G. Form of Government and the Median Voter. *Soc. Sci. Quart.*, September 1987, *68*(3), pp. 569–82.   [G: U.S.]

Feldman, David Lewis. The Defeat of the Blue Ridge Pump–Storage Project as Microcosm of Environmental Policy Change. *Policy Sci.*, 1987, *20*(3), pp. 235–58.   [G: U.S.]

Fiorina, Morris P. Comment: Alternative Rationales for Restrictive Procedures [Collective Decisionmaking and Standing Committees: An Informational Rationale for Restrictive Amendment Procedures]. *J. Law, Econ., Organ.*, Fall 1987, *3*(2), pp. 337–43.

Fiorina, Morris P. The Case of the Vanishing Marginals: The Bureaucracy Did It. *McCubbins, M. D. and Sullivan, T., eds.*, 1987, *1977*, pp. 30–38.   [G: U.S.]

Fuchs, Edward Paul and Anderson, James. Institutionalizing Cost–Benefit Analysis in Regulatory Agencies. *Nagel, S. S., ed.*, 1987, pp. 187–211.   [G: U.S.]

Fung, K. K. Surplus Seeking and Rent Seeking through Back-Door Deals in Mainland China: Price Control and Central Planning Fix Prices below Market Clearance, Creating a Contrived Surplus. *Amer. J. Econ. Soc.*, July 1987, *46*(3), pp. 299–317.   [G: China]

Goff, Brian L. and Tollison, Robert D. The Allocation of Death in the Vietnam War: A Public Choice Perspective. *Southern Econ. J.*, October 1987, *54*(2), pp. 316–21.   [G: U.S.]

Goudriaan, René; De Groot, Hans and van Tulder, Frank. Public Sector Productivity: Recent Empirical Findings and Policy Applications. *van de Kar, H. M. and Wolfe, B. L., eds.*, 1987, pp. 193–209.   [G: U.S.; Netherlands]

Grier, Kevin Blaine. Presidential Elections and Federal Reserve Policy: An Empirical Test.

Southern Econ. J., October 1987, 54(2), pp. 475–86. [G: U.S.]

Grimm, Curtis M. and Holcomb, John M. Choices among Encompassing Organizations: Business and the Budget Deficit. *Marcus, A. A.; Kaufman, A. M. and Beam, D. R., eds.,* 1987, pp. 105–18. [G: U.S.]

Gupta, Dipak K. Economic Behavior and the Analysis of Violent Collective Actions. *J. Behav. Econ.,* Summer 1987, 16(2), pp. 33–44.

Hannaway, Jane. Supply Creates Demands: An Organizational Process View of Administrative Expansion. *J. Policy Anal. Manage.,* Fall 1987, 7(1), pp. 118–34. [G: U.S.]

Heath, Anthony F. The Economic Theory of Democracy: The Rise of the Liberals in Britain. *Radnitzky, G. and Bernholz, P., eds.,* 1987, pp. 105–30. [G: U.K.]

Hetzner, C. N., III and Westin, Stu. Legislative Ratings as a Metric of Goal Cohesion within Interest Groups: Business vs. Labor. *Public Choice,* 1987, 53(1), pp. 21–39. [G: U.S.]

Hibbs, Douglas A., Jr. Economics and Politics in France: Economic Performance and Mass Political Support for Presidents Pompidou and Giscard d'Estaing. *Hibbs, D. A., Jr.,* 1987, 1981, pp. 224–40. [G: France]

Hibbs, Douglas A., Jr. On the Demand for Economic Outcomes: Macroeconomic Performance and Mass Political Support in the United States, Great Britain, and Germany. *Hibbs, D. A., Jr.,* 1987, 1982, pp. 193–223. [G: U.S.; U.K.; W. Germany]

Hibbs, Douglas A., Jr. Political Parties and Macroeconomic Policy. *Hibbs, D. A., Jr.,* 1987, 1977, pp. 290–321. [G: U.K.; U.S.]

Hibbs, Douglas A., Jr. President Reagan's Mandate from the 1980 Elections: A Shift to the Right? *Hibbs, D. A., Jr.,* 1987, 1982, pp. 164–90. [G: U.S.]

Hibbs, Douglas A., Jr. and Madsen, Henrik Jess. The Impact of Economic Performance on Electoral Support in Sweden, 1967–1978. *Hibbs, D. A., Jr.,* 1987, 1981, pp. 241–57. [G: Sweden]

Holcomb, John M. Citizen Group Agendas during the Reagan Era. *Bloom, P. N., ed.,* 1987, pp. 137–86. [G: U.S.]

Jacobson, Gary C. Running Scared: Elections and Congressional Politics in the 1980s. *McCubbins, M. D. and Sullivan, T., eds.,* 1987, pp. 39–81. [G: U.S.]

Janssens, Ilse; Moesen, Wim and Pauwels, Wilfried. Publieke voorzieningen: Welvaart, poliltiek en sanering. (With English summary.) *Cah. Écon. Bruxelles,* Third Trimester 1987, (115), pp. 77–110.

Johnston, R. J. and Pattie, C. J. A Dividing Nation? An Initial Exploration of the Changing Electoral Geography of Great Britain, 1979–1987. *Environ. Planning A,* August 1987, 19(8), pp. 1001–13. [G: U.K.]

Jones, Charles O. Joseph G. Cannon and Howard W. Smith: An Essay on the Limits of Leadership in the House of Representatives. *McCub-*

bins, M. D. and Sullivan, T., eds., 1987, 1968, pp. 260–85. [G: U.S.]

Jones, Woodrow, Jr. and Keiser, K. Robert. Issue Visibility and the Effects of PAC Money. *Soc. Sci. Quart.,* March 1987, 68(1), pp. 170–76. [G: U.S.]

Jonung, Lars and Wadensjö, Eskil. Rational, Adaptive and Learning Behavior of Voters: Evidence from Disaggregated Popularity Functions for Sweden. *Public Choice,* August 1987, 54(3), pp. 197–210. [G: Sweden]

Kamlet, Mark S. and Mowery, David C. Influences on Executive and Congressional Budgetary Priorities, 1955–1981. *Amer. Polit. Sci. Rev.,* March 1987, 81(1), pp. 155–78. [G: U.S.]

Kau, James B. and Rubin, Paul H. The Political Economy of Urban Land Use. *Jaffe, A. J., ed.,* 1987, pp. 5–26. [G: U.S.]

Kaufman, Allen M.; Karson, Marvin J. and Sohl, Jeffrey. Business Fragmentation and Solidarity: An Analysis of PAC Donations in the 1980 and 1982 Elections. *Marcus, A. A.; Kaufman, A. M. and Beam, D. R., eds.,* 1987, pp. 119–35. [G: U.S.]

Kaufman, Allen M.; Marcus, Alfred A. and Zacharias, Larry. How Business Manages Politics. *Marcus, A. A.; Kaufman, A. M. and Beam, D. R., eds.,* 1987, pp. 293–312. [G: U.S.]

Kimenyi, Mwangi S. Bureaucratic Rents and Political Institutions. *Econ. Scelte Pubbliche/J. Public Finance Public Choice,* Sept.-Dec. 1987, 5(3), pp. 189–99. [G: Global]

Kirchgässner, Gebhard. Granger-Kausalität und Rationale Erwartungen. (With English summary.) *Kyklos,* 1987, 40(1), pp. 21–42. [G: W. Germany]

Krehbiel, Keith. Sophisticated Committees and Structure-Induced Equilibria in Congress. *McCubbins, M. D. and Sullivan, T., eds.,* 1987, pp. 376–402. [G: U.S.]

Laband, David N. and Sophocleus, John P. The Social Cost of Rent-Seeking: First Estimates. *Econ. Scelte Pubbliche/J. Public Finance Public Choice,* May-Aug. 1987, 5(2), pp. 127–33. [G: U.S.]

Lempert, David. A Demographic–Economic Explanation of Political Stabilty: Mauritius as a Microcosm. *Eastern Afr. Econ. Rev.,* June 1987, 3(1), pp. 77–90. [G: Mauritus]

Lesbirel, S. Hayden. The Political Economy of Project Delay. *Policy Sci.,* 1987, 20(2), pp. 153–71. [G: Japan]

Lipford, Jody and Yandle, Bruce. Political Dominance and State Unemployment Benefits. *Public Choice,* 1987, 53(2), pp. 175–80. [G: U.S.]

Lott, John R., Jr. Political Cheating. *Public Choice,* 1987, 52(2), pp. 169–86. [G: U.S.]

Lott, John R., Jr. The Effect of Nontransferable Property Rights on the Efficiency of Political Markets: Some Evidence. *J. Public Econ.,* March 1987, 32(2), pp. 231–46. [G: U.S.]

Lovik, Lawrence W. Bureaucracy, Privatization,

and the Supply of Public Goods. *Kent, C. A., ed.*, 1987, pp. 23–34.

Mackay, Robert J. The FTC Budget Process: Zero-Based Budgeting by Committee. *MacKay, R. J.; Miller, J. C., III and Yandle, B., eds.*, 1987, pp. 295–321. **[G: U.S.]**

Mahon, John F. and Post, James E. The Evolution of Political Strategies during the 1980 Superfund Debate. *Marcus, A. A.; Kaufman, A. M. and Beam, D. R., eds.*, 1987, pp. 61–78. **[G: U.S.]**

Maitland, Ian. Collective versus Individual Lobbying: How Business Ends Up the Loser. *Marcus, A. A.; Kaufman, A. M. and Beam, D. R., eds.*, 1987, pp. 95–104. **[G: U.S.]**

Masters, Marick F. Corporations, Human Resources Management, and Political Action. *Rowland, K. M. and Ferris, G. R., eds.*, 1987, pp. 357–93.

Masters, Marick F. and Zardkoohi, Asghar. Labor Unions and the U.S. Congress: PAC Allocations and Legislative Voting. *Lewin, D.; Lipsky, D. B. and Sockell, D., eds.*, 1987, pp. 79–117. **[G: U.S.]**

Mayer, Wolfgang. Endogenous Tariff Formation. *Bhagwati, J. N., ed.*, 1987, *1984*, pp. 329–52.

McCallum, John and Blais, André. Government, Special Interest Groups, and Economic Growth. *Public Choice*, 1987, *54*(1), pp. 3–18. **[G: OECD]**

McCubbins, Mathew D. and Page, Talbot. A Theory of Congressional Delegation. *McCubbins, M. D. and Sullivan, T., eds.*, 1987, pp. 409–25. **[G: U.S.]**

McCubbins, Mathew D. and Schwartz, Thomas. Congressional Oversight Overlooked: Police Patrols versus Fire Alarms. *McCubbins, M. D. and Sullivan, T., eds.*, 1987, *1984*, pp. 426–40. **[G: U.S.]**

McCubbins, Mathew D. and Sullivan, Terry. Congress: Structure and Policy: Introduction: Institutional Aspects of Decision Processes. *McCubbins, M. D. and Sullivan, T., eds.*, 1987, pp. 1–11. **[G: U.S.]**

McKinney, Scott. Crowding and the Club Membership Margin. *J. Urban Econ.*, November 1987, *22*(3), pp. 312–23. **[G: U.S.]**

Mehay, Stephen L. and Gonzalez, Rodolfo A. Outside Information and the Monopoly Power of a Public Bureau: An Empirical Analysis. *Public Finance Quart.*, January 1987, *15*(1), pp. 61–75. **[G: U.S.]**

Mikesell, John L. A Note on Senatorial Mass Mailing Expenditure and the Quest for Reelection. *Public Choice*, 1987, *53*(3), pp. 257–65. **[G: U.S.]**

Mills, Edwin S. Bureaucratic Corruption as a Constraint on Voter Choice: Comments. *Public Choice*, September 1987, *55*(1–2), pp. 161–62.

Mohai, Paul. Public Participation and Natural Resource Decision-Making: The Case of the RARE II Decisions. *Natural Res. J.*, Winter 1987, *27*(1), pp. 123–55. **[G: U.S.]**

Mueller, Dennis C. The Growth of Government: A Public Choice Perspective. *Int. Monet. Fund*

Staff Pap., March 1987, *34*(1), pp. 115–49. **[G: OECD]**

Murashima, Eiji. Local Elections and Leadership in Thailand: A Case Study of Nakhon Sawan Province. *Devel. Econ.*, December 1987, *25*(4), pp. 363–85. **[G: Thailand]**

Nanetti, Raffaella Y.; Leonardi, Robert and Putnam, Robert D. The Management of Regional Policies: Endogenous Explanations of Performance. *Picard, L. A. and Zariski, R., eds.*, 1987, pp. 103–18. **[G: Italy]**

Nelson, Douglas and Silberberg, Eugene. Ideology and Legislator Shirking. *Econ. Inquiry*, January 1987, *25*(1), pp. 15–25. **[G: U.S.]**

Neumann, Manfred J. M. and Lohmann, Susanne. Political Business Cycles in Industrialized Democratic Countries: A Comment. *Kyklos*, 1987, *40*(4), pp. 568–72. **[G: OECD]**

Niemi, Richard G. and Wright, J. R. Voting Cycles and the Structure of Individual Preferences. *Soc. Choice Welfare*, September 1987, *4*(3), pp. 173–83. **[G: U.S.]**

North, Douglass C. The Lessons of 1787: Comment. *Public Choice*, September 1987, *55*(1–2), pp. 35–39. **[G: U.S.]**

Pack, Janet Rothenberg. The Political Policy Cycle: Presidential Effort vs. Presidential Control. *Public Choice*, August 1987, *54*(3), pp. 231–59. **[G: U.S.]**

Paldam, Martin. Inflation and Political Instability in Eight Latin American Countries 1946–83. *Public Choice*, 1987, *52*(2), pp. 143–68. **[G: Latin America]**

Parent, T. Wayne; Jillson, Calvin C. and Weber, Ronald E. Voting Outcomes in the 1984 Democratic Party Primaries and Caucuses. *Amer. Polit. Sci. Rev.*, March 1987, *81*(1), pp. 67–84. **[G: U.S.]**

Peltzman, Sam. Economic Conditions and Gubernatorial Elections. *Amer. Econ. Rev.*, May 1987, *77*(2), pp. 293–97. **[G: U.S.]**

Polsby, Nelson W. The Institutionalization of the U.S. House of Representatives. *McCubbins, M. D. and Sullivan, T., eds.*, 1987, *1968*, pp. 91–130. **[G: U.S.]**

Poole, Keith T.; Romer, Thomas and Rosenthal, Howard. The Revealed Preferences of Political Action Committees. *Amer. Econ. Rev.*, May 1987, *77*(2), pp. 298–302. **[G: U.S.]**

Quiggin, John. Egoistic Rationality and Public Choice: A Critical Review of Theory and Evidence. *Econ. Rec.*, March 1987, *63*(180), pp. 10–21.

Renaud, Paul S. A. and van Winden, Frans A. A. M. Political Accountability for Price Stability and Unemployment in a Multi-party System with Coalition Governments. *Public Choice*, 1987, *53*(2), pp. 181–86. **[G: Netherlands]**

Ricketts, Martin. Rent Seeking, Entrepreneurship, Subjectivism, and Property Rights. *J. Inst. Theoretical Econ.*, September 1987, *143*(3), pp. 457–66.

Riker, William H. The Lessons of 1787. *Public Choice*, September 1987, *55*(1–2), pp. 5–34. **[G: U.S.]**

Rivlin, Alice M. Economics and the Political Process. *Amer. Econ. Rev.*, March 1987, 77(1), pp. 1–10. **[G: U.S.]**

Rogowski, Ronald. Trade and the Variety of Democratic Institutions. *Int. Organ.*, Spring 1987, 41(2), pp. 203–23. **[G: OECD]**

Rohde, David A. and Shepsle, Kenneth A. Democratic Committee Assignments in the House of Representatives: Strategic Aspects of a Social Choice Process. *McCubbins, M. D. and Sullivan, T., eds.*, 1987, 1973, pp. 179–206. **[G: U.S.]**

Saltzman, Gregory M. Congressional Voting on Labor Issues: The Role of PACs. *Ind. Lab. Relat. Rev.*, January 1987, 40(2), pp. 163–79. **[G: U.S.]**

Samuelson, Larry. A Test of the Revealed-Preference Phenomenon in Congressional Elections. *Public Choice*, 1987, 54(2), pp. 141–69. **[G: U.S.]**

Schneider, Mark and Ji, Byung Moon. The Flypaper Effect and Competition in the Local Market for Public Goods. *Public Choice*, 1987, 54(1), pp. 27–39.

Seidmann, Daniel J. The Distribution of Power in Dáil Éireann. *Econ. Soc. Rev.*, October 1987, 19(1), pp. 61–68. **[G: Ireland]**

Sheehan, Dennis and Winston, Clifford. Expectations and Automobile Policy. *Winston, C., et al.*, 1987, pp. 89–102. **[G: U.S.]**

Sullivan, Terry. Presidential Leadership in Congress: Securing Commitments. *McCubbins, M. D. and Sullivan, T., eds.*, 1987, pp. 286–308. **[G: U.S.]**

Tosini, Suzanne C. and Tower, Edward. The Textile Bill of 1985: The Determinants of Congressional Voting Patterns. *Public Choice*, 1987, 54(1), pp. 19–25. **[G: U.S.]**

Verbon, H. A. A. The Rise and Evolution of Public Pension Systems. *Public Choice*, 1987, 52(1), pp. 75–100. **[G: Netherlands]**

Wade, Robert. The Management of Common Property Resources: Finding a Cooperative Solution. *World Bank Res. Observer*, July 1987, 2(2), pp. 219–34. **[G: India]**

Weingast, Barry R. A Rational Choice Perspective on Congressional Norms. *McCubbins, M. D. and Sullivan, T., eds.*, 1987, 1979, pp. 131–46. **[G: U.S.]**

Wilhite, Allen and Theilmann, John. Labor PAC Contributions and Labor Legislation: A Simultaneous Logit Approach. *Public Choice*, 1987, 53(3), pp. 267–76. **[G: U.S.]**

Willison, David. Agency Audits and Congressional Oversight: The Impact of State Tax Burdens on GAO Audit Requests. *Public Choice*, August 1987, 54(3), pp. 277–81. **[G: U.S.]**

Wintrobe, Ronald. The Market for Corporate Control and the Market for Political Control. *J. Law, Econ., Organ.*, Fall 1987, 3(2), pp. 435–48. **[G: U.S.]**

Yandle, Bruce. Regulatory Reform in the Realm of the Rent Seekers. *MacKay, R. J.; Miller, J. C., III and Yandle, B., eds.*, 1987, pp. 121–42. **[G: U.S.]**

Yoffie, David B. Corporate Strategies for Political Action: A Rational Model. *Marcus, A. A.; Kauf-*

man, A. M. and Beam, D. R., eds., 1987, pp. 43–60. **[G: U.S.]**

026 Economics of Uncertainty and Information; Game Theory and Bargaining Theory

0260 General

Aoki, Masahiko. Incentive-Compatible Approximation of a Nashlike Solution under Nonconvex Technology. *[Hurwicz, L.]*, 1987, pp. 295–307.

Brandenburger, Adam and Dekel, Eddie. Common Knowledge with Probability 1. *J. Math. Econ.*, 1987, 16(3), pp. 237–45.

Cho, In-Koo and Kreps, David M. Signaling Games and Stable Equilibria. *Quart. J. Econ.*, May 1987, 102(2), pp. 179–221.

Engers, Maxim and Fernandez, Luis F. Market Equilibrium with Hidden Knowledge and Self-selection. *Econometrica*, March 1987, 55(2), pp. 425–39.

Groves, Theodore and Ledyard, John O. Incentive Compatibility since 1972. *[Hurwicz, L.]*, 1987, pp. 48–111.

Hagerty, Kathleen M. and Rogerson, William P. Robust Trading Mechanisms. *J. Econ. Theory*, June 1987, 42(1), pp. 94–107.

Hahn, Frank H. Information, Dynamics and Equilibrium. *Scot. J. Polit. Econ.*, November 1987, 34(4), pp. 321–34.

Hellwig, Martin. Some Recent Developments in the Theory of Competition in Markets with Adverse Selection. *Europ. Econ. Rev.*, Feb./Mar. 1987, 31(1/2), pp. 319–25.

Jovanovic, Boyan. Micro Shocks and Aggregate Risk. *Quart. J. Econ.*, May 1987, 102(2), pp. 395–409.

Nakamura, Yutaka. Expected Utility with a Threshold Function. *Sawaragi, Y.; Inoue, K. and Nakayama, H., eds.*, 1987, pp. 170–79.

Roberds, William. Models of Policy under Stochastic Replanning. *Int. Econ. Rev.*, October 1987, 28(3), pp. 731–55.

Sonnenschein, Hugo. Theory and Method—Second-Generation Perspective: An Interview. *Feiwel, G. R., ed. (I)*, 1987, pp. 325–39.

0261 Theory of Uncertainty and Information

Abrams, Burton A. and Lewis, Kenneth A. The Effect of Information Costs on Regulatory Outcomes. *J. Econ. Bus.*, May 1987, 39(2), pp. 159–70.

Admati, Anat R. and Pfleiderer, Paul. Viable Allocations of Information in Financial Markets. *J. Econ. Theory*, October 1987, 43(1), pp. 76–115.

Aghion, Philippe and Bolton, Patrick. Contracts as a Barrier to Entry. *Amer. Econ. Rev.*, June 1987, 77(3), pp. 388–401.

Akiba, Hiroya. Resource Allocation with Factor Price Differentials in a Simple Two-Sector Model with Production Risk. *Ricerche Econ.*, Apr.-June 1987, 41(2), pp. 174–89.

Allen, Beth. Smooth Preferences and the Approximate Expected Utility Hypothesis. *J. Econ. Theory*, April 1987, *41*(2), pp. 340–55.

Andersen, Torben M. Effective Demand, Differential Information and the Multiplier. *Econ. J.*, June 1987, 97(386), pp. 353–71.

Andersen, Torben M. The Information Content of Quantity Signals and Downward Inflexible Prices. *Scand. J. Econ.*, 1987, 89(4), pp. 451–68.

Ang, James S. and Lai, Tsong-Yue. Insurance Premium Pricing and Ratemaking in Competitive Insurance and Capital Asset Markets. *J. Risk Ins.*, December 1987, 54(4), pp. 767–79.

Anglin, Paul M. and Baye, Michael R. Information, Multiprice Search, and Cost-of-Living Index Theory. *J. Polit. Econ.*, December 1987, 95(6), pp. 1179–95.

Antonovitz, Frances and Roe, Terry. Economic Efficiency and Market Information. *Kilmer, R. L. and Armbruster, W. J., eds.*, 1987, pp. 181–204.   [G: U.S.]

Appelbaum, Elie and Katz, Eliakim. Asymmetric Taxation and the Theory of the Competitive Firm under Uncertainty. *Can. J. Econ.*, May 1987, 20(2), pp. 357–69.

Appleby, Lynda and Starmer, Chris. Individual Choice under Uncertainty: A Review of Experimental Evidence, Past and Present. *Hey, J. D. and Lambert, P. J., eds.*, 1987, pp. 25–45.

Arnott, Richard J. Essai sur le risque moral. (An Essay on Moral Hazard. With English summary.) *L'Actual. Econ.*, June-September 1987, 63(2–3), pp. 74–97.

Arouh, Albert. The Mumpsimus of Economists and the Role of Time and Uncertainty in the Progress of Economic Knowledge. *J. Post Keynesian Econ.*, Spring 1987, 9(3), pp. 395–423.

Arrow, Kenneth J. Technical Information, Returns to Scale, and the Existence of Competitive Equilibrium. *[Hurwicz, L.]*, 1987, pp. 243–55.

Asch, Peter and Quandt, Richard E. Efficiency and Profitability in Exotic Bets. *Economica*, August 1987, 54(215), pp. 289–98.

d'Aspremont, Claude; Jacquemin, Alexis and Gabszewicz, Jean Jaskold. Imperfect Information and Market Organization. *Europ. Econ. Rev.*, June 1987, 31(4), pp. 825–26.

Băcescu, M.; Stroe, R. and Tamaş, I. Production of Information Component of Social Production System. *Econ. Computat. Cybern. Stud. Res.*, 1987, 22(3), pp. 23–30.

Backhaus, Jürgen. On Intercepting the Flow of Ideas: An Economic Analysis. *Int. J. Soc. Econ.*, 1987, 14(7/8/9), pp. 99–114.

Bamberg, Günter. Risk Sharing and Subcontracting. *Bamberg, G. and Spremann, K., eds.*, 1987, pp. 61–79.

Baron, David P. and Besanko, David. Commitment and Fairness in a Dynamic Regulatory Relationship. *Rev. Econ. Stud.*, July 1987, 54(3), pp. 413–36.

Baron, David P. and Besanko, David. Monitoring, Moral Hazard, Asymmetric Information,

and Risk Sharing in Procurement Contracting. *Rand J. Econ.*, Winter 1987, 18(4), pp. 509–32.

Barrett, C. R. and Pattanaik, Prasanta K. Aggregation of Probability Judgements. *Econometrica*, September 1987, 55(5), pp. 1237–41.

Barzel, Yoram. Knight's "Moral Hazard" Theory of Organization. *Econ. Inquiry*, January 1987, 25(1), pp. 117–20.

Bassett, Gilbert W., Jr. The St. Petersburg Paradox and Bounded Utility. *Hist. Polit. Econ.*, Winter 1987, 19(4), pp. 517–23.

Basu, Kaushik. Monopoly, Quality Uncertainty and 'Status' Goods. *Int. J. Ind. Organ.*, December 1987, 5(4), pp. 435–46.

Berman, Lawrence E. and Dunn, Donald A. Service Bundling and Strategic Equilibrium in the Information Services Industry. *J. Econ. Bus.*, May 1987, 39(2), pp. 115–29.

Bhattacharya, Gautam. Notes on Optimality of Rational Expectations Equilibrium with Incomplete Markets. *J. Econ. Theory*, August 1987, 42(2), pp. 191–208.

Blanc, Gérard. The Grain Traders: Masters of the Intelligence Game. *Dedijer, S. and Jéquier, N., eds.*, 1987, pp. 139–57.

Blickle, Marina. Information Systems and the Design of Optimal Contracts. *Bamberg, G. and Spremann, K., eds.*, 1987, pp. 93–103.

Border, Kim C. and Sobel, Joel. Samurai Accountant: A Theory of Auditing and Plunder. *Rev. Econ. Stud.*, October 1987, 54(4), pp. 525–40.

Borm, Peter. Games with Incomplete Information. *Peters, H. J. M. and Vrieze, O. J., eds.*, 1987, pp. 71–102.

Bray, Margaret. Rational Expectations, Information and Asset Markets: An Introduction. *Sinclair, P. J. N., ed.*, 1987, 1985, pp. 248–82.

Bray, Margaret and Kreps, David M. Rational Learning and Rational Expectations. *Feiwel, G. R., ed. (I)*, 1987, pp. 597–625.

Briys, Eric. Demande d'assurance, décisions de consommation et de portefeuille: Une analyse en temps continu. (Insurance Demand, Consumption and Portfolio Decisions. With English summary.) *L'Actual. Econ.*, June-September 1987, 63(2–3), pp. 200–212.

Brockett, Patrick L., et al. Cost–Volume–Utility Analysis with Partial Stochastic Information. *Quart. Rev. Econ. Bus.*, Autumn 1987, 27(3), pp. 70–90.

Buccola, Steven T. and Smith, Vernon L. Uncertainty and Partial Adjustment in Double-Auction Markets. *J. Econ. Behav. Organ.*, December 1987, 8(4), pp. 587–601.

Budescu, David V. and Wallsten, Thomas S. Subjective Estimation of Precise and Vague Uncertainties. *Wright, G. and Ayton, P., eds.*, 1987, pp. 63–82.

Calsamiglia, Xavier. Informational Requirements of Parametric Resource Allocation Processes. *[Hurwicz, L.]*, 1987, pp. 115–31.

Chan, Yuk-Shee and Thakor, Anjan V. Collateral and Competitive Equilibria with Moral Hazard and Private Information. *J. Finance*, June 1987, 42(2), pp. 345–63.

Chatterjee, Kalyan and Samuelson, Larry. Bargaining with Two-Sided Incomplete Information: An Infinite Horizon Model with Alternating Offers. *Rev. Econ. Stud.*, April 1987, *54*(2), pp. 175–92.

Chavas, Jean-Paul. Constrained Choices under Risk. *Southern Econ. J.*, January 1987, *53*(3), pp. 662–76.

Cheng, Hsueh-Cheng; Magill, Michael J. P. and Shafer, Wayne J. Some Results on Comparative Statics under Uncertainty. *Int. Econ. Rev.*, June 1987, *28*(2), pp. 493–507.

Chew, Soo Hong; Karni, Edi and Safra, Zvi. Risk Aversion in the Theory of Expected Utility with Rank Dependent Probabilities. *J. Econ. Theory*, August 1987, *42*(2), pp. 370–81.

Chew, Soo Hong and Mao, M. H. Portfolio Risk Aversion and Weighted Utility Theory. *Sawaragi, Y.; Inoue, K. and Nakayama, H., eds.*, 1987, pp. 162–69.

Choi, Eun Kwan and Johnson, Stanley R. Consumer's Surplus and Price Uncertainty. *Int. Econ. Rev.*, June 1987, *28*(2), pp. 407–11.

Clarida, Richard H. Consumption, Liquidity Constraints and Asset Accumulation in the Presence of Random Income Fluctuations. *Int. Econ. Rev.*, June 1987, *28*(2), pp. 339–51.

Cochran, Mark J. and Raskin, Rob. Interpretations and Transformations of Scale for the Pratt–Arrow Absolute Risk Aversion Coefficient: Implications for Generalized Stochastic Dominance: Reply. *Western J. Agr. Econ.*, December 1987, *12*(2), pp. 231–32.

Colby, William E. Comprehensive Intelligence for Advancement. *Dedijer, S. and Jéquier, N., eds.*, 1987, pp. 41–48.

Cooper, Russell and Hayes, Beth. Multi-period Insurance Contracts. *Int. J. Ind. Organ.*, June 1987, *5*(2), pp. 211–31.

Cotter, Kevin D. Convergence of Information, Random Variables and Noise. *J. Math. Econ.*, 1987, *16*(1), pp. 39–51.

Covello, Vincent T. and Merkhofer, Miley. The Inexact Science of Chemical Hazard Risk Assessment: A Description and Critical Evaluation of Available Methods. *Kleindorfer, P. R. and Kunreuther, H. C., ed.*, 1987, pp. 229–76.

Cowell, Frank A. The Economic Analysis of Tax Evasion. *Hey, J. D. and Lambert, P. J., eds.*, 1987, *1985*, pp. 173–203.

Cressy, Robert C. Equilibrium Costs and Prices in a Market with Imperfect Information and Technological Change. *Greek Econ. Rev.*, 1987, *9*(2), pp. 162–82.

Cressy, Robert C. Equilibrium Price Dispersion: An Extension of Reinganum's 'Simple Model.' *Bull. Econ. Res.*, July 1987, *39*(3), pp. 235–41.

Cresta, Jean-Paul and Laffont, Jean-Jacques. Incentive Compatibility of Insurance Contracts and the Value of Information. *J. Risk Ins.*, September 1987, *54*(3), pp. 520–40.

Dahlby, B. G. Monopoly versus Competition in an Insurance Market with Adverse Selection. *J. Risk Ins.*, June 1987, *54*(2), pp. 325–31.

Dasgupta, Partha and David, Paul A. Information Disclosure and the Economics of Science and Technology. *Feiwel, G. R., ed. (1)*, 1987, pp. 519–42.

Daub, M. An Institutional Approach to the Rationality of Expectations. *Appl. Econ.*, October 1987, *19*(10), pp. 1303–16. [G: Canada]

Davidson, Carl; Martin, Lawrence W. and Matusz, Steven J. Search, Unemployment, and the Production of Jobs. *Econ. J.*, December 1987, *97*(388), pp. 857–76.

De Vany, Arthur. Institutions for Stochastic Markets. *J. Inst. Theoretical Econ.*, March 1987, *143*(1), pp. 91–103.

Detemple, Jerome B. and Kihlstrom, Richard E. Acquisition d'information dans un modèle intertemporel en temps continu. (Information acquisition in an Intertemporal Continuous Time Model. With English summary.) *L'Actual. Econ.*, June-September 1987, *63*(2–3), pp. 118–37.

Diamond, Peter. Consumer Differences and Prices in a Search Model. *Quart. J. Econ.*, May 1987, *102*(2), pp. 429–36.

Dionne, Georges. Incertain et information: Où en sommes-nous trente-cinq ans après le colloque de Paris? (Uncertainty and Information: Where Do We Stand Thirty-five Years after the Paris Symposium. With English summary.) *L'Actual. Econ.*, June-September 1987, *63*(2–3), pp. 5–39.

Dionne, Georges and Eeckhoudt, Louis. Proportional Risk Aversion, Taxation and Labor Supply under Uncertainty. *J. Econ. (Z. Nationalökon.)*, 1987, *47*(4), pp. 353–66.

Dionne, Georges and Lasserre, Pierre. Adverse Selection and Finite-Horizon Insurance Contracts. *Europ. Econ. Rev.*, June 1987, *31*(4), pp. 843–61.

Dionne, Georges and Pellerin, Marc. Investissement en incertitude: Extension du problème de la taille optimale d'une usine. (Investment under Uncertainty. With English summary.) *L'Actual. Econ.*, June-September 1987, *63*(2–3), pp. 256–81.

Dixit, Avinash K. Trade and Insurance with Moral Hazard. *J. Int. Econ.*, November 1987, *23*(3/4), pp. 201–20.

Drèze, Jacques H. (Uncertainty and) the Firm in General Equilibrium Theory. *Drèze, J. H.*, 1987, *1985*, pp. 321–43.

Drèze, Jacques H. A Paradox in Information Theory. *Drèze, J. H.*, 1987, pp. 105–12.

Drèze, Jacques H. Axiomatic Theories of Choice, Cardinal Utility and Subjective Probability: A Review. *Drèze, J. H.*, 1987, *1974*, pp. 3–22.

Drèze, Jacques H. Decision Criteria for Business Firms. *Drèze, J. H.*, 1987, *1982*, pp. 298–320.

Drèze, Jacques H. Decision Theory with Moral Hazard and State-Dependent Preferences. *Drèze, J. H.*, 1987, pp. 23–89.

Drèze, Jacques H. Demand Estimation, Risk Aversion and Sticky Prices. *Drèze, J. H.*, 1987, *1979*, pp. 144–49.

Drèze, Jacques H. Econometrics and Decision Theory. *Drèze, J. H.*, 1987, *1972*, pp. 401–19.

Drèze, Jacques H. Espérance morale avec risque moral. (Moral Expectation with Moral Hazard. With English summary.) *L'Actual. Econ.*, June-September 1987, *63*(2–3), pp. 40–57.

Drèze, Jacques H. Human Capital and Risk-Bearing. *Drèze, J. H.*, 1987, *1979*, pp. 347–65.

Drèze, Jacques H. Inferring Risk Tolerance from Deductibles in Insurance Contracts. *Drèze, J. H.*, 1987, *1981*, pp. 113–16.

Drèze, Jacques H. Logical Foundations of Cardinal Utility and Subjective Probability. *Drèze, J. H.*, 1987, pp. 90–104.

Drèze, Jacques H. Market Allocation under Uncertainty. *Drèze, J. H.*, 1987, *1971*, pp. 119–43.

Drèze, Jacques H. and Dehez, Pierre. State-Dependent Utility, the Demand for Insurance and the Value of Safety. *Drèze, J. H.*, 1987, *1982*, pp. 153–81.

Drèze, Jacques H. and Modigliani, Franco. Consumption Decisions under Uncertainty. *Drèze, J. H.*, 1987, *1972*, pp. 182–212.

Drèze, Jacques H. and Sheshinski, Eytan. Demand Fluctuations, Capacity Utilisation and Costs. *Drèze, J. H.*, 1987, *1976*, pp. 234–49.

Drèze, Jacques H. and Sheshinski, Eytan. On Industry Equilibrium under Uncertainty. *Drèze, J. H.*, 1987, *1984*, pp. 250–58.

Duffie, Darrell. Stochastic Equilibria with Incomplete Financial Markets. *J. Econ. Theory*, April 1987, *41*(2), pp. 405–16.

Dyer, James S. and Ravinder, H. V. A Rationale for Additive Decomposition in Multiattribute Utility Assessment. *Sawaragi, Y.; Inoue, K. and Nakayama, H., eds.*, 1987, pp. 277–85.

Eeckhoudt, Louis; Bauwens, Luc and Lebrun, Thérèse. Théorie de l'information et diagnostic médical: Une analyse coût-efficacité. (Information Theory and Medical Diagnosis: A Cost-Efficiency Analysis. With English summary.) *L'Actual. Econ.*, June-September 1987, *63*(2–3), pp. 243–55.

Eeckhoudt, Louis; Sneessens, Henri R. and Calcoen, Francis. L'épargne de précaution et les changements de risque. (Precautionary Saving and Changes in Risk. With English summary.) *L'Actual. Econ.*, June-September 1987, *63*(2–3), pp. 213–24.

Eichenbaum, Martin S. and Peled, Dan. Capital Accumulation and Annuities in an Adverse Selection Economy. *J. Polit. Econ.*, April 1987, *95*(2), pp. 334–54.

Encarnación, J. Preference Paradoxes and Lexicographic Choice. *J. Econ. Behav. Organ.*, June 1987, *8*(2), pp. 231–48.

Engers, Maxim. Signalling with Many Signals. *Econometrica*, May 1987, *55*(3), pp. 663–74.

Farrell, Joseph. Information and the Coase Theorem. *J. Econ. Perspectives*, Fall 1987, *1*(2), pp. 113–29.

Feiwel, George R. The Potentials and Limits of Economic Analysis: The Contributions of Kenneth J. Arrow. *Feiwel, G. R., ed. (I)*, 1987, pp. 1–187.

Feldman, Mark D. Bayesian Learning and Convergence to Rational Expectations. *J. Math.*

Econ., 1987, *16*(3), pp. 297–313.

Finsinger, Jörg and von der Schulenburg, J.-Matthias Graf. Nachfragerverhalten bei unvollständigen Preisinformationen—eine Marktanalyse am Beispiel der Kraftfahrzeugversicherung. (Consumer Behavior under Incomplete Price Information—Survey Results from the Automobile Insurance Market. With English summary.) *Jahr. Nationalökon. Statist.*, May 1987, *203*(3), pp. 244–56. **[G: W. Germany]**

Firchau, Volker. Information Systems for Principal–Agent Problems. *Bamberg, G. and Spremann, K., eds.*, 1987, pp. 81–92.

Fishburn, Peter C. Reconsiderations in the Foundations of Decision under Uncertainty. *Econ. J.*, December 1987, *97*(388), pp. 825–41.

Fishe, Raymond P. H. and McAfee, R. Preston. Nonlinear Contracts, Zero Profits and Moral Hazard. *Economica*, February 1987, *54*(213), pp. 97–101.

Friedman, Benjamin M. and Roley, V. Vance. Aspects of Investor Behaviour under Risk. *Feiwel, G. R., ed. (I)*, 1987, pp. 626–53. **[G: U.S.]**

Froyen, Richard T. and Waud, Roger N. An Examination of Aggregate Price Uncertainty in Four Countries and Some Implications for Real Output. *Int. Econ. Rev.*, June 1987, *28*(2), pp. 353–72. **[G: U.S.; U.K.; Canada; W. Germany]**

Fuhrer, Jeffrey C. Information Gathering and Expectation Formation under Model Uncertainty. *Southern Econ. J.*, January 1987, *53*(3), pp. 685–701.

Gal-Or, Esther. First Mover Disadvantages with Private Information. *Rev. Econ. Stud.*, April 1987, *54*(2), pp. 279–92.

Gilboa, Itzhak. Expected Utility with Purely Subjective Non-additive Probabilities. *J. Math. Econ.*, 1987, *16*(1), pp. 65–88.

Giuseppi, Russo. Disoccupazione e incertezza. Una applicazione della teoria dell'utilità attesa. (Unemployment and Uncertainty. An Application the the Expected Utility Theory. With English summary.) *Giorn. Econ.*, May-June 1987, *46*(5–6), pp. 317–46.

Gollier, Christian. The Design of Optimal Insurance Contracts without the Nonnegativity Constraint on Claims. *J. Risk Ins.*, June 1987, *54*(2), pp. 314–24.

Gougeon, Patrick. Assurance et diversification. (Insurance and Diversification. With English summary.) *L'Actual. Econ.*, June-September 1987, *63*(2–3), pp. 187–99.

Grandmont, Jean-Michel and Laroque, Guy. Stability of Cycles and Expectations. *Grandmont, J.-M., ed.*, 1987, *1986*, pp. 138–51.

Green, Jerry R. "Making Book against Oneself," the Independence Axiom, and Nonlinear Utility Theory. *Quart. J. Econ.*, November 1987, *102*(4), pp. 785–96.

Green, Jerry R. and Laffont, Jean-Jacques. Limited Communication and Incentive Compatibility. *[Hurwicz, L.]*, 1987, pp. 308–29.

Green, Jerry R. and Laffont, Jean-Jacques. Posterior Implementability in a Two-Person Decision Problem. *Econometrica*, January 1987, 55(1), pp. 69–94.

Greenwald, Bruce C. and Stiglitz, Joseph E. Imperfect Information, Credit Markets and Unemployment. *Europ. Econ. Rev.*, Feb./Mar. 1987, 31(1/2), pp. 444–56.

de Grolier, Eric. Government, the Information Industry and Social Intelligence. *Dedijer, S. and Jéquier, N., eds.*, 1987, pp. 79–92.

Gruber, Andreas. Signalling and Market Behavior. *Bamberg, G. and Spremann, K., eds.*, 1987, pp. 205–27.

Guasch, J. Luis and Weiss, Andrew. Existence of an Optimal Random Monitor: The Labor Market Case. *Invest. Ecón.*, January 1987, 11(1), pp. 95–99.

Hadar, Josef and Seo, Tae Kun. Consistent Planning under Uncertain Lifetime. *Int. Econ. J.*, Summer 1987, 1(2), pp. 95–108.

Hahm, Sangmoon. Information Acquisition in an Incomplete Information Model of Business Cycle. *J. Monet. Econ.*, July 1987, 20(1), pp. 123–40.

Hargreaves Heap, Shaun P. Risk and Culture: A Missing Link in the Post Keynesian Tradition. *J. Post Keynesian Econ.*, Winter 1986-87, 9(2), pp. 267–78.

Harpaz, Giora and Thomadakis, Stavros B. Valuation under Imperfect Information: Bayesian Learning from the Performance of the Firm and the Market. *Managerial Dec. Econ.*, September 1987, 8(3), pp. 229–34.

Harrington, Joseph E., Jr. Oligopolistic Entry Deterrence under Incomplete Information. *Rand J. Econ.*, Summer 1987, 18(2), pp. 211–31.

Harris, Christopher and Vickers, John. Racing with Uncertainty. *Rev. Econ. Stud.*, January 1987, 54(1), pp. 1–21.

Harris, Milton and Holmstrom, Bengt. On the Duration of Agreements. *Int. Econ. Rev.*, June 1987, 28(2), pp. 389–406.

Harsanyi, John C. Von Neumann–Morgenstern Utilities, Risk Taking, and Welfare. *Feiwel, G. R., ed. (I)*, 1987, pp. 545–58.

Hartman, Richard and Plummer, Mark L. Option Value under Income and Price Uncertainty. *J. Environ. Econ. Manage.*, September 1987, 14(3), pp. 212–25.

Hartmann-Wendels, Thomas. Dividend Policy under Asymmetric Information. *Bamberg, G. and Spremann, K., eds.*, 1987, pp. 229–53.

Haruna, Shoji. Random Input Price and the Theory of the Competitive Cooperative Firm. *J. Compar. Econ.*, March 1987, 11(1), pp. 81–95.

Hax, Herbert. Institutions for Stochastic Markets: Comment. *J. Inst. Theoretical Econ.*, March 1987, 143(1), pp. 107–09.

Henderson, Dennis R. Economic Efficiency and Market Information: A Discussion. *Kilmer, R. L. and Armbruster, W. J., eds.*, 1987, pp. 205–08.

Hendricks, Kenneth; Porter, Robert H. and Boudreau, Bryan. Information, Returns, and Bidding Behavior in OCS Auctions: 1954–1969. *J. Ind. Econ.*, June 1987, 35(4), pp. 517–42.
[G: U.S.]

Henriet, Dominique and Rochet, Jean-Charles. Some Reflections on Insurance Pricing. *Europ. Econ. Rev.*, June 1987, 31(4), pp. 863–85.
[G: France]

Hey, John D. Still Searching [Search for Rules for Search]. *J. Econ. Behav. Organ.*, March 1987, 8(1), pp. 137–44.

Hey, John D. The Dynamic Competitive Firm under Spot Price Uncertainty. *Manchester Sch. Econ. Soc. Stud.*, March 1987, 55(1), pp. 1–12.

Hjorth-Andersen, Chr. Forbrugeroplysning spgsm om milliarder. (The Economic Importance of Imperfect Consumer Information. With English summary.) *Nationaløkon. Tidsskr.*, 1987, 125(1), pp. 78–94.
[G: Denmark]

Holmstrom, Bengt and Milgrom, Paul R. Aggregation and Linearity in the Provision of Intertemporal Incentives. *Econometrica*, March 1987, 55(2), pp. 303–28.

Hoogduin, Lex. On the Difference between the Keynesian, Knightian and the 'Classical' Analysis of Uncertainty and the Development of a More General Monetary Theory. *De Economist*, 1987, 135(1), pp. 52–65.

Horowitz, Ann R. Loss Functions and Public Policy. *J. Macroecon.*, Fall 1987, 9(4), pp. 489–504.

Isaac, R. Mark. The Value of Information in Resource Exploration: The Interaction of Strategic Plays and Institutional Rules. *J. Environ. Econ. Manage.*, December 1987, 14(4), pp. 313–22.

Itoh, Hideshi. Information Processing Capacities of the Firm. *J. Japanese Int. Economies*, September 1987, 1(3), pp. 299–326. [G: Japan; U.S.]

Jewitt, Ian. Risk Aversion and the Choice between Risky Prospects: The Preservation of Comparative Statics Results. *Rev. Econ. Stud.*, January 1987, 54(1), pp. 73–85.

Jordan, James S. The Informational Requirements of Local Stability in Decentralized Allocation Mechanisms. *[Hurwicz, L.]*, 1987, pp. 183–212.

Jose, Manuel L. and Stevens, Jerry L. Product Market Structure, Capital Intensity, and Systematic Risk: Empirical Results from the Theory of the Firm. *J. Finan. Res.*, Summer 1987, 10(2), pp. 161–75. [G: U.S.]

Karni, Edi. Generalized Expected Utility Analysis of Risk Aversion with State-Dependent Preference. *Int. Econ. Rev.*, February 1987, 28(1), pp. 229–40.

Katz, Eliakim and Stark, Oded. Migration, Information and the Costs and Benefits of Signalling. *Reg. Sci. Urban Econ.*, August 1987, 17(3), pp. 323–31.

Katzner, Donald W. More on the Distinction between Potential Confirmation and Probability. *J. Post Keynesian Econ.*, Fall 1987, 10(1), pp. 65–83.

Kaylen, Michael S.; Preckel, Paul V. and Loehman, Edna T. Risk Modeling via Direct Utility Maximization Using Numerical Quadrature. *Amer. J. Agr. Econ.*, August 1987, *69*(3), pp. 701–06.

Keck, Otto. The Information Dilemma: Private Information as a Cause of Transaction Failure in Markets, Regulation, Hierarchy, and Politics. *J. Conflict Resolution*, March 1987, *31*(1), pp. 139–63.

Kim, Jong Seok. Optimal Price–Quality Schedules and Sustainability. *J. Ind. Econ.*, December 1987, *36*(2), pp. 231–44.

Kim, Young Chin and Yoon, Bong Joon. Risk Behavior under Linear Utility Function. *Int. Econ. J.*, Autumn 1987, *1*(3), pp. 49–56.

Kmenta, Jan. Institutions for Stochastic Markets: Comment. *J. Inst. Theoretical Econ.*, March 1987, *143*(1), pp. 104–06.

Krahnen, Jan P. and Meran, Georg. Why Leasing? An Introduction to Comparative Contractual Analysis. *Bamberg, G. and Spremann, K., eds.*, 1987, pp. 255–80.

Kuenne, Robert E. Oligopolistic Uncertainty and Optimal Bidding in Government Procurement: A Subjective Probability Approach. *Feiwel, G. R., ed. (I)*, 1987, pp. 654–74.

Laffont, Jean-Jacques. Toward a Normative Theory of Incentive Contracts between Government and Private Firms. *Econ. J.*, Supplement 1987, *97*, pp. 17–31.

Lawrence, David B. The Assessment of the Expected Value of Information in the Binary Decision Model. *Managerial Dec. Econ.*, December 1987, *8*(4), pp. 301–06.

Leibenstein, Harvey. On Some Economic Aspects of a Fragile Input: Trust. *Feiwel, G. R., ed. (II)*, 1987, pp. 600–612.

LeRoy, Stephen F. and Singell, Larry D., Jr. Knight on Risk and Uncertainty. *J. Polit. Econ.*, April 1987, *95*(2), pp. 394–406.

Li, Lode; McKelvey, Richard D. and Page, Talbot. Optimal Research for Cournot Oligopolists. *J. Econ. Theory*, June 1987, *42*(1), pp. 140–66.

Loewenstein, George. Anticipation and the Valuation of Delayed Consumption. *Econ. J.*, September 1987, *97*(387), pp. 666–84.

Löfgren, Karl-Gustaf and Ranneby, Bo. Behavioral Modes for a Firm Facing an Uncertain Supply or Demand Curve. *Scand. J. Econ.*, 1987, *89*(1), pp. 39–54.

Loomes, Graham and Sugden, Robert. Some Implications of a More General Form of Regret Theory. *J. Econ. Theory*, April 1987, *41*(2), pp. 270–87.

Loomes, Graham and Sugden, Robert. Testing for Regret and Disappointment in Choice under Uncertainty. *Econ. J.*, Supplement 1987, *97*, pp. 118–29.

Machina, Mark J. Choice under Uncertainty: Problems Solved and Unsolved. *J. Econ. Perspectives*, Summer 1987, *1*(1), pp. 121–54.

Machina, Mark J. and Neilson, William S. The Ross Characterization of Risk Aversion: Strengthening and Extension. *Econometrica*,

September 1987, *55*(5), pp. 1139–49.

MacMinn, Richard D. Insurance and Corporate Risk Management. *J. Risk Ins.*, December 1987, *54*(4), pp. 658–77.

Marrelli, M. The Economic Analysis of Tax Evasion: Empirical Aspects. *Hey, J. D. and Lambert, P. J., eds.*, 1987, pp. 204–28. [G: U.S.; W. Europe]

Maskin, Eric and Tirole, Jean. Correlated Equilibria and Sunspots. *J. Econ. Theory*, December 1987, *43*(2), pp. 364–73.

Matthews, Steven. Comparing Auctions for Risk Averse Buyers: A Buyer's Point of View. *Econometrica*, May 1987, *55*(3), pp. 633–46.

Matthews, Steven and Moore, John. Monopoly Provision of Quality and Warranties: An Exploration in the Theory of Multidimensional Screening. *Econometrica*, March 1987, *55*(2), pp. 441–67.

McAfee, R. Preston and McMillan, John. Auctions and Bidding. *J. Econ. Lit.*, June 1987, *25*(2), pp. 699–738.

McAfee, R. Preston and McMillan, John. Auctions with a Stochastic Number of Bidders. *J. Econ. Theory*, October 1987, *43*(1), pp. 1–19.

McCarl, Bruce A. Interpretations and Transformations of Scale for the Pratt–Arrow Absolute Risk Aversion Coefficient: Implications for Generalized Stochastic Dominance: Comment. *Western J. Agr. Econ.*, December 1987, *12*(2), pp. 228–30.

McCarl, Bruce A., et al. Stochastic Dominance over Potential Portfolios: Caution Regarding Covariance. *Amer. J. Agr. Econ.*, November 1987, *69*(4), pp. 804–12.

McKenna, Christopher J. Models of Search Market Equilibrium. *Hey, J. D. and Lambert, P. J., eds.*, 1987, pp. 110–23.

McKenna, Christopher J. Theories of Individual Search Behaviour. *Hey, J. D. and Lambert, P. J., eds.*, 1987, *1986*, pp. 91–109.

McNulty, James E. Measuring Interest Rate Risk: What Do We Really Know? *Wilcox, J. A., ed.*, 1987, *1986*, pp. 37–46.

Melody, William H. Information: An Emerging Dimension of Institutional Analysis. *J. Econ. Issues*, September 1987, *21*(3), pp. 1313–39.

Mendelson, Haim. Quantile-Preserving Spread. *J. Econ. Theory*, August 1987, *42*(2), pp. 334–51.

Merton, Robert C. A Simple Model of Capital Market Equilibrium with Incomplete Information. *J. Finance*, July 1987, *42*(3), pp. 483–510.

Meyer, Jack. Two-moment Decision Models and Expected Utility Maximization. *Amer. Econ. Rev.*, June 1987, *77*(3), pp. 421–30.

Meyer, Margaret A. and Mookherjee, Dilip. Incentives, Compensation, and Social Welfare. *Rev. Econ. Stud.*, April 1987, *54*(2), pp. 209–26.

de Meza, David and Webb, David C. Too Much Investment: A Problem of Asymmetric Information. *Quart. J. Econ.*, May 1987, *102*(2), pp. 281–92.

Milde, Hellmuth. Managerial Contracting with Public and Private Information. *Bamberg, G.*

and Spremann, K., eds., 1987, pp. 39–59.

Milne, Frank and Shefrin, H. M. Information and Securities: A Note on Pareto Dominance and the Second Best. *J. Econ. Theory*, December 1987, *43*(2), pp. 314–28.

Moffet, Denis. Axiomes de rationalité en contexte d'incertitude. (Axioms of Rationality under Uncertainty. With English summary.) *L'Actual. Econ.*, June-September 1987, *63*(2–3), pp. 58–73.

Montesano, Aldo. Utility and Uncertainty in Intertemporal Choice. *Carraro, C. and Sartore, D., eds.*, 1987, pp. 135–42.

Mount, Kenneth R. and Reiter, Stanley. On the Existence of a Locally Stable Dynamic Process with a Statically Minimal Message Space. *[Hurwicz, L.]*, 1987, pp. 213–40.

Mura, Alberto. Verso una generalizzazione della teoria bayesiana delle decisioni. (Toward a Generalization of the Bayesian Decision Theory. With English summary.) *Econ. Scelte Pubbliche/J. Public Finance Public Choice*, Jan.-Apr. 1987, *5*(1), pp. 53–67.

Nalebuff, Barry and Scharfstein, David. Testing in Models of Asymmetric Information. *Rev. Econ. Stud.*, April 1987, *54*(2), pp. 265–77.

Nielsen, Lars Tyge. Corrigenda [Unbounded Expected Utility and Continuity]. *Math. Soc. Sci.*, October 1987, *14*(2), pp. 193–94.

Ondrich, Jan. Job Search: The Choice of Intensity: A Comment. *J. Polit. Econ.*, October 1987, *95*(5), pp. 1098–1102.

Palfrey, Thomas R. and Srivastava, Sanjay. On Bayesian Implementable Allocations. *Rev. Econ. Stud.*, April 1987, *54*(2), pp. 193–208.

Pelloni, Gianluigi. Atteggiamento neo-bayesiano e aspettative razionali: alcune considerazioni. (Rational Expectations and the Neo-Bayesian Approach. With English summary.) *Econ. Polit.*, December 1987, *4*(3), pp. 357–79.

Pfingsten, Andreas. Incentives to Forecast Honestly. *Bamberg, G. and Spremann, K., eds.*, 1987, pp. 117–33.

Picard, Pierre. On the Design of Incentive Schemes under Moral Hazard and Adverse Selection. *J. Public Econ.*, August 1987, *33*(3), pp. 305–31.

Pitchik, Carolyn and Schotter, Andrew. Honesty in a Model of Strategic Information Transmission. *Amer. Econ. Rev.*, December 1987, *77*(5), pp. 1032–36.

van der Ploeg, Frederick. Inefficiency of Credible Strategies in Oligopolistic Resource Markets with Uncertainty. *J. Econ. Dynam. Control*, March 1987, *11*(1), pp. 123–45.

Pope, Rulon D. An Analogy between Risk Aversion and Homothetic Production under Certainty. *Amer. J. Agr. Econ.*, May 1987, *69*(2), pp. 378–81.

Postlewaite, Andrew and Schmeidler, David. Differential Information and Strategic Behavior in Economic Environments: A General Equilibrium Approach. *[Hurwicz, L.]*, 1987, pp. 330–48.

Pratt, John W. Multiattribute Utility and Derived Utility. *Sawaragi, Y.; Inoue, K. and Naka-*

yama, H., eds., 1987, pp. 149–54.

Pratt, John W. and Zeckhauser, Richard J. Incentive-Based Decentralization: Expected-Externality Payments Induce Efficient Behaviour in Groups. *Feiwel, G. R., ed. (I)*, 1987, pp. 439–83.

Pratt, John W. and Zeckhauser, Richard J. Proper Risk Aversion. *Econometrica*, January 1987, *55*(1), pp. 143–54.

Preckel, Paul V.; Loehman, Edna T. and Kaylen, Michael S. The Value of Public Information for Microeconomic Production Decisions. *Western J. Agr. Econ.*, December 1987, *12*(2), pp. 193–97.   [G: U.S.]

Quiggin, John. Decision Weights in Anticipated Utility Theory: Response [A Theory of Anticipated Utility]. *J. Econ. Behav. Organ.*, December 1987, *8*(4), pp. 641–45.

Radner, Roy. Decentralization and Incentives. *[Hurwicz, L.]*, 1987, *1983*, pp. 3–47.

Rafiquzzaman, M. The Optimal Patent Term under Uncertainty. *Int. J. Ind. Organ.*, June 1987, *5*(2), pp. 233–46.

Rasmusen, Eric. Moral Hazard in Risk-Averse Teams. *Rand J. Econ.*, Autumn 1987, *18*(3), pp. 428–35.

Rea, Samuel A., Jr. The Market Response to the Elimination of Sex-Based Annuities. *Southern Econ. J.*, July 1987, *54*(1), pp. 55–63.

Riordan, Michael H. and Sappington, David E. M. Awarding Monopoly Franchises. *Amer. Econ. Rev.*, June 1987, *77*(3), pp. 375–87.

Riordan, Michael H. and Sappington, David E. M. Information, Incentives, and Organizational Mode. *Quart. J. Econ.*, May 1987, *102*(2), pp. 243–63.

Rob, Rafael. Entry, Fixed Costs and the Aggregation of Private Information. *Rev. Econ. Stud.*, October 1987, *54*(4), pp. 619–30.

Roberts, John. Incentives, Information, and Iterative Planning. *[Hurwicz, L.]*, 1987, pp. 349–74.

Rochet, Jean-Charles. Some Recent Results in Bargaining Theory. *Europ. Econ. Rev.*, Feb./Mar. 1987, *31*(1/2), pp. 326–35.

Röell, Ailsa A. Risk Aversion in Quiggin and Yaari's Rank–Order Model of Choice under Uncertainty. *Econ. J.*, Supplement 1987, *97*, pp. 143–59.

Rogerson, William P. A Note on the Existence of Single Price Equilibrium Price Distributions in Sequential Search Models. *Rev. Econ. Stud.*, April 1987, *54*(2), pp. 339–42.

Rowley, Robin and Hamouda, Omar. Troublesome Probability and Economics. *J. Post Keynesian Econ.*, Fall 1987, *10*(1), pp. 44–64.

Rubinstein, Ariel and Wolinsky, Asher. Middlemen. *Quart. J. Econ.*, August 1987, *102*(3), pp. 581–93.

Saari, Donald G. The Source of Some Paradoxes from Social Choice and Probability. *J. Econ. Theory*, February 1987, *41*(1), pp. 1–22.

Saari, Donald G. and Williams, Steven R. On the Local Convergence of Economic Mechanisms. *Grandmont, J.-M., ed.*, 1987, *1986*, pp. 152–67.

Salop, Steven C. Evaluating Uncertain Evidence with Sir Thomas Bayes: A Note for Teachers. *J. Econ. Perspectives,* Summer 1987, *1*(1), pp. 155–59.

Salop, Steven C. and Stiglitz, Joseph E. Information, Welfare, and Product Diversity. *Feiwel, G. R., ed. (II),* 1987, pp. 328–40.

Samuelson, Larry. On the Restrictiveness of Monotonic Scalable Choice in Probabilistic Choice Models. *Math. Soc. Sci.,* August 1987, *14*(1), pp. 19–38.

Schlesinger, Harris and von der Schulenburg, J.-Matthias Graf. Risk Aversion and the Purchase of Risky Insurance. *J. Econ. (Z. Nationalökon.),* 1987, *47*(3), pp. 309–14.

von der Schulenburg, J.-Matthias Graf. Marktgeschehen bei unvollständigen Nachfragerinformationen. Die Auswirkungen von Anbieterwechselkosten und Informationskosten in dynamischen Markprozessen. (With English summary.) *Z. Betriebswirtshaft,* July 1987, *57*(7), pp. 699–719. **[G: W. Germany]**

Segal, Uzi. Some Remarks on Quiggin's Anticipated Utility [A Theory of Anticipated Utility]. *J. Econ. Behav. Organ.,* March 1987, *8*(1), pp. 145–54.

Segal, Uzi. The Ellsberg Paradox and Risk Aversion: An Anticipated Utility Approach. *Int. Econ. Rev.,* February 1987, *28*(1), pp. 175–202.

Seidmann, Daniel J. Incentives for Information Production and Disclosure: Comment [The Strategic Role of Information on the Demand Function in an Oligopolistic Market]. *Quart. J. Econ.,* May 1987, *102*(2), pp. 445–52.

Shaw, Graham K. Rational Expectations. *Bull. Econ. Res.,* July 1987, *39*(3), pp. 187–209.

Siebert, Horst. Risk Allocation in Large-scale Resource Ventures. *Kyklos,* 1987, *40*(4), pp. 476–95.

Smith, Michael L. and Buser, Stephen A. Risk Aversion, Insurance Costs and Optimal Property-Liability Coverages. *J. Risk Ins.,* June 1987, *54*(2), pp. 226–45.

Smith, V. Kerry and Desvousges, William H. An Empirical Analysis of the Economic Value of Risk Changes. *J. Polit. Econ.,* February 1987, *95*(1), pp. 89–114. **[G: U.S.]**

Soubiran-Zone, Danièla. Les effets de l'asymétrie informationnelle dans l'appréciation des qualités et des opportunités. (Informational Asymmetries Effects in Quality and Opportunities Appreciations. With English summary.) *Écon. Soc.,* January 1987, *21*(1), pp. 129–47.

Spremann, Klaus. Agent and Principal. *Bamberg, G. and Spremann, K., eds.,* 1987, pp. 3–37.

Sproule, Robert A. The Owner-Managed Firm under Output-Price Uncertainty: A Model Based on a Synthesis of Sandmo (1971), Block and Heineke (1973), and Ishii (1977). *J. Econ. (Z. Nationalökon.),* 1987, *47*(2), pp. 125–41.

Stein, Jeremy C. Informational Externalities and Welfare-Reducing Speculation. *J. Polit. Econ.,* December 1987, *95*(6), pp. 1123–45.

Stiglitz, Joseph E. The Causes and Consequences of the Dependence of Quality on Price. *J.*

Econ. Lit., March 1987, *25*(1), pp. 1–48.

Strand, Jon. The Relationship between Wages and Firm Size: An Information Theoretic Analysis. *Int. Econ. Rev.,* February 1987, *28*(1), pp. 51–68.

Suppes, Patrick. Maximizing Freedom of Decision: An Axiomatic Analysis. *Feiwel, G. R., ed. (II),* 1987, pp. 243–54.

Tamura, H.; Mori, Y. and Nakamura, Y. On a Measurable Value Function under Risk: A Descriptive Model of Preferences Resolving the Expected Utility Paradoxes. *Sawaragi, Y.; Inoue, K. and Nakayama, H., eds.,* 1987, pp. 210–19.

Taylor, Mark P. Further Developments in the Theory of Implicit Labour Contracts. *Hey, J. D. and Lambert, P. J., eds.,* 1987, pp. 151–72.

Taylor, Mark P. The Simple Analytics of Implicit Labour Contracts. *Bull. Econ. Res.,* January 1987, *39*(1), pp. 1–27.

Taylor, Mark P. The Simple Analytics of Implicit Labour Contracts. *Hey, J. D. and Lambert, P. J., eds.,* 1987, pp. 124–50.

Thomson, William. The Vulnerability to Manipulative Behavior of Resource Allocation Mechanisms Designed to Select Equitable and Efficient Outcomes. *[Hurwicz, L.],* 1987, pp. 375–96.

Townsend, Robert M. Economic Organization with Limited Communication. *Amer. Econ. Rev.,* December 1987, *77*(5), pp. 954–71.

Townsend, Robert M. Taking Pure Theory to Data: Arrow's Seminal Contribution. *Feiwel, G. R., ed. (I),* 1987, pp. 675–81.

Vannini, Marco. Modeling Uncertainty beyond Mathematical Risk: Heiner's C–D Gap Hypothesis. *Stud. Econ.,* 1987, *42*(32), pp. 155–78.

Vazquez-Presedo, Vicente. Expectativas, predicciones keynesianas y otras predicciones. (Expectations, Keynesian Predictions and Other Predictions. With English summary.) *Económica (La Plata),* July-Dec. 1987, *33*(2), pp. 305–22.

Vickers, John. Signalling in a Model of Monetary Policy with Incomplete Information. *Sinclair, P. J. N., ed.,* 1987, *1986,* pp. 471–83.

Viscusi, W. Kip; Magat, Wesley A. and Huber, Joel C. An Investigation of the Rationality of Consumer Valuations of Multiple Health Risks. *Rand J. Econ.,* Winter 1987, *18*(4), pp. 465–79. **[G: U.S.]**

Wagenhofer, Alfred. Investigation Strategies with Costly Perfect Information. *Bamberg, G. and Spremann, K., eds.,* 1987, pp. 347–77.

Wakker, Peter. From Decision Making under Uncertainty to Game Theory. *Peters, H. J. M. and Vrieze, O. J., eds.,* 1987, pp. 163–80.

Wakker, Peter. Subjective Probabilities for State Dependent Continuous Utility. *Math. Soc. Sci.,* December 1987, *14*(3), pp. 289–98.

Wan, Henry, Jr. Arrow and the Theory of Discrimination. *Feiwel, G. R., ed. (I),* 1987, pp. 484–97.

Webb, David C. The Importance of Incomplete

Information in Explaining the Existence of Costly Bankruptcy. *Economica*, August 1987, 54(215), pp. 279–88.

Weymark, John A. Comparative Static Properties of Optimal Nonlinear Income Taxes. *Econometrica*, September 1987, 55(5), pp. 1165–85.

Wilde, Louis L. Consumer Behavior under Imperfect Information: A Review of Psychological and Marketing Research as It Relates to Economic Theory. *Green, L. and Kagel, J. H., eds.*, 1987, pp. 219–48.

Williams, Jeffrey. Futures Markets: A Consequences of Risk Aversion or Transactions Costs? *J. Polit. Econ.*, October 1987, 95(5), pp. 1000–1023.

Williamson, Stephen D. Costly Monitoring, Loan Contracts, and Equilibrium Credit Rationing. *Quart. J. Econ.*, February 1987, 102(1), pp. 135–45.

Wilman, Elizabeth A. A Note on Supply Side Option Value. *Land Econ.*, August 1987, 63(3), pp. 284–89.

Wu, Ho-mou. On the Theory of Effective Demand under Stochastic Rationing. *Econ. J.*, June 1987, 97(386), pp. 487–92.

Yaari, Menahem E. The Dual Theory of Choice under Risk. *Econometrica*, January 1987, 55(1), pp. 95–115.

Zilcha, Itzhak. Characterizing the Efficient Set When Preferences Are State-Dependent. *J. Econ. Theory*, April 1987, 41(2), pp. 417–23.

0262 Game Theory and Bargaining Theory

Abdou, Joseph. Stable Effectivity Functions with an Infinity of Players and Alternatives. *J. Math. Econ.*, 1987, 16(3), pp. 291–95.

Abou-Kandil, H. and Bertrand, P. Government–Private Sector Relations as a Stackelberg Game: A Degenerate Case. *J. Econ. Dynam. Control*, December 1987, 11(4), pp. 513–17.

Admati, Anat R. and Perry, Motty. Strategic Delay in Bargaining. *Rev. Econ. Stud.*, July 1987, 54(3), pp. 345–64.

Aivazian, Varouj A.; Callen, Jeffrey L. and Lipnowski, Irwin. The Coase Theorem and Coalitional Stability. *Economica*, November 1987, 54(216), pp. 517–20.

Alesina, Alberto. Macroeconomic Policy in a Two-Party System as a Repeated Game. *Quart. J. Econ.*, August 1987, 102(3), pp. 651–78.

Alesina, Alberto. Rules, Discretion and Reputation in a Two-Party System. *Giorn. Econ.*, Jan.-Feb. 1987, 46(1–2), pp. 3–27.

Anderson, M. and Harary, F. Achievement and Avoidance Games for Generating Abelian Groups. *Int. J. Game Theory*, 1987, 16(4), pp. 321–25.

d'Aspremont, Claude; Jacquemin, Alexis and Mertens, J.-F. A Measure of Aggregate Power in Organizations. *J. Econ. Theory*, October 1987, 43(1), pp. 184–91.

Atkinson, Scott E.; Sandler, Todd and Tschirhart, John. Terrorism in a Bargaining Framework. *J. Law Econ.*, April 1987, 30(1), pp. 1–21.   [G: Global]

Aumann, Robert J. Correlated Equilibrium as an Expression of Bayesian Rationality. *Econometrica*, January 1987, 55(1), pp. 1–18.

Aumann, Robert J.; Kurz, Mordecai and Neyman, Abraham. Power and Public Goods. *J. Econ. Theory*, June 1987, 42(1), pp. 108–27.

Baba, Norio. Microcomputer-Based Games for the Purposes of Environmental Protection and Managemental Training. *Sawaragi, Y.; Inoue, K. and Nakayama, H., eds.*, 1987, pp. 403–11.

Badke, Michael. Corrigendum [Optimal Cartel Trigger Price Strategies]. *J. Econ. Theory*, February 1987, 41(1), pp. 216–17.

Bae, Hyung. A Price-Setting Supergame between Two Heterogeneous Firms. *Europ. Econ. Rev.*, August 1987, 31(6), pp. 1159–71.

Bagwell, Kyle. Introductory Price as a Signal of Cost in a Model of Repeat Business. *Rev. Econ. Stud.*, July 1987, 54(3), pp. 365–84.

Baldwin, Robert E. and Clarke, Richard N. Game-Modeling Multilateral Trade Negotiations. *J. Policy Modeling*, Summer 1987, 9(2), pp. 257–84.

Banks, Jeffrey S. and Gasmi, F. Endogenous Agenda Formation in Three-Person Committees. *Soc. Choice Welfare*, June 1987, 4(2), pp. 133–52.

Banks, Jeffrey S. and Sobel, Joel. Equilibrium Selection in Signaling Games. *Econometrica*, May 1987, 55(3), pp. 647–61.

Bartos, Otomar J. How Predictable Are Negotiations? *Zartman, I. W., ed. (I)*, 1987, 1967, pp. 485–509.

Başar, Tamer. Relaxation Techniques and Asynchronous Algorithms for On-Line Computation of Non-cooperative Equilibria. *J. Econ. Dynam. Control*, December 1987, 11(4), pp. 531–49.

Baston, V. J. D. and Bostock, F. A. Discrete Hamstrung Squad Car Games. *Int. J. Game Theory*, 1987, 16(4), pp. 253–61.

Bendor, Jonathan and Mookherjee, Dilip. Institutional Structure and the Logic of Ongoing Collective Action. *Amer. Polit. Sci. Rev.*, March 1987, 81(1), pp. 129–54.

Benoit, Jean-Pierre and Krishna, Vijay. Dynamic Duopoly: Prices and Quantities. *Rev. Econ. Stud.*, January 1987, 54(1), pp. 23–35.

Bernheim, B. Douglas; Peleg, Bezalel and Whinston, Michael D. Coalition-Proof Nash Equilibria: Concepts. *J. Econ. Theory*, June 1987, 42(1), pp. 1–12.

Bernheim, B. Douglas and Whinston, Michael D. Coalition-Proof Nash Equilibria: Applications. *J. Econ. Theory*, June 1987, 42(1), pp. 13–29.

Binmore, Ken. Bargaining Models. *Golombek, R.; Hoel, M. and Vislie, J., eds.*, 1987, pp. 239–52.

Binmore, Ken. Modeling Rational Players: Part 1. *Econ. Philos.*, October 1987, 3(2), pp. 179–214.

Blackburn, Keith. International Policy Games in a Simple Macroeconomic Model with Incomplete Information: Some Problems of Credibility, Secrecy and Cooperation. *Ricerche Econ.*, July-Dec. 1987, *41*(3–4), pp. 419–38.

Blackburn, Keith and Christensen, Michael. Macroeconomic Policy Games and Reputational Equilibria in a Contracting Model. *Ricerche Econ.*, Apr.-June 1987, *41*(2), pp. 190–209.

Blalock, Hubert M., Jr. A Power Analysis of Conflict Processes. *Lawler, E. J. and Markovsky, B., eds.*, 1987, pp. 1–40.

Bonanno, Giacomo. Location Choice, Product Proliferation and Entry Deterrence. *Rev. Econ. Stud.*, January 1987, *54*(1), pp. 37–45.

Borm, Peter. Games with Incomplete Information. *Peters, H. J. M. and Vrieze, O. J., eds.*, 1987, pp. 71–102.

Brams, Steven J. and Kilgour, D. Marc. Winding Down If Preemption or Escalation Occurs: A Game-Theoretic Analysis. *J. Conflict Resolution*, December 1987, *31*(4), pp. 547–72.

Brandenburger, Adam and Dekel, Eddie. Rationalizability and Correlated Equilibria. *Econometrica*, November 1987, *55*(6), pp. 1391–1402.

Bryant, John. The Paradox of Thrift, Liquidity Preference and Animal Spirits. *Econometrica*, September 1987, *55*(5), pp. 1231–35.

Buiter, Willem H. Approaches to the Analysis of Policy Coordination: Overview. *Bryant, R. C. and Portes, R., eds.*, 1987, pp. 66–72.

Bull, Clive. The Existence of Self-Enforcing Implicit Contracts. *Quart. J. Econ.*, February 1987, *102*(1), pp. 147–59.

Cadot, Olivier. Corruption as a Gamble. *J. Public Econ.*, July 1987, *33*(2), pp. 223–44.

Calvert, Randall L. Reputation and Legislative Leadership. *Public Choice*, September 1987, *55*(1–2), pp. 81–119.

Carraro, Carlo. Hierarchical Games for Macroeconomic Policy Analysis. *Carraro, C. and Sartore, D., eds.*, 1987, pp. 215–38.

Carraro, Carlo. Stackelberg Games and the Problem of Time-Inconsistency. *Econ. Notes*, 1987, (3), pp. 5–19.

Carraro, Carlo and Giavazzi, Francesco. Policy Instruments and Coalitions in International Games. *Ricerche Econ.*, July-Dec. 1987, *41*(3–4), pp. 293–314.

Cave, Jonathan. Long-term Competition in a Dynamic Game: The Cold Fish War. *Rand J. Econ.*, Winter 1987, *18*(4), pp. 596–610.

Chatterjee, Kalyan and Samuelson, Larry. Bargaining with Two-Sided Incomplete Information: An Infinite Horizon Model with Alternating Offers. *Rev. Econ. Stud.*, April 1987, *54*(2), pp. 175–92.

Cheng, Harrison H. C. The Coalitional Approach to Core Theory. *J. Math. Econ.*, 1987, *16*(3), pp. 247–58.

Cho, In-Koo. A Refinement of Sequential Equilibrium. *Econometrica*, November 1987, *55*(6), pp. 1367–89.

Clemenz, Gerhard. Adverse Selection and Imperfect Monitoring in a Labour Market: Some Game-Theoretic Remarks. *Empirica*, 1987, *14*(2), pp. 213–26.

Correa, Hector and Gruver, Gene W. Teacher–Student Interaction: A Game Theoretic Extension of the Economic Theory of Education. *Math. Soc. Sci.*, February 1987, *13*(1), pp. 19–47.

Cramton, Peter; Gibbons, Robert and Klemperer, Paul. Dissolving a Partnership Efficiently. *Econometrica*, May 1987, *55*(3), pp. 615–32.

Crémer, Jacques and Riordan, Michael H. On Governing Multilateral Transactions with Bilateral Contracts. *Rand J. Econ.*, Autumn 1987, *18*(3), pp. 436–51.

Curiel, Imma J. A Class of Non-normalized Power Indices for Simple Games. *Math. Soc. Sci.*, April 1987, *13*(2), pp. 141–52.

Curiel, Imma J. Combinatorial Games. *Peters, H. J. M. and Vrieze, O. J., eds.*, 1987, pp. 229–50.

van Damme, Eric. Equilibria in Noncooperative Games. *Peters, H. J. M. and Vrieze, O. J., eds.*, 1987, pp. 1–35.

Dana, Rose-Anne and Montrucchio, Luigi. Dynamic Complexity in Duopoly Games. *Grandmont, J.-M., ed.*, 1987, *1986*, pp. 40–56.

De Fraja, Giovanni and Flavio, Delboni. Oligopoly, Public Firm and Welfare Maximization: A Game-Theoretic Analysis. *Giorn. Econ.*, July-August 1987, *46*(7–8), pp. 416–35.

DeGraba, Patrick J. The Effects of Price Restrictions on Competition between National and Local Firms. *Rand J. Econ.*, Autumn 1987, *18*(3), pp. 333–47.

Demange, Gabrielle. Nonmanipulable Cores. *Econometrica*, September 1987, *55*(5), pp. 1057–74.

Derks, Jean. On the Extreme Elements of the Class of (0,1)-Normalized Superadditive Games. *Peters, H. J. M. and Vrieze, O. J., eds.*, 1987, pp. 215–28.

Dixit, Avinash K. Strategic Aspects of Trade Policy. *Bewley, T. F., ed.*, 1987, pp. 329–62.

Dixit, Avinash K. Strategic Behavior in Contests. *Amer. Econ. Rev.*, December 1987, *77*(5), pp. 891–98.

Domowitz, Ian; Hubbard, R. Glenn and Petersen, Bruce C. Oligopoly Supergames: Some Empirical Evidence on Prices and Margins. *J. Ind. Econ.*, June 1987, *35*(4), pp. 379–98. [G: U.S.]

Drèze, Jacques H. Espérance morale avec risque moral. (Moral Expectation with Moral Hazard. With English summary.) *L'Actual. Econ.*, June-September 1987, *63*(2–3), pp. 40–57.

Driessen, Theo. The τ-Value: A Survey. *Peters, H. J. M. and Vrieze, O. J., eds.*, 1987, pp. 209–13.

Driessen, Theo. The Core of a Cooperative Game: Bounds and Characterizations. *Peters, H. J. M. and Vrieze, O. J., eds.*, 1987, pp. 181–208.

Driffill, John. Credibility and Reputation in Macroeconomic Policy. *Brit. Rev. Econ. Issues*, Spring 1987, *9*(20), pp. 1–25.

Dubey, Pradeep; Geanakoplos, John and Shubik, Martin. The Revelation of Information in Strategic Market Games: A Critique of Rational

Expectations Equilibrium. *J. Math. Econ.*, 1987, *16*(2), pp. 105–37.

Economides, Nicholas S. On Nash Equilibrium Existence and Optimality in Oligopolistic Competition in Prices and Varieties. *Greek Econ. Rev.*, 1987, *9*(2), pp. 198–209.

Encaoua, David and Moreaux, Michel. Concurrence et monopole naturel: une approche par la théorie des jeux. (Competition and Natural Monopoly: A Game Theoretic Approach. With English summary.) *Ann. Écon. Statist.*, Oct./Dec. 1987, (8), pp. 89–116.

Epple, Dennis and Riordan, Michael H. Cooperation and Punishment under Repeated Majority Voting. *Public Choice*, September 1987, *55*(1–2), pp. 41–73.

Farm, Ante and Weibull, Jörgen W. Perfectly Flexible Pricing in a Homogeneous Market. *Scand. J. Econ.*, 1987, *89*(4), pp. 487–95.

Feichtinger, Gustav and Sorger, Gerhard. Intertemporal Sharecropping: A Differential Game Approach. *Bamberg, G. and Spremann, K., eds.*, 1987, pp. 415–38.

Fershtman, Chaim. Alternative Approaches to Dynamic Games. *Bryant, R. C. and Portes, R., eds.*, 1987, pp. 43–57.

Fershtman, Chaim and Kamien, Morton I. Dynamic Duopolistic Competition with Sticky Prices. *Econometrica*, September 1987, *55*(5), pp. 1151–64.

Fluck, Zsuzsanna; Okuguchi, Koji and Szidarovszky, Ferenc. Contribution to Oligopoly Theory: The Case of Uncertain Collusions. *Keio Econ. Stud.*, 1987, *24*(1), pp. 13–23.

Fudenberg, Drew and Kreps, David M. Reputation in the Simultaneous Play of Multiple Opponents. *Rev. Econ. Stud.*, October 1987, *54*(4), pp. 541–68.

Fudenberg, Drew; Levine, David K. and Tirole, Jean. Incomplete Information Bargaining with Outside Opportunities. *Quart. J. Econ.*, February 1987, *102*(1), pp. 37–50.

Fudenberg, Drew and Tirole, Jean. Understanding Rent Dissipation: On the Use of Game Theory in Industrial Organization. *Amer. Econ. Rev.*, May 1987, *77*(2), pp. 176–83.

Gal-Or, Esther. First Mover Disadvantages with Private Information. *Rev. Econ. Stud.*, April 1987, *54*(2), pp. 279–92.

Gal-Or, Esther. Strategic and Non-strategic Differentiation. *Can. J. Econ.*, May 1987, *20*(2), pp. 340–56.

Gardner, Roy J. A Theory of the Spoils System. *Public Choice*, 1987, *54*(2), pp. 171–85.

Graham, John L. A Theory of Interorganizational Negotiations. *Sheth, J. N., ed.*, 1987, pp. 163–83.

Green, Edward J. Cooperation and Punishment under Repeated Majority Voting: A Comment. *Public Choice*, September 1987, *55*(1–2), pp. 75–79.

Gul, Faruk. Noncooperative Collusion in Durable Goods Oligopoly. *Rand J. Econ.*, Summer 1987, *18*(2), pp. 248–54.

Hammond, Peter J. Markets as Constraints: Multilateral Incentive Compatibility in Continuum

Economies. *Rev. Econ. Stud.*, July 1987, *54*(3), pp. 399–412.

Hampton, Jean. Free-Rider Problems in the Production of Collective Goods. *Econ. Philos.*, October 1987, *3*(2), pp. 245–73.

Harker, Patrick T. The Core of a Spatial Price Equilibrium Game. *J. Reg. Sci.*, August 1987, *27*(3), pp. 369–89. **[G: U.S.]**

Harrington, Joseph E., Jr. Collusion in Multiproduct Oligopoly Games under a Finite Horizon. *Int. Econ. Rev.*, February 1987, *28*(1), pp. 1–14.

Haurie, Alain and Pohjola, Matti. Efficient Equilibria in a Differential Game of Capitalism. *J. Econ. Dynam. Control*, March 1987, *11*(1), pp. 65–78.

Hegtvedt, Karen A. and Cook, Karen S. The Role of Justice in Conflict Situations. *Lawler, E. J. and Markovsky, B., eds.*, 1987, pp. 109–36.

Hellwig, Martin and Leininger, Wolfgang. On the Existence of Subgame-perfect Equilibrium in Infinite-action Games of Perfect Information. *J. Econ. Theory*, October 1987, *43*(1), pp. 55–75.

Hillman, Arye L. and Samet, Dov. Characterizing Equilibrium Rent-Seeking Behavior: A Reply. *Public Choice*, 1987, *54*(1), pp. 85–87.

Hillman, Arye L. and Samet, Dov. Dissipation of Contestable Rents by Small Numbers of Contenders. *Public Choice*, 1987, *54*(1), pp. 63–82.

Hirshleifer, Jack. Evolutionary Models in Economics and Law: Cooperation versus Conflict Strategies. *Hirshleifer, J.*, 1987, *1982*, pp. 211–72.

Hirshleifer, Jack. The Economic Approach to Conflict. *Radnitzky, G. and Bernholz, P., eds.*, 1987, pp. 335–64.

Hirshleifer, Jack. The Economic Approach to Conflict. *Hirshleifer, J.*, 1987, *1986*, pp. 273–301.

Hoel, Michael and Vislie, Jon. Bargaining, Bilateral Monopoly and Exhaustible Resources. *Golombek, R.; Hoel, M. and Vislie, J., eds.*, 1987, pp. 253–65.

Holly, Sean. Non-cooperative Dynamic Games with Rational Observers. *J. Econ. Dynam. Control*, June 1987, *11*(2), pp. 159–61.

Holzman, R. Sub-core Solutions of the Problem of Strong Implementation. *Int. J. Game Theory*, 1987, *16*(4), pp. 263–89.

Hubbard, R. Glenn and Weiner, Robert J. Natural Gas Contracting in Practice: Evidence from the United States. *Golombek, R.; Hoel, M. and Vislie, J., eds.*, 1987, pp. 279–313. **[G: U.S.]**

Hughes Hallett, Andrew J. Autonomy and the Choice of Policy in Asymmetrically Dependent Economies. *Sinclair, P. J. N., ed.*, 1987, *1986*, pp. 349–77. **[G: U.S.; EEC]**

Ichiishi, Tatsuro. Strong Equilibria of a Repeated Game with Randomized Strategies. *Math. Soc. Sci.*, December 1987, *14*(3), pp. 201–24.

Ingberman, Daniel E. Reputation and Legislative Leadership: Comment. *Public Choice*, September 1987, *55*(1–2), pp. 121–26.

Intriligator, Michael D. and Brito, Dagobert L.

A Game-Theoretic Analysis of the Role of the Arms Industry in the International Security System. *Borner, S. and Taylor, A., eds.*, 1987, pp. 219–31.

Jansen, Mathijs. Equilibrium Points of Bimatrix Games. *Peters, H. J. M. and Vrieze, O. J., eds.*, 1987, pp. 37–69.

Jensen, Lloyd. Soviet–American Behavior in Disarmament Negotiations. *Zartman, I. W., ed. (I),* 1987, *1963,* pp. 288–321.   [G: U.S.; U.S.S.R.]

Kahn, J.; Lagarias, J. C. and Witsenhausen, H. S. Single-Suit Two-Person Card Play. *Int. J. Game Theory,* 1987, *16*(4), pp. 291–320.

Kaneko, Mamoru. The Conventionally Stable Sets in Non-cooperative Games with Limited Observations I: Definitions and Introductory Arguments. *Math. Soc. Sci.,* April 1987, *13*(2), pp. 93–128.

Kapoor, Ashok. International Business–Government Negotiations: A Study in India. *Zartman, I. W., ed. (I),* 1987, pp. 430–51.   [G: India]

Kotlikoff, Laurence J.; Shoven, John B. and Spivak, Avia. Annuity Markets, Savings, and the Capital Stock. *Bodie, Z.; Shoven, J. B. and Wise, D. A., eds.,* 1987, pp. 211–34.

Kreps, David M. and Ramey, Garey. Structural Consistency, Consistency, and Sequential Rationality. *Econometrica,* November 1987, *55*(6), pp. 1331–48.

Kumar, K. Ravi. The Relationship between Mixed Strategies and Strategic Groups. *Managerial Dec. Econ.,* September 1987, *8*(3), pp. 235–42.

Laing, James D. and Slotznick, Benjamin. Viable Alternatives to the Status Quo: A Game-Theoretic and Laboratory Study of Four-Fifths Majority Rule. *J. Conflict Resolution,* March 1987, *31*(1), pp. 63–85.

Lambelet, Jean-Christian and Luterbacher, Urs. Conflicts, Arms Races and War: A Synthetic Approach. *Schmidt, C. and Blackaby, F., eds.,* 1987, pp. 85–103.

Lambson, Val Eugene. Dynamic Behaviour in Large Markets for Differentiated Products. *Rev. Econ. Stud.,* April 1987, *54*(2), pp. 293–300.

Lambson, Val Eugene. Optimal Penal Codes in Price-Setting Supergames with Capacity Constraints. *Rev. Econ. Stud.,* July 1987, *54*(3), pp. 385–97.

Le Breton, Michel. On the Core of Voting Games. *Soc. Choice Welfare,* December 1987, *4*(4), pp. 295–305.

Le Breton, Michel. On the Generic Nonexistence of Pure Strategy Nash Equilibria in Continuous Games. *J. Econ. Theory,* December 1987, *43*(2), pp. 374–82.

Le Breton, Michel and Salles, M. On the Generic Emptiness of the Local Core of Voting Games. *Soc. Choice Welfare,* December 1987, *4*(4), pp. 287–94.

Leech, Dennis. Ownership Concentration and the Theory of the Firm: A Simple-Game-Theoretic Approach. *J. Ind. Econ.,* March 1987, *35*(3), pp. 225–40.

Leeds, Michael A. Bargaining as Search Behavior under Mutual Uncertainty. *Southern Econ. J.,* January 1987, *53*(3), pp. 677–84.

Legros, Patrick. Disadvantageous Syndicates and Stable Cartels: The Case of the Nucleolus. *J. Econ. Theory,* June 1987, *42*(1), pp. 30–49.

Levine, Paul. Three Themes from Game Theory and International Macroeconomic Policy Formation. *Ricerche Econ.,* July-Dec. 1987, *41*(3–4), pp. 392–418.

Levine, Paul and Currie, David. Does International Macroeconomic Policy Coordination Pay and Is It Sustainable? A Two Country Analysis. *Oxford Econ. Pap.,* March 1987, *39*(1), pp. 38–74.

Levine, Paul and Currie, David. Does International Macroeconomic Policy Coordination Pay and Is It Sustainable? A Two Country Analysis. *Sinclair, P. J. N., ed.,* 1987, pp. 38–74.

Lippman, Steven A.; Mamer, John W. and McCardle, Kevin F. Comparative Statics in Non-cooperative Games via Transfinitely Iterated Play. *J. Econ. Theory,* April 1987, *41*(2), pp. 288–303.

Lippman, Steven A. and McCardle, Kevin F. Dropout Behavior in R&D Races with Learning. *Rand J. Econ.,* Summer 1987, *18*(2), pp. 287–95.

MacLeod, W. Bentley; Norman, G. and Thisse, Jacques-François. Competition, Tacit Collusion and Free Entry. *Econ. J.,* March 1987, *97*(385), pp. 189–98.

Madrigal, Vicente; Tan, Tommy C. C. and da Costa Werlang, Sérgio Ribeiro. Support Restrictions and Sequential Equilibria. *J. Econ. Theory,* December 1987, *43*(2), pp. 329–34.

Mailath, George J. Incentive Compatibility in Signaling Games with a Continuum of Types. *Econometrica,* November 1987, *55*(6), pp. 1349–65.

Makowski, Louis and Ostroy, Joseph M. Vickrey–Clarke–Groves Mechanisms and Perfect Competition. *J. Econ. Theory,* August 1987, *42*(2), pp. 244–61.

Manasse, Paolo. Microfoundations of Fiscal Policy Games under Flexible Exchange Rates: An Example. *Giorn. Econ.,* Jan.-Feb. 1987, *46*(1–2), pp. 55–84.

Manning, Alan. An Integration of Trade Union Models in a Sequential Bargaining Framework. *Econ. J.,* March 1987, *97*(385), pp. 121–39.

Marchi, Ezio and Quintas, Luis G. About Extreme Equilibrium Points: Note. *Math. Soc. Sci.,* June 1987, *13*(3), pp. 273–76.

McKelvey, Richard D. and Ordeshook, Peter C. Elections with Limited Information: A Multidimensional Model. *Math. Soc. Sci.,* August 1987, *14*(1), pp. 77–99.

McKelvey, Richard D. and Schofield, Norman. Generalized Symmetry Conditions at a Core Point. *Econometrica,* July 1987, *55*(4), pp. 923–33.

Meister, Helmut. On the Existence of Approximate Equilibrium in Pure Strategies for a Game with Incomplete Information. *Math. Soc. Sci.,* April 1987, *13*(2), pp. 129–39.

Milgrom, Paul R. and Roberts, John. Informational Asymmetries, Strategic Behavior, and Industrial Organization. *Amer. Econ. Rev.*, May 1987, 77(2), pp. 184–93.

Mirman, Leonard J. Alternative Approaches to Dynamic Games: Discussion. *Bryant, R. C. and Portes, R., eds.*, 1987, pp. 58–63.

Molm, Linda D. Power-Dependence Theory: Power Processes and Negative Outcomes. *Lawler, E. J. and Markovsky, B., eds.*, 1987, pp. 171–98.

Moore, Clement Henry. Prisoners' Financial Dilemmas: A Consociational Future for Lebanon? *Amer. Polit. Sci. Rev.*, March 1987, 81(1), pp. 201–18. [G: Lebanon]

Moore, John and Repullo, Rafael. Implementation by Stage Mechanisms: An Introduction. *Europ. Econ. Rev.*, Feb./Mar. 1987, 31(1/2), pp. 336–41.

Morse, Edward L. The Bargaining Structure of NATO: Multi-issue Negotiations in an Interdependent World. *Zartman, I. W., ed. (I)*, 1987, pp. 66–97.

Moulin, Hervé J. A Core Selection for Regulating a Single-Output Monopoly. *Rand J. Econ.*, Autumn 1987, 18(3), pp. 397–407.

Moulin, Hervé J. Egalitarian-Equivalent Cost Sharing of a Public Good. *Econometrica*, July 1987, 55(4), pp. 963–76.

Mueller, Ulrich. Optimal Retaliation for Optimal Cooperation. *J. Conflict Resolution*, December 1987, 31(4), pp. 692–724.

Murnighan, J. Keith; Roth, Alvin E. and Schoumaker, Françoise. Risk Aversion and Bargaining: Some Preliminary Results. *Europ. Econ. Rev.*, Feb./Mar. 1987, 31(1/2), pp. 265–71.

Nakamori, Y. Interactive Modeling and Gaming-Simulation for Group Decision Making. *Sawaragi, Y.; Inoue, K. and Nakayama, H., eds.*, 1987, pp. 412–21.

Nalebuff, Barry. Credible Pretrial Negotiation. *Rand J. Econ.*, Summer 1987, 18(2), pp. 198–210.

Neck, Reinhard and Dockner, Engelbert. Conflict and Cooperation in a Model of Stabilization Policies: A Differential Game Approach. *J. Econ. Dynam. Control*, June 1987, 11(2), pp. 153–58.

Niou, Emerson M. S. and Ordeshook, Peter C. Preventative War and the Balance of Power: A Game-Theoretic Approach. *J. Conflict Resolution*, September 1987, 31(3), pp. 387–419.

Nogee, Joseph L. Propaganda and Negotiation: The Ten-Nation Disarmament Committee. *Zartman, I. W., ed. (I)*, 1987, 1963, pp. 322–42.

Orkin, Michael. Balanced Strategies for Prisoner's Dilemma. *J. Conflict Resolution*, March 1987, 31(1), pp. 186–91.

Osborne, Martin J. and Pitchik, Carolyn. Equilibrium in Hotelling's Model of Spatial Competition. *Econometrica*, July 1987, 55(4), pp. 911–22.

Patchen, Martin. Strategies for Eliciting Cooperation from an Adversary: Laboratory and International Findings. *J. Conflict Resolution*, March

1987, 31(1), pp. 164–85.

Peleg, Bezalel. Cores and Capacities of Compound Simple Games. *Soc. Choice Welfare*, December 1987, 4(4), pp. 307–16.

Peleg, Bezalel. On the Reduced Game Property and Its Converse: A Correction. *Int. J. Game Theory*, 1987, 16(4), pp. 290.

Peters, Hans. Nonsymmetric Nash Bargaining Solutions. *Peters, H. J. M. and Vrieze, O. J., eds.*, 1987, pp. 277–305.

Petith, Howard C. Strike Costs, Ability to Win and the Determination of Wage Settlements. *Rech. Écon. Louvain*, 1987, 53(4), pp. 345–55.

Potters, Jos. Linear Optimalization Games. *Peters, H. J. M. and Vrieze, O. J., eds.*, 1987, pp. 251–76.

Raskin, A. H. The Newspaper Strike: A Step-by-Step Account. *Zartman, I. W., ed. (I)*, 1987, 1963, pp. 452–80. [G: U.S.]

Reynolds, Stanley S. Capacity Investment, Preemption and Commitment in an Infinite Horizon Model. *Int. Econ. Rev.*, February 1987, 28(1), pp. 69–88.

Roberts, John. Battles for Market Share: Incomplete Information, Aggressive Strategic Pricing, and Competitive Dynamics. *Bewley, T. F., ed.*, 1987, pp. 157–95.

Roberts, John. The Complexity of Strategies and the Resolution of Conflict: An Introduction: Discussion. *Bryant, R. C. and Portes, R., eds.*, 1987, pp. 33–40.

Rochet, Jean-Charles. Some Recent Results in Bargaining Theory. *Europ. Econ. Rev.*, Feb./Mar. 1987, 31(1/2), pp. 326–35.

Romer, Thomas and Rosenthal, Howard. Modern Political Economy and the Study of Regulation. *Bailey, E. E., ed.*, 1987, pp. 73–116. [G: U.S.]

Rosenmüller, Joachim. The Rôle of Nondegeneracy and Homogeneity in n-Person Game Theory: An Equivalence Theorem. *J. Econ. (Z. Nationalökon.)*, 1987, 47(4), pp. 367–89.

Roth, Alvin E. Bargaining Phenomena and Bargaining Theory. *Roth, A. E., ed.*, 1987, pp. 14–41.

Rothchild, Donald. Racial Stratification and Bargaining: The Kenya Experience. *Zartman, I. W., ed. (I)*, 1987, 1973, pp. 235–54. [G: Kenya]

Rothschild, Michael. Annuity Markets, Savings, and the Capital Stock: Comment. *Bodie, Z.; Shoven, J. B. and Wise, D. A., eds.*, 1987, pp. 234–36.

Rubinstein, Ariel. A Sequential Strategic Theory of Bargaining. *Bewley, T. F., ed.*, 1987, pp. 197–224.

Rubinstein, Ariel. The Complexity of Strategies and the Resolution of Conflict: An Introduction. *Bryant, R. C. and Portes, R., eds.*, 1987, pp. 17–32.

Rustem, Berc. Methods for the Simultaneous Use of Multiple Models in Optimal Policy Design. *Carraro, C. and Sartore, D., eds.*, 1987, pp. 157–86.

Salonen, Hannu. Partially Monotonic Bargaining

Solutions. *Soc. Choice Welfare*, March 1987, 4(1), pp. 1–8.

Sanders, Elizabeth. The Regulatory Surge of the 1970s in Historical Perspective. *Bailey, E. E., ed.*, 1987, pp. 117–50. **[G: U.S.]**

Schuler, G. Henry M. The International Oil Negotiations. *Zartman, I. W., ed. (I)*, 1987, pp. 124–207. **[G: OPEC]**

Selten, Reinhard. Equity and Coalition Bargaining in Experimental Three-Person Games. *Roth, A. E., ed.*, 1987, pp. 42–98.

Seo, Fumiko. Socio-economic Interpretation of Multiple Agents Decision Making by Game Theory. *Sawaragi, Y.; Inoue, K. and Nakayama, H., eds.*, 1987, pp. 393–402.

Sertel, Murat R. Explorations in Aggregating Choices. *Math. Soc. Sci.*, December 1987, 14(3), pp. 251–62.

Shiozawa, Shuhei. Pareto Optimality, Core and Equilibria in a Cooperative Super Game without Side Payments. *Keio Econ. Stud.*, 1987, 24(1), pp. 25–41.

Shubik, Martin. The Uses, Value and Limitations of Game Theoretic Methods in Defence Analysis. *Schmidt, C. and Blackaby, F., eds.*, 1987, pp. 53–84. **[G: U.S.; U.S.S.R.]**

Siegel, Carole; Laska, Eugene and Lin, Shang. Decision Theory Models for Choosing Prospective Payment Schemes: A Negotiated Approach between Payers and Providers. *McGuire, T. G. and Scheffler, R. M., eds.*, 1987, pp. 143–55. **[G: U.S.]**

Simon, Leo K. Bertrand Price Competition with Differentiated Commodities. *J. Econ. Theory*, April 1987, 41(2), pp. 304–32.

Simon, Leo K. Games with Discontinuous Payoffs. *Rev. Econ. Stud.*, October 1987, 54(4), pp. 569–97.

Simon, Leo K. Local Perfection. *J. Econ. Theory*, October 1987, 43(1), pp. 134–56.

Slade, Margaret E. Interfirm Rivalry in a Repeated Game: An Empirical Test of Tacit Collusion. *J. Ind. Econ.*, June 1987, 35(4), pp. 499–516. **[G: Canada]**

Smith, James L. The Common Pool, Bargaining, and the Rule of Capture. *Econ. Inquiry*, October 1987, 25(4), pp. 631–44.

Storcken, Ton. Some Social Choice Problems. *Peters, H. J. M. and Vrieze, O. J., eds.*, 1987, pp. 307–30.

Strauss, Anselm, et al. The Hospital and Its Negotiated Order. *Zartman, I. W., ed. (I)*, 1987, 1963, pp. 98–117.

Sutton, John. Bargaining Experiments. *Europ. Econ. Rev.*, Feb./Mar. 1987, 31(1/2), pp. 272–84.

Szidarovszky, Ferenc and Okuguchi, Koji. Notes on the Stability of Quadratic Games. *Keio Econ. Stud.*, 1987, 24(2), pp. 33–45.

Tedeschi, Piero. Teorie assiomatiche e strategiche della contrattazione: risultati comparati. (Axiomatic and Strategic Theories of Bargaining: A Comparison of Results. With English summary.) *Rivista Int. Sci. Econ. Com.*, March 1987, 34(3), pp. 195–211.

Thomson, William. Individual and Collective Opportunities. *Int. J. Game Theory*, 1987, 16(4), pp. 245–52.

Thomson, William. Monotonicity of Bargaining Solutions with Respect to the Disagreement Point. *J. Econ. Theory*, June 1987, 42(1), pp. 50–58.

Thuijsman, Frank. Non-zerosum Stochastic Games. *Peters, H. J. M. and Vrieze, O. J., eds.*, 1987, pp. 133–61.

Tijs, Stef H. An Axiomatization of the τ-Value: Note. *Math. Soc. Sci.*, April 1987, 13(2), pp. 177–81.

Travaglini, Guido. Optimal Control and Differential Games. A Comparative Analysis of an Expectations-Augmented Phillips Curve Model. *Rivista Int. Sci. Econ. Com.*, September 1987, 34(9), pp. 801–21.

Tullock, Gordon. Another Part of the Swamp. *Public Choice*, 1987, 54(1), pp. 83–84.

Ulph, Alistair M. Recent Advances in Oligopoly Theory from a Game Theory Perspective. *J. Econ. Surveys*, 1987, 1(2), pp. 149–72.

Valdés Prieto, Salvador. Negociación Vertical y Subinversión. (With English summary.) *Cuadernos Econ.*, August 1987, 24(72), pp. 225–42.

Velasco, Andrés. Políticas de estabilización y teoría de juegos. (Stabilization Policies and Game Theory. With English summary.) *Colección Estud. CIEPLAN*, June 1987, (21), pp. 49–75.

Vislie, Jon. Long-term Bilateral Contracts for Natural Gas. *Golombek, R.; Hoel, M. and Vislie, J., eds.*, 1987, pp. 267–77.

Vrieze, Koos. Zero-sum Stochastic Games. *Peters, H. J. M. and Vrieze, O. J., eds.*, 1987, pp. 103–32.

Wakker, Peter. From Decision Making under Uncertainty to Game Theory. *Peters, H. J. M. and Vrieze, O. J., eds.*, 1987, pp. 163–80.

Waldman, Michael. Noncooperative Entry Deterrence, Uncertainty, and the Free Rider Problem. *Rev. Econ. Stud.*, April 1987, 54(2), pp. 301–10.

Waller, Christopher J. Deficit Financing and the Role of the Central Bank—A Game Theoretic Approach. *Atlantic Econ. J.*, July 1987, 15(2), pp. 25–32.

Wieczorek, Andrzej. Pseudo-utilities. *Jahn, J. and Krabs, W., eds.*, 1987, pp. 241–53.

Willer, David and Patton, Travis. The Development of Network Exchange Theory. *Lawler, E. J. and Markovsky, B., eds.*, 1987, pp. 199–242.

Williams, Steven R. Efficient Performance in Two Agent Bargaining. *J. Econ. Theory*, February 1987, 41(1), pp. 154–72.

Wilson, Robert B. Game-Theoretic Analyses of Trading Processes. *Bewley, T. F., ed.*, 1987, pp. 33–70.

Wilson, Robert B. On Equilibria of Bid–Ask Markets. *Feiwel, G. R., ed. (I)*, 1987, pp. 375–414.

Wolinsky, Asher. Matching, Search, and Bargaining. *J. Econ. Theory*, August 1987, 42(2), pp. 311–33.

Wooders, Myrna Holtz and Zame, William R. Large Games: Fair and Stable Outcomes. *J. Econ. Theory*, June 1987, *42*(1), pp. 59–93.

Yannelis, Nicholas C. Equilibria in Noncooperative Models of Competition. *J. Econ. Theory*, February 1987, *41*(1), pp. 96–111.

Zartman, I. William. The Analysis of Negotiation. *Zartman, I. W., ed. (I)*, 1987, pp. 2–41.

027 Economics of Centrally Planned Economies

0270 General

Abalkin, Leonid I. The New Model of Economic Management. *Soviet Econ.*, October-December 1987, *3*(4), pp. 298–312. [G: U.S.S.R.]

Aganbegyan, Abel G. Basic Directions of *Perestroyka. Soviet Econ.*, October-December 1987, *3*(4), pp. 277–97. [G: U.S.S.R.]

Altaev, V. Modeling Economic Growth of a Socialist Economy. *Rivista Int. Sci. Econ. Com.*, October 1987, *34*(10), pp. 971–87. [G: U.S.S.R.]

Cherkovets, V. Theoretical Issues in Restructuring the System of Economic Management. *Prob. Econ.*, May 1987, *30*(1), pp. 64–80. [G: U.S.S.R.]

Chunze, Jiang. The Development of Socialist Economic Models. *Comp. Econ. Stud.*, Spring 1987, *29*(1), pp. 81–105. [G: E. Europe; China]

Deriabin, A. Principles in the Restructuring of Price Formation. *Prob. Econ.*, July 1987, *30*(3), pp. 54–69. [G: U.S.S.R.]

Desai, Padma and Bhagwati, Jagdish N. Three Alternative Concepts of Foreign Exchange Difficulties in Centrally Planned Economies. *Desai, P.*, 1987, *1979*, pp. 163–72.

Desai, Padma and Martin, Ricardo. Efficiency Loss from Resource Misallocation in Soviet Industry. *Desai, P.*, 1987, *1983*, pp. 117–29. [G: U.S.S.R.]

Ebbersbach, Annette. The Development of Socialist Foreign Trade Theory in the Conditions of the 1980s. *Soviet E. Europ. Foreign Trade*, Summer 1987, *23*(2), pp. 94–117. [G: CMEA]

Gajęcki, R. and Kasiewicz, S. Provision of Services in Poland: A Theoretical and Statistical Study. *Rev. Income Wealth*, September 1987, *33*(3), pp. 273–304. [G: Poland]

Harmstone, R. C. Possible Divergence of Results with Micro and Macro Replacement Criteria. *Indian Econ. J.*, July-Sept. 1987, *35*(1), pp. 60–65. [G: U.S.S.R.]

Homos, Tudor and Constantin, Dumitru. Specialization, Cooperation, and Integration in Production and Intensive Economic Development. *Eastern Europ. Econ.*, Spring 1987, *25*(3), pp. 109–16.

Iun', O. M. Planning Methods—Areas of Improvement. *Matekon*, Winter 1987-88, *24*(2), pp. 26–48. [G: U.S.S.R.]

Józefiak, Cezary. The Road to the Barriers of Demand. *Eastern Europ. Econ.*, Winter 1987-88,

26(2), pp. 84–91. [G: Poland]

Kantorovich, L.; Albegov, M. and Bezrukov, V. Toward the Wider Use of Optimizing Methods in the National Economy. *Prob. Econ.*, February 1987, *29*(10), pp. 5–20. [G: U.S.S.R.]

Kazakevich, D. M. Economic Theory, Mathematical Economics, and Plan Management. *Matekon*, Fall 1987, *24*(1), pp. 3–20. [G: U.S.S.R.]

Latsis, Otto R. "To Take a New Look": Reflections of an Economist. *Prob. Econ.*, June 1987, *30*(2), pp. 22–42. [G: U.S.S.R.]

Mainwaring, Lynn. Foreign Trade in the Kaleckian Perspective Plan. *Econ. Planning*, 1987, *21*(2–3), pp. 101–14.

Malafeev, A. Commodity–Monetary Relations and the Restructuring of the Economic Mechanism. *Prob. Econ.*, July 1987, *30*(3), pp. 22–37. [G: U.S.S.R.]

Petrakov, Nikolay. Soviet Pricing and Fiscal-Credit System: Prospects for Economic Policy Changes. *Rivista Int. Sci. Econ. Com.*, October 1987, *34*(10), pp. 903–12. [G: U.S.S.R.]

Petrakov, Nikolay. The Plan Price in the National Economy's System of Management. *Prob. Econ.*, July 1987, *30*(3), pp. 38–53. [G: U.S.S.R.]

Sah, Raaj Kumar and Stiglitz, Joseph E. Price Scissors and the Structure of the Economy. *Quart. J. Econ.*, February 1987, *102*(1), pp. 109–34.

Szul, Roman and Kirejczyk, Edward. Dilemmas of Economic Reform and Self-management in Poland. *Econ. Anal. Workers' Manage.*, 1987, *21*(3), pp. 373–91. [G: Poland]

Toms, Miroslav and Hájek, Mojmír. The Measurement of Overall Efficiency. *Czech. Econ. Pap.*, 1987, (24), pp. 35–58. [G: Czechoslovakia]

Valenta, František. Intensive Development of Socialist Economy. (The Evolution of Theoretical Approach) *Czech. Econ. Pap.*, 1987, (24), pp. 7–33. [G: Czechoslovakia]

Wanless, P. T. The Efficiency of Central Planning: A Perspective from 'Markets vs Hierarchies.' *Scot. J. Polit. Econ.*, February 1987, *34*(1), pp. 52–68.

0271 Microeconomic Theory

Alexeev, Michael. Microeconomic Modeling of Parallel Markets: The Case of Agricultural Goods in the USSR. *J. Compar. Econ.*, December 1987, *11*(4), pp. 543–57. [G: U.S.S.R.]

Băcescu, M.; Stroe, R. and Tamaş, I. Production of Information Component of Social Production System. *Econ. Computat. Cybern. Stud. Res.*, 1987, *22*(3), pp. 23–30.

Bain, James A., Jr., et al. The Ratchet, Tautness, and Managerial Behavior in Soviet-Type Economies. *Europ. Econ. Rev.*, August 1987, *31*(6), pp. 1173–1201.

Barskii, L. A., et al. Techniques for Ecological and Economic Appraisal of the Development of Waste-Free Factories. *Matekon*, Fall 1987, *24*(1), pp. 70–85. [G: U.S.S.R.]

Bartlett, Will. Capital Accumulation and Employment in a Self-Financed Worker Cooperative. *Int. J. Ind. Organ.*, September 1987, *5*(3), pp. 277–87.

Bartlett, Will. Enterprise Investment and Public Consumption in a Self-managed Economy. *Jones, D. C. and Svejnar, J., eds.*, 1987, pp. 165–81.   [G: Yugoslavia]

Bennett, John. The Choice of Final Signals in Malinvaud's Model of Decentralized Planning. *Europ. Econ. Rev.*, August 1987, *31*(6), pp. 1203–10.

Bonin, John P. and Fukuda, Wataru. Controlling a Risk-Averse, Effort-Selecting Manager in the Soviet Incentive Model. *J. Compar. Econ.*, June 1987, *11*(2), pp. 221–33.   [G: U.S.S.R.]

Breyer, Friedrich. The "Homothetic" Firm in Illyria: Comment. *J. Compar. Econ.*, December 1987, *11*(4), pp. 603–05.

Brown, Pamela Clark; Miller, Jeffrey B. and Thornton, James R. An Optimal Incentive Scheme for Planning with Targets: Comment. *J. Compar. Econ.*, December 1987, *11*(4), pp. 596–600.

Byrd, William A. China's Industrial Reform: The Role and Impact of Markets. *Tidrick, G. and Jiyuan, C., eds.*, 1987, pp. 237–75.
                                             [G: China]

Cable, John. Some Tests of Employee Participation Indices. *Jones, D. C. and Svejnar, J., eds.*, 1987, pp. 79–90.

Danilov-Danil'ian, V. I. Methodological Aspects of Calculating and Using Limit Costs. *Matekon*, Winter 1987-88, *24*(2), pp. 3–25.
                                             [G: U.S.S.R.]

Darvish, Tikva and Kahana, Nava. The Ratchet Principle: A Diagrammatic Interpretation. *J. Compar. Econ.*, June 1987, *11*(2), pp. 245–49.
                                             [G: U.S.S.R.]

Desai, Padma and Martin, Ricardo. Measuring Resource-Allocational Efficiency in Centrally Planned Economies: A Theoretical Analysis. *Desai, P.*, 1987, *1983*, pp. 101–16.

Diao, Xinshen. The Role of the Two-Tier Price System. *Reynolds, B. L.*, 1987, pp. 35–46.
                                             [G: China]

Don, Yehuda and Paroush, Jacob. Cooperatives with Cost Saving. *Jones, D. C. and Svejnar, J., eds.*, 1987, pp. 183–99.

Egiazarian, G. A. From the Experiment to an Integral System. *Prob. Econ.*, March 1987, *29*(11), pp. 47–61.   [G: U.S.S.R.]

Faerman, E. Iu. Coordinating Forecasts in Hierarchically Organized Units. *Matekon*, Spring 1987, *23*(3), pp. 28–49.

Galasi, Péter and Kertesi, Gábor. The Spread of Bribery in a Centrally Planned Economy. *Acta Oecon.*, 1987, *38*(3–4), pp. 371–89.

Gorodetskii, E. and Gorodetskii, A. Theoretical Prerequisites to the Systematic Restructuring of Prices. *Prob. Econ.*, September 1987, *30*(5), pp. 43–60.   [G: U.S.S.R.]

Guran, M. The Concept of Industrial Cybernetic System under the Impact Production Flexible Systems. *Econ. Computat. Cybern. Stud. Res.*, 1987, *22*(3), pp. 89–95.

Haruna, Shoji. Random Input Price and the Theory of the Competitive Cooperative Firm. *J. Compar. Econ.*, March 1987, *11*(1), pp. 81–95.

Hodgson, Geoffrey M. Economic Pluralism and Self-management. *Jones, D. C. and Svejnar, J., eds.*, 1987, pp. 129–42.

Hollander, Abraham; Huarie, Alain and L'Ecuyer, Pierre. Ratchet Effects and the Cost of Incremental Incentive Schemes. *J. Econ. Dynam. Control*, September 1987, *11*(3), pp. 373–89.

Houthakker, Hendrik S. and Tobin, James. Estimates of the Free Demand for Rationed Foodstuffs. *Tobin, J. (II)*, 1987, *1952*, pp. 379–96.

Hua, Sheng, et al. A Restructuring of the Microeconomic Foundation: More on China's Further Reform and Some Related Thoughts. *Chinese Econ. Stud.*, Summer 1987, *20*(4), pp. 3–26.   [G: China]

Kahana, Nava. The Multifactor Illyrian Firm Revisited: Comment. *J. Compar. Econ.*, December 1987, *11*(4), pp. 611–12.

Kahana, Nava and Spiegel, Uriel. Do Egalitarian Labour-Managed Enterprises Respond Perversely? *Econ. Anal. Workers' Manage.*, 1987, *21*(4), pp. 465–67.

Kornai, János. The Dual Dependence of the State-Owned Firm in Hungary. *Tidrick, G. and Jiyuan, C., eds.*, 1987, pp. 317–38.
                                             [G: Hungary]

Liu, Pak-Wai. Optimal Incentive Schemes with Targets: First-Best or Second-Best? Reply. *J. Compar. Econ.*, December 1987, *11*(4), pp. 601–02.

Martin, Robert E. Long-run Supply in Competitive Labor-Managed Industries. *Jones, D. C. and Svejnar, J., eds.*, 1987, pp. 113–28.

Melzer, Manfred. The Pricing System of the GDR: Principles and Problems. *Jeffries, I. and Melzer, M., eds.*, 1987, pp. 141–48.
                                             [G: E. Germany]

Meran, Georg and Wolfstetter, Elmar. Optimal Risk Shifting vs Efficient Employment in Illyria: The Labor-Managed Firm under Asymmetric Information. *J. Compar. Econ.*, June 1987, *11*(2), pp. 163–79.

Moskalenko, V. P. Cost-Accounting Interest in High Final Results. *Prob. Econ.*, March 1987, *29*(11), pp. 28–46.   [G: U.S.S.R.]

Nitzan, Shmuel and Schnytzer, Adi. Diligence and Laziness in the Chinese Countryside Revisited. *J. Devel. Econ.*, August 1987, *26*(2), pp. 407–18.   [G: China]

Osband, Kent. Speak Softly, but Carry a Big Stick: On Optimal Targets under Moral Hazard. *J. Compar. Econ.*, December 1987, *11*(4), pp. 584–95.

Oxenstierna, Susanne. Bonuses, Factor Demand, and Technical Efficiency in the Soviet Enterprise. *J. Compar. Econ.*, June 1987, *11*(2), pp. 234–44.   [G: U.S.S.R.]

Putterman, Louis. The Incentive Problem and the Demise of Team Farming in China. *J. Devel. Econ.*, June 1987, *26*(1), pp. 103–27.
                                             [G: China]

Rosefielde, Steven and Pfouts, Ralph W. The Effect of Radially Parallel Technologies on the Behavior of the Illyrian Firm: Reply. *J. Compar. Econ.*, December 1987, *11*(4), pp. 606–10.

Rozenova, L. Price as the Cost–Benefit Norm. *Prob. Econ.*, December 1987, *30*(8), pp. 93–107. [G: U.S.S.R.]

Rutgaizer, V. M. and Sheviakhov, Iu. E. Distribution According to One's Labor. *Prob. Econ.*, November 1987, *30*(7), pp. 31–46. [G: CMEA]

Sabolčík, Michal. Prices and Value Instruments. *Czech. Econ. Digest.*, October 1987, (7), pp. 78–87.

Scitovski, Rudolf. Ispodgodišnje ukamaćivanje. (On Determining Less-than-Annual Interest. With English summary.) *Econ. Anal. Workers' Manage.*, 1987, *21*(2), pp. 243–57. [G: Yugoslavia]

Smith, Stephen C. and Ye, Meng-Hua. The Behavior of Labor-Managed Firms under Uncertainty: Product Diversification, Income Insurance and Layoff Policy. *Ann. Pub. Co-op. Econ.*, Jan.-Mar. 1987, *58*(1), pp. 65–82.

Sokolovskii, L. E. On Individual and Collective Forms of Labor Organization and Incentives. *Matekon*, Summer 1987, *23*(4), pp. 3–27. [G: U.S.S.R.]

Soós, Karoly Attila. Informal Pressures, Mobilization, and Campaigns in the Management of Centrally Planned Economies. *Econ. Planning*, 1987, *21*(1), pp. 39–48. [G: Hungary]

Timofeev, S. A. Where Does the System of Priorities Push the Enterprise? *Prob. Econ.*, September 1987, *30*(5), pp. 24–42. [G: U.S.S.R.]

Tobin, James. A Survey of the Theory of Rationing. *Tobin, J. (II)*, 1987, *1952*, pp. 321–58.

Tobin, James and Houthakker, Hendrik S. The Effects of Rationing on Demand Elasticities. *Tobin, J. (II)*, 1987, *1951*, pp. 359–77.

Vanek, Jaroslav. Toward a Just, Efficient, and Fully Democratic Society. *Jones, D. C. and Svejnar, J.*, eds., 1987, pp. 13–78.

Vavilov, Andrei P., et al. Methods for Incorporating Rent in Prices and Plans. *Matekon*, Spring 1987, *23*(3), pp. 3–27. [G: U.S.S.R.]

Volkonskii, Victor A.; Vavilov, Andrei P. and Pavlov, Nikolai V. Optimization of Branch Price Level Relations in Planned Economy. [*Marrama, V.*], Vol. 2, 1987, pp. 651–75. [G: U.S.S.R.]

Žigič, Krešimir. Decentralizacija i cijene proizvodnje—Cijene proizvodnje kao dualne varijable u procesu decentralizacije. (Decentralization and Production Prices—Prices of Production as a Dual Variable in Decentralization Process. With English summary.) *Econ. Anal. Workers' Manage.*, 1987, *21*(4), pp. 443–63.

0272 Macroeconomic Theory

Batizi, E. E., et al. Problems of Proportionality in a Socialist Economy. *Soviet E. Europ. Foreign Trade*, Summer 1987, *23*(2), pp. 6–23. [G: CMEA]

Bogomolov, Oleg T. Monetary Institutions in a Planned Economy. *de Cecco, M. and Fitoussi, J.-P.*, eds., 1987, pp. 209–21. [G: U.S.S.R.; CMEA]

Desai, Padma. The Rate of Return on Foreign Capital Inflow to the Soviet Economy. *Desai, P.*, 1987, pp. 133–52. [G: U.S.S.R.]

Ershov, E. B. and Sadykov, I. S. Aggregational Analysis of Production Possibility Frontiers for Industrial Branches in the USSR. *Matekon*, Summer 1987, *23*(4), pp. 28–47. [G: U.S.S.R.]

Feltenstein, Andrew and Farhadian, Ziba. Fiscal Policy, Monetary Targets, and the Price Level in a Centrally Planned Economy: An Application to the Case of China. *J. Money, Credit, Banking*, May 1987, *19*(2), pp. 137–56. [G: China]

Grosfeld, Irena. Modeling Planners' Investment Behavior: Poland, 1956–1981. *J. Compar. Econ.*, June 1987, *11*(2), pp. 180–91. [G: Poland]

Hare, Paul. Supply Multipliers in a Centrally Planned Economy with a Private Sector. *Econ. Planning*, 1987, *21*(2–3), pp. 53–61.

Holzman, Franklyn D. Internal and External Balance in a Centrally Planned Economy: Commentary. *Holzman, F. D.*, 1987, *1980*, pp. 83–88. [G: CMEA]

Hrnčíř, Miroslav. Macroeconomic Proportionality in an Open Planned Economy. *Soviet E. Europ. Foreign Trade*, Summer 1987, *23*(2), pp. 37–59.

Kowalski, Jan S. Rational Expectations in Centrally Planned Economies. *Pejovich, S.*, ed., 1987, pp. 175–207.

Kulikov, V. Commodity–Monetary Relations in the Concept of Acceleration. *Prob. Econ.*, June 1987, *30*(2), pp. 43–59. [G: U.S.S.R.]

Leeds, Eva Marikova and Kmenta, Jan. On the Similarity of Macro-econometric Models of Market and Planned Economies: The First Models of Czechoslovakia. *Comp. Econ. Stud.*, Spring 1987, *29*(1), pp. 63–80. [G: Czechoslovakia]

Li, Chengrui. An Important Question in Macroeconomic Management: Strict State Control of the Amount of Currency in Circulation. *Chinese Econ. Stud.*, Winter 1986-87, *20*(2), pp. 3–12. [G: China]

Liu, Guoguang, et al. Economic Reform and Macroeconomic Management: Commentaries on the International Conference on Macroeconomic Management. *Chinese Econ. Stud.*, Spring 1987, *20*(3), pp. 3–45. [G: China]

Makarov, V. L. On Dynamic Models of the Economy and the Development of L. V. Kantorovich's Ideas. *Matekon*, Summer 1987, *23*(4), pp. 48–74.

Malle, Silvana. Capacity Utilization and the Shift Coefficient in Soviet Planning. *Econ. Planning*, 1987, *21*(2–3), pp. 63–86. [G: U.S.S.R.]

Mstislavskii, P. Optimizing the Relationship of Consumption and Accumulation. *Prob. Econ.*,

027 Economics of Centrally Planned Economies

February 1987, *29*(10), pp. 21–37.
[G: U.S.S.R.]

Portes, Richard. The Impact of External Shocks on Centrally Planned Economies: Theoretical Considerations. *Pasinetti, L. and Lloyd, P., eds.*, 1987, pp. 409–25. [G: CMEA]

Portes, Richard, et al. Macroeconomic Planning and Disequilibrium: Estimates for Poland, 1955–1980. *Econometrica*, January 1987, *55*(1), pp. 19–41. [G: Poland]

Simonovits, András. Investment Cycles: A New Interpretation of an Old Model. *Acta Oecon.*, 1987, *38*(1–2), pp. 155–64.

030 HISTORY OF THOUGHT; METHODOLOGY

031 History of Economic Thought

0310 General

Albelda, Randy; Gunn, Christopher and Waller, William T., Jr. The Resurgence of Political Economy. *Albelda, R.; Gunn, C. and Waller, W., eds.*, 1987, pp. 3–17.

Ault, Richard W. and Ekelund, Robert B., Jr. The Problem of Unnecessary Originality in Economics. *Southern Econ. J.*, January 1987, *53*(3), pp. 650–61.

Brandis, Royall. Marx *and* Keynes? Marx *or* Keynes? A Reply. *J. Econ. Issues*, March 1987, *21*(1), pp. 470–73.

Breit, William. Biography and the Making of Economic Worlds. *Southern Econ. J.*, April 1987, *53*(4), pp. 823–33.

Brems, Hans. Frequently Wrong but Rarely in Doubt. *Challenge*, Nov./Dec. 1987, *30*(5), pp. 51–56.

Craver, Earlene and Leijonhufvud, Axel. Economics in America: The Continental Influence. *Hist. Polit. Econ.*, Summer 1987, *19*(2), pp. 173–82. [G: U.S.; W. Germany]

Perlman, Mark. An Essay on Karl Pribram's A History of Economic Reasoning. *Revue Écon.*, January 1987, *38*(1), pp. 171–76.

Wolff, Robert Paul. Piero Sraffa and the Rehabilitation of Classical Political Economy. *Albelda, R.; Gunn, C. and Waller, W., eds.*, 1987, *1982*, pp. 157–74.

0311 Ancient, Medieval

Campbell, William F. The Old Art of Political Economy: Commentary [The Greek Heritage in Economic Thought]. *Lowry, S. T., ed.*, 1987, pp. 31–42.

Essid, M. Yassine. Islamic Economic Thought. *Lowry, S. T., ed.*, 1987, pp. 77–102.

Gordon, Barry. Biblical and Early Judeo–Christian Thought: Genesis to Augustine. *Lowry, S. T., ed.*, 1987, pp. 43–67.

Kleiman, Ephraim. 'Just Price' in Talmudic Literature. *Hist. Polit. Econ.*, Spring 1987, *19*(1), pp. 23–45.

Kuran, Timur. Continuity and Change in Islamic Economic Thought: Commentary. *Lowry, S. T., ed.*, 1987, pp. 103–13.

Langholm, Odd. Scholastic Economics. *Lowry, S. T., ed.*, 1987, pp. 115–35.

Lapidus, André. La propriété de la monnaie: doctrine de l'usure et théorie de l'intérêt. (The Property of Money: Theory of Interest and Doctrine of Usury. With English summary.) *Revue Écon.*, November 1987, *38*(6), pp. 1095–1109.

Lowry, S. Todd. Pre-classical Economic Thought: From the Greeks to the Scottish Enlightenment: Introduction. *Lowry, S. T., ed.*, 1987, pp. 1–6.

Lowry, S. Todd. The Greek Heritage in Economic Thought. *Lowry, S. T., ed.*, 1987, pp. 7–30.

Ohrenstein, Roman A. Some Socioeconomic Aspects of Judaic Thought: Commentary [Biblical and Early Judeo–Christian Thought: Genesis to Augustine]. *Lowry, S. T., ed.*, 1987, pp. 68–76.

Popescu, Oreste. Price Theory in the Hispanic American Scholastics. *Int. J. Soc. Econ.*, 1987, *14*(3/4/5), pp. 132–39.

Worland, Stephen T. Scholastic Economics: Commentary. *Lowry, S. T., ed.*, 1987, pp. 136–46.

0312 Preclassical

Backhaus, Jürgen and Wagner, Richard E. The Cameralists: A Public Choice Perspective. *Public Choice*, 1987, *53*(1), pp. 3–20.

Endres, Anthony M. The King–Davenant 'Law' in Classical Economics. *Hist. Polit. Econ.*, Winter 1987, *19*(4), pp. 621–38.

Groenewegen, Peter D. The International Foundations of Classical Political Economy in the Eighteenth Century: An Alternative Perspective: Commentary [In Search of Economic Order: French Predecessors of Adam Smith]. *Lowry, S. T., ed.*, 1987, pp. 211–20.

Hébert, Robert F. In Search of Economic Order: French Predecessors of Adam Smith. *Lowry, S. T., ed.*, 1987, pp. 185–210.

Lowry, S. Todd. Pre-classical Economic Thought: From the Greeks to the Scottish Enlightenment: Introduction. *Lowry, S. T., ed.*, 1987, pp. 1–6.

Staum, Martin S. The Institute Economists: From Physiocracy to Entrepreneurial Capitalism. *Hist. Polit. Econ.*, Winter 1987, *19*(4), pp. 525–50.

Steiner, Philippe. Le projet physiocratique: théorie de la propriété et lien social. (The Physiocratic Project: Theory of Property and Social Link. With English summary.) *Revue Écon.*, November 1987, *38*(6), pp. 1111–28.

0313 Mercantilist

Baron, Samuel H. Was Križanić a Mercantilist? *Hist. Polit. Econ.*, Spring 1987, *19*(1), pp. 67–86.

Magnusson, Lars. Mercantilism and "Reform" Mercantilism: The Rise of Economic Discourse in Sweden during the Eighteenth Century. *Hist. Polit. Econ.*, Fall 1987, *19*(3), pp. 415–33.

Magnusson, Lars. The Language of Mercantilism: Commentary [The Development of Mercantilist Economic Thought]. *Lowry, S. T., ed.,* 1987, pp. 174–84.

Wiles, Richard C. The Development of Mercantilist Economic Thought. *Lowry, S. T., ed.,* 1987, pp. 147–73.

0314 Classical

Arnon, Arie. Banking between the Invisible and Visible Hands: A Reinterpretation of Ricardo's Place within the Classical School. *Oxford Econ. Pap.,* June 1987, *39*(2), pp. 268–81.

Bhaduri, Amit and Harris, Donald J. The Complex Dynamics of the Simple Ricardian System. *Quart. J. Econ.,* November 1987, *102*(4), pp. 893–901.

Brown, Vivienne. Value and Property in the History of Economic Thought: An Analysis of the Emergence of Scarcity. *Écon. Soc.,* March 1987, *21*(3), pp. 85–112.

Coats, A. W. Samuel Hollander's Mill: A Review Article. *Manchester Sch. Econ. Soc. Stud.,* September 1987, *55*(3), pp. 310–16.

Evensky, Jerry M. The Two Voices of Adam Smith: Moral Philosopher and Social Critic. *Hist. Polit. Econ.,* Fall 1987, *19*(3), pp. 447–68.

Fukiharu, Toshitaka. The Classical Economics from the Neo-classical Viewpoint. *Kobe Univ. Econ.,* 1987, *33*, pp. 71–99.

Gramm, Warren S. Unproductive Labour and Unproductive Consumption: Historical Review, Contemporary Relevance. *Int. J. Soc. Econ.,* 1987, *14*(3/4/5), pp. 154–66. [G: U.S.]

Grampp, William D. Peace and Trade: The Classical vs. the Marxian View. *Visser, H. and Schoor, E., eds.,* 1987, pp. 17–31.

Hennipman, Piet. A Tale of Two Schools: Comments on a New View of the Ordinalist Revolution. *De Economist,* 1987, *135*(2), pp. 141–62.

Humphrey, Thomas M. Classical and Neoclassical Roots of the Theory of Optimum Tariffs. *Fed. Res. Bank Richmond Econ. Rev.,* July/Aug. 1987, *73*(4), pp. 17–28.

Levy, David T. Adam Smith's Case for Usury Laws. *Hist. Polit. Econ.,* Fall 1987, *19*(3), pp. 387–400.

Lowe, Adolph. The Classical Theory of Economic Growth. *Lowe, A.,* 1987, *1954*, pp. 107–31.

Niehans, Jürg. Classical Monetary Theory, New and Old. *J. Money, Credit, Banking,* November 1987, *19*(4), pp. 409–24.

Petrella, Frank. Daniel Raymond, Adam Smith, and Classical Growth Theory: An Inquiry into the Nature and Causes of the Wealth of America. *Hist. Polit. Econ.,* Summer 1987, *19*(2), pp. 239–59.

Prendergast, Renee. James Anderson's Political Economy—His Influence on Smith and Malthus. *Scot. J. Polit. Econ.,* November 1987, *34*(4), pp. 388–409.

Pullen, John M. Lord Grenville's Manuscript Notes on Malthus. *Hist. Polit. Econ.,* Summer 1987, *19*(2), pp. 217–37.

Rashid, Salim. Political Economy as Moral Philosophy: Dugald Stewart of Edinburgh. *Australian Econ. Pap.,* June 1987, *26*(48), pp. 145–56.

Rashid, Salim. The Scottish Enlightenment: Evaluation of Origins: Commentary. *Lowry, S. T., ed.,* 1987, pp. 256–63.

Rebeyrol, Antoine. Gravitation et marché du travail. Un essai d'interprétation. (Gravitation and Labour Market: Essay of Interpretation. With English summary.) *Écon. Soc.,* March 1987, *21*(3), pp. 53–84.

Reid, Gavin C. Disequilibrium and Increasing Returns in Adam Smith's Analysis of Growth and Accumulation. *Hist. Polit. Econ.,* Spring 1987, *19*(1), pp. 87–106.

Thomson, Herbert F. The Scottish Enlightenment and Political Economy. *Lowry, S. T., ed.,* 1987, pp. 221–55.

Thweatt, William O. James and John Mill on Comparative Advantage: Sraffa's Account Corrected. *Visser, H. and Schoor, E., eds.,* 1987, pp. 33–43.

0315 Austrian, Marshallian, Neoclassical

Baird, Charles W. *The Economics of Time and Ignorance:* A Review. *Rothbard, M. N., ed.,* 1987, pp. 189–206.

Beach, E. F. Marshallian Methodology. *Int. J. Soc. Econ.,* 1987, *14*(7/8/9), pp. 19–26.

Brems, Hans. Dansk økonomisk teori efter 1870— var svenskerne bedre? (Danish Economic Theory after 1870—Were the Swedes Better? With English summary.) *Nationaløkon. Tidsskr.,* 1987, *125*(2), pp. 244–52. [G: Denmark]

Brown, Vivienne. Value and Property in the History of Economic Thought: An Analysis of the Emergence of Scarcity. *Écon. Soc.,* March 1987, *21*(3), pp. 85–112.

Cubeddu, Raimondo. Popper et l'Ecole Autrichienne. (Popper and the Austrian School: Menger, Boehm-Bauerk, Wieser, Mises. With English summary.) *Écon. Soc.,* October 1987, *21*(10), pp. 41–62.

Endres, Anthony M. The Origins of Böhm-Bawerk's 'Greatest Error': Theoretical Points of Separation from Menger. *J. Inst. Theoretical Econ.,* June 1987, *143*(2), pp. 291–309.

Evensky, Jerry M. Expanding the Scope of the Neoclassical Vision. *Rev. Soc. Econ.,* October 1987, *45*(2), pp. 178–91.

Gallaway, Lowell and Vedder, Richard K. Wages, Prices, and Employment: Von Mises and the Progressives. *Rothbard, M. N., ed.,* 1987, pp. 33–80. [G: U.S.; U.K.]

Gallegati, Mauro. Era Alfred Marshall un economista neoclassico? A Proposito di Recenti Studi di Storia dell'economia politica. (With English summary.) *Stud. Econ.,* 1987, *42*(31), pp. 153–71.

Garrison, Roger W. Full Employment and Intertemporal Coordination: A Rejoinder [Intertemporal Coordination and the Invisible Hand: An Austrian Perspective on the Keynesian Vision]. *Hist. Polit. Econ.,* Summer 1987, *19*(2), pp. 335–41.

Gramm, Warren S. Unproductive Labour and Unproductive Consumption: Historical Review, Contemporary Relevance. *Int. J. Soc. Econ.*, 1987, *14*(3/4/5), pp. 154–66. [G: U.S.]

Hedlund-Nyström, Torun; Jonung, Lars and Sandelin, Bo. Opublicerat manuskript av Knut Wicksell med en kapitalteoretisk modell. (An Unpublished Manuscript by Knut Wicksell on a Capital-Theoretical Model. With English summary.) *Ekon. Samfundets Tidskr.*, 1987, *40*(3), pp. 123–37.

Hennipman, Piet. A Tale of Two Schools: Comments on a New View of the Ordinalist Revolution. *De Economist*, 1987, *135*(2), pp. 141–62.

Holland, Thomas E. On Parallelism in Neo-Classical Economic Theory. *Int. J. Soc. Econ.*, 1987, *14*(3/4/5), pp. 191–98.

Humphrey, Thomas M. Classical and Neoclassical Roots of the Theory of Optimum Tariffs. *Fed. Res. Bank Richmond Econ. Rev.*, July/Aug. 1987, *73*(4), pp. 17–28.

Jensen, Hans E. J. M. Keynes as a Marshallian: Reply. *J. Econ. Issues*, March 1987, *21*(1), pp. 457–67.

Keizer, William. Two Forgotten Articles by Ludwig von Mises on the Rationality of Socialist Economic Calculation. *Rothbard, M. N., ed.*, 1987, pp. 109–22.

Khalil, Elias L. Kuhn, Lakatos, and the History of Economic Thought. *Int. J. Soc. Econ.*, 1987, *14*(3/4/5), pp. 118–31.

Krelle, Wilhelm. Von Thünen-Vorlesung. (Von Thünen Lecture. With English summary.) *Z. Wirtschaft. Sozialwissen.*, 1987, *107*(1), pp. 5–28.

Larson, Bruce. Edgeworth, Samuelson, and Operationally Meaningful Theorems. *Hist. Polit. Econ.*, Fall 1987, *19*(3), pp. 351–57.

Myrdal, Gunnar. Utilitarianism and Modern Economics. *Feiwel, G. R., ed. (II)*, 1987, pp. 273–78.

Pack, Spencer J. Schumpeter Plus Optimism Equals Gilder (*ceteris paribus*). *Hist. Polit. Econ.*, Fall 1987, *19*(3), pp. 469–80.

Reinhardt, Paul G. Demand Analysis and the Flow of Time in Consumption. *Int. J. Soc. Econ.*, 1987, *14*(3/4/5), pp. 199–206.

Rothbard, Murray N. Breaking Out of the Walrasian Box: The Cases of Schumpeter and Hansen. *Rothbard, M. N., ed.*, 1987, pp. 97–108.

Rotheim, Roy J. Equilibrium in Walras's and Marx's Theories of Capital Accumulation. *Int. J. Soc. Econ.*, 1987, *14*(7/8/9), pp. 27–43.

Smiley, Gene. Some Austrian Perspectives on Keynesian Fiscal Policy and the Recovery in the Thirties. *Rothbard, M. N., ed.*, 1987, pp. 145–79. [G: U.S.]

Snippe, J. Intertemporal Coordination and the Economics of Keynes: Comment. *Hist. Polit. Econ.*, Summer 1987, *19*(2), pp. 329–34.

Timberlake, Richard H., Jr. A Critique of Monetarist and Austrian Doctrines on the Utility and Value of Money. *Rothbard, M. N., ed.*, 1987, pp. 81–96.

Tisdell, Clem A. Neo-Classical Economics: Relevance, Irrelevance and Rugina's Methodology.
Int. J. Soc. Econ., 1987, *14*(3/4/5), pp. 37–49.

Trescott, Paul B. J. M. Keynes as a Marshallian: Comment. *J. Econ. Issues*, March 1987, *21*(1), pp. 452–57.

Walker, Donald A. Edgeworth versus Walras on the Theory of Tatonnement. *Eastern Econ. J.*, Apr.-June 1987, *13*(2), pp. 155–65.

Whalen, Charles J. A Reason to Look beyond Neoclassical Economics: Some Major Shortcomings of Orthodox Theory. *J. Econ. Issues*, March 1987, *21*(1), pp. 259–80.

Yeager, Leland B. The Review of Austrian Economics: Why Subjectivism? *Rothbard, M. N., ed.*, 1987, pp. 5–31.

0316 General Equilibrium until 1945

Boland, Lawrence A. On the Relevance of Neo-Walrasian Economic Theory: A Review. *Hist. Polit. Econ.*, Winter 1987, *19*(4), pp. 659–66.

Brems, Hans. Dansk økonomisk teori efter 1870—var svenskerne bedre? (Danish Economic Theory after 1870—Were the Swedes Better? With English summary.) *Nationaløkon. Tidsskr.*, 1987, *125*(2), pp. 244–52. [G: Denmark]

Niman, Neil B. Keynes and the Invisible Hand Theorem. *J. Post Keynesian Econ.*, Fall 1987, *10*(1), pp. 105–15.

Rothbard, Murray N. Breaking Out of the Walrasian Box: The Cases of Schumpeter and Hansen. *Rothbard, M. N., ed.*, 1987, pp. 97–108.

Thomas, Mark. General Equilibrium Models and Research in Economic History. *Field, A. J., ed.*, 1987, pp. 121–83.

0317 Socialist and Marxian until 1945

Buick, Adam. Bordigism. *Rubel, M. and Crump, J., eds.*, 1987, pp. 127–50.

Burkett, John P. Soviet Socioeconomic Development: A Fold Catastrophe? *Comp. Econ. Stud.*, Fall 1987, *29*(3), pp. 70–93.

Coleman, Stephen. Impossibilism. *Rubel, M. and Crump, J., eds.*, 1987, pp. 83–103.

Crump, John. The Thin Red Line: Non-market Socialism in the Twentieth Century. *Rubel, M. and Crump, J., eds.*, 1987, pp. 35–59.

Davis, John B. Marx's Conception of Ethics in Capitalist Society. *Samuels, W. J., ed.*, 1987, pp. 51–90.

Day, Richard B. Democratic Control and the Dignity of Politics—An Analysis of *The Revolution Betrayed*. *Comp. Econ. Stud.*, Fall 1987, *29*(3), pp. 4–29. [G: U.S.S.R.]

Eldred, Michael. The Unreflected Historicity of Historical Materialism. *Sci. Soc.*, Winter 1987-1988, *51*(4), pp. 475–77.

Elliott, John E. Justice and Freedom in Marx's Moral Critique of Capitalism. *Samuels, W. J., ed.*, 1987, pp. 1–49.

England, Richard W. Form vs. Content: A Critique of Morishima's Mathematical Marxism. *England, R. W., ed.*, 1987, pp. 20–34.

Grampp, William D. Peace and Trade: The Classical vs. the Marxian View. *Visser, H. and Schoor, E., eds.*, 1987, pp. 17–31.

Groll, Shalom and Orzech, Ze'ev B. Technical Progress and Values in Marx's Theory of the Decline in the Rate of Profit: An Exegetical Approach. *Hist. Polit. Econ.*, Winter 1987, *19*(4), pp. 591–613.

Gurley, John G. Marx and the Critique of Capitalism. *Albelda, R.; Gunn, C. and Waller, W., eds.*, 1987, *1980*, pp. 273–96.

Haines, Walter W. A Society without Money: Reflections on Jacques Maritain. *Int. J. Soc. Econ.*, 1987, *14*(3/4/5), pp. 97–104.

Horvat, Branko. Sraffa Systematized and Marx Vindicated. *Econ. Anal. Workers' Manage.*, 1987, *21*(3), pp. 289–97.

Howard, Michael C. and King, John E. Friedrich Engels and the Prize Essay Competition in the Marxian Theory of Value. *Hist. Polit. Econ.*, Winter 1987, *19*(4), pp. 571–89.

Indart, Gustavo. Marx's Law of Market Value. *Sci. Soc.*, Winter 1987-1988, *51*(4), pp. 458–67.

Keizer, William. Two Forgotten Articles by Ludwig von Mises on the Rationality of Socialist Economic Calculation. *Rothbard, M. N., ed.*, 1987, pp. 109–22.

Klitgaard, Kent A. and Ellis, Valarie D. Accumulation and Crisis. *England, R. W., ed.*, 1987, pp. 89–106.

Kuczynski, Thomas. Marx and Engels on Long Waves. *Vasko, T., ed.*, 1987, pp. 35–45.

Lazonick, William. Theory and History in Marxian Economics. *Field, A. J., ed.*, 1987, pp. 255–312.

Lysandrou, P. On Marx's Contribution to a 'Complete' Theory of Price. *Brit. Rev. Econ. Issues*, Autumn 1987, *9*(21), pp. 65–89.

Menshikov, Stanislav. Structural Crisis as a Phase in Long-term Economic Fluctuations. *Vasko, T., ed.*, 1987, pp. 66–75.

Milenkovitch, Deborah Duff. Trotsky's *The Revolution Betrayed*: A Contemporary Look. *Comp. Econ. Stud.*, Fall 1987, *29*(3), pp. 40–44.

Nove, Alec. Trotsky, Markets, and East European Reforms. *Comp. Econ. Stud.*, Fall 1987, *29*(3), pp. 30–39. [G: U.S.S.R.; E. Europe]

O'Brien, John C. The Instauration of the New Man of Marxism: A Critique. *Int. J. Soc. Econ.*, 1987, *14*(3/4/5), pp. 22–32.

Pengam, Alain. Anarcho-communism. *Rubel, M. and Crump, J., eds.*, 1987, pp. 60–82.

Rotheim, Roy J. Equilibrium in Walras's and Marx's Theories of Capital Accumulation. *Int. J. Soc. Econ.*, 1987, *14*(7/8/9), pp. 27–43.

Rubel, Maximilien. Non-market Socialism in the Nineteenth Century. *Rubel, M. and Crump, J., eds.*, 1987, pp. 10–34.

Shaikh, Anwar. The Poverty of Algebra. *Albelda, R.; Gunn, C. and Waller, W., eds.*, 1987, *1981*, pp. 297–322.

Shapiro, J. C. On the Accuracy of Economic Observations of *Chto Takoe SSSR* in Historical Retrospect. *Comp. Econ. Stud.*, Fall 1987, *29*(3), pp. 45–69.

Shipway, Mark. Council Communism. *Rubel, M. and Crump, J., eds.*, 1987, pp. 104–26.

Shipway, Mark. Situationism. *Rubel, M. and*

Crump, J., eds., 1987, pp. 151–72.

Steedman, Ian. Value, Price, and Profit. *Albelda, R.; Gunn, C. and Waller, W., eds.*, 1987, *1975*, pp. 175–85.

Valdés, Benigno. Technical Change and Profitability: The "Law of the Tendency of the Rate of Profit to Fall" Reconsidered. *England, R. W., ed.*, 1987, pp. 107–17.

Webber, M. J. Quantitative Measurement of Some Marxist Categories. *Environ. Planning A*, October 1987, *19*(10), pp. 1303–21.

Young, James J. H. M. Hyndman and Daniel De Leon: The Two Souls of Socialism. *Labor Hist.*, Fall 1987, *28*(4), pp. 534–56. [G: U.S.; U.K.]

0318 Historical and Institutional

Adams, John. Trade and Payments as Instituted Process: The Institutional Theory of the External Sector. *J. Econ. Issues*, December 1987, *21*(4), pp. 1839–60.

Atkinson, Glen W. Instrumentalism and Economic Policy: The Quest for Reasonable Value. *J. Econ. Issues*, March 1987, *21*(1), pp. 189–202.

Averitt, Robert T. The Dual Economy Twenty Years Later. *J. Econ. Issues*, June 1987, *21*(2), pp. 795–802. [G: U.S.]

Barzelay, Michael and Smith, Rogers M. The One Best System? A Political Analysis of Neoclassical Institutionalist Perspectives on the Modern Corporation. *Samuels, W. J. and Miller, A. S., eds.*, 1987, pp. 81–110. [G: U.S.]

Basu, Kaushik; Jones, Eric and Schlicht, Ekkehart. The Growth and Decay of Custom: The Role of the New Institutional Economics in Economic History. *Exploration Econ. Hist.*, January 1987, *24*(1), pp. 1–21.

Bodily, Christopher L. Henry David Thoreau: The Instrumental Transcendentalist? *J. Econ. Issues*, March 1987, *21*(1), pp. 203–18.

Brown, Doug. A Hungarian Connection: Karl Polanyi's Influence on the Budapest School. *J. Econ. Issues*, March 1987, *21*(1), pp. 339–47.

Bush, Paul D. The Theory of Institutional Change. *J. Econ. Issues*, September 1987, *21*(3), pp. 1075–1116.

Dillard, Dudley. The Evolutionary Economics of a Monetary Economy: Remarks upon Receipt of the Veblen–Commons Award. *J. Econ. Issues*, June 1987, *21*(2), pp. 575–85.

Dugger, William M. An Institutionalist Theory of Economic Planning. *J. Econ. Issues*, December 1987, *21*(4), pp. 1649–75.

Eichner, Alfred S. Prices and Pricing. *J. Econ. Issues*, December 1987, *21*(4), pp. 1555–84.

Eliasson, Gunnar. The Economics of Institutions and Markets—The Organization of Research at IUI. *Eliasson, G., ed.*, 1987, pp. 15–26.

Hamilton, David. A Theory of the Social Origin of Factors of Production. *Albelda, R.; Gunn, C. and Waller, W., eds.*, 1987, *1955*, pp. 244–52.

Hamilton, David. Institutional Economics and

Consumption. *J. Econ. Issues*, December 1987, *21*(4), pp. 1531–54.

Hamilton, Walton H. The Institutional Approach to Economic Theory. *Albelda, R.; Gunn, C. and Waller, W., eds.*, 1987, *1919*, pp. 204–12.

Hayden, F. Gregory. Evolution of Time Constructs and Their Impact on Socioeconomic Planning. *J. Econ. Issues*, September 1987, *21*(3), pp. 1281–1312.

Hickerson, Steven R. Instrumental Valuation: The Normative Compass of Institutional Economics. *J. Econ. Issues*, September 1987, *21*(3), pp. 1117–43.

Jensen, Hans E. The Theory of Human Nature. *J. Econ. Issues*, September 1987, *21*(3), pp. 1039–73.

Klein, Philip A. Power and Economic Performance: The Institutionalist View. *J. Econ. Issues*, September 1987, *21*(3), pp. 1341–77.

Krabbe, Jacob Jan. Organistic Theory in Economics: The Contribution of the Historical School. *Int. J. Soc. Econ.*, 1987, *14*(3/4/5), pp. 105–17.

Lowe, Adolph. What Is Evolutionary Economics? Remarks upon Receipt of the Veblen–Commons Award. *Lowe, A.*, 1987, *1980*, pp. 226–33.

Lower, Milton D. The Concept of Technology within the Institutionalist Perspective. *J. Econ. Issues*, September 1987, *21*(3), pp. 1147–76.

Martin, David A. and Mayhew, Anne. Bronfenbrenner on Institutionalists and the Critical Tradition in American Economics: Comment. *J. Econ. Issues*, March 1987, *21*(1), pp. 375–80.

Mattson, Vernon and Tilman, Rick. Thorstein Veblen, Frederick Jackson Turner, and the American Experience. *J. Econ. Issues*, March 1987, *21*(1), pp. 219–35.

Mayhew, Anne. The Beginnings of Institutionalism. *J. Econ. Issues*, September 1987, *21*(3), pp. 971–98.

McClintock, Brent. Institutional Transaction Analysis. *J. Econ. Issues*, June 1987, *21*(2), pp. 673–81.

Melody, William H. Information: An Emerging Dimension of Institutional Analysis. *J. Econ. Issues*, September 1987, *21*(3), pp. 1313–39.

Mirowski, Philip. The Philosophical Bases of Institutionalist Economics. *J. Econ. Issues*, September 1987, *21*(3), pp. 1001–38.

Munkirs, John R. and Knoedler, Janet T. The Dual Economy: An Empirical Analysis. *J. Econ. Issues*, June 1987, *21*(2), pp. 803–11. [G: U.S.]

Munkirs, John R. and Knoedler, Janet T. The Existence and Exercise of Corporate Power: An Opaque Fact. *J. Econ. Issues*, December 1987, *21*(4), pp. 1679–1706. [G: U.S.]

Neale, Walter C. Institutions. *J. Econ. Issues*, September 1987, *21*(3), pp. 1177–1206.

O'Brien, John C. The Social Economics of Hugo Eisenhart Gustav von Schmoller. *Int. J. Soc. Econ.*, 1987, *14*(11), pp. 26–47.

Peach, James T. Distribution and Economic Progress. *J. Econ. Issues*, December 1987, *21*(4), pp. 1495–1529. [G: U.S.]

Peterson, Wallace C. Macroeconomic Theory and Policy in an Institutionalist Perspective. *J. Econ. Issues*, December 1987, *21*(4), pp. 1587–1621. [G: U.S.]

Ramstad, Yngve. Institutional Existentialism: More on Why John R. Commons Has So Few Followers. *J. Econ. Issues*, June 1987, *21*(2), pp. 661–71.

Ranson, Baldwin. The Institutionalist Theory of Capital Formation. *J. Econ. Issues*, September 1987, *21*(3), pp. 1265–78.

Rutherford, Malcolm. Wesley Mitchell: Institutions and Quantitative Methods. *Eastern Econ. J.*, Jan.-Mar. 1987, *13*(1), pp. 63–73.

Scaperlanda, Anthony. Institutionalist Methodology and Social Economics. *Int. J. Soc. Econ.*, 1987, *14*(3/4/5), pp. 146–53.

Singh, Harinder. The Rationalist Conception of Action: Comment. *J. Econ. Issues*, March 1987, *21*(1), pp. 441–51.

Soble, Irvin. Adam Smith: What Kind of an Institutionalist Was He? Old Wine in New Bottles. *Rivista Int. Sci. Econ. Com.*, Jan.-Feb. 1987, *34*(1–2), pp. 87–108.

Stabile, Donald R. Veblen and the Political Economy of Technocracy: The Herald of Technological Revolution Developed an Ideology of 'Scientific' Collectivism. *Amer. J. Econ. Soc.*, January 1987, *46*(1), pp. 35–48.

Stevenson, Rodney E. Institutional Economics and the Theory of Production. *J. Econ. Issues*, December 1987, *21*(4), pp. 1471–93.

Street, James H. The Institutionalist Theory of Economic Development. *J. Econ. Issues*, December 1987, *21*(4), pp. 1861–87.

Street, James H. The Latin American Structuralists and the Institutionalists: Convergence in Development Theory. *Dietz, J. L. and Street, J. H., eds.*, 1987, pp. 101–14. [G: Latin America]

Swaney, James A. Elements of a Neoinstitutional Environmental Economics. *J. Econ. Issues*, December 1987, *21*(4), pp. 1739–79.

Tilman, Rick. Grace Jaffé and Richard Ely on Thorstein Veblen: An Unknown Chapter in American Economic Thought. *Hist. Polit. Econ.*, Spring 1987, *19*(1), pp. 141–62.

Tilman, Rick. Some Recent Interpretations of Thorstein Veblen's Theory of Institutional Change. *J. Econ. Issues*, June 1987, *21*(2), pp. 683–90.

Tilman, Rick. The Neoinstrumental Theory of Democracy. *J. Econ. Issues*, September 1987, *21*(3), pp. 1379–1401.

Tool, Marc R. Evolutionary Economics I: Foundations of Institutional Thought: Introduction. *J. Econ. Issues*, September 1987, *21*(3), pp. 951–67.

Tool, Marc R. Value and Its Corollaries. *Albelda, R.; Gunn, C. and Waller, W., eds.*, 1987, *1979*, pp. 225–43.

Trebing, Harry M. Regulation of Industry: An Institutionalist Approach. *J. Econ. Issues*, December 1987, *21*(4), pp. 1707–37.

Waller, William T., Jr. The Evolution of the Veblenian Dichotomy: Veblen, Hamilton, Ayres, and Foster. *Albelda, R.; Gunn, C. and Waller, W., eds.*, 1987, *1982*, pp. 213–24.

Williamson, Oliver E. Kenneth Arrow and the New Institutional Economics. *Feiwel, G. R., ed. (II)*, 1987, pp. 584–99.

Woodbury, Stephen A. Power in the Labor Market: Institutionalist Approaches to Labor Problems. *J. Econ. Issues*, December 1987, *21*(4), pp. 1781–1807.

032 History of Economic Thought (continued)

0321 Other Schools since 1800

Amadeo, Edward J. and Dutt, Amitava Krishna. Os keynesianos neo-ricardianos e os pós-keynesianos. (With English summary.) *Pesquisa Planejamento Econ.*, December 1987, *17*(3), pp. 561–603.

Breit, William. Creating the "Virginia School": Charlottesville as an Academic Environment in the 1960s. *Econ. Inquiry*, October 1987, *25*(4), pp. 645–57.   [G: U.S.]

Dow, Sheila C. The Scottish Political Economy Tradition. *Scot. J. Polit. Econ.*, November 1987, *34*(4), pp. 335–48.   [G: U.K.]

Finoia, Massimo. Founders of Modern Economic Thought in Italy. *Int. J. Soc. Econ.*, 1987, *14*(7/8/9), pp. 182–94.   [G: Italy]

Hill, Lewis E. A Pragmatic Methodology for Social Economics: A Preliminary Proposal. *Int. J. Soc. Econ.*, 1987, *14*(3/4/5), pp. 140–45.

Houmanidis, Lazaros. Keynesianism and Stagflation. *Int. J. Soc. Econ.*, 1987, *14*(7/8/9), pp. 211–20.

Jonung, Lars. The Stockholm School After Fifty Years: A Conversation with Lars Jonung. *Eastern Econ. J.*, Apr.-June 1987, *13*(2), pp. 93–97.

Khalil, Elias L. Kuhn, Lakatos, and the History of Economic Thought. *Int. J. Soc. Econ.*, 1987, *14*(3/4/5), pp. 118–31.

Maier, Charles S. Political Economy and History. *Maier, C. S.*, 1987, pp. 1–16.

Meijer, Gerrit. The History of Neo-liberalism: Affinity to Some Developments in Economics in Germany. *Int. J. Soc. Econ.*, 1987, *14*(7/8/9), pp. 142–55.

Niedercorn, John H. Parable of the Minas: A Caricature of Zealot Political Economy. *Int. J. Soc. Econ.*, 1987, *14*(6), pp. 39–45.

Nitsch, Thomas O. Social Economics: From Search for Identity to Quest for Roots; or, Social Economics: The First 100 Years (or So). *Int. J. Soc. Econ.*, 1987, *14*(3/4/5), pp. 70–90.

Pellanda, Anna. Angelo Messedaglia on Money and the Nineteenth Century Italian Economic School. *Int. J. Soc. Econ.*, 1987, *14*(7/8/9), pp. 170–81.   [G: Italy]

0322 Individuals

Alchian, Armen A.
Brunner, Karl. Armen A. Alchian. *J. Inst. Theoretical Econ.*, March 1987, *143*(1), pp. 229–31.

Demsetz, Harold. An Appreciation of Armen A. Alchian's Contribution to the Theory of the Firm. *J. Inst. Theoretical Econ.*, March 1987, *143*(1), pp. 3–6.

Anderson, James
Prendergast, Renee. James Anderson's Political Economy—His Influence on Smith and Malthus. *Scot. J. Polit. Econ.*, November 1987, *34*(4), pp. 388–409.

Anderson, William
Pullen, John M. William Anderson (fl. 1797–1832), on Banking, the Money Supply, and Public Expenditure: A Forgotten Interventionist. *Hist. Polit. Econ.*, Fall 1987, *19*(3), pp. 359–85.

Aquinas, Thomas
Lapidus, André. La propriété de la monnaie: doctrine de l'usure et théorie de l'intérêt. (The Property of Money: Theory of Interest and Doctrine of Usury. With English summary.) *Revue Écon.*, November 1987, *38*(6), pp. 1095–1109.

Arrow, Kenneth J.
Anderson, Theodore W. The Young Scholar: An Interview. *Feiwel, G. R., ed. (II)*, 1987, pp. 666–71.

Arrow, Kenneth J. Arrow and the Ascent of Modern Economic Theory: Oral History I: An Interview. *Feiwel, G. R., ed. (I)*, 1987, pp. 191–242.

Arrow, Kenneth J. Arrow on Arrow: An Interview. *Feiwel, G. R., ed. (II)*, 1987, pp. 637–57.

Aumann, Robert J. Arrow—The Breadth, Depth, and Conscience of the Scholar: An Interview. *Feiwel, G. R., ed. (II)*, 1987, pp. 658–62.

Aumann, Robert J. Economic Theory and Mathematical Method: An Interview. *Feiwel, G. R., ed. (I)*, 1987, pp. 306–16.

Bliss, Christopher. Arrow's Vision of the Economic Process. *Feiwel, G. R., ed. (I)*, 1987, pp. 295–305.

Feiwel, George R. Arrow's Weltanschauung. *Rivista Int. Sci. Econ. Com.*, Jan.-Feb. 1987, *34*(1–2), pp. 1–50.

Feiwel, George R. The Many Dimensions of Kenneth J. Arrow. *Feiwel, G. R., ed. (II)*, 1987, pp. 1–115.

Feiwel, George R. The Potentials and Limits of Economic Analysis: The Contributions of Kenneth J. Arrow. *Feiwel, G. R., ed. (I)*, 1987, pp. 1–187.

Feiwel, George R. There Is Music in Economics. *Feiwel, G. R., ed. (II)*, 1987, pp. 713–24.

Green, Jerry R. A Younger Colleague's View from Harvard: An Interview. *Feiwel, G. R., ed. (II)*, 1987, pp. 678–79.

Hurwicz, Leonid. 'Partners in Crime': An Interview. *Feiwel, G. R., ed. (II)*, 1987, pp. 663–65.

Intriligator, Michael D. The Impact of Arrow's Contribution to Economic Analysis. *Feiwel, G. R., ed. (II)*, 1987, pp. 683–91.

Kelly, Jerry S. An Interview with Kenneth J.

Arrow. *Soc. Choice Welfare*, March 1987, *4*(1), pp. 43–62.

Kennedy, Donald. The University Citizen: An Interview. *Feiwel, G. R., ed. (II)*, 1987, pp. 701–04.

Lieberman, Gerald J. Making Music at Stanford: An Interview. *Feiwel, G. R., ed. (II)*, 1987, pp. 705–11.

Lipset, Seymour Martin. Ken Arrow—Success without Pressure: An Interview. *Feiwel, G. R., ed. (II)*, 1987, pp. 692–700.

Mas-Colell, Andreu. Transformation in General Equilibrium Theory and Methods: An Interview. *Feiwel, G. R., ed. (I)*, 1987, pp. 317–24.

Raiffa, Howard. Axiomatic Soul Searching. *Feiwel, G. R., ed. (II)*, 1987, pp. 672–77.

Sonnenschein, Hugo. Theory and Method—Second-Generation Perspective: An Interview. *Feiwel, G. R., ed. (I)*, 1987, pp. 325–39.

Starrett, David A. *Production and Capital: Kenneth Arrow's Contribution in Perspective—A Review Article. J. Econ. Lit.*, March 1987, *25*(1), pp. 92–102.

Williamson, Oliver E. Kenneth Arrow and the New Institutional Economics. *Feiwel, G. R., ed. (II)*, 1987, pp. 584–99.

Ayres, Clarence E.
Pickens, Donald K. Clarence E. Ayres and the Legacy of German Idealism. *Amer. J. Econ. Soc.*, July 1987, *46*(3), pp. 287–98.

Waller, William T., Jr. The Evolution of the Veblenian Dichotomy: Veblen, Hamilton, Ayres, and Foster. *Albelda, R.; Gunn, C. and Waller, W., eds.*, 1987, *1982*, pp. 213–24.

Bagiotti, Tullio
Montesano, Aldo. The Life and Works of Tullio Bagiotti (1921–1983). *Int. J. Soc. Econ.*, 1987, *14*(7/8/9), pp. 156–59.

Barone, Enrico
Maneschi, Andrea and Thweatt, William O. Barone's 1908 Representation of an Economy's Trade Equilibrium and the Gains from Trade. *J. Int. Econ.*, May 1987, *22*(3/4), pp. 375–82.

Bauer, Peter
Yamey, Basil S. Peter Bauer: Economist and Scholar. *Cato J.*, Spring/Summer 1987, *7*(1), pp. 21–27.

Bentham, Jeremy
Elliott, John E. and Scott, Joanna V. Theories of Liberal Capitalist Democracy: Alternative Perspectives. *Int. J. Soc. Econ.*, 1987, *14*(7/8/9), pp. 52–87.   [G: U.S.]

Bergson, Abram
Bergson, Abram. Recollections and Reflections of a Comparativist. *Amer. Econ.*, Spring 1987, *31*(1), pp. 3–8.

Bickerdike, Charles F.
Larson, Bruce. Bickerdike's Life and Work. *Hist. Polit. Econ.*, Spring 1987, *19*(1), pp. 1–21.

Bodin, Jean
Tortajada, Ramon. M. de Malestroit et la théorie quantitative de la monnaie. (M. de Malestroit and the Quantity Theory of Money. With English summary.) *Revue Écon.*, July 1987, *38*(4), pp. 853–76.

Böhm-Bawerk, Eugene
Endres, Anthony M. The Origins of Böhm-Bawerk's 'Greatest Error': Theoretical Points of Separation from Menger. *J. Inst. Theoretical Econ.*, June 1987, *143*(2), pp. 291–309.

von Bortkiewicz, Ladislaus
Meldolesi, Luca. Ladislaus von Bortkiewicz and the Origin of Interest. *Stud. Econ.*, 1987, *42*(31), pp. 145–52.

Buchanan, James M.
Aranson, Peter H. Calculus and Consent. *[Tullock, G.]*, 1987, pp. 60–65.

Atkinson, Anthony B. James M. Buchanan's Contributions to Economics. *Scand. J. Econ.*, 1987, *89*(1), pp. 5–15.

Eusepi, Giuseppe. General Implications of Subjectivism and Dynamics in Buchanan's Works. *Econ. Int.*, February 1987, *40*(1), pp. 55–66.

Mitchell, William C. The Calculus of Consent: Notes in Retrospection. *[Tullock, G.]*, 1987, pp. 66–73.

Rowley, Charles K. The Calculus of Consent. *[Tullock, G.]*, 1987, pp. 41–59.

Rowley, Charles K. The Economic Philosophy of James McGill Buchanan. *Econ. Scelte Pubbliche/J. Public Finance Public Choice*, Sept.-Dec. 1987, *5*(3), pp. 171–87.

Čajanov, A. V.
Stanziani, Alessandro. L'impresa familiare nel pensiero di A. V. Čajanov. (With English summary.) *Stud. Econ.*, 1987, *42*(32), pp. 61–117.

Cantillon, Richard
Murphy, Antoin E. Richard Cantillon and John Law. *Écon. Soc.*, March 1987, *21*(3), pp. 3–37.

Chamberlin, Edward H.
Rothschild, R. The Theory of Monopolistic Competition: E. H. Chamberlin's Influence on Industrial Organisation Theory over Sixty Years. *J. Econ. Stud.*, 1987, *14*(1), pp. 34–54.

Champernowne, David Gawen
Campano, Fred. A Fresh Look at Champernowne's Five-Parameter Formula. *Écon. Appl.*, 1987, *40*(1), pp. 161–75.   [G: U.S.]

Commons, John R.
Ramstad, Yngve. Free Trade versus Fair Trade: Import Barriers as a Problem of Reasonable Value. *J. Econ. Issues*, March 1987, *21*(1), pp. 5–32.   [G: U.S.]

Ramstad, Yngve. Institutional Existentialism: More on Why John R. Commons Has So Few Followers. *J. Econ. Issues*, June 1987, *21*(2), pp. 661–71.

Cossa, Luigi
  Finoia, Massimo. Founders of Modern Economic Thought in Italy. *Int. J. Soc. Econ.*, 1987, *14*(7/8/9), pp. 182–94.　　**[G: Italy]**
Debreu, Gerard
  Debreu, Gerard. Arrow and the Ascent of Modern Economic Theory: Oral History II: An Interview. *Feiwel, G. R., ed.* (I), 1987, pp. 243–57.
Díaz-Alejandro, Carlos F.
  Kindleberger, Charles P. Carlos F. Díaz-Alejandro: An Appreciation. *J. Devel. Econ.*, October 1987, *27*(1–2), pp. 1–4.
  Kindleberger, Charles P. Carlos F. Díaz-Alejandro: An Appreciation. *[Diaz-Alejandro, C. F.]*, 1987, pp. 1–4.
Downey, Ezekial H.
  Downey, Ezekial H. The Futility of Marginal Utility. *Albelda, R.; Gunn, C. and Waller, W., eds.*, 1987, *1910*, pp. 48–59.
Edgeworth, Francis Ysidro
  Larson, Bruce. Edgeworth, Samuelson, and Operationally Meaningful Theorems. *Hist. Polit. Econ.*, Fall 1987, *19*(3), pp. 351–57.
Ely, Richard
  Tilman, Rick. Grace Jaffé and Richard Ely on Thorstein Veblen: An Unknown Chapter in American Economic Thought. *Hist. Polit. Econ.*, Spring 1987, *19*(1), pp. 141–62.
Engels, Friedrich
  Wolf, Eric K. The Peasant War in Germany: Friedrich Engels as Social Historian. *Sci. Soc.*, Spring 1987, *51*(1), pp. 82–92.
Erhard, Ludwig
  Wünsche, Horst Friedrich. Does Industrial Policy Comply with Ludwig Erhard's Conception of the Social Market Economy? *Gemper, B. B., ed.*, 1987, pp. 37–43.
Eucken, Walter
  Meijer, Gerrit. The History of Neo-liberalism: Affinity to Some Developments in Economics in Germany. *Int. J. Soc. Econ.*, 1987, *14*(7/8/9), pp. 142–55.
de Finetti, Bruno
  Gillies, D. A. and Ietto-Gillies, G. Probability and Economics in the Works of Bruno de Finetti. *Econ. Int.*, May-Aug. 1987, *40*(2–3), pp. 192–209.
Fisher, Irving
  Hotson, John H. The Keynesian Revolution and the Aborted Fisher–Simons Revolution or the Road Not Taken. *Écon. Soc.*, September 1987, *21*(9), pp. 185–219.
Foster, J. Fagg
  Waller, William T., Jr. The Evolution of the Veblenian Dichotomy: Veblen, Hamilton, Ayres, and Foster. *Albelda, R.; Gunn, C. and Waller, W., eds.*, 1987, *1982*, pp. 213–24.
Friedman, Milton
  Mongin, Philippe. L'Instrumentalisme dans l'Essai de M. Friedman. (Instrumentalism in M. Friedman's Essay. With English summary.) *Écon. Soc.*, October 1987, *21*(10), pp. 73–106.

Webb, James L. Is Friedman's Methodological Instrumentalism a Special Case of Dewey's Instrumental Philosophy? A Comment [Friedman's Positive Economics and the Philosophy of Science]. *J. Econ. Issues*, March 1987, *21*(1), pp. 393–429.
Wible, James R. Criticism and the Validity of the Special-Case Interpretation of Friedman's Essay: Reply [Friedman's Positive Economics and the Philosophy of Science]. *J. Econ. Issues*, March 1987, *21*(1), pp. 430–40.
Galiani, Ferdinando
  Porta, Pier Luigi. Ferdinando Galiani on Population and Economic Growth. *Écon. Soc.*, March 1987, *21*(3), pp. 39–52.
George, Henry
  Bonaparte, T. H. Henry George's Impact at Home and Abroad: He Won the Workers of Marx's Adopted Country but through Leninism Marxism Has Won Half the World. *Amer. J. Econ. Soc.*, January 1987, *46*(1), pp. 109–24.
  Johannsen, Oscar B. Henry George and His Philosophy: He Sought Equality of Opportunity to Use the Earth's Resources as Well as the End of Land Monopoly. *Amer. J. Econ. Soc.*, July 1987, *46*(3), pp. 379–82.
  Kamerschen, David R. Some Surviving Elements in the Work of Henry George. *Amer. J. Econ. Soc.*, October 1987, *46*(4), pp. 489–93.
  Silagi, Michael. Henry George and Europe: Ireland, the First Target of His Efforts to Spread His Doctrines Internationally, Disappointed Him. *Amer. J. Econ. Soc.*, October 1987, *46*(4), pp. 495–501.
  Steele, E. Springs. Henry George on Chattel and Wage Slavery: The American Social Philosopher Condemned Both Forms as Immoral, Irrational Denials of Equality. *Amer. J. Econ. Soc.*, July 1987, *46*(3), pp. 367–78.
Gilder, George
  Pack, Spencer J. Schumpeter Plus Optimism Equals Gilder (*ceteris paribus*). *Hist. Polit. Econ.*, Fall 1987, *19*(3), pp. 469–80.
Graaff, J. de V.
  Melck, A. P. *Theoretical Welfare Economics* after Thirty Years. *S. Afr. J. Econ.*, September 1987, *55*(3), pp. 259–66.
　　　　　　　　　　　　[G: S. Africa]
Grenville, William Wyndham [Lord]
  Pullen, John M. Lord Grenville's Manuscript Notes on Malthus. *Hist. Polit. Econ.*, Summer 1987, *19*(2), pp. 217–37.
Hamilton, Walton H.
  Hamilton, Walton H. The Institutional Approach to Economic Theory. *Albelda, R.; Gunn, C. and Waller, W., eds.*, 1987, *1919*, pp. 204–12.
  Waller, William T., Jr. The Evolution of the Veblenian Dichotomy: Veblen, Hamilton, Ayres, and Foster. *Albelda, R.; Gunn, C.*

and Waller, W., eds., 1987, *1982*, pp. 213–24.

Hansen, Alvin H.
  Barber, William J. The Career of Alvin H. Hansen in the 1920s and 1930s: A Study in Intellectual Transformation. *Hist. Polit. Econ.*, Summer 1987, *19*(2), pp. 191–205.

Harris, Abram
  Darity, William A., Jr. Abram Harris: An Odyssey from Howard to Chicago. *Rev. Black Polit. Econ.*, Winter 1987, *15*(3), pp. 4–40.

von Hayek, Friedrich A.
  Cubeddu, Raimondo. Popper et l'Ecole Autrichienne. (Popper and the Austrian School: Menger, Boehm-Bawerk, Wieser, Mises. With English summary.) *Écon. Soc.*, October 1987, *21*(10), pp. 41–62.
  Schmidtchen, Dieter. Hayek on Liberty and the Rule of Law: The Road to Serfdom Revisited. *Pejovich, S., ed.*, 1987, pp. 115–44.
  Sicard, François. Popper et Hayek: économie et politique. (Popper and Hayek: Economics and Politics. With English summary.) *Écon. Soc.*, October 1987, *21*(10), pp. 63–72.

Heller, Walter
  Tobin, James. Remembering Walter Heller. *Challenge*, Nov./Dec. 1987, *30*(5), pp. 59–63.

Hensel, K. P.
  Meijer, Gerrit. The History of Neo-liberalism: Affinity to Some Developments in Economics in Germany. *Int. J. Soc. Econ.*, 1987, *14*(7/8/9), pp. 142–55.

Hicks, John R.
  Malinvaud, Edmond. Reflecting on the Theory of Capital and Growth. *Sinclair, P. J. N., ed.*, 1987, *1986*, pp. 395–413.

Hollander, Samuel
  Coats, A. W. Samuel Hollander's Mill: A Review Article. *Manchester Sch. Econ. Soc. Stud.*, September 1987, *55*(3), pp. 310–16.

Hume, David
  Perlman, Morris. Of a Controversial Passage in Hume. *J. Polit. Econ.*, April 1987, *95*(2), pp. 274–89.

Hyndman, Henry M.
  Young, James J. H. M. Hyndman and Daniel De Leon: The Two Souls of Socialism. *Labor Hist.*, Fall 1987, *28*(4), pp. 534–56. **[G: U.S.; U.K.]**

Jaffé, Grace
  Tilman, Rick. Grace Jaffé and Richard Ely on Thorstein Veblen: An Unknown Chapter in American Economic Thought. *Hist. Polit. Econ.*, Spring 1987, *19*(1), pp. 141–62.

Jevons, W. Stanley
  Aldrich, John. Jevons as Statistician: The Role of Probability. *Manchester Sch. Econ. Soc. Stud.*, September 1987, *55*(3), pp. 233–56.
  Bostaph, Samuel and Shieh, Yeung-Nan. Jevons's Demand Curve. *Hist. Polit. Econ.*, Spring 1987, *19*(1), pp. 107–26.

Johannsen, Nicholas
  Hagemann, Harald and Rühl, Christof. Nicholas Johannsen's Early Analysis of the Saving–Investment Process and the Multiplier. *Stud. Econ.*, 1987, *42*(31), pp. 99–143.

Kalecki, Michal
  Sebastiani, Mario. Kalecki e l'economia capitalistica: una nota sulla recente pubblicazione in Italia degli Essays. (Kalecki on the Capitalist Economy: A Note on the Recent Publication in Italy of the *Essays*. With English summary.) *Econ. Polít.*, April 1987, *4*(1), pp. 113–22.

Kantorovich, Leonid V.
  Makarov, V. L. On Dynamic Models of the Economy and the Development of L. V. Kantorovich's Ideas. *Matekon*, Summer 1987, *23*(4), pp. 48–74.

Keynes, John Maynard
  Amadeo, Edward J. and Dutt, Amitava Krishna. Os keynesianos neo-ricardianos e os pós-keynesianos. (With English summary.) *Pesquisa Planejamento Econ.*, December 1987, *17*(3), pp. 561–603.
  Bateman, Bradley W. Keynes's Changing Conception of Probability. *Econ. Philos.*, April 1987, *3*(1), pp. 97–119.
  Bhattacharjea, Aditya. Keynes and the Long-Period Theory of Employment: A Note. *Cambridge J. Econ.*, September 1987, *11*(3), pp. 275–84.
  Bird, Graham. Bancor and the Developing Countries: How Much Difference Would It Have Made? Discussion. *Thirlwall, A. P., ed.*, 1987, pp. 107–16.
  Brandis, Royall. Marx *and* Keynes? Marx *or* Keynes? A Reply. *J. Econ. Issues*, March 1987, *21*(1), pp. 470–73.
  Burkett, Paul and Wohar, Mark E. Keynes on Investment and the Business Cycle. *Rev. Radical Polit. Econ.*, Winter 1987, *19*(4), pp. 39–54.
  Chandavarkar, Anand G. Keynes and the International Monetary System Revisited (A Contextual and Conjectural Essay). *World Devel.*, December 1987, *15*(12), pp. 1395–1405. **[G: LDCs]**
  Chick, Victoria. Are *The General Theory's* Central Contributions Still Valid? *J. Econ. Stud.*, 1987, *14*(4), pp. 5–12.
  Dimsdale, N. H. Keynes on British Budgetary Policy 1914–46. *Boskin, M. J.; Fleming, J. S. and Gorini, S., eds.*, 1987, pp. 208–33. **[G: U.K.]**
  Ditz, Gerhard W. Smith and Keynes: Religious Differences in Economic Philosophy. *Economia (Portugal)*, October 1987, *11*(3), pp. 399–431.
  Dutt, Amitava Krishna. Keynes with a Perfectly Competitive Goods Market. *Australian Econ. Pap.*, December 1987, *26*(49), pp. 275–93.
  Elliott, John E. and Clark, Barry S. Keynes's *General Theory* and Social Justice. *J. Post Keynesian Econ.*, Spring 1987, *9*(3), pp. 381–94.

Fichtenbaum, Rudy and Shahidi, Hushang. Marx and Keynes? Marx or Keynes? A Comment. *J. Econ. Issues*, March 1987, *21*(1), pp. 467–70.

Galbraith, John Kenneth. Keynes, Roosevelt, and the Complementary Revolutions. *Challenge*, Special Issue 1987, *30*(6), pp. 19–23. [G: U.S.]

Garrison, Roger W. Full Employment and Intertemporal Coordination: A Rejoinder [Intertemporal Coordination and the Invisible Hand: An Austrian Perspective on the Keynesian Vision]. *Hist. Polit. Econ.*, Summer 1987, *19*(2), pp. 335–41.

Goux, Jean-François. La théorie monétaire de la "finance" chez Keynes: une réinterprétation. (With English summary.) *Revue Écon. Polit.*, Sept.-Oct. 1987, *97*(5), pp. 592–612.

Graziani, Augusto. Keynes' Finance Motive. *Écon. Soc.*, September 1987, *21*(9), pp. 23–42.

Houmanidis, Lazaros. Keynesianism and Stagflation. *Int. J. Soc. Econ.*, 1987, *14*(7/8/9), pp. 211–20.

Jensen, Hans E. J. M. Keynes as a Marshallian: Reply. *J. Econ. Issues*, March 1987, *21*(1), pp. 457–67.

Kregel, Jan A. Keynes's Given Degree of Competition: Comment. *J. Post Keynesian Econ.*, Summer 1987, *9*(4), pp. 490–95.

Kregel, Jan A. The Changing Place of Money in Keynes's Theory from the *Treatise* to the *General Theory*. [Marrama, V.], Vol. 1, 1987, pp. 97–114.

Lawlor, Michael S.; Darity, William A., Jr. and Horn, Bobbie L. Was Keynes a Chapter Two Keynesian? *J. Post Keynesian Econ.*, Summer 1987, *9*(4), pp. 516–28.

McCallum, Bennett T. The Development of Keynesian Macroeconomics. *Amer. Econ. Rev.*, May 1987, *77*(2), pp. 125–29.

Motley, Brian. Ricardo or Keynes: Does the Government Debt Affect Consumption? *Fed. Res. Bank San Francisco Econ. Rev.*, Winter 1987, (1), pp. 47–62.

Niman, Neil B. Keynes and the Invisible Hand Theorem. *J. Post Keynesian Econ.*, Fall 1987, *10*(1), pp. 105–15.

Peden, G. C. The Policy Debate: Keynes. *Glynn, S. and Booth, A., eds.*, 1987, pp. 97–108. [G: U.K.]

Pheby, John. A New Perspective on Shackle's Keynesian Fundamentalism. *J. Econ. Stud.*, 1987, *14*(4), pp. 24–35.

Poulon, F. Keynes et Robertson: naissance d'un désaccord sur la fonction de l'épargne dans la théorie monétaire. (Keynes and Robertson: The Beginning of a Disagreement about the Role of Saving in Monetary Theory. With English summary.) *Écon. Soc.*, September 1987, *21*(9), pp. 9–22.

Pressman, Steven. The Policy Relevance of *The General Theory*. *J. Econ. Stud.*, 1987, *14*(4), pp. 13–23. [G: U.S.]

Roychowdhury, Krishna Ch. Keynes, Expectation and Employment. *Indian Econ. J.*, July-Sept. 1987, *35*(1), pp. 54–59.

Rutherford, R. P. Malthus and Keynes. *Sinclair, P. J. N., ed.*, 1987, pp. 175–89.

Rutherford, R. P. Malthus and Keynes. *Oxford Econ. Pap.*, March 1987, *39*(1), pp. 175–89.

Sinclair, P. J. N. Prices, Quantities and Expectations: Keynes and Macroeconomics in the Fifty Years since the Publication of the *General Theory*: Preface. *Sinclair, P. J. N., ed.*, 1987, pp. vii–xxiv.

Singer, Hans W. Discussion [Keynes, Economic Development and the Developing Countries] [Some Reflections by a Keynesian Economist on the Problems of Developing Countries]. *Thirlwall, A. P., ed.*, 1987, pp. 66–69.

Singer, Hans W. What Keynes and Keynesianism Can Teach Us about Less Developed Countries. *Thirlwall, A. P., ed.*, 1987, pp. 70–89.

Snippe, J. Intertemporal Coordination and the Economics of Keynes: Comment. *Hist. Polit. Econ.*, Summer 1987, *19*(2), pp. 329–34.

Thirlwall, A. P. Keynes, Economic Development and the Developing Countries. *Thirlwall, A. P., ed.*, 1987, pp. 3–35.

Tobin, James. On the Theoretical Foundations of Keynesian Economics (Comment on Lord Kaldor's 'Keynesian Economics after Fifty Years'). *Tobin, J. (III)*, 1987, *1983*, pp. 40–49.

Trescott, Paul B. J. M. Keynes as a Marshallian: Comment. *J. Econ. Issues*, March 1987, *21*(1), pp. 452–57.

Ulmer, Melville J. Fifty Years of Keynes. *Atlantic Econ. J.*, September 1987, *15*(3), pp. 3–8.

Wells, Paul. Keynes's Employment Function and the Marginal Productivity of Labor. *J. Post Keynesian Econ.*, Summer 1987, *9*(4), pp. 507–15.

Williamson, John. Bancor and the Developing Countries: How Much Difference Would It Have Made? *Thirlwall, A. P., ed.*, 1987, pp. 92–106.

Williamson, John. Keynes and the International Economic Order. *Williamson, J.*, 1987, *1983*, pp. 37–59.

Kitamura, Hiroshi

El-Agraa, Ali M. Hiroshi Kitamura: A Short Personal History. [Kitamura, H.], 1987, pp. 1–19.

Knight, Frank

Kern, William S. Frank Knight's Three Commandments. *Hist. Polit. Econ.*, Winter 1987, *19*(4), pp. 639–46.

LeRoy, Stephen F. and Singell, Larry D., Jr. Knight on Risk and Uncertainty. *J. Polit. Econ.*, April 1987, *95*(2), pp. 394–406.

Križanić, Juraj

Baron, Samuel H. Was Križanić a Mercantilist? *Hist. Polit. Econ.*, Spring 1987, *19*(1), pp. 67–86.

Lebergott, Stanley
   Kilby, Peter. Stanley Lebergott: An Appreciation. *Kilby, P., ed.*, 1987, pp. xv–xxiii.
   [G: U.S.]
De Leon, Daniel
   Young, James J. H. M. Hyndman and Daniel De Leon: The Two Souls of Socialism. *Labor Hist.*, Fall 1987, *28*(4), pp. 534–56.
   [G: U.S.; U.K.]
List, Friedrich
   Henderson, W. O. Friedrich List and England. *Jahr. Nationalökon. Statist.*, October 1987, *203*(5–6), pp. 532–46.   [G: U.K.; Germany]
Lowe, Adolph
   Oakley, Allen. Adolph Lowe's Contribution to the Development of a Political Economics. *Lowe, A.*, 1987, pp. 1–24.
de Malestroit, M.
   Tortajada, Ramon. M. de Malestroit et la théorie quantitative de la monnaie. (M. de Malestroit and the Quantity Theory of Money. With English summary.) *Revue Écon.*, July 1987, *38*(4), pp. 853–76.
Malinvaud, Edmond
   Malinvaud, Edmond. The Challenge of Macroeconomic Understanding. *Banca Naz. Lavoro Quart. Rev.*, September 1987, (162), pp. 219–38.
Malthus, Thomas Robert
   Behar, Cem L. Malthus and the Development of Demographic Analysis. *Population Stud.*, July 1987, *41*(2), pp. 269–81.
   Lee, Maw Lin and Loschky, David. Malthusian Population Oscillations. *Econ. J.*, September 1987, *97*(387), pp. 727–39.
   [G: U.S.]
   Malthus, Thomas Robert. An Essay on the Principle of Population. *Menard, S. W. and Moen, E. W., eds.*, 1987, *1798*, pp. 97–103.
   Prendergast, Renee. James Anderson's Political Economy—His Influence on Smith and Malthus. *Scot. J. Polit. Econ.*, November 1987, *34*(4), pp. 388–409.
   Pullen, John M. Lord Grenville's Manuscript Notes on Malthus. *Hist. Polit. Econ.*, Summer 1987, *19*(2), pp. 217–37.
   Pullen, John M. Some New Information on the Rev. T. R. Malthus. *Hist. Polit. Econ.*, Spring 1987, *19*(1), pp. 127–40.
   Rutherford, R. P. Malthus and Keynes. *Sinclair, P. J. N., ed.*, 1987, pp. 175–89.
   Rutherford, R. P. Malthus and Keynes. *Oxford Econ. Pap.*, March 1987, *39*(1), pp. 175–89.
   Waterman, A. M. C. On the Malthusian Theory of Long Swings. *Can. J. Econ.*, May 1987, *20*(2), pp. 257–70.
Mandeville, Bernard
   Moss, Laurence S. The Subjectivist Mercantilism of Bernard Mandeville. *Int. J. Soc. Econ.*, 1987, *14*(3/4/5), pp. 167–84.
Maritain, Jacques
   Haines, Walter W. A Society without Money: Reflections on Jacques Maritain. *Int. J. Soc.

Econ.*, 1987, *14*(3/4/5), pp. 97–104.
Marrama, Vittorio
   Gandolfo, Giancarlo. The Life and Works of Vittorio Marrama. *[Marrama, V.], Vol. 1*, 1987, pp. xiii–xxv.
Marshall, Alfred
   Beach, E. F. Marshall and His Critics. *Indian Econ. J.*, July-Sept. 1987, *35*(1), pp. 1–53.
   Beach, E. F. Marshallian Methodology. *Int. J. Soc. Econ.*, 1987, *14*(7/8/9), pp. 19–26.
   Gallegati, Mauro. Era Alfred Marshall un economista neoclassico? A Proposito di Recenti Studi di Storia dell'economia politica. (With English summary.) *Stud. Econ.*, 1987, *42*(31), pp. 153–71.
   Jensen, Hans E. Alfred Marshall as a Social Economist. *Rev. Soc. Econ.*, April 1987, *45*(1), pp. 14–36.
Marx, Karl
   Arnold, N. Scott. Final Reply to Professor Schweickart [Marx and Disequilibrium in Market Socialist Relations of Production]. *Econ. Philos.*, October 1987, *3*(2), pp. 335–38.
   Arnold, N. Scott. Further Thoughts on the Degeneration of Market Socialism: A Reply to Schweickart [Marx and Disequilibrium in Market Socialist Relations of Production]. *Econ. Philos.*, October 1987, *3*(2), pp. 320–30.
   Arnold, N. Scott. Marx and Disequilibrium in Market Socialist Relations of Production. *Econ. Philos.*, April 1987, *3*(1), pp. 23–47.
   Bandyopadhyay, Pradeep. Value and Post-Sraffa Marxian Analysis. *Albelda, R.; Gunn, C. and Waller, W., eds.*, 1987, *1984*, pp. 186–94.
   Bellofiore, Riccardo. Moneta, produzione e prezzi. In margine ad un recente convegno. (With English summary.) *Stud. Econ.*, 1987, *42*(33), pp. 107–15.
   Brandis, Royall. Marx *and* Keynes? Marx *or* Keynes? A Reply. *J. Econ. Issues*, March 1987, *21*(1), pp. 470–73.
   Clark, Barry S. Solitude and Solidarity in the Just Society: A Reappraisal of Marx's Vision. *Int. J. Soc. Econ.*, 1987, *14*(7/8/9), pp. 44–51.
   Colodny, Robert G. The Problem of the Ruling Class in Marxist Theory: A Comment. *Sci. Soc.*, Spring 1987, *51*(1), pp. 93–96.
   Davis, John B. Marx's Conception of Ethics in Capitalist Society. *Samuels, W. J., ed.*, 1987, pp. 51–90.
   Elliott, John E. Justice and Freedom in Marx's Moral Critique of Capitalism. *Samuels, W. J., ed.*, 1987, pp. 1–49.
   Elliott, John E. Moral and Ethical Considerations in Karl Marx's Robust Vision of the Future Society. *Int. J. Soc. Econ.*, 1987, *14*(10), pp. 3–26.
   Fichtenbaum, Rudy and Shahidi, Hushang. Marx and Keynes? Marx or Keynes? A Comment. *J. Econ. Issues*, March 1987, *21*(1), pp. 467–70.

Glick, Mark and Ehrbar, Hans G. The Transformation Problem: An Obituary. *Australian Econ. Pap.*, December 1987, *26*(49), pp. 294–317.

Hixson, William F. Marxism and "Monetary Policy." *Écon. Soc.*, September 1987, *21*(9), pp. 43–63.

Horvat, Branko. Sraffa Systematized and Marx Vindicated. *Econ. Anal. Workers' Manage.*, 1987, *21*(3), pp. 289–97.

Lebowitz, Michael A. The Political Economy of Wage Labor. *Sci. Soc.*, Fall 1987, *51*(3), pp. 262–86.

Martinius, Sture. Capitalism: A Threat against Freehold Farms around the Middle of the Nineteenth Century? *Scand. Econ. Hist. Rev.*, 1987, *35*(2), pp. 178–90.
                                  [G: W. Europe]

O'Brien, John C. The Instauration of the New Man of Marxism: A Critique. *Int. J. Soc. Econ.*, 1987, *14*(3/4/5), pp. 22–32.

Rodríguez Braun, Carlos. *Capital*'s Last Chapter. *Hist. Polit. Econ.*, Summer 1987, *19*(2), pp. 299–310.

Rotheim, Roy J. Equilibrium in Walras's and Marx's Theories of Capital Accumulation. *Int. J. Soc. Econ.*, 1987, *14*(7/8/9), pp. 27–43.

Schweickart, David. A Reply to Arnold's Reply [Marx and Disequilibrium in Market Socialist Relations of Production]. *Econ. Philos.*, October 1987, *3*(2), pp. 331–34.

Schweickart, David. Market Socialist Capitalist Roaders: A Comment on Arnold [Marx and Disequilibrium in Market Socialist Relations of Production]. *Econ. Philos.*, October 1987, *3*(2), pp. 308–19.

Meade, James
Darity, William A., Jr. and Cottrell, Allin F. Meade's *General Theory* Model: A Geometric Reprise. *J. Money, Credit, Banking*, May 1987, *19*(2), pp. 210–21.

Solow, Robert M. James Meade at Eighty. *Econ. J.*, December 1987, *97*(388), pp. 986–88.

Menger, Carl
Cubeddu, Raimondo. Popper et l'Ecole Autrichienne. (Popper and the Austrian School: Menger, Boehm-Bawerk, Wieser, Mises. With English summary.) *Écon. Soc.*, October 1987, *21*(10), pp. 41–62.

Messedaglia, Angelo
Finoia, Massimo. Founders of Modern Economic Thought in Italy. *Int. J. Soc. Econ.*, 1987, *14*(7/8/9), pp. 182–94.   [G: Italy]

Pellanda, Anna. Angelo Messedaglia on Money and the Nineteenth Century Italian Economic School. *Int. J. Soc. Econ.*, 1987, *14*(7/8/9), pp. 170–81.   [G: Italy]

Mill, JamesStuart
Elliott, John E. and Scott, Joanna V. Theories of Liberal Capitalist Democracy: Alternative Perspectives. *Int. J. Soc. Econ.*, 1987, *14*(7/8/9), pp. 52–87.   [G: U.S.]

Mitchell, Wesley C.
Rutherford, Malcolm. Wesley Mitchell: Institutions and Quantitative Methods. *Eastern Econ. J.*, Jan.-Mar. 1987, *13*(1), pp. 63–73.

Modigliani, Franco
Merton, Robert C. In Honor of Nobel Laureate, Franco Modigliani. *J. Econ. Perspectives*, Fall 1987, *1*(2), pp. 145–55.

Samuelson, Paul A. The 1985 Nobel Prize in Economics. [*Modigliani, F.*], 1987, *1986*, pp. 29–35.

Mueller, Willard F.
Clodius, Robert L. A Personal View of the Contributions of Willard F. Mueller. *Wills, R. L.; Caswell, J. A. and Culbertson, J. D., eds.*, 1987, pp. 12–17.   [G: U.S.]

Hoffman, A. C. Recollections of a Friend and Colleague. *Wills, R. L.; Caswell, J. A. and Culbertson, J. D., eds.*, 1987, pp. 18–22.
                                  [G: U.S.]

Mühlpfort, Wolfgang
Howard, Michael C. and King, John E. Dr Mühlpfort, Professor von Bortkiewicz and the 'Transformation Problem.' *Cambridge J. Econ.*, September 1987, *11*(3), pp. 265–68.

Myrdal, Gunnar
Kindleberger, Charles P. Gunnar Myrdal, 1898–1987. *Scand. J. Econ.*, 1987, *89*(4), pp. 393–403.

Neurath, Otto
Rosier, Michel. Otto Neurath, économiste et leader du Cercle de Vienne. (Otto Neurath, Economist and Leader of the Vienna Circle. With English summary.) *Écon. Soc.*, March 1987, *21*(3), pp. 113–45.

Nicholson, J. Shield
Deans, Robert H. and Deans, Janet S. J. Shield Nicholson's Project of Empire: The Edinburgh Economist Evolved from a Free Trader into a Premier Apologist for Imperialism. *Amer. J. Econ. Soc.*, July 1987, *46*(3), pp. 319–40.

Okun, Arthur
Tobin, James. Okun on Macroeconomic Policy. *Tobin, J. (III)*, 1987, *1983*, pp. 415–18.

Pasinetti, Luigi
Falkinger, Josef. Technological Unemployment: A Note. *J. Post Keynesian Econ.*, Fall 1987, *10*(1), pp. 37–43.

Pedersen, H. Winding
Brems, Hans. En disputats om finanspolitiske ideer i Danmark 1930–1945. (With English summary.) *Nationaløkon. Tidsskr.*, 1987, *125*(3), pp. 287–98.   [G: Denmark]

Pedersen, Jørgen
Brems, Hans. En disputats om finanspolitiske ideer i Danmark 1930–1945. (With English summary.) *Nationaløkon. Tidsskr.*, 1987, *125*(3), pp. 287–98.   [G: Denmark]

Penrose, Ernest Francis
Dore, Ronald and Sinha, Radha. E. F. Penrose: The Record. [*Penrose, E. F.*], 1987, pp. xvii–xxi.

Penrose, Edith. In Memoriam: Ernest Francis Penrose. *[Penrose, E. F.]*, 1987, pp. xiii–xvi.

Polanyi, Karl

Brown, Doug. A Hungarian Connection: Karl Polanyi's Influence on the Budapest School. *J. Econ. Issues*, March 1987, *21*(1), pp. 339–47.

Popper, Karl

Boyer, Alain. Karl Popper face aux sciences sociales. (Karl Popper and Social Sciences. With English summary.) *Écon. Soc.*, October 1987, *21*(10), pp. 5–24.

Cubeddu, Raimondo. Popper et l'Ecole Autrichienne. (Popper and the Austrian School: Menger, Boehm-Bauerk, Wieser, Mises. With English summary.) *Écon. Soc.*, October 1987, *21*(10), pp. 41–62.

Lallement, Jérôme. Popper et le principe de rationalité . (Popper and the Rationality Principle. With English summary.) *Écon. Soc.*, October 1987, *21*(10), pp. 25–40.

Sicard, François. Popper et Hayek: économie et politique. (Popper and Hayek: Economics and Politics. With English summary.) *Écon. Soc.*, October 1987, *21*(10), pp. 63–72.

Prebisch, Raúl

Love, Joseph L. Raúl Prebisch and the Origins of the Doctrine of Unequal Exchange. *Dietz, J. L. and Street, J. H., eds.*, 1987, pp. 78–100.   **[G: Argentina]**

Street, James H. Raúl Prebisch, 1901–1986: An Appreciation. *J. Econ. Issues*, June 1987, *21*(2), pp. 649–59.

Quesney, François

Steiner, Philippe. Le projet physiocratique: théorie de la propriété et lien social. (The Physiocratic Project: Theory of Property and Social Link. With English summary.) *Revue Écon.*, November 1987, *38*(6), pp. 1111–28.

Raguet, Condy

Martin, Thomas L. Neglected Aspects of the Economic Thought and the Method of Condy Raguet. *Hist. Polit. Econ.*, Fall 1987, *19*(3), pp. 401–13.

Raymond, Daniel

Petrella, Frank. Daniel Raymond, Adam Smith, and Classical Growth Theory: An Inquiry into the Nature and Causes of the Wealth of America. *Hist. Polit. Econ.*, Summer 1987, *19*(2), pp. 239–59.

Ricardo, David

Burgstaller, André. Demand and Relative Price in Ricardo: An Examination of Outstanding Issues. *Hist. Polit. Econ.*, Summer 1987, *19*(2), pp. 207–15.

Motley, Brian. Ricardo or Keynes: Does the Government Debt Affect Consumption? *Fed. Res. Bank San Francisco Econ. Rev.*, Winter 1987, (1), pp. 47–62.

Richardson, Lewis Fry

Intriligator, Michael D. Semantic Variations on Richardson's Armaments Dynamics: Note. *Schmidt, C., ed.*, 1987, pp. 176–79.

Schmidt, Christian. Semantic Variations on Richardson's Armaments Dynamics. *Schmidt, C., ed.*, 1987, pp. 141–75.

Robbins, Lionel

Aslanbeigui, Nahid. Some Inconsistencies in Lionel Robbins' Methodology. *Revue Écon. Polit.*, Nov.-Dec. 1987, *97*(6), pp. 325–35.

Robertson, Dennis H.

Poulon, F. Keynes et Robertson: naissance d'un désaccord sur la fonction de l'épargne dans la théorie monétaire. (Keynes and Robertson: The Beginning of a Disagreement about the Role of Saving in Monetary Theory. With English summary.) *Écon. Soc.*, September 1987, *21*(9), pp. 9–22.

Robinson, Joan

Feiwel, George R. Intellectual Revolutions in Modern Economic Theory: Joan Robinson's Contributions and Challenges. *Keio Econ. Stud.*, 1987, *24*(2), pp. 47–86.

Roscher, Wilhelm

Krabbe, Jacob Jan. Organistic Theory in Economics: The Contribution of the Historical School. *Int. J. Soc. Econ.*, 1987, *14*(3/4/5), pp. 105–17.

Rugina, Anghel N.

Balabkins, Nicholas W. Value and Value-Judgements in Economics: Rugina's Contribution. *Int. J. Soc. Econ.*, 1987, *14*(3/4/5), pp. 50–62.

Karsten, Siegfried G. Rugina's Contribution to Social Economics. *Int. J. Soc. Econ.*, 1987, *14*(3/4/5), pp. 63–69.

O'Brien, John C. To an Original Thinker—The Meed of Praise: Introduction. *Int. J. Soc. Econ.*, 1987, *14*(3/4/5), pp. 9–13.

Thanawala, Kishor. Nature and Scope of Rugina's Social Economics. *Int. J. Soc. Econ.*, 1987, *14*(3/4/5), pp. 91–96.

Tisdell, Clem A. Neo-Classical Economics: Relevance, Irrelevance and Rugina's Methodology. *Int. J. Soc. Econ.*, 1987, *14*(3/4/5), pp. 37–49.

Scheler, Max

Stikkers, Kenneth W. Max Scheler's Contributions to Social Economics. *Rev. Soc. Econ.*, December 1987, *45*(3), pp. 223–42.

von Schmoller, Gustav

Balabkins, Nicholas W. Line by Line: Schmoller's *Grundriss:* Its Meaning for the 1980s. *Int. J. Soc. Econ.*, 1987, *14*(1), pp. 22–31.

Krabbe, Jacob Jan. Organistic Theory in Economics: The Contribution of the Historical School. *Int. J. Soc. Econ.*, 1987, *14*(3/4/5), pp. 105–17.

O'Brien, John C. The Social Economics of Hugo Eisenhart Gustav von Schmoller. *Int. J. Soc. Econ.*, 1987, *14*(11), pp. 26–47.

Schultz, Theodore

Lundahl, Mats. 'Efficient but Poor'—Schultz' Theory of Traditional Agriculture. *Scand. Econ. Hist. Rev.*, 1987, *35*(1), pp. 108–29.

Schumpeter, Joseph A.

Jensen, Hans E. New Lights on J. A. Schumpeter's Theory of the History of Economics? *Samuels, W. J., ed.*, 1987, pp. 117–48.

Pack, Spencer J. Schumpeter Plus Optimism Equals Gilder (*ceteris paribus*). *Hist. Polit. Econ.*, Fall 1987, *19*(3), pp. 469–80.

Sufrin, Sidney C. Schumpeter–Walras and Pragmatism. *Rivista Int. Sci. Econ. Com.*, September 1987, *34*(9), pp. 823–28.

Schwartz, Anna J.

Bordo, Michael D. and Friedman, Milton. Money in Historical Perspective: Introduction. *Schwartz, A. J.*, 1987, pp. xiii–xvii.

Shackle, George L.

Pheby, John. A New Perspective on Shackle's Keynesian Fundamentalism. *J. Econ. Stud.*, 1987, *14*(4), pp. 24–35.

Smith, Adam

Ditz, Gerhard W. Smith and Keynes: Religious Differences in Economic Philosophy. *Economia (Portugal)*, October 1987, *11*(3), pp. 399–431.

Evensky, Jerry M. The Two Voices of Adam Smith: Moral Philosopher and Social Critic. *Hist. Polit. Econ.*, Fall 1987, *19*(3), pp. 447–68.

Levy, David T. Adam Smith's Case for Usury Laws. *Hist. Polit. Econ.*, Fall 1987, *19*(3), pp. 387–400.

Petrella, Frank. Daniel Raymond, Adam Smith, and Classical Growth Theory: An Inquiry into the Nature and Causes of the Wealth of America. *Hist. Polit. Econ.*, Summer 1987, *19*(2), pp. 239–59.

Prendergast, Renee. James Anderson's Political Economy—His Influence on Smith and Malthus. *Scot. J. Polit. Econ.*, November 1987, *34*(4), pp. 388–409.

Rashid, Salim. Adam Smith's Interpretation of the History of Economics and Its Influence in the 18th and 19th Centuries. *Quart. Rev. Econ. Bus.*, Autumn 1987, *27*(3), pp. 56–69.

Reid, Gavin C. Disequilibrium and Increasing Returns in Adam Smith's Analysis of Growth and Accumulation. *Hist. Polit. Econ.*, Spring 1987, *19*(1), pp. 87–106.

Soble, Irvin. Adam Smith: What Kind of an Institutionalist Was He? Old Wine in New Bottles. *Rivista Int. Sci. Econ. Com.*, Jan.-Feb. 1987, *34*(1–2), pp. 87–108.

Sraffa, Piero

Amadeo, Edward J. and Dutt, Amitava Krishna. Os keynesianos neo-ricardianos e os pós-keynesianos. (With English summary.) *Pesquisa Planejamento Econ.*, December 1987, *17*(3), pp. 561–603.

Bandyopadhyay, Pradeep. Value and Post-Sraffa Marxian Analysis. *Albelda, R.; Gunn, C. and Waller, W.*, eds., 1987, *1984*, pp. 186–94.

Catz, F. L'étalon des prix: sens. et non-sens. (The Concept of Standard Commodity: Meaningful and Meaningless. With English summary.) *Écon. Appl.*, 1987, *40*(1), pp. 177–84.

Griffin, Robert A. Thorstein Veblen and Piero Sraffa: A New Level of Economic Theory.

Int. J. Soc. Econ., 1987, *14*(7/8/9), pp. 136–41.

Horvat, Branko. Sraffa Systematized and Marx Vindicated. *Econ. Anal. Workers' Manage.*, 1987, *21*(3), pp. 289–97.

Thweatt, William O. James and John Mill on Comparative Advantage: Sraffa's Account Corrected. *Visser, H. and Schoor, E.*, eds., 1987, pp. 33–43.

Wolff, Robert Paul. Piero Sraffa and the Rehabilitation of Classical Political Economy. *Albelda, R.; Gunn, C. and Waller, W.*, eds., 1987, *1982*, pp. 157–74.

Steuart, James [Sir]

Khalil, Elias L. Sir James Steuart vs. Professor James Buchanan: Critical Notes on Modern Public Choice. *Rev. Soc. Econ.*, October 1987, *45*(2), pp. 113–32.

Stewart, Dugald

Rashid, Salim. Political Economy as Moral Philosophy: Dugald Stewart of Edinburgh. *Australian Econ. Pap.*, June 1987, *26*(48), pp. 145–56.

Thoreau, Henry David

Bodily, Christopher L. Henry David Thoreau: The Instrumental Transcendentalist? *J. Econ. Issues*, March 1987, *21*(1), pp. 203–18.

Thornton, Henry

Hetzel, Robert L. Henry Thornton: Seminal Monetary Theorist and Father of the Modern Central Bank. *Fed. Res. Bank Richmond Econ. Rev.*, July/Aug. 1987, *73*(4), pp. 3–16.

von Thünen, Johann Heinrich

Krelle, Wilhelm. Von Thünen-Vorlesung. (Von Thünen Lecture. With English summary.) *Z. Wirtschaft. Sozialwissen.*, 1987, *107*(1), pp. 5–28.

Tinbergen, Jan

Thanawala, Kishor. Tinbergen's Contribution to Social Economics. *Rivista Int. Sci. Econ. Com.*, August 1987, *34*(8), pp. 751–59.

Trotsky, Leon

Burkett, John P. Soviet Socioeconomic Development: A Fold Catastrophe? *Comp. Econ. Stud.*, Fall 1987, *29*(3), pp. 70–93.

Day, Richard B. Democratic Control and the Dignity of Politics—An Analysis of *The Revolution Betrayed*. *Comp. Econ. Stud.*, Fall 1987, *29*(3), pp. 4–29. [G: U.S.S.R.]

Milenkovitch, Deborah Duff. Trotsky's *The Revolution Betrayed*: A Contemporary Look. *Comp. Econ. Stud.*, Fall 1987, *29*(3), pp. 40–44.

Nove, Alec. Trotsky, Markets, and East European Reforms. *Comp. Econ. Stud.*, Fall 1987, *29*(3), pp. 30–39. [G: U.S.S.R.; E. Europe]

Shapiro, J. C. On the Accuracy of Economic Observations of *Chto Takoe SSSR* in Historical Retrospect. *Comp. Econ. Stud.*, Fall 1987, *29*(3), pp. 45–69.

Woodward, Susan L. A Symposium on Leon Trotsky's *The Revolution Betrayed*: Fifty Years Later: Editor's Preface. *Comp. Econ.*

Stud., Fall 1987, *29*(3), pp. 1–3.

Tullock, Gordon

Aranson, Peter H. Calculus and Consent. *[Tullock, G.]*, 1987, pp. 60–65.

Buchanan, James M. The Qualities of a Natural Economist. *[Tullock, G.]*, 1987, pp. 9–19.

Mitchell, William C. The Calculus of Consent: Notes in Retrospection. *[Tullock, G.]*, 1987, pp. 66–73.

Niskanen, William A. Bureaucracy. *[Tullock, G.]*, 1987, pp. 135–40.

Rowley, Charles K. Natural Economist or Popperian Logician? *[Tullock, G.]*, 1987, pp. 20–26.

Rowley, Charles K. The Calculus of Consent. *[Tullock, G.]*, 1987, pp. 41–59.

Seldon, Arthur. Public Choice and the Choices of the Public. *[Tullock, G.]*, 1987, pp. 122–34.

Wagner, Richard E. Gordon Tullock as Rhetorical Economist. *[Tullock, G.]*, 1987, pp. 27–38.

Turgot, Anne Robert Jacques

Brewer, Anthony A. Turgot: Founder of Classical Economics. *Economica*, November 1987, *54*(216), pp. 417–28.

Desai, Meghnad. A Pioneering Analysis of the Core: Turgot's Essay on Value. *Rech. Écon. Louvain*, 1987, *53*(2), pp. 191–98.

Turner, Frederick Jackson

Mattson, Vernon and Tilman, Rick. Thorstein Veblen, Frederick Jackson Turner, and the American Experience. *J. Econ. Issues*, March 1987, *21*(1), pp. 219–35.

Veblen, Thorstein

Foster, Gladys Parker and Ranson, Baldwin. Thorstein Veblen on Money and Production. *Écon. Soc.*, September 1987, *21*(9), pp. 221–28.

Griffin, Robert A. Thorstein Veblen and Piero Sraffa: A New Level of Economic Theory. *Int. J. Soc. Econ.*, 1987, *14*(7/8/9), pp. 136–41.

Mattson, Vernon and Tilman, Rick. Thorstein Veblen, Frederick Jackson Turner, and the American Experience. *J. Econ. Issues*, March 1987, *21*(1), pp. 219–35.

Phillips, Ron. Veblen and the "Wobblies": A Note. *Rev. Radical Polit. Econ.*, Spring 1987, *19*(1), pp. 98–103.

Stabile, Donald R. Veblen and the Political Economy of Technocracy: The Herald of Technological Revolution Developed an Ideology of 'Scientific' Collectivism. *Amer. J. Econ. Soc.*, January 1987, *46*(1), pp. 35–48.

Tilman, Rick. Grace Jaffé and Richard Ely on Thorstein Veblen: An Unknown Chapter in American Economic Thought. *Hist. Polit. Econ.*, Spring 1987, *19*(1), pp. 141–62.

Waller, William T., Jr. The Evolution of the Veblenian Dichotomy: Veblen, Hamilton, Ayres, and Foster. *Albelda, R.; Gunn, C. and Waller, W.*, eds., 1987, *1982*, pp. 213–24.

Walker, Francis Amasa

Backhouse, Roger E. F. A. Walker's Theory of Hard Times. *Hist. Polit. Econ.*, Fall 1987, *19*(3), pp. 435–46.

Solow, Robert M. What Do We Know that Francis Amasa Walker Didn't? *Hist. Polit. Econ.*, Summer 1987, *19*(2), pp. 183–89.

Walras, Léon

Bidard, Christian and Franke, Reiner. On Walras' Model of General Equilibrium: A Simpler Way to Demonstrate Existence. *J. Econ. (Z. Nationalökon.)*, 1987, *47*(3), pp. 315–19.

Potestio, Paola. Investment and Social Categories in Walrasian Analysis. *Écon. Appl.*, 1987, *40*(1), pp. 79–96.

Rotheim, Roy J. Equilibrium in Walras's and Marx's Theories of Capital Accumulation. *Int. J. Soc. Econ.*, 1987, *14*(7/8/9), pp. 27–43.

Sufrin, Sidney C. Schumpeter–Walras and Pragmatism. *Rivista Int. Sci. Econ. Com.*, September 1987, *34*(9), pp. 823–28.

Walker, Donald A. Bibliography of the Writings of Léon Walras. *Hist. Polit. Econ.*, Winter 1987, *19*(4), pp. 667–702.

Walker, Donald A. Walras's Theories of Tatonnement. *J. Polit. Econ.*, August 1987, *95*(4), pp. 758–74.

Warburton, Clark

Bordo, Michael D. and Schwartz, Anna J. Clark Warburton: Pioneer Monetarist. *Schwartz, A. J.*, 1987, *1979*, pp. 234–54.
[G: U.S.]

Wicksell, Knut

Buchanan, James M. Costituzione e politica economica. (The Constitution of Economic Policy. With English summary.) *Econ. Scelte Pubbliche/J. Public Finance Public Choice*, Jan.-Apr. 1987, *5*(1), pp. 3–14.

Hedlund-Nyström, Torun; Jonung, Lars and Sandelin, Bo. Opublicerat manuskript av Knut Wicksell med en kapitalteoretisk modell. (An Unpublished Manuscript by Knut Wicksell on a Capital-Theoretical Model. With English summary.) *Ekon. Samfundets Tidskr.*, 1987, *40*(3), pp. 123–37.

Williams, Eric

Sheridan, Richard B. Eric Williams and *Capitalism and Slavery*: A Biographical and Historiographical Essay. *Solow, B. L. and Engerman, S. L.*, eds., 1987, pp. 317–45.

Temperley, Howard. Eric Williams and Abolition: The Birth of a New Orthodoxy. *Solow, B. L. and Engerman, S. L.*, eds., 1987, pp. 229–57.

0329 Other Special Topics

Aldrich, John. Jevons as Statistician: The Role of Probability. *Manchester Sch. Econ. Soc. Stud.*, September 1987, *55*(3), pp. 233–56.

Allais, Maurice. The Equimarginal Principle: Meaning, Limits, and Generalization. *Rivista Int. Sci. Econ. Com.*, August 1987, *34*(8), pp. 689–750.

Arnon, Arie. Banking between the Invisible and Visible Hands: A Reinterpretation of Ricardo's Place within the Classical School. *Oxford Econ. Pap.*, June 1987, *39*(2), pp. 268–81.

Ashikaga, Sueo. Über die Eigenständigkeit der deutschen Sozialstatistik—zur Rolle der Frankfurter Schule in der deutschen Statistik. (The Self-Reliance of German Social Statistics—The Importance of the "Frankfurter Schule" in German Statistics. With English summary.) *Jahr. Nationalökon. Statist.*, October 1987, *203*(5–6), pp. 456–66.

Backhouse, Roger E. F. A. Walker's Theory of Hard Times. *Hist. Polit. Econ.*, Fall 1987, *19*(3), pp. 435–46.

Barbalet, J. M. The "Labor Aristocracy" in Context. *Sci. Soc.*, Summer 1987, *51*(2), pp. 133–53.

Barzel, Yoram. Knight's "Moral Hazard" Theory of Organization. *Econ. Inquiry*, January 1987, *25*(1), pp. 117–20.

Bassett, Gilbert W., Jr. The St. Petersburg Paradox and Bounded Utility. *Hist. Polit. Econ.*, Winter 1987, *19*(4), pp. 517–23.

Bateman, Bradley W. Keynes's Changing Conception of Probability. *Econ. Philos.*, April 1987, *3*(1), pp. 97–119.

Benassi, Corrado. An Input–Output Formulation of the "Coefficient of Money Transactions": A Note on Hayek's Trade Cycle Theory. *Econ. Int.*, February 1987, *40*(1), pp. 1–19.

Beranek, William and Timberlake, Richard H., Jr. The Liquidity Trap Theory: A Critique. *Southern Econ. J.*, October 1987, *54*(2), pp. 387–96.

Berti, Lapo. Stoccolma e Cambridge: storia di una controversia. (With English summary.) *Stud. Econ.*, 1987, *42*(32), pp. 3–59.

Bleaney, Michael F. Macroeconomic Theory and the Great Depression Revisited. *Scot. J. Polit. Econ.*, May 1987, *34*(2), pp. 105–19. [G: U.S.]

Bostaph, Samuel and Shieh, Yeung-Nan. Jevons's Demand Curve. *Hist. Polit. Econ.*, Spring 1987, *19*(1), pp. 107–26.

Brems, Hans. En disputats om finanspolitiske ideer i Danmark 1930–1945. (With English summary.) *Nationaløkon. Tidsskr.*, 1987, *125*(3), pp. 287–98. [G: Denmark]

Brewer, Anthony A. Turgot: Founder of Classical Economics. *Economica*, November 1987, *54*(216), pp. 417–28.

Brown, Vivienne. Value and Property in the History of Economic Thought: An Analysis of the Emergence of Scarcity. *Écon. Soc.*, March 1987, *21*(3), pp. 85–112.

Brunner, Karl. The Perception of Man and the Conception of Society: Two Approaches to Understanding Society. *Econ. Inquiry*, July 1987, *25*(3), pp. 367–88.

Buchanan, James M. "La Scienza delle Finanze": The Italian Tradition in Fiscal Theory. *Buchanan, J. M. (II)*, 1987, *1960*, pp. 317–56. [G: Italy]

Buchanan, James M. The Domain of Subjective Economics: Between Predictive Science and Moral Philosophy. *Buchanan, J. M. (II)*, 1987, *1982*, pp. 67–80.

Burgstaller, André. Demand and Relative Price in Ricardo: An Examination of Outstanding Issues. *Hist. Polit. Econ.*, Summer 1987, *19*(2), pp. 207–15.

Bush, Paul D. The Theory of Institutional Change. *J. Econ. Issues*, September 1987, *21*(3), pp. 1075–1116.

Catz, F. L'étalon des prix: sens. et non-sens. (The Concept of Standard Commodity: Meaningful and Meaningless. With English summary.) *Écon. Appl.*, 1987, *40*(1), pp. 177–84.

Chang, James L. Y. History of Chinese Economic Thought: Overview and Recent Works. *Hist. Polit. Econ.*, Fall 1987, *19*(3), pp. 481–502.

Chick, Victoria. Are *The General Theory's* Central Contributions Still Valid? *J. Econ. Stud.*, 1987, *14*(4), pp. 5–12.

Cookingham, Mary E. Social Economists and Reform: Berkeley, 1906–1961. *Hist. Polit. Econ.*, Spring 1987, *19*(1), pp. 47–65.

Cowen, Tyler and Kroszner, Randall. The Development of the New Monetary Economics. *J. Polit. Econ.*, June 1987, *95*(3), pp. 567–90.

Darity, William A., Jr. The Hume Process, Laws of Returns, and the Anglo–Portuguese Trade. *Southern Econ. J.*, July 1987, *54*(1), pp. 119–33.

Davis, John B. The Science of Happiness and the Marginalization of Ethics. *Rev. Soc. Econ.*, December 1987, *45*(3), pp. 298–312.

Desai, Meghnad. A Pioneering Analysis of the Core: Turgot's Essay on Value. *Rech. Écon. Louvain*, 1987, *53*(2), pp. 191–98.

Duménil, Gérard and Lévy, Dominique. The Dynamics of Competition: A Restoration of the Classical Analysis. *Cambridge J. Econ.*, June 1987, *11*(2), pp. 133–64.

Duménil, Gérard and Lévy, Dominique. Value and Natural Prices Trapped in Joint Production Pitfalls. *J. Econ. (Z. Nationalökon.)*, 1987, *47*(1), pp. 15–46.

Endres, Anthony M. The Origins of Böhm-Bawerk's 'Greatest Error': Theoretical Points of Separation from Menger. *J. Inst. Theoretical Econ.*, June 1987, *143*(2), pp. 291–309.

Foster, Gladys Parker and Ranson, Baldwin. Thorstein Veblen on Money and Production. *Écon. Soc.*, September 1987, *21*(9), pp. 221–28.

Giorgi, Giorgio. On the Linearity of the Distribution Function and the Fundamental Marxian Theorem in Simple Sraffa's Models. *Econ. Notes*, 1987, (2), pp. 48–59.

Goux, Jean-François. La théorie monétaire de la "finance" chez Keynes: une réinterprétation. (With English summary.) *Revue Écon. Polit.*, Sept.-Oct. 1987, *97*(5), pp. 592–612.

Gramm, Warren S. Unproductive Labour and Unproductive Consumption: Historical Review, Contemporary Relevance. *Int. J. Soc. Econ.*, 1987, *14*(3/4/5), pp. 154–66. [G: U.S.]

Graziani, Augusto. Keynes' Finance Motive. *Écon. Soc.*, September 1987, *21*(9), pp. 23–42.

Griffin, Robert A. Thorstein Veblen and Piero Sraffa: A New Level of Economic Theory. *Int. J. Soc. Econ.*, 1987, *14*(7/8/9), pp. 136–41.

Hagemann, Harald and Rühl, Christof. Nicholas Johannsen's Early Analysis of the Saving–Investment Process and the Multiplier. *Stud. Econ.*, 1987, *42*(31), pp. 99–143.

Hahn, Frank H. "Of Marx and Keynes and Many Things": A Review Article. Sinclair, P. J. N., ed., 1987, *1986*, pp. 378–85.

Hayden, F. Gregory. Evolution of Time Constructs and Their Impact on Socioeconomic Planning. *J. Econ. Issues*, September 1987, *21*(3), pp. 1281–1312.

Hennipman, Piet. A Tale of Two Schools: Comments on a New View of the Ordinalist Revolution. *De Economist*, 1987, *135*(2), pp. 141–62.

Hixson, William F. Marxism and "Monetary Policy." *Écon. Soc.*, September 1987, *21*(9), pp. 43–63.

Hotson, John H. The Keynesian Revolution and the Aborted Fisher–Simons Revolution or the Road Not Taken. *Écon. Soc.*, September 1987, *21*(9), pp. 185–219.

Humphrey, Thomas M. Classical and Neoclassical Roots of the Theory of Optimum Tariffs. *Fed. Res. Bank Richmond Econ. Rev.*, July/Aug. 1987, *73*(4), pp. 17–28.

Humphrey, Thomas M. The Theory of Multiple Expansion of Deposits: What It Is and Whence It Came. *Fed. Res. Bank Richmond Econ. Rev.*, Mar./Apr. 1987, *73*(2), pp. 3–11.

Jensen, Hans E. Alfred Marshall as a Social Economist. *Rev. Soc. Econ.*, April 1987, *45*(1), pp. 14–36.

Karayiannis, Anastasios D. Twentieth Century Greek Economists and the Quantity Theory of Money. *Int. J. Soc. Econ.*, 1987, *14*(7/8/9), pp. 221–32.

Karsten, Siegfried G. Nature in Economic Theories: Hans Immler Traces Recognition of the Environment—and Its Neglect—in Various Classics. *Amer. J. Econ. Soc.*, January 1987, *46*(1), pp. 61–70.

Kleiman, Ephraim. Opportunity Cost, Human Capital, and Some Related Economic Concepts in Talmudic Literature. *Hist. Polit. Econ.*, Summer 1987, *19*(2), pp. 261–87.

Köllner, Lutz. Bemerkungen zur Finanzsoziologie heute. (Notes on the Sociology of Finance Today. With English summary.) *Jahr. Nationalökon. Statist.*, January 1987, *203*(1), pp. 26–42.

Krelle, Wilhelm. Von Thünen-Vorlesung. (Von Thünen Lecture. With English summary.) *Z. Wirtschaft. Sozialwissen.*, 1987, *107*(1), pp. 5–28.

Larceneux, André. Previsions et rationnement dans une logique Keynésienne. (Expectations and Rationing Constraint in a Keynesian Logical Framework. With English summary.) *Écon. Soc.*, September 1987, *21*(9), pp. 121–47.

Larson, Bruce. Edgeworth, Samuelson, and Operationally Meaningful Theorems. *Hist. Polit. Econ.*, Fall 1987, *19*(3), pp. 351–57.

Lavoie, Marc. Monnaie et production: une synthèse de la théorie du circuit. (Money and Production: A Synthesis of the Circuit Theory. With English summary.) *Écon. Soc.*, September 1987, *21*(9), pp. 65–101.

Lawlor, Michael S.; Darity, William A., Jr. and Horn, Bobbie L. Was Keynes a Chapter Two Keynesian? *J. Post Keynesian Econ.*, Summer 1987, *9*(4), pp. 516–28.

LeRoy, Stephen F. and Singell, Larry D., Jr. Knight on Risk and Uncertainty. *J. Polit. Econ.*, April 1987, *95*(2), pp. 394–406.

Levy, David T. Adam Smith's Case for Usury Laws. *Hist. Polit. Econ.*, Fall 1987, *19*(3), pp. 387–400.

Lianos, Theodore P. Marx on the Rate of Interest. *Rev. Radical Polit. Econ.*, Fall 1987, *19*(3), pp. 34–55.

Liebhafsky, Herbert H. Law and Economics from Different Perspectives. *J. Econ. Issues*, December 1987, *21*(4), pp. 1809–36.

Littleboy, Bruce and Mehta, Ghanshyam. Patinkin on Keynes' Theory of Effective Demand. *Hist. Polit. Econ.*, Summer 1987, *19*(2), pp. 311–28.

Machan, Tibor R. A New Individualist Basis for the Free Market. *Int. J. Soc. Econ.*, 1987, *14*(10), pp. 27–39.

Magnusson, Lars. Mercantilism and "Reform" Mercantilism: The Rise of Economic Discourse in Sweden during the Eighteenth Century. *Hist. Polit. Econ.*, Fall 1987, *19*(3), pp. 415–33.

Malinvaud, Edmond. Reflecting on the Theory of Capital and Growth. Sinclair, P. J. N., ed., 1987, *1986*, pp. 395–413.

Meemken, Hermann. Keynes Entrepreneur or Money Wage Economy. *Stud. Econ.*, 1987, *42*(33), pp. 67–105.

Meijer, Gerrit. The History of Neo-liberalism: Affinity to Some Developments in Economics in Germany. *Int. J. Soc. Econ.*, 1987, *14*(7/8/9), pp. 142–55.

Meijer, Gerrit. The History of Neo-liberalism: A General View and Developments in Several Countries. *Rivista Int. Sci. Econ. Com.*, July 1987, *34*(7), pp. 577–91. **[G: W. Europe]**

Melody, William H. Information: An Emerging Dimension of Institutional Analysis. *J. Econ. Issues*, September 1987, *21*(3), pp. 1313–39.

Moss, Laurence S. The Subjectivist Mercantilism of Bernard Mandeville. *Int. J. Soc. Econ.*, 1987, *14*(3/4/5), pp. 167–84.

Ohrenstein, Roman A. and Gordon, Barry. Some Aspects of Human Capital in Talmudic Literature. *Int. J. Soc. Econ.*, 1987, *14*(3/4/5), pp. 185–90.

Patinkin, Don. Keynes' Theory of Effective Demand: A Reply. *Hist. Polit. Econ.*, Winter 1987, *19*(4), pp. 647–58.

Perlman, Morris. Of a Controversial Passage in Hume. *J. Polit. Econ.*, April 1987, *95*(2), pp. 274–89.

Petrella, Frank. Daniel Raymond, Adam Smith, and Classical Growth Theory: An Inquiry into the Nature and Causes of the Wealth of America. *Hist. Polit. Econ.*, Summer 1987, *19*(2), pp. 239–59.

Pheby, John. A New Perspective on Shackle's Keynesian Fundamentalism. *J. Econ. Stud.*, 1987, *14*(4), pp. 24–35.

Popescu, Oreste. Price Theory in the Hispanic American Scholastics. *Int. J. Soc. Econ.*, 1987, *14*(3/4/5), pp. 132–39.

Potestio, Paola. Investment and Social Categories in Walrasian Analysis. *Écon. Appl.*, 1987, *40*(1), pp. 79–96.

Poulon, F. Keynes et Robertson: naissance d'un désaccord sur la fonction de l'épargne dans la théorie monétaire. (Keynes and Robertson: The Beginning of a Disagreement about the Role of Saving in Monetary Theory. With English summary.) *Écon. Soc.*, September 1987, *21*(9), pp. 9–22.

Power, Simon. The Origins of the Heckscher–Ohlin Concept. *Hist. Polit. Econ.*, Summer 1987, *19*(2), pp. 289–98.

Rebeyrol, Antoine. Gravitation et marché du travail. Un essai d'interprétation. (Gravitation and Labour Market: Essay of Interpretation. With English summary.) *Écon. Soc.*, March 1987, *21*(3), pp. 53–84.

Reid, Joseph D., Jr. The Theory of Sharecropping: Occam's Razor and Economic Analysis. *Hist. Polit. Econ.*, Winter 1987, *19*(4), pp. 551–69.

Reinhardt, Paul G. Demand Analysis and the Flow of Time in Consumption. *Int. J. Soc. Econ.*, 1987, *14*(3/4/5), pp. 199–206.

Rodríguez Braun, Carlos. *Capital*'s Last Chapter. *Hist. Polit. Econ.*, Summer 1987, *19*(2), pp. 299–310.

Rostow, Walt W. The Rich Country–Poor Country Problem: From the Eighteenth to the Twenty-first Centuries. *Steinherr, A. and Weiserbs, D., eds.*, 1987, pp. 47–83.
[G: Global]

Rotheim, Roy J. Equilibrium in Walras's and Marx's Theories of Capital Accumulation. *Int. J. Soc. Econ.*, 1987, *14*(7/8/9), pp. 27–43.

Rutherford, R. P. Malthus and Keynes. *Oxford Econ. Pap.*, March 1987, *39*(1), pp. 175–89.

Rutherford, R. P. Malthus and Keynes. *Sinclair, P. J. N., ed.*, 1987, pp. 175–89.

Schilirò, Daniele. Il modello IS–LM e la reinterpretazione di Hicks: una nota. (IS-LM Model and Its Reinterpretation by Hicks: A Note. With English summary.) *Econ. Polít.*, December 1987, *4*(3), pp. 421–35.

Schmidt, Christian. Peace and War Economics in Retrospect: Some Reflections on the Historical Background of Defence Economics. *Schmidt, C. and Blackaby, F., eds.*, 1987, pp. 20–39.

Schwartz, Pedro. The Market and the Metamarket: A Review of the Contributions of the Economic Theory of Property Rights. *Pejovich, S., ed.*, 1987, pp. 11–32.

Sicard, François. Popper et Hayek: économie et politique. (Popper and Hayek: Economics and Politics. With English summary.) *Écon. Soc.*,

October 1987, *21*(10), pp. 63–72.

Starr, Paul. The Sociology of Official Statistics. *Alonso, W. and Starr, P., eds.*, 1987, pp. 7–57. [G: U.S.]

Suttle, Bruce B. The Passion of Self-interest: The Development of the Idea and Its Changing Status. *Amer. J. Econ. Soc.*, October 1987, *46*(4), pp. 459–72.

Taurand, Francis and Hung, Nguyen Manh. Pitfalls in a Received Idea: Ricardian Decreasing Returns at the Extensive Margin of a Natural Resource. *Can. J. Econ.*, February 1987, *20*(1), pp. 61–73.

Taylor, T. W. and Evans, J. W. Islamic Banking and the Prohibition of Usury in Western Economic Thought. *Nat. Westminster Bank Quart. Rev.*, November 1987, pp. 15–27.

Tilman, Rick. The Neoinstrumental Theory of Democracy. *J. Econ. Issues*, September 1987, *21*(3), pp. 1379–1401.

Tortajada, Ramon. M. de Malestroit et la théorie quantitative de la monnaie. (M. de Malestroit and the Quantity Theory of Money. With English summary.) *Revue Écon.*, July 1987, *38*(4), pp. 853–76.

Walker, Donald A. Walras's Theories of Tatonnement. *J. Polit. Econ.*, August 1987, *95*(4), pp. 758–74.

Weintraub, E. Roy. Stability Theory via Liapunov's Method: A Note on the Contribution of Takuma Yasui. *Hist. Polit. Econ.*, Winter 1987, *19*(4), pp. 615–20.

Wells, Paul. Keynes's Employment Function and the Marginal Productivity of Labor. *J. Post Keynesian Econ.*, Summer 1987, *9*(4), pp. 507–15.

White, Michael. Porter's 'Hint'? A Note. *Australian Econ. Pap.*, December 1987, *26*(49), pp. 328–31.

036 Economic Methodology

0360 Economic Methodology

Ancil, Ralph E. On the Rhetoric of Economics. *Rev. Soc. Econ.*, December 1987, *45*(3), pp. 259–75.

Arouh, Albert. The Mumpsimus of Economists and the Role of Time and Uncertainty in the Progress of Economic Knowledge. *J. Post Keynesian Econ.*, Spring 1987, *9*(3), pp. 395–423.

Aslanbeigui, Nahid. Some Inconsistencies in Lionel Robbins' Methodology. *Revue Écon. Polit.*, Nov.-Dec. 1987, *97*(6), pp. 325–35.

Balabkins, Nicholas W. Value and Value-Judgements in Economics: Rugina's Contribution. *Int. J. Soc. Econ.*, 1987, *14*(3/4/5), pp. 50–62.

Bazerman, Charles. Codifying the Social Scientific Style: The APA *Publication Manual* as a Behaviorist Rhetoric. *Nelson, J. S.; Megill, A. and McCloskey, D. N., eds.*, 1987, pp. 125–44.

Beach, E. F. Marshallian Methodology. *Int. J. Soc. Econ.*, 1987, *14*(7/8/9), pp. 19–26.

Becker, William E. "Measurement" or Finding Things Out in Economics: A Comment. *J. Econ. Educ.*, Spring 1987, *18*(2), pp. 208–12. [G: U.S.]

Bergmann, Barbara R. "Measurement" or Finding Things Out in Economics. *J. Econ. Educ.*, Spring 1987, *18*(2), pp. 191–201.

Bienaymé, Alain. Une économie politique pour l'entreprise. (With English summary.) *Revue Écon. Polit.*, May-June 1987, *97*(3), pp. 285–300.

Boland, Lawrence A. Boland on Friedman's Methodology: A Summation [A Critique of Friedman's Critics]. *J. Econ. Issues,* March 1987, *21*(1), pp. 380–88.

Boyer, Alain. Karl Popper face aux sciences sociales. (Karl Popper and Social Sciences. With English summary.) *Écon. Soc.*, October 1987, *21*(10), pp. 5–24.

Brochier, Hubert. Les théories économiques sont-elles réfutables? (Are Economic Theories Falsifiable? With English summary.) *Écon. Soc.*, October 1987, *21*(10), pp. 107–18.

Bruter, C. P. Symétrie, économie et inflation. (Symmetry, Economics and Inflation. With English summary.) *Écon. Soc.*, January 1987, *21*(1), pp. 109–18.

Buchanan, James M. Markets, States, and the Extent of Morals. *Buchanan, J. M. (II)*, 1987, *1978*, pp. 269–75.

Buchanan, James M. The Domain of Subjective Economics: Between Predictive Science and Moral Philosophy. *Buchanan, J. M. (II)*, 1987, *1982*, pp. 67–80.

Buchanan, James M. The Related but Distinct 'Sciences' of Economics and of Political Economy. *Buchanan, J. M. (I)*, 1987, *1982*, pp. 87–97.

Butos, William N. Rhetoric and Rationality: A Review Essay. *Eastern Econ. J.*, July-Sept. 1987, *13*(3), pp. 295–304.

Chanier, Paul. Les limites des postulats de symétrie et d'invariance dans les sciences et en économique. (On the Limits of Symmetry and Invariance Postulates in Science and Economics. With English summary.) *Écon. Soc.*, January 1987, *21*(1), pp. 5–84.

Coats, A. W. and Pressman, Steven. The Rhetoric of Economics: Further Comments. *Eastern Econ. J.*, July-Sept. 1987, *13*(3), pp. 305–07.

Cubeddu, Raimondo. Popper et l'Ecole Autrichienne. (Popper and the Austrian School: Menger, Boehm-Bauerk, Wieser, Mises. With English summary.) *Écon. Soc.*, October 1987, *21*(10), pp. 41–62.

Davis, John B. Three Principles of Post Keynesian Methodology. *J. Post Keynesian Econ.*, Summer 1987, *9*(4), pp. 552–64.

De Alessi, Louis. Nature and Methodological Foundations of Some Recent Extensions of Economic Theory. *Radnitzky, G. and Bernholz, P., eds.*, 1987, pp. 51–76.

Deane, Phyllis. The Scope and Method of Economic Science. *Albelda, R.; Gunn, C. and Waller, W., eds.*, 1987, *1983*, pp. 35–47.

Dennis, Ken. Boland on Boland: A Further Rebuttal [A Critique of Friedman's Critics]. *J. Econ. Issues,* March 1987, *21*(1), pp. 388–93.

Dow, Sheila C. The Scottish Political Economy Tradition. *Scot. J. Polit. Econ.*, November 1987, *34*(4), pp. 335–48. [G: U.K.]

Dwyer, Larry. Some Implications of a Pragmatist Conception of the Aims of Economic Enquiry. *Int. J. Soc. Econ.*, 1987, *14*(6), pp. 22–35.

Eliasson, Gunnar. The Economics of Institutions and Markets—The Organization of Research at IUI. *Eliasson, G., ed.*, 1987, pp. 15–26.

England, Richard W. Form vs. Content: A Critique of Morishima's Mathematical Marxism. *England, R. W., ed.*, 1987, pp. 20–34.

Eusepi, Giuseppe. General Implications of Subjectivism and Dynamics in Buchanan's Works. *Econ. Int.*, February 1987, *40*(1), pp. 55–66.

Evensky, Jerry M. Expanding the Scope of the Neoclassical Vision. *Rev. Soc. Econ.*, October 1987, *45*(2), pp. 178–91.

Finn, Daniel Rush. When Are Economic Explanations Persuasive? A View from Social Economics. *Rev. Soc. Econ.*, April 1987, *45*(1), pp. 1–13.

Guitton, Henri. The Rational and the Non-rational in Economics. *Int. J. Soc. Econ.*, 1987, *14*(3/4/5), pp. 33–36.

Guthrie, William. The Roles of Intellectual Pedigrees in Economic Science. *Amer. J. Econ. Soc.*, January 1987, *46*(1), pp. 49–60.

Henley, Andrew. Economic Orthodoxy and the Free Market System: A Christian Critique. *Int. J. Soc. Econ.*, 1987, *14*(10), pp. 56–66.

Hill, Lewis E. A Pragmatic Methodology for Social Economics: A Preliminary Proposal. *Int. J. Soc. Econ.*, 1987, *14*(3/4/5), pp. 140–45.

Holland, Thomas E. On Parallelism in Neo-Classical Economic Theory. *Int. J. Soc. Econ.*, 1987, *14*(3/4/5), pp. 191–98.

Johnson, Glenn L. Holistic Modeling of Multidisciplinary Subject Matter and Problem Domains. *Fox, K. A. and Miles, D. G., eds.*, 1987, pp. 85–109.

Khalil, Elias L. Kuhn, Lakatos, and the History of Economic Thought. *Int. J. Soc. Econ.*, 1987, *14*(3/4/5), pp. 118–31.

Khalil, Elias L. Sir James Steuart vs. Professor James Buchanan: Critical Notes on Modern Public Choice. *Rev. Soc. Econ.*, October 1987, *45*(2), pp. 113–32.

Klamer, Arjo. As if Economists and Their Subject Were Rational. *Nelson, J. S.; Megill, A. and McCloskey, D. N., eds.*, 1987, pp. 163–83.

Kozlov, Nicholas N. Dialectic of Matter vs. Dialectic of History: A Critique of Lucio Colletti's Materialism. *England, R. W., ed.*, 1987, pp. 3–19.

Lallement, Jérôme. Popper et le principe de rationalité . (Popper and the Rationality Principle. With English summary.) *Écon. Soc.*, October 1987, *21*(10), pp. 25–40.

Lawson, Tony. The Relative/Absolute Nature of Knowledge and Economic Analysis. *Econ. J.*, December 1987, *97*(388), pp. 951–70.

Le Pen, Claude. "Falsifiabilite" et theorie economique ou comment rendre une theorie scientifique infalsifiable. ("Falsifiability" and Economic Theory or How to Make a Scientific Theory Unfalsifiable. With English summary.) *Écon. Soc.*, October 1987, *21*(10), pp. 119–28.

Lea, S. E. G. Animal Experiments in Economic Psychology. *Green, L. and Kagel, J. H., eds.*, 1987, *1981*, pp. 95–116.

McCloskey, Donald N. The Rhetoric of Economics: Response to My Critics. *Eastern Econ. J.*, July-Sept. 1987, *13*(3), pp. 308–11.

Meidinger, Claude. L'empirisme et le statut des hypotheses "Ad Hoc" en physique et en économie. (Empiricism and "Ad hoc" Hypotheses in Physics and Economics. With English summary.) *Écon. Soc.*, October 1987, *21*(10), pp. 129–52.

Meller, Patricio. Una Revisión de la Crisis de la Ciencia Económica. (A Review of the Crisis of the Economic Science. With English summary.) *Colección Estud. CIEPLAN*, December 1987, (22), pp. 153–72.

Mirowski, Philip. Shall I Compare Thee to a Minkowski–Ricardo–Leontief–Metzler Matrix of the Mosak–Hicks Type? Or, Rhetoric, Mathematics, and the Nature of Neoclassical Economic Theory. *Econ. Philos.*, April 1987, *3*(1), pp. 67–95.

Mirowski, Philip. The Philosophical Bases of Institutionalist Economics. *J. Econ. Issues*, September 1987, *21*(3), pp. 1001–38.

Mongin, Philippe. L'Instrumentalisme dans l'Essai de M. Friedman. (Instrumentalism in M. Friedman's Essay. With English summary.) *Écon. Soc.*, October 1987, *21*(10), pp. 73–106.

Oswald, Donald J. Metaphysical Beliefs and the Foundations of Modern Economics. *Rev. Soc. Econ.*, December 1987, *45*(3), pp. 276–97.

Pelloni, Gianluigi. A Note on Friedman and the Neo-Bayesian Approach. *Manchester Sch. Econ. Soc. Stud.*, December 1987, *55*(4), pp. 407–18.

Perlman, Mark. Concerning Winters of Discontent: Does Methodology or Rhetoric Contain the Answer to a Possible Malaise? *Int. J. Soc. Econ.*, 1987, *14*(7/8/9), pp. 9–18.

Pheby, John. A New Perspective on Shackle's Keynesian Fundamentalism. *J. Econ. Stud.*, 1987, *14*(4), pp. 24–35.

Reid, Joseph D., Jr. The Theory of Sharecropping: Occam's Razor and Economic Analysis. *Hist. Polit. Econ.*, Winter 1987, *19*(4), pp. 551–69.

Rosenberg, Alexander. Weintraub's Aims: A Brief Rejoinder [Lakatosian Consolations for Economists]. *Econ. Philos.*, April 1987, *3*(1), pp. 143–44.

Rosier, Michel. Otto Neurath, économiste et leader du Cercle de Vienne. (Otto Neurath, Economist and Leader of the Vienna Circle. With English summary.) *Écon. Soc.*, March 1987, *21*(3), pp. 113–45.

Rugina, Anghel N. How a New Research Programme Was Born and Developed: A Long Journey to the Third Revolution in Social Economics. *Int. J. Soc. Econ.*, 1987, *14*(3/4/5), pp. 14–21.

Rugina, Anghel N. The Third Revolution in Economic Thinking: A New Methodology of Orientation, Clarification and Development of New Knowledge. *Rivista Int. Sci. Econ. Com.*, June 1987, *34*(6), pp. 487–512.

Rutherford, Malcolm. Wesley Mitchell: Institutions and Quantitative Methods. *Eastern Econ. J.*, Jan.-Mar. 1987, *13*(1), pp. 63–73.

Salanti, Andrea. Falsificationism and Fallibilism as Epistemic Foundations of Economics: A Critical View. *Kyklos*, 1987, *40*(3), pp. 368–392.

Scaperlanda, Anthony. Institutionalist Methodology and Social Economics. *Int. J. Soc. Econ.*, 1987, *14*(3/4/5), pp. 146–53.

Sicard, François. Popper et Hayek: économie et politique. (Popper and Hayek: Economics and Politics. With English summary.) *Écon. Soc.*, October 1987, *21*(10), pp. 63–72.

Sufrin, Sidney C. Schumpeter–Walras and Pragmatism. *Rivista Int. Sci. Econ. Com.*, September 1987, *34*(9), pp. 823–28.

Thistle, Paul D. The Rationale for Experiments in Economics. *J. Behav. Econ.*, Winter 1987, *16*(4), pp. 41–53.

Truu, M. L. Confused Thinking, Intellectual Fashion and Received Knowledge in Economics Today. *S. Afr. J. Econ.*, December 1987, *55*(4), pp. 319–32.

Vaughan, William, Jr. and Herrnstein, R. J. Stability, Melioration, and Natural Selection. *Green, L. and Kagel, J. H., eds.*, 1987, pp. 185–215.

Vredeveld, George M. Economics: Musing or Reality—Some Thoughts on Bergmann's Methodology. *J. Econ. Educ.*, Spring 1987, *18*(2), pp. 203–07.

Wagner, Richard E. Gordon Tullock as Rhetorical Economist. *[Tullock, G.]*, 1987, pp. 27–38.

Walliser, Bernard. Le problème de l'induction et de la réfutation en économétrie. (Induction Problem and Refutation in Econometrics. With English summary.) *Écon. Soc.*, October 1987, *21*(10), pp. 153–64.

Webb, James L. Is Friedman's Methodological Instrumentalism a Special Case of Dewey's Instrumental Philosophy? A Comment [Friedman's Positive Economics and the Philosophy of Science]. *J. Econ. Issues*, March 1987, *21*(1), pp. 393–429.

Weintraub, E. Roy. Rosenberg's "Lakatosian Consolations for Economists": Comment. *Econ. Philos.*, April 1987, *3*(1), pp. 139–42.

Wible, James R. Criticism and the Validity of the Special-Case Interpretation of Friedman's Essay: Reply [Friedman's Positive Economics and the Philosophy of Science]. *J. Econ. Issues*, March 1987, *21*(1), pp. 430–40.

Wisman, Jon D. Human Interests, Modes of Rationality and the Social Foundations of Economic Science. *Int. J. Soc. Econ.*, 1987, *14*(7/8/9), pp. 88–98.

Wulwick, Nancy J. The Phillips Curve: Which? Whose? To Do What? How? *Southern Econ. J.*, April 1987, *53*(4), pp. 834–57.

040 ECONOMIC HISTORY

041 Economic History: General

0410 General

Ault, Richard W.; Ekelund, Robert B., Jr. and Tollison, Robert D. The Pope and the Price of Meat: A Public Choice Perspective. *Kyklos*, 1987, *40*(3), pp. 399–413.

Barbalet, J. M. The "Labor Aristocracy" in Context. *Sci. Soc.*, Summer 1987, *51*(2), pp. 133–53.

Charnovitz, Steve. The Influence of International Labour Standards on the World Trading Regime. A Historical Overview. *Int. Lab. Rev.*, Sept.-Oct. 1987, *126*(5), pp. 565–84.

Fraser, Maryna. International Archives in South Africa. *Atack, J., ed.*, 1987, pp. 163–73.
[G: S. Africa]

Gottlieb, Roger S. Historical Materialism, Historical Laws and Social Primacy: Further Discussion of the Transition Debate. *Sci. Soc.*, Summer 1987, *51*(2), pp. 188–99.

Haines, Michael R. Economic History and Historical Demography: Past, Present, and Future. *Field, A. J., ed.*, 1987, pp. 185–253.

Hawkins, Richard; Partridge, Michael and Ville, Simon. List of Publications on the Economic and Social History of Great Britain and Ireland: Published in 1986. *Econ. Hist. Rev., 2nd Ser.*, November 1987, *40*(4), pp. 603–47.

Laibman, David. Modes and Transitions: Replies. *Sci. Soc.*, Summer 1987, *51*(2), pp. 179–88.

Megill, Allan and McCloskey, Donald N. The Rhetoric of History. *Nelson, J. S.; Megill, A. and McCloskey, D. N., eds.*, 1987, pp. 221–38.

Meldolesi, Luca. Historical Hierarchies and the "Complication" of Economics: An Outline. *J. Europ. Econ. Hist.*, Fall 1987, *16*(2), pp. 357–62.

Rodra, Ashok. The Transition Debate: Lessons for Third World Marxists. *Sci. Soc.*, Summer 1987, *51*(2), pp. 170–78.

Rostow, Walt W. Reflections on the Drive to Technological Maturity. *Banca Naz. Lavoro Quart. Rev.*, June 1987, (161), pp. 115–46.
[G: Global]

Schwartz, Anna J. Secular Price Change in Historical Perspective. *Schwartz, A. J.*, 1987, *1973*, pp. 78–109.

Van Camp, Anne. The International Records of Corporations. *Atack, J., ed.*, 1987, pp. 175–80.

0411 Development of the Discipline

Basu, Kaushik; Jones, Eric and Schlicht, Ekkehart. The Growth and Decay of Custom: The Role of the New Institutional Economics in Economic History. *Exploration Econ. Hist.*,

January 1987, *24*(1), pp. 1–21.

Bédarida, François. The Modern Historian's Dilemma: Conflicting Pressures from Science and Society. *Econ. Hist. Rev., 2nd Ser.*, August 1987, *40*(3), pp. 335–48.

Crafts, N. F. R. Cliometrics, 1971–1986: A Survey. *J. Appl. Econometrics*, July 1987, *2*(3), pp. 171–92.

Eichengreen, Barry. Macroeconomics and History. *Field, A. J., ed.*, 1987, pp. 43–90.

Feeny, David. The Exploration of Economic Change: The Contribution of Economic History to Development Economics. *Field, A. J., ed.*, 1987, pp. 91–119.

Field, Alexander J. The Future of Economic History. *Field, A. J., ed.*, 1987, pp. 1–41.

Lazonick, William. Theory and History in Marxian Economics. *Field, A. J., ed.*, 1987, pp. 255–312.

Meiners, Roger E. Economic Considerations in History: Theory and a Little Practice. *Radnitzky, G. and Bernholz, P., eds.*, 1987, pp. 79–103.

North, Douglass C. Institutions, Transaction Costs and Economic Growth. *Econ. Inquiry*, July 1987, *25*(3), pp. 419–28.

Parker, William N. Quantity and Quiddity: Historical Introduction. *Kilby, P., ed.*, 1987, pp. 3–16.
[G: U.S.]

Thomas, Mark. General Equilibrium Models and Research in Economic History. *Field, A. J., ed.*, 1987, pp. 121–83.

Wright, Gavin. Labor History and Labor Economics. *Field, A. J., ed.*, 1987, pp. 313–48.

Zeitlin, Jonathan. From Labour History to the History of Industrial Relations. *Econ. Hist. Rev., 2nd Ser.*, May 1987, *40*(2), pp. 159–84.
[G: U.K.]

0412 Comparative Intercountry or Intertemporal Economic History

Alonso, William. Population North and South. *Alonso, W., ed.*, 1987, pp. 1–11.

Burgstaller, André. Europe's Industrialization and Colonial Underdevelopment in the Light of Ricardo's Corn Model. *J. Int. Econ.*, February 1987, *22*(1/2), pp. 157–69.

Chandler, Alfred D., Jr. A Framework for Analyzing the Modern Multinational Enterprise and Its Competitive Advantage. *Atack, J., ed.*, 1987, pp. 3–17.
[G: U.S.]

Clark, Gregory. Why Isn't the Whole World Developed? Lessons from the Cotton Mills. *J. Econ. Hist.*, March 1987, *47*(1), pp. 141–73.

Davis, Kingsley. Low Fertility in Evolutionary Perspective. *Davis, K.; Bernstam, M. S. and Ricardo-Campbell, R., eds.*, 1987, *1986*, pp. 48–65.
[G: OECD]

Drescher, Seymour. Paradigms Tossed: Capitalism and the Political Sources of Abolition. *Solow, B. L. and Engerman, S. L., eds.*, 1987, pp. 191–208.

Duchêne, François and Shepherd, Geoffrey. Western Europe: A Family of Contrasts. *Duchêne, F. and Shepherd, G., eds.*, 1987, pp. 21–40.
[G: W. Europe]

Dunning, John H. The Organisation of International Economic Interdependence: An Historical Excursion. *Dunning, J. H. and Usui, M., eds.*, 1987, pp. 3–18.

Gerhart, Barry A. and Jarley, Paul. Comment [A Tale of Employment Decline in Two Cities: How Bad Was the Worst of Times?]. *Ind. Lab. Relat. Rev.*, January 1987, 40(2), pp. 280–84. [G: U.S.]

Hohemberg, Paul M. Urbanization and Population Dynamics in History: Review Article. *J. Europ. Econ. Hist.*, Spring 1987, 16(1), pp. 171–77.

Inikori, Joseph E. Slavery and the Development of Industrial Capitalism in England. *Solow, B. L. and Engerman, S. L., eds.*, 1987, pp. 79–101. [G: U.K.]

Kuznets, Simon. Population, Income and Capital. *Dupriez, L. H., ed.*, 1987, 1955, pp. 3–20. [G: Global]

Maier, Charles S. Society as Factory. *Maier, C. S.*, 1987, pp. 19–69. [G: U.S.; Germany; Italy]

Menard, Scott. Regional Variations in Population Histories. *Menard, S. W. and Moen, E. W., eds.*, 1987, pp. 10–15.

Nossal, Kim Richard. Economic Sanctions in the League of Nations and the United Nations. *Leyton-Brown, D., ed.*, 1987, pp. 7–21.

Rostow, Walt W. The Rich Country–Poor Country Problem: From the Eighteenth to the Twenty-first Century. *Rostow, W. W.*, 1987, pp. 49–78. [G: Global]

Rostow, Walt W. The World Economy since 1945: A Stylized Historical Analysis. *Rostow, W. W.*, 1987, 1985, pp. 19–48. [G: Global]

Schwartz, Anna J. Alternative Monetary Regimes: The Gold Standard. *Schwartz, A. J.*, 1987, 1986, pp. 364–90. [G: U.S.; U.K.; W. Germany; France]

Schwartz, Anna J. Real and Pseudo-financial Crises. *Schwartz, A. J.*, 1987, 1986, pp. 271–88. [G: U.S.; U.K.]

Solow, Barbara L. Capitalism and Slavery in the Exceedingly Long Run. *Solow, B. L. and Engerman, S. L., eds.*, 1987, pp. 51–77.

Soltow, Lee C. Inequalities on the Eve of Mass Migration: Agricultural Holdings in Sweden and the United States in 1845–1850. *Scand. Econ. Hist. Rev.*, 1987, 35(3), pp. 219–36. [G: U.S.; Sweden]

Sutton, Francis X. Refugees and Mass Exoduses: The Search for a Humane, Effective Policy. *Alonso, W., ed.*, 1987, pp. 201–26.

Tolliday, Steven and Zeitlin, Jonathan. The Automobile Industry and Its Workers: Between Fordism and Flexibility: Introduction. *Tolliday, S. and Zeitlin, J., eds.*, 1987, pp. 1–25. [G: U.S.; Europe; Japan]

Van Huyck, John B. A Retrospective on the Classical Gold Standard, 1821–1931: A Review Essay. *J. Monet. Econ.*, May 1987, 19(3), pp. 451–56.

Wilkins, Mira. Efficiency and Management: A Comment on Gregory Clark's "Why Isn't the Whole World Developed?" *J. Econ. Hist.*, De-cember 1987, 47(4), pp. 981–88.

Yonekawa, Shin'ichi. Flotation Booms in the Cotton Spinning Industry, 1870–1890: A Comparative Study. *Bus. Hist. Rev.*, Winter 1987, 61(4), pp. 551–81. [G: Japan; U.S.; U.K.; India]

042 Economic History: United States and Canada

0420 General

Atack, Jeremy. Economies of Scale and Efficiency Gains in the Rise of the Factory in America, 1820–1900. *Kilby, P., ed.*, 1987, pp. 286–335. [G: U.S.]

Bleaney, Michael F. Macroeconomic Theory and the Great Depression Revisited. *Scot. J. Polit. Econ.*, May 1987, 34(2), pp. 105–19. [G: U.S.]

Bordo, Michael D. and Marcotte, Ivan A. Purchasing Power Parity in Colonial America: Some Evidence for South Carolina 1732–1774: A Comment. *Carnegie–Rochester Conf. Ser. Public Policy*, Autumn 1987, 27, pp. 311–23. [G: U.S.]

Bruchey, Stuart. Economy and Society in an Earlier America. *J. Econ. Hist.*, June 1987, 47(2), pp. 299–319. [G: U.S.; W. Europe]

Cagan, Phillip and Schwartz, Anna J. How Feasible Is a Flexible Monetary Policy? *Schwartz, A. J.*, 1987, 1975, pp. 183–208. [G: U.S.]

Davis, Lance E.; Gallman, Robert E. and Hutchins, Teresa D. The Structure of the Capital Stock in Economic Growth and Decline: The New Bedford Whaling Fleet in the Nineteenth Century. *Kilby, P., ed.*, 1987, pp. 336–98. [G: U.S.]

Duménil, Gérard; Glick, Mark and Rangel, Jose. Does Rajani Kanth's Comment Matter? *Rev. Radical Polit. Econ.*, Winter 1987, 19(4), pp. 75. [G: U.S.]

Duménil, Gérard; Glick, Mark and Rangel, Jose. Theories of the Great Depression: Why Did Profitability Matter? *Rev. Radical Polit. Econ.*, Summer 1987, 19(2), pp. 16–42. [G: U.S.]

Eichengreen, Barry. Agricultural Mortgages in the Populist Era: Reply. *J. Econ. Hist.*, September 1987, 47(3), pp. 757–60. [G: U.S.]

French, Michael J. and Wilson, Thomas. Depression and Protection: The Early Thirties and the Early Eighties Compared. *[Penrose, E. F.]*, 1987, pp. 14–31. [G: OECD]

George, Peter J. Ontario's Mining Industry, 1870–1940. *Drummond, I. M.*, 1987, pp. 52–76. [G: Canada]

Gorton, Gary B. and Mullineaux, Donald J. The Joint Production of Confidence: Endogenous Regulation and Nineteenth Century Commercial-Bank Clearinghouses. *J. Money, Credit, Banking*, November 1987, 19(4), pp. 457–68. [G: U.S.]

Greenspan, Alan. The Great Malaise. *Challenge*, Special Issue 1987, 30(6), pp. 11–14. [G: U.S.]

Habakkuk, H. J. The Historical Experience of the Basic Conditions of Economic Progress. *Dupriez, L. H., ed.*, 1987, pp. 85–102.
[G: U.S.; U.S.S.R.; W. Europe; Japan]

Harris, Howell John. Give Us Some Less of the Old-time Corporate History: Review Essay. *Labor Hist.*, Winter 1987, *28*(1), pp. 75–83.
[G: U.S.]

Heller, Walter W. Can There Be Another Crash? *Challenge*, Special Issue 1987, *30*(6), pp. 6–10.
[G: U.S.]

Hirshleifer, Jack. Disaster and Recovery: An Historical Survey. *Hirshleifer, J.*, 1987, *1963*, pp. 5–94.
[G: U.S.; Japan; W. Germany]

Hoch, Charles. A Brief History of the Homeless Problem in the United States. *Bingham, R. D.; Green, R. E. and White, S. B., eds.*, 1987, pp. 16–32.
[G: U.S.]

Inwood, Kris. Progress without Planning: The Economic History of Ontario from Confederation to the Second World War: The Iron and Steel Industry. *Drummond, I. M.*, 1987, pp. 185–207.
[G: Canada]

Kanth, Rajani. Why Does the Duménil–Glick–Rangel Thesis Matter? A Comment. *Rev. Radical Polit. Econ.*, Winter 1987, *19*(4), pp. 73–74.
[G: U.S.]

Klingaman, David C. The Nature of Midwest Manufacturing in 1890. *Klingaman, D. C. and Vedder, R. K., eds.*, 1987, pp. 275–98.
[G: U.S.]

Komlos, John. The Height and Weight of West Point Cadets: Dietary Change in Antebellum America. *J. Econ. Hist.*, December 1987, *47*(4), pp. 897–927.
[G: U.S.]

Laidler, David. Wicksell and Fisher on the "Backing" of Money and the Quantity Theory: A Comment on the Debate between Bruce Smith and Ronald Michener. *Carnegie–Rochester Conf. Ser. Public Policy*, Autumn 1987, *27*, pp. 325–34.
[G: U.S.]

Livingston, James. The Social Analysis of Economic History and Theory: Conjectures on Late Nineteenth-Century American Development. *Amer. Hist. Rev.*, February 1987, *92*(1), pp. 69–95.
[G: U.S.]

Mason, Karen Oppenheim and Cope, Lisa G. Sources of Age and Date-of-Birth Misreporting in the 1900 U.S. Census. *Demography*, November 1987, *24*(4), pp. 563–73.
[G: U.S.]

Michener, Ronald. Fixed Exchange Rates and the Quantity Theory in Colonial America. *Carnegie–Rochester Conf. Ser. Public Policy*, Autumn 1987, *27*, pp. 233–307.
[G: U.S.]

O'Brien, David J. The Economic Thought of the American Hierarchy. *Gannon, T. M., ed.*, 1987, pp. 27–41.
[G: U.S.]

Parker, William N. Native Origins of Modern Industry: Heavy Industrialization in the Old Northwest before 1900. *Klingaman, D. C. and Vedder, R. K., eds.*, 1987, pp. 243–74.
[G: U.S.]

Parker, William N. New England's Early Industrialization: A Sketch. *Kilby, P., ed.*, 1987, pp. 17–46.
[G: U.S.]

Parker, William N. Quantity and Quiddity: Historical Introduction. *Kilby, P., ed.*, 1987, pp. 3–16.
[G: U.S.]

Rubinstein, W. D. Entrepreneurial Effort and Entrepreneurial Success: Peak Wealth-Holding in Three Societies, 1850–1939. *Rubinstein, W. D.*, 1987, *1983*, pp. 119–42.
[G: U.K.; U.S.; Australia]

Schwartz, Anna J. Understanding 1929–1933. *Schwartz, A. J.*, 1987, *1981*, pp. 110–51.
[G: U.S.]

Sinclair, Peter W. The North and the North-west: Forestry and Agriculture. *Drummond, I. M.*, 1987, pp. 77–90.
[G: Canada]

Snowden, Kenneth A. Mortgage Rates and American Capital Market Development in the Late Nineteenth Century. *J. Econ. Hist.*, September 1987, *47*(3), pp. 771–91.
[G: U.S.]

Soltow, Lee C. Tocqueville's View of the Northwest in 1835: Ohio a Generation after Settlement. *Klingaman, D. C. and Vedder, R. K., eds.*, 1987, pp. 131–55.
[G: U.S.]

Stevens, Edward W., Jr. Structural and Ideological Dimensions of Literacy and Education in the Old Northwest. *Klingaman, D. C. and Vedder, R. K., eds.*, 1987, pp. 157–85.
[G: U.S.]

Tiffany, Paul. Opportunity Denied: The Abortive Attempt to Internationalize the American Steel Industry, 1903–1929. *Atack, J., ed.*, 1987, pp. 229–47.
[G: U.S.]

Timberlake, Richard H., Jr. Private Production of Scrip-Money in the Isolated Community. *J. Money, Credit, Banking*, November 1987, *19*(4), pp. 437–47.
[G: U.S.]

Traves, Tom. The Development of the Ontario Automobile Industry to 1939. *Drummond, I. M.*, 1987, pp. 208–23.
[G: Canada]

Vedder, Richard K. and Gallaway, Lowell. Economic Growth and Decline in the Old Northwest. *Klingaman, D. C. and Vedder, R. K., eds.*, 1987, pp. 299–318.
[G: U.S.]

Walton, Gary M. River Transportation and the Old Northwest Territory. *Klingaman, D. C. and Vedder, R. K., eds.*, 1987, pp. 225–42.
[G: U.S.]

Weiman, David F. Farmers and the Market in Antebellum America: A View from the Georgia Upcountry. *J. Econ. Hist.*, September 1987, *47*(3), pp. 627–47.
[G: U.S.]

0421 History of Product Prices and Markets

Altman, Morris. A Revision of Canadian Economic Growth: 1870–1910 (A Challenge to the Gradualist Interpretation). *Can. J. Econ.*, February 1987, *20*(1), pp. 86–113.
[G: Canada]

Broadberry, Stephen N. Purchasing Power Parity and the Pound–Dollar Rate in the 1930s. *Economica*, February 1987, *54*(213), pp. 69–78.
[G: U.S.; U.K.]

Cohen, Avi J. Factor Substitution and Induced Innovation in North American Kraft Pulping: 1914–1940. *Exploration Econ. Hist.*, April 1987, *24*(2), pp. 197–217. [G: U.S.; Canada]

Corley, T. A. B. Interactions between the British and American Patent Medicine Industries 1708–1914. *Atack, J., ed.*, 1987, pp. 111–29.
[G: U.S.; U.K.]

Davis, Lance E.; Gallman, Robert E. and Hutchins, Teresa D. Technology, Productivity, and Profits: British–American Whaling Competition in the North Atlantic, 1816–1842. *Oxford Econ. Pap.*, December 1987, *39*(4), pp. 738–59. [G: U.S.; U.K.]

Duménil, Gérard; Glick, Mark and Rangel, Jose. The Rate of Profit in the United States. *Cambridge J. Econ.*, December 1987, *11*(4), pp. 331–59. [G: U.S.]

Field, Alexander J. Modern Business Enterprise as a Capital-Saving Innovation. *J. Econ. Hist.*, June 1987, *47*(2), pp. 473–85. [G: U.S.]

French, Michael J. The Emergence of a U.S. Multinational Enterprise: The Goodyear Tire and Rubber Company, 1910–1939. *Econ. Hist. Rev.*, 2nd Ser., February 1987, *40*(1), pp. 64–79. [G: U.S.]

George, Peter J. and Preston, Richard J. "Going in Between": The Impact of European Technology on the Work Patterns of the West Main Cree of Northern Ontario. *J. Econ. Hist.*, June 1987, *47*(2), pp. 447–60. [G: Canada]

Godley, Michael R. The China Business: Review Article. *Bus. Hist. Rev.*, Winter 1987, *61*(4), pp. 606–14. [G: U.S.]

Hirshleifer, Jack. Disaster Behavior: Altruism or Alliance? *Hirshleifer, J.*, 1987, pp. 134–41. [G: U.S.]

Hoke, Donald. British and American Horology: Time to Test Factor-Substitution Models. *J. Econ. Hist.*, June 1987, *47*(2), pp. 321–27. [G: U.S.; U.K.]

Laffargue, Jean-Pierre. Croissance et endettement externe. (With English summary.) *Revue Écon. Polit.*, July-Aug. 1987, *97*(4), pp. 409–18. [G: New Zealand; U.S.]

Lewis, Frank and MacKinnon, Mary. Government Loan Guarantees and the Failure of the Canadian Northern Railway. *J. Econ. Hist.*, March 1987, *47*(1), pp. 175–96. [G: Canada]

Mullineaux, Donald J. Competitive Monies and the Suffolk Bank System: A Contractual Perspective. *Southern Econ. J.*, April 1987, *53*(4), pp. 884–98. [G: U.S.]

Nelson, Daniel. Mass Production and the U.S. Tire Industry. *J. Econ. Hist.*, June 1987, *47*(2), pp. 329–39. [G: U.S.]

Price, Jacob M. and Clemens, Paul G. E. A Revolution of Scale in Overseas Trade: British Firms in the Chesapeake Trade, 1675–1775. *J. Econ. Hist.*, March 1987, *47*(1), pp. 1–43. [G: U.S.; U.K.]

Pudup, Mary Beth. From Farm to Factory: Structuring and Location of the U.S. Farm Machinery Industry. *Econ. Geogr.*, July 1987, *63*(3), pp. 203–22. [G: U.S.]

Ransom, Roger L. and Sutch, Richard. Tontine Insurance and the Armstrong Investigation: A Case of Stifled Innovation, 1868–1905. *J. Econ. Hist.*, June 1987, *47*(2), pp. 379–90. [G: U.S.]

Reich, Leonard S. Edison, Coolidge, and Langmuir: Evolving Approaches to American Industrial Research. *J. Econ. Hist.*, June 1987, *47*(2), pp. 341–51. [G: U.S.]

Rider, Christine. Early U.S. Industrialization: A Pre-industrial Divide? *Rev. Soc. Econ.*, October 1987, *45*(2), pp. 133–51. [G: U.S.]

Rucker, Randal R. and Alston, Lee J. Farm Failures and Government Intervention: A Case Study of the 1930's. *Amer. Econ. Rev.*, September 1987, *77*(4), pp. 724–30. [G: U.S.]

Santoni, G. J. The Great Bull Markets 1924–29 and 1982–87: Speculative Bubbles or Economic Fundamentals? *Fed. Res. Bank St. Louis Rev.*, November 1987, *69*(9), pp. 16–30. [G: U.S.]

Selgin, George A. and White, Lawrence H. The Evaluation of a Free Banking System. *Econ. Inquiry*, July 1987, *25*(3), pp. 439–57. [G: U.S.]

Thomson, Ross. Learning by Selling and Invention: The Case of the Sewing Machine. *J. Econ. Hist.*, June 1987, *47*(2), pp. 433–45. [G: U.S.]

Veenendaal, Augustus J., Jr. The Kansas City Southern Railway and the Dutch Connection. *Bus. Hist. Rev.*, Summer 1987, *61*(2), pp. 291–316. [G: U.S.]

Willcox, Walter F. Negro Criminality. *Rev. Black Polit. Econ.*, Summer-Fall 1987, *16*(1–2), pp. 33–45. [G: U.S.]

Wilson, Jack W. and Jones, Charles P. A Comparison of Annual Common Stock Returns: 1871–1925 with 1926–85. *J. Bus.*, April 1987, *60*(2), pp. 239–58. [G: U.S.]

Woolf, Arthur G. The Residential Adoption of Electricity in Early Twentieth-Century America. *Energy J.*, April 1987, *8*(2), pp. 19–30.

0422 History of Factor Prices and Markets

Allen, Steven G. Relative Wage Variability in the United States, 1860–1983. *Rev. Econ. Statist.*, November 1987, *69*(4), pp. 617–26. [G: U.S.]

Arnesen, Eric. To Rule or Ruin: New Orleans Dock Workers' Struggle for Control 1902–1903. *Labor Hist.*, Spring 1987, *28*(2), pp. 139–66. [G: U.S.]

Ashworth, John. The Relationship between Capitalism and Humanitarianism. *Amer. Hist. Rev.*, October 1987, *92*(4), pp. 813–28. [G: U.K.; U.S.]

Barsky, Robert B. The Fisher Hypothesis and the Forecastability and Persistence of Inflation. *J. Monet. Econ.*, January 1987, *19*(1), pp. 3–24. [G: U.S.]

Brody, David. Elements of Paradox in U.S. Labor History. *Mon. Lab. Rev.*, August 1987, *110*(8), pp. 48–50. [G: U.S.]

Brown, Clair. Consumption Norms, Work Roles, and Economic Growth, 1918–80. *Brown, C. and Pechman, J. A., eds.*, 1987, pp. 13–49. [G: U.S.]

Brown, Martin and Nuwer, Michael. Strategic Jobs and Wage Structure in the Steel Industry: 1910–1930. *Ind. Relat.*, Fall 1987, *26*(3), pp. 253–66. [G: U.S.]

Carter, Susan B. Consumption Norms, Work Roles, and Economic Growth, 1918–80: Comments. *Brown, C. and Pechman, J. A., eds.*, 1987, pp. 49–54. [G: U.S.]

Cloud, Patricia and Galenson, David W. Chinese Immigration and Contract Labor in the Late Nineteenth Century. *Exploration Econ. Hist.*, January 1987, *24*(1), pp. 22–42. [G: U.S.]

Cohn, Jan. The Business Ethic for Boys: *The Saturday Evening Post* and the Post Boys. *Bus. Hist. Rev.*, Summer 1987, *61*(2), pp. 185–215. [G: U.S.]

Cohn, Raymond L. The Determinants of Individual Immigrant Mortality on Sailing Ships, 1836–1853. *Exploration Econ. Hist.*, October 1987, *24*(4), pp. 371–91. [G: U.S.]

Crew, Spencer R. The Great Migration of Afro-Americans, 1915–40. *Mon. Lab. Rev.*, March 1987, *110*(3), pp. 34–36. [G: U.S.]

Cross, Gary and Shergold, Peter R. "We Think We Are of the Oppressed": Gender, White Collar Work, and Grievances of Late Nineteenth-Century Women. *Labor Hist.*, Winter 1987, *28*(1), pp. 23–53. [G: U.S.]

David, Paul A. Industrial Labor Market Adjustments in a Region of Recent Settlement: Chicago, 1848–1868. *Kilby, P., ed.*, 1987, pp. 47–97. [G: U.S.]

Davis, David Brion. Reflections on Abolitionism and Ideological Hegemony. *Amer. Hist. Rev.*, October 1987, *92*(4), pp. 797–812. [G: U.K.; U.S.]

Dillon, Patricia and Gang, Ira N. Earnings Effects of Labor Organizations in 1890. *Ind. Lab. Relat. Rev.*, July 1987, *40*(4), pp. 516–27. [G: U.S.]

Du Bois, W. E. B. The Negro Criminal. *Rev. Black Polit. Econ.*, Summer-Fall 1987, *16*(1–2), pp. 17–31. [G: U.S.]

Dudden, Faye. Small Town Knights: The Knights of Labor in Homer, New York. *Labor Hist.*, Summer 1987, *28*(3), pp. 307–27. [G: U.S.]

Eichengreen, Barry. The Impact of Late Nineteenth-Century Unions on Labor Earnings and Hours: Iowa in 1894. *Ind. Lab. Relat. Rev.*, July 1987, *40*(4), pp. 501–15. [G: U.S.]

Emmons, David. An Aristocracy of Labor: The Irish Miners of Butte, 1880–1914. *Labor Hist.*, Summer 1987, *28*(3), pp. 275–306. [G: U.S.]

von Ende, Eleanor and Weiss, Thomas. Labor Force Changes in the Old Northwest. *Klingaman, D. C. and Vedder, R. K., eds.*, 1987, pp. 103–30. [G: U.S.]

Englander, Ernest J. The Inside Contract System of Production and Organization: A Neglected Aspect of the History of the Firm. *Labor Hist.*, Fall 1987, *28*(4), pp. 429–46. [G: U.S.]

Foner, Philip S. Women and the American Labor Movement: A Historical Perspective. *Koziara, K. S.; Moskow, M. H. and Tanner, L. D., eds.*, 1987, pp. 154–86. [G: U.S.]

Gallman, Robert E. Investment Flows and Capital Stocks: U.S. Experience in the Nineteenth Century. *Kilby, P., ed.*, 1987, pp. 214–54. [G: U.S.]

Goldin, Claudia. The Gender Gap in Historical Perspective. *Kilby, P., ed.*, 1987, pp. 135–70. [G: U.S.]

Goldin, Claudia. Women's Employment and Technological Change: A Historical Perspec-

tive. *Hartmann, H. I., ed.*, 1987, pp. 185–222. [G: U.S.]

Gottlieb, Peter. Black Miners and the 1925–28 Bituminous Coal Strike: The Colored Committee of Non-Union Miners, Montour Mine No. 1, Pittsburgh Coal Company. *Labor Hist.*, Spring 1987, *28*(2), pp. 233–37. [G: U.S.]

Green, William A. Race and Slavery: Considerations on the Williams Thesis. *Solow, B. L. and Engerman, S. L., eds.*, 1987, pp. 25–49. [G: Caribbean; U.S.]

Grubb, Farley. Colonial Immigrant Literacy: An Economic Analysis of Pennsylvania—German Evidence, 1727–1775. *Exploration Econ. Hist.*, January 1987, *24*(1), pp. 63–76. [G: U.S.]

Grubb, Farley. Colonial Labor Markets and the Length of Indenture: Further Evidence. *Exploration Econ. Hist.*, January 1987, *24*(1), pp. 101–06.

Harris, Robert L., Jr. The Flowering of Afro-American History: Review Article. *Amer. Hist. Rev.*, December 1987, *92*(5), pp. 1150–61. [G: U.S.]

Haskell, Thomas L. Convention and Hegemonic Interest in the Debate over Antislavery: A Reply. *Amer. Hist. Rev.*, October 1987, *92*(4), pp. 829–78. [G: U.S.; U.K.]

Henderson, Alexa Benson. Herman E. Perry and Black Enterprise in Atlanta, 1908–1925. *Bus. Hist. Rev.*, Summer 1987, *61*(2), pp. 216–42. [G: U.S.]

Jacoby, Sanford M. The Development of Cost-of-Living Escalators in the United States. *Labor Hist.*, Fall 1987, *28*(4), pp. 515–33. [G: U.S.]

James, John A. and Skinner, Jonathan S. Sources of Savings in the Nineteenth Century United States. *Kilby, P., ed.*, 1987, pp. 255–85. [G: U.S.]

Janick, Herbert. Yale Blue: Unionization at Yale University, 1931–1985. *Labor Hist.*, Summer 1987, *28*(3), pp. 349–69. [G: U.S.]

Kazin, Michael. Struggling with Class Struggle: Marxism and the Search for a Synthesis of U.S. Labor History. *Labor Hist.*, Fall 1987, *28*(4), pp. 497–514. [G: U.S.]

Krueger, Alan B. and Summers, Lawrence H. Reflections on the Inter-industry Wage Structure. *Lang, K. and Leonard, J. S., eds.*, 1987, pp. 17–47. [G: Global]

Kunitz, Stephen J. Explanations and Ideologies of Mortality Patterns. *Population Devel. Rev.*, September 1987, *13*(3), pp. 379–408. [G: U.S.]

Lasser, Carol. The Domestic Balance of Power: Relations between Mistress and Maid in Nineteenth-Century New England. *Labor Hist.*, Winter 1987, *28*(1), pp. 5–22. [G: U.S.]

Laumas, G. S. and Fackler, James S. Economic Instability and the Demand for Money, 1908–1980. *Eastern Econ. J.*, July-Sept. 1987, *13*(3), pp. 249–57. [G: U.S.]

Lebergott, Stanley. "O Pioneers": Land Speculation and the Growth of the Midwest. *Klinga-*

man, D. C. and Vedder, R. K., eds., 1987, pp. 37–57. [G: U.S.]

Lebergott, Stanley. Consumption Norms, Work Roles, and Economic Growth, 1918–80: Comments. *Brown, C. and Pechman, J. A., eds.*, 1987, pp. 54–58. [G: U.S.]

Lee, Maw Lin and Loschky, David. Malthusian Population Oscillations. *Econ. J.*, September 1987, 97(387), pp. 727–39. [G: U.S.]

Margo, Robert A. and Villaflor, Georgia C. The Growth of Wages in Antebellum America: New Evidence. *J. Econ. Hist.*, December 1987, 47(4), pp. 873–95. [G: U.S.]

Mason, Karen Oppenheim; Weinstein, Maxine and Laslett, Barbara. The Decline of Fertility in Los Angeles, California, 1880–1900. *Population Stud.*, November 1987, 41(3), pp. 483–99. [G: U.S.]

Mills, Herb and Wellman, David. Contractually Sanctioned Job Action and Workers' Control: The Case of San Francisco Longshoremen. *Labor Hist.*, Spring 1987, 28(2), pp. 167–95. [G: U.S.]

Moen, Jon. The Labor of Older Men: A Comment. *J. Econ. Hist.*, September 1987, 47(3), pp. 761–67. [G: U.S.]

Palladino, Grace. When Militancy Isn't Enough: The Impact of Automation on New York City Building Service Workers, 1934–1970. *Labor Hist.*, Spring 1987, 28(2), pp. 196–220. [G: U.S.]

Percy, Michael B. and Woroby, Tamara. American Homesteaders and the Canadian Prairies, 1899 and 1909. *Exploration Econ. Hist.*, January 1987, 24(1), pp. 77–100. [G: U.S.]

Piore, Michael J. Historical Perspectives and the Interpretation of Unemployment. *J. Econ. Lit.*, December 1987, 25(4), pp. 1834–50. [G: U.S.; Europe]

Power, Marilyn. From Home Production to Wage Labor: Women as a Reserve Army of Labor. *England, R. W., ed.*, 1987, pp. 157–77. [G: U.S.]

Raff, Daniel M. G. and Summers, Lawrence H. Did Henry Ford Pay Efficiency Wages? *J. Lab. Econ.*, Part 2, Oct. 1987, 5(4), pp. S57–86. [G: U.S.]

Rubinstein, W. D. New Men of Wealth and the Purchase of Land in Nineteenth-Century Britain. *Rubinstein, W. D.*, 1987, 1981, pp. 145–71. [G: U.K.]

Sanderson, Warren C. Below-Replacement Fertility in Nineteenth Century America. *Population Devel. Rev.*, June 1987, 13(2), pp. 305–13. [G: U.S.]

Santos, Michael W. Laboring on the Periphery: Managers and Workers at the A. M. Byers Company, 1900–1956. *Bus. Hist. Rev.*, Spring 1987, 61(1), pp. 113–33. [G: U.S.]

Schaefer, Donald F. A Model of Migration and Wealth Accumulation: Farmers at the Antebellum Southern Frontier. *Exploration Econ. Hist.*, April 1987, 24(2), pp. 130–57. [G: U.S.]

Schwartz, Anna J. The Beginning of Competitive Banking in Philadelphia, 1782–1809. *Schwartz,*

A. J., 1987, 1947, pp. 3–23. [G: U.S.]

Screpanti, Ernesto. Long Cycles in Strike Activity: An Empirical Investigation. *Brit. J. Ind. Relat.*, March 1987, 25(1), pp. 99–124. [G: France; Italy; U.K.; U.S.; W. Germany]

Smiley, Gene. Postbellum Banking and Financial Markets in the Old Northwest. *Klingaman, D. C. and Vedder, R. K., eds.*, 1987, pp. 187–223. [G: U.S.]

Snowden, Kenneth A. American Stock Market Development and Performance, 1871–1929. *Exploration Econ. Hist.*, October 1987, 24(4), pp. 327–53. [G: U.S.]

Stabile, Donald R. The Du Pont Experiments in Scientific Management: Efficiency and Safety, 1911–1919. *Bus. Hist. Rev.*, Autumn 1987, 61(3), pp. 365–86. [G: U.S.]

Strom, Sharon Hartman. "Machines Instead of Clerks": Technology and the Feminization of Bookkeeping, 1910–1950. *Hartmann, H. I., ed.*, 1987, pp. 63–97. [G: U.S.]

Swanson, Dorothy. Annual Bibliography on American Labor History, 1986: Periodicals, Dissertations, and Research in Progress. *Labor Hist.*, Fall 1987, 28(4), pp. 484–96. [G: U.S.]

Tobin, James. The Monetary Interpretation of History: A Review Article. *Tobin, J. (I)*, 1987, pp. 471–96. [G: U.S.]

Tomlins, Christopher L. Criminal Conspiracy and Early Labor Combinations: Massachusetts, 1824–1840. *Labor Hist.*, Summer 1987, 28(3), pp. 370–85. [G: U.S.]

Tripp, Joseph F. Law and Social Control: Historians' Views of Progressive-Era Labor Legislation. *Labor Hist.*, Fall 1987, 28(4), pp. 447–83. [G: U.S.]

Ward, David C. Industrial Workers in the Mid-Nineteenth Century South: Family and Labor in the Graniteville (SC) Textile Mill, 1845–1880. *Labor Hist.*, Summer 1987, 28(3), pp. 328–48. [G: U.S.]

Weiss, Thomas. Demographic Aspects of the Urban Population, 1800–1840. *Kilby, P., ed.*, 1987, pp. 171–213. [G: U.S.]

Whatley, Warren C. Southern Agrarian Labor Contracts as Impediments to Cotton Mechanization. *J. Econ. Hist.*, March 1987, 47(1), pp. 45–70. [G: U.S.]

Whiteside, Noel. Counting the Cost: Sickness and Disability among Working People in an Era of Industrial Recession, 1920–39. *Econ. Hist. Rev., 2nd Ser.*, May 1987, 40(2), pp. 228–46. [G: U.S.]

Wright, Gavin. Capitalism and Slavery on the Islands: A Lesson from the Mainland. *Solow, B. L. and Engerman, S. L., eds.*, 1987, pp. 283–302. [G: Caribbean; U.S.]

Wright, Gavin. Postbellum Southern Labor Markets. *Kilby, P., ed.*, 1987, pp. 98–134. [G: U.S.]

Zolberg, Aristide R. Wanted But Not Welcome: Alien Labor in Western Development. *Alonso, W., ed.*, 1987, pp. 36–73. [G: Europe; N. America]

0423 History of Public Economic Policy (all levels)

Anderson, Gary Michael and Martin, Dolores T. The Public Domain and Nineteenth Century Transfer Policy. *Cato J.*, Winter 1987, 6(3), pp. 905–23. [G: U.S.]

Anderson, Terry L. The First Privatization Movement. *Klingaman, D. C. and Vedder, R. K., eds.*, 1987, pp. 59–75. [G: U.S.]

Anderson, Terry L. and Hill, Peter J. Privatizing the Commons: Reply. *Southern Econ. J.*, July 1987, 54(1), pp. 225–26.

Atack, Jeremy and Bateman, Fred. Yankee Farming and Settlement in the Old Northwest: A Comparative Analysis. *Klingaman, D. C. and Vedder, R. K., eds.*, 1987, pp. 77–102. [G: U.S.]

Berkowitz, Edward D. The First Advisory Council and the 1939 Amendments. *Berkowitz, E. D., ed.*, 1987, pp. 55–78. [G: U.S.]

Blanchard, Margaret A. The Associated Press Antitrust Suit: A Philosophical Clash over Ownership of First Amendment Rights. *Bus. Hist. Rev.*, Spring 1987, 61(1), pp. 43–85.

Bordo, Michael D. and Redish, Angela. Why Did the Bank of Canada Emerge in 1935? *J. Econ. Hist.*, June 1987, 47(2), pp. 405–17. [G: Canada]

Brady, David; Cooper, Joseph and Hurley, Patricia A. The Decline of Party in the U.S. House of Representatives, 1887–1968. *McCubbins, M. D. and Sullivan, T., eds.*, 1987, 1979, pp. 235–59. [G: U.S.]

Brady, David and Morgan, Mark A. Reforming the Structure of the House Appropriations Process: The Effects of the 1885 and 1919–20 Reforms on Money Decisions. *McCubbins, M. D. and Sullivan, T., eds.*, 1987, pp. 207–34. [G: U.S.]

Breen, William J. Administrative Politics and Labor Policy in the First World War: The U.S. Employment Service and the Seattle Labor Market Experiment. *Bus. Hist. Rev.*, Winter 1987, 61(4), pp. 582–605. [G: U.S.]

Bromfield, David H. Women and the Law of Property in Early America. *Mich. Law Rev.*, Apr.-May 1987, 85(5–6), pp. 1109–16.

Cagan, Phillip. A Compensated Dollar: Better or More Likely Than Gold? *Dorn, J. A. and Schwartz, A. J., eds.*, 1987, pp. 261–77. [G: U.S.; U.K.]

Cooper, Richard N. Trade Policy as Foreign Policy. *Stern, R. M., ed.*, 1987, pp. 291–322. [G: U.S.]

England, Richard W. Capital Accumulation, Class Struggle, and School Finance Reform. *England, R. W., ed.*, 1987, pp. 203–25. [G: U.S.]

Fischer, Wolfram. Swings between Protection and Free Trade in History. *Giersch, H., ed.*, 1987, pp. 20–32. [G: U.S.; W. Europe]

Flynn, John J. The Jurisprudence of Corporate Personhood: The Misuse of a Legal Concept. *Samuels, W. J. and Miller, A. S., eds.*, 1987, pp. 131–59. [G: U.S.]

Friedman, Milton and Schwartz, Anna J. Money and Business Cycles. *Schwartz, A. J.*, 1987, 1963, pp. 24–77. [G: U.S.]

Furubotn, Eirik G. Privatizing the Commons: Comment. *Southern Econ. J.*, July 1987, 54(1), pp. 219–24.

Galbraith, John Kenneth. Keynes, Roosevelt, and the Complementary Revolutions. *Challenge*, Special Issue 1987, 30(6), pp. 19–23. [G: U.S.]

Hamilton, Carl. The Political Economy of U.S. Protection: Comment. *Giersch, H., ed.*, 1987, pp. 403–06. [G: U.S.]

Hamilton, James D. Monetary Factors in the Great Depression. *J. Monet. Econ.*, March 1987, 19(2), pp. 145–69. [G: U.S.]

Horwitz, Morton J. *Santa Clara* Revisited: The Development of Corporate Theory. *Samuels, W. J. and Miller, A. S., eds.*, 1987, pp. 13–63. [G: U.S.]

Hufbauer, Gary Clyde. Trade Policy as Foreign Policy: Comment. *Stern, R. M., ed.*, 1987, pp. 323–26. [G: U.S.]

Hughes, Jonathan. The Great Land Ordinances: Colonial America's Thumbprint on History. *Klingaman, D. C. and Vedder, R. K., eds.*, 1987, pp. 1–18. [G: U.S.]

Jones, Charles O. Joseph G. Cannon and Howard W. Smith: An Essay on the Limits of Leadership in the House of Representatives. *McCubbins, M. D. and Sullivan, T., eds.*, 1987, 1968, pp. 260–85. [G: U.S.]

Keller, Robert R. The Role of the State in the U.S. Economy during the 1920s. *J. Econ. Issues*, June 1987, 21(2), pp. 877–84. [G: U.S.]

Kelman, Steven. The Political Foundations of American Statistical Policy. *Alonso, W. and Starr, P., eds.*, 1987, pp. 275–302. [G: U.S.]

Kindleberger, Charles P. An Excerpt from an Oral History, Truman Library. *Kindleberger, C. P.*, 1987, pp. 106–19. [G: U.S.; W. Europe]

Kindleberger, Charles P. Did Dollars Save the World? *Kindleberger, C. P.*, 1987, pp. 245–65. [G: U.S.; Global]

Kindleberger, Charles P. Excerpts from the Cleveland–Moore–Kindleberger Memorandum of 12 June 1947, on a European Recovery Program. *Kindleberger, C. P.*, 1987, pp. 1–24. [G: U.S.; W. Europe]

Kindleberger, Charles P. Memorandum for the Files: Origins of the Marshall Plan. *Kindleberger, C. P.*, 1987, 1972, pp. 25–32. [G: U.S.; W. Europe]

Kindleberger, Charles P. The American Origins of the Marshall Plan: A View from the State Department. *Kindleberger, C. P.*, 1987, 1984, pp. 154–60. [G: U.S.; W. Europe]

Kindleberger, Charles P. Toward the Marshall Plan: A Memoir of Policy Development in Germany, 1945–47. *Kindleberger, C. P.*, 1987, pp. 161–208. [G: U.S.; W. Europe]

Kirkby, Diane. "The Wage-Earning Woman and the State": The National Women's Trade Union League and Protective Labor Legislation,

1903–1923. *Labor Hist.*, Winter 1987, *28*(1), pp. 54–74. [G: U.S.]

Knodell, Jane. Open Market Operations: Evolution and Significance. *J. Econ. Issues*, June 1987, *21*(2), pp. 691–99. [G: U.S.]

Krasner, Stephen D. Trade Policy as Foreign Policy: Comment. *Stern, R. M., ed.*, 1987, pp. 327–36. [G: U.S.]

Leamer, Edward E. Endogenous Protection in the United States, 1900–1984: Comment. *Stern, R. M., ed.*, 1987, pp. 196–200. [G: U.S.]

Leff, Mark H. Historical Perspectives on Old-Age Insurance: The State of the Art on the Art of the State. *Berkowitz, E. D., ed.*, 1987, pp. 29–53. [G: U.S.]

Little, Ian M. D. Swings between Protection and Free Trade in History: Comment. *Giersch, H., ed.*, 1987, pp. 33–34.

Lovett, William A. Theory and Practice of Antitrust. *Wills, R. L.; Caswell, J. A. and Culbertson, J. D., eds.*, 1987, pp. 41–60. [G: U.S.]

Magee, Stephen P. The Political Economy of U.S. Protection. *Giersch, H., ed.*, 1987, pp. 368–402. [G: U.S.]

Magee, Stephen P. and Young, Leslie. Endogenous Protection in the United States, 1900–1984. *Stern, R. M., ed.*, 1987, pp. 145–95. [G: U.S.]

Mankiw, N. Gregory; Miron, Jeffrey A. and Weil, David N. The Adjustment of Expectations to a Change in Regime: A Study of the Founding of the Federal Reserve. *Amer. Econ. Rev.*, June 1987, *77*(3), pp. 358–74. [G: U.S.]

Margo, Robert A. Accounting for Racial Differences in School Attendance in the American South, 1900: The Role of Separate-but-Equal. *Rev. Econ. Statist.*, November 1987, *69*(4), pp. 661–66. [G: U.S.]

Martin, David Dale. The Corporation and Antitrust Law Policy: Double Standards. *Samuels, W. J. and Miller, A. S., eds.*, 1987, pp. 193–217. [G: U.S.]

Meyer, Charles W. Social Security: Past, Present, and Future. *Meyer, C. W., ed.*, 1987, pp. 1–34. [G: U.S.]

Miller, Arthur S. Corporations and Our Two Constitutions. *Samuels, W. J. and Miller, A. S., eds.*, 1987, pp. 241–62. [G: U.S.]

Mills, Geofrey and Rockoff, Hugh. Compliance with Price Controls in the United States and the United Kingdom during World War II. *J. Econ. Hist.*, March 1987, *47*(1), pp. 197–213. [G: U.S.; U.K.]

Neary, J. Peter. Endogenous Protection in the United States, 1900–1984: Comment. *Stern, R. M., ed.*, 1987, pp. 201–06. [G: U.S.]

Neufeld, John L. Price Discrimination and the Adoption of the Electricity Demand Charge. *J. Econ. Hist.*, September 1987, *47*(3), pp. 693–709. [G: U.S.]

North, Douglass C. and Rutten, Andrew R. The Northwest Ordinance in Historical Perspec-

tive. *Klingaman, D. C. and Vedder, R. K., eds.*, 1987, pp. 19–35. [G: U.S.]

Olasky, Marvin N. Anticompetitive Campaigns by Big Business in the Pre–World War II Period. *Marcus, A. A.; Kaufman, A. M. and Beam, D. R., eds.*, 1987, pp. 239–53. [G: U.S.]

Pecquet, Gary M. Money in the Trans-Mississippi Confederacy and the Confederate Currency Reform Act of 1864. *Exploration Econ. Hist.*, April 1987, *24*(2), pp. 218–43. [G: U.S.]

Perkins, Edwin J. Lost Opportunities for Compromise in the Bank War: A Reassessment of Jackson's Veto Message. *Bus. Hist. Rev.*, Winter 1987, *61*(4), pp. 531–50. [G: U.S.]

Phillips, Ron. Veblen and the "Wobblies": A Note. *Rev. Radical Polit. Econ.*, Spring 1987, *19*(1), pp. 98–103.

Rodriguez, Rita M. Exim's Mission and Accomplishments: 1934–84. *Rodriguez, R. M., ed.*, 1987, pp. 1–33. [G: U.S.]

Rolnick, Arthur J. The Benefits of Bank Deposit Rate Ceilings: New Evidence on Bank Rates and Risk in the 1920s. *Fed. Res. Bank Minn. Rev.*, Summer 1987, *11*(3), pp. 2–18. [G: U.S.]

Sanders, Elizabeth. The Regulatory Surge of the 1970s in Historical Perspective. *Bailey, E. E., ed.*, 1987, pp. 117–50. [G: U.S.]

Shughart, William F., II and Tollison, Robert D. Antitrust Recidivism in Federal Trade Commission Data: 1914–1982. *MacKay, R. J.; Miller, J. C., III and Yandle, B., eds.*, 1987, pp. 255–80. [G: U.S.]

Sklar, Martin J. The Sherman Antitrust Act and the Corporate Reconstruction of American Capitalism, 1890–1914. *Samuels, W. J. and Miller, A. S., eds.*, 1987, pp. 65–80. [G: U.S.]

Soifer, Aviam. The Paradox of Paternalism and Laissez-Faire Constitutionalism: The U.S. Supreme Court, 1888–1921. *Samuels, W. J. and Miller, A. S., eds.*, 1987, pp. 161–90. [G: U.S.]

Sylla, Richard; Legler, John B. and Wallis, John Joseph. Banks and State Public Finance in the New Republic: The United States, 1790–1860. *J. Econ. Hist.*, June 1987, *47*(2), pp. 391–403. [G: U.S.]

Tripp, Joseph F. Law and Social Control: Historians' Views of Progressive-Era Labor Legislation. *Labor Hist.*, Fall 1987, *28*(4), pp. 447–83. [G: U.S.]

Wallis, John Joseph. Employment, Politics, and Economic Recovery during the Great Depression. *Rev. Econ. Statist.*, August 1987, *69*(3), pp. 516–20. [G: U.S.]

Weaver, Carolyn L. Support of the Elderly before the Depression: Individual and Collective Arrangements. *Cato J.*, Fall 1987, *7*(2), pp. 503–25. [G: U.S.]

Wigmore, Barrie A. Was the Bank Holiday of 1933 Caused by a Run on the Dollar? *J. Econ. Hist.*, September 1987, *47*(3), pp. 739–55. [G: U.S.]

Wills, Robert L. Economists and Competition Policy: A Case Study. *Wills, R. L.; Caswell, J. A. and Culbertson, J. D., eds.*, 1987, pp. 3–8.   **[G: U.S.]**

043 Economic History: Ancient and Medieval (until 1453)

0430 General

Bruchey, Stuart. Economy and Society in an Earlier America. *J. Econ. Hist.*, June 1987, *47*(2), pp. 299–319.   **[G: U.S.; W. Europe]**

Caroselli, M. R. The Economic Development of the Region of Lazio in the Middle Ages. *J. Europ. Econ. Hist.*, Spring 1987, *16*(1), pp. 101–43.   **[G: Italy]**

Day, John. Crises and Trends in the Late Middle Ages. *Day, J.*, 1987, pp. 185–224.
[G: Europe]

Day, John. Late Medieval Price Movements and the 'Crisis of Feudalism.' *Day, J.*, 1987, pp. 90–107.   **[G: Europe]**

Day, John. Medieval Merchants and Financiers. *Day, J.*, 1987, pp. 162–84.   **[G: Europe]**

Day, John. Monetary Colonialism in the Medieval Mediterranean. *Day, J.*, 1987, pp. 116–28.
[G: Europe]

Day, John. The Decline of a Money Economy: Sardinia under Catalan Rule. *Day, J.*, 1987, *1978*, pp. 72–89.   **[G: Italy]**

Day, John. The Fisher Equation and Medieval Monetary History. *Day, J.*, 1987, *1984*, pp. 108–15.   **[G: Europe]**

Day, John. The Great Bullion Famine of the Fifteenth Century. *Day, J.*, 1987, *1973*, pp. 1–54.   **[G: Europe]**

Day, John. The Question of Monetary Contraction in Late Medieval Europe. *Day, J.*, 1987, *1981*, pp. 55–71.   **[G: Europe]**

French, Michael J. and Wilson, Thomas. Depression and Protection: The Early Thirties and the Early Eighties Compared. *[Penrose, E. F.]*, 1987, pp. 14–31.   **[G: OECD]**

McNeill, William H. Migration in Premodern Times. *Alonso, W., ed.*, 1987, pp. 15–35.

McNeill, William H. The Eccentricity of Wheels, or Eurasian Transportation in Historical Perspective. *Amer. Hist. Rev.*, December 1987, *92*(5), pp. 1111–26.

Stow, Kenneth R. The Jewish Family in the Rhineland in the High Middle Ages: Form and Function. *Amer. Hist. Rev.*, December 1987, *92*(5), pp. 1085–1110.   **[G: Germany]**

0431 History of Product Prices and Markets

Chorley, Patrick. The Cloth Exports of Flanders and Northern France during the Thirteenth Century: A Luxury Trade? *Econ. Hist. Rev.*, *2nd Ser.*, August 1987, *40*(3), pp. 349–79.
[G: France; Flanders]

Gustafsson, Bo. The Rise and Economic Behaviour of Medieval Craft Guilds. An Economic–Theoretical Interpretation. *Scand. Econ. Hist. Rev.*, 1987, *35*(1), pp. 1–40. **[G: W. Europe]**

Mate, Mavis. Pastoral Farming in South-east England in the Fifteenth Century. *Econ. Hist. Rev.*, *2nd Ser.*, November 1987, *40*(4), pp. 523–36.   **[G: U.K.]**

Taub, B. A Model of Medieval Grain Prices: Comment [Corn at Interest: The Extent and Cost of Grain Storage in Medieval England]. *Amer. Econ. Rev.*, December 1987, *77*(5), pp. 1048–53.   **[G: U.K.]**

0432 History of Factor Prices and Markets

Leneman, Leah and Mitchison, Rosalind. Scottish Illegitimacy Ratios in the Early Modern Period. *Econ. Hist. Rev.*, *2nd Ser.*, February 1987, *40*(1), pp. 41–63.   **[G: Scotland]**

0433 History of Public Economic Policy (all levels)

Day, John. Money and Credit in Medieval and Renaissance Italy. *Day, J.*, 1987, pp. 141–61.
[G: Italy]

Day, John. The Monetary Circulation in Tuscany in the Age of Dante. *Day, J.*, 1987, pp. 129–40.   **[G: Italy]**

Hamshere, J. D. Domesday Book, Cliometric Analysis and Taxation Assessments [Were the Tax Assessments of Domesday England Artificial? The Case of Essex]. *Econ. Hist. Rev.*, *2nd Ser.*, May 1987, *40*(2), pp. 262–66.
[G: U.K.]

Hamshere, J. D. Regressing Domesday Book: Tax Assessments of Domesday England: Comments [Were the Tax Assessments of Domesday England Artificial? The Case of Essex]. *Econ. Hist. Rev.*, *2nd Ser.*, May 1987, *40*(2), pp. 247–51.   **[G: U.K.]**

Krüger, Kersten. Public Finance and Modernisation: The Change from Domain State to Tax State in Hesse in the Sixteenth and Seventeenth Centuries—A Case Study. *Witt, P.-C., ed.*, 1987, pp. 49–62. **[G: Germany; Europe]**

McDonald, John and Snooks, G. D. The Suitability of Domesday Book for Cliometric Analysis [Were the Tax Assessments of Domesday England Artificial? The Case of Essex]. *Econ. Hist. Rev.*, *2nd Ser.*, May 1987, *40*(2), pp. 252–61.   **[G: U.K.]**

Ormrod, W. M. The English Crown and the Customs, 1349–63. *Econ. Hist. Rev.*, *2nd Ser.*, February 1987, *40*(1), pp. 27–40.   **[G: U.K.]**

Wunder, Heide. Finance in the 'Economy of Old Europe': The Example of Peasant Credit from the Late Middle Ages to the Thirty Years War. *Witt, P.-C., ed.*, 1987, pp. 19–47.
[G: Europe]

044 Economic History: Europe

0440 General

Aldrich, Robert. Late-Comer or Early-Starter? New Views on French Economic History. *J. Europ. Econ. Hist.*, Spring 1987, *16*(1), pp. 89–100.   **[G: France]**

Barras, Richard. Technical Change and the Urban Development Cycle. *Urban Stud.*, February 1987, *24*(1), pp. 5–30. **[G: U.K.]**

Baumol, William J. Rebirth of a Fallen Leader: Italy and the Long Period Data. *[Marrama, V.], Vol. 1*, 1987, pp. 135–60.

Brüninghaus, Beate. A Review of the New Literature on Business History. *Pohl, H. and Rudolph, B., eds.*, 1987, pp. 117–39. **[G: W. Germany]**

Cain, P. J. and Hopkins, A. G. Gentlemanly Capitalism and British Expansion Overseas. II: New Imperialism, 1850–1945. *Econ. Hist. Rev., 2nd Ser.*, February 1987, *40*(1), pp. 1–26. **[G: U.K.]**

Crafts, N. F. R. British Economic Growth, 1700–1850; Some Difficulties of Interpretation. *Exploration Econ. Hist.*, July 1987, *24*(3), pp. 245–68. **[G: U.K.]**

Davis, David Brion. Capitalism, Abolitionism, and Hegemony. *Solow, B. L. and Engerman, S. L., eds.*, 1987, pp. 209–27.

Dunning, John H. and Archer, Howard. The Eclectic Paradigm and the Growth of UK Multinational Enterprise 1870–1983. *Atack, J., ed.*, 1987, pp. 19–49. **[G: U.K.]**

Faroqhi, Suraiya. The Venetian Presence in the Ottoman Empire, 1600–30. *Islamoglu-Inan, H., ed.*, 1987, pp. 311–44. **[G: Ottoman Empire; Italy]**

Findlay, Ronald. Intermediate Goods, Export Taxation and Resource-Based Industrialization. *[Corden, W. M.]*, 1987, pp. 162–71.

Genç, Mehmet. A Study of the Feasibility of Using Eighteenth-Century Ottoman Financial Records as an Indicator of Economic Activity. *Islamoglu-Inan, H., ed.*, 1987, pp. 345–73. **[G: Ottoman Empire]**

Habakkuk, H. J. The Historical Experience of the Basic Conditions of Economic Progress. *Dupriez, L. H., ed.*, 1987, pp. 85–102. **[G: U.S.; U.S.S.R.; W. Europe; Japan]**

Hayes, Peter. Carl Bosch and Carl Krauch: Chemistry and the Political Economy of Germany, 1925–1945. *J. Econ. Hist.*, June 1987, *47*(2), pp. 353–63. **[G: Germany]**

Hirshleifer, Jack. Disaster and Recovery: An Historical Survey. *Hirshleifer, J., 1963*, pp. 5–94. **[G: U.S.; Japan; W. Germany]**

Hirshleifer, Jack. Disaster and Recovery: The Black Death in Western Europe. *Hirshleifer, J., 1966*, pp. 95–115. **[G: W. Europe]**

Hocevar, Toussaint. The Albanian Economy 1912–1944: A Survey. *J. Europ. Econ. Hist.*, Winter 1987, *16*(3), pp. 561–68. **[G: Albania]**

Hundert, Gershon David. The Role of the Jews in Commerce in Early Modern Poland–Lithuania. *J. Europ. Econ. Hist.*, Fall 1987, *16*(2), pp. 245–75. **[G: Poland; Lithuania]**

Islamoğlu-Inan, Huri. 'Oriental Despotism' in World-System Perspective. *Islamoglu-Inan, H., ed.*, 1987, pp. 1–24. **[G: Ottoman Empire]**

Islamoğlu-Inan, Huri. State and Peasants in the Ottoman Empire: A Study of Peasant Economy in North-central Anatolia during the Sixteenth Century. *Islamoglu-Inan, H., ed.*, 1987, pp. 101–59. **[G: Ottoman Empire]**

Islamoğlu-Inan, Huri and Keyder, Çağlar. Agenda for Ottoman History. *Islamoglu-Inan, H., ed., 1987, 1977*, pp. 42–62. **[G: Ottoman Empire]**

Joshi, P. C. Technological Potentialities of Peasant Agriculture: East–West Parallels and Contrasts. *Joshi, P. C.*, 1987, pp. 159–89. **[G: Asia; W. Europe]**

Kellenbenz, Hermann. The Valet, a Typus of the Court Society. His Entrepreneurial Role. *Pohl, H. and Rudolph, B., eds.*, 1987, pp. 13–40. **[G: Europe]**

Klein, P. W. Trade in Transit: World Trade and World Economy—Past, Present, and Future: Opening Lecture. *Visser, H. and Schoor, E., eds.*, 1987, pp. 3–16. **[G: Europe]**

Kurmuş, Orhan. The Cotton Famine and Its Effects on the Ottoman Empire. *Islamoglu-Inan, H., ed.*, 1987, pp. 160–69. **[G: Ottoman Empire]**

Landers, J. Mortality and Metropolis: The Case of London 1675–1825. *Population Stud.*, March 1987, *41*(1), pp. 59–76. **[G: U.K.]**

Lee, Chi-Wen Jevons and Petruzzi, Christopher R. A Test of the Shiller–Siegel Hypothesis of the Gibson Paradox [The Gibson Paradox and Historical Movements in Real Interest Rates]. *Australian Econ. Pap.*, June 1987, *26*(48), pp. 157–64. **[G: U.K.]**

Maier, Charles S. "Fictitious Bonds . . . of Wealth and law": On the Theory and Practice of Interest Representation. *Maier, C. S., 1987, 1981*, pp. 225–60. **[G: W. Europe]**

Maier, Charles S. The Two Postwar Eras and the Conditions for Stability in Twentieth-Century Western Europe. *Maier, C. S., 1987, 1981*, pp. 153–84. **[G: W. Europe]**

Margulies, Ronnie and Yildizoğlu, Ergin. Agrarian Change: 1923–70. *Schick, I. C. and Tonak, E. A., eds.*, 1987, pp. 269–92. **[G: Turkey]**

Martinius, Sture. Capitalism: A Threat against Freehold Farms around the Middle of the Nineteenth Century? *Scand. Econ. Hist. Rev.*, 1987, *35*(2), pp. 178–90. **[G: W. Europe]**

McElligott, Anthony. Mobilising the Unemployed: The KPD and the Unemployed Workers' Movement in Hamburg-Altona during the Weimar Republic. *Evans, R. J. and Geary, D., eds.*, 1987, pp. 228–60. **[G: Germany]**

McGowan, Bruce. The Middle Danube *Cul-de-sac. Islamoglu-Inan, H., ed.*, 1987, pp. 170–77. **[G: Ottoman Empire]**

Metz, Rainer. Kondratieff and the Theory of Linear Filters. *Vasko, T., ed.*, 1987, pp. 390–404. **[G: U.K.; France; Germany]**

Mogensen, Gunnar Viby. Nyere forskning i dansk økonomisk historie—en oversigt. (Danish Literature on Economic History—A Survey Article. With English summary.) *Nationaløkon. Tidsskr.*, 1987, *125*(2), pp. 153–70. **[G: Denmark]**

Mokyr, Joel. Has the Industrial Revolution Been Crowded Out? Some Reflections on Crafts and Williamson. *Exploration Econ. Hist.*, July

1987, *24*(3), pp. 293–325.

Morineau, Michel. A Rejoinder. *J. Europ. Econ. Hist.*, Spring 1987, *16*(1), pp. 145–48.
[G: France]

Nicholas, Stephen. Empirical Tests of the Transaction Cost Model: The Evolution of the Pre-1939 British Manufacturing Multinational. *Atack, J., ed.*, 1987, pp. 133–45. [G: U.K.]

Pamuk, Şevket. Commodity Production for World-Markets and Relations of Production in Ottoman Agriculture, 1840–1913. *Islamoglu-Inan, H., ed.*, 1987, pp. 178–202.
[G: Ottoman Empire]

Phillips, Carla Rahn. Time and Duration: A Model for the Economy of Early Modern Spain. *Amer. Hist. Rev.*, June 1987, *92*(3), pp. 531–62. [G: Spain]

Pohl, Hans. Cooperation between Business and Science in the Third Reich: The Association for the Promotion of German Industry of 1942. *Pohl, H. and Rudolph, B., eds.*, 1987, pp. 65–91. [G: Germany]

Rosenhaft, Eve. The Unemployed in the Neighbourhood: Social Dislocation and Political Mobilisation in Germany 1929–33. *Evans, R. J. and Geary, D., eds.*, 1987, pp. 194–227.
[G: Germany]

Roszkowski, Wojciech. Large Estates and Small Farms in the Polish Agrarian Economy between the Wars (1918–1938). *J. Europ. Econ. Hist.*, Spring 1987, *16*(1), pp. 75–88.
[G: Poland]

Rubinstein, W. D. British Radicalism and the 'Dark Side' of Populism. *Rubinstein, W. D.*, 1987, pp. 339–73. [G: U.K.]

Rubinstein, W. D. Education and the Social Origins of British Elites, 1880–1970. *Rubinstein, W. D.*, 1987, *1986*, pp. 172–221. [G: U.K.]

Rubinstein, W. D. Elites and the Wealthy in Modern British History: Introduction. *Rubinstein, W. D.*, 1987, pp. 1–14. [G: U.K.]

Rubinstein, W. D. Entrepreneurial Effort and Entrepreneurial Success: Peak Wealth-Holding in Three Societies, 1850–1939. *Rubinstein, W. D.*, 1987, *1983*, pp. 119–42. [G: U.K.; U.S.; Australia]

Rubinstein, W. D. The Evolution of the British Honours System since the Mid–Nineteenth Century. *Rubinstein, W. D.*, 1987, pp. 222–61. [G: U.K.]

Rubinstein, W. D. The Victorian Middle Classes: Wealth, Occupation and Geography. *Rubinstein, W. D.*, 1987, *1977*, pp. 17–50.
[G: U.K.]

Rubinstein, W. D. Wealth, Elites and the Class Structure of Modern Britain. *Rubinstein, W. D.*, 1987, pp. 51–82. [G: U.K.]

Saraceno, Pasquale. La questione meridionale nel 1987. (The "Southern Question" Today. With English summary.) *Ricerche Econ.*, Apr.-June 1987, *41*(2), pp. 163–73. [G: Italy]

Schick, Irvin C. and Tonak, E. Ahmet. Turkey in Transition: Conclusion. *Schick, I. C. and Tonak, E. A., eds.*, 1987, pp. 365–78.
[G: Turkey]

Shapiro, J. C. On the Accuracy of Economic Observations of *Chto Takoe SSSR* in Historical Retrospect. *Comp. Econ. Stud.*, Fall 1987, *29*(3), pp. 45–69.

Street, Donald R. The Economic Societies: Springboard to the Spanish Enlightenment. *J. Europ. Econ. Hist.*, Winter 1987, *16*(3), pp. 569–85. [G: Spain]

Timur, Taner. The Ottoman Heritage. *Schick, I. C. and Tonak, E. A., eds.*, 1987, pp. 3–26.
[G: Turkey]

Tucci, Ugo. Venetian Ship-Owners in the XVIth Century. *J. Europ. Econ. Hist.*, Fall 1987, *16*(2), pp. 277–96. [G: Italy]

Vandenbroeke, Christian. The Regional Economy of Flanders and Industrial Modernization in the Eighteenth Century: A Discussion. *J. Europ. Econ. Hist.*, Spring 1987, *16*(1), pp. 149–70. [G: Flanders]

Wallerstein, Immanuel; Decdeli, Hale and Kasaba, Reşat. The Incorporation of the Ottoman Empire into the World-Economy. *Islamoglu-Inan, H., ed.*, 1987, pp. 88–97.
[G: Ottoman Empire]

Webb, Steven B. The German Inflation and Foreign Business Cycles, 1920–1922. *Exploration Econ. Hist.*, October 1987, *24*(4), pp. 409–33.
[G: W. Germany]

White, Lawrence H. Accounting for Non-interest-Bearing Currency: A Critique of the Legal Restrictions Theory of Money. *J. Money, Credit, Banking*, November 1987, *19*(4), pp. 448–56.

Williamson, Jeffrey G. Debating the British Industrial Revolution. *Exploration Econ. Hist.*, July 1987, *24*(3), pp. 269–92. [G: U.S.]

0441 History of Product Prices and Markets

Åström, Sven-Erik. Northeastern Europe's Timber Trade between the Napoleonic and Crimean Wars: A Preliminary Survey. *Scand. Econ. Hist. Rev.*, 1987, *35*(2), pp. 170–77.
[G: Finland; U.S.S.R.]

Broadberry, Stephen N. Cheap Money and the Housing Boom in Interwar Britain: An Econometric Appraisal. *Manchester Sch. Econ. Soc. Stud.*, December 1987, *55*(4), pp. 378–91.
[G: U.K.]

Broadberry, Stephen N. Purchasing Power Parity and the Pound–Dollar Rate in the 1930s. *Economica*, February 1987, *54*(213), pp. 69–78.
[G: U.S.; U.K.]

Burmeister, Edwin and Wall, Kent D. Unobserved Rational Expectations and the German Hyperinflation with Endogenous Money Supply. *Int. Econ. Rev.*, February 1987, *28*(1), pp. 15–32. [G: Germany]

Chapman, S. D. Investment Groups in India and South Africa [British-based Investment Groups before 1914]. *Econ. Hist. Rev., 2nd Ser.*, May 1987, *40*(2), pp. 275–80. [G: U.K.]

Christiano, Lawrence J. Cagan's Model of Hyperinflation under Rational Expectations. *Int. Econ. Rev.*, February 1987, *28*(1), pp. 33–49.
[G: Germany]

Corley, T. A. B. Interactions between the British and American Patent Medicine Industries

1708–1914. *Atack, J., ed.*, 1987, pp. 111–29. [G: U.S.; U.K.]

Davis, Lance E.; Gallman, Robert E. and Hutchins, Teresa D. Technology, Productivity, and Profits: British–American Whaling Competition in the North Atlantic, 1816–1842. *Oxford Econ. Pap.*, December 1987, 39(4), pp. 738–59. [G: U.S.; U.K.]

Dellheim, Charles. The Creation of a Company Culture: *Cadburys*, 1861–1931. *Amer. Hist. Rev.*, February 1987, 92(1), pp. 13–44. [G: U.K.]

Di Vittorio, Antonio. A Multinational Bank: The Bank of Rome. *J. Europ. Econ. Hist.*, Fall 1987, 16(2), pp. 389–98. [G: Italy]

Feldenkirchen, Wilfried. Big Business in Interwar Germany: Organizational Innovation at Vereinigte Stahlwerke, IG Farben, and Siemens. *Bus. Hist. Rev.*, Autumn 1987, 61(3), pp. 417–51.

Fenoaltea, Stefano. Construction in Italy, 1861–1913. *Rivista Storia Econ.*, S.S., Int. Issue, 1987, 4, pp. 21–53. [G: Italy]

Foreman-Peck, J. S. Natural Monopoly and Railway Policy in the Nineteenth Century. *Oxford Econ. Pap.*, December 1987, 39(4), pp. 699–718. [G: U.K.]

Franco, Gustavo H. B. The Rentenmark "Miracle." *Rivista Storia Econ.*, S.S., Int. Issue, 1987, 4, pp. 96–117. [G: W. Germany]

Habakkuk, H. J. The Agrarian History of England and Wales: Regional Farming Systems and Agrarian Change, 1640–1750. *Econ. Hist. Rev.*, 2nd Ser., May 1987, 40(2), pp. 281–96. [G: U.K.]

Harvey, Charles and Taylor, Peter. Mineral Wealth and Economic Development: Foreign Direct Investment in Spain, 1851–1913. *Econ. Hist. Rev.*, 2nd Ser., May 1987, 40(2), pp. 185–207. [G: Spain]

Hausman, William J. The English Coastal Coal Trade, 1691–1910: How Rapid Was Productivity Growth? [Total Factor Productivity in the English Shipping Industry: The North-east Coal Trade, 1700–1850]. *Econ. Hist. Rev.*, 2nd Ser., November 1987, 40(4), pp. 588–96. [G: U.K.]

Heikkinen, Sakari and Hjerppe, Riitta. The Growth of Finnish Industry in 1860–1913. Causes and Linkages. *J. Europ. Econ. Hist.*, Fall 1987, 16(2), pp. 227–44. [G: Finland]

Heim, Carol E. R&D, Defense, and Spatial Divisions of Labor in Twentieth-Century Britain. *J. Econ. Hist.*, June 1987, 47(2), pp. 365–78. [G: U.K.]

Hennart, Jean-Francois. Transaction Costs and the Multinational Enterprise: The Case of Tin. *Atack, J., ed.*, 1987, pp. 147–59. [G: U.K.]

Hoke, Donald. British and American Horology: Time to Test Factor-Substitution Models. *J. Econ. Hist.*, June 1987, 47(2), pp. 321–27. [G: U.S.; U.K.]

Klovland, Jan Tore. The Demand for Money in the United Kingdom, 1875–1913. *Oxford Bull. Econ. Statist.*, August 1987, 49(3), pp. 251–71. [G: U.K.]

Lazonick, William. Stubborn Mules: Some Comments [New Evidence of the Stubborn English Mule and the Cotton Industry, 1878–1920]. *Econ. Hist. Rev.*, 2nd Ser., February 1987, 40(1), pp. 80–86. [G: U.K.]

Lloyd-Jones, Roger. Innovation, Industrial Structure and the Long Wave: The British Economy c. 1873–1914. *J. Europ. Econ. Hist.*, Fall 1987, 16(2), pp. 315–53. [G: U.K.]

Lyons, John S. Powerloom Profitability and Steam Power Costs: Britain in the 1830s. *Exploration Econ. Hist.*, October 1987, 24(4), pp. 392–408. [G: U.K.]

Malanima, Paolo. Pisa and the Trade Routes to the Near East in the Late Middle Ages. *J. Europ. Econ. Hist.*, Fall 1987, 16(2), pp. 335–56. [G: Italy]

Marcuzzo, Maria Cristina and Rosselli, Annalisa. Profitability in the International Gold Market in the Early History of the Gold Standard. *Economica*, August 1987, 54(215), pp. 367–80. [G: U.K.]

Martellaro, Joseph A. The Nineteenth Century Development of the Russian Petroleum Industry. *Rivista Int. Sci. Econ. Com.*, August 1987, 34(8), pp. 777–92. [G: U.S.S.R.]

Mate, Mavis. Pastoral Farming in South-east England in the Fifteenth Century. *Econ. Hist. Rev.*, 2nd Ser., November 1987, 40(4), pp. 523–36. [G: U.K.]

Matthews, Derek. The Technical Transformation of the Late Nineteenth-Century Gas Industry. *J. Econ. Hist.*, December 1987, 47(4), pp. 967–80. [G: U.K.]

McNeill, William H. The Eccentricity of Wheels, or Eurasian Transportation in Historical Perspective. *Amer. Hist. Rev.*, December 1987, 92(5), pp. 1111–26.

Mendoza, Antonio Gómez. Oligopoly and Economic Efficiency: Portland Cement in Spain (1899–1935). *Rivista Storia Econ.*, S.S., Int. Issue, 1987, 4, pp. 76–95. [G: Spain]

Millward, Robert and Ward, Robert. The Costs of Public and Private Gas Enterprises in Late 19th Century Britain. *Oxford Econ. Pap.*, December 1987, 39(4), pp. 719–37. [G: U.K.]

Murat, Çizakça. Price History and the Bursa Silk Industry: A Study in Ottoman Industrial Decline, 1550–1650. *Islamoglu-Inan, H., ed.*, 1987, 1980, pp. 247–61 [G: Ottoman Empire]

Nguyen, Duc Tin and Rose, M. Demand for Tea in the UK 1874–1938: An Econometric Study. *J. Devel. Stud.*, October 1987, 24(1), pp. 43–59. [G: U.K.]

Nordvik, Helge W. The Bergen Shipping Industry in the 19th and 20th Centuries. *Scand. Econ. Hist. Rev.*, 1987, 35(1), pp. 130–34. [G: Norway]

Nye, John Vincent. Firm Size and Economic Backwardness: A New Look at the French Industrialization Debate. *J. Econ. Hist.*, September 1987, 47(3), pp. 649–69. [G: France]

Okyar, Osman. A New Look at the Problem of Economic Growth in the Ottoman Empire

(1800–1914). *J. Europ. Econ. Hist.*, Spring 1987, *16*(1), pp. 7–49. [G: Ottoman Empire]

Price, Jacob M. and Clemens, Paul G. E. A Revolution of Scale in Overseas Trade: British Firms in the Chesapeake Trade, 1675–1775. *J. Econ. Hist.*, March 1987, *47*(1), pp. 1–43.
[G: U.S.; U.K.]

Riden, Philip. An English Factor at Stockholm in the 1680's. *Scand. Econ. Hist. Rev.*, 1987, *35*(2), pp. 191–207. [G: U.K.; Sweden]

Saxonhouse, Gary R. and Wright, Gavin. Stubborn Mules and Vertical Integration: The Disappearing Constraint? [New Evidence of the Stubborn English Mule and the Cotton Industry, 1878–1920]. *Econ. Hist. Rev.*, 2nd Ser., February 1987, *40*(1), pp. 87–94. [G: U.K.]

Subrahmanyam, Sanjay. "Um bom Homem de Tratar": Piero Strozzi, a Florentine in Portuguese Asia, 1510–1522. *J. Europ. Econ. Hist.*, Winter 1987, *16*(3), pp. 511–26. [G: Italy; Portugal]

Tignor, Robert. British Textile Companies and the Egyptian Economy. *Atack, J., ed.*, 1987, pp. 53–67. [G: U.K.; Egypt]

Turnbull, Gerard. Canals, Coal and Regional Growth during the Industrial Revolution. *Econ. Hist. Rev.*, 2nd Ser., November 1987, *40*(4), pp. 537–60. [G: U.K.]

Turner, Michael. Towards an Agricultural Prices Index for Ireland 1850–1914. *Econ. Soc. Rev.*, January 1987, *18*(2), pp. 123–36.
[G: Ireland]

Turrell, Robert Vicat and Van-Helten, Jean Jacques. The Investment Group: The Missing Link in British Overseas Expansion before 1914? [British-based Investment Groups before 1914]. *Econ. Hist. Rev.*, 2nd Ser., May 1987, *40*(2), pp. 267–74. [G: U.K.]

Ville, Simon. Defending Productivity Growth in the English Coal Trade during the Eighteenth and Nineteenth Centuries. *Econ. Hist. Rev.*, 2nd Ser., November 1987, *40*(4), pp. 597–602.
[G: U.K.]

0442 History of Factor Prices and Markets

Ashworth, John. The Relationship between Capitalism and Humanitarianism. *Amer. Hist. Rev.*, October 1987, *92*(4), pp. 813–28. [G: U.K.; U.S.]

Beenstock, Michael. Real Wages and Unemployment in the 1930s: A Reply [Wages and Unemployment in Interwar Britain]. *Nat. Inst. Econ. Rev.*, February 1987, (119), pp. 76–78.
[G: U.K.]

Benedictow, O. J. Morbidity in Historical Plague Epidemics. *Population Stud.*, November 1987, *41*(3), pp. 401–31. [G: Europe]

Berg, Maxine. Women's Work, Mechanisation and the Early Phases of Industrialisation in England. *Joyce, P., ed.*, 1987, pp. 64–98.
[G: U.K.]

Bessel, Richard. Unemployment and Demobilisation in Germany after the First World War. *Evans, R. J. and Geary, D., eds.*, 1987, pp. 23–43. [G: Germany]

Bigazzi, Duccio. Management Strategies in the Italian Car Industry 1906–1945: Fiat and Alfa Romeo. *Tolliday, S. and Zeitlin, J., eds.*, 1987, pp. 76–96. [G: Italy]

Booth, Alan. The War and the White Paper. *Glynn, S. and Booth, A., eds.*, 1987, pp. 175–95. [G: U.K.]

Booth, Alan. Unemployment and Interwar Politics. *Glynn, S. and Booth, A., eds.*, 1987, pp. 43–56. [G: U.K.]

Boserup, Ester. Population and Technology in Preindustrial Europe. *Population Devel. Rev.*, December 1987, *13*(4), pp. 691–701.
[G: Europe]

Botham, F. W. and Hunt, E. H. Wages in Britain during the Industrial Revolution. *Econ. Hist. Rev.*, 2nd Ser., August 1987, *40*(3), pp. 380–99. [G: U.K.]

Capie, Forrest H. Unemployment and Real Wages. *Glynn, S. and Booth, A., eds.*, 1987, pp. 57–69. [G: U.K.]

Carrington, Selwyn H. H. The American Revolution and the British West Indies' Economy. *Solow, B. L. and Engerman, S. L., eds.*, 1987, pp. 135–61. [G: Caribbean; U.K.]

Clark, Gregory. Productivity Growth without Technical Change in European Agriculture before 1850. *J. Econ. Hist.*, June 1987, *47*(2), pp. 419–32. [G: Europe; U.S.]

Crafts, N. F. R. Long-term Unemployment in Britain in the 1930s. *Econ. Hist. Rev.*, 2nd Ser., August 1987, *40*(3), pp. 418–32.
[G: U.K.]

Davis, David Brion. Reflections on Abolitionism and Ideological Hegemony. *Amer. Hist. Rev.*, October 1987, *92*(4), pp. 797–812. [G: U.K.; U.S.]

Deacon, Alan. Systems of Interwar Unemployment Relief. *Glynn, S. and Booth, A., eds.*, 1987, pp. 31–42. [G: U.K.]

Eichengreen, Barry. Unemployment in Interwar Britain: Dole or Doldrums? *Oxford Econ. Pap.*, December 1987, *39*(4), pp. 597–623.
[G: U.K.]

Eichengreen, Barry and Portes, Richard. The Anatomy of Financial Crises. *Portes, R. and Swoboda, A. K., eds.*, 1987, pp. 10–58.
[G: Global]

Evans, Richard J. The Experience of Unemployment in the Weimar Republic. *Evans, R. J. and Geary, D., eds.*, 1987, pp. 1–22.
[G: Germany]

Evans, Richard J. and Geary, Dick. The German Unemployed: Experiences and Consequences of Mass Unemployment from the Weimar Republic to the Third Reich: Preface. *Evans, R. J. and Geary, D., eds.*, 1987, pp. xiii–xviii.
[G: Germany]

Faroqhi, Suraiya. Notes on the Production of Cotton and Cotton Cloth in Sixteenth- and Seventeenth-Century Anatolia. *Islamoglu-Inan, H., ed.*, 1987, *1979*, pp. 262–70.
[G: Ottoman Empire]

Fischer, Lewis R. and Nordvik, Helge W. From Namsos to Halden: Myths and Realities in the History of Norwegian Seamen's Wages, 1850–

1914. *Scand. Econ. Hist. Rev.*, 1987, 35(1), pp. 41–66. **[G: Norway]**

Garside, W. R. The Real Wage Debate and British Interwar Unemployment. *Glynn, S. and Booth, A., eds.*, 1987, pp. 70–81. **[G: U.K.]**

Geary, Dick. Unemployment and Working-Class Solidarity: The Germany Experience 1929–33. *Evans, R. J. and Geary, D., eds.*, 1987, pp. 261–80. **[G: Germany]**

Gemmill, Robert F. The Anatomy of Financial Crises: Discussion. *Portes, R. and Swoboda, A. K., eds.*, 1987, pp. 58–61. **[G: Global]**

Glynn, Sean. The Road to Full Employment: The Scale and Nature of the Problem. *Glynn, S. and Booth, A., eds.*, 1987, pp. 3–16.
[G: U.K.]

Haskell, Thomas L. Convention and Hegemonic Interest in the Debate over Antislavery: A Reply. *Amer. Hist. Rev.*, October 1987, 92(4), pp. 829–78. **[G: U.S.; U.K.]**

Hennock, E. P. The Measurement of Urban Poverty: From the Metropolis to the Nation, 1880–1920. *Econ. Hist. Rev., 2nd Ser.*, May 1987, 40(2), pp. 208–27. **[G: U.K.]**

Hirsch, Barry T. and Hausman, William J. Labouring: A Reply [Labour Productivity in the British and South Wales Coal Industry, 1874–1914]. *Economica*, November 1987, 54(216), pp. 525. **[G: U.K.]**

Humphries, Jane. "…The Most Free From Objection…" The Sexual Division of Labor and Women's Work in Nineteenth-Century England. *J. Econ. Hist.*, December 1987, 47(4), pp. 929–49. **[G: U.K.]**

Jackson, R. V. The Structure of Pay in Nineteenth-century Britain. *Econ. Hist. Rev., 2nd Ser.*, November 1987, 40(4), pp. 561–70.
[G: U.K.]

Johansson, S. Ryan. Status Anxiety and Demographic Contraction of Privileged Populations. *Population Devel. Rev.*, September 1987, 13(3), pp. 439–70. **[G: W. Europe]**

Jones, S. R. H. Technology, Transaction Costs, and the Transition to Factory Production in the British Silk Industry, 1700–1870. *J. Econ. Hist.*, March 1987, 47(1), pp. 71–96.
[G: U.K.]

Joyce, Patrick. The Historical Meanings of Work. *Joyce, P., ed.*, 1987, pp. 1–30. **[G: U.K.]**

Komlos, John. Financial Innovation and the Demand for Money in Austria–Hungary, 1867–1913. *J. Europ. Econ. Hist.*, Winter 1987, 16(3), pp. 587–605. **[G: Austria–Hungary]**

Kramer, Helgard. Frankfurt's Working Women: Scapegoats or Winners of the Great Depression? *Evans, R. J. and Geary, D., eds.*, 1987, pp. 108–41. **[G: Germany]**

Lutz, Wolfgang. Factors Associated with the Finnish Fertility Decline since 1776. *Population Stud.*, November 1987, 41(3), pp. 463–82.
[G: Finland]

Matthews, Kent G. P. Unemployment in Interwar Britain: An Equilibrium Approach. *Bull. Econ. Res.*, April 1987, 39(2), pp. 151–69.
[G: U.K.]

McCaffray, Susan P. Origins of Labor Policy in

the Russian Coal and Steel Industry, 1874–1900. *J. Econ. Hist.*, December 1987, 47(4), pp. 951–65. **[G: Russia]**

McClelland, Keith. Time to Work, Time to Live: Some Aspects of Work and the Re-formation of Class in Britain, 1850–1880. *Joyce, P., ed.*, 1987, pp. 180–209. **[G: U.K.]**

Mirowski, Philip. What Do Markets Do? Efficiency Tests of the 18th-Century London Stock Market. *Exploration Econ. Hist.*, April 1987, 24(2), pp. 107–29. **[G: U.K.]**

Morell, Mats. Eli F. Heckscher, the 'Food Budgets' and Swedish Food Consumption from the 16th to the 19th Century: The Summing Up and Conclusions of a Long Debate. *Scand. Econ. Hist. Rev.*, 1987, 35(1), pp. 67–107.
[G: Sweden]

Mulert, Jürgen. Wealth Sharing and Capital Formation for Employees of the Robert Bosch Company between 1886 and 1945. *Pohl, H. and Rudolph, B., eds.*, 1987, pp. 41–64.
[G: Germany]

Neal, Larry. The Integration and Efficiency of the London and Amsterdam Stock Markets in the Eighteenth Century. *J. Econ. Hist.*, March 1987, 47(1), pp. 97–115. **[G: U.K.; Netherlands]**

Nicholas, Stephen and Shergold, Peter R. Human Capital and the Pre-famine Irish Emigration to England. *Exploration Econ. Hist.*, April 1987, 24(2), pp. 158–77. **[G: U.K.; Ireland]**

Nummela, Ilkka and Laitinen, Erkki K. Distribution of Income in Kuopio 1880–1910. *Scand. Econ. Hist. Rev.*, 1987, 35(3), pp. 237–53.
[G: Finland]

Peukert, Detlev. The Lost Generation: Youth Unemployment at the End of the Weimar Republic. *Evans, R. J. and Geary, D., eds.*, 1987, pp. 172–93. **[G: Germany]**

Pierenkemper, Toni. The Standard of Living and Employment in Germany, 1850–1980: An Overview. *J. Europ. Econ. Hist.*, Spring 1987, 16(1), pp. 51–73. **[G: Germany]**

Piore, Michael J. Historical Perspectives and the Interpretation of Unemployment. *J. Econ. Lit.*, December 1987, 25(4), pp. 1834–50.
[G: U.S.; Europe]

Pollard, Sidney. Comment on Peter Temin's Comment [Capital Exports: 1870–1914: Harmful or Beneficial?]. *Econ. Hist. Rev., 2nd Ser.*, August 1987, 40(3), pp. 459–60. **[G: U.K.]**

Quataert, Donald. A Provisional Report Concerning the Impact of European Capital on Ottoman Port Workers, 1880–1909. *Islamoglu-Inan, H., ed.*, 1987, 1983, pp. 300–308.
[G: Ottoman Empire]

Richardson, David. The Costs of Survival: The Transport of Slaves in the Middle Passage and the Profitability of the 18th-Century British Slave Trade. *Exploration Econ. Hist.*, April 1987, 24(2), pp. 178–96. **[G: U.K.]**

Richardson, David. The Slave Trade, Sugar, and British Economic Growth, 1748–1776. *Solow, B. L. and Engerman, S. L., eds.*, 1987, pp. 103–33. **[G: U.K.; Caribbean]**

Roche, William K. Leisure, Insecurity and Union

Policy in Britain: A Critical Extension of Biene-feld's Theory of Hours Rounds. *Brit. J. Ind. Relat.*, March 1987, *25*(1), pp. 1–17.
[G: U.K.]

Rosenberg, William G. and Koenker, Diane P. The Limits of Formal Protest: Worker Activism and Social Polarization in Petrograd and Moscow, March to October, 1917. *Amer. Hist. Rev.*, April 1987, *92*(2), pp. 296–326.
[G: U.S.S.R.]

Rosenhaft, Eve. The Unemployed in the Neighbourhood: Social Dislocation and Political Mobilisation in Germany 1929–33. *Evans, R. J. and Geary, D., eds.*, 1987, pp. 194–227.
[G: Germany]

Rubinstein, W. D. The Geographical Distribution of Middle-Class Income in Britain, 1800–1914. *Rubinstein, W. D.*, 1987, pp. 85–118.
[G: U.K.]

Rule, John. The Property of Skill in the Period of Manufacture. *Joyce, P., ed.*, 1987, pp. 99–118.
[G: U.K.]

Rybczynski, Tad M. The Anatomy of Financial Crises: Discussion. *Portes, R. and Swoboda, A. K., eds.*, 1987, pp. 61–66. [G: Global]

Schwartz, Anna J. A Century of British Market Interest Rates, 1874–1975. *Schwartz, A. J.*, 1987, *1981*, pp. 152–64. [G: U.K.]

Scott, Joan W. 'L'ouvrière! Mot impie, sordide . . .': Women Workers in the Discourse of French Political Economy, 1840–1860. *Joyce, P., ed.*, 1987, pp. 119–42. [G: France]

Screpanti, Ernesto. Long Cycles in Strike Activity: An Empirical Investigation. *Brit. J. Ind. Relat.*, March 1987, *25*(1), pp. 99–124.
[G: France; Italy; U.K.; U.S.; W. Germany]

Sella, Domenico. Household, Land Tenure, and Occupation in North Italy in the Late Sixteenth Century. *J. Europ. Econ. Hist.*, Winter 1987, *16*(3), pp. 487–509. [G: Italy]

Sonenscher, Michael. Mythical Work: Workshop Production and the *Compagnonnages* of Eighteenth-Century France. *Joyce, P., ed.*, 1987, pp. 31–63. [G: France]

St. Seidenfus, Hellmuth. From the "Rhine–Main–Danube Canal" to the "Main–Danube Connection." *Tismer, J. F.; Ambler, J. and Symons, L., eds.*, 1987, pp. 429–48.
[G: W. Germany; E. Europe]

Temin, Peter. Capital Exports, 1870–1914: An Alternative Model: Comment [Capital Exports: 1870–1914: Harmful or Beneficial?]. *Econ. Hist. Rev., 2nd Ser.*, August 1987, *40*(3), pp. 453–58. [G: U.K.]

Temperley, Howard. Eric Williams and Abolition: The Birth of a New Orthodoxy. *Solow, B. L. and Engerman, S. L., eds.*, 1987, pp. 229–57.

Thomas, W. A. The Evolution of a Capital Market: The Case of Ireland. *J. Europ. Econ. Hist.*, Winter 1987, *16*(3), pp. 527–60. [G: Ireland]

Tolliday, Steven. Management and Labour in Britain 1896–1939. *Tolliday, S. and Zeitlin, J., eds.*, 1987, pp. 29–56. [G: U.K.]

Treble, John G. Sliding Scales and Conciliation Boards: Risk-Sharing in the Late 19th Century

British Coal Industry. *Oxford Econ. Pap.*, December 1987, *39*(4), pp. 679–98. [G: U.K.]

Van de Casteele-Schweitzer, Sylvie. Management and Labour in France 1914–39. *Tolliday, S. and Zeitlin, J., eds.*, 1987, pp. 57–75.
[G: France]

Wardley, Peter. Labouring over Productivity Estimates: A Comment on Hirsch and Hausman's Model of Coal Miners' Productivity, 1874–1914 [Labour Productivity in the British and South Wales Coal Industry, 1874–1914]. *Economica*, November 1987, *54*(216), pp. 521–24. [G: U.K.]

Weisser, Michael R. Rural Crisis and Rural Credit in XVIIth-Century Castile. *J. Europ. Econ. Hist.*, Fall 1987, *16*(2), pp. 297–313.
[G: Spain]

Whipp, Richard. 'A Time to Every Purpose': An Essay on Time and Work. *Joyce, P., ed.*, 1987, pp. 210–36. [G: U.K.]

Whiteside, Noel. The Social Consequences of Interwar Unemployment. *Glynn, S. and Booth, A., eds.*, 1987, pp. 17–30. [G: U.K.]

Williamson, Jeffrey G. Did English Factor Markets Fail during the Industrial Revolution? *Oxford Econ. Pap.*, December 1987, *39*(4), pp. 641–78. [G: U.K.]

Woods, R. I. Approaches to the Fertility Transition in Victorian England. *Population Stud.*, July 1987, *41*(2), pp. 283–311. [G: U.K.]

Wrege, Charles D.; Greenwood, Ronald G. and Hata, Sakae. The International Management Institute and Political Opposition to Its Efforts in Europe, 1925–1934. *Atack, J., ed.*, 1987, pp. 249–65. [G: Europe; U.S.]

Zeitlin, Jonathan. From Labour History to the History of Industrial Relations. *Econ. Hist. Rev., 2nd Ser.*, May 1987, *40*(2), pp. 159–84.
[G: U.K.]

Zimmerman, William. Mobilized Participation and the Nature of the Soviet Dictatorship. *Millar, J. R., ed.*, 1987, pp. 332–53.
[G: U.S.S.R.]

Zolberg, Aristide R. Wanted But Not Welcome: Alien Labor in Western Development. *Alonso, W., ed.*, 1987, pp. 36–73. [G: Europe; N. America]

0443 History of Public Economic Policy (all levels)

Ahmed, Shaghil. Government Spending, the Balance of Trade and the Terms of Trade in British History. *J. Monet. Econ.*, September 1987, *20*(2), pp. 195–220. [G: U.K.]

Barro, Robert J. Government Spending, Interest Rates, Prices, and Budget Deficits in the United Kingdom, 1701–1918. *J. Monet. Econ.*, September 1987, *20*(2), pp. 221–47.
[G: U.K.]

Booth, Alan. Britain in the 1930s: A Managed Economy? *Econ. Hist. Rev., 2nd Ser.*, November 1987, *40*(4), pp. 499–522. [G: U.K.]

Booth, Alan. The War and the White Paper. *Glynn, S. and Booth, A., eds.*, 1987, pp. 175–95. [G: U.K.]

Booth, Alan. Unemployment and Interwar Politics. *Glynn, S. and Booth, A., eds.*, 1987, pp. 43–56. **[G: U.K.]**

Brandt, Harm-Hinrich. Public Finances of Neo-absolutism in Austria in the 1850s: Integration and Modernisation. *Witt, P.-C., ed.*, 1987, pp. 81–109. **[G: Austria]**

Brems, Hans. En disputats om finanspolitiske ideer i Danmark 1930–1945. (With English summary.) *Nationaløkon. Tidsskr.*, 1987, *125*(3), pp. 287–98. **[G: Denmark]**

Cagan, Phillip. A Compensated Dollar: Better or More Likely Than Gold? *Dorn, J. A. and Schwartz, A. J., eds.*, 1987, pp. 261–77. **[G: U.S.; U.K.]**

Day, John. Money and Credit in Medieval and Renaissance Italy. *Day, J.*, 1987, pp. 141–61. **[G: Italy]**

Delbeke, Jos. Long-term Trends in the Belgian Money Supply, 1877–1984. *Vasko, T., ed.*, 1987, pp. 313–25. **[G: Belgium]**

Dimsdale, N. H. Keynes on British Budgetary Policy 1914–46. *Boskin, M. J.; Fleming, J. S. and Gorini, S., eds.*, 1987, pp. 208–33. **[G: U.K.]**

Dornbusch, Rudiger. Lessons from the German Inflation Experience of the 1920s. *[Modigliani, F.]*, 1987, pp. 337–66. **[G: Germany]**

Egginton, Don M. A Historical Analysis of Labour Supply Incentives. *Beenstock, M., et al.*, 1987, pp. 76–123. **[G: U.K.]**

Eichengreen, Barry. Conducting the International Orchestra: Bank of England Leadership under the Classical Gold Standard. *J. Int. Money Finance*, March 1987, *6*(1), pp. 5–29. **[G: U.K.]**

Fischer, Wolfram. Swings between Protection and Free Trade in History. *Giersch, H., ed.*, 1987, pp. 20–32. **[G: U.S.; W. Europe]**

Forbes, Neil. London Banks, the German Standstill Agreements, and 'Economic Appeasement' in the 1930s. *Econ. Hist. Rev., 2nd Ser.*, November 1987, *40*(4), pp. 571–87. **[G: U.K.]**

Foreman-Peck, J. S. Natural Monopoly and Railway Policy in the Nineteenth Century. *Oxford Econ. Pap.*, December 1987, *39*(4), pp. 699–718. **[G: U.K.]**

Glynn, Sean. Real Policy Options. *Glynn, S. and Booth, A., eds.*, 1987, pp. 154–74. **[G: U.K.]**

Grampp, William D. Britain and Free Trade: In Whose Interest? *Public Choice*, October 1987, *55*(3), pp. 245–56. **[G: U.K.]**

Grampp, William D. How Britain Turned to Free Trade. *Bus. Hist. Rev.*, Spring 1987, *61*(1), pp. 86–112. **[G: U.K.]**

Gray, Robert. The Languages of Factory Reform in Britain, c. 1830–1860. *Joyce, P., ed.*, 1987, pp. 143–79. **[G: U.K.]**

Harvey, Elizabeth. Youth Unemployment and the State: Public Policies towards Unemployed Youth in Hamburg during the World Economic Crisis. *Evans, R. J. and Geary, D., eds.*, 1987, pp. 142–71. **[G: Germany]**

Hatton, T. J. The Outlines of a Keynesian Solution. *Glynn, S. and Booth, A., eds.*, 1987, pp. 82–94. **[G: U.K.]**

Heim, Carol E. and Mirowski, Philip. Interest Rates and Crowding-Out during Britain's Industrial Revolution. *J. Econ. Hist.*, March 1987, *47*(1), pp. 117–39. **[G: U.K.]**

Henderson, W. O. Friedrich List and England. *Jahr. Nationalökon. Statist.*, October 1987, *203*(5–6), pp. 532–46. **[G: U.K.; Germany]**

Hodne, Fritz and Basberg, Bjørn. Public Infrastructure, Its Indispensability for Economic Growth: The Case of Norwegian Public Health Measures 1850–1940. *Scand. Econ. Hist. Rev.*, 1987, *35*(2), pp. 145–69. **[G: Norway]**

Holtfrerich, Carl-Ludwig. The Modernisation of the Tax System in the First World War and the Great Inflation, 1914–23. *Witt, P.-C., ed.*, 1987, pp. 125–35. **[G: Germany]**

Homburg, Heidrun. From Unemployment Insurance to Compulsory Labour: The Transformation of the Benefit System in Germany 1927–33. *Evans, R. J. and Geary, D., eds.*, 1987, pp. 73–107. **[G: Germany]**

Howson, Susan. The Origins of Cheaper Money, 1945–7. *Econ. Hist. Rev., 2nd Ser.*, August 1987, *40*(3), pp. 433–52. **[G: U.K.]**

Keyder, Çağlar. The Political Economy of Turkish Democracy. *Schick, I. C. and Tonak, E. A., eds.*, 1987, pp. 27–65. **[G: Turkey]**

Kidd, Alan J. Historians or Polemicists? How the Webbs Wrote Their History of the English Poor Laws. *Econ. Hist. Rev., 2nd Ser.*, August 1987, *40*(3), pp. 400–417. **[G: U.K.]**

Kindleberger, Charles P. Belgium after World War II: An Experiment in Supply-Side Economics. *Kindleberger, C. P.*, 1987, pp. 230–44. **[G: Belgium]**

Kindleberger, Charles P. Excerpts from the Cleveland–Moore–Kindleberger Memorandum of 12 June 1947, on a European Recovery Program. *Kindleberger, C. P.*, 1987, pp. 1–24. **[G: U.S.; W. Europe]**

Kindleberger, Charles P. Financial Deregulation and Economic Performance: An Attempt to Relate European Financial History to Current LDC Issues. *[Diaz-Alejandro, C. F.]*, 1987, pp. 339–53. **[G: U.K.; France; W. Germany; Italy]**

Kindleberger, Charles P. Financial Deregulation and Economic Performance: An Attempt to Relate European Financial History to Current LDC Issues. *J. Devel. Econ.*, October 1987, *27*(1–2), pp. 339–53. **[G: U.K.; France; W. Germany; Italy]**

Kindleberger, Charles P. Germany and the Economic Recovery of Europe. *Kindleberger, C. P.*, 1987, *1949*, pp. 33–45. **[G: U.S.; W. Germany; W. Europe]**

Kindleberger, Charles P. Memorandum for the Files: Origins of the Marshall Plan. *Kindleberger, C. P.*, 1987, *1972*, pp. 25–32. **[G: U.S.; W. Europe]**

Kirby, M. W. The Policy Debate: Industrial Policy. *Glynn, S. and Booth, A., eds.*, 1987, pp. 125–39. **[G: U.K.]**

von Kruedener, Jürgen. The Franckenstein Paradox in the Intergovernmental Fiscal Relations of Imperial Germany. *Witt, P.-C., ed.*, 1987, pp. 111–23. **[G: Germany]**

Little, Ian M. D. Swings between Protection and Free Trade in History: Comment. *Giersch, H., ed.*, 1987, pp. 33–34.

Lowe, Rodney. The Policy Debate: Labour Policy. *Glynn, S. and Booth, A., eds.*, 1987, pp. 140–53. **[G: U.K.]**

MacKinnon, Mary. English Poor Law Policy and the Crusade against Outrelief. *J. Econ. Hist.*, September 1987, *47*(3), pp. 603–25.

Maier, Charles S. The Economics of Fascism and Nazism. *Maier, C. S.*, 1987, pp. 70–120. **[G: Italy; Germany]**

Middleton, Roger. Treasury Policy on Unemployment. *Glynn, S. and Booth, A., eds.*, 1987, pp. 109–24. **[G: U.K.]**

Mills, Geoffrey and Rockoff, Hugh. Compliance with Price Controls in the United States and the United Kingdom during World War II. *J. Econ. Hist.*, March 1987, *47*(1), pp. 197–213. **[G: U.S.; U.K.]**

Modigliani, Franco and Jappelli, Tullio. Fiscal Policy and Saving in Italy since 1860. *Boskin, M. J.; Fleming, J. S. and Gorini, S., eds.*, 1987, pp. 126–70. **[G: Italy]**

Niehuss, Merith. From Welfare Provision to Social Insurance: The Unemployment in Augsburg 1918–27. *Evans, R. J. and Geary, D., eds.*, 1987, pp. 44–72. **[G: Germany]**

Peden, G. C. The Policy Debate: Keynes. *Glynn, S. and Booth, A., eds.*, 1987, pp. 97–108. **[G: U.K.]**

Pullen, John M. William Anderson (fl. 1797–1832), on Banking, the Money Supply, and Public Expenditure: A Forgotten Interventionist. *Hist. Polit. Econ.*, Fall 1987, *19*(3), pp. 359–85.

Rohrlich, Paul Egon. Economic Culture and Foreign Policy: The Cognitive Analysis of Economic Policy Making. *Int. Organ.*, Winter 1987, *41*(1), pp. 61–92. **[G: U.K.]**

Rosen, Josef. Two Municipal Accounts: Frankfurt and Basel in 1428. *J. Europ. Econ. Hist.*, Fall 1987, *16*(2), pp. 363–88. **[G: Europe]**

Rubinstein, W. D. The End of 'Old Corruption' in Britain, 1780–1860. *Rubinstein, W. D.*, 1987, *1983*, pp. 265–303. **[G: U.K.]**

Serra, Enrico. Financial and Economic Factors in Foreign Policy: The Italian Example. *J. Europ. Econ. Hist.*, Winter 1987, *16*(3), pp. 607–20. **[G: Italy]**

Sommariva, Andrea and Tullio, Giuseppe. A Note on the Real Exchange Rate, Differential Productivity Growth and Protectionism in Gold Standard Germany, 1878–1913. *Weltwirtsch. Arch.*, 1987, *123*(2), pp. 354–62. **[G: W. Germany]**

Spaventa, Luigi. Lessons from the German Inflation Experience of the 1920s: Comments. *[Modigliani, F.]*, 1987, pp. 367–71. **[G: Germany]**

Sunar, Ilkay. State and Economy in the Ottoman Empire. *Islamoglu-Inan, H., ed.*, 1987, pp. 63–87. **[G: Ottoman Empire]**

Ullmann, Hans-Peter. The Emergence of Modern Public Debts in Bavaria and Baden between 1780 and 1820. *Witt, P.-C., ed.*, 1987, pp. 63–79. **[G: Germany]**

Westcott, Nicholas. Stabilizing Commodity Prices: State Control of Colonial Commodity Trade, 1930–1950. *Dewey, C., ed.*, 1987, pp. 262–87. **[G: U.S.; Europe]**

Williamson, Jeffrey G. Has Crowding Out Really Been Given a Fair Test? A Comment [Interest Rates and Crowding-Out during Britain's Industrial Revolution]. *J. Econ. Hist.*, March 1987, *47*(1), pp. 214–15. **[G: U.K.]**

Witt, Peter-Christian. History and Sociology of Public Finance—Problems and Topics. *Witt, P.-C., ed.*, 1987, pp. 1–18. **[G: Germany]**

Witt, Peter-Christian. Tax Policies, Tax Assessment and Inflation: Towards a Sociology of Public Finances in the German Inflation, 1914–23. *Witt, P.-C., ed.*, 1987, pp. 137–60. **[G: Germany]**

Wulff, Birgit. The Third Reich and the Unemployed: National Socialist Work-Creation Schemes in Hamburg 1933–4. *Evans, R. J. and Geary, D., eds.*, 1987, pp. 281–302. **[G: Germany]**

Yerasimos, Stéphane. The Monoparty Period. *Schick, I. C. and Tonak, E. A., eds.*, 1987, pp. 66–100. **[G: Turkey]**

045 Economic History: Asia

0450 General

Bakker, Hans. Class Relations in Java in the Nineteenth Century: A Weberian Perspective. *Can. J. Devel. Stud.*, 1987, *8*(1), pp. 137–56. **[G: Java]**

Bates, Crispin. Tribalism, Dependency and the Sub-regional Dynamics of Economic Change in Central India, 1820–1930. *Dewey, C., ed.*, 1987, pp. 105–25. **[G: India]**

Blumenthal, Tuvia. Depressions in Japan: The 1930s and the 1970s. *[Penrose, E. F.]*, 1987, pp. 68–82. **[G: Japan]**

Bronfenbrenner, Martin. Japan and Two World Economic Depressions. *[Penrose, E. F.]*, 1987, pp. 32–51. **[G: Japan]**

Dore, Ronald. How Fragile a Super State? *[Penrose, E. F.]*, 1987, pp. 83–110. **[G: Japan]**

French, Michael J. and Wilson, Thomas. Depression and Protection: The Early Thirties and the Early Eighties Compared. *[Penrose, E. F.]*, 1987, pp. 14–31. **[G: OECD]**

Habakkuk, H. J. The Historical Experience of the Basic Conditions of Economic Progress. *Dupriez, L. H., ed.*, 1987, pp. 85–102. **[G: U.S.; U.S.S.R.; W. Europe; Japan]**

Hanley, Susan B. How Well Did the Japanese Live in the Tokugawa Period? A Historian's Reappraisal. *Econ. Stud. Quart.*, December 1987, *38*(4), pp. 309–22. **[G: Japan]**

Hirshleifer, Jack. Disaster and Recovery: An Historical Survey. *Hirshleifer, J.*, 1987, *1963*, pp. 5–94. **[G: U.S.; Japan; W. Germany]**

Hjejle, Benedicte. Social Stratification in a Rice-Irrigated Economy: South Vizagapatam, 1870–1905. *Dewey, C., ed.*, 1987, pp. 126–54. **[G: India]**

Howe, Christopher. Japan's Economic Experience in China before the Establishment of the People's Republic of China: A Retrospective Balance-Sheet. *[Penrose, E. F.]*, 1987, pp. 155–77. **[G: Japan; China]**

Inalcik, Halil. When and How British Cotton Goods Invaded the Levant Markets. *Islamoglu-Inan, H., ed.*, 1987, pp. 374–83. **[G: Middle East]**

Joshi, P. C. Agrarian Retrogression under British Rule: The Colonial Legacy. *Joshi, P. C.*, 1987, pp. 3–15. **[G: India]**

Joshi, P. C. Colonial Modernisation and Agricultural Stagnation: The Case of Bengal under Colonial Impact. *Joshi, P. C.*, 1987, pp. 16–27. **[G: India]**

Joshi, P. C. Conflicting Pulls of Productivity and Employment: Contemporary Choices in the Light of Historical Experience. *Joshi, P. C.*, 1987, pp. 135–58. **[G: India; Japan]**

Joshi, P. C. Pre-independence Thinking on Agrarian Policy: Landlords versus Peasants as Agents of Agricultural Development. *Joshi, P. C.*, 1987, *1967*, pp. 28–45. **[G: India]**

Joshi, P. C. Technological Potentialities of Peasant Agriculture: East–West Parallels and Contrasts. *Joshi, P. C.*, 1987, pp. 159–89. **[G: Asia; W. Europe]**

Lehmann, Jean-Pierre. Variations on a Pan-Asianist Theme: The 'Special Relationship' between Japan and Thailand. *[Penrose, E. F.]*, 1987, pp. 178–201. **[G: Japan; Thailand]**

Mason, Mark. Foreign Direct Investment and Japanese Economic Development, 1899–1931. *Atack, J., ed.*, 1987, pp. 93–107. **[G: Japan]**

Nakamura, Takafusa. The Japanese Economy in the Interwar Period: A Brief Summary. *[Penrose, E. F.]*, 1987, pp. 52–67. **[G: Japan]**

Nish, Ian. Britain's View of the Japanese Economy in the Early Showa Period. *[Penrose, E. F.]*, 1987, pp. 135–48. **[G: Japan; U.K.]**

Nishikawa, Shunsaku. The Economy of Chōshū on the Eve of Industrialization. *Econ. Stud. Quart.*, December 1987, 38(4), pp. 323–37. **[G: Japan]**

Nove, Alec. Soviet–Japanese Relations, Past and Present. *[Penrose, E. F.]*, 1987, pp. 149–54. **[G: Japan; U.S.S.R.]**

Owen, Roger. The Silk-Reeling Industry of Mount Lebanon, 1840–1914: A Study of the Possibilities and Limitations of Factory Production in the Periphery. *Islamoglu-Inan, H., ed.*, 1987, *1984*, pp. 271–83. **[G: Lebanon]**

Penrose, Ernest Francis. Memoirs of Japan, 1925–30. *[Penrose, E. F.]*, 1987, pp. 6–13. **[G: Japan]**

Quataert, Donald. The Silk Industry of Bursa, 1880–1914. *Islamoglu-Inan, H., ed.*, 1987, pp. 284–99. **[G: Middle East]**

Rao, J. Mohan. Class Relations in an 'Asiatic' Regime. *Cambridge J. Econ.*, September 1987, 11(3), pp. 229–50. **[G: India]**

Reddy, M. Atchi. Rich Lands and Poor Lords: Temple Lands and Tenancy in Nellore District, 1860–1986. *Indian Econ. Soc. Hist. Rev.*, Jan.-Mar. 1987, 24(1), pp. 1–33. **[G: India]**

Sharma, R. R. Class and Social–Agrarian Transformation in Soviet Central Asia: A Historical–Cultural Context. *Gidadhubli, R. G., ed.*, 1987, pp. 116–36. **[G: U.S.S.R.]**

Shimizu, Hajime. *Nanshin-ron:* Its Turning Point in World War I. *Devel. Econ.*, December 1987, 25(4), pp. 386–402. **[G: Japan]**

Siddiqi, Majid Hayat. Bluff, Doubt and Fear: The Kheiri Brothers and the Colonial State, 1904–45. *Indian Econ. Soc. Hist. Rev.*, July-Sept. 1987, 24(3), pp. 233–63. **[G: India]**

Tuma, Elias H. Technology Transfer and Economic Development: Lessons of History. *J. Devel. Areas*, July 1987, 21(4), pp. 403–27. **[G: Middle East]**

Yasuba, Yasukichi. The Tokugawa Legacy: A Survey. *Econ. Stud. Quart.*, December 1987, 38(4), pp. 290–308. **[G: Japan]**

0451 History of Product Prices and Markets

Cochran, Sherman. Losing Money Abroad: The Swedish Match Company in China during the 1930s. *Atack, J., ed.*, 1987, pp. 83–91. **[G: China]**

Kako, Toshiyuki. Development of the Farm Machinery Industry in Japan: A Case Study of the Walking Type Tractor. *Hitotsubashi J. Econ.*, December 1987, 28(2), pp. 155–71. **[G: Japan]**

Kiyokawa, Yukihiko. Transplantation of the European Factory System and Adaptations in Japan: The Experience of the Tomioka Model Filature. *Hitotsubashi J. Econ.*, June 1987, 28(1), pp. 27–39. **[G: Japan]**

Kiyokawa, Yukihiko and Ishikawa, Shigeru. The Significance of Standardization in the Development of the Machine-Tool Industry: The Cases of Japan and China (Part 1). *Hitotsubashi J. Econ.*, December 1987, 28(2), pp. 123–54. **[G: China; Japan]**

Pauer, Erich. Traditional Technology and its Impact on Japan's Industry During the Early Period of the Industrial Revolution. *Econ. Stud. Quart.*, December 1987, 38(4), pp. 354–71. **[G: Japan]**

Prakash, Om. Opium Monopoly in India and Indonesia in the Eighteenth Century. *Indian Econ. Soc. Hist. Rev.*, Jan.-Mar. 1987, 24(1), pp. 63–80. **[G: India; Indonesia]**

Saith, Ashwani. Contrasting Experiences in Rural Industrialisation: Are the East Asian Successes Transferable? *Islam, R., ed.*, 1987, pp. 241–303. **[G: Japan; Taiwan; S. Korea]**

Subrahmanyam, Sanjay. Notes on the Sixteenth Century Bengal Trade. *Indian Econ. Soc. Hist. Rev.*, July-Sept. 1987, 24(3), pp. 265–89. **[G: India]**

Sugiyama, Shinya. The Impact of the Opening of the Ports on Domestic Japanese Industry: The Case of Silk and Cotton. *Econ. Stud. Quart.*, December 1987, 38(4), pp. 338–53. **[G: Japan]**

White, David L. Parsis in the Commercial World of Western India, 1700–1750. *Indian Econ. Soc. Hist. Rev.*, Apr.-June 1987, 24(2), pp. 183–203. **[G: India]**

0452 History of Factor Prices and Markets

Alam, M. Shahid. Some European Perceptions of Japan's Work-Ethos in the Tokugawa Era: A Limited Survey of Observations from the West's First Encounters Offers Parallels to Today's. *Amer. J. Econ. Soc.*, April 1987, *46*(2), pp. 229–43. **[G: Japan]**

Brandt, Loren. Farm Household Behavior, Factor Markets, and the Distributive Consequences of Commercialization in Early Twentieth-Century China. *J. Econ. Hist.*, September 1987, *47*(3), pp. 711–37. **[G: China]**

Gottschang, Thomas R. Economic Change, Disasters, and Migration: The Historical Case of Manchuria. *Econ. Develop. Cult. Change*, April 1987, *35*(3), pp. 461–90. **[G: China]**

Guha, Sumit. The Land Market in Upland Maharashtra c. 1820–1960—II. *Indian Econ. Soc. Hist. Rev.*, July-Sept. 1987, *24*(3), pp. 291–322. **[G: India]**

Guha, Sumit. The Land Market in Upland Maharashtra c. 1820–1960—I. *Indian Econ. Soc. Hist. Rev.*, Apr.-June 1987, *24*(2), pp. 117–44. **[G: India]**

Jones, Geoffrey. The Imperial Bank of Iran and Iranian Economic Development, 1890–1952. *Atack, J., ed.*, 1987, pp. 69–80. **[G: Iran]**

Kozlowski, Gregory C. Muslim Women and the Control of Property in North India. *Indian Econ. Soc. Hist. Rev.*, Apr.-June 1987, *24*(2), pp. 163–81. **[G: India]**

Krishnamurty, Sunanda. Real Wages of Agricultural Labourers in the Bombay Deccan, 1874–1922. *Indian Econ. Soc. Hist. Rev.*, Jan.-Mar. 1987, *24*(1), pp. 81–98. **[G: India]**

Owen, Roger. The Middle Eastern Factory as a Site for the Application of New Technology in the Nineteenth Century. *Dewey, C., ed.*, 1987, pp. 192–205. **[G: Middle East]**

Pant, Rashmi. The Cognitive Status of Caste in Colonial Ethnography: A Review of Some Literature on the North West Provinces and Oudh. *Indian Econ. Soc. Hist. Rev.*, Apr.-June 1987, *24*(2), pp. 145–62. **[G: India]**

Shlomowitz, Ralph. Fertility and Fiji's Indian Migrants, 1879–1919. *Indian Econ. Soc. Hist. Rev.*, Apr.-June 1987, *24*(2), pp. 205–17. **[G: India]**

0453 History of Public Economic Policy (all levels)

Heitzman, James. State Formation in South India, 850–1250. *Indian Econ. Soc. Hist. Rev.*, Jan.-Mar. 1987, *24*(1), pp. 35–61. **[G: India]**

Muraleedharan, V. R. Rural Health Care in Madras Presidency: 1919–39. *Indian Econ. Soc. Hist. Rev.*, July-Sept. 1987, *24*(3), pp. 323–34. **[G: India]**

Osterhammel, Jürgen. State Control of Foreign Trade in Nationalist China, 1927–1937. *Dewey, C., ed.*, 1987, pp. 209–37. **[G: China]**

Ravallion, Martin. Trade and Stabilization: Another Look at British India's Controversial Foodgrain Exports. *Exploration Econ. Hist.*, October 1987, *24*(4), pp. 354–70. **[G: India]**

046 Economic History: Africa

0460 General

Gran, Peter. Late–Eighteenth- Early–Nineteenth-Century Egypt: Merchant Capitalism or Modern Capitalism? *Islamoglu-Inan, H., ed.*, 1987, *1982*, pp. 27–41. **[G: Egypt]**

MacKenzie, John M. Chivalry, Social Darwinism and Ritualised Killing: The Hunting Ethos in Central Africa up to 1914. *Anderson, D. and Grove, R., eds.*, 1987, pp. 41–61. **[G: Africa]**

McCracken, John. Colonialism, Capitalism and the Ecological Crisis in Malawi: A Reassessment. *Anderson, D. and Grove, R., eds.*, 1987, pp. 63–77. **[G: Malawi]**

Müller, A. L. The Economic Awakening of the Eastern Cape, 1795–1820. *S. Afr. J. Econ.*, March 1987, *55*(1), pp. 40–52. **[G: S. Africa]**

Reyna, Stephen P. Wars without End: Reproduction of Class Relations through Predatory Accumulation in Precolonial Bagirmi. *England, R. W., ed.*, 1987, pp. 37–60. **[G: Sudan]**

Richards, Alan R. Primitive Accumulation in Egypt, 1798–1882. *Islamoglu-Inan, H., ed.*, 1987, *1977*, pp. 203–43. **[G: Egypt]**

0461 History of Product Prices and Markets

Eldredge, Elizabeth A. Drought, Famine and Disease in Nineteenth-Century Lesotho. *African Econ. Hist.*, 1987, (16), pp. 61–93. **[G: Africa]**

Fitzgerald, Peter. Markets, Commodity Production and Indigenous Farmers in Colonial Algeria. *Dewey, C., ed.*, 1987, pp. 47–65. **[G: Algeria]**

Gyimah-Brempong, Kwabena and Apraku, Kofi Konadu. Structural Change in Supply Response of Ghanaian Cocoa Production: 1933–1983. *J. Devel. Areas*, October 1987, *22*(1), pp. 59–70. **[G: Ghana]**

Klein, Martin A. and Roberts, Richard. The Resurgence of Pawning in French West Africa during the Depression of the 1930s. *African Econ. Hist.*, 1987, (16), pp. 23–37. **[G: W. Africa]**

van der Laan, Laurens. Selling Tropical Africa's Export Crops: The Experience of the Interwar Period. *Dewey, C., ed.*, 1987, pp. 238–61. **[G: Africa]**

Newbury, Colin. Technology, Capital, and Consolidation: The Performance of De Beers Mining Company Limited, 1880–1889. *Bus. Hist. Rev.*, Spring 1987, *61*(1), pp. 1–42. **[G: S. Africa]**

Roberts, Richard. French Colonialism, Imported Technology, and the Handicraft Textile Industry in the Western Sudan, 1898–1918. *J. Econ. Hist.*, June 1987, *47*(2), pp. 461–72. **[G: Sudan]**

Tignor, Robert. British Textile Companies and the Egyptian Economy. *Atack, J., ed.*, 1987, pp. 53–67. **[G: U.K.; Egypt]**

0462 History of Factor Prices and Markets

Falola, Toyin. Power Relations and Social Interactions among Ibadan Slaves, 1850–1900. *African*

Econ. Hist., 1987, (16), pp. 95–114.
[G: Africa]

Feder, Gershon and Noronha, Raymond. Land Rights Systems and Agricultural Development in Sub-Saharan Africa. *World Bank Res. Observer*, July 1987, *2*(2), pp. 143–69. [G: Sub-Saharan Africa]

James, Wilmot G. Grounds for a Strike: South African Gold Mining in the 1940s. *African Econ. Hist.*, 1987, (16), pp. 1–22.
[G: S. Africa]

La Rue, G. Michael. Land and Social Stratification in the Dār Fūr Region of the Sudan, 1785–1875: The Hākūra System. *Dewey, C., ed.*, 1987, pp. 24–44. [G: Sudan]

Phimister, Ian. Peasant Differentiation in Southern Rhodesia, 1898–1938. *Dewey, C., ed.*, 1987, pp. 66–104. [G: Rhodesia]

0463 History of Public Economic Policy (all levels)

Anderson, David M. Managing the Forest: The Conservation History of Lembus, Kenya, 1904–63. *Anderson, D. and Grove, R., eds.*, 1987, pp. 249–68. [G: Kenya]

Bates, Robert H. The Commercialization of Agriculture and the Rise of Rural Political Protest. *Bates, R. H.*, 1987, *1979*, pp. 92–104.
[G: Africa]

Bates, Robert II. The Nature and Origins of Agricultural Policies in Africa. *Bates, R. H.*, 1987, pp. 107–33. [G: Africa]

Campbell, Gwyn. The Role of the Merina State in the Decline of the Imperial Merina Economy, 1875–1895. *Dewey, C., ed.*, 1987, pp. 3–23. [G: Madagascar]

Grove, Richard. Early Themes in African Conservation: The Cape in the Nineteenth Century. *Anderson, D. and Grove, R., eds.*, 1987, pp 21–39. [G: Africa]

Millington, Andrew C. Environmental Degradation, Soil Conservation and Agricultural Policies in Sierra Leone, 1895–1984. *Anderson, D. and Grove, R., eds.*, 1987, pp. 229–48. [G: Sierra Leone]

Roberts, Richard. French Colonialism, Imported Technology, and the Handicraft Textile Industry in the Western Sudan, 1898–1918. *J. Econ. Hist.*, June 1987, *47*(2), pp. 461–72.
[G: Sudan]

047 Economic History: Latin America and Caribbean

0470 General

Carrington, Selwyn H. H. The American Revolution and the British West Indies' Economy. *Solow, B. L. and Engerman, S. L., eds.*, 1987, pp. 135–61. [G: Caribbean; U.K.]

Di Tella, Torcuato S. Las huelgas en la minería mexicana, 1826–1828. (With English summary.) *Desarrollo Econ.*, Jan.-Mar. 1987, *26*(104), pp. 579–608. [G: Mexico]

Esteva, Gustavo. Food Needs and Capacities: Four Centuries of Conflict. *Austin, J. E. and*

Esteva, G., eds., 1987, pp. 23–47.
[G: Mexico]

Love, Joseph L. Raúl Prebisch and the Origins of the Doctrine of Unequal Exchange. *Dietz, J. L. and Street, J. H., eds.*, 1987, pp. 78–100. [G: Argentina]

Miller, Rory. Transferring Techniques: Railway Building and Management on the West Coast of South America. *Dewey, C., ed.*, 1987, pp. 155–91. [G: Peru; Chile; Bolivia; Argentina]

Thorp, Rosemary. Trends and Cycles in the Peruvian Economy. *J. Devel. Econ.*, October 1987, *27*(1–2), pp. 355–74. [G: Peru]

Thorp, Rosemary. Trends and Cycles in the Peruvian Economy. *[Diaz-Alejandro, C. F.]*, 1987, pp. 355–74. [G: Peru]

0471 History of Product Prices and Markets

Brown, Jonathan C. Domestic Politics and Foreign Investment: British Development of Mexican Petroleum, 1889–1911. *Bus. Hist. Rev.*, Autumn 1987, *61*(3), pp. 387–416.
[G: Mexico]

Minchinton, Walter E. Bristol's Trade with the West Indies and South America, 1780–1830. *Rivista Storia Econ.*, S.S., Int. Issue, 1987, *4*, pp. 54–75. [G: West Indies; S. America; U.K.]

0472 History of Factor Prices and Markets

Beckles, Hilary McD. "The Williams Effect": Eric Williams's *Capitalism and Slavery* and the Growth of West Indian Political Economy. *Solow, B. L. and Engerman, S. L., eds.*, 1987, pp. 303–16. [G: Caribbean]

Carrington, Selwyn H. H. The American Revolution and the British West Indies' Economy. *Solow, B. L. and Engerman, S. L., eds.*, 1987, pp. 135–61. [G: Caribbean; U.K.]

Craton, Michael. What and Who to Whom and What: The Significance of Slave Resistance. *Solow, B. L. and Engerman, S. L., eds.*, 1987, pp. 259–82. [G: Caribbean]

Dunn, Richard S. "Dreadful Idlers" in the Cane Fields: The Slave Labor Pattern on a Jamaican Sugar Estate, 1762–1831. *Solow, B. L. and Engerman, S. L., eds.*, 1987, pp. 163–90.
[G: Jamaica]

Eichengreen, Barry and Portes, Richard. The Anatomy of Financial Crises. *Portes, R. and Swoboda, A. K., eds.*, 1987, pp. 10–58.
[G: Global]

Gemmill, Robert F. The Anatomy of Financial Crises: Discussion. *Portes, R. and Swoboda, A. K., eds.*, 1987, pp. 58–61. [G: Global]

Green, William A. Race and Slavery: Considerations on the Williams Thesis. *Solow, B. L. and Engerman, S. L., eds.*, 1987, pp. 25–49. [G: Caribbean; U.S.]

Rybczynski, Tad M. The Anatomy of Financial Crises: Discussion. *Portes, R. and Swoboda, A. K., eds.*, 1987, pp. 61–66. [G: Global]

Solow, Barbara L. and Engerman, Stanley L. British Capitalism and Caribbean Slavery: The

Legacy of Eric Williams: An Introduction. *Solow, B. L. and Engerman, S. L., eds.*, 1987, pp. 1–23. [G: Caribbean]

Wright, Gavin. Capitalism and Slavery on the Islands: A Lesson from the Mainland. *Solow, B. L. and Engerman, S. L., eds.*, 1987, pp. 283–302. [G: Caribbean; U.S.]

0473 History of Public Economic Policy (all levels)

Cárdenas, Enrique and Manns, Carlos. Inflation and Monetary Stabilization in Mexico during the Revolution. *[Diaz-Alejandro, C. F.]*, 1987, pp. 375–94. [G: Mexico]

Cárdenas, Enrique and Manns, Carlos. Inflation and Monetary Stabilization in Mexico During the Revolution. *J. Devel. Econ.*, October 1987, 27(1–2), pp. 375–94. [G: Mexico]

Finch, Henry. Technology Policy and the State in Uruguay, 1900–1935. *Dewey, C., ed.*, 1987, pp. 288–318. [G: Uruguay]

Fishlow, Albert. Lições da década de 1890 para a de 1980. (With English summary.) *Pesquisa Planejamento Econ.*, December 1987, 17(3), pp. 497–532. [G: Argentina; Brazil]

048 Economic History: Oceania

0480 General

Maddock, Rodney and McLean, Ian W. The Australian Economy in the Very Long Run. *Maddock, R. and McLean, I. W., eds.*, 1987, pp. 5–29. [G: Australia]

Maddock, Rodney and McLean, Ian W. The Australian Economy in the Long Run: Epilogue: A Comparative Perspective. *Maddock, R. and McLean, I. W., eds.*, 1987, pp. 344–52. [G: Australia]

Pope, David. Population and Australian Economic Development 1900–1930. *Maddock, R. and McLean, I. W., eds.*, 1987, pp. 33–60. [G: Australia]

Rubinstein, W. D. Entrepreneurial Effort and Entrepreneurial Success: Peak Wealth-Holding in Three Societies, 1850–1939. *Rubinstein, W. D.*, 1987, *1983*, pp. 119–42. [G: U.K.; U.S.; Australia]

Schedvin, C. B. The Australian Economy on the Hinge of History. *Australian Econ. Rev.*, First Quarter 1987, (77), pp. 20–30. [G: Australia]

Valentine, Tom J. The Australian Economy in the Long Run: The Depression of the 1930s. *Maddock, R. and McLean, I. W., eds.*, 1987, pp. 61–78. [G: Australia]

Valentine, Tom J. The Causes of the Depression in Australia. *Exploration Econ. Hist.*, January 1987, 24(1), pp. 43–62. [G: Australia]

0481 History of Product Prices and Markets

Freebairn, John W. The Australian Economy in the Long Run: Natural Resource Industries. *Maddock, R. and McLean, I. W., eds.*, 1987, pp. 133–64. [G: Australia]

Laffargue, Jean-Pierre. Croissance et endette-ment externe. (With English summary.) *Revue Écon. Polit.*, July-Aug. 1987, 97(4), pp. 409–18. [G: New Zealand; U.S.]

Lougheed, Alan. The Cyanide Process and God Extraction in Australia and New Zealand 1888–1913. *Australian Econ. Hist. Rev.*, March 1987, 27(1), pp. 44–60. [G: Australia; New Zealand]

Richardson, Peter. The Origins and Development of the Collins House Group, 1915–1951. *Australian Econ. Hist. Rev.*, March 1987, 27(1), pp. 3–29. [G: Australia]

Siriwardana, A. M. An Input–Output Table for the Colony of Victoria in 1880. *Australian Econ. Hist. Rev.*, March 1987, 27(1), pp. 61–85. [G: Australia]

Whittred, Greg. Taxation and the Evolution of Holding Company Form in Australia. *Australian Econ. Hist. Rev.*, September 1987, 27(2), pp. 77–86. [G: Australia]

0482 History of Factor Prices and Markets

Butlin, Matthew W. The Australian Economy in the Long Run: Capital Markets. *Maddock, R. and McLean, I. W., eds.*, 1987, pp. 229–47. [G: Australia]

Carter, Michael G. and Maddock, Rodney. Leisure and Australian Wellbeing 1911–81. *Australian Econ. Hist. Rev.*, March 1987, 27(1), pp. 30–43. [G: Australia]

Jones, F. L. Occupational Statistics Revisited: The Female Labour Force in Early British and Australian Censuses. *Australian Econ. Hist. Rev.*, September 1987, 27(2), pp. 56–76. [G: U.K.; Australia]

Nicholas, Stephen and Shergold, Peter R. Inter-county Labour Mobility during the Industrial Revolution: Evidence from Australian Transportation Records. *Oxford Econ. Pap.*, December 1987, 39(4), pp. 624–40. [G: Australia]

Nyland, Chris. Worktime in the 1920s. *Australian Econ. Hist. Rev.*, September 1987, 27(2), pp. 37–55. [G: U.S.]

Withers, Glenn. The Australian Economy in the Long Run: Labour. *Maddock, R. and McLean, I. W., eds.*, 1987, pp. 248–88. [G: Australia]

0483 History of Public Economic Policy (all levels)

Pincus, Jonathan J. The Australian Economy in the Long Run: Government. *Maddock, R. and McLean, I. W., eds.*, 1987, pp. 291–318. [G: Australia]

050 ECONOMIC SYSTEMS

0500 General

Boulding, Kenneth E. The Economy as an Ecosystem: Economics in the General System of the World. *Fox, K. A. and Miles, D. G., eds.*, 1987, pp. 3–18.

Fan, Liang-Shing. Institutional Design and Innovation: Discussion. *Amer. J. Agr. Econ.*, May 1987, 69(2), pp. 418–19.

Feeny, David. Institutional Design and Innovation: Discussion. *Amer. J. Agr. Econ.*, May 1987, *69*(2), pp. 416–17.

Gottlieb, Roger S. Historical Materialism, Historical Laws and Social Primacy: Further Discussion of the Transition Debate. *Sci. Soc.*, Summer 1987, *51*(2), pp. 188–99.

Laibman, David. Modes and Transitions: Replies. *Sci. Soc.*, Summer 1987, *51*(2), pp. 179–88.

Rodra, Ashok. The Transition Debate: Lessons for Third World Marxists. *Sci. Soc.*, Summer 1987, *51*(2), pp. 170–78.

Tinbergen, Jan. The Optimum Order Revisited. *Feiwel, G. R., ed. (II)*, 1987, pp. 281–327.

051 Capitalist Economic Systems: Market Economies

0510 Capitalist Economic Systems: Market Economies

Abraham, H. and Gurzynski, Z. S. A. The Entrepreneur as a Non-factor. *S. Afr. J. Econ.*, June 1987, *55*(2), pp. 114–20.

Adams, Walter. Economic Power and the Constitution: Interview. *Challenge*, July/Aug. 1987, *30*(3), pp. 17–25.   [G: U.S.]

Al-Jarhi, Mabid Ali Muhamed Mahmoud. The Relative Efficiency of Interest-Free Monetary Economies: The Fiat Money Case. *Khan, M. S. and Mirakhor, A., eds.*, 1987, *1981*, pp. 37–73.

Albert, Hans. Is Socialism Inevitable? Historical Prophecy and the Possibilities of Reason. *Pejovich, S., ed.*, 1987, pp. 55–88.

Alcorn, John H. and Gleicher, David. Workers, Inputs and Exploitation: A Note on Roemer. *Rev. Radical Polit. Econ.*, Summer 1987, *19*(2), pp. 77–82.

Amin, Samir. SADCC Prospects for Disengagement and Development in Southern Africa: Preface. *Amin, S.; Chitala, D. and Mandaza, I., eds.*, 1987, pp. 1–7.   [G: S. Africa]

Anderson, Terry L. and Hill, Peter J. Privatizing the Commons: Reply. *Southern Econ. J.*, July 1987, *54*(1), pp. 225–26.

Ashworth, John. The Relationship between Capitalism and Humanitarianism. *Amer. Hist. Rev.*, October 1987, *92*(4), pp. 813–28. [G: U.K.; U.S.]

Averitt, Robert T. The Dual Economy Twenty Years Later. *J. Econ. Issues*, June 1987, *21*(2), pp. 795–802.   [G: U.S.]

Bakker, Hans. Class Relations in Java in the Nineteenth Century: A Weberian Perspective. *Can. J. Devel. Stud.*, 1987, *8*(1), pp. 137–56. [G: Java]

Balassa, Bela and Tyson, Laura. Adjustment to External Shocks in Socialist and Private Market Economies. *Pasinetti, L. and Lloyd, P., eds.*, 1987, pp. 439–64.   [G: Global]

Bandyopadhyay, Pradeep. Value and Post-Sraffa Marxian Analysis. *Albelda, R.; Gunn, C. and Waller, W., eds.*, 1987, *1984*, pp. 186–94.

Bar-El, Raphael. Rural Industrialization in Israel: A Summary of Experiences. *Bar-El, R., ed.*, 1987, pp. 1–20.   [G: Israel]

Bar-El, Raphael; Erickson, Eugene and Nesher, Ariela. Rural Industrialization in Israel: Concluding Considerations. *Bar-El, R., ed.*, 1987, pp. 169–89.   [G: Israel]

Bates, Robert H. The Centralization of African Societies. *Bates, R. H.*, 1987, pp. 21–58. [G: Africa]

Bates, Robert H. The Preservation of Order in Stateless Societies: A Reinterpretation of Evans-Pritchard's *The Nuer. Bates, R. H.*, *1979*, pp. 7–20.   [G: Africa]

Baumol, William J. Entrepreneurship: Creative, Unproductive and Destructive. *Schweiz. Z. Volkswirtsch. Statist.*, September 1987, *123*(3), pp. 415–23.

Becker, David G. Postimperialism: A First Quarterly Report. *Becker, D. G., et al.*, 1987, pp. 203–25.

Becker, David G. and Sklar, Richard L. Why Postimperialism? *Becker, D. G., et al.*, 1987, pp. 1–18.

Beckford, George L. The Social Economy of Bauxite in the Jamaican Man–Space. *Soc. Econ. Stud.*, March 1987, *36*(1), pp. 1–55. [G: Jamaica]

Bienaymé, Alain. Une économie politique pour l'entreprise. (With English summary.) *Revue Écon. Polit.*, May-June 1987, *97*(3), pp. 285–300.

Biewener, Carole. Class and Socialist Politics in France. *Rev. Radical Polit. Econ.*, Summer 1987, *19*(2), pp. 61–76.   [G: France]

Binford, Leigh and Cook, Scott. Toward a Marxist Rethinking of Third World Rural Industrialization. *England, R. W., ed.*, 1987, pp. 61–85. [G: Mexico; LDCs]

Blanchflower, David G. and Oswald, Andrew J. Profit Sharing—Can It Work? *Sinclair, P. J. N., ed.*, 1987, pp. 1–19.   [G: U.K.]

Blanchflower, David G. and Oswald, Andrew J. Profit Sharing—Can It Work? *Oxford Econ. Pap.*, March 1987, *39*(1), pp. 1–19. [G: U.K.]

Block, Fred. Social Policy and Accumulation: A Critique of the New Consensus. *Rein, M.; Esping-Andersen, G. and Rainwater, L., eds.*, 1987, pp. 13–31.   [G: U.S.]

Bradley, Keith and Gelb, Alan. Cooperative Labour Relations: Mondragon's Response to Recession. *Brit. J. Ind. Relat.*, March 1987, *25*(1), pp. 77–97.   [G: Spain]

Buchanan, James M. Man and the State. *Pejovich, S., ed.*, 1987, pp. 3–9.

Buchanan, James M. Markets, States, and the Extent of Morals. *Buchanan, J. M. (II)*, 1987, *1978*, pp. 269–75.

Buchanan, James M. What Is the State? *Buchanan, J. M. (I)*, 1987, pp. 51–55.

Cain, P. J. and Hopkins, A. G. Gentlemanly Capitalism and British Expansion Overseas. II: New Imperialism, 1850–1945. *Econ. Hist. Rev., 2nd Ser.*, February 1987, *40*(1), pp. 1–26. [G: U.K.]

Canterbery, E. Ray. A Theory of Supra-surplus Capitalism. *Eastern Econ. J.*, October-December 1987, *13*(4), pp. 315–32.

Cataife, Daniel. Across Capital and Labor Power, Within Workers' Distinctive and Collective Socioeconomic Space. *Écon. Soc.*, November 1987, *21*(11), pp. 127–46.

Chakravarty, Sukhamoy. Marxist Economics and Contemporary Developing Economies. *Cambridge J. Econ.*, March 1987, *11*(1), pp. 3–22. **[G: Selected Countries]**

Chernomas, Robert. Is Supply-Side Economics Rational for Capital? *Rev. Radical Polit. Econ.*, Fall 1987, *19*(3), pp. 1–17. **[G: U.S.]**

Clark, Barry S. Solitude and Solidarity in the Just Society: A Reappraisal of Marx's Vision. *Int. J. Soc. Econ.*, 1987, *14*(7/8/9), pp. 44–51.

Craton, Michael. What and Who to Whom and What: The Significance of Slave Resistance. *Solow, B. L. and Engerman, S. L., eds.*, 1987, pp. 259–82. **[G: Caribbean]**

Dandekar, Vinayak M. Economies as Differentiated Systems. *J. Econ. Issues*, June 1987, *21*(2), pp. 813–25. **[G: India]**

Davis, David Brion. Reflections on Abolitionism and Ideological Hegemony. *Amer. Hist. Rev.*, October 1987, *92*(4), pp. 797–812. **[G: U.K.; U.S.]**

Detremmerie, Hubert. Le financement des entreprises cooperatives. (Financing Cooperative Firms. With English summary.) *Ann. Pub. Co-op. Econ.*, July-Sept. 1987, *58*(3), pp. 267–73. **[G: Belgium]**

Dillard, Dudley. Money as an Institution of Capitalism. *J. Econ. Issues*, December 1987, *21*(4), pp. 1623–47.

Diwan, Romesh. Mahatma Gandhi and the Economics of Non-exploitation. *Int. J. Soc. Econ.*, 1987, *14*(2), pp. 39–52.

Don, Yehuda and Leviatan, Uri. Kibbutz Industrialization. *Bar-El, R., ed.*, 1987, pp. 21–55. **[G: Israel]**

Don, Yehuda and Paroush, Jacob. Cooperatives with Cost Saving. *Jones, D. C. and Svejnar, J., eds.*, 1987, pp. 183–99.

Downe, Edward A. Minsky's Model of Financial Fragility: A Suggested Addition. *J. Post Keynesian Econ.*, Spring 1987, *9*(3), pp. 440–54.

Drescher, Seymour. Paradigms Tossed: Capitalism and the Political Sources of Abolition. *Solow, B. L. and Engerman, S. L., eds.*, 1987, pp. 191–208.

Dugger, William M. Corporate Hegemony and Market Mythology. *Challenge*, Jan./Feb. 1987, *29*(6), pp. 55–58. **[G: OECD]**

Dugger, William M. Three Modes of Income Distribution: Market, Hierarchy, and Industry. *J. Econ. Issues*, June 1987, *21*(2), pp. 723–31.

Duménil, Gérard; Glick, Mark and Rangel, Jose. Does Rajani Kanth's Comment Matter? *Rev. Radical Polit. Econ.*, Winter 1987, *19*(4), pp. 75. **[G: U.S.]**

Duménil, Gérard; Glick, Mark and Rangel, Jose. The Rate of Profit in the United States. *Cambridge J. Econ.*, December 1987, *11*(4), pp. 331–59. **[G: U.S.]**

Duménil, Gérard; Glick, Mark and Rangel, Jose. Theories of the Great Depression: Why Did

Profitability Matter? *Rev. Radical Polit. Econ.*, Summer 1987, *19*(2), pp. 16–42. **[G: U.S.]**

Dutt, Amitava Krishna. Competition, Monopoly Power and the Uniform Rate of Profit. *Rev. Radical Polit. Econ.*, Winter 1987, *19*(4), pp. 55–72.

Elliott, John E. and Scott, Joanna V. Theories of Liberal Capitalist Democracy: Alternative Perspectives. *Int. J. Soc. Econ.*, 1987, *14*(7/8/9), pp. 52–87. **[G: U.S.]**

England, Richard W. Ecology, Social Class, and Political Conflict. *England, R. W., ed.*, 1987, pp. 118–53. **[G: U.S.; Global]**

Epstein, Richard A. The Public Trust Doctrine. *Cato J.*, Fall 1987, *7*(2), pp. 411–30. **[G: U.S.]**

Esping-Andersen, Gøsta. Citizenship and Socialism: De-commodification and Solidarity in the Welfare State. *Rein, M.; Esping-Andersen, G. and Rainwater, L., eds.*, 1987, pp. 78–101. **[G: W. Europe]**

Esping-Andersen, Gøsta. The Comparison of Policy Regimes: An Introduction. *Rein, M.; Esping-Andersen, G. and Rainwater, L., eds.*, 1987, pp. 3–12.

Essid, M. Yassine. Islamic Economic Thought. *Lowry, S. T., ed.*, 1987, pp. 77–102.

Estrin, Saul; Jones, Derek C. and Svejnar, Jan. The Productivity Effects of Worker Participation: Producer Cooperatives in Western Economies. *J. Compar. Econ.*, March 1987, *11*(1), pp. 40–61. **[G: Spain; Italy; U.K.; France]**

Etzioni, Amitai. Entrepreneurship, Adaptation and Legitimation: A Macro-behavioral Perspective. *J. Econ. Behav. Organ.*, June 1987, *8*(2), pp. 175–89.

Ferreira da Costa, Fernando. Origine et evolution des cooperatives dans l'economie sociale portugaise. (The Origin and Evolution of Cooperatives in the Portuguese Economy. With English summary.) *Ann. Pub. Co-op. Econ.*, Jan.-Mar. 1987, *58*(1), pp. 49–64. **[G: Portugal]**

Freeman, R. D. The State and the Private Sector: Comment. *Levitt, M. S., ed.*, 1987, pp. 43–47. **[G: U.K.]**

Frieden, Jeff. International Capital and National Development: Comments on Postimperialism. *Becker, D. G., et al.*, 1987, pp. 179–91.

Furubotn, Eirik G. Privatizing the Commons: Comment. *Southern Econ. J.*, July 1987, *54*(1), pp. 219–24.

Garello, Jacques. Economic and Social Consequences of Socialist Policies in France. *Pejovich, S., ed.*, 1987, pp. 251–76. **[G: France]**

Garnier, Jean-Pierre. Les nouvelles technologies de l'aliénation. (The New Technologies of Alienation. With English summary.) *Écon. Soc.*, August 1987, *21*(8), pp. 129–52.

Gerschenkron, Alexander. Social Attitudes, Entrepreneurship and Economic Development. *Dupriez, L. H., ed.*, 1987, *1955*, pp. 256–74. **[G: U.S.S.R.; France]**

Glasberg, Davita Silfen. Control of Capital Flows and Class Relations. *Soc. Sci. Quart.*, March 1987, *68*(1), pp. 51–69. **[G: U.S.]**

Goodin, Robert E. and Le Grand, Julian. Creeping Universalism in the Australian Welfare State. *Goodin, R. E. and Le Grand, J.*, 1987, pp. 108–26. **[G: Australia]**

Gordon, Myron J. Insecurity, Growth, and the Rise of Capitalism. *J. Post Keynesian Econ.*, Summer 1987, *9*(4), pp. 529–51.

Gramm, Warren S. Unproductive Labour and Unproductive Consumption: Historical Review, Contemporary Relevance. *Int. J. Soc. Econ.*, 1987, *14*(3/4/5), pp. 154–66. **[G: U.S.]**

Gran, Peter. Late–Eighteenth- Early–Nineteenth-Century Egypt: Merchant Capitalism or Modern Capitalism? *Islamoglu-Inan, H., ed.*, 1987, *1982*, pp. 27–41. **[G: Egypt]**

Grubel, Herbert G. Capitalism Needs Risk-, Not Profit-Sharing. *Kyklos*, 1987, *40*(2), pp. 163–75.

Gulalp, Haldun. Capital Accumulation, Classes and the Relative Autonomy of the State. *Sci. Soc.*, Fall 1987, *51*(3), pp. 287–313.

Gunn, Bruce. Competruism and the Steady State Economy. *J. Behav. Econ.*, Fall 1987, *16*(3), pp. 13–22.

Gurley, John G. Marx and the Critique of Capitalism. *Albelda, R.; Gunn, C. and Waller, W., eds.*, 1987, *1980*, pp. 273–96.

Haqiqi, Abdul Wassay and Pomeranz, Felix. Accounting Needs of Islamic Banking. *Most, Kenneth S., ed.*, 1987, pp. 153–68. **[G: Arab Countries]**

Haque, Nadeem Ul and Mirakhor, Abbas. Optimal Profit-Sharing Contracts and Investment in an Interest-Free Islamic Economy. *Khan, M. S. and Mirakhor, A., eds.*, 1987, pp. 141–61.

Haque, Nadeem Ul and Mirakhor, Abbas. Saving Behavior in an Economy without Fixed Interest. *Khan, M. S. and Mirakhor, A., eds.*, 1987, pp. 125–39.

Harrison, Bennett. Cold Bath or Restructuring? An Expansion of the Weisskopf–Bowles–Gordon Framework. *Sci. Soc.*, Spring 1987, *51*(1), pp. 72–82. **[G: U.S.]**

Haskell, Thomas L. Convention and Hegemonic Interest in the Debate over Antislavery: A Reply. *Amer. Hist. Rev.*, October 1987, *92*(4), pp. 829–78. **[G: U.S.; U.K.]**

Haurie, Alain and Pohjola, Matti. Efficient Equilibria in a Differential Game of Capitalism. *J. Econ. Dynam. Control*, March 1987, *11*(1), pp. 65–78.

Henley, Andrew. Labour's Shares and Profitability Crisis in the U.S.: Recent Experience and Post-war Trends. *Cambridge J. Econ.*, December 1987, *11*(4), pp. 315–30. **[G: U.S.]**

Heuss, Ernst. Gerechtigkeit und Marktwirtschaft. (Justice in the Market Economy. With English summary.) *Lenel, H. O., et al., eds.*, 1987, pp. 3–19.

Hibbs, Douglas A., Jr. On the Political Economy of Long-run Trends in Strike Activity. *Hibbs, D. A., Jr.*, 1987, *1978*, pp. 52–76. **[G: W. Europe; Canada; U.S.]**

Higgs, Robert and Twight, Charlotte. National Emergency and the Erosion of Private Prop-

erty Rights. *Cato J.*, Winter 1987, *6*(3), pp. 747–73. **[G: U.S.]**

Hirshleifer, Jack. Privacy: Its Origin, Function, and Future. *Hirshleifer, J.*, 1987, *1980*, pp. 194–210.

Hodgson, Geoffrey M. Economic Pluralism and Self-management. *Jones, D. C. and Svejnar, J., eds.*, 1987, pp. 129–42.

Houston, David and Paus, Eva. The Theory of Unequal Exchange: An Indictment. *Rev. Radical Polit. Econ.*, Spring 1987, *19*(1), pp. 90–97.

Hurwicz, Leonid. Inventing New Institutions: The Design Perspective. *Amer. J. Agr. Econ.*, May 1987, *69*(2), pp. 395–402.

Inikori, Joseph E. Slavery and the Development of Industrial Capitalism in England. *Solow, B. L. and Engerman, S. L., eds.*, 1987, pp. 79–101. **[G: U.K.]**

Islamoğlu-Inan, Huri. 'Oriental Despotism' in World-System Perspective. *Islamoglu-Inan, H., ed.*, 1987, pp. 1–24. **[G: Ottoman Empire]**

Jankowski, Richard. The Profit-Squeeze and Tax Policy: Can the State Actively Intervene? *Rev. Radical Polit. Econ.*, Fall 1987, *19*(3), pp. 18–33. **[G: U.S.]**

Kanth, Rajani. Against "Surplus" Theorizing: A Comment. *Rev. Radical Polit. Econ.*, Summer 1987, *19*(2), pp. 83–85. **[G: LDCs]**

Kanth, Rajani. Why Does the Duménil–Glick–Rangel Thesis Matter? A Comment. *Rev. Radical Polit. Econ.*, Winter 1987, *19*(4), pp. 73–74. **[G: U.S.]**

Kebbede, Girma. State Capitalism and Development: The Case of Ethiopia. *J. Devel. Areas*, October 1987, *22*(1), pp. 1–23. **[G: Ethiopia]**

Kelleher, Patricia. Familism in Irish Capitalism in the 1950s. *Econ. Soc. Rev.*, January 1987, *18*(2), pp. 75–94. **[G: Ireland]**

Kent, Calvin A. and Wooten, Sandra P. Privatization: The Entrepreneurial Response. *Kent, C. A., ed.*, 1987, pp. 145–57. **[G: U.S.]**

Khan, Mohsin S. Islamic Interest-Free Banking: A Theoretical Analysis. *Khan, M. S. and Mirakhor, A., eds.*, 1987, pp. 201–06.

Khan, Mohsin S. and Mirakhor, Abbas. The Financial System and Monetary Policy in an Islamic Economy. *Khan, M. S. and Mirakhor, A., eds.*, 1987, pp. 163–84.

Khan, Mohsin S. and Mirakhor, Abbas. The Framework and Practice of Islamic Banking. *Khan, M. S. and Mirakhor, A., eds.*, 1987, *1986*, pp. 1–13.

Khan, Mohsin S. and Mirakhor, Abbas. Theoretical Studies in Islamic Banking and Finance: Introduction. *Khan, M. S. and Mirakhor, A., eds.*, 1987, pp. ix–xvi.

Khan, Shahrukh Rafi. An Economic Analysis of a PLS Model for the Financial Sector. *Khan, M. S. and Mirakhor, A., eds.*, 1987, *1984*, pp. 107–24.

Khan, Waqar Masood. Towards an Interest Free Islamic Economic System. *Khan, M. S. and Mirakhor, A., eds.*, 1987, pp. 75–105.

Khan, Waqar Masood. Towards an Interest-Free

Islamic Economic System. *Khan, M. S. and Mirakhor, A., eds.*, 1987, pp. 215–20.

Khan, Waqar Masood. Towards and Interest-Free Islamic Economic System. *Khan, M. S. and Mirakhor, A., eds.*, 1987, pp. 207–13.

Kliemt, Hartmut. On Leland Yeager's Utilitarianism: A Comment [Rights, Contract, and Utility in Policy Espousal]. *Cato J.*, Spring/Summer 1987, 7(1), pp. 259–67.

Klitgaard, Kent A. and Ellis, Valarie D. Accumulation and Crisis. *England, R. W., ed.*, 1987, pp. 89–106.

Kotz, David M. Long Waves and Social Structures of Accumulation: A Critique and Reinterpretation. *Rev. Radical Polit. Econ.*, Winter 1987, 19(4), pp. 16–38. **[G: U.S.]**

Kregel, Jan A. Markets and Institutions as Features of a Capitalistic Production System. *Albelda, R.; Gunn, C. and Waller, W., eds.*, 1987, 1980, pp. 111–23.

Kuran, Timur. Continuity and Change in Islamic Economic Thought: Commentary. *Lowry, S. T., ed.*, 1987, pp. 103–13.

Le Grand, Julian and Winter, David. The Middle Classes and the Defence of the British Welfare State. *Goodin, R. E. and Le Grand, J.*, 1987, pp. 147–68. **[G: U.K.]**

Lebowitz, Michael A. The Political Economy of Wage Labor. *Sci. Soc.*, Fall 1987, 51(3), pp. 262–86.

Lee, Dwight R. The *Calculus of Consent* and the Constitution of Capitalism. *Cato J.*, Fall 1987, 7(2), pp. 331–36. **[G: U.S.]**

Lindbeck, Assar. Is the Welfare State in Trouble? *Eastern Econ. J.*, October-December 1987, 13(4), pp. 345–51.

Lippit, Victor D. Surplus Theorizing Reaffirmed. *Rev. Radical Polit. Econ.*, Summer 1987, 19(2), pp. 86–88. **[G: LDCs]**

Lowe, Adolph. The Classical Theory of Economic Growth. *Lowe, A.*, 1987, 1954, pp. 107–31.

Machan, Tibor R. A New Individualist Basis for the Free Market. *Int. J. Soc. Econ.*, 1987, 14(10), pp. 27–39.

Machan, Tibor R. Are Teleological Rights Theories Utilitarian? [Rights, Contracts, and Utility in Policy Espousal]. *Cato J.*, Spring/Summer 1987, 7(1), pp. 255–58.

MacLeod, W. Bentley. Behavior and the Organization of the Firm. *J. Compar. Econ.*, June 1987, 11(2), pp. 207–20.

Maier, Charles S. "Fictitious Bonds . . . of Wealth and law": On the Theory and Practice of Interest Representation. *Maier, C. S.*, 1987, 1981, pp. 225–60. **[G: W. Europe]**

Martinius, Sture. Capitalism: A Threat against Freehold Farms around the Middle of the Nineteenth Century? *Scand. Econ. Hist. Rev.*, 1987, 35(2), pp. 178–90. **[G: W. Europe]**

Menshikov, Stanislav. Structural Crisis as a Phase in Long-term Economic Fluctuations. *Vasko, T., ed.*, 1987, pp. 66–75.

Mirakhor, Abbas. Short-term Asset Concentration and Islamic Banking. *Khan, M. S. and Mirakhor, A., eds.*, 1987, pp. 185–99.

Mitchell, Daniel J. B. The Share Economy and

Industrial Relations. *Ind. Relat.*, Winter 1987, 26(1), pp. 1–17. **[G: U.S.]**

Monzon Campos, Jose Luis. L'economie sociale et cooperative en Espagne. (Social and Cooperative Economy in Spain. With English summary.) *Ann. Pub. Co-op. Econ.*, Jan.-Mar. 1987, 58(1), pp. 23–29. **[G: Spain]**

Moseley, Fred. The Profit Share and the Rate of Surplus Value in the U.S. Economy, 1975–85 [Marxian Crisis Theory and the Rate of Profit in the Postwar U.S. Economy]. *Cambridge J. Econ.*, December 1987, 11(4), pp. 393–399. **[G: U.S.]**

Nattrass, Nicoli Jean. Street Trading in Transkei—A Struggle against Poverty, Persecution, and Prosecution. *World Devel.*, July 1987, 15(7), pp. 861–75. **[G: S. Africa]**

Noël, Alain. Accumulation, Regulation, and Social Change: An Essay on French Political Economy. *Int. Organ.*, Spring 1987, 41(2), pp. 303–33. **[G: France]**

Nuti, Domenico Mario. Profit-Sharing and Employment: Claims and Overclaims. *Ind. Relat.*, Winter 1987, 26(1), pp. 18–29.

Pack, Spencer J. Schumpeter Plus Optimism Equals Gilder (*ceteris paribus*). *Hist. Polit. Econ.*, Fall 1987, 19(3), pp. 469–80.

Pantin, Dennis A. Long Waves and Caribbean Development. *Soc. Econ. Stud.*, June 1987, 36(2), pp. 1–20. **[G: Caribbean]**

Pascha, Werner. Do Advanced Economies Turn into Casinos?—A Note on the "Paper Economy." *Rivista Int. Sci. Econ. Com.*, Nov.-Dec. 1987, 34(11–12), pp. 1041–52.

Peet, Richard. Industrial Devolution, Underconsumption and the Third World Debt Crisis. *World Devel.*, June 1987, 15(6), pp. 777–88. **[G: Global]**

Pelikan, Pavel. Why Private Enterprise? Towards a Dynamic Analysis of Economic Institutions and Policies. *Eliasson, G., ed.*, 1987, pp. 133–46.

Pérotin, Virginie. Conditions of Survival and Closure of French Worker Cooperatives: Some Preliminary Findings. *Jones, D. C. and Svejnar, J., eds.*, 1987, pp. 201–24. **[G: France]**

Petr, Jerry L. The Nature and Necessity of the Mixed Economy. *J. Econ. Issues*, December 1987, 21(4), pp. 1445–68.

Pickles, A. R. and O'Farrell, P. N. An Analysis of Entrepreneurial Behaviour from Male Work Histories. *Reg. Stud.*, October 1987, 21(5), pp. 425–44. **[G: Ireland]**

Pinto S. C., Aníbal. La ofensiva contra el Estado-económico. (The Offensive against the Economic State. With English summary.) *Colección Estud. CIEPLAN*, June 1987, (21), pp. 117–27. **[G: Chile]**

Pottenger, John R. Mormonism and the American Industrial State. *Int. J. Soc. Econ.*, 1987, 14(2), pp. 25–38. **[G: U.S.]**

Power, Marilyn. Unity and Division among Women: Feminist Theories of Gender and Class in Capitalist Society. *England, R. W., ed.*, 1987, 1984, pp. 178–99. **[G: U.S.]**

Rao, J. Mohan. Class Relations in an 'Asiatic' Regime. *Cambridge J. Econ.*, September 1987, *11*(3), pp. 229–50. **[G: India]**

Reyna, Stephen P. Wars without End: Reproduction of Class Relations through Predatory Accumulation in Precolonial Bagirmi. *England, R. W., ed.*, 1987, pp. 37–60. **[G: Sudan]**

Ribeiro, Gustavo Lins. Cuánto más grande mejor? Proyectos de gran escala: una forma de producción vinculada a la expansión de sistemas económicos. (With English summary.) *Desarrollo Econ.*, Apr.-June 1987, *27*(105), pp. 3–27.

Richards, Alan R. Primitive Accumulation in Egypt, 1798–1882. *Islamoglu-Inan, H., ed.*, 1987, *1977*, pp. 203–43. **[G: Egypt]**

Rock, Charles P. Recent Reforms Democratizing Swedish Economic Institutions. *J. Econ. Issues*, June 1987, *21*(2), pp. 837–45. **[G: Sweden]**

Rodrigues, Maria João. Le système d'emploi comme alternative aux approches du marché du travail. (The Employment System as an Alternative to Labor Market Approaches. With English summary.) *Écon. Soc.*, November 1987, *21*(11), pp. 3–39.

Ronen, Joshua. Comments [Entrepreneurship, Adaption and Legitimation: A Macro-behavioral Perspective] [Entrepreneurship, Entrepreneurial Training, and X-Efficiency Theory]. *J. Econ. Behav. Organ.*, June 1987, *8*(2), pp. 207–12.

Rosholt, A. M. Has South Africa a Free Enterprise Future? *Managerial Dec. Econ.*, March 1987, *8*(1), pp. 81–84. **[G: S. Africa]**

Roth, Gabriel. The Role of Property Rights in Development [Economic Growth and the Property Rights Regime]. *Cato J.*, Spring/Summer 1987, *7*(1), pp. 117–20. **[G: LDCs]**

Rubinstein, W. D. Entrepreneurial Effort and Entrepreneurial Success: Peak Wealth-Holding in Three Societies, 1850–1939. *Rubinstein, W. D.*, 1987, *1983*, pp. 119–42. **[G: U.K.; U.S.; Australia]**

Sachs, Ignacy. The Crisis of the Welfare State and the Exercise of Social Rights to Development. *Sachs, I.*, 1987, pp. 69–78.

Schatz, Sayre P. Postimperialism and the Great Competition. *Becker, D. G., et al.*, 1987, 193–201.

Schatz, Sayre P. Socializing Adaptation: A Perspective on World Capitalism. *Becker, D. G., et al.*, 1987, *1983*, pp. 161–77. **[G: Global]**

Schmidt, Herbert. Labororiented Management-policy in Industry within a Social Market Economy. *Gemper, B. B., ed.*, 1987, pp. 187–200. **[G: W. Germany]**

Schmidtchen, Dieter. Hayek on Liberty and the Rule of Law: The Road to Serfdom Revisited. *Pejovich, S., ed.*, 1987, pp. 115–44.

Silipo, Damiano. La teoria dell'instabilita' del capitalismo: la posizione di Hyman Minsky. (With English summary.) *Stud. Econ.*, 1987, *42*(32), pp. 119–53.

Sklar, Richard L. Postimperialism: A Class Analysis of Multinational Corporate Expansion. *Becker, D. G., et al.*, 1987, *1976*, pp. 19–40.

Skocpol, Theda. America's Incomplete Welfare State: The Limits of New Deal Reforms and the Origins of the Present Crisis. *Rein, M.; Esping-Andersen, G. and Rainwater, L., eds.*, 1987, pp. 35–58. **[G: U.S.]**

Solow, Barbara L. Capitalism and Slavery in the Exceedingly Long Run. *Solow, B. L. and Engerman, S. L., eds.*, 1987, pp. 51–77.

Soref, Michael and Zeitlin, Maurice. Finance Capital and the Internal Structure of the Capitalist Class in the United States. *Mizruchi, M. S. and Schwartz, M., eds.*, 1987, pp. 56–84. **[G: U.S.]**

Soulage, François. Le financement des entreprises d'economie sociale en France. (The Financing of Social and Co-operative Enterprises in France. With English summary.) *Ann. Pub. Co-op. Econ.*, July-Sept. 1987, *58*(3), pp. 259–66. **[G: France]**

Streit, Manfred E. Economic Order and Public Policy—Market, Constitution and the Welfare State. *Pethig, R. and Schlieper, U., eds.*, 1987, pp. 1–21.

Studlar, Donley T. Policy Convergence? Political Economy in the United States and Britain. *Waltman, J. L. and Studlar, D. T., eds.*, 1987, pp. 3–15. **[G: U.S.; U.K.]**

Suarez-Villa, Luis. Entrepreneurship and the International Diffusion of Innovations in Manufacturing: A General Approach. *Rivista Int. Sci. Econ. Com.*, May 1987, *34*(5), pp. 369–91. **[G: Global]**

Sweezy, Paul M. Corporations, the State, and Imperialism. *Albelda, R.; Gunn, C. and Waller, W., eds.*, 1987, *1978*, pp. 339–45.

Thordarson, Bodil. A Comparison of Worker-Owned Firms and Conventionally Owned Firms in Sweden. *Jones, D. C. and Svejnar, J., eds.*, 1987, pp. 225–42. **[G: Sweden]**

Tinbergen, Jan. A European Socialist on Japan: Some Brief Reflections. *[Kitamura, H.]*, 1987, pp. 85–88. **[G: Japan]**

Tonak, E. Ahmet. The U.S. Welfare State and the Working Class, 1952–1980. *Rev. Radical Polit. Econ.*, Spring 1987, *19*(1), pp. 47–72. **[G: U.S.]**

Valdés, Benigno. Technical Change and Profitability: The "Law of the Tendency of the Rate of Profit to Fall" Reconsidered. *England, R. W., ed.*, 1987, pp. 107–17.

Vaubel, Roland. The Philosophical Basis of the Free Society. *Lenel, H. O., et al., eds.*, 1987, pp. 21–29.

Vorst, Karen S. A Note on Central Planning Core Banks and Correspondent Bank Balances [Centralized Private Sector Planning: An Institutionalist's Perspective on the Contemporary U.S. Economy]. *J. Econ. Issues*, March 1987, *21*(1), pp. 482–92. **[G: U.S.]**

Wade, Robert. The Management of Common Property Resources: Collective Action as an Alternative to Privatisation or State Regulation. *Cambridge J. Econ.*, June 1987, *11*(2), pp. 95–106.

Walker, Jill and Moore, Roger. The Impact of Privatization on the United Kingdom Local

Government Labour Market. *Tarling, R., ed.,* 1987, pp. 197–223. **[G: U.K.]**

Waller, William T., Jr. Ceremonial Encapsulation and Corporate Cultural Hegemony. *J. Econ. Issues,* March 1987, *21*(1), pp. 321–28.

Waltman, Jerold L. The Strength of Policy Inheritance. *Waltman, J. L. and Studlar, D. T., eds.,* 1987, pp. 259–69. **[G: U.K.; U.S.]**

Waterman, A. M. C. On the Malthusian Theory of Long Swings. *Can. J. Econ.,* May 1987, *20*(2), pp. 257–70.

Waters, Alan Rufus. Economic Growth and the Property Rights Regime. *Cato J.,* Spring/Summer 1987, *7*(1), pp. 99–115. **[G: LDCs]**

Watrin, Christian. The Case of Codetermination in West Germany. *Pejovich, S., ed.,* 1987, pp. 277–314. **[G: W. Germany]**

Webber, M. J. Quantitative Measurement of Some Marxist Categories. *Environ. Planning A,* October 1987, *19*(10), pp. 1303–21.

White, Geoff. The State and the Private Sector. *Levitt, M. S., ed.,* 1987, pp. 30–42.

Williams, Walter E. How Business Transcends Politics. *Managerial Dec. Econ.,* March 1987, *8*(1), pp. 15–20.

Williamson, Oliver E. Kenneth Arrow and the New Institutional Economics. *Feiwel, G. R., ed. (II),* 1987, pp. 584–99.

Windisch, Rupert. Economic Order and Public Policy—Market, Constitution and the Welfare State: Comment. *Pethig, R. and Schlieper, U., eds.,* 1987, pp. 23–26.

Winther, Gorm. Future Prospects for Self-management in Greenland? *Econ. Anal. Workers' Manage.,* 1987, *21*(2), pp. 265–78. **[G: Denmark]**

Wolfson, Dirk J. Controlling the Welfare State: A Case Study of Retrenchment in the Netherlands. *Public Finance,* 1987, *42*(2), pp. 165–80. **[G: Netherlands]**

Wünsche, Horst Friedrich. Does Industrial Policy Comply with Ludwig Erhard's Conception of the Social Market Economy? *Gemper, B. B., ed.,* 1987, pp. 37–43.

Yaron, Dan; Ratner, Aaron and Wijler, Johanan. Integrating Industrial Plants into the Moshav Economy—Benefits and Conflicts. *Econ. Anal. Workers' Manage.,* 1987, *21*(3), pp. 353–72. **[G: Israel]**

Yeager, Leland B. Reply [Rights, Contracts, and Utility in Policy Espousal]. *Cato J.,* Spring/Summer 1987, *7*(1), pp. 269–71.

052 Socialist and Communist Economic Systems

0520 Socialist and Communist Economic Systems

Abalkin, Leonid I. The New Model of Economic Management. *Soviet Econ.,* October-December 1987, *3*(4), pp. 298–312. **[G: U.S.S.R.]**

Abalkin, Leonid I., et al. Reflections on Technology in Postwar Reconstruction. *Soviet Econ.,* October-December 1987, *3*(4), pp. 353–59. **[G: U.S.S.R.]**

Aganbegyan, Abel G. Basic Directions of *Perestroyka. Soviet Econ.,* October-December 1987, *3*(4), pp. 277–97. **[G: U.S.S.R.]**

Aganbegyan, Abel G. The New Economic Strategy of the USSR and Its Social Dimensions. *Int. Lab. Rev.,* Jan.-Feb. 1987, *126*(1), pp. 95–109. **[G: U.S.S.R.]**

Angyal, Á. Change and Reform: Comments and Contributions. *Acta Oecon.,* 1987, *38*(3–4), pp. 215–24. **[G: Hungary]**

Antal, László, et al. Change and Reform. *Acta Oecon.,* 1987, *38*(3–4), pp. 187–213. **[G: Hungary]**

Arnold, N. Scott. Final Reply to Professor Schweickart [Marx and Disequilibrium in Market Socialist Relations of Production]. *Econ. Philos.,* October 1987, *3*(2), pp. 335–38.

Arnold, N. Scott. Further Thoughts on the Degeneration of Market Socialism: A Reply to Schweickart [Marx and Disequilibrium in Market Socialist Relations of Production]. *Econ. Philos.,* October 1987, *3*(2), pp. 320–30.

Arnold, N. Scott. Marx and Disequilibrium in Market Socialist Relations of Production. *Econ. Philos.,* April 1987, *3*(1), pp. 23–47.

Åslund, Anders. Gorbachev's Economic Advisors. *Soviet Econ.,* July-Sept. 1987, *3*(3), pp. 246–69. **[G: U.S.S.R.]**

Auzan, A. A. The Leninist Idea of Increasing the Role of Consumers in a Planned Economy. *Prob. Econ.,* November 1987, *30*(7), pp. 5–17. **[G: U.S.S.R.]**

Balassa, Bela. China's Economic Reforms in a Comparative Perspective. *J. Compar. Econ.,* September 1987, *11*(3), pp. 410–26. **[G: China]**

Balassa, Bela and Tyson, Laura. Adjustment to External Shocks in Socialist and Private Market Economies. *Pasinetti, L. and Lloyd, P., eds.,* 1987, pp. 439–64. **[G: Global]**

Baoming, Chen. Individual Businesses and Their Challenge to Conventional Concepts. *Chinese Econ. Stud.,* Fall 1987, *21*(1), pp. 93–101. **[G: China]**

Baranson, Jack. Ideology versus Innovation in Soviet Industry. *World Econ.,* March 1987, *10*(1), pp. 85–95. **[G: U.S.S.R.]**

Batizi, E. E., et al. Problems of Proportionality in a Socialist Economy. *Soviet E. Europ. Foreign Trade,* Summer 1987, *23*(2), pp. 6–23. **[G: CMEA]**

Bauer, Tamás. Perfecting or Reforming the Economic Mechanism? *Eastern Europ. Econ.,* Winter 1987-88, *26*(2), pp. 5–34.

Bauer, Tamás. Reforming or Perfecting the Economic Mechanism. *Europ. Econ. Rev.,* Feb./Mar. 1987, *31*(1/2), pp. 132–38. **[G: CMEA]**

Bechtold, Hartmut and Helfer, Andreas. Stagflation Problems in Socialist Economies. *Gey, P.; Kosta, J. and Quaisser, W., eds.,* 1987, pp. 11–31. **[G: Hungary; Yugoslavia]**

Beksiak, Janusz. Enterprise and Reform: The Polish Experience. *Europ. Econ. Rev.,* Feb./Mar. 1987, *31*(1/2), pp. 118–24. **[G: Poland]**

Bergson, Abram. The Gorbachev Revolution.

Challenge, Sept./Oct. 1987, *30*(4), pp. 26–33. [G: U.S.S.R.]

Berliner, Joseph S. Politics, Work, and Daily Life in the USSR: Foreword. *Millar, J. R., ed.,* 1987, pp. vii–xii. [G: U.S.S.R.]

Bernholz, Peter. Information, Motivation, and the Problem of Rational Economic Calculation in Socialism. *Pejovich, S., ed.,* 1987, pp. 147–74.

Bim, A. and Shokhin, A. The Distribution System: On the Road to Restructuring. *Prob. Econ.,* May 1987, *30*(1), pp. 47–63. [G: U.S.S.R.]

Bogomolov, Oleg T. Monetary Institutions in a Planned Economy. *de Cecco, M. and Fitoussi, J.-P., eds.,* 1987, pp. 209–21. [G: U.S.S.R.; CMEA]

Bogomolov, Oleg T. The Socialist Countries at a Critical Stage in World Economic Development. *Prob. Econ.,* December 1987, *30*(8), pp. 38–54. [G: CMEA]

Boisot, Max H. Industrial Feudalism and Enterprise Reform—Could the Chinese Use Some More Bureaucracy? *Warner, M., ed.,* 1987, pp. 217–37. [G: China]

Boldyrev, Boris; Ilyin, Vladimir and Sichev, Nikolai. The Role of Public Finance in Socialist Economies. *van de Kar, H. M. and Wolfe, B. L., eds.,* 1987, pp. 259–63.

Bolton, Roger. Regional Aspects of the Chinese Economic Reforms: Introduction to the Special Issue. *Int. Reg. Sci. Rev.,* 1987, *11*(1), pp. 1–3. [G: China]

Bonin, John P. and Fukuda, Wataru. Controlling a Risk-Averse, Effort-Selecting Manager in the Soviet Incentive Model. *J. Compar. Econ.,* June 1987, *11*(2), pp. 221–33. [G: U.S.S.R.]

Boot, Pieter. Incentive Systems and Unemployment: The East European Experience. *Comp. Econ. Stud.,* Spring 1987, *29*(1), pp. 37–61. [G: E. Europe]

Brezinski, Horst. The Second Economies in Eastern Europe. *Marer, P. and van Veen, P., eds.,* 1987, pp. 23–33. [G: E. Europe]

Bryson, Phillip J. GDR Economic Planning and Social Policy in the 1980s. *Comp. Econ. Stud.,* Summer 1987, *29*(2), pp. 19–38. [G: E. Germany]

Bryson, Phillip J. and Melzer, Manfred. The *Kombinat* in GDR Economic Organisation. *Jeffries, I. and Melzer, M., eds.,* 1987, pp. 51–68. [G: E. Germany]

Buchanan, James M. Notes for an Economic Theory of Socialism. *Buchanan, J. M. (II),* 1987, *1970,* pp. 237–50.

Bukhval'd, E. M. and Pogrebinskaia, V. A. Socioeconomic Factors in the Intensification of Social Labor. *Prob. Econ.,* November 1987, *30*(7), pp. 18–30. [G: U.S.S.R.]

Burkett, John P. Soviet Socioeconomic Development: A Fold Catastrophe? *Comp. Econ. Stud.,* Fall 1987, *29*(3), pp. 70–93.

Buza, M. Change and Reform: Comments and Contributions. *Acta Oecon.,* 1987, *38*(3–4), pp. 224–32. [G: Hungary]

Byrd, William A. The Impact of the Two-Tier Plan/Market System in Chinese Industry. *J.*

Compar. Econ., September 1987, *11*(3), pp. 295–308. [G: China]

Červinka, Antonín. The State Enterprise Act. *Czech. Econ. Digest.,* August 1987, (6), pp. 3–12. [G: Czechoslovakia]

Chang, Pei-kang and Lin, Shao-kung. China's Modernization: Stability, Efficiency, and the Price Mechanism. *Dutta, M., ed. (I),* 1987, pp. 103–18. [G: China]

Chen, Yizi and Wang, Xiaoqiang. Reform: Results and Lessons from the 1985 CESRRI Survey. *J. Compar. Econ.,* September 1987, *11*(3), pp. 462–78. [G: China]

Cherkovets, V. Theoretical Issues in Restructuring the System of Economic Management. *Prob. Econ.,* May 1987, *30*(1), pp. 64–80. [G: U.S.S.R.]

Chubakov, G. Avenues for Improving Retail Prices. *Prob. Econ.,* July 1987, *30*(3), pp. 70–84. [G: U.S.S.R.]

Chunze, Jiang. The Development of Socialist Economic Models. *Comp. Econ. Stud.,* Spring 1987, *29*(1), pp. 81–105. [G: E. Europe; China]

Codina Jiménez, Alexis. Workers Incentives in Cuba. *World Devel.,* January 1987, *15*(1), pp. 127–38. [G: Cuba]

Colton, Timothy J. Approaches to the Politics of Systemic Economic Reform in the Soviet Union. *Soviet Econ.,* April-June 1987, *3*(2), pp. 145–70. [G: U.S.S.R.]

Crosnier, Marie-Agnès. La protection sociale en Union Soviétique. (Welfare Benefits in the Soviet Union. With English summary.) *Écon. Soc.,* February 1987, *21*(2), pp. 29–75. [G: U.S.S.R.]

Day, Richard B. Democratic Control and the Dignity of Politics—An Analysis of *The Revolution Betrayed. Comp. Econ. Stud.,* Fall 1987, *29*(3), pp. 4–29. [G: U.S.S.R.]

Declercq, D. Management in China. *Tijdschrift Econ. Manage.,* 1987, *32*(3), pp. 321–35. [G: China]

Dědek, Oldřich. Scientific Debate on the Publication by Miroslav Toms "The Measurement of Effects in Socialist Eoncomy." *Czech. Econ. Pap.,* 1987, (24), pp. 141–47.

Deriabin, A. Principles in the Restructuring of Price Formation. *Prob. Econ.,* July 1987, *30*(3), pp. 54–69. [G: U.S.S.R.]

Donleavy, Gabriel D. Aspects of Hungarian Accounting. *Most, Kenneth S., ed.,* 1987, pp. 85–109. [G: Hungary]

Duchêne, Gérard. Les transferts sociaux dans les économies centralement planifiées. (Welfare Benefits in the Centrally Planned Economies. With English summary.) *Écon. Soc.,* February 1987, *21*(2), pp. 5–27. [G: E. Europe]

Dyker, David A. Restructuring and "Radical Reform": The Articulation of Investment Demand. *Comp. Econ. Stud.,* Winter 1987, *29*(4), pp. 103–27. [G: U.S.S.R.]

Fei, John and Reynolds, Bruce L. A Tentative Plan for the Rational Sequencing of Overall Reform in China's Economic System. *J. Com-*

par. Econ., September 1987, *11*(3), pp. 490–502. **[G: China]**

Ferge, Zsuzsa. Change and Reform: Comments and Contributions. *Acta Oecon.*, 1987, *38*(3–4), pp. 232–38. **[G: Hungary]**

Ferge, Zsuzsa. The Crisis and the 'Welfare State' in Eastern Europe with a Focus on Hungary. *Europ. Econ. Rev.*, Feb./Mar. 1987, *31*(1/2), pp. 212–19. **[G: Hungary]**

Fung, K. K. Surplus Seeking and Rent Seeking through Back-Door Deals in Mainland China: Price Control and Central Planning Fix Prices below Market Clearance, Creating a Contrived Surplus. *Amer. J. Econ. Soc.*, July 1987, *46*(3), pp. 299–317. **[G: China]**

Galasi, Péter and Kertesi, Gábor. The Spread of Bribery in a Centrally Planned Economy. *Acta Oecon.*, 1987, *38*(3–4), pp. 371–89.

Gergely, Istvá. Personal Income Tax, Yes—But How? (Contribution to Debated Issues). *Acta Oecon.*, 1987, *38*(3–4), pp. 275–87. **[G: Hungary]**

Gey, Peter and Kosta, Jiří. Diversity and Transitions in Socialist Economic Systems: A Comparative Introduction. *Gey, P.; Kosta, J. and Quaisser, W., eds.*, 1987, pp. 1–10. **[G: U.S.S.R.; E. Europe; China]**

Gliński, Bohdan. Variants of the Socialist Economic Management System in Eastern Europe. *Child, J. and Bate, P., eds.*, 1987, pp. 151–62. **[G: E. Europe]**

Gorodetskii, E. and Gorodetskii, A. Theoretical Prerequisites to the Systematic Restructuring of Prices. *Prob. Econ.*, September 1987, *30*(5), pp. 43–60. **[G: U.S.S.R.]**

Grancelli, Bruno. Managerial Practices and Patterns of Employee Behaviour in the Soviet Enterprise. *Child, J. and Bate, P., eds.*, 1987, pp. 205–20. **[G: U.S.S.R.]**

Granick, David. The Industrial Environment in China and the CMEA Countries. *Tidrick, G. and Jiyuan, C., eds.*, 1987, pp. 103–31. **[G: China; CMEA]**

Hamel, Hannelore and Leipold, Helmut. Economic Reform in the GDR: Causes and Effects. *Jeffries, I. and Melzer, M., eds.*, 1987, pp. 280–304. **[G: E. Germany]**

Hanson, Philip. The Soviet Economy: A Look Ahead from 1985. *[Marrama, V.], Vol. 2*, 1987, pp. 559–75. **[G: U.S.S.R.]**

Hare, Paul. Economic Reform in Eastern Europe. *J. Econ. Surveys*, 1987, *1*(1), pp. 25–58. **[G: E. Europe]**

Hauslohner, Peter. Gorbachev's Social Contract. *Soviet Econ.*, Jan.-Mar. 1987, *3*(1), pp. 54–89. **[G: U.S.S.R.]**

Havasi, Ferenc. Change and Reform: Stand Taken by the Economic Panel of the Central Committee of the HSWP. *Acta Oecon.*, 1987, *38*(3–4), pp. 263–72. **[G: Hungary]**

Hoch, R. Change and Reform: Comments and Contributions. *Acta Oecon.*, 1987, *38*(3–4), pp. 238–48. **[G: Hungary]**

Höhmann, Hans-Hermann. Soviet Economic Policies under Gorbachev: Problems and Pro-

spects. *Gey, P.; Kosta, J. and Quaisser, W., eds.*, 1987, pp. 33–48. **[G: U.S.S.R.]**

Holzman, Franklyn D. The Economics of Soviet Bloc Trade and Finance: Introduction. *Holzman, F. D.*, 1987, pp. 1–29. **[G: U.S.S.R.; CMEA]**

Homos, Tudor and Constantin, Dumitru. Specialization, Cooperation, and Integration in Production and Intensive Economic Development. *Eastern Europ. Econ.*, Spring 1987, *25*(3), pp. 109–16.

Hong, Hai. The Service Sector in China's Economic Reform Policy. *Singapore Econ. Rev.*, October 1987, *32*(2), pp. 16–27. **[G: China]**

Hua, Sheng, et al. A Restructuring of the Microeconomic Foundation: More on China's Further Reform and Some Related Thoughts. *Chinese Econ. Stud.*, Summer 1987, *20*(4), pp. 3–26. **[G: China]**

Ishihara, Kyōichi. Planning and the Market in China. *Devel. Econ.*, December 1987, *25*(4), pp. 287–309. **[G: China]**

Jeffries, Ian. The GDR in Historical and International Perspective. *Jeffries, I. and Melzer, M., eds.*, 1987, pp. 1–11. **[G: E. Germany]**

Jeffries, Ian and Melzer, Manfred. Command Planning and the Production Unit. *Jeffries, I. and Melzer, M., eds.*, 1987, pp. 12–25. **[G: E. Germany]**

Jeffries, Ian and Melzer, Manfred. The Economic Strategy of the 1980s and the Limits to Possible Reforms. *Jeffries, I. and Melzer, M., eds.*, 1987, pp. 41–50. **[G: E. Germany]**

Jeffries, Ian and Melzer, Manfred. The New Economic System of Planning and Management 1963–70 and Recentralisation in the 1970s. *Jeffries, I. and Melzer, M., eds.*, 1987, pp. 26–40. **[G: E. Germany]**

Józefiak, Cezary. The Road to the Barriers of Demand. *Eastern Europ. Econ.*, Winter 1987-88, *26*(2), pp. 84–91. **[G: Poland]**

Karsai, Gábor. The Market-Building Process Is Uncompleted: The Organization of Domestic Trade in the First Half of the 1980s. *Eastern Europ. Econ.*, Winter 1987-88, *26*(2), pp. 35–63. **[G: Hungary]**

Kasimovskii, E. Social Justice and the Improvement of Distribution Relations in the USSR. *Prob. Econ.*, September 1987, *30*(5), pp. 61–81. **[G: U.S.S.R.]**

Kemenes, E. Change and Reform: Comments and Contributions. *Acta Oecon.*, 1987, *38*(3–4), pp. 248–55. **[G: Hungary]**

Khalil, Elias L. The Process of Capitalist Accumulation: A Review Essay of David Levine's Contribution. *Rev. Radical Polit. Econ.*, Winter 1987, *19*(4), pp. 76–85.

Klein, Bohuslav. Joint Enterprises in Czechoslovakia. *Czech. Econ. Digest.*, August 1987, (6), pp. 36–46. **[G: Czechoslovakia]**

Kołodko, Grzegorz W. Development Goals and Economic Macroproportions. *Eastern Europ. Econ.*, Spring 1987, *25*(3), pp. 72–85. **[G: CMEA]**

Kosta, Jiří. The Chinese Economic Reform: Approaches, Results and Prospects. *Gey, P.;*

Kosta, J. and Quaisser, W., eds., 1987, pp. 145–71. [G: China]

Kowalski, Jan S. Rational Expectations in Centrally Planned Economies. Pejovich, S., ed., 1987, pp. 175–207.

Koziolek, Helmut. The Economic Strategy of the Eleventh Party Congress of the SED and the New Stage in Science-Production Relations. Eastern Europ. Econ., Winter 1987-88, 26(2), pp. 64–83. [G: E. Germany]

Kulikov, V. Commodity–Monetary Relations in the Concept of Acceleration. Prob. Econ., June 1987, 30(2), pp. 43–59. [G: U.S.S.R.]

Kupa, Mihály. Personal Income Tax: Principles and Debates. Acta Oecon., 1987, 38(3–4), pp. 289–302. [G: Hungary]

Kushnirsky, F. I. Soviet Economic Reform: An Analysis and a Model. Comp. Econ. Stud., Winter 1987, 29(4), pp. 54–85. [G: U.S.S.R.]

Kuznetsova, T. Cooperative Relations in a Socialist Economy. Prob. Econ., September 1987, 30(5), pp. 6–23. [G: U.S.S.R.]

Laptev, Vladimir. Legal Problems in the Restructuring of the Economic Mechanism. Prob. Econ., December 1987, 30(8), pp. 75–92. [G: U.S.S.R.]

Latsis, Otto R. "To Take a New Look": Reflections of an Economist. Prob. Econ., June 1987, 30(2), pp. 22–42. [G: U.S.S.R.]

Latsis, Otto R. Individual Labor in a Modern Socialist Economy. Prob. Econ., August 1987, 30(4), pp. 37–49. [G: U.S.S.R.]

Lavigne, Marie. Economic Prospects in the Eastern Bloc Countries. Marer, P. and van Veen, P., eds., 1987, pp. 17–21. [G: E. Europe]

Leggett, Robert E. Gorbachev's Reform Program: "Radical" or More of the Same? Comp. Econ. Stud., Winter 1987, 29(4), pp. 29–53. [G: U.S.S.R.]

Leibbrandt, M. V. Rethinking Socialist Economics (Review Note). S. Afr. J. Econ., September 1987, 55(3), pp. 286–91. [G: U.K.]

Levine, Herbert S. Anatomy of Gorbachev's Economic Reform: Comment. Soviet Econ., July-Sept. 1987, 3(3), pp. 242–45. [G: U.S.S.R.]

Lin, Justin Yifu. The Household Responsibility System Reform in China: A Peasant's Institutional Choice. Amer. J. Agr. Econ., May 1987, 69(2), pp. 410–15. [G: China]

Linz, Susan J. Reorganization and Reform in the Soviet Economy. Comp. Econ. Stud., Winter 1987, 29(4), pp. 1–6. [G: U.S.S.R.]

Linz, Susan J. The Impact of Soviet Economic Reform: Evidence from the Soviet Interview Project. Comp. Econ. Stud., Winter 1987, 29(4), pp. 150–72. [G: U.S.S.R.]

Liu, Guoguang. Problems in the Reform of Ownership Relations in China. Warner, M., ed., 1987, pp. 165–75. [G: China]

Liu, Guoguang, et al. Economic Reform and Macroeconomic Management: Commentaries on the International Conference on Macroeconomic Management. Chinese Econ. Stud., Spring 1987, 20(3), pp. 3–45. [G: China]

Lockett, Martin. Technical Innovation and Eco-nomic Reform in Socialist Economies with Special Reference to China. Child, J. and Bate, P., eds., 1987, pp. 191–203. [G: China]

Ma, Bin and Hong, Zhunyan. Enlivening Large State Enterprises: Where Is the Motive Force? J. Compar. Econ., September 1987, 11(3), pp. 503–08. [G: China]

Mach, Miloš. Some Questions Concerning the Essence and Function of the Socialist Economic Mechanism. Czech. Econ. Pap., 1987, (24), pp. 59–81. [G: Czechoslovakia]

Manevich, E. Means of Restructuring the Economic Mechanism. Prob. Econ., May 1987, 30(1), pp. 81–97. [G: U.S.S.R.]

Marzano, Ferruccio. Keynesian Theory Planning Models and Quantitative Economics: An Overview of the Essays. [Marrama, V.], Vol. 1, 1987, pp. xxviii–liv.

Maximova, M. M. World Markets and Socialist Economies. Pasinetti, L. and Lloyd, P., eds., 1987, pp. 427–37. [G: CMEA]

Melzer, Manfred. The Perfecting of the Planning and Steering Mechanisms. Jeffries, I. and Melzer, M., eds., 1987, pp. 99–118. [G: E. Germany]

Mencinger, Jože. The Crisis and the Reform of the Yugoslav Economic System in the Eighties. Gey, P.; Kosta, J. and Quaisser, W., eds., 1987, pp. 99–119. [G: Yugoslavia]

Merkel, Konrad. The East German Economy: Agriculture. Jeffries, I. and Melzer, M., eds., 1987, pp. 202–34. [G: E. Germany]

Mojžišková, Soňa. Foreign Exchange Regulations in the Socialist Countries. Soviet E. Europ. Foreign Trade, Winter 1987-1988, 23(4), pp. 22–66. [G: CMEA]

Nitzan, Shmuel and Schnytzer, Adi. Diligence and Laziness in the Chinese Countryside Revisited. J. Devel. Econ., August 1987, 26(2), pp. 407–18. [G: China]

Nováček, Vladimír. Czechoslovakia in the International Division of Labour. Czech. Econ. Digest., October 1987, (7), pp. 61–68. [G: Czechoslovakia]

Nove, Alec. Trotsky, Markets, and East European Reforms. Comp. Econ. Stud., Fall 1987, 29(3), pp. 30–39. [G: U.S.S.R.; E. Europe]

Oldak, P. G. Changing the Paradigm of Economic Thought. Prob. Econ., October 1987, 30(6), pp. 51–71. [G: U.S.S.R.]

Pejovich, Steve. Freedom, Property Rights and Innovation in Socialism. Kyklos, 1987, 40(4), pp. 461–75. [G: Yugoslavia]

Pejovich, Svetozar. The Case of Self-management in Yugoslavia. Pejovich, S., ed., 1987, pp. 239–49. [G: Yugoslavia]

Péter, Sándor. Reform and Paternalism in China: Some Theoretical Concerns. Int. Reg. Sci. Rev., 1987, 11(1), pp. 59–73. [G: China]

Petrakov, Nikolay. Prospects for Change in the Systems of Price Formation, Finance and Credit in the USSR. Soviet Econ., April-June 1987, 3(2), pp. 135–44. [G: U.S.S.R.]

Petrakov, Nikolay. The Plan Price in the National Economy's System of Management. Prob.

Econ., July 1987, *30*(3), pp. 38–53.
[G: U.S.S.R.]

Pryor, Frederic L. Marxist Regimes Series: Review Article. *J. Compar. Econ.*, March 1987, *11*(1), pp. 124–32.

Pysz, Piotr. The Polish Economic Reform: Central Planning or Socialist Markets? *Gey, P.; Kosta, J. and Quaisser, W., eds.*, 1987, pp. 49–69.
[G: Poland]

Rohlíček, Rudolf. Fundamental Principles of the Restructuring of the Economic Mechanism. *Czech. Econ. Digest.*, October 1987, (7), pp. 17–32.
[G: Czechoslovakia]

Rong, Wenzuo. Establishing Socialist Joint Stock Companies: A Report of a Study on the Joint-Development Company of the China Tourism Souvenirs Enterprise. *Chinese Econ. Stud.*, Spring 1987, *20*(3), pp. 46–62. [G: China]

Rong, Yiren. Observations on Some Questions in the Building of a Socialist Economy with Chinese Characteristics: Reflections on Rereading the Constitution. *Chinese Econ. Stud.*, Winter 1986-87, *20*(2), pp. 13–25.
[G: China]

Rosen, Stanley. The Private Economy (I): Editor's Introduction. *Chinese Econ. Stud.*, Fall 1987, *21*(1), pp. 3–9. [G: China]

Ruble, Blair A. The Social Dimensions of *Perestroyka*. *Soviet Econ.*, April-June 1987, *3*(2), pp. 171–83. [G: U.S.S.R.]

Rutgaizer, V. M. and Sheviakhov, Iu. E. Distribution According to One's Labor. *Prob. Econ.*, November 1987, *30*(7), pp. 31–46.
[G: CMEA]

Schrenk, Martin. The Self-managed Firm in Yugoslavia. *Tidrick, G. and Jiyuan, C., eds.*, 1987, pp. 339–69. [G: Yugoslavia; China]

Schroeder, Gertrude E. Anatomy of Gorbachev's Economic Reform. *Soviet Econ.*, July-Sept. 1987, *3*(3), pp. 219–41. [G: U.S.S.R.]

Schroeder, Gertrude E. Organizations and Hierarchies: The Perennial Search for Solutions. *Comp. Econ. Stud.*, Winter 1987, *29*(4), pp. 7–28. [G: U.S.S.R.]

Schweickart, David. A Reply to Arnold's Reply [Marx and Disequilibrium in Market Socialist Relations of Production]. *Econ. Philos.*, October 1987, *3*(2), pp. 331–34.

Schweickart, David. Market Socialist Capitalist Roaders: A Comment on Arnold [Marx and Disequilibrium in Market Socialist Relations of Production]. *Econ. Philos.*, October 1987, *3*(2), pp. 308–19.

Šedivý, Zdenk. Improvement of the Economic Mechanism and the Transition to Intensive Development. *Eastern Europ. Econ.*, Spring 1987, *25*(3), pp. 50–62. [G: CMEA]

Senchagov, V. The Collective Experience in Improving Economic Management. *Prob. Econ.*, January 1987, *29*(9), pp. 56–78. [G: CMEA]

Sha, Ye. The Role of China's Managing Directors in the Current Economic Reform. *Int. Lab. Rev.*, Nov.-Dec. 1987, *126*(6), pp. 691–701.
[G: China]

Shapiro, J. C. On the Accuracy of Economic Observations of *Chto Takoe SSSR* in Historical

Retrospect. *Comp. Econ. Stud.*, Fall 1987, *29*(3), pp. 45–69.

Shatalin, S. S. Social Development and Economic Growth. *Prob. Econ.*, May 1987, *30*(1), pp. 27–46. [G: U.S.S.R.]

Shatalin, S. S. The Effective Utilization of Resources: Interests and Stimuli. *Prob. Econ.*, August 1987, *30*(4), pp. 6–21. [G: U.S.S.R.]

Shi, Ling. Xue Muqiao Expresses New Views on the Question of Ownership: Possible Formation of Socialist Public Ownership with Multiple Tiers and Modes of Administration. *Chinese Econ. Stud.*, Winter 1986-87, *20*(2), pp. 64–66. [G: China]

Sitarian, Stepan A. Aspects of Political Economy in the Concept of Acceleration. *Prob. Econ.*, November 1987, *30*(7), pp. 74–90.
[G: U.S.S.R.]

Sklair, Leslie. Capitalist Efficiency without Capitalist Exploitation—Some Indications from Shenzhen. *Warner, M., ed.*, 1987, pp. 176–97. [G: China]

Sun, Li-teh. Confucianism and the Recent Chinese Economic Reform. *J. Econ. Devel.*, June 1987, *12*(1), pp. 7–32. [G: China]

Sung, Yun-wing and Chan, Thomas M. H. China's Economic Reforms I: The Debates in China. *Asian-Pacific Econ. Lit.*, May 1987, *1*(1), pp. 1–24. [G: China]

Szelenyi, Ivan and Manchin, Robert. Social Policy under State Socialism: Market Redistribution and Social Inequalities in East European Socialist Societies. *Rein, M.; Esping-Andersen, G. and Rainwater, L., eds.*, 1987, pp. 102–39. [G: E. Europe]

Szita, Éva. New Types of Entrepreneurial and Organizational Forms in the Hungarian Economy. *Alessandrini, S. and Dallago, B., eds.*, 1987, pp. 181–93. [G: Hungary]

Tarafás, I. Change and Reform: Comments and Contributions. *Acta Oecon.*, 1987, *38*(3–4), pp. 255–63. [G: Hungary]

Tardos, Márton. The Role of Money in Hungary. *Europ. Econ. Rev.*, Feb./Mar. 1987, *31*(1/2), pp. 125–31. [G: Hungary]

Telegdy, I. Stephen. Doing Business in Eastern Europe: A Manager's Perspective on the Practical Aspects. *Marer, P. and van Veen, P., eds.*, 1987, pp. 99–106. [G: E. Europe]

Theen, Rolf H. W. Hierarchical Reform: The Case of Agriculture. *Comp. Econ. Stud.*, Winter 1987, *29*(4), pp. 86–102. [G: U.S.S.R.]

Tidrick, Gene and Chen, Jiyuan. China's Industrial Reform: The Essence of the Industrial Reforms. *Tidrick, G. and Jiyuan, C., eds.*, 1987, pp. 1–10. [G: China]

Tong, Dalin and Song, Yanming. Horizontal Economic Integration Is a Beachhead to Launch Urban Reform. *Chinese Econ. Stud.*, Winter 1986-87, *20*(2), pp. 26–35. [G: China]

Torkanovskii, E. The Participation of Working People in the Management of Production as a Factor in Heightening Labor Activism. *Prob. Econ.*, June 1987, *30*(2), pp. 60–70.

Toumanoff, Peter. Economic Reform and Industrial Performance in the Soviet Union: 1950–

1984. *Comp. Econ. Stud.*, Winter 1987, *29*(4), pp. 128–49. **[G: U.S.S.R.]**

Tröder, Manfred. The 1981–85 Order of Planning (Planungsordnung). *Jeffries, I. and Melzer, M., eds.*, 1987, pp. 69–98. **[G: E. Germany]**

Turysov, K. The Human Factor in the Strategy of Acceleration. *Prob. Econ.*, October 1987, *30*(6), pp. 6–18. **[G: U.S.S.R.]**

Valenta, František. Intensive Development of Socialist Economy. (The Evolution of Theoretical Approach) *Czech. Econ. Pap.*, 1987, (24), pp. 7–33. **[G: Czechoslovakia]**

Vaubel, Roland. Socialism: Do the Ends Justify the Means? *Pejovich, S., ed.*, 1987, pp. 89–113.

Veretennikov, V. G. The Economic Mechanism and Self-management. *Prob. Econ.*, October 1987, *30*(6), pp. 19–33. **[G: U.S.S.R.]**

Volkonskii, Victor A.; Vavilov, Andrei P. and Pavlov, Nikolai V. Optimization of Branch Price Level Relations in Planned Economy. *[Marrama, V.], Vol. 2*, 1987, pp. 651–75. **[G: U.S.S.R.]**

Walker, Ignacio. Socialismo y democracia: algunas experiencias europeas. (Socialism and Democracy: Some European Experiences. With English summary.) *Colección Estud. CIEPLAN*, June 1987, (21), pp. 23–48. **[G: Europe]**

Wanless, P. T. The Efficiency of Central Planning: A Perspective from 'Markets vs Hierarchies.' *Scot. J. Polit. Econ.*, February 1987, *34*(1), pp. 52–68.

Wass von Czege, Andreas. Hungary's "New Economic Mechanism": Upheaval or Continuity? *Gey, P.; Kosta, J. and Quaisser, W., eds.*, 1987, pp. 121–44. **[G: Hungary]**

Xu, Jing'an. The Stock-Share System: A New Avenue for China's Economic Reform. *J. Compar. Econ.*, September 1987, *11*(3), pp. 509–14. **[G: China]**

Youzhi,Tao. A Brief Discussion of the Consolidation and Development of the Individual Economy. *Chinese Econ. Stud.*, Fall 1987, *21*(1), pp. 37–42. **[G: China]**

Zaslavskaia, Tatiana I. Creative Activity of the Masses: Social Reserves of Growth. *Prob. Econ.*, March 1987, *29*(11), pp. 5–27. **[G: U.S.S.R.]**

Zaslavskaia, Tatiana I. Social Justice and the Human Factor in Economic Development. *Prob. Econ.*, May 1987, *30*(1), pp. 5–26. **[G: U.S.S.R.]**

Zaslavskaia, Tatiana I. Socioeconomic Aspects of *Perestroyka. Soviet Econ.*, October-December 1987, *3*(4), pp. 313–31. **[G: U.S.S.R.]**

Zdeněk, Mošna. The Principles of Activity. *Czech. Econ. Digest.*, August 1987, (6), pp. 13–35.

Zhongrui, Xia; Wanzhen, Wang and Zhi, Jin. Strengthening Guidance and Management; Expanding Individual Economy: Shanghai Forum on Individual Economy. *Chinese Econ. Stud.*, Fall 1987, *21*(1), pp. 102–17. **[G: China]**

Zimbalist, Andrew. Cuba's Socialist Economy toward the 1990s: Introduction. *Zimbalist, A., ed.*, 1987, pp. 1–5. **[G: Cuba]**

Zimbalist, Andrew and Eckstein, Susan. Patterns of Cuban Development: The First Twenty-five Years. *Zimbalist, A., ed.*, 1987, pp. 7–24. **[G: Cuba]**

Zuo, Mu. An Exploration into Several Problems Related to the Restructuring of the System of Ownership. *Chinese Econ. Stud.*, Spring 1987, *20*(3), pp. 63–77. **[G: China]**

053 Comparative Economic Systems

0530 Comparative Economic Systems

Amirahmadi, Hooshang. The Non-capitalist Way of Development. *Rev. Radical Polit. Econ.*, Spring 1987, *19*(1), pp. 22–46.

Bate, Paul and Child, John. Paradigms and Understandings in Comparative Organizational Research. *Child, J. and Bate, P., eds.*, 1987, pp. 19–49.

Ben-Ner, Avner. Preferences in a Communal Economic System. *Economica*, May 1987, *54*(214), pp. 207–21. **[G: Israel]**

Bergson, Abram. Comparative Productivity: The USSR, Eastern Europe, and the West. *Amer. Econ. Rev.*, June 1987, *77*(3), pp. 342–57. **[G: OECD; CMEA]**

Bognár, József. Impact of External Market Fluctuations on Centrally Planned and Market Economies: Discussion and Conclusions. *Pasinetti, L. and Lloyd, P., eds.*, 1987, pp. 479–83. **[G: CMEA]**

Boyd, Michael L. The Performance of Private and Cooperative Socialist Organization: Postwar Yugoslav Agriculture. *Rev. Econ. Statist.*, May 1987, *69*(2), pp. 205–14. **[G: Yugoslavia]**

Cassel, Dieter and Cichy, Ulrich. The Shadow Economy and Economic Policy in East and West: A Comparative System Approach. *Alessandrini, S. and Dallago, B., eds.*, 1987, pp. 127–46.

Dallago, Bruno. The Underground Economy in the West and the East: A Comparative Approach. *Alessandrini, S. and Dallago, B., eds.*, 1987, pp. 147–63.

Gintis, Herbert. The Nature of Labor Exchange and the Theory of Capitalist Production. *Albelda, R.; Gunn, C. and Waller, W., eds.*, 1987, 1976, pp. 68–88.

Holzman, Franklyn D. A Comparative View of Foreign Trade Behavior: Market versus Centrally Planned Economies. *Holzman, F. D.*, 1987, 1985, pp. 91–112.

Kolodko, Grzegorz W. and McMahon, Walter W. Stagflation and Shortageflation: A Comparative Approach. *Kyklos*, 1987, *40*(2), pp. 176–97. **[G: OECD; CMEA]**

Komiya, Ryutaro. Japanese Firms, Chinese Firms: Problems for Economic Reform in China: Part I. *J. Japanese Int. Economies*, March 1987, *1*(1), pp. 31–61. **[G: Japan; China]**

Komiya, Ryutaro. Japanese Firms, Chinese Firms: Problems for Economic Reform in China: Part II. *J. Japanese Int. Economies*,

June 1987, *1*(2), pp. 229–47.   **[G: Japan; China]**

Laaksonen, Oiva. Capitalist–Socialist Dialogue on Organizational Behaviour. *Child, J. and Bate, P., eds.*, 1987, pp. 1–15.

Pejovich, Steve. Freedom, Property Rights and Innovation in Socialism. *Kyklos*, 1987, *40*(4), pp. 461–75.   **[G: Yugoslavia]**

Srinivasan, T. N. Economic Liberalization in China and India: Issues and an Analytical Framework. *J. Compar. Econ.*, September 1987, *11*(3), pp. 427–43.   **[G: China; India]**

Stollar, Andrew J. and Thompson, G. Rodney. Sectoral Employment Shares: A Comparative Systems Context. *J. Compar. Econ.*, March 1987, *11*(1), pp. 62–80.

Sydow, Jörg. Information Technology and Organizational Choice. *Child, J. and Bate, P., eds.*, 1987, pp. 85–100.

Trzeciakowski, Witold. Impact of External Market Fluctuations on Centrally Planned and Market Economies: A Systematic Comparative Approach. *Pasinetti, L. and Lloyd, P., eds.*, 1987, pp. 465–77.   **[G: CMEA]**

Wood, Stephen. Towards Socialist–Capitalist Comparisons of the Organizational Problem. *Child, J. and Bate, P., eds.*, 1987, pp. 51–71.

Zamfir, Cătălin. Four Structural Problems of the Modern Enterprise: Similarities and Differences in Capitalist and Socialist Countries. *Child, J. and Bate, P., eds.*, 1987, pp. 73–83.

100 Economic Growth; Development; Planning; Fluctuations

110 ECONOMIC GROWTH; DEVELOPMENT; PLANNING THEORY AND POLICY

111 Economic Growth Theory and Models

1110 Growth Theories

Akin, Ethan. Competitive Growth of Firms in an Industry. *Batten, D.; Casti, J. and Johansson, B., eds.*, 1987, pp. 86–115.

Altaev, V. Modeling Economic Growth of a Socialist Economy. *Rivista Int. Sci. Econ. Com.*, October 1987, *34*(10), pp. 971–87. **[G: U.S.S.R.]**

Frey, René L. Wirtschaftswachstum und Umweltqualität: Auf der Suche nach einer neuen Wachstumspolitik. (Economic Growth and Environmental Quality: In Search of a New Growth Policy. With English summary.) *Schweiz. Z. Volkswirtsch. Statist.*, September 1987, *123*(3), pp. 289–315.

Funke, Michael. A Generated Goodwin Model Incorporating Technical Progress and Variable Prices. *Econ. Notes*, 1987, (2), pp. 36–47.

Gini, Corrado. Occidental and Oriental Conceptions of Economic Progress. *Dupriez, L. H., ed.*, 1987, *1955*, pp. 182–92.

Glombowski, Jorg and Krüger, Michael. Generalizations of Goodwin's Growth Cycle Model.

Batten, D.; Casti, J. and Johansson, B., eds., 1987, pp. 260–90.

Gordon, Myron J. Insecurity, Growth, and the Rise of Capitalism. *J. Post Keynesian Econ.*, Summer 1987, *9*(4), pp. 529–51.

Greenwood, David. Note on the Impact of Military Expenditure on Economic Growth and Performance. *Schmidt, C., ed.*, 1987, pp. 98–103.

de Haan, Hendrik. Military Expenditures and Economic Growth: Some Theoretical Remarks. *Schmidt, C., ed.*, 1987, pp. 87–97.

Habakkuk, H. J. The Historical Experience of the Basic Conditions of Economic Progress. *Dupriez, L. H., ed.*, 1987, pp. 85–102.   **[G: U.S.; U.S.S.R.; W. Europe; Japan]**

Hahn, Frank H. "Of Marx and Keynes and Many Things": A Review Article. *Sinclair, P. J. N., ed.*, 1987, *1986*, pp. 378–85.

Johansson, Börje; Batten, David F. and Casti, John. Economic Dynamics, Evolution and Structural Adjustment. *Batten, D.; Casti, J. and Johansson, B., eds.*, 1987, pp. 1–23.

Laibman, David. Growth, Technical Change, and Cycles: Simulation Models in Marxist Economic Theory. *Sci. Soc.*, Winter 1987-1988, *51*(4), pp. 414–38.

Lowe, Adolph. Structural Analysis of Real-Capital Formation. *Lowe, A.*, 1987, *1955*, pp. 60–106.

Lowe, Adolph. The Classical Theory of Economic Growth. *Lowe, A.*, 1987, *1954*, pp. 107–31.

Majumdar, Mukul K. and Zilcha, Itzhak. Optimal Growth in a Stochastic Environment: Some Sensitivity and Turnpike Results. *J. Econ. Theory*, October 1987, *43*(1), pp. 116–33.

Malinvaud, Edmond. Reflecting on the Theory of Capital and Growth. *Sinclair, P. J. N., ed.*, 1987, *1986*, pp. 395–413.

Melese, Francois and Transue, William. Unscrambling Chaos through Thick and Thin: An Explanation. *Quart. J. Econ.*, February 1987, *102*(1), pp. 171.

Metcalfe, J. S. and Gibbons, Michael. On the Economics of Structural Change and the Evolution of Technology. *Pasinetti, L. and Lloyd, P., eds.*, 1987, pp. 91–102.

Nicolau, Ed. Growth Models. *Econ. Computat. Cybern. Stud. Res.*, 1987, *22*(2), pp. 39–44.

Nikaido, Hukukane. No Growth, No Fluctuations. *Feiwel, G. R., ed. (II)*, 1987, pp. 421–45.

North, Douglass C. Institutions, Transaction Costs and Economic Growth. *Econ. Inquiry*, July 1987, *25*(3), pp. 419–28.

O'Connell, Joan. Kaldor's Distribution Theory. *J. Post Keynesian Econ.*, Summer 1987, *9*(4), pp. 572–75.

Pasinetti, Luigi L. "Satisfactory" versus "Optimal" Economic Growth. *Rivista Int. Sci. Econ. Com.*, October 1987, *34*(10), pp. 989–99.

Pasinetti, Luigi L. Economic Growth with Structural Change: An Introduction. *Pasinetti, L. and Lloyd, P., eds.*, 1987, pp. 7–12.

Prescott, Edward C. and Boyd, John H. Dynamic Coalitions: Engines of Growth. *Amer. Econ. Rev.*, May 1987, *77*(2), pp. 63–67.

Ranson, Baldwin. The Institutionalist Theory of

Capital Formation. *J. Econ. Issues*, September 1987, *21*(3), pp. 1265–78.

Reid, Gavin C. Disequilibrium and Increasing Returns in Adam Smith's Analysis of Growth and Accumulation. *Hist. Polit. Econ.*, Spring 1987, *19*(1), pp. 87–106.

Solow, Robert M. Second Thoughts on Growth Theory. *Steinherr, A. and Weiserbs, D., eds.*, 1987, pp. 13–28.

Tobin, James. Economic Growth as an Objective of Government Policy. *Tobin, J. (I)*, 1987, *1964*, pp. 174–94.

Vasko, Tibor. The Long-Wave Debate: Preface. *Vasko, T., ed.*, 1987, pp. v–xi.

Willis, Robert J. Externalities and Population. *Johnson, D. G. and Lee, R. D., eds.*, 1987, pp. 661–702.

1112 One and Two Sector Growth Models and Related Topics

Albin, Peter S. Microeconomic Foundations of Cyclical Irregularities or 'Chaos.' *Math. Soc. Sci.*, June 1987, *13*(3), pp. 185–214.

Andersson, Åke. Creativity and Economic Dynamics Modelling. *Batten, D.; Casti, J. and Johansson, B., eds.*, 1987, pp. 27–45.

Batten, David F. The Balanced Path of Economic Development: A Fable for Growth Merchants. *Batten, D.; Casti, J. and Johansson, B., eds.*, 1987, pp. 64–85.

Bernheim, B. Douglas and Ray, Debraj. Economic Growth with Intergenerational Altruism. *Rev. Econ. Stud.*, April 1987, *54*(2), pp. 227–41.

Bidard, Christian and Franke, Reiner. On the Existence of Long-term Equilibria in the Two-Class Pasinetti–Morishima Model. *Ricerche Econ.*, Jan.–Mar. 1987, *41*(1), pp. 3–21.

Boldrin, Michele and Montrucchio, Luigi. On the Indeterminacy of Capital Accumulation Paths. *Grandmont, J.-M., ed.*, 1987, *1986*, pp. 26–39.

Cairncross, Alec. The Place of Capital in Economic Progress. *Dupriez, L. H., ed.*, 1987, *1955*, pp. 197–209.

Canavese, Alfredo Juan. Estancamiento e inflación en un modelo de crecimiento desequilibrado. (Stagflation in a Three Sector Model of Unbalanced Growth. With English summary.) *Económica (La Plata)*, January–June 1987, *33*(1), pp. 39–50.

Chang, Fwu-Ranq and Malliaris, A. G. Asymptotic Growth under Uncertainty: Existence and Uniqueness. *Rev. Econ. Stud.*, January 1987, *54*(1), pp. 169–74.

Deneckere, Raymond J. and Pelikan, Steve. Competitive Chaos. *Grandmont, J.-M., ed.*, 1987, *1986*, pp. 13–25.

Dutta, Prajit K. Capital Deepening and Impatience Equivalence in Stochastic Aggregative Growth Models. *J. Econ. Dynam. Control*, December 1987, *11*(4), pp. 519–30.

Friesz, Terry L. and Luque, Javier. Optimal Regional Growth Models: Multiple Objectives, Singular Controls, and Sufficiency Conditions. *J. Reg. Sci.*, May 1987, *27*(2), pp. 201–24.

Ginsburgh, Victor; Henin, P. Y. and Michel, Philippe. A Dual Decision Approach to Disequilibrium Growth. *Sinclair, P. J. N., ed.*, 1987, *1985*, pp. 386–94.

Laitner, John. The Dynamic Analysis of Continuous-Time Life-Cycle Savings Growth Models. *J. Econ. Dynam. Control*, September 1987, *11*(3), pp. 331–57.

Peters, Wolfgang. Steady State Growth Paths in a Continuously Overlapping Generations Model. *Z. Wirtschaft. Sozialwissen.*, 1987, *107*(4), pp. 581–94.

Rama, Martín. L'endettement extérieur dans un modèle de croissance en déséquilibre. (With English summary.) *Revue Écon.*, September 1987, *38*(5), pp. 933–48.

Romer, Paul M. Growth Based on Increasing Returns Due to Specialization. *Amer. Econ. Rev.*, May 1987, *77*(2), pp. 56–62.

Seidman, Laurence S. The Government Deficit in a Growth Model: Consequences and Trade-offs. *J. Macroecon.*, Fall 1987, *9*(4), pp. 593–611.

Shea, Koon-Lam and Lau, Man-Lui. A Choice Theoretic Model of the Kaldorian Growth Analysis. *Hong Kong Econ. Pap.*, 1987, (18), pp. 15–22.

Smith, M. Alasdair M. Capital Accumulation in the Open Two-Sector Economy. *Bhagwati, J. N., ed.*, 1987, *1977*, pp. 395–406.

Sotomayor, Marilda de Oliveira. On Income Fluctuations and Capital Gains with a Convex Production Function. *J. Econ. Dynam. Control*, September 1987, *11*(3), pp. 285–312.

Stiglitz, Joseph E. Learning to Learn, Localized Learning and Technological Progress. *Dasgupta, P. and Stoneman, P., eds.*, 1987, pp. 125–53.

Takekuma, Shin-Ichi. Support Prices for Optimal Programs of Capital Accumulation in a General Reduced Model under Uncertainty. *Hitotsubashi J. Econ.*, December 1987, *28*(2), pp. 183–89.

Tobin, James. A Dynamic Aggregative Model. *Tobin, J. (I)*, 1987, pp. 115–32.

Tobin, James. Life Cycle Saving and Balanced Growth. *Tobin, J. (II)*, 1987, *1967*, pp. 127–53.

Zilcha, Itzhak. Uncertain Horizon and Stability: Analysis in an Optimal Growth Model. *J. Econ. Dynam. Control*, September 1987, *11*(3), pp. 445–53.

1113 Multisector Growth Models and Related Topics

Andersson, Åke. Creativity and Economic Dynamics Modelling. *Batten, D.; Casti, J. and Johansson, B., eds.*, 1987, pp. 27–45.

Becker, Robert A. and Foias, Ciprian. A Characterization of Ramsey Equilibrium. *J. Econ. Theory*, February 1987, *41*(1), pp. 173–84.

Benhabib, J.; Majumdar, Mukul K. and Nishimura, K. Global Equilibrium Dynamics with Stationary Recursive Preferences. *J. Econ. Behav. Organ.*, September 1987, *8*(3), pp. 429–52.

111 Economic Growth Theory and Models

Bidard, Christian and Hosoda, Eiji. On Consumption Baskets in a Generalized von Neumann Model. *Int. Econ. Rev.*, June 1987, 28(2), pp. 509–19.

Epstein, Larry G. A Simple Dynamic General Equilibrium Model. *J. Econ. Theory*, February 1987, 41(1), pp. 68–95.

Epstein, Larry G. The Global Stability of Efficient Intertemporal Allocations. *Econometrica*, March 1987, 55(2), pp. 329–55.

Flåm, Sjur D. and Wets, Roger J.-B. Existence Results and Finite Horizon Approximates for Infinite Horizon Optimization Problems. *Econometrica*, September 1987, 55(5), pp. 1187–1209.

Hori, Hajime. A Turnpike Theorem for Rolling Plans. *J. Math. Econ.*, 1987, 16(3), pp. 223–35.

Medio, Alfredo. Oscillations in Optimal Growth Models. *J. Econ. Behav. Organ.*, September 1987, 8(3), pp. 413–27.

Medio, Alfredo. Oscillations in Optimal Growth Models. *J. Econ. Dynam. Control*, June 1987, 11(2), pp. 201–06.

Teubal, Morris. The Engineering Sector in a Model of Economic Development. *Teubal, M.*, 1987, pp. 280–94.

1114 Monetary Growth Models

Aiyagari, S. Rao. Optimality and Monetary Equilibria in Stationary Overlapping Generations Models with Long-Lived Agents: Growth versus Discounting. *J. Econ. Theory*, December 1987, 43(2), pp. 292–313.

Danthine, Jean-Pierre; Donaldson, John B. and Smith, Lance. On the Superneutrality of Money in a Stochastic Dynamic Macroeconomic Model. *J. Monet. Econ.*, December 1987, 20(3), pp. 475–99.

Tobin, James. Money and Economic Growth. *Tobin, J. (I)*, 1987, pp. 133–45.

Tobin, James. Notes on Optimal Monetary Growth. *Tobin, J. (I)*, 1987, 1968, pp. 146–73.

Turnovsky, Stephen J. Monetary Growth, Inflation, and Economic Activity in a Dynamic Macro Model. *Int. Econ. Rev.*, October 1987, 28(3), pp. 707–30.

112 Economic Development Models and Theories

1120 Economic Development Models and Theories

Abdul Aziz, Abdul Rahman. Identification of Structural Constraints in Sectoral Development using the Diamond–Laumas Key Sector Method: With West Malaysian Case Study. *Singapore Econ. Rev.*, April 1987, 32(1), pp. 32–45. [G: Malaysia]

Abella, Manolo I. Asian Labour Mobility: New Dimensions and Implications for Development. *Pakistan Devel. Rev.*, Autumn 1987, 26(3), pp. 363–77. [G: Asia]

Adedeji, Adebayo. An Ecology for Economic Change. *Challenge*, Jan./Feb. 1987, 29(6), pp. 4–8. [G: Africa]

Agbonyitor, Alberto D. K. On Import Substitution, Quality Uncertainty and Development Policy. *J. Econ. Devel.*, June 1987, 12(1), pp. 33–47.

Aggarwal, Mangat Ram. Transnational Corporations, Economic Development and Income Distribution in Less Developed Countries. *Indian Econ. J.*, Jan.-Mar. 1987, 34(3), pp. 4–50. [G: LDCs]

Alagh, Yoginder K. Employment and Structural Change in the Indian Economy. *Amjad, R., ed.*, 1987, pp. 285–303. [G: India]

Albagli, Claude. Structures sociales, besoins et pouvoir: le verrou agricole. (Social Structures, Needs and Power: The Agricultural Deadlock. With English summary.) *Écon. Soc.*, July 1987, 21(7), pp. 149–68. [G: Africa]

Ali, Shanti Sadiq. Africa: Dimensions of the Economic Crisis: The International Environment. *Ali, S. S. and Gupta, A., eds.*, 1987, pp. 20–33. [G: Africa]

Amirahmadi, Hooshang. The Non-capitalist Way of Development. *Rev. Radical Polit. Econ.*, Spring 1987, 19(1), pp. 22–46.

Anglade, Christian and Fortin, Carlos. The Role of the State in Latin America's Strategic Options. *CEPAL Rev.*, April 1987, (31), pp. 211–34. [G: Latin America]

Arida, Persio and Bacha, Edmar Lisboa. Balance of Payments: A Disequilibrium Analysis for Semi-industrialized Economies. *J. Devel. Econ.*, October 1987, 27(1–2), pp. 85–108. [G: Latin America]

Arida, Persio and Bacha, Edmar Lisboa. Balance of Payments: A Disequilibrium Analysis for Semi-industrialized Economies. *[Diaz-Alejandro, C. F.]*, 1987, pp. 85–108. [G: Latin America]

Arora, Harjit K. Monetary Stabilization Policy and Its Effects—A Case Study of India. *Indian J. Quant. Econ.*, 1987, 3(1), pp. 1–13. [G: India]

Arrow, Kenneth J. General Economic Theory and the Emergency of Theories of Economic Development. *Indian Econ. J.*, Apr.-June 1987, 34(4), pp. 1–8.

Awanohara, Susumu. 'Look East'—The Japan Model. *Asian-Pacific Econ. Lit.*, May 1987, 1(1), pp. 75–89. [G: Asia]

Balassa, Bela. The Importance of Trade for Developing Countries. *Banca Naz. Lavoro Quart. Rev.*, December 1987, (163), pp. 437–69. [G: LDCs]

Barling, J. Kurt. Aid and African Development. *Akinrinade, O. and Barling, J. K., eds.*, 1987, pp. 19–51. [G: Africa]

Barling, J. Kurt and Akinrinade, Olusola. Economic Development in Africa: Introduction. *Akinrinade, O. and Barling, J. K., eds.*, 1987, pp. 1–18. [G: Africa]

Batra, Raveendra N. and Lahiri, Sajal. Imported Technologies, Urban Unemployment and the North–South Dialogue. *J. Devel. Econ.*, February 1987, 25(1), pp. 21–32.   [G: LDCs]

Becker, Charles M. Urban Sector Income Distribution and Economic Development. *J. Urban Econ.*, March 1987, 21(2), pp. 127–45.
     [G: LDCs]

Becker, David G. Development, Democracy, and Dependency in Latin America: A Postimperialist View. *Becker, D. G., et al.*, 1987, pp. 41–62.   [G: Latin America]

Becker, David G. Postimperialism: A First Quarterly Report. *Becker, D. G., et al.*, 1987, pp. 203–25.

Bentick, B. L. A Development Gains Tax Will Accelerate the Time of Development unless There Is Also a Tax on Redevelopment [The Neutrality of a Development Gains Tax]. *Public Finance*, 1987, 42(2), pp. 320–24.   [G: U.K.]

Berberoglu, Berch. The Contradictions of Export-Oriented Development in the Third World. *Soc. Econ. Stud.*, December 1987, 36(4), pp. 85–112.   [G: LDCs]

Berlinski, Julio. Choice of Growth Strategy: Trade Regimes and Export Promotion. *Martirena-Mantel, A. M., ed.*, 1987, pp. 95–114.
     [G: Latin America]

Berry, Albert. The Labour Market and Human Capital in LDCs. *Gemmell, N., ed.*, 1987, pp. 205–35.

Beza, Sterie T. Choice of Growth Strategy: Trade Regimes and Export Promotion: Comment. *Martirena-Mantel, A. M., ed.*, 1987, pp. 114–19.   [G: Latin America]

Bhaduri, Amit. Dependent and Self-reliant Growth with Foreign Borrowing. *Cambridge J. Econ.*, September 1987, 11(3), pp. 269–73.

Bianchi, Giuliano; Casini-Benvenuti, Stefano and Maltinti, Giovanni. Long Waves and Regional Take-Offs in Italy and Great Britain: Preliminary Investigations into Multiregional Disparities of Development. *Vasko, T., ed.*, 1987, pp. 187–97.   [G: Italy; U.K.]

Bigsten, Arne. Poverty, Inequality and Development. *Gemmell, N., ed.*, 1987, pp. 135–71.
     [G: LDCs]

Binford, Leigh and Cook, Scott. Toward a Marxist Rethinking of Third World Rural Industrialization. *England, R. W., ed.*, 1987, pp. 61–85.
     [G: Mexico; LDCs]

Blejer, Mario I. and Liviatan, Nissan. Fighting Hyperinflation: Stabilization Strategies in Argentina and Israel, 1985–86. *Int. Monet. Fund Staff Pap.*, September 1987, 34(3), pp. 409–38.   [G: Israel; Argentina]

Boeri, Tito. Modelling Foreign Aid, Capital Inflows and Economic Development. *Rivista Int. Sci. Econ. Com.*, July 1987, 34(7), pp. 623–47.

Boisier, Sergio. Decentralization and Regional Development in Latin America Today. *CEPAL Rev.*, April 1987, (31), pp. 133–44.
     [G: Latin America]

Bourne, L. S. Urbanization, Migration and Urban Research in Comparative Context: An Urban Systems Perspective. *Can. J. Devel. Stud.*, 1987, 8(1), pp. 69–80.

Boussard, J.-M. Le progrès technique et l'équili-

bre agriculture–industrie dans les modèles calculables d'équilibre général. (The Consequences of Technical Progress for Agriculture/Industry Balance as Described by Computable General Equilibrium Models. With English summary.) *Écon. Soc.*, July 1987, 21(7), pp. 7–36.

Bradford, Colin I., Jr. Trade and Structural Change: NICs and Next Tier NICs as Transitional Economies. *World Devel.*, March 1987, 15(3), pp. 299–316.   [G: LDCs]

Bray, Mark. Small Countries in International Development: Review Article. *J. Devel. Stud.*, January 1987, 23(2), pp. 295–300.

Brodhead, Tim. NGOs: In One Year, Out the Other? *World Devel.*, Supp. Autumn 1987, 15, pp. 1–6.   [G: Global]

Bruton, Henry. Technology Choice and Factor Proportions Problems in LDCs. *Gemmell, N., ed.*, 1987, pp. 236–65.

Buffie, Edward F. Labor Market Distortions, the Structure of Protection and Direct Foreign Investment. *[Diaz-Alejandro, C. F.]*, 1987, pp. 149–63.

Buffie, Edward F. Labor Market Distortions, the Structure of Protection and Direct Foreign Investment. *J. Devel. Econ.*, October 1987, 27(1–2), pp. 149–63.

Buffie, Edward F. Real Wage Rigidity and Optimal Commercial Policy in Less Developed Countries. *J. Devel. Econ.*, August 1987, 26(2), pp. 321–41.   [G: LDCs]

Burkett, Paul. Financial "Repression" and Financial "Liberalization" in the Third World: A Contribution to the Critique of Neoclassical Development Theory. *Rev. Radical Polit. Econ.*, Spring 1987, 19(1), pp. 1–21.
     [G: LDCs]

Burney, Nadeem A. Asian Labour Mobility: New Dimensions and Implications for Development: Comments. *Pakistan Devel. Rev.*, Autumn 1987, 26(3), pp. 380–81.   [G: Asia]

Byres, Terence J. Sukhamoy Chakravarty on Marxist Economics and Contemporary Developing Economies: Some Comments. *Cambridge J. Econ.*, June 1987, 11(2), pp. 173–78.

Cairncross, Alec. The Neoclassical Resurgence in Development Economics: Its Strength and Limitations: Comment. *Meier, G. M., ed.*, 1987, pp. 137–43.

Cairncross, Alec. The Place of Capital in Economic Progress. *Dupriez, L. H., ed.*, 1987, 1955, pp. 197–209.

Campbell, Burnham O. Foreign Trade Regimes and Economic Growth in Developing Countries: Comment. *Giersch, H., ed.*, 1987, pp. 236–49.   [G: LDCs]

Canavese, Alfredo Juan. Estancamiento e inflación en un modelo de crecimiento desequilibrado. (Stagflation in a Three Sector Model of Unbalanced Growth. With English summary.) *Económica (La Plata)*, January-June 1987, 33(1), pp. 39–50.

Casetti, Emilio and Pandit, Kavita. The Non Linear Dynamics of Sectoral Shifts. *Econ. Geogr.*,

July 1987, 63(3), pp. 241–58.

Chakravarty, Sukhamoy. Development Dialogue in the 1980s and Beyond. *Indian Econ. J.*, Jan.-Mar. 1987, 34(3), pp. 1–12. **[G: LDCs]**

Chakravarty, Sukhamoy. Marxist Economics and Contemporary Developing Economies. *Cambridge J. Econ.*, March 1987, 11(1), pp. 3–22. **[G: Selected Countries]**

Chakravarty, Sukhamoy. The State of Development Economics. *Manchester Sch. Econ. Soc. Stud.*, June 1987, 55(2), pp. 125–43.

Chandhoke, Neera. Regional Hegemonic and Peripheral States: The Case of Mozambique. *Ali, S. S. and Gupta, A., eds.*, 1987, pp. 182–99. **[G: Mozambique]**

Chen, John-ren. Unsicherheit und Entwicklung der neolklassischen Dualökonomie. (Uncertainty and the Development of the Neoclassical Dual Economy. With English summary.) *Jahr. Nationalökon. Statist.*, January 1987, 203(1), pp. 65–83.

Chen, Tain-Jy and Tang, De-Piao. Comparing Technical Efficiency between Import-Substitution-Oriented and Export-Oriented Foreign Firms in a Developing Economy. *J. Devel. Econ.*, August 1987, 26(2), pp. 277–89. **[G: Taiwan]**

Cohen, Suleiman I. Input–Output versus Social Accounting in the Macro-analysis of Development Policy. *Industry Devel.*, 1987, (22), pp. 93–129. **[G: Colombia; Pakistan; S. Korea]**

Cohen, Suleiman I. Stabilization and Economic Growth in Developing Countries: Comments. *Pakistan Devel. Rev.*, Autumn 1987, 26(3), pp. 356–59.

Colby, William E. Comprehensive Intelligence for Advancement. *Dedijer, S. and Jéquier, N., eds.*, 1987, pp. 41–48.

Corbo, Vittorio. Underdevelopment: To Conform or Reform: Comment. *Meier, G. M., ed.*, 1987, pp. 228–36. **[G: Brazil]**

Corden, W. Max. Liberal and Illiberal Development Policy: Comment. *Meier, G. M., ed.*, 1987, pp. 84–91.

Corden, W. Max. The Relevance for Developing Countries of Recent Developments in Macroeconomic Theory. *World Bank Res. Observer*, July 1987, 2(2), pp. 171–88. **[G: LDCs]**

Costa-Filho, Alfredo. International Colloquium on New Directions for Development Planning in Market Economies: Address. *CEPAL Rev.*, April 1987, (31), pp. 12–18.

Dahiya, Bhagwan S. On the Evolution of Development Planning. *[Marrama, V.], Vol. 1*, 1987, pp. 161–223.

Darrat, Ali F. Are Exports an Engine of Growth? Another Look at the Evidence. *Appl. Econ.*, February 1987, 19(2), pp. 277–83. **[G: Hong Kong; S. Korea; Singapore; Taiwan]**

Das-Gupta, Arindam. A Note on the Effects of Tax-Subsidy Policies on the Personal Distribution of Income in Dual Economies. *Indian Econ. Rev.*, Jan.-June 1987, 22(1), pp. 95–105. **[G: LDCs]**

Day, Richard H., et al. Instability in Rural–Urban Migration. *Econ. J.*, December 1987, 97(388), pp. 940–50.

Demery, Lionel and Addison, Tony. Stabilization Policy and Income Distribution in Developing Countries. *World Devel.*, December 1987, 15(12), pp. 1483–98. **[G: LDCs]**

Desai, Meghnad. Marxist Economics and Contemporary Developing Economies: Comments. *Cambridge J. Econ.*, June 1987, 11(2), pp. 179–81.

Dholakia, Nikhilesh and Sherry, John F., Jr. Marketing and Development: A Resynthesis of Knowledge. *Sheth, J. N., ed.*, 1987, pp. 119–43.

Dieng, Adama. Background to and Growth of the Right to Development: The Role of Law and Lawyers in Development. *Nobel, P., ed.*, 1987, pp. 55–60. **[G: Senegal]**

Dietz, James L. and Street, James H. Latin America's Economic Development. *Dietz, J. L. and Street, J. H., eds.*, 1987, pp. 2–12. **[G: Latin America]**

Dooley, Michael P. An Analysis of the Management of the Currency Composition of Reserve Assets and External Liabilities of Developing Countries. *Aliber, R. Z., ed.*, 1987, pp. 262–80. **[G: LDCs]**

Dorn, James A. Development Economics after 40 Years: Introduction. *Cato J.*, Spring/Summer 1987, 7(1), pp. 1–19.

Drabek, Anne Gordon. Development Alternatives: The Challenge for NGOs—An Overview of the Issues. *World Devel.*, Supp. Autumn 1987, 15, pp. ix–xv. **[G: Global]**

Dunlevy, James A. and Seiver, Daniel A. Foreign Finance, Wealth Effects and Economic Development. *Appl. Econ.*, April 1987, 19(4), pp. 467–81. **[G: LDCs]**

Dutt, Amitava Krishna. As relações de troca e o desenvolvimento desigual: Resultados de um modelo de comércio Norte-Sul. (With English summary.) *Pesquisa Planejamento Econ.*, December 1987, 17(3), pp. 533–59.

Esfahani, Hadi Salehi. The Resurgence of Inflation in Latin America: Discussion. *World Devel.*, August 1987, 15(8), pp. 1141–43. **[G: S. America; Peru; Chile]**

Etim, Ekei U. ECA: Towards a Sub-regional Economic Cooperation. *Akinrinade, O. and Barling, J. K., eds.*, 1987, pp. 77–98. **[G: Africa]**

Evans, A. W. The Effect of a Development Gains Tax on the Timing of Development [The Neutrality of a Development Gains Tax]. *Public Finance*, 1987, 42(2), pp. 325–31.

Faroque, Akhter and Butterfield, David W. Impacts on Growth of the Structure of Demand and Income Distribution in Less Developed Countries: An Application to Bangladesh. *J. Econ. Devel.*, June 1987, 12(1), pp. 161–93. **[G: Bangladesh]**

Feeny, David. The Exploration of Economic Change: The Contribution of Economic History to Development Economics. *Field, A. J., ed.*, 1987, pp. 91–119.

Fields, Gary S. Measuring Inequality Change in an Economy with Income Growth. *J. Devel.*

Econ., August 1987, *26*(2), pp. 357–74.

Findlay, Ronald. Liberal and Illiberal Development Policy: Comment. *Meier, G. M., ed.*, 1987, pp. 92–103.

Foders, Federico and Glismann, Hans H. Long Waves in Argentine Economic Development. *Vasko, T., ed.*, 1987, pp. 12–26. [G: Argentina]

Frieden, Jeff. International Capital and National Development: Comments on Postimperialism. *Becker, D. G., et al.*, 1987, pp. 179–91.

Fry, Maxwell J. Neo-classical and Neo-structuralist Models of Financial Development: Theories and Evidence. *Greek Econ. Rev.*, 1987, *9*(1), pp. 1–37. [G: LDCs]

Fry, Maxwell J. Neo-classical and Neo-structuralist Models of Financial Development: Theories and Evidence. *Greek Econ. Rev.*, 1987, *9*(1), pp. 1–37. [G: LDCs]

Furtado, Celso. Underdevelopment: To Conform or Reform. *Meier, G. M., ed.*, 1987, pp. 205–27. [G: Brazil]

Gang, Ira N. Distribution and Development Effects of Tariff Cum Subsidy Policies. *Singapore Econ. Rev.*, April 1987, *32*(1), pp. 71–86. [G: LDCs]

Gang, Ira N. and Gangopadhyay, Shubhashis. Employment, Output and the Choice of Techniques: The Trade-Off Revisited. *J. Devel. Econ.*, April 1987, *25*(2), pp. 321–27. [G: LDCs]

Gang, Ira N. and Gangopadhyay, Shubhashis. Optimal Policies in a Dual Economy with Open Unemployment and Surplus Labour. *Oxford Econ. Pap.*, June 1987, *39*(2), pp. 378–87.

Gang, Ira N. and Gangopadhyay, Shubhashis. Welfare Aspects of a Harris–Todaro Economy with Underemployment and Variable Prices. *Devel. Econ.*, September 1987, *25*(3), pp. 203–19.

Gaude, J., et al. Rural Development and Labour-Intensive Schemes: Impact Studies of Some Pilot Programmes. *Int. Lab. Rev.*, July-Aug. 1987, *126*(4), pp. 423–46. [G: Burkina Faso; Burundi; Rwanda; Nepal; Tanzania]

Gemmell, Norman. Surveys in Development Economics: Introduction. *Gemmell, N., ed.*, 1987, pp. 1–7.

Gemmell, Norman. Taxation and Development. *Gemmell, N., ed.*, 1987, pp. 269–306. [G: LDCs]

Gereffi, Gary and Evans, Peter. Transnational Corporations, Dependent Development, and State Policy in the Semiperiphery: A Comparison of Brazil and Mexico. *Dietz, J. L. and Street, J. H., eds.*, 1987, *1981*, pp. 159–90. [G: Brazil; Mexico]

Ghatak, Subrata. Agriculture and Economic Development. *Gemmell, N., ed.*, 1987, pp. 341–72.

Ghosh, Dipak. A Theoretical Model of Behaviour of Marketed Surplus in a Partially Monetized Economy. *Indian Econ. J.*, Apr.-June 1987, *34*(4), pp. 39–54. [G: India]

Giersch, Herbert. Stages and Spurts of Economic Development. *Dupriez, L. H., ed.*, 1987, *1955*, pp. 103–25.

Gini, Corrado. Occidental and Oriental Conceptions of Economic Progress. *Dupriez, L. H., ed.*, 1987, *1955*, pp. 182–92.

Glewwe, Paul. Unemployment in Developing Countries: Economist's Models in Light of Evidence from Sri Lanka. *Int. Econ. J.*, Winter 1987, *1*(4), pp. 1–17. [G: Sri Lanka]

Glewwe, Paul and Bhalla, Surjit S. A Response to Comment [The Distribution of Income in Sri Lanka in 1969–70 and 1980–81: Sri Lankan Experience]. *World Bank Econ. Rev.*, May 1987, *1*(3), pp. 533–36. [G: Sri Lanka; LDCs]

de Grauwe, Paul. Financial Deregulation in Developing Countries. *Tijdschrift Econ. Manage.*, 1987, *32*(4), pp. 381–401. [G: LDCs]

Greenaway, David and Milner, Chris. 'True Protection' Concepts and Their Role in Evaluating Trade Policies in LDCs. *J. Devel. Stud.*, January 1987, *23*(2), pp. 200–219. [G: Selected LDCs]

Greenaway, David and Milner, Chris. Trade Theory and the Less Developed Countries. *Gemmell, N., ed.*, 1987, pp. 11–55. [G: LDCs]

Gupta, Manash Ranjan. Harris–Todaro Migration-Mechanism and the Optimum Development of the Urban Sector. *Indian Econ. Rev.*, July-Dec. 1987, *22*(2), pp. 179–94. [G: LDCs]

Gupta, Manash Ranjan. Rural–Urban Migration and Urban Unemployment: A Note. *Scot. J. Polit. Econ.*, August 1987, *34*(3), pp. 295–305.

Gupta, Manash Ranjan. The Shadow Wage: A Note. *Math. Soc. Sci.*, June 1987, *13*(3), pp. 289–95.

Gupta, Vijay. Dialectics of Southern African Crisis: Basic Contradictions. *Ali, S. S. and Gupta, A., eds.*, 1987, pp. 164–81. [G: Southern Africa]

Haberler, Gottfried. Liberal and Illiberal Development Policy. *Meier, G. M., ed.*, 1987, pp. 51–83.

Harwood, Richard R. Low Input Technologies for Sustainable Agricultural Systems. *Ruttan, V. W. and Pray, C. E., eds.*, 1987, pp. 319–31.

Haustein, Heinz-Dieter. The Pathway of Dynamic Efficiency: Economic Trajectory of a Technical Revolution. *Vasko, T., ed.*, 1987, pp. 198–215.

Heady, Christopher. Designing Taxes with Migration. *Econ. J.*, Supplement 1987, *97*, pp. 87–98. [G: LDCs]

Helleiner, Gerald K. Stabilization, Adjustment, and the Poor. *World Devel.*, December 1987, *15*(12), pp. 1499–1513. [G: Tanzania]

Henry, C. Michael. Economic Growth and Economic Development: A Distinction without a Difference. *Soc. Econ. Stud.*, December 1987, *36*(4), pp. 67–84. [G: LDCs]

Herrera-Lasso, Luis. Economic Growth, Military Expenditure, Arms Industry and Arms Transfer in Latin America. *Schmidt, C., ed.*, 1987, pp. 113–34. **[G: Latin America]**

Horowitz, David. Monetary Policy, Capital Movements and Underdevelopment. *Ciocca, P., ed.*, 1987, *1958*, pp. 299–312.

Hosier, Richard H. The Informal Sector in Kenya: Spatial Variation and Development Alternatives. *J. Devel. Areas*, July 1987, *21*(4), pp. 383–402. **[G: Kenya]**

Houston, David and Paus, Eva. The Theory of Unequal Exchange: An Indictment. *Rev. Radical Polit. Econ.*, Spring 1987, *19*(1), pp. 90–97.

Huff, W. G. Patterns in the Economic Development of Singapore. *J. Devel. Areas*, April 1987, *21*(3), pp. 305–25. **[G: Singapore]**

Ingelstam, Lars. Long-Range Development Planning: Notes on Its Substance and Methodology. *CEPAL Rev.*, April 1987, (31), pp. 69–74.

Irfan, M. Asian Labour Mobility: New Dimensions and Implications for Development: Comments. *Pakistan Devel. Rev.*, Autumn 1987, *26*(3), pp. 378–79. **[G: Asia]**

Isenman, Paul. Growth and Equity in Developing Countries: A Reinterpretation of the Sri Lankan Experience: A Comment. *World Bank Econ. Rev.*, May 1987, *1*(3), pp. 521–31. **[G: Sri Lanka; LDCs]**

Islam, Nurul. Tensions between Economics and Politics in Dealing with Agriculture: Comment. *Meier, G. M., ed.*, 1987, pp. 39–48.

Itagaki, Takao. Optimal Tariffs for a Large and a Small Country under Uncertain Terms of Trade: Reply and Reinterpretation. *Oxford Econ. Pap.*, June 1987, *39*(2), pp. 418.

James, Jeffrey. Positional Goods, Conspicuous Consumption and the International Demonstration Effect Reconsidered. *World Devel.*, April 1987, *15*(4), pp. 449–62.

Jéquier, Nicolas and Dedijer, Stevan. Information, Knowledge and Intelligence: A General Overview. *Dedijer, S. and Jéquier, N., eds.*, 1987, pp. 1–23.

Johnson, D. Gale. Is Population Growth the Dominant Force in Development? [Population Growth, Economic Growth, and Foreign Aid]. *Cato J.*, Spring/Summer 1987, *7*(1), pp. 187–93. **[G: LDCs]**

Jones, Edwin. *The Dynamics of Development and Development Administration:* Review Article. *Soc. Econ. Stud.*, December 1987, *36*(4), pp. 209–22. **[G: LDCs]**

Joshi, P. C. From Semi-feudalism to Structural Dualism: Towards an Institutional Approach to Agricultural Development. *Joshi, P. C.*, 1987, *1986*, pp. 252–86. **[G: India]**

Joshi, P. C. Perspectives of Agrarian Reconstruction: India in the Asian Context. *Joshi, P. C.*, 1987, *1986*, pp. 68–103. **[G: India]**

Kähkönen, Juha. Liberalization Policies and Welfare in a Financially Repressed Economy. *Int. Monet. Fund Staff Pap.*, September 1987, *34*(3), pp. 531–47. **[G: LDCs]**

Kanth, Rajani. Against "Surplus" Theorizing: A Comment. *Rev. Radical Polit. Econ.*, Summer 1987, *19*(2), pp. 83–85. **[G: LDCs]**

Katzman, Martin T. Ecology, Natural Resources, and Economic Growth: Underdeveloping the Amazon: Review Article. *Econ. Develop. Cult. Change*, January 1987, *35*(2), pp. 425–36. **[G: Brazil]**

Kebbede, Girma. State Capitalism and Development: The Case of Ethiopia. *J. Devel. Areas*, October 1987, *22*(1), pp. 1–23. **[G: Ethiopia]**

Kemal, A. R. Pakistan's Experience in Employment and Manpower Planning. *Amjad, R., ed.*, 1987, pp. 234–56. **[G: Pakistan]**

Khan, Mohsin S. Macroeconomic Adjustment in Developing Countries: A Policy Perspective. *World Bank Res. Observer*, January 1987, *2*(1), pp. 23–42. **[G: LDCs]**

Khan, Mohsin S. Stabilization and Economic Growth in Developing Countries. *Pakistan Devel. Rev.*, Autumn 1987, *26*(3), pp. 341–55.

Khang, Chulsoon. Export-led Economic Growth: The Case of Technology Transfer. *Econ. Stud. Quart.*, June 1987, *38*(2), pp. 131–47. **[G: S. Korea; Hong Kong; Singapore; Taiwan]**

Kharas, Homi J. and Shishido, Hisanobu. Foreign Borrowing and Macroeconomic Adjustment to External Shocks. *J. Devel. Econ.*, February 1987, *25*(1), pp. 125–48.

Kirkpatrick, Colin. Trade Policy and Industrialization in LDCs. *Gemmell, N., ed.*, 1987, pp. 56–89. **[G: LDCs]**

Kirkpatrick, Colin and Nixson, Frederick. Inflation and Stabilization Policy in LDCs. *Gemmell, N., ed.*, 1987, pp. 172–202.

Kitchen, Richard and Weiss, John. Prices and Government Interventions in Developing Countries. *Industry Devel.*, 1987, (20), pp. 51–99. **[G: LDCs]**

Kleiman, Ephraim. The Resurgence of Inflation in Latin America: Discussion. *World Devel.*, August 1987, *15*(8), pp. 1143–45. **[G: Peru]**

Kockläuner, Gerhard. Eine nichtlineare Analyse der sozioökonom.schen Entwicklung von Nationen. (A Nonlinear Analysis of Socioeconomic Development of Nations. With English summary.) *Z. Wirtschaft. Sozialwissen.*, 1987, *107*(3), pp. 417–30.

Kraus, Willy. Stages of Development, Cultural Context and the Problem of International Interdependence. *[Kitamura, H.]*, 1987, pp. 190–203. **[G: LDCs]**

Lächler, Ulrich and Nunnenkamp, Peter. The Effects of Debt versus Equity Inflows on Savings and Growth in Developing Economies. *Weltwirtsch. Arch.*, 1987, *123*(4), pp. 631–50. **[G: LDCs]**

Lahiri, Sajal and Batra, Raveendra N. Imported Technologies, North–South Dialogue and the Optimal Subsidy Policy. *Indian Econ. J.*, Jan.-Mar. 1987, *34*(3), pp. 81–85.

Lai, Ching-chong and Chang, Wen-ya. Flexible Exchange Rates, Capital Mobility Control and Macroeconomic Policies. *J. Econ. Devel.*, December 1987, *12*(2), pp. 183–88.

Lal, Deepak. The Political Economy of Economic Liberalization. *World Bank Econ. Rev.*, January 1987, *1*(2), pp. 273–99. **[G: LDCs]**

Lal, Deepak and Rajapatirana, Sarath. Foreign Trade Regimes and Economic Growth in Developing Countries. *World Bank Res. Observer*, July 1987, *2*(2), pp. 189–217. [G: LDCs]

Lal, Deepak and Rajapatirana, Sarath. Foreign Trade Regimes and Economic Growth in Developing Countries. *Giersch, H., ed.*, 1987, pp. 204–35. [G: LDCs]

Lam, David. Distribution Issues in the Relationship between Population Growth and Economic Development. *Johnson, D. G. and Lee, R. D., eds.*, 1987, pp. 589–627. [G: Selected Countries]

Lebovic, James H. and Ishaq, Ashfaq. Military Burden, Security Needs, and Economic Growth in the Middle East. *J. Conflict Resolution*, March 1987, *31*(1), pp. 106–38. [G: Middle East]

Levy, Santiago. A Short-run General Equilibrium Model for a Small, Open Economy. *J. Devel. Econ.*, February 1987, *25*(1), pp. 63–88. [G: LDCs]

Lewis, Jeffrey D.; de Melo, Jaime and Robinson, Sherman. Simulating Alternative Development Strategies: Some Suggestions from Korea's Experience. *Int. Econ. J.*, Autumn 1987, *1*(3), pp. 1–17. [G: S. Korea]

Lippit, Victor D. Surplus Theorizing Reaffirmed. *Rev. Radical Polit. Econ.*, Summer 1987, *19*(2), pp. 86–88. [G: LDCs]

Lombardini, Siro. Prolegomena to a Theory of Economic Development. *Rivista Int. Sci. Econ. Com.*, October 1987, *34*(10), pp. 1001–23.

Love, James. Export Instability in Less Developed Countries: Consequences and Causes. *J. Econ. Stud.*, 1987, *14*(2), pp. 3–80. [G: LDCs]

Love, Joseph L. Raúl Prebisch and the Origins of the Doctrine of Unequal Exchange. *Dietz, J. L. and Street, J. H., eds.*, 1987, pp. 78–100. [G: Argentina]

Lundahl, Mats. 'Efficient but Poor'—Schultz' Theory of Traditional Agriculture. *Scand. Econ. Hist. Rev.*, 1987, *35*(1), pp. 108–29.

Mackenzie, Fiona and Taylor, D. R. F. District Focus as a Strategy for Rural Development in Kenya: The Case of Murang'a District, Central Province. *Can. J. Devel. Stud.*, 1987, *8*(2), pp. 299–316. [G: Kenya]

Maizels, Alfred. Commodities in Crisis: An Overview of the Main Issues. *World Devel.*, May 1987, *15*(5), pp. 537–49. [G: Global]

Mantel, Rolf R. and Martirena-Mantel, Ana María. Liberalizacion del crecimiento y equidad en la economia abierta. (Growth Liberalization and Equity in the Open Economy. With English summary.) *Económica (La Plata)*, July-Dec. 1987, *33*(2), pp. 245–68. [G: Latin America]

Marsden, Keith. The Reappraisal of Development Strategies [Taxation, Economic Growth, and Liberty]. *Cato J.*, Spring/Summer 1987, *7*(1), pp. 149–52. [G: LDCs]

Martin, Linda G. Human Resources and Economic Development. *Martin, L. G., ed.*, 1987, pp. 92–96. [G: ASEAN]

Martirena-Mantel, Ana María. External Debt, Savings, and Growth in Latin America: Introduction and Overview. *Martirena-Mantel, A. M., ed.*, 1987, pp. 1–25. [G: Latin America]

Marzano, Ferruccio. Keynesian Theory Planning Models and Quantitative Economics: An Overview of the Essays. *[Marrama, V.], Vol. 1*, 1987, pp. xxviii–liv.

McKloskey, Donald N. The Rhetoric of Economic Development. *Cato J.*, Spring/Summer 1987, *7*(1), pp. 249–54.

Mehta, Vinod. Development Experience of Soviet Central Asia and the Countries of the Third World. *Gidadhubli, R. G., ed.*, 1987, pp. 219–38. [G: U.S.S.R.; LDCs]

Meier, Gerald M. On Getting Policies Right. *Meier, G. M., ed.*, 1987, pp. 3–11.

Meier, Gerald M. Towards More Effective Development Policy-making. *[Kitamura, H.]*, 1987, pp. 204–11. [G: LDCs]

Melkote, Rama S. West Africa: Problems of Dependent Development. *Ali, S. S. and Gupta, A., eds.*, 1987, pp. 114–27. [G: W. Africa]

Menzel, Ulrich and Senghaas, Dieter. Para una definición de los países de industrialización reciente. Propuesta de indicadores para evaluar los países que se encuentran en el umbral de la industrialización. (With English summary.) *Desarrollo Econ.*, Oct.-Dec. 1987, *27*(107), pp. 323–46. [G: LDCs]

Metcalfe, J. S. and Gibbons, Michael. On the Economics of Structural Change and the Evolution of Technology. *Pasinetti, L. and Lloyd, P., eds.*, 1987, pp. 91–102.

de Meza, David. The Optimum Tariff and Quota when the Terms of Trade Are Random. *Oxford Econ. Pap.*, June 1987, *39*(2), pp. 412–17.

Mitra, Soumya and Ali, Shanti Sadiq. The Sahel: Drought, Desertification and Man-Made Problems. *Ali, S. S. and Gupta, A., eds.*, 1987, pp. 128–45. [G: Africa]

Mohtadi, Hamid. Industrialization and Urban Inequality in LDCs: A Theoretical Analysis with Evidence from Prerevolutionary Iran. *J. Devel. Areas*, October 1987, *22*(1), pp. 41–57. [G: Iran]

Mongula, Benedict S. and Ng'andwe, Chiselebwe. Limits to Development in Southern Africa: Energy, Transport and Communications in SADCC Countries. *Amin, S.; Chitala, D. and Mandaza, I., eds.*, 1987, pp. 85–108. [G: Southern Africa]

Moreno, Sergio Martín. La hipótesis de la estructura dual de la industria: el caso de la economía mexicana. (The Dual Industrial Structure Hypothesis: The Case of the Mexican Economy. With English summary.) *Estud. Econ.*, Jan.-June 1987, *2*(1), pp. 81–112. [G: Mexico]

Morley, Samuel A. and Fishlow, Albert. Deficits, Debt and Destabilization: The Perversity of High Interest Rates. *[Diaz-Alejandro, C. F.]*, 1987, pp. 227–44. [G: LDCs]

Morley, Samuel A. and Fishlow, Albert. Deficits, Debt and Destabilization: The Perversity of

High Interest Rates. *J. Devel. Econ.*, October 1987, 27(1–2), pp. 227–44.   [G: LDCs]

Mosley, Paul; Hudson, John and Horrell, Sara. Aid, the Public Sector and the Market in Less Developed Countries. *Econ. J.*, September 1987, 97(387), pp. 616–41.   [G: LDCs]

Myint, Hla. The Neoclassical Resurgence in Development Economics: Its Strength and Limitations. *Meier, G. M., ed.*, 1987, pp. 107–36.

Nanjundan, S. Small and Medium Enterprises: Some Basic Development Issues. *Industry Devel.*, 1987, (20), pp. 1–50.   [G: LDCs]

Naqvi, Syed Nawab Haider. The Anatomy of 'Failures'. *Pakistan Devel. Rev.*, Autumn 1987, 26(3), pp. 257–72.

Nelson, Richard R. Innovation and Economic Development Theoretical Retrospect and Prospect. *Katz, J. M., ed.*, 1987, pp. 78–93.

das Neves, João César. Desenvolvimento e Solidariedade. (With English summary.) *Economia (Portugal)*, May 1987, 11(2), pp. 253–61.

Nobel, Peter. Notes on the Right to Development. *Nobel, P., ed.*, 1987, pp. 47–52.   [G: Africa]

Ocampo, José Antonio. The Macroeconomic Effect of Import Controls: A Keynesian Analysis. *[Diaz-Alejandro, C. F.]*, 1987, pp. 285–305.

Ocampo, José Antonio. The Macroeconomic Effect of Import Controls: A Keynesian Analysis. *J. Devel. Econ.*, October 1987, 27(1–2), pp. 285–305.

Ohno, Koichi and Imaoka, Hideki. The Experience of Dual-Industrial Growth: Korea and Taiwan. *Devel. Econ.*, December 1987, 25(4), pp. 310–24.   [G: S. Korea; Taiwan]

Olanrewaju, S. A. and Falola, Toyin. Development through Integration: The Politics and Problems of ECOWAS. *Akinrinade, O. and Barling, J. K., eds.*, 1987, pp. 52–76.   [G: W. Africa]

Olson, Mancur. Diseconomies of Scale and Development. *Cato J.*, Spring/Summer 1987, 7(1), pp. 77–97.

Öniş, Ziya. Markets and Planning in Development Theory: An Interpretation and an Assessment. *METU*, 1987, 14(2), pp. 179–200.

Ortona, Guido. Il lavoro superfluo può non essere superfluo. (Excess Employment May Be not in Excess. With English summary.) *Rivista Storia Econ.*, S.S., October 1987, 4(3), pp. 887–96.   [G: LDCs]

Padoan, Pier Carlo. Growth, Debt, Country Risk and Financial Instability. *[Marrama, V.]*, *Vol. 1*, 1987, pp. 269–93.

Padron, Mario. Non-governmental Development Organizations: From Development Aid to Development Cooperation. *World Devel.*, Supp. Autumn 1987, 15, pp. 69–77.   [G: Latin America]

Palazzi, Paolo and Sardoni, Claudio. Public Expenditure and Socio-economic Structure in the Developed and LDCs. *Stud. Econ.*, 1987, 42(32), pp. 179–216.   [G: LDCs]

Papanek, Gustav F. and Kyn, Oldrich. Flattening the Kuznets Curve: The Consequences for Income Distribution of Development Strategy, Government Intervention, Income and Rate of Growth. *Pakistan Devel. Rev.*, Spring 1987, 26(1), pp. 1–54.   [G: Selected Countries]

Papps, Ivy. Techniques of Project Appraisal. *Gemmell, N., ed.*, 1987, pp. 307–38.

Parai, Amar K. and Batra, Raveendra N. Customs Union and Unemployment in LDCs. *J. Devel. Econ.*, August 1987, 26(2), pp. 311–19.   [G: LDCs]

Park, Hui-Jong. The Effects of Foreign Capital Inflow on Economic Growth in Korea: The Reevaluation of Griffin and Enos's Hypotheses. *Int. Econ. J.*, Summer 1987, 1(2), pp. 79–93.   [G: S. Korea]

Patel, Jayanti K. Central Africa: Crisis of Growth and Development in Malawi, Zambia and Zimbabwe. *Ali, S. S. and Gupta, A., eds.*, 1987, pp. 81–102. [G: Malawi; Zambia; Zimbabwe]

Pazos, Felipe. Import Substitution Policies, Tariffs, and Competition. *Dietz, J. L. and Street, J. H., eds.*, 1987, pp. 147–55.   [G: Latin America]

Pearson, Charles and Hufschmidt, Maynard. Incorporating the Environment in Development Planning. *Borner, S. and Taylor, A., eds.*, 1987, pp. 19–34.

Peattie, Lisa. An Idea in Good Currency and How It Grew: The Informal Sector. *World Devel.*, July 1987, 15(7), pp. 851–60.

Piganiol, Pierre. Intelligence in Science and Technology Policy. *Dedijer, S. and Jéquier, N., eds.*, 1987, pp. 183–96.   [G: LDCs]

Pyatt, Graham. Growth and Equity in Developing Countries: A Reinterpretation of the Sri Lankan Experience: A Comment. *World Bank Econ. Rev.*, May 1987, 1(3), pp. 515–20.   [G: Sri Lanka; LDCs]

Qadir, Asghar. Stabilization and Economic Growth in Developing Countries: Comments. *Pakistan Devel. Rev.*, Autumn 1987, 26(3), pp. 360–61.

Rabushka, Alvin. Taxation, Economic Growth, and Liberty. *Cato J.*, Spring/Summer 1987, 7(1), pp. 121–48.   [G: LDCs]

Raffer, Kunibert. Unfavorable Specialization and Dependence: The Case of Peripheral Raw Material Exporters. *World Devel.*, May 1987, 15(5), pp. 701–12.   [G: LDCs]

Rajapatirana, Sarath. Industrialization and Foreign Trade. *Finance Develop.*, September 1987, 24(3), pp. 2–5.   [G: LDCs]

Ram, Rati. Exports and Economic Growth in Developing Countries: Evidence from Time-Series and Cross-Section Data. *Econ. Develop. Cult. Change*, October 1987, 36(1), pp. 51–72.   [G: LDCs]

Ranis, Gustav. The Neoclassical Resurgence in Development Economics: Its Strength and Limitations: Comment. *Meier, G. M., ed.*, 1987, pp. 144–50.

Rao, M. J. Manohar. Development Planning Theory and the Use of Prior Information to Obtain a Benchmark Estimate of Capital-Stock: Case Study for India. *Indian J. Quant. Econ.*, 1987, 3(2), pp. 21–33.   [G: India]

Reddaway, W. B. Some Reflections by a Keynesian Economist on the Problems of Developing Countries. *Thirlwall, A. P., ed.*, 1987, pp. 36–65.

Richards, Donald G. An Empirical Examination of the Dependency Approach to Underdevelopment. *Singapore Econ. Rev.*, April 1987, 32(1), pp. 1–23. **[G: LDCs]**

Rivlin, Paul. The Burden of Defence in Developing Countries. *Schmidt, C., ed.*, 1987, pp. 104–12. **[G: LDCs]**

Roberts, Paul Craig. Third World Debt: Legacy of Development Experts. *Cato J.*, Spring/Summer 1987, 7(1), pp. 231–40. **[G: LDCs]**

Robinson, Warren C. and Schutjer, Wayne A. Reply to Djavad Salehi-Isfahani's Clarifications [Agricultural Development and Demographic Change: A Generalization of the Boserup Model]. *Econ. Develop. Cult. Change*, July 1987, 35(4), pp. 883. **[G: LDCs]**

Rodrik, Dani. Trade and Capital-Account Liberalization in a Keynesian Economy. *J. Int. Econ.*, August 1987, 23(1/2), pp. 113–29.

Rojas-Suarez, Liliana. Devaluation and Monetary Policy in Developing Countries: A General Equilibrium Model for Economies Facing Financial Constraints. *Int. Monet. Fund Staff Pap.*, September 1987, 34(3), pp. 439–70. **[G: LDCs]**

Rong, Yiren. Observations on Some Questions in the Building of a Socialist Economy with Chinese Characteristics: Reflections on Rereading the Constitution. *Chinese Econ. Stud.*, Winter 1986-87, 20(2), pp. 13–25. **[G: China]**

Rostow, Walt W. Reflections on the Drive to Technological Maturity. *Banca Naz. Lavoro Quart. Rev.*, June 1987, (161), pp. 115–46. **[G: Global]**

Rostow, Walt W. The Rich Country–Poor Country Problem: From the Eighteenth to the Twenty-first Centuries. *Steinherr, A. and Weiserbs, D., eds.*, 1987, pp. 47–83. **[G: Global]**

Rostow, Walt W. Toward a New Hemispheric Partnership. *Rostow, W. W.*, 1987, pp. 120–33. **[G: Latin America]**

Rotemberg, Julio J. Export Promotion as a Development Strategy. *J. Devel. Econ.*, August 1987, 26(2), pp. 343–55.

Roth, Gabriel. The Role of Property Rights in Development [Economic Growth and the Property Rights Regime]. *Cato J.*, Spring/Summer 1987, 7(1), pp. 117–20. **[G: LDCs]**

Roy, Raj and Rassuli, Ali. Transfer Models Using Mixed Keynesian-Classical Assumptions. *Rivista Int. Sci. Econ. Com.*, June 1987, 34(6), pp. 513–22.

Sachs, Ignacy. Development or Misdevelopment: A Plea for Anthropological Economics. *Sachs, I.*, 1987, pp. 59–68.

Sachs, Ignacy. Endogenous Development Potential. *Sachs, I.*, 1987, pp. 79–94.

Sachs, Ignacy. Local Development and Ways Out of the Crisis. *Sachs, I.*, 1987, pp. 105–11.

Sachs, Ignacy. The Logic of Development. *Sachs, I.*, 1987, pp. 12–18.

Sachs, Ignacy. The Time-Spaces of Development. *Sachs, I.*, 1987, pp. 52–58.

Sagasti, Francisco R. Techno-economic Intelligence for Development. *Dedijer, S. and Jéquier, N., eds.*, 1987, pp. 173–82. **[G: LDCs]**

Sah, Raaj Kumar and Stiglitz, Joseph E. Price Scissors and the Structure of the Economy. *Quart. J. Econ.*, February 1987, 102(1), pp. 109–34.

Sahn, David E. and von Braun, Joachim. The Relationship between Food Production and Consumption Variability: Policy Implications for Developing Countries. *J. Agr. Econ.*, May 1987, 38(2), pp. 315–27. **[G: LDCs]**

Saith, Ashwani. Contrasting Experiences in Rural Industrialisation: Are the East Asian Successes Transferable? *Islam, R., ed.*, 1987, pp. 241–303. **[G: Japan; Taiwan; S. Korea]**

Salehi-Isfahani, Djavad. On the Generalization of the Boserup Model: Some Clarifications. *Econ. Develop. Cult. Change*, July 1987, 35(4), pp. 875–81.

Samuelson, Larry. Inflation, Indexing and Economic Development. *World Devel.*, August 1987, 15(8), pp. 1119–30.

Sattar, Zaidi. Non-competitive Imports in Planning Models: The Bangladesh Case. *Bangladesh Devel. Stud.*, September 1987, 15(3), pp. 95–99. **[G: Bangladesh]**

Sauvy, Alfred. Occupational Migration and Training as Conditions and Consequences of Progress. *Dupriez, L. H., ed.*, 1987, pp. 277–90. **[G: France]**

Schatz, Sayre P. Postimperialism and the Great Competition. *Becker, D. G., et al.*, 1987, pp. 193–201.

Schubert, Renate. Interne Migration in Entwicklungsländern. Zur Rationalität von Land-Stadt Wanderungen. (Internal Migration in Developing Countries—Rationality of Rural–Urban Migration. With English summary.) *Z. Wirtschaft. Sozialwissen.*, 1987, 107(2), pp. 207–23.

Schultz, Theodore W. Tensions between Economics and Politics in Dealing with Agriculture. *Meier, G. M., ed.*, 1987, pp. 17–38.

Sen, Amartya K. Goods and People. *Urquidi, V. L., ed.*, 1987, pp. 153–77.

Sercovich, Francisco C. Política technológica y reestructuración industrial: los temas centrales. (With English summary.) *Desarrollo Econ.*, Jan.-Mar. 1987, 26(104), pp. 561–78. **[G: LDCs]**

Shahid, M. Alam. Savings and Industrialization: Some Hypotheses Suggested by Lewis and Others. *Singapore Econ. Rev.*, October 1987, 32(2), pp. 56–65. **[G: LDCs]**

Sheth, V. S. The Horn of Africa: Problems of Security and Development. *Ali, S. S. and Gupta, A., eds.*, 1987, pp. 71–80. **[G: Ethiopia; Somalia; Djibouti]**

Shrestha, Nanda R. Institutional Policies and Migration Behavior: A Selective Review. *World Devel.*, March 1987, 15(3), pp. 329–45. **[G: LDCs]**

Simon, Julian L. Population Growth, Economic Growth, and Foreign Aid. *Cato J.*, Spring/Summer 1987, 7(1), pp. 159–86. **[G: LDCs]**

Singer, Hans W. Discussion [Keynes, Economic Development and the Developing Countries] [Some Reflections by a Keynesian Economist on the Problems of Developing Countries]. *Thirlwall, A. P., ed.*, 1987, pp. 66–69.

Singer, Hans W. Problems of Industrialisation of Underdeveloped Countries. *Dupriez, L. H., ed.*, 1987, 1955, pp. 134–52. **[G: LDCs]**

Singer, Hans W. What Keynes and Keynesianism Can Teach Us about Less Developed Countries. *[Kitamura, H.]*, 1987, pp. 229–45. **[G: LDCs]**

Singer, Hans W. What Keynes and Keynesianism Can Teach Us about Less Developed Countries. *Thirlwall, A. P., ed.*, 1987, pp. 70–89.

Snowden, P. N. Financial Market Liberalisation in LDCs: The Incidence of Risk Allocation Effects of Interest Rate Increases. *J. Devel. Stud.*, October 1987, 24(1), pp. 83–93. **[G: LDCs]**

Stevens, Christopher. The EC and Development Efforts in Africa. *Akinrinade, O. and Barling, J. K., eds.*, 1987, pp. 129–48. **[G: EEC; Africa]**

Stewart, Frances. Macro-policies for Appropriate Technology: An Introductory Classification. *Stewart, F., ed.*, 1987, pp. 1–21. **[G: LDCs]**

Stewart, Frances. Macro-policies for Appropriate Technology in Developing Countries: Overview and Conclusions. *Stewart, F., ed.*, 1987, pp. 271–99. **[G: LDCs]**

Street, James H. The Institutionalist Theory of Economic Development. *J. Econ. Issues*, December 1987, 21(4), pp. 1861–87.

Street, James H. The Latin American Structuralists and the Institutionalists: Convergence in Development Theory. *Dietz, J. L. and Street, J. H., eds.*, 1987, pp. 101–14. **[G: Latin America]**

Streeten, Paul. Structural Adjustment: A Survey of the Issues and Options. *World Devel.*, December 1987, 15(12), pp. 1469–82. **[G: LDCs]**

Succar, Patricia. International Technology Transfer: A Model of Endogenous Technological Assimilation. *J. Devel. Econ.*, August 1987, 26(2), pp. 375–95. **[G: LDCs]**

Succar, Patricia. The Need for Industrial Policy in LDC's—A Re-statement of the Infant Industry Argument. *Int. Econ. Rev.*, June 1987, 28(2), pp. 521–34.

Taylor, Lance. Macro Policy in the Tropics: How Sensible People Stand. *World Devel.*, December 1987, 15(12), pp. 1407–35. **[G: LDCs]**

Teubal, Morris. Innovation and Development: A Review of Some Work at the IDB/ECLA/UNDP Programme. *Katz, J. M., ed.*, 1987, pp. 481–98. **[G: Latin America]**

Thirlwall, A. P. Keynes, Economic Development and the Developing Countries. *Thirlwall, A. P., ed.*, 1987, pp. 3–35.

Thomas, Scott. Dying Separately or Living Together: Regional Security and Economic Cooperation in Southern Africa. *Akinrinade, O. and*

Barling, J. K., eds., 1987, pp. 99–128. **[G: Southern Africa]**

Turner, Charlie G. Two Simple Measures of Dynamic Efficiency in the Global Economy. *Quart. Rev. Econ. Bus.*, Autumn 1987, 27(3), pp. 40–55. **[G: Global]**

Twose, Nigel. European NGOs: Growth or Partnership? *World Devel.*, Supp. Autumn 1987, 15, pp. 7–10. **[G: Europe]**

Vakil, C. N. and Brahmananda, P. R. Technical Knowledge and Managerial Capacity as Limiting Factors on Industrial Expansion in Underdeveloped Countries. *Dupriez, L. H., ed.*, 1987, 1955, pp. 153–72.

Valenta, František. Intensive Development of Socialist Economy. (The Evolution of Theoretical Approach) *Czech. Econ. Pap.*, 1987, (24), pp. 7–33. **[G: Czechoslovakia]**

Van Der Willigen, Tessa A. Cash Crop Production and the Balance of Trade in a Less Developed Economy: A Model of Temporary Equilibrium with Rationing. *Sinclair, P. J. N., ed.*, 1987, 1986, pp. 452–70.

Veit, Lawrence A. Time of the New Asian Tigers. *Challenge*, July/Aug. 1987, 30(3), pp. 49–55. **[G: S.E. Asia]**

Velasco, Andrés. Financial Crises and Balance of Payments Crises: A Simple Model of the Southern Cone Experience. *J. Devel. Econ.*, October 1987, 27(1–2), pp. 263–83. **[G: Chile; Argentina; Uruguay]**

Velasco, Andrés. Financial Crises and Balance of Payments Crises: A Simple Model of the Southern Cone Experience. *[Diaz-Alejandro, C. F.]*, 1987, pp. 263–83. **[G: Chile; Argentina; Uruguay]**

Wasylenko, Michael. Fiscal Decentralization and Economic Development. *Public Budg. Finance*, Winter 1987, 7(4), pp. 57–71. **[G: Global]**

Waters, Alan Rufus. Economic Growth and the Property Rights Regime. *Cato J.*, Spring/Summer 1987, 7(1), pp. 99–115. **[G: LDCs]**

Weiss, Dieter. Der informelle Sektor in den Metropolen der Entiwicklungsländer—Kunzeptionelle Ansätze zu einerr Neuorientierung von Regelungspolitiken. (On the Informal Sector in Developing Countries' Cities. With English summary.) *Konjunkturpolitik*, 1987, 33(2), pp. 99–115. **[G: LDCs]**

Werneck, Rogério L. Furquim. Retomada do crescimento e esforço de poupança: limitações e possibilidades. (With English summary.) *Pesquisa Planejamento Econ.*, April 1987, 17(1), pp. 1–18. **[G: Brazil]**

Williamson, John. A Survey of the Literature on the Optimal Peg. *Williamson, J.*, 1987, 1982, pp. 94–116.

Wolfe, Marshall. Agents of "Development." *CEPAL Rev.*, April 1987, (31), pp. 107–13.

Wu, Yuan-li. Models of Development: A Comparative Study of Economic Growth in South Korea and Taiwan—A Review. *Weltwirtsch. Arch.*, 1987, 123(2), pp. 377–80. **[G: S. Korea; Taiwan]**

Wulf, Herbert. Arms Production in Third World

Countries, Effects on Industrialisation. *Schmidt, C., ed.*, 1987, pp. 357–83.
[G: LDCs]

Yotopoulos, Pan A. The Anatomy of 'Failures': Comments. *Pakistan Devel. Rev.*, Autumn 1987, 26(3), pp. 273–74.

Young, Leslie. Intermediate Goods and the Formation of Duty-Free Zones. *J. Devel. Econ.*, April 1987, 25(2), pp. 369–84.
[G: LDCs]

Young, Leslie and Miyagiwa, Kaz F. Unemployment and the Formation of Duty-Free Zones. *J. Devel. Econ.*, August 1987, 26(2), pp. 397–405.
[G: LDCs]

Zimbalist, Andrew and Eckstein, Susan. Patterns of Cuban Development: The First Twenty-five Years. *World Devel.*, January 1987, 15(1), pp. 5–22.
[G: Cuba]

113 Economic Planning Theory and Policy

1130 Economic Planning Theory and Policy

Blazyca, George. The New Round of Economic Reform in Eastern Europe. *Nat. Westminster Bank Quart. Rev.*, November 1987, pp. 41–53.
[G: E. Europe]

Chen, Yizi. Social Scientific Research Serves Reform. *Reynolds, B. L.*, 1987, pp. xxii–xxiv.
[G: China]

Cohen, Suleiman I. Modelling the Prospects of Economic Growth and Social Development: Results of Circular Flow Planning Models Applied to Pakistan 1980–1993. *Pakistan Devel. Rev.*, Winter 1987, 26(4), pp. 609–26.
[G: Pakistan]

Colton, Timothy J. Approaches to the Politics of Systemic Economic Reform in the Soviet Union. *Soviet Econ.*, April–June 1987, 3(2), pp. 145–70.
[G: U.S.S.R.]

Dugger, William M. An Institutionalist Theory of Economic Planning. *J. Econ. Issues*, December 1987, 21(4), pp. 1649–75.

Dugger, William M. Democratic Economic Planning and Worker Ownership. *J. Econ. Issues*, March 1987, 21(1), pp. 87–99.
[G: U.S.]

Dyker, David A. Restructuring and "Radical Reform": The Articulation of Investment Demand. *Comp. Econ. Stud.*, Winter 1987, 29(4), pp. 103–27.
[G: U.S.S.R.]

Egiazarian, G. A. From the Experiment to an Integral System. *Prob. Econ.*, March 1987, 29(11), pp. 47–61.
[G: U.S.S.R.]

Grémion, Catherine. Decentralization in France: A Historical Perspective. *Ross, G.; Hoffmann, S. and Malzacher, S., eds.*, 1987, pp. 237–47.
[G: France]

Hegedüs, Andras. Some Problems of the Expansion of the Second Economy in Hungary. *Alessandrini, S. and Dallago, B., eds.*, 1987, pp. 297–301.
[G: Hungary]

Höhmann, Hans-Hermann. Soviet Economic Policies under Gorbachev: Problems and Prospects. *Gey, P.; Kosta, J. and Quaisser, W., eds.*, 1987, pp. 33–48.
[G: U.S.S.R.]

Holland, Stuart. Beyond Indicative Planning. *CEPAL Rev.*, April 1987, (31), pp. 75–89.
[G: France]

Ishihara, Kyōichi. Planning and the Market in China. *Devel. Econ.*, December 1987, 25(4), pp. 287–309.
[G: China]

Kantorovich, L.; Albegov, M. and Bezrukov, V. Toward the Wider Use of Optimizing Methods in the National Economy. *Prob. Econ.*, February 1987, 29(10), pp. 5–20. [G: U.S.S.R.]

Kazakevich, D. M. Economic Theory, Mathematical Economics, and Plan Management. *Matekon*, Fall 1987, 24(1), pp. 3–20.
[G: U.S.S.R.]

Kovalev, A. Improving Distribution Relations in the Present Stage. *Prob. Econ.*, November 1987, 30(7), pp. 47–58. [G: U.S.S.R.]

Lockett, Martin. Technical Innovation and Economic Reform in Socialist Economies with Special Reference to China. *Child, J. and Bate, P., eds.*, 1987, pp. 191–203. [G: China]

Marzano, Ferruccio. Keynesian Theory Planning Models and Quantitative Economics: An Overview of the Essays. *[Marrama, V.], Vol. 1*, 1987, pp. xxviii–liv.

Patel, Indraprasad G. Foreign Capital and Domestic Planning. *Ciocca, P., ed.*, 1987, 1967, pp. 277–97.

Petrakov, Nikolay. Soviet Pricing and Fiscal-Credit System: Prospects for Economic Policy Changes. *Rivista Int. Sci. Econ. Com.*, October 1987, 34(10), pp. 903–12. [G: U.S.S.R.]

Portes, Richard, et al. Macroeconomic Planning and Disequilibrium: Estimates for Poland, 1955–1980. *Econometrica*, January 1987, 55(1), pp. 19–41. [G: Poland]

Sachs, Ignacy. Inventing the Future: Future Studies and Planning. *Sachs, I.*, 1987, pp. 1–11.

Sachs, Ignacy. Lifestyles and Planning. *Sachs, I.*, 1987, pp. 33–51.

Sachs, Ignacy. Planning and Local Autonomy. *Sachs, I.*, 1987, pp. 19–24.

Tidrick, Gene and Chen, Jiyuan. China's Industrial Reform: The Essence of the Industrial Reforms. *Tidrick, G. and Jiyuan, C., eds.*, 1987, pp. 1–10.
[G: China]

Tomlinson, Jim. To Plan or Not to Plan: Review Article. *J. Econ. Stud.*, 1987, 14(1), pp. 60–65.
[G: OECD]

Vavilov, Andrei P., et al. Methods for Incorporating Rent in Prices and Plans. *Matekon*, Spring 1987, 23(3), pp. 3–27. [G: U.S.S.R.]

Wang, Xiaoqiang and Zhang, Gang. An Overview of the CESRRI Survey. *Reynolds, B. L.*, 1987, pp. xxv–xxxii.
[G: China]

White, Gordon. Cuban Planning in the Mid-1980s: Centralization, Decentralization, and Participation. *World Devel.*, January 1987, 15(1), pp. 153–61.
[G: Cuba]

Wu, Jinglian; Hu, Ji and Li, Jiange. On Controlling Demand and Improving Supply. *Chinese Econ. Stud.*, Winter 1986-87, 20(2), pp. 36–45.
[G: China]

Zhang, Shaojie and Zhang, Amei. The Present Management Environment in China's Industrial Enterprises. *Reynolds, B. L.*, 1987, pp. 47–58.
[G: China]

113 Economic Planning Theory and Policy

1132 Economic Planning Theory

Bennett, John. The Choice of Final Signals in Malinvaud's Model of Decentralized Planning. *Europ. Econ. Rev.*, August 1987, *31*(6), pp. 1203–10.

Bogaert, Henri; de Biolley, Tanguy and Maldague, Robert. Between Theory and Policy: Is the Planner a Necessary Go-Between? *Steinherr, A. and Weiserbs, D., eds.*, 1987, pp. 213–38. **[G: Belgium]**

Brillet, Jean-Louis, et al. Planning and Optimization: The French Experience. *[Marrama, V.],* Vol. 2, 1987, pp. 525–38. **[G: France]**

Brown, Pamela Clark; Miller, Jeffrey B. and Thornton, James R. An Optimal Incentive Scheme for Planning with Targets: Comment. *J. Compar. Econ.*, December 1987, *11*(4), pp. 596–600.

Browning, Martin. Prices vs. Quantities vs. Laissez-faire. *Rev. Econ. Stud.*, October 1987, *54*(4), pp. 691–94.

Dahiya, Bhagwan S. On the Evolution of Development Planning. *[Marrama, V.],* Vol. 1, 1987, pp. 161–223.

Dong, Fureng. China's Industrial Reform: Increasing the Vitality of Enterprises. *Tidrick, G. and Jiyuan, C., eds.*, 1987, pp. 44–59. **[G: China]**

Dror, Yehezkel. Governability, Participation and Social Aspects of Planning. *CEPAL Rev.*, April 1987, (31), pp. 95–105.

Gao, Shangquan. The Reform of China's Industrial System. *Tidrick, G. and Jiyuan, C., eds.*, 1987, pp. 132–42. **[G: China]**

García d'Acuña, Eduardo. New Directions in Planning: An Interpretive Balance. *CEPAL Rev.*, April 1987, (31), pp. 25–31. **[G: Latin America]**

Guesnerie, Roger and Penz, Ph. L'évaluation des effets macroéconomiques des projets: une introduction critique. (Evaluating "Macroeconomic Effects" of Projects: A Critical Introduction. With English summary.) *Écon. Soc.*, April 1987, *21*(4), pp. 19–44.

Gurrieri, Adolfo. The Validity of the State-as-Planner in the Current Crisis. *CEPAL Rev.*, April 1987, (31), pp. 193–209. **[G: Latin America]**

Hamel, Hannelore and Leipold, Helmut. Economic Reform in the GDR: Causes and Effects. *Jeffries, I. and Melzer, M., eds.*, 1987, pp. 280–304. **[G: E. Germany]**

Harker, Trevor. Agricultural Sector Policy and Macro-economic Planning. *CEPAL Rev.*, December 1987, (33), pp. 69–75. **[G: Caribbean]**

Holzman, Franklyn D. Internal and External Balance in a Centrally Planned Economy: Commentary. *Holzman, F. D.*, 1987, *1980*, pp. 83–88. **[G: CMEA]**

Ingelstam, Lars. Long-Range Development Planning: Notes on Its Substance and Methodology. *CEPAL Rev.*, April 1987, (31), pp. 69–74.

Iun', O. M. Planning Methods—Areas of Im-

provement. *Matekon*, Winter 1987-88, *24*(2), pp. 26–48. **[G: U.S.S.R.]**

Jeffries, Ian and Melzer, Manfred. Command Planning and the Production Unit. *Jeffries, I. and Melzer, M., eds.*, 1987, pp. 12–25. **[G: E. Germany]**

Joshi, P. C. Institutional and Technological Factors in Agricultural Planning: Reflections on the Mahalanobis Approach. *Joshi, P. C.*, 1987, *1982*, pp. 104–31. **[G: India]**

Keizer, William. Two Forgotten Articles by Ludwig von Mises on the Rationality of Socialist Economic Calculation. *Rothbard, M. N., ed.*, 1987, pp. 109–22.

Kosta, Jiří. The Chinese Economic Reform: Approaches, Results and Prospects. *Gey, P.; Kosta, J. and Quaisser, W., eds.*, 1987, pp. 145–71. **[G: China]**

Linstone, Harold A. The Need for Multiple Perspectives in Planning. *CEPAL Rev.*, April 1987, (31), pp. 43–49.

Liu, Pak-Wai. Optimal Incentive Schemes with Targets: First-Best or Second-Best? Reply. *J. Compar. Econ.*, December 1987, *11*(4), pp. 601–02.

Matus, Carlos. Planning and Government. *CEPAL Rev.*, April 1987, (31), pp. 153–69.

Meijer, Gerrit. The History of Neo-liberalism: Affinity to Some Developments in Economics in Germany. *Int. J. Soc. Econ.*, 1987, *14*(7/8/9), pp. 142–55.

Mstislavskii, P. Optimizing the Relationship of Consumption and Accumulation. *Prob. Econ.*, February 1987, *29*(10), pp. 21–37. **[G: U.S.S.R.]**

Osband, Kent. Speak Softly, but Carry a Big Stick: On Optimal Targets under Moral Hazard. *J. Compar. Econ.*, December 1987, *11*(4), pp. 584–95.

Peek, Thomas R. Overcoming Fragmentary Analysis: An Integrative Approach to Policy Studies. *Reg. Stud.*, August 1987, *21*(4), pp. 363–72. **[G: U.S.]**

Sklair, Leslie. Capitalist Efficiency without Capitalist Exploitation—Some Indications from Shenzhen. *Warner, M., ed.*, 1987, pp. 176–97. **[G: China]**

Tröder, Manfred. The 1981–85 Order of Planning (Planungsordnung). *Jeffries, I. and Melzer, M., eds.*, 1987, pp. 69–98. **[G: E. Germany]**

Van Arkadie, Brian. A Note on New Directions in Planning. *CEPAL Rev.*, April 1987, (31), pp. 33–41.

Villarreal, René. Planning in Mixed Market Economies and the Paradigms of Development: Problems and Options. *CEPAL Rev.*, April 1987, (31), pp. 51–58. **[G: Latin America]**

Wass von Czege, Andreas. Hungary's "New Economic Mechanism": Upheaval or Continuity? *Gey, P.; Kosta, J. and Quaisser, W., eds.*, 1987, pp. 121–44. **[G: Hungary]**

Zaslavskaia, Tatiana I. Socioeconomic Aspects of Perestroyka. *Soviet Econ.*, October-December 1987, *3*(4), pp. 313–31. **[G: U.S.S.R.]**

Zheng, Guangliang. China's Industrial Reform:

The Leadership System. *Tidrick, G. and Ji-yuan, C., eds.*, 1987, pp. 297–312.
[G: China]

1136 Economic Planning Policy

Aganbegyan, Abel G. The New Economic Strategy of the USSR and Its Social Dimensions. *Int. Lab. Rev.*, Jan.-Feb. 1987, *126*(1), pp. 95–109. [G: U.S.S.R.]

Anglade, Christian and Fortin, Carlos. The Role of the State in Latin America's Strategic Options. *CEPAL Rev.*, April 1987, (31), pp. 211–34. [G: Latin America]

Bácskai, Tamás. Foreign Trade, Investments, and Economic Reforms in Hungary. *Marer, P. and van Veen, P., eds.*, 1987, pp. 139–52. [G: Hungary]

Balassa, Bela. China's Economic Reforms in a Comparative Perspective. *J. Compar. Econ.*, September 1987, *11*(3), pp. 410–26. [G: China]

Bauchet, Pierre. L'avenir des plans nationaux. (With English summary.) *Revue Écon. Polit.*, Mar.-Apr. 1987, *97*(2), pp. 133–55. [G: France]

Boisier, Sergio. Decentralization and Regional Development in Latin America Today. *CEPAL Rev.*, April 1987, (31), pp. 133–44. [G: Latin America]

Boisot, Max H. Industrial Feudalism and Enterprise Reform—Could the Chinese Use Some More Bureaucracy? *Warner, M., ed.*, 1987, pp. 217–37. [G: China]

Bryson, Phillip J. GDR Economic Planning and Social Policy in the 1980s. *Comp. Econ. Stud.*, Summer 1987, *29*(2), pp. 19–38. [G: E. Germany]

Bryson, Phillip J. and Melzer, Manfred. The *Kombinat* in GDR Economic Organisation. *Jeffries, I. and Melzer, M., eds.*, 1987, pp. 51–68. [G: E. Germany]

Byrd, William A. The Impact of the Two-Tier Plan/Market System in Chinese Industry. *J. Compar. Econ.*, September 1987, *11*(3), pp. 295–308. [G: China]

Byrd, William A. and Tidrick, Gene. China's Industrial Reform: Factor Allocation and Enterprise Incentives. *Tidrick, G. and Jiyuan, C., eds.*, 1987, pp. 60–102. [G: China]

Chen, Jiyuan. China's Industrial Reform: The Planning System. *Tidrick, G. and Jiyuan, C., eds.*, 1987, pp. 148–74. [G: China]

Collier, Irwin L. The GDR Five-Year Plan 1986–1990. *Comp. Econ. Stud.*, Summer 1987, *29*(2), pp. 39–53. [G: E. Germany]

Dubois, Paul. Macroeconomic Models and Planning in the Context of an Uncertain Future: The French Experience. *CEPAL Rev.*, April 1987, (31), pp. 59–67. [G: France]

Dušek, Stanislav and Hindls, Richard. Long-term Planning in the Czech Socialist Republic. *Czech. Econ. Digest.*, January 1987, (2), pp. 49–74. [G: Czechoslovakia]

Garland, John. The Economic Situation in Poland: Prospects for Recovery. *Marer, P. and van Veen, P., eds.*, 1987, pp. 109–29. [G: Poland]

Georgiev, Iliia. Improving the Management of the National Economy. *Eastern Europ. Econ.*, Spring 1987, *25*(3), pp. 93–108. [G: Bulgaria]

Gey, Peter. The Cuban Economy under the New "System of Management and Planning": Success or Failure? *Gey, P.; Kosta, J. and Quaisser, W., eds.*, 1987, pp. 71–98. [G: Cuba]

Gouni, Lucien. Reflections on Energy Planning in France. *Maillet, P.; Hague, D. and Rowland, C., eds.*, 1987, pp. 235–57. [G: France]

Griffin, Keith. Industrial Reforms in China. *Griffin, K.*, 1987, pp. 109–46. [G: China]

Grosfeld, Irena. Modeling Planners' Investment Behavior: Poland, 1956–1981. *J. Compar. Econ.*, June 1987, *11*(2), pp. 180–91. [G: Poland]

Gupta, S. Indian Plans: Retrospects and Prospects. *Indian Econ. J.*, Apr.-June 1987, *34*(4), pp. 87–111. [G: India]

Hall, Peter A. The Evolution of Economic Policy under Mitterrand. *Ross, G.; Hoffmann, S. and Malzacher, S., eds.*, 1987, pp. 54–72. [G: France]

Heinrichs, Wolfgang. Symposium on the German Democratic Republic: Comments. *Comp. Econ. Stud.*, Summer 1987, *29*(2), pp. 54–61. [G: E. Germany]

Hvorecký, Jozef. The Material Balance of the National Economic Plan. *Eastern Europ. Econ.*, Spring 1987, *25*(3), pp. 63–71. [G: Czechoslovakia]

Jeffries, Ian and Melzer, Manfred. The Economic Strategy of the 1980s and the Limits to Possible Reforms. *Jeffries, I. and Melzer, M., eds.*, 1987, pp. 41–50. [G: E. Germany]

Jeffries, Ian and Melzer, Manfred. The New Economic System of Planning and Management 1963–70 and Recentralisation in the 1970s. *Jeffries, I. and Melzer, M., eds.*, 1987, pp. 26–40. [G: E. Germany]

Kogane, Yoshihiro. Planning Today. *CEPAL Rev.*, April 1987, (31), pp. 91–94. [G: Japan]

Kołodko, Grzegorz W. Development Goals and Economic Macroproportions. *Eastern Europ. Econ.*, Spring 1987, *25*(3), pp. 72–85. [G: CMEA]

Kornai, János. The Dual Dependence of the State-Owned Firm in Hungary. *Tidrick, G. and Jiyuan, C., eds.*, 1987, pp. 317–38. [G: Hungary]

Koziolek, Helmut. The Economic Strategy of the Eleventh Party Congress of the SED and the New Stage in Science-Production Relations. *Eastern Europ. Econ.*, Winter 1987-88, *26*(2), pp. 64–83. [G: E. Germany]

Kushnirsky, F. I. Soviet Economic Reform: An Analysis and a Model. *Comp. Econ. Stud.*, Winter 1987, *29*(4), pp. 54–85. [G: U.S.S.R.]

Leggett, Robert E. Gorbachev's Reform Program: "Radical" or More of the Same? *Comp. Econ.*

113 Economic Planning Theory and Policy

Stud., Winter 1987, *29*(4), pp. 29–53.
[G: U.S.S.R.]

Levine, Herbert S. Anatomy of Gorbachev's Economic Reform: Comment. *Soviet Econ.*, July-Sept. 1987, *3*(3), pp. 242–45. [G: U.S.S.R.]

Lockett, Martin. The Economic Environment of Management. *Warner, M., ed.,* 1987, pp. 8–23. [G: China]

Malle, Silvana. Capacity Utilization and the Shift Coefficient in Soviet Planning. *Econ. Planning,* 1987, *21*(2–3), pp. 63–86. [G: U.S.S.R.]

de Mattos, Carlos A. The State, Decision-Making and Planning in Latin America. *CEPAL Rev.,* April 1987, (31), pp. 115–31.
[G: Latin America]

Melzer, Manfred. The Perfecting of the Planning and Steering Mechanisms. *Jeffries, I. and Melzer, M., eds.,* 1987, pp. 99–118.
[G: E. Germany]

Melzer, Manfred and Stahnke, Arthur A. Product and Process Renewal in GDR Economic Strategy: Goals, Problems and Prospects. *Jeffries, I. and Melzer, M., eds.,* 1987, pp. 119–40. [G: E. Germany]

Minhas, B. S. The Planning Process and the Annual Budgets: Some Reflections on Recent Indian Experience. *Indian Econ. Rev.,* July-Dec. 1987, *22*(2), pp. 115–49. [G: India]

Moskalenko, V. P. Cost-Accounting Interest in High Final Results. *Prob. Econ.,* March 1987, *29*(11), pp. 28–46. [G: U.S.S.R.]

Nachane, D. M. Regional Planning in the USSR: A Case Study of Soviet Central Asia. *Gidadhubli, R. G., ed.,* 1987, pp. 137–63.
[G: U.S.S.R.]

Ngau, Peter M. Tensions in Empowerment: The Experience of the *Harambee* (Self-Help) Movement in Kenya. *Econ. Develop. Cult. Change,* April 1987, *35*(3), pp. 523–38. [G: Kenya]

Okuniewski, Jósef. The Use of Planning and of the Market to Achieve a Growth of Agricultural Production in Poland. *Kettunen, L., ed.,* 1987, pp. 169–81. [G: Poland]

Potáč, Svatopluk. The Law on the State Plan of Development of the National Economy of the Czechoslovak Socialist Republic in the 8th Five-Year Plan (1986–1990). *Czech. Econ. Digest.,* Apr.-May 1987, (3), pp. 4–26.
[G: Czechoslovakia]

Pysz, Piotr. The Polish Economic Reform: Central Planning or Socialist Markets? *Gey, P.; Kosta, J. and Quaisser, W., eds.,* 1987, pp. 49–69.
[G: Poland]

Ramos, Joseph. Planning and the Market during the Next Ten Years in Latin America. *CEPAL Rev.,* April 1987, (31), pp. 145–52.
[G: Latin America]

Roca, Sergio G. Planners in Wonderland: A Reply [State Enterprises in Cuba under the New System of Planning and Management]. *Mesa-Lago, C., ed.,* 1987, pp. 167–72. [G: Cuba]

Rzheshevskii, V. Application of the New Methods of Management in 1986. *Prob. Econ.,* April 1987, *29*(12), pp. 73–86. [G: U.S.S.R.]

Schroeder, Gertrude E. Anatomy of Gorbachev's

Economic Reform. *Soviet Econ.*, July-Sept. 1987, *3*(3), pp. 219–41. [G: U.S.S.R.]

Schroeder, Gertrude E. Organizations and Hierarchies: The Perennial Search for Solutions. *Comp. Econ. Stud.,* Winter 1987, *29*(4), pp. 7–28. [G: U.S.S.R.]

Sebestyén, Mária. The Management of Agricultural Supply in a Centrally Planned Country: The Case of Hungary. *Kettunen, L., ed.,* 1987, pp. 221–30. [G: Hungary]

Streeten, Paul. From Growth to Basic Needs. *Dietz, J. L. and Street, J. H., eds.,* 1987, *1979,* pp. 33–41.

Tang, Zongkun. China's Industrial Reform: Supply and Marketing. *Tidrick, G. and Jiyuan, C., eds.,* 1987, pp. 210–36. [G: China]

Tidrick, Gene. China's Industrial Reform: Planning and Supply. *Tidrick, G. and Jiyuan, C., eds.,* 1987, pp. 175–209. [G: China]

Timofeev, S. A. Where Does the System of Priorities Push the Enterprise? *Prob. Econ.,* September 1987, *30*(5), pp. 24–42.
[G: U.S.S.R.]

Tröder, Manfred. The 1981–85 Order of Planning (Planungsordnung). *Jeffries, I. and Melzer, M., eds.,* 1987, pp. 69–98. [G: E. Germany]

Ward, Ian and Kulkarni, Anand. The Rise and Fall of National Allocative Planning in Australia. *Australian Econ. Rev.,* Second Quarter 1987, (78), pp. 37–48. [G: Australia]

White, Gordon. Cuban Planning in the Mid-1980s: Centralization, Decentralization, and Participation. *Zimbalist, A., ed.,* 1987, pp. 155–63. [G: Cuba]

White, Gordon. Labour Market Reform in Chinese Industry. *Warner, M., ed.,* 1987, pp. 113–26. [G: China]

Wong, Christine P. W. Between Plan and Market: The Role of the Local Sector in Post-Mao China. *J. Compar. Econ.,* September 1987, *11*(3), pp. 385–98. [G: China]

Wu, Jinglian and Zhao, Renwei. The Dual Pricing System in China's Industry. *J. Compar. Econ.,* September 1987, *11*(3), pp. 309–18.
[G: China]

Xia, Xiaosun and Li, Jun. Consumption Expansion: A Grave Challenge to Reform and Development. *Reynolds, B. L.,* 1987, pp. 89–107.
[G: China]

Yang, Jinbai. Market Mechanism and Macroeconomic Control. *Chinese Econ. Stud.,* Winter 1986-87, *20*(2), pp. 75–82. [G: China]

Zhan, Wu. Proper Attention Should Be Paid to the Supplementary Role of Microeconomic Regulation in Enterprises. *Chinese Econ. Stud.,* Winter 1986-87, *20*(2), pp. 83–89.
[G: China]

Zhang, Shaojie, et al. Investment: Initial Changes in the Mechanism and Preliminary Ideas about Reform. *Reynolds, B. L.,* 1987, pp. 108–29.
[G: China]

Zimbalist, Andrew. Analyzing Cuban Planning: A Response [State Enterprises in Cuba under the New System of Planning and Management]. *Mesa-Lago, C., ed.*, 1987, pp. 159–65. [G: Cuba]

114 Economics of War, Defense, and Disarmament

1140 Economics of War, Defense, and Disarmament

Aben, Jacques and Smith, Ron P. Defence and Employment in the UK and France: A Comparative Study of the Existing Results. *Schmidt, C. and Blackaby, F., eds.*, 1987, pp. 384–98. [G: France; U.K.]

Adams, Gordon. Conversion: A Dead-end Strategy? *Lynch, J. E., ed.*, 1987, pp. 219–32. [G: U.S.]

Adams, Gordon and Gold, D. A. The Economics of Military Spending: Is the Military Dollar Really Different? *Schmidt, C. and Blackaby, F., eds.*, 1987, pp. 266–300. [G: U.S.]

Ady, Robert. Normal Industrial Plant Redevelopment Process. *Lynch, J. E., ed.*, 1987, pp. 137–54. [G: U.S.]

Albrecht, Ulrich. The Current Warfare/Welfare Alternative and the Evidence from Technology. *Schmidt, C. and Blackaby, F., eds.*, 1987, pp. 233–49.

Anglin, Douglas G. United Nations Economic Sanctions against South Africa and Rhodesia. *Leyton-Brown, D., ed.*, 1987, pp. 23–56. [G: Rhodesia; S. Africa]

Anton, James J. and Yao, Dennis A. Second Sourcing and the Experience Curve: Price Competition in Defense Procurement. *Rand J. Econ.*, Spring 1987, *18*(1), pp. 57–76.

Apostolakis, Bobby E. The Buy-American Practices of the U.S. Defence Department and Their Repercussions. *J. Econ. Stud.*, 1987, *11*(3), pp. 61–74. [G: U.S.]

Barro, Robert J. Government Spending, Interest Rates, Prices, and Budget Deficits in the United Kingdom, 1701–1918. *J. Monet. Econ.*, September 1987, *20*(2), pp. 221–47. [G: U.K.]

van Bergeijk, Peter A. G. A Formal Treatment of Threats: A Note on the Economics of Deterrence. *De Economist*, 1987, *135*(3), pp. 298–315.

Bessel, Richard. Unemployment and Demobilisation in Germany after the First World War. *Evans, R. J. and Geary, D., eds.*, 1987, pp. 23–43. [G: Germany]

Blackaby, Frank. A Note on the International Comparison of Military Expenditures: Note. *Schmidt, C., ed.*, 1987, pp. 44–46. [G: Global]

Blackaby, Frank. Peace, Defense and Economic Analysis: Preface. *Schmidt, C. and Blackaby, F., eds.*, 1987, pp. xv–xviii.

Blackaby, Frank and Ohlson, Thomas. Military Expenditure and the Arms Trade: Problems of the Data. *Schmidt, C., ed.*, 1987, pp. 3–24. [G: Global]

Boulding, Kenneth E. Unilateral National Defence Organisations: An Economic Analysis of Non-economic Structures. *Schmidt, C. and Blackaby, F., eds.*, 1987, pp. 3–19. [G: U.S.]

Brady, Lawrence J. The Utility of Economic Sanctions as a Policy Instrument. *Leyton-Brown, D., ed.*, 1987, pp. 297–302.

Brams, Steven J. and Kilgour, D. Marc. Winding Down If Preemption or Escalation Occurs: A Game-Theoretic Analysis. *J. Conflict Resolution*, December 1987, *31*(4), pp. 547–72.

Braun, Bertram and Lynch, John E. Economic Adjustment and Conversion of Defense Industries: Annotated Bibliography. *Lynch, J. E., ed.*, 1987, pp. 245–304.

Brennan, Geoffrey. Methodological Individualism under Fire: A Reply [An Economic Theory of Military Tactics: Methodological Individualism at War]. *J. Econ. Behav. Organ.*, December 1987, *8*(4), pp. 627–35.

Brito, Dagobert L. and Intriligator, Michael D. Arms Races and the Outbreak of War: Application of Principal–Agent Relationships and Asymmetric Information. *Schmidt, C. and Blackaby, F., eds.*, 1987, pp. 104–20.

Bródy, András. Defence Spending as a Priority. *Schmidt, C. and Blackaby, F., eds.*, 1987, pp. 40–44.

Brown, Charles C. Comment [Military Hiring and Youth Employment] [Uncle Sam Wants You—Sometimes: Military Enlistments and the Youth Labor Market] [Military Service and Civilian Earnings of Youths]. *Wise, D. A., ed.*, 1987, pp. 140–45. [G: U.S.]

Buchanan, Timothy. U.S.–Japan Defense Cooperation: Interoperability—A Two-Way Street? *Finn, R. B., ed.*, 1987, pp. 151–61. [G: U.S.; Japan]

Bueno de Mesquita, Bruce. Conceptualizing War: Reply. *J. Conflict Resolution*, June 1987, *31*(2), pp. 370–82.

Buhofer, Heinz and Frey, Bruno S. Lösegeld für Gefangene. (Ransom for Prisoners. With English summary.) *Konjunkturpolitik*, 1987, *33*(1), pp. 27–46. [G: Europe]

Burnett, William B. Competition in the Weapons Acquisition Process: The Case of U.S. Warplanes. *J. Policy Anal. Manage.*, Fall 1987, *7*(1), pp. 17–39. [G: U.S.]

Cars, Hans Christian. Negotiations to Reduce Military Expenditures—Problems and Possibilities. *Schmidt, C., ed.*, 1987, pp. 69–84. [G: Global]

Cars, Hans Christian and Fontanel, Jacques. Military Expenditure Comparisons. *Schmidt, C. and Blackaby, F., eds.*, 1987, pp. 250–65. [G: Global; W. Europe; U.S.]

Cartwright, Joseph V. and Trott, Edward A., Jr. Defense-Related Employment for Selected Weapon Systems. *Lynch, J. E., ed.*, 1987, pp. 51–58. [G: U.S.]

Clark, Rolf. Defense Budget Instability and Weapon System Acquisition. *Public Budg. Finance*, Summer 1987, *7*(2), pp. 24–36. [G: U.S.]

Cohany, Sharon R. Labor Force Status of Vietnam-Era Veterans. *Mon. Lab. Rev.*, February

1987, *110*(2), pp. 11–17.   [G: U.S.]

Craig, Paul P. and Watt, Kenneth E. F. Dynamic Programming of Socioeconomics and War: A Computer Experiment. *Vasko, T., ed.,* 1987, pp. 420–26.

Crane, Jon R. and Wise, David A. Military Service and Civilian Earnings of Youths. *Wise, D. A., ed.,* 1987, pp. 119–37.   [G: U.S.]

Cypher, James M. Military Spending, Technical Change, and Economic Growth: A Disguised Form of Industrial Policy? *J. Econ. Issues,* March 1987, *21*(1), pp. 33–59.   [G: U.S.]

Cyr, Arthur and Kosobud, Richard F. Rational Security Expectations of Stability in Northeast Asia: Can They Be Fulfilled? *Dutta, M., ed. (II),* 1987, pp. 297–308.   [G: Asia]

Decker, Wayne. Japanese Decision Criteria on the Strategic Defense Initiative. *Finn, R. B., ed.,* 1987, pp. 163–73.   [G: U.S.; Japan]

Deger, Saadet and Sen, S. Defence Industrialisation, Technology Transfer and Choice of Techniques in LDCs. *Borner, S. and Taylor, A., eds.,* 1987, pp. 233–54.   [G: LDCs]

DeGrasse, Robert W., Jr. Corporate Diversification and Conversion Experience. *Lynch, J. E., ed.,* 1987, pp. 91–120.   [G: U.S.]

Demski, Joel S.; Sappington, David E. M. and Spiller, Pablo T. Managing Supplier Switching. *Rand J. Econ.,* Spring 1987, *18*(1), pp. 77–97.

Desai, Padma. The Soviet Union and Cancún. *Desai, P.,* 1987, *1982,* pp. 249–55.
                        [G: U.S.S.R.]

Deutsch, Edwin. Efficiency, Industry and Alternative Weapons Procurement Policies: Note. *Schmidt, C., ed.,* 1987, pp. 301–03.
                        [G: U.S.; EEC]

Deutsch, Edwin and Schöpp, Wolfgang. Civil versus Military R&D Expenditures and Industrial Productivity. *Schmidt, C., ed.,* 1987, pp. 336–56.   [G: OECD]

Dewitt, David B. The Arab Boycott of Israel. *Leyton-Brown, D., ed.,* 1987, pp. 149–66.
                  [G: Israel; Arab Countries]

Dudkin, Lev and Vasilevsky, Anatol. The Soviet Military Burden: A Critical Analysis of Current Research. *Hitotsubashi J. Econ.,* June 1987, *28*(1), pp. 41–61.   [G: U.S.S.R.]

Dumas, Lloyd J. National Security and Economic Delusion. *Challenge,* Mar./Apr. 1987, *30*(1), pp. 28–33.   [G: U.S.]

Dussauge, Pierre. The Conversion of Military Activities: A Strategic Management of the Firm Perspective. *Schmidt, C. and Blackaby, F., eds.,* 1987, pp. 424–37.   [G: U.S.]

Ellwood, David T. and Wise, David A. Military Hiring and Youth Employment. *Wise, D. A., ed.,* 1987, pp. 79–95.   [G: U.S.]

Ellwood, David T. and Wise, David A. Uncle Sam Wants You—Sometimes: Military Enlistments and the Youth Labor Market. *Wise, D. A., ed.,* 1987, pp. 97–118.   [G: U.S.]

Evans, Paul M. Caging the Dragon: Post-war Economic Sanctions against the People's Republic of China. *Leyton-Brown, D., ed.,* 1987, pp. 59–85.   [G: China]

Faber, Jan. Measuring Cooperation, Conflict, and the Social Network of Nations. *J. Conflict Resolution,* September 1987, *31*(3), pp. 438–64.

Falkenheim, Peggy L. Post-Afghanistan Sanctions. *Leyton-Brown, D., ed.,* 1987, pp. 105–30.   [G: U.S.S.R.]

Fontanel, Jacques. A Note on the International Comparison of Military Expenditures. *Schmidt, C., ed.,* 1987, pp. 29–43.
                        [G: Global]

Fontanel, Jacques. Military Expenditure and the Arms Trade: Problems of the Data: Note. *Schmidt, C., ed.,* 1987, pp. 25–28.
                        [G: Global]

Friedman, Miles and Culbertson, Deborah. State–Local Economic Development Programs. *Lynch, J. E., ed.,* 1987, pp. 175–90.
                        [G: U.S.]

Gigengack, A. R.; de Haan, Hendrik and Jepma, Catherine J. Military Expenditure Dynamics and a World Model. *Schmidt, C. and Blackaby, F., eds.,* 1987, pp. 321–41.

Goff, Brian L. and Tollison, Robert D. The Allocation of Death in the Vietnam War: A Public Choice Perspective. *Southern Econ. J.,* October 1987, *54*(2), pp. 316–21.   [G: U.S.]

Goldstein, Joshua S. Long Waves in War, Production, Prices, and Wages. *J. Conflict Resolution,* December 1987, *31*(4), pp. 573–600.
                   [G: Selected MDCs]

Greenwood, David. Note on the Impact of Military Expenditure on Economic Growth and Performance. *Schmidt, C., ed.,* 1987, pp. 98–103.

Greenwood, Michael J.; Hunt, Gary L. and Pfalzgraff, Ellen L. The Economic Effects of Space Science Activities on Colorado and the Western United States. *Ann. Reg. Sci.,* July 1987, *21*(2), pp. 21–44.   [G: U.S.]

Gregerman, Alan and Penne, R. Leo. Community Economic Adjustment to Defense Industrial Cutbacks. *Lynch, J. E., ed.,* 1987, pp. 59–80.   [G: U.S.]

Greilsammer, Ilan. Reflections on the Capability of the European Community to Play an Active Role in an International Crisis: The Case of the Israeli Action in Lebanon. *Greilsammer, I. and Weiler, J. H. H., eds.,* 1987, pp. 283–302.   [G: EEC; Israel]

Grusky, Sara. The Changing Role of the U.S. Military in Puerto Rico. *Soc. Econ. Stud.,* September 1987, *36*(3), pp. 37–76.   [G: U.S.; Puerto Rico]

de Haan, Hendrik. Military Expenditures and Economic Growth: Some Theoretical Remarks. *Schmidt, C., ed.,* 1987, pp. 87–97.

Harkavy, R. E. Arms Resupply *during* Conflict: A Framework for Analysis. *Schmidt, C., ed.,* 1987, pp. 239–79.   [G: Global]

Hartley, Keith. Efficiency, Industry and Alternative Weapons Procurement Policies. *Schmidt, C., ed.,* 1987, pp. 283–300.   [G: U.S.; EEC]

Hartley, Keith. Public Procurement and Competitiveness: A Community Market for Military Hardware and Technology? *J. Common Market*

Stud., March 1987, 25(3), pp. 237–47.
[G: EEC]

Hartley, Keith. Reducing Defence Expenditure: A Public Choice Analysis and a Case Study of the UK. *Schmidt, C. and Blackaby, F., eds.*, 1987, pp. 399–423. [G: U.K.]

Hartley, Keith. The Evaluation of Efficiency in the Arms Industry. *Borner, S. and Taylor, A., eds.*, 1987, pp. 181–201.

Heim, Carol E. R&D, Defense, and Spatial Divisions of Labor in Twentieth-Century Britain. *J. Econ. Hist.*, June 1987, 47(2), pp. 365–78. [G: U.K.]

Helpman, Elhanan. The National Defense Argument for Government Intervention in Foreign Trade: Comment. *Stern, R. M., ed.*, 1987, pp. 370–73. [G: U.S.]

Henry, David K. and Oliver, Richard P. The Defense Buildup, 1977–85: Effects on Production and Employment. *Mon. Lab. Rev.*, August 1987, 110(8), pp. 3–11. [G: U.S.]

Herek, Gregory M.; Janis, Irving L. and Huth, Paul. Decision Making during International Crises: Is Quality of Process Related to Outcome? *J. Conflict Resolution*, June 1987, 31(2), pp. 203–26. [G: U.S.]

Herrera-Lasso, Luis. Economic Growth, Military Expenditure, Arms Industry and Arms Transfer in Latin America. *Schmidt, C., ed.*, 1987, pp. 113–34. [G: Latin America]

Hirsch, Seev. Trade Regimes and the Middle East Peace Process. *World Econ.*, March 1987, 10(1), pp. 61–74. [G: Israel; Egypt]

Hirshleifer, Jack. Disaster and Recovery: An Historical Survey. *Hirshleifer, J.*, 1987, 1963, pp. 5–94. [G: U.S.; Japan; W. Germany]

Hirshleifer, Jack. Disaster and Recovery: The Black Death in Western Europe. *Hirshleifer, J.*, 1987, 1966, pp. 95–115. [G: W. Europe]

Hirshleifer, Jack. War Damage Insurance. *Hirshleifer, J.*, 1987, 1953, pp. 116–33. [G: U.S.]

Holtfrerich, Carl-Ludwig. The Modernisation of the Tax System in the First World War and the Great Inflation, 1914–23. *Witt, P.-C., ed.*, 1987, pp. 125–35. [G: Germany]

Howorth, Jolyon. Of Budgets and Strategic Choices: Defense Policy under François Mitterrand. *Ross, G.; Hoffmann, S. and Malzacher, S., eds.*, 1987, pp. 306–23.
[G: France]

Im, Eric Iksoon; Cauley, Jon and Sandler, Todd. Cycles and Substitutions in Terrorist Activities: A Spectral Approach. *Kyklos*, 1987, 40(2), pp. 238–55. [G: Global]

Intriligator, Michael D. Semantic Variations on Richardson's Armaments Dynamics: Note. *Schmidt, C., ed.*, 1987, pp. 176–79.

Intriligator, Michael D. The National Defense Argument for Government Intervention in Foreign Trade: Comment. *Stern, R. M., ed.*, 1987, pp. 364–69. [G: U.S.]

Intriligator, Michael D. and Brito, Dagobert L. A Game-Theoretic Analysis of the Role of the Arms Industry in the International Security System. *Borner, S. and Taylor, A., eds.*, 1987, pp. 219–31.

Intriligator, Michael D. and Brito, Dagobert L. Can Arms Races Lead to the Outbreak of War? *Schmidt, C., ed.*, 1987, pp. 180–96.

Jackson, M. W. Chocolate-Box Soldiers: A Critique of 'An Economic Theory of Military Tactics.' *J. Econ. Behav. Organ.*, March 1987, 8(1), pp. 1–11. [G: U.S.]

Jensen, Lloyd. Soviet–American Behavior in Disarmament Negotiations. *Zartman, I. W., ed. (I)*, 1987, 1963, pp. 288–321. [G: U.S.; U.S.S.R.]

Karier, Thomas. A Note on Wage Rates in Defense Industries. *Ind. Relat.*, Spring 1987, 26(2), pp. 195–200. [G: U.S.]

Kindleberger, Charles P. An Excerpt from an Oral History, Truman Library. *Kindleberger, C. P.*, 1987, pp. 106–19. [G: U.S.; W. Europe]

Kindleberger, Charles P. Did Dollars Save the World? *Kindleberger, C. P.*, 1987, pp. 245–65. [G: U.S.; Global]

Kindleberger, Charles P. Excerpts from the Cleveland–Moore–Kindleberger Memorandum of 12 June 1947, on a European Recovery Program. *Kindleberger, C. P.*, 1987, pp. 1–24. [G: U.S.; W. Europe]

Kindleberger, Charles P. Finnish War Reparations. *Kindleberger, C. P.*, 1987, pp. 209–29. [G: Finland; U.S.S.R.]

Kindleberger, Charles P. The American Origins of the Marshall Plan: A View from the State Department. *Kindleberger, C. P.*, 1987, 1984, pp. 154–60. [G: U.S.; W. Europe]

Kindleberger, Charles P. The Marshall Plan and the Cold War. *Kindleberger, C. P.*, 1987, 1968, pp. 92–105. [G: U.S.; W. Europe]

King, Alexander. Science, Technology and International Relations: Some Comments and a Speculation. *Hieronymi, O., ed.*, 1987, pp. 9–24.

Kirton, John. Economic Sanctions and Alliance Consultations: Canada, the United States and the Strains of 1979–82. *Leyton-Brown, D., ed.*, 1987, pp. 269–93. [G: U.S.; Canada]

Kolodziej, Edward A. Re-evaluating Economic and Technological Variables to Explain Global Arms Production and Sales. *Schmidt, C., ed.*, 1987, pp. 304–35. [G: LDCs]

Kolodziej, Edward A. Whither Modernisation and Militarisation? Implications for International Security and Arms Control. *Schmidt, C. and Blackaby, F., eds.*, 1987, pp. 206–32.

Kondo, Shigekatsu. U.S.–Japan Security Relations in the Changing International Environment of East Asia. *Finn, R. B., ed.*, 1987, pp. 135–49. [G: U.S.; Japan]

Kulik, Jane and Fairchild, Charles. Worker Assistance and Placement Experience. *Lynch, J. E., ed.*, 1987, pp. 191–218. [G: U.S.]

Lamare, James W. International Conflict: Anzus and New Zealand Public Opinion. *J. Conflict Resolution*, September 1987, 31(3), pp. 420–37. [G: New Zealand]

Lambelet, Jean-Christian and Luterbacher, Urs. Conflicts, Arms Races and War: A Synthetic

Approach. *Schmidt, C. and Blackaby, F., eds.*, 1987, pp. 85–103.

Lawson, James. Civilian Market Opportunities for Defense Industry. *Lynch, J. E., ed.*, 1987, pp. 155–74.   **[G: U.S.]**

Lawson, James. Industrial Plant Reuse and Conversion. *Lynch, J. E., ed.*, 1987, pp. 129–36.   **[G: U.S.]**

Lebovic, James H. and Ishaq, Ashfaq. Military Burden, Security Needs, and Economic Growth in the Middle East. *J. Conflict Resolution*, March 1987, *31*(1), pp. 106–38.   **[G: Middle East]**

Lee, Douglas and Stekler, H. O. Modeling High Levels of Defense Expenditures: A Vietnam. *J. Policy Modeling*, Fall 1987, *9*(3), pp. 437–53.   **[G: U.S.]**

Lee, L. Douglas. Time to Rethink Defense. *Challenge*, Mar./Apr. 1987, *30*(1), pp. 15–20.   **[G: U.S.]**

Leonard, Herman B. Investing in the Defense Work Force: The Debt and Structure of Military Pensions. *Wise, D. A., ed.*, 1987, pp. 47–73.   **[G: U.S.]**

Leyton-Brown, David. Extraterritoriality in United States Trade Sanctions. *Leyton-Brown, D., ed.*, 1987, pp. 255–67.   **[G: U.S.]**

Leyton-Brown, David. Lessons and Policy Considerations about Economic Sanctions. *Leyton-Brown, D., ed.*, 1987, pp. 303–10.

Leyton-Brown, David. The Utility of International Economic Sanctions: Introduction. *Leyton-Brown, D., ed.*, 1987, pp. 1–4.

Licklider, Roy. The Arab Oil Weapon of 1973–74. *Leyton-Brown, D., ed.*, 1987, pp. 167–81.   **[G: OPEC]**

Looney, Robert E. Impact of Military Expenditures on Third World Debt. *Can. J. Devel. Stud.*, 1987, *8*(1), pp. 7–26.   **[G: LDCs]**

Lynch, John E. Adjustment and Conversion Policy Issues. *Lynch, J. E., ed.*, 1987, pp. 29–50.   **[G: U.S.]**

Lynch, John E. Defense Spending in the Economy. *Lynch, J. E., ed.*, 1987, pp. 13–28.   **[G: U.S.]**

Lynch, John E. Economic Adjustment and Conversion of Defense Industries: Introduction. *Lynch, J. E., ed.*, 1987, pp. 1–12.   **[G: U.S.]**

Lynch, John E. Economic Adjustment and Conversion of Defense Industries: Conclusion: Dealing with Major Plant Closures. *Lynch, J. E., ed.*, 1987, pp. 233–44.   **[G: U.S.]**

Lynch, John E. Military Base Civilian Reuse Experience. *Lynch, J. E., ed.*, 1987, pp. 81–90.   **[G: U.S.]**

Maier, Charles S. The Politics of Productivity: Foundations of American International Economic Policy after World War II. *Maier, C. S.*, 1987, *1977*, pp. 121–52.   **[G: U.S.]**

Mandel, Robert. An Evaluation of the "Balance of Power" Simulation. *J. Conflict Resolution*, June 1987, *31*(2), pp. 333–45.

Marantz, Paul. Economic Sanctions in the Polish Crisis. *Leyton-Brown, D., ed.*, 1987, pp. 131–46.   **[G: Poland]**

Martin, Stephen; Smith, Ron P. and Fontanel,

Jacques. Time-Series Estimates of the Macroeconomic Impact of Defence Spending in France and the UK. *Schmidt, C. and Blackaby, F., eds.*, 1987, pp. 342–61.   **[G: France; U.K.]**

McGuire, Martin C. Economic Considerations in the Comparison between Assured Destruction and Assured Survival. *Schmidt, C. and Blackaby, F., eds.*, 1987, pp. 122–49.   **[G: U.S.]**

McGuire, Martin C. Foreign Assistance, Investment, and Defense: A Methodological Study with an Application to Israel, 1960–1979. *Econ. Develop. Cult. Change*, July 1987, *35*(4), pp. 847–73.   **[G: Israel]**

McGuire, Martin C. U.S. Foreign Assistance, Israeli Resource Allocation and the Arms Race in the Middle East: An Analysis of Three Interdependent Resource Allocation Processes. *Schmidt, C., ed.*, 1987, pp. 197–238.   **[G: U.S.; Israel; Middle East]**

McNaught, William and Ratner, Jonathan. Budgeting for Inflation in the Department of Defense. *Public Budg. Finance*, Winter 1987, *7*(4), pp. 24–35.   **[G: U.S.]**

McWilliams Tullberg, Rita. Military-Related Debt in Non-oil Developing Countries, 1972–82. *Schmidt, C. and Blackaby, F., eds.*, 1987, pp. 302–16.   **[G: LDCs]**

Mickolus, Edward F. Comment—Terrorists, Governments, and Numbers: Counting Things versus Things That Count. *J. Conflict Resolution*, March 1987, *31*(1), pp. 54–62.

Mills, Geofrey and Rockoff, Hugh. Compliance with Price Controls in the United States and the United Kingdom during World War II. *J. Econ. Hist.*, March 1987, *47*(1), pp. 197–213.   **[G: U.S.; U.K.]**

Morse, Edward L. The Bargaining Structure of NATO: Multi-issue Negotiations in an Interdependent World. *Zartman, I. W., ed. (I)*, 1987, pp. 66–97.

Nicholson, Michael. The Conceptual Bases of the *The War Trap*. *J. Conflict Resolution*, June 1987, *31*(2), pp. 346–69.

Niou, Emerson M. S. and Ordeshook, Peter C. Preventative War and the Balance of Power: A Game-Theoretic Approach. *J. Conflict Resolution*, September 1987, *31*(3), pp. 387–419.

Nishikawa, Jun. Note on the Impact of Military Expenditure on the Japanese Economy. *Schmidt, C., ed.*, 1987, pp. 135–37.   **[G: Japan]**

Nogee, Joseph L. Propaganda and Negotiation: The Ten-Nation Disarmament Committee. *Zartman, I. W., ed. (I)*, 1987, *1963*, pp. 322–42.

Nourzad, Farrokh. A Reexamination of the Effect of Rapid Military Spending on Inflation. *Quart. J. Bus. Econ.*, Summer 1987, *26*(3), pp. 57–66.   **[G: U.S.]**

O'Neill, Barry. A Measure for Crisis Instability with an Application to Space-Based Antimissile Systems. *J. Conflict Resolution*, December 1987, *31*(4), pp. 631–72.

Paarlberg, Robert L. The 1980–81 U.S. Grain

Embargo: Consequences for the Participants. *Leyton-Brown, D., ed.*, 1987, pp. 185–206. **[G: U.S.; U.S.S.R.]**

Passadeos, Christos. The Economics of Military Spending: Is the Military Dollar Really Different? Comment. *Schmidt, C. and Blackaby, F., eds.*, 1987, pp. 301. **[G: U.S.]**

Phillips, Douglas W. and Wise, David A. Military versus Civilian Pay: A Descriptive Discussion. *Wise, D. A., ed.*, 1987, pp. 19–46. **[G: U.S.]**

Pilandon, Louis. Quantitative and Causal Analysis of Military Expenditures. *Schmidt, C., ed.*, 1987, pp. 47–68. **[G: Global]**

Plous, S. Perceptual Illusions and Military Realities: Results from a Computer-Simulated Arms Race. *J. Conflict Resolution*, March 1987, *31*(1), pp. 5–33.

Quester, George H. Through the Nuclear Strategic Looking Glass, or Reflections off the Window of Vulnerability. *J. Conflict Resolution*, December 1987, *31*(4), pp. 725–37. **[G: U.S.]**

Rietman, Mark. Toward the Global Optimization Model of Peace Defense. *J. Conflict Resolution*, September 1987, *31*(3), pp. 525–42.

Rivlin, Paul. The Burden of Defence in Developing Countries. *Schmidt, C., ed.*, 1987, pp. 104–12. **[G: LDCs]**

Rizzo, Robert F. Moral Debate on the Arms Race and Its Economic Implications. *Int. J. Soc. Econ.*, 1987, *14*(12), pp. 19–30.

Robertson, Marjorie J. Homeless Veterans: An Emerging Problem? *Bingham, R. D.; Green, R. E. and White, S. B., eds.*, 1987, pp. 64–81. **[G: U.S.]**

Roca, Sergio G. Economic Sanctions against Cuba. *Leyton-Brown, D., ed.*, 1987, pp. 87–104. **[G: U.S.; Cuba]**

Rosen, Harvey S. Comment [Military versus Civilian Pay: A Descriptive Discussion] [Investing in the Defense Work Force: The Debt and Structure of Military Pensions]. *Wise, D. A., ed.*, 1987, pp. 73–77. **[G: U.S.]**

Rostow, Walt W. How the Cold War Might End. *Rostow, W. W.*, 1987, pp. 175–87. **[G: U.S.; U.S.S.R.]**

Rostow, Walt W. On Ending the Cold War. *Foreign Aff.*, Spring 1987, *65*(4), pp. 831–51. **[G: U.S.; U.S.S.R.]**

Rothschild, Kurt W. Economic Considerations in the Comparison between Assured Destruction and Assured Survival: Comment. *Schmidt, C. and Blackaby, F., eds.*, 1987, pp. 150–54. **[G: U.S.]**

Russett, Bruce. Economic Change as a Cause of International Conflict. *Schmidt, C. and Blackaby, F., eds.*, 1987, pp. 185–205.

Sandler, Todd. NATO Burden-Sharing: Rules or Reality? *Schmidt, C. and Blackaby, F., eds.*, 1987, pp. 363–83. **[G: U.S.; EEC]**

Sandler, Todd and Scott, John L. Terrorist Success in Hostage-Taking Incidents. *J. Conflict Resolution*, March 1987, *31*(1), pp. 35–53.

Scheetz, Thomas. Public Sector Expenditures and Financial Crisis in Chile. *World Devel.*, August 1987, *15*(8), pp. 1053–75. **[G: Chile]**

Schmidt, Christian. Alternative Approaches to the Arms Industry: Some Suggestions for a Research Programme. *Borner, S. and Taylor, A., eds.*, 1987, pp. 255–63.

Schmidt, Christian. Economic Impact of the Arms Industry: Introduction. *Borner, S. and Taylor, A., eds.*, 1987, pp. 175–80.

Schmidt, Christian. Peace and War Economics in Retrospect: Some Reflections on the Historical Background of Defence Economics. *Schmidt, C. and Blackaby, F., eds.*, 1987, pp. 20–39.

Schmidt, Christian. Peace, Defense and Economic Analysis: Introduction. *Schmidt, C. and Blackaby, F., eds.*, 1987, pp. xix–xxiv.

Schmidt, Christian. Semantic Variations on Richardson's Armaments Dynamics. *Schmidt, C., ed.*, 1987, pp. 141–75.

Schmidt, Christian. The Economics of Military Expenditures: Introduction. *Schmidt, C., ed.*, 1987, pp. xvii–xxiii.

Sen, Amartya K. Defence Spending as a Priority: Comment. *Schmidt, C. and Blackaby, F., eds.*, 1987, pp. 45–49.

Shubik, Martin. The Uses, Value and Limitations of Game Theoretic Methods in Defence Analysis. *Schmidt, C. and Blackaby, F., eds.*, 1987, pp. 53–84. **[G: U.S.; U.S.S.R.]**

Smith, D. Alton. Military Service and Civilian Earnings of Youths: Comment. *Wise, D. A., ed.*, 1987, pp. 138–40. **[G: U.S.]**

Smith, Ron P. The Demand for Military Expenditure: A Correction. *Econ. J.*, December 1987, *97*(388), pp. 989–90. **[G: U.K.]**

Springer, Bernard. Can Arms Races Lead to the Outbreak of War? Comments. *J. Conflict Resolution*, September 1987, *31*(3), pp. 543–44.

Srinivasan, T. N. The National Defense Argument for Government Intervention in Foreign Trade: Postscript. *Stern, R. M., ed.*, 1987, pp. 374–75.

Srinivasan, T. N. The National Defense Argument for Government Intervention in Foreign Trade. *Stern, R. M., ed.*, 1987, pp. 337–63. **[G: U.S.]**

Stanislawski, Howard. The Impact of the Arab Boycott of Israel on the United States and Canada. *Leyton-Brown, D., ed.*, 1987, pp. 223–54. **[G: U.S.; Canada]**

Stockwin, J. A. A. Japanese Public Opinion and Policies on Security and Defence. *[Penrose, E. F.]*, 1987, pp. 111–34. **[G: Japan]**

Tannen, Michael B. Is the Army College Fund Meeting Its Objectives? *Ind. Lab. Relat. Rev.*, October 1987, *41*(1), pp. 50–62. **[G: U.S.]**

Thies, Wallace J. Alliances and Collective Goods. *J. Conflict Resolution*, June 1987, *31*(2), pp. 298–332.

Thompson, Fred. Managing Defense Expenditures. *Thai, K. V., ed.*, 1987, *1985*, pp. 129–46. **[G: U.S.]**

Tinbergen, Jan. Integration of Security Issues into Economic Policy. *Indian J. Quant. Econ.*, 1987, *3*(1), pp. 27–33.

Tinbergen, Jan. Peace, Defence and Economic Analysis: Opening Presentation: World Peace

Policy. *Schmidt, C. and Blackaby, F., eds.*, 1987, pp. xxvi–xxxiii.

Tullock, Gordon. Jackson and the Prisoner's Dilemma [Chocolate-box Soldiers: A critique of 'An Economic Theory of Military Tactics']. *J. Econ. Behav. Organ.*, December 1987, *8*(4), pp. 637–40. **[G: U.S.]**

Udis, Bernard. European Conversion Experience. *Lynch, J. E., ed.*, 1987, pp. 121–28. **[G: W. Europe]**

Urquidi, Victor L. Military-Related Debt in Non-oil Developing Countries, 1972–82: Comment. *Schmidt, C. and Blackaby, F., eds.*, 1987, pp. 317–18. **[G: LDCs]**

Urquidi, Victor L. The Economics of Military Expenditures: Introductory Remarks. *Schmidt, C., ed.*, 1987, pp. xiii–xvi.

Vernon, Raymond. The Politics of Comparative Economic Statistics: Three Cultures and Three Cases. *Alonso, W. and Starr, P., eds.*, 1987, pp. 61–82.

Ward, Michael D. and Mintz, Alex. Dynamics of Military Spending in Israel: A Computer Simulation. *J. Conflict Resolution*, March 1987, *31*(1), pp. 86–105. **[G: Israel]**

Wells, P. The Military Scientific Infrastructure and Regional Development. *Environ. Planning A*, December 1987, *19*(12), pp. 1631–58. **[G: U.K.]**

Wionczek, Miguel S. The Growth of Military Industries in Developing Countries and Their Impact on the Development Process. *[Kitamura, H.]*, 1987, pp. 212–28. **[G: LDCs]**

Wise, David A. Public Sector Payrolls: Overview. *Wise, D. A., ed.*, 1987, pp. 1–18. **[G: U.S.]**

Wolf, Bernard M. Economic Impact on the United States of the Pipeline Sanctions. *Leyton-Brown, D., ed.*, 1987, pp. 207–20. **[G: U.S.]**

Wolfson, Murray. A Theorem on the Existence of Zones of Initiation and Deterrence in Intriligator–Brito Arms Race Models [Strategic Considerations in the Richardson Model of the Arms Race] [Nuclear Proliferation and the Probability of Nuclear War]. *Public Choice*, August 1987, *54*(3), pp. 291–97. **[G: U.S.; U.S.S.R.]**

Wolfson, Murray and Farrell, John P. Economic Warfare between the Superpowers. *Schmidt, C. and Blackaby, F., eds.*, 1987, pp. 155–81. **[G: U.S.; U.S.S.R.]**

Wulf, Herbert. Arms Industry Unlimited: The Economic Impact of the Arms Sector in Developing Countries. *Borner, S. and Taylor, A., eds.*, 1987, pp. 203–217. **[G: LDCs]**

Wulf, Herbert. Arms Production in Third World Countries, Effects on Industrialisation. *Schmidt, C., ed.*, 1987, pp. 357–83. **[G: LDCs]**

120 COUNTRY STUDIES

121 Economic Studies of Developing Countries

1210 General

Bacha, Edmar Lisboa. Balance of Payments Experience and Growth Prospects of Developing Countries: Terms of Reference for the Country Studies. *Dell, S., ed., Pt. 3*, 1987, pp. 1012–30.

Bacha, Edmar Lisboa. IMF Conditionality: Conceptual Problems and Policy Alternatives. *World Devel.*, December 1987, *15*(12), pp. 1457–67. **[G: LDCs]**

Bartoli, Henri. La matrise des cots humains du travail. Condition de la matrise des transformations technologiques dans les pays du Tiers Monde. (Mastering the Human Cost of Labour: An Essential Condition for Mastery of Technological Change in the third world. With English summary.) *Écon. Soc.*, November 1987, *21*(11), pp. 101–26. **[G: LDCs]**

Casson, Mark and Pearce, Robert D. Multinational Enterprises in LDCs. *Gemmell, N., ed.*, 1987, pp. 90–132.

Chow, Peter C. Y. Causality between Export Growth and Industrial Development: Empirical Evidence from the NICs. *J. Devel. Econ.*, June 1987, *26*(1), pp. 55–63. **[G: LDCs]**

Fisher, Sethard. Economic Development and Crime: Two May Be Associated as an Adaptation to Industrialism in Social Revolution. *Amer. J. Econ. Soc.*, January 1987, *46*(1), pp. 17–34.

Levy, Victor. Anticipated Development Assistance, Temporary Relief Aid, and Consumption Behaviour of Low-Income Countries. *Econ. J.*, June 1987, *97*(386), pp. 446–58. **[G: Africa]**

Lim, David. Export Instability, Investment and Economic Growth in Developing Countries. *Australian Econ. Pap.*, December 1987, *26*(49), pp. 318–27. **[G: LDCs]**

Lloyd, Peter J. Structural Change in a Selection of Countries: Discussion and Conclusions. *Pasinetti, L. and Lloyd, P., eds.*, 1987, pp. 263–66.

Love, James. Export Instability in Less Developed Countries: Consequences and Causes. *J. Econ. Stud.*, 1987, *14*(2), pp. 3–80. **[G: LDCs]**

McCarthy, F. Desmond; Taylor, Lance and Talati, Cyrus. Trade Patterns in Developing Countries, 1964–82. *[Diaz-Alejandro, C. F.]*, 1987, pp. 5–39. **[G: LDCs]**

McCarthy, F. Desmond; Taylor, Lance and Talati, Cyrus. Trade Patterns in Developing Countries, 1964–82. *J. Devel. Econ.*, October 1987, *27*(1–2), pp. 5–39. **[G: LDCs]**

McWilliams Tullberg, Rita. Military-Related Debt in Non-oil Developing Countries, 1972–82. *Schmidt, C. and Blackaby, F., eds.*, 1987, pp. 302–16. **[G: LDCs]**

Mirakhor, Abbas and Montiel, Peter J. Adjustment and the Import Intensity of Output. *Finance Develop.*, December 1987, *24*(4), pp. 17–19. **[G: LDCs]**

Morgan, John B. A Note on Eaton and Gersovitz's Model of Borrowing [LDC Participation in International Financial Markets] [Debt with Potential Repudiation: Theoretical and Empirical Analysis]. *J. Devel. Econ.*, February 1987, *25*(1), pp. 251–61. **[G: LDCs]**

Nwanna, Gladson I. Devaluation, Unanticipated Inflation and Output Growth: A Comparative Aggregate Analysis. *Econ. Int.*, November 1987, *40*(4), pp. 329–44. [G: LDCs]

Riddle, Dorothy I. The Role of the Service Sector in Economic Development: Similarities and Differences by Development Category. *Giarini, O., ed.*, 1987, pp. 83–104. [G: LDCs]

Selowsky, Marcelo. Adjustment in the 1980s: An Overview of Issues. *Finance Develop.*, June 1987, *24*(2), pp. 11–14. [G: LDCs]

Terweduwe, D. The Newly and Semi-industrialized Countries: A Critical Appraisal of the Country Classifications. *Tijdschrift Econ. Manage.*, 1987, *32*(1), pp. 55–71. [G: Selected LDCs]

1211 Comparative Country Studies

Berberoglu, Berch. The Contradictions of Export-Oriented Development in the Third World. *Soc. Econ. Stud.*, December 1987, *36*(4), pp. 85–112. [G: LDCs]

Bradford, Colin I., Jr. NICs and the Next-Tier NICs as Transitional Economies. *Bradford, C. I., Jr. and Branson, W. H., eds.*, 1987, pp. 173–204. [G: Asia; LDCs]

Bradford, Colin I., Jr. Trade and Structural Change: NICs and Next Tier NICs as Transitional Economies. *World Devel.*, March 1987, *15*(3), pp. 299–316. [G: LDCs]

Cornia, Giovanni Andrea. Adjustment Policies 1980–1985: Effects on Child Welfare. *Cornia, G. A.; Jolly, R. and Stewart, F., eds.*, 1987, pp. 48–72. [G: LDCs]

Cornia, Giovanni Andrea and Stewart, Frances. Country Experience with Adjustment. *Cornia, G. A.; Jolly, R. and Stewart, F., eds.*, 1987, pp. 105–27. [G: LDCs]

Dervis, Kemal and Petri, Peter A. The Macroccomomics of Successful Development: What Are the Lessons? *Fischer, S., ed.*, 1987, pp. 211–54. [G: LDCs]

Devarajan, Shantayanan and de Melo, Jaime. Evaluating Participation in African Monetary Unions: A Statistical Analysis of the CFA Zones. *World Devel.*, April 1987, *15*(4), pp. 483–96. [G: W. Africa; LDCs]

Gonçalves, Reinaldo and Richtering, Jürgen. Intercountry Comparison of Export Performance and Output Growth. *Devel. Econ.*, March 1987, *25*(1), pp. 3–18. [G: LDCs]

Harberger, Arnold C. The Macroeconomics of Successful Development: What Are the Lessons? Comment. *Fischer, S., ed.*, 1987, pp. 255–58.

van der Hoeven, Rolph. External Shocks and Stabilisation Policies: Spreading the Load. *Int. Lab. Rev.*, Mar.-Apr. 1987, *126*(2), pp. 133–50. [G: Africa; Latin America]

Jha, L. K. Do Outward-Oriented Polices Really Favor Growth? *Finance Develop.*, December 1987, *24*(4), pp. 44–46. [G: LDCs]

Krueger, Anne O. Origins of the Developing Countries' Debt Crisis 1970 to 1982. *[Diaz-Alejandro, C. F.]*, 1987, pp. 165–87. [G: LDCs]

Krueger, Anne O. Origins of the Developing Countries' Debt Crisis 1970 to 1982. *J. Devel. Econ.*, October 1987, *27*(1–2), pp. 165–87. [G: LDCs]

Krueger, Anne O. The Importance of Economic Policy in Development: Contrasts between Korea and Turkey. *[Corden, W. M.]*, 1987, pp. 172–203. [G: S. Korea; Turkey]

Lal, Deepak and Rajapatirana, Sarath. Foreign Trade Regimes and Economic Growth in Developing Countries. *World Bank Res. Observer*, July 1987, *2*(2), pp. 189–217. [G: LDCs]

Looney, Robert E. Determinants of Third World Mineral-Oil Economies External Debt. *J. Econ. Devel.*, December 1987, *12*(2), pp. 39–56. [G: LDCs]

Macomber, John D. East Asia's Lessons for Latin American Resurgence. *World Econ.*, December 1987, *10*(4), pp. 469–82. [G: Latin America; E. Asia]

Menzel, Ulrich and Senghaas, Dieter. Para una definición de los países de industrialización reciente. Propuesta de indicadores para evaluar los países que se encuentran en el umbral de la industrialización. (With English summary.) *Desarrollo Econ.*, Oct.-Dec. 1987, *27*(107), pp. 323–46. [G: LDCs]

Montiel, Peter J. and Zaidi, Iqbal. Cross-Regime Tests of the Lucas Supply Function in Developing Countries. *Int. Monet. Fund Staff Pap.*, December 1987, *34*(4), pp. 760–69. [G: LDCs]

Rabushka, Alvin. Taxation, Economic Growth, and Liberty. *Cato J.*, Spring/Summer 1987, *7*(1), pp. 121–48. [G: LDCs]

Rajapatirana, Sarath. Industrialization and Foreign Trade. *Finance Develop.*, September 1987, *24*(3), pp. 2–5. [G: LDCs]

Ram, Rati. Exports and Economic Growth in Developing Countries: Evidence from Time-Series and Cross-Section Data. *Econ. Develop. Cult. Change*, October 1987, *36*(1), pp. 51–72. [G: LDCs]

Urrutia, Miguel. The Macroeconomics of Successful Development: What Are the Lessons? Comment. *Fischer, S., ed.*, 1987, pp. 258–61.

1213 European Countries

Bajt, Aleksander. Economic Growth and Factor Substitution: What Happened to the Yugoslav Miracle? A Post-Festum Comment. *Econ. Anal. Workers' Manage.*, 1987, *21*(4), pp. 469–71. [G: Yugoslavia]

Keyder, Çağlar. Economic Development and Crisis: 1950–80. *Schick, I. C. and Tonak, E. A., eds.*, 1987, pp. 293–308. [G: Turkey]

Keyder, Çağlar. The Political Economy of Turkish Democracy. *Schick, I. C. and Tonak, E. A., eds.*, 1987, pp. 27–65. [G: Turkey]

Krueger, Anne O. The Importance of Economic Policy in Development: Contrasts between Korea and Turkey. *[Corden, W. M.]*, 1987, pp. 172–203. [G: S. Korea; Turkey]

Mencinger, Jože. The Crisis and the Reform of

the Yugoslav Economic System in the Eighties. *Gey, P.; Kosta, J. and Quaisser, W., eds.*, 1987, pp. 99–119.   [G: Yugoslavia]

1214 Asian Countries

Abdul Aziz, Abdul Rahman. Identification of Structural Constraints in Sectoral Development Using the Diamond–Laumas Key Sector Method: With West Malaysian Case Study. *Singapore Econ. Rev.*, October 1987, *32*(2), pp. 75–91.   [G: Malaysia]

Aghevli, Bijan B.; Kim, In-Su and Neiss, Hubert. Growth and Adjustment in South Asia. *Finance Develop.*, September 1987, *24*(3), pp. 12–16.
[G: Bangladesh; India; Pakistan; Sri Lanka]

Aghevli, Bijan B. and Márquez-Ruarte, Jorge. A Case of Successful Adjustment in a Developing Country: Korea's Experience during 1980–84. *Holmes, F., ed.*, 1987, pp. 91–113.
[G: S. Korea]

Agrawal, Govind R. Special Problems of Low Income Countries in South Asia. *Agrawal, G. R., et al. (I)*, 1987, pp. 24–27.   [G: S. Asia]

Ajanant, Juanjai. Trade Patterns and Trends of Thailand. *Bradford, C. I., Jr. and Branson, W. H., eds.*, 1987, pp. 467–84.
[G: Thailand]

Alburo, Florian A. Manufactured Exports and Industrialization: Trade Patterns and Trends of the Philippines. *Bradford, C. I., Jr. and Branson, W. H., eds.*, 1987, pp. 485–513.
[G: Philippines]

Amin, A. T. M. Nurul. The Role of the Informal Sector in Economic Development: Some Evidence from Dhaka, Bangladesh. *Int. Lab. Rev.*, Sept.-Oct. 1987, *126*(5), pp. 611–23.
[G: Bangladesh]

Arndt, H. W. Industrial Policy in East Asia. *Industry Devel.*, 1987, (22), pp. 1–66.
[G: E. Asia]

Beals, Ralph E. Trade Patterns and Trends of Indonesia. *Bradford, C. I., Jr. and Branson, W. H., eds.*, 1987, pp. 515–45.
[G: Indonesia]

Bhatty, I. Z., et al. Issues in Financial Investment. *Margin*, Apr.-June 1987, *19*(3), pp. 32–47.   [G: India]

Chee, Peng Lim. Changes in the Malaysian Economy and Trade Trends and Prospects. *Bradford, C. I., Jr. and Branson, W. H., eds.*, 1987, pp. 435–66.   [G: Malaysia]

Chia, Siow-Yue. Industrial Restructuring in a Newly Industrialising Country: The Case of Singapore. *Pasinetti, L. and Lloyd, P., eds.*, 1987, pp. 213–32.   [G: Singapore]

Collins, Susan M. Korean Growth Policy: Comment. *Brookings Pap. Econ. Act.*, 1987, (2), pp. 445–50.   [G: S. Korea]

Corbo, Vittorio. Korean Growth Policy: Comment. *Brookings Pap. Econ. Act.*, 1987, (2), pp. 450–52.   [G: S. Korea]

Curry, Robert L., Jr. Poverty and Mass Unemployment in Mineral-Rich Botswana. *Amer. J. Econ. Soc.*, January 1987, *46*(1), pp. 71–87.
[G: Botswana]

Darrat, Ali F. Are Exports an Engine of Growth? Another Look at the Evidence. *Appl. Econ.*, February 1987, *19*(2), pp. 277–83.
[G: Hong Kong; S. Korea; Singapore; Taiwan]

Dhar, P. N. The Political Economy of Development in India. *Indian Econ. Rev.*, Jan.-June 1987, *22*(1), pp. 1–18.   [G: India]

Dornbusch, Rudiger and Park, Yung Chul. Korean Growth Policy. *Brookings Pap. Econ. Act.*, 1987, (2), pp. 389–444.   [G: S. Korea]

Faroque, Akhter and Butterfield, David W. Impacts on Growth of the Structure of Demand and Income Distribution in Less Developed Countries: An Application to Bangladesh. *J. Econ. Devel.*, June 1987, *12*(1), pp. 161–93.
[G: Bangladesh]

Fong, Chan-Onn. ASEAN Industrialization: Structural Changes and Adjustments. *Dutta, M., ed. (II)*, 1987, pp. 267–93.   [G: ASEAN]

Glewwe, Paul and Bhalla, Surjit S. A Response to Comment [The Distribution of Income in Sri Lanka in 1969–70 and 1980–81: Sri Lankan Experience]. *World Bank Econ. Rev.*, May 1987, *1*(3), pp. 533–36.   [G: Sri Lanka; LDCs]

Grais, W. M. Coping with a Decline in World Energy Prices: Macroeconomic and Income Distribution Effects in Thailand. *J. Devel. Econ.*, August 1987, *26*(2), pp. 235–55.
[G: Thailand]

Hill, Hal. Survey of Recent Developments. *Bull. Indonesian Econ. Stud.*, December 1987, *23*(3), pp. 1–33.   [G: Indonesia]

Hitam, Dato Musa. ASEAN and the Pacific Basin. *Martin, L. G., ed.*, 1987, pp. 8–13.
[G: ASEAN]

Hobohm, Sarwar O. H. Survey of Recent Developments. *Bull. Indonesian Econ. Stud.*, August 1987, *23*(2), pp. 1–37.   [G: Indonesia]

Hsiao, Mei-chu W. Tests of Causality and Exogeneity Between Exports and Economic Growth: The Case of Asian NICs. *J. Econ. Devel.*, December 1987, *12*(2), pp. 143–59.
[G: Asia]

Huff, W. G. Patterns in the Economic Development of Singapore. *J. Devel. Areas*, April 1987, *21*(3), pp. 305–25.   [G: Singapore]

Isenman, Paul. Growth and Equity in Developing Countries: A Reinterpretation of the Sri Lankan Experience: A Comment. *World Bank Econ. Rev.*, May 1987, *1*(3), pp. 521–31.
[G: Sri Lanka; LDCs]

Karunaratne, Neil Dias. An Analysis of Papua New Guinea's Hard Currency Regime. *Econ. Int.*, May-Aug. 1987, *40*(2–3), pp. 210–23.
[G: New Guinea]

Kazi, Shahnaz. Intersectoral Terms of Trade for Pakistan's Economy: 1970-71–1981-82. *Pakistan Devel. Rev.*, Spring 1987, *26*(1), pp. 81–105.   [G: Pakistan]

Kim, Youn-Suk. External Debt and Economic Development: The Case of Korea. *Dutta, M., ed. (II)*, 1987, pp. 151–61.   [G: S. Korea]

Kohsaka, Akira. Financial Liberalization in Asian NICs: A Comparative Study of Korea and Taiwan in the 1980s. *Devel. Econ.*, December 1987, *25*(4), pp. 325–45. **[G: S. Korea; Taiwan]**

Kopits, George. Turkey's Adjustment Experience, 1980–85. *Finance Develop.*, September 1987, *24*(3), pp. 8–11. **[G: Turkey]**

Krueger, Anne O. The Importance of Economic Policy in Development: Contrasts between Korea and Turkey. *[Corden, W. M.]*, 1987, pp. 172–203. **[G: S. Korea; Turkey]**

Kwack, Sung Y. External Influences on the Korean Economy and Their Policy Implications. *Dutta, M., ed. (I)*, 1987, pp. 195–217. **[G: S. Korea]**

Lim, Joseph. The New Structuralist Critique of the Monetarist Theory of Inflation: The Case of the Philippines. *J. Devel. Econ.*, February 1987, *25*(1), pp. 45–61. **[G: Philippines]**

Lye, J. N. Stochastic Simulation of the Reserve Bank's Model of the New Zealand Economy. *New Zealand Econ. Pap.*, 1987, *21*, pp. 17–29. **[G: New Zealand]**

Minhas, B. S. The Planning Process and the Annual Budgets: Some Reflections on Recent Indian Experience. *Indian Econ. Rev.*, July-Dec. 1987, *22*(2), pp. 115–49. **[G: India]**

Miyawaki, T. The Pacific Basin, Recent Economic and Financial Developments. *Visser, H. and Schoor, E., eds.*, 1987, pp. 263–80. **[G: Asia-Pacific]**

Mukherji, Smriti. Exports and Economic Growth in India (1950-51–1980-81): An Empirical Investigation. *Margin*, Jan.-Mar. 1987, *19*(2), pp. 50–59. **[G: India]**

Nam, Sang Woo. A Case of Successful Adjustment in a Developing Country: Korea's Experience during 1980–84: Comment. *Holmes, F., ed.*, 1987, pp. 114–19. **[G: S. Korea]**

Narayana, N. S. S.; Parikh, Kirit S. and Srinivasan, T. N. Indian Agricultural Policy: An Applied General Equilibrium Model. *J. Policy Modeling*, Winter 1987, *9*(4), pp. 527–58. **[G: India]**

Naya, Seiji. Economic Performance and Growth Factors of the ASEAN Countries. *Martin, L. G., ed.*, 1987, pp. 47–87. **[G: ASEAN]**

Ohno, Koichi and Imaoka, Hideki. The Experience of Dual-Industrial Growth: Korea and Taiwan. *Devel. Econ.*, December 1987, *25*(4), pp. 310–24. **[G: S. Korea; Taiwan]**

Pangestu, Mari. Survey of Recent Developments. *Bull. Indonesian Econ. Stud.*, April 1987, *23*(1), pp. 1–39. **[G: Indonesia]**

Park, Wookyu. An Example of Using the BVAR Model and not Violating the "Lucas Critique:" An Explanation of the Recent Korean Economic Boom. *J. Econ. Devel.*, December 1987, *12*(2), pp. 115–41. **[G: Korea]**

Pinto, Brian. Nigeria during and after the Oil Boom: A Policy Comparison with Indonesia. *World Bank Econ. Rev.*, May 1987, *1*(3), pp. 419–45. **[G: Nigeria; Indonesia]**

Pyatt, Graham. Growth and Equity in Developing Countries: A Reinterpretation of the Sri Lankan Experience: A Comment. *World Bank Econ. Rev.*, May 1987, *1*(3), pp. 515–20. **[G: Sri Lanka; LDCs]**

Sahn, David E. Changes in the Living Standards of the Poor in Sri Lanka during a Period of Macroeconomic Restructuring. *World Devel.*, June 1987, *15*(6), pp. 809–30. **[G: Sri Lanka]**

Tinsulanonda, Prem. ASEAN: Meeting the Challenges of Asia and the Pacific. *Martin, L. G., ed.*, 1987, pp. 3–7. **[G: ASEAN]**

Veit, Lawrence A. Time of the New Asian Tigers. *Challenge*, July/Aug. 1987, *30*(3), pp. 49–55. **[G: S.E. Asia]**

Warr, Peter G. and Nijathaworn, Bandid. Thai Economic Performance: Some Thai Perspectives. *Asian-Pacific Econ. Lit.*, May 1987, *1*(1), pp. 60–74. **[G: Thailand]**

Wattoo, Mian Muhammad Yasin Khan. Fourth Annual General Meeting of the Pakistan Society of Development Economists: Inaugural Address. *Pakistan Devel. Rev.*, Autumn 1987, *26*(3), pp. 241–53. **[G: Pakistan]**

Wong, Aline K. and Cheung, Paul P. L. Demographic and Social Development: Taking Stock for the Morrow. *Martin, L. G., ed.*, 1987, pp. 17–36. **[G: ASEAN]**

1215 African Countries

Adedeji, Adebayo. An Ecology for Economic Change. *Challenge*, Jan./Feb. 1987, *29*(6), pp. 4–8. **[G: Africa]**

Aliouche, El-Hachemi. Heavy Industrialization: The Algerian Experience. *England, R. W., ed.*, 1987, pp. 257–90. **[G: Algeria]**

Amin, Samir. SADCC Prospects for Disengagement and Development in Southern Africa: Preface. *Amin, S.; Chitala, D. and Mandaza, I., eds.*, 1987, pp. 1–7. **[G: S. Africa]**

Ayittey, George B. N. Economic Atrophy in Black Africa. *Cato J.*, Spring/Summer 1987, *7*(1), pp. 195–222. **[G: Africa]**

Barve, Arvind. Financial and Monetary Aspects of Trade Promotion in the Context of Co-operation among Developing Countries, with Special Reference to Africa. *Dell, S., ed., Pt. 2*, 1987, pp. 611–38. **[G: Africa; LDCs]**

Bevan, D. L.; Collier, P. and Gunning, J. W. Consequences of a Commodity Boom in a Controlled Economy: Accumulation and Redistribution in Kenya 1975–83. *World Bank Econ. Rev.*, May 1987, *1*(3), pp. 489–513. **[G: Kenya]**

Chitala, Derrick. The Political Economy of the SADCC and Imperialism's Response. *Amin, S.; Chitala, D. and Mandaza, I., eds.*, 1987, pp. 13–36. **[G: Southern Africa; S. Africa]**

Curry, Robert L., Jr. Botswana's Macroeconomic Management of Its Mineral-Based Growth: It Used Mining Revenues for Development and Services but Must Now Broaden the Beneficiaries. *Amer. J. Econ. Soc.*, October 1987, *46*(4), pp. 473–88. **[G: Botswana]**

Dalal, K. L. New Dimensions in Indo–African Relations in Sub-Saharan Africa. *Ali, S. S. and Gupta, A., eds.*, 1987, pp. 203–14. **[G: India; Sub-Saharan Africa]**

Griffin, Keith. The Economic Crisis in Ethiopia. *Griffin, K.*, 1987, pp. 183–202. **[G: Ethiopia]**

Gupta, Anirudha. Africa: Dimensions of the Economic Crisis: Introduction. *Ali, S. S. and Gupta, A., eds.*, 1987, pp. 1–14. **[G: Africa]**

Kebbede, Girma. State Capitalism and Development: The Case of Ethiopia. *J. Devel. Areas*, October 1987, 22(1), pp. 1–23. **[G: Ethiopia]**

Kherbachi, Hamid and Diwan, Romesh. Technical and Structural Change in Algerian Economy: 1969–74. *Indian J. Quant. Econ.*, 1987, 3(1), pp. 14–26. **[G: Algeria]**

Kilby, Peter. The Internal Forces Afflicting Africa [Economic Atrophy in Black Africa]. *Cato J.*, Spring/Summer 1987, 7(1), pp. 223–29. **[G: Africa]**

Kiwanuka, Richard N. The Thirteenth UN General Assembly Special Session: Lessons for Africa. *J. World Trade Law*, April 1987, 21(2), pp. 65–78. **[G: Africa]**

McMahon, Gary. Does a Small Developing Country Benefit from International Commodity Agreements? The Case of Coffee and Kenya. *Econ. Develop. Cult. Change*, January 1987, 35(2), pp. 409–23. **[G: Kenya]**

Mitra, Soumya and Ali, Shanti Sadiq. The Sahel: Drought, Desertification and Man-Made Problems. *Ali, S. S. and Gupta, A., eds.*, 1987, pp. 128–45. **[G: Africa]**

Ngau, Peter M. Tensions in Empowerment: The Experience of the *Harambee* (Self-Help) Movement in Kenya. *Econ. Develop. Cult. Change*, April 1987, 35(3), pp. 523–38. **[G: Kenya]**

Olopoenia, Razaq A. Fiscal Policy and Economic Instability in an Oil-Dependent Economy: The Nigerian Experience during the Oil Boom of the Seventies. *Pakistan J. Appl. Econ.*, Summer 1987, 6(1), pp. 41–60. **[G: Nigeria]**

Ortmann, G. F. Land Rents and Production Costs in the South African Sugar Industry. *S. Afr. J. Econ.*, September 1987, 55(3), pp. 249–58. **[G: S. Africa]**

Patel, Jayanti K. Central Africa: Crisis of Growth and Development in Malawi, Zambia and Zimbabwe. *Ali, S. S. and Gupta, A., eds.*, 1987, pp. 81–102. **[G: Malawi; Zambia; Zimbabwe]**

Pinto, Brian. Nigeria during and after the Oil Boom: A Policy Comparison with Indonesia. *World Bank Econ. Rev.*, May 1987, 1(3), pp. 419–45. **[G: Nigeria; Indonesia]**

Ramchandani, R. R. Internal Factors of Africa's Economic Crisis. *Ali, S. S. and Gupta, A., eds.*, 1987, pp. 34–47. **[G: Africa]**

Rao, V. L. South Asian Regional Cooperation: Problems and Prospects. *Agrawal, G. R., et al. (II)*, 1987, pp. 116–54. **[G: S. Asia]**

Richardson, Richard W. and Ahmed, Osman S. Challenge for Africa's Private Sector. *Challenge*, Jan./Feb. 1987, 29(6), pp. 16–25. **[G: Africa]**

Rwegasira, Delphin G. Balance-of-Payments Adjustment in Low-Income Developing Countries: The Experiences of Kenya and Tanzania in the 1970s. *World Devel.*, Oct./Nov. 1987, 15(10/11), pp. 1321–35. **[G: Kenya; Tanzania]**

Schware, Robert and Trembour, Alice. Rethinking Microcomputer Technology Transfer to Third World Countries. *Ruth, S. R. and Mann, C. K., eds.*, 1987, 1985, pp. 23–37. **[G: Tunisia; Egypt]**

Sharma, Veena. East Africa: Crisis of Many Dimensions. *Ali, S. S. and Gupta, A., eds.*, 1987, pp. 51–70. **[G: E. Africa]**

Tallroth, Nils Borje. Structural Adjustment in Nigeria. *Finance Develop.*, September 1987, 24(3), pp. 20–22. **[G: Nigeria]**

Titilola, Sunday O. Low Income Countries in West Africa. *Agrawal, G. R., et al. (I)*, 1987, pp. 28–30. **[G: W. Africa]**

Watanabe, Susumu. Technological Capability and Industrialisation. Effects of Aid and Sanctions in the United Republic of Tanzania and Zimbabwe. *Int. Lab. Rev.*, Sept.-Oct. 1987, 126(5), pp. 525–41. **[G: Zimbabwe; Tanzania]**

1216 Latin American and Caribbean Countries

Aboagye, A.; Gozo, K. and Ahmed, Iftikhar. World Recession and Global Interdependence: Sub-Saharan Africa. *International Labour Office.*, 1987, pp. 75–98. **[G: Sub-Saharan Africa]**

Baer, Werner. The Resurgence of Inflation in Brazil, 1974–86. *World Devel.*, August 1987, 15(8), pp. 1007–34. **[G: Brazil]**

Baer, Werner; da Fonseca, Manuel A. R. and Guilhoto, Joaquim J. M. Structural Changes in Brazil's Industrial Economy, 1960–80. *World Devel.*, February 1987, 15(2), pp. 275–86. **[G: Brazil]**

Barbone, Luca and Rivera-Batiz, Francisco. Foreign Capital and the Contractionary Impact of Currency Devaluation, with an Application to Jamaica. *J. Devel. Econ.*, June 1987, 26(1), pp. 1–15. **[G: Jamaica]**

Becker, David G. "Bonanza Development" and the "New Bourgeoisie": Peru under Military Rule. *Becker, D. G., et al.*, 1987, pp. 63–105. **[G: Peru]**

Bourne, Compton. Financial Deepening, Domestic Resource Mobilisation and Economic Growth: Jamaica 1955–1982. *Salazar-Carrillo, J. and Tirado de Alonzo, I., eds.*, 1987, pp. 1–26. **[G: Jamaica]**

Caballeros, Rómulo. External Debt in Central America. *CEPAL Rev.*, August 1987, (32), pp. 123–48. **[G: Central America]**

Cardoso, Eliana A. Latin America's Debt: Which Way Now? *Challenge*, May/June 1987, 30(2), pp. 11–17. **[G: Latin America]**

Centeno, Máximo Vega. Nature and Determinants of Technical Change: The Peruvian Industrial Sector. *Katz, J. M., ed.*, 1987, pp. 431–45. **[G: Peru]**

Colburn, Forrest D. and Leguizamón, Francisco A. Deteriorating Public and Private Sector Relations in Central America. *J. Policy Anal. Manage.*, Winter 1987, 6(2), pp. 220–29. **[G: Central America]**

Corbo, Vittorio and de Melo, Jaime. Lessons from

the Southern Cone Policy Reforms. *World Bank Res. Observer*, July 1987, *2*(2), pp. 111–42.   [G: Argentina; Chile; Uruguay]

Cuccia, Luis R. and Navajas, Fernando H. Argentina: Crisis, Adjustment Policies and Agricultural Development, 1980–1985. *CEPAL Rev.*, December 1987, (33), pp. 77–82.   [G: Argentina]

Da Silva, Ednaldo Araquem. Wage–Profit Trade-offs in Brazil: In Input/Output Analysis, 1970–1975. *Sci. Soc.*, Fall 1987, *51*(3), pp. 347–54.   [G: Brazil]

Devlin, Robert. Economic Restructuring in Latin America in the Face of the Foreign Debt and the External Transfer Problem. *CEPAL Rev.*, August 1987, (32), pp. 75–101.   [G: Latin America]

Díaz-Alejandro, Carlos F. Some Aspects of the Development Crisis in Latin America. *Thorp, R. and Whitehead, L.*, eds., 1987, pp. 9–27.   [G: Latin America]

Epstein, Edward C. Recent Stabilization Programs in Argentina, 1973–86. *World Devel.*, August 1987, *15*(8), pp. 991–1005.   [G: Argentina]

Eyzaguirre, Nicolás and Valdivia, Mario. External Restriction and Adjustment. Options and Policies in Latin America. *CEPAL Rev.*, August 1987, (32), pp. 149–68.   [G: Latin America]

Fitzgerald, Frank T. The "Sovietization of Cuba Thesis" Revisited. *Sci. Soc.*, Winter 1987-1988, *51*(4), pp. 439–57.   [G: Cuba]

Foxley, Alejandro. Latin American Development After the Debt Crisis. *J. Devel. Econ.*, October 1987, *27*(1–2), pp. 201–25.   [G: Latin America]

Foxley, Alejandro. Latin American Development After the Debt Crisis. *[Diaz-Alejandro, C. F.]*, 1987, pp. 201–25.   [G: Latin America]

Frenkel, Roberto. Heterodox Theory and Policy: The Plan Austral in Argentina. *J. Devel. Econ.*, October 1987, *27*(1–2), pp. 307–38.   [G: Argentina]

Frenkel, Roberto. Heterodox Theory and Policy: The Plan Austral in Argentina. *[Diaz-Alejandro, C. F.]*, 1987, pp. 307–38.   [G: Argentina]

Garcia Rocha, Adalberto. Inequality and Growth in Mexico. *Salazar-Carrillo, J. and Tirado de Alonzo, I.*, eds., 1987, pp. 1–6.   [G: Mexico]

Gereffi, Gary and Evans, Peter. Transnational Corporations, Dependent Development, and State Policy in the Semiperiphery: A Comparison of Brazil and Mexico. *Dietz, J. L. and Street, J. H.*, eds., 1987, *1981*, pp. 159–90.   [G: Brazil; Mexico]

Gollas, Manuel. Comments on the Mexican Economy in 1984. *Salazar-Carrillo, J. and Tirado de Alonzo, I.*, eds., 1987, pp. 1–5.   [G: Mexico]

Griffith, Winston H. Can CARICOM Countries Replicate the Singapore Experience? *J. Devel. Stud.*, October 1987, *24*(1), pp. 60–82.   [G: Caribbean]

Herold, Marc W. Development in a Peripheral Socialist Economy: Grenada, 1979–83. *En-gland, R. W.*, ed., 1987, pp. 291–318.   [G: Grenada]

Herrera, Felipe. Structural Change, Economic Interdependence and World Development: A Latin American Perspective. *Urquidi, V. L.*, ed., 1987, pp. 53–77.   [G: Latin America]

Holland, Dorothy C. and Crane, Julia G. Adapting to an Industrializing Nation: The Shango Cult in Trinidad. *Soc. Econ. Stud.*, December 1987, *36*(4), pp. 41–66.   [G: Trinidad and Tobago]

Landim, Leilah. Non-governmental Organizations in Latin America. *World Devel.*, Supp. Autumn 1987, *15*, pp. 29–38.   [G: Latin America]

Lustig, Nora. Crisis económica y niveles de vida en México: 1982–1985. (Economic Crisis and Living Standards in Mexico. With English summary.) *Estud. Econ.*, July-December 1987, *2*(2), pp. 227–49.   [G: Mexico]

Massad, Carlos. Internal Debt, External Debt and Economic Transformation: Introduction. *CEPAL Rev.*, August 1987, (32), pp. 7–9.   [G: Latin America]

Massad, Carlos and Zahler, Roberto. Another View of the Latin American Crisis: Domestic Debt. *CEPAL Rev.*, August 1987, (32), pp. 11–25.   [G: Latin America]

Maxwell, Philip. Technical Change and Appropriate Technology: A Review of Some Latin American Case Studies. *Stewart, F.*, ed., 1987, pp. 248–70.   [G: Latin America]

Mertens, L. and Richards, P. J. Recession and Employment in Mexico. *Int. Lab. Rev.*, Mar.-Apr. 1987, *126*(2), pp. 229–43.   [G: Mexico]

Nunnenkamp, Peter. Latin American Debt and Development: A Review. *Weltwirtsch. Arch.*, 1987, *123*(4), pp. 734–38.   [G: Latin America]

Ocampo, José Antonio. Crisis and Economic Policy in Colombia, 1980–5. *Thorp, R. and Whitehead, L.*, eds., 1987, pp. 239–70.   [G: Colombia]

de Pablo, Juan Carlos. Transición hacia las urnas, confusión inicial y plan austral: Argentina, 1982–87. (Transition to Democracy, Initial Confusion and Austral Plan: Argentina: 1982–87. With English summary.) *Económica (La Plata)*, July-Dec. 1987, *33*(2), pp. 213–44.   [G: Argentina]

Pantin, Dennis A. Long Waves and Caribbean Development. *Soc. Econ. Stud.*, June 1987, *36*(2), pp. 1–20.   [G: Caribbean]

Roca, Santiago and Priale, Rodrigo. Devaluation, Inflationary Expectations and Stabilisation in Peru. *J. Econ. Stud.*, 1987, *14*(1), pp. 5–33.   [G: Peru]

Ros, Jaime. Mexico from the Oil Boom to the Debt Crisis: An Analysis of Policy Responses to External Shocks, 1978–85. *Thorp, R. and Whitehead, L.*, eds., 1987, pp. 68–116.   [G: Mexico]

Rostow, Walt W. Toward a New Hemispheric Partnership. *Rostow, W. W.*, 1987, pp. 120–33.   [G: Latin America]

Scheetz, Thomas. Public Sector Expenditures and

Financial Crisis in Chile. *World Devel.*, August 1987, *15*(8), pp. 1053–75. **[G: Chile]**

Skidmore, Thomas E. The Resurgence of Inflation in Latin America: Discussion. *World Devel.*, August 1987, *15*(8), pp. 1148–49. **[G: Brazil; Argentina]**

Smith, Russell E. The Resurgence of Inflation in Latin America: Discussion. *World Devel.*, August 1987, *15*(8), pp. 1146–48. **[G: Argentina; Brazil]**

Solimano, Andrés. Emprego e salários reais: Uma análise macroeconômica de desequilíbrio para o Chile e o Brasil. (With English summary.) *Pesquisa Planejamento Econ.*, December 1987, *17*(3), pp. 605–31. **[G: Chile; Brazil]**

Street, James H. The Ayres–Kuznets Framework and Argentine Dependency. *Dietz, J. L. and Street, J. H.*, eds., 1987, *1974*, pp. 54–73. **[G: Argentina]**

Street, James H. The Technological Frontier in Latin America: Creativity and Productivity. *Dietz, J. L. and Street, J. H.*, eds., 1987, pp. 200–216. **[G: Latin America]**

di Tella, Guido. Argentina's Most Recent Inflationary Cycle, 1975–85. *Thorp, R. and Whitehead, L.*, eds., 1987, pp. 162–207. **[G: Argentina]**

Thorp, Rosemary. Peruvian Adjustment Policies, 1978–85: The Effects of Prolonged Crisis. *Thorp, R. and Whitehead, L.*, eds., 1987, pp. 208–38. **[G: Peru]**

Thorp, Rosemary. Trends and Cycles in the Peruvian Economy. *J. Devel. Econ.*, October 1987, *27*(1–2), pp. 355–74. **[G: Peru]**

Thorp, Rosemary. Trends and Cycles in the Peruvian Economy. *[Diaz-Alejandro, C. F.]*, 1987, pp. 355–74. **[G: Peru]**

Thorp, Rosemary and Whitehead, Laurence. Latin American Debt and the Adjustment Crisis: Review and Conclusions. *Thorp, R. and Whitehead, L.*, eds., 1987, pp. 318–54. **[G: Latin America]**

Villanueva, Javier. Crecimiento y coyuntura en América Latina: Un enfoque sectorial. (Growth and Juncture in Latin America. A Sectoral Approach. With English summary.) *Económica (La Plata)*, January-June 1987, *33*(1), pp. 113–56. **[G: Latin America]**

Webb, Richard. Internal Debt and Financial Adjustment in Peru. *CEPAL Rev.*, August 1987, (32), pp. 55–74. **[G: Peru]**

Werneck, Rogério L. Furquim. A Multisectoral Analysis of the Structural Adjustment of the Brazilian Economy in the 1980s. *Pasinetti, L. and Lloyd, P.*, eds., 1987, pp. 233–61. **[G: Brazil]**

Werneck, Rogério L. Furquim. Retomada do crescimento e esforço de poupança: limitações e possibilidades. (With English summary.) *Pesquisa Planejamento Econ.*, April 1987, *17*(1), pp. 1–18. **[G: Brazil]**

Whitehead, Laurence. The Adjustment Process in Chile: A Comparative Perspective. *Thorp, R. and Whitehead, L.*, eds., 1987, pp. 117–61. **[G: Chile]**

Zimbalist, Andrew and Eckstein, Susan. Patterns of Cuban Development: The First Twenty-five Years. *World Devel.*, January 1987, *15*(1), pp. 5–22. **[G: Cuba]**

1217 Oceanic Countries

Paderanga, Cayetano, Jr. A Review of Land Settlements in the Philippines, 1900–1975. *Philippine Rev. Econ. Bus.*, Mar.-June 1987, *24*(1–2), pp. 1–54. **[G: Philippines]**

122 Economic Studies of Developed Countries

1220 General

Baumol, William J. Rebirth of a Fallen Leader: Italy and the Long Period Data. *[Marrama, V.]*, Vol. 1, 1987, pp. 135–60.

Didier, Michel. Micro Initiatives and Macroeconomic Adjustments in the Industrialised Countries. *Pasinetti, L. and Lloyd, P.*, eds., 1987, pp. 159–75. **[G: Global]**

van Gemert, Henk G. Structural Change in Industrial Countries. *Macmillen, M.; Mayes, D. G. and van Veen, P.*, eds., 1987, pp. 89–118. **[G: U.S.; EEC]**

Jungenfelt, Karl. Structural Adjustment in Industrially Advanced Countries: Discussion and Conclusions. *Pasinetti, L. and Lloyd, P.*, eds., 1987, pp. 177–85. **[G: MDCs]**

Wren-Lewis, Simon and Eastwood, Fiona. The World Economy. *Nat. Inst. Econ. Rev.*, May 1987, (120), pp. 21–41. **[G: U.S.; Japan; W. Germany; Canada; France]**

1221 Comparative Country Studies

Adams, Charles; Fenton, Paul R. and Larsen, Flemming. Potential Output in Major Industrial Countries. *International Monetary Fund Research Department.*, 1987, pp. 1–38. **[G: OECD]**

Baeck, Louis. O desequilíbrio da economia internacional dos anos 80. (With English summary.) *Pesquisa Planejamento Econ.*, April 1987, *17*(1), pp. 221–49. **[G: U.S.; Japan; W. Europe]**

Baeck, Louis. The Imbalance of the Western Economy. *Tijdschrift Econ. Manage.*, 1987, *32*(2), pp. 221–47. **[G: EEC; U.S.; Japan]**

Budd, Alan. The Conservative Revolution: A Roundtable Discussion. *De Menil, G. and Portes, R.*, eds., 1987, pp. 185–91. **[G: Europe; U.S.]**

Fagerberg, Jan and Sollie, Gunnar. The Method of Constant Market Shares Analysis Reconsidered. *Appl. Econ.*, December 1987, *19*(12), pp. 1571–83. **[G: OECD]**

van Gemert, Henk G. Structural Change in OECD Countries: A Normal Pattern Analysis. *De Economist*, 1987, *135*(1), pp. 29–51. **[G: OECD]**

Maddison, Angus. Growth and Slowdown in Advanced Capitalist Economies: Techniques of Quantitative Assessment. *J. Econ. Lit.*, June 1987, *25*(2), pp. 649–98. **[G: OECD]**

Paldam, Martin. How Much Does One Percent of Growth Change the Unemployment Rate? A Study of 17 OECD Countries, 1948–1985. *Europ. Econ. Rev.*, Feb./Mar. 1987, *31*(1/2), pp. 306–13. **[G: OECD]**

Ransom, Michael R. Economic Growth and the Size Distribution of Income; a Longitudinal Analysis. *Heijmans, R. and Neudecker, H., eds.*, 1987, pp. 165–77. **[G: MDCs]**

Solow, Robert M. The Conservative Revolution: A Roundtable Discussion. *De Menil, G. and Portes, R., eds.*, 1987, pp. 181–85. **[G: Europe; U.S.]**

Suzuki, Yoshio. Comparative Studies of Financial Innovation, Deregulation, and Reform in Japan and United States. *Patrick, H. T. and Tachi, R., eds.*, 1987, pp. 156–67. **[G: Japan; U.S.]**

Tatom, John A. The Macroeconomic Effects of the Recent Fall in Oil Prices. *Fed. Res. Bank St. Louis Rev.*, June/July 1987, *69*(6), pp. 34–45. **[G: OECD]**

Wegner, Manfred. Scope and Limits of International Economic Policy Coordination. *World Econ.*, September 1987, *10*(3), pp. 283–306. **[G: OECD]**

von Weizsacker, Christian. The Conservative Revolution: A Roundtable Discussion. *De Menil, G. and Portes, R., eds.*, 1987, pp. 191–95. **[G: U.S.; Europe]**

1223 European Countries

Barker, Terry. The Cambridge Multisectoral Dynamic Model of the British Economy: Introduction. *Barker, T. and Peterson, W., eds.*, 1987, pp. 1–9. **[G: U.K.]**

Bauchet, Pierre. L'avenir des plans nationaux. (With English summary.) *Revue Écon. Polit.*, Mar.-Apr. 1987, *97*(2), pp. 133–55. **[G: France]**

Bean, Charles R. The Performance of the British Economy: The Impact of North Sea Oil. *Dornbusch, R. and Layard, R., eds.*, 1987, pp. 64–96. **[G: U.K.]**

Begg, David K. H. Long-run Implications of the Increase in Taxation and Public Debt for Employment and Economic Growth in Europe: Comments. *Europ. Econ. Rev.*, April 1987, *31*(3), pp. 775–77. **[G: W. Europe]**

Berthélemy, Jean-Claude and Devezeaux de Lavergne, Jean-Guy. L'impact des chocs pétroliers. Une simulation rétrospective: 1973–1982. (Oil Shocks Effects: A Retrospective Simulation: 1973–1982. With English summary.) *Revue Écon.*, July 1987, *38*(4), pp. 877–96. **[G: France]**

Bianchi, Giuliano; Casini-Benvenuti, Stefano and Maltinti, Giovanni. Long Waves and Regional Take-Offs in Italy and Great Britain: Preliminary Investigations into Multiregional Disparities of Development. *Vasko, T., ed.*, 1987, pp. 187–97. **[G: Italy; U.K.]**

Bosworth, Barry P. and Lawrence, Robert Z. Adjusting to Slower Economic Growth: The Domestic Economy. *Bosworth, B. P. and Rivlin, A. M., eds.*, 1987, pp. 22–54. **[G: Sweden]**

Bosworth, Barry P. and Lawrence, Robert Z. Economic Goals and the Policy Mix. *Bosworth, B. P. and Rivlin, A. M., eds.*, 1987, pp. 97–124. **[G: Sweden]**

Budd, Alan. The Conservative Revolution: A Roundtable Discussion. *De Menil, G. and Portes, R., eds.*, 1987, pp. 185–91. **[G: Europe; U.S.]**

Christensen, Michael. Disinflation, Credibility and Price Inertia: A Danish Exposition. *Appl. Econ.*, October 1987, *19*(10), pp. 1353–66. **[G: Denmark]**

Cipolletta, A. Heimler and Calcagnini, G. Restructuring and Adjustment in Italian Industry. *Rev. Econ. Cond. Italy*, Sept.-Dec. 1987, (3), pp. 341–81. **[G: Italy]**

Clements, Michael; Walker, John and Rossi, Vanessa. The UK Economy: Analysis and Prospects. *Oxford Rev. Econ. Policy*, Summer 1987, *3*(2), pp. xxii–xxxii. **[G: U.K.]**

Crafts, N. F. R. British Economic Growth, 1700–1850; Some Difficulties of Interpretation. *Exploration Econ. Hist.*, July 1987, *24*(3), pp. 245–68. **[G: U.K.]**

Dahrendorf, Ralf. Slow Growth in Europe: Conceptual Issues: Comment. *Lawrence, R. Z. and Schultze, C. L., eds.*, 1987, pp. 76–79. **[G: W. Europe]**

Danthine, Jean-Pierre. Restoring Europe's Prosperity: A Review Essay. *J. Monet. Econ.*, December 1987, *20*(3), pp. 521–26. **[G: W. Europe]**

Danthine, Jean-Pierre and Lambelet, Jean-Christian. The Swiss Case. *De Menil, G. and Portes, R., eds.*, 1987, pp. 147–74. **[G: Switzerland]**

De Rita, Giuseppe. The Culture of Development and the Legacy of the Submerged Economy. *Rev. Econ. Cond. Italy*, Jan.-Apr. 1987, (1), pp. 9–19. **[G: Italy]**

Deaglio, Mario. Submergence in the Italian Economy 1970–85. *Rev. Econ. Cond. Italy*, Jan.-Apr. 1987, (1), pp. 49–77. **[G: Italy]**

Drèze, Jacques H. Slow Growth in Europe: Conceptual Issues: Comment. *Lawrence, R. Z. and Schultze, C. L., eds.*, 1987, pp. 79–93. **[G: W. Europe]**

Duwendag, Dieter. Towards Sustainable Growth: The 1986/87 Report of the German Council of Economic Experts. *J. Inst. Theoretical Econ.*, September 1987, *143*(3), pp. 497–504.

Feldstein, Martin S. Long-run Implications of the Increase in Taxation and Public Debt for Employment and Economic Growth in Europe: Comments. *Europ. Econ. Rev.*, April 1987, *31*(3), pp. 778–80. **[G: W. Europe]**

Genberg, Hans; Salemi, Michael K. and Swoboda, Alexander K. The Relative Importance of Foreign and Domestic Disturbances for Aggregate Fluctuations in the Open Economy: Switzerland, 1964–1981. *J. Monet. Econ.*, January 1987, *19*(1), pp. 45–67. **[G: Switzerland]**

George, Kenneth D. and Mainwaring, Lynn. The Welsh Economy in the 1980s. *Day, G. and Rees, G., eds.*, 1987, pp. 7–37. **[G: U.K.]**

Giavazzi, Francesco. The Performance of the British Economy: The Impact of EEC Membership. *Dornbusch, R. and Layard, R., eds.,* 1987, pp. 97–130. **[G: U.K.]**

de Grauwe, Paul. International Trade and Economic Growth in the European Monetary System. *Europ. Econ. Rev.,* Feb./Mar. 1987, *31*(1/2), pp. 389–98. **[G: W. Europe]**

Gutowski, Armin. Slow Growth in Europe: Conceptual Issues: Comment. *Lawrence, R. Z. and Schultze, C. L., eds.,* 1987, pp. 93–98. **[G: W. Europe]**

Hall, S. G. Analysing Economic Behaviour 1975–85 with a Model Incorporating Consistent Expectations. *Nat. Inst. Econ. Rev.,* May 1987, (120), pp. 75–80. **[G: U.K.]**

Hellwig, Martin and Neumann, Manfred J. M. Economic Policy in Germany: Was There a Turnaround? *De Menil, G. and Portes, R., eds.,* 1987, pp. 103–40. **[G: W. Germany]**

Helpman, Elhanan. Mrs Thatcher's Economic Policies 1979–87: Discussion. *De Menil, G. and Portes, R., eds.,* 1987, pp. 96–98. **[G: U.S.]**

Henry, E. W. The Impact of the Agriculture and Dependent Food Processing Sectors on the Irish Economy during 1982. *Irish J. Agr. Econ. Rural Soc.,* 1987, *12*, pp. 1–17. **[G: Ireland]**

Honkapohja, Seppo. The Swiss Case: Discussion. *De Menil, G. and Portes, R., eds.,* 1987, pp. 175–77. **[G: Switzerland]**

Kindleberger, Charles P. Belgium after World War II: An Experiment in Supply Side Economics. *Steinherr, A. and Weiserbs, D., eds.,* 1987, pp. 167–84. **[G: Belgium]**

Krugman, Paul R. Slow Growth in Europe: Conceptual Issues. *Lawrence, R. Z. and Schultze, C. L., eds.,* 1987, pp. 48–76. **[G: W. Europe]**

Kuisel, Richard F. French Post-war Economic Growth: A Historical Perspective on the *Trente Glorieuses. Ross, G.; Hoffmann, S. and Malzacher, S., eds.,* 1987, pp. 18–32. **[G: France]**

La Malfa, Giorgio and Lecaldano Sasso la Terza, Edoardo. Modigliani–La Malfa Revisited: The Italian Economy from the Sixties to the Eighties. *[Modigliani, F.],* 1987, pp. 373–97. **[G: Italy]**

Lawrence, Robert Z. and Bosworth, Barry P. Adjusting to Slower Economic Growth: The External Sector. *Bosworth, B. P. and Rivlin, A. M., eds.,* 1987, pp. 55–96. **[G: Sweden]**

Lesourne, Jacques. World Economic Interdependence and Structural Change: The Specific Problems of the European Community. *Urquidi, V. L., ed.,* 1987, pp. 78–102. **[G: EEC]**

Matthews, Kent G. P. and Minford, Patrick. Mrs Thatcher's Economic Policies 1979–87. *De Menil, G. and Portes, R., eds.,* 1987, pp. 57–92. **[G: U.K.]**

Miller, Marcus H. Economic Policy in Germany: Was There a Turnaround? Discussion. *De Menil, G. and Portes, R., eds.,* 1987, pp. 143–44. **[G: W. Germany]**

Mitek, Lars. Denmark: Unsustainable Recovery. *Vartia, P., et al.,* 1987, pp. 61–103. **[G: Denmark]**

Mokyr, Joel. Has the Industrial Revolution Been Crowded Out? Some Reflections on Crafts and Williamson. *Exploration Econ. Hist.,* July 1987, *24*(3), pp. 293–325.

Nickell, Stephen J. Mrs Thatcher's Economic Policies 1979–87: Discussion. *De Menil, G. and Portes, R., eds.,* 1987, pp. 93–95. **[G: U.K.]**

Nilsson, Ronny. OECD Leading Indicators. *OECD Econ. Stud.,* Autumn 1987, (9), pp. 105–45. **[G: OECD]**

Ollila, Esko. Strukturomvandling i Finland—ett debattinlägg. (Structural Change in Finland: A Contribution to the Debate. With English summary.) *Ekon. Samfundets Tidskr.,* 1987, *40*(2), pp. 63–70. **[G: Finland]**

Oxelheim, Lars. Sweden: Is Something Wrong with the Growth Engine? *Vartia, P., et al.,* 1987, pp. 171–205. **[G: Sweden]**

Rivlin, Alice M. The Swedish Economy: Overview. *Bosworth, B. P. and Rivlin, A. M., eds.,* 1987, pp. 1–21. **[G: Sweden]**

Scheide, Joachim. Die deutsche Konjunkturpolitik in den fünfziger Jahren—Beginn der Globalsteuerung? (German Economic Policy in the Fifties—Beginning of Demand Management? With English summary.) *Konjunkturpolitik,* 1987, *33*(5), pp. 243–67. **[G: W. Germany]**

Solow, Robert M. The Conservative Revolution: A Roundtable Discussion. *De Menil, G. and Portes, R., eds.,* 1987, pp. 181–85. **[G: Europe; U.S.]**

Tullio, Giuseppe. Long-run Implications of the Increase in Taxation and Public Debt for Employment and Economic Growth in Europe. *Europ. Econ. Rev.,* April 1987, *31*(3), pp. 741–74. **[G: W. Europe]**

Tvedt, Karl-Ove. Norway: On the Brink of Recession. *Vartia, P., et al.,* 1987, pp. 141–69. **[G: Norway]**

Vartia, Pentti, et al. Growth Policies in a Nordic Perspective. *Vartia, P., et al.,* 1987, pp. 7–48. **[G: Norway; Finland; Denmark; Sweden]**

Vaubel, Roland. Economic Policy in Germany: Was There a Turnaround? Discussion. *De Menil, G. and Portes, R., eds.,* 1987, pp. 141–43. **[G: W. Germany]**

Waelbroeck, Jean. Ability to Adjust and the Problems of European Market Economies. *Pasinetti, L. and Lloyd, P., eds.,* 1987, pp. 109–21. **[G: Europe]**

Webb, Steven B. The German Inflation and Foreign Business Cycles, 1920–1922. *Exploration Econ. Hist.,* October 1987, *24*(4), pp. 409–33. **[G: W. Germany]**

von Weizsacker, Christian. The Conservative Revolution: A Roundtable Discussion. *De Menil, G. and Portes, R., eds.,* 1987, pp. 191–95. **[G: U.S.; Europe]**

Williamson, Jeffrey G. Debating the British Industrial Revolution. *Exploration Econ. Hist.,* July 1987, *24*(3), pp. 269–92. **[G: U.S.]**

Ylä-Anttila, Pekka. Finland: Can the Good Macroeconomic Performance Continue? *Vartia, P., et al.,* 1987, pp. 105–39. **[G: Finland]**

1224 Asian Countries

Aoki, Masahiko. The Political Economy of Japan: The Japanese Firm in Transition. *Yamamura, K. and Yasuba, Y., eds.*, 1987, pp. 263–88.
[G: Japan]

Bergsten, C. Fred. The U.S.-Japan Economic Problem: Next Steps. *Patrick, H. T. and Tachi, R., eds.*, 1987, pp. 9–17. [G: U.S.; Japan]

Bronfenbrenner, Martin. Japan and Two World Economic Depressions. *[Penrose, E. F.]*, 1987, pp. 32–51. [G: Japan]

Bronfenbrenner, Martin and Yasuba, Yasukichi. The Political Economy of Japan: Economic Welfare. *Yamamura, K. and Yasuba, Y., eds.*, 1987, pp. 93–136. [G: Japan]

Dore, Ronald. How Fragile a Super State? *[Penrose, E. F.]*, 1987, pp. 83–110. [G: Japan]

Drucker, Peter F. Japan's Choices. *Foreign Aff.*, Summer 1987, *65*(5), pp. 923–41.
[G: Japan]

Fujita, Natsuki and James, William E. Exports and Technological Changes in the Adjustment Process of the Japanese Economy in the 1970s. *Hitotsubashi J. Econ.*, December 1987, *28*(2), pp. 107–22. [G: Japan]

Kosai, Yutaka. The Political Economy of Japan: The Politics of Economic Management. *Yamamura, K. and Yasuba, Y., eds.*, 1987, pp. 555–92. [G: Japan]

Miyawaki, T. The Pacific Basin, Recent Economic and Financial Developments. *Visser, H. and Schoor, E., eds.*, 1987, pp. 263–80. [G: Asia-Pacific]

Murakami, Yasusuke. The Japanese Model of Political Economy. *Yamamura, K. and Yasuba, Y., eds.*, 1987, pp. 33–90. [G: Japan]

Murakami, Yasusuke and Patrick, Hugh T. The Political Economy of Japan: The Domestic Transformation: Preface. *Yamamura, K. and Yasuba, Y., eds.*, 1987, pp. xxi–xxvi.
[G: Japan]

Muramatsu, Michio and Krauss, Ellis S. The Political Economy of Japan: The Conservative Policy Line and the Development of Patterned Pluralism. *Yamamura, K. and Yasuba, Y., eds.*, 1987, pp. 516–54. [G: Japan]

Nakamura, Takafusa. The Japanese Economy in the Interwar Period: A Brief Summary. *[Penrose, E. F.]*, 1987, pp. 52–67. [G: Japan]

Patrick, Hugh T. and Tachi, Ryuichiro. Japan and the United States Today: Exchange Rates, Macroeconomic Policies, and Financial Market Innovations. *Patrick, H. T. and Tachi, R., eds.*, 1987, pp. 1–8. [G: U.S.; Japan]

Ridley, William P. Japan: An Uneasy Transition to a Rentier Society. *[Marjolin, R.]*, 1987, pp. 169–89. [G: Japan]

Sato, Kazuo. The Political Economy of Japan: Saving and Investment. *Yamamura, K. and Yasuba, Y., eds.*, 1987, pp. 137–85.
[G: Japan]

Yamamura, Kozo and Yasuba, Yasukichi. The Political Economy of Japan: The Domestic Transformation: Introduction. *Yamamura, K. and Yasuba, Y., eds.*, 1987, pp. 1–29. [G: Japan]

1227 Oceanic Countries

Fallon, John and Thompson, Lynne. An Analysis of the Effects of Recent Changes in the Exchange Rate and the Terms of Trade on the Level and Composition of Economic Activity. *Australian Econ. Rev.*, Second Quarter 1987, (78), pp. 24–36. [G: Australia]

James, Colin. Economic Adjustment in New Zealand: A Developed Country Case Study of Policies and Problems: Comment. *Holmes, F., ed.*, 1987, pp. 85–90. [G: New Zealand]

Lattimore, Ralph. Economic Adjustment in New Zealand: A Developed Country Case Study of Policies and Problems. *Holmes, F., ed.*, 1987, pp. 34–84. [G: New Zealand]

Maddock, Rodney. The Australian Economy in the Long Run: The Long Boom 1940–1970. *Maddock, R. and McLean, I. W., eds.*, 1987, pp. 79–105. [G: Australia]

Maddock, Rodney and McLean, Ian W. The Australian Economy in the Long Run: Epilogue: A Comparative Perspective. *Maddock, R. and McLean, I. W., eds.*, 1987, pp. 344–52.
[G: Australia]

Maddock, Rodney and McLean, Ian W. The Australian Economy in the Very Long Run. *Maddock, R. and McLean, I. W., eds.*, 1987, pp. 5–29. [G: Australia]

McDonald, Daina and Dixon, Peter B. Economic Developments in Australia: 1986–87 and 1987–88. *Australian Econ. Rev.*, Second Quarter 1987, (78), pp. 3–23.

McDonald, Daina and Dixon, Peter B. The Australian Economy in 1987–88 and 1988–89. *Australian Econ. Rev.*, Fourth Quarter 1987, (80), pp. 3–30. [G: Australia]

Pagan, Adrian R. The Australian Economy in the Long Run: The End of the Long Boom. *Maddock, R. and McLean, I. W., eds.*, 1987, pp. 106–30. [G: Australia]

Schedvin, C. B. The Australian Economy on the Hinge of History. *Australian Econ. Rev.*, First Quarter 1987, (77), pp. 20–30.
[G: Australia]

1228 North American Countries

Anastasopoulos, A. Removal of the Canadian Tariffs on Imports from the United States Regional Impacts in the Short Run. *Tremblay, R., ed.*, 1987, pp. 419–61. [G: Canada; U.S.]

Bergsten, C. Fred. The U.S.-Japan Economic Problem: Next Steps. *Patrick, H. T. and Tachi, R., eds.*, 1987, pp. 9–17. [G: U.S.; Japan]

Blanchard, Olivier Jean. Reaganomics. *De Menil, G. and Portes, R., eds.*, 1987, pp. 15–48.
[G: U.S.]

Branson, William H. Reaganomics: Discussion. *De Menil, G. and Portes, R., eds.*, 1987, pp. 48–52. [G: U.S.]

Budd, Alan. The Conservative Revolution: A Roundtable Discussion. *De Menil, G. and Portes, R., eds.*, 1987, pp. 185–91.
[G: Europe; U.S.]

Canton, Richard and Wenninger, John. Current Labor Market Trends and Inflation. *Fed. Res.*

Bank New York Quart. Rev., Autumn 1987, *12*(3), pp. 36–48. [G: U.S.]

Coulombe, Serge. Dette publique, endettement envers l'éetranger et l'effet d'éviction dans une économie ouverte: le cas canadien. (Public Debt, National Foreign Indebtedness and the Crowding-Out Effect in an Open Economy: The Case of Canada. With English summary.) *Écon. Soc.*, September 1987, *21*(9), pp. 169–84. [G: Canada]

Currie, David. Reaganomics: Discussion. *De Menil, G. and Portes, R., eds.*, 1987, pp. 52–53. [G: U.S.]

Hamilton, James D. Monetary Factors in the Great Depression. *J. Monet. Econ.*, March 1987, *19*(2), pp. 145–69. [G: U.S.]

Keyserling, Leon H. Will It Be Progress or Poverty? *Challenge*, May/June 1987, *30*(2), pp. 30–36. [G: U.S.]

Matejko, Alexander J. The Fate of Canada: Between Underdevelopment and Postindustrialism. *Indian J. Quant. Econ.*, 1987, *3*(1), pp. 67–86. [G: Canada]

Mishkin, Frederic S. U.S. Macroeconomic Policy and Performance in the 1980s: An Overview. *Patrick, H. T. and Tachi, R., eds.*, 1987, pp. 37–53. [G: U.S.; Global]

Ott, Mack. The Growing Share of Services in the U.S. Economy— Degeneration or Evolution? *Fed. Res. Bank St. Louis Rev.*, June/July 1987, *69*(6), pp. 5–22. [G: U.S.]

Patrick, Hugh T. and Tachi, Ryuichiro. Japan and the United States Today: Exchange Rates, Macroeconomic Policies, and Financial Market Innovations. *Patrick, H. T. and Tachi, R., eds.*, 1987, pp. 1–8. [G: U.S.; Japan]

Plourde, André. The Impact of $(US)15 Oil on the Canadian Economy: Evidence from the MACE Model. *Can. Public Policy*, March 1987, *13*(1), pp. 19–25. [G: Canada]

Solow, Robert M. The Conservative Revolution: A Roundtable Discussion. *De Menil, G. and Portes, R., eds.*, 1987, pp. 181–85. [G: Europe; U.S.]

Stein, Herbert. The United States Economy in Transition. *Visser, H. and Schoor, E., eds.*, 1987, pp. 111–23. [G: U.S.]

Tatom, John A. Will a Weaker Dollar Mean a Stronger Economy? *J. Int. Money Finance*, December 1987, *6*(4), pp. 433–47. [G: U.S.]

Volcker, Paul A. Statement to the U.S. Senate Subcommittee on International Finance and Monetary Policy, Committee on Banking, Housing, and Urban Affairs, April 7, 1987. *Fed. Res. Bull.*, June 1987, *73*(6), pp. 425–30. [G: U.S.]

Waverman, Leonard. The Impact of $(US)15 Oil: Good News and/or Bad News? *Can. Public Policy*, March 1987, *13*(1), pp. 1–18. [G: Canada]

von Weizsacker, Christian. The Conservative Revolution: A Roundtable Discussion. *De Menil, G. and Portes, R., eds.*, 1987, pp. 191–95. [G: U.S.; Europe]

123 Comparative Studies of Developing, Developed, and/or Centrally Planned Economies

1230 Comparative Studies of Developing, Developed, and/or Centrally Planned Economies

Brewer, Thomas L. Instability in Developing and Industrial Countries: Methodological and Theoretical Issues: Reply [A Comparative Analysis of the Fiscal Policies of Industrial and Developing Countries—Policy Instability and Governmental-Regime Instability]. *J. Compar. Econ.*, March 1987, *11*(1), pp. 120–23.

Chatterjee, Pranab Kumar. Relative Economic Levels, Characters and Interdependence: A Study of Selected Countries in Asia and the United States. *Dutta, M., ed. (II)*, 1987, pp. 105–32. [G: U.S.; Asia]

Cornia, Giovanni Andrea. Economic Decline and Human Welfare in the First Half of the 1980s. *Cornia, G. A.; Jolly, R. and Stewart, F., eds.*, 1987, pp. 11–47. [G: Global]

Dooley, Michael P.; Frankel, Jeffrey A. and Mathieson, Donald J. International Capital Mobility: What Do Saving–Investment Correlations Tell Us? *Int. Monet. Fund Staff Pap.*, September 1987, *34*(3), pp. 503–30. [G: Selected Countries]

Erol, Umit and Yu, Eden S. H. On the Causal Relationship between Energy and Income for Industrialized Countries. *J. Energy Devel.*, Autumn 1987, *13*(1), pp. 113–22. [G: Europe; Canada; U.K.; Japan]

Hill, Lawrence J. Modeling the Macroeconomy/ Energy Economy Relationship in Developing Countries: The Case of Liberia. *J. Devel. Areas*, October 1987, *22*(1), pp. 71–84. [G: Liberia]

Johnson, D. Gale. Is Population Growth the Dominant Force in Development? [Population Growth, Economic Growth, and Foreign Aid]. *Cato J.*, Spring/Summer 1987, *7*(1), pp. 187–93. [G: LDCs]

Krelle, Wilhelm. Long-term Fluctuations of Technical Progress and Growth. *J. Inst. Theoretical Econ.*, September 1987, *143*(3), pp. 379–401. [G: OECD; CMEA]

Krueger, Alan B. and Summers, Lawrence H. Reflections on the Inter-industry Wage Structure. *Lang, K. and Leonard, J. S., eds.*, 1987, pp. 17–47. [G: Global]

Kux, Jaroslav. International Comparisons of Economic Activity of the Population. *Czech. Econ. Digest.*, June 1987, (4), pp. 61–79. [G: Europe]

Lizondo, José Saúl and Mathieson, Donald J. The Stability of the Demand for International Reserves. *J. Int. Money Finance*, September 1987, *6*(3), pp. 251–82. [G: Selected Countries]

Looney, Robert E. Impact of Military Expenditures on Third World Debt. *Can. J. Devel.*

Stud., 1987, *8*(1), pp. 7–26.　　　**[G: LDCs]**

Papanek, Gustav F. and Kyn, Oldrich. Flattening the Kuznets Curve: The Consequences for Income Distribution of Development Strategy, Government Intervention, Income and Rate of Growth. *Pakistan Devel. Rev.*, Spring 1987, *26*(1), pp. 1–54.　　　**[G: Selected Countries]**

Ram, Rati. Economic Growth and Structure of Domestic Absorption: Evidence from Internationally Comparable Data. *J. Devel. Econ.*, August 1987, *26*(2), pp. 291–300.

Richardson, Harry W. The Costs of Urbanization: A Four-Country Comparison. *Econ. Develop. Cult. Change*, April 1987, *35*(3), pp. 561–80.
　　[G: Bangladesh; Egypt; Pakistan; Indonesia]

Riddle, Dorothy I. The Role of the Service Sector in Economic Development: Similarities and Differences by Development Category. *Giarini, O., ed.*, 1987, pp. 83–104.　　　**[G: LDCs]**

Rostow, Walt W. The Rich Country–Poor Country Problem: From the Eighteenth to the Twenty-first Century. *Rostow, W. W.*, 1987, pp. 49–78.　　　**[G: Global]**

Sarantides, Stylianos A. International Income Inequality and *per capita* Income Rates of Growth: A Cross-Section Analysis. *Int. J. Soc. Econ.*, 1987, *14*(7/8/9), pp. 195–210.
　　　[G: Selected Countries]

Shinohara, Miyohei. Patterns and Backgrounds of Dynamics in the Asia-Pacific Economies. *Dutta, M., ed. (I)*, 1987, pp. 23–48.
　　　[G: Asia-Pacific]

Simon, Julian L. Population Growth, Economic Growth, and Foreign Aid. *Cato J.*, Spring/Summer 1987, *7*(1), pp. 159–86.　**[G: LDCs]**

Srinivasan, T. N. Economic Liberalization in China and India: Issues and an Analytical Framework. *J. Compar. Econ.*, September 1987, *11*(3), pp. 427–43.　**[G: China; India]**

Stollar, Andrew J. and Thompson, G. Rodney. Sectoral Employment Shares: A Comparative Systems Context. *J. Compar. Econ.*, March 1987, *11*(1), pp. 62–80.

Szakolczai, György. The Asia-Pacific Market: A Review. *Dutta, M., ed. (I)*, 1987, pp. 289–308.
　　　[G: Asia-Pacific]

Teitel, Simón. Science and Technology Indicators, Country Size and Economic Development: An International Comparison. *World Devel.*, September 1987, *15*(9), pp. 1225–35.
　　　[G: Global]

Tuma, Elias H. Technology Transfer and Economic Development: Lessons of History. *J. Devel. Areas*, July 1987, *21*(4), pp. 403–27.
　　　[G: Middle East]

Venieris, Y. P. and Stewart, D. B. Sociopolitical Instability, Inequality and Consumption Behavior. *J. Econ. Devel.*, December 1987, *12*(2), pp. 7–20.　　　**[G: Selected Countries]**

Yu, Chwo-Ming. A Reconsideration of Measures of Instability: Comment [A Comparative Analysis of the Fiscal Policies of Industrial and Developing Countries—Policy Instability and Governmental-Regime Instability]. *J. Compar. Econ.*, March 1987, *11*(1), pp. 116–19.

124 Economic Studies of Centrally Planned Economies

1240 General

Bauer, Tamás. Reforming or Perfecting the Economic Mechanism. *Europ. Econ. Rev.*, Feb./Mar. 1987, *31*(1/2), pp. 132–38.　**[G: CMEA]**

1241 Comparative Country Studies

Granick, David. The Industrial Environment in China and the CMEA Countries. *Tidrick, G. and Jiyuan, C., eds.*, 1987, pp. 103–31.
　　　[G: China; CMEA]

1243 European Countries

Abalkin, Leonid I. The New Model of Economic Management. *Soviet Econ.*, October-December 1987, *3*(4), pp. 298–312.　**[G: U.S.S.R.]**

Abalkin, Leonid I., et al. Reflections on Technology in Postwar Reconstruction. *Soviet Econ.*, October-December 1987, *3*(4), pp. 353–59.
　　　[G: U.S.S.R.]

Aganbegyan, Abel G. Basic Directions of *Perestroyka*. *Soviet Econ.*, October-December 1987, *3*(4), pp. 277–97.　**[G: U.S.S.R.]**

Aganbegyan, Abel G. The New Economic Strategy of the USSR and Its Social Dimensions. *Int. Lab. Rev.*, Jan.-Feb. 1987, *126*(1), pp. 95–109.　　　**[G: U.S.S.R.]**

Andreff, Wladimir and Lavigne, Marie. A Way Out of the Crisis for the CMEA Economies? *Soviet E. Europ. Foreign Trade*, Fall 1987, *23*(3), pp. 8–43.　　　**[G: CMEA]**

Angyal, A. Change and Reform: Comments and Contributions. *Acta Oecon.*, 1987, *38*(3–4), pp. 215–24.　　　**[G: Hungary]**

Antal, László, et al. Change and Reform. *Acta Oecon.*, 1987, *38*(3–4), pp. 187–213.
　　　[G: Hungary]

Boretsky, Michael. The Tenability of the CIA Estimates of Soviet Economic Growth. *J. Compar. Econ.*, December 1987, *11*(4), pp. 517–42.　**[G: U.S.S.R.; U.S.; W. Germany]**

Brzeski, Andrzej. The Case of Central Planning in the USSR. *Pejovich, S., ed.*, 1987, pp. 209–37.　　　**[G: U.S.S.R.]**

Burkett, John P. Soviet Socioeconomic Development: A Fold Catastrophe? *Comp. Econ. Stud.*, Fall 1987, *29*(3), pp. 70–93.

Buza, M. Change and Reform: Comments and Contributions. *Acta Oecon.*, 1987, *38*(3–4), pp. 224–32.　　　**[G: Hungary]**

Csaba, László. Die Investitions- und Innovationspolitischen Befugnisse der Unternehmung in der DDR, der Sowjetunion und in Ungarn. (Freedom of Enterprises in Innovation and in Investment Decisions in the Post-Reform Period: Experiences of the GDR, the Soviet Union and Hungary. With English summary.) *Konjunkturpolitik*, 1987, *33*(3), pp. 167–84.
　　[G: U.S.S.R.; Hungary; E. Germany]

Desai, Padma. The Production Function and Technical Change in Postwar Soviet Industry: A Reexamination. *Desai, P.*, 1987, *1976*, pp. 63–77. **[G: U.S.S.R.]**

Drechsler, László. Hungarian Economic Performance, 1960–1980. *Marer, P. and van Veen, P., eds.*, 1987, pp. 131–37. **[G: Hungary]**

Dyba, Karel and Kupka, Václav. Accommodating the Czechoslovak Economy to External Blows (A Macroeconomic Analysis for 1973–1981). *Soviet E. Europ. Foreign Trade*, Spring 1987, *23*(1), pp. 6–30. **[G: Czechoslovakia]**

Dyba, Karel and Kupka, Václav. The Adjustment of Czechoslovak Economy to External Disturbances (Macro-economic Analysis for 1973–1981. *Czech. Econ. Pap.*, 1987, (24), pp. 99–117. **[G: Czechoslovakia]**

Ferge, Zsuzsa. Change and Reform: Comments and Contributions. *Acta Oecon.*, 1987, *38*(3–4), pp. 232–38. **[G: Hungary]**

Ferge, Zsuzsa. The Crisis and the 'Welfare State' in Eastern Europe with a Focus on Hungary. *Europ. Econ. Rev.*, Feb./Mar. 1987, *31*(1/2), pp. 212–19. **[G: Hungary]**

Garland, John. The Economic Situation in Poland: Prospects for Recovery. *Marer, P. and van Veen, P., eds.*, 1987, pp. 109–29. **[G: Poland]**

Glaser, Václav and Ungerman, Jaroslav. Some Aspects of a New Cycle of a Work on a Long-term Outlook. *Czech. Econ. Digest.*, January 1987, (2), pp. 20–33. **[G: Czechoslovakia]**

Hanson, Philip. The Soviet Economy: A Look Ahead from 1985. *[Marrama, V.], Vol. 2*, 1987, pp. 559–75. **[G: U.S.S.R.]**

Hare, Paul. Economic Reform in Eastern Europe. *J. Econ. Surveys*, 1987, *1*(1), pp. 25–58. **[G: E. Europe]**

Hauslohner, Peter. Gorbachev's Social Contract. *Soviet Econ.*, Jan.-Mar. 1987, *3*(1), pp. 54–89. **[G: U.S.S.R.]**

Havasi, Ferenc. Change and Reform: Stand Taken by the Economic Panel of the Central Committee of the HSWP. *Acta Oecon.*, 1987, *38*(3–4), pp. 263–72. **[G: Hungary]**

Heinrichs, Wolfgang. Symposium on the German Democratic Republic: Comments. *Comp. Econ. Stud.*, Summer 1987, *29*(2), pp. 54–61. **[G: E. Germany]**

Hoch, R. Change and Reform: Comments and Contributions. *Acta Oecon.*, 1987, *38*(3–4), pp. 238–48. **[G: Hungary]**

Kasimovskii, E. Social Justice and the Improvement of Distribution Relations in the USSR. *Prob. Econ.*, September 1987, *30*(5), pp. 61–81. **[G: U.S.S.R.]**

Kemenes, E. Change and Reform: Comments and Contributions. *Acta Oecon.*, 1987, *38*(3–4), pp. 248–55. **[G: Hungary]**

Košař, Josef. Economic Research on the Intensification of the Reproduction Process in Czechoslovakia. *Eastern Europ. Econ.*, Spring 1987, *25*(3), pp. 6–49. **[G: Czechoslovakia]**

Kushnirsky, F. I. Soviet Economic Reform: An Analysis and a Model. *Comp. Econ. Stud.*, Winter 1987, *29*(4), pp. 54–85. **[G: U.S.S.R.]**

Leggett, Robert E. Gorbachev's Reform Program: "Radical" or More of the Same? *Comp. Econ. Stud.*, Winter 1987, *29*(4), pp. 29–53. **[G: U.S.S.R.]**

Melzer, Manfred and Stahnke, Arthur A. Product and Process Renewal in GDR Economic Strategy: Goals, Problems and Prospects. *Jeffries, I. and Melzer, M., eds.*, 1987, pp. 119–40. **[G: E. Germany]**

Ofer, Gur. Soviet Economic Growth: 1928–1985. *J. Econ. Lit.*, December 1987, *25*(4), pp. 1767–1833. **[G: U.S.S.R.]**

Petrakov, Nikolay. Prospects for Change in the Systems of Price Formation, Finance and Credit in the USSR. *Soviet Econ.*, April-June 1987, *3*(2), pp. 135–44. **[G: U.S.S.R.]**

Shcherbakov, V. I. The Wholesale Restructuring of Wages. *Prob. Econ.*, October 1987, *30*(6), pp. 72–88. **[G: U.S.S.R.]**

Simatupang, Batara. Economic Recovery in Poland? The Polish Economy 1982–1984. *[Marrama, V.], Vol. 2*, 1987, pp. 603–27. **[G: Poland]**

Šujan, Ivan. An Analysis of Factors Contributing to the Deceleration in the Growth Rate of the Czechoslovak Economy in the Period 1975–1980: A Simulation Analysis Using an Econometric Model. *Soviet E. Europ. Foreign Trade*, Spring 1987, *23*(1), pp. 31–53. **[G: Czechoslovakia]**

Szul, Roman and Kirejczyk, Edward. Dilemmas of Economic Reform and Self-management in Poland. *Econ. Anal. Workers' Manage.*, 1987, *21*(3), pp. 373–91. **[G: Poland]**

Tarafás, I. Change and Reform: Comments and Contributions. *Acta Oecon.*, 1987, *38*(3–4), pp. 255–63. **[G: Hungary]**

Toumanoff, Peter. Economic Reform and Industrial Performance in the Soviet Union: 1950–1984. *Comp. Econ. Stud.*, Winter 1987, *29*(4), pp. 128–49. **[G: U.S.S.R.]**

Urban, Luděk. Long-term Trends in the Economic Development of the Socialist Countries. *Czech. Econ. Digest.*, October 1987, (7), pp. 3–16. **[G: CMEA]**

Vanous, Jan. The GDR within CMEA. *Comp. Econ. Stud.*, Summer 1987, *29*(2), pp. 1–6. **[G: CMEA; E. Germany]**

Winiecki, Jan. Überdimensionierung des industriellen Sektors bei zentraler Planung: Empirische Evidenz und Auswirkungen auf Allokation und Wachstum. (The Oversized Industrial Sector in Centrally Planned Economies: Empirical Evidence and Effects on Resource Allocation and Growth. With English summary.) *Ifo-Studien*, 1987, *33*(4), pp. 251–75. **[G: E. Europe]**

Zaslavskaia, Tatiana I. Social Factors of Speeding-Up the Development of the Soviet Economy. *Europ. Econ. Rev.*, Feb./Mar. 1987, *31*(1/2), pp. 111–17. **[G: U.S.S.R.]**

Zaslavskaia, Tatiana I. Socioeconomic Aspects of Perestroyka. *Soviet Econ.*, October-December 1987, *3*(4), pp. 313–31. **[G: U.S.S.R.]**

1244 Asian Countries

Adelman, Irma and Sunding, David. Economic Policy and Income Distribution in China. *J. Compar. Econ.*, September 1987, *11*(3), pp. 444–61. **[G: China]**

Byrd, William A. The Impact of the Two-Tier Plan/Market System in Chinese Industry. *J. Compar. Econ.*, September 1987, *11*(3), pp. 295–308. **[G: China]**

Chen, Yizi and Wang, Xiaoqiang. Reform: Results and Lessons from the 1985 CESRRI Survey. *J. Compar. Econ.*, September 1987, *11*(3), pp. 462–78. **[G: China]**

Fei, John and Reynolds, Bruce L. A Tentative Plan for the Rational Sequencing of Overall Reform in China's Economic System. *J. Compar. Econ.*, September 1987, *11*(3), pp. 490–502. **[G: China]**

Griffin, Keith. The Chinese Economy after Mao. *Griffin, K.*, 1987, pp. 92–108. **[G: China]**

Komiya, Ryutaro. Japanese Firms, Chinese Firms: Problems for Economic Reform in China: Part II. *J. Japanese Int. Economies*, June 1987, *1*(2), pp. 229–47. **[G: Japan; China]**

Komiya, Ryutaro. Japanese Firms, Chinese Firms: Problems for Economic Reform in China: Part I. *J. Japanese Int. Economies*, March 1987, *1*(1), pp. 31–61. **[G: Japan; China]**

Lin, Justin Yifu. The Household Responsibility System Reform in China: A Peasant's Institutional Choice. *Amer. J. Agr. Econ.*, May 1987, *69*(2), pp. 410–15. **[G: China]**

Lockett, Martin. The Economic Environment of Management. *Warner, M., ed.*, 1987, pp. 8–23. **[G: China]**

Lyons, Thomas P. Interprovincial Trade and Development in China, 1957–1979. *Econ. Develop. Cult. Change*, January 1987, *35*(2), pp. 223–56. **[G: China]**

Martellaro, Joseph A. and Chen, Jing-Yau. Some Aspects of Growth and Technical Progress in the People's Republic of China. *Econ. Int.*, November 1987, *40*(4), pp. 301–16. **[G: China]**

Naughton, Barry. Macroeconomic Policy and Response in the Chinese Economy: The Impact of the Reform Process. *J. Compar. Econ.*, September 1987, *11*(3), pp. 334–53. **[G: China]**

Rosen, Stanley. The Private Economy (I): Editor's Introduction. *Chinese Econ. Stud.*, Fall 1987, *21*(1), pp. 3–9. **[G: China]**

Sun, Li-teh. Confucianism and the Recent Chinese Economic Reform. *J. Econ. Devel.*, June 1987, *12*(1), pp. 7–32. **[G: China]**

Sung, Yun-wing and Chan, Thomas M. H. China's Economic Reforms I: The Debates in China. *Asian-Pacific Econ. Lit.*, May 1987, *1*(1), pp. 1–24. **[G: China]**

Tidrick, Gene and Chen, Jiyuan. China's Industrial Reform: The Essence of the Industrial Reforms. *Tidrick, G. and Jiyuan, C., eds.*, 1987, pp. 1–10. **[G: China]**

Urata, Shujiro. Sources of Economic Growth and Structural Change in China: 1956–1981. *J. Compar. Econ.*, March 1987, *11*(1), pp. 96–115. **[G: China]**

1246 Latin American and Caribbean Countries

Gey, Peter. The Cuban Economy under the New "System of Management and Planning": Success or Failure? *Gey, P.; Kosta, J. and Quaisser, W., eds.*, 1987, pp. 71–98. **[G: Cuba]**

Zimbalist, Andrew. Cuba's Socialist Economy toward the 1990s: Introduction. *Zimbalist, A., ed.*, 1987, pp. 1–5. **[G: Cuba]**

Zimbalist, Andrew and Eckstein, Susan. Patterns of Cuban Development: The First Twenty-five Years. *Zimbalist, A., ed.*, 1987, pp. 7–24. **[G: Cuba]**

130 ECONOMIC FLUCTUATIONS; FORECASTING; STABILIZATION; INFLATION

131 Economic Fluctuations

1310 Economic Fluctuations: General

Fichtenbaum, Rudy and Shahidi, Hushang. Marx and Keynes? Marx or Keynes? A Comment. *J. Econ. Issues*, March 1987, *21*(1), pp. 467–70.

Melese, Francois and Transue, William. Unscrambling Chaos through Thick and Thin: An Explanation. *Quart. J. Econ.*, February 1987, *102*(1), pp. 171.

Tobin, James. Money and Income: Post Hoc Ergo Propter Hoc? *Tobin, J. (I)*, 1987, *1970*, pp. 497–514.

1312 Economic Fluctuations: Theory

Ahmed, Shaghil. Wage Stickiness and the Non-neutrality of Money: A Cross-Industry Analysis. *J. Monet. Econ.*, July 1987, *20*(1), pp. 25–50. **[G: Canada]**

Alesina, Alberto. Macroeconomic Policy in a Two-Party System as a Repeated Game. *Quart. J. Econ.*, August 1987, *102*(3), pp. 651–78.

Alesina, Alberto. Rules, Discretion and Reputation in a Two-Party System. *Giorn. Econ.*, Jan.-Feb. 1987, *46*(1–2), pp. 3–27.

Andersen, Torben M. Effective Demand, Differential Information and the Multiplier. *Econ. J.*, June 1987, *97*(386), pp. 353–71.

Asada, Toichiro. Government Finance and Wealth Effect in a Kaldorian Cycle Model. *J. Econ. (Z. Nationalökon.)*, 1987, *47*(2), pp. 143–66.

Aukutsionek, S. P. On Theories of Cycles in Technical Progress. *Matekon*, Spring 1987, *23*(3), pp. 50–75.

Baaske, Wolfgang; Hussain, Mushtaq and Millendorfer, Johann. Long Waves, Growth-Retarding Factors, and Paradigms of the New Upswing. *Vasko, T., ed.*, 1987, pp. 239–56. **[G: Global]**

Baslé, Maurice. Les salaires et le cycle: fondements micro-économiques et analyse macro-économique des flexibilités. (Wages and the Cycle: Micro-economics' Foundations and Macro-economic Analysis of Flexibilities. With English summary.) *Écon. Soc.*, November 1987, *21*(11), pp. 57–81.   [G: OECD]

Becketti, Sean and Haltiwanger, John. Limited Countercyclical Policies: An Exploratory Study. *J. Public Econ.*, December 1987, *34*(3), pp. 311–28.   [G: U.S.]

Benassi, Corrado. An Input–Output Formulation of the "Coefficient of Money Transactions": A Note on Hayek's Trade Cycle Theory. *Econ. Int.*, February 1987, *40*(1), pp. 1–19.

Bhaduri, Amit and Harris, Donald J. The Complex Dynamics of the Simple Ricardian System. *Quart. J. Econ.*, November 1987, *102*(4), pp. 893–901.

Brainard, William C. and Tobin, James. Pitfalls in Financial Model Building. *Tobin, J. (I)*, 1987, *1968*, pp. 352–77.   [G: U.S.]

Brock, W. A. Distinguishing Random and Deterministic Systems: Abridged Version. *Grandmont, J.-M., ed.*, 1987, *1986*, pp. 168–95.

Bródy, András and Farkas, Miklós. Forms of Economic Motion. *Acta Oecon.*, 1987, *38*(3–4), pp. 361–70.   [G: Hungary]

Bruckmann, Gerhart. Will There Be a Fifth Kondratieff? *Vasko, T., ed.*, 1987, pp. 3–4.

Buffie, Edward F. Input Price Shocks in the Small Open Economy. *Sinclair, P. J. N., ed.*, 1987, *1986*, pp. 233–47.

Burkett, Paul and Wohar, Mark E. Keynes on Investment and the Business Cycle. *Rev. Radical Polit. Econ.*, Winter 1987, *19*(4), pp. 39–54.

Cantor, Richard and Mark, Nelson C. International Debt and World Business Fluctuations. *J. Int. Money Finance*, June 1987, *6*(2), pp. 153–65.

Caskey, John and Fazzari, Steven M. Aggregate Demand Contractions with Nominal Debt Commitments: Is Wage Flexibility Stabilizing? *Econ. Inquiry*, October 1987, *25*(4), pp. 583–97.

Chizhov, Y. A. Problems of Model Estimation of Long-term Economic Oscillations. *Vasko, T., ed.*, 1987, pp. 5–11.

Dahmen, Erik. Technology, Innovation and International Industrial Transformation. *Dupriez, L. H., ed.*, 1987, *1955*, pp. 241–52.   [G: Sweden]

Davis, Steven J. Allocative Disturbances and Specific Capital in Real Business Cycle Theories. *Amer. Econ. Rev.*, May 1987, *77*(2), pp. 326–32.

Day, Richard H. and Shafer, Wayne J. Ergodic Fluctuations in Deterministic Economic Models. *J. Econ. Behav. Organ.*, September 1987, *8*(3), pp. 339–61.

Dellas, Harris. Cyclical Co-movements of Output and Trade in the World Economy. *Can. J. Econ.*, November 1987, *20*(4), pp. 855–69.

Dendrinos, Dimitrios S. and Sonis, Michael. The Onset of Turbulence in Discrete Relative Multiple Spatial Dynamics. *Batten, D.; Casti, J.*

and Johansson, B., eds., 1987, pp. 349–67.

Devine, James N. Cyclical Over-Investment and Crisis in a Labor-Scarce Economy. *Eastern Econ. J.*, July-Sept. 1987, *13*(3), pp. 271–80.   [G: U.S.]

Di Matteo, Massimo. Relative Prices and Technical Change: A Suggested Approach to Long Waves. *Vasko, T., ed.*, 1987, pp. 326–32.

Dow, Sheila C. Post Keynesian Monetary Theory for an Open Economy. *J. Post Keynesian Econ.*, Winter 1986-87, *9*(2), pp. 237–57.

Downe, Edward A. Minsky's Model of Financial Fragility: A Suggested Addition. *J. Post Keynesian Econ.*, Spring 1987, *9*(3), pp. 440–54.

Duménil, Gérard and Lévy, Dominique. Équilibre de long terme déséquilibre stationnaire et crise. (With English summary.) *Revue Écon.*, September 1987, *38*(5), pp. 949–93.   [G: U.S.]

Duménil, Gérard and Lévy, Dominique. The Macroeconomics of Disequilibrium. *J. Econ. Behav. Organ.*, September 1987, *8*(3), pp. 377–95.

Eichenbaum, Martin S. and Singleton, Kenneth J. Do Equilibrium Real Business Cycle Theories Explain Postwar U.S. Business Cycles? Erratum. *Fischer, S., ed.*, 1987, pp. 317–21.

Entov, R. M. and Poletayev, A. V. On the Long-term Dynamics of the Rate of Return. *Vasko, T., ed.*, 1987, pp. 105–18.

Farmer, Roger E. A. Deficits and Cycles. *Grandmont, J.-M., ed.*, 1987, *1986*, pp. 77–88.

Flemming, John S. The Economics of Worldwide Stagflation: A Review. *Sinclair, P. J. N., ed.*, 1987, pp. 223–32.   [G: Global]

Flemming, John S. The Economics of Worldwide Stagflation: A Review. *Oxford Econ. Pap.*, March 1987, *39*(1), pp. 223–32.

Foley, Duncan K. Liquidity–Profit Rate Cycles in a Capitalist Economy. *J. Econ. Behav. Organ.*, September 1987, *8*(3), pp. 363–76.

Freeman, Christopher. Technical Innovation, Diffusion, and Long Cycles of Economic Development. *Vasko, T., ed.*, 1987, pp. 295–309.

Funke, Michael. A Generated Goodwin Model Incorporating Technical Progress and Variable Prices. *Econ. Notes*, 1987, (2), pp. 36–47.

Gabisch, Günter. Nonlinearities in Dynamic Economic Systems. *Atlantic Econ. J.*, December 1987, *15*(4), pp. 22–31.

Gapinski, James H. Capital Theoretics, Business Cycles, and Feedback Policy: An Experiment in Macroeconomic Control. *Carraro, C. and Sartore, D., eds.*, 1987, pp. 305–26.

Giannaros, Demetrios S. and Lashgari, Malek K. Business Cycles, Inflation and the Price of Gold: An Empirical Investigation. *Tremblay, R., ed.*, 1987, pp. 111–21.

Giannelli, Gianna C. Implicit Contracts, Asymmetric Information and the Business Cycle. *Econ. Lavoro*, Jan.-Mar. 1987, *21*(1), pp. 35–45.

Glombowski, Jorg and Krüger, Michael. Generalizations of Goodwin's Growth Cycle Model.

Batten, D.; Casti, J. and Johansson, B., eds., 1987, pp. 260–90.

Goodwin, Richard M. The Economy as an Evolutionary Pulsator. Vasko, T., ed., 1987, pp. 27–34.

Goodwin, Richard M. The Nonlinear Theory of the Cycle Revisited. [Marrama, V.], Vol. 1, 1987, pp. 247–53.

Grandmont, Jean-Michel. Stabilizing Competitive Business Cycles. Grandmont, J.-M., ed., 1987, 1986, pp. 57–76.

Grandmont, Jean-Michel and Laroque, Guy. Stability of Cycles and Expectations. Grandmont, J.-M., ed., 1987, 1986, pp. 138–51.

Grandmont, Jean-Michel and Malgrange, Pierre. Nonlinear Economic Dynamics: Introduction. Grandmont, J.-M., ed., 1987, 1986, pp. 3–12.

Guesnerie, Roger. Stationary Sunspot Equilibria in an N Commodity World. Grandmont, J.-M., ed., 1987, 1986, pp. 103–27.

Haag, Günter; Weidlich, Wolfgang and Mensch, Gerhard O. The Schumpeter Clock. Batten, D.; Casti, J. and Johansson, B., eds., 1987, pp. 187–226. [G: W. Germany]

Hahm, Sangmoon. Information Acquisition in an Incomplete Information Model of Business Cycle. J. Monet. Econ., July 1987, 20(1), pp. 123–40.

Hibbs, Douglas A., Jr. The Dynamics of Political Support for American Presidents among Occupational and Partisan Groups. Hibbs, D. A., Jr., 1987, 1982, pp. 143–63. [G: U.S.]

Hillinger, Claude. Business Cycle Stylized Facts and Explanatory Models. J. Econ. Dynam. Control, June 1987, 11(2), pp. 257–63. [G: OECD]

Hillinger, Claude. Keynes and Business Cycles. [Marrama, V.], Vol. 1, 1987, pp. 77–95.

Johansson, Börje; Batten, David F. and Casti, John. Economic Dynamics, Evolution and Structural Adjustment. Batten, D.; Casti, J. and Johansson, B., eds., 1987, pp. 1–23.

Jones, Stephen R. G. and Stock, James H. Demand Disturbances and Aggregate Fluctuations: The Implications of Near Rationality. Econ. J., March 1987, 97(385), pp. 49–64.

Jovanovic, Boyan. Work, Rest, and Search: Unemployment, Turnover, and the Cycle. J. Lab. Econ., April 1987, 5(2), pp. 131–48.

Kempf, Hubert. Irregular Staggered Contracts and Monetary Policy. Europ. Econ. Rev., August 1987, 31(6), pp. 1247–66.

King, Robert G. and Plosser, Charles I. Nominal Surprises, Real Factors, and Propagation Mechanisms. Barnett, W. A. and Singleton, K. J., eds., 1987, pp. 273–92. [G: U.S.]

Kleinknecht, Alfred. Rates of Innovations and Profits in the Long Wave. Vasko, T., ed., 1987, pp. 216–38.

Klimenko, L. and Menshikov, Stanislav. Catastrophe Theory Applied to the Analysis of Long Waves. Vasko, T., ed., 1987, pp. 345–58.

Korpinen, Pekka. A Monetary Model of Long Cycles. Vasko, T., ed., 1987, pp. 333–41.

Kraft, M. and Weise, P. Eine Formalisierung von Spiethoffs Theorie der wirtschaftlichen Wechsellagen. (A Formalization of Spiethoff's Business Cycle Theory. With English summary.) Schweiz. Z. Volkswirtsch. Statist., December 1987, 123(4), pp. 531–42.

Krelle, Wilhelm, et al. Structural Change and Long-term Fluctuations in Economic Growth. Vasko, T., ed., 1987, pp. 359–72.

Kuczynski, Thomas. Marx and Engels on Long Waves. Vasko, T., ed., 1987, pp. 35–45.

Laibman, David. Growth, Technical Change, and Cycles: Simulation Models in Marxist Economic Theory. Sci. Soc., Winter 1987-1988, 51(4), pp. 414–38.

Lavoie, Marc. Systemic Financial Fragility: A Simplified View. J. Post Keynesian Econ., Winter 1986-87, 9(2), pp. 258–66.

Levy, Amnon and Bar-Niv, Ran. Macroeconomic Aspects of Firm Bankruptcy Analysis. J. Macroecon., Summer 1987, 9(3), pp. 407–15. [G: U.S.]

Loef, Hans-Edi. Reale Wechselkurse und realer zyklischer Output. Theoretisches Modell und empirische Analyse für die Bundesrepublik Deutschland. (Real Exchange Rates and Real Cyclical Output. With English summary.) Kredit Kapital, 1987, 20(1), pp. 22–47. [G: W. Germany]

Lorenz, Hans-Walter. Goodwin's Nonlinear Accelerator and Chaotic Motion. J. Econ. (Z. Nationalökon.), 1987, 47(4), pp. 413–18.

Lorenz, Hans-Walter. Strange Attractors in a Multisector Business Cycle Model. J. Econ. Behav. Organ., September 1987, 8(3), pp. 397–411.

Maier, Harry. Basic Innovations and the Next Long Wave of Productivity Growth: Socioeconomic Implications and Consequences. Vasko, T., ed., 1987, pp. 46–65.

Marchal, André. Short-period and Long-period Analysis. Dupriez, L. H., ed., 1987, 1955, pp. 349–64.

Martin, John D. and Keown, Arthur J. One-Bank Holding Company Formation and the 1970 Bank Holding Company Act Amendment: An Empirical Examination Allowing for Industry Group Effects. J. Banking Finance, June 1987, 11(2), pp. 213–21. [G: U.S.]

McCallum, Bennett T. The Development of Keynesian Macroeconomics. Amer. Econ. Rev., May 1987, 77(2), pp. 125–29.

Medio, Alfredo. A Multisector Model of the Trade Cycle. Batten, D.; Casti, J. and Johansson, B., eds., 1987, pp. 291–312.

Mensch, Gerhard O.; Weidlich, Wolfgang and Haag, Günter. Outline of a Formal Theory of Long-term Economic Cycles. Vasko, T., ed., 1987, pp. 373–89.

Menshikov, Stanislav. Structural Crisis as a Phase in Long-term Economic Fluctuations. Vasko, T., ed., 1987, pp. 66–75.

Metz, Rainer. Kondratieff and the Theory of Linear Filters. Vasko, T., ed., 1987, pp. 390–404. [G: U.K.; France; Germany]

Mosekilde, Erik; Rasmussen, Steen and Zebrowski, Maciej. Technoeconomic Succession and the Economic Long Wave. *Vasko, T., ed.,* 1987, pp. 257–73.

O'Driscoll, Gerald P., Jr. Money, Deregulation, and the Business Cycle. *Dorn, J. A. and Schwartz, A. J., eds.,* 1987, *1986,* pp. 319–37. **[G: U.S.]**

Ondrich, Jan. Job Search in a Cyclical Economy. *Southern Econ. J.,* July 1987, *54*(1), pp. 81–94.

van Paridon, C. W. A. M. The Crucial Influence of Structural Change on Long-term Fluctuations in Economic Growth. *Vasko, T., ed.,* 1987, pp. 162–75.

van der Ploeg, Frederick. Growth Cycles, Induced Technical Change, and Perpetual Conflict over the Distribution of Income. *J. Macroecon.,* Winter 1987, *9*(1), pp. 1–12.

Puu, Tönu. Complex Dynamics in Continuous Models of the Business Cycle. *Batten, D.; Casti, J. and Johansson, B., eds.,* 1987, pp. 227–59.

Ray, George F. On Long Cycles: Kondratiev and All That. *Hieronymi, O., ed.,* 1987, pp. 43–52.

Raynauld, Jacques. The Transmission of U.S. Business Cycles to Canada: A Regional Perspective. *Tremblay, R., ed.,* 1987, pp. 187–98. **[G: U.S.; Canada]**

Reichlin, Pietro. Equilibrium Cycles in an Overlapping Generations Economy with Production. *Grandmont, J.-M., ed.,* 1987, *1986,* pp. 89–102.

Rosecrance, Richard. Long Cycle Theory and International Relations. *Int. Organ.,* Spring 1987, *41*(2), pp. 283–301. **[G: Global]**

Schwert, G. William. Effects of Model Specification on Tests for Unit Roots in Macroeconomic Data. *J. Monet. Econ.,* July 1987, *20*(1), pp. 73–103.

Semmler, Willi. A Macroeconomic Limit Cycle with Financial Perturbations. *J. Econ. Behav. Organ.,* September 1987, *8*(3), pp. 469–95.

Shiller, Robert J. Ultimate Sources of Aggregate Variability. *Amer. Econ. Rev.,* May 1987, *77*(2), pp. 87–92. **[G: U.S.]**

Silipo, Damiano. La teoria dell'instabilita' del capitalismo: la posizione di Hyman Minsky. (With English summary.) *Stud. Econ.,* 1987, *42*(32), pp. 119–53.

Singleton, Kenneth J. Asset Prices in a Time-Series Model with Disparately Informed, Competitive Traders. *Barnett, W. A. and Singleton, K. J., eds.,* 1987, pp. 249–72.

Spivak, Avia; Weinblatt, J. and Zilberfarb, Ben-Zion. Inflation and Wage Indexation with Multiperiod Contracts. *Europ. Econ. Rev.,* August 1987, *31*(6), pp. 1299–1312. **[G: OECD]**

Sterman, John D. The Economic Long Wave: Theory and Evidence. *Vasko, T., ed.,* 1987, pp. 127–61.

Stock, James H. Measuring Business Cycle Time. *J. Polit. Econ.,* December 1987, *95*(6), pp. 1240–61. **[G: U.S.]**

Tran, Dang T. A Conflict Model of Stagflation. *Eastern Econ. J.,* Jan.-Mar. 1987, *13*(1), pp. 7–18. **[G: U.S.]**

Turnovsky, Stephen J. Supply Shocks and Optimal Monetary Policy. *Oxford Econ. Pap.,* March 1987, *39*(1), pp. 20–37.

Turnovsky, Stephen J. Supply Shocks and Optimal Monetary Policy. *Sinclair, P. J. N., ed.,* 1987, pp. 20–37.

Vasko, Tibor. The Long-Wave Debate: Preface. *Vasko, T., ed.,* 1987, pp. v–xi.

Waterman, A. M. C. On the Malthusian Theory of Long Swings. *Can. J. Econ.,* May 1987, *20*(2), pp. 257–70.

Williamson, Stephen D. Financial Intermediation, Business Failures, and Real Business Cycles. *J. Polit. Econ.,* December 1987, *95*(6), pp. 1196–1216.

Williamson, Stephen D. Recent Developments in Modeling Financial Intermediation. *Fed. Res. Bank Minn. Rev.,* Summer 1987, *11*(3), pp. 19–29.

Wold, Herman and Kaasch, Klaus. Transfers between Industrial Branches in the Course of Schumpeter–Mensch Long Swings. *Vasko, T., ed.,* 1987, pp. 405–19.

Woodford, Michael. Stationary Sunspot Equilibria in a Finance Constrained Economy. *Grandmont, J.-M., ed.,* 1987, *1986,* pp. 128–37.

Woodford, Michael. Three Questions about Sunspot Equilibria as an Explanation of Economic Fluctuations. *Amer. Econ. Rev.,* May 1987, *77*(2), pp. 93–98.

1313 Economic Fluctuations: Studies

Abaan, Ernur Demir. Parasal Şok ve Reel Ekonomik Etkinlik. (With English summary.) *METU,* 1987, *14*(3), pp. 271–82. **[G: Turkey]**

Amacher, Ryan C., et al. The Behavior of Regulatory Activity over the Business Cycle: An Empirical Test. *MacKay, R. J.; Miller, J. C., III and Yandle, B., eds.,* 1987, *1985,* pp. 145–53. **[G: U.S.]**

Andresen, Svein and Everaert, Luc. International Macroeconomic Interdependence. *Ann. Écon. Statist.,* Apr./Sept. 1987, (6/7), pp. 161–81. **[G: OECD]**

Asimakopulos, Athanasios. The Profits–Investment Relation, Cyclical and Structural Changes, Canada, 1950–1983. *Écon. Appl.,* 1987, *40*(4), pp. 631–54. **[G: Canada]**

Baaske, Wolfgang; Hussain, Mushtaq and Millendorfer, Johann. Long Waves, Growth-Retarding Factors, and Paradigms of the New Upswing. *Vasko, T., ed.,* 1987, pp. 239–56. **[G: Global]**

Barras, Richard. Technical Change and the Urban Development Cycle. *Urban Stud.,* February 1987, *24*(1), pp. 5–30. **[G: U.K.]**

Barras, Richard and Ferguson, D. Dynamic Modelling of the Building Cycle: 2: Empirical Results. *Environ. Planning A,* April 1987, *19*(4), pp. 493–520. **[G: U.K.]**

Barras, Richard and Ferguson, D. Dynamic Modelling of the Building Cycle: 1. Theoretical Framework. *Environ. Planning A,* March 1987, *19*(3), pp. 353–67.

Bils, Mark. The Cyclical Behavior of Marginal

Cost and Price. *Amer. Econ. Rev.*, December 1987, 77(5), pp. 838–55. **[G: U.S.]**

Bleaney, Michael F. Macroeconomic Theory and the Great Depression Revisited. *Scot. J. Polit. Econ.*, May 1987, 34(2), pp. 105–19. **[G: U.S.]**

Blumenthal, Tuvia. Depressions in Japan: The 1930s and the 1970s. *[Penrose, E. F.]*, 1987, pp. 68–82. **[G: Japan]**

Bognár, József. World Economic Crisis, Adjustment Policies and Global Questions: An Introduction. *Pasinetti, L. and Lloyd, P., eds.*, 1987, pp. 405–08. **[G: Global]**

Booth, Douglas E. Regional Long Waves and Urban Policy. *Urban Stud.*, December 1987, 24(6), pp. 447–59. **[G: U.S.]**

Boyer, Robert. The Current Economic Crisis: Its Dynamics and Its Implications for France. *Ross, G.; Hoffmann, S. and Malzacher, S., eds.*, 1987, pp. 33–53. **[G: France]**

Bronfenbrenner, Martin. Japan and Two World Economic Depressions. *[Penrose, E. F.]*, 1987, pp. 32–51. **[G: Japan]**

Bruno, Michael. Stagflation in the Industrial Countries: An Updated Overview. *Hitotsubashi J. Econ.*, October 1987, 27, pp. 57–74. **[G: OECD]**

Bull, Clive. Business Cycle and Wage Determination in the United States. *Nalbantian, H. R., ed.*, 1987, pp. 213–28. **[G: U.S.]**

Cagan, Phillip and Schwartz, Anna J. How Feasible Is a Flexible Monetary Policy? *Schwartz, A. J.*, 1987, 1975, pp. 183–208. **[G: U.S.]**

Campbell, John Y. and Mankiw, N. Gregory. Are Output Fluctuations Transitory? *Quart. J. Econ.*, November 1987, 102(4), pp. 857–80. **[G: U.S.]**

Campbell, John Y. and Mankiw, N. Gregory. Permanent and Transitory Components in Macroeconomic Fluctuations. *Amer. Econ. Rev.*, May 1987, 77(2), pp. 111–17. **[G: U.S.]**

Chen, Chien-Hsun and Steindl, Frank G. Anticipated Monetary and Fiscal Policy Effects on Output. *J. Macroecon.*, Spring 1987, 9(2), pp. 255–74. **[G: U.S.]**

Christiano, Lawrence J. Why is Consumption Less Volatile than Income? *Fed. Res. Bank Minn. Rev.*, Fall 1987, 11(4), pp. 2–20. **[G: U.S.]**

Clark, Peter K. The Cyclical Component of U.S. Economic Activity. *Quart. J. Econ.*, November 1987, 102(4), pp. 797–814. **[G: U.S.]**

Connaughton, John E. and Madsen, Ronald A. Measuring Cyclical Sensitivity in State Performance: 1969–1984. *Reg. Sci. Persp.*, 1987, 17(2), pp. 34–40. **[G: U.S.]**

Coombs, R. W. Long Waves, Depression and Innovation: Comment. *De Economist*, 1987, 135(3), pp. 385–87. **[G: Global]**

Cornwall, John. Structural Change and Economic Breakdown. *Écon. Appl.*, 1987, 40(4), pp. 655–80.

Craig, Paul P. and Watt, Kenneth E. F. Dynamic Programming of Socioeconomics and War: A

Computer Experiment. *Vasko, T., ed.*, 1987, pp. 420–26.

Cuddington, John T. and Winters, L. Alan. The Beveridge–Nelson Decomposition of Economic Time Series: A Quick Computational Method. *J. Monet. Econ.*, January 1987, 19(1), pp. 125–27.

Cummins, J. David and Outreville, J. François. An International Analysis of Underwriting Cycles in Property-Liability Insurance. *J. Risk Ins.*, June 1987, 54(2), pp. 246–62. **[G: OECD]**

Davis, Steven J. Fluctuations in the Pace of Labor Reallocations. *Carnegie–Rochester Conf. Ser. Public Policy*, Autumn 1987, 27, pp. 335–402. **[G: U.S.]**

Day, John. Crises and Trends in the Late Middle Ages. *Day, J.*, 1987, pp. 185–224. **[G: Europe]**

Duménil, Gérard; Glick, Mark and Rangel, Jose. Does Rajani Kanth's Comment Matter? *Rev. Radical Polit. Econ.*, Winter 1987, 19(4), pp. 75. **[G: U.S.]**

Duménil, Gérard; Glick, Mark and Rangel, Jose. Theories of the Great Depression: Why Did Profitability Matter? *Rev. Radical Polit. Econ.*, Summer 1987, 19(2), pp. 16–42. **[G: U.S.]**

Eden, Benjamin. Trading Uncertainty, Markups, and Productivity: A Comment [Productivity and the Business Cycle]. *Carnegie–Rochester Conf. Ser. Public Policy*, Autumn 1987, 27, pp. 445–52. **[G: U.S.]**

Ferson, Wayne E. and Merrick, John J., Jr. Non-stationarity and Stage-of-the-Business-Cycle Effects in Consumption-Based Asset Pricing Relations. *J. Finan. Econ.*, March 1987, 18(1), pp. 127–46. **[G: U.S.]**

Foders, Federico and Glismann, Hans H. Long Waves in Argentine Economic Development. *Vasko, T., ed.*, 1987, pp. 12–26. **[G: Argentina]**

Forman, Leonard; Groves, Miles and Eichner, Alfred S. The Cyclical Dynamics of the American Economy: Preliminary Results from a Post-Keynesian Econometric Model. *Écon. Appl.*, 1987, 40(4), pp. 681–708. **[G: U.S.]**

Freeman, Richard B. How Do Public Sector Wages and Employment Respond to Economic Conditions? *Wise, D. A., ed.*, 1987, pp. 183–207. **[G: U.S.]**

French, Michael J. and Wilson, Thomas. Depression and Protection: The Early Thirties and the Early Eighties Compared. *[Penrose, E. F.]*, 1987, pp. 14–31. **[G: OECD]**

Friedman, Milton and Schwartz, Anna J. Money and Business Cycles. *Schwartz, A. J.*, 1987, 1963, pp. 24–77. **[G: U.S.]**

Gallaway, Lowell and Vedder, Richard K. Wages, Prices, and Employment: Von Mises and the Progressives. *Rothbard, M. N., ed.*, 1987, pp. 33–80. **[G: U.S.; U.K.]**

Giannaros, Demetrios S. and Lashgari, Malek K. Business Cycles, Inflation and the Price of Gold: An Empirical Investigation. *Tremblay, R., ed.*, 1987, pp. 111–21.

Goldstein, Joshua S. Long Waves in War, Produc-

tion, Prices, and Wages. *J. Conflict Resolution*, December 1987, *31*(4), pp. 573–600.
[G: Selected MDCs]

Gordon, Robert J. The Wage and Price Adjustment Process in Six Large OECD Countries. *Aliber, R. Z., ed.*, 1987, pp. 70–91.
[G: OECD]

Greenspan, Alan. The Great Malaise. *Challenge*, Special Issue 1987, *30*(6), pp. 11–14.
[G: U.S.]

Hall, Robert E. Productivity and the Business Cycle. *Carnegie–Rochester Conf. Ser. Public Policy*, Autumn 1987, *27*, pp. 421–44.
[G: U.S.]

Hamilton, James D. Monetary Factors in the Great Depression. *J. Monet. Econ.*, March 1987, *19*(2), pp. 145–69.
[G: U.S.]

Heller, Walter W. Can There Be Another Crash? *Challenge*, Special Issue 1987, *30*(6), pp. 6–10.
[G: U.S.]

Henschel, Rudolf. Einflüsse Öffentlicher Meinungsbildung auf die Einkommensverteilung. (The Influence of Public Opinion on the Distribution of Income. With English summary.) *Ifo-Studien*, 1987, *33*(1), pp. 1–26.
[G: W. Germany]

Hibbs, Douglas A., Jr. Economics and Politics in France: Economic Performance and Mass Political Support for Presidents Pompidou and Giscard d'Estaing. *Hibbs, D. A., Jr., 1987, 1981*, pp. 224–40.
[G: France]

Hibbs, Douglas A., Jr. On the Demand for Economic Outcomes: Macroeconomic Performance and Mass Political Support in the United States, Great Britain, and Germany. *Hibbs, D. A., Jr., 1987, 1982*, pp. 193–223.
[G: U.S.; U.K.; W. Germany]

Hibbs, Douglas A., Jr. President Reagan's Mandate from the 1980 Elections: A Shift to the Right? *Hibbs, D. A., Jr., 1987, 1982*, pp. 164–90.
[G: U.S.]

Hibbs, Douglas A., Jr. and Madsen, Henrik Jess. The Impact of Economic Performance on Electoral Support in Sweden, 1967–1978. *Hibbs, D. A., Jr., 1987, 1981*, pp. 241–57.
[G: Sweden]

Hillinger, Claude; Reich, Utz-Peter and Wehner, G. Konjunkturschwankungen der Aggregate der VGR in 10 OECD Ländern. (Cyclical Fluctuations of the Components of Gross Domestic Product in 10 OECD Countries. With English summary.) *Jahr. Nationalökon. Statist.*, May 1987, *203*(3), pp. 217–24.
[G: OECD]

Hochstein, Alan. Changes in Loan Practices by Banks: An Explanation of Canada's Economic Decline in the Early 1980's. *Tremblay, R., ed.*, 1987, pp. 263–72.
[G: Canada]

van der Hoeven, Rolph and Richards, P. J. Depression and Adjustment. *International Labour Office.*, 1987, pp. 1–19.
[G: OECD; LDCs]

Holloway, Thomas M. Measuring the Sensitivity of Net Interest Paid to the Business Cycle and to Inflation. *Public Finance Quart.*, July 1987, *15*(3), pp. 235–58.
[G: U.S.]

Kanth, Rajani. Why Does the Duménil–Glick–

Rangel Thesis Matter? A Comment. *Rev. Radical Polit. Econ.*, Winter 1987, *19*(4), pp. 73–74.
[G: U.S.]

Kindleberger, Charles P. 1929: Ten Lessons for Today. *Challenge*, Special Issue 1987, *30*(6), pp. 15–18.

Kirk, Robert. Are Business Services Immune to the Business Cycle? *Growth Change*, Spring 1987, *18*(2), pp. 15–23.
[G: U.S.]

Kleinknecht, Alfred. Reply [Long Waves, Depression and Innovation]. *De Economist*, 1987, *135*(3), pp. 387–88.
[G: Global]

König, Heinz and Nerlove, Marc. Saisonale und konjunkturelle Komponenten in der Beziehung zwischen Erwartungen, Plänen und Realisationen in Konjunkturtests. (Seasonal and Cyclical Variations in Relationship among Expectations, Plans and Realizations in Business Test Surveys. With English summary.) *Ifo-Studien*, 1987, *33*(3), pp. 161–93.
[G: W. Germany; France]

Kotz, David M. Long Waves and Social Structures of Accumulation: A Critique and Reinterpretation. *Rev. Radical Polit. Econ.*, Winter 1987, *19*(4), pp. 16–38.
[G: U.S.]

Kozlowski, Paul J. Regional Cyclical Volatility: Tests of a Growth-Buffer Hypothesis. *Reg. Sci. Persp.*, 1987, *17*(2), pp. 41–56.
[G: U.S.]

Krelle, Wilhelm. Long-term Fluctuations of Technical Progress and Growth. *J. Inst. Theoretical Econ.*, September 1987, *143*(3), pp. 379–401.
[G: OECD; CMEA]

Kuntjoro-Jakti, Dorodjatun. The Global Crisis of the 1980s and Indonesia's Response. *Hitotsubashi J. Econ.*, October 1987, *27*, pp. 101–13.

Layton, Allan P. A Spectral Analysis of Australia's Leading and Coincident Indexes of Cyclical Economic Growth. *Australian Econ. Rev.*, First Quarter 1987, (77), pp. 39–45.
[G: Australia]

Layton, Allan P. Australian and U.S. Growth Cycle Linkages, 1967–1983. *J. Macroecon.*, Winter 1987, *9*(1), pp. 31–44.
[G: Australia; U.S.]

Lecaillon, Jacques and Grangeas, Geneviève. Salaires, répartition et cycles. (With English summary.) *Revue Écon. Polit.*, July-Aug. 1987, *97*(4), pp. 363–80.
[G: France]

Lee, Chi-Wen Jevons and Petruzzi, Christopher R. A Test of the Shiller–Siegel Hypothesis of the Gibson Paradox [The Gibson Paradox and Historical Movements in Real Interest Rates]. *Australian Econ. Pap.*, June 1987, *26*(48), pp. 157–64.
[G: U.K.]

Liebling, Herman I. The Keynesian Recovery Myth: A Rejoinder. *J. Macroecon.*, Summer 1987, *9*(3), pp. 473–74.
[G: U.S.]

Lloyd-Jones, Roger. Innovation, Industrial Structure and the Long Wave: The British Economy c. 1873–1914. *J. Europ. Econ. Hist.*, Fall 1987, *16*(2), pp. 315–53.
[G: U.K.]

Long, John B., Jr. and Plosser, Charles I. Sectoral vs. Aggregate Shocks in the Business Cycle. *Amer. Econ. Rev.*, May 1987, *77*(2), pp. 333–36.
[G: U.S.]

Luigi, Guiso and Sestito, Paolo. Fluttuazione cicliche e curva di offerta "À la" Lucas: Una verifica empirica diretta. (Cyclical Fluctuations and the Lucas Supply Function: A Direct Empirical Test. With English summary.) *Giorn. Econ.*, July-August 1987, *46*(7–8), pp. 401–15. **[G: Italy]**

Mario, Deaglio. Alla Ricerca dei cicli lunghi. (The Search for Long Waves. With English summary.) *Giorn. Econ.*, July-August 1987, *46*(7–8), pp. 365–99.

Martin, Vance L. Leads and Lags in the Australian Business Cycle: A Canonical Approach in the Frequency Domain. *Australian Econ. Pap.*, December 1987, *26*(49), pp. 188–96. **[G: Australia]**

May, Ann Mari. The Political Business Cycle: An Institutional Critique and Reconstruction. *J. Econ. Issues*, June 1987, *21*(2), pp. 713–22. **[G: U.S.]**

McGavin, Brian H. The Political Business Cycle: A Reexamination of Some Empirical Evidence. *Quart. J. Bus. Econ.*, Winter 1987, *26*(1), pp. 36–49. **[G: U.S.]**

McNees, Stephen K. Forecasting Cyclical Turning Points: The Record in the Past Three Recessions. *New Eng. Econ. Rev.*, Mar./Apr. 1987, pp. 31–40. **[G: U.S.]**

Mennes, L. B. M. World Priorities for Structural Change, Economic Interdependence and World Development. *Urquidi, V. L., ed.*, 1987, pp. 195–99.

Moore, Goeffrey H. The Service Industries and the Business Cycle. *Bus. Econ.*, April 1987, *22*(2), pp. 12–17. **[G: U.S.]**

Myers, Samuel L., Jr. and Sabol, William J. Business Cycles and Racial Disparities in Punishment. *Contemp. Policy Issues*, October 1987, *5*(4), pp. 46–58. **[G: U.S.]**

Nakicenovic, Nebojsa. Technological Substitution and Long Waves in the USA. *Vasko, T., ed.*, 1987, pp. 76–103. **[G: U.S.]**

Nam, Sang Woo. A Case of Successful Adjustment in a Developing Country: Korea's Experience during 1980–84: Comment. *Holmes, F., ed.*, 1987, pp. 114–19. **[G: S. Korea]**

Neelin, Janet. Sectoral Shifts and Canadian Unemployment. *Rev. Econ. Statist.*, November 1987, *69*(4), pp. 718–23. **[G: Canada]**

Neumann, Manfred J. M. and Lohmann, Susanne. Political Business Cycles in Industrialized Democratic Countries: A Comment. *Kyklos*, 1987, *40*(4), pp. 568–72. **[G: OECD]**

Nilsson, Ronny. OECD Leading Indicators. *OECD Econ. Stud.*, Autumn 1987, (9), pp. 105–45. **[G: OECD]**

Nolan, Brian. Cyclical Fluctuations in Factor Shares and the Size Distribution of Income. *Rev. Income Wealth*, June 1987, *33*(2), pp. 193–210. **[G: U.K.]**

Odagiri, Hiroyuki and Yamashita, Takashi. Price Mark-Ups, Market Structure, and Business Fluctuation in Japanese Manufacturing Industries. *J. Ind. Econ.*, March 1987, *35*(3), pp. 317–31. **[G: Japan]**

Oi, Walter Y. Comment on the Relation between Unemployment and Sectoral Shifts [Fluctua-

tions in the Pace of Labor Reallocations]. *Carnegie–Rochester Conf. Ser. Public Policy*, Autumn 1987, *27*, pp. 403–20. **[G: U.S.]**

Ortona, Guido. A Model of Political Business Cycle in a Soviet-Type Economy. *Econ. Notes*, 1987, (1), pp. 107–18.

Owen, Susan J. and Joshi, Heather E. Does Elastic Retract: The Effect of Recession on Women's Labour Force Participation. *Brit. J. Ind. Relat.*, March 1987, *25*(1), pp. 125–43. **[G: U.K.]**

Pack, Janet Rothenberg. The Political Policy Cycle: Presidential Effort vs. Presidential Control. *Public Choice*, August 1987, *54*(3), pp. 231–59. **[G: U.S.]**

Pagan, Adrian R. The Australian Economy in the Long Run: The End of the Long Boom. *Maddock, R. and McLean, I. W., eds.*, 1987, pp. 106–30. **[G: Australia]**

Pantin, Dennis A. Long Waves and Caribbean Development. *Soc. Econ. Stud.*, June 1987, *36*(2), pp. 1–20. **[G: Caribbean]**

Pauly, Ralf. Messung von Wachstumsschwankungen ökonomischer Variablen. (A New Procedure for Measuring Growth Cycles. With English summary.) *Jahr. Nationalökon. Statist.*, January 1987, *203*(1), pp. 43–57. **[G: W. Germany]**

Peltzman, Sam. How Do Public Sector Wages and Employment Respond to Economic Conditions? Comment. *Wise, D. A., ed.*, 1987, pp. 207–13. **[G: U.S.]**

Peterson, Wallace C. and Estenson, Paul S. The Myth of Keynesian Recovery: Response. *J. Macroecon.*, Summer 1987, *9*(3), pp. 469–72. **[G: U.S.]**

Poole, William. Monetary Control and the Political Business Cycle. *Dorn, J. A. and Schwartz, A. J., eds.*, 1987, 1986, pp. 31–45. **[G: U.S.]**

Rayack, Wendy. Sources and Centers of Cyclical Movement in Real Wages: Evidence from Panel Data. *J. Post Keynesian Econ.*, Fall 1987, *10*(1), pp. 3–21. **[G: U.S.]**

Raynauld, Jacques. The Transmission of U.S. Business Cycles to Canada: A Regional Perspective. *Tremblay, R., ed.*, 1987, pp. 187–98. **[G: U.S.; Canada]**

Roland, Gérard. Investment Growth Fluctuations in the Soviet Union: An Econometric Analysis. *J. Compar. Econ.*, June 1987, *11*(2), pp. 192–206. **[G: U.S.S.R.]**

Rossana, Robert J. Interrelated Demands for Labor and Buffer Stocks: An Empirical Test. *J. Macroecon.*, Winter 1987, *9*(1), pp. 13–30. **[G: U.S.]**

Rostow, Walt W. Long Cycles and Policy. *Rostow, W. W.*, 1987, pp. 79–104.

Sapsford, David. A Simple Model of Primary Commodity Price Determination: 1900–80. *J. Devel. Stud.*, January 1987, *23*(2), pp. 265–74.

Scarfe, Brian L. Economic Fluctuations and Stabilization Policy in Canada: The State of the Art. *Can. Public Policy*, March 1987, *13*(1), pp. 75–85. **[G: Canada]**

van Schaik, A. B. T. M. and Mulder, R. J. On

Superimposed Recurrent Cycles. *J. Econ. (Z. Nationalökon.)*, 1987, *47*(3), pp. 253–72.
[G: U.S.]

Schwartz, Anna J. Understanding 1929–1933. *Schwartz, A. J.*, 1987, *1981*, pp. 110–51.
[G: U.S.]

Screpanti, Ernesto. Long Cycles in Strike Activity: An Empirical Investigation. *Brit. J. Ind. Relat.*, March 1987, *25*(1), pp. 99–124.
[G: France; Italy; U.K.; U.S.; W. Germany]

Shapiro, Matthew D. Are Cyclical Fluctuation in Productivity Due More to Supply Shocks or Demand Shocks? *Amer. Econ. Rev.*, May 1987, *77*(2), pp. 118–24. [G: U.S.]

Siklos, P. L. Cyclical Fluctuations in U.S. Monetary Policy and Output: A Test of Their Relationship. *J. Stud. Econ. Econometrics*, July 1987, *11*(2), pp. 69–94. [G: U.S.]

Sipos, Béla. Empirical Research and Forecasting Based on Hungarian and World Economic Data Series. *Vasko, T., ed.*, 1987, pp. 119–26.
[G: Hungary; Global]

Steinherr, Alfred. The Great Depression: A Repeat in the 1980s? *[Marrama, V.], Vol. 1*, 1987, pp. 295–364.

Suba-Varga, Judit. "Cycles" in Hungary's Trade with the Developed Western Countries. *Acta Oecon.*, 1987, *38*(3–4), pp. 339–60.
[G: Hungary]

Thorp, Rosemary. Trends and Cycles in the Peruvian Economy. *[Diaz-Alejandro, C. F.]*, 1987, pp. 355–74. [G: Peru]

Thorp, Rosemary. Trends and Cycles in the Peruvian Economy. *J. Devel. Econ.*, October 1987, *27*(1–2), pp. 355–74. [G: Peru]

Val'tukh, Konstantin K. The Law of Value and Structural Shifts in a National Economy. *Vasko, T., ed.*, 1987, pp. 176–84. [G: U.S.]

Valentine, Tom J. The Australian Economy in the Long Run: The Depression of the 1930s. *Maddock, R. and McLean, I. W., eds.*, 1987, pp. 61–78. [G: Australia]

Valentine, Tom J. The Causes of the Depression in Australia. *Exploration Econ. Hist.*, January 1987, *24*(1), pp. 43–62. [G: Australia]

Vasko, Tibor. The Long-Wave Debate: Preface. *Vasko, T., ed.*, 1987, pp. v–xi.

Webb, Steven B. The German Inflation and Foreign Business Cycles, 1920–1922. *Exploration Econ. Hist.*, October 1987, *24*(4), pp. 409–33.
[G: W. Germany]

Woods, Ronald N. Keynesian Recovery: Reality Down Under. *J. Macroecon.*, Summer 1987, *9*(3), pp. 463–67. [G: Australia]

Yoshikawa, Hiroshi and Ohtake, Fumio. Postwar Business Cycles in Japan: A Quest for the Right Explanation. *J. Japanese Int. Economies*, December 1987, *1*(4), pp. 373–407. [G: Japan]

132 Forecasting; Econometric Models

1320 General

Bovenberg, A. Lans. The General Equilibrium Approach: Relevant for Public Policy? *van de Kar, H. M. and Wolfe, B. L., eds.*, 1987, pp. 33–43.

Braat, Leon C. and van Lierop, Wal F. J. Economic–Ecological Modeling: Evaluation. *Braat, L. C. and van Lierop, W. F. J., eds.*, 1987, pp. 282–85.

Cilke, James M. and Wyscarver, Roy A. The Individual Income Tax Simulation Model. *U.S. Treasury, Office of Tax Analysis.*, 1987, pp. 43–75. [G: U.S.]

Cusack, Thomas R. The GLOBUS Model: Computer Simulation of Worldwide Political and Economic Development: Government Budget Processes. *Bremer, S. A., ed.*, 1987, pp. 325–458. [G: Global]

Daub, M. An Institutional Approach to the Rationality of Expectations. *Appl. Econ.*, October 1987, *19*(10), pp. 1303–16. [G: Canada]

Deardorff, Alan V. Trade and Capital Mobility in a World of Diverging Populations. *Johnson, D. G. and Lee, R. D., eds.*, 1987, pp. 561–88. [G: LDCs; MDCs]

Dworin, Lowell. Impact of the Corporate Alternative Minimum Tax: A Monte Carlo Simulation Study. *U.S. Treasury, Office of Tax Analysis.*, 1987, pp. 253–78. [G: U.S.]

Eberwein, Wolf-Dieter. The GLOBUS Model: Computer Simulation of Worldwide Political and Economic Development: Domestic Political Processes. *Bremer, S. A., ed.*, 1987, pp. 159–282. [G: Global]

Fase, Martin M. G. Modelling Multivariate Stochastic Time Series for Prediction: Another Look at the Lydia Pinkham Data. *Heijmans, R. and Neudecker, H., eds.*, 1987, pp. 205–22. [G: U.S.]

Fullerton, Don; Gillette, Robert and Mackie, James. Investment Incentives under the Tax Reform Act of 1986. *U.S. Treasury, Office of Tax Analysis.*, 1987, pp. 131–71. [G: U.S.]

Fullerton, Don; Henderson, Yolanda Kodrzycki and Mackie, James. Investment Allocation and Growth under the Tax Reform Act of 1986. *U.S. Treasury, Office of Tax Analysis.*, 1987, pp. 173–201. [G: U.S.]

Gerardi, Geraldine, et al. The Treasury Depreciation Model. *U.S. Treasury, Office of Tax Analysis.*, 1987, pp. 203–27. [G: U.S.]

Gigengack, A. R.; de Haan, Hendrik and Jepma, Catherine J. Military Expenditure Dynamics and a World Model. *Schmidt, C. and Blackaby, F., eds.*, 1987, pp. 321–41.

Grubert, Harry and Mutti, John. The Impact of the Tax Reform Act of 1986 on Trade and Capital Flows. *U.S. Treasury, Office of Tax Analysis.*, 1987, pp. 229–52. [G: U.S.]

Henry, Ken R., et al. Implementing Computable General Equilibrium Models: Data Preparation, Calibration and Replication. *New Zealand Econ. Pap.*, 1987, *21*, pp. 129.
[G: New Zealand]

Narayana, N. S. S.; Parikh, Kirit S. and Srinivasan, T. N. Indian Agricultural Policy: An Applied General Equilibrium Model. *J. Policy Modeling*, Winter 1987, *9*(4), pp. 527–58.
[G: India]

Neubig, Thomas S. and Sullivan, Martin A. The Effect of the Tax Reform Act of 1986 on Commercial Banks. *U.S. Treasury, Office of Tax Analysis.*, 1987, pp. 279–305. **[G: U.S.]**

Nguyen, Dung and Olson, Josephine E. U.S. Budget Deficits: Empirical and Policy Issues. *Thai, K. V., ed.*, 1987, *1986*, pp. 47–63. **[G: U.S.]**

Nijkamp, Peter. Economic Modeling: Shortcomings and Perspectives. *Braat, L. C. and van Lierop, W. F. J., eds.*, 1987, pp. 20–35.

Passet, René. Prévision à long terme et mutation des systémes économiques. (With English summary.) *Revue Écon. Polit.*, Sept.-Oct. 1987, *97*(5), pp. 532–55.

Polishchuck, Leonid I. On Some Applications of Stochastic Dominance in Multiobjective Decision-Making. *Jahn, J. and Krabs, W., eds.*, 1987, pp. 208–21.

Prescott, James R. Community Dynamics: Microanalytical Simulation Models with Behavior Settings as Basic Units. *Fox, K. A. and Miles, D. G., eds.*, 1987, pp. 158–79.

Smith, Dale L. The GLOBUS Model: Computer Simulation of Worldwide Political and Economic Development: International Political Processes. *Bremer, S. A., ed.*, 1987, pp. 569–721. **[G: Global]**

Zagamé, Paul. L'expérience française de modélisation macro-économétrique: bilan et perspectives. (With English summary.) *Revue Écon. Polit.*, Sept.-Oct. 1987, *97*(5), pp. 485–528. **[G: France]**

1322 General Forecasts and Models

Ågren, Goran I. Models for Forestry. *Braat, L. C. and van Lierop, W. F. J., eds.*, 1987, pp. 87–99.

Anderson, Robert and Enzler, Jared J. Toward Realistic Policy Design: Policy Reaction Functions That Rely on Economic Forecasts. *[Modigliani, F.]*, 1987, pp. 291–330. **[G: U.S.]**

Andresen, Svein and Everaert, Luc. International Macroeconomic Interdependence. *Ann. Écon. Statist.*, Apr./Sept. 1987, (6/7), pp. 161–81. **[G: OECD]**

Aoki, Masanao. Studies of Economic Interdependence by State Space Modeling of Time Series: U.S.–Japan Example. *Ann. Écon. Statist.*, Apr./Sept. 1987, (6/7), pp. 225–52. **[G: U.S.; Japan]**

Barbolla, Rosa and Gomez Pérez, José Patricio. Control de sistemas macroeconómicos. Estudio de un caso para la economía española. (With English summary.) *Invest. Ecón.*, January 1987, *11*(1), pp. 101–31. **[G: Spain]**

Barker, Terry. The Cambridge Multisectoral Dynamic Model of the British Economy: The Complete Model. *Barker, T. and Peterson, W., eds.*, 1987, pp. 47–86. **[G: U.K.]**

Barker, Terry. The Cambridge Multisectoral Dynamic Model of the British Economy: Introduction. *Barker, T. and Peterson, W., eds.*, 1987, pp. 1–9. **[G: U.K.]**

Barker, Terry. The Cambridge Multisectoral Dynamic Model of the British Economy: Export and Import Prices. *Barker, T. and Peterson,*

W., eds., 1987, pp. 311–39. **[G: U.K.]**

Barker, Terry. The Cambridge Multisectoral Dynamic Model of the British Economy: Exports and Imports. *Barker, T. and Peterson, W., eds.*, 1987, pp. 201–45. **[G: U.K.]**

Barker, Terry and Peterson, William. The Cambridge Multisectoral Dynamic Model of the British Economy: Theory and Method. *Barker, T. and Peterson, W., eds.*, 1987, pp. 13–24. **[G: U.K.]**

Barker, Terry and Weale, Martin. The Cambridge Multisectoral Dynamic Model of the British Economy: The Accounting Framework and the Data. *Barker, T. and Peterson, W., eds.*, 1987, pp. 25–46. **[G: U.K.]**

Baum, Christopher F. The Effects of Price- and Output-Stabilising Policies in an Interdependent World Economy. *J. Econ. Dynam. Control*, June 1987, *11*(2), pp. 195–200. **[G: OECD]**

Bennett, Adam. Wealth and the Dynamics of Macroeconomic Adjustment. *Econ. Modelling*, January 1987, *4*(1), pp. 3–18. **[G: U.K.]**

Bianchi, Carlo; Brillet, Jean-Louis and Panattoni, Lorenzo. Uncertainty and Stability in a Macroeconometric Model. *Ann. Écon. Statist.*, Apr./Sept. 1987, (6/7), pp. 347–67. **[G: France]**

Biørn, Erik; Jensen, Morten and Reymert, Morten. KVARTS—A Quarterly Model of the Norwegian Economy. *Econ. Modelling*, January 1987, *4*(1), pp. 77–109. **[G: Norway]**

Bogardi, Istvan. Water Resources Models. *Braat, L. C. and van Lierop, W. F. J., eds.*, 1987, pp. 117–34.

Borooah, Vani. The Cambridge Multisectoral Dynamic Model of the British Economy: Consumers' Expenditure. *Barker, T. and Peterson, W., eds.*, 1987, pp. 125–49. **[G: U.K.]**

Boynton, G. R. and Deissenberg, Christophe. Models of the Economy Implicit in Public Discourse. *Policy Sci.*, 1987, *20*(2), pp. 129–51.

Braat, Leon C. and van Lierop, Wal F. J. Integrated Economic–Ecological Modeling. *Braat, L. C. and van Lierop, W. F. J., eds.*, 1987, pp. 49–68.

Brahmananda, P. R. New Classical Macro-econometric Model Variants for the Indian Economy. *Indian Econ. J.*, Oct.-Dec. 1987, *35*(2), pp. 23–37. **[G: India]**

Brayton, Flint and Mauskopf, Eileen. Structure and Uses of the MPS Quarterly Econometric Model of the United States. *Fed. Res. Bull.*, February 1987, *73*(2), pp. 93–109. **[G: U.S.]**

Bremer, Stuart A. The GLOBUS Model: Computer Simulation of Worldwide Political and Economic Development: Demographic Processes. *Bremer, S. A., ed.*, 1987, pp. 283–324. **[G: Global]**

Bremer, Stuart A. The GLOBUS Model: Computer Simulation of Worldwide Political and Economic Development: Introduction. *Bremer, S. A., ed.*, 1987, pp. 1–38.

Britton, Andrew; Gurney, Andrew and Herbert, Rhys. The Home Economy. *Nat. Inst. Econ. Rev.*, February 1987, (119), pp. 6–16. **[G: U.K.]**

Britton, Andrew; Gurney, Andrew and Joyce, Michael. Chapter I: The Home Economy. *Nat. Inst. Econ. Rev.*, August 1987, (121), pp. 6–20. [G: U.K.]

Britton, Andrew; Gurney, Andrew and Joyce, Michael. The Home Economy. *Nat. Inst. Econ. Rev.*, November 1987, (122), pp. 7–23. [G: U.K.]

Canzoneri, Matthew B. The Gains from Policy Coordination: Overview. *Bryant, R. C. and Portes, R., eds.*, 1987, pp. 185–90.

Card, David and Farber, Henry S. Semiparametric Estimation of Employment Duration Models: Comments. *Econometric Rev.*, 1987, 6(1), pp. 41–54.

Carraro, Carlo. Preferenze rivelate e giochi di Nash: Gli obiettivi impliciti di politiche monetarie e fiscali in Italia. (Preference Revelation and Nash Equilibria: The Implicit Objective Function of Italian Macroeconomic Policy. With English summary.) *Econ. Lavoro*, Apr.-June 1987, 21(2), pp. 47–58. [G: Italy]

Chiarini, Bruno. Different Assumptions about Fiscal and Monetary Authority Behaviour in an Optimal Control Framework. Experiments with a Medium-size Nonlinear Econometric Model. *Econ. Notes*, 1987, (3), pp. 59–86. [G: Italy]

Chunze, Jiang. The Development of Socialist Economic Models. *Comp. Econ. Stud.*, Spring 1987, 29(1), pp. 81–105. [G: E. Europe; China]

Cohen, Suleiman I. Modelling the Prospects of Economic Growth and Social Development: Results of Circular Flow Planning Models Applied to Pakistan 1980–1993. *Pakistan Devel. Rev.*, Winter 1987, 26(4), pp. 609–26. [G: Pakistan]

Currie, David; Levine, Paul and Vidalis, Nic. International Cooperation and Reputation in an Empirical Two-Bloc Model. *Bryant, R. C. and Portes, R., eds.*, 1987, pp. 75–121. [G: U.S.]

Dalamagas, Basil A. Government Deficits, Crowding Out, and Inflation: Some International Evidence. *Public Finance*, 1987, 42(1), pp. 65–84. [G: OECD]

Davis, E. P. A Stock-flow Consistent Macroeconometric Model of the UK Economy—Part II. *J. Appl. Econometrics*, October 1987, 2(4), pp. 259–307. [G: U.K.]

Davis, E. P. A Stock-Flow Consistent Macroeconometric Model of the UK Economy—Part I. *J. Appl. Econometrics*, April 1987, 2(2), pp. 111–32. [G: U.K.]

Drachman, Rául and Zilberfarb, Ben-Zion. An Econometric Annual Model of the Real Sector in Israel. *Econ. Modelling*, July 1987, 4(3), pp. 370–76. [G: Israel]

Dubois, Paul. Macroeconomic Models and Planning in the Context of an Uncertain Future: The French Experience. *CEPAL Rev.*, April 1987, (31), pp. 59–67. [G: France]

Easton, Bill and Patterson, Kerry David. Interest Rates in Five Macroeconomic Models of the UK: Survey, Analysis and Simulation. *Econ.*

Modelling, January 1987, 4(1), pp. 19–64. [G: U.K.]

Edison, Hali J.; Marquez, Jaime R. and Tryon, Ralph W. The Structure and Properties of the Federal Reserve Baord Multicountry Model. *Econ. Modelling*, April 1987, 4(2), pp. 115–315. [G: U.S.; Canada; W. Germany; Japan; U.K.]

Eggert, Jim. Consensus Forecasting—A Ten-Year Report Card. *Challenge*, July/Aug. 1987, 30(3), pp. 59–62. [G: U.S.]

Fair, Ray C. Properties of a Multicountry Econometric Model. *J. Policy Modeling*, Spring 1987, 9(1), pp. 83–123. [G: Global]

Forman, Leonard; Groves, Miles and Eichner, Alfred S. The Cyclical Dynamics of the American Economy: Preliminary Results from a Post-Keynesian Econometric Model. *Écon. Appl.*, 1987, 40(4), pp. 681–708. [G: U.S.]

Friedman, Benjamin M. Toward Realistic Policy Design: Policy Reaction Functions That Rely on Economic Forecasts: Comments. *[Modigliani, F.]*, 1987, pp. 331–36. [G: U.S.]

Gandolfo, Giancarlo and Petit, Maria Luisa. Optimization in Continuous Time and Policy Design in the Italian Economy. *Ann. Écon. Statist.*, Apr./Sept. 1987, (6/7), pp. 311–33. [G: Italy]

Goudie, Andrew; Meeks, Geoffrey and Weale, Martin. The Cambridge Multisectoral Dynamic Model of the British Economy: The Company Sector. *Barker, T. and Peterson, W., eds.*, 1987, pp. 389–410. [G: U.K.]

Grais, W. M. Coping with a Decline in World Energy Prices: Macroeconomic and Income Distribution Effects in Thailand. *J. Devel. Econ.*, August 1987, 26(2), pp. 235–55. [G: Thailand]

de Grauwe, Paul and Rosiers, Marc. Real Exchange Rate Variability and Monetary Disturbances. *Weltwirtsch. Arch.*, 1987, 123(3), pp. 430–48. [G: Global]

Gruhn, Walter L. The GLOBUS Simulation Package. *Bremer, S. A., ed.*, 1987, pp. 777–802. [G: Global]

Hall, S. G. An Investigation of Time Inconsistency and Optimal Policy Formulation in the Presence of Rational Expectations Using the National Institute's Model 7. *Appl. Econ.*, September 1987, 19(9), pp. 1175–85. [G: U.K.]

Hall, S. G. Analysing Economic Behaviour 1975–85 with a Model Incorporating Consistent Expectations. *Nat. Inst. Econ. Rev.*, May 1987, (120), pp. 75–80. [G: U.K.]

Hanssens, Dominique M. and Vanden Abeele, Pierre M. A Time-Series Study of the Formation and Predictive Performance of EEC Production Survey Expectations. *J. Bus. Econ. Statist.*, October 1987, 5(4), pp. 507–19. [G: EEC]

Harnos, Zsolt. Agricultural Models. *Braat, L. C. and van Lierop, W. F. J., eds.*, 1987, pp. 100–116.

Hasan, M. Aynul. A Rational Expectations Macroeconometric Model of Pakistan's Monetary Policy since 1970s. *Pakistan Devel. Rev.*, Winter

1987, *26*(4), pp. 513–23. **[G: Pakistan]**
Heilemann, Ullrich and Neuhaus, Ralph. ARIMA-Modelle: Eine Alternative zu ökonometrischen Konjunkturmodellen? Eine empirische Untersuchung für das Jahr 1983. (ARIMA Models—An Alternative to Econometric Short-term Models? With English summary.) *Jahr. Nationalökon. Statist.*, March 1987, *203*(2), pp. 167–87. **[G: W. Germany]**
Helliwell, John F., et al. Supply Oriented Macroeconomics: The MACE Model of Canada. *Econ. Modelling*, July 1987, *4*(3), pp. 318–40.
[G: Canada]
Henry, E. W. Estimating and Testing CES Production Functions on Irish 12-Sector Input–Output Data. *Econ. Soc. Rev.*, July 1987, *18*(4), pp. 223–35. **[G: Ireland]**
Henry, Samuel G. Brian. Dynamic Modelling and Rational Expectations. *Ann. Écon. Statist.*, Apr./Sept. 1987, (6/7), pp. 183–206.
[G: U.K.]
Hoffman, Dennis L. Two-Step Generalized Least Squares Estimators in Multi-equation Generated Regressor Models. *Rev. Econ. Statist.*, May 1987, *69*(2), pp. 336–46. **[G: U.S.; W. Germany; U.K.]**
Holden, Karen C.; Peel, David A. and Sandhu, B. The Accuracy of OECD Forecasts. *Empirical Econ.*, 1987, *12*(3), pp. 175–86.
[G: OECD]
Holtham, Gerald and Hughes Hallett, Andrew J. International Policy Cooperation and Model Uncertainty. *Bryant, R. C. and Portes, R., eds.*, 1987, pp. 128–77.
Horowitz, Joel L. and Neumann, George R. Semiparametric Estimation of Employment Duration Models. *Econometric Rev.*, 1987, *6*(1), pp. 5–40. **[G: U.S.]**
Horowitz, Joel L. and Neumann, George R. Semiparametric Estimation of Employment Duration Models: Reply. *Econometric Rev.*, 1987, *6*(1), pp. 79–81. **[G: U.S.]**
Howard, James A. Government Economic Projections: A Comparison between CBO and OMB Forecasts. *Public Budg. Finance*, Autumn 1987, *7*(3), pp. 14–25. **[G: U.S.]**
Hughes, Barry B. The GLOBUS Model: Computer Simulation of Worldwide Political and Economic Development: Domestic Economic Processes. *Bremer, S. A., ed.*, 1987, pp. 39–157. **[G: Global]**
Hughes Hallett, Andrew J. International Competitiveness and Economic Recovery: Examples of the Risk-Ambition Trade-Off in Dutch Economic Policies. *Manchester Sch. Econ. Soc. Stud.*, March 1987, *55*(1), pp. 38–59.
[G: Netherlands]
Ikeda, Saburo. Economic–Ecological Models in Regional Total Systems. *Braat, L. C. and van Lierop, W. F. J., eds.*, 1987, pp. 185–202.
Ito, Yukio. Adaptive Control of Econometric Models with Unknown Parameters. *J. Econ. Dynam. Control*, June 1987, *11*(2), pp. 269–73.
[G: Japan]
de Janvry, Alain and Sadoulet, Elisabeth. Agricultural Price Policy in General Equilibrium

Models: Results and Comparisons. *Amer. J. Agr. Econ.*, May 1987, *69*(2), pp. 230–46.
[G: Selected LDCs]
Jonson, Peter D. and Rankin, Robert W. Continuous Time Modelling: A Report from "Down Under." *[Marrama, V.], Vol. 2*, 1987, pp. 799–826. **[G: Australia]**
Joyeux, Roselyne. Evaluation of the Forecasting Performance of the Real Private Sector Output Variable of the Reserve Bank of New Zealand Core Model. *New Zealand Econ. Pap.*, 1987, *21*, pp. 31–39. **[G: New Zealand]**
Kamlet, Mark S.; Mowery, David C. and Su, Tsai-Tsu. Whom Do You Trust? An Analysis of Executive and Congressional Economic Forecasts. *J. Policy Anal. Manage.*, Spring 1987, *6*(3), pp. 365–84. **[G: U.S.]**
Khan, Mohsin S. A Rational Expectations Macroeconometric Model of Pakistan's Monetary Policy since 1970s: Comments. *Pakistan Devel. Rev.*, Winter 1987, *26*(4), pp. 524–27.
[G: Pakistan]
Kirkpatrick, Grant. Structural Modelling of Dynamic Macro-economic Systems: General Considerations, Techniques and an Application to the Federal Republic of Germany. *Ann. Écon. Statist.*, Apr./Sept. 1987, (6/7), pp. 71–99.
[G: W. Germany]
Klein, Lawrence R. The South Asian and Pacific Far East Countries in Project LINK. *Bradford, C. I., Jr. and Branson, W. H., eds.*, 1987, pp. 157–69. **[G: S. Asia; Pacific Basin]**
Kohers, Theodor and Simpson, W. Gary. A Comparison of the Forecasting Accuracy of the Futures and Forward Markets for Foreign Exchange. *Appl. Econ.*, July 1987, *19*(7), pp. 961–67. **[G: OECD]**
Kohli, Ulrich and Ryan, Christopher J. Investment and Interest Rates: An Econometric Dissection. *J. Macroecon.*, Summer 1987, *9*(3), pp. 373–89. **[G: Australia]**
Krishnamurty, K. Inflation and Growth: Some Experiments on a Model for India. *Pasinetti, L. and Lloyd, P., eds.*, 1987, pp. 305–22.
[G: India]
Kutscher, Ronald E. Overview and Implications of the Projections to 2000. *Mon. Lab. Rev.*, September 1987, *110*(9), pp. 3–9. **[G: U.S.]**
Lancaster, Tony. Semiparametric Estimation of Employment Duration Models: Comment. *Econometric Rev.*, 1987, *6*(1), pp. 55–57.
Landesmann, Michael. The Cambridge Multisectoral Dynamic Model of the British Economy: Stockbuilding. *Barker, T. and Peterson, W., eds.*, 1987, pp. 185–200. **[G: U.K.]**
Lawson, Tony. The Cambridge Multisectoral Dynamic Model of the British Economy: Incomes Policy and Earnings. *Barker, T. and Peterson, W., eds.*, 1987, pp. 341–72. **[G: U.K.]**
Leeds, Eva Marikova and Kmenta, Jan. On the Similarity of Macro-econometric Models of Market and Planned Economies: The First Models of Czechoslovakia. *Comp. Econ. Stud.*, Spring 1987, *29*(1), pp. 63–80.
[G: Czechoslovakia]
Levy, Santiago. A Short-run General Equilibrium

Model for a Small, Open Economy. *J. Devel. Econ.*, February 1987, *25*(1), pp. 63–88. [G: LDCs]

Lewis, Jeffrey D.; de Melo, Jaime and Robinson, Sherman. Simulating Alternative Development Strategies: Some Suggestions from Korea's Experience. *Int. Econ. J.*, Autumn 1987, *1*(3), pp. 1–17. [G: S. Korea]

Litterman, Robert. The Limits of Counter-Cyclical Monetary Policy: An Analysis Based on Optimal Control Theory and Vector Autoregressions. *Ann. Écon. Statist.*, Apr./Sept. 1987, (6/7), pp. 125–60.

Lloyd, Peter J. Structural Change in a Selection of Countries: Discussion and Conclusions. *Pasinetti, L. and Lloyd, P., eds.*, 1987, pp. 263–66.

Lye, J. N. Stochastic Simulation of the Reserve Bank's Model of the New Zealand Economy. *New Zealand Econ. Pap.*, 1987, *21*, pp. 17–29. [G: New Zealand]

Majumder, Amita. Use of Pooled Data—An Empirical Note on Demand Analysis. *Indian Econ. Rev.*, Jan.-June 1987, *22*(1), pp. 79–93. [G: India]

Manski, Charles F. Semiparametric Estimation of Employment Duration Models: Comment. *Econometric Rev.*, 1987, *6*(1), pp. 59–64.

Marquez, Jaime R. and Pauly, Peter H. International Policy Coordination and Growth Prospects of Developing Countries: An Optimal Control Application. *J. Devel. Econ.*, February 1987, *25*(1), pp. 89–104.

Masson, Paul R. International Cooperation and Reputation in an Empirical Two-Bloc Model: Discussion. *Bryant, R. C. and Portes, R., eds.*, 1987, pp. 122–25. [G: U.S.]

Masson, Paul R. The Dynamics of a Two-Country Minimodel under Rational Expectations. *Ann. Écon. Statist.*, Apr./Sept. 1987, (6/7), pp. 37–69. [G: U.S.]

McDonald, Daina and Dixon, Peter B. Economic Developments in Australia: 1986–87 and 1987–88. *Australian Econ. Rev.*, Second Quarter 1987, (78), pp. 3–23.

McNees, Stephen K. Forecasting Cyclical Turning Points: The Record in the Past Three Recessions. *New Eng. Econ. Rev.*, Mar./Apr. 1987, pp. 31–40. [G: U.S.]

Meltzer, Allan H. Limits of Short-run Stabilization Policy: Presidential Address to the Western Economic Association, July 3, 1986. *Econ. Inquiry*, January 1987, *25*(1), pp. 1–14. [G: U.S.]

Metwally, M. M. and Daghistani, A. I. The Interaction between the Economies of the Member States of the Gulf Co-operation Council and the Industrialised Economies. *Indian Econ. J.*, Jan.-Mar. 1987, *34*(3), pp. 51–59. [G: Persian Gulf]

Mork, Knut Anton. Ain't Behavin': Forecast Errors and Measurement Errors in Early GNP Estimates. *J. Bus. Econ. Statist.*, April 1987, *5*(2), pp. 165–75. [G: U.S.]

Müller, J. A. Further Development of Macroeconometric Modelling by the Application of the Self-Organization of Mathematical Models. *Econ. Computat. Cybern. Stud. Res.*, 1987, *22*(2), pp. 51–75. [G: E. Germany]

Naughton, Barry. Macroeconomic Policy and Response in the Chinese Economy: The Impact of the Reform Process. *J. Compar. Econ.*, September 1987, *11*(3), pp. 334–53. [G: China]

Neary, J. Peter. ARMOD: A Small Numberical Macroeconomic World Model with Non-clearing Markets: Comment. *Scand. J. Econ.*, 1987, *89*(3), pp. 247–50. [G: OECD]

Odum, Howard T. Models for National, International, and Global Systems Policy. *Braat, L. C. and van Lierop, W. F. J., eds.*, 1987, pp. 203–51.

Okyere, William A. and Johnson, Stanley R. Variability in Forecasts in a Nonlinear Model of the U.S. Beef Sector. *Appl. Econ.*, November 1987, *19*(11), pp. 1457–70. [G: U.S.]

Otter, Pieter W. and Van Dal, René. State–Space and Distributed Lag Modelling of Dynamic Economic Processes Based on Singular Value Decompositions (With an Application to the Dutch Economy). *Ann. Écon. Statist.*, Apr./Sept. 1987, (6/7), pp. 253–77. [G: Netherlands]

Oudiz, Gilles. International Policy Cooperation and Model Uncertainty: Discussion. *Bryant, R. C. and Portes, R., eds.*, 1987, pp. 178–82.

Pagan, Adrian R. and Shannon, J. H. How Reliable Are ORANI Conclusions? *Econ. Rec.*, March 1987, *63*(180), pp. 33–45. [G: Australia]

Pandit, V. and Bhattacharya, B. B. Resource Mobilization, Growth, and Inflation: A Trade-Off Analysis for India. *Dutta, M., ed. (I)*, 1987, pp. 119–41. [G: India]

Park, Wookyu. An Example of Using the BVAR Model and not Violating the "Lucas Critique:" An Explanation of the Recent Korean Economic Boom. *J. Econ. Devel.*, December 1987, *12*(2), pp. 115–41. [G: Korea]

Patterson, Kerry David. The Development of Expectations Generating Schemes Which Are Asymptotically Rational. *Scot. J. Polit. Econ.*, February 1987, *34*(1), pp. 1–18. [G: U.S.; U.K.]

Patterson, Kerry David, et al. The Bank of England Quarterly Model of the UK Economy. *Econ. Modelling*, October 1987, *4*(4), pp. 398–529. [G: U.K.]

Pearse, Peter H. and Walters, Carl J. Perspectives on the Application of Economic–Ecological Models. *Braat, L. C. and van Lierop, W. F. J., eds.*, 1987, pp. 269–81.

Personick, Valerie A. Industry Output and Employment through the End of the Century. *Mon. Lab. Rev.*, September 1987, *110*(9), pp. 30–45. [G: U.S.]

Peterson, William. The Cambridge Multisectoral Dynamic Model of the British Economy: Estimation. *Barker, T. and Peterson, W., eds.*, 1987, pp. 87–103. [G: U.K.]

Peterson, William. The Cambridge Multisectoral Dynamic Model of the British Economy: Fixed

Investment. *Barker, T. and Peterson, W., eds.*, 1987, pp. 151–83. **[G: U.K.]**

Peterson, William. The Cambridge Multisectoral Dynamic Model of the British Economy: The Demand for Energy. *Barker, T. and Peterson, W., eds.*, 1987, pp. 275–91. **[G: U.K.]**

Peterson, William. The Cambridge Multisectoral Dynamic Model of the British Economy: Employment. *Barker, T. and Peterson, W., eds.*, 1987, pp. 247–74. **[G: U.K.]**

Peterson, William. The Cambridge Multisectoral Dynamic Model of the British Economy: Computer Software for a Large Econometric Model. *Barker, T. and Peterson, W., eds.*, 1987, pp. 105–21. **[G: U.K.]**

Pethe, Abhay. Robust Modelling: An Application to the Indian Economy. *J. Quant. Econ.*, July 1987, *3*(2), pp. 259–85. **[G: India]**

van der Ploeg, S. W. Floris. Models for Outdoor Recreation. *Braat, L. C. and van Lierop, W. F. J., eds.*, 1987, pp. 149–65.

Portes, Richard, et al. Macroeconomic Planning and Disequilibrium: Estimates for Poland, 1955–1980. *Econometrica*, January 1987, *55*(1), pp. 19–41. **[G: Poland]**

Powell, James L. Semiparametric Estimation of Employment Duration Models: Comment. *Econometric Rev.*, 1987, *6*(1), pp. 65–78. **[G: U.S.]**

Rabeau, Yves. Déficit du gouvernement canadien: à quelle vitesse les autorités budgétaires doivent-elles réagir. (With English summary.) *Can. Public Policy*, December 1987, *13*(4), pp. 423–34. **[G: Canada]**

Rattso, Jorn. The Macroeconomic Performance in India 1980–85: An Applied General Equilibrium Model Analysis. *J. Quant. Econ.*, July 1987, *3*(2), pp. 225–58. **[G: India]**

Reichenstein, William and Elliott, J. Walter. A Comparison of Models of Long-term Inflationary Expectations. *J. Monet. Econ.*, May 1987, *19*(3), pp. 405–25. **[G: U.S.]**

Rindfuss, Peter. Mathematical Aspects of GLOBUS. *Bremer, S. A., ed.*, 1987, pp. 803–19. **[G: Global]**

Roberds, William and Todd, Richard M. Forecasting and Modeling the U.S. Economy in 1986–88. *Fed. Res. Bank Minn. Rev.*, Winter 1987, *11*(1), pp. 7–20. **[G: U.S.]**

Saunders, Norman C. Economic Projections to the Year 2000. *Mon. Lab. Rev.*, September 1987, *110*(9), pp. 10–18. **[G: U.S.]**

Schlesinger, Helmut and Jahnke, Wilfried. Geldmenge, Preise und Sozialprodukt: Interdependenzzusammenhänge im Lichte Ökonometrischer Forschungsergebnisse für die Bundesrepublik Deutschland. (Money, Prices, and Production: Interdependencies in the Light Econometric Results for the Federal Republic of Germany. With English summary.) *Jahr. Nationalökon. Statist.*, October 1987, *203*(5–6), pp. 576–90. **[G: W. Germany]**

Schoonbeek, Lambert. On the Eigenvectors of Macro-economic Models. *Ann. Écon. Statist.*, Apr./Sept. 1987, (6/7), pp. 335–45.

Sharpe, Don. The Cambridge Multisectoral Dy-

namic Model of the British Economy: Social Security Benefits and Personal Income Tax. *Barker, T. and Peterson, W., eds.*, 1987, pp. 373–87. **[G: U.K.]**

Snell, Andrew. The Cambridge Multisectoral Dynamic Model of the British Economy: Sterling Exchange Rate. *Barker, T. and Peterson, W., eds.*, 1987, pp. 433–54. **[G: U.K.]**

de Sousa, Maria da Conceição Sampaio. Avaliação econômica do Programa Nacional do Álcool (PROÁLCOOL): uma análise de equilíbrio geral. (With English summary.) *Pesquisa Planejamento Econ.*, August 1987, *17*(2), pp. 381–410. **[G: Brazil]**

Staley, Michael. The Practice of Resource Modeling. *Braat, L. C. and van Lierop, W. F. J., eds.*, 1987, pp. 257–68.

Steigum, Erling S., Jr. ARMOD: A Small Numerical Macroeconomic World Model with Nonclearing Markets. *Scand. J. Econ.*, 1987, *89*(3), pp. 227–46. **[G: OECD]**

Stekler, H. O. Who Forecasts Better? [Economic Forecasts and Their Assessment]. *J. Bus. Econ. Statist.*, January 1987, *5*(1), pp. 155–58. **[G: U.S.]**

Sundararajan, V. The Debt–Equity Ratio of Firms and the Effectiveness of Interest Rate Policy: Analysis with a Dynamic Model of Saving, Investment, and Growth in Korea. *Int. Monet. Fund Staff Pap.*, June 1987, *34*(2), pp. 260–310. **[G: S. Korea]**

Szakolczai, György; Bagdy, Gábor and Vindics, József. The Dependence of the Hungarian Economy on the World Economy: Facts and Consequences. *Soviet E. Europ. Foreign Trade*, Spring 1987, *23*(1), pp. 54–88. **[G: Hungary]**

Tsao, James T. H. An Econometric Model of the People's Republic of China. *Dutta, M., ed. (II)*, 1987, pp. 79–89. **[G: China]**

Vishwakarma, Keshav P. Forecasting and Stabilization of Multiple Economic Time Series in the State Space. *J. Econ. Dynam. Control*, June 1987, *11*(2), pp. 265–68. **[G: U.S.]**

Wallis, Kenneth F. and Whitley, John D. Long-Run Properties of Large-scale Macroeconometric Models. *Ann. Écon. Statist.*, Apr./Sept. 1987, (6/7), pp. 207–24. **[G: U.K.]**

Weale, Martin. The Cambridge Multisectoral Dynamic Model of the British Economy: Financial Stocks and Returns. *Barker, T. and Peterson, W., eds.*, 1987, pp. 411–31. **[G: U.K.]**

Weale, Martin. The Cambridge Multisectoral Dynamic Model of the British Economy: Industrial Prices and Profits. *Barker, T. and Peterson, W., eds.*, 1987, pp. 293–309. **[G: U.K.]**

Werneck, Rogério L. Furquim. A Multisectoral Analysis of the Structural Adjustment of the Brazilian Economy in the 1980s. *Pasinetti, L. and Lloyd, P., eds.*, 1987, pp. 233–61. **[G: Brazil]**

Werneck, Rogério L. Furquim. Retomada do crescimento e esforço de poupança: limitações e possibilidades. (With English summary.) *Pesquisa Planejamento Econ.*, April 1987, *17*(1), pp. 1–18. **[G: Brazil]**

Winters, L. Alan. An Empirical Intertemporal Model of Developing Countries' Imports. *Weltwirtsch. Arch.*, 1987, *123*(1), pp. 58–80. [G: Malaysia; Colombia; Kenya]

Wren-Lewis, Simon. Introducing Exchange-Rate Equations into a World Econometric Model. *Nat. Inst. Econ. Rev.*, February 1987, (119), pp. 57–69. [G: OECD]

Wren-Lewis, Simon and Eastwood, Fiona. Chapter II. The World Economy. *Nat. Inst. Econ. Rev.*, August 1987, (121), pp. 21–39. [G: Global]

Wren-Lewis, Simon and Eastwood, Fiona. The World Economy. *Nat. Inst. Econ. Rev.*, February 1987, (119), pp. 24–39. [G: Global]

Wren-Lewis, Simon and Eastwood, Fiona. The World Economy. *Nat. Inst. Econ. Rev.*, November 1987, (122), pp. 24–40. [G: Global]

1323 Specific Forecasts and Models

Adams, Charles; Fenton, Paul R. and Larsen, Flemming. Potential Output in Major Industrial Countries. *International Monetary Fund Research Department.*, 1987, pp. 1–38. [G: OECD]

Aitkin, M. and Healey, R. Statistical Modelling of the EEC Labour Force Survey: A Project History. *Hand, D. J. and Everitt, B. S., eds.*, 1987, pp. 171–79. [G: EEC]

Alexander, Don and Thomas, Lee R., III. Monetary/Asset Models of Exchange Rate Determination: How Well Have They Performed in the 1980s? *Int. J. Forecasting*, 1987, *3*(1), pp. 53–63. [G: U.S.]

Alfsen, Knut H. and Glomsrød, Solveig. Future Emissions to Air in Norway: Forecasts Based on the Macroeconomic Model MSG-4E. *Statist. J.*, May 1987, *4*(3), pp. 219–36. [G: Norway]

Amano, Akihiro. A Small Forecasting Model of the World Oil Market. *J. Policy Modeling*, Winter 1987, *9*(4), pp. 615–35.

Anderson, Kym and Warr, Peter G. General Equilibrium Effects of Agricultural Price Distortions: A Simple Model for Korea. *Food Res. Inst. Stud.*, 1987, *20*(3), pp. 245–63. [G: S. Korea]

Anderson, Oskar. Zur Treffsicherheit der Antizipationen im Ifo-Konjunkturtest (KT) in Abhängigkeit von der Betriebsgrösse. (The Accuracy of Anticipations in the Ifo-Business-Test Dependent on the Firm Size. With English summary.) *Jahr. Nationalökon. Statist.*, October 1987, *203*(5–6), pp. 451–55. [G: W. Germany]

Anderton, R. and Dunnett, A. Modelling the Behaviour of Export Volumes of Manufacturers: An Evaluation of the Performance of Different Measures of International Competitiveness. *Nat. Inst. Econ. Rev.*, August 1987, (121), pp. 46–52. [G: U.K.]

Andrews, Laurel M. INDEPTH Level I Results: Econometric Forecast Models for 20 Industries. *Faruqui, A. and Broehl, J., eds.*, 1987, pp. 395–409. [G: U.S.]

Andrews, Martyn J. The Aggregate Labour Market: An Empirical Investigation into Market-Clearing for the UK. *Econ. J.*, March 1987, *97*(385), pp. 157–76. [G: U.K.]

Aradhyula, Satheesh V. Rational Expectations and Policy Modeling: The Case of Wheat in India. *J. Policy Modeling*, Winter 1987, *9*(4), pp. 667–70. [G: India]

Baillie, Richard T. and Selover, David D. Cointegration and Models of Exchange Rate Determination. *Int. J. Forecasting*, 1987, *3*(1), pp. 43–51.

Balintfy, Joseph L. and Taj, Shahram. A Utility Maximization-Based Decision Support System for USDA Family Food Plans. *Schultz, R. L., ed.*, 1987, pp. 1–22. [G: U.S.]

Baumgartner, J. P. Looking Back at Transport Forecasts. *Int. J. Transport Econ.*, February 1987, *14*(1), pp. 45–56. [G: Switzerland]

Baumgartner, Thomas and Midttun, Atle. Energy Forecasting and Political Structure: Some Comparative Notes. *Baumgartner, T. and Midttun, A., eds.*, 1987, pp. 267–89. [G: OECD]

Baumgartner, Thomas and Midttun, Atle. Energy Forecasting: Science, Art, and Politics. *Baumgartner, T. and Midttun, A., eds.*, 1987, pp. 3–10.

Baumgartner, Thomas and Midttun, Atle. Modelling and Forecasting in Self-reactive Policy Contexts: Some Meta-methodological Comments. *Baumgartner, T. and Midttun, A., eds.*, 1987, pp. 290–308.

Baumgartner, Thomas and Midttun, Atle. The Socio-political Context of Energy Forecasting. *Baumgartner, T. and Midttun, A., eds.*, 1987, pp. 11–29.

Becker, William E. Building Theoretical Models. *Becker, W. E. and Walstad, W. B., eds.*, 1987, pp. 19–26.

Becker, William E. Measuring Intervention, Interaction, and Distribution Effects with Dummy Variables. *Becker, W. E. and Walstad, W. B., eds.*, 1987, pp. 27–49. [G: U.S.]

Belongia, Michael T. Predicting Interest Rates: A Comparison of Professional and Market-Based Forecasts. *Fed. Res. Bank St. Louis Rev.*, March 1987, *69*(3), pp. 9–15. [G: U.S.]

Bergman, Lars. Oil Price Increases and Macroeconomic Instability: General Equilibrium Calculations on the Basis of Swedish Data. *Maillet, P.; Hague, D. and Rowland, C., eds.*, 1987, pp. 208–25. [G: Sweden]

Berthélemy, Jean-Claude and Devezeaux de Lavergne, Jean-Guy. L'impact des chocs pétroliers. Une simulation rétrospective: 1973–1982. (Oil Shocks Effects: A Retrospective Simulation: 1973–1982. With English summary.) *Revue Écon.*, July 1987, *38*(4), pp. 877–96. [G: France]

Berthélemy, Jean-Claude and Devezeaux de Lavergne, Jean-Guy. Le modèle mélodie: un modèle énergétique de long terme pour l'écomomie française. (With English summary.) *Revue Écon. Polit.*, Sept.-Oct. 1987, *97*(5), pp. 649–72. [G: France]

Bessler, David A. and Babula, Ronald A. Forecasting Wheat Exports: Do Exchange Rates Matter? *J. Bus. Econ. Statist.*, July 1987, 5(3), pp. 397–406. **[G: U.S.]**

Blocher, Edward. A General Bayesian Model of the Misstatement in an Accounting Population. *Schultz, R. L., ed.*, 1987, pp. 23–60.

Bomhoff, Eduard J. and Koedijk, Kees G. A Portfolio Balance Model of Bilateral Exchange Rates. *Chrystal, K. A. and Sedgwick, R., eds.*, 1987, pp. 54–71.

Bond, Marian E. An Econometric Study of Primary Commodity Exports from Developing Country Regions to the World. *Int. Monet. Fund Staff Pap.*, June 1987, 34(2), pp. 191–227. **[G: Global]**

Boothe, Paul M. and Glassman, Debra A. Comparing Exchange Rate Forecasting Models: Accuracy versus Profitability. *Int. J. Forecasting*, 1987, 3(1), pp. 65–79. **[G: U.S.]**

Brakman, Steven and Joosten, Geert. On a Two Regime Model of the Dutch Export Market. *De Economist*, 1987, 135(3), pp. 279–97. **[G: Netherlands]**

Brenner, Menachem and Galai, Dan. On the Prediction of the Implied Standard Deviation. *Fabozzi, F. J., ed.*, 1987, pp. 167–77. **[G: U.S.]**

Broehl, John H. INDEPTH Level II Results. *Faruqui, A. and Broehl, J., eds.*, 1987, pp. 417–30. **[G: U.S.]**

Brown, Lawrence D.; Richardson, Gordon D. and Schwager, Steven J. An Information Interpretation of Financial Analyst Superiority in Forecasting Earnings. *J. Acc. Res.*, Spring 1987, 25(1), pp. 49–67. **[G: U.S.]**

Browne, F. X. Sluggish Quantity Adjustment in a Non-clearing Market—A Disequilibrium Econometric Application to the Loan Market. *J. Appl. Econometrics*, October 1987, 2(4), pp. 335–49. **[G: Ireland]**

Buchenroth, Sherree and Jennings, Robert. A Descriptive Analysis of the Time Series Behavior of Financial Analysts' Earnings Forecasts. *Quart. J. Bus. Econ.*, Summer 1987, 26(3), pp. 22–41. **[G: U.S.]**

Büttler, Hans-Jürg and Schips, Bernd. Equilibrium Exchange Rates in a Multi-country Model: An Econometric Study. *Weltwirtsch. Arch.*, 1987, 123(1), pp. 1–23. **[G: Global]**

Byers, J. D. and Peel, David A. Forecasting Livestock Slaughter: An Empirical Assessment of MLC Forecasts. *J. Agr. Econ.*, May 1987, 38(2), pp. 235–41. **[G: U.K.]**

Carlevaro, Fabrizio; Chaze, Jean-Paul and Spierer, Charles. Le déterminants de l'évolution annuelle de la consommation d'énergie en Suisse. (The Determinants of the Evolution of the Annual Energy Consumption in Switzerland. With English summary.) *Schweiz. Z. Volkswirtsch. Statist.*, March 1987, 123(1), pp. 1–22. **[G: Switzerland]**

Chan, K. Hung and Ho, Kwok. Forecasting Seasonal and Cyclical Financial Variables: The Wiener–Kolmogorov Method vs. the Box–Jenkins Method. *Lee, C. F., ed.*, 1987, pp. 103–18. **[G: U.S.]**

Chizhov, Y. A. Problems of Model Estimation of Long-term Economic Oscillations. *Vasko, T., ed.*, 1987, pp. 5–11.

Christodoulakis, Nicos and Weale, Martin. The Stock Exchange in a Macroeconometric Model. *Econ. Modelling*, July 1987, 4(3), pp. 341–54. **[G: U.K.]**

Clark, John A. A Vintage–Capital Simulation Model. *Freeman, C. and Soete, L., eds.*, 1987, pp. 86–98.

Clark, John A.; Patel, Pari and Soete, Luc. Future Employment Trends in UK Manufacturing Using a Capital–Vintage Simulation Model. *Freeman, C. and Soete, L., eds.*, 1987, pp. 99–118. **[G: U.K.]**

Cozanet, Eric and Gensollen, Michel. Les modèles de prévision de la demande téléphonique en France. (The Econometric Modeling of Telephone Access in France. With English summary.) *Revue Écon.*, March 1987, 38(2), pp. 257–305. **[G: France]**

Dickens, Rodney. Variability in Some Major UK Asset Markets since the Mid-1960s: An Application of the ARCH Model. *Goodhart, C.; Currie, D. and Llewellyn, D. T., eds.*, 1987, pp. 231–70. **[G: U.K.]**

Diefenbacher, Hans and Johnson, Jeffrey. Energy Forecasting in West Germany: Confrontation and Convergence. *Baumgartner, T. and Midttun, A., eds.*, 1987, pp. 61–84. **[G: W. Germany]**

Doukas, John. The Performance of Euromoney Currency Report Hedging Recommendations. *Appl. Econ.*, June 1987, 19(6), pp. 845–52. **[G: OECD]**

Dudley, Leonard. Explaining Forecasting Bias: The Case of Real Exchange Rate Variance. *Appl. Econ.*, September 1987, 19(9), pp. 1249–60. **[G: OECD]**

Eastwood, Robert. Forecasting Investment in the Medium Term. *Freeman, C. and Soete, L., eds.*, 1987, pp. 73–85.

Eliasson, Gunnar. Dynamic Micro–Macro Co-ordination, Technical Change and Trade. *Eliasson, G.*, 1987, pp. 81–118. **[G: Sweden]**

Elliott, J. Walter and Reichenstein, William. A Monetary Approach to Measuring Long-run Inflationary Expectations. *J. Econ. Bus.*, November 1987, 39(4), pp. 327–38. **[G: U.S.]**

Faerman, E. Iu. Coordinating Forecasts in Hierarchically Organized Units. *Matekon*, Spring 1987, 23(3), pp. 28–49.

Fair, Ray C. International Evidence on the Demand for Money. *Rev. Econ. Statist.*, August 1987, 69(3), pp. 473–80. **[G: OECD; LDCs]**

Feibig, Denzil G. and Bewley, Ronald. International Telecommunications Forecasting: An Investigation of Alternative Functional Forms. *Appl. Econ.*, July 1987, 19(7), pp. 949–60. **[G: Australia]**

Fuller, J. David. The Impact of $(US)15 Oil Prices on Canadian Energy Markets. *Can. Public Policy*, March 1987, 13(1), pp. 34–40. **[G: Canada]**

Fullerton, Howard N., Jr. Labor Force Projections: 1986 to 2000. *Mon. Lab. Rev.*, Sep-

tember 1987, *110*(9), pp. 19–29. [G: U.S.]
Garcia-Ferrer, Antonio, et al. Macroeconomic Forecasting Using Pooled International Data. *J. Bus. Econ. Statist.*, January 1987, *5*(1), pp. 53–67. [G: OECD]
Gentry, James A. and Lee, Cheng F. Financial Forecasting and the X-11 Model: Preliminary Evidence. *Lee, C. F., ed.*, 1987, pp. 27–49. [G: U.S.]
Golabi, Kamal. Assessing the Uranium Resources of the United States. *Schultz, R. L., ed.*, 1987, pp. 197–235. [G: U.S.]
Gray, Dale. Framework for Projecting Petroleum Product Demand Including the Effect of Energy Prices. *Pachauri, R. K., ed.*, 1987, pp. 1009–34.
Greenberger, Martin and Hogan, William W. Energy-Policy Modelling in the U.S.: Competing Societal Alternatives. *Baumgartner, T. and Midttun, A., eds.*, 1987, pp. 241–63. [G: U.S.]
Gregory, Allan W. and Sampson, Michael. Testing the Independence of Forecast Errors in the Forward Foreign Exchange Market Using Markov Chains: A Cross-Country Comparison. *Int. J. Forecasting*, 1987, *3*(1), pp. 97–113.
Grosfeld, Irena. Modeling Planners' Investment Behavior: Poland, 1956–1981. *J. Compar. Econ.*, June 1987, *11*(2), pp. 180–91. [G: Poland]
Haaland, Jan I., et al. VEMOD: A Ricardo–Heckscher–Ohlin–Jones Model of World Trade. *Scand. J. Econ.*, 1987, *89*(3), pp. 251–70. [G: Global]
Hall, S. G. An Empirical Model of the Exchange Rate Incorporating Rational Expectations. *Chrystal, K. A. and Sedgwick, R., eds.*, 1987, pp. 91–112.
Hall, S. G. and Henry, Samuel G. Brian. Wage Models. *Nat. Inst. Econ. Rev.*, February 1987, (119), pp. 70–75. [G: U.K.]
Hanson, Kenneth. On New Firm Entry and Macro Stability. *Eliasson, G., ed.*, 1987, pp. 63–72. [G: Sweden]
Hegrenes, Agnar and Norum, Leopold. Macromodel Calculations of Effects of Different Policy Instruments on Agricultural Output, Resource Use, and Farm Income. *Kettunen, L., ed.*, 1987, pp. 331–41. [G: Norway]
Hickman, Bert G. Macroeconomic Impacts of Energy Shocks and Policy Responses: A Structural Comparison of Fourteen Models. *Hickman, B. G.; Huntington, H. G. and Sweeney, J. L., eds.*, 1987, pp. 125–98. [G: U.S.]
Hickman, Bert G. Real Wages, Aggregate Demand, and Unemployment. *Europ. Econ. Rev.*, December 1987, *31*(8), pp. 1531–60. [G: U.S.]
Hickman, Bert G. and Huntington, Hillard G. EMF 7 Study Design. *Hickman, B. G.; Huntington, H. G. and Sweeney, J. L., eds.*, 1987, pp. 237–67. [G: U.S.]
Huntington, Hillard G. and Eschbach, Joseph E. Macroeconomic Models and Energy Policy Issues. *Hickman, B. G.; Huntington, H. G.*

and Sweeney, J. L., eds., 1987, pp. 199–236. [G: U.S.]
Husted, Steven and Kollintzas, Tryphon. Linear Rational Expectations Equilibrium Laws of Motion for Selected U.S. Raw Material Imports. *Int. Econ. Rev.*, October 1987, *28*(3), pp. 651–70. [G: U.S.]
Jennings, Robert. Unsystematic Security Price Movements, Management Earnings Forecasts, and Revisions in Consensus Analyst Earnings Forecasts. *J. Acc. Res.*, Spring 1987, *25*(1), pp. 90–110. [G: U.S.]
Jolly, L. O. and Wong, Gordon. Composite Forecasting: Some Empirical Results Using BAE Short-term Forecasts. *Rev. Marketing Agr. Econ.*, April 1987, *55*(1), pp. 51–73. [G: Australia]
Katzman, Martin T. Multiattribute Utility Elicitation Techniques and Public Policy: A Meta-analysis of Empirical Applications. *Schultz, R. L., ed.*, 1987, pp. 237–303. [G: U.S.]
Keepin, Bill and Wynne, Brian. The Roles of Models—What Can We Expect from Science? A Study of the IIASA World Energy Model. *Baumgartner, T. and Midttun, A., eds.*, 1987, pp. 33–57.
Keyzer, M. A. Consequences of Increased Foodgrain Production on the Bangladesh Economy. *Talman, D. and van der Laan, G., eds.*, 1987, pp. 59–83. [G: Bangladesh]
Kiss, Ferenc and Lefebvre, Bernard. Econometric Models of Telecommunications Firms. *Revue Écon.*, March 1987, *38*(2), pp. 307–73. [G: Canada]
Klein, Lawrence R.; Pauly, Peter H. and Petersen, Christian E. Empirical Aspects of Protectionism: Results from Project LINK. *Salvatore, D., ed.*, 1987, pp. 69–94. [G: Global]
Lahiri, Kajal and Zaporowski, Mark. More Flexible Use of Survey Data on Expectations in Macroeconomic Models. *J. Bus. Econ. Statist.*, January 1987, *5*(1), pp. 68–76. [G: U.S.]
Lau, Knud Lindholm. Electricity Forecasting in Denmark: Conflicts between Ministries and Utilities. *Baumgartner, T. and Midttun, A., eds.*, 1987, pp. 155–79. [G: Denmark]
Laumas, G. S. and Fackler, James S. Economic Instability and the Demand for Money, 1908–1980. *Eastern Econ. J.*, July-Sept. 1987, *13*(3), pp. 249–57. [G: U.S.]
Lee, Carie E. and Sugiyama, Samuel O. IN-DEPTH Case Study: Pulp and Paper Process Model. *Faruqui, A. and Broehl, J., eds.*, 1987, pp. 435–49. [G: U.S.]
Levy, Santiago. Short Run Responses to Foreign Exchange Crises. *J. Policy Modeling*, Winter 1987, *9*(4), pp. 577–614. [G: LDCs]
Li, Ze-Gao. China's Modernization and Manpower Base: Forecasts of Experts and Professionals in the Year 2000 in China—A Technical Note. *Dutta, M., ed. (II)*, 1987, pp. 45–52. [G: China]
Lunde, Tormod and Midttun, Atle. Electricity Forecasting in Norway: Administrative Centralism. *Baumgartner, T. and Midttun, A., eds.*, 1987, pp. 137–54. [G: Norway]

Machak, Joseph A.; Spivey, W. Allen and Wrobleski, William J. A Multiple Time Series Approach to Analyzing and Forecasting the Major French Monetary Aggregates. *Ann. Écon. Statist.*, Jan./Mar. 1987, (5), pp. 89–107. [G: France]

Maddala, G. S. Limited Dependent Variable Models Using Panel Data. *J. Human Res.*, Summer 1987, *22*(3), pp. 307–38.

Mahmud, S. F.; Robb, A. L. and Scarth, William M. On Estimating Dynamic Factor Demands. *J. Appl. Econometrics*, January 1987, *2*(1), pp. 69–75. [G: U.S.]

Mahmud, S. Fakre and Nishat, Mohammed. Short-term Forecasting: An Application of Box–Jenkins Methods. *Pakistan J. Appl. Econ.*, Summer 1987, *6*(1), pp. 61–65. [G: Pakistan]

de Man, Reinier. The Dutch Energy Scenario Game: Corporatist Search for Consensus. *Baumgartner, T. and Midttun, A., eds.*, 1987, pp. 85–109. [G: Netherlands]

de Man, Reinier. United Kingdom Energy Policy and Forecasting: Technocratic Conflict Resolution. *Baumgartner, T. and Midttun, A., eds.*, 1987, pp. 110–34. [G: U.K.]

Mathiesen, Lars. International Trade in Grains: Domestic Policies and Trade Impacts: Comment. *Scand. J. Econ.*, 1987, *89*(3), pp. 285–86. [G: Global]

McKenzie, George W. and Thomas, Steven H. Dominant Factors in Dollar–Sterling Exchange Rates Movements, 1965–1981. *Chrystal, K. A. and Sedgwick, R., eds.*, 1987, pp. 113–36. [G: U.S.; U.K.]

Mills, Terence C. and Stephenson, Michael J. A Time Series Forecasting System for the UK Money Supply. *Econ. Modelling*, July 1987, *4*(3), pp. 355–69. [G: U.S.]

Moen, Elizabeth W. Voodoo Forecasting: Technical, Political, and Ethical Issues Regarding the Projection of Local Population Growth. *Menard, S. W. and Moen, E. W., eds.*, 1987, *1984*, pp. 446–60. [G: U.S.]

Moxnes, Erling. Uncertainty in Future Oil Price Predictions. *Pachauri, R. K., ed.*, 1987, pp. 1105–21.

Murphy, Mary Zimmerman. The Importance of Sample Selection Bias in the Estimation of Medical Care Demand Equations. *Eastern Econ. J.*, Jan.-Mar. 1987, *13*(1), pp. 19–29. [G: U.S.]

Nordhaus, William D. Forecasting Efficiency: Concepts and Applications. *Rev. Econ. Statist.*, November 1987, *69*(4), pp. 667–74. [G: U.S.]

O'Mara, L. P. The Contribution of the Farm Sector to Annual Variations in Gross Domestic Product in Australia. *Econ. Rec.*, September 1987, *63*(182), pp. 255–69. [G: Australia]

Osten, James A. The Impact of $(US)15 Oil Prices on Canadian Energy Markets. *Can. Public Policy*, March 1987, *13*(1), pp. 26–33. [G: Canada]

Plourde, André. The Impact of $(US)15 Oil on the Canadian Economy: Evidence from the MACE Model. *Can. Public Policy*, March

1987, *13*(1), pp. 19–25. [G: Canada]

Pollins, Brian M. and Brecke, Peter K. The GLOBUS Model: Computer Simulation of Worldwide Political and Economic Development: International Economic Processes. *Bremer, S. A., ed.*, 1987, pp. 459–567. [G: Global]

Prat, Georges. Prévisions de la tendance du cours moyen des actions dans le cadre d'une formulation États-Unis, 1981–1984. (With English summary.) *Revue Écon. Polit.*, Sept.-Oct. 1987, *97*(5), pp. 575–91. [G: U.S.]

Puiseux, Louis. The Ups and Downs of Electricity Forecasting in France: Technocratic Elitism. *Baumgartner, T. and Midttun, A., eds.*, 1987, pp. 180–207. [G: France]

Rahman, Sultan Hafeez. A Macro-econometric Energy Policy Model for Oil Importing Developing Countries. *Pachauri, R. K., ed.*, 1987, pp. 1201–11. [G: Selected LDCs]

Rainford, P. and Masser, Ian. Population Forecasting and Urban Planning Practice: A Case Study. *Environ. Planning A*, November 1987, *19*(11), pp. 1463–75. [G: U.K.]

Ratick, Samuel J. and Kuby, Michael J. Regional Assessment of Coal Utilization Technologies Using Mathematical Programming. *Schultz, R. L., ed.*, 1987, pp. 155–95. [G: U.S.]

Reister, David B. Validating Allocation Functions in Energy Models: A Comment. *Energy J.*, January 1987, *8*(1), pp. 151–52.

Rios, Sandra Maria C. Polônia. Exportações brasileiras de produtos manufaturados: uma avaliação econométrica para o período 1964/84. (With English summary.) *Pesquisa Planejamento Econ.*, August 1987, *17*(2), pp. 299–332. [G: Brazil]

Robinson, John B. and Hooker, Clifford A. Future Imperfect: Energy Policy and Modelling in Canada Institutional Mandates and Constitutional Conflict. *Baumgartner, T. and Midttun, A., eds.*, 1987, pp. 211–40. [G: Canada]

Rogers, J. S. Some Long-term Impacts of $(US)15 Oil on Energy Policy and on Engineering R&D Policy: Results from the EMCAN Model. *Can. Public Policy*, March 1987, *13*(1), pp. 41–48. [G: Canada]

Roland, Gérard. Investment Growth Fluctuations in the Soviet Union: An Econometric Analysis. *J. Compar. Econ.*, June 1987, *11*(2), pp. 192–206. [G: U.S.S.R.]

Rosengren, Eric S. Forecasting Changes in Inflation Using the Treasury Bill Futures Market. *New Eng. Econ. Rev.*, Mar./Apr. 1987, pp. 41–48. [G: U.S.]

Salinas, Jose A. and Weyant, John P. A Comparison of Macroeconomic Model Structures. *Hickman, B. G.; Huntington, H. G. and Sweeney, J. L., eds.*, 1987, pp. 269–331. [G: U.S.]

Samson, Danny and Thomas, Howard. Linear Models as Decision Aids in Insurance Decision-making: The Case of Estimation of Automobile Insurance Claims. *Wright, G. and Ayton, P., eds.*, 1987, pp. 215–28.

Schroeder, Larry D. Forecasting Local Revenues and Expenditures. *Aronson, J. R. and*

Schwartz, E., eds., 1987, pp. 93–117.
[G: U.S.]

Shaikh, Abdul Hafeez and Zaman, Asad. Short-term Forecasting: An Application of Box–Jenkins Methods—A Reply. *Pakistan J. Appl. Econ.*, Winter 1987, 6(2), pp. 125–29.
[G: Pakistan]

Shortle, James S. and Willett, Keith D. A Computable Market Equilibrium Model with Markets for Transferable Discharge Permits. *Managerial Dec. Econ.*, December 1987, 8(4), pp. 263–70.

Silvestri, George T. and Lukasiewicz, John M. A Look at Occupational Employment Trends to the Year 2000. *Mon. Lab. Rev.*, September 1987, 110(9), pp. 46–63. [G: U.S.]

Sipos, Béla. Empirical Research and Forecasting Based on Hungarian and World Economic Data Series. *Vasko, T., ed.*, 1987, pp. 119–26.
[G: Hungary; Global]

Smith, V. Kerry and Hill, Lawrence J. On Straw Men, Free Parameters, and Validating Allocation Functions: A Reply [Validating Allocation Functions in Energy Models: An Experimental Methodology]. *Energy J.*, January 1987, 8(1), pp. 153–56.

Srinivasan, T. N. Population and Food. *Johnson, D. G. and Lee, R. D., eds.*, 1987, pp. 3–26.
[G: Global]

Stanislaw, Joe. The Need for All Available Sources of Energy. *Maillet, P.; Hague, D. and Rowland, C., eds.*, 1987, pp. 119–45.
[G: OECD; LDCs]

Stockman, Alan C. Economic Theory and Exchange Rate Forecasts. *Int. J. Forecasting*, 1987, 3(1), pp. 3–15.

Stockton, David J. and Glassman, James E. An Evaluation of the Forecast Performance of Alternative Models of Inflation. *Rev. Econ. Statist.*, February 1987, 69(1), pp. 108–17.
[G: U.S.]

Taylor, Stephen J. Forecasting the Volatility of Currency Exchange Rates. *Int. J. Forecasting*, 1987, 3(1), pp. 159–70. [G: U.S.]

Tomczyk, Paweł. CMEA Foreign Trade Forecast: 1985–1990. *Soviet E. Europ. Foreign Trade*, Fall 1987, 23(3), pp. 44–73. [G: CMEA]

Trela, Irene; Whalley, John and Wigle, Randall. International Trade in Grains: Domestic Policies and Trade Impacts. *Scand. J. Econ.*, 1987, 89(3), pp. 271–83. [G: Global]

Turner, David S.; Wallis, Kenneth F. and Whitley, John D. Evaluating Special Employment Measures with Macroeconometric Models. *Oxford Rev. Econ. Policy*, Autumn 1987, 3(3), pp. xxv–xxxvi. [G: U.K.]

Ursprung, Heinrich W. On the Value of Free Foreign-Exchange Forecasts. *Managerial Dec. Econ.*, June 1987, 8(2), pp. 161–65.
[G: OECD]

Vlek, Charles and Otten, Wilma. Judgmental Handling of Energy Scenarios: A Psychological Analysis and Experiment. *Wright, G. and Ayton, P., eds.*, 1987, pp. 267–89.

de Vos, Aart F. Forecasting the Daily Balance of the Dutch Giro. *Heijmans, R. and Neu-decker, H., eds.*, 1987, pp. 131–48.
[G: Netherlands]

Waverman, Leonard. The Impact of $(US)15 Oil: Good News and/or Bad News? *Can. Public Policy*, March 1987, 13(1), pp. 1–18.
[G: Canada]

Weller, Barry R. and Kurre, James A. Applicability of the Transfer Function Approach to Forecasting Employment Levels in Small Regions. *Ann. Reg. Sci.*, March 1987, 21(1), pp. 34–43. [G: U.S.]

Welsch, Heinz. An Aggregate Import Demand Model for Long-term Projections. *Jahr. Nationalökon. Statist.*, July 1987, 203(4), pp. 372–89. [G: OECD]

Winters, L. Alan. Models of Primary Price Indices. *Oxford Bull. Econ. Statist.*, August 1987, 49(3), pp. 307–22. [G: LDCs]

Wixon, Bernard; Bridges, Benjamin, Jr. and Pattison, David. Policy Analysis through Microsimulation: The STATS Model. *Soc. Sec. Bull.*, December 1987, 50(12), pp. 4–12. [G: U.S.]

Wolff, Christian C. P. Time-Varying Parameters and the Out-of-Sample Forecasting Performance of Structural Exchange Rate Models. *J. Bus. Econ. Statist.*, January 1987, 5(1), pp. 87–97. [G: U.S.; U.K.; Japan]

Zlatoper, Thomas J. Testing for Functional Form and Autocorrelation in the Analysis of Motor Vehicle Deaths. *Quart. Rev. Econ. Bus.*, Winter 1987, 27(4), pp. 6–17. [G: U.S.]

1324 Forecasting and Econometric Models: Theory and Methodology

Ahlburg, Dennis A. The Impact of Population Growth on Economic Growth in Developing Nations: The Evidence from Macroeconomic–Demographic Models. *Johnson, D. G. and Lee, R. D., eds.*, 1987, pp. 479–521. [G: LDCs]

Armstrong, J. Scott. Forecasting Methods for Conflict Situations. *Wright, G. and Ayton, P., eds.*, 1987, pp. 157–76.

Baillie, Richard T. and McMahon, Patrick C. Rational Forecasts in Models of the Term Structure of Interest Rates. *Goodhart, C.; Currie, D. and Llewellyn, D. T., eds.*, 1987, pp. 189–206.

Beach, Lee Roy; Christensen-Szalanski, Jay and Barnes, Valerie. Assessing Human Judgment: Has It Been Done, Can It Be Done, Should It Be Done? *Wright, G. and Ayton, P., eds.*, 1987, pp. 49–62.

Blanchard, Olivier Jean. Vector Autoregressions and Reality: Comment. *J. Bus. Econ. Statist.*, October 1987, 5(4), pp. 449–51. [G: U.S.]

Bohara, Alok K.; McNown, Robert F. and Batts, John T. A Re-evaluation of the Combination and Adjustment of Forecasts. *Appl. Econ.*, April 1987, 19(4), pp. 437–45. [G: U.S.]

Brehmer, Berndt. Social Judgment Theory and Forecasting. *Wright, G. and Ayton, P., eds.*, 1987, pp. 199–214.

Bremer, Stuart A. Evaluating GLOBUS. *Bremer, S. A., ed.*, 1987, pp. 723–76.

Bremer, Stuart A. The GLOBUS Model: Computer Simulation of Worldwide Political and Economic Development: Introduction. *Bremer, S. A., ed.*, 1987, pp. 1–38.

Brock, Horace W. Arrow–Bayes Equilibria: A New Theory of Price Forecasting. *Feiwel, G. R., ed. (I)*, 1987, pp. 559–96.

Budescu, David V. and Wallsten, Thomas S. Subjective Estimation of Precise and Vague Uncertainties. *Wright, G. and Ayton, P., eds.*, 1987, pp. 63–82.

Bunn, Derek. Expert Use of Forecasts: Bootstrapping and Linear Models. *Wright, G. and Ayton, P., eds.*, 1987, pp. 229–41.

Chiarini, Bruno. "Instrument Instability" in Large-Scale Econometric Models. *Giorn. Econ.*, Sept.-Oct. 1987, *46*(9–10), pp. 525–32.

Dewatripont, Mathias and Michel, Gilles. On Closure Rules, Homogeneity and Dynamics in Applied General Equilibrium Models. *J. Devel. Econ.*, June 1987, *26*(1), pp. 65–76.

Dixon, Peter B. On Using Applied General Equilibrium Models for Analysing Structural Change. *Pasinetti, L. and Lloyd, P., eds.*, 1987, pp. 149–58.

Domazlicky, Bruce R. A Comparison of Monthly Forecasting Methods for a Small Region. *Reg. Sci. Persp.*, 1987, *17*(2), pp. 3–17. [G: U.S.]

Evans, Jonathan St. B. T. Beliefs and Expectations as Causes of Judgmental Bias. *Wright, G. and Ayton, P., eds.*, 1987, pp. 31–47.

Farrell, Claude and Hall, William W., Jr. Tracking and Forecasting Local Economic Activity. *Rev. Reg. Stud.*, Fall 1987, *17*(3), pp. 31–36. [G: U.S.]

Geistauts, George A. and Eschenbach, Ted G. Bridging the Gap between Forecasting and Action. *Wright, G. and Ayton, P., eds.*, 1987, pp. 177–95.

Hasbrouck, Joel. A Note on Forecaster Discord and Consensus Prediction Error. *J. Bus. Econ. Statist.*, January 1987, *5*(1), pp. 151–54. [G: U.S.]

Heilemann, Ullrich and Neuhaus, Ralph. ARIMA-Modelle: Eine Alternative zu ökonometrischen Konjunkturmodellen? Eine empirische Untersuchung für das Jahr 1983. (ARIMA Models—An Alternative to Econometric Short-term Models? With English summary.) *Jahr. Nationalökon. Statist.*, March 1987, *203*(2), pp. 167–87. [G: W. Germany]

Hughes, Barry B. The GLOBUS Model: Computer Simulation of Worldwide Political and Economic Development: Domestic Economic Processes. *Bremer, S. A., ed.*, 1987, pp. 39–157. [G: Global]

Jolly, L. O. and Wong, Gordon. Composite Forecasting: Some Empirical Results Using BAE Short-term Forecasts. *Rev. Marketing Agr. Econ.*, April 1987, *55*(1), pp. 51–73. [G: Australia]

Jungermann, Helmut and Thüring, Manfred. The Use of Mental Models for Generating Scenarios. *Wright, G. and Ayton, P., eds.*, 1987, pp. 245–66.

Keen, Howard, Jr. Economists and Their Forecasts: Have the Projections Been That Bad? *Bus. Econ.*, January 1987, *22*(1), pp. 37–40. [G: U.S.]

Keyfitz, Nathan. The Social and Political Context of Population Forecasting. *Alonso, W. and Starr, P., eds.*, 1987, pp. 235–58. [G: U.S.]

Lock, Andy. Integrating Group Judgments in Subjective Forecasts. *Wright, G. and Ayton, P., eds.*, 1987, pp. 109–27.

McNees, Stephen K. Consensus Forecasts: Tyranny of the Majority? *New Eng. Econ. Rev.*, Nov./Dec. 1987, pp. 15–21. [G: U.S.]

Odum, Howard T. Models for National, International, and Global Systems Policy. *Braat, L. C. and van Lierop, W. F. J., eds.*, 1987, pp. 203–51.

Oliver, Robert M. Bayesian Forecasting with Stable Seasonal Patterns. *J. Bus. Econ. Statist.*, January 1987, *5*(1), pp. 77–85.

Parenté, Frederick J. and Anderson-Parenté, Janet K. Delphi Inquiry Systems. *Wright, G. and Ayton, P., eds.*, 1987, pp. 129–56. [G: U.S.]

Parke, William R. Macroeconometric Model Comparison and Evaluation Techniques: A Practical Appraisal. *J. Appl. Econometrics*, April 1987, *2*(2), pp. 133–44. [G: U.S.]

Peña, Daniel. Observaciones influyentes en modelos econométricos. (With English summary.) *Invest. Econ.*, January 1987, *11*(1), pp. 3–24. [G: OECD]

Phillips, Lawrence D. On the Adequacy of Judgmental Forecasts. *Wright, G. and Ayton, P., eds.*, 1987, pp. 11–30.

Phillips, Robert F. Composite Forecasting: An Integrated Approach and Optimality Reconsidered. *J. Bus. Econ. Statist.*, July 1987, *5*(3), pp. 389–95. [G: U.S.]

Runkle, David E. Vector Autoregressions and Reality: Reply. *J. Bus. Econ. Statist.*, October 1987, *5*(4), pp. 454. [G: U.S.]

Runkle, David E. Vector Autoregressions and Reality. *J. Bus. Econ. Statist.*, October 1987, *5*(4), pp. 437–42. [G: U.S.]

van Schaik, A. B. T. M. and Mulder, R. J. On Superimposed Recurrent Cycles. *J. Econ. (Z. Nationalökon.)*, 1987, *47*(3), pp. 253–72. [G: U.S.]

Scott, M. J. and Goldsmith, Oliver Scott. Assessing Regional Econometric Models: A Discussion and Application. *Ann. Reg. Sci.*, March 1987, *21*(1), pp. 1–21. [G: U.S.]

Sims, Christopher A. Vector Autoregressions and Reality: Comment. *J. Bus. Econ. Statist.*, October 1987, *5*(4), pp. 443–49. [G: U.S.]

Sklarz, Michael A.; Miller, Norman G. and Gersch, Will. Forecasting Using Long-Order Autoregressive Processes: An Example Using Housing Starts. *Amer. Real Estate Urban Econ. Assoc. J.*, Winter 1987, *15*(4), pp. 374–88. [G: U.S.]

Stekler, H. O. Who Forecasts Better? [Economic Forecasts and Their Assessment]. *J. Bus. Econ. Statist.*, January 1987, *5*(1), pp. 155–58. [G: U.S.]

Taylor, Mark P. On Long-run Solutions to Dynamic Econometric Equations under Rational

Expectations [A Cautionary Note on the Interpretation of Long-run Equilibrium Solutions in Conventional Macro Models]. *Econ. J.*, March 1987, 97(385), pp. 215–18.

Tikhomirov, N. P. Measuring the Accuracy of Population Forecasts. *Matekon*, Winter 1987-88, 24(2), pp. 49–68. **[G: U.S.S.R.]**

Walstad, William B. Applying Two-Stage Least Squares. *Becker, W. E. and Walstad, W. B., eds.*, 1987, pp. 111–34.

Watson, Mark W. Vector Autoregressions and Reality: Comment. *J. Bus. Econ. Statist.*, October 1987, 5(4), pp. 451–53. **[G: U.S.]**

Webb, Roy H. The Irrelevance of Tests for Bias in Series of Macroeconomic Forecasts. *Fed. Res. Bank Richmond Econ. Rev.*, Nov./Dec. 1987, 73(6), pp. 3–9. **[G: U.S.]**

Wright, George and Ayton, Peter. Judgmental Forecasting: Introduction. *Wright, G. and Ayton, P., eds.*, 1987, pp. 1–8.

Wright, George and Ayton, Peter. The Psychology of Forecasting. *Wright, G. and Ayton, P., eds.*, 1987, pp. 83–105.

Zarnowitz, Victor and Lambros, Louis A. Consensus and Uncertainty in Economic Prediction. *J. Polit. Econ.*, June 1987, 95(3), pp. 591–621. **[G: U.S.]**

133 General Outlook and Stabilization Theories and Policies

1330 General Outlook and General Economic Policy Discussions

Arndt, Sven W. The Role of Domestic Policy in Addressing Trade Problems. *Barfield, C. E. and Makin, J. H., eds.*, 1987, pp. 39–42. **[G: U.S.]**

Baka, Władysław. The Reform Has Taken Root. *Soviet E. Europ. Foreign Trade*, Fall 1987, 23(3), pp. 124–35. **[G: Poland]**

Bazdresch P., Carlos. World Economic Outlook and Prospects for Latin America: Comment. *Martirena-Mantel, A. M., ed.*, 1987, pp. 51–55. **[G: Latin America]**

Berger, Suzanne. French Business from Transition to Transition. *Ross, G.; Hoffmann, S. and Malzacher, S., eds.*, 1987, pp. 187–98. **[G: France]**

Bergsten, C. Fred. Economic Imbalances and World Politics. *Foreign Aff.*, Spring 1987, 65(4), pp. 770–94. **[G: Global]**

Biewener, Carole. Class and Socialist Politics in France. *Rev. Radical Polit. Econ.*, Summer 1987, 19(2), pp. 61–76. **[G: France]**

Blanchard, Olivier Jean. Reaganomics. *De Menil, G. and Portes, R., eds.*, 1987, pp. 15–48. **[G: U.S.]**

Branson, William H. Reaganomics: Discussion. *De Menil, G. and Portes, R., eds.*, 1987, pp. 48–52. **[G: U.S.]**

Brittan, Samuel. The Role of Domestic U.S. Economy and Financial Policy in the World Economy: Cures That Could Be Worse Than the Disease. *Visser, H. and Schoor, E., eds.*, 1987, pp. 125–37. **[G: U.S.; Global]**

Britton, Andrew; Gurney, Andrew and Herbert, Rhys. The Home Economy. *Nat. Inst. Econ. Rev.*, February 1987, (119), pp. 6–16. **[G: U.K.]**

Brown, Lester R. and Wolf, Edward C. Charting a Sustainable Course. *Brown, L. R., et al.*, 1987, pp. 196–213. **[G: Global]**

Brunner, Karl. The Limits of Economic Policy. *Pejovich, S., ed.*, 1987, 1985, pp. 33–52.

Bruno, Michael. Stagflation in the Industrial Countries: An Updated Overview. *Hitotsubashi J. Econ.*, October 1987, 27, pp. 57–74. **[G: OECD]**

Budd, Alan. The Conservative Revolution: A Roundtable Discussion. *De Menil, G. and Portes, R., eds.*, 1987, pp. 185–91. **[G: Europe; U.S.]**

Cardoso, Eliana A. Latin America's Debt: Which Way Now? *Challenge*, May/June 1987, 30(2), pp. 11–17. **[G: Latin America]**

Chandhoke, Neera. The Apartheid State: Crisis of Legitimacy. *Ali, S. S. and Gupta, A., eds.*, 1987, pp. 146–63. **[G: S. Africa]**

Chandler, William U. Designing Sustainable Economies. *Brown, L. R., et al.*, 1987, pp. 177–95. **[G: Global]**

Chernomas, Robert. Is Supply-Side Economics Rational for Capital? *Rev. Radical Polit. Econ.*, Fall 1987, 19(3), pp. 1–17. **[G: U.S.]**

Cho, Lee-Jay. ASEAN: The Challenges Ahead. *Martin, L. G., ed.*, 1987, pp. 211–17. **[G: ASEAN]**

Clancy, Peter. The Politics of Economic Policy. *Can. Public Policy*, June 1987, 13(2), pp. 232–37. **[G: Canada]**

Clements, Michael; Walker, John and Rossi, Vanessa. The UK Economy: Analysis and Prospects. *Oxford Rev. Econ. Policy*, Summer 1987, 3(2), pp. xxii–xxxii. **[G: U.K.]**

Cornwall, John. Structural Change and Economic Breakdown. *Écon. Appl.*, 1987, 40(4), pp. 655–80.

Corrigan, E. Gerald. International Economic Prospects: A Case Study in Mutuality. *Fed. Res. Bank New York Quart. Rev.*, Winter 1987-88, 12(4), pp. 1–5. **[G: U.S.]**

Currie, David. Reaganomics: Discussion. *De Menil, G. and Portes, R., eds.*, 1987, pp. 52–53. **[G: U.S.]**

Danthine, Jean-Pierre and Lambelet, Jean-Christian. The Swiss Case. *De Menil, G. and Portes, R., eds.*, 1987, pp. 147–74. **[G: Switzerland]**

Day, Graham and Rees, Gareth. Images of Contemporary Wales: Researching Social and Economic Change. *Day, G. and Rees, G., eds.*, 1987, pp. 1–6. **[G: U.K.]**

Dell, Sidney and Lawrence, Roger. The Balance of Payments Adjustment Process in Developing Countries. *Dell, S., ed., Pt. 1*, 1987, 1980, pp. 1–154. **[G: Global]**

Didier, Michel. Micro Initiatives and Macroeconomic Adjustments in the Industrialised Countries. *Pasinetti, L. and Lloyd, P., eds.*, 1987, pp. 159–75. **[G: Global]**

Dixon, Peter B. and Parmenter, Brian R. Foreign

Debts, the Exchange Rate and Australia's Economic Prospects. *Australian Econ. Rev.*, Third Quarter 1987, (79), pp. 36–42. **[G: Australia]**

Dollery, B. E. and Wallis, J. Economic Reality and Economic Policy in South Africa: Foundation for Confidence or Cause for Alarm? *J. Stud. Econ. Econometrics*, July 1987, *11*(2), pp. 1–18. **[G: S. Africa]**

Dore, Ronald. How Fragile a Super State? *[Penrose, E. F.]*, 1987, pp. 83–110. **[G: Japan]**

Dornbusch, Rudiger. Prosperity or Price Stability. *Oxford Rev. Econ. Policy*, Autumn 1987, *3*(3), pp. 9–19. **[G: OECD]**

Duisenberg, W. F. The Financial Conditions for Sustaining the Present Recovery. *Visser, H. and Schoor, E.*, eds., 1987, pp. 47–55. **[G: Global]**

Duwendag, Dieter. Towards Sustainable Growth: The 1986/87 Report of the German Council of Economic Experts. *J. Inst. Theoretical Econ.*, September 1987, *143*(3), pp. 497–504.

Ferleger, Lou and Mandle, Jay R. Democracy and Productivity in the Future American Economy. *Rev. Radical Polit. Econ.*, Winter 1987, *19*(4), pp. 1–15. **[G: U.S.]**

Fratianni, Michele. Italy in the Eighties: Opportunities and Prospects. *Rev. Econ. Cond. Italy*, May-August 1987, (2), pp. 253–77. **[G: Italy]**

Fritsch, Winston. World Economic Outlook and Prospects for Latin America: Comment. *Martirena-Mantel, A. M.*, ed., 1987, pp. 55–59. **[G: Latin America]**

Galbraith, James K. The Case for Shock Treatment. *Challenge*, July/Aug. 1987, *30*(3), pp. 4–10. **[G: U.S.]**

Garrett, John R. Macroeconomic Policy and History. *Cambridge J. Econ.*, December 1987, *11*(4), pp. 375–92. **[G: U.S.; U.K.]**

George, Kenneth D. and Mainwaring, Lynn. The Welsh Economy in the 1980s. *Day, G. and Rees, G.*, eds., 1987, pp. 7–37. **[G: U.K.]**

Giersch, Herbert. Economic Policies in the Age of Schumpeter. *Europ. Econ. Rev.*, Feb./Mar. 1987, *31*(1/2), pp. 35–52. **[G: OECD]**

Gleysteen, William H., Jr. and Romberg, Alan D. Korea: Asian Paradox. *Foreign Aff.*, Summer 1987, *65*(5), pp. 1037–54. **[G: S. Korea]**

Gordon, Robert J. U.S. Fiscal Deficits and the World Imbalance of Payments. *Hitotsubashi J. Econ.*, October 1987, *27*, pp. 7–41. **[G: U.S.]**

Gramley, Lyle E. The Economic and Financial Outlook. *J. Bus. Econ. Statist.*, January 1987, *5*(1), pp. 1–4. **[G: U.S.]**

Greenspan, Alan. The Great Malaise. *Challenge*, Special Issue 1987, *30*(6), pp. 11–14. **[G: U.S.]**

Ground, Richard L. Agricultural Development and Macroeconomic Balance in Latin America: An Overview of Some Basic Policy Issues. *CEPAL Rev.*, December 1987, (33), pp. 29–38. **[G: Latin America]**

Gupta, Anirudha. Africa: Dimensions of the Economic Crisis: Introduction. *Ali, S. S. and Gupta, A.*, eds., 1987, pp. 1–14. **[G: Africa]**

Gupta, Vijay. Dialectics of Southern African Crisis: Basic Contradictions. *Ali, S. S. and Gupta, A.*, eds., 1987, pp. 164–81. **[G: Southern Africa]**

Hämäläinen, Timo. International Outlook: Recovery in the Medium Term. *Vartia, P.*, et al., 1987, pp. 49–59. **[G: OECD]**

Harberger, Arnold C. A Primer on the Chilean Economy: 1973–83. *Connolly, M. and González-Vega, C.*, eds., 1987, pp. 219–27. **[G: Chile]**

Hauslohner, Peter. Gorbachev's Social Contract. *Soviet Econ.*, Jan.-Mar. 1987, *3*(1), pp. 54–89. **[G: U.S.S.R.]**

Heike, Hans-Dieter and Blazejczak, Jürgen. Brauchen wir eine andere Wirtschaftspolitik zur Bekämpfung der Arbeitslosigkeit? Kommentar zu einer rhetorischen Übung des Sachverständigenrates zur Begutachtung der gesamtwirtschaftlichen Entwicklung. (Do We Need a Different Economic Policy for Fighting Unemployment? With English summary.) *Konjunkturpolitik*, 1987, *33*(3), pp. 127–45. **[G: W. Germany]**

Heller, Walter W. Can There Be Another Crash? *Challenge*, Special Issue 1987, *30*(6), pp. 6–10. **[G: U.S.]**

Hellwig, Martin and Neumann, Manfred J. M. Economic Policy in Germany: Was There a Turnaround? *De Menil, G. and Portes, R.*, eds., 1987, pp. 103–40. **[G: W. Germany]**

Helpman, Elhanan. Mrs Thatcher's Economic Policies 1979–87: Discussion. *De Menil, G. and Portes, R.*, eds., 1987, pp. 96–98. **[G: U.S.]**

Hernandez, Carolina G. The Philippines: Implications for Regional Order. *Martin, L. G.*, ed., 1987, pp. 170–81. **[G: Philippines; ASEAN]**

Hill, Hal. Survey of Recent Developments. *Bull. Indonesian Econ. Stud.*, December 1987, *23*(3), pp. 1–33. **[G: Indonesia]**

Hobohm, Sarwar O. H. Survey of Recent Developments. *Bull. Indonesian Econ. Stud.*, August 1987, *23*(2), pp. 1–37. **[G: Indonesia]**

van der Hoeven, Rolph and Richards, P. J. Depression and Adjustment. *International Labour Office.*, 1987, pp. 1–19. **[G: OECD; LDCs]**

Hoffmann, Stanley. The Mitterrand Experiment: Continuity and Change in Modern France: Conclusion. *Ross, G.; Hoffmann, S. and Malzacher, S.*, eds., 1987, pp. 341–53. **[G: France]**

Honkapohja, Seppo. The Swiss Case: Discussion. *De Menil, G. and Portes, R.*, eds., 1987, pp. 175–77. **[G: Switzerland]**

Horne, Jocelyn P. and Masson, Paul R. International Economic Cooperation and Policy Coordination. *Finance Develop.*, June 1987, *24*(2), pp. 28–31. **[G: OECD]**

Howitt, Peter. Disinflation and Exchange Rate Stabilization: Canada, 1980–1985. *J. Policy Modeling*, Winter 1987, *9*(4), pp. 637–59. **[G: Canada]**

Hughes Hallett, Andrew J. The Impact of Interdependence on Economic Policy Design: The Case of the USA, EEC and Japan. *Econ.*

Modelling, July 1987, *4*(3), pp. 377–96.
[G: U.S.; EEC; Japan]

Hughes, Kent. Transferring Authority to the Trade Representative. *Barfield, C. E. and Makin, J. H., eds.,* 1987, pp. 17–18. [G: U.S.]

Jenkins, Simon. Reflections on a Siege Economy. *Managerial Dec. Econ.,* March 1987, *8*(1), pp. 11–14. [G: S. Africa]

Jezioranski, Tomasz. The Economic Reform Commission Assesses Three Years of the New System. *Soviet E. Europ. Foreign Trade,* Fall 1987, *23*(3), pp. 116–23. [G: Poland]

Jungenfelt, Karl. Structural Adjustment in Industrially Advanced Countries: Discussion and Conclusions. *Pasinetti, L. and Lloyd, P., eds.,* 1987, pp. 177–85. [G: MDCs]

Kaldor, Nicholas. Economic Prospects of the 1980s. *de Cecco, M. and Fitoussi, J.-P., eds.,* 1987, pp. 326–43. [G: Global]

Karl, Kurt. Long-term U.S. Economic Outlook. *Faruqui, A. and Broehl, J., eds.,* 1987, pp. 127–37. [G: U.S.]

Kindleberger, Charles P. 1929: Ten Lessons for Today. *Challenge,* Special Issue 1987, *30*(6), pp. 15–18.

Klein, Lawrence R. Asia-Pacific Economies: Challenges and Prospects. *Dutta, M., ed. (I),* 1987, pp. 3–8. [G: Asia-Pacific]

Klein, Lawrence R. The Changing World Economic Situation and Its Impact on International Trade. *Rodriguez, R. M., ed.,* 1987, pp. 37–53. [G: U.S.; Global]

Kuntjoro-Jakti, Dorodjatun. The Global Crisis of the 1980s and Indonesia's Response. *Hitotsubashi J. Econ.,* October 1987, *27*, pp. 101–13.

Kutscher, Ronald E. Overview and Implications of the Projections to 2000. *Mon. Lab. Rev.,* September 1987, *110*(9), pp. 3–9. [G: U.S.]

Lancelot, Alain and Lancelot, Marie-Thérèse. The Evolution of the French Electorate: 1981–86. *Ross, G.; Hoffmann, S. and Malzacher, S., eds.,* 1987, pp. 77–99. [G: France]

Lanyi, Anthony. World Economic Outlook and Prospects for Latin America. *Martirena-Mantel, A. M., ed.,* 1987, pp. 26–50.
[G: Latin America]

Lawrence, Robert Z. Is Deindustrialization a Myth? [The Myth of U.S. Deindustrialization]. *Staudohar, P. D. and Brown, H. E.,* 1987, *1983,* pp. 25–40. [G: U.S.; OECD]

Lehmann, Jean-Pierre. Variations on a Pan-Asianist Theme: The 'Special Relationship' between Japan and Thailand. *[Penrose, E. F.],* 1987, pp. 178–201. [G: Japan; Thailand]

Lekachman, Robert. America's Morning after Reagan. *Challenge,* Mar./Apr. 1987, *30*(1), pp. 34–44. [G: U.S.]

Lisi, E. and Poscetti, M. Highlights of the 20th CENSIS Report on Italy's Social Situation. *Rev. Econ. Cond. Italy,* Jan.-Apr. 1987, (1), pp. 81–90. [G: Italy]

Liu, Guoguang, et al. Economic Reform and Macroeconomic Management: Commentaries on the International Conference on Macroeconomic Management. *Chinese Econ. Stud.,* Spring 1987, *20*(3), pp. 3–45. [G: China]

López Cordovez, Luis. Crisis, Adjustment Policies and Agriculture. *CEPAL Rev.,* December 1987, (33), pp. 7–28. [G: Latin America]

Malamud, Bernard. Ominous Parallels...Heartening Differences. *Challenge,* Mar./Apr. 1987, *30*(1), pp. 59–60. [G: OECD]

Malinvaud, Edmond. The Legacy of European Stagflation. *Europ. Econ. Rev.,* Feb./Mar. 1987, *31*(1/2), pp. 53–65. [G: W. Europe]

Mandelbaum, Thomas B. A Review of the Eighth District's Business Economy in 1986. *Fed. Res. Bank St. Louis Rev.,* April 1987, *69*(4), pp. 22–31. [G: U.S.]

Marston, Richard C. Japanese–U.S. Current Accounts and Exchange Rates before and after the G5 Agreement: Discussion. *Sato, R. and Wachtel, P., eds.,* 1987, pp. 152–56.
[G: Japan; U.S.]

Martínez, Astrid. Colombia: Effects of the Adjustment Policy on Agricultural Development. *CEPAL Rev.,* December 1987, (33), pp. 91–105. [G: Colombia]

Martirena-Mantel, Ana María. External Debt, Savings, and Growth in Latin America: Introduction and Overview. *Martirena-Mantel, A. M., ed.,* 1987, pp. 1–25. [G: Latin America]

Matejko, Alexander J. The Fate of Canada: Between Underdevelopment and Postindustrialism. *Indian J. Quant. Econ.,* 1987, *3*(1), pp. 67–86. [G: Canada]

Matthews, Kent G. P. and Minford, Patrick. Mrs Thatcher's Economic Policies 1979–87. *De Menil, G. and Portes, R., eds.,* 1987, pp. 57–92. [G: U.K.]

McCracken, Paul W. Reluctant to Prosper. *Bus. Econ.,* January 1987, *22*(1), pp. 7–12.
[G: U.S.; W. Europe; Japan]

McDonald, Daina and Dixon, Peter B. The Australian Economy in 1987–88 and 1988–89. *Australian Econ. Rev.,* Fourth Quarter 1987, (80), pp. 3–30. [G: Australia]

Melkote, Rama S. Zaire: Crisis of Neo-colonialism. *Ali, S. S. and Gupta, A., eds.,* 1987, pp. 103–13. [G: Zaire]

Miller, Marcus H. Economic Policy in Germany: Was There a Turnaround? Discussion. *De Menil, G. and Portes, R., eds.,* 1987, pp. 143–44. [G: W. Germany]

de Miramon, J. Countertrade: A Disruptive Phenomenon in International Trade. *Visser, H. and Schoor, E., eds.,* 1987, pp. 197–205.
[G: Global]

Miyawaki, T. The Pacific Basin, Recent Economic and Financial Developments. *Visser, H. and Schoor, E., eds.,* 1987, pp. 263–80. [G: Asia-Pacific]

Mjøset, Lars. Nordic Economic Policies in the 1970s and 1980s. *Int. Organ.,* Summer 1987, *41*(3), pp. 403–56. [G: Norway; Finland; Denmark; Iceland]

Müller, Anton P. Reaganomics. Eine keynesianische Interrpretation. (Reaganomics: A Keynesian Interpretation. With English summary.) *Konjunkturpolitik,* 1987, *33*(2), pp. 71–98. [G: OECD]

Nickell, Stephen J. Mrs Thatcher's Economic Policies 1979–87: Discussion. *De Menil, G. and Portes, R., eds.*, 1987, pp. 93–95. **[G: U.K.]**

Nováček, Vladimír. Czechoslovakia in the International Division of Labour. *Czech. Econ. Digest.*, October 1987, (7), pp. 61–68.
[G: Czechoslovakia]

Okimoto, Daniel I. and Saxonhouse, Gary R. The Political Economy of Japan: Technology and the Future of the Economy. *Yamamura, K. and Yasuba, Y., eds.*, 1987, pp. 385–419.
[G: Japan]

Osaki, Kazumasa. End of an Era: OPEC's Temporary Retreat. *Finn, R. B., ed.*, 1987, pp. 119–34. **[G: OPEC; U.S.; Japan]**

Pangestu, Mari. Survey of Recent Developments. *Bull. Indonesian Econ. Stud.*, April 1987, 23(1), pp. 1–39. **[G: Indonesia]**

Patrick, Hugh T. Japan and the United States Today: Exchange Rates, Macroeconomic Policies, and Financial Market Innovations: Concluding Comments. *Patrick, H. T. and Tachi, R., eds.*, 1987, pp. 209–13. **[G: Japan; U.S.]**

Pollard, Sidney. Stagflation, Fiscal Deficits and Balance of Payments—Great Britain and Germany. *Hitotsubashi J. Econ.*, October 1987, 27, pp. 42–56. **[G: U.K.; W. Germany]**

Potáč, Svatopluk. The Law on the State Plan of Development of the National Economy of the Czechoslovak Socialist Republic in the 8th Five-Year Plan (1986–1990). *Czech. Econ. Digest.*, Apr.-May 1987, (3), pp. 4–26.
[G: Czechoslovakia]

Reinhardt, Uwe E. The Political Economy of "Feeling Good": True Confession of a Supply-Sider. *Aussenwirtschaft*, December 1987, 42(4), pp. 443–69. **[G: U.S.]**

Rémond, René. The Right as Opposition and Future Majority. *Ross, G.; Hoffmann, S. and Malzacher, S., eds.*, 1987, pp. 128–39.
[G: France]

Richardson, Richard W. and Ahmed, Osman S. Challenge for Africa's Private Sector. *Challenge*, Jan./Feb. 1987, 29(6), pp. 16–25.
[G: Africa]

Rivlin, Alice M. Economics and the Political Process. *Amer. Econ. Rev.*, March 1987, 77(1), pp. 1–10. **[G: U.S.]**

Roca, Sergio G. Planners in Wonderland: A Reply [State Enterprises in Cuba under the New System of Planning and Management]. *Mesa-Lago, C., ed.*, 1987, pp. 167–72. **[G: Cuba]**

Rosholt, A. M. Has South Africa a Free Enterprise Future? *Managerial Dec. Econ.*, March 1987, 8(1), pp. 81–84. **[G: S. Africa]**

Ross, George. The Mitterrand Experiment: Continuity and Change in Modern France: Introduction. *Ross, G.; Hoffmann, S. and Malzacher, S., eds.*, 1987, pp. 3–14. **[G: France]**

Rostow, Walt W. The World Economy since 1945: A Stylized Historical Analysis. *Rostow, W. W.*, 1987, *1985*, pp. 19–48. **[G: Global]**

Samuelson, Paul A. Evaluating Reaganomics. *Challenge*, Special Issue 1987, 30(6), pp. 58–65. **[G: U.S.]**

Saraceno, Pasquale. La questione meridionale nel 1987. (The "Southern Question" Today. With

English summary.) *Ricerche Econ.*, Apr.-June 1987, 41(2), pp. 163–73. **[G: Italy]**

Saulnier, Raymond J. The President's Economic Report: A Critique. *J. Portfol. Manage.*, Summer 1987, 13(4), pp. 83–84. **[G: U.S.]**

Scarth, William M. Unemployment, Inflation and Deficits: A Review Essay. *Can. Public Policy*, June 1987, 13(2), pp. 222–31. **[G: Canada]**

Schapers, J. J. Success Factors for the Next Ten Years: An Approach to the Development of International Trading. *Visser, H. and Schoor, E., eds.*, 1987, pp. 291–99. **[G: Global]**

Scheide, Joachim. Die deutsche Konjunkturpolitik in den fünfziger Jahren—Beginn der Globalsteuerung? (German Economic Policy in the Fifties—Beginning of Demand Management? With English summary.) *Konjunkturpolitik*, 1987, 33(5), pp. 243–67. **[G: W. Germany]**

Schenkel, Marina. La misurazione del conflitto: necessità di una teoria e insufficienza delle formulazioni esistenti. (Gauging the Conflict: The Necessity of a Theory and the Inadequacy of the Existing Formulae. With English summary.) *Econ. Lavoro*, Apr.-June 1987, 21(2), pp. 87–102. **[G: Italy]**

Schick, Irvin C. and Tonak, E. Ahmet. Turkey in Transition: Conclusion. *Schick, I. C. and Tonak, E. A., eds.*, 1987, pp. 365–78.
[G: Turkey]

Schwarz, Gerhard. Die schwierige Geburt: Neun Monate bürgerliche Regierung in Frankreich. Eine Zwischenbilanz aus liberaler Sicht. (A Difficult Start: Nine Months of Conservative Government in France: An Assessment from a Liberal Point of View. With English summary.) *Aussenwirtschaft*, April 1987, 42(1), pp. 85–108. **[G: France]**

Scitovsky, Tibor. Growth in the Affluent Society. *Lloyds Bank Rev.*, January 1987, (163), pp. 1–14. **[G: U.K.; U.S.]**

Selowsky, Marcelo. Adjustment in the 1980s: An Overview of Issues. *Finance Develop.*, June 1987, 24(2), pp. 11–14. **[G: LDCs]**

Shields, Roger E. The Export–Import Bank: A Changing Mission? *Rodriguez, R. M., ed.*, 1987, pp. 157–65. **[G: U.S.]**

Shimizu, Hikaru. Long-run Economic Policy: A Positive Appraisal. *Finn, R. B., ed.*, 1987, pp. 31–43. **[G: U.S.; Japan]**

Shishido, Shuntaro. Remarks on Growth, Inflation and Employment. *Pasinetti, L. and Lloyd, P., eds.*, 1987, pp. 301–03. **[G: Global]**

Silk, Leonard. The United States and the World Economy. *Foreign Aff.*, 1987, 65(3), pp. 458–76. **[G: Global]**

Skok, Charles D. Key Theological Positions Underlying the Bishops' Pastoral Letter on Catholic Social Teaching and the U.S. Economy. *Int. J. Soc. Econ.*, 1987, 14(1), pp. 3–15.
[G: U.S.]

Sloan, Judith and Wooden, Mark. The Australian Labour Market, December 1987. *Australian Bull. Lab.*, December 1987, 14(1), pp. 295–320. **[G: Australia]**

Solow, Robert M. The Conservative Revolution: A Roundtable Discussion. *De Menil, G. and*

Portes, R., eds., 1987, pp. 181–85.
[G: Europe; U.S.]
Sommaruga, Cornelio. Die schweizerische Aussenwirtschaftspolitik im wirtschaftspolitischen Spannungsfeld. (Swiss International Economic Policy Options and Implications. With English summary.) *Aussenwirtschaft*, April 1987, *42*(1), pp. 23–40. **[G: Switzerland]**
Srivastava, P. N. Africa: Dimensions of the Economic Crisis: Focus on Issues. *Ali, S. S. and Gupta, A., eds.*, 1987, pp. 17–19. **[G: Africa]**
Stein, Herbert. The United States Economy in Transition. *Visser, H. and Schoor, E., eds.*, 1987, pp. 111–23. **[G: U.S.]**
Stein, Herbert. U.S. Macroeconomic Policy and Trade Relations with Japan. *Sato, R. and Wachtel, P., eds.*, 1987, pp. 100–109.
[G: U.S.; Japan]
Stewart, Marion B. The Economics of Oil Prices: How Long Will World Supply Exceed Demand? *Stewart, M. B., ed.*, 1987, pp. 17–20.
[G: OPEC]
Strigel, W. H. On the World's Short- and Longer-term Economic Development as Expected by Entrepreneurs. *J. Stud. Econ. Econometrics*, November 1987, *11*(3), pp. 1–23.
[G: OECD]
Thurow, Lester C. Can America Compete in the World Economy? *Shetty, Y. K. and Buehler, V. M., eds.*, 1987, pp. 11–32. **[G: U.S.]**
Tobin, James. Make Jobs, Cut Deficits. *Tobin, J. (III)*, 1987, *1983*, pp. 186–88. **[G: U.S.]**
Tobin, James. The Fiscal Revolution: Disturbing Prospects. *Tobin, J. (III)*, 1987, *1985*, pp. 133–41. **[G: U.S.]**
Tobin, James. The Fiscal Revolution: Disturbing Prospects. *Challenge*, Special Issue 1987, *30*(6), pp. 45–49. **[G: U.S.]**
Tokman, Víctor E. and Wurgaft, J. The Recession and the Workers of Latin America. *International Labour Office.*, 1987, pp. 37–74.
[G: Latin America]
Trapp, Peter. West Germany: Why Reflation Does Not Work. *Econ. Int.*, May-Aug. 1987, *40*(2–3), pp. 237–46. **[G: U.S.; W. Germany]**
Trapp, Peter. West Germany's Economic Policy: What Direction? *Cato J.*, Winter 1987, *6*(3), pp. 837–50. **[G: W. Germany]**
Ueda, Kazuo. Japanese–U.S. Current Accounts and Exchange Rates before and after the G5 Agreement. *Sato, R. and Wachtel, P., eds.*, 1987, pp. 127–47. **[G: Japan; U.S.]**
Vaubel, Roland. Economic Policy in Germany: Was There a Turnaround? Discussion. *De Menil, G. and Portes, R., eds.*, 1987, pp. 141–43. **[G: W. Germany]**
Viraphol, Sarasin. Political Development in Thailand and the Kampuchea Problem. *Martin, L. G., ed.*, 1987, pp. 182–86. **[G: Thailand; ASEAN; Kampuchea]**
Volcker, Paul A. Facing up to the Twin Deficits. *Challenge*, Special Issue 1987, *30*(6), pp. 31–36. **[G: U.S.]**
Volcker, Paul A. Statement to the Joint Economic Committee of the U.S. Congress, February 2, 1987. *Fed. Res. Bull.*, April 1987, 73(4), pp. 275–79. **[G: U.S.]**

Volcker, Paul A. Statement to the U.S. Senate Committee on Banking, Housing, and Urban Affairs, February 19, 1987. *Fed. Res. Bull.*, April 1987, 73(4), pp. 282–89. **[G: U.S.]**
Volcker, Paul A. Statement to the U.S. Senate Committee on the Budget, February 24, 1987. *Fed. Res. Bull.*, April 1987, 73(4), pp. 290–95. **[G: U.S.]**
Waelbroeck, Jean. Ability to Adjust and the Problems of European Market Economies. *Pasinetti, L. and Lloyd, P., eds.*, 1987, pp. 109–21. **[G: Europe]**
Walker, John; Rossi, Vanessa and Clements, Michael. The World and UK Economy: Analysis and Prospects. *Oxford Rev. Econ. Policy*, Spring 1987, *3*(1), pp. xx–xxxiii. **[G: U.K.; U.S.]**
Warr, Peter G. and Nijathaworn, Bandid. Thai Economic Performance: Some Thai Perspectives. *Asian-Pacific Econ. Lit.*, May 1987, *1*(1), pp. 60–74. **[G: Thailand]**
Weaver, R. Kent. Political Foundations of Swedish Economic Policy. *Bosworth, B. P. and Rivlin, A. M., eds.*, 1987, pp. 289–324.
[G: Sweden]
von Weizsacker, Christian. The Conservative Revolution: A Roundtable Discussion. *De Menil, G. and Portes, R., eds.*, 1987, pp. 191–95. **[G: U.S.; Europe]**
Willett, Thomas D. A New Monetary Constitution. *Dorn, J. A. and Schwartz, A. J., eds.*, 1987, pp. 145–60. **[G: U.S.]**
Wojnilower, Albert M. Japan and the United States: Some Observations on Economic Policy. *Patrick, H. T. and Tachi, R., eds.*, 1987, pp. 76–83. **[G: Japan; U.S.]**
Worswick, David. The IMF's World Economic Outlook: A Critique. *Dell, S., ed., Pt. 3*, 1987, pp. 723–41.
Wren-Lewis, Simon and Eastwood, Fiona. The World Economy. *Nat. Inst. Econ. Rev.*, May 1987, (120), pp. 21–41. **[G: U.S.; Japan; W. Germany; Canada; France]**
Wren-Lewis, Simon and Eastwood, Fiona. The World Economy. *Nat. Inst. Econ. Rev.*, February 1987, (119), pp. 24–39. **[G: Global]**
Wyplosz, Charles. La France en 1986: bilan et perspectives macro-économiques. (France in 1986: Macroeconomic Assessment and Perspectives. With English summary.) *Revue Écon.*, May 1987, *38*(3), pp. 677–702.
[G: France]
Yamamura, Kozo and Yasuba, Yasukichi. The Political Economy of Japan: The Domestic Transformation: Introduction. *Yamamura, K. and Yasuba, Y., eds.*, 1987, pp. 1–29.
[G: Japan]
Yang, Jinbai. Market Mechanism and Macroeconomic Control. *Chinese Econ. Stud.*, Winter 1986-87, *20*(2), pp. 75–82. **[G: China]**
Zandi, Mark. What Impact Will Energy Price Changes Have on Economic Growth in the United States? *Stewart, M. B., ed.*, 1987, pp. 41–54. **[G: U.S.]**
Zhou, Daojiong. Macro Control and Micro Self-Regulating Investment. *Chinese Econ. Stud.*, Winter 1986-87, *20*(2), pp. 90–96.
[G: China]

Zimbalist, Andrew. Analyzing Cuban Planning: A Response [State Enterprises in Cuba under the New System of Planning and Management]. *Mesa-Lago, C., ed.*, 1987, pp. 159–65. **[G: Cuba]**

Zimbalist, Andrew. Cuba's Socialist Economy toward the 1990s. *World Devel.*, January 1987, 15(1), pp. 1–4. **[G: Cuba]**

1331 Stabilization Theories and Policies

Abou-Kandil, H. and Bertrand, P. Government–Private Sector Relations as a Stackelberg Game: A Degenerate Case. *J. Econ. Dynam. Control*, December 1987, 11(4), pp. 513–17.

Aghevli, Bijan B. and Márquez-Ruarte, Jorge. A Case of Successful Adjustment in a Developing Country: Korea's Experience during 1980–84. *Holmes, F., ed.*, 1987, pp. 91–113. **[G: S. Korea]**

Alesina, Alberto and Tabellini, Guido. Rules and Discretion with Noncoordinated Monetary and Fiscal Policies. *Econ. Inquiry*, October 1987, 25(4), pp. 619–30.

Allsopp, Christopher and Graham, Andrew. The Assessment: Policy Options for the UK. *Oxford Rev. Econ. Policy*, Autumn 1987, 3(3), pp. i–xxiv. **[G: U.K.]**

Amman, Hans M. and Jager, Henk. Optimal Economic Policies under a Crawling-Peg Exchange-Rate System. *Carraro, C. and Sartore, D., eds.*, 1987, pp. 105–26.

Andersen, Torben M. Pre-set Prices, Differential Information and Monetary Policy. *Sinclair, P. J. N., ed.*, 1987, 1986, pp. 283–307.

Arora, Harjit K. Monetary Stabilization Policy and Its Effects—A Case Study of India. *Indian J. Quant. Econ.*, 1987, 3(1), pp. 1–13. **[G: India]**

Atkinson, Glen W. Instrumentalism and Economic Policy: The Quest for Reasonable Value. *J. Econ. Issues*, March 1987, 21(1), pp. 189–202.

Auernheimer, Leonardo. On the Outcome of Inconsistent Programs under Exchange Rate and Monetary Rules. *J. Monet. Econ.*, March 1987, 19(2), pp. 279–305.

Bacha, Edmar Lisboa. IMF Conditionality: Conceptual Problems and Policy Alternatives. *World Devel.*, December 1987, 15(12), pp. 1457–67. **[G: LDCs]**

Backus, David and Driffill, John. Credible Disinflation in Closed and Open Economies. *Ricerche Econ.*, July-Dec. 1987, 41(3–4), pp. 326–40. **[G: Canada]**

Baer, Werner. The Resurgence of Inflation in Brazil, 1974–86. *World Devel.*, August 1987, 15(8), pp. 1007–34. **[G: Brazil]**

Barbosa, A. P. Stabilization under Rigidity. *Greek Econ. Rev.*, 1987, 9(2), pp. 147–61.

Bartlett, Will. The Problem of Indebtedness in Yugoslavia: Causes and Consequences. *Rivista Int. Sci. Econ. Com.*, Nov.-Dec. 1987, 34(11–12), pp. 1179–95. **[G: Yugoslavia]**

Baum, Christopher F. The Effects of Price- and

Output-Stabilising Policies in an Interdependent World Economy. *J. Econ. Dynam. Control*, June 1987, 11(2), pp. 195–200. **[G: OECD]**

Becketti, Sean and Haltiwanger, John. Limited Countercyclical Policies: An Exploratory Study. *J. Public Econ.*, December 1987, 34(3), pp. 311–28. **[G: U.S.]**

Bjerre-Nielsen, Henrik. Fordelene ved en international koordination af den økonomiske politik. (The Gains of International Economic Policy Coordination. With English summary.) *Nationaløkon. Tidsskr.*, 1987, 125(1), pp. 129–45. **[G: OECD]**

Blackburn, Keith. International Policy Games in a Simple Macroeconomic Model with Incomplete Information: Some Problems of Credibility, Secrecy and Cooperation. *Ricerche Econ.*, July-Dec. 1987, 41(3–4), pp. 419–38.

Blackburn, Keith and Christensen, Michael. Macroeconomic Policy Games and Reputational Equilibria in a Contracting Model. *Ricerche Econ.*, Apr.-June 1987, 41(2), pp. 190–209.

Blinder, Alan S. The Rules-versus-Discretion Debate in the Light of Recent Experience. *Weltwirtsch. Arch.*, 1987, 123(3), pp. 399–414. **[G: OECD]**

Blyth, Conrad. The Economists' Perspective of Economic Liberalisation. *Bollard, A. and Buckle, R., eds.*, 1987, pp. 3–24. **[G: New Zealand]**

Booth, Alan. Britain in the 1930s: A Managed Economy? *Econ. Hist. Rev.*, 2nd Ser., November 1987, 40(4), pp. 499–522. **[G: U.K.]**

Booth, Alan. The War and the White Paper. *Glynn, S. and Booth, A., eds.*, 1987, pp. 175–95. **[G: U.K.]**

Bosworth, Barry P. and Lawrence, Robert Z. Economic Goals and the Policy Mix. *Bosworth, B. P. and Rivlin, A. M., eds.*, 1987, pp. 97–124. **[G: Sweden]**

Boyer, Robert. The Current Economic Crisis: Its Dynamics and Its Implications for France. *Ross, G.; Hoffmann, S. and Malzacher, S., eds.*, 1987, pp. 33–53. **[G: France]**

Brandsma, Andries S. Risk Reduction and the Robustness of Economic Policies. *Carraro, C. and Sartore, D., eds.*, 1987, pp. 83–104.

Brandsma, Andries S.; Hughes Hallett, Andrew J. and Swank, J. The Robustness of Economic Policy Selections and the Incentive to Cooperate. *J. Econ. Dynam. Control*, June 1987, 11(2), pp. 163–70. **[G: U.S.; E. Europe]**

Brandsma, Andries S. and Siebrand, Jan C. Latent Transversality Conditions in Macroeconomic Stabilization Policies. *J. Econ. Dynam. Control*, June 1987, 11(2), pp. 235–39. **[G: Netherlands]**

Brunner, Karl. The Limits of Economic Policy. *Pejovich, S., ed.*, 1987, 1985, pp. 33–52.

Canzoneri, Matthew B. The Gains from Policy Coordination: Overview. *Bryant, R. C. and Portes, R., eds.*, 1987, pp. 185–90.

Caravani, Paolo. Modeling Economic Policy with Non-symmetric Losses and Risk Aversion. *J.*

Econ. Behav. Organ., September 1987, *8*(3), pp. 453–67.

Cardoso, Eliana A. and Dornbusch, Rudiger. Brazil's Tropical Plan. *Amer. Econ. Rev.*, May 1987, 77(2), pp. 288–92. **[G: Brazil]**

Carraro, Carlo. Hierarchical Games for Macroeconomic Policy Analysis. *Carraro, C. and Sartore, D.*, eds., 1987, pp. 215–38.

Carraro, Carlo. Preferenze rivelate e giochi di Nash: Gli obiettivi impliciti di politiche monetarie e fiscali in Italia. (Preference Revelation and Nash Equilibria: The Implicit Objective Function of Italian Macroeconomic Policy. With English summary.) *Econ. Lavoro,* Apr.-June 1987, *21*(2), pp. 47–58. **[G: Italy]**

Carraro, Carlo. Stackelberg Games and the Problem of Time-Inconsistency. *Econ. Notes*, 1987, (3), pp. 5–19.

Carraro, Carlo. Strategie punitive, annunci ottimali e politiche dei redditi. (Threats, Optimal Announcements, and Income Policy. With English summary.) *Ricerche Econ.*, Apr.-June 1987, *41*(2), pp. 210–30.

Carraro, Carlo and Giavazzi, Francesco. Policy Instruments and Coalitions in International Games. *Ricerche Econ.*, July-Dec. 1987, *41*(3–4), pp. 293–314.

Chen, Chau-nan; Lai, Ching-chong and Chang, Wen-ya. The Tight Money Effect, Wage Indexation and Macroeconomic Policy: The Fleming Model Revisited. *J. Econ. Stud.*, 1987, *14*(5), pp. 54–62.

Chen, Chien-Hsun and Steindl, Frank G. Anticipated Monetary and Fiscal Policy Effects on Output. *J. Macroecon.*, Spring 1987, *9*(2), pp. 255–74. **[G: U.S.]**

Chiarini, Bruno. Different Assumptions about Fiscal and Monetary Authority Behaviour in an Optimal Control Framework. Experiments with a Medium-size Nonlinear Econometric Model. *Econ. Notes*, 1987, (3), pp. 59–86. **[G: Italy]**

Chow, Gregory C. Development of Control Theory in Macroeconomics. *Carraro, C. and Sartore, D.*, eds., 1987, pp. 3–19.

Christensen, Michael. Disinflation, Credibility and Price Inertia: A Danish Exposition. *Appl. Econ.*, October 1987, *19*(10), pp. 1353–66. **[G: Denmark]**

Christodoulakis, Nicos and Levine, Paul. The Trade-off between Simplicity and Optimality in Macroeconomic Policy Design. *J. Econ. Dynam. Control*, June 1987, *11*(2), pp. 173–78.

Cohen, Suleiman I. Stabilization and Economic Growth in Developing Countries: Comments. *Pakistan Devel. Rev.*, Autumn 1987, *26*(3), pp. 356–59.

Congdon, Tim G. The Link between Budget Deficits and Inflation: Some Contrasts between Developed and Developing Countries. *Boskin, M. J.; Fleming, J. S. and Gorini, S.*, eds., 1987, pp. 72–91. **[G: LDCs; MDCs]**

Corbo, Vittorio and de Melo, Jaime. Lessons from the Southern Cone Policy Reforms. *World Bank Res. Observer*, July 1987, *2*(2), pp. 111–42. **[G: Argentina; Chile; Uruguay]**

Cornia, Giovanni Andrea. Adjustment Policies 1980–1985: Effects on Child Welfare. *Cornia, G. A.; Jolly, R. and Stewart, F.*, eds., 1987, pp. 48–72. **[G: LDCs]**

Cornia, Giovanni Andrea; Jolly, Richard and Stewart, Frances. Adjustment with a Human Face: Protecting the Vulnerable and Promoting Growth: An Overview of the Alternative Approach. *Cornia, G. A.; Jolly, R. and Stewart, F.*, eds., 1987, pp. 131–46.

Cornia, Giovanni Andrea; Jolly, Richard and Stewart, Frances. Adjustment with a Human Face: Protecting the Vulnerable and Promoting Growth: Summary and Conclusions. *Cornia, G. A.; Jolly, R. and Stewart, F.*, eds., 1987, pp. 287–97.

Cornwall, John. Structural Change and Economic Breakdown. *Écon. Appl.*, 1987, *40*(4), pp. 655–80.

Cornwall, John and Cornwall, Wendy. The Political Economy of Stagnation. *J. Econ. Issues*, June 1987, *21*(2), pp. 785–93.

Cukierman, Alex and Meltzer, Allan H. Errata [A Positive Theory of Discretionary Policy, the Cost of Democratic Government and the Benefits of a Constitution]. *Econ. Inquiry*, April 1987, *25*(2), pp. 363–65.

Currie, David. Options for UK Macroeconomic Policy. *Oxford Rev. Econ. Policy*, Autumn 1987, *3*(3), pp. 1–8. **[G: U.K.]**

Currie, David and Levine, Paul. Credibility and Time Consistency in a Stochastic World. *J. Econ. (Z. Nationalökon.)*, 1987, *47*(3), pp. 225–52.

Currie, David; Levine, Paul and Vidalis, Nic. International Cooperation and Reputation in an Empirical Two-Bloc Model. *Bryant, R. C. and Portes, R.*, eds., 1987, pp. 75–121. **[G: U.S.]**

Dagnino Pastore, José María. Las tasas de interés bajo distintos contextos cambiario y financiero. (With English summary.) *Desarrollo Econ.*, Apr.-June 1987, *27*(105), pp. 61–85. **[G: Argentina]**

Darby, Michael R. International Economic Policy Coordination and Transmission: A Review. *Sinclair, P. J. N.*, ed., 1987, *1986*, pp. 343–48.

Dell, Sidney, et al. Determination of Quotas and the Relative Position of Developing Countries in the International Monetary Fund: Structural Adjustment Policies. *Dell, S.*, ed., Pt. 2, 1987, pp. 541–56. **[G: U.K.]**

Demery, Lionel and Addison, Tony. Stabilization Policy and Income Distribution in Developing Countries. *World Devel.*, December 1987, *15*(12), pp. 1483–98. **[G: LDCs]**

Dias Carneiro, Dionísio. Long-run Adjustment, the Debt Crisis and the Changing Role of Stabilisation Policies in the Recent Brazilian Experience. *Thorp, R. and Whitehead, L.*, eds., 1987, pp. 28–67. **[G: Brazil]**

Dornbusch, Rudiger. Lessons from the German Inflation Experience of the 1920s. *[Modigliani, F.]*, 1987, pp. 337–66. **[G: Germany]**

Doukas, John. LDC Stabilization Policies, Price and Output Adjustment: Theory and Evidence,

1974–83. *Appl. Econ.*, April 1987, *19*(4), pp. 447–58. [G: LDCs]

Downe, Edward A. Minsky's Model of Financial Fragility: A Suggested Addition. *J. Post Keynesian Econ.*, Spring 1987, *9*(3), pp. 440–54.

Drazen, Allan and Helpman, Elhanan. Stabilization with Exchange Rate Management. *Quart. J. Econ.*, November 1987, *102*(4), pp. 835–55.

Driffill, John. Credibility and Reputation in Macroeconomic Policy. *Brit. Rev. Econ. Issues*, Spring 1987, *9*(20), pp. 1–25.

Edison, Hali J.; Marquez, Jaime R. and Tryon, Ralph W. The Structure and Properties of the Federal Reserve Baord Multicountry Model. *Econ. Modelling*, April 1987, *4*(2), pp. 115–315. [G: U.S.; Canada; W. Germany; Japan; U.K.]

Epstein, Edward C. Recent Stabilization Programs in Argentina, 1973–86. *World Devel.*, August 1987, *15*(8), pp. 991–1005. [G: Argentina]

Eroğul, Cem. The Establishment of Multiparty Rule: 1945–71. *Schick, I. C. and Tonak, E. A., eds.*, 1987, pp. 101–43. [G: Turkey]

Filc, Wolfgang. Bestandsorientierte Wechselkurstheorien und Wirtschaftspolitik. (Asset Market-Oriented Exchange Rate Theories and Economic Policy. With English summary.) *Kredit Kapital*, 1987, *20*(1), pp. 48–72.

Fischer, Stanley. The Israeli Stabilization Program, 1985–86. *Amer. Econ. Rev.*, May 1987, *77*(2), pp. 275–78. [G: Israel]

Flemming, John S. Wage Flexibility and Employment Stability. *Sinclair, P. J. N., ed.*, 1987, pp. 161–74.

Freeman, R. D. The State and the Private Sector: Comment. *Levitt, M. S., ed.*, 1987, pp. 43–47. [G: U.K.]

Frenkel, Roberto. Heterodox Theory and Policy: The Plan Austral in Argentina. *[Diaz-Alejandro, C. F.]*, 1987, pp. 307–38. [G: Argentina]

Frenkel, Roberto. Heterodox Theory and Policy: The Plan Austral in Argentina. *J. Devel. Econ.*, October 1987, *27*(1–2), pp. 307–38. [G: Argentina]

Gapinski, James H. Capital Lessons in Leaning against the Wind. *J. Money, Credit, Banking*, May 1987, *19*(2), pp. 235–45.

Gapinski, James H. Capital Theoretics, Business Cycles, and Feedback Policy: An Experiment in Macroeconomic Control. *Carraro, C. and Sartore, D., eds.*, 1987, pp. 305–26.

Garay S., Luis Jorge. Fiscal Policy, Growth, and Design of Stabilization Programs: Comment. *Martirena-Mantel, A. M., ed.*, 1987, pp. 141–47. [G: LDCs]

Garello, Jacques. Economic and Social Consequences of Socialist Policies in France. *Pejovich, S., ed.*, 1987, pp. 251–76. [G: France]

Gedeon, Shirley J. Neomonetarism and Stabilization. *Econ. Anal. Workers' Manage.*, 1987, *21*(2), pp. 259–63. [G: Yugoslavia]

Glynn, Sean. Real Policy Options. *Glynn, S. and Booth, A., eds.*, 1987, pp. 154–74. [G: U.K.]

Gonzalez, Norberto. International Price Fluctuations and Inflation: Discussion and Conclusions. *Pasinetti, L. and Lloyd, P., eds.*, 1987, pp. 395–402. [G: Global]

Guiliani Cury, Hugo. Economic Reform and Stabilization in Latin America: Preface. *Connolly, M. and González-Vega, C., eds.*, 1987, pp. xiii–xvii. [G: Dominican Republic]

Gylfason, Thorvaldur. Does Exchange Rate Really Matter? *Europ. Econ. Rev.*, Feb./Mar. 1987, *31*(1/2), pp. 375–81.

Hall, Peter A. The Evolution of Economic Policy under Mitterrand. *Ross, G.; Hoffmann, S. and Malzacher, S., eds.*, 1987, pp. 54–72. [G: France]

Hall, S. G. An Investigation of Time Inconsistency and Optimal Policy Formulation in the Presence of Rational Expectations Using the National Institute's Model 7. *Appl. Econ.*, September 1987, *19*(9), pp. 1175–85. [G: U.K.]

Hardouvelis, Gikas A. Optimal Wage Indexation and Monetary Policy in an Economy with Imported Raw Materials. *J. Int. Money Finance*, December 1987, *6*(4), pp. 419–32.

Hatton, T. J. The Outlines of a Keynesian Solution. *Glynn, S. and Booth, A., eds.*, 1987, pp. 82–94. [G: U.K.]

Hausmann, Ricardo. Fiscal Policy, Growth, and Design of Stabilization Programs: Comment. *Martirena-Mantel, A. M., ed.*, 1987, pp. 147–53. [G: LDCs]

Helleiner, Gerald K. Stabilization, Adjustment, and the Poor. *World Devel.*, December 1987, *15*(12), pp. 1499–1513. [G: Tanzania]

Heymann, Daniel. The Austral Plan. *Amer. Econ. Rev.*, May 1987, *77*(2), pp. 284–87. [G: Argentina]

Hibbs, Douglas A., Jr. Economics and Politics in France: Economic Performance and Mass Political Support for Presidents Pompidou and Giscard d'Estaing. *Hibbs, D. A., Jr., 1987, 1981*, pp. 224–40. [G: France]

Hibbs, Douglas A., Jr. On the Demand for Economic Outcomes: Macroeconomic Performance and Mass Political Support in the United States, Great Britain, and Germany. *Hibbs, D. A., Jr., 1987, 1982*, pp. 193–223. [G: U.S.; U.K.; W. Germany]

Hibbs, Douglas A., Jr. Political Parties and Macroeconomic Policy. *Hibbs, D. A., Jr., 1987, 1977*, pp. 290–321. [G: U.K.; U.S.]

Hibbs, Douglas A., Jr. The Mass Public and Macroeconomic Performance: Dynamics of Public Opinion toward Unemployment and Inflation. *Hibbs, D. A., Jr., 1987, 1979*, pp. 117–42. [G: U.S.]

Hibbs, Douglas A., Jr. The Political Economy of Industrial Democracies: Introduction. *Hibbs, D. A., Jr., 1987*, pp. 1–13.

Higgins, Christopher. Fiscal and Monetary Policies: Their Role in the Adjustment Process: Comment. *Holmes, F., ed.*, 1987, pp. 185–91. [G: W. Germany; Japan; Belgium; U.S.]

van der Hoeven, Rolph. External Shocks and Stabilisation Policies: Spreading the Load. *Int.*

Lab. Rev., Mar.-Apr. 1987, *126*(2), pp. 133–50. **[G: Africa; Latin America]**

Hof, Franz Xaver. The Lucas Supply Function and the Feasibility of Monetary Stabilization Policy with Rational Expectations. *Empirica*, 1987, *14*(2), pp. 227–48.

Hoffman, Ronald. Macroeconomic Analysis and Stabilization Policy: Searching for Consensus. *van de Kar, H. M. and Wolfe, B. L., eds.*, 1987, pp. 13–31. **[G: U.S.]**

Holtham, Gerald and Hughes Hallett, Andrew J. International Policy Cooperation and Model Uncertainty. *Bryant, R. C. and Portes, R., eds.*, 1987, pp. 128–77.

Horowitz, Ann R. Loss Functions and Public Policy. *J. Macroecon.*, Fall 1987, *9*(4), pp. 489–504.

Hughes Hallett, Andrew J. Autonomy and the Choice of Policy in Asymmetrically Dependent Economies. *Sinclair, P. J. N., ed.*, 1987, *1986*, pp. 349–77. **[G: U.S.; EEC]**

Hughes Hallett, Andrew J. How Robust Are the Gains to Policy Coordination to Variations in the Model and Objectives? *Ricerche Econ.*, July-Dec. 1987, *41*(3–4), pp. 341–72.

Hughes Hallett, Andrew J. Optimal Policy Design in Interdependent Economies. *Carraro, C. and Sartore, D., eds.*, 1987, pp. 187–214.

Jackman, Richard and Layard, Richard. Innovative Supply-Side Policies to Reduce Unemployment. *Begg, D. K. H., et al.*, 1987, pp. 93–117. **[G: U.K.]**

Jung, W. S. Optimal Stabilization Policy with Instruments of Differing Frequency. *Math. Soc. Sci.*, June 1987, *13*(3), pp. 231–41.

Kanbur, S. M. Ravi. Structural Adjustment, Macroeconomic Adjustment and Poverty: A Methodology for Analysis. *World Devel.*, December 1987, *15*(12), pp. 1515–26.

Keyder, Çağlar. The Political Economy of Turkish Democracy. *Schick, I. C. and Tonak, E. A., eds.*, 1987, pp. 27–65. **[G: Turkey]**

Khan, Mohsin S. Stabilization and Economic Growth in Developing Countries. *Pakistan Devel. Rev.*, Autumn 1987, *26*(3), pp. 341–55.

Kindleberger, Charles P. Belgium after World War II: An Experiment in Supply Side Economics. *Steinherr, A. and Weiserbs, D., eds.*, 1987, pp. 167–84. **[G: Belgium]**

Klein, Lawrence R. Growth, Inflation and Employment: Discussion and Conclusions. *Pasinetti, L. and Lloyd, P., eds.*, 1987, pp. 323–25.

Klein, Lawrence R. Growth, Inflation and Employment: An Introduction. *Pasinetti, L. and Lloyd, P., eds.*, 1987, pp. 269–74. **[G: Global]**

Körner, Heiko. Some Econometric Evidence on the Relative Importance of Monetary and Fiscal Policy in Pakistan: Comments. *Pakistan Devel. Rev.*, Winter 1987, *26*(4), pp. 550–51. **[G: Pakistan]**

Krelle, Wilhelm. Growth, Inflation and Employment. *Pasinetti, L. and Lloyd, P., eds.*, 1987, pp. 275–91.

Krueger, Anne O. The Importance of Economic

Policy in Development: Contrasts between Korea and Turkey. *[Corden, W. M.]*, 1987, pp. 172–203. **[G: S. Korea; Turkey]**

La Malfa, Giorgio and Lecaldano Sasso la Terza, Edoardo. Modigliani–La Malfa Revisited: The Italian Economy from the Sixties to the Eighties. *[Modigliani, F.]*, 1987, pp. 373–97. **[G: Italy]**

Laskar, Daniel. The "Rules of the Game" and Sterilization under a Fixed Exchange Rate System: A Strategic Argument. *Ricerche Econ.*, July-Dec. 1987, *41*(3–4), pp. 439–56.

Lawrence, Robert Z. and Schultze, Charles L. Barriers to European Growth: Overview. *Lawrence, R. Z. and Schultze, C. L., eds.*, 1987, pp. 1–47. **[G: W. Europe]**

Lawson, Tony. The Cambridge Multisectoral Dynamic Model of the British Economy: Incomes Policy and Earnings. *Barker, T. and Peterson, W., eds.*, 1987, pp. 341–72. **[G: U.K.]**

Levačic, Rosalind. The Analysis of Economic Management: The Aggregate Demand and Supply Model. *Thompson, G.; Brown, V. and Levačić, R., eds.*, 1987, pp. 38–76. **[G: U.K.]**

Levine, Paul. Three Themes from Game Theory and International Macroeconomic Policy Formation. *Ricerche Econ.*, July-Dec. 1987, *41*(3–4), pp. 392–418.

Levine, Paul and Currie, David. Does International Macroeconomic Policy Coordination Pay and Is It Sustainable? A Two Country Analysis. *Oxford Econ. Pap.*, March 1987, *39*(1), pp. 38–74.

Levine, Paul and Currie, David. Does International Macroeconomic Policy Coordination Pay and Is It Sustainable? A Two Country Analysis. *Sinclair, P. J. N., ed.*, 1987, pp. 38–74.

Li, Chengrui. An Important Question in Macroeconomic Management: Strict State Control of the Amount of Currency in Circulation. *Chinese Econ. Stud.*, Winter 1986-87, *20*(2), pp. 3–12. **[G: China]**

Llach, Juan J. La naturaleza institucional e internacional de las hiperestabilizaciones. El caso de Alemania desde 1923 y algunas lecciones para la Argentina de 1985. (With English summary.) *Desarrollo Econ.*, Jan.-Mar. 1987, *26*(104), pp. 527–60. **[G: Germany; Argentina]**

Lopez Murphy, Ricardo H. La política fiscal compensatoria. (The Compensatory Fiscal Policy. With English summary.) *Económica (La Plata)*, January-June 1987, *33*(1), pp. 85–112.

Lowe, Adolph. Is the Glass Half Full or Half Empty? A Self-critique. *Lowe, A.*, 1987, *1982*, pp. 234–50.

Maier, Charles S. In Search of Stability: Explorations in Historical Political Economy: Conclusion: Why Stability? *Maier, C. S.*, 1987, pp. 261–73.

Malinvaud, Edmond. Monetary and Fiscal Policies for Economic Recovery in Europe. *Europ. Econ. Rev.*, Feb./Mar. 1987, *31*(1/2), pp. 73–75. **[G: W. Europe]**

Malley, James R. and Hady, Thomas F. The Impact of Macroeconomic Policies on Rural Em-

ployment. *U.S.D.A.*, *Econ. Res. Serv.*, *Agr. and Rural Econ. Div.*, 1987, pp. 10.1–19.
[G: U.S.]

Marcella, Mulino. Politiche di stabilizzazione in mercato aperto: due approcci alternativi. (Stabilization Policies in an Open Market: Two Alternative Approaches. With English summary.) *Giorn. Econ.*, May-June 1987, *46*(5–6), pp. 257–90.

Marini, Giancarlo. Determinatezza dei prezzi ed effetti di stabilizzazione di manovre anticicliche del tasso d'interesse. (Interest Rate Rules, Price Level Determinancy and Stabilization Policy. With English summary.) *Econ. Polit.*, December 1987, *4*(3), pp. 343–55.

Marini, Giancarlo. Price Variability, Supply-Side Policies and Monetary Rules. *Economica*, February 1987, *54*(213), pp. 109–11.

Marquez, Jaime R. and Pauly, Peter H. International Policy Coordination and Growth Prospects of Developing Countries: An Optimal Control Application. *J. Devel. Econ.*, February 1987, *25*(1), pp. 89–104.

Mason, Will E. Happy-Face Economics versus the 'Dismal Science': Is the Borrowed Lunch Really Free? *[Marjolin, R.]*, 1987, pp. 137–51.
[G: U.S.]

Masson, Paul R. International Cooperation and Reputation in an Empirical Two-Bloc Model: Discussion. *Bryant, R. C. and Portes, R., eds.*, 1987, pp. 122–25.
[G: U.S.]

McNelis, Paul D. The Preferential Option for the Poor and the Evolution of Latin American Macroeconomic Orthodoxies. *Gannon, T. M., ed.*, 1987, pp. 138–50.
[G: U.S.; Latin America]

Meller, Patricio and Solimano, Andrés. A Simple Macro Model for a Small Open Economy Facing a Binding External Constraint (Chile). *J. Devel. Econ.*, June 1987, *26*(1), pp. 25–35.
[G: Chile]

de Melo, Jaime. Financial Reforms, Stabilization, and Growth under High Capital Mobility: Uruguay 1974–83. *Connolly, M. and González-Vega, C., eds.*, 1987, pp. 229–49.
[G: Uruguay]

Meltzer, Allan H. Limits of Short-run Stabilization Policy: Presidential Address to the Western Economic Association, July 3, 1986. *Econ. Inquiry*, January 1987, *25*(1), pp. 1–14.
[G: U.S.]

Messner, Zbigniew. Some Problems of Poland's Economic Policy in 1986–1990. *Soviet E. Europ. Foreign Trade*, Fall 1987, *23*(3), pp. 87–96.
[G: Poland]

Middleton, Roger. Treasury Policy on Unemployment. *Glynn, S. and Booth, A., eds.*, 1987, pp. 109–24.
[G: U.K.]

Mishkin, Frederic S. U.S. Macroeconomic Policy and Performance in the 1980s: An Overview. *Patrick, H. T. and Tachi, R., eds.*, 1987, pp. 37–53.
[G: U.S.; Global]

Modigliani, Franco, et al. Reducing Unemployment in Europe: The Role of Capital Formation. *Layard, R. and Calmfors, L., eds.*, 1987, pp. 11–47.
[G: W. Europe]

Monticelli, Carlo. Stabilization Priorities and Op-

timal Monetary Policy. *Greek Econ. Rev.*, 1987, *9*(2), pp. 210–23.

Montiel, Peter J. Output and Unanticipated Money in the Dependent Economy Model. *Int. Monet. Fund Staff Pap.*, June 1987, *34*(2), pp. 228–59.
[G: Mexico]

Morley, Samuel A. and Fishlow, Albert. Deficits, Debt and Destabilization: The Perversity of High Interest Rates. *J. Devel. Econ.*, October 1987, *27*(1–2), pp. 227–44.
[G: LDCs]

Morley, Samuel A. and Fishlow, Albert. Deficits, Debt and Destabilization: The Perversity of High Interest Rates. *[Diaz-Alejandro, C. F.]*, 1987, pp. 227–44.
[G: LDCs]

Mussa, Michael. Macroeconomic Policy and Trade Liberalization: Some Guidelines. *World Bank Res. Observer*, January 1987, *2*(1), pp. 61–77.
[G: LDCs]

Mutoh, Takahiko. On the Relation between Monetary Interdependence and Exchange Rate Volatility. *J. Japanese Int. Economies*, December 1987, *1*(4), pp. 351–72.

Myatt, Anthony E. and Scarth, William M. Fiscal Policy, Interest Sensitive Aggregate Supply and the Costs of Disinflation. *Manchester Sch. Econ. Soc. Stud.*, June 1987, *55*(2), pp. 144–57.

Neck, Reinhard and Dockner, Engelbert. Can the Gains from International Cooperation be Secured without Policy Coordination? *Ricerche Econ.*, July-Dec. 1987, *41*(3–4), pp. 373–91.

Neck, Reinhard and Dockner, Engelbert. Conflict and Cooperation in a Model of Stabilization Policies: A Differential Game Approach. *J. Econ. Dynam. Control*, June 1987, *11*(2), pp. 153–58.

Nicholl, Peter. Some Aspects of Economic Adjustment in Small Island Economies: Comment. *Holmes, F., ed.*, 1987, pp. 263–72.
[G: S. Pacific]

Nyers, R.; Révész, G. and Sipos, A. Report on the Project "Scientific Foundations of the Further Development of Economic Policy." *Acta Oecon.*, 1987, *38*(3–4), pp. 391–94.
[G: Hungary]

Odedokun, Matthew O. A Flow-of-Funds Framework for Evaluating the Behaviours of Fiscal and Monetary Authorities Using Nigerian Data. *Public Finance*, 1987, *42*(2), pp. 193–213.
[G: Nigeria]

Öller, Lars-Erik. Stabiliseringspolitik och prognoser. (Stabilization Policy and Forecasts. With English summary.) *Ekon. Samfundets Tidskr.*, 1987, *40*(1), pp. 23–27.
[G: Finland]

Olopoenia, Razaq A. Fiscal Policy and Economic Instability in an Oil-Dependent Economy: The Nigerian Experience during the Oil Boom of the Seventies. *Pakistan J. Appl. Econ.*, Summer 1987, *6*(1), pp. 41–60.
[G: Nigeria]

Oudiz, Gilles. International Policy Cooperation and Model Uncertainty: Discussion. *Bryant, R. C. and Portes, R., eds.*, 1987, pp. 178–82.

Pastor, Manuel, Jr. The Effects of IMF Programs in the Third World: Debate and Evidence from Latin America. *World Devel.*, February 1987, *15*(2), pp. 249–62.
[G: Latin America]

Penha Cysne, Rubens; Simonsen Leal, Carlos Ivan and da Costa Werlang, Sérgio Ribeiro. Macroeconomia com racionamento: um modelo simplificado para economia aberta. (With English summary.) *Pesquisa Planejamento Econ.*, August 1987, *17*(2), pp. 265–99.

Perkins, James O. N. and Tran, Van Hoa. Towards the Formulation and Testing of a More General Theory of Macroeconomic Policy. *Weltwirtsch. Arch.*, 1987, *123*(2), pp. 199–215. [G: OECD]

Peterson, Wallace C. Macroeconomic Theory and Policy in an Institutionalist Perspective. *J. Econ. Issues*, December 1987, *21*(4), pp. 1587–1621. [G: U.S.]

Petit, Maria Luisa. A System-Theoretic Approach to the Theory of Economic Policy. *Carraro, C. and Sartore, D., eds.*, 1987, pp. 31–45.

Pincus, Jonathan J. The Australian Economy in the Long Run: Government. *Maddock, R. and McLean, I. W., eds.*, 1987, pp. 291–318. [G: Australia]

Pinstrup-Andersen, Per; Jaramillo, Maurice and Stewart, Frances. Adjustment with a Human Face: Protecting the Vulnerable and Promoting Growth: The Impact on Government Expenditure. *Cornia, G. A.; Jolly, R. and Stewart, F., eds.*, 1987, pp. 73–89. [G: LDCs]

Pinto, Brian. Nigeria during and after the Oil Boom: A Policy Comparison with Indonesia. *World Bank Econ. Rev.*, May 1987, *1*(3), pp. 419–45. [G: Nigeria; Indonesia]

Pitchford, John David and Vousden, Neil J. Exchange Rates, Policy Rules and Inflation. *Australian Econ. Pap.*, June 1987, *26*(48), pp. 43–57.

van der Ploeg, Frederick. Optimal Government Policy in a Small Open Economy with Rational Expectations and Uncertain Election Outcomes. *Int. Econ. Rev.*, June 1987, *28*(2), pp. 469–91.

Potáč, Svatopluk. The Economic Policy of the Czechoslovak Socialist Republic. *Czech. Econ. Digest.*, June 1987, (5), pp. 3–7. [G: Czechoslovakia]

Prachowny, Martin F. J. Macroeconomic Policy in a Conflict Environment. *J. Inst. Theoretical Econ.*, June 1987, *143*(2), pp. 244–60.

Pressman, Steven. The Policy Relevance of *The General Theory*. *J. Econ. Stud.*, 1987, *14*(4), pp. 13–23. [G: U.S.]

Qadir, Asghar. Stabilization and Economic Growth in Developing Countries: Comments. *Pakistan Devel. Rev.*, Autumn 1987, *26*(3), pp. 360–61.

Reichlin, Pietro. Equilibrium Cycles in an Overlapping Generations Economy with Production. *Grandmont, J.-M., ed.*, 1987, *1986*, pp. 89–102.

Roberds, William. Models of Policy under Stochastic Replanning. *Int. Econ. Rev.*, October 1987, *28*(3), pp. 731–55.

Robertson, John D. Guiding and Making Policy: Ideas and Institutions. *Waltman, J. L. and Studlar, D. T., eds.*, 1987, pp. 16–43. [G: U.K.; U.S.]

Roca, Santiago and Priale, Rodrigo. Devaluation, Inflationary Expectations and Stabilisation in Peru. *J. Econ. Stud.*, 1987, *14*(1), pp. 5–33. [G: Peru]

Rogoff, Kenneth. Reputational Constraints on Monetary Policy. *Carnegie–Rochester Conf. Ser. Public Policy*, Spring 1987, *26*, pp. 141–81.

Rohrlich, Paul Egon. Economic Culture and Foreign Policy: The Cognitive Analysis of Economic Policy Making. *Int. Organ.*, Winter 1987, *41*(1), pp. 61–92. [G: U.K.]

Ross, George. From One Left to Another: *Le Social* in Mitterrand's France. *Ross, G.; Hoffmann, S. and Malzacher, S., eds.*, 1987, pp. 199–216. [G: France]

Rustem, Berc and Velupillai, K. Objective Functions and the Complexity of Policy Design. *J. Econ. Dynam. Control*, June 1987, *11*(2), pp. 185–92.

Rwegasira, Delphin G. Balance-of-Payments Adjustment in Low-Income Developing Countries: The Experiences of Kenya and Tanzania in the 1970s. *World Devel.*, Oct./Nov. 1987, *15*(10/11), pp. 1321–35. [G: Kenya; Tanzania]

Sachs, Jeffrey D. The Bolivian Hyperinflation and Stabilization. *Amer. Econ. Rev.*, May 1987, *77*(2), pp. 279–83. [G: Bolivia]

Saqib, Najam us and Yasmin, Attiya. Some Econometric Evidence on the Relative Importance of Monetary and Fiscal Policy in Pakistan. *Pakistan Devel. Rev.*, Winter 1987, *26*(4), pp. 541–49. [G: Pakistan]

Scarfe, Brian L. Economic Fluctuations and Stabilization Policy in Canada: The State of the Art. *Can. Public Policy*, March 1987, *13*(1), pp. 75–85. [G: Canada]

Scarth, William M. Unemployment, Inflation and Deficits: A Review Essay. *Can. Public Policy*, June 1987, *13*(2), pp. 222–31. [G: Canada]

Schlieper, Ulrich. Macroeconomic Policy, Rent Seeking and Economic Order. *Pethig, R. and Schlieper, U., eds.*, 1987, pp. 27–34.

Shupp, Franklin R. Policy Effectiveness and the Divergence of Objectives of Private Agents and Public Authorities. *[Marrama, V.], Vol. 2*, 1987, pp. 899–917.

Skidmore, Thomas E. The Resurgence of Inflation in Latin America: Discussion. *World Devel.*, August 1987, *15*(8), pp. 1148–49. [G: Brazil; Argentina]

Smith, Bruce J. Some Aspects of Economic Adjustment in Small Island Economies. *Holmes, F., ed.*, 1987, pp. 237–62. [G: S. Pacific]

Smith, Russell E. The Resurgence of Inflation in Latin America: Discussion. *World Devel.*, August 1987, *15*(8), pp. 1146–48. [G: Argentina; Brazil]

Spaventa, Luigi. Lessons from the German Inflation Experience of the 1920s: Comments. *[Modigliani, F.]*, 1987, pp. 367–71. [G: Germany]

Spencer, Grant H. and Clements, Robin T. Fiscal and Monetary Policies: Their Role in the Adjustment Process. *Holmes, F., ed.*, 1987, pp. 154–84. **[G: Japan; Belgium; W. Germany]**

Stewart, Frances. Adjustment with a Human Face: Protecting the Vulnerable and Promoting Growth: Alternative Macro Policies, Meso Policies, and Vulnerable Groups. *Cornia, G. A.; Jolly, R. and Stewart, F., eds.*, 1987, pp. 147–64. **[G: LDCs]**

Street, James H. Values in Conflict: Developing Countries as Social Laboratories. *Dietz, J. L. and Street, J. H., eds.*, 1987, *1984*, pp. 261–69. **[G: Mexico; Argentina; Chile; Brazil; Uruguay]**

Tabellini, Guido. Reputational Constraints on Monetary Policy: A Comment. *Carnegie–Rochester Conf. Ser. Public Policy*, Spring 1987, *26*, pp. 183–90.

Tabellini, Guido. The Politics of Inflation and Economic Stagnation: A Review Essay. *J. Monet. Econ.*, May 1987, *19*(3), pp. 457–61.

Tanzi, Vito. Fiscal Policy, Growth, and Stabilization Programs. *Finance Develop.*, June 1987, *24*(2), pp. 15–17.

Tanzi, Vito. Fiscal Policy, Growth, and Design of Stabilization Programs. *Martirena-Mantel, A. M., ed.*, 1987, pp. 121–41. **[G: LDCs]**

Taylor, Lance. Macro Policy in the Tropics: How Sensible People Stand. *World Devel.*, December 1987, *15*(12), pp. 1407–35. **[G: LDCs]**

Thompson, Grahame. Managing the UK Economy: Current Controversies: Introduction. *Thompson, G.; Brown, V. and Levačić, R., eds.*, 1987, pp. xii–xxvii. **[G: U.K.]**

Thompson, Grahame. Objectives and Instruments of Economic Management. *Thompson, G.; Brown, V. and Levačić, R., eds.*, 1987, pp. 1–37. **[G: U.K.]**

Thygesen, Niels. Monetary and Fiscal Policies for Economic Recovery in Europe. *Europ. Econ. Rev.*, Feb./Mar. 1987, *31*(1/2), pp. 67–73. **[G: W. Europe]**

Tobin, James. Deposit Interest Ceilings as a Monetary Control. *Tobin, J. (I)*, 1987, *1970*, pp. 339–51. **[G: U.S.]**

Tobin, James. Economic Growth as an Objective of Government Policy. *Tobin, J. (I)*, 1987, *1964*, pp. 174–94.

Tobin, James. Economic Stabilization Policies in the United States. *Tobin, J. (III)*, 1987, *1976*, pp. 439–53. **[G: U.S.]**

Tobin, James. Fiscal and Monetary Policy under the Employment Act. *Tobin, J. (III)*, 1987, *1986*, pp. 24–39.

Tobin, James. Macroeconomic Diagnosis and Prescription. *Gunderson, M.; Meltz, N. M. and Ostry, S., eds.*, 1987, pp. 12–40. **[G: OECD]**

Tobin, James. Monetarism: An Ebbing Tide? *Tobin, J. (III)*, 1987, *1985*, pp. 265–74. **[G: U.S.]**

Tobin, James. Okun on Macroeconomic Policy. *Tobin, J. (III)*, 1987, *1983*, pp. 415–18.

Tobin, James. Reaganomics in Retrospect. *Tobin, J. (III)*, 1987, pp. 69–88. **[G: U.S.]**

Tobin, James. Remembering Walter Heller. *Challenge*, Nov./Dec. 1987, *30*(5), pp. 59–63.

Tobin, James. Running the Economy with Less

Unemployment and Poverty (Comments on the Bishops' Pastoral Letter on Catholic Social Teaching and the Economy). *Tobin, J. (III)*, 1987, *1985*, pp. 488–94. **[G: U.S.]**

Tobin, James. The Conservative Counter-revolution in Economic Policy. *Tobin, J. (III)*, 1987, *1981*, pp. 89–99. **[G: U.S.]**

Tobin, James. The Monetary–Fiscal Mix in the United States. *Tobin, J. (III)*, 1987, pp. 142–67. **[G: U.S.]**

Tobin, James. The Political Economy of the 1960s. *Tobin, J. (III)*, 1987, *1977*, pp. 422–38. **[G: U.S.]**

Tobin, James. Unemployment in the 1980s: Macroeconomic Diagnosis and Prescription. *Tobin, J. (III)*, 1987, *1984*, pp. 386–414. **[G: U.S.; OECD]**

Towe, Christopher M. Transactions Technology and the Time Consistency of Optimal Policy. *J. Public Econ.*, October 1987, *34*(1), pp. 121–28.

Turner, Paul. The Inefficiency of Uncoordinated Stabilisation Policy in Multicountry Models. *Chrystal, K. A. and Sedgwick, R., eds.*, 1987, pp. 229–38.

Turnovsky, Stephen J. Optimal Monetary Policy and Wage Indexation under Alternative Disturbances and Information Structures. *J. Money, Credit, Banking*, May 1987, *19*(2), pp. 157–80.

Turnovsky, Stephen J. Supply Shocks and Optimal Monetary Policy. *Sinclair, P. J. N., ed.*, 1987, pp. 20–37.

Turnovsky, Stephen J. Supply Shocks and Optimal Monetary Policy. *Oxford Econ. Pap.*, March 1987, *39*(1), pp. 20–37.

Van Poeck, A. Labour Market Characteristics, Stabilization Policy and Real Wage Rigidity. *Tijdschrift Econ. Manage.*, 1987, *32*(2), pp. 189–213. **[G: OECD]**

Van Rompuy, G. The Laffer Curve Proposition in a Unionized Economy. *Tijdschrift Econ. Manage.*, 1987, *32*(1), pp. 39–54. **[G: U.S.]**

Vane, Howard and Caslin, Terry. The Appropriate Economic Strategy for the UK Economy. *Vane, H. and Caslin, T., eds.*, 1987, pp. 293–315. **[G: U.K.]**

Velasco, Andrés. Financial Crises and Balance of Payments Crises: A Simple Model of the Southern Cone Experience. *J. Devel. Econ.*, October 1987, *27*(1–2), pp. 263–83. **[G: Chile; Argentina; Uruguay]**

Velasco, Andrés. Financial Crises and Balance of Payments Crises: A Simple Model of the Southern Cone Experience. *[Diaz-Alejandro, C. F.]*, 1987, pp. 263–83. **[G: Chile; Argentina; Uruguay]**

Velasco, Andrés. Políticas de estabilización y teoría de juegos. (Stabilization Policies and Game Theory. With English summary.) *Colección Estud. CIEPLAN*, June 1987, (21), pp. 49–75.

Villa, Pierre. Règles de gestion du taux d'intérêt. (Interest Rate Policy as a Stabilization Tool. With English summary.) *Ann. Écon. Statist.*, Jan./Mar. 1987, (5), pp. 49–76.

de la Vinelle, Louis Duquesne. Economic Policy as an Instrument of Progress. *Dupriez, L. H., ed.*, 1987, *1955*, pp. 313–27.

Ward, Ian and Kulkarni, Anand. The Rise and Fall of National Allocative Planning in Australia. *Australian Econ. Rev.*, Second Quarter 1987, (78), pp. 37–48. [G: Australia]

Watrin, Christian. The Case of Codetermination in West Germany. *Pejovich, S., ed.*, 1987, pp. 277–314. [G: W. Germany]

Welfens, Paul J. J. Angebotsorientierte Stabilitätspolitik: Probleme, Erfahrungen, Perspektiven. (Supply-Side Oriented Stabilization Policy: Problems, Experience, Perspectives. With English summary.) *Konjunkturpolitik*, 1987, *33*(4), pp. 185–210.

White, Geoff. The State and the Private Sector. *Levitt, M. S., ed.*, 1987, pp. 30–42.

Whitehead, Laurence. The Adjustment Process in Chile: A Comparative Perspective. *Thorp, R. and Whitehead, L., eds.*, 1987, pp. 117–61. [G: Chile]

Wilkinson, Frank. Deregulation, Structured Labour Markets and Unemployment. *Pedersen, P. J. and Lund, R., eds.*, 1987, pp. 167–85. [G: W. Europe]

Williamson, John. Can the Economy Be Managed? *Williamson, J.*, 1987, pp. 231–45.

Williamson, John. Global Macroeconomic Strategy. *Williamson, J.*, 1987, *1982*, pp. 258–75. [G: Global]

Wymer, Clifford R. Sensitivity Analysis of Economic Policy. *[Marrama, V.], Vol. 2*, 1987, pp. 953–65.

Ziemes, Georg. Macroeconomic Policy, Rent Seeking and Economic Order: Comment. *Pethig, R. and Schlieper, U., eds.*, 1987, pp. 35–37.

Zimmermann, Klaus F. Transfers, Perfect Foresight and the Efficacy of Demand Policy. *J. Inst. Theoretical Econ.*, December 1987, *143*(4), pp. 652–57.

1332 Wage and Price Controls

Arnott, Richard J. Rent Control: The International Experience. *Arnott, R. J. and Mintz, J. M., eds.*, 1987, pp. 3–14. [G: Global]

Axell, Bo. Can Inflation Be Prohibited. *Eliasson, G., ed.*, 1987, pp. 129–31. [G: Sweden]

Belchamber, G. D. The Impact of Wages and Industrial Policy on the Performance of the Agricultural Sector from an ACTU Perspective. *Rev. Marketing Agr. Econ.*, April 1987, *55*(1), pp. 88–97. [G: Australia]

Blejer, Mario I. and Liviatan, Nissan. Fighting Hyperinflation: Stabilization Strategies in Argentina and Israel, 1985–86. *Int. Monet. Fund Staff Pap.*, September 1987, *34*(3), pp. 409–38. [G: Israel; Argentina]

Booth, Alan. Britain in the 1930s: A Managed Economy? *Econ. Hist. Rev., 2nd Ser.*, November 1987, *40*(4), pp. 499–522. [G: U.K.]

Bresser Pereira, Luiz. Inertial Inflation and the Cruzado Plan. *World Devel.*, August 1987, *15*(8), pp. 1035–44. [G: Brazil]

Brittan, Samuel. Innovative Supply-Side Policies to Reduce Unemployment: Commentary. *Begg, D. K. H., et al.*, 1987, pp. 122–27. [G: U.K.]

Carmody, G. F. Alternative Wages and Industrial Relations Policies: Pressures for Change. *Rev. Marketing Agr. Econ.*, April 1987, *55*(1), pp. 98–109. [G: Australia]

Cloete, J. J. A Role for Incomes Policy (Review Article). *S. Afr. J. Econ.*, September 1987, *55*(3), pp. 267–77. [G: OECD]

Coes, Donald V. Inertial Inflation and the Cruzado Plan: Discussion. *World Devel.*, August 1987, *15*(8), pp. 1139–41. [G: Brazil]

Cohen, Daniel and Michel, Philippe. Théorie et pratique du chômage en France. (Theory and Practice of French Unemployment. With English summary.) *Revue Écon.*, May 1987, *38*(3), pp. 661–75. [G: France]

Coleman, David. Rent Control: The British Experience and Policy Response. *Arnott, R. J. and Mintz, J. M., eds.*, 1987, pp. 77–98. [G: U.K.]

Diao, Xinshen. The Role of the Two-Tier Price System. *Reynolds, B. L.*, 1987, pp. 35–46. [G: China]

Erlich, S.; Ginsburgh, Victor and Van der Heyden, Ludo. Where Do Real Wage Policies Lead Belgium? A General Equilibrium Analysis. *Europ. Econ. Rev.*, October 1987, *31*(7), pp. 1369–83. [G: Belgium]

Fallis, George. Rent Control: The Citizen, the Market and the State. *Arnott, R. J. and Mintz, J. M., eds.*, 1987, pp. 163–74.

Franco, Gustavo H. B. The Rentenmark "Miracle." *Rivista Storia Econ.*, S.S., Int. Issue, 1987, *4*, pp. 96–117. [G: W. Germany]

Giambiagi, Fabio. A aritmética da escala móvel: Uma análise do comportamento do salário real num regime de reajustes com periodicidade Endógena. (With English summary.) *Pesquisa Planejamento Econ.*, December 1987, *17*(3), pp. 743–66. [G: Brazil]

Koford, Kenneth J. Some Short-run Microeconomic Effects of a Market Incentive Anti-inflation Plan. *Public Finance Quart.*, April 1987, *15*(2), pp. 199–218.

Lacroix, Robert and Robert, Jacques. Money-Wage Rigidities and the Effects of Wage Controls: An Analysis of Canadian Experience. *Steinherr, A. and Weiserbs, D., eds.*, 1987, pp. 185–212. [G: Canada]

Layard, Richard and Nickell, Stephen J. The Performance of the British Economy: The Labour Market. *Dornbusch, R. and Layard, R., eds.*, 1987, pp. 131–79. [G: U.K.]

Levine, A. L. A Further Note on Prices Policy from a Sraffian Perspective. *Math. Soc. Sci.*, June 1987, *13*(3), pp. 283–88.

Lewis, Philip E. T. and Kirby, Michael G. The Impact of Incomes Policy on Aggregate Wage Determination in Australia. *Econ. Rec.*, June 1987, *63*(181), pp. 156–61. [G: Australia]

McDermott, John H.; Bain, James A., Jr. and Miller, Jeffrey B. Price Control and Input Inventory: The Firm under Disequilibrium Trading. *J. Econ. Bus.*, August 1987, *39*(3), pp. 239–50.

Mills, Geofrey and Rockoff, Hugh. Compliance with Price Controls in the United States and the United Kingdom during World War II. *J. Econ. Hist.*, March 1987, *47*(1), pp. 197–213. **[G: U.S.; U.K.]**

Minford, Patrick. The Performance of the British Economy: The Labour Market: Comment. *Dornbusch, R. and Layard, R., eds.*, 1987, pp. 260–62. **[G: U.K.]**

Murray, Michael P., et al. Analyzing Rent Control: The Case of Los Angeles. *Arnott, R. J. and Mintz, J. M., eds.*, 1987, pp. 17–53. **[G: U.S.]**

Olsen, Edgar O. What Do Economists Know about the Effect of Rent Control on Housing Maintenance? *Arnott, R. J. and Mintz, J. M., eds.*, 1987, pp. 143–58.

Palokangas, Tapio. Optimal Taxation and Employment Policy with a Centralized Wage Setting. *Oxford Econ. Pap.*, December 1987, *39*(4), pp. 799–812.

Peel, David A. Innovative Supply-Side Policies to Reduce Unemployment: Commentary. *Begg, D. K. H., et al.*, 1987, pp. 118–21. **[G: U.K.]**

Sarris, Alexander H. Domestic Price Policies and International Distortions: The Cases of Wheat and Rice. *Econ. Notes*, 1987, (2), pp. 5–35. **[G: LDCs; MDCs]**

Sigurdsson, Brynjólfur. Prisdannelse og priskontrol. (Price Controls and Price Equilibrium. With English summary.) *Nationaløkon. Tidsskr.*, 1987, *125*(1), pp. 95–112.

Skidmore, Thomas E. The Resurgence of Inflation in Latin America: Discussion. *World Devel.*, August 1987, *15*(8), pp. 1148–49. **[G: Brazil; Argentina]**

Smith, Lawrence B. An Economic Assessment of Rent Controls: The Ontario Experience. *Arnott, R. J. and Mintz, J. M., eds.*, 1987, pp. 57–72. **[G: Canada]**

Smith, Russell E. Política salarial, mercado de trabajo y salarios industriales en San Pablo, 1960–1976: análisis sugn tamaño de las empresas y su condición de nacionales o extranjeras. (With English summary.) *Desarrollo Econ.*, Oct.-Dec. 1987, *27*(107), pp. 399–421. **[G: Brazil]**

Smith, Russell E. The Resurgence of Inflation in Latin America: Discussion. *World Devel.*, August 1987, *15*(8), pp. 1146–48. **[G: Argentina; Brazil]**

Solimano, Andrés. Emprego e salários reais: Uma análise macroeconômica de desequilíbrio para o Chile e o Brasil. (With English summary.) *Pesquisa Planejamento Econ.*, December 1987, *17*(3), pp. 605–31. **[G: Chile; Brazil]**

Stegman, Trevor. Incomes Policy: Some Issues. *Stegman, T., et al.*, 1987, pp. 1–24. **[G: Australia]**

Tobin, James. After Disinflation, Then What? *Tobin, J. (III)*, 1987, *1984*, pp. 348–67. **[G: U.S.]**

Tobin, James. Incentive-Based Incomes Policies:

Foreword. *Tobin, J. (III)*, 1987, *1986*, pp. 382–85. **[G: U.S.]**

Tobin, James. Inflation Control as Social Priority. *Tobin, J. (III)*, 1987, pp. 340–47. **[G: U.S.]**

Tobin, James. Inflation: Monetary and Structural Causes and Cures. *Tobin, J. (III)*, 1987, *1983*, pp. 324–39.

Tobin, James. Strategy for Disinflation (Fellner on 'The State of Monetary Policy'). *Tobin, J. (III)*, 1987, *1981*, pp. 368–74. **[G: U.S.]**

Tobin, James. The Case for Incomes Policies. *Tobin, J. (III)*, 1987, *1984*, pp. 375–81. **[G: U.S.]**

Turner, Bengt. Economic and Political Aspects of Negotiated Rents in the Swedish Housing Market. *Arnott, R. J. and Mintz, J. M., eds.*, 1987, pp. 101–20. **[G: Sweden]**

Walters, Alan. The Mischief of Moving Average Pricing. *Cato J.*, Spring/Summer 1987, *7*(1), pp. 241–48. **[G: LDCs]**

Werczberger, Elia. Rent Control in Israel. *Arnott, R. J. and Mintz, J. M., eds.*, 1987, pp. 123–39. **[G: Israel]**

Williamson, John. The Problem of Indexation. *Williamson, J.*, 1987, pp. 246–57.

Yang, Guansan; Yang, Xiaodong and Xuan, Mingdong. The Public Response to Price Reform. *Reynolds, B. L.*, 1987, pp. 59–73. **[G: China]**

134 Inflation and Deflation

1340 General

Barbera, Anthony J. Inflation, Tax Rules, and Investment: Some Additional Evidence. *J. Post Keynesian Econ.*, Spring 1987, *9*(3), pp. 315–26.

Batchelor, Roy A. Monetary Indicators and Operating Targets: Some Recent Issues in the UK. *Begg, D. K. H., et al.*, 1987, pp. 55–82. **[G: U.K.]**

Begg, David K. H. Fiscal Policy in Britain: Placing the Medium-term Financial Strategy in Context. *Begg, D. K. H., et al.*, 1987, pp. 17–43. **[G: U.K.]**

Bernholz, Peter. The Implementation and Maintenance of a Monetary Constitution. *Dorn, J. A. and Schwartz, A. J., eds.*, 1987, *1986*, pp. 83–117. **[G: OECD]**

Buchanan, James M. Constitutional Strategy and the Monetary Regime: Comment [The Implementation and Maintenance of a Monetary Constitution]. *Dorn, J. A. and Schwartz, A. J., eds.*, 1987, pp. 119–27. **[G: OECD]**

Budd, Alan. Fiscal Policy in Britain: Placing the Medium-term Financial Strategy in Context: Commentary. *Begg, D. K. H., et al.*, 1987, pp. 44–49. **[G: U.K.]**

Cameron, Norman E. Inflation and Nominal Policy Yields on Participating Life Insurance. *J. Risk Ins.*, September 1987, *54*(3), pp. 542–56. **[G: U.S.]**

Cardoso, Eliana A. and Dornbusch, Rudiger. Brazil's Tropical Plan. *Amer. Econ. Rev.*, May 1987, *77*(2), pp. 288–92. **[G: Brazil]**

Chang, Pei-kang and Lin, Shao-kung. China's

134 Inflation and Deflation

Modernization: Stability, Efficiency, and the Price Mechanism. *Dutta, M., ed. (I)*, 1987, pp. 103–18. **[G: China]**

Corbo, Vittorio. Impact on Debtor Countries of World Economic Conditions: Comment. *Martirena-Mantel, A. M., ed.*, 1987, pp. 87–90. **[G: Latin America]**

Currie, David. Fiscal Policy in Britain: Placing the Medium-term Financial Strategy in Context: Commentary. *Begg, D. K. H., et al.*, 1987, pp. 50–53. **[G: U.K.]**

Dornbusch, Rudiger. Impact on Debtor Countries of World Economic Conditions. *Martirena-Mantel, A. M., ed.*, 1987, pp. 60–87. **[G: Latin America]**

Dornbusch, Rudiger. Lessons from the German Inflation Experience of the 1920s. *[Modigliani, F.]*, 1987, pp. 337–66. **[G: Germany]**

Doupnik, Timothy S. The Brazilian System of Monetary Correction. *Most, Kenneth S., ed.*, 1987, pp. 111–35. **[G: Brazil]**

Eckstein, Zvi. Inflation and the Government Budget Constraint: Comments. *Razin, A. and Sadka, E., eds.*, 1987, pp. 201–02.

Fischer, Stanley. Inflation and the Government Budget Constraint: Comments. *Razin, A. and Sadka, E., eds.*, 1987, pp. 203–07.

Fischer, Stanley. The Israeli Stabilization Program, 1985–86. *Amer. Econ. Rev.*, May 1987, 77(2), pp. 275–78. **[G: Israel]**

Franco, Gustavo H. B. The Rentenmark "Miracle." *Rivista Storia Econ.*, S.S., Int. Issue, 1987, 4, pp. 96–117. **[G: W. Germany]**

Freeman, Scott. Reserve Requirements and Optimal Seigniorage. *J. Monet. Econ.*, March 1987, 19(2), pp. 307–14.

Goodhart, Charles A. E. Monetary Indicators and Operating Targets: Some Recent Issues in the UK: Commentary. *Begg, D. K. H., et al.*, 1987, pp. 83–88.

Hagelmayer, István. The Causes of Inflation in Hungary and the Prospects for Its Reduction. *Acta Oecon.*, 1987, 38(1–2), pp. 1–15. **[G: Hungary]**

Hazlitt, Henry. The Review of Austrian Economics: Editorial: The Inflationary Chaos Ahead. *Rothbard, M. N., ed.*, 1987, pp. 1–3. **[G: U.S.]**

Hester, Donald D. Inflation and Intermediation by Depository Institutions. *de Cecco, M. and Fitoussi, J.-P., eds.*, 1987, pp. 163–81. **[G: U.S.]**

Heymann, Daniel. Impact on Debtor Countries of World Economic Conditions: Comment. *Martirena-Mantel, A. M., ed.*, 1987, pp. 90–94. **[G: Latin America]**

Heymann, Daniel. The Austral Plan. *Amer. Econ. Rev.*, May 1987, 77(2), pp. 284–87. **[G: Argentina]**

Hibbs, Douglas A., Jr. The Mass Public and Macroeconomic Performance: Dynamics of Public Opinion toward Unemployment and Inflation. *Hibbs, D. A., Jr.*, 1987, 1979, pp. 117–42. **[G: U.S.]**

Kelton, Christina M. L. The Inflationary Contribution of Market Structure in Food and Tobacco Manufacturing. *Wills, R. L.; Caswell, J. A. and Culbertson, J. D., eds.*, 1987, pp. 345–59.

Lee, Chi-Wen Jevons and Petruzzi, Christopher R. A Test of the Shiller–Siegel Hypothesis of the Gibson Paradox [The Gibson Paradox and Historical Movements in Real Interest Rates]. *Australian Econ. Pap.*, June 1987, 26(48), pp. 157–64. **[G: U.K.]**

McFadden, Lynn. Government Revenue from Money Creation in Latin America: 1977–81. *Connolly, M. and González-Vega, C., eds.*, 1987, pp. 341–48. **[G: Latin America]**

McKinnon, Ronald I. Protectionism and the Misaligned Dollar: The Case for Monetary Coordination. *Salvatore, D., ed.*, 1987, pp. 367–88. **[G: Global]**

Nadiri, M. Ishaq. Price Inertia and Inflation: Evidence and Theoretical Rationale. *Pasinetti, L. and Lloyd, P., eds.*, 1987, pp. 329–57. **[G: U.S.]**

Nourzad, Farrokh. A Reexamination of the Effect of Rapid Military Spending on Inflation. *Quart. J. Bus. Econ.*, Summer 1987, 26(3), pp. 57–66. **[G: U.S.]**

Pandit, V. and Bhattacharya, B. B. Resource Mobilization, Growth, and Inflation: A Trade-Off Analysis for India. *Dutta, M., ed. (I)*, 1987, pp. 119–41. **[G: India]**

Perraudin, W. R. M. Inflation and Portfolio Choice. *Int. Monet. Fund Staff Pap.*, December 1987, 34(4), pp. 739–59. **[G: U.K.]**

Rose, Harold. Monetary Indicators and Operating Targets: Some Recent Issues in the UK: Commentary. *Begg, D. K. H., et al.*, 1987, pp. 89–91. **[G: U.K.]**

Sami, Heibatollah and Trapnell, Jerry E. Inflation-Adjusted Data and Security Prices: Some Empirical Evidence. *Schwartz, B. N., ed.*, 1987, pp. 39–57. **[G: U.S.]**

Sargent, Thomas J. and Wallace, Neil. Inflation and the Government Budget Constraint. *Razin, A. and Sadka, E., eds.*, 1987, pp. 170–200.

Schwartz, Anna J. Secular Price Change in Historical Perspective. *Schwartz, A. J.*, 1987, 1973, pp. 78–109.

Schwert, G. William. Effects of Model Specification on Tests for Unit Roots in Macroeconomic Data. *J. Monet. Econ.*, July 1987, 20(1), pp. 73–103.

Siklos, P. L. Additional Thoughts on the Hungarian Hyperinflation of 1945–46. *S. Afr. J. Econ.*, March 1987, 55(1), pp. 83–85.

Spaventa, Luigi. Lessons from the German Inflation Experience of the 1920s: Comments. *[Modigliani, F.]*, 1987, pp. 367–71. **[G: Germany]**

Sweeney, James L. The Response of Energy Demand to Higher Prices: What Have We Learned? *Pachauri, R. K., ed.*, 1987, pp. 573–84.

Thorp, Rosemary. Peruvian Adjustment Policies, 1978–85: The Effects of Prolonged Crisis. *Thorp, R. and Whitehead, L., eds.*, 1987, pp. 208–38. **[G: Peru]**

Tobin, James. Inflation and Unemployment. *Tobin, J. (II),* 1987, *1972,* pp. 33–59.

Tobin, James. The Case for Incomes Policies. *Tobin, J. (III),* 1987, *1984,* pp. 375–81.
[G: U.S.]

Vane, Howard. The Importance of Controlling Inflation. *Vane, H. and Caslin, T., eds.,* 1987, pp. 81–102. [G: U.K.]

1342 Inflation Theories; Studies Illustrating Inflation Theories

Abraham, Jesse M. Income Redistribution during a Disinflation. *J. Macroecon.,* Spring 1987, 9(2), pp. 203–21. [G: U.S.]

Adachi, Hideyuki. The Role of Commodity Prices in the Worldwide Inflation and Disinflation. *Kobe Univ. Econ.,* 1987, *33,* pp. 17–31.

Ahmad, J. Inflationary Expectations and Price Interdependence under Floating Exchange Rates. *Borner, S. and Taylor, A., eds.,* 1987, pp. 395–404.

Andersen, Torben M. Pre-set Prices, Differential Information and Monetary Policy. *Sinclair, P. J. N., ed.,* 1987, *1986,* pp. 283–307.

Argimon, Isabel and González-Páramo, José Manuel. Una medición de la rémora inflacionaria del IRPF, 1979–1985. (With English summary.) *Invest. Econ.,* May 1987, *11*(2), pp. 345–66. [G: Spain]

Arize, Augustine. Inflation and Import Prices in Some Developing Countries: An Instrumental Variable Procedure. *Pakistan Econ. Soc. Rev.,* Summer 1987, *25*(1), pp. 39–57. [G: Africa]

Arize, Augustine. Past Inflation Variability and the Stability of the Demand-for-Money Function in Nigeria. *Atlantic Econ. J.,* March 1987, *15*(1), pp. 31–41. [G: Nigeria]

Backus, David and Driffill, John. Credible Disinflation in Closed and Open Economies. *Ricerche Econ.,* July-Dec. 1987, *41*(3–4), pp. 326–40. [G: Canada]

Baer, Werner. The Resurgence of Inflation in Brazil, 1974–86. *World Devel.,* August 1987, *15*(8), pp. 1007–34. [G: Brazil]

Baer, Werner and Welch, John H. The Resurgence of Inflation in Latin America: Editors' Introduction. *World Devel.,* August 1987, *15*(8), pp. 989–90. [G: Latin America]

Bahr, Richard C. Inflation Fueled by Oil Prices in First 9 Months of 1987. *Mon. Lab. Rev.,* December 1987, *110*(12), pp. 3–6. [G: U.S.]

Barsky, Robert B. The Fisher Hypothesis and the Forecastability and Persistence of Inflation. *J. Monet. Econ.,* January 1987, *19*(1), pp. 3–24. [G: U.S.]

Batchelor, Roy A. and Dua, P. The Accuracy and Rationality of UK Inflation Expectations: Some Quantitative Evidence. *Appl. Econ.,* June 1987, *19*(6), pp. 819–28. [G: U.K.]

Bechtold, Hartmut and Helfer, Andreas. Stagflation Problems in Socialist Economies. *Gey, P.; Kosta, J. and Quaisser, W., eds.,* 1987, pp. 11–31. [G: Hungary; Yugoslavia]

Beckerman, Paul. Inflation and Dollar Accounts in Peru's Banking System, 1978–84. *World Devel.,* August 1987, *15*(8), pp. 1087–1106.
[G: Peru]

Black, Robert P. The Fed's Anti-inflationary Strategy: Is It Adequate? *Fed. Res. Bank Richmond Econ. Rev.,* Sept./Oct. 1987, *73*(5), pp. 3–9. [G: U.S.]

Blanchard, Olivier Jean. Aggregate and Individual Price Adjustment. *Brookings Pap. Econ. Act.,* 1987, (1), pp. 57–109. [G: U.S.]

Blejer, Mario I. and Liviatan, Nissan. Fighting Hyperinflation: Stabilization Strategies in Argentina and Israel, 1985–86. *Int. Monet. Fund Staff Pap.,* September 1987, *34*(3), pp. 409–38. [G: Israel; Argentina]

Booth, Laurence D.; Finkelstein, John M. and Lee, Wayne Y. A Note on the Demand for Labor by Firms and the Phillips Curve Phenomenon. *J. Econ. Bus.,* November 1987, *39*(4), pp. 349–56.

Boskin, Michael J. Deficits, Public Debt, Interest Rates and Private Saving: Perspectives and Reflections on Recent Analyses and on U.S. Experience. *Boskin, M. J.; Fleming, J. S. and Gorini, S., eds.,* 1987, pp. 255–86. [G: U.S.]

Bresser Pereira, Luiz. Inertial Inflation and the Cruzado Plan. *World Devel.,* August 1987, *15*(8), pp. 1035–44. [G: Brazil]

Bruno, Michael. Stagflation in the Industrial Countries: An Updated Overview. *Hitotsubashi J. Econ.,* October 1987, *27,* pp. 57–74.
[G: OECD]

Bruter, C. P. Inflation et théorie des singularités. Pour François Perroux, en hommage fidèle. (Inflation and Theory of Singularities. With English summary.) *Écon. Appl.,* 1987, *40*(3), pp. 565–79.

Bruter, C. P. Symétrie, économie et inflation. (Symmetry, Economics and Inflation. With English summary.) *Écon. Soc.,* January 1987, *21*(1), pp. 109–18.

Buffie, Edward F. Input Price Shocks in the Small Open Economy. *Sinclair, P. J. N., ed.,* 1987, *1986,* pp. 233–47.

Buiter, Willem H. A Fiscal Theory of Hyperdeflations? Some Surprising Monetarist Arithmetic. *Oxford Econ. Pap.,* March 1987, *39*(1), pp. 111–18.

Buiter, Willem H. A Fiscal Theory of Hyperdeflations? Some Surprising Monetarist Arithmetic. *Sinclair, P. J. N., ed.,* 1987, pp. 111–18.

Burdekin, Richard C. K. Swiss Monetary Policy: Central Bank Independence and Stabilization Goals. *Kredit Kapital,* 1987, *20*(4), pp. 454–66. [G: Switzerland]

Burmeister, Edwin and Wall, Kent D. Unobserved Rational Expectations and the German Hyperinflation with Endogenous Money Supply. *Int. Econ. Rev.,* February 1987, *28*(1), pp. 15–32. [G: Germany]

Burns, Arthur F. The Anguish of Central Banking. *Ciocca, P., ed.,* 1987, *1979,* pp. 147–66.
[G: U.S.]

Burns, Arthur F. The Anguish of Central Banking. *Fed. Res. Bull.,* September 1987, *73*(9), pp. 687–98. [G: U.S.]

Cagan, Phillip. Disinflation, the Dollar, and Ve-

locity. *Cagan, P., ed.*, 1987, pp. 129–52.
[G: U.S.]

Canto, Victor A.; Nickelsburg, Gerald and Rizos, Paul. The Effect of Fiscal Policy on the Short-run Relation between Nominal Interest Rates and Inflation. *Econ. Inquiry*, January 1987, 25(1), pp. 27–42. [G: U.S.]

Canton, Richard and Wenninger, John. Current Labor Market Trends and Inflation. *Fed. Res. Bank New York Quart. Rev.*, Autumn 1987, 12(3), pp. 36–48. [G: U.S.]

Caplin, Andrew S. and Spulber, Daniel F. Menu Costs and the Neutrality of Money. *Quart. J. Econ.*, November 1987, 102(4), pp. 703–25.

Cárdenas, Enrique and Manns, Carlos. Inflation and Monetary Stabilization in Mexico During the Revolution. *J. Devel. Econ.*, October 1987, 27(1–2), pp. 375–94. [G: Mexico]

Cárdenas, Enrique and Manns, Carlos. Inflation and Monetary Stabilization in Mexico during the Revolution. *[Diaz-Alejandro, C. F.]*, 1987, pp. 375–94. [G: Mexico]

Carrington, Samantha and Crouch, Robert. Interest Rate Differentials on Short-term Securities and Rational Expectations of Inflation. *J. Banking Finance*, December 1987, 11(4), pp. 571–79. [G: U.S.]

Carter, Michael G. and Maddock, Rodney. Inflation: The Invisible Foot of Macroeconomics. *Econ. Rec.*, June 1987, 63(181), pp. 120–28.

Chambers, E. J. and Hsu, Andy. Some Findings on Relative Price Change Variance and Inflation Rate Uncertainty in the Canadian CPI. *Appl. Econ.*, March 1987, 19(3), pp. 285–303. [G: Canada]

Chang, Eric C. and Pinegar, J. Michael. Risk and Inflation. *J. Finan. Quant. Anal.*, March 1987, 22(1), pp. 89–99. [G: U.S.]

Christensen, Michael. Disinflation, Credibility and Price Inertia: A Danish Exposition. *Appl. Econ.*, October 1987, 19(10), pp. 1353–66. [G: Denmark]

Christiano, Lawrence J. Cagan's Model of Hyperinflation under Rational Expectations. *Int. Econ. Rev.*, February 1987, 28(1), pp. 33–49. [G: Germany]

Clements, Kenneth W. and Izan, H. Y. The Measurement of Inflation: A Stochastic Approach. *J. Bus. Econ. Statist.*, July 1987, 5(3), pp. 339–50. [G: Australia]

Coes, Donald V. Inertial Inflation and the Cruzado Plan: Discussion. *World Devel.*, August 1987, 15(8), pp. 1139–41. [G: Brazil]

Congdon, Tim G. The Link between Budget Deficits and Inflation: Some Contrasts between Developed and Developing Countries. *Boskin, M. J.; Fleming, J. S. and Gorini, S., eds.*, 1987, pp. 72–91. [G: LDCs; MDCs]

Cooper, Kathleen M. Real Interest Rates: The Unpuzzle. *Bus. Econ.*, January 1987, 22(1), pp. 13–17. [G: U.S.; U.K.]

Cross, Rod B. Hysteresis and Instability in the Natural Rate of Unemployment. *Scand. J. Econ.*, 1987, 89(1), pp. 71–89.

Danziger, Leif. Inflation, Fixed Cost of Price Adjustment, and Measurement of Relative-Price

Variability: Theory and Evidence. *Amer. Econ. Rev.*, September 1987, 77(4), pp. 704–13. [G: Israel]

Danziger, Leif. On Inflation and Real Price Variability. *Econ. Inquiry*, April 1987, 25(2), pp. 285–98.

De Freitas, A. J. M. and Solnik, Bruno. L'anticipation de l'inflation et le taux d'intérêt à court term. (Expected Inflation and Short Term Interest Rates. With English summary.) *Finance*, December 1987, 8(2), pp. 77–89. [G: OECD; Brazil; Mexico]

Devereux, Michael. The Effect of Monetary Variability on Welfare in a Simple Macroeconomic Model. *J. Monet. Econ.*, May 1987, 19(3), pp. 427–35.

Domberger, Simon. Relative Price Variability and Inflation: A Disaggregated Analysis. *J. Polit. Econ.*, June 1987, 95(3), pp. 547–66. [G: U.K.]

Elliott, J. Walter and Reichenstein, William. A Monetary Approach to Measuring Long-run Inflationary Expectations. *J. Econ. Bus.*, November 1987, 39(4), pp. 327–38. [G: U.S.]

Epstein, Edward C. Recent Stabilization Programs in Argentina, 1973–86. *World Devel.*, August 1987, 15(8), pp. 991–1005. [G: Argentina]

Esfahani, Hadi Salehi. The Resurgence of Inflation in Latin America: Discussion. *World Devel.*, August 1987, 15(8), pp. 1141–43. [G: S. America; Peru; Chile]

Flemming, John S. The Economics of Worldwide Stagflation: A Review. *Oxford Econ. Pap.*, March 1987, 39(1), pp. 223–32.

Flemming, John S. The Economics of Worldwide Stagflation: A Review. *Sinclair, P. J. N., ed.*, 1987, pp. 223–32. [G: Global]

Fortune, J. Neill. Some Determinants of Labour Productivity. *Appl. Econ.*, June 1987, 19(6), pp. 839–43. [G: U.S.]

Franz, Wolfgang. Hysteresis, Persistence, and the NAIRU: An Empirical Analysis for the Federal Republic of Germany. *Layard, R. and Calmfors, L., eds.*, 1987, pp. 91–122. [G: W. Germany]

Frenkel, Jacob A. Optimal Currency Substitution Policy and Public Finance: Comments. *Razin, A. and Sadka, E., eds.*, 1987, pp. 165–69.

Froyen, Richard T. and Waud, Roger N. An Examination of Aggregate Price Uncertainty in Four Countries and Some Implications for Real Output. *Int. Econ. Rev.*, June 1987, 28(2), pp. 353–72. [G: U.S.; U.K.; Canada; W. Germany]

Fullerton, Don. The Indexation of Interest, Depreciation, and Capital Gains and Tax Reform in the United States. *J. Public Econ.*, February 1987, 32(1), pp. 25–51. [G: U.S.]

Garber, Peter M. Monetary History and Monetary Policy: A Review Essay. *J. Monet. Econ.*, July 1987, 20(1), pp. 177–82.

Garrett, John R. Macroeconomic Policy and History. *Cambridge J. Econ.*, December 1987, 11(4), pp. 375–92. [G: U.S.; U.K.]

Giambiagi, Fabio. A aritmética da escala móvel:

Uma análise do comportamento do salário real num regime de reajustes com periodicidade Endógena. (With English summary.) *Pesquisa Planejamento Econ.*, December 1987, *17*(3), pp. 743–66. **[G: Brazil]**

Giannaros, Demetrios S. and Lashgari, Malek K. Business Cycles, Inflation and the Price of Gold: An Empirical Investigation. *Tremblay, R., ed.*, 1987, pp. 111–21.

Glezakos, Constantine and Nugent, Jeffrey B. The Relationship between the Rate of Inflation and Its Unpredictability in High Inflation Latin American Countries. *World Devel.*, February 1987, *15*(2), pp. 291–93. **[G: Latin America]**

Golden, John M.; Orescovich, Robert and Ostafin, David. Optimality on the Short-run Phillips Curve: A "Misery Index" Criterion, a Note. *Amer. Econ.*, Fall 1987, *31*(2), pp. 72.

Gonzalez, Norberto. International Price Fluctuations and Inflation: Discussion and Conclusions. *Pasinetti, L. and Lloyd, P., eds.*, 1987, pp. 395–402. **[G: Global]**

Gordon, Robert J. Aggregate and Individual Price Adjustment: Comments. *Brookings Pap. Econ. Act.*, 1987, (1), pp. 110–17. **[G: U.S.]**

Green, Steven L. Theories of Inflation: A Review Essay. *J. Monet. Econ.*, July 1987, *20*(1), pp. 169–75.

Greenwood, Jeremy and Huffman, Gregory W. A Dynamic Equilibrium Model of Inflation and Unemployment. *J. Monet. Econ.*, March 1987, *19*(2), pp. 203–28.

Grubb, David. Wage Behaviour and Macroeconomic Policy. *Gunderson, M.; Meltz, N. M. and Ostry, S., eds.*, 1987, pp. 103–07. **[G: U.S.; W. Europe; Canada]**

Guerberoff, Simón L. Flexibilidad de precios, variaciones de stocks e incertidumbre: la política antinflacionaria después del Plan Austral. (With English summary.) *Desarrollo Econ.*, July-Sept. 1987, *27*(106), pp. 171–200. **[G: Argentina]**

Gunderson, Morley; Meltz, Noah M. and Ostry, Sylvia. Unemployment: International Perspectives: Introduction: A Summary of the Issues. *Gunderson, M.; Meltz, N. M. and Ostry, S., eds.*, 1987, pp. 1–10.

Hall, Thomas E. and Fields, T. Windsor. Anticipated Nominal Demand Shocks and the Speed of Aggregate Price Adjustment. *Rev. Econ. Statist.*, February 1987, *69*(1), pp. 140–44. **[G: U.S.]**

Haltiwanger, John and Plant, Mark. Alternative Measures of Slackness in the Labor Market and Their Relationship to Wage and Price Inflation. *Lang, K. and Leonard, J. S., eds.*, 1987, pp. 212–33. **[G: U.S.]**

Handler, Heinz. Short-run Relations between the Real Sector and Inflation. *Empirica*, 1987, *14*(2), pp. 187–212. **[G: Austria]**

Hardouvelis, Gikas A. Optimal Wage Indexation and Monetary Policy in an Economy with Imported Raw Materials. *J. Int. Money Finance*, December 1987, *6*(4), pp. 419–32.

Hartzell, David J.; Hekman, John S. and Miles, Mike E. Real Estate Returns and Inflation. *Amer. Real Estate Urban Econ. Assoc. J.*, Spring 1987, *15*(1), pp. 617–37. **[G: U.S.]**

Henry, Samuel G. Brian and Karakitsos, Elias. Inflation, Unemployment and Indirect Taxation. *Bull. Econ. Res.*, January 1987, *39*(1), pp. 29–47.

Hercowitz, Zvi and Sadka, Efraim. On Optimal Currency Substitution Policy and Public Finance. *Razin, A. and Sadka, E., eds.*, 1987, pp. 147–64.

Hetzel, Robert L. Will Recent High Growth Rates of Money Revive Inflation? *Contemp. Policy Issues*, January 1987, *5*(1), pp. 41–53. **[G: U.S.]**

Hibbs, Douglas A., Jr. Trade Union Power, Wage Inflation, and Labor Militancy: A Comparative Analysis. *Hibbs, D. A., Jr.*, 1987, *1977*, pp. 77–114. **[G: Italy; France; U.K.; U.S.]**

Hickman, Bert G. Growth, Inflation and Unemployment in the United States. *Pasinetti, L. and Lloyd, P., eds.*, 1987, pp. 293–300. **[G: U.S.]**

Himarios, Daniel. Devaluation, Devaluation Expectations and Price Dynamics. *Economica*, August 1987, *54*(215), pp. 299–313. **[G: Selected Countries]**

de Holanda Barbosa, Fernando. Domestic and International Sources of Brazilian Inflation: 1947–80. *Pasinetti, L. and Lloyd, P., eds.*, 1987, pp. 381–93. **[G: Brazil]**

Holmlund, Bertil. Unemployment and the Real Wage: Comment. *Siven, C.-H., ed.*, 1987, pp. 69–70.

Holtfrerich, Carl-Ludwig. The Modernisation of the Tax System in the First World War and the Great Inflation, 1914–23. *Witt, P.-C., ed.*, 1987, pp. 125–35. **[G: Germany]**

Hossain, Akhtar. Impact of Inflation on Fiscal Deficits in the Bangladesh Economy. *Pakistan Devel. Rev.*, Summer 1987, *26*(2), pp. 179–200. **[G: Bangladesh]**

Howe, Keith M. and Lapan, Harvey. Inflation and Asset Life: The Darby versus the Fisher Effect. *J. Finan. Quant. Anal.*, June 1987, *22*(2), pp. 249–58.

Howell, Craig; Burns, Roger and Clem, Andrew G. Sharp Drop in Energy Prices Holds Inflation in Check during 1986. *Mon. Lab. Rev.*, May 1987, *110*(5), pp. 3–9. **[G: U.S.]**

Hu, Sheng Cheng. Uncertain Inflation and Social Security Indexation. *J. Econ. Dynam. Control*, September 1987, *11*(3), pp. 359–72.

Hvidding, James M. Measurement Error and Tests for Expectational Rationality Using Survey Data. *Southern Econ. J.*, July 1987, *54*(1), pp. 110–18. **[G: U.S.]**

Jones, Jonathan D. and Uri, Noel D. Money, Inflation and Causality (Another Look at the Empirical Evidence for the USA, 1953–84). *Appl. Econ.*, May 1987, *19*(5), pp. 619–34. **[G: U.S.]**

Kaufman, Roger T. and Woglom, Geoffrey. The Conformity of Wage Indexation Models with the "Stylized Facts": A Comment. *Amer. Econ.*

Rev., September 1987, *77*(4), pp. 747–49.
[**G: Canada; W. Germany; Japan; U.S.; U.K.**]

Kaul, Gautam. Stock Returns and Inflation: The Role of the Monetary Sector. *J. Finan. Econ.*, June 1987, *18*(2), pp. 253–76.   [**G: U.S.; U.K.; Canada; W. Germany**]

Kirkpatrick, Colin and Nixson, Frederick. Inflation and Stabilization Policy in LDCs. *Gemmell, N., ed.*, 1987, pp. 172–202.

Kleiman, Ephraim. The Resurgence of Inflation in Latin America: Discussion. *World Devel.*, August 1987, *15*(8), pp. 1143–45.   [**G: Peru**]

Klein, Lawrence R. Growth, Inflation and Employment: Discussion and Conclusions. *Pasinetti, L. and Lloyd, P., eds.*, 1987, pp. 323–25.

Klein, Lawrence R. Growth, Inflation and Employment: An Introduction. *Pasinetti, L. and Lloyd, P., eds.*, 1987, pp. 269–74.
[**G: Global**]

Koford, Kenneth J. Some Short-run Microeconomic Effects of a Market Incentive Anti-inflation Plan. *Public Finance Quart.*, April 1987, *15*(2), pp. 199–218.

Kolodko, Grzegorz W. International Transmission of Inflation: Its Economics and Its Politics. *World Devel.*, August 1987, *15*(8), pp. 1131–38.   [**G: Global**]

Kolodko, Grzegorz W. and McMahon, Walter W. Stagflation and Shortageflation: A Comparative Approach. *Kyklos*, 1987, *40*(2), pp. 176–97.   [**G: OECD; CMEA**]

Koluri, Bharat R. and Giannaros, Demetrios S. Deficit and External Debt Effects on Money and Inflation in Brazil and Mexico: Some Evidence. *Eastern Econ. J.*, July-Sept. 1987, *13*(3), pp. 243–48.   [**G: Brazil; Mexico**]

Koskela, Erkki and Virén, Matti. Inflation, Hedging and the Demand for Money: Some Empirical Evidence. *Econ. Inquiry*, April 1987, *25*(2), pp. 251–65.   [**G: U.S.**]

Kosters, Marvin H. and Ross, Murray N. The Influence of Employment Shifts and New Job Opportunities on the Growth and Distribution of Real Wages. *Cagan, P., ed.*, 1987, pp. 209–42.   [**G: U.S.**]

Kravis, Irving B. and Lipsey, Robert E. The Assessment of National Price Levels. *Arndt, S. W. and Richardson, J. D. eds.*, 1987, pp. 97–134.   [**G: Selected Countries**]

Kregel, Jan A. The Effective Demand Approach to Employment and Inflation Analysis. *J. Post Keynesian Econ.*, Fall 1987, *10*(1), pp. 133–45.

Krelle, Wilhelm. Growth, Inflation and Employment. *Pasinetti, L. and Lloyd, P., eds.*, 1987, pp. 275–91.

Krishnamurty, K. Inflation and Growth: Some Experiments on a Model for India. *Pasinetti, L. and Lloyd, P., eds.*, 1987, pp. 305–22.
[**G: India**]

Kuczynski, Michael. Inflation and Monetary Institutions in Developing Countries. *de Cecco, M. and Fitoussi, J.-P., eds.*, 1987, pp. 222–40.
[**G: LDCs**]

Lacroix, Robert and Robert, Jacques. Money-Wage Rigidities and the Effects of Wage Controls: An Analysis of Canadian Experience. *Steinherr, A. and Weiserbs, D., eds.*, 1987, pp. 185–212.   [**G: Canada**]

Lahiri, Kajal and Zaporowski, Mark. More Flexible Use of Survey Data on Expectations in Macroeconomic Models. *J. Bus. Econ. Statist.*, January 1987, *5*(1), pp. 68–76.   [**G: U.S.**]

Leijonhufvud, Axel. Constitutional Constraints on the Monetary Powers of Government. *Dorn, J. A. and Schwartz, A. J., eds.*, 1987, pp. 129–43.   [**G: U.S.**]

Leijonhufvud, Axel. Rational Expectations and Monetary Institutions. *de Cecco, M. and Fitoussi, J.-P., eds.*, 1987, pp. 44–65.

Leonard, David C. and Solt, Michael E. Stock Market Signals of Changes in Expected Inflation. *J. Finan. Res.*, Spring 1987, *10*(1), pp. 57–63.   [**G: U.S.**]

LeRoy, Stephen F. and Raymon, Neil. A Monetarist Model of Inflation. *J. Econ. Theory*, August 1987, *42*(2), pp. 275–310.

Levačic, Rosalind. Inflation and Unemployment. *Thompson, G.; Brown, V. and Levaćić, R., eds.*, 1987, pp. 161–95.

Lim, Joseph. The New Structuralist Critique of the Monetarist Theory of Inflation: The Case of the Philippines. *J. Devel. Econ.*, February 1987, *25*(1), pp. 45–61.   [**G: Philippines**]

Machlup, Fritz. The Political Economy of Inflation. *Dorn, J. A. and Schwartz, A. J., eds.*, 1987, pp. 291–96.

Maier, Charles S. The Politics of Inflation in the Twentieth Century. *Maier, C. S.*, 1987, *1978*, pp. 187–224.

Mair, Douglas. Prices and Income Distribution in Manufacturing Industry: Comment. *J. Post Keynesian Econ.*, Fall 1987, *10*(1), pp. 154–60.   [**G: Italy; U.S.**]

Malamud, Bernard. Ominous Parallels...Heartening Differences. *Challenge*, Mar./Apr. 1987, *30*(1), pp. 59–60.   [**G: OECD**]

Malcomson, James M. and Sartor, Nicola. Tax Push Inflation in a Unionized Labour Market. *Europ. Econ. Rev.*, December 1987, *31*(8), pp. 1581–96.   [**G: Italy**]

Malinvaud, Edmond. Investment and the Inflation–Unemployment Tradeoff in a Macroeconomic Rationing Model with Monopolistic Competition: Comments. *Europ. Econ. Rev.*, April 1987, *31*(3), pp. 808–11.

Manchester, Joyce. Mortgage Contracts in a General Equilibrium Model when There Are Inflation Shocks. *J. Macroecon.*, Summer 1987, *9*(3), pp. 327–49.

Mankiw, N. Gregory. The Optimal Collection of Seigniorage: Theory and Evidence. *J. Monet. Econ.*, September 1987, *20*(2), pp. 327–41.
[**G: U.S.**]

Manski, Charles F. and Goldin, Ephraim. The Denomination-Specific Demand for Currency in a High-Inflation Setting: The Israeli Experience. *Heijmans, R. and Neudecker, H., eds.*, 1987, pp. 99–120.   [**G: Israel**]

Mates, Neven. Some Specific Features of Inflation

in a Heavily-Indebted Socialist Country. *Econ. Anal. Workers' Manage.*, 1987, *21*(4), pp. 419–31. **[G: Yugoslavia]**

McCallum, Bennett T. The Optimal Inflation Rate in an Overlapping-Generations Economy with Land. *Barnett, W. A. and Singleton, K. J., eds.*, 1987, pp. 325–39.

McNelis, Paul D. Indexing, Exchange Rate Policy and Inflationary Feedback Effects in Latin America. *World Devel.*, August 1987, *15*(8), pp. 1107–17. **[G: S. America]**

McNelis, Paul D. Indexing, Exchange Rate Policy and Inflationary Feedback Effects in Latin America: Discussion. *World Devel.*, August 1987, *15*(8), pp. 1145–46. **[G: S. America]**

Mencinger, Jože. Acceleration of Inflation into Hyperinflation—The Yugoslav Experience in the 1980's. *Econ. Anal. Workers' Manage.*, 1987, *21*(4), pp. 399–418. **[G: Yugoslavia]**

Mistri, Maurizio. Comportamenti innovativi di impresa con aspettative inflazionistiche dualistiche e struttura del mercato del lavoro. (Innovative Behaviours with Dualistic Inflationary Expectations and Labour Market Structure. With English summary.) *Rivista Int. Sci. Econ. Com.*, July 1987, *34*(7), pp. 609–21.

Monticelli, Carlo. Inflation and Liquidity Preference. *Giorn. Econ.*, Sept.-Oct. 1987, *46*(9–10), pp. 481–90.

Morrison, Rodney J. Inflation in Portugal, 1953–1980: An Econometric Analysis. *Kyklos*, 1987, *40*(2), pp. 219–37. **[G: Portugal]**

Morse, Jeremy [Sir]. The Great Inflation and Its Aftermath. *Lloyds Bank Rev.*, October 1987, (166), pp. 1–6.

Myatt, Anthony E. and Scarth, William M. Fiscal Policy, Interest Sensitive Aggregate Supply and the Costs of Disinflation. *Manchester Sch. Econ. Soc. Stud.*, June 1987, *55*(2), pp. 144–57.

Nickell, Stephen J. Unemployment and the Real Wage. *Siven, C.-H., ed.*, 1987, pp. 45–68.

Nickell, Stephen J. Why Is Wage Inflation in Britain So High? *Oxford Bull. Econ. Statist.*, February 1987, *49*(1), pp. 103–28. **[G: U.K.]**

Nickelsburg, Gerald. Inflation, Expectations and Qualitative Government Policy in Ecuador, 1970–82. *World Devel.*, August 1987, *15*(8), pp. 1077–85. **[G: Ecuador]**

Ohyama, Michihiro. Unemployment and Inflation: Natural Wage Rate Hypothesis. *Keio Econ. Stud.*, 1987, *24*(2), pp. 11–26.

Paldam, Martin. Inflation and Political Instability in Eight Latin American Countries 1946–83. *Public Choice*, 1987, *52*(2), pp. 143–68. **[G: Latin America]**

Pauls, B. Dianne. Comovements in Aggregate and Relative Prices: Some Evidence on Neutrality. *J. Monet. Econ.*, July 1987, *20*(1), pp. 155–68. **[G: U.S.]**

Pearce, Douglas K. Short-term Inflation Expectations: Evidence from a Monthly Survey: A Note. *J. Money, Credit, Banking*, August 1987, *19*(3), pp. 388–95. **[G: U.S.]**

Peek, Joe. The Distorting Effects of the Inflation Premium on Personal Income and Expendi-

tures. *New Eng. Econ. Rev.*, Sept./Oct. 1987, pp. 10–24. **[G: U.S.]**

Pikoulakis, Emmanuel. The Cost of Disinflation Reexamined. *Economia (Portugal)*, May 1987, *11*(2), pp. 215–30.

Pitchford, John David and Vousden, Neil J. Exchange Rates, Policy Rules and Inflation. *Australian Econ. Pap.*, June 1987, *26*(48), pp. 43–57.

Portes, Richard. Investment and the Inflation–Unemployment Tradeoff in a Macroeconomic Rationing Model with Monopolistic Competition: Comments. *Europ. Econ. Rev.*, April 1987, *31*(3), pp. 812–15.

Pourgerami, Abbas and Maskus, Keith E. The Effects of Inflation on the Predictability of Price Changes in Latin America: Some Estimates and Policy Implications. *World Devel.*, February 1987, *15*(2), pp. 287–90. **[G: Latin America]**

Pozdena, Randall Johnston. Inflation, Age, and Wealth. *Fed. Res. Bank San Francisco Econ. Rev.*, Winter 1987, (1), pp. 17–30. **[G: U.S.]**

Prachowny, Martin F. J. Conflict in the Labor Market: Seniority Rules and Unemployment. *J. Macroecon.*, Fall 1987, *9*(4), pp. 527–34. **[G: U.S.]**

Protopapadakis, Aris A. and Siegel, Jeremy J. Are Money Growth and Inflation Related to Government Deficits? Evidence from Ten Industrialized Economies. *J. Int. Money Finance*, March 1987, *6*(1), pp. 31–48. **[G: Selected OECD]**

Rabeau, Yves. L'expérience de déflation au Canada et le comportement des salaires. (With English summary.) *Revue Écon. Polit.*, Sept.-Oct. 1987, *97*(5), pp. 556–74.

Rabin, Alan. A Reexamination of the Acceleration of Worldwide Inflation in the Early 1970s. *J. Macroecon.*, Spring 1987, *9*(2), pp. 275–85. **[G: Global]**

Raczkowski, Stanislaw. The Influence of International Price Movements and Inflation on the Centrally Planned Economies. *Pasinetti, L. and Lloyd, P., eds.*, 1987, pp. 359–80. **[G: CMEA]**

Reichenstein, William and Elliott, J. Walter. A Comparison of Models of Long-term Inflationary Expectations. *J. Monet. Econ.*, May 1987, *19*(3), pp. 405–25. **[G: U.S.]**

Richter, Rudolf and Diener, Frank. Phillips Curves in West-Germany 1975–1985: On the Role of the Deutsche Bundesbank as an Expectation Determining Institution. *Weltwirtsch. Arch.*, 1987, *123*(2), pp. 346–53. **[G: W. Germany]**

Robinson, Kenneth J. Estimating the Inflationary Consequences of Discretionary Central Bank Behavior. *Fed. Res. Bank Dallas Econ. Rev.*, May 1987, pp. 17–28. **[G: U.S.]**

Rosengren, Eric S. Forecasting Changes in Inflation Using the Treasury Bill Futures Market. *New Eng. Econ. Rev.*, Mar./Apr. 1987, pp. 41–48. **[G: U.S.]**

Sachs, Jeffrey D. The Bolivian Hyperinflation and Stabilization. *Amer. Econ. Rev.*, May 1987, *77*(2), pp. 279–83. **[G: Bolivia]**

Samuelson, Larry. Inflation, Indexing and Economic Development. *World Devel.*, August 1987, *15*(8), pp. 1119–30.

Sanguinetti, Pablo. La hipótesis monetarista del proceso inflacionario en el caso argentino: Dinero exógeno vs. dinero endógeno. (The Monetarist Approach to the Inflationary Process in the Argentine: Exogenous vs. Endogenous Money. With English summary.) *Económica (La Plata)*, July-Dec. 1987, *33*(2), pp. 269–304. **[G: Argentina]**

Schott, Kerry. Lessons for Australia. *Stegman, T., et al.*, 1987, pp. 25–52. **[G: Australia; W. Europe; U.K.; Japan]**

Sertel, Murat R. On Conquering Stagflation. *Econ. Anal. Workers' Manage.*, 1987, *21*(4), pp. 433–41.

Sheen, Jeffrey. Inflation Debt and Fiscal Policy Attitudes. *Sinclair, P. J. N., ed.*, 1987, pp. 90–110.

Sheen, Jeffrey. Inflation Debt and Fiscal Policy Attitudes. *Oxford Econ. Pap.*, March 1987, *39*(1), pp. 90–110.

Shishido, Shuntaro. Remarks on Growth, Inflation and Employment. *Pasinetti, L. and Lloyd, P., eds.*, 1987, pp. 301–03. **[G: Global]**

Shupp, Franklin R. Disinflation and Sectoral Productivity Gains. *J. Econ. Dynam. Control*, June 1987, *11*(2), pp. 207–12. **[G: U.S.]**

Sims, Christopher A. Aggregate and Individual Price Adjustment: Comments. *Brookings Pap. Econ. Act.*, 1987, (1), pp. 117–20. **[G: U.S.]**

Skidmore, Thomas E. The Resurgence of Inflation in Latin America: Discussion. *World Devel.*, August 1987, *15*(8), pp. 1148–49. **[G: Brazil; Argentina]**

Smith, Andrew and MacKinnon, Neil J. Inflation and Relative Price Variability: The U.K. Experience over the Last 30 Years. *Scot. J. Polit. Econ.*, May 1987, *34*(2), pp. 145–60. **[G: U.K.]**

Smith, Russell E. The Resurgence of Inflation in Latin America: Discussion. *World Devel.*, August 1987, *15*(8), pp. 1146–48. **[G: Argentina; Brazil]**

Sneessens, Henri R. Investment and the Inflation–Unemployment Tradeoff in a Macroeconomic Rationing Model with Monopolistic Competition. *Europ. Econ. Rev.*, April 1987, *31*(3), pp. 781–808.

Spiro, Peter S. New Findings on the Effects of Inflation on Interest Rates. *Bus. Econ.*, April 1987, *22*(2), pp. 38–42. **[G: U.S.]**

Spivak, Avia; Weinblatt, J. and Zilberfarb, Ben-Zion. Inflation and Wage Indexation with Multiperiod Contracts. *Europ. Econ. Rev.*, August 1987, *31*(6), pp. 1299–1312. **[G: OECD]**

Stein, Jerome L. Short and Long-run Effects of Monetary and Fiscal Policy upon Real Output and Inflation. *[Marrama, V.], Vol. 1*, 1987, pp. 479–97.

Sterman, John D. The Economic Long Wave: Theory and Evidence. *Vasko, T., ed.*, 1987, pp. 127–61.

Stockton, David J. and Glassman, James E. An Evaluation of the Forecast Performance of Al-ternative Models of Inflation. *Rev. Econ. Statist.*, February 1987, *69*(1), pp. 108–17. **[G: U.S.]**

Sweeney, Richard J. Some Macro Implications of Risk. *J. Money, Credit, Banking*, May 1987, *19*(2), pp. 222–34.

Sylos-Labini, Paolo. Reply [Prices and Income Distribution in Manufacturing Industry]. *J. Post Keynesian Econ.*, Fall 1987, *10*(1), pp. 161–62. **[G: U.S.; Italy]**

Tabellini, Guido. The Politics of Inflation and Economic Stagnation: A Review Essay. *J. Monet. Econ.*, May 1987, *19*(3), pp. 457–61.

Tanzi, Vito; Blejer, Mario I. and Teijeiro, Mario O. Inflation and the Measurement of Fiscal Deficits. *Int. Monet. Fund Staff Pap.*, December 1987, *34*(4), pp. 711–38.

Tarantelli, Ezio. Monetary Policy and the Regulation of Inflation and Unemployment. *Gunderson, M.; Meltz, N. M. and Ostry, S., eds.*, 1987, pp. 94–102. **[G: W. Europe]**

Tatom, John A. The Macroeconomic Effects of the Recent Fall in Oil Prices. *Fed. Res. Bank St. Louis Rev.*, June/July 1987, *69*(6), pp. 34–45. **[G: OECD]**

Taylor, John B. Externalities Associated with Nominal Price and Wage Rigidities. *Barnett, W. A. and Singleton, K. J., eds.*, 1987, pp. 350–67.

Taylor, Lance. Macro Policy in the Tropics: How Sensible People Stand. *World Devel.*, December 1987, *15*(12), pp. 1407–35. **[G: LDCs]**

di Tella, Guido. Argentina's Most Recent Inflationary Cycle, 1975–85. *Thorp, R. and Whitehead, L., eds.*, 1987, pp. 162–207. **[G: Argentina]**

Thornton, John. Inflation and Output Growth: A Note on Some Time Series Evidence. *S. Afr. J. Econ.*, December 1987, *55*(4), pp. 425–27.

Tobin, James. After Disinflation, Then What? *Tobin, J. (III)*, 1987, *1984*, pp. 348–67. **[G: U.S.]**

Tobin, James. Inflation. *Tobin, J. (III)*, 1987, *1982*, pp. 301–19.

Tobin, James. Inflation Control as Social Priority. *Tobin, J. (III)*, 1987, pp. 340–47. **[G: U.S.]**

Tobin, James. Inflation: Monetary and Structural Causes and Cures. *Tobin, J. (III)*, 1987, *1983*, pp. 324–39.

Tobin, James. Phillips Curve Algebra. *Tobin, J. (II)*, 1987, pp. 11–15.

Tobin, James. Strategy for Disinflation (Fellner on 'The State of Monetary Policy'). *Tobin, J. (III)*, 1987, *1981*, pp. 368–74. **[G: U.S.]**

Tobin, James. Taxes, Saving and Inflation. *Tobin, J. (I)*, 1987, *1949*, pp. 99–108.

Tobin, James. The Cruel Dilemma. *Tobin, J. (II)*, 1987, *1967*, pp. 3–10. **[G: U.S.]**

Tobin, James. The Wage–Price Mechanism. *Tobin, J. (II)*, 1987, *1973*, pp. 17–32.

Tobin, James. There Are Three Types of Inflation: We Have Two. *Tobin, J. (III)*, 1987, *1974*, pp. 320–23. **[G: U.S.]**

Tobin, James. Unemployment in the 1980s: Macroeconomic Diagnosis and Prescription. *Tobin,*

J. (III), 1987, *1984*, pp. 386–414. **[G: U.S.; OECD]**

Togan, Sübidey. The Influence of Money and the Rate of Interest on the Rate of Inflation in a Financially Repressed Economy: The Case of Turkey. *Appl. Econ.*, December 1987, *19*(12), pp. 1585–1601. **[G: Turkey]**

Tran, Dang T. A Conflict Model of Stagflation. *Eastern Econ. J.*, Jan.-Mar. 1987, *13*(1), pp. 7–18. **[G: U.S.]**

Turnovsky, Stephen J. Monetary Growth, Inflation, and Economic Activity in a Dynamic Macro Model. *Int. Econ. Rev.*, October 1987, *28*(3), pp. 707–30.

Turnovsky, Stephen J. Optimal Monetary Policy and Wage Indexation under Alternative Disturbances and Information Structures. *J. Money, Credit, Banking*, May 1987, *19*(2), pp. 157–80.

Van Rompuy, Paul. Hysteresis, Persistence, and the NAIRU: An Empirical Analysis for the Federal Republic of Germany: Comments. *Layard, R. and Calmfors, L., eds.*, 1987, pp. 132–38. **[G: W. Germany]**

Vinod, H. D. New Techniques for Estimation of Rational Expectation Models and Volcker Deflation. *Empirical Econ.*, 1987, *12*(3), pp. 157–74. **[G: U.S.]**

Virén, Matti. Inflation and Interest Rates: Some Time Series Evidence from 6 OECD Countries. *Empirical Econ.*, 1987, *12*(1), pp. 51–66. **[G: Selected OECD]**

Visco, Ignazio. The Use of Italian Survey Data in the Analysis of Inflation Expectations. *Giorn. Econ.*, Nov.-Dec. 1987, *46*(11–12), pp. 561–89. **[G: Italy]**

Wadhwani, Sushil B. The Effects of Inflation and Real Wages on Employment. *Economica*, February 1987, *54*(213), pp. 21–40. **[G: U.K.]**

Wadhwani, Sushil B. The Macroeconomic Implications of Profit Sharing: Some Empirical Evidence. *Econ. J.*, Supplement 1987, *97*, pp. 171–83. **[G: OECD]**

Walsh, Carl E. Monetary Targeting and Inflation: 1976–1984. *Fed. Res. Bank San Francisco Econ. Rev.*, Winter 1987, (1), pp. 5–16. **[G: U.S.]**

Webb, Steven B. The German Inflation and Foreign Business Cycles, 1920–1922. *Exploration Econ. Hist.*, October 1987, *24*(4), pp. 409–33. **[G: W. Germany]**

Weicher, John C. Mismeasuring Poverty and Progress. *Cato J.*, Winter 1987, *6*(3), pp. 715–30. **[G: U.S.]**

Weiermair, Klaus. Unemployment: Western Europe: Comment. *Gunderson, M.; Meltz, N. M. and Ostry, S., eds.*, 1987, pp. 108–10. **[G: W. Europe]**

Weil, Philippe. Permanent Budget Deficits and Inflation. *J. Monet. Econ.*, September 1987, *20*(2), pp. 393–410.

Williams, Arlington W. The Formation of Price Forecasts in Experimental Markets. *J. Money, Credit, Banking*, February 1987, *19*(1), pp. 1–18.

Williamson, John. The Problem of Indexation.

Williamson, J., 1987, pp. 246–57.

Williamson, Stephen D. Transactions Costs, Inflation, and the Variety of Intermediation Services. *J. Money, Credit, Banking*, November 1987, *19*(4), pp. 484–98.

Witt, Peter-Christian. Tax Policies, Tax Assessment and Inflation: Towards a Sociology of Public Finances in the German Inflation, 1914–23. *Witt, P.-C., ed.*, 1987, pp. 137–60. **[G: Germany]**

Wulwick, Nancy J. The Phillips Curve: Which? Whose? To Do What? How? *Southern Econ. J.*, April 1987, *53*(4), pp. 834–57.

Wyplosz, Charles. Hysteresis, Persistence, and the NAIRU: An Empirical Analysis for the Federal Republic of Germany: Comments. *Layard, R. and Calmfors, L., eds.*, 1987, pp. 123–31. **[G: W. Germany]**

200 Quantitative Economic Methods and Data

210 ECONOMETRIC, STATISTICAL, AND MATHEMATICAL METHODS AND MODELS

211 Econometric and Statistical Methods and Models

2110 General

Andrews, Donald W. K. Consistency in Nonlinear Econometric Models: A Generic Uniform Law of Large Numbers [On Unification of the Asymptotic Theory of Nonlinear Econometric Models]. *Econometrica*, November 1987, *55*(6), pp. 1465–71.

Antle, John M. Econometric Estimation of Producers' Risk Attitudes. *Amer. J. Agr. Econ.*, August 1987, *69*(3), pp. 509–22. **[G: India]**

Arnold, Barry C., et al. Generating Ordered Families of Lorenz Curves by Strongly Unimodal Distributions. *J. Bus. Econ. Statist.*, April 1987, *5*(2), pp. 305–08.

Ashikaga, Sueo. Über die Eigenständigkeit der deutschen Sozialstatistik—zur Rolle der Frankfurter Schule in der deutschen Statistik. (The Self-Reliance of German Social Statistics—The Importance of the "Frankfurter Schule" in German Statistics. With English summary.) *Jahr. Nationalökon. Statist.*, October 1987, *203*(5–6), pp. 456–66.

Bera, Anil K. and McKenzie, C. R. Additivity and Separability of the Lagrange Multiplier, Likelihood Ratio and Wald Tests. *J. Quant. Econ.*, January 1987, *3*(1), pp. 53–63.

Bookstaber, Richard M. and McDonald, James B. A General Distribution for Describing Security Price Returns. *J. Bus.*, July 1987, *60*(3), pp. 401–24. **[G: U.S.]**

Brandenburger, Adam and Dekel, Eddie. Common Knowledge with Probability 1. *J. Math. Econ.*, 1987, *16*(3), pp. 237–45.

Brockett, Patrick L., et al. Cost–Volume–Utility Analysis with Partial Stochastic Information.

Quart. Rev. Econ. Bus., Autumn 1987, 27(3), pp. 70–90.

Brunner, Ronald D., et al. Improving Data Utilization: The Case-Wise Alternative. *Policy Sci.*, 1987, 20(4), pp. 365–94.

Chakravarty, Satya Ranjan and Dutta, Bhaskar. A Note on Measures of Distance between Income Distributions. *J. Econ. Theory*, February 1987, 41(1), pp. 185–88.

Crafts, N. F. R. Cliometrics, 1971–1986: A Survey. *J. Appl. Econometrics*, July 1987, 2(3), pp. 171–92.

Davidson, Russell and MacKinnon, James G. Implicit Alternatives and the Local Power of Test Statistics. *Econometrica*, November 1987, 55(6), pp. 1305–29.

Drèze, Jacques H. Econometrics and Decision Theory. *Drèze, J. H.*, 1987, 1972, pp. 401–19.

Dudewicz, Edward J. Nonparametric Methods: The History, the Reality, and the Future (with Special Reference to Statistical Selection Problems). *[Eberl, W., Sr.]*, 1987, pp. 63–83.

Durbin, J. Statistics and Statistical Science. *J. Roy. Statist. Soc.*, 1987, 150(3), pp. 177–89. [G: U.K.]

Edwards, David and Havránek, Tomáš. A Fast Model Selection Procedure for Large Families of Models. *J. Amer. Statist. Assoc.*, March 1987, 82(397), pp. 205–13.

Ferschl, Franz. Information und bedingte Wahrscheinlichkeiten. (Information and Conditional Probabilities. With English summary.) *Jahr. Nationalökon. Statist.*, October 1987, 203(5–6), pp. 498–506.

Gambetta, Guido. Teoria e practica in econometria. Ovvero "Tutto quello che avreste voluto sapere sull'econometria (ma non avete mai osato chiedere)." (Theory and Practice in Econometrics. Or "Everything You Always Wanted to Know about Econometrics [but Were Afraid to Ask]." With English summary.) *Econ. Polit.*, December 1987, 4(3), pp. 437–67.

Gastwirth, Joseph L. and Greenhouse, Samuel W. Estimating a Common Relative Risk: Application in Equal Employment. *J. Amer. Statist. Assoc.*, March 1987, 82(397), pp. 38–45. [G: U.S.]

Gillies, D. A. and Ietto-Gillies, G. Probability and Economics in the Works of Bruno de Finetti. *Econ. Int.*, May-Aug. 1987, 40(2–3), pp. 192–209.

Hendry, David F. Econometrics in Action. *Empirica*, 1987, 14(2), pp. 135–56. [G: U.S.]

Hendry, David F. and Neale, Adrian J. Monte Carlo Experimentation Using PC-NAIVE. *Fomby, T. B. and Rhodes, G. F., Jr., eds.*, 1987, pp. 91–125.

Hodges, James S. Assessing the Accuracy of Normal Approximations. *J. Amer. Statist. Assoc.*, March 1987, 82(397), pp. 149–54.

Marquardt, Donald W. The Importance of Statisticians. *J. Amer. Statist. Assoc.*, March 1987, 82(397), pp. 1–7.

Marron, J. S. Partitioned Cross-Validation. *Econometric Rev.*, 1987-88, 6(2), pp. 271–83.

McDonald, James B. and Butler, Richard J. Some Generalized Mixture Distributions with an Application to Unemployment Duration. *Rev. Econ. Statist.*, May 1987, 69(2), pp. 232–40. [G: U.S.]

Mendelson, Haim. Quantile-Preserving Spread. *J. Econ. Theory*, August 1987, 42(2), pp. 334–51.

Molina, David J. and Slottje, D. J. The Gamma Distribution and the Size Distribution of Income Reconsidered. *Atlantic Econ. J.*, July 1987, 15(2), pp. 86.

Pagan, Adrian R. Three Econometric Methodologies: A Critical Appraisal. *J. Econ. Surveys*, 1987, 1(1), pp. 3–24.

Pollastri, Angiola. Le curve di concentrazione L_p e Z_p nella distribuzione lognormale generalizzata. (The Concentration Curves L_p and Z_p in the Generalized Lognormal Distribution. With English summary.) *Giorn. Econ.*, Nov.-Dec. 1987, 46(11–12), pp. 639–63.

Power, Simon and Ullah, Aman. Nonparametric Monte Carlo Density Estimation of Rational Expectations Estimators and Their t Ratios. *Fomby, T. B. and Rhodes, G. F., Jr., eds.*, 1987, pp. 157–86.

Rhodes, George F., Jr. Validating Simulation Studies. *Fomby, T. B. and Rhodes, G. F., Jr., eds.*, 1987, pp. 187–213.

Riese, Martin. An Extension of the Lorenz-Diagram with Special Reference to Survival Analysis. *Oxford Bull. Econ. Statist.*, May 1987, 49(2), pp. 245–50.

Rissanen, Jorma. Stochastic Complexity and the MDL Principle. *Econometric Rev.*, 1987, 6(1), pp. 85–102.

Săcuiu, I. and Du, Xiaolin. Some Asymptotical Results Concerning the p Rank Normal Distribution. *Econ. Computat. Cybern. Stud. Res.*, 1987, 22(1), pp. 67–75.

Sargan, J. Denis. The Method of Iterative Maximization. *[Cochrane, D.]*, 1987, pp. 353–54.

Ştefănescu, V. An Algorithm for Generating Random Variables with a Normal Distribution of Order p. *Econ. Computat. Cybern. Stud. Res.*, 1987, 22(3), pp. 61–66.

Takahashi, Hajime. Some Thoughts in Sequential Two Sample Problems with Data Dependent Allocation Rule. *Hitotsubashi J. Econ.*, December 1987, 28(2), pp. 173–81.

Tse, Y. K. A Note on Sargan Densities. *J. Econometrics*, March 1987, 34(3), pp. 349–54.

Văduva, I. Homogeneousness Measures of a Statistical Collectivity. *Econ. Computat. Cybern. Stud. Res.*, 1987, 22(2), pp. 81–90.

Walliser, Bernard. Le problème de l'induction et de la réfutation en économétrie. (Induction Problem and Refutation in Econometrics. With English summary.) *Écon. Soc.*, October 1987, 21(10), pp. 153–64.

Zarnowitz, Victor and Lambros, Louis A. Consensus and Uncertainty in Economic Prediction. *J. Polit. Econ.*, June 1987, 95(3), pp. 591–621. [G: U.S.]

2112 Inferential Problems in Simultaneous Equation Systems

Bekker, Paul; Kapteyn, Arie and Wansbeek, Tom. Consistent Sets of Estimates for Regressions with Correlated or Uncorrelated Measurement Errors in Arbitrary Subsets of All Variables. *Econometrica,* September 1987, 55(5), pp. 1223–30.

Bewley, Ronald and Theil, Henri. Monte Carlo Testing for Heteroscedasticity in Equation Systems. *Fomby, T. B. and Rhodes, G. F., Jr., eds.,* 1987, pp. 1–15.

Bhargava, Alok. Wald Tests and Systems of Stochastic Equations. *Int. Econ. Rev.,* October 1987, 28(3), pp. 789–808.

Calzolari, Giorgio. Forecast Variance in Dynamic Simulation of Simultaneous Equation Models. *Econometrica,* November 1987, 55(6), pp. 1473–76.

Calzolari, Giorgio and Panattoni, Lorenzo. Gradient Methods in FIML Estimation of Econometric Models. *Carraro, C. and Sartore, D., eds.,* 1987, pp. 143–53.

Calzolari, Giorgio; Panattoni, Lorenzo and Weihs, Claus. Computational Efficiency of FIML Estimation. *J. Econometrics,* November 1987, 36(3), pp. 299–310.

Charemza, Wojciech. Maximum Likelihood Methods of Estimation for Disequilibrium Models in a Centrally Planned Economy. *Econ. Planning,* 1987, 21(2–3), pp. 87–99.

Dastoor, Naorayex K. and McAleer, Michael. On the Consistency of Joint and Paired Tests for Non-nested Regression Models. *J. Quant. Econ.,* January 1987, 3(1), pp. 65–84.

Deistler, Manfred. An Introduction to Linear Dynamic Errors-in-Variables Models. *[Eberl, W., Sr.],* 1987, pp. 28–37.

Deville, Hervé. Econométrie des modèles dynamiques d'équilibre avec rationnement. (With English summary.) *Cah. Écon. Bruxelles,* Third Trimester 1987, (115), pp. 111–27.

Duncan, Gregory M. A Simplified Approach to *M*-Estimation with Application to Two-Stage Estimators. *J. Econometrics,* March 1987, 34(3), pp. 373–89.

Fischer, Manfred M. and Nijkamp, Peter. From Static Towards Dynamic Discrete Choice Modelling: A State of the Art Review. *Reg. Sci. Urban Econ.,* February 1987, 17(1), pp. 3–27.

Hasan, M. Aynul. Rational Expectations Estimation of Macroeconomic Models: Some Monte Carlo Results. *J. Macroecon.,* Spring 1987, 9(2), pp. 297–315.

Hausman, Jerry A.; Newey, Whitney K. and Taylor, William E. Efficient Estimation and Identification of Simultaneous Equation Models with Covariance Restrictions. *Econometrica,* July 1987, 55(4), pp. 849–74.

Hoffman, Dennis L. Two-Step Generalized Least Squares Estimators in Multi-equation Generated Regressor Models. *Rev. Econ. Statist.,* May 1987, 69(2), pp. 336–46. [G: U.S.; W. Germany; U.K.]

Holly, Alberto. Testing for Exogeneity: A Survey. *Econ. Notes,* 1987, (3), pp. 108–30.

Huang, Cliff J.; Sloan, Frank A. and Adamache, Killard W. Estimation of Seemingly Unrelated Tobit Regressions via the EM Algorithm. *J. Bus. Econ. Statist.,* July 1987, 5(3), pp. 425–30. [G: U.S.]

Joyeux, Roselyne. Misspecification Tests on Taylor's Version of a Keynesian Macromodel. *Southern Econ. J.,* July 1987, 54(1), pp. 159–67. [G: U.S.]

Khatri, C. G. The First Two Moments of the Forecast from Partially Restricted Reduced Form. *J. Quant. Econ.,* January 1987, 3(1), pp. 85–100.

Kiviet, Jan F. and Ridder, Geert. On the Rationale for and Scope of Regression Models in Econometrics. *Heijmans, R. and Neudecker, H., eds.,* 1987, pp. 223–46.

Klepper, Steven and Stapleton, David C. Consistent Sets of Estimates for Restricted Regressions with Errors in All Variables. *Int. Econ. Rev.,* June 1987, 28(2), pp. 445–57.

Krasker, William S. and Pratt, John W. Bounding the Effects of Proxy Variables on Instrumental-Variables Coefficients. *J. Econometrics,* July 1987, 35(2/3), pp. 233–52.

Mallela, Parthasaradhi. Necessary and Sufficient Conditions for the Consistency of the OLS Estimates in Simultaneous Equations: Generalized Recursivity. *J. Quant. Econ.,* January 1987, 3(1), pp. 39–52.

Manning, Willard G.; Duan, Naihua and Rogers, W. H. Monte Carlo Evidence on the Choice between Sample Selection and Two-Part Models. *J. Econometrics,* May 1987, 35(1), pp. 59–82.

Mauleon, Ignacio. Problemas prácticos en el tratamiento econométrico de datos "cross-section." (With English summary.) *Invest. Econ.,* January 1987, 11(1), pp. 41–94.

McCarthy, Michael D. Exact Finite Sample Test Statistics for Restricted Reduced Forms: A Generalization of "Students" Result. *Int. Econ. Rev.,* February 1987, 28(1), pp. 259–69.

Newey, Whitney K. Efficient Estimation of Limited Dependent Variable Models with Endogenous Explanatory Variables. *J. Econometrics,* November 1987, 36(3), pp. 231–50.

Newey, Whitney K. and West, Kenneth D. Hypothesis Testing with Efficient Method of Moments Estimation. *Int. Econ. Rev.,* October 1987, 28(3), pp. 777–87.

Orcutt, Guy H. and Cochrane, Donald. A Sampling Study of the Merits of Autoregressive and Reduced Form Transformations in Regression Analysis. *[Cochrane, D.],* 1987, pp. 335–52.

Palm, Franz C. Time Series and Econometric Models with Unobservables. *Econ. Notes,* 1987, (1), pp. 22–38.

Pollock, Stephen. The Classical Econometric Model. *Heijmans, R. and Neudecker, H., eds.,* 1987, pp. 247–62.

Prucha, Ingmar R. The Variance–Covariance Matrix of the Maximum Likelihood Estimator in

Triangular Structural Systems: Consistent Estimation. *Econometrica*, July 1987, *55*(4), pp. 977–78.

Salemi, Michael K. and Tauchen, George E. Simultaneous Nonlinear Learning Models. *Becker, W. E. and Walstad, W. B., eds.*, 1987, pp. 207–23.

Schulze, Peter M. Once Again: Testing for Regional Homogeneity. *J. Reg. Sci.*, February 1987, *27*(1), pp. 129–33. [G: W. Germany]

Smith, Richard J. Testing the Normality Assumption in Multivariate Simultaneous Limited Dependent Variable Models. *J. Econometrics*, Jan./Feb. 1987, *34*(1/2), pp. 105–23.

Swan, Craig. Simultaneous Equations Estimation. *Becker, W. E. and Walstad, W. B., eds.*, 1987, pp. 99–109.

Tse, Y. K. A Diagnostic Test for the Multinomial Logit Model. *J. Bus. Econ. Statist.*, April 1987, *5*(2), pp. 283–86.

Velu, Raja P. and Reinsel, Gregory C. Reduced Rank Regression with Autoregressive Errors. *J. Econometrics*, July 1987, *35*(2/3), pp. 317–35. [G: U.K.]

Walstad, William B. Applying Two-Stage Least Squares. *Becker, W. E. and Walstad, W. B., eds.*, 1987, pp. 111–34.

Weerahandi, Samaradasa. Testing Regression Equality with Unequal Variances. *Econometrica*, September 1987, *55*(5), pp. 1211–15.

Zellner, Arnold and Park, Soo-Bin. Bayesian Prediction with Random Regressors. *[Cochrane, D.]*, 1987, pp. 234–49.

2113 Distributed Lags and Serially Correlated Disturbance Terms; Inferential Problems in Single Equation Models

Ali, Mukhtar M. Durbin–Watson and Generalized Durbin–Watson Tests for Autocorrelations and Randomness. *J. Bus. Econ. Statist.*, April 1987, *5*(2), pp. 195–203.

Amemiya, Takeshi and Vuong, Quang H. A Comparison of Two Consistent Estimators in the Choice-based Sampling Qualitative Response Model. *Econometrica*, May 1987, *55*(3), pp. 699–702.

Anderson, Gordon J. Prediction Tests in Limited Dependent Variable Models. *J. Econometrics*, Jan./Feb. 1987, *34*(1/2), pp. 253–61.

Andrews, Donald W. K. and Phillips, Peter C. B. Best Median-Unbiased Estimation in Linear Regression with Bounded Asymmetric Loss Functions. *J. Amer. Statist. Assoc.*, September 1987, *82*(399), pp. 886–93.

Arellano, M. Computing Robust Standard Errors for Within-Groups Estimators. *Oxford Bull. Econ. Statist.*, November 1987, *49*(4), pp. 431–34.

Aznar, Antonio. Contenido informativo y selección de modelos econométricos. (With English summary.) *Invest. Econ.*, January 1987, *11*(1), pp. 25–39. [G: Spain]

Azzam, Azzeddine and Yanagida, John F. A Cautionary Note on Polynomial Distributed Lag Formulations of Supply Response. *Western J.*

Agr. Econ., July 1987, *12*(1), pp. 60–64. [G: U.S.]

Barten, Anton P. The Coefficient of Determination for Regression without a Constant Term. *Heijmans, R. and Neudecker, H., eds.*, 1987, pp. 181–89.

Becker, William E. Measuring Intervention, Interaction, and Distribution Effects with Dummy Variables. *Becker, W. E. and Walstad, W. B., eds.*, 1987, pp. 27–49. [G: U.S.]

Becker, William E. and Waldman, Donald M. The Probit Model. *Becker, W. E. and Walstad, W. B., eds.*, 1987, pp. 135–40.

Bhargava, Alok. Towards a Theory of Point Optimal Testing: Comment. *Econometric Rev.*, 1987-88, *6*(2), pp. 241–47.

Bierens, Herman J. Towards a Theory of Point Optimal Testing: Comment. *Econometric Rev.*, 1987-88, *6*(2), pp. 231–33.

Blundell, Richard and Meghir, Costas. Bivariate Alternatives to the Tobit Model. *J. Econometrics*, Jan./Feb. 1987, *34*(1/2), pp. 179–200. [G: U.K.]

Blundell, Richard and Meghir, Costas. Engel Curve Estimation with Individual Data. *Heijmans, R. and Neudecker, H., eds.*, 1987, pp. 3–14. [G: U.K.]

Bockstael, Nancy E. and Strand, Ivar E., Jr. The Effect of Common Sources of Regression Error on Benefit Estimates. *Land Econ.*, February 1987, *63*(1), pp. 11–20.

Breusch, Trevor S. Maximum Likelihood Estimation of Random Effects Models. *J. Econometrics*, November 1987, *36*(3), pp. 383–89.

Burt, Oscar R. The Fallacy of Differencing to Reduce Multicollinearity. *Amer. J. Agr. Econ.*, August 1987, *69*(3), pp. 697–700.

Burt, Oscar R.; Frank, Michael D. and Beattie, Bruce R. Prior Information and Heuristic Ridge Regression for Production Function Estimation. *Western J. Agr. Econ.*, December 1987, *12*(2), pp. 135–43. [G: U.S.]

Cameron, Trudy Ann. The Impact of Grouping Coarseness in Alternative Grouped-Data Regression Models. *J. Econometrics*, May 1987, *35*(1), pp. 37–57.

Cassidy, H. J. and Chung, Jae Wan. A Model of Collinearity and Specification Error. *J. Stud. Econ. Econometrics*, April 1987, *11*(1), pp. 1–34.

Caudill, Steven B. and Holcombe, Randall G. Coefficient Bias Due to Specification Search in Econometric Models. *Atlantic Econ. J.*, September 1987, *15*(3), pp. 30–34.

Chamberlain, Gary. Asymptotic Efficiency in Estimation with Conditional Moment Restrictions. *J. Econometrics*, March 1987, *34*(3), pp. 305–34.

Chesher, Andrew and Irish, Margaret. Residual Analysis in the Grouped and Censored Normal Linear Model. *J. Econometrics*, Jan./Feb. 1987, *34*(1/2), pp. 33–61. [G: U.K.]

Chesher, Andrew and Jewitt, Ian. The Bias of a Heteroskedasticity Consistent Covariance Matrix Estimator. *Econometrica*, September 1987, *55*(5), pp. 1217–22.

Chin, C. F. and Kennedy, Peter E. On Inferring the True Model's Direction. *Can. J. Econ.*, November 1987, *20*(4), pp. 876–79.

Choudhury, Askar H.; Chaudhury, Mohammed M. and Power, Simon. A New Approximate GLS Estimator for the Regression Model with MA(1) Disturbances. *Bull. Econ. Res.*, April 1987, *39*(2), pp. 171–77.

Chowdhury, Abdur R. Are Causal Relationships Sensitive to Causality Tests? *Appl. Econ.*, April 1987, *19*(4), pp. 449–65. [G: U.S.]

Chowdhury, Gopa. A Note on Correcting Biases in Dynamic Panel Models. *Appl. Econ.*, January 1987, *19*(1), pp. 31–37.

Clarke, Judith A.; Giles, David E. A. and Wallace, T. Dudley. Estimating the Error Variance in Regression after a Preliminary Test of Restrictions on the Coefficients. *J. Econometrics*, March 1987, *34*(3), pp. 293–304.

Cochrane, Donald and Orcutt, Guy H. Application of Least Squares Regression to Relationships Containing Auto-correlated Error Terms. *[Cochrane, D.]*, 1987, pp. 307–34.

Cooley, Thomas F. and Parke, William R. Likelihood and Other Approaches to Prediction in Dynamic Models. *J. Econometrics*, May 1987, *35*(1), pp. 119–42.

Cosslett, Stephen R. Efficiency Bounds for Distribution-free Estimators of the Binary Choice and the Censored Regression Models. *Econometrica*, May 1987, *55*(3), pp. 559–85.

Cramer, J. S. Men and Variance of R^2 in Small and Moderate Samples. *J. Econometrics*, July 1987, *35*(2/3), pp. 253–66.

Dastoor, Naorayex K. and Fisher, Gordon. The Theory and Practice of Point-Optimal Testing: Comment [Towards a Theory of Point Optimal Testing]. *Econometric Rev.*, 1987-88, *6*(2), pp. 219–29.

Dastoor, Naorayex K. and McAleer, Michael. On the Consistency of Joint and Paired Tests for Non-nested Regression Models. *J. Quant. Econ.*, January 1987, *3*(1), pp. 65–84.

Davidian, M. and Carroll, R. J. Variance Function Estimation. *J. Amer. Statist. Assoc.*, December 1987, *82*(400), pp. 1079–91.

De Gruttola, Victor; Ware, James H. and Louis, Thomas A. Influence Analysis of Generalized Least Squares Estimators. *J. Amer. Statist. Assoc.*, September 1987, *82*(399), pp. 911–17.

Dhrymes, Phoebus J. and Schwarz, Samuel. On the Invariance of Estimators for Singular Systems of Equations. *Greek Econ. Rev.*, 1987, *9*(1), pp. 88–108.

Dhrymes, Phoebus J. and Schwarz, Samuel. On the Invariance of Estimators for Singular Systems of Equations. *Greek Econ. Rev.*, 1987, *9*(1), pp. 88–107.

van Dijk, Herman K. Some Advances in Bayesian Estimation Methods Using Monte Carlo Integration. *Fomby, T. B. and Rhodes, G. F., Jr., eds.*, 1987, pp. 215–61.

Duan, Naihua and Li, Ker-Chau. Distribution-Free and Link-Free Estimation for the Sample Selection Model. *J. Econometrics*, May 1987, *35*(1), pp. 25–35.

Dufour, Jean-Marie and Hallin, Marc. Tests non paramétriques optimaux pour le modèle autorégressif d'orde un. (Optimal Nonparametric Tests for First Order Autoregressive Model. With English summary.) *Ann. Écon. Statist.*, Apr./Sept. 1987, (6/7), pp. 411–34.

Duncan, Gregory M. A Simplified Approach to M-Estimation with Application to Two-Stage Estimators. *J. Econometrics*, March 1987, *34*(3), pp. 373–89.

Engle, Robert F.; Lilien, David M. and Robins, Russell P. Estimating Time Varying Risk Premia in the Term Structure: The Arch-M Model. *Econometrica*, March 1987, *55*(2), pp. 391–407.

Erlat, Haluk. Computing Heteroscedasticity-Robust Tests of Linear Restrictions. *Oxford Bull. Econ. Statist.*, November 1987, *49*(4), pp. 439–46.

Farebrother, Richard W. Independent Conditions for the Stability of a Dynamic Linear Model. *Manchester Sch. Econ. Soc. Stud.*, September 1987, *55*(3), pp. 305–09.

Farebrother, Richard W. The Statistical Foundations of a Class of Parametric Tests for Heteroscedasticity. *J. Econometrics*, November 1987, *36*(3), pp. 359–68.

Fischer, Manfred M. and Nijkamp, Peter. From Static Towards Dynamic Discrete Choice Modelling: A State of the Art Review. *Reg. Sci. Urban Econ.*, February 1987, *17*(1), pp. 3–27.

Fomby, Thomas B. The Ridge Regression Monte Carlo Controversy: Where Do We Stand? *Fomby, T. B. and Rhodes, G. F., Jr., eds.*, 1987, pp. 17–49.

Gallant, A. Ronald and Nychka, Douglas W. Semi-nonparametric Maximum Likelihood Estimation. *Econometrica*, March 1987, *55*(2), pp. 363–90.

Ghali, Moheb A. and Snow, Marcellus S. Specification Error: A Generalized Test. *Econ. Modelling*, January 1987, *4*(1), pp. 65–76.

Giles, David E. A. and Beattie, Murray. Autocorrelation Pre-test Estimation in Models with a Lagged Dependent Variable. *[Cochrane, D.]*, 1987, pp. 99–116.

Godfrey, Leslie G. Discriminating between Autocorrelation and Misspecification in Regression Analysis: An Alternative Test Strategy. *Rev. Econ. Statist.*, February 1987, *69*(1), pp. 128–34.

Gourieroux, Christian, et al. Generalised Residuals. *J. Econometrics*, Jan./Feb. 1987, *34*(1/2), pp. 5–32.

Gourieroux, Christian, et al. Simulated Residuals. *J. Econometrics*, Jan./Feb. 1987, *34*(1/2), pp. 201–52.

Gregory, Allan W. and Veall, Michael R. Formulating Wald Tests of the Restrictions Implied by the Rational Expectations Hypothesis. *J. Appl. Econometrics*, January 1987, *2*(1), pp. 61–68. [G: Canada]

Griffiths, William E.; Hill, R. Carter and Pope, Peter J. Small Sample Properties of Probit Model Estimators. *J. Amer. Statist. Assoc.*,

September 1987, 82(399), pp. 929–37.

Gruber, Josef; Fusek, Ivo and Fusková, Lidmila. Evaluating the Relative Performance of Estimators by Means of Combined Response Surfaces: The Case of TWE and OLS in the Simple Errors-in-Variables Model. *Jahr. Nationalökon. Statist.*, October 1987, 203(5–6), pp. 507–16.

Hall, Alastair. The Information Matrix Test for the Linear Model. *Rev. Econ. Stud.*, April 1987, 54(2), pp. 257–63.

Han, Aaron K. A Non-parametric Analysis of Transformations. *J. Econometrics*, July 1987, 35(2/3), pp. 191–209.

Han, Aaron K. Non-parametric Analysis of a Generalized Regression Model: The Maximum Rank Correlation Estimator. *J. Econometrics*, July 1987, 35(2/3), pp. 303–16.

Hannan, Edward J. The Cochrane and Orcutt Papers. *[Cochrane, D.]*, 1987, pp. 9–18.

Hansen, Gerd. Multikollinearität und Prognosefehler. (Forecasting Error and Multicollinearity. With English summary.) *Jahr. Nationalökon. Statist.*, October 1987, 203(5–6), pp. 517–31.

Hartung, Joachim and Voet, Bernard. An Asymptotic x^2-Test for Variance Components. *[Eberl, W., Sr.]*, 1987, pp. 153–63.

Hasan, M. Aynul. Rational Expectations Estimation of Macroeconomic Models: Some Monte Carlo Results. *J. Macroecon.*, Spring 1987, 9(2), pp. 297–315.

Hausman, Jerry A. and Ruud, Paul A. Specifying and Testing Econometric Models for Rank-Ordered Data. *J. Econometrics*, Jan./Feb. 1987, 34(1/2), pp. 83–104.

Heijmans, Risto D. H. and Magnus, Jan R. Corrigenda [Consistent Maximum-Likelihood Estimation with Dependent Observations: The General (Non-normal) Case and the Normal Case]. *J. Econometrics*, July 1987, 35(2/3), pp. 395.

Heijmans, Risto D. H. and Neudecker, Heinz. The Coefficient of Determination Revisited. *Heijmans, R. and Neudecker, H., eds.*, 1987, pp. 191–204.

Hill, R. Carter. Modeling Multicollinearity and Extrapolation in Monte Carlo Experiments on Regression. *Fomby, T. B. and Rhodes, G. F., Jr., eds.*, 1987, pp. 127–55.

Hill, R. Carter and Judge, George. Improved Prediction in the Presence of Multicollinearity. *J. Econometrics*, May 1987, 35(1), pp. 83–100.

Hillier, Grant H. and King, Maxwell L. Linear Regression with Correlated Errors: Bounds and Coefficient Estimates and t-Values. *[Cochrane, D.]*, 1987, pp. 74–80.

Holly, Alberto. Testing for Exogeneity: A Survey. *Econ. Notes*, 1987, (3), pp. 108–30.

Honda, Yuzo. On Hausman's Specification Test. *Econ. Stud. Quart.*, June 1987, 38(2), pp. 172–83.

Horowitz, Joel L. Specification Tests for Nested Logit Models. *Environ. Planning A*, March 1987, 19(3), pp. 395–402.

Jarque, Carlos M. Sample Splitting and Applied Econometric Modeling. *J. Bus. Econ. Statist.*, April 1987, 5(2), pp. 267–74. [G: Mexico]

Johnson, Thomas. The Analysis of Qualitative and Limited Responses. *Becker, W. E. and Walstad, W. B., eds.*, 1987, pp. 141–84.

Johnson, Wesley. The Detection of Influential Observations for Allocation, Separation, and the Determination of Probabilities in a Bayesian Framework. *J. Bus. Econ. Statist.*, July 1987, 5(3), pp. 369–81.

Judge, George, et al. The Extended Stein Procedure for Simultaneous Model Selection and Parameter Estimation. *J. Econometrics*, July 1987, 35(2/3), pp. 375–91.

King, Maxwell L. An Alternative Test for Regression Coefficient Stability [Testing for Regression Coefficient Stability with a Stationary AR(1) Alternative]. *Rev. Econ. Statist.*, May 1987, 69(2), pp. 379–81.

King, Maxwell L. Testing for Autocorrelation in Linear Regression Models: A Survey. *[Cochrane, D.]*, 1987, pp. 19–73.

King, Maxwell L. Towards a Theory of Point Optimal Testing. *Econometric Rev.*, 1987-88, 6(2), pp. 169–218.

King, Maxwell L. Towards a Theory of Point Optimal Testing: Reply. *Econometric Rev.*, 1987-88, 6(2), pp. 249–55.

King, Maxwell L. and Giles, David E. A. Specification Analysis in the Linear Model: Introduction. *[Cochrane, D.]*, 1987, pp. 1–5.

King, Maxwell L. and McAleer, Michael. Further Results on Testing AR (1) against MA (1) Disturbances in the Linear Regression Model. *Rev. Econ. Stud.*, October 1987, 54(4), pp. 649–63.

Kiviet, Jan F. and Ridder, Geert. On the Rationale for and Scope of Regression Models in Econometrics. *Heijmans, R. and Neudecker, H., eds.*, 1987, pp. 223–46.

Klepper, Steven and Stapleton, David C. Consistent Sets of Estimates for Restricted Regressions with Errors in All Variables. *Int. Econ. Rev.*, June 1987, 28(2), pp. 445–57.

Koenker, Roger and Portnoy, Stephen. L-Estimation for Linear Models. *J. Amer. Statist. Assoc.*, September 1987, 82(399), pp. 851–57.

Krämer, Walter and Donninger, Christian. Spatial Autocorrelation among Errors and the Relative Efficiency of OLS in the Linear Regression Model. *J. Amer. Statist. Assoc.*, June 1987, 82(398), pp. 577–79.

Krasker, William S. and Pratt, John W. Bounding the Effects of Proxy Variables on Instrumental-Variables Coefficients. *J. Econometrics*, July 1987, 35(2/3), pp. 233–52.

Krishnamurthi, Lakshman and Rangaswamy, Arvind. The Equity Estimator for Marketing Research. *Marketing Sci.*, Fall 1987, 6(4), pp. 336–57.

Kumbhakar, Subal C. The Specification of Technical and Allocative Inefficiency in Stochastic Production and Profit Frontiers. *J. Econometrics*, March 1987, 34(3), pp. 335–48.

Lawless, J. F. Regression Methods for Poisson Process Data. *J. Amer. Statist. Assoc.*, September 1987, 82(399), pp. 808–15.

Leamer, Edward E. Errors in Variables in Linear Systems. *Econometrica*, July 1987, 55(4), pp. 893–909.

Lee, Lung-Fei. Non-parametric Testing of Discrete Panel Data Models. *J. Econometrics*, Jan./Feb. 1987, 34(1/2), pp. 147–77.

Legendre, François. Dynamic Adjustment When the Target Is Nonstationary: A Comment. *Int. Econ. Rev.*, October 1987, 28(3), pp. 809–11.

Lien, Da-Hsiang Donald and Vuong, Quang H. Selecting the Best Linear Regression Model: A Classical Approach. *J. Econometrics*, May 1987, 35(1), pp. 3–23.

Maasoumi, Esfandiar and Ullah, Aman. Specification Analysis in Special Rational Distributed Lag and Other Dynamic Models. *J. Quant. Econ.*, July 1987, 3(2), pp. 203–11.

Maddala, G. S. Limited Dependent Variable Models Using Panel Data. *J. Human Res.*, Summer 1987, 22(3), pp. 307–38.

Maeshiro, Asatoshi. OLS and a Dynamic Model with Autocorrelated Disturbances. *Atlantic Econ. J.*, September 1987, 15(3), pp. 78.

Magee, Lonnie J. A Note on Cochrane–Orcutt Estimation. *J. Econometrics*, July 1987, 35(2/3), pp. 211–18.

Magee, Lonnie J.; Ullah, Aman and Srivastava, Virendra K. Efficiency of Estimators in the Regression Model with First-Order Autoregressive Errors. *[Cochrane, D.]*, 1987, pp. 81–98.

Manning, Willard G.; Duan, Naihua and Rogers, W. H. Monte Carlo Evidence on the Choice between Sample Selection and Two-Part Models. *J. Econometrics*, May 1987, 35(1), pp. 59–82.

Manski, Charles F. Semiparametric Analysis of Random Effects Linear Models from Binary Panel Data. *Econometrica*, March 1987, 55(2), pp. 357–62.

Mauleon, Ignacio. Problemas prácticos en el tratamiento econométrico de datos "cross-section." (With English summary.) *Invest. Econ.*, January 1987, 11(1), pp. 41–94.

McAleer, Michael. Specification Tests for Separate Models: A Survey. *[Cochrane, D.]*, 1987, pp. 146–96.

McFadden, Daniel L. Regression-Based Specification Tests for the Multinomial Logit Model. *J. Econometrics*, Jan./Feb. 1987, 34(1/2), pp. 63–82.

Megdal, Sharon Bernstein. The Flypaper Effect Revisited: An Econometric Explanation. *Rev. Econ. Statist.*, May 1987, 69(2), pp. 347–51.

Melfi, Catherine A. and Waldman, Donald M. Limited and Discrete Dependent Variable Models: Use, Applications, and Comparisons. *Becker, W. E. and Walstad, W. B., eds.*, 1987, pp. 185–205.

Moulton, Brent R. Diagnostics for Group Effects in Regression Analysis. *J. Bus. Econ. Statist.*, April 1987, 5(2), pp. 275–82. **[G: U.S.]**

Mwabu, Germano M. Expositional Note on Use of Dummy Variables in the Estimation of a Multinomial Logit Model. *Eastern Afr. Econ.*

Rev., June 1987, 3(1), pp. 7–14.

Nakervis, J. C. and Savin, N. E. Corrigendum [Testing the Autoregressive Parameter with the *t* Statistic]. *J. Econometrics*, March 1987, 34(3), pp. 391.

Newey, Whitney K. Specification Tests for Distributional Assumptions in the Tobit Model. *J. Econometrics*, Jan./Feb. 1987, 34(1/2), pp. 125–45. **[G: U.K.]**

Newey, Whitney K. and Powell, James L. Asymmetric Least Squares Estimation and Testing. *Econometrica*, July 1987, 55(4), pp. 819–47.

Newey, Whitney K. and West, Kenneth D. A Simple, Positive Semi-definite, Heteroskedasticity and Autocorrelation Consistent Covariance Matrix. *Econometrica*, May 1987, 55(3), pp. 703–08.

Newey, Whitney K. and West, Kenneth D. Hypothesis Testing with Efficient Method of Moments Estimation. *Int. Econ. Rev.*, October 1987, 28(3), pp. 777–87.

Ohtani, Kazuhiro. On Pooling Disturbance Variances when the Goal Is Testing Restrictions on Regression Coefficients. *J. Econometrics*, July 1987, 35(2/3), pp. 219–31.

Oksanen, E. H. On Sign Changes upon Deletion of a Variable in Linear Regression Analysis. *Oxford Bull. Econ. Statist.*, May 1987, 49(2), pp. 227–29.

Orcutt, Guy H. Joint Conditional Probability Functions for Modeling National Economies. *[Cochrane, D.]*, 1987, pp. 133–45.

Orcutt, Guy H. and Cochrane, Donald. A Sampling Study of the Merits of Autoregressive and Reduced Form Transformations in Regression Analysis. *[Cochrane, D.]*, 1987, pp. 335–52.

Palm, Franz C. Time Series and Econometric Models with Unobservables. *Econ. Notes*, 1987, (1), pp. 22–38.

Patterson, Kerry David. Growth Coefficients in Dynamic Time Series Models. *Oxford Econ. Pap.*, June 1987, 39(2), pp. 282–92.

Peracchi, Franco. Robust M-Estimators of Regression. *Giorn. Econ.*, Sept.-Oct. 1987, 46(9–10), pp. 533–45.

Pokropp, Fritz. Zur Begründung einiger Schätzer mit Hilfe von Vorkenntnissen in der Stichprobentheorie. (Conventional Justification for Estimators Using Auxiliary Information in Finite Sampling. With English summary.) *Jahr. Nationalökon. Statist.*, October 1987, 203(5–6), pp. 554–68.

Pötscher, Benedikt M. Towards a Theory of Point Optimal Testing: Comment. *Econometric Rev.*, 1987-88, 6(2), pp. 235–39.

Power, Simon and Bishopp, William. A Note on the Computation of the Correct Estimated Covariance Matrix for a Ridge Regression Shortcut. *Oxford Bull. Econ. Statist.*, August 1987, 49(3), pp. 343–45.

Praetz, Peter. Some Aspects of Mis-specification in the Linear Model. *[Cochrane, D.]*, 1987, pp. 117–30.

Robinson, P. M. Asymptotically Efficient Estimation in the Presence of Heteroskedasticity of

Unknown Form. *Econometrica*, July 1987, 55(4), pp. 875–91.

Schafer, Daniel W. Measurement-Error Diagnostics and the Sex Discrimination Problem. *J. Bus. Econ. Statist.*, October 1987, 5(4), pp. 529–37.   [G: U.S.]

Schneeweiss, Hans. Correlated Measurement Errors in Repeated Measurements. *Jahr. Nationalökon. Statist.*, October 1987, 203(5–6), pp. 600–610.

Schwarz, Gideon. Least-Absolute-Value Prediction Lines in Closed Form. *J. Amer. Statist. Assoc.*, December 1987, 82(400), pp. 1150–52.

Shin, Jeong-Shik. Aggregation and the Endogeneity Problem. *Int. Econ. J.*, Spring 1987, 1(1), pp. 57–65.

Siu, Alan K. F. Applications of Influence Analysis. *Hong Kong Econ. Pap.*, 1987, (18), pp. 23–42.   [G: U.S.]

Small, Kenneth A. A Discrete Choice Model for Ordered Alternatives. *Econometrica*, March 1987, 55(2), pp. 409–24.

Smith, Richard J. Alternative Asymptotically Optimal Tests and Their Application to Dynamic Specification. *Rev. Econ. Stud.*, October 1987, 54(4), pp. 665–80.

Smith, Richard J. Testing for Exogeneity in Limited Dependent Variable Models Using a Simplified Likelihood Ratio Statistic. *J. Appl. Econometrics*, July 1987, 2(3), pp. 237–45.

Souvaine, Diane L. and Steele, J. Michael. Time- and Space-Efficient Algorithms for Least Median of Squares Regression. *J. Amer. Statist. Assoc.*, September 1987, 82(399), pp. 794–801.

Spanos, Aris. Error Autocorrelation Revisited: The AR(1) Case. *Econometric Rev.*, 1987-88, 6(2), pp. 285–94.

Stine, Robert A. Estimating Properties of Autoregressive Forecasts. *J. Amer. Statist. Assoc.*, December 1987, 82(400), pp. 1072–78.

Stock, James H. Asymptotic Properties of Least Squares Estimators of Cointegrating Vectors. *Econometrica*, September 1987, 55(5), pp. 1035–56.

Teräsvirta, Timo. Usefulness of Proxy Variables in Linear Models with Stochastic Regressors. *J. Econometrics*, November 1987, 36(3), pp. 377–82.

Terza, Joseph V. Estimating Linear Models with Ordinal Qualitative Regressors. *J. Econometrics*, March 1987, 34(3), pp. 275–91.

Thornton, Daniel L. A Note on the Efficiency of the Cochrane–Orcutt Estimator of the AR(1) Regression Model. *J. Econometrics*, November 1987, 36(3), pp. 369–76.

Thursby, Jerry G. OLS or GLS in the Presence of Specification Error? An Expected Loss Approach. *J. Econometrics*, July 1987, 35(2/3), pp. 359–74.

Trognon, Alain. Les méthodes du pseudo-maximum de vraisemblance. (The Pseudo-maximum Likelihood Methods. With English summary.) *Ann. Écon. Statist.*, Oct./Dec. 1987, (8), pp. 117–34.

Vanhonacker, Wilfried R. and Day, Diana. Cross-sectional Estimation in Marketing: Di-

rect versus Reverse Regression. *Marketing Sci.*, Summer 1987, 6(3), pp. 254–67.
                    [G: U.S.]

Vijverberg, Wim P. M. Non-normality as Distributional Misspecification in Single-Equation Limited Dependent Variable Models. *Oxford Bull. Econ. Statist.*, November 1987, 49(4), pp. 417–30.

Weerahandi, Samaradasa. Testing Regression Equality with Unequal Variances. *Econometrica*, September 1987, 55(5), pp. 1211–15.

Wills, Hugh. A Note on Specification Tests for the Multinomial Logit Model. *J. Econometrics*, Jan./Feb. 1987, 34(1/2), pp. 263–74.

Wolack, Frank A. An Exact Test for Multiple Inequality and Equality Constraints in the Linear Regression Model. *J. Amer. Statist. Assoc.*, September 1987, 82(399), pp. 782–93.

2114 Multivariate Analysis, Statistical Information Theory, and Other Special Inferential Problems; Queuing Theory; Markov Chains

Chua, Tin Chiu and Fuller, Wayne A. A Model for Multinomial Response Error Applied to Labor Flows. *J. Amer. Statist. Assoc.*, March 1987, 82(397), pp. 46–51.   [G: U.S.]

Dumitrescu, D. Divisive Hierarchical Classification. *Econ. Computat. Cybern. Stud. Res.*, 1987, 22(3), pp. 31–38.

Fraisse, Anne-Marie; Robert, Christian and Roy, Madeleine. Estimateurs à rétrécisseur matriciel différentiable, pour un coût quadratique général. (Shrinkage Estimators with Differentiable Shrinking Functions for Arbitrary Quadratic Loss. With English summary.) *Ann. Écon. Statist.*, Oct./Dec. 1987, (8), pp. 161–75.

Friedman, Jerome H. Exploratory Projection Pursuit. *J. Amer. Statist. Assoc.*, March 1987, 82(397), pp. 249–66.

Hausman, Jerry A. and Ruud, Paul A. Specifying and Testing Econometric Models for Rank-Ordered Data. *J. Econometrics*, Jan./Feb. 1987, 34(1/2), pp. 83–104.

Kodde, David A. and Palm, Franz C. A Parametric Test of the Negativity of the Substitution Matrix. *J. Appl. Econometrics*, July 1987, 2(3), pp. 227–35.   [G: W. Germany]

Lee, Lung-Fei. Non-parametric Testing of Discrete Panel Data Models. *J. Econometrics*, Jan./Feb. 1987, 34(1/2), pp. 147–77.

Narula, Subhash C. and Wellington, John F. Multicriteria Optimization Problems in Statistics. *Sawaragi, Y.; Inoue, K. and Nakayama, H., eds.*, 1987, pp. 348–57.

Purcaru, I. On Unilateral Entropic Correlation Factor. *Econ. Computat. Cybern. Stud. Res.*, 1987, 22(3), pp. 39–43.

Wills, Hugh. A Note on Specification Tests for the Multinomial Logit Model. *J. Econometrics*, Jan./Feb. 1987, 34(1/2), pp. 263–74.

2115 Bayesian Statistics and Bayesian Econometrics

Atkinson, Scott E. and Crocker, Thomas D. A Bayesian Approach to Assessing the Robustness of Hedonic Property Value Studies. *J. Appl. Econometrics*, January 1987, *2*(1), pp. 27–45. [G: U.S.]

Berger, James O. and Sellke, Thomas. Testing a Point Null Hypothesis: The Irreconcilability of *P* Values and Evidence: Rejoinder. *J. Amer. Statist. Assoc.*, March 1987, *82*(397), pp. 135–39.

Berger, James O. and Sellke, Thomas. Testing a Point Null Hypothesis: The Irreconcilability of *P* Values and Evidence. *J. Amer. Statist. Assoc.*, March 1987, *82*(397), pp. 112–22.

Brock, Horace W. Arrow–Bayes Equilibria: A New Theory of Price Forecasting. *Feiwel, G. R., ed. (I)*, 1987, pp. 559–96.

Burgstahler, David. Inference from Empirical Research. *Accounting Rev.*, January 1987, *62*(1), pp. 203–14.

Casella, George and Berger, Roger L. Reconciling Bayesian and Frequentist Evidence in the One-Sided Testing Problem. *J. Amer. Statist. Assoc.*, March 1987, *82*(397), pp. 106–11.

Casella, George and Berger, Roger L. Testing a Point Null Hypothesis: The Irreconcilability of *P* Values and Evidence: Rejoinder. *J. Amer. Statist. Assoc.*, March 1987, *82*(397), pp. 133–35.

Caves, Douglas W., et al. A Bayesian Approach to Combining Conditional Demand and Engineering Models of Electricity Usage. *Rev. Econ. Statist.*, August 1987, *69*(3), pp. 438–48. [G: U.S.]

Dempster, A. P. The Calculation of Posterior Distributions by Data Augmentation: Comment. *J. Amer. Statist. Assoc.*, June 1987, *82*(398), pp. 541.

Dickey, James M. Testing a Point Null Hypothesis: The Irreconcilability of *P* Values and Evidence: Comment. *J. Amer. Statist. Assoc.*, March 1987, *82*(397), pp. 129–30.

Dickey, James M.; Jiang, Jhy-Ming and Kadane, Joseph B. Bayesian Methods for Censored Categorical Data. *J. Amer. Statist. Assoc.*, September 1987, *82*(399), pp. 773–81.

Ehrman, Chaim Meyer; Krieger, Abba M. and Miescke, Klaus J. Subset Selection toward Optimizing the Best Performance at a Second Stage. *J. Bus. Econ. Statist.*, April 1987, *5*(2), pp. 295–303. [G: U.S.]

Good, I. J. Testing a Point Null Hypothesis: The Irreconcilability of *P* Values and Evidence: Comment. *J. Amer. Statist. Assoc.*, March 1987, *82*(397), pp. 125–28.

Haberman, Shelby J. The Calculation of Posterior Distributions by Data Augmentation: Comment. *J. Amer. Statist. Assoc.*, June 1987, *82*(398), pp. 547.

Hinkley, David V. Testing a Point Null Hypothesis: The Irreconcilability of *P* Values and Evidence: Comment. *J. Amer. Statist. Assoc.*, March 1987, *82*(397), pp. 128–29.

Johnson, Wesley. The Detection of Influential Observations for Allocation, Separation, and the Determination of Probabilities in a Bayesian Framework. *J. Bus. Econ. Statist.*, July 1987, *5*(3), pp. 369–81.

Kadane, Joseph B. Corrigenda [Is Victimization Chronic? A Bayesian Analysis of Multinomial Missing Data]. *J. Econometrics*, July 1987, *35*(2/3), pp. 393. [G: U.S.]

Kennedy, Peter E. Using Bayesian Analysis. *Becker, W. E. and Walstad, W. B., eds.*, 1987, pp. 225–46.

Lee, Jack C. and Sabavala, Darius J. Bayesian Estimation and Prediction for the Beta-Binomial Model. *J. Bus. Econ. Statist.*, July 1987, *5*(3), pp. 357–67.

Morris, C. N. Simulation in Hierarchical Models: Comment [The Calculation of Posterior Distributions by Data Augmentation]. *J. Amer. Statist. Assoc.*, June 1987, *82*(398), pp. 542–43.

Morris, C. N. Testing a Point Null Hypothesis: The Irreconcilability of *P* Values and Evidence: Comment. *J. Amer. Statist. Assoc.*, March 1987, *82*(397), pp. 131–33.

O'Hagan, A. The Calculation of Posterior Distributions by Data Augmentation: Comment. *J. Amer. Statist. Assoc.*, June 1987, *82*(398), pp. 546.

Parmigiani, Giovanni. Decisioni e modelli statistici: quale confine? (Decision Making and Statistical Model: Which Boundary? With English summary.) *Giorn. Econ.*, Jan.-Feb. 1987, *46*(1–2), pp. 97–107.

Peck, Stephen C. and Richels, Richard G. The Value of Information to the Acidic Deposition Debates. *J. Bus. Econ. Statist.*, April 1987, *5*(2), pp. 205–17.

Pratt, John W. Testing a Point Null Hypothesis: The Irreconcilability of *P* Values and Evidence: Comment. *J. Amer. Statist. Assoc.*, March 1987, *82*(397), pp. 123–25.

Rubin, Donald B. A Noniterative Sampling/Importance Resampling Alternative to the Data Augmentation Algorithm for Creating a Few Imputations when Fractions of Missing Information Are Modest: The SIR Algorithm: Comment [The Calculation of Posterior Distributions by Data Augmentation]. *J. Amer. Statist. Assoc.*, June 1987, *82*(398), pp. 543–46.

Salop, Steven C. Evaluating Uncertain Evidence with Sir Thomas Bayes: A Note for Teachers. *J. Econ. Perspectives*, Summer 1987, *1*(1), pp. 155–59.

Tanner, Martin A. and Wong, Wing Hung. The Calculation of Posterior Distributions by Data Augmentation: Rejoinder. *J. Amer. Statist. Assoc.*, June 1987, *82*(398), pp. 548–50.

Tanner, Martin A. and Wong, Wing Hung. The Calculation of Posterior Distributions by Data Augmentation. *J. Amer. Statist. Assoc.*, June 1987, *82*(398), pp. 528–40.

Vardeman, Stephen B. Testing a Point Null Hypothesis: The Irreconcilability of *P* Values and Evidence: Comment. *J. Amer. Statist. Assoc.*, March 1987, *82*(397), pp. 130–31.

Viertl, Reinhard. Bayesian Statistics in the Regional and Information Sciences. *[Eberl, W., Sr.]*, 1987, pp. 236–47.

Zellner, Arnold and Park, Soo-Bin. Bayesian Prediction with Random Regressors. *[Cochrane, D.]*, 1987, pp. 234–49.

2116 Time Series and Spectral Analysis

Ali, Mukhtar M. Durbin–Watson and Generalized Durbin–Watson Tests for Autocorrelations and Randomness. *J. Bus. Econ. Statist.*, April 1987, *5*(2), pp. 195–203.

Baillie, Richard T. Inference in Dynamic Models Containing 'Surprise' Variables. *J. Econometrics*, May 1987, *35*(1), pp. 101–17.

Baltagi, Badi H. On Estimating from a More General Time-Series cum Cross-section Data Structure. *Amer. Econ.*, Fall 1987, *31*(2), pp. 69–71.

Bell, William. A Note on Overdifferencing and the Equivalence of Seasonal Time Series Models with Monthly Means and Models with (0, 1, 1)$_{12}$ Seasonal Parts when $\Theta = 1$. *J. Bus. Econ. Statist.*, July 1987, *5*(3), pp. 383–87.

Bierens, Herman J. ARMAX Model Specification Testing, with an Application to Unemployment in the Netherlands. *J. Econometrics*, May 1987, *35*(1), pp. 161–90. [G: Netherlands]

Blanchard, Olivier Jean. Vector Autoregressions and Reality: Comment. *J. Bus. Econ. Statist.*, October 1987, *5*(4), pp. 449–51. [G: U.S.]

Box, George E. P.; Pierce, David A. and Newbold, Paul. Estimating Trend and Growth Rates in Seasonal Time Series. *J. Amer. Statist. Assoc.*, March 1987, *82*(397), pp. 276–82.

Brock, W. A. Distinguishing Random and Deterministic Systems: Abridged Version. *Grandmont, J.-M., ed.,* 1987, *1986*, pp. 168–95.

Carraro, Carlo and Sartore, Domenico. Square Root Iterative Filter: Theory and Applications to Econometric Models. *Ann. Écon. Statist.*, Apr./Sept. 1987, (6/7), pp. 435–59.

Chowdhury, Abdur R. Are Causal Relationships Sensitive to Causality Tests? *Appl. Econ.*, April 1987, *19*(4), pp. 449–65. [G: U.S.]

Chowdhury, Gopa. A Note on Correcting Biases in Dynamic Panel Models. *Appl. Econ.*, January 1987, *19*(1), pp. 31–37.

Christiano, Lawrence J. and Eichenbaum, Martin S. Temporal Aggregation and Structural Inference in Macroeconomics. *Carnegie–Rochester Conf. Ser. Public Policy*, Spring 1987, *26*, pp. 63–130. [G: U.S.]

Colletaz, Gilbert. La prévision optimale des taux d'intérêt. (With English summary.) *Revue Écon. Polit.*, May-June 1987, *97*(3), pp. 301–20. [G: France]

Cooley, Thomas F. and Parke, William R. Likelihood and Other Approaches to Prediction in Dynamic Models. *J. Econometrics*, May 1987, *35*(1), pp. 119–42.

Coulson, N. Edward and Robins, Russell P. A Test of the First Difference Transformation in Time Series Models. *Rev. Econ. Statist.*, November 1987, *69*(4), pp. 723–26. [G: U.S.]

Cuddington, John T. and Winters, L. Alan. The Beveridge–Nelson Decomposition of Economic Time Series: A Quick Computational Method. *J. Monet. Econ.*, January 1987, *19*(1), pp. 125–27.

Dagum, Estela Bee and Laniel, Normand. Revisions of Trend-Cycle Estimators of Moving Average Seasonal Adjustment Methods. *J. Bus. Econ. Statist.*, April 1987, *5*(2), pp. 177–89.

Dickey, David A. and Pantula, Sastry G. Determining the Ordering of Differencing in Autoregressive Processes. *J. Bus. Econ. Statist.*, October 1987, *5*(4), pp. 455–61.

Engle, Robert F. and Granger, Clive W. J. Co-integration and Error Correction: Representation, Estimation, and Testing. *Econometrica*, March 1987, *55*(2), pp. 251–76. [G: U.S.]

Engle, Robert F. and Yoo, Byung Sam. Forecasting and Testing in Co-integrated Systems. *J. Econometrics*, May 1987, *35*(1), pp. 143–59.

Evans, George W. The Structure of ARMA Solutions to a General Linear Model with Rational Expectations. *J. Econ. Dynam. Control*, March 1987, *11*(1), pp. 79–91.

Fernández Macho, F. J.; Harvey, A. C. and Stock, James H. Forecasting and Interpolation Using Vector Autoregressions with Common Trends. *Ann. Écon. Statist.*, Apr./Sept. 1987, (6/7), pp. 279–87.

Florens, Jean-Pierre; Mouchart, Michel and Richard, Jean-François. Dynamic Error-in-Variables Models and Limited Information Analysis. *Ann. Écon. Statist.*, Apr./Sept. 1987, (6/7), pp. 289–310.

Ghysels, Eric. Seasonal Extraction in the Presence of Feedback. *J. Bus. Econ. Statist.*, April 1987, *5*(2), pp. 191–94.

Giannini, Carlo and Mosconi, Rocco. Predictions from Unrestricted and Restricted VAR Models. *Giorn. Econ.*, May-June 1987, *46*(5–6), pp. 291–316.

Giorgio, Ardeni Pier and Diego, Lubian. Cointegrazione nelle serie storiche macroeconomiche. (Cointegration in Macroeconomic Time Series. With English summary.) *Giorn. Econ.*, July-August 1987, *46*(7–8), pp. 437–65.

Gonçalves, Esmeralda. Une généralisation des processus ARMA. (A Generalization of ARMA Processes. With English summary.) *Ann. Écon. Statist.*, Jan./Mar. 1987, (5), pp. 109–45.

Gourieroux, Christian. Une approche géométrique des processus ARMA. (A Geometric Approach of ARMA Processes. With English summary.) *Ann. Écon. Statist.*, Oct./Dec. 1987, (8), pp. 135–59.

Gourieroux, Christian; Monfort, Alain and Renault, Eric. Kullback Causality Measures. *Ann. Écon. Statist.*, Apr./Sept. 1987, (6/7), pp. 369–410.

Granger, Clive W. J. Equilibrium, Causality and Error-Correction Models. *Econ. Notes*, 1987, (1), pp. 5–21.

Hannan, Edward J. The Cochrane and Orcutt Papers. *[Cochrane, D.],* 1987, pp. 9–18.

Hillmer, Steven C. and Tabelsi, Abdelwahed. Benchmarking of Economic Time Series. *J. Amer. Statist. Assoc.*, December 1987, *82*(400), pp. 1064–71.

Izenman, Alan J. and Sarkar, Sanat K. Simultaneous Confidence Regions for the Frequency Analysis of Multiple Time Series. *J. Amer. Statist. Assoc.*, March 1987, *82*(397), pp. 271–75.

de Jong, Piet. Rational Economic Data Revisions. *J. Bus. Econ. Statist.*, October 1987, *5*(4), pp. 539–48. **[G: Canada]**

King, Maxwell L. An Alternative Test for Regression Coefficient Stability [Testing for Regression Coefficient Stability with a Stationary AR(1) Alternative]. *Rev. Econ. Statist.*, May 1987, *69*(2), pp. 379–81.

King, Maxwell L. and McAleer, Michael. Further Results on Testing AR (1) against MA (1) Disturbances in the Linear Regression Model. *Rev. Econ. Stud.*, October 1987, *54*(4), pp. 649–63.

Kitagawa, Genshiro. Non-Guassian State–Space Modeling of Nonstationary Time Series: Rejoinder. *J. Amer. Statist. Assoc.*, December 1987, *82*(400), pp. 1060–63.

Kitagawa, Genshiro. Non-Guassian State–Space Modeling of Nonstationary Time Series. *J. Amer. Statist. Assoc.*, December 1987, *82*(400), pp. 1032–41.

Kling, John L. Predicting the Turning Points of Business and Economic Time Series. *J. Bus.*, April 1987, *60*(2), pp. 201–38. **[G: U.S.]**

Kohn, Robert and Ansley, Craig F. Non-Guassian State–Space Modeling of Nonstationary Time Series: Comment. *J. Amer. Statist. Assoc.*, December 1987, *82*(400), pp. 1041–44.

Ladiray, Dominique and Roth, Nicole. Lissage robuste de séries chronologiques. Une étude expérimentale. (Non-linear Smoothers, a Monte Carlo Study. With English summary.) *Ann. Écon. Statist.*, Jan./Mar. 1987, (5), pp. 147–81.

Le Van, Cuong. Stationary Uncertainty Frontiers in Macroeconometric Models and Existence and Uniqueness of Solutions to Matrix Riccati Equations. *J. Econ. Dynam. Control*, March 1987, *11*(1), pp. 93–116.

Maravall, Agustín. Minimum Mean Squared Error Estimation of the Noise in Unobserved Component Models. *J. Bus. Econ. Statist.*, January 1987, *5*(1), pp. 115–20.

Martin, R. Douglas and Raftery, Adrian E. Robustness, Computation, and Non-Euclidean Models: Comment [Non-Guassian State–Space Modeling of Nonstationary Time Series]. *J. Amer. Statist. Assoc.*, December 1987, *82*(400), pp. 1044–50.

Nakervis, J. C. and Savin, N. E. Corrigendum [Testing the Autoregressive Parameter with the *t* Statistic]. *J. Econometrics*, March 1987, *34*(3), pp. 391.

O'Sullivan, Finbarr. Non-Guassian State–Space Modeling of Nonstationary Time Series: Comment. *J. Amer. Statist. Assoc.*, December 1987, *82*(400), pp. 1051–55.

Oliver, Robert M. Bayesian Forecasting with Stable Seasonal Patterns. *J. Bus. Econ. Statist.*, January 1987, *5*(1), pp. 77–85.

Orcutt, Guy H. and Cochrane, Donald. A Sampling Study of the Merits of Autoregressive and Reduced Form Transformations in Regression Analysis. *[Cochrane, D.]*, 1987, pp. 335–52.

Palm, Franz C. Time Series and Econometric Models with Unobservables. *Econ. Notes*, 1987, (1), pp. 22–38.

Pecican, E. Crossed Spectral Analysis Regarding the Correlated Evolution of Economic Processes. *Econ. Computat. Cybern. Stud. Res.*, 1987, *22*(3), pp. 45–52.

Peña, Daniel and Box, George E. P. Identifying a Simplifying Structure in Time Series. *J. Amer. Statist. Assoc.*, September 1987, *82*(399), pp. 836–43.

Phillips, Peter C. B. Time Series Regression with a Unit Root. *Econometrica*, March 1987, *55*(2), pp. 277–301.

Pierce, David A. and McKenzie, Sandra K. On Concurrent Seasonal Adjustment. *J. Amer. Statist. Assoc.*, September 1987, *82*(399), pp. 720–32.

Runkle, David E. Vector Autoregressions and Reality. *J. Bus. Econ. Statist.*, October 1987, *5*(4), pp. 437–42. **[G: U.S.]**

Runkle, David E. Vector Autoregressions and Reality: Reply. *J. Bus. Econ. Statist.*, October 1987, *5*(4), pp. 454. **[G: U.S.]**

Salinas, Teresita S. and Hillmer, Steven C. Multicollinearity Problems in Modeling Time Series with Trading-Day Variation. *J. Bus. Econ. Statist.*, July 1987, *5*(3), pp. 431–36.

Schwert, G. William. Effects of Model Specification on Tests for Unit Roots in Macroeconomic Data. *J. Monet. Econ.*, July 1987, *20*(1), pp. 73–103.

Sen, D. L. and Dickey, David A. Symmetric Test for Second Differencing in Univariate Time Series. *J. Bus. Econ. Statist.*, October 1987, *5*(4), pp. 463–73. **[G: U.S.]**

Sims, Christopher A. Vector Autoregressions and Reality: Comment. *J. Bus. Econ. Statist.*, October 1987, *5*(4), pp. 443–49. **[G: U.S.]**

Stekler, H. O. The Effect of Data Revisions and Additional Observations on Time-Series Estimates. *Appl. Econ.*, March 1987, *19*(3), pp. 347–53. **[G: U.K.]**

Stine, Robert A. Estimating Properties of Autoregressive Forecasts. *J. Amer. Statist. Assoc.*, December 1987, *82*(400), pp. 1072–78.

Stock, James H. Asymptotic Properties of Least Squares Estimators of Cointegrating Vectors. *Econometrica*, September 1987, *55*(5), pp. 1035–56.

Stock, James H. Temporal Aggregation and Structural Inference in Macroeconomics: A Comment. *Carnegie–Rochester Conf. Ser. Public Policy*, Spring 1987, *26*, pp. 131–39. **[G: U.S.]**

Tsay, Ruey S. Conditional Heteroscedastic Time Series Models. *J. Amer. Statist. Assoc.*, June 1987, *82*(398), pp. 590–604.

Tsay, Ruey S. Detecting and Modeling Changes in Time Series: Comment [Non-Guassian State–Space Modeling of Non Stationary Time Series]. *J. Amer. Statist. Assoc.*, December 1987, *82*(400), pp. 1056–59.

de Vos, Aart F. Forecasting the Daily Balance of the Dutch Giro. *Heijmans, R. and Neudecker, H., eds.*, 1987, pp. 131–48. **[G: Netherlands]**

Wahba, Grace. Non-Guassian State–Space Modeling of Nonstationary Time Series: Comment. *J. Amer. Statist. Assoc.*, December 1987, 82(400), pp. 1055–56.

Watson, Geoffrey S. Asymptotic Spectral Analysis of Cross-Product Matrices. *[Cochrane, D.]*, 1987, pp. 219–33.

Watson, Mark W. Uncertainty in Model-Based Seasonal Adjustment Procedures and Construction of Minimax Filters. *J. Amer. Statist. Assoc.*, June 1987, 82(398), pp. 395–408. [G: U.S.]

Watson, Mark W. Vector Autoregressions and Reality: Comment. *J. Bus. Econ. Statist.*, October 1987, 5(4), pp. 451–53. [G: U.S.]

2117 Survey Methods; Sampling Methods

Anderson, Barbara A. and Silver, Brian D. The SIP General Survey Sample. *Millar, J. R., ed.*, 1987, pp. 354–71. [G: U.S.S.R.]

Berliner, Joseph S. Politics, Work, and Daily Life in the USSR: Foreword. *Millar, J. R., ed.*, 1987, pp. vii–xii. [G: U.S.S.R.]

Blair, Edward and Burton, Scot. Cognitive Processes Used by Survey Respondents to Answer Behavioral Frequency Questions. *J. Cons. Res.*, September 1987, 14(2), pp. 280–88. [G: U.S.]

Bowden, Roger J. Repeated Sampling in the Presence of Publication Effects. *J. Amer. Statist. Assoc.*, June 1987, 82(398), pp. 476–84.

Buchanan, Bruce and Morrison, Donald G. Sampling Properties of Rate Questions with Implications for Survey Research. *Marketing Sci.*, Summer 1987, 6(3), pp. 286–98.

Cahoon, Lawrence S. Repeated Sampling in the Presence of Publication Effects: Comment. *J. Amer. Statist. Assoc.*, June 1987, 82(398), pp. 484–86.

Collins, Martin and Sykes, Wendy. The Problems of Non-coverage and Unlisted Numbers in Telephone Surveys in Britain. *J. Roy. Statist. Soc.*, 1987, 150(3), pp. 241–53. [G: U.K.]

Cressie, Noel. Census Undercount Adjustment and the Quality of Geographic Population Distributions: Comment. *J. Amer. Statist. Assoc.*, December 1987, 82(400), pp. 980–83. [G: U.S.]

Deville, Jean-Claude. Sur la durée d'observation dans les enquêtes à carnets de compte. (On the Observation Periods in Surveys of Household Spending Records. With English summary.) *Ann. Écon. Statist.*, Jan./Mar. 1987, (5), pp. 183–95.

Dickie, Mark; Fisher, Ann and Gerking, Shelby. Market Transactions and Hypothetical Demand Data: A Comparative Study. *J. Amer. Statist. Assoc.*, March 1987, 82(397), pp. 69–75. [G: U.S.]

Karmel, T. S. and Jain, Malti. Comparison of Purposive and Random Sampling Schemes for Estimating Capital Expenditure. *J. Amer. Statist. Assoc.*, March 1987, 82(397), pp. 52–57. [G: Australia]

Kott, Phillip S. Nonresponse in a Periodic Sample

Survey. *J. Bus. Econ. Statist.*, April 1987, 5(2), pp. 287–93. [G: U.S.]

Millar, James R. Politics, Work, and Daily Life in the USSR: History, Method, and the Problem of Bias. *Millar, J. R., ed.*, 1987, pp. 3–30. [G: U.S.S.R.]

O'Brien, L. G. User Control versus Randomisation in Geographical Probability Sampling: A Compromise Solution Using Controlled Sampling. *Environ. Planning A*, July 1987, 19(7), pp. 949–58. [G: U.K.]

Ordeshook, Peter C. Repeated Sampling in the Presence of Publication Effects: Public Opinion Polls and Democratic Processes: Comment. *J. Amer. Statist. Assoc.*, June 1987, 82(398), pp. 486–91.

Schäffer, Karl-August. Wirkung von Antwortausfällen infolge Freiwilligkeit der Auskunftserteilung. (The Effect of Non-response in Voluntary Surveys. With English summary.) *Jahr. Nationalökon. Statist.*, October 1987, 203(5–6), pp. 569–75. [G: W. Germany]

Schirm, Allen L. and Preston, Samuel H. Census Undercount Adjustment and the Quality of Geographic Population Distributions: Rejoinder. *J. Amer. Statist. Assoc.*, December 1987, 82(400), pp. 986–90.

Schirm, Allen L. and Preston, Samuel H. Census Undercount Adjustment and the Quality of Geographic Population Distributions. *J. Amer. Statist. Assoc.*, December 1987, 82(400), pp. 965–78. [G: U.S.]

Spencer, Bruce D. Census Undercount Adjustment and the Quality of Geographic Population Distributions: Comment. *J. Amer. Statist. Assoc.*, December 1987, 82(400), pp. 984–86. [G: U.S.]

Stenger, Horst. Post-stratification in Replicative Designs. *Jahr. Nationalökon. Statist.*, October 1987, 203(5–6), pp. 611–19.

Swafford, Michael, et al. Response Effects in SIP's General Survey of Soviet Emigrants. *Millar, J. R., ed.*, 1987, pp. 372–405. [G: U.S.S.R.]

Tobin, James. Estimation of Relationships for Limited Dependent Variables. *Tobin, J. (II)*, 1987, 1958, pp. 467–83.

Tobin, James. Multiple Probit Regression of Dichotomous Economic Variables. *Tobin, J. (II)*, 1987, pp. 447–66. [G: U.S.]

Wilson, P. R. and Elliot, D. J. An Evaluation of the Postcode Address File as a Sampling Frame and Its Use within OPCS. *J. Roy. Statist. Soc.*, 1987, 150(3), pp. 230–40.

Wolter, Kirk M. Census Undercount Adjustment and the Quality of Geographic Population Distributions: Comment. *J. Amer. Statist. Assoc.*, December 1987, 82(400), pp. 978–80. [G: U.S.]

2118 Theory of Index Numbers and Aggregation

Al, Pieter G., et al. The Use of Chain Indices for Deflating the National Accounts. *Statist. J.*, July 1987, 4(4), pp. 347–68.

Anglin, Paul M. and Baye, Michael R. Information, Multiprice Search, and Cost-of-Living Index Theory. *J. Polit. Econ.*, December 1987, *95*(6), pp. 1179–95.

Barnett, William A. The Microeconomic Theory of Monetary Aggregation. *Barnett, W. A. and Singleton, K. J., eds.*, 1987, pp. 115–68.

Beckman, Barry A. and Tapscott, Tracy R. Composite Indexes of Leading, Coincident, and Lagging Indicators. *Surv. Curr. Bus.*, November 1987, *67*(11), pp. 24–28. **[G: U.S.]**

Berrebi, Zeev M. and Silber, Jacques G. Dispersion, Asymmetry and the Gini Index of Inequality. *Int. Econ. Rev.*, June 1987, *28*(2), pp. 331–38.

Berrebi, Zeev M. and Silber, Jacques G. Interquantile Differences, Income Inequality Measurement and the Gini Concentration Index. *Math. Soc. Sci.*, February 1987, *13*(1), pp. 67–72. **[G: Selected Countries]**

Clements, Kenneth W. and Izan, H. Y. The Measurement of Inflation: A Stochastic Approach. *J. Bus. Econ. Statist.*, July 1987, *5*(3), pp. 339–50. **[G: Australia]**

Serletis, Apostolos. Monetary Asset Separability Tests. *Barnett, W. A. and Singleton, K. J., eds.*, 1987, pp. 169–82.

2119 Experimental Design; Social Experiments

Coyle, Dennis J. and Wildavsky, Aaron. Social Experimentation in the Face of Formidable Fables. *Munnell, A. H., ed.*, 1987, pp. 167–84. **[G: U.S.]**

Hausman, Jerry A. Evaluating the Methodology of Social Experiments: Discussion. *Munnell, A. H., ed.*, 1987, pp. 158–61. **[G: U.S.]**

Heclo, Hugh. Social Experimentation in the Face of Formidable Fables: Discussion. *Munnell, A. H., ed.*, 1987, pp. 185–88. **[G: U.S.]**

Mead, Lawrence M. Social Experimentation in the Face of Formidable Fables: Discussion. *Munnell, A. H., ed.*, 1987, pp. 189–93. **[G: U.S.]**

Metcalf, Charles E. Evaluating the Methodology of Social Experiments: Discussion. *Munnell, A. H., ed.*, 1987, pp. 162–66. **[G: U.S.]**

Zellner, Arnold and Rossi, Peter E. Evaluating the Methodology of Social Experiments. *Munnell, A. H., ed.*, 1987, pp. 131–57. **[G: U.S.]**

212 Construction, Analysis, and Use of Econometric Models

2120 Construction, Analysis, and Use of Econometric Models

Ahmad, Ehtisham; Stern, Nicholas H. and Leung, H.-M. The Demand for Wheat under Non-linear Pricing in Pakistan. *J. Econometrics*, Sept./Oct. 1987, *36*(1/2), pp. 55–65. **[G: Pakistan]**

Ahumada, Hildegart. Econometría Dinámica: Una aplicación a la demanda de billetes y monedas en poder del público. (Dynamic Econometric: An Application to the Demand for Notes and Coins in the Hands of the Public.

With English summary.) *Económica (La Plata)*, July-Dec. 1987, *33*(2), pp. 159–84.

Akiyama, T. and Trivedi, Pravin K. Vintage Production Approach to Perennial Crop Supply: An Application to Tea in Major Producing Countries. *J. Econometrics*, Sept./Oct. 1987, *36*(1/2), pp. 133–61. **[G: India; Sri Lanka; Kenya]**

Alaouze, Chris M. Empirical Evidence on the Sign of the Slope of the Hazard Rate from Unemployment from a Fixed Effects Model. *J. Appl. Econometrics*, April 1987, *2*(2), pp. 159–68. **[G: U.S.]**

Almon, Clopper. Principles and Practices of the INFORUM Interindustry Macro Model. *Tchijov, I. and Tomaszewicz, L., eds.*, 1987, pp. 7–25. **[G: U.S.]**

Altonji, Joseph G. and Siow, Aloysius. Testing the Response of Consumption to Income Changes with (Noisy) Panel Data. *Quart. J. Econ.*, May 1987, *102*(2), pp. 293–328. **[G: U.S.]**

Amemiya, Takeshi and Vuong, Quang H. A Comparison of Two Consistent Estimators in the Choice-based Sampling Qualitative Response Model. *Econometrica*, May 1987, *55*(3), pp. 699–702.

Amman, Hans M. and Jager, Henk. Optimal Economic Policies under a Crawling-Peg Exchange-Rate System. *Carraro, C. and Sartore, D., eds.*, 1987, pp. 105–26.

Anandalingam, G. and Kulatilaka, Nalin. Decomposing Production Efficiency into Technical, Allocative and Structural Components. *J. Roy. Statist. Soc.*, 1987, *150*(2), pp. 143–51.

Anderson, Gary. A Procedure for Differentiating Perfect-Foresight-Model Reduced-Form Coefficients. *J. Econ. Dynam. Control*, December 1987, *11*(4), pp. 465–81.

Anderson, Gordon J. Prediction Tests in Limited Dependent Variable Models. *J. Econometrics*, Jan./Feb. 1987, *34*(1/2), pp. 253–61.

Anderson, Robert and Enzler, Jared J. Toward Realistic Policy Design: Policy Reaction Functions That Rely on Economic Forecasts. *[Modigliani, F.]*, 1987, pp. 291–330. **[G: U.S.]**

Andrews, Donald W. K. Consistency in Nonlinear Econometric Models: A Generic Uniform Law of Large Numbers [On Unification of the Asymptotic Theory of Nonlinear Econometric Models]. *Econometrica*, November 1987, *55*(6), pp. 1465–71.

Antonini, Alberto and Kwack, Sung Y. Price and Inventory Dynamics of Primary Commodities. *Int. Econ. J.*, Spring 1987, *1*(1), pp. 43–55.

Aoki, Masanao. Studies of Economic Interdependence by State Space Modeling of Time Series: U.S.–Japan Example. *Ann. Écon. Statist.*, Apr./Sept. 1987, (6/7), pp. 225–52. **[G: U.S.; Japan]**

Aznar, Antonio. Contenido informativo y selección de modelos econométricos. (With English summary.) *Invest. Econ.*, January 1987, *11*(1), pp. 25–39. **[G: Spain]**

Barnett, William A.; Lee, Yul W. and Wolfe, Michael D. The Global Properties of the Two

Miniflex Laurent Flexible Functional Forms. *J. Econometrics*, November 1987, *36*(3), pp. 281–98.

Barras, Richard and Ferguson, D. Dynamic Modelling of the Building Cycle: 1. Theoretical Framework. *Environ. Planning A*, March 1987, *19*(3), pp. 353–67.

Bartik, Timothy J. Estimating Hedonic Demand Parameters with Single Market Data: The Problems Caused by Unobserved Tastes. *Rev. Econ. Statist.*, February 1987, *69*(1), pp. 178–80.

Bartik, Timothy J. The Estimation of Demand Parameters in Hedonic Price Models. *J. Polit. Econ.*, February 1987, *95*(1), pp. 81–88. [G: U.S.]

Baxter, M. J. Testing for Misspecification in Models of Spatial Flows. *Environ. Planning A*, September 1987, *19*(9), pp. 1153–60.

Becker, William E. and Waldman, Donald M. The Probit Model. *Becker, W. E. and Walstad, W. B., eds.*, 1987, pp. 135–40.

Behrman, Jere R. and Wolfe, Barbara L. How Does Mother's Schooling Affect Family Health, Nutrition, Medical Care Usage, and Household Sanitation? *J. Econometrics*, Sept./Oct. 1987, *36*(1/2), pp. 185–204. [G: Nicaragua]

Belongia, Michael T. and Sheehan, Richard G. The Informational Efficiency of Weekly Money Announcements: An Econometric Critique. *J. Bus. Econ. Statist.*, July 1987, *5*(3), pp. 351–56. [G: U.S.]

Bergstrom, A. R. Optimal Control in Wide-Sense Stationary Continuous-Time Stochastic Models. *J. Econ. Dynam. Control*, September 1987, *11*(3), pp. 425–43.

Bernard, Victor L. Cross-Sectional Dependence and Problems in Inference in Market-Based Accounting Research. *J. Acc. Res.*, Spring 1987, *25*(1), pp. 1–48. [G: U.S.]

Bewley, Ronald and Young, Trevor. Applying Thiel's Multinomial Extension of the Linear Logit Model to Meat Expenditure Data. *Amer. J. Agr. Econ.*, February 1987, *69*(1), pp. 151–57. [G: U.K.]

Bhargava, Alok. Towards a Theory of Point Optimal Testing: Comment. *Econometric Rev.*, 1987-88, *6*(2), pp. 241–47.

Bianchi, Carlo; Brillet, Jean-Louis and Panattoni, Lorenzo. Uncertainty and Stability in a Macroeconometric Model. *Ann. Écon. Statist.*, Apr./Sept. 1987, (6/7), pp. 347–67. [G: France]

Bierens, Herman J. ARMAX Model Specification Testing, with an Application to Unemployment in the Netherlands. *J. Econometrics*, May 1987, *35*(1), pp. 161–90. [G: Netherlands]

Bierens, Herman J. Towards a Theory of Point Optimal Testing: Comment. *Econometric Rev.*, 1987-88, *6*(2), pp. 231–33.

Binswanger, Hans P., et al. On the Determinants of Cross-country Aggregate Agricultural Supply. *J. Econometrics*, Sept./Oct. 1987, *36*(1/2), pp. 111–31. [G: LDCs]

Björklund, Anders and Moffitt, Robert. The Estimation of Wage Gains and Welfare Gains in Self-selection Models. *Rev. Econ. Statist.*,

February 1987, *69*(1), pp. 42–49. [G: Sweden]

Blackburn, Keith. Macroeconomic Policy Evaluation and Optimal Control Theory: A Critical Review of Some Recent Developments. *J. Econ. Surveys*, 1987, *1*(2), pp. 113–48.

Blanchard, Olivier Jean. Vector Autoregressions and Reality: Comment. *J. Bus. Econ. Statist.*, October 1987, *5*(4), pp. 449–51. [G: U.S.]

Blundell, Richard. Econometric Approaches to the Specification of Life-Cycle Labour Supply and Commodity Demand Behaviour. *Econometric Rev.*, 1987, *6*(1), pp. 103–65.

Blundell, Richard and Meghir, Costas. Bivariate Alternatives to the Tobit Model. *J. Econometrics*, Jan./Feb. 1987, *34*(1/2), pp. 179–200. [G: U.K.]

Bollerslev, Tim. A Conditionally Heteroskedastic Time Series Model for Speculative Prices and Rates of Return. *Rev. Econ. Statist.*, August 1987, *69*(3), pp. 542–47. [G: U.S.; U.K.; W. Germany]

Borgers, Aloys and Timmermans, Harry. Choice Model Specification, Substitution and Spatial Structure Effects: A Simulation Experiment. *Reg. Sci. Urban Econ.*, February 1987, *17*(1), pp. 29–47.

Botha, J. P. Data: Die aard, kwaliteit en aanwending daarvan. (With English summary.) *J. Stud. Econ. Econometrics*, November 1987, *11*(3), pp. 83–109.

Brandsma, Andries S. Risk Reduction and the Robustness of Economic Policies. *Carraro, C. and Sartore, D., eds.*, 1987, pp. 83–104.

Brandsma, Andries S. and Siebrand, Jan C. Latent Transversality Conditions in Macroeconomic Stabilization Policies. *J. Econ. Dynam. Control*, June 1987, *11*(2), pp. 235–39. [G: Netherlands]

Brock, Horace W. Arrow–Bayes Equilibria: A New Theory of Price Forecasting. *Feiwel, G. R., ed. (I)*, 1987, pp. 559–96.

Burmeister, Edwin and Wall, Kent D. Unobserved Rational Expectations and the German Hyperinflation with Endogenous Money Supply. *Int. Econ. Rev.*, February 1987, *28*(1), pp. 15–32. [G: Germany]

Calzolari, Giorgio. Forecast Variance in Dynamic Simulation of Simultaneous Equation Models. *Econometrica*, November 1987, *55*(6), pp. 1473–76.

Calzolari, Giorgio and Panattoni, Lorenzo. Gradient Methods in FIML Estimation of Econometric Models. *Carraro, C. and Sartore, D., eds.*, 1987, pp. 143–53.

Cameron, Trudy Ann and James, Michelle D. Efficient Estimation Methods for "Closed-ended" Contingent Valuation Surveys. *Rev. Econ. Statist.*, May 1987, *69*(2), pp. 269–76. [G: Canada]

Campbell, John Y. and Mankiw, N. Gregory. Permanent and Transitory Components in Macroeconomic Fluctuations. *Amer. Econ. Rev.*, May 1987, *77*(2), pp. 111–17. [G: U.S.]

Caravani, Paolo. Modeling Economic Policy with

Non-symmetric Losses and Risk Aversion. *J. Econ. Behav. Organ.*, September 1987, *8*(3), pp. 453–67.

Card, David and Farber, Henry S. Semiparametric Estimation of Employment Duration Models: Comments. *Econometric Rev.*, 1987, *6*(1), pp. 41–54.

Carota, Cinzia. Dati e modello statistico: Quale confine? (Data and Statistical Model: Which Boundary? With English summary.) *Giorn. Econ.*, Jan.-Feb. 1987, *46*(1–2), pp. 85–96.

Caves, Douglas W., et al. A Bayesian Approach to Combining Conditional Demand and Engineering Models of Electricity Usage. *Rev. Econ. Statist.*, August 1987, *69*(3), pp. 438–48. **[G: U.S.]**

Chalfant, James A. A Globally Flexible, Almost Ideal Demand System. *J. Bus. Econ. Statist.*, April 1987, *5*(2), pp. 233–42. **[G: U.S.]**

Charemza, Wojciech. Maximum Likelihood Methods of Estimation for Disequilibrium Models in a Centrally Planned Economy. *Econ. Planning*, 1987, *21*(2–3), pp. 87–99.

Chavas, Jean-Paul and Segerson, Kathleen. Stochastic Specification and Estimation of Share Equation Systems. *J. Econometrics*, July 1987, *35*(2/3), pp. 337–58.

Chesher, Andrew and Irish, Margaret. Residual Analysis in the Grouped and Censored Normal Linear Model. *J. Econometrics*, Jan./Feb. 1987, *34*(1/2), pp. 33–61. **[G: U.K.]**

Chiarini, Bruno. "Instrument Instability" in Large-Scale Econometric Models. *Giorn. Econ.*, Sept.-Oct. 1987, *46*(9–10), pp. 525–32.

Chin, C. F. and Kennedy, Peter E. On Inferring the True Model's Direction. *Can. J. Econ.*, November 1987, *20*(4), pp. 876–79.

Chow, Gregory C. Development of Control Theory in Macroeconomics. *Carraro, C. and Sartore, D., eds.*, 1987, pp. 3–19.

Christiano, Lawrence J. Cagan's Model of Hyperinflation under Rational Expectations. *Int. Econ. Rev.*, February 1987, *28*(1), pp. 33–49. **[G: Germany]**

Christiano, Lawrence J. and Eichenbaum, Martin S. Temporal Aggregation and Structural Inference in Macroeconomics. *Carnegie–Rochester Conf. Ser. Public Policy*, Spring 1987, *26*, pp. 63–130. **[G: U.S.]**

Christodoulakis, Nicos and Levine, Paul. The Trade-off between Simplicity and Optimality in Macroeconomic Policy Design. *J. Econ. Dynam. Control*, June 1987, *11*(2), pp. 173–78.

Chua, Tin Chiu and Fuller, Wayne A. A Model for Multinomial Response Error Applied to Labor Flows. *J. Amer. Statist. Assoc.*, March 1987, *82*(397), pp. 46–51. **[G: U.S.]**

Chung, Jae Wan. On the Estimation of Factor Substitution in the Translog Model. *Rev. Econ. Statist.*, August 1987, *69*(3), pp. 409–17. **[G: U.S.]**

Çinar, E. Miné. The Sensitivity of Extended Linear Expenditure System Household Scales to Income Declaration Errors. *J. Econometrics*, March 1987, *34*(3), pp. 361–72. **[G: U.S.; Turkey]**

Clark, Colin W. Behavioral Modelling and Resource Management. *Vincent, T. L., et al., eds.*, 1987, pp. 11–19.

Clements, Kenneth W. and Taylor, John C. The Pattern of Financial Asset Holdings in Australia. *[Cochrane, D.]*, 1987, pp. 268–88. **[G: Australia]**

Cohen, Yosef. Approaches to Adaptive Policy Design for Harvest Management: Comment. *Vincent, T. L., et al., eds.*, 1987, pp. 123.

Cohen, Yosef. Identification and Control of Stochastic Linear Multispecies Ecosystem Models. *Vincent, T. L., et al., eds.*, 1987, pp. 66–79.

Conrad, Klaus and Unger, Ralph. Ex post Tests for Short- and Long-run Optimization. *J. Econometrics*, November 1987, *36*(3), pp. 339–58. **[G: W. Germany]**

Coomes, Paul A. PLEM: A Computer Program for Passive Learning, Stochastic Control Experiments. *J. Econ. Dynam. Control*, June 1987, *11*(2), pp. 223–27.

Coondoo, Dipankor and Majumder, Amita. A System of Demand Equations Based on Price Independent Generalized Linearity. *Int. Econ. Rev.*, February 1987, *28*(1), pp. 213–28. **[G: India]**

Cosslett, Stephen R. Efficiency Bounds for Distribution-free Estimators of the Binary Choice and the Censored Regression Models. *Econometrica*, May 1987, *55*(3), pp. 559–85.

Currie, David and Levine, Paul. Credibility and Time Consistency in a Stochastic World. *J. Econ. (Z. Nationalökon.)*, 1987, *47*(3), pp. 225–52.

Dastoor, Naorayex K. and Fisher, Gordon. The Theory and Practice of Point-Optimal Testing: Comment [Towards a Theory of Point Optimal Testing]. *Econometric Rev.*, 1987-88, *6*(2), pp. 219–29.

Davis, E. P. A Stock-flow Consistent Macroeconometric Model of the UK Economy—Part II. *J. Appl. Econometrics*, October 1987, *2*(4), pp. 259–307. **[G: U.K.]**

Davis, E. P. A Stock-Flow Consistent Macroeconometric Model of the UK Economy—Part I. *J. Appl. Econometrics*, April 1987, *2*(2), pp. 111–32. **[G: U.K.]**

Davis, M. H. A. and Gómez, G. L. The Martingale Maximum Principle and the Allocation of Labour Surplus. *J. Econ. Dynam. Control*, June 1987, *11*(2), pp. 241–47.

Deaton, Angus. Estimation of Own- and Cross-price Elasticities from Household Survey Data. *J. Econometrics*, Sept./Oct. 1987, *36*(1/2), pp. 7–30. **[G: Ivory Coast]**

Deissenberg, Christophe. On the Minmax Lyapunov Stabilization of Uncertain Economies. *J. Econ. Dynam. Control*, June 1987, *11*(2), pp. 229–34.

Dewatripont, Mathias and Michel, Gilles. On Closure Rules, Homogeneity and Dynamics in Applied General Equilibrium Models. *J. Devel. Econ.*, June 1987, *26*(1), pp. 65–76.

Dickie, Mark; Fisher, Ann and Gerking, Shelby. Market Transactions and Hypothetical Demand Data: A Comparative Study. *J. Amer. Statist. Assoc.*, March 1987, 82(397), pp. 69–75. **[G: U.S.]**

Diewert, Walter Erwin and Wales, Terence J. Flexible Functional Forms and Global Curvature Conditions. *Econometrica*, January 1987, 55(1), pp. 43–68. **[G: U.S.]**

Dixon, Bruce L.; Garcia, Philip and Anderson, Margot. Usefulness of Pretests for Estimating Underlying Technologies Using Dual Profit Functions. *Int. Econ. Rev.*, October 1987, 28(3), pp. 623–33.

Dixon, Peter B. On Using Applied General Equilibrium Models for Analysing Structural Change. *Pasinetti, L. and Lloyd, P., eds.*, 1987, pp. 149–58.

Dudewicz, Edward J. Nonparametric Methods: The History, the Reality, and the Future (with Special Reference to Statistical Selection Problems). *[Eberl, W., Sr.]*, 1987, pp. 63–83.

Edwards, David and Havránek, Tomáš. A Fast Model Selection Procedure for Large Families of Models. *J. Amer. Statist. Assoc.*, March 1987, 82(397), pp. 205–13.

Engle, Robert F.; Lilien, David M. and Robins, Russell P. Estimating Time Varying Risk Premia in the Term Structure: The Arch-M Model. *Econometrica*, March 1987, 55(2), pp. 391–407.

Eppers, J. and Leserer, M. Some Remarks on Forward Programming. *Carraro, C. and Sartore, D., eds.*, 1987, pp. 127–34.

Epple, Dennis. Hedonic Prices and Implicit Markets: Estimating Demand and Supply Functions for Differentiated Products. *J. Polit. Econ.*, February 1987, 95(1), pp. 59–80.

Fernández Macho, F. J.; Harvey, A. C. and Stock, James H. Forecasting and Interpolation Using Vector Autoregressions with Common Trends. *Ann. Écon. Statist.*, Apr./Sept. 1987, (6/7), pp. 279–87.

Fischer, Manfred M. and Nijkamp, Peter. From Static Towards Dynamic Discrete Choice Modelling: A State of the Art Review. *Reg. Sci. Urban Econ.*, February 1987, 17(1), pp. 3–27.

Fisher, P. G. and Hughes Hallett, Andrew J. The Convergence Characteristics of Iterative Techniques for Solving Econometric Models. *Oxford Bull. Econ. Statist.*, May 1987, 49(2), pp. 231–44. **[G: U.K.]**

Florens, Jean-Pierre; Mouchart, Michel and Richard, Jean-François. Dynamic Error-in-Variables Models and Limited Information Analysis. *Ann. Écon. Statist.*, Apr./Sept. 1987, (6/7), pp. 289–310.

Friedman, Benjamin M. Toward Realistic Policy Design: Policy Reaction Functions That Rely on Economic Forecasts: Comments. *[Modigliani, F.]*, 1987, pp. 331–36. **[G: U.S.]**

Gambetta, Guido. Teoria e practica in econometria. Ovvero "Tutto quello che avreste voluto sapere sull'econometria (ma non avete mai osato chiedere)." (Theory and Practice in Econometrics. Or "Everything You Always Wanted to Know about Econometrics [but Were Afraid to Ask]." With English summary.) *Econ. Polit.*, December 1987, 4(3), pp. 437–67.

Gandolfo, Giancarlo and Petit, Maria Luisa. Optimization in Continuous Time and Policy Design in the Italian Economy. *Ann. Écon. Statist.*, Apr./Sept. 1987, (6/7), pp. 311–33. **[G: Italy]**

Gertler, Paul; Locay, Luis and Sanderson, Warren C. Are User Fees Regressive? The Welfare Implications of Health Care Financing Proposals in Peru. *J. Econometrics*, Sept./Oct. 1987, 36(1/2), pp. 67–88. **[G: Peru]**

Giannini, Carlo and Mosconi, Rocco. Predictions from Unrestricted and Restricted VAR Models. *Giorn. Econ.*, May-June 1987, 46(5–6), pp. 291–316.

Gibbons, Michael R. and Shanken, Jay. Subperiod Aggregation and the Power of Multivariate Tests of Portfolio Efficiency. *J. Finan. Econ.*, December 1987, 19(2), pp. 389–94.

Gourieroux, Christian, et al. Generalised Residuals. *J. Econometrics*, Jan./Feb. 1987, 34(1/2), pp. 5–32.

Granger, Clive W. J. Equilibrium, Causality and Error-Correction Models. *Econ. Notes*, 1987, (1), pp. 5–21.

Green, Richard; Hahn, William and Rocke, David. Standard Errors for Elasticities: A Comparison of Bootstrap and Asymptotic Standard Errors. *J. Bus. Econ. Statist.*, January 1987, 5(1), pp. 145–49. **[G: Canada]**

Gregory, Allan W. and Veall, Michael R. Formulating Wald Tests of the Restrictions Implied by the Rational Expectations Hypothesis. *J. Appl. Econometrics*, January 1987, 2(1), pp. 61–68. **[G: Canada]**

Gruber, Josef. Interactive Vector Optimization as a Complement to Optimal Control in Econometric Models. *Carraro, C. and Sartore, D., eds.*, 1987, pp. 63–82.

Hajivassiliou, Vassilis A. The External Debt Repayments Problems of LDC's: An Econometric Model Based on Panel Data. *J. Econometrics*, Sept./Oct. 1987, 36(1/2), pp. 205–30. **[G: LDCs]**

Hall, S. G. An Investigation of Time Inconsistency and Optimal Policy Formulation in the Presence of Rational Expectations Using the National Institute's Model 7. *Appl. Econ.*, September 1987, 19(9), pp. 1175–85. **[G: U.K.]**

Han, Aaron K. A Non-parametric Analysis of Transformations. *J. Econometrics*, July 1987, 35(2/3), pp. 191–209.

Hanna, Susan S. Behavioral Modelling and Resource Management: Comment. *Vincent, T. L., et al., eds.*, 1987, pp. 20–21.

Hansen, Gerd. Multikollinearität und Prognosefehler. (Forecasting Error and Multicollinearity. With English summary.) *Jahr. Nationalökon. Statist.*, October 1987, 203(5–6), pp. 517–31.

Hansen, Lars Peter and Richard, Scott F. The Role of Conditioning Information in Deducing Testable Restrictions Implied by Dynamic Asset Pricing Models. *Econometrica*, May 1987, 55(3), pp. 587–613.

Hart, Myra K. Specification Tests of the Lucas–Rapping Model. *Amer. Econ. Rev.*, June 1987, 77(3), pp. 442–45. **[G: U.S.]**

Hasan, M. Aynul. Rational Expectations Estimation of Macroeconomic Models: Some Monte Carlo Results. *J. Macroecon.*, Spring 1987, 9(2), pp. 297–315.

Hausman, Jerry A. and Ruud, Paul A. Specifying and Testing Econometric Models for Rank-Ordered Data. *J. Econometrics*, Jan./Feb. 1987, 34(1/2), pp. 83–104.

Hendry, David F. Econometrics in Action. *Empirica*, 1987, 14(2), pp. 135–56. **[G: U.S.]**

Henry, Samuel G. Brian. Dynamic Modelling and Rational Expectations. *Ann. Écon. Statist.*, Apr./Sept. 1987, (6/7), pp. 183–206.
[G: U.K.]

Hensher, David A. and Milthorpe, Frank W. Selectivity Correction in Discrete-Continuous Choice Analysis: With Empirical Evidence for Vehicle Choice and Use. *Reg. Sci. Urban Econ.*, February 1987, 17(1), pp. 123–50.
[G: U.S.]

Hillier, Brian. Forecasting and Policy Evaluation When Expectations Are Rational: The Discrete Time Case—A Comment. *Bull. Econ. Res.*, January 1987, 39(1), pp. 71–78.

Horowitz, Ann R. Loss Functions and Public Policy. *J. Macroecon.*, Fall 1987, 9(4), pp. 489–504.

Horowitz, Joel L. Identification and Stochastic Specification in Rosen's Hedonic Price Model. *J. Urban Econ.*, September 1987, 22(2), pp. 165–73.

Horowitz, Joel L. Specification Tests for Nested Logit Models. *Environ. Planning A*, March 1987, 19(3), pp. 395–402.

Horowitz, Joel L. and Neumann, George R. Semiparametric Estimation of Employment Duration Models: Reply. *Econometric Rev.*, 1987, 6(1), pp. 79–81. **[G: U.S.]**

Horowitz, Joel L. and Neumann, George R. Semiparametric Estimation of Employment Duration Models. *Econometric Rev.*, 1987, 6(1), pp. 5–40. **[G: U.S.]**

Huang, Cliff J.; Sloan, Frank A. and Adamache, Killard W. Estimation of Seemingly Unrelated Tobit Regressions via the EM Algorithm. *J. Bus. Econ. Statist.*, July 1987, 5(3), pp. 425–30. **[G: U.S.]**

Hughes Hallett, Andrew J. Forecasting and Policy Evaluation in Economies with Rational Expectations: The Discrete Time Case. *Bull. Econ. Res.*, January 1987, 39(1), pp. 49–70.

Hughes Hallett, Andrew J. Optimal Policy Design in Interdependent Economies. *Carraro, C. and Sartore, D., eds.*, 1987, pp. 187–214.

Isaic-Maniu, Al. and Voda, V. G. A Method for the Analysis of Sub-unitary Values—An Uniparametric Distribution. *Econ. Computat. Cybern. Stud. Res.*, 1987, 22(3), pp. 53–60.

Ito, Yukio. Adaptive Control of Econometric Models with Unknown Parameters. *J. Econ. Dy-*

nam. Control, June 1987, 11(2), pp. 269–73.
[G: Japan]

Jarque, Carlos M. An Application of LDV Models to Household Expenditure Analysis in Mexico. *J. Econometrics*, Sept./Oct. 1987, 36(1/2), pp. 31–53. **[G: Mexico]**

Jarque, Carlos M. Sample Splitting and Applied Econometric Modeling. *J. Bus. Econ. Statist.*, April 1987, 5(2), pp. 267–74. **[G: Mexico]**

Johnson, Thomas. The Analysis of Qualitative and Limited Responses. *Becker, W. E. and Walstad, W. B., eds.*, 1987, pp. 141–84.

Jonson, Peter D. and Rankin, Robert W. Continuous Time Modelling: A Report from "Down Under." *[Marrama, V.], Vol. 2*, 1987, pp. 799–826. **[G: Australia]**

Jorgenson, Dale W. and Slesnick, Daniel T. Aggregate Consumer Behavior and Household Equivalence Scales. *J. Bus. Econ. Statist.*, April 1987, 5(2), pp. 219–32. **[G: U.S.]**

Joyeux, Roselyne. Misspecification Tests on Taylor's Version of a Keynesian Macromodel. *Southern Econ. J.*, July 1987, 54(1), pp. 159–67. **[G: U.S.]**

Jung, W. S. Optimal Stabilization Policy with Instruments of Differing Frequency. *Math. Soc. Sci.*, June 1987, 13(3), pp. 231–41.

Kendrick, David. Software for Economic Optimal Control Models. *Carraro, C. and Sartore, D., eds.*, 1987, pp. 47–59.

King, Maxwell L. Towards a Theory of Point Optimal Testing: Reply. *Econometric Rev.*, 1987-88, 6(2), pp. 249–55.

King, Maxwell L. Towards a Theory of Point Optimal Testing. *Econometric Rev.*, 1987-88, 6(2), pp. 169–218.

Kirkpatrick, Grant. Structural Modelling of Dynamic Macro-economic Systems: General Considerations, Techniques and an Application to the Federal Republic of Germany. *Ann. Écon. Statist.*, Apr./Sept. 1987, (6/7), pp. 71–99.
[G: W. Germany]

Kirkwood, Geoff P. Approaches to Adaptive Policy Design for Harvest Management: Comment. *Vincent, T. L., et al., eds.*, 1987, pp. 124.

Kiss, Ferenc and Lefebvre, Bernard. Econometric Models of Telecommunications Firms. *Revue Écon.*, March 1987, 38(2), pp. 307–73.
[G: Canada]

Kling, John L. Predicting the Turning Points of Business and Economic Time Series. *J. Bus.*, April 1987, 60(2), pp. 201–38. **[G: U.S.]**

Kulatilaka, Nalin. The Specification of Partial Static Equilibrium Models. *Rev. Econ. Statist.*, May 1987, 69(2), pp. 327–35. **[G: U.S.]**

Kumbhakar, Subal C. Production Frontiers and Panel Data: An Application to U.S. Class 1 Railroads. *J. Bus. Econ. Statist.*, April 1987, 5(2), pp. 249–55. **[G: U.S.]**

Kumbhakar, Subal C. The Specification of Technical and Allocative Inefficiency of Multi-product Firms in Stochastic Production and Profit Frontiers. *J. Quant. Econ.*, July 1987, 3(2), pp. 213–23.

Kumbhakar, Subal C. The Specification of Technical and Allocative Inefficiency in Stochastic Production and Profit Frontiers. *J. Econometrics*, March 1987, *34*(3), pp. 335–48.

Laban, Raul. El teorema de extracción de señales y la estimación de parámetros variables: Una nota. (With English summary.) *Cuadernos Econ.*, December 1987, *24*(73), pp. 399–412.

Lancaster, Tony. Semiparametric Estimation of Employment Duration Models: Comment. *Econometric Rev.*, 1987, *6*(1), pp. 55–57.

Lawrence, David B. The Application of Censored Regression Techniques to the Analysis of Tax Reform. *J. Econometrics*, July 1987, *35*(2/3), pp. 287–302. [G: U.S.]

Le Van, Cuong. Stationary Uncertainty Frontiers in Macroeconometric Models and Existence and Uniqueness of Solutions to Matrix Riccati Equations. *J. Econ. Dynam. Control*, March 1987, *11*(1), pp. 93–116.

Lee, Lung-Fei and Pitt, Mark M. Microeconometric Models of Rationing, Imperfect Markets, and Non-negativity Constraints. *J. Econometrics*, Sept./Oct. 1987, *36*(1/2), pp. 89–110. [G: Indonesia]

Legendre, François. Dynamic Adjustment When the Target Is Nonstationary: A Comment. *Int. Econ. Rev.*, October 1987, *28*(3), pp. 809–11.

Levine, Paul and Currie, David. The Design of Feedback Rules in Linear Stochastic Rational Expectations Models. *J. Econ. Dynam. Control*, March 1987, *11*(1), pp. 1–28.

Lewbel, Arthur. Characterizing Some Gorman Engel Curves. *Econometrica*, November 1987, *55*(6), pp. 1451–59.

Lewbel, Arthur. Fractional Demand Systems. *J. Econometrics*, November 1987, *36*(3), pp. 311–37.

Liaw, Kao-Lee and Ledent, Jacques. Nested Logit Model and Maximum Quasi-likelihood Method: A Flexible Methodology for Analyzing Interregional Migration Patterns. *Reg. Sci. Urban Econ.*, February 1987, *17*(1), pp. 67–88. [G: Canada]

Maasoumi, Esfandiar. Experimental and Nonexperimental Approaches to Statistical Research. *Becker, W. E. and Walstad, W. B., eds.*, 1987, pp. 51–72.

Maasoumi, Esfandiar and Ullah, Aman. Specification Analysis in Special Rational Distributed Lag and Other Dynamic Models. *J. Quant. Econ.*, July 1987, *3*(2), pp. 203–11.

MacKinlay, A. Craig. On Multivariate Tests of the CAPM. *J. Finan. Econ.*, June 1987, *18*(2), pp. 341–71. [G: U.S.]

Maddala, G. S. Limited Dependent Variable Models Using Panel Data. *J. Human Res.*, Summer 1987, *22*(3), pp. 307–38.

Mahmud, S. F.; Robb, A. L. and Scarth, William M. On Estimating Dynamic Factor Demands. *J. Appl. Econometrics*, January 1987, *2*(1), pp. 69–75. [G: U.S.]

Manning, Willard G.; Duan, Naihua and Rogers, W. H. Monte Carlo Evidence on the Choice between Sample Selection and Two-Part Models. *J. Econometrics*, May 1987, *35*(1), pp. 59–82.

Manski, Charles F. Semiparametric Estimation of Employment Duration Models: Comment. *Econometric Rev.*, 1987, *6*(1), pp. 59–64.

Manski, Charles F. and Salomon, Ilan. The Demand for Teleshopping: An Application of Discrete Choice Models. *Reg. Sci. Urban Econ.*, February 1987, *17*(1), pp. 109–21.

Marshall, Robert C. and Zarkin, Gary A. Price-Tenure Regressions with Censored Data. *Oxford Bull. Econ. Statist.*, August 1987, *49*(3), pp. 335–41. [G: U.S.]

Mauleon, Ignacio. Problemas prácticos en el tratamiento econométrico de datos "cross-section." (With English summary.) *Invest. Ecón.*, January 1987, *11*(1), pp. 41–94.

McAleer, Michael. Specification Tests for Separate Models: A Survey. *[Cochrane, D.]*, 1987, pp. 146–96.

McConnell, Kenneth E. and Phipps, T. T. Identification of Preference Parameters in Hedonic Models: Consumer Demands with Nonlinear Budgets. *J. Urban Econ.*, July 1987, *22*(1), pp. 35–52.

McDonald, Bill. Event Studies and Systems Methods: Some Additional Evidence. *J. Finan. Quant. Anal.*, December 1987, *22*(4), pp. 495–504. [G: U.S.]

McDonald, James B. and Butler, Richard J. Some Generalized Mixture Distributions with an Application to Unemployment Duration. *Rev. Econ. Statist.*, May 1987, *69*(2), pp. 232–40. [G: U.S.]

McElroy, Marjorie B. Additive General Error Models for Production, Cost, and Derived Demand or Share Systems. *J. Polit. Econ.*, August 1987, *95*(4), pp. 737–57. [G: U.S.]

McFadden, Daniel L. Regression-Based Specification Tests for the Multinomial Logit Model. *J. Econometrics*, Jan./Feb. 1987, *34*(1/2), pp. 63–82.

McFadden, Daniel L. and Han, Aaron K. Comment on Joel Horowitz and George Neumann "Semiparametric Estimation of Employment Duration Models." *Econometric Rev.*, 1987-88, *6*(2), pp. 257–70.

McHugh, Richard and Lane, Julia. The Age of Capital, the Age of Utilized Capital, and Tests of the Embodiment Hypothesis. *Rev. Econ. Statist.*, May 1987, *69*(2), pp. 362–67. [G: U.S.]

McLaren, Keith R. and Cooper, Russel J. Functional Forms in Intertemporal Duality. *[Cochrane, D.]*, 1987, pp. 197–216.

Megdal, Sharon Bernstein. The Econometrics of Piecewise–Linear Budget Constraints: A Monte Carlo Study. *J. Bus. Econ. Statist.*, April 1987, *5*(2), pp. 243–48.

Megdal, Sharon Bernstein. The Flypaper Effect Revisited: An Econometric Explanation. *Rev. Econ. Statist.*, May 1987, *69*(2), pp. 347–51.

Melfi, Catherine A. and Waldman, Donald M. Limited and Discrete Dependent Variable Models: Use, Applications, and Comparisons. *Becker, W. E. and Walstad, W. B., eds.*, 1987, pp. 185–205.

Mendelsohn, Robert. A Review of Identification

of Hedonic Supply and Demand Functions. *Growth Change*, Winter 1987, *18*(1), pp. 82–92.

Moulton, Brent R. Diagnostics for Group Effects in Regression Analysis. *J. Bus. Econ. Statist.*, April 1987, *5*(2), pp. 275–82. **[G: U.S.]**

Mroz, Thomas A. The Sensitivity of an Empirical Model of Married Women's Hours of Work to Economic and Statistical Assumptions. *Econometrica*, July 1987, *55*(4), pp. 765–99. **[G: U.S.]**

Müller, J. A. Further Development of Macroeconometric Modelling by the Application of the Self-Organization of Mathematical Models. *Econ. Computat. Cybern. Stud. Res.*, 1987, *22*(2), pp. 51–75. **[G: E. Germany]**

Newey, Whitney K. Specification Tests for Distributional Assumptions in the Tobit Model. *J. Econometrics*, Jan./Feb. 1987, *34*(1/2), pp. 125–45. **[G: U.K.]**

Nordhaus, William D. Forecasting Efficiency: Concepts and Applications. *Rev. Econ. Statist.*, November 1987, *69*(4), pp. 667–74. **[G: U.S.]**

Odhiambo, Mark Ollunga. An Application of Stochastic Econometric Production Risk Model: The Case of Egyptian Cotton Production. *Eastern Afr. Econ. Rev.*, December 1987, *3*(2), pp. 131–42. **[G: Egypt]**

Orcutt, Guy H. Joint Conditional Probability Functions for Modeling National Economies. *[Cochrane, D.]*, 1987, pp. 133–45.

Oren, Shmuel S.; Smith, Stephen A. and Wilson, Robert B. Multi-product Pricing for Electric Power. *Energy Econ.*, April 1987, *9*(2), pp. 104–14.

Otter, Pieter W. and Van Dal, René. State–Space and Distributed Lag Modelling of Dynamic Economic Processes Based on Singular Value Decompositions (With an Application to the Dutch Economy). *Ann. Écon. Statist.*, Apr./Sept. 1987, (6/7), pp. 253–77. **[G: Netherlands]**

Pagan, Adrian R. Three Econometric Methodologies: A Critical Appraisal. *J. Econ. Surveys*, 1987, *1*(1), pp. 3–24.

Pagan, Adrian R. and Shannon, J. H. How Reliable Are ORANI Conclusions? *Econ. Rec.*, March 1987, *63*(180), pp. 33–45. **[G: Australia]**

Palm, Franz C. Time Series and Econometric Models with Unobservables. *Econ. Notes*, 1987, (1), pp. 22–38.

Park, Wookyu. An Example of Using the BVAR Model and not Violating the "Lucas Critique:" An Explanation of the Recent Korean Economic Boom. *J. Econ. Devel.*, December 1987, *12*(2), pp. 115–41. **[G: Korea]**

Parke, William R. Macroeconometric Model Comparison and Evaluation Techniques: A Practical Appraisal. *J. Appl. Econometrics*, April 1987, *2*(2), pp. 133–44. **[G: U.S.]**

Parmigiani, Giovanni. Decisioni e modelli statistici: quale confine? (Decision Making and Statistical Model: Which Boundary? With English summary.) *Giorn. Econ.*, Jan.-Feb. 1987, *46*(1–2), pp. 97–107.

Patterson, Kerry David. Growth Coefficients in Dynamic Time Series Models. *Oxford Econ. Pap.*, June 1987, *39*(2), pp. 282–92.

Patterson, Kerry David. The Development of Expectations Generating Schemes Which Are Asymptotically Rational. *Scot. J. Polit. Econ.*, February 1987, *34*(1), pp. 1–18. **[G: U.S.; U.K.]**

Peña, Daniel. Observaciones influyentes en modelos econométricos. (With English summary.) *Invest. Econ.*, January 1987, *11*(1), pp. 3–24. **[G: OECD]**

Petit, Maria Luisa. A System-Theoretic Approach to the Theory of Economic Policy. *Carraro, C. and Sartore, D., eds.*, 1987, pp. 31–45.

Petkovski, Djordjija B. Time-Domain Robustness Criteria for Large-scale Economic Systems. *J. Econ. Dynam. Control*, June 1987, *11*(2), pp. 249–54.

Phillips, Robert F. Composite Forecasting: An Integrated Approach and Optimality Reconsidered. *J. Bus. Econ. Statist.*, July 1987, *5*(3), pp. 389–95. **[G: U.S.]**

Polachek, Solomon W. and Yoon, Bong Joon. A Two-tiered Earnings Frontier Estimation of Employer and Employee Information in the Labor Market. *Rev. Econ. Statist.*, May 1987, *69*(2), pp. 296–302. **[G: U.S.]**

Pollak, Robert A. and Wales, Terence J. Pooling International Consumption Data. *Rev. Econ. Statist.*, February 1987, *69*(1), pp. 90–99. **[G: Belgium; U.S.; U.K.]**

Pollak, Robert A. and Wales, Terence J. Specification and Estimation of Nonseparable Two-Stage Technologies: The Leontief CES and the Cobb–Douglas CES. *J. Polit. Econ.*, April 1987, *95*(2), pp. 311–33. **[G: U.S.]**

Powell, James L. Semiparametric Estimation of Employment Duration Models: Comment. *Econometric Rev.*, 1987, *6*(1), pp. 65–78. **[G: U.S.]**

Power, Simon and Ullah, Aman. Nonparametric Monte Carlo Density Estimation of Rational Expectations Estimators and Their *t* Ratios. *Fomby, T. B. and Rhodes, G. F., Jr., eds.*, 1987, pp. 157–86.

Prescott, David M. and Stengos, Thanasis. Bootstrapping Confidence Intervals: An Application to Forecasting the Supply of Pork. *Amer. J. Agr. Econ.*, May 1987, *69*(2), pp. 266–73. **[G: U.S.]**

Quandt, Richard E. and Rosen, Harvey S. Unemployment, Disequilibrium and the Short-run Phillips Curve: Correction and Extension. *J. Appl. Econometrics*, July 1987, *2*(3), pp. 247–49. **[G: U.S.]**

Ransom, Michael R. A Comment on Consumer Demand Systems with Binding Non-negativity Constraints. *J. Econometrics*, March 1987, *34*(3), pp. 355–59.

Ransom, Michael R. An Empirical Model of Discrete and Continuous Choice in Family Labor Supply. *Rev. Econ. Statist.*, August 1987, *69*(3), pp. 465–72. **[G: U.S.]**

Rhodes, George F., Jr. Validating Simulation Studies. *Fomby, T. B. and Rhodes, G. F., Jr., eds.*, 1987, pp. 187–213.

Richard, Jean-François. Exogeneity and Control in Econometric Time Series Modelling. *Carraro, C. and Sartore, D., eds.*, 1987, pp. 327–39.

Richards, Donald G. An Empirical Examination of the Dependency Approach to Underdevelopment. *Singapore Econ. Rev.*, April 1987, 32(1), pp. 1–23. **[G: LDCs]**

Rosenzweig, Mark R. and Schultz, T. Paul. Fertility and Investments in Human Capital: Estimates of the Consequence of Imperfect Fertility Control in Malaysia. *J. Econometrics*, Sept./Oct. 1987, 36(1/2), pp. 163–84. **[G: Malaysia]**

Rosenzweig, Michael L. Behavioral Modelling and Resource Management: Comment. *Vincent, T. L., et al., eds.*, 1987, pp. 19–20.

Rossi, Nicola. An Intertemporally Quasi Separable Demand System. *Rev. Econ. Statist.*, August 1987, 69(3), pp. 449–57. **[G: U.K.]**

Runkle, David E. Vector Autoregressions and Reality. *J. Bus. Econ. Statist.*, October 1987, 5(4), pp. 437–42. **[G: U.S.]**

Runkle, David E. Vector Autoregressions and Reality: Reply. *J. Bus. Econ. Statist.*, October 1987, 5(4), pp. 454. **[G: U.S.]**

Rust, John. Optimal Replacement of GMC Bus Engines: An Empirical Model of Harold Zurcher. *Econometrica*, September 1987, 55(5), pp. 999–1033. **[G: U.S.]**

Rustem, Berc. Methods for the Simultaneous Use of Multiple Models in Optimal Policy Design. *Carraro, C. and Sartore, D., eds.*, 1987, pp. 157–86.

Rustem, Berc and Velupillai, K. Objective Functions and the Complexity of Policy Design. *J. Econ. Dynam. Control*, June 1987, 11(2), pp. 185–92.

Salemi, Michael K. and Tauchen, George E. Simultaneous Nonlinear Learning Models. *Becker, W. E. and Walstad, W. B., eds.*, 1987, pp. 207–23.

Sandblom, Carl-Louis. Smoothing Optimal Economic Policies. *J. Econ. Dynam. Control*, June 1987, 11(2), pp. 179–84. **[G: Canada]**

Schoonbeek, Lambert. On the Eigenvectors of Macro-economic Models. *Ann. Écon. Statist.*, Apr./Sept. 1987, (6/7), pp. 335–45.

Schwert, G. William. Effects of Model Specification on Tests for Unit Roots in Macroeconomic Data. *J. Monet. Econ.*, July 1987, 20(1), pp. 73–103.

Sengupta, Jati K. Production Frontier Estimation to Measure Efficiency: A Critical Evaluation in Light of Data Envelopment Analysis. *Managerial Dec. Econ.*, June 1987, 8(2), pp. 93–99. **[G: U.S.]**

Shanken, Jay. A Bayesian Approach to Testing Portfolio Efficiency. *J. Finan. Econ.*, December 1987, 19(2), pp. 195–215.

Sims, Christopher A. A Rational Expectations Framework for Short-run Policy Analysis. *Barnett, W. A. and Singleton, K. J., eds.*, 1987, pp. 293–308.

Sims, Christopher A. Vector Autoregressions and Reality: Comment. *J. Bus. Econ. Statist.*, October 1987, 5(4), pp. 443–49. **[G: U.S.]**

Smith, Tony E. A Threshold Theory of Discretionary Interaction Behavior. *Reg. Sci. Urban Econ.*, November 1987, 17(4), pp. 495–517.

Steel, Mark F. J. Testing for Exogeneity: An Application to Consumption Behaviour. *Europ. Econ. Rev.*, October 1987, 31(7), pp. 1443–63. **[G: Belgium]**

Sternthal, Brian; Tybout, Alice M. and Calder, Bobby J. Confirmatory versus Comparative Approaches to Judging Theory Tests. *J. Cons. Res.*, June 1987, 14(1), pp. 114–25.

Stock, James H. Temporal Aggregation and Structural Inference in Macroeconomics: A Comment. *Carnegie–Rochester Conf. Ser. Public Policy*, Spring 1987, 26, pp. 131–39. **[G: U.S.]**

Swan, Craig. Simultaneous Equations Estimation. *Becker, W. E. and Walstad, W. B., eds.*, 1987, pp. 99–109.

Taylor, Mark P. On Long-run Solutions to Dynamic Econometric Equations under Rational Expectations [A Cautionary Note on the Interpretation of Long-run Equilibrium Solutions in Conventional Macro Models]. *Econ. J.*, March 1987, 97(385), pp. 215–18.

Teeples, Ronald K. and Glyer, David. Cost of Water Delivery Systems: Specification and Ownership Effects. *Rev. Econ. Statist.*, August 1987, 69(3), pp. 399–408. **[G: U.S.]**

Ţigănescu, E. and Oprescu, G. Generalized Analysis of the Economic–Cybernetic Systems. *Econ. Computat. Cybern. Stud. Res.*, 1987, 22(2), pp. 5–10.

Tinbergen, Jan. Learning from Errors. *[Marrama, V.], Vol. 2*, 1987, pp. 919–31.

Trivedi, Pravin K. Applications of Econometrics to Problems and Issues of the LDCs: Editor's Introduction. *J. Econometrics*, Sept./Oct. 1987, 36(1/2), pp. 1–6.

Veall, Michael R. Bootstrapping the Probability Distribution of Peak Electricity Demand. *Int. Econ. Rev.*, February 1987, 28(1), pp. 203–12. **[G: Canada]**

Vinod, H. D. New Techniques for Estimation of Rational Expectation Models and Volcker Deflation. *Empirical Econ.*, 1987, 12(3), pp. 157–74. **[G: U.S.]**

Vishwakarma, Keshav P. Forecasting and Stabilization of Multiple Economic Time Series in the State Space. *J. Econ. Dynam. Control*, June 1987, 11(2), pp. 265–68. **[G: U.S.]**

Wallis, Kenneth F. and Whitley, John D. Long-Run Properties of Large-scale Macroeconometric Models. *Ann. Écon. Statist.*, Apr./Sept. 1987, (6/7), pp. 207–24. **[G: U.K.]**

Walters, Carl J. Approaches to Adaptive Policy Design for Harvest Management. *Vincent, T. L., et al., eds.*, 1987, pp. 114–22.

Watson, Patrick Kent. On the Abuse of Statistical Criteria in the Evaluation of Econometric Models (with Special Reference to the Caribbean). *Soc. Econ. Stud.*, September 1987, *36*(3), pp. 119–48.   [G: Caribbean]

Webb, Roy H. The Irrelevance of Tests for Bias in Series of Macroeconomic Forecasts. *Fed. Res. Bank Richmond Econ. Rev.*, Nov./Dec. 1987, *73*(6), pp. 3–9.   [G: U.S.]

Williams, Ross A. Dwelling Commencements in Australia: Lags and Autocorrelation. *[Cochrane, D.]*, 1987, pp. 289–301. [G: Australia]

Wills, Hugh. A Note on Specification Tests for the Multinomial Logit Model. *J. Econometrics*, Jan./Feb. 1987, *34*(1/2), pp. 263–74.

Wymer, Clifford R. Sensitivity Analysis of Economic Policy. *[Marrama, V.]*, Vol. 2, 1987, pp. 953–65.

Xu, Shubo and Liu, Bao. The New Dynamic Priorities Model and an Analysis of China's Energy Strategy for the Future. *Sawaragi, Y.; Inoue, K. and Nakayama, H.*, eds., 1987, pp. 249–56.   [G: China]

Ziebart, David A. The Effects of Annual Accounting Data on Stock Returns and Trading Activity: A Causal Model Study. *J. Amer. Statist. Assoc.*, September 1987, *82*(399), pp. 733–38.   [G: U.S.]

213 Mathematical Methods and Models

2130 General

Barbu, G. On the Simulation of a System Reliability. *Econ. Computat. Cybern. Stud. Res.*, 1987, *22*(2), pp. 23–28.

Gardner, Roy J. Systems Theory in Mathematical Economics. *Fox, K. A. and Miles, D. G.*, eds., 1987, pp. 50–66.

Gensemer, Susan H. Continuous Semiorder Representations. *J. Math. Econ.*, 1987, *16*(3), pp. 275–89.

Gensemer, Susan H. On Relationships between Numerical Representations of Interval Orders and Semiorders. *J. Econ. Theory*, October 1987, *43*(1), pp. 157–69.

Jeffers, J. N. R. Ecological Modeling: Shortcomings and Perspectives. *Braat, L. C. and van Lierop, W. F. J.*, eds., 1987, pp. 36–48.

Kazakevich, D. M. Economic Theory, Mathematical Economics, and Plan Management. *Matekon*, Fall 1987, *24*(1), pp. 3–20.   [G: U.S.S.R.]

Larson, Bruce. Edgeworth, Samuelson, and Operationally Meaningful Theorems. *Hist. Polit. Econ.*, Fall 1987, *19*(3), pp. 351–57.

Le Breton, Michel. Stochastic Dominance: A Bibliographical Rectification and a Restatement of Whitmore's Theorem. *Math. Soc. Sci.*, February 1987, *13*(1), pp. 73–79.

Le Van, Cuong. Stationary Uncertainty Frontiers in Macroeconometric Models and Existence and Uniqueness of Solutions to Matrix Riccati Equations. *J. Econ. Dynam. Control*, March 1987, *11*(1), pp. 93–116.

Lewis, Alain A. On the Construction of Subinvariant Weakly Additive Set-Functions. *Math. Soc. Sci.*, February 1987, *13*(1), pp. 81–86.

Roy, B. and Vincke, Ph. Pseudo-orders: Defini-

tion, Properties and Numerical Representation. *Math. Soc. Sci.*, December 1987, *14*(3), pp. 263–74.

Silva Reus, José Angel. Una generalización del teorema de Frobenius bajo hipótesis débiles. (With English summary.) *Invest. Ecón.*, January 1987, *11*(1), pp. 191–98.

Ţigănescu, E. and Oprescu, G. Generalized Analysis of the Economic–Cybernetic Systems. *Econ. Computat. Cybern. Stud. Res.*, 1987, *22*(2), pp. 5–10.

2132 Optimization Techniques

Bednarczuk, Ewa. Well Posedness of Vector Optimization Problems. *Jahn, J. and Krabs, W.*, eds., 1987, pp. 51–61.

Bergstrom, A. R. Optimal Control in Wide-Sense Stationary Continuous-Time Stochastic Models. *J. Econ. Dynam. Control*, September 1987, *11*(3), pp. 425–43.

Borwein, J. M. Convex Cones, Minimality Notions, and Consequences. *Jahn, J. and Krabs, W.*, eds., 1987, pp. 62–85.

Carraro, Carlo and Sartore, Domenico. Developments of Control Theory for Economic Analysis: Introduction. *Carraro, C. and Sartore, D.*, eds., 1987, pp. xi–xxiii.

Casti, John. Singularity Theory for Nonlinear Optimization Problems. *Kurzhanski, A. B. and Sigmund, K.*, eds., 1987, pp. 106–28.

Chadha, S. S. Hyperbolic Programming—A New Criteria. *Econ. Computat. Cybern. Stud. Res.*, 1987, *22*(4), pp. 83–88.

Chernousko, F. L. State Estimation for Dynamical Systems by Means of Ellipsoids. *Kurzhanski, A. B. and Sigmund, K.*, eds., 1987, pp. 95–105.

Conti, R. Linear Controllability Results and Open Questions. *Carraro, C. and Sartore, D.*, eds., 1987, pp. 21–30.

Deissenberg, Christophe. On the Minmax Lyapunov Stabilization of Uncertain Economies. *J. Econ. Dynam. Control*, June 1987, *11*(2), pp. 229–34.

Dolecki, S. and Malivert, C. Polarities and Stability in Vector Optimization. *Jahn, J. and Krabs, W.*, eds., 1987, pp. 96–113.

Dumitru, V. and Luban, Florica. On the Monotone Functionals in Multicriteria Optimization. *Econ. Computat. Cybern. Stud. Res.*, 1987, *22*(1), pp. 77–83.

Durier, Roland. Sets of Efficiency in a Normed Space and Inner Product. *Jahn, J. and Krabs, W.*, eds., 1987, pp. 114–28.

Elster, K.-H. and Göpfert, A. Recent Results on Duality in Vector Optimization. *Jahn, J. and Krabs, W.*, eds., 1987, pp. 129–36.

Eppers, J. and Leserer, M. Some Remarks on Forward Programming. *Carraro, C. and Sartore, D.*, eds., 1987, pp. 127–34.

Ester, Jochen. A Fuzzy Concept of Efficiency. *Jahn, J. and Krabs, W.*, eds., 1987, pp. 257–64.

Flåm, Sjur D. and Wets, Roger J.-B. Existence Results and Finite Horizon Approximates for

Infinite Horizon Optimization Problems. *Econometrica*, September 1987, *55*(5), pp. 1187–1209.

Gidas, Basilis. Simulations and Global Optimization. *Papanicolaou, G., ed.*, 1987, pp. 129–45.

Gwinner, Joachim. A Result of Farkas Type and Duality in Vector Optimization. *Jahn, J. and Krabs, W., eds.*, 1987, pp. 137–45.

Hartl, Richard F. A Simple Proof of the Monotonicity of the State Trajectories in Autonomous Control Problems. *J. Econ. Theory*, February 1987, *41*(1), pp. 211–15.

Helbig, Siegfried. Parametric Optimization with a Bottleneck Objective and Vector Optimization. *Jahn, J. and Krabs, W., eds.*, 1987, pp. 146–59.

Jahn, Johannes. Duality in Partially Ordered Sets. *Jahn, J. and Krabs, W., eds.*, 1987, pp. 160–72.

Kaliszewski, Ignacy. Generating Nested Subsets of Efficient Solutions. *Jahn, J. and Krabs, W., eds.*, 1987, pp. 173–82.

Kirsten, H. and Tichatschke, R. The Efficiency of a Method of Feasible Directions for Solving Variational Inequalities. *Jahn, J. and Krabs, W., eds.*, 1987, pp. 379–99.

Léonard, Daniel. Co-state Variables Correctly Value Stocks at Each Instant: A Proof. *J. Econ. Dynam. Control*, March 1987, *11*(1), pp. 117–22.

Levine, Paul and Currie, David. The Design of Feedback Rules in Linear Stochastic Rational Expectations Models. *J. Econ. Dynam. Control*, March 1987, *11*(1), pp. 1–28.

Lucchetti, Roberto. Well Posedness, Towards Vector Optimization. *Jahn, J. and Krabs, W., eds.*, 1987, pp. 194–207.

Montesano, Aldo. Utility and Uncertainty in Intertemporal Choice. *Carraro, C. and Sartore, D., eds.*, 1987, pp. 135–42.

Petit, Maria Luisa. A System-Theoretic Approach to the Theory of Economic Policy. *Carraro, C. and Sartore, D., eds.*, 1987, pp. 31–45.

Robinson, P. D. and Yuen, P. K. Bivariational Bounding Methods. *Jahn, J. and Krabs, W., eds.*, 1987, pp. 400–405.

Şerban, R. Algorithms of Unidimensional Optimization. *Econ. Computat. Cybern. Stud. Res.*, 1987, *22*(1), pp. 41–56.

Şerban, R. Solving Some Systems of Non-linear Equations by Means of Function Optimizing Algorithms. *Econ. Computat. Cybern. Stud. Res.*, 1987, *22*(4), pp. 45–49.

Sierra, Hector and Condon, Timothy. An Approximation Technique for Computing Optimal Dynamic Paths. *J. Econ. Dynam. Control*, September 1987, *11*(3), pp. 405–23.

da Silva, A. R. Evaluation Functionals Are the Extreme Points of a Basis for the Dual of C†[a,b]. *Jahn, J. and Krabs, W., eds.*, 1987, pp. 86–95.

Stadler, W. Initiators of Multicriteria Optimization. *Jahn, J. and Krabs, W., eds.*, 1987, pp. 3–47.

Sterna-Karwat, Alicia. On the Existence of Cone-Efficient Points. *Jahn, J. and Krabs, W., eds.*, 1987, pp. 233–40.

Weistroffer, H. Roland. A Flexible Model for Multi-objective Optimization. *Jahn, J. and Krabs, W., eds.*, 1987, pp. 311–16.

Wieczorek, Andrzej. Pseudo-utilities. *Jahn, J. and Krabs, W., eds.*, 1987, pp. 241–53.

Willems, J. C. Modeling, Approximation, and Complexity of Linear Systems. *Kurzhanski, A. B. and Sigmund, K., eds.*, 1987, pp. 129–36.

Yu, P. L. and Chien, I. S. Foundation of Effective Goal Setting. *Jahn, J. and Krabs, W., eds.*, 1987, pp. 317–42.

2133 Existence and Stability Conditions of Equilibrium

Aubin, J.-P. and Frankowska, H. A Viability Approach to Ljapunov's Second Method. *Kurzhanski, A. B. and Sigmund, K., eds.*, 1987, pp. 31–38.

Cavagnac, M.; Kephaliacos, C. and Marfaing, R. Efficience, rareté et domination dans une technologie de Von Neumann. (Efficiency, Scarcity and Domination in a Von Neumann Type Technology: A Twin Example. With English summary.) *Écon. Appl.*, 1987, *40*(1), pp. 35–47.

Chateauneuf, Alain. Continuous Representation of a Preference Relation on a Connected Topological Space. *J. Math. Econ.*, 1987, *16*(2), pp. 139–46.

Froeschlé, Claude and Longhi, A. Connectance et stabilité locale d'un équilibre général. (Connectance and Local Stability of General Equilibrium. With English summary.) *Écon. Appl.*, 1987, *40*(1), pp. 49–78.

Fujimoto, Takao. A Simple Proof of the Nonsubstitution Theorem. *J. Quant. Econ.*, January 1987, *3*(1), pp. 35–38.

de la Grandville, Olivier. On Two-Regime Discrete-Time Models: A Methodological Note. *J. Econ. Behav. Organ.*, September 1987, *8*(3), pp. 513–30.

Howe, Roger. Sections and Extensions of Concave Functions. *J. Math. Econ.*, 1987, *16*(1), pp. 53–64.

Jones, Larry E. Existence of Equilibria with Infinitely Many Commodities: Banach Lattices Reconsidered. *J. Math. Econ.*, 1987, *16*(2), pp. 89–104.

Mehta, Ghanshyam and Tarafdar, Enayet. Infinite-Dimensional Gale–Nikaido–Debreu Theorem and a Fixed-Point Theorem of Tarafdar. *J. Econ. Theory*, April 1987, *41*(2), pp. 333–39.

Milota, J. Stability for a Linear Functional Differential Equation with Infinite Delay. *Kurzhanski, A. B. and Sigmund, K., eds.*, 1987, pp. 50–54.

Montrucchio, Luigi. Lipschitz Continuous Policy Functions for Strongly Concave Optimization Problems. *J. Math. Econ.*, 1987, *16*(3), pp. 259–73.

Rochet, Jean-Charles. A Necessary and Sufficient Condition for Rationalizability in a Quasi-linear

Context. *J. Math. Econ.*, 1987, *16*(2), pp. 191–200.

Yamamoto, Yoshitsugu. Competitive Equilibria in the Market with Indivisibility. *Talman, D. and van der Laan, G., eds.*, 1987, pp. 193–204.

2134 Computational Techniques

Anderson, Gary. A Procedure for Differentiating Perfect-Foresight-Model Reduced-Form Coefficients. *J. Econ. Dynam. Control*, December 1987, *11*(4), pp. 465–81.

Başar, Tamer. Relaxation Techniques and Asynchronous Algorithms for On-Line Computation of Non-cooperative Equilibria. *J. Econ. Dynam. Control*, December 1987, *11*(4), pp. 531–49.

Calzolari, Giorgio and Panattoni, Lorenzo. Gradient Methods in FIML Estimation of Econometric Models. *Carraro, C. and Sartore, D., eds.*, 1987, pp. 143–53.

Doup, T. M.; van den Elzen, A. H. and Talman, A. J. J. Simplicial Algorithms for Solving the Nonlinear Complementarity Problem on the Simplotope. *Talman, D. and van der Laan, G., eds.*, 1987, pp. 125–53.

Eaves, B. Curtis. Thoughts on Computing Market Equilibrium with SLCP. *Talman, D. and van der Laan, G., eds.*, 1987, pp. 1–17.

Fisher, P. G. and Hughes Hallett, Andrew J. The Convergence Characteristics of Iterative Techniques for Solving Econometric Models. *Oxford Bull. Econ. Statist.*, May 1987, *49*(2), pp. 231–44. **[G: U.K.]**

Forster, W. Computing "All" Solutions of Systems of Polynomial Equations by Simplicial Fixed Point Algorithms. *Talman, D. and van der Laan, G., eds.*, 1987, pp. 39–57.

Khilnani, Arvind and Tse, Edison T. S. A Response [A Fixed Point Algorithm with Economic Applications]. *J. Econ. Dynam. Control*, September 1987, *11*(3), pp. 461–63.

van der Laan, Gerard and Talman, A. J. J. Adjustment Processes for Finding Economic Equilibria. *Talman, D. and van der Laan, G., eds.*, 1987, pp. 85–123.

van Maaren, Hans. Generalized Pivoting and Coalitions. *Talman, D. and van der Laan, G., eds.*, 1987, pp. 155–76.

Marcotte, Patrice. A Note on Khilnani and Tse's USA Algorithm [A Fixed Point Algorithm with Economic Applications]. *J. Econ. Dynam. Control*, September 1987, *11*(3), pp. 455–59.

Nagurney, Anna. Computational Comparisons of Spatial Price Equilibrium Methods. *J. Reg. Sci.*, February 1987, *27*(1), pp. 55–76.

Ruys, Pieter H. M. and van der Laan, Gerard. Computation of an Industrial Equilibrium. *Talman, D. and van der Laan, G., eds.*, 1987, pp. 205–29.

Serafini, Paolo. Some Considerations about Computational Complexity for Multi Objective Combinatorial Problems. *Jahn, J. and Krabs, W., eds.*, 1987, pp. 222–32.

Sierra, Hector and Condon, Timothy. An Approximation Technique for Computing Optimal

Dynamic Paths. *J. Econ. Dynam. Control*, September 1987, *11*(3), pp. 405–23.

Todd, Michael J. Reformulations of Economic Equilibrium Problems for Solution by Quasi-Newton and Simplicial Algorithms. *Talman, D. and van der Laan, G., eds.*, 1987, pp. 19–37.

Van der Heyden, Ludo. On a Theorem of Scarf. *Talman, D. and van der Laan, G., eds.*, 1987, pp. 177–92.

2135 Construction, Analysis, and Use of Mathematical Programming Models

Batterham, R. L. Data Entry Programmes for Mathematical Programming Models. *Rev. Marketing Agr. Econ.*, August 1987, *55*(2), pp. 178–80.

Bouzaher, Aziz and Mendoza, Guillermo A. Goal Programming: Potential and Limitations for Agricultural Economics. *Can. J. Agr. Econ.*, March 1987, *35*(1), pp. 89–107.

Burton, Robert O., Jr., et al. Nearly Optimal Linear Programming Solutions: Some Conceptual Issues and a Farm Management Application. *Amer. J. Agr. Econ.*, November 1987, *69*(4), pp. 813–18. **[G: U.S.]**

Chandra, Suresh and Saxena, P. K. Cost/Completion-Date Tradeoffs in Quadratic Fractional Transportation Problem. *Econ. Computat. Cybern. Stud. Res.*, 1987, *22*(3), pp. 67–72.

Drynan, Ross G. A Generalised Concept of Dominance in Linear Programming Models. *Rev. Marketing Agr. Econ.*, August 1987, *55*(2), pp. 140–46.

Drynan, Ross G. Allocative vs. Technical Efficiency, and Related Matters in Linear Programming. *Rev. Marketing Agr. Econ.*, August 1987, *55*(2), pp. 147–54.

Gineo, Wayne M. A Graphic Interpretation of Risk Programming Models. *Can. J. Agr. Econ.*, March 1987, *35*(1), pp. 155–67.

Intrator, Jacob and Weiss, Joseph. Exhaustive Iterations—An Improving Approach for Long Transportation Problems. *Econ. Computat. Cybern. Stud. Res.*, 1987, *22*(3), pp. 73–87.

Islei, Gerd. An Approach to Measuring Consistency of Preference Vector Derivations Using Least Square Distance. *Jahn, J. and Krabs, W., eds.*, 1987, pp. 265–84.

Krause, Ulrich. Hierarchical Structures in Multicriteria Decision Making. *Jahn, J. and Krabs, W., eds.*, 1987, pp. 183–93.

McSweeny, William T.; Kenyon, David and Kramer, Randall A. Toward an Appropriate Measure of Uncertainty in a Risk Programming Model. *Amer. J. Agr. Econ.*, February 1987, *69*(1), pp. 87–96. **[G: U.S.]**

Megiddo, Nimrod. On the Complexity of Linear Programming. *Bewley, T. F., ed.*, 1987, pp. 225–68.

Mihalyi, Margareta and Raischi, C. An Algorithm for Optimal Ordering of the Arcs of a Network. *Econ. Computat. Cybern. Stud. Res.*, 1987, *22*(2), pp. 29–32.

Preckel, Paul V.; Featherstone, Allen M. and Baker, Timothy G. Interpreting Dual Variables for Optimization with Nonmonetary Objectives. *Amer. J. Agr. Econ.*, November 1987, 69(4), pp. 849–51.

Romero, Carlos and Rehman, Tahir. Natural Resource Management and the Use of Multiple Criteria Decision-Making Techniques: A Review. *Europ. Rev. Agr. Econ.*, 1987, 14(1), pp. 61–89.

Sakawa, Masatoshi. An Interactive Fuzzy Satisficing Method for Multiobjective Linear Fractional Programming Problems with Fuzzy Parameters. *Sawaragi, Y.; Inoue, K. and Nakayama, H., eds.*, 1987, pp. 338–47.

Vereskov, A. I. and Gol'shtein, E. G. On a Linear Programming Problem in Broadened Formulation. *Matekon*, Summer 1987, 23(4), pp. 75–103.

Vincze, István. Inequalities for Convex Functions. *[Eberl, W., Sr.]*, 1987, pp. 248–53.

Vlačić, Lj.; Wierzbicki, A. and Matić, B. Aggregation Procedures for Hierarchically Grouped Decision Attributes with Application to Control System Performance Evaluation. *Jahn, J. and Krabs, W., eds.*, 1987, pp. 285–310.

214 Computer Programs

2140 Computer Programs

Batterham, R. L. Data Entry Programmes for Mathematical Programming Models. *Rev. Marketing Agr. Econ.*, August 1987, 55(2), pp. 178–80.

Birchenhall, Chris. STATA: The Data Tool. *J. Econ. Surveys*, 1987, 1(2), pp. 173–80.

Bleymüller, Josef. Menügesteuerte PC-Programmpakete für höhere Stichprobenverfahren. (Menu-Driven Microcomputer Programs for Statistical Sampling. With English summary.) *Jahr. Nationalökon. Statist.*, October 1987, 203(5–6), pp. 485–97.

Calzolari, Giorgio; Panattoni, Lorenzo and Weihs, Claus. Computational Efficiency of FIML Estimation. *J. Econometrics*, November 1987, 36(3), pp. 299–310.

Carruth, Alan A. Multi-user Access of PC-GIVE Versions 4.1 and 4.2. *Oxford Bull. Econ. Statist.*, November 1987, 49(4), pp. 435–37.

Clarke, M. and Openshaw, S. The AGW Spatial Interaction Workstation. *Environ. Planning A*, September 1987, 19(9), pp. 1261–68.

Coomes, Paul A. PLEM: A Computer Program for Passive Learning, Stochastic Control Experiments. *J. Econ. Dynam. Control*, June 1987, 11(2), pp. 223–27.

Dobre, V., et al. On Modelling Interactive Systems of Computer-Aided Design. *Econ. Computat. Cybern. Stud. Res.*, 1987, 22(1), pp. 19–27.

Falk, Constance L.; Tilley, Daniel S. and Schatzer, R. Joe. The Packing Simulation Model. *Southern J. Agr. Econ.*, December 1987, 19(2), pp. 211–15.

Gruhn, Walter L. The GLOBUS Simulation Package. *Bremer, S. A., ed.*, 1987, pp. 777–802. [G: Global]

Hall, James A. Management Policies in Local Government Finance: Computer Applications. *Aronson, J. R. and Schwartz, E., eds.*, 1987, pp. 176–97. [G: U.S.]

Hayes, Kathy J.; Hirschberg, Joseph G. and Slottje, D. J. Computer Algebra: Symbolic and Algebraic Computation in Economic/Econometric Applications. *Fomby, T. B. and Rhodes, G. F., Jr., eds.*, 1987, pp. 51–89.

Hendry, David F. and Neale, Adrian J. Monte Carlo Experimentation Using PC-NAIVE. *Fomby, T. B. and Rhodes, G. F., Jr., eds.*, 1987, pp. 91–125.

Kendrick, David. Software for Economic Optimal Control Models. *Carraro, C. and Sartore, D., eds.*, 1987, pp. 47–59.

Mandel, Robert. An Evaluation of the "Balance of Power" Simulation. *J. Conflict Resolution*, June 1987, 31(2), pp. 333–45.

Peterson, William. The Cambridge Multisectoral Dynamic Model of the British Economy: Computer Software for a Large Econometric Model. *Barker, T. and Peterson, W., eds.*, 1987, pp. 105–21. [G: U.K.]

Rindfuss, Peter. Mathematical Aspects of GLOBUS. *Bremer, S. A., ed.*, 1987, pp. 803–19. [G: Global]

Roberts, Colin J. User-Friendly Econometric Software: A Review. *Scot. J. Polit. Econ.*, November 1987, 34(4), pp. 410–16.

Spircu, Liliana, et al. An Interactive System of Programmes for the Analysis and Processing of Statistical Data in Agriculture. *Econ. Computat. Cybern. Stud. Res.*, 1987, 22(1), pp. 29–39.

Turner, Paul and Podivinsky, Jan. PC GIVE © David Hendry Version 4.1 July 1986. *J. Econ. Surveys*, 1987, 1(1), pp. 92–96.

Walker, Ian. Cross-Section Econometrics Software: LIMDEP and SST. *J. Econ. Surveys*, 1987, 1(1), pp. 81–91.

215 Experimental Economic Methods

2150 Experimental Economic Methods

Alger, Dan. Laboratory Tests of Equilibrium Predictions with Disequilibrium Data. *Rev. Econ. Stud.*, January 1987, 54(1), pp. 105–45.

Appleby, Lynda and Starmer, Chris. Individual Choice under Uncertainty: A Review of Experimental Evidence, Past and Present. *Hey, J. D. and Lambert, P. J., eds.*, 1987, pp. 25–45.

Battalio, Raymond C.; Dwyer, Gerald P., Jr. and Kagel, John H. Tests of Competing Theories of Consumer Choice and the Representative Consumer Hypothesis. *Econ. J.*, December 1987, 97(388), pp. 842–56.

Battalio, Raymond C.; Kagel, John H. and Phillips, Owen R. Optimal Prices and Animal Consumers in Congested Markets: A Reply. *Econ. Inquiry*, October 1987, 25(4), pp. 721–22.

Becker, Winfried; Büchner, Heinz-Jürgen and Sleeking, Simon. The Impact of Public Transfer Expenditures on Tax Evasion: An Experimental Approach. *J. Public Econ.*, November 1987, *34*(2), pp. 243–52.

Bennett, Jeffrey W. Strategic Behaviour: Some Experimental Evidence. *J. Public Econ.*, April 1987, *32*(3), pp. 355–68. **[G: Australia]**

Berk, Richard A., et al. Social Policy Experimentation: A Position Paper. *Cordray, D. S. and Lipsey, M. W., eds.*, 1987, *1985*, pp. 630–72.

Binmore, Ken. Experimental Economics. *Europ. Econ. Rev.*, Feb./Mar. 1987, *31*(1/2), pp. 257–64.

Brann, Peter and Foddy, Margaret. Trust and the Consumption of a Deteriorating Common Resource. *J. Conflict Resolution*, December 1987, *31*(4), pp. 615–30.

Brookshire, David S.; Coursey, Don L. and Schulze, William D. The External Validity of Experimental Economics Techniques: Analysis of Demand Behavior. *Econ. Inquiry*, April 1987, *25*(2), pp. 239–50. **[G: U.S.]**

Bull, Clive; Schotter, Andrew and Weigelt, Keith. Tournaments and Piece Rates: An Experimental Study. *J. Polit. Econ.*, February 1987, *95*(1), pp. 1–33. **[G: U.S.]**

Butler, David J. and Hey, John D. Experimental Economics: An Introduction. *Empirica*, 1987, *14*(2), pp. 157–86.

Camerer, Colin F. Do Biases in Probability Judgment Matter in Markets? Experimental Evidence. *Amer. Econ. Rev.*, December 1987, *77*(5), pp. 981–97.

Collier, Kenneth E., et al. Retrospective Voting: An Experimental Study. *Public Choice*, 1987, *53*(2), pp. 101–30.

Coursey, Don L. Markets and the Measurement of Value. *Public Choice*, October 1987, *55*(3), pp. 291–97.

Coursey, Don L.; Hovis, John L. and Schulze, William D. The Disparity between Willingness to Accept and Willingness to Pay Measures of Value. *Quart. J. Econ.*, August 1987, *102*(3), pp. 679–90.

Coursey, Don L. and Mason, Charles. Investigations Concerning the Dynamics of Consumer Behavior in Uncertain Environments. *Econ. Inquiry*, October 1987, *25*(4), pp. 549–64.

Cox, James C. and Isaac, R. Mark. Mechanisms for Incentive Regulation: Theory and Experiment. *Rand J. Econ.*, Autumn 1987, *18*(3), pp. 348–59.

Daughety, Andrew F. and Forsythe, Robert. Industrywide Regulation and the Formation of Reputations: A Laboratory Analysis. *Bailey, E. E., ed.*, 1987, pp. 347–98.

Davis, Douglas D. Maximal Quality Selection and Discrimination in Employment. *J. Econ. Behav. Organ.*, March 1987, *8*(1), pp. 97–112. **[G: U.S.]**

DuBose, Philip B. and Bigoness, William J. A Test of Wheeler's Closed-Offer Arbitration System: An Experimental Study. *J. Lab. Res.*, Fall 1987, *8*(4), pp. 385–93. **[G: U.S.]**

Faminow, Merle D. and Benson, Bruce L. Price Reporting in Experimental Markets. *Can. J. Agr. Econ.*, July 1987, *35*(2), pp. 357–71.

Graham, John L. and Lin, Chi-Yuan. A Compari-

son of Marketing Negotiations in the Republic of China (Taiwan) and the United States. *Cavusgil, S. T., ed.*, 1987, pp. 23–46. **[G: Taiwan; U.S.]**

Gregory, Robin and Furby, Lita. Auctions, Experiments and Contingent Valuation. *Public Choice*, October 1987, *55*(3), pp. 273–89.

Harrison, Glenn W. Experimental Evaluation of the Contestable Markets Hypothesis. *Bailey, E. E., ed.*, 1987, pp. 191–225.

Harrison, Glenn W., et al. Coasian Solutions to the Externality Problem in Experimental Markets. *Econ. J.*, June 1987, *97*(386), pp. 388–402.

Herhold, Susan; Parry, Robert W., Jr. and Patton, James M. Behavioral Research in Municipal Accounting. *Chan, J. L., ed., Pt. B*, 1987, pp. 71–109.

Holcomb, James H. and Evans, Dorla A. The Effect of Sunk Costs on Uncertain Decisions in Experimental Markets. *J. Behav. Econ.*, Fall 1987, *16*(3), pp. 59–66.

Johnson, Michael D. and Fornell, Claes. The Nature and Methodological Implications of the Cognitive Representation of Products. *J. Cons. Res.*, September 1987, *14*(2), pp. 214–28.

Kagel, John H. Economics According to the Rats (and Pigeons Too): What Have We Learned and What Can We Hope to Learn? *Roth, A. E., ed.*, 1987, pp. 155–92.

Kagel, John H. and Green, Leonard. Intertemporal Choice Behavior: Evaluation of Economic and Psychological Models. *Green, L. and Kagel, J. H., eds.*, 1987, pp. 166–84.

Kagel, John H.; Harstad, Ronald M. and Levin, Dan. Information Impact and Allocation Rules in Auctions with Affiliated Private Values: A Laboratory Study. *Econometrica*, November 1987, *55*(6), pp. 1275–1304.

Karni, Edi and Safra, Zvi. "Preference Reversal" and the Observability of Preferences by Experimental Methods. *Econometrica*, May 1987, *55*(3), pp. 675–85.

Knez, Marc and Smith, Vernon L. Hypothetical Valuations and Preference Reversals in the Context of Asset Trading. *Roth, A. E., ed.*, 1987, pp. 131–54.

Laing, James D. and Slotznick, Benjamin. Viable Alternatives to the Status Quo: A Game-Theoretic and Laboratory Study of Four-Fifths Majority Rule. *J. Conflict Resolution*, March 1987, *31*(1), pp. 63–85.

Lea, S. E. G. Animal Experiments in Economic Psychology. *Green, L. and Kagel, J. H., eds.*, 1987, *1981*, pp. 95–116.

Leuthold, Jane N. A Public Goods Experiment for the Classroom. *J. Econ. Educ.*, Winter 1987, *18*(1), pp. 58–65. **[G: U.S.]**

Loomes, Graham and Sugden, Robert. Testing for Regret and Disappointment in Choice under Uncertainty. *Econ. J.*, Supplement 1987, *97*, pp. 118–29.

Manning, Willard G., et al. Health Insurance and the Demand for Medical Care: Evidence from a Randomized Experiment. *Amer. Econ. Rev.*, June 1987, *77*(3), pp. 251–77. **[G: U.S.]**

Mestelman, Stuart; Welland, Deborah and Welland, Douglas. Advance Production in Posted Offer Markets. *J. Econ. Behav. Organ.*, June 1987, 8(2), pp. 249–64.

Murnighan, J. Keith; Roth, Alvin E. and Schoumaker, Françoise. Risk Aversion and Bargaining: Some Preliminary Results. *Europ. Econ. Rev.*, Feb./Mar. 1987, 31(1/2), pp. 265–71.

Patchen, Martin. Strategies for Eliciting Cooperation from an Adversary: Laboratory and International Findings. *J. Conflict Resolution*, March 1987, 31(1), pp. 164–85.

Plott, Charles R. Dimensions of Parallelism: Some Policy Applications of Experimental Methods. *Roth, A. E., ed.*, 1987, pp. 193–219. [G: U.S.]

Roth, Alvin E. Bargaining Phenomena and Bargaining Theory. *Roth, A. E., ed.*, 1987, pp. 14–41.

Roth, Alvin E. Laboratory Experimentation in Economics: Introduction and Overview. *Roth, A. E., ed.*, 1987, pp. 1–13.

Roth, Alvin E. Laboratory Experimentation in Economics. *Bewley, T. F., ed.*, 1987, pp. 269–99.

Rycroft, Robert S. Econometric and Forecasting Software for the IBM PC and Compatibles. *J. Econ. Educ.*, Summer 1987, 18(3), pp. 331–44.

Sandler, Todd. On Optimal Prices and Animal Consumers in Congested Markets. *Econ. Inquiry*, October 1987, 25(4), pp. 715–20.

Selten, Reinhard. Equity and Coalition Bargaining in Experimental Three-Person Games. *Roth, A. E., ed.*, 1987, pp. 42–98.

Sutton, John. Bargaining Experiments. *Europ. Econ. Rev.*, Feb./Mar. 1987, 31(1/2), pp. 272–84.

Taylor, Dalmas A. and Moriarty, Beatrice F. Ingroup Bias as a Function of Competition and Race. *J. Conflict Resolution*, March 1987, 31(1), pp. 192–99.

Thaler, Richard H. The Psychology of Choice and the Assumptions of Economics. *Roth, A. E., ed.*, 1987, pp. 99–130.

Thistle, Paul D. The Rationale for Experiments in Economics. *J. Behav. Econ.*, Winter 1987, 16(4), pp. 41–53.

Veugelers, Reinhilde. The Role of Information in a Duopoly Setting: Some Experimental Results. *Rech. Écon. Louvain*, 1987, 53(4), pp. 357–77.

Viscusi, W. Kip; Magat, Wesley A. and Huber, Joel C. An Investigation of the Rationality of Consumer Valuations of Multiple Health Risks. *Rand J. Econ.*, Winter 1987, 18(4), pp. 465–79. [G: U.S.]

Walker, Joe. Experimental Economics in the Classroom. *J. Econ. Educ.*, Winter 1987, 18(1), pp. 51–57.

Williams, Arlington W. The Formation of Price Forecasts in Experimental Markets. *J. Money, Credit, Banking*, February 1987, 19(1), pp. 1–18.

220 ECONOMIC AND SOCIAL STATISTICAL DATA AND ANALYSIS

2200 General

Allen, Bryant J. A Review of Smallholder Data Sources in PNG Relevant to the Export Tree Crops Sector. *Barker, P.; Bodman, P. and Remenyl, J., eds.*, 1987, pp. 14–54. [G: Papua New Guinea]

Bartelmus, Peter. Beyond GDP—New Approaches to Applied Statistics. *Rev. Income Wealth*, December 1987, 33(4), pp. 347–58.

Bartholomew, R. B. and Densley, D. R. J. Data Needs, Output and Options: Smallholder Component—PNG Export Tree Crop Study. *Barker, P.; Bodman, P. and Remenyl, J., eds.*, 1987, pp. 55–63. [G: Papua New Guinea]

Bobst, Barry W., et al. Data Sources for Demand Analyses. *Raunikar, R. and Huang, C.-L., eds.*, 1987, pp. 33–53. [G: U.S.]

Botha, J. P. Data: Die aard, kwaliteit en aanwending daarvan. (With English summary.) *J. Stud. Econ. Econometrics*, November 1987, 11(3), pp. 83–109.

Conway, Gordon. Rapid Rural Appraisal Strategies for Collecting and Analysing Data. *Barker, P.; Bodman, P. and Remenyl, J., eds.*, 1987, pp. 64–82. [G: Papua New Guinea]

DeBrock, Larry M. Selected Current Data Sources. *J. Econ. Educ.*, Summer 1987, 18(3), pp. 345–50.

Duncan, Joseph W. Technology, Costs, and the New Economics of Statistics. *Alonso, W. and Starr, P., eds.*, 1987, pp. 395–413. [G: U.S.]

Fox, Karl A. The Eco-behavioral View of Human Societies: Behavior Settings, Time-Allocation Matrices, and Social System Accounts. *Fox, K. A. and Miles, D. G., eds.*, 1987, pp. 118–42.

Fox, Karl A. and Miles, Don G. Systems Economics: Summary and Overview. *Fox, K. A. and Miles, D. G., eds.*, 1987, pp. 180–93.

Hauser, Philip M. The U.S. Census Undercount. *Menard, S. W. and Moen, E. W., eds.*, 1987, 1981, pp. 434–40. [G: U.S.]

Havinga, Ivo C., et al. A Social Accounting Matrix for the Agricultural Sector of Pakistan. *Pakistan Devel. Rev.*, Winter 1987, 26(4), pp. 627–39. [G: Pakistan]

Jéquier, Nicolas and Dedijer, Stevan. Information, Knowledge and Intelligence: A General Overview. *Dedijer, S. and Jéquier, N., eds.*, 1987, pp. 1–23.

Kelman, Steven. The Political Foundations of American Statistical Policy. *Alonso, W. and Starr, P., eds.*, 1987, pp. 275–302. [G: U.S.]

Malinvaud, Edmond. Produzione Statistica e Progresso della Conoscenza. (Statistical Production and the Progress of Knowledge. With English summary.) *Econ. Lavoro*, July-Sept. 1987, 21(3), pp. 3–22. [G: Italy]

Martinotti, Guido. Bisogni conoscitivi per la società italiana degli anni '90. (Information Needs in the Italian Society of the Nineties. With

English summary.) *Econ. Lavoro*, Apr.-June 1987, *21*(2), pp. 3–29. [G: Italy]

Maunder, W. F. and Fleming, M. C. Review of United Kingdom Statistical Sources: A Progress Report. *J. Roy. Statist. Soc.*, 1987, *150*(2), pp. 138–42. [G: U.K.]

van Moeseke, Paul. The Dollar Values of Social Variables: Two Models of Social Income. *Fox, K. A. and Miles, D. G., eds.*, 1987, pp. 143–57.

Mohammad, Faiz. A Social Accounting Matrix for the Agricultural Sector of Pakistan: Comments. *Pakistan Devel. Rev.*, Winter 1987, *26*(4), pp. 640–41. [G: Pakistan]

de Neufville, Judith Innes. Federal Statistics in Local Governments. *Alonso, W. and Starr, P., eds.*, 1987, pp. 343–62.

Pedullà, Giovanna. Concetti e metodi utilizzati in contabilità nazionale per la stima delle unità di lavoro. (Concepts and Methods Utilized in National Accounting for Estimating Work. With English summary.) *Econ. Lavoro*, July-Sept. 1987, *21*(3), pp. 23–37. [G: Italy]

Prescott, James R. Community Dynamics: Microanalytical Simulation Models with Behavior Settings as Basic Units. *Fox, K. A. and Miles, D. G., eds.*, 1987, pp. 158–79.

Prewitt, Kenneth. Public Statistics and Democratic Politics. *Alonso, W. and Starr, P., eds.*, 1987, pp. 261–74. [G: U.S.]

Rapaport, Edmund. Indentitätsschutz in der statistischen Tätigkeit. Gesetze, ethische Regeln und die Einstellung der Bevölkerung aus internationaler Perspektive. (Laws, Ethics and the Attitude of the General Population as Seen from an International Perspective. With English summary.) *Jahr. Nationalökon. Statist.*, May 1987, *203*(3), pp. 295–305.

Rey, Guido Mario. L'informazione statistica e i processi decisionali. (Statistical Information and the Decision Making Procedures. With English summary.) *Econ. Lavoro*, Jan.-Mar. 1987, *21*(1), pp. 3–18.

Starr, Paul. The Sociology of Official Statistics. *Alonso, W. and Starr, P., eds.*, 1987, pp. 7–57. [G: U.S.]

Starr, Paul and Corson, Ross. Who Will Have the Numbers? The Rise of the Statistical Services Industry and the Politics of Public Data. *Alonso, W. and Starr, P., eds.*, 1987, pp. 415–47. [G: U.S.]

Stekler, H. O. The Effect of Data Revisions and Additional Observations on Time-Series Estimates. *Appl. Econ.*, March 1987, *19*(3), pp. 347–53. [G: U.K.]

221 National Income Accounting

2210 National Income Accounting Theory and Procedures

Aanestad, James M. Measurement Problems of the Service Sector. *Bus. Econ.*, April 1987, *22*(2), pp. 32–37. [G: U.S.]

Al, Pieter G. Dual Sectoring in National Accounts. *Statist. J.*, July 1987, *4*(4), pp. 323–45.

Al, Pieter G., et al. The Use of Chain Indices for Deflating the National Accounts. *Statist. J.*, July 1987, *4*(4), pp. 347–68.

Barker, Terry and Weale, Martin. The Cambridge Multisectoral Dynamic Model of the British Economy: The Accounting Framework and the Data. *Barker, T. and Peterson, W., eds.*, 1987, pp. 25–46. [G: U.K.]

Bélanger, Gérard. L'univers du secteur public et les règles comptables utilisées dans les systèmes statistiques canadiens. (The Public Sector Universe and the Accounting Rules Used in the Canadian Statistical Systems. With English summary.) *L'Actual. Econ.*, December 1987, *63*(4), pp. 402–23. [G: Canada]

Carson, Carol S. GNP: An Overview of Source Data and Estimating Methods. *Surv. Curr. Bus.*, July 1987, *67*(7), pp. 103–26. [G: U.S.]

Colijn, Leendert. Some Proposed Methodologies to Quantify the Influence of Macroeconomic Disequilibrium on the Size of the Second Economy in Poland. *Alessandrini, S. and Dallago, B., eds.*, 1987, pp. 337–45. [G: Poland]

Cortázar, René and Meller, Patricio. Los dos Chiles. O la importancia de revisar las estadísticas oficiales. (Two Countries Called Chile or the Importance of Reviewing Official Statistics. With English summary.) *Colección Estud. CIEPLAN*, June 1987, (21), pp. 5–21. [G: Chile]

Feige, Edgar L. The Anatomy of the Underground Economy. *Alessandrini, S. and Dallago, B., eds.*, 1987, pp. 83–106. [G: U.S.]

Gajęcki, R. and Kasiewicz, S. Provision of Services in Poland: A Theoretical and Statistical Study. *Rev. Income Wealth*, September 1987, *33*(3), pp. 273–304. [G: Poland]

Goldschmidt-Clermont, Luisella. Assessing the Economic Significance of Domestic and Related Activities. *Statist. J.*, December 1987, *5*(1), pp. 81–93.

Heertje, Arnold. Some Observations on the Welfare Economic Aspects of the Unofficial Economy. *Alessandrini, S. and Dallago, B., eds.*, 1987, pp. 303–10.

Ilieva, Jana and Varjonen, Seppo. Comparison of the Balance Sheets of Bulgaria and the National Accounts of Finland. *Statist. J.*, July 1987, *4*(4), pp. 395–410. [G: Bulgaria; Finland]

Ivanov, Youri. Possibilities and Problems of Reconciliation of the SNA and the MPS. *Rev. Income Wealth*, March 1987, *33*(1), pp. 1–18.

Jessen, J., et al. The Informal Work of Industrial Workers: Present Situation, Trend Prognosis and Policy Implications. *Alessandrini, S. and Dallago, B., eds.*, 1987, pp. 271–82.

Kanth, Rajani. Against "Surplus" Theorizing: A Comment. *Rev. Radical Polit. Econ.*, Summer 1987, *19*(2), pp. 83–85. [G: LDCs]

Kenessey, Zoltan. The Primary, Secondary, Tertiery and Quaternary Sectors of the Economy. *Rev. Income Wealth*, December 1987, *33*(4), pp. 359–85. [G: U.S.]

Landesmann, Michael. The Cambridge Multisectoral Dynamic Model of the British Economy:

Stockbuilding. *Barker, T. and Peterson, W.*, eds., 1987, pp. 185–200. **[G: U.K.]**

Leipert, Christian. A Critical Appraisal of Gross National Product: The Measurement of Net National Welfare and Environmental Accounting: Impressions and Reflections in the Wake of Discussions Conducted during a Visit to the United States in May 1985. *J. Econ. Issues*, March 1987, *21*(1), pp. 357–73. **[G: U.S.]**

Lippit, Victor D. Surplus Theorizing Reaffirmed. *Rev. Radical Polit. Econ.*, Summer 1987, *19*(2), pp. 86–88. **[G: LDCs]**

Mamalakis, Markos J. The Treatment of Interest and Financial Intermediaries in the National Accounts: The Old "Bundle" versus the New "Unbundle" Approach. *Rev. Income Wealth*, June 1987, *33*(2), pp. 169–92.

Martynov, V. A Short Note on International Comparisons of Main Indicators of National Accounts and Balances. *Statist. J.*, July 1987, *4*(4), pp. 391–94. **[G: U.S.; U.S.S.R.]**

Peterson, William. The Cambridge Multisectoral Dynamic Model of the British Economy: Fixed Investment. *Barker, T. and Peterson, W., eds.*, 1987, pp. 151–83. **[G: U.K.]**

Quah, Euston. Household Production and the GNP: A Model for Use in Valuation. *Econ. Int.*, November 1987, *40*(4), pp. 345–61.

Quah, Euston. Valuing Family Household Production: A Contingent Evaluation Approach. *Appl. Econ.*, July 1987, *19*(7), pp. 875–89.

Reich, Utz-Peter. Does Consumption Entail Income? Implications of the Dual Classification of Consumption Expenditure for the Income Side of the Household Sector in the National Accounts. *Rev. Income Wealth*, June 1987, *33*(2), pp. 157–68.

Ruggles, Nancy D. Financial Accounts and Balance Sheets: Issues for the Revision of SNA. *Rev. Income Wealth*, March 1987, *33*(1), pp. 39–62.

Rugman, Alan M. Multinationals and Trade in Services: A Transaction Cost Approach. *Weltwirtsch. Arch.*, 1987, *123*(4), pp. 651–67. **[G: Canada]**

Rushbrook, Tony and Wells, Jack. National and Sector Balance Sheets in Concept and in Practice. *Rev. Income Wealth*, March 1987, *33*(1), pp. 19–37.

Sachs, Ignacy. The Crisis, Technological Progress and the Hidden Economy. *Sachs, I.*, 1987, pp. 95–104.

Schimmler, Harry. On Rents and Interest. *Rev. Income Wealth*, June 1987, *33*(2), pp. 229–30.

Schlitz, M. T. A New Method of Assessment of the Insurance Service Production. *Rev. Income Wealth*, December 1987, *33*(4), pp. 431–37.

Skolka, Jiri. A Few Facts about the Hidden Economy. *Alessandrini, S. and Dallago, B., eds.*, 1987, pp. 35–59. **[G: U.S.]**

Sunga, Preetom S. Adjusting Net Worth for Price Changes with Reference to the Canadian System of National Accounts. *Rev. Income Wealth*, March 1987, *33*(1), pp. 83–108. **[G: Canada]**

Szybisz, Boguslaw. Towards the Integration of Input–Output Tables with National Accounts.

Statist. J., July 1987, *4*(4), pp. 313–22.

Valovoi, D. Measuring and Assessing Production Activity. *Prob. Econ.*, March 1987, *29*(11), pp. 78–96.

Van Bochove, C. A. and Bloem, A. M. The Structure of the Next SNA: Review of the Basic Options. *Statist. J.*, July 1987, *4*(4), pp. 369–90.

Weale, Martin. The Cambridge Multisectoral Dynamic Model of the British Economy: Industrial Prices and Profits. *Barker, T. and Peterson, W., eds.*, 1987, pp. 293–309. **[G: U.K.]**

Wiles, Peter. The Second Economy, Its Definitional Problems. *Alessandrini, S. and Dallago, B., eds.*, 1987, pp. 21–33.

2212 National Income Accounts

Altman, Morris. A Revision of Canadian Economic Growth: 1870–1910 (A Challenge to the Gradualist Interpretation). *Can. J. Econ.*, February 1987, *20*(1), pp. 86–113. **[G: Canada]**

Batemarco, Robert. GNP, PPR, and the Standard of Living. *Rothbard, M. N., ed.*, 1987, pp. 181–86. **[G: U.S.]**

Beeton, D. J. On the Size of the Public Sector. *Appl. Econ.*, July 1987, *19*(7), pp. 927–36. **[G: U.K.]**

Bićanić, Ivo. The Inequality Impact of the Unofficial Economy in Yugoslavia. *Alessandrini, S. and Dallago, B., eds.*, 1987, pp. 323–36. **[G: Yugoslavia]**

Blades, Derek. Goods and Services in OECD Countries. *OECD Econ. Stud.*, Spring 1987, (8), pp. 159–84. **[G: OECD]**

Blinder, Alan S. Why Is U.S. National Saving So Low? Comments. *Brookings Pap. Econ. Act.*, 1987, (2), pp. 636–38. **[G: U.S.]**

Bonke, Jens. Husholdningernes økonomi. (Household Production. With English summary.) *Nationaløkon. Tidsskr.*, 1987, *125*(2), pp. 223–33. **[G: Denmark]**

Boretsky, Michael. The Tenability of the CIA Estimates of Soviet Economic Growth. *J. Compar. Econ.*, December 1987, *11*(4), pp. 517–42. **[G: U.S.S.R.; U.S.; W. Germany]**

Brezinski, Horst. The Second Economies in Eastern Europe. *Marer, P. and van Veen, P., eds.*, 1987, pp. 23–33. **[G: E. Europe]**

Brzeski, Andrzej. The Case of Central Planning in the USSR. *Pejovich, S., ed.*, 1987, pp. 209–37. **[G: U.S.S.R.]**

Cassel, Dieter and Cichy, Ulrich. The Shadow Economy and Economic Policy in East and West: A Comparative System Approach. *Alessandrini, S. and Dallago, B., eds.*, 1987, pp. 127–46.

Chakraborti, Sibaji. Growth Pattern of National Income: A Time-Series Study. *Indian Econ. J.*, Apr.-June 1987, *34*(4), pp. 18–24. **[G: India]**

Clark, Peter K. The Cyclical Component of U.S. Economic Activity. *Quart. J. Econ.*, November 1987, *102*(4), pp. 797–814. **[G: U.S.]**

Contador, Claudio R. and dos Santos Filho, Wilber A. C. Produto Interno Bruto trimestral:

Bases metodológicas e estimativas. (With English summary.) *Pesquisa Planejamento Econ.*, December 1987, *17*(3), pp. 711–42.
[G: Brazil]

Da Silva, Ednaldo Araquem. Wage–Profit Trade-offs in Brazil: In Input/Output Analysis, 1970–1975. *Sci. Soc.*, Fall 1987, *51*(3), pp. 347–54.
[G: Brazil]

Dallago, Bruno. The Underground Economy in the West and the East: A Comparative Approach. *Alessandrini, S. and Dallago, B., eds.*, 1987, pp. 147–63.

Deaglio, Mario. Submergence in the Italian Economy 1970–85. *Rev. Econ. Cond. Italy*, Jan.-Apr. 1987, (1), pp. 49–77. [G: Italy]

Dilullo, Anthony J. U.S. International Transactions, Third Quarter 1987. *Surv. Curr. Bus.*, December 1987, *67*(12), pp. 20–44.
[G: U.S.]

Divila, Emil and Goulli, Rochdi. The Relationship of Personal and Social Consumption of the Population—Prerequisites for Rationalization. *Czech. Econ. Pap.*, 1987, (24), pp. 119–39. [G: Czechoslovakia]

Dobosiewicz, Zbigniew. The Role of Unofficial Economy in North African Countries. *Alessandrini, S. and Dallago, B., eds.*, 1987, pp. 165–74. [G: N. Africa]

Dooley, Michael P.; Frankel, Jeffrey A. and Mathieson, Donald J. International Capital Mobility: What Do Saving–Investment Correlations Tell Us? *Int. Monet. Fund Staff Pap.*, September 1987, *34*(3), pp. 503–30.
[G: Selected Countries]

Duchêne, Gérard. Les transferts sociaux dans les économies centralement planifiées. (Welfare Benefits in the Centrally Planned Economies. With English summary.) *Écon. Soc.*, February 1987, *21*(2), pp. 5–27. [G: E. Europe]

Duménil, Gérard; Glick, Mark and Rangel, Jose. The Rate of Profit in the United States. *Cambridge J. Econ.*, December 1987, *11*(4), pp. 331–59. [G: U.S.]

Farber, Kit D. and Rutledge, Gary L. Pollution Abatement and Control Expenditures, 1982–85. *Surv. Curr. Bus.*, May 1987, *67*(5), pp. 21–26. [G: U.S.]

Feige, Edgar L. Sweden's "Underground Economy." *Eliasson, G., ed.*, 1987, pp. 113–28.
[G: Sweden]

Feige, Edgar L. The Anatomy of the Underground Economy. *Alessandrini, S. and Dallago, B., eds.*, 1987, pp. 83–106. [G: U.S.]

Feldstein, Martin S. and Jun, Joosung. The Effects of Tax Rules on Nonresidential Fixed Investment: Some Preliminary Evidence from the 1980s. *Feldstein, M., ed. (I)*, 1987, pp. 101–56. [G: U.S.]

Gordon, Roger H. The Effects of Tax Rules on Nonresidential Fixed Investment: Some Preliminary Evidence from the 1980s: Comment. *Feldstein, M., ed. (I)*, 1987, pp. 156–61.
[G: U.S.]

Grossman, Gregory and Treml, Vladimir G. Measuring Hidden Personal Incomes in the

USSR. *Alessandrini, S. and Dallago, B., eds.*, 1987, pp. 285–96. [G: U.S.S.R.]

Guissarri, Adrián C. La Demanda de Circulante y la Informalidad en la Argentina: 1930–1983. (With English summary.) *Cuadernos Econ.*, August 1987, *24*(72), pp. 197–224.
[G: Argentina]

Gutiérrez U., Mario A. Ahorro interno y crecimiento económico: Un enfoque de cuentas nacionales. (With English summary.) *Cuadernos Econ.*, December 1987, *24*(73), pp. 331–57.
[G: Chile]

Hegedüs, Andras. Some Problems of the Expansion of the Second Economy in Hungary. *Alessandrini, S. and Dallago, B., eds.*, 1987, pp. 297–301. [G: Hungary]

Hendershott, Patric H. Tax Changes and Capital Allocation in the 1980s. *Feldstein, M., ed. (I)*, 1987, pp. 259–90. [G: U.S.]

Henley, Andrew. Labour's Shares and Profitability Crisis in the U.S.: Recent Experience and Post-war Trends. *Cambridge J. Econ.*, December 1987, *11*(4), pp. 315–30. [G: U.S.]

Herr, Ellen M. Capital Expenditures by Majority-Owned Foreign Affiliates of U.S. Companies, 1987. *Surv. Curr. Bus.*, March 1987, *67*(3), pp. 26–31. [G: U.S.]

Herr, Ellen M. Capital Expenditures by Majority-Owned Foreign Affiliates of U.S. Companies, 1987 and 1988. *Surv. Curr. Bus.*, September 1987, *67*(9), pp. 26–31. [G: U.S.]

Ilieva, Jana and Varjonen, Seppo. Comparison of the Balance Sheets of Bulgaria and the National Accounts of Finland. *Statist. J.*, July 1987, *4*(4), pp. 395–410. [G: Bulgaria; Finland]

Jankowski, Richard. The Profit-Squeeze and Tax Policy: Can the State Actively Intervene? *Rev. Radical Polit. Econ.*, Fall 1987, *19*(3), pp. 18–33. [G: U.S.]

Jencks, Christopher. The Politics of Income Measurement. *Alonso, W. and Starr, P., eds.*, 1987, pp. 83–131. [G: U.S.]

Jenkins, C. M. Disinvestment: Effects on the Rate of Growth of GDP. *S. Afr. J. Econ.*, December 1987, *55*(4), pp. 395–406. [G: S. Africa]

Keller, Wouter J., et al. Real Income Changes of Households in the Netherlands, 1977–1983. *Rev. Income Wealth*, September 1987, *33*(3), pp. 257–71. [G: Netherlands]

Kuznets, Simon. Population, Income and Capital. *Dupriez, L. H., ed.*, 1987, *1955*, pp. 3–20.
[G: Global]

Lambooy, Jan G. and Renooy, P. H. Informal Economy and the Labour Market: Relations with the Economic Order. *Gordon, I., ed.*, 1987, pp. 172–91. [G: Netherlands]

Landau, Zbigniew. Selected Problems of Unofficial Economy in Poland. *Alessandrini, S. and Dallago, B., eds.*, 1987, pp. 175–79.
[G: Poland]

Lemaire, Maryvonne. Satellite Accounts: A Relevant Framework for Analysis in Social Fields. *Rev. Income Wealth*, September 1987, *33*(3), pp. 305–25. [G: France]

Maddison, Angus. Growth and Slowdown in Ad-

221 National Income Accounting

vanced Capitalist Economies: Techniques of Quantitative Assessment. *J. Econ. Lit.*, June 1987, *25*(2), pp. 649–98. **[G: OECD]**

Marrelli, M. The Economic Analysis of Tax Evasion: Empirical Aspects. *Hey, J. D. and Lambert, P. J., eds.*, 1987, pp. 204–28. **[G: U.S.; W. Europe]**

McUsic, Molly. U.S. Manufacturing: Any Cause for Alarm? *New Eng. Econ. Rev.*, Jan./Feb. 1987, pp. 3–17. **[G: U.S.]**

Mork, Knut Anton. Ain't Behavin': Forecast Errors and Measurement Errors in Early GNP Estimates. *J. Bus. Econ. Statist.*, April 1987, *5*(2), pp. 165–75. **[G: U.S.]**

van Nieuwkerk, Marius. In Search of 100 Billion Dollars. *Heijmans, R. and Neudecker, H., eds.*, 1987, pp. 121–30. **[G: Global]**

Nolan, Brian. Cyclical Fluctuations in Factor Shares and the Size Distribution of Income. *Rev. Income Wealth*, June 1987, *33*(2), pp. 193–210. **[G: U.K.]**

O'Mara, L. P. The Contribution of the Farm Sector to Annual Variations in Gross Domestic Product in Australia. *Econ. Rec.*, September 1987, *63*(182), pp. 255–69. **[G: Australia]**

Ott, Mack. The Growing Share of Services in the U.S. Economy— Degeneration or Evolution? *Fed. Res. Bank St. Louis Rev.*, June/July 1987, *69*(6), pp. 5–22. **[G: U.S.]**

Otto, Lars. Konstruktion af erhvervsfordelte kapitaldata for Danmark. (Construction of Capital Equipment Data for the Danish Economy. With English summary.) *Nationaløkon. Tidsskr.*, 1987, *125*(3), pp. 378–89. **[G: Denmark]**

Park, Thae S. Relationship between Personal Income and Adjusted Gross Income, 1983–85. *Surv. Curr. Bus.*, May 1987, *67*(5), pp. 18–20. **[G: U.S.]**

Patton, Spiro G. and Reilly, Bernard J. The Role of Private Services in the American Economy. *Bus. Econ.*, April 1987, *22*(2), pp. 7–11. **[G: U.S.]**

Peek, Joe. The Distorting Effects of the Inflation Premium on Personal Income and Expenditures. *New Eng. Econ. Rev.*, Sept./Oct. 1987, pp. 10–24. **[G: U.S.]**

Perlman, Mark. Political Purpose and the National Accounts. *Alonso, W. and Starr, P., eds.*, 1987, pp. 133–51. **[G: U.S.]**

Peterson, Milo O. Gross Product by Industry, 1986. *Surv. Curr. Bus.*, April 1987, *67*(4), pp. 25–27. **[G: U.S.]**

Petrović, Pavle. The Deviation of Production Prices from Labour Values: Some Methodology and Empirical Evidence. *Cambridge J. Econ.*, September 1987, *11*(3), pp. 197–210. **[G: Yugoslavia]**

Reynolds, Peter J. Wage Rises and Income Distribution—A Note. *Manchester Sch. Econ. Soc. Stud.*, March 1987, *55*(1), pp. 77–87. **[G: U.K.]**

Roland, Gérard. Investment Growth Fluctuations in the Soviet Union: An Econometric Analysis. *J. Compar. Econ.*, June 1987, *11*(2), pp. 192–206. **[G: U.S.S.R.]**

Rosen, Harvey S. Tax Changes and Capital Allocation in the 1980s: Comment. *Feldstein, M., ed. (I)*, 1987, pp. 290–94. **[G: U.S.]**

Rutledge, Gary L. and Stergioulas, Nikolaos. Plant and Equipment Expenditures by Business for Pollution Abatement, 1986 and 1987. *Surv. Curr. Bus.*, October 1987, *67*(10), pp. 23–26. **[G: U.S.]**

Sato, Kazuo. The Political Economy of Japan: Saving and Investment. *Yamamura, K. and Yasuba, Y., eds.*, 1987, pp. 137–85. **[G: Japan]**

Schultze, Charles L. Saving, Investment, and Profitability in Europe. *Lawrence, R. Z. and Schultze, C. L., eds.*, 1987, pp. 508–39. **[G: W. Europe]**

Seskin, Eugene P. and Sullivan, David F. Plant and Equipment Expenditures. *Surv. Curr. Bus.*, December 1987, *67*(12), pp. 16–19. **[G: U.S.]**

Seskin, Eugene P. and Sullivan, David F. Plant and Equipment Expenditures, the Four Quarters of 1987. *Surv. Curr. Bus.*, September 1987, *67*(9), pp. 20–25. **[G: U.S.]**

Seskin, Eugene P. and Sullivan, David F. Plant and Equipment Expenditures, the Four Quarters of 1987. *Surv. Curr. Bus.*, June 1987, *67*(6), pp. 19–22. **[G: U.S.]**

Seskin, Eugene P. and Sullivan, David F. Plant and Equipment Expenditures, First and Second Quarters and Second Half of 1987. *Surv. Curr. Bus.*, April 1987, *67*(4), pp. 28–32. **[G: U.S.]**

Siesto, Vincenzo. Macroeconomic Statistics and the Submerged Economy. *Rev. Econ. Cond. Italy*, Jan.-Apr. 1987, (1), pp. 21–47. **[G: OECD]**

Slade, John. The Ways Cigarettes Contribute to GNP. *Eastern Econ. J.*, October-December 1987, *13*(4), pp. 353–59. **[G: U.S.]**

Söderström, Hans Tson. Sectoral Saving and Investment Patterns in 16 OECD Countries, 1965–82. *Boskin, M. J.; Fleming, J. S. and Gorini, S., eds.*, 1987, pp. 3–39. **[G: OECD]**

Stollar, Andrew J.; Grubaugh, Stephen G. and Thompson, G. Rodney. Utilisation of Direct and Indirect Estimates of Real GDP Per Capita: Implications of the Errors in the Variables Model. *Econ. J.*, June 1987, *97*(386), pp. 468–78. **[G: U.S.]**

Stone, Richard. How Accurate Are the British National Accounts? *[Cochrane, D.]*, 1987, pp. 253–67. **[G: U.K.]**

Summers, Lawrence H. and Carroll, Chris. Why Is U.S. National Saving So Low? *Brookings Pap. Econ. Act.*, 1987, (2), pp. 607–35. **[G: U.S.]**

Vernon, Raymond. The Politics of Comparative Economic Statistics: Three Cultures and Three Cases. *Alonso, W. and Starr, P., eds.*, 1987, pp. 61–82.

Visser, Hans; Eijgenhuijsen, Hans and Koelewijn, Jaap. Capital Ratios, Own Funds and Investment in The Netherlands. *Nat. Westminster Bank Quart. Rev.*, February 1987, pp. 39–50. **[G: Netherlands]**

Wakefield, Joseph C. The Tax Reform Act of 1986.

240

Surv. Curr. Bus., March 1987, 67(3), pp. 18–25. [G: U.S.]

Weiss, Mary A. Macroeconomic Insurance Output Estimation. *J. Risk Ins.*, September 1987, 54(3), pp. 582–93. [G: U.S.]

Witte, Ann D. The Nature and Extent of Unrecorded Activity: A Survey Concentrating on Recent U.S. Research. *Alessandrini, S. and Dallago, B., eds.*, 1987, pp. 61–81. [G: U.S.]

Young, Allan H. Evaluation of the GNP Estimates. *Surv. Curr. Bus.*, August 1987, 67(8), pp. 18–42. [G: U.S.]

2213 Income Distribution

Abraham, Jesse M. Income Redistribution during a Disinflation. *J. Macroecon.*, Spring 1987, 9(2), pp. 203–21. [G: U.S.]

Adelman, Irma and Sunding, David. Economic Policy and Income Distribution in China. *J. Compar. Econ.*, September 1987, 11(3), pp. 444–61. [G: China]

Aggarwal, Mangat Ram. Transnational Corporations, Economic Development and Income Distribution in Less Developed Countries. *Indian Econ. J.*, Jan.-Mar. 1987, 34(3), pp. 4–50. [G: LDCs]

Altimer, Oscar. Income Distribution Statistics in Latin America and Their Reliability. *Rev. Income Wealth*, June 1987, 33(2), pp. 111–55. [G: Latin America]

Arsalanbod, Mohamadreza. Farm Size Structure and the Distribution of Income in the Rural Areas of Iran. *Léon, Y. and Mahé, L., eds.*, 1987, pp. 137–44. [G: Iran]

Arun Kumar, K. S., et al. Income Inequality in Rural India 1965–1983. *Léon, Y. and Mahé, L., eds.*, 1987, pp. 129–36. [G: India]

Asimakopulos, Athanasios. The Profits–Investment Relation, Cyclical and Structural Changes, Canada, 1950–1983. *Écon. Appl.*, 1987, 40(4), pp. 631–54. [G: Canada]

Atkinson, Anthony B. and Bourguignon, François. Income Distribution and Differences in Needs. *Feiwel, G. R., ed. (II)*, 1987, pp. 350–70.

Bawa, R. S. and Kainth, Gursharan Singh. Income Inequalities in Urban Areas: Measurement and Determinant. *Margin*, Jan.-Mar. 1987, 19(2), pp. 60–73. [G: India]

Becker, Charles M. Urban Sector Income Distribution and Economic Development. *J. Urban Econ.*, March 1987, 21(2), pp. 127–45. [G: LDCs]

Berrebi, Zeev M. and Silber, Jacques G. Dispersion, Asymmetry and the Gini Index of Inequality. *Int. Econ. Rev.*, June 1987, 28(2), pp. 331–38.

Berrebi, Zeev M. and Silber, Jacques G. Interquantile Differences, Income Inequality Measurement and the Gini Concentration Index. *Math. Soc. Sci.*, February 1987, 13(1), pp. 67–72. [G: Selected Countries]

Berry, Albert. Evidence on Relationships among Alternative Measures of Concentration: A Tool for Analysis of LDC Inequality. *Rev. Income Wealth*, December 1987, 33(4), pp. 417–29. [G: LDCs]

Bićanić, Ivo. The Inequality Impact of the Unofficial Economy in Yugoslavia. *Alessandrini, S. and Dallago, B., eds.*, 1987, pp. 323–36. [G: Yugoslavia]

Blackburn, McKinley L. and Bloom, David E. Earnings and Income Inequality in the United States. *Population Devel. Rev.*, December 1987, 13(4), pp. 575–609. [G: U.S.]

Bosanquet, N. The Distribution and Redistribution of Income in the United Kingdom, 1971–84: Comment. *Levitt, M. S., ed.*, 1987, pp. 65–69. [G: U.K.]

Briquel, Vincent and Baschet, Jean-François. Les disparités catégorielles de revenus: quelques facteurs d'évolution. (With English summary.) *Léon, Y. and Mahé, L., eds.*, 1987, pp. 145–56. [G: France]

Butault, Jean-Pierre; Lerouvillois, Philippe and Rousselle, Jean-Marc. Les facteurs de dispersion des revenus agricoles (RICA—France 1979). (With English summary.) *Léon, Y. and Mahé, L., eds.*, 1987, pp. 157–75. [G: France]

Butler, Richard J. and McDonald, James B. Interdistributional Income Inequality. *J. Bus. Econ. Statist.*, January 1987, 5(1), pp. 13–18. [G: U.S.]

Butt, Abdul Rauf. Impact of Population Planning on the Size Distribution of Income: A Theoretical and Methodological Framework. *Pakistan Econ. Soc. Rev.*, Winter 1987, 25(2), pp. 59–72. [G: Pakistan]

Campano, Fred. A Fresh Look at Champernowne's Five-Parameter Formula. *Écon. Appl.*, 1987, 40(1), pp. 161–75. [G: U.S.]

Chakravarty, Satya Ranjan and Dutta, Bhaskar. A Note on Measures of Distance between Income Distributions. *J. Econ. Theory*, February 1987, 41(1), pp. 185–88.

Chipman, John S. When Is a Fixed Income Distribution Optimal? *Feiwel, G. R., ed. (II)*, 1987, pp. 371–81.

Chowdhury, Nuimuddin. Urban Rationing in Bangladesh in Mid-1980s: The Distribution of Its Benefits. *Bangladesh Devel. Stud.*, December 1987, 15(4), pp. 53–84. [G: Bangladesh]

Cloutier, Norman R. Who Gains from Racism? The Impact of Racial Inequality on White Income Distribution. *Rev. Soc. Econ.*, October 1987, 45(2), pp. 152–62. [G: U.S.]

Cordellier, Christian. Les revenus des familles d'agriculteurs en 1978: composition et disparités. (With English summary.) *Léon, Y. and Mahé, L., eds.*, 1987, pp. 217–36. [G: France]

Cornelisse, Peter A. A 'World' Distribution of Income and of Real Poverty and Affluence: Comments. *Pakistan Devel. Rev.*, Autumn 1987, 26(3), pp. 300–302. [G: Global]

Curry, L. Areal Heterogeneity and Labour Returns. *Gordon, I., ed.*, 1987, pp. 101–15.

Dagum, Camilo. Measuring the Economic Affluence between Populations of Income Receivers. *J. Bus. Econ. Statist.*, January 1987, 5(1), pp. 5–12. [G: U.S.]

Downes, Andrew S. The Distribution of Household Income in Barbados. *Soc. Econ. Stud.*, December 1987, 36(4), pp. 127–55.
[G: Barbados]

Dugger, William M. Three Modes of Income Distribution: Market, Hierarchy, and Industry. *J. Econ. Issues*, June 1987, 21(2), pp. 723–31.

Dumondel, Michel. Pluriactivité et disparités socio-économiques au niveau communal suisse. (With English summary.) *Léon, Y. and Mahé, L., eds.*, 1987, pp. 237–53. [G: Switzerland]

Fecher, Fabienne. Politique d'austérité et récession économique. Incidence sur la distribution du revenu des belges de 1980 à 1984. (With English summary.) *Cah. Écon. Bruxelles*, Second Trimester 1987, (114), pp. 397–420.
[G: Belgium]

Fields, Gary S. Measuring Inequality Change in an Economy with Income Growth. *J. Devel. Econ.*, August 1987, 26(2), pp. 357–74.

Gang, Ira N. Distribution and Development Effects of Tariff Cum Subsidy Policies. *Singapore Econ. Rev.*, April 1987, 32(1), pp. 71–86.
[G: LDCs]

Gibson, Bill; Lustig, Nora and Taylor, Lance. SAM's Impact on Income Distribution. *Austin, J. E. and Esteva, G., eds.*, 1987, pp. 298–311.
[G: Mexico]

Greenwood, Daphne T. Age, Income, and Household Size: Their Relation to Wealth Distribution in the United States. *Wolff, E. N., ed.*, 1987, pp. 121–40. [G: U.S.]

Greenwood, Michael J. and Ladman, Jerry R. Intertemporal and Intersectoral Aspects of Income and Distribution in Mexico. *Rev. Soc. Econ.*, April 1987, 45(1), pp. 48–63.
[G: Mexico]

Haller, Max. Positional and Sectoral Differences in Income: The Federal Republic, France, and the United States. *Teckenberg, W., ed.*, 1987, pp. 172–90. [G: W. Germany; France; U.S.]

Henschel, Rudolf. Einflüsse Öffentlicher Meinungsbildung auf die Einkommensverteilung. (The Influence of Public Opinion on the Distribution of Income. With English summary.) *Ifo-Studien*, 1987, 33(1), pp. 1–26.
[G: W. Germany]

Herrero, Carmen. Teorías alternativas de la utilidad esperada: Una interpretación en términos de bienestar social. (With English summary.) *Invest. Econ.*, September 1987, 11(3), pp. 375–98.

Higgins, James. The Distribution of Income on Irish Farms. *Léon, Y. and Mahé, L., eds.*, 1987, pp. 255–70. [G: Ireland]

Hill, Berkeley. Income Disparities in UK Agriculture: Information and Inference. *Léon, Y. and Mahé, L., eds.*, 1987, pp. 415–32. [G: U.K.]

Ikemoto, Yukio and Limskul, Kitti. Income Inequality and Regional Disparity in Thailand, 1962–81. *Devel. Econ.*, September 1987, 25(3), pp. 249–69. [G: Thailand]

Jegouzo, Guenhaël. Les sources non agricoles des revenus de ménage chez les petits paysans et

les autres agriculteurs français. (With English summary.) *Léon, Y. and Mahé, L., eds.*, 1987, pp. 271–96. [G: France]

Jorgensen, Aage Walter. Measuring Income, Income Distribution and Economic Return in Danish Agriculture. *Léon, Y. and Mahé, L., eds.*, 1987, pp. 109–26. [G: Denmark]

Keller, Wouter J., et al. Real Income Changes of Households in the Netherlands, 1977–1983. *Rev. Income Wealth*, September 1987, 33(3), pp. 257–71. [G: Netherlands]

Kemal, A. R. Sources of Income Inequality in Pakistan: Comments. *Pakistan Devel. Rev.*, Winter 1987, 26(4), pp. 670–72.
[G: Pakistan]

Kessler, Peter and Gantner, Urs. Disparités des revenus des familles d'agriculteurs en Suisse. (With English summary.) *Léon, Y. and Mahé, L., eds.*, 1987, pp. 433–47. [G: Switzerland]

Khan, Ashfaque H. Aggregate Consumption Function and Income Distribution Effect: Some Evidence from Developing Countries. *World Devel.*, Oct./Nov. 1987, 15(10/11), pp. 1369–74. [G: LDCs]

Khan, Mahmood Hasan. A 'World' Distribution of Income and of Real Poverty and Affluence: Comments. *Pakistan Devel. Rev.*, Autumn 1987, 26(3), pp. 303–04. [G: Global]

Klank, Leszek. Income Disparities among Farm Households and Agricultural Policy in Poland. *Léon, Y. and Mahé, L., eds.*, 1987, pp. 449–62. [G: Poland]

de Kruijk, Hans. Sources of Income Inequality in Pakistan. *Pakistan Devel. Rev.*, Winter 1987, 26(4), pp. 659–69. [G: Pakistan]

Kula, Erhun. Prospects for Farmers to Improve Incomes by Switching Crops in N. Ireland: An Analysis to Improve Government Support Schemes. *Léon, Y. and Mahé, L., eds.*, 1987, pp. 297–307. [G: U.K.]

Lam, David. Distribution Issues in the Relationship between Population Growth and Economic Development. *Johnson, D. G. and Lee, R. D., eds.*, 1987, pp. 589–627.
[G: Selected Countries]

Levy, Amnon. Income Inequality and the Distribution of Ownership of Productive Resources: Theory and Application with Lognormal Distribution. *J. Policy Modeling*, Summer 1987, 9(2), pp. 321–36. [G: Israel]

Livernois, John R. The Redistributive Effects of Lotteries: Evidence from Canada. *Public Finance Quart.*, July 1987, 15(3), pp. 339–51.
[G: Canada]

Malik, Muhammad Hussain. A 'World' Distribution of Income and of Real Poverty and Affluence: Comments. *Pakistan Devel. Rev.*, Autumn 1987, 26(3), pp. 305–06.

Matthews, Alan. Agricultural Income Distribution and Public Policy: A Dynamic Analysis. *Léon, Y. and Mahé, L., eds.*, 1987, pp. 463–76. [G: Ireland]

Merkies, Arnold H. Q. M. Inductive Analysis from Empirical Income Distributions. *Heijmans, R. and Neudecker, H., eds.*, 1987, pp. 151–64.

Michel, Richard C., et al. Are We Better Off in 1984? *Challenge*, Special Issue 1987, *30*(6), pp. 37–44. **[G: U.S.]**

Milanovic, Branko. Remittances and Income Distribution. *J. Econ. Stud.*, 1987, *14*(5), pp. 24–37. **[G: Yugoslavia]**

Molina, David J. and Slottje, D. J. The Gamma Distribution and the Size Distribution of Income Reconsidered. *Atlantic Econ. J.*, July 1987, *15*(2), pp. 86.

Niessler, Rudolf. Income Distribution in Austrian Agriculture (Empirical Findings, Theories and Strategies Concerning Income Policy). *Léon, Y. and Mahé, L.*, eds., 1987, pp. 325–38. **[G: Austria]**

Nolan, Brian. Cyclical Fluctuations in Factor Shares and the Size Distribution of Income. *Rev. Income Wealth*, June 1987, *33*(2), pp. 193–210. **[G: U.K.]**

Nummela, Ilkka and Laitinen, Erkki K. Distribution of Income in Kuopio 1880–1910. *Scand. Econ. Hist. Rev.*, 1987, *35*(3), pp. 237–53. **[G: Finland]**

O'Higgins, Michael. The Distribution and Redistribution of Income in the United Kingdom, 1971–84. *Levitt, M. S.*, ed., 1987, pp. 50–65. **[G: U.K.]**

Papanek, Gustav F. and Kyn, Oldrich. Flattening the Kuznets Curve: The Consequences for Income Distribution of Development Strategy, Government Intervention, Income and Rate of Growth. *Pakistan Devel. Rev.*, Spring 1987, *26*(1), pp. 1–54. **[G: Selected Countries]**

Peach, James T. Distribution and Economic Progress. *J. Econ. Issues*, December 1987, *21*(4), pp. 1495–1529. **[G: U.S.]**

Piachaud, David. The Distribution of Income and Work. *Oxford Rev. Econ. Policy*, Autumn 1987, *3*(3), pp. 41–61. **[G: U.K.]**

Plankl, Reiner. Identification and Estimation of the Number of Low-income Farmers in Federal Republic of Germany by Means of a Sample of Bookkeeping Test Farmers. *Léon, Y. and Mahé, L.*, eds., 1987, pp. 339–60. **[G: W. Germany]**

Pollastri, Angiola. Le curve di concentrazione L_p e Z_p nella distribuzione lognormale generalizzata. (The Concentration Curves L_p and Z_p in the Generalized Lognormal Distribution. With English summary.) *Giorn. Econ.*, Nov.-Dec. 1987, *46*(11–12), pp. 639–63.

Poppe, Krijn J. and Zachariasse, Vinus. Income Disparities among Farm Households and Agricultural Policy Case: The Netherlands. *Léon, Y. and Mahé, L.*, eds., 1987, pp. 361–76. **[G: Netherlands]**

Powell, Irene. The Effect of Reductions in Concentration on Income Distribution. *Rev. Econ. Statist.*, February 1987, *69*(1), pp. 75–82.

Quinn, Joseph F. The Economic Status of the Elderly: Beware of the Mean. *Rev. Income Wealth*, March 1987, *33*(1), pp. 63–82.

Radner, Daniel B. Money Incomes of Aged and Nonaged Family Units, 1967–84. *Soc. Sec. Bull.*, August 1987, *50*(8), pp. 9–28. **[G: U.S.]**

Radner, Daniel B. and Vaughan, Denton R. Wealth, Income, and the Economic Status of Aged Households. *Wolff, E. N.*, ed., 1987, pp. 93–120. **[G: U.S.]**

Ransom, Michael R. Economic Growth and the Size Distribution of Income; a Longitudinal Analysis. *Heijmans, R. and Neudecker, H.*, eds., 1987, pp. 165–77. **[G: MDCs]**

Rubinstein, W. D. The Geographical Distribution of Middle-Class Income in Britain, 1800–1914. *Rubinstein, W. D.*, 1987, pp. 85–118. **[G: U.K.]**

Sarantides, Stylianos A. International Income Inequality and *per capita* Income Rates of Growth: A Cross-Section Analysis. *Int. J. Soc. Econ.*, 1987, *14*(7/8/9), pp. 195–210. **[G: Selected Countries]**

Satchell, Stephen E. Source and Subgroup Decomposition Inequalities for the Lorenz Curve. *Int. Econ. Rev.*, June 1987, *28*(2), pp. 323–29.

Shackett, Joyce R. and Slottje, D. J. Labor Supply Decisions, Human Capital Attributes, and Inequality in the Size Distribution of Earnings in the U.S., 1952–81. *J. Human Res.*, Winter 1987, *22*(1), pp. 82–100. **[G: U.S.]**

Slottje, D. J. Relative Price Changes and Inequality in the Size Distribution of Various Components of Income: A Multidemensional Approach. *J. Bus. Econ. Statist.*, January 1987, *5*(1), pp. 19–26. **[G: U.S.]**

Smith, Steve. The Degree of Inequality in the Distribution of Personal Incomes. *Vane, H. and Caslin, T.*, eds., 1987, pp. 169–92. **[G: U.K.]**

Soares, Fernando B. Regional Disparities on Farm Income in Portugal: Will EEC Membership Be a Remedial or Aggravating Factor? *Léon, Y. and Mahé, L.*, eds., 1987, pp. 477–88. **[G: Portugal]**

Soltow, Lee C. The Distribution of Income in the United States in 1798: Estimates Based on the Federal Housing Inventory. *Rev. Econ. Statist.*, February 1987, *69*(1), pp. 181–85. **[G: U.S.]**

Terwey, Michael. Class Position and Income Inequality: Comparing Results for the Federal Republic with Current U.S. Research. *Teckenberg, W.*, ed., 1987, pp. 119–71. **[G: W. Germany; U.S.]**

Thompson, Shelley J. and von Witzke, Harald. Income Inequality within Agriculture: Relevant Dimensions and Methods of Analysis. *Léon, Y. and Mahé, L.*, eds., 1987, pp. 81–94. **[G: W. Germany]**

Tillieut, Michel. Disparité des revenus en agriculture dans la Communauté Européenne. (With English summary.) *Léon, Y. and Mahé, L.*, eds., 1987, pp. 199–214. **[G: EEC]**

Venieris, Y. P. and Stewart, D. B. Sociopolitical Instability, Inequality and Consumption Behavior. *J. Econ. Devel.*, December 1987, *12*(2), pp. 7–20. **[G: Selected Countries]**

Vert, Eric. Les revenus des agriculteurs. Comparaison avec les autres catégories sociales et rôle des revenus non agricoles. (With English summary.) *Léon, Y. and Mahé, L.*, eds., 1987, pp. 377–91. [G: France]

Vinokur, Aaron and Ofer, Gur. Inequality of Earnings, Household Income, and Wealth in the Soviet Union in the 1970s. *Millar, J. R.*, ed., 1987, pp. 171–202. [G: U.S.S.R.]

Winegarden, C. R. Women's Labour Force Participation and the Distribution of Household Incomes: Evidence from Cross-national Data. *Economica*, May 1987, *54*(214), pp. 223–36. [G: U.S.; U.K.]

Yaron, Dan; Ratner, Aaron and Wijler, Johanan. Integrating Industrial Plants into the Moshav Economy—Benefits and Conflicts. *Econ. Anal. Workers' Manage.*, 1987, *21*(3), pp. 353–72. [G: Israel]

Yoo, Jong G. and Kwon, Jene K. Welfare Inequality among Urban Households in South Korea: 1965–83. *Appl. Econ.*, April 1987, *19*(4), pp. 497–510.

Yotopoulos, Pan A. A 'World' Distribution of Income and of Real Poverty and Affluence. *Pakistan Devel. Rev.*, Autumn 1987, *26*(3), pp. 275–99. [G: Global]

Zachariasse, Vinus. Income Disparities among Farm Households and Agricultural Policy: Concluding Comments. *Léon, Y. and Mahé, L.*, eds., 1987, pp. 499–505.

222 Input–Output

2220 Input–Output

Adams, F. Gerard. Industrial Modeling with Input–Output: An Application to the Italian Metal Mechanical Industry. *Tchijov, I. and Tomaszewicz, L.*, eds., 1987, pp. 125–37. [G: Italy]

Almon, Clopper. Principles and Practices of the INFORUM Interindustry Macro Model. *Tchijov, I. and Tomaszewicz, L.*, eds., 1987, pp. 7–25. [G: U.S.]

Antille, Gabrielle and Laplanche, Bernadette. Impact of Constraints in Energy Imports and Energy Production of Final Domestic Demand. *Tchijov, I. and Tomaszewicz, L.*, eds., 1987, pp. 169–83. [G: Switzerland]

Batey, P. W. J.; Madden, M. and Weeks, M. J. Household Income and Expenditure in Extended Input–Output Models: A Comparative Theoretical and Empirical Analysis. *J. Reg. Sci.*, August 1987, *27*(3), pp. 341–56. [G: U.S.]

Bourque, Philip J. Synthetic I–O Models: A Comment [Regional Input–Output Analyis: A Comparison of Five "Ready-Made" Model Systems]. *Rev. Reg. Stud.*, Spring 1987, *17*(2), pp. 28–29.

Brautzsch, Hans-Ulrich. The Input–Output Model of the GDR Forest Sector. *Tchijov, I. and Tomaszewicz, L.*, eds., 1987, pp. 153–62. [G: E. Germany]

Brucker, Sharon M.; Hastings, Steven E. and Latham, William R., III. Regional Input–Output Analysis: A Comparison of Five "Ready-Made" Model Systems. *Rev. Reg. Stud.*,

Spring 1987, *17*(2), pp. 1–16. [G: U.S.]

Cassetti, Mario. Gli effetti moltiplicativi degli investimenti per settore di destinazione sulla produzione, sulle importazioni e sull'occupazione in Italia, dal 1970 al 1982. Un'analisi intersettoriale. (The Effect of Investment Demands by Destination on Total Production, Imports and Employment in Italy, since 1970 to 1982. An Intersectoral Analysis. With English summary.) *Ricerche Econ.*, Apr.-June 1987, *41*(2), pp. 231–61. [G: Italy]

Chawluk, Antoni. Is Soviet Capital Too Old? *Economica*, August 1987, *54*(215), pp. 335–54. [G: U.S.S.R.]

Cohen, Suleiman I. Input–Output versus Social Accounting in the Macro-analysis of Development Policy. *Industry Devel.*, 1987, (22), pp. 93–129. [G: Colombia; Pakistan; S. Korea]

Conti, Vittorio and Silvani, Marco. Foreign Trade and Industrial Structure in Italy: An Input–Output Multiplier Analysis. *Saunders, C. T.*, ed., 1987, pp. 183–203. [G: Italy]

Corsetti, Giancarlo. Taxes and Subsidies in Input–Output Analysis: A Comment. *Ricerche Econ.*, Apr.-June 1987, *41*(2), pp. 262–73.

Crown, William H. An Approach to Estimating a Consistent Aggregate Input–Output Model. *Growth Change*, Fall 1987, *18*(4), pp. 1–9.

Czyzewski, Adam B.; Tomaszewicz, Andrzej and Tomaszewicz, Lucja. Intra-CMEA Trade Share Matrices: Reconstruction and Analysis for 1971–1980. *Tchijov, I. and Tomaszewicz, L.*, eds., 1987, pp. 113–18. [G: CMEA]

Da Silva, Ednaldo Araquem. Wage-Profit Trade-offs in Brazil: In Input/Output Analysis, 1970–1975. *Sci. Soc.*, Fall 1987, *51*(3), pp. 347–54. [G: Brazil]

Deimezis, Nikitas. A Projection of the Input–Output Tables of the Belgian Economy. *Cah. Écon. Bruxelles*, Second Trimester 1987, (114), pp. 421–47. [G: Belgium]

Divay, J. F. and Meunier, F. An Easy Econometric Way of Constructing Input–Output Tables. *Tchijov, I. and Tomaszewicz, L.*, eds., 1987, pp. 79–89.

Erdösi, P. Special Input–Output Model for Analyzing the Effectiveness of the Energy Supply Systems. *Tchijov, I. and Tomaszewicz, L.*, eds., 1987, pp. 185–94. [G: Hungary]

Feldman, Stanley J.; McClain, David and Palmer, Karen. Sources of Structural Change in the United States, 1963–78: An Input–Output Perspective. *Rev. Econ. Statist.*, August 1987, *69*(3), pp. 503–10. [G: U.S.]

Filip-Köhn, Renate and Stäglin, Reiner. On Policy Applications of Input–Output Models in the Federal Republic of Germany. *Tchijov, I. and Tomaszewicz, L.*, eds., 1987, pp. 45–58. [G: W. Germany]

Garhart, Robert E. and Giarratani, Frank. Nonsurvey Input–Output Estimation Techniques: Evidence on the Structure of Errors. *J. Reg. Sci.*, May 1987, *27*(2), pp. 245–53. [G: U.S.]

Gios, Geremia and Miglierina, Claudio. Cost Structure and Integration in the Agro-food Sectors: A Comparative Study in EC Countries.

Europ. Rev. Agr. Econ., 1987, *14*(2), pp. 179–94.   [G: EEC]

Gowdy, John M. and Miller, Jack L. Technological and Demand Change in Energy Use: An Input–Output Analysis. *Environ. Planning A*, October 1987, *19*(10), pp. 1387–98.   [G: U.S.]

Groenewold, Nicolaas; Hagger, A. J. and Madden, J. R. The Measurement of Industry Employment Contribution in an Input–Output Model. *Reg. Stud.*, June 1987, *21*(3), pp. 255–63.

Haji, J. A. Key Sectors and the Structure of Production in Kuwait—An Input–Output Approach. *Appl. Econ.*, September 1987, *19*(9), pp. 1187–1200.   [G: Kuwait]

Halvorson, Alan L. Alternative Approaches to the Estimation of Economic Impacts Resulting from Supply Constraints: Comment and Elaboration. *Ann. Reg. Sci.*, March 1987, *21*(1), pp. 80–83.

Harrison, Glenn W. and Manning, Richard. Best Approximate Aggregation of Input–Output Systems. *J. Amer. Statist. Assoc.*, December 1987, *82*(400), pp. 1027–31.   [G: Australia]

Harthoorn, R. and Wossink, G. A. A. Backward and Forward Effects of Dutch Agriculture. *Europ. Rev. Agr. Econ.*, 1987, *14*(3), pp. 325–33.   [G: Netherlands]

Henry, E. W. Estimating and Testing CES Production Functions on Irish 12-Sector Input–Output Data. *Econ. Soc. Rev.*, July 1987, *18*(4), pp. 223–35.   [G: Ireland]

Henry, E. W. The Impact of the Agriculture and Dependent Food Processing Sectors on the Irish Economy during 1982. *Irish J. Agr. Econ. Rural Soc.*, 1987, *12*, pp. 1–17.   [G: Ireland]

Jensen, R. C. On the Concept of Ready-Made Regional Input–Output Models. *Rev. Reg. Stud.*, Spring 1987, *17*(2), pp. 20–25.

Karasz, Pavol. INFORUM-Type Model for Czechoslovakia. *Tchijov, I. and Tomaszewicz, L., eds.*, 1987, pp. 67–78.
     [G: Czechoslovakia]

Katz, Joseph L. and Burford, Roger L. Shortcut Multiplier Formulas for Interregional Input–Output Models. *Rev. Reg. Stud.*, Spring 1987, *17*(2), pp. 31–45.   [G: Netherlands]

Kazantzev, Sergei V. Financial Restrictions in Optimizing Dynamic Input–Output Model. *Tchijov, I. and Tomaszewicz, L., eds.*, 1987, pp. 91–97.   [G: U.S.S.R.]

Kherbachi, Hamid and Diwan, Romesh. Technical and Structural Change in Algerian Economy: 1969–74. *Indian J. Quant. Econ.*, 1987, *3*(1), pp. 14–26.   [G: Algeria]

Knox, Hugh W. I–O to Go: A Comment on Ready-Made Multipliers. *Rev. Reg. Stud.*, Spring 1987, *17*(2), pp. 25–26.

Kuboniwa, Masaaki. Input–Output Analysis of the Structure of Soviet Foreign Trade—A Comparative View. *Hitotsubashi J. Econ.*, June 1987, *28*(1), pp. 63–85.   [G: U.S.S.R.]

Lipinski, Czeslaw. Changes of Output Capacity Utilization Caused by Structural Changes of Material Inputs. *Tchijov, I. and Tomaszewicz,*

L., eds., 1987, pp. 99–106.   [G: Poland]

Lorenzen, Gunter. On Input–Output Type Output Multipliers from Incomplete Information. *Econ. Planning*, 1987, *21*(1), pp. 31–37.

Maier, Theo. Intervall-Input–Output-Analyse als Grundlage eines Preissystems bei ungenauem Datenmaterial. (Interval-Input–Output-Analysis as the Basis of a Price System with Inexact Data Material. With English summary.) *Jahr. Nationalökon. Statist.*, May 1987, *203*(3), pp. 274–94.

Merrifield, John D. A Note on the General Mathematical Equivalence of Economic Base and Aggregate Input–Output Multipliers: Fact or Fiction. *J. Reg. Sci.*, November 1987, *27*(4), pp. 651–54.

Miernyk, William H. Regional Input–Output Analysis: A Comparison of Five "Ready-Made" Model Systems: Comment. *Rev. Reg. Stud.*, Spring 1987, *17*(2), pp. 17.

Möhr, Malte; Crown, William H. and Polenske, Karen R. A Linear Programming Approach to Solving Infeasible RAS Problems. *J. Reg. Sci.*, November 1987, *27*(4), pp. 587–603.

Ngo, T. W.; Jazayeri, A. and Richardson, Harry W. Regional Policy Simulations with an Interregional Input–Output Model of the Philippines. *Reg. Stud.*, April 1987, *21*(2), pp. 121–29.   [G: Philippines]

Nyhus, Douglas. Exchange Rates: How They Effect Prices and Quantities in the INFORUM-ERI International System of Macroeconomic Input–Output Models. *Tchijov, L. and Tomaszewicz, L., eds.*, 1987, pp. 107–12.   [G: U.S.; Canada; Japan; W. Europe]

Okuguchi, Koji and Szidarovszky, Ferenc. On a Nonlinear Input–Output System: Note. *Math. Soc. Sci.*, June 1987, *13*(3), pp. 277–81.

Petrović, Slavica P. Input–Output prilaz modeliranju i ispitivanju sistema cena radne organizacije. (An Input–Output Approach to Modelling and Examining the Price System of Work Organization. With English summary.) *Econ. Anal. Workers' Manage.*, 1987, *21*(4), pp. 473–89.   [G: Yugoslavia]

Petrović, Slavica P. Matrica tehničkih koeficijenata—analitička i ekonomski instrumentarium istraživanja jednog aspekta strukture proizvodnog sistema radne organizacije. (A Matrix of Technical Coefficients—An Analytical and Economic Instrument for Research into One Aspect of the Structure of the Production System of a Work Organization. With English summary.) *Econ. Anal. Workers' Manage.*, 1987, *21*(1), pp. 95–112.

Pintz, Peter and Havinga, Ivo C. An Energy Input–Output Table of Pakistan for 1979–80 and Some Applications. *Pakistan Devel. Rev.*, Winter 1987, *26*(4), pp. 593–606.   [G: Pakistan]

Planting, Mark A. Input–Output Accounts of the U.S. Economy, 1981. *Surv. Curr. Bus.*, January 1987, *67*(1), pp. 42–58.   [G: U.S.]

Qurashi, M. M. An Energy Input–Output Table of Pakistan for 1979–80 and Some Applications: Comments. *Pakistan Devel. Rev.*, Winter 1987, *26*(4), pp. 607–08.   [G: Pakistan]

Revesz, T. Input–Output Model for Analyzing National Economics of Varying Energy Intensities. *Tchijov, I. and Tomaszewicz, L., eds.,* 1987, pp. 163–67. **[G: Hungary]**

Richter, Josef. Industrial Use of Input–Output Models—Austrian Experiences. *Tchijov, I. and Tomaszewicz, L., eds.,* 1987, pp. 119–24. **[G: Austria]**

Ringwald, Karl. Estimating Input–Output Multipliers from Incomplete I–O Tables. *J. Econ. (Z. Nationalökon.),* 1987, *47*(4), pp. 391–406. **[G: W. Germany]**

Round, Jeffery I. A Note on "Ready-Made" Regional Input–Output Models. *Rev. Reg. Stud.,* Spring 1987, *17*(2), pp. 26–27.

Roy, Dilip Kumar. Employment Linkages in Bangladesh Industries. *Industry Devel.,* 1987, (21), pp. 63–74. **[G: Bangladesh]**

Săcuiu, I. and Enăchescu, Maria. Input–Output Models and Amount of Included Information. *Econ. Computat. Cybern. Stud. Res.,* 1987, *22*(2), pp. 11–22.

Sand, Paal. The Use of Impact Tables in Policy Applications of Input–Output Models. *Tchijov, I. and Tomaszewicz, L., eds.,* 1987, pp. 27–44. **[G: Norway]**

Segura, Julio and Restoy, Fernando. Notas sobre el cambio en la estructura productiva de la economía española 1975–1980. (With English summary.) *Invest. Econ.,* September 1987, *11*(3), pp. 521–52. **[G: Spain]**

Senn, Lanfranco and Miglierina, Claudio. Empirical Tests of the Stochastic Estimation of Technical Coefficients. *Ricerche Econ.,* Jan.-Mar. 1987, *41*(1), pp. 62–81. **[G: Italy]**

Simon, András. An Input–Output Analysis of Prices in the Hungarian Economy between 1981–1985. *Acta Oecon.,* 1987, *38*(1–2), pp. 17–33. **[G: Hungary]**

Siriwardana, A. M. An Input–Output Table for the Colony of Victoria in 1880. *Australian Econ. Hist. Rev.,* March 1987, *27*(1), pp. 61–85. **[G: Australia]**

Smyshlayev, Anatoli. Supply Rigidities in Input–Output Modeling of the Wood and Paper Industry Development. *Tchijov, I. and Tomaszewicz, L., eds.,* 1987, pp. 139–52. **[G: U.S.S.R.]**

Soares, Maria Isabel R. T. L'utilisation de l'énergie dans un contexte interindustriel: analyse du profil enérgétique de l'inudstrie portugaise des textiles et de l'habillement. (With English summary.) *Economia (Portugal),* May 1987, *11*(2), pp. 157–70. **[G: Portugal]**

Stevens, Benjamin H. "Ready-Made" Regional Input–Output Model Systems: Model Accuracy and the Value of Limited Surveys: Comments. *Rev. Reg. Stud.,* Spring 1987, *17*(2), pp. 17–20.

Swenson, Charles W. and Moore, Michael L. Use of Input–Ouput Analysis in Tax Research. *Jones, S. M., ed.,* 1987, pp. 49–83. **[G: U.S.]**

Szybisz, Boguslaw. Towards the Integration of Input–Output Tables with National Accounts. *Statist. J.,* July 1987, *4*(4), pp. 313–22.

Tchijov, Iouri and Sytchova, Irene. Technological

Progress Analysis: Some Input–Output Approaches. *Tchijov, I. and Tomaszewicz, L., eds.,* 1987, pp. 59–65. **[G: Japan]**

Tchijov, Iouri and Tomaszewicz, Lucja. Input–Output Modeling: Introduction. *Tchijov, I. and Tomaszewicz, L., eds.,* 1987, pp. 1–5.

Thomas, Mark. General Equilibrium Models and Research in Economic History. *Field, A. J., ed.,* 1987, pp. 121–83.

Willis, K. G. Spatially Disaggregated Input–Output Tables: An Evaluation and Comparison of Survey and Nonsurvey Results. *Environ. Planning A,* January 1987, *19*(1), pp. 107–16.

Yokokura, Hiroyuki. Interindustry Analysis and Unit Structure in the Yugoslav Economy. *Econ. Anal. Workers' Manage.,* 1987, *21*(3), pp. 313–32. **[G: Yugoslavia]**

223 Financial Accounts

2230 Financial Accounts; Financial Statistics; Empirical Analyses of Capital Adequacy

Barbera, Anthony J. Inflation, Tax Rules, and Investment: Some Additional Evidence. *J. Post Keynesian Econ.,* Spring 1987, *9*(3), pp. 315–26.

Blinder, Alan S. Why Is U.S. National Saving So Low? Comments. *Brookings Pap. Econ. Act.,* 1987, (2), pp. 636–38. **[G: U.S.]**

Byrd, William A. and Tidrick, Gene. China's Industrial Reform: Factor Allocation and Enterprise Incentives. *Tidrick, G. and Jiyuan, C., eds.,* 1987, pp. 60–102. **[G: China]**

Horvei, Tore, et al. Financial Markets in the Nordic Countries. *Vartia, P., et al.,* 1987, pp. 237–301. **[G: Denmark; Sweden; Finland; Norway]**

Kopcke, Richard W. Financial Assets, Interest Rates, and Money Growth. *New Eng. Econ. Rev.,* Mar./Apr. 1987, pp. 17–30. **[G: U.S.]**

Pitelis, Christos N. Corporate Retained Earnings and the 'Kaldorian' Hypothesis of Saving. *Brit. Rev. Econ. Issues,* Spring 1987, *9*(20), pp. 79–95. **[G: U.K.]**

Ruggles, Nancy D. Financial Accounts and Balance Sheets: Issues for the Revision of SNA. *Rev. Income Wealth,* March 1987, *33*(1), pp. 39–62.

Sarcinelli, Mario. Financial Assets, Public Debt and Monetary Policy: An International Integration Perspective. *Banca Naz. Lavoro Quart. Rev.,* September 1987, (162), pp. 263–372. **[G: Italy]**

Sato, Kazuo. The Political Economy of Japan: Saving and Investment. *Yamamura, K. and Yasuba, Y., eds.,* 1987, pp. 137–85. **[G: Japan]**

Summers, Lawrence H. and Carroll, Chris. Why Is U.S. National Saving So Low? *Brookings Pap. Econ. Act.,* 1987, (2), pp. 607–35. **[G: U.S.]**

Terzi, Andrea. The Independence of Finance from Saving: A Flow-of-Funds Interpretation. *J. Post Keynesian Econ.,* Winter 1986-87, *9*(2), pp. 188–97.

Visser, Hans; Eijgenhuijsen, Hans and Koelewijn, Jaap. Capital Ratios, Own Funds and Investment in The Netherlands. *Nat. Westminster Bank Quart. Rev.*, February 1987, pp. 39–50. **[G: Netherlands]**

224 National Wealth and Balance Sheets

2240 National Wealth and Balance Sheets

Bennett, Adam. Wealth and the Dynamics of Macroeconomic Adjustment. *Econ. Modelling*, January 1987, *4*(1), pp. 3–18. **[G: U.K.]**

Bernheim, B. Douglas. Dissaving after Retirement: Testing the Pure Life Cycle Hypothesis. *Bodie, Z.; Shoven, J. B. and Wise, D. A., eds.*, 1987, pp. 237–74. **[G: U.S.]**

Bhatia, Kul B. Real Estate Assets and Consumer Spending. *Quart. J. Econ.*, May 1987, *102*(2), pp. 437–44. **[G: U.S.]**

Buyst, Erik. Investeringen in woongebouwen in België tijdens de grote depressie van de jaren dertig en gedurende de huidige economische crisis: Een verkennende vergelijking. (With English summary.) *Cah. Écon. Bruxelles*, Fourth Trimester 1987, (116), pp. 99–116. **[G: Belgium]**

Chawluk, Antoni. Is Soviet Capital Too Old? *Economica*, August 1987, *54*(215), pp. 335–54. **[G: U.S.S.R.]**

Davis, Lance E.; Gallman, Robert E. and Hutchins, Teresa D. The Structure of the Capital Stock in Economic Growth and Decline: The New Bedford Whaling Fleet in the Nineteenth Century. *Kilby, P., ed.*, 1987, pp. 336–98. **[G: U.S.]**

Domar, Evsey D. The Interrelation between Capital and Output in the American Economy. *Dupriez, L. H., ed.*, 1987, pp. 210–26. **[G: U.S.]**

Duncan, William A.; O'Dell, Michael A. and Panich, Richard L. Potential Personal Wealth Redistribution Effects of Structural Income Tax Reform. *Jones, S. M., ed.*, 1987, pp. 1–21. **[G: U.S.]**

Gallman, Robert E. Investment Flows and Capital Stocks: U.S. Experience in the Nineteenth Century. *Kilby, P., ed.*, 1987, pp. 214–54. **[G: U.S.]**

Greenwood, Daphne T. Age, Income, and Household Size: Their Relation to Wealth Distribution in the United States. *Wolff, E. N., ed.*, 1987, pp. 121–40. **[G: U.S.]**

Gutiérrez U., Mario A. Ahorro interno y crecimiento económico: Un enfoque de cuentas nacionales. (With English summary.) *Cuadernos Econ.*, December 1987, *24*(73), pp. 331–57. **[G: Chile]**

Harbury, C. D. and Hitchens, D. M. W. N. The Influence of Relative Prices on the Distribution of Wealth and the Measurement of Inheritance. *Wolff, E. N., ed.*, 1987, pp. 248–75. **[G: U.K.]**

Hurd, Michael D. Dissaving after Retirement: Testing the Pure Life Cycle Hypothesis: Comment. *Bodie, Z.; Shoven, J. B. and Wise, D. A., eds.*, 1987, pp. 275–79. **[G: U.S.]**

Ioannides, Yannis M. and Sato, Ryuzo. On the Distribution of Wealth and Intergenerational Transfers. *J. Lab. Econ.*, July 1987, *5*(3), pp. 366–85.

James, John A. and Skinner, Jonathan S. Sources of Savings in the Nineteenth Century United States. *Kilby, P., ed.*, 1987, pp. 255–85. **[G: U.S.]**

Jenkins, Stephen. The Implications of 'Stochastic' Demographic Assumptions for Models of the Distribution of Inherited Wealth: Correction. *Bull. Econ. Res.*, April 1987, *39*(2), pp. 185.

Kessler, Denis and Masson, André. Personal Wealth Distribution in France: Cross-Sectional Evidence and Extensions. *Wolff, E. N., ed.*, 1987, pp. 141–76. **[G: France]**

Kokoski, Mary F. Indices of Household Welfare and the Value of Leisure Time. *Rev. Econ. Statist.*, February 1987, *69*(1), pp. 83–89. **[G: U.S.]**

Levy, Béatrice. Le patrimoine des agriculteurs en France. (With English summary.) *Léon, Y. and Mahé, L., eds.*, 1987, pp. 309–23. **[G: France]**

Maddison, Angus. Growth and Slowdown in Advanced Capitalist Economies: Techniques of Quantitative Assessment. *J. Econ. Lit.*, June 1987, *25*(2), pp. 649–98. **[G: OECD]**

McCants, Blaine E. Projecting Soviet Energy Requirements Using a Vintage Capital Model. *J. Compar. Econ.*, December 1987, *11*(4), pp. 572–83. **[G: U.S.S.R.]**

Otto, Lars. Konstruktion af erhvervsfordelte kapitaldata for Danmark. (Construction of Capital Equipment Data for the Danish Economy. With English summary.) *Nationaløkon. Tidsskr.*, 1987, *125*(3), pp. 378–89. **[G: Denmark]**

Piggott, John. The Nation's Private Wealth—Some New Calculations for Australia. *Econ. Rec.*, March 1987, *63*(180), pp. 61–79. **[G: Australia]**

Pozdena, Randall Johnston. Inflation, Age, and Wealth. *Fed. Res. Bank San Francisco Econ. Rev.*, Winter 1987, (1), pp. 17–30. **[G: U.S.]**

Radner, Daniel B. and Vaughan, Denton R. Wealth, Income, and the Economic Status of Aged Households. *Wolff, E. N., ed.*, 1987, pp. 93–120. **[G: U.S.]**

Rao, M. J. Manohar. Development Planning Theory and the Use of Prior Information to Obtain a Benchmark Estimate of Capital-Stock: Case Study for India. *Indian J. Quant. Econ.*, 1987, *3*(2), pp. 21–33. **[G: India]**

Sato, Kazuo. The Political Economy of Japan: Saving and Investment. *Yamamura, K. and Yasuba, Y., eds.*, 1987, pp. 137–85. **[G: Japan]**

Shorrocks, Anthony F. UK Wealth Distribution: Current Evidence and Future Prospects. *Wolff, E. N., ed.*, 1987, pp. 29–50. **[G: U.K.]**

Smith, Alasdair. A Current Cost Accounting Measure of Britain's Stock of Equipment. *Nat. Inst. Econ. Rev.*, May 1987, (120), pp. 42–57. **[G: U.K.]**

Smith, James D. Recent Trends in the Distribution of Wealth in the U.S.: Data, Research Problems, and Prospects. *Wolff, E. N., ed.,* 1987, pp. 72–89. [G: U.S.]

Spånt, Roland. Wealth Distribution in Sweden: 1920–1983. *Wolff, E. N., ed.,* 1987, pp. 51–71. [G: Sweden]

Weale, Martin. The Cambridge Multisectoral Dynamic Model of the British Economy: Financial Stocks and Returns. *Barker, T. and Peterson, W., eds.,* 1987, pp. 411–31. [G: U.K.]

Wolff, Edward N. Estimates of Household Wealth Inequality in the U.S., 1962–1983. *Rev. Income Wealth,* September 1987, *33*(3), pp. 231–56. [G: U.S.]

Wolff, Edward N. The Effects of Pensions and Social Security on the Distribution of Wealth in the U.S. *Wolff, E. N., ed.,* 1987, pp. 208–47. [G: U.S.]

Wolff, Edward N. and Marley, Marcia. International Comparisons of the Distribution of Household Wealth: Introduction and Overview. *Wolff, E. N., ed.,* 1987, pp. 1–26. [G: Canada; France; Sweden; U.K.; U.S.]

225 Social Indicators: Data and Analysis

2250 Social Indicators: Data and Analysis

Bailly, Antoine S. Les indicateurs sociaux: des mesures objectives des sciences dures aux évaluations subjectives des sciences molles. (Social Indicators: From Objective Indicators of the Hard Sciences to Subjective Evaluation of Soft Sciences. With English summary.) *Schweiz. Z. Volkswirtsch. Statist.,* September 1987, *123*(3), pp. 341–51.

Bronfenbrenner, Martin and Yasuba, Yasukichi. The Political Economy of Japan: Economic Welfare. *Yamamura, K. and Yasuba, Y., eds.,* 1987, pp. 93–136. [G: Japan]

Cornia, Giovanni Andrea. Economic Decline and Human Welfare in the First Half of the 1980s. *Cornia, G. A.; Jolly, R. and Stewart, F., eds.,* 1987, pp. 11–47. [G: Global]

Dixon, William J. Progress in the Provision of Basic Human Needs: Latin America, 1960–1980. *J. Devel. Areas,* January 1987, *21*(2), pp. 129–39. [G: Latin America]

Fox, Karl A. The Eco-behavioral View of Human Societies: Behavior Settings, Time-Allocation Matrices, and Social System Accounts. *Fox, K. A. and Miles, D. G., eds.,* 1987, pp. 118–42.

Jamal, Haroon and Malik, Salman. Working with Statistics of Quality of Life: Pakistan, 1960 to 1983. *Devel. Econ.,* September 1987, *25*(3), pp. 270–80. [G: Pakistan]

Marcus, Solomon. Semiotics and the System of Social Indicators—A Few Landmarks. *Econ. Computat. Cybern. Stud. Res.,* 1987, *22*(2), pp. 77–80.

Martellaro, Joseph A. Investment in Human Resources: The Experience of Five Third World Nations. *Rivista Int. Sci. Econ. Com.,* April 1987, *34*(4), pp. 273–90. [G: Egypt; Ethiopia; Mongolia; Pakistan; Paraguay]

van Moeseke, Paul. The Dollar Values of Social Variables: Two Models of Social Income. *Fox, K. A. and Miles, D. G., eds.,* 1987, pp. 143–57.

Stewart, Frances. Monitoring and Statistics for Adjustment with a Human Face. *Cornia, G. A.; Jolly, R. and Stewart, F., eds.,* 1987, pp. 257–72.

Thernstrom, Abigail. Statistics and the Politics of Minority Representation: The Evolution of the Voting Rights Act since 1965. *Alonso, W. and Starr, P., eds.,* 1987, pp. 303–27.

Thomas, Mark. General Equilibrium Models and Research in Economic History. *Field, A. J., ed.,* 1987, pp. 121–83.

Weiss, Janet A. and Gruber, Judith E. The Managed Irrelevance of Federal Education Statistics. *Alonso, W. and Starr, P., eds.,* 1987, pp. 363–91. [G: U.S.]

226 Productivity and Growth: Theory and Data

2260 Productivity and Growth: Theory and Data

Aboagye, A.; Gozo, K. and Ahmed, Iftikhar. World Recession and Global Interdependence: Sub-Saharan Africa. *International Labour Office.,* 1987, pp. 75–98. [G: Sub-Saharan Africa]

Adams, Charles; Fenton, Paul R. and Larsen, Flemming. Potential Output in Major Industrial Countries. *International Monetary Fund Research Department.,* 1987, pp. 1–38. [G: OECD]

Ahlburg, Dennis A. The Impact of Population Growth on Economic Growth in Developing Nations: The Evidence from Macroeconomic–Demographic Models. *Johnson, D. G. and Lee, R. D., eds.,* 1987, pp. 479–521. [G: LDCs]

Aldrich, Robert. Late-Comer or Early-Starter? New Views on French Economic History. *J. Europ. Econ. Hist.,* Spring 1987, *16*(1), pp. 89–100. [G: France]

Aliber, Robert Z. Financial Markets and the Growth of Europe. *Lawrence, R. Z. and Schultze, C. L., eds.,* 1987, pp. 384–409. [G: W. Europe; U.S.]

Atack, Jeremy. Economies of Scale and Efficiency Gains in the Rise of the Factory in America, 1820–1900. *Kilby, P., ed.,* 1987, pp. 286–335. [G: U.S.]

Baily, Martin Neil. Crazy Explanations for the Productivity Slowdown: Comment. *Fischer, S., ed.,* 1987, pp. 205–08.

Bairam, Erkin I. The Verdoorn Law, Returns to Scale and Industrial Growth: A Review of the Literature. *Australian Econ. Pap.,* June 1987, *26*(48), pp. 20–42. [G: OECD]

Bechtold, Hartmut and Helfer, Andreas. Stagflation Problems in Socialist Economies. *Gey, P.; Kosta, J. and Quaisser, W., eds.,* 1987, pp. 11–31. [G: Hungary; Yugoslavia]

Begg, David K. H. Long-run Implications of the Increase in Taxation and Public Debt for Employment and Economic Growth in Europe: Comments. *Europ. Econ. Rev.*, April 1987, *31*(3), pp. 775–77.   **[G: W. Europe]**

Bernanke, Ben S. Crazy Explanations for the Productivity Slowdown: Comment. *Fischer, S., ed.*, 1987, pp. 202–05.

Berndt, Ernst R. and Wood, David O. Energy Price Shocks and Productivity Growth: A Survey. *[Adelman, M. A.]*, 1987, pp. 305–42.

Bispham, J. A. Rising Public-Sector Indebtedness: Some More Unpleasant Arithmetic. *Boskin, M. J.; Fleming, J. S. and Gorini, S., eds.*, 1987, pp. 40–71.   **[G: OECD]**

Bond, Marian E. and Milne, Elizabeth. Export Diversification in Developing Countries: Recent Trends and Policy Impact. *International Monetary Fund Research Department.*, 1987, pp. 98–144.   **[G: LDCs]**

Boretsky, Michael. The Tenability of the CIA Estimates of Soviet Economic Growth. *J. Compar. Econ.*, December 1987, *11*(4), pp. 517–42.   **[G: U.S.S.R.; U.S.; W. Germany]**

Borpujari, Jitendra G. Consumption and Productivity Patterns and Their Implications for the Production Structure. *Pasinetti, L. and Lloyd, P., eds.*, 1987, pp. 75–90. **[G: Global]**

Bosworth, Barry P. and Lawrence, Robert Z. Adjusting to Slower Economic Growth: The Domestic Economy. *Bosworth, B. P. and Rivlin, A. M., eds.*, 1987, pp. 22–54.
                    [G: Sweden]

Boyer, Robert. The Current Economic Crisis: Its Dynamics and Its Implications for France. *Ross, G.; Hoffmann, S. and Malzacher, S., eds.*, 1987, pp. 33–53.   **[G: France]**

Brinkman, Richard L. Democratic Planning in a Market Economy and Social Values. *Gemper, B. B., ed.*, 1987, pp. 21–36.   **[G: U.S.; W. Germany; Japan; U.K.]**

Brown, Clair. Consumption Norms, Work Roles, and Economic Growth, 1918–80. *Brown, C. and Pechman, J. A., eds.*, 1987, pp. 13–49.
                    [G: U.S.]

Bruno, Michael. Stagflation in the Industrial Countries: An Updated Overview. *Hitotsubashi J. Econ.*, October 1987, *27*, pp. 57–74.
                    [G: OECD]

Byrd, William A. and Tidrick, Gene. China's Industrial Reform: Factor Allocation and Enterprise Incentives. *Tidrick, G. and Jiyuan, C., eds.*, 1987, pp. 60–102.   **[G: China]**

Carter, Susan B. Consumption Norms, Work Roles, and Economic Growth, 1918–80: Comments. *Brown, C. and Pechman, J. A., eds.*, 1987, pp. 49–54.   **[G: U.S.]**

Chakraborti, Sibaji. Growth Pattern of National Income: A Time-Series Study. *Indian Econ. J.*, Apr.-June 1987, *34*(4), pp. 18–24.
                    [G: India]

Chen, Edward K. Y. Foreign Trade and Economic Growth in Hong Kong: Experience and Prospects. *Bradford, C. I., Jr. and Branson, W. H., eds.*, 1987, pp. 333–78. **[G: Hong Kong]**

Dahrendorf, Ralf. Slow Growth in Europe: Conceptual Issues: Comment. *Lawrence, R. Z. and*

Schultze, C. L., eds., 1987, pp. 76–79.
                    [G: W. Europe]

Daly, Herman E. The Economic Growth Debate: What Some Economists Have Learned but Many Have Not. *J. Environ. Econ. Manage.*, December 1987, *14*(4), pp. 323–36.

Dervis, Kemal and Petri, Peter A. The Macroeconomics of Successful Development: What Are the Lessons? *Fischer, S., ed.*, 1987, pp. 211–54.   **[G: LDCs]**

Desai, Padma. Soviet Growth Retardation: Causes and Consequences. *Desai, P.*, 1987, pp. 7–60.   **[G: U.S.S.R.]**

Desai, Padma. The Rate of Return on Foreign Capital Inflow to the Soviet Economy. *Desai, P.*, 1987, pp. 133–52.   **[G: U.S.S.R.]**

Desai, Padma. Total Factor Productivity in Postwar Soviet Industry and Its Branches. *Desai, P.*, 1987, *1985*, pp. 78–98.   **[G: U.S.S.R.]**

Desai, Padma and Martin, Ricardo. Efficiency Loss from Resource Misallocation in Soviet Industry. *Desai, P.*, 1987, *1983*, pp. 117–29.
                    [G: U.S.S.R.]

Domar, Evsey D. The Interrelation between Capital and Output in the American Economy. *Dupriez, L. H., ed.*, 1987, pp. 210–26.
                    [G: U.S.]

Dornbusch, Rudiger and Layard, Richard. The Performance of the British Economy: Introduction. *Dornbusch, R. and Layard, R., eds.*, 1987, pp. 1–5.   **[G: U.K.]**

Drèze, Jacques H. Slow Growth in Europe: Conceptual Issues: Comment. *Lawrence, R. Z. and Schultze, C. L., eds.*, 1987, pp. 79–93.
                    [G: W. Europe]

Duchêne, François and Shepherd, Geoffrey. Western Europe: A Family of Contrasts. *Duchêne, F. and Shepherd, G., eds.*, 1987, pp. 21–40.   **[G: W. Europe]**

Dudler, Hermann-Josef. Financial Markets and the Growth of Europe: Comment. *Lawrence, R. Z. and Schultze, C. L., eds.*, 1987, pp. 409–14.   **[G: W. Europe; U.S.]**

Dupriez, Léon H. Principles of a Theory of Secular Economic Movement. *Dupriez, L. H., ed.*, 1987, *1955*, pp. 365–79.

Eastwood, Robert. Forecasting Investment in the Medium Term. *Freeman, C. and Soete, L., eds.*, 1987, pp. 73–85.

Eliasson, Gunnar. Dynamic Micro–Macro Co-ordination, Technical Change and Trade. *Eliasson, G.*, 1987, pp. 81–118.   **[G: Sweden]**

Ergas, Henry. Does Technology Policy Matter? *Guile, B. R. and Brooks, H., eds.*, 1987, pp. 191–245.   **[G: U.K.; U.S.; France; Japan]**

Feldman, Stanley J. Impact of Final Demand Changes on Interindustry Growth Prospects. *Faruqui, A. and Broehl, J., eds.*, 1987, pp. 143–59.   **[G: U.S.]**

Feldstein, Martin S. Long-run Implications of the Increase in Taxation and Public Debt for Employment and Economic Growth in Europe: Comments. *Europ. Econ. Rev.*, April 1987, *31*(3), pp. 778–80.   **[G: W. Europe]**

Fennema, Meindert and van der Pijl, Kees. International Bank Capital and the New Liberalism. *Mizruchi, M. S. and Schwartz, M., eds.*, 1987, pp. 298–319.   [G: EEC; Japan; U.S.]

Fourastié, Jean. The Statistical Measurement of Various Material Aspects of Economic Progress. *Dupriez, L. H., ed.*, 1987, *1955*, pp. 21–36.

Goldstein, Joshua S. Long Waves in War, Production, Prices, and Wages. *J. Conflict Resolution*, December 1987, *31*(4), pp. 573–600.
[G: Selected MDCs]

Gollop, Frank M. Modeling Aggregate Productivity Growth: The Importance of Intersectoral Transfer Prices and International Trade. *Rev. Income Wealth*, June 1987, *33*(2), pp. 211–27.
[G: OECD]

Gonçalves, Reinaldo and Richtering, Jürgen. Intercountry Comparison of Export Performance and Output Growth. *Devel. Econ.*, March 1987, *25*(1), pp. 3–18.   [G: LDCs]

Gupta, Pradeep C. and Faruqui, Ahmad. Assessing the Future Competitiveness of American Industry in World Markets: Some Preliminary Results. *Faruqui, A. and Broehl, J., eds.*, 1987, pp. 199–218.   [G: U.S.]

Gutowski, Armin. Slow Growth in Europe: Conceptual Issues: Comment. *Lawrence, R. Z. and Schultze, C. L., eds.*, 1987, pp. 93–98.
[G: W. Europe]

Hahn, Frank H. "Of Marx and Keynes and Many Things": A Review Article. *Sinclair, P. J. N., ed.*, 1987, *1986*, pp. 378–85.

Hale, David D. Twilight of Anglo-American Power. *Challenge*, Sept./Oct. 1987, *30*(4), pp. 52–55.   [G: OECD]

Harberger, Arnold C. The Macroeconomics of Successful Development: What Are the Lessons? Comment. *Fischer, S., ed.*, 1987, pp. 255–58.

Heitger, Bernhard. Corporatism, Technological Gaps and Growth in OECD Countries. *Weltwirtsch. Arch.*, 1987, *123*(3), pp. 463–73.
[G: OECD]

Heitger, Bernhard. Import Protection and Export Performance—Their Impact on Economic Growth. *Weltwirtsch. Arch.*, 1987, *123*(2), pp. 249–61.   [G: Global]

Hickman, Bert G. Growth, Inflation and Unemployment in the United States. *Pasinetti, L. and Lloyd, P., eds.*, 1987, pp. 293–300.
[G: U.S.]

Hieronymi, Otto. Reflections on Technology, International Order and Economic Growth. *Hieronymi, O., ed.*, 1987, pp. 69–95. [G: OECD]

Hong, Wontack. Export-Oriented Growth and Trade Patterns of Korea. *Bradford, C. I., Jr. and Branson, W. H., eds.*, 1987, pp. 273–305.
[G: S. Korea]

Hong, Wontack. Trade, Growth and Economic Problems of Asian NICs. *Hitotsubashi J. Econ.*, October 1987, *27*, pp. 79–100.
[G: Asian NICs]

Hufbauer, Gary Clyde. The Competitiveness Gap. *Barfield, C. E. and Makin, J. H., eds.*, 1987, pp. 43–45.   [G: U.S.]

Jacquemin, Alexis. Trade Performance as a Constraint on European Growth: Comment. *Lawrence, R. Z. and Schultze, C. L., eds.*, 1987, pp. 374–81.   [G: W. Europe]

James, Jeffrey. Population and Technical Change in the Manufacturing Sector of Developing Countries. *Johnson, D. G. and Lee, R. D., eds.*, 1987, pp. 225–56.   [G: LDCs]

Jorgenson, Dale W.; Kuroda, Masahiro and Nishimizu, Mieko. Japan–U.S. Industry-Level Productivity Comparisons, 1960–1979. *J. Japanese Int. Economies*, March 1987, *1*(1), pp. 1–30.   [G: U.S.; Japan]

Kasman, Bruce. Japan's Growth Performance over the Last Decade. *Fed. Res. Bank New York Quart. Rev.*, Summer 1987, *12*(2), pp. 45–55.   [G: Japan]

Kemme, David M. Productivity Growth in Polish Industry. *J. Compar. Econ.*, March 1987, *11*(1), pp. 1–20.   [G: Poland]

Klein, Lawrence R. Growth, Inflation and Employment: Discussion and Conclusions. *Pasinetti, L. and Lloyd, P., eds.*, 1987, pp. 323–25.

Klein, Lawrence R. Growth, Inflation and Employment: An Introduction. *Pasinetti, L. and Lloyd, P., eds.*, 1987, pp. 269–74.
[G: Global]

Krelle, Wilhelm. Long-term Fluctuations of Technical Progress and Growth. *J. Inst. Theoretical Econ.*, September 1987, *143*(3), pp. 379–401.
[G: OECD; CMEA]

Krishnamurty, K. Inflation and Growth: Some Experiments on a Model for India. *Pasinetti, L. and Lloyd, P., eds.*, 1987, pp. 305–22.
[G: India]

Krugman, Paul R. Slow Growth in Europe: Conceptual Issues. *Lawrence, R. Z. and Schultze, C. L., eds.*, 1987, pp. 48–76.
[G: W. Europe]

Kuisel, Richard F. French Post-war Economic Growth: A Historical Perspective on the *Trente Glorieuses*. *Ross, G.; Hoffmann, S. and Malzacher, S., eds.*, 1987, pp. 18–32.
[G: France]

Kuznets, Simon. Population, Income and Capital. *Dupriez, L. H., ed.*, 1987, *1955*, pp. 3–20.
[G: Global]

Lawrence, Robert Z. Trade Performance as a Constraint on European Growth. *Lawrence, R. Z. and Schultze, C. L., eds.*, 1987, pp. 303–74.   [G: W. Europe]

Lawrence, Robert Z. and Schultze, Charles L. Barriers to European Growth: Overview. *Lawrence, R. Z. and Schultze, C. L., eds.*, 1987, pp. 1–47.   [G: W. Europe]

Lebergott, Stanley. Consumption Norms, Work Roles, and Economic Growth, 1918–80: Comments. *Brown, C. and Pechman, J. A., eds.*, 1987, pp. 54–58.   [G: U.S.]

Lee, E. World Recession and Developing Economies in Asia. *International Labour Office.*, 1987, pp. 99–132.   [G: Asia]

MacCharles, D. C. International Knowledge Transfers and Competitiveness: Canada as a Case Study. *Safarian, A. E. and Bertin, G. Y., eds.*, 1987, pp. 53–69.   [G: Canada]

Maddison, Angus. Growth and Slowdown in Advanced Capitalist Economies: Techniques of Quantitative Assessment. *J. Econ. Lit.*, June 1987, 25(2), pp. 649–98. [G: OECD]

Maddock, Rodney. The Australian Economy in the Long Run: The Long Boom 1940–1970. *Maddock, R. and McLean, I. W., eds.*, 1987, pp. 79–105. [G: Australia]

Maier, Charles S. The Politics of Productivity: Foundations of American International Economic Policy after World War II. *Maier, C. S.*, 1987, *1977*, pp. 121–52. [G: U.S.]

Marston, Richard C. Real Exchange Rates and Productivity Growth in the United States and Japan. *Arndt, S. W. and Richardson, J. D. eds.*, 1987, pp. 71–96. [G: U.S.; Japan]

Martellaro, Joseph A. and Chen, Jing-Yau. Some Aspects of Growth and Technical Progress in the People's Republic of China. *Econ. Int.*, November 1987, 40(4), pp. 301–16. [G: China]

Mathur, Ashok. 'Why Growth Rates Differ' within India: An Alternative Approach. *J. Devel. Stud.*, January 1987, 23(2), pp. 167–99. [G: India]

McCallum, John and Blais, André. Government, Special Interest Groups, and Economic Growth. *Public Choice*, 1987, 54(1), pp. 3–18. [G: OECD]

Mirakhor, Abbas and Montiel, Peter J. Import Intensity of Output Growth in Developing Countries, 1970–85. *International Monetary Fund Research Department.*, 1987, pp. 59–97. [G: LDCs]

Mitek, Lars. Denmark: Unsustainable Recovery. *Vartia, P., et al.*, 1987, pp. 61–103. [G: Denmark]

Monti, Mario. Financial Markets and the Growth of Europe: Comment. *Lawrence, R. Z. and Schultze, C. L., eds.*, 1987, pp. 414–18. [G: W. Europe; U.S.]

Nagel, Stuart S. The New Productivity. *Nagel, S. S., ed.*, 1987, pp. 271–84. [G: U.S.]

Naya, Seiji. Economic Performance and Growth Factors of the ASEAN Countries. *Martin, L. G., ed.*, 1987, pp. 47–87. [G: ASEAN]

Nwanna, Gladson I. Devaluation, Unanticipated Inflation and Output Growth: A Comparative Aggregate Analysis. *Econ. Int.*, November 1987, 40(4), pp. 329–44. [G: LDCs]

Ofer, Gur. Soviet Economic Growth: 1928–1985. *J. Econ. Lit.*, December 1987, 25(4), pp. 1767–1833. [G: U.S.S.R.]

Okyar, Osman. A New Look at the Problem of Economic Growth in the Ottoman Empire (1800–1914). *J. Europ. Econ. Hist.*, Spring 1987, 16(1), pp. 7–49. [G: Ottoman Empire]

Oxelheim, Lars. Sweden: Is Something Wrong with the Growth Engine? *Vartia, P., et al.*, 1987, pp. 171–205. [G: Sweden]

Pollard, Sidney. Comment on Peter Temin's Comment [Capital Exports: 1870–1914: Harmful or Beneficial?]. *Econ. Hist. Rev., 2nd Ser.*, August 1987, 40(3), pp. 459–60. [G: U.K.]

Proulx, Pierre-Paul. A Review of Studies of Sectoral Impacts of Bilateral and Multilateral Trade

Liberalization on Canada. *Tremblay, R., ed.*, 1987, pp. 463–530. [G: Canada; U.S.]

Ram, Rati. Economic Growth and Structure of Domestic Absorption: Evidence from Internationally Comparable Data. *J. Devel. Econ.*, August 1987, 26(2), pp. 291–300.

Ram, Rati. Exports and Economic Growth in Developing Countries: Evidence from Time-Series and Cross-Section Data. *Econ. Develop. Cult. Change*, October 1987, 36(1), pp. 51–72. [G: LDCs]

Ransom, Michael R. Economic Growth and the Size Distribution of Income; a Longitudinal Analysis. *Heijmans, R. and Neudecker, H., eds.*, 1987, pp. 165–77. [G: MDCs]

Riaz, T. Energy and Economic Growth: A Case Study of Pakistan. *Energy Econ.*, July 1987, 9(3), pp. 195–204. [G: Pakistan]

Ridley, William P. Japan: An Uneasy Transition to a Rentier Society. *[Marjolin, R.]*, 1987, pp. 169–89. [G: Japan]

Romer, Paul M. Crazy Explanations for the Productivity Slowdown. *Fischer, S., ed.*, 1987, pp. 163–202.

Rostow, Walt W. The Rich Country–Poor Country Problem: From the Eighteenth to the Twenty-first Century. *Rostow, W. W.*, 1987, pp. 49–78. [G: Global]

Rostow, Walt W. The Rich Country–Poor Country Problem: From the Eighteenth to the Twenty-first Centuries. *Steinherr, A. and Weiserbs, D., eds.*, 1987, pp. 47–83. [G: Global]

Rostow, Walt W. The World Economy since 1945: A Stylized Historical Analysis. *Rostow, W. W.*, 1987, *1985*, pp. 19–48. [G: Global]

Rostow, Walt W. Trends in the Allocation of Resources in Secular Growth. *Dupriez, L. H., ed.*, 1987, *1955*, pp. 294–307.

Sachs, Ignacy. Development or Misdevelopment: A Plea for Anthropological Economics. *Sachs, I.*, 1987, pp. 59–68.

Schott, Kerry. Lessons for Australia. *Stegman, T., et al.*, 1987, pp. 25–52. [G: Australia; W. Europe; U.K.; Japan]

Schultze, Charles L. Saving, Investment, and Profitability in Europe. *Lawrence, R. Z. and Schultze, C. L., eds.*, 1987, pp. 508–39. [G: W. Europe]

Scitovsky, Tibor. Growth in the Affluent Society. *Lloyds Bank Rev.*, January 1987, (163), pp. 1–14. [G: U.K.; U.S.]

Searl, Milton F. The Relationship of Electricity to Aggregate Economic Activity in Industrial Economies—Some Empirical Observations. *Pachauri, R. K., ed.*, 1987, pp. 601–20. [G: MDCs]

Shishido, Shuntaro. Remarks on Growth, Inflation and Employment. *Pasinetti, L. and Lloyd, P., eds.*, 1987, pp. 301–03. [G: Global]

Sinnett, M. W. Method versus Methodology: A Note on *The Ultimate Resource. Rothbard, M. N., ed.*, 1987, pp. 207–23.

Sneessens, Henri R. and Drèze, Jacques H. A Discussion of Belgian Unemployment, Combining Traditional Concepts and Disequi-

librium Econometrics. *Steinherr, A. and Weiserbs, D., eds.*, 1987, pp. 239–82.
[G: Belgium]

Stavrinos, Vasilios G. The Intertemporal Stability of Kaldor's First and Second Growth Laws in the UK. *Appl. Econ.*, September 1987, *19*(9), pp. 1201–09. [G: U.K.]

Šujan, Ivan. An Analysis of Factors Contributing to the Deceleration in the Growth Rate of the Czechoslovak Economy in the Period 1975–1980: A Simulation Analysis Using an Econometric Model. *Soviet E. Europ. Foreign Trade*, Spring 1987, *23*(1), pp. 31–53.
[G: Czechoslovakia]

Syrquin, Moshe. Growth Accounting with Intermediate Inputs and the Transmission of Technical Change. *J. Devel. Econ.*, June 1987, *26*(1), pp. 17–23.

Temin, Peter. Capital Exports, 1870–1914: An Alternative Model: Comment [Capital Exports: 1870–1914: Harmful or Beneficial?]. *Econ. Hist. Rev., 2nd Ser.*, August 1987, *40*(3), pp. 453–58. [G: U.K.]

Thompson, Grahame. Objectives and Instruments of Economic Management. *Thompson, G.; Brown, V. and Levačić, R., eds.*, 1987, pp. 1–37. [G: U.K.]

Thompson, Grahame. The Supply Side and Industrial Policy. *Thompson, G.; Brown, V. and Levačić, R., eds.*, 1987, pp. 254–92.
[G: U.S.; U.K.; W. Europe]

Thurow, Lester C. Can America Compete in the World Economy? *Shetty, Y. K. and Buehler, V. M., eds.*, 1987, pp. 11–32. [G: U.S.]

Thurow, Lester C. Economic Paradigms and Slow American Productivity Growth. *Eastern Econ. J.*, October-December 1987, *13*(4), pp. 333–43. [G: U.S.]

Tullio, Giuseppe. Long-run Implications of the Increase in Taxation and Public Debt for Employment and Economic Growth in Europe. *Europ. Econ. Rev.*, April 1987, *31*(3), pp. 741–74. [G: W. Europe]

Turner, Stephen. The Swedish Model: What Went Wrong? *Eliasson, G., ed.*, 1987, pp. 73–84. [G: Sweden]

Tvedt, Karl-Ove. Norway: On the Brink of Recession. *Vartia, P., et al.*, 1987, pp. 141–69.
[G: Norway]

Urata, Shujiro. Sources of Economic Growth and Structural Change in China: 1956–1981. *J. Compar. Econ.*, March 1987, *11*(1), pp. 96–115. [G: China]

Urrutia, Miguel. The Macroeconomics of Successful Development: What Are the Lessons? Comment. *Fischer, S., ed.*, 1987, pp. 258–61.

Vartia, Pentti, et al. Growth Policies in a Nordic Perspective. *Vartia, P., et al.*, 1987, pp. 7–48. [G: Norway; Finland; Denmark; Sweden]

Vernon, Raymond. The Politics of Comparative Economic Statistics: Three Cultures and Three Cases. *Alonso, W. and Starr, P., eds.*, 1987, pp. 61–82.

Wu, Jinglian; Li, Jiange and Ding, Ningning. Keep the Growth Rate of the National Economy within Proper Limits. *Chinese Econ.*

Stud., Winter 1986-87, *20*(2), pp. 46–54.
[G: China]

Yamaguchi, Mitoshi and Kennedy, George. A Comparison of Conventional and General Equilibrium Growth Accounting: The Case of Japanese Agriculture, 1880–1970. *Kobe Univ. Econ.*, 1987, *33*, pp. 49–69. [G: Japan]

Ylä-Anttila, Pekka. Finland: Can the Good Macroeconomic Performance Continue? *Vartia, P., et al.*, 1987, pp. 105–39. [G: Finland]

227 Prices

2270 Prices

Abadia, Antonio. Indice de precios de consumo, coste de vida y distribución del bienestar: 1976–1985. (With English summary.) *Invest. Econ.*, January 1987, *11*(1), pp. 179–90.
[G: Spain]

Al, Pieter G., et al. The Use of Chain Indices for Deflating the National Accounts. *Statist. J.*, July 1987, *4*(4), pp. 347–68.

Alexeev, Michael. Microeconomic Modeling of Parallel Markets: The Case of Agricultural Goods in the USSR. *J. Compar. Econ.*, December 1987, *11*(4), pp. 543–57.
[G: U.S.S.R.]

Alston, Julian M. and Chalfant, James A. A Note on Causality between Money, Wages and Prices in Australia. *Econ. Rec.*, June 1987, *63*(181), pp. 115–19. [G: Australia]

Antonini, Alberto and Kwack, Sung Y. Price and Inventory Dynamics of Primary Commodities. *Int. Econ. J.*, Spring 1987, *1*(1), pp. 43–55.

Baer, Werner. The Resurgence of Inflation in Brazil, 1974–86. *World Devel.*, August 1987, *15*(8), pp. 1007–34. [G: Brazil]

Bahr, Richard C. Inflation Fueled by Oil Prices in First 9 Months of 1987. *Mon. Lab. Rev.*, December 1987, *110*(12), pp. 3–6. [G: U.S.]

Barker, Terry. The Cambridge Multisectoral Dynamic Model of the British Economy: Export and Import Prices. *Barker, T. and Peterson, W., eds.*, 1987, pp. 311–39. [G: U.K.]

Batchelor, Roy A. and Dua, P. The Accuracy and Rationality of UK Inflation Expectations: Some Quantitative Evidence. *Appl. Econ.*, June 1987, *19*(6), pp. 819–28. [G: U.K.]

Bernholz, Peter. The Implementation and Maintenance of a Monetary Constitution. *Dorn, J. A. and Schwartz, A. J., eds.*, 1987, *1986*, pp. 83–117. [G: OECD]

Bhujangarao, C. Determinants of Foodgrain Prices in India: An Empirical Study, 1961–83. *Indian Econ. Rev.*, Jan.-June 1987, *22*(1), pp. 51–77. [G: India]

Bils, Mark. The Cyclical Behavior of Marginal Cost and Price. *Amer. Econ. Rev.*, December 1987, *77*(5), pp. 838–55. [G: U.S.]

Bird, Peter J. W. N. Continuity and Reversal in Oil Spot Price Movements. *Energy Econ.*, April 1987, *9*(2), pp. 73–81. [G: Global]

Blades, Derek and Roberts, David. A Note on the New OECD Benchmark Purchasing Power Parities for 1985. *OECD Econ. Stud.*, Autumn 1987, (9), pp. 183–97. [G: OECD]

Blanchard, Olivier Jean. Aggregate and Individual Price Adjustment. *Brookings Pap. Econ. Act.*, 1987, (1), pp. 57–109. **[G: U.S.]**

Blang, Hans-Georg and Schöler, Klaus. Informationsgrundlagen und Preiserwartungen. Eine empirische Untersuchung der Verkaufspreiserwartungen in der deutschen Industrie. (Information Sets and Price Expectations. An Empirical Investigation of the German Industrial Selling Price Expectations. With English summary.) *Ifo-Studien*, 1987, *33*(2), pp. 133–51. **[G: W. Germany]**

Blank, Steven C. Evaluating International Price Relationships Using Causal Models. *Europ. Rev. Agr. Econ.*, 1987, *14*(3), pp. 305–23. **[G: OECD]**

Bornstein, Morris. Soviet Price Policies. *Soviet Econ.*, April-June 1987, *3*(2), pp. 96–134. **[G: U.S.S.R.]**

van Brabant, Jozef M. Socialist and World Market Prices: An Ingrowth? *J. Compar. Econ.*, March 1987, *11*(1), pp. 21–39. **[G: Hungary]**

Bradburd, Ralph M. and Caves, Richard E. Transaction-Cost Influences on the Adjustment of Industries' Prices and Outputs. *Rev. Econ. Statist.*, November 1987, *69*(4), pp. 575–83. **[G: U.S.]**

Branson, William H. Productivity, Wages, and Prices inside and outside Manufacturing in the U.S., Japan, and Europe: Comments. *Europ. Econ. Rev.*, April 1987, *31*(3), pp. 733–36. **[G: U.S.; Japan; Europe]**

Brenton, Paul and Parikh, Ashok. Price Behaviour in European Countries: Testing the Law of One Price in the Short- and Long-Run at Various Levels of Aggregation. *Appl. Econ.*, November 1987, *19*(11), pp. 1533–59. **[G: W. Europe]**

Buchanan, James M. Constitutional Strategy and the Monetary Regime: Comment [The Implementation and Maintenance of a Monetary Constitution]. *Dorn, J. A. and Schwartz, A. J., eds.*, 1987, pp. 119–27. **[G: OECD]**

Chambers, E. J. and Hsu, Andy. Some Findings on Relative Price Change Variance and Inflation Rate Uncertainty in the Canadian CPI. *Appl. Econ.*, March 1987, *19*(3), pp. 285–303. **[G: Canada]**

Chan, M. W. Luke and Okasanen, E. H. Regional Energy Input Prices in Canadian Manufacturing: An Index Number Approach. *Energy Econ.*, April 1987, *9*(2), pp. 66–72. **[G: Canada]**

Chekhlov, N. I. Prices and Rates in Industry. *Prob. Econ.*, March 1987, *29*(11), pp. 62–77. **[G: U.S.S.R.]**

Chow, Gregory C. Money and Price Level Determination in China. *J. Compar. Econ.*, September 1987, *11*(3), pp. 319–33. **[G: China]**

Clem, Andrew G. and Thomas, William D. New Weight Structure Being Used in Producer Price Index. *Mon. Lab. Rev.*, August 1987, *110*(8), pp. 12–21. **[G: U.S.]**

Clements, Kenneth W. and Izan, H. Y. The Measurement of Inflation: A Stochastic Approach. *J. Bus. Econ. Statist.*, July 1987, *5*(3), pp. 339–50. **[G: Australia]**

Cobb, Stephen A. Interarea Cost of Living Measurement with Nonmarket Goods: A Demand Systems Approach. *J. Urban Econ.*, September 1987, *22*(2), pp. 174–89. **[G: U.S.]**

Corsetti, Giancarlo. Taxes and Subsidies in Input–Output Analysis: A Comment. *Ricerche Econ.*, Apr.-June 1987, *41*(2), pp. 262–73.

Danielsen, Albert L. Issues in the Indexation of Crude Oil and Natural Gas Prices. *Pachauri, R. K., ed.*, 1987, pp. 1049–61.

Danziger, Leif. Inflation, Fixed Cost of Price Adjustment, and Measurement of Relative-Price Variability: Theory and Evidence. *Amer. Econ. Rev.*, September 1987, *77*(4), pp. 704–13. **[G: Israel]**

Day, John. Late Medieval Price Movements and the 'Crisis of Feudalism.' *Day, J.*, 1987, pp. 90–107. **[G: Europe]**

Devadoss, S. and Meyers, William H. Relative Prices and Money: Further Results for the United States. *Amer. J. Agr. Econ.*, November 1987, *69*(4), pp. 838–42. **[G: U.S.]**

Di Matteo, Massimo. Relative Prices and Technical Change: A Suggested Approach to Long Waves. *Vasko, T., ed.*, 1987, pp. 326–32.

Domberger, Simon. Relative Price Variability and Inflation: A Disaggregated Analysis. *J. Polit. Econ.*, June 1987, *95*(3), pp. 547–66. **[G: U.K.]**

Dornbusch, Rudiger. Exchange Rates and Prices. *Amer. Econ. Rev.*, March 1987, *77*(1), pp. 93–106.

Dryden, John; Reut, Katrina and Slater, Barbara. Comparison of Purchasing Power Parity between the United States and Canada. *Mon. Lab. Rev.*, December 1987, *110*(12), pp. 7–24. **[G: U.S.; Canada]**

Fortune, J. Neill. The Inflation Rate of the Price of Gold, Expected Prices and Interest Rates. *J. Macroecon.*, Winter 1987, *9*(1), pp. 71–82. **[G: U.S.]**

Froyen, Richard T. and Waud, Roger N. An Examination of Aggregate Price Uncertainty in Four Countries and Some Implications for Real Output. *Int. Econ. Rev.*, June 1987, *28*(2), pp. 353–72. **[G: U.S.; U.K.; Canada; W. Germany]**

Genberg, Hans and Salemi, Michael K. The Effects of Foreign Shocks on Prices of Swiss Goods and Credit: An Analysis Based on VAR Methods. *Ann. Écon. Statist.*, Apr./Sept. 1987, (6/7), pp. 101–24. **[G: Switzerland]**

Giavazzi, Francesco and Giovannini, Alberto. Exchange Rates and Prices in Europe. *Weltwirtsch. Arch.*, 1987, *123*(4), pp. 592–605. **[G: France; U.K.; W. Germany; Italy; Netherlands]**

Gibbons, Elizabeth and Halpin, Gerald F. Import Price Declines in 1986 Reflected Reduced Oil Prices. *Mon. Lab. Rev.*, April 1987, *110*(4), pp. 3–17. **[G: U.S.]**

Gillingham, Robert and Greenlees, John S. The Impact of Direct Taxes on the Cost of Living. *J. Polit. Econ.*, August 1987, *95*(4), pp. 775–96. **[G: U.S.]**

Gilmour, Brad and Fawcett, Peter. The Relationship between U.S. and Canadian Wheat Prices. *Can. J. Agr. Econ.*, November 1987, *35*(3), pp. 571–89. **[G: U.S.; Canada]**

Glezakos, Constantine and Nugent, Jeffrey B. The Relationship between the Rate of Inflation and Its Unpredictability in High Inflation Latin American Countries. *World Devel.*, February 1987, *15*(2), pp. 291–93. **[G: Latin America]**

Goldstein, Joshua S. Long Waves in War, Production, Prices, and Wages. *J. Conflict Resolution*, December 1987, *31*(4), pp. 573–600. **[G: Selected MDCs]**

Gonzalez, Norberto. International Price Fluctuations and Inflation: Discussion and Conclusions. *Pasinetti, L. and Lloyd, P., eds.*, 1987, pp. 395–402. **[G: Global]**

Gordon, Robert J. Aggregate and Individual Price Adjustment: Comments. *Brookings Pap. Econ. Act.*, 1987, (1), pp. 110–17. **[G: U.S.]**

Gordon, Robert J. Productivity, Wages, and Prices inside and outside of Manufacturing in the U.S., Japan, and Europe. *Europ. Econ. Rev.*, April 1987, *31*(3), pp. 685–733. **[G: U.S.; Japan; Europe]**

Gorodetskii, E. and Gorodetskii, A. Theoretical Prerequisites to the Systematic Restructuring of Prices. *Prob. Econ.*, September 1987, *30*(5), pp. 43–60. **[G: U.S.S.R.]**

Guerberoff, Simón L. Flexibilidad de precios, variaciones de stocks e incertidumbre: la política antiinflacionaria después del Plan Austral. (With English summary.) *Desarrollo Econ.*, July-Sept. 1987, *27*(106), pp. 171–200. **[G: Argentina]**

Hall, Thomas E. and Fields, T. Windsor. Anticipated Nominal Demand Shocks and the Speed of Aggregate Price Adjustment. *Rev. Econ. Statist.*, February 1987, *69*(1), pp. 140–44. **[G: U.S.]**

Hamaui, Rony and Rinaldi, Roberto. I prezzi all'importazione italiani dei beni manufatti: un'analisi preliminare. (With English summary.) *Polit. Econ.*, April 1987, *3*(1), pp. 81–104. **[G: Italy]**

Harbury, C. D. and Hitchens, D. M. W. N. The Influence of Relative Prices on the Distribution of Wealth and the Measurement of Inheritance. *Wolff, E. N., ed.*, 1987, pp. 248–75. **[G: U.K.]**

Howell, Craig; Burns, Roger and Clem, Andrew G. Sharp Drop in Energy Prices Holds Inflation in Check during 1986. *Mon. Lab. Rev.*, May 1987, *110*(5), pp. 3–9. **[G: U.S.]**

Jones, Charles P. and Wilson, Jack W. Stocks, Bonds, Paper, and Inflation: 1870–1985. *J. Portfol. Manage.*, Fall 1987, *14*(1), pp. 20–24. **[G: U.S.]**

Kazi, Shahnaz. Intersectoral Terms of Trade for Pakistan's Economy: 1970-71–1981-82. *Pakistan Devel. Rev.*, Spring 1987, *26*(1), pp. 81–105. **[G: Pakistan]**

Kirchgässner, Gebhard. Zur Anpassung der schweizerischen Mineralölpreise an die internationale Entwicklung. Empirische Tests einiger Hypothesen. (On the Adjustment of Swiss Oil Prices to the International Development. With English summary.) *Schweiz. Z. Volk-*

swirtsch. Statist., June 1987, *123*(2), pp. 123–46. **[G: Switzerland]**

Kitchen, John and Denbaly, Mark. Commodity Prices, Money Surprises, and Fed Credibility: A Comment. *J. Money, Credit, Banking*, May 1987, *19*(2), pp. 246–51. **[G: U.S.]**

König, Heinz. Productivity, Wages, and Prices inside and outside of Manufacturing in the U.S., Japan, and Europe: Comments. *Europ. Econ. Rev.*, April 1987, *31*(3), pp. 736–39.

Kordos, Jan and Czajka, Bozena. Consumer Price Indices in Poland. *Statist. J.*, December 1987, *5*(1), pp. 53–66. **[G: Poland]**

Kreinin, Mordechai E.; Martin, Stephen and Sheehey, Edmund J. Differential Response of U.S. Import Prices and Quantities to Exchange-Rate Adjustments. *Weltwirtsch. Arch.*, 1987, *123*(3), pp. 449–62. **[G: U.S.]**

Lee, Chi-Wen Jevons and Petruzzi, Christopher R. A Test of the Shiller–Siegel Hypothesis of the Gibson Paradox [The Gibson Paradox and Historical Movements in Real Interest Rates]. *Australian Econ. Pap.*, June 1987, *26*(48), pp. 157–64. **[G: U.K.]**

Mason, Charles and Butler, Clifford. Errata [New Basket of Goods and Services Being Priced in Revised CPI]. *Mon. Lab. Rev.*, February 1987, *110*(2), pp. 17.

Mason, Charles and Butler, Clifford. New Basket of Goods and Services Being Priced in Revised CPI. *Mon. Lab. Rev.*, January 1987, *110*(1), pp. 3–22. **[G: U.S.]**

Minhas, B. S., et al. On the Choice of Appropriate Consumer Price Indices and Data Sets for Estimating the Incidence of Poverty in India. *Indian Econ. Rev.*, Jan.-June 1987, *22*(1), pp. 19–49. **[G: India]**

Moxnes, Erling. Uncertainty in Future Oil Price Predictions. *Pachauri, R. K., ed.*, 1987, pp. 1105–21.

Nadiri, M. Ishaq. Price Inertia and Inflation: Evidence and Theoretical Rationale. *Pasinetti, L. and Lloyd, P., eds.*, 1987, pp. 329–57. **[G: U.S.]**

Ohta, Makoto. Gasoline Cost and Hedonic Price Indexes of U.S. Used Cars for 1970–1983. *J. Bus. Econ. Statist.*, October 1987, *5*(4), pp. 521–28. **[G: U.S.]**

Ohta, Makoto. Hedonic Price Indexes of Japanese Passenger Cars Over 1970–83: A Note. *Econ. Stud. Quart.*, September 1987, *38*(3), pp. 264–74. **[G: Japan]**

Pauls, B. Dianne. Comovements in Aggregate and Relative Prices: Some Evidence on Neutrality. *J. Monet. Econ.*, July 1987, *20*(1), pp. 155–68. **[G: U.S.]**

Petrakov, Nikolay. Prospects for Change in the Systems of Price Formation, Finance and Credit in the USSR. *Soviet Econ.*, April-June 1987, *3*(2), pp. 135–44. **[G: U.S.S.R.]**

Petrakov, Nikolay. Soviet Pricing and Fiscal-Credit System: Prospects for Economic Policy Changes. *Rivista Int. Sci. Econ. Com.*, October 1987, *34*(10), pp. 903–12. **[G: U.S.S.R.]**

Petrović, Pavle. The Deviation of Production Prices from Labour Values: Some Methodology and Empirical Evidence. *Cambridge J. Econ.*,

September 1987, *11*(3), pp. 197–210.
[G: Yugoslavia]
Pourgerami, Abbas and Maskus, Keith E. The Effects of Inflation on the Predictability of Price Changes in Latin America: Some Estimates and Policy Implications. *World Devel.*, February 1987, *15*(2), pp. 287–90. [G: Latin America]
Raczkowski, Stanislaw. The Influence of International Price Movements and Inflation on the Centrally Planned Economies. *Pasinetti, L. and Lloyd, P., eds.*, 1987, pp. 359–80.
[G: CMEA]
Rahman, Sultan Hafeez. An Analysis of Seasonal Jute Price Behaviour. *Bangladesh Devel. Stud.*, September 1987, *15*(3), pp. 43–61.
[G: Bangladesh]
Raj, Baldev. Did the Cost of Living in Canada Increase Faster for the Rich during the Period 1950–1980? *Empirical Econ.*, 1987, *12*(1), pp. 19–28. [G: Canada]
Ray, George F. The Decline of Primary Producer Power. *Nat. Inst. Econ. Rev.*, August 1987, (121), pp. 40–45. [G: Global]
Recalde de Bernardi, María Luisa. Precio sostén o subsidio al fertilizante beneficios y costos. (Price Support or Fertilizer Subsidy: Benefits and Costs. With English summary.) *Económica (La Plata)*, July-Dec. 1987, *33*(2), pp. 185–212.
[G: Argentina]
Rozenova, L. Price as the Cost–Benefit Norm. *Prob. Econ.*, December 1987, *30*(8), pp. 93–107. [G: U.S.S.R.]
Sabolčík, Michal. Prices and Value Instruments. *Czech. Econ. Digest.*, October 1987, (7), pp. 78–87.
Sapsford, David. A Simple Model of Primary Commodity Price Determination: 1900–80. *J. Devel. Stud.*, January 1987, *23*(2), pp. 265–74.
Sapsford, David and Varoufakis, Y. An ARIMA Analysis of Tea Prices. *J. Agr. Econ.*, May 1987, *38*(2), pp. 329–34. [G: U.K.]
Schmidt, Mary Lynn. Comparison of the Revised and the Old CPI. *Mon. Lab. Rev.*, November 1987, *110*(11), pp. 3–6. [G: U.S.]
Simon, András. An Input–Output Analysis of Prices in the Hungarian Economy between 1981–1985. *Acta Oecon.*, 1987, *38*(1–2), pp. 17–33. [G: Hungary]
Sims, Christopher A. Aggregate and Individual Price Adjustment: Comments. *Brookings Pap. Econ. Act.*, 1987, (1), pp. 117–20. [G: U.S.]
Skidmore, Thomas E. The Resurgence of Inflation in Latin America: Discussion. *World Devel.*, August 1987, *15*(8), pp. 1148–49. [G: Brazil; Argentina]
Smith, Andrew and MacKinnon, Neil J. Inflation and Relative Price Variability: The U.K. Experience over the Last 30 Years. *Scot. J. Polit. Econ.*, May 1987, *34*(2), pp. 145–60.
[G: U.K.]
Smith, Russell E. The Resurgence of Inflation in Latin America: Discussion. *World Devel.*, August 1987, *15*(8), pp. 1146–48.
[G: Argentina; Brazil]
Thomas, Vinod. Differences in Income and Poverty with in Brazil. *World Devel.*, February

1987, *15*(2), pp. 263–73. [G: Brazil]
Turner, Michael. Towards an Agricultural Prices Index for Ireland 1850–1914. *Econ. Soc. Rev.*, January 1987, *18*(2), pp. 123–36.
[G: Ireland]
Val'tukh, Konstantin K. Statistical Verification of the Theory of Value: An Analysis of Price Indices. *[Marrama, V.], Vol. 2*, 1987, pp. 629–49. [G: U.S.]
Verma, P. C. Domestic Demand for Jute Goods in India. *Margin*, Jan.-Mar. 1987, *19*(2), pp. 43–49. [G: India]
Visco, Ignazio. The Use of Italian Survey Data in the Analysis of Inflation Expectations. *Giorn. Econ.*, Nov.-Dec. 1987, *46*(11–12), pp. 561–89. [G: Italy]
Vomfelde, Werner. Modelling Price Inflation: A Response [Die Determinanten der Preisentwicklung in der Bundesrepublik Deutschland]. *Jahr. Nationalökon. Statist.*, May 1987, *203*(3), pp. 306–10. [G: W. Germany]
Walters, Alan. The Mischief of Moving Average Pricing. *Cato J.*, Spring/Summer 1987, *7*(1), pp. 241–48. [G: LDCs]
Weale, Martin. The Cambridge Multisectoral Dynamic Model of the British Economy: Industrial Prices and Profits. *Barker, T. and Peterson, W., eds.*, 1987, pp. 293–309. [G: U.K.]
Webster, Allan. Purchasing Power Parity as a Theory of International Arbitrage in Manufactured Goods: An Empirical View of UK/US Prices in the 1970s. *Appl. Econ.*, November 1987, *19*(11), pp. 1433–56. [G: U.K.; U.S.]
Weicher, John C. Mismeasuring Poverty and Progress. *Cato J.*, Winter 1987, *6*(3), pp. 715–30. [G: U.S.]
Winters, L. Alan. Models of Primary Price Indices. *Oxford Bull. Econ. Statist.*, August 1987, *49*(3), pp. 307–22. [G: LDCs]
Xue, Muqiao. Price Fluctuations and Changes in People's Livelihood in China in the Past Six Years. *Chinese Econ. Stud.*, Winter 1986-87, *20*(2), pp. 55–63. [G: China]

228 Regional Statistics

2280 Regional Statistics

Cressie, Noel. Census Undercount Adjustment and the Quality of Geographic Population Distributions: Comment. *J. Amer. Statist. Assoc.*, December 1987, *82*(400), pp. 980–83.
[G: U.S.]
DePass, Rudolph E. State Personal Income, First Quarter 1987. *Surv. Curr. Bus.*, July 1987, *67*(7), pp. 129–34. [G: U.S.]
Friendenberg, Howard L. Regional Nonfarm Personal Income in the Current Economic Expansion. *Surv. Curr. Bus.*, October 1987, *67*(10), pp. 27–41. [G: U.S.]
Hill, Edward W. What Is the Effect of Random Variation in State Unemployment Rates? *Mon. Lab. Rev.*, December 1987, *110*(12), pp. 41–46. [G: U.S.]
Hjerppe, Reino T.; Niitamo, Olavi E. and Suur-Kujala, Markku. Regional Policy-Making and Regional Data Bases. *Rev. Income Wealth*, De-

cember 1987, *33*(4), pp. 387–400.

Nair, K. R. G. Regional Income Estimation. *Indian Econ. J.*, Apr.-June 1987, *34*(4), pp. 55–59.

Rajalakshmi, K. Composition of State Domestic Products of India (An Indepth Analysis for the Period between 1971 to 1982). *Indian Econ. J.*, Apr.-June 1987, *34*(4), pp. 60–78.
[G: India]

Schirm, Allen L. and Preston, Samuel H. Census Undercount Adjustment and the Quality of Geographic Population Distributions: Rejoinder. *J. Amer. Statist. Assoc.*, December 1987, *82*(400), pp. 986–90.

da Silva Costa, Jose; Ellson, Richard W. and Martin, Randolph C. Public Capital, Regional Output, and Development: Some Empirical Evidence. *J. Reg. Sci.*, August 1987, *27*(3), pp. 419–37.
[G: U.S.]

Spencer, Bruce D. Census Undercount Adjustment and the Quality of Geographic Population Distributions: Comment. *J. Amer. Statist. Assoc.*, December 1987, *82*(400), pp. 984–86.
[G: U.S.]

Walters, R. J. A Framework for Regional Accounts: An Australian Perspective. *Rev. Income Wealth*, December 1987, *33*(4), pp. 401–15.
[G: Australia]

Wolter, Kirk M. Census Undercount Adjustment and the Quality of Geographic Population Distributions: Comment. *J. Amer. Statist. Assoc.*, December 1987, *82*(400), pp. 978–80.
[G: U.S.]

229 Microdata and Database Analysis

2290 Microdata and Database Analysis

Juster, F. Thomas. The Role of Microdata in the Production of Economic Knowledge. *Green, L. and Kagel, J. H., eds.*, 1987, pp. 67–90.

Nunns, James R. Tabulations from the Treasury Tax Reform Data Base. *U.S. Treasury, Office of Tax Analysis.*, 1987, pp. 101–29. [G: U.S.]

Rubinstein, Mark and Vijh, Anand M. The Berkeley Options Data Base: A Tool for Empirical Research. *Fabozzi, F. J., ed.*, 1987, pp. 209–21.
[G: U.S.]

St-Hilaire, France and Whalley, John. A Microconsistent Data Set for Canada for Use in Regional General Equilibrium Policy Analysis. *Rev. Income Wealth*, September 1987, *33*(3), pp. 327–43.
[G: Canada]

300 Domestic Monetary and Fiscal Theory and Institutions

310 DOMESTIC MONETARY AND FINANCIAL THEORY AND INSTITUTIONS

3100 General

Antal, László and Surányi, György. The Prehistory of the Reform of Hungary's Banking System. *Acta Oecon.*, 1987, *38*(1–2), pp. 35–48.
[G: Hungary]

Avery, Robert B., et al. Changes in the Use of Transaction Accounts and Cash from 1984 to 1986. *Fed. Res. Bull.*, March 1987, *73*(3), pp. 179–96.
[G: U.S.]

Bofinger, Peter. Geldpolitische Regulierungen und Finanzinnovationen. (Monetary Regulation and Financial Innovation. With English summary.) *Aussenwirtschaft*, September 1987, *42*(2/3), pp. 251–73. [G: U.S.; W. Germany]

Bokros, Lajos. The Conditions of the Development of Businesslike Behaviour in a Two-Tier Banking System (An *"ex ante"* Evaluation of the Hungarian Banking Reform). *Acta Oecon.*, 1987, *38*(1–2), pp. 49–60. [G: Hungary]

Bolnick, Bruce R. Financial Liberalization with Imperfect Markets: Indonesia during the 1970s. *Econ. Develop. Cult. Change*, April 1987, *35*(3), pp. 581–99. [G: Indonesia]

Burkett, Paul. Financial "Repression" and Financial "Liberalization" in the Third World: A Contribution to the Critique of Neoclassical Development Theory. *Rev. Radical Polit. Econ.*, Spring 1987, *19*(1), pp. 1–21.
[G: LDCs]

Chino, Yoshitoki. Thoughts on Japanese Financial Liberalization. *Patrick, H. T. and Tachi, R., eds.*, 1987, pp. 178–83. [G: Japan]

Corrigan, E. Gerald. A Framework for Reform of the Financial System. *Fed. Res. Bank New York Quart. Rev.*, Summer 1987, *12*(2), pp. 1–8. [G: U.S.]

Corrigan, E. Gerald. A Perspective on the Globalization of Financial Markets and Institutions. *Fed. Res. Bank New York Quart. Rev.*, Spring 1987, *12*(1), pp. 1–9.
[G: U.S.; Japan; U.K.]

Corrigan, E. Gerald. Statement to the U.S. Senate Committee on the Budget, May 6, 1987. *Fed. Res. Bull.*, July 1987, *73*(7), pp. 569–77.
[G: U.S.; U.K.; Japan]

Cumming, Christine M. and Sweet, Lawrence M. Financial Structure of the G-10 Countries: How Does the United States Compare? *Fed. Res. Bank New York Quart. Rev.*, Winter 1987-88, *12*(4), pp. 14–25. [G: OECD]

Dooley, Michael P. and Mathieson, Donald J. Financial Liberalization in Developing Countries. *Finance Develop.*, September 1987, *24*(3), pp. 31–34.

Edwards, Franklin R. The Dark Side of Financial Innovation. *Patrick, H. T. and Tachi, R., eds.*, 1987, pp. 147–55. [G: U.S.]

Fischer, Bernhard. Finanzwirtschaftliche Rahmenbedingungen und Bankleistungen in Entwicklungsländern auf dem Prüfstand. (Financial Policies and the Performance of Finanacial Institutions in Developing Countries: A Critical Assessment. With English summary.) *Z. Wirtschaft. Sozialwissen.*, 1987, *107*(4), pp. 553–80. [G: LDCs]

Freund, William C. Industry Perspective: The Securities Industry in the Financial Services Marketplace: A Review of Dynamic Trends. *Bus. Econ.*, April 1987, *22*(2), pp. 48–53.
[G: U.S.]

Fry, Maxwell J. Neo-classical and Neo-structuralist Models of Financial Development: Theories and Evidence. *Greek Econ. Rev.*, 1987, 9(1), pp. 1–37. **[G: LDCs]**

Fukao, Mitsuhiro and Hanazaki, Masaharu. Internationalisation of Financial Markets and the Allocation of Capital. *OECD Econ. Stud.*, Spring 1987, (8), pp. 35–92. **[G: OECD]**

de Grauwe, Paul. Financial Deregulation in Developing Countries. *Tijdschrift Econ. Manage.*, 1987, 32(4), pp. 381–401. **[G: LDCs]**

Hamada, Koichi and Horiuchi, Akiyoshi. The Political Economy of Japan: The Political Economy of the Financial Market. *Yamamura, K. and Yasuba, Y., eds.*, 1987, pp. 223–60. **[G: Japan]**

Hansen, Hans Ejvind. Brancheglidning i den finansielle sektor—hvad nu? (Structural Changes in the Financial Sector of Denmark. With English summary.) *Nationaløkon. Tidsskr.*, 1987, 125(3), pp. 299–315. **[G: Denmark]**

Harrigan, Frank J. and McGregor, Peter G. Interregional Arbitrage and the Supply of Loanable Funds: A Model of Intermediate Financial Capital Mobility. *J. Reg. Sci.*, August 1987, 27(3), pp. 357–67.

Kindleberger, Charles P. Financial Deregulation and Economic Performance: An Attempt to Relate European Financial History to Current LDC Issues. *J. Devel. Econ.*, October 1987, 27(1–2), pp. 339–53. **[G: U.K.; France; W. Germany; Italy]**

Kindleberger, Charles P. Financial Deregulation and Economic Performance: An Attempt to Relate European Financial History to Current LDC Issues. *[Diaz-Alejandro, C. F.],* 1987, pp. 339–53. **[G: U.K.; France; W. Germany; Italy]**

Kohsaka, Akira. Financial Liberalization in Asian NICs: A Comparative Study of Korea and Taiwan in the 1980s. *Devel. Econ.*, December 1987, 25(4), pp. 325–45. **[G: S. Korea; Taiwan]**

Kusukawa, Toru. Japan's Financial Market: Present Conditions and Outlook. *Patrick, H. T. and Tachi, R., eds.*, 1987, pp. 131–35. **[G: Japan; U.S.]**

Leveson, Irving. Globalization of Financial Services. *Bus. Econ.*, October 1987, 22(4), pp. 40–44. **[G: U.S.; U.K.; Canada; Japan]**

Llewellyn, David T. Competition and the Regulatory Mix. *Nat. Westminster Bank Quart. Rev.*, August 1987, pp. 4–13. **[G: U.K.]**

Looney, Robert E. Consequences of Financial Underdevelopment in Saudi Arabia. *Rivista Int. Sci. Econ. Com.*, Nov.-Dec. 1987, 34(11–12), pp. 1197–1216. **[G: Suadi Arabia]**

Marimon, Ramon and Wallace, Neil. Trade Using Assets Divisible at a Cost. *J. Econ. Theory*, December 1987, 43(2), pp. 223–51.

Mochizuki, Hiroshi and Murata, Satoshi. The Impact of Deregulation on Financial Markets in the United States and Japan: Is the Market Always Right? *Finn, R. B., ed.*, 1987, pp. 97–108. **[G: U.S.; Japan]**

Odano, Sumimaru. The Evolution of the Japanese Monetary System: Liberalisation and Integration. *[Kitamura, H.],* 1987, pp. 99–113. **[G: Japan]**

Parry, Robert T. Major Trends in the U.S. Financial System: Implications and Issues. *Fed. Res. Bank San Francisco Econ. Rev.*, Spring 1987, (2), pp. 5–19. **[G: U.S.]**

Patrick, Hugh T. Japan and the United States Today: Exchange Rates, Macroeconomic Policies, and Financial Market Innovations: Concluding Comments. *Patrick, H. T. and Tachi, R., eds.*, 1987, pp. 209–13. **[G: Japan; U.S.]**

Prindl, A. R. The Internationalisation of Japanese Financial Institutions. *Trevor, M., ed.*, 1987, pp. 111–19. **[G: Japan]**

Sarcinelli, Mario. Determinants and Trends of Italian Financial Policy. *Banca Naz. Lavoro Quart. Rev.*, March 1987, (160), pp. 3–29. **[G: Italy]**

Sarcinelli, Mario. Financial Assets, Public Debt and Monetary Policy: An International Integration Perspective. *Banca Naz. Lavoro Quart. Rev.*, September 1987, (162), pp. 263–372. **[G: Italy]**

Shafer, Jeffrey R. Managing Crises in the Emerging Financial Landscape. *OECD Econ. Stud.*, Autumn 1987, (9), pp. 55–77. **[G: Global]**

Shinohara, Naoyuki. Tokyo as an International Finance Center: Financial Liberalization and International Standardization. *Finn, R. B., ed.*, 1987, pp. 75–95. **[G: Japan; U.S.]**

Suzuki, Yoshio. Comparative Studies of Financial Innovation, Deregulation, and Reform in Japan and United States. *Patrick, H. T. and Tachi, R., eds.*, 1987, pp. 156–67. **[G: Japan; U.S.]**

Swanson, Peggy E. Capital Market Integration over the Past Decade: The Case of the U.S. Dollar. *J. Int. Money Finance*, June 1987, 6(2), pp. 215–25. **[G: U.S.]**

Teranishi, Juro. The "Catch-up" Process, Financial System, and Japan's Rise as a Capital Exporter. *Hitotsubashi J. Econ.*, October 1987, 27, pp. 133–46. **[G: Japan]**

Vichit-Vadakan, Vinyu. Finance and Banking. *Martin, L. G., ed.*, 1987, pp. 132–34. **[G: ASEAN]**

Whittemore, Frederick. The Internationalization of Investment Banking. *Patrick, H. T. and Tachi, R., eds.*, 1987, pp. 136–46. **[G: Global]**

Yang, Peixin. On Building a Socialist Capital Market in China. *Chinese Econ. Stud.*, Winter 1986-87, 20(2), pp. 67–74. **[G: China]**

Zhou, Xiaochuan and Zhu, Li. China's Banking System: Current Status, Perspective on Reform. *J. Compar. Econ.*, September 1987, 11(3), pp. 399–409. **[G: China]**

311 Domestic Monetary and Financial Theory and Policy

3110 Domestic Monetary Theory and Policy

Basu, Kaushik. Disneyland Monopoly, Interlinkage and Usurious Interest Rates. *J. Public Econ.*, October 1987, 34(1), pp. 1–17.

Beckman, Steven. A Microcomputer Program That Simulates the Baumol–Tobin Transactions Demand for Money. *J. Econ. Educ.*, Summer 1987, *18*(3), pp. 309–17.

Bernholz, Peter. The Implementation and Maintenance of a Monetary Constitution. *Dorn, J. A. and Schwartz, A. J., eds.*, 1987, *1986*, pp. 83–117. **[G: OECD]**

Bordo, Michael D. and Schwartz, Anna J. Clark Warburton: Pioneer Monetarist. *Schwartz, A. J.*, 1987, *1979*, pp. 234–54. **[G: U.S.]**

Bosworth, Barry P. and Lawrence, Robert Z. Economic Goals and the Policy Mix. *Bosworth, B. P. and Rivlin, A. M., eds.*, 1987, pp. 97–124. **[G: Sweden]**

Brunner, Karl and Meltzer, Allan H. Bubbles and Other Essays. *Carnegie–Rochester Conf. Ser. Public Policy*, Spring 1987, *26*, pp. 1–8.

Brunner, Karl and Meltzer, Allan H. Empirical Studies of Velocity, Real Exchange Rates, Unemployment, and Productivity. *Carnegie–Rochester Conf. Ser. Public Policy*, Autumn 1987, *27*, pp. 1–8.

Buchanan, James M. Constitutional Strategy and the Monetary Regime: Comment [The Implementation and Maintenance of a Monetary Constitution]. *Dorn, J. A. and Schwartz, A. J., eds.*, 1987, pp. 119–27. **[G: OECD]**

Burdekin, Richard C. K. Cross-country Evidence on the Relationship Between Central Banks and Governments. *J. Macroecon.*, Summer 1987, *9*(3), pp. 391–405. **[G: Canada; U.K.; France; W. Germany]**

Caeser, Rolf. Internationaler Zinszusammenhang und deutsche Zinspolitik im Europäischen Währungssystem. (International Interdependence of Interest Rates and German Interest Rate Policy within the European Monetary System. With English summary.) *Konjunkturpolitik*, 1987, *33*(1), pp. 47–70. **[G: EEC]**

Cagan, Phillip. A Compensated Dollar: Better or More Likely Than Gold? *Dorn, J. A. and Schwartz, A. J., eds.*, 1987, pp. 261–77. **[G: U.S.; U.K.]**

Cagan, Phillip and Schwartz, Anna J. Has the Growth of Money Substitutes Hindered Monetary Policy? *Schwartz, A. J.*, 1987, *1975*, pp. 209–33. **[G: U.S.]**

Campbell, John Y. and Shiller, Robert J. Cointegration and Tests of Present Value Models. *J. Polit. Econ.*, October 1987, *95*(5), pp. 1062–88. **[G: U.S.]**

Cooper, Kathleen M. Real Interest Rates: The Unpuzzle. *Bus. Econ.*, January 1987, *22*(1), pp. 13–17. **[G: U.S.; U.K.]**

Cooper, Richard N. The Gold Standard: Historical Facts and Future Prospects. *Cooper, R. N.*, 1987, *1982*, pp. 43–86.

Deville, Volker and Gebauer, Wolfgang. Zinssätze und Preisindizes in ECU: Ein Beitrag zur Arithmetik von Währungskörben. (Interest Rates and Price Indices in ECU: Remarks on the Arithmetic of Currency Baskets. With English summary.) *Kredit Kapital*, 1987, *20*(4), pp. 439–53. **[G: EEC]**

Dillard, Dudley. Money as an Institution of Capitalism. *J. Econ. Issues*, December 1987, *21*(4), pp. 1623–47.

Fase, Martin M. G. and Steel, K. On Interest Rates in Belgium and the Netherlands: A Comparative Analysis of Interest Rate, Developments and Financial Innovations, 1980–1984. *De Economist*, 1987, *135*(3), pp. 316–39. **[G: Belgium; Netherlands]**

Friedman, Milton. The Case for Overhauling the Federal Reserve. *Wilcox, J. A., ed.*, 1987, *1985*, pp. 243–51. **[G: U.S.]**

Friedman, Milton and Schwartz, Anna J. Has Government Any Role in Money? *Schwartz, A. J.*, 1987, *1986*, pp. 289–314.

Greenfield, Robert L. Federal Reserve Fallacies: Comment [Monetary Reform in an Uncertain Environment]. *Dorn, J. A. and Schwartz, A. J., eds.*, 1987, pp. 221–28. **[G: U.S.]**

Hayek, Friedrich A. Toward a Free-Market Monetary System. *Dorn, J. A. and Schwartz, A. J., eds.*, 1987, pp. 383–90.

Healey, Nigel M. The UK 1979–82 "Monetarist Experiment": Why Economists still Disagree. *Banca Naz. Lavoro Quart. Rev.*, December 1987, (163), pp. 471–99. **[G: U.K.]**

Hetzel, Robert L. Henry Thornton: Seminal Monetary Theorist and Father of the Modern Central Bank. *Fed. Res. Bank Richmond Econ. Rev.*, July/Aug. 1987, *73*(4), pp. 3–16.

Kudlow, Lawrence A. Loose Money and the Dollar's Crash. *Challenge*, Mar./Apr. 1987, *30*(1), pp. 52–55. **[G: U.S.]**

Machlup, Fritz. The Political Economy of Inflation. *Dorn, J. A. and Schwartz, A. J., eds.*, 1987, pp. 291–96.

Mankiw, N. Gregory; Miron, Jeffrey A. and Weil, David N. The Adjustment of Expectations to a Change in Regime: A Study of the Founding of the Federal Reserve. *Amer. Econ. Rev.*, June 1987, *77*(3), pp. 358–74. **[G: U.S.]**

McNees, Stephen K. Prospective Nominal GNP Targeting: An Alternative Framework for Monetary Policy. *New Eng. Econ. Rev.*, Sept./Oct. 1987, pp. 3–9.

Meiselman, David I. Is Gold the Answer? Comment [Gold Standards: True and False]. *Dorn, J. A. and Schwartz, A. J., eds.*, 1987, pp. 257–60.

Meltzer, Allan H. Monetary Reform in an Uncertain Environment. *Dorn, J. A. and Schwartz, A. J., eds.*, 1987, *1983*, pp. 201–20. **[G: U.S.]**

Mills, Terence C. Uncertainty in the U.K. Monetary Aggregates: Modelling Data Revisions in Economic Time Series. *Manchester Sch. Econ. Soc. Stud.*, December 1987, *55*(4), pp. 337–52. **[G: U.K.]**

Mullineux, Andrew W. Monopoly of Money or Monopoly Money. *Nat. Westminster Bank Quart. Rev.*, August 1987, pp. 35–44. **[G: EEC; U.S.]**

Pecquet, Gary M. Money in the Trans-Mississippi Confederacy and the Confederate Currency

Reform Act of 1864. *Exploration Econ. Hist.*, April 1987, *24*(2), pp. 218–43. **[G: U.S.]**

Salerno, Joseph T. Gold Standards: True and False. *Dorn, J. A. and Schwartz, A. J., eds.*, 1987, pp. 241–55. **[G: U.S.]**

Sundararajan, V. The Debt–Equity Ratio of Firms and the Effectiveness of Interest Rate Policy: Analysis with a Dynamic Model of Saving, Investment, and Growth in Korea. *Int. Monet. Fund Staff Pap.*, June 1987, *34*(2), pp. 260–310. **[G: S. Korea]**

Tardos, Márton. The Role of Money in Hungary. *Europ. Econ. Rev.*, Feb./Mar. 1987, *31*(1/2), pp. 125–31. **[G: Hungary]**

Thornton, Daniel L. Why Does Velocity Matter? *Wilcox, J. A., ed.*, 1987, *1983*, pp. 219–27. **[G: U.S.]**

Timberlake, Richard H., Jr. Private Production of Scrip-Money in the Isolated Community. *J. Money, Credit, Banking*, November 1987, *19*(4), pp. 437–47. **[G: U.S.]**

Tobin, James. Deposit Interest Ceilings as a Monetary Control. *Tobin, J. (1)*, 1987, *1970*, pp. 339–51. **[G: U.S.]**

Wachtel, Paul and Young, John. Deficit Announcements and Interest Rates. *Amer. Econ. Rev.*, December 1987, *77*(5), pp. 1007–12. **[G: U.S.]**

White, Lawrence H. Competitive Money, Inside and Out. *Dorn, J. A. and Schwartz, A. J., eds.*, 1987, pp. 339–57. **[G: U.S.]**

Willett, Thomas D. A New Monetary Constitution. *Dorn, J. A. and Schwartz, A. J., eds.*, 1987, pp. 145–60. **[G: U.S.]**

Zhou, Xiaochuan and Zhu, Li. China's Banking System: Current Status, Perspective on Reform. *J. Compar. Econ.*, September 1987, *11*(3), pp. 399–409. **[G: China]**

3112 Monetary Theory; Empirical Studies Illustrating Theory

Abaan, Ernur Demir. Parasal Şok ve Reel Ekonomik Etkinlik. (With English summary.) *METU*, 1987, *14*(3), pp. 271–82. **[G: Turkey]**

Abel, Andrew B. Optimal Monetary Growth. *J. Monet. Econ.*, May 1987, *19*(3), pp. 437–50.

Abraham, Jesse M. Income Redistribution during a Disinflation. *J. Macroecon.*, Spring 1987, *9*(2), pp. 203–21. **[G: U.S.]**

Ahmed, Ather Maqsood and Rafiq, Mohammad. Monetary Anticipations and the Demand for Money: An Application for the South Asian Region. *Pakistan Devel. Rev.*, Winter 1987, *26*(4), pp. 529–37. **[G: Pakistan; India; Sri Lanka]**

Ahmed, Shaghil. Wage Stickiness and the Non-neutrality of Money: A Cross-Industry Analysis. *J. Monet. Econ.*, July 1987, *20*(1), pp. 25–50. **[G: Canada]**

Ahumada, Hildegart. Econometría Dinámica: Una aplicación a la demanda de billetes y monedas en poder del público. (Dynamic Econometric: An Application to the Demand for Notes and Coins in the Hands of the Public. With English summary.) *Económica (La Plata)*,

July-Dec. 1987, *33*(2), pp. 159–84.

Al-Jarhi, Mabid Ali Muhamed Mahmoud. The Relative Efficiency of Interest-Free Monetary Economies: The Fiat Money Case. *Khan, M. S. and Mirakhor, A., eds.*, 1987, *1981*, pp. 37–73.

Alesina, Alberto and Tabellini, Guido. Rules and Discretion with Noncoordinated Monetary and Fiscal Policies. *Econ. Inquiry*, October 1987, *25*(4), pp. 619–30.

Alexander, Volbert. Die Funktion der Geldpolitik im Rahmen moderner Konzepte zur gesamtwirtschaftlichen Stabilisierung. (The Role of Monetary Policy within Modern Concepts for Economic Stabilization. With English summary.) *Konjunkturpolitik*, 1987, *33*(5), pp. 268–84.

Ali, Shaukat. Monetary Anticipations and the Demand for Money: An Application for the South Asian Region: Comments. *Pakistan Devel. Rev.*, Winter 1987, *26*(4), pp. 538–39. **[G: Pakistan; India; Sri Lanka]**

Aliber, Robert Z. Gold in the International Monetary System: A Catalog of the Options. *Aliber, R. Z., ed.*, 1987, pp. 168–82. **[G: U.S.]**

Allais, Maurice. The Credit Mechanism and Its Implications. *Feiwel, G. R., ed. (II)*, 1987, pp. 491–561.

Alston, Julian M. and Chalfant, James A. A Note on Causality between Money, Wages and Prices in Australia. *Econ. Rec.*, June 1987, *63*(181), pp. 115–19. **[G: Australia]**

Amano, Masanori. Endogenous Money Supply and Monetary Policy in Asset Markets with Alternative Rationing Schemes. *J. Japanese Int. Economies*, March 1987, *1*(1), pp. 110–29. **[G: Japan]**

Andersen, Torben M. Pre-set Prices, Differential Information and Monetary Policy. *Sinclair, P. J. N., ed.*, 1987, *1986*, pp. 283–307.

Anderson, Robert and Enzler, Jared J. Toward Realistic Policy Design: Policy Reaction Functions That Rely on Economic Forecasts. *[Modigliani, F.]*, 1987, pp. 291–330. **[G: U.S.]**

Anyadike-Danes, Michael and Godley, Wynne. A Stock Adjustment Model of Income Determination with Inside Money and Private Debt with Some Preliminary Empirical Results for the United States. *de Cecco, M. and Fitoussi, J.-P., eds.*, 1987, pp. 95–120. **[G: U.S.]**

Arize, Augustine. Past Inflation Variability and the Stability of the Demand-for-Money Function in Nigeria. *Atlantic Econ. J.*, March 1987, *15*(1), pp. 31–41. **[G: Nigeria]**

Arnon, Arie. Banking between the Invisible and Visible Hands: A Reinterpretation of Ricardo's Place within the Classical School. *Oxford Econ. Pap.*, June 1987, *39*(2), pp. 268–81.

Arora, Harjit K. Monetary Stabilization Policy and Its Effects—A Case Study of India. *Indian J. Quant. Econ.*, 1987, *3*(1), pp. 1–13. **[G: India]**

Artus, Patrick. Fixation de l'objectif monétaire et réputation de la Banque Centrale. (The

Choice of the Intermediate Monetary Target and the Reputation of the Central Bank. With English summary.) *Revue Écon.*, July 1987, *38*(4), pp. 807–35.

Artus, Patrick. Hétérogénéité des banques et des circuits de financement et régulation monétaire. (Banks' Heterogeneity and Monetary Policy. With English summary.) *Ann. Écon. Statist.*, Oct./Dec. 1987, (8), pp. 27–41.

Artus, Patrick. Politique monétaire, fonctionnement du marché du crédit et innovations financières. (With English summary.) *Revue Écon. Polit.*, Jan.-Feb. 1987, *97*(1), pp. 27–50.

Asako, Kazumi. On the Optimal Short-run Money Supply Management under the Monetarist Long-run Money Supply Rule. *Econ. Stud. Quart.*, March 1987, *38*(1), pp. 46–60.

Aschheim, Joseph and Tavlas, George S. Inconsistency in Correcting for Serial Correlation in Money-Demand Models. *Atlantic Econ. J.*, December 1987, *15*(4), pp. 16–21. **[G: U.S.]**

Auernheimer, Leonardo. On the Outcome of Inconsistent Programs under Exchange Rate and Monetary Rules. *J. Monet. Econ.*, March 1987, *19*(2), pp. 279–305.

d'Autume, Antoine and Michel, Philippe. 'Transversality Conditions', Budget Constraints and the Determinancy of a Perfect Foresight Equilibrium in a Monetary Growth Model. *Europ. Econ. Rev.*, October 1987, *31*(7), pp. 1343–67.

Bailey, Ralph W., et al. Monnaie, demande globale et inertie des rythmes d'inflation dans les principaux pays européens. (Money, Aggregate Demand and Price Inertia in the Major European Countries. With English summary.) *Écon. Appl.*, 1987, *40*(3), pp. 483–538.
[G: Europe]

Baillie, Richard T. and McMahon, Patrick C. Rational Forecasts in Models of the Term Structure of Interest Rates. *Goodhart, C.; Currie, D. and Llewellyn, D. T., eds.,* 1987, pp. 189–206.

Baker, Wayne E. What Is Money? A Social Structural Interpretation. *Mizruchi, M. S. and Schwartz, M., eds.,* 1987, pp. 109–44.
[G: U.S.]

Bana, Ismail Mahomed and Handa, Jagdish. Currency Substitution: A Multicurrency Study for Canada. *Int. Econ. J.*, Autumn 1987, *1*(3), pp. 71–86.

Barge, Jim. Interest Rate Exposure. *Gardener, E. P. M., ed.,* 1987, pp. 7–22.

Barnett, William A. The Microeconomic Theory of Monetary Aggregation. *Barnett, W. A. and Singleton, K. J., eds.,* 1987, pp. 115–68.

Barro, Robert J. Government Spending, Interest Rates, Prices, and Budget Deficits in the United Kingdom, 1701–1918. *J. Monet. Econ.*, September 1987, *20*(2), pp. 221–47.
[G: U.K.]

Barsky, Robert B. The Fisher Hypothesis and the Forecastability and Persistence of Inflation. *J. Monet. Econ.*, January 1987, *19*(1), pp. 3–24. **[G: U.S.]**

Batchelor, Roy A. Monetary Indicators and Oper-

ating Targets: Some Recent Issues in the UK. *Begg, D. K. H., et al.,* 1987, pp. 55–82.
[G: U.K.]

Belongia, Michael T. The Link between Monetary Uncertainty and GNP: Some Direct Estimates. *Appl. Econ.*, August 1987, *19*(8), pp. 1059–64. **[G: U.S.]**

Benassi, Corrado. An Input–Output Formulation of the "Coefficient of Money Transactions": A Note on Hayek's Trade Cycle Theory. *Econ. Int.*, February 1987, *40*(1), pp. 1–19.

Benassy, Jean-Pascal. Imperfect Competition, Unemployment and Policy. *Europ. Econ. Rev.*, Feb./Mar. 1987, *31*(1/2), pp. 417–26.

Benveniste, Lawrence M. Incomplete Market Participation and the Optimal Exchange of Credit. *Prescott, E. C. and Wallace, N., eds.,* 1987, pp. 121–45.

Benveniste, Lawrence M. and Berger, Allen N. Securitization with Recourse: An Instrument that Offers Uninsured Bank Depositors Sequential Claims. *J. Banking Finance*, September 1987, *11*(3), pp. 403–24.

Beranek, William and Timberlake, Richard H., Jr. The Liquidity Trap Theory: A Critique. *Southern Econ. J.*, October 1987, *54*(2), pp. 387–96.

Bernanke, Ben S. and Gertler, Mark. Banking and Macroeconomic Equilibrium. *Barnett, W. A. and Singleton, K. J., eds.,* 1987, pp. 89–111.

Besanko, David and Thakor, Anjan V. Collateral and Rationing: Sorting Equilibria in Monopolistic and Competitive Credit Markets. *Int. Econ. Rev.*, October 1987, *28*(3), pp. 671–89.

Bester, Helmut. The Role of Collateral in Credit Markets with Imperfect Information. *Europ. Econ. Rev.*, June 1987, *31*(4), pp. 887–99.

Bester, Helmut and Hellwig, Martin. Moral Hazard and Equilibrium Credit Rationing: An Overview of the Issues. *Bamberg, G. and Spremann, K., eds.,* 1987, pp. 135–66.

Bhattacharya, Sudipto and Gale, Douglas M. Preference Shocks, Liquidity, and Central Bank Policy. *Barnett, W. A. and Singleton, K. J., eds.,* 1987, pp. 69–88.

Birchler, Urs W. and Kästli, René. Finanzinnovationen und schweizerische Geldpolitik. (Financial Innovations and Swiss Monetary Policy. With English summary.) *Aussenwirtschaft*, September 1987, *42*(2/3), pp. 275–303.
[G: Switzerland]

Blackburn, Keith. Interest Parity, the Degree of Capital Mobility and the Information Contents of the Exchange Rate and the Interest Rate: Clarifications and Extensions. *Manchester Sch. Econ. Soc. Stud.*, March 1987, *55*(1), pp. 60–76.

Blinder, Alan S. Credit Rationing and Effective Supply Failures. *Econ. J.*, June 1987, *97*(386), pp. 327–52.

Bogomolov, Oleg T. Monetary Institutions in a Planned Economy. *de Cecco, M. and Fitoussi, J.-P., eds.,* 1987, pp. 209–21. **[G: U.S.S.R.; CMEA]**

Bohanon, Cecil E. and Van Cott, T. Norman.

Patinkin on a Money-Financed Increase in Government Expenditures: What Happened to Seigniorage? *Public Finance*, 1987, *42*(2), pp. 332–35.

Bond, Michael T. and Smolen, Gerald E. Nominal Interest Rates and Marginal Tax Rates. *Quart. J. Bus. Econ.*, Spring 1987, *26*(2), pp. 104–09.   [G: U.S.]

Boot, Arnoud; Thakor, Anjan V. and Udell, Gregory F. Competition, Risk Neutrality and Loan Commitments. *J. Banking Finance*, September 1987, *11*(3), pp. 449–71.

Bordo, Michael D.; Choudhri, Ehsan U. and Schwartz, Anna J. The Behavior of Money Stock under Interest Rate Control: Some Evidence for Canada. *J. Money, Credit, Banking*, May 1987, *19*(2), pp. 181–97.   [G: Canada]

Bordo, Michael D. and Marcotte, Ivan A. Purchasing Power Parity in Colonial America: Some Evidence for South Carolina 1732–1774: A Comment. *Carnegie–Rochester Conf. Ser. Public Policy*, Autumn 1987, *27*, pp. 311–23.   [G: U.S.]

Bordo, Michael D. and Schwartz, Anna J. The Importance of Stable Money: Theory and Evidence. *Schwartz, A. J.*, 1987, *1983*, pp. 255–70.   [G: U.S.]

Bordo, Michael D. and Schwartz, Anna J. The Importance of Stable Money: Theory and Evidence. *Dorn, J. A. and Schwartz, A. J., eds.*, 1987, pp. 53–72.   [G: U.S.]

Boskin, Michael J. Deficits, Public Debt, Interest Rates and Private Saving: Perspectives and Reflections on Recent Analyses and on U.S. Experience. *Boskin, M. J.; Fleming, J. S. and Gorini, S., eds.*, 1987, pp. 255–86.   [G: U.S.]

Bosshardt, Donald I. A Model of Intertemporal Discount Rates in the Presence of Real and Inflationary Autocorrelations. *J. Finance*, September 1987, *42*(4), pp. 1049–70.   [G: U.S.]

Boyer, Russell S. and Kingston, Geoffrey H. Currency Substitution under Finance Constraints. *J. Int. Money Finance*, September 1987, *6*(3), pp. 235–50.

Brainard, William C. and Tobin, James. Pitfalls in Financial Model Building. *Tobin, J. (I)*, 1987, *1968*, pp. 352–77.   [G: U.S.]

Breece, James H. Rational Expectations, Currency Substitution, and the Demand for Money during the German Hyperinflation. *METU*, 1987, *14*(1), pp. 65–74.   [G: Germany]

Brown, Z. M. Interest Margin Analysis Revisited Yet Again. *Gardener, E. P. M., ed.*, 1987, pp. 73–132.

Browne, F. X. Sluggish Quantity Adjustment in a Non-clearing Market—A Disequilibrium Econometric Application to the Loan Market. *J. Appl. Econometrics*, October 1987, *2*(4), pp. 335–49.   [G: Ireland]

Brunner, Karl. Has Monetarism Failed? *Dorn, J. A. and Schwartz, A. J., eds.*, 1987, pp. 163–99.   [G: U.S.]

Buchanan, James M. and Roback, Jennifer. The Incidence and Effects of Public Debt in the Absence of Fiscal Illusion. *Public Finance Quart.*, January 1987, *15*(1), pp. 5–26.

Buiter, Willem H. A Fiscal Theory of Hyperdeflations? Some Surprising Monetarist Arithmetic. *Sinclair, P. J. N., ed.*, 1987, pp. 111–18.

Buiter, Willem H. A Fiscal Theory of Hyperdeflations? Some Surprising Monetarist Arithmetic. *Oxford Econ. Pap.*, March 1987, *39*(1), pp. 111–18.

Burkett, Paul and Vogel, Robert C. Microeconomic Foundations of Financial Liberalization: Interest Rates, Transactions Costs, and Financial Savings. *Connolly, M. and González-Vega, C., eds.*, 1987, pp. 305–21.

Burmeister, Edwin and Wall, Kent D. Unobserved Rational Expectations and the German Hyperinflation with Endogenous Money Supply. *Int. Econ. Rev.*, February 1987, *28*(1), pp. 15–32.   [G: Germany]

Cagan, Phillip and Schwartz, Anna J. How Feasible Is a Flexible Monetary Policy? *Schwartz, A. J.*, 1987, *1975*, pp. 183–208.   [G: U.S.]

Campbell, John Y. Macroeconomic Lessons from Britain: A Review Essay. *J. Monet. Econ.*, March 1987, *19*(2), pp. 315–24.   [G: U.K.]

Campbell, John Y. Money Announcements, the Demand for Bank Reserves, and the Behavior of the Federal Funds Rate within the Statement Week. *J. Money, Credit, Banking*, February 1987, *19*(1), pp. 56–67.   [G: U.S.]

Campbell, John Y. and Clarida, Richard H. The Dollar and Real Interest Rates. *Carnegie–Rochester Conf. Ser. Public Policy*, Autumn 1987, *27*, pp. 103–39.   [G: U.S.]

Canto, Victor A. Monetary Policy, "Dollarization," and Parallel Market Exchange Rates: The Case of the Dominican Republic. *Connolly, M. and González-Vega, C., eds.*, 1987, pp. 177–94.   [G: Dominican Republic]

Canto, Victor A.; Nickelsburg, Gerald and Rizos, Paul. The Effect of Fiscal Policy on the Short-run Relation between Nominal Interest Rates and Inflation. *Econ. Inquiry*, January 1987, *25*(1), pp. 27–42.   [G: U.S.]

Caplin, Andrew S. and Spulber, Daniel F. Menu Costs and the Neutrality of Money. *Quart. J. Econ.*, November 1987, *102*(4), pp. 703–25.

Carhill, M. Effective Demand Failure: Critique of an Anti-monetary Theory: A Note. *S. Afr. J. Econ.*, March 1987, *55*(1), pp. 86–89.

Carraro, Carlo. Strategie punitive, annunci ottimali e politiche dei redditi. (Threats, Optimal Announcements, and Income Policy. With English summary.) *Ricerche Econ.*, Apr.-June 1987, *41*(2), pp. 210–30.

Carrington, Samantha and Crouch, Robert. Interest Rate Differentials on Short-term Securities and Rational Expectations of Inflation. *J. Banking Finance*, December 1987, *11*(4), pp. 571–79.   [G: U.S.]

Caskey, John and Fazzari, Steven M. Aggregate Demand Contractions with Nominal Debt Commitments: Is Wage Flexibility Stabilizing? *Econ. Inquiry*, October 1987, *25*(4), pp. 583–97.

Cecchetti, Stephen G. Testing Short-run Neutrality: International Evidence. *Rev. Econ. Sta-*

tist., February 1987, *69*(1), pp. 135–40.
[G: U.S.; Canada; W. Europe]

de Cecco, Marcello. Financial Innovations and Monetary Theory. *de Cecco, M., ed.*, 1987, pp. 1–9.

de Cecco, Marcello and Fitoussi, Jean-Paul. From the Use to the Production of Money: Monetary Theory and Economic Institutions— Theme and Outline of the Conference. *de Cecco, M. and Fitoussi, J.-P., eds.*, 1987, pp. 1–17.

Chadha, Binky. Contract Length, Monetary Policy and Exchange Rate Variability. *J. Int. Money Finance*, December 1987, *6*(4), pp. 491–504. [G: U.S.]

Chan, Yuk-Shee and Thakor, Anjan V. Collateral and Competitive Equilibria with Moral Hazard and Private Information. *J. Finance*, June 1987, *42*(2), pp. 345–63.

Chen, Chau-nan; Lai, Ching-chong and Chang, Wen-ya. The Tight Money Effect, Wage Indexation and Macroeconomic Policy: The Fleming Model Revisited. *J. Econ. Stud.*, 1987, *14*(5), pp. 54–62.

Chen, Chien-Hsun and Steindl, Frank G. Anticipated Monetary and Fiscal Policy Effects on Output. *J. Macroecon.*, Spring 1987, *9*(2), pp. 255–74. [G: U.S.]

Chick, Victoria. Speculation, the Rate of Interest, and the Rate of Profit. *J. Post Keynesian Econ.*, Fall 1987, *10*(1), pp. 124–32.

Chow, Gregory C. Money and Price Level Determination in China. *J. Compar. Econ.*, September 1987, *11*(3), pp. 319–33. [G: China]

Christensen, Anders Møller and Jensen, Hugo Frey. Den danske pengeefterspørgsel 1975– 86. (The Demand for Money in Demark, 1975– 86. With English summary.) *Nationaløkon. Tidsskr.*, 1987, *125*(2), pp. 185–96.
[G: Denmark]

Christiano, Lawrence J. Cagan's Model of Hyperinflation under Rational Expectations. *Int. Econ. Rev.*, February 1987, *28*(1), pp. 33–49.
[G: Germany]

Chrystal, K. Alec and Chatterji, Monojit. Money and Disaggregate Supply in the United States, 1950–1982. *Europ. Econ. Rev.*, August 1987, *31*(6), pp. 1211–28. [G: U.S.]

Colletaz, Gilbert. Les taux d'intérêt observés sur le marché monétaire sont-ils trop volatils? Un test de la rationalité des prévisions dans le cadre de la théorie des anticipations de la structure par échéance. (Do French Money Market Interest Rates Move Too Much? Test of the Rational Expectations Model of the Term Structure of Interest Rates. With English summary.) *Revue Écon.*, July 1987, *38*(4), pp. 837– 52. [G: France]

Cooper, Richard N. Gold: Does It Provide a Viable Basis for the Monetary System? *Aliber, R. Z., ed.*, 1987, pp. 151–67.

Cooper, Russell. Gale on Monetary Theory: A Review Essay. *J. Monet. Econ.*, March 1987, *19*(2), pp. 325–32.

Corden, W. Max. The Relevance for Developing Countries of Recent Developments in Macro-

economic Theory. *World Bank Res. Observer*, July 1987, *2*(2), pp. 171–88. [G: LDCs]

Cosimano, Thomas F. Reserve Accounting and Variability in the Federal Funds Market. *J. Money, Credit, Banking*, May 1987, *19*(2), pp. 198–209. [G: U.S.]

Cosimano, Thomas F. The Federal Funds Market under Bank Deregulation. *J. Money, Credit, Banking*, August 1987, *19*(3), pp. 326–39.
[G: U.S.]

Cothren, Richard. Asymmetric Information and Optimal Bank Reserves. *J. Money, Credit, Banking*, February 1987, *19*(1), pp. 68–77.

Courakis, Anthony S. In What Sense Do Compulsory Ratios Reduce the Volume of Deposits? *Goodhart, C.; Currie, D. and Llewellyn, D. T., eds.*, 1987, pp. 150–86.

Cover, James Peery and Keeler, James P. Estimating Money Demand in Log–First-Difference Form. *Southern Econ. J.*, January 1987, *53*(3), pp. 751–67. [G: U.S.]

Cowen, Tyler and Kroszner, Randall. The Development of the New Monetary Economics. *J. Polit. Econ.*, June 1987, *95*(3), pp. 567– 90.

Croushore, Dean D. Government Financial Policy and Capital. *Southern Econ. J.*, October 1987, *54*(2), pp. 435–48.

Cukierman, Alex. Central Bank Behavior and Credibility: Some Recent Theoretical Developments. *Wilcox, J. A., ed.*, 1987, *1986*, pp. 280– 92.

Cuthbertson, Keith and Taylor, Mark P. Buffer-Stock Money: An Appraisal. *Goodhart, C.; Currie, D. and Llewellyn, D. T., eds.*, 1987, pp. 103–24. [G: U.K.]

Cuthbertson, Keith and Taylor, Mark P. Monetary Anticipations and the Demand for Money: Some Evidence for the U.K. *Weltwirtsch. Arch.*, 1987, *123*(3), pp. 509–20. [G: U.K.]

Cuthbertson, Keith and Taylor, Mark P. The Demand for Money: A Dynamic Rational Expectations Model. *Econ. J.*, Supplement 1987, *97*, pp. 65–76. [G: U.K.]

Danthine, Jean-Pierre; Donaldson, John B. and Smith, Lance. On the Superneutrality of Money in a Stochastic Dynamic Macroeconomic Model. *J. Monet. Econ.*, December 1987, *20*(3), pp. 475–99.

Dauhajre, Andrés. Financial Reform in a Small Open Economy with a Flexible Exchange Rate. *Connolly, M. and González-Vega, C., eds.*, 1987, pp. 283–304.

Dauhajre, Andrés. Some Warnings Concerning Possible Financial Reform in the Dominican Republic. *Salazar-Carrillo, J. and Tirado de Alonzo, I., eds.*, 1987, pp. 1–12.
[G: Dominican Republic]

Davidson, James. Disequilibrium Money: Some Further Results with a Monetary Model of the UK. *Goodhart, C.; Currie, D. and Llewellyn, D. T., eds.*, 1987, pp. 125–49. [G: U.K.]

Davidson, James and Ireland, Jonathan. Buffer Stock Models of the Monetary Sector. *Nat. Inst. Econ. Rev.*, August 1987, (121), pp. 67– 71. [G: U.K.]

Davidson, Paul. Sensible Expectations and the Long-run Non-neutrality of Money. *J. Post Keynesian Econ.*, Fall 1987, *10*(1), pp. 146–53.

Day, John. Monetary Colonialism in the Medieval Mediterranean. *Day, J.*, 1987, pp. 116–28.
[G: Europe]

Day, John. The Decline of a Money Economy: Sardinia under Catalan Rule. *Day, J.*, 1987, *1978*, pp. 72–89. [G: Italy]

Day, John. The Fisher Equation and Medieval Monetary History. *Day, J.*, 1987, *1984*, pp. 108–15. [G: Europe]

Day, John. The Great Bullion Famine of the Fifteenth Century. *Day, J.*, 1987, *1973*, pp. 1–54. [G: Europe]

Day, John. The Monetary Circulation in Tuscany in the Age of Dante. *Day, J.*, 1987, pp. 129–40. [G: Italy]

Day, John. The Question of Monetary Contraction in Late Medieval Europe. *Day, J.*, 1987, *1981*, pp. 55–71. [G: Europe]

De Freitas, A. J. M. and Solnik, Bruno. L'anticipation de l'inflation et le taux d'intérêt à court term. (Expected Inflation and Short Term Interest Rates. With English summary.) *Finance*, December 1987, *8*(2), pp. 77–89.
[G: OECD; Brazil; Mexico]

De Vroey, Michel. La possibilité d'une économie décentralisée. Esquisse d'une alternative à la théorie de l'équilibre général. (The Possibility of a Decentralized Economy. An Alternative to the General Equilibrium Framework. With English summary.) *Revue Écon.*, July 1987, *38*(4), pp. 773–805.

Deaves, Richard; Melino, Angelo and Pesando, James E. The Response of Interest Rates to the Federal Reserve's Weekly Money Announcements: The 'Puzzle' of Anticipated Money. *J. Monet. Econ.*, May 1987, *19*(3), pp. 393–404. [G: Canada; U.S.]

Deravi, M. Keivan. Endogeneity of the Money Supply: The Monetarists Proposition Revisited. *Atlantic Econ. J.*, September 1987, *15*(3), pp. 79.

Deshons, Michel and Freixas, Xavier. Le rôle de la garantie dans le contrat de prêt bancaire. (The Role of Collateral in the Bank's Debt Contract. With English summary.) *Finance*, June 1987, *8*(1), pp. 7–32.

Devereux, Michael. The Effect of Monetary Variability on Welfare in a Simple Macroeconomic Model. *J. Monet. Econ.*, May 1987, *19*(3), pp. 427–35.

Dewes, Leonard D. The Mechanics of the Short-term Interbank ECU Market. *Levich, R. M. and Sommariva, A., eds.*, 1987, pp. 73–87. [G: EEC]

Diamond, Peter. Multiple Equilibria in Models of Credit. *Amer. Econ. Rev.*, May 1987, *77*(2), pp. 82–86.

Diamond, Peter and Yellin, Joel. Pricing and the Distribution of Money Holdings in a Search Economy, II. *Barnett, W. A. and Singleton, K. J., eds.*, 1987, pp. 311–24.

Dokko, Yoon and Edelstein, Robert. The Empiri-

cal Interrelationships among the Mundell and Darby Hypotheses and Expected Stock Market Returns. *Rev. Econ. Statist.*, February 1987, *69*(1), pp. 161–66. [G: U.S.]

Domowitz, Ian and Elbadawi, Ibrahim. An Error-Correction Approach to Money Demand: The Case of Sudan. *J. Devel. Econ.*, August 1987, *26*(2), pp. 257–75. [G: Sudan]

Dooley, Michael P. An Analysis of the Management of the Currency Composition of Reserve Assets and External Liabilities of Developing Countries. *Aliber, R. Z., ed.*, 1987, pp. 262–80. [G: LDCs]

Dorn, James A. and Schwartz, Anna J. The Search for Stable Money: Preface. *Dorn, J. A. and Schwartz, A. J., eds.*, 1987, pp. xi–xvii.

Dornbusch, Rudiger. Collapsing Exchange Rate Regimes. *[Diaz-Alejandro, C. F.]*, 1987, pp. 71–83.

Dornbusch, Rudiger. Collapsing Exchange Rate Regimes. *J. Devel. Econ.*, October 1987, *27*(1–2), pp. 71–83.

Dotsey, Michael. Monetary Policy, Secrecy, and Federal Funds Rate Behavior. *J. Monet. Econ.*, December 1987, *20*(3), pp. 463–74.
[G: U.S.]

Dow, Sheila C. Post Keynesian Monetary Theory for an Open Economy. *J. Post Keynesian Econ.*, Winter 1986-87, *9*(2), pp. 237–57.

Dow, Sheila C. The Treatment of Money in Regional Economics. *J. Reg. Sci.*, February 1987, *27*(1), pp. 13–24.

Dutkowsky, Donald H. Unanticipated Money Growth, Interest Rate Volatility, and Unemployment in the United States. *Rev. Econ. Statist.*, February 1987, *69*(1), pp. 144–48.
[G: U.S.]

Edwards, J. R. The Value of Money, Monetary Equilibrium and the Cambridge Effect: A Reply [Effective Demand Failure: Critique of an Anti-monetary Theory]. *S. Afr. J. Econ.*, September 1987, *55*(3), pp. 300–303.

Eichengreen, Barry. Conducting the International Orchestra: Bank of England Leadership under the Classical Gold Standard. *J. Int. Money Finance*, March 1987, *6*(1), pp. 5–29.
[G: U.K.]

Elliott, J. Walter and Reichenstein, William. A Monetary Approach to Measuring Long-run Inflationary Expectations. *J. Econ. Bus.*, November 1987, *39*(4), pp. 327–38. [G: U.S.]

Entov, R. M. and Poletayev, A. V. On the Long-term Dynamics of the Rate of Return. *Vasko, T., ed.*, 1987, pp. 105–18.

Erol, Umit; Richardson, James A. and Gulledge, Thomas R., Jr. Spectral Analysis of Nominal Interest Rates. *J. Econ. Dynam. Control*, June 1987, *11*(2), pp. 275–81. [G: U.S.]

Evans, Paul. Do Budget Deficits Raise Nominal Interest Rates? Evidence from Six Countries. *J. Monet. Econ.*, September 1987, *20*(2), pp. 281–300. [G: N. America; France; W. Germany; Japan; U.K.]

Evans, Paul D. Interest Rates and Expected Fu-

ture Budget Deficits in the United States. *J. Polit. Econ.*, February 1987, *95*(1), pp. 34–58.
[G: U.S.]

Fair, Ray C. International Evidence on the Demand for Money. *Rev. Econ. Statist.*, August 1987, *69*(3), pp. 473–80. [G: OECD; LDCs]

Feige, Edgar L. The Theory and Measurement of Cash Payments: A Case Study of the Netherlands. *Heijmans, R. and Neudecker, H., eds.*, 1987, pp. 67–98. [G: Netherlands]

Feltenstein, Andrew and Farhadian, Ziba. Fiscal Policy, Monetary Targets, and the Price Level in a Centrally Planned Economy: An Application to the Case of China. *J. Money, Credit, Banking*, May 1987, *19*(2), pp. 137–56.
[G: China]

Fender, John. Monetary and Exchange Rate Policies in an Open Macroeconomic Model with Unemployment and Rational Expectations. *Sinclair, P. J. N., ed.*, 1987, *1986*, pp. 328–42.

Fethke, Gary and Policano, Andrew. Monetary Policy and the Timing of Wage Negotiations. *J. Monet. Econ.*, January 1987, *19*(1), pp. 89–105.

Flood, Robert P. and Garber, Peter M. Gold Monetization and Gold Discipline. *Aliber, R. Z., ed.*, 1987, pp. 183–211.

Foster, Gladys Parker and Ranson, Baldwin. Thorstein Veblen on Money and Production. *Écon. Soc.*, September 1987, *21*(9), pp. 221–28.

Frankel, Jeffrey A. Expectations and Commodity Price Dynamics: The Overshooting Model: Reply. *Amer. J. Agr. Econ.*, November 1987, *69*(4), pp. 856.

Fratianni, Michele; Hur, Hyung-Doh and Kang, Heejoon. Random Walk and Monetary Causality in Five Exchange Markets. *J. Int. Money Finance*, December 1987, *6*(4), pp. 505–14.
[G: U.S.]

Freeman, Scott. Reserve Requirements and Optimal Seigniorage. *J. Monet. Econ.*, March 1987, *19*(2), pp. 307–14.

Friedman, Benjamin M. Toward Realistic Policy Design: Policy Reaction Functions That Rely on Economic Forecasts: Comments. *[Modigliani, F.]*, 1987, pp. 331–36. [G: U.S.]

Friedman, Milton. Monetary Policy: Tactics versus Strategy. *Dorn, J. A. and Schwartz, A. J., eds.*, 1987, *1984*, pp. 361–82. [G: U.S.]

Fry, Maxwell J. Neo-classical and Neo-structuralist Models of Financial Development: Theories and Evidence. *Greek Econ. Rev.*, 1987, *9*(1), pp. 1–37. [G: LDCs]

Frydman, Roman and Rappoport, Peter. Is the Distinction between Anticipated and Unanticipated Money Growth Relevant in Explaining Aggregate Output? *Amer. Econ. Rev.*, September 1987, *77*(4), pp. 693–703.
[G: U.S.]

Fumagalli, Andrea. Instabilità del mercato creditizio e prezzo relativo del credito: un'analisi teorica. (Instability of the Credit Market and Credit Relative Price: A Theoretical Analysis.

With English summary.) *Econ. Polít.*, August 1987, *4*(2), pp. 213–45.

von Furstenberg, George M. Internationally Managed Money Supply. *Aliber, R. Z., ed.*, 1987, pp. 117–26.

von Furstenberg, George M. Stock/Flow Ratios with Money and Debt: What Can Be Learned from the Breakup of Past Relationships in the United States? *Kredit Kapital*, 1987, *20*(4), pp. 415–38. [G: U.S.]

Garber, Peter M. Monetary History and Monetary Policy: A Review Essay. *J. Monet. Econ.*, July 1987, *20*(1), pp. 177–82.

Gardener, Edward P. M. Interest Rate Risk and the Banking Firm: Interest Margin Analysis Revisited. *Gardener, E. P. M., ed.*, 1987, pp. 23–71.

Gedeon, Shirley J. Neomonetarism and Stabilization. *Econ. Anal. Workers' Manage.*, 1987, *21*(2), pp. 259–63. [G: Yugoslavia]

Gibson-Asner, Rajna. Del modéles d'équilibre de là structure des taux d'intérêt: un essai de synthèse. (Equilibrium Models of the Term Structure of Interest Rates: A Synthesis. With English summary.) *Finance*, December 1987, *8*(2), pp. 133–71.

Gilles, Christian and LeRoy, Stephen F. A Note on the Local Expectations Hypothesis: A Discrete-Time Exposition—Erratum. *J. Finance*, June 1987, *42*(2), pp. 473.

Glick, Reuven. Interest Rate Linkages in the Pacific Basin. *Fed. Res. Bank San Francisco Econ. Rev.*, Summer 1987, (3), pp. 31–42.
[G: OECD; Hong Kong; Singapore; Taiwan; Malaysia]

Goldfeld, Stephen M. and Sichel, Daniel E. Money Demand: The Effects of Inflation and Alternative Adjustment Mechanisms. *Rev. Econ. Statist.*, August 1987, *69*(3), pp. 511–15. [G: U.S.]

Goodfriend, Marvin. A Model of Money Stock Determination with Loan Demand and a Banking System Balance Sheet Constraint. *Goodfriend, M.*, 1987, *1982*, pp. 3–16. [G: U.S.]

Goodfriend, Marvin. Interest Rate Smoothing and Price Level Trend-Stationarity. *J. Monet. Econ.*, May 1987, *19*(3), pp. 335–48.

Goodfriend, Marvin, et al. A Weekly Rational Expectations Model of the Nonborrowed Reserve Operating Procedure. *Goodfriend, M.*, 1987, *1986*, pp. 17–34. [G: U.S.]

Goodhart, Charles A. E. Monetary Indicators and Operating Targets: Some Recent Issues in the UK: Commentary. *Begg, D. K. H., et al.*, 1987, pp. 83–88.

Goodhart, Charles A. E. Why Do Banks Need a Central Bank? *Sinclair, P. J. N., ed.*, 1987, pp. 75–89.

Goodhart, Charles A. E. Why Do Banks Need a Central Bank? *Oxford Econ. Pap.*, March 1987, *39*(1), pp. 75–89.

Gordon, J. Douglas. Expectations and Commodity Price Dynamics: The Overshooting Model: Comment. *Amer. J. Agr. Econ.*, November 1987, *69*(4), pp. 852–55.

Gottinger, Hans W. Decision Costs and Microeconomic Demand for Money. *Z. Wirtschaft. Sozialwissen.*, 1987, *107*(3), pp. 361–78.

Goux, Jean-François. La théorie monétaire de la "finance" chez Keynes: une réinterprétation. (With English summary.) *Revue Écon. Polit.*, Sept.-Oct. 1987, *97*(5), pp. 592–612.

Grandmont, Jean-Michel. Classical and Keynesian Unemployment in the IS–LM Model. *de Cecco, M. and Fitoussi, J.-P., eds.*, 1987, pp. 66–94.

de Grauwe, Paul and Rosiers, Marc. Real Exchange Rate Variability and Monetary Disturbances. *Weltwirtsch. Arch.*, 1987, *123*(3), pp. 430–48. **[G: Global]**

de Grauwe, Paul and Rosiers, Marc. Real Exchange Rate Variability and Monetary Disturbances. *Chrystal, K. A. and Sedgwick, R., eds.*, 1987, pp. 30–53. **[G: Global]**

Graziani, Augusto. Keynes' Finance Motive. *Écon. Soc.*, September 1987, *21*(9), pp. 23–42.

Green, Christopher J. Did High-Powered Money Rule the Roost? Monetary Policy, Private Behaviour and the Structure of Interest Rates in the United Kingdom: 1972–77. *Goodhart, C.; Currie, D. and Llewellyn, D. T., eds.*, 1987, pp. 207–30. **[G: U.K.]**

Green, Christopher J. Money Market Arbitrage and Commercial Banks' Base Rate Adjustments in the United Kingdom. *Bull. Econ. Res.*, October 1987, *39*(4), pp. 273–96. **[G: U.K.]**

Green, Steven L. Theories of Inflation: A Review Essay. *J. Monet. Econ.*, July 1987, *20*(1), pp. 169–75.

Gregory, Allan W. Testing Interest Rate Parity and Rational Expectations for Canada and the United States. *Can. J. Econ.*, May 1987, *20*(2), pp. 289–305. **[G: Canada; U.S.]**

Gregory, Allan W. and Veall, Michael R. Formulating Wald Tests of the Restrictions Implied by the Rational Expectations Hypothesis. *J. Appl. Econometrics*, January 1987, *2*(1), pp. 61–68. **[G: Canada]**

Gros, Daniel. The Effectiveness of Capital Controls: Implications for Monetary Autonomy in the Presence of Incomplete Market Separation. *Int. Monet. Fund Staff Pap.*, December 1987, *34*(4), pp. 621–42. **[G: Italy]**

Grossman, Sanford J. Monetary Dynamics with Proportional Transaction Costs and Fixed Payment Periods. *Barnett, W. A. and Singleton, K. J., eds.*, 1987, pp. 3–41.

Gualandri, Elisabetta. Italian Banks and Interest Rate Risk: A Survey for the Decade 1975–1984. *Gardener, E. P. M., ed.*, 1987, pp. 149–60. **[G: Italy]**

Gupta, Kanhaya L. Aggregate Savings, Financial Intermediation, and Interest Rate. *Rev. Econ. Statist.*, May 1987, *69*(2), pp. 303–11. **[G: Latin America; Asia]**

Haberler, Gottfried. Money, Markets, and Stability: Comment [The Importance of Stable Money: Theory and Evidence]. *Dorn, J. A. and Schwartz, A. J., eds.*, 1987, *1983*, pp. 73–80. **[G: U.S.]**

von Hagen, Jürgen. Money Stock Targeting with Alternative Reserve Requirement Systems. *Z. Wirtschaft. Sozialwissen.*, 1987, *107*(3), pp. 379–95.

Hahm, Sangmoon. Information Acquisition in an Incomplete Information Model of Business Cycle. *J. Monet. Econ.*, July 1987, *20*(1), pp. 123–40.

Hahn, Frank H. The Foundations of Monetary Theory. *de Cecco, M. and Fitoussi, J.-P., eds.*, 1987, pp. 21–43.

Hamburger, Michael J. A Stable Money Demand Function. *Contemp. Policy Issues*, January 1987, *5*(1), pp. 34–40. **[G: U.S.]**

Hamilton, James D. Monetary Factors in the Great Depression. *J. Monet. Econ.*, March 1987, *19*(2), pp. 145–69. **[G: U.S.]**

Hancock, Diana. Aggregation of Monetary Goods: A Production Model. *Barnett, W. A. and Singleton, K. J., eds.*, 1987, pp. 200–218. **[G: U.S.]**

Haque, Nadeem Ul and Mirakhor, Abbas. Optimal Profit-Sharing Contracts and Investment in an Interest-Free Islamic Economy. *Khan, M. S. and Mirakhor, A., eds.*, 1987, pp. 141–61.

Haque, Nadeem Ul and Mirakhor, Abbas. Saving Behavior in an Economy without Fixed Interest. *Khan, M. S. and Mirakhor, A., eds.*, 1987, pp. 125–39.

Hardouvelis, Gikas A. Optimal Wage Indexation and Monetary Policy in an Economy with Imported Raw Materials. *J. Int. Money Finance*, December 1987, *6*(4), pp. 419–32.

Hardouvelis, Gikas A. Reserves Announcements and Interest Rates: Does Monetary Policy Matter? *J. Finance*, June 1987, *42*(2), pp. 407–22. **[G: U.S.]**

Harris, Frederick H. deB. Security and Penalty in Debt Contracts: Comment. *J. Inst. Theoretical Econ.*, March 1987, *143*(1), pp. 168–74.

Hartman, Richard. Monetary Uncertainty and Investment in an Optimizing, Rational Expectations Model with Income Taxes and Government Debt. *Econometrica*, January 1987, *55*(1), pp. 169–76.

Hasan, M. Aynul. Rational Expectations Estimation of Money Demand for South Asian Countries. *Atlantic Econ. J.*, July 1987, *15*(2), pp. 87. **[G: S Asia]**

Havrilesky, Thomas M. A Partisanship Theory of Fiscal and Monetary Regimes. *J. Money, Credit, Banking*, August 1987, *19*(3), pp. 308–25.

Havrilesky, Thomas M. Monetary Modeling in a World of Financial Innovation. *Solomon, E. H., ed.*, 1987, pp. 159–87. **[G: U.S.]**

Hein, Scott E. Monetary Announcements and Interest Rate Responses. *Southern Econ. J.*, January 1987, *53*(3), pp. 615–26. **[G: U.S.]**

Heinsohn, Gunnar and Steiger, Otto. Private Ownership and the Foundations of Monetary Theory. *Écon. Soc.*, September 1987, *21*(9), pp. 229–43.

Hendry, David F. Econometrics in Action. *Empirica*, 1987, *14*(2), pp. 135–56. **[G: U.S.]**

Herr, Hansjörg. Ansätze monetärer Währungstheorie—eine keynesianische Kritik der orthodoxen Theorie. (Rudiments of International Monetary Theory—A Keynesian Criticism of Orthodox Theory. With English summary.) *Konjunkturpolitik*, 1987, *33*(1), pp. 1–26.

Hess, James D. and Knoeber, Charles R. Security and Penalty in Debt Contracts. *J. Inst. Theoretical Econ.*, March 1987, *143*(1), pp. 149–67.

Himarios, Daniel. Has There Been a Shift in the Greek Money Demand Function? [Inflationary Expectations and the Demand for Money: The Greek Experience]. *Kredit Kapital*, 1987, *20*(1), pp. 106–15.   [G: Greece]

Hixson, William F. Marxism and "Monetary Policy." *Écon. Soc.*, September 1987, *21*(9), pp. 43–63.

Hof, Franz Xaver. The Lucas Supply Function and the Feasibility of Monetary Stabilization Policy with Rational Expectations. *Empirica*, 1987, *14*(2), pp. 227–48.

Holland, A. Steven. Real Interest Rates: What Accounts for Their Recent Rise? *Wilcox, J. A., ed.*, 1987, *1984*, pp. 67–78.   [G: U.S.]

Hong, Wontack. A Theory of Interest and the Steady-State Rate of Return on Capital. *Int. Econ. J.*, Autumn 1987, *1*(3), pp. 87–90.

Hoogduin, Lex. On the Difference between the Keynesian, Knightian and the 'Classical' Analysis of Uncertainty and the Development of a More General Monetary Theory. *De Economist*, 1987, *135*(1), pp. 52–65.

Hotson, John H. The Keynesian Revolution and the Aborted Fisher–Simons Revolution or the Road Not Taken. *Écon. Soc.*, September 1987, *21*(9), pp. 185–219.

Howe, Keith M. and Lapan, Harvey. Inflation and Asset Life: The Darby versus the Fisher Effect. *J. Finan. Quant. Anal.*, June 1987, *22*(2), pp. 249–58.

Huizinga, John and Leiderman, Leonardo. The Signalling Role of Base and Money Announcements and Their Effects on Interest Rates. *J. Monet. Econ.*, December 1987, *20*(3), pp. 439–62.   [G: U.S.]

Humphrey, Thomas M. The Theory of Multiple Expansion of Deposits: What It Is and Whence It Came. *Fed. Res. Bank Richmond Econ. Rev.*, Mar./Apr. 1987, *73*(2), pp. 3–11.

Ito, Takatoshi and Roley, V. Vance. News from the U.S. and Japan: Which Moves the Yen/ Dollar Exchange Rate? *J. Monet. Econ.*, March 1987, *19*(2), pp. 255–77.   [G: U.S.; Japan]

Jacklin, Charles J. Demand Deposits, Trading Restrictions, and Risk Sharing. *Prescott, E. C. and Wallace, N., eds.*, 1987, pp. 26–47.

Jenkins, Paul and Walsh, Carl E. Real Interest Rates, Credit Markets and Economic Stabilization. *J. Macroecon.*, Winter 1987, *9*(1), pp. 95–108.

Jensen, Keith Christian and Kamath, Shyam J. Liquidity in the Production Function: A Reexamination. *Indian Econ. J.*, Oct.-Dec. 1987, *35*(2), pp. 91–114.   [G: U.S.]

Jones, Jonathan D. and Uri, Noel D. Money, Inflation and Causality (Another Look at the Empirical Evidence for the USA, 1953–84). *Appl. Econ.*, May 1987, *19*(5), pp. 619–34.   [G: U.S.]

Jones, Jonathan D. and Uri, Noel D. The Money Supply, Stock Returns and Causality. *Econ. Notes*, 1987, (1), pp. 39–51.   [G: U.S.]

Judd, John P. and Trehan, Bharat. Portfolio Substitution and the Reliability of M1, M2 and M3 as Monetary Policy Indicators. *Fed. Res. Bank San Francisco Econ. Rev.*, Summer 1987, (3), pp. 5–29.   [G: U.S.]

Kabir, M. and Mangla, I. Financial Innovations in Canada and Forecasting Money Stocks: An Econometric Analysis (1967–1985). *Tremblay, R., ed.*, 1987, pp. 299–314.   [G: Canada]

Kähkönen, Juha. Liberalization Policies and Welfare in a Financially Repressed Economy. *Int. Monet. Fund Staff Pap.*, September 1987, *34*(3), pp. 531–47.   [G: LDCs]

Kaldor, Nicholas. The Rise and Decline of Monetarism. *Steinherr, A. and Weiserbs, D., eds.*, 1987, pp. 87–97.   [G: U.S.; U.K.]

Kamaiah, Bandi, et al. An ARIMA Model of Velocity of Money in India. *Margin*, Jan.-Mar. 1987, *19*(2), pp. 32–42.   [G: India]

Kanatas, George. Commercial Paper, Bank Reserve Requirements, and the Informational Role of Loan Commitments. *J. Banking Finance*, September 1987, *11*(3), pp. 425–48.

Kang, Myung Hun. Money, Income and Causality: Korea and Japan. *Int. Econ. J.*, Autumn 1987, *1*(3), pp. 57–70.   [G: S. Korea; Japan]

Karacaoglu, Girol. Fitting Money into Conventional Macroeconomic Models. *Australian Econ. Pap.*, June 1987, *26*(48), pp. 83–100.

Karayiannis, Anastasios D. Twentieth Century Greek Economists and the Quantity Theory of Money. *Int. J. Soc. Econ.*, 1987, *14*(7/8/9), pp. 221–32.

Kareken, John H. The Emergence and Regulation of Contingent Commitment Banking. *J. Banking Finance*, September 1987, *11*(3), pp. 359–77.   [G: U.S.]

Karunaratne, Neil Dias. An Analysis of Papua New Guinea's Hard Currency Regime. *Econ. Int.*, May-Aug. 1987, *40*(2–3), pp. 210–23.   [G: New Guinea]

Katsaitis, Odysseus. The Crowding Out Debate [Comment]. *J. Post Keynesian Econ.*, Spring 1987, *9*(3), pp. 473–76.   [G: U.S.]

Kaufman, Roger T. and Woglom, Geoffrey. The Conformity of Wage Indexation Models with the "Stylized Facts": A Comment. *Amer. Econ. Rev.*, September 1987, *77*(4), pp. 747–49.   [G: Canada; W. Germany; Japan; U.S.; U.K.]

Kaul, Gautam. Stock Returns and Inflation: The Role of the Monetary Sector. *J. Finan. Econ.*, June 1987, *18*(2), pp. 253–76.   [G: U.S.; U.K.; Canada; W. Germany]

Kempf, Hubert. Irregular Staggered Contracts and Monetary Policy. *Europ. Econ. Rev.*, August 1987, *31*(6), pp. 1247–66.

Keyder, Nur. Türkiye'de Değişen Para Politikasi

Işığinda Para Arzinin Belirlenmesi, 1984–1987. (The Determination of Money Supply in Turkey in the Light of Changing Monetary Policy, 1984–1987. With English summary.) *METU*, 1987, *14*(4), pp. 315–37. **[G: Turkey]**

Khan, Mohsin S. Islamic Interest-Free Banking: A Theoretical Analysis. *Khan, M. S. and Mirakhor, A., eds.*, 1987, pp. 201–06.

Khan, Mohsin S. Islamic Interest-Free Banking: A Theoretical Analysis. *Khan, M. S. and Mirakhor, A., eds.*, 1987, *1986*, pp. 15–35.

Khan, Mohsin S. and Mirakhor, Abbas. The Financial System and Monetary Policy in an Islamic Economy. *Khan, M. S. and Mirakhor, A., eds.*, 1987, pp. 163–84.

Khan, Shahrukh Rafi. An Economic Analysis of a PLS Model for the Financial Sector. *Khan, M. S. and Mirakhor, A., eds.*, 1987, *1984*, pp. 107–24.

Khan, Waqar Masood. Towards an Interest Free Islamic Economic System. *Khan, M. S. and Mirakhor, A., eds.*, 1987, pp. 75–105.

Khan, Waqar Masood. Towards an Interest-Free Islamic Economic System. *Khan, M. S. and Mirakhor, A., eds.*, 1987, pp. 215–20.

Khan, Waqar Masood. Towards and Interest-Free Islamic Economic System. *Khan, M. S. and Mirakhor, A., eds.*, 1987, pp. 207–13.

Kiguel, Miguel A. The Non-dynamic Equivalence of Monetary and Exchange Rate Rules under Imperfect Capital Mobility and Rational Expectations. *J. Int. Money Finance*, June 1987, *6*(2), pp. 207–14.

Kirchgässner, Gebhard. Granger-Kausalität und Rationale Erwartungen. (With English summary.) *Kyklos*, 1987, *40*(1), pp. 21–42. **[G: W. Germany]**

Kitagawa, Masaaki. Intermediate Target Policy and Financial Structure (In Japanese. With English summary.) *Econ. Stud. Quart.*, September 1987, *38*(3), pp. 234–44.

Kitchen, John and Denbaly, Mark. Commodity Prices, Money Surprises, and Fed Credibility: A Comment. *J. Money, Credit, Banking*, May 1987, *19*(2), pp. 246–51. **[G: U.S.]**

Klovland, Jan Tore. The Demand for Money in the United Kingdom, 1875–1913. *Oxford Bull. Econ. Statist.*, August 1987, *49*(3), pp. 251–71. **[G: U.K.]**

Koenig, Evan F. The Short-run "Tobin Effect" in a Monetary Optimizing Model. *Econ. Inquiry*, January 1987, *25*(1), pp. 43–53.

Kohli, Ulrich. Exogenous Money, Monetary (Dis)equilibrium and Expectational Lags. *Kredit Kapital*, 1987, *20*(2), pp. 179–99. **[G: Switzerland]**

Kolluri, Bharat R. and Giannaros, Demetrios S. Budget Deficits and Short-term Real Interest Rate Forecasting. *J. Macroecon.*, Winter 1987, *9*(1), pp. 109–25.

Komlos, John. Financial Innovation and the Demand for Money in Austria–Hungary, 1867–1913. *J. Europ. Econ. Hist.*, Winter 1987, *16*(3), pp. 587–605. **[G: Austria–Hungary]**

Korpinen, Pekka. A Monetary Model of Long Cycles. *Vasko, T., ed.*, 1987, pp. 333–41.

Koskela, Erkki and Virén, Matti. Inflation, Hedging and the Demand for Money: Some Empirical Evidence. *Econ. Inquiry*, April 1987, *25*(2), pp. 251–65. **[G: U.S.]**

Kotlikoff, Laurence J. Consumer Spending and the After-Tax Real Interest Rate: Comment. *Feldstein, M., ed. (I)*, 1987, pp. 67–68. **[G: U.S.]**

Krashinsky, Michael. Option Demand Revisited. *Public Finance Quart.*, October 1987, *15*(4), pp. 460–71.

Kregel, Jan A. The Changing Place of Money in Keynes's Theory from the *Treatise* to the *General Theory*. *[Marrama, V.], Vol. 1*, 1987, pp. 97–114.

Krugman, Paul R. The Narrow Moving Band, the Dutch Disease, and the Competitive Consequences of Mrs. Thatcher: Notes on Trade in the Presence of Dynamic Scale Economies. *[Diaz-Alejandro, C. F.]*, 1987, pp. 41–55. **[G: U.K.]**

Krugman, Paul R. The Narrow Moving Band, the Dutch Disease, and the Competitive Consequences of Mrs. Thatcher. *J. Devel. Econ.*, October 1987, *27*(1–2), pp. 41–55. **[G: U.K.]**

Kuczynski, Michael. Inflation and Monetary Institutions in Developing Countries. *de Cecco, M. and Fitoussi, J.-P., eds.*, 1987, pp. 222–40. **[G: LDCs]**

Kugler, Peter. Die geldpolitische Zielsetzung und die Erwartungstheorie der Zinsstruktur: Empirische Implikationen. (Monetary Policy and the Expectations Theory of the Term Structure: Empirical Implications. With English summary.) *Aussenwirtschaft*, September 1987, *42*(2/3), pp. 335–46. **[G: Switzerland]**

Laban, Raul. Evolución de la Demanda por Dinero en Chile (1974–86): Una Aplicación del Filtro de Kalman. (The Evolution of Money Demand in Chile (1974–86) A Kalman Filter Approach.) *Colección Estud. CIEPLAN*, December 1987, (22), pp. 77–109. **[G: Chile]**

Laidler, David. Wicksell and Fisher on the "Backing" of Money and the Quantity Theory: A Comment on the Debate between Bruce Smith and Ronald Michener. *Carnegie–Rochester Conf. Ser. Public Policy*, Autumn 1987, *27*, pp. 325–34. **[G: U.S.]**

Lambelet, Jean-Christian and Nilles, Délia. Statistique monétaire et demande de monnaie en Suisse. (The Money Stock Statistic and Money Demand in Switzerland. With English summary.) *Schweiz. Z. Volkswirtsch. Statist.*, December 1987, *123*(4), pp. 449–66. **[G: Switzerland]**

Lamdany, Ruben and Dorlhiac, Jorge. The Dollarization of a Small Economy. *Scand. J. Econ.*, 1987, *89*(1), pp. 91–102.

Landi, Andrea. Interest Rate Risk and Protection of the Interest Margin in the Italian Banking System. *Gardener, E. P. M., ed.*, 1987, pp. 161–81. **[G: Italy]**

Laudadio, Leonard. Commercial Banks: Market Structure and Short-term Interest Rates [A

Markup Theory of Bank Loan Rates]. *J. Post Keynesian Econ.*, Summer 1987, *9*(4), pp. 633–41. **[G: U.S.]**

Läufer, Nikolaus K. A. Eine portfoliotheoretische Analyse der Friedmanschen Neuformulierung der Quantitütstheorie. (A Portfolio Theory Analysis of Friedman's Reformulation of the Quantity Theory of Money. With English summary.) *Z. Wirtschaft. Sozialwissen.*, 1987, *107*(1), pp. 29–49.

Laumas, G. S. and Fackler, James S. Economic Instability and the Demand for Money, 1908–1980. *Eastern Econ. J.*, July-Sept. 1987, *13*(3), pp. 249–57. **[G: U.S.]**

Lavoie, Marc. Monnaie et production: une synthèse de la théorie du circuit. (Money and Production: A Synthesis of the Circuit Theory. With English summary.) *Écon. Soc.*, September 1987, *21*(9), pp. 65–101.

Lavoie, Marc. Systemic Financial Fragility: A Simplified View. *J. Post Keynesian Econ.*, Winter 1986-87, *9*(2), pp. 258–66.

Leach, John E. Optimal Portfolio and Savings Decisions in an Intergenerational Economy. *Int. Econ. Rev.*, February 1987, *28*(1), pp. 123–34.

Lee, Chi-Wen Jevons and Petruzzi, Christopher R. A Test of the Shiller–Siegel Hypothesis of the Gibson Paradox [The Gibson Paradox and Historical Movements in Real Interest Rates]. *Australian Econ. Pap.*, June 1987, *26*(48), pp. 157–64. **[G: U.K.]**

Lee, Chi-Wen Jevons and Petruzzi, Christopher R. Prices, Interest Rates, and the Monetary Standard: A Study of the Gibson–Kitchin Phenomenon. *J. Macroecon.*, Spring 1987, *9*(2), pp. 185–202. **[G: U.K.]**

Leijonhufvud, Axel. Constitutional Constraints on the Monetary Powers of Government. *Dorn, J. A. and Schwartz, A. J., eds.*, 1987, pp. 129–43. **[G: U.S.]**

Leijonhufvud, Axel. Rational Expectations and Monetary Institutions. *de Cecco, M. and Fitoussi, J.-P., eds.*, 1987, pp. 44–65.

Leon, H. and Molana, Hasan. Testing the Monetary Approach to Balance of Payments in Developing Countries. *Chrystal, K. A. and Sedgwick, R., eds.*, 1987, pp. 137–63.
[G: Latin America; Thailand; India; Sri Lanka]

Leonard, Jacques. Le paradoxe de l'intérêt et la crise de l'économie monétaire de production. (The Paradox of Interest and the Crisis of the Monetary Production Economy. With English summary.) *Écon. Soc.*, September 1987, *21*(9), pp. 149–68.

LeRoy, Stephen F. and Raymon, Neil. A Monetarist Model of Inflation. *J. Econ. Theory*, August 1987, *42*(2), pp. 275–310.

Levačic, Rosalind. The Analysis of Economic Management: The Aggregate Demand and Supply Model. *Thompson, G.; Brown, V. and Levačić, R., eds.*, 1987, pp. 38–76. **[G: U.K.]**

Levi, Maurice and Shapiro, Alan C. A Market-Based Test of the Effect of Monetary Policy. *Econ. Inquiry*, April 1987, *25*(2), pp. 341–49. **[G: U.S.]**

Levine, Paul and Currie, David. The Design of Feedback Rules in Linear Stochastic Rational Expectations Models. *J. Econ. Dynam. Control*, March 1987, *11*(1), pp. 1–28.

Levine, Philip and Loeb, Peter D. Nonrandom Behavior of the Prime Rate of Interest. *Atlantic Econ. J.*, March 1987, *15*(1), pp. 119. **[G: U.S.]**

Lianos, Theodore P. Marx on the Rate of Interest. *Rev. Radical Polit. Econ.*, Fall 1987, *19*(3), pp. 34–55.

Litterman, Robert. The Limits of Counter-Cyclical Monetary Policy: An Analysis Based on Optimal Control Theory and Vector Autoregressions. *Ann. Écon. Statist.*, Apr./Sept. 1987, (6/7), pp. 125–60.

Llewellyn, David T. The Operation and Regulation of Financial Markets: Introduction. *Goodhart, C.; Currie, D. and Llewellyn, D. T., eds.*, 1987, pp. xi–xvii. **[G: U.K.]**

Lucas, Deborah and McDonald, Robert L. Bank Portfolio Choice with Private Information about Loan Quality: Theory and Implications for Regulation. *J. Banking Finance*, September 1987, *11*(3), pp. 473–97.

Lucas, Robert E., Jr. and Stokey, Nancy L. La monnaie et l'intérêt sous contrainte de transaction. (Money and Interest in a Cash-in-Advance Economy. With English summary.) *Ann. Écon. Statist.*, Oct./Dec. 1987, (8), pp. 1–26.

Lucas, Robert E., Jr. and Stokey, Nancy L. Money and Interest in a Cash-in-Advance Economy. *Econometrica*, May 1987, *55*(3), pp. 491–513.

MacDonald, Ronald and Peel, David A. Consumer Expenditure, the Demand for Money, and the Hall Hypothesis. *Empirical Econ.*, 1987, *12*(1), pp. 3–17. **[G: OECD]**

MacKinnon, Keith T. More on the Inflation Tax and the Value of Equity. *Can. J. Econ.*, November 1987, *20*(4), pp. 823–31.

Maling, Charles. On the Consumers' Surplus of Money Holders and the Measuring of Money's Services. *J. Money, Credit, Banking*, November 1987, *19*(4), pp. 469–83.

Malinvaud, Edmond. Monetary and Fiscal Policies for Economic Recovery in Europe. *Europ. Econ. Rev.*, Feb./Mar. 1987, *31*(1/2), pp. 73–75. **[G: W. Europe]**

Manchester, Joyce. Mortgage Contracts in a General Equilibrium Model when There Are Inflation Shocks. *J. Macroecon.*, Summer 1987, *9*(3), pp. 327–49.

Mankiw, N. Gregory. Consumer Spending and the After-Tax Real Interest Rate. *Feldstein, M., ed. (II)*, 1987, pp. 97–99. **[G: U.S.]**

Mankiw, N. Gregory. Consumer Spending and the After-Tax Real Interest Rate. *Feldstein, M., ed. (I)*, 1987, pp. 53–67. **[G: U.S.]**

Mankiw, N. Gregory. Government Purchases and Real Interest Rates. *J. Polit. Econ.*, April 1987, *95*(2), pp. 407–19.

Mankiw, N. Gregory. The Optimal Collection of Seigniorage: Theory and Evidence. *J. Monet.*

Econ., September 1987, *20*(2), pp. 327–41.
[G: U.S.]

Manski, Charles F. and Goldin, Ephraim. The Denomination-Specific Demand for Currency in a High-Inflation Setting: The Israeli Experience. *Heijmans, R. and Neudecker, H., eds.,* 1987, pp. 99–120. [G: Israel]

Marini, Giancarlo. Determinatezza dei prezzi ed effetti di stabilizzazione di manovre anticicliche del tasso d'interesse. (Interest Rate Rules, Price Level Determinancy and Stabilization Policy. With English summary.) *Econ. Polit.,* December 1987, *4*(3), pp. 343–55.

Marquez, Jaime R. Money Demand in Open Economies: A Currency Substitution Model for Venezuela. *J. Int. Money Finance,* June 1987, *6*(2), pp. 167–78. [G: Venezuela]

Marquez, Jaime R. Money Demand in Open Economies: A Divisia Application to the U.S. Case. *Barnett, W. A. and Singleton, K. J., eds.,* 1987, pp. 183–99. [G: U.S.]

Marshall, John M.; Sonstelie, Jon and Gilles, Christian. Money and Redistribution: Revisionist Notes on a Problem of Samuelson. *J. Monet. Econ.,* July 1987, *20*(1), pp. 3–23.

Mascaro, Angelo R. M1–Velocity and Money-Demand Functions: Do Stable Relationships Exist? Comments. *Carnegie–Rochester Conf. Ser. Public Policy,* Autumn 1987, 27, pp. 89–101. [G: U.S.]

Massad, Carlos. Internal Debt, External Debt and Economic Transformation: Introduction. *CEPAL Rev.,* August 1987, (32), pp. 7–9. [G: Latin America]

McCallum, Bennett T. The Case for Rules in the Conduct of Monetary Policy: A Concrete Example. *Fed. Res. Bank Richmond Econ. Rev.,* Sept./Oct. 1987, *73*(5), pp. 10–18. [G: U.S.]

McCallum, Bennett T. The Optimal Inflation Rate in an Overlapping-Generations Economy with Land. *Barnett, W. A. and Singleton, K. J., eds.,* 1987, pp. 325–39.

McDermott, John H. Adding Exhaustibility to the Traditional Theory of the Gold Standard. *J. Macroecon.,* Fall 1987, *9*(4), pp. 545–66.

Mehra, Yash. Money Growth Volatility and High Nominal Interest Rates. *Fed. Res. Bank Richmond Econ. Rev.,* Nov./Dec. 1987, *73*(6), pp. 10–19. [G: U.S.]

Menichella, Donato. The Contribution of the Banking System to Monetary Equilibrium and Economic Stability: Italian Experience. *Ciocca, P., ed.,* 1987, *1956*, pp. 95–119. [G: Italy]

Michener, Ronald. Fixed Exchange Rates and the Quantity Theory in Colonial America. *Carnegie–Rochester Conf. Ser. Public Policy,* Autumn 1987, 27, pp. 233–307. [G: U.S.]

Milbourne, Ross D. Re-examining the Buffer-Stock Model of Money. *Econ. J.,* Supplement 1987, 97, pp. 130–42. [G: U.S.]

Mills, Terence C. and Stephenson, Michael J. The Behaviour of Expected Short-term Real Interest Rates in the UK. *Appl. Econ.,* March 1987, *19*(3), pp. 331–46. [G: U.K.]

Mirakhor, Abbas. Short-term Asset Concentration and Islamic Banking. *Khan, M. S. and Mirakhor, A., eds.,* 1987, pp. 185–99.

Mishkin, Frederic S. The Dollar and Real Interest Rates: A Comment. *Carnegie–Rochester Conf. Ser. Public Policy,* Autumn 1987, 27, pp. 141–48. [G: U.S.]

Mistri, Maurizio. Preferenze per la liquiditá in inflazione ed equilibri generali temporanei. Una critica a Friedman. (With English summary.) *Stud. Econ.,* 1987, *42*(31), pp. 51–65.

Modigliani, Franco. Conventional Valuation and the Term Structure of Interest Rates: Comments. *[Modigliani, F.],* 1987, pp. 89–92. [G: U.K.; U.S.]

Modigliani, Franco and Papademos, Lucas. Money, Credit and the Monetary Mechanism. *de Cecco, M. and Fitoussi, J.-P., eds.,* 1987, pp. 121–60.

Modjtahedi, Bagher. An Empirical Investigation into the International Real Interest Rate Linkages. *Can. J. Econ.,* November 1987, *20*(4), pp. 832–54. [G: OECD]

Monticelli, Carlo. Inflation and Liquidity Preference. *Giorn. Econ.,* Sept.-Oct. 1987, *46*(9–10), pp. 481–90.

Monticelli, Carlo. Stabilization Priorities and Optimal Monetary Policy. *Greek Econ. Rev.,* 1987, *9*(2), pp. 210–23.

Montiel, Peter J. Output and Unanticipated Money in the Dependent Economy Model. *Int. Monet. Fund Staff Pap.,* June 1987, *34*(2), pp. 228–59. [G: Mexico]

Montiel, Peter J. and Zaidi, Iqbal. Cross-Regime Tests of the Lucas Supply Function in Developing Countries. *Int. Monet. Fund Staff Pap.,* December 1987, *34*(4), pp. 760–69. [G: LDCs]

Moreno, Ramon. The Eurodollar Market and U.S. Residents. *Fed. Res. Bank San Francisco Econ. Rev.,* Summer 1987, (3), pp. 43–59. [G: U.S.]

Mossetti, Giovanna. Loanable Funds and Output in a Model of the Firm. *Giorn. Econ.,* Nov.-Dec. 1987, *46*(11–12), pp. 617–38.

Motley, Brian. Should Money Be Redefined? *Wilcox, J. A., ed.,* 1987, *1986*, pp. 164–66. [G: U.S.]

Murata, Yasuo. A Correspondence Principle in the Tobin–Buiter Model. *[Marrama, V.], Vol. 2,* 1987, pp. 827–48.

Neldner, Manfred. Currency Substitution in West Germany. An Empirical Estimation of the Substitution Effect Using Slutsky-Elasticities. *J. Inst. Theoretical Econ.,* December 1987, *143*(4), pp. 630–42. [G: W. Germany]

Nickelsburg, Gerald. Inflation, Expectations and Qualitative Government Policy in Ecuador, 1970–82. *World Devel.,* August 1987, *15*(8), pp. 1077–85. [G: Ecuador]

Nickerson, David. The Neutrality and Optimality of Counter-cyclical Monetary Policy in Equilibrium Models with a Wealth Effect. *Can. J. Econ.,* August 1987, *20*(3), pp. 612–24.

Niehans, Jürg. Classical Monetary Theory, New and Old. *J. Money, Credit, Banking,* November 1987, *19*(4), pp. 409–24.

Niehans, Jürg. Monetary Policy and Investment Dynamics in Interdependent Economies. *J. Money, Credit, Banking*, February 1987, *19*(1), pp. 33–45.

Niehans, Jürg. Monetary Policy in an Open Economy. *de Cecco, M. and Fitoussi, J.-P., eds.*, 1987, pp. 243–68.

Niggle, Christopher J. A Comment on the Markup Theory of Bank Loan Rates. *J. Post Keynesian Econ.*, Summer 1987, *9*(4), pp. 629–31. [G: U.S.]

Norman, Alfred Lorn. A Theory of Monetary Exchange. *Rev. Econ. Stud.*, July 1987, *54*(3), pp. 499–517.

O'Driscoll, Gerald P., Jr. Money, Deregulation, and the Business Cycle. *Dorn, J. A. and Schwartz, A. J., eds.*, 1987, *1986*, pp. 319–37. [G: U.S.]

Onado, Marco. Interest Rate Risk in the Italian Banking System. *Gardener, E. P. M., ed.*, 1987, pp. 133–47. [G: Italy]

Parguez, Alain. Introduction à l'économie de rentiers. (Introduction to the Rentiers Economy. With English summary.) *Écon. Soc.*, September 1987, *21*(9), pp. 103–19.

Parkin, Michael. The Quantity Theory of Money, Rational Expectations and the Relationship between Money, Income and Prices. *Greek Econ. Rev.*, 1987, *9*(1), pp. 57–87.

Parkin, Michael. The Quantity Theory of Money, Rational Expectations and the Relationship between Money, Income and Prices. *Greek Econ. Rev.*, 1987, *9*(1), pp. 57–87.

Patterson, Kerry David. The Specification and Stability of the Demand for Money in the United Kingdom. *Economica*, February 1987, *54*(213), pp. 41–55. [G: U.K.]

Pauls, B. Dianne. Comovements in Aggregate and Relative Prices: Some Evidence on Neutrality. *J. Monet. Econ.*, July 1987, *20*(1), pp. 155–68. [G: U.S.]

Peek, Joe and Wilcox, James A. Monetary Policy Regimes and the Reduced Form for Interest Rates. *J. Money, Credit, Banking*, August 1987, *19*(3), pp. 273–91. [G: U.S.]

Peel, David A. and Pope, P. F. On Testing the Relationship between Exchange Rate Movements and Monetary Surprises: A Comment. *Manchester Sch. Econ. Soc. Stud.*, June 1987, *55*(2), pp. 197–202. [G: U.S.; U.K.]

Pellanda, Anna. Angelo Messedaglia on Money and the Nineteenth Century Italian Economic School. *Int. J. Soc. Econ.*, 1987, *14*(7/8/9), pp. 170–81. [G: Italy]

Perlman, Morris. Of a Controversial Passage in Hume. *J. Polit. Econ.*, April 1987, *95*(2), pp. 274–89.

Persson, Mats; Persson, Torsten and Svensson, Lars E. O. Time Consistency of Fiscal and Monetary Policy. *Econometrica*, November 1987, *55*(6), pp. 1419–31.

Pietra, Tito and Siconolfi, Paolo. Sul ruolo della moneta interna e della moneta esterna. (On the Role of Inside Money and Outside Money. With English summary.) *Econ. Polít.*, April 1987, *4*(1), pp. 49–88.

Pitchford, John David and Vousden, Neil J. Exchange Rates, Policy Rules and Inflation. *Australian Econ. Pap.*, June 1987, *26*(48), pp. 43–57.

Pizzutto, Giorgio. Un contronto tra modelli macroeconomici. (A Comparison between Macroeconomic Models. With English summary.) *Rivista Int. Sci. Econ. Com.*, May 1987, *34*(5), pp. 393–409.

van der Ploeg, Frederick. Benefits of Contingent Rules for Optimal Taxation of a Monetary Economy: A Note. *J. Money, Credit, Banking*, May 1987, *19*(2), pp. 252–59.

Plosser, Charles I. Fiscal Policy and the Term Structure. *J. Monet. Econ.*, September 1987, *20*(2), pp. 343–67.

Portes, Richard and Santorum, Anita. Money and the Consumption Goods Market in China. *J. Compar. Econ.*, September 1987, *11*(3), pp. 354–71. [G: China]

Postlewaite, Andrew and Vives, Xavier. Bank Runs as an Equilibrium Phenomenon. *J. Polit. Econ.*, June 1987, *95*(3), pp. 485–91.

Poterba, James M. and Rotemberg, Julio J. Money in the Utility Function: An Empirical Implementation. *Barnett, W. A. and Singleton, K. J., eds.*, 1987, pp. 219–40. [G: U.S.]

Poulon, F. Keynes et Robertson: naissance d'un désaccord sur la fonction de l'épargne dans la théorie monétaire. (Keynes and Robertson: The Beginning of a Disagreement about the Role of Saving in Monetary Theory. With English summary.) *Écon. Soc.*, September 1987, *21*(9), pp. 9–22.

Prescott, Edward C. A Multiple Means-of-Payment Model. *Barnett, W. A. and Singleton, K. J., eds.*, 1987, pp. 42–51.

Protopapadakis, Aris A. and Siegel, Jeremy J. Are Money Growth and Inflation Related to Government Deficits? Evidence from Ten Industrialized Economies. *J. Int. Money Finance*, March 1987, *6*(1), pp. 31–48. [G: Selected OECD]

Radecki, Lawrence J. and Garver, Cecily C. The Household Demand for Money: Estimates from Cross-sectional Data. *Fed. Res. Bank New York Quart. Rev.*, Spring 1987, *12*(1), pp. 29–34. [G: U.S.]

Ram, Rati. A Broader Multicountry Perspective on the Gibson Paradox and Fisher's Hypothesis. *De Economist*, 1987, *135*(2), pp. 219–30. [G: Global]

Rasche, Robert H. M1–Velocity and Money-Demand Functions: Do Stable Relationships Exist? *Carnegie–Rochester Conf. Ser. Public Policy*, Autumn 1987, *27*, pp. 9–88. [G: U.S.]

Raymond, Robert. La monnaie: transmutation des concepts. (With English summary.) *Revue Écon. Polit.*, July-Aug. 1987, *97*(4), pp. 451–61.

Reichenstein, William. The Impact of Money on Short-term Interest Rates. *Econ. Inquiry*, January 1987, *25*(1), pp. 67–82. [G: U.S.]

Riese, Hajo. Keynes als Kapitaltheoretiker. (Keynes as a Capital Theorist. With English summary.) *Kredit Kapital*, 1987, *20*(2), pp. 153–78.

Riley, John G. Credit Rationing: A Further Remark [Credit Rationing in Markets with Imperfect Information] [Incentives Effects of Terminations: Applications to the Credit and Labor Markets]. *Amer. Econ. Rev.*, March 1987, *77*(1), pp. 224–27.

Rogoff, Kenneth. Reputational Constraints on Monetary Policy. *Carnegie–Rochester Conf. Ser. Public Policy*, Spring 1987, *26*, pp. 141–81.

Rojas-Suarez, Liliana. Devaluation and Monetary Policy in Developing Countries: A General Equilibrium Model for Economies Facing Financial Constraints. *Int. Monet. Fund Staff Pap.*, September 1987, *34*(3), pp. 439–70. [G: LDCs]

Roley, V. Vance. The Effects of Money Announcements under Alternative Monetary Control Procedures. *J. Money, Credit, Banking*, August 1987, *19*(3), pp. 292–307. [G: U.S.]

Romer, David. The Monetary Transmission Mechanism in a General Equilibrium Version of the Baumol–Tobin Model. *J. Monet. Econ.*, July 1987, *20*(1), pp. 105–22.

Rose, Harold. Monetary Indicators and Operating Targets: Some Recent Issues in the UK: Commentary. *Begg, D. K. H., et al.*, 1987, pp. 89–91. [G: U.K.]

Rossi, Enzo and Stolfa, Fabio. The Control of Bank Liquidity: A Theoretical Model and Empirical Verifications. *Rev. Econ. Cond. Italy*, May-August 1987, (2), pp. 209–50. [G: Italy]

Rossiter, Rosemary and Lee, Tong Hun. Implicit Returns on Conventional Demand Deposits: An Empirical Comparison. *J. Macroecon.*, Fall 1987, *9*(4), pp. 613–24. [G: U.S.]

Rousseas, Stephen. Rejoinder [A Markup Theory of Bank Loan Rates]. *J. Post Keynesian Econ.*, Summer 1987, *9*(4), pp. 642–43. [G: U.S.]

Saleem, Samir Taha. On the Determination of Interest Rates in Rural Credit Markets: A Case Study from the Sudan. *Cambridge J. Econ.*, June 1987, *11*(2), pp. 165–72. [G: Sudan]

Sanguinetti, Pablo. La hipótesis monetarista del proceso inflacionario en el caso argentino: Dinero exógeno vs. dinero endógeno. (The Monetarist Approach to the Inflationary Process in the Argentine: Exogenous vs. Endogenous Money. With English summary.) *Económica (La Plata)*, July-Dec. 1987, *33*(2), pp. 269–304. [G: Argentina]

Santoni, G. J. Changes in Wealth and the Velocity of Money. *Fed. Res. Bank St. Louis Rev.*, March 1987, *69*(3), pp. 16–26. [G: U.S.]

Sargent, Thomas J. and Smith, Bruce D. Irrelevance of Open Market Operations in Some Economies with Government Currency Being Dominated in Rate of Return. *Amer. Econ. Rev.*, March 1987, *77*(1), pp. 78–92.

Scarth, William M. Can Economic Growth Make Monetarist Arithmetic Pleasant? *Southern Econ. J.*, April 1987, *53*(4), pp. 1028–36.

Schebeck, Fritz and Thury, Gerhard. Dynamic Specification of the Demand for Money in Austria. *Empirica*, 1987, *14*(1), pp. 25–53. [G: Austria]

Schlesinger, Helmut and Jahnke, Wilfried. Geldmenge, Preise und Sozialprodukt: Interdependenzzusammenhänge im Lichte Ökonometrischer Forschungsergebnisse für die Bundesrepublik Deutschland. (Money, Prices, and Production: Interdependencies in the Light Econometric Results for the Federal Republic of Germany. With English summary.) *Jahr. Nationalökon. Statist.*, October 1987, *203*(5–6), pp. 576–90. [G: W. Germany]

Schumann, Jochen. Security and Penalty in Debt Contracts: Comment. *J. Inst. Theoretical Econ.*, March 1987, *143*(1), pp. 175–79.

Schwartz, Anna J. A Century of British Market Interest Rates, 1874–1975. *Schwartz, A. J.*, 1987, *1981*, pp. 152–64. [G: U.K.]

Schwartz, Anna J. Why Money Matters. *Schwartz, A. J.*, 1987, pp. 167–82. [G: U.K.; U.S.-X1 - 1969]

Selgin, George A. The Stability and Efficiency of Money Supply under Free Banking. *J. Inst. Theoretical Econ.*, September 1987, *143*(3), pp. 435–56.

Semmler, Willi. A Macroeconomic Limit Cycle with Financial Perturbations. *J. Econ. Behav. Organ.*, September 1987, *8*(3), pp. 469–95.

Sephton, Peter S. The Choice of Monetary Policy Instruments in Canada: An Extension. *Can. J. Econ.*, February 1987, *20*(1), pp. 55–60. [G: Canada]

Serletis, Apostolos. Monetary Asset Separability Tests. *Barnett, W. A. and Singleton, K. J., eds.*, 1987, pp. 169–82.

Serletis, Apostolos. On the Demand for Money in the United States. *Empirical Econ.*, 1987, *12*(4), pp. 249–55. [G: U.S.]

Serletis, Apostolos. The Demand for Divisia M_1, M_2, and M_3 in the United States. *J. Macroecon.*, Fall 1987, *9*(4), pp. 567–91. [G: U.S.]

Shafer, Jeffrey R. The Theory of the Lender of Last Resort and the Eurocurrency Markets. *Aliber, R. Z., ed.*, 1987, pp. 281–304. [G: EEC]

Shiller, Robert J. Conventional Valuation and the Term Structure of Interest Rates. *[Modigliani, F.]*, 1987, pp. 63–88. [G: U.S.; U.K.]

Siegloff, Eric S. and Groenewold, Nicolaas. Policy Ineffectiveness: Tests with Australian Data. *Australian Econ. Pap.*, December 1987, *26*(49), pp. 179–87. [G: Australia]

Siklos, P. L. Cyclical Fluctuations in U.S. Monetary Policy and Output: A Test of Their Relationship. *J. Stud. Econ. Econometrics*, July 1987, *11*(2), pp. 69–94. [G: U.S.]

Sims, Grant E.; Takayama, Akira and Chao, Chi-chur. A Dual Approach to Measuring the Nearness of Near-Monies. *Rev. Econ. Statist.*, February 1987, *69*(1), pp. 118–27. [G: U.S.]

Singleton, Kenneth J. Asset Prices in a Time-Series Model with Disparately Informed, Competitive Traders. *Barnett, W. A. and Singleton, K. J., eds.*, 1987, pp. 249–72.

Smeets, Heinz-Dieter. Finanzinnovationen und Geldpolitik. (Financial Innovations and Monetary Policy. With English summary.) *Lenel, H. O., et al., eds.*, 1987, pp. 91–112.

[G: W. Germany]

Smith, Bruce D. Private Information, the Real Bills Doctrine, and the Quantity Theory: An Alternative Approach. *Prescott, E. C. and Wallace, N., eds.*, 1987, pp. 48–80.

Smith, Janet Kiholm. Trade Credit and Informational Asymmetry. *J. Finance*, September 1987, *42*(4), pp. 863–72.

Snippe, J. Monetary Equilibrium versus the Wicksell Connection. *Banca Naz. Lavoro Quart. Rev.*, June 1987, (161), pp. 197–212.

Snowden, P. N. Financial Market Liberalisation in LDCs: The Incidence of Risk Allocation Effects of Interest Rate Increases. *J. Devel. Stud.*, October 1987, *24*(1), pp. 83–93. [G: LDCs]

Sørensen, Anette. Finansielle innovationer og pengepolitikkens effektivitet. (The Impact of Financial Innovations on the Efficiency of Monetary Policy. With English summary.) *Nationaløkon. Tidsskr.*, 1987, *125*(2), pp. 213–22.

Spaventa, Luigi. Public Debt and Rules of Monetary Growth: An Exercise in Monetarist Arithmetic. *de Cecco, M. and Fitoussi, J.-P., eds.*, 1987, pp. 269–85.

Spaventa, Luigi. The Growth of Public Debt: Sustainability, Fiscal Rules, and Monetary Rules. *Int. Monet. Fund Staff Pap.*, June 1987, *34*(2), pp. 374–99.

Spiro, Peter S. The Elusive Effect of Fiscal Deficits on Interest Rates: Comment. *Int. Monet. Fund Staff Pap.*, June 1987, *34*(2), pp. 400–403. [G: U.S.]

Stemp, Peter J. and Turnovsky, Stephen J. Optimal Monetary Policy in an Open Economy. *Europ. Econ. Rev.*, July 1987, *31*(5), pp. 1113–35.

Stiglitz, Joseph E. and Weiss, Andrew. Credit Rationing: Reply [Credit Rationing in Markets with Imperfect Information] [Incentives Effects of Terminations: Applications to the Credit and Labor Markets]. *Amer. Econ. Rev.*, March 1987, *77*(1), pp. 228–31.

Stone, Courtenay C. and Thornton, Daniel L. Solving the 1980s' Velocity Puzzle: A Progress Report. *Fed. Res. Bank St. Louis Rev.*, Aug./Sept. 1987, *69*(7), pp. 5–23. [G: U.S.]

Sweeney, Richard J. Some Macro Implications of Risk. *J. Money, Credit, Banking*, May 1987, *19*(2), pp. 222–34.

Sykes, David; Smith, W. James and Formby, John P. On the Measurement of Tax Progressivity: An Implication of the Atkinson Theorem. *Southern Econ. J.*, January 1987, *53*(3), pp. 768–77.

Tabellini, Guido. Central Bank Reputation and the Monetization of Deficits: The 1981 Italian Monetary Reform. *Econ. Inquiry*, April 1987, *25*(2), pp. 185–200. [G: Italy]

Tabellini, Guido. Optimal Monetary Instruments and Policy Games. *Ricerche Econ.*, July-Dec. 1987, *41*(3–4), pp. 315–25.

Tabellini, Guido. Reputational Constraints on Monetary Policy: A Comment. *Carnegie–*

Rochester Conf. Ser. Public Policy, Spring 1987, *26*, pp. 183–90.

Tabellini, Guido. Secrecy of Monetary Policy and the Variability of Interest Rates. *J. Money, Credit, Banking*, November 1987, *19*(4), pp. 425–36. [G: U.S.]

Tanigawa, Yasuhiko. On the Existence of Financial Intermediaries. *Econ. Stud. Quart.*, March 1987, *38*(1), pp. 61–75.

Tanzi, Vito. The Effect of Fiscal Deficits on Interest Rates: Reply. *Int. Monet. Fund Staff Pap.*, June 1987, *34*(2), pp. 404–07. [G: U.S.]

Tavlas, George S. Inflationary Finance and the Demand for Money in Greece. *Kredit Kapital*, 1987, *20*(2), pp. 245–57. [G: Greece]

Taylor, Lance. Macro Policy in the Tropics: How Sensible People Stand. *World Devel.*, December 1987, *15*(12), pp. 1407–35. [G: LDCs]

Taylor, Mark P. Financial Innovation, Inflation and the Stability of the Demand for Broad Money in the United Kingdom. *Bull. Econ. Res.*, July 1987, *39*(3), pp. 225–33. [G: U.K.]

Terzi, Andrea. The Independence of Finance from Saving: A Flow-of-Funds Interpretation. *J. Post Keynesian Econ.*, Winter 1986-87, *9*(2), pp. 188–97.

Thakor, Anjan V. and Udell, Gregory F. An Economic Rationale for the Pricing Structure of Bank Loan Commitments. *J. Banking Finance*, June 1987, *11*(2), pp. 271–89.

Thomson, James B. The Use of Market Information in Pricing Deposit Insurance. *J. Money, Credit, Banking*, November 1987, *19*(4), pp. 528–37. [G: U.S.]

Thygesen, Niels. Monetary and Fiscal Policies for Economic Recovery in Europe. *Europ. Econ. Rev.*, Feb./Mar. 1987, *31*(1/2), pp. 67–73.

[G: W. Europe]

Timberlake, Richard H., Jr. A Critique of Monetarist and Austrian Doctrines on the Utility and Value of Money. *Rothbard, M. N., ed.*, 1987, pp. 81–96.

Tindall, Michael and Spencer, Roger W. A Monthly Model of Bank Reserve Aggregates. *Atlantic Econ. J.*, September 1987, *15*(3), pp. 35–42. [G: U.S.]

Tobin, James. A General Equilibrium Approach to Monetary Theory. *Tobin, J. (I)*, 1987, *1969*, pp. 322–38.

Tobin, James. Asset Holdings and Spending Decisions. *Tobin, J. (I)*, 1987, *1952*, pp. 83–98.

Tobin, James. Commercial Banks as Creators of "Money." *Tobin, J. (I)*, 1987, *1963*, pp. 272–82.

Tobin, James. Liquidity Preference and Monetary Policy. *Tobin, J. (I)*, 1987, *1947*, pp. 27–46.

[G: U.S.]

Tobin, James. Liquidity Preference as Behavior towards Risk. *Tobin, J. (I)*, 1987, pp. 242–71.

Tobin, James. Money and Economic Growth. *Tobin, J. (I)*, 1987, pp. 133–45.

Tobin, James. Money and Income: Post Hoc Ergo Propter Hoc? *Tobin, J. (I)*, 1987, *1970*, pp. 497–514.

Tobin, James. Money, Capital, and Other Stores

of Value. *Tobin, J. (I)*, 1987, *1961*, pp. 217–28.

Tobin, James. Notes on Optimal Monetary Growth. *Tobin, J. (I)*, 1987, *1968*, pp. 146–73.

Tobin, James. The Interest Elasticity of Transactions Demand for Cash. *Tobin, J. (I)*, 1987, *1956*, pp. 229–41.

Tobin, James and Brainard, William C. Financial Intermediaries and the Effectiveness of Monetary Controls. *Tobin, J. (I)*, 1987, *1963*, pp. 283–321.

Togan, Sübidey. The Influence of Money and the Rate of Interest on the Rate of Inflation in a Financially Repressed Economy: The Case of Turkey. *Appl. Econ.*, December 1987, *19*(12), pp. 1585–1601. **[G: Turkey]**

Torre, Dominique. Effet d'encaisse réelle et équilibre général dans une économie monétaire: les enseignements d'une controverse. (Real Balance Effect and General Equilibrium in a Monetary Economy: The Outcome of a Controversy. With English summary.) *Écon. Soc.*, March 1987, *21*(3), pp. 177–204.

Tortajada, Ramon. M. de Malestroit et la théorie quantitative de la monnaie. (M. de Malestroit and the Quantity Theory of Money. With English summary.) *Revue Écon.*, July 1987, *38*(4), pp. 853–76.

Towe, Christopher M. Transactions Technology and the Time Consistency of Optimal Policy. *J. Public Econ.*, October 1987, *34*(1), pp. 121–28.

Townsend, Robert M. Asset-Return Anomalies in a Monetary Economy. *J. Econ. Theory*, April 1987, *41*(2), pp. 219–47.

Townsend, Robert M. and Wallace, Neil. Circulating Private Debt: An Example with a Coordination Problem. *Prescott, E. C. and Wallace, N., eds.*, 1987, pp. 105–20.

Trehan, Bharat and Walsh, Carl E. Examining the Recent Surge in M1. *Wilcox, J. A., ed.*, 1987, *1985*, pp. 161–63. **[G: U.S.]**

Turnovsky, Stephen J. Monetary Growth, Inflation, and Economic Activity in a Dynamic Macro Model. *Int. Econ. Rev.*, October 1987, *28*(3), pp. 707–30.

Turnovsky, Stephen J. Optimal Monetary Growth with Accommodating Fiscal Policy in a Small Open Economy. *J. Int. Money Finance*, June 1987, *6*(2), pp. 179–93.

Turnovsky, Stephen J. Supply Shocks and Optimal Monetary Policy. *Sinclair, P. J. N., ed.*, 1987, pp. 20–37.

Turnovsky, Stephen J. Supply Shocks and Optimal Monetary Policy. *Oxford Econ. Pap.*, March 1987, *39*(1), pp. 20–37.

Turnovsky, Stephen J. and Wohar, Mark E. Alternative Modes of Deficit Financing and Endogeneous Monetary and Fiscal Policy in the U.S.A. 1923–1982. *J. Appl. Econometrics*, January 1987, *2*(1), pp. 1–25. **[G: U.S.]**

Urquidi, Victor L. Structural Change and Monetary Policy in Latin America—Possible Lessons for Other Developing Countries. *de Cecco, M.*

and Fitoussi, J.-P., eds., 1987, pp. 305–25. **[G: Latin America]**

VanHoose, David D. A "Penalty" Discount Rate, Bank Behavior, and Price and Output Stability. *J. Macroecon.*, Spring 1987, *9*(2), pp. 165–83.

VanHoose, David D. A Note on Discount Rate Policy and the Variability of Discount Window Borrowing. *J. Banking Finance*, December 1987, *11*(4), pp. 563–70. **[G: U.S.]**

Vaubel, Roland. Competing Currencies: The Case for Free Entry. *Dorn, J. A. and Schwartz, A. J., eds.*, 1987, pp. 281–96.

Velasco, Andrés. Financial Crises and Balance of Payments Crises: A Simple Model of the Southern Cone Experience. *J. Devel. Econ.*, October 1987, *27*(1–2), pp. 263–83. **[G: Chile; Argentina; Uruguay]**

Velasco, Andrés. Financial Crises and Balance of Payments Crises: A Simple Model of the Southern Cone Experience. *[Diaz-Alejandro, C. F.]*, 1987, pp. 263–83. **[G: Chile; Argentina; Uruguay]**

Vickers, John. Signalling in a Model of Monetary Policy with Incomplete Information. *Sinclair, P. J. N., ed.*, 1987, *1986*, pp. 471–83.

Villa, Pierre. Règles de gestion du taux d'intérêt. (Interest Rate Policy as a Stabilization Tool. With English summary.) *Ann. Écon. Statist.*, Jan./Mar. 1987, (5), pp. 49–76.

Virén, Matti. Inflation and Interest Rates: Some Time Series Evidence from 6 OECD Countries. *Empirical Econ.*, 1987, *12*(1), pp. 51–66. **[G: Selected OECD]**

Virén, Matti. Inflation, Hedging, and the Fisher Hypothesis. *J. Macroecon.*, Winter 1987, *9*(1), pp. 45–57. **[G: U.S.; U.K.; Canada]**

de Vos, Aart F. Forecasting the Daily Balance of the Dutch Giro. *Heijmans, R. and Neudecker, H., eds.*, 1987, pp. 131–48. **[G: Netherlands]**

Wallace, Neil. Some Unsolved Problems for Monetary Theory. *Barnett, W. A. and Singleton, K. J., eds.*, 1987, pp. 340–49.

Waller, Christopher J. Deficit Financing and the Role of the Central Bank—A Game Theoretic Approach. *Atlantic Econ. J.*, July 1987, *15*(2), pp. 25–32.

Waller, Christopher J. Reputation Building in a Monetary Policy Game. *J. Macroecon.*, Summer 1987, *9*(3), pp. 351–71.

Walsh, Carl E. Three Questions Concerning Nominal and Real Interest Rates. *Fed. Res. Bank San Francisco Econ. Rev.*, Fall 1987, (4), pp. 5–19. **[G: U.S.]**

Warschauer, Thomas and Cherin, Antony C. Optimal Liquidity in Personal Financial Planning. *Financial Rev.*, November 1987, *22*(4), pp. 355–68.

Weil, Philippe. Confidence and the Real Value of Money in an Overlapping Generations Economy. *Quart. J. Econ.*, February 1987, *102*(1), pp. 1–22.

Weil, Philippe. Permanent Budget Deficits and Inflation. *J. Monet. Econ.*, September 1987, *20*(2), pp. 393–410.

Weinberg, David. Monetary Versions of the Balanced Budget Multiplier. *J. Macroecon.*, Summer 1987, *9*(3), pp. 429–38.

Wenninger, John and Klitgaard, Thomas. Exploring the Effects of Capital Movements on M1 and the Economy. *Fed. Res. Bank New York Quart. Rev.*, Summer 1987, *12*(2), pp. 21–31. [G: U.S.]

White, Lawrence H. Accounting for Non-interest-Bearing Currency: A Critique of the Legal Restrictions Theory of Money. *J. Money, Credit, Banking*, November 1987, *19*(4), pp. 448–56.

Willett, Thomas D. Currency Substitution, U.S. Money Demand, and International Interdependence. *Contemp. Policy Issues*, July 1987, *5*(3), pp. 76–82. [G: U.S.]

Williamson, Stephen D. Costly Monitoring, Loan Contracts, and Equilibrium Credit Rationing. *Quart. J. Econ.*, February 1987, *102*(1), pp. 135–45.

Williamson, Stephen D. Financial Intermediation, Business Failures, and Real Business Cycles. *J. Polit. Econ.*, December 1987, *95*(6), pp. 1196–1216.

Williamson, Stephen D. Transactions Costs, Inflation, and the Variety of Intermediation Services. *J. Money, Credit, Banking*, November 1987, *19*(4), pp. 484–98.

Wood, Geoffrey E. Properties of Monetary Systems: Comment. *Res, Z. and Motamen, S., eds.*, 1987, pp. 105–11. [G: U.S.]

Woodford, Michael. Credit Policy and the Price Level in a Cash-in-Advance Economy. *Barnett, W. A. and Singleton, K. J., eds.*, 1987, pp. 52–66.

Yeager, Leland B. Stable Money and Free-Market Currencies. *Dorn, J. A. and Schwartz, A. J., eds.*, 1987, pp. 297–317.

3116 Monetary Policy, Including All Central Banking Topics

Aftalion, Florin. Factors Affecting French Monetary Policy. *Hodgman, D. R. and Wood, G. E., eds.*, 1987, pp. 49–68. [G: France]

Aguirre, Ubaldo and Feldman, Ernesto. The Argentine Financial Sector. *Portes, R. and Swoboda, A. K., eds.*, 1987, pp. 293–302. [G: Argentina]

Akerholm, Johnny. The Role of Public Policy in Ensuring Financial Stability in Finland. *Portes, R. and Swoboda, A. K., eds.*, 1987, pp. 288–92. [G: Finland]

Al-Jarhi, Mabid Ali Muhamed Mahmoud. The Relative Efficiency of Interest-Free Monetary Economies: The Fiat Money Case. *Khan, M. S. and Mirakhor, A., eds.*, 1987, *1981*, pp. 37–73.

Angell, Wayne D. Statement to the U.S. House Subcommittee on Domestic Monetary Policy of the Committee on Banking, Finance and Urban Affairs and the Subcommittee on Procurement, Innovation, and Minority Enterprise Development of the Committee on Small Business, October 30, 1987. *Fed. Res. Bull.*, December 1987, *73*(12), pp. 913–14. [G: U.S.]

Angell, Wayne D. Statement to the U.S. House Subcommittee on Domestic Monetary Policy of the Committee on Banking, Finance and Urban Affairs, May 6, 1987. *Fed. Res. Bull.*, July 1987, *73*(7), pp. 563–69. [G: U.S.]

Angell, Wayne D. Statement to the U.S. House Committee on Banking, Finance and Urban Affairs, January 27, 1987. *Fed. Res. Bull.*, March 1987, *73*(3), pp. 205–08. [G: U.S.]

Arcelli, Mario. New Monetary Policy Trends in the Leading Western Countries. *Rev. Econ. Cond. Italy*, May-August 1987, (2), pp. 147–54. [G: EEC; U.S.]

Baillie, Richard T. and McMahon, Patrick C. Rational Forecasts in Models of the Term Structure of Interest Rates. *Goodhart, C.; Currie, D. and Llewellyn, D. T., eds.*, 1987, pp. 189–206.

Baltensperger, Ernst and Dermine, Jean. The Role of Public Policy in Ensuring Financial Stability: A Cross-Country, Comparative Perspective. *Portes, R. and Swoboda, A. K., eds.*, 1987, pp. 67–90. [G: Global]

Barbato, Michele. The Evolution of Monetary Policy and its Impact on Banks. *Rev. Econ. Cond. Italy*, May-August 1987, (2), pp. 165–208. [G: Italy]

Barth, James R. and Keleher, Robert E. "Financial Crises" and the Role of the Lender of Last Resort. *Wilcox, J. A., ed.*, 1987, *1984*, pp. 209–18. [G: U.S.]

Basevi, Giorgio. Reshaping Monetary Policy: Comments. *[Modigliani, F.]*, 1987, pp. 287–90. [G: Italy]

Batchelor, Roy A. Monetary Indicators and Operating Targets: Some Recent Issues in the UK. *Begg, D. K. H., et al.*, 1987, pp. 55–82. [G: U.K.]

Beckerman, Paul. Inflation and Dollar Accounts in Peru's Banking System, 1978–84. *World Devel.*, August 1987, *15*(8), pp. 1087–1106. [G: Peru]

Begg, David K. H. Fiscal Policy in Britain: Placing the Medium-term Financial Strategy in Context. *Begg, D. K. H., et al.*, 1987, pp. 17–43. [G: U.K.]

Belongia, Michael T. and Sheehan, Richard G. The Informational Efficiency of Weekly Money Announcements: An Econometric Critique. *J. Bus. Econ. Statist.*, July 1987, *5*(3), pp. 351–56. [G: U.S.]

Belton, Terrence M., et al. Daylight Overdrafts and Payments System Risk. *Fed. Res. Bull.*, November 1987, *73*(11), pp. 839–52. [G: U.S.]

Bench, Robert R. The Design of Bank Regulation and Supervision: Some Lessons from the Theory of Finance: Discussion. *Portes, R. and Swoboda, A. K., eds.*, 1987, pp. 104–07. [G: U.K.]

Benston, George J. Deposit Insurance and Bank Failures. *Wilcox, J. A., ed.*, 1987, *1983*, pp. 117–30. [G: U.S.]

Bergström, Stig-Erik. Föröndringarna i penningpolitiken. (Monetary Policy Changes: Comments. With English summary.) *Ekon. Sam-*

fundets Tidskr., 1987, *40*(1), pp. 19–21.
[G: Finland]
Black, Robert P. A Proposal to Clarify the Fed's Policy Mandate. *Dorn, J. A. and Schwartz, A. J., eds.*, 1987, *1986*, pp. 229–37.
[G: U.S.]
Black, Robert P. The Fed's Anti-inflationary Strategy: Is It Adequate? *Fed. Res. Bank Richmond Econ. Rev.*, Sept./Oct. 1987, *73*(5), pp. 3–9.
[G: U.S.]
Blejer, Mario I. and Sagari, Silvia. The Structure of the Banking Sector and the Sequence of Financial Liberalization. *Connolly, M. and González-Vega, C., eds.*, 1987, pp. 93–107.
[G: Latin America]
Blinder, Alan S. The Rules-versus-Discretion Debate in the Light of Recent Experience. *Weltwirtsch. Arch.*, 1987, *123*(3), pp. 399–414.
[G: OECD]
Bockelmann, Horst. Neue Finanzierungsformen aus der Sicht der Notenbanken. (New Forms of Financing from the Central Bank's Point of View. With English summary.) *Kredit Kapital*, 1987, *20*(4), pp. 486–95. [G: W. Germany]
Bogomolov, Oleg T. Monetary Institutions in a Planned Economy. *de Cecco, M. and Fitoussi, J.-P., eds.*, 1987, pp. 209–21. [G: U.S.S.R.; CMEA]
Bohara, Alok K.; Bradley, Michael C. and McNown, Robert F. New Evidence on Targets for Monetary Policy. *Southern Econ. J.*, January 1987, *53*(3), pp. 591–604. [G: U.S.]
Bourne, Compton. Financial Deepening, Domestic Resource Mobilisation and Economic Growth: Jamaica 1955–1982. *Salazar-Carrillo, J. and Tirado de Alonzo, I., eds.*, 1987, pp. 1–26. [G: Jamaica]
Brayton, Flint and Mauskopf, Eileen. Structure and Uses of the MPS Quarterly Econometric Model of the United States. *Fed. Res. Bull.*, February 1987, *73*(2), pp. 93–109. [G: U.S.]
Broaddus, Alfred and Goodfriend, Marvin. Base Drift and the Longer Run Growth of M1: Experience from a Decade of Monetary Targeting. *Goodfriend, M.*, 1987, *1984*, pp. 63–74.
[G: U.S.]
Brocato, Joseph M. The 1979 Federal Reserve Policy Shift: Some Evidence Using Causality Tests. *Southern Econ. J.*, July 1987, *54*(1), pp. 134–44. [G: U.S.]
Buck, Hannsjörg F. The GDR Financial System. *Jeffries, I. and Melzer, M., eds.*, 1987, pp. 149–201. [G: E. Germany]
Budd, Alan. Fiscal Policy in Britain: Placing the Medium-term Financial Strategy in Context: Commentary. *Begg, D. K. H., et al.*, 1987, pp. 44–49. [G: U.K.]
Burdekin, Richard C. K. Swiss Monetary Policy: Central Bank Independence and Stabilization Goals. *Kredit Kapital*, 1987, *20*(4), pp. 454–66. [G: Switzerland]
Burns, Arthur F. The Anguish of Central Banking. *Fed. Res. Bull.*, September 1987, *73*(9), pp. 687–98. [G: U.S.]
Burns, Arthur F. The Anguish of Central Bank-

ing. *Ciocca, P., ed.*, 1987, *1979*, pp. 147–66.
[G: U.S.]
Cairncross, Alec. Prelude to Radcliffe: Monetary Policy in the United Kingdom 1948–57. *Rivista Storia Econ.*, S.S., Int. Issue, 1987, *4*, pp. 1–20. [G: U.K.]
Canner, Glenn B. and Fergus, James T. The Economic Effects of Proposed Ceilings on Credit Card Interest Rates. *Fed. Res. Bull.*, January 1987, *73*(1), pp. 1–13. [G: U.S.]
Canner, Glenn B. and Fergus, James T. The Effects on Consumers and Creditors of Proposed Ceilings on Credit Card Interest Rates. *Fed. Res. Bull.*, October 1987, *73*(10), pp. 783–84.
[G: U.S.]
Capie, Forrest H. and Wood, Geoffrey E. Policy Makers in Crisis: A Study of Two Devaluations. *Hodgman, D. R. and Wood, G. E., eds.*, 1987, pp. 166–92. [G: U.K.]
Caramazza, Francesco. International Real Interest Rate Linkages in the 1970s and 1980s. *Tremblay, R., ed.*, 1987, pp. 123–50.
Cárdenas, Enrique and Manns, Carlos. Inflation and Monetary Stabilization in Mexico During the Revolution. *J. Devel. Econ.*, October 1987, *27*(1–2), pp. 375–94. [G: Mexico]
Cárdenas, Enrique and Manns, Carlos. Inflation and Monetary Stabilization in Mexico during the Revolution. *[Diaz-Alejandro, C. F.]*, 1987, pp. 375–94. [G: Mexico]
Chandavarkar, Anand G. Developmental Role of Central Banks. *Finance Develop.*, December 1987, *24*(4), pp. 34–37.
Chowdhury, Abdur R. Monetary Aggregates as a Target Variable: Comment [Monetary vs. Credit Aggregates: An Evaluation of Monetary Policy Targets]. *Southern Econ. J.*, July 1987, *54*(1), pp. 227–31.
Ciampi, Carlo A. The Functions of the Central Bank in Today's Economy. *Ciocca, P., ed.*, 1987, pp. 79–91.
Ciocca, Pierluigi. Between 'a Science' and 'an Art': Central Banks and the Political Economy of Money. *Ciocca, P., ed.*, 1987, pp. 3–44.
Cobbold, Cameron F. [Lord]. Some Thoughts on Central Banking. *Ciocca, P., ed.*, 1987, *1962*, pp. 47–56.
Cobham, David. Controlling the Money Supply. *Thompson, G.; Brown, V. and Levačić, R., eds.*, 1987, pp. 196–223. [G: U.K.]
Cobham, David and Serre, Jean-Marin. The Variability of Monetary Growth in France and the UK, 1970–84. *Goodhart, C.; Currie, D. and Llewellyn, D. T., eds.*, 1987, pp. 78–100.
[G: France; U.K.]
Cook, Timothy and Hahn, Thomas. The Reaction of Interest Rates to Unanticipated Federal Reserve Actions and Statements: Implications for the Money Announcement Controversy. *Econ. Inquiry*, July 1987, *25*(3), pp. 511–34.
[G: U.S.]
Cross, Sam Y. Treasury and Federal Reserve Foreign Exchange Operations. *Fed. Res. Bull.*, October 1987, *73*(10), pp. 779–82. [G: U.S.]
Cross, Sam Y. Treasury and Federal Reserve Foreign Exchange Operations. *Fed. Res. Bull.*,

May 1987, 73(5), pp. 330–35.   [G: U.S.]

Cross, Sam Y. Treasury and Federal Reserve Foreign Exchange Operations. *Fed. Res. Bull.*, July 1987, 73(7), pp. 552–57.   [G: U.S.]

Cross, Sam Y. Treasury and Federal Reserve Foreign Exchange Operations: August–October 1987. *Fed. Res. Bank New York Quart. Rev.*, Winter 1987-88, 12(4), pp. 48–53.   [G: U.S.]

Cross, Sam Y. Treasury and Federal Reserve Foreign Exchange Operations: May–June 1987. *Fed. Res. Bank New York Quart. Rev.*, Autumn 1987, 12(3), pp. 49–54.   [G: U.S.]

Cross, Sam Y. Treasury and Federal Reserve Foreign Exchange Operations: February–April 1987. *Fed. Res. Bank New York Quart. Rev.*, Spring 1987, 12(1), pp. 57–63.   [G: U.S.]

Cross, Sam Y. Treasury and Federal Reserve Foreign Exchange Operations. *Fed. Res. Bull.*, January 1987, 73(1), pp. 14–19.   [G: U.S.]

Cross, Sam Y. Treasury and Federal Reserve Foreign Exchange Operations: November 1987–January 1988. *Fed. Res. Bank New York Quart. Rev.*, Winter 1987-88, 12(4), pp. 54–59.
          [G: U.S.]

Cross, Sam Y. Treasury and Federal Reserve Foreign Exchange Operations: November 1986–January 1987. *Fed. Res. Bank New York Quart. Rev.*, Spring 1987, 12(1), pp. 64–70.
          [G: U.S.]

Cumby, Robert E. Japanese–U.S. Current Accounts and Exchange Rates before and after the G5 Agreement: Discussion. *Sato, R. and Wachtel, P., eds.*, 1987, pp. 148–52.
          [G: Japan; U.S.]

Currie, David. Fiscal Policy in Britain: Placing the Medium-term Financial Strategy in Context: Commentary. *Begg, D. K. H., et al.*, 1987, pp. 50–53.   [G: U.K.]

Cuthbertson, Keith and Taylor, Mark P. Buffer-Stock Money: An Appraisal. *Goodhart, C.; Currie, D. and Llewellyn, D. T., eds.*, 1987, pp. 103–24.   [G: U.K.]

Davidson, James. Disequilibrium Money: Some Further Results with a Monetary Model of the UK. *Goodhart, C.; Currie, D. and Llewellyn, D. T., eds.*, 1987, pp. 125–49.   [G: U.K.]

Delbeke, Jos. Long-term Trends in the Belgian Money Supply, 1877–1984. *Vasko, T., ed.*, 1987, pp. 313–25.   [G: Belgium]

Demopoulos, George D.; Katsimbris, George M. and Miller, Stephen M. Monetary Policy and Central-Bank Financing of Government Budget Deficits: A Cross-Country Comparison. *Europ. Econ. Rev.*, July 1987, 31(5), pp. 1023–50.   [G: OECD]

Devadoss, S. and Meyers, William H. Relative Prices and Money: Further Results for the United States. *Amer. J. Agr. Econ.*, November 1987, 69(4), pp. 838–42.   [G: U.S.]

Dolde, Walter and Tobin, James. Monetary and Fiscal Effects on Consumption. *Tobin, J. (II)*, 1987, 1971, pp. 175–215.   [G: U.S.]

Dotsey, Michael. The Australian Money Market and the Operations of the Reserve Bank of Australia: A Comparative Analysis. *Fed. Res. Bank*

Richmond Econ. Rev., Sept./Oct. 1987, 73(5), pp. 19–31.   [G: Australia]

Dow, Christopher. A Critique of Monetary Policy. *Lloyds Bank Rev.*, October 1987, (166), pp. 20–32.   [G: U.K.]

Eichengreen, Barry. Conducting the International Orchestra: Bank of England Leadership under the Classical Gold Standard. *J. Int. Money Finance*, March 1987, 6(1), pp. 5–29.
          [G: U.K.]

Einaudi, Luigi. Experience with Monetary Management: 'Noise.' *Ciocca, P., ed.*, 1987, 1960, pp. 121–25.   [G: Italy]

Eisenberg, Meyer. The Current Status of the Regulation of Financial Services and Products in the United States: Developments and Trends. *de Cecco, M., ed.*, 1987, pp. 28–76.
          [G: U.S.]

Ellis, Howard S. Monetary Policy as an Instrument of Progress. *Dupriez, L. H., ed.*, 1987, 1955, pp. 327–40.

Ellis, Larry V. The Privatization of Money: A Survey of the Issues. *Kent, C. A., ed.*, 1987, pp. 135–44.

Emminger, Otmar. The Dollar's Borrowed Strength. *Salvatore, D., ed.*, 1987, pp. 450–68.   [G: U.S.]

Emminger, Otmar. Thirty Years of the Deutschmark. *Ciocca, P., ed.*, 1987, 1978, pp. 127–46.   [G: W. Germany]

Esfahani, Hadi Salehi. The Resurgence of Inflation in Latin America: Discussion. *World Devel.*, August 1987, 15(8), pp. 1141–43.
          [G: S. America; Peru; Chile]

Feltenstein, Andrew and Farhadian, Ziba. Fiscal Policy, Monetary Targets, and the Price Level in a Centrally Planned Economy: An Application to the Case of China. *J. Money, Credit, Banking*, May 1987, 19(2), pp. 137–56.
          [G: China]

Fischer, Stanley. The Performance of the British Economy: Monetary Policy. *Dornbusch, R. and Layard, R., eds.*, 1987, pp. 6–28.
          [G: U.K.]

Friedman, Milton. Monetary Policy: Tactics versus Strategy. *Dorn, J. A. and Schwartz, A. J., eds.*, 1987, 1984, pp. 361–82.   [G: U.S.]

Friedman, Milton and Schwartz, Anna J. Money and Business Cycles. *Schwartz, A. J.*, 1987, 1963, pp. 24–77.   [G: U.S.]

Fuchs, Michael. Udviklingstendenser i centralbankernes likvikitetsstyring. (Developments in Central Bank Liquidity Management. With English summary.) *Nationaløkon. Tidsskr.*, 1987, 125(2), pp. 197–212.   [G: OECD]

Gidlow, R. M. Instability in the Rand–Dollar Market: Cause and Cures. *S. Afr. J. Econ.*, June 1987, 55(2), pp. 136–49.   [G: S. Africa]

Gilbert, R. Alton. A Revision in the Monetary Base. *Fed. Res. Bank St. Louis Rev.*, Aug./Sept. 1987, 69(7), pp. 24–29.   [G: U.S.]

Gleske, Leonhard. Monetary Policy: Priorities and Limitations. *[Wallich, H. C.]*, 1987, pp. 16–22.   [G: W. Germany]

González-Vega, Claudio and Zinser, James E. Regulated and Nonregulated Financial and

Foreign Exchange Markets and Income Inequality in the Dominican Republic. *Connolly, M. and González-Vega, C., eds.*, 1987, pp. 195–216. **[G: Dominican Republic]**

Goodfriend, Marvin. Federal Funds: Instrument of Federal Reserve Policy. *Goodfriend, M.,* 1987, *1986*, pp. 54–62. **[G: U.S.]**

Goodfriend, Marvin. Monetary Policy in Practice: Introduction: Topics, Methods, and Themes. *Goodfriend, M.,* 1987, pp. 1–2. **[G: U.S.]**

Goodfriend, Marvin. The Promises and Pitfalls of Contemporaneous Reserve Requirements for the Implementation of Monetary Policy. *Goodfriend, M.,* 1987, *1984*, pp. 75–84. **[G: U.S.]**

Goodfriend, Marvin and Hargraves, Monica. A Historical Assessment of the Rationales and Functions of Reserve Requirements. *Goodfriend, M.,* 1987, *1983*, pp. 35–53. **[G: U.S.]**

Goodhart, Charles A. E. Monetary Indicators and Operating Targets: Some Recent Issues in the UK: Commentary. *Begg, D. K. H., et al.,* 1987, pp. 83–88.

Goodhart, Charles A. E. The Performance of the British Economy: Monetary Policy: Comment. *Dornbusch, R. and Layard, R., eds.,* 1987, pp. 253–55. **[G: U.K.]**

Green, Christopher J. Did High-Powered Money Rule the Roost? Monetary Policy, Private Behaviour and the Structure of Interest Rates in the United Kingdom: 1972–77. *Goodhart, C.; Currie, D. and Llewellyn, D. T., eds.,* 1987, pp. 207–30. **[G: U.K.]**

Grier, Kevin Blaine. Presidential Elections and Federal Reserve Policy: An Empirical Test. *Southern Econ. J.,* October 1987, *54*(2), pp. 475–86. **[G: U.S.]**

Grier, Kevin Blaine and Neiman, Howard E. Deficits, Politics and Money Growth. *Econ. Inquiry,* April 1987, *25*(2), pp. 201–14. **[G: U.S.]**

Guttmann, Robert. Changing of the Guard at the Fed. *Challenge,* Nov./Dec. 1987, *30*(5), pp. 4–9. **[G: U.S.]**

Hall, Maximilian J. B. UK Banking Supervision and the Johnson Matthey Affair. *Goodhart, C.; Currie, D. and Llewellyn, D. T., eds.,* 1987, pp. 3–30. **[G: U.K.]**

Hall, Thomas E. and Noble, Nicholas R. Velocity and the Variability of Money Growth: Evidence from Granger-Causality Tests: A Note. *J. Money, Credit, Banking,* February 1987, *19*(1), pp. 112–16. **[G: U.S.]**

Havrilesky, Thomas M. Monetary Modeling in a World of Financial Innovation. *Solomon, E. H., ed.,* 1987, pp. 159–87. **[G: U.S.]**

Hester, Donald D. On the Empirical Detection of Financial Innovation. *de Cecco, M., ed.,* 1987, pp. 77–111. **[G: U.S.]**

Hetzel, Robert L. Will Recent High Growth Rates of Money Revive Inflation? *Contemp. Policy Issues,* January 1987, *5*(1), pp. 41–53. **[G: U.S.]**

Higgins, Christopher. Fiscal and Monetary Policies: Their Role in the Adjustment Process:

Comment. *Holmes, F., ed.,* 1987, pp. 185–91. **[G: W. Germany; Japan; Belgium; U.S.]**

Hodgman, Donald R. and Resek, Robert W. Central Bank Exchange Rate Policy. *Hodgman, D. R. and Wood, G. E., eds.,* 1987, pp. 136–65. **[G: EEC]**

Hoffmeyer, Erik. The International Capital Market and the International Monetary System. *Ciocca, P., ed.,* 1987, *1978*, pp. 245–61. **[G: Denmark]**

Horstmann, Theo. "The Worst Banking Practice in the World": Inter-allied Discussion over American Plans to Reform the German Banking System in 1945/46. *Pohl, H. and Rudolph, B., eds.,* 1987, pp. 93–115. **[G: W. Germany]**

Howitt, Peter. Disinflation and Exchange Rate Stabilization: Canada, 1980–1985. *J. Policy Modeling,* Winter 1987, *9*(4), pp. 637–59. **[G: Canada]**

Howson, Susan. The Origins of Cheaper Money, 1945–7. *Econ. Hist. Rev., 2nd Ser.,* August 1987, *40*(3), pp. 433–52. **[G: U.K.]**

Islam, Sadequal. Monetary Policy in a Developing Economy: The Case of Bangladesh. *Indian Econ. J.,* Oct.-Dec. 1987, *35*(2), pp. 38–47. **[G: Bangladesh]**

Ito, Takatoshi. The Intradaily Exchange Rate Dynamics and Monetary Policies after the Group of Five Agreement. *J. Japanese Int. Economies,* September 1987, *1*(3), pp. 275–98. **[G: Japan]**

Jones, David D. On the Fed Board of Governors: Eroding Political Insularity... *Challenge,* Jan./Feb. 1987, *29*(6), pp. 53–54. **[G: U.S.]**

Jones, Geoffrey. The Imperial Bank of Iran and Iranian Economic Development, 1890–1952. *Atack, J., ed.,* 1987, pp. 69–80. **[G: Iran]**

Judd, John P. and Trehan, Bharat. Portfolio Substitution and the Reliability of M1, M2 and M3 as Monetary Policy Indicators. *Fed. Res. Bank San Francisco Econ. Rev.,* Summer 1987, (3), pp. 5–29. **[G: U.S.]**

Kamitz, Reinhard. Banks and Economic Policy. *Ciocca, P., ed.,* 1987, *1963*, pp. 187–96.

Khan, Mohsin S. and Mirakhor, Abbas. The Financial System and Monetary Policy in an Islamic Economy. *Khan, M. S. and Mirakhor, A., eds.,* 1987, pp. 163–84.

Kleiman, Ephraim. The Resurgence of Inflation in Latin America: Discussion. *World Devel.,* August 1987, *15*(8), pp. 1143–45. **[G: Peru]**

Knodell, Jane. Open Market Operations: Evolution and Significance. *J. Econ. Issues,* June 1987, *21*(2), pp. 691–99. **[G: U.S.]**

Koluri, Bharat R. and Giannaros, Demetrios S. Deficit and External Debt Effects on Money and Inflation in Brazil and Mexico: Some Evidence. *Eastern Econ. J.,* July-Sept. 1987, *13*(3), pp. 243–48. **[G: Brazil; Mexico]**

Kopcke, Richard W. Financial Assets, Interest Rates, and Money Growth. *New Eng. Econ. Rev.,* Mar./Apr. 1987, pp. 17–30. **[G: U.S.]**

Kretzmer, Peter E. and Porter, Richard D. Total Transaction Measures and M1 Growth. *Contemp. Policy Issues,* January 1987, *5*(1), pp. 64–75. **[G: U.S.]**

Kuczynski, Michael. Inflation and Monetary Institutions in Developing Countries. *de Cecco, M. and Fitoussi, J.-P., eds.*, 1987, pp. 222–40. **[G: LDCs]**

Leijonhufvud, Axel. Constitutional Constraints on the Monetary Powers of Government. *Dorn, J. A. and Schwartz, A. J., eds.*, 1987, pp. 129–43. **[G: U.S.]**

Libby, Barbara. Changes in the Decision-Making Structure of the Federal Reserve System. *J. Econ. Issues*, June 1987, *21*(2), pp. 701–12. **[G: U.S.]**

Llewellyn, David T. The Operation and Regulation of Financial Markets: Introduction. *Goodhart, C.; Currie, D. and Llewellyn, D. T., eds.*, 1987, pp. xi–xvii. **[G: U.K.]**

Lusser, Markus. Policy and Financial Innovation: Will There Be a Switch from Deregulation to Reregulation? *Portes, R. and Swoboda, A. K., eds.*, 1987, pp. 257–62.

MacDonald, Ronald and Torrance, Thomas S. £M3 Surprises and Asset Prices. *Economica*, November 1987, *54*(216), pp. 505–15. **[G: U.K.]**

Machak, Joseph A.; Spivey, W. Allen and Wrobleski, William J. A Multiple Time Series Approach to Analyzing and Forecasting the Major French Monetary Aggregates. *Ann. Écon. Statist.*, Jan./Mar. 1987, (5), pp. 89–107. **[G: France]**

Mates, Neven. Some Specific Features of Inflation in a Heavily-Indebted Socialist Country. *Econ. Anal. Workers' Manage.*, 1987, *21*(4), pp. 419–31. **[G: Yugoslavia]**

Mayer, Thomas. Replacing the FOMC by a PC. *Contemp. Policy Issues*, April 1987, *5*(2), pp. 31–43. **[G: U.S.]**

McCallum, Bennett T. The Case for Rules in the Conduct of Monetary Policy: A Concrete Example. *Weltwirtsch. Arch.*, 1987, *123*(3), pp. 415–29. **[G: OECD]**

McFadden, Lynn. Government Revenue from Money Creation in Latin America: 1977–81. *Connolly, M. and González-Vega, C., eds.*, 1987, pp. 341–48. **[G: Latin America]**

McKinnon, R. J. Exchange Stability, International Monetary Coordination, and the U.S. Federal Reserve System. *Visser, H. and Schoor, E., eds.*, 1987, pp. 139–67. **[G: U.S.; Global]**

McMillin, W. Douglas and Fackler, James S. Monetary Aggregates as a Target Variable: Reply [Monetary vs. Credit Aggregates: An Evaluation of Monetary Policy Targets]. *Southern Econ. J.*, July 1987, *54*(1), pp. 232–34.

McNulty, James E. Measuring Interest Rate Risk: What Do We Really Know? *Wilcox, J. A., ed.*, 1987, *1986*, pp. 37–46.

Mehra, Yash. Money Growth Volatility and High Nominal Interest Rates. *Fed. Res. Bank Richmond Econ. Rev.*, Nov./Dec. 1987, *73*(6), pp. 10–19. **[G: U.S.]**

Meltzer, Allan H. Properties of Monetary Systems. *Res, Z. and Motamen, S., eds.*, 1987, pp. 83–104. **[G: U.S.]**

Mengle, David L. The Discount Window. *Wilcox, J. A., ed.*, 1987, *1986*, pp. 200–208. **[G: U.S.]**

Menichella, Donato. The Contribution of the Banking System to Monetary Equilibrium and Economic Stability: Italian Experience. *Ciocca, P., ed.*, 1987, *1956*, pp. 95–119. **[G: Italy]**

Mills, Terence C. and Stephenson, Michael J. A Time Series Forecasting System for the UK Money Supply. *Econ. Modelling*, July 1987, *4*(3), pp. 355–69. **[G: U.S.]**

Modigliani, Franco and Papademos, Lucas. Money, Credit and the Monetary Mechanism. *de Cecco, M. and Fitoussi, J.-P., eds.*, 1987, pp. 121–60.

Mookerjee, Rajen. Monetary Policy and the Informational Efficiency of the Stock Market: The Evidence from Many Countries. *Appl. Econ.*, November 1987, *19*(11), pp. 1521–32. **[G: OECD]**

Niehans, Jürg. Monetary Policy in an Open Economy. *de Cecco, M. and Fitoussi, J.-P., eds.*, 1987, pp. 243–68.

Nuetzel, Philip A. The FOMC in 1986: Flexible Policy for Uncertain Times. *Fed. Res. Bank St. Louis Rev.*, February 1987, *69*(2), pp. 15–29. **[G: U.S.]**

O'Brien, Leslie Kenneth [Lord]. The Banking Act 1979. *Ciocca, P., ed.*, 1987, *1979*, pp. 197–213. **[G: U.K.]**

Odedokun, Matthew O. A Flow-of-Funds Framework for Evaluating the Behaviours of Fiscal and Monetary Authorities Using Nigerian Data. *Public Finance*, 1987, *42*(2), pp. 193–213. **[G: Nigeria]**

Odedokun, Matthew O. Fungibility and Effectiveness of Selective Credit Policies: Evidence from Nigerian Data. *Devel. Econ.*, September 1987, *25*(3), pp. 234–48. **[G: Nigeria]**

Ogata, Shijuro. Maintaining a Sound Financial System in Japan. *Portes, R. and Swoboda, A. K., eds.*, 1987, pp. 282–87. **[G: Japan]**

Padoa-Schioppa, Tommaso. Reshaping Monetary Policy. *[Modigliani, F.]*, 1987, pp. 265–86. **[G: Italy]**

Pennacchi, George G. A Reexamination of the Over- (or Under-) Pricing of Deposit Insurance. *J. Money, Credit, Banking*, August 1987, *19*(3), pp. 340–60. **[G: U.S.]**

Pennacchi, George G. Alternative Forms of Deposit Insurance: Pricing and Bank Incentive Issues. *J. Banking Finance*, June 1987, *11*(2), pp. 291–312.

Poole, William. Monetary Control and the Political Business Cycle. *Dorn, J. A. and Schwartz, A. J., eds.*, 1987, *1986*, pp. 31–45. **[G: U.S.]**

Price, Lionel D. D. UK Public Policy on Ensuring Financial Stability. *Portes, R. and Swoboda, A. K., eds.*, 1987, pp. 271–74. **[G: U.K.]**

Puntila, Markku. Penningpolitiken under förändring. (Monetary Policy Changes. With English summary.) *Ekon. Samfundets Tidskr.*, 1987, *40*(1), pp. 11–18. **[G: Finland]**

Rasminsky, Louis. The Role of the Central Banker Today. *Ciocca, P., ed.*, 1987, *1966*, pp. 57–78.

Rich, Georg. Swiss and United States Monetary Policy: Has Monetarism Failed? *Fed. Res. Bank Richmond Econ. Rev.*, May/June 1987, 73(3), pp. 3–16. **[G: U.S.; Switzerland]**

Robinson, Kenneth J. Estimating the Inflationary Consequences of Discretionary Central Bank Behavior. *Fed. Res. Bank Dallas Econ. Rev.*, May 1987, pp. 17–28. **[G: U.S.]**

Roley, V. Vance. U.S. Money Announcements and Covered Interest Parity: The Case of Japan. *J. Int. Money Finance*, March 1987, 6(1), pp. 57–70. **[G: Japan; U.S.]**

Rolnick, Arthur J. The Benefits of Bank Deposit Rate Ceilings: New Evidence on Bank Rates and Risk in the 1920s. *Fed. Res. Bank Minn. Rev.*, Summer 1987, 11(3), pp. 2–18. **[G: U.S.]**

Roos, Lawrence K. Inherent Conflicts of U.S. Monetary Policymaking. *Dorn, J. A. and Schwartz, A. J., eds.*, 1987, 1986, pp. 47–52. **[G: U.S.]**

Rose, Harold. Monetary Indicators and Operating Targets: Some Recent Issues in the UK: Commentary. *Begg, D. K. H., et al.*, 1987, pp. 89–91. **[G: U.K.]**

Rose, Harold. The Design of Bank Regulation and Supervision: Some Lessons from the Theory of Finance: Discussion. *Portes, R. and Swoboda, A. K., eds.*, 1987, pp. 107–10. **[G: U.K.]**

Roth, Howard L. Federal Reserve Open Market Techniques. *Wilcox, J. A., ed.*, 1987, 1986, pp. 187–99. **[G: U.S.]**

Sarcinelli, Mario. Financial Assets, Public Debt and Monetary Policy: An International Integration Perspective. *Banca Naz. Lavoro Quart. Rev.*, September 1987, (162), pp. 263–372. **[G: Italy]**

Saubari, Moh. Reflections on Economic Policy Making: 1945–51. *Bull. Indonesian Econ. Stud.*, August 1987, 23(2), pp. 118–21. **[G: Indonesia]**

Savage, Donald T. Interstate Banking Developments. *Fed. Res. Bull.*, February 1987, 73(2), pp. 79–92. **[G: U.S.]**

Schaefer, Stephen M. The Design of Bank Regulation and Supervision: Some Lessons from the Theory of Finance. *Portes, R. and Swoboda, A. K., eds.*, 1987, pp. 91–104. **[G: U.K.]**

Schmid, Peter. The Role of Public Policy in Ensuring Financial Stability in Germany. *Portes, R. and Swoboda, A. K., eds.*, 1987, pp. 275–81. **[G: W. Germany]**

Schwartz, Anna J. The Lender of Last Resort and the Federal Safety Net. *J. Finan. Services Res.*, September 1987, 1(1), pp. 1–17. **[G: U.S.]**

Schwartz, Anna J. The Postwar Institutional Evolution of the International Monetary System. *Schwartz, A. J.*, 1987, 1983, pp. 333–63. **[G: OECD]**

Schwartz, Anna J. Understanding 1929–1933. *Schwartz, A. J.*, 1987, 1981, pp. 110–51. **[G: U.S.]**

Seger, Martha R. Statement to the U.S. House Subcommittee on Consumer Affairs and Coinage of the Committee on Banking, Finance and Urban Affairs, March 18, 1987. *Fed. Res. Bull.*, May 1987, 73(5), pp. 338–41. **[G: U.S.]**

Selgin, George A. Central Banking: Myth and Reality. *Hong Kong Econ. Pap.*, 1987, (18), pp. 1–13. **[G: Hong Kong]**

Shafer, Jeffrey R. The Theory of the Lender of Last Resort and the Eurocurrency Markets. *Aliber, R. Z., ed.*, 1987, pp. 281–304. **[G: EEC]**

Sheehan, Richard G. Does U.S. Money Growth Determine Money Growth in Other Nations? *Fed. Res. Bank St. Louis Rev.*, January 1987, 69(1), pp. 5–14. **[G: OECD]**

Smeets, Heinz-Dieter. Finanzinnovationen und Geldpolitik. (Financial Innovations and Monetary Policy. With English summary.) *Lenel, H. O., et al., eds.*, 1987, pp. 91–112. **[G: W. Germany]**

Soss, Neal M. On the Fed Board of Governors: ...And Growing Short on Experience. *Challenge*, Jan./Feb. 1987, 29(6), pp. 54–55. **[G: U.S.]**

Spaventa, Luigi. Public Debt and Rules of Monetary Growth: An Exercise in Monetarist Arithmetic. *de Cecco, M. and Fitoussi, J.-P., eds.*, 1987, pp. 269–85.

Spencer, Grant H. and Clements, Robin T. Fiscal and Monetary Policies: Their Role in the Adjustment Process. *Holmes, F., ed.*, 1987, pp. 154–84. **[G: Japan; Belgium; W. Germany]**

Spindt, Paul A. and Tarhan, Vefa. The Federal Reserve's New Operating Procedures: A Post Mortem. *J. Monet. Econ.*, January 1987, 19(1), pp. 107–23. **[G: U.S.]**

Sprinkel, Beryl W. Confronting Monetary Policy Dilemmas: The Legacy of Homer Jones. *Fed. Res. Bank St. Louis Rev.*, March 1987, 69(3), pp. 5 8. **[C: U.S.]**

Sterman, John D. The Economic Long Wave: Theory and Evidence. *Vasko, T., ed.*, 1987, pp. 127–61.

Tandon, Kishore and Urich, Thomas. International Market Response to Announcements of U.S. Macroeconomic Data. *J. Int. Money Finance*, March 1987, 6(1), pp. 71–83. **[G: U.S.; Selected OECD]**

Tanzi, Vito and Ter-Minassian, Teresa. The European Monetary System and Fiscal Policies. *Cnossen, S., ed.*, 1987, pp. 337–57. **[G: EEC]**

Tarantelli, Ezio. Monetary Policy and the Regulation of Inflation and Unemployment. *Gunderson, M.; Meltz, N. M. and Ostry, S., eds.*, 1987, pp. 94–102. **[G: W. Europe]**

Taylor, Herb. What Has Happened to M1? *Wilcox, J. A., ed.*, 1987, 1986, pp. 228–39. **[G: U.S.]**

Thomson, James B. Alternative Methods for Assessing Risk-Based Deposit-Insurance Premiums. *Wilcox, J. A., ed.*, 1987, 1986, pp. 131–36. **[G: U.S.]**

Throop, Adrian W. Three Views of Real Interest. *Wilcox, J. A., ed.*, 1987, 1986, pp. 79–81. **[G: U.S.]**

Tobin, James. A Case for Preserving Regulatory

Distinctions. *Challenge*, Nov./Dec. 1987, *30*(5), pp. 10–17. [G: U.S.]

Tobin, James. After Disinflation, Then What? *Tobin, J. (III)*, 1987, *1984*, pp. 348–67. [G: U.S.]

Tobin, James. An Essay on the Principles of Debt Management. *Tobin, J. (I)*, 1987, *1963*, pp. 378–455. [G: U.S.]

Tobin, James. Financial Innovation and Deregulation in Perspective. *Tobin, J. (III)*, 1987, *1985*, pp. 255–64. [G: U.S.]

Tobin, James. Fiscal and Monetary Policy under the Employment Act. *Tobin, J. (III)*, 1987, *1986*, pp. 24–39.

Tobin, James. Inflation, Interest Rates, and Stock Values. *Tobin, J. (III)*, 1987, *1974*, pp. 275–81. [G: U.S.]

Tobin, James. Monetarism: An Ebbing Tide? *Tobin, J. (III)*, 1987, *1985*, pp. 265–74. [G: U.S.]

Tobin, James. Monetary Policy and the Management of the Public Debt: The Patman Inquiry. *Tobin, J. (I)*, 1987, *1953*, pp. 456–70. [G: U.S.]

Tobin, James. Monetary Policy in an Uncertain World. *Tobin, J. (III)*, 1987, *1983*, pp. 240–54. [G: U.S.]

Tobin, James. Monetary Rules and Control in Brave New World. *Solomon, E. H., ed.*, 1987, pp. 137–57.

Tobin, James. Strategy for Disinflation (Fellner on 'The State of Monetary Policy'). *Tobin, J. (III)*, 1987, *1981*, pp. 368–74. [G: U.S.]

Tobin, James. The Monetary Interpretation of History: A Review Article. *Tobin, J. (I)*, 1987, pp. 471–96. [G: U.S.]

Tobin, James. The Monetary–Fiscal Mix in the United States. *Tobin, J. (III)*, 1987, pp. 142–67. [G: U.S.]

Tobin, James. The Reagan Economic Plan—Supply-Side, Budget, and Inflation. *Tobin, J. (III)*, 1987, *1981*, pp. 106–19. [G: U.S.]

Tobin, James. Unemployment, Interest, Deficits, and Money. *Tobin, J. (III)*, 1987, pp. 189–214. [G: U.S.]

Trehan, Bharat and Walsh, Carl E. Portfolio Substitution and Recent M1 Behavior. *Contemp. Policy Issues*, January 1987, *5*(1), pp. 54–63. [G: U.S.]

Triffin, Robert. A European Monetary Bank with Central Bank Functions. *Steinherr, A. and Weiserbs, D., eds.*, 1987, pp. 119–32. [G: W. Europe]

Urquidi, Victor L. Structural Change and Monetary Policy in Latin America—Possible Lessons for Other Developing Countries. *de Cecco, M. and Fitoussi, J.-P., eds.*, 1987, pp. 305–25. [G: Latin America]

Vastrup, Claus. Pengepolitik og dansk økonomi. (Monetary Policy in Denmark. With English summary.) *Nationaløkon. Tidsskr.*, 1987, *125*(1), pp. 113–28. [G: Denmark]

Volcker, Paul A. Facing up to the Twin Deficits. *Challenge*, Special Issue 1987, *30*(6), pp. 31–36. [G: U.S.]

Volcker, Paul A. Statement to the U.S. Senate Committee on Banking, Housing, and Urban Affairs, February 19, 1987. *Fed. Res. Bull.*, April 1987, *73*(4), pp. 282–89. [G: U.S.]

Volcker, Paul A. Statement to U.S. House Committee on Banking, Finance and Urban Affairs, July 21, 1987. *Fed. Res. Bull.*, September 1987, *73*(9), pp. 703–05. [G: U.S.]

Wall, Larry D. Has Bank Holding Companies' Diversification Affected Their Risk of Failure? *J. Econ. Bus.*, November 1987, *39*(4), pp. 313–26. [G: U.S.]

Wallich, Henry C. Central Banks as Regulators and Lenders of Last Resort in an International Context: A View from the United States. *Ciocca, P., ed.*, 1987, *1982*, pp. 231–42. [G: U.S.]

Walsh, Carl E. Monetary Targeting and Inflation: 1976–1984. *Fed. Res. Bank San Francisco Econ. Rev.*, Winter 1987, (1), pp. 5–16. [G: U.S.]

Weaver, R. Kent. Political Foundations of Swedish Economic Policy. *Bosworth, B. P. and Rivlin, A. M., eds.*, 1987, pp. 289–324. [G: Sweden]

Welker, Donald L. IPC or Total Deposits? There Is a Difference! *Fed. Res. Bank Richmond Econ. Rev.*, Mar./Apr. 1987, *73*(2), pp. 31–38. [G: U.S.]

Whittaker, J. and Theunissen, A. J. Why Does the Reserve Bank Set the Interest Rate? *S. Afr. J. Econ.*, March 1987, *55*(1), pp. 16–33. [G: S. Africa]

Whitwell, Jan L. Monetary Policy with a Deregulated Financial Sector. *Bollard, A. and Buckle, R., eds.*, 1987, pp. 261–82. [G: New Zealand]

Wigmore, Barrie A. Was the Bank Holiday of 1933 Caused by a Run on the Dollar? *J. Econ. Hist.*, September 1987, *47*(3), pp. 739–55. [G: U.S.]

Willms, Manfred. The DM/Dollar Rate and the Exchange Market Intervention Policy of the Deutsche Bundesbank 1974–1984. *Hodgman, D. R. and Wood, G. E., eds.*, 1987, pp. 193–219. [G: U.S.; W. Germany]

Woolley, John T. The Political Uses of Monetary Targets. *Hodgman, D. R. and Wood, G. E., eds.*, 1987, pp. 69–98. [G: U.S.; W. Germany; U.K.; France; Italy]

Wulwick, Nancy J. The Radcliffe Central Bankers. *J. Econ. Stud.*, 1987, *14*(4), pp. 36–50. [G: U.K.]

Zijlstra, Jelle. Central Banking with the Benefit of Hindsight. *Ciocca, P., ed.*, 1987, *1981*, pp. 167–83.

312 Commercial Banking

3120 Commercial Banking

Aach, David L. Designing Citibank's Computer Support System. *Shetty, Y. K. and Buehler, V. M., eds.*, 1987, pp. 197–206. [G: U.S.]

Abrams, Burton A. and Huang, Cliff J. Predicting Bank Failures: The Role of Structure in Affecting Recent Failure Experiences in the USA.

Appl. Econ., October 1987, *19*(10), pp. 1291–1302. [G: U.S.]

Aguirre, Ubaldo and Feldman, Ernesto. The Argentine Financial Sector. *Portes, R. and Swoboda, A. K., eds.*, 1987, pp. 293–302. [G: Argentina]

Akerholm, Johnny. The Role of Public Policy in Ensuring Financial Stability in Finland. *Portes, R. and Swoboda, A. K., eds.*, 1987, pp. 288–92. [G: Finland]

Aliber, Robert Z. Financial Innovation and the Boundaries of Banking. *Managerial Dec. Econ.*, March 1987, *8*(1), pp. 67–73.

Allais, Maurice. The Credit Mechanism and Its Implications. *Feiwel, G. R., ed. (II)*, 1987, pp. 491–561.

Amano, Masanori. Endogenous Money Supply and Monetary Policy in Asset Markets with Alternative Rationing Schemes. *J. Japanese Int. Economies*, March 1987, *1*(1), pp. 110–29. [G: Japan]

Angell, Wayne D. Statement to the U.S. House Committee on Banking, Finance and Urban Affairs, January 27, 1987. *Fed. Res. Bull.*, March 1987, *73*(3), pp. 205–08. [G: U.S.]

Angell, Wayne D. Statement to the U.S. Senate Subcommittee on Consumer Affairs of the Committee on Banking, Housing, and Urban Affairs, February 5, 1987. *Fed. Res. Bull.*, April 1987, *73*(4), pp. 279–82. [G: U.S.]

Arruñada Sanchez, Benito. Los excedentes de productividad de la Banca Privada. (With English summary.) *Invest. Econ.*, January 1987, *11*(1), pp. 151–78. [G: Spain]

Arshadi, Nasser and Lawrence, Edward C. An Empirical Investigation of New Bank Performance. *J. Banking Finance*, March 1987, *11*(1), pp. 33–48. [G: U.S.]

Artus, Patrick. Hétérogénéité des banques et des circuits de financement et régulation monétaire. (Banks' Heterogeneity and Monetary Policy. With English summary.) *Ann. Écon. Statist.*, Oct./Dec. 1987, (8), pp. 27–41.

Baker, James C. and Severiens, Jacobus T. Geographic Diversification and Concentration in U.S. Commercial Banking and Thrift Markets: A Regional Analysis. *Tremblay, R., ed.*, 1987, pp. 273–81. [G: U.S.]

Baltensperger, Ernst and Dermine, Jean. The Role of Public Policy in Ensuring Financial Stability: A Cross-Country, Comparative Perspective. *Portes, R. and Swoboda, A. K., eds.*, 1987, pp. 67–90. [G: Global]

Barbato, Michele. The Evolution of Monetary Policy and its Impact on Banks. *Rev. Econ. Cond. Italy*, May-August 1987, (2), pp. 165–208. [G: Italy]

Bardos, Jeffrey. The Risk-based Capital Agreement: A Further Step towards Policy Convergence. *Fed. Res. Bank New York Quart. Rev.*, Winter 1987-88, *12*(4), pp. 26–34. [G: OECD]

Barge, Jim. Interest Rate Exposure. *Gardener, E. P. M., ed.*, 1987, pp. 7–22.

Barry, Lynn M. A Review of the Eighth District's Banking Economy in 1986. *Fed. Res. Bank St. Louis Rev.*, April 1987, *69*(4), pp. 16–21. [G: U.S.]

Belongia, Michael T. and Santoni, G. J. Hedging Interest Rate Risk with Financial Futures: Some Basic Principles. *Wilcox, J. A., ed.*, 1987, *1984*, pp. 47–57. [G: U.S.]

Belton, Terrence M., et al. Daylight Overdrafts and Payments System Risk. *Fed. Res. Bull.*, November 1987, *73*(11), pp. 839–52. [G: U.S.]

Bench, Robert R. The Design of Bank Regulation and Supervision: Some Lessons from the Theory of Finance: Discussion. *Portes, R. and Swoboda, A. K., eds.*, 1987, pp. 104–07. [G: U.K.]

Benston, George J. Deposit Insurance and Bank Failures. *Wilcox, J. A., ed.*, 1987, *1983*, pp. 117–30. [G: U.S.]

Benveniste, Lawrence M. and Berger, Allen N. Securitization with Recourse: An Instrument that Offers Uninsured Bank Depositors Sequential Claims. *J. Banking Finance*, September 1987, *11*(3), pp. 403–24.

Berger, Allen N.; Hanweck, Gerald A. and Humphrey, David B. Competitive Viability in Banking: Scale, Scope, and Product Mix Economies. *J. Monet. Econ.*, December 1987, *20*(3), pp. 501–20. [G: U.S.]

Bernanke, Ben S. and Gertler, Mark. Banking and Macroeconomic Equilibrium. *Barnett, W. A. and Singleton, K. J., eds.*, 1987, pp. 89–111.

Bertoni, Albeto. How a Major Banking Group Can Deal with Structural Changes (Real and Financial) in Companies. *Rev. Econ. Cond. Italy*, Sept.-Dec. 1987, (3), pp. 455–78. [G: Italy]

Besanko, David and Thakor, Anjan V. Collateral and Rationing: Sorting Equilibria in Monopolistic and Competitive Credit Markets. *Int. Econ. Rev.*, October 1987, *28*(3), pp. 671–89.

Bester, Helmut. The Role of Collateral in Credit Markets with Imperfect Information. *Europ. Econ. Rev.*, June 1987, *31*(4), pp. 887–99.

de Boissieu, Christian. Lessons from the French Experience as Compared with Some Other OECD Countries. *de Cecco, M., ed.*, 1987, pp. 212–28. [G: France; OECD]

Bordo, Michael D.; Choudhri, Ehsan U. and Schwartz, Anna J. The Behavior of Money Stock under Interest Rate Control: Some Evidence for Canada. *J. Money, Credit, Banking*, May 1987, *19*(2), pp. 181–97. [G: Canada]

Boskin, Michael J., et al. The Federal Budget and Federal Insurance Programs. *[Harberger, A.]*, 1987, pp. 14–39. [G: U.S.]

Braun, Hanne. A Review of the New Literature on Banking History. *Pohl, H. and Rudolph, B., eds.*, 1987, pp. 141–49. [G: W. Germany]

Brickley, James A. and James, Christopher M. The Takeover Market, Corporate Board Composition, and Ownership Structure: The Case of Banking. *J. Law Econ.*, April 1987, *30*(1), pp. 161–80. [G: U.S.]

Brown, Z. M. Interest Margin Analysis Revisited

Yet Again. *Gardener, E. P. M., ed.*, 1987, pp. 73–132.

Bruner, Robert F. and Simms, John M., Jr. The International Debt Crisis and Bank Security Returns in 1982. *J. Money, Credit, Banking*, February 1987, *19*(1), pp. 46–55.   [G: U.S.]

Campbell, John Y. Money Announcements, the Demand for Bank Reserves, and the Behavior of the Federal Funds Rate within the Statement Week. *J. Money, Credit, Banking*, February 1987, *19*(1), pp. 56–67.   [G: U.S.]

Canner, Glenn B. and Maland, Ellen. Basic Banking. *Fed. Res. Bull.*, April 1987, *73*(4), pp. 255–69.   [G: U.S.]

Caprara, Ugo. Se si può parlare per la banca di un "eccesso di liquidité." (Can We Talk of a Bank having Excess Liquidity? With English summary.) *Rivista Int. Sci. Econ. Com.*, Nov.-Dec. 1987, *34*(11–12), pp. 1083–88.
    [G: Italy]

Caranza, Cesare and Cottarelli, Carlo. Financial Innovation in Italy: A Lop-Sided Process. *de Cecco, M., ed.*, 1987, pp. 172–211. [G: Italy]

Carli, Guido. Why Banks Are Unpopular. *Ciocca, P., ed.*, 1987, *1976*, pp. 215–30.   [G: Italy]

Carrizosa, Mauricio and Urdinola, Antonio. Private Internal Debt in Colombia, 1970–1985. *CEPAL Rev.*, August 1987, (32), pp. 27–53.
    [G: Colombia]

dalla Chiesa, Romeo. Banking and the Transformation of Italy's Productive Base: Introductory Address. *Rev. Econ. Cond. Italy*, Sept.-Dec. 1987, (3), pp. 337–39.   [G: Italy]

Christensen, Anders Møller and Jensen, Hugo Frey. Den danske pengeefterspørgsel 1975–86. (The Demand for Money in Demark, 1975–86. With English summary.) *Nationaløkon. Tidsskr.*, 1987, *125*(2), pp. 185–96.
    [G: Denmark]

Clair, Robert T. Branch Banking in Texas: Implications for Bank Structure. *Fed. Res. Bank Dallas Econ. Rev.*, September 1987, pp. 1–12.
    [G: U.S.]

Clair, Robert T. Financial Strategies of Top-Performance Banks in the Eleventh District. *Fed. Res. Bank Dallas Econ. Rev.*, January 1987, pp. 1–14.   [G: U.S.]

Clair, Robert T. and Gunther, Jeffery W. Problem Loans and the Profitability of Eleventh District Commercial Banks in 1986. *Fed. Res. Bank Dallas Econ. Rev.*, November 1987, (11), pp. 15–27.   [G: U.S.]

Clark, Jeffrey A. The Efficient Structure Hypothesis: More Evidence from Banking. *Quart. Rev. Econ. Bus.*, Autumn 1987, *27*(3), pp. 25–39.   [G: U.S.]

Corrigan, E. Gerald. Keep Banking Apart. *Challenge*, Nov./Dec. 1987, *30*(5), pp. 28–35.
    [G: U.S.]

Cosimano, Thomas F. Reserve Accounting and Variability in the Federal Funds Market. *J. Money, Credit, Banking*, May 1987, *19*(2), pp. 198–209.   [G: U.S.]

Cosimano, Thomas F. The Federal Funds Market under Bank Deregulation. *J. Money, Credit,*

Banking, August 1987, *19*(3), pp. 326–39.
    [G: U.S.]

Cothren, Richard. Asymmetric Information and Optimal Bank Reserves. *J. Money, Credit, Banking*, February 1987, *19*(1), pp. 68–77.

Courakis, Anthony S. In What Sense Do Compulsory Ratios Reduce the Volume of Deposits? *Goodhart, C.; Currie, D. and Llewellyn, D. T., eds.*, 1987, pp. 150–86.

Cumming, Christine M. The Economics of Securitization. *Fed. Res. Bank New York Quart. Rev.*, Autumn 1987, *12*(3), pp. 11–23.
    [G: U.S.]

Curtis, Carole and Baker, James C. The Evolution of the Super Edge: Regulation and Operations of Edge Act Banks. *J. World Trade Law*, December 1987, *21*(6), pp. 25–36. [G: U.S.]

Cyrnak, Anthony W. Recent Bank Failures. *Wilcox, J. A., ed.*, 1987, *1986*, pp. 114–16.
    [G: U.S.]

Danker, Deborah J. and McLaughlin, Mary M. The Profitability of U.S.-Chartered Insured Commercial Banks in 1986. *Fed. Res. Bull.*, July 1987, *73*(7), pp. 537–51.   [G: U.S.]

Day, John. Medieval Merchants and Financiers. *Day, J.*, 1987, pp. 162–84.   [G: Europe]

Dermine, Jean. Measuring the Market Value of a Bank, a Primer. *Finance*, December 1987, *8*(2), pp. 91–108.

Desai, Meghnad and Low, William. Measuring the Opportunity for Product Innovation. *de Cecco, M., ed.*, 1987, pp. 112–40.   [G: U.S.]

DeSarbo, Wayne S., et al. A Friction Model for Describing and Forecasting Price Changes. *Marketing Sci.*, Fall 1987, *6*(4), pp. 299–319.
    [G: U.S.]

Deshons, Michel and Freixas, Xavier. Le rôle de la garantie dans le contrat de prêt bancaire. (The Role of Collateral in the Bank's Debt Contract. With English summary.) *Finance*, June 1987, *8*(1), pp. 7–32.

Di Vittorio, Antonio. A Multinational Bank: The Bank of Rome. *J. Europ. Econ. Hist.*, Fall 1987, *16*(2), pp. 389–98.   [G: Italy]

Doukas, John and Melhem, Melhem. Canadian Banks: Risk Reduction by International Diversification. *Appl. Econ.*, December 1987, *19*(12), pp. 1561–69.   [G: Canada]

Dudler, Hermann-Josef. Financial Innovation in Germany. *de Cecco, M., ed.*, 1987, pp. 158–71.   [G: W. Germany]

Eisenberg, Meyer. The Current Status of the Regulation of Financial Services and Products in the United States: Developments and Trends. *de Cecco, M., ed.*, 1987, pp. 28–76.
    [G: U.S.]

Evanoff, Douglas D. and Fortier, Diana. The Impact of Geographic Expansion in Banking: Some Axioms to Grind. *Wilcox, J. A., ed.*, 1987, *1986*, pp. 99–113.   [G: U.S.]

Felgran, Steven D. Interest Rate Swaps: Use, Risk, and Prices. *New Eng. Econ. Rev.*, Nov./Dec. 1987, pp. 22–32.

Felgran, Steven D. and Ferguson, R. Edward. The Evolution of Retail EFT Networks. *Wil-*

cox, J. A., ed., 1987, 1986, pp. 170–84.
[G: U.S.]

Fischer, Herbert and Sydow, Peter. Agricultural Development in the German Democratic Republic. *Saunders, C. T., ed.*, 1987, pp. 348–53. [G: E. Germany]

Forsyth, John H. Financial Innovation in Britain. *de Cecco, M., ed.*, 1987, pp. 141–57.
[G: U.K.]

Foweraker, Joe. What's Good for Citicorp... *Challenge*, Jan./Feb. 1987, 29(6), pp. 47–50.
[G: U.S.]

Fung, W. K. F. and Theobald, M. F. Taxes, Unequal Access, Public Debt and Corporate Financial Policy in the United Kingdom. *J. Banking Finance*, March 1987, 11(1), pp. 65–78.
[G: U.K.]

Furlong, Frederick T. and Keeley, Michael C. Bank Capital Regulation and Asset Risk. *Fed. Res. Bank San Francisco Econ. Rev.*, Spring 1987, (2), pp. 20–40. [G: U.S.]

Gardener, Edward P. M. Interest Rate Risk and the Banking Firm: Interest Margin Analysis Revisited. *Gardener, E. P. M., ed.*, 1987, pp. 23–71.

Gelfand, Matthew D. and Spiller, Pablo T. Entry Barriers and Multiproduct Oligopolies: Do They Forebear or Spoil? *Int. J. Ind. Organ.*, March 1987, 5(1), pp. 101–13. [G: Uruguay]

Geller, Henry. Telecommunications Policy Issues: The New Money Delivery Modes. *Solomon, E. H., ed.*, 1987, pp. 63–78. [G: U.S.]

Gemmill, Robert F. The Role of Public Policy in Ensuring Financial Stability in the United States. *Portes, R. and Swoboda, A. K., eds.*, 1987, pp. 263–70. [G: U.S.]

Gerke, Wolfgang and Kayser, Ottmar. Bewertung eines Rückversicherungskonzepts für die Deckung von Kreditausfallrisiken der Kreditinstitute. (With English summary.) *Z. Betriebswirtshaft*, July 1987, 57(7), pp. 662–83.

Goldfarb, David R. Hedging Interest Rate Risk in Banking. *J. Futures Markets*, February 1987, 7(1), pp. 35–47.

Goodfriend, Marvin. Federal Funds: Instrument of Federal Reserve Policy. *Goodfriend, M.*, 1987, 1986, pp. 54–62. [G: U.S.]

Goodhart, Charles A. E. Financial Regulation and Supervision: A Review of Three Books. *Nat. Westminster Bank Quart. Rev.*, August 1987, pp. 55–64. [G: U.S.; U.K.]

Gooptu, Sudarshan and Lombra, Raymond. Aggregation across Heterogeneous Depository Institutions. *Financial Rev.*, November 1987, 22(4), pp. 369–78. [G: U.S.]

Gorton, Gary B. and Haubrich, Joseph G. Assessing Deregulation: Further Considerations: A Reply. *Carnegie–Rochester Conf. Ser. Public Policy*, Spring 1987, 26, pp. 345–48.
[G: U.S.]

Gorton, Gary B. and Haubrich, Joseph G. Bank Deregulation, Credit Markets, and the Control of Capital. *Carnegie–Rochester Conf. Ser. Public Policy*, Spring 1987, 26, pp. 289–333.
[G: U.S.]

Gorton, Gary B. and Mullineaux, Donald J. The Joint Production of Confidence: Endogenous Regulation and Nineteenth Century Commercial-Bank Clearinghouses. *J. Money, Credit, Banking*, November 1987, 19(4), pp. 457–68.
[G: U.S.]

Green, Christopher J. Money Market Arbitrage and Commercial Banks' Base Rate Adjustments in the United Kingdom. *Bull. Econ. Res.*, October 1987, 39(4), pp. 273–96. [G: U.K.]

Greenbaum, Stuart I. and Thakor, Anjan V. Bank Funding Modes: Securitization versus Deposits. *J. Banking Finance*, September 1987, 11(3), pp. 379–401.

Greenspan, Alan. Statement to the U.S. House Subcommittee on Telecommunications and Finance of the Committee on Energy and Commerce, October 5, 1987. *Fed. Res. Bull.*, December 1987, 73(12), pp. 907–10. [G: U.S.]

Gualandri, Elisabetta. Italian Banks and Interest Rate Risk: A Survey for the Decade 1975–1984. *Gardener, E. P. M., ed.*, 1987, pp. 149–60.
[G: Italy]

Guttmann, Robert. Changing of the Guard at the Fed. *Challenge*, Nov./Dec. 1987, 30(5), pp. 4–9. [G: U.S.]

Haberman, Gary. Capital Requirements of Commercial and Investment Banks: Contrasts in Regulation. *Fed. Res. Bank New York Quart. Rev.*, Autumn 1987, 12(3), pp. 1–10.
[G: U.S.]

Hall, Maximilian J. B. The Deposit Protection Scheme: The Case for Reform. *Nat. Westminster Bank Quart. Rev.*, August 1987, pp. 45–54. [G: U.K.]

Hall, Maximilian J. B. UK Banking Supervision and the Johnson Matthey Affair. *Goodhart, C.; Currie, D. and Llewellyn, D. T., eds.*, 1987, pp. 3–30. [G: U.K.]

Hancock, Diana. Aggregation of Monetary Goods: A Production Model. *Barnett, W. A. and Singleton, K. J., eds.*, 1987, pp. 200–218.
[G: U.S.]

Hannan, Timothy H. and McDowell, John M. Rival Precedence and the Dynamics of Technology Adoption: An Empirical Analysis. *Economica*, May 1987, 54(214), pp. 155–71.
[G: U.S.]

Hannan, Timothy H. and Rhoades, Stephen A. Acquisition Targets and Motives: The Case of the Banking Industry. *Rev. Econ. Statist.*, February 1987, 69(1), pp. 67–74. [G: U.S.]

Haqiqi, Abdul Wassay and Pomeranz, Felix. Accounting Needs of Islamic Banking. *Most, Kenneth S., ed.*, 1987, pp. 153–68.
[G: Arab Countries]

Haque, Nadeem Ul and Mirakhor, Abbas. Optimal Profit-Sharing Contracts and Investment in an Interest-Free Islamic Economy. *Khan, M. S. and Mirakhor, A., eds.*, 1987, pp. 141–61.

Haque, Nadeem Ul and Mirakhor, Abbas. Saving Behavior in an Economy without Fixed Interest. *Khan, M. S. and Mirakhor, A., eds.*, 1987, pp. 125–39.

Haraf, William S. Maintaining Financial Stability: Financial Strains and Public Policy. *Cagan, P.*, *ed.*, 1987, pp. 181–208.   [G: U.S.]

Harper, David A. and Karacaoglu, Girol. Financial Policy Reform in New Zealand. *Bollard, A. and Buckle, R., eds.*, 1987, pp. 206–35.
[G: New Zealand]

Havrilesky, Thomas M. Monetary Modeling in a World of Financial Innovation. *Solomon, E. H., ed.*, 1987, pp. 159–87.   [G: U.S.]

Henderson, Paul B., Jr. Modern Money. *Solomon, E. H., ed.*, 1987, pp. 17–37. [G: U.S.]

Henderson, Yolanda Kodrzycki. The Taxation of Banks: Particular Privileges or Objectional Burdens? *New Eng. Econ. Rev.*, May/June 1987, pp. 3–18.   [G: U.S.]

Herring, Richard J. and Vankudre, Prashant. Growth Opportunities and Risk-Taking by Financial Intermediaries. *J. Finance*, July 1987, *42*(3), pp. 583–99.   [G: U.S.]

Hester, Donald D. Inflation and Intermediation by Depository Institutions. *de Cecco, M. and Fitoussi, J.-P., eds.*, 1987, pp. 163–81.
[G: U.S.]

Hester, Donald D. On the Empirical Detection of Financial Innovation. *de Cecco, M., ed.*, 1987, pp. 77–111.   [G: U.S.]

Hochstein, Alan. Changes in Loan Practices by Banks: An Explanation of Canada's Economic Decline in the Early 1980's. *Tremblay, R., ed.*, 1987, pp. 263–72.   [G: Canada]

Hoffman, Lorey Arthur; Poddar, S. N. and Whalley, John. Taxation of Banking Services under a Consumption Type, Destination Basis VAT. *Nat. Tax J.*, December 1987, *40*(4), pp. 547–54.   [G: U.S.]

Holly, B. P. Regulation, Competition, and Technology: The Restructuring of the U.S. Commercial Banking System. *Environ. Planning A*, May 1987, *19*(5), pp. 633–52.   [G: U.S.]

Hölscher, Reinhold. Die Messung bankbetrieblicher Risikokosten unter Berücksichtigung von Risikoverbundeffekten. (Measuring the Cost of Banking while Taking Account of Related Risks. With English summary.) *Kredit Kapital*, 1987, *20*(4), pp. 522–58.

Horstmann, Theo. "The Worst Banking Practice in the World": Inter-allied Discussion over American Plans to Reform the German Banking System in 1945/46. *Pohl, H. and Rudolph, B., eds.*, 1987, pp. 93–115. [G: W. Germany]

Humphrey, David B. Cost Dispersion and the Measurement of Economies in Banking. *Fed. Res. Bank Richmond Econ. Rev.*, May/June 1987, *73*(3), pp. 24–38.   [G: U.S.]

Humphrey, David B. Payments System Risk, Market Failure, and Public Policy. *Solomon, E. H., ed.*, 1987, pp. 83–109.

Humphrey, Thomas M. The Theory of Multiple Expansion of Deposits: What It Is and Whence It Came. *Fed. Res. Bank Richmond Econ. Rev.*, Mar./Apr. 1987, *73*(2), pp. 3–11.

Jain, Arvind K. and Gupta, Satyadev. Some Evidence on "Herding" Behavior of U.S. Banks. *J. Money, Credit, Banking*, February 1987, *19*(1), pp. 78–89.   [G: U.S.]

James, Christopher M. Off-Balance Sheet Banking. *Fed. Res. Bank San Francisco Econ. Rev.*,
Fall 1987, (4), pp. 21–36.   [G: U.S.]

James, Christopher M. Some Evidence on the Uniqueness of Bank Loans. *J. Finan. Econ.*, December 1987, *19*(2), pp. 217–35.
[G: U.S.]

James, Christopher M. and Wier, Peggy. An Analysis of FDIC Failed Bank Auctions. *J. Monet. Econ.*, July 1987, *20*(1), pp. 141–53.
[G: U.S.]

James, Christopher M. and Wier, Peggy. Returns to Acquirers and Competition in the Acquisition Market: The Case of Banking. *J. Polit. Econ.*, April 1987, *95*(2), pp. 355–70.
[G: U.S.]

Jani, B. M. Portfolio Management in Indian Scheduled Commercial Banks. *Indian Econ. J.*, Oct.-Dec. 1987, *35*(2), pp. 77–90.
[G: India]

Johnson, Manuel H., Jr. Statement to the U.S. House Subcommittee on Financial Institutions, Supervision, Regulation and Insurance of the Committee on Banking, Finance and Urban Affairs, March 24, 1987. *Fed. Res. Bull.*, May 1987, *73*(5), pp. 341–46.   [G: U.S.]

Johnson, Manuel H., Jr. Statement to the U.S. House Subcommittee on Financial Institutions Supervision, Regulation and Insurance of the Committee on Banking, Finance and Urban Affairs, June 9, 1987. *Fed. Res. Bull.*, August 1987, *73*(8), pp. 649–54.   [G: U.S.]

Johnson, Manuel H., Jr. Statement to the U.S. Senate Committee on Banking, Housing, and Urban Affairs, May 21, 1987. *Fed. Res. Bull.*, July 1987, *73*(7), pp. 577–87.   [G: U.S.]

Kamitz, Reinhard. Banks and Economic Policy. *Ciocca, P., ed.*, 1987, *1963*, pp. 187–96.

Kanatas, George. Commercial Paper, Bank Reserve Requirements, and the Informational Role of Loan Commitments. *J. Banking Finance*, September 1987, *11*(3), pp. 425–48.

Kane, Edward J. Competitive Financial Reregulation: An International Perspective. *Portes, R. and Swoboda, A. K., eds.*, 1987, pp. 111–45.
[G: OECD]

Kane, Edward J. No Room for Weak Links in the Chain of Deposit-Insurance Reform. *J. Finan. Services Res.*, September 1987, *1*(1), pp. 77–111.   [G: U.S.]

Kannan, R. Banking Development and Regional Disparities. *Indian Econ. J.*, Oct.-Dec. 1987, *35*(2), pp. 58–76.   [G: India]

Kareken, John H. The Emergence and Regulation of Contingent Commitment Banking. *J. Banking Finance*, September 1987, *11*(3), pp. 359–77.   [G: U.S.]

Kaufman, George G. Bank Capital Forbearance and Public Policy. *Contemp. Policy Issues*, January 1987, *5*(1), pp. 84–91.   [G: U.S.]

Khalily, M. A. Baqui; Meyer, Richard L. and Hushak, Leroy J. Deposit Mobilization in Bangladesh: Implications for Rural Financial Institutions and Financial Policies. *Bangladesh Devel. Stud.*, December 1987, *15*(4), pp. 85–117.   [G: Bangladesh]

Khan, Mohsin S. Islamic Interest-Free Banking: A Theoretical Analysis. *Khan, M. S. and Mira-*

khor, A., eds., 1987, *1986*, pp. 15–35.

Khan, Mohsin S. and Mirakhor, Abbas. The Framework and Practice of Islamic Banking. *Khan, M. S. and Mirakhor, A., eds.*, 1987, *1986*, pp. 1–13.

Khan, Mohsin S. and Mirakhor, Abbas. Theoretical Studies in Islamic Banking and Finance: Introduction. *Khan, M. S. and Mirakhor, A., eds.*, 1987, pp. ix–xvi.

Khan, Shahrukh Rafi. An Economic Analysis of a PLS Model for the Financial Sector. *Khan, M. S. and Mirakhor, A., eds.*, 1987, *1984*, pp. 107–24.

Khan, Shahrukh Rafi. The Pakistani Experiment with Islamic (Profit-and-Loss Sharing) Banking. *Bangladesh Devel. Stud.*, December 1987, *15*(4), pp. 131–48. **[G: Pakistan]**

Khan, Waqar Masood. Towards an Interest Free Islamic Economic System. *Khan, M. S. and Mirakhor, A., eds.*, 1987, pp. 75–105.

Kim, Kyung Moo. A Short-run Variable Adjustment Model for Bank Loans. *J. Econ. Devel.*, December 1987, *12*(2), pp. 73–87. **[G: U.S.]**

King, Stephen R. and Remolona, Eli M. The Pricing and Hedging of Market Index Deposits. *Fed. Res. Bank New York Quart. Rev.*, Summer 1987, *12*(2), pp. 9–20. **[G: U.S.]**

Kon, Yoshinori. Bank Customer Relationship in a Corporate Growth Model (In Japanese. With English summary.) *Econ. Stud. Quart.*, September 1987, *38*(3), pp. 223–33.

Koppenhaver, G. D. and Lee, Cheng F. Alternative Instruments for Hedging Inflation Risk in the Banking Industry. *J. Futures Markets*, December 1987, *7*(6), pp. 619–36. **[G: U.S.]**

Landi, Andrea. Interest Rate Risk and Protection of the Interest Margin in the Italian Banking System. *Gardener, E. P. M., ed.*, 1987, pp. 161–81. **[G: Italy]**

Langevoort, Donald C. Statutory Obsolescence and the Judicial Process: The Revisionist Role of the Courts in Federal Banking Regulation. *Mich. Law Rev.*, February 1987, *85*(4), pp. 672–733. **[G: U.S.]**

Larcker, David F. Short-term Compensation Contracts and Executive Expenditure Decisions: The Case of Commercial Banks. *J. Finan. Quant. Anal.*, March 1987, *22*(1), pp. 33–50. **[G: U.S.]**

Laudadio, Leonard. Commercial Banks: Market Structure and Short-term Interest Rates [A Markup Theory of Bank Loan Rates]. *J. Post Keynesian Econ.*, Summer 1987, *9*(4), pp. 633–41. **[G: U.S.]**

Leiderman, Leonardo and Blejer, Mario I. The Term Structure of Interest Rates during a Financial Reform: Argentina 1977–81. *J. Devel. Econ.*, April 1987, *25*(2), pp. 285–99. **[G: Argentina]**

Lewis, Mervyn K. International and Multinational Banking. *Brit. Rev. Econ. Issues*, Spring 1987, *9*(20), pp. 27–55. **[G: Global]**

Lewis, Mervyn K. Personal Financial Services in the United States: A Transatlantic Perspective. *Goodhart, C.; Currie, D. and Llewellyn, D. T., eds.*, 1987, pp. 54–77. **[G: U.S.; U.K.]**

Litan, Robert E. Which Way for Congress? *Challenge*, Nov./Dec. 1987, *30*(5), pp. 36–43. **[G: U.S.]**

Lomax, David F. Risk Asset Ratios—A New Departure in Supervisory Policy. *Nat. Westminster Bank Quart. Rev.*, August 1987, pp. 14–25. **[G: U.K.]**

Lown, Cara S. Money Market Deposit Accounts versus Money Market Mutual Funds. *Fed. Res. Bank Dallas Econ. Rev.*, November 1987, (11), pp. 29–38. **[G: U.S.]**

Lucas, Deborah and McDonald, Robert L. Bank Portfolio Choice with Private Information about Loan Quality: Theory and Implications for Regulation. *J. Banking Finance*, September 1987, *11*(3), pp. 473–97.

Lumpkin, Stephen A. Repurchase and Reverse Repurchase Agreements. *Fed. Res. Bank Richmond Econ. Rev.*, Jan./Feb. 1987, *73*(1), pp. 15–23. **[G: U.S.]**

Lusser, Markus. Policy and Financial Innovation: Will There Be a Switch from Deregulation to Reregulation? *Portes, R. and Swoboda, A. K., eds.*, 1987, pp. 257–62.

Markley, Deborah Morentz. Impacts of Banking Deregulation on Rural Capital Markets: Evidence from Virginia and Tennessee. *Rev. Reg. Stud.*, Fall 1987, *17*(3), pp. 14–22. **[G: U.S.]**

Marshall R., Enrique. Interacción entre la tasa de interés por los depósitos a plazo y la calidad de los servicios en cuenta corriente. (With English summary.) *Cuadernos Econ.*, December 1987, *24*(73), pp. 375–98. **[G: Chile]**

Martin, John D. and Keown, Arthur J. One-Bank Holding Company Formation and the 1970 Bank Holding Company Act Amendment: An Empirical Examination Allowing for Industry Group Effects. *J. Banking Finance*, June 1987, *11*(2), pp. 213–21. **[G: U.S.]**

Meeker, Larry G. and Gray, Laura. A Note on Non-performing Loans as an Indicator of Asset Quality. *J. Banking Finance*, March 1987, *11*(1), pp. 161–68. **[G: U.S.]**

Melnik, Arie and Plaut, Steven E. Interest Rate Indexation and the Pricing of Loan Commitment Contracts. *J. Banking Finance*, March 1987, *11*(1), pp. 137–45.

Mengle, David L.; Humphrey, David B. and Summers, Bruce J. Intraday Credit: Risk, Value, and Pricing. *Fed. Res. Bank Richmond Econ. Rev.*, Jan./Feb. 1987, *73*(1), pp. 3–14. **[G: U.S.]**

Mirakhor, Abbas. Short-term Asset Concentration and Islamic Banking. *Khan, M. S. and Mirakhor, A., eds.*, 1987, pp. 185–99.

Moore, Clement Henry. Prisoners' Financial Dilemmas: A Consociational Future for Lebanon? *Amer. Polit. Sci. Rev.*, March 1987, *81*(1), pp. 201–18. **[G: Lebanon]**

Moore, Linda K. S. Payments and the Economic Transaction Chain. *Solomon, E. H., ed.*, 1987, pp. 39–62. **[G: U.S.]**

Morgan, George Emir and Smith, Stephen D. Maturity Intermediation and Intertemporal Lending Policies of Financial Intermediaries.

J. Finance, September 1987, *42*(4), pp. 1023–34.

Morgan, George Emir and Smith, Stephen D. The Role of Capital Adequacy Regulation in the Hedging Decisions of Financial Intermediaries. *J. Finan. Res.*, Spring 1987, *10*(1), pp. 33–46.

Motley, Brian. Should Money Be Redefined? *Wilcox, J. A., ed.*, 1987, *1986*, pp. 164–66. [G: U.S.]

Mullineaux, Donald J. Competitive Monies and the Suffolk Bank System: A Contractual Perspective. *Southern Econ. J.*, April 1987, *53*(4), pp. 884–98. [G: U.S.]

Neubig, Thomas S. and Sullivan, Martin A. The Effect of the Tax Reform Act of 1986 on Commercial Banks. *U.S. Treasury, Office of Tax Analysis.*, 1987, pp. 279–305. [G: U.S.]

Neubig, Thomas S. and Sullivan, Martin A. The Implications of Tax Reform for Bank Holdings of Tax-Exempt Securities. *Nat. Tax J.*, September 1987, *40*(3), pp. 403–18. [G: U.S.]

Niggle, Christopher J. A Comment on the Markup Theory of Bank Loan Rates. *J. Post Keynesian Econ.*, Summer 1987, *9*(4), pp. 629–31. [G: U.S.]

Ogata, Shijuro. Maintaining a Sound Financial System in Japan. *Portes, R. and Swoboda, A. K., eds.*, 1987, pp. 282–87. [G: Japan]

Onado, Marco. Interest Rate Risk in the Italian Banking System. *Gardener, E. P. M., ed.*, 1987, pp. 133–47. [G: Italy]

Pantalone, Coleen C. and Platt, Marjorie B. Predicting Commercial Bank Failure since Deregulation. *New Eng. Econ. Rev.*, July/Aug. 1987, pp. 37–47. [G: U.S.]

Patalinghug, Epictetus E. Rediscounting, Savings Mobilization, and the Rural Banking System. *Philippine Rev. Econ. Bus.*, Mar.-June 1987, *24*(1–2), pp. 103–23. [G: Philippines]

Pennacchi, George G. A Reexamination of the Over- (or Under-) Pricing of Deposit Insurance. *J. Money, Credit, Banking*, August 1987, *19*(3), pp. 340–60. [G: U.S.]

Pennacchi, George G. Alternative Forms of Deposit Insurance: Pricing and Bank Incentive Issues. *J. Banking Finance*, June 1987, *11*(2), pp. 291–312.

Perkins, Edwin J. Lost Opportunities for Compromise in the Bank War: A Reassessment of Jackson's Veto Message. *Bus. Hist. Rev.*, Winter 1987, *61*(4), pp. 531–50. [G: U.S.]

Phillips, Almarin. The New Money and the Old Monopoly Problem. *Solomon, E. H., ed.*, 1987, pp. 193–209. [G: U.S.]

Phillips, Almarin. The Role of Standardization in Shared Bank Card Systems. *Gabel, H. L., ed.*, 1987, pp. 263–82. [G: U.S.]

Polo, Yolanda. Determinantes empresariales de la adopción de innovaciones: Terminales de teleproceso en el sector bancario español. (With English summary.) *Invest. Ecón.*, May 1987, *11*(2), pp. 243–60. [G: Spain]

Postlewaite, Andrew and Vives, Xavier. Bank Runs as an Equilibrium Phenomenon. *J. Polit. Econ.*, June 1987, *95*(3), pp. 485–91.

Pozdena, Randall Johnston. Securitization and Banking. *Wilcox, J. A., ed.*, 1987, *1986*, pp. 34–36. [G: U.S.]

Price, Lionel D. D. UK Public Policy on Ensuring Financial Stability. *Portes, R. and Swoboda, A. K., eds.*, 1987, pp. 271–74. [G: U.K.]

Pyle, David H. Competitive Financial Reregulation: An International Perspective: Discussion. *Portes, R. and Swoboda, A. K., eds.*, 1987, pp. 145–49. [G: OECD]

Rhoades, Stephen A. Determinants of Premiums Paid in Bank Acquisitions. *Atlantic Econ. J.*, March 1987, *15*(1), pp. 20–30. [G: U.S.]

Rhoades, Stephen A. The Effect of Nonbank Thrift Institutions on Commercial Bank Profit Performance in Local Markets. *Quart. Rev. Econ. Bus.*, Spring 1987, *27*(1), pp. 16–28. [G: U.S.]

Rhoades, Stephen A. The Operating Performance of Acquired Firms in Banking. *Wills, R. L.; Caswell, J. A. and Culbertson, J. D., eds.*, 1987, pp. 277–92. [G: U.S.]

Rolnick, Arthur J. The Benefits of Bank Deposit Rate Ceilings: New Evidence on Bank Rates and Risk in the 1920s. *Fed. Res. Bank Minn. Rev.*, Summer 1987, *11*(3), pp. 2–18. [G: U.S.]

Romer, David. Bank Deregulation, Credit Markets, and the Control of Capital: Comments. *Carnegie–Rochester Conf. Ser. Public Policy*, Spring 1987, *26*, pp. 335–43. [G: U.S.]

Ronn, Ehud I. and Verma, Avinash K. A Multiattribute Comparative Evaluation of Relative Risk for a Sample of Banks. *J. Banking Finance*, September 1987, *11*(3), pp. 499–523. [G: U.S.]

Rose, Harold. The Design of Bank Regulation and Supervision: Some Lessons from the Theory of Finance: Discussion. *Portes, R. and Swoboda, A. K., eds.*, 1987, pp. 107–10. [G: U.K.]

Rose, John T. and Savage, Donald T. Interstate Banking and the Viability of Small, Independent Banks: Further Evidence on Market Share Accumulation by New Banks. *Antitrust Bull.*, Winter 1987, *32*(4), pp. 1007–18. [G: U.S.]

Rose, Peter S. The Impact of Financial Services Deregulation: The Hypotheses and the Evidence from 240 U.S. Metropolitan Banking Markets. *Quart. J. Bus. Econ.*, Spring 1987, *26*(2), pp. 55–88. [G: U.S.]

Rose, Peter S. The Impact of Mergers in Banking: Evidence from a Nationwide Sample of Federally Chartered Banks. *J. Econ. Bus.*, November 1987, *39*(4), pp. 289–312. [G: U.S.]

Rossi, Enzo and Stolfa, Fabio. The Control of Bank Liquidity: A Theoretical Model and Empirical Verifications. *Rev. Econ. Cond. Italy*, May-August 1987, (2), pp. 209–50. [G: Italy]

Rotella, Elyce J. The Dynamics of Occupational Segregation among Bank Tellers: Comments. *Brown, C. and Pechman, J. A., eds.*, 1987, pp. 149–54. [G: U.S.]

Rousseas, Stephen. Rejoinder [A Markup Theory of Bank Loan Rates]. *J. Post Keynesian Econ.*,

Summer 1987, *9*(4), pp. 642–43.   [G: U.S.]

Sachs, Jeffrey D. and Huizinga, Harry. U.S. Commercial Banks and the Developing-Country Debt Crisis. *Brookings Pap. Econ. Act.*, 1987, (2), pp. 555–601.   [G: U.S.]

Saubari, Moh. Reflections on Economic Policy Making: 1945–51. *Bull. Indonesian Econ. Stud.*, August 1987, *23*(2), pp. 118–21.   [G: Indonesia]

Saunders, Anthony and Smirlock, Michael. Intra- and Interindustry Effects of Bank Securities Market Activities: The Case of Discount Brokerage. *J. Finan. Quant. Anal.*, December 1987, *22*(4), pp. 467–82.   [G: U.S.]

Savage, Donald T. Interstate Banking Developments. *Fed. Res. Bull.*, February 1987, *73*(2), pp. 79–92.   [G: U.S.]

Schaefer, Stephen M. The Design of Bank Regulation and Supervision: Some Lessons from the Theory of Finance. *Portes, R. and Swoboda, A. K., eds.*, 1987, pp. 91–104.   [G: U.K.]

Schmid, Peter. The Role of Public Policy in Ensuring Financial Stability in Germany. *Portes, R. and Swoboda, A. K., eds.*, 1987, pp. 275–81.   [G: W. Germany]

Schwartz, Anna J. The Beginning of Competitive Banking in Philadelphia, 1782–1809. *Schwartz, A. J.*, 1987, *1947*, pp. 3–23.   [G: U.S.]

Schwartz, Anna J. The Lender of Last Resort and the Federal Safety Net. *J. Finan. Services Res.*, September 1987, *1*(1), pp. 1–17.   [G: U.S.]

Scott, Kenneth E. The Defective Design of Federal Deposit Insurance. *Contemp. Policy Issues*, January 1987, *5*(1), pp. 92–99.   [G: U.S.]

Seidman, L. William. Safe and Sound Banking behind the Wall. *Challenge*, Nov./Dec. 1987, *30*(5), pp. 18–27.   [G: U.S.]

Selgin, George A. and White, Lawrence H. The Evaluation of a Free Banking System. *Econ. Inquiry*, July 1987, *25*(3), pp. 439–57.   [G: U.S.]

Sheldon, Ian M. Testing for Weak Form Efficiency in New Agricultural Futures Markets: Some UK Evidence. *J. Agr. Econ.*, January 1987, *38*(1), pp. 51–64.   [G: U.K.]

Short, Eugenie D. Bank Problems and Financial Safety Nets. *Fed. Res. Bank Dallas Econ. Rev.*, March 1987, pp. 17–28.   [G: U.S.]

Shoven, John B. U.S. Commercial Banks and the Developing-Country Debt Crisis: Comment. *Brookings Pap. Econ. Act.*, 1987, (2), pp. 602–04.   [G: U.S.]

Sinkey, Joseph F., Jr.; Terza, Joseph V. and Dince, Robert R. A Zeta Analysis of Failed Commercial Banks. *Quart. J. Bus. Econ.*, Autumn 1987, *26*(4), pp. 35–49.   [G: U.S.]

Smiley, Gene. Postbellum Banking and Financial Markets in the Old Northwest. *Klingaman, D. C. and Vedder, R. K., eds.*, 1987, pp. 187–223.   [G: U.S.]

Smirlock, Michael and Kaufold, Howard. Bank Foreign Lending, Mandatory Disclosure Rules, and the Reaction of Bank Stock Prices to the Mexican Debt Crisis. *J. Bus.*, July 1987, *60*(3), pp. 347–64.   [G: U.S.]

Smith, Hilary H. Agricultural Lending: Bank Closures and Branch Banking. *Fed. Res. Bank Dallas Econ. Rev.*, September 1987, pp. 27–38.   [G: U.S.]

Smith, Stephen D.; Gregory, Deborah Wright and Weiss, Kathleen A. A Note on Quantity versus Price Risk and the Theory of Financial Intermediation. *J. Finance*, December 1987, *42*(5), pp. 1377–83.

Snowden, P. N. Chicago Schism on Banking Reforms and the Debt Crisis. *World Econ.*, June 1987, *10*(2), pp. 219–26.   [G: LDCs]

Soldatos, Gerasimos T. Electronic Banking Services and the Pattern of the Firm's Operations. *Greek Econ. Rev.*, 1987, *9*(1), pp. 131–40.

Soldatos, Gerasimos T. Electronic Banking Services and the Pattern of the Firm's Operations. *Greek Econ. Rev.*, 1987, *9*(1), pp. 131–40.

Solomon, Elinor Harris. Electronic Funds Transfers and Payments: The Public Policy Issues: Introduction. *Solomon, E. H., ed.*, 1987, pp. 1–11.

Solomon, Elinor Harris. EFT: A Consumer's View. *Solomon, E. H., ed.*, 1987, pp. 211–37.   [G: U.S.]

Sprenkle, Case M. Liability and Asset Uncertainty for Banks. *J. Banking Finance*, March 1987, *11*(1), pp. 147–59.

Storck, Ekkehard. Innovative Instrumente des Euro-Kreditmarktes. (With English summary.) *Z. Betriebswirtshaft*, February 1987, *57*(2), pp. 176–88.   [G: W. Europe]

Strober, Myra H. and Arnold, Carolyn L. The Dynamics of Occupational Segregation among Bank Tellers. *Brown, C. and Pechman, J. A., eds.*, 1987, pp. 107–48.   [G: U.S.]

Suzuki, Yoshio. Financial Innovation in Japan: Its Origins, Diffusion and Impacts. *de Cecco, M., ed.*, 1987, pp. 229–59.   [G: Japan]

Tarhan, Vefa. Unanticipated Interest Rates, Bank Stock Returns and the Nominal Contracting Hypothesis. *J. Banking Finance*, March 1987, *11*(1), pp. 99–115.   [G: U.S.]

Taylor, T. W. and Evans, J. W. Islamic Banking and the Prohibition of Usury in Western Economic Thought. *Nat. Westminster Bank Quart. Rev.*, November 1987, pp. 15–27.

Thomson, James B. Alternative Methods for Assessing Risk-Based Deposit-Insurance Premiums. *Wilcox, J. A., ed.*, 1987, *1986*, pp. 131–36.   [G: U.S.]

Thomson, James B. The Use of Market Information in Pricing Deposit Insurance. *J. Money, Credit, Banking*, November 1987, *19*(4), pp. 528–37.   [G: U.S.]

Thornton, John. The Demand for Borrowed Reserves: Some Evidence from West Germany. *Amer. Econ.*, Fall 1987, *31*(2), pp. 41–43.   [G: W. Germany]

Tobin, James. A Case for Preserving Regulatory Distinctions. *Challenge*, Nov./Dec. 1987, *30*(5), pp. 10–17.   [G: U.S.]

Tobin, James. Commercial Banks as Creators of "Money." *Tobin, J. (I),* 1987, *1963*, pp. 272–82.

Tobin, James. Financial Innovation and Deregulation in Perspective. *Tobin, J. (III)*, 1987, *1985*, pp. 255–64. [G: U.S.]

Tobin, James. Monetary Rules and Control in Brave New World. *Solomon, E. H., ed.*, 1987, pp. 137–57.

Tobin, James and Brainard, William C. Financial Intermediaries and the Effectiveness of Monetary Controls. *Tobin, J. (I)*, 1987, *1963*, pp. 283–321.

Tonnel-Martinache, Mariette. Degré de développement des systèmes financiers et redéploiement géographique des banques. Une interprétation en termes d'avantages comparés de pays et de secteur. (The Current Development of Financial Systems and Geographical Trends in Banking: A Comparative Analysis of the Advantages by Country and by Sector. With English summary.) *Revue Écon.*, January 1987, *38*(1), pp. 117–47. [G: Global]

Trifts, Jack W. and Scanlon, Kevin P. Interstate Bank Mergers: The Early Evidence. *J. Finan. Res.*, Winter 1987, *10*(4), pp. 305–11. [G: U.S.]

Ulman, Lloyd. The Dynamics of Occupational Segregation among Bank Tellers: Comments. *Brown, C. and Pechman, J. A., eds.*, 1987, pp. 154–57. [G: U.S.]

VanHoose, David D. A Note on Discount Rate Policy and the Variability of Discount Window Borrowing. *J. Banking Finance*, December 1987, *11*(4), pp. 563–70. [G: U.S.]

Volcker, Paul A. Statement to the U.S. House Subcommittee on General Oversight and Investigations of the Committee on Banking, Finance and Urban Affairs, April 30, 1987. *Fed. Res. Bull.*, June 1987, *73*(6), pp. 435–40. [G: U.S.; U.K.]

Volcker, Paul A. Statement to the U.S. Senate Committee on Banking, Housing, and Urban Affairs, January 21, 1987. *Fed. Res. Bull.*, March 1987, *73*(3), pp. 199–205. [G: U.S.]

Vorst, Karen S. A Note on Central Planning Core Banks and Correspondent Bank Balances [Centralized Private Sector Planning: An Institutionalist's Perspective on the Contemporary U.S. Economy]. *J. Econ. Issues*, March 1987, *21*(1), pp. 482–92. [G: U.S.]

Wall, Larry D. Has Bank Holding Companies' Diversification Affected Their Risk of Failure? *J. Econ. Bus.*, November 1987, *39*(4), pp. 313–26. [G: U.S.]

Wall, Larry D. Regulation of Banks' Equity Capital. *Wilcox, J. A., ed.*, 1987, *1985*, pp. 137–49. [G: U.S.]

Wall, Larry D. and Peterson, David R. The Effect of Capital Adequacy Guidelines on Large Bank Holding Companies. *J. Banking Finance*, December 1987, *11*(4), pp. 581–600. [G: U.S.]

Walter, John R. and Mengle, David L. A Review of Bank Performance in the Fifth District, 1986. *Fed. Res. Bank Richmond Econ. Rev.*, July/Aug. 1987, *73*(4), pp. 29–37. [G: U.S.]

Welker, Donald L. IPC or Total Deposits? There Is a Difference! *Fed. Res. Bank Richmond*

Econ. Rev., Mar./Apr. 1987, *73*(2), pp. 31–38. [G: U.S.]

White, Lawrence H. Privatization of Financial Sectors. *Hanke, S. H., ed.*, 1987, pp. 149–60.

Wilson, J. S. G. The Indian Money Market. *Banca Naz. Lavoro Quart. Rev.*, December 1987, (163), pp. 501–21. [G: India]

Wojnilower, Albert M. Financial Change in the United States. *de Cecco, M., ed.*, 1987, pp. 10–27. [G: U.S.]

Zaman, Raquibuz. Factors Determining the Survival of the Relatively Small Size U.S. Banks in the Late Eighties. *Tremblay, R., ed.*, 1987, pp. 283–97. [G: U.S.]

Zimmerman, Gary C. and Keeley, Michael C. Interest Checking. *Wilcox, J. A., ed.*, 1987, *1986*, pp. 167–69. [G: U.S.]

313 Capital Markets

3130 General

Aliber, Robert Z. Financial Markets and the Growth of Europe. *Lawrence, R. Z. and Schultze, C. L., eds.*, 1987, pp. 384–409. [G: W. Europe; U.S.]

Belongia, Michael T. and Sheehan, Richard G. The Informational Efficiency of Weekly Money Announcements: An Econometric Critique. *J. Bus. Econ. Statist.*, July 1987, *5*(3), pp. 351–56. [G: U.S.]

Berglund, Tom. Aktieomsättning och spekulation. (Share Dealing and Speculation. With English summary.) *Ekon. Samfundets Tidskr.*, 1987, *40*(1), pp. 33–38.

Clements, Peter. The New City: Geared for the Wider World. *Brit. Rev. Econ. Issues*, Autumn 1987, *9*(21), pp. 51–64. [G: U.K.]

Cumming, Christine M. The Economics of Securitization. *Fed. Res. Bank New York Quart. Rev.*, Autumn 1987, *12*(3), pp. 11–23. [G: U.S.]

Daigler, Robert T. Futures Bibliography. *J. Futures Markets*, December 1987, *7*(6), pp. 721–26.

De Vany, Arthur. Institutions for Stochastic Markets. *J. Inst. Theoretical Econ.*, March 1987, *143*(1), pp. 91–103.

Dudler, Hermann-Josef. Financial Markets and the Growth of Europe: Comment. *Lawrence, R. Z. and Schultze, C. L., eds.*, 1987, pp. 409–14. [G: W. Europe; U.S.]

Ewell, C. Daniel. Rule 10b-5 and the Duty to Disclose Merger Negotiations in Corporate Statements. *Yale Law J.*, January 1987, *96*(3), pp. 547–68. [G: U.S.]

Grieves, Robin and Singleton, J. Clay. Analytic Methods of the All-America Research Team. *J. Portfol. Manage.*, Fall 1987, *14*(1), pp. 4–8. [G: U.S.]

Grout, Paul A. Wider Share Ownership and Economic Performance. *Oxford Rev. Econ. Policy*, Winter 1987, *3*(4), pp. 13–29. [G: U.K.]

Hax, Herbert. Institutions for Stochastic Markets: Comment. *J. Inst. Theoretical Econ.*, March 1987, *143*(1), pp. 107–09.

Herzel, Leo and Katz, Leo. Insider Trading: Who Loses? *Lloyds Bank Rev.*, July 1987, (165), pp. 15–26. **[G: U.S.]**

Horvei, Tore, et al. Financial Markets in the Nordic Countries. *Vartia, P., et al.*, 1987, pp. 237–301. **[G: Denmark; Sweden; Finland; Norway]**

Johnson, Lewis D. Growth Prospects and Share Prices: A Systematic View. *J. Portfol. Manage.*, Winter 1987, *13*(2), pp. 58–60.

Kmenta, Jan. Institutions for Stochastic Markets: Comment. *J. Inst. Theoretical Econ.*, March 1987, *143*(1), pp. 104–06.

Kritzman, Mark. How to Build a Normal Portfolio in Three Easy Steps. *J. Portfol. Manage.*, Summer 1987, *13*(4), pp. 21–23.

Massad, Carlos. Internal Debt, External Debt and Economic Transformation: Introduction. *CEPAL Rev.*, August 1987, (32), pp. 7–9. **[G: Latin America]**

Massad, Carlos and Zahler, Roberto. Another View of the Latin American Crisis: Domestic Debt. *CEPAL Rev.*, August 1987, (32), pp. 11–25. **[G: Latin America]**

McDonald, Bill. Event Studies and Systems Methods: Some Additional Evidence. *J. Finan. Quant. Anal.*, December 1987, *22*(4), pp. 495–504. **[G: U.S.]**

Miller, Edward M. Bounded Efficient Markets: A New Wrinkle to the EMH. *J. Portfol. Manage.*, Summer 1987, *13*(4), pp. 4–13.

Monti, Mario. Financial Markets and the Growth of Europe: Comment. *Lawrence, R. Z. and Schultze, C. L., eds.*, 1987, pp. 414–18. **[G: W. Europe; U.S.]**

Morley, Alfred C. Ethical Standards for Investment Professionals. *Bus. Econ.*, October 1987, *22*(4), pp. 27–34. **[G: U.S.]**

Plosser, Charles I. Fiscal Policy and the Term Structure. *J. Monet. Econ.*, September 1987, *20*(2), pp. 343–67.

Santoni, G. J. The Great Bull Markets 1924–29 and 1982–87: Speculative Bubbles or Economic Fundamentals? *Fed. Res. Bank St. Louis Rev.*, November 1987, *69*(9), pp. 16–30. **[G: U.S.]**

Schwartz, Anna J. Real and Pseudo-financial Crises. *Schwartz, A. J.*, 1987, *1986*, pp. 271–88. **[G: U.S.; U.K.]**

Snowden, P. N. Financial Market Liberalisation in LDCs: The Incidence of Risk Allocation Effects of Interest Rate Increases. *J. Devel. Stud.*, October 1987, *24*(1), pp. 83–93. **[G: LDCs]**

Thaler, Richard H. The January Effect. *J. Econ. Perspectives*, Summer 1987, *1*(1), pp. 197–201.

Tobin, James. On the Efficiency of the Financial System. *Tobin, J. (III)*, 1987, *1984*, pp. 282–96. **[G: U.S.]**

White, Frederick L. Legal and Regulatory Developments: The Exchange-Trading Requirement of the Commodity Exchange Act. *J. Futures Markets*, February 1987, *7*(1), pp. 109–10.

White, Frederick L. and Stein, William L. Broker–Customer Arbitration: An Attractive Alternative to Litigation. *J. Futures Markets*, August 1987, *7*(4), pp. 459–60. **[G: U.S.]**

Williamson, Stephen D. Recent Developments in Modeling Financial Intermediation. *Fed. Res. Bank Minn. Rev.*, Summer 1987, *11*(3), pp. 19–29.

Zimmermann, Heinz. Zur ökonomischen Bedeutung von Finanzmarktinnovationen. (On the Economic Relevance of Innovation in Financial Markets. With English summary.) *Aussenwirtschaft*, September 1987, *42*(2/3), pp. 163–98. **[G: Switzerland; U.S.]**

3131 Capital Markets: Theory, Including Portfolio Selection, and Empirical Studies Illustrating Theory

Abel, Ulrich and Boing, Georg. Addendum [Stock Price Distribution versus Time to Maturity of Associated Options]. *Z. Wirtschaft. Sozialwissen.*, 1987, *107*(4), pp. 595–96.

Abel, Ulrich and Boing, Georg. Stock Price Distribution versus Time to Maturity of Associated Options. *Z. Wirtschaft. Sozialwissen.*, 1987, *107*(2), pp. 201–05.

Admati, Anat R. and Pfleiderer, Paul. Viable Allocations of Information in Financial Markets. *J. Econ. Theory*, October 1987, *43*(1), pp. 76–115.

Affleck-Graves, J. F. and Blomerus, H. J. The Effect of Different Indices on Beta Estimates for Securities Listed on the JSE. *J. Stud. Econ. Econometrics*, April 1987, *11*(1), pp. 65–89. **[G: S. Africa]**

Alexander, Gordon J.; Eun, Cheol S. and Janakiramanan, S. Asset Pricing and Dual Listing on Foreign Capital Markets: A Note. *J. Finance*, March 1987, *42*(1), pp. 151–58.

Ambarish, Ramasastry; John, Kose and Williams, Joseph T. Efficient Signalling with Dividends and Investments. *J. Finance*, June 1987, *42*(2), pp. 321–43.

Andrikopoulos, Andreas A.; Brox, James A. and Matthews, D. The Demand for Financial Assets in Canada. *Tremblay, R., ed.*, 1987, pp. 249–62. **[G: Canada]**

Ang, James S. and Lai, Tsong-Yue. Insurance Premium Pricing and Ratemaking in Competitive Insurance and Capital Asset Markets. *J. Risk Ins.*, December 1987, *54*(4), pp. 767–79.

Artus, Patrick. Marché à terme, options, et stabilté du marché au comptant de taux d'intérêt. (Futures and Options Contracts and the Stability of the Spot Price of Bonds. With English summary.) *Finance*, December 1987, *8*(2), pp. 25–54.

Baek, Yong-Ho. A Modified Version of Breeden's Capital Asset Pricing Model. *J. Econ. Devel.*, June 1987, *12*(1), pp. 137–47.

Balcer, Yves and Judd, Kenneth L. Effects of Capital Gains Taxation on Life-Cycle Investment and Portfolio Management. *J. Finance*, July 1987, *42*(3), pp. 743–58.

Barnea, Amir; Talmor, Eli and Haugen, Robert A. Debt and Taxes: A Multiperiod Investigation. *J. Banking Finance*, March 1987, *11*(1), pp. 79–97.

Barone-Adesi, Giovanni and Whaley, Robert E. Efficient Analytic Approximation of American

Option Values. *J. Finance*, June 1987, *42*(2), pp. 301–20.

Basu, Parantap. An Adjustment Cost Model of Asset Pricing. *Int. Econ. Rev.*, October 1987, *28*(3), pp. 609–21.

Batlin, Carl A. Hedging Mortgage-Backed Securities with Treasury Bond Futures. *J. Futures Markets*, December 1987, *7*(6), pp. 675–93. [G: U.S.]

Belongia, Michael T. and Santoni, G. J. Interest Rate Risk, Market Value, and Hedging Financial Portfolios. *J. Finan. Res.*, Spring 1987, *10*(1), pp. 47–55.

Bench, Robert R. The Design of Bank Regulation and Supervision: Some Lessons from the Theory of Finance: Discussion. *Portes, R. and Swoboda, A. K., eds.*, 1987, pp. 104–07. [G: U.K.]

Benveniste, Lawrence M. Incomplete Market Participation and the Optimal Exchange of Credit. *Prescott, E. C. and Wallace, N., eds.*, 1987, pp. 121–45.

Bernstein, Peter L. The Discomforts of Efficiency. *J. Portfol. Manage.*, Fall 1987, *14*(1), pp. 1.

Bick, Avi. On the Consistency of the Black–Scholes Model with a General Equilibrium Framework. *J. Finan. Quant. Anal.*, September 1987, *22*(3), pp. 259–75.

Bierwag, Gerald O. Bond Returns, Discrete Stochastic Processes, and Duration. *J. Finan. Res.*, Fall 1987, *10*(3), pp. 191–209.

Bierwag, Gerald O., et al. Duration: Response to Critics [Alternative Duration Specifications and the Measurement of Basis Risk: Empirical Tests]. *J. Portfol. Manage.*, Winter 1987, *13*(2), pp. 48–52. [G: U.S.]

Bird, Ron; McCrae, Michael and Beggs, John J. Are Gamblers Really Risk Takers? *Australian Econ. Pap.*, December 1987, *26*(49), pp. 237–53. [G: Australia]

Bomhoff, Eduard J. and Koedijk, Kees G. A Portfolio Balance Model of Bilateral Exchange Rates. *Chrystal, K. A. and Sedgwick, R., eds.*, 1987, pp. 54–71.

Bond, Gary E.; Thompson, Stanley R. and Lee, Benny M. S. Application of a Simplified Hedging Rule. *J. Futures Markets*, February 1987, *7*(1), pp. 65–72.

Booth, James R. and Smith, Richard L. An Examination of the Small-Firm Effect on the Basis of Skewness Preference. *J. Finan. Res.*, Spring 1987, *10*(1), pp. 77–86.

Booth, Laurence D. The Dividend Tax Credit and Canadian Ownership Objectives. *Can. J. Econ.*, May 1987, *20*(2), pp. 321–39. [G: Canada]

Bosshardt, Donald I. A Model of Intertemporal Discount Rates in the Presence of Real and Inflationary Autocorrelations. *J. Finance*, September 1987, *42*(4), pp. 1049–70. [G: U.S.]

Botha, D.; Bosch, J. K. and van Zyl, G. J. J. The Effect of Dividend Policy on Changes in Shareholders' Wealth. *S. Afr. J. Econ.*, June 1987, *55*(2), pp. 101–13. [G: S. Africa]

Bray, Margaret. Rational Expectations, Informa-

tion and Asset Markets: An Introduction. *Sinclair, P. J. N., ed.*, 1987, *1985*, pp. 248–82.

Brenner, Menachem and Galai, Dan. On the Prediction of the Implied Standard Deviation. *Fabozzi, F. J., ed.*, 1987, pp. 167–77. [G: U.S.]

Bulow, Jeremy I.; Mørck, Randall and Summers, Lawrence H. How Does the Market Value Unfunded Pension Liabilities? *Bodie, Z.; Shoven, J. B. and Wise, D. A., eds.*, 1987, pp. 81–104. [G: U.S.]

Burdett, Kenneth and O'Hara, Maureen. Building Blocks: An Introduction to Block Trading. *J. Banking Finance*, June 1987, *11*(2), pp. 193–212.

Campbell, John Y. and Shiller, Robert J. Cointegration and Tests of Present Value Models. *J. Polit. Econ.*, October 1987, *95*(5), pp. 1062–88. [G: U.S.]

Cargill, Thomas F. and Meyer, Robert A. Multiperiod Portfolio Optimization and the Value of Risk Information. *Lee, C. F., ed.*, 1987, pp. 245–67. [G: U.S.]

Carr, Peter. A Note on the Pricing of Commodity-Linked Bonds. *J. Finance*, September 1987, *42*(4), pp. 1071–76.

Carrington, Samantha and Crouch, Robert. A Theorem on Interest Rate Differentials, Risk and Anticipated Inflation. *Appl. Econ.*, December 1987, *19*(12), pp. 1675–83. [G: U.S.]

Chance, Don M. Parity Tests of Index Options. *Fabozzi, F. J., ed.*, 1987, pp. 47–64. [G: U.S.]

Chang, Eric C. and Pinegar, J. Michael. Risk and Inflation. *J. Finan. Quant. Anal.*, March 1987, *22*(1), pp. 89–99. [G: U.S.]

Chang, Jack S. K. and Loo, Jean C. H. Marking-to-Market, Stochastic Interest Rates and Discounts on Stock Index Futures. *J. Futures Markets*, February 1987, *7*(1), pp. 15–20.

Chang, Jack S. K. and Shanker, Latha. A Risk-Return Measure of Hedging Effectiveness: A Comment. *J. Finan. Quant. Anal.*, September 1987, *22*(3), pp. 373–76.

Chang, Jack S. K. and Shanker, Latha. Option Pricing and Arbitrage Pricing Theory. *J. Finan. Res.*, Spring 1987, *10*(1), pp. 1–16. [G: U.S.]

Chen, Son-Nan. Simple Optimal Asset Allocation under Uncertainty. *J. Portfol. Manage.*, Summer 1987, *13*(4), pp. 69–76.

Chew, Soo Hong; Karni, Edi and Safra, Zvi. Risk Aversion in the Theory of Expected Utility with Rank Dependent Probabilities. *J. Econ. Theory*, August 1987, *42*(2), pp. 370–81.

Chew, Soo Hong and Mao, M. H. Portfolio Risk Aversion and Weighted Utility Theory. *Sawaragi, Y.; Inoue, K. and Nakayama, H., eds.*, 1987, pp. 162–69.

Chiang, Raymond. Some Results on Bond Yield and Default Probability. *Southern Econ. J.*, April 1987, *53*(4), pp. 1037–51.

Chick, Victoria. Speculation, the Rate of Interest, and the Rate of Profit. *J. Post Keynesian Econ.*, Fall 1987, *10*(1), pp. 124–32.

Christensen, Peter Ove and Nielsen, Jørgen Aase. The Bond-Type Effect on Yield to Maturity. *Scand. J. Econ.*, 1987, *89*(2), pp. 193–208.

Clarke, Roger G. Stochastic Dominance Properties of Option Strategies. *Fabozzi, F. J., ed.,* 1987, pp. 1–18.

Colletaz, Gilbert. Les taux d'intérêt observés sur le marché monétaire sont-ils trop volatils? Un test de la rationalité des prévisions dans le cadre de la théorie des anticipations de la structure par échéance. (Do French Money Market Interest Rates Move Too Much? Test of the Rational Expectations Model of the Term Structure of Interest Rates. With English summary.) *Revue Écon.*, July 1987, *38*(4), pp. 837–52. **[G: France]**

de la Cuadra G., Rodrigo and García O., Víctor. Modelo de valuación de activos de capital y riesgo financiero. (With English summary.) *Cuadernos Econ.*, December 1987, *24*(73), pp. 359–74.

Cumby, Robert E. and Modest, David M. Testing for Market Timing Ability: A Framework for Forecast Evaluation. *J. Finan. Econ.*, September 1987, *19*(1), pp. 169–89.

Dammon, Robert M. and Green, Richard C. Tax Arbitrage and the Existence of Equilibrium Prices for Financial Assets. *J. Finance*, December 1987, *42*(5), pp. 1143–66.

Damodaran, Aswath. The Impact of Information Structure on Stock Returns. *J. Portfol. Manage.*, Spring 1987, *13*(3), pp. 53–58.

Danthine, Jean-Pierre. Financial and Futures Markets: Introduction. *Europ. Econ. Rev.*, Feb./Mar. 1987, *31*(1/2), pp. 221–25.

Dawson, Steven M. Initial Public Offer Underpricing: The Issuer's View—A Note. *J. Finance*, March 1987, *42*(1), pp. 159–62.

Điacogiannis, George P. The Mean-Standard Deviation Efficient Set Theorem: A Note. *Managerial Dec. Econ.*, September 1987, *8*(3), pp. 217–19.

Diamond, Douglas W. and Verrecchia, Robert E. Constraints on Short-Selling and Asset Price Adjustment to Private Information. *J. Finan. Econ.*, June 1987, *18*(2), pp. 277–311.

Diba, Behzad T. and Grossman, Herschel I. On the Inception of Rational Bubbles. *Quart. J. Econ.*, August 1987, *102*(3), pp. 697–700.

Dickens, Rodney. Variability in Some Major UK Asset Markets since the Mid-1960s: An Application of the ARCH Model. *Goodhart, C.; Currie, D. and Llewellyn, D. T., eds.,* 1987, pp. 231–70. **[G: U.K.]**

Dothan, Michael U. A Random Volatility Correction for the Black–Scholes Option-Pricing Formula. *Fabozzi, F. J., ed.,* 1987, pp. 97–115.

Drèze, Jacques H. Investment under Private Ownership: Optimality, Equilibrium and Stability. *Drèze, J. H.,* 1987, *1974*, pp. 261–97.

Drèze, Jacques H. and Modigliani, Franco. Earnings, Assets and Savings: A Model of Interdependent Choice. *Drèze, J. H.,* 1987, pp. 213–19.

Dubois, Michel and Dumontier, Pascal. La sous-evaluation des actions lors de leur introduction en bourse: motifs et consequences. (The

Underpricing of Unseasoned New Issues: Reason and Results. With English summary.) *Écon. Soc.*, December 1987, *21*(12), pp. 43–56. **[G: France]**

Duffie, Darrell. Stochastic Equilibria with Incomplete Financial Markets. *J. Econ. Theory*, April 1987, *41*(2), pp. 405–16.

Easley, David and O'Hara, Maureen. Price, Trade Size, and Information in Securities Markets. *J. Finan. Econ.*, September 1987, *19*(1), pp. 69–90.

Echchihab, Slimane and Jacquillat, Bertrand. Consommation, aversion au risque et rendement des actions: théorie et tests. (Consumption, Risk Aversion and Equity Returns: Theory and Tests. With English summary.) *Finance*, June 1987, *8*(1), pp. 105–24. **[G: France]**

Ehrhardt, Michael C. A Mean-Variance Derivation of a Multi-factor Equilibrium Model. *J. Finan. Quant. Anal.*, June 1987, *22*(2), pp. 227–36.

Ehrhardt, Michael C. Arbitrage Pricing Models: The Sufficient Number of Factors and Equilibrium Conditions. *J. Finan. Res.*, Summer 1987, *10*(2), pp. 111–20. **[G: U.S.]**

Eichenbaum, Martin S. and Peled, Dan. Capital Accumulation and Annuities in an Adverse Selection Economy. *J. Polit. Econ.*, April 1987, *95*(2), pp. 334–54.

Eldor, Rafael and Zilcha, Itzhak. Discriminating Monopoly, Forward Markets and International Trade. *Int. Econ. Rev.*, June 1987, *28*(2), pp. 459–68.

Engle, Robert F.; Lilien, David M. and Robins, Russell P. Estimating Time Varying Risk Premia in the Term Structure: The Arch-M Model. *Econometrica*, March 1987, *55*(2), pp. 391–407.

Entov, R. M. and Poletayev, A. V. On the Long-term Dynamics of the Rate of Return. *Vasko, T., ed.,* 1987, pp. 105–18.

Fellingham, John C.; Limberg, Stephen T. and Wilkie, Patrick J. Tax Rates, Tax Shelters and Optimal Portfolios. *Jones, S. M., ed.,* 1987, pp. 23–47.

Ferson, Wayne E.; Kandel, Shmuel and Stambaugh, Robert F. Tests of Asset Pricing with Time-Varying Expected Risk Premiums and Market Betas. *J. Finance*, June 1987, *42*(2), pp. 201–20. **[G: U.S.]**

Ferson, Wayne E. and Merrick, John J., Jr. Nonstationarity and Stage-of-the-Business-Cycle Effects in Consumption-Based Asset Pricing Relations. *J. Finan. Econ.*, March 1987, *18*(1), pp. 127–46. **[G: U.S.]**

Flowers, Marilyn R. Price Level Uncertainty and Indexed Bonds: Note. *Quart. Rev. Econ. Bus.*, Winter 1987, *27*(4), pp. 100–103.

Forsythe, Robert and Suchanek, Gerry L. Decentralizing Constrained Pareto Optimal Allocations in Stock Ownership Economies: An Impossibility Theorem. *Int. Econ. Rev.*, June 1987, *28*(2), pp. 299–313.

Franke, Günter. Costless Signalling in Financial

Markets. *J. Finance*, September 1987, *42*(4), pp. 809–22.

Frankfurter, George M. and Lamoureux, Christopher G. The Relevance of the Distributional Form of Common Stock Returns to the Construction of Optimal Portfolios. *J. Finan. Quant. Anal.*, December 1987, *22*(4), pp. 505–11.

French, Kenneth R.; Schwert, G. William and Stambaugh, Robert F. Expected Stock Returns and Volatility. *J. Finan. Econ.*, September 1987, *19*(1), pp. 3–29. [G: U.S.]

Friedman, Benjamin M. and Roley, V. Vance. Aspects of Investor Behaviour under Risk. *Feiwel, G. R., ed. (I)*, 1987, pp. 626–53. [G: U.S.]

Friedman, Jeffrey F. Is Time Travel Impossible? Comment. *J. Portfol. Manage.*, Spring 1987, *13*(3), pp. 83.

Garman, Mark B. Perpetual Currency Options. *Int. J. Forecasting*, 1987, *3*(1), pp. 179–84.

Gendron, Michel. Mesures de performance et économie de l'information, une synthèse de la littérature théorique. (Performance Measurement and Information Economics, a Synthesis of Theoretical Literature. With English summary.) *L'Actual. Econ.*, June-September 1987, *63*(2–3), pp. 169–86.

Gibbons, Michael R. and Shanken, Jay. Subperiod Aggregation and the Power of Multivariate Tests of Portfolio Efficiency. *J. Finan. Econ.*, December 1987, *19*(2), pp. 389–94.

Gibson-Asner, Rajna. Del modéles d'équilibre de la structure des taux d'intérêt: un essai de synthèse. (Equilibrium Models of the Term Structure of Interest Rates: A Synthesis. With English summary.) *Finance*, December 1987, *8*(2), pp. 133–71.

Gilles, Christian and LeRoy, Stephen F. A Note on the Local Expectations Hypothesis: A Discrete-Time Exposition—Erratum. *J. Finance*, June 1987, *42*(2), pp. 473.

Gjerde, Øystein. Measuring Hedging Effectiveness in a Traditional One-Periodic Portfolio Framework. *J. Futures Markets*, December 1987, *7*(6), pp. 663–74.

Glosten, Lawrence R. Components of the Bid–Ask Spread and the Statistical Properties of Transaction Prices. *J. Finance*, December 1987, *42*(5), pp. 1293–1307.

Gooptu, Sudarshan and Lombra, Raymond. Aggregation across Heterogeneous Depository Institutions. *Financial Rev.*, November 1987, *22*(4), pp. 369–78. [G: U.S.]

Gorton, Gary B. and Haubrich, Joseph G. Assessing Deregulation: Further Considerations: A Reply. *Carnegie–Rochester Conf. Ser. Public Policy*, Spring 1987, *26*, pp. 345–48. [G: U.S.]

Gorton, Gary B. and Haubrich, Joseph G. Bank Deregulation, Credit Markets, and the Control of Capital. *Carnegie–Rochester Conf. Ser. Public Policy*, Spring 1987, *26*, pp. 289–333. [G: U.S.]

Green, Richard C. and Jarrow, Robert A. Spanning and Completeness in Markets with Con-

tingent Claims. *J. Econ. Theory*, February 1987, *41*(1), pp. 202–10.

Grinblatt, Mark and Titman, Sheridan. How Clients Can Win the Gaming Game. *J. Portfol. Manage.*, Summer 1987, *13*(4), pp. 14–20.

Grinblatt, Mark and Titman, Sheridan. The Relation between Mean-Variance Efficiency and Arbitrage Pricing. *J. Bus.*, January 1987, *60*(1), pp. 97–112.

Gruber, Andreas. Signalling and Market Behavior. *Bamberg, G. and Spremann, K., eds.*, 1987, pp. 205–27.

Haddock, David D. and Macey, Jonathan R. Regulation on Demand: A Private Interest Model, with an Application to Insider Trading Regulation. *J. Law Econ.*, October 1987, *30*(2), pp. 311–52. [G: U.S.]

Hagigi, Moshe and Kluger, Brian. Safety First: An Alternative Performance Measure. *J. Portfol. Manage.*, Summer 1987, *13*(4), pp. 34–40. [G: U.S.]

Hamada, Robert S. Differential Taxes and the Structure of Equilibrium Rates of Return: Managerial Implications and Remaining Conundrums. *Lee, C. F., ed.*, 1987, pp. 1–25.

Hamilton, Jonathan H. Taxation, Savings, and Portfolio Choice in a Continuous Time Model. *Public Finance*, 1987, *42*(2), pp. 264–82.

Hansen, Lars Peter and Richard, Scott F. The Role of Conditioning Information in Deducing Testable Restrictions Implied by Dynamic Asset Pricing Models. *Econometrica*, May 1987, *55*(3), pp. 587–613.

Heath, David C. and Jarrow, Robert A. Arbitrage, Continuous Trading, and Margin Requirements. *J. Finance*, December 1987, *42*(5), pp. 1129–42.

Hendershott, Patric H. and Van Order, Robert. Pricing Mortgages: An Interpretation of the Models and Results. *J. Finan. Services Res.*, September 1987, *1*(1), pp. 19–55.

Henn, Rudolf and Kischka, Peter. On the Use of Predictive Distributions in Portfolio Theory. *[Eberl, W., Sr.]*, 1987, pp. 175–83.

Herring, Richard J. and Vankudre, Prashant. Growth Opportunities and Risk-Taking by Financial Intermediaries. *J. Finance*, July 1987, *42*(3), pp. 583–99. [G: U.S.]

Hochman, Shalom and Palmon, Oded. Expected Inflation and the Real Rates of Interest on Taxable and Tax-Exempt Bonds. *J. Money, Credit, Banking*, February 1987, *19*(1), pp. 90–103.

Hodrick, Robert J. and Srivastava, Sanjay. Foreign Currency Futures. *J. Int. Econ.*, February 1987, *22*(1/2), pp. 1–24. [G: U.S.]

Howard, Charles T. and D'Antonio, Louis J. A Risk-Return Measure of Hedging Effectiveness: A Reply. *J. Finan. Quant. Anal.*, September 1987, *22*(3), pp. 377–81.

Hsieh, David A. and Huizinga, John. Gold in the Optimal Portfolio. *Aliber, R. Z., ed.*, 1987, pp. 212–61. [G: N. America; U.K.; W. Germany; Belgium; Switzerland]

Huang, Chi-fu. An Intertemporal General Equilibrium Asset Pricing Model: The Case of Diffusion Information. *Econometrica*, January

1987, 55(1), pp. 117–42.

Hubbes, Hans H. Pricing of Caps and Floors: A Simplified Approach. *Kredit Kapital*, 1987, 20(1), pp. 1–21.

Huberman, Gur and Kandel, Shmuel. Mean–Variance Spanning. *J. Finance*, September 1987, 42(4), pp. 873–88. **[G: U.S.]**

Huberman, Gur; Kandel, Shmuel and Stambaugh, Robert F. Mimicking Portfolios and Exact Arbitrage Pricing. *J. Finance*, March 1987, 42(1), pp. 1–9.

Huffman, Gregory W. A Dynamic Equilibrium Model of Asset Prices and Transaction Volume. *J. Polit. Econ.*, February 1987, 95(1), pp. 138–59.

Hull, John C. and White, Alan D. Hedging the Risks from Writing Foreign Currency Options. *J. Int. Money Finance*, June 1987, 6(2), pp. 131–52. **[G: U.S.]**

Hull, John C. and White, Alan D. The Pricing of Options on Assets with Stochastic Volatilities. *J. Finance*, June 1987, 42(2), pp. 281–300.

Jain, Prem C. The Time-Series Behavior of Annual Accounting Earnings: A Comparison of the Random Walk and the Random–Percentage-Growth Models. *Lee, C. F., ed.*, 1987, pp. 179–204. **[G: U.S.]**

Jarrow, Robert A. The Pricing of Commodity Options with Stochastic Interest Rates. *Fabozzi, F. J., ed.*, 1987, pp. 19–45.

Johnson, Herb. Options on the Maximum or the Minimum of Several Assets. *J. Finan. Quant. Anal.*, September 1987, 22(3), pp. 277–83.

Johnson, Herb and Shanno, David. Option Pricing When the Variance Is Changing. *J. Finan. Quant. Anal.*, June 1987, 22(2), pp. 143–51.

Johnson, Herb and Stulz, René M. The Pricing of Options with Default Risk. *J. Finance*, June 1987, 42(2), pp. 267–80.

Jorion, Philippe. The ECU and Efficient Portfolio Choice. *Levich, R. M. and Sommariva, A., eds.*, 1987, pp. 119–39. **[G: EEC]**

Junkus, Joan C. Hedge Ratios in Up and Down Equity Markets. *Fabozzi, F. J., ed.*, 1987, pp. 279–89. **[G: U.S.]**

Jüttner, D. Johannes. Spekulation—immer segensreich? (Speculation—Good or Evil? With English summary.) *Jahr. Nationalökon. Statist.*, January 1987, 203(1), pp. 1–11.

Kalaba, Robert E., et al. Implied Parameter Estimation in Contingent Claim Models. *Fabozzi, F. J., ed.*, 1987, pp. 65–95.

Kamara, Avraham and Siegel, Andrew F. Optimal Hedging in Futures Markets with Multiple Delivery Specifications. *J. Finance*, September 1987, 42(4), pp. 1007–21. **[G: U.S.]**

Kandel, Shmuel. Orthogonal Frontiers and Alternative Mean–Variance Efficiency Tests: Discussion. *J. Finance*, July 1987, 42(3), pp. 620–22.

Kandel, Shmuel and Stambaugh, Robert F. On Correlations and Inferences about Mean-Variance Efficiency. *J. Finan. Econ.*, March 1987, 18(1), pp. 61–90. **[G: U.S.]**

Karp, Larry S. Methods for Selecting the Optimal

Dynamic Hedge when Production Is Stochastic. *Amer. J. Agr. Econ.*, August 1987, 69(3), pp. 647–57. **[G: U.S.]**

Kau, James B., et al. The Valuation and Securitization of Commercial and Multifamily Mortgages. *J. Banking Finance*, September 1987, 11(3), pp. 525–46.

Kawaller, Ira G. A Note: Debunking the Myth of the Risk-Free Return. *J. Futures Markets*, June 1987, 7(3), pp. 327–31.

Kolari, James W. An Analytical Model of Risky Yield Curves. *J. Finan. Res.*, Winter 1987, 10(4), pp. 295–303.

Kormendi, Roger and Lipe, Robert. Earnings Innovations, Earnings Persistence, and Stock Returns. *J. Bus.*, July 1987, 60(3), pp. 323–45. **[G: U.S.]**

Kryzanowski, Lawrence and To, Minh Chau. The *E–V* Stationarity of Secure Returns: Some Empirical Evidence. *J. Banking Finance*, March 1987, 11(1), pp. 117–35. **[G: U.S.]**

de La Bruslerie, Hubert. Le statut theorique de la prime de risque dans la structure a terme des taux. (The Theoretical Status of the Risk Premium in the Term Structure of Rates. With English summary.) *Écon. Soc.*, December 1987, 21(12), pp. 5–42.

Leape, Jonathan I. Taxes and Transaction Costs in Asset Market Equilibrium. *J. Public Econ.*, June 1987, 33(1), pp. 1–20.

Lee, Cheng F.; Bubnys, Edward L. and Lin, Yun. Stock Index Futures Hedge Ratios: Tests on Horizon Effects and Functional Form. *Fabozzi, F. J., ed.*, 1987, pp. 291–311. **[G: U.S.]**

Lehmann, Bruce N. Orthogonal Frontiers and Alternative Mean–Variance Efficiency Tests. *J. Finance*, July 1987, 42(3), pp. 601–19.

Levy, Haim and Levy, Azriel. Equilibrium under Uncertain Inflation: A Discrete Time Approach. *J. Finan. Quant. Anal.*, September 1987, 22(3), pp. 285–97.

Lippens, Robert E. Multimaturity Efficient Market Hypotheses: Sorting Out Rejections in International Interest and Exchange Rate Markets. *Int. J. Forecasting*, 1987, 3(1), pp. 149–58. **[G: U.S.]**

Livingston, Miles. Flattening of Bond Yield Curves. *J. Finan. Res.*, Spring 1987, 10(1), pp. 17–24. **[G: U.S.]**

Livingston, Miles. The Delivery Option of Forward Contracts. *J. Finan. Quant. Anal.*, March 1987, 22(1), pp. 79–87.

Llerena, Patrick. Décisions temporairement irréversibles un modèle de valeur d'option relative. (With English summary.) *Revue Écon. Polit.*, Sept.-Oct. 1987, 97(5), pp. 613–30. **[G: France]**

Lo, Andrew W. Semi-parametric Upper Bounds for Option Prices and Expected Payoffs. *J. Finan. Econ.*, December 1987, 19(2), pp. 373–87.

MacKinlay, A. Craig. On Multivariate Tests of the CAPM. *J. Finan. Econ.*, June 1987, 18(2), pp. 341–71. **[G: U.S.]**

MacMinn, Richard D. Forward Markets, Stock Markets, and the Theory of the Firm. *J. Fi-*

nance, December 1987, *42*(5), pp. 1167–85.

McCurdy, Thomas H. and Morgan, Ieuan G. Tests of the Martingale Hypothesis for Foreign Currency Futures with Time-Varying Volatility. *Int. J. Forecasting,* 1987, *3*(1), pp. 131–48.

McMillin, W. Douglas and Laumas, G. S. Economic Policy and Consumption and Investment Expenditures: An Empirical Examination. *Appl. Econ.,* February 1987, *19*(2), pp. 167–77.   **[G: U.S.]**

Meisner, James F. and Labuszewski, John W. The Cox–Ross–Rubinstein Option-Pricing Model for Alternative Underlying Instruments. *Fabozzi, F. J., ed.,* 1987, pp. 263–78.   **[G: U.S.]**

Mendelson, Haim. Consolidation, Fragmentation, and Market Performance. *J. Finan. Quant. Anal.,* June 1987, *22*(2), pp. 189–207.

Merton, Robert C. A Simple Model of Capital Market Equilibrium with Incomplete Information. *J. Finance,* July 1987, *42*(3), pp. 483–510.

Merton, Robert C. On the Current State of the Stock Market Rationality Hypothesis. *[Modigliani, F.],* 1987, pp. 93–124.

Miller, Merton H. The Informational Content of Dividends. *[Modigliani, F.],* 1987, pp. 37–58.

Milne, Frank. The Induced Preference Approach to Arbitrage and Diversification Arguments in Finance. *Europ. Econ. Rev.,* Feb./Mar. 1987, *31*(1/2), pp. 235–45.

Morgan, George Emir and Smith, Stephen D. The Role of Capital Adequacy Regulation in the Hedging Decisions of Financial Intermediaries. *J. Finan. Res.,* Spring 1987, *10*(1), pp. 33–46.

Morris, Victor F. Is Time Travel Impossible? A Financial Proof: Comment. *J. Portfol. Manage.,* Summer 1987, *13*(4), pp. 85–86.

Moses, Edward A.; Cheyney, John M. and Veit, E. Theodore. A New and More Complete Performance Measure. *J. Portfol. Manage.,* Summer 1987, *13*(4), pp. 24–33.   **[G: U.S.]**

Müller, Urs. A Translog Portfolio Choice Model. *Rivista Int. Sci. Econ. Com.,* Nov.-Dec. 1987, *34*(11–12), pp. 1113–22.

Myers, Stewart C. The Informational Content of Dividends: Comments. *[Modigliani, F.],* 1987, pp. 59–61.

Nachman, David C. Efficient Funds for Meager Asset Spaces. *J. Econ. Theory,* December 1987, *43*(2), pp. 335–47.

Nairay, Alain. Stochastic Equilibrium Discounting. *J. Econ. Dynam. Control,* September 1987, *11*(3), pp. 391–404.

Narayanaswamy, C. R. and Phillips, Herbert E. CAPM, Valuation of Firms, and Financial Leverage. *Quart. J. Bus. Econ.,* Winter 1987, *26*(1), pp. 86–93.

Nermuth, Manfred. Futures Markets, Information Structures, and the Allocation of Resources: An Introduction. *Europ. Econ. Rev.,* Feb./Mar. 1987, *31*(1/2), pp. 226–34.

Newbery, David M. When Do Futures Destabilize Spot Prices? *Int. Econ. Rev.,* June 1987, *28*(2), pp. 291–97.

Nielsen, Lars Tyge. Portfolio Selection in the Mean-Variance Model: A Note. *J. Finance,* December 1987, *42*(5), pp. 1371–76.

Nielsen, Lars Tyge. Positively Weighted Frontier Portfolios: A Note. *J. Finance,* June 1987, *42*(2), pp. 471.

Ofer, Aharon R. and Thakor, Anjan V. A Theory of Stock Price Responses to Alternative Corporate Cash Disbursement Methods: Stock Repurchases and Dividends. *J. Finance,* June 1987, *42*(2), pp. 365–94.

Ogden, Joseph P. An Analysis of Yield Curve Notes. *J. Finance,* March 1987, *42*(1), pp. 99–110.

Oldfield, George S. and Rogalski, Richard J. The Stochastic Properties of Term Structure Movements. *J. Monet. Econ.,* March 1987, *19*(2), pp. 229–54.   **[G: U.S.]**

Omberg, Edward. A Note on the Convergence of Binomial-Pricing and Compound-Option Models. *J. Finance,* June 1987, *42*(2), pp. 463–69.

Omberg, Edward. The Valuation of American Put Options with Exponential Exercise Policies. *Fabozzi, F. J., ed.,* 1987, pp. 117–42.   **[G: U.S.]**

Park, Won-Am. Crawling Peg, Inflation Hedges, and Exchange Rate Dynamics. *J. Int. Econ.,* August 1987, *23*(1/2), pp. 131–50.   **[G: Argentina]**

Parkinson, John M. The Explanatory Power of the Market Model: An International Comparison. *Appl. Econ.,* December 1987, *19*(12), pp. 1625–37.   **[G: OECD; Kuwait; Kenya]**

Perrakis, Stylianos. Option Bounds in Discrete Time and the Pricing of Corporate Debt. *Fabozzi, F. J., ed.,* 1987, pp. 179–207.

Peterson, Paul E. and Leuthold, Raymond M. A Portfolio Approach to Optimal Hedging for a Commercial Cattle Feedlot. *J. Futures Markets,* August 1987, *7*(4), pp. 443–57.   **[G: U.S.]**

Pieptea, Dan R. Leveraged Bond Portfolio Optimization under Uncertainty. *Financial Rev.,* February 1987, *22*(1), pp. 87–109.

Piros, Christopher D. Taxable vs. Tax-Exempt Bonds: A Note on the Effect of Uncertain Taxable Income. *J. Finance,* June 1987, *42*(2), pp. 447–51.

Polinsky, A. Mitchell. Fixed Price versus Spot Price Contracts: A Study in Risk Allocation. *J. Law, Econ., Organ.,* Spring 1987, *3*(1), pp. 27–46.   **[G: U.S.]**

Poncet, Patrice and Portait, Roland. Les marchés à terme d'instruments financiers: quelques mises au point sur les théories de la couverture et de l'équilibre. (Futures Markets: Clarifications on the Theories of Hedging and Equilibrium. With English summary.) *Finance,* December 1987, *8*(2), pp. 55–76.

Putnam, Bluford H. and Mullaney, Brian V. The ECU and Efficient Portfolio Choice: Discussion. *Levich, R. M. and Sommariva, A., eds.,* 1987, pp. 140–43.   **[G: EEC]**

Rashid, Muhammad and Amoako-Adu, Ben. Personal Taxes, Inflation and Market Valuation.

J. Finan. Res., Winter 1987, *10*(4), pp. 341–51.

Romer, David. Bank Deregulation, Credit Markets, and the Control of Capital: Comments. *Carnegie–Rochester Conf. Ser. Public Policy*, Spring 1987, *26*, pp. 335–43.   [G: U.S.]

Rose, Harold. The Design of Bank Regulation and Supervision: Some Lessons from the Theory of Finance: Discussion. *Portes, R. and Swoboda, A. K., eds.*, 1987, pp. 107–10.   [G: U.K.]

Ross, Stephen A. Arbitrage and Martingales with Taxation. *J. Polit. Econ.*, April 1987, *95*(2), pp. 371–93.

Ross, Stephen A. The Interrelations of Finance and Economics: Theoretical Perspectives. *Amer. Econ. Rev.*, May 1987, *77*(2), pp. 29–34.

Rubinstein, Mark. Derivative Assets Analysis. *J. Econ. Perspectives*, Fall 1987, *1*(2), pp. 73–93.

Sami, Heibatollah and Trapnell, Jerry E. Inflation-Adjusted Data and Security Prices: Some Empirical Evidence. *Schwartz, B. N., ed.*, 1987, pp. 39–57.   [G: U.S.]

Schneider, Dieter. Agency Costs and Transaction Costs: Flops in the Principal-Agent–Theory of Financial Markets. *Bamberg, G. and Spremann, K., eds.*, 1987, pp. 481–94.

Scholes, Myron S. How Does the Market Value Unfunded Pension Liabilities? Comment. *Bodie, Z.; Shoven, J. B. and Wise, D. A., eds.*, 1987, pp. 104–09.   [G: U.S.]

Scott, Louis O. Option Pricing When the Variance Changes Randomly: Theory, Estimation, and an Application. *J. Finan. Quant. Anal.*, December 1987, *22*(4), pp. 419–38.

Shanken, Jay. A Bayesian Approach to Testing Portfolio Efficiency. *J. Finan. Econ.*, December 1987, *19*(2), pp. 195–215.

Shanken, Jay. Multivariate Proxies and Asset Pricing Relations: Living with the Roll Critique. *J. Finan. Econ.*, March 1987, *18*(1), pp. 91–110.   [G: U.S.]

Simonds, Richard R. Modern Financial Theory. *Wilcox, J. A., ed.*, 1987, *1978*, pp. 5–14.

Singleton, Kenneth J. Asset Prices in a Time-Series Model with Disparately Informed, Competitive Traders. *Barnett, W. A. and Singleton, K. J., eds.*, 1987, pp. 249–72.

Singleton, Kenneth J. Speculation and the Volatility of Foreign Currency Exchange Rates. *Carnegie–Rochester Conf. Ser. Public Policy*, Spring 1987, *26*, pp. 9–56.

Sondermann, Dieter. Currency Options: Hedging and Social Value. *Europ. Econ. Rev.*, Feb./Mar. 1987, *31*(1/2), pp. 246–56.

Spatt, Chester S. Effects of Capital Gains Taxation on Life-Cycle Investment and Portfolio Management: Discussion. *J. Finance*, July 1987, *42*(3), pp. 758–61.

Starks, Laura T. Performance Incentive Fees: An Agency Theoretic Approach. *J. Finan. Quant. Anal.*, March 1987, *22*(1), pp. 17–32.

Stein, Jeremy C. Informational Externalities and Welfare-Reducing Speculation. *J. Polit. Econ.*, December 1987, *95*(6), pp. 1123–45.

Stein, William E.; Pfaffenberger, Roger C. and French, Dan W. Sampling Error in First Order Stochastic Dominance. *J. Finan. Res.*, Fall 1987, *10*(3), pp. 259–68.

Stulz, René M. Time-Varying Risk Premia, Imperfect Information and the Forward Exchange Rate. *Int. J. Forecasting*, 1987, *3*(1), pp. 171–77.

Tew, Bernard V. and Reid, Donald W. More Evidence on Expected Value-Variance Analysis versus Direct Utility Maximization. *J. Finan. Res.*, Fall 1987, *10*(3), pp. 249–57.   [G: U.S.]

Tobin, James. Liquidity Preference as Behavior towards Risk. *Tobin, J. (I)*, 1987, pp. 242–71.

Tobin, James. On the Current State of the Stock Market Rationality Hypothesis: Comments. *[Modigliani, F.]*, 1987, pp. 125–29.

Townsend, Robert M. Asset-Return Anomalies in a Monetary Economy. *J. Econ. Theory*, April 1987, *41*(2), pp. 219–47.

Townsend, Robert M. and Wallace, Neil. Circulating Private Debt: An Example with a Coordination Problem. *Prescott, E. C. and Wallace, N., eds.*, 1987, pp. 105–20.

Varian, Hal R. The Arbitrage Principle in Financial Economics. *J. Econ. Perspectives*, Fall 1987, *1*(2), pp. 55–72.

Vila, Jean-Luc. Spéculation et intérêt collectif. (Speculation and the Public Interest. With English summary.) *L'Actual. Econ.*, June-September 1987, *63*(2–3), pp. 138–52.

Warschauer, Thomas and Cherin, Antony C. Optimal Liquidity in Personal Financial Planning. *Financial Rev.*, November 1987, *22*(4), pp. 355–68.

Webb, David C. Conflict of Interest, Bond Rating and the Value Maximization Rule. *Economica*, November 1987, *54*(216), pp. 455–63.

Webb, Robert I. A Note on Volatility and Pricing of Futures Options during Choppy Markets. *J. Futures Markets*, June 1987, *7*(3), pp. 333–37.

Weller, Paul and Yano, Makoto. Forward Exchange, Futures Trading, and Spot Price Variability: A General Equilibrium Approach. *Econometrica*, November 1987, *55*(6), pp. 1433–50.

Wiggins, James B. Option Values under Stochastic Volatility: Theory and Empirical Estimates. *J. Finan. Econ.*, December 1987, *19*(2), pp. 351–72.   [G: U.S.]

Williams, Jeffrey. Futures Markets: A Consequences of Risk Aversion or Transactions Costs? *J. Polit. Econ.*, October 1987, *95*(5), pp. 1000–1023.

Wolf, Avner S. Optimal Hedging with Futures Options. *J. Econ. Bus.*, May 1987, *39*(2), pp. 141–58.

Womer, Norman Keith and Cantrell, R. Stephen. The Demand for Risky Assets under Uncertain Inflation: An Examination of Some Widely Used Assumptions. *J. Econ. Bus.*, November 1987, *39*(4), pp. 357–62.

van Zijl, Tony. Risk Decomposition: Variance or Standard Deviation—A Reexamination and Extension. *J. Finan. Quant. Anal.*, June 1987, *22*(2), pp. 237–47.

Zimmermann, Heinz. Emissionspreis und Bezugsrechtswert bei Aktienemissionen. (Offer Price, Rights Value, and New Stock Issues. With English summary.) *Kredit Kapital*, 1987, *20*(2), pp. 236–44. **[G: Switzerland]**

3132 Capital Markets: Empirical Studies, Including Regulation

Adams, Paul D. and Wyatt, Steve B. Biases in Option Prices. *J. Banking Finance*, December 1987, *11*(4), pp. 549–62. **[G: U.S.]**

Adams, Paul D. and Wyatt, Steve B. On the Pricing of European and American Foreign Currency Call Options. *J. Int. Money Finance*, September 1987, *6*(3), pp. 315–38. **[G: U.S.]**

Aggarwal, Raj and Sundararaghavan, P. S. Efficiency of the Silver Futures Market: An Empirical Study Using Daily Data. *J. Banking Finance*, March 1987, *11*(1), pp. 49–64. **[G: U.S.]**

Akgiray, Vedat and Booth, G. Geoffrey. Compound Distribution Models of Stock Returns: An Empirical Comparison. *J. Finan. Res.*, Fall 1987, *10*(3), pp. 269–80. **[G: U.S.]**

Aldrich, Peter C. Active versus Passive: A New Look. *J. Portfol. Manage.*, Fall 1987, *14*(1), pp. 9–11. **[G: U.S.]**

Allen, Paul R. and Sirmans, C. F. An Analysis of Gains to Acquiring Firm's Shareholders: The Special Case of REITs. *J. Finan. Econ.*, March 1987, *18*(1), pp. 175–84. **[G: U.S.]**

Amihud, Yakov and Mendelson, Haim. Are Trading Rule Profits Feasible? *J. Portfol. Manage.*, Fall 1987, *14*(1), pp. 77–78.

Amihud, Yakov and Mendelson, Haim. Trading Mechanisms and Stock Returns: An Empirical Investigation. *J. Finance*, July 1987, *42*(3), pp. 533–53. **[G: U.S.]**

Anderson, Gary and Chiang, Raymond. Interest Rate Risk Hedging for Due-on-Sale Mortgages with Early Termination. *J. Finan. Res.*, Summer 1987, *10*(2), pp. 133–42. **[G: U.S.]**

Anderson, Seth Copeland. An Analysis of Trading Strategies for Closed-End Equity Funds. *Quart. J. Bus. Econ.*, Winter 1987, *26*(1), pp. 3–19. **[G: U.S.]**

Andrikopoulos, Andreas A.; Brox, James A. and Matthews, D. The Demand for Financial Assets in Canada. *Tremblay, R., ed.*, 1987, pp. 249–62. **[G: Canada]**

Arak, Marcelle and Goodman, Laurie S. Treasury Bond Futures: Valuing the Delivery Options. *J. Futures Markets*, June 1987, *7*(3), pp. 269–86. **[G: U.S.]**

Arak, Marcelle, et al. The Municipal-Treasury Futures Spread. *J. Futures Markets*, August 1987, *7*(4), pp. 355–71. **[G: U.S.]**

Ariel, Robert A. A Monthly Effect in Stock Returns. *J. Finan. Econ.*, March 1987, *18*(1), pp. 161–74. **[G: U.S.]**

Arnott, Robert D. Structural Inefficiencies in Municipal Bond Futures. *Fabozzi, F. J., ed.*, 1987, pp. 313–19. **[G: U.S.]**

Atchison, Michael D.; Butler, Kirt C. and Simonds, Richard R. Nonsynchronous Security Trading and Market Index Autocorrelation. *J. Finance*, March 1987, *42*(1), pp. 111–18. **[G: U.S.]**

Atchison, Michael D. and Sanborn, Robert. Current Classification Criteria of New Financial Instruments. *Schwartz, B. N., ed.*, 1987, pp. 99–109. **[G: U.S.]**

Atiase, Rowland Kwame. Market Implications of Predisclosure Information: Size and Exchange Effects. *J. Acc. Res.*, Spring 1987, *25*(1), pp. 168–76. **[G: U.S.]**

Austin, Robert P. Regulatory Principles and the Internationalization of Securities Markets. *Law Contemp. Probl.*, Summer 1987, *50*(3), pp. 221–50. **[G: U.S.]**

Baginski, Stephen P. Intraindustry Information Transfers Associated with Management Forecasts of Earnings. *J. Acc. Res.*, Autumn 1987, *25*(2), pp. 196–216. **[G: U.S.]**

Bailey, Warren Bernard. An Empirical Investigation of the Market for Comex Gold Futures Options. *J. Finance*, December 1987, *42*(5), pp. 1187–94. **[G: U.S.]**

Baillie, Richard T. and McMahon, Patrick C. Rational Forecasts in Models of the Term Structure of Interest Rates. *Goodhart, C.; Currie, D. and Llewellyn, D. T., eds.*, 1987, pp. 189–206.

Bamber, Linda Smith. Unexpected Earnings, Firm Size, and Trading Volume around Quarterly Earnings Announcements. *Accounting Rev.*, July 1987, *62*(3), pp. 510–32. **[G: U.S.]**

Bar-Yosef, Sasson; Callen, Jeffrey L. and Livnat, Joshua. Autoregressive Modeling of Earnings–Investment Causality. *J. Finance*, March 1987, *42*(1), pp. 11–28. **[G: U.S.]**

Barclay, Michael J. Dividends, Taxes, and Common Stock Prices: The Ex-dividend Day Behavior of Common Stock Prices before the Income Tax. *J. Finan. Econ.*, September 1987, *19*(1), pp. 31–44. **[G: U.S.]**

Barnes, Tom and Burnie, David A. The Estimation of Corporate Bond Yield Curves as a Function of Term to Maturity and Coupon. *Quart. J. Bus. Econ.*, Autumn 1987, *26*(4), pp. 50–64.

Barnhill, Theodore M.; Jordan, James V. and Seale, William E. Maturity and Refunding Effects on Treasury-Bond Futures Price Variance. *J. Finan. Res.*, Summer 1987, *10*(2), pp. 121–31. **[G: U.S.]**

Barr, G. D. I. and Affleck-Graves, J. F. Diversification in Foreign Assets—A Comment. *J. Stud. Econ. Econometrics*, July 1987, *11*(2), pp. 95–113. **[G: S. Africa]**

Barrett, W. Brian, et al. The Adjustment of Stock Prices to Completely Unanticipated Events. *Financial Rev.*, November 1987, *22*(4), pp. 345–54. **[G: U.S.]**

Bauer, Richard J., Jr.; Hays, Patrick A. and Upton, David E. Parameter Instability in Mutual Fund Portfolios: A Shifting Regimes Test. *Quart. J. Bus. Econ.*, Winter 1987, *26*(1), pp. 50–62. **[G: U.S.]**

Beatty, Randolph P. Estimation of Convertible Security Systematic Risk: The Marginal Effect of Time, Price, Premium over Bond Value, and Conversion Value/Call Price. *Lee, C. F., ed.*, 1987, pp. 135–54. [G: U.S.]

Beaver, William H.; Lambert, Richard A. and Ryan, Stephen G. The Information Content of Security Prices: A Second Look. *J. Acc. Econ.*, July 1987, 9(2), pp. 139–57. [G: U.S.]

Becker, Brian E. Concession Bargaining: The Impact of Shareholders' Equity. *Ind. Lab. Relat. Rev.*, January 1987, 40(2), pp. 268–79. [G: U.S.]

Belongia, Michael T. Predicting Interest Rates: A Comparison of Professional and Market-Based Forecasts. *Fed. Res. Bank St. Louis Rev.*, March 1987, 69(3), pp. 9–15. [G: U.S.]

Belongia, Michael T. and Santoni, G. J. Hedging Interest Rate Risk with Financial Futures: Some Basic Principles. *Wilcox, J. A., ed.*, 1987, 1984, pp. 47–57. [G: U.S.]

Benelli, Giuseppe and Wyttenbach, Bernhard. Der schweizerische Aktienmarkt in internationaler Perspektive. (With English summary.) *Aussenwirtschaft*, September 1987, 42(2/3), pp. 305–33. [G: U.S.; Switzerland; W. Germany]

Benesh, Gary A. and Pari, Robert A. Performance of Stocks Recommended on the Basis of Insider Trading Activity. *Financial Rev.*, February 1987, 22(1), pp. 145–58. [G: U.S.]

Berglund, Tom; Liljeblom, Eva and Wahlroos, Björn. Stock Price Reactions to Announcements of Stock Dividends and Rights Issues: A Test of Liquidity and Signalling Hypotheses on the Helsinki Stock Exchange. *Finance*, December 1987, 8(2), pp. 109–32. [G: Finland]

Berkowitz, Stephen A. and Logue, Dennis E. The Portfolio Turnover Explosion Explored. *J. Portfol. Manage.*, Spring 1987, 13(3), pp. 38–45. [G: U.S.]

Bernard, Victor L. Cross-Sectional Dependence and Problems in Inference in Market-Based Accounting Research. *J. Acc. Res.*, Spring 1987, 25(1), pp. 1–48. [G: U.S.]

Bernard, Victor L. and Frecka, Thomas J. Commodity Contracts and Common Stocks as Hedges against Relative Consumer Price Risk. *J. Finan. Quant. Anal.*, June 1987, 22(2), pp. 169–88. [G: U.S.]

Bhagat, Sanjai; Brickley, James A. and Coles, Jeffrey L. Managerial Indemnification and Liability Insurance: The Effect on Shareholder Wealth. *J. Risk Ins.*, December 1987, 54(4), pp. 721–36. [G: U.S.]

Bhagat, Sanjai; Brickley, James A. and Loewenstein, Uri. The Pricing Effects of Interfirm Cash Tender Offers. *J. Finance*, September 1987, 42(4), pp. 965–86.

Bhattacharya, Anand K. Option Expirations and Treasury Bond Futures Prices. *J. Futures Markets*, February 1987, 7(1), pp. 49–64. [G: U.S.]

Bhattacharya, Mihir. Price Changes of Related Securities: The Case of Call Options and Stocks. *J. Finan. Quant. Anal.*, March 1987, 22(1), pp. 1–15. [G: U.S.]

Biasco, Salvatore. Currency Cycles and the International Economy. *Banca Naz. Lavoro Quart. Rev.*, March 1987, (160), pp. 31–60. [G: U.S.; W. Germany]

Bierwag, Gerald O.; Kaufman, George G. and Latta, Cynthia M. Bond Portfolio Immunization: Tests of Maturity, One- and Two-Factor Duration Matching Strategies. *Financial Rev.*, May 1987, 22(2), pp. 203–19. [G: U.S.]

Bilson, John F. O. and Hsieh, David A. The Profitability of Currency Speculation. *Int. J. Forecasting*, 1987, 3(1), pp. 115–30. [G: U.S.]

Bird, Peter J. W. N. Futures Trading and the European Oil Market. *Energy J.*, July 1987, 8(3), pp. 149–55. [G: W. Europe]

Bito, Christian. Les options sur contrats futures. Introduction d'un processus de diffusion mixte et application aux devises. (Options on Futures Contracts: Introduction of a Mixed Stochastic Process and an Application to the Foreign Exchange Markets. With English summary.) *Finance*, December 1987, 8(2), pp. 7–24.

Black, Fischer and Jones, Robert. Simplifying Portfolio Insurance. *J. Portfol. Manage.*, Fall 1987, 14(1), pp. 48–51.

Bland, Robert L. The Interest Cost Savings from Municipal Bond Insurance: The Implications for Privatization. *J. Policy Anal. Manage.*, Winter 1987, 6(2), pp. 207–19. [G: U.S.]

Bodurtha, James N., Jr. and Courtadon, Georges R. Tests of an American Option Pricing Model on the Foreign Currency Options Market. *J. Finan. Quant. Anal.*, June 1987, 22(2), pp. 153–67. [G: U.S.]

Bohi, Douglas R. and Toman, Michael A. Futures Trading and Oil Market Conditions. *J. Futures Markets*, April 1987, 7(2), pp. 203–21. [G: Global]

Bond, Michael T. and Smolen, Gerald E. Nominal Interest Rates and Marginal Tax Rates. *Quart. J. Bus. Econ.*, Spring 1987, 26(2), pp. 104–09. [G: U.S.]

Bookstaber, Richard M. and McDonald, James B. A General Distribution for Describing Security Price Returns. *J. Bus.*, July 1987, 60(3), pp. 401–24. [G: U.S.]

Bopp, Anthony E. and Sitzer, Scott. Are Petroleum Futures Prices Good Predictors of Cash Value? *J. Futures Markets*, December 1987, 7(6), pp. 705–19. [G: U.S.]

Borensztein, Eduardo R. Alternative Hypotheses about the Excess Return on Dollar Assets, 1980–84. *Int. Monet. Fund Staff Pap.*, March 1987, 34(1), pp. 29–59. [G: U.S.; W. Europe; Japan]

Borensztein, Eduardo R. and Dooley, Michael P. Options on Foreign Exchange and Exchange Rate Expectations. *Int. Monet. Fund Staff Pap.*, December 1987, 34(4), pp. 643–80. [G: U.S.]

Bowlin, Lyle and Rozeff, Michael S. Do Specialists' Short Sales Predict Returns? *J. Portfol. Manage.*, Spring 1987, 13(3), pp. 59–63. [G: U.S.]

Brenner, Menachem and Galai, Dan. On the Prediction of the Implied Standard Deviation. *Fabozzi, F. J., ed.*, 1987, pp. 167–77. [G: U.S.]

Bressand, Albert. Wealth Creation and the Role of Financial Markets in the Early Twenty-first Century. *[Marjolin, R.]*, 1987, pp. 35–47.

Brick, John R. A Primer on Mortgage-Backed Securities. *Wilcox, J. A., ed.*, 1987, *1984*, pp. 25–33. [G: U.S.]

Brown, Keith C. and Brown, Gregory D. Does the Composition of the Market Portfolio *Really* Matter? *J. Portfol. Manage.*, Winter 1987, *13*(2), pp. 26–32. [G: U.S.]

Brown, Keith C. and Statman, Meir. The Benefits of Insured Stocks for Corporate Cash Management. *Fabozzi, F. J., ed.*, 1987, pp. 243–61. [G: U.S.]

Brown, Lawrence D., et al. An Evaluation of Alternative Proxies for the Market's Assessment of Unexpected Earnings. *J. Acc. Econ.*, July 1987, *9*(2), pp. 159–93. [G: U.S.]

Brown, Lawrence D., et al. Security Analyst Superiority Relative to Univariate Time-Series Models in Forecasting Quarterly Earnings. *J. Acc. Econ.*, April 1987, *9*(1), pp. 61–87. [G: U.S.]

Browne, Lynn E. and Rosengren, Eric S. Should States Restrict Takeovers? *New Eng. Econ. Rev.*, July/Aug. 1987, pp. 13–21. [G: U.S.]

Bruner, Robert F. and Simms, John M., Jr. The International Debt Crisis and Bank Security Returns in 1982. *J. Money, Credit, Banking*, February 1987, *19*(1), pp. 46–55. [G: U.S.]

Buchenroth, Sherree and Jennings, Robert. A Descriptive Analysis of the Time Series Behavior of Financial Analysts' Earnings Forecasts. *Quart. J. Bus. Econ.*, Summer 1987, *26*(3), pp. 22–41. [G: U.S.]

Burns, Malcolm R. New Evidence on the Value Additivity Principle. *J. Finan. Quant. Anal.*, March 1987, *22*(1), pp. 65–77. [G: U.S.]

Buthelezi, Mangosuthu G. Discerning the Divestment Debate. *Sethi, S. P., ed.*, 1987, pp. 165–69. [G: S. Africa]

Butlin, Matthew W. The Australian Economy in the Long Run: Capital Markets. *Maddock, R. and McLean, I. W., eds.*, 1987, pp. 229–47. [G: Australia]

Cabanilla, Nathaniel B. Life Insurers in the Public and Private Security Markets. *J. Risk Ins.*, June 1987, *54*(2), pp. 348–56. [G: U.S.]

Calvet, A. L. and Lefoll, J. Information Asymmetry and Wealth Effect of Canadian Corporate Acquisitions. *Financial Rev.*, November 1987, *22*(4), pp. 415–31. [G: Canada]

Campbell, John Y. Stock Returns and the Term Structure. *J. Finan. Econ.*, June 1987, *18*(2), pp. 373–99. [G: U.S.]

Campbell, John Y. and Clarida, Richard H. The Term Structure of Euromarket Interest Rates: An Empirical Investigation. *J. Monet. Econ.*, January 1987, *19*(1), pp. 25–44.

Canto, Victor A. Monetary Policy, "Dollarization," and Parallel Market Exchange Rates: The Case of the Dominican Republic. *Connolly,*

M. and González-Vega, C., eds., 1987, pp. 177–94. [G: Dominican Republic]

Cartwright, Phillip A. and Lee, Cheng F. Time Aggregation and the Estimation of the Market Model: Empirical Evidence. *J. Bus. Econ. Statist.*, January 1987, *5*(1), pp. 131–43. [G: U.S.]

Cavanaugh, Kenneth L. Price Dynamics in Foreign Currency Futures Markets. *J. Int. Money Finance*, September 1987, *6*(3), pp. 295–314. [G: U.S.]

Chance, Don M. and Ferris, Stephen P. The Effect of Aviation Disasters on the Air Transport Industry: A Financial Market Perspective. *J. Transp. Econ. Policy*, May 1987, *21*(2), pp. 151–65. [G: Global]

Chang, Philip C. Merger Waves and Stock Market Fluctuations: A Test of Causality. *Atlantic Econ. J.*, March 1987, *15*(1), pp. 122.

Chen, K. C.; Sears, R. Stephen and Tzang, Dah-Nein. Oil Prices and Energy Futures. *J. Futures Markets*, October 1987, *7*(5), pp. 501–18. [G: U.S.]

Chen, Nai-Fu; Copeland, Thomas E. and Mayers, David. A Comparison of Single and Multi-factor Portfolio Performance Methodologies. *J. Finan. Quant. Anal.*, December 1987, *22*(4), pp. 401–17. [G: U.S.]

Chesney, Marc and Loubergé, Henri. The Pricing of European Currency Options: Empirical Tests Based on Swiss Data. *Aussenwirtschaft*, September 1987, *42*(2/3), pp. 213–28. [G: Switzerland; U.S.]

Cho, David Chinhyung and Taylor, William M. The Seasonal Stability of the Factor Structure of Stock Returns. *J. Finance*, December 1987, *42*(5), pp. 1195–1211. [G: U.S.]

Cleeton, David L. and Reeder, Paul A. Stock and Option Markets: Are Insider Trading Regulations Effective? *Quart. Rev. Econ. Bus.*, Spring 1987, *27*(1), pp. 63–76. [G: U.S.]

Clements, Kenneth W. and Taylor, John C. The Pattern of Financial Asset Holdings in Australia. *[Cochrane, D.]*, 1987, pp. 268–88. [G: Australia]

Clinch, Greg J. and Sinclair, Norman A. Intra-industry Information Releases: A Recursive Systems Approach. *J. Acc. Econ.*, April 1987, *9*(1), pp. 89–106. [G: Australia]

Coggin, T. Daniel and Hunter, John E. A Meta-Analysis of Pricing "Risk" Factors in APT. *J. Portfol. Manage.*, Fall 1987, *14*(1), pp. 35–38. [G: U.S.]

Colletaz, Gilbert. La prévision optimale des taux d'intérêt. (With English summary.) *Revue Écon. Polit.*, May-June 1987, *97*(3), pp. 301–20. [G: France]

Collins, Daniel W.; Kothari, S. P. and Rayburn, Judy Dawson. Firm Size and the Information Content of Prices with Respect to Earnings. *J. Acc. Econ.*, July 1987, *9*(2), pp. 111–38. [G: U.S.]

Collins, Daniel W.; Ledolter, Johannes and Rayburn, Judy Dawson. Some Further Evidence on the Stochastic Properties of Systematic Risk.

J. Bus., July 1987, *60*(3), pp. 425–48.
[G: U.S.]

Connelly, Mark Q. Multinational Securities Offerings: A Canadian Perspective. *Law Contemp. Probl.*, Summer 1987, *50*(3), pp. 251–69.
[G: Canada]

Connock, Michael and Hillier, Harry. Long Bond Yields and Inflation Rates in OECD Countries: A Cross-section Study. *Appl. Econ.*, March 1987, *19*(3), pp. 407–15.   [G: OECD]

Conroy, Robert M. and Rendleman, Richard J., Jr. A Test of Market Efficiency in Government Bonds. *J. Portfol. Manage.*, Summer 1987, *13*(4), pp. 57–64.   [G: U.S.]

Coons, Christopher. Divestment Steamroller Seeks to Bury Apartheid. *Sethi, S. P., ed.*, 1987, pp. 295–306.   [G: S. Africa]

Cooper, Kathleen M. Real Interest Rates: The Unpuzzle. *Bus. Econ.*, January 1987, *22*(1), pp. 13–17.   [G: U.S.; U.K.]

Copeland, Thomas E. and Friedman, Daniel. The Effect of Sequential Information Arrival on Asset Prices: An Experimental Study. *J. Finance*, July 1987, *42*(3), pp. 763–97.
[G: U.S.]

Corgel, John B. and Gay, Gerald D. Local Economic Base, Geographic Diversification, and Risk Management of Mortgage Portfolios. *Amer. Real Estate Urban Econ. Assoc. J.*, Fall 1987, *15*(3), pp. 256–67.   [G: U.S.]

Corhay, Albert; Hawawini, Gabriel and Michel, Pierre. Seasonality in the Risk–Return Relationship: Some International Evidence. *J. Finance*, March 1987, *42*(1), pp. 49–68.
[G: U.S.; U.K.; France; Belgium]

Corner, D. C. and Tonks, I. The Impact of the Internationalisation of World Stock Markets on the Integration of EC Securities Markets. *Macmillen, M.; Mayes, D. G. and van Veen, P., eds.*, 1987, pp. 229–46.   [G: EEC]

Cotner, John S. and Seitz, Neil E. A Simplified Approach to Short-term International Diversification. *Financial Rev.*, May 1987, *22*(2), pp. 249–66.

Courtenay, Stephen M. and Millar, James A. Accounting Earnings and Convertible Calls. *Tremblay, R., ed.*, 1987, pp. 579–93.

Cready, William M. and Shank, John K. Understanding Accounting Changes in an Efficient Market—A Comment, Replication, and Re-interpretation. *Accounting Rev.*, July 1987, *62*(3), pp. 589–96.   [G: U.S.]

Crouhy, Michel. Gains from International Diversification: 1968–85 Returns on Portfolios of Stocks and Bonds: Discussion. *J. Finance*, July 1987, *42*(3), pp. 739–41.   [G: U.S.; W. Europe; Japan; Australia; Canada]

Da Silva, Roberto and Dellva, Wilfred L. Evidence of the Size Effect on Stock Returns in the Chemical Industry. *Quart. J. Bus. Econ.*, Spring 1987, *26*(2), pp. 22–40.   [G: U.S.]

Darrat, Ali F. Money and Stock Prices in West Germany and the United Kingdom: Is the Stock Market Efficient? *Quart. J. Bus. Econ.*, Winter 1987, *26*(1), pp. 20–35.   [G: U.K.; W. Germany]

Davidson, Wallace N., III; Chandy, P. R. and Cross, Mark. Large Losses, Risk Management and Stock Returns in the Airline Industry. *J. Risk Ins.*, March 1987, *54*(1), pp. 162–72.
[G: U.S.]

Davidson, Wallace N., III; Garrison, Sharon Hatten and Henderson, Glenn V., Jr. Examining Merger Synergy with the Capital Asset Pricing Model. *Financial Rev.*, May 1987, *22*(2), pp. 233–47.   [G: U.S.]

Davis, Carolyn D. and White, Alice P. Stock Market Volatility. *Fed. Res. Bull.*, September 1987, *73*(9), pp. 699–700.   [G: U.S.]

De Bondt, Werner F. M. and Thaler, Richard H. Further Evidence on Investor Overreaction and Stock Market Seasonality. *J. Finance*, July 1987, *42*(3), pp. 557–81.   [G: U.S.]

Dickens, Rodney. Variability in Some Major UK Asset Markets since the Mid-1960s: An Application of the ARCH Model. *Goodhart, C.; Currie, D. and Llewellyn, D. T., eds.*, 1987, pp. 231–70.   [G: U.K.]

Dokko, Yoon and Edelstein, Robert. The Empirical Interrelationships among the Mundell and Darby Hypotheses and Expected Stock Market Returns. *Rev. Econ. Statist.*, February 1987, *69*(1), pp. 161–66.   [G: U.S.]

Doukas, John and Rahman, Abdul H. Unit Roots Tests: Evidence from the Foreign Exchange Futures Market. *J. Finan. Quant. Anal.*, March 1987, *22*(1), pp. 101–08.   [G: U.S.; Canada; Japan; W. Europe]

Dowen, Richard J. and Bauman, W. Scott. Residual Returns and Extramarket Risk. *Quart. J. Bus. Econ.*, Spring 1987, *26*(2), pp. 41–54.
[G: U.S.]

Downs, Thomas and Hendershott, Patric H. Tax Policy and Stock Prices. *Nat. Tax J.*, June 1987, *40*(2), pp. 183 90.   [G: U.S.]

Dravid, Ajay R. A Note on the Behavior of Stock Returns around Ex-dates of Stock Distributions. *J. Finance*, March 1987, *42*(1), pp. 163–68.   [G: U.S.]

Dubofsky, David A. Hedging Dividend Capture Strategies with Stock Index Futures. *J. Futures Markets*, October 1987, *7*(5), pp. 471–81.
[G: U.S.]

Dukes, William P.; Bowlin, Oswald D. and MacDonald, S. Scott. The Performance of Beta in Forecasting Portfolio Returns in Bull and Bear Markets Using Alternative Market Proxies. *Quart. J. Bus. Econ.*, Spring 1987, *26*(2), pp. 89–103.   [G: U.S.]

Eaker, Mark R. and Grant, Dwight M. Cross-hedging Foreign Currency Risk. *J. Int. Money Finance*, March 1987, *6*(1), pp. 85–105.
[G: Selected OECD; S. Africa]

Edelman, Richard B. and Baker, H. Kent. The Dynamics of Neglect and Return. *J. Portfol. Manage.*, Fall 1987, *14*(1), pp. 52–55.
[G: U.S.]

Ederington, Louis H.; Yawitz, Jess B. and Roberts, Brian E. The Informational Content of Bond Ratings. *J. Finan. Res.*, Fall 1987, *10*(3), pp. 211–26.   [G: U.S.]

Ehrhardt, Michael C.; Jordan, James V. and

Walkling, Ralph A. An Application of Arbitrage Pricing Theory to Futures Markets: Tests of Normal Backwardation. *J. Futures Markets*, February 1987, 7(1), pp. 21–34. [G: U.S.]

Elgers, Pieter; Callahan, Carolyn and Strock, Elizabeth. The Effect of Earnings Yields upon the Association between Unexpected Earnings and Security Returns: A Re-examination. *Accounting Rev.*, October 1987, 62(4), pp. 763–73. [G: U.S.]

Elton, Edwin J.; Gruber, Martin J. and Rentzler, Joel C. Professionally Managed, Publicly Traded Commodity Funds. *J. Bus.*, April 1987, 60(2), pp. 175–99. [G: U.S.]

Errunza, Vihang and Losq, Etienne. How Risky Are Emerging Markets? *J. Portfol. Manage.*, Fall 1987, 14(1), pp. 62–67. [G: LDCs]

Estep, Tony. Manager Style and the Sources of Equity Returns. *J. Portfol. Manage.*, Winter 1987, 13(2), pp. 4–10. [G: U.S.]

Evnine, Jeremy and Henriksson, Roy. Asset Allocation and Options. *J. Portfol. Manage.*, Fall 1987, 14(1), pp. 56–61. [G: U.S.]

Fama, Eugene F. and Bliss, Robert R. The Information in Long-Maturity Forward Rates. *Amer. Econ. Rev.*, September 1987, 77(4), pp. 680–92. [G: U.S.]

Fama, Eugene F. and French, Kenneth R. Commodity Futures Prices: Some Evidence on Forecast Power, Premiums, and the Theory of Storage. *J. Bus.*, January 1987, 60(1), pp. 55–73. [G: U.S.]

Feinman, David. The Mechanics of the ECU Bond Market. *Levich, R. M. and Sommariva, A., eds.*, 1987, pp. 89–92. [G: EEC; U.S.]

Feinstone, Lauren J. Minute to Minute: Efficiency, Normality, and Randomness in Intradaily Asset Prices. *J. Appl. Econometrics*, July 1987, 2(3), pp. 193–214. [G: U.S.; W. Germany]

Fekrat, M. Ali. Accounting for Forward Exchange Contracts: Theory and Implications for Practice. *Most, Kenneth S., ed.*, 1987, pp. 249–62. [G: U.S.]

Ferris, Stephen P. and Chance, Don M. Trading Time Effects in Financial and Commodity Futures Markets. *Financial Rev.*, May 1987, 22(2), pp. 281–94. [G: U.S.]

Fons, Jerome S. The Default Premium and Corporate Bond Experience. *J. Finance*, March 1987, 42(1), pp. 81–97. [G: U.S.]

Fortune, J. Neill. The Inflation Rate of the Price of Gold, Expected Prices and Interest Rates. *J. Macroecon.*, Winter 1987, 9(1), pp. 71–82. [G: U.S.]

Frantzmann, Hans-Jörg. Der Montagseffekt am deutschen Aktienmarkt. (With English summary.) *Z. Betriebswirtshaft*, July 1987, 57(7), pp. 611–35. [G: W. Germany]

Freeman, Robert N. The Association between Accounting Earnings and Security Returns for Large and Small Firms. *J. Acc. Econ.*, July 1987, 9(2), pp. 195–228. [G: U.S.]

Froland, Charles. What Determines Cap Rates on Real Estate? *J. Portfol. Manage.*, Summer 1987, 13(4), pp. 77–82. [G: U.S.]

Fukao, Mitsuhiro. A Risk Premium Model of the Yen–Dollar and DM–Dollar Exchange Rates. *OECD Econ. Stud.*, Autumn 1987, (9), pp. 79–104. [G: U.S.]

Furtado, Eugene P. H. and Rozeff, Michael S. The Wealth Effects of Company Initiated Management Changes. *J. Finan. Econ.*, March 1987, 18(1), pp. 147–60. [G: U.S.]

Garland, James P. Taxable Portfolios: Value and Performance. *J. Portfol. Manage.*, Winter 1987, 13(2), pp. 19–24.

Gaumnitz, Bruce R. and Thompson, Joel E. Establishing the Common Stock Equivalence of Convertible Bonds. *Accounting Rev.*, July 1987, 62(3), pp. 601–22.

Gay, Gerald D. and Kim, Tae-Hyuk. An Investigation into Seasonality in the Futures Market. *J. Futures Markets*, April 1987, 7(2), pp. 169–81.

Giannaros, Demetrios S. and Lashgari, Malek K. Business Cycles, Inflation and the Price of Gold: An Empirical Investigation. *Tremblay, R., ed.*, 1987, pp. 111–21.

Gibbons, Michael R. The Interrelations of Finance and Economics: Empirical Perspectives. *Amer. Econ. Rev.*, May 1987, 77(2), pp. 35–41.

Giovannini, Alberto and Jorion, Philippe. Interest Rates and Risk Premia in the Stock Market and in the Foreign Exchange Market. *J. Int. Money Finance*, March 1987, 6(1), pp. 107–23. [G: U.S.; Selected OECD]

Glascock, John L.; Davidson, Wallace N., III and Henderson, Glenn V., Jr. Announcement Effects of Moody's Bond Rating Changes on Equity Returns. *Quart. J. Bus. Econ.*, Summer 1987, 26(3), pp. 67–78. [G: U.S.]

Glassman, Debra A. Exchange Rate Risk and Transactions Costs: Evidence from Bid–Ask Spreads. *J. Int. Money Finance*, December 1987, 6(4), pp. 479–90. [G: U.S.]

Glassman, Debra A. The Efficiency of Foreign Exchange Futures Markets in Turbulent and Non-turbulent Periods. *J. Futures Markets*, June 1987, 7(3), pp. 245–67. [G: U.K.; U.S.; Canada; W. Germany; Switzerland]

Glick, Reuven. Interest Rate Linkages in the Pacific Basin. *Fed. Res. Bank San Francisco Econ. Rev.*, Summer 1987, (3), pp. 31–42. [G: OECD; Hong Kong; Singapore; Taiwan; Malaysia]

Goodhart, Charles A. E. Structural Changes in the British Markets. *Goodhart, C.; Currie, D. and Llewellyn, D. T., eds.*, 1987, pp. 31–53. [G: U.K.]

Goss, Barry A. Wool Prices and Publicly Available Information. *Australian Econ. Pap.*, December 1987, 26(49), pp. 225–36. [G: Australia]

Graham, David and Jennings, Robert. Systematic Risk, Dividend Yield and the Hedging Performance of Stock Index Futures. *J. Futures Markets*, February 1987, 7(1), pp. 1–13. [G: U.S.]

Granito, Michael R. The Problem with Bond Index Funds. *J. Portfol. Manage.*, Summer 1987, 13(4), pp. 41–47. [G: U.S.]

Grauer, Robert R. and Hakansson, Nils H. Gains from International Diversification: 1968–85 Returns on Portfolios of Stocks and Bonds. *J. Finance*, July 1987, *42*(3), pp. 721–39.
[G: W. Europe; Japan; Australia; U.S.; Canada]

Green, Christopher J. Did High-Powered Money Rule the Roost? Monetary Policy, Private Behaviour and the Structure of Interest Rates in the United Kingdom: 1972–77. *Goodhart, C.; Currie, D. and Llewellyn, D. T., eds.*, 1987, pp. 207–30. [G: U.K.]

Grissom, Terry V.; Kuhle, James L. and Walther, Carl H. Diversification Works in Real Estate, Too. *J. Portfol. Manage.*, Winter 1987, *13*(2), pp. 66–71. [G: U.S.]

Grossman, Sanford J.; Melino, Angelo and Shiller, Robert J. Estimating the Continuous-Time Consumption-Based Asset-Pricing Model. *J. Bus. Econ. Statist.*, July 1987, *5*(3), pp. 315–27. [G: U.S.]

Grube, R. Corwin; Joy, O. Maurice and Howe, John S. Some Empirical Evidence on Stock Returns and Security Credit Regulation in the OTC Equity Market. *J. Banking Finance*, March 1987, *11*(1), pp. 17–31. [G: U.S.]

Gultekin, Mustafa N. and Gultekin, N. Bulent. Stock Return Anomalies and the Tests of the APT. *J. Finance*, December 1987, *42*(5), pp. 1213–24. [G: U.S.]

Haar, Lawrence. The Role and Importance of Crude and Product Futures Markets. *Pachauri, R. K., ed.*, 1987, pp. 683–701.

Hall, Maximilian J. B. Reform of the London Stock Exchange: The Prudential Issues. *Banca Naz. Lavoro Quart. Rev.*, June 1987, (161), pp. 167–81. [G: U.K.]

Hamilton, James L. Market Information and Price Dispersion: Unlisted Stocks and NASDAQ. *J. Econ. Bus.*, February 1987, *39*(1), pp. 67–80. [G: U.S.]

Hamilton, James L. Off-Board Trading of NYSE-Listed Stocks: The Effects of Degregulation and the National Market System. *J. Finance*, December 1987, *42*(5), pp. 1331–45. [G: U.S.]

Hardouvelis, Gikas A. Macroeconomic Information and Stock Prices. *J. Econ. Bus.*, May 1987, *39*(2), pp. 131–40. [G: U.S.]

Harris, Lawrence. Transaction Data Tests of the Mixture of Distributions Hypothesis. *J. Finan. Quant. Anal.*, June 1987, *22*(2), pp. 127–41. [G: U.S.]

Hartzmark, Michael L. Returns to Individual Traders of Futures: Aggregate Results. *J. Polit. Econ.*, December 1987, *95*(6), pp. 1292–1306. [G: U.S.]

Hasbrouck, Joel and Ho, Thomas S. Y. Order Arrival, Quote Behavior, and the Return-Generating Process. *J. Finance*, September 1987, *42*(4), pp. 1035–48. [G: U.S.]

Hauch, Jeanne M. Insider Trading by Intermediaries: A Contract Remedy for Acquirers' Increased Costs of Takeovers. *Yale Law J.*, November 1987, *97*(1), pp. 115–34. [G: U.S.]

Hauser, Robert J. and Andersen, Dane K. Hedg-

ing with Options under Variance Uncertainty: An Illustration of Pricing New-Crop Soybeans. *Amer. J. Agr. Econ.*, February 1987, *69*(1), pp. 38–45. [G: U.S.]

Heinkel, Robert and Kraus, Alan. The Effect of Insider Trading on Average Rates of Return. *Can. J. Econ.*, August 1987, *20*(3), pp. 588–611. [G: Canada]

Helfat, Constance E. and Teece, David J. Vertical Integration and Risk Reduction. *J. Law, Econ., Organ.*, Spring 1987, *3*(1), pp. 47–67. [G: U.S.]

Heller, H. Robert. The ECU and the Choice of an Invoice Currency: Discussion. *Levich, R. M. and Sommariva, A., eds.*, 1987, pp. 156–59. [G: EEC]

Herbst, Anthony F.; McCormack, Joseph P. and West, Elizabeth N. Investigation of a Lead-Lag Relationship between Spot Indices and Their Futures Contracts. *J. Futures Markets*, August 1987, *7*(4), pp. 373–81. [G: U.S.]

Hetherington, Norriss S. High Return and Low Risk in Called Preferreds. *J. Portfol. Manage.*, Spring 1987, *13*(3), pp. 81–82. [G: U.S.]

Hirschfeld, David J. Development of ECU Futures Markets: An Institutional Perspective. *Levich, R. M. and Sommariva, A., eds.*, 1987, pp. 93–102. [G: EEC]

Hirst, Ian. Restrictions on Outward Portfolio Investment and Domestic Equity Markets. *Managerial Dec. Econ.*, March 1987, *8*(1), pp. 75–80. [G: U.S.; Japan; U.K.; S. Africa; W. Germany]

Hirtle, Beverly. The Growth of the Financial Guarantee Market. *Fed. Res. Bank New York Quart. Rev.*, Spring 1987, *12*(1), pp. 10–28. [G: U.S.]

Hite, Gailen L.; Owers, James E. and Rogers, Ronald C. The Market for Interfirm Asset Sales: Partial Sell-offs and Total Liquidations. *J. Finan. Econ.*, June 1987, *18*(2), pp. 229–52. [G: U.S.]

Hoffer, George E.; Pruitt, Stephen W. and Reilly, Robert J. Automotive Recalls and Informational Efficiency. *Financial Rev.*, November 1987, *22*(4), pp. 433–42. [G: U.S.]

Holthausen, Robert W.; Leftwich, Richard W. and Mayers, David. The Effect of Large Block Transactions on Security Prices: A Cross-sectional Analysis. *J. Finan. Econ.*, December 1987, *19*(2), pp. 237–67. [G: U.S.]

Horsky, Dan and Swyngedouw, Patrick. Does It Pay to Change Your Company's Name? A Stock Market Perspective. *Marketing Sci.*, Fall 1987, *6*(4), pp. 320–35.

Hoshi, Takeo. Stock Market Rationality and Price Volatility: Tests Using Japanese Data. *J. Japanese Int. Economies*, December 1987, *1*(4), pp. 441–62. [G: Japan]

Huang, Yen-Sheng and Walkling, Ralph A. Target Abnormal Returns Associated with Acquisition Announcements: Payment, Acquisition Form, and Managerial Resistance. *J. Finan. Econ.*, December 1987, *19*(2), pp. 329–49. [G: U.S.]

Huberman, Gur and Kandel, Shmuel. Value Line

Rank and Firm Size. *J. Bus.*, October 1987, *60*(4), pp. 577–89.   [G: U.S.]

Hudson, Michael A.; Leuthold, Raymond M. and Sarassoro, Gboroton F. Commodity Futures Price Changes: Recent Evidence for Wheat, Soybeans and Live Cattle. *J. Futures Markets*, June 1987, *7*(3), pp. 287–301.

Hughes, John S. and Ricks, William E. Associations between Forecast Errors and Excess Returns Near to Earnings Announcements. *Accounting Rev.*, January 1987, *62*(1), pp. 158–75.   [G: U.S.]

Huizinga, John and Leiderman, Leonardo. The Signalling Role of Base and Money Announcements and Their Effects on Interest Rates. *J. Monet. Econ.*, December 1987, *20*(3), pp. 439–62.   [G: U.S.]

Ingram, Robert W.; Raman, Krishnamurthy K. and Wilson, Earl R. Governmental Capital Markets Research in Accounting: A Review. *Chan, J. L., ed., Pt. B*, 1987, pp. 111–126.

Irwin, Scott H. and Brorsen, B. Wade. A Note on the Factors Affecting Technical Trading System Returns. *J. Futures Markets*, October 1987, *7*(5), pp. 591–95.   [G: U.S.]

Irwin, Scott H. and Landa, Diego. Real Estate, Futures, and Gold as Portfolio Assets. *J. Portfol. Manage.*, Fall 1987, *14*(1), pp. 29–34.   [G: U.S.]

Ithurbide, Philippe. Le marché de l'or et les bulles rationnelles. (The Gold Market and Rational Bubbles. With English summary.) *L'Actual. Econ.*, December 1987, *63*(4), pp. 331–56.

Jahera, John S., Jr.; Lloyd, William P. and Page, Daniel E. Firm Diversification and Financial Performance. *Quart. Rev. Econ. Bus.*, Spring 1987, *27*(1), pp. 51–62.   [G: U.S.]

Jahera, John S., Jr.; Lloyd, William P. and Page, Daniel E. The Relationship between Financial Performance and Stock Market Based Measures of Corporate Diversification. *Financial Rev.*, November 1987, *22*(4), pp. 379–89.   [G: U.S.]

Jahnke, Gregg; Klaffke, Stephen J. and Oppenheimer, Henry R. Price–Earnings Ratios and Security Performance. *J. Portfol. Manage.*, Fall 1987, *14*(1), pp. 39–46.   [G: U.S.]

James, Christopher M. Some Evidence on the Uniqueness of Bank Loans. *J. Finan. Econ.*, December 1987, *19*(2), pp. 217–35.   [G: U.S.]

James, Christopher M. and Wier, Peggy. Returns to Acquirers and Competition in the Acquisition Market: The Case of Banking. *J. Polit. Econ.*, April 1987, *95*(2), pp. 355–70.   [G: U.S.]

Jani, B. M. Portfolio Management in Indian Scheduled Commercial Banks. *Indian Econ. J.*, Oct.-Dec. 1987, *35*(2), pp. 77–90.   [G: India]

Jarrell, Gregg A. and Poulsen, Annette B. Shark Repellents and Stock Prices: The Effects of Antitakeover Amendments since 1980. *J. Finan. Econ.*, September 1987, *19*(1), pp. 127–68.

Johnson, Larry J. and Wofford, Larry E. On

Contracts as Options: Some Evidence from Condominium Developments: Comment. *Amer. Real Estate Urban Econ. Assoc. J.*, Spring 1987, *15*(1), pp. 739–41.   [G: U.S.]

Johnson, W. Bruce. Discussion of Management Compensation Contracts and Merger-Induced Abnormal Returns. *J. Acc. Res.*, Supplement 1987, *25*, pp. 77–84.   [G: U.S.]

Jones, Charles P.; Pearce, Douglas K. and Wilson, Jack W. Can Tax-Loss Selling Explain the January Effect? A Note. *J. Finance*, June 1987, *42*(2), pp. 453–61.   [G: U.S.]

Jones, Charles P. and Wilson, Jack W. Stocks, Bonds, Paper, and Inflation: 1870–1985. *J. Portfol. Manage.*, Fall 1987, *14*(1), pp. 20–24.   [G: U.S.]

Jones, Jonathan D. and Uri, Noel D. The Money Supply, Stock Returns and Causality. *Econ. Notes*, 1987, (1), pp. 39–51.   [G: U.S.]

Jordan, James V., et al. Transactions Data Tests of the Black Model for Soybean Futures Options. *J. Futures Markets*, October 1987, *7*(5), pp. 535–54.   [G: U.S.]

Jorion, Philippe. The ECU and Efficient Portfolio Choice. *Levich, R. M. and Sommariva, A., eds.*, 1987, pp. 119–39.   [G: EEC]

Junkus, Joan C. Hedge Ratios in Up and Down Equity Markets. *Fabozzi, F. J., ed.*, 1987, pp. 279–89.   [G: U.S.]

Kalay, Avner and Shimrat, Adam. Firm Value and Seasoned Equity Issues: Price Pressure, Wealth Redistribution, or Negative Information. *J. Finan. Econ.*, September 1987, *19*(1), pp. 109–26.   [G: U.S.]

Kane, Alex and Marks, Stephen Gary. The Rocking Horse Analyst. *J. Portfol. Manage.*, Spring 1987, *13*(3), pp. 32–37.

Kantor, Jeffrey and Pike, Richard. Valuing Unlisted Shares: A Dual Approach to the Major Information Determinants. *Managerial Dec. Econ.*, September 1987, *8*(3), pp. 221–27.   [G: Canada]

Karathanassis, G. and Philippas, N. Estimation of Share Valuation Parameters from Time Series and Cross Section Data. Some Results Using Data from the Athens Stock Exchange. *Rivista Int. Sci. Econ. Com.*, Nov.-Dec. 1987, *34*(11–12), pp. 1167–77.   [G: Greece]

Karpoff, Jonathan M. The Relation between Price Changes and Trading Volume: A Survey. *J. Finan. Quant. Anal.*, March 1987, *22*(1), pp. 109–26.   [G: U.S.]

Kaul, Gautam. Stock Returns and Inflation: The Role of the Monetary Sector. *J. Finan. Econ.*, June 1987, *18*(2), pp. 253–76.   [G: U.S.; U.K.; Canada; W. Germany]

Kawaller, Ira G.; Koch, Paul D. and Koch, Timothy W. The Temporal Price Relationship between S&P 500 Futures and the S&P 500 Index. *J. Finance*, December 1987, *42*(5), pp. 1309–29.   [G: U.S.]

Keeley, Terrence R. Financial Innovation and Social Benefit. *[Marjolin, R.]*, 1987, pp. 117–35.   [G: U.S.]

Keim, Donald B. Daily Returns and Size-Related Premiums: One More Time. *J. Portfol. Man-*

age., Winter 1987, *13*(2), pp. 41–47.
[G: U.S.]

Keim, Donald B. and Smirlock, Michael. The Behavior of Intraday Stock Index Futures Prices. *Fabozzi, F. J., ed.*, 1987, pp. 143–66.
[G: U.S.]

Kelly, William A., Jr.; Nardinelli, Clark and Wallace, Myles S. Regulation of Insider Trading: Rethinking SEC Policy Rules. *Cato J.*, Fall 1987, *7*(2), pp. 441–48.
[G: U.S.]

Kenyon, David and Clay, John. Analysis of Profit Margin Hedging Strategies for Hog Producers. *J. Futures Markets*, April 1987, *7*(2), pp. 183–202.
[G: U.S.]

Kenyon, David, et al. Factors Affecting Agricultural Futures Price Variance. *J. Futures Markets*, February 1987, *7*(1), pp. 73–91.
[G: U.S.]

Kidwell, David S.; Koch, Timothy W. and Stock, Duane R. Issue Size and Term-structure Segmentation Effects on Regional Yield Differentials in the Municipal Bond Market. *J. Econ. Bus.*, November 1987, *39*(4), pp. 339–47.
[G: U.S.]

Kidwell, David S.; Marr, M. Wayne and Thompson, G. Rodney. Shelf Registration: Competition and Market Flexibility. *J. Law Econ.*, April 1987, *30*(1), pp. 181–206. [G: U.S.]

Kidwell, David S.; Sorensen, Eric H. and Wachowicz, John M., Jr. Estimating the Signaling Benefits of Debt Insurance: The Case of Municipal Bonds. *J. Finan. Quant. Anal.*, September 1987, *22*(3), pp. 299–313. [G: U.S.]

Kim, E. Han and Schatzberg, John D. Voluntary Corporate Liquidations. *J. Finan. Econ.*, December 1987, *19*(2), pp. 311–28. [G: U.S.]

Kim, Moon K. and Wu, Chunchi. Macro-economic Factors and Stock Returns. *J. Finan. Res.*, Summer 1987, *10*(2), pp. 87–98.
[G: U.S.]

King, Stephen R. and Remolona, Eli M. The Pricing and Hedging of Market Index Deposits. *Fed. Res. Bank New York Quart. Rev.*, Summer 1987, *12*(2), pp. 9–20. [G: U.S.]

Kirchgässner, Gebhard and Wolters, Jürgen. U.S.–European Interest Rate Linkage: A Time Series Analysis for West Germany, Switzerland, and the United States. *Rev. Econ. Statist.*, November 1987, *69*(4), pp. 675–84.
[G: W. Germany; U.S.; Switzerland]

Klein, April and Rosenfeld, James. The Influence of Market Conditions on Event-Study Residuals. *J. Finan. Quant. Anal.*, September 1987, *22*(3), pp. 345–51. [G: U.S.]

Koedijk, Kees G. and Ott, Mack. Risk Aversion, Efficient Markets and the Forward Exchange Rate. *Fed. Res. Bank St. Louis Rev.*, December 1987, *69*(10), pp. 5–13. [G: U.S.]

Kohers, Theodor and Simpson, W. Gary. A Comparison of the Forecasting Accuracy of the Futures and Forward Markets for Foreign Exchange. *Appl. Econ.*, July 1987, *19*(7), pp. 961–67. [G: OECD]

Kolb, Robert W. and Rodriguez, Ricardo J. Friday the Thirteenth: 'Part VII'—A Note. *J. Fi-*

nance, December 1987, *42*(5), pp. 1385–87.
[G: U.S.]

Krol, Robert. The Term Structure of Eurodollar Interest Rates and Its Relationship to the U.S. Treasury-Bill Market. *J. Int. Money Finance*, September 1987, *6*(3), pp. 339–54. [G: U.S.]

de La Bruslerie, Hubert and Gellusseau, Laurence. La mise en évidence empirique de la structure à terme des taux d'intérêt. (Empirical Tests of the Term Structure of Interest Rates. With English summary.) *Finance*, June 1987, *8*(1), pp. 55–74. [G: France]

Laber, Gene. Effects of the Bell System Breakup on the Cost of Debt. *J. Econ. Bus.*, August 1987, *39*(3), pp. 185–97. [G: U.S.]

Lakonishok, Josef and Lev, Baruch. Stock Splits and Stock Dividends: Why, Who, and When. *J. Finance*, September 1987, *42*(4), pp. 913–32. [G: U.S.]

Lamoureux, Christopher G. and Poon, Percy. The Market Reaction to Stock Splits. *J. Finance*, December 1987, *42*(5), pp. 1347–70.
[G: U.S.]

Lamoureux, Christopher G. and Wansley, James W. Market Effects of Changes in the Standard & Poor's 500 Index. *Financial Rev.*, February 1987, *22*(1), pp. 53–69. [G: U.S.]

Larcker, David F. and Lys, Thomas. An Empirical Analysis of the Incentives to Engage in Costly Information Acquisition: The Case of Risk Arbitrage. *J. Finan. Econ.*, March 1987, *18*(1), pp. 111–26. [G: U.S.]

Larson, John C. and Morse, Joel N. Intervalling Effects in Hong Kong Stocks. *J. Finan. Res.*, Winter 1987, *10*(4), pp. 353–62.
[G: Hong Kong]

Lasser, Dennis J. Influence of Treasury Bill Futures Trading on the Primary Sale of the Deliverable Treasury Bill. *Financial Rev.*, November 1987, *22*(4), pp. 391–402. [G: U.S.]

Lee, Adrian F. International Asset and Currency Allocation. *J. Portfol. Manage.*, Fall 1987, *14*(1), pp. 68–73. [G: U.S.]

Lee, Cheng F.; Bubnys, Edward L. and Lin, Yun. Stock Index Futures Hedge Ratios: Tests on Horizon Effects and Functional Form. *Fabozzi, F. J., ed.*, 1987, pp. 291–311. [G: U.S.]

Lee, Cheng F. and Kau, James B. Dividend Payment Behavior and Dividend Policy on REITs. *Quart. Rev. Econ. Bus.*, Summer 1987, *27*(2), pp. 6–21. [G: U.S.]

Lee, Cheng F.; Wort, Donald H. and Han, Doug. The Relationship between Dividend Yield and Earnings Yield and Its Implication for Forecasting. *Lee, C. F., ed.*, 1987, pp. 155–77.
[G: U.S.]

Lehmann, Bruce N. and Modest, David M. Mutual Fund Performance Evaluation: A Comparison of Benchmarks and Benchmark Comparisons. *J. Finance*, June 1987, *42*(2), pp. 233–65. [G: U.S.]

Leibowitz, Martin L. Liability Returns: A New Look at Asset Allocation. *J. Portfol. Manage.*, Winter 1987, *13*(2), pp. 11–18. [G: U.S.]

Leiderman, Leonardo and Blejer, Mario I. The Term Structure of Interest Rates during a Fi-

nancial Reform: Argentina 1977–81. *J. Devel. Econ.*, April 1987, *25*(2), pp. 285–99.
[G: Argentina]

Leonard, David C. and Solt, Michael E. Stock Market Signals of Changes in Expected Inflation. *J. Finan. Res.*, Spring 1987, *10*(1), pp. 57–63. [G: U.S.]

Leuthold, Raymond M. and Peterson, Paul E. A Portfolio Approach to Optimal Hedging for a Commercial Cattle Feedlot. *J. Futures Markets*, April 1987, *7*(2), pp. 119–33. [G: U.S.]

Levich, Richard M. Development of the ECU Markets: Perspectives on Financial Innovation. *Levich, R. M. and Sommariva, A., eds.*, 1987, pp. 103–16. [G: EEC]

Levin, Jay H. The Simultaneous Determination of Spot and Forward Exchange Rates: An Asset Market Approach. *Kredit Kapital*, 1987, *20*(4), pp. 467–85.

Levis, Mario. Market Size and Seasonalities: The Case of the UK Investment Trust Industry. *Managerial Dec. Econ.*, June 1987, *8*(2), pp. 101–11. [G: U.K.]

Levy, Haim. Futures, Spots, Stocks and Bonds: Multi-asset Portfolio Analysis. *J. Futures Markets*, August 1987, *7*(4), pp. 383–95.
[G: U.S.]

Lien, Da-Hsiang Donald. The Inventory Effect in Commodity Futures Markets: An Empirical Study. *J. Futures Markets*, December 1987, *7*(6), pp. 637–52. [G: U.S.]

Lindley, James T.; Helms, Billy P. and Haddad, Mahmoud. A Measurement of the Errors in Intra-period Compounding and Bond Valuation. *Financial Rev.*, February 1987, *22*(1), pp. 33–51. [G: U.S.]

Liu, Pu and Moore, William T. The Impact of Split Bond Ratings on Risk Premia. *Financial Rev.*, February 1987, *22*(1), pp. 71–85.
[G: U.S.]

Livingston, Miles. The Effect of Coupon Level on Treasury Bond Futures Delivery. *J. Futures Markets*, June 1987, *7*(3), pp. 303–09.
[G: U.S.]

Lumpkin, Stephen A. Repurchase and Reverse Repurchase Agreements. *Fed. Res. Bank Richmond Econ. Rev.*, Jan./Feb. 1987, *73*(1), pp. 15–23. [G: U.S.]

Luskin, Donald L. The Marketplace for "Composite Assets" *J. Portfol. Manage.*, Fall 1987, *14*(1), pp. 12–19. [G: U.S.]

Maberly, Edwin D. An Analysis of Trading and Nontrading Period Returns for the Value Line Composite Index; Spot versus Futures: A Note. *J. Futures Markets*, October 1987, *7*(5), pp. 497–500. [G: U.S.]

MacDonald, Ronald and Ta, Guy. The Singapore Dollar: Tests of the Efficient Markets Hypothesis and the Role of 'News.' *Appl. Econ.*, May 1987, *19*(5), pp. 569–79. [G: Singapore]

MacDonald, Ronald and Torrance, Thomas S. £M3 Surprises and Asset Prices. *Economica*, November 1987, *54*(216), pp. 505–15.
[G: U.K.]

Maher, John J. Pension Obligations and the Bond Credit Market: An Empirical Analysis of Ac-

counting Numbers. *Accounting Rev.*, October 1987, *62*(4), pp. 785–98. [G: U.S.]

Malick, William M. and Ward, Ronald W. Stock Effects and Seasonality in the FCOJ Futures Basis. *J. Futures Markets*, April 1987, *7*(2), pp. 157–67. [G: U.S.]

Marcus, Richard D.; Swidler, Steve and Zivney, Terry L. An Explanation of Why Shareholders' Losses Are So Large after Drug Recalls. *Managerial Dec. Econ.*, December 1987, *8*(4), pp. 295–300. [G: U.S.]

Marlin, Alice Tepper. Social Investing: Potent Force for Political Change. *Sethi, S. P., ed.*, 1987, pp. 307–16. [G: U.S.; S. Africa]

Marsh, Terry A. and Merton, Robert C. Dividend Behavior for the Aggregate Stock Market. *J. Bus.*, January 1987, *60*(1), pp. 1–40.
[G: U.S.]

Martell, Terrence F. and Wolf, Avner S. Determinants of Trading Volume in Futures Markets. *J. Futures Markets*, June 1987, *7*(3), pp. 233–44. [G: U.S.]

Martin, Deryl W. and French, Dan W. The Characteristics of Interest Rates and Stock Variances Implied in Option Prices. *J. Econ. Bus.*, August 1987, *39*(3), pp. 279–88.
[G: U.S.]

Mayers, David and Smith, Clifford W., Jr. Death and Taxes: The Market for Flower Bonds. *J. Finance*, July 1987, *42*(3), pp. 685–98.
[G: U.S.]

McCauley, Robert N. and Hargraves, Lauren A. Eurocommercial Paper and U.S. Commercial Paper: Converging Money Markets? *Fed. Res. Bank New York Quart. Rev.*, Autumn 1987, *12*(3), pp. 24–35. [G: U.S.]

McConnell, John J. and Sanger, Gary C. The Puzzle in Post-listing Common Stock Returns. *J. Finance*, March 1987, *42*(1), pp. 119–40.
[G: U.S.]

McCulloch, J. Huston. The Monotonicity of the Term Premium: A Closer Look [Term Premium in Bond Returns]. *J. Finan. Econ.*, March 1987, *18*(1), pp. 185–92.

McFarland, James W.; Pettit, R. Richardson and Sung, Sam K. The Distribution of Foreign Exchange Price Changes: Trading Day Effects and Risk Measurement—A Reply. *J. Finance*, March 1987, *42*(1), pp. 189–94. [G: U.S.]

McKeown, James C. Understanding Accounting Changes in an Efficient Market: Analysis of Variance Issues. *Accounting Rev.*, July 1987, *62*(3), pp. 597–600. [G: U.S.]

McKillop, D. G. and Hutchinson, R. W. The Relevance of a "Beta Book" for Irish Equities. *Econ. Soc. Rev.*, July 1987, *18*(4), pp. 257–69. [G: Ireland]

McRae, Hamish. The Implications of an International Equity Market. *[Marjolin, R.]*, 1987, pp. 99–115. [G: U.K.]

Meisner, James F. and Labuszewski, John W. The Cox–Ross–Rubinstein Option-Pricing Model for Alternative Underlying Instruments. *Fabozzi, F. J., ed.*, 1987, pp. 263–78.
[G: U.S.]

Merino, Barbara D.; Koch, Bruce S. and Mac-

Ritchie, Kenneth L. Historical Analysis—A Diagnostic Tool for "Events" Studies: The Impact of the Securities Act of 1933. *Accounting Rev.*, October 1987, *62*(4), pp. 748–62. **[G: U.S.]**

Merrick, John J., Jr. Volume Determination in Stock and Stock Index Futures Markets: An Analysis of Arbitrage and Volatility Effects. *J. Futures Markets*, October 1987, *7*(5), pp. 483–96. **[G: U.S.]**

Michel, Allen and Shaked, Israel. Trucking Deregulation and Motor-Carrier Performance: The Shareholders' Perspective. *Financial Rev.*, May 1987, *22*(2), pp. 295–311. **[G: U.S.]**

Mikdashi, Z. Oil Funding and International Financial Markets. *Rees, J. and Odell, P., eds.*, 1987, pp. 88–106. **[G: Global]**

Miller, Girard. The Investment of Public Funds: A Research Agenda. *Public Budg. Finance*, Autumn 1987, *7*(3), pp. 47–56. **[G: U.K.]**

Milonas, Nikolaos T. The Effects of USDA Crop Announcements on Commodity Prices. *J. Futures Markets*, October 1987, *7*(5), pp. 571–89. **[G: U.S.]**

Mirowski, Philip. What Do Markets Do? Efficiency Tests of the 18th-Century London Stock Market. *Exploration Econ. Hist.*, April 1987, *24*(2), pp. 107–29. **[G: U.K.]**

Modigliani, Franco. Conventional Valuation and the Term Structure of Interest Rates: Comments. *[Modigliani, F.]*, 1987, pp. 89–92. **[G: U.K.; U.S.]**

Mookerjee, Rajen. Monetary Policy and the Informational Efficiency of the Stock Market: The Evidence from Many Countries. *Appl. Econ.*, November 1987, *19*(11), pp. 1521–32. **[G: OECD]**

Morgan, Alison and Morgan, Ieuan G. Measurement of Abnormal Returns from Small Firms. *J. Bus. Econ. Statist.*, January 1987, *5*(1), pp. 121–29. **[G: U.S.]**

Mossavar-Rahmani, Sharmin. Customized Benchmarks in Structured Management. *J. Portfol. Manage.*, Summer 1987, *13*(4), pp. 65–68. **[G: U.S.]**

Muller, Frederick L. and Fielitz, Bruce D. Standard & Poor's Quality Rankings Revisited. *J. Portfol. Manage.*, Spring 1987, *13*(3), pp. 64–68. **[G: U.S.]**

Munnell, Alicia H. Pension Contributions and the Stock Market. *New Eng. Econ. Rev.*, Nov./Dec. 1987, pp. 3–14. **[G: U.S.]**

Murphy, J. Austin. Stable Distributions, Futures Prices, and the Measurement of Trading Performance: A Reply. *J. Futures Markets*, February 1987, *7*(1), pp. 103–07. **[G: U.S.]**

Murphy, J. Austin. The Seasonality of Risk and Return on Agricultural Futures Positions. *Amer. J. Agr. Econ.*, August 1987, *69*(3), pp. 639–46. **[G: U.S.]**

Murphy, Joseph. The Apartheid Debate on American Campuses. *Sethi, S. P., ed.*, 1987, pp. 285–93. **[G: U.S.; S. Africa]**

Nauss, Robert M. Generating Optimal True Interest Cost Bids for New Municipal Bond Competitive Issues. *J. Banking Finance*, June 1987, *11*(2), pp. 329–43. **[G: U.S.]**

Neal, Larry. The Integration and Efficiency of the London and Amsterdam Stock Markets in the Eighteenth Century. *J. Econ. Hist.*, March 1987, *47*(1), pp. 97–115. **[G: U.K.; Netherlands]**

Neal, Robert. Potential Competition and Actual Competition in Equity Options. *J. Finance*, July 1987, *42*(3), pp. 511–31. **[G: U.S.]**

Nelson, Charles R. and Siegel, Andrew F. Parsimonious Modeling of Yield Curves. *J. Bus.*, October 1987, *60*(4), pp. 473–89. **[G: U.S.]**

Nishina, Kazuhiko and Funaoka, Fumio. The Role of the Market Price of Risk in the Investment Decision. *Econ. Rev. (Keizai Kenkyu)*, April 1987, *38*(2), pp. 139–52. **[G: Japan]**

O'Hara, Maureen. Trading Mechanisms and Stock Returns: An Empirical Investigation: Discussion. *J. Finance*, July 1987, *42*(3), pp. 554–55. **[G: U.S.]**

Ofer, Aharon R. and Natarajan, Ashok. Convertible Call Policies: An Empirical Analysis of an Information-signaling Hypothesis. *J. Finan. Econ.*, September 1987, *19*(1), pp. 91–108. **[G: U.S.]**

Ofer, Aharon R. and Siegel, Daniel R. Corporate Financial Policy, Information, and Market Expectations: An Empirical Investigation of Dividends. *J. Finance*, September 1987, *42*(4), pp. 889–911. **[G: U.S.]**

Officer, Dennis T. and Hoffmeister, J. Ronald. ADRs: A Substitute for the Real Thing? *J. Portfol. Manage.*, Winter 1987, *13*(2), pp. 61–65. **[G: U.S.]**

Ogden, Joseph P. Determinants of the Ratings and Yields on Corporate Bonds: Tests of the Contingent Claims Model. *J. Finan. Res.*, Winter 1987, *10*(4), pp. 329–39. **[G: U.S.]**

Ogden, Joseph P. The End of the Month as a Preferred Habitat: A Test of Operational Efficiency in the Money Market. *J. Finan. Quant. Anal.*, September 1987, *22*(3), pp. 329–43. **[G: U.S.]**

Ogden, Joseph P. and Tucker, Alan L. Empirical Tests of the Efficiency of the Currency Futures Options Market. *J. Futures Markets*, December 1987, *7*(6), pp. 695–703. **[G: U.S.]**

Östermark, Ralf. On the Relationship between the Empirical Market Line for the Finnish Stock Exchange and International Evidence. *Liiketaloudellinen Aikak.*, 1987, *36*(3), pp. 244–59. **[G: Finland]**

Overdahl, James A. The Use of Crude Oil Futures by the Governments of Oil-Producing States. *J. Futures Markets*, December 1987, *7*(6), pp. 603–17. **[G: U.S.]**

Page, Frank H., Jr. On Equilibrium in Hart's Securities Exchange Model. *J. Econ. Theory*, April 1987, *41*(2), pp. 392–404.

Palmén, Henrik. Äänipreemiot vallan hinnan mittana Helsingin pörssissä. (Empirical Study of the Voting Premium on the Helsinki Stock Exchange. With English summary.) *Liiketaloudellinen Aikak.*, 1987, *36*(3), pp. 294–316. **[G: Finland]**

Pari, Robert A. Wall $treet Week Recommendations: Yes or No? *J. Portfol. Manage.*, Fall

1987, *14*(1), pp. 74–76.   [G: U.S.]

Park, Hun Y.; Lee, Angela and Lee, Hei W. Cross-Hedging Performance of the U.S. Currency Futures Market: The European Monetary System Currencies. *Fabozzi, F. J., ed.*, 1987, pp. 223–42.   [G: U.S.]

Parkinson, John M. The Explanatory Power of the Market Model: An International Comparison. *Appl. Econ.*, December 1987, *19*(12), pp. 1625–37.   [G: OECD; Kuwait; Kenya]

Parkinson, John M. The EMH and the CAPM on the Nairobi Stock Exchange. *Eastern Afr. Econ. Rev.*, December 1987, *3*(2), pp. 105–10.   [G: Kenya]

Peavy, John W., III and Hempel, George H. The Effect of the WPPSS Crisis on the Tax-Exempt Bond Market. *J. Finan. Res.*, Fall 1987, *10*(3), pp. 239–47.

Peck, Anne E. Futures Markets and Intertemporal Commodity Pricing. *Kilmer, R. L. and Armbruster, W. J., eds.*, 1987, pp. 256–69.   [G: U.S.]

Peck, Anne E. and Budge, Carlos C. The Effects of Extraordinary Speculative Margins in the 1947–48 Grain Futures Markets. *Food Res. Inst. Stud.*, 1987, *20*(2), pp. 165–80.   [G: U.S.]

Penman, Stephen H. The Distribution of Earnings News over Time and Seasonalities in Aggregate Stock Returns. *J. Finan. Econ.*, June 1987, *18*(2), pp. 199–228.   [G: U.S.]

Perraudin, W. R. M. Inflation and Portfolio Choice. *Int. Monet. Fund Staff Pap.*, December 1987, *34*(4), pp. 739–59.   [G: U.K.]

Petersen, John E. Examining the Impacts of the 1986 Tax Reform Act on the Municipal Securities Market. *Nat. Tax J.*, September 1987, *40*(3), pp. 393–402.   [G: U.S.]

Peterson, David R. Security Price Reactions to Initial Reviews of Common Stock by the Value Line Investment Survey. *J. Finan. Quant. Anal.*, December 1987, *22*(4), pp. 483–94.   [G: U.S.]

Peterson, Pamela P.; Peterson, David R. and Moore, Norman H. The Adoption of New-Issue Dividend Reinvestment Plans and Shareholder Wealth. *Financial Rev.*, May 1987, *22*(2), pp. 221–32.   [G: U.S.]

Pettway, Richard H. and Jordan, Bradford D. APT vs. CAPM Estimates of the Return-Generating Function Parameters for Regulated Public Utilities. *J. Finan. Res.*, Fall 1987, *10*(3), pp. 227–38.   [G: U.S.]

Poitras, Geoffrey. "Golden Turtle Tracks": In Search of Unexploited Profits in Gold Spreads. *J. Futures Markets*, August 1987, *7*(4), pp. 397–412.   [G: U.S.]

Pound, John and Shiller, Robert J. Are Institutional Investors Speculators? *J. Portfol. Manage.*, Spring 1987, *13*(3), pp. 46–52.   [G: U.S.]

Pozdena, Randall Johnston. Securitization and Banking. *Wilcox, J. A., ed.*, 1987, *1986*, pp. 34–36.   [G: U.S.]

Prat, Georges. Prévisions de la tendance du cours moyen des actions dans le cadre d'une formula-

tion États-Unis, 1981–1984. (With English summary.) *Revue Écon. Polit.*, Sept.-Oct. 1987, *97*(5), pp. 575–91.   [G: U.S.]

Pruitt, Stephen W.; Tawarangkoon, Wuttipan and Wei, K. C. John. Chernobyl, Commodities, and Chaos: An Examination of the Reaction of Commodity futures Prices to Evolving Information. *J. Futures Markets*, October 1987, *7*(5), pp. 555–69.   [G: U.S.]

Putnam, Bluford H. and Mullaney, Brian V. The ECU and Efficient Portfolio Choice: Discussion. *Levich, R. M. and Sommariva, A., eds.*, 1987, pp. 140–43.   [G: EEC]

Rahman, Abdul H. Memory in Commodity Futures Prices in Canada: Using Akaike Information Criterion under Heteroskedasticity. *Can. J. Agr. Econ.*, March 1987, *35*(1), pp. 229–40.

Rahman, Abdul H.; Kryzanowski, Lawrence and Sim, Ah Boon. Simultaneous Estimation of the Parameters of the Black–Scholes Option Pricing Model. *Rev. Econ. Statist.*, November 1987, *69*(4), pp. 727–32.   [G: U.S.]

Rahman, Abdul H.; Kryzanowski, Lawrence and Sim, Ah Boon. Systematic Risk in a Purely Random Market Model: Some Empirical Evidence for Individual Public Utilities. *J. Finan. Res.*, Summer 1987, *10*(2), pp. 143–52.   [G: U.S.]

Ramaswami, Murali. Stock Market Perception of Industrial Firm Bankruptcy. *Financial Rev.*, May 1987, *22*(2), pp. 267–79.   [G: U.S.]

Rayburn, William; Devaney, Michael and Evans, Richard. A Test of Weak-Form Efficiency in Residential Real Estate Returns. *Amer. Real Estate Urban Econ. Assoc. J.*, Fall 1987, *15*(3), pp. 220–33.   [G: U.S.]

Reichenstein, William. On Standard Deviation and Risk. *J. Portfol. Manage.*, Winter 1987, *13*(2), pp. 39–40.   [G: U.S.]

Reinganum, Marc R. and Shapiro, Alan C. Taxes and Stock Return Seasonality: Evidence from the London Stock Exchange. *J. Bus.*, April 1987, *60*(2), pp. 281–95.   [G: U.K.]

Rendleman, Richard J., Jr.; Jones, Charles P. and Latané, Henry A. Further Insight into the Standarized Unexpected Earnings Anomaly: Size and Serial Correlation Effects. *Financial Rev.*, February 1987, *22*(1), pp. 131–44.   [G: U.S.]

Ritter, Jay R. The Costs of Going Public. *J. Finan. Econ.*, December 1987, *19*(2), pp. 269–81.   [G: U.S.]

Roley, V. Vance. U.S. Money Announcements and Covered Interest Parity: The Case of Japan. *J. Int. Money Finance*, March 1987, *6*(1), pp. 57–70.   [G: Japan; U.S.]

Ronn, Ehud I. A New Linear Programming Approach to Bond Portfolio Management. *J. Finan. Quant. Anal.*, December 1987, *22*(4), pp. 439–66.   [G: U.S.]

Rosengren, Eric S. Forecasting Changes in Inflation Using the Treasury Bill Futures Market. *New Eng. Econ. Rev.*, Mar./Apr. 1987, pp. 41–48.   [G: U.S.]

Rubinstein, Mark and Vijh, Anand M. The Berkeley Options Data Base: A Tool for Empirical Research. *Fabozzi, F. J., ed.*, 1987, pp. 209–21. [G: U.S.]

Rubio Irigoyen, Gonzalo. El contenido informativo de los derechos de suscripcion e información asimétrica en los mercados primarios. (With English summary.) *Invest. Ecón.*, May 1987, *11*(2), pp. 219–42. [G: Spain]

Rzepczynski, Mark S. Risk Premiums in Financial Futures Markets: The Case of Treasury Bond Futures. *J. Futures Markets*, December 1987, *7*(6), pp. 653–62. [G: U.S.]

Samuelson, Paul A. Paradise Lost and Refound: The Harvard ABC Barometers. *J. Portfol. Manage.*, Spring 1987, *13*(3), pp. 4–9. [G: U.S.]

Santoni, G. J. Has Programmed Trading Made Stock Prices More Volatile? *Fed. Res. Bank St. Louis Rev.*, May 1987, *69*(5), pp. 18–29. [G: U.S.]

Saunders, Anthony and Smirlock, Michael. Intra- and Interindustry Effects of Bank Securities Market Activities: The Case of Discount Brokerage. *J. Finan. Quant. Anal.*, December 1987, *22*(4), pp. 467–82. [G: U.S.]

Schaefer, Stephen M. The Design of Bank Regulation and Supervision: Some Lessons from the Theory of Finance. *Portes, R. and Swoboda, A. K., eds.*, 1987, pp. 91–104. [G: U.K.]

Schaefer, Stephen M. and Schwartz, Eduardo S. Time-Dependent Variance and the Pricing of Bond Options. *J. Finance*, December 1987, *42*(5), pp. 1113–28. [G: U.K.]

Schipper, Katherine; Thompson, Rex and Weil, Roman L. Disentangling Interrelated Effects of Regulatory Changes on Shareholder Wealth: The Case of Motor Carrier Deregulation. *J. Law Econ.*, April 1987, *30*(1), pp. 67–100. [G: U.S.]

Seaquist, Gwen. An Inquiry into the Enforceability of the Insider Trading Sanctions Act (ITSA) of 1984: The Record of Prosecution Thus Far and the Prospects for the Future. *Tremblay, R., ed.*, 1987, pp. 617–29. [G: U.S.]

Sengupta, Jati K. and Sfeir, Raymond E. Evaluation of Investment Portfolios: Some Tests of Robustness and Diversification. *Appl. Econ.*, February 1987, *19*(2), pp. 179–89. [G: U.S.]

Sethi, S. Prakash. South Africa Beyond Apartheid Reformation of Institutions and Instruments of Change. *Sethi, S. P., ed.*, 1987, pp. 1–37. [G: S. Africa]

Severn, Alan K.; Mills, James Charles and Copeland, Basil L., Jr. Capital Gains Taxes after Tax Reform. *J. Portfol. Manage.*, Spring 1987, *13*(3), pp. 69–75. [G: U.S.]

Shanken, Jay. Nonsynchronous Data and the Co-variance-Factor Structure of Returns. *J. Finance*, June 1987, *42*(2), pp. 221–31. [G: U.S.]

Shastri, Kuldeep and Tandon, Kishore. Valuation of American Options on Foreign Currency. *J. Banking Finance*, June 1987, *11*(2), pp. 245–69. [G: U.S.]

Shastri, Kuldeep and Wethyavivorn, Kulpatra. The Valuation of Currency Options for Alter-nate Stochastic Processes. *J. Finan. Res.*, Winter 1987, *10*(4), pp. 283–93. [G: U.S.; W. Europe; Canada; Japan]

Shaviro, Frieda W. An Analysis of Cash and Futures Prices in the Delivery Period of Maturing Contracts in the Coffee "C" Market, 1972–1981. *J. Futures Markets*, August 1987, *7*(4), pp. 413–41. [G: U.S.]

Sheales, Terence C. and Tomek, William G. Hedging Australian Wheat Exports Using Futures Markets. *J. Futures Markets*, October 1987, *7*(5), pp. 519–33. [G: Australia]

Shiller, Robert J. Conventional Valuation and the Term Structure of Interest Rates. *[Modigliani, F.]*, 1987, pp. 63–88. [G: U.S.; U.K.]

Shilling, James D.; Sirmans, C. F. and Benjamin, John D. On Option-Pricing Models in Real Estate: A Critique: Reply [Contracts as Options: Some Evidence from Condominium Developments]. *Amer. Real Estate Urban Econ. Assoc. J.*, Spring 1987, *15*(1), pp. 742–52. [G: U.S.]

Sicherman, Neil W. and Pettway, Richard H. Acquisition of Divested Assets and Shareholders' Wealth. *J. Finance*, December 1987, *42*(5), pp. 1261–73. [G: U.S.]

Sirmans, G. Stacy and Sirmans, C. F. The Historical Perspective of Real Estate Returns. *J. Portfol. Manage.*, Spring 1987, *13*(3), pp. 22–31.

Skantz, Terrance R. and Marchesini, Roberto. The Effect of Voluntary Corporate Liquidation on Shareholder Wealth. *J. Finan. Res.*, Spring 1987, *10*(1), pp. 65–75. [G: U.S.]

Smirlock, Michael and Kaufold, Howard. Bank Foreign Lending, Mandatory Disclosure Rules, and the Reaction of Bank Stock Prices to the Mexican Debt Crisis. *J. Bus.*, July 1987, *60*(3), pp. 347–64. [G: U.S.]

Smith, Donald J. Risk-Efficient Lottery Bets?! *J. Portfol. Manage.*, Fall 1987, *14*(1), pp. 25–28. [G: U.S.]

Snowden, Kenneth A. American Stock Market Development and Performance, 1871–1929. *Exploration Econ. Hist.*, October 1987, *24*(4), pp. 327–53. [G: U.S.]

Snowden, P. N. International Equity Investment in Less Developed Countries' Stockmarkets: The Replacement for Bank Lending? *Nat. Westminster Bank Quart. Rev.*, February 1987, pp. 29–38. [G: LDCs]

So, Jacky C. Commodity Futures Risk Premium and Unstable Systematic Risk. *J. Futures Markets*, June 1987, *7*(3), pp. 311–26. [G: U.S.]

So, Jacky C. The Distribution of Foreign Exchange Price Changes: Trading Day Effects and Risk Measurement—A Comment. *J. Finance*, March 1987, *42*(1), pp. 181–88. [G: U.S.]

So, Jacky C. The Sub-Gaussian Distribution of Currency Futures: Stable Peretian or Nonstationary? *Rev. Econ. Statist.*, February 1987, *69*(1), pp. 100–107. [G: Japan; Canada; W. Germany; U.K.; Switzerland]

Statman, Meir. How Many Stocks Make a Diversified Portfolio? *J. Finan. Quant. Anal.*, September 1987, *22*(3), pp. 353–63. [G: U.S.]

Statman, Meir and Ushman, Neal L. Bonds versus Stocks: Another Look. *J. Portfol. Manage.*, Winter 1987, *13*(2), pp. 33–38.   [**G: U.S.**]

Stenius, Marianne. Floatation Procedures, Market Microstructure and Efficiency: Evidence from Financial Markets in Finland. *Liiketaloudellinen Aikak.*, 1987, *36*(2), pp. 144–57.
[**G: Finland**]

Stoll, Hans R. Effects of Options on Underlying Assets. *Aussenwirtschaft*, September 1987, *42*(2/3), pp. 199–212.   [**G: U.S.**]

Strong, John S. and Meyer, John R. Asset Writedowns: Managerial Incentives and Security Returns. *J. Finance*, July 1987, *42*(3), pp. 643–61.   [**G: U.S.**]

Suzuki, Yoshio. Financial Innovation in Japan: Its Origins, Diffusion and Impacts. *de Cecco, M.*, ed., 1987, pp. 229–59.   [**G: Japan**]

Syron, Richard and Tschinkel, Sheila L. The Government Securities Market: Playing Field for Repos. *Wilcox, J. A.*, ed., 1987, *1985*, pp. 15–24.   [**G: U.S.**]

Takagi, Shinji. Transactions Costs and the Term Structure of Interest Rates in the OTC Bond Market in Japan. *J. Money, Credit, Banking*, November 1987, *19*(4), pp. 515–27.
[**G: Japan**]

Tarhan, Vefa. Unanticipated Interest Rates, Bank Stock Returns and the Nominal Contracting Hypothesis. *J. Banking Finance*, March 1987, *11*(1), pp. 99–115.   [**G: U.S.**]

Taylor, Mark P. Learning and Rationality: An Empirical Study of Investment Managers' Stock Market Predictions. *Ann. Écon. Statist.*, Oct./Dec. 1987, (8), pp. 43–57.   [**G: U.K.**]

Taylor, Stephen J. Forecasting the Volatility of Currency Exchange Rates. *Int. J. Forecasting*, 1987, *3*(1), pp. 159–70.   [**G: U.S.**]

Tehranian, Hassan, et al. Management Compensation Contracts and Merger-Induced Abnormal Returns. *J. Acc. Res.*, Supplement 1987, *25*, pp. 51–76.   [**G: U.S.**]

Tehranian, Hassan; Travlos, Nickolaos G. and Waegelein, James F. The Effect of Long-term Performance Plans on Corporate Sell-Off-Induced Abnormal Returns. *J. Finance*, September 1987, *42*(4), pp. 933–42.   [**G: U.S.**]

Thakor, Anjan V. Asset Writedowns: Managerial Incentives and Security Returns: Discussion. *J. Finance*, July 1987, *42*(3), pp. 661–63.
[**G: U.S.**]

Thaler, Richard H. Seasonal Movements in Security Prices II: Weekend, Holiday, Turn of the Month, and Intraday Effects. *J. Econ. Perspectives*, Fall 1987, *1*(2), pp. 169–77.   [**G: U.S.**]

Thompson, Sarahelen R. Futures Markets and Intertemporal Commodity Pricing: A Discussion. *Kilmer, R. L. and Armbruster, W. J.*, eds., 1987, pp. 270–73.   [**G: U.S.**]

Thompson, Sarahelen R. and Waller, Mark L. The Execution Cost of Trading in Commodity Futures Markets. *Food Res. Inst. Stud.*, 1987, *20*(2), pp. 141–63.   [**G: U.S.**]

Thompson, Stanley R. and Bond, Gary E. Offshore Commodity Hedging under Floating Exchange Rates. *Amer. J. Agr. Econ.*, February 1987, *69*(1), pp. 46–55.   [**G: U.S.; Australia**]

Tinic, Seha M.; Barone-Adesi, Giovanni and West, Richard R. Seasonality in Canadian Stock Prices: A Test of the "Tax-Loss–Selling" Hypothesis. *J. Finan. Quant. Anal.*, March 1987, *22*(1), pp. 51–63.   [**G: Canada**]

Tobin, James. Inflation, Interest Rates, and Stock Values. *Tobin, J. (III)*, 1987, *1974*, pp. 275–81.   [**G: U.S.**]

Travlos, Nickolaos G. Corporate Takeover Bids, Methods of Payment, and Bidding Firms' Stock Returns. *J. Finance*, September 1987, *42*(4), pp. 943–63.   [**G: U.S.**]

Tschoegl, Adrian E. Seasonality in Asset Returns: Evidence from the Gold Market. *Managerial Dec. Econ.*, September 1987, *8*(3), pp. 251–54.   [**G: U.S.**]

Tucker, Alan L. Foreign Exchange Option Prices as Predictors of Equilibrium Forward Exchange Rates. *J. Int. Money Finance*, September 1987, *6*(3), pp. 283–94.   [**G: U.S.**]

Tucker, Alan L. and Scott, Elton. A Study of Diffusion Processes for Foreign Exchange Rates. *J. Int. Money Finance*, December 1987, *6*(4), pp. 465–78.   [**G: U.S.**]

Tueting, William F. and King, Christopher Q. Funds Protections: An Overview of What Happens When a Commodity Broker Becomes Insolvent. *J. Futures Markets*, February 1987, *7*(1), pp. 93–101.   [**G: U.S.**]

Turvey, Calum Greig and Driver, H. C. Systematic and Nonsystematic Risks in Agriculture. *Can. J. Agr. Econ.*, July 1987, *35*(2), pp. 387–401.   [**G: U.S.**]

Van Horne, James C. Call Risk in Municipal Bonds. *J. Portfol. Manage.*, Winter 1987, *13*(2), pp. 53–57.   [**G: U.S.**]

VanDerhei, Jack L. The Effect of Voluntary Termination of Overfunded Pension Plans on Shareholder Wealth. *J. Risk Ins.*, March 1987, *54*(1), pp. 132–56.   [**G: U.S.**]

Vanthienen, Lambert and Vermaelen, Theo. The Effect of Personal Taxes on Common Stock Prices: The Case of a Belgian Tax Reform. *J. Banking Finance*, June 1987, *11*(2), pp. 223–44.   [**G: Belgium**]

Veeman, Michele M. and Taylor, Ellen Moreau. Two Tests of Pricing Efficiency in the Rapeseed Futures Market. *Can. J. Agr. Econ.*, March 1987, *35*(1), pp. 21–32.

Virén, Matti. Inflation, Hedging, and the Fisher Hypothesis. *J. Macroecon.*, Winter 1987, *9*(1), pp. 45–57.   [**G: U.S.; U.K.; Canada**]

Vlahos, George, et al. Empirical Tests of Parity-Based Option Pricing Models: The Case of Options on Japanese Yen Futures. *Rivista Int. Sci. Econ. Com.*, Nov.-Dec. 1987, *34*(11–12), pp. 1123–38.   [**G: U.S.**]

Wansley, James W.; Lane, William R. and Yang, Ho C. Gains to Bidder Firms in Cash and Securities Transactions. *Financial Rev.*, November 1987, *22*(4), pp. 403–14.   [**G: U.S.**]

Webb, James R. and Rubens, Jack H. How Much in Real Estate? A Surprising Answer. *J. Portfol. Manage.*, Spring 1987, *13*(3), pp. 10–14.
[**G: U.S.**]

Weinstein, Mark I. A Curmudgeon's View of Junk

Bonds. *J. Portfol. Manage.*, Spring 1987, *13*(3), pp. 76–80. [G: U.S.]

West, Kenneth D. A Specification Test for Speculative Bubbles. *Quart. J. Econ.*, August 1987, *102*(3), pp. 553–80. [G: U.S.]

Wiggins, James B. Option Values under Stochastic Volatility: Theory and Empirical Estimates. *J. Finan. Econ.*, December 1987, *19*(2), pp. 351–72. [G: U.S.]

Wilson, G. Peter. The Incremental Information Content of the Accrual and Funds Components of Earnings after Controlling for Earnings. *Accounting Rev.*, April 1987, *62*(2), pp. 293–322. [G: U.S.]

Wilson, Jack W. and Jones, Charles P. A Comparison of Annual Common Stock Returns: 1871–1925 with 1926–85. *J. Bus.*, April 1987, *60*(2), pp. 239–58. [G: U.S.]

Witt, Harvey J.; Schroeder, Ted C. and Hayenga, Marvin L. Comparison of Analytical Approaches for Estimating Hedge Ratios for Agricultural Commodities. *J. Futures Markets*, April 1987, *7*(2), pp. 135–46. [G: U.S.]

Witt, Robert C. Death and Taxes: The Market for Flower Bonds: Discussion. *J. Finance*, July 1987, *42*(3), pp. 698–702. [G: U.S.]

Wolf, Avner S.; Castelino, Mark and Francis, Jack Clark. Hedging Mispriced Options. *J. Futures Markets*, April 1987, *7*(2), pp. 147–56. [G: U.S.]

Woo, Wing Thye. Some Evidence of Speculative Bubbles in the Foreign Exchange Markets. *J. Money, Credit, Banking*, November 1987, *19*(4), pp. 499–514. [G: U.S.]

Woodward, R. S. Interest Rate Arbitrage Using the Forwards and Futures Markets, 1977–85. *Appl. Econ.*, October 1987, *19*(10), pp. 1329–35. [G: OECD]

Yawitz, Jess B., et al. The Pricing and Duration of Floating Rate Bonds. *J. Portfol. Manage.*, Summer 1987, *13*(4), pp. 49–56. [G: U.S.]

Yitzhaki, Shlomo. The Relation between Return and Income. *Quart. J. Econ.*, February 1987, *102*(1), pp. 77–95. [G: U.S.]

Yli-Olli, Paavo and Virtanen, Ilkka. Predictability of Stock Returns in a Thin Security Market: Empirical Evidence with Data from Helsinki Stock Exchange 1975–1986. *Liiketaloudellinen Aikak.*, 1987, *36*(3), pp. 226–43. [G: Finland]

Zacharias, Thomas P., et al. A Producer-level Cross-hedge for Rough Rice Using Wheat Futures. *Southern J. Agr. Econ.*, December 1987, *19*(2), pp. 75–82. [G: U.S.]

Ziebart, David A. The Effects of Annual Accounting Data on Stock Returns and Trading Activity: A Causal Model Study. *J. Amer. Statist. Assoc.*, September 1987, *82*(399), pp. 733–38. [G: U.S.]

Ziebart, David A. and Kim, David H. An Examination of the Market Reactions Associated with SFAS No. 8 and SFAS No. 52. *Accounting Rev.*, April 1987, *62*(2), pp. 343–57. [G: U.S.]

Zivney, Terry L. and Thompson, Donald J., II. Relative Stock Prices and the Firm Size Effect.

J. Finan. Res., Summer 1987, *10*(2), pp. 99–110. [G: U.S.]

314 Financial Intermediaries

3140 Financial Intermediaries

Al-Jarhi, Mabid Ali Muhamed Mahmoud. The Relative Efficiency of Interest-Free Monetary Economies: The Fiat Money Case. *Khan, M. S. and Mirakhor, A., eds.*, 1987, *1981*, pp. 37–73.

Angell, Wayne D. Statement to the U.S. Senate Subcommitee on Consumer Affairs of the Committee on Banking, Housing, and Urban Affairs, February 5, 1987. *Fed. Res. Bull.*, April 1987, *73*(4), pp. 279–82. [G: U.S.]

Barth, James R., et al. The Thrift Industry's Rough Road Ahead. *Wilcox, J. A., ed.*, 1987, *1986*, pp. 150–55. [G: U.S.]

Basch, Donald L. Rivalry and Expense-Preference Behavior among Savings Banks: The Role of Deposit Rate Ceilings. *J. Econ. Bus.*, August 1987, *39*(3), pp. 225–38. [G: U.S.]

Belongia, Michael T. and Santoni, G. J. Hedging Interest Rate Risk with Financial Futures: Some Basic Principles. *Wilcox, J. A., ed.*, 1987, *1984*, pp. 47–57. [G: U.S.]

Black, Harold A. and Schweitzer, Robert L. The Effect of Common Bond on Credit Union Performance: The Case of Black-Controlled Credit Unions. *Rev. Black Polit. Econ.*, Spring 1987, *15*(4), pp. 89–98. [G: U.S.]

de Boissieu, Christian. Lessons from the French Experience as Compared with Some Other OECD Countries. *de Cecco, M., ed.*, 1987, pp. 212–28. [G: France; OECD]

Boleat, Mark. Building Societies: The New Supervisory Framework. *Nat. Westminster Bank Quart. Rev.*, August 1987, pp. 26–34. [G: U.K.]

Brewer, Elijah, III and Garcia, Gillian G. A Discriminant Analysis of Savings and Loan Accounting Profits, 1976–1981. *Lee, C. F., ed.*, 1987, pp. 205–44. [G: U.S.]

Brooks, Stephen. The State as Financier: A Comparison of the Caisse de dépôt et placement du Québec and Alberta Heritage Savings Trust Fund. *Can. Public Policy*, September 1987, *13*(3), pp. 318–29. [G: Canada]

Brumbaugh, R. Dan, Jr. and Carron, Andrew S. Thrift Industry Crisis: Causes and Solutions. *Brookings Pap. Econ. Act.*, 1987, (2), pp. 349–77. [G: U.S.]

Caranza, Cesare and Cottarelli, Carlo. Financial Innovation in Italy: A Lop-Sided Process. *de Cecco, M., ed.*, 1987, pp. 172–211. [G: Italy]

Chan, M. W. Luke and Mountain, Dean C. Technological Change and Economies of Scale in Canadian Financial Institutions: A Selection from Competing Hypotheses. *J. Econ. Bus.*, February 1987, *39*(1), pp. 57–66. [G: Canada]

Corrigan, E. Gerald. Keep Banking Apart. *Challenge*, Nov./Dec. 1987, *30*(5), pp. 28–35. [G: U.S.]

D'Arcy, Stephen P. and Lee, Keun Chang. Universal/Variable Life Insurance versus Similar Unbundled Investment Strategies. *J. Risk Ins.*, September 1987, *54*(3), pp. 452–77.
[G: U.S.]

Desai, Meghnad and Low, William. Measuring the Opportunity for Product Innovation. *de Cecco, M., ed.*, 1987, pp. 112–40. [G: U.S.]

Dudler, Hermann-Josef. Financial Innovation in Germany. *de Cecco, M., ed.*, 1987, pp. 158–71. [G: W. Germany]

Eisenberg, Meyer. The Current Status of the Regulation of Financial Services and Products in the United States: Developments and Trends. *de Cecco, M., ed.*, 1987, pp. 28–76.
[G: U.S.]

Ferris, Stephen P. and Chance, Don M. The Effect of 12b-1 Plans on Mutual Fund Expense Ratios: A Note. *J. Finance*, September 1987, *42*(4), pp. 1077–82. [G: U.S.]

Forsyth, John H. Financial Innovation in Britain. *de Cecco, M., ed.*, 1987, pp. 141–57.
[G: U.K.]

Francis, Jere R. and Reiter, Sara Ann. Determinants of Corporate Pension Funding Strategy. *J. Acc. Econ.*, April 1987, *9*(1), pp. 35–59.
[G: U.S.]

Fung, W. K. F. and Theobald, M. F. Taxes, Unequal Access, Public Debt and Corporate Financial Policy in the United Kingdom. *J. Banking Finance*, March 1987, *11*(1), pp. 65–78.
[G: U.K.]

Furlong, Frederick T. "Recapitalizing" the FSLIC. *Wilcox, J. A., ed.*, 1987, *1986*, pp. 156–58. [G: U.S.]

Goldfarb, David R. Hedging Interest Rate Risk in Banking. *J. Futures Markets*, February 1987, *7*(1), pp. 35–47.

Goldstein, Steven J.; McNulty, James E. and Verbrugge, James A. Scale Economies in the Savings and Loan Industry before Diversification. *J. Econ. Bus.*, August 1987, *39*(3), pp. 199–207. [G: U.S.]

González-Vega, Claudio and Zinser, James E. Regulated and Nonregulated Financial and Foreign Exchange Markets and Income Inequality in the Dominican Republic. *Connolly, M. and González-Vega, C., eds.*, 1987, pp. 195–216. [G: Dominican Republic]

Gooptu, Sudarshan and Lombra, Raymond. Aggregation across Heterogeneous Depository Institutions. *Financial Rev.*, November 1987, *22*(4), pp. 369–78. [G: U.S.]

Greenspan, Alan. Statement to the U.S. House Subcommittee on Telecommunications and Finance of the Committee on Energy and Commerce, October 5, 1987. *Fed. Res. Bull.*, December 1987, *73*(12), pp. 907–10. [G: U.S.]

Haberman, Gary. Capital Requirements of Commercial and Investment Banks: Contrasts in Regulation. *Fed. Res. Bank New York Quart. Rev.*, Autumn 1987, *12*(3), pp. 1–10.
[G: U.S.]

Hancock, Diana. Aggregation of Monetary Goods: A Production Model. *Barnett, W. A. and Sin-*

gleton, K. J., eds., 1987, pp. 200–218.
[G: U.S.]

Haraf, William S. Maintaining Financial Stability: Financial Strains and Public Policy. *Cagan, P., ed.*, 1987, pp. 181–208. [G: U.S.]

Harper, David A. and Karacaoglu, Girol. Financial Policy Reform in New Zealand. *Bollard, A. and Buckle, R., eds.*, 1987, pp. 206–35.
[G: New Zealand]

Hess, Alan C. Could Thrifts Be Profitable? Theoretical and Empirical Evidence. *Carnegie–Rochester Conf. Ser. Public Policy*, Spring 1987, *26*, pp. 223–81. [G: U.S.]

Hester, Donald D. Inflation and Intermediation by Depository Institutions. *de Cecco, M. and Fitoussi, J.-P., eds.*, 1987, pp. 163–81.
[G: U.S.]

Hester, Donald D. On the Empirical Detection of Financial Innovation. *de Cecco, M., ed.*, 1987, pp. 77–111. [G: U.S.]

Jaffee, Dwight M. Thrift Industry Crisis: Causes and Solutions: Comment. *Brookings Pap. Econ. Act.*, 1987, (2), pp. 378–81. [G: U.S.]

Joffrion, Theresa and Rose, Peter S. Savings and Loans' Response to Deregulation: Evidence from Multivariate Models and a National Survey. *Housing Finance Rev.*, Spring 1987, *6*(1), pp. 17–38. [G: U.S.]

Kane, Edward J. Dangers of Capital Forbearance: The Case of the FSLIC and "Zombie" S&Ls. *Contemp. Policy Issues*, January 1987, *5*(1), pp. 77–83. [G: U.S.]

Kane, Edward J. No Room for Weak Links in the Chain of Deposit-Insurance Reform. *J. Finan. Services Res.*, September 1987, *1*(1), pp. 77–111. [G: U.S.]

Kane, Edward J. Technological and Regulatory Forces in the Developing Fusion of Financial-Services Competition. *Wilcox, J. A., ed.*, 1987, *1984*, pp. 85–98. [G: U.S.]

Kaufman, George G. Could Thrifts Be Profitable? Theoretical and Empirical Evidence: Comment. *Carnegie–Rochester Conf. Ser. Public Policy*, Spring 1987, *26*, pp. 283–87.
[G: U.S.]

Litan, Robert E. Which Way for Congress? *Challenge*, Nov./Dec. 1987, *30*(5), pp. 36–43.
[G: U.S.]

Lockhart, Julie A.; Long, Michael S. and Sefcik, Stephan E. Regulatory Accounting Principles, Forbearance, and the Perpetuation of the Savings and Loan Industry. *Housing Finance Rev.*, Spring 1987, *6*(1), pp. 79–91. [G: U.S.]

Lown, Cara S. Money Market Deposit Accounts versus Money Market Mutual Funds. *Fed. Res. Bank Dallas Econ. Rev.*, November 1987, (11), pp. 29–38. [G: U.S.]

Martin, John D. and Keown, Arthur J. One-Bank Holding Company Formation and the 1970 Bank Holding Company Act Amendment: An Empirical Examination Allowing for Industry Group Effects. *J. Banking Finance*, June 1987, *11*(2), pp. 213–21. [G: U.S.]

Masulis, Ronald W. Changes in Ownership Structure: Conversions of Mutual Savings and Loans to Stock Charter. *J. Finan. Econ.*, March 1987, *18*(1), pp. 29–59. **[G: U.S.]**

Mester, Loretta J. A Multiproduct Cost Study of Savings and Loans. *J. Finance*, June 1987, *42*(2), pp. 423–45. **[G: U.S.]**

Mester, Loretta J. Multiple Market Contact between Savings and Loans: A Note. *J. Money, Credit, Banking*, November 1987, *19*(4), pp. 538–49. **[G: U.S.]**

Modigliani, Franco and Papademos, Lucas. Money, Credit and the Monetary Mechanism. *de Cecco, M. and Fitoussi, J.-P., eds.*, 1987, pp. 121–60.

Morgan, George Emir and Smith, Stephen D. Maturity Intermediation and Intertemporal Lending Policies of Financial Intermediaries. *J. Finance*, September 1987, *42*(4), pp. 1023–34.

Morgan, George Emir and Smith, Stephen D. The Role of Capital Adequacy Regulation in the Hedging Decisions of Financial Intermediaries. *J. Finan. Res.*, Spring 1987, *10*(1), pp. 33–46.

Neely, Walter P. and Rochester, David P. Operating Performance and Merger Benefits: The Savings and Loan Experience. *Financial Rev.*, February 1987, *22*(1), pp. 111–30. **[G: U.S.]**

Pantalone, Coleen C. and Platt, Marjorie B. Predicting Failure of Savings & Loan Associations. *Amer. Real Estate Urban Econ. Assoc. J.*, Summer 1987, *15*(2), pp. 46–64. **[G: U.S.]**

Pesando, James E. Discontinuities in Pension Benefit Formulas and the Spot Model of the Labor Market: Implications for Financial Economists. *Econ. Inquiry*, April 1987, *25*(2), pp. 215–38. **[G: U.S.]**

Poole, William. Thrift Industry Crisis: Causes and Solutions: Comment. *Brookings Pap. Econ. Act.*, 1987, (2), pp. 381–86. **[G: U.S.]**

Rhoades, Stephen A. The Effect of Nonbank Thrift Institutions on Commercial Bank Profit Performance in Local Markets. *Quart. Rev. Econ. Bus.*, Spring 1987, *27*(1), pp. 16–28. **[G: U.S.]**

Saunders, Anthony and Smirlock, Michael. Intra- and Interindustry Effects of Bank Securities Market Activities: The Case of Discount Brokerage. *J. Finan. Quant. Anal.*, December 1987, *22*(4), pp. 467–82. **[G: U.S.]**

Schwartz, Anna J. The Lender of Last Resort and the Federal Safety Net. *J. Finan. Services Res.*, September 1987, *1*(1), pp. 1–17. **[G: U.S.]**

Scott, Kenneth E. The Defective Design of Federal Deposit Insurance. *Contemp. Policy Issues*, January 1987, *5*(1), pp. 92–99. **[G: U.S.]**

Smith, Stephen D.; Gregory, Deborah Wright and Weiss, Kathleen A. A Note on Quantity versus Price Risk and the Theory of Financial Intermediation. *J. Finance*, December 1987, *42*(5), pp. 1377–83.

Starr, Ross M. On the Theoretical Foundations of Financial Intermediation and Secondary Financial Markets. *[Wallich, H. C.]*, 1987, pp. 53–60.

Storck, Ekkehard. Innovative Instrumente des

Euro-Kreditmarktes. (With English summary.) *Z. Betriebswirtshaft*, February 1987, *57*(2), pp. 176–88. **[G: W. Europe]**

Suzuki, Yoshio. Financial Innovation in Japan: Its Origins, Diffusion and Impacts. *de Cecco, M., ed.*, 1987, pp. 229–59. **[G: Japan]**

Tanigawa, Yasuhiko. On the Existence of Financial Intermediaries. *Econ. Stud. Quart.*, March 1987, *38*(1), pp. 61–75.

Thomson, James B. The Use of Market Information in Pricing Deposit Insurance. *J. Money, Credit, Banking*, November 1987, *19*(4), pp. 528–37. **[G: U.S.]**

Tobin, James. Financial Innovation and Deregulation in Perspective. *Tobin, J. (III)*, 1987, *1985*, pp. 255–64. **[G: U.S.]**

Tobin, James and Brainard, William C. Financial Intermediaries and the Effectiveness of Monetary Controls. *Tobin, J. (I)*, 1987, *1963*, pp. 283–321.

Volcker, Paul A. Statement to the U.S. Senate Committee on Banking, Housing, and Urban Affairs, January 21, 1987. *Fed. Res. Bull.*, March 1987, *73*(3), pp. 199–205. **[G: U.S.]**

Welker, Donald L. IPC or Total Deposits? There Is a Difference! *Fed. Res. Bank Richmond Econ. Rev.*, Mar./Apr. 1987, *73*(2), pp. 31–38. **[G: U.S.]**

White, Lawrence H. Privatization of Financial Sectors. *Hanke, S. H., ed.*, 1987, pp. 149–60.

Wojnilower, Albert M. Financial Change in the United States. *de Cecco, M., ed.*, 1987, pp. 10–27. **[G: U.S.]**

315 Credit to Business, Consumer, etc. (including mortgages)

3150 General

Allais, Maurice. The Credit Mechanism and Its Implications. *Feiwel, G. R., ed. (II)*, 1987, pp. 491–561.

Benveniste, Lawrence M. Incomplete Market Participation and the Optimal Exchange of Credit. *Prescott, E. C. and Wallace, N., eds.*, 1987, pp. 121–45.

Besanko, David and Thakor, Anjan V. Collateral and Rationing: Sorting Equilibria in Monopolistic and Competitive Credit Markets. *Int. Econ. Rev.*, October 1987, *28*(3), pp. 671–89.

Besanko, David and Thakor, Anjan V. Competitive Equilibrium in the Credit Market under Asymmetric Information. *J. Econ. Theory*, June 1987, *42*(1), pp. 167–82.

Bester, Helmut and Hellwig, Martin. Moral Hazard and Equilibrium Credit Rationing: An Overview of the Issues. *Bamberg, G. and Spremann, K., eds.*, 1987, pp. 135–66.

de Boissieu, Christian. Lessons from the French Experience as Compared with Some Other OECD Countries. *de Cecco, M., ed.*, 1987, pp. 212–28. **[G: France; OECD]**

Boot, Arnoud; Thakor, Anjan V. and Udell, Gregory F. Competition, Risk Neutrality and Loan Commitments. *J. Banking Finance*, September

1987, *11*(3), pp. 449–71.

Caranza, Cesare and Cottarelli, Carlo. Financial Innovation in Italy: A Lop-Sided Process. *de Cecco, M., ed.*, 1987, pp. 172–211. **[G: Italy]**

Chan, Yuk-Shee and Thakor, Anjan V. Collateral and Competitive Equilibria with Moral Hazard and Private Information. *J. Finance*, June 1987, *42*(2), pp. 345–63.

Day, John. Medieval Merchants and Financiers. *Day, J.*, 1987, pp. 162–84. **[G: Europe]**

Desai, Meghnad and Low, William. Measuring the Opportunity for Product Innovation. *de Cecco, M., ed.*, 1987, pp. 112–40. **[G: U.S.]**

Dudler, Hermann-Josef. Financial Innovation in Germany. *de Cecco, M., ed.*, 1987, pp. 158–71. **[G: W. Germany]**

Eisenberg, Meyer. The Current Status of the Regulation of Financial Services and Products in the United States: Developments and Trends. *de Cecco, M., ed.*, 1987, pp. 28–76. **[G: U.S.]**

Forsyth, John H. Financial Innovation in Britain. *de Cecco, M., ed.*, 1987, pp. 141–57. **[G: U.K.]**

Guntermann, Karl L. and Smith, Richard L. Derivation of Cost of Capital and Equity Rates from Market Data. *Amer. Real Estate Urban Econ. Assoc. J.*, Summer 1987, *15*(2), pp. 98–109. **[G: U.S.]**

Hester, Donald D. Inflation and Intermediation by Depository Institutions. *de Cecco, M. and Fitoussi, J.-P., eds.*, 1987, pp. 163–81. **[G: U.S.]**

Hester, Donald D. On the Empirical Detection of Financial Innovation. *de Cecco, M., ed.*, 1987, pp. 77–111. **[G: U.S.]**

Horvei, Tore, et al. Financial Markets in the Nordic Countries. *Vartia, P., et al.*, 1987, pp. 237–301. **[G: Denmark; Sweden; Finland; Norway]**

Jiang, Sidong and Xu, Xiaopo. The Financial "Two-Track System": Strengthen Credit and Open Up the Nonbank Market. *Reynolds, B. L.*, 1987, pp. 188–207. **[G: China]**

Kanatas, George. Commercial Paper, Bank Reserve Requirements, and the Informational Role of Loan Commitments. *J. Banking Finance*, September 1987, *11*(3), pp. 425–48.

Lewis, Mervyn K. Personal Financial Services in the United States: A Transatlantic Perspective. *Goodhart, C.; Currie, D. and Llewellyn, D. T., eds.*, 1987, pp. 54–77. **[G: U.S.; U.K.]**

Massad, Carlos and Zahler, Roberto. Another View of the Latin American Crisis: Domestic Debt. *CEPAL Rev.*, August 1987, (32), pp. 11–25. **[G: Latin America]**

Modigliani, Franco and Papademos, Lucas. Money, Credit and the Monetary Mechanism. *de Cecco, M. and Fitoussi, J.-P., eds.*, 1987, pp. 121–60.

Riley, John G. Credit Rationing: A Further Remark [Credit Rationing in Markets with Imperfect Information] [Incentives Effects of Terminations: Applications to the Credit and Labor Markets]. *Amer. Econ. Rev.*, March 1987, *77*(1), pp. 224–27.

Smith, Donald J. The Borrower's Choice between Fixed and Adjustable Rate Loan Contracts. *Amer. Real Estate Urban Econ. Assoc. J.*, Summer 1987, *15*(2), pp. 110–16.

Stiglitz, Joseph E. and Weiss, Andrew. Credit Rationing: Reply [Credit Rationing in Markets with Imperfect Information] [Incentives Effects of Terminations: Applications to the Credit and Labor Markets]. *Amer. Econ. Rev.*, March 1987, *77*(1), pp. 228–31.

Suzuki, Yoshio. Financial Innovation in Japan: Its Origins, Diffusion and Impacts. *de Cecco, M., ed.*, 1987, pp. 229–59. **[G: Japan]**

Tobin, James. Consumer Debt and Spending: Some Evidence from Analysis of a Survey. *Tobin, J. (II)*, 1987, pp. 217–45. **[G: U.S.]**

Townsend, Robert M. and Wallace, Neil. Circulating Private Debt: An Example with a Coordination Problem. *Prescott, E. C. and Wallace, N., eds.*, 1987, pp. 105–20.

Wunder, Heide. Finance in the 'Economy of Old Europe': The Example of Peasant Credit from the Late Middle Ages to the Thirty Years War. *Witt, P.-C., ed.*, 1987, pp. 19–47. **[G: Europe]**

3151 Consumer Finance

Avery, Robert B.; Elliehausen, Gregory E. and Kennickell, Arthur B. Changes in Consumer Installment Debt: Evidence Form the 1983 and 1986 Surveys of Consumer Finances. *Fed. Res. Bull.*, October 1987, *73*(10), pp. 761–78. **[G: U.S.]**

Canner, Glenn B. and Fergus, James T. The Economic Effects of Proposed Ceilings on Credit Card Interest Rates. *Fed. Res. Bull.*, January 1987, *73*(1), pp. 1–13. **[G: U.S.]**

Canner, Glenn B. and Fergus, James T. The Effects on Consumers and Creditors of Proposed Ceilings on Credit Card Interest Rates. *Fed. Res. Bull.*, October 1987, *73*(10), pp. 783–84. **[G: U.S.]**

Christelow, Dorothy B. Converging Household Debt Ratios of Four Industrial Countries. *Fed. Res. Bank New York Quart. Rev.*, Winter 1987-88, *12*(4), pp. 35–47. **[G: U.S.; Japan; Germany; U.K.]**

Lerman, Donald L. Perspectives on Household Portfolios, 1977–83. *Eastern Econ. J.*, October-December 1987, *13*(4), pp. 399–410. **[G: U.S.]**

Seger, Martha R. Statement to the U.S. House Subcommittee on Consumer Affairs and Coinage of the Committee on Banking, Finance and Urban Affairs, March 18, 1987. *Fed. Res. Bull.*, May 1987, *73*(5), pp. 338–41. **[G: U.S.]**

Seger, Martha R. Statement to the U.S. House Subcommittee on Consumer Affairs and Coinage of the Committee on Banking, Finance and Urban Affairs, October 6, 1987. *Fed. Res. Bull.*, December 1987, *73*(12), pp. 910–13. **[G: U.S.]**

Seger, Martha R. Statement to the U.S. Senate Subcommittee on Consumer Affairs of the Committee on Banking, Housing, and Urban

Affairs, April 21, 1987. *Fed. Res. Bull.*, June 1987, *73*(6), pp. 430–35. [G: U.S.]

3152 Mortgage Market

Alm, James and Follain, James R. Consumer Demand for Adjustable Rate Mortgages. *Housing Finance Rev.*, Spring 1987, *6*(1), pp. 1–16. [G: U.S.]

Anderson, Gary and Chiang, Raymond. Interest Rate Risk Hedging for Due-on-Sale Mortgages with Early Termination. *J. Finan. Res.*, Summer 1987, *10*(2), pp. 133–42. [G: U.S.]

Ang, James S.; Chiang, Raymond and Corgel, John B. Illustrations of Financing and Tax Transfers in Owner Financed Real Estate Sales. *J. Econ. Bus.*, November 1987, *39*(4), pp. 363–72. [G: U.S.]

Archer, Wayne R. and Nye, David J. An Insurance Approach to Risk Analysis of Debt Home Equity Conversion Programs. *Amer. Real Estate Urban Econ. Assoc. J.*, Fall 1987, *15*(3), pp. 185–98. [G: U.S.]

Benjamin, John D. and Sirmans, C. F. Who Benefits from Mortgage Revenue Bonds? *Nat. Tax J.*, March 1987, *40*(1), pp. 115–20. [G: U.S.]

Brick, John R. A Primer on Mortgage-Backed Securities. *Wilcox, J. A., ed.*, 1987, *1984*, pp. 25–33. [G: U.S.]

Christelow, Dorothy B. Converging Household Debt Ratios of Four Industrial Countries. *Fed. Res. Bank New York Quart. Rev.*, Winter 1987-88, *12*(4), pp. 35–47. [G: U.S.; Japan; Germany; U.K.]

Clauretie, Terrence M. The Impact of Interstate Foreclosure Cost Differences and the Value of Mortgages on Default Rates. *Amer. Real Estate Urban Econ. Assoc. J.*, Fall 1987, *15*(3), pp. 152–67. [G: U.S.]

Corgel, John B. and Gay, Gerald D. Local Economic Base, Geographic Diversification, and Risk Management of Mortgage Portfolios. *Amer. Real Estate Urban Econ. Assoc. J.*, Fall 1987, *15*(3), pp. 256–67. [G: U.S.]

Dale-Johnson, David; Dietrich, J. Kimball and Langetieg, Terence C. A Legal and Economic Analysis of the Due-on-Sale Clause: A Retrospective Examination. *Jaffe, A. J., ed.*, 1987, pp. 105–27. [G: U.S.]

DeSarbo, Wayne S., et al. A Friction Model for Describing and Forecasting Price Changes. *Marketing Sci.*, Fall 1987, *6*(4), pp. 299–319. [G: U.S.]

Dhillon, Upinder S.; Shilling, James D. and Sirmans, C. F. Choosing between Fixed and Adjustable Rate Mortgages: A Note. *J. Money, Credit, Banking*, May 1987, *19*(2), pp. 260–67. [G: U.S.]

Durning, Dan. The Efficiency and Distribution of Mortgage Revenue Bond Subsidies: The Effects of Behavioral Responses. *J. Policy Anal. Manage.*, Fall 1987, *7*(1), pp. 74–93. [G: U.S.]

Eichengreen, Barry. Agricultural Mortgages in the Populist Era: Reply. *J. Econ. Hist.*, September 1987, *47*(3), pp. 757–60. [G: U.S.]

Gabriel, Stuart A. Housing and Mortgage Markets: The Post-1982 Expansion. *Fed. Res. Bull.*, December 1987, *73*(12), pp. 893–903. [G: U.S.]

Hartzell, David J. and Fernald, Julia D. A Recent Innovation: Creating High-Yielding Synthetic Commercial Mortgage-Backed Floating Rate Bonds through Interest Rate Swaps. *Housing Finance Rev.*, Spring 1987, *6*(1), pp. 73–77. [G: U.S.]

Hendershott, Patric H. and Van Order, Robert. Pricing Mortgages: An Interpretation of the Models and Results. *J. Finan. Services Res.*, September 1987, *1*(1), pp. 19–55.

Jones, Colin and Maclennan, Duncan. Building Societies and Credit Rationing: An Empirical Examination of Redlining. *Urban Stud.*, June 1987, *24*(3), pp. 205–16. [G: Scotland]

Kau, James B. and Keenan, Donald. Taxes, Points and Rationality in the Mortgage Market. *Amer. Real Estate Urban Econ. Assoc. J.*, Fall 1987, *15*(3), pp. 168–84. [G: U.S.]

Kau, James B., et al. The Valuation and Securitization of Commercial and Multifamily Mortgages. *J. Banking Finance*, September 1987, *11*(3), pp. 525–46.

Kent, Richard J. Dynamic Credit Rationing in the Home Mortgage Market. *Amer. Real Estate Urban Econ. Assoc. J.*, Winter 1987, *15*(4), pp. 300–320. [G: U.S.]

Kim, Taewon. A Contingent Claims Analysis of Price Level-Adjusted Mortgages. *Amer. Real Estate Urban Econ. Assoc. J.*, Fall 1987, *15*(3), pp. 117–31.

Leeds, Eva Marikova. Why Are Mortgage Rates So Uniform? *Atlantic Econ. J.*, July 1987, *15*(2), pp. 33–41.

Manchester, Joyce. Mortgage Contracts in a General Equilibrium Model when There Are Inflation Shocks. *J. Macroecon.*, Summer 1987, *9*(3), pp. 327–49.

Moore, James S. An Investigation of the Major Influences of Residential Liquidity: A Multivariate Approach. *Amer. Real Estate Urban Econ. Assoc. J.*, Spring 1987, *15*(1), pp. 684–703. [G: U.S.]

Mulherin, J. Harold and Muller, Walter J., III. Volatile Interest Rates and the Divergence of Incentives in Mortgage Contracts. *J. Law, Econ., Organ.*, Spring 1987, *3*(1), pp. 99–115.

Park, Hun Y. and Bera, Anil K. Interest-Rate Volatility, Basis Risk and Heteroscedasticity in Hedging Mortgages. *Amer. Real Estate Urban Econ. Assoc. J.*, Summer 1987, *15*(2), pp. 79–97. [G: U.S.]

Quigley, John M. Interest Rate Variations, Mortgage Prepayments and Household Mobility. *Rev. Econ. Statist.*, November 1987, *69*(4), pp. 636–43. [G: U.S.]

Rosen, Kenneth T., et al. Housing and Mortgage Market Review. *Housing Finance Rev.*, Spring 1987, *6*(1), pp. 41–72. [G: U.S.]

Sa-Aadu, Jarjisu. Consumer Welfare under the Adjustable-Rate Mortgage: Some Empirical Evidence. *Amer. Real Estate Urban Econ. As-*

soc. J., Fall 1987, *15*(3), pp. 132–51.
[G: U.S.]

Shilling, James D. and Sirmans, C. F. Pricing Fast-Pay Mortgages: Some Simulation Results. *J. Finan. Res.*, Spring 1987, *10*(1), pp. 25–32.
[G: U.S.]

Sirmans, G. Stacy; Sirmans, C. F. and Smith, Stanley D. Creative Financing, House Prices, and Property Tax Inequities. *Urban Stud.*, October 1987, *24*(5), pp. 409–15. [G: U.S.]

Snowden, Kenneth A. Mortgage Rates and American Capital Market Development in the Late Nineteenth Century. *J. Econ. Hist.*, September 1987, *47*(3), pp. 771–91. [G: U.S.]

Vaghari, Jila. Has Removal of the Mortgage Ceiling Rates Helped the Home-Buyers? *Indian Econ. J.*, Oct.-Dec. 1987, *35*(2), pp. 126–31.
[G: U.S.]

Weinrobe, Maurice. An Analysis of Home Equity Conversion in the RAM Program. *Amer. Real Estate Urban Econ. Assoc. J.*, Summer 1987, *15*(2), pp. 65–78. [G: U.S.]

3153 Business Credit

Artus, Patrick. Politique monétaire, fonctionnement du marché du crédit et innovations financières. (With English summary.) *Revue Écon. Polit.*, Jan.-Feb. 1987, *97*(1), pp. 27–50.

Bertoni, Albeto. How a Major Banking Group Can Deal with Structural Changes (Real and Financial) in Companies. *Rev. Econ. Cond. Italy*, Sept.-Dec. 1987, (3), pp. 455–78. [G: Italy]

Bester, Helmut. The Role of Collateral in Credit Markets with Imperfect Information. *Europ. Econ. Rev.*, June 1987, *31*(4), pp. 887–99.

Browne, F. X. Sluggish Quantity Adjustment in a Non-clearing Market—A Disequilibrium Econometric Application to the Loan Market. *J. Appl. Econometrics*, October 1987, *2*(4), pp. 335–49. [G: Ireland]

Carrizosa, Mauricio and Urdinola, Antonio. Private Internal Debt in Colombia, 1970–1985. *CEPAL Rev.*, August 1987, (32), pp. 27–53.
[G: Colombia]

Deshons, Michel and Freixas, Xavier. Le rôle de la garantie dans le contrat de prêt bancaire. (The Role of Collateral in the Bank's Debt Contract. With English summary.) *Finance*, June 1987, *8*(1), pp. 7–32.

Felgran, Steven D. Interest Rate Swaps: Use, Risk, and Prices. *New Eng. Econ. Rev.*, Nov./Dec. 1987, pp. 22–32. [G: U.S.]

Ham, John C. and Melnik, Arie. Loan Demand: An Empirical Analysis Using Micro Data. *Rev. Econ. Statist.*, November 1987, *69*(4), pp. 704–09. [G: U.S.]

James, Christopher M. Off-Balance Sheet Banking. *Fed. Res. Bank San Francisco Econ. Rev.*, Fall 1987, (4), pp. 21–36. [G: U.S.]

James, Christopher M. Some Evidence on the Uniqueness of Bank Loans. *J. Finan. Econ.*, December 1987, *19*(2), pp. 217–35.
[G: U.S.]

Kareken, John H. The Emergence and Regulation of Contingent Commitment Banking. *J. Bank-*

ing Finance, September 1987, *11*(3), pp. 359–77. [G: U.S.]

Kim, Kyung Moo. A Short-run Variable Adjustment Model for Bank Loans. *J. Econ. Devel.*, December 1987, *12*(2), pp. 73–87. [G: U.S.]

Kugler, Peter. Credit Rationing and the Adjustment of the Loan Rate: An Empirical Investigation. *J. Macroecon.*, Fall 1987, *9*(4), pp. 505–25. [G: U.K.; U.S.; W. Germany; Switzerland]

Mengle, David L.; Humphrey, David B. and Summers, Bruce J. Intraday Credit: Risk, Value, and Pricing. *Fed. Res. Bank Richmond Econ. Rev.*, Jan./Feb. 1987, *73*(1), pp. 3–14.
[G: U.S.]

Ngend-Ngend, Sam. Un outil de selection des credits-clients: l'analyse en composantes principales. (Accounts Receivable Policy Selection: The Factor Analysis Method. With English summary.) *Écon. Soc.*, December 1987, *21*(12), pp. 57–82.

Odedokun, Matthew O. Fungibility and Effectiveness of Selective Credit Policies: Evidence from Nigerian Data. *Devel. Econ.*, September 1987, *25*(3), pp. 234–48. [G: Nigeria]

Smith, Janet Kiholm. Trade Credit and Informational Asymmetry. *J. Finance*, September 1987, *42*(4), pp. 863–72.

Thakor, Anjan V. and Udell, Gregory F. An Economic Rationale for the Pricing Structure of Bank Loan Commitments. *J. Banking Finance*, June 1987, *11*(2), pp. 271–89.

Webb, Richard. Internal Debt and Financial Adjustment in Peru. *CEPAL Rev.*, August 1987, (32), pp. 55–74. [G: Peru]

320 FISCAL THEORY AND POLICY; PUBLIC FINANCE

3200 General

Ackley, Gardner. The Size and Economic Role of Government. *[Marrama, V.], Vol. 1*, 1987, pp. 387–407. [G: U.S.; Japan; W. Germany; France; U.K.]

Afxentiou, Panayiotis C. Displacement Effect: An Econometric Test for Cyprus. *Greek Econ. Rev.*, 1987, *9*(1), pp. 113–30. [G: Cyprus]

Beeton, D. J. On the Size of the Public Sector. *Appl. Econ.*, July 1987, *19*(7), pp. 927–36.
[G: U.K.]

Bélanger, Gérard. L'univers du secteur public et les règles comptables utilisées dans les systèmes statistiques canadiens. (The Public Sector Universe and the Accounting Rules Used in the Canadian Statistical Systems. With English summary.) *L'Actual. Econ.*, December 1987, *63*(4), pp. 402–23. [G: Canada]

Bish, Robert L. Federalism: A Market Economics Perspective. *Cato J.*, Fall 1987, *7*(2), pp. 377–96.

Bordo, Michael D. and Landau, Daniel. The Growth of Government: A Protection Explanation. *Public Choice*, 1987, *53*(2), pp. 167–74.
[G: U.S.]

Buchanan, James M. The Moral Dimension of Debt Financing. *Fink, R. H. and High, J. C., eds.*, 1987, *1985*, pp. 102–07.

Dorn, James A. Government, the Economy, and the Constitution: Introduction. *Cato J.*, Fall 1987, *7*(2), pp. 283–303. **[G: U.S.]**

Faulhaber, Gerald R. The Role of Government in a Mixed Economy: Reprise. *J. Policy Anal. Manage.*, Summer 1987, *6*(4), pp. 557–61.

Gemmell, Norman. A Model of Unbalanced Growth: The Market versus the Non-market Sector of the Economy. *Oxford Econ. Pap.*, June 1987, *39*(2), pp. 253–67.

Grémion, Catherine. Decentralization in France: A Historical Perspective. *Ross, G.; Hoffmann, S. and Malzacher, S., eds.*, 1987, pp. 237–47. **[G: France]**

Harbeson, John W. Grass-roots Development and Development Administration in East Africa. *Picard, L. A. and Zariski, R., eds.*, 1987, pp. 196–207. **[G: E. Africa]**

Ho, Yin-Ping. Endogenous Government Expenditure: A Test of Wagner's Hypothesis for Hong Kong. *Int. Econ. J.*, Autumn 1987, *1*(3), pp. 31–47. **[G: Hong Kong]**

Hughes, Gordon A. Fiscal Federalism in the UK. *Oxford Rev. Econ. Policy*, Summer 1987, *3*(2), pp. 1–23. **[G: U.K.]**

Jackson, P. M. Public Expenditure: Trends and Prospects: Comment. *Levitt, M. S., ed.*, 1987, pp. 23–27. **[G: U.K.]**

King, Victor E. The African Public Services: Problems and Challenges. *Soc. Econ. Stud.*, June 1987, *36*(2), pp. 207–15. **[G: Africa]**

Kosai, Yutaka. The Political Economy of Japan: The Politics of Economic Management. *Yamamura, K. and Yasuba, Y., eds.*, 1987, pp. 555–92. **[G: Japan]**

Kunreuther, Howard. Roles of Government in a Mixed Economy: Comment. *J. Policy Anal. Manage.*, Summer 1987, *6*(4), pp. 562–66.

Leonard, David K. The Political Realities of African Management. *World Devel.*, July 1987, *15*(7), pp. 899–910. **[G: Africa]**

Levitt, M. S. and Joyce, Michael. Public Expenditure: Trends and Prospects. *Levitt, M. S., ed.*, 1987, pp. 6–23. **[G: U.K.]**

Meiners, Roger E. Economic Considerations in History: Theory and a Little Practice. *Radnitzky, G. and Bernholz, P., eds.*, 1987, pp. 79–103.

Mény, Yves. The Socialist Decentralization. *Ross, G.; Hoffmann, S. and Malzacher, S., eds.*, 1987, pp. 248–62. **[G: France]**

Meyer, Peter B. and Fitzgerald, Joan. Political Cohesion and Local Economic Control: An Analytical Framework and Pennsylvania Evidence. *Picard, L. A. and Zariski, R., eds.*, 1987, pp. 178–95. **[G: U.S.]**

Muramatsu, Michio and Krauss, Ellis S. The Political Economy of Japan: The Conservative Policy Line and the Development of Patterned Pluralism. *Yamamura, K. and Yasuba, Y., eds.*, 1987, pp. 516–54. **[G: Japan]**

Nelson, Richard R. Roles of Government in a Mixed Economy. *J. Policy Anal. Manage.*,

Summer 1987, *6*(4), pp. 541–57.

Rasmussen, David W. Federalism from a Market Perspective. *Cato J.*, Fall 1987, *7*(2), pp. 397–402.

Renaud, Paul S. A. and van Winden, Frans A. A. M. Tax Rate and Government Expenditure. *Kyklos*, 1987, *40*(3), pp. 349–67. **[G: Netherlands]**

Salmon, Pierre. Decentralisation as an Incentive Scheme. *Oxford Rev. Econ. Policy*, Summer 1987, *3*(2), pp. 24–43. **[G: France]**

Sbragia, Alberta M. Public-Sector Politics, Capital Markets, and Economic Development: Public Investment in Great Britain and the United States. *Picard, L. A. and Zariski, R., eds.*, 1987, pp. 161–77. **[G: U.K.; U.S.]**

Stroup, Richard L. Reflections on Freedom, Fairness, and the Constitution. *Cato J.*, Fall 1987, *7*(2), pp. 403–11.

Tobin, James. Who Is Crowding Out What? *Tobin, J. (III)*, 1987, *1975*, pp. 215–17. **[G: U.S.]**

321 Fiscal Theory and Policy

3210 Fiscal Theory and Policy

Anand, Sudhir and Nalebuff, Barry. Issues in the Application of Cost–Benefit Analysis to Energy Projects in Developing Countries. *Sinclair, P. J. N., ed.*, 1987, pp. 190–222. **[G: LDCs]**

Atkinson, Anthony B. James M. Buchanan's Contributions to Economics. *Scand. J. Econ.*, 1987, *89*(1), pp. 5–15.

Baccouche, Mounir. L'existence du phénomène fiscal dans les régimes de type soviétique. (The Existence of the Fiscal Phenomenon in Soviet Type Systems. With English summary.) *Public Finance*, 1987, *42*(3), pp. 415–30.

Bell, Clive and Devarajan, Shantayanan. Intertemporally Consistent Shadow Prices in an Open Economy: Estimates for Cyprus. *J. Public Econ.*, April 1987, *32*(3), pp. 263–85. **[G: Cyprus]**

Biger, Nahum and Kuhn, Tillo E. Precision Assessment of the Economic Impact of Public Projects: An Analysis of the Expenditures. *Int. J. Transport Econ.*, October 1987, *14*(3), pp. 223–38.

Boettke, Peter and Ellig, Jerome. The Business of Government and Government as a Business. *Fink, R. H. and High, J. C., eds.*, 1987, pp. 272–86. **[G: U.S.]**

Bosworth, Barry P. and Lawrence, Robert Z. Economic Goals and the Policy Mix. *Bosworth, B. P. and Rivlin, A. M., eds.*, 1987, pp. 97–124. **[G: Sweden]**

Brems, Hans. En disputats om finanspolitiske ideer i Danmark 1930–1945. (With English summary.) *Nationaløkon. Tidsskr.*, 1987, *125*(3), pp. 287–98. **[G: Denmark]**

Brown, Stephen P. A. The Fairness of Discounting: A Majority Rule Approach. *Public Choice*, October 1987, *55*(3), pp. 215–26.

Buchanan, James M. The Constitution of Economic Policy. *Buchanan, J. M. (II)*, 1987, pp. 303–14.

Buchanan, James M. The Constitution of Economic Policy. *Amer. Econ. Rev.*, June 1987, 77(3), pp. 243–50.

Buchanan, James M. The Pure Theory of Government Finance: A Suggested Approach. *Buchanan, J. M. (I)*, 1987, *1949*, pp. 101–12.

Buchanan, James M. and Lee, Dwight R. Politics, Time, and the Laffer Curve. *Buchanan, J. M. (II)*, 1987, *1982*, pp. 409–13.

Buffie, Edward F. Shadow Prices and Substitution in Trade Distorted Economies. *J. Public Econ.*, November 1987, 34(2), pp. 211–42.

Coursey, Don L. Markets and the Measurement of Value. *Public Choice*, October 1987, 55(3), pp. 291–97.

Coverdale, A. G. and Healey, J. M. Project Appraisal and Project Aid: A Decade of Experience in Rural Development. *J. Agr. Econ.*, January 1987, 38(1), pp. 99–105. [G: Africa]

Dinwiddy, Caroline L. and Teal, Francis J. Project Appraisal and Foreign Exchange Constraints: A Comment. *Econ. J.*, June 1987, 97(386), pp. 479–86.

Donaldson, Graham. Community Participation in Northern Pakistan. *Finance Develop.*, December 1987, 24(4), pp. 23–25. [G: Pakistan]

Findlay, Ronald and Wilson, John Douglas. The Political Economy of Leviathan. *Razin, A. and Sadka, E., eds.*, 1987, pp. 289–304.

Flanders, M. June. The Political Economy of Leviathan: Comments. *Razin, A. and Sadka, E., eds.*, 1987, pp. 305–06.

Freixas, Xavier. L'effet d'irréversibilité dans le choix de grands projets. (The Irreversibility Effect in the Choice among Large Projects. With English summary.) *Revue Écon.*, January 1987, 38(1), pp. 149–55.

Gan, Khuan-Poh and Tower, Edward. A General Equilibrium Cost–Benefit Approach to Policy Reform and Project Evaluation in Malaysia. *Singapore Econ. Rev.*, April 1987, 32(1), pp. 46–61. [G: Malaysia]

Gregory, Robin and Furby, Lita. Auctions, Experiments and Contingent Valuation. *Public Choice*, October 1987, 55(3), pp. 273–89.

Guesnerie, Roger and Penz, Ph. L'évaluation des effets macroéconomiques des projets: une introduction critique. (Evaluating "Macroeconomic Effects" of Projects: A Critical Introduction. With English summary.) *Écon. Soc.*, April 1987, 21(4), pp. 19–44.

Hewett, Roger S. Public Finance, Public Economics, and Public Choice: A Survey of Undergraduate Textbooks. *J. Econ. Educ.*, Fall 1987, 18(4), pp. 425–35. [G: U.S.]

Howe, Charles W. Project Benefits and Costs from National and Regional Viewpoints: Methodological Issues and Case Study of the Colorado–Big Thompson Project. *Natural Res. J.*, Winter 1987, 27(1), pp. 5–20. [G: U.S.]

Ihori, Toshihiro. The Size of Government Spending and the Private Sector's Evaluation. *J. Japanese Int. Economies*, March 1987, 1(1), pp. 82–96. [G: Japan]

Irwin, Alan. Technical Expertise and Risk Conflict: An Institutional Study of the British Compulsory Seat Belt Debate. *Policy Sci.*, 1987, 20(4), pp. 339–64. [G: U.K.]

Kanemoto, Yoshitsugu. Asymmetric Information in the Credit Market and Discount Rates for Public Investment. *J. Public Econ.*, December 1987, 34(3), pp. 291–309.

King, Ronald F. The Politics of Denial: The Use of Funding Penalties as an Implementation Device for Social Policy. *Policy Sci.*, 1987, 20(4), pp. 307–37. [G: U.S.]

Mullins, D. Supporting Measures to Cost–Benefit Analysis in Project Evaluation in the Public Sector—An Application of Input–Output Analysis. *J. Stud. Econ. Econometrics*, April 1987, 11(1), pp. 35–64. [G: S. Africa]

Musgrave, Richard A. Fifty Years of Public Finance. *Roskamp, K. W., ed.*, 1987, pp. 19–50.

Nelson, Michael A. Searching for Leviathan: Comment and Extension. *Amer. Econ. Rev.*, March 1987, 77(1), pp. 198–204.

Nentjes, Andries and Zuidema, Thijs. A Determination of the Opportunity Costs of Government Projects: A Neo-classical versus a Keynesian Approach. *Public Finance*, 1987, 42(1), pp. 119–36.

Nuti, Domenico Mario. Economic and Financial Evaluation of Investment Projects: General Principles and E.C. Procedures. *[Marrama, V.], Vol. 1*, 1987, pp. 457–78.

Papps, Ivy. Techniques of Project Appraisal. *Gemmell, N., ed.*, 1987, pp. 307–38.

Paul, Samuel. Community Participation in World Bank Projects. *Finance Develop.*, December 1987, 24(4), pp. 20–23. [G: LDCs]

Smith, Alasdair. Shadow Price Calculations in Distorted Economies. *Scand. J. Econ.*, 1987, 89(3), pp. 287–302.

Starrett, David A. *Production and Capital:* Kenneth Arrow's Contribution in Perspective—A Review Article. *J. Econ. Lit.*, March 1987, 25(1), pp. 92–102.

Tower, Edward and Pursell, Garry G. On Shadow Pricing Labour and Foreign Exchange. *Oxford Econ. Pap.*, June 1987, 39(2), pp. 318–32.

Weiss, John. Some Comments on Estimating Economic Parameters for Jamaica. *Industry Devel.*, 1987, (21), pp. 75–98. [G: Jamaica]

Wergeland, Tor. Shadow Price Calculations in Distorted Economies: Comment. *Scand. J. Econ.*, 1987, 89(3), pp. 303–04.

Zuidema, Thijs. Cost–Benefit Analysis in a Situation of Unemployment: Calculating the Decline in Unemployment as a Result of the Realization of a Government Project. *Public Finance Quart.*, January 1987, 15(1), pp. 105–15.

3212 Fiscal Theory; Empirical Studies Illustrating Fiscal Theory

Abel, Andrew B. Anticipated Tax Changes and the Timing of Investment: Comment. *Feld-*

stein, M., ed. (I), 1987, pp. 196–200.
[G: U.S.]

Abel, Andrew B. Operative Gift and Bequest Motives. *Amer. Econ. Rev.,* December 1987, 77(5), pp. 1037–47.

Abel, Andrew B. Optimal Monetary Growth. *J. Monet. Econ.,* May 1987, 19(3), pp. 437–50.

Adams, Roy D. and McCormick, Ken. Private Goods, Club Goods, and Public Goods as a Continuum. *Rev. Soc. Econ.,* October 1987, 45(2), pp. 192–99.

Ahmed, Shaghil. Government Spending, the Balance of Trade and the Terms of Trade in British History. *J. Monet. Econ.,* September 1987, 20(2), pp. 195–220. [G: U.K.]

Aivazian, Varouj A. and Turnbull, Stuart M. Taxation and Capital Structure: A Selected Review. *Mintz, J. M. and Purvis, D. D., eds.,* 1987, pp. 230–62.

Aiyagari, S. Rao. Intergenerational Linkages and Government Budget Policies. *Fed. Res. Bank Minn. Rev.,* Spring 1987, 11(2), pp. 14–23.

Alesina, Alberto and Tabellini, Guido. Rules and Discretion with Noncoordinated Monetary and Fiscal Policies. *Econ. Inquiry,* October 1987, 25(4), pp. 619–30.

Allen, Stephen P. Taxes, Redistribution, and the Minimum Wage: A Theoretical Analysis. *Quart. J. Econ.,* August 1987, 102(3), pp. 477–89.

Alworth, Julian S. Taxation and the Cost of Capital: A Comparison of Six EC Countries. *Cnossen, S., ed.,* 1987, pp. 253–83. [G: EEC]

Apostolakis, Bobby E. The Subsidy Incidence on Industrialization. *Rivista Int. Sci. Econ. Com.,* April 1987, 34(4), pp. 291–307.

Appelbaum, Elie and Katz, Eliakim. Asymmetric Taxation and the Theory of the Competitive Firm under Uncertainty. *Can. J. Econ.,* May 1987, 20(2), pp. 357–69.

Artana, Daniel. Incentivos fiscales a la inversión industrial. (Fiscal Incentives to the Industrial Investment. With English summary.) *Económica (La Plata),* January-June 1987, 33(1), pp. 3–38. [G: Argentina]

Artis, M. J. Deficit Financing: Keynes, the Keynesians and the New Approach, with Special Reference to the UK. *Boskin, M. J.; Fleming, J. S. and Gorini, S., eds.,* 1987, pp. 234–51. [G: U.K.]

Atkinson, Anthony B. The Collected Papers of Richard A. Musgrave: A Review Article. *J. Public Econ.,* August 1987, 33(3), pp. 389–98.

Auerbach, Alan J. The Theory and Measurement of Effective Tax Rates: Comment. *Mintz, J. M. and Purvis, D. D., eds.,* 1987, pp. 99–101.

Auerbach, Alan J. Weighted-Average Discount Rates in Public Expenditure Analysis: A Generalization. *[Harberger, A.],* 1987, pp. 40–60.

Auerbach, Alan J. and Hines, James R., Jr. Anticipated Tax Changes and the Timing of Investment. *Feldstein, M., ed. (II),* 1987, pp. 85–87. [G: U.S.]

Auerbach, Alan J. and Hines, James R., Jr. Anticipated Tax Changes and the Timing of Investment. *Feldstein, M., ed. (I),* 1987, pp. 163–96. [G: U.S.]

Auerbach, Alan J. and Kotlikoff, Laurence J. Evaluating Fiscal Policy with a Dynamic Simulation Model. *Amer. Econ. Rev.,* May 1987, 77(2), pp. 49–55.

Auerbach, Alan J. and Poterba, James M. Tax-Loss Carryforwards and Corporate Tax Incentives. *Feldstein, M., ed. (II),* 1987, pp. 89–92. [G: U.S.]

Aumann, Robert J.; Kurz, Mordecai and Neyman, Abraham. Power and Public Goods. *J. Econ. Theory,* June 1987, 42(1), pp. 108–27.

Backhaus, Jürgen; Holcombe, Randall G. and Zardkoohi, Asghar. Public Investment and Its Effects on the Burden of the Public Debt. *Southern Econ. J.,* July 1987, 54(1), pp. 145–58. [G: U.S.]

Bagella, Michele. Debt Neutrality and Fiscal Illusion: Theoretical Underpinnings and Empirical Studies: A Comment. *Boskin, M. J.; Fleming, J. S. and Gorini, S., eds.,* 1987, pp. 287–97. [G: U.S.]

Baker, Wayne E. What Is Money? A Social Structural Interpretation. *Mizruchi, M. S. and Schwartz, M., eds.,* 1987, pp. 109–44. [G: U.S.]

Baldani, Jeffrey P. and Michl, Thomas R. A Balanced Budget Multiplier for Interest Payments. *J. Post Keynesian Econ.,* Spring 1987, 9(3), pp. 424–39.

Baldry, Jonathan C. Income Tax Evasion and the Tax Schedule: Some Experimental Results. *Public Finance,* 1987, 42(3), pp. 357–83.

Ballard, Charles L.; Scholz, John Karl and Shoven, John B. The Value-Added Tax: A General Equilibrium Look at Its Efficiency and Incidence. *Feldstein, M., ed. (II),* 1987, pp. 105–07. [G: U.S.]

Ballard, Charles L. and Shoven, John B. The Value-Added Tax: The Efficiency Cost of Achieving Progressivity by Using Exemptions. *[Harberger, A.],* 1987, pp. 109–29.

Ballentine, J. Gregory. The Impact of Fundamental Tax Reform on the Allocation of Resources: Comment. *Feldstein, M., ed. (I),* 1987, pp. 437–43. [G: U.S.]

Barnett, Richard R. and Bone, John. A Note on Fiscal Preferences. *Scot. J. Polit. Econ.,* August 1987, 34(3), pp. 285–90.

Barro, Robert J. The Economic Effects of Budget Deficits and Government Spending: Introduction. *J. Monet. Econ.,* September 1987, 20(2), pp. 191–93.

Barry, Frank G. A Note on the Employment Effects of Investment Subsidies. *Econ. Soc. Rev.,* July 1987, 18(4), pp. 307–14.

Barry, Frank G. Fiscal Policy in a Small Open Economy: An Integration of the Short-run, Heckscher–Ohlin and Capital Accumulation Models. *J. Int. Econ.,* February 1987, 22(1/2), pp. 103–21.

Basu, Kaushik. Disneyland Monopoly, Interlinkage and Usurious Interest Rates. *J. Public Econ.,* October 1987, 34(1), pp. 1–17.

Batina, Raymond G. The Consumption Tax in

the Presence of Altruistic Cash and Human Capital Bequests with Endogenous Fertility Decisions. *J. Public Econ.*, December 1987, 34(3), pp. 329–54.

Beck, John H. User Charges as a Delegation Mechanism: Comment. *Nat. Tax J.*, June 1987, 40(2), pp. 275–78.

Becketti, Sean and Haltiwanger, John. Limited Countercyclical Policies: An Exploratory Study. *J. Public Econ.*, December 1987, 34(3), pp. 311–28. **[G: U.S.]**

Beenstock, Michael. Budget Lines and Labour Supply Incentives. *Beenstock, M., et al.*, 1987, pp. 1–24. **[G: U.K.]**

Behrman, Jere R. and Craig, Steven G. The Distribution of Public Services: An Exploration of Local Governmental Preferences. *Amer. Econ. Rev.*, March 1987, 77(1), pp. 37–49. **[G: U.S.]**

Bennett, Jeffrey W. Strategic Behaviour: Some Experimental Evidence. *J. Public Econ.*, April 1987, 32(3), pp. 355–68. **[G: Australia]**

Bennett, John. The Second-Best Lump-Sum Taxation of Observable Characteristics. *Public Finance*, 1987, 42(2), pp. 227–35.

Bernheim, B. Douglas. Ricardian Equivalence: An Evaluation of Theory and Evidence. *Fischer, S., ed.*, 1987, pp. 263–304.

Bernstein, Jeffrey I. and Nadiri, M. Ishaq. Corporate Taxes and Incentives and the Structure of Production: A Selected Survey. *Mintz, J. M. and Purvis, D. D., eds.*, 1987, pp. 178–208.

Bertocchi, Graziella. Il debito pubblico in un modello generazionale. (Government Debt in an Overlapping Generations Model. With English summary.) *Ricerche Econ.*, Jan.-Mar. 1987, 41(1), pp. 22–40.

Birch, Thomas D. Basic Needs: Paternalistic Government Welfare Policy with Distortionary Taxation. *Public Finance Quart.*, July 1987, 15(3), pp. 298–321.

Blanchard, Olivier Jean and Summers, Lawrence H. Fiscal Increasing Returns, Hysteresis, Real Wages and Unemployment. *Europ. Econ. Rev.*, April 1987, 31(3), pp. 543–66. **[G: OECD]**

Boadway, Robin W. The Theory and Measurement of Effective Tax Rates. *Mintz, J. M. and Purvis, D. D., eds.*, 1987, pp. 60–98.

Bohanon, Cecil E. and Van Cott, T. Norman. Patinkin on a Money-Financed Increase in Government Expenditures: What Happened to Seigniorage? *Public Finance*, 1987, 42(2), pp. 332–35.

Boldyrev, Boris; Ilyin, Vladimir and Sichev, Nikolai. The Role of Public Finance in Socialist Economies. *van de Kar, H. M. and Wolfe, B. L., eds.*, 1987, pp. 259–63.

Boskin, Michael J. Tax Policy and the International Location of Investment. *Feldstein, M., ed. (II)*, 1987, pp. 73–81. **[G: U.S.]**

Boskin, Michael J. and Gale, William G. New Results on the Effects of Tax Policy on the International Location of Investment. *Feldstein, M., ed. (I)*, 1987, pp. 201–19. **[G: U.S.]**

Braid, Ralph M. The Spatial Incidence of Local Retail Taxation. *Quart. J. Econ.*, November 1987, 102(4), pp. 881–91.

Brito, Dagobert L. and Intriligator, Michael D. Stock Externalities, Pigovian Taxation and Dynamic Stability. *J. Public Econ.*, June 1987, 33(1), pp. 59–72.

Brito, Dagobert L. and Sheshinski, Eytan. Effects of Capital Gain Taxation on Non-Austrian Assets: Comments. *Razin, A. and Sadka, E., eds.*, 1987, pp. 340–42. **[G: Austria]**

Bródy, András. Defence Spending as a Priority. *Schmidt, C. and Blackaby, F., eds.*, 1987, pp. 40–44.

Brookshire, David S. and Coursey, Don L. Measuring the Value of a Public Good: An Empirical Comparison of Elicitation Procedures. *Amer. Econ. Rev.*, September 1987, 77(4), pp. 554–66. **[G: U.S.]**

Browning, Edgar K. On the Marginal Welfare Cost of Taxation. *Amer. Econ. Rev.*, March 1987, 77(1), pp. 11–23. **[G: U.S.]**

Bruce, Neil. Will the Neoclassical Theory of Investment Please Rise? The General Structure of Investment Models and Their Implications for Tax Policy: Comment. *Mintz, J. M. and Purvis, D. D., eds.*, 1987, pp. 168–70.

Buchanan, James M. "La Scienza delle Finanze": The Italian Tradition in Fiscal Theory. *Buchanan, J. M. (II)*, 1987, 1960, pp. 317–56. **[G: Italy]**

Buchanan, James M. Concerning Future Generations. *Buchanan, J. M. (I)*, 1987, 1958, pp. 113–19.

Buchanan, James M. Fiscal Institutions and Efficiency in Collective Outlay. *Buchanan, J. M. (II)*, 1987, 1964, pp. 357–66.

Buchanan, James M. and Brennan, Geoffrey. The Normative Purpose of Economic "Science": Rediscovery of an Eighteenth Century Method. *Buchanan, J. M. (II)*, 1987, 1981, pp. 51–65.

Buchanan, James M. and Brennan, Geoffrey. Towards a Tax Constitution for Leviathan. *Buchanan, J. M. (II)*, 1987, 1977, pp. 367–87.

Buchanan, James M. and Faith, Roger L. Secession and the Limits of Taxation: Toward a Theory of Internal Exit. *Amer. Econ. Rev.*, December 1987, 77(5), pp. 1023–31.

Buiter, Willem H. A Fiscal Theory of Hyperdeflations? Some Surprising Monetarist Arithmetic. *Sinclair, P. J. N., ed.*, 1987, pp. 111–18.

Buiter, Willem H. A Fiscal Theory of Hyperdeflations? Some Surprising Monetarist Arithmetic. *Oxford Econ. Pap.*, March 1987, 39(1), pp. 111–18.

Buiter, Willem H. Fiscal Policy in Open, Interdependent Economies. *Razin, A. and Sadka, E., eds.*, 1987, pp. 101–44.

Burtless, Gary and Haveman, Robert H. Taxes, Transfers, and Labor Supply: The Evolving Views of U.S. Economists. *van de Kar, H. M. and Wolfe, B. L., eds.*, 1987, pp. 127–45. **[G: U.S.]**

Campbell, John Y. Macroeconomic Lessons from Britain: A Review Essay. *J. Monet. Econ.*,

March 1987, *19*(2), pp. 315–24. [G: U.K.]

Cebula, Richard J. Federal Deficits and the Real Rate of Interest in the United States: A Note. *Public Choice*, 1987, *53*(1), pp. 97–100.
[G: U.S.]

Chamley, Christophe and Wright, Brian D. Fiscal Incidence in an Overlapping Generations Model with a Fixed Asset. *J. Public Econ.*, February 1987, *32*(1), pp. 3–24.

Chan, James L. and Rubin, Marc A. The Role of Information in a Democracy and in Government Operations: The Public Choice Methodology. *Chan, J. L., ed., Pt. B*, 1987, pp. 3–27.

Chirinko, Robert S. Will the Neoclassical Theory of Investment Please Rise? The General Structure of Investment Models and Their Implications for Tax Policy. *Mintz, J. M. and Purvis, D. D., eds.*, 1987, pp. 109–67.

Choi, Kwang. Tax Policy and Corporate Financial Structure in Korea. *Int. Econ. J.*, Winter 1987, *1*(4), pp. 61–76. [G: S. Korea]

Cooley, Thomas F. and Salyer, Kevin D. The Effects of Inflation-Induced Tax Increases on Stock and Housing Prices. *Scand. J. Econ.*, 1987, *89*(4), pp. 421–34. [G: U.S.]

Corden, W. Max. The Relevance for Developing Countries of Recent Developments in Macroeconomic Theory. *World Bank Res. Observer*, July 1987, *2*(2), pp. 171–88. [G: LDCs]

Cowell, Frank A. The Economic Analysis of Tax Evasion. *Hey, J. D. and Lambert, P. J., eds.*, 1987, *1985*, pp. 173–203.

Craig, Steven G. The Impact of Congestion on Local Public Good Production. *J. Public Econ.*, April 1987, *32*(3), pp. 331–53. [G: U.S.]

Cremer, Helmuth; Kessler, Denis and Pestieau, Pierre. Fertility Differentials and the Regressive Effect of Public Debt. *Economica*, February 1987, *54*(213), pp. 79–87.

Croushore, Dean D. Government Financial Policy and Capital. *Southern Econ. J.*, October 1987, *54*(2), pp. 435–48.

Croushore, Dean D. The Neutrality of Optimal Government Financial Policy: Supplying the Intergenerational Free Lunch. *Eastern Econ. J.*, Apr.-June 1987, *13*(2), pp. 123–36.

Cunningham, Thomas J. Growing Out of Deficits: Debt Dynamics in a Disequilibrium Model. *J. Post Keynesian Econ.*, Winter 1986-87, *9*(2), pp. 297–306. [G: U.S.]

Dalamagas, Basil A. A Flow of Funds Analysis of Crowding Out: Some International Evidence. *Southern Econ. J.*, April 1987, *53*(4), pp. 997–1010. [G: OECD]

Dalamagas, Basil A. Government Deficits, Crowding Out, and Inflation: Some International Evidence. *Public Finance*, 1987, *42*(1), pp. 65–84. [G: OECD]

Dalton, Thomas R. Public Expenditure and the Optimal Commodity Tax Structure. *Atlantic Econ. J.*, July 1987, *15*(2), pp. 88–89.

Das-Gupta, Arindam. A Note on the Effects of Tax-Subsidy Policies on the Personal Distribution of Income in Dual Economies. *Indian*

Econ. Rev., Jan.-June 1987, *22*(1), pp. 95–105.
[G: LDCs]

Devereux, Michael. Fiscal Spending, the Terms of Trade, and Real Interest Rates. *J. Int. Econ.*, May 1987, *22*(3/4), pp. 219–35.

Dierker, Egbert. Increasing Returns, Efficiency, and the Distribution of Wealth. *Europ. Econ. Rev.*, Feb./Mar. 1987, *31*(1/2), pp. 475–82.

Diewert, Walter Erwin. Corporate Taxes and Incentives and the Structure of Production: A Selected Survey: Comment. *Mintz, J. M. and Purvis, D. D., eds.*, 1987, pp. 209–24.

Dinwiddy, Caroline L. and Teal, Francis J. Shadow Prices for Non-traded Goods in a Tax-Distorted Economy: Formulae and Values. *J. Public Econ.*, July 1987, *33*(2), pp. 207–21.

Dixit, Avinash K. On Pareto-Improving Redistributions of Aggregate Economic Gains. *J. Econ. Theory*, February 1987, *41*(1), pp. 133–53.

Djajić, Slobodan. Effects of Budgetary Policies in Open Economies: The Role of Intertemporal Consumption Substitution. *J. Int. Money Finance*, September 1987, *6*(3), pp. 373–83.

Djajić, Slobodan. Government Spending and the Optimal Rates of Consumption and Capital Accumulation. *Can. J. Econ.*, August 1987, *20*(3), pp. 544–54.

Driessen, Patrick A. A Qualification Concerning the Efficiency of Tax Expenditures [A Contribution to the Theory of Tax Expenditures: The Case of Charitable Giving]. *J. Public Econ.*, June 1987, *33*(1), pp. 125–31.

Eckstein, Zvi. Inflation and the Government Budget Constraint: Comments. *Razin, A. and Sadka, E., eds.*, 1987, pp. 201–02.

Egginton, Don M. Case Studies of Labour Supply Incentives and Budget Lines. *Beenstock, M., et al.*, 1987, pp. 25–75. [G: U.K.]

Esfahani, Hadi Salehi. The Resurgence of Inflation in Latin America: Discussion. *World Devel.*, August 1987, *15*(8), pp. 1141–43.
[G: S. America; Peru; Chile]

Evans, Paul. Do Budget Deficits Raise Nominal Interest Rates? Evidence from Six Countries. *J. Monet. Econ.*, September 1987, *20*(2), pp. 281–300. [G: N. America; France; W. Germany; Japan; U.K.]

Fane, G. Neutral Taxation under Uncertainty. *J. Public Econ.*, June 1987, *33*(1), pp. 95–105.

Feenberg, Daniel R. The Cash Flow Corporate Income Tax: Comment. *Feldstein, M., ed. (I)*, 1987, pp. 398–400. [G: U.S.]

Feldstein, Martin S. Tax Rules and Business Investment. *Feldstein, M., ed. (II)*, 1987, pp. 63–72. [G: U.S.]

Feldstein, Martin S. The Efficiency of Tax Expenditures: Reply [A Contribution to the Theory of Tax Expenditures: The Case of Charitable Giving]. *J. Public Econ.*, June 1987, *33*(1), pp. 133–36. [G: U.S.]

Feldstein, Martin S. and Jun, Joosung. The Effects of Tax Rules on Nonresidential Fixed Investment: Some Preliminary Evidence from the 1980s. *Feldstein, M., ed. (I)*, 1987, pp. 101–56. [G: U.S.]

Fender, John. Fiscal Policy in a Two Good Open

Economy [Expansionary Fiscal Policy and the Exchange Rate: A Review]. *Australian Econ. Pap.*, June 1987, *26*(48), pp. 71–82.

Fischer, Stanley. Inflation and the Government Budget Constraint: Comments. *Razin, A. and Sadka, E., eds.*, 1987, pp. 203–07.

Flaig, Gebhard. Staatsausgaben, Staatsverschuldung und die makroökonomische Konsumfunktion. (Government Expenditure, Public Debt, and Macroeconomic Consumption Function. With English summary.) *Z. Wirtschaft. Sozialwissen.*, 1987, *107*(3), pp. 337–59.
[G: W. Germany]

Flavin, Marjorie. Ricardian Equivalence: An Evaluation of Theory and Evidence: Comment. *Fischer, S., ed.*, 1987, pp. 304–09.

Flemming, John S. Debt and Taxes in War and Peace: The Case of a Small Open Economy. *Boskin, M. J.; Fleming, J. S. and Gorini, S., eds.*, 1987, pp. 373–91.

Fluet, Claude. Fraude fiscale et offre de travail au noir. (Tax Evasion and the Supply of Unofficial Labour. With English summary.) *L'Actual. Econ.*, June-September 1987, *63*(2–3), pp. 225–42.

Formby, John P.; Smith, W. James and Thistle, Paul D. Difficulties in the Measurement of Tax Progressivity: Further Analysis. *Public Finance*, 1987, *42*(3), pp. 438–45. [G: Canada; Australia; U.K.; U.S.]

Forte, Francesco. The Laffer Curve and the Theory of Fiscal Bureaucracy. *Public Choice*, 1987, *52*(2), pp. 101–24.

Frenkel, Jacob A. Optimal Currency Substitution Policy and Public Finance: Comments. *Razin, A. and Sadka, E., eds.*, 1987, pp. 165–69.

Frenkel, Jacob A. and Razin, Assaf. The Mundell–Fleming Model a Quarter Century Later. *Int. Monet. Fund Staff Pap.*, December 1987, *34*(4), pp. 567–620.

Fullerton, Don and Henderson, Yolanda Kodrzycki. The Impact of Fundamental Tax Reform on the Allocation of Resources. *Feldstein, M., ed. (I)*, 1987, pp. 401–37. [G: U.S.]

Fullerton, Don and Henderson, Yolanda Kodrzycki. The Impact of Fundamental Tax Reform on the Allocation of Resources. *Feldstein, M., ed. (II)*, 1987, pp. 101–03. [G: U.S.]

Funke, Helmut. Incentive Compatible Mechanisms for the Allocation of Public Goods. *Bamberg, G. and Spremann, K., eds.*, 1987, pp. 105–16.

Fuss, Melvyn A. Corporate Taxes and Incentives and the Structure of Production: A Selected Survey: Comment. *Mintz, J. M. and Purvis, D. D., eds.*, 1987, pp. 225–27.

Giersch, Herbert. Economic Policies in the Age of Schumpeter. *Europ. Econ. Rev.*, Feb./Mar. 1987, *31*(1/2), pp. 35–52. [G: OECD]

Goetze, David. Identifying Appropriate Institutions for Efficient Use of Common Pools. *Natural Res. J.*, Winter 1987, *27*(1), pp. 187–99.

Gordon, Roger H. Taxation and Capital Structure: A Selected Review: Comment. *Mintz, J. M. and Purvis, D. D., eds.*, 1987, pp. 263–66.

Gordon, Roger H. The Effects of Tax Rules on

Nonresidential Fixed Investment: Some Preliminary Evidence from the 1980s: Comment. *Feldstein, M., ed. (I)*, 1987, pp. 156–61.
[G: U.S.]

Gordon, Roger H.; Hines, James R., Jr. and Summers, Lawrence H. Notes on the Tax Treatment of Structures. *Feldstein, M., ed. (I)*, 1987, pp. 223–54. [G: U.S.]

Gorini, Stefano. The Neoclassical Theory of Public Debt and the Theory of a Long-run Full-Employment Deficit. *Boskin, M. J.; Fleming, J. S. and Gorini, S., eds.*, 1987, pp. 347–72.

Gramlich, Edward M. Subnational Fiscal Policy. *Quigley, J. M., ed.*, 1987, pp. 3–27.
[G: U.S.]

Grandmont, Jean-Michel. Stabilizing Competitive Business Cycles. *Grandmont, J.-M., ed.*, 1987, *1986*, pp. 57–76.

Grossman, Philip J. The Optimal Size of Government. *Public Choice*, 1987, *53*(2), pp. 131–47.
[G: U.S.]

Hamilton, Jonathan H. Optimal Wage and Income Taxation with Wage Uncertainty. *Int. Econ. Rev.*, June 1987, *28*(2), pp. 373–88.

Hamilton, Jonathan H. Taxation, Savings, and Portfolio Choice in a Continuous Time Model. *Public Finance*, 1987, *42*(2), pp. 264–82.

Hands, D. Wade and Mann, Bruce D. Urban Industrial Tax Subsidies: A Non-cooperative Equilibrium Approach. *Reg. Sci. Urban Econ.*, May 1987, *17*(2), pp. 179–90.

Hansson, Ingemar. Effects of Capital Taxation on Capital Formation, Distribution, and Efficiency. *van de Kar, H. M. and Wolfe, B. L., eds.*, 1987, pp. 147–63. [G: OECD]

Hansson, Ingemar. Optimal Income Taxation and the Untaxed Sector. *Alessandrini, S. and Dallago, B., eds.*, 1987, pp. 311–21.

Hansson, Ingemar and Stuart, Charles. The Welfare Costs of Deficit Finance. *Econ. Inquiry*, July 1987, *25*(3), pp. 479–96. [G: U.S.]

Hartman, David G. New Results on the Effects of Tax Policy on the International Location of Investment: Comment. *Feldstein, M., ed. (I)*, 1987, pp. 219–22. [G: U.S.]

Hartman, Richard. Monetary Uncertainty and Investment in an Optimizing, Rational Expectations Model with Income Taxes and Government Debt. *Econometrica*, January 1987, *55*(1), pp. 169–76.

Havrilesky, Thomas M. A Partisanship Theory of Fiscal and Monetary Regimes. *J. Money, Credit, Banking*, August 1987, *19*(3), pp. 308–25.

Heady, Christopher. A Diagrammatic Approach to Optimal Commodity Taxation. *Public Finance*, 1987, *42*(2), pp. 250–63.

Helliwell, John F. The Effect of Taxation on Business Activity: Concluding Remarks. *Mintz, J. M. and Purvis, D. D., eds.*, 1987, pp. 280–87.

Hendershott, Patric H. Tax Changes and Capital Allocation in the 1980s. *Feldstein, M., ed. (I)*, 1987, pp. 259–90. [G: U.S.]

Hendershott, Patric H. Tax Reform and the Slope

of the Playing Field. *Feldstein, M., ed. (II)*, 1987, pp. 51–61. **[G: U.S.]**

Henderson, Yolanda Kodrzycki. A General Equilibrium Evaluation of Corporate Income Tax Reform. *Econ. Inquiry*, October 1987, *25*(4), pp. 565–81.

Hercowitz, Zvi and Sadka, Efraim. On Optimal Currency Substitution Policy and Public Finance. *Razin, A. and Sadka, E., eds.*, 1987, pp. 147–64.

Hewitt, Daniel P. The Benefit Incidence of Consumption Public Goods. *Public Finance Quart.*, April 1987, *15*(2), pp. 138–65. **[G: U.S.]**

Hillier, Brian and Lunati, M. Teresa. On Nash versus Stackelberg Strategies and the Conditions for Operative Intergenerational Transfers. *Scot. J. Polit. Econ.*, February 1987, *34*(1), pp. 91–96.

Hines, James R., Jr. The Tax Treatment of Structures. *Feldstein, M., ed. (II)*, 1987, pp. 37–50. **[G: U.S.]**

Hoffman, Ronald. Macroeconomic Analysis and Stabilization Policy: Searching for Consensus. *van de Kar, H. M. and Wolfe, B. L., eds.*, 1987, pp. 13–31. **[G: U.S.]**

Honohan, Patrick and Irvine, Ian. The Marginal Social Cost of Taxation in Ireland. *Econ. Soc. Rev.*, October 1987, *19*(1), pp. 15–41. **[G: Ireland]**

Hunter, William J. and Scott, Charles E. Statutory Changes in State Income Taxes: An Indirect Test of Fiscal Illusion. *Public Choice*, 1987, *53*(1), pp. 41–51. **[G: U.S.]**

Hutchison, Michael M. and Pigott, Charles A. Real and Financial Linkages in the Macroeconomic Response to Budget Deficits: An Empirical Investigation. *Arndt, S. W. and Richardson, J. D. eds.*, 1987, pp. 139–66. **[G: U.S.; W. Germany; Japan; U.K.]**

Ihori, Toshihiro. Spillover Effects and the Terms of Trade within a Two-Country Model. *J. Int. Econ.*, May 1987, *22*(3/4), pp. 203–18.

Ihori, Toshihiro. Tax Reform and Intergeneration Incidence. *J. Public Econ.*, August 1987, *33*(3), pp. 377–87.

Ihori, Toshihiro. The Optimal Linear Income Tax: A Diagrammatic Analysis. *J. Public Econ.*, December 1987, *34*(3), pp. 379–90.

Ize, Alain and Ortiz, Guillermo. Fiscal Rigidities, Public Debt, and Capital Flight. *Int. Monet. Fund Staff Pap.*, June 1987, *34*(2), pp. 311–32. **[G: Mexico]**

Jones, Philip R. and Cullis, John G. Fiscal Preferences and Tax-Prices: A Rejoinder. *Scot. J. Polit. Econ.*, August 1987, *34*(3), pp. 291–94.

Judd, Kenneth L. A Dynamic Theory of Factor Taxation. *Amer. Econ. Rev.*, May 1987, *77*(2), pp. 42–48.

Judd, Kenneth L. Debt and Distortionary Taxation in a Simple Perfect Foresight Model. *J. Monet. Econ.*, July 1987, *20*(1), pp. 51–72.

Judd, Kenneth L. The Welfare Cost of Factor Taxation in a Perfect-Foresight Model. *J. Polit. Econ.*, August 1987, *95*(4), pp. 675–709.

Kakwani, Nanak. Measures of Tax Progressivity and Redistribution Effect: A Comment. *Public Finance*, 1987, *42*(3), pp. 431–34.

van de Kar, Hans M. and Wolfe, Barbara L. The Nature and Relevance of Public Finance. *van de Kar, H. M. and Wolfe, B. L., eds.*, 1987, pp. 1–10.

Karacaoglu, Girol. Fitting Money into Conventional Macroeconomic Models. *Australian Econ. Pap.*, June 1987, *26*(48), pp. 83–100.

Kay, John A. and Keen, Michael. Commodity Taxation for Maximum Revenue. *Public Finance Quart.*, October 1987, *15*(4), pp. 371–85.

Keen, Michael. Welfare Effects of Commodity Tax Harmonisation. *J. Public Econ.*, June 1987, *33*(1), pp. 107–14.

Kehoe, Patrick J. Coordination of Fiscal Policies in a World Economy. *J. Monet. Econ.*, May 1987, *19*(3), pp. 349–76.

Kelly, William A., Jr.; Ferris, James M. and Miles, James A. The Expenditure Tax and Savings Incentives: Design Matters. *Growth Change*, Winter 1987, *18*(1), pp. 32–43.

Khan, Mohsin S. and Lizondo, José Saúl. Devaluation, Fiscal Deficits, and the Real Exchange Rate. *World Bank Econ. Rev.*, January 1987, *1*(2), pp. 357–74.

Kim, Moshe and Spiegel, Menahem. The Effects of Lump-Sum Subsidies on the Structure of Production and Productivity in Regulated Industries. *J. Public Econ.*, October 1987, *34*(1), pp. 105–19. **[G: Israel]**

Kimball, Miles S. Making Sense of Two-Sided Altruism. *J. Monet. Econ.*, September 1987, *20*(2), pp. 301–26.

King, Mervyn A. The Cash Flow Corporate Income Tax. *Feldstein, M., ed. (II)*, 1987, pp. 109–10. **[G: U.S.]**

King, Mervyn A. The Cash Flow Corporate Income Tax. *Feldstein, M., ed. (I)*, 1987, pp. 377–98. **[G: U.S.]**

Kleiman, Ephraim. The Resurgence of Inflation in Latin America: Discussion. *World Devel.*, August 1987, *15*(8), pp. 1143–45. **[G: Peru]**

Koford, Kenneth J. Some Short-run Microeconomic Effects of a Market Incentive Anti-inflation Plan. *Public Finance Quart.*, April 1987, *15*(2), pp. 199–218.

Kofuji, Yasuo. Wealth Effects and Fiscal Policy in the Context of a Flexible Price Level—A Reply. *Public Finance*, 1987, *42*(1), pp. 160–63.

Kolluri, Bharat R. and Giannaros, Demetrios S. Budget Deficits and Short-term Real Interest Rate Forecasting. *J. Macroecon.*, Winter 1987, *9*(1), pp. 109–25.

Koskela, Erkki. Changes in Tax Progression and Labour Supply under Wage Rate Uncertainty. *Public Finance*, 1987, *42*(2), pp. 214–26.

Kotlikoff, Laurence J. The Theory and Measurement of Effective Tax Rates: Comment. *Mintz, J. M. and Purvis, D. D., eds.*, 1987, pp. 102–04.

Kovenock, Daniel J. and Rothschild, Michael. Notes on the Effect of Capital Gain Taxation on Non-Austrian Assets. *Razin, A. and Sadka,*

E., eds., 1987, pp. 309–39.   [G: Austria]

Krause-Junk, Gerold. Optimal Taxation: A Beautiful Cul-de-sac? *van de Kar, H. M. and Wolfe, B. L., eds.*, 1987, pp. 55–66.

Kreutzer, David and Lee, Dwight R. Joint Products and a Positive Response to a Profit Tax. *Public Finance Quart.*, January 1987, *15*(1), pp. 98–104.

Kwong, Kai-Sun. The Excess Burden of a Selective Consumption Tax: A Formal Proof. *Hong Kong Econ. Pap.*, 1987, (18), pp. 53–55.

Laffont, Jean-Jacques. Optimal Taxation of a Nonlinear Pricing Monopolist. *J. Public Econ.*, July 1987, *33*(2), pp. 137–55.

Laffont, Jean-Jacques. Toward a Normative Theory of Incentive Contracts between Government and Private Firms. *Econ. J.*, Supplement 1987, *97*, pp. 17–31.

Lal, Deepak. The Political Economy of Economic Liberalization. *World Bank Econ. Rev.*, January 1987, *1*(2), pp. 273–99.   [G: LDCs]

Leape, Jonathan I. Taxes and Transaction Costs in Asset Market Equilibrium. *J. Public Econ.*, June 1987, *33*(1), pp. 1–20.

Lerda, Juan Carlos. A dinâmica da dívida pública: de Domar–Lerner a Tobin–Simonsen. (With English summary.) *Pesquisa Planejamento Econ.*, August 1987, *17*(2), pp. 343–68.

Lindbeck, Assar and Snower, Dennis J. Strike and Lock-Out Threats and Fiscal Policy. *Oxford Econ. Pap.*, December 1987, *39*(4), pp. 760–84.

Lindsey, Lawrence B. Capital Gains Rates, Realizations, and Revenues. *Feldstein, M., ed. (I)*, 1987, pp. 69–97.   [G: U.S.]

Lindsey, Lawrence B. Rates, Realizations, and Revenues of Capital Gains. *Feldstein, M., ed. (II)*, 1987, pp. 17–25.   [G: U.S.]

Liu, Pak-Wai. Measuring Global Tax Progressivity as Weighted Deviations from Proportional Tax: A Comment. *Public Finance*, 1987, *42*(3), pp. 435–37.

Llau, Pierre and Gilbert, Guy. De la "Théorie" au "Conseil" et à la "Politique": l'experience Française du Conseil des impôts. (With English summary.) *van de Kar, H. M. and Wolfe, B. L., eds.*, 1987, pp. 277–92.   [G: France]

Lopez Murphy, Ricardo H. La política fiscal compensatoria. (The Compensatory Fiscal Policy. With English summary.) *Económica (La Plata)*, January-June 1987, *33*(1), pp. 85–112.

Lord, William A. Welfare Effects of Capital Income Taxation under Variable and Fixed Labor Supply. *Southern Econ. J.*, July 1987, *54*(1), pp. 48–54.

Majd, Saman and Myers, Stewart C. Tax Asymmetries and Corporate Income Tax Reform. *Feldstein, M., ed. (II)*, 1987, pp. 93–95.   [G: U.S.]

Majd, Saman and Myers, Stewart C. Tax Asymmetries and Corporate Income Tax Reform. *Feldstein, M., ed. (I)*, 1987, pp. 343–73.   [G: U.S.]

Makin, John H. Capital Gains Rates, Realizations, and Revenues: Comment. *Feldstein, M., ed. (I)*, 1987, pp. 98–100.   [G: U.S.]

Malinvaud, Edmond. Monetary and Fiscal Policies for Economic Recovery in Europe. *Europ. Econ. Rev.*, Feb./Mar. 1987, *31*(1/2), pp. 73–75.   [G: W. Europe]

Manasse, Paolo. Microfoundations of Fiscal Policy Games under Flexible Exchange Rates: An Example. *Giorn. Econ.*, Jan.-Feb. 1987, *46*(1–2), pp. 55–84.

Mankiw, N. Gregory. Consumer Spending and the After-Tax Real Interest Rate. *Feldstein, M., ed. (II)*, 1987, pp. 97–99.   [G: U.S.]

Mankiw, N. Gregory. Government Purchases and Real Interest Rates. *J. Polit. Econ.*, April 1987, *95*(2), pp. 407–19.

Mankiw, N. Gregory. The Optimal Collection of Seigniorage: Theory and Evidence. *J. Monet. Econ.*, September 1987, *20*(2), pp. 327–41.   [G: U.S.]

Marchand, Maurice and Pestieau, Pierre. Public Production and Employment Policies in a Two-Region Economy with Unemployment. *Reg. Sci. Urban Econ.*, August 1987, *17*(3), pp. 345–55.

Marchand, Maurice and Pestieau, Pierre. Should Employment Policy Making Be Entrusted to Regions? *Reg. Sci. Urban Econ.*, August 1987, *17*(3), pp. 357–65.

Marfán, Manuel. Reactivación y Restricción Externa: El Rol de la Política Fiscal. (Economic Recovery Under Payments Constraints: The Role of Short-run Fiscal Policy. With English summary.) *Colección Estud. CIEPLAN*, December 1987, (22), pp. 5–40.

Marrelli, M. The Economic Analysis of Tax Evasion: Empirical Aspects. *Hey, J. D. and Lambert, P. J., eds.*, 1987, pp. 204–28. [G: U.S.; W. Europe]

Martinich, Joseph S. and Hurter, Arthur P., Jr. A Note on Income Taxes and Degree One Production Homogeneity. *J. Reg. Sci.*, August 1987, *27*(3), pp. 477–82.

Maussner, Alfred. Public Consumption, Optimal Capital Accumulation and the Social Rate of Time Preference. *J. Inst. Theoretical Econ.*, June 1987, *143*(2), pp. 324–33.

McClure, Charles E., Jr. Reflections on Recent Proposals to Rationalize the U.S. Income Tax. *van de Kar, H. M. and Wolfe, B. L., eds.*, 1987, pp. 97–112.   [G: U.S.]

McGuire, Martin C. Economic Considerations in the Comparison between Assured Destruction and Assured Survival. *Schmidt, C. and Blackaby, F., eds.*, 1987, pp. 122–49.   [G: U.S.]

McGuire, Robert A.; Ohsfeldt, Robert L. and Van Cott, T. Norman. The Determinants of the Choice between Public and Private Production of a Publicly Funded Service. *Public Choice*, August 1987, *54*(3), pp. 211–30.   [G: U.S.]

McKinney, Scott. Crowding and the Club Membership Margin. *J. Urban Econ.*, November 1987, *22*(3), pp. 312–23.   [G: U.S.]

Mestelman, Stuart. Corrective Taxes and Uniform Standards: Different Policies and Different Targets. *Econ. Scelte Pubbliche/J. Public*

Finance Public Choice, Jan.-Apr. 1987, 5(1), pp. 27–44.

Miller, Preston J. Higher Deficit Policies Lead to Higher Inflation. *Wilcox, J. A., ed.*, 1987, *1983*, pp. 293–304. **[G: U.S.]**

Mintz, Jack M. and Purvis, Douglas D. Taxation and Business Activity: Introduction. *Mintz, J. M. and Purvis, D. D., eds.*, 1987, pp. 2–57.

Misiolek, Walter S. and Elder, Harold W. Cost-Effective Redistribution: Implications of a Basic Needs Approach to Public Assistance. *Public Finance Quart.*, January 1987, 15(1), pp. 76–97.

Moffitt, Robert and Rothschild, Michael. Variable Earnings and Nonlinear Taxation. *J. Human Res.*, Summer 1987, 22(3), pp. 405–21. **[G: U.S.]**

Monaco, Margaret A. and Rowley, Charles K. A Political Economy of Budget Deficits. *[Tullock, G.]*, 1987, pp. 223–42. **[G: U.S.]**

Moore, Michael J. The Irish Consumption Function and Ricardian Equivalence. *Econ. Soc. Rev.*, October 1987, 19(1), pp. 43–60. **[G: Ireland]**

Morley, Samuel A. and Fishlow, Albert. Deficits, Debt and Destabilization: The Perversity of High Interest Rates. *J. Devel. Econ.*, October 1987, 27(1–2), pp. 227–44. **[G: LDCs]**

Morley, Samuel A. and Fishlow, Albert. Deficits, Debt and Destabilization: The Perversity of High Interest Rates. *[Diaz-Alejandro, C. F.]*, 1987, pp. 227–44. **[G: LDCs]**

Motley, Brian. Ricardo or Keynes: Does the Government Debt Affect Consumption? *Fed. Res. Bank San Francisco Econ. Rev.*, Winter 1987, (1), pp. 47–62.

Mumy, Gene E. What Does Nozick's Minimal State Do? *Econ. Philos.*, October 1987, 3(2), pp. 275–305.

Musgrave, Richard A. Equity Principles in Public Finance. *van de Kar, H. M. and Wolfe, B. L., eds.*, 1987, pp. 113–23.

Myatt, Anthony E. and Scarth, William M. Fiscal Policy, Interest Sensitive Aggregate Supply and the Costs of Disinflation. *Manchester Sch. Econ. Soc. Stud.*, June 1987, 55(2), pp. 144–57.

Myles, Gareth D. Tax Design in the Presence of Imperfect Competition: An Example. *J. Public Econ.*, December 1987, 34(3), pp. 367–78.

Ng, Yew-Kwang. Diamonds Are a Government's Best Friend: Burden-Free Taxes on Goods Valued for Their Values. *Amer. Econ. Rev.*, March 1987, 77(1), pp. 186–91.

Ng, Yew-Kwang. Relative-Income Effects and the Appropriate Level of Public Expenditure. *Oxford Econ. Pap.*, June 1987, 39(2), pp. 293–300.

Ohlsson, Henry. Cost–Benefit Rules in a Regionalized Disequilibrium Model. *Scand. J. Econ.*, 1987, 89(2), pp. 165–82.

Padoa Schioppa, Fiorella. Wealth Effects and Fiscal Policy in the Context of a Flexible Price Level—A Comment. *Public Finance*, 1987, 42(1), pp. 156–59.

Palokangas, Tapio. Optimal Taxation and Employment Policy with a Centralized Wage Setting. *Oxford Econ. Pap.*, December 1987, 39(4), pp. 799–812.

Papageorgiou, Y. Y. Spatial Public Goods. 1: Theory. *Environ. Planning A*, March 1987, 19(3), pp. 331–52.

Papageorgiou, Y. Y. Spatial Public Goods: 2. Applications. *Environ. Planning A*, April 1987, 19(4), pp. 471–92.

Paulsen, Jim W. and Adams, Roy D. Optimal Taxation of a Monopoly. *Nat. Tax J.*, March 1987, 40(1), pp. 121–25.

Peacock, Alan. Some Gratuitous Advice to Fiscal Advisers. *van de Kar, H. M. and Wolfe, B. L., eds.*, 1987, pp. 265–76.

Penati, Alessandro. Government Spending and the Real Exchange Rate. *J. Int. Econ.*, May 1987, 22(3/4), pp. 237–67.

Perasso, Giancarlo. The Ricardian Equivalence Theorem and the Consumption Function: A Survey of the Literature. *Rivista Int. Sci. Econ. Com.*, July 1987, 34(7), pp. 649–74.

Perroni, Carlo. Valutazione degli effetti di politiche fiscali in presenza di razionamento. (Evaluation of the Effects of Fiscal Policies under a Rational Mechanism. With English summary.) *Giorn. Econ.*, Mar.-Apr. 1987, 46(3–4), pp. 185–204.

Persson, Mats; Persson, Torsten and Svensson, Lars E. O. Time Consistency of Fiscal and Monetary Policy. *Econometrica*, November 1987, 55(6), pp. 1419–31.

Pfähler, Wilhelm. Redistributive Effects of Tax Progressivity: Evaluating a General Class of Aggregate Measures. *Public Finance*, 1987, 42(1), pp. 1–31.

Pfähler, Wilhelm. Redistributive Effects of Tax Progressivity: A Reply. *Public Finance*, 1987, 42(3), pp. 446–47.

Pfingsten, Andreas. Axiomatically Based Local Measures of Tax Progression. *Bull. Econ. Res.*, July 1987, 39(3), pp. 211–23.

Pinstrup-Andersen, Per; Jaramillo, Maurice and Stewart, Frances. Adjustment with a Human Face: Protecting the Vulnerable and Promoting Growth: The Impact on Government Expenditure. *Cornia, G. A.; Jolly, R. and Stewart, F., eds.*, 1987, pp. 73–89. **[G: LDCs]**

van der Ploeg, Frederick. Benefits of Contingent Rules for Optimal Taxation of a Monetary Economy: A Note. *J. Money, Credit, Banking*, May 1987, 19(2), pp. 252–59.

Plosser, Charles I. Fiscal Policy and the Term Structure. *J. Monet. Econ.*, September 1987, 20(2), pp. 343–67.

Plosser, Charles I. Ricardian Equivalence: An Evaluation of Theory and Evidence: Comment. *Fischer, S., ed.*, 1987, pp. 309–13.

Plummer, Mark L. Supply Uncertainty and Option Value: Reply. *Land Econ.*, November 1987, 63(4), pp. 408.

Poterba, James M. Taxation and Capital Structure: A Selected Review: Comment. *Mintz, J. M. and Purvis, D. D., eds.*, 1987, pp. 267–74.

Poterba, James M. and Summers, Lawrence H.

Finite Lifetimes and the Effects of Budget Deficits on National Saving. *J. Monet. Econ.*, September 1987, *20*(2), pp. 369–91.   [G: U.S.]

Prakken, Joel L. The Macroeconomics of Tax Reform. *Walker, C. E. and Bloomfield, M. A., eds.*, 1987, pp. 117–66.   [G: U.S.]

Protopapadakis, Aris A. and Siegel, Jeremy J. Are Money Growth and Inflation Related to Government Deficits? Evidence from Ten Industrialized Economies. *J. Int. Money Finance*, March 1987, *6*(1), pp. 31–48.
[G: Selected OECD]

Rankin, Neil. Debt Policy under Fixed and Flexible Prices. *Sinclair, P. J. N., ed.*, 1987, *1986*, pp. 308–27.

Rankin, Neil. Disequilibrium and the Welfare-Maximising Levels of Government Spending, Taxation and Debt. *Econ. J.*, March 1987, *97*(385), pp. 65–85.

Richter, Wolfram F. Taxation as Insurance and the Case of Rate Differentiation According to Consanguinity under Inheritance Taxation. *J. Public Econ.*, August 1987, *33*(3), pp. 363–76.
[G: W. Germany]

Riordan, Michael H. and Sappington, David E. M. Awarding Monopoly Franchises. *Amer. Econ. Rev.*, June 1987, *77*(3), pp. 375–87.

Roberts, Russell D. Financing Public Goods. *J. Polit. Econ.*, April 1987, *95*(2), pp. 420–37.

Robinson, Marc S. The Welfare Cost of Resource Taxation. *[Harberger, A.]*, 1987, pp. 95–108.

Rogers, Carol Ann. Expenditure Taxes, Income Taxes, and Time-Inconsistency. *J. Public Econ.*, March 1987, *32*(2), pp. 215–30.

Rosen, Harvey S. Tax Changes and Capital Allocation in the 1980s: Comment. *Feldstein, M., ed. (I)*, 1987, pp. 290–94.   [G: U.S.]

Roskamp, Karl W. Optimal Lifetime Consumption Paths under Equal Yield Income and Consumption Taxes. *Public Finance*, 1987, *42*(1), pp. 32–41.

Ross, Stephen A. Arbitrage and Martingales with Taxation. *J. Polit. Econ.*, April 1987, *95*(2), pp. 371–93.

Rossi, José W. A dívida pública no Brasil e a aritmética da instabilidade. (With English summary.) *Pesquisa Planejamento Econ.*, August 1987, *17*(2), pp. 369–79.   [G: Brazil]

Rothschild, Kurt W. Economic Considerations in the Comparison between Assured Destruction and Assured Survival: Comment. *Schmidt, C. and Blackaby, F., eds.*, 1987, pp. 150–54.
[G: U.S.]

Russell, A. M. and Rickard, J. A. A Model of Tax Evasion Incorporating Income Variation and Retroactive Penalities. *Australian Econ. Pap.*, December 1987, *26*(49), pp. 254–64.

Samuelson, Larry. Inflation, Indexing and Economic Development. *World Devel.*, August 1987, *15*(8), pp. 1119–30.

Sandler, Todd; Sterbenz, Frederic P. and Posnett, John. Free Riding and Uncertainty. *Europ. Econ. Rev.*, December 1987, *31*(8), pp. 1605–17.

Sandmo, Agnar. A Reinterpretation of Elasticity Formulae in Optimum Tax Theory. *Econo-*

mica, February 1987, *54*(213), pp. 89–96.

Sargent, Thomas J. and Wallace, Neil. Inflation and the Government Budget Constraint. *Razin, A. and Sadka, E., eds.*, 1987, pp. 170–200.

Sauernheimer, K. Interest Rates, Exchange Rates, and Aggregate Supply. *J. Macroecon.*, Summer 1987, *9*(3), pp. 451–55.

Scarth, William M. Can Economic Growth Make Monetarist Arithmetic Pleasant? *Southern Econ. J.*, April 1987, *53*(4), pp. 1028–36.

Schwab, Robert M. and Zampelli, Ernest M. Disentangling the Demand Function from the Production Function for Local Public Services: The Case of Public Safety. *J. Public Econ.*, July 1987, *33*(2), pp. 245–60.   [G: U.S.]

Schwallie, Daniel P. A Theory of Intergovernmental Grants and Their Effect on Aggregate Grantor–Recipient Spending. *Public Finance Quart.*, July 1987, *15*(3), pp. 322–38.

Scotchmer, Suzanne. Audit Classes and Tax Enforcement Policy. *Amer. Econ. Rev.*, May 1987, *77*(2), pp. 229–33.

Segerson, Kathleen. Supply Uncertainty and Option Value: Comment. *Land Econ.*, November 1987, *63*(4), pp. 406–07.

Seidman, Laurence S. Relativity and Efficient Taxation. *Southern Econ. J.*, October 1987, *54*(2), pp. 463–74.

Seidman, Laurence S. The Government Deficit in a Growth Model: Consequences and Trade-offs. *J. Macroecon.*, Fall 1987, *9*(4), pp. 593–611.

Sen, Amartya K. Defence Spending as a Priority: Comment. *Schmidt, C. and Blackaby, F., eds.*, 1987, pp. 45–49.

Shaw, Graham K. Macroeconomic Implications of Fiscal Deficits: An Expository Note. *Scot. J. Polit. Econ.*, May 1987, *34*(2), pp. 192–98.

Sheen, Jeffrey. Inflation Debt and Fiscal Policy Attitudes. *Sinclair, P. J. N., ed.*, 1987, pp. 90–110.

Sheen, Jeffrey. Inflation Debt and Fiscal Policy Attitudes. *Oxford Econ. Pap.*, March 1987, *39*(1), pp. 90–110.

Shibata, Hirofumi and Shibata, Aiko. Rent Redistribution through Provision of Public Goods. *[Kitamura, H.]*, 1987, pp. 268–84.

Shughart, William F., II; Tollison, Robert D. and Higgins, Richard S. Rational Self-Taxation: Complementary Inputs and Excise Taxation. *Can. J. Econ.*, August 1987, *20*(3), pp. 527–32.

Shupp, Franklin R. Policy Effectiveness and the Divergence of Objectives of Private Agents and Public Authorities. *[Marrama, V.], Vol. 2*, 1987, pp. 899–917.

Singh, Nirvikar and Thomas, Ravi. User Charges as a Delegation Mechanism: Response. *Nat. Tax J.*, June 1987, *40*(2), pp. 279–82.

Slemrod, Joel. On Effective Tax Rates and Steady-State Tax Revenues. *Nat. Tax J.*, March 1987, *40*(1), pp. 127–32.

Slemrod, Joel and Yitzhaki, Shlomo. The Optimal Size of a Tax Collection Agency. *Scand. J. Econ.*, 1987, *89*(2), pp. 183–92.

Smiley, Gene. Some Austrian Perspectives on Keynesian Fiscal Policy and the Recovery in the Thirties. *Rothbard, M. N., ed.*, 1987, pp. 145–79. [G: U.S.]

Smolensky, Eugene; Hoyt, William and Danziger, Sheldon. A Critical Survey of Efforts to Measure Budget Incidence. *van de Kar, H. M. and Wolfe, B. L., eds.*, 1987, pp. 165–79.

Söderström, Hans Tson. Sectoral Saving and Investment Patterns in 16 OECD Countries, 1965–82. *Boskin, M. J.; Fleming, J. S. and Gorini, S., eds.*, 1987, pp. 3–39. [G: OECD]

Spaventa, Luigi. Public Debt and Rules of Monetary Growth: An Exercise in Monetarist Arithmetic. *de Cecco, M. and Fitoussi, J.-P., eds.*, 1987, pp. 269–85.

Spaventa, Luigi. The Growth of Public Debt: Sustainability, Fiscal Rules, and Monetary Rules. *Int. Monet. Fund Staff Pap.*, June 1987, 34(2), pp. 374–99.

Spiro, Peter S. New Findings on the Effects of Inflation on Interest Rates. *Bus. Econ.*, April 1987, 22(2), pp. 38–42. [G: U.S.]

Stern, Gary H. The Federal Budget's Effects on Intergenerational Equity: Undone or Not Undone? *Fed. Res. Bank Minn. Rev.*, Winter 1987, 11(1), pp. 2–6. [G: U.S.]

Stern, Nicholas H. The Effects of Taxation, Price Control and Government Contracts in Oligopoly and Monopolistic Competition. *J. Public Econ.*, March 1987, 32(2), pp. 133–58.

Stiglitz, Joseph E. Tax Asymmetries and Corporate Income Tax Reform: Comment. *Feldstein, M., ed. (I)*, 1987, pp. 374–76. [G: U.S.]

Subrahmanyam, Ganti. Wealth Effects, IS–LM Stability, and the Efficacy of Economic Policies: A Comment. *J. Macroecon.*, Spring 1987, 9(2), pp. 293–96.

Summers, Lawrence H. Corporate Capital Budgeting Practices and the Effects of Tax Policies on Investment. *Feldstein, M., ed. (II)*, 1987, pp. 27–36. [G: U.S.]

Summers, Lawrence H. Taxation and the Size and Composition of the Capital Stock: An Asset Price Approach. *[Harberger, A.]*, 1987, pp. 61–94.

Summers, Lawrence H. Will the Neoclassical Theory of Investment Please Rise? The General Structure of Investment Models and Their Implications for Tax Policy: Comment. *Mintz, J. M. and Purvis, D. D., eds.*, 1987, pp. 171–73.

Sunley, Emil M. Notes on the Tax Treatment of Structures: Comment. *Feldstein, M., ed. (I)*, 1987, pp. 254–57. [G: U.S.]

Svensson, Lars E. O. International Fiscal Policy Transmission. *Scand. J. Econ.*, 1987, 89(3), pp. 305–34.

Svensson, Lars-Gunnar and Weibull, Jörgen W. Constrained Pareto-Optimal Taxation of Labour and Capital Incomes. *J. Public Econ.*, December 1987, 34(3), pp. 355–66.

Tabellini, Guido. Central Bank Reputation and the Monetization of Deficits: The 1981 Italian Monetary Reform. *Econ. Inquiry*, April 1987, 25(2), pp. 185–200. [G: Italy]

Tanzi, Vito. Fiscal Policy, Growth, and Stabilization Programs. *Finance Develop.*, June 1987, 24(2), pp. 15–17.

Tanzi, Vito; Blejer, Mario I. and Teijeiro, Mario O. Inflation and the Measurement of Fiscal Deficits. *Int. Monet. Fund Staff Pap.*, December 1987, 34(4), pp. 711–38.

Théret, Bruno and Uri, Didier. Pression fiscale limite, prélèvements obligatoires et production marchande: à propos de récentes estimations économétriques d'une courbe de Laffer pour la France. (Limit of the Tax Rate, Public Levies and Productive Sector. About Some Recent Econometric Estimations of a Laffer Curve for France. With English summary.) *Écon. Appl.*, 1987, 40(1), pp. 115–59. [G: France]

Thon, Dominique. Redistributive Properties of Progressive Taxation: Note. *Math. Soc. Sci.*, October 1987, 14(2), pp. 185–91.

Thygesen, Niels. Monetary and Fiscal Policies for Economic Recovery in Europe. *Europ. Econ. Rev.*, Feb./Mar. 1987, 31(1/2), pp. 67–73. [G: W. Europe]

Tobin, James. An Essay on the Principles of Debt Management. *Tobin, J. (I)*, 1987, 1963, pp. 378–455. [G: U.S.]

Tobin, James. Does Fiscal Policy Matter? *Tobin, J. (III)*, 1987, pp. 175–85. [G: U.S.]

Tobin, James. Supply-Side Economics: What Is It? Will It Work? *Tobin, J. (III)*, 1987, 1981, pp. 126–32. [G: U.S.]

Tobin, James. Unemployment, Interest, Deficits, and Money. *Tobin, J. (III)*, 1987, pp. 189–214. [G: U.S.]

Tobin, James. Yes, Virginia, There Are Laffer Curves. *Tobin, J. (III)*, 1987, pp. 120–25. [G: U.S.]

Tobin, James and Hall, Challis A. Income Taxation, Output and Prices. *Tobin, J. (I)*, 1987, 1955, pp. 47–82.

Towe, Christopher M. Transactions Technology and the Time Consistency of Optimal Policy. *J. Public Econ.*, October 1987, 34(1), pp. 121–28.

Tsukamoto, Jun. Bequest Behavior and the Steady-State Interest Rate. *Econ. Stud. Quart.*, September 1987, 38(3), pp. 258–63.

Tsuneki, Atsushi. The Measurement of Waste in a Public Goods Economy. *J. Public Econ.*, June 1987, 33(1), pp. 73–94.

Turnbull, Geoffrey K. Land Taxes, Income Taxes, and Land Use. *Nat. Tax J.*, June 1987, 40(2), pp. 265–69.

Turnbull, Geoffrey K. Reply [On the Interpretation of Reduced Form Public Demand Parameter Estimates]. *Nat. Tax J.*, March 1987, 40(1), pp. 137–38.

Turnovsky, Stephen J. Optimal Monetary Growth with Accommodating Fiscal Policy in a Small Open Economy. *J. Int. Money Finance*, June 1987, 6(2), pp. 179–93.

Turnovsky, Stephen J. and Scarth, William M. Non-uniqueness and Instability under Rational Expectations: The Case of a Bond-Financed Government Deficit. *[Marrama, V.]*, Vol. 2, 1987, pp. 933–52.

Turnovsky, Stephen J. and Wohar, Mark E. Alternative Modes of Deficit Financing and Endogeneous Monetary and Fiscal Policy in the U.S.A. 1923–1982. *J. Appl. Econometrics*, January 1987, *2*(1), pp. 1–25.　　　　[G: U.S.]

Turunen, Arja H. Economic Inequality and Public Policy in a Small Open Economy. *Scand. J. Econ.*, 1987, *89*(4), pp. 405–19.

Vaghari, Jila. The Private Sector's Perception of Fiscal Actions. *J. Macroecon.*, Spring 1987, *9*(2), pp. 287–92.　　　　[G: U.S.]

Van Imhoff, Evert. On the Independence of Financing Methods and Redistributive Aspects of Public Pensions: A Comment. *Public Finance*, 1987, *42*(3), pp. 448–53.

Veall, Michael R. A Note on the Expenditure Tax and Progressivity. *Nat. Tax J.*, June 1987, *40*(2), pp. 259–63.

Verbon, H. A. A. On the Independence of Financing Methods and Redistributive Aspects of Pension Schemes: A Reply. *Public Finance*, 1987, *42*(3), pp. 454–56.

Vohra, Rajiv. Local Public Goods as Individual Commodities. *Reg. Sci. Urban Econ.*, May 1987, *17*(2), pp. 191–208.

Waller, Christopher J. Deficit Financing and the Role of the Central Bank—A Game Theoretic Approach. *Atlantic Econ. J.*, July 1987, *15*(2), pp. 25–32.

Weil, Philippe. Love Thy Children: Reflections on the Barro Debt Neutrality Theorem. *J. Monet. Econ.*, May 1987, *19*(3), pp. 377–91.

Weil, Philippe. Permanent Budget Deficits and Inflation. *J. Monet. Econ.*, September 1987, *20*(2), pp. 393–410.

Welch, John H.; Primo Braga, Carlos Alberto and Afonso de André, Paulo de Tarso. Brazilian Public Sector Disequilibrium. *World Devel.*, August 1987, *15*(8), pp. 1045–52.　　　　[G: Brazil]

Weymark, John A. Comparative Static Properties of Optimal Nonlinear Income Taxes. *Econometrica*, September 1987, *55*(5), pp. 1165–85.

Wibaut, Serge R. A Model of Tax Reform for Belgium. *J. Public Econ.*, February 1987, *32*(1), pp. 53–77.　　　　[G: Belgium]

Wilson, John Douglas. Trade in a Tiebout Economy. *Amer. Econ. Rev.*, June 1987, *77*(3), pp. 431–41.

Wilson, John Douglas. Trade, Capital Mobility, and Tax Competition. *J. Polit. Econ.*, August 1987, *95*(4), pp. 835–56.

van Winden, Frans A. A. M. Man in the Public Sector. *De Economist*, 1987, *135*(1), pp. 1–28.

Witt, Peter-Christian. History and Sociology of Public Finance—Problems and Topics. *Witt, P.-C., ed.*, 1987, pp. 1–18.　　[G: Germany]

Wyckoff, Paul Gary. A Note on the Effect of a Common Misspecification of the Median Voter Model [On the Interpretation of Reduced Form Public Demand Parameter Estimates]. *Nat. Tax J.*, March 1987, *40*(1), pp. 133–35.

Yitzhaki, Shlomo. On the Excess Burden of Tax Evasion. *Public Finance Quart.*, April 1987, *15*(2), pp. 123–37.

Yotsuzuka, Toshiki. Ricardian Equivalence in the Presence of Capital Market Imperfections. *J. Monet. Econ.*, September 1987, *20*(2), pp. 411–36.

Young, H. P. Progressive Taxation and the Equal Sacrifice Principle. *J. Public Econ.*, March 1987, *32*(2), pp. 203–14.

Zee, Howell H. Government Debt, Capital Accumulation, and the Terms of Trade in a Model of Interdependent Economies. *Econ. Inquiry*, October 1987, *25*(4), pp. 599–618.

3216 Fiscal Policy

Aaron, Henry J. The Impact of a Value-Added Tax on U.S. Competitiveness. *Walker, C. E. and Bloomfield, M. A., eds.*, 1987, pp. 206–13.　　　　[G: U.S.]

Adams, Gordon and Gold, D. A. The Economics of Military Spending: Is the Military Dollar Really Different? *Schmidt, C. and Blackaby, F., eds.*, 1987, pp. 266–300.　　[G: U.S.]

Aoki, Torao. Ongoing Tax Reform I: Japan. *Bull. Int. Fiscal Doc.*, March 1987, *41*(3), pp. 111–16.　　　　[G: Japan]

Arellano, José Pablo and Marfán, Manuel. 25 años de política fiscal en Chile. (25 Years of Fiscal Policy in Chile. With English summary.) *Colección Estud. CIEPLAN*, June 1987, (21), pp. 129–62.　　　　[G: Chile]

Auerbach, Alan J. and Poterba, James M. Tax-Loss Carryforwards and Corporate Tax Incentives. *Feldstein, M., ed. (I)*, 1987, pp. 305–38.　　　　[G: U.S.]

Bale, Harvey E., Jr. The Consumption Tax: A Better Alternative? The International Trade Issues. *Walker, C. E. and Bloomfield, M. A., eds.*, 1987, pp. 213–21.　　[G: U.S.]

Ballentine, J. Gregory. The Administrability of a Value-Added Tax. *Walker, C. E. and Bloomfield, M. A., eds.*, 1987, pp. 296–300.　　　　[G: U.S.]

Baucus, Max. A Congressional Perspective on Competitiveness. *Walker, C. E. and Bloomfield, M. A., eds.*, 1987, pp. 221–24.　　　　[G: U.S.]

Begg, David K. H. Fiscal Policy in Britain: Placing the Medium-term Financial Strategy in Context. *Begg, D. K. H., et al.*, 1987, pp. 17–43.　　　　[G: U.K.]

Begg, David K. H. The Performance of the British Economy: Fiscal Policy. *Dornbusch, R. and Layard, R., eds.*, 1987, pp. 29–63. [G: U.K.]

Bell, Stephen E. A Political Strategy for a Consumption Tax: The Political Context. *Walker, C. E. and Bloomfield, M. A., eds.*, 1987, pp. 353–56.　　　　[G: U.S.]

Bernheim, B. Douglas and Shoven, John B. Taxation and the Cost of Capital: An International Comparison. *Walker, C. E. and Bloomfield, M. A., eds.*, 1987, pp. 61–85.　　[G: Global]

Bhargava, Surendra N. India–Canada Treaty for the Avoidance of Double Taxation. *Bull. Int. Fiscal Doc.*, March 1987, *41*(3), pp. 117–18.　　　　[G: India; Canada]

Bogaert, Henri; de Biolley, Tanguy and Maldague, Robert. Between Theory and Policy:

Is the Planner a Necessary Go-Between? *Steinherr, A. and Weiserbs, D., eds.*, 1987, pp. 213–38. **[G: Belgium]**

Bosanquet, N. The Distribution and Redistribution of Income in the United Kingdom, 1971–84: Comment. *Levitt, M. S., ed.*, 1987, pp. 65–69. **[G: U.K.]**

Bradford, David F. On the Incidence of Consumption Taxes. *Walker, C. E. and Bloomfield, M. A., eds.*, 1987, pp. 243–61. **[G: U.S.]**

Bradford, David F. Tax-Loss Carryforwards and Corporate Tax Incentives: Comment. *Feldstein, M., ed. (I)*, 1987, pp. 339–42. **[G: U.S.]**

Brewer, Thomas L. Instability in Developing and Industrial Countries: Methodological and Theoretical Issues: Reply [A Comparative Analysis of the Fiscal Policies of Industrial and Developing Countries—Policy Instability and Governmental-Regime Instability]. *J. Compar. Econ.*, March 1987, *11*(1), pp. 120–23.

Bruno, Michael. The Economics of Public Deficits: Comments. *Razin, A. and Sadka, E., eds.*, 1987, pp. 45–46. **[G: U.S.]**

Buchanan, James M. and Wagner, Richard E. The Political Biases of Keynesian Economics. *Buchanan, J. M. (II)*, 1987, *1978*, pp. 389–408.

Budd, Alan. Fiscal Policy in Britain: Placing the Medium-term Financial Strategy in Context: Commentary. *Begg, D. K. H., et al.*, 1987, pp. 44–49. **[G: U.K.]**

Buiter, Willem H. Fiscal Policy and European Economic Growth: Comment. *Lawrence, R. Z. and Schultze, C. L., eds.*, 1987, pp. 492–501. **[G: W. Europe]**

Burman, Leonard E.; Neubig, Thomas S. and Wilson, D. Gordon. The Use and Abuse of Rental Project Models. *U.S. Treasury, Office of Tax Analysis.*, 1987, pp. 307–49. **[G: U.S.]**

Canto, Victor A.; Nickelsburg, Gerald and Rizos, Paul. The Effect of Fiscal Policy on the Short-run Relation between Nominal Interest Rates and Inflation. *Econ. Inquiry*, January 1987, *25*(1), pp. 27–42. **[G: U.S.]**

Carlson, George N. A Federal Consumption Tax: Design and Administrative Issues. *Walker, C. E. and Bloomfield, M. A., eds.*, 1987, pp. 375–95. **[G: U.S.]**

Carlson, Keith M. Federal Fiscal Policy since the Employment Act of 1946. *Fed. Res. Bank St. Louis Rev.*, December 1987, *69*(10), pp. 14–29. **[G: U.S.]**

Carroll, Chris and Summers, Lawrence H. Why Have Private Savings Rates in the United States and Canada Diverged? *J. Monet. Econ.*, September 1987, *20*(2), pp. 249–79. **[G: U.S.; Canada]**

Casanegra de Jantscher, Milka. Problems in Administering a Consumption Tax. *Walker, C. E. and Bloomfield, M. A., eds.*, 1987, pp. 300–305. **[G: U.S.]**

Christian, Ernest S., Jr. Consumption Taxes Are Not Regressive. *Walker, C. E. and Bloomfield, M. A., eds.*, 1987, pp. 329–32. **[G: U.S.]**

Cohen, Edwin S. The Consumption Tax: A Better Alternative? Lessons from the European VAT Experience. *Walker, C. E. and Bloomfield, M. A., eds.*, 1987, pp. 305–08. **[G: U.S.]**

Courant, Paul N. Fiscal Policy and European Economic Growth. *Lawrence, R. Z. and Schultze, C. L., eds.*, 1987, pp. 423–92. **[G: W. Europe]**

Cukierman, Alex. The Economics of Public Deficits: Comments. *Razin, A. and Sadka, E., eds.*, 1987, pp. 47–50. **[G: U.S.]**

Cumby, Robert E. Japanese–U.S. Current Accounts and Exchange Rates before and after the G5 Agreement: Discussion. *Sato, R. and Wachtel, P., eds.*, 1987, pp. 148–52. **[G: Japan; U.S.]**

Currie, David. Fiscal Policy in Britain: Placing the Medium-term Financial Strategy in Context: Commentary. *Begg, D. K. H., et al.*, 1987, pp. 50–53. **[G: U.K.]**

Curtis, Douglas C. A. Quantitative Estimates of Canadian Fiscal Policy 1970–1983. *Public Finance*, 1987, *42*(1), pp. 42–64. **[G: Canada]**

Dimsdale, N. H. Keynes on British Budgetary Policy 1914–46. *Boskin, M. J.; Fleming, J. S. and Gorini, S., eds.*, 1987, pp. 208–33. **[G: U.K.]**

Dolde, Walter and Tobin, James. Monetary and Fiscal Effects on Consumption. *Tobin, J. (II)*, 1987, *1971*, pp. 175–215. **[G: U.S.]**

Durenberger, Dave. The Consumption Tax Alternative. *Walker, C. E. and Bloomfield, M. A., eds.*, 1987, pp. 167–72.

Dworin, Lowell. Impact of the Corporate Alternative Minimum Tax: A Monte Carlo Simulation Study. *U.S. Treasury, Office of Tax Analysis.*, 1987, pp. 253–78. **[G: U.S.]**

FitzGerald, E. V. K. Looney and Frederiksen on Mexican Fiscal Policy: A Reply. *World Devel.*, March 1987, *15*(3), pp. 405–06. **[G: Mexico]**

Flippo, Ronnie G. A U.S. Consumption Tax: Comments from a Legislator. *Walker, C. E. and Bloomfield, M. A., eds.*, 1987, pp. 308–10. **[G: U.S.]**

Fowler, Henry H. A Historical Perspective on Tax Policy. *Walker, C. E. and Bloomfield, M. A., eds.*, 1987, pp. 3–23. **[G: U.S.]**

Fullerton, Don; Gillette, Robert and Mackie, James. Investment Incentives under the Tax Reform Act of 1986. *U.S. Treasury, Office of Tax Analysis.*, 1987, pp. 131–71. **[G: U.S.]**

Fullerton, Don; Henderson, Yolanda Kodrzycki and Mackie, James. Investment Allocation and Growth under the Tax Reform Act of 1986. *U.S. Treasury, Office of Tax Analysis.*, 1987, pp. 173–201. **[G: U.S.]**

Galbraith, John Kenneth. The Budget and the Bust. *Fink, R. H. and High, J. C., eds.*, 1987, *1982*, pp. 136–42. **[G: U.S.]**

Garcia Rocha, Adalberto. Inequality and Growth in Mexico. *Salazar-Carrillo, J. and Tirado de Alonzo, I., eds.*, 1987, pp. 1–6. **[G: Mexico]**

Gerardi, Geraldine, et al. The Treasury Depreciation Model. *U.S. Treasury, Office of Tax Analysis.*, 1987, pp. 203–27. **[G: U.S.]**

Gordon, Robert J. The Performance of the British

Economy: Fiscal Policy: Comment. *Dornbusch, R. and Layard, R.*, eds., 1987, pp. 256–59. [G: U.K.]

Gradison, Bill. A U.S. Consumption Tax: A Congressional Response. *Walker, C. E. and Bloomfield, M. A.*, eds., 1987, pp. 262–65. [G: U.S.]

Grubert, Harry and Mutti, John. The Impact of the Tax Reform Act of 1986 on Trade and Capital Flows. *U.S. Treasury, Office of Tax Analysis.*, 1987, pp. 229–52. [G: U.S.]

Higgins, Christopher. Fiscal and Monetary Policies: Their Role in the Adjustment Process: Comment. *Holmes, F.*, ed., 1987, pp. 185–91. [G: W. Germany; Japan; Belgium; U.S.]

Holtham, Gerald. Fiscal Policy and European Economic Growth: Comment. *Lawrence, R. Z. and Schultze, C. L.*, eds., 1987, pp. 501–04. [G: W. Europe]

Hong, Lee Fook. Tax Incentives to Become a Financial Centre: Singapore. *Bull. Int. Fiscal Doc.*, March 1987, *41*(3), pp. 103–10. [G: Singapore]

Hufbauer, Gary Clyde. The Consumption Tax and International Competitiveness. *Walker, C. E. and Bloomfield, M. A.*, eds., 1987, pp. 179–205. [G: U.S.]

Jankowski, Richard. The Profit-Squeeze and Tax Policy: Can the State Actively Intervene? *Rev. Radical Polit. Econ.*, Fall 1987, *19*(3), pp. 18–33. [G: U.S.]

Katsaitis, Odysseus. The Crowding Out Debate [Comment]. *J. Post Keynesian Econ.*, Spring 1987, *9*(3), pp. 473–76. [G: U.S.]

Kay, John A. Tax Reform in Retrospect: The Role of Inquiries. *van de Kar, H. M. and Wolfe, B. L.*, eds., 1987, pp. 67–81. [G: U.S.; U.K.; Canada; Australia; New Zealand]

Knight, Malcolm and Masson, Paul R. Transmission of the Effects of Fiscal Policies among Industrial Countries. *Finance Develop.*, March 1987, *24*(1), pp. 41–44. [G: U.S.; Japan; W. Germany]

Köllner, Lutz. Bemerkungen zur Finanzsoziologie heute. (Notes on the Sociology of Finance Today. With English summary.) *Jahr. Nationalökon. Statist.*, January 1987, *203*(1), pp. 26–42.

Kuttner, Robert. The Liberal Case for a Value-Added Tax. *Walker, C. E. and Bloomfield, M. A.*, eds., 1987, pp. 337–46. [G: U.S.]

LeLoup, Lance T.; Graham, Barbara Luck and Barwick, Stacey. Deficit Politics and Constitutional Government: The Impact of Gramm–Rudman–Hollings. *Public Budg. Finance*, Spring 1987, *7*(1), pp. 83–103. [G: U.S.]

Lerner, Abba P. Functional Finance and the Federal Debt. *Fink, R. H. and High, J. C.*, eds., 1987, *1983*, pp. 58–66.

Looney, Robert E. and Frederiksen, P. C. Fiscal Policy in Mexico: The FitzGerald Thesis Reexamined. *World Devel.*, March 1987, *15*(3), pp. 399–404. [G: Mexico]

Lynch, Thomas D. A Line-Item Veto for the American President. *Thai, K. V.*, ed., 1987, pp. 261–94. [G: U.S.]

Makin, John H. Income Tax Reform and the Con-

sumption Tax. *Walker, C. E. and Bloomfield, M. A.*, eds., 1987, pp. 87–115. [G: U.S.]

Makin, John H. and Shoven, John B. Are There Lessons for the United States in the Japanese Tax System? *Cagan, P.*, ed., 1987, pp. 305–29. [G: U.S.; Japan]

Marris, Stephen. Growth Gaps, Exchange Rates and Asymmetry: Comments. *Patrick, H. T. and Tachi, R.*, eds., 1987, pp. 30–36. [G: Japan; U.S.]

Martin, Stephen; Smith, Ron P. and Fontanel, Jacques. Time-Series Estimates of the Macroeconomic Impact of Defence Spending in France and the UK. *Schmidt, C. and Blackaby, F.*, eds., 1987, pp. 342–61. [G: France; U.K.]

Masera, Rainer S. Four Arguments for Fiscal Recovery in Italy. *Boskin, M. J.; Fleming, J. S. and Gorini, S.*, eds., 1987, pp. 171–207. [G: Italy]

Matsui, Robert T. Issues of the Regressivity of a Consumption Tax: The Political Dynamics. *Walker, C. E. and Bloomfield, M. A.*, eds., 1987, pp. 333–36. [G: U.S.]

McLure, Charles E., Jr. The Optimal Consumption Tax for the United States. *Walker, C. E. and Bloomfield, M. A.*, eds., 1987, pp. 265–71. [G: U.S.]

Modigliani, Franco. The Economics of Public Deficits. *Razin, A. and Sadka, E.*, eds., 1987, pp. 3–44. [G: U.S.]

Modigliani, Franco and Jappelli, Tullio. Fiscal Policy and Saving in Italy since 1860. *Boskin, M. J.; Fleming, J. S. and Gorini, S.*, eds., 1987, pp. 126–70. [G: Italy]

Neubig, Thomas S. and Sullivan, Martin A. The Effect of the Tax Reform Act of 1986 on Commercial Banks. *U.S. Treasury, Office of Tax Analysis.*, 1987, pp. 279–305. [G: U.S.]

O'Higgins, Michael. The Distribution and Redistribution of Income in the United Kingdom, 1971–84. *Levitt, M. S.*, ed., 1987, pp. 50–65. [G: U.K.]

Odedokun, Matthew O. A Flow-of-Funds Framework for Evaluating the Behaviours of Fiscal and Monetary Authorities Using Nigerian Data. *Public Finance*, 1987, *42*(2), pp. 193–213. [G: Nigeria]

Olopoenia, Razaq A. Fiscal Policy and Economic Instability in an Oil-Dependent Economy: The Nigerian Experience during the Oil Boom of the Seventies. *Pakistan J. Appl. Econ.*, Summer 1987, *6*(1), pp. 41–60. [G: Nigeria]

Parry, Charles W. An Industrialist Looks at the Consumption Tax. *Walker, C. E. and Bloomfield, M. A.*, eds., 1987, pp. 29–33. [G: U.S.]

Passadeos, Christos. The Economics of Military Spending: Is the Military Dollar Really Different? Comment. *Schmidt, C. and Blackaby, F.*, eds., 1987, pp. 301. [G: U.S.]

Pechman, Joseph A. A Consumption Tax Is Not Desirable for the United States. *Walker, C. E. and Bloomfield, M. A.*, eds., 1987, pp. 271–74. [G: U.S.]

Penner, Rudolph G. The Consumption Tax: A Better Alternative? The Federal Budget Con-

text. *Walker, C. E. and Bloomfield, M. A.,
eds.*, 1987, pp. 35–40.   [G: U.S.]
Phelps, Edmund S. Appraising the American Fiscal Stance. *Boskin, M. J.; Fleming, J. S. and Gorini, S., eds.*, 1987, pp. 95–104. [G: U.S.]
Phillips, Kevin P. A Political Strategy for a Consumption Tax. *Walker, C. E. and Bloomfield, M. A., eds.*, 1987, pp. 347–52.   [G: U.S.]
Posner, Michael V. Private Saving and Public Debt: A Survey of the Debate. *Boskin, M. J.; Fleming, J. S. and Gorini, S., eds.*, 1987, pp. 395–414.
Prakken, Joel L. The Macroeconomics of Tax Reform. *Walker, C. E. and Bloomfield, M. A., eds.*, 1987, pp. 117–66.   [G: U.S.]
Pressman, Steven. A Tale of Two Taxpayers: The Effects of the Economic Recovery and Tax Act of 1981. *J. Post Keynesian Econ.*, Winter 1986-87, 9(2), pp. 226–36.   [G: U.S.]
Rostenkowski, Dan. The Consumption Tax: A Better Alternative? A View from the Ways and Means Committee. *Walker, C. E. and Bloomfield, M. A., eds.*, 1987, pp. 25–28. [G: U.S.]
Sapounas, George S. Allocation of Goods and Services in VAT: The Case of Greece. *Europ. Econ. Rev.*, August 1987, 31(6), pp. 1285–98.
                                        [G: Greece]
Schulze, Dick. The Consumption Tax: A Better Alternative? A Congressional View. *Walker, C. E. and Bloomfield, M. A., eds.*, 1987, pp. 240–42.   [G: U.S.]
Sheffrin, Steven M. Fiscal Policy Tied to the Mast: What Has Gramm–Rudman Wrought? *Contemp. Policy Issues*, April 1987, 5(2), pp. 44–56.   [G: U.S.]
Smiley, Gene. Some Austrian Perspectives on Keynesian Fiscal Policy and the Recovery in the Thirties. *Rothbard, M. N., ed.*, 1987, pp. 145–79.   [G: U.S.]
Spencer, Grant H. and Clements, Robin T. Fiscal and Monetary Policies: Their Role in the Adjustment Process. *Holmes, F., ed.*, 1987, pp. 154–84. [G: Japan; Belgium; W. Germany]
Stein, Herbert. The Significance of Budget Deficits. *Fink, R. H. and High, J. C., eds.*, 1987, 1984, pp. 235–42.   [G: U.S.]
Stockfisch, J. A. The Value-Added Tax as a "Money Machine." *Walker, C. E. and Bloomfield, M. A., eds.*, 1987, pp. 225–37.
                                        [G: OECD]
Summers, Lawrence H. Investment Incentives and the Discounting of Depreciation Allowances. *Feldstein, M., ed. (I)*, 1987, pp. 295–304.   [G: U.S.]
Summers, Lawrence H. The Impact of Tax Policy on Savings. *Walker, C. E. and Bloomfield, M. A., eds.*, 1987, pp. 172–77.   [G: U.S.]
Tanzi, Vito and Ter-Minassian, Teresa. The European Monetary System and Fiscal Policies. *Cnossen, S., ed.*, 1987, pp. 337–57.
                                        [G: EEC]
Thai, Khi V. President Reagan's Tax Reform. *Thai, K. V., ed.*, 1987, pp. 193–220.
                                        [G: U.S.]
Tobin, James. A Keynesian View of the Budget

Deficit. *Fink, R. H. and High, J. C., eds.*, 1987, 1984, pp. 75–82.   [G: U.S.]
Tobin, James. Comment from an Academic Scribbler (on *Democracy in Deficit*). *Tobin, J. (III)*, 1987, 1978, pp. 226–36.   [G: U.S.]
Tobin, James. Fiscal and Monetary Policy under the Employment Act. *Tobin, J. (III)*, 1987, 1986, pp. 24–39.
Tobin, James. Reagan: Recovery or Reaction? *Tobin, J. (III)*, 1987, 1981, pp. 100–105.
                                        [G: U.S.]
Tobin, James. Reaganomics in Retrospect. *Tobin, J. (III)*, 1987, pp. 69–88.   [G: U.S.]
Tobin, James. The Fiscal Revolution: Disturbing Prospects. *Tobin, J. (III)*, 1987, 1985, pp. 133–41.   [G: U.S.]
Tobin, James. The Fiscal Revolution: Disturbing Prospects. *Challenge*, Special Issue 1987, 30(6), pp. 45–49.   [G: U.S.]
Tobin, James. The Monetary–Fiscal Mix in the United States. *Tobin, J. (III)*, 1987, pp. 142–67.   [G: U.S.]
Tobin, James. The Reagan Economic Plan—Supply-Side, Budget, and Inflation. *Tobin, J. (III)*, 1987, 1981, pp. 106–19.   [G: U.S.]
Tobin, James. The Reagan Legacy. *Tobin, J. (III)*, 1987, 1984, pp. 168–70.   [G: U.S.]
Tobin, James. Unemployment, Interest, Deficits, and Money. *Tobin, J. (III)*, 1987, pp. 189–214.
                                        [G: U.S.]
Trías Fargas, Ramón and Raga, José. Public Finance and Governance in a New Democracy: Opportunities and Problems. *van de Kar, H. M. and Wolfe, B. L., eds.*, 1987, pp. 251–57.
                                        [G: Spain]
Vasquez, Thomas E. Addressing Issues of the Regressivity of a Consumption Tax. *Walker, C. E. and Bloomfield, M. A., eds.*, 1987, pp. 311–28.   [G: U.S.]
Waltman, Jerold L. Changing the Course of Tax Policy: Convergence in Intent, Divergence in Practice. *Waltman, J. L. and Studlar, D. T., eds.*, 1987, pp. 98–119.   [G: U.K.; U.S.]
Weaver, R. Kent. Political Foundations of Swedish Economic Policy. *Bosworth, B. P. and Rivlin, A. M., eds.*, 1987, pp. 289–324.
                                        [G: Sweden]
Wells, Graeme. The Changing Focus of Fiscal Policy. *Bollard, A. and Buckle, R., eds.*, 1987, pp. 283–98.   [G: New Zealand]
West, Edwin G. Public Debt Burden and Cost Theory. *Fink, R. H. and High, J. C., eds.*, 1987, 1975, pp. 108–18.
Will, George F. Economic Growth: Growing Up. *Walker, C. E. and Bloomfield, M. A., eds.*, 1987, pp. 49–57.   [G: U.S.]
Wilson, Michael H. Canada Considers a Business Transfer Tax. *Walker, C. E. and Bloomfield, M. A., eds.*, 1987, pp. 41–48. [G: Canada]
Yoshitomi, Masaru. Growth Gaps, Exchange Rates and Asymmetry: Is it Possible to Unwind Current-Account Imbalances without Fiscal Expansion in Japan? *Patrick, H. T. and Tachi, R., eds.*, 1987, pp. 18–29. [G: Japan; U.S.]
Yu, Chwo-Ming. A Reconsideration of Measures of Instability: Comment [A Comparative Analy-

sis of the Fiscal Policies of Industrial and Developing Countries—Policy Instability and Governmental-Regime Instability]. *J. Compar. Econ.*, March 1987, *11*(1), pp. 116–19.

322 National Government Expenditures and Budgeting

3220 General

Afxentiou, Panayiotis C. Displacement Effect: An Econometric Test for Cyprus. *Greek Econ. Rev.*, 1987, *9*(1), pp. 113–30. **[G: Cyprus]**

Arnold, R. Douglas. Legislators, Bureaucrats, and Locational Decisions. *McCubbins, M. D. and Sullivan, T., eds.*, 1987, *1981*, pp. 523–48. **[G: U.S.]**

Beeton, D. J. and Peston, M. H. A Note on the Definition, Provision and Financing of Public Expenditure. *Brit. Rev. Econ. Issues,* Spring 1987, *9*(20), pp. 69–78.

Begg, David K. H. Long-run Implications of the Increase in Taxation and Public Debt for Employment and Economic Growth in Europe: Comments. *Europ. Econ. Rev.*, April 1987, *31*(3), pp. 775–77. **[G: W. Europe]**

Berry, Maureen. Financial Accountability in West German Government. *Most, Kenneth S., ed.*, 1987, pp. 39–84. **[G: W. Germany]**

Brown, Richard E. and Sprohge, Hans-Dieter. Governmental Managerial Accounting: What and Where Is It? *Public Budg. Finance,* Autumn 1987, *7*(3), pp. 35–46.

Buchanan, James M. The Moral Dimension of Debt Financing. *Fink, R. H. and High, J. C., eds.*, 1987, *1985*, pp. 102–07.

Buck, Hannsjörg F. The GDR Financial System. *Jeffries, I. and Melzer, M., eds.*, 1987, pp. 149–201. **[G: E. Germany]**

Burstein, Carolyn and Fisk, Donald M. The Federal Government Productivity Improvement Program: Status and Agenda. *Public Budg. Finance,* Winter 1987, *7*(4), pp. 36–47. **[G: U.S.]**

Byatt, I. C. R. Public Expenditure: The International Dimension: Comment. *Levitt, M. S., ed.*, 1987, pp. 119–22. **[G: U.K.]**

Cullis, John G. and Jones, Philip R. Fiscal Illusion and "Excessive" Budgets: Some Indirect Evidence. *Public Finance Quart.*, April 1987, *15*(2), pp. 219–28. **[G: U.K.]**

Curtis, Douglas C. A. Quantitative Estimates of Canadian Fiscal Policy 1970–1983. *Public Finance,* 1987, *42*(1), pp. 42–64. **[G: Canada]**

Dobbs, David T. and Ziemer, Richard C. Federal Fiscal Programs. *Surv. Curr. Bus.*, February 1987, *67*(2), pp. 19–24. **[G: U.S.]**

Feldstein, Martin S. Long-run Implications of the Increase in Taxation and Public Debt for Employment and Economic Growth in Europe: Comments. *Europ. Econ. Rev.*, April 1987, *31*(3), pp. 778–80. **[G: W. Europe]**

Fountain, James R. Governmental Accounting: Where Is It Heading. *Public Budg. Finance,* Winter 1987, *7*(4), pp. 95–103. **[G: U.S.]**

Freeman, R. D. The State and the Private Sector: Comment. *Levitt, M. S., ed.*, 1987, pp. 43–47. **[G: U.K.]**

Goldman, Stephanie, et al. AABPA Symposium: Capital Budgets—Expanded Use in Federal Sector. *Public Budg. Finance,* Autumn 1987, *7*(3), pp. 4–13. **[G: U.S.]**

Gramlich, Edward M. Rethinking the Role of the Public Sector. *Bosworth, B. P. and Rivlin, A. M., eds.*, 1987, pp. 250–88. **[G: Sweden]**

Grossman, Philip J. The Optimal Size of Government. *Public Choice*, 1987, *53*(2), pp. 131–47. **[G: U.S.]**

Hepworth, N. Developments in Management and Control: Comment. *Levitt, M. S., ed.*, 1987, pp. 100–104. **[G: U.K.]**

Katsaitis, Odysseus. On the Substitutability between Private Consumer Expenditure and Government Spending in Canada. *Can. J. Econ.*, August 1987, *20*(3), pp. 533–43. **[G: Canada]**

Keller, Robert R. The Role of the State in the U.S. Economy during the 1920s. *J. Econ. Issues*, June 1987, *21*(2), pp. 877–84. **[G: U.S.]**

Mamet, L. W. Tax Aspects of Joint Ventures: U.S.S.R. *Bull. Int. Fiscal Doc.*, October 1987, *41*(10), pp. 452–59. **[G: U.S.S.R.]**

McCallum, John and Blais, André. Government, Special Interest Groups, and Economic Growth. *Public Choice*, 1987, *54*(1), pp. 3–18. **[G: OECD]**

McNaught, William and Ratner, Jonathan. Budgeting for Inflation in the Department of Defense. *Public Budg. Finance,* Winter 1987, *7*(4), pp. 24–35. **[G: U.S.]**

Moore, Michael J. The Irish Consumption Function and Ricardian Equivalence. *Econ. Soc. Rev.*, October 1987, *19*(1), pp. 43–60. **[G: Ireland]**

Mueller, Dennis C. The Growth of Government: A Public Choice Perspective. *Int. Monet. Fund Staff Pap.*, March 1987, *34*(1), pp. 115–49. **[G: OECD]**

Noguchi, Yukio. The Political Economy of Japan: Public Finance. *Yamamura, K. and Yasuba, Y., eds.*, 1987, pp. 186–222. **[G: Japan]**

Palazzi, Paolo and Sardoni, Claudio. Public Expenditure and Socio-economic Structure in the Developed and LDCs. *Stud. Econ.*, 1987, *42*(32), pp. 179–216. **[G: LDCs]**

Pinto S. C., Aníbal. La ofensiva contra el Estadoeconómico. (The Offensive against the Economic State. With English summary.) *Colección Estud. CIEPLAN,* June 1987, (21), pp. 117–27. **[G: Chile]**

Ram, Rati. Wagner's Hypothesis in Time-Series and Cross-section Perspectives: Evidence from "Real" Data for 115 Countries. *Rev. Econ. Statist.*, May 1987, *69*(2), pp. 194–204. **[G: Global]**

Ruggles, Patricia and O'Higgins, Michael. Retrenchment and the New Right: A Comparative Analysis of the Impacts of the Thatcher and Reagan Administrations. *Rein, M.; Esping-Andersen, G. and Rainwater, L., eds.*, 1987, pp. 160–90. **[G: U.S.; U.K.]**

Sumner, Michael. The Economics of the Public Sector: Getting and Spending without Laying Waste Our Powers. *Bull. Econ. Res.*, October 1987, *39*(4), pp. 309–20.

Tullio, Giuseppe. Long-run Implications of the Increase in Taxation and Public Debt for Employment and Economic Growth in Europe. *Europ. Econ. Rev.*, April 1987, *31*(3), pp. 741–74. **[G: W. Europe]**

Wallace, W. J. L. Public Expenditure: The International Dimension. *Levitt, M. S., ed.*, 1987, pp. 107–19. **[G: U.K.]**

Wasylenko, Michael. Fiscal Decentralization and Economic Development. *Public Budg. Finance*, Winter 1987, *7*(4), pp. 57–71. **[G: Global]**

White, Geoff. The State and the Private Sector. *Levitt, M. S., ed.*, 1987, pp. 30–42.

Willis, Robin. Developments in Management and Control. *Levitt, M. S., ed.*, 1987, pp. 92–100. **[G: U.K.]**

3221 National Government Expenditures

Adams, Gordon and Gold, D. A. The Economics of Military Spending: Is the Military Dollar Really Different? *Schmidt, C. and Blackaby, F., eds.*, 1987, pp. 266–300. **[G: U.S.]**

Apostolakis, Bobby E. The Buy-American Practices of the U.S. Defence Department and Their Repercussions. *J. Econ. Stud.*, 1987, *14*(3), pp. 61–74. **[G: U.S.]**

Arroyo, Gloria M. An Investigation of the Real Effects of Government Expenditures. *Philippine Rev. Econ. Bus.*, Mar.-June 1987, *24*(1–2), pp. 55–77. **[G: Philippines]**

Avadhani, V. A. Real and Monetary Effects of Government Expenditure in India. *Indian Econ. J.*, Oct.-Dec. 1987, *35*(2), pp. 1–22. **[G: India]**

Blackaby, Frank. A Note on the International Comparison of Military Expenditures: Note. *Schmidt, C., ed.*, 1987, pp. 44–46. **[G: Global]**

Blackaby, Frank and Ohlson, Thomas. Military Expenditure and the Arms Trade: Problems of the Data. *Schmidt, C., ed.*, 1987, pp. 3–24. **[G: Global]**

Bradshaw, Ted K. and Blakely, Edward J. Unanticipated Consequences of Government Programs on Rural Economic Development. *U.S.D.A., Econ. Res. Serv., Agr. and Rural Econ. Div.*, 1987, pp. 11.1–17. **[G: U.S.]**

Brandt, Harm-Hinrich. Public Finances of Neoabsolutism in Austria in the 1850s: Integration and Modernisation. *Witt, P.-C., ed.*, 1987, pp. 81–109. **[G: Austria]**

Bródy, András. Defence Spending as a Priority. *Schmidt, C. and Blackaby, F., eds.*, 1987, pp. 40–44.

Buiter, Willem H. Fiscal Policy and European Economic Growth: Comment. *Lawrence, R. Z. and Schultze, C. L., eds.*, 1987, pp. 492–501. **[G: W. Europe]**

Cars, Hans Christian. Negotiations to Reduce Military Expenditures—Problems and Possibilities. *Schmidt, C., ed.*, 1987, pp. 69–84. **[G: Global]**

Cars, Hans Christian and Fontanel, Jacques. Military Expenditure Comparisons. *Schmidt, C. and Blackaby, F., eds.*, 1987, pp. 250–65. **[G: Global; W. Europe; U.S.]**

Courant, Paul N. Fiscal Policy and European Economic Growth. *Lawrence, R. Z. and Schultze, C. L., eds.*, 1987, pp. 423–92. **[G: W. Europe]**

Deiaco, Enrico. Why Is Government Spending Outgrowing GDP? *Eliasson, G., ed.*, 1987, pp. 85–93. **[G: Sweden]**

Dittman, David A.; Krasniewski, Raymond J. and Smith, Margaret. Contracting Strategies for Maximum Benefit in Sales Contracts with Government: The Installment Sale Alternative. *Chan, J. L., ed., Pt. A*, 1987, pp. 107–30. **[G: U.S.]**

Ergas, Henry. The Importance of Technology Policy. *Dasgupta, P. and Stoneman, P., eds.*, 1987, pp. 51–96. **[G: OECD]**

Fontanel, Jacques. A Note on the International Comparison of Military Expenditures. *Schmidt, C., ed.*, 1987, pp. 29–43. **[G: Global]**

Fontanel, Jacques. Military Expenditure and the Arms Trade: Problems of the Data: Note. *Schmidt, C., ed.*, 1987, pp. 25–28. **[G: Global]**

George, K. K. Discretionary Budgetary Transfers: A Review. *Gulati, I. S., ed.*, 1987, *1986*, pp. 247–64. **[G: India]**

Goodin, Robert E. and Dryzek, John. Risk-Sharing and Social Justice: The Motivational Foundations of the Post-war Welfare State. *Goodin, R. E. and Le Grand, J.*, 1987, pp. 37–73. **[G: U.K.]**

Greenwood, David. Note on the Impact of Military Expenditure on Economic Growth and Performance. *Schmidt, C., ed.*, 1987, pp. 98–103.

de Haan, Hendrik. Military Expenditures and Economic Growth: Some Theoretical Remarks. *Schmidt, C., ed.*, 1987, pp. 87–97.

Hammes, David L. and Wills, Douglas T. Public Debt, Interest and Fiscal Incidence. *Rev. Income Wealth*, December 1987, *33*(4), pp. 439–42.

Hartley, Keith. Reducing Defence Expenditure: A Public Choice Analysis and a Case Study of the UK. *Schmidt, C. and Blackaby, F., eds.*, 1987, pp. 399–423. **[G: U.K.]**

Herrera-Lasso, Luis. Economic Growth, Military Expenditure, Arms Industry and Arms Transfer in Latin America. *Schmidt, C., ed.*, 1987, pp. 113–34. **[G: Latin America]**

Ho, Yin-Ping. Endogenous Government Expenditure: A Test of Wagner's Hypothesis for Hong Kong. *Int. Econ. J.*, Autumn 1987, *1*(3), pp. 31–47. **[G: Hong Kong]**

Holloway, Thomas M. Measuring the Sensitivity of Net Interest Paid to the Business Cycle and to Inflation. *Public Finance Quart.*, July 1987, *15*(3), pp. 235–58. **[G: U.S.]**

Holtham, Gerald. Fiscal Policy and European

Economic Growth: Comment. *Lawrence, R. Z. and Schultze, C. L., eds.*, 1987, pp. 501–04. **[G: W. Europe]**

Hur, Jaewan. An Indirect Approach to Measure Governmental Perceptions of Regional Welfare Inequalities. *J. Econ. Devel.*, June 1987, *12*(1), pp. 195–209. **[G: U.S.]**

Ihori, Toshihiro. The Size of Government Spending and the Private Sector's Evaluation. *J. Japanese Int. Economies*, March 1987, *1*(1), pp. 82–96. **[G: Japan]**

Intriligator, Michael D. Semantic Variations on Richardson's Armaments Dynamics: Note. *Schmidt, C., ed.*, 1987, pp. 176–79.

Intriligator, Michael D. and Brito, Dagobert L. Can Arms Races Lead to the Outbreak of War? *Schmidt, C., ed.*, 1987, pp. 180–96.

Jackson, P. M. Public Expenditure: Trends and Prospects: Comment. *Levitt, M. S., ed.*, 1987, pp. 23–27. **[G: U.K.]**

Karavitis, Nicholas. The Causal Factors of Government Expenditure Growth in Greece, 1950–80. *Appl. Econ.*, June 1987, *19*(6), pp. 789–807. **[G: Greece]**

Kolodziej, Edward A. Re-evaluating Economic and Technological Variables to Explain Global Arms Production and Sales. *Schmidt, C., ed.*, 1987, pp. 304–35. **[G: LDCs]**

Le Grand, Julian and Winter, David. The Middle Classes and the Defence of the British Welfare State. *Goodin, R. E. and Le Grand, J.*, 1987, pp. 147–68. **[G: U.K.]**

Levitt, M. S. and Joyce, Michael. Public Expenditure: Trends and Prospects. *Levitt, M. S., ed.*, 1987, pp. 6–23. **[G: U.K.]**

Lynch, John E. Defense Spending in the Economy. *Lynch, J. E., ed.*, 1987, pp. 13–28. **[G: U.S.]**

MacLaury, Bruce K. The Relationship of Tax Revenues to Government Spending. *Walker, C. E. and Bloomfield, M. A., eds.*, 1987, pp. 238–40. **[G: U.S.]**

Madhusudhan, Ranjana G. and Burkhead, Jesse. Expenditure Trends in Selected Industrialized Countries. *Public Budg. Finance*, Winter 1987, *7*(4), pp. 49–56. **[G: OECD]**

McGuire, Martin C. Foreign Assistance, Investment, and Defense: A Methodological Study with an Application to Israel, 1960–1979. *Econ. Develop. Cult. Change*, July 1987, *35*(4), pp. 847–73. **[G: Israel]**

McGuire, Martin C. U.S. Foreign Assistance, Israeli Resource Allocation and the Arms Race in the Middle East: An Analysis of Three Interdependent Resource Allocation Processes. *Schmidt, C., ed.*, 1987, pp. 197–238. **[G: U.S.; Israel; Middle East]**

Nishikawa, Jun. Note on the Impact of Military Expenditure on the Japanese Economy. *Schmidt, C., ed.*, 1987, pp. 135–37. **[G: Japan]**

Passadeos, Christos. The Economics of Military Spending: Is the Military Dollar Really Different? Comment. *Schmidt, C. and Blackaby, F., eds.*, 1987, pp. 301. **[G: U.S.]**

Piggott, John and Whalley, John. Interpreting Net Fiscal Incidence Calculations. *Rev. Econ. Statist.*, November 1987, *69*(4), pp. 685–94. **[G: Australia]**

Pilandon, Louis. Quantitative and Causal Analysis of Military Expenditures. *Schmidt, C., ed.*, 1987, pp. 47–68. **[G: Global]**

Rivlin, Paul. The Burden of Defence in Developing Countries. *Schmidt, C., ed.*, 1987, pp. 104–12. **[G: LDCs]**

Rizzo, Ilde and Peacock, Alan. Government Debt and Growth in Public Spending. *Public Finance*, 1987, *42*(2), pp. 283–91.

Sandler, Todd. NATO Burden-Sharing: Rules or Reality? *Schmidt, C. and Blackaby, F., eds.*, 1987, pp. 363–83. **[G: U.S.; EEC]**

Scheetz, Thomas. Public Sector Expenditures and Financial Crisis in Chile. *World Devel.*, August 1987, *15*(8), pp. 1053–75. **[G: Chile]**

Schick, Allen. Controlling the "Uncontrollables": Budgeting for Health Care in an Age of Megadeficits. *Meyer, J. A. and Lewin, M. E., eds.*, 1987, pp. 13–34. **[G: U.S.]**

Schmidt, Christian. Semantic Variations on Richardson's Armaments Dynamics. *Schmidt, C., ed.*, 1987, pp. 141–75.

Schmidt, Christian. The Economics of Military Expenditures: Introduction. *Schmidt, C., ed.*, 1987, pp. xvii–xxiii.

Sen, Amartya K. Defence Spending as a Priority: Comment. *Schmidt, C. and Blackaby, F., eds.*, 1987, pp. 45–49.

Shibata, Hirofumi and Kimura, Yoko. Government Debt and Growth in Public Spending: A Reply [Economics of Representative Democracy: A Model of Skewed Representation]. *Public Finance*, 1987, *42*(2), pp. 292–96.

Smith, Ron P. The Demand for Military Expenditure: A Correction. *Econ. J.*, December 1987, *97*(388), pp. 989–90. **[G: U.K.]**

Thompson, Fred. Managing Defense Expenditures. *Thai, K. V., ed.*, 1987, *1985*, pp. 129–46. **[G: U.S.]**

Urquidi, Victor L. Military-Related Debt in Nonoil Developing Countries, 1972–82: Comment. *Schmidt, C. and Blackaby, F., eds.*, 1987, pp. 317–18. **[G: LDCs]**

Urquidi, Victor L. The Economics of Military Expenditures: Introductory Remarks. *Schmidt, C., ed.*, 1987, pp. xiii–xvi.

Weaver, R. Kent. Political Foundations of Swedish Economic Policy. *Bosworth, B. P. and Rivlin, A. M., eds.*, 1987, pp. 289–324. **[G: Sweden]**

3226 National Government Budgeting and Deficits

Artis, M. J. Deficit Financing: Keynes, the Keynesians and the New Approach, with Special Reference to the UK. *Boskin, M. J.; Fleming, J. S. and Gorini, S., eds.*, 1987, pp. 234–51. **[G: U.K.]**

Backhaus, Jürgen; Holcombe, Randall G. and Zardkoohi, Asghar. Public Investment and Its Effects on the Burden of the Public Debt. *Southern Econ. J.*, July 1987, *54*(1), pp. 145–58. **[G: U.S.]**

Bagella, Michele. Debt Neutrality and Fiscal Illusion: Theoretical Underpinnings and Empirical Studies: A Comment. *Boskin, M. J.; Fleming, J. S. and Gorini, S., eds.,* 1987, pp. 287–97. [G: U.S.]

Bernheim, B. Douglas. Ricardian Equivalence: An Evaluation of Theory and Evidence. *Fischer, S., ed.,* 1987, pp. 263–304.

Bhatty, I. Z., et al. Issues in Financial Investment. *Margin,* Apr.-June 1987, *19*(3), pp. 32–47. [G: India]

Bispham, J. A. Rising Public-Sector Indebtedness: Some More Unpleasant Arithmetic. *Boskin, M. J.; Fleming, J. S. and Gorini, S., eds.,* 1987, pp. 40–71. [G: OECD]

Boettke, Peter and Ellig, Jerome. The Business of Government and Government as a Business. *Fink, R. H. and High, J. C., eds.,* 1987, pp. 272–86. [G: U.S.]

Boskin, Michael J. Deficits, Public Debt, Interest Rates and Private Saving: Perspectives and Reflections on Recent Analyses and on U.S. Experience. *Boskin, M. J.; Fleming, J. S. and Gorini, S., eds.,* 1987, pp. 255–86. [G: U.S.]

Boskin, Michael J., et al. The Federal Budget and Federal Insurance Programs. *[Harberger, A.],* 1987, pp. 14–39. [G: U.S.]

Bowsher, Charles A. Restructuring the Federal Budgeting and Accounting System. *Thai, K. V., ed.,* 1987, *1985,* pp. 223–43. [G: U.S.]

Brewer, Thomas L. Instability in Developing and Industrial Countries: Methodological and Theoretical Issues: Reply [A Comparative Analysis of the Fiscal Policies of Industrial and Developing Countries—Policy Instability and Governmental-Regime Instability]. *J. Compar. Econ.,* March 1987, *11*(1), pp. 120–23.

Brimmer, Andrew F. Dim Prospects for the Federal Budget Deficit. *Challenge,* May/June 1987, *30*(2), pp. 58–60. [G: U.S.]

Britton, Andrew. Public Sector Borrowing and the Public Sector Balance Sheet. *Nat. Inst. Econ. Rev.,* August 1987, (121), pp. 64–66. [G: U.K.]

Britton, Andrew. Taxpayers' Capital: The Public Sector Balance Sheet. *Fisc. Stud.,* May 1987, *8*(2), pp. 24–34. [G: U.K.]

Bruno, Michael. The Economics of Public Deficits: Comments. *Razin, A. and Sadka, E., eds.,* 1987, pp. 45–46. [G: U.S.]

Bulmer-Thomas, Victor. The Balance-of-Payments Crisis and Adjustment Programmes in Central America. *Thorp, R. and Whitehead, L., eds.,* 1987, pp. 271–317. [G: Central America]

Cebula, Richard J. Federal Deficits and the Real Rate of Interest in the United States: A Note. *Public Choice,* 1987, *53*(1), pp. 97–100. [G: U.S.]

Chrystal, K. Alec and Dowd, Kevin. Would a Higher Fiscal Deficit Stimulate the Economy? *Fisc. Stud.,* February 1987, *8*(1), pp. 17–23. [G: U.K.]

Clark, Rolf. Defense Budget Instability and Weapon System Acquisition. *Public Budg. Fi-*nance, Summer 1987, *7*(2), pp. 24–36. [G: U.S.]

Clark, Timothy B. Stiff Tax Hikes Will Be Key to Future Efforts to Close the Budget Deficit. *Fink, R. H. and High, J. C., eds.,* 1987, *1984,* pp. 243–53. [G: U.S.]

Congdon, Tim G. The Link between Budget Deficits and Inflation: Some Contrasts between Developed and Developing Countries. *Boskin, M. J.; Fleming, J. S. and Gorini, S., eds.,* 1987, pp. 72–91. [G: LDCs; MDCs]

Cukierman, Alex. The Economics of Public Deficits: Comments. *Razin, A. and Sadka, E., eds.,* 1987, pp. 47–50. [G: U.S.]

Cusack, Thomas R. The GLOBUS Model: Computer Simulation of Worldwide Political and Economic Development: Government Budget Processes. *Bremer, S. A., ed.,* 1987, pp. 325–458. [G: Global]

Dalamagas, Basil A. Government Deficits, Crowding Out, and Inflation: Some International Evidence. *Public Finance,* 1987, *42*(1), pp. 65–84. [G: OECD]

Dean, Peter N. Performance Budgeting in India. *Public Finance,* 1987, *42*(2), pp. 181–92. [G: India]

Demopoulos, George D.; Katsimbris, George M. and Miller, Stephen M. Monetary Policy and Central-Bank Financing of Government Budget Deficits: A Cross-Country Comparison. *Europ. Econ. Rev.,* July 1987, *31*(5), pp. 1023–50. [G: OECD]

Dicks, Geoffrey. The 1987 Budget: A Forecaster's Perspective. *Fisc. Stud.,* May 1987, *8*(2), pp. 1–10. [G: U.K.]

Dilnot, Andrew, et al. The 1987 Budget in Perspective. *Fisc. Stud.,* May 1987, *8*(2), pp. 48–57. [G: U.K.]

Dimsdale, N. H. Keynes on British Budgetary Policy 1914–46. *Boskin, M. J.; Fleming, J. S. and Gorini, S., eds.,* 1987, pp. 208–33. [G: U.K.]

Doss, C. Bradley, Jr. The Use of Capital Budgeting Procedures in U.S. Cities. *Public Budg. Finance,* Autumn 1987, *7*(3), pp. 57–69. [G: U.S.]

Eckstein, Zvi. Inflation and the Government Budget Constraint: Comments. *Razin, A. and Sadka, E., eds.,* 1987, pp. 201–02.

Eisner, Robert and Pieper, Paul J. Errata [Dette et déficit gouvernementaux. (Measurement and Effects of Government Debt and Deficits.)]. *Ann. Écon. Statist.,* Jan./Mar. 1987, (5), pp. 197. [G: Japan; U.S.; W. Germany]

Eisner, Robert and Pieper, Paul J. How to Make Sense of the Deficit. *Fink, R. H. and High, J. C., eds.,* 1987, *1985,* pp. 87–101. [G: U.S.]

Elliott, E. Donald. Regulating the Deficit after *Bowsher v. Synar. Yale J. Regul.,* Spring 1987, *4*(2), pp. 317–62. [G: U.S.]

Eltis, Walter. Some Implications of Deficit-Financed Tax Cuts: These Will Always Increase Demand, but Will They Reduce Supply? *Boskin, M. J.; Fleming, J. S. and Gorini, S., eds.,* 1987, pp. 318–46. [G: U.S.]

Evans, Paul D. Interest Rates and Expected Future Budget Deficits in the United States. *J. Polit. Econ.*, February 1987, *95*(1), pp. 34–58. **[G: U.S.]**

Feldstein, Martin S. The Job of Reducing the Federal Deficit. *Fink, R. H. and High, J. C., eds.*, 1987, *1982*, pp. 254–57. **[G: U.S.]**

Fieleke, Norman S. The Budget Deficit: Are the International Consequences Unfavorable? *Fink, R. H. and High, J. C., eds.*, 1987, *1984*, pp. 171–80. **[G: U.S.]**

Fischer, Stanley. Inflation and the Government Budget Constraint: Comments. *Razin, A. and Sadka, E., eds.*, 1987, pp. 203–07.

Flavin, Marjorie. Ricardian Equivalence: An Evaluation of Theory and Evidence: Comment. *Fischer, S., ed.*, 1987, pp. 304–09.

Fratianni, Michele. Can Belgium Borrow Itself out of the Budget Deficit? *Rech. Écon. Louvain*, 1987, *53*(1), pp. 89–96. **[G: Belgium]**

Frenkel, Jacob A. and Razin, Assaf. The International Transmission of Fiscal Expenditures and Budget Deficits in the World Economy. *Razin, A. and Sadka, E., eds.*, 1987, pp. 51–96.

Gopalakrishnan, S. Effect of Government Borrowing on Private Investment in India. *Indian Econ. J.*, Oct.-Dec. 1987, *35*(2), pp. 48–57. **[G: India]**

Gordon, Robert J. U.S. Fiscal Deficits and the World Imbalance of Payments. *Hitotsubashi J. Econ.*, October 1987, *27*, pp. 7–41. **[G: U.S.]**

Gramlich, Edward M. Federalism and Federal Deficit Reduction. *Nat. Tax J.*, September 1987, *40*(3), pp. 299–313. **[G: U.S.]**

Grier, Kevin Blaine and Neiman, Howard E. Deficits, Politics and Money Growth. *Econ. Inquiry*, April 1987, *25*(2), pp. 201–14. **[G: U.S.]**

Grimm, Curtis M. and Holcomb, John M. Choices among Encompassing Organizations: Business and the Budget Deficit. *Marcus, A. A.; Kaufman, A. M. and Beam, D. R., eds.*, 1987, pp. 105–18. **[G: U.S.]**

de Haan, J. The (Un)importance of Public Debt: A Review Essay. *De Economist*, 1987, *135*(3), pp. 367–84. **[G: OECD]**

Hansson, Ingemar and Stuart, Charles. The Welfare Costs of Deficit Finance. *Econ. Inquiry*, July 1987, *25*(3), pp. 479–96. **[G: U.S.]**

Hazlitt, Henry. A Proposal for Two Constitutional Amendments. *Fink, R. H. and High, J. C., eds.*, 1987, *1983*, pp. 231–34. **[G: U.S.]**

Hoffman, Ronald. Macroeconomic Analysis and Stabilization Policy: Searching for Consensus. *van de Kar, H. M. and Wolfe, B. L., eds.*, 1987, pp. 13–31. **[G: U.S.]**

Hong, Lee Fook. A Summary of the 1987 Budget's Tax Clauses: Singapore. *Bull. Int. Fiscal Doc.*, May 1987, *41*(5), pp. 232–34. **[G: Singapore]**

Hossain, Akhtar. Impact of Inflation on Fiscal Deficits in the Bangladesh Economy. *Pakistan Devel. Rev.*, Summer 1987, *26*(2), pp. 179–200. **[G: Bangladesh]**

Howard, James A. Government Economic Projections: A Comparison between CBO and OMB Forecasts. *Public Budg. Finance*, Autumn 1987, *7*(3), pp. 14–25. **[G: U.S.]**

Humbert, Thomas M. Understanding the Federal Deficit: Putative Impact on Trade. *Fink, R. H. and High, J. C., eds.*, 1987, *1984*, pp. 162–70. **[G: U.S.]**

Hutchison, Michael M. and Pigott, Charles A. Real and Financial Linkages in the Macroeconomic Response to Budget Deficits: An Empirical Investigation. *Arndt, S. W. and Richardson, J. D. eds.*, 1987, pp. 139–66. **[G: U.S.; W. Germany; Japan; U.K.]**

Iqbal, Zubair. Instability of Federal Government Revenues and Expenditures in Pakistan: Comments. *Pakistan Devel. Rev.*, Winter 1987, *26*(4), pp. 510–11. **[G: Pakistan]**

Janssens, Ilse; Moesen, Wim and Pauwels, Wilfried. Publieke voorzieningen: Welvaart, poliltiek en sanering. (With English summary.) *Cah. Écon. Bruxelles*, Third Trimester 1987, (115), pp. 77–110.

Jones, Jonathan D. Are Future Taxes Anticipated by Consumers? More Evidence for the U.S., 1946–1985. *Econ. Notes*, 1987, (2), pp. 141–44. **[G: U.S.]**

Kee, James Edwin. President Reagan's FY 88 Budget: The Deficit Drives the Debate. *Public Budg. Finance*, Summer 1987, *7*(2), pp. 3–23. **[G: U.S.]**

Kremers, J. J. M. Financing Budget Deficits in the Netherlands. *De Economist*, 1987, *135*(3), pp. 340–66. **[G: Netherlands]**

LeLoup, Lance T.; Graham, Barbara Luck and Barwick, Stacey. Deficit Politics and Constitutional Government: The Impact of Gramm–Rudman–Hollings. *Public Budg. Finance*, Spring 1987, *7*(1), pp. 83–103. **[G: U.S.]**

Lerda, Juan Carlos. A dinâmica da dívida pública: de Domar–Lerner a Tobin–Simonsen. (With English summary.) *Pesquisa Planejamento Econ.*, August 1987, *17*(2), pp. 343–68.

Lerner, Abba P. Functional Finance and the Federal Debt. *Fink, R. H. and High, J. C., eds.*, 1987, *1983*, pp. 58–66.

Looney, Robert E. The Impact of Political Change, Debt Servicing and Fiscal Deficits on Argentinian Budgetary Priorities. *J. Econ. Stud.*, 1987, *14*(3), pp. 23–40. **[G: Argentina]**

Malik, Muhammad Hussain and Yasmin, Attiya. Instability of Federal Government Revenues and Expenditures in Pakistan. *Pakistan Devel. Rev.*, Winter 1987, *26*(4), pp. 501–09. **[G: Pakistan]**

Martin, Bill. The 1987 Budget. *Fisc. Stud.*, May 1987, *8*(2), pp. 11–23. **[G: U.K.]**

Masera, Rainer S. Four Arguments for Fiscal Recovery in Italy. *Boskin, M. J.; Fleming, J. S. and Gorini, S., eds.*, 1987, pp. 171–207. **[G: Italy]**

Mickwitz, Gösta. Investering i vetenskap. (Investment in Sciences. With English summary.) *Ekon. Samfundets Tidskr.*, 1987, *40*(2), pp. 59–61. **[G: Finland]**

Mickwitz, Gösta. Skall statsobligationer öronmärkas? (Should Central Government Bonds Be

Earmarked? With English summary.) *Ekon. Samfundets Tidskr.*, 1987, *40*(3), pp. 111–13. [G: Finland]

Mills, Gregory B. Prospects for the Restraint of Federal Expenditures. *Thai, K. V., ed.*, 1987, *1984*, pp. 67–93. [G: U.S.]

Minhas, B. S. The Planning Process and the Annual Budgets: Some Reflections on Recent Indian Experience. *Indian Econ. Rev.*, July-Dec. 1987, *22*(2), pp. 115–49. [G: India]

Modigliani, Franco. Budget Deficits and Rates of Interest in the World Economy: Comments. *Razin, A. and Sadka, E., eds.*, 1987, pp. 97–100.

Modigliani, Franco. The Economics of Public Deficits. *Razin, A. and Sadka, E., eds.*, 1987, pp. 3–44. [G: U.S.]

Monaco, Margaret A. and Rowley, Charles K. A Political Economy of Budget Deficits. *[Tullock, G.]*, 1987, pp. 223–42. [G: U.S.]

Moran, Donald W. Perspectives on Proposals for Budget Process Reform. *Thai, K. V., ed.*, 1987, *1984*, pp. 245–59. [G: U.S.]

Nguyen, Dung and Olson, Josephine E. U.S. Budget Deficits: Empirical and Policy Issues. *Thai, K. V., ed.*, 1987, *1986*, pp. 47–63. [G: U.S.]

Öller, Lars-Erik. Stabiliseringspolitik och prognoser. (Stabilization Policy and Forecasts. With English summary.) *Ekon. Samfundets Tidskr.*, 1987, *40*(1), pp. 23–27. [G: Finland]

Orzechowski, William P. and Conda, Cesar V. The Future of Federal Budget Reform. *Fink, R. H. and High, J. C., eds.*, 1987, pp. 287–300. [G: U.S.]

Paganetto, Luigi. Public Debt, Private Savings and Supply-Side Policies. *Boskin, M. J.; Fleming, J. S. and Gorini, S., eds.*, 1987, pp. 298–317. [G: U.S.]

Palmer, John L. The Changing Structure of the Deficit. *Nat. Tax J.*, September 1987, *40*(3), pp. 285–97. [G: U.S.]

Penner, Rudolph G. Government Deficits: The Case of the United States. *Boskin, M. J.; Fleming, J. S. and Gorini, S., eds.*, 1987, pp. 105–25. [G: U.S.]

Penner, Rudolph G. The Consumption Tax: A Better Alternative? The Federal Budget Context. *Walker, C. E. and Bloomfield, M. A., eds.*, 1987, pp. 35–40. [G: U.S.]

Plosser, Charles I. Ricardian Equivalence: An Evaluation of Theory and Evidence: Comment. *Fischer, S., ed.*, 1987, pp. 309–13.

Plotnick, Robert D. and Lidman, Russell M. Forecasting Welfare Caseloads: A Tool to Improve Budgeting. *Public Budg. Finance*, Autumn 1987, *7*(3), pp. 70–81. [G: U.S.]

Pollard, Sidney. Stagflation, Fiscal Deficits and Balance of Payments—Great Britain and Germany. *Hitotsubashi J. Econ.*, October 1987, *27*, pp. 42–56. [G: U.K.; W. Germany]

Posner, Michael V. Private Saving and Public Debt: A Survey of the Debate. *Boskin, M. J.; Fleming, J. S. and Gorini, S., eds.*, 1987, pp. 395–414.

Premchand, A. Managing the Budget. *Finance*

Develop., September 1987, *24*(3), pp. 39–42. [G: U.S.]

Rabeau, Yves. Déficit du gouvernement canadien: à quelle vitesse les autorités budgétaires doivent-elles réagir. (With English summary.) *Can. Public Policy*, December 1987, *13*(4), pp. 423–34. [G: Canada]

Rabushka, Alvin. A Compelling Case for a Constitutional Amendment to Balance the Budget and Limit Taxes. *Fink, R. H. and High, J. C., eds.*, 1987, *1982*, pp. 212–30. [G: U.S.]

Reinhardt, Uwe E. The Political Economy of "Feeling Good": True Confession of a Supply-Sider. *Aussenwirtschaft*, December 1987, *42*(4), pp. 443–69. [G: U.S.]

Rivlin, Alice M. Why and How to Cut the Deficit. *Fink, R. H. and High, J. C., eds.*, 1987, *1984*, pp. 258–65. [G: U.S.]

Robinson, Bill. How Buoyant Is Public Revenue? *Fisc. Stud.*, May 1987, *8*(2), pp. 35–47. [G: U.K.]

Rossi, José W. A dívida pública no Brasil e a aritmética da instabilidade. (With English summary.) *Pesquisa Planejamento Econ.*, August 1987, *17*(2), pp. 369–79. [G: Brazil]

Rutayisire, Laurean W. Measurement of Government Budget Deficit and Fiscal Stance in a Less Developed Economy: The Case of Tanzania, 1966–84. *World Devel.*, Oct./Nov. 1987, *15*(10/11), pp. 1337–51. [G: Tanzania]

Sargent, Thomas J. and Wallace, Neil. Inflation and the Government Budget Constraint. *Razin, A. and Sadka, E., eds.*, 1987, pp. 170–200.

Savage, James. Federal R&D Budget Policy in the Reagan Administration. *Public Budg. Finance*, Summer 1987, *7*(2), pp. 37–51. [G: U.S.]

Sewell, John W. and Contee, Christine E. Foreign Aid and Gramm–Rudman. *Foreign Aff.*, Summer 1987, *65*(5), pp. 1015–36. [G: U.S.]

Sheffrin, Steven M. Fiscal Policy Tied to the Mast: What Has Gramm–Rudman Wrought? *Contemp. Policy Issues*, April 1987, *5*(2), pp. 44–56. [G: U.S.]

Söderström, Hans Tson. Sectoral Saving and Investment Patterns in 16 OECD Countries, 1965–82. *Boskin, M. J.; Fleming, J. S. and Gorini, S., eds.*, 1987, pp. 3–39. [G: OECD]

Spiro, Peter S. The Elusive Effect of Fiscal Deficits on Interest Rates: Comment. *Int. Monet. Fund Staff Pap.*, June 1987, *34*(2), pp. 400–403. [G: U.S.]

Tanzi, Vito. The Effect of Fiscal Deficits on Interest Rates: Reply. *Int. Monet. Fund Staff Pap.*, June 1987, *34*(2), pp. 404–07. [G: U.S.]

Tanzi, Vito; Blejer, Mario I. and Teijeiro, Mario O. Inflation and the Measurement of Fiscal Deficits. *Int. Monet. Fund Staff Pap.*, December 1987, *34*(4), pp. 711–38.

Tarschys, Daniel. From Expansion to Restraint: Recent Developments in Budgeting. *van de Kar, H. M. and Wolfe, B. L., eds.*, 1987, pp. 307–20. [G: OECD]

Thai, Khi V. Structural Budget Deficits: Concepts

and Facts. *Thai, K. V., ed.*, 1987, pp. 7–28. [G: U.S.]

Thai, Khi V. and Cao, Le T. Structural Budget Deficits in the Federal Government: A Theoretical Perspective. *Thai, K. V., ed.*, 1987, pp. 29–46. [G: U.S.; OECD]

Thompson, Fred. Managing Defense Expenditures. *Thai, K. V., ed.*, 1987, 1985, pp. 129–46. [G: U.S.]

Tobin, James. A Keynesian View of the Budget Deficit. *Fink, R. H. and High, J. C., eds.*, 1987, 1984, pp. 75–82. [G: U.S.]

Tobin, James. Against the Balanced Budget and Tax Limitation Amendment. *Tobin, J. (III)*, 1987, 1983, pp. 218–25. [G: U.S.]

Tobin, James. Does Fiscal Policy Matter? *Tobin, J. (III)*, 1987, pp. 175–85. [G: U.S.]

Tobin, James. Reagan: Recovery or Reaction? *Tobin, J. (III)*, 1987, 1981, pp. 100–105. [G: U.S.]

Tobin, James. The Reagan Economic Plan—Supply-Side, Budget, and Inflation. *Tobin, J. (III)*, 1987, 1981, pp. 106–19. [G: U.S.]

Volcker, Paul A. Facing Up to the Twin Deficits. *Fink, R. H. and High, J. C., eds.*, 1987, 1984, pp. 154–61. [G: U.S.]

Wachtel, Paul and Young, John. Deficit Announcements and Interest Rates. *Amer. Econ. Rev.*, December 1987, 77(5), pp. 1007–12. [G: U.S.]

Waller, Christopher J. Deficit Financing and the Role of the Central Bank—A Game Theoretic Approach. *Atlantic Econ. J.*, July 1987, 15(2), pp. 25–32.

Weicher, John C. The Domestic Budget after Gramm–Rudman—and after Reagan. *Cagan, P., ed.*, 1987, pp. 243–73. [G: U.S.]

Yu, Chwo-Ming. A Reconsideration of Measures of Instability: Comment [A Comparative Analysis of the Fiscal Policies of Industrial and Developing Countries—Policy Instability and Governmental-Regime Instability]. *J. Compar. Econ.*, March 1987, 11(1), pp. 116–19.

3228 National Government Debt Management

Artis, M. J. Deficit Financing: Keynes, the Keynesians and the New Approach, with Special Reference to the UK. *Boskin, M. J.; Fleming, J. S. and Gorini, S., eds.*, 1987, pp. 234–51. [G: U.K.]

Bagella, Michele. Debt Neutrality and Fiscal Illusion: Theoretical Underpinnings and Empirical Studies: A Comment. *Boskin, M. J.; Fleming, J. S. and Gorini, S., eds.*, 1987, pp. 287–97. [G: U.S.]

Bispham, J. A. Rising Public-Sector Indebtedness: Some More Unpleasant Arithmetic. *Boskin, M. J.; Fleming, J. S. and Gorini, S., eds.*, 1987, pp. 40–71. [G: OECD]

Boskin, Michael J. Deficits, Public Debt, Interest Rates and Private Saving: Perspectives and Reflections on Recent Analyses and on U.S. Experience. *Boskin, M. J.; Fleming, J. S. and Gorini, S., eds.*, 1987, pp. 255–86. [G: U.S.]

Buchanan, James M. Concerning Future Genera-

tions. *Buchanan, J. M. (I)*, 1987, 1958, pp. 113–19.

Congdon, Tim G. The Link between Budget Deficits and Inflation: Some Contrasts between Developed and Developing Countries. *Boskin, M. J.; Fleming, J. S. and Gorini, S., eds.*, 1987, pp. 72–91. [G: LDCs; MDCs]

Coulombe, Serge. Dette publique, endettement envers l'éetranger et l'effet d'éviction dans une économie ouverte: le cas canadien. (Public Debt, National Foreign Indebtedness and the Crowding-Out Effect in an Open Economy: The Case of Canada. With English summary.) *Écon. Soc.*, September 1987, 21(9), pp. 169–84. [G: Canada]

Cremer, Helmuth; Kessler, Denis and Pestieau, Pierre. Fertility Differentials and the Regressive Effect of Public Debt. *Economica*, February 1987, 54(213), pp. 79–87.

Cunningham, Thomas J. Growing Out of Deficits: Debt Dynamics in a Disequilibrium Model. *J. Post Keynesian Econ.*, Winter 1986-87, 9(2), pp. 297–306. [G: U.S.]

Dimsdale, N. H. Keynes on British Budgetary Policy 1914–46. *Boskin, M. J.; Fleming, J. S. and Gorini, S., eds.*, 1987, pp. 208–33. [G: U.K.]

Eisner, Robert and Pieper, Paul J. Errata [Dette et déficit gouvernementaux. (Measurement and Effects of Government Debt and Deficits.)]. *Ann. Écon. Statist.*, Jan./Mar. 1987, (5), pp. 197. [G: Japan; U.S.; W. Germany]

Eltis, Walter. Some Implications of Deficit-Financed Tax Cuts: These Will Always Increase Demand, but Will They Reduce Supply? *Boskin, M. J.; Fleming, J. S. and Gorini, S., eds.*, 1987, pp. 318–46. [G: U.S.]

Flemming, John S. Debt and Taxes in War and Peace: The Case of a Small Open Economy. *Boskin, M. J.; Fleming, J. S. and Gorini, S., eds.*, 1987, pp. 373–91.

Gorini, Stefano. The Neoclassical Theory of Public Debt and the Theory of a Long-run Full-Employment Deficit. *Boskin, M. J.; Fleming, J. S. and Gorini, S., eds.*, 1987, pp. 347–72.

Heim, Carol E. and Mirowski, Philip. Interest Rates and Crowding-Out during Britain's Industrial Revolution. *J. Econ. Hist.*, March 1987, 47(1), pp. 117–39. [G: U.K.]

Hotson, John H. The Keynesian Revolution and the Aborted Fisher–Simons Revolution or the Road Not Taken. *Écon. Soc.*, September 1987, 21(9), pp. 185–219.

Ize, Alain and Ortiz, Guillermo. Fiscal Rigidities, Public Debt, and Capital Flight. *Int. Monet. Fund Staff Pap.*, June 1987, 34(2), pp. 311–32. [G: Mexico]

Koray, Faik. Government Debt, Economic Activity, and Transmission of Economic Disturbances. *J. Money, Credit, Banking*, August 1987, 19(3), pp. 361–75. [G: U.S.]

Lynch, Thomas D. A Line-Item Veto for the American President. *Thai, K. V., ed.*, 1987, pp. 261–94. [G: U.S.]

Masera, Rainer S. Four Arguments for Fiscal Recovery in Italy. *Boskin, M. J.; Fleming, J. S.*

and Gorini, S., eds., 1987, pp. 171–207.
[G: Italy]

Mason, Will E. Happy-Face Economics versus the 'Dismal Science': Is the Borrowed Lunch Really Free? *[Marjolin, R.]*, 1987, pp. 137–51. [G: U.S.]

McWilliams Tullberg, Rita. Military-Related Debt in Non-oil Developing Countries, 1972–82. *Schmidt, C. and Blackaby, F., eds.*, 1987, pp. 302–16. [G: LDCs]

Minhas, B. S. The Planning Process and the Annual Budgets: Some Reflections on Recent Indian Experience. *Indian Econ. Rev.*, July-Dec. 1987, *22*(2), pp. 115–49. [G: India]

Morley, Samuel A. and Fishlow, Albert. Deficits, Debt and Destabilization: The Perversity of High Interest Rates. *J. Devel. Econ.*, October 1987, *27*(1–2), pp. 227–44. [G: LDCs]

Morley, Samuel A. and Fishlow, Albert. Deficits, Debt and Destabilization: The Perversity of High Interest Rates. *[Diaz-Alejandro, C. F.]*, 1987, pp. 227–44. [G: LDCs]

Paganetto, Luigi. Public Debt, Private Savings and Supply-Side Policies. *Boskin, M. J.; Fleming, J. S. and Gorini, S., eds.*, 1987, pp. 298–317. [G: U.S.]

Posner, Michael V. Private Saving and Public Debt: A Survey of the Debate. *Boskin, M. J.; Fleming, J. S. and Gorini, S., eds.*, 1987, pp. 395–414.

Rizzo, Ilde and Peacock, Alan. Government Debt and Growth in Public Spending. *Public Finance*, 1987, *42*(2), pp. 283–91.

Sarcinelli, Mario. Financial Assets, Public Debt and Monetary Policy: An International Integration Perspective. *Banca Naz. Lavoro Quart. Rev.*, September 1987, (162), pp. 263–372.
[G: Italy]

Shibata, Hirofumi and Kimura, Yoko. Government Debt and Growth in Public Spending: A Reply [Economics of Representative Democracy: A Model of Skewed Representation]. *Public Finance*, 1987, *42*(2), pp. 292–96.

Söderström, Hans Tson. Sectoral Saving and Investment Patterns in 16 OECD Countries, 1965–82. *Boskin, M. J.; Fleming, J. S. and Gorini, S., eds.*, 1987, pp. 3–39. [G: OECD]

Spaventa, Luigi. Public Debt and Rules of Monetary Growth: An Exercise in Monetarist Arithmetic. *de Cecco, M. and Fitoussi, J.-P., eds.*, 1987, pp. 269–85.

Spaventa, Luigi. The Growth of Public Debt: Sustainability, Fiscal Rules, and Monetary Rules. *Int. Monet. Fund Staff Pap.*, June 1987, *34*(2), pp. 374–99.

Spiro, Peter S. The Elusive Effect of Fiscal Deficits on Interest Rates: Comment. *Int. Monet. Fund Staff Pap.*, June 1987, *34*(2), pp. 400–403. [G: U.S.]

Tanzi, Vito. The Effect of Fiscal Deficits on Interest Rates: Reply. *Int. Monet. Fund Staff Pap.*, June 1987, *34*(2), pp. 404–07. [G: U.S.]

Tanzi, Vito; Blejer, Mario I. and Teijeiro, Mario O. Inflation and the Measurement of Fiscal Deficits. *Int. Monet. Fund Staff Pap.*, December 1987, *34*(4), pp. 711–38.

Tobin, James. An Essay on the Principles of Debt Management. *Tobin, J. (I)*, 1987, *1963*, pp. 378–455. [G: U.S.]

Tobin, James. Monetary Policy and the Management of the Public Debt: The Patman Inquiry. *Tobin, J. (I)*, 1987, *1953*, pp. 456–70.
[G: U.S.]

Tobin, James. Unemployment, Interest, Deficits, and Money. *Tobin, J. (III)*, 1987, pp. 189–214.
[G: U.S.]

Ullmann, Hans-Peter. The Emergence of Modern Public Debts in Bavaria and Baden between 1780 and 1820. *Witt, P.-C., ed.*, 1987, pp. 63–79. [G: Germany]

Urquidi, Victor L. Military-Related Debt in Non-oil Developing Countries, 1972–82: Comment. *Schmidt, C. and Blackaby, F., eds.*, 1987, pp. 317–18. [G: LDCs]

Weil, Philippe. Love Thy Children: Reflections on the Barro Debt Neutrality Theorem. *J. Monet. Econ.*, May 1987, *19*(3), pp. 377–91.

Welch, John H.; Primo Braga, Carlos Alberto and Afonso de André, Paulo de Tarso. Brazilian Public Sector Disequilibrium. *World Devel.*, August 1987, *15*(8), pp. 1045–52.
[G: Brazil]

West, Edwin G. Public Debt Burden and Cost Theory. *Fink, R. H. and High, J. C., eds.*, 1987, *1975*, pp. 108–18.

Williamson, Jeffrey G. Has Crowding Out Really Been Given a Fair Test? A Comment [Interest Rates and Crowding-Out during Britain's Industrial Revolution]. *J. Econ. Hist.*, March 1987, *47*(1), pp. 214–15. [G: U.K.]

323 National Taxation, Revenue, and Subsidies

3230 National Taxation, Revenue, and Subsidies

Aarbakke, Magnus. Tax Problems of the Liquidation of Corporations: Norway. *International Fiscal Association, ed. (II)*, 1987, pp. 383–94.
[G: Norway]

Aaron, Henry J. Symposium on Tax Reform. *J. Econ. Perspectives*, Summer 1987, *1*(1), pp. 7–10. [G: U.S.]

Aaron, Henry J. The Impact of a Value-Added Tax on U.S. Competitiveness. *Walker, C. E. and Bloomfield, M. A., eds.*, 1987, pp. 206–13. [G: U.S.]

Aaron, Henry J. The Impossible Dream Comes True. *Pechman, J. A., ed.*, 1987, pp. 10–22.
[G: U.S.]

Abel, Andrew B. Anticipated Tax Changes and the Timing of Investment: Comment. *Feldstein, M., ed. (I)*, 1987, pp. 196–200.
[G: U.S.]

Adams, Walter and Brock, James W. Corporate Size and the Bailout Factor. *J. Econ. Issues*, March 1987, *21*(1), pp. 61–85. [G: U.S.]

Aivazian, Varouj A. and Callen, Jeffrey L. Miller's Irrelevance Mechanism: A Note. *J. Finance*, March 1987, *42*(1), pp. 169–80.

Aivazian, Varouj A. and Turnbull, Stuart M. Taxation and Capital Structure: A Selected Review. *Mintz, J. M. and Purvis, D. D., eds.*, 1987, pp. 230–62.

Albeseder, Werner. Taxation of Eastern European Source Income: Austria. *Bull. Int. Fiscal Doc.*, July 1987, *41*(7), pp. 326–28.
[G: Austria]

Alderighi, Massimo. Tax Problems of the Liquidation of Corporations: Italy. *International Fiscal Association, ed. (II)*, 1987, pp. 321–35.
[G: Italy]

Alonso, Aurora and Tusell, Fernando. Impuesto sobre el Valor Añadido y estabilización automótica. (With English summary.) *Invest. Econ.*, May 1987, *11*(2), pp. 327–43. [G: Spain]

Alworth, Julian S. Taxation and the Cost of Capital: A Comparison of Six EC Countries. *Cnossen, S., ed.*, 1987, pp. 253–83. [G: EEC]

Andel, Norbert. Determination of Company Profits. *Cnossen, S., ed.*, 1987, pp. 287–304.
[G: EEC]

Ang, James S.; Chiang, Raymond and Corgel, John B. Illustrations of Financing and Tax Transfers in Owner Financed Real Estate Sales. *J. Econ. Bus.*, November 1987, *39*(4), pp. 363–72. [G: U.S.]

Aoki, Torao. Ongoing Tax Reform I: Japan. *Bull. Int. Fiscal Doc.*, March 1987, *41*(3), pp. 111–16. [G: Japan]

Aoki, Torao. Ongoing Tax Reform II: Japan. *Bull. Int. Fiscal Doc.*, May 1987, *41*(5), pp. 224–31. [G: Japan]

Apostolakis, Bobby E. Output and Input Subsidies as a Means of Industrial Decentralization: The Greek Case. *Devel. Econ.*, June 1987, *25*(2), pp. 171–87. [G: Greece]

Apostolakis, Bobby E. The Subsidy Incidence on Industrialization. *Rivista Int. Sci. Econ. Com.*, April 1987, *34*(4), pp. 291–307.

Argimon, Isabel and González-Páramo, José Manuel. Una medición de la rémora inflacionaria del IRPF, 1979–1985. (With English summary.) *Invest. Econ.*, May 1987, *11*(2), pp. 345–66. [G: Spain]

Arnold, Brian J. Once More into the Breach: Recent Developments in Canadian Tax Reform. *Australian Tax Forum*, 1987, *4*(2), pp. 197–215. [G: Canada]

Arnott, Robert D. Structural Inefficiencies in Municipal Bond Futures. *Fabozzi, F. J., ed.*, 1987, pp. 313–19. [G: U.S.]

Arsić, Miodrag. Relevant Aspects in Tax Laws and Treaties Concerning the Taxing of Foreign Persons: Yugoslavia. *Bull. Int. Fiscal Doc.*, October 1987, *41*(10), pp. 472–76.
[G: Yugoslavia]

Asher, Mukul G. Tax Reform in Singapore. *Indian Econ. J.*, Oct.-Dec. 1987, *35*(2), pp. 132–51.
[G: Singapore]

Ashworth, Mark and Dilnot, Andrew. Company Cars Taxation. *Fisc. Stud.*, November 1987, *8*(4), pp. 24–38. [G: U.K.]

Askholt, Steen and Michelsen, Aage. The Fiscal Residence of Companies: Denmark. *International Fiscal Association, ed. (I)*, 1987, pp. 273–86. [G: Denmark]

Auerbach, Alan J. Corporate Taxation in the U.S. *Razin, A. and Sadka, E., eds.*, 1987, pp. 375–430. [G: U.S.]

Auerbach, Alan J. The Tax Reform Act of 1986 and the Cost of Capital. *J. Econ. Perspectives*, Summer 1987, *1*(1), pp. 73–86. [G: U.S.]

Auerbach, Alan J. The Theory and Measurement of Effective Tax Rates: Comment. *Mintz, J. M. and Purvis, D. D., eds.*, 1987, pp. 99–101.

Auerbach, Alan J. and Hines, James R., Jr. Anticipated Tax Changes and the Timing of Investment. *Feldstein, M., ed. (II)*, 1987, pp. 85–87. [G: U.S.]

Auerbach, Alan J. and Hines, James R., Jr. Anticipated Tax Changes and the Timing of Investment. *Feldstein, M., ed. (I)*, 1987, pp. 163–96. [G: U.S.]

Auerbach, Alan J. and Kotlikoff, Laurence J. Evaluating Fiscal Policy with a Dynamic Simulation Model. *Amer. Econ. Rev.*, May 1987, *77*(2), pp. 49–55.

Auerbach, Alan J. and Poterba, James M. Tax-Loss Carryforwards and Corporate Tax Incentives. *Feldstein, M., ed. (I)*, 1987, pp. 305–38. [G: U.S.]

Auerbach, Alan J. and Poterba, James M. Why Have Corporate Tax Revenues Declined? *Summers, L. H., ed.*, 1987, pp. 1–28. [G: U.S.]

Autenne, J. Tax Incentives for Scientific Research Activities: Belgium. *Bull. Int. Fiscal Doc.*, Aug.-Sept. 1987, *41*(8–9), pp. 407–09.
[G: Belgium]

Bahl, Roy. Urban Government Finance and Federal Income Tax Reform. *Nat. Tax J.*, March 1987, *40*(1), pp. 1–18. [G: U.S.]

Bakeš, Milan. Conventions on the Avoidance of Double Taxation: Czechoslovakia. *Bull. Int. Fiscal Doc.*, April 1987, *41*(4), pp. 181–85.
[G: Czechoslovakia]

Balcer, Yves and Judd, Kenneth L. Effects of Capital Gains Taxation on Life-Cycle Investment and Portfolio Management. *J. Finance*, July 1987, *42*(3), pp. 743–58.

Baldry, Jonathan C. Income Tax Evasion and the Tax Schedule: Some Experimental Results. *Public Finance*, 1987, *42*(3), pp. 357–83.

Bale, Harvey E., Jr. The Consumption Tax: A Better Alternative? The International Trade Issues. *Walker, C. E. and Bloomfield, M. A., eds.*, 1987, pp. 213–21. [G: U.S.]

Ballard, Charles L. Tax Policy and Consumer Foresight: A General Equilibrium Simulation Study. *Econ. Inquiry*, April 1987, *25*(2), pp. 267–84. [G: U.S.]

Ballard, Charles L.; Scholz, John Karl and Shoven, John B. The Value-Added Tax: A General Equilibrium Look at Its Efficiency and Incidence. *Feldstein, M., ed. (I)*, 1987, pp. 445–74.

Ballard, Charles L.; Scholz, John Karl and Shoven, John B. The Value-Added Tax: A General Equilibrium Look at Its Efficiency and Incidence. *Feldstein, M., ed. (II)*, 1987, pp. 105–07. [G: U.S.]

Ballard, Charles L. and Shoven, John B. The Value-Added Tax: The Efficiency Cost of Achieving Progressivity by Using Exemptions. *[Harberger, A.]*, 1987, pp. 109–29.

Ballentine, J. Gregory. The Administrability of

a Value-Added Tax. *Walker, C. E. and Bloomfield, M. A., eds.*, 1987, pp. 296–300.
[G: U.S.]

Ballentine, J. Gregory. The Impact of Fundamental Tax Reform on the Allocation of Resources: Comment. *Feldstein, M., ed. (I)*, 1987, pp. 437–43. **[G: U.S.]**

Barber, John and White, Geoff. Current Policy Practice and Problems from a UK Perspective. *Dasgupta, P. and Stoneman, P., eds.*, 1987, pp. 24–50. **[G: U.K.]**

Barclay, Michael J. Dividends, Taxes, and Common Stock Prices: The Ex-dividend Day Behavior of Common Stock Prices before the Income Tax. *J. Finan. Econ.*, September 1987, *19*(1), pp. 31–44. **[G: U.S.]**

Barham, Vicky; Poddar, S. N. and Whalley, John. The Tax Treatment of Insurance under a Consumption Type, Destination Basis VAT. *Nat. Tax J.*, June 1987, *40*(2), pp. 171–82.

Barnea, Amir; Talmor, Eli and Haugen, Robert A. Debt and Taxes: A Multiperiod Investigation. *J. Banking Finance*, March 1987, *11*(1), pp. 79–97.

Bassichis, William H.; Crumbley, D. Larry and Stolle Carlton D. Caution: Teaching and Research Awards Ahead. *Jones, S. M., ed.*, 1987, pp. 199–210. **[G: U.S.]**

Batina, Raymond G. The Consumption Tax in the Presence of Altruistic Cash and Human Capital Bequests with Endogenous Fertility Decisions. *J. Public Econ.*, December 1987, *34*(3), pp. 329–54.

Baucus, Max. A Congressional Perspective on Competitiveness. *Walker, C. E. and Bloomfield, M. A., eds.*, 1987, pp. 221–24.
[G: U.S.]

Baum, Sandra R. On the Measurement of Tax Progressivity: Relative Share Adjustment. *Public Finance Quart.*, April 1987, *15*(2), pp. 166–87. **[G: U.S.]**

Bayar, Ali and Frank, Max. The Erosion of the Different Tax Bases. *Public Finance*, 1987, *42*(3), pp. 341–56. **[G: OECD]**

Becker, Winfried; Büchner, Heinz-Jürgen and Sleeking, Simon. The Impact of Public Transfer Expenditures on Tax Evasion: An Experimental Approach. *J. Public Econ.*, November 1987, *34*(2), pp. 243–52.

Beenstock, Michael. Budget Lines and Labour Supply Incentives. *Beenstock, M., et al.*, 1987, pp. 1–24. **[G: U.K.]**

Begg, David K. H. Long-run Implications of the Increase in Taxation and Public Debt for Employment and Economic Growth in Europe: Comments. *Europ. Econ. Rev.*, April 1987, *31*(3), pp. 775–77. **[G: W. Europe]**

Beighton, Leonard. Tax Policy and Management: The Role of the Inland Revenue. *Fisc. Stud.*, February 1987, *8*(1), pp. 1–16. **[G: U.K.]**

Bell, Stephen E. A Political Strategy for a Consumption Tax: The Political Context. *Walker, C. E. and Bloomfield, M. A., eds.*, 1987, pp. 353–56. **[G: U.S.]**

Bennett, John. The Second-Best Lump-Sum Taxation of Observable Characteristics. *Public Fi-*

nance, 1987, *42*(2), pp. 227–35.

Bennett, Robert J. A General Accounting Model of Intergovernmental Tax and Benefit Effects on Business. *Environ. Planning A*, November 1987, *19*(11), pp. 1495–1510. **[G: U.K.; W. Germany]**

Bentick, B. L. A Development Gains Tax Will Accelerate the Time of Development unless There Is Also a Tax on Redevelopment [The Neutrality of a Development Gains Tax]. *Public Finance*, 1987, *42*(2), pp. 320–24. **[G: U.K.]**

Bernheim, B. Douglas. Does the Estate Tax Raise Revenue? *Summers, L. H., ed.*, 1987, pp. 113–38. **[G: U.S.]**

Bernheim, B. Douglas and Shoven, John B. Taxation and the Cost of Capital: An International Comparison. *Walker, C. E. and Bloomfield, M. A., eds.*, 1987, pp. 61–85. **[G: Global]**

Bernstein, Jeffrey I. and Nadiri, M. Ishaq. Corporate Taxes and Incentives and the Structure of Production: A Selected Survey. *Mintz, J. M. and Purvis, D. D., eds.*, 1987, pp. 178–208.

Bhargava, Surendra N. India–Canada Treaty for the Avoidance of Double Taxation. *Bull. Int. Fiscal Doc.*, March 1987, *41*(3), pp. 117–18. **[G: India; Canada]**

Birch, Thomas D. Basic Needs: Paternalistic Government Welfare Policy with Distortionary Taxation. *Public Finance Quart.*, July 1987, *15*(3), pp. 298–321.

Bird, Richard M. A New Look at Indirect Taxation in Developing Countries. *World Devel.*, September 1987, *15*(9), pp. 1151–61. **[G: LDCs]**

Bird, Richard M. Corporate–Personal Tax Integration. *Cnossen, S., ed.*, 1987, pp. 227–51. **[G: EEC]**

Bird, Richard M. Imputation and the Foreign Tax Credit: Some Critical Notes from an International Perspective. *Australian Tax Forum*, 1987, *4*(1), pp. 1–34. **[G: Australia]**

Birnbaum, Jeffrey H. Showdown at Gucci Gulch. *Nat. Tax J.*, September 1987, *40*(3), pp. 357–61. **[G: U.S.]**

Blaug, Mark. Declining Subsidies to Higher Education: An Economic Analysis. *Blaug, M., 1987, 1983*, pp. 227–43. **[G: OECD]**

Blaug, Mark. Education Vouchers—It All Depends on What You Mean. *Blaug, M., 1987, 1985*, pp. 244–61.

Blaug, Mark. The Distributional Effects of Higher Education Subsidies. *Blaug, M., 1987, 1982*, pp. 204–26. **[G: U.S.]**

Blaug, Mark and Woodhall, Maureen. Patterns of Subsidies to Higher Education in Europe. *Blaug, M., 1987, 1979*, pp. 166–96. **[G: W. Europe]**

Blouet, J. F. La résidence fiscale des sociétés: France. (The Fiscal Residence of Companies: France. With English summary.) *International Fiscal Association, ed. (I)*, 1987, pp. 321–31. **[G: France]**

Boadway, Robin W. The Theory and Measurement of Effective Tax Rates. *Mintz, J. M. and Purvis, D. D., eds.*, 1987, pp. 60–98.

Boadway, Robin W., et al. Marginal Effective Tax Rates for Capital in the Canadian Mining Industry. *Can. J. Econ.*, February 1987, *20*(1), pp. 1–16. [G: Canada]

Bomchil, Máximo, Jr. Taxation of Royalties: Argentina. *Bull. Int. Fiscal Doc.*, May 1987, *41*(5), pp. 236–39. [G: Argentina]

Bonafide, Robert T. A View from the Trenches. *Nat. Tax J.*, September 1987, *40*(3), pp. 465–67. [G: U.S.]

Bond, Michael T. and Smolen, Gerald E. Nominal Interest Rates and Marginal Tax Rates. *Quart. J. Bus. Econ.*, Spring 1987, *26*(2), pp. 104–09. [G: U.S.]

Booth, Laurence D. The Dividend Tax Credit and Canadian Ownership Objectives. *Can. J. Econ.*, May 1987, *20*(2), pp. 321–39. [G: Canada]

Bosco, Bruno. Dividend Taxes and Corporate Dividend Policy: Further Econometric Results. *Rivista Int. Sci. Econ. Com.*, Nov.-Dec. 1987, *34*(11–12), pp. 1139–65. [G: Italy]

Boskin, Michael J. and Gale, William G. New Results on the Effects of Tax Policy on the International Location of Investment. *Feldstein, M., ed. (I)*, 1987, pp. 201–19. [G: U.S.]

Bossons, John. The Impact of the 1986 Tax Reform Act on Tax Reform in Canada. *Nat. Tax J.*, September 1987, *40*(3), pp. 331–38. [G: U.S.; Canada]

Bovenberg, A. Lans. Indirect Taxation in Developing Countries: A General Equilibrium Approach. *Int. Monet. Fund Staff Pap.*, June 1987, *34*(2), pp. 333–73. [G: Thailand]

Bovenberg, A. Lans. The General Equilibrium Approach: Relevant for Public Policy? *van de Kar, H. M. and Wolfe, B. L., eds.*, 1987, pp. 33–43.

Boyne, George A. Median Voters, Political Systems and Public Policies: An Empirical Test. *Public Choice*, 1987, *53*(3), pp. 201–19. [G: U.K.]

Boynton, Charles E., IV and Robison, Jack. Factors Empirically Associated with Federal Tax Trial Case Loads. *Jones, S. M., ed.*, 1987, pp. 169–82. [G: U.S.]

Bradford, David F. On the Incidence of Consumption Taxes. *Walker, C. E. and Bloomfield, M. A., eds.*, 1987, pp. 243–61. [G: U.S.]

Bradford, David F. Tax-Loss Carryforwards and Corporate Tax Incentives: Comment. *Feldstein, M., ed. (I)*, 1987, pp. 339–42. [G: U.S.]

Branco da Silva, Rubens. Tax Problems of the Liquidation of Corporations: Brazil. *International Fiscal Association, ed. (II)*, 1987, pp. 221–27. [G: Brazil]

Brandt, Harm-Hinrich. Public Finances of Neoabsolutism in Austria in the 1850s: Integration and Modernisation. *Witt, P.-C., ed.*, 1987, pp. 81–109. [G: Austria]

Brick, Ivan E. and Fisher, Lawrence. Effects of Classifying Equity or Debt on the Value of the Firm under Tax Asymmetry. *J. Finan. Quant. Anal.*, December 1987, *22*(4), pp. 383–99. [G: U.S.]

Bright, Geoff. Tax Changes and Machinery Investment. *J. Agr. Econ.*, January 1987, *38*(1), pp. 39–49. [G: U.K.]

Brito, Dagobert L. and Intriligator, Michael D. Stock Externalities, Pigovian Taxation and Dynamic Stability. *J. Public Econ.*, June 1987, *33*(1), pp. 59–72.

Brito, Dagobert L. and Sheshinski, Eytan. Effects of Capital Gain Taxation on Non-Austrian Assets: Comments. *Razin, A. and Sadka, E., eds.*, 1987, pp. 340–42. [G: Austria]

Brown, Eleanor. Tax Incentives and Charitable Giving: Evidence from New Survey Data. *Public Finance Quart.*, October 1987, *15*(4), pp. 386–96. [G: U.S.]

Brown, James N. and Rosen, Harvey S. Taxation, Wage Variation, and Job Choice. *J. Lab. Econ.*, Part 1, Oct. 1987, *5*(4), pp. 430–51. [G: U.S.]

Browning, Edgar K. On the Marginal Welfare Cost of Taxation. *Amer. Econ. Rev.*, March 1987, *77*(1), pp. 11–23. [G: U.S.]

Buchanan, James M. Tax Reform as Political Choice. *J. Econ. Perspectives*, Summer 1987, *1*(1), pp. 29–35. [G: U.S.]

Buchanan, James M. and Brennan, Geoffrey. Towards a Tax Constitution for Leviathan. *Buchanan, J. M. (II)*, 1987, 1977, pp. 367–87.

Buchanan, James M. and Faith, Roger L. Secession and the Limits of Taxation: Toward a Theory of Internal Exit. *Amer. Econ. Rev.*, December 1987, *77*(5), pp. 1023–31.

Buchanan, James M. and Lee, Dwight R. Politics, Time, and the Laffer Curve. *Buchanan, J. M. (II)*, 1987, 1982, pp. 409–13.

Buiter, Willem H. Fiscal Policy and European Economic Growth: Comment. *Lawrence, R. Z. and Schultze, C. L., eds.*, 1987, pp. 492–501. [G: W. Europe]

Burman, Leonard E.; Neubig, Thomas S. and Wilson, D. Gordon. The Use and Abuse of Rental Project Models. *U.S. Treasury, Office of Tax Analysis.*, 1987, pp. 307–49. [G: U.S.]

Burtless, Gary. Taxes, Transfers, and Swedish Labor Supply. *Bosworth, B. P. and Rivlin, A. M., eds.*, 1987, pp. 185–249. [G: Sweden]

Burtless, Gary and Haveman, Robert H. Taxes and Transfers: How Much Economic Loss? *Challenge*, Mar./Apr. 1987, *30*(1), pp. 45–51. [G: U.S.]

Burtless, Gary and Haveman, Robert H. Taxes, Transfers, and Labor Supply: The Evolving Views of U.S. Economists. *van de Kar, H. M. and Wolfe, B. L., eds.*, 1987, pp. 127–45. [G: U.S.]

Cain, Charles. Your "User-Friendly" Offshore Centre: The Isle of Man. *Bull. Int. Fiscal Doc.*, January 1987, *41*(1), pp. 37–40. [G: U.K.]

Campbell, Dennis. Joint Ventures between East and West. *Bull. Int. Fiscal Doc.*, July 1987, *41*(7), pp. 299–303. [G: E. Europe; OECD]

Carlson, George N. A Federal Consumption Tax: Design and Administrative Issues. *Walker, C. E. and Bloomfield, M. A., eds.*, 1987, pp. 375–95. [G: U.S.]

Carlson, J. Lon and Bausell, Charles W., Jr. Financing Superfund: An Evaluation of Alternative Tax Mechanisms. *Natural Res. J.*, Winter 1987, *27*(1), pp. 103–22. [G: U.S.]

Carroll, Chris and Summers, Lawrence H. Why Have Private Savings Rates in the United States and Canada Diverged? *J. Monet. Econ.*, September 1987, *20*(2), pp. 249–79.
[G: U.S.; Canada]

de Carvalho, António Joaquim. Régime de liquidation des sociétés: Portugal. (Tax Problems of the Liquidation of Corporations: Portugal. With English summary.) *International Fiscal Association, ed. (II)*, 1987, pp. 435–43.
[G: Portugal]

Casanegra de Jantscher, Milka. Problems in Administering a Consumption Tax. *Walker, C. E. and Bloomfield, M. A., eds.*, 1987, pp. 300–305. [G: U.S.]

Casas Sánchez, Roberto. The Fiscal Residence of Companies: Mexico. *International Fiscal Association, ed. (I)*, 1987, pp. 403–12.
[G: Mexico]

Cha, Jae-Neung. Tax Problems of the Liquidation of Corporations: Republic of Korea. *International Fiscal Association, ed. (II)*, 1987, pp. 445–54. [G: S. Korea]

Chambers, Robert G. and Lopez, Ramon E. Tax Policies and the Financially Constrained Farm Household. *Amer. J. Agr. Econ.*, May 1987, *69*(2), pp. 369–77.

Chandra, Subodh. The Fiscal Residence of Companies: India. *International Fiscal Association, ed. (I)*, 1987, pp. 345–52. [G: India]

Chernick, Howard A.; Holmer, Martin R. and Weinberg, Daniel H. Tax Policy toward Health Insurance and the Demand for Medical Services. *J. Health Econ.*, March 1987, *6*(1), pp. 1–25. [G: U.S.]

Chernick, Howard A. and Reschovsky, Andrew. The Deductibility of State and Local Taxes: Comment. *Nat. Tax J.*, March 1987, *40*(1), pp. 95–102. [G: U.S.]

Cheung, Joseph K. Depreciation, Debt, and Equilibrium Tax Rates: A Reconsideration. *Quart. Rev. Econ. Bus.*, Spring 1987, *27*(1), pp. 6–15.

Chirinko, Robert S. The Ineffectiveness of Effective Tax Rates on Business Investment: A Critique of Feldstein's Fisher–Schultz Lecture. *J. Public Econ.*, April 1987, *32*(3), pp. 369–87. [G: U.S.]

Christian, Ernest S., Jr. Consumption Taxes Are Not Regressive. *Walker, C. E. and Bloomfield, M. A., eds.*, 1987, pp. 329–32. [G: U.S.]

Chu, C. Y. Cyrus. The Effect of Social Security on the Steady State Distribution of Consumption. *J. Public Econ.*, November 1987, *34*(2), pp. 189–210.

Cilke, James M. and Wyscarver, Roy A. The Individual Income Tax Simulation Model. *U.S. Treasury, Office of Tax Analysis.*, 1987, pp. 43–75. [G: U.S.]

Clark, Timothy B. Stiff Tax Hikes Will Be Key to Future Efforts to Close the Budget Deficit. *Fink, R. H. and High, J. C., eds.*, 1987, *1984*, pp. 243–53. [G: U.S.]

Cnossen, Sijbren. Tax Coordination in the European Community: Introduction. *Cnossen, S., ed.*, 1987, pp. 1–15. [G: EEC]

Cnossen, Sijbren. Tax Structure Developments. *Cnossen, S., ed.*, 1987, pp. 19–55. [G: EEC]

Cnossen, Sijbren. The Technical Superiority of VAT over RST. *Australian Tax Forum*, 1987, *4*(4), pp. 419–64. [G: OECD]

Cnossen, Sijbren and Shoup, Carl S. Coordination of Value-Added Taxes. *Cnossen, S., ed.*, 1987, pp. 59–84. [G: EEC]

Cohen, Edwin S. The Consumption Tax: A Better Alternative? Lessons from the European VAT Experience. *Walker, C. E. and Bloomfield, M. A., eds.*, 1987, pp. 305–08. [G: U.S.]

Collins, David J. Taxation of Fringe Benefits— An Economist's Perspective. *Australian Tax Forum*, 1987, *4*(1), pp. 95–121.
[G: Australia]

Condor, Ioan. Taxation of Joint Ventures and Non-residents: Romania. *Bull. Int. Fiscal Doc.*, July 1987, *41*(7), pp. 337–42.
[G: Romania]

Cook, Eric W. and O'Hare, John F. Issues Relating to the Taxation of Capital Gains. *Nat. Tax J.*, September 1987, *40*(3), pp. 473–88.
[G: U.S.]

Cooley, Thomas F. and Salyer, Kevin D. The Effects of Inflation-Induced Tax Increases on Stock and Housing Prices. *Scand. J. Econ.*, 1987, *89*(4), pp. 421–34. [G: U.S.]

Cordes, Joseph J.; Watson, Harry S. and Hauger, J. Scott. Effects of Tax Reform on High Technology Firms. *Nat. Tax J.*, September 1987, *40*(3), pp. 373–91. [G: U.S.]

Corsetti, Giancarlo. Taxes and Subsidies in Input–Output Analysis: A Comment. *Ricerche Econ.*, Apr.-June 1987, *41*(2), pp. 262–73.

Courant, Paul N. Fiscal Policy and European Economic Growth. *Lawrence, R. Z. and Schultze, C. L., eds.*, 1987, pp. 423–92.
[G: W. Europe]

Courant, Paul N. and Rubinfeld, Daniel L. Tax Reform: Implications for the State–Local Public Sector. *J. Econ. Perspectives*, Summer 1987, *1*(1), pp. 87–100. [G: U.S.]

Cowell, Frank A. The Economic Analysis of Tax Evasion. *Hey, J. D. and Lambert, P. J., eds.*, 1987, *1985*, pp. 173–203.

Coyle, Dennis J. and Wildavsky, Aaron. Requisites of Radical Reform: Income Maintenance versus Tax Preferences. *J. Policy Anal. Manage.*, Fall 1987, *7*(1), pp. 1–16. [G: U.S.]

Crane, Steven E. and Nourzad, Farrokh. On the Treatment of Income Tax Rates in Empirical Analysis of Tax Evasion. *Kyklos*, 1987, *40*(3), pp. 338–48.

Czamanski, Daniel Z. The Effect of Location Subsidies on Corporate Decisions. *Reg. Sci. Urban Econ.*, August 1987, *17*(3), pp. 411–21.

D'Avino, Carey R. The Fiscal Residence of Companies: United States. *International Fiscal Association, ed. (I)*, 1987, pp. 299–312.
[G: U.S.]

Daly, Michael J. and Jung, Jack. The Taxation of Corporate Investment Income in Canada:

An Analysis of Marginal Effective Tax Rates. *Can. J. Econ.*, August 1987, *20*(3), pp. 555–87. [G: Canada]

Dammon, Robert M. and Green, Richard C. Tax Arbitrage and the Existence of Equilibrium Prices for Financial Assets. *J. Finance*, December 1987, *42*(5), pp. 1143–66.

Dart, Robert J. and Minzberg, Samuel. Tax Problems of the Liquidation of Corporations: Canada. *International Fiscal Association, ed. (II)*, 1987, pp. 229–46. [G: Canada]

Defoort, Jos. Régime de liquidation des sociétés: Belgique. (Tax Problems of the Liquidation of Corporations: Belgium. With English summary.) *International Fiscal Association, ed. (II)*, 1987, pp. 201–20. [G: Belgium]

Denys, L. A. The Proposed Belgian Tax Reform: Aspects of International Taxation. *Bull. Int. Fiscal Doc.*, Aug.-Sept. 1987, *41*(8–9), pp. 383–90. [G: Belgium]

Deutsch, Antal and Zowall, Hanna. Inequalities in the Tax Impact of Compulsory Retirement Savings in Singapore. *Singapore Econ. Rev.*, October 1987, *32*(2), pp. 28–42.
[G: Singapore]

Deutsch, Robert L. Foreign Tax Credits. *Australian Tax Forum*, 1987, *4*(2), pp. 161–96.
[G: Australia]

Devereux, Michael. On the Growth of Corporation Tax Revenues. *Fisc. Stud.*, May 1987, *8*(2), pp. 77–85. [G: U.K.]

Devereux, Michael. Taxation and the Cost of Capital: The UK Experience. *Oxford Rev. Econ. Policy*, Winter 1987, *3*(4), pp. xvii–xxxii.
[G: U.K.]

Diewert, Walter Erwin. Corporate Taxes and Incentives and the Structure of Production: A Selected Survey: Comment. *Mintz, J. M. and Purvis, D. D., eds.*, 1987, pp. 209–24.

Dildine, Larry L. Tax Reform and the U.S. Economy: Effects on Industry. *Pechman, J. A., ed.*, 1987, pp. 31–44. [G: U.S.]

Dilnot, Andrew; Stark, Graham and Webb, Steven J. The Targeting of Benefits: Two Approaches. *Fisc. Stud.*, February 1987, *8*(1), pp. 83–93. [G: U.K.]

Dilnot, Andrew, et al. The 1987 Budget in Perspective. *Fisc. Stud.*, May 1987, *8*(2), pp. 48–57. [G: U.K.]

Dixon, Daryl A. and Vann, Richard J. An Examination of the Imputation System in the Context of the Erosion of the Company Tax Base. *Australian Tax Forum*, 1987, *4*(1), pp. 63–93.

Dore, M. H. I. Mineral Taxation in Jamaica: An Oligopoly Confronts Taxes on Resource Rents—and Prevails. *Amer. J. Econ. Soc.*, April 1987, *46*(2), pp. 179–204.
[G: Jamaica]

Downs, Thomas and Hendershott, Patric H. Tax Policy and Stock Prices. *Nat. Tax J.*, June 1987, *40*(2), pp. 183–90. [G: U.S.]

Driessen, Patrick A. A Qualification Concerning the Efficiency of Tax Expenditures [A Contribution to the Theory of Tax Expenditures: The Case of Charitable Giving]. *J. Public Econ.*, June 1987, *33*(1), pp. 125–31.

Dubin, Jeffrey A.; Graetz, Michael J. and Wilde,

Louis L. Are We a Nation of Tax Cheaters? New Econometric Evidence on Tax Compliance. *Amer. Econ. Rev.*, May 1987, *77*(2), pp. 240–45. [G: U.S.]

Dudley, Leonard and Montmarquette, Claude. Bureaucratic Corruption as a Constraint on Voter Choice. *Public Choice*, September 1987, *55*(1–2), pp. 127–60. [G: Selected Countries]

Duggal, Vijaya G. and Adams, F. Gerard. Corporate Tax Reform and Business Investment: Empirical Estimates for Structures and Equipment. *Empirical Econ.*, 1987, *12*(3), pp. 187–95. [G: U.S.]

Duncan, William A.; O'Dell, Michael A. and Panich, Richard L. Potential Personal Wealth Redistribution Effects of Structural Income Tax Reform. *Jones, S. M., ed.*, 1987, pp. 1–21.
[G: U.S.]

Durenberger, Dave. The Consumption Tax Alternative. *Walker, C. E. and Bloomfield, M. A., eds.*, 1987, pp. 167–72.

Durning, Dan. The Efficiency and Distribution of Mortgage Revenue Bond Subsidies: The Effects of Behavioral Responses. *J. Policy Anal. Manage.*, Fall 1987, *7*(1), pp. 74–93.
[G: U.S.]

Dworin, Lowell. Impact of the Corporate Alternative Minimum Tax. *Nat. Tax J.*, September 1987, *40*(3), pp. 505–13. [G: U.S.]

Dworin, Lowell. Impact of the Corporate Alternative Minimum Tax: A Monte Carlo Simulation Study. *U.S. Treasury, Office of Tax Analysis.*, 1987, pp. 253–78. [G: U.S.]

Eckbo, Paul Leo. Worldwide Petroleum Taxation: The Pressure for Revision. *[Adelman, M. A.]*, 1987, pp. 215–33. [G: Global]

Edgar, Tim. The Corporate Interest Deduction and the Financing of Foreign Subsidiaries. *Australian Tax Forum*, 1987, *4*(4), pp. 491–528. [G: Canada; Australia]

Edvardsson, Leif. Tax Problems of the Liquidation of Corporations: Sweden. *International Fiscal Association, ed. (II)*, 1987, pp. 475–89.
[G: Sweden]

Edwards, P. S. A. The Fiscal Residence of Companies: Hong Kong. *International Fiscal Association, ed. (I)*, 1987, pp. 333–43.
[G: Hong Kong]

Egginton, Don M. Case Studies of Labour Supply Incentives and Budget Lines. *Beenstock, M., et al.*, 1987, pp. 25–75. [G: U.K.]

Elegido, J. M. Taxation of Dividends: Nigeria. *Bull. Int. Fiscal Doc.*, June 1987, *41*(6), pp. 271–77. [G: Nigeria]

Espenshade, Thomas J. and Minarik, Joseph J. Demographic Implications of the 1986 U.S. Tax Reform. *Population Devel. Rev.*, March 1987, *13*(1), pp. 115–27. [G: U.S.]

Etherington, K. E. Hidden Distributions of Profit: United Kingdom. *Bull. Int. Fiscal Doc.*, November 1987, *41*(11), pp. 509–13, 516.
[G: U.K.]

Evans, A. W. The Effect of a Development Gains Tax on the Timing of Development [The Neutrality of a Development Gains Tax]. *Public Finance*, 1987, *42*(2), pp. 325–31.

Eyskens, Mark. Recent Measures and Future

Prospects: Taxation in Belgium. *Bull. Int. Fiscal Doc.*, Aug.-Sept. 1987, *41*(8–9), pp. 356–58. **[G: Belgium]**

Faivre, Michel. Régime de liquidation des sociétés: France. (Tax Problems of the Liquidation of Corporations: France. With English summary.) *International Fiscal Association*, ed. (II), 1987, pp. 279–94. **[G: France]**

Fane, G. Neutral Taxation under Uncertainty. *J. Public Econ.*, June 1987, *33*(1), pp. 95–105.

Fazzari, Steven M. Tax Reform and Investment: Blessing or Curse? *Fed. Res. Bank St. Louis Rev.*, June/July 1987, *69*(6), pp. 23–33. **[G: U.S.]**

Fazzari, Steven M. Tax Reform and Investment: How Big an Impact? *Fed. Res. Bank St. Louis Rev.*, January 1987, *69*(1), pp. 15–27. **[G: U.S.]**

Feenberg, Daniel R. Are Tax Price Models Really Identified: The Case of Charitable Giving. *Nat. Tax J.*, December 1987, *40*(4), pp. 629–33. **[G: U.S.]**

Feenberg, Daniel R. The Cash Flow Corporate Income Tax: Comment. *Feldstein, M., ed. (I)*, 1987, pp. 398–400. **[G: U.S.]**

Feldstein, Martin S. Long-run Implications of the Increase in Taxation and Public Debt for Employment and Economic Growth in Europe: Comments. *Europ. Econ. Rev.*, April 1987, *31*(3), pp. 778–80. **[G: W. Europe]**

Feldstein, Martin S. Tax Rates and Business Investment: Reply [Inflation, Tax Rules and Investment: Some Econometric Evidence]. *J. Public Econ.*, April 1987, *32*(3), pp. 389–96. **[G: U.S.]**

Feldstein, Martin S. Tax Rules and Business Investment. *Feldstein, M., ed. (II)*, 1987, pp. 63–72. **[G: U.S.]**

Feldstein, Martin S. The Efficiency of Tax Expenditures: Reply [A Contribution to the Theory of Tax Expenditures: The Case of Charitable Giving]. *J. Public Econ.*, June 1987, *33*(1), pp. 133–36. **[G: U.S.]**

Feldstein, Martin S. and Jun, Joosung. The Effects of Tax Rules on Nonresidential Fixed Investment: Some Preliminary Evidence from the 1980s. *Feldstein, M., ed. (I)*, 1987, pp. 101–56. **[G: U.S.]**

Feldstein, Martin S. and Metcalf, Gilbert E. The Effect of Federal Tax Deductibility on State and Local Taxes and Spending. *J. Polit. Econ.*, August 1987, *95*(4), pp. 710–36. **[G: U.S.]**

Fellingham, John C.; Limberg, Stephen T. and Wilkie, Patrick J. Tax Rates, Tax Shelters and Optimal Portfolios. *Jones, S. M., ed.*, 1987, pp. 23–47.

Finger, J. Michael and Nogués, Julio. International Control of Subsidies and Countervailing Duties. *World Bank Econ. Rev.*, September 1987, *1*(4), pp. 707–25. **[G: Global]**

Flippo, Ronnie G. A U.S. Consumption Tax: Comments from a Legislator. *Walker, C. E. and Bloomfield, M. A., eds.*, 1987, pp. 308–10. **[G: U.S.]**

Fluet, Claude. Fraude fiscale et offre de travail au noir. (Tax Evasion and the Supply of Unoffi-

cial Labour. With English summary.) *L'Actual. Econ.*, June-September 1987, *63*(2–3), pp. 225–42.

Follain, James R.; Hendershott, Patric H. and Ling, David C. Understanding the Real Estate Provisions of Tax Reform: Motivation and Impact. *Nat. Tax J.*, September 1987, *40*(3), pp. 363–72. **[G: U.S.]**

Fong, Nellie. Tax Problems of the Liquidation of Corporations: Hong Kong. *International Fiscal Association*, ed. (II), 1987, pp. 295–303. **[G: Hong Kong]**

Formby, John P.; Smith, W. James and Thistle, Paul D. Difficulties in the Measurement of Tax Progressivity: Further Analysis. *Public Finance*, 1987, *42*(3), pp. 438–45. **[G: Canada; Australia; U.K.; U.S.]**

Forte, Francesco. The Laffer Curve and the Theory of Fiscal Bureaucracy. *Public Choice*, 1987, *52*(2), pp. 101–24.

Fowler, Henry H. A Historical Perspective on Tax Policy. *Walker, C. E. and Bloomfield, M. A., eds.*, 1987, pp. 3–23. **[G: U.S.]**

van Fraeyenhoven, Guy. Tax Problems of the Liquidation of Corporations: General Report. *International Fiscal Association*, ed. (II), 1987, pp. 37–56.

Frankel, Marvin. Taxes, Pollution, and Optimal Abatement in an Urban Economy. *J. Urban Econ.*, September 1987, *22*(2), pp. 117–35.

Franks, Julian R. and Hodges, Stewart D. Lease Valuation When Taxable Earnings Are a Scarce Resource. *J. Finance*, September 1987, *42*(4), pp. 987–1005. **[G: U.K.]**

Fraser, Peter M. Tax Problems of the Liquidation of Corporations: Australia. *International Fiscal Association*, ed. (II), 1987, pp. 173–86. **[G: Australia]**

Freimüller, Hans-Ulrich and Burki, Nico H. Steuerliche Probleme der Liquidation von Körperschaften: Schweiz. (Tax Problems of the Liquidation of Corporations: Switzerland. With English summary.) *International Fiscal Association*, ed. (II), 1987, pp. 491–513. **[G: Switzerland]**

Fukao, Mitsuhiro and Hanazaki, Masaharu. Internationalisation of Financial Markets and the Allocation of Capital. *OECD Econ. Stud.*, Spring 1987, (8), pp. 35–92. **[G: OECD]**

Fullerton, Don. The Indexation of Interest, Depreciation, and Capital Gains and Tax Reform in the United States. *J. Public Econ.*, February 1987, *32*(1), pp. 25–51. **[G: U.S.]**

Fullerton, Don; Gillette, Robert and Mackie, James. Investment Incentives under the Tax Reform Act of 1986. *U.S. Treasury, Office of Tax Analysis.*, 1987, pp. 131–71. **[G: U.S.]**

Fullerton, Don and Henderson, Yolanda Kodrzycki. The Impact of Fundamental Tax Reform on the Allocation of Resources. *Feldstein, M., ed. (II)*, 1987, pp. 101–03. **[G: U.S.]**

Fullerton, Don and Henderson, Yolanda Kodrzycki. The Impact of Fundamental Tax Reform on the Allocation of Resources. *Feldstein, M., ed. (I)*, 1987, pp. 401–37. **[G: U.S.]**

Fullerton, Don; Henderson, Yolanda Kodrzycki

and Mackie, James. Investment Allocation and Growth under the Tax Reform Act of 1986. *U.S. Treasury, Office of Tax Analysis.*, 1987, pp. 173–201. [G: U.S.]

Fuss, Melvyn A. Corporate Taxes and Incentives and the Structure of Production: A Selected Survey: Comment. *Mintz, J. M. and Purvis, D. D., eds.*, 1987, pp. 225–27.

Gabrielli, A. R. The Fiscal Residence of Companies: Argentina. *International Fiscal Association, ed. (I),* 1987, pp. 177–99.
[G: Argentina]

Gagnon, Jean-Marie; Suret, Jean-Marc and St-Pierre, Josée. Asymétrie de l'information, fiscalité et endettement au Canada. (Information Asymmetry, Taxes and Debt-Equity Ratios in Canada. With English summary.) *Finance,* June 1987, 8(1), pp. 75–103. [G: Canada]

Gaier, Richard. Steuerliche Probleme der Liquidation von Körperschaften: Österreich. (Tax Problems of the Liquidation of Corporations: Austria. With English summary.) *International Fiscal Association, ed. (II),* 1987, pp. 187–200.
[G: Austria]

Galli, Giovanni B. The Fiscal Residence of Companies: Italy. *International Fiscal Association, ed. (I),* 1987, pp. 369–87. [G: Italy]

Galper, Harvey. The Value-Added Tax: A General Equilibrium Look at Its Efficiency and Incidence: Comment. *Feldstein, M., ed. (I),* 1987, pp. 475–80. [G: U.S.]

Garland, James P. Taxable Portfolios: Value and Performance. *J. Portfol. Manage.*, Winter 1987, 13(2), pp. 19–24.

Gassner, Wolfgang. Die steuerliche Ansässigkeit von Kapitalgesellschaften: Österreich. (The Fiscal Residence of Companies: Austria. With English summary.) *International Fiscal Association, ed. (I),* 1987, pp. 217–29. [G: Austria]

Gemmell, Norman. Taxation and Development. *Gemmell, N., ed.*, 1987, pp. 269–306.
[G: LDCs]

Gerard, Marcel. Autour du débat fiscal belge: neutralité à l'égard des choix financiers et imposition effective des revenus de l'investissement. (With English summary.) *Cah. Écon. Bruxelles,* Fourth Trimester 1987, (116), pp. 25–63. [G: Belgium]

Gerardi, Geraldine, et al. The Treasury Depreciation Model. *U.S. Treasury, Office of Tax Analysis.*, 1987, pp. 203–27. [G: U.S.]

Gergely, Istvá. Personal Income Tax, Yes—But How? (Contribution to Debated Issues). *Acta Oecon.,* 1987, 38(3–4), pp. 275–87.
[G: Hungary]

Ghaus, Aisha. Is the Abolition of Capital Gains Tax Justified? *Pakistan J. Appl. Econ.*, Winter 1987, 6(2), pp. 103–24. [G: Pakistan]

Gillingham, Robert and Greenlees, John S. The Impact of Direct Taxes on the Cost of Living. *J. Polit. Econ.*, August 1987, 95(4), pp. 775–96. [G: U.S.]

Giordano, Robert M. Tax Reform and the U.S. Economy: Effects on Financial Decisionmaking: Comments. *Pechman, J. A., ed.,* 1987, pp. 66–70. [G: U.S.]

Gladstone, Robert. Tax Reform and the U.S. Economy: Effects on Real Estate: Comments. *Pechman, J. A., ed.,* 1987, pp. 94–97.
[G: U.S.]

Głuchowski, Jan. Tax Aspects of Joint Ventures with Western Companies Taking into Account Tax Treaties Concluded with Other Countries: Poland. *Bull. Int. Fiscal Doc.,* October 1987, 41(10), pp. 467–71. [G: Poland]

Gold, Steven D. The State Government Response to Federal Income Tax Reform: Indications from the States That Completed Their Work Early. *Nat. Tax J.,* September 1987, 40(3), pp. 431–44. [G: U.S.]

Gomez de Parada, Rodolfo Garcia. Tax Problems of the Liquidation of Corporations: Mexico. *International Fiscal Association, ed. (II),* 1987, pp. 369–82. [G: Mexico]

Goode, Richard. Disappointed Expectations and Tax Reform. *Nat. Tax J.,* June 1987, 40(2), pp. 159–69. [G: U.S.]

Goode, Richard. Obstacles to Tax Reform in Developing Countries. *van de Kar, H. M. and Wolfe, B. L., eds.,* 1987, pp. 213–23.
[G: LDCs]

Gordon, Roger H. Taxation and Capital Structure: A Selected Review: Comment. *Mintz, J. M. and Purvis, D. D., eds.,* 1987, pp. 263–66.

Gordon, Roger H. The Effects of Tax Rules on Nonresidential Fixed Investment: Some Preliminary Evidence from the 1980s: Comment. *Feldstein, M., ed. (I),* 1987, pp. 156–61.
[G: U.S.]

Gordon, Roger H.; Hines, James R., Jr. and Summers, Lawrence H. Notes on the Tax Treatment of Structures. *Feldstein, M., ed. (I),* 1987, pp. 223–54.

Govind, Har. Tax Approaches to Energy Management: India. *Bull. Int. Fiscal Doc.,* February 1987, 41(2), pp. 80–88. [G: India]

Govind, Har. Tax Treatment of Payments under Foreign Collaboration Agreements: India. *Bull. Int. Fiscal Doc.,* Aug.-Sept. 1987, 41(8–9), pp. 420–25.

Gradison, Bill. A U.S. Consumption Tax: A Congressional Response. *Walker, C. E. and Bloomfield, M. A., eds.,* 1987, pp. 262–65.
[G: U.S.]

Gramlich, Edward M. Rethinking the Role of the Public Sector. *Bosworth, B. P. and Rivlin, A. M., eds.,* 1987, pp. 250–88. [G: Sweden]

Greene, Kenneth V. and Balkan, Erol M. A Comparative Analysis of Tax Progressivity in the United States. *Public Finance Quart.*, October 1987, 15(4), pp. 397–416. [G: U.S.]

Grout, Paul A. Wider Share Ownership and Economic Performance. *Oxford Rev. Econ. Policy,* Winter 1987, 3(4), pp. 13–29. [G: U.K.]

Grubert, Harry and Mutti, John. Taxes, International Capital Flows and Trade: The International Implications of the Tax Reform Act of 1986. *Nat. Tax J.,* September 1987, 40(3), pp. 315–29. [G: U.S.]

Grubert, Harry and Mutti, John. The Impact of the Tax Reform Act of 1986 on Trade and Capital Flows. *U.S. Treasury, Office of Tax Analysis.*, 1987, pp. 229–52. **[G: U.S.]**

Guieu, Pierre and Bonnet, Claire. Completion of the Internal Market and Indirect Taxation. *J. Common Market Stud.*, March 1987, 25(3), pp. 209–22. **[G: EEC]**

Gupta, Vinod K. Removal of Poverty and Commodity Taxation: A Suggested Approach. *Indian Econ. J.*, July–Sept. 1987, 35(1), pp. 83–96. **[G: India]**

Haase, Herwig E. Direct Taxes in East and West. *Bull. Int. Fiscal Doc.*, July 1987, 41(7), pp. 304–17. **[G: OECD; E. Europe]**

Hacker, George A. Taxing Booze for Health and Wealth. *J. Policy Anal. Manage.*, Summer 1987, 6(4), pp. 701–08. **[G: U.S.]**

Hall, Robert E. Tax Policy and Corporate Saving: Comment. *Brookings Pap. Econ. Act.*, 1987, (2), pp. 504–06. **[G: U.S.]**

Halperin, Robert M. and Lanen, William N. The Effects of the *Thor Power Tool* Decision on the LIFO/FIFO Choice. *Accounting Rev.*, April 1987, 62(2), pp. 378–84.

Halperin, Robert M. and Srinidhi, Bin. The Effects of the U.S. Income Tax Regulations' Transfer Pricing Rules on Allocative Efficiency. *Accounting Rev.*, October 1987, 62(4), pp. 686–706. **[G: U.S.]**

Halpern, T. Lionel. Tax Problems of the Liquidation of Corporations: United Kingdom. *International Fiscal Association, ed. (II)*, 1987, pp. 455–74. **[G: U.K.]**

Hamilton, Jonathan H. Taxation, Savings, and Portfolio Choice in a Continuous Time Model. *Public Finance*, 1987, 42(2), pp. 264–82.

Hammer, Richard M. and Rohrer, William D. U.S. Branch Taxation: A Venture into the Unknown. *Bull. Int. Fiscal Doc.*, January 1987, 41(1), pp. 3–12. **[G: U.S.]**

Hamshere, J. D. Domesday Book, Cliometric Analysis and Taxation Assessments [Were the Tax Assessments of Domesday England Artificial? The Case of Essex]. *Econ. Hist. Rev.*, 2nd Ser., May 1987, 40(2), pp. 262–66. **[G: U.K.]**

Hamshere, J. D. Regressing Domesday Book: Tax Assessments of Domesday England: Comments [Were the Tax Assessments of Domesday England Artificial? The Case of Essex]. *Econ. Hist. Rev.*, 2nd Ser., May 1987, 40(2), pp. 247–51. **[G: U.K.]**

Hansmann, Henry. The Effect of Tax Exemption and Other Factors on the Market Share of Nonprofit versus For-Profit Firms. *Nat. Tax J.*, March 1987, 40(1), pp. 71–82. **[G: U.S.]**

Hansson, Ingemar. Effects of Capital Taxation on Capital Formation, Distribution, and Efficiency. *van de Kar, H. M. and Wolfe, B. L., eds.*, 1987, pp. 147–63. **[G: OECD]**

Hansson, Ingemar. Optimal Income Taxation and the Untaxed Sector. *Alessandrini, S. and Dallago, B., eds.*, 1987, pp. 311–21.

Hardesty, Sermin D.; Carman, Hoy F. and Moore, Charles V. Dynamic Analysis of Income Taxes on Farm Firms. *Amer. J. Agr.*

Econ., May 1987, 69(2), pp. 358–68. **[G: U.S.]**

Harley, Geoffrey John. The Fiscal Residence of Companies: New Zealand. *International Fiscal Association, ed. (I)*, 1987, pp. 423–37. **[G: New Zealand]**

Harris, Jeffrey E. The 1983 Increase in the Federal Cigarette Excise Tax. *Summers, L. H., ed.*, 1987, pp. 87–111. **[G: U.S.]**

Hartman, David G. New Results on the Effects of Tax Policy on the International Location of Investment: Comment. *Feldstein, M., ed. (I)*, 1987, pp. 219–22. **[G: U.S.]**

Hausman, James S. and Tamaki, George T. The Fiscal Residence of Companies: Canada. *International Fiscal Association, ed. (I)*, 1987, pp. 263–72. **[G: Canada]**

Hausman, Jerry A. Evaluating the Methodology of Social Experiments: Discussion. *Munnell, A. H., ed.*, 1987, pp. 158–61. **[G: U.S.]**

Hausman, Jerry A. and Poterba, James M. Household Behavior and the Tax Reform Act of 1986. *J. Econ. Perspectives*, Summer 1987, 1(1), pp. 101–19. **[G: U.S.]**

Head, John G. Capital Gains Tax and Capital Income Taxation. *Australian Tax Forum*, 1987, 4(1), pp. 35–62. **[G: Australia]**

Head, John G. The Carter Legacy: An International Perspective. *Australian Tax Forum*, 1987, 4(2), pp. 143–59. **[G: Australia; New Zealand; U.S.; Canada]**

Heady, Christopher. A Diagrammatic Approach to Optimal Commodity Taxation. *Public Finance*, 1987, 42(2), pp. 250–63.

Heady, Christopher. Designing Taxes with Migration. *Econ. J.*, Supplement 1987, 97, pp. 87–98. **[G: LDCs]**

Heaton, Hal. On the Bias of the Corporate Tax against High-Risk Projects. *J. Finan. Quant. Anal.*, September 1987, 22(3), pp. 365–71.

Helfrich-Laubrock, Jacoba. Critical Review of the OECD/Council of Europe Multilateral (Draft) Convention on Mutual Administrative Assistance in Tax Matters. *Bull. Int. Fiscal Doc.*, Aug.-Sept. 1987, 41(8–9), pp. 410–13. **[G: OECD]**

Helliwell, John F. The Effect of Taxation on Business Activity: Concluding Remarks. *Mintz, J. M. and Purvis, D. D., eds.*, 1987, pp. 280–87.

Hendershott, Patric H. Tax Changes and Capital Allocation in the 1980s. *Feldstein, M., ed. (I)*, 1987, pp. 259–90. **[G: U.S.]**

Hendershott, Patric H. Tax Reform and the Slope of the Playing Field. *Feldstein, M., ed. (II)*, 1987, pp. 51–61. **[G: U.S.]**

Hendershott, Patric H.; Follain, James R. and Ling, David C. Tax Reform and the U.S. Economy: Effects on Real Estate. *Pechman, J. A., ed.*, 1987, pp. 71–94. **[G: U.S.]**

Henderson, Yolanda Kodrzycki. A General Equilibrium Evaluation of Corporate Income Tax Reform. *Econ. Inquiry*, October 1987, 25(4), pp. 565–81.

Henderson, Yolanda Kodrzycki. The Taxation of Banks: Particular Privileges or Objectional

Burdens? *New Eng. Econ. Rev.*, May/June 1987, pp. 3–18.   [G: U.S.]

Henry, Samuel G. Brian and Karakitsos, Elias. Inflation, Unemployment and Indirect Taxation. *Bull. Econ. Res.*, January 1987, 39(1), pp. 29–47.

Hernandez Berenguel, Luis, et al. The Fiscal Residence of Companies: Peru. *International Fiscal Association, ed. (I)*, 1987, pp. 459–74.   [G: Peru]

Hinnekens, Luc. International Aspects of Taxation of Executive Remuneration: Belgium. *Bull. Int. Fiscal Doc.*, Aug.-Sept. 1987, 41(8–9), pp. 400–406.   [G: Belgium]

Hite, Peggy A. An Application of Attribution Theory in Taxpayer Noncompliance Research. *Public Finance*, 1987, 42(1), pp. 105–18.   [G: U.S.]

Hite, Peggy A. Qualifications for a Tax Specialist: Some Tax Partners' Views. *Jones, S. M., ed.*, 1987, pp. 183–98.   [G: U.S.]

Hoffman, Lorey Arthur; Poddar, S. N. and Whalley, John. Taxation of Banking Services under a Consumption Type, Destination Basis VAT. *Nat. Tax J.*, December 1987, 40(4), pp. 547–54.   [G: U.S.]

Holland, J. C. The Nature of VAT. *Bull. Int. Fiscal Doc.*, January 1987, 41(1), pp. 22–28.   [G: E. Europe]

Holtfrerich, Carl-Ludwig. The Modernisation of the Tax System in the First World War and the Great Inflation, 1914–23. *Witt, P.-C., ed.*, 1987, pp. 125–35.   [G: Germany]

Holtham, Gerald. Fiscal Policy and European Economic Growth: Comment. *Lawrence, R. Z. and Schultze, C. L., eds.*, 1987, pp. 501–04.   [G: W. Europe]

Hong, Lee Fook. A Summary of the 1987 Budget's Tax Clauses: Singapore. *Bull. Int. Fiscal Doc.*, May 1987, 41(5), pp. 232–34. [G: Singapore]

Hong, Lee Fook. Tax Incentives to Become a Financial Centre: Singapore. *Bull. Int. Fiscal Doc.*, March 1987, 41(3), pp. 103–10.   [G: Singapore]

Hongskrailers, Montri. Taxation of Joint Ventures: Thailand. *Bull. Int. Fiscal Doc.*, December 1987, 41(12), pp. 557–60. [G: Thailand]

Honohan, Patrick and Irvine, Ian. The Marginal Social Cost of Taxation in Ireland. *Econ. Soc. Rev.*, October 1987, 19(1), pp. 15–41.   [G: Ireland]

Howard, Michael. Income Tax Reform: Barbados. *Bull. Int. Fiscal Doc.*, April 1987, 41(4), pp. 151–60.   [G: Barbados]

Hubbard, R. Glenn. Tax Policy and Corporate Saving: Comment. *Brookings Pap. Econ. Act.*, 1987, (2), pp. 504–13.   [G: U.S.]

Hufbauer, Gary Clyde. The Consumption Tax and International Competitiveness. *Walker, C. E. and Bloomfield, M. A., eds.*, 1987, pp. 179–205.   [G: U.S.]

Hulten, Charles R. Tax Reform and the U.S. Economy: Effects on Industry: Comments. *Pechman, J. A., ed.*, 1987, pp. 46–51.   [G: U.S.]

Hund, D. Taxation of Eastern European-Source Income: The Netherlands. *Bull. Int. Fiscal Doc.*, July 1987, 41(7), pp. 319–25.   [G: Netherlands]

Hunt, Herbert G., III. Federal Tax Reform: Analysis of Two Consumption Taxes. *Jones, S. M., ed.*, 1987, pp. 109–30.   [G: U.S.]

Hunter, William J. and Scott, Charles E. The Impact of Income Tax Progressivity on Tax Revenue. *Public Finance Quart.*, April 1987, 15(2), pp. 188–98.   [G: U.S.]

Hutchison, Gary and Winslade, Ralph S. After-Tax Costs of Capital Purchases. *Can. J. Agr. Econ.*, May 1987, 34, pp. 40–61.

Hwang, Hong and Mai, Chao-Cheng. Business Taxation and Industrial Location. *Rivista Int. Sci. Econ. Com.*, March 1987, 34(3), pp. 241–48.

Ihori, Toshihiro. Tax Reform and Intergeneration Incidence. *J. Public Econ.*, August 1987, 33(3), pp. 377–87.

Ihori, Toshihiro. The Optimal Linear Income Tax: A Diagrammatic Analysis. *J. Public Econ.*, December 1987, 34(3), pp. 379–90.

Iqbal, Zubair. Instability of Federal Government Revenues and Expenditures in Pakistan: Comments. *Pakistan Devel. Rev.*, Winter 1987, 26(4), pp. 510–11.   [G: Pakistan]

Ishi, Hiromitsu. The Impact of the Shoup Mission. *van de Kar, H. M. and Wolfe, B. L., eds.*, 1987, pp. 237–49.   [G: Japan]

Itaba, Yoshio and Tachibanaki, Toshiaki. Measurement of Tax Progressivity When the Forms of Both Income Distribution and Tax Function Are Given. *Econ. Stud. Quart.*, June 1987, 38(2), pp. 97–106.   [G: Japan; U.S.]

Itoh, Motoshige and Kiyono, Kazuharu. Welfare-Enhancing Export Subsidies. *J. Polit. Econ.*, February 1987, 95(1), pp. 115–37.

Jankowski, Richard. The Profit-Squeeze and Tax Policy: Can the State Actively Intervene? *Rev. Radical Polit. Econ.*, Fall 1987, 19(3), pp. 18–33.   [G: U.S.]

Jeffcote, B. M. The Fiscal Residence of Companies: United Kingdom. *International Fiscal Association, ed. (I)*, 1987, pp. 503–22.   [G: U.K.]

Johnson, Omotunde E. G. Trade Tax and Exchange Rate Coordination in the Context of Border Trading: A Theoretical Analysis. *Int. Monet. Fund Staff Pap.*, September 1987, 34(3), pp. 548–64.   [G: Africa]

Jones, Charles P.; Pearce, Douglas K. and Wilson, Jack W. Can Tax-Loss Selling Explain the January Effect? A Note. *J. Finance*, June 1987, 42(2), pp. 453–61.   [G: U.S.]

Jones, Jonathan D. Are Future Taxes Anticipated by Consumers? More Evidence for the U.S., 1946–1985. *Econ. Notes*, 1987, (2), pp. 141–44.   [G: U.S.]

Judd, Kenneth L. A Dynamic Theory of Factor Taxation. *Amer. Econ. Rev.*, May 1987, 77(2), pp. 42–48.

Kahn, Edward and Goldman, Charles A. Impact of Tax Reform on Renewable Energy and Cogeneration Projects. *Energy Econ.*, October 1987, 9(4), pp. 215–26.   [G: U.S.]

Kajas, Ilkka. The Fiscal Residence of Companies: Finland. *International Fiscal Association, ed. (I)*, 1987, pp. 313–19. **[G: Finland]**

Kakwani, Nanak. Measures of Tax Progressivity and Redistribution Effect: A Comment. *Public Finance*, 1987, *42*(3), pp. 431–34.

Kanemoto, Yoshitsugu; Hayashi, Fumio and Wago, Hajime. An Econometric Analysis of a Capital Gains Tax on Land. *Econ. Stud. Quart.*, June 1987, *38*(2), pp. 159–71. **[G: Japan]**

Kaufmann, Daniel and Quigley, John M. The Consumption Benefits of Investment in Infrastructure: The Evaluation of Sites-and-Services Programs in Underdeveloped Countries. *J. Devel. Econ.*, April 1987, *25*(2), pp. 263–84. **[G: El Salvador]**

Kay, John A. Tax Reform in Retrospect: The Role of Inquiries. *van de Kar, H. M. and Wolfe, B. L., eds.*, 1987, pp. 67–81. **[G: U.S.; U.K.; Canada; Australia; New Zealand]**

Kay, John A. and Keen, Michael. Alcohol and Tobacco Taxes: Criteria for Harmonisation. *Cnossen, S., ed.*, 1987, pp. 85–111. **[G: EEC]**

Kay, John A. and Keen, Michael. Commodity Taxation for Maximum Revenue. *Public Finance Quart.*, October 1987, *15*(4), pp. 371–85.

Keeley, Michael C. The Effects of Experimental Negative Income Tax Programs on Marital Dissolution: Evidence from the Seattle and Denver Income Maintenance Experiments. *Int. Econ. Rev.*, February 1987, *28*(1), pp. 241–57. **[G: U.S.]**

Keen, Michael. Welfare Effects of Commodity Tax Harmonisation. *J. Public Econ.*, June 1987, *33*(1), pp. 107–14.

Kelly, William A., Jr.; Ferris, James M. and Miles, James A. The Expenditure Tax and Savings Incentives: Design Matters. *Growth Change*, Winter 1987, *18*(1), pp. 32–43.

Kelly, William A., Jr. and Miles, James A. A Fisherian Analysis of Individual Retirement Accounts. *Atlantic Econ. J.*, July 1987, *15*(2), pp. 1–10.

Kim, Moshe and Spiegel, Menahem. The Effects of Lump-Sum Subsidies on the Structure of Production and Productivity in Regulated Industries. *J. Public Econ.*, October 1987, *34*(1), pp. 105–19. **[G: Israel]**

King, Mervyn A. The Cash Flow Corporate Income Tax. *Feldstein, M., ed. (II)*, 1987, pp. 109–10. **[G: U.S.]**

King, Mervyn A. The Cash Flow Corporate Income Tax. *Feldstein, M., ed. (I)*, 1987, pp. 377–98. **[G: U.S.]**

Kirwan, Richard M. Fiscal Policy and the Price of Land and Housing in Japan. *Urban Stud.*, October 1987, *24*(5), pp. 345–60. **[G: Japan]**

Klemperer, W. David and O'Neil, Cherie J. Effects of an Inflation-Adjusted Basis on Asset Values after Capital Gains Taxes. *Land Econ.*, November 1987, *63*(4), pp. 386–95.

Knauthe, Erhardt and Spiller, Hans. The Structure of Obligatory Payments to the National Budget and the Management of the Socialist Economy: German Democratic Republic. *Bull. Int. Fiscal Doc.*, July 1987, *41*(7), pp. 329–36. **[G: E. Germany]**

Knoester, Anthonie and van der Windt, Nico. Real Wages and Taxation in Ten OECD Countries. *Oxford Bull. Econ. Statist.*, February 1987, *49*(1), pp. 151–69. **[G: OECD]**

Kohn, Robert E. The Technology of Pollution Avoidance by Firms. *Public Finance*, 1987, *42*(3), pp. 384–94.

Kornhuaser, Marjorie E. The Rhetoric of the Antic-Progressive Income Tax Movement: A Typical Male Reaction. *Mich. Law Rev.*, December 1987, *86*(3), pp. 465–523. **[G: U.S.]**

Koskela, Erkki. Changes in Tax Progression and Labour Supply under Wage Rate Uncertainty. *Public Finance*, 1987, *42*(2), pp. 214–26.

Kotlikoff, Laurence J. The Theory and Measurement of Effective Tax Rates: Comment. *Mintz, J. M. and Purvis, D. D., eds.*, 1987, pp. 102–04.

Kovenock, Daniel J. and Rothschild, Michael. Notes on the Effect of Capital Gain Taxation on Non-Austrian Assets. *Razin, A. and Sadka, E., eds.*, 1987, pp. 309–39. **[G: Austria]**

Krause-Junk, Gerold. Optimal Taxation: A Beautiful Cul-de-sac? *van de Kar, H. M. and Wolfe, B. L., eds.*, 1987, pp. 55–66.

Kreutzer, David and Lee, Dwight R. Joint Products and a Positive Response to a Profit Tax. *Public Finance Quart.*, January 1987, *15*(1), pp. 98–104.

Krüger, Kersten. Public Finance and Modernisation: The Change from Domain State to Tax State in Hesse in the Sixteenth and Seventeenth Centuries—A Case Study. *Witt, P.-C., ed.*, 1987, pp. 49–62. **[G: Germany; Europe]**

Kuiper, Willem G. East–West Tax Treaties. *Bull. Int. Fiscal Doc.*, October 1987, *41*(10), pp. 477–83. **[G: CMEA; OECD]**

Kumar, Raj and Radetzki, Marian. Alternative Fiscal Regimes for Mining in Developing Countries. *World Devel.*, May 1987, *15*(5), pp. 741–58. **[G: LDCs]**

Kupa, Mihály. Personal Income Tax: Principles and Debates. *Acta Oecon.*, 1987, *38*(3–4), pp. 289–302. **[G: Hungary]**

Kuttner, Robert. The Liberal Case for a Value-Added Tax. *Walker, C. E. and Bloomfield, M. A., eds.*, 1987, pp. 337–46. **[G: U.S.]**

Laffont, Jean-Jacques. Optimal Taxation of a Nonlinear Pricing Monopolist. *J. Public Econ.*, July 1987, *33*(2), pp. 137–55.

Lagae, Jean-Pierre. Coordination Centers: Belgium. *Bull. Int. Fiscal Doc.*, Aug.-Sept. 1987, *41*(8–9), pp. 359–70. **[G: Belgium]**

Lambert, Peter J. and Pfähler, Wilhelm. Intersecting Tax Concentration Curves and the Measurement of Tax Progressivity: A Rejoinder [On the Regressivity of State-Operated Numbers Games]. *Nat. Tax J.*, December 1987, *40*(4), pp. 635–38.

Lanthier, Allan R. Proposals for Tax Reform: Canada. *Bull. Int. Fiscal Doc.*, November 1987, *41*(11), pp. 495–504. **[G: Canada]**

Lapidoth, Arye. The Fiscal Residence of Companies: Israel. *International Fiscal Association, ed. (I)*, 1987, pp. 353–67.   **[G: Israel]**

Lapidoth, Arye. The 1987 Tax Reform: Israel. *Bull. Int. Fiscal Doc.*, December 1987, *41*(12), pp. 561–63.   **[G: Israel]**

Laroche, Christian. Twists and Turns in the Tax Rules for Foreign Companies Owning Real Estate in France. *Bull. Int. Fiscal Doc.*, March 1987, *41*(3), pp. 120–36.

Lawrence, David B. The Application of Censored Regression Techniques to the Analysis of Tax Reform. *J. Econometrics*, July 1987, *35*(2/3), pp. 287–302.   **[G: U.S.]**

Leape, Jonathan I. Taxes and Transaction Costs in Asset Market Equilibrium. *J. Public Econ.*, June 1987, *33*(1), pp. 1–20.

Leavy, James. New Tax Developments: Colombia. *Bull. Int. Fiscal Doc.*, January 1987, *41*(1), pp. 36–37.   **[G: Colombia]**

Leavy, James. Tax Reform Adopted by Congress: Colombia. *Bull. Int. Fiscal Doc.*, March 1987, *41*(3), pp. 142–43.

Leavy, James. Tax Reform Changes to Existing Rules: Colombia. *Bull. Int. Fiscal Doc.*, May 1987, *41*(5), pp. 235.   **[G: Colombia]**

Lee, Chul Song and Kim, Woo Taik. The Fiscal Residence of Companies: Republic of Korea. *International Fiscal Association, ed. (I)*, 1987, pp. 497–501.   **[G: S. Korea]**

Lefebvre, Pierre and Mayer, Francine. Une T.V.A. ou une T.V. fédérale au Québec? Quelques réponses tirées d'une analyse d'équilibre général. (A Federal V.A.T. or Sales Tax in Quebec? Some Answers from an Applied General Equilibrium Analysis. With English summary.) *L'Actual. Econ.*, December 1987, *63*(4), pp. 373–401.   **[G: Canada]**

Lemgruber, Rolando C. The Fiscal Residence of Companies: Brazil. *International Fiscal Association, ed. (I)*, 1987, pp. 245–61.   **[G: Brazil]**

Lewis, Frank and MacKinnon, Mary. Government Loan Guarantees and the Failure of the Canadian Northern Railway. *J. Econ. Hist.*, March 1987, *47*(1), pp. 175–96.   **[G: Canada]**

Li, Jinyan. The New Regulatory Tax on Individual Income: People's Republic of China. *Bull. Int. Fiscal Doc.*, April 1987, *41*(4), pp. 167–71.   **[G: China]**

Liebman, Howard M. Taxation of East European-Source Joint Venture Income: United States. *Bull. Int. Fiscal Doc.*, October 1987, *41*(10), pp. 460–66.   **[G: U.S.]**

Liebman, Howard M. and Kunze, Carol A. An Update on Taxation: The Mariana Islands. *Bull. Int. Fiscal Doc.*, December 1987, *41*(12), pp. 549–53.   **[G: Mariana Islands]**

Lindsey, Lawrence B. Capital Gains Rates, Realizations, and Revenues. *Feldstein, M., ed. (I)*, 1987, pp. 69–97.   **[G: U.S.]**

Lindsey, Lawrence B. Capital Gains Taxes under the Tax Reform Act of 1986: Revenue Estimates under Various Assumptions. *Nat. Tax J.*, September 1987, *40*(3), pp. 489–504.   **[G: U.S.]**

Lindsey, Lawrence B. Individual Taxpayer Response to Tax Cuts: 1824–1984: With Implica-

tions for the Revenue Maximizing Tax Rates. *J. Public Econ.*, July 1987, *33*(2), pp. 173–206.   **[G: U.S.]**

Lindsey, Lawrence B. Rates, Realizations, and Revenues of Capital Gains. *Feldstein, M., ed. (II)*, 1987, pp. 17–25.   **[G: U.S.]**

Lipka, Roland. Effects of Taxation of Social Security Benefits on Portfolio Revisions. *J. Risk Ins.*, December 1987, *54*(4), pp. 737–51.   **[G: U.S.]**

Liu, Pak-Wai. Measuring Global Tax Progressivity as Weighted Deviations from Proportional Tax: A Comment. *Public Finance*, 1987, *42*(3), pp. 435–37.

Llontop Chavarri, Carlos Enrique; Francesqui, Manuel Eduardo and Buckley, Tomas O. Branches of Foreign Companies—Income and Patrimony Tax Regimes: Peru. *Bull. Int. Fiscal Doc.*, January 1987, *41*(1), pp. 29–34.   **[G: Peru]**

Long, James E. and Caudill, Steven B. The Usage and Benefits of Paid Tax Return Preparation. *Nat. Tax J.*, March 1987, *40*(1), pp. 35–46.   **[G: U.S.]**

Long, James E. and Gwartney, James D. Income Tax Avoidance: Evidence from Individual Tax Returns. *Nat. Tax J.*, December 1987, *40*(4), pp. 517–32.   **[G: U.S.]**

Lord, William A. Welfare Effects of Capital Income Taxation under Variable and Fixed Labor Supply. *Southern Econ. J.*, July 1987, *54*(1), pp. 48–54.

Lowenberg-DeBoer, J. and Turvey, Calum Greig. A Note on the Changing Tax Treatment of Farmland Capital Gains and Losses in Canada and the United States. *Can. J. Agr. Econ.*, November 1987, *35*(3), pp. 605–13.   **[G: U.S.; Canada]**

Lucke, Robert and Toder, Eric. Assessing the U.S. Federal Tax Burden on Oil and Gas Extraction. *Energy J.*, October 1987, *8*(4), pp. 51–64.   **[G: U.S.]**

Lukács, József. The Introduction of VAT in 1988: Hungary. *Bull. Int. Fiscal Doc.*, October 1987, *41*(10), pp. 446–51.

Lynch, Anthony and Ziegler, Peter. Graphical Analysis of Amendments to the Income Tax Assessment Act (1936–87). *Australian Tax Forum*, 1987, *4*(4), pp. 529–46.   **[G: Canada]**

MacLaury, Bruce K. The Relationship of Tax Revenues to Government Spending. *Walker, C. E. and Bloomfield, M. A., eds.*, 1987, pp. 238–40.   **[G: U.S.]**

Madeo, Silvia A.; Schepanski, Albert and Uecker, Wilfred C. Modeling Judgments of Taxpayer Compliance. *Accounting Rev.*, April 1987, *62*(2), pp. 323–42.   **[G: U.S.]**

Majd, Saman and Myers, Stewart C. Tax Asymmetries and Corporate Income Tax Reform. *Feldstein, M., ed. (I)*, 1987, pp. 343–73.   **[G: U.S.]**

Makin, John H. Capital Gains Rates, Realizations, and Revenues: Comment. *Feldstein, M., ed. (I)*, 1987, pp. 98–100.   **[G: U.S.]**

Makin, John H. Income Tax Reform and the Consumption Tax. *Walker, C. E. and Bloomfield,*

M. A., eds., 1987, pp. 87–115. [G: U.S.]

Makin, John H. and Shoven, John B. Are There Lessons for the United States in the Japanese Tax System? *Cagan, P., ed.*, 1987, pp. 305–29. [G: U.S.; Japan]

Malcomson, James M. and Sartor, Nicola. Tax Push Inflation in a Unionized Labour Market. *Europ. Econ. Rev.*, December 1987, *31*(8), pp. 1581–96. [G: Italy]

Malherbe, Jacques. Simulation, Fraus Legis and Business Purpose under Belgian Tax Law: Belgium. *Bull. Int. Fiscal Doc.*, Aug.-Sept. 1987, *41*(8–9), pp. 396–99, 409. [G: Belgium]

Malik, Muhammad Hussain and Yasmin, Attiya. Instability of Federal Government Revenues and Expenditures in Pakistan. *Pakistan Devel. Rev.*, Winter 1987, *26*(4), pp. 501–09. [G: Pakistan]

Mankiw, N. Gregory. Consumer Spending and the After-Tax Real Interest Rate. *Feldstein, M., ed. (II)*, 1987, pp. 97–99. [G: U.S.]

Manning, Ian G. Income Tax—An Institution to Reform? *Australian Tax Forum*, 1987, *4*(3), pp. 313–26. [G: Australia]

Marcus, Richard D. Transferable Tax Liabilities on Real Estate. *Land Econ.*, February 1987, *63*(1), pp. 102–06. [G: U.S.]

Marin Arias, Manuel. La résidence fiscale des sociétés: Espagne. (The Fiscal Residence of Companies: Spain. With English summary.) *International Fiscal Association, ed. (I)*, 1987, pp. 287–97. [G: Spain]

Marrelli, M. The Economic Analysis of Tax Evasion: Empirical Aspects. *Hey, J. D. and Lambert, P. J., eds.*, 1987, pp. 204–28. [G: U.S.; W. Europe]

Marsden, Keith. The Reappraisal of Development Strategies [Taxation, Economic Growth, and Liberty]. *Cato J.*, Spring/Summer 1987, *7*(1), pp. 149–52. [G: LDCs]

Martinich, Joseph S. and Hurter, Arthur P., Jr. A Note on Income Taxes and Degree One Production Homogeneity. *J. Reg. Sci.*, August 1987, *27*(3), pp. 477–82.

Matsui, Robert T. Issues of the Regressivity of a Consumption Tax: The Political Dynamics. *Walker, C. E. and Bloomfield, M. A., eds.*, 1987, pp. 333–36. [G: U.S.]

Matsumura, Hideo. The Fiscal Residence of Companies: Japan. *International Fiscal Association, ed. (I)*, 1987, pp. 389–401. [G: Japan]

Mayo, Stephen K. and Gross, David J. Sites and Services—and Subsidies: The Economics of Low-Cost Housing in Developing Countries. *World Bank Econ. Rev.*, January 1987, *1*(2), pp. 301–35. [G: LDCs]

Mayo, Wayne. Interest, Exempt Income and Inter-corporate Dividends. *Australian Tax Forum*, 1987, *4*(1), pp. 123–42. [G: Australia]

McClure, Charles E., Jr. Reflections on Recent Proposals to Rationalize the U.S. Income Tax. *van de Kar, H. M. and Wolfe, B. L., eds.*, 1987, pp. 97–112. [G: U.S.]

McDaniel, Paul R. Personal Income Taxes: The Treatment of Tax Expenditures. *Cnossen, S., ed.*, 1987, pp. 319–33. [G: EEC]

McDermott, John E. and Sherman, William B. Tax Problems of the Liquidation of Corporations: United States. *International Fiscal Association, ed. (II)*, 1987, pp. 269–77. [G: U.S.]

McDonald, John and Snooks, G. D. The Suitability of Domesday Book for Cliometric Analysis [Were the Tax Assessments of Domesday England Artificial? The Case of Essex]. *Econ. Hist. Rev., 2nd Ser.*, May 1987, *40*(2), pp. 252–61. [G: U.K.]

McLay, David. Tax Problems of the Liquidation of Corporations: New Zealand. *International Fiscal Association, ed. (II)*, 1987, pp. 395–402. [G: New Zealand]

McLure, Charles E., Jr. The Optimal Consumption Tax for the United States. *Walker, C. E. and Bloomfield, M. A., eds.*, 1987, pp. 265–71. [G: U.S.]

McLure, Charles E., Jr. U.S. Tax Reform. *Australian Tax Forum*, 1987, *4*(3), pp. 293–312. [G: U.S.]

McLure, Charles E., Jr. and Zodrow, George R. Treasury I and the Tax Reform Act of 1986: The Economics and Politics of Tax Reform. *J. Econ. Perspectives*, Summer 1987, *1*(1), pp. 37–58. [G: U.S.]

Messere, K. C. and Owens, Jeffrey P. International Comparisons of Tax Levels: Pitfalls and Insights. *OECD Econ. Stud.*, Spring 1987, (8), pp. 93–119. [G: OECD]

Metcalf, Charles E. Evaluating the Methodology of Social Experiments: Discussion. *Munnell, A. H., ed.*, 1987, pp. 162–66. [G: U.S.]

Mills, Edwin S. Bureaucratic Corruption as a Constraint on Voter Choice: Comments. *Public Choice*, September 1987, *55*(1–2), pp. 161–62.

Mintz, Jack M. and Purvis, Douglas D. Taxation and Business Activity: Introduction. *Mintz, J. M. and Purvis, D. D., eds.*, 1987, pp. 2–57.

Modi, Jitendra R. Major Features of Corporate Profits Taxes in Selected Developing Countries. *Bull. Int. Fiscal Doc.*, February 1987, *41*(2), pp. 65–74. [G: LDCs]

Moffitt, Robert and Rothschild, Michael. Variable Earnings and Nonlinear Taxation. *J. Human Res.*, Summer 1987, *22*(3), pp. 405–21. [G: U.S.]

Mohammad, Faiz. Agricultural Taxation in Pakistan Revisited. *Pakistan Devel. Rev.*, Winter 1987, *26*(4), pp. 419–29. [G: Pakistan]

Moore, Norman H. and Pruitt, Stephen W. The Market Pricing of Net Operating Loss Carryforwards: Implications of the Tax Motivations of Mergers. *J. Finan. Res.*, Summer 1987, *10*(2), pp. 153–60. [G: U.S.]

Morgan, Eleanor J. The UK Corporate Tax Reform and Business Investment Decisions. *Managerial Dec. Econ.*, June 1987, *8*(2), pp. 149–59. [G: U.K.]

Morris, Michael H. and Wittenbach, James L. The First Year of Safe Harbor Leasing Activity: A Look Back at Objectives and Results. *Jones, S. M., ed.*, 1987, pp. 131–52. [G: U.S.]

Muellbauer, John. The Community Charge, Rates and Tax Reform. *Lloyds Bank Rev.*, October 1987, (166), pp. 7–19. [G: U.K.]

Murfin, Andy. Price Discrimination and Tax Differences in the European Motor Industry. *Cnossen, S., ed.*, 1987, pp. 171–94.
[G: EEC]

Musgrave, Peggy B. Interjurisdictional Coordination of Taxes on Capital Income. *Cnossen, S., ed.*, 1987, pp. 197–225. [G: EEC]

Musgrave, Richard A. Fifty Years of Public Finance. *Roskamp, K. W., ed.*, 1987, pp. 19–50.

Musgrave, Richard A. Short of Euphoria. *J. Econ. Perspectives*, Summer 1987, *1*(1), pp. 59–71.
[G: U.S.]

Myles, Gareth D. Tax Design in the Presence of Imperfect Competition: An Example. *J. Public Econ.*, December 1987, *34*(3), pp. 367–78.

Nagy, Tibor. Changes in the Tax System: Viet-Nam. *Bull. Int. Fiscal Doc.*, December 1987, *41*(12), pp. 554–56. [G: Vietnam]

Nagy, Tibor. Current Trends in Income Taxation in Eastern Europe. *Bull. Int. Fiscal Doc.*, October 1987, *41*(10), pp. 439–45.
[G: E. Europe]

Nakatani, Iwao. Japan–U.S. Relations: Asymmetry of Institutional Features as a Source of Trade Frictions. *Patrick, H. T. and Tachi, R., eds.*, 1987, pp. 184–95. [G: Japan; U.S.]

Nam, Chong-Hyun. Export-Promoting Subsidies, Countervailing Threats, and the General Agreement of Tariffs and Trade. *World Bank Econ. Rev.*, September 1987, *1*(4), pp. 727–43. [G: Global]

Nauta, Klaas. The Fiscal Residence of Companies: Netherlands. *International Fiscal Association, ed. (I)*, 1987, pp. 439–58.
[G: Netherlands]

Nellor, David C. L. Sovereignty and Natural Resource Taxation in Developing Countries. *Econ. Develop. Cult. Change*, January 1987, *35*(2), pp. 367–92. [G: LDCs]

Nelson, Michael A. Searching for Leviathan: Comment and Extension. *Amer. Econ. Rev.*, March 1987, *77*(1), pp. 198–204.

Nelson, Susan C. Family Economic Income and Other Income Concepts Used in Analyzing Tax Reform. *U.S. Treasury, Office of Tax Analysis.*, 1987, pp. 77–99. [G: U.S.]

Nester, Howard W. A Guide to Interpreting the Dynamic Elements of Revenue Estimates. *U.S. Treasury, Office of Tax Analysis.*, 1987, pp. 13–41. [G: U.S.]

Neubig, Thomas S. The Impossible Dream Comes True: Comments. *Pechman, J. A., ed.*, 1987, pp. 22–25. [G: U.S.]

Neubig, Thomas S. and Sullivan, Martin A. The Effect of the Tax Reform Act of 1986 on Commercial Banks. *U.S. Treasury, Office of Tax Analysis.*, 1987, pp. 279–305. [G: U.S.]

Neubig, Thomas S. and Sullivan, Martin A. The Implications of Tax Reform for Bank Holdings of Tax-Exempt Securities. *Nat. Tax J.*, September 1987, *40*(3), pp. 403–18. [G: U.S.]

Nevile, J. W., et al. A Simple Model of Recent Changes in the Residential Property Market. *Econ. Rec.*, September 1987, *63*(182), pp. 270–80. [G: Australia]

Newman, Sandra J. and Reschovsky, James D. An Evaluation of the One-Time Capital Gains Exclusion for Older Homeowners. *Amer. Real Estate Urban Econ. Assoc. J.*, Spring 1987, *15*(1), pp. 704–24. [G: U.S.]

Ng, Yew-Kwang. Taxation Policies: Some Neglected Essential Issues. *Australian Tax Forum*, 1987, *4*(3), pp. 347–55.

Noguchi, Yukio. The Political Economy of Japan: Public Finance. *Yamamura, K. and Yasuba, Y., eds.*, 1987, pp. 186–222. [G: Japan]

Nolan, Brian. Direct Taxation, Transfers and Reranking: Some Empirical Results for the UK. *Oxford Bull. Econ. Statist.*, August 1987, *49*(3), pp. 273–90. [G: U.K.]

Nomura, Shigeru. Impact on the Japanese Tax System. *Bull. Int. Fiscal Doc.*, June 1987, *41*(6), pp. 259–61. [G: Japan]

Noriega del Valle, Enrique; Carrión, Hugo Paniague and Dueñas, César Rodríguez. Tax Problems of the Liquidation of Corporations: Peru. *International Fiscal Association, ed. (II)*, 1987, pp. 423–34. [G: Peru]

Nourse, Hugh O. The "Cap Rate," 1966–1984: A Test of the Impact of Income Tax Changes on Income Property. *Land Econ.*, May 1987, *63*(2), pp. 147–52. [G: U.S.]

Nunns, James R. Tabulations from the Treasury Tax Reform Data Base. *U.S. Treasury, Office of Tax Analysis.*, 1987, pp. 101–29. [G: U.S.]

Nystad, Arild N. Petroleum Taxes and Resource Management. *Pachauri, R. K., ed.*, 1987, pp. 19–34.

O'Neil, Cherie J. and Thompson, G. Rodney. Participation in Individual Retirement Accounts: An Empirical Investigation. *Nat. Tax J.*, December 1987, *40*(4), pp. 617–24.
[G: U.S.]

Oates, Wallace E. Fiscal Structure in the Federal System. *Aronson, J. R. and Schwartz, E., eds.*, 1987, pp. 51–73. [G: U.S.]

Officer, Robert R. The Required Rate of Return and Tax Imputation: Estimating the Effect of the Imputation Tax on Investment Appraisal. *Australian Tax Forum*, 1987, *4*(3), pp. 405–17.

Ohde, Bjorn. The Fiscal Residence of Companies: Sweden. *International Fiscal Association, ed. (I)*, 1987, pp. 535–42. [G: Sweden]

Ormrod, W. M. The English Crown and the Customs, 1349–63. *Econ. Hist. Rev., 2nd Ser.*, February 1987, *40*(1), pp. 27–40. [G: U.K.]

Owens, Jeffrey P. Tax Reform: An International Perspective. *Nat. Westminster Bank Quart. Rev.*, May 1987, pp. 2–13. [G: OECD]

Palm, Alexis and Thiry, Bernard. La réforme des impôts indirects: l'effet de quelques propositions de réforme sur le poids de la fiscalité indirecte dans le revenu des ménages belges. (With English summary.) *Cah. Écon. Bruxelles*, Fourth Trimester 1987, (116), pp. 65–97. [G: Belgium]

Palokangas, Tapio. Optimal Taxation and Employment Policy with a Centralized Wage Setting. *Oxford Econ. Pap.*, December 1987, *39*(4), pp. 799–812.

Park, Thae S. Federal Personal Income Taxes: Liabilities and Payments, 1981–85. *Surv. Curr. Bus.*, June 1987, *67*(6), pp. 17–18. **[G: U.S.]**

Parmenter, Brian R. and Seyfort, Anthony. The Imputation System of Company Tax: Context, Characteristics, Critique. *Australian Econ. Rev.*, First Quarter 1987, (77), pp. 3–8. **[G: Australia]**

Parry, Charles W. An Industrialist Looks at the Consumption Tax. *Walker, C. E. and Bloomfield, M. A., eds.*, 1987, pp. 29–33. **[G: U.S.]**

Parsons, Ross W. A Survey of the General Provisions of Part IIIA of the Income Tax Assessment Act. *Australian Tax Forum*, 1987, *4*(3), pp. 357–404. **[G: Australia]**

Paulsen, Jim W. and Adams, Roy D. Optimal Taxation of a Monopoly. *Nat. Tax J.*, March 1987, *40*(1), pp. 121–25.

Pechman, Joseph A. A Consumption Tax Is Not Desirable for the United States. *Walker, C. E. and Bloomfield, M. A., eds.*, 1987, pp. 271–74. **[G: U.S.]**

Pechman, Joseph A. Pechman's Tax Incidence Study: A Response. *Amer. Econ. Rev.*, March 1987, *77*(1), pp. 232–34. **[G: U.S.]**

Pechman, Joseph A. Tax Reform and the U.S. Economy: Introduction. *Pechman, J. A., ed.*, 1987, pp. 1–9. **[G: U.S.]**

Pechman, Joseph A. Tax Reform: Theory and Practice. *J. Econ. Perspectives*, Summer 1987, *1*(1), pp. 11–28. **[G: U.S.]**

Penner, Rudolph G. The Consumption Tax: A Better Alternative? The Federal Budget Context. *Walker, C. E. and Bloomfield, M. A., eds.*, 1987, pp. 35–40. **[G: U.S.]**

Petersen, Carol D.; Shear, William and Vehorn, Charles L. Cash Accounting Rules for Farmers: Differential Benefits and Federal Costs. *J. Econ. Issues*, June 1987, *21*(2), pp. 639–47. **[G: U.S.]**

Petersen, John E. Examining the Impacts of the 1986 Tax Reform Act on the Municipal Securities Market. *Nat. Tax J.*, September 1987, *40*(3), pp. 393–402. **[G: U.S.]**

Pfähler, Wilhelm. Redistributive Effects of Tax Progressivity: A Reply. *Public Finance*, 1987, *42*(3), pp. 446–47.

Pfähler, Wilhelm. Redistributive Effects of Tax Progressivity: Evaluating a General Class of Aggregate Measures. *Public Finance*, 1987, *42*(1), pp. 1–31.

Pfingsten, Andreas. Axiomatically Based Local Measures of Tax Progression. *Bull. Econ. Res.*, July 1987, *39*(3), pp. 211–23.

Philipose, Susy. A Macroeconomic Model for Income Tax Assessment for India. *J. Econ. Dynam. Control*, June 1987, *11*(2), pp. 213–19. **[G: India]**

Phillips, Kevin P. A Political Strategy for a Consumption Tax. *Walker, C. E. and Bloomfield, M. A., eds.*, 1987, pp. 347–52. **[G: U.S.]**

Phypers, Dean P. Tax Reform and the U.S. Economy: Effects on Industry: Comments. *Pechman, J. A., ed.*, 1987, pp. 51–54. **[G: U.S.]**

Piggott, John and Whalley, John. Interpreting Net Fiscal Incidence Calculations. *Rev. Econ. Statist.*, November 1987, *69*(4), pp. 685–94. **[G: Australia]**

Piros, Christopher D. Taxable vs. Tax-Exempt Bonds: A Note on the Effect of Uncertain Taxable Income. *J. Finance*, June 1987, *42*(2), pp. 447–51.

Plasschaert, Sylvain R. F. The Weak Case for Dualistic (Composite) Types of Income Taxation. *Bull. Int. Fiscal Doc.*, April 1987, *41*(4), pp. 161–66. **[G: Global]**

Pollard, William B. and Speer, Charles C. An Analysis of the Impact of Recent Social Security Legislation on Marginal Tax Rates. *Public Budg. Finance*, Spring 1987, *7*(1), pp. 104–10. **[G: U.S.]**

Poterba, James M. How Burdensome Are Capital Gains Taxes? Evidence from the United States. *J. Public Econ.*, July 1987, *33*(2), pp. 157–72. **[G: U.S.]**

Poterba, James M. Tax Evasion and Capital Gains Taxation. *Amer. Econ. Rev.*, May 1987, *77*(2), pp. 234–39. **[G: U.S.]**

Poterba, James M. Tax Policy and Corporate Saving. *Brookings Pap. Econ. Act.*, 1987, (2), pp. 455–503. **[G: U.S.]**

Poterba, James M. Taxation and Capital Structure: A Selected Review: Comment. *Mintz, J. M. and Purvis, D. D., eds.*, 1987, pp. 267–74.

Poterba, James M. and Summers, Lawrence H. Finite Lifetimes and the Effects of Budget Deficits on National Saving. *J. Monet. Econ.*, September 1987, *20*(2), pp. 369–91. **[G: U.S.]**

Pozdena, Randall Johnston. Tax Policy and Corporate Capital Structure. *Fed. Res. Bank San Francisco Econ. Rev.*, Fall 1987, (4), pp. 37–51. **[G: U.S.]**

Prakken, Joel L. The Macroeconomics of Tax Reform. *Walker, C. E. and Bloomfield, M. A., eds.*, 1987, pp. 117–66. **[G: U.S.]**

Prebble, John. Canadian and Swedish Procedures for Advance Rulings in Income Tax Cases. *Australian Tax Forum*, 1987, *4*(2), pp. 217–40. **[G: Canada; Sweden]**

Pressman, Steven. A Tale of Two Taxpayers: The Effects of the Economic Recovery and Tax Act of 1981. *J. Post Keynesian Econ.*, Winter 1986-87, *9*(2), pp. 226–36. **[G: U.S.]**

Pressman, Steven. The Myths and Realities of Tax Bracket Creep. *Eastern Econ. J.*, Jan.-Mar. 1987, *13*(1), pp. 31–39. **[G: U.S.]**

Qianli, Ma. Management of the "Stupid Melon Seed Dealer" and Its Evasion of Taxes and Other Tax Problems. *Chinese Econ. Stud.*, Fall 1987, *21*(1), pp. 76–83. **[G: China]**

Qureshi, A. H. The Freedom of a State to Legislate in Fiscal Matters under General International Law. *Bull. Int. Fiscal Doc.*, January 1987, *41*(1), pp. 14–21.

Qureshi, A. H. Unitary Taxation and General International Law. *Bull. Int. Fiscal Doc.*, February 1987, *41*(2), pp. 56–64, 88.

Qureshi, Sarfraz Khan. Agricultural Taxation in Pakistan Revisited: Comments. *Pakistan*

Devel. Rev., Winter 1987, *26*(4), pp. 430–32. [G: Pakistan]

Rabushka, Alvin. Taxation, Economic Growth, and Liberty. *Cato J.*, Spring/Summer 1987, *7*(1), pp. 121–48. [G: LDCs]

Rafael, Amnon. Tax Problems of the Liquidation of Corporations: Israel. *International Fiscal Association, ed. (II)*, 1987, pp. 305–19. [G: Israel]

Rao, Hemlata. Income Tax Proceeds: Are the States Getting Their Due Share? *Gulati, I. S., ed.*, 1987, *1985*, pp. 185–94. [G: India]

Reinganum, Marc R. and Shapiro, Alan C. Taxes and Stock Return Seasonality: Evidence from the London Stock Exchange. *J. Bus.*, April 1987, *60*(2), pp. 281–95. [G: U.K.]

Resk, Carlos H. Tax Problems of the Liquidation of Corporations: Argentina. *International Fiscal Association, ed. (II)*, 1987, pp. 153–71. [G: Argentina]

Rica, Narciso Amorós. Problemas fiscales de la liquidación de sociedades: Espagne. (Tax Problems of the Liquidation of Corporations: Spain. With English summary.) *International Fiscal Association, ed. (II)*, 1987, pp. 259–68. [G: Spain]

Richardson, G. V. C. The Fiscal Residence of Companies: South Africa. *International Fiscal Association, ed. (I)*, 1987, pp. 147–59. [G: S. Africa]

Richter, Wolfram F. Taxation as Insurance and the Case of Rate Differentiation According to Consanguinity under Inheritance Taxation. *J. Public Econ.*, August 1987, *33*(3), pp. 363–76. [G: W. Germany]

Rivier, Jean-Marc. The Fiscal Residence of Companies: General Report. *International Fiscal Association, ed. (I)*, 1987, pp. 47–143. [G: Global]

Robinson, Bill. How Buoyant Is Public Revenue? *Fisc. Stud.*, May 1987, *8*(2), pp. 35–47. [G: U.K.]

Robinson, Marc S. The Welfare Cost of Resource Taxation. *[Harberger, A.]*, 1987, pp. 95–108.

Rock, Steven M. Repealing Deductibility and the Aggregate Incidence of State and Local Income Taxes. *Amer. Econ.*, Fall 1987, *31*(2), pp. 35–40. [G: U.S.]

Rodrigues Pardal, Francisco. La résidence fiscale des sociétés: Portugal. (The Fiscal Residence of Companies: Portugal. With English summary.) *International Fiscal Association, ed. (I)*, 1987, pp. 475–96. [G: Portugal]

Rogers, Carol Ann. Expenditure Taxes, Income Taxes, and Time-Inconsistency. *J. Public Econ.*, March 1987, *32*(2), pp. 215–30.

Rolt, Sidney C. and Burgum, Kathleen J. The Fiscal Residence of Companies: Singapore. *International Fiscal Association, ed. (I)*, 1987, pp. 523–33. [G: Singapore]

Ronn, Ehud I. A New Linear Programming Approach to Bond Portfolio Management. *J. Finan. Quant. Anal.*, December 1987, *22*(4), pp. 439–66. [G: U.S.]

Rose, Manfred. Optimal Tax Perspective on Tax

Coordination. *Cnossen, S., ed.*, 1987, pp. 113–38. [G: EEC]

Rosen, Harvey S. Tax Changes and Capital Allocation in the 1980s: Comment. *Feldstein, M., ed. (I)*, 1987, pp. 290–94. [G: U.S.]

Rosen, Harvey S. The Marriage Tax Is Down but Not Out. *Nat. Tax J.*, December 1987, *40*(4), pp. 567–75. [G: U.S.]

Roskamp, Karl W. Optimal Lifetime Consumption Paths under Equal Yield Income and Consumption Taxes. *Public Finance*, 1987, *42*(1), pp. 32–41.

Ross, A. D. Living with Anti-tax Haven Legislation: Three Years of U.K. Experience: United Kingdom. *Bull. Int. Fiscal Doc.*, June 1987, *41*(6), pp. 263–70. [G: U.K.]

Ross, Stephen A. Arbitrage and Martingales with Taxation. *J. Polit. Econ.*, April 1987, *95*(2), pp. 371–93.

Rostenkowski, Dan. The Consumption Tax: A Better Alternative? A View from the Ways and Means Committee. *Walker, C. E. and Bloomfield, M. A., eds.*, 1987, pp. 25–28. [G: U.S.]

Rousslang, Donald J. The Effects of Recent Corporate Tax Changes on U.S. International Trade. *Nat. Tax J.*, December 1987, *40*(4), pp. 603–15. [G: U.S.]

Rousslang, Donald J. The Opportunity Cost of Import Tariffs. *Kyklos*, 1987, *40*(1), pp. 88–102. [G: U.S.]

Rubin, Rose M.; Riney, Bobye J. and Johansen, Todd. Tax Effects on the Net Income of Wives in Dual-Earner Households, 1980–1983. *Public Finance Quart.*, October 1987, *15*(4), pp. 441–59. [G: U.S.]

Ruggles, Patricia and O'Higgins, Michael. Retrenchment and the New Right: A Comparative Analysis of the Impacts of the Thatcher and Reagan Administrations. *Rein, M.; Esping-Andersen, G. and Rainwater, L., eds.*, 1987, pp. 160–90. [G: U.S.; U.K.]

Runge, Berndt. Die steuerliche Ansässigkeit von Kapitalgesellschaften: Deutschland. (The Fiscal Residence of Companies: Germany. With English summary.) *International Fiscal Association, ed. (I)*, 1987, pp. 161–76. [G: W. Germany]

Russell, A. M. and Rickard, J. A. A Model of Tax Evasion Incorporating Income Variation and Retroactive Penalities. *Australian Econ. Pap.*, December 1987, *26*(49), pp. 254–64.

Salvatici, S. and Vieceli, A. Incentives for Private Forestry in Italy. *Merlo, M., et al., eds.*, 1987, pp. 491–99. [G: Italy]

Sandmo, Agnar. A Reinterpretation of Elasticity Formulae in Optimum Tax Theory. *Economica*, February 1987, *54*(213), pp. 89–96.

Sandford, Cedric. Death Duties: Taxing Estates or Inheritances. *Fisc. Stud.*, November 1987, *8*(4), pp. 15–23. [G: U.K.]

Sapounas, George S. Allocation of Goods and Services in VAT: The Case of Greece. *Europ. Econ. Rev.*, August 1987, *31*(6), pp. 1285–98. [G: Greece]

Saunders, Michael. Oil Taxation: The Cross-Field

Allowance. *Fisc. Stud.*, November 1987, *8*(4), pp. 55–68. **[G: U.K.]**

Saunders, Michael. Tax-Privileged Government Debt: Low Coupon Gilts. *Fisc. Stud.*, May 1987, *8*(2), pp. 86–108. **[G: U.K.]**

Sav, G. Thomas. Tax Incentives for Innovative Energy Sources: Extensions of E–K Complementarity. *Public Finance Quart.*, October 1987, *15*(4), pp. 417–27. **[G: U.S.]**

Schulze, Dick. The Consumption Tax: A Better Alternative? A Congressional View. *Walker, C. E. and Bloomfield, M. A., eds.*, 1987, pp. 240–42. **[G: U.S.]**

Scotchmer, Suzanne. Audit Classes and Tax Enforcement Policy. *Amer. Econ. Rev.*, May 1987, *77*(2), pp. 229–33.

Scott, M. F. G. A Note on King and Fullerton's Formulae to Estimate the Taxation of Income from Capital. *J. Public Econ.*, November 1987, *34*(2), pp. 253–63. **[G: U.K.]**

Seeger, Norbert. Tax Reform in Liechtenstein. *Bull. Int. Fiscal Doc.*, Aug.-Sept. 1987, *41*(8–9), pp. 414–19. **[G: Liechtenstein]**

Seidman, Laurence S. Relativity and Efficient Taxation. *Southern Econ. J.*, October 1987, *54*(2), pp. 463–74.

Sen, Nandita. Losses May Be Set Off against Foreign-Source Dividends Exempt under a Tax Treaty: India. *Bull. Int. Fiscal Doc.*, May 1987, *41*(5), pp. 221–23. **[G: India]**

Severn, Alan K.; Mills, James Charles and Copeland, Basil L., Jr. Capital Gains Taxes after Tax Reform. *J. Portfol. Manage.*, Spring 1987, *13*(3), pp. 69–75. **[G: U.S.]**

Sharpe, Don. The Cambridge Multisectoral Dynamic Model of the British Economy: Social Security Benefits and Personal Income Tax. *Barker, T. and Peterson, W., eds.*, 1987, pp. 373–87. **[G: U.K.]**

Shaw, Wayne H. Safe Harbor or Muddy Waters. *Accounting Rev.*, April 1987, *62*(2), pp. 385–400.

Sherman, H. A. The Argentine Wealth Tax and Its Transborder Effects: Or Tax Foreigners—They Have No Vote. *Bull. Int. Fiscal Doc.*, December 1987, *41*(12), pp. 536–41. **[G: Argentina]**

Shioda, Shigenori. Tax Problems of the Liquidation of Corporations: Japan. *International Fiscal Association, ed. (II)*, 1987, pp. 337–54. **[G: Japan]**

Shoven, John B. The Tax Consequences of Share Repurchases and Other Non-dividend Cash Payments to Equity Owners. *Summers, L. H., ed.*, 1987, pp. 29–54. **[G: U.S.]**

Shughart, William F., II. Durable Tax Reform. *Cato J.*, Spring/Summer 1987, *7*(1), pp. 273–81. **[G: U.S.]**

Sibille, Charles and Fryt, Michael D. Planning for Coordination Centers: After U.S. Tax Reform: Belgium. *Bull. Int. Fiscal Doc.*, Aug.-Sept. 1987, *41*(8–9), pp. 371–82. **[G: Belgium; U.S.]**

Siebens, H. Some Special Aspects of Foreign Source Profits and Losses in Corporate Income Taxation: Belgium. *Bull. Int. Fiscal Doc.*,

Aug.-Sept. 1987, *41*(8–9), pp. 391–95.

de Silva, R. G. L. Recent Changes in the Tax Law: Sri Lanka. *Bull. Int. Fiscal Doc.*, November 1987, *41*(11), pp. 514–16. **[G: Sri Lanka]**

Skou, Jørgen and Ancher, Tom. Tax Problems of the Liquidation of Corporations: Denmark. *International Fiscal Association, ed. (II)*, 1987, pp. 247–58. **[G: Denmark]**

Slemrod, Joel. On Effective Tax Rates and Steady-State Tax Revenues. *Nat. Tax J.*, March 1987, *40*(1), pp. 127–32.

Slemrod, Joel and Yitzhaki, Shlomo. The Optimal Size of a Tax Collection Agency. *Scand. J. Econ.*, 1987, *89*(2), pp. 183–92.

Smeets, G. C. A. The New Ship Registration Tax Act: The Netherlands Antilles. *Bull. Int. Fiscal Doc.*, November 1987, *41*(11), pp. 505–08. **[G: Netherlands]**

Smith, Roger S. Motor Vehicle Tax Harmonization. *Cnossen, S., ed.*, 1987, pp. 141–70. **[G: EEC]**

Smolensky, Eugene; Hoyt, William and Danziger, Sheldon. A Critical Survey of Efforts to Measure Budget Incidence. *van de Kar, H. M. and Wolfe, B. L., eds.*, 1987, pp. 165–79.

Solem, James J. Housing Provisions of the 1986 Tax Reform Act: Can the States Make Them Work? *Nat. Tax J.*, September 1987, *40*(3), pp. 419–29. **[G: U.S.]**

Sommers, Paul M. Tax Reform and the Repeal of Deductibility. *Atlantic Econ. J.*, March 1987, *15*(1), pp. 120. **[G: U.S.]**

Sondhi, H. K. Income Tax Incentives—Harnessing Corporate Skills for Rural Development: India. *Bull. Int. Fiscal Doc.*, June 1987, *41*(6), pp. 283–87.

Spatt, Chester S. Effects of Capital Gains Taxation on Life-Cycle Investment and Portfolio Management: Discussion. *J. Finance*, July 1987, *42*(3), pp. 758–61.

Spicer, Michael W. The Effect of Tax Evasion on Tax Rates under Leviathan. *Nat. Tax J.*, December 1987, *40*(4), pp. 625–28.

Stark, Richard C. An IRS View of Tax Reform Implementation. *Nat. Tax J.*, September 1987, *40*(3), pp. 461–64. **[G: U.S.]**

Stephens, Robert J. Tax Reform in New Zealand. *Australian Tax Forum*, 1987, *4*(3), pp. 327–46. **[G: New Zealand]**

Stern, Nicholas H. The Effects of Taxation, Price Control and Government Contracts in Oligopoly and Monopolistic Competition. *J. Public Econ.*, March 1987, *32*(2), pp. 133–58.

Steuerle, Eugene. Tax Reform and the U.S. Economy: Effects on Financial Decisionmaking. *Pechman, J. A., ed.*, 1987, pp. 55–66. **[G: U.S.]**

Steuerle, Eugene. The New Tax Law. *Cagan, P., ed.*, 1987, pp. 275–303. **[G: U.S.]**

Stiglitz, Joseph E. Tax Asymmetries and Corporate Income Tax Reform: Comment. *Feldstein, M., ed. (I)*, 1987, pp. 374–76.

Stockfisch, J. A. The Value-Added Tax as a "Money Machine." *Walker, C. E. and Bloomfield, M. A., eds.*, 1987, pp. 225–37. **[G: OECD]**

Storm-Nielsen, Truls. The Fiscal Residence of Companies: Norway. *International Fiscal Association, ed. (I),* 1987, pp. 413–21.
[G: Norway]

Strauss, Robert P. and Wittenberg, Uriel. Price and Quantity Effects of Tax Reform: An Application to West Virginia. *Nat. Tax J.,* March 1987, *40*(1), pp. 83–94. **[G: U.S.]**

Summers, Lawrence H. Corporate Capital Budgeting Practices and the Effects of Tax Policies on Investment. *Feldstein, M., ed. (II),* 1987, pp. 27–36. **[G: U.S.]**

Summers, Lawrence H. The Impact of Tax Policy on Savings. *Walker, C. E. and Bloomfield, M. A., eds.,* 1987, pp. 172–77. **[G: U.S.]**

Sunley, Emil M. Notes on the Tax Treatment of Structures: Comment. *Feldstein, M., ed. (I),* 1987, pp. 254–57. **[G: U.S.]**

Sury, M. M. Decline of Direct Taxes: India. *Bull. Int. Fiscal Doc.,* June 1987, *41*(6), pp. 279–82. **[G: India]**

Svensson, Lars-Gunnar and Weibull, Jörgen W. Constrained Pareto-Optimal Taxation of Labour and Capital Incomes. *J. Public Econ.,* December 1987, *34*(3), pp. 355–66.

Swaine, G. D. Impact on the Tax Policies of the United Kingdom. *Bull. Int. Fiscal Doc.,* June 1987, *41*(6), pp. 251–56. **[G: U.K.]**

Swenson, Charles W. An Analysis of ACRS during Inflationary Periods. *Accounting Rev.,* January 1987, *62*(1), pp. 117–36. **[G: U.S.]**

Swenson, Charles W. and Moore, Michael L. Use of Input–Ouput Analysis in Tax Research. *Jones, S. M., ed.,* 1987, pp. 49–83. **[G: U.S.]**

Sykes, David; Smith, W. James and Formby, John P. On the Measurement of Tax Progressivity: An Implication of the Atkinson Theorem. *Southern Econ. J.,* January 1987, *53*(3), pp. 768–77.

Tannenwald, Robert. The Effects of Federal Tax Reform on New England's State Income Tax Revenues. *Nat. Tax J.,* September 1987, *40*(3), pp. 445–59. **[G: U.S.]**

Tannewald, Robert. State Response in New England to Federal Tax Reform. *New Eng. Econ. Rev.,* Sept./Oct. 1987, pp. 25–44. **[G: U.S.]**

Tanzi, Vito. A Review of Major Tax Policy Missions in Developing Countries. *van de Kar, H. M. and Wolfe, B. L., eds.,* 1987, pp. 225–36. **[G: LDCs]**

Tanzi, Vito. The Response of Other Industrial Countries to the U.S. Tax Reform Act. *Nat. Tax J.,* September 1987, *40*(3), pp. 339–55. **[G: U.S.; OECD]**

Thai, Khi V. President Reagan's Tax Reform. *Thai, K. V., ed.,* 1987, pp. 193–220. **[G: U.S.]**

Théret, Bruno and Uri, Didier. Pression fiscale limite, prélèvements obligatoires et production marchande: à propos de récentes estimations économétriques d'une courbe de Laffer pour la France. (Limit of the Tax Rate, Public Levies and Productive Sector. About Some Recent Econometric Estimations of a Laffer Curve for France. With English summary.) *Écon. Appl.,*

1987, *40*(1), pp. 115–59. **[G: France]**

Thirsk, Wayne R. The Value-Added Tax in Canada: Saviour or Siren Song? *Can. Public Policy,* September 1987, *13*(3), pp. 259–83. **[G: Canada]**

Thomas, Peter. The Legal and Tax Considerations of Privatization. *Hanke, S. H., ed.,* 1987, pp. 87–100.

Thon, Dominique. Redistributive Properties of Progressive Taxation: Note. *Math. Soc. Sci.,* October 1987, *14*(2), pp. 185–91.

Tirard, Jean-Marc. Present Status of Taxation Including Recent Tax Reform: Morocco. *Bull. Int. Fiscal Doc.,* December 1987, *41*(12), pp. 542–47, 53. **[G: Morocco]**

Tirard, Jean-Marc. Taxation of Foreign Companies Doing Business in Algeria. *Bull. Int. Fiscal Doc.,* February 1987, *41*(2), pp. 51–55. **[G: Algeria]**

Tobin, James. Against the Balanced Budget and Tax Limitation Amendment. *Tobin, J. (III),* 1987, *1983,* pp. 218–25. **[G: U.S.]**

Tobin, James. Considerations Regarding Taxation and Inequality. *Tobin, J. (III),* 1987, *1977,* pp. 479–87. **[G: U.S.]**

Tobin, James. Supply-Side Economics: What Is It? Will It Work? *Tobin, J. (III),* 1987, *1981,* pp. 126–32. **[G: U.S.]**

Tobin, James. Taxes, Saving and Inflation. *Tobin, J. (I),* 1987, *1949,* pp. 99–108.

Tobin, James. Yes, Virginia, There Are Laffer Curves. *Tobin, J. (III),* 1987, pp. 120–25. **[G: U.S.]**

Tobin, James and Hall, Challis A. Income Taxation, Output and Prices. *Tobin, J. (I),* 1987, *1955,* pp. 47–82.

Tonak, E. Ahmet. The U.S. Welfare State and the Working Class, 1952–1980. *Rev. Radical Polit. Econ.,* Spring 1987, *19*(1), pp. 47–72. **[G: U.S.]**

Townsend, Joy L. Cigarette Tax, Economic Welfare and Social Class Patterns of Smoking. *Appl. Econ.,* March 1987, *19*(3), pp. 355–65. **[G: U.K.]**

Trías Fargas, Ramón and Raga, José. Public Finance and Governance in a New Democracy: Opportunities and Problems. *van de Kar, H. M. and Wolfe, B. L., eds.,* 1987, pp. 251–57. **[G: Spain]**

Tullio, Giuseppe. Long-run Implications of the Increase in Taxation and Public Debt for Employment and Economic Growth in Europe. *Europ. Econ. Rev.,* April 1987, *31*(3), pp. 741–74. **[G: W. Europe]**

Turnbull, Geoffrey K. Land Taxes, Income Taxes, and Land Use. *Nat. Tax J.,* June 1987, *40*(2), pp. 265–69.

Turner, Robert W. Are Taxes Responsible for the Growth in Fringe Benefits? *Nat. Tax J.,* June 1987, *40*(2), pp. 205–20. **[G: U.S.]**

Turner, Robert W. Taxes and the Number of Fringe Benefits Received. *J. Public Econ.,* June 1987, *33*(1), pp. 41–57. **[G: U.S.]**

Ulph, David T. Tax Harmonisation and Labour Mobility. *Cnossen, S., ed.,* 1987, pp. 305–17. **[G: EEC]**

Vaillancourt, François. The Compliance Costs of Taxes on Businesses and Individuals: A Review of the Evidence. *Public Finance*, 1987, 42(3), pp. 395–414.

Van Rompuy, G. The Laffer Curve Proposition in a Unionized Economy. *Tijdschrift Econ. Manage.*, 1987, 32(1), pp. 39–54.   [G: U.S.]

Vanthienen, Lambert and Vermaelen, Theo. The Effect of Personal Taxes on Common Stock Prices: The Case of a Belgian Tax Reform. *J. Banking Finance*, June 1987, 11(2), pp. 223–44.   [G: Belgium]

Vasche, Jon David. Tax Expenditure Reporting—A Comment. *Nat. Tax J.*, June 1987, 40(2), pp. 255–57.   [G: U.S.]

Vasquez, Thomas E. Addressing Issues of the Regressivity of a Consumption Tax. *Walker, C. E. and Bloomfield, M. A., eds.*, 1987, pp. 311–28.   [G: U.S.]

Veall, Michael R. A Note on the Expenditure Tax and Progressivity. *Nat. Tax J.*, June 1987, 40(2), pp. 259–63.

Vella, Edwin A. The Malta/Libya Double Taxation Convention—Treaty Shopping in Unexpected Quarters? *Bull. Int. Fiscal Doc.*, February 1987, 41(2), pp. 75–79.   [G: Malta; Libya]

Wachtel, Michael H. The Fiscal Residence of Companies: Australia. *International Fiscal Association, ed. (I)*, 1987, pp. 201–16.   [G: Australia]

Wakefield, Joseph C. The Tax Reform Act of 1986. *Surv. Curr. Bus.*, March 1987, 67(3), pp. 18–25.   [G: U.S.]

Walker, Charls E. Tax Reform and the U.S. Economy: Effects on Industry: Comments. *Pechman, J. A., ed.*, 1987, pp. 44–46.   [G: U.S.]

Warren, Alvin C., Jr. Taxing Corporate Income in the U.S. Twenty Years after the Carter Commission: Integration or Disintegration? *Australian Tax Forum*, 1987, 4(4), pp. 465–89.   [G: U.S.]

Watanabe, Judith E.; Bean, Virginia L. and Stolen, Justin D. An Empirical Study of Complexity Experienced by Taxpayers. *Jones, S. M., ed.*, 1987, pp. 153–68.   [G: U.S.]

Wattel, Peter J. Tax Problems of the Liquidation of Corporations: Netherlands. *International Fiscal Association, ed. (II)*, 1987, pp. 403–21.   [G: Netherlands]

Webb, Richard. Internal Debt and Financial Adjustment in Peru. *CEPAL Rev.*, August 1987, (32), pp. 55–74.   [G: Peru]

Weinberg, Daniel H. The Distributional Implications of Tax Expenditures and Comprehensive Income Taxation. *Nat. Tax J.*, June 1987, 40(2), pp. 237–53.   [G: U.S.]

Weiss, Randall D. The Impossible Dream Comes True: Comments. *Pechman, J. A., ed.*, 1987, pp. 25–30.   [G: U.S.]

Wellmann, Richard. Steuerliche Probleme der Liquidation von Körperschaften: Deutschland. (Tax Problems of the Liquidation of Corporations: Germany. With English summary.) *International Fiscal Association, ed. (II)*, 1987, pp. 133–51.   [G: W. Germany]

Wells, F. Eugene. A View from Proctor & Gam-

ble. *Nat. Tax J.*, September 1987, 40(3), pp. 469–72.   [G: U.S.]

Wenehed, Lars-Erik. Taxes and Computers. *Bull. Int. Fiscal Doc.*, Aug.-Sept. 1987, 41(8–9), pp. 426–28.   [G: U.S.]

Weymark, John A. Comparative Static Properties of Optimal Nonlinear Income Taxes. *Econometrica*, September 1987, 55(5), pp. 1165–85.

White, Frederic E. Taxation of Foreign Currency Transactions under the Tax Reform Act of 1986: U.S.A. *Bull. Int. Fiscal Doc.*, May 1987, 41(5), pp. 206–14.   [G: U.S.]

Wibaut, Serge R. A Model of Tax Reform for Belgium. *J. Public Econ.*, February 1987, 32(1), pp. 53–77.   [G: Belgium]

Will, George F. Economic Growth: Growing Up. *Walker, C. E. and Bloomfield, M. A., eds.*, 1987, pp. 49–57.   [G: U.S.]

Wilson, Michael H. Canada Considers a Business Transfer Tax. *Walker, C. E. and Bloomfield, M. A., eds.*, 1987, pp. 41–48.   [G: Canada]

Wingert, K. D. Impact on the German Tax System. *Bull. Int. Fiscal Doc.*, June 1987, 41(6), pp. 256–59.   [G: W. Germany]

Wise, David A. Individual Retirement Accounts and Saving. *Feldstein, M., ed. (II)*, 1987, pp. 3–15.   [G: U.S.]

Witt, Peter-Christian. History and Sociology of Public Finance—Problems and Topics. *Witt, P.-C., ed.*, 1987, pp. 1–18.   [G: Germany]

Witt, Peter-Christian. Tax Policies, Tax Assessment and Inflation: Towards a Sociology of Public Finances in the German Inflation, 1914–23. *Witt, P.-C., ed.*, 1987, pp. 137–60.   [G: Germany]

Wixon, Bernard; Bridges, Benjamin, Jr. and Pattison, David. Policy Analysis through Microsimulation: The STATS Model. *Soc. Sec. Bull.*, December 1987, 50(12), pp. 4–12.   [G: U.S.]

Woellner, Robin H. An Analysis of the New Taxation Appeal Process. *Australian Tax Forum*, 1987, 4(2), pp. 241–91.   [G: Australia]

Wright, Randall D. and Loberg, Janine. Unemployment Insurance, Taxes, and Unemployment. *Can. J. Econ.*, February 1987, 20(1), pp. 36–54.

Yinger, John. Tax Reform and the U.S. Economy: Effects on Real Estate: Comments. *Pechman, J. A., ed.*, 1987, pp. 97–102.   [G: U.S.]

Yitzhaki, Shlomo. On the Excess Burden of Tax Evasion. *Public Finance Quart.*, April 1987, 15(2), pp. 123–37.

Ylä-Liedenpohja, Jouko. Korot verolle—miksi ja miten? (Imposing Tax on Interest Rates—Why and How? With English summary.) *Liiketaloudellinen Aikak.*, April 1987, 36(4), pp. 389–403.   [G: Finland]

Yoingco, Angel Q. Experience with Tax Amnesty Legislation: Philippines. *Bull. Int. Fiscal Doc.*, April 1987, 41(4), pp. 172–80.   [G: Philippines]

Young, H. P. Progressive Taxation and the Equal Sacrifice Principle. *J. Public Econ.*, March 1987, 32(2), pp. 203–14.

Yücel, Mine Kuban. A Revised Tax Code—Impact on Oil and Gas Producers and Consumers. *J.*

Policy Modeling, Winter 1987, 9(4), pp. 661–66. [G: U.S.]

Zellner, Arnold and Rossi, Peter E. Evaluating the Methodology of Social Experiments. *Munnell, A. H., ed.*, 1987, pp. 131–57. [G: U.S.]

Zimmerman, Silvia. Die steuerliche Ansässigkeit von Kapitalgesellschaften: Schweiz. (The Fiscal Residence of Companies: Switzerland. With English summary.) *International Fiscal Association, ed. (I)*, 1987, pp. 543–58.
[G: Switzerland]

324 State and Local Government Finance

3240 General

Baum, Donald N. The Economic Effects of State and Local Business Incentives. *Land Econ.*, November 1987, 63(4), pp. 348–60.

Beck, John H. User Charges as a Delegation Mechanism: Comment. *Nat. Tax J.*, June 1987, 40(2), pp. 275–78.

Behrman, Jere R. and Craig, Steven G. The Distribution of Public Services: An Exploration of Local Governmental Preferences. *Amer. Econ. Rev.*, March 1987, 77(1), pp. 37–49.
[G: U.S.]

Blackley, Paul R. and DeBoer, Larry. Measuring Basic Wants for State and Local Public Goods: A Preference Independence Transformation Approach. *Rev. Econ. Statist.*, August 1987, 69(3), pp. 418–25. [G: U.S.]

Blecha, Betty J. The Crowding Parameter and Samuelsonian Publicness [Micro Estimates of Public Spending Demand Functions and Tests of the Tiebout and Median-Voter Hypotheses]. *J. Polit. Econ.*, June 1987, 95(3), pp. 622–31.
[G: U.S.]

Brandt, Harm-Hinrich. Public Finances of Neo-absolutism in Austria in the 1850s: Integration and Modernisation. *Witt, P.-C., ed.*, 1987, pp. 81–109. [G: Austria]

Butt, Henry A. Value for Money: The Experience of Local Government in the United Kingdom. *Public Budg. Finance*, Winter 1987, 7(4), pp. 5–11. [G: U.K.]

Canto, Victor A. and Webb, Robert I. The Effect of State Fiscal Policy on State Relative Economic Performance. *Southern Econ. J.*, July 1987, 54(1), pp. 186–202. [G: U.S.]

Courant, Paul N. and Rubinfeld, Daniel L. Tax Reform: Implications for the State–Local Public Sector. *J. Econ. Perspectives*, Summer 1987, 1(1), pp. 87–100. [G: U.S.]

Craig, Steven G. The Impact of Congestion on Local Public Good Production. *J. Public Econ.*, April 1987, 32(3), pp. 331–53. [G: U.S.]

Craig, Steven G. and Sailors, Joel W. Interstate Trade Barriers and the Constitution. *Cato J.*, Winter 1987, 6(3), pp. 819–35. [G: U.S.]

Datta, Bhabatosh. An Evaluation of the Seventh Award. *Gulati, I. S., ed.*, 1987, 1979, pp. 154–76. [G: India]

Enis, Charles R.; Stuart, William T. and Hourihan, John J. Local Revenue Policy in Less Developed Countries: The Case for Energy Con-

sumption Taxation. *Jones, S. M., ed.*, 1987, pp. 85–107. [G: Philippines]

Feldstein, Martin S. and Metcalf, Gilbert E. The Effect of Federal Tax Deductibility on State and Local Taxes and Spending. *J. Polit. Econ.*, August 1987, 95(4), pp. 710–36. [G: U.S.]

Friedman, Miles and Culbertson, Deborah. State–Local Economic Development Programs. *Lynch, J. E., ed.*, 1987, pp. 175–90.
[G: U.S.]

Gollub, James O. Increasing Employment Opportunities for Older Workers: Emerging State and Local Initiatives. *Sandell, S. H., ed.*, 1987, pp. 143–64. [G: U.S.]

Gonzalez, Rodolfo A. and Mehay, Stephen L. Economies of City Size in a Price Searcher Model of Local Government. *Public Finance*, 1987, 42(2), pp. 236–49. [G: U.S.]

Gramlich, Edward M. Subnational Fiscal Policy. *Quigley, J. M., ed.*, 1987, pp. 3–27.
[G: U.S.]

Hall, James A. Management Policies in Local Government Finance: Computer Applications. *Aronson, J. R. and Schwartz, E., eds.*, 1987, pp. 176–97. [G: U.S.]

Hayes, Kathy J. and Slottje, D. J. Measures of Publicness Based on Demographic Scaling. *Rev. Econ. Statist.*, November 1987, 69(4), pp. 713–18. [G: U.S.]

Helm, Dieter and Smith, Stephen. The Assessment: Decentralisation and the Economics of Local Government. *Oxford Rev. Econ. Policy*, Summer 1987, 3(2), pp. i–xxi. [G: U.K.]

Holder, William W. Management Policies in Local Government Finance: Financial Accounting, Reporting, and Auditing. *Aronson, J. R. and Schwartz, E., eds.*, 1987, pp. 158–75.
[G: U.S.]

Hughes, Gordon A. Fiscal Federalism in the UK. *Oxford Rev. Econ. Policy*, Summer 1987, 3(2), pp. 1–23. [G: U.K.]

Ingham, Michael D. Local Government Demand for Labour in England and Wales. *Scot. J. Polit. Econ.*, August 1987, 34(3), pp. 267–84.
[G: U.K.]

Islam, Muhammed N. and Sahni, Balbir S. Property Taxation and Regional Public Services in Canada: A Causality Analysis. *Ann. Pub. Coop. Econ.*, July–Sept. 1987, 58(3), pp. 275–86.
[G: Canada]

Krüger, Kersten. Public Finance and Modernisation: The Change from Domain State to Tax State in Hesse in the Sixteenth and Seventeenth Centuries—A Case Study. *Witt, P.-C., ed.*, 1987, pp. 49–62. [G: Germany; Europe]

Lankford, R. Hamilton. A Note on Measuring Flypaper Effects [Income and Grant Effects on Local Expenditure: The Flypaper Effect and Other Difficulties]. *J. Urban Econ.*, July 1987, 22(1), pp. 113–15. [G: U.S.]

Lauth, Thomas P. Exploring the Budgetary Base in Georgia. *Public Budg. Finance*, Winter 1987, 7(4), pp. 72–82. [G: U.S.]

Levin, David J. State and Local Government Fiscal Position in 1986. *Surv. Curr. Bus.*, February 1987, 67(2), pp. 25–28. [G: U.S.]

Levin, David J. and Peters, Donald L. Receipts and Expenditures of State Governments and of Local Governments: Revised and Updated Estimates, 1983–86. *Surv. Curr. Bus.*, November 1987, *67*(11), pp. 29–37. [G: U.S.]

Lowery, David. Fiscal Illusion and Revenue Yield in the American States: An Empirical Assessment. *Soc. Sci. Quart.*, December 1987, *68*(4), pp. 857–65. [G: U.S.]

Margolis, Julius. The Fiscal Problems of the Fragmented Metropolis. *Aronson, J. R. and Schwartz, E., eds.*, 1987, pp. 30–50. [G: U.S.]

McGuire, Therese J. The Effect of New Firm Locations on Local Property Taxes. *J. Urban Econ.*, September 1987, *22*(2), pp. 223–29. [G: U.S.]

McKinney, Scott. Crowding and the Club Membership Margin. *J. Urban Econ.*, November 1987, *22*(3), pp. 312–23. [G: U.S.]

Morelle, H. Lévy. La résidence fiscale des sociétés: Belgique. (The Fiscal Residence of Companies: Belgium. With English summary.) *International Fiscal Association, ed. (I)*, 1987, pp. 231–43. [G: Belgium]

Murray, Richard. The Dynamics of Local Government Behavior. *Eliasson, G., ed.*, 1987, pp. 95–100. [G: Sweden]

Raczynski, Dagmar and Serrano, Claudia. Administración y Gestión Local: La Experiencia de Algunos Municipios en Santiago. (Local Administration and Management: The Experience of some Municipalities in Santiago. With English summary.) *Colección Estud. CIEPLAN*, December 1987, (22), pp. 129–51. [G: Chile]

Razzolini, Laura. L'analisi della domanda dei servizi pubblici locali: Una stima dell'efficacia. (With English summary.) *Stud. Econ.*, 1987, *42*(33), pp. 41–65. [G: Italy]

Rubinfeld, Daniel L.; Shapiro, Perry and Roberts, Judith. Tiebout Bias and the Demand for Local Public Schooling. *Rev. Econ. Statist.*, August 1987, *69*(3), pp. 426–37. [G: U.S.]

Ruchelman, Leonard I. The Finance Function in Local Government. *Aronson, J. R. and Schwartz, E., eds.*, 1987, pp. 3–29. [G: U.S.]

Schwab, Robert M. and Zampelli, Ernest M. Disentangling the Demand Function from the Production Function for Local Public Services: The Case of Public Safety. *J. Public Econ.*, July 1987, *33*(2), pp. 245–60. [G: U.S.]

Schwartz, Eli. Management Policies in Local Government Finance: Inventory and Cash Management. *Aronson, J. R. and Schwartz, E., eds.*, 1987, pp. 342–63. [G: U.S.]

Shoulders, Craig D. Criteria for Identifying the Municipal Organizational Reporting Entity. *Chan, J. L., ed., Pt. A*, 1987, pp. 181–206. [G: U.S.]

Singh, Nirvikar and Thomas, Ravi. User Charges as a Delegation Mechanism: Response. *Nat. Tax J.*, June 1987, *40*(2), pp. 279–82.

Steen, Robert C. Effects of Governmental Structure in Urban Areas. *J. Urban Econ.*, March 1987, *21*(2), pp. 166–79. [G: U.S.]

Swallow, Brent M. and Johnson, Thomas G. A Fiscal Impact Model for Virginia Counties. *Rev. Reg. Stud.*, Spring 1987, *17*(2), pp. 67–74. [G: U.S.]

Swartz, Thomas R. A New Urban Crisis in the Making. *Challenge*, Sept./Oct. 1987, *30*(4), pp. 34–41. [G: U.S.]

Sylla, Richard; Legler, John B. and Wallis, John Joseph. Banks and State Public Finance in the New Republic: The United States, 1790–1860. *J. Econ. Hist.*, June 1987, *47*(2), pp. 391–403. [G: U.S.]

Twomey, J. Local Authority Fiscal Stance and the Pattern of Residential Migration in the North West of England. *Appl. Econ.*, October 1987, *19*(10), pp. 1391–1401. [G: U.K.]

Vithal, B. P. R. States' Plan Outlays and Resource Mobilisation: Criterion for Central Assistance. *Gulati, I. S., ed.*, 1987, *1969*, pp. 224–35. [G: India]

Vohra, Rajiv. Local Public Goods as Individual Commodities. *Reg. Sci. Urban Econ.*, May 1987, *17*(2), pp. 191–208.

Wilson, John Douglas. Trade in a Tiebout Economy. *Amer. Econ. Rev.*, June 1987, *77*(3), pp. 431–41.

Wilson, John Douglas. Trade, Capital Mobility, and Tax Competition. *J. Polit. Econ.*, August 1987, *95*(4), pp. 835–56.

Wu, Sen-Yuan and Korman, Hyman. Socioeconomic Impacts of Disinvestment on Communities in New York State. *Amer. J. Econ. Soc.*, July 1987, *46*(3), pp. 261–71. [G: U.S.]

3241 State and Local Government Expenditures and Budgeting

Ahsan, Syed M. and Sahni, Balbir S. La relation entre les dépenses et les recettes publiques dans un économie régionale: le Québec, 1955–82. (Relationship between Public Expenditure and Income in a Regional Economy: Quebec 1955–82. With English summary.) *L'Actual. Econ.*, December 1987, *63*(4), pp. 295–310. [G: Canada]

Arnold, David S. Management Policies in Local Government Finance: Purchasing and Risk Management. *Aronson, J. R. and Schwartz, E., eds.*, 1987, pp. 364–82. [G: U.S.]

Aronson, J. Richard and Schwartz, Eli. Capital Budgeting. *Aronson, J. R. and Schwartz, E., eds.*, 1987, pp. 400–421. [G: U.S.]

Bahl, Roy. Local Government Expenditures and Revenues. *Aronson, J. R. and Schwartz, E., eds.*, 1987, pp. 74–90. [G: U.S.]

Bland, Robert L. The Interest Cost Savings from Municipal Bond Insurance: The Implications for Privatization. *J. Policy Anal. Manage.*, Winter 1987, *6*(2), pp. 207–19. [G: U.S.]

Botner, Stanley B. Utilization and Impact of Microcomputers in State Central Budget Offices. *Public Budg. Finance*, Autumn 1987, *7*(3), pp. 99–111. [G: U.S.]

Brazer, Harvey E. and McCarty, Therese A. Interaction between Demand for Education and for Municipal Services. *Nat. Tax J.*, December

1987, *40*(4), pp. 555–66. [G: U.S.]

Brown, Stephen P. A. New Directions for Economic Growth: Redesigning Fiscal Policies in Louisiana, New Mexico, and Texas. *Fed. Res. Bank Dallas Econ. Rev.*, July 1987, pp. 13–20. [G: U.S.]

Burke, Michael P. and Dowling, Michael. Promoting High-Technology Industry: Initiatives and Policies for State Governments: Introduction. *Schmandt, J. and Wilson, R., eds.*, 1987, pp. 1–10. [G: U.S.]

Cameron, Samuel. Hidden Costs of Unemployment: The Case of Excess Fire Service Expenditures. *Appl. Econ.*, November 1987, *19*(11), pp. 1421–31. [G: U.K.]

Cavin, Edward S.; Murnane, Richard J. and Brown, Randall S. How Enrollment Declines Affect per Pupil Expenditure Levels in Public School Districts. *Quigley, J. M., ed.*, 1987, pp. 159–96. [G: U.S.]

Deno, Kevin T. and Mehay, Stephen L. Municipal Management Structure and Fiscal Performance: Do City Managers Make a Difference? *Southern Econ. J.*, January 1987, *53*(3), pp. 627–42. [G: U.S.]

Dolan, L. W.; Wolpert, J. and Seley, J. E. Dynamic Municipal Allocation Analysis. *Environ. Planning A*, January 1987, *19*(1), pp. 93–105. [G: U.S.]

Duncombe, Sydney and Kinney, Richard. Agency Budget Success: How It Is Defined by Budget Officials in Five Western States. *Public Budg. Finance*, Spring 1987, *7*(1), pp. 24–37. [G: U.S.]

Feenberg, Daniel R. and Rosen, Harvey S. Tax Structure and Public Sector Growth. *J. Public Econ.*, March 1987, *32*(2), pp. 185–201. [G: U.S.]

Felder, Stefan and Finsinger, Jörg. Auswirkungen protektionistischer und preisstützender Submissionsvorschriften auf die Baubranche. (The Consequences of Non-competitive and Protectionist Government Purchasing Behavior. With English summary.) *Schweiz. Z. Volkswirtsch. Statist.*, June 1987, *123*(2), pp. 147–73. [G: Switzerland]

Gold, Steven D. Developments in State Finances, 1983 to 1986. *Public Budg. Finance*, Spring 1987, *7*(1), pp. 5–23. [G: U.S.]

Gosling, James J. The State Budget Office and Policy Making. *Public Budg. Finance*, Spring 1987, *7*(1), pp. 51–65. [G: U.S.]

Gyimah-Brempong, Kwabena. Economies of Scale in Municipal Police Departments: The Case of Florida. *Rev. Econ. Statist.*, May 1987, *69*(2), pp. 352–56. [G: U.S.]

Gyimah-Brempong, Kwabena. Elasticity of Factor Substitution in Police Agencies: Evidence from Florida. *J. Bus. Econ. Statist.*, April 1987, *5*(2), pp. 257–65. [G: U.S.]

Ingham, Michael D. Local Government Pay Drift: The Search for Causality. *Appl. Econ.*, January 1987, *19*(1), pp. 83–100. [G: U.K.]

Krane, Dale A. Does the Federal–Unitary Dichotomy Make Any Difference? One Answer

Derived from Macrocomparative Analysis. *Picard, L. A. and Zariski, R., eds.*, 1987, pp. 35–54. [G: U.S.]

Marlow, Michael L. and Manage, Neela. Expenditures and Receipts: Testing for Causality in State and Local Government Finances. *Public Choice*, 1987, *53*(3), pp. 243–55. [G: U.S.]

Muller, Brian and Dowling, Michael. Promoting High-Technology Industry: Initiatives and Policies for State Governments: Texas. *Schmandt, J. and Wilson, R., eds.*, 1987, pp. 231–57. [G: U.S.]

Murthy, N. R. Vasudeva. Bureaucracy and the Divisibility of Local Public Output: Further Econometric Evidence. *Public Choice*, October 1987, *55*(3), pp. 265–72. [G: U.S.]

Petersen, John E. Public Pension Fund Administration. *Aronson, J. R. and Schwartz, E., eds.*, 1987, pp. 318–41. [G: U.S.]

Quan, Nguyen T. and Beck, John H. Public Education Expenditures and State Economic Growth: Northeast and Sunbelt Regions. *Southern Econ. J.*, October 1987, *54*(2), pp. 361–76. [G: U.S.]

Rosen, Josef. Two Municipal Accounts: Frankfurt and Basel in 1428. *J. Europ. Econ. Hist.*, Fall 1987, *16*(2), pp. 363–88. [G: Europe]

Rubin, Irene S. Estimated and Actual Urban Revenues: Exploring the Gap. *Public Budg. Finance*, Winter 1987, *7*(4), pp. 83–94. [G: U.S.]

Sallack, David and Allen, David N. From Impact to Output: Pennsylvania's Planning-Programming Budgeting System in Transition. *Public Budg. Finance*, Spring 1987, *7*(1), pp. 38–50. [G: U.S.]

Schneider, Mark and Ji, Byung Moon. The Flypaper Effect and Competition in the Local Market for Public Goods. *Public Choice*, 1987, *54*(1), pp. 27–39.

Schokkaert, Erik. Preferences and Demand for Local Public Spending. *J. Public Econ.*, November 1987, *34*(2), pp. 175–88. [G: Belgium]

Schroeder, Larry D. Forecasting Local Revenues and Expenditures. *Aronson, J. R. and Schwartz, E., eds.*, 1987, pp. 93–117. [G: U.S.]

Smith, Peter N. Optimal Local Authority Budgeting Strategies under Block Grant. *Appl. Econ.*, July 1987, *19*(7), pp. 891–905. [G: U.K.]

Solano, Paul L. and Brams, Marvin R. Management Policies in Local Government Finance: Budgeting. *Aronson, J. R. and Schwartz, E., eds.*, 1987, pp. 118–57. [G: U.S.]

Stutzer, Michael J. Improving Intergovernmental Finance: A Message from the Northland. *Fed. Res. Bank Minn. Rev.*, Spring 1987, *11*(2), pp. 2–13. [G: U.S.]

Turnbull, Geoffrey K. Alternative Local Public Education Expenditure Functions: An Econometric Evaluation. *Public Finance Quart.*, January 1987, *15*(1), pp. 45–60. [G: U.S.]

Vasche, Jon David. Tax Expenditure Reporting— A Comment. *Nat. Tax J.*, June 1987, *40*(2), pp. 255–57. [G: U.S.]

Vasche, Jon David and Williams, Brad. Optimal Governmental Budgeting Contingency Reserve Funds. *Public Budg. Finance,* Spring 1987, *7*(1), pp. 66–82. **[G: U.S.]**

Wolkoff, Michael. An Evaluation of Municipal Rainy Day Funds. *Public Budg. Finance,* Summer 1987, *7*(2), pp. 52–63. **[G: U.S.]**

Zhao, Yujiang. Management of Extrabudgetary Funds. *Reynolds, B. L.,* 1987, pp. 130–41. **[G: China]**

3242 State and Local Government Taxation, Subsidies, and Revenue

Alm, James and Zubrow, Reuben A. Who Benefits from Indexation? *Public Finance Quart.,* January 1987, *15*(1), pp. 27–44. **[G: U.S.]**

Anderson, Gary Michael; Martin, Dolores T. and Tollison, Robert D. Do Loopholes Decrease or Increase Tax Revenue? *Econ. Scelte Pubbliche/J. Public Finance Public Choice,* May-Aug. 1987, *5*(2), pp. 83–95. **[G: U.S.]**

Bahl, Roy. Local Government Expenditures and Revenues. *Aronson, J. R. and Schwartz, E., eds.,* 1987, pp. 74–90. **[G: U.S.]**

Bahl, Roy. Urban Government Finance and Federal Income Tax Reform. *Nat. Tax J.,* March 1987, *40*(1), pp. 1–18. **[G: U.S.]**

Bahl, Roy; Weist, Dana and Schulman, Wanda. The Fiscal Implications of Industrial Restructuring: The Case of Northeastern Ohio. *McKee, D. L. and Bennett, R. E., eds.,* 1987, pp. 155–202. **[G: U.S.]**

Beck, Paul Allen, et al. Citizen Views of Taxes and Services: A Tale of Three Cities. *Soc. Sci. Quart.,* June 1987, *68*(2), pp. 223–43. **[G: U.S.]**

Bell, Michael E. and Bowman, John H. The Effect of Various Intergovernmental Aid Types on Local Own-Source Revenues: The Case of Property Taxes in Minnesota Cities. *Public Finance Quart.,* July 1987, *15*(3), pp. 282–97. **[G: U.S.]**

Benjamin, John D. and Sirmans, C. F. Who Benefits from Mortgage Revenue Bonds? *Nat. Tax J.,* March 1987, *40*(1), pp. 115–20. **[G: U.S.]**

Bennett, Robert J. A General Accounting Model of Intergovernmental Tax and Benefit Effects on Business. *Environ. Planning A,* November 1987, *19*(11), pp. 1495–1510. **[G: U.K.; W. Germany]**

Bennett, Robert J. Local Business Taxes: Theory and Practice. *Oxford Rev. Econ. Policy,* Summer 1987, *3*(2), pp. 60–80. **[G: U.K.; W. Germany]**

Blackley, Paul R. and DeBoer, Larry. Tax Base Choice by Local Governments. *Land Econ.,* August 1987, *63*(3), pp. 227–36. **[G: U.S.]**

Blair, Andrew R.; Giarratani, Frank and Spiro, Michael H. Incidence of the Amusement Tax. *Nat. Tax J.,* March 1987, *40*(1), pp. 61–69. **[G: U.S.]**

Borland, Melvin V. An Alternative Measure of the Degree of Inequity in Assessed Values for Individual Properties: A Theoretic Perspective. *Public Finance Quart.,* July 1987, *15*(3), pp. 352–65.

Bourassa, Steven C. Land Value Taxation and New Housing Development in Pittsburgh. *Growth Change,* Fall 1987, *18*(4), pp. 44–56. **[G: U.S.]**

Bradbury, Katharine L. and Ladd, Helen F. City Property Taxes: The Effects of Economic Change and Competitive Pressures. *New Eng. Econ. Rev.,* July/Aug. 1987, pp. 22–36. **[G: U.S.]**

Braid, Ralph M. The Spatial Incidence of Local Retail Taxation. *Quart. J. Econ.,* November 1987, *102*(4), pp. 881–91. **[G: U.S.]**

Brown, Stephen P. A. New Directions for Economic Growth: Redesigning Fiscal Policies in Louisiana, New Mexico, and Texas. *Fed. Res. Bank Dallas Econ. Rev.,* July 1987, pp. 13–20. **[G: U.S.]**

Buckley, Robert M. and Simonson, John. Effective Property Tax Rates and Capital Formation Issues: Manvel, Acton and Darby. *Amer. Real Estate Urban Econ. Assoc. J.,* Spring 1987, *15*(1), pp. 725–38. **[G: U.S.]**

Cebula, Richard J. Was Proposition 4 Really a Tax Reduction Mirage? A Correction and Reinterpretation of Previous Findings. *Amer. J. Econ. Soc.,* January 1987, *46*(1), pp. 107–08. **[G: U.S.]**

Chernick, Howard A. and Reschovsky, Andrew. The Deductibility of State and Local Taxes: Comment. *Nat. Tax J.,* March 1987, *40*(1), pp. 95–102. **[G: U.S.]**

Clotfelter, Charles T. and Cook, Philip J. Implicit Taxation in Lottery Finance. *Nat. Tax J.,* December 1987, *40*(4), pp. 533–46. **[G: U.S.]**

Cohn, Elchanan. Federal and State Grants to Education: Are They Stimulative or Substitutive? *Econ. Educ. Rev.,* 1987, *6*(4), pp. 339–44. **[G: U.S.]**

Cohn, Elchanan. Revenue and Formula Effects of School Finance Reform on Wealth Neutrality. *Appl. Econ.,* December 1987, *19*(12), pp. 1685–95. **[G: U.S.]**

Connors, Donald L. and High, Michael E. The Expanding Circle of Exactions: From Dedication to Linkage. *Law Contemp. Probl.,* Winter 1987, *50*(1), pp. 69–83. **[G: U.S.]**

Curwen, Peter. Comment [Local Taxation and Housing Finance: A Proposal for Reform]. *Lloyds Bank Rev.,* January 1987, (163), pp. 47. **[G: U.K.]**

DiMasi, Joseph A. The Effects of Site Value Taxation in an Urban Area: A General Equilibrium Computational Approach. *Nat. Tax J.,* December 1987, *40*(4), pp. 577–90. **[G: U.S.]**

Downing, Paul B. and DiLorenzo, Thomas J. User Charges and Special Districts. *Aronson, J. R. and Schwartz, E., eds.,* 1987, pp. 260–84. **[G: U.S.]**

Durning, Dan. The Efficiency and Distribution of Mortgage Revenue Bond Subsidies: The Effects of Behavioral Responses. *J. Policy Anal. Manage.,* Fall 1987, *7*(1), pp. 74–93. **[G: U.S.]**

Erickson, Rodney A. and Wollover, David R. Local Tax Burdens and the Supply of Business Sites in Suburban Municipalities. *J. Reg. Sci.,*

February 1987, 27(1), pp. 25–37.   [G: U.S.]

Fahning, Hans. Finanzierungsformen der regionalen und örtlichen öffentlichen Unternehmen in der B.R.D. (Forms of Financing of the Regional and Local Public Enterprises in Germany. With English summary.) *Ann. Pub. Coop. Econ.*, Apr.-June 1987, 58(2), pp. 185–94.
[G: W. Germany]

Feenberg, Daniel R. and Rosen, Harvey S. Tax Structure and Public Sector Growth. *J. Public Econ.*, March 1987, 32(2), pp. 185–201.
[G: U.S.]

Fender, John. Reply [Local Taxation and Housing Finance: A Proposal for Reform]. *Lloyds Bank Rev.*, January 1987, (163), pp. 47–48.
[G: U.K.]

Fischel, William A. The Economics of Land Use Exactions: A Property Rights Analysis. *Law Contemp. Probl.*, Winter 1987, 50(1), pp. 101–13.   [G: U.S.]

Frankel, Marvin. Taxes, Pollution, and Optimal Abatement in an Urban Economy. *J. Urban Econ.*, September 1987, 22(2), pp. 117–35.

Fullerton, Thomas M., Jr. Rational Reactions to Temporary Sales Tax Legislation: An Idaho Case Study. *Public Budg. Finance*, Summer 1987, 7(2), pp. 64–71.   [G: U.S.]

Funkhouser, Richard and Lorenz, Edward. Fiscal and Employment Impacts of Enterprise Zones. *Atlantic Econ. J.*, July 1987, 15(2), pp. 62–76.   [G: U.S.]

Gaur, Achal Kumar. Financial Autonomy of States: Emerging Trends. *Margin*, July-Sept. 1987, 19(4), pp. 62–77.   [G: India]

Gerber, Robert I. and Hewitt, Daniel P. Decentralized Tax Competition for Business Capital and National Economic Efficiency. *J. Reg. Sci.*, August 1987, 27(3), pp. 451–60.

Gerber, Robert I. and Hewitt, Daniel P. Tax Competition and Redistribution Policy of Local Governments Competing for Business Capital. *J. Urban Econ.*, January 1987, 21(1), pp. 69–82.

Gillingham, Robert and Greenlees, John S. The Impact of Direct Taxes on the Cost of Living. *J. Polit. Econ.*, August 1987, 95(4), pp. 775–96.   [G: U.S.]

Gold, Steven D. Developments in State Finances, 1983 to 1986. *Public Budg. Finance*, Spring 1987, 7(1), pp. 5–23.   [G: U.S.]

Gold, Steven D. The State Government Response to Federal Income Tax Reform: Indications from the States That Completed Their Work Early. *Nat. Tax J.*, September 1987, 40(3), pp. 431–44.   [G: U.S.]

Gyourko, Joseph. Effects of Local Tax Structures on the Factor Intensity Composition of Manufacturing Activity across Cities. *J. Urban Econ.*, September 1987, 22(2), pp. 151–64.
[G: U.S.]

Hands, D. Wade and Mann, Bruce D. Urban Industrial Tax Subsidies: A Non-cooperative Equilibrium Approach. *Reg. Sci. Urban Econ.*, May 1987, 17(2), pp. 179–90.

Harriss, C. L. Use of Income from Urban Land: Thoughts from U.S. Experience. *Econ. Scelte*

Pubbliche/J. Public Finance Public Choice, Sept.-Dec. 1987, 5(3), pp. 213–17.   [G: U.S.]

Hofflander, Alfred E. and Nye, Blaine F. An Analysis of Premium Tax Revenue and Rate in California: The Case of Structured Settlement Annuities. *J. Risk Ins.*, December 1987, 54(4), pp. 760–66.   [G: U.S.]

Hunter, William J. and Scott, Charles E. Statutory Changes in State Income Taxes: An Indirect Test of Fiscal Illusion. *Public Choice*, 1987, 53(1), pp. 41–51.   [G: U.S.]

Kaiser, Ronald A. and Fletcher, James E. State Policies and Practices in Coal Severance Taxation. *Natural Res. J.*, Summer 1987, 27(3), pp. 591–604.   [G: U.S.]

Kemp, Roger L. Raising Revenues without Increasing Taxes through Cooperation between Local Bodies and Private Sector: A Note. *Pakistan Econ. Soc. Rev.*, Winter 1987, 25(2), pp. 109–14.

Késenne, Stefan and Butzen, Paul. Subsidizing Sports Facilities: The Shadow Price-Elasticities of Sports. *Appl. Econ.*, January 1987, 19(1), pp. 101–10.   [G: Belgium]

Kirwan, Richard M. Fiscal Policy and the Price of Land and Housing in Japan. *Urban Stud.*, October 1987, 24(5), pp. 345–60.   [G: Japan]

Leonard, Herman B. and Zeckhauser, Richard J. Amnesty, Enforcement, and Tax Policy. *Summers, L. H., ed.*, 1987, pp. 55–85.
[G: U.S.]

Livernois, John R. The Redistributive Effects of Lotteries: Evidence from Canada. *Public Finance Quart.*, July 1987, 15(3), pp. 339–51.
[G: Canada]

Livesey, David A. Central Control of Local Authority Expenditure. *Oxford Rev. Econ. Policy*, Summer 1987, 3(2), pp. 44–59.
[G: U.K.]

MacKinnon, Mary. English Poor Law Policy and the Crusade against Outrelief. *J. Econ. Hist.*, September 1987, 47(3), pp. 603–25.

Marlow, Michael L. and Manage, Neela. Expenditures and Receipts: Testing for Causality in State and Local Government Finances. *Public Choice*, 1987, 53(3), pp. 243–55.   [G: U.S.]

Martinez-Vazquez, Jorge and Ihlanfeldt, Keith R. Why Property Tax Capitalization Rates Differ: A Critical Analysis. *Quigley, J. M., ed.*, 1987, pp. 127–56.   [G: U.S.]

McGuire, Therese J. The Effect of New Firm Locations on Local Property Taxes. *J. Urban Econ.*, September 1987, 22(2), pp. 223–29.
[G: U.S.]

McHone, W. Warren. Factors in the Adoption of Industrial Development Incentives by States. *Appl. Econ.*, January 1987, 19(1), pp. 17–29.   [G: U.S.]

Mikesell, John L. The Effect of Maturity and Competition on State Lottery Markets. *J. Policy Anal. Manage.*, Winter 1987, 6(2), pp. 251–53.   [G: U.S.]

Mikesell, John L. and Zorn, C. Kurt. State Lottery Sales: Separating the Influence of Markets and Game Structure. *Growth Change*, Fall 1987, 18(4), pp. 10–19.   [G: U.S.]

Misiolek, Walter S. and Perdue, D. Grady. The Portfolio Approach to State and Local Tax Structures. *Nat. Tax J.*, March 1987, *40*(1), pp. 111–14.   [G: U.S.]

Moore, Michael L.; Steece, Bert M. and Swenson, Charles W. An Analysis of the Impact of State Income Tax Rates and Bases on Foreign Investment. *Accounting Rev.*, October 1987, *62*(4), pp. 671–85.   [G: U.S.]

Nelson, Michael A. Searching for Leviathan: Comment and Extension. *Amer. Econ. Rev.*, March 1987, *77*(1), pp. 198–204.

Nicholas, James C. Impact Exactions: Economic Theory, Practice, and Incidence. *Law Contemp. Probl.*, Winter 1987, *50*(1), pp. 85–100.   [G: U.S.]

Papke, Leslie E. Subnational Taxation and Capital Mobility: Estimates of Tax–Price Elasticities. *Nat. Tax J.*, June 1987, *40*(2), pp. 191–203.   [G: U.S.]

Peppard, Donald M., Jr. Government as Bookie: Explaining the Rise of Lotteries for Revenue. *Rev. Radical Polit. Econ.*, Fall 1987, *19*(3), pp. 56–68.

Pillai, Vel. Property Tax Assessment Reform: A Source of Local Revenue Windfall or Fiscal Retrenchment? *Amer. J. Econ. Soc.*, July 1987, *46*(3), pp. 341–53.   [G: U.S.]

Pillai, Vel. Property Taxation in Thailand: An Uncommon Combination of a Land Tax and a Rental Tax. *Singapore Econ. Rev.*, October 1987, *32*(2), pp. 43–55.   [G: Thailand]

Raphaelson, Arnold H. The Property Tax. *Aronson, J. R. and Schwartz, E., eds.*, 1987, pp. 201–28.   [G: U.S.]

Rock, Steven M. Repealing Deductibility and the Aggregate Incidence of State and Local Income Taxes. *Amer. Econ.*, Fall 1987, *31*(2), pp. 35–40.   [G: U.S.]

Rodgers, James D. Sales Taxes, Income Taxes, and Other Nonproperty Tax Revenues. *Aronson, J. R. and Schwartz, E., eds.*, 1987, pp. 229–59.   [G: U.S.]

Rosen, Josef. Two Municipal Accounts: Frankfurt and Basel in 1428. *J. Europ. Econ. Hist.*, Fall 1987, *16*(2), pp. 363–88.   [G: Europe]

Rowntree, John T. and Rolph, Earl R. Efficient Community Management: A Profit-Maximizing Approach. *Quigley, J. M., ed.*, 1987, pp. 87–109.   [G: U.S.]

de Rus Mendoza, Ginés. Discriminación de precios y subvenciones cruzadas en transporte público. (With English summary.) *Invest. Econ.*, May 1987, *11*(2), pp. 201–18.
                    [G: Spain]

Sarti, Armando. Le financement des entreprises publiques locales en Italie. (The Financing of Local Public Enterprises in Italy. With English summary.) *Ann. Pub. Co-op. Econ.*, Apr.-June 1987, *58*(2), pp. 195–212.   [G: Italy]

Schroeder, Larry D. Forecasting Local Revenues and Expenditures. *Aronson, J. R. and Schwartz, E., eds.*, 1987, pp. 93–117.
                    [G: U.S.]

Sexton, Terri A. Forecasting Property Taxes: A Comparison and Evaluation of Methods. *Nat.*

Tax J., March 1987, *40*(1), pp. 47–59.
                    [G: U.S.]

Sherwood-Call, Carolyn. Tax Revolt or Tax Reform? The Effects of Local Government Limitation Measures in California. *Fed. Res. Bank San Francisco Econ. Rev.*, Spring 1987, (2), pp. 57–67.   [G: U.S.]

Simmons, Susan A. and Sharp, Robert. State Lotteries' Effects on Thoroughbred Horse Racing. *J. Policy Anal. Manage.*, Spring 1987, *6*(3), pp. 446–48.   [G: U.S.]

Sirmans, G. Stacy; Sirmans, C. F. and Smith, Stanley D. Creative Financing, House Prices, and Property Tax Inequities. *Urban Stud.*, October 1987, *24*(5), pp. 409–15.   [G: U.S.]

Solem, James J. Housing Provisions of the 1986 Tax Reform Act: Can the States Make Them Work? *Nat. Tax J.*, September 1987, *40*(3), pp. 419–29.   [G: U.S.]

Steen, Robert C. Effects of the Property Tax in Urban Areas. *J. Urban Econ.*, March 1987, *21*(2), pp. 146–65.

Stover, Mark Edward. Revenue Potential of State Lotteries. *Public Finance Quart.*, October 1987, *15*(4), pp. 428–40.   [G: U.S.]

Sullivan, Arthur M. Efficient Taxation in an Isolated City: Variable-Rate Taxes on Property and Income. *Quigley, J. M., ed.*, 1987, pp. 111–25.   [G: U.S.]

Sullivan, Arthur M. The Spatial Effects of a General Capital Tax: Property Taxes and Urban Labor Markets. *Reg. Sci. Urban Econ.*, May 1987, *17*(2), pp. 209–22.

Swenson, Charles W. and Moore, Michael L. Use of Input–Ouput Analysis in Tax Research. *Jones, S. M., ed.*, 1987, pp. 49–83. [G: U.S.]

Tannenwald, Robert. Rating Massachusetts' Tax Competitiveness. *New Eng. Econ. Rev.*, Nov./Dec. 1987, pp. 33–45.   [G: U.S.]

Tannenwald, Robert. The Effects of Federal Tax Reform on New England's State Income Tax Revenues. *Nat. Tax J.*, September 1987, *40*(3), pp. 445–59.   [G: U.S.]

Tannewald, Robert. State Response in New England to Federal Tax Reform. *New Eng. Econ. Rev.*, Sept./Oct. 1987, pp. 25–44.   [G: U.S.]

Tanzer, Ellen P. Effects of the Property Tax on Operating and Investment Decisions of Rental Property Owners: An Empirical Test. *Reg. Sci. Urban Econ.*, November 1987, *17*(4), pp. 535–47.   [G: U.S.]

Tanzer, Ellen P. Housing Quality and the Structure Tax: Evidence from Microdata. *Amer. Real Estate Urban Econ. Assoc. J.*, Summer 1987, *15*(2), pp. 32–45.   [G: U.S.]

Turnbull, Geoffrey K. Land Taxes, Income Taxes, and Land Use. *Nat. Tax J.*, June 1987, *40*(2), pp. 265–69.

Wildasin, David E. The Demand for Public Goods in the Presence of Tax Exporting. *Nat. Tax J.*, December 1987, *40*(4), pp. 591–601.

Willison, David. Agency Audits and Congressional Oversight: The Impact of State Tax Burdens on GAO Audit Requests. *Public Choice*, August 1987, *54*(3), pp. 277–81.   [G: U.S.]

Wren, Colin. The Relative Effects of Local Au-

thority Financial Assistance Policies. *Urban Stud.*, August 1987, *24*(4), pp. 268–78.
[G: U.K.]

3243 State and Local Government Borrowing

Arnott, Robert D. Structural Inefficiencies in Municipal Bond Futures. *Fabozzi, F. J., ed.*, 1987, pp. 313–19. [G: U.S.]

Beck, John H. Municipal Government Use of Short-term Debt: The Case of Cleveland. *Quigley, J. M., ed.*, 1987, pp. 65–83.
[G: U.S.]

Buchanan, James M. Concerning Future Generations. *Buchanan, J. M. (I)*, 1987, *1958*, pp. 113–19.

Ingram, Robert W.; Raman, Krishnamurthy K. and Wilson, Earl R. Governmental Capital Markets Research in Accounting: A Review. *Chan, J. L., ed., Pt. B*, 1987, pp. 111–126.

Karvelis, Leon J., Jr. The Use and Usefulness of Governmental Financial Reports: The Perspective of Municipal Investors. *Chan, J. L., ed., Pt. B*, 1987, pp. 175–88. [G: U.S.]

Kaufman, George G. and Fischer, Philip J. Management Policies in Local Government Finance: Debt Management. *Aronson, J. R. and Schwartz, E., eds.*, 1987, pp. 287–317.
[G: U.S.]

Kidwell, David S.; Sorensen, Eric H. and Wachowicz, John M., Jr. Estimating the Signaling Benefits of Debt Insurance: The Case of Municipal Bonds. *J. Finan. Quant. Anal.*, September 1987, *22*(3), pp. 299–313. [G: U.S.]

Livesey, David A. Central Control of Local Authority Expenditure. *Oxford Rev. Econ. Policy*, Summer 1987, *3*(2), pp. 44–59.
[G: U.K.]

Nauss, Robert M. Generating Optimal True Interest Cost Bids for New Municipal Bond Competitive Issues. *J. Banking Finance*, June 1987, *11*(2), pp. 329–43. [G: U.S.]

Peavy, John W., III and Hempel, George H. The Effect of the WPPSS Crisis on the Tax-Exempt Bond Market. *J. Finan. Res.*, Fall 1987, *10*(3), pp. 239–47.

Petersen, John E. Examining the Impacts of the 1986 Tax Reform Act on the Municipal Securities Market. *Nat. Tax J.*, September 1987, *40*(3), pp. 393–402. [G: U.S.]

Ullmann, Hans-Peter. The Emergence of Modern Public Debts in Bavaria and Baden between 1780 and 1820. *Witt, P.-C., ed.*, 1987, pp. 63–79. [G: Germany]

325 Intergovernmental Financial Relationships

3250 Intergovernmental Financial Relationships

Ansari, M. M. Financing of the States' Plans: A Perspective for Regional Development. *Gulati, I. S., ed.*, 1987, *1983*, pp. 211–23. [G: India]

Auld, D. A. L. and Eden, Lorraine. A Comparative Evaluation of Provincial–Local Equalization. *Can. Public Policy*, December 1987, *13*(4), pp. 515–28. [G: Canada]

Bahl, Roy. Industrial Policy and the States. *Goldstein, H. A., ed.*, 1987, pp. 176–88.
[G: U.S.]

Bell, Michael E. and Bowman, John H. The Effect of Various Intergovernmental Aid Types on Local Own-Source Revenues: The Case of Property Taxes in Minnesota Cities. *Public Finance Quart.*, July 1987, *15*(3), pp. 282–97.
[G: U.S.]

Bird, Richard M. Federalism and Regional Disparities: A Review Essay. *Can. Public Policy*, September 1987, *13*(3), pp. 380–83.
[G: Canada]

Brown, Charles C. and Oates, Wallace E. Assistance to the Poor in a Federal System. *J. Public Econ.*, April 1987, *32*(3), pp. 307–30.
[G: U.S.; U.K.]

Brunel, Andre and Burke, Michael P. Promoting High-Technology Industry: Initiatives and Policies for State Governments: Pennsylvania. *Schmandt, J. and Wilson, R., eds.*, 1987, pp. 191–229. [G: U.S.]

Buchanan, James M. and Brennan, Geoffrey. The Normative Purpose of Economic "Science": Rediscovery of an Eighteenth Century Method. *Buchanan, J. M. (II)*, 1987, *1981*, pp. 51–65.

Burke, Michael P. and Dowling, Michael. Promoting High-Technology Industry: Initiatives and Policies for State Governments: Introduction. *Schmandt, J. and Wilson, R., eds.*, 1987, pp. 1–10. [G: U.S.]

Caputo, David A. Political, Social, and Economic Aspects of the "Old" and the "New" New Federalism. *Picard, L. A. and Zariski, R., eds.*, 1987, pp. 21–34. [G: U.S.]

Cohn, Elchanan. Federal and State Grants to Education: Are They Stimulative or Substitutive? *Econ. Educ. Rev.*, 1987, *6*(4), pp. 339–44.
[G: U.S.]

Cohn, Elchanan. Revenue and Formula Effects of School Finance Reform on Wealth Neutrality. *Appl. Econ.*, December 1987, *19*(12), pp. 1685–95. [G: U.S.]

Dafflon, Bernard and Solari, Paolo. Les parts des cantons aux recettes fédérales: évolution et incidences en 1983. (The System of Revenue-Sharing between the Federal Government and the Cantons of Switzerland: Evolution and Incidence in 1983. With English summary.) *Schweiz. Z. Volkswirtsch. Statist.*, March 1987, *123*(1), pp. 71–86. [G: Switzerland]

Dandekar, Vinayak M. Inter-state Allocation of Central Excise: Below the Poverty Line. *Gulati, I. S., ed.*, 1987, *1979*, pp. 177–84.
[G: India]

Datta, Bhabatosh. An Evaluation of the Seventh Award. *Gulati, I. S., ed.*, 1987, *1979*, pp. 154–76. [G: India]

Derbyshire, M. E. Statistical Rationale for Grant-Related Expenditure Assessment (GREA) Concerning Personal Social Services. *J. Roy. Statist. Soc.*, 1987, *150*(4), pp. 309–25.
[G: U.K.]

Dye, Thomas R. Targeting Intergovernmental

Aid. *Soc. Sci. Quart.*, September 1987, *68*(3), pp. 443–46. [G: U.S.]

Elazar, Daniel J. Federalism, Intergovernmental Relations, and Changing Models of the Polity. *Picard, L. A. and Zariski, R., eds.*, 1987, pp. 5–20. [G: U.S.]

Fischer, Harald and Peck, Amy Miriam. Promoting High-Technology Industry: Initiatives and Policies for State Governments: New York. *Schmandt, J. and Wilson, R., eds.*, 1987, pp. 129–62. [G: U.S.]

Freudenberg, Michael and Henderson, Tracy L. Promoting High-Technology Industry: Initiatives and Policies for State Governments: Florida. *Schmandt, J. and Wilson, R., eds.*, 1987, pp. 35–64. [G: U.S.]

Gaur, Achal Kumar. Financial Autonomy of States: Emerging Trends. *Margin*, July-Sept. 1987, *19*(4), pp. 62–77. [G: India]

George, K. K. Discretionary Budgetary Transfers: A Review. *Gulati, I. S., ed.*, 1987, *1986*, pp. 247–64. [G: India]

Graham, Lawrence S. The Role of the States in the Brazilian Federation. *Picard, L. A. and Zariski, R., eds.*, 1987, pp. 119–39. [G: Brazil]

Gramlich, Edward M. Federalism and Federal Deficit Reduction. *Nat. Tax J.*, September 1987, *40*(3), pp. 299–313. [G: U.S.]

Guhan, S. Devolution Criteria of Financing and Planning Commissions: From Gamble to Policy. *Gulati, I. S., ed.*, 1987, *1984*, pp. 283–312. [G: India]

Gulati, I. S. Approach of the Finance Commissions. *Gulati, I. S., ed.*, 1987, *1973*, pp. 63–85. [G: India]

Gulati, I. S. Centre–State Budgetary Transfers: Introduction. *Gulati, I. S., ed.*, 1987, pp. 1–19. [G: India]

Gulati, I. S. Possible Routes of Change. *Gulati, I. S., ed.*, 1987, *1973*, pp. 121–53. [G: India]

Gulati, I. S. and George, K. K. Inter-state Redistribution through the Budget. *Gulati, I. S., ed.*, 1987, *1978*, pp. 267–82. [G: India]

Gunlicks, Arthur B. The German Federal System Today: National, State, and Local Relations in an Era of Cooperative Federalism. *Picard, L. A. and Zariski, R., eds.*, 1987, pp. 89–102. [G: W. Germany]

Hacker, Sidney Bailey and Sommerfeld, Robert D. Promoting High-Technology Industry: Initiatives and Policies for State Governments: Minnesota. *Schmandt, J. and Wilson, R., eds.*, 1987, pp. 97–127. [G: U.S.]

Hammes, David L. and Wills, Douglas T. Fiscal Illusion and the Grantor Government in Canada. *Econ. Inquiry*, October 1987, *25*(4), pp. 707–13. [G: Canada]

Harbeson, John W. Grass-roots Development and Development Administration in East Africa. *Picard, L. A. and Zariski, R., eds.*, 1987, pp. 196–207. [G: E. Africa]

Haughwout, Andrew F. and Richardson, Charles J. Federal Grants to State and Local Governments in the 1980s. *Public Budg. Finance*, Winter 1987, *7*(4), pp. 12–23. [G: U.S.]

Helm, Dieter and Smith, Stephen. The Assessment: Decentralisation and the Economics of Local Government. *Oxford Rev. Econ. Policy*, Summer 1987, *3*(2), pp. i–xxi. [G: U.K.]

Howard, Mark and Kragie, Mary. Promoting High-Technology Industry: Initiatives and Policies for State Governments: North Carolina. *Schmandt, J. and Wilson, R., eds.*, 1987, pp. 163–90. [G: U.S.]

Hughes, Gordon A. Fiscal Federalism in the UK. *Oxford Rev. Econ. Policy*, Summer 1987, *3*(2), pp. 1–23. [G: U.K.]

Jhaveri, N. J. Distribution of Non-plan Transfers: Needed an Alternative Approach. *Gulati, I. S., ed.*, 1987, *1969*, pp. 111–20. [G: India]

Khatkhate, Deena R. and Bhatt, V. V. Accommodating the Planning Dimension. *Gulati, I. S., ed.*, 1987, *1970*, pp. 41–59. [G: India]

King, Ronald F. The Politics of Denial: The Use of Funding Penalties as an Implementation Device for Social Policy. *Policy Sci.*, 1987, *20*(4), pp. 307–37. [G: U.S.]

Krane, Dale A. Does the Federal–Unitary Dichotomy Make Any Difference? One Answer Derived from Macrocomparative Analysis. *Picard, L. A. and Zariski, R., eds.*, 1987, pp. 35–54. [G: U.S.]

von Kruedener, Jürgen. The Franckenstein Paradox in the Intergovernmental Fiscal Relations of Imperial Germany. *Witt, P.-C., ed.*, 1987, pp. 111–23. [G: Germany]

Lakdawala, D. T. Eighth Finance Commission's Recommendations. *Gulati, I. S., ed.*, 1987, *1984*, pp. 195–207. [G: India]

Lankford, R. Hamilton. A Note on Measuring Flypaper Effects [Income and Grant Effects on Local Expenditure: The Flypaper Effect and Other Difficulties]. *J. Urban Econ.*, July 1987, *22*(1), pp. 113–15. [G: U.S.]

Leach, Richard H. Governmental Institutions and Areawide Problems: The United States and Canada—An Intergovernmental Perspective. *Picard, L. A. and Zariski, R., eds.*, 1987, pp. 55–67. [G: U.S.; Canada]

Livesey, David A. Central Control of Local Authority Expenditure. *Oxford Rev. Econ. Policy*, Summer 1987, *3*(2), pp. 44–59. [G: U.K.]

Lyons, William and Fitzgerald, Michael R. Intergovernmental Aid and Ratio Measurement. *Soc. Sci. Quart.*, September 1987, *68*(3), pp. 478–86. [G: U.S.]

Lyons, William and Fitzgerald, Michael R. Measurement and Theory in Urban Policy Research: A Reply. *Soc. Sci. Quart.*, September 1987, *68*(3), pp. 491–93. [G: U.S.]

Marando, Vincent L. and Reeves, Mavis Mann. States and Metropolitan Structural Reorganization. *Picard, L. A. and Zariski, R., eds.*, 1987, pp. 73–88. [G: U.S.]

Margolis, Julius. The Fiscal Problems of the Fragmented Metropolis. *Aronson, J. R. and Schwartz, E., eds.*, 1987, pp. 30–50. [G: U.S.]

Megdal, Sharon Bernstein. The Flypaper Effect Revisited: An Econometric Explanation. *Rev.*

Econ. Statist., May 1987, *69*(2), pp. 347–51.

Merrigan, Kathleen A. and Smith, Suzanne E.
Promoting High-Technology Industry: Initiatives and Policies for State Governments: Massachusetts. *Schmandt, J. and Wilson, R., eds.*, 1987, pp. 65–96. **[G: U.S.]**

Meyer, Peter B. and Fitzgerald, Joan. Political Cohesion and Local Economic Control: An Analytical Framework and Pennsylvania Evidence. *Picard, L. A. and Zariski, R., eds.*, 1987, pp. 178–95. **[G: U.S.]**

Meyers, Harry G. Displacement Effects of Federal Highway Grants. *Nat. Tax J.*, June 1987, *40*(2), pp. 221–35. **[G: U.S.]**

Mitra, Ashok. Will Growth and Centralised Fiscal Arrangements Do? *Gulati, I. S., ed.*, 1987, *1975*, pp. 23–40. **[G: India]**

Nanetti, Raffaella Y.; Leonardi, Robert and Putnam, Robert D. The Management of Regional Policies: Endogenous Explanations of Performance. *Picard, L. A. and Zariski, R., eds.*, 1987, pp. 103–18. **[G: Italy]**

Nanjundappa, D. M. and Rao, G. V. K. Re-examining the Bases of Plan Assistance. *Gulati, I. S., ed.*, 1987, *1973*, pp. 236–43. **[G: India]**

Nathan, Richard P. The Politics of Printouts: The Use of Official Numbers to Allocate Federal Grants-in-Aid. *Alonso, W. and Starr, P., eds.*, 1987, pp. 331–42. **[G: U.S.]**

de Neufville, Judith Innes. Federal Statistics in Local Governments. *Alonso, W. and Starr, P., eds.*, 1987, pp. 343–62. **[G: U.S.]**

Oates, Wallace E. Fiscal Structure in the Federal System. *Aronson, J. R. and Schwartz, E., eds.*, 1987, pp. 51–73. **[G: U.S.]**

Palumbo, George M. The Report on Federal–State–Local Fiscal Relations: A Review. *Public Budg. Finance*, Autumn 1987, *7*(3), pp. 26–34. **[G: U.S.]**

Pelissero, John P. and Morgan, David R. Intergovernmental Aid for Cities and Schools: A Comment on Research Methods. *Soc. Sci. Quart.*, September 1987, *68*(3), pp. 487–90. **[G: U.S.]**

Peterson, George E. Infrastructure Support for Industrial Policy. *Goldstein, H. A., ed.*, 1987, pp. 95–104. **[G: U.S.]**

Raczynski, Dagmar and Serrano, Claudia. Administración y Gestión Local: La Experiencia de Algunos Municipios en Santiago. (Local Administration and Management: The Experience of some Municipalities in Santiago. With English summary.) *Colección Estud. CIEPLAN*, December 1987, (22), pp. 129–51. **[G: Chile]**

Rao, Hemlata. Income Tax Proceeds: Are the States Getting Their Due Share? *Gulati, I. S., ed.*, 1987, *1985*, pp. 185–94. **[G: India]**

Rao, V. K. R. V. Scope for Rationalisation within the System. *Gulati, I. S., ed.*, 1987, *1973*, pp. 86–110. **[G: India]**

Ruchelman, Leonard I. The Finance Function in Local Government. *Aronson, J. R. and Schwartz, E., eds.*, 1987, pp. 3–29. **[G: U.S.]**

Sbragia, Alberta M. Public-Sector Politics, Capital Markets, and Economic Development: Pub-

lic Investment in Great Britain and the United States. *Picard, L. A. and Zariski, R., eds.*, 1987, pp. 161–77. **[G: U.K.; U.S.]**

Schneider, Mark and Ji, Byung Moon. The Flypaper Effect and Competition in the Local Market for Public Goods. *Public Choice*, 1987, *54*(1), pp. 27–39.

Schwallie, Daniel P. A Theory of Intergovernmental Grants and Their Effect on Aggregate Grantor–Recipient Spending. *Public Finance Quart.*, July 1987, *15*(3), pp. 322–38.

Silbert, Lance. Promoting High-Technology Industry: Initiatives and Policies for State Governments: California. *Schmandt, J. and Wilson, R., eds.*, 1987, pp. 11–33. **[G: U.S.]**

Smith, Peter N. Optimal Local Authority Budgeting Strategies under Block Grant. *Appl. Econ.*, July 1987, *19*(7), pp. 891–905. **[G: U.K.]**

Stein, Robert M. and Hamm, Keith E. A Comparative Analysis of the Targeting Capacity of State and Federal Intergovernmental Aid Allocations: 1977, 1982. *Soc. Sci. Quart.*, September 1987, *68*(3), pp. 347–65. **[G: U.S.]**

Steinberg, Richard S. Voluntary Donations and Public Expenditures in a Federalist System. *Amer. Econ. Rev.*, March 1987, *77*(1), pp. 24–36.

Stutzer, Michael J. Improving Intergovernmental Finance: A Message from the Northland. *Fed. Res. Bank Minn. Rev.*, Spring 1987, *11*(2), pp. 2–13. **[G: U.S.]**

Swartz, Thomas R. A New Urban Crisis in the Making. *Challenge*, Sept./Oct. 1987, *30*(4), pp. 34–41. **[G: U.S.]**

Vithal, B. P. R. States' Plan Outlays and Resource Mobilisation: Criterion for Central Assistance. *Gulati, I. S., ed.*, 1987, *1969*, pp. 224–35. **[G: India]**

Wildasin, David E. Federal–State–Local Fiscal Relations: A Review of the Treasury Report. *Public Finance Quart.*, October 1987, *15*(4), pp. 472–99. **[G: U.S.]**

Wolman, Harold and Page, Edward. The Impact of Intergovernmental Grants on Subnational Resource Disparities: A Cross-National Comparison. *Public Budg. Finance*, Autumn 1987, *7*(3), pp. 82–98. **[G: U.S.; W. Europe; Canada; Australia]**

Obermann, Gabriel. Capital Intensity and the Federal Sector: Some Further Evidence. *Public Choice*, 1987, *52*(2), pp. 193–99. **[G: U.S.]**

400 International Economics

4000 General

Becker, David G. Postimperialism: A First Quarterly Report. *Becker, D. G., et al.*, 1987, pp. 203–25.

Bognár, József. World Economic Crisis, Adjustment Policies and Global Questions: An Introduction. *Pasinetti, L. and Lloyd, P., eds.*, 1987, pp. 405–08. **[G: Global]**

Bogomolov, Oleg T. Interdependence, Structural Change and Conflict in the World Economy.

Urquidi, V. L., ed., 1987, pp. 33–52.

Boon, Gerard K. North–South Interdependence: An Economic–Physical Interpretation. *De Economist,* 1987, *135*(1), pp. 66–93.
[G: Global]

Brooks, Harvey and Guile, Bruce R. Technology and Global Industry: Overview. *Guile, B. R. and Brooks, H., eds.,* 1987, pp. 1–15.

Buiter, Willem H. Approaches to the Analysis of Policy Coordination: Overview. *Bryant, R. C. and Portes, R., eds.,* 1987, pp. 66–72.

Culbertson, John M. A Realistic International Economics. *J. Econ. Educ.,* Spring 1987, *18*(2), pp. 161–75.

Duisenberg, W. F. The Financial Conditions for Sustaining the Present Recovery. *Visser, H. and Schoor, E., eds.,* 1987, pp. 47–55.
[G: Global]

Dunning, John H. The Organisation of International Economic Interdependence: An Historical Excursion. *Dunning, J. H. and Usui, M., eds.,* 1987, pp. 3–18.

Emmerij, L. The Future of North–South Relations: Alternative Approaches. *Visser, H. and Schoor, E., eds.,* 1987, pp. 179–96.
[G: Global]

Fousek, Peter. World Economy in Transition? *Kaushik, S. K., ed.,* 1987, pp. 107–14.

Frieden, Jeff. International Capital and National Development: Comments on Postimperialism. *Becker, D. G., et al.,* 1987, pp. 179–91.

Friedheim, Robert L. The Third United Nations Conference on the Law of the Sea: North–South Bargaining on Ocean Issues. *Zartman, I. W., ed. (II),* 1987, pp. 73–114.

Fujino, Shozaburo. International Symposium on World Economy and Japan: Introduction. *Hitotsubashi J. Econ.,* October 1987, 27, pp. 1–3.
[G: Global]

Haggard, Stephen and Simmons, Beth A. Theories of International Regimes. *Int. Organ.,* Summer 1987, *41*(3), pp. 491–517.
[G: Global]

Herrera, Felipe. Structural Change, Economic Interdependence and World Development: A Latin American Perspective. *Urquidi, V. L., ed.,* 1987, pp. 53–77. [G: Latin America]

Hieronymi, Otto. Reflections on Technology, International Order and Economic Growth. *Hieronymi, O., ed.,* 1987, pp. 69–95.
[G: OECD]

Hieronymi, Otto. Technology and International Relations: Introduction. *Hieronymi, O., ed.,* 1987, pp. 5–8.

Hirsch, Seev. The Political Economy of Interdependence. *Dunning, J. H. and Usui, M., eds.,* 1987, pp. 31–43.

Horowitz, David. Monetary Policy, Capital Movements and Underdevelopment. *Ciocca, P., ed.,* 1987, *1958,* pp. 299–312.

Keohane, Robert O. and Nye, Joseph S., Jr. *Power and Interdependence* Revisited. *Int. Organ.,* Autumn 1987, *41*(4), pp. 725–53.
[G: Global]

Kindleberger, Charles P. Economic Development and International Responsibility. *[Kita-*

mura, H.], 1987, pp. 89–98.

Kraus, Willy. Stages of Development, Cultural Context and the Problem of International Interdependence. *[Kitamura, H.],* 1987, pp. 190–203. [G: LDCs]

Krelle, Wilhelm. Growth, Inflation and Employment. *Pasinetti, L. and Lloyd, P., eds.,* 1987, pp. 275–91.

de Lattre, Andre. International Equilibrium— Some Longer-term Issues. *Visser, H. and Schoor, E., eds.,* 1987, pp. 87–94.
[G: Global]

Lewis, John P. Promoting Positive North–South Interdependence and Adjustment in the Medium Term, in a Context of Nation-State Politics. *Urquidi, V. L., ed.,* 1987, pp. 103–24.
[G: LDCs]

Meltzer, Ronald I. The Committee of the Whole: Initiative and Impasse in North–South Negotiations. *Zartman, I. W., ed. (II),* 1987, pp. 48–72.

Onitiri, Herbert M. A. Structural Change, Economic Interdependence and World Development: Implications for Economic Analysis and Policy. *Urquidi, V. L., ed.,* 1987, pp. 125–38.
[G: LDCs]

Ozawa, Terutomo. Can the Market Alone Manage Structural Upgrading? A Challenge Posed by Economic Interdependence. *Dunning, J. H. and Usui, M., eds.,* 1987, pp. 45–61.

Pajestka, Józef. Towards Greater Global Rationality. *Urquidi, V. L., ed.,* 1987, pp. 181–94.

Rostow, Walt W. A Perspective on the Global Economic Agenda. *Rostow, W. W.,* 1987, pp. 105–19.

Rostow, Walt W. Is There Need for Economic Leadership? Japanese or U.S.? *Rostow, W. W.,* 1987, *1985,* pp. 165–74. [G: Japan; U.S.]

Rostow, Walt W. The Pacific Basin and the World Economy. *Rostow, W. W.,* 1987, *1985,* pp. 151–64. [G: U.S.S.R.; U.S.; Japan]

Rushing, Francis W. In Defense of Realistic International Economics: Free Trade. *J. Econ. Educ.,* Spring 1987, *18*(2), pp. 185–90.

Schatz, Sayre P. Postimperialism and the Great Competition. *Becker, D. G., et al.,* 1987, pp. 193–201.

Schatz, Sayre P. Socializing Adaptation: A Perspective on World Capitalism. *Becker, D. G., et al.,* 1987, *1983,* pp. 161–77. [G: Global]

Segura, Julio. Structural Change, Economic Interdependence and World Development: General Conclusions of the Congress. *Urquidi, V. L., ed.,* 1987, pp. 203–08.

Simpson, Mark S. C. South–South Cooperation: Africa's Brazilian Option. *Akinrinade, O. and Barling, J. K., eds.,* 1987, pp. 199–217.
[G: Africa; Brazil]

Strange, Susan. The Persistent Myth of Lost Hegemony. *Int. Organ.,* Autumn 1987, *41*(4), pp. 551–74. [G: U.S.]

Streeten, Paul. Interdependence: A North–South Perspective. *Dunning, J. H. and Usui, M., eds.,* 1987, pp. 19–29.

Usui, Mikoto. Technological Development and Economic Interdependence: Introduction.

Dunning, J. H. and Usui, M., eds., 1987, pp. 83–94.   [G: LDCs]

Weidenaar, Dennis J. Teaching International Economics: A Response and Suggested Approach. *J. Econ. Educ.*, Spring 1987, *18*(2), pp. 177–84.

Wendt, Alexander E. The Agent–Structure Problem in International Relations Theory. *Int. Organ.*, Summer 1987, *41*(3), pp. 335–70.
                                               [G: Global]

Zartman, I. William. Positive Sum: Improving North–South Negotiations: Introduction: Explaining North–South Negotiations. *Zartman, I. W., ed. (II)*, 1987, pp. 1–14.

Zartman, I. William. Positive Sum: Improving North–South Negotiations: Conclusions: Importance of North–South Negotiations. *Zartman, I. W., ed. (II)*, 1987, pp. 278–301.

410 INTERNATIONAL TRADE THEORY

411 International Trade Theory

4110 General

Bhagwati, Jagdish N.; Brecher, Richard A. and Srinivasan, T. N. DUP Activities and Economic Theory. *Bhagwati, J. N., ed.*, 1987, *1984*, pp. 311–28.

Deardorff, Alan V. Trade and Capital Mobility in a World of Diverging Populations. *Johnson, D. G. and Lee, R. D., eds.*, 1987, pp. 561–88.   [G: LDCs; MDCs]

Eliasson, Gunnar. Dynamic Micro–Macro Co-ordination, Technical Change and Trade. *Eliasson, G.*, 1987, pp. 81–118.   [G: Sweden]

Eliasson, Gunnar. Technological Competition and Trade in the Experimentally Organized Economy—The Themes. *Eliasson, G.*, 1987, pp. 9–18.

Grampp, William D. Peace and Trade: The Classical vs. the Marxian View. *Visser, H. and Schoor, E., eds.*, 1987, pp. 17–31.

Olson, Mancur. Economic Nationalism and Economic Progress. *World Econ.*, September 1987, *10*(3), pp. 241–64.   [G: OECD]

Richardson, John B. A Sub-sectoral Approach to Services' Trade Theory. *Giarini, O., ed.*, 1987, pp. 59–82.

Thweatt, William O. James and John Mill on Comparative Advantage: Sraffa's Account Corrected. *Visser, H. and Schoor, E., eds.*, 1987, pp. 33–43.

Venkateswarlu, Tadiboyina. International Economics: Survey of Course Reading Materials in Universities in Canada and the United States of America. *Amer. Econ.*, Spring 1987, *31*(1), pp. 66–84.   [G: U.S.; Canada]

4112 Theory of International Trade

Abd-el-Rahman, K. S. Hypothèses concernant le rôle des avantages comparatifs des pays èt des avantages spécifiques des firmes dans l'explication des échanges croisés des produits similaires. (With English summary.) *Revue Écon.*

Polit., Mar.-Apr. 1987, *97*(2), pp. 165–92.
                                               [G: France]

Adams, John. Trade and Payments as Instituted Process: The Institutional Theory of the External Sector. *J. Econ. Issues*, December 1987, *21*(4), pp. 1839–60.

Altenburg, Lutz. Production Possibilities with a Public Intermediate Good. *Can. J. Econ.*, November 1987, *20*(4), pp. 715–34.

Asheim, G. B. Erratum [Hartwick's Rule in Open Economies]. *Can. J. Econ.*, February 1987, *20*(1), pp. 177.

Ballance, Robert H.; Forstner, Helmut and Murray, Tracy. Consistency Tests of Alternative Measures of Comparative Advantage. *Rev. Econ. Statist.*, February 1987, *69*(1), pp. 157–61.   [G: Global]

Barry, Frank G. Fiscal Policy in a Small Open Economy: An Integration of the Short-run, Heckscher–Ohlin and Capital Accumulation Models. *J. Int. Econ.*, February 1987, *22*(1/2), pp. 103–21.

Bartel, Ann P. and Lichtenberg, Frank R. The Skill Distribution and Competitive Trade Advantage of High-Technology Industries. *Lewin, D.; Lipsky, D. B. and Sockell, D., eds.*, 1987, pp. 161–76.   [G: U.S.]

Batra, Raveendra N. and Naqvi, Nadeem. Urban Unemployment and the Gains from Trade. *Economica*, August 1987, *54*(215), pp. 381–95.

Beladi, Hamid and Naqvi, Nadeem. An Analysis of Wage Differentials for a Small Open Economy. *Southern Econ. J.*, January 1987, *53*(3), pp. 605–14.

Beladi, Hamid and Naqvi, Nadeem. The Theory of Interindustry Wage Differentials: An Intertemporal Analysis. *Can. J. Econ.*, May 1987, *20*(2), pp. 245–56.

Berthélemy, Jean-Claude. Endettement international et théorie des transferts. (With English summary.) *Revue Écon. Polit.*, May-June 1987, *97*(3), pp. 253–81.   [G: LDCs]

Bhagwati, Jagdish N.; Brecher, Richard A. and Hatta, Tatsuo. The Generalized Theory of Transfers and Welfare: Bilateral Transfers in a Multilateral World. *Bhagwati, J. N., ed.*, 1987, *1983*, pp. 431–52.

Bhagwati, Jagdish N.; Brecher, Richard A. and Hatta, Tatsuo. The Global Correspondence Principle: A Generalization. *Amer. Econ. Rev.*, March 1987, *77*(1), pp. 124–32.

Bhagwati, Jagdish N., et al. Quid pro Quo Foreign Investment and Welfare: A Political-Economy–Theoretic Model. *[Diaz-Alejandro, C. F.]*, 1987, pp. 127–38.

Bhagwati, Jagdish N., et al. Quid Pro Quo Foreign Investment and Welfare: A Political-Economy–Theoretic Model. *J. Devel. Econ.*, October 1987, *27*(1–2), pp. 127–38.

Bikker, Jacob A. An International Trade Flow Model with Substitution: An Extension of the Gravity Model. *Kyklos*, 1987, *40*(3), pp. 315–37.   [G: Global]

Bliss, Christopher. The New Trade Theory and Economic Policy. *Oxford Rev. Econ. Policy*, Spring 1987, *3*(1), pp. 20–36.

Bond, Eric W. and Chen, Tain-Jy. The Welfare Effects of Illegal Immigration. *J. Int. Econ.*, November 1987, *23*(3/4), pp. 315–28.

Borsook, Ian. Earnings, Ability and International Trade. *J. Int. Econ.*, May 1987, *22*(3/4), pp. 281–95.

Bowen, Harry P.; Leamer, Edward E. and Sveikauskas, Leo. Multicountry, Multifactor Tests of the Factor Abundance Theory. *Amer. Econ. Rev.*, December 1987, *77*(5), pp. 791–809. [G: Global]

Brakman, Steven and Jepma, Catrinus J. The Impact of the Composition of Exports on Export Performance. *De Economist*, 1987, *135*(2), pp. 163–81.

Brecher, Richard A. and Choudhri, Ehsan U. International Migration versus Foreign Investment in the Presence of Unemployment. *J. Int. Econ.*, November 1987, *23*(3/4), pp. 329–42.

Bronfenbrenner, Martin. Some 'Scandals' of International Economics. *[Kitamura, H.]*, 1987, pp. 285–300.

Buffie, Edward F. Labor Market Distortions, the Structure of Protection and Direct Foreign Investment. *[Diaz-Alejandro, C. F.]*, 1987, pp. 149–63.

Buffie, Edward F. Labor Market Distortions, the Structure of Protection and Direct Foreign Investment. *J. Devel. Econ.*, October 1987, *27*(1–2), pp. 149–63.

Burgstaller, André. Europe's Industrialization and Colonial Underdevelopment in the Light of Ricardo's Corn Model. *J. Int. Econ.*, February 1987, *22*(1/2), pp. 157–69.

Burgstaller, André. Industrialization, Deindustrialization, and North–South Trade. *Amer. Econ. Rev.*, December 1987, *77*(5), pp. 1017–18.

Burney, Nadeem A. Unilateral International Transfers and Their Effects on the Welfare of the Recipient and Donor Countries. *Pakistan Devel. Rev.*, Summer 1987, *26*(2), pp. 135–59.

Calaza, J. R. L'élargissement du modèle de Pasinetti: "roundaboutness" et paradoxe de Leontief. (On the Expansion of the Pasinetti Model: Roundaboutness and Leontief Paradox. With English summary.) *Écon. Appl.*, 1987, *40*(3), pp. 581–601.

Campos e Cunha, Luís. More Goods Than Factors in International Trade Once Again. *Greek Econ. Rev.*, 1987, *9*(2), pp. 183–97.

Casas, F. R. and Choi, Eun Kwan. Trade Imbalance, the Factor Proportions Theory and the Resource Content of International Trade. *Rivista Int. Sci. Econ. Com.*, March 1987, *34*(3), pp. 213–30. [G: U.S.]

Chaudhuri, T. Datta; Khan, M. Ali and Tang, Min. Technical Progress and Structural Change. *J. Inst. Theoretical Econ.*, June 1987, *143*(2), pp. 310–23.

Cheng, Leonard K. Optimal Trade and Technology Policies: Dynamic Linkages. *Int. Econ. Rev.*, October 1987, *28*(3), pp. 757–76.

Cheng, Leonard K. Uncertainty and Economic Self-sufficiency. *J. Int. Econ.*, August 1987, *23*(1/2), pp. 167–78.

Chichilnisky, Graciela and Thomson, William. The Walrasian Mechanism from Equal Division Is Not Monotonic with Respect to Variations in the Number of Consumers. *J. Public Econ.*, February 1987, *32*(1), pp. 119–24.

Choi, Jai-Young. Nontraded Goods, Variable Returns to Scale and Welfare. *Southern Econ. J.*, April 1987, *53*(4), pp. 874–83.

Choi, Jai-Young and Yu, Eden S. H. Immiserizing Transfer under Variable Returns to Scale. *Can. J. Econ.*, August 1987, *20*(3), pp. 634–45.

Choi, Jai-Young and Yu, Eden S. H. Technical Progress and Outputs under Variable Returns to Scale. *Economica*, May 1987, *54*(214), pp. 249–53.

Clarete, Ramon L. and Whalley, John. Comparing the Marginal Welfare Costs of Commodity and Trade Taxes. *J. Public Econ.*, August 1987, *33*(3), pp. 357–62. [G: Philippines]

Colombo, Caterina. Exchange Rate and Prices: Firms' Behaviour in the Open Economy. *Giorn. Econ.*, Mar.-Apr. 1987, *46*(3–4), pp. 149–74.

Corden, W. Max. Why Trade Is Not Free: Is There a Clash between Theory and Practice? *Giersch, H., ed.*, 1987, pp. 1–19.

Darity, William A., Jr. The Hume Process, Laws of Returns, and the Anglo–Portuguese Trade. *Southern Econ. J.*, July 1987, *54*(1), pp. 119–33.

Deardorff, Alan V. Weak Links in the Chain of Comparative Advantage. *Bhagwati, J. N., ed.*, 1987, *1979*, pp. 101–14.

Devereux, Michael. Fiscal Spending, the Terms of Trade, and Real Interest Rates. *J. Int. Econ.*, May 1987, *22*(3/4), pp. 219–35.

Diewert, Walter Erwin. The Effects of an Innovation: A Trade Theory Approach. *Can. J. Econ.*, November 1987, *20*(4), pp. 694–714.

Dixit, Avinash K. On Pareto-Improving Redistributions of Aggregate Economic Gains. *J. Econ. Theory*, February 1987, *41*(1), pp. 133–53.

Dixit, Avinash K. Strategic Aspects of Trade Policy. *Bewley, T. F., ed.*, 1987, pp. 329–62.

Dixit, Avinash K. The Theory of International Trade: Comment. *Officer, L. H., ed.*, 1987, pp. 58–63.

Djajić, Slobodan. Illegal Aliens, Unemployment and Immigration Policy. *J. Devel. Econ.*, February 1987, *25*(1), pp. 235–49. [G: U.S.]

Donnenfeld, Shabtai and Mayer, Wolfgang. The Quality of Export Products and Optimal Trade Policy. *Int. Econ. Rev.*, February 1987, *28*(1), pp. 159–74.

Dornbusch, Rudiger. North–South Interdependence: Overview. *Bryant, R. C. and Portes, R., eds.*, 1987, pp. 338–43.

Drudi, Francesco. Supply and Demand Shocks in a Dependent Economy: The Case of the Dutch Disease. *Rivista Int. Sci. Econ. Com.*, April 1987, *34*(4), pp. 319–36.

Dutt, Amitava Krishna. As relações de troca e o desenvolvimento desigual: Resultados de um modelo de comércio Norte-Sul. (With English summary.) *Pesquisa Planejamento Econ.*, December 1987, *17*(3), pp. 533–59.

Eaton, Jonathan. A Dynamic Specific-Factors Model of International Trade. *Rev. Econ. Stud.*, April 1987, *54*(2), pp. 325–38.

Eaton, Jonathan and Grossman, Gene M. Optimal Trade and Industrial Policy under Oligopoly. *Bhagwati, J. N., ed.*, 1987, *1986*, pp. 161–82.

Ebbersbach, Annette. The Development of Socialist Foreign Trade Theory in the Conditions of the 1980s. *Soviet E. Europ. Foreign Trade*, Summer 1987, *23*(2), pp. 94–117.
[G: CMEA]

Edwards, Sebastian and van Wijnbergen, Sweder. Tariffs, The Real Exchange Rate and the Terms of Trade: On Two Popular Propositions in International Economics. *Oxford Econ. Pap.*, September 1987, *39*(3), pp. 458–64.

Ethier, Wilfred J. Bundled International Factor Mobility. *[Corden, W. M.]*, 1987, pp. 99–111.

Ethier, Wilfred J. The Theory of International Trade. *Officer, L. H., ed.*, 1987, pp. 1–57.

Falvey, Rodney E. and Kierzkowski, Henryk. Product Quality, Intra-industry Trade and (Im)perfect Competition. *[Corden, W. M.]*, 1987, pp. 143–61.

Findlay, Ronald. Factor Proportions and Comparative Advantage in the Long Run. *Bhagwati, J. N., ed.*, 1987, *1970*, pp. 93–100.

Flam, Harry and Helpman, Elhanan. Vertical Product Differentiation and North–South Trade. *Amer. Econ. Rev.*, December 1987, *77*(5), pp. 810–22.

Flückiger, Yves. La notion de rareté factorielle dans la théorie du commerce international. (The Notion of Factorial Scarcity in the Pure Theory of International Trade. With English summary.) *Rivista Int. Sci. Econ. Com.*, March 1987, *34*(3), pp. 231–39.

Galor, O. and Polemarchakis, H. M. Intertemporal Equilibrium and the Transfer Paradox. *Rev. Econ. Stud.*, January 1987, *54*(1), pp. 147–56.

de Grauwe, Paul and de Bellefroid, Bernard. Long-run Exchange Rate Variability and International Trade. *Arndt, S. W. and Richardson, J. D. eds.*, 1987, pp. 193–212.

Greenaway, David. The New Theories of Intra-industry Trade. *Bull. Econ. Res.*, April 1987, *39*(2), pp. 95–120.

Greenaway, David and Milner, Chris. Intra-industry Trade: Current Perspectives and Unresolved Issues. *Weltwirtsch. Arch.*, 1987, *123*(1), pp. 39–57.

Greenaway, David and Milner, Chris. Theories of Intra-industry Trade: A Review of the 'State of the Art.' *Andersson, J. O., ed.*, 1987, pp. 11–34.

Grinols, Earl L. Transfers and the Generalized Theory of Distortions and Welfare. *Economica*, November 1987, *54*(216), pp. 477–91.

Gros, Daniel. A Note on the Optimal Tariff, Retaliation and the Welfare Loss from Tariff Wars in a Framework with Intra-industry Trade. *J.*

Int. Econ., November 1987, *23*(3/4), pp. 357–67.

Gros, Daniel. Protectionism in a Framework with Intra-industry Trade: Tariffs, Quotas, Retaliation, and Welfare Losses. *Int. Monet. Fund Staff Pap.*, March 1987, *34*(1), pp. 86–114.

Haaland, Jan I. and Norman, Victor D. Modelling Trade and Trade Policy: Introduction. *Scand. J. Econ.*, 1987, *89*(3), pp. 217–26.

Haaland, Jan I., et al. VEMOD: A Ricardo–Heckscher–Ohlin–Jones Model of World Trade. *Scand. J. Econ.*, 1987, *89*(3), pp. 251–70.
[G: Global]

Helpman, Elhanan. A Simple Theory of International Trade with Multinational Corporations. *Bhagwati, J. N., ed.*, 1987, *1984*, pp. 477–97.

Hoel, Michael and Strøm, Steinar. Supply Security and Import Diversification of Natural Gas. *Golombek, R.; Hoel, M. and Vislie, J., eds.*, 1987, pp. 151–72. [G: W. Europe; Norway; U.S.S.R.]

Hong, Wontack. A Comparative Static Application of the Heckscher–Ohlin Model of Factor Proportions: Korean Experience. *Weltwirtsch. Arch.*, 1987, *123*(2), pp. 309–24.
[G: S. Korea]

Hwang, Hong; Liu, Jung-Chao and Mai, Chao-Cheng. Price, Profit and Market Share Effects of Tariffs, Volume Quotas and Ratio Quotas. *Manchester Sch. Econ. Soc. Stud.*, September 1987, *55*(3), pp. 274–86.

Ihori, Toshihiro. Spillover Effects and the Terms of Trade within a Two-Country Model. *J. Int. Econ.*, May 1987, *22*(3/4), pp. 203–18.

Isard, W. and Dean, W. The Projection of World (Multiregional) Trade Matrices. *Environ. Planning A*, August 1987, *19*(8), pp. 1059–66.

Jones, Ronald W. Tax Wedges and Mobile Capital. *Scand. J. Econ.*, 1987, *89*(3), pp. 335–46.

Jones, Ronald W. The Population Monotonicity Property and the Transfer Paradox. *J. Public Econ.*, February 1987, *32*(1), pp. 125–32.

Jones, Ronald W.; Neary, J. Peter and Ruane, Frances P. International Capital Mobility and the Dutch Disease. *[Corden, W. M.]*, 1987, pp. 86–98.

Joshi, Pravin R. Heckscher–Ohlin Trade Model and Factor Price Equalisation Theorem under Alternative Conditions—A Geometrical Exposition. *Indian Econ. J.*, Jan.-Mar. 1987, *34*(3), pp. 92–108.

Kierzkowski, Henryk. Recent Advances in International Trade Theory: A Selective Survey. *Oxford Rev. Econ. Policy*, Spring 1987, *3*(1), pp. 1–19.

Kletzer, Kenneth and Bardhan, Pranab. Credit Markets and Patterns of International Trade. *[Diaz-Alejandro, C. F.]*, 1987, pp. 57–70.

Kletzer, Kenneth and Bardhan, Pranab. Credit Markets and Patterns of International Trade. *J. Devel. Econ.*, October 1987, *27*(1–2), pp. 57–70.

Kojima, Kiyoshi. Agreed Specialisation and Cross Direct Investment. *Hitotsubashi J. Econ.*, December 1987, *28*(2), pp. 87–105. [G: Japan; U.S.]

Kotlikoff, Laurence J. and Leamer, Edward E. Empirical Tests of Alternative Models of International Growth. *Bradford, C. I., Jr. and Branson, W. H., eds.*, 1987, pp. 227–69. **[G: U.S.; LDCs; MDCs]**

Krugman, Paul R. Increasing Returns and the Theory of International Trade. *Bewley, T. F., ed.*, 1987, pp. 301–28.

Krugman, Paul R. Increasing Returns, Monopolistic Competition, and International Trade. *Bhagwati, J. N., ed.*, 1987, *1979*, pp. 129–40.

Krugman, Paul R. Is Free Trade Passé? *J. Econ. Perspectives*, Fall 1987, *1*(2), pp. 131–44.

Krugman, Paul R. Pricing to Market When the Exchange Rate Changes. *Arndt, S. W. and Richardson, J. D. eds.*, 1987, pp. 49–70. **[G: U.S.]**

Krugman, Paul R. The Narrow Moving Band, the Dutch Disease, and the Competitive Consequences of Mrs. Thatcher. *J. Devel. Econ.*, October 1987, *27*(1–2), pp. 41–55. **[G: U.K.]**

Krugman, Paul R. The Narrow Moving Band, the Dutch Disease, and the Competitive Consequences of Mrs. Thatcher: Notes on Trade in the Presence of Dynamic Scale Economies. *[Diaz-Alejandro, C. F.]*, 1987, pp. 41–55. **[G: U.K.]**

Kuhn, Peter J. and Wooton, Ian. International Factor Movements in the Presence of a Fixed Factor. *J. Int. Econ.*, February 1987, *22*(1/2), pp. 123–40.

Lassudrie-Duchene, Bernard. Un retour à Ricardiana: les fonctions du commerce extérieur. (With English summary.) *Revue Écon. Polit.*, July-Aug. 1987, *97*(4), pp. 419–34.

Lawler, P. Short and Long-run Effects of a Resource Discovery on the Sectoral Distribution of Output. *Scot. J. Polit. Econ.*, August 1987, *34*(3), pp. 209–29.

Leamer, Edward E. Paths of Development in the Three-Factor, *n*-Good General Equilibrium Model. *J. Polit. Econ.*, October 1987, *95*(5), pp. 961–99. **[G: Selected Countries]**

Leamer, Edward E. The Leontief Paradox, Reconsidered. *Bhagwati, J. N., ed.*, 1987, *1980*, pp. 115–24. **[G: U.S.]**

Lo Cascio, Martino. Technology and the Terms of Trade. *Hieronymi, O., ed.*, 1987, pp. 157–68.

López, Elena and Pagoulatos, Emilio. A Model of International Trade with Differentiated Products. *Rivista Int. Sci. Econ. Com.*, September 1987, *34*(9), pp. 853–68.

Mainardi, Stefano. An Appraisal of Different Theoretical Approaches and Models of Foreign Direct Investment and International Trade. *Rivista Int. Sci. Econ. Com.*, May 1987, *34*(5), pp. 431–52.

Maneschi, Andrea. Shadow Pricing in a Specific-factors Model: Rejoinder. *Can. J. Econ.*, May 1987, *20*(2), pp. 403–04.

Maneschi, Andrea and Thweatt, William O. Barone's 1908 Representation of an Economy's Trade Equilibrium and the Gains from Trade. *J. Int. Econ.*, May 1987, *22*(3/4), pp. 375–82.

Marjit, Sugata. Trade in Intermediates and the Colonial Pattern of Trade. *Economica*, May 1987, *54*(214), pp. 173–84.

Menzler-Hokkanen, I. Competitive Advantage: How to Measure It Empirically? *Liiketaloudellinen Aikak.*, 1987, *36*(2), pp. 116–27.

van Mourik, Aad. Testing the Factor Price Equalization Theorem in the EC: An Alternative Approach: A Comment. *J. Common Market Stud.*, September 1987, *26*(1), pp. 79–86. **[G: EEC]**

Mundell, Robert A. International Trade and Factor Mobility. *Bhagwati, J. N., ed.*, 1987, *1957*, pp. 21–36.

Mussa, Michael. The Two-Sector Model in Terms of Its Dual: A Geometric Exposition. *Bhagwati, J. N., ed.*, 1987, *1979*, pp. 55–70.

Naqvi, Nadeem. Endogenous Investment, Current Account and the Rybczynski Theorem. *Southern Econ. J.*, April 1987, *53*(4), pp. 925–33.

Opocher, Arrigo. Technical Change in a Neo-Ricardian Model of the Small Open Economy. A Dual Approach. *Econ. Notes*, 1987, (3), pp. 20–36.

Perasso, Giancarlo. Alcuni toeremi fondamentali della teoria pura del commercio internazionale: Un approccio non tradizionale. (Some Fundamental Issues of the Pure Theory of International Trade: A Non Traditional Approach. With English summary.) *Giorn. Econ.*, Mar.-Apr. 1987, *46*(3–4), pp. 175–83.

Popović, Danica. Neorikardijanski pristup u čistoj teoriji spoljne trgovine. (The Neoricardian Analysis of the Pure Theory of International Trade. With English summary.) *Econ. Anal. Workers' Manage.*, 1987, *21*(2), pp. 221–42.

Power, Simon. The Origins of the Heckscher–Ohlin Concept. *Hist. Polit. Econ.*, Summer 1987, *19*(2), pp. 289–98.

Rauscher, Michael. Trade with an Exhaustible Resource When Demand Reactions Are Lagged. *Europ. Econ. Rev.*, December 1987, *31*(8), pp. 1597–1604.

Rieber, William J. A Further Look at Dumping in International Markets. *Rivista Int. Sci. Econ. Com.*, April 1987, *34*(4), pp. 309–18.

Rodrik, Dani. The Economics of Export-Performance Requirements. *Quart. J. Econ.*, August 1987, *102*(3), pp. 633–50.

Rugman, Alan M. Strategies for International Competitiveness. *Tremblay, R., ed.*, 1987, pp. 315–25. **[G: U.S.]**

Samuelson, Paul A. International Factor-Price Equalisation Once Again. *Bhagwati, J. N., ed.*, 1987, *1949*, pp. 5–20.

Sandmo, Agnar. Tax Wedges and Mobile Capital: Comment. *Scand. J. Econ.*, 1987, *89*(3), pp. 347–48.

Sarkar, Abhirup. Pattern of Trade in a Neo-Austrian Model of Production. *J. Quant. Econ.*, July 1987, *3*(2), pp. 177–88.

Sau, Ranjit. A Neo-Ricardo–Viner Theory of International Trade. *Econ. Int.*, May-Aug. 1987, *40*(2–3), pp. 224–36.

Sgro, Pasquale M. A Note on Minimum Wages, Non-traded Goods, Terms of Trade, Welfare and Unemployment. *Econ. Notes*, 1987, (1), pp. 100–106.

Shelburne, Robert C. A Ratio Test of Trade Intensity and Per-capita-Income Similarity. *Weltwirtsch. Arch.*, 1987, *123*(3), pp. 474–87.
[G: OECD]

Smith, Alasdair. Factor Shadow Prices in Distorted Open Economies. *[Corden, W. M.]*, 1987, pp. 54–67.

Staiger, Robert W. Heckscher–Ohlin Theory in the Presence of Market Power. *Europ. Econ. Rev.*, Feb./Mar. 1987, *31*(1/2), pp. 97–102.

Staiger, Robert W.; Deardorff, Alan V. and Stern, Robert M. An Evaluation of Factor Endowments and Protection as Determinants of Japanese and American Foreign Trade. *Can. J. Econ.*, August 1987, *20*(3), pp. 449–63.
[G: U.S.; Japan]

Staiger, Robert W. and Tabellini, Guido. Discretionary Trade Policy and Excessive Protection. *Amer. Econ. Rev.*, December 1987, *77*(5), pp. 823–37.

Stenbacka, Rune. Horizontal and Vertical Product Differentiation—A Comparison of the Consequences for International Trade. *Andersson, J. O., ed.*, 1987, pp. 171–84.

Tamor, Kenneth L. An Empirical Examination of the Factor Endowments Hypothesis. *Can. J. Econ.*, May 1987, *20*(2), pp. 387–98.

Thompson, Henry. A Review of Advancements in the General Equilibrium Theory of Production and Trade. *Keio Econ. Stud.*, 1987, *24*(1), pp. 43–62.

Thursby, Jerry G. and Thursby, Marie C. Bilateral Trade Flows, the Linder Hypothesis, and Exchange Risk. *Rev. Econ. Statist.*, August 1987, *69*(3), pp. 488–95. [G: OECD]

Tower, Edward; Pursell, Garry G. and Han, Ki-youn. Shadow Pricing in a Specific-factors Model: Comment. *Can. J. Econ.*, May 1987, *20*(2), pp. 399–402.

Tsai, Pan-long. The Welfare Impact of Foreign Investment in the Presence of Specific Factors and Non-traded Goods. *Weltwirtsch. Arch.*, 1987, *123*(3), pp. 496–508.

Venables, Anthony J. Trade and Trade Policy with Differentiated Products: A Chamberlinian–Ricardian Model. *Econ. J.*, September 1987, *97*(387), pp. 700–717.

Viaene, Jean-Marie. Factor Accumulation in a Minimum-Wage Economy. *Europ. Econ. Rev.*, August 1987, *31*(6), pp. 1313–28.
[G: Netherlands]

Vines, David. Protectionism and the Debt Crisis: Discussion. *Bryant, R. C. and Portes, R., eds.*, 1987, pp. 331–36.

Webster, Allan. Patterns of Bilateral Trade Flows within the Characteristics Approach to Trade. *J. Econ. Stud.*, 1987, *14*(5), pp. 3–23.

van Wijnbergen, Sweder. Protectionism and the Debt Crisis. *Bryant, R. C. and Portes, R., eds.*, 1987, pp. 307–30.

Wong, Kar-yiu. Are International Trade and Factor Mobility Substitutes? *Bhagwati, J. N., ed.*, 1987, *1986*, pp. 37–53.

Wu, Ho-mou. The Equalization of Factor Prices

in General Equilibrium When Commodities Outnumber Factors. *J. Int. Econ.*, November 1987, *23*(3/4), pp. 343–56.

Yabuuchi, Shigemi and Kakimoto, Sumio. Higher Dimensional Issues in the Rybczynski Theorem with Nontraded Goods and Interindustry Flows. *Econ. Stud. Quart.*, September 1987, *38*(3), pp. 193–98.

Yeh, Yeong-Her. International Trade vs. Factor Mobility under Domestic Distortions. *Amer. Econ.*, Fall 1987, *31*(2), pp. 73–75.

Yeh, Yeong-Her. The Effect of Consumption Taxes and Production Subsidies. *Atlantic Econ. J.*, July 1987, *15*(2), pp. 57–61.

Ylönen, Sakari. Factor Demand and Substitution under Decreasing Returns to Scale. An Application to the Rybczynski Theorem. *Scand. J. Econ.*, 1987, *89*(2), pp. 209–16.

Yu, Eden S. H. Inter-industrial Externalities, Technical Progress and Welfare. *Southern Econ. J.*, October 1987, *54*(2), pp. 412–21.

4113 Theory of Protection

Abraham, Filip; Deardorff, Alan V. and Stern, Robert M. The Economic Consequences of an Import Surcharge: Theory and Empirical Evidence for the U.S. Economy. *J. Policy Modeling*, Summer 1987, *9*(2), pp. 285–309.
[G: U.S.]

Anderson, James E. Quotas as Options: Optimality and Quota License Pricing under Uncertainty. *J. Int. Econ.*, August 1987, *23*(1/2), pp. 21–39.

Axelrod, Robert. How Should the United States Respond to Other Countries' Trade Policies? Comment. *Stern, R. M., ed.*, 1987, pp. 283–86.
[G: U.S.]

Balassa, Bela and Michalopoulos, Constantine. The Extent and the Cost of Protection in Developed–Developing-Country Trade. *Salvatore, D., ed.*, 1987, pp. 482–504. [G: LDCs; MDCs]

Baldwin, Robert E. The New Protectionism: A Response to Shifts in National Economic Power. *Salvatore, D., ed.*, 1987, pp. 95–112.
[G: U.S.]

Bark, Taeho. Distortions and Intertemporal Welfare in a Small Open Economy. *J. Int. Econ.*, August 1987, *23*(1/2), pp. 151–66.

Bark, Taeho and de Melo, Jaime. Export Mix Adjustment to the Imposition of VERs: Alternative License Allocation Schemes. *Weltwirtsch. Arch.*, 1987, *123*(4), pp. 668–78.

Benson, Bruce L. and Hartigan, James C. Tariffs and Location Specific Income Redistribution. *Reg. Sci. Urban Econ.*, May 1987, *17*(2), pp. 223–43.

Bhagwati, Jagdish N. Protectionism: Old Wine in New Bottles. *Salvatore, D., ed.*, 1987, pp. 31–44.

Bhagwati, Jagdish N. The Generalized Theory of Distortions and Welfare. *Bhagwati, J. N., ed.*, 1987, *1971*, pp. 265–86.

Bhagwati, Jagdish N. VERs, Quid Pro Quo DFI and VIEs: Political-Economy–Theoretic Analyses. *Int. Econ. J.*, Spring 1987, *1*(1), pp. 1–14.

Bhagwati, Jagdish N., et al. Quid pro Quo Foreign Investment and Welfare: A Political-Economy–Theoretic Model. *[Diaz-Alejandro, C. F.]*, 1987, pp. 127–38.

Bhagwati, Jagdish N., et al. Quid Pro Quo Foreign Investment and Welfare: A Political-Economy–Theoretic Model. *J. Devel. Econ.*, October 1987, *27*(1–2), pp. 127–38.

Bigman, David. The Theory of Variable Levies. *Oxford Econ. Pap.*, June 1987, *39*(2), pp. 357–77.

Black, P. A. and Cooper, J. H. On the Welfare and Employment Effects of Economic Sanctions. *S. Afr. J. Econ.*, March 1987, *55*(1), pp. 1–15. **[G: S. Africa]**

Black, P. A. and Cooper, J. H. On the Welfare and Employment Effects of Economic Sanctions: Reply. *S. Afr. J. Econ.*, September 1987, *55*(3), pp. 297–99. **[G: S. Africa]**

Bliss, Christopher. The New Trade Theory and Economic Policy. *Oxford Rev. Econ. Policy*, Spring 1987, *3*(1), pp. 20–36.

Brander, James A. and Spencer, Barbara J. Foreign Direct Investment with Unemployment and Endogenous Taxes and Tariffs. *J. Int. Econ.*, May 1987, *22*(3/4), pp. 257–79.

Brander, James A. and Spencer, Barbara J. Tariffs and the Extraction of Foreign Monopoly Rents under Potential Entry. *Bhagwati, J. N., ed.*, 1987, *1981*, pp. 141–60.

Brecher, Richard A. and Bhagwati, Jagdish N. Voluntary Export Restrictions versus Import Restrictions: A Welfare-Theoretic Comparison. *[Corden, W. M.]*, 1987, pp. 41–53.

Brecher, Richard A. and Díaz-Alejandro, Carlos F. Tariffs, Foreign Capital, and Immiserizing Growth. *Bhagwati, J. N., ed.*, 1987, *1977*, pp. 389–94.

Britten-Jones, Mark; Nettle, Richard S. and Anderson, Kym. On Optimal Second-Best Trade Intervention in the Presence of a Domestic Divergence. *Australian Econ. Pap.*, December 1987, *26*(49), pp. 332–36.

Bronfenbrenner, Martin. Some 'Scandals' of International Economics. *[Kitamura, H.]*, 1987, pp. 285–300.

Brown, Drusilla K. Tariffs, the Terms of Trade, and National Product Differentiation. *J. Policy Modeling*, Fall 1987, *9*(3), pp. 503–26.

Buffie, Edward F. Labor Market Distortions, the Structure of Protection and Direct Foreign Investment. *J. Devel. Econ.*, October 1987, *27*(1–2), pp. 149–63.

Buffie, Edward F. Labor Market Distortions, the Structure of Protection and Direct Foreign Investment. *[Diaz-Alejandro, C. F.]*, 1987, pp. 149–63.

Buffie, Edward F. Real Wage Rigidity and Optimal Commercial Policy in Less Developed Countries. *J. Devel. Econ.*, August 1987, *26*(2), pp. 321–41. **[G: LDCs]**

Calvo, Guillermo A. On the Costs of Temporary Policy. *[Diaz-Alejandro, C. F.]*, 1987, pp. 245–61.

Calvo, Guillermo A. On the Costs of Temporary Policy. *J. Devel. Econ.*, October 1987, *27*(1–2), pp. 245–61.

Carmichael, Calum M. The Control of Export Credit Subsidies and Its Welfare Consequences. *J. Int. Econ.*, August 1987, *23*(1/2), pp. 1–19. **[G: U.S.]**

Cassing, James H. The Issue of Protection: Comment. *Officer, L. H., ed.*, 1987, pp. 103–17.

Caves, Richard E. Industrial Policy and Trade Policy: The Connections. *[Corden, W. M.]*, 1987, pp. 68–85.

Choi, Jai-Young and Yu, Eden S. H. Nominal and Optimum Tariffs under Variable Returns to Scale. *Oxford Econ. Pap.*, December 1987, *39*(4), pp. 785–98.

Clarete, Ramon L. and Roumasset, James A. A Shoven–Whalley Model of a Small Open Economy: An Illustration with Philippine Tariffs. *J. Public Econ.*, March 1987, *32*(2), pp. 247–61. **[G: Philippines]**

Clarete, Ramon L. and Whalley, John. Comparing the Marginal Welfare Costs of Commodity and Trade Taxes. *J. Public Econ.*, August 1987, *33*(3), pp. 357–62. **[G: Philippines]**

Corden, W. Max. The Revival of Protectionism in Developed Countries. *Salvatore, D., ed.*, 1987, pp. 45–68. **[G: OECD]**

Corden, W. Max. Why Trade Is Not Free: Is There a Clash between Theory and Practice? *Giersch, H., ed.*, 1987, pp. 1–19.

Das, Satya P. and Donnenfeld, Shabtai. Trade Policy and Its Impact on Quality of Imports: A Welfare Analysis. *J. Int. Econ.*, August 1987, *23*(1/2), pp. 77–95.

Das, Satya P. and Mohanty, Adwait K. Welfare of the Dumping Country: A Comprehensive Ranking of Policies. *J. Quant. Econ.*, January 1987, *3*(1), pp. 13–34.

Deardorff, Alan V. Safeguards Policy and the Conservative Social Welfare Function. *[Corden, W. M.]*, 1987, pp. 22–40.

Deardorff, Alan V. Why Do Governments Prefer Nontariff Barriers? *Carnegie–Rochester Conf. Ser. Public Policy*, Spring 1987, *26*, pp. 191–216.

Deardorff, Alan V. and Stern, Robert M. Current Issues in Trade Policy: An Overview. *Stern, R. M., ed.*, 1987, pp. 15–68. **[G: U.S.]**

DeRosa, Dean A. A Positive View of Duty Remission Schemes. *Quart. Rev. Econ. Bus.*, Summer 1987, *27*(2), pp. 42–49.

DeRosa, Dean A. and Nye, William W. Industrial Targeting and International Competitiveness in a Two Country Model of Monopolistic Competition. *Amer. Econ.*, Spring 1987, *31*(1), pp. 9–18.

Dixit, Avinash K. How Should the United States Respond to Other Countries' Trade Policies? *Stern, R. M., ed.*, 1987, pp. 245–82. **[G: U.S.]**

Dixit, Avinash K. Issues of Strategic Trade Policy for Small Countries. *Scand. J. Econ.*, 1987, *89*(3), pp. 349–67.

Dixit, Avinash K. Trade and Insurance with Moral

Hazard. *J. Int. Econ.*, November 1987, *23*(3/4), pp. 201–20.

Djajić, Slobodan. Temporary Import Quota and the Current Account. *J. Int. Econ.*, May 1987, *22*(3/4), pp. 349–62.

Dollar, David. Import Quotas and the Product Cycle. *Quart. J. Econ.*, August 1987, *102*(3), pp. 615–32.

Dollery, B. E. and Leibbrandt, M. V. On the Welfare and Employment Effects of Economic Sanctions: Comment. *S. Afr. J. Econ.*, September 1987, *55*(3), pp. 292–96.
[G: S. Africa]

Donnenfeld, Shabtai and Mayer, Wolfgang. The Quality of Export Products and Optimal Trade Policy. *Int. Econ. Rev.*, February 1987, *28*(1), pp. 159–74.

Dung, Tran Huu. Optimal Countervailing Intervention. *Int. Econ. J.*, Autumn 1987, *1*(3), pp. 19–29.

Eaton, Jonathan and Grossman, Gene M. Optimal Trade and Industrial Policy under Oligopoly. *Bhagwati, J. N., ed.*, 1987, *1986*, pp. 161–82.

Edwards, Sebastian and van Wijnbergen, Sweder. Tariffs, The Real Exchange Rate and the Terms of Trade: On Two Popular Propositions in International Economics. *Oxford Econ. Pap.*, September 1987, *39*(3), pp. 458–64.

Eliasson, Gunnar. Industrial Targeting: Defensive or Offensive Strategies in a Neo-Schumpeterian Perspective. *Giersch, H., ed.*, 1987, pp. 333–60.

Eliasson, Gunnar. Industrial Targeting: Defensive or Offensive Strategies in a Neo-Schumpeterian Perspective. *Eliasson, G.*, 1987, pp. 21–48.

Fan, Liang-Shing and Fan, Chuen-Mei. On the Welfare Effects of Rent Seeking. *Indian Econ. J.*, July-Sept. 1987, *35*(1), pp. 136–39.

Feenstra, Robert C. Incentive Compatible Trade Policies. *Scand. J. Econ.*, 1987, *89*(3), pp. 373–87.

Feldman, David H. Tariffs and Compensation Payments in General Equilibrium: A Consumer Surplus Approach. *Rivista Int. Sci. Econ. Com.*, May 1987, *34*(5), pp. 419–30.

Findlay, Ronald. Current Issues in Trade Policy: An Overview: Comment. *Stern, R. M., ed.*, 1987, pp. 73–76. [G: U.S.]

Findlay, Ronald. Intermediate Goods, Export Taxation and Resource-Based Industrialization. *[Corden, W. M.]*, 1987, pp. 162–71.

Flam, Harry. Reverse Dumping. *Europ. Econ. Rev.*, Feb./Mar. 1987, *31*(1/2), pp. 82–88.

Flam, Harry and Helpman, Elhanan. Industrial Policy under Monopolistic Competition. *J. Int. Econ.*, February 1987, *22*(1/2), pp. 79–102.

Fung, K. C. Industry Structure, Antitrust and Tariffs. *Int. J. Ind. Organ.*, December 1987, *5*(4), pp. 447–56.

Gang, Ira N. Tariff Policy and Poverty Alleviation in a Harris–Todaro Type Economy. *Indian Econ. J.*, July-Sept. 1987, *35*(1), pp. 97–115.

Gray, H. Peter and Walter, Ingo. The Issue of

Protection. *Officer, L. H., ed.*, 1987, pp. 65–102.

Greenaway, David and Milner, Chris. 'True Protection' Concepts and Their Role in Evaluating Trade Policies in LDCs. *J. Devel. Stud.*, January 1987, *23*(2), pp. 200–219.
[G: Selected LDCs]

Greenaway, David and Milner, Chris. Effective Protection and Intra-industry Trade: Some Positive and Normative Issues. *J. Econ. Stud.*, 1987, *14*(5), pp. 38–53.

Greenaway, David and Milner, Chris. Trade Theory and the Less Developed Countries. *Gemmell, N., ed.*, 1987, pp. 11–55.
[G: LDCs]

Grinols, Earl L. Transfers and the Generalized Theory of Distortions and Welfare. *Economica*, November 1987, *54*(216), pp. 477–91.

Gros, Daniel. A Note on the Optimal Tariff, Retaliation and the Welfare Loss from Tariff Wars in a Framework with Intra-industry Trade. *J. Int. Econ.*, November 1987, *23*(3/4), pp. 357–67.

Gros, Daniel. Protectionism in a Framework with Intra-industry Trade: Tariffs, Quotas, Retaliation, and Welfare Losses. *Int. Monet. Fund Staff Pap.*, March 1987, *34*(1), pp. 86–114.

Haaland, Jan I. and Norman, Victor D. Modelling Trade and Trade Policy: Introduction. *Scand. J. Econ.*, 1987, *89*(3), pp. 217–26.

Hagen, Kåre P. Incentive Compatible Trade Policies: Comment. *Scand. J. Econ.*, 1987, *89*(3), pp. 389–91.

Heady, Christopher and Mitra, Pradeep K. Distributional and Revenue Raising Arguments for Tariffs. *J. Devel. Econ.*, June 1987, *26*(1), pp. 77–101. [G: Brazil; Turkey]

Hollander, Abraham. Content Protection and Transnational Monopoly. *J. Int. Econ.*, November 1987, *23*(3/4), pp. 283–97.

Holzman, Franklyn D. Countervailing Foreign Use of Monopoly Power: Commentary. *Holzman, F. D.*, 1987, *1979*, pp. 137–42.
[G: U.S.S.R.]

Humphrey, Thomas M. Classical and Neoclassical Roots of the Theory of Optimum Tariffs. *Fed. Res. Bank Richmond Econ. Rev.*, July/Aug. 1987, *73*(4), pp. 17–28.

Ihori, Toshihiro. Spillover Effects and the Terms of Trade within a Two-Country Model. *J. Int. Econ.*, May 1987, *22*(3/4), pp. 203–18.

Itagaki, Takao. Optimal Tariffs for a Large and a Small Country under Uncertain Terms of Trade: Reply and Reinterpretation. *Oxford Econ. Pap.*, June 1987, *39*(2), pp. 418.

Ithurbide, Philippe. Les restrictions volontaires d'exportations: Une analyse macro-économique en régime de changes flexibles. (The Voluntary Export Restraints: A Macroeconomic Analysis under Flexible Exchanges Rates. With English summary.) *Revue Écon.*, January 1987, *38*(1), pp. 25–54.

Itoh, Motoshige and Kiyono, Kazuharu. Welfare-Enhancing Export Subsidies. *J. Polit. Econ.*, February 1987, *95*(1), pp. 115–37.

Johansson, Per-Olov and Löfgren, Karl-Gustaf.

Tariff Policy and Real Wage Adjustments in a Small Open Economy. *Siven, C.-H., ed.*, 1987, pp. 155–78.

Johnson, Harry G. Optimal Trade Intervention in the Presence of Domestic Distortions. *Bhagwati, J. N., ed.*, 1987, *1965*, pp. 235–63.

Johnson, Harry G. The Possibility of Income Losses from Increased Efficiency or Factor Accumulation in the Presence of Tariffs. *Bhagwati, J. N., ed.*, 1987, *1967*, pp. 385–87.

Jones, Ronald W. Current Issues in Trade Policy: An Overview: Comment. *Stern, R. M., ed.*, 1987, pp. 69–72. **[G: U.S.]**

Jones, Ronald W. Tax Wedges and Mobile Capital. *Scand. J. Econ.*, 1987, 89(3), pp. 335–46.

Kaempfer, William H. and Willett, Thomas D. Why an Import Surcharge Wouldn't Help America's Trade Deficit. *World Econ.*, March 1987, 10(1), pp. 27–38. **[G: U.S.]**

Kähkönen, Juha. Liberalization Policies and Welfare in a Financially Repressed Economy. *Int. Monet. Fund Staff Pap.*, September 1987, 34(3), pp. 531–47. **[G: LDCs]**

Karp, Larry S. Consistent Tariffs with Dynamic Supply Response. *J. Int. Econ.*, November 1987, 23(3/4), pp. 369–76.

Kierzkowski, Henryk. Issues of Strategic Trade Policy for Small Countries: Comment. *Scand. J. Econ.*, 1987, 89(3), pp. 369–71.

Klein, Lawrence R.; Pauly, Peter H. and Petersen, Christian E. Empirical Aspects of Protectionism: Results from Project LINK. *Salvatore, D., ed.*, 1987, pp. 69–94. **[G: Global]**

Krishna, Kala. Tariffs versus Quotas with Endogenous Quality. *J. Int. Econ.*, August 1987, 23(1/2), pp. 97–112.

Krueger, Anne O. The Political Economy of the Rent-Seeking Society. *Bhagwati, J. N., ed.*, 1987, *1974*, pp. 291–309.

Krugman, Paul R. Market Access and Competition in High Technology Industries: A Simulation Exercise. *[Corden, W. M.]*, 1987, pp. 128–42.

Krugman, Paul R. Strategic Sectors and International Competition. *Stern, R. M., ed.*, 1987, pp. 207–32. **[G: U.S.]**

Leamer, Edward E. Endogenous Protection in the United States, 1900–1984: Comment. *Stern, R. M., ed.*, 1987, pp. 196–200. **[G: U.S.]**

Levy, Santiago. A Short-run General Equilibrium Model for a Small, Open Economy. *J. Devel. Econ.*, February 1987, 25(1), pp. 63–88. **[G: LDCs]**

Lloyd, Peter J. Protection Policy and the Assignment Rule. *[Corden, W. M.]*, 1987, pp. 4–21.

Lucas, Robert E. B. On the Theory of DRC Criteria: Reply. *J. Devel. Econ.*, June 1987, 26(1), pp. 169–71.

Lucas, Robert E. B.; Pursell, Garry G. and Tower, Edward. Ex Ante versus Ex Post DRC's and the Possibility of Negative Shadow Prices: Resolution. *J. Devel. Econ.*, June 1987, 26(1), pp. 173–74.

de Macedo, Jorge Braga. Currency Inconvertibil-

ity, Trade Taxes and Smuggling. *J. Devel. Econ.*, October 1987, 27(1–2), pp. 109–25.

de Macedo, Jorge Braga. Currency Inconvertibility, Trade Taxes and Smuggling. *[Diaz-Alejandro, C. F.]*, 1987, pp. 109–25.

Magee, Stephen P. and Young, Leslie. Endogenous Protection in the United States, 1900–1984. *Stern, R. M., ed.*, 1987, pp. 145–95. **[G: U.S.]**

Mayer, Wolfgang. Endogenous Tariff Formation. *Bhagwati, J. N., ed.*, 1987, *1984*, pp. 329–52.

Mayer, Wolfgang and Riezman, Raymond G. Endogenous Choice of Trade Policy Instruments. *J. Int. Econ.*, November 1987, 23(3/4), pp. 377–81.

McCulloch, Rachel. Why Do Governments Prefer Nontariff Barriers? A Comment. *Carnegie–Rochester Conf. Ser. Public Policy*, Spring 1987, 26, pp. 217–21.

McLeod, Darryl L. and Salvatore, Dominick. The Employment Effects of Barriers to North–South Trade with and without Indexed Debt Service Payments. *Salvatore, D., ed.*, 1987, pp. 551–70. **[G: Global]**

Mercenier, Jean. Tariff Change, Foreign Capital and Immiserization: A General Equilibrium Evaluation of the Latin American Case. *J. Devel. Econ.*, June 1987, 26(1), pp. 145–62. **[G: Latin America]**

de Meza, David. The Optimum Tariff and Quota when the Terms of Trade Are Random. *Oxford Econ. Pap.*, June 1987, 39(2), pp. 412–17.

Michaely, Michael. The Demand for Protection against Exports of Newly Industrializing Countries. *Salvatore, D., ed.*, 1987, pp. 471–81. **[G: Brazil; Hong Kong; S. Korea; Mexico; Singapore]**

Mundell, Robert A. International Trade and Factor Mobility. *Bhagwati, J. N., ed.*, 1987, *1957*, pp. 21–36.

Mussa, Michael. Average Protection and Economic Policy. *Salvatore, D., ed.*, 1987, pp. 389–407. **[G: U.S.]**

Neary, J. Peter. Endogenous Protection in the United States, 1900–1984: Comment. *Stern, R. M., ed.*, 1987, pp. 201–06. **[G: U.S.]**

Nettle, Richard S.; Britten-Jones, Mark and Anderson, Kym. Optimal Policy Intervention to Reduce Import Dependence. *Int. Econ. J.*, Winter 1987, 1(4), pp. 101–06.

Portes, Richard. Industrial Targeting: Defensive or Offensive Strategies in a Neo-Schumpeterian Perspective: Comment. *Giersch, H., ed.*, 1987, pp. 361–65.

Pursell, Garry G. and Tower, Edward. DRC Criteria: Comment. *J. Devel. Econ.*, June 1987, 26(1), pp. 163–67.

Reiber, William J. The Non-equivalence of Tariffs and Quotas: An Extension. *J. Econ. Stud.*, 1987, 14(1), pp. 55–59.

Richardson, J. David. How Should the United States Respond to Other Countries' Trade Policies? Comment. *Stern, R. M., ed.*, 1987, pp. 287–90. **[G: U.S.]**

Rodriguez, Carlos Alfredo. The Non-equivalence of Tariffs and Quotas under Retaliation. *Bhag-*

wati, J. N., ed., 1987, *1974*, pp. 197–201.

Rodrik, Dani. Policy Targeting with Endogenous Distortions: Theory of Optimum Subsidy Revisited. *Quart. J. Econ.*, November 1987, *102*(4), pp. 903–11.

Rodrik, Dani. Trade and Capital-Account Liberalization in a Keynesian Economy. *J. Int. Econ.*, August 1987, *23*(1/2), pp. 113–29.

Samuelson, Paul A. Joint Authorship in Science: Serendipity with Wolfgang Stolper. *J. Inst. Theoretical Econ.*, June 1987, *143*(2), pp. 235–43.

Sandmo, Agnar. Tax Wedges and Mobile Capital: Comment. *Scand. J. Econ.*, 1987, *89*(3), pp. 347–48.

Sato, Mitsuaki. Costs and Benefits to the United States of the 1985 Steel Import Quota Program: Discussion. *Sato, R. and Wachtel, P., eds.*, 1987, pp. 181–83. **[G: U.S.; Japan]**

Saxonhouse, Gary R. Strategic Sectors and International Competition: Comment. *Stern, R. M., ed.*, 1987, pp. 239–43. **[G: U.S.]**

Smith, Alasdair. Shadow Price Calculations in Distorted Economies. *Scand. J. Econ.*, 1987, *89*(3), pp. 287–302.

Smith, Alasdair. Strategic Investment, Multinational Corporations and Trade Policy. *Europ. Econ. Rev.*, Feb./Mar. 1987, *31*(1/2), pp. 89–96.

Snape, Richard H. The Importance of Frontier Barriers. *[Corden, W. M.]*, 1987, pp. 215–32.

Spinelli, Franco. Labor Market Rigidities and Protectionism. *Salvatore, D., ed.*, 1987, pp. 181–200.

Staiger, Robert W.; Deardorff, Alan V. and Stern, Robert M. Employment Effects of Japanese and American Protectionism. *Salvatore, D., ed.*, 1987, pp. 164–80. **[G: U.S.; Japan]**

Staiger, Robert W. and Tabellini, Guido. Discretionary Trade Policy and Excessive Protection. *Amer. Econ. Rev.*, December 1987, *77*(5), pp. 823–37.

Tange, Toshiko. United States–Japan Trade Frictions and Competitiveness. *Salvatore, D., ed.*, 1987, pp. 201–15. **[G: U.S.; Japan]**

Tarr, David G. Costs and Benefits to the United States of the 1985 Steel Import Quota Program. *Sato, R. and Wachtel, P., eds.*, 1987, pp. 159–77. **[G: Japan; U.S.]**

Tarr, David G. and Morkre, Morris E. Aggregate Costs to the United States of Tariffs and Quotas on Imports. *Salvatore, D., ed.*, 1987, pp. 216–29. **[G: U.S.]**

Tullock, Gordon. The Opportunity Cost of Import Tariffs—A Comment. *Kyklos*, 1987, *40*(4), pp. 573–74.

Turunen, Arja H. Economic Inequality and Public Policy in a Small Open Economy. *Scand. J. Econ.*, 1987, *89*(4), pp. 405–19.

Venables, Anthony J. Trade and Trade Policy with Differentiated Products: A Chamberlinian–Ricardian Model. *Econ. J.*, September 1987, *97*(387), pp. 700–717.

Viaene, Jean-Marie. Factor Accumulation in a Minimum-Wage Economy. *Europ. Econ.*

Rev., August 1987, *31*(6), pp. 1313–28. **[G: Netherlands]**

Vousden, Neil J. Content Protection and Tariffs under Monopoly and Competition. *J. Int. Econ.*, November 1987, *23*(3/4), pp. 263–82.

Wadensjö, Eskil. Tariff Policy and Real Wage Adjustments in a Small Open Economy: Comment. *Siven, C.-H., ed.*, 1987, pp. 179–81.

Wagner, Joachim. Zur politischen Ökonomie der Protektion in der Bundesrepublik Deutschland. (With English summary.) *Kyklos*, 1987, *40*(4), pp. 548–67. **[G: W. Germany]**

Webb, Michael A. Anti-dumping Laws, Production Location and Prices. *J. Int. Econ.*, May 1987, *22*(3/4), pp. 363–68.

Wergeland, Tor. Shadow Price Calculations in Distorted Economies: Comment. *Scand. J. Econ.*, 1987, *89*(3), pp. 303–04.

White, Lawrence J. Costs and Benefits to the United States of the 1985 Steel Import Quota Program: Discussion. *Sato, R. and Wachtel, P., eds.*, 1987, pp. 177–81. **[G: U.S.; Japan]**

Whitman, Marina von Neumann. Strategic Sectors and International Competition: Comment. *Stern, R. M., ed.*, 1987, pp. 233–38. **[G: U.S.]**

van Wijnbergen, Sweder. Tariffs, Employment and the Current Account: Real Wage Resistance and the Macroeconomics of Protectionism. *Int. Econ. Rev.*, October 1987, *28*(3), pp. 691–706.

Young, Leslie. Intermediate Goods and the Formation of Duty-Free Zones. *J. Devel. Econ.*, April 1987, *25*(2), pp. 369–84. **[G: LDCs]**

Young, Leslie and Miyagiwa, Kaz F. Unemployment and the Formation of Duty-Free Zones. *J. Devel. Econ.*, August 1987, *26*(2), pp. 397–405. **[G: LDCs]**

4114 Theory of International Trade and Economic Development

Agbonyitor, Alberto D. K. On Import Substitution, Quality Uncertainty and Development Policy. *J. Econ. Devel.*, June 1987, *12*(1), pp. 33–47.

Alexander, Robert J. The Import Substitution Strategy of Economic Development. *Dietz, J. L. and Street, J. H., eds.*, 1987, pp. 118–27.

Anderson, Kym and Warr, Peter G. General Equilibrium Effects of Agricultural Price Distortions: A Simple Model for Korea. *Food Res. Inst. Stud.*, 1987, *20*(3), pp. 245–63. **[G: S. Korea]**

Atsain, Achi. Food Policy and the Choice of Trade Regime: Commentary. *Mellor, J. W.; Delgado, C. L. and Blackie, M. J., eds.*, 1987, pp. 274–75. **[G: Africa]**

Balassa, Bela and Michalopoulos, Constantine. The Extent and the Cost of Protection in Developed–Developing-Country Trade. *Salvatore, D., ed.*, 1987, pp. 482–504. **[G: LDCs; MDCs]**

Banerji, Kalyan. Financial Cooperation for Trade Expansion. *Agrawal, G. R., et al. (II)*, 1987, pp. 66–73.

Batra, Raveendra N. and Naqvi, Nadeem. Urban Unemployment and the Gains from Trade. *Economica*, August 1987, *54*(215), pp. 381–95.

Berlinski, Julio. Choice of Growth Strategy: Trade Regimes and Export Promotion. *Martirena-Mantel, A. M., ed.*, 1987, pp. 95–114. **[G: Latin America]**

Beza, Sterie T. Choice of Growth Strategy: Trade Regimes and Export Promotion: Comment. *Martirena-Mantel, A. M., ed.*, 1987, pp. 114–19. **[G: Latin America]**

Bhagwati, Jagdish N. International Trade in Services and Its Relevance for Economic Development. *Giarini, O., ed.*, 1987, pp. 3–34.

Boeri, Tito. Modelling Foreign Aid, Capital Inflows and Economic Development. *Rivista Int. Sci. Econ. Com.*, July 1987, *34*(7), pp. 623–47.

Bond, Marian E. and Milne, Elizabeth. Export Diversification in Developing Countries: Recent Trends and Policy Impact. *International Monetary Fund Research Department.*, 1987, pp. 98–144. **[G: LDCs]**

Botero A., Germán. Choice of Growth Strategy: Trade Regimes and Export Promotion: Comment. *Martirena-Mantel, A. M., ed.*, 1987, pp. 119–20. **[G: Latin America]**

Brock, Philip and Tower, Edward. Economic Liberalization in Less Developed Countries: Guidelines from the Empirical Evidence and Clarification of the Theory. *Connolly, M. and González-Vega, C., eds.*, 1987, pp. 19–43. **[G: LDCs]**

Buffie, Edward F. Real Wage Rigidity and Optimal Commercial Policy in Less Developed Countries. *J. Devel. Econ.*, August 1987, *26*(2), pp. 321–41. **[G: LDCs]**

Buffie, Edward F. Shadow Prices and Substitution in Trade Distorted Economies. *J. Public Econ.*, November 1987, *34*(2), pp. 211–42.

Cairncross, Alec. The Neoclassical Resurgence in Development Economics: Its Strength and Limitations: Comment. *Meier, G. M., ed.*, 1987, pp. 137–43.

Calvo, Guillermo A. On the Costs of Temporary Liberalization/Stabilization Experiments. *Connolly, M. and González-Vega, C., eds.*, 1987, pp. 3–17.

Campbell, Burnham O. Foreign Trade Regimes and Economic Growth in Developing Countries: Comment. *Giersch, H., ed.*, 1987, pp. 236–49. **[G: LDCs]**

Cassing, James H.; Wells, Jerome C. and Zamalloa, Edgar L. On Resource Booms and Busts: Some Aspects of the Dutch Disease in Six Developing Economies. *Eastern Econ. J.*, October-December 1987, *13*(4), pp. 373–87. **[G: LDCs]**

Cimoli, Mario. Modelli "Nord–Sud": Una valutazione critica. (With English summary.) *Stud. Econ.*, 1987, *42*(31), pp. 67–97.

Corden, W. Max. Liberal and Illiberal Development Policy: Comment. *Meier, G. M., ed.*, 1987, pp. 84–91.

Deger, Saadet and Sen, S. Defence Industrialisation, Technology Transfer and Choice of Tech-

niques in LDCs. *Borner, S. and Taylor, A., eds.*, 1987, pp. 233–54. **[G: LDCs]**

Díaz-Alejandro, Carlos F. and Helleiner, Gerald K. Developing Countries and Reform of the World Trading System. *Salvatore, D., ed.*, 1987, pp. 505–25. **[G: LDCs]**

Dung, Tran Huu. Commodity versus Capital Transfers. *J. Econ. Devel.*, December 1987, *12*(2), pp. 189–95.

Dutt, Amitava Krishna. As relações de troca e o desenvolvimento desigual: Resultados de um modelo de comércio Norte-Sul. (With English summary.) *Pesquisa Planejamento Econ.*, December 1987, *17*(3), pp. 533–59.

Edwards, Sebastian and van Wijnbergen, Sweder. On the Appropriate Timing and Speed of Economic Liberalization in Developing Countries. *Connolly, M. and González-Vega, C., eds.*, 1987, pp. 71–92.

Feder, Gershon and Uy, Lily V. Policy Implications of International Creditworthiness in Trade-Gap and Savings-Gap Economies. *Salvatore, D., ed.*, 1987, pp. 526–50. **[G: LDCs]**

Findlay, Ronald. Liberal and Illiberal Development Policy: Comment. *Meier, G. M., ed.*, 1987, pp. 92–103.

Greenaway, David and Milner, Chris. 'True Protection' Concepts and Their Role in Evaluating Trade Policies in LDCs. *J. Devel. Stud.*, January 1987, *23*(2), pp. 200–219. **[G: Selected LDCs]**

Greenaway, David and Milner, Chris. Trade Theory and the Less Developed Countries. *Gemmell, N., ed.*, 1987, pp. 11–55. **[G: LDCs]**

Greenaway, David and Sapsford, David. Further Econometric Analysis of the Relationship between Fiscal Dependence on Trade Taxes and Economic Development [A Statistical Analysis of Fiscal Dependence on Trade Taxes and Economic Development]. *Public Finance*, 1987, *42*(2), pp. 309–19.

Haberler, Gottfried. Liberal and Illiberal Development Policy. *Meier, G. M., ed.*, 1987, pp. 51–83.

Heath, Edward. International Keynesianism: The Problem of the North–South Divide: Discussion. *Thirlwall, A. P., ed.*, 1987, pp. 133–35.

Heath, Edward. International Keynesianism: The Problem of the North–South Divide. *Thirlwall, A. P., ed.*, 1987, pp. 118–29.

Hindley, Brian. International Trade in Services and Its Relevance for Economic Development: Comment. *Giarini, O., ed.*, 1987, pp. 35–39.

Hitiris, T. and Weekes, A. J. Fiscal Dependence on Trade Taxes and Economic Development: An Econometric Investigation. *Public Finance*, 1987, *42*(2), pp. 297–308.

Holzman, Franklyn D. Some Theories of the Hard Currency Shortages of Centrally Planned Economies. *Holzman, F. D.*, 1987, *1979*, pp. 33–57. **[G: CMEA]**

Houston, David and Paus, Eva. The Theory of Unequal Exchange: An Indictment. *Rev. Radi-*

cal Polit. Econ., Spring 1987, *19*(1), pp. 90–97.

James, Jeffrey. Positional Goods, Conspicuous Consumption and the International Demonstration Effect Reconsidered. *World Devel.*, April 1987, *15*(4), pp. 449–62.

Jensen, Richard and Thursby, Marie C. A Decision Theoretic Model of Innovation, Technology Transfer, and Trade. *Rev. Econ. Stud.*, October 1987, *54*(4), pp. 631–47.

Katz, Jorge M. Domestic Technological Innovations and Dynamic Comparative Advantages: Further Reflections on a Comparative Case Study Programme. *Dunning, J. H. and Usui, M., eds.*, 1987, pp. 135–55.   [G: LDCs]

Khan, Mohsin S. and Zahler, Roberto. The Liberalization of Trade and Capital Flows in Developing Countries: Some Theoretical and Empirical Issues. *Connolly, M. and González-Vega, C., eds.*, 1987, pp. 45–67.

Khang, Chulsoon. Export-led Economic Growth: The Case of Technology Transfer. *Econ. Stud. Quart.*, June 1987, *38*(2), pp. 131–47.
          [G: S. Korea; Hong Kong; Singapore; Taiwan]

Kierzkowski, Henryk. International Trade in Services and Its Relevance for Economic Development: Comment. *Giarini, O., ed.*, 1987, pp. 39–43.

Kirkpatrick, Colin. Trade Policy and Industrialization in LDCs. *Gemmell, N., ed.*, 1987, pp. 56–89.   [G: LDCs]

Kolisevski, Mitre. GSTP: An Instrument for the Intensification of ECDC. *Agrawal, G. R., et al. (II)*, 1987, pp. 36–49.

Krueger, Anne O. The Stake of the Developing Countries in the International Economy. *Rodriguez, R. M., ed.*, 1987, pp. 63–75.

Krugman, Paul R. The Narrow Moving Band, the Dutch Disease, and the Competitive Consequences of Mrs. Thatcher. *J. Devel. Econ.*, October 1987, *27*(1–2), pp. 41–55.
          [G: U.K.]

Krugman, Paul R. The Narrow Moving Band, the Dutch Disease, and the Competitive Consequences of Mrs. Thatcher: Notes on Trade in the Presence of Dynamic Scale Economies. *[Diaz-Alejandro, C. F.]*, 1987, pp. 41–55.   [G: U.K.]

Lahiri, Sajal and Batra, Raveendra N. Imported Technologies, North–South Dialogue and the Optimal Subsidy Policy. *Indian Econ. J.*, Jan.-Mar. 1987, *34*(3), pp. 81–85.

Lal, Deepak and Rajapatirana, Sarath. Foreign Trade Regimes and Economic Growth in Developing Countries. *Giersch, H., ed.*, 1987, pp. 204–35.   [G: LDCs]

Lawrence, Colin and Spiller, Pablo T. International Technological Diffusion, Product Differentiation and Economies of Scale. *Dunning, J. H. and Usui, M., eds.*, 1987, pp. 95–115.
          [G: LDCs]

Leamer, Edward E. Paths of Development in the Three-Factor, *n*-Good General Equilibrium Model. *J. Polit. Econ.*, October 1987, *95*(5), pp. 961–99.   [G: Selected Countries]

Little, Ian M. D. International Keynesianism: The Problem of the North–South Divide: Discussion. *Thirlwall, A. P., ed.*, 1987, pp. 130–33.

Lyons, Bruce. International Trade and Technology Policy. *Dasgupta, P. and Stoneman, P., eds.*, 1987, pp. 169–205.

Mainwaring, Lynn. Foreign Trade in the Kaleckian Perspective Plan. *Econ. Planning*, 1987, *21*(2–3), pp. 101–14.

Mantel, Rolf R. and Martirena-Mantel, Ana María. Liberalizacion del crecimiento y equidad en la economia abierta. (Growth Liberalization and Equity in the Open Economy. With English summary.) *Económica (La Plata)*, July-Dec. 1987, *33*(2), pp. 245–68.
          [G: Latin America]

McLeod, Darryl L. and Salvatore, Dominick. The Employment Effects of Barriers to North–South Trade with and without Indexed Debt Service Payments. *Salvatore, D., ed.*, 1987, pp. 551–70.   [G: Global]

Mirakhor, Abbas and Montiel, Peter J. Import Intensity of Output Growth in Developing Countries, 1970–85. *International Monetary Fund Research Department.*, 1987, pp. 59–97.
          [G: LDCs]

Modwel, S. K. GSTP: Some Issues in Implementation. *Agrawal, G. R., et al. (II)*, 1987, pp. 49–65.   [G: LDCs]

Myint, Hla. The Neoclassical Resurgence in Development Economics: Its Strength and Limitations. *Meier, G. M., ed.*, 1987, pp. 107–36.

Norman, Victor D. and Strandenes, Siri P. International Trade in Services and Its Relevance for Economic Development: Comment. *Giarini, O., ed.*, 1987, pp. 44–49.

Oyejide, T. Ademola. Food Policy and the Choice of Trade Regime. *Mellor, J. W.; Delgado, C. L. and Blackie, M. J., eds.*, 1987, pp. 257–73.   [G: Africa]

Raipuria, K. M. South–South Trade Cooperation: The Conceptual Basis. *Agrawal, G. R., et al. (II)*, 1987, pp. 23–35.   [G: LDCs]

Ranis, Gustav. The Neoclassical Resurgence in Development Economics: Its Strength and Limitations: Comment. *Meier, G. M., ed.*, 1987, pp. 144–50.

Richards, Donald G. An Empirical Examination of the Dependency Approach to Underdevelopment. *Singapore Econ. Rev.*, April 1987, *32*(1), pp. 1–23.   [G: LDCs]

Rojo, Luis A. Interdependence and Development. *Urquidi, V. L., ed.*, 1987, pp. 139–52.

Rotemberg, Julio J. Export Promotion as a Development Strategy. *J. Devel. Econ.*, August 1987, *26*(2), pp. 343–55.

Sapir, André. International Trade in Services and Its Relevance for Economic Development: Comment. *Giarini, O., ed.*, 1987, pp. 49–54.

Srinivasan, T. N. International Trade of Developing Countries in the 1980s: Problems and Prospects. *Dunning, J. H. and Usui, M., eds.*, 1987, pp. 247–66.   [G: LDCs]

Tshibaka, Tshikala B. Food Policy and the Choice of Trade Regime: Commentary. *Mellor, J. W.;*

Delgado, C. L. and Blackie, M. J., eds., 1987, pp. 276–77. **[G: Africa]**

Waelbroeck, Jean. International Trade in Services and Its Relevance for Economic Development: Comment. *Giarini, O., ed.*, 1987, pp. 54–57.

Young, Leslie. Intermediate Goods and the Formation of Duty-Free Zones. *J. Devel. Econ.*, April 1987, *25*(2), pp. 369–84. **[G: LDCs]**

Zakariya, Hasan S. The Third World Perspective on Petroleum: The Travails of the 'Haves' and the Plight of the 'Have-Nots.' *Rees, J. and Odell, P., eds.*, 1987, pp. 107–28. **[G: LDCs]**

420 TRADE RELATIONS; COMMERCIAL POLICY; INTERNATIONAL ECONOMIC INTEGRATION

4200 General

Corden, W. Max. Why Trade Is Not Free: Is There a Clash between Theory and Practice? *Giersch, H., ed.*, 1987, pp. 1–19.

Hämäläinen, Timo. International Outlook: Recovery in the Medium Term. *Vartia, P., et al.*, 1987, pp. 49–59. **[G: OECD]**

Johnson, Omotunde E. G. Trade Tax and Exchange Rate Coordination in the Context of Border Trading: A Theoretical Analysis. *Int. Monet. Fund Staff Pap.*, September 1987, *34*(3), pp. 548–64. **[G: Africa]**

Olson, Mancur. Economic Nationalism and Economic Progress. *World Econ.*, September 1987, *10*(3), pp. 241–64. **[G: OECD]**

Williamson, John. Keynes and the International Economic Order. *Williamson, J.*, 1987, *1983*, pp. 37–59.

421 Trade Relations

4210 Trade Relations

Abd-el-Rahman, K. S. Hypothèses concernant le rôle des avantages comparatifs des pays et des avantages spécifiques des firmes dans l'explication des échanges croisés des produits similaires. (With English summary.) *Revue Écon. Polit.*, Mar.-Apr. 1987, *97*(2), pp. 165–92. **[G: France]**

Abe, Kiyoshi. Trade Flows among the United States and Asian Countries: Interdependence and Inter- vs. Intra-industry Trade. *Dutta, M., ed. (II)*, 1987, pp. 3–27. **[G: U.S.; Asia]**

Adkins, Roger L. Competitive Decline: Views of Two Disciplines. *J. Econ. Issues*, June 1987, *21*(2), pp. 869–76. **[G: U.S.]**

Agrawal, Govind R. Economic Dimensions of South Asian Regional Cooperation. *Agrawal, G. R., et al. (II)*, 1987, pp. 154–78. **[G: S. Asia]**

Ahmed, Shaghil. Government Spending, the Balance of Trade and the Terms of Trade in British History. *J. Monet. Econ.*, September 1987, *20*(2), pp. 195–220. **[G: U.K.]**

Ahuja, Kanta and Pahariya, N. C. Changes in Determinants and Structure of India's Foreign Trade. *Indian Econ. J.*, Jan.-Mar. 1987, *34*(3), pp. 13–33. **[G: India]**

Ajanant, Juanjai. Trade Patterns and Trends of Thailand. *Bradford, C. I., Jr. and Branson, W. H., eds.*, 1987, pp. 467–84. **[G: Thailand]**

Alburo, Florian A. Manufactured Exports and Industrialization: Trade Patterns and Trends of the Philippines. *Bradford, C. I., Jr. and Branson, W. H., eds.*, 1987, pp. 485–513. **[G: Philippines]**

Ali, Ifzal. India's Manufactured Exports: An Analysis of Supply Factors. *Devel. Econ.*, June 1987, *25*(2), pp. 152–70. **[G: India]**

Allen, D. E.; Carse, S. and Fujio, K. Trade Financing Procedures in Britain and Japan. *Appl. Econ.*, June 1987, *19*(6), pp. 711–28. **[G: U.K.; Japan]**

Amine, Lyn S. Toward a Conceptualization of Export Trading Companies in World Markets. *Cavusgil, S. T., ed.*, 1987, pp. 199–238. **[G: Japan; S. Korea; Brazil; U.S.]**

Anderson, Kym and Tyers, Rodney. Economic Growth and Market Liberalization in China: Implications for Agricultural Trade. *Devel. Econ.*, June 1987, *25*(2), pp. 124–51. **[G: China]**

Andersson, Jan Otto. Integration and Intra-industry Trade: A Study of the Nordic Countries Using LISREL-Estimates. *Andersson, J. O., ed.*, 1987, pp. 131–47. **[G: N. Europe]**

Anderton, R. and Dunnett, A. Modelling the Behaviour of Export Volumes of Manufacturers: An Evaluation of the Performance of Different Measures of International Competitiveness. *Nat. Inst. Econ. Rev.*, August 1987, (121), pp. 46–52. **[G: U.K.]**

Antille, Gabrielle and Laplanche, Bernadette. Impact of Constraints in Energy Imports and Energy Production of Final Domestic Demand. *Tchijov, I. and Tomaszewicz, L., eds.*, 1987, pp. 169–83. **[G: Switzerland]**

Arestis, Philip and Driver, Ciaran. The Effects of Income Distribution on Consumer Imports. *J. Macroecon.*, Winter 1987, *9*(1), pp. 83–94. **[G: U.K.]**

Ariff, Mohamed, et al. Economic Relations between ASEAN and Australia. *Econ. Rec.*, March 1987, *63*(180), pp. 1–9. **[G: Australia; ASEAN]**

Arize, Augustine. The Elasticities and Structural Stability of Import Demand Function for Nigeria (1960–1977). *Soc. Econ. Stud.*, June 1987, *36*(2), pp. 171–86. **[G: Nigeria]**

Arize, Augustine. The Supply and Demand for Imports and Exports in a Simultaneous Model. *Appl. Econ.*, September 1987, *19*(9), pp. 1233–47. **[G: Africa]**

Arize, Augustine and Afifi, Rasoul. An Econometric Examination of Import Demand Function in Thirty Developing Countries. *J. Post Keynesian Econ.*, Summer 1987, *9*(4), pp. 604–16. **[G: LDCs]**

Arndt, H. W. and Dorrance, G. The J-Curve. *Australian Econ. Rev.*, First Quarter 1987, (77), pp. 9–19. **[G: Australia]**

Arriola, Salvador. Some Ideas on Financial and Monetary Co-operation among Developing

Countries. *Dell, S., ed., Pt. 2*, 1987, pp. 639–64. **[G: LDCs]**

Artus, Patrick. Les exportations industrielles sont-elles déterminées par l'offre ou par la demande. (With English summary.) *Revue Écon.*, September 1987, *38*(5), pp. 995–1015.
[G: France]

Asai, Motofumi. The ASEAN Success Story: Social, Economic, and Political Dimensions: Japan. *Martin, L. G., ed.*, 1987, pp. 192–99.
[G: Japan; ASEAN]

Ascher, Bernard and Whichard, Obie G. Improving Services Trade Data. *Giarini, O., ed.*, 1987, pp. 255–81. **[G: U.S.]**

Aschheim, Joseph; Bailey, Martin J. and Tavlas, George S. Dollar Variability, the New Protectionism, Trade and Financial Performance. *Salvatore, D., ed.*, 1987, pp. 424–49.
[G: OECD]

Åström, Sven-Erik. Northeastern Europe's Timber Trade between the Napoleonic and Crimean Wars: A Preliminary Survey. *Scand. Econ. Hist. Rev.*, 1987, *35*(2), pp. 170–77.
[G: Finland; U.S.S.R.]

Avramovic, Dragoslav. Commodity Problem: What Next? *World Devel.*, May 1987, *15*(5), pp. 645–55. **[G: LDCs]**

Axelrod, Robert. How Should the United States Respond to Other Countries' Trade Policies? Comment. *Stern, R. M., ed.*, 1987, pp. 283–86. **[G: U.S.]**

Babula, Ronald A. An Armington Model of U.S. Cotton Exports. *J. Agr. Econ. Res.*, Fall 1987, *39*(4), pp. 12–22. **[G: U.S.]**

Bach, Christopher L. U.S. International Transactions, Fourth Quarter and Year 1986. *Surv. Curr. Bus.*, March 1987, *67*(3), pp. 32–62.
[G: U.S.]

Baeck, Louis. O desequilíbrio da economia internacional dos anos 80. (With English summary.) *Pesquisa Planejamento Econ.*, April 1987, *17*(1), pp. 221–49. **[G: U.S.; Japan; W. Europe]**

Baer, Werner and Birch, Melissa. The International Economic Relations of a Small Country: The Case of Paraguay. *Econ. Develop. Cult. Change*, April 1987, *35*(3), pp. 601–27.
[G: Paraguay; Selected Countries]

Bailey, Martin J.; Tavlas, George S. and Ulan, Michael. The Impact of Exchange-Rate Volatility on Export Growth: Some Theoretical Considerations and Empirical Results. *J. Policy Modeling*, Spring 1987, *9*(1), pp. 225–43.
[G: OECD]

Bajo, Oscar. Organización industrial y comportamiento exportador de los sectores industriales españoles ante la C.E.E. (With English summary.) *Invest. Econ.*, September 1987, *11*(3), pp. 497–520. **[G: EEC; Spain]**

Baker, C. B. Changes in Financial Markets and Their Effects on Agriculture. *Fed. Res. Bank St. Louis Rev.*, October 1987, *69*(8), pp. 13–19. **[G: U.S.]**

Balassa, Bela. Japan's Trade Policies. *Giersch, H., ed.*, 1987, pp. 111–70. **[G: Japan]**

Balassa, Bela. The Importance of Trade for Devel-

oping Countries. *Banca Naz. Lavoro Quart. Rev.*, December 1987, (163), pp. 437–69.
[G: LDCs]

Balassa, Bela. Trends in International Trade in Manufactured Goods and Structural Change in the Industrial Countries. *Pasinetti, L. and Lloyd, P., eds.*, 1987, pp. 123–47.
[G: Global]

Balassa, Bela and Bauwens, Luc. Intra-industry Specialisation in a Multi-country and Multi-industry Framework. *Econ. J.*, December 1987, *97*(388), pp. 923–39. **[G: Global]**

Balassa, Bela and Michalopoulos, Constantine. The Extent and the Cost of Protection in Developed–Developing-Country Trade. *Salvatore, D., ed.*, 1987, pp. 482–504. **[G: LDCs; MDCs]**

Baldwin, Robert E. and Richardson, J. David. Recent U.S. Trade Policy and Its Global Implications. *Bradford, C. I., Jr. and Branson, W. H., eds.*, 1987, pp. 121–55. **[G: Global; U.S.]**

Bale, Harvey E., Jr. The Consumption Tax: A Better Alternative? The International Trade Issues. *Walker, C. E. and Bloomfield, M. A., eds.*, 1987, pp. 213–21. **[G: U.S.]**

Balisacan, Arsenio M.; Lee, Chung H. and Roumasset, James A. National Food Policies of the Asia-Pacific Region and Their International Implications. *Dutta, M., ed. (I)*, 1987, pp. 221–41. **[G: Asia-Pacific]**

Balkay, Bálint. The Third World and the CMEA Group in the World Economy of Raw and Basic Materials. *World Devel.*, May 1987, *15*(5), pp. 685–700. **[G: CMEA; LDCs]**

Baranson, Jack. Trade Liberalization and the New Generation of Manufacturing Technologies: Implications for Canadian Industry in North American Markets. *Tremblay, R., ed.*, 1987, pp. 407–17. **[G: Canada; U.S.]**

Barjon, Michel. Integrating Economic Strategy with Science and Technology. *Hieronymi, O., ed.*, 1987, pp. 189–92.

Barker, Terry. The Cambridge Multisectoral Dynamic Model of the British Economy: Export and Import Prices. *Barker, T. and Peterson, W., eds.*, 1987, pp. 311–39. **[G: U.K.]**

Barker, Terry. The Cambridge Multisectoral Dynamic Model of the British Economy: Exports and Imports. *Barker, T. and Peterson, W., eds.*, 1987, pp. 201–45. **[G: U.K.]**

Bartholomew, R. B. and Densley, D. R. J. Data Needs, Output and Options: Smallholder Component—PNG Export Tree Crop Study. *Barker, P.; Bodman, P. and Remenyl, J., eds.*, 1987, pp. 55–63. **[G: Papua New Guinea]**

Barve, Arvind. Financial and Monetary Aspects of Trade Promotion in the Context of Co-operation among Developing Countries, with Special Reference to Africa. *Dell, S., ed., Pt. 2*, 1987, pp. 611–38. **[G: Africa; LDCs]**

Beals, Ralph E. Trade Patterns and Trends of Indonesia. *Bradford, C. I., Jr. and Branson, W. H., eds.*, 1987, pp. 515–45.
[G: Indonesia]

Becker, David G. "Bonanza Development" and the "New Bourgeoisie": Peru under Military

Rule. *Becker, D. G., et al.*, 1987, pp. 63–105.
[G: Peru]

Behrman, Jere R. Commodity Price Instability and Economic Goal Attainment in Developing Countries. *World Devel.*, May 1987, *15*(5), pp. 559–73. [G: Chile; Zambia; Brazil; Ivory Coast; El Salvador]

Beladi, Hamid and Biswas, Basudeb. The Impact of Effective Exchange Rates and Domestic Absorption on Sectoral Exports: An Application to Indian Tea Exports. *Indian Econ. J.*, Jan.-Mar. 1987, *34*(3), pp. 73–80. [G: India]

Bell, Trevor. International Competition and Industrial Decentralization in South Africa. *World Devel.*, Oct./Nov. 1987, *15*(10/11), pp. 1291–1307. [G: S. Africa]

Benvignati, Anita M. Domestic Profit Advantages of Multinational Firms. *J. Bus.*, July 1987, *60*(3), pp. 449–61. [G: U.S.]

Berg, Hartmut. Internationaler Wettbewerb— Nationale Wettbewerbspolitik: Zielkonflikte unvermeidbar! (International Competitiveness—National Competition Policy: Conflicts Unavoidable! With English summary.) *Lenel, H. O., et al., eds.*, 1987, pp. 131–42.
[G: W. Germany]

Bergsten, C. Fred. The U.S.-Japan Economic Problem: Next Steps. *Patrick, H. T. and Tachi, R., eds.*, 1987, pp. 9–17. [G: U.S.; Japan]

Bergstrand, Jeffrey H. The U.S. Trade Deficit: A Perspective from Selected Bilateral Trade Models. *New Eng. Econ. Rev.*, May/June 1987, pp. 19–31. [G: U.S.]

Bertrand, Jean-Pierre. L'impact des variables "macroéconomiques" sur les marchés internationaux des grains. With English summary.) *Écon. Soc.*, April 1987, *21*(4), pp. 103–26.
[G: U.S.; Brazil]

Bessler, David A. and Babula, Ronald A. Forecasting Wheat Exports: Do Exchange Rates Matter? *J. Bus. Econ. Statist.*, July 1987, *5*(3), pp. 397–406. [G: U.S.]

Bethkenhagen, Jochen. Economic and Political Relations between the Two Germanies. *Marer, P. and van Veen, P., eds.*, 1987, pp. 91–98.
[G: E. Germany; W. Germany]

Bevan, D. L.; Collier, P. and Gunning, J. W. Consequences of a Commodity Boom in a Controlled Economy: Accumulation and Redistribution in Kenya 1975–83. *World Bank Econ. Rev.*, May 1987, *1*(3), pp. 489–513.
[G: Kenya]

Bhagwati, Jagdish N. International Trade in Services and Its Relevance for Economic Development. *Giarini, O., ed.*, 1987, pp. 3–34.

Bhagwati, Jagdish N. Trade in Services and the Multilateral Trade Negotiations. *World Bank Econ. Rev.*, September 1987, *1*(4), pp. 549–69. [G: LDCs; OECD]

Bhagwati, Jagdish N. and Irwin, Douglas A. The Return of the Reciprocitarians—U.S. Trade Policy Today. *World Econ.*, June 1987, *10*(2), pp. 109–30. [G: U.S.]

Bhagwati, Jagdish N.; Krueger, Anne O. and Snape, Richard H. A Symposium Issue on the Multilateral Trade Negotiations and Develop-

ing-Country Interests: Introduction. *World Bank Econ. Rev.*, September 1987, *1*(4), pp. 539–47. [G: LDCs]

Bhatt, P. R. India's Trade Relations with Japan: A Quantitative Analysis. *Margin*, July-Sept. 1987, *19*(4), pp. 29–40. [G: Japan; India]

Bikker, Jacob A. An International Trade Flow Model with Substitution: An Extension of the Gravity Model. *Kyklos*, 1987, *40*(3), pp. 315–37. [G: Global]

Bilkey, Warren J. Toward a Theory of the Export Marketing Mix. *Cavusgil, S. T., ed.*, 1987, pp. 157–76.

Binkley, James K. Trade Instability and Distance between Trading Countries. *Oxford Bull. Econ. Statist.*, November 1987, *49*(4), pp. 401–15. [G: U.S.]

Blackaby, Frank and Ohlson, Thomas. Military Expenditure and the Arms Trade: Problems of the Data. *Schmidt, C., ed.*, 1987, pp. 3–24. [G: Global]

Blake, Rebecca P. The Evolution of International Trade in Alabama. *Spencer, S. I., ed.*, 1987, pp. 46–53. [G: U.S.]

Blanc, Gérard. The Grain Traders: Masters of the Intelligence Game. *Dedijer, S. and Jéquier, N., eds.*, 1987, pp. 139–57.

Blank, Steven C. Evaluating International Price Relationships Using Causal Models. *Europ. Rev. Agr. Econ.*, 1987, *14*(3), pp. 305–23.
[G: OECD]

Bond, Marian E. An Econometric Study of Primary Commodity Exports from Developing Country Regions to the World. *Int. Monet. Fund Staff Pap.*, June 1987, *34*(2), pp. 191–227. [G: Global]

Bond, Marian E. and Milne, Elizabeth. Export Diversification in Developing Countries: Recent Trends and Policy Impact. *International Monetary Fund Research Department.*, 1987, pp. 98–144. [G: LDCs]

Bonnici, Josef. Imports in Keynesian Models. *Econ. Rec.*, December 1987, *63*(183), pp. 352–54.

Boon, Gerard K. North–South Interdependence: An Economic–Physical Interpretation. *De Economist*, 1987, *135*(1), pp. 66–93.
[G: Global]

ter Borg, F. A. East–West Trade and the Role of the Western Government. *Visser, H. and Schoor, E., eds.*, 1987, pp. 213–25.
[G: OECD; CMEA]

Bosworth, Barry P. The Persistence of the U.S. Trade Deficit: Comments. *Brookings Pap. Econ. Act.*, 1987, (1), pp. 44–47. [G: U.S.]

Boucher, Carlston B. and Siebeck, Wolfgang E. UNCTAD VII: New Spirit in North–South Relations? *Finance Develop.*, December 1987, *24*(4), pp. 14–16. [G: Global]

Bowen, Harry P. Is the Japan Problem Over? Discussion. *Sato, R. and Wachtel, P., eds.*, 1987, pp. 40–44. [G: U.S.; Japan]

Bowen, Harry P.; Leamer, Edward E. and Sveikauskas, Leo. Multicountry, Multifactor Tests of the Factor Abundance Theory. *Amer. Econ.*

Rev., December 1987, 77(5), pp. 791–809.
[G: Global]

Boylan, T. A. and Cuddy, M. P. Elasticities of Import Demand and Economic Development: The Irish Experience. *J. Devel. Econ.*, August 1987, 26(2), pp. 301–09. [G: Ireland]

van Brabant, Jozef M. Socialist and World Market Prices: An Ingrowth? *J. Compar. Econ.*, March 1987, 11(1), pp. 21–39. [G: Hungary]

Bradford, Colin I., Jr. NICs and the Next-Tier NICs as Transitional Economies. *Bradford, C. I., Jr. and Branson, W. H., eds.*, 1987, pp. 173–204. [G: Asia; LDCs]

Bradford, Colin I., Jr. Trade and Structural Change: NICs and Next Tier NICs as Transitional Economies. *World Devel.*, March 1987, 15(3), pp. 299–316. [G: LDCs]

Bradford, Colin I., Jr. and Branson, William H. Patterns of Trade and Structural Change. *Bradford, C. I., Jr. and Branson, W. H., eds.*, 1987, pp. 3–24. [G: Global]

Brakman, Steven and Jepma, Catrinus J. The Impact of the Composition of Exports on Export Performance. *De Economist*, 1987, 135(2), pp. 163–81.

Brakman, Steven and Joosten, Geert. On a Two Regime Model of the Dutch Export Market. *De Economist*, 1987, 135(3), pp. 279–97. [G: Netherlands]

Brandt, Jon A., et al. Live Hog and Pork Imports: Past and Projected Consequences for the U.S. Pork Sector. *Southern J. Agr. Econ.*, December 1987, 19(2), pp. 133–44. [G: U.S.]

Branson, William H. Macroeconomics and Protection: Comment. *Stern, R. M., ed.*, 1987, pp. 131–36. [G: OECD]

Branson, William H. The Changing Structure of U.S. Trade: Implications for Research and Policy. *Salvatore, D., ed.*, 1987, pp. 153–63. [G: U.S.]

Branson, William H. Trade and Structural Interdependence between the United States and the Newly Industrializing Countries. *Bradford, C. I., Jr. and Branson, W. H., eds.*, 1987, pp. 27–60. [G: Asia; U.S.]

Brilmayer, Lea. The Extraterritorial Application of American Law: A Methodological and Constitutional Appraisal. *Law Contemp. Probl.*, Summer 1987, 50(3), pp. 11–38. [G: U.S.]

Brinkman, George L. The Competitive Position of Canadian Agriculture. *Can. J. Agr. Econ.*, July 1987, 35(2), pp. 263–88. [G: Canada]

Brittan, Samuel. The Role of Domestic U.S. Economy and Financial Policy in the World Economy: Cures That Could Be Worse Than the Disease. *Visser, H. and Schoor, E., eds.*, 1987, pp. 125–37. [G: U.S.; Global]

Browder, John O. Brazil's Export Promotion Policy (1980–1984): Impacts on the Amazon's Industrial Wood Sector. *J. Devel. Areas*, April 1987, 21(3), pp. 285–304. [G: Brazil]

Burgstaller, André. Industrialization, Deindustrialization, and North–South Trade. *Amer. Econ. Rev.*, December 1987, 77(5), pp. 1017–18.

Burton, F. N. and Saelens, F. H. Trade Barriers

and Japanese Foreign Direct Investment in the Colour Television Industry. *Managerial Dec. Econ.*, December 1987, 8(4), pp. 285–93. [G: Japan]

Byerlee, Derek. The Political Economy of Third World Food Imports: The Case of Wheat. *Econ. Develop. Cult. Change*, January 1987, 35(2), pp. 307–28. [G: LDCs]

Cable, Vincent. The Impact of EEC Trade Policies on Developing Countries. *Giersch, H., ed.*, 1987, pp. 294–326. [G: EEC; LDCs]

Campbell, Burnham O. Foreign Trade Regimes and Economic Growth in Developing Countries: Comment. *Giersch, H., ed.*, 1987, pp. 236–49. [G: LDCs]

Campbell, John Y. Macroeconomic Lessons from Britain: A Review Essay. *J. Monet. Econ.*, March 1987, 19(2), pp. 315–24. [G: U.K.]

Carrada-Bravo, Francisco. International Trade, Investment, Regional Security, and the Prospects of the Mexico–U.S. Relations. *Tremblay, R., ed.*, 1987, pp. 531–48. [G: Mexico; U.S.]

Carrington, Selwyn H. H. The American Revolution and the British West Indies' Economy. *Solow, B. L. and Engerman, S. L., eds.*, 1987, pp. 135–61. [G: Caribbean; U.K.]

Casas, F. R. and Choi, Eun Kwan. Trade Imbalance, the Factor Proportions Theory and the Resource Content of International Trade. *Rivista Int. Sci. Econ. Com.*, March 1987, 34(3), pp. 213–30. [G: U.S.]

Chard, John S. European Competition Policy and the Pricing of Cars: An Economic Analysis of the Motor Vehicle Block Exemption Regulation. *Macmillen, M.; Mayes, D. G. and van Veen, P., eds.*, 1987, pp. 152–93. [G: EEC]

Chatterjee, Pranab Kumar. Relative Economic Levels, Characters and Interdependence: A Study of Selected Countries in Asia and the United States. *Dutta, M., ed. (II)*, 1987, pp. 105–32. [G: U.S.; Asia]

Chatterjee, Srikanta and Ray, Ranjan. Net Import Content of Consumption in Rural and Urban India. *Indian Econ. J.*, Jan.-Mar. 1987, 34(3), pp. 109–15. [G: India]

Chee, Peng Lim. Changes in the Malaysian Economy and Trade Trends and Prospects. *Bradford, C. I., Jr. and Branson, W. H., eds.*, 1987, pp. 435–66. [G: Malaysia]

Chen, Edward K. Y. Foreign Trade and Economic Growth in Hong Kong: Experience and Prospects. *Bradford, C. I., Jr. and Branson, W. H., eds.*, 1987, pp. 333–78. [G: Hong Kong]

Cheng, Bifan. The ASEAN Success Story: Social, Economic, and Political Dimensions: China. *Martin, L. G., ed.*, 1987, pp. 189–91. [G: ASEAN; China]

Chia, Siow-Yue. Industrial Restructuring in a Newly Industrialising Country: The Case of Singapore. *Pasinetti, L. and Lloyd, P., eds.*, 1987, pp. 213–32. [G: Singapore]

Chitala, Derrick. The Political Economy of the SADCC and Imperialism's Response. *Amin, S.; Chitala, D. and Mandaza, I., eds.*, 1987, pp. 13–36. [G: Southern Africa; S. Africa]

Chmura, Christine. The Effect of Exchange Rate Variation on U.S. Textile and Apparel Imports. *Fed. Res. Bank Richmond Econ. Rev.*, May/June 1987, *73*(3), pp. 17–23. [G: U.S.]

Chorley, Patrick. The Cloth Exports of Flanders and Northern France during the Thirteenth Century: A Luxury Trade? *Econ. Hist. Rev.*, *2nd Ser.*, August 1987, *40*(3), pp. 349–79. [G: France; Flanders]

Chow, Peter C. Y. Causality between Export Growth and Industrial Development: Empirical Evidence from the NICs. *J. Devel. Econ.*, June 1987, *26*(1), pp. 55–63. [G: LDCs]

Chung, Ming Wong. Trends and Patterns of Singapore's Trade in Manufactures. *Bradford, C. I., Jr. and Branson, W. H., eds.*, 1987, pp. 379–432. [G: Singapore]

Clark, Don P. Regulation of International Trade: The United States' Generalized System of Preferences Scheme [The Kennedy Round: Evidence on the Regulation of International Trade in the United States]. *Weltwirtsch. Arch.*, 1987, *123*(4), pp. 697–704. [G: U.S.]

Coffin, H. Garth. The Internationalization of Canadian Agriculture. *Can. J. Agr. Econ.*, December 1987, *35*(4), pp. 691–707. [G: Canada]

Collins, Susan M. Korean Growth Policy: Comment. *Brookings Pap. Econ. Act.*, 1987, (2), pp. 445–50. [G: S. Korea]

Conti, Vittorio and Silvani, Marco. Foreign Trade and Industrial Structure in Italy: An Input–Output Multiplier Analysis. *Saunders, C. T., ed.*, 1987, pp. 183–203. [G: Italy]

Conway, Roger K. An Examination of the 'Schuh Controversy': Is the Demand for U.S. Agricultural Exports Elastic? *Appl. Econ.*, July 1987, *19*(7), pp. 853–73. [G: U.S.]

Corbo, Vittorio. Korean Growth Policy: Comment. *Brookings Pap. Econ. Act.*, 1987, (2), pp. 450–52. [G: S. Korea]

Corley, T. A. B. Interactions between the British and American Patent Medicine Industries 1708–1914. *Atack, J., ed.*, 1987, pp. 111–29. [G: U.S.; U.K.]

Costa, Antonio Maria. The Need for New Multilateral Trade Negotiations: Why Is It Urgent to Complete the GATT Round Successfully? *Salvatore, D., ed.*, 1987, pp. 113–49. [G: OECD]

Côté, Agathe. The Link between the U.S. Dollar Real Exchange Rate, Real Primary Commodity Prices, and LDCs' Terms of Trade. *Rev. Econ. Statist.*, August 1987, *69*(3), pp. 547–51. [G: U.S.; LDCs]

Coughlin, Cletus C. International Trade in the United States: Past, Present, and Future: Introduction. *Spencer, S. I., ed.*, 1987, pp. 41–45. [G: U.S.]

Coughlin, Cletus C. The Evolution of International Trade in Georgia. *Spencer, S. I., ed.*, 1987, pp. 64–72. [G: U.S.]

Crum, Roy L. The Evolution of International Trade in Florida. *Spencer, S. I., ed.*, 1987, pp. 54–63. [G: U.S.]

Culem, Claudy G. Foreign Trade Behavior in a Small Open Economy (Belgium 1970–1980). *Scand. J. Econ.*, 1987, *89*(1), pp. 55–70. [G: Belgium]

Cumby, Robert E. Japanese–U.S. Current Accounts and Exchange Rates before and after the G5 Agreement: Discussion. *Sato, R. and Wachtel, P., eds.*, 1987, pp. 148–52. [G: Japan; U.S.]

Curtis, Gerald L. Trade, Yen, and Politics: Comments on the Political Implications of U.S.-Japan Economic Relations. *Patrick, H. T. and Tachi, R., eds.*, 1987, pp. 196–202. [G: U.S.; Japan]

Curzon, Gerard and Curzon, Victoria. Follies in European Trade Relations with Japan. *World Econ.*, June 1987, *10*(2), pp. 155–76. [G: EEC; Japan]

Czyzewski, Adam B.; Tomaszewicz, Andrzej and Tomaszewicz, Lucja. Intra-CMEA Trade Share Matrices: Reconstruction and Analysis for 1971–1980. *Tchijov, I. and Tomaszewicz, L., eds.*, 1987, pp. 113–18. [G: CMEA]

Darrat, Ali F. Are Exports an Engine of Growth? Another Look at the Evidence. *Appl. Econ.*, February 1987, *19*(2), pp. 277–83. [G: Hong Kong; S. Korea; Singapore; Taiwan]

De Boer, Paul M. C.; Harkema, Rins and Van Heeswijk, Brigitte J. Estimating Foreign Trade Functions: A Comment and a Correction. *J. Int. Econ.*, May 1987, *22*(3/4), pp. 369–73.

Dean, Andrew and Koromzay, Val. Current-Account Imbalances and Adjustment Mechanisms. *OECD Econ. Stud.*, Spring 1987, (8), pp. 7–33. [G: OECD]

Deardorff, Alan V. and Stern, Robert M. Current Issues in Trade Policy: An Overview. *Stern, R. M., ed.*, 1987, pp. 15–68. [G: U.S.]

Dekker, W. High-Tech and the Changing Shape of World Trade. *Visser, H. and Schoor, E., eds.*, 1987, pp. 77–86. [G: Global]

Dell, Sidney and Lawrence, Roger. The Balance of Payments Adjustment Process in Developing Countries. *Dell, S., ed., Pt. 1*, 1987, *1980*, pp. 1–154. [G: Global]

Dell, Sidney, et al. Determination of Quotas and the Relative Position of Developing Countries in the International Monetary Fund: Structural Adjustment Policies. *Dell, S., ed., Pt. 2*, 1987, pp. 541–56. [G: U.K.]

Desai, Padma. Soviet Grain and Wheat Import Demands in 1981–1985. *Desai, P.*, 1987, *1982*, pp. 175–91. [G: U.S.S.R.]

Desai, Padma. The Soviet Union and the Third World: A Faltering Partnership? *Desai, P.*, 1987, *1984*, pp. 256–73. [G: U.S.S.R.; LDCs]

Desai, Padma. The Soviet Union and Cancún. *Desai, P.*, 1987, *1982*, pp. 249–55. [G: U.S.S.R.]

Díaz-Alejandro, Carlos F. and Helleiner, Gerald K. Developing Countries and Reform of the World Trading System. *Salvatore, D., ed.*, 1987, pp. 505–25. [G: LDCs]

Dichtl, Erwin, et al. Ulkomaille suuntautuminen

vientimenestyksen edellytyksenä. (Foreign Orientation as a Precondition of Successful Export. With English summary.) *Liiketaloudellinen Aikak.*, 1987, *36*(3), pp. 260–73.
[G: Finland]

Dieckhoff, Alain. Motives, Developments and Hindrances for a European Policy towards the Arab–Israeli Conflict. *Greilsammer, I. and Weiler, J. H. H.*, eds., 1987, pp. 256–82.
[G: Israel; W. Europe]

Dilullo, Anthony J. U.S. International Transactions, Third Quarter 1987. *Surv. Curr. Bus.*, December 1987, *67*(12), pp. 20–44.
[G: U.S.]

Dixit, Avinash K. How Should the United States Respond to Other Countries' Trade Policies? *Stern, R. M.*, ed., 1987, pp. 245–82.
[G: U.S.]

Dombois, Rainer. The New International Division of Labour, Labour Market and Automobile Production: The Case of Mexico. *Tolliday, S. and Zeitlin, J.*, eds., 1987, pp. 244–57.
[G: Mexico]

Dornbusch, Rudiger and Frankel, Jeffrey A. Macroeconomics and Protection. *Stern, R. M.*, ed., 1987, pp. 77–130. **[G: OECD]**

Dornbusch, Rudiger and Park, Yung Chul. Korean Growth Policy. *Brookings Pap. Econ. Act.*, 1987, (2), pp. 389–444. **[G: S. Korea]**

Doroodian, Khosrow. The Permanent Income Theory of Demand for Imports of Finished Manufactured Goods: The Case of the United States. *Quart. J. Bus. Econ.*, Winter 1987, *26*(1), pp. 78–85. **[G: U.S.]**

Dorosh, Paul A. International Trade in Corn. *Timmer, C. P.*, ed., 1987, pp. 235–50.
[G: Indonesia]

Doz, Yves. International Industries: Fragmentation versus Globalization. *Guile, B. R. and Brooks, H.*, eds., 1987, pp. 96–118.

Drucker, Peter F. Japan's Choices. *Foreign Aff.*, Summer 1987, *65*(5), pp. 923–41. **[G: Japan]**

Duchêne, François. Israel in the Eyes of Europeans: A Speculative Essay. *Greilsammer, I. and Weiler, J. H. H.*, eds., 1987, pp. 11–32.
[G: Israel; W. Europe]

Dudley, Leonard. Explaining Forecasting Bias: The Case of Real Exchange Rate Variance. *Appl. Econ.*, September 1987, *19*(9), pp. 1249–60. **[G: OECD]**

Durand, Martine and Giorno, Claude. Indicators of International Competitiveness: Conceptual Aspects and Evaluation. *OECD Econ. Stud.*, Autumn 1987, (9), pp. 147–82. **[G: OECD]**

Durham, Stephen E. and Lee, David R. An Evaluation of Alternative Approaches to Market Share Analysis with Application to the Kuwaiti Poultry Market. *J. Agr. Econ.*, January 1987, *38*(1), pp. 85–97. **[G: Kuwait]**

Dyba, Karel and Kupka, Václav. Accommodating the Czechoslovak Economy to External Blows (A Macroeconomic Analysis for 1973–1981). *Soviet E. Europ. Foreign Trade*, Spring 1987, *23*(1), pp. 6–30. **[G: Czechoslovakia]**

Ebbersbach, Annette. Experiences and Tasks in Improving the Planning and Economic Stimu-

lation of Foreign Trade for the Furtherance of Economic Strategy. *Soviet E. Europ. Foreign Trade*, Fall 1987, *23*(3), pp. 74–86.
[G: CMEA]

Ebbersbach, Annette. The Development of Socialist Foreign Trade Theory in the Conditions of the 1980s. *Soviet E. Europ. Foreign Trade*, Summer 1987, *23*(2), pp. 94–117.
[G: CMEA]

Edwards, Clark. The Exchange Rate and U.S. Agricultural Exports. *Agr. Econ. Res.*, Winter 1987, *39*(1), pp. 1–12. **[G: U.S.]**

Edwards, Geoff W. U.S. Farm Policy: An Australian Perspective. *Fed. Res. Bank St. Louis Rev.*, October 1987, *69*(8), pp. 20–31.
[G: U.S.; Australia]

Ehlermann, Claus Dieter. The Institutional Context of EEC–Israel Economic Relations. *Greilsammer, I. and Weiler, J. H. H.*, eds., 1987, pp. 215–29. **[G: EEC; Israel]**

Ellis, Mark S. Yugoslavia's Exports to the European Economic Community—An Analysis of the 1980 Cooperation Agreement. *Econ. Anal. Workers' Manage.*, 1987, *21*(1), pp. 49–94.
[G: Yugoslavia; EEC]

Emmerij, L. The Future of North–South Relations: Alternative Approaches. *Visser, H. and Schoor, E.*, eds., 1987, pp. 179–96.
[G: Global]

Evans, David. The Long-run Determinants of North–South Terms of Trade and Some Recent Empirical Evidence. *World Devel.*, May 1987, *15*(5), pp. 657–71. **[G: Global]**

Fagerberg, Jan. Diffusion of Technology, Structural Change and Intra-industry Trade: The Case of the Nordic Countries 1961–1983. *Andersson, J. O.*, ed., 1987, pp. 73–102.
[G: N. Europe]

Fagerberg, Jan and Sollie, Gunnar. The Method of Constant Market Shares Analysis Reconsidered. *Appl. Econ.*, December 1987, *19*(12), pp. 1571–83. **[G: OECD]**

Fallon, John and Thompson, Lynne. An Analysis of the Effects of Recent Changes in the Exchange Rate and the Terms of Trade on the Level and Composition of Economic Activity. *Australian Econ. Rev.*, Second Quarter 1987, (78), pp. 24–36. **[G: Australia]**

Farness, Donald H. The Evolution of International Trade in Oregon. *Spencer, S. I.*, ed., 1987, pp. 90–98. **[G: U.S.]**

Faroqhi, Suraiya. The Venetian Presence in the Ottoman Empire, 1600–30. *Islamoglu-Inan, H.*, ed., 1987, pp. 311–44.
[G: Ottoman Empire; Italy]

Feenstra, Robert C. Automobile Prices and Protection: The U.S.–Japan Trade Restraint. *Salvatore, D.*, ed., 1987, pp. 333–51. **[G: U.S.; Japan]**

Fekete, J. Some Thoughts about East–West Economic Relations and the World Economy. *Visser, H. and Schoor, E.*, eds., 1987, pp. 227–36. **[G: OECD; CMEA]**

Feketekuty, Geza. About Trade in Tourism Services. *Giarini, O.*, ed., 1987, pp. 245–51.
[G: Global]

Feldstein, Martin S. Correcting the Trade Deficit. *Foreign Aff.*, Spring 1987, 65(4), pp. 795–806. **[G: U.S.]**

Fels, Gerhard. United States Trade Policy: From Multilateralism to Bilateralism? Comments. *Giersch, H., ed.*, 1987, pp. 105–09. **[G: U.S.]**

Fennema, Meindert and van der Pijl, Kees. International Bank Capital and the New Liberalism. *Mizruchi, M. S. and Schwartz, M., eds.*, 1987, pp. 298–319. **[G: EEC; Japan; U.S.]**

Filho, Ugo Fasano. Uma comparação entre o índice de vantagem comparativa de Bowen e o tradicional índice de vantagem comparativa revelada: o caso brasileiro—1964/81. (With English summary.) *Pesquisa Planejamento Econ.*, August 1987, 17(2), pp. 457–69. **[G: Brazil]**

Findlay, Ronald. Current Issues in Trade Policy: An Overview: Comment. *Stern, R. M., ed.*, 1987, pp. 73–76. **[G: U.S.]**

Finger, J. Michael and Olechowski, Andrzej. Trade Barriers: Who Does What to Whom. *Giersch, H., ed.*, 1987, pp. 37–71. **[G: Global]**

Fiorentini, Riccardo. Il deficit commerciale USA: Interpretazioni alternative. (Alternative Explanations of USA Trade Deficit. With English summary.) *Rivista Int. Sci. Econ. Com.*, Nov.-Dec. 1987, 34(11–12), pp. 1069–82. **[G: U.S.]**

Fischer, Wolfram. Swings between Protection and Free Trade in History. *Giersch, H., ed.*, 1987, pp. 20–32. **[G: U.S.; W. Europe]**

Fitzgerald, Bruce. Countertrade Reconsidered. *Finance Develop.*, June 1987, 24(2), pp. 46–49. **[G: Indonesia]**

Flowers, Edward B. and Lees, Francis A. A Survey of the Changing Patterns of World Trade: The High Export Growth Countries. *Tremblay, R., ed.*, 1987, pp. 367–75. **[G: Global]**

Fontanel, Jacques. Military Expenditure and the Arms Trade: Problems of the Data: Note. *Schmidt, C., ed.*, 1987, pp. 25–28. **[G: Global]**

Fraser, R. W. and Salerian, Soy Nia. Agricultural Exports and the Western Australian Economy. *Australian J. Agr. Econ.*, April 1987, 31(1), pp. 74–82. **[G: Australia]**

Freebairn, John W. Implications of Wages and Industrial Policies on the Competitiveness of Agricultural Export Industries. *Rev. Marketing Agr. Econ.*, April 1987, 55(1), pp. 79–87. **[G: Australia]**

French, Michael J. and Wilson, Thomas. Depression and Protection: The Early Thirties and the Early Eighties Compared. *[Penrose, E. F.]*, 1987, pp. 14–31. **[G: OECD]**

Frey, Bruno S. and Pommerehne, Werner W. International Trade in Art: Attitudes and Behaviour. *Rivista Int. Sci. Econ. Com.*, June 1987, 34(6), pp. 465–86. **[G: U.S.; Europe]**

Gann, Pamela B. Issues in Extraterritoriality. *Law Contemp. Probl.*, Summer 1987, 50(3), pp. 1–10. **[G: U.S.]**

Garland, John and Brezinski, Horst. U.S. and West German Policies on Trade with the USSR. *Marer, P. and van Veen, P., eds.*, 1987, pp. 65–89. **[G: U.S.; W. Germany; U.S.S.R.]**

Ghartey, Edward E. Devaluation as a Balance of Payments Corrective Measure in Developing Countries: A Study Relating to Ghana. *Appl. Econ.*, July 1987, 19(7), pp. 937–47. **[G: Ghana]**

Ghoshal, Animesh. Floating Exchange Rates and U.S.—Canadian Trade. *Tremblay, R., ed.*, 1987, pp. 151–60. **[G: Canada; U.S.]**

Gibbons, Elizabeth and Halpin, Gerald F. Import Price Declines in 1986 Reflected Reduced Oil Prices. *Mon. Lab. Rev.*, April 1987, 110(4), pp. 3–17. **[G: U.S.]**

Gilbert, Christopher L. International Commodity Agreements: Design and Performance. *World Devel.*, May 1987, 15(5), pp. 591–616. **[G: LDCs]**

Girvan, Norman P. Transnational Corporations and Non-fuel Primary Commodities in Developing Countries. *World Devel.*, May 1987, 15(5), pp. 713–40. **[G: LDCs]**

Godley, Michael R. The China Business: Review Article. *Bus. Hist. Rev.*, Winter 1987, 61(4), pp. 606–14. **[G: U.S.]**

Gollop, Frank M. Modeling Aggregate Productivity Growth: The Importance of Intersectoral Transfer Prices and International Trade. *Rev. Income Wealth*, June 1987, 33(2), pp. 211–27. **[G: OECD]**

Gonçalves, Reinaldo. Competitividade internacional, vantagem comparativa e empresas multinancionais: o caso das exportações brasileiras de manufaturados. (With English summary.) *Pesquisa Planejamento Econ.*, August 1987, 17(2), pp. 411–36. **[G: Brazil]**

Gonçalves, Reinaldo and Richtering, Jürgen. Intercountry Comparison of Export Performance and Output Growth. *Devel. Econ.*, March 1987, 25(1), pp. 3–18. **[G: LDCs]**

de Gorter, Harry and Meilke, Karl D. The EEC's Wheat Price Policies and International Trade in Differentiated Products. *Amer. J. Agr. Econ.*, May 1987, 69(2), pp. 223–29. **[G: EEC]**

Gould, Peter. Agricultural Issues in a Comprehensive Canada–U.S. Trade Agreement: A Canadian Perspective: A Response. *Can. J. Agr. Econ.*, May 1987, 34, pp. 230–32. **[G: Canada]**

Graham, Douglas H.; Gauthier, Howard and Mendonça de Barros, José Roberto. Thirty Years of Agricultural Growth in Brazil: Crop Performance, Regional Profile, and Recent Policy Review. *Econ. Develop. Cult. Change*, October 1987, 36(1), pp. 1–34. **[G: Brazil]**

Granell, Francesco. Spain and the Enlargement of the EEC. *Greilsammer, I. and Weiler, J. H. H., eds.*, 1987, pp. 159–72. **[G: EEC; Spain]**

de Grauwe, Paul. Did the Exchange Rate Stability within the EMS Contribute to More Trade? *Visser, H. and Schoor, E., eds.*, 1987, pp. 237–48. **[G: EEC; U.S.]**

de Grauwe, Paul. International Trade and Economic Growth in the European Monetary System. *Europ. Econ. Rev.*, Feb./Mar. 1987, *31*(1/2), pp. 389–98. **[G: W. Europe]**

Green, Robert T. and Srivastava, Rajendra K. Classification of Export Markets Based on Product Mix. *Cavusgil, S. T., ed.*, 1987, pp. 139–55.

Greenaway, David. Intra-industry Trade, Intrafirm Trade and European Integration: Evidence, Gains and Policy Aspects. *J. Common Market Stud.*, December 1987, *26*(2), pp. 153–72. **[G: EEC]**

Greenaway, David and Milner, Chris. Intra-industry Trade: Current Perspectives and Unresolved Issues. *Weltwirtsch. Arch.*, 1987, *123*(1), pp. 39–57.

Greenaway, David and Milner, Chris. Theories of Intra-industry Trade: A Review of the 'State of the Art.' *Andersson, J. O., ed.*, 1987, pp. 11–34.

Greilsammer, Ilan and Weiler, Joseph H. H. Europe and Israel: Troubled Neighbours: An Introduction. *Greilsammer, I. and Weiler, J. H. H., eds.*, 1987, pp. 1–7. **[G: Israel; EEC]**

Griffith-Jones, Stephany. Compensatory Financing Facility: A Review of Its Operation and Proposals for Improvement. *Dell, S., ed., Pt. 2*, 1987, pp. 691–712.

Griffith, Winston H. Can CARICOM Countries Replicate the Singapore Experience? *J. Devel. Stud.*, October 1987, *24*(1), pp. 60–82. **[G: Caribbean]**

Grubel, Herbert G. All Traded Services Are Embodied in Materials or People. *World Econ.*, September 1987, *10*(3), pp. 319–30. **[G: OECD]**

Grubert, Harry and Mutti, John. Taxes, International Capital Flows and Trade: The International Implications of the Tax Reform Act of 1986. *Nat. Tax J.*, September 1987, *40*(3), pp. 315–29. **[G: U.S.]**

Guerrieri, Paulo and Padoan, Pier Carlo. The Political Economy Approach to International Cooperation: A Critical Survey. *Econ. Notes*, 1987, (2), pp. 67–88.

Gupta, Pradeep C. and Faruqui, Ahmad. Assessing the Future Competitiveness of American Industry in World Markets: Some Preliminary Results. *Faruqui, A. and Broehl, J., eds.*, 1987, pp. 199–218. **[G: U.S.]**

Gylfason, Thorvaldur. Does Exchange Rate Really Matter? *Europ. Econ. Rev.*, Feb./Mar. 1987, *31*(1/2), pp. 375–81.

Gyooten, Toyoo. Internationalization of the Yen: Its Implication for U.S.–Japan Relations. *Patrick, H. T. and Tachi, R., eds.*, 1987, pp. 84–89. **[G: U.S.; Japan]**

Haaland, Jan I., et al. VEMOD: A Ricardo–Heckscher–Ohlin–Jones Model of World Trade. *Scand. J. Econ.*, 1987, *89*(3), pp. 251–70. **[G: Global]**

Hager, Wolfgang. The Community as Israel's Trading Partner: A Look at the Future. *Greilsammer, I. and Weiler, J. H. H., eds.*, 1987, pp. 43–55. **[G: Israel; EEC]**

Hamaui, Rony and Rinaldi, Roberto. I prezzi all'importazione italiani dei beni manufatti: un-'analisi preliminare. (With English summary.) *Polit. Econ.*, April 1987, *3*(1), pp. 81–104. **[G: Italy]**

Hamilton, Colleen and Whalley, John. Relaciones con el Norte: Los países en desarrollo y las negociaciones comerciales a nivel mundial. (Dealing with the North: Developing Countries and Global Trade Negotions. With English summary.) *Estud. Econ.*, July-December 1987, *2*(2), pp. 151–225. **[G: LDCs]**

Hampton, Gerald M. and Buske, Erwin. The Global Marketing Perspective. *Cavusgil, S. T., ed.*, 1987, pp. 259–77. **[G: Global]**

Hanink, Dean M. A Comparative Analysis of the Competitive Geographical Trade Performances of the USA, FRG, and Japan: The Markets and Marketers Hypothesis. *Econ. Geogr.*, October 1987, *63*(4), pp. 293–305. **[G: U.S.; W. Germany; Japan]**

Harkavy, R. E. Arms Resupply *during* Conflict: A Framework for Analysis. *Schmidt, C., ed.*, 1987, pp. 239–79. **[G: Global]**

Hasegawa, Toshiaki, et al. U.S.–Japan Economic Coordination: A Global Solution for Mutual Prosperity. *Finn, R. B., ed.*, 1987, pp. 1–29. **[G: U.S.; Japan]**

Hayden, Rose L. Foreign Languages and International Trade: Preface. *Spencer, S. I., ed.*, 1987, pp. ix–xiv. **[G: U.S.]**

Helpman, Elhanan. Imperfect Competition and International Trade: Evidence from Fourteen Industrial Countries. *J. Japanese Int. Economies*, March 1987, *1*(1), pp. 62–81. **[G: MDCs]**

Helpman, Elhanan. The National Defense Argument for Government Intervention in Foreign Trade: Comment. *Stern, R. M., ed.*, 1987, pp. 370–73. **[G: U.S.]**

Herrera-Lasso, Luis. Economic Growth, Military Expenditure, Arms Industry and Arms Transfer in Latin America. *Schmidt, C., ed.*, 1987, pp. 113–34. **[G: Latin America]**

Hesse, Helmut. Protection in Germany: Toward Industrial Selectivity: Comment. *Giersch, H., ed.*, 1987, pp. 192–203. **[G: W. Germany]**

Hietarinta, Kai. Oljepriset och östhandelns utveckling. (The Price of Oil and the Development Trade with Eastern Europe. With English summary.) *Ekon. Samfundets Tidskr.*, 1987, *40*(1), pp. 7–10. **[G: Finland; U.S.S.R.]**

Hillman, Jimmye S. Domestic and Export Demand for U.S. Agricultural Products: Discussion. *Amer. J. Agr. Econ.*, May 1987, *69*(2), pp. 459–60. **[G: U.S.]**

Hindley, Brian. International Trade in Services and Its Relevance for Economic Development: Comment. *Giarini, O., ed.*, 1987, pp. 35–39.

Hindley, Brian. Trade in Services within the European Community. *Giersch, H., ed.*, 1987, pp. 468–86. **[G: EEC]**

Hirsch, Seev. The Impact of EEC Trade Policies on Developing Countries: Comment. *Giersch, H., ed.*, 1987, pp. 327–31. **[G: EEC; LDCs]**

Hirsch, Seev. Trade Regimes and the Middle East

Peace Process. *World Econ.*, March 1987, *10*(1), pp. 61–74.   [G: Israel; Egypt]

Hitiris, T. and Bedrossian, Arakel. Import Penetration, Export Competitiveness, and the Pattern of UK Intra-industry Trade: A Note. *Appl. Econ.*, February 1987, *19*(2), pp. 215–20.   [G: U.K.]

Hobkhoo, Ahmad. Les industries agro-alimentaires ivoiriennes: évolution et prospective. (The Ivorian Food and Aricultural Industries: Evolution and Prospective. With English summary.) *Écon. Soc.*, July 1987, *21*(7), pp. 209–25.   [G: Ivory Coast]

van der Hoeven, Rolph and Richards, P. J. International Linkages. *International Labour Office.*, 1987, pp. 21–36.   [G: OECD; LDCs]

Hogan, William T. Protectionism in the Steel Industry: A Historical Perspective. *Salvatore, D., ed.*, 1987, pp. 352–64.   [G: Global]

Holland, Martin. Three Approaches for Understanding European Political Co-operation: A Case-Study of EC–South African Policy. *J. Common Market Stud.*, June 1987, *25*(4), pp. 295–313.   [G: EEC; S. Africa]

Holmes, Frank [Sir]. Economic Adjustment: Policies and Problems: Introduction. *Holmes, F., ed.*, 1987, pp. 1–7.   [G: ASEAN]

Holzman, Franklyn D. A Comparative View of Foreign Trade Behavior: Market versus Centrally Planned Economies. *Holzman, F. D.*, 1987, *1985*, pp. 91–112.

Holzman, Franklyn D. and Portes, Richard. Trade, Technology, and Leverage: The Limits of Pressure. *Holzman, F. D.*, 1987, *1978*, pp. 113–20.

Hong, Wontack. A Comparative Static Application of the Heckscher–Ohlin Model of Factor Proportions: Korean Experience. *Weltwirtsch. Arch.*, 1987, *123*(2), pp. 309–24.   [G: S. Korea]

Hong, Wontack. Export-Oriented Growth and Trade Patterns of Korea. *Bradford, C. I., Jr. and Branson, W. H., eds.*, 1987, pp. 273–305.   [G: S. Korea]

Hong, Wontack. Trade, Growth and Economic Problems of Asian NICs. *Hitotsubashi J. Econ.*, October 1987, *27*, pp. 79–100.   [G: Asian NICs]

Honko, Jaakko. Kansainvälinen kilpailukyky ja tieteellinen tutkimus. (International Competitiveness and Scientific Research. With English summary.) *Liiketaloudellinen Aikak.*, 1987, *36*(2), pp. 107–15.   [G: Finland]

Hooper, Peter. The Persistence of the U.S. Trade Deficit: Comments. *Brookings Pap. Econ. Act.*, 1987, (1), pp. 47–51.   [G: U.S.]

Hopkins, Raymond F. The Wheat Negotiations: Loss or Gain in North–South Relations? *Zartman, I. W., ed. (II)*, 1987, pp. 115–48.

Horn, Ernst-Jürgen. Trade in Services within the European Community: Comment. *Giersch, H., ed.*, 1987, pp. 487–91.   [G: EEC]

Horridge, Mark; Parmenter, Brian R. and Warr, Peter G. Buying Australian. *Econ. Rec.*, September 1987, *63*(182), pp. 231–46.   [G: Australia]

Horwitz, Eva Christina. Export Competitiveness among the Nordic Countries. *Andersson, J. O., ed.*, 1987, pp. 149–69.   [G: N. Europe]

Houston, David and Paus, Eva. The Theory of Unequal Exchange: An Indictment. *Rev. Radical Polit. Econ.*, Spring 1987, *19*(1), pp. 90–97.

Howe, Christopher. Japan's Economic Experience in China before the Establishment of the People's Republic of China: A Retrospective Balance-Sheet. *[Penrose, E. F.]*, 1987, pp. 155–77.   [G: Japan; China]

Howell, Thomas. Steel and the State in Romania. *Comp. Econ. Stud.*, Summer 1987, *29*(2), pp. 71–100.   [G: Romania]

Hoyt, Ronald E. and Legault, Michel. A Discriminant Analysis of Soviet Decision-Making Behavior in Selecting United States Suppliers of Goods and Services. *Most, Kenneth S., ed.*, 1987, pp. 263–85.   [G: U.S.S.R.; U.S.]

Hsiao, Mei-chu W. Tests of Causality and Exogeneity Between Exports and Economic Growth: The Case of Asian NICs. *J. Econ. Devel.*, December 1987, *12*(2), pp. 143–59.   [G: Asia]

Hughes Hallett, Andrew J. International Competitiveness and Economic Recovery: Examples of the Risk-Ambition Trade-Off in Dutch Economic Policies. *Manchester Sch. Econ. Soc. Stud.*, March 1987, *55*(1), pp. 38–59.   [G: Netherlands]

Humbert, Thomas M. Understanding the Federal Deficit: Putative Impact on Trade. *Fink, R. H. and High, J. C., eds.*, 1987, *1984*, pp. 162–70.   [G: U.S.]

Husted, Steven and Kollintzas, Tryphon. Linear Rational Expectations Equilibrium Laws of Motion for Selected U.S. Raw Material Imports. *Int. Econ. Rev.*, October 1987, *28*(3), pp. 651–70.   [G: U.S.]

Inalcik, Halil. When and How British Cotton Goods Invaded the Levant Markets. *Islamoglu-Inan, H., ed.*, 1987, pp. 374–83.   [G: Middle East]

Inikori, Joseph E. Slavery and the Development of Industrial Capitalism in England. *Solow, B. L. and Engerman, S. L., eds.*, 1987, pp. 79–101.   [G: U.K.]

Intriligator, Michael D. The National Defense Argument for Government Intervention in Foreign Trade: Comment. *Stern, R. M., ed.*, 1987, pp. 364–69.   [G: U.S.]

Iran Ministry Econ. Aff. and Finance. Trade Co-operation and Collective Self-reliance. *Agrawal, G. R., et al. (II)*, 1987, pp. 7–22.   [G: LDCs]

Isard, W. and Dean, W. The Projection of World (Multiregional) Trade Matrices. *Environ. Planning A*, August 1987, *19*(8), pp. 1059–66.

Ivanov, Ivan D. Restructuring the Mechanism of Foreign Economic Relations in the USSR. *Soviet Econ.*, July-Sept. 1987, *3*(3), pp. 192–218.   [G: U.S.S.R.]

Jabara, Cathy L. and Schwartz, Nancy E. Flexible Exchange Rates and Commodity Price Changes: The Case of Japan. *Amer. J. Agr.*

Econ., August 1987, *69*(3), pp. 580–90.
[G: Japan]

Jacobsen, Hanns-Dieter. The Foreign Trade and Payments of the GDR in a Changing World Economy. *Jeffries, I. and Melzer, M., eds.,* 1987, pp. 235–60. **[G: E. Germany]**

Jacquemin, Alexis. Trade Performance as a Constraint on European Growth: Comment. *Lawrence, R. Z. and Schultze, C. L., eds.,* 1987, pp. 374–81. **[G: W. Europe]**

Jain, Subhash C. Perspectives on International Strategic Alliances. *Cavusgil, S. T., ed.,* 1987, pp. 103–20.

Jeffries, Ian and Melzer, Manfred. The Economic Strategy of the 1980s and the Limits to Possible Reforms. *Jeffries, I. and Melzer, M., eds.,* 1987, pp. 41–50. **[G: E. Germany]**

Jelliss, Arvin D. and Kuo, Chun-Yan. On Measuring the Economic Subsidy of Export Sales Financing. *Econ. Develop. Cult. Change,* July 1987, *35*(4), pp. 832–46. **[G: Canada]**

Ježek, Jiří. Czechoslovak Foreign Trade in 1986. *Czech. Econ. Digest.,* June 1987, (5), pp. 21–24. **[G: Czechoslovakia]**

Ježek, Jiří. Czechoslovakia's Trade with Advanced Capitalist Countries. *Czech. Econ. Digest.,* June 1987, (5), pp. 28–30.
[G: Czechoslovakia]

Ježek, Jiří. Space for Development of Direct Relations (Czechoslovakia–CMEA) *Czech. Econ. Digest.,* June 1987, (5), pp. 25–27.
[G: CMEA]

Jha, L. K. Do Outward-Oriented Polices Really Favor Growth? *Finance Develop.,* December 1987, *24*(4), pp. 44–46. **[G: LDCs]**

Johnson, Manuel H., Jr. and Loopesko, Bonnie E. The Yen–Dollar Relationship: A Recent Historical Perspective. *Patrick, H. T. and Tachi, R., eds.,* 1987, pp. 95–116. **[G: U.S.; Japan]**

Johnson, Omotunde E. G. Currency Depreciation and Imports. *Finance Develop.,* June 1987, *24*(2), pp. 18–21.

Johnson, Omotunde E. G. Currency Depreciation and Export Expansion. *Finance Develop.,* March 1987, *24*(1), pp. 23–26.

Jones, Ronald W. Current Issues in Trade Policy: An Overview: Comment. *Stern, R. M., ed.,* 1987, pp. 69–72. **[G: U.S.]**

Jones, William I. Agriculture's Changing Role in International Trade and Aid: Tastes and Techniques. *Hieronymi, O., ed.,* 1987, pp. 53–68.

Juenger, Friedrich K. Constitutional Control of Extraterritoriality? A Comment. *Law Contemp. Probl.,* Summer 1987, *50*(3), pp. 39–46.
[G: U.S.]

Kahn, S. B. Import Penetration and Import Demands in the South African Economy. *S. Afr. J. Econ.,* September 1987, *55*(3), pp. 238–48.
[G: S. Africa]

Kaldor, Nicholas. The Role of Commodity Prices in Economic Recovery. *World Devel.,* May 1987, *15*(5), pp. 551–58. **[G: EEC; U.S.]**

Kalyala, Denny H. and Mudenda, Gilbert N. The Effects of the World Economic Recession on the Mining Sector in the SADCC Region.

Amin, S.; Chitala, D. and Mandaza, I., eds., 1987, pp. 109–27. **[G: Southern Africa]**

Katayama, Sei-ichi; Ohtani, Kazuhiro and Toyoda, Toshihisa. Estimation of Structural Change in the Import and Export Equations: An International Comparison. *Econ. Stud. Quart.,* June 1987, *38*(2), pp. 148–58.
[G: OECD; Korea]

Kerr, William A. The Recent Findings of the Canadian Import Tribunal Regarding Beef Originating in the European Economic Community. *J. World Trade Law,* October 1987, *21*(5), pp. 55–65. **[G: EEC; Canada]**

Kessler, Richard J. Multilateral Attempts at Managing Energy Resources: The Responses from the North and the South. *Pachauri, R. K., ed.,* 1987, pp. 857–80.

Kierzkowski, Henryk. International Trade in Services and Its Relevance for Economic Development: Comment. *Giarini, O., ed.,* 1987, pp. 39–43.

Kim, C. S.; Bolling, Christine and Wainio, John. Import Demand for Feed Grains in Venezuela. *J. Agr. Econ. Res.,* Summer 1987, *39*(3), pp. 12–19. **[G: Venezuela; U.S.]**

Kindleberger, Charles P. Finnish War Reparations. *Kindleberger, C. P.,* 1987, pp. 209–29.
[G: Finland; U.S.S.R.]

Klein, Lawrence R. The South Asian and Pacific Far East Countries in Project LINK. *Bradford, C. I., Jr. and Branson, W. H., eds.,* 1987, pp. 157–69. **[G: S. Asia; Pacific Basin]**

Klepper, Gernot; Weiss, Frank D. and Witteler, Doris. Protection in Germany: Toward Industrial Selectivity. *Giersch, H., ed.,* 1987, pp. 171–91. **[G: W. Germany]**

Koekkoek, Ad. The Competitive Position of the EC in Hi-tech. *Weltwirtsch. Arch.,* 1987, *123*(1), pp. 159–68. **[G: EEC; OECD]**

Kohler, Wilhelm. The Factor Content of Austria's Foreign Trade 1976. *Empirica,* 1987, *14*(1), pp. 3–24. **[G: Austria]**

Kol, Jacob. Exports from Developing Countries: Some Facts and Scope. *Europ. Econ. Rev.,* Feb./Mar. 1987, *31*(1/2), pp. 466–74.
[G: LDCs; OECD]

Kollert, Antonín. The Role and Problems of External Economic Relations in the Period of the 8th Five-Year Plan. *Czech. Econ. Digest.,* October 1987, (7), pp. 48–60.
[G: Czechoslovakia]

Kolodziej, Edward A. Re-evaluating Economic and Technological Variables to Explain Global Arms Production and Sales. *Schmidt, C., ed.,* 1987, pp. 304–35. **[G: LDCs]**

Kostecki, Michel. Should One Countertrade? *J. World Trade Law,* April 1987, *21*(2), pp. 7–21. **[G: Global]**

Kotlikoff, Laurence J. and Leamer, Edward E. Empirical Tests of Alternative Models of International Growth. *Bradford, C. I., Jr. and Branson, W. H., eds.,* 1987, pp. 227–69.
[G: U.S.; LDCs; MDCs]

Köves, András. The Import Restriction Squeeze and Import-Maximizing Ambitions: Some Connections of East–West vs. Intra-CMEA Trade.

Soviet E. Europ. Foreign Trade, Summer 1987, *23*(2), pp. 78–93. **[G: CMEA]**

Kraus, Josef. Can Contract Prices Be Based on Regional Prices? *Soviet E. Europ. Foreign Trade*, Winter 1987-1988, *23*(4), pp. 5–21. **[G: EEC]**

Krause, Lawrence B. The Structure of Trade in Manufactured Goods in the East and Southeast Asian Region. *Bradford, C. I., Jr. and Branson, W. H., eds.*, 1987, pp. 205–25. **[G: Asia]**

Kreinin, Mordechai E. Comparative Advantage and Possible Trade Restrictions in High-Technology Products. *Salvatore, D., ed.*, 1987, pp. 297–332. **[G: U.S.]**

Kreinin, Mordechai E.; Martin, Stephen and Sheehey, Edmund J. Differential Response of U.S. Import Prices and Quantities to Exchange-Rate Adjustments. *Weltwirtsch. Arch.*, 1987, *123*(3), pp. 449–62. **[G: U.S.]**

Kristensen, Thorkil. Landbrugets fremtid. (The Prospects for Danish Agriculture. With English summary.) *Nationaløkon. Tidsskr.*, 1987, *125*(3), pp. 316–20. **[G: Denmark]**

Krommenacker, Raymond. Services and Space Technology: The Emergence of Space Generated, Highly Integrated Goods and Services (IGS). *Giarini, O., ed.*, 1987, pp. 173–92.

Krueger, Anne O. Origins of the Developing Countries' Debt Crisis 1970 to 1982. *J. Devel. Econ.*, October 1987, *27*(1–2), pp. 165–87. **[G: LDCs]**

Krueger, Anne O. Origins of the Developing Countries' Debt Crisis 1970 to 1982. *[Diaz-Alejandro, C. F.]*, 1987, pp. 165–87. **[G: LDCs]**

Krueger, Russell C. U.S. International Transactions, First Quarter 1987. *Surv. Curr. Bus.*, June 1987, *67*(6), pp. 46–84. **[G: U.S.]**

Krueger, Russell C. U.S. International Transaction, Second Quarter 1987. *Surv. Curr. Bus.*, September 1987, *67*(9), pp. 32–55. **[G: U.S.]**

Krugman, Paul R. Imports in Japan: Closed Markets or Minds? Comment. *Brookings Pap. Econ. Act.*, 1987, (2), pp. 549–52. **[G: Japan]**

Krugman, Paul R. Is the Japan Problem Over? *Sato, R. and Wachtel, P., eds.*, 1987, pp. 16–37. **[G: U.S.; Japan]**

Krugman, Paul R. Strategic Sectors and International Competition. *Stern, R. M., ed.*, 1987, pp. 207–32. **[G: U.S.]**

Krugman, Paul R. Targeted Industrial Policies: Theory and Evidence. *Salvatore, D., ed.*, 1987, pp. 266–96. **[G: Japan; U.S.]**

Krugman, Paul R. and Baldwin, Richard E. The Persistence of the U.S. Trade Deficit. *Brookings Pap. Econ. Act.*, 1987, (1), pp. 1–43. **[G: U.S.]**

Krugman, Paul R. and Hatsopoulos, George N. The Problem of U.S. Competitiveness in Manufacturing. *New Eng. Econ. Rev.*, Jan./Feb. 1987, pp. 18–29. **[G: U.S.]**

Kuboniwa, Masaaki. Input–Output Analysis of the Structure of Soviet Foreign Trade—A Comparative View. *Hitotsubashi J. Econ.*,

June 1987, *28*(1), pp. 63–85. **[G: U.S.S.R.]**

Kumagai, Naohiro. The Outlook for International Trade Relations. *Bus. Econ.*, January 1987, *22*(1), pp. 18–21. **[G: Global]**

Kumar, Rajiv. Performance of Foreign and Domestic Firms in Export Processing Zones. *World Devel.*, Oct./Nov. 1987, *15*(10/11), pp. 1309–19. **[G: India]**

Kunst, Robert and Marin, Dalia. The Export-Productivity Relationship: A Time Series Representation for Austria. *Empirica*, 1987, *14*(1), pp. 55–75. **[G: Austria]**

van der Laan, Laurens. Selling Tropical Africa's Export Crops: The Experience of the Interwar Period. *Dewey, C., ed.*, 1987, pp. 238–61. **[G: Africa]**

Laird, Samuel. Trade Barriers: Who Does What to Whom: Comment. *Giersch, H., ed.*, 1987, pp. 72–77. **[G: Global]**

Lal, Deepak and Rajapatirana, Sarath. Foreign Trade Regimes and Economic Growth in Developing Countries. *Giersch, H., ed.*, 1987, pp. 204–35. **[G: LDCs]**

Lal, Deepak and Rajapatirana, Sarath. Foreign Trade Regimes and Economic Growth in Developing Countries. *World Bank Res. Observer*, July 1987, *2*(2), pp. 189–217. **[G: LDCs]**

Lall, Sanjaya; Khanna, Ashok and Alikhani, Iradj. Determinants of Manufactured Export Performance in Low-Income Africa: Kenya and Tanzania. *World Devel.*, September 1987, *15*(9), pp. 1219–24. **[G: Kenya; Tanzania]**

Landefeld, J. Steven. International Trade in Services: Its Composition, Importance and Links to Merchandise Trade. *Bus. Econ.*, April 1987, *22*(2), pp. 25–31. **[G: U.S.]**

Langdale, John. Transborder Data Flows and National Sovereignty. *Barr, T., ed.*, 1987, pp. 137–45.

Langhammer, Rolf J. The EEC Trade Policies in Manufactures, the Mediterranean Market. *Greilsammer, I. and Weiler, J. H. H., eds.*, 1987, pp. 195–211. **[G: EEC; Israel]**

de Lattre, Andre. International Equilibrium— Some Longer-term Issues. *Visser, H. and Schoor, E., eds.*, 1987, pp. 87–94. **[G: Global]**

Lawrence, Robert Z. Imports in Japan: Closed Markets or Minds? *Brookings Pap. Econ. Act.*, 1987, (2), pp. 517–48. **[G: Japan]**

Lawrence, Robert Z. International Competitiveness and Its Impact on Industrial Structure. *Faruqui, A. and Broehl, J., eds.*, 1987, pp. 181–92. **[G: U.S.]**

Lawrence, Robert Z. Trade Performance as a Constraint on European Growth. *Lawrence, R. Z. and Schultze, C. L., eds.*, 1987, pp. 303–74. **[G: W. Europe]**

Lawrence, Robert Z. and Bosworth, Barry P. Adjusting to Slower Economic Growth: The External Sector. *Bosworth, B. P. and Rivlin, A. M., eds.*, 1987, pp. 55–96. **[G: Sweden]**

Le, Can D. The Role of R&D in High-Technology Trade: An Empirical Analysis. *Atlantic Econ.*

J., December 1987, *15*(4), pp. 32–38.
[G: OECD]
Leach, Russell A. The Evolution of International Trade in Michigan. *Spencer, S. I., ed.*, 1987, pp. 82–89. [G: U.S.]
Leamer, Edward E. Endogenous Protection in the United States, 1900–1984: Comment. *Stern, R. M., ed.*, 1987, pp. 196–200.
[G: U.S.]
Leamer, Edward E. The Leontief Paradox, Reconsidered. *Bhagwati, J. N., ed.*, 1987, *1980*, pp. 115–24. [G: U.S.]
Lee, E. World Recession and Developing Economies in Asia. *International Labour Office.*, 1987, pp. 99–132. [G: Asia]
Lee, K. and Dutta, M. Shifting Patterns of International Trade—The United States, Japan, Korea, and the Row. *Dutta, M., ed. (II)*, 1987, pp. 163–84. [G: U.S.; Japan; S. Korea]
Lee, Young Sun. Intra-industry Trade in the Pacific Basin. *Int. Econ. J.*, Spring 1987, *1*(1), pp. 75–90. [G: U.S.; Japan; Taiwan; S. Korea; Canada]
Lehmann, Jean-Pierre. Variations on a Pan-Asianist Theme: The 'Special Relationship' between Japan and Thailand. *[Penrose, E. F.]*, 1987, pp. 178–201. [G: Japan; Thailand]
Lenel, Hans Otto. Ist zur Förderung der internationalen Wettbewerbsfähigkeit externes Unternehmenswachstum erstrebenswert? (Are Mergers Necessary to Secure International Competitiveness? With English summary.) *Lenel, H. O., et al., eds.*, 1987, pp. 113–29.
[G: W. Germany]
Lenz, Allen J. Overview of the U.S. Competitive Position Today. *Barfield, C. E. and Makin, J. H., eds.*, 1987, pp. 27–35. [G: U.S.]
Liander, Bertil and Keller, John F. The Evolution of International Trade in Massachusetts. *Spencer, S. I., ed.*, 1987, pp. 73–81.
[G: U.S.]
Lim, David. Ability of the IMF-CFF to Stabilize Export Earnings. *J. World Trade Law*, October 1987, *21*(5), pp. 91–95.
Lim, David. Export Instability, Investment and Economic Growth in Developing Countries. *Australian Econ. Pap.*, December 1987, *26*(49), pp. 318–27. [G: LDCs]
Lindemann, Beate. Votes of EC Members at the United Nations on Questions Related to Israel. *Greilsammer, I. and Weiler, J. H. H., eds.*, 1987, pp. 303–12. [G: EEC; Israel]
Lipsey, Robert E. and Kravis, Irving B. The Competitiveness and Comparative Advantage of U.S. Multinationals 1957–1984. *Banca Naz. Lavoro Quart. Rev.*, June 1987, (161), pp. 147–65. [G: U.S.]
Little, Ian M. D. Swings between Protection and Free Trade in History: Comment. *Giersch, H., ed.*, 1987, pp. 33–34.
Little, Jane Sneddon. Intra-firm Trade: An Update. *New Eng. Econ. Rev.*, May/June 1987, pp. 46–51. [G: U.S.]
van Loggerenberg, Bazil J. A Deterministic Analysis of Change in International Unit Labor Costs: Import Implications for U.S. Industry.

Managerial Dec. Econ., December 1987, *8*(4), pp. 339–42. [G: U.S.]
López, Elena and Pagoulatos, Emilio. A Model of International Trade with Differentiated Products. *Rivista Int. Sci. Econ. Com.*, September 1987, *34*(9), pp. 853–68.
Lorenz, Detlef. Motive und Möglichkeiten einer engeren wirtschaftlichen Kooperation EG–EA-SEAN in der Zukunft. (Issues of Closer Economic Cooperation between EC and ASEAN in the Future. With English summary.) *Konjunkturpolitik*, 1987, *33*(5), pp. 285–302.
[G: EEC; ASEAN]
Love, James. Export Instability in Less Developed Countries: Consequences and Causes. *J. Econ. Stud.*, 1987, *14*(2), pp. 3–80.
[G: LDCs]
Lundberg, Lars and Hansson, Pär. The Country Pattern of Swedish Trade in Manufactured Products: An Econometric Analysis. *Andersson, J. O., ed.*, 1987, pp. 103–29.
[G: Sweden]
Lutz, James M. Foreign Investment in the United States: Effects on Export Performance. *Soc. Sci. Quart.*, December 1987, *68*(4), pp. 816–33. [G: U.S.]
MacBean, Alasdair and Nguyen, Duc Tin. International Commodity Agreements: Shadow and Substance. *World Devel.*, May 1987, *15*(5), pp. 575–90. [G: LDCs]
MacCharles, D. C. Canadian Foreign Subsidiaries: Productivity and Trade Performance. *Tremblay, R., ed.*, 1987, pp. 331–50.
[G: Canada]
MacCharles, D. C. International Knowledge Transfers and Competitiveness: Canada as a Case Study. *Safarian, A. E. and Bertin, G. Y., eds.*, 1987, pp. 53–69. [G: Canada]
MacPhee, Craig R. The Consistency of Partial Equilibrium Estimates of Trade Creation and Diversion. *Weltwirtsch. Arch.*, 1987, *123*(1), pp. 81–92.
Madeuf, Bernadette. Trends in Technological Competitiveness within the OECD, 1970–80. *Safarian, A. E. and Bertin, G. Y., eds.*, 1987, pp. 34–52. [G: OECD]
Madian, Alan L. Technology and the Changing Industrial Balance. *Thorup, C. L., ed.*, 1987, pp. 41–66. [G: Mexico; U.S.]
Madsen, Tage Koed. Empirical Export Performance Studies: A Review of Conceptualizations and Findings. *Cavusgil, S. T., ed.*, 1987, pp. 177–98.
Maes, Denise. Transboundary Waste Dumping: The United States and Mexico Take a Stand. *Natural Res. J.*, Fall 1987, *27*(4), pp. 941–48.
[G: U.S.; Mexico]
Magee, Stephen P. and Young, Leslie. Endogenous Protection in the United States, 1900–1984. *Stern, R. M., ed.*, 1987, pp. 145–95.
[G: U.S.]
Mahmud, S. Fakre and Nishat, Mohammed. Short-term Forecasting: An Application of Box–Jenkins Methods. *Pakistan J. Appl. Econ.*, Summer 1987, *6*(1), pp. 61–65. [G: Pakistan]
Maizels, Alfred. Commodities in Crisis: An Over-

view of the Main Issues. *World Devel.*, May 1987, *15*(5), pp. 537–49. **[G: Global]**

Malanima, Paolo. Pisa and the Trade Routes to the Near East in the Late Middle Ages. *J. Europ. Econ. Hist.*, Fall 1987, *16*(2), pp. 335–56. **[G: Italy]**

Manrique, Gabriel G. Foreign Export Orientation and Regional Growth in the U.S. *Growth Change*, Winter 1987, *18*(1), pp. 1–12. **[G: U.S.]**

Manrique, Gabriel G. Intra-industry Trade between Developed and Developing Countries: The United States and the NICs. *J. Devel. Areas*, July 1987, *21*(4), pp. 481–93. **[G: U.S.; OECD]**

Marquez, Jaime R. and Pauly, Peter H. International Policy Coordination and Growth Prospects of Developing Countries: An Optimal Control Application. *J. Devel. Econ.*, February 1987, *25*(1), pp. 89–104.

Marris, Stephen. Growth Gaps, Exchange Rates and Asymmetry: Comments. *Patrick, H. T. and Tachi, R., eds.*, 1987, pp. 30–36. **[G: Japan; U.S.]**

Marston, Richard C. Japanese–U.S. Current Accounts and Exchange Rates before and after the G5 Agreement: Discussion. *Sato, R. and Wachtel, P., eds.*, 1987, pp. 152–56. **[G: Japan; U.S.]**

Martellaro, Joseph A. United States–Taiwan Trade Relations and the Trade Deficit. *Bus. Econ.*, July 1987, *22*(3), pp. 28–33. **[G: U.S.; Taiwan]**

Martin, Fernand and Tremblay, Rodrigue. The Canadian Industries of Telecommunication Equipments and Computers, and North American Trade Liberalization. *Tremblay, R., ed.*, 1987, pp. 377–405. **[G: Canada; U.S.]**

Martin, S. K. and Zwart, A. C. Marketing Agencies and the Economics of Market Segmentation. *Australian J. Agr. Econ.*, December 1987, *31*(3), pp. 242–55. **[G: New Zealand]**

Marvel, Howard P. and Ray, Edward John. Intraindustry Trade: Sources and Effects on Protection. *J. Polit. Econ.*, December 1987, *95*(6), pp. 1278–91.

Maskus, Keith E. The View of Trade Problems from Washington's Capitol Hill. *World Econ.*, December 1987, *10*(4), pp. 409–23. **[G: U.S.]**

Mathiesen, Lars. International Trade in Grains: Domestic Policies and Trade Impacts: Comment. *Scand. J. Econ.*, 1987, *89*(3), pp. 285–86. **[G: Global]**

Mayes, David G. The Role of Exchange Rate and Other Pricing Policies in the Adjustment Process: Comment. *Holmes, F., ed.*, 1987, pp. 210–16. **[G: New Zealand]**

Mazier, Jacques. Politique sélective des importations et relance de l'investissement industriel: un essai d'évaluation. (Import Policy on Industrial Investment: An Evaluation Attempt. With English summary.) *Écon. Soc.*, April 1987, *21*(4), pp. 73–100. **[G: OECD]**

McCarthy, F. Desmond; Taylor, Lance and Talati, Cyrus. Trade Patterns in Developing Countries, 1964–82. *J. Devel. Econ.*, October 1987, *27*(1–2), pp. 5–39. **[G: LDCs]**

McCarthy, F. Desmond; Taylor, Lance and Talati, Cyrus. Trade Patterns in Developing Countries, 1964–82. *[Diaz-Alejandro, C. F.]*, 1987, pp. 5–39. **[G: LDCs]**

McCulloch, Rachel. Macroeconomics and Protection: Comment. *Stern, R. M., ed.*, 1987, pp. 137–43. **[G: OECD]**

McStocker, Robert. The Indonesian Coffee Industry. *Bull. Indonesian Econ. Stud.*, April 1987, *23*(1), pp. 40–69. **[G: Indonesia]**

Meessen, Karl M. Conflicts of Jurisdiction under the New Restatement. *Law Contemp. Probl.*, Summer 1987, *50*(3), pp. 47–69. **[G: U.S.]**

Mehta, Pradeep Kumar. Trade Complementarity between India and ASEAN Countries. *Indian J. Quant. Econ.*, 1987, *3*(2), pp. 57–80. **[G: India; ASEAN]**

Mendelsohn, M. S. World Trade and International Finance: Lessons from the Past. *Visser, H. and Schoor, E., eds.*, 1987, pp. 57–64. **[G: Global]**

Menzler-Hokkanen, I. Competitive Advantage: How to Measure It Empirically? *Liiketaloudellinen Aikak.*, 1987, *36*(2), pp. 116–27.

Merz, Hans-Peter. The Internationalisation of the Japanese Economy: The Example of the Federal Republic of Germany. *Trevor, M., ed.*, 1987, pp. 36–49. **[G: Japan; W. Germany]**

Messerlin, Patrick A. International Investment, Protection and Technical Transfer: A Preliminary Examination of the Franco–Japanese Case. *Safarian, A. E. and Bertin, G. Y., eds.*, 1987, pp. 167–79. **[G: France; Japan]**

Metwally, M. M. Determinants of the External Surplus of the Member States of the Gulf Co-operation Council. *Appl. Econ.*, March 1987, *19*(3), pp. 305–16. **[G: Middle East]**

Metwally, M. M. and Arab, A. T. Price Elasticity of Demand for Oil and the Terms of Trade of the OPEC Countries. *Energy J.*, January 1987, *8*(1), pp. 53–67. **[G: OPEC]**

Metwally, M. M. and Daghistani, A. I. The Interaction between the Economies of the Member States of the Gulf Co-operation Council and the Industrialised Economies. *Indian Econ. J.*, Jan.-Mar. 1987, *34*(3), pp. 51–59. **[G: Persian Gulf]**

Michaely, Michael. The Demand for Protection against Exports of Newly Industrializing Countries. *Salvatore, D., ed.*, 1987, pp. 471–81. **[G: Brazil; Hong Kong; S. Korea; Mexico; Singapore]**

Michalski, Wolfgang. Trade Barriers: Who Does What to Whom: Comment. *Giersch, H., ed.*, 1987, pp. 77–84. **[G: Global]**

Mikami, Yoshiki. Exchange of Ideas and People: Cooperation in Science and Technology between the United States and Japan. *Finn, R. B., ed.*, 1987, pp. 45–58. **[G: U.S.; Japan]**

Miller, Dennis D. U.S.–Soviet Grain Trade: A Broken Promise. *Challenge*, Mar./Apr. 1987, *30*(1), pp. 55–56. **[G: U.S.; U.S.S.R.]**

Minchinton, Walter E. Bristol's Trade with the West Indies and South America, 1780–1830.

Rivista Storia Econ., S.S., Int. Issue, 1987, 4, pp. 54–75.   [G: West Indies; S. America; U.K.]

Mintjes, H. Doing Business Crossculturally: International Trade and the Resurgence of Islam. *Visser, H. and Schoor, E., eds.*, 1987, pp. 327–38.   [G: Islamic Countries]

Mirakhor, Abbas and Montiel, Peter J. Adjustment and the Import Intensity of Output. *Finance Develop.*, December 1987, 24(4), pp. 17–19.   [G: LDCs]

Mirakhor, Abbas and Montiel, Peter J. Import Intensity of Output Growth in Developing Countries, 1970–85. *International Monetary Fund Research Department.*, 1987, pp. 59–97.   [G: LDCs]

de Miramon, J. Countertrade: A Disruptive Phenomenon in International Trade. *Visser, H. and Schoor, E., eds.*, 1987, pp. 197–205.   [G: Global]

Mirus, Rolf and Yeung, Bernard. Countertrade and Foreign Exchange Shortages: A Preliminary Assessment. *Weltwirtsch. Arch.*, 1987, 123(3), pp. 535–44.

Mitchell, Donald O. and Duncan, Ronald C. Market Behavior of Grains Exporters. *World Bank Res. Observer*, January 1987, 2(1), pp. 3–21.   [G: Selected Countries]

Miyawaki, T. The Pacific Basin, Recent Economic and Financial Developments. *Visser, H. and Schoor, E., eds.*, 1987, pp. 263–80. [G: Asia-Pacific]

Miyoshi, Masaya. The Japanese–U.S. Trade Friction: Some Perspectives from the Japanese Business Community. *Sato, R. and Wachtel, P., eds.*, 1987, pp. 45–49.   [G: U.S.; Japan]

Modwel, S. K. GSTP: Some Issues in Implementation. *Agrawal, G. R., et al. (II)*, 1987, pp. 49–65.   [G: LDCs]

Mody, Ashoka and Wheeler, David. Towards a Vanishing Middle: Competition in the World Garment Industry. *World Devel.*, Oct./Nov. 1987, 15(10/11), pp. 1269–84.   [G: LDCs]

Morello, G. The Consumer in World Trade. *Visser, H. and Schoor, E., eds.*, 1987, pp. 303–13.   [G: Global]

Mukherji, Smriti. Exports and Economic Growth in India (1950-51–1980-81): An Empirical Investigation. *Margin*, Jan.-Mar. 1987, 19(2), pp. 50–59.   [G: India]

Mwase, Ngila R. L. Reflections on the Proposed Botswana–Namibia Trans-Kalahari Railway. *Eastern Afr. Econ. Rev.*, June 1987, 3(1), pp. 65–75.   [G: Botswana; Namibia]

Myers, Lester H.; Blaylock, James R. and White, T. Kelly. Domestic and Export Demand for U.S. Agricultural Products. *Amer. J. Agr. Econ.*, May 1987, 69(2), pp. 443–47.   [G: U.S.]

Nakatani, Iwao. Japan–U.S. Relations: Asymmetry of Institutional Features as a Source of Trade Frictions. *Patrick, H. T. and Tachi, R., eds.*, 1987, pp. 184–95.   [G: Japan; U.S.]

Nakatani, Iwao. Towards the New International Economic Order—The Role of Japan in the World Economy. *Hitotsubashi J. Econ.*, Octo-

ber 1987, 27, pp. 121–32.   [G: Japan; U.S.]

Nash, D. Barter: The Misunderstood Alternative. *Visser, H. and Schoor, E., eds.*, 1987, pp. 207–12.

Natke, Paul A. Foreign Ownership and Firm-Level Import Performance in Brazilian Manufacturing Industries. *Atlantic Econ. J.*, December 1987, 15(4), pp. 39–48.   [G: Brazil]

Neary, J. Peter. Endogenous Protection in the United States, 1900–1984: Comment. *Stern, R. M., ed.*, 1987, pp. 201–06.   [G: U.S.]

Nicholl, Peter. Some Aspects of Economic Adjustment in Small Island Economies: Comment. *Holmes, F., ed.*, 1987, pp. 263–72.   [G: S. Pacific]

Noland, Marcus. Newly Industrializing Countries' Comparative Advantage in Manufactured Goods. *Weltwirtsch. Arch.*, 1987, 123(4), pp. 679–96.   [G: NICs]

Norman, Victor D. and Strandenes, Siri P. International Trade in Services and Its Relevance for Economic Development: Comment. *Giarini, O., ed.*, 1987, pp. 44–49.

Nove, Alec. Soviet–Japanese Relations, Past and Present. *[Penrose, E. F.]*, 1987, pp. 149–54.   [G: Japan; U.S.S.R.]

Noyce, Robert N. Intel's Leader Looks at the Computer Evolution in the 21st Century. *Shetty, Y. K. and Buehler, V. M., eds.*, 1987, pp. 223–34.   [G: U.S.]

Nyankori, James C. O. and Nodine, Stephen K. Implications of Restrictions on Imports of Canadian Softwood Lumber to the Southern Softwood Lumber Industry. *Rev. Reg. Stud.*, Winter 1987, 17(1), pp. 45–52.   [G: U.S.; Canada]

O'Connor, K. The Location of Services Involved with International Trade. *Environ. Planning A*, May 1987, 19(5), pp. 687–700.   [G: U.S.; Australia]

Okawara, Yoshio. Restructuring the Japanese Economy from a Global Perspective. *Sato, R. and Wachtel, P., eds.*, 1987, pp. 11–15.   [G: Japan; U.S.]

Okita, Saburo. Pacific Development and Cooperation. *[Kitamura, H.]*, 1987, pp. 114–26.   [G: ASEAN; Pacific]

Oleson, Brian T. World Grain Trade: An Economic Perspective of the Current Price War. *Can. J. Agr. Econ.*, November 1987, 35(3), pp. 501–14.   [G: Global]

Oort, C. J. The Influences of International Capital Flows on World Trade. *Visser, H. and Schoor, E., eds.*, 1987, pp. 65–76.   [G: Global]

Packard, George R. The Coming U.S.–Japan Crisis. *Foreign Aff.*, Winter 1987/88, 66(2), pp. 348–67.   [G: U.S.; Japan]

Parikh, Ashok. The Application of the CES Utility Approach to the Estimation of Bilateral Flows in a Trade Matrix. *Pakistan J. Appl. Econ.*, Winter 1987, 6(2), pp. 71–101.   [G: Global]

Parsons, John E. Forms of GDR Economic Cooperation with the Nonsocialist World. *Comp. Econ. Stud.*, Summer 1987, 29(2), pp. 7–18.   [G: E. Germany]

Patrick, Hugh T. Japan and the United States

Today: Exchange Rates, Macroeconomic Policies, and Financial Market Innovations: Concluding Comments. *Patrick, H. T. and Tachi, R., eds.*, 1987, pp. 209–13. [G: Japan; U.S.]

Pazos, Felipe. Import Substitution Policies, Tariffs, and Competition. *Dietz, J. L. and Street, J. H., eds.*, 1987, pp. 147–55.
[G: Latin America]

Pelkmans, Jacques. Liberalization of Product Markets in the European Community. *Giersch, H., ed.*, 1987, pp. 429–61.
[G: EEC]

Pérez-López, Jorge F. Cuban Oil Reexports: Significance and Prospects. *Energy J.*, January 1987, 8(1), pp. 1–16. [G: Cuba]

Perna, Nicholas S. The Shift from Manufacturing to Services: A Concerned View. *New Eng. Econ. Rev.*, Jan./Feb. 1987, pp. 30–38.

Petersson, Lennart. Growth and Determinants of Intraindustry Trade in Sweden, 1871–1980. *Andersson, J. O., ed.*, 1987, pp. 35–72.
[G: Sweden]

Pollins, Brian M. and Brecke, Peter K. The GLOBUS Model: Computer Simulation of Worldwide Political and Economic Development: International Economic Processes. *Bremer, S. A., ed.*, 1987, pp. 459–567. [G: Global]

Pomfret, Richard. Liberalization of Product Markets in the European Community: Comment. *Giersch, H., ed.*, 1987, pp. 462–67.
[G: EEC]

Pomfret, Richard. Main Economic Trends in EC–Israel Economic Relations since the Creation of the Common Market. *Greilsammer, I. and Weiler, J. H. H., eds.*, 1987, pp. 56–72.
[G: Israel; EEC]

Praet, Peter. Structural Developments and Euro–Asian Cooperation. *[Kitamura, H.]*, 1987, pp. 127–39. [G: EEC; Asia]

Prasad, Kamta and Sinha, Pramod Kumar. Allocative Efficiency, Policy Shifts and Trade Flows in the Context of Indo–U.S. Trade. *Dutta, M., ed. (II)*, 1987, pp. 95–104. [G: India; U.S.]

Prentice, Barry E. Agricultural Issues in a Comprehensive Canada–U.S. Trade Agreement: A Canadian Perspective: A Discussion. *Can. J. Agr. Econ.*, May 1987, 34, pp. 228–29.
[G: Canada]

Price, Jacob M. and Clemens, Paul G. E. A Revolution of Scale in Overseas Trade: British Firms in the Chesapeake Trade, 1675–1775. *J. Econ. Hist.*, March 1987, 47(1), pp. 1–43.
[G: U.S.; U.K.]

Proulx, Pierre-Paul. A Review of Studies of Sectoral Impacts of Bilateral and Multilateral Trade Liberalization on Canada. *Tremblay, R., ed.*, 1987, pp. 463–530. [G: Canada; U.S.]

Pugel, Thomas A. Limits of Trade Policy toward High Technology Industries: The Case of Semiconductors. *Sato, R. and Wachtel, P., eds.*, 1987, pp. 184–223. [G: U.S.; Japan]

Rácz, Margit. The Mechanism of Hungarian–Soviet Economic Relations. *Acta Oecon.*, 1987, 38(3–4), pp. 323–37. [G: Hungary; U.S.S.R.]

Raczkowski, Stanislaw. The Influence of International Price Movements and Inflation on the Centrally Planned Economies. *Pasinetti, L. and Lloyd, P., eds.*, 1987, pp. 359–80.
[G: CMEA]

Rada, Juan F. Information Technology and Services. *Giarini, O., ed.*, 1987, pp. 127–71.
[G: U.S.; Canada; W. Europe]

Raffer, Kunibert. Unfavorable Specialization and Dependence: The Case of Peripheral Raw Material Exporters. *World Devel.*, May 1987, 15(5), pp. 701–12. [G: LDCs]

Rajapatirana, Sarath. Industrialization and Foreign Trade. *Finance Develop.*, September 1987, 24(3), pp. 2–5. [G: LDCs]

Ram, Rati. Exports and Economic Growth in Developing Countries: Evidence from Time-Series and Cross-Section Data. *Econ. Develop. Cult. Change*, October 1987, 36(1), pp. 51–72. [G: LDCs]

Ramachandran, Rama V. Limits of Trade Policy toward High Technology Industries: The Case of Semiconductors: Discussion. *Sato, R. and Wachtel, P., eds.*, 1987, pp. 223–30.
[G: U.S.; Japan]

Ramchandani, R. R. India–Africa Economic Relations. *Agrawal, G. R., et al. (II)*, 1987, pp. 221–55. [G: India; Africa]

Ranis, Gustav. Challenges and Opportunities Posed by Asia's Superexporters: Implications for Manufactured Exports from Latin America. *Dietz, J. L. and Street, J. H., eds.*, 1987, 1981, pp. 128–46. [G: E. Asia; Latin America]

Rao, V. L. South Asian Regional Cooperation: Problems and Prospects. *Agrawal, G. R., et al. (II)*, 1987, pp. 116–54. [G: S. Asia]

Raubitschek, Ruth S. Limits of Trade Policy toward High Technology Industries: The Case of Semiconductors: Discussion. *Sato, R. and Wachtel, P., eds.*, 1987, pp. 230–37.
[G: Japan; U.S.]

Ravallion, Martin. Trade and Stabilization: Another Look at British India's Controversial Foodgrain Exports. *Exploration Econ. Hist.*, October 1987, 24(4), pp. 354–70. [G: India]

Raworth, Philip. Canada–U.S. Free Trade: A Legal Perspective. *Can. Public Policy*, September 1987, 13(3), pp. 350–65. [G: Canada; U.S.]

Ray, Edward John. The Impact of Special Interests on Preferential Tariff Concessions by the United States. *Rev. Econ. Statist.*, May 1987, 69(2), pp. 187–93. [G: U.S.]

Redmond, John. Trade between China and the European Community: A New Relationship? *Nat. Westminster Bank Quart. Rev.*, May 1987, pp. 31–46. [G: EEC; China]

Reilly, Bernard J. and DiAngelo, Joseph A., Jr. The Internationalized Environment of Business. *Bus. Econ.*, January 1987, 22(1), pp. 26–30. [G: OECD]

Reynolds, Bruce L. Trade, Employment, and Inequality in Postreform China. *J. Compar. Econ.*, September 1987, 11(3), pp. 479–89.
[G: China]

Richardson, David. The Slave Trade, Sugar, and British Economic Growth, 1748–1776. *Solow, B. L. and Engerman, S. L., eds.*, 1987, pp. 103–33. [G: U.K.; Caribbean]

Richardson, J. David. How Should the United States Respond to Other Countries' Trade Policies? Comment. *Stern, R. M., ed.*, 1987, pp. 287–90. **[G: U.S.]**

Richardson, John B. A Sub-sectoral Approach to Services' Trade Theory. *Giarini, O., ed.*, 1987, pp. 59–82.

Richter, Sándor. The Development of Hungarian–Soviet Economic Relations. *Acta Oecon.*, 1987, 38(3–4), pp. 303–22. **[G: Hungary; U.S.S.R.]**

Riden, Philip. An English Factor at Stockholm in the 1680's. *Scand. Econ. Hist. Rev.*, 1987, 35(2), pp. 191–207. **[G: U.K.; Sweden]**

Riedel, James. United States Trade Policy: From Multilateralism to Bilateralism? *Giersch, H., ed.*, 1987, pp. 85–104. **[G: U.S.]**

Rios, Sandra Maria C. Polônia. Exportações brasileiras de produtos manufaturados: uma avaliação econométrica para o período 1964/84. (With English summary.) *Pesquisa Planejamento Econ.*, August 1987, 17(2), pp. 299–332. **[G: Brazil]**

Roarty, Michael J. The Impact of the Common Agricultural Policy on Agricultural Trade and Development. *Nat. Westminster Bank Quart. Rev.*, February 1987, pp. 12–28. **[G: EEC]**

Rogowski, Ronald. Trade and the Variety of Democratic Institutions. *Int. Organ.*, Spring 1987, 41(2), pp. 203–23. **[G: OECD]**

Román, Zoltán and Bayer, Kurt. Structural Policy in Hungary and Austria. *Saunders, C. T., ed.*, 1987, pp. 79–99. **[G: Hungary; Austria]**

Rostow, Walt W. The Pacific Basin and the World Economy. *Rostow, W. W.*, 1987, 1985, pp. 151–64. **[G: U.S.S.R.; U.S.; Japan]**

Rostow, Walt W. The Rich Country–Poor Country Problem: From the Eighteenth to the Twenty-first Centuries. *Steinherr, A. and Weiserbs, D., eds.*, 1987, pp. 47–83. **[G: Global]**

Rostow, Walt W. The World Economy since 1945: A Stylized Historical Analysis. *Rostow, W. W.*, 1987, 1985, pp. 19–48. **[G: Global]**

Rousslang, Donald J. The Effects of Recent Corporate Tax Changes on U.S. International Trade. *Nat. Tax J.*, December 1987, 40(4), pp. 603–15. **[G: U.S.]**

Rowse, John. Canadian Natural Gas Exports, Domestic Gas Prices, and Future Gas Supply Costs. *Energy J.*, April 1987, 8(2), pp. 43–62. **[G: Canada]**

Roy, Dilip Kumar. Exports and Labour Absorption: The Case of Bangladesh Manufactures. *Industry Devel.*, 1987, (22), pp. 67–92. **[G: Bangladesh]**

Rugman, Alan M. Multinationals and Trade in Services: A Transaction Cost Approach. *Weltwirtsch. Arch.*, 1987, 123(4), pp. 651–67. **[G: Canada]**

Rugman, Alan M. Strategies for International Competitiveness. *Tremblay, R., ed.*, 1987, pp. 315–25. **[G: U.S.]**

Rwegasira, Delphin G. Balance-of-Payments Adjustment in Low-Income Developing Countries: The Experiences of Kenya and Tanzania in the 1970s. *World Devel.*, Oct./Nov. 1987, 15(10/11), pp. 1321–35. **[G: Kenya; Tanzania]**

Sabel, Hermann. Gegenwärtige Probleme des Managements in der chinesischen Wirtschaft. (With English summary.) *Z. Betriebswirtshaft*, February 1987, 57(2), pp. 124–44. **[G: W. Germany; China]**

Saelens, F. H. Japanese Strategies for Serving Overseas Markets: The Case of Electronics. *Trevor, M., ed.*, 1987, pp. 50–62. **[G: Japan]**

Samli, A. Coskun. An Alternative International Marketing Strategy: The "J" Model. *Cavusgil, S. T., ed.*, 1987, pp. 239–57.

Samuelson, Paul A. The U.S. and Japanese Economies in the Remaining Reagan Years. *Sato, R. and Wachtel, P., eds.*, 1987, pp. 89–99. **[G: U.S.; Japan]**

Samulewicz, Wincenty W. Some Qualitative Changes in the East–West Economic Relations: An Outline. *Econ. Int.*, February 1987, 40(1), pp. 78–89. **[G: Europe]**

Santiago, Carlos E. The Impact of Foreign Direct Investment on Export Structure and Employment Generation. *World Devel.*, March 1987, 15(3), pp. 317–28. **[G: Puerto Rico]**

Sapir, André. International Trade in Services and Its Relevance for Economic Development: Comment. *Giarini, O., ed.*, 1987, pp. 49–54.

Sapsford, David. A Simple Model of Primary Commodity Price Determination: 1900–80. *J. Devel. Stud.*, January 1987, 23(2), pp. 265–74.

Sapsford, David. Primary Commodities in International Trade: An Analysis of Real Prices. *Appl. Econ.*, March 1987, 19(3), pp. 317–21. **[G: Global]**

Sapsford, David. The Determinants of the Demand for Internationally Traded Primary Commodities: An Empirical Analysis. *J. Econ. Stud.*, 1987, 14(3), pp. 55–60.

Sarkar, Prabirjit. The Long-term Behaviour of Terms Trade between Primary Products and Manufacturers: From the Classical Idea to the Prebisch–Singer Hypothesis. *Indian Econ. J.*, Jan.-Mar. 1987, 34(3), pp. 34–42.

Sarmad, Khwaja and Mahmood, Riaz. Disaggregated Import Demand Functions for Pakistan. *Pakistan Devel. Rev.*, Spring 1987, 26(1), pp. 71–80. **[G: Pakistan]**

Sarris, Alexander H. Domestic Price Policies and International Distortions: The Cases of Wheat and Rice. *Econ. Notes*, 1987, (2), pp. 5–35. **[G: LDCs; MDCs]**

Sato, Kazuo and Lii, Sheng-Yann. The Exchange Rate, Trade Balance, and Capital Flows: The Case of Japan. *Dutta, M., ed. (1)*, 1987, pp. 145–70. **[G: Japan]**

Sato, Mitsuaki. Costs and Benefits to the United States of the 1985 Steel Import Quota Program: Discussion. *Sato, R. and Wachtel, P., eds.*, 1987, pp. 181–83. **[G: U.S.; Japan]**

Sattar, Zaidi. Non-competitive Imports in Planning Models: The Bangladesh Case. *Bangladesh Devel. Stud.*, September 1987, 15(3), pp. 95–99. **[G: Bangladesh]**

Saunders, Christopher. Industrial Policies and Structural Change: Introduction. *Saunders, C. T., ed.*, 1987, pp. 1–19.

Saxonhouse, Gary R. Strategic Sectors and International Competition: Comment. *Stern, R. M., ed.*, 1987, pp. 239–43. **[G: U.S.]**

Schäfer, Henry. Schaden flexible Wechselkurse der Weltwirtschaft? Ein Überblick zum aktuellen theoretischen und empirischen Forschungsstand. (Do Flexible Exchange Rates Disadvantage the World Economy? A Survey of Current Theoretical and Empirical Research. With English summary.) *Konjunkturpolitik*, 1987, *33*(4), pp. 219–41.

Schedvin, C. B. The Australian Economy on the Hinge of History. *Australian Econ. Rev.*, First Quarter 1987, (77), pp. 20–30. **[G: Australia]**

Schick, Irvin C. and Tonak, E. Ahmet. The International Dimension: Trade, Aid, and Debt. *Schick, I. C. and Tonak, E. A., eds.*, 1987, pp. 333–63. **[G: Turkey]**

Schive, Chi. Trade Patterns and Trends of Taiwan. *Bradford, C. I., Jr. and Branson, W. H., eds.*, 1987, pp. 307–31. **[G: Taiwan]**

Schuh, G. Edward. The Changing Context of Food and Agricultural Development Policy. *Gittinger, J. P.; Leslie, J. and Hoisington, C., eds.*, 1987, pp. 72–88. **[G: Global]**

Schware, Robert. Software Industry Development in the Third World: Policy Guidelines, Institutional Options, and Constraints. *World Devel.*, Oct./Nov. 1987, *15*(10/11), pp. 1249–67. **[G: LDCs]**

Seringhaus, F. H. Rolf. Do Experienced Exporters Have Market Entry Problems? *Liiketaloudellinen Aikak.*, April 1987, *36*(4), pp. 376–88. **[G: Canada]**

Serruya, Michel and Librowicz, Michel. Countertrade: A Partial Solution to Liquidity Crisis of Mexico. *Tremblay, R., ed.*, 1987, pp. 203–25. **[G: Mexico; Canada]**

Shachmurove, Yochanan. The Integration of the Israeli Economy into the EEC: Recent Trends and a Forecast. *Greilsammer, I. and Weiler, J. H. H., eds.*, 1987, pp. 73–112. **[G: Israel; EEC]**

Sharp, Margaret. Europe: Collaboration in the High Technology Sectors. *Oxford Rev. Econ. Policy*, Spring 1987, *3*(1), pp. 52–65. **[G: W. Europe; Japan; U.S.]**

Shelburne, Robert C. A Ratio Test of Trade Intensity and Per-capita-Income Similarity. *Weltwirtsch. Arch.*, 1987, *123*(3), pp. 474–87. **[G: OECD]**

Silber, Jacques G. and Berrebi, Zeev M. The 1975 Free Trade Agreement and Its Impact on Israeli Exports to the EEC. *Greilsammer, I. and Weiler, J. H. H., eds.*, 1987, pp. 136–55. **[G: Israel; EEC]**

Simpson, Mark S. C. South–South Cooperation: Africa's Brazilian Option. *Akinrinade, O. and Barling, J. K., eds.*, 1987, pp. 199–217. **[G: Africa; Brazil]**

Smith, Bruce J. Some Aspects of Economic Adjustment in Small Island Economies. *Holmes, F., ed.*, 1987, pp. 237–62. **[G: S. Pacific]**

Smith, Roy C. New Financial Aspects of the U.S.–Japanese Trade Relationship. *Sato, R. and Wachtel, P., eds.*, 1987, pp. 110–26. **[G: U.S.; Japan]**

Smith, Valdemar. En empirisk model for grænsehandel. (An Empirical Model of Trade across the Danish–German Frontier. With English summary.) *Nationaløkon. Tidsskr.*, 1987, *125*(2), pp. 234–43. **[G: Denmark; W. Germany]**

Sosin, Kim and Fairchild, Loretta. Capital Intensity and Export Propensity in Some Latin American Countries. *Oxford Bull. Econ. Statist.*, May 1987, *49*(2), pp. 191–208. **[G: Latin America]**

Soulié, Daniel. Technology Transfers in the Automotive Equipment Industry: The French Case. *Safarian, A. E. and Bertin, G. Y., eds.*, 1987, pp. 180–90. **[G: France]**

Spinanger, Dean. Will the Multi-fibre Arrangement Keep Bangladesh Humble? *World Econ.*, March 1987, *10*(1), pp. 75–84. **[G: Bangladesh]**

Srinivasan, T. N. The National Defense Argument for Government Intervention in Foreign Trade. *Stern, R. M., ed.*, 1987, pp. 337–63. **[G: U.S.]**

Srinivasan, T. N. The National Defense Argument for Government Intervention in Foreign Trade: Postscript. *Stern, R. M., ed.*, 1987, pp. 374–75. **[G: U.S.]**

Staiger, Robert W.; Deardorff, Alan V. and Stern, Robert M. An Evaluation of Factor Endowments and Protection as Determinants of Japanese and American Foreign Trade. *Can. J. Econ.*, August 1987, *20*(3), pp. 449–63. **[G: U.S.; Japan]**

Staiger, Robert W.; Deardorff, Alan V. and Stern, Robert M. Employment Effects of Japanese and American Protectionism. *Salvatore, D., ed.*, 1987, pp. 164–80. **[G: U.S.; Japan]**

Stein, Herbert. U.S. Macroeconomic Policy and Trade Relations with Japan. *Sato, R. and Wachtel, P., eds.*, 1987, pp. 100–109. **[G: U.S.; Japan]**

Stern, Robert M. and Hoekman, Bernard M. Issues and Data Needs for GATT Negotiations on Services. *World Econ.*, March 1987, *10*(1), pp. 39–60.

Stevens, Christopher. The EC and Development Efforts in Africa. *Akinrinade, O. and Barling, J. K., eds.*, 1987, pp. 129–48. **[G: EEC; Africa]**

Stone, Charles F. and Sawhill, Isabel V. Trade's Impact on U.S. Jobs. *Challenge*, Sept./Oct. 1987, *30*(4), pp. 12–18. **[G: U.S.]**

Strydom, P. D. F. South Africa in World Trade. *S. Afr. J. Econ.*, September 1987, *55*(3), pp. 203–18. **[G: S. Africa]**

Suba-Varga, Judit. "Cycles" in Hungary's Trade with the Developed Western Countries. *Acta Oecon.*, 1987, *38*(3–4), pp. 339–60. **[G: Hungary]**

Subrahmanyam, Sanjay. Notes on the Sixteenth Century Bengal Trade. *Indian Econ. Soc. Hist.*

Rev., July-Sept. 1987, *24*(3), pp. 265–89.
[G: India]
Swann, G. M. P. International Differences in Product Design and Their Economic Significance. *Appl. Econ.*, February 1987, *19*(2), pp. 201–13. [G: U.K.]
Szakolczai, György; Bagdy, Gábor and Vindics, József. The Dependence of the Hungarian Economy on the World Economy: Facts and Consequences. *Soviet E. Europ. Foreign Trade*, Spring 1987, *23*(1), pp. 54–88.
[G: Hungary]
Tabaczyński, Eugeniusz. Export-Oriented Changes in Polish Industry. *Eastern Europ. Econ.*, Spring 1987, *25*(3), pp. 86–92.
[G: Poland]
Tamor, Kenneth L. An Empirical Examination of the Factor Endowments Hypothesis. *Can. J. Econ.*, May 1987, *20*(2), pp. 387–98.
Tange, Toshiko. United States–Japan Trade Frictions and Competitiveness. *Salvatore, D., ed.*, 1987, pp. 201–15. [G: U.S.; Japan]
Tansel, Aysit and Togan, Sübidey. Price and Income Effects in Turkish Foreign Trade. *Weltwirtsch. Arch.*, 1987, *123*(3), pp. 521–34.
[G: Turkey]
Tarr, David G. Costs and Benefits to the United States of the 1985 Steel Import Quota Program. *Sato, R. and Wachtel, P., eds.*, 1987, pp. 159–77. [G: Japan; U.S.]
Tarr, David G. and Morkre, Morris E. Aggregate Costs to the United States of Tariffs and Quotas on Imports. *Salvatore, D., ed.*, 1987, pp. 216–29. [G: U.S.]
Teitel, Simón and Thoumi, Francisco E. De la sustitución de importaciones a las exportaciones: la experiencia de las exportaciones manufactureras de la Argentina y el Brasil. (With English summary.) *Desarrollo Econ.*, Apr.-June 1987, *27*(105), pp. 29–60.
[G: Argentina; Brazil]
Telegdy, I. Stephen. Doing Business in Eastern Europe: A Manager's Perspective on the Practical Aspects. *Marer, P. and van Veen, P., eds.*, 1987, pp. 99–106. [G: E. Europe]
Terweduwe, D. The Newly and Semi-industrialized Countries: A Critical Appraisal of the Country Classifications. *Tijdschrift Econ. Manage.*, 1987, *32*(1), pp. 55–71.
[G: Selected LDCs]
Teubal, Morris. The Role of Technological Learning in the Exports of Manufactured Goods: The Case of Selected Capital Goods in Brazil. *Teubal, M.*, 1987, pp. 104–30. [G: Brazil]
Thomas, Charles P. U.S. International Transactions in 1986. *Fed. Res. Bull.*, May 1987, *73*(5), pp. 321–29. [G: U.S.]
Thorp, Rosemary. Trends and Cycles in the Peruvian Economy. *[Diaz-Alejandro, C. F.]*, 1987, pp. 355–74. [G: Peru]
Thorp, Rosemary. Trends and Cycles in the Peruvian Economy. *J. Devel. Econ.*, October 1987, *27*(1–2), pp. 355–74. [G: Peru]
Thursby, Jerry G. and Thursby, Marie C. Bilateral Trade Flows, the Linder Hypothesis, and Exchange Risk. *Rev. Econ. Statist.*, August

1987, *69*(3), pp. 488–95. [G: OECD]
Timmer, C. Peter. Corn Marketing. *Timmer, C. P., ed.*, 1987, pp. 201–34. [G: Indonesia]
Tokdemir, Ertuğrul. Türkiye'nin Isviçre ile Ticaretinde Bazi Egilimler (1970–1983). (With English summary.) *METU*, 1987, *14*(1), pp. 49–63. [G: Turkey; Sweden]
Tokman, Víctor E. and Wurgaft, J. The Recession and the Workers of Latin America. *International Labour Office.*, 1987, pp. 37–74.
[G: Latin America]
Tomczyk, Paweł. CMEA Foreign Trade Forecast: 1985–1990. *Soviet E. Europ. Foreign Trade*, Fall 1987, *23*(3), pp. 44–73. [G: CMEA]
Toren, Benny. The Impact of the FTA Agreement with the EEC on Israeli Industry: A Follow-Up. *Greilsammer, I. and Weiler, J. H. H., eds.*, 1987, pp. 113–35. [G: Israel; EEC]
Torricelli, Robert G. The ASEAN Success Story: Social, Economic, and Political Dimensions: The United States. *Martin, L. G., ed.*, 1987, pp. 200–207. [G: U.S.; ASEAN]
Tovias, Alfred. The Impact of the Second Enlargement of the EC upon Israel's Balance of Payments. *Greilsammer, I. and Weiler, J. H. H., eds.*, 1987, pp. 173–94. [G: EEC; Israel]
Trela, Irene; Whalley, John and Wigle, Randall. International Trade in Grains: Domestic Policies and Trade Impacts. *Scand. J. Econ.*, 1987, *89*(3), pp. 271–83. [G: Global]
Trevor, Malcolm. Japanese Companies in the UK. *Trevor, M., ed.*, 1987, pp. 13–27.
[G: Japan; U.K.]
Trevor, Malcolm. What Is Internationalisation? *Trevor, M., ed.*, 1987, pp. 2–12. [G: Japan]
Truett, Dale B. and Truett, Lila J. The Response of Tourism to International Economic Conditions: Greece, Mexico, and Spain. *J. Devel. Areas*, January 1987, *21*(2), pp. 177–89.
[G: Greece; Mexico; Spain]
Truett, Lila J. and Truett, Dale B. The Mexican Automobile Industry and International Trade, 1970–1983. *J. Econ. Devel.*, June 1987, *12*(1), pp. 65–85. [G: Mexico]
Tsutsui, Shunichi. Is the Japan Problem Over? Discussion. *Sato, R. and Wachtel, P., eds.*, 1987, pp. 37–39. [G: U.S.; Japan]
Tuan, Chyau. U.S. Influence on the Hong Kong Economy and Prospect. *Dutta, M., ed. (II)*, 1987, pp. 199–221. [G: Hong Kong]
Turits, Richard. Trade, Debt, and the Cuban Economy. *Zimbalist, A., ed.*, 1987, pp. 165–82. [G: Cuba]
Ueda, Kazuo. Japanese–U.S. Current Accounts and Exchange Rates before and after the G5 Agreement. *Sato, R. and Wachtel, P., eds.*, 1987, pp. 127–47. [G: Japan; U.S.]
Ueda, Kazuo. Prospects for Japan's Current-Account Surplus. *Patrick, H. T. and Tachi, R., eds.*, 1987, pp. 54–57. [G: Japan]
Urban, Bohumil. Objective World Market Criteria Must Be Used. *Czech. Econ. Digest.*, December 1987, (8), pp. 35–49.
[G: Czechoslovakia]
Urban, Bohumil. World Criteria of Effectiveness

and Quality. *Czech. Econ. Digest.*, June 1987, (4), pp. 10–22. **[G: Czechoslovakia]**

Vaidya, Kalyan. Selected Measures of Financial Co-operation among Developing Countries. *Dell, S., ed., Pt. 2*, 1987, pp. 569–609. **[G: LDCs]**

Valdés, Alberto. Agriculture in the Uruguay Round: Interests of Developing Countries. *World Bank Econ. Rev.*, September 1987, *1*(4), pp. 571–93. **[G: LDCs]**

Valdés, Alberto and León A., Javier. Política Comercial, Industrialización y su Sesgo Antiexportador: Peru 1940–1983. (With English summary.) *Cuadernos Econ.*, April 1987, *24*(71), pp. 3–28. **[G: Peru]**

Veeman, Michele M. Hedonic Price Functions for Wheat in the World Market: Implications for Canadian Wheat Export Strategy. *Can. J. Agr. Econ.*, November 1987, *35*(3), pp. 535–52.

Vellai-Posta, Györgyi and Veliczky, József. A Statistical Analysis of the "Openness" of Our Economic Processes. *Soviet E. Europ. Foreign Trade*, Spring 1987, *23*(1), pp. 89–110. **[G: Hungary]**

Vernon, Raymond. Coping with Technological Change: U.S. Problems and Prospects. *Guile, B. R. and Brooks, H., eds.*, 1987, pp. 160–90. **[G: U.S.]**

Voráček, Michal. Czechoslovakia and the Restructuring of the CMEA Mechanism. *Czech. Econ. Digest.*, December 1987, (8), pp. 29–34. **[G: Czechoslovakia]**

Vošický, Emilián. Still Too Many Obstacles. *Czech. Econ. Digest.*, June 1987, (4), pp. 56–60. **[G: Czechoslovakia]**

de Vries, Rimmer and Hargreaves, Derek. The Dollar's Decline and Trade: Mission Accomplished? *Challenge*, Jan./Feb. 1987, *29*(6), pp. 37–46. **[G: Global]**

Wachtel, Paul. Trade Friction and Economic Policy: Problems and Prospects for Japan and the United States: Introduction. *Sato, R. and Wachtel, P., eds.*, 1987, pp. 1–8. **[G: U.S.; Japan]**

Waelbroeck, Jean. Exports of Manufactures from Developing Countries to the European Community. *Bradford, C. I., Jr. and Branson, W. H., eds.*, 1987, pp. 61–92. **[G: LDCs; W. Europe]**

Waelbroeck, Jean. International Trade in Services and Its Relevance for Economic Development: Comment. *Giarini, O., ed.*, 1987, pp. 54–57.

Wagao, Jumanne H. Trade Relations among SADCC Countries. *Amin, S.; Chitala, D. and Mandaza, I., eds.*, 1987, pp. 147–80. **[G: Southern Africa]**

Wagner, Joachim and Bellmann, Lutz. Importdruck, Anpassungsstrategien und Qualifikationsstruktur: Eineökonometrische Untersuchung für Industrien des Verarbeitenden Gewerbes in der Bundesrepublik Deutschland 1976–1983. (Import Pressure, Adjustment Strategies, and Structure of Employment—An Econometric Study for Manufacturing Indus-

tries in the Federal Republic of Germany, 1976–1983. With English summary.) *Z. Wirtschaft. Sozialwissen.*, 1987, *107*(4), pp. 513–35. **[G: W. Germany]**

Walker, John; Rossi, Vanessa and Clements, Michael. The World and UK Economy: Analysis and Prospects. *Oxford Rev. Econ. Policy*, Spring 1987, *3*(1), pp. xx–xxxiii. **[G: U.K.; U.S.]**

Warley, T. K. and Barichello, R. R. Agricultural Issues in a Comprehensive Canada–U.S. Trade Agreement: A Canadian Perspective. *Can. J. Agr. Econ.*, May 1987, *34*, pp. 213–27. **[G: Canada]**

Warr, Peter G. Structural Effects of Increasing Australia's Imports from Less Developed Countries. *Pasinetti, L. and Lloyd, P., eds.*, 1987, pp. 189–211. **[G: Australia]**

Watson, William G. Canada–U.S. Free Trade: Why Now? *Can. Public Policy*, September 1987, *13*(3), pp. 337–49. **[G: U.S.; Canada]**

Weiler, Joseph H. H. The Evolution of a European Foreign Policy: Mechanisms and Institutions. *Greilsammer, I. and Weiler, J. H. H., eds.*, 1987, pp. 233–54. **[G: Israel; EEC]**

Welsch, Heinz. An Aggregate Import Demand Model for Long-term Projections. *Jahr. Nationalökon. Statist.*, July 1987, *203*(4), pp. 372–89. **[G: OECD]**

Westoby, Jack C. Prospects for Expanding Forest Products Exports from Developing Countries. *Westoby, J.*, 1987, *1964*, pp. 71–114. **[G: LDCs]**

Whichard, Obie G. U.S. Sales of Services to Foreigners. *Surv. Curr. Bus.*, January 1987, *67*(1), pp. 22–41. **[G: U.S.]**

White, David L. Parsis in the Commercial World of Western India, 1700–1750. *Indian Econ. Soc. Hist. Rev.*, Apr.-June 1987, *24*(2), pp. 183–203. **[G: India]**

White, Lawrence J. Costs and Benefits to the United States of the 1985 Steel Import Quota Program: Discussion. *Sato, R. and Wachtel, P., eds.*, 1987, pp. 177–81. **[G: U.S.; Japan]**

Whitman, Marina von Neumann. Strategic Sectors and International Competition: Comment. *Stern, R. M., ed.*, 1987, pp. 233–38. **[G: U.S.]**

Whitman, Marina von Neumann. The Impact of the Debt Problem on International Trade. *Rodriguez, R. M., ed.*, 1987, pp. 87–96. **[G: LDCs]**

Winters, L. Alan. An Empirical Intertemporal Model of Developing Countries' Imports. *Weltwirtsch. Arch.*, 1987, *123*(1), pp. 58–80. **[G: Malaysia; Colombia; Kenya]**

Winters, L. Alan. Britain in Europe: A Survey of Quantitative Trade Studies. *J. Common Market Stud.*, June 1987, *25*(4), pp. 315–35. **[G: EEC]**

Winters, L. Alan. Models of Primary Price Indices. *Oxford Bull. Econ. Statist.*, August 1987, *49*(3), pp. 307–22. **[G: LDCs]**

Winters, L. Alan. The Economic Consequences of Agricultural Support: A Survey. *OECD Econ. Stud.*, Autumn 1987, (9), pp. 7–54.

Wojnilower, Albert M. Japan and the United States: Some Observations on Economic Policy. *Patrick, H. T. and Tachi, R., eds.*, 1987, pp. 76–83.   **[G: Japan; U.S.]**

Wolf, Bernard M. The Reaction of U.S.-Based Multinational Enterprises to Free Trade between Canada and the United States: Impediments to Empirical Verification. *Tremblay, R., ed.*, 1987, pp. 351–66.   **[G: U.S.; Canada]**

Wolf, Martin. An Unholy Alliance: The European Community and Developing Countries in the International Trading Sysem. *Aussenwirtschaft*, April 1987, *42*(1), pp. 41–64.
                                                      [G: EEC; LDCs]

Wolf, Thomas A. On the Conversion of Ruble Trade Flows into Dollars. *J. Compar. Econ.*, December 1987, *11*(4), pp. 558–71.
                                                      [G: CMEA]

van Wolferen, Karel G. The Japan Problem. *Foreign Aff.*, Winter 1986/87, *65*(2), pp. 288–303.
                                                      [G: Japan; U.S.]

Wren-Lewis, Simon and Eastwood, Fiona. The World Economy. *Nat. Inst. Econ. Rev.*, May 1987, (120), pp. 21–41.   **[G: U.S.; Japan; W. Germany; Canada; France]**

Wulf, Herbert. Arms Industry Unlimited: The Economic Impact of the Arms Sector in Developing Countries. *Borner, S. and Taylor, A., eds.*, 1987, pp. 203–217.   **[G: LDCs]**

Yamazawa, Ippei. Japan and Her Asian Neighbors in a Dynamic Perspective. *Bradford, C. I., Jr. and Branson, W. H., eds.*, 1987, pp. 93–119.   **[G: Asia]**

Yanagihara, Tōru. Pacific Basin Economic Relations: Japan's New Role? *Devel. Econ.*, December 1987, *25*(4), pp. 403–20.
                                          [G: Pacific Basin; Japan]

Yang, Bong M. The Supply and Demand for Exports for Industrialized Countries: A Disequilibrium Analysis. *Appl. Econ.*, September 1987, *19*(9), pp. 1137–48.   **[G: OECD]**

Yannopoulos, George N. United States Trade Interests and EC Enlargement. *J. World Trade Law*, August 1987, *21*(4), pp. 49–65.
                                                      [G: EEC; U.S.]

Yeats, Alexander J. A Note on the Functioning of International Commodity Price Stabilisation Agreements in Periods of Fluctuating Monetary Exchange Rates. *J. Devel. Stud.*, April 1987, *23*(3), pp. 382–401.

Yoshitomi, Masaru. Growth Gaps, Exchange Rates and Asymmetry: Is it Possible to Unwind Current-Account Imbalances without Fiscal Expansion in Japan? *Patrick, H. T. and Tachi, R., eds.*, 1987, pp. 18–29. **[G: Japan; U.S.]**

Zacher, Mark W. Trade Gaps, Analytical Gaps: Regime Analysis and International Commodity Trade Regulation. *Int. Organ.*, Spring 1987, *41*(2), pp. 173–202.   **[G: Global]**

Zanias, George P. Adjustment Costs and Rational Expectations: An Application to a Tobacco Export Model. *Amer. J. Agr. Econ.*, February 1987, *69*(1), pp. 22–29.   **[G: Greece]**

Zilberfarb, Ben-Zion. The Effect of Relative Exchange and Market Growth Rates on the Geographic Allocation of Exports: More Empirical

Evidence. *Quart. J. Bus. Econ.*, Summer 1987, *26*(3), pp. 96–101.   **[G: Israel]**

Zimmermann, Klaus F. Trade and Dynamic Efficiency. *Kyklos*, 1987, *40*(1), pp. 73–87.
                                                 [G: W. Germany]

422 Commercial Policy

4220 Commercial Policy

Aaron, Henry J. The Impact of a Value-Added Tax on U.S. Competitiveness. *Walker, C. E. and Bloomfield, M. A., eds.*, 1987, pp. 206–13.   **[G: U.S.]**

Abbott, Kenneth W. Collective Goods, Mobile Resources, and Extraterritorial Trade Controls. *Law Contemp. Probl.*, Summer 1987, *50*(3), pp. 117–52.   **[G: U.S.]**

Abraham, Filip; Deardorff, Alan V. and Stern, Robert M. The Economic Consequences of an Import Surcharge: Theory and Empirical Evidence for the U.S. Economy. *J. Policy Modeling*, Summer 1987, *9*(2), pp. 285–309.
                                                      [G: U.S.]

Ahmadi-Esfahani, Fredoun Z. and Carter, Colin A. A Dynamic Analysis of U.S. Export Wheat Pricing and Market Shares. *Australian J. Agr. Econ.*, December 1987, *31*(3), pp. 191–203.
                                                      [G: U.S.]

Ali, Ifzal. India's Manufactured Exports: An Analysis of Supply Factors. *Devel. Econ.*, June 1987, *25*(2), pp. 152–70.   **[G: India]**

Amstutz, Daniel G. Agricultural Reform Efforts in the United States and Japan: Remarks. *Johnson, D. G., ed.*, 1987, pp. 82–87.   **[G: U.S.; Japan]**

Anastasopoulos, A. Removal of the Canadian Tariffs on Imports from the United States Regional Impacts in the Short Run. *Tremblay, R., ed.*, 1987, pp. 419–61.   **[G: Canada; U.S.]**

Anderson, Kym. The Australian Economy in the Long Run: Tariffs and the Manufacturing Sector. *Maddock, R. and McLean, I. W., eds.*, 1987, pp. 165–94.   **[G: Australia]**

Anderson, Kym and Baldwin, Robert E. The Political Market for Protection in Industrial Countries. *[Kitamura, H.]*, 1987, pp. 20–36.
                                      [G: U.S.; Japan; Australia]

Anglin, Douglas G. United Nations Economic Sanctions against South Africa and Rhodesia. *Leyton-Brown, D., ed.*, 1987, pp. 23–56.
                                         [G: Rhodesia; S. Africa]

Anjaria, Shailendra J. Balance of Payments and Related Issues in the Uruguay Round of Trade Negotiations. *World Bank Econ. Rev.*, September 1987, *1*(4), pp. 669–88.   **[G: LDCs]**

Ariff, Mohamed, et al. Economic Relations between ASEAN and Australia. *Econ. Rec.*, March 1987, *63*(180), pp. 1–9. **[G: Australia; ASEAN]**

Arndt, H. W. GATT and the Developing World: Agenda for a New Trade Round. *Weltwirtsch. Arch.*, 1987, *123*(4), pp. 705–18. **[G: Global]**

Arndt, Sven W. The Role of Domestic Policy in Addressing Trade Problems. *Barfield, C. E. and Makin, J. H., eds.*, 1987, pp. 39–42.
                                                      [G: U.S.]

Atwood, James R. Conflicts of Jurisdiction in the Antitrust Field: The Example of Export Cartels. *Law Contemp. Probl.*, Summer 1987, *50*(3), pp. 153–64. [G: U.S.]

Avramovic, Dragoslav. Commodity Problem: What Next? *World Devel.*, May 1987, *15*(5), pp. 645–55. [G: LDCs]

Axelrod, Robert. How Should the United States Respond to Other Countries' Trade Policies? Comment. *Stern, R. M., ed.*, 1987, pp. 283–86. [G: U.S.]

Bácskai, Tamás. Foreign Trade, Investments, and Economic Reforms in Hungary. *Marer, P. and van Veen, P., eds.*, 1987, pp. 139–52. [G: Hungary]

van Bael, Ivo. Creeping Protectionism: Editorial. *J. World Trade Law*, December 1987, *21*(6), pp. 5–7. [G: U.S.; EEC]

Baker, Antony M. Liberalization of Trade in Services—The World Insurance Industry. *Giarini, O., ed.*, 1987, pp. 193–211. [G: Global]

Baker, James A., III. Renewing America's Competitiveness. *Barfield, C. E. and Makin, J. H., eds.*, 1987, pp. 3–10. [G: U.S.]

Balassa, Bela. Japan's Trade Policies. *Giersch, H., ed.*, 1987, pp. 111–70. [G: Japan]

Balassa, Bela. Japanese Trade Policies toward Developing Countries. *Dutta, M., ed. (I)*, 1987, pp. 49–68. [G: Japan]

Balassa, Bela and Michalopoulos, Constantine. The Extent and the Cost of Protection in Developed–Developing-Country Trade. *Salvatore, D., ed.*, 1987, pp. 482–504. [G: LDCs; MDCs]

Baldwin, John R. and Gorecki, Paul K. The Impact of High Tariffs and Imperfect Market Structure on Plant Scale Inefficiency in Canadian Manufacturing Industries in the 1970's. *Rech. Écon. Louvain*, 1987, *53*(1), pp. 51–73. [G: Canada]

Baldwin, Robert E. Alternative Liberalization Strategies. *Giersch, H., ed.*, 1987, pp. 579–604.

Baldwin, Robert E. GATT Reform: Selected Issues. *[Corden, W. M.]*, 1987, pp. 204–14.

Baldwin, Robert E. The New Protectionism: A Response to Shifts in National Economic Power. *Salvatore, D., ed.*, 1987, pp. 95–112. [G: U.S.]

Baldwin, Robert E. and Clarke, Richard N. Game-Modeling Multilateral Trade Negotiations. *J. Policy Modeling*, Summer 1987, *9*(2), pp. 257–84.

Baldwin, Robert E. and Richardson, J. David. Recent U.S. Trade Policy and Its Global Implications. *Bradford, C. I., Jr. and Branson, W. H., eds.*, 1987, pp. 121–55. [G: Global; U.S.]

Bale, Harvey E., Jr. The Consumption Tax: A Better Alternative? The International Trade Issues. *Walker, C. E. and Bloomfield, M. A., eds.*, 1987, pp. 213–21. [G: U.S.]

Balisacan, Arsenio M.; Lee, Chung H. and Roumasset, James A. National Food Policies of the Asia-Pacific Region and Their International Implications. *Dutta, M., ed. (I)*, 1987, pp. 221–41. [G: Asia-Pacific]

Balisacan, Arsenio M. and Roumasset, James A. Public Choice of Economic Policy: The Growth of Agricultural Protection. *Weltwirtsch. Arch.*, 1987, *123*(2), pp. 232–48. [G: Global]

Baranson, Jack. Trade Liberalization and the New Generation of Manufacturing Technologies: Implications for Canadian Industry in North American Markets. *Tremblay, R., ed.*, 1987, pp. 407–17. [G: Canada; U.S.]

Bark, Taeho and de Melo, Jaime. Export Mix Adjustment to the Imposition of VERs: Alternative License Allocation Schemes. *Weltwirtsch. Arch.*, 1987, *123*(4), pp. 668–78.

Baron, David P. Exim at Fifty: At a Crossroads? *Rodriguez, R. M., ed.*, 1987, pp. 107–32. [G: U.S.]

Barratt, C. John A. Can External Leverage Pressure South Africa? *Sethi, S. P., ed.*, 1987, pp. 205–17. [G: S. Africa]

Baucus, Max. A Congressional Perspective on Competitiveness. *Walker, C. E. and Bloomfield, M. A., eds.*, 1987, pp. 221–24. [G: U.S.]

Baumann, Renato and Moreira, Heloiza C. Os incentivos às exportações brasileiras de produtos manufaturados—1969/85. (With English summary.) *Pesquisa Planejamento Econ.*, August 1987, *17*(2), pp. 471–89. [G: Brazil]

Bautista, Romeo M. The Recent Recession and Rising Protectionism in Developed Countries: Some Thoughts on the ASEAN Economies. *Dutta, M., ed. (I)*, 1987, pp. 83–91. [G: ASEAN]

Beckmann, Dennis G. On Estimating the Static Effects of Preferential Tariffs. *Eastern Econ. J.*, October-December 1987, *13*(4), pp. 389–97. [G: U.S.]

Behney, Thomas Amos, Jr. Extraterritoriality of Economic Legislation: Bibliography *Law Contemp. Probl.*, Summer 1987, *50*(3), pp. 303–47.

Bennett, Karl. The Caribbean Basin Initiative and Its Implications for CARICOM Exports. *Soc. Econ. Stud.*, June 1987, *36*(2), pp. 21–40. [G: Caribbean]

Berger, Mark C. and Webb, Michael A. Commercial Policy and the Brain Drain. *Appl. Econ.*, February 1987, *19*(2), pp. 143–53. [G: U.S.]

Bergsten, C. Fred. Reform Trade Policy with Auction Quotas. *Challenge*, May/June 1987, *30*(2), pp. 4–10. [G: U.S.]

Berlinski, Julio. Choice of Growth Strategy: Trade Regimes and Export Promotion. *Martirena-Mantel, A. M., ed.*, 1987, pp. 95–114. [G: Latin America]

Bernholz, Peter. The Political Economy of Revaluation-Induced Protectionism under Discretionary Monetary Regimes with Flexible Exchange Rates. *Giersch, H., ed.*, 1987, pp. 407–24. [G: U.S.]

Bethkenhagen, Jochen. Economic and Political Relations between the Two Germanies. *Marer, P. and van Veen, P., eds.*, 1987, pp. 91–98. [G: E. Germany; W. Germany]

Beza, Sterie T. Choice of Growth Strategy: Trade

Regimes and Export Promotion: Comment. *Martirena-Mantel, A. M., ed.*, 1987, pp. 114–19.   [G: Latin America]

Bhagwati, Jagdish N. Protectionism: Old Wine in New Bottles. *Salvatore, D., ed.*, 1987, pp. 31–44.

Bhagwati, Jagdish N. Trade in Services and the Multilateral Trade Negotiations. *World Bank Econ. Rev.*, September 1987, *1*(4), pp. 549–69.   [G: LDCs; OECD]

Bhagwati, Jagdish N. and Irwin, Douglas A. The Return of the Reciprocitarians—U.S. Trade Policy Today. *World Econ.*, June 1987, *10*(2), pp. 109–30.   [G: U.S.]

Bhagwati, Jagdish N.; Krueger, Anne O. and Snape, Richard H. A Symposium Issue on the Multilateral Trade Negotiations and Developing-Country Interests: Introduction. *World Bank Econ. Rev.*, September 1987, *1*(4), pp. 539–47.   [G: LDCs]

Bizer, David S. and Stuart, Charles. The Public Finance of a Protective Tariff: The Case of an Oil Import Fee. *Amer. Econ. Rev.*, December 1987, *77*(5), pp. 1019–22.

Blackhurst, R. The Trend in World Protectionism. *Visser, H. and Schoor, E., eds.*, 1987, pp. 95–107.   [G: Global]

Boltho, Andrea and Allsopp, Christopher. The Assessment: Trade and Trade Policy. *Oxford Rev. Econ. Policy*, Spring 1987, *3*(1), pp. i–xix.   [G: Global]

Boonekamp, Clemens F. J. Voluntary Export Restraints. *Finance Develop.*, December 1987, *24*(4), pp. 2–5.   [G: OECD]

Bossak, Jan. CMEA at the Threshold of Fundamental Reforms. *Econ. Rev. (Keizai Kenkyu)*, July 1987, *38*(3), pp. 217–21.   [G: CMEA]

Botero A., Germán. Choice of Growth Strategy: Trade Regimes and Export Promotion: Comment. *Martirena-Mantel, A. M., ed.*, 1987, pp. 119–20.   [G: Latin America]

Boucher, Carlston B. and Siebeck, Wolfgang E. UNCTAD VII: New Spirit in North–South Relations? *Finance Develop.*, December 1987, *24*(4), pp. 14–16.   [G: Global]

Bowen, Harry P. Is the Japan Problem Over? Discussion. *Sato, R. and Wachtel, P., eds.*, 1987, pp. 40–44.   [G: U.S.; Japan]

Boyd, Roy G. and Krutilla, Kerry. The Welfare Impacts of U.S. Trade Restrictions against the Canadian Softwood Lumber Industry: A Spatial Equilibrium Analysis. *Can. J. Econ.*, February 1987, *20*(1), pp. 17–35.   [G: Canada]

Brada, Josef C. and Dunn, Robin L. Industrial Policies in East and West Europe Compared. *Saunders, C. T., ed.*, 1987, pp. 57–77.   [G: Europe]

Brady, Lawrence J. The Utility of Economic Sanctions as a Policy Instrument. *Leyton-Brown, D., ed.*, 1987, pp. 297–302.

Brand, Simon S. How Economic Sanctions Could Cripple Reform. *Sethi, S. P., ed.*, 1987, pp. 197–203.   [G: S. Africa]

Brander, James A. and Spencer, Barbara J. Tariffs and the Extraction of Foreign Monopoly Rents under Potential Entry. *Bhagwati, J. N.,*

ed., 1987, *1981*, pp. 141–60.

Branson, William H. Macroeconomics and Protection: Comment. *Stern, R. M., ed.*, 1987, pp. 131–36.   [G: OECD]

Branson, William H. The Changing Structure of U.S. Trade: Implications for Research and Policy. *Salvatore, D., ed.*, 1987, pp. 153–63.   [G: U.S.]

Bredahl, Maury E.; Schmitz, Andrew and Hillman, Jimmye S. Rent Seeking in International Trade: The Great Tomato War. *Amer. J. Agr. Econ.*, February 1987, *69*(1), pp. 1–10.   [G: U.S.; Mexico]

Bronfenbrenner, Martin. Japan and Two World Economic Depressions. *[Penrose, E. F.]*, 1987, pp. 32–51.   [G: Japan]

Browder, John O. Brazil's Export Promotion Policy (1980–1984): Impacts on the Amazon's Industrial Wood Sector. *J. Devel. Areas*, April 1987, *21*(3), pp. 285–304.   [G: Brazil]

Brown, Drusilla K. General Equilibrium Effects of the U.S. Generalized System of Preferences. *Southern Econ. J.*, July 1987, *54*(1), pp. 27–47.

Brown, Drusilla K. Tariffs, the Terms of Trade, and National Product Differentiation. *J. Policy Modeling*, Fall 1987, *9*(3), pp. 503–26.

Brown, Kenneth M. Changes in Industrial Structure and Foreign Competition—The Policy Arguments. *Cagan, P., ed.*, 1987, pp. 97–128.   [G: U.S.]

Brown, Stuart S. Nonmarket Economies, Multiple Exchange Rates and the Countervailing Duty Law: The Case of Polish and Czech Steel. *J. World Trade Law*, December 1987, *21*(6), pp. 89–111.   [G: Poland; Czechoslovakia]

Bulajic, Milan. International Protection of Intellectual Property and Foreign Investment. *Dicke, D. C., ed.*, 1987, pp. 42–67.   [G: Global]

Byerlee, Derek. The Political Economy of Third World Food Imports: The Case of Wheat. *Econ. Develop. Cult. Change*, January 1987, *35*(2), pp. 307–28.   [G: LDCs]

Cable, Vincent. Textiles and Clothing in a New Round of Trade Negotiations. *World Bank Econ. Rev.*, September 1987, *1*(4), pp. 619–46.   [G: Global]

Cable, Vincent. The Impact of EEC Trade Policies on Developing Countries. *Giersch, H., ed.*, 1987, pp. 294–326.   [G: EEC; LDCs]

Campbell, Dennis. Joint Ventures between East and West. *Bull. Int. Fiscal Doc.*, July 1987, *41*(7), pp. 299–303.   [G: E. Europe; OECD]

Carmichael, Calum M. The Control of Export Credit Subsidies and Its Welfare Consequences. *J. Int. Econ.*, August 1987, *23*(1/2), pp. 1–19.   [G: U.S.]

Carrada-Bravo, Francisco. International Trade, Investment, Regional Security, and the Prospects of the Mexico–U.S. Relations. *Tremblay, R., ed.*, 1987, pp. 531–48.   [G: Mexico; U.S.]

Carter, Colin A. and Mooney, W. Japanese Tariff Protection of Rapeseed and Soybean Processing. *Can. J. Agr. Econ.*, July 1987, *35*(2), pp. 305–15. **[G: Japan]**

Castro, Emilio. Church Groups Lead the Battle against Apartheid: International Campaign. *Sethi, S. P., ed.*, 1987, pp. 271–78.
[G: S. Africa; U.S.]

Černý, Milan. Will a Constructive Approach Prevail? *Czech. Econ. Digest.*, June 1987, (5), pp. 39–45. **[G: Czechoslovakia]**

Chang, Eui Tae. Protective Effects of Discriminatory Quantitative Restrictions. *Int. Econ. J.*, Spring 1987, *1*(1), pp. 15–28. **[G: U.S.]**

Charnovitz, Steve. The Influence of International Labour Standards on the World Trading Regime. A Historical Overview. *Int. Lab. Rev.*, Sept.-Oct. 1987, *126*(5), pp. 565–84.

Chen, Tain-Jy and Tang, De-Piao. Comparing Technical Efficiency between Import-Substitution-Oriented and Export-Oriented Foreign Firms in a Developing Economy. *J. Devel. Econ.*, August 1987, *26*(2), pp. 277–89.
[G: Taiwan]

Cho, Yoon-Je. How the United States Broke into Korea's Insurance Market. *World Econ.*, December 1987, *10*(4), pp. 483–96. **[G: U.S.; S. Korea]**

Christodoulakis, Nicos and Godley, Wynne. Macroeconomic Consequences of Alternative Trade Policy Options. *J. Policy Modeling*, Fall 1987, *9*(3), pp. 405–36. **[G: U.K.]**

Cieślik, Jerzy; Grolig, Otto and Bogaert, Peter. The Newly-Amended EEC Anti-dumping Regulation: Black Holes in the Common Market? *J. World Trade Law*, December 1987, *21*(6), pp. 79–87. **[G: EEC]**

Clark, Don P. Regulation of International Trade: The United States' Generalized System of Preferences Scheme [The Kennedy Round: Evidence on the Regulation of International Trade in the United States]. *Weltwirtsch. Arch.*, 1987, *123*(4), pp. 697–704. **[G: U.S.]**

Clark, Don P. Regulation of International Trade in the United States: The Tokyo Round. *J. Bus.*, April 1987, *60*(2), pp. 297–306.
[G: U.S.]

Clements, Benedict J. and Kim, Kwan S. The Distributional and Employment Consequences of Export Promotion and Import Substitution in Brazil. *Eastern Econ. J.*, October-December 1987, *13*(4), pp. 435–46. **[G: Brazil]**

Collyns, Charles and Dunaway, Steven. The Cost of Trade Restraints: The Case of Japanese Automobile Exports to the United States. *Int. Monet. Fund Staff Pap.*, March 1987, *34*(1), pp. 150–75. **[G: Japan; U.S.]**

Coloma, Fernando and González, Pablo. Credibilidad de la Política Comercial: Chile 1974–1979. (With English summary.) *Cuadernos Econ.*, August 1987, *24*(72), pp. 143–64.
[G: Chile]

Cooper, Richard N. Industrial Policy and Trade Distortion. *Salvatore, D., ed.*, 1987, pp. 233–65. **[G: W. Europe; U.S.; Japan]**

Cooper, Richard N. Industrial Policy and Trade

Distortion: A Policy Perspective. *[Kitamura, H.]*, 1987, pp. 37–69. **[G: U.S.; Japan; LDCs]**

Cooper, Richard N. Trade Policy as Foreign Policy. *Stern, R. M., ed.*, 1987, pp. 291–322.
[G: U.S.]

Corbo, Vittorio and de Melo, Jaime. Lessons from the Southern Cone Policy Reforms. *World Bank Res. Observer*, July 1987, *2*(2), pp. 111–42. **[G: Argentina; Chile; Uruguay]**

Corden, W. Max. On Making Rules for International Trading System. *Stern, R. M., ed.*, 1987, pp. 413–26. **[G: U.S.]**

Corden, W. Max. The Revival of Protectionism in Developed Countries. *Salvatore, D., ed.*, 1987, pp. 45–68. **[G: OECD]**

Costa, Antonio Maria. The Need for New Multilateral Trade Negotiations: Why Is It Urgent to Complete the GATT Round Successfully? *Salvatore, D., ed.*, 1987, pp. 113–49.
[G: OECD]

Coughlin, Cletus C. and Cartwright, Phillip A. An Examination of State Foreign Export Promotion and Manufacturing Exports. *J. Reg. Sci.*, August 1987, *27*(3), pp. 439–49.
[G: U.S.]

Crandall, Robert W. The Effects of U.S. Trade Protection for Autos and Steel. *Brookings Pap. Econ. Act.*, 1987, (1), pp. 271–88. **[G: U.S.]**

Csikos-Nagy, Béla. Export-Oriented Policies under Severe Import Regimes: A Case Study for Hungary. *Saunders, C. T., ed.*, 1987, pp. 239–49. **[G: Hungary]**

Culbert, Jay. War-Time Anglo–American Talks and the Making of the GATT. *World Econ.*, December 1987, *10*(4), pp. 381–99.
[G: U.K.; U.S.]

Cumby, Robert E. Japanese–U.S. Current Accounts and Exchange Rates before and after the G5 Agreement: Discussion. *Sato, R. and Wachtel, P., eds.*, 1987, pp. 148–52.
[G: Japan; U.S.]

Czepurko, Aleksander. Industrial Policies and Structural Change: Overall Assessments and Comparisons: Comment. *Saunders, C. T., ed.*, 1987, pp. 99–101.

Dalal, K. L. New Dimensions in Indo–African Relations in Sub-Saharan Africa. *Ali, S. S. and Gupta, A., eds.*, 1987, pp. 203–14.
[G: India; Sub-Saharan Africa]

De Bandt, Jacques. Des mesures combinées de politique commerciale et de politique industrielle: tendance ou non au protectionnisme? (Combined Trade and Industrial Policy Measures: More Protectionism or Not? With English summary.) *Écon. Soc.*, April 1987, *21*(4), pp. 47–71. **[G: Global]**

Deardorff, Alan V. Why Do Governments Prefer Nontariff Barriers? *Carnegie–Rochester Conf. Ser. Public Policy*, Spring 1987, *26*, pp. 191–216.

Deardorff, Alan V. and Stern, Robert M. Current Issues in Trade Policy: An Overview. *Stern, R. M., ed.*, 1987, pp. 15–68. **[G: U.S.]**

Deardorff, Alan V. and Stern, Robert M. Tariff and Defensive Responses: A Computational

Analysis. *Int. Econ. J.*, Summer 1987, *1*(2), pp. 1–23. **[G: U.S.; Global]**

DeLay, Tom. Trade Policy: A Republican's View. *Barfield, C. E. and Makin, J. H., eds.*, 1987, pp. 61–64. **[G: U.S.]**

Dell, Sidney and Lawrence, Roger. The Balance of Payments Adjustment Process in Developing Countries. *Dell, S., ed., Pt. 1*, 1987, *1980*, pp. 1–154. **[G: Global]**

Denman, Roy [Sir]. Trade Legislation: A View from the European Community. *Barfield, C. E. and Makin, J. H., eds.*, 1987, pp. 70–72. **[G: EEC; U.S.]**

DeRosa, Dean A. A Positive View of Duty Remission Schemes. *Quart. Rev. Econ. Bus.*, Summer 1987, 27(2), pp. 42–49.

Desai, Padma. The Soviet Union and the Third World: A Faltering Partnership? *Desai, P.*, 1987, *1984*, pp. 256–73. **[G: U.S.S.R.; LDCs]**

Dewitt, David B. The Arab Boycott of Israel. *Leyton-Brown, D., ed.*, 1987, pp. 149–66. **[G: Israel; Arab Countries]**

Dholakia, Nikhilesh. Industrial Policy, Competitiveness, and the Restructuring of World Markets. *Bloom, P. N., ed.*, 1987, pp. 187–216.

Díaz-Alejandro, Carlos F. and Helleiner, Gerald K. Developing Countries and Reform of the World Trading System. *Salvatore, D., ed.*, 1987, pp. 505–25. **[G: LDCs]**

Diebold, William. Western Industrial Policies and East–West Economic Relations. *Saunders, C. T., ed.*, 1987, pp. 21–44.

Dieckhoff, Alain. Motives, Developments and Hindrances for a European Policy towards the Arab–Israeli Conflict. *Greilsammer, I. and Weiler, J. H. H., eds.*, 1987, pp. 256–82. **[G: Israel; W. Europe]**

Dirksen, Erik. What If the Soviet Union Applies to Join the GATT? *World Econ.*, June 1987, 10(2), pp. 229–30. **[G: U.S.S.R.]**

Dixit, Avinash K. How Should the United States Respond to Other Countries' Trade Policies? *Stern, R. M., ed.*, 1987, pp. 245–82. **[G: U.S.]**

Dixit, Avinash K. Issues of Strategic Trade Policy for Small Countries. *Scand. J. Econ.*, 1987, 89(3), pp. 349–67.

Dixit, Avinash K. Strategic Aspects of Trade Policy. *Bewley, T. F., ed.*, 1987, pp. 329–62.

Dixit, Avinash K. Tariffs and Subsidies under Oligopoly: The Case of the U.S. Automobile Industry. *[Corden, W. M.]*, 1987, pp. 112–27. **[G: U.S.]**

Donges, Juergen B. International Migration and the International Division of Labor. *Alonso, W., ed.*, 1987, pp. 129–48.

Dornbusch, Rudiger. External Balance Correction: Depreciation or Protection? *Brookings Pap. Econ. Act.*, 1987, (1), pp. 248–69. **[G: U.S.]**

Dornbusch, Rudiger and Frankel, Jeffrey A. Macroeconomics and Protection. *Stern, R. M., ed.*, 1987, pp. 77–130. **[G: OECD]**

Dunkel, Arthur. The Uruguay Round and the World Economy. *Aussenwirtschaft*, April 1987, *42*(1), pp. 7–10. **[G: Global]**

Dunn, James A., Jr. Automobiles in International Trade: Regime Change or Persistence? *Int. Organ.*, Spring 1987, *41*(2), pp. 225–52. **[G: Global]**

Dutta, M. The Asia-Pacific Economic Community: Some Comments. *Dutta, M., ed. (I)*, 1987, pp. 93–100. **[G: Asia-Pacific]**

Eberle, William D. Trade Policy and the Trade Representative. *Barfield, C. E. and Makin, J. H., eds.*, 1987, pp. 22–23. **[G: U.S.]**

Edwards, Sebastian. Sequencing Economic Liberalization in Developing Countries. *Finance Develop.*, March 1987, 24(1), pp. 26–29. **[G: LDCs]**

Eglin, Richard. Surveillance of Balance-of-Payments Measures in the GATT. *World Econ.*, March 1987, 10(1), pp. 1–26. **[G: LDCs]**

Ehlermann, Claus Dieter. The Institutional Context of EEC–Israel Economic Relations. *Greilsammer, I. and Weiler, J. H. H., eds.*, 1987, pp. 215–29. **[G: EEC; Israel]**

Erb, Richard D. International Debt and Adjustment—Setting the Issues in a Global Perspective. *Tremblay, R., ed.*, 1987, pp. 1–3. **[G: Global]**

Evans, Paul M. Caging the Dragon: Post-war Economic Sanctions against the People's Republic of China. *Leyton-Brown, D., ed.*, 1987, pp. 59–85. **[G: China]**

Falkenheim, Peggy L. Post-Afghanistan Sanctions. *Leyton-Brown, D., ed.*, 1987, pp. 105–30. **[G: U.S.S.R.]**

Faminow, Merle D. and Hillman, Jimmye S. Embargoes and the Emergence of Brazil's Soyabean Industry. *World Econ.*, September 1987, 10(3), pp. 351–66. **[G: Brazil]**

Fan, Liang-Shing and Fan, Chuen-Mei. On the Welfare Effects of Rent Seeking. *Indian Econ. J.*, July-Sept. 1987, 35(1), pp. 136–39.

Feenstra, Robert C. Automobile Prices and Protection: The U.S.–Japan Trade Restraint. *Salvatore, D., ed.*, 1987, pp. 333–51. **[G: U.S.; Japan]**

Feenstra, Robert C. Incentive Compatible Trade Policies. *Scand. J. Econ.*, 1987, 89(3), pp. 373–87.

Feenstra, Robert C. Voluntary Export Restraint in U.S. Autos, 1980–81: Quality, Employment, and Welfare Effects. *Bhagwati, J. N., ed.*, 1987, *1984*, pp. 203–30. **[G: U.S.; Japan]**

Feinberg, Richard E. and Tucker, Stuart K. Export Credits in U.S. Trade, Development, and Industrial Policy. *Rodriguez, R. M., ed.*, 1987, pp. 133–43. **[G: U.S.]**

Fekete, J. Some Thoughts about East–West Economic Relations and the World Economy. *Visser, H. and Schoor, E., eds.*, 1987, pp. 227–36. **[G: OECD; CMEA]**

Fels, Gerhard. United States Trade Policy: From Multilateralism to Bilateralism? Comments. *Giersch, H., ed.*, 1987, pp. 105–09. **[G: U.S.]**

Fernández Kelly, M. Patricia. Technology and Employment along the U.S.–Mexican Border.

Thorup, C. L., ed., 1987, pp. 149–66.
[G: U.S.; Mexico]

Findlay, Ronald. Current Issues in Trade Policy: An Overview: Comment. *Stern, R. M., ed.*, 1987, pp. 73–76. [G: U.S.]

Finger, J. Michael and Laird, Samuel. Protection in Developed and Developing Countries—An Overview. *J. World Trade Law*, December 1987, *21*(6), pp. 9–23. [G: Global]

Finger, J. Michael and Nogués, Julio. International Control of Subsidies and Countervailing Duties. *World Bank Econ. Rev.*, September 1987, *1*(4), pp. 707–25. [G: Global]

Finger, J. Michael and Olechowski, Andrzej. Trade Barriers: Who Does What to Whom. *Giersch, H., ed.*, 1987, pp. 37–71.
[G: Global]

Finlayson, Grant E. Rethinking the Overlapping Jurisdictions of Section 337 and the U.S. Courts. *J. World Trade Law*, April 1987, *21*(2), pp. 41–63. [G: U.S.]

Fischer, Wolfram. Swings between Protection and Free Trade in History. *Giersch, H., ed.*, 1987, pp. 20–32. [G: U.S.; W. Europe]

Fischer-Zernin, Justus. GATT versus Tax Treaties? The Basic Conflicts between International Taxation Methods and the Rules and Concepts of GATT. *J. World Trade Law*, June 1987, *21*(3), pp. 39–62. [G: Global]

Fitzgerald, Bruce. Countertrade Reconsidered. *Finance Develop.*, June 1987, *24*(2), pp. 46–49. [G: Indonesia]

Flam, Harry. Reverse Dumping. *Europ. Econ. Rev.*, Feb./Mar. 1987, *31*(1/2), pp. 82–88.

Flam, Harry and Helpman, Elhanan. Industrial Policy under Monopolistic Competition. *J. Int. Econ.*, February 1987, *22*(1/2), pp. 79–102.

Fleisig, Heywood and Hill, Catharine. Some Issues Surrounding Government-Subsidized Export Credit. *Rodriguez, R. M., ed.*, 1987, pp. 145–55. [G: U.S.]

Fliess, Barbara A. The World Administrative Radio Conference 1979 Negotiations: Toward More Equitable Sharing of the Global Radio Resources. *Zartman, I. W., ed. (II)*, 1987, pp. 171–212. [G: Global]

Frank, Isaiah. Import Quotas, the Balance of Payments and the GATT. *World Econ.*, September 1987, *10*(3), pp. 307–18. [G: Global]

Franzmeyer, Fritz. Concepts of Industrial Policy in the Industrial West: Are Mutual Trade Relations in Danger? Reply. *Saunders, C. T., ed.*, 1987, pp. 103–04.

Franzmeyer, Fritz. Concepts of Industrial Policy in the Industrial West: Are Mutual Trade Relations in Danger? *Saunders, C. T., ed.*, 1987, pp. 45–56.

French, Michael J. and Wilson, Thomas. Depression and Protection: The Early Thirties and the Early Eighties Compared. *[Penrose, E. F.]*, 1987, pp. 14–31. [G: OECD]

Galbraith, James K. U.S. Macroeconomic Strategy and the Advanced Developing Countries. *Thorup, C. L., ed.*, 1987, pp. 83–99.
[G: U.S.; Mexico]

Gan, Khuan-Poh and Tower, Edward. A General

Equilibrium Cost–Benefit Approach to Policy Reform and Project Evaluation in Malaysia. *Singapore Econ. Rev.*, April 1987, *32*(1), pp. 46–61. [G: Malaysia]

Gang, Ira N. Distribution and Development Effects of Tariff Cum Subsidy Policies. *Singapore Econ. Rev.*, April 1987, *32*(1), pp. 71–86.
[G: LDCs]

Garland, John and Brezinski, Horst. U.S. and West German Policies on Trade with the USSR. *Marer, P. and van Veen, P., eds.*, 1987, pp. 65–89. [G: U.S.; W. Germany; U.S.S.R.]

Geha, Susan. International Regulation of Whaling: The United States' Compromise. *Natural Res. J.*, Fall 1987, *27*(4), pp. 931–40.
[G: U.S.]

Genç, Mehmet. A Study of the Feasibility of Using Eighteenth-Century Ottoman Financial Records as an Indicator of Economic Activity. *Islamoglu-Inan, H., ed.*, 1987, pp. 345–73.
[G: Ottoman Empire]

Ghosh, A. Tariff and Non-tariff Protection through a Social Accounting Matrix—Case Study of an African Economy. *Indian Econ. Rev.*, July–Dec. 1987, *22*(2), pp. 195–211.
[G: Tanzania]

Gibbs, J. Murray. The Uruguay Round and the International Trading System: Editorial. *J. World Trade Law*, October 1987, *21*(5), pp. 5–12. [G: Global]

Giersch, Herbert. Economic Policies in the Age of Schumpeter. *Europ. Econ. Rev.*, Feb./Mar. 1987, *31*(1/2), pp. 35–52. [G: OECD]

Giese, Jill L. The Special Import Measures Act: Balancing the Interests of Foreign Exporters and Canadian Industries. *J. World Trade Law*, June 1987, *21*(3), pp. 9–25. [G: Canada]

Gilbert, Christopher L. International Commodity Agreements: Design and Performance. *World Devel.*, May 1987, *15*(5), pp. 591–616.
[G: LDCs]

Glismann, Hans H. The Political Economy of Revaluation-Induced Protectionism under Discretionary Monetary Regimes with Flexible Exchange Rates: Comment. *Giersch, H., ed.*, 1987, pp. 425–28. [G: U.S.]

de Gorter, Harry. Agricultural Policies and International Trade Negotiations: Research Issues. *Can. J. Agr. Econ.*, May 1987, *34*, pp. 280–94. [G: Canada; U.S.; EEC]

Graham, Edward M. World Trade Law and Government Subsidies to Industrial Innovation. *Hieronymi, O., ed.*, 1987, pp. 25–41.
[G: MDCs]

Grampp, William D. Britain and Free Trade: In Whose Interest? *Public Choice*, October 1987, *55*(3), pp. 245–56. [G: U.K.]

Grampp, William D. How Britain Turned to Free Trade. *Bus. Hist. Rev.*, Spring 1987, *61*(1), pp. 86–112. [G: U.K.]

Granell, Francesco. Spain and the Enlargement of the EEC. *Greilsammer, I. and Weiler, J. H. H., eds.*, 1987, pp. 159–72. [G: EEC; Spain]

Greenaway, David. Intra-industry Trade, Intra-firm Trade and European Integration: Evidence, Gains and Policy Aspects. *J. Common Market Stud.*, December 1987, *26*(2), pp. 153–72. [G: EEC]

Greenaway, David and Milner, Chris. 'True Protection' Concepts and Their Role in Evaluating Trade Policies in LDCs. *J. Devel. Stud.*, January 1987, *23*(2), pp. 200–219. [G: Selected LDCs]

Greenaway, David and Sapsford, David. Further Econometric Analysis of the Relationship between Fiscal Dependence on Trade Taxes and Economic Development [A Statistical Analysis of Fiscal Dependence on Trade Taxes and Economic Development]. *Public Finance*, 1987, *42*(2), pp. 309–19.

Greenwald, Joseph A. Dealing with the Agricultural Trade Crisis in the Uruguay Round Negotiations. *World Econ.*, June 1987, *10*(2), pp. 227–28. [G: Global]

Greilsammer, Ilan. Reflections on the Capability of the European Community to Play an Active Role in an International Crisis: The Case of the Israeli Action in Lebanon. *Greilsammer, I. and Weiler, J. H. H., eds.*, 1987, pp. 283–302. [G: EEC; Israel]

Greilsammer, Ilan and Weiler, Joseph H. H. Europe and Israel: Troubled Neighbours: An Introduction. *Greilsammer, I. and Weiler, J. H. H., eds.*, 1987, pp. 1–7. [G: Israel; EEC]

Griffith-Jones, Stephany. Compensatory Financing Facility: A Review of Its Operation and Proposals for Improvement. *Dell, S., ed., Pt. 2*, 1987, pp. 691–712.

Gros, Daniel. Protectionism in a Framework with Intra-industry Trade: Tariffs, Quotas, Retaliation, and Welfare Losses. *Int. Monet. Fund Staff Pap.*, March 1987, *34*(1), pp. 86–114.

Grubel, Herbert G. All Traded Services Are Embodied in Materials or People. *World Econ.*, September 1987, *10*(3), pp. 319–30. [G: OECD]

Guillaumont, Patrick. From Export Instability Effects to International Stabilization Policies. *World Devel.*, May 1987, *15*(5), pp. 633–43. [G: LDCs]

Haaland, Jan I. and Norman, Victor D. Modelling Trade and Trade Policy: Introduction. *Scand. J. Econ.*, 1987, *89*(3), pp. 217–26.

Hagen, Kåre P. Incentive Compatible Trade Policies: Comment. *Scand. J. Econ.*, 1987, *89*(3), pp. 389–91.

Hager, Wolfgang. The Community as Israel's Trading Partner: A Look at the Future. *Greilsammer, I. and Weiler, J. H. H., eds.*, 1987, pp. 43–55. [G: Israel; EEC]

Hamilton, Carl. The Political Economy of U.S. Protection: Comment. *Giersch, H., ed.*, 1987, pp. 403–06. [G: U.S.]

Hamilton, Colleen and Whalley, John. Relaciones con el Norte: Los países en desarrollo y las negociaciones comerciales a nivel mundial. (Dealing with the North: Developing Countries and Global Trade Negotions. With English summary.) *Estud. Econ.*, July-December 1987, *2*(2), pp. 151–225. [G: LDCs]

Hansen, Patricia I. Defining Unreasonableness in International Trade: Section 301 of the Trade Act of 1974. *Yale Law J.*, April 1987, *96*(5), pp. 1122–46. [G: U.S.]

Hart, Michael M. The Mercantilist's Lament: National Treatment and Modern Trade Negotiations. *J. World Trade Law*, December 1987, *21*(6), pp. 37–61. [G: Global]

Hasegawa, Toshiaki, et al. U.S.–Japan Economic Coordination: A Global Solution for Mutual Prosperity. *Finn, R. B., ed.*, 1987, pp. 1–29. [G: U.S.; Japan]

Hazledine, Tim and Wigington, Ian. Canadian Auto Policy. *Can. Public Policy*, December 1987, *13*(4), pp. 490–501. [G: Canada]

Heady, Christopher and Mitra, Pradeep K. Distributional and Revenue Raising Arguments for Tariffs. *J. Devel. Econ.*, June 1987, *26*(1), pp. 77–101. [G: Brazil; Turkey]

Heitger, Bernhard. Import Protection and Export Performance—Their Impact on Economic Growth. *Weltwirtsch. Arch.*, 1987, *123*(2), pp. 249–61. [G: Global]

Hellström, Mats. Den nya GATT-rundan: implikationer för protektionism och jordbruk. (The New GATT Round: Implications for Protectionism and Agriculture. With English summary.) *Ekon. Samfundets Tidskr.*, 1987, *40*(2), pp. 71–79. [G: Global]

Helpman, Elhanan. The National Defense Argument for Government Intervention in Foreign Trade: Comment. *Stern, R. M., ed.*, 1987, pp. 370–73. [G: U.S.]

Hemmi, Kenzo. Agricultural Reform Efforts in Japan: Political Feasibility and Consequences for Trade with the United States and Third Countries. *Johnson, D. G., ed.*, 1987, pp. 24–46. [G: Japan; U.S.]

Hesse, Helmut. Protection in Germany: Toward Industrial Selectivity: Comment. *Giersch, H., ed.*, 1987, pp. 192–203. [G: W. Germany]

Hessel, Stéphane. Mitterrand's France and the Third World. *Ross, G.; Hoffmann, S. and Malzacher, S., eds.*, 1987, pp. 324–37. [G: France; LDCs]

Hewitt, Adrian P. Stabex and Commodity Export Compensation Schemes: Prospects for Globalization. *World Devel.*, May 1987, *15*(5), pp. 617–31. [G: EEC; LDCs]

Hindley, Brian. GATT Safeguards and Voluntary Export Restraints: What Are the Interests of Developing Countries? *World Bank Econ. Rev.*, September 1987, *1*(4), pp. 689–705. [G: LDCs]

Hindley, Brian. Trade in Services within the European Community. *Giersch, H., ed.*, 1987, pp. 468–86. [G: EEC]

Hirsch, Seev. The Impact of EEC Trade Policies on Developing Countries: Comment. *Giersch, H., ed.*, 1987, pp. 327–31. [G: EEC; LDCs]

Hirsch, Seev. Trade Regimes and the Middle East Peace Process. *World Econ.*, March 1987, *10*(1), pp. 61–74. [G: Israel; Egypt]

Hitiris, T. and Weekes, A. J. Fiscal Dependence on Trade Taxes and Economic Development: An Econometric Investigation. *Public Finance*,

1987, *42*(2), pp. 297–308.

Hoffmann, Stanley. Mitterrand's Foreign Policy, or Gaullism by Any Other Name. *Ross, G.; Hoffmann, S. and Malzacher, S., eds.*, 1987, pp. 294–305. **[G: France]**

Hogan, William T. Protectionism in the Steel Industry: A Historical Perspective. *Salvatore, D., ed.*, 1987, pp. 352–64. **[G: Global]**

Hognestad, Gunnar. The Role of the Norwegian Government When Selling Natural Gas. *Golombek, R.; Hoel, M. and Vislie, J., eds.*, 1987, pp. 173–80. **[G: Norway]**

Holladay, J. Douglas. The Limits of American Influence. *Sethi, S. P., ed.*, 1987, pp. 63–71. **[G: S. Africa; U.S.]**

Holmer, Alan F. Congress and the President— The Issues. *Barfield, C. E. and Makin, J. H., eds.*, 1987, pp. 13–16. **[G: U.S.]**

Holzman, Franklyn D. Countervailing Foreign Use of Monopoly Power: Commentary. *Holzman, F. D.*, 1987, *1979*, pp. 137–42. **[G: U.S.S.R.]**

Holzman, Franklyn D. Dumping by Centrally Planned Economies: The Polish Golf Cart Case. *Holzman, F. D.*, 1987, *1983*, pp. 121–36. **[G: U.S.; Poland]**

Holzman, Franklyn D. The Economics of Soviet Bloc Trade and Finance: Introduction. *Holzman, F. D.*, 1987, pp. 1–29. **[G: U.S.S.R.; CMEA]**

Horn, Ernst-Jürgen. Trade in Services within the European Community: Comment. *Giersch, H., ed.*, 1987, pp. 487–91. **[G: EEC]**

Hufbauer, Gary Clyde. Symposium on World Trade: Comments. *Brookings Pap. Econ. Act.*, 1987, (1), pp. 337–45. **[G: U.S.]**

Hufbauer, Gary Clyde. The Competitiveness Gap. *Barfield, C. E. and Makin, J. H., eds.*, 1987, pp. 43–45. **[G: U.S.]**

Hufbauer, Gary Clyde. The Consumption Tax and International Competitiveness. *Walker, C. E. and Bloomfield, M. A., eds.*, 1987, pp. 179–205. **[G: U.S.]**

Hufbauer, Gary Clyde. Trade Policy as Foreign Policy: Comment. *Stern, R. M., ed.*, 1987, pp. 323–26. **[G: U.S.]**

Hughes, Kent. Transferring Authority to the Trade Representative. *Barfield, C. E. and Makin, J. H., eds.*, 1987, pp. 17–18. **[G: U.S.]**

Intriligator, Michael D. The National Defense Argument for Government Intervention in Foreign Trade: Comment. *Stern, R. M., ed.*, 1987, pp. 364–69. **[G: U.S.]**

Iran Ministry Econ. Aff. and Finance. Trade Cooperation and Collective Self-reliance. *Agrawal, G. R., et al. (II)*, 1987, pp. 7–22. **[G: LDCs]**

Ithurbide, Philippe. Les restrictions volontaires d'exportations: Une analyse macro-économique en régime de changes flexibles. (The Voluntary Export Restraints: A Macroeconomic Analysis under Flexible Exchanges Rates. With English summary.) *Revue Écon.*, January 1987, *38*(1), pp. 25–54.

Ivens, Michael. The Corporate Role in Fighting

Apartheid: British Style. *Sethi, S. P., ed.*, 1987, pp. 319–31. **[G: S. Africa]**

Jackson, John H. Multilateral and Bilateral Negotiating Approaches for the Conduct of U.S. Trade Policies. *Stern, R. M., ed.*, 1987, pp. 377–401. **[G: U.S.]**

Jacquemin, Alexis. Trade Performance as a Constraint on European Growth: Comment. *Lawrence, R. Z. and Schultze, C. L., eds.*, 1987, pp. 374–81. **[G: W. Europe]**

Jain, Subhash C. Perspectives on International Strategic Alliances. *Cavusgil, S. T., ed.*, 1987, pp. 103–20.

Jamal, Haroon. Support Prices in the Context of International Trade: The Case of Cotton in Pakistan. *Bangladesh Devel. Stud.*, March 1987, *15*(1), pp. 143–56. **[G: Pakistan]**

James, Colin. Economic Adjustment in New Zealand: A Developed Country Case Study of Policies and Problems: Comment. *Holmes, F., ed.*, 1987, pp. 85–90. **[G: New Zealand]**

Jelliss, Arvin D. and Kuo, Chun-Yan. On Measuring the Economic Subsidy of Export Sales Financing. *Econ. Develop. Cult. Change*, July 1987, *35*(4), pp. 832–46. **[G: Canada]**

Jenkins, Glenn P. Costs and Consequences of the New Protectionism. The Case of Canada's Clothing Sector. *[Harberger, A.]*, 1987, pp. 217–53. **[G: Canada]**

Johnson, D. Gale. Agricultural Reform Efforts in the United States and Japan: Concluding Comments. *Johnson, D. G., ed.*, 1987, pp. 88–90. **[G: U.S.; Japan]**

Johnson, D. Gale. Agricultural Reform Efforts in the United States and Japan: Introduction. *Johnson, D. G., ed.*, 1987, pp. 1–4. **[G: U.S.; Japan]**

Johnson, Manuel H., Jr. Statement to the U.S. House Subcommittee on Financial Institutions, Supervision, Regulation and Insurance of the Committee on Banking, Finance and Urban Affairs, March 24, 1987. *Fed. Res. Bull.*, May 1987, *73*(5), pp. 341–46. **[G: U.S.]**

Jones, Ronald W. Current Issues in Trade Policy: An Overview: Comment. *Stern, R. M., ed.*, 1987, pp. 69–72. **[G: U.S.]**

Kaempfer, William H. and Willett, Thomas D. Why an Import Surcharge Wouldn't Help America's Trade Deficit. *World Econ.*, March 1987, *10*(1), pp. 27–38. **[G: U.S.]**

Karsenty, Guy and Laird, Samuel. The GSP, Policy Options and the New Round. *Weltwirtsch. Arch.*, 1987, *123*(2), pp. 262–96. **[G: Global]**

Keene, Karlyn H. What the Polls Tell Us. *Barfield, C. E. and Makin, J. H., eds.*, 1987, pp. 127–30. **[G: U.S.]**

Kemal, A. R. Effective Protection Rates—A Guide to Tariff Making. *Pakistan Devel. Rev.*, Winter 1987, *26*(4), pp. 775–83. **[G: Pakistan]**

Kennedy, Kevin C. The Accession of the Soviet Union to GATT. *J. World Trade Law*, April 1987, *21*(2), pp. 23–39. **[G: U.S.S.R.]**

Keohane, Robert O. Multilateral and Bilateral Negotiating Approaches for the Conduct of

422 Commercial Policy

U.S. Trade Policies: Comment. *Stern, R. M.*, *ed.*, 1987, pp. 402–07. **[G: U.S.]**

Kerr, William A. The Recent Findings of the Canadian Import Tribunal Regarding Beef Originating in the European Economic Community. *J. World Trade Law*, October 1987, *21*(5), pp. 55–65. **[G: EEC; Canada]**

Kettunen, Lauri. Experiences in Controlling Milk Supply in Finland. *Kettunen, L., ed.*, 1987, pp. 147–57. **[G: Finland]**

Kierzkowski, Henryk. Issues of Strategic Trade Policy for Small Countries: Comment. *Scand. J. Econ.*, 1987, *89*(3), pp. 369–71.

Kindleberger, Charles P. Belgium after World War II: An Experiment in Supply-Side Economics. *Kindleberger, C. P.*, 1987, pp. 230–44. **[G: Belgium]**

Kindleberger, Charles P. The OECD and the Third World. *Kindleberger, C. P.*, 1987, *1978*, pp. 120–40. **[G: OECD]**

Kirkpatrick, Colin. Trade Policy and Industrialization in LDCs. *Gemmell, N., ed.*, 1987, pp. 56–89. **[G: LDCs]**

Kirton, John. Economic Sanctions and Alliance Consultations: Canada, the United States and the Strains of 1979–82. *Leyton-Brown, D., ed.*, 1987, pp. 269–93. **[G: U.S.; Canada]**

Klein, Lawrence R. The Changing World Economic Situation and Its Impact on International Trade. *Rodriguez, R. M., ed.*, 1987, pp. 37–53. **[G: U.S.; Global]**

Klein, Saul. Export Promotion: The Trading House Option Revisited. *Can. Public Policy*, September 1987, *13*(3), pp. 284–93. **[G: Canada]**

Klepper, Gernot; Weiss, Frank D. and Witteler, Doris. Protection in Germany: Toward Industrial Selectivity. *Giersch, H., ed.*, 1987, pp. 171–91. **[G: W. Germany]**

Koekkoek, Ad and de Leeuw, Jeroen. The Applicability of GATT to International Trade in Services: General Considerations and the Interest of Developing Countries. *Aussenwirtschaft*, April 1987, *42*(1), pp. 65–84. **[G: LDCs]**

Koester, Ulrich. How to Open the Common Agricultural Market. *Giersch, H., ed.*, 1987, pp. 515–31. **[G: EEC]**

Kohona, Palitha T. B. Investment Protection Agreements: An Australian Perspective. *J. World Trade Law*, April 1987, *21*(2), pp. 79–103. **[G: Australia]**

Kol, Jacob. Exports from Developing Countries: Some Facts and Scope. *Europ. Econ. Rev.*, Feb./Mar. 1987, *31*(1/2), pp. 466–74. **[G: LDCs; OECD]**

Kolisevski, Mitre. GSTP: An Instrument for the Intensification of ECDC. *Agrawal, G. R., et al. (II)*, 1987, pp. 36–49.

Kostecki, Michel. Export-Restraint Arrangements and Trade Liberalization. *World Econ.*, December 1987, *10*(4), pp. 425–53. **[G: Global]**

Köves, András. The Import Restriction Squeeze and Import-Maximizing Ambitions: Some Connections of East–West vs. Intra-CMEA Trade. *Soviet E. Europ. Foreign Trade*, Summer 1987, *23*(2), pp. 78–93. **[G: CMEA]**

Krasner, Stephen D. Trade Policy as Foreign Policy: Comment. *Stern, R. M., ed.*, 1987, pp. 327–36. **[G: U.S.]**

Kraus, Willy. Stages of Development, Cultural Context and the Problem of International Interdependence. *[Kitamura, H.]*, 1987, pp. 190–203. **[G: LDCs]**

Krause, Lawrence B. A Second-Best Strategy for Pacific Dynamism. *Dutta, M., ed. (I)*, 1987, pp. 11–22. **[G: Asia-Pacific]**

Krause, Lawrence B. The Structure of Trade in Manufactured Goods in the East and Southeast Asian Region. *Bradford, C. I., Jr. and Branson, W. H., eds.*, 1987, pp. 205–25. **[G: Asia]**

Kreinin, Mordechai E. Comparative Advantage and Possible Trade Restrictions in High-Technology Products. *Salvatore, D., ed.*, 1987, pp. 297–332. **[G: U.S.]**

Krueger, Anne O. The Political Economy of the Rent-Seeking Society. *Bhagwati, J. N., ed.*, 1987, *1974*, pp. 291–309.

Krugman, Paul R. Imports in Japan: Closed Markets or Minds? Comment. *Brookings Pap. Econ. Act.*, 1987, (2), pp. 549–52. **[G: Japan]**

Krugman, Paul R. Is the Japan Problem Over? *Sato, R. and Wachtel, P., eds.*, 1987, pp. 16–37. **[G: U.S.; Japan]**

Krugman, Paul R. Strategic Sectors and International Competition. *Stern, R. M., ed.*, 1987, pp. 207–32. **[G: U.S.]**

Krugman, Paul R. Targeted Industrial Policies: Theory and Evidence. *Salvatore, D., ed.*, 1987, pp. 266–96. **[G: Japan; U.S.]**

Kumagai, Naohiro. The Outlook for International Trade Relations. *Bus. Econ.*, January 1987, *22*(1), pp. 18–21. **[G: Global]**

Kumar, Nagesh. India's Economic and Technical Cooperation with the Co-developing Countries. *Agrawal, G. R., et al. (II)*, 1987, pp. 181–220. **[G: India]**

Kumar, Rajiv. Performance of Foreign and Domestic Firms in Export Processing Zones. *World Devel.*, Oct./Nov. 1987, *15*(10/11), pp. 1309–19. **[G: India]**

Kumcu, M. Ercan. The Trade Liberalization and Exchange Rate Determination in a Small Open Economy. *METU*, 1987, *14*(3), pp. 205–13.

Laird, Samuel. Trade Barriers: Who Does What to Whom: Comment. *Giersch, H., ed.*, 1987, pp. 72–77. **[G: Global]**

Laird, Samuel and Sampson, Gary P. Case for Evaluating Protection in an Economy-Wide Perspective. *World Econ.*, June 1987, *10*(2), pp. 177–92. **[G: OECD]**

Laird, Samuel and Yeats, Alexander J. Empirical Evidence Concerning the Magnitude and Effects of Developing Country Tariff Escalation. *Devel. Econ.*, June 1987, *25*(2), pp. 99–123. **[G: LDCs]**

Laird, Samuel and Yeats, Alexander J. On the Potential Contribution of Trade Policy Initiatives for Alleviating the International Debt Crisis. *J. Econ. Bus.*, August 1987, *39*(3), pp. 209–24. **[G: OECD; LDCs]**

Lal, Deepak and Rajapatirana, Sarath. Foreign Trade Regimes and Economic Growth in Developing Countries. *World Bank Res. Observer*, July 1987, *2*(2), pp. 189–217.
[G: LDCs]

Langhammer, Rolf J. The EEC Trade Policies in Manufactures, the Mediterranean Market. *Greilsammer, I. and Weiler, J. H. H., eds.*, 1987, pp. 195–211. [G: EEC; Israel]

Lattimore, Ralph. Economic Adjustment in New Zealand: A Developed Country Case Study of Policies and Problems. *Holmes, F., ed.*, 1987, pp. 34–84. [G: New Zealand]

Lawrence, Robert Z. Imports in Japan: Closed Markets or Minds? *Brookings Pap. Econ. Act.*, 1987, (2), pp. 517–48. [G: Japan]

Lawrence, Robert Z. Trade Performance as a Constraint on European Growth. *Lawrence, R. Z. and Schultze, C. L., eds.*, 1987, pp. 303–74. [G: W. Europe]

Lawrence, Robert Z. and Litan, Robert E. The Protectionist Prescription: Errors in Diagnosis and Cure. *Brookings Pap. Econ. Act.*, 1987, (1), pp. 289–310. [G: U.S.]

Leamer, Edward E. Endogenous Protection in the United States, 1900–1984: Comment. *Stern, R. M., ed.*, 1987, pp. 196–200. [G: U.S.]

Lecraw, Donald J. Japanese Standards: A Barrier to Trade? *Gabel, H. L., ed.*, 1987, pp. 29–46. [G: Japan]

Levin, Sander M. The Need and the Prospects for a Trade Bill in 1987. *Barfield, C. E. and Makin, J. H., eds.*, 1987, pp. 58–60. [G: U.S.]

Levy, Santiago. A Short-run General Equilibrium Model for a Small, Open Economy. *J. Devel. Econ.*, February 1987, *25*(1), pp. 63–88. [G: LDCs]

Leyton-Brown, David. Extraterritoriality in United States Trade Sanctions. *Leyton-Brown, D., ed.*, 1987, pp. 255–67. [G: U.S.]

Leyton-Brown, David. Lessons and Policy Considerations about Economic Sanctions. *Leyton-Brown, D., ed.*, 1987, pp. 303–10.

Leyton-Brown, David. The Utility of International Economic Sanctions: Introduction. *Leyton-Brown, D., ed.*, 1987, pp. 1–4.

Li, Chung-chou. Resumption of China's GATT Membership. *J. World Trade Law*, August 1987, *21*(4), pp. 25–48. [G: China]

Lien, Da-Hsiang Donald and Bates, Robert H. Political Behavior in the Coffee Agreement. *Econ. Develop. Cult. Change*, April 1987, *35*(3), pp. 629–36. [G: Selected Countries]

Lilley, William, III. Successful Exporting: What the Private Sector Can Do. *Barfield, C. E. and Makin, J. H., eds.*, 1987, pp. 46–49. [G: U.S.]

Linder, Staffan Burenstam. Economic and Political Consequences of Asia-Pacific Dynamism. *Dutta, M., ed. (I)*, 1987, pp. 69–84. [G: Asia-Pacific]

Little, Ian M. D. Swings between Protection and Free Trade in History: Comment. *Giersch, H., ed.*, 1987, pp. 33–34.

Lloyd, Peter J. Trade Policies and Their Impact on Individual Economies. *Holmes, F., ed.*, 1987, pp. 8–29. [G: Australia]

Lukaszewicz, Aleksander. Industrial Policies and Structural Change: Overall Assessments and Comparisons: Comment. *Saunders, C. T., ed.*, 1987, pp. 102–03.

MacBean, Alasdair and Nguyen, Duc Tin. International Commodity Agreements: Shadow and Substance. *World Devel.*, May 1987, *15*(5), pp. 575–90. [G: LDCs]

MacCharles, D. C. Canadian Foreign Subsidiaries: Productivity and Trade Performance. *Tremblay, R., ed.*, 1987, pp. 331–50. [G: Canada]

MacPhee, Craig R. The Consistency of Partial Equilibrium Estimates of Trade Creation and Diversion. *Weltwirtsch. Arch.*, 1987, *123*(1), pp. 81–92.

Magee, Stephen P. The Political Economy of U.S. Protection. *Giersch, H., ed.*, 1987, pp. 368–402. [G: U.S.]

Magee, Stephen P. and Young, Leslie. Endogenous Protection in the United States, 1900–1984. *Stern, R. M., ed.*, 1987, pp. 145–95. [G: U.S.]

Maizels, Alfred. Commodities in Crisis: An Overview of the Main Issues. *World Devel.*, May 1987, *15*(5), pp. 537–49. [G: Global]

Mandaza, Ibbo. Perspectives on Economic Cooperation and Autonomous Development in Southern Africa. *Amin, S.; Chitala, D. and Mandaza, I., eds.*, 1987, pp. 210–30. [G: Southern Africa]

Mann, Catherine L. Protection and Retaliation: Changing the 'Rules of the Game.' *Brookings Pap. Econ. Act.*, 1987, (1), pp. 311–35. [G: U.S.]

Mannering, Fred and Winston, Clifford. Economic Effects of Voluntary Export Restrictions. *Winston, C., et al.*, 1987, pp. 61–67. [G: U.S.]

Marantz, Paul. Economic Sanctions in the Polish Crisis. *Leyton-Brown, D., ed.*, 1987, pp. 131–46. [G: Poland]

Marston, Richard C. Japanese–U.S. Current Accounts and Exchange Rates before and after the G5 Agreement: Discussion. *Sato, R. and Wachtel, P., eds.*, 1987, pp. 152–56. [G: Japan; U.S.]

Martin, David Dale. The Evolution of Industrial Policies: A World Perspective. *Wills, R. L.; Caswell, J. A. and Culbertson, J. D., eds.*, 1987, pp. 115–30. [G: U.S.]

Martin, Fernand and Tremblay, Rodrigue. The Canadian Industries of Telecommunication Equipments and Computers, and North American Trade Liberalization. *Tremblay, R., ed.*, 1987, pp. 377–405. [G: Canada; U.S.]

Marvel, Howard P. and Ray, Edward John. Intraindustry Trade: Sources and Effects on Protection. *J. Polit. Econ.*, December 1987, *95*(6), pp. 1278–91.

Maskus, Keith E. The View of Trade Problems from Washington's Capitol Hill. *World Econ.*,

December 1987, *10*(4), pp. 409–23.
[G: U.S.]

Mathiesen, Lars. International Trade in Grains: Domestic Policies and Trade Impacts: Comment. *Scand. J. Econ.*, 1987, *89*(3), pp. 285–86. [G: Global]

Matsui, Robert T. Trade Policy: A Democrat's View. *Barfield, C. E. and Makin, J. H., eds.*, 1987, pp. 55–57. [G: U.S.]

Mayer, Wolfgang and Riezman, Raymond G. Endogenous Choice of Trade Policy Instruments. *J. Int. Econ.*, November 1987, *23*(3/4), pp. 377–81.

Mazier, Jacques. Politique sélective des importations et relance de l'investissement industriel: un essai d'évaluation. (Import Policy on Industrial Investment: An Evaluation Attempt. With English summary.) *Écon. Soc.*, April 1987, *21*(4), pp. 73–100. [G: OECD]

McCulloch, Rachel. Macroeconomics and Protection: Comment. *Stern, R. M., ed.*, 1987, pp. 137–43. [G: OECD]

McCulloch, Rachel. Why Do Governments Prefer Nontariff Barriers? A Comment. *Carnegie–Rochester Conf. Ser. Public Policy*, Spring 1987, *26*, pp. 217–21.

McDonnell, J. E. D. China's Move to Rejoin the GATT System: An Epic Transition. *World Econ.*, September 1987, *10*(3), pp. 331–50.
[G: China]

McKenzie, Richard B. and Smith, Stephen D. Loss of Textile and Apparel Jobs: Is Protectionism Warranted? *Cato J.*, Winter 1987, *6*(3), pp. 731–46. [G: U.S.]

McMahon, Gary. Does a Small Developing Country Benefit from International Commodity Agreements? The Case of Coffee and Kenya. *Econ. Develop. Cult. Change*, January 1987, *35*(2), pp. 409–23. [G: Kenya]

Meade, James. James Meade's War-Time Proposal for a Liberal Trade Regime. *World Econ.*, December 1987, *10*(4), pp. 399–407.
[G: U.K.]

Meessen, Karl M. Intellectual Property Rights in International Trade. *J. World Trade Law*, February 1987, *21*(1), pp. 67–74.
[G: OECD]

Mendelsohn, M. S. World Trade and International Finance: Lessons from the Past. *Visser, H. and Schoor, E., eds.*, 1987, pp. 57–64.
[G: Global]

Mészáros, Sándor. Possibility of an Export Oriented Price Policy as a Tool of Supply Management. *Kettunen, L., ed.*, 1987, pp. 205–19.
[G: Hungary]

Meyers, William H.; Devadoss, S. and Helmar, Michael D. Agricultural Trade Liberalization: Cross-Commodity and Cross-Country Impact Products. *J. Policy Modeling*, Fall 1987, *9*(3), pp. 455–82.

Michaely, Michael. The Demand for Protection against Exports of Newly Industrializing Countries. *Salvatore, D., ed.*, 1987, pp. 471–94.
[G: Brazil; Hong Kong; S. Korea; Mexico; Singapore]

Michalski, Wolfgang. Trade Barriers: Who Does

What to Whom: Comment. *Giersch, H., ed.*, 1987, pp. 77–84. [G: Global]

Milner, Helen. Resisting the Protectionist Temptation: Industry and the Making of Trade Policy in France and the United States during the 1970s. *Int. Organ.*, Autumn 1987, *41*(4), pp. 639–65. [G: France; U.S.]

de Miramon, J. Countertrade: A Disruptive Phenomenon in International Trade. *Visser, H. and Schoor, E., eds.*, 1987, pp. 197–205.
[G: Global]

Miyoshi, Masaya. The Japanese–U.S. Trade Friction: Some Perspectives from the Japanese Business Community. *Sato, R. and Wachtel, P., eds.*, 1987, pp. 45–49. [G: U.S.; Japan]

Modwel, S. K. GSTP: Some Issues in Implementation. *Agrawal, G. R., et al. (II)*, 1987, pp. 49–65. [G: LDCs]

Monke, Eric A.; Pearson, Scott R. and Silva-Carvalho, José-Paulo. Welfare Effects of a Processing Cartel: Flour Milling in Portugal. *Econ. Develop. Cult. Change*, January 1987, *35*(2), pp. 393–407. [G: Portugal]

Morgan, Ivor P. The U.S. Experience with Airline Deregulation: International Consequences. *Meyer, J. R. and Oster, C. V., Jr.*, 1987, pp. 137–57. [G: U.S.; Global]

Mork, Knut Anton. Some General-Equilibrium Considerations for the Analysis of Oil Import Restrictions. *Energy J.*, October 1987, *8*(4), pp. 79–84.

Murali, R. Demand Uncertainty and Input Constraints. *Quart. Rev. Econ. Bus.*, Summer 1987, *27*(2), pp. 22–41.

Mussa, Michael. Average Protection and Economic Policy. *Salvatore, D., ed.*, 1987, pp. 389–407. [G: U.S.]

Mussa, Michael. Macroeconomic Policy and Trade Liberalization: Some Guidelines. *World Bank Res. Observer*, January 1987, *2*(1), pp. 61–77. [G: LDCs]

Nakatani, Iwao. Towards the New International Economic Order—The Role of Japan in the World Economy. *Hitotsubashi J. Econ.*, October 1987, *27*, pp. 121–32. [G: Japan; U.S.]

Nam, Chong-Hyun. Export-Promoting Subsidies, Countervailing Threats, and the General Agreement of Tariffs and Trade. *World Bank Econ. Rev.*, September 1987, *1*(4), pp. 727–43. [G: Global]

Neary, J. Peter. Endogenous Protection in the United States, 1900–1984: Comment. *Stern, R. M., ed.*, 1987, pp. 201–06. [G: U.S.]

Ng'andwe, Chiselebwe. Financial Integration and Development in SADCC and PTA Countries. *Amin, S.; Chitala, D. and Mandaza, I., eds.*, 1987, pp. 181–209. [G: Southern Africa]

Nickel, Herman. Will Sanctions Harm the Oppressed or the Oppressor? *Sethi, S. P., ed.*, 1987, pp. 179–88. [G: S. Africa]

Nicolaides, Phedon. How Fair Is Fair Trade? *J. World Trade Law*, August 1987, *21*(4), pp. 147–62. [G: Global]

Nyankori, James C. O. and Nodine, Stephen K. Implications of Restrictions on Imports of Canadian Softwood Lumber to the Southern Softwood Lumber Industry. *Rev. Reg. Stud.*, Winter 1987, *17*(1), pp. 45–52. **[G: U.S.; Canada]**

Nyankori, James C. O.; Rosson, C. Parr and Rathwell, P. J. Estimates of the Effects of Canadian Tariff on Fresh Peach Imports from the United States. *Can. J. Agr. Econ.*, March 1987, *35*(1), pp. 75–87. **[G: Canada; U.S.]**

Ocampo, José Antonio. The Macroeconomic Effect of Import Controls: A Keynesian Analysis. *J. Devel. Econ.*, October 1987, *27*(1–2), pp. 285–305.

Ocampo, José Antonio. The Macroeconomic Effect of Import Controls: A Keynesian Analysis. *[Diaz-Alejandro, C. F.]*, 1987, pp. 285–305.

Okada, Katsuya. U.S.–Japan Cooperative Efforts to Protect Intellectual Property Rights. *Finn, R. B., ed.*, 1987, pp. 59–74. **[G: U.S.; Japan]**

Okawara, Yoshio. Restructuring the Japanese Economy from a Global Perspective. *Sato, R. and Wachtel, P., eds.*, 1987, pp. 11–15. **[G: Japan; U.S.]**

Oliver, Daniel. Protectionism. *Barfield, C. E. and Makin, J. H., eds.*, 1987, pp. 81–85. **[G: U.S.]**

Ormrod, W. M. The English Crown and the Customs, 1349–63. *Econ. Hist. Rev.*, 2nd Ser., February 1987, *40*(1), pp. 27–40. **[G: U.K.]**

Oskam, Arie J. and van der Stelt-Scheele, D. D. Two Years of Experience with the EC Super Levy System: A Quantitative Analysis of Recent and Future Policy Alternatives. *Kettunen, L., ed.*, 1987, pp. 77–103. **[G: EEC]**

Osmani, S. R. The Impact of Economic Liberalisation on the Small-Scale and Rural Industries of Sri Lanka. *Islam, R., ed.*, 1987, pp. 171–209. **[G: Sri Lanka]**

Østeras, Magne. The GATT International Dairy Arrangement. *Kettunen, L., ed.*, 1987, pp. 231–48.

Osterhammel, Jürgen. State Control of Foreign Trade in Nationalist China, 1927–1937. *Dewey, C., ed.*, 1987, pp. 209–37. **[G: China]**

Osunbor, Oserheimen A. Law and Policy on the Registration of Technology Transfer Transactions in Nigeria. *J. World Trade Law*, October 1987, *21*(5), pp. 13–30. **[G: Nigeria]**

Page, Sheila. The Rise in Protection since 1974. *Oxford Rev. Econ. Policy*, Spring 1987, *3*(1), pp. 37–51. **[G: Global]**

Palmeter, N. David. Dumping Margins and Material Injury: The USITC Is Free to Choose. *J. World Trade Law*, August 1987, *21*(4), pp. 173–75. **[G: U.S.]**

Palmeter, N. David. Injury Determinations in Antidumping and Countervailing Duty Cases—A Commentary on U.S. Practice. *J. World Trade Law*, February 1987, *21*(1), pp. 7–45. **[G: U.S.]**

Palmeter, N. David. Material Retardation in the Establishment of an Industry Standard in Antidumping Cases. *J. World Trade Law*, December 1987, *21*(6), pp. 113–15. **[G: U.S.]**

Patrick, Hugh T. Japan and the United States Today: Exchange Rates, Macroeconomic Policies, and Financial Market Innovations: Con-

cluding Comments. *Patrick, H. T. and Tachi, R., eds.*, 1987, pp. 209–13. **[G: Japan; U.S.]**

Patterson, Gardner. Multilateral and Bilateral Negotiating Approaches for the Conduct of U.S. Trade Policies: Comment. *Stern, R. M., ed.*, 1987, pp. 408–12. **[G: U.S.]**

Pazos, Felipe. Import Substitution Policies, Tariffs, and Competition. *Dietz, J. L. and Street, J. H., eds.*, 1987, pp. 147–55. **[G: Latin America]**

Pease, Don J. Reform of Section 201 Import Relief. *Barfield, C. E. and Makin, J. H., eds.*, 1987, pp. 77–80. **[G: U.S.]**

Pelkmans, Jacques. Liberalization of Product Markets in the European Community. *Giersch, H., ed.*, 1987, pp. 429–61. **[G: EEC]**

Pelzman, Joseph. The Multifiber Arrangement: The Third Reincarnation. *Zartman, I. W., ed. (II)*, 1987, pp. 149–70. **[G: U.S.]**

Pharo, Helge. Conflict and Cooperation in the Indo–Norwegian Fisheries Project 1952–1972. *Dewey, C., ed.*, 1987, pp. 319–51. **[G: Norway; India]**

Pickford, M. Industry Inefficiency, Monopoly and Import Liberalization in New Zealand—An Assessment of the Static Welfare Effects. *Econ. Rec.*, June 1987, *63*(181), pp. 162–74. **[G: New Zealand]**

Pickford, M. Measuring the Welfare Effects of the Tariff Cuts of 19th December 1985. *New Zealand Econ. Pap.*, 1987, *21*, pp. 75–82. **[G: New Zealand]**

Pindyck, Robert S. and Rotemberg, Julio J. Are Imports to Blame? Attribution of Injury under the 1974 Trade Act. *J. Law Econ.*, April 1987, *30*(1), pp. 101–22. **[G: U.S.]**

Piontek, Eugeniusz. Anti-dumping in the EEC—Some Observations by an Outsider. *J. World Trade Law*, August 1987, *21*(4), pp. 67–93. **[G: EEC]**

Polach, Jay G. The Industry Structure and Pricing Policies in Oil International Transactions. *Pachauri, R. K., ed.*, 1987, pp. 35–57. **[G: Global]**

Pollins, Brian M. and Brecke, Peter K. The GLOBUS Model: Computer Simulation of Worldwide Political and Economic Development: International Economic Processes. *Bremer, S. A., ed.*, 1987, pp. 459–567. **[G: Global]**

Pomfret, Richard. Liberalization of Product Markets in the European Community: Comment. *Giersch, H., ed.*, 1987, pp. 462–67. **[G: EEC]**

Pomfret, Richard. Long-term Consequences of Temporary Trade Measures. *Challenge*, Nov./Dec. 1987, *30*(5), pp. 57–59. **[G: U.S.]**

Pomfret, Richard. Main Economic Trends in EC–Israel Economic Relations since the Creation of the Common Market. *Greilsammer, I. and Weiler, J. H. H., eds.*, 1987, pp. 56–72. **[G: Israel; EEC]**

Praet, Peter. Structural Developments and Euro–Asian Cooperation. *[Kitamura, H.]*, 1987, pp. 127–39. **[G: EEC; Asia]**

Price, Jacob M. and Clemens, Paul G. E. A Revo-

lution of Scale in Overseas Trade: British Firms in the Chesapeake Trade, 1675–1775. *J. Econ. Hist.*, March 1987, *47*(1), pp. 1–43.
[G: U.S.; U.K.]

Proulx, Pierre-Paul. A Review of Studies of Sectoral Impacts of Bilateral and Multilateral Trade Liberalization on Canada. *Tremblay, R., ed.,* 1987, pp. 463–530. [G: Canada; U.S.]

Pugel, Thomas A. Limits of Trade Policy toward High Technology Industries: The Case of Semiconductors. *Sato, R. and Wachtel, P., eds.,* 1987, pp. 184–223. [G: U.S.; Japan]

Raipuria, K. M. South–South Trade Cooperation: The Conceptual Basis. *Agrawal, G. R., et al. (II),* 1987, pp. 23–35. [G: LDCs]

Ramachandran, Rama V. Limits of Trade Policy toward High Technology Industries: The Case of Semiconductors: Discussion. *Sato, R. and Wachtel, P., eds.,* 1987, pp. 223–30.
[G: U.S.; Japan]

Ramchandani, R. R. India–Africa Economic Relations. *Agrawal, G. R., et al. (II),* 1987, pp. 221–55. [G: India; Africa]

Ramstad, Yngve. Free Trade versus Fair Trade: Import Barriers as a Problem of Reasonable Value. *J. Econ. Issues*, March 1987, *21*(1), pp. 5–32. [G: U.S.]

Randhawa, P. S. Punta del Este and after: Negotiations on Trade in Services and the Uruguay Round. *J. World Trade Law*, August 1987, *21*(4), pp. 163–71. [G: Global]

Ranis, Gustav. Challenges and Opportunities Posed by Asia's Superexporters: Implications for Manufactured Exports from Latin America. *Dietz, J. L. and Street, J. H., eds.,* 1987, 1981, pp. 128–46. [G: E. Asia; Latin America]

Rasul, Ghulam. Effective Protection Rates—A Guide to Tariff Making: Comments. *Pakistan Devel. Rev.*, Winter 1987, *26*(4), pp. 784–85.
[G: Pakistan]

Raubitschek, Ruth S. Limits of Trade Policy toward High Technology Industries: The Case of Semiconductors: Discussion. *Sato, R. and Wachtel, P., eds.,* 1987, pp. 230–37.
[G: Japan; U.S.]

Ravenhill, John. Negotiating the Lomé Conventions: A Little Is Preferable to Nothing. *Zartman, I. W., ed. (II),* 1987, pp. 213–58.

Raworth, Philip. Canada–U.S. Free Trade: A Legal Perspective. *Can. Public Policy*, September 1987, *13*(3), pp. 350–65. [G: Canada; U.S.]

Ray, Edward John. The Impact of Special Interests on Preferential Tariff Concessions by the United States. *Rev. Econ. Statist.*, May 1987, *69*(2), pp. 187–93. [G: U.S.]

Ray, Edward John. Trade Liberalization, Preferential Agreements, and Their Impact on U.S. Imports from Latin America. *Connolly, M. and González-Vega, C., eds.,* 1987, pp. 253–79.
[G: U.S.]

Reeves, George W. World Agricultural Trade and the New GATT Round. *J. Agr. Econ.*, September 1987, *38*(3), pp. 393–405. [G: Global]

Richardson, J. David. How Should the United States Respond to Other Countries' Trade Poli-

cies? Comment. *Stern, R. M., ed.,* 1987, pp. 287–90. [G: U.S.]

Riedel, James. United States Trade Policy: From Multilateralism to Bilateralism? *Giersch, H., ed.,* 1987, pp. 85–104. [G: U.S.]

Riezman, Raymond G. and Slemrod, Joel. Tariffs and Collection Costs. *Weltwirtsch. Arch.*, 1987, *123*(3), pp. 545–49. [G: Global]

Roca, Sergio G. Economic Sanctions against Cuba. *Leyton-Brown, D., ed.,* 1987, pp. 87–104. [G: U.S.; Cuba]

Rodriguez, Rita M. Exim's Mission and Accomplishments: 1934–84. *Rodriguez, R. M., ed.,* 1987, pp. 1–33. [G: U.S.]

Rodriguez, Rita M. The Export–Import Bank at Fifty: Preface. *Rodriguez, R. M., ed.,* 1987, pp. xi–xii. [G: U.S.]

Roessler, Frieder. The Competence of GATT. *J. World Trade Law*, June 1987, *21*(3), pp. 73–83. [G: Global]

Roger, C. L'évaluation de la protection d'une agriculture. (Protection Evaluation in Agriculture. With English summary.) *Écon. Soc.*, April 1987, *21*(4), pp. 127–66. [G: OECD]

Rogowski, Ronald. Trade and the Variety of Democratic Institutions. *Int. Organ.*, Spring 1987, *41*(2), pp. 203–23. [G: OECD]

Rollins, Edward J. A Republican's View. *Barfield, C. E. and Makin, J. H., eds.,* 1987, pp. 122–26. [G: U.S.]

Rondinelli, Dennis A. Export Processing Zones and Economic Development in Asia: A Review and Reassessment of a Means of Promoting Growth and Jobs. *Amer. J. Econ. Soc.*, January 1987, *46*(1), pp. 89–105. [G: Asia]

Rosenthal, Paul C. Making Relief Conditional on Adjustment. *Barfield, C. E. and Makin, J. H., eds.,* 1987, pp. 90–91. [G: U.S.]

Rothstein, Robert L. Commodity Bargaining: The Political Economy of Regime Creation. *Zartman, I. W., ed. (II),* 1987, pp. 15–47.

Rousslang, Donald J. The Opportunity Cost of Import Tariffs. *Kyklos*, 1987, *40*(1), pp. 88–102.
[G: U.S.]

Rugman, Alan M. and Anderson, Andrew. A Fishy Business: The Abuse of American Trade Law in the Atlantic Groundfish Case of 1985–1986. *Can. Public Policy*, June 1987, *13*(2), pp. 152–64. [G: U.S.; Canada]

Salvatore, Dominick. Import Penetration, Exchange Rates, and Protectionism in the United States. *J. Policy Modeling*, Spring 1987, *9*(1), pp. 125–41. [G: U.S.]

Salvatore, Dominick. The New Protectionist Threat to World Welfare: Introduction. *Salvatore, D., ed.,* 1987, pp. 1–27. [G: Global]

Sampson, Gary P. Pseudo-economics of the MFA—A Proposal for Reform. *World Econ.*, December 1987, *10*(4), pp. 455–68.

Samuel, Howard D. Myths Surrounding Displaced Workers. *Barfield, C. E. and Makin, J. H., eds.,* 1987, pp. 104–06. [G: U.S.]

Samuelson, Paul A. The U.S. and Japanese Economies in the Remaining Reagan Years. *Sato, R. and Wachtel, P., eds.,* 1987, pp. 89–99.
[G: U.S.; Japan]

Sanderson, Fred H. United States–Japan Negotiating Issues and Opportunities in the GATT. *Johnson, D. G., ed.*, 1987, pp. 47–76. [G: U.S.; Japan]

Sanderson, Susan Walsh. Automated Manufacturing and Offshore Assembly in Mexico. *Thorup, C. L., ed.*, 1987, pp. 127–48. [G: Mexico]

Santana, Carlos Augusto Mattos. Efeitos das Políticas Econômicas Brasileiras sobre o Setor Doméstico de soja em Grão. (With English summary.) *Pesquisa Planejamento Econ.*, December 1987, *17*(3), pp. 633–78. [G: Brazil]

Sathirathai, Surakiart and Siamwalla, Ammar. GATT Law, Agricultural Trade, and Developing Countries: Lessons from Two Case Studies. *World Bank Econ. Rev.*, September 1987, *1*(4), pp. 595–618. [G: Thailand; U.S.; EEC]

Sato, Mitsuaki. Costs and Benefits to the United States of the 1985 Steel Import Quota Program: Discussion. *Sato, R. and Wachtel, P., eds.*, 1987, pp. 181–83. [G: U.S.; Japan]

Sato, Takashi. Agricultural Reform Efforts in the United States and Japan: Remarks. *Johnson, D. G., ed.*, 1987, pp. 77–81. [G: U.S.; Japan]

Saunders, Christopher. Industrial Policies and Structural Change: Introduction. *Saunders, C. T., ed.*, 1987, pp. 1–19.

Saxonhouse, Gary R. Strategic Sectors and International Competition: Comment. *Stern, R. M., ed.*, 1987, pp. 239–43. [G: U.S.]

Schnittker, John A. Agricultural Reform Efforts in the United States: Feasibility and Consequences for Japan and Third Countries. *Johnson, D. G., ed.*, 1987, pp. 5–23. [G: U.S.; Japan]

Sethi, S. Prakash. South Africa Beyond Apartheid Reformation of Institutions and Instruments of Change. *Sethi, S. P., ed.*, 1987, pp. 1–37. [G: S. Africa]

Shachmurove, Yochanan. The Integration of the Israeli Economy into the EEC: Recent Trends and a Forecast. *Greilsammer, I. and Weiler, J. H. H., eds.*, 1987, pp. 73–112. [G: Israel; EEC]

Shelton, Joanna. The Congressional Perspective. *Barfield, C. E. and Makin, J. H., eds.*, 1987, pp. 19–21. [G: U.S.]

Shields, Roger E. The Export–Import Bank: A Changing Mission? *Rodriguez, R. M., ed.*, 1987, pp. 157–65. [G: U.S.]

Sicat, Gerardo P. Economic Structure, Trade, and Cooperation. *Martin, L. G., ed.*, 1987, pp. 126–31. [G: ASEAN]

Silber, Jacques G. and Berrebi, Zeev M. The 1975 Free Trade Agreement and Its Impact on Israeli Exports to the EEC. *Greilsammer, I. and Weiler, J. H. H., eds.*, 1987, pp. 136–55. [G: Israel; EEC]

Silk, Leonard. The United States and the World Economy. *Foreign Aff.*, 1987, *65*(3), pp. 458–76. [G: Global]

Sjaastad, Larry A. Commercial Policy for Panama in the 1980s. *[Harberger, A.]*, 1987, pp. 166–216. [G: Panama]

Skipper, Harold D., Jr. Protectionism in the Provision of International Insurance Services. *J. Risk Ins.*, March 1987, *54*(1), pp. 56–85.

Smith, N. Craig. How the West Gains from Apartheid: The Case of the United Kingdom. *Sethi, S. P., ed.*, 1987, pp. 333–52. [G: U.K.; S. Africa]

Smith, Roy C. New Financial Aspects of the U.S.–Japanese Trade Relationship. *Sato, R. and Wachtel, P., eds.*, 1987, pp. 110–26. [G: U.S.; Japan]

Snape, Richard H. The Importance of Frontier Barriers. *[Corden, W. M.]*, 1987, pp. 215–32.

Sommaruga, Cornelio. Die schweizerische Aussenwirtschaftspolitik im wirtschaftspolitischen Spannungsfeld. (Swiss International Economic Policy Options and Implications. With English summary.) *Aussenwirtschaft*, April 1987, *42*(1), pp. 23–40. [G: Switzerland]

Soon, Cho. Trade Policies and Their Impact on Individual Economies: Comment. *Holmes, F., ed.*, 1987, pp. 30–33. [G: Australia]

Spinanger, Dean. Handmaiden under Harassment: The Multi-fibre Arrangement as an Obstacle to Development: Comment. *Giersch, H., ed.*, 1987, pp. 286–93.

Spinanger, Dean. Will the Multi-fibre Arrangement Keep Bangladesh Humble? *World Econ.*, March 1987, *10*(1), pp. 75–84. [G: Bangladesh]

Srinivasan, T. N. Economic Liberalization in China and India: Issues and an Analytical Framework. *J. Compar. Econ.*, September 1987, *11*(3), pp. 427–43. [G: China; India]

Srinivasan, T. N. The National Defense Argument for Government Intervention in Foreign Trade. *Stern, R. M., ed.*, 1987, pp. 337–63. [G: U.S.]

Srinivasan, T. N. The National Defense Argument for Government Intervention in Foreign Trade: Postscript. *Stern, R. M., ed.*, 1987, pp. 374–75. [G: U.S.]

Staiger, Robert W.; Deardorff, Alan V. and Stern, Robert M. Employment Effects of Japanese and American Protectionism. *Salvatore, D., ed.*, 1987, pp. 164–80. [G: U.S.; Japan]

Stam, J. A. The Internationalization of Japanese Business: European and Japanese Perspectives: Conclusion. *Trevor, M., ed.*, 1987, pp. 203–07. [G: Japan]

Stein, Herbert. U.S. Macroeconomic Policy and Trade Relations with Japan. *Sato, R. and Wachtel, P., eds.*, 1987, pp. 100–109. [G: U.S.; Japan]

Steinberg, Gerald M. Science and Politics: The Links between Israel and the European Community. *Greilsammer, I. and Weiler, J. H. H., eds.*, 1987, pp. 337–48. [G: EEC; Israel]

Stern, Robert M. U.S. Trade Policies in a Changing World Economy: Introduction. *Stern, R. M., ed.*, 1987, pp. 1–13. [G: U.S.]

Stern, Robert M. and Hoekman, Bernard M. Issues and Data Needs for GATT Negotiations on Services. *World Econ.*, March 1987, *10*(1), pp. 39–60.

Streit, Manfred E. Industrial Policies and Structural Change: Overall Assessments and Comparisons: Comment. *Saunders, C. T., ed.*, 1987, pp. 101–02.

Sutcliffe, Michael O. Plenty of Propaganda to Prop Up Pretoria. *Sethi, S. P., ed.*, 1987, pp. 171–78. **[G: S. Africa]**

Suzman, Helen. The Folly of Economic Sanctions. *Sethi, S. P., ed.*, 1987, pp. 189–95. **[G: S. Africa]**

Szakolczai, György. The Asia-Pacific Market: A Review. *Dutta, M., ed. (I)*, 1987, pp. 289–308. **[G: Asia-Pacific]**

Takase, Tamotsu. The Role of Concessions in the GATT Trading System and Their Implications for Developing Countries. *J. World Trade Law*, October 1987, *21*(5), pp. 67–89. **[G: Global]**

Tange, Toshiko. United States–Japan Trade Frictions and Competitiveness. *Salvatore, D., ed.*, 1987, pp. 201–15. **[G: U.S.; Japan]**

Tangermann, Stefan. How to Open the Common Agricultural Market: Comment. *Giersch, H., ed.*, 1987, pp. 532–38. **[G: EEC]**

Tangermann, Stefan; Josling, Timothy and Pearson, Scott R. Multilateral Negotiations on Farm-Support Levels. *World Econ.*, September 1987, *10*(3), pp. 265–82.

Tarr, David G. Costs and Benefits to the United States of the 1985 Steel Import Quota Program. *Sato, R. and Wachtel, P., eds.*, 1987, pp. 159–77. **[G: Japan; U.S.]**

Tarr, David G. Effects of Restraining Steel Exports from the Republic of Korea and Other Countries to the United States and the European Economic Community. *World Bank Econ. Rev.*, May 1987, *1*(3), pp. 397–418. **[G: S. Korea; U.S.; EEC]**

Tarr, David G. and Morkre, Morris E. Aggregate Costs to the United States of Tariffs and Quotas on Imports. *Salvatore, D., ed.*, 1987, pp. 216–29. **[G: U.S.]**

Tiffany, Paul. Opportunity Denied: The Abortive Attempt to Internationalize the American Steel Industry, 1903–1929. *Atack, J., ed.*, 1987, pp. 229–47. **[G: U.S.]**

Toren, Benny. The Impact of the FTA Agreement with the EEC on Israeli Industry: A Follow-Up. *Greilsammer, I. and Weiler, J. H. H., eds.*, 1987, pp. 113–35. **[G: Israel; EEC]**

Tovias, Alfred. The Impact of the Second Enlargement of the EC upon Israel's Balance of Payments. *Greilsammer, I. and Weiler, J. H. H., eds.*, 1987, pp. 173–94. **[G: EEC; Israel]**

Tower, Edward. International Trade Regimes and Private Property Rights: Comments. *Contemp. Policy Issues*, April 1987, *5*(2), pp. 13–15. **[G: Global]**

Tower, Edward and Willett, Thomas D. Enforceability and the Resolution of International Jurisdictional Conflicts: Comments. *Law Contemp. Probl.*, Summer 1987, *50*(3), pp. 189–93. **[G: U.S.]**

Trela, Irene; Whalley, John and Wigle, Randall. International Trade in Grains: Domestic Policies and Trade Impacts. *Scand. J. Econ.*, 1987, *89*(3), pp. 271–83. **[G: Global]**

Treumann, T. P. Export Finance from a Keynes-

ian Point of View. *Visser, H. and Schoor, E., eds.*, 1987, pp. 315–25.

Trevor, Malcolm. Japanese Companies in the UK. *Trevor, M., ed.*, 1987, pp. 13–27. **[G: Japan; U.K.]**

Tsutsui, Shunichi. Is the Japan Problem Over? Discussion. *Sato, R. and Wachtel, P., eds.*, 1987, pp. 37–39. **[G: U.S.; Japan]**

Tumlir, Jan. International Commercial Relations: Crisis or a New Beginning? *Rodriguez, R. M., ed.*, 1987, pp. 55–62. **[G: OECD]**

Tumlir, Jan. International Trade Regimes and Private Property Rights. *Contemp. Policy Issues*, April 1987, *5*(2), pp. 1–12. **[G: Global]**

Tutu, Desmond. A Plea for International Sanctions. *Sethi, S. P., ed.*, 1987, pp. 161–64. **[G: S. Africa]**

Ueda, Kazuo. Japanese–U.S. Current Accounts and Exchange Rates before and after the G5 Agreement. *Sato, R. and Wachtel, P., eds.*, 1987, pp. 127–47. **[G: Japan; U.S.]**

UNCTAD Secretariat. Export Financing in Developing Countries. *Dell, S., ed., Pt. 2*, 1987, pp. 665–90.

Urban, Bohumil. Objective World Market Criteria Must Be Used. *Czech. Econ. Digest.*, December 1987, (8), pp. 35–49. **[G: Czechoslovakia]**

Urban, Bohumil. World Criteria of Effectiveness and Quality. *Czech. Econ. Digest.*, June 1987, (4), pp. 10–22. **[G: Czechoslovakia]**

Uusitalo, Matti. GATT-rundan och Finlands jordbruk. (The GATT Round and Finnish Agriculture. With English summary.) *Ekon. Samfundets Tidskr.*, 1987, *40*(2), pp. 81–83. **[G: Finland]**

Valdés, Alberto. Agriculture in the Uruguay Round: Interests of Developing Countries. *World Bank Econ. Rev.*, September 1987, *1*(4), pp. 571–93. **[G: LDCs]**

Valdés, Alberto and León A., Javier. Política Comercial, Industrialización y su Sesgo Antiexportador: Peru 1940–1983. (With English summary.) *Cuadernos Econ.*, April 1987, *24*(71), pp. 3–28. **[G: Peru]**

Valdés, Alberto and Zietz, Joachim. Export Subsidies and Minimum Access Guarantees in Agricultural Trade: A Developing Country Perspective. *World Devel.*, May 1987, *15*(5), pp. 673–83. **[G: Global]**

Ventura, Arnaldo K. Jamaica's Bauxite Battle. *Dedijer, S. and Jéquier, N., eds.*, 1987, pp. 110–27. **[G: Jamaica]**

Vošický, Emilián. Czechoslovakia's Trade Policy towards Advanced Capitalist States. *Czech. Econ. Digest.*, June 1987, (5), pp. 31–38. **[G: Czechoslovakia]**

de Vries, Rimmer and Hargreaves, Derek. The Dollar's Decline and Trade: Mission Accomplished? *Challenge*, Jan./Feb. 1987, *29*(6), pp. 37–46. **[G: Global]**

Wachtel, Paul. Trade Friction and Economic Policy: Problems and Prospects for Japan and the United States: Introduction. *Sato, R. and Wachtel, P., eds.*, 1987, pp. 1–8. **[G: U.S.; Japan]**

Waelbroeck, Jean. The Causes of Protection: From Economic to Historical Determinism? *Giersch, H., ed.,* 1987, pp. 605–21.

Wagner, Joachim. Zur politischen Ökonomie der Protektion in der Bundesrepublik Deutschland. (With English summary.) *Kyklos,* 1987, *40*(4), pp. 548–67. **[G: W. Germany]**

Waldman, Andrea K. Natural Gas Imports: Federal Policy and Competition for U.S. Markets. *Natural Res. J.,* Fall 1987, *27*(4), pp. 789–98. **[G: U.S.]**

Wallen, Axel. The OECD Arrangement on Guidelines for Officially Supported Export Credit: Past and Future. *Rodriguez, R. M., ed.,* 1987, pp. 97–104. **[G: OECD]**

Walters, David A. Competitiveness and Trade Policy: A View from the Administration. *Barfield, C. E. and Makin, J. H., eds.,* 1987, pp. 65–69. **[G: U.S.]**

Warley, T. K. Issues Facing Agriculture in the GATT Negotiations. *Can. J. Agr. Econ.,* November 1987, *35*(3), pp. 515–34. **[G: OECD]**

Warr, Peter G. Export Promotion via Industrial Enclaves: The Philippines' Bataan Export Processing Zone. *J. Devel. Stud.,* January 1987, *23*(2), pp. 220–41. **[G: Philippines]**

Warr, Peter G. Malaysia's Industrial Enclaves: Benefits and Costs. *Devel. Econ.,* March 1987, *25*(1), pp. 30–55. **[G: Malaysia]**

Watson, William G. Canada–U.S. Free Trade: Why Now? *Can. Public Policy,* September 1987, *13*(3), pp. 337–49. **[G: U.S.; Canada]**

Weiler, Joseph H. H. The Evolution of a European Foreign Policy: Mechanisms and Institutions. *Greilsammer, I. and Weiler, J. H. H., eds.,* 1987, pp. 233–54. **[G: Israel; EEC]**

Weiss, John. Some Comments on Estimating Economic Parameters for Jamaica. *Industry Devel.,* 1987, (21), pp. 75–98. **[G: Jamaica]**

Wellons, Philip A. Banks and the Export Credit Wars: Mixed Credits in the Sicartsa Financing. *Rodriguez, R. M., ed.,* 1987, pp. 167–203. **[G: U.K.; Mexico]**

Westcott, Nicholas. Stabilizing Commodity Prices: State Control of Colonial Commodity Trade, 1930–1950. *Dewey, C., ed.,* 1987, pp. 262–87. **[G: U.S.; Europe]**

Westlake, M. J. The Measurement of Agricultural Price Distortion in Developing Countries. *J. Devel. Stud.,* April 1987, *23*(3), pp. 367–81. **[G: Kenya]**

White, Lawrence J. Costs and Benefits to the United States of the 1985 Steel Import Quota Program: Discussion. *Sato, R. and Wachtel, P., eds.,* 1987, pp. 177–81. **[G: U.S.; Japan]**

Whitman, Marina von Neumann. Strategic Sectors and International Competition: Comment. *Stern, R. M., ed.,* 1987, pp. 233–38. **[G: U.S.]**

Winston, Clifford. Blind Intersection? Policy and the Automobile Industry: Introduction and Summary. *Winston, C., et al.,* 1987, pp. 1–5. **[G: U.S.]**

Winters, L. Alan. Negotiating the Abolition of Non-tariff Barriers. *Oxford Econ. Pap.,* September 1987, *39*(3), pp. 465–80. **[G: Global]**

Winters, L. Alan. The Economic Consequences of Agricultural Support: A Survey. *OECD Econ. Stud.,* Autumn 1987, (9), pp. 7–54.

Wolf, Bernard M. The Reaction of U.S.-Based Multinational Enterprises to Free Trade between Canada and the United States: Impediments to Empirical Verification. *Tremblay, R., ed.,* 1987, pp. 351–66. **[G: U.S.; Canada]**

Wolf, Martin. An Unholy Alliance: The European Community and Developing Countries in the International Trading Sysem. *Aussenwirtschaft,* April 1987, *42*(1), pp. 41–64. **[G: EEC; LDCs]**

Wolf, Martin. Differential and More Favorable Treatment of Developing Countries and the International Trading System. *World Bank Econ. Rev.,* September 1987, *1*(4), pp. 647–68. **[G: LDCs]**

Wolf, Martin. Fiddling While GATT Burns. *[Kitamura, H.],* 1987, pp. 246–67. **[G: OECD]**

Wolf, Martin. Handmaiden under Harassment: The Multi-fibre Arrangement as an Obstacle to Development. *Giersch, H., ed.,* 1987, pp. 252–85.

Wolff, Alan. The Importance of Process. *Barfield, C. E. and Makin, J. H., eds.,* 1987, pp. 86–89. **[G: U.S.]**

Wolpe, Howard. The Double Standard of American Foreign Policy. *Sethi, S. P., ed.,* 1987, pp. 53–61. **[G: S. Africa; U.S.]**

Wolter, Frank. Trade Liberalization within the GATT Framework? *Giersch, H., ed.,* 1987, pp. 540–73.

Wong, Edy L. Recent Developments in China's Special Economic Zones: Problems and Prognosis. *Devel. Econ.,* March 1987, *25*(1), pp. 73–86. **[G: China]**

Wonnacott, Ronald J. Economic Imperatives of a Trade Agreement with the U.S. *Tremblay, R., ed.,* 1987, pp. 327–29. **[G: U.S.; Canada]**

Wooding, Paul. Liberalising the International Trade Regime. *Bollard, A. and Buckle, R., eds.,* 1987, pp. 86–101. **[G: New Zealand]**

Woronoff, Jon. Japan: Comments: How Are the Products Kept Out of Japan? *Dutta, M., ed. (II),* 1987, pp. 41–42. **[G: Japan]**

Yamazawa, Ippei. Japan and Her Asian Neighbors in a Dynamic Perspective. *Bradford, C. I., Jr. and Branson, W. H., eds.,* 1987, pp. 93–119. **[G: Asia]**

Yannopoulos, George N. European Community Tariff Preferences and Foreign Direct Investment. *Banca Naz. Lavoro Quart. Rev.,* March 1987, (160), pp. 93–109. **[G: EEC]**

Yannopoulos, George N. United States Trade Interests and EC Enlargement. *J. World Trade Law,* August 1987, *21*(4), pp. 49–65. **[G: EEC; U.S.]**

Yarbrough, Beth V. and Yarbrough, Robert M. Cooperation in the Liberalization of International Trade: After Hegemony, What? *Int. Organ.,* Winter 1987, *41*(1), pp. 1–26. **[G: Global]**

Yarbrough, Beth V. and Yarbrough, Robert M. Institutions for the Governance of Opportunism in International Trade. *J. Law, Econ., Or-*

gan., Spring 1987, *3*(1), pp. 129–39.
[G: Global]
Yarrow, George. Economic Aspects of Anti-dumping Policies. *Oxford Rev. Econ. Policy*, Spring 1987, *3*(1), pp. 66–79. [G: Global]
Yeats, Alexander J. A Note on the Functioning of International Commodity Price Stabilisation Agreements in Periods of Fluctuating Monetary Exchange Rates. *J. Devel. Stud.*, April 1987, *23*(3), pp. 382–401.
Young, Soogil. Trade Liberalization within the GATT Framework? Comment. *Giersch, H., ed.*, 1987, pp. 574–78.
Zacher, Mark W. Trade Gaps, Analytical Gaps: Regime Analysis and International Commodity Trade Regulation. *Int. Organ.*, Spring 1987, *41*(2), pp. 173–202. [G: Global]
Zheng, Tuobin. The Problem of Reforming China's Foreign Trade System. *Chinese Econ. Stud.*, Summer 1987, *20*(4), pp. 27–49.
[G: China]
Zschau, Ed. Meeting the Global Competitive Challenge. *Shetty, Y. K. and Buehler, V. M., eds.*, 1987, pp. 45–56. [G: U.S.]

423 Economic Integration

4230 General

Bryant, Ralph C.; Driffill, John and Portes, Richard. Global Macroeconomics: Introduction. *Bryant, R. C. and Portes, R., eds.*, 1987, pp. 1–13.
Holzman, Franklyn D. A Comparative View of Foreign Trade Behavior: Market versus Centrally Planned Economies. *Holzman, F. D.*, 1987, *1985*, pp. 91–112.
Hong, Lee Fook. Tax Incentives to Become a Financial Centre: Singapore. *Bull. Int. Fiscal Doc.*, March 1987, *41*(3), pp. 103–10.
[G: Singapore]
Kaldor, Nicholas. The Role of Commodity Prices in Economic Recovery. *World Devel.*, May 1987, *15*(5), pp. 551–58. [G: EEC; U.S.]
Kindleberger, Charles P. European Economic Integration. *Kindleberger, C. P.*, 1987, *1951*, pp. 46–63. [G: W. Europe; U.S.]
Kindleberger, Charles P. Machlup on Integration. *Kindleberger, C. P.*, 1987, *1978*, pp. 141–53. [G: U.S.; W. Europe]
Salgado, Germánico. Economic Integration Processes: Introduction. *Dunning, J. H. and Usui, M., eds.*, 1987, pp. 243–45. [G: LDCs]
Wangwe, Samuel M. Economic Co-operation among Developing Countries: Status and Prospects. *Dunning, J. H. and Usui, M., eds.*, 1987, pp. 337–53. [G: LDCs]

4232 Theory of Economic Integration

Desai, Padma. Is the Soviet Union Subsidizing Eastern Europe? *Desai, P.*, 1987, *1985*, pp. 153–62. [G: CMEA]
Kemp, Murray C. and Wan, Henry, Jr. An Elementary Proposition Concerning the Formation of Customs Unions. *Bhagwati, J. N., ed.*,

1987, *1976*, pp. 377–80.
Lipsey, Richard G. The Theory of Customs Unions: A General Survey. *Bhagwati, J. N., ed.*, 1987, *1960*, pp. 357–76.
Mullei, Andrew K. Determinants of the Effects of Economic Integration among African Countries. *Eastern Afr. Econ. Rev.*, June 1987, *3*(1), pp. 21–25. [G: Africa]
Nicolaides, Phedon. Customs Unions and Preferential Trading: The (In)Significance of Reciprocity. *Weltwirtsch. Arch.*, 1987, *123*(3), pp. 488–95.
Parai, Amar K. and Batra, Raveendra N. Customs Union and Unemployment in LDCs. *J. Devel. Econ.*, August 1987, *26*(2), pp. 311–19.
[G: LDCs]
Patterson, Seymour. Economic Expansion and the Theory of Customs Unions. *Rivista Int. Sci. Econ. Com.*, May 1987, *34*(5), pp. 411–17.
Venables, Anthony J. Customs Union and Tariff Reform under Imperfect Competition. *Europ. Econ. Rev.*, Feb./Mar. 1987, *31*(1/2), pp. 103–10.

4233 Economic Integration: Policy and Empirical Studies

Agrawal, Govind R. Economic Dimensions of South Asian Regional Cooperation. *Agrawal, G. R., et al. (II)*, 1987, pp. 154–78.
[G: S. Asia]
Ahmad, Zakaria Haji. ASEAN and Malaysian Political Development. *Martin, L. G., ed.*, 1987, pp. 166–69. [G: Malaysia; ASEAN]
Akrasanee, Narongchai. ASEAN Economic Cooperation. *Martin, L. G., ed.*, 1987, pp. 99–125. [G: ASEAN]
Alworth, Julian S. Taxation and the Cost of Capital: A Comparison of Six EC Countries. *Cnossen, S., ed.*, 1987, pp. 253–83. [G: EEC]
Amin, Samir; Chitala, Derrick and Mandaza, Ibbo. SADCC Prospects for Disengagement and Development in Southern Africa: Introduction. *Amin, S.; Chitala, D. and Mandaza, I., eds.*, 1987, pp. 8–12.
[G: Southern Africa]
Andel, Norbert. Determination of Company Profits. *Cnossen, S., ed.*, 1987, pp. 287–304.
[G: EEC]
Andreff, Wladimir and Lavigne, Marie. A Way Out of the Crisis for the CMEA Economies? *Soviet E. Europ. Foreign Trade*, Fall 1987, *23*(3), pp. 8–43. [G: CMEA]
Artis, M. J. The European Monetary System: An Evaluation. *J. Policy Modeling*, Spring 1987, *9*(1), pp. 175–98. [G: EEC]
Asai, Motofumi. The ASEAN Success Story: Social, Economic, and Political Dimensions: Japan. *Martin, L. G., ed.*, 1987, pp. 192–99.
[G: Japan; ASEAN]
Bartoli, Pierre. L'agriculture dans le développement économique et les politiques communautaires en Méditerranée. (Agriculture in the Economic Development and E.E.C. Policies in the Mediterranean. With English summary.)

Écon. Soc., July 1987, *21*(7), pp. 111–48.
[G: EEC]
Batizi, E. E., et al. Problems of Proportionality in a Socialist Economy. *Soviet E. Europ. Foreign Trade*, Summer 1987, *23*(2), pp. 6–23.
[G: CMEA]
Bautista, Romeo M. The Recent Recession and Rising Protectionism in Developed Countries: Some Thoughts on the ASEAN Economies. *Dutta, M., ed. (I)*, 1987, pp. 83–91.
[G: ASEAN]
Bird, Richard M. Corporate–Personal Tax Integration. *Cnossen, S., ed.*, 1987, pp. 227–51.
[G: EEC]
Blair, Andrew R. The Relative Distribution of United States Direct Investment: The U.K./EEC Experience. *Europ. Econ. Rev.*, July 1987, *31*(5), pp. 1137–44. **[G: EEC; U.S.]**
Bossak, Jan. CMEA at the Threshold of Fundamental Reforms. *Econ. Rev. (Keizai Kenkyu)*, July 1987, *38*(3), pp. 217–21. **[G: CMEA]**
van Brabant, Jozef M. Socialist and World Market Prices: An Ingrowth? *J. Compar. Econ.*, March 1987, *11*(1), pp. 21–39. **[G: Hungary]**
Brewin, Christopher. The European Community: A Union of States without Unity of Government. *J. Common Market Stud.*, September 1987, *26*(1), pp. 1–23. **[G: EEC]**
Brewin, Christopher and McAllister, Richard. Annual Review of the Activities of the European Communities in 1986. *J. Common Market Stud.*, June 1987, *25*(4), pp. 337–72.
[G: EEC]
Buckley, Peter J. and Artisien, Patrick. Policy Issues of Intra-EC Direct Investment: British, French and German Multinationals in Greece, Portugal and Spain, with Special Reference to Employment Effects. *J. Common Market Stud.*, December 1987, *26*(2), pp. 207–30.
[G: EEC]
Burniaux, Jean Marc. Does the European Agricultural Lobby Retard Economic Recovery? A General Equilibrium Approach. *Econ. Notes*, 1987, (1), pp. 72–99. **[G: EEC]**
Cable, Vincent. The Impact of EEC Trade Policies on Developing Countries. *Giersch, H., ed.*, 1987, pp. 294–326. **[G: EEC; LDCs]**
Caeser, Rolf. Internationaler Zinszusammenhang und deutsche Zinspolitik im Europäischen Währungssystem. (International Interdependence of Interest Rates and German Interest Rate Policy within the European Monetary System. With English summary.) *Konjunkturpolitik*, 1987, *33*(1), pp. 47–70. **[G: EEC]**
Cantwell, John. The Reorganization of European Industries After Integration: Selected Evidence on the Role of Multinational Enterprise Activities. *J. Common Market Stud.*, December 1987, *26*(2), pp. 127–51. **[G: EEC]**
Caraveli-Ioannidis, Helen. Farm Income Disparity in Greece and Membership of the EC. *Europ. Rev. Agr. Econ.*, 1987, *14*(2), pp. 239–49. **[G: Greece; EEC]**
Chard, John S. European Competition Policy and the Pricing of Cars: An Economic Analysis of the Motor Vehicle Block Exemption Regula-

tion. *Macmillen, M.; Mayes, D. G. and van Veen, P., eds.*, 1987, pp. 152–93. **[G: EEC]**
Chee, Peng Lim. A Malaysian View of Economic Cooperation. *Martin, L. G., ed.*, 1987, pp. 135–39. **[G: Malaysia; ASEAN]**
Cheng, Bifan. The ASEAN Success Story: Social, Economic, and Political Dimensions: China. *Martin, L. G., ed.*, 1987, pp. 189–91.
[G: ASEAN; China]
Chitala, Derrick. The Political Economy of the SADCC and Imperialism's Response. *Amin, S.; Chitala, D. and Mandaza, I., eds.*, 1987, pp. 13–36. **[G: Southern Africa; S. Africa]**
Cho, Lee-Jay. ASEAN: The Challenges Ahead. *Martin, L. G., ed.*, 1987, pp. 211–17.
[G: ASEAN]
Cieślik, Jerzy; Grolig, Otto and Bogaert, Peter. The Newly-Amended EEC Anti-dumping Regulation: Black Holes in the Common Market? *J. World Trade Law*, December 1987, *21*(6), pp. 79–87. **[G: EEC]**
Cnossen, Sijbren. Tax Coordination in the European Community: Introduction. *Cnossen, S., ed.*, 1987, pp. 1–15. **[G: EEC]**
Cnossen, Sijbren. Tax Structure Developments. *Cnossen, S., ed.*, 1987, pp. 19–55. **[G: EEC]**
Cnossen, Sijbren and Shoup, Carl S. Coordination of Value-Added Taxes. *Cnossen, S., ed.*, 1987, pp. 59–84. **[G: EEC]**
Cohen, Benjamin J. Implications of the European Monetary System for Developing Nations. *Dell, S., ed., Pt. 1*, 1987, pp. 295–339.
[G: W. Europe; LDCs]
Croxford, G. J.; Wise, M. and Chalkley, B. S. The Reform of the European Regional Development Fund: A Preliminary Assessment. *J. Common Market Stud.*, September 1987, *26*(1), pp. 25–38. **[G: EEC]**
Desai, Padma. Is the Soviet Union Subsidizing Eastern Europe? *Desai, P.*, 1987, *1985*, pp. 153–62. **[G: CMEA]**
Diejomaoh, V. P. The Economic Integration Process in Africa: Experience, Problems and Prospects. *Dunning, J. H. and Usui, M., eds.*, 1987, pp. 321–36. **[G: Africa]**
Dunning, John H. and Robson, Peter. Multinational Corporate Integration and Regional Economic Integration. *J. Common Market Stud.*, December 1987, *26*(2), pp. 103–25.
[G: EEC]
Econ. and Soc. Commiss. for Asia and the Pacific. Experiences in Promoting ECDC in Asia. *Agrawal, G. R., et al. (II)*, 1987, pp. 89–97.
[G: Asia]
El-Agraa, Ali M. An Equitable Budget for the European Community? *[Kitamura, H.]*, 1987, pp. 174–89. **[G: EEC]**
Etim, Ekei U. ECA: Towards a Sub-regional Economic Cooperation. *Akinrinade, O. and Barling, J. K., eds.*, 1987, pp. 77–98. **[G: Africa]**
Fennell, Rosemary. Reform of the CAP: Shadow or Substance? *J. Common Market Stud.*, September 1987, *26*(1), pp. 61–77. **[G: EEC]**
Franzmeyer, Fritz. Was kostet die Vollendung des europäischen Binnenmarktes? Eine Bewertung aus wirtschaftlicher, sozialer und poli-

tischer Sicht. (The Completion of the Common Internal Market—What Are the Costs. A Valuation from the Economic, Social, and Political Points of View. With English summary.) *Konjunkturpolitik*, 1987, 33(3), pp. 146–66.

Giavazzi, Francesco. The Performance of the British Economy: The Impact of EEC Membership. *Dornbusch, R. and Layard, R., eds.*, 1987, pp. 97–130. **[G: U.K.]**

Gleske, Leonhard. Die währungspolitische Zusammenarbeit im Rahmen der neuverfassten Europäischen Gemeinschaft. (Monetary Cooperation after the Single European Act. With English summary.) *Konjunkturpolitik*, 1987, 33(6), pp. 311–22. **[G: W. Germany]**

Granell, Francesco. Spain and the Enlargement of the EEC. *Greilsammer, I. and Weiler, J. H. H., eds.*, 1987, pp. 159–72. **[G: EEC; Spain]**

de Grauwe, Paul. Did the Exchange Rate Stability within the EMS Contribute to More Trade? *Visser, H. and Schoor, E., eds.*, 1987, pp. 237–48. **[G: EEC; U.S.]**

de Grauwe, Paul. International Trade and Economic Growth in the European Monetary System. *Europ. Econ. Rev.*, Feb./Mar. 1987, 31(1/2), pp. 389–98. **[G: W. Europe]**

Greenaway, David. Intra-industry Trade, Intra-firm Trade and European Integration: Evidence, Gains and Policy Aspects. *J. Common Market Stud.*, December 1987, 26(2), pp. 153–72. **[G: EEC]**

Guieu, Pierre and Bonnet, Claire. Completion of the Internal Market and Indirect Taxation. *J. Common Market Stud.*, March 1987, 25(3), pp. 209–22. **[G: EEC]**

Hartley, Keith. Public Procurement and Competitiveness: A Community Market for Military Hardware and Technology? *J. Common Market Stud.*, March 1987, 25(3), pp. 237–47. **[G: EEC]**

Hernandez, Carolina G. The Philippines: Implications for Regional Order. *Martin, L. G., ed.*, 1987, pp. 170–81. **[G: Philippines; ASEAN]**

Hindley, Brian. Trade in Services within the European Community. *Giersch, H., ed.*, 1987, pp. 468–86. **[G: EEC]**

Hirsch, Seev. The Impact of EEC Trade Policies on Developing Countries: Comment. *Giersch, H., ed.*, 1987, pp. 327–31. **[G: EEC; LDCs]**

Hitam, Dato Musa. ASEAN and the Pacific Basin. *Martin, L. G., ed.*, 1987, pp. 8–13. **[G: ASEAN]**

Holland, Martin. Three Approaches for Understanding European Political Co-operation: A Case-Study of EC–South African Policy. *J. Common Market Stud.*, June 1987, 25(4), pp. 295–313. **[G: EEC; S. Africa]**

Holzman, Franklyn D. Comecon: A "Trade-Destroying" Customs Union? *Holzman, F. D.*, 1987, 1985, pp. 171–86. **[G: CMEA]**

Holzman, Franklyn D. Further Thoughts on the Significance of Soviet Subsidies to Eastern Europe. *Holzman, F. D.*, 1987, 1986, pp. 203–08. **[G: CMEA]**

Holzman, Franklyn D. The Significance of Soviet Subsidies to Eastern Europe. *Holzman, F. D.*, 1987, 1986, pp. 187–201. **[G: CMEA]**

Hood, Neil and Young, Stephen. Inward Investment and the EC: UK Evidence on Corporate Integration Strategies. *J. Common Market Stud.*, December 1987, 26(2), pp. 193–206. **[G: U.K.; EEC]**

Horn, Ernst-Jürgen. Trade in Services within the European Community: Comment. *Giersch, H., ed.*, 1987, pp. 487–91. **[G: EEC]**

Inukai, Ichiro. Regional Integration and Development in Eastern and Southern Africa. *[Kitamura, H.]*, 1987, pp. 140–58. **[G: Africa]**

Ivanov, Ivan D. Restructuring the Mechanism of Foreign Economic Relations in the USSR. *Soviet Econ.*, July-Sept. 1987, 3(3), pp. 192–218. **[G: U.S.S.R.]**

Jager, Henk and de Jong, Eelke. The Viability of the ECU. *Visser, H. and Schoor, E., eds.*, 1987, pp. 249–62. **[G: EEC]**

Ježek, Jiří. Direct Relations in Economic and Scientific–Technological Cooperation. *Czech. Econ. Digest.*, June 1987, (5), pp. 8–20. **[G: CMEA]**

Ježek, Jiří. Space for Development of Direct Relations (Czechoslovakia–CMEA) *Czech. Econ. Digest.*, June 1987, (5), pp. 25–27. **[G: CMEA]**

de Jong, Henk Wouter. Market Structures in the European Economic Community. *Macmillen, M.; Mayes, D. G. and van Veen, P., eds.*, 1987, pp. 40–88. **[G: EEC]**

Kaufmann, Peter J. The Community Trademark; Its Role in Making the Internal Market Effective. *J. Common Market Stud.*, March 1987, 25(3), pp. 223–35. **[G: EEC]**

Kay, John A. and Keen, Michael. Alcohol and Tobacco Taxes: Criteria for Harmonisation. *Cnossen, S., ed.*, 1987, pp. 85–111. **[G: EEC]**

Klein, Werner. The Role of the GDR in Comecon: Some Economic Aspects. *Jeffries, I. and Melzer, M., eds.*, 1987, pp. 261–79. **[G: E. Germany; CMEA]**

Kng, Chng Meng. The Policy Framework of ASEAN Economic Cooperation. *Agrawal, G. R., et al. (II)*, 1987, pp. 98–115. **[G: ASEAN]**

Koester, Ulrich. How to Open the Common Agricultural Market. *Giersch, H., ed.*, 1987, pp. 515–31. **[G: EEC]**

Kraus, Josef. Can Contract Prices Be Based on Regional Prices? *Soviet E. Europ. Foreign Trade*, Winter 1987-1988, 23(4), pp. 5–21. **[G: EEC]**

Krause, Lawrence B. A Second-Best Strategy for Pacific Dynamism. *Dutta, M., ed. (I)*, 1987, pp. 11–22. **[G: Asia-Pacific]**

Kříž, Karel and Voráček, Michal. CMEA: Prerequisites of Higher Effectiveness. *Czech. Econ. Digest.*, January 1987, (2), pp. 13–19. **[G: CMEA]**

Lavigne, Marie. Is Eastern Europe an Asset or a Liability to the USSR? *Marer, P. and van Veen, P., eds.*, 1987, pp. 55–64. **[G: U.S.S.R.; CMEA]**

Lopez-Claros, Augusto. The European Community: On the Road to Integration. *Finance Develop.*, September 1987, *24*(3), pp. 35–38. [G: EC]

Luft, C. and Maier, Lutz. International Investment Cooperation within the CMEA Area. *Borner, S. and Taylor, A., eds.,* 1987, pp. 301–20. [G: CMEA]

Mahé, Louis and Moreddu, Catherine. An Illustrative Trade Model to Analyse CAP Changes: Unilateral Moves and Interaction with USA. *Econ. Notes*, 1987, (1), pp. 52–71. [G: EEC; U.S.]

Mandaza, Ibbo. Perspectives on Economic Cooperation and Autonomous Development in Southern Africa. *Amin, S.; Chitala, D. and Mandaza, I., eds.,* 1987, pp. 210–30. [G: Southern Africa]

Marer, Paul. Soviet–East European Economic Relations: A Historical Perspective. *Marer, P. and van Veen, P., eds.,* 1987, pp. 45–53. [G: CMEA]

Martin, Linda G. Human Resources and Economic Development. *Martin, L. G., ed.,* 1987, pp. 92–96. [G: ASEAN]

Maximova, M. M. World Markets and Socialist Economies. *Pasinetti, L. and Lloyd, P., eds.,* 1987, pp. 427–37. [G: CMEA]

Mayes, David G. European Industrial Policy. *Macmillen, M.; Mayes, D. G. and van Veen, P., eds.,* 1987, pp. 247–67. [G: EEC]

McAleese, Dermot and Matthews, Alan. The Single European Act and Ireland: Implications for a Small Member State. *J. Common Market Stud.*, September 1987, *26*(1), pp. 39–60. [G: EEC]

McCorriston, S. and Sheldon, Ian M. EC Integration and the Agricultural Supply Industries. *Macmillen, M.; Mayes, D. G. and van Veen, P., eds.,* 1987, pp. 119–51. [G: EEC]

McDaniel, Paul R. Personal Income Taxes: The Treatment of Tax Expenditures. *Cnossen, S., ed.,* 1987, pp. 319–33. [G: EEC]

Mélitz, Jacques. Discipline monétaire, République fédérale allemande et Système monétaire européen. (Monetary Discipline, Germany, and the European Monetary System. With English summary.) *Ann. Écon. Statist.*, Oct./Dec. 1987, (8), pp. 59–87. [G: Europe]

Mennes, L. B. M. World Priorities for Structural Change, Economic Interdependence and World Development. *Urquidi, V. L., ed.,* 1987, pp. 195–99.

Monti, Mario. Integration of Financial Markets in Europe. *Giersch, H., ed.,* 1987, pp. 492–503. [G: EEC]

Mudenda, Gilbert N. The Development of a Local Technological Capacity in the SADCC Region. *Amin, S.; Chitala, D. and Mandaza, I., eds.,* 1987, pp. 128–46. [G: Southern Africa]

Murfin, Andy. Price Discrimination and Tax Differences in the European Motor Industry. *Cnossen, S., ed.,* 1987, pp. 171–94. [G: EEC]

Musgrave, Peggy B. Interjurisdictional Coordination of Taxes on Capital Income. *Cnossen, S.,*

ed., 1987, pp. 197–225. [G: EEC]

Mytelka, Lynn Krieger and Delapierre, Michel. The Alliance Strategies of European Firms in the Information Technology Industry and the Role of ESPRIT. *J. Common Market Stud.*, December 1987, *26*(2), pp. 231–53. [G: EEC]

Naranjo L., Edgar. The Andean Pact. *Bull. Int. Fiscal Doc.*, February 1987, *41*(2), pp. 89–90. [G: Andean]

Naya, Seiji. Economic Performance and Growth Factors of the ASEAN Countries. *Martin, L. G., ed.,* 1987, pp. 47–87. [G: ASEAN]

Ndlela, Daniel B. The Manufacturing Sector in the East and Southern African Subregion, with Emphasis on the SADCC. *Amin, S.; Chitala, D. and Mandaza, I., eds.,* 1987, pp. 37–61. [G: E. Africa; Southern Africa]

Ng'andwe, Chiselebwe. Financial Integration and Development in SADCC and PTA Countries. *Amin, S.; Chitala, D. and Mandazc, I., eds.,* 1987, pp. 181–209. [G: Southern Africa]

Okita, Saburo. Pacific Development and Cooperation. *[Kitamura, H.],* 1987, pp. 114–26. [G: ASEAN; Pacific]

Olanrewaju, S. A. and Falola, Toyin. Development through Integration: The Politics and Problems of ECOWAS. *Akinrinade, O. and Barling, J. K., eds.,* 1987, pp. 52–76. [G: W. Africa]

Pelkmans, Jacques. Liberalization of Product Markets in the European Community. *Giersch, H., ed.,* 1987, pp. 429–61. [G: EEC]

Pelkmans, Jacques. Market Integration in the Community: Industrial Product Markets and the White Paper. *Macmillen, M.; Mayes, D. G. and van Veen, P., eds.,* 1987, pp. 7–39. [G: EEC]

Pelkmans, Jacques. The Community's Vivid Core: Integration Processes in Industrial Product Market. *Dunning, J. H. and Usui, M., eds.,* 1987, pp. 267–98. [G: EEC]

Pelkmans, Jacques. The New Approach to Technical Harmonization and Standardization. *J. Common Market Stud.*, March 1987, *25*(3), pp. 249–69. [G: EEC]

Pelkmans, Jacques and Robson, Peter. The Aspirations of the White Paper. *J. Common Market Stud.*, March 1987, *25*(3), pp. 181–92. [G: EEC]

Pomfret, Richard. Liberalization of Product Markets in the European Community: Comment. *Giersch, H., ed.,* 1987, pp. 462–67. [G: EEC]

Přib, Jan. Direct Relations in the Development of Industrial Specialization and Cooperation with CMEA Countries. *Czech. Econ. Digest.*, October 1987, (7), pp. 69–77. [G: CMEA]

Rácz, Margit. The Mechanism of Hungarian–Soviet Economic Relations. *Acta Oecon.*, 1987, *38*(3–4), pp. 323–37. [G: Hungary; U.S.S.R.]

Rao, V. L. South Asian Regional Cooperation: Problems and Prospects. *Agrawal, G. R., et al. (II),* 1987, pp. 116–54. [G: S. Asia]

Richter, Sándor. The Development of Hungarian–Soviet Economic Relations. *Acta Oecon.*, 1987, *38*(3–4), pp. 303–22. **[G: Hungary; U.S.S.R.]**

Robson, Peter. Variable Geometry and Automaticity: Strategies for Experience of Regional Integration in West Africa. *[Kitamura, H.]*, 1987, pp. 159–73. **[G: W. Africa]**

Rose, Manfred. Optimal Tax Perspective on Tax Coordination. *Cnossen, S., ed.*, 1987, pp. 113–38. **[G: EEC]**

Rosenthal, Gert. Some Lessons of Economic Integration in Latin America: The Case of Central America. *Dunning, J. H. and Usui, M., eds.*, 1987, pp. 299–320. **[G: Central America]**

Schäfers, Alfons. The Luxembourg Patent Convention, the Best Option for the Internal Market. *J. Common Market Stud.*, March 1987, *25*(3), pp. 193–207. **[G: EEC]**

Schlecht, Otto. Die Vollendung des europäischen Binnenmarktes Ziele, Voraussetzungen und Chancen. (The Completion of the European Internal Market—Goals, Prerequisites, and Opportunities. With English summary.) *Konjunkturpolitik*, 1987, *33*(6), pp. 303–10. **[G: W. Europe]**

Sicat, Gerardo P. Economic Structure, Trade, and Cooperation. *Martin, L. G., ed.*, 1987, pp. 126–31. **[G: ASEAN]**

Sleuwaegen, Leo. Multinationals, the European Community and Belgium: Recent Developments. *J. Common Market Stud.*, December 1987, *26*(2), pp. 255–72. **[G: Belgium]**

Smith, Peter C. Micro-level Aspects of Demographic Change. *Martin, L. G., ed.*, 1987, pp. 37–39. **[G: ASEAN]**

Smith, Roger S. Motor Vehicle Tax Harmonization. *Cnossen, S., ed.*, 1987, pp. 141–70. **[G: EEC]**

Soares, Fernando B. Regional Disparities on Farm Income in Portugal: Will EEC Membership Be a Remedial or Aggravating Factor? *Léon, Y. and Mahé, L., eds.*, 1987, pp. 477–88. **[G: Portugal]**

Szakolczai, György. The Asia-Pacific Market: A Review. *Dutta, M., ed. (I)*, 1987, pp. 289–308. **[G: Asia-Pacific]**

Tangermann, Stefan. How to Open the Common Agricultural Market: Comment. *Giersch, H., ed.*, 1987, pp. 532–38. **[G: EEC]**

Tanzi, Vito and Ter-Minassian, Teresa. The European Monetary System and Fiscal Policies. *Cnossen, S., ed.*, 1987, pp. 337–57. **[G: EEC]**

Thomas, Scott. Dying Separately or Living Together: Regional Security and Economic Cooperation in Southern Africa. *Akinrinade, O. and Barling, J. K., eds.*, 1987, pp. 99–128. **[G: Southern Africa]**

Tinsulanonda, Prem. ASEAN: Meeting the Challenges of Asia and the Pacific. *Martin, L. G., ed.*, 1987, pp. 3–7. **[G: ASEAN]**

Tomczyk, Paweł. CMEA Foreign Trade Forecast: 1985–1990. *Soviet E. Europ. Foreign Trade*, Fall 1987, *23*(3), pp. 44–73. **[G: CMEA]**

Torricelli, Robert G. The ASEAN Success Story: Social, Economic, and Political Dimensions:

The United States. *Martin, L. G., ed.*, 1987, pp. 200–207. **[G: U.S.; ASEAN]**

Ulph, David T. Tax Harmonisation and Labour Mobility. *Cnossen, S., ed.*, 1987, pp. 305–17. **[G: EEC]**

Urban, Luděk. Long-term Trends in the Economic Development of the Socialist Countries. *Czech. Econ. Digest.*, October 1987, (7), pp. 3–16. **[G: CMEA]**

Válek, Vratislav. The Restructuring of Foreign Exchange Financial Relations: The Czechoslovak Approach. *Czech. Econ. Digest.*, October 1987, (7), pp. 33–47. **[G: Czechoslovakia; CMEA]**

Vanous, Jan. The GDR within CMEA. *Comp. Econ. Stud.*, Summer 1987, *29*(2), pp. 1–6. **[G: CMEA; E. Germany]**

Vichit-Vadakan, Vinyu. Finance and Banking. *Martin, L. G., ed.*, 1987, pp. 132–34. **[G: ASEAN]**

Viraphol, Sarasin. Political Development in Thailand and the Kampuchea Problem. *Martin, L. G., ed.*, 1987, pp. 182–86. **[G: Thailand; ASEAN; Kampuchea]**

Vollebergh, Ad. The European Steel Industry—A Model for European Co-operation? *Macmillen, M.; Mayes, D. G. and van Veen, P., eds.*, 1987, pp. 194–228. **[G: EEC]**

Voráček, Michal. Concrete Forms of Cooperation. *Czech. Econ. Digest.*, December 1987, (8), pp. 16–20. **[G: CMEA]**

Voráček, Michal. Czechoslovakia and the Restructuring of the CMEA Mechanism. *Czech. Econ. Digest.*, December 1987, (8), pp. 29–34. **[G: Czechoslovakia]**

Vošický, Emilián. Mutually Beneficial Progress. *Czech. Econ. Digest.*, December 1987, (8), pp. 9–15. **[G: CMEA]**

Vratusa, Anton. Role of South–South Cooperation: A Comment. *Agrawal, G. R., et al. (I)*, 1987, pp. 15–17. **[G: LDCs]**

Wagao, Jumanne H. Trade Relations among SADCC Countries. *Amin, S.; Chitala, D. and Mandaza, I., eds.*, 1987, pp. 147–80. **[G: Southern Africa]**

Walter, Ingo. Integration of Financial Markets in Europe: Comment. *Giersch, H., ed.*, 1987, pp. 504–14. **[G: EEC]**

Wanandi, Jusuf. Political Development and Regional Order. *Martin, L. G., ed.*, 1987, pp. 143–65. **[G: ASEAN]**

Wang, Gungwu. Ethnicity and Religion in Social Development. *Martin, L. G., ed.*, 1987, pp. 40–43. **[G: ASEAN]**

Weiss, Frank D. A Political Economy of European Community Trade Policy against the Less Developed Countries? *Europ. Econ. Rev.*, Feb./Mar. 1987, *31*(1/2), pp. 457–65. **[G: EEC; LDCs]**

Winters, L. Alan. Britain in Europe: A Survey of Quantitative Trade Studies. *J. Common Market Stud.*, June 1987, *25*(4), pp. 315–35. **[G: EEC]**

Wong, Aline K. and Cheung, Paul P. L. Demographic and Social Development: Taking Stock for the Morrow. *Martin, L. G., ed.*, 1987, pp. 17–36. **[G: ASEAN]**

Yannopoulos, George N. Trade Effects from the Extension of Customs Unions on Third Countries: A Case Study of the Spanish Accession to the EEC. *Appl. Econ.*, January 1987, *19*(1), pp. 39–50. **[G: Spain; EEC]**

430 INTERNATIONAL FINANCE

4300 General

Venkateswarlu, Tadiboyina. International Economics: Survey of Course Reading Materials in Universities in Canada and the United States of America. *Amer. Econ.*, Spring 1987, *31*(1), pp. 66–84. **[G: U.S.; Canada]**

431 Open Economy Macroeconomics; Exchange Rates

4310 General

Bognár, József. World Economic Crisis, Adjustment Policies and Global Questions: An Introduction. *Pasinetti, L. and Lloyd, P., eds.*, 1987, pp. 405–08. **[G: Global]**

Darby, Michael R. International Economic Policy Coordination and Transmission: A Review. *Sinclair, P. J. N., ed.*, 1987, *1986*, pp. 343–48.

Demery, Lionel and Addison, Tony. Stabilization Policy and Income Distribution in Developing Countries. *World Devel.*, December 1987, *15*(12), pp. 1483–98. **[G: LDCs]**

El-Naggar, Said. Adjustment Policies and Development Strategies in the Arab World: Summary of the Seminar. *El-Naggar, S., ed.*, 1987, pp. 1–23. **[G: Middle East]**

Fukao, Mitsuhiro and Hanazaki, Masaharu. Internationalisation of Financial Markets and the Allocation of Capital. *OECD Econ. Stud.*, Spring 1987, (8), pp. 35–92. **[G: OECD]**

Guerrieri, Paulo and Padoan, Pier Carlo. The Political Economy Approach to International Cooperation: A Critical Survey. *Econ. Notes*, 1987, (2), pp. 67–88.

Hassan, Izzadin Ibrahim. Adjustment Challenges and Strategies Facing Arab Countries in Light of Recent Experience and New Initiatives: Comment. *El-Naggar, S., ed.*, 1987, pp. 44–48. **[G: Middle East]**

van der Hoeven, Rolph and Richards, P. J. World Recession and Global Interdependence: Conclusions. *International Labour Office.*, 1987, pp. 133–39.

Khan, Mohsin S. Macroeconomic Adjustment in Developing Countries: A Policy Perspective. *World Bank Res. Observer*, January 1987, *2*(1), pp. 23–42. **[G: LDCs]**

Kindleberger, Charles P. The European Recovery Program. *Kindleberger, C. P.*, 1987, *1953*, pp. 64–91. **[G: U.S.; W. Europe]**

Schäfer, Henry. Schaden flexible Wechselkurse der Weltwirtschaft? Ein Überblick zum aktuellen theoretischen und empirischen Forschungsstand. (Do Flexible Exchange Rates Disadvantage the World Economy? A Survey of Current Theoretical and Empirical Research. With English summary.) *Konjunkturpolitik*, 1987, *33*(4), pp. 219–41.

Shaalan, A. Shakour. Adjustment Challenges and Strategies Facing Arab Countries in Light of Recent Experience and New Initiatives. *El-Naggar, S., ed.*, 1987, pp. 24–43. **[G: Middle East]**

Williamson, John. The Failure of World Monetary Reform: A Reassessment. *Williamson, J.*, 1987, *1982*, pp. 201–11.

4312 Open Economy Macroeconomic Theory: Balance of Payments and Adjustment Mechanisms

Adachi, Hideyuki. The Role of Commodity Prices in the Worldwide Inflation and Disinflation. *Kobe Univ. Econ.*, 1987, *33*, pp. 17–31.

Ahmed, Shaghil. Government Spending, the Balance of Trade and the Terms of Trade in British History. *J. Monet. Econ.*, September 1987, *20*(2), pp. 195–220. **[G: U.K.]**

Ahtiala, K. Pekka. The Effects of Foreign Disturbances under Flexible Exchange Rates. *J. Int. Money Finance*, December 1987, *6*(4), pp. 387–400. **[G: W. Europe]**

Albornoz, Hugo E. Procesos de endeudamiento externo y ajuste de precios. (With English summary.) *Cuadernos Econ.*, December 1987, *24*(73), pp. 319–30.

Aoki, Masanao. A Convenient Framework to Analyze a Two-Country World Model: An Illustrative Analysis of Anticipated Real Supply Shocks on the Exchange Rate and the Interest Rate Difference. *[Marrama, V.]*, Vol. 2, 1987, pp. 679–702.

Arida, Persio and Bacha, Edmar Lisboa. Balance of Payments: A Disequilibrium Analysis for Semi-industrialized Economies. *[Diaz-Alejandro, C. F.]*, 1987, pp. 85–108. **[G: Latin America]**

Arida, Persio and Bacha, Edmar Lisboa. Balance of Payments: A Disequilibrium Analysis for Semi-industrialized Economies. *J. Devel. Econ.*, October 1987, *27*(1–2), pp. 85–108. **[G: Latin America]**

Arndt, Sven W. and Richardson, J. David. Real–Financial Linkages among Open Economies: An Overview. *Arndt, S. W. and Richardson, J. D. eds.*, 1987, pp. 5–32.

Auernheimer, Leonardo. On the Outcome of Inconsistent Programs under Exchange Rate and Monetary Rules. *J. Monet. Econ.*, March 1987, *19*(2), pp. 279–305.

Avila, L. and Bacha, Edmar Lisboa. Balance of Payments Experience and Growth Prospects of Developing Countries: Methodological Note. *Dell, S., ed.*, Pt. 3, 1987, pp. 1005–11.

Awad, Mohamed Hashim. Structural Adjustment in Selected Arab Countries: Need, Challenge, and Approaches: Comment. *El-Naggar, S., ed.*, 1987, pp. 68–72. **[G: Middle East]**

Bacha, Edmar Lisboa. IMF Conditionality: Conceptual Problems and Policy Alternatives.

World Devel., December 1987, *15*(12), pp. 1457–67. **[G: LDCs]**

Backus, David and Driffill, John. Credible Disinflation in Closed and Open Economies. *Ricerche Econ.*, July-Dec. 1987, *41*(3–4), pp. 326–40. **[G: Canada]**

Bark, Taeho. Distortions and Intertemporal Welfare in a Small Open Economy. *J. Int. Econ.*, August 1987, *23*(1/2), pp. 151–66.

Barry, Frank G. Fiscal Policy in a Small Open Economy: An Integration of the Short-run, Heckscher–Ohlin and Capital Accumulation Models. *J. Int. Econ.*, February 1987, *22*(1/2), pp. 103–21.

Basevi, Giorgio and Giavazzi, Francesco. Conflicts and Coordination in the European Monetary System. *Steinherr, A. and Weiserbs, D., eds.*, 1987, pp. 133–64. **[G: W. Europe]**

Baxter, Marianne. International Linkages, Exchange-Rate Regimes, and the International Transmission Process: Perspectives from Optimizing Models: Comment. *Officer, L. H., ed.*, 1987, pp. 197–202.

Beladi, Hamid and Naqvi, Nadeem. An Analysis of Wage Differentials for a Small Open Economy. *Southern Econ. J.*, January 1987, *53*(3), pp. 605–14.

Bhandari, Jagdeep S. and Decaluwe, Bernard. A Stochastic Model of Incomplete Separation between Commercial and Financial Exchange Markets. *J. Int. Econ.*, February 1987, *22*(1/2), pp. 25–55.

Black, Stanley W. and Salemi, Michael K. Government Policy and the Risk Premium in Foreign Exchange Markets. *Chrystal, K. A. and Sedgwick, R., eds.*, 1987, pp. 72–90. **[G: W. Germany]**

Blackburn, Keith. Interest Parity, the Degree of Capital Mobility and the Information Contents of the Exchange Rate and the Interest Rate: Clarifications and Extensions. *Manchester Sch. Econ. Soc. Stud.*, March 1987, *55*(1), pp. 60–76.

Blackburn, Keith. International Policy Games in a Simple Macroeconomic Model with Incomplete Information: Some Problems of Credibility, Secrecy and Cooperation. *Ricerche Econ.*, July-Dec. 1987, *41*(3–4), pp. 419–38.

Blejer, Mario I. and Sagari, Silvia. The Structure of the Banking Sector and the Sequence of Financial Liberalization. *Connolly, M. and González-Vega, C., eds.*, 1987, pp. 93–107. **[G: Latin America]**

Boyer, Russell S. and Kingston, Geoffrey H. Currency Substitution under Finance Constraints. *J. Int. Money Finance*, September 1987, *6*(3), pp. 235–50.

Brandsma, Andries S.; Hughes Hallett, Andrew J. and Swank, J. The Robustness of Economic Policy Selections and the Incentive to Cooperate. *J. Econ. Dynam. Control*, June 1987, *11*(2), pp. 163–70. **[G: U.S.; E. Europe]**

Branson, William H. Macroeconomics and Protection: Comment. *Stern, R. M., ed.*, 1987, pp. 131–36. **[G: OECD]**

Breece, James H. A Seemingly Unrelated Currency Area. *METU*, 1987, *14*(3), pp. 283–90.

Breece, James H. Devaluation, Money and Currency Substitution. *Econ. Int.*, May-Aug. 1987, *40*(2–3), pp. 172–91.

Bronfenbrenner, Martin. Some 'Scandals' of International Economics. *[Kitamura, H.]*, 1987, pp. 285–300.

Bryant, Ralph C.; Driffill, John and Portes, Richard. Global Macroeconomics: Introduction. *Bryant, R. C. and Portes, R., eds.*, 1987, pp. 1–13.

Buffie, Edward F. Input Price Shocks in the Small Open Economy. *Sinclair, P. J. N., ed.*, 1987, *1986*, pp. 233–47.

Buiter, Willem H. Borrowing to Defend the Exchange Rate and the Timing and Magnitude of Speculative Attacks. *J. Int. Econ.*, November 1987, *23*(3/4), pp. 221–39.

Burkett, Paul; Ramirez, Javier and Wohar, Mark E. The Determinants of International Reserves in the Small Open Economy: The Case of Honduras. *J. Macroecon.*, Summer 1987, *9*(3), pp. 439–50. **[G: Honduras]**

Cadsby, Charles Bram. Exchange Rate Instability in a Two-Country Portfolio Balance Model. *J. Macroecon.*, Spring 1987, *9*(2), pp. 223–38.

Calvo, Guillermo A. Balance of Payments Crises in a Cash-in-Advance Economy. *J. Money, Credit, Banking*, February 1987, *19*(1), pp. 19–32.

Calvo, Guillermo A. On the Costs of Temporary Liberalization/Stabilization Experiments. *Connolly, M. and González-Vega, C., eds.*, 1987, pp. 3–17.

Campbell, John Y. Macroeconomic Lessons from Britain: A Review Essay. *J. Monet. Econ.*, March 1987, *19*(2), pp. 315–24. **[G: U.K.]**

Cantor, Richard and Mark, Nelson C. International Debt and World Business Fluctuations. *J. Int. Money Finance*, June 1987, *6*(2), pp. 153–65.

Carraro, Carlo and Giavazzi, Francesco. Policy Instruments and Coalitions in International Games. *Ricerche Econ.*, July-Dec. 1987, *41*(3–4), pp. 293–314.

Chaudhuri, T. Datta; Khan, M. Ali and Tang, Min. Technical Progress and Structural Change. *J. Inst. Theoretical Econ.*, June 1987, *143*(2), pp. 310–23.

Chen, Chau-nan; Lai, Ching-chong and Chang, Wen-ya. The Tight Money Effect, Wage Indexation and Macroeconomic Policy: The Fleming Model Revisited. *J. Econ. Stud.*, 1987, *14*(5), pp. 54–62.

Chrystal, K. Alec and Sedgwick, Robert. Exchange Rates and Open Economy Macroeconomics: An Introduction. *Chrystal, K. A. and Sedgwick, R., eds.*, 1987, pp. 1–6.

Cobham, David. Managing the Open Economy. *Thompson, G.; Brown, V. and Levačić, R., eds.*, 1987, pp. 224–53. **[G: U.K.]**

Coes, Donald V. Exchange Rate Intervention and Imperfect Capital Mobility. *Hodgman, D. R. and Wood, G. E., eds.*, 1987, pp. 99–135. **[G: W. Germany; U.K.]**

Cooper, Richard N. The Balance-of-Payments

Adjustment Process. *Cooper, R. N.*, 1987, pp. 119–38.

Danker, Deborah J., et al. Small Empirical Models of Exchange Market Intervention: Applications to Germany, Japan, and Canada. *J. Policy Modeling*, Spring 1987, 9(1), pp. 143–73.
[G: W. Germany; Japan; Canada]

Darity, William A., Jr. Debt, Finance, Production and Trade in a North–South Model: The Surplus Approach. *Cambridge J. Econ.*, September 1987, 11(3), pp. 211–27.

Darity, William A., Jr. The Hume Process, Laws of Returns, and the Anglo–Portuguese Trade. *Southern Econ. J.*, July 1987, 54(1), pp. 119–33.

Dauhajre, Andrés. Some Warnings Concerning Possible Financial Reform in the Dominican Republic. *Salazar-Carrillo, J. and Tirado de Alonzo, I., eds.*, 1987, pp. 1–12.
[G: Dominican Republic]

Dellas, Harris. Cyclical Co-movements of Output and Trade in the World Economy. *Can. J. Econ.*, November 1987, 20(4), pp. 855–69.

Desai, Padma and Bhagwati, Jagdish N. Three Alternative Concepts of Foreign Exchange Difficulties in Centrally Planned Economies. *Desai, P.*, 1987, 1979, pp. 163–72.

Djajić, Slobodan. Effects of Budgetary Policies in Open Economies: The Role of Intertemporal Consumption Substitution. *J. Int. Money Finance*, September 1987, 6(3), pp. 373–83.

Dornbusch, Rudiger. Exchange Rate Economics: 1986. *Econ. J.*, March 1987, 97(385), pp. 1–18.
[G: U.S.]

Dornbusch, Rudiger. External Balance Correction: Depreciation or Protection? *Brookings Pap. Econ. Act.*, 1987, (1), pp. 248–69.
[G: U.S.]

Dornbusch, Rudiger and Frankel, Jeffrey A. Macroeconomics and Protection. *Stern, R. M., ed.*, 1987, pp. 77–130. [G: OECD]

Dow, Sheila C. Post Keynesian Monetary Theory for an Open Economy. *J. Post Keynesian Econ.*, Winter 1986-87, 9(2), pp. 237–57.

Drazen, Allan and Helpman, Elhanan. Stabilization with Exchange Rate Management. *Quart. J. Econ.*, November 1987, 102(4), pp. 835–55.

Driskill, Robert and McCafferty, Stephen. Exchange-Rate Determination: An Equilibrium Approach with Imperfect Capital Substitutability. *J. Int. Econ.*, November 1987, 23(3/4), pp. 241–61.

Eaton, Jonathan. Public Debt Guarantees and Private Capital Flight. *World Bank Econ. Rev.*, May 1987, 1(3), pp. 377–95. [G: LDCs]

Edwards, Sebastian and van Wijnbergen, Sweder. On the Appropriate Timing and Speed of Economic Liberalization in Developing Countries. *Connolly, M. and González-Vega, C., eds.*, 1987, pp. 71–92.

Ellis, Christopher J. and Fender, John. Bargaining and Wage Resistance in an Open Macroeconomic Model. *Econ. J.*, March 1987, 97(385), pp. 106–20.

Eyzaguirre, Nicolás and Valdivia, Mario. External Restriction and Adjustment. Options and Policies in Latin America. *CEPAL Rev.*, August 1987, (32), pp. 149–68. [G: Latin America]

Fair, Ray C. Properties of a Multicountry Econometric Model. *J. Policy Modeling*, Spring 1987, 9(1), pp. 83–123. [G: Global]

Fender, John. Fiscal Policy in a Two Good Open Economy [Expansionary Fiscal Policy and the Exchange Rate: A Review]. *Australian Econ. Pap.*, June 1987, 26(48), pp. 71–82.

Fender, John. Monetary and Exchange Rate Policies in an Open Macroeconomic Model with Unemployment and Rational Expectations. *Sinclair, P. J. N., ed.*, 1987, 1986, pp. 328–42.

Fender, John and Nandakumar, Parameswar. Oil in an Intertemporal Macroeconomic Model. *Greek Econ. Rev.*, 1987, 9(1), pp. 38–56.

Fender, John and Nandakumar, Parameswar. Oil in an Intertemporal Macroeconomic Model. *Greek Econ. Rev.*, 1987, 9(1), pp. 38–56.

Frenkel, Jacob A. and Razin, Assaf. The International Transmission of Fiscal Expenditures and Budget Deficits in the World Economy. *Razin, A. and Sadka, E., eds.*, 1987, pp. 51–96.

Frenkel, Jacob A. and Razin, Assaf. The Mundell–Fleming Model a Quarter Century Later. *Int. Monet. Fund Staff Pap.*, December 1987, 34(4), pp. 567–620.

Goodfriend, Marvin. Exchange Rate Policy and the Dual Role of Exchange Rate Movements in International Adjustment. *Goodfriend, M.*, 1987, 1979, pp. 92–102.

Goodhart, Charles A. E. Exchange Rate Economics 1986: A Comment. *Econ. J.*, March 1987, 97(385), pp. 19–22. [G: U.S.]

de Grauwe, Paul and de Bellefroid, Bernard. Long-run Exchange Rate Variability and International Trade. *Arndt, S. W. and Richardson, J. D. eds.*, 1987, pp. 193–212.

Greenwood, Jeremy and Kimbrough, Kent P. An Investigation in the Theory of Foreign Exchange Controls. *Can. J. Econ.*, May 1987, 20(2), pp. 271–88.

Gros, Daniel. The Effectiveness of Capital Controls: Implications for Monetary Autonomy in the Presence of Incomplete Market Separation. *Int. Monet. Fund Staff Pap.*, December 1987, 34(4), pp. 621–42. [G: Italy]

Grubert, Harry and Mutti, John. Taxes, International Capital Flows and Trade: The International Implications of the Tax Reform Act of 1986. *Nat. Tax J.*, September 1987, 40(3), pp. 315–29. [G: U.S.]

Harck, Søren. Løn, produktivitet og bytteforhold i en lille åben økonomi. (Wages, Productivity, and Terms of Trade in a Small Open Economy. With English summary.) *Nationaløkon. Tidsskr.*, 1987, 125(3), pp. 390–404.

Hardouvelis, Gikas A. Optimal Wage Indexation and Monetary Policy in an Economy with Imported Raw Materials. *J. Int. Money Finance*, December 1987, 6(4), pp. 419–32.

Hasan, Parvez. Structural Adjustment in Selected Arab Countries: Need, Challenge, and Approaches. *El-Naggar, S., ed.*, 1987, pp. 49–67. [G: Middle East]

Helpman, Elhanan and Razin, Assaf. Exchange Rate Management: Intertemporal Tradeoffs. *Amer. Econ. Rev.*, March 1987, 77(1), pp. 107–23. [G: Argentina; Chile; Israel]

Henry, Samuel G. Brian and Karakitsos, Elias. Inflation, Unemployment and Indirect Taxation. *Bull. Econ. Res.*, January 1987, 39(1), pp. 29–47.

Herr, Hansjörg. Ansätze monetärer Währungstheorie—eine keynesianische Kritik der orthodoxen Theorie. (Rudiments of International Monetary Theory—A Keynesian Criticism of Orthodox Theory. With English summary.) *Konjunkturpolitik*, 1987, 33(1), pp. 1–26.

Holzman, Franklyn D. Creditworthiness and Balance-of-Payments Adjustment Mechanisms of Centrally Planned Economies. *Holzman, F. D.*, 1987, 1981, pp. 59–81. [G: E. Europe]

Holzman, Franklyn D. Internal and External Balance in a Centrally Planned Economy: Commentary. *Holzman, F. D.*, 1987, 1980, pp. 83–88. [G: CMEA]

Holzman, Franklyn D. Some Theories of the Hard Currency Shortages of Centrally Planned Economies. *Holzman, F. D.*, 1987, 1979, pp. 33–57. [G: CMEA]

Hrnčíř, Miroslav. Macroeconomic Proportionality in an Open Planned Economy. *Soviet E. Europ. Foreign Trade*, Summer 1987, 23(2), pp. 37–59.

Hughes Hallett, Andrew J. Autonomy and the Choice of Policy in Asymmetrically Dependent Economies. *Sinclair, P. J. N., ed.*, 1987, 1986, pp. 349–77. [G: U.S.; EEC]

Hughes Hallett, Andrew J. Optimal Policy Design in Interdependent Economies. *Carraro, C. and Sartore, D., eds.*, 1987, pp. 187–214.

Humbert, Thomas M. Understanding the Federal Deficit: Putative Impact on Trade. *Fink, R. H. and High, J. C., eds.*, 1987, 1984, pp. 162–70. [G: U.S.]

Ithurbide, Philippe. Les restrictions volontaires d'exportations: Une analyse macro-économique en régime de changes flexibles. (The Voluntary Export Restraints: A Macroeconomic Analysis under Flexible Exchanges Rates. With English summary.) *Revue Écon.*, January 1987, 38(1), pp. 25–54.

Johansson, Per-Olov and Löfgren, Karl-Gustaf. Tariff Policy and Real Wage Adjustments in a Small Open Economy. *Siven, C.-H., ed.*, 1987, pp. 155–78.

Jones, Michael. IMF Surveillance, Policy Coordination, and Time Consistency. *Int. Econ. Rev.*, February 1987, 28(1), pp. 135–58.

Jones, Ronald W.; Neary, J. Peter and Ruane, Frances P. International Capital Mobility and the Dutch Disease. *[Corden, W. M.]*, 1987, pp. 86–98.

Kaldor, Nicholas. The Role of Devaluation in the Adjustment of Balance-of-Payments Deficits. *Dell, S., ed., Pt. 2*, 1987, pp. 557–67.

Kehoe, Patrick J. Coordination of Fiscal Policies in a World Economy. *J. Monet. Econ.*, May 1987, 19(3), pp. 349–76.

Kenen, Peter B. Global Policy Optimization and the Exchange-Rate Regime. *J. Policy Modeling*, Spring 1987, 9(1), pp. 19–63. [G: Global]

Khan, Mohsin S. and Lizondo, José Saúl. Devaluation, Fiscal Deficits, and the Real Exchange Rate. *World Bank Econ. Rev.*, January 1987, 1(2), pp. 357–74.

Khan, Mohsin S. and Montiel, Peter J. Real Exchange Rate Dynamics in a Small, Primary-Exporting Country. *Int. Monet. Fund Staff Pap.*, December 1987, 34(4), pp. 681–710. [G: LDCs]

Khan, Mohsin S. and Zahler, Roberto. The Liberalization of Trade and Capital Flows in Developing Countries: Some Theoretical and Empirical Issues. *Connolly, M. and González-Vega, C., eds.*, 1987, pp. 45–67.

Kharas, Homi J. and Shishido, Hisanobu. Foreign Borrowing and Macroeconomic Adjustment to External Shocks. *J. Devel. Econ.*, February 1987, 25(1), pp. 125–48.

Kiguel, Miguel A. The Non-dynamic Equivalence of Monetary and Exchange Rate Rules under Imperfect Capital Mobility and Rational Expectations. *J. Int. Money Finance*, June 1987, 6(2), pp. 207–14.

Kimbrough, Kent P. International Linkages, Exchange-Rate Regimes, and the International Transmission Process: Perspectives from Optimizing Models. *Officer, L. H., ed.*, 1987, pp. 119–96.

Klein, Martin. Real Exchange Rate Fluctuations in a Small Open Economy under Fixed and Flexible Exchange Rates. *Z. Wirtschaft. Sozialwissen.*, 1987, 107(1), pp. 51–66.

Koray, Faik. Government Debt, Economic Activity, and Transmission of Economic Disturbances. *J. Money, Credit, Banking*, August 1987, 19(3), pp. 361–75. [G: U.S.]

Korkman, Sixten. Devaluation Policy and Employment. *Siven, C.-H., ed.*, 1987, pp. 195–200.

Kouri, Pentti J. K. Real Wage, World Demand, and Unemployment in a Customer Market Model of a Small Open Economy. *Siven, C.-H., ed.*, 1987, pp. 183–94.

Kravis, Irving B. and Lipsey, Robert E. The Assessment of National Price Levels. *Arndt, S. W. and Richardson, J. D. eds.*, 1987, pp. 97–134. [G: Selected Countries]

Krugman, Paul R. Pricing to Market When the Exchange Rate Changes. *Arndt, S. W. and Richardson, J. D. eds.*, 1987, pp. 49–70. [G: U.S.]

Kumcu, M. Ercan. The Trade Liberalization and Exchange Rate Determination in a Small Open Economy. *METU*, 1987, 14(3), pp. 205–13.

LaCivita, Charles J. Currency, Trade, and Capital Flows in General Equilibrium. *J. Bus.*, January 1987, 60(1), pp. 113–35.

Laffargue, Jean-Pierre. Croissance et endettement externe. (With English summary.) *Revue Écon. Polit.*, July-Aug. 1987, 97(4), pp. 409–18. [G: New Zealand; U.S.]

Lai, Ching-chong and Chang, Wen-ya. Currency Devaluation with Flexible Wages: An Application of the Cebula Model. *J. Macroecon.*, Fall 1987, *9*(4), pp. 625–35.

Lai, Ching-chong and Chang, Wen-ya. Flexible Exchange Rates, Capital Mobility Control and Macroeconomic Policies. *J. Econ. Devel.*, December 1987, *12*(2), pp. 183–88.

Lamdany, Ruben and Dorlhiac, Jorge. The Dollarization of a Small Economy. *Scand. J. Econ.*, 1987, *89*(1), pp. 91–102.

Laskar, Daniel. The "Rules of the Game" and Sterilization under a Fixed Exchange Rate System: A Strategic Argument. *Ricerche Econ.*, July-Dec. 1987, *41*(3–4), pp. 439–56.

Laussel, Didier and Soubeyran, Antoine. Le retour optimal à la solvabilité d'une économie endettée: Une introduction. (Optimal Adjustment Policies of a Small Open Indebted Economy: An Introduction. With English summary.) *Revue Écon.*, January 1987, *38*(1), pp. 55–73.

Lawler, P. Short and Long-run Effects of a Resource Discovery on the Sectoral Distribution of Output. *Scot. J. Polit. Econ.*, August 1987, *34*(3), pp. 209–29.

Lawrence, Colin. The Impact of Supply Shocks on Exchange Rates and Interest Rates: Does the Marshall–Lerner Condition Matter? *J. Int. Econ.*, May 1987, *22*(3/4), pp. 321–37.

Levine, Paul. Three Themes from Game Theory and International Macroeconomic Policy Formation. *Ricerche Econ.*, July-Dec. 1987, *41*(3–4), pp. 392–418.

Levine, Paul and Currie, David. Does International Macroeconomic Policy Coordination Pay and Is It Sustainable? A Two Country Analysis. *Sinclair, P. J. N., ed.*, 1987, pp. 38–74.

Levine, Paul and Currie, David. Does International Macroeconomic Policy Coordination Pay and Is It Sustainable? A Two Country Analysis. *Oxford Econ. Pap.*, March 1987, *39*(1), pp. 38–74.

Lizondo, José Saúl. Exchange Rate Differential and Balance of Payments under Dual Exchange Markets. *J. Devel. Econ.*, June 1987, *26*(1), pp. 37–53.

Lizondo, José Saúl. Unification of Dual Exchange Markets. *J. Int. Econ.*, February 1987, *22*(1/2), pp. 57–77.

Lizondo, José Saúl and Mathieson, Donald J. The Stability of the Demand for International Reserves. *J. Int. Money Finance*, September 1987, *6*(3), pp. 251–82. **[G: Selected Countries]**

Loef, Hans-Edi. Reale Wechselkurse und realer zyklischer Output. Theoretisches Modell und empirische Analyse für die Bundesrepublik Deutschland. (Real Exchange Rates and Real Cyclical Output. With English summary.) *Kredit Kapital*, 1987, *20*(1), pp. 22–47. **[G: W. Germany]**

Mantel, Rolf R. and Martirena-Mantel, Ana María. Liberalizacion del crecimiento y equidad en la economia abierta. (Growth Liberalization and Equity in the Open Economy. With English summary.) *Económica (La Plata)*, July-Dec. 1987, *33*(2), pp. 245–68. **[G: Latin America]**

Marcella, Mulino. Politiche di stabilizzazione in mercato aperto: due approcci alternativi. (Stabilization Policies in an Open Market: Two Alternative Approaches. With English summary.) *Giorn. Econ.*, May-June 1987, *46*(5–6), pp. 257–90.

Marfán, Manuel. Reactivación y Restricción Externa: El Rol de la Política Fiscal. (Economic Recovery Under Payments Constraints: The Role of Short-run Fiscal Policy. With English summary.) *Colección Estud. CIEPLAN*, December 1987, (22), pp. 5–40.

Marjit, Sugata. Economic Growth and the Current Account in Large Countries. *Keio Econ. Stud.*, 1987, *24*(2), pp. 27–31.

Masson, Paul R. The Dynamics of a Two-Country Minimodel under Rational Expectations. *Ann. Écon. Statist.*, Apr./Sept. 1987, (6/7), pp. 37–69. **[G: U.S.]**

Matsuyama, Kiminori. Current Account Dynamics in a Finite Horizon Model. *J. Int. Econ.*, November 1987, *23*(3/4), pp. 299–313.

Mayes, David G. The Role of Exchange Rate and Other Pricing Policies in the Adjustment Process: Comment. *Holmes, F., ed.*, 1987, pp. 210–16. **[G: New Zealand]**

McCulloch, Rachel. Macroeconomics and Protection: Comment. *Stern, R. M., ed.*, 1987, pp. 137–43. **[G: OECD]**

McDermott, John H. Adding Exhaustibility to the Traditional Theory of the Gold Standard. *J. Macroecon.*, Fall 1987, *9*(4), pp. 545–66.

McDermott, John H. Employment in a Controlled, Open Economy. *Connolly, M. and González-Vega, C., eds.*, 1987, pp. 325–39.

Meller, Patricio. Review of the Theoretical Approaches to External Adjustment and Their Relevance for Latin America. *CEPAL Rev.*, August 1987, (32), pp. 169–208. **[G: Latin America]**

Meller, Patricio and Solimano, Andrés. A Simple Macro Model for a Small Open Economy Facing a Binding External Constraint (Chile). *J. Devel. Econ.*, June 1987, *26*(1), pp. 25–35. **[G: Chile]**

Modigliani, Franco. Budget Deficits and Rates of Interest in the World Economy: Comments. *Razin, A. and Sadka, E., eds.*, 1987, pp. 97–100.

Montiel, Peter J. Output and Unanticipated Money in the Dependent Economy Model. *Int. Monet. Fund Staff Pap.*, June 1987, *34*(2), pp. 228–59. **[G: Mexico]**

Morley, Samuel A. and Fishlow, Albert. Deficits, Debt and Destabilization: The Perversity of High Interest Rates. *J. Devel. Econ.*, October 1987, *27*(1–2), pp. 227–44. **[G: LDCs]**

Morley, Samuel A. and Fishlow, Albert. Deficits, Debt and Destabilization: The Perversity of High Interest Rates. *[Diaz-Alejandro, C. F.]*, 1987, pp. 227–44. **[G: LDCs]**

Mussa, Michael. Average Protection and Economic Policy. *Salvatore, D., ed.*, 1987, pp. 389–407.   **[G: U.S.]**

Mussa, Michael. Macroeconomic Policy and Trade Liberalization: Some Guidelines. *World Bank Res. Observer*, January 1987, *2*(1), pp. 61–77.   **[G: LDCs]**

Mutoh, Takahiko. On the Relation between Monetary Interdependence and Exchange Rate Volatility. *J. Japanese Int. Economies*, December 1987, *1*(4), pp. 351–72.

Neary, J. Peter. ARMOD: A Small Numberical Macroeconomic World Model with Non-clearing Markets: Comment. *Scand. J. Econ.*, 1987, *89*(3), pp. 247–50.   **[G: OECD]**

Neck, Reinhard and Dockner, Engelbert. Can the Gains from International Cooperation Be Secured without Policy Coordination? *Ricerche Econ.*, July-Dec. 1987, *41*(3–4), pp. 373–91.

Niehans, Jürg. Monetary Policy and Investment Dynamics in Interdependent Economies. *J. Money, Credit, Banking*, February 1987, *19*(1), pp. 33–45.

Niehans, Jürg. Monetary Policy in an Open Economy. *de Cecco, M. and Fitoussi, J.-P., eds.*, 1987, pp. 243–68.

Ocampo, José Antonio. The Macroeconomic Effect of Import Controls: A Keynesian Analysis. *[Diaz-Alejandro, C. F.]*, 1987, pp. 285–305.

Ocampo, José Antonio. The Macroeconomic Effect of Import Controls: A Keynesian Analysis. *J. Devel. Econ.*, October 1987, *27*(1–2), pp. 285–305.

Okishio, Nobuo. Theoretical Foundations of International Macro-economic Model. *Kobe Univ. Econ.*, 1987, *33*, pp. 1–16.

Penati, Alessandro. Government Spending and the Real Exchange Rate. *J. Int. Econ.*, May 1987, *22*(3/4), pp. 237–67.

Pikoulakis, Emmanuel. The Cost of Disinflation Reexamined. *Economia (Portugal)*, May 1987, *11*(2), pp. 215–30.

Pitchford, John David and Vousden, Neil J. Exchange Rates, Policy Rules and Inflation. *Australian Econ. Pap.*, June 1987, *26*(48), pp. 43–57.

van der Ploeg, Frederick. Optimal Government Policy in a Small Open Economy with Rational Expectations and Uncertain Election Outcomes. *Int. Econ. Rev.*, June 1987, *28*(2), pp. 469–91.

van der Ploeg, Frederick. Rationing in Open Economy and Dynamic Macroeconomics: A Survey. *De Economist*, 1987, *135*(4), pp. 488–519.

Portes, Richard. The Impact of External Shocks on Centrally Planned Economies: Theoretical Considerations. *Pasinetti, L. and Lloyd, P., eds.*, 1987, pp. 409–25.   **[G: CMEA]**

Rama, Martín. L'endettement extérieur dans un modèle de croissance en déséquilibre. (With English summary.) *Revue Écon.*, September 1987, *38*(5), pp. 933–48.

Reddaway, W. B. Some Reflections by a Keynesian Economist on the Problems of Developing Countries. *Thirlwall, A. P., ed.*, 1987, pp. 36–65.

Risager, Ole. The Effects of Currency Depreciation in a Model with Capital Formation. *Europ. Econ. Rev.*, Feb./Mar. 1987, *31*(1/2), pp. 399–406.   **[G: Denmark]**

Rodrik, Dani. Trade and Capital-Account Liberalization in a Keynesian Economy. *J. Int. Econ.*, August 1987, *23*(1/2), pp. 113–29.

Rogerson, Richard. The Economics of Worldwide Stagflation: A Review Essay. *J. Monet. Econ.*, January 1987, *19*(1), pp. 129–36.

Rojas-Suarez, Liliana. Devaluation and Monetary Policy in Developing Countries: A General Equilibrium Model for Economies Facing Financial Constraints. *Int. Monet. Fund Staff Pap.*, September 1987, *34*(3), pp. 439–70.
                                                [G: LDCs]

Roy, Raj and Rassuli, Ali. Transfer Models Using Mixed Keynesian-Classical Assumptions. *Rivista Int. Sci. Econ. Com.*, June 1987, *34*(6), pp. 513–22.

Rübel, Gerhard. International Interdependencies with Fiscal Policy Measures. *J. Econ. (Z. Nationalökon.)*, 1987, *47*(1), pp. 47–67.

Sauernheimer, K. Interest Rates, Exchange Rates, and Aggregate Supply. *J. Macroecon.*, Summer 1987, *9*(3), pp. 451–55.

Schittko, Ulrich K. Keynesian and Classical Unemployment in a Two-Country Model with Asset Markets. *[Marrama, V.]*, Vol. 2, 1987, pp. 857–97.

Sephton, Peter S. The Choice of Monetary Policy Instruments in Canada: An Extension. *Can. J. Econ.*, February 1987, *20*(1), pp. 55–60.
                                                [G: Canada]

Siebert, Horst. Foreign Debt and Capital Accumulation. *Weltwirtsch. Arch.*, 1987, *123*(4), pp. 618–30.

Singer, Hans W. Discussion [Keynes, Economic Development and the Developing Countries] [Some Reflections by a Keynesian Economist on the Problems of Developing Countries]. *Thirlwall, A. P., ed.*, 1987, pp. 66–69.

Smith, Alasdair. Factor Shadow Prices in Distorted Open Economies. *[Corden, W. M.]*, 1987, pp. 54–67.

Smith, M. Alasdair M. Capital Accumulation in the Open Two-Sector Economy. *Bhagwati, J. N., ed.*, 1987, *1977*, pp. 395–406.

Smith, Peter N. Current Account Movements, Wealth Effects and the Determination of the Real Exchange Rate. *Manchester Sch. Econ. Soc. Stud.*, December 1987, *55*(4), pp. 353–77.   **[G: U.K.]**

Spinelli, Franco. Labor Market Rigidities and Protectionism. *Salvatore, D., ed.*, 1987, pp. 181–200.

Steigum, Erling S., Jr. ARMOD: A Small Numerical Macroeconomic World Model with Non-clearing Markets. *Scand. J. Econ.*, 1987, *89*(3), pp. 227–46.   **[G: OECD]**

Stemp, Peter J. and Turnovsky, Stephen J. Optimal Monetary Policy in an Open Economy. *Europ. Econ. Rev.*, July 1987, *31*(5), pp. 1113–35.

Stockman, Alan C. Some Interactions between Goods Markets and Asset Markets in Open

Economies. *Arndt, S. W. and Richardson, J. D. eds.*, 1987, pp. 33–44.

Stockman, Alan C. The Equilibrium Approach to Exchange Rates. *Fed. Res. Bank Richmond Econ. Rev.*, Mar./Apr. 1987, *73*(2), pp. 12–30. **[G: OECD]**

Stockman, Alan C. and Svensson, Lars E. O. Capital Flows, Investment, and Exchange Rates. *J. Monet. Econ.*, March 1987, *19*(2), pp. 171–201.

Stulz, René M. An Equilibrium Model of Exchange Rate Determination and Asset Pricing with Nontraded Goods and Imperfect Information. *J. Polit. Econ.*, October 1987, *95*(5), pp. 1024–40.

Svensson, Lars E. O. International Fiscal Policy Transmission. *Scand. J. Econ.*, 1987, *89*(3), pp. 305–34.

Taylor, Lance. Macro Policy in the Tropics: How Sensible People Stand. *World Devel.*, December 1987, *15*(12), pp. 1407–35. **[G: LDCs]**

Taylor, Mark P. On Granger Causality and the Monetary Approach to the Balance of Payments. *J. Macroecon.*, Spring 1987, *9*(2), pp. 239–53. **[G: U.K.]**

Tower, Edward and Pursell, Garry G. On Shadow Pricing Labour and Foreign Exchange. *Oxford Econ. Pap.*, June 1987, *39*(2), pp. 318–32.

Trapp, Peter. West Germany: Why Reflation Does Not Work. *Econ. Int.*, May-Aug. 1987, *40*(2–3), pp. 237–46. **[G: U.S.; W. Germany]**

Turnovsky, Stephen J. Optimal Monetary Growth with Accommodating Fiscal Policy in a Small Open Economy. *J. Int. Money Finance*, June 1987, *6*(2), pp. 179–93.

Turnovsky, Stephen J. Optimal Monetary Policy and Wage Indexation under Alternative Disturbances and Information Structures. *J. Money, Credit, Banking*, May 1987, *19*(2), pp. 157–80.

Van Der Willigen, Tessa A. Cash Crop Production and the Balance of Trade in a Less Developed Economy: A Model of Temporary Equilibrium with Rationing. *Sinclair, P. J. N., ed.*, 1987, *1986*, pp. 452–70.

Van Huyck, John B. A Retrospective on the Classical Gold Standard, 1821–1931: A Review Essay. *J. Monet. Econ.*, May 1987, *19*(3), pp. 451–56.

Velasco, Andrés. Financial Crises and Balance of Payments Crises: A Simple Model of the Southern Cone Experience. *[Diaz-Alejandro, C. F.]*, 1987, pp. 263–83. **[G: Chile; Argentina; Uruguay]**

Velasco, Andrés. Financial Crises and Balance of Payments Crises: A Simple Model of the Southern Cone Experience. *J. Devel. Econ.*, October 1987, *27*(1–2), pp. 263–83. **[G: Chile; Argentina; Uruguay]**

Wadensjö, Eskil. Tariff Policy and Real Wage Adjustments in a Small Open Economy: Comment. *Siven, C.-H., ed.*, 1987, pp. 179–81.

Wang, Leonard F. S. The Effect of Devaluation When the *IS* Curve is Positively-Sloped: Does It Make a Difference? *Rivista Int. Sci. Econ.*

Com., Nov.-Dec. 1987, *34*(11–12), pp. 1089–94.

Weller, Paul and Yano, Makoto. Forward Exchange, Futures Trading, and Spot Price Variability: A General Equilibrium Approach. *Econometrica*, November 1987, *55*(6), pp. 1433–50.

Wickham, Peter. The Role of Exchange Rate and Other Pricing Policies in the Adjustment Process. *Holmes, F., ed.*, 1987, pp. 192–209.

van Wijnbergen, Sweder. Government Deficits, Private Investment and the Current Account: An Intertemporal Disequilibrium Analysis. *Econ. J.*, September 1987, *97*(387), pp. 596–615.

van Wijnbergen, Sweder. Tariffs, Employment and the Current Account: Real Wage Resistance and the Macroeconomics of Protectionism. *Int. Econ. Rev.*, October 1987, *28*(3), pp. 691–706.

Williamson, John. International Liquidity: Are the Supply and Composition Appropriate? *Williamson, J.*, 1987, *1984*, pp. 119–39.

Williamson, John. International Monetary Reform: An Agenda for the 1980s. *Williamson, J.*, 1987, *1983*, pp. 212–27.

Williamson, John. Resource Transfer and the International Monetary System. *Williamson, J.*, 1987, pp. 157–77. **[G: LDCs]**

Williamson, John. The Crawling Peg in Historical Perspective. *Williamson, J.*, 1987, *1981*, pp. 63–93. **[G: OECD; Selected LDCs]**

Zee, Howell H. Government Debt, Capital Accumulation, and the Terms of Trade in a Model of Interdependent Economies. *Econ. Inquiry*, October 1987, *25*(4), pp. 599–618.

Zeira, Joseph. Risk and Capital Accumulation in a Small Open Economy. *Quart. J. Econ.*, May 1987, *102*(2), pp. 265–79.

4313 Open Economy Macroeconomic Studies: Balance of Payments and Adjustment Mechanisms

Amin, Galal A. Adjustment and Development: The Case of Egypt. *El-Naggar, S., ed.*, 1987, pp. 92–116. **[G: Egypt]**

Amman, Hans M. and Jager, Henk. Optimal Economic Policies under a Crawling-Peg Exchange-Rate System. *Carraro, C. and Sartore, D., eds.*, 1987, pp. 105–26.

Anani, Jawad. Adjustment and Development: The Case of Jordan. *El-Naggar, S., ed.*, 1987, pp. 124–48. **[G: Jordan]**

Andresen, Svein and Everaert, Luc. International Macroeconomic Interdependence. *Ann. Écon. Statist.*, Apr./Sept. 1987, (6/7), pp. 161–81. **[G: OECD]**

Anjaria, Shailendra J. Balance of Payments and Related Issues in the Uruguay Round of Trade Negotiations. *World Bank Econ. Rev.*, September 1987, *1*(4), pp. 669–88. **[G: LDCs]**

Aoki, Masanao. Studies of Economic Interdependence by State Space Modeling of Time Series: U.S.–Japan Example. *Ann. Écon. Statist.*, Apr./Sept. 1987, (6/7), pp. 225–52. **[G: U.S.; Japan]**

Arellano, José Pablo and Ramos, Joseph. Fuga de Capitales en Chile: Magnitud Y Causas. (Capital Flight in Chile: Magnitude and Causes. With English summary.) *Colección Estud. CIEPLAN*, December 1987, (22), pp. 63–76. **[G: Chile]**

Arndt, H. W. and Dorrance, G. The J-Curve. *Australian Econ. Rev.*, First Quarter 1987, (77), pp. 9–19. **[G: Australia]**

Bach, Christopher L. U.S. International Transactions, Fourth Quarter and Year 1986. *Surv. Curr. Bus.*, March 1987, 67(3), pp. 32–62. **[G: U.S.]**

Bacha, Edmar Lisboa. Balance of Payments Experience and Growth Prospects of Developing Countries: Terms of Reference for the Country Studies. *Dell, S., ed., Pt. 3*, 1987, pp. 1012–30.

Bacha, Edmar Lisboa. Balance-of-Payments Experience and Growth Prospects of Developing Countries: A Synthesis: Terms of Reference for the Country Studies. *United Nations Conference on Trade and Development.*, 1987, pp. 183–206. **[G: LDCs]**

Baeck, Louis. O desequilíbrio da economia internacional dos anos 80. (With English summary.) *Pesquisa Planejamento Econ.*, April 1987, 17(1), pp. 221–49. **[G: U.S.; Japan; W. Europe]**

Baeck, Louis. The Imbalance of the Western Economy. *Tijdschrift Econ. Manage.*, 1987, 32(2), pp. 221–47. **[G: EEC; U.S.; Japan]**

Baer, Werner and Birch, Melissa. The International Economic Relations of a Small Country: The Case of Paraguay. *Econ. Develop. Cult. Change*, April 1987, 35(3), pp. 601–27. **[G: Paraguay; Selected Countries]**

Bahmani-Oskooee, Mohsen. Demand for International Reserves: Corrections for Serial Correlation and Heteroscedasticity. *Appl. Econ.*, May 1987, 19(5), pp. 609–18.

Bahmani-Oskooee, Mohsen. Effects of Rising Price of Gold on the LDCs' Demand for International Reserves. *Int. Econ. J.*, Winter 1987, 1(4), pp. 35–44. **[G: LDCs]**

Balassa, Bela. Mexico's Debt Problem and Policies for the Future. *Tremblay, R., ed.*, 1987, pp. 11–29. **[G: Mexico]**

Balassa, Bela and Tyson, Laura. Adjustment to External Shocks in Socialist and Private Market Economies. *Pasinetti, L. and Lloyd, P., eds.*, 1987, pp. 439–64. **[G: Global]**

Bangura, Yusuf. IMF/World Bank Conditionality and Nigeria's Structural Adjustment Programme. *Havnevik, K. J., ed.*, 1987, pp. 95–116. **[G: Nigeria]**

Barbone, Luca and Rivera-Batiz, Francisco. Foreign Capital and the Contractionary Impact of Currency Devaluation, with an Application to Jamaica. *J. Devel. Econ.*, June 1987, 26(1), pp. 1–15. **[G: Jamaica]**

Baum, Christopher F. The Effects of Price- and Output-Stabilising Policies in an Interdependent World Economy. *J. Econ. Dynam. Control*, June 1987, 11(2), pp. 195–200. **[G: OECD]**

Behrman, Jere R. Commodity Price Instability and Economic Goal Attainment in Developing Countries. *World Devel.*, May 1987, 15(5), pp. 559–73. **[G: Chile; Zambia; Brazil; Ivory Coast; El Salvador]**

Benjamin, Nancy C.; Devarajan, Shantayanan and Weiner, Robert J. Oil Revenues, Capital Expenditure, and the "Dutch Disease": The Case of Cameroon. *Pachauri, R. K., ed.*, 1987, pp. 59–74. **[G: Cameroon]**

Bergsten, C. Fred. The Second Debt Crisis is Coming. *Challenge*, Special Issue 1987, 30(6), pp. 50–57. **[G: U.S.]**

Bergstrand, Jeffrey H. The U.S. Trade Deficit: A Perspective from Selected Bilateral Trade Models. *New Eng. Econ. Rev.*, May/June 1987, pp. 19–31. **[G: U.S.]**

Bognár, József. Impact of External Market Fluctuations on Centrally Planned and Market Economies: Discussion and Conclusions. *Pasinetti, L. and Lloyd, P., eds.*, 1987, pp. 479–83. **[G: CMEA]**

Boltho, Andrea. External Constraints on European Growth: Comment. *Lawrence, R. Z. and Schultze, C. L., eds.*, 1987, pp. 591–96. **[G: W. Europe]**

Bosworth, Barry P. The Persistence of the U.S. Trade Deficit: Comments. *Brookings Pap. Econ. Act.*, 1987, (1), pp. 44–47. **[G: U.S.]**

Brittan, Samuel. The Role of Domestic U.S. Economy and Financial Policy in the World Economy: Cures That Could Be Worse Than the Disease. *Visser, H. and Schoor, E., eds.*, 1987, pp. 125–37. **[G: U.S.; Global]**

Brock, Philip and Tower, Edward. Economic Liberalization in Less Developed Countries: Guidelines from the Empirical Evidence and Clarification of the Theory. *Connolly, M. and González-Vega, C., eds.*, 1987, pp. 19–43. **[G: LDCs]**

Bulmer-Thomas, Victor. The Balance-of-Payments Crisis and Adjustment Programmes in Central America. *Thorp, R. and Whitehead, L., eds.*, 1987, pp. 271–317. **[G: Central America]**

Byatt, I. C. R. Public Expenditure: The International Dimension: Comment. *Levitt, M. S., ed.*, 1987, pp. 119–22. **[G: U.K.]**

Canzoneri, Matthew B. The Gains from Policy Coordination: Overview. *Bryant, R. C. and Portes, R., eds.*, 1987, pp. 185–90.

Christodoulakis, Nicos and Godley, Wynne. Macroeconomic Consequences of Alternative Trade Policy Options. *J. Policy Modeling*, Fall 1987, 9(3), pp. 405–36. **[G: U.K.]**

Cobham, David. Managing the Open Economy. *Thompson, G.; Brown, V. and Levačić, R., eds.*, 1987, pp. 224–53. **[G: U.K.]**

Collins, Susan M. Korean Growth Policy: Comment. *Brookings Pap. Econ. Act.*, 1987, (2), pp. 445–50. **[G: S. Korea]**

Cooney, Stephen. The Impact of the U.S. Trade Deficit on Future Investment Flows. *[Marjolin, R.]*, 1987, pp. 153–67. **[G: U.S.]**

Cooper, Richard N. External Constraints on European Growth. *Lawrence, R. Z. and Schultze,*

C. L., eds., 1987, pp. 540–91.
[G: W. Europe]

Corbo, Vittorio. Impact on Debtor Countries of World Economic Conditions: Comment. *Martirena-Mantel, A. M., ed.*, 1987, pp. 87–90.
[G: Latin America]

Corbo, Vittorio. The Use of the Exchange Rate for Stabilization Purposes: The Case of Chile. *Connolly, M. and González-Vega, C., eds.*, 1987, pp. 111–37. [G: Chile]

Corden, W. Max. The Revival of Protectionism in Developed Countries. *Salvatore, D., ed.*, 1987, pp. 45–68. [G: OECD]

Costa, Antonio Maria. The Need for New Multilateral Trade Negotiations: Why Is It Urgent to Complete the GATT Round Successfully? *Salvatore, D., ed.*, 1987, pp. 113–49.
[G: OECD]

Coulombe, Serge. Dette publique, endettement envers l'éetranger et l'effet d'éviction dans une économie ouverte: le cas canadien. (Public Debt, National Foreign Indebtedness and the Crowding-Out Effect in an Open Economy: The Case of Canada. With English summary.) *Écon. Soc.*, September 1987, *21*(9), pp. 169–84. [G: Canada]

Cuddington, John T. Capital Flight. *Europ. Econ. Rev.*, Feb./Mar. 1987, *31*(1/2), pp. 382–88.
[G: Latin America; S. Korea]

Culem, Claudy G. Foreign Trade Behavior in a Small Open Economy (Belgium 1970–1980). *Scand. J. Econ.*, 1987, *89*(1), pp. 55–70.
[G: Belgium]

Cumby, Robert E. Japanese–U.S. Current Accounts and Exchange Rates before and after the G5 Agreement: Discussion. *Sato, R. and Wachtel, P., eds.*, 1987, pp. 148–52.
[G: Japan; U.S.]

Currie, David; Levine, Paul and Vidalis, Nic. International Cooperation and Reputation in an Empirical Two-Bloc Model. *Bryant, R. C. and Portes, R., eds.*, 1987, pp. 75–121.
[G: U.S.]

Darby, Michael R. National Policies and the International Monetary System: Comment. *Officer, L. H., ed.*, 1987, pp. 271–74.
[G: Global]

Dean, Andrew and Koromzay, Val. Current-Account Imbalances and Adjustment Mechanisms. *OECD Econ. Stud.*, Spring 1987, (8), pp. 7–33. [G: OECD]

Dell, Sidney, et al. Determination of Quotas and the Relative Position of Developing Countries in the International Monetary Fund: Structural Adjustment Policies. *Dell, S., ed., Pt. 2*, 1987, pp. 541–56. [G: U.K.]

Devarajan, Shantayanan and de Melo, Jaime. Adjustment with a Fixed Exchange Rate: Cameroon, Côte d'Ivoire, and Senegal. *World Bank Econ. Rev.*, May 1987, *1*(3), pp. 447–87. [G: Cameroon; Ivory Coast; Senegal]

Dias Carneiro, Dionísio. Long-run Adjustment, the Debt Crisis and the Changing Role of Stabilisation Policies in the Recent Brazilian Experience. *Thorp, R. and Whitehead, L., eds.*, 1987, pp. 28–67. [G: Brazil]

Dilullo, Anthony J. U.S. International Transactions, Third Quarter 1987. *Surv. Curr. Bus.*, December 1987, *67*(12), pp. 20–44.
[G: U.S.]

Dooley, Michael P. An Analysis of the Management of the Currency Composition of Reserve Assets and External Liabilities of Developing Countries. *Aliber, R. Z., ed.*, 1987, pp. 262–80. [G: LDCs]

Dornbusch, Rudiger. Impact on Debtor Countries of World Economic Conditions. *Martirena-Mantel, A. M., ed.*, 1987, pp. 60–87.
[G: Latin America]

Dornbusch, Rudiger and Park, Yung Chul. Korean Growth Policy. *Brookings Pap. Econ. Act.*, 1987, (2), pp. 389–444. [G: S. Korea]

Dyba, Karel and Kupka, Václav. Accommodating the Czechoslovak Economy to External Blows (A Macroeconomic Analysis for 1973–1981). *Soviet E. Europ. Foreign Trade*, Spring 1987, *23*(1), pp. 6–30. [G: Czechoslovakia]

Edwards, Sebastian. Sequencing Economic Liberalization in Developing Countries. *Finance Develop.*, March 1987, *24*(1), pp. 26–29.
[G: LDCs]

Emminger, Otmar. The Dollar's Borrowed Strength. *Salvatore, D., ed.*, 1987, pp. 450–68. [G: U.S.]

Faaland, Just. Economic Disarray and Dependence: The Case of the Sudan. *Havnevik, K. J., ed.*, 1987, pp. 117–26. [G: Sudan]

Feldstein, Martin S. Correcting the Trade Deficit. *Foreign Aff.*, Spring 1987, *65*(4), pp. 795–806. [G: U.S.]

Fieleke, Norman S. The Budget Deficit: Are the International Consequences Unfavorable? *Fink, R. H. and High, J. C., eds.*, 1987, *1984*, pp. 171–80. [G: U.S.]

Fishlow, Albert. Lições da década de 1890 para a de 1980. (With English summary.) *Pesquisa Planejamento Econ.*, December 1987, *17*(3), pp. 497–532. [G: Argentina; Brazil]

Frieden, Jeff. Third World Indebted Industrialization: International Finance and State Capitalism in Mexico, Brazil, Algeria, and South Korea. *Becker, D. G., et al.*, 1987, *1981*, pp. 131–59. [G: Mexico; Brazil; Algeria; S. Korea]

Genberg, Hans and Salemi, Michael K. The Effects of Foreign Shocks on Prices of Swiss Goods and Credit: An Analysis Based on VAR Methods. *Ann. Écon. Statist.*, Apr./Sept. 1987, (6/7), pp. 101–24. [G: Switzerland]

Genberg, Hans; Salemi, Michael K. and Swoboda, Alexander K. The Relative Importance of Foreign and Domestic Disturbances for Aggregate Fluctuations in the Open Economy: Switzerland, 1964–1981. *J. Monet. Econ.*, January 1987, *19*(1), pp. 45–67.
[G: Switzerland]

Ghartey, Edward E. Devaluation as a Balance of Payments Corrective Measure in Developing Countries: A Study Relating to Ghana. *Appl. Econ.*, July 1987, *19*(7), pp. 937–47.
[G: Ghana]

Giavazzi, Francesco. The Performance of the

British Economy: The Impact of EEC Membership. *Dornbusch, R. and Layard, R., eds.*, 1987, pp. 97–130. **[G: U.K.]**

Girardin, E. and Marois, W. Déficit budgétaire et déficit externe: une analyse empirique. (With English summary.) *Revue Écon. Polit.*, Jan.-Feb. 1987, 97(1), pp. 51–78. **[G: U.S.; U.K.; France]**

Glick, Reuven. Interest Rate Linkages in the Pacific Basin. *Fed. Res. Bank San Francisco Econ. Rev.*, Summer 1987, (3), pp. 31–42. **[G: OECD; Hong Kong; Singapore; Taiwan; Malaysia]**

Gonzalez, Norberto. International Price Fluctuations and Inflation: Discussion and Conclusions. *Pasinetti, L. and Lloyd, P., eds.*, 1987, pp. 395–402. **[G: Global]**

Gordon, Robert J. U.S. Fiscal Deficits and the World Imbalance of Payments. *Hitotsubashi J. Econ.*, October 1987, 27, pp. 7–41. **[G: U.S.]**

Gray, H. Peter. "International Crowding Out": Concept and Policy Implications. *Eastern Econ. J.*, July-Sept. 1987, 13(3), pp. 193–203. **[G: U.S.]**

Hamada, Koichi and Horiuchi, Akiyoshi. Monetary, Financial, and Real Effects of Yen Internationalization. *Arndt, S. W. and Richardson, J. D. eds.*, 1987, pp. 167–91. **[G: Japan]**

Hamdouch, Bachir. Adjustment and Development: The Case of Morocco. *El-Naggar, S., ed.*, 1987, pp. 156–87. **[G: Morocco]**

Hasegawa, Toshiaki, et al. U.S.–Japan Economic Coordination: A Global Solution for Mutual Prosperity. *Finn, R. B., ed.*, 1987, pp. 1–29. **[G: U.S.; Japan]**

Helleiner, Gerald K. Balance of Payments Experience and Growth Prospects of Developing Countries. *Dell, S., ed., Pt. 3*, 1987, pp. 961–1004. **[G: LDCs]**

Helleiner, Gerald K. Balance-of-Payments Experience and Growth Prospects of Developing Countries: A Synthesis. *United Nations Conference on Trade and Development.*, 1987, pp. 125–82. **[G: LDCs]**

Helleiner, Gerald K. Direct Foreign Investment and Alternative Forms of External Non-concessional Finance for Developing Countries. *Borner, S. and Taylor, A., eds.*, 1987, pp. 445–66. **[G: LDCs]**

Heymann, Daniel. Impact on Debtor Countries of World Economic Conditions: Comment. *Martirena-Mantel, A. M., ed.*, 1987, pp. 90–94. **[G: Latin America]**

Holtham, Gerald and Hughes Hallett, Andrew J. International Policy Cooperation and Model Uncertainty. *Bryant, R. C. and Portes, R., eds.*, 1987, pp. 128–77.

Holzman, Franklyn D. CMEA's Hard Currency Deficits and Rouble Convertibility. *Holzman, F. D.*, 1987, 1978, pp. 145–67. **[G: CMEA]**

Holzman, Franklyn D. The Economics of Soviet Bloc Trade and Finance: Introduction. *Holzman, F. D.*, 1987, pp. 1–29. **[G: U.S.S.R.; CMEA]**

Hooper, Peter. The Persistence of the U.S. Trade

Deficit: Comments. *Brookings Pap. Econ. Act.*, 1987, (1), pp. 47–51. **[G: U.S.]**

Hughes Hallett, Andrew J. How Robust Are the Gains to Policy Coordination to Variations in the Model and Objectives? *Ricerche Econ.*, July-Dec. 1987, 41(3–4), pp. 341–72.

Hughes Hallett, Andrew J. International Competitiveness and Economic Recovery: Examples of the Risk-Ambition Trade-Off in Dutch Economic Policies. *Manchester Sch. Econ. Soc. Stud.*, March 1987, 55(1), pp. 38–59. **[G: Netherlands]**

Hughes Hallett, Andrew J. The Impact of Interdependence on Economic Policy Design: The Case of the USA, EEC and Japan. *Econ. Modelling*, July 1987, 4(3), pp. 377–96. **[G: U.S.; EEC; Japan]**

Hutchison, Michael M. and Pigott, Charles A. Real and Financial Linkages in the Macroeconomic Response to Budget Deficits: An Empirical Investigation. *Arndt, S. W. and Richardson, J. D. eds.*, 1987, pp. 139–66. **[G: U.S.; W. Germany; Japan; U.K.]**

Islam, Shafiqul. What's Causing America's Capital Imports? *Challenge*, Sept./Oct. 1987, 30(4), pp. 4–11. **[G: U.S.]**

Ize, Alain and Ortiz, Guillermo. Fiscal Rigidities, Public Debt, and Capital Flight. *Int. Monet. Fund Staff Pap.*, June 1987, 34(2), pp. 311–32. **[G: Mexico]**

Jacobsen, Hanns-Dieter. The Foreign Trade and Payments of the GDR in a Changing World Economy. *Jeffries, I. and Melzer, M., eds.*, 1987, pp. 235–60. **[G: E. Germany]**

Karunaratne, Neil Dias. An Analysis of Papua New Guinea's Hard Currency Regime. *Econ. Int.*, May-Aug. 1987, 40(2–3), pp. 210–23. **[G: New Guinea]**

Kenen, Peter B. Changing Views about the Role of the SDR and Implications for Its Attributes. *Dell, S., ed., Pt. 2*, 1987, pp. 373–85.

Khan, Mohsin S. and Ul-Haque, Nadeem. Capital Flight from Developing Countries. *Finance Develop.*, March 1987, 24(1), pp. 2–5. **[G: LDCs]**

Killick, Tony. Unsettled Questions about Adjustment with Growth. *United Nations Conference on Trade and Development.*, 1987, pp. 207–58. **[G: Latin America]**

Kim, Kwan S. Mexico's Debt Crisis and Adjustment Policies. *Tremblay, R., ed.*, 1987, pp. 55–70. **[G: Mexico]**

Kirchgässner, Gebhard and Wolters, Jürgen. U.S.–European Interest Rate Linkage: A Time Series Analysis for West Germany, Switzerland, and the United States. *Rev. Econ. Statist.*, November 1987, 69(4), pp. 675–84. **[G: W. Germany; U.S.; Switzerland]**

Krueger, Russell C. U.S. International Transactions, First Quarter 1987. *Surv. Curr. Bus.*, June 1987, 67(6), pp. 46–84. **[G: U.S.]**

Krugman, Paul R. and Baldwin, Richard E. The Persistence of the U.S. Trade Deficit. *Brookings Pap. Econ. Act.*, 1987, (1), pp. 1–43. **[G: U.S.]**

Kuntjoro-Jakti, Dorodjatun. The Global Crisis of

the 1980s and Indonesia's Response. *Hitotsu-bashi J. Econ.*, October 1987, *27*, pp. 101–13.

Lal, Deepak. The Political Economy of Economic Liberalization. *World Bank Econ. Rev.*, January 1987, *1*(2), pp. 273–99.   [G: LDCs]

de Lattre, Andre. International Equilibrium—Some Longer-term Issues. *Visser, H. and Schoor, E., eds.*, 1987, pp. 87–94.
[G: Global]

Lee, E. World Recession and Developing Economies in Asia. *International Labour Office.*, 1987, pp. 99–132.   [G: Asia]

Lenz, Allen J. Overview of the U.S. Competitive Position Today. *Barfield, C. E. and Makin, J. H., eds.*, 1987, pp. 27–35.   [G: U.S.]

Leon, H. and Molana, Hasan. Testing the Monetary Approach to Balance of Payments in Developing Countries. *Chrystal, K. A. and Sedgwick, R., eds.*, 1987, pp. 137–63.
[G: Latin America; Thailand; India; Sri Lanka]

Levy, Santiago. Short Run Responses to Foreign Exchange Crises. *J. Policy Modeling*, Winter 1987, *9*(4), pp. 577–614.   [G: LDCs]

Lizondo, José Saúl and Mathieson, Donald J. The Stability of the Demand for International Reserves. *J. Int. Money Finance*, September 1987, *6*(3), pp. 251–82.
[G: Selected Countries]

Lustig, Nora. Crisis económica y niveles de vida en México: 1982–1985. (Economic Crisis and Living Standards in Mexico. With English summary.) *Estud. Econ.*, July-December 1987, *2*(2), pp. 227–49.   [G: Mexico]

Maenner, Ulrike. Verschuldung und aussenwirtschaftliche Anpassung von Entwicklungsländern—Erfolgsfall Indonesien? (Debt Problems and External Adjustment in Developing Countries: Indonesia, a Case of Success? With English summary.) *Konjunkturpolitik*, 1987, *33*(6), pp. 357–76.   [G: Indonesia]

Marcano, Jorge. Adjustment, Indebtedness, and Economic Growth: Recent Experience: Comment. *Martirena-Mantel, A. M., ed.*, 1987, pp. 175–77.   [G: Latin America]

Marer, Paul. East Europe's Balance of Payment Crisis and Consequences. *Marer, P. and van Veen, P., eds.*, 1987, pp. 11–16.
[G: E. Europe]

Marquez, Jaime R. Money Demand in Open Economies: A Divisia Application to the U.S. Case. *Barnett, W. A. and Singleton, K. J., eds.*, 1987, pp. 183–99.   [G: U.S.]

Marris, Stephen. Growth Gaps, Exchange Rates and Asymmetry: Comments. *Patrick, H. T. and Tachi, R., eds.*, 1987, pp. 30–36.
[G: Japan; U.S.]

Marston, Richard C. Japanese–U.S. Current Accounts and Exchange Rates before and after the G5 Agreement: Discussion. *Sato, R. and Wachtel, P., eds.*, 1987, pp. 152–56.
[G: Japan; U.S.]

Marston, Richard C. Real Exchange Rates and Productivity Growth in the United States and Japan. *Arndt, S. W. and Richardson, J. D. eds.*, 1987, pp. 71–96.   [G: U.S.; Japan]

Martirena-Mantel, Ana María. External Debt, Savings, and Growth in Latin America: Introduction and Overview. *Martirena-Mantel, A. M., ed.*, 1987, pp. 1–25.   [G: Latin America]

Marwah, Kanta. On Managing the Exchange Rate of the Indian Rupee: Modelling Post-Bretton Woods Experience. *J. Quant. Econ.*, January 1987, *3*(1), pp. 137–63.   [G: India]

Masson, Paul R. International Cooperation and Reputation in an Empirical Two-Bloc Model: Discussion. *Bryant, R. C. and Portes, R., eds.*, 1987, pp. 122–25.   [G: U.S.]

de Melo, Jaime. Financial Reforms, Stabilization, and Growth under High Capital Mobility: Uruguay 1974–83. *Connolly, M. and González-Vega, C., eds.*, 1987, pp. 229–49.
[G: Uruguay]

Mendelsohn, M. S. World Trade and International Finance: Lessons from the Past. *Visser, H. and Schoor, E., eds.*, 1987, pp. 57–64.
[G: Global]

Metwally, M. M. Determinants of the External Surplus of the Member States of the Gulf Cooperation Council. *Appl. Econ.*, March 1987, *19*(3), pp. 305–16.   [G: Middle East]

Modjtahedi, Bagher. An Empirical Investigation into the International Real Interest Rate Linkages. *Can. J. Econ.*, November 1987, *20*(4), pp. 832–54.   [G: OECD]

Morgan, John B. A Note on Eaton and Gersovitz's Model of Borrowing [LDC Participation in International Financial Markets] [Debt with Potential Repudiation: Theoretical and Empirical Analysis]. *J. Devel. Econ.*, February 1987, *25*(1), pp. 251–61.   [G: LDCs]

Murphy, J. Carter. National Policies and the International Monetary System. *Officer, L. H., ed.*, 1987, pp. 203–70.   [G: Global]

Nabulsi, M. Said. Adjustment and Development: The Case of Egypt: Comment. *El-Naggar, S., ed.*, 1987, pp. 117–23.   [G: Egypt]

Nawaz, Shuja. Why the World Current Account Does Not Balance. *Finance Develop.*, September 1987, *24*(3), pp. 43–45.   [G: Global]

Ncube, P. D.; Sakala, M. and Ndulo, M. The International Monetary Fund and the Zambian Economy—A Case. *Havnevik, K. J., ed.*, 1987, pp. 127–48.   [G: Zambia]

van Nieuwkerk, Marius. In Search of 100 Billion Dollars. *Heijmans, R. and Neudecker, H., eds.*, 1987, pp. 121–30.   [G: Global]

O'Mara, L. P.; Wallace, N. A. and Meshios, H. The Current Account, Monetary Policy, Market Sentiment and the Real Exchange Rate: Some Implications for the Farm Sector. *Australian J. Agr. Econ.*, December 1987, *31*(3), pp. 219–41.   [G: Australia]

Ocampo, José Antonio. Crisis and Economic Policy in Colombia, 1980–5. *Thorp, R. and Whitehead, L., eds.*, 1987, pp. 239–70.
[G: Colombia]

Oort, C. J. The Influences of International Capital Flows on World Trade. *Visser, H. and Schoor, E., eds.*, 1987, pp. 65–76.   [G: Global]

Oppenheimer, Peter M. The Endogeneity of International Liquidity. *Aliber, R. Z., ed.*, 1987, pp. 305–23.

Ortega, Leonidas. Adjustment, Indebtedness, and Economic Growth: Recent Experience: Comment. *Martirena-Mantel, A. M., ed.*, 1987, pp. 177–79. **[G: Latin America]**

Ortiz, Guillermo. Adjustment, Indebtedness, and Economic Growth: Recent Experience. *Martirena-Mantel, A. M., ed.*, 1987, pp. 154–75. **[G: Latin America]**

Oudiz, Gilles. External Constraints on European Growth: Comment. *Lawrence, R. Z. and Schultze, C. L., eds.*, 1987, pp. 596–99. **[G: W. Europe]**

Oudiz, Gilles. International Policy Cooperation and Model Uncertainty: Discussion. *Bryant, R. C. and Portes, R., eds.*, 1987, pp. 178–82.

Park, Hui-Jong. The Effects of Foreign Capital Inflow on Economic Growth in Korea: The Reevaluation of Griffin and Enos's Hypotheses. *Int. Econ. J.*, Summer 1987, *1*(2), pp. 79–93. **[G: S. Korea]**

Pastor, Manuel, Jr. The Effects of IMF Programs in the Third World: Debate and Evidence from Latin America. *World Devel.*, February 1987, *15*(2), pp. 249–62. **[G: Latin America]**

Pollard, Sidney. Stagflation, Fiscal Deficits and Balance of Payments—Great Britain and Germany. *Hitotsubashi J. Econ.*, October 1987, *27*, pp. 42–56. **[G: U.K.; W. Germany]**

Rabin, Alan. A Reexamination of the Acceleration of Worldwide Inflation in the Early 1970s. *J. Macroecon.*, Spring 1987, *9*(2), pp. 275–85. **[G: Global]**

Raczkowski, Stanislaw. The Influence of International Price Movements and Inflation on the Centrally Planned Economies. *Pasinetti, L. and Lloyd, P., eds.*, 1987, pp. 359–80. **[G: CMEA]**

Rada, Juan F. Information Technology and Services. *Giarini, O., ed.*, 1987, pp. 127–71. **[G: U.S.; Canada; W. Europe]**

Ridley, William P. Japan: An Uneasy Transition to a Rentier Society. *[Marjolin, R.]*, 1987, pp. 169–89. **[G: Japan]**

Roca, Santiago and Priale, Rodrigo. Devaluation, Inflationary Expectations and Stabilisation in Peru. *J. Econ. Stud.*, 1987, *14*(1), pp. 5–33. **[G: Peru]**

Ros, Jaime. Mexico from the Oil Boom to the Debt Crisis: An Analysis of Policy Responses to External Shocks, 1978–85. *Thorp, R. and Whitehead, L., eds.*, 1987, pp. 68–116. **[G: Mexico]**

Saba, Elias. Adjustment and Development: The Case of Jordan: Comment. *El-Naggar, S., ed.*, 1987, pp. 149–55. **[G: Jordan]**

Sadik, Mohammed T. Adjustment and Development: The Case of Morocco: Comment. *El-Naggar, S., ed.*, 1987, pp. 188–94. **[G: Morocco]**

Sarcinelli, Mario. Towards Financial Integration in a European and International Context: Exchange Liberalization in Italy. *Rev. Econ. Cond. Italy*, May-August 1987, (2), pp. 125–46. **[G: Italy]**

Scarfe, Brian L. Economic Fluctuations and Stabilization Policy in Canada: The State of the Art. *Can. Public Policy*, March 1987, *13*(1), pp. 75–85. **[G: Canada]**

Scholl, Russell B. The International Investment Position of the United States in 1986. *Surv. Curr. Bus.*, June 1987, *67*(6), pp. 38–45. **[G: U.S.]**

Seth, Rama and McCauley, Robert N. Financial Consequences of New Asian Surpluses. *Fed. Res. Bank New York Quart. Rev.*, Summer 1987, *12*(2), pp. 32–44. **[G: Japan; Taiwan; Korea]**

Snowden, P. N. International Equity Investment in Less Developed Countries' Stockmarkets: The Replacement for Bank Lending? *Nat. Westminster Bank Quart. Rev.*, February 1987, pp. 29–38. **[G: LDCs]**

Szakolczai, György; Bagdy, Gábor and Vindics, József. The Dependence of the Hungarian Economy on the World Economy: Facts and Consequences. *Soviet E. Europ. Foreign Trade*, Spring 1987, *23*(1), pp. 54–88. **[G: Hungary]**

Taylor, Mark P. Testing the Exogeneity Specification Underlying the Monetary Approach to the Balance of Payments: Some UK Evidence. *Appl. Econ.*, May 1987, *19*(5), pp. 651–61. **[G: U.K.]**

di Tella, Guido. Argentina's Most Recent Inflationary Cycle, 1975–85. *Thorp, R. and Whitehead, L., eds.*, 1987, pp. 162–207. **[G: Argentina]**

Thomas, Charles P. U.S. International Transactions in 1986. *Fed. Res. Bull.*, May 1987, *73*(5), pp. 321–29. **[G: U.S.]**

Thompson, Grahame. Objectives and Instruments of Economic Management. *Thompson, G.; Brown, V. and Levačić, R., eds.*, 1987, pp. 1–37. **[G: U.K.]**

Thorp, Rosemary. Peruvian Adjustment Policies, 1978–85: The Effects of Prolonged Crisis. *Thorp, R. and Whitehead, L., eds.*, 1987, pp. 208–38. **[G: Peru]**

Thorp, Rosemary and Whitehead, Laurence. Latin American Debt and the Adjustment Crisis: Review and Conclusions. *Thorp, R. and Whitehead, L., eds.*, 1987, pp. 318–54. **[G: Latin America]**

Tovias, Alfred. The Impact of the Second Enlargement of the EC upon Israel's Balance of Payments. *Greilsammer, I. and Weiler, J. H. H., eds.*, 1987, pp. 173–94. **[G: EEC; Israel]**

Triffin, Robert. The IMS (International Monetary System... or Scandal?) and the EMS (European Monetary System). *Banca Naz. Lavoro Quart. Rev.*, September 1987, (162), pp. 239–61.

Trzeciakowski, Witold. Impact of External Market Fluctuations on Centrally Planned and Market Economies: A Systematic Comparative Approach. *Pasinetti, L. and Lloyd, P., eds.*, 1987, pp. 465–77. **[G: CMEA]**

Turits, Richard. Trade, Debt, and the Cuban Economy. *Zimbalist, A., ed.*, 1987, pp. 165–82. **[G: Cuba]**

Turner, Paul. The Inefficiency of Uncoordinated

Stabilisation Policy in Multicountry Models. *Chrystal, K. A. and Sedgwick, R., eds.*, 1987, pp. 229–38.

Ueda, Kazuo. Japanese–U.S. Current Accounts and Exchange Rates before and after the G5 Agreement. *Sato, R. and Wachtel, P., eds.*, 1987, pp. 127–47. **[G: Japan; U.S.]**

Ueda, Kazuo. Prospects for Japan's Current-Account Surplus. *Patrick, H. T. and Tachi, R., eds.*, 1987, pp. 54–57. **[G: Japan]**

Várhegyi, Éva. Some Macroeconomic Components in the Hungarian Economy's Balance of Trade during the Seventies. *Soviet E. Europ. Foreign Trade*, Summer 1987, *23*(2), pp. 60–77. **[G: Hungary]**

Vellai-Posta, Györgyi and Veliczky, József. A Statistical Analysis of the "Openness" of Our Economic Processes. *Soviet E. Europ. Foreign Trade*, Spring 1987, *23*(1), pp. 89–110. **[G: Hungary]**

de Vries, Rimmer. International Imbalances and the Search for Exchange-Rate Stability. *Patrick, H. T. and Tachi, R., eds.*, 1987, pp. 117–20. **[G: U.S.; Japan; W. Germany]**

Wallace, W. J. L. Public Expenditure: The International Dimension. *Levitt, M. S., ed.*, 1987, pp. 107–19. **[G: U.K.]**

Wangwe, Samuel M. Impact of the IMF/World Bank Philosophy, the Case of Tanzania. *Havnevik, K. J., ed.*, 1987, pp. 149–60. **[G: Tanzania]**

Wegner, Manfred. Scope and Limits of International Economic Policy Coordination. *World Econ.*, September 1987, *10*(3), pp. 283–306. **[G: OECD]**

Wenninger, John and Klitgaard, Thomas. Exploring the Effects of Capital Movements on M1 and the Economy. *Fed. Res. Bank New York Quart. Rev.*, Summer 1987, *12*(2), pp. 21–31. **[G: U.S.]**

Whichard, Obie G. U.S. Sales of Services to Foreigners. *Surv. Curr. Bus.*, January 1987, *67*(1), pp. 22–41. **[G: U.S.]**

Whitehead, Laurence. The Adjustment Process in Chile: A Comparative Perspective. *Thorp, R. and Whitehead, L., eds.*, 1987, pp. 117–61. **[G: Chile]**

Williamson, John. Global Macroeconomic Strategy. *Williamson, J.*, 1987, *1982*, pp. 258–75. **[G: Global]**

Winters, L. Alan. An Empirical Intertemporal Model of Developing Countries' Imports. *Weltwirtsch. Arch.*, 1987, *123*(1), pp. 58–80. **[G: Malaysia; Colombia; Kenya]**

Yoshitomi, Masaru. Growth Gaps, Exchange Rates and Asymmetry: Is it Possible to Unwind Current-Account Imbalances without Fiscal Expansion in Japan? *Patrick, H. T. and Tachi, R., eds.*, 1987, pp. 18–29. **[G: Japan; U.S.]**

4314 Exchange Rates and Markets: Theory and Studies

Adams, Paul D. and Wyatt, Steve B. Biases in Option Prices. *J. Banking Finance*, December 1987, *11*(4), pp. 549–62. **[G: U.S.]**

Adams, Paul D. and Wyatt, Steve B. On the Pricing of European and American Foreign Currency Call Options. *J. Int. Money Finance*, September 1987, *6*(3), pp. 315–38. **[G: U.S.]**

Ahking, Francis W. and Miller, Stephen M. A Comparison of the Stochastic Processes of Structural and Time-Series Exchange-Rate Models. *Rev. Econ. Statist.*, August 1987, *69*(3), pp. 496–502. **[G: OECD]**

Ahmad, J. Inflationary Expectations and Price Interdependence under Floating Exchange Rates. *Borner, S. and Taylor, A., eds.*, 1987, pp. 395–404.

Alexander, Don and Thomas, Lee R., III. Monetary/Asset Models of Exchange Rate Determination: How Well Have They Performed in the 1980s? *Int. J. Forecasting*, 1987, *3*(1), pp. 53–63. **[G: U.S.]**

Aliber, Robert Z. Gold in the International Monetary System: A Catalog of the Options. *Aliber, R. Z., ed.*, 1987, pp. 168–82. **[G: U.S.]**

Allen, Polly Reynolds. Is the ECU an Optimal Currency Basket? Discussion. *Levich, R. M. and Sommariva, A., eds.*, 1987, pp. 210–13. **[G: EEC]**

Allsopp, Christopher. The Rise and Fall of the Dollar: A Comment. *Econ. J.*, March 1987, *97*(385), pp. 44–48. **[G: U.S.; U.K.]**

Alterman, William; Johnson, David S. and Goth, John. BLS Publishes Average Exchange Rate and Foreign Currency Price Indexes. *Mon. Lab. Rev.*, December 1987, *110*(12), pp. 47–49. **[G: U.S.]**

Artis, M. J. The European Monetary System: An Evaluation. *J. Policy Modeling*, Spring 1987, *9*(1), pp. 175–98. **[G: EEC]**

Artus, Jacques R. Toward a More Orderly Exchange Rate System. *Aliber, R. Z., ed.*, 1987, pp. 46–69. **[G: U.S.; U.K.; Japan; W. Germany]**

Aschheim, Joseph; Bailey, Martin J. and Tavlas, George S. Dollar Variability, the New Protectionism, Trade and Financial Performance. *Salvatore, D., ed.*, 1987, pp. 424–49. **[G: OECD]**

Auernheimer, Leonardo. On the Outcome of Inconsistent Programs under Exchange Rate and Monetary Rules. *J. Monet. Econ.*, March 1987, *19*(2), pp. 279–305.

Baer, Werner and Birch, Melissa. The International Economic Relations of a Small Country: The Case of Paraguay. *Econ. Develop. Cult. Change*, April 1987, *35*(3), pp. 601–27. **[G: Paraguay; Selected Countries]**

Baffi, Paolo. The European Monetary System and Italian Participation. *Ciocca, P., ed.*, 1987, *1978*, pp. 263–76. **[G: EEC]**

Bailey, Martin J.; Tavlas, George S. and Ulan, Michael. The Impact of Exchange-Rate Volatility on Export Growth: Some Theoretical Considerations and Empirical Results. *J. Policy Modeling*, Spring 1987, *9*(1), pp. 225–43. **[G: OECD]**

Baillie, Richard T. and McMahon, Patrick C. Empirical Regularities in Exchange Rate Be-

haviour. *Chrystal, K. A. and Sedgwick, R.,
eds.*, 1987, pp. 7–29.   **[G: OECD]**

Baillie, Richard T. and Selover, David D. Cointegration and Models of Exchange Rate Determination. *Int. J. Forecasting*, 1987, 3(1), pp. 43–51.

Balassa, Bela. Mexico's Debt Problem and Policies for the Future. *Tremblay, R., ed.*, 1987, pp. 11–29.   **[G: Mexico]**

Bana, Ismail Mahomed and Handa, Jagdish. Currency Substitution: A Multicurrency Study for Canada. *Int. Econ. J.*, Autumn 1987, 1(3), pp. 71–86.

Basevi, Giorgio; Cocchi, Daniela and Lischi, Pier Luigi. The Choice of Currency in the Foreign Trade of Italy. *Hodgman, D. R. and Wood, G. E., eds.*, 1987, pp. 1–48.   **[G: Italy]**

Basevi, Giorgio and Giavazzi, Francesco. Conflicts and Coordination in the European Monetary System. *Steinherr, A. and Weiserbs, D., eds.*, 1987, pp. 133–64.   **[G: W. Europe]**

Batten, Dallas S. and Belongia, Michael T. Do the New Exchange Rate Indexes Offer Better Answers to Old Questions? *Fed. Res. Bank St. Louis Rev.*, May 1987, 69(5), pp. 5–17.
                                          [G: U.S.]

de Beaufort Wijnholds, J. H. A. Surveillance over Exchange Rate Policies. *Visser, H. and Schoor, E., eds.*, 1987, pp. 169–75.

Beckerman, Paul. Inflation and Dollar Accounts in Peru's Banking System, 1978–84. *World Devel.*, August 1987, 15(8), pp. 1087–1106.
                                          [G: Peru]

Bernholz, Peter. The Political Economy of Revaluation-Induced Protectionism under Discretionary Monetary Regimes with Flexible Exchange Rates. *Giersch, H., ed.*, 1987, pp. 407–24.   **[G: U.S.]**

Bessler, David A. and Babula, Ronald A. Forecasting Wheat Exports: Do Exchange Rates Matter? *J. Bus. Econ. Statist.*, July 1987, 5(3), pp. 397–406.   **[G: U.S.]**

Bhandari, Jagdeep S. and Decaluwe, Bernard. A Stochastic Model of Incomplete Separation between Commercial and Financial Exchange Markets. *J. Int. Econ.*, February 1987, 22(1/2), pp. 25–55.

Biasco, Salvatore. Currency Cycles and the International Economy. *Banca Naz. Lavoro Quart. Rev.*, March 1987, (160), pp. 31–60.
                            [G: U.S.; W. Germany]

Bilson, John F. O. Foreign Exchange Intervention as an Alternative to Protectionism. *Salvatore, D., ed.*, 1987, pp. 408–23. **[G: OECD]**

Bilson, John F. O. The ECU and the Choice of an Invoice Currency. *Levich, R. M. and Sommariva, A., eds.*, 1987, pp. 145–55.
                                          [G: EEC]

Bilson, John F. O. and Hsieh, David A. The Profitability of Currency Speculation. *Int. J. Forecasting*, 1987, 3(1), pp. 115–30.   **[G: U.S.]**

Bird, Graham. Bancor and the Developing Countries: How Much Difference Would It Have Made? Discussion. *Thirlwall, A. P., ed.*, 1987, pp. 107–16.

Bito, Christian. Les options sur contrats futures.

Introduction d'un processus de diffusion mixte et application aux devises. (Options on Futures Contracts: Introduction of a Mixed Stochastic Process and an Application to the Foreign Exchange Markets. With English summary.) *Finance*, December 1987, 8(2), pp. 7–24.

Black, Stanley W. and Salemi, Michael K. Government Policy and the Risk Premium in Foreign Exchange Markets. *Chrystal, K. A. and Sedgwick, R., eds.*, 1987, pp. 72–90.
                                    [G: W. Germany]

Blackburn, Keith. Interest Parity, the Degree of Capital Mobility and the Information Contents of the Exchange Rate and the Interest Rate: Clarifications and Extensions. *Manchester Sch. Econ. Soc. Stud.*, March 1987, 55(1), pp. 60–76.

Blades, Derek and Roberts, David. A Note on the New OECD Benchmark Purchasing Power Parities for 1985. *OECD Econ. Stud.*, Autumn 1987, (9), pp. 183–97.   **[G: OECD]**

Bodurtha, James N., Jr. and Courtadon, Georges R. Tests of an American Option Pricing Model on the Foreign Currency Options Market. *J. Finan. Quant. Anal.*, June 1987, 22(2), pp. 153–67.   **[G: U.S.]**

Bollerslev, Tim. A Conditionally Heteroskedastic Time Series Model for Speculative Prices and Rates of Return. *Rev. Econ. Statist.*, August 1987, 69(3), pp. 542–47.   **[G: U.S.; U.K.; W. Germany]**

Bomhoff, Eduard J. and Koedijk, Kees G. A Portfolio Balance Model of Bilateral Exchange Rates. *Chrystal, K. A. and Sedgwick, R., eds.*, 1987, pp. 54–71.

Booth, Elizabeth B. and Booth, G. Geoffrey. Exchange Rate Bubbles: Some New Evidence. *Rivista Int. Sci. Econ. Com.*, Nov.-Dec. 1987, 34(11–12), pp. 1053–68.

Boothe, Paul M. and Glassman, Debra A. Comparing Exchange Rate Forecasting Models: Accuracy versus Profitability. *Int. J. Forecasting*, 1987, 3(1), pp. 65–79.   **[G: U.S.]**

Boothe, Paul M. and Glassman, Debra A. Off the Mark: Lessons for Exchange Rate Modelling. *Oxford Econ. Pap.*, September 1987, 39(3), pp. 443–57.   **[G: W. Germany; U.S.]**

Boothe, Paul M. and Glassman, Debra A. The Statistical Distribution of Exchange Rates: Empirical Evidence and Economic Implications. *J. Int. Econ.*, May 1987, 22(3/4), pp. 297–319.
                  [G: U.K.; Canada; Japan; W. Germany]

Bordo, Michael D. and Marcotte, Ivan A. Purchasing Power Parity in Colonial America: Some Evidence for South Carolina 1732–1774: A Comment. *Carnegie–Rochester Conf. Ser. Public Policy*, Autumn 1987, 27, pp. 311–23.
                                          [G: U.S.]

Borensztein, Eduardo R. Alternative Hypotheses about the Excess Return on Dollar Assets, 1980–84. *Int. Monet. Fund Staff Pap.*, March 1987, 34(1), pp. 29–59.   **[G: U.S.; W. Europe; Japan]**

Borensztein, Eduardo R. and Dooley, Michael P. Options on Foreign Exchange and Exchange Rate Expectations. *Int. Monet. Fund Staff*

Pap., December 1987, *34*(4), pp. 643–80. **[G: U.S.]**

Bosco, Luigi. Determinants of the Exchange Rate Regimes in LDCs: Some Empirical Evidence. *Econ. Notes*, 1987, (1), pp. 119–43. **[G: LDCs]**

Bosworth, Barry P. The Persistence of the U.S. Trade Deficit: Comments. *Brookings Pap. Econ. Act.*, 1987, (1), pp. 44–47. **[G: U.S.]**

Boughton, James M. Tests of the Performance of Reduced-Form Exchange Rate Models. *J. Int. Econ.*, August 1987, *23*(1/2), pp. 41–56. **[G: U.S.; Japan; W. Germany]**

Boyer, Russell S. and Kingston, Geoffrey H. Currency Substitution under Finance Constraints. *J. Int. Money Finance*, September 1987, *6*(3), pp. 235–50.

Breece, James H. Rational Expectations, Currency Substitution, and the Demand for Money during the German Hyperinflation. *METU*, 1987, *14*(1), pp. 65–74. **[G: Germany]**

Brenton, Paul and Parikh, Ashok. Price Behaviour in European Countries: Testing the Law of One Price in the Short- and Long-Run at Various Levels of Aggregation. *Appl. Econ.*, November 1987, *19*(11), pp. 1533–59. **[G: W. Europe]**

Broadberry, Stephen N. Purchasing Power Parity and the Pound–Dollar Rate in the 1930s. *Economica*, February 1987, *54*(213), pp. 69–78. **[G: U.S.; U.K.]**

Brock, Philip and Tower, Edward. Economic Liberalization in Less Developed Countries: Guidelines from the Empirical Evidence and Clarification of the Theory. *Connolly, M. and González-Vega, C., eds.*, 1987, pp. 19–43. **[G: LDCs]**

Brown, Stuart S. Nonmarket Economies, Multiple Exchange Rates and the Countervailing Duty Law: The Case of Polish and Czech Steel. *J. World Trade Law*, December 1987, *21*(6), pp. 89–111. **[G: Poland; Czechoslovakia]**

Brunner, Karl and Meltzer, Allan H. Empirical Studies of Velocity, Real Exchange Rates, Unemployment, and Productivity. *Carnegie–Rochester Conf. Ser. Public Policy*, Autumn 1987, *27*, pp. 1–8.

Buckle, Robert A. Sequencing and the Role of the Foreign Exchange Market. *Bollard, A. and Buckle, R., eds.*, 1987, pp. 236–60. **[G: New Zealand]**

Buira, Ariel. The Nature and Direction of International Monetary Reform. *Dell, S., ed., Pt. 3*, 1987, pp. 765–84.

Buiter, Willem H. An Empirical Investigation of the Long-run Behavior of Real Exchange Rates: Comment. *Carnegie–Rochester Conf. Ser. Public Policy*, Autumn 1987, *27*, pp. 215–23. **[G: OECD]**

Buiter, Willem H. Borrowing to Defend the Exchange Rate and the Timing and Magnitude of Speculative Attacks. *J. Int. Econ.*, November 1987, *23*(3/4), pp. 221–39.

Büttler, Hans-Jürg and Schips, Bernd. Equilibrium Exchange Rates in a Multi-country Model: An Econometric Study. *Weltwirtsch.*

Arch., 1987, *123*(1), pp. 1–23. **[G: Global]**

Cadsby, Charles Bram. Exchange Rate Instability in a Two-Country Portfolio Balance Model. *J. Macroecon.*, Spring 1987, *9*(2), pp. 223–38.

Cagan, Phillip. Disinflation, the Dollar, and Velocity. *Cagan, P., ed.*, 1987, pp. 129–52. **[G: U.S.]**

Calvo, Guillermo A. On the Costs of Temporary Policy. *J. Devel. Econ.*, October 1987, *27*(1–2), pp. 245–61.

Calvo, Guillermo A. On the Costs of Temporary Policy. *[Diaz-Alejandro, C. F.]*, 1987, pp. 245–61.

Calvo, Guillermo A. Real Exchange Rate Dynamics with Nominal Parities: Structural Change and Overshooting. *J. Int. Econ.*, February 1987, *22*(1/2), pp. 141–55.

Campbell, John Y. and Clarida, Richard H. The Dollar and Real Interest Rates. *Carnegie–Rochester Conf. Ser. Public Policy*, Autumn 1987, *27*, pp. 103–39. **[G: U.S.]**

Campbell, John Y. and Clarida, Richard H. The Term Structure of Euromarket Interest Rates: An Empirical Investigation. *J. Monet. Econ.*, January 1987, *19*(1), pp. 25–44.

Canto, Victor A. Monetary Policy, "Dollarization," and Parallel Market Exchange Rates: The Case of the Dominican Republic. *Connolly, M. and González-Vega, C., eds.*, 1987, pp. 177–94. **[G: Dominican Republic]**

Capie, Forrest H. and Wood, Geoffrey E. Policy Makers in Crisis: A Study of Two Devaluations. *Hodgman, D. R. and Wood, G. E., eds.*, 1987, pp. 166–92. **[G: U.K.]**

Caramazza, Francesco. International Real Interest Rate Linkages in the 1970s and 1980s. *Tremblay, R., ed.*, 1987, pp. 123–50.

Carstens, Agustín G. Paridad de tasas de interés y riesgo político. El caso de México. (Interest Rate Parity and Political Risk: The Mexican Case. With English summary.) *Estud. Econ.*, July–December 1987, *2*(2), pp. 269–94. **[G: Mexico]**

Cavanaugh, Kenneth L. Price Dynamics in Foreign Currency Futures Markets. *J. Int. Money Finance*, September 1987, *6*(3), pp. 295–314. **[G: U.S.]**

Chadha, Binky. Contract Length, Monetary Policy and Exchange Rate Variability. *J. Int. Money Finance*, December 1987, *6*(4), pp. 491–504. **[G: U.S.]**

Chandavarkar, Anand G. Keynes and the International Monetary System Revisited (A Contextual and Conjectural Essay). *World Devel.*, December 1987, *15*(12), pp. 1395–1405. **[G: LDCs]**

Chesney, Marc and Loubergé, Henri. The Pricing of European Currency Options: Empirical Tests Based on Swiss Data. *Aussenwirtschaft*, September 1987, *42*(2/3), pp. 213–28. **[G: Switzerland; U.S.]**

Chino, Yoshitoki. Thoughts on Japanese Financial Liberalization. *Patrick, H. T. and Tachi, R., eds.*, 1987, pp. 178–83. **[G: Japan]**

Chmura, Christine. The Effect of Exchange Rate Variation on U.S. Textile and Apparel Imports.

Fed. Res. Bank Richmond Econ. Rev., May/June 1987, *73*(3), pp. 17–23. [G: U.S.]

Chrystal, K. Alec. A Guide to Foreign Exchange Markets. *Wilcox, J. A., ed.*, 1987, *1984*, pp. 307–20.

Chrystal, K. Alec. Changing Perceptions of International Money and International Reserves in the World Economy. *Aliber, R. Z., ed.*, 1987, pp. 127–50.

Chrystal, K. Alec. International Liquidity and the Position of Developing Countries in the 1980s. *Dell, S., ed., Pt. 2*, 1987, pp. 358–72.

Chrystal, K. Alec and Sedgwick, Robert. Exchange Rates and Open Economy Macroeconomics: An Introduction. *Chrystal, K. A. and Sedgwick, R., eds.*, 1987, pp. 1–6.

Cobham, David. Managing the Open Economy. *Thompson, G.; Brown, V. and Levačić, R., eds.*, 1987, pp. 224–53. [G: U.K.]

Coes, Donald V. Exchange Rate Intervention and Imperfect Capital Mobility. *Hodgman, D. R. and Wood, G. E., eds.*, 1987, pp. 99–135. [G: W. Germany; U.K.]

Connolly, Michael and Fernández-Pérez, Arturo. Speculation against the Preannounced Exchange Rate in Mexico: January 1983 to June 1985. *Connolly, M. and González-Vega, C., eds.*, 1987, pp. 161–74. [G: Mexico]

Cooper, Richard N. Flexible Exchange Rates, 1973–1980: How Bad Have They Really Been? *Cooper, R. N.*, 1987, *1982*, pp. 103–17.

Cooper, Richard N. Flexing the International Monetary System: The Case of Gliding Parities. *Cooper, R. N.*, 1987, *1970*, pp. 87–101.

Cooper, Richard N. IMF Surveillance over Floating Exchange Rates. *Cooper, R. N.*, 1987, *1977*, pp. 139–51.

Cooper, Richard N. The Future of the Dollar. *Cooper, R. N.*, 1987, *1973*, pp. 173–88. [G: U.S.; Global]

Corbo, Vittorio. Korean Growth Policy: Comment. *Brookings Pap. Econ. Act.*, 1987, (2), pp. 450–52. [G: S. Korea]

Corbo, Vittorio. The Use of the Exchange Rate for Stabilization Purposes: The Case of Chile. *Connolly, M. and González-Vega, C., eds.*, 1987, pp. 111–37. [G: Chile]

Corbo, Vittorio and de Melo, Jaime. Lessons from the Southern Cone Policy Reforms. *World Bank Res. Observer*, July 1987, *2*(2), pp. 111–42. [G: Argentina; Chile; Uruguay]

Costa, Antonio Maria. The Need for New Multilateral Trade Negotiations: Why Is It Urgent to Complete the GATT Round Successfully? *Salvatore, D., ed.*, 1987, pp. 113–49. [G: OECD]

Côté, Agathe. The Link between the U.S. Dollar Real Exchange Rate, Real Primary Commodity Prices, and LDCs' Terms of Trade. *Rev. Econ. Statist.*, August 1987, *69*(3), pp. 547–51. [G: U.S.; LDCs]

Cotner, John S. and Seitz, Neil E. A Simplified Approach to Short-term International Diversification. *Financial Rev.*, May 1987, *22*(2), pp. 249–66.

Coulbois, Paul. Le changes pervertis. (With English summary.) *Revue Écon. Polit.*, July-Aug. 1987, *97*(4), pp. 397–408. [G: U.S.]

Cox, W. Michael. A Comprehensive New Real Dollar Exchange Rate Index. *Fed. Res. Bank Dallas Econ. Rev.*, March 1987, pp. 1–14. [G: U.S.]

Cross, Sam Y. Treasury and Federal Reserve Foreign Exchange Operations: November 1987–January 1988. *Fed. Res. Bank New York Quart. Rev.*, Winter 1987-88, *12*(4), pp. 54–59. [G: U.S.]

Cross, Sam Y. Treasury and Federal Reserve Foreign Exchange Operations: November 1986–January 1987. *Fed. Res. Bank New York Quart. Rev.*, Spring 1987, *12*(1), pp. 64–70. [G: U.S.]

Cross, Sam Y. Treasury and Federal Reserve Foreign Exchange Operations. *Fed. Res. Bull.*, October 1987, *73*(10), pp. 779–82. [G: U.S.]

Cross, Sam Y. Treasury and Federal Reserve Foreign Exchange Operations. *Fed. Res. Bull.*, January 1987, *73*(1), pp. 14–19. [G: U.S.]

Cross, Sam Y. Treasury and Federal Reserve Foreign Exchange Operations. *Fed. Res. Bull.*, May 1987, *73*(5), pp. 330–35. [G: U.S.]

Cross, Sam Y. Treasury and Federal Reserve Foreign Exchange Operations: August–October 1987. *Fed. Res. Bank New York Quart. Rev.*, Winter 1987-88, *12*(4), pp. 48–53. [G: U.S.]

Cross, Sam Y. Treasury and Federal Reserve Foreign Exchange Operations: February–April 1987. *Fed. Res. Bank New York Quart. Rev.*, Spring 1987, *12*(1), pp. 57–63. [G: U.S.]

Cross, Sam Y. Treasury and Federal Reserve Foreign Exchange Operations: May–June 1987. *Fed. Res. Bank New York Quart. Rev.*, Autumn 1987, *12*(3), pp. 49–54. [G: U.S.]

Cross, Sam Y. Treasury and Federal Reserve Foreign Exchange Operations. *Fed. Res. Bull.*, July 1987, *73*(7), pp. 552–57. [G: U.S.]

de la Cuadra, Sergio. Exchange Rate Policies in Chile: 1933–82. *Connolly, M. and González-Vega, C., eds.*, 1987, pp. 139–59. [G: Chile]

Cumby, Robert E. Japanese–U.S. Current Accounts and Exchange Rates before and after the G5 Agreement: Discussion. *Sato, R. and Wachtel, P., eds.*, 1987, pp. 148–52. [G: Japan; U.S.]

Dagnino Pastore, José María. Las tasas de interés bajo distintos contextos cambiario y finaciero. (With English summary.) *Desarrollo Econ.*, Apr.-June 1987, *27*(105), pp. 61–85. [G: Argentina]

Danker, Deborah J., et al. Small Empirical Models of Exchange Market Intervention: Applications to Germany, Japan, and Canada. *J. Policy Modeling*, Spring 1987, *9*(1), pp. 143–73. [G: W. Germany; Japan; Canada]

Dauhajre, Andrés. Financial Reform in a Small Open Economy with a Flexible Exchange Rate. *Connolly, M. and González-Vega, C., eds.*, 1987, pp. 283–304.

Dauhajre, Andrés. Some Warnings Concerning Possible Financial Reform in the Dominican Republic. *Salazar-Carrillo, J. and Tirado de*

Alonzo, I., eds., 1987, pp. 1–12.
[G: Dominican Republic]
Dehem, Roger. The Canadian Dollar: The Odd Currency. *Tremblay, R., ed.*, 1987, pp. 199–201. [G: Canada]
Dell, Sidney and Lawrence, Roger. The Balance of Payments Adjustment Process in Developing Countries. *Dell, S., ed., Pt. 1*, 1987, *1980*, pp. 1–154. [G: Global]
Desai, Padma and Bhagwati, Jagdish N. Three Alternative Concepts of Foreign Exchange Difficulties in Centrally Planned Economies. *Desai, P.*, 1987, *1979*, pp. 163–72.
Devarajan, Shantayanan and de Melo, Jaime. Adjustment with a Fixed Exchange Rate: Cameroon, Côte d'Ivoire, and Senegal. *World Bank Econ. Rev.*, May 1987, *1*(3), pp. 447–87. [G: Cameroon; Ivory Coast; Senegal]
Dewes, Leonard D. The Mechanics of the Short-term Interbank ECU Market. *Levich, R. M. and Sommariva, A., eds.*, 1987, pp. 73–87. [G: EEC]
Diba, Behzad T. A Critique of Variance Bounds Tests for Monetary Exchange Rate Models: A Note. *J. Money, Credit, Banking*, February 1987, *19*(1), pp. 104–11. [G: U.S.]
Dinwiddy, Caroline L. and Teal, Francis J. Project Appraisal and Foreign Exchange Constraints: A Comment. *Econ. J.*, June 1987, *97*(386), pp. 479–86.
Dixon, Peter B. and Parmenter, Brian R. Foreign Debts, the Exchange Rate and Australia's Economic Prospects. *Australian Econ. Rev.*, Third Quarter 1987, (79), pp. 36–42. [G: Australia]
Dooley, Michael P. and Isard, Peter. Country Preferences, Currency Values and Policy Issues. *J. Policy Modeling*, Spring 1987, *9*(1), pp. 65–81.
Dornbusch, Rudiger. Collapsing Exchange Rate Regimes. *[Diaz-Alejandro, C. F.]*, 1987, pp. 71–83.
Dornbusch, Rudiger. Collapsing Exchange Rate Regimes. *J. Devel. Econ.*, October 1987, *27*(1–2), pp. 71–83.
Dornbusch, Rudiger. Exchange Rate Economics: 1986. *Econ. J.*, March 1987, *97*(385), pp. 1–18. [G: U.S.]
Dornbusch, Rudiger. Exchange Rates and Prices. *Amer. Econ. Rev.*, March 1987, *77*(1), pp. 93–106.
Dornbusch, Rudiger. External Balance Correction: Depreciation or Protection? *Brookings Pap. Econ. Act.*, 1987, (1), pp. 248–69. [G: U.S.]
Doukas, John. The Performance of Euromoney Currency Report Hedging Recommendations. *Appl. Econ.*, June 1987, *19*(6), pp. 845–52. [G: OECD]
Doukas, John and Rahman, Abdul H. Unit Roots Tests: Evidence from the Foreign Exchange Futures Market. *J. Finan. Quant. Anal.*, March 1987, *22*(1), pp. 101–08. [G: U.S.; Canada; Japan; W. Europe]
Drazen, Allan and Helpman, Elhanan. Stabilization with Exchange Rate Management. *Quart. J. Econ.*, November 1987, *102*(4), pp. 835–55.

Dreyer, Jacob S. The Behavior of the Dollar: Causes and Consequences. *Cagan, P., ed.*, 1987, pp. 5–61. [G: U.S.]
Driskill, Robert and McCafferty, Stephen. Exchange-Rate Determination: An Equilibrium Approach with Imperfect Capital Substitutability. *J. Int. Econ.*, November 1987, *23*(3/4), pp. 241–61.
Dryden, John; Reut, Katrina and Slater, Barbara. Comparison of Purchasing Power Parity between the United States and Canada. *Mon. Lab. Rev.*, December 1987, *110*(12), pp. 7–24. [G: U.S.; Canada]
Dudley, Leonard. Explaining Forecasting Bias: The Case of Real Exchange Rate Variance. *Appl. Econ.*, September 1987, *19*(9), pp. 1249–60. [G: OECD]
Dutton, John and Grennes, Thomas. Alternative Measures of Effective Exchange Rates for Agricultural Trade. *Europ. Rev. Agr. Econ.*, 1987, *14*(4), pp. 427–42. [G: U.S.]
Eaker, Mark R. and Grant, Dwight M. Cross-hedging Foreign Currency Risk. *J. Int. Money Finance*, March 1987, *6*(1), pp. 85–105. [G: Selected OECD; S. Africa]
Edison, Hali J. Is the ECU an Optimal Currency Basket? *Levich, R. M. and Sommariva, A., eds.*, 1987, pp. 191–209. [G: EEC]
Edison, Hali J. Purchasing Power Parity in the Long Run: A Test of the Dollar/Pound Exchange Rate (1890–1978). *J. Money, Credit, Banking*, August 1987, *19*(3), pp. 376–87. [G: U.S.]
Edison, Hali J. and Klovland, Jan Tore. A Quantitative Reassessment of the Purchasing Power Parity Hypothesis: Evidence from Norway and the United Kingdom. *J. Appl. Econometrics*, October 1987, *2*(4), pp. 309–33. [G: U.K.; Norway]
Edison, Hali J.; Miller, Marcus H. and Williamson, John. On Evaluating and Extending the Target Zone Proposal. *J. Policy Modeling*, Spring 1987, *9*(1), pp. 199–224. [G: U.S.; U.K.; Canada; Japan; W. Germany]
Edison, Hali J. and Vårdal, Erling. Optimal Currency Basket in a World of Generalized Floating: An Application to the Nordic Countries. *Int. J. Forecasting*, 1987, *3*(1), pp. 81–96.
Edwards, Clark. The Exchange Rate and U.S. Agricultural Exports. *Agr. Econ. Res.*, Winter 1987, *39*(1), pp. 1–12. [G: U.S.]
Edwards, Sebastian. Real Exchange Rate Variability: An Empirical Analysis of the Developing Countries Case. *Int. Econ. J.*, Spring 1987, *1*(1), pp. 91–106.
Eichengreen, Barry and Portes, Richard. The Anatomy of Financial Crises. *Portes, R. and Swoboda, A. K., eds.*, 1987, pp. 10–58. [G: Global]
El-Erian, Mohamed A. Foreign Currency Deposits in LDCs. *Finance Develop.*, December 1987, *24*(4), pp. 38–40. [G: LDCs]
Emminger, Otmar. The Dollar's Borrowed Strength. *Salvatore, D., ed.*, 1987, pp. 450–68. [G: U.S.]
Emminger, Otmar. Thirty Years of the Deutsch-

mark. *Ciocca, P., ed.*, 1987, *1978*, pp. 127–46. **[G: W. Germany]**

Esfahani, Hadi Salehi. The Resurgence of Inflation in Latin America: Discussion. *World Devel.*, August 1987, *15*(8), pp. 1141–43. **[G: S. America; Peru; Chile]**

Fallon, John and Thompson, Lynne. An Analysis of the Effects of Recent Changes in the Exchange Rate and the Terms of Trade on the Level and Composition of Economic Activity. *Australian Econ. Rev.*, Second Quarter 1987, (78), pp. 24–36. **[G: Australia]**

Feldstein, Martin S. and Bacchetta, Philippe. How Far Has the Dollar Fallen? *Bus. Econ.*, October 1987, *22*(4), pp. 35–39. **[G: U.S.]**

Fender, John. Monetary and Exchange Rate Policies in an Open Macroeconomic Model with Unemployment and Rational Expectations. *Sinclair, P. J. N., ed.*, 1987, *1986*, pp. 328–42.

Fernandes, Abel L. Costa. Testing the Validity of the PPP Theory in the Case of the Portuguese Escudo/French Franc Rate. *Economia (Portugal)*, January 1987, *11*(1), pp. 3–13. **[G: Portugal; France]**

Filc, Wolfgang. Bestandsorientierte Wechselkurstheorien und Wirtschaftspolitik. (Asset Market-Oriented Exchange Rate Theories and Economic Policy. With English summary.) *Kredit Kapital*, 1987, *20*(1), pp. 48–72.

Flood, Robert P. Are Exchange Rates Excessively Variable? Comment. *Fischer, S., ed.*, 1987, pp. 153–57.

Flood, Robert P. Speculation and the Volatility of Foreign Currency Exchange Rates: Comments. *Carnegie–Rochester Conf. Ser. Public Policy*, Spring 1987, *26*, pp. 57–62.

Frankel, Allen B. and Marquardt, Jeffrey C. International Payments and EFT Links. *Solomon, E. H., ed.*, 1987, pp. 111–30.

Frankel, Jeffrey A. and Froot, Kenneth A. Short-term and Long-term Expectations of the Yen/Dollar Exchange Rate: Evidence from Survey Data. *J. Japanese Int. Economies*, September 1987, *1*(3), pp. 249–74. **[G: U.S.; Japan]**

Frankel, Jeffrey A. and Froot, Kenneth A. Using Survey Data to Test Standard Propositions Regarding Exchange Rate Expectations. *Amer. Econ. Rev.*, March 1987, *77*(1), pp. 133–53. **[G: U.S.; W. Europe; Japan]**

Frankel, Jeffrey A. and Meese, Richard. Are Exchange Rates Excessively Variable? *Fischer, S., ed.*, 1987, pp. 117–53.

Frankel, Jeffrey A. and Stock, James H. Regression vs. Volatility Tests of the Efficiency of Foreign Exchange Markets. *J. Int. Money Finance*, March 1987, *6*(1), pp. 49–56.

Fratianni, Michele; Hur, Hyung-Doh and Kang, Heejoon. Random Walk and Monetary Causality in Five Exchange Markets. *J. Int. Money Finance*, December 1987, *6*(4), pp. 505–14. **[G: U.S.]**

Frenkel, Jacob A. Is the European Economic Community an Optimal Currency Area? Discussion. *Levich, R. M. and Sommariva, A., eds.*, 1987, pp. 186–89. **[G: EEC]**

Frenkel, Jacob A. Optimal Currency Substitution Policy and Public Finance: Comments. *Razin, A. and Sadka, E., eds.*, 1987, pp. 165–69.

Fukao, Mitsuhiro. A Risk Premium Model of the Yen–Dollar and DM–Dollar Exchange Rates. *OECD Econ. Stud.*, Autumn 1987, (9), pp. 79–104. **[G: U.S.]**

von Furstenberg, George M. Internationally Managed Money Supply. *Aliber, R. Z., ed.*, 1987, pp. 117–26.

Garbers, Hermann. A Misspecification Analysis of the Relationship between Spot and Forward Exchange Rates. *Europ. Econ. Rev.*, October 1987, *31*(7), pp. 1407–17. **[G: U.S.; Switzerland]**

Garman, Mark B. Perpetual Currency Options. *Int. J. Forecasting*, 1987, *3*(1), pp. 179–84.

Gärtner, Manfred. Intervention Policy under Floating Exchange Rates: An Analysis of the Swiss Case. *Economica*, November 1987, *54*(216), pp. 439–53. **[G: Switzerland]**

Gärtner, Manfred. Normative und Politische Ökonomie flexibler Wechselkurse. (Normative and Political Economy of Flexible Exchange Rates. Wtih English summary.) *Aussenwirtschaft*, December 1987, *42*(4), pp. 471–89.

Gemmill, Robert F. The Anatomy of Financial Crises: Discussion. *Portes, R. and Swoboda, A. K., eds.*, 1987, pp. 58–61. **[G: Global]**

Genberg, Hans and Salemi, Michael K. The Effects of Foreign Shocks on Prices of Swiss Goods and Credit: An Analysis Based on VAR Methods. *Ann. Écon. Statist.*, Apr./Sept. 1987, (6/7), pp. 101–24. **[G: Switzerland]**

Genberg, Hans and Swoboda, Alexander K. Fixed Exchange Rates, Flexible Exchange Rates, or the Middle of the Road: A Re-examination of the Arguments in View of Recent Experience. *Aliber, R. Z., ed.*, 1987, pp. 92–113.

Gerlach, Stefan. Exchange Rates: A Review Essay. *J. Monet. Econ.*, January 1987, *19*(1), pp. 137–42.

Ghosh, Dilip K. Some Comments on the Economics of Exchange Rate. *Dutta, M., ed. (I)*, 1987, pp. 191–93. **[G: Japan; India]**

Ghoshal, Animesh. Floating Exchange Rates and U.S.—Canadian Trade. *Tremblay, R., ed.*, 1987, pp. 151–60. **[G: Canada; U.S.]**

Giavazzi, Francesco and Giovannini, Alberto. Exchange Rates and Prices in Europe. *Weltwirtsch. Arch.*, 1987, *123*(4), pp. 592–605. **[G: France; U.K.; W. Germany; Italy; Netherlands]**

Gidlow, R. M. Instability in the Rand–Dollar Market: Cause and Cures. *S. Afr. J. Econ.*, June 1987, *55*(2), pp. 136–49. **[G: S. Africa]**

Giovannetti, Giorgia. Testing Purchasing Power Parity as a Long Run Equilibrium Condition. *Giorn. Econ.*, Sept.-Oct. 1987, *46*(9–10), pp. 491–508. **[G: Selected MDCs]**

Giovannini, Alberto and Jorion, Philippe. Interest Rates and Risk Premia in the Stock Market and in the Foreign Exchange Market. *J. Int. Money Finance*, March 1987, *6*(1), pp. 107–23. **[G: U.S.; Selected OECD]**

Glassman, Debra A. Exchange Rate Risk and Transactions Costs: Evidence from Bid–Ask Spreads. *J. Int. Money Finance*, December 1987, 6(4), pp. 479–90. **[G: U.S.]**

Glassman, Debra A. The Efficiency of Foreign Exchange Futures Markets in Turbulent and Non-turbulent Periods. *J. Futures Markets*, June 1987, 7(3), pp. 245–67. **[G: U.K.; U.S.; Canada; W. Germany; Switzerland]**

Glismann, Hans H. The Political Economy of Re-valuation-Induced Protectionism under Discretionary Monetary Regimes with Flexible Exchange Rates: Comment. *Giersch, H., ed.*, 1987, pp. 425–28. **[G: U.S.]**

González-Vega, Claudio and Zinser, James E. Regulated and Nonregulated Financial and Foreign Exchange Markets and Income Inequality in the Dominican Republic. *Connolly, M. and González-Vega, C., eds.*, 1987, pp. 195–216. **[G: Dominican Republic]**

Goodfriend, Marvin. Exchange Rate Policy and the Dual Role of Exchange Rate Movements in International Adjustment. *Goodfriend, M., 1987, 1979*, pp. 92–102.

Goodhart, Charles A. E. Exchange Rate Economics 1986: A Comment. *Econ. J.*, March 1987, 97(385), pp. 19–22. **[G: U.S.]**

Gordon, Robert J. U.S. Fiscal Deficits and the World Imbalance of Payments. *Hitotsubashi J. Econ.*, October 1987, 27, pp. 7–41. **[G: U.S.]**

de Grauwe, Paul. Did the Exchange Rate Stability within the EMS Contribute to More Trade? *Visser, H. and Schoor, E., eds.*, 1987, pp. 237–48. **[G: EEC; U.S.]**

de Grauwe, Paul. International Trade and Economic Growth in the European Monetary System. *Europ. Econ. Rev.*, Feb./Mar. 1987, 31(1/2), pp. 389–98. **[G: W. Europe]**

de Grauwe, Paul and de Bellefroid, Bernard. Long-run Exchange Rate Variability and International Trade. *Arndt, S. W. and Richardson, J. D. eds.*, 1987, pp. 193–212.

de Grauwe, Paul and Rosiers, Marc. Real Exchange Rate Variability and Monetary Disturbances. *Weltwirtsch. Arch.*, 1987, 123(3), pp. 430–48. **[G: Global]**

de Grauwe, Paul and Rosiers, Marc. Real Exchange Rate Variability and Monetary Disturbances. *Chrystal, K. A. and Sedgwick, R., eds.*, 1987, pp. 30–53. **[G: Global]**

Greenwood, Jeremy and Kimbrough, Kent P. An Investigation in the Theory of Foreign Exchange Controls. *Can. J. Econ.*, May 1987, 20(2), pp. 271–88.

Greenwood, Jeremy and Kimbrough, Kent P. Foreign Exchange Controls in a Black Market Economy. *J. Devel. Econ.*, June 1987, 26(1), pp. 129–43.

Gregory, Allan W. Testing Interest Rate Parity and Rational Expectations for Canada and the United States. *Can. J. Econ.*, May 1987, 20(2), pp. 289–305. **[G: Canada; U.S.]**

Gregory, Allan W. and Sampson, Michael. Testing the Independence of Forecast Errors in the Forward Foreign Exchange Market Using

Markov Chains: A Cross-Country Comparison. *Int. J. Forecasting*, 1987, 3(1), pp. 97–113.

Guglielmotto, Enrica and Passatore, Giuseppe. The Private ECU Market: A Case of International Financial Innovation. *de Cecco, M., ed.*, 1987, pp. 260–319. **[G: W. Europe]**

Gylfason, Thorvaldur. Does Exchange Rate Really Matter? *Europ. Econ. Rev.*, Feb./Mar. 1987, 31(1/2), pp. 375–81.

Gyooten, Toyoo. Internationalization of the Yen: Its Implication for U.S.–Japan Relations. *Patrick, H. T. and Tachi, R., eds.*, 1987, pp. 84–89. **[G: U.S.; Japan]**

Haberler, Gottfried. The International Monetary System and Proposals for International Policy Coordination. *Cagan, P., ed.*, 1987, pp. 63–96. **[G: U.S.]**

Hall, S. G. A Forward Looking Model of the Exchange Rate. *J. Appl. Econometrics*, January 1987, 2(1), pp. 47–60. **[G: U.K.]**

Hall, S. G. An Empirical Model of the Exchange Rate Incorporating Rational Expectations. *Chrystal, K. A. and Sedgwick, R., eds.*, 1987, pp. 91–112.

Hamada, Koichi and Horiuchi, Akiyoshi. Monetary, Financial, and Real Effects of Yen Internationalization. *Arndt, S. W. and Richardson, J. D. eds.*, 1987, pp. 167–91. **[G: Japan]**

Hatton, T. J. The Outlines of a Keynesian Solution. *Glynn, S. and Booth, A., eds.*, 1987, pp. 82–94. **[G: U.K.]**

Heitger, Bernhard. Purchasing Power Parity under Flexible Exchange Rates—The Impact of Structural Change. *Weltwirtsch. Arch.*, 1987, 123(1), pp. 149–58. **[G: U.S.; W. Germany; Japan]**

Helleiner, Gerald K. The Impact of the Exchange Rate System on the Developing Countries. *Dell, S., ed., Pt. 2*, 1987, pp. 407–510. **[G: LDCs]**

Helpman, Elhanan and Razin, Assaf. Exchange Rate Management: Intertemporal Tradeoffs. *Amer. Econ. Rev.*, March 1987, 77(1), pp. 107–23. **[G: Argentina; Chile; Israel]**

Hepp, Stefan and McMahon, Patrick C. The Efficiency of the Forward Exchange Markets—A Reinterpretation with Sfr and DM Data. *Aussenwirtschaft*, September 1987, 42(2/3), pp. 347–67. **[G: W. Germany; Switzerland]**

Hercowitz, Zvi and Sadka, Efraim. On Optimal Currency Substitution Policy and Public Finance. *Razin, A. and Sadka, E., eds.*, 1987, pp. 147–64.

Heyndels, B. and Vuchelen, J. De valutasamenstelling van de Belgische Korte termijn buitenlandse schuld. (With English summary.) *Cah. Écon. Bruxelles*, Second Trimester 1987, (114), pp. 375–95. **[G: Belgium]**

Himarios, Daniel. Devaluation, Devaluation Expectations and Price Dynamics. *Economica*, August 1987, 54(215), pp. 299–313. **[G: Selected Countries]**

Hodgman, Donald R. and Resek, Robert W. Central Bank Exchange Rate Policy. *Hodgman, D. R. and Wood, G. E., eds.*, 1987, pp. 136–65. **[G: EEC]**

Hodrick, Robert J. and Srivastava, Sanjay. Foreign Currency Futures. *J. Int. Econ.*, February 1987, *22*(1/2), pp. 1–24. **[G: U.S.]**

Hoffmeyer, Erik. The International Capital Market and the International Monetary System. *Ciocca, P., ed.*, 1987, *1978*, pp. 245–61. **[G: Denmark]**

Holzman, Franklyn D. CMEA's Hard Currency Deficits and Rouble Convertibility. *Holzman, F. D.*, 1987, *1978*, pp. 145–67. **[G: CMEA]**

Hooper, Peter. The Persistence of the U.S. Trade Deficit: Comments. *Brookings Pap. Econ. Act.*, 1987, (1), pp. 47–51. **[G: U.S.]**

Howitt, Peter. Disinflation and Exchange Rate Stabilization: Canada, 1980–1985. *J. Policy Modeling*, Winter 1987, *9*(4), pp. 637–59. **[G: Canada]**

Hsu, John C. Hong Kong Exchange Rate System and the Money Supply. *Hong Kong Econ. Pap.*, 1987, (18), pp. 43–52. **[G: Hong Kong]**

Huang, Roger D. Expectations of Exchange Rates and Differential Inflation Rates: Further Evidence on Purchasing Power Parity in Efficient Markets. *J. Finance*, March 1987, *42*(1), pp. 69–79. **[G: OECD]**

Huizinga, John. An Empirical Investigation of the Long-run Behavior of Real Exchange Rates. *Carnegie–Rochester Conf. Ser. Public Policy*, Autumn 1987, *27*, pp. 149–214. **[G: OECD]**

Huizinga, John. An Empirical Investigation of the Long-run Behavior of Real Exchange Rates: Reply. *Carnegie–Rochester Conf. Ser. Public Policy*, Autumn 1987, *27*, pp. 225–31. **[G: OECD]**

Hull, John C. and White, Alan D. Hedging the Risks from Writing Foreign Currency Options. *J. Int. Money Finance*, June 1987, *6*(2), pp. 131–52. **[G: U.S.]**

Hutchison, Michael M. and Pigott, Charles A. Real and Financial Linkages in the Macroeconomic Response to Budget Deficits: An Empirical Investigation. *Arndt, S. W. and Richardson, J. D. eds.*, 1987, pp. 139–66. **[G: U.S.; W. Germany; Japan; U.K.]**

Isard, Peter. Lessons from Empirical Models of Exchange Rates. *Int. Monet. Fund Staff Pap.*, March 1987, *34*(1), pp. 1–28. **[G: W. Europe; U.S.; Japan]**

Ishiyama, Yoshihide. The Yen–Dollar Exchange Rate: Test of a Simple General Model. *Econ. Stud. Quart.*, March 1987, *38*(1), pp. 33–45. **[G: Japan; U.S.]**

Ito, Takatoshi. The Intradaily Exchange Rate Dynamics and Monetary Policies after the Group of Five Agreement. *J. Japanese Int. Economies*, September 1987, *1*(3), pp. 275–98. **[G: Japan]**

Ito, Takatoshi and Roley, V. Vance. News from the U.S. and Japan: Which Moves the Yen/Dollar Exchange Rate? *J. Monet. Econ.*, March 1987, *19*(2), pp. 255–77. **[G: U.S.; Japan]**

Ize, Alain and Ortiz, Guillermo. Fiscal Rigidities, Public Debt, and Capital Flight. *Int. Monet. Fund Staff Pap.*, June 1987, *34*(2), pp. 311–32. **[G: Mexico]**

Jager, Henk and de Jong, Eelke. The Exchange-Rate Mechanism of the EMS and the ECU as a Reserve Asset: An Impending Incompatibility. *Europ. Econ. Rev.*, July 1987, *31*(5), pp. 1071–91. **[G: EEC]**

Jager, Henk and de Jong, Eelke. The Viability of the ECU. *Visser, H. and Schoor, E., eds.*, 1987, pp. 249–62. **[G: EEC]**

Johnson, Manuel H., Jr. and Loopesko, Bonnie E. The Yen–Dollar Relationship: A Recent Historical Perspective. *Patrick, H. T. and Tachi, R., eds.*, 1987, pp. 95–116. **[G: U.S.; Japan]**

Johnson, Omotunde E. G. Currency Depreciation and Export Expansion. *Finance Develop.*, March 1987, *24*(1), pp. 23–26.

Johnson, Omotunde E. G. Currency Depreciation and Imports. *Finance Develop.*, June 1987, *24*(2), pp. 18–21.

Kaempfer, William H. and Willett, Thomas D. Why an Import Surcharge Wouldn't Help America's Trade Deficit. *World Econ.*, March 1987, *10*(1), pp. 27–38. **[G: U.S.]**

Kaldor, Nicholas. The Role of Devaluation in the Adjustment of Balance-of-Payments Deficits. *Dell, S., ed., Pt. 2*, 1987, pp. 557–67.

Karakitsos, Elias. Exchange Rate Dynamics and the Labour Market. *Chrystal, K. A. and Sedgwick, R., eds.*, 1987, pp. 164–98.

Kawaller, Ira G. Management of Foreign-Exchange–Rate Risk. *Kaushik, S. K., ed.*, 1987, pp. 97–105.

Kenen, Peter B. Exchange Rate Management: What Role for Intervention? *Amer. Econ. Rev.*, May 1987, *77*(2), pp. 194–99. **[G: U.S.]**

Kenen, Peter B. Global Policy Optimization and the Exchange-Rate Regime. *J. Policy Modeling*, Spring 1987, *9*(1), pp. 19–63. **[G: Global]**

Kenen, Peter B. What Role for IMF Surveillance? *World Devel.*, December 1987, *15*(12), pp. 1445–56.

Kercheval, Michael P. Another Look at the Dollar's Trade-Weighted Value. *Bus. Econ.*, April 1987, *22*(2), pp. 43–47. **[G: U.S.]**

Khatkhate, Deena R. International Monetary System—Which Way? Editor's Perspective. *World Devel.*, December 1987, *15*(12), pp. vii–xvi. **[G: Global]**

Kleiman, Ephraim. The Resurgence of Inflation in Latin America: Discussion. *World Devel.*, August 1987, *15*(8), pp. 1143–45. **[G: Peru]**

Klein, Lawrence R. The Choice among Alternative Exchange-Rate Regimes. *J. Policy Modeling*, Spring 1987, *9*(1), pp. 7–18. **[G: Global]**

Klein, Martin. Real Exchange Rate Fluctuations in a Small Open Economy under Fixed and Flexible Exchange Rates. *Z. Wirtschaft. Sozialwissen.*, 1987, *107*(1), pp. 51–66.

Koedijk, Kees G. and Ott, Mack. Risk Aversion, Efficient Markets and the Forward Exchange Rate. *Fed. Res. Bank St. Louis Rev.*, December 1987, *69*(10), pp. 5–13. **[G: U.S.]**

Kohers, Theodor and Simpson, W. Gary. A Comparison of the Forecasting Accuracy of the Futures and Forward Markets for Foreign Exchange. *Appl. Econ.*, July 1987, *19*(7), pp. 961–67. **[G: OECD]**

Kohli, Ulrich. A Simple Structural Model of the Swiss Franc–U.S. Dollar Exchange Rate. *Appl. Econ.*, March 1987, *19*(3), pp. 381–92. [G: Switzerland; U.S.]

Kolodko, Grzegorz W. International Transmission of Inflation: Its Economics and Its Politics. *World Devel.*, August 1987, *15*(8), pp. 1131–38. [G: Global]

Komiya, Ryutaro. Recent Developments in the Yen–Dollar Exchange-Rate Relationship. *Patrick, H. T. and Tachi, R., eds.*, 1987, pp. 90–94. [G: U.S.; Japan]

Korkman, Sixten. Devaluation Policy and Employment. *Siven, C.-H., ed.*, 1987, pp. 195–200.

Koromzay, Val; Llewellyn, John and Potter, Stephen. The Rise and Fall of the Dollar: Some Explanations, Consequences and Lessons. *Econ. J.*, March 1987, *97*(385), pp. 23–43. [G: U.S.]

Kravis, Irving B. and Lipsey, Robert E. The Assessment of National Price Levels. *Arndt, S. W. and Richardson, J. D. eds.*, 1987, pp. 97–134. [G: Selected Countries]

Kregel, Jan A. I tassi di cambio tra teoria e practica. (Exchange Rates between Theory and Practice. With English summary.) *Econ. Polít.*, December 1987, *4*(3), pp. 337–42.

Kreinin, Mordechai E.; Martin, Stephen and Sheehey, Edmund J. Differential Response of U.S. Import Prices and Quantities to Exchange-Rate Adjustments. *Weltwirtsch. Arch.*, 1987, *123*(3), pp. 449–62. [G: U.S.]

Krugman, Paul R. Pricing to Market When the Exchange Rate Changes. *Arndt, S. W. and Richardson, J. D. eds.*, 1987, pp. 49–70. [G: U.S.]

Krugman, Paul R. and Baldwin, Richard E. The Persistence of the U.S. Trade Deficit. *Brookings Pap. Econ. Act.*, 1987, (1), pp. 1–43. [G: U.S.]

Kudlow, Lawrence A. Loose Money and the Dollar's Crash. *Challenge*, Mar./Apr. 1987, *30*(1), pp. 52–55. [G: U.S.]

Kumcu, M. Ercan. The Trade Liberalization and Exchange Rate Determination in a Small Open Economy. *METU*, 1987, *14*(3), pp. 205–13.

de La Bruslerie, Hubert. Le statut theorique de la prime de risque dans la structure a terme des taux. (The Theoretical Status of the Risk Premium in the Term Structure of Rates. With English summary.) *Écon. Soc.*, December 1987, *21*(12), pp. 5–42.

Laidler, David. Wicksell and Fisher on the "Backing" of Money and the Quantity Theory: A Comment on the Debate between Bruce Smith and Ronald Michener. *Carnegie–Rochester Conf. Ser. Public Policy*, Autumn 1987, *27*, pp. 325–34. [G: U.S.]

Lamfalussy, Alexandre. Current-Account Imbalances in the Industrial World: Why They Matter. *[Wallich, H. C.]*, 1987, pp. 31–37.

Lamfalussy, Alexandre. International Financial Integration: Policy Implications. *Steinherr, A. and Weiserbs, D., eds.*, 1987, pp. 99–117.

Le Fort V., Guillermo R. and Ross K., Cristián. La Devaluación Esperada. Una Aproximación Bayesiana: Chile 1974–1984. (With English summary.) *Cuadernos Econ.*, April 1987, *24*(71), pp. 45–76. [G: Chile]

Lee, Adrian F. International Asset and Currency Allocation. *J. Portfol. Manage.*, Fall 1987, *14*(1), pp. 68–73. [G: U.S.]

Leroux, François. Currency Baskets: Can the SDR Match the ECU's Success? *Tremblay, R., ed.*, 1987, pp. 161–71.

Leventakis, John A. Exchange Rate Models: Do They Work? *Weltwirtsch. Arch.*, 1987, *123*(2), pp. 363–76. [G: U.S.; W. Germany]

Levin, Jay H. The Simultaneous Determination of Spot and Forward Exchange Rates: An Asset Market Approach. *Kredit Kapital*, 1987, *20*(4), pp. 467–85.

Levy, Mickey D. Corporate Profits and the U.S. Dollar Exchange Rate. *Bus. Econ.*, January 1987, *22*(1), pp. 31–36. [G: U.S.]

Lippens, Robert E. Multimaturity Efficient Market Hypotheses: Sorting Out Rejections in International Interest and Exchange Rate Markets. *Int. J. Forecasting*, 1987, *3*(1), pp. 149–58. [G: U.S.]

Lizondo, José Saúl. Exchange Rate Differential and Balance of Payments under Dual Exchange Markets. *J. Devel. Econ.*, June 1987, *26*(1), pp. 37–53.

Lizondo, José Saúl. Unification of Dual Exchange Markets. *J. Int. Econ.*, February 1987, *22*(1/2), pp. 57–77.

Loef, Hans-Edi. Reale Wechselkurse und realer zyklischer Output. Theoretisches Modell und empirische Analyse für die Bundesrepublik Deutschland. (Real Exchange Rates and Real Cyclical Output. With English summary.) *Kredit Kapital*, 1987, *20*(1), pp. 22–47. [G: W. Germany]

Logan, Kevin. The Evolution of the ECU Market: A Private Sector View: Discussion. *Levich, R. M. and Sommariva, A., eds.*, 1987, pp. 29–32. [G: EEC]

Lomax, David F. The Evolution of the ECU Market: A Private Sector View. *Levich, R. M. and Sommariva, A., eds.*, 1987, pp. 9–28. [G: EEC]

Lothian, James R. The Behavior of Real Exchange Rates. *Int. J. Forecasting*, 1987, *3*(1), pp. 17–42. [G: U.S.]

Lowe, Philip W. and Trevor, Robert G. The Performance of Exchange Rate Forecasts. *Australian Econ. Rev.*, Fourth Quarter 1987, (80), pp. 31–44. [G: Australia]

MacDonald, Ronald and Ta, Guy. The Singapore Dollar: Tests of the Efficient Markets Hypothesis and the Role of 'News.' *Appl. Econ.*, May 1987, *19*(5), pp. 569–79. [G: Singapore]

de Macedo, Jorge Braga. Currency Inconvertibility, Trade Taxes and Smuggling. *J. Devel. Econ.*, October 1987, *27*(1–2), pp. 109–25.

de Macedo, Jorge Braga. Currency Inconvertibility, Trade Taxes and Smuggling. *[Diaz-Alejandro, C. F.]*, 1987, pp. 109–25.

Maennig, Wolfgang G. Ch. and Tease, Warren J. Covered Interest Parity in Non-dollar Euro-markets. *Weltwirtsch. Arch.*, 1987, *123*(4), pp. 606–17. **[G: U.S.; Italy; W. Germany; France]**

Maila, Michel G. Diversifiable Exchange Risk under Floating Exchange Rates: Does the Paris Accord Really Matter? *[Marjolin, R.]*, 1987, pp. 21–33.

Marcuzzo, Maria Cristina and Rosselli, Annalisa. Profitability in the International Gold Market in the Early History of the Gold Standard. *Economica*, August 1987, *54*(215), pp. 367–80. **[G: U.K.]**

Marquez, Jaime R. Money Demand in Open Economies: A Currency Substitution Model for Venezuela. *J. Int. Money Finance*, June 1987, *6*(2), pp. 167–78. **[G: Venezuela]**

Marris, Stephen. Growth Gaps, Exchange Rates and Asymmetry: Comments. *Patrick, H. T. and Tachi, R., eds.*, 1987, pp. 30–36. **[G: Japan; U.S.]**

Marston, Richard C. Japanese–U.S. Current Accounts and Exchange Rates before and after the G5 Agreement: Discussion. *Sato, R. and Wachtel, P., eds.*, 1987, pp. 152–56. **[G: Japan; U.S.]**

Marston, Richard C. Real Exchange Rates and Productivity Growth in the United States and Japan. *Arndt, S. W. and Richardson, J. D. eds.*, 1987, pp. 71–96. **[G: U.S.; Japan]**

Marwah, Kanta. On Managing the Exchange Rate of the Indian Rupee: Modeling Post–Bretton Woods Experience. *Dutta, M., ed. (I)*, 1987, pp. 171–90. **[G: India]**

Marwah, Kanta. On Managing the Exchange Rate of the Indian Rupee: Modelling Post-Bretton Woods Experience. *J. Quant. Econ.*, January 1987, *3*(1), pp. 137–63. **[G: India]**

Masera, Rainer S. An Increasing Role for the ECU: A Character in Search of a Script. *Levich, R. M. and Sommariva, A., eds.*, 1987, pp. 33–67. **[G: EEC]**

Mayes, David G. The Role of Exchange Rate and Other Pricing Policies in the Adjustment Process: Comment. *Holmes, F., ed.*, 1987, pp. 210–16. **[G: New Zealand]**

McCulloch, Rachel. Unexpected Real Consequences of Floating Exchange Rates. *Aliber, R. Z., ed.*, 1987, pp. 21–45.

McCurdy, Thomas H. and Morgan, Ieuan G. Tests of the Martingale Hypothesis for Foreign Currency Futures with Time-Varying Volatility. *Int. J. Forecasting*, 1987, *3*(1), pp. 131–48.

McFarland, James W.; Pettit, R. Richardson and Sung, Sam K. The Distribution of Foreign Exchange Price Changes: Trading Day Effects and Risk Measurement—A Reply. *J. Finance*, March 1987, *42*(1), pp. 189–94. **[G: U.S.]**

McKenzie, George W. and Thomas, Steven H. Dominant Factors in Dollar–Sterling Exchange Rates Movements, 1965–1981. *Chrystal, K. A. and Sedgwick, R., eds.*, 1987, pp. 113–36. **[G: U.S.; U.K.]**

McKinnon, R. J. Exchange Stability, International Monetary Coordination, and the U.S. Federal Reserve System. *Visser, H. and*

Schoor, E., eds., 1987, pp. 139–67. **[G: U.S.; Global]**

McKinnon, Ronald I. Objectives for International Negotiations to Harmonize Monetary, Trade, and Exchange Rate Policies. *Kaushik, S. K., ed.*, 1987, pp. 83–90.

McKinnon, Ronald I. Protectionism and the Misaligned Dollar: The Case for Monetary Coordination. *Salvatore, D., ed.*, 1987, pp. 367–88. **[G: Global]**

Meltzer, Allan H. Properties of Monetary Systems. *Res, Z. and Motamen, S., eds.*, 1987, pp. 83–104. **[G: U.S.]**

Mendelsohn, M. S. World Trade and International Finance: Lessons from the Past. *Visser, H. and Schoor, E., eds.*, 1987, pp. 57–64. **[G: Global]**

Michener, Ronald. Fixed Exchange Rates and the Quantity Theory in Colonial America. *Carnegie–Rochester Conf. Ser. Public Policy*, Autumn 1987, *27*, pp. 233–307. **[G: U.S.]**

Milhøj, Anders. A Conditional Variance Model for Daily Deviations of an Exchange Rate. *J. Bus. Econ. Statist.*, January 1987, *5*(1), pp. 99–103. **[G: U.S.]**

Minford, Patrick. Are Exchange Rates Excessively Variable? Comment. *Fischer, S., ed.*, 1987, pp. 157–60.

Mirus, Rolf and Yeung, Bernard. The Relevance of the Invoicing Currency in Intra-firm Trade Transactions. *J. Int. Money Finance*, December 1987, *6*(4), pp. 449–64. **[G: Canada]**

Mishkin, Frederic S. The Dollar and Real Interest Rates: A Comment. *Carnegie–Rochester Conf. Ser. Public Policy*, Autumn 1987, *27*, pp. 141–48. **[G: U.S.]**

Mocan, Naci H. Marshall–Lerner Condition, Expected Market Change and Exchange Rate Determination. *Atlantic Econ. J.*, March 1987, *15*(1), pp. 121.

Mojžišková, Soňa. Foreign Exchange Regulations in the Socialist Countries. *Soviet E. Europ. Foreign Trade*, Winter 1987-1988, *23*(4), pp. 22–66. **[G: CMEA]**

Mussa, Michael. Average Protection and Economic Policy. *Salvatore, D., ed.*, 1987, pp. 389–407. **[G: U.S.]**

Nascimento, Jean-Claude. The Choice of an Optimum Exchange Currency Regime for a Small Economy: An Econometric Analysis. *J. Devel. Econ.*, February 1987, *25*(1), pp. 149–65. **[G: W. Africa]**

Nickelsburg, Gerald. Inflation, Expectations and Qualitative Government Policy in Ecuador, 1970–82. *World Devel.*, August 1987, *15*(8), pp. 1077–85. **[G: Ecuador]**

Niehans, Jürg. Monetary Policy in an Open Economy. *de Cecco, M. and Fitoussi, J.-P., eds.*, 1987, pp. 243–68.

Nwanna, Gladson I. Devaluation, Unanticipated Inflation and Output Growth: A Comparative Aggregate Analysis. *Econ. Int.*, November 1987, *40*(4), pp. 329–44. **[G: LDCs]**

Nyhus, Douglas. Exchange Rates: How They Effect Prices and Quantities in the INFORUM-ERI International System of Macroeconomic

Input–Output Models. *Tchijov, I. and Tomasz-ewicz, L., eds.*, 1987, pp. 107–12. [G: U.S.; Canada; Japan; W. Europe]

O'Mara, L. P.; Wallace, N. A. and Meshios, H. The Current Account, Monetary Policy, Market Sentiment and the Real Exchange Rate: Some Implications for the Farm Sector. *Australian J. Agr. Econ.*, December 1987, *31*(3), pp. 219–41. [G: Australia]

Ogawa, Kazuo. Some Evidence on the Structure of the Forward Exchange Markets. *Econ. Stud. Quart.*, March 1987, *38*(1), pp. 15–32. [G: Japan; U.S.]

Ogden, Joseph P. and Tucker, Alan L. Empirical Tests of the Efficiency of the Currency Futures Options Market. *J. Futures Markets*, December 1987, *7*(6), pp. 695–703. [G: U.S.]

Ohr, Renate. Notenbankinterventionen und Effizienz der Devisenmärkte. Überlegungen zur Dollarkursentwicklung. (Intervention Policy and the Efficiency of Foreign Exchange Markets Reflections to the Fluctuating Dollar. With English summary.) *Kredit Kapital*, 1987, *20*(2), pp. 200–214. [G: W. Germany; U.S.]

Ott, Mack. The Dollar's Effective Exchange Rate: Assessing the Impact of Alternative Weighting Schemes. *Fed. Res. Bank St. Louis Rev.*, February 1987, *69*(2), pp. 5–14. [G: U.S.]

Palmer, David W. Exchange-Rate Movements: A Practitioner's View. *Kaushik, S. K., ed.*, 1987, pp. 91–95.

Park, Hun Y.; Lee, Angela and Lee, Hei W. Cross-Hedging Performance of the U.S. Currency Futures Market: The European Monetary System Currencies. *Fabozzi, F. J., ed.*, 1987, pp. 223–42. [G: U.S.]

Park, Won-Am. Crawling Peg, Inflation Hedges, and Exchange Rate Dynamics. *J. Int. Econ.*, August 1987, *23*(1/2), pp. 131–50. [G: Argentina]

Patrick, Hugh T. Japan and the United States Today: Exchange Rates, Macroeconomic Policies, and Financial Market Innovations: Concluding Comments. *Patrick, H. T. and Tachi, R., eds.*, 1987, pp. 209–13. [G: Japan; U.S.]

Pauls, B. Dianne. Measuring the Foreign-Exchange Value of the Dollar. *Fed. Res. Bull.*, June 1987, *73*(6), pp. 411–22. [G: U.S.]

Peel, David A. and Pope, P. F. On Testing the Relationship between Exchange Rate Movements and Monetary Surprises: A Comment. *Manchester Sch. Econ. Soc. Stud.*, June 1987, *55*(2), pp. 197–202. [G: U.S.; U.K.]

Rieffel, Alexis. Exchange Controls: A Dead-end for Advanced Developing Countries? *[Marjolin, R.]*, 1987, pp. 1–19.

Roley, V. Vance. U.S. Money Announcements and Covered Interest Parity: The Case of Japan. *J. Int. Money Finance*, March 1987, *6*(1), pp. 57–70. [G: Japan; U.S.]

Rybczynski, Tad M. The Anatomy of Financial Crises: Discussion. *Portes, R. and Swoboda, A. K., eds.*, 1987, pp. 61–66. [G: Global]

Salvatore, Dominick. Import Penetration, Exchange Rates, and Protectionism in the United States. *J. Policy Modeling*, Spring 1987, *9*(1), pp. 125–41. [G: U.S.]

Salvatore, Dominick. The New Protectionist Threat to World Welfare: Introduction. *Salvatore, D., ed.*, 1987, pp. 1–27. [G: Global]

Samuelson, Paul A. The U.S. and Japanese Economies in the Remaining Reagan Years. *Sato, R. and Wachtel, P., eds.*, 1987, pp. 89–99. [G: U.S.; Japan]

Sarantis, Nicholas. A Dynamic Asset Market Model for the Exchange Rate of the Pound Sterling. *Weltwirtsch. Arch.*, 1987, *123*(1), pp. 24–38. [G: Selected OECD]

Sarcinelli, Mario. Financial Assets, Public Debt and Monetary Policy: An International Integration Perspective. *Banca Naz. Lavoro Quart. Rev.*, September 1987, (162), pp. 263–372. [G: Italy]

Sarcinelli, Mario. Towards Financial Integration in a European and International Context: Exchange Liberalization in Italy. *Rev. Econ. Cond. Italy*, May-August 1987, (2), pp. 125–46. [G: Italy]

Sato, Kazuo and Lii, Sheng-Yann. The Exchange Rate, Trade Balance, and Capital Flows: The Case of Japan. *Dutta, M., ed. (I)*, 1987, pp. 145–70. [G: Japan]

Sawyer, W. Charles and Sprinkle, Richard L. Contractionary Effects of Devaluation in Mexico. *Soc. Sci. Quart.*, December 1987, *68*(4), pp. 885–93. [G: Mexico]

Schwartz, Anna J. Alternative Monetary Regimes: The Gold Standard. *Schwartz, A. J.*, 1987, *1986*, pp. 364–90. [G: U.S.; U.K.; W. Germany; France]

Schwartz, Anna J. Lessons of the Gold Standard Era and the Bretton Woods System for the Prospects of an International Monetary System Constitution. *Schwartz, A. J.*, 1987, *1986*, pp. 391–406.

Schwartz, Anna J. The Postwar Institutional Evolution of the International Monetary System. *Schwartz, A. J.*, 1987, *1983*, pp. 333–63. [G: OECD]

Shastri, Kuldeep and Tandon, Kishore. Valuation of American Options on Foreign Currency. *J. Banking Finance*, June 1987, *11*(2), pp. 245–69. [G: U.S.]

Shastri, Kuldeep and Wethyavivorn, Kulpatra. The Valuation of Currency Options for Alternate Stochastic Processes. *J. Finan. Res.*, Winter 1987, *10*(4), pp. 283–93. [G: U.S.; W. Europe; Canada; Japan]

Singleton, Kenneth J. Speculation and the Volatility of Foreign Currency Exchange Rates. *Carnegie–Rochester Conf. Ser. Public Policy*, Spring 1987, *26*, pp. 9–56.

Smith, Peter N. Current Account Movements, Wealth Effects and the Determination of the Real Exchange Rate. *Manchester Sch. Econ. Soc. Stud.*, December 1987, *55*(4), pp. 353–77. [G: U.K.]

Snell, Andrew. The Cambridge Multisectoral Dynamic Model of the British Economy: Sterling Exchange Rate. *Barker, T. and Peterson, W., eds.*, 1987, pp. 433–54. [G: U.K.]

So, Jacky C. The Distribution of Foreign Exchange Price Changes: Trading Day Effects and Risk Measurement—A Comment. *J. Finance*, March 1987, *42*(1), pp. 181–88.   [G: U.S.]

So, Jacky C. The Sub-Gaussian Distribution of Currency Futures: Stable Peretian or Nonstationary? *Rev. Econ. Statist.*, February 1987, *69*(1), pp. 100–107.   [G: Japan; Canada; W. Germany; U.K.; Switzerland]

Sobhan, Rehman and Ahsan, Ahmad. The Effect of Exchange Rate Depreciation on the Loan Repayment Performance of Private Enterprise in Bangladesh. *Bangladesh Devel. Stud.*, December 1987, *15*(4), pp. 1–52.   [G: Bangladesh]

Solnik, Bruno. Using Financial Prices to Test Exchange Rate Models: A Note. *J. Finance*, March 1987, *42*(1), pp. 141–49.   [G: OECD]

Sommariva, Andrea. An Increasing Role for the ECU: A Character in Search of a Script: Discussion. *Levich, R. M. and Sommariva, A., eds.*, 1987, pp. 68–70.   [G: EEC]

Sommariva, Andrea and Tullio, Giuseppe. A Note on the Real Exchange Rate, Differential Productivity Growth and Protectionism in Gold Standard Germany, 1878–1913. *Weltwirtsch. Arch.*, 1987, *123*(2), pp. 354–62.   [G: W. Germany]

Son, Iltae. The Choice of an Optimal Exchange Rate System for a Small Country under the Three Good and Three Country Model. *Int. Econ. J.*, Summer 1987, *1*(2), pp. 25–45.   [G: S. Korea]

Sondermann, Dieter. Currency Options: Hedging and Social Value. *Europ. Econ. Rev.*, Feb./Mar. 1987, *31*(1/2), pp. 246–56.

Špaček, Petr. Exchange Rates and the Effectiveness of Foreign Tourist Traffic in CMEA Member-Countries. *Soviet E. Europ. Foreign Trade*, Winter 1987-1988, *23*(4), pp. 67–93.   [G: CMEA]

Stadermann, Hans-Joachim. Der unaufhaltsame Abstieg eines Leitwährungslandes. (The Unstoppable Decline of a Reserve-Currency Country. With English summary.) *Kredit Kapital*, 1987, *20*(2), pp. 215–35.   [G: U.S.]

Stockman, Alan C. Economic Theory and Exchange Rate Forecasts. *Int. J. Forecasting*, 1987, *3*(1), pp. 3–15.

Stockman, Alan C. Exchange Rate Systems and Relative Prices. *J. Policy Modeling*, Spring 1987, *9*(1), pp. 245–56.

Stockman, Alan C. The Equilibrium Approach to Exchange Rates. *Fed. Res. Bank Richmond Econ. Rev.*, Mar./Apr. 1987, *73*(2), pp. 12–30.   [G: OECD]

Stulz, René M. An Equilibrium Model of Exchange Rate Determination and Asset Pricing with Nontraded Goods and Imperfect Information. *J. Polit. Econ.*, October 1987, *95*(5), pp. 1024–40.

Stulz, René M. Time-Varying Risk Premia, Imperfect Information and the Forward Exchange Rate. *Int. J. Forecasting*, 1987, *3*(1), pp. 171–77.

Swanson, Peggy E. A Preliminary Assessment of the Impact of Floating Exchange Rates on International and Vehicle Currency Uses of U.S. Dollars. *Quart. J. Bus. Econ.*, Spring 1987, *26*(2), pp. 3–21.   [G: U.S.]

Swanson, Peggy E. Capital Market Integration over the Past Decade: The Case of the U.S. Dollar. *J. Int. Money Finance*, June 1987, *6*(2), pp. 215–25.   [G: U.S.]

Swanson, Peggy E. The International Role of the U.S. Dollar under Fixed versus Flexible Exchange Rates. *Amer. Econ.*, Spring 1987, *31*(1), pp. 48–55.   [G: U.S.]

Takagi, Shinji. Testing the Multilateral Version of Purchasing Power Parity: An Application to Burma and Jordan under the SDR Peg, 1981–5. *Appl. Econ.*, March 1987, *19*(3), pp. 367–80.   [G: Burma; Jordan]

Tandon, Kishore and Urich, Thomas. International Market Response to Announcements of U.S. Macroeconomic Data. *J. Int. Money Finance*, March 1987, *6*(1), pp. 71–83.   [G: U.S.; Selected OECD]

Tatom, John A. Will a Weaker Dollar Mean a Stronger Economy? *J. Int. Money Finance*, December 1987, *6*(4), pp. 433–47.   [G: U.S.]

Tavlas, George S. Policy Aspects of Alternative Exchange-Rate Regimes: Introduction. *J. Policy Modeling*, Spring 1987, *9*(1), pp. 1–5.

Taylor, Mark P. Covered Interest Parity: A High-Frequency, High-Quality Data Study. *Economica*, November 1987, *54*(216), pp. 429–38.   [G: U.S.; U.K.; W. Germany]

Taylor, Mark P. Risk Premia and Foreign Exchange: A Multiple Time Series Approach to Testing Uncovered Interest-Rate Parity. *Weltwirtsch. Arch.*, 1987, *123*(4), pp. 579–91.   [G: W. Europe; U.S.; Japan]

Taylor, Mark P. The Role of Speculation in the Forward Exchange Market: Some Consistent Estimates Assuming Rational Expectations. *Oxford Bull. Econ. Statist.*, August 1987, *49*(3), pp. 323–33.   [G: U.S.; U.K.; France]

Taylor, Stephen J. Forecasting the Volatility of Currency Exchange Rates. *Int. J. Forecasting*, 1987, *3*(1), pp. 159–70.   [G: U.S.]

Thompson, Stanley R. and Bond, Gary E. Offshore Commodity Hedging under Floating Exchange Rates. *Amer. J. Agr. Econ.*, February 1987, *69*(1), pp. 46–55.   [G: U.S.; Australia]

Thursby, Jerry G. and Thursby, Marie C. Bilateral Trade Flows, the Linder Hypothesis, and Exchange Risk. *Rev. Econ. Statist.*, August 1987, *69*(3), pp. 488–95.   [G: OECD]

Thygesen, Niels. Is the European Economic Community an Optimal Currency Area? *Levich, R. M. and Sommariva, A., eds.*, 1987, pp. 163–85.   [G: EEC]

Tower, Edward and Pursell, Garry G. On Shadow Pricing Labour and Foreign Exchange. *Oxford Econ. Pap.*, June 1987, *39*(2), pp. 318–32.

Triffin, Robert. The Paper-Exchange Standard: 1971–19??. *[Wallich, H. C.]*, 1987, pp. 70–85.   [G: U.S.]

Triffin, Robert. W.M.S.: The World Monetary

System or Scandal? *Kaushik, S. K., ed.*, 1987, pp. 31–46.

Troberg, Pontus Henrik. Foreign Currency Translation: A Comparative Analysis of Approaches. *Most, Kenneth S., ed.*, 1987, pp. 317–56.

Tronzano, Marco. Purchasing Power Parity and Exchange-Rate Dynamics: An Empirical Investigation. *Econ. Notes*, 1987, (3), pp. 87–107. **[G: Italy]**

Tucker, Alan L. Foreign Exchange Option Prices as Predictors of Equilibrium Forward Exchange Rates. *J. Int. Money Finance*, September 1987, 6(3), pp. 283–94. **[G: U.S.]**

Tucker, Alan L. and Scott, Elton. A Study of Diffusion Processes for Foreign Exchange Rates. *J. Int. Money Finance*, December 1987, 6(4), pp. 465–78. **[G: U.S.]**

Ueda, Kazuo. Japanese–U.S. Current Accounts and Exchange Rates before and after the G5 Agreement. *Sato, R. and Wachtel, P., eds.*, 1987, pp. 127–47. **[G: Japan; U.S.]**

Ueda, Kazuo. Prospects for Japan's Current-Account Surplus. *Patrick, H. T. and Tachi, R., eds.*, 1987, pp. 54–57. **[G: Japan]**

Ulin, Robert P. The Search for a Dollar–Yen Parity. *Bus. Econ.*, July 1987, 22(3), pp. 25–27. **[G: U.S.; Japan]**

UNCTAD Secretariat. The Exchange-Rate System. *United Nations Conference on Trade and Development.*, 1987, pp. 77–123.

von Ungern-Sternberg, Thomas. Does the Swiss National Bank Stabilize the Swiss Franc Exchange Rates? *J. Bus. Econ. Statist.*, January 1987, 5(1), pp. 105–13. **[G: Switzerland]**

Ursprung, Heinrich W. On the Value of Free Foreign-Exchange Forecasts. *Managerial Dec. Econ.*, June 1987, 8(2), pp. 161–65. **[G: OECD]**

Válek, Vratislav. The Restructuring of Foreign Exchange Financial Relations: The Czechoslovak Approach. *Czech. Econ. Digest.*, October 1987, (7), pp. 33–47. **[G: Czechoslovakia; CMEA]**

Vlahos, George, et al. Empirical Tests of Parity-Based Option Pricing Models: The Case of Options on Japanese Yen Futures. *Rivista Int. Sci. Econ. Com.*, Nov.-Dec. 1987, 34(11–12), pp. 1123–38. **[G: U.S.]**

Volcker, Paul A. Statement to the U.S. Senate Subcommittee on International Finance and Monetary Policy, Committee on Banking, Housing, and Urban Affairs, April 7, 1987. *Fed. Res. Bull.*, June 1987, 73(6), pp. 425–30. **[G: U.S.]**

de Vries, Rimmer. International Imbalances and the Search for Exchange-Rate Stability. *Patrick, H. T. and Tachi, R., eds.*, 1987, pp. 117–20. **[G: U.S.; Japan; W. Germany]**

de Vries, Rimmer and Hargreaves, Derek. The Dollar's Decline and Trade: Mission Accomplished? *Challenge*, Jan./Feb. 1987, 29(6), pp. 37–46. **[G: Global]**

Wadhwani, Sushil B. Are Exchange Rates 'Excessively' Volatile? *J. Int. Econ.*, May 1987, 22(3/4), pp. 339–48. **[G: U.K.]**

Webster, Allan. Purchasing Power Parity as a Theory of International Arbitrage in Manufactured Goods: An Empirical View of UK/US Prices in the 1970s. *Appl. Econ.*, November 1987, 19(11), pp. 1433–56. **[G: U.K.; U.S.]**

Weil, Gordon. The "Pegging Practices" of LDC's: A Look at Recent Behavior. *Eastern Econ. J.*, Jan.-Mar. 1987, 13(1), pp. 49–53. **[G: LDCs]**

Weller, Paul and Yano, Makoto. Forward Exchange, Futures Trading, and Spot Price Variability: A General Equilibrium Approach. *Econometrica*, November 1987, 55(6), pp. 1433–50.

Werner, Frank-Bernhard and Cornelius, Peter. Zur Bedeutung von Zentralbankinterventionen auf Optionsmärkten. (On Central Bank Interventions in the Options Market. With English summary.) *Konjunkturpolitik*, 1987, 33(6), pp. 323–37. **[G: Europe]**

West, Kenneth D. A Standard Monetary Model and the Variability of the Deutschemark–Dollar Exchange Rate. *J. Int. Econ.*, August 1987, 23(1/2), pp. 57–76. **[G: U.S.]**

Wickham, Peter. The Role of Exchange Rate and Other Pricing Policies in the Adjustment Process. *Holmes, F., ed.*, 1987, pp. 192–209.

Wigmore, Barrie A. Was the Bank Holiday of 1933 Caused by a Run on the Dollar? *J. Econ. Hist.*, September 1987, 47(3), pp. 739–55. **[G: U.S.]**

Willett, Thomas D. Currency Substitution, U.S. Money Demand, and International Interdependence. *Contemp. Policy Issues*, July 1987, 5(3), pp. 76–82. **[G: U.S.]**

Williamson, John. A Survey of the Literature on the Optimal Peg. *Williamson, J.*, 1987, 1982, pp. 94–116.

Williamson, John. Bancor and the Developing Countries: How Much Difference Would It Have Made? *Thirlwall, A. P., ed.*, 1987, pp. 92–106.

Williamson, John. Exchange Rate Flexibility, Target Zones, and Policy Coordination. *World Devel.*, December 1987, 15(12), pp. 1437–43. **[G: OECD]**

Williamson, John. Exchange Rate Management: The Role of Target Zones. *Amer. Econ. Rev.*, May 1987, 77(2), pp. 200–204.

Williamson, John. The Crawling Peg in Historical Perspective. *Williamson, J.*, 1987, 1981, pp. 63–93. **[G: OECD; Selected LDCs]**

Williamson, John. The Theorists and the Real World. *Williamson, J.*, 1987, 1985, pp. 15–36.

Willms, Manfred. The DM/Dollar Rate and the Exchange Market Intervention Policy of the Deutsche Bundesbank 1974–1984. *Hodgman, D. R. and Wood, G. E., eds.*, 1987, pp. 193–219. **[G: U.S.; W. Germany]**

Wolff, Christian C. P. Forward Foreign Exchange Rates, Expected Spot Rates, and Premia: A Signal-Extraction Approach. *J. Finance*, June 1987, 42(2), pp. 395–406. **[G: U.S.; U.K.; Japan; W. Germany]**

Wolff, Christian C. P. Time-Varying Parameters and the Out-of-Sample Forecasting Performance of Structural Exchange Rate Models.

J. Bus. Econ. Statist., January 1987, 5(1), pp. 87–97. **[G: U.S.; U.K.; Japan]**

Woo, Wing Thye. Some Evidence of Speculative Bubbles in the Foreign Exchange Markets. *J. Money, Credit, Banking,* November 1987, 19(4), pp. 499–514. **[G: U.S.]**

Wood, Geoffrey E. Properties of Monetary Systems: Comment. *Res, Z. and Motamen, S., eds.,* 1987, pp. 105–11. **[G: U.S.]**

Woodward, R. S. Interest Rate Arbitrage Using the Forwards and Futures Markets, 1977–85. *Appl. Econ.,* October 1987, 19(10), pp. 1329–35. **[G: OECD]**

Wren-Lewis, Simon. Introducing Exchange-Rate Equations into a World Econometric Model. *Nat. Inst. Econ. Rev.,* February 1987, (119), pp. 57–69. **[G: OECD]**

Wren-Lewis, Simon and Eastwood, Fiona. The World Economy. *Nat. Inst. Econ. Rev.,* May 1987, (120), pp. 21–41. **[G: U.S.; Japan; W. Germany; Canada; France]**

Yoshitomi, Masaru. Growth Gaps, Exchange Rates and Asymmetry: Is it Possible to Unwind Current-Account Imbalances without Fiscal Expansion in Japan? *Patrick, H. T. and Tachi, R., eds.,* 1987, pp. 18–29. **[G: Japan; U.S.]**

Yuravlivker, David E. Political Shocks, International Reserves and the Real Exchange Rate—The Argentine Case. *J. Int. Money Finance,* December 1987, 6(4), pp. 401–17. **[G: Argentina]**

Zervoyianni, Athina. Currency Substitution, Flexible Exchange Rates and the International Transmission of Disturbances. *Chrystal, K. A. and Sedgwick, R., eds.,* 1987, pp. 199–228.

Zijlstra, Jelle. Central Banking with the Benefit of Hindsight. *Ciocca, P., ed.,* 1987, *1981,* pp. 167–83.

432 International Monetary Arrangements

4320 International Monetary Arrangements

Akyüz, Yilmaz and Dell, Sidney. Issues in International Monetary Reform. *United Nations Conference on Trade and Development.,* 1987, pp. 33–75. **[G: Global]**

Aliber, Robert Z. Gold in the International Monetary System: A Catalog of the Options. *Aliber, R. Z., ed.,* 1987, pp. 168–82. **[G: U.S.]**

Aliber, Robert Z. The Reconstruction of International Monetary Arrangements. *Aliber, R. Z., ed.,* 1987, pp. 1–4.

Allen, Polly Reynolds. Is the ECU an Optimal Currency Basket? Discussion. *Levich, R. M. and Sommariva, A., eds.,* 1987, pp. 210–13. **[G: EEC]**

Arriola, Salvador. Some Ideas on Financial and Monetary Co-operation among Developing Countries. *Dell, S., ed., Pt. 2,* 1987, pp. 639–64. **[G: LDCs]**

Artis, M. J. The European Monetary System: An Evaluation. *J. Policy Modeling,* Spring 1987, 9(1), pp. 175–98. **[G: EEC]**

Artus, Jacques R. Toward a More Orderly Exchange Rate System. *Aliber, R. Z., ed.,* 1987, pp. 46–69. **[G: U.S.; U.K.; Japan; W. Germany]**

Baeck, Louis. O desequilíbrio da economia internacional dos anos 80. (With English summary.) *Pesquisa Planejamento Econ.,* April 1987, 17(1), pp. 221–49. **[G: U.S.; Japan; W. Europe]**

Baffi, Paolo. The European Monetary System and Italian Participation. *Ciocca, P., ed.,* 1987, *1978,* pp. 263–76. **[G: EEC]**

Barve, Arvind. Financial and Monetary Aspects of Trade Promotion in the Context of Co-operation among Developing Countries, with Special Reference to Africa. *Dell, S., ed., Pt. 2,* 1987, pp. 611–38. **[G: Africa; LDCs]**

Basevi, Giorgio and Giavazzi, Francesco. Conflicts and Coordination in the European Monetary System. *Steinherr, A. and Weiserbs, D., eds.,* 1987, pp. 133–64. **[G: W. Europe]**

Begg, David K. H. and Wyplosz, Charles. Why the EMS? Dynamic Games and the Equilibrium Policy Regime. *Bryant, R. C. and Portes, R., eds.,* 1987, pp. 193–232. **[G: W. Europe]**

Bilson, John F. O. The ECU and the Choice of an Invoice Currency. *Levich, R. M. and Sommariva, A., eds.,* 1987, pp. 145–55. **[G: EEC]**

de Boissieu, Christian. L'ÉCU et la libéralisation financière en Europe. (With English summary.) *Revue Écon. Polit.,* July-Aug. 1987, 97(4), pp. 435–50. **[G: EEC]**

Boltho, Andrea. External Constraints on European Growth: Comment. *Lawrence, R. Z. and Schultze, C. L., eds.,* 1987, pp. 591–96. **[G: W. Europe]**

Branson, William H. Why the EMS? Dynamic Games and the Equilibrium Policy Regime: Discussion. *Bryant, R. C. and Portes, R., eds.,* 1987, pp. 233–35. **[G: W. Europe]**

Brillembourg, Arturo. The Inter-bank Market, Contagion Effects and International Financial Crises: Discussion. *Portes, R. and Swoboda, A. K., eds.,* 1987, pp. 232–34. **[G: Global]**

Bryant, Ralph C. Intergovernmental Coordination of Economic Policies: An Interim Stocktaking. *[Wallich, H. C.],* 1987, pp. 4–15.

Buira, Ariel. The Nature and Direction of International Monetary Reform. *Dell, S., ed., Pt. 3,* 1987, pp. 765–84.

Buira, Ariel. The Role of the IMF in the 1980s. *Dell, S., ed., Pt. 3,* 1987, pp. 713–21.

Cáceres Sandoval, Carlos. Garantía Oficial Implícita y Créditos Externos. (With English summary.) *Cuadernos Econ.,* August 1987, 24(72), pp. 127–42. **[G: LDCs]**

Caeser, Rolf. Internationaler Zinszusammenhang und deutsche Zinspolitik im Europäischen Währungssystem. (International Interdependence of Interest Rates and German Interest Rate Policy within the European Monetary System. With English summary.) *Konjunkturpolitik,* 1987, 33(1), pp. 47–70. **[G: EEC]**

Cagan, Phillip. A Compensated Dollar: Better or More Likely Than Gold? *Dorn, J. A. and*

Schwartz, A. J., eds., 1987, pp. 261–77.
[G: U.S.; U.K.]
Capie, Forrest H. and Wood, Geoffrey E. Policy Makers in Crisis: A Study of Two Devaluations. *Hodgman, D. R. and Wood, G. E., eds.*, 1987, pp. 166–92. **[G: U.K.]**
de Cecco, Marcello. Inflation and Structural Change in the Euro-dollar Market. *de Cecco, M. and Fitoussi, J.-P., eds.*, 1987, pp. 182–208. **[G: U.S.; EEC]**
Chandavarkar, Anand G. Keynes and the International Monetary System Revisited (A Contextual and Conjectural Essay). *World Devel.*, December 1987, *15*(12), pp. 1395–1405.
[G: LDCs]
Chrystal, K. Alec. Changing Perceptions of International Money and International Reserves in the World Economy. *Aliber, R. Z., ed.*, 1987, pp. 127–50.
Chrystal, K. Alec. International Liquidity and the Position of Developing Countries in the 1980s. *Dell, S., ed., Pt. 2*, 1987, pp. 358–72.
Cohen, Benjamin J. Implications of the European Monetary System for Developing Nations. *Dell, S., ed., Pt. 1*, 1987, pp. 295–339.
[G: W. Europe; LDCs]
Cooper, Richard N. A Monetary System for the Future. *Cooper, R. N.*, 1987, *1984*, pp. 259–78. **[G: Global]**
Cooper, Richard N. Does the International Financial System Need Reform? *Kaushik, S. K., ed.*, 1987, pp. 7–13.
Cooper, Richard N. Eurodollars, Reserve Dollars, and Asymmetries in the International Monetary System. *Cooper, R. N.*, 1987, *1972*, pp. 153–71.
Cooper, Richard N. External Constraints on European Growth. *Lawrence, R. Z. and Schultze, C. L., eds.*, 1987, pp. 540–91.
[G: W. Europe]
Cooper, Richard N. Flexible Exchange Rates, 1973–1980: How Bad Have They Really Been? *Cooper, R. N.*, 1987, *1982*, pp. 103–17.
Cooper, Richard N. Flexing the International Monetary System: The Case of Gliding Parities. *Cooper, R. N.*, 1987, *1970*, pp. 87–101.
Cooper, Richard N. Gold: Does It Provide a Viable Basis for the Monetary System? *Aliber, R. Z., ed.*, 1987, pp. 151–67.
Cooper, Richard N. IMF Surveillance over Floating Exchange Rates. *Cooper, R. N.*, 1987, *1977*, pp. 139–51.
Cooper, Richard N. Prolegomena to the Choice of an International Monetary System. *Cooper, R. N.*, 1987, *1975*, pp. 1–41.
Cooper, Richard N. Sterling, European Monetary Unification, and the International Monetary System. *Cooper, R. N.*, 1987, *1972*, pp. 189–214. **[G: U.K.; EEC]**
Cooper, Richard N. The Evolution of the International Monetary Fund toward a World Central Bank. *Cooper, R. N.*, 1987, *1983*, pp. 239–57.
Cooper, Richard N. The Future of the Dollar. *Cooper, R. N.*, 1987, *1973*, pp. 173–88.
[G: U.S.; Global]

Cooper, Richard N. The Future of the SDR. *Cooper, R. N.*, 1987, *1983*, pp. 215–21.
Cooper, Richard N. The Gold Standard: Historical Facts and Future Prospects. *Cooper, R. N.*, 1987, *1982*, pp. 43–86.
Cooper, Richard N. The International Monetary System in the 1980s. *Cooper, R. N.*, 1987, pp. 223–37.
Cornelius, Peter. Eine kombinierte Querschnitts/Zeitreihenanalyse zur Kreditnachfrage der Nicht-Öl-Entwicklungsländer beim Internationalen Währungsfonds. (A Combined Cross-Section/Time Series Analysis of the Demand for IMF Credit by the Non-oil Developing Nations. With English summary.) *Kredit Kapital*, 1987, *20*(1), pp. 88–105. **[G: LDCs]**
Dadzie, K. K. S. International Monetary and Financial Issues for the Developing Countries. *United Nations Conference on Trade and Development.*, 1987, pp. i–v.
Darby, Michael R. National Policies and the International Monetary System: Comment. *Officer, L. H., ed.*, 1987, pp. 271–74.
[G: Global]
Dell, Sidney. Proposal for the Establishment of a Medium-term Facility within the Framework of the International Monetary Fund. *Dell, S., ed., Pt. 1*, 1987, pp. 173–77.
Dell, Sidney and Lawrence, Roger. The Balance of Payments Adjustment Process in Developing Countries. *Dell, S., ed., Pt. 1*, 1987, *1980*, pp. 1–154. **[G: Global]**
Devarajan, Shantayanan and de Melo, Jaime. Evaluating Participation in African Monetary Unions: A Statistical Analysis of the CFA Zones. *World Devel.*, April 1987, *15*(4), pp. 483–96. **[G: W. Africa; LDCs]**
Deville, Volker and Gebauer, Wolfgang. Zinssätze und Preisindizes in ECU: Ein Beitrag zur Arithmetik von Währungskörben. (Interest Rates and Price Indices in ECU: Remarks on the Arithmetic of Currency Baskets. With English summary.) *Kredit Kapital*, 1987, *20*(4), pp. 439–53. **[G: EEC]**
Dewes, Leonard D. The Mechanics of the Short-term Interbank ECU Market. *Levich, R. M. and Sommariva, A., eds.*, 1987, pp. 73–87.
[G: EEC]
Díaz-Alejandro, Carlos F. International Financial and Goods Markets in 1982–3 and Beyond. *Borner, S. and Taylor, A., eds.*, 1987, pp. 429–43.
Dornbusch, Rudiger. Collapsing Exchange Rate Regimes. *J. Devel. Econ.*, October 1987, *27*(1–2), pp. 71–83.
Dornbusch, Rudiger. Collapsing Exchange Rate Regimes. *[Diaz-Alejandro, C. F.]*, 1987, pp. 71–83.
Edison, Hali J. Is the ECU an Optimal Currency Basket? *Levich, R. M. and Sommariva, A., eds.*, 1987, pp. 191–209. **[G: EEC]**
Eichengreen, Barry. Conducting the International Orchestra: Bank of England Leadership under the Classical Gold Standard. *J. Int. Money Finance*, March 1987, *6*(1), pp. 5–29.
[G: U.K.]

Fairbairn, Te'o I. J. Long-term Structural Adjustment Policies: Comment. *Holmes, F., ed.*, 1987, pp. 232–36.

Feinman, David. The Mechanics of the ECU Bond Market. *Levich, R. M. and Sommariva, A., eds.*, 1987, pp. 89–92. **[G: EEC; U.S.]**

Fitzgerald, D. The Costs and Benefits of International Banking: Comments. *Res, Z. and Motamen, S., eds.*, 1987, pp. 136–38.

Flood, Robert P. and Garber, Peter M. Gold Monetization and Gold Discipline. *Aliber, R. Z., ed.*, 1987, pp. 183–211.

Frenkel, Jacob A. Is the European Economic Community an Optimal Currency Area? Discussion. *Levich, R. M. and Sommariva, A., eds.*, 1987, pp. 186–89. **[G: EEC]**

Frenkel, Jacob A. The International Monetary System: Should It Be Reformed? *Amer. Econ. Rev.*, May 1987, 77(2), pp. 205–10. **[G: Global]**

Friedman, Irving S. Moderator's Opening Remarks: Exchange Rate Policy Formation in Historical Perspective. *Kaushik, S. K., ed.*, 1987, pp. 77–81.

von Furstenberg, George M. Internationally Managed Money Supply. *Aliber, R. Z., ed.*, 1987, pp. 117–26.

Garay S., Luis Jorge. Fiscal Policy, Growth, and Design of Stabilization Programs: Comment. *Martirena-Mantel, A. M., ed.*, 1987, pp. 141–47. **[G: LDCs]**

Genberg, Hans and Swoboda, Alexander K. Fixed Exchange Rates, Flexible Exchange Rates, or the Middle of the Road: A Re-examination of the Arguments in View of Recent Experience. *Aliber, R. Z., ed.*, 1987, pp. 92–113.

Giavazzi, Francesco and Giovannini, Alberto. Models of the EMS: Is Europe a Greater Deutschmark Area? *Bryant, R. C. and Portes, R., eds.*, 1987, pp. 237–66. **[G: W. Europe]**

Gleske, Leonhard. Die währungspolitische Zusammenarbeit im Rahmen der neuverfassten Europäischen Gemeinschaft. (Monetary Cooperation after the Single European Act. With English summary.) *Konjunkturpolitik*, 1987, 33(6), pp. 311–22. **[G: W. Germany]**

Goodfriend, Marvin. Eurodollars. *Wilcox, J. A., ed.*, 1987, 1986, pp. 330–41.

Goodfriend, Marvin. Eurodollars. *Goodfriend, M.*, 1987, 1986, pp. 85–91.

Goreux, Louis M. Responses by Representatives from the IMF and the World Bank. *Havnevik, K. J., ed.*, 1987, pp. 85–87.

de Grauwe, Paul. International Trade and Economic Growth in the European Monetary System. *Europ. Econ. Rev.*, Feb./Mar. 1987, 31(1/2), pp. 389–98. **[G: W. Europe]**

Griffith-Jones, Stephany. Compensatory Financing Facility: A Review of Its Operation and Proposals for Improvement. *Dell, S., ed., Pt. 2*, 1987, pp. 691–712.

Griffith-Jones, Stephany and Lipton, Michael. International Lenders of Last Resort: Are Changes Required? *Res, Z. and Motamen, S., eds.*, 1987, pp. 141–63.

Grubel, Herbert G. The Evolving International Monetary System: Past Plans and Optimality. *Aliber, R. Z., ed.*, 1987, pp. 7–20.

Guglielmotto, Enrica and Passatore, Giuseppe. The Private ECU Market: A Case of International Financial Innovation. *de Cecco, M., ed.*, 1987, pp. 260–319. **[G: W. Europe]**

Guitián, Manuel. External Debt Management and the International Monetary Fund. *Tremblay, R., ed.*, 1987, pp. 5–10.

Gulhati, Ravi. Responses by Representatives from the IMF and the World Bank. *Havnevik, K. J., ed.*, 1987, pp. 88–92.

Gyooten, Toyoo. Internationalization of the Yen: Its Implication for U.S.–Japan Relations. *Patrick, H. T. and Tachi, R., eds.*, 1987, pp. 84–89. **[G: U.S.; Japan]**

Haberler, Gottfried. Further Thoughts on International Policy Coordination. *[Wallich, H. C.]*, 1987, pp. 23–30.

Haberler, Gottfried. The International Monetary System: Recent Developments in Historic Perspective. *Aussenwirtschaft*, December 1987, 42(4), pp. 373–85. **[G: Global]**

Hausmann, Ricardo. Fiscal Policy, Growth, and Design of Stabilization Programs: Comment. *Martirena-Mantel, A. M., ed.*, 1987, pp. 147–53. **[G: LDCs]**

Havnevik, Kjell J. The IMF and the World Bank in Africa: Introduction. *Havnevik, K. J., ed.*, 1987, pp. 9–23. **[G: Africa]**

Haxthausen, Ulrik. Nordic View on the IMF/World Bank: Discussion. *Havnevik, K. J., ed.*, 1987, pp. 173–74. **[G: N. Europe]**

Hayek, Friedrich A. Toward a Free-Market Monetary System. *Dorn, J. A. and Schwartz, A. J., eds.*, 1987, pp. 383–90.

Heffernan, Shelagh A. The Costs and Benefits of International Banking: Reply. *Res, Z. and Motamen, S., eds.*, 1987, pp. 139–40.

Heffernan, Shelagh A. The Costs and Benefits of International Banking. *Res, Z. and Motamen, S., eds.*, 1987, pp. 113–35.

Helleiner, Gerald K. The Impact of the Exchange Rate System on the Developing Countries. *Dell, S., ed., Pt. 2*, 1987, pp. 407–510. **[G: LDCs]**

Heller, H. Robert. The ECU and the Choice of an Invoice Currency: Discussion. *Levich, R. M. and Sommariva, A., eds.*, 1987, pp. 156–59. **[G: EEC]**

Hirschfeld, David J. Development of ECU Futures Markets: An Institutional Perspective. *Levich, R. M. and Sommariva, A., eds.*, 1987, pp. 93–102. **[G: EEC]**

Hoffmeyer, Erik. The International Capital Market and the International Monetary System. *Ciocca, P., ed.*, 1987, 1978, pp. 245–61. **[G: Denmark]**

Horne, Jocelyn P. and Masson, Paul R. International Economic Cooperation and Policy Coordination. *Finance Develop.*, June 1987, 24(2), pp. 28–31. **[G: OECD]**

Jager, Henk and de Jong, Eelke. The Exchange-Rate Mechanism of the EMS and the ECU as a Reserve Asset: An Impending Incompatibility. *Europ. Econ. Rev.*, July 1987, *31*(5), pp. 1071–91. **[G: EEC]**

Jager, Henk and de Jong, Eelke. The Viability of the ECU. *Visser, H. and Schoor, E., eds.*, 1987, pp. 249–62. **[G: EEC]**

Jalal, Mahsoun. The Role of the Fund and the World Bank in Adjustment and Development: Comment. *El-Naggar, S., ed.*, 1987, pp. 88–91.

Jorion, Philippe. The ECU and Efficient Portfolio Choice. *Levich, R. M. and Sommariva, A., eds.*, 1987, pp. 119–39. **[G: EEC]**

Kadam, V. B. Implications for Developing Countries of Current Proposals for a Substitution Account. *Dell, S., ed., Pt. 1*, 1987, pp. 155–72.

Kaushik, S. K. The Changing Nature of International Financing. *Pachauri, R. K., ed.*, 1987, pp. 821–34. **[G: Global]**

Kees, Andreas. The Monetary Committee of the European Community. *Kredit Kapital*, 1987, *20*(2), pp. 258–67. **[G: EEC]**

Kenen, Peter B. Changing Views about the Role of the SDR and Implications for Its Attributes. *Dell, S., ed., Pt. 2*, 1987, pp. 373–85.

Kenen, Peter B. What Role for IMF Surveillance? *World Devel.*, December 1987, *15*(12), pp. 1445–56.

Khatkhate, Deena R. International Monetary System—Which Way? Editor's Perspective. *World Devel.*, December 1987, *15*(12), pp. vii–xvi. **[G: Global]**

Kindleberger, Charles P. Belgium after World War II: An Experiment in Supply-Side Economics. *Kindleberger, C. P.*, 1987, pp. 230–44. **[G: Belgium]**

Klein, Lawrence R. The Choice among Alternative Exchange-Rate Regimes. *J. Policy Modeling*, Spring 1987, *9*(1), pp. 7–18. **[G: Global]**

Klopstock, Fred H. Euro-currency Market Regulation: Its Potential Effects on Third World Access to the Market. *Dell, S., ed., Pt. 1*, 1987, pp. 279–94. **[G: Global; W. Europe]**

Klopstock, Fred H. Implications of a Substitution Account for the Eurocurrency Markets. *Dell, S., ed., Pt. 1*, 1987, pp. 205–20.

Korpinen, Pekka. Nordic View on the IMF/World Bank: Discussion. *Havnevik, K. J., ed.*, 1987, pp. 167–69. **[G: N. Europe]**

Lamfalussy, Alexandre. International Financial Integration: Policy Implications. *Steinherr, A. and Weiserbs, D., eds.*, 1987, pp. 99–117.

Legarda, Benito. Issues Arising in Making the SDR the Principal International Reserve Asset. *Dell, S., ed., Pt. 2*, 1987, pp. 387–91.

Leroux, François. Currency Baskets: Can the SDR Match the ECU's Success? *Tremblay, R., ed.*, 1987, pp. 161–71.

Levich, Richard M. Development of the ECU Markets: Perspectives on Financial Innovation. *Levich, R. M. and Sommariva, A., eds.*, 1987, pp. 103–16. **[G: EEC]**

Llach, Juan J. La naturaleza institucional e internacional de las hiperestabilizaciones. El caso de Alemania desde 1923 y algunas lecciones para la Argentina de 1985. (With English sum-

mary.) *Desarrollo Econ.*, Jan.-Mar. 1987, *26*(104), pp. 527–60. **[G: Germany; Argentina]**

Logan, Kevin. The Evolution of the ECU Market: A Private Sector View: Discussion. *Levich, R. M. and Sommariva, A., eds.*, 1987, pp. 29–32. **[G: EEC]**

Lomax, David F. The Evolution of the ECU Market: A Private Sector View. *Levich, R. M. and Sommariva, A., eds.*, 1987, pp. 9–28. **[G: EEC]**

Lopez-Claros, Augusto. The European Community: On the Road to Integration. *Finance Develop.*, September 1987, *24*(3), pp. 35–38. **[G: EC]**

Loxley, John. Responses by Representatives from the IMF and the World Bank: Comment. *Havnevik, K. J., ed.*, 1987, pp. 92–94.

Loxley, John. The IMF, the World Bank, and Sub-Saharan Africa: Policies and Politics. *Havnevik, K. J., ed.*, 1987, pp. 47–63. **[G: Sub-Saharan Africa]**

de Luca, Mario. Financial Innovation in East–West Relations. *Rev. Econ. Cond. Italy*, May-August 1987, (2), pp. 155–64. **[G: EEC; CMEA; U.S.]**

Lundström, Hans. Nordic View on the IMF/World Bank: Discussion. *Havnevik, K. J., ed.*, 1987, pp. 170–72. **[G: N. Europe]**

Maier, Charles S. The Politics of Productivity: Foundations of American International Economic Policy after World War II. *Maier, C. S.*, 1987, *1977*, pp. 121–52. **[G: U.S.]**

Marston, Richard C. Models of the EMS: Is Europe a Greater Deutschmark Area? Discussion. *Bryant, R. C. and Portes, R., eds.*, 1987, pp. 266–70. **[G: W. Europe]**

Masera, Rainer S. An Increasing Role for the ECU: A Character in Search of a Script. *Levich, R. M. and Sommariva, A., eds.*, 1987, pp. 33–67. **[G: EEC]**

Masera, Rainer S. European Currency: An Italian View. *Econ. Int.*, November 1987, *40*(4), pp. 317–28. **[G: W. Europe]**

McCulloch, Rachel. Unexpected Real Consequences of Floating Exchange Rates. *Aliber, R. Z., ed.*, 1987, pp. 21–45.

McDermott, John H. Adding Exhaustibility to the Traditional Theory of the Gold Standard. *J. Macroecon.*, Fall 1987, *9*(4), pp. 545–66.

McKinnon, R. J. Exchange Stability, International Monetary Coordination, and the U.S. Federal Reserve System. *Visser, H. and Schoor, E., eds.*, 1987, pp. 139–67. **[G: U.S.; Global]**

McKinnon, Ronald I. Protectionism and the Misaligned Dollar: The Case for Monetary Coordination. *Salvatore, D., ed.*, 1987, pp. 367–88. **[G: Global]**

McLeod, Alex N. The Domestic Roots of Chronic International Problems. *Tremblay, R., ed.*, 1987, pp. 173–85.

Meiselman, David I. Is Gold the Answer? Comment [Gold Standards: True and False]. *Dorn, J. A. and Schwartz, A. J., eds.*, 1987, pp. 257–60.

Mélitz, Jacques. Discipline monétaire, République fédérale allemande et Système monétaire européen. (Monetary Discipline, Germany, and the European Monetary System. With English summary.) *Ann. Écon. Statist.*, Oct./Dec. 1987, (8), pp. 59–87. **[G: Europe]**

Meltzer, Allan H. Properties of Monetary Systems. *Res, Z. and Motamen, S., eds.*, 1987, pp. 83–104. **[G: U.S.]**

Miller, Marcus H. The European Monetary System: Overview. *Bryant, R. C. and Portes, R., eds.*, 1987, pp. 273–76.

Mohammed, Azizali F. The Role of the Fund and the World Bank in Adjustment and Development. *El-Naggar, S., ed.*, 1987, pp. 73–87.

Monti, Mario. Integration of Financial Markets in Europe. *Giersch, H., ed.*, 1987, pp. 492–503. **[G: EEC]**

Müller, Burkhardt. Konstruktion und Berechnung von Währungskörben. (Construction and Commutation of Currency Baskets. With English summary.) *Jahr. Nationalökon. Statist.*, March 1987, 203(2), pp. 188–99.

Murphy, J. Carter. National Policies and the International Monetary System. *Officer, L. H., ed.*, 1987, pp. 203–70. **[G: Global]**

Narasimham, M. Shortcomings and Inequities of the Present International Monetary and Financial System. *Dell, S., ed., Pt. 3*, 1987, pp. 797–811.

Narasimham, M. Transfer of Resources to Developing Countries: Nature and Direction of Reform in the International Financial System. *Dell, S., ed., Pt. 3*, 1987, pp. 813–26. **[G: LDCs]**

Nascimento, Jean-Claude. The Choice of an Optimum Exchange Currency Regime for a Small Economy: An Econometric Analysis. *J. Devel. Econ.*, February 1987, 25(1), pp. 149–65. **[G: W. Africa]**

Ncube, P. D.; Sakala, M. and Ndulo, M. The International Monetary Fund and the Zambian Economy—A Case. *Havnevik, K. J., ed.*, 1987, pp. 127–48. **[G: Zambia]**

Nossal, Kìm Richard. Economic Sanctions in the League of Nations and the United Nations. *Leyton-Brown, D., ed.*, 1987, pp. 7–21.

Nwankwo, G. O. Africa and the International Monetary System. *Borner, S. and Taylor, A., eds.*, 1987, pp. 337–57. **[G: Africa]**

Nwankwo, G. O. Low-Income Countries and the International Monetary and Financial System. *Dell, S., ed., Pt. 3*, 1987, pp. 785–96. **[G: LDCs]**

Ogata, Shijuro. How to Cope with the Present International Monetary System. *[Wallich, H. C.]*, 1987, pp. 38–43.

Oppenheimer, Peter M. Impact of a Substitution Account on Euro-currency and Related Lending to Developing Countries. *Dell, S., ed., Pt. 1*, 1987, pp. 221–26. **[G: LDCs]**

Oppenheimer, Peter M. The Endogeneity of International Liquidity. *Aliber, R. Z., ed.*, 1987, pp. 305–23.

Oudiz, Gilles. External Constraints on European Growth: Comment. *Lawrence, R. Z. and*

Schultze, C. L., eds., 1987, pp. 596–99. **[G: W. Europe]**

Payer, Cheryl. The IMF and India. *Havnevik, K. J., ed.*, 1987, pp. 65–83. **[G: India]**

Phylatkis, K. International Lenders of Last Resort: Are Changes Required? Comment. *Res, Z. and Motamen, S., eds.*, 1987, pp. 164–66.

Please, Stanley. Long-term Structural Adjustment Policies. *Holmes, F., ed.*, 1987, pp. 217–31.

Pozo, Susan. The ECU as International Money. *J. Int. Money Finance*, June 1987, 6(2), pp. 195–206. **[G: Global]**

Price, Lionel D. D. The Inter-bank Market, Contagion Effects and International Financial Crises: Discussion. *Portes, R. and Swoboda, A. K., eds.*, 1987, pp. 234–38. **[G: Global]**

Putnam, Bluford H. and Mullaney, Brian V. The ECU and Efficient Portfolio Choice: Discussion. *Levich, R. M. and Sommariva, A., eds.*, 1987, pp. 140–43. **[G: EEC]**

Rangarajan, C. and Hasib, A. Financial Problems of Low Income and Least Developed Countries. *Agrawal, G. R., et al. (I)*, 1987, pp. 35–58. **[G: LDCs]**

Res, Zannis and Motamen, Sima. International Debt and Central Banking in the 1980s: Introduction. *Res, Z. and Motamen, S., eds.*, 1987, pp. 1–17. **[G: Global]**

Ribe, Halvor and Schneider, Friedrich. Finanzinnovationen an den Euromärkten. (Financial Innovations in the Eurocurrency Market. With English summary.) *Kredit Kapital*, 1987, 20(1), pp. 116–39.

Rybczynski, Tad M. The Approaches towards the Reform of the International Monetary System. *Nat. Westminster Bank Quart. Rev.*, February 1987, pp. 2–11. **[G: Global]**

Salerno, Joseph T. Gold Standards: True and False. *Dorn, J. A. and Schwartz, A. J., eds.*, 1987, pp. 241–55. **[G: U.S.]**

Saunders, Anthony. The Inter-bank Market, Contagion Effects and International Financial Crises. *Portes, R. and Swoboda, A. K., eds.*, 1987, pp. 196–232. **[G: Global]**

Schwartz, Anna J. Lessons of the Gold Standard Era and the Bretton Woods System for the Prospects of an International Monetary System Constitution. *Schwartz, A. J.*, 1987, *1986*, pp. 391–406.

Schwartz, Anna J. Prospects of an International Monetary System Constitution. *Contemp. Policy Issues*, April 1987, 5(2), pp. 16–30. **[G: Global]**

Schwartz, Anna J. Reflections on the Gold Commission *Report. Schwartz, A. J.*, 1987, *1982*, pp. 317–32. **[G: U.S.]**

Schwartz, Anna J. The Postwar Institutional Evolution of the International Monetary System. *Schwartz, A. J.*, 1987, *1983*, pp. 333–63. **[G: OECD]**

Sengupta, Arjun. The Allocation of Special Drawing Rights Linked to the Reserve Needs of Countries. *United Nations Conference on Trade and Development.*, 1987, pp. 311–28.

Shafer, Jeffrey R. Managing Crises in the Emerging Financial Landscape. *OECD Econ. Stud.*, Autumn 1987, (9), pp. 55–77. **[G: Global]**

Shafer, Jeffrey R. The Theory of the Lender of Last Resort and the Eurocurrency Markets. *Aliber, R. Z., ed.*, 1987, pp. 281–304.
[G: EEC]

Snowden, P. N. International Equity Investment in Less Developed Countries' Stockmarkets: The Replacement for Bank Lending? *Nat. Westminster Bank Quart. Rev.*, February 1987, pp. 29–38. **[G: LDCs]**

Sobhan, Rehman. Characteristics of LICs. *Agrawal, G. R., et al. (I)*, 1987, pp. 20–23.

Sommariva, Andrea. An Increasing Role for the ECU: A Character in Search of a Script: Discussion. *Levich, R. M. and Sommariva, A., eds.*, 1987, pp. 68–70. **[G: EEC]**

Stewart, Frances. Should Conditionality Change? *Havnevik, K. J., ed.*, 1987, pp. 29–45.

Stewart, Michael. A Survey of Some Recent Proposals for New International Facilities. *Dell, S., ed., Pt. 1*, 1987, pp. 179–98.

Stewart, Michael. An Elaboration of a Proposal for a Long-term Facility for Financing Purchases of Capital Goods by Developing Countries (Mexican Proposal). *Dell, S., ed., Pt. 1*, 1987, pp. 199–203. **[G: LDCs]**

Svendsen, Knud Erik. The Nordic Countries and the IMF/World Bank. *Havnevik, K. J., ed.*, 1987, pp. 161–65. **[G: N. Europe]**

Swanson, Peggy E. A Preliminary Assessment of the Impact of Floating Exchange Rates on International and Vehicle Currency Uses of U.S. Dollars. *Quart. J. Bus. Econ.*, Spring 1987, 26(2), pp. 3–21. **[G: U.S.]**

Tandon, Kishore and Urich, Thomas. International Market Response to Announcements of U.S. Macroeconomic Data. *J. Int. Money Finance*, March 1987, 6(1), pp. 71–83.
[G: U.S.; Selected OECD]

Tanzi, Vito. Fiscal Policy, Growth, and Design of Stabilization Programs. *Martirena-Mantel, A. M., ed.*, 1987, pp. 121–41. **[G: LDCs]**

Tanzi, Vito and Ter-Minassian, Teresa. The European Monetary System and Fiscal Policies. *Cnossen, S., ed.*, 1987, pp. 337–57.
[G: EEC]

Tavlas, George S. Policy Aspects of Alternative Exchange-Rate Regimes: Introduction. *J. Policy Modeling*, Spring 1987, 9(1), pp. 1–5.

Taylor, Alwyn. Foreign Indebtedness, Exchange Rates and the Monetary System: Introduction. *Borner, S. and Taylor, A., eds.*, 1987, pp. 323–35.

Thygesen, Niels. Is the European Economic Community an Optimal Currency Area? *Levich, R. M. and Sommariva, A., eds.*, 1987, pp. 163–85. **[G: EEC]**

Tobin, James. Agenda for International Coordination of Macroeconomic Policies. *[Wallich, H. C.]*, 1987, pp. 61–69.

Triffin, Robert. A European Monetary Bank with Central Bank Functions. *Steinherr, A. and Weiserbs, D., eds.*, 1987, pp. 119–32.
[G: W. Europe]

Triffin, Robert. The *IMS* (International Monetary

System... or Scandal?) and the *EMS* (European Monetary *System*). *Banca Naz. Lavoro Quart. Rev.*, September 1987, (162), pp. 239–61.

Triffin, Robert. W.M.S.: The World Monetary System or Scandal? *Kaushik, S. K., ed.*, 1987, pp. 31–46.

Triffin, Robert. Worldwide and European Monetary Reforms: Long-run Blueprints and Short-run Arrangements. *Levich, R. M. and Sommariva, A., eds.*, 1987, pp. 217–31. **[G: EEC; Global]**

UNCTAD Secretariat. Determination of Quotas and the Relative Position of Developing Countries in the International Monetary Fund: Introduction. *Dell, S., ed., Pt. 2*, 1987, pp. 511–40.

UNCTAD Secretariat. Export Financing in Developing Countries. *Dell, S., ed., Pt. 2*, 1987, pp. 665–90.

Vaidya, Kalyan. Selected Measures of Financial Co-operation among Developing Countries. *Dell, S., ed., Pt. 2*, 1987, pp. 569–609.
[G: LDCs]

Van Huyck, John B. A Retrospective on the Classical Gold Standard, 1821–1931: A Review Essay. *J. Monet. Econ.*, May 1987, 19(3), pp. 451–56.

Vaubel, Roland. Competing Currencies: The Case for Free Entry. *Dorn, J. A. and Schwartz, A. J., eds.*, 1987, pp. 281–96.

Wallich, Henry C. Central Banks as Regulators and Lenders of Last Resort in an International Context: A View from the United States. *Ciocca, P., ed.*, 1987, 1982, pp. 231–42.
[G: U.S.]

Walter, Ingo. Integration of Financial Markets in Europe: Comment. *Giersch, H., ed.*, 1987, pp. 504–14. **[G: EEC]**

Wangwe, Samuel M. Impact of the IMF/World Bank Philosophy, the Case of Tanzania. *Havnevik, K. J., ed.*, 1987, pp. 149–60.
[G: Tanzania]

Wegner, Manfred. Scope and Limits of International Economic Policy Coordination. *World Econ.*, September 1987, 10(3), pp. 283–306.
[G: OECD]

Williamson, John. Exchange Rate Flexibility, Target Zones, and Policy Coordination. *World Devel.*, December 1987, 15(12), pp. 1437–43.
[G: OECD]

Williamson, John. International Liquidity: Are the Supply and Composition Appropriate? *Williamson, J.*, 1987, 1984, pp. 119–39.

Williamson, John. International Monetary Reform: An Agenda for the 1980s. *Williamson, J.*, 1987, 1983, pp. 212–27.

Williamson, John. International Monetary Reform: A Survey of the Options. *Dell, S., ed., Pt. 1*, 1987, pp. 227–78. **[G: LDCs]**

Williamson, John. Keynes and the International Economic Order. *Williamson, J.*, 1987, 1983, pp. 37–59.

Williamson, John. Resource Transfer and the International Monetary System. *Williamson, J.*, 1987, pp. 157–77. **[G: LDCs]**

Williamson, John. The Failure of World Monetary

Reform: A Reassessment. *Williamson, J.*, 1987, *1982*, pp. 201–11.

Williamson, John. The Growth of Official Reserves and the Issue of World Monetary Control. *Williamson, J.*, 1987, *1982*, pp. 140–53.

Williamson, John. The Theorists and the Real World. *Williamson, J.*, 1987, *1985*, pp. 15–36.

Williamson, John. Valuation of the SDR: The Case for a Standard Five-Currency Logarithmic Basket. *Dell, S., ed., Pt. 2*, 1987, pp. 393–406.

Williamson, John and Gavin, Michael. International Monetary Issues in 1985. *United Nations Conference on Trade and Development.*, 1987, pp. 1–32. **[G: Global]**

Wood, Geoffrey E. Properties of Monetary Systems: Comment. *Res, Z. and Motamen, S., eds.*, 1987, pp. 105–11. **[G: U.S.]**

Yeager, Leland B. Stable Money and Free-Market Currencies. *Dorn, J. A. and Schwartz, A. J., eds.*, 1987, pp. 297–317.

Zervoyianni, Athina. Currency Substitution, Flexible Exchange Rates and the International Transmission of Disturbances. *Chrystal, K. A. and Sedgwick, R., eds.*, 1987, pp. 199–228.

Zijlstra, Jelle. Central Banking with the Benefit of Hindsight. *Ciocca, P., ed.*, 1987, *1981*, pp. 167–83.

433 Private International Lending

4330 Private International Lending

Aliber, Robert Z. Financial Innovation and the Boundaries of Banking. *Managerial Dec. Econ.*, March 1987, *8*(1), pp. 67–73.

Bacha, Edmar Lisboa. O sistema de condicionalidades do FMI: uma proposta de reforma. (With English summary.) *Pesquisa Planejamento Econ.*, August 1987, *17*(2), pp. 333–42.

Balassa, Bela. Mexico's Debt Problem and Policies for the Future. *Tremblay, R., ed.*, 1987, pp. 11–29. **[G: Mexico]**

Bardos, Jeffrey. The Risk-based Capital Agreement: A Further Step towards Policy Convergence. *Fed. Res. Bank New York Quart. Rev.*, Winter 1987-88, *12*(4), pp. 26–34. **[G: OECD]**

Batchelor, Roy A. Country Risk: A Model for Predicting Debt Servicing Problems in Developing Countries: Comments. *Res, Z. and Motamen, S., eds.*, 1987, pp. 224–27. **[G: LDCs]**

Beenstock, Michael. Emergency Liquidity Assistance for International Banks: Discussion. *Portes, R. and Swoboda, A. K., eds.*, 1987, pp. 186–88.

Beenstock, Michael. The Theory of Last Resort Lending. *Res, Z. and Motamen, S., eds.*, 1987, pp. 167–83.

Berger, Thomas J. The U.S. Debt Initiative: A Status Report. *Tremblay, R., ed.*, 1987, pp. 51–54. **[G: U.S.; LDCs]**

Bergsten, C. Fred. The Second Debt Crisis is Coming. *Challenge*, Special Issue 1987, *30*(6), pp. 50–57. **[G: U.S.]**

Bernal, Richard L. Default as a Negotiating Tactic in Debt Rescheduling Strategies of Developing

Countries: A Preliminary Note. *Salazar-Carrillo, J. and Tirado de Alonzo, I., eds.*, 1987, pp. 1–32. **[G: Ghana; Latin America]**

Bird, Graham. Debt Conversion in Principle and Practice. *Banca Naz. Lavoro Quari. Rev.*, June 1987, (161), pp. 183–95. **[G: LDCs]**

Bird, Graham. Interest Rate Compensation and Debt: Would a Cap Fit? *World Devel.*, September 1987, *15*(9), pp. 1237–42.

Blejer, Mario I. and Sagari, Silvia. The Structure of the Banking Sector and the Sequence of Financial Liberalization. *Connolly, M. and González-Vega, C., eds.*, 1987, pp. 93–107. **[G: Latin America]**

Brainard, Lawrence J. Current Illusions about the International Debt Crisis. *Wilcox, J. A., ed.*, 1987, *1985*, pp. 321–29. **[G: Global]**

Brainard, Lawrence J. Managing the International Debt Crisis: The Future of the Baker Plan. *Contemp. Policy Issues*, July 1987, *5*(3), pp. 66–75. **[G: U.S.]**

Brainard, Lawrence J. and Shelton-Colby, Sally. Prospects for Cooperation between Commercial Banks and Multilateral Financial Institutions: The Future of the Baker Plan. *Myers, R. J., ed.*, 1987, pp. 159–67.

Brillembourg, Arturo. The Inter-bank Market, Contagion Effects and International Financial Crises: Discussion. *Portes, R. and Swoboda, A. K., eds.*, 1987, pp. 232–34. **[G: Global]**

Bruner, Robert F. and Simms, John M., Jr. The International Debt Crisis and Bank Security Returns in 1982. *J. Money, Credit, Banking*, February 1987, *19*(1), pp. 46–55. **[G: U.S.]**

Carrada-Bravo, Francisco. International Trade, Investment, Regional Security, and the Prospects of the Mexico–U.S. Relations. *Tremblay, R., ed.*, 1987, pp. 531–48. **[G: Mexico; U.S.]**

Chakravarty, Shanti P. The Latin American Debt. *Scot. J. Polit. Econ.*, May 1987, *34*(2), pp. 120–44. **[G: Latin America]**

Citron, Joel-Tomas and Nickelsburg, Gerald. Country Risk and Political Instability. *J. Devel. Econ.*, April 1987, *25*(2), pp. 385–92. **[G: Latin America; Spain; Sweden]**

Cline, William R. International Financial Rescue: Viability and Modalities. *Dell, S., ed., Pt. 3*, 1987, pp. 875–905. **[G: LDCs]**

Conway, Patrick. Baker Plan and International Indebtedness. *World Econ.*, June 1987, *10*(2), pp. 193–204. **[G: LDCs]**

Corrigan, E. Gerald. A Perspective on the Globalization of Financial Markets and Institutions. *Fed. Res. Bank New York Quart. Rev.*, Spring 1987, *12*(1), pp. 1–9. **[G: U.S.; Japan; U.K.]**

Corrigan, E. Gerald. Statement to the U.S. Senate Committee on the Budget, May 6, 1987. *Fed. Res. Bull.*, July 1987, *73*(7), pp. 569–77. **[G: U.S.; U.K.; Japan]**

Curtis, Carole and Baker, James C. The Evolution of the Super Edge: Regulation and Operations of Edge Act Banks. *J. World Trade Law*, December 1987, *21*(6), pp. 25–36. **[G: U.S.]**

Darity, William A., Jr. Debt, Finance, Production and Trade in a North–South Model: The

Surplus Approach. *Cambridge J. Econ.*, September 1987, *11*(3), pp. 211–27.

Devlin, Robert. Economic Restructuring in Latin America in the Face of the Foreign Debt and the External Transfer Problem. *CEPAL Rev.*, August 1987, (32), pp. 75–101.
[G: Latin America]

Di Vittorio, Antonio. A Multinational Bank: The Bank of Rome. *J. Europ. Econ. Hist.*, Fall 1987, *16*(2), pp. 389–98. [G: Italy]

Dietz, James L. Debt and Development: The Future of Latin America. *Dietz, J. L. and Street, J. H., eds.*, 1987, pp. 273–92.
[G: Latin America]

Dietz, James L. The Latin American Economies and Debt: Institutional and Structural Response to Crisis. *J. Econ. Issues*, June 1987, *21*(2), pp. 827–36. [G: Latin America]

Dooley, Michael P. Market Valuation of External Debt. *Finance Develop.*, March 1987, *24*(1), pp. 6–9. [G: LDCs]

Dornbusch, Rudiger and Fischer, Stanley. The World Debt Problem. *Dell, S., ed., Pt. 3*, 1987, pp. 907–59. [G: Selected LDCs]

Doukas, John and Melhem, Melhem. Canadian Banks: Risk Reduction by International Diversification. *Appl. Econ.*, December 1987, *19*(12), pp. 1561–69. [G: Canada]

Eichengreen, Barry and Portes, Richard. The Anatomy of Financial Crises. *Portes, R. and Swoboda, A. K., eds.*, 1987, pp. 10–58.
[G: Global]

Erb, Richard D. International Debt and Adjustment—Setting the Issues in a Global Perspective. *Tremblay, R., ed.*, 1987, pp. 1–3.
[G: Global]

Feinberg, Richard E. Multilateral Lending and Latin America. *World Econ.*, June 1987, *10*(2), pp. 205–17. [G: Latin America]

Ferrer, A. Latin American Foreign Debt: Problems and Prospects. *Borner, S. and Taylor, A., eds.*, 1987, pp. 381–93. [G: Argentina]

Ffrench-Davis, Ricardo. Conversión de Pagarés de la Deuda Externa en Chile. (Conversion of Chilean Foreign Debt. With English summary.) *Colección Estud. CIEPLAN*, December 1987, (22), pp. 41–62. [G: Chile]

Findlay, Christopher. The Role of Aid and Private Capital Inflows in Economic Development: Comment. *Holmes, F., ed.*, 1987, pp. 147–53.
[G: LDCs]

Fischer, Stanley. Sharing the Burden of the International Debt Crisis. *Amer. Econ. Rev.*, May 1987, *77*(2), pp. 165–70. [G: LDCs]

Forbes, Neil. London Banks, the German Standstill Agreements, and 'Economic Appeasement' in the 1930s. *Econ. Hist. Rev.*, *2nd Ser.*, November 1987, *40*(4), pp. 571–87. [G: U.K.]

Foweraker, Joe. What's Good for Citicorp... *Challenge*, Jan./Feb. 1987, *29*(6), pp. 47–50.
[G: U.S.]

Foxley, Alejandro. El problema de la deuda externa desde una perspectiva latinoamericana. (With English summary.) *Desarrollo Econ.*, July-Sept. 1987, *27*(106), pp. 223–43.

Freedman, Charles. Emergency Liquidity Assistance for International Banks: Discussion.

Portes, R. and Swoboda, A. K., eds., 1987, pp. 189–94.

Gemmill, Robert F. The Anatomy of Financial Crises: Discussion. *Portes, R. and Swoboda, A. K., eds.*, 1987, pp. 58–61. [G: Global]

Gennotte, Gerard; Kharas, Homi J. and Sadeq, Sayeed. A Valuation Model of Developing-Country Debt with Endogenous Rescheduling. *World Bank Econ. Rev.*, January 1987, *1*(2), pp. 237–71. [G: LDCs]

Griffith-Jones, Stephany and Lipton, Michael. International Lenders of Last Resort: Are Changes Required? *Res, Z. and Motamen, S., eds.*, 1987, pp. 141–63.

Guttentag, Jack and Herring, Richard J. Emergency Liquidity Assistance for International Banks. *Portes, R. and Swoboda, A. K., eds.*, 1987, pp. 150–86.

Hajivassiliou, Vassilis A. The External Debt Repayments Problems of LDC's: An Econometric Model Based on Panel Data. *J. Econometrics*, Sept./Oct. 1987, *36*(1/2), pp. 205–30.
[G: LDCs]

Haley, John C. Debt Crisis, Exchange Rates, the U.S. Deficit, and Electronic Reaction to the World Events. *Kaushik, S. K., ed.*, 1987, pp. 63–70.

Hanke, Steve H. The Anatomy of a Successful Debt Swap. *Hanke, S. H., ed.*, 1987, pp. 161–68. [G: Chile]

Heller, H. Robert. The Debt Crisis and the Future of International Bank Lending. *Amer. Econ. Rev.*, May 1987, *77*(2), pp. 171–75.
[G: LDCs]

Hewitt, Adrian P. Stabex and Commodity Export Compensation Schemes: Prospects for Globalization. *World Devel.*, May 1987, *15*(5), pp. 617–31. [G: EEC; LDCs]

Hojman, David E. Why the Latin American Countries Will Never Form a Debtors' Cartel. *Kyklos*, 1987, *40*(2), pp. 198–218.
[G: Latin America]

Hughes, Helen. The Role of Aid and Private Capital Inflows in Economic Development. *Holmes, F., ed.*, 1987, pp. 120–46.
[G: LDCs]

Jain, Arvind K. and Gupta, Satyadev. Some Evidence on "Herding" Behavior of U.S. Banks. *J. Money, Credit, Banking*, February 1987, *19*(1), pp. 78–89. [G: U.S.]

Kane, Edward J. Competitive Financial Reregulation: An International Perspective. *Portes, R. and Swoboda, A. K., eds.*, 1987, pp. 111–45.
[G: OECD]

Kaushik, S. K. The Changing Nature of International Financing. *Pachauri, R. K., ed.*, 1987, pp. 821–34. [G: Global]

Kim, In Kie. Foreign Participation in Korean Money Markets. *Dutta, M., ed. (II)*, 1987, pp. 135–50. [G: S. Korea]

Kim, Kwan S. Mexico's Debt Crisis and Adjustment Policies. *Tremblay, R., ed.*, 1987, pp. 55–70. [G: Mexico]

Krueger, Anne O. Debt, Capital Flows, and LDC Growth. *Amer. Econ. Rev.*, May 1987, *77*(2), pp. 159–64. [G: LDCs]

Kuczynski, Pedro-Pablo. The Outlook for Latin American Debt. *Foreign Aff.*, Fall 1987, *66*(1), pp. 129–49. **[G: Latin America]**

Lächler, Ulrich and Nunnenkamp, Peter. The Effects of Debt versus Equity Inflows on Savings and Growth in Developing Economies. *Weltwirtsch. Arch.*, 1987, *123*(4), pp. 631–50. **[G: LDCs]**

Lahera, Eugenio. The Conversion of Foreign Debt Viewed from Latin America. *CEPAL Rev.*, August 1987, (32), pp. 103–22. **[G: Latin America]**

Laird, Samuel and Yeats, Alexander J. On the Potential Contribution of Trade Policy Initiatives for Alleviating the International Debt Crisis. *J. Econ. Bus.*, August 1987, *39*(3), pp. 209–24. **[G: OECD; LDCs]**

Laney, Leroy O. The Secondary Market in Developing Country Debt: Some Observations and Policy Implications. *Fed. Res. Bank Dallas Econ. Rev.*, July 1987, pp. 1–12. **[G: LDCs]**

Langoni, Carlos Geraldo. The Lessons of the Crisis: A Developing Country View. *Res, Z. and Motamen, S., eds.*, 1987, *1983*, pp. 41–55.

Lanyi, Anthony. Issues in Capital Flows to Developing Countries. *Finance Develop.*, September 1987, *24*(3), pp. 27–30. **[G: LDCs]**

de Larosière, J. Progress on the International Debt Strategy. *Finance Develop.*, March 1987, *24*(1), pp. 10–11. **[G: LDCs]**

Lavigne, Marie. External Finance as a Factor of Internal Regulation in Eastern European Economies. *Soviet E. Europ. Foreign Trade*, Summer 1987, *23*(2), pp. 24–36. **[G: CMEA]**

Madura, Jeff and Veit, E. Theodore. Intertemporal Exposure to Country Risk. *Rivista Int. Sci. Econ. Com.*, Nov.-Dec. 1987, *34*(11–12), pp. 1095–1102. **[G: Selected Countries]**

McCauley, Robert N. and Hargraves, Lauren A. Eurocommercial Paper and U.S. Commercial Paper: Converging Money Markets? *Fed. Res. Bank New York Quart. Rev.*, Autumn 1987, *12*(3), pp. 24–35. **[G: U.S.]**

Milanović, Branko. On Grants and Lending. *Econ. Anal. Workers' Manage.*, 1987, *21*(3), pp. 299–312.

Moreno, Ramon. The Eurodollar Market and U.S. Residents. *Fed. Res. Bank San Francisco Econ. Rev.*, Summer 1987, (3), pp. 43–59. **[G: U.S.]**

Morgan, John B. A Note on Eaton and Gersovitz's Model of Borrowing [LDC Participation in International Financial Markets] [Debt with Potential Repudiation: Theoretical and Empirical Analysis]. *J. Devel. Econ.*, February 1987, *25*(1), pp. 251–61. **[G: LDCs]**

Muffett, Mark. Credit Risk on Swaps. *Aussenwirtschaft*, September 1987, *42*(2/3), pp. 229–50.

Narasimham, M. Transfer of Resources to Developing Countries: Nature and Direction of Reform in the International Financial System. *Dell, S., ed., Pt. 3*, 1987, pp. 813–26. **[G: LDCs]**

Nogueira Batista, Paulo, Jr. International Debt Rescheduling since Mid-1982: Rescue Operations and Their Implications for Commercial Banks and Debtor Countries. *Dell, S., ed., Pt. 3*, 1987, pp. 828–74. **[G: Latin America]**

Nunnenkamp, Peter. Latin American Debt and Development: A Review. *Weltwirtsch. Arch.*, 1987, *123*(4), pp. 734–38. **[G: Latin America]**

Oppenheimer, Peter M. Impact of a Substitution Account on Euro-currency and Related Lending to Developing Countries. *Dell, S., ed., Pt. 1*, 1987, pp. 221–26. **[G: LDCs]**

Padoan, Pier Carlo. Growth, Debt, Country Risk and Financial Instability. *[Marrama, V.], Vol. 1*, 1987, pp. 269–93.

Panić, M. and Kumar, M. S. International Interdependence and the Debt Problem. *Borner, S. and Taylor, A., eds.*, 1987, pp. 359–80. **[G: LDCs]**

Phylatkis, K. International Lenders of Last Resort: Are Changes Required? Comment. *Res, Z. and Motamen, S., eds.*, 1987, pp. 164–66.

Price, Lionel D. D. The Inter-bank Market, Contagion Effects and International Financial Crises: Discussion. *Portes, R. and Swoboda, A. K., eds.*, 1987, pp. 234–38. **[G: Global]**

Price, Lionel D. D. The Theory of Last Resort Lending: Comment. *Res, Z. and Motamen, S., eds.*, 1987, pp. 184–86.

Prindl, A. R. The Internationalisation of Japanese Financial Institutions. *Trevor, M., ed.*, 1987, pp. 111–19. **[G: Japan]**

Pyle, David H. Competitive Financial Reregulation: An International Perspective: Discussion. *Portes, R. and Swoboda, A. K., eds.*, 1987, pp. 145–49. **[G: OECD]**

Ranis, Gustav. Latin American Debt and Adjustment. *J. Devel. Econ.*, October 1987, *27*(1–2), pp. 189–99. **[G: Latin America]**

Ranis, Gustav. Latin American Debt and Adjustment. *[Diaz-Alejandro, C. F.]*, 1987, pp. 189–99. **[G: Latin America]**

Rieke, Wolfgang. Jahresversammlung von IWF und Weltbank 1987. (1987 IMF/World Bank Annual Meeting. With English Summary) *Kredit Kapital*, 1987, *20*(4), pp. 559–71.

Rybczynski, Tad M. The Anatomy of Financial Crises: Discussion. *Portes, R. and Swoboda, A. K., eds.*, 1987, pp. 61–66. **[G: Global]**

Sachs, Jeffrey D. and Huizinga, Harry. U.S. Commercial Banks and the Developing-Country Debt Crisis. *Brookings Pap. Econ. Act.*, 1987, (2), pp. 555–601. **[G: U.S.]**

Saunders, Anthony. The Inter-bank Market, Contagion Effects and International Financial Crises. *Portes, R. and Swoboda, A. K., eds.*, 1987, pp. 196–232. **[G: Global]**

Savvides, Andreas. Bank Loan Rate Indexation in the Eurocurrency Market. *J. Int. Money Finance*, September 1987, *6*(3), pp. 355–71. **[G: LDCs]**

Seger, Martha R. Statement to the U.S. House Subcommittee on Financial Institutions Supervision, Regulation and Insurance of the Committee on Banking, Finance and Urban Affairs, May 6, 1987. *Fed. Res. Bull.*, July 1987, *73*(7), pp. 560–63. **[G: U.S.]**

Shariff, Ismael. External Debt and Policy Issues in the Developing Countries. *Indian Econ. J.*, Jan.-Mar. 1987, *34*(3), pp. 86–91. **[G: LDCs]**

Shinn, Chang Min. Capital Imports in Economic Development: The Korean Case, 1962–85. *J. Econ. Devel.*, June 1987, *12*(1), pp. 49–63.
[G: Korea]

Shinohara, Naoyuki. Tokyo as an International Finance Center: Financial Liberalization and International Standardization. *Finn, R. B., ed.*, 1987, pp. 75–95. **[G: Japan; U.S.]**

Shoven, John B. U.S. Commercial Banks and the Developing-Country Debt Crisis: Comment. *Brookings Pap. Econ. Act.*, 1987, (2), pp. 602–04. **[G: U.S.]**

Smirlock, Michael and Kaufold, Howard. Bank Foreign Lending, Mandatory Disclosure Rules, and the Reaction of Bank Stock Prices to the Mexican Debt Crisis. *J. Bus.*, July 1987, *60*(3), pp. 347–64. **[G: U.S.]**

Smith, Roy C. New Financial Aspects of the U.S.– Japanese Trade Relationship. *Sato, R. and Wachtel, P., eds.*, 1987, pp. 110–26.
[G: U.S.; Japan]

Snowden, P. N. Chicago Schism on Banking Reforms and the Debt Crisis. *World Econ.*, June 1987, *10*(2), pp. 219–26. **[G: LDCs]**

Street, James H. Solutions for Mexico's External Debt Problem. *Tremblay, R., ed.*, 1987, pp. 31–41. **[G: Mexico]**

Taffler, R. J. and Abassi, B. Country Risk: A Model for Predicting Debt Servicing Problems in Developing Countries. *Res, Z. and Motamen, S., eds.*, 1987, pp. 187–223. **[G: LDCs]**

Teranishi, Juro. The "Catch-up" Process, Financial System, and Japan's Rise as a Capital Exporter. *Hitotsubashi J. Econ.*, October 1987, *27*, pp. 133–46. **[G: Japan]**

Tonnel-Martinache, Mariette. Degré de développement des systèmes financiers et redéploiement géographique des banques. Une interprétation en termes d'avantages comparés de pays et de secteur. (The Current Development of Financial Systems and Geographical Trends in Banking: A Comparative Analysis of the Advantages by Country and by Sector. With English summary.) *Revue Écon.*, January 1987, *38*(1), pp. 117–47. **[G: Global]**

Volcker, Paul A. Statement to the U.S. House Subcommittee on General Oversight and Investigations of the Committee on Banking, Finance and Urban Affairs, April 30, 1987. *Fed. Res. Bull.*, June 1987, *73*(6), pp. 435–40.
[G: U.S.; U.K.]

Walter, Ingo. Country Risk, Portfolio Decisions and Regulation in International Bank Lending. *Wilcox, J. A., ed.*, 1987, *1981*, pp. 342–56.

Warren, Stanton A. and Romans, J. Thomas. The Debtor/Creditor Status of Latin American Countries and the Issue of Repudiation or Forgiveness of Debt. *Tremblay, R., ed.*, 1987, pp. 71–78. **[G: Latin America]**

Weaving, Rachel. Measuring Developing Countries' External Debt. *Finance Develop.*, March 1987, *24*(1), pp. 16–19. **[G: LDCs]**

Zecher, J. Richard. Emergency Liquidity Assis-

tance for International Banks: Discussion. *Portes, R. and Swoboda, A. K., eds.*, 1987, pp. 194–95.

Zombanakis, Minos. The International Debt Threat: A Way to Avoid a Crash. *Res, Z. and Motamen, S., eds.*, 1987, pp. 69–79.
[G: Global]

440 INTERNATIONAL INVESTMENT AND FOREIGN AID

441 International Investment and Long-term Capital Movements

4410 General

Donges, Juergen B. Capital Needs and Capital Markets: Introduction. *Borner, S. and Taylor, A., eds.*, 1987, pp. 267–73.

Findlay, Ronald and Lundahl, Mats. Racial Discrimination, Dualistic Labor Markets and Foreign Investment. *J. Devel. Econ.*, October 1987, *27*(1–2), pp. 139–48. **[G: S. Africa]**

Findlay, Ronald and Lundahl, Mats. Racial Discrimination, Dualistic Labor Markets and Foreign Investment. *[Diaz-Alejandro, C. F.]*, 1987, pp. 139–48. **[G: S. Africa]**

Hormats, Robert D. International Capital Markets and Financial Flows. *Kaushik, S. K., ed.*, 1987, pp. 15–21.

Kindleberger, Charles P. Finnish War Reparations. *Kindleberger, C. P.*, 1987, pp. 209–29.
[G: Finland; U.S.S.R.]

Prindl, A. R. The Internationalisation of Japanese Financial Institutions. *Trevor, M., ed.*, 1987, pp. 111–19. **[G: Japan]**

Stam, J. A. Japanese Direct Foreign Investment in the Netherlands: An Overview. *Trevor, M., ed.*, 1987, pp. 198–202. **[G: Japan; Netherlands]**

Streeten, Paul. "New" Directions for Private Resource Transfers. *Banca Naz. Lavoro Quart. Rev.*, March 1987, (160), pp. 61–76.

Triffin, Robert. W.M.S.: The World Monetary System or Scandal? *Kaushik, S. K., ed.*, 1987, pp. 31–46.

4411 International Investment and Long-term Capital Movements: Theory

Arndt, Sven W. and Richardson, J. David. Real–Financial Linkages among Open Economies: An Overview. *Arndt, S. W. and Richardson, J. D. eds.*, 1987, pp. 5–32.

Bhagwati, Jagdish N.; Brecher, Richard A. and Hatta, Tatsuo. The Generalized Theory of Transfers and Welfare: Bilateral Transfers in a Multilateral World. *Bhagwati, J. N., ed.*, 1987, *1983*, pp. 431–52.

Bhagwati, Jagdish N., et al. Quid pro Quo Foreign Investment and Welfare: A Political-Economy–Theoretic Model. *[Diaz-Alejandro, C. F.]*, 1987, pp. 127–38.

Bhagwati, Jagdish N., et al. Quid Pro Quo Foreign Investment and Welfare: A Political-Economy–Theoretic Model. *J. Devel. Econ.*, October 1987, 27(1–2), pp. 127–38.

Boeri, Tito. Modelling Foreign Aid, Capital Inflows and Economic Development. *Rivista Int. Sci. Econ. Com.*, July 1987, 34(7), pp. 623–47.

Brander, James A. and Spencer, Barbara J. Foreign Direct Investment with Unemployment and Endogenous Taxes and Tariffs. *J. Int. Econ.*, May 1987, 22(3/4), pp. 257–79.

Brecher, Richard A. and Díaz-Alejandro, Carlos F. Tariffs, Foreign Capital, and Immiserizing Growth. *Bhagwati, J. N., ed.*, 1987, 1977, pp. 389–94.

Broadman, Harry G. Petroleum Firm Foreign Investment in Non-OPEC Developing Countries: A Theoretical Perspective. *Pachauri, R. K., ed.*, 1987, pp. 547–60.   [G: LDCs]

Buffie, Edward F. Labor Market Distortions, the Structure of Protection and Direct Foreign Investment. *[Diaz-Alejandro, C. F.]*, 1987, pp. 149–63.

Buffie, Edward F. Labor Market Distortions, the Structure of Protection and Direct Foreign Investment. *J. Devel. Econ.*, October 1987, 27(1–2), pp. 149–63.

Burgstaller, André. Europe's Industrialization and Colonial Underdevelopment in the Light of Ricardo's Corn Model. *J. Int. Econ.*, February 1987, 22(1/2), pp. 157–69.

Cozier, Barry V. An Analysis of Foreign Asset Behaviour in Jamaica: 1957–1981. *Tremblay, R., ed.*, 1987, pp. 227–48.   [G: Jamaica]

Culem, Claudy G. Pourquoi les multinationales? Une revue de la littérature sur les motivations de la croissance multinationale des firmes. (With English summary.) *Cah. Écon. Bruxelles*, Third Trimester 1987, (115), pp. 3–33.

Deardorff, Alan V. Trade and Capital Mobility in a World of Diverging Populations. *Johnson, D. G. and Lee, R. D., eds.*, 1987, pp. 561–88.   [G: LDCs; MDCs]

Desai, Padma. The Rate of Return on Foreign Capital Inflow to the Soviet Economy. *Desai, P.*, 1987, pp. 133–52.   [G: U.S.S.R.]

Dornbusch, Rudiger and Fischer, Stanley. International Capital Flows and the World Debt Problem. *Razin, A. and Sadka, E., eds.*, 1987, pp. 211–54.   [G: Global]

Eckstein, Zvi. Aspects of Capital Flows between Developing and Developed Countries: Comments. *Razin, A. and Sadka, E., eds.*, 1987, pp. 283–85.   [G: LDCs]

Emminger, Otmar. The Dollar's Borrowed Strength. *Salvatore, D., ed.*, 1987, pp. 450–68.   [G: U.S.]

Ethier, Wilfred J. Bundled International Factor Mobility. *[Corden, W. M.]*, 1987, pp. 99–111.

Horstmann, Ignatius J. and Markusen, James R. Licensing versus Direct Investment: A Model of Internalization by the Multinational Enterprise. *Can. J. Econ.*, August 1987, 20(3), pp. 464–81.

Hughes, Helen. Capital Needs of the Developing Countries in the Eighties. *Borner, S. and Taylor, A., eds.*, 1987, pp. 275–99.   [G: LDCs]

Jones, Ronald W.; Neary, J. Peter and Ruane,

Frances P. International Capital Mobility and the Dutch Disease. *[Corden, W. M.]*, 1987, pp. 86–98.

Krueger, Anne O. Aspects of Capital Flows between Developing and Developed Countries. *Razin, A. and Sadka, E., eds.*, 1987, pp. 255–82.   [G: LDCs]

Mainardi, Stefano. An Appraisal of Different Theoretical Approaches and Models of Foreign Direct Investment and International Trade. *Rivista Int. Sci. Econ. Com.*, May 1987, 34(5), pp. 431–52.

Mercenier, Jean. Tariff Change, Foreign Capital and Immiserization: A General Equilibrium Evaluation of the Latin American Case. *J. Devel. Econ.*, June 1987, 26(1), pp. 145–62.   [G: Latin America]

Niehans, Jürg. Monetary Policy and Investment Dynamics in Interdependent Economies. *J. Money, Credit, Banking*, February 1987, 19(1), pp. 33–45.

Patel, Indraprasad G. Foreign Capital and Domestic Planning. *Ciocca, P., ed.*, 1987, 1967, pp. 277–97.

Stockman, Alan C. Some Interactions between Goods Markets and Asset Markets in Open Economies. *Arndt, S. W. and Richardson, J. D. eds.*, 1987, pp. 33–44.

Tsai, Pan-long. The Welfare Impact of Foreign Investment in the Presence of Specific Factors and Non-traded Goods. *Weltwirtsch. Arch.*, 1987, 123(3), pp. 496–508.

Wong, Kar-yiu. Are International Trade and Factor Mobility Substitutes? *Bhagwati, J. N., ed.*, 1987, 1986, pp. 37–53.

4412 International Investment and Long-term Capital Movements: Studies

Aggarwal, Raj and Soenen, Luc A. Changing Benefits of International Diversification of Real Assets. *Rivista Int. Sci. Econ. Com.*, Nov.-Dec. 1987, 34(11–12), pp. 1103–12.   [G: U.S.]

Aslam, Naheed. The Impact of Foreign Capital Inflow on Savings and Investment: The Case of Pakistan. *Pakistan Devel. Rev.*, Winter 1987, 26(4), pp. 787–89.   [G: Pakistan]

Bentham, Richard W. Questions of Hardship in Transnational Agreements. *Dicke, D. C., ed.*, 1987, pp. 163–76.

Bird, Richard M. Imputation and the Foreign Tax Credit: Some Critical Notes from an International Perspective. *Australian Tax Forum*, 1987, 4(1), pp. 1–34.   [G: Australia]

Bitros, George C. Foreign Direct Investment in Manufacturing: A Note. *Greek Econ. Rev.*, 1987, 9(1), pp. 108–12.

Bitros, George C. Foreign Direct Investment in Manufacturing: A Note. *Greek Econ. Rev.*, 1987, 9(1), pp. 108–12.

Blair, Andrew R. The Relative Distribution of United States Direct Investment: The U.K./EEC Experience. *Europ. Econ. Rev.*, July 1987, 31(5), pp. 1137–44.   [G: EEC; U.S.]

Boskin, Michael J. Tax Policy and the International Location of Investment. *Feldstein, M.,* *ed. (II)*, 1987, pp. 73–81.   [G: U.S.]

Boskin, Michael J. and Gale, William G. New Results on the Effects of Tax Policy on the International Location of Investment. *Feldstein, M., ed. (I)*, 1987, pp. 201–19.   [G: U.S.]

Broadman, Harry G. Corporate Strategies of Foreign Investment in Oil Exploration outside North America. *J. Energy Devel.*, Autumn 1987, *13*(1), pp. 27–44.   [G: U.S.; Canada]

Bulajic, Milan. International Protection of Intellectual Property and Foreign Investment. *Dicke, D. C., ed.*, 1987, pp. 42–67.
                [G: Global]

Burton, F. N. and Saelens, F. H. Trade Barriers and Japanese Foreign Direct Investment in the Colour Television Industry. *Managerial Dec. Econ.*, December 1987, *8*(4), pp. 285–93.
                [G: Japan]

Chevassus, Emmanuelle and Green, Raúl H. Les investissements croisés France–États-Unis dans l'agro-alimentaire. (U.S.–French Crossed Investment in Food Industry. With English summary.) *Écon. Soc.*, July 1987, *21*(7), pp. 57–90.   [G: U.S.; France]

Chowdhury, Subrata Roy. Reasonable Expectations of the Foreign Investor and the Host State. *Dicke, D. C., ed.*, 1987, pp. 259–67.

Cooney, Stephen. The Impact of the U.S. Trade Deficit on Future Investment Flows. *[Marjolin, R.]*, 1987, pp. 153–67.   [G: U.S.]

Coughlin, Cletus C. International Trade in the United States: Past, Present, and Future: Introduction. *Spencer, S. I., ed.*, 1987, pp. 41–45.   [G: U.S.]

Cozier, Barry V. An Analysis of Foreign Asset Behaviour in Jamaica: 1957–1981. *Tremblay, R., ed.*, 1987, pp. 227–48.   [G: Jamaica]

Cushman, David O. The Effects of Real Wages and Labor Productivity on Foreign Direct Investment. *Southern Econ. J.*, July 1987, *54*(1), pp. 174–85.   [G: U.S.]

Deppler, Michael and Williamson, Martin. Capital Flight: Concepts, Measurement, and Issues. *International Monetary Fund Research Department.*, 1987, pp. 39–58.   [G: LDCs; MDCs]

Dicke, Detlev Chr. Unjust Enrichment and Compensation. *Dicke, D. C., ed.*, 1987, pp. 268–80.

Dooley, Michael P.; Frankel, Jeffrey A. and Mathieson, Donald J. International Capital Mobility: What Do Saving–Investment Correlations Tell Us? *Int. Monet. Fund Staff Pap.*, September 1987, *34*(3), pp. 503–30.
                [G: Selected Countries]

Dunlevy, James A. and Seiver, Daniel A. Foreign Finance, Wealth Effects and Economic Development. *Appl. Econ.*, April 1987, *19*(4), pp. 467–81.   [G: LDCs]

Evans, Keith R. Canada for Sale: The Investment Canada Act. *J. World Trade Law*, June 1987, *21*(3), pp. 85–97.   [G: Canada]

Feldman, Mario. MIGA, Critical Remarks from a South American Point of View. *Dicke, D. C., ed.*, 1987, pp. 347–53.

Fouch, Gregory G. Foreign Direct Investment

in the United States: Detail for Position and Balance of Payments Flows, 1986. *Surv. Curr. Bus.*, August 1987, *67*(8), pp. 85–103.
                [G: U.S.]

Fukao, Mitsuhiro and Hanazaki, Masaharu. Internationalisation of Financial Markets and the Allocation of Capital. *OECD Econ. Stud.*, Spring 1987, (8), pp. 35–92.   [G: OECD]

Gaudard, Gaston. Foreign Investment and Transnational Corporations. *Dicke, D. C., ed.*, 1987, pp. 33–41.

Gomez-Samper, Henry and Villalba, Julian. A Venezuelan Paradox: The Prospects for Attracting (or Repatriating) Foreign Investment. *Salazar-Carrillo, J. and Tirado de Alonzo, I., eds.*, 1987, pp. 1–10.   [G: Venezuela]

Griffin, Keith. Doubts about Aid. *Griffin, K.*, 1987, *1986*, pp. 235–54.   [G: LDCs]

Grubaugh, Stephen G. Determinants of Direct Foreign Investment. *Rev. Econ. Statist.*, February 1987, *69*(1), pp. 149–52.   [G: U.S.]

Grubaugh, Stephen G. The Process of Direct Foreign Investment. *Southern Econ. J.*, October 1987, *54*(2), pp. 351–60.   [G: U.S.]

Hartman, David G. New Results on the Effects of Tax Policy on the International Location of Investment: Comment. *Feldstein, M., ed. (I)*, 1987, pp. 219–22.   [G: U.S.]

Harvie, Charles. The Structural Effects of North Sea Oil upon the U.K. Economy: Alternative Viewpoints and Evidence. *J. Energy Devel.*, Autumn 1987, *13*(1), pp. 45–86.   [G: U.K.]

Haschek, Helmut H. Austrian Foreign Investments and Investment-Protection Agreements. *Dicke, D. C., ed.*, 1987, pp. 3–6.
                [G: Austria]

Helleiner, Gerald K. Direct Foreign Investment and Alternative Forms of External Non-concessional Finance for Developing Countries. *Borner, S. and Taylor, A., eds.*, 1987, pp. 445–66.   [G: LDCs]

Herr, Ellen M. U.S. Business Enterprises Acquired or Established by Foreign Direct Investors in 1986. *Surv. Curr. Bus.*, May 1987, *67*(5), pp. 27–35.   [G: U.S.]

Hiemenz, Ulrich. Foreign Direct Investment and Industrialization in ASEAN Countries. *Weltwirtsch. Arch.*, 1987, *123*(1), pp. 121–39.
                [G: ASEAN]

Hill, Hal and Lindsey, C. W. Multinationals from Large and Small Countries: A Philippine Case Study. *Banca Naz. Lavoro Quart. Rev.*, March 1987, (160), pp. 77–92.   [G: Philippines]

Hossain, Kamal. Foreign Investment in the Present and a New International Economic Order: Introduction. *Dicke, D. C., ed.*, 1987, pp. 7–12.   [G: Global]

Hughes, Helen. Capital Needs of the Developing Countries in the Eighties. *Borner, S. and Taylor, A., eds.*, 1987, pp. 275–99.   [G: LDCs]

Jaenicke, Günther. Consequences of a Breach of an Investment Agreement Governed by International Law, by General Principles of Law, or by Domestic Law of the Host State. *Dicke, D. C., ed.*, 1987, pp. 177–93.

Jenkins, C. M. Disinvestment: Effects on the Rate

of Growth of GDP. *S. Afr. J. Econ.*, December 1987, *55*(4), pp. 395–406. **[G: S. Africa]**

Jun, Yongwook. The Reverse Direct Investment: The Case of the Korean Consumer Electronics Industry. *Int. Econ. J.*, Autumn 1987, *1*(3), pp. 91–104. **[G: S. Korea]**

Kaempfer, William H.; Lehman, James A. and Lowenberg, Anton D. Divestment, Investment Sanctions, and Disinvestment: An Evaluation of Anti-apartheid Policy Instruments. *Int. Organ.*, Summer 1987, *41*(3), pp. 457–73. **[G: S. Africa]**

Killick, Tony. Unsettled Questions about Adjustment with Growth. *United Nations Conference on Trade and Development.*, 1987, pp. 207–58. **[G: Latin America]**

Kojima, Kiyoshi. Agreed Specialisation and Cross Direct Investment. *Hitotsubashi J. Econ.*, December 1987, *28*(2), pp. 87–105. **[G: Japan; U.S.]**

Kozlow, Ralph. U.S. Direct Investment Abroad: Detail for Position and Balance of Payments Flows, 1986. *Surv. Curr. Bus.*, August 1987, *67*(8), pp. 58–84. **[G: U.S.]**

Krafft, Matthias. Bilateral Foreign Investment Agreements. *Dicke, D. C., ed.*, 1987, pp. 96–101.

Kudo, Akira. From Commercial Controversy to Industrial and Technological Cooperation between Japan and the EC: The New Role of Japanese Direct Investment in the EC. *Trevor, M., ed.*, 1987, pp. 63–72. **[G: Japan; EEC]**

Kumar, Nagesh. Intangible Assets, Internalisation and Foreign Production: Direct Investments and Licensing in Indian Manufacturing. *Weltwirtsch. Arch.*, 1987, *123*(2), pp. 325–45. **[G: India]**

Lebrowski, Maciej and Monkiewicz, Jan. CMEA Direct Investments in the Western Countries: The Case of Poland. *J. World Trade Law*, June 1987, *21*(3), pp. 27–38. **[G: Poland; CMEA]**

Lillich, Richard B. Lump Sum Agreements: Standards Therein and Impact Thereof. *Dicke, D. C., ed.*, 1987, pp. 239–58. **[G: U.S.; Global]**

Loibl, Gerhard. Foreign Investment Insurance Systems. *Dicke, D. C., ed.*, 1987, pp. 102–15. **[G: Global]**

Luft, C. and Maier, Lutz. International Investment Cooperation within the CMEA Area. *Borner, S. and Taylor, A., eds.*, 1987, pp. 301–20. **[G: CMEA]**

Lutz, James M. Foreign Investment in the United States: Effects on Export Performance. *Soc. Sci. Quart.*, December 1987, *68*(4), pp. 816–33. **[G: U.S.]**

Mayer, Helmut W. Financial Flows to Developing Countries: Trends, Problems and Future Outlook. *Borner, S. and Taylor, A., eds.*, 1987, pp. 411–27. **[G: LDCs]**

Meyer, Hermann S. Foreign Investment Planning and Consequences. *Dicke, D. C., ed.*, 1987, pp. 13–32. **[G: Latin America]**

van Nieuwkerk, Marius. In Search of 100 Billion Dollars. *Heijmans, R. and Neudecker, H., eds.*, 1987, pp. 121–30. **[G: Global]**

Park, Hui-Jong. The Effects of Foreign Capital

Inflow on Economic Growth in Korea: The Reevaluation of Griffin and Enos's Hypotheses. *Int. Econ. J.*, Summer 1987, *1*(2), pp. 79–93. **[G: S. Korea]**

Parry, Thomas G. The Australian Development Assistance Bureau's South Pacific Joint Venture Scheme. *J. World Trade Law*, June 1987, *21*(3), pp. 63–72. **[G: Australia]**

Pazos, Felipe. Foreign Investment Revisited. *Salazar-Carrillo, J. and Tirado de Alonzo, I., eds.*, 1987, pp. 1–20. **[G: Latin America]**

Petersmann, Ernst-Ulrich. Sovereignty, International Law and the United Nations Code of Conduct on Transnational Corporations. *Dicke, D. C., ed.*, 1987, pp. 310–36.

Pollard, Sidney. Comment on Peter Temin's Comment [Capital Exports: 1870–1914: Harmful or Beneficial?]. *Econ. Hist. Rev., 2nd Ser.*, August 1987, *40*(3), pp. 459–60. **[G: U.K.]**

Rothgeb, John M., Jr. Trojan Horse, Scapegoat, or Non-foreign Entity: Foreign Policy and Investment Penetration in Poor Countries. *J. Conflict Resolution*, June 1987, *31*(2), pp. 227–65. **[G: LDCs]**

Rugman, Alan M. Canadian Foreign Direct Investment. *Safarian, A. E. and Bertin, G. Y., eds.*, 1987, pp. 120–34. **[G: Canada; U.S.]**

Sacerdoti, Giorgio. Foreign and Foreign-Owned Corporations in International Economic Law. *Dicke, D. C., ed.*, 1987, pp. 289–309.

Salazar-Carrillo, Jorge and Tirado de Alonso, Irma. Foreign Investment and Economic Development in Latin America: Introduction. *Salazar-Carrillo, J. and Tirado de Alonzo, I., eds.*, 1987, pp. 1–7. **[G: Latin America]**

Santiago, Carlos E. The Impact of Foreign Direct Investment on Export Structure and Employment Generation. *World Devel.*, March 1987, *15*(3), pp. 317–28. **[G: Puerto Rico]**

Sato, Kazuo and Lii, Sheng-Yann. The Exchange Rate, Trade Balance, and Capital Flows: The Case of Japan. *Dutta, M., ed. (I)*, 1987, pp. 145–70. **[G: Japan]**

Scholl, Russell B. The International Investment Position of the United States in 1986. *Surv. Curr. Bus.*, June 1987, *67*(6), pp. 38–45. **[G: U.S.]**

Seidl-Hohenveldern, Ignaz. Semantics of Wealth Deprivation and Their Legal Significance. *Dicke, D. C., ed.*, 1987, pp. 218–38.

Shihata, Ibrahim F. I. The Multilateral Investment Guarantee Agency (MIGA). *Dicke, D. C., ed.*, 1987, pp. 137–52. **[G: LDCs]**

Shinn, Chang Min. Capital Imports in Economic Development: The Korean Case, 1962–85. *J. Econ. Devel.*, June 1987, *12*(1), pp. 49–63. **[G: Korea]**

Temin, Peter. Capital Exports, 1870–1914: An Alternative Model: Comment [Capital Exports: 1870–1914: Harmful or Beneficial?]. *Econ. Hist. Rev., 2nd Ser.*, August 1987, *40*(3), pp. 453–58. **[G: U.K.]**

Trooboff, Peter D. The Revised Restatement of the Foreign Relations Law of the United States: Reaffirmation of Established International Legal Principles Governing State Responsibility toward Foreign-Owned Investment. *Dicke, D. C., ed.*, 1987, pp. 201–17. **[G: U.S.]**

Tuan, Chyau. U.S. Influence on the Hong Kong Economy and Prospect. *Dutta, M., ed. (II)*, 1987, pp. 199–221. **[G: Hong Kong]**

de Waart, Paul J. I. M. ICSID and Other Forms of Arbitration and Conciliation: Institutionalization of Dispute Settlement in the Context of the Right of Development. *Dicke, D. C., ed.*, 1987, pp. 116–36. **[G: U.S.]**

Wonghanchao, Warin and Pongpissanupichit, Jeerasak. Contribution of Direct U.S. Investment to the Thai Economy. *Dutta, M., ed. (II)*, 1987, pp. 225–52. **[G: Thailand]**

Wu, Rong-I. U.S. Direct Investment in Taiwan: An Economic Appraisal. *Dutta, M., ed. (II)*, 1987, pp. 185–98. **[G: Taiwan]**

Yannopoulos, George N. European Community Tariff Preferences and Foreign Direct Investment. *Banca Naz. Lavoro Quart. Rev.*, March 1987, (160), pp. 93–109. **[G: EEC]**

442 International Business and Multinational Enterprises

4420 International Business and Multinational Enterprises

Abbott, Kenneth W. Collective Goods, Mobile Resources, and Extraterritorial Trade Controls. *Law Contemp. Probl.*, Summer 1987, *50*(3), pp. 117–52. **[G: U.S.]**

Abe, Y. Japanese Market Entry Strategy. The Case of Yamanouchi Pharmaceuticals in Western Europe. *Trevor, M., ed.*, 1987, pp. 150–55. **[G: Japan; W. Europe]**

Aggarwal, Mangat Ram. Transnational Corporations, Economic Development and Income Distribution in Less Developed Countries. *Indian Econ. J.*, Jan.-Mar. 1987, *34*(3), pp. 4–50. **[G: LDCs]**

Aggarwal, Raj. Foreign Operations of Singapore Industrial Firms: A Study of Emerging Multinationals from a Newly Industrializing Country. *Dutta, M., ed. (II)*, 1987, pp. 253–65. **[G: Singapore]**

Akhter, Humayun and Lusch, Robert F. Political Risk: A Structural Analysis. *Cavusgil, S. T., ed.*, 1987, pp. 81–101.

Amine, Lyn S. Toward a Conceptualization of Export Trading Companies in World Markets. *Cavusgil, S. T., ed.*, 1987, pp. 199–238. **[G: Japan; S. Korea; Brazil; U.S.]**

An, Tang. The Law Applicable to a Transnational Economic Development Contract. *J. World Trade Law*, August 1987, *21*(4), pp. 95–146. **[G: Global]**

Askholt, Steen and Michelsen, Aage. The Fiscal Residence of Companies: Denmark. *International Fiscal Association, ed. (I)*, 1987, pp. 273–86. **[G: Denmark]**

Atwood, James R. Conflicts of Jurisdiction in the Antitrust Field: The Example of Export Cartels. *Law Contemp. Probl.*, Summer 1987, *50*(3), pp. 153–64. **[G: U.S.]**

Austin, Robert P. Regulatory Principles and the

Internationalization of Securities Markets. *Law Contemp. Probl.*, Summer 1987, *50*(3), pp. 221–50. **[G: U.S.]**

Barbone, Luca and Rivera-Batiz, Francisco. Foreign Capital and the Contractionary Impact of Currency Devaluation, with an Application to Jamaica. *J. Devel. Econ.*, June 1987, *26*(1), pp. 1–15. **[G: Jamaica]**

Barratt, C. John A. Can External Leverage Pressure South Africa? *Sethi, S. P., ed.*, 1987, pp. 205–17. **[G: S. Africa]**

Basevi, Giorgio; Cocchi, Daniela and Lischi, Pier Luigi. The Choice of Currency in the Foreign Trade of Italy. *Hodgman, D. R. and Wood, G. E., eds.*, 1987, pp. 1–48. **[G: Italy]**

Becker, David G. "Bonanza Development" and the "New Bourgeoisie": Peru under Military Rule. *Becker, D. G., et al.*, 1987, pp. 63–105. **[G: Peru]**

Becker, David G. Development, Democracy, and Dependency in Latin America: A Postimperialist View. *Becker, D. G., et al.*, 1987, pp. 41–62. **[G: Latin America]**

Becker, David G. and Sklar, Richard L. Why Postimperialism? *Becker, D. G., et al.*, 1987, pp. 1–18.

Beckford, George L. The Social Economy of Bauxite in the Jamaican Man–Space. *Soc. Econ. Stud.*, March 1987, *36*(1), pp. 1–55. **[G: Jamaica]**

Behney, Thomas Amos, Jr. Extraterritoriality of Economic Legislation: Bibliography. *Law Contemp. Probl.*, Summer 1987, *50*(3), pp. 303–47.

Behrman, Jack N. International Industrial Integration through Multinational Enterprises. *Dunning, J. H. and Usui, M., eds.*, 1987, pp. 63–76.

Bennett, Karl. The Caribbean Basin Initiative and Its Implications for CARICOM Exports. *Soc. Econ. Stud.*, June 1987, *36*(2), pp. 21–40. **[G: Caribbean]**

Benvignati, Anita M. Domestic Profit Advantages of Multinational Firms. *J. Bus.*, July 1987, *60*(3), pp. 449–61. **[G: U.S.]**

Bertin, Gilles Y. Multinational Enterprises: Transfer Partners and Transfer Policies. *Safarian, A. E. and Bertin, G. Y., eds.*, 1987, pp. 85–100. **[G: OECD]**

Blouet, J. F. La résidence fiscale des sociétés: France. (The Fiscal Residence of Companies: France. With English summary.) *International Fiscal Association, ed. (I)*, 1987, pp. 321–31. **[G: France]**

Boltuck, Richard D. An Economic Analysis of Dumping. *J. World Trade Law*, October 1987, *21*(5), pp. 45–54. **[G: U.S.]**

Bonin, Bernard. Contractual Agreements and International Technology Transfers: The Empirical Studies. *Safarian, A. E. and Bertin, G. Y., eds.*, 1987, pp. 73–84.

Bourlakis, Constantine A. Mutinational Corporations and Domestic Market Structure: The Case of Greek Manufacturing Industries. *Weltwirtsch. Arch.*, 1987, *123*(4), pp. 719–33. **[G: Greece]**

Brand, Simon S. How Economic Sanctions Could Cripple Reform. *Sethi, S. P., ed.*, 1987, pp. 197–203. **[G: S. Africa]**

Brereton, Barbara F. U.S. Multinational Companies: Operations in 1985. *Surv. Curr. Bus.*, June 1987, *67*(6), pp. 26–37. **[G: U.S.]**

Broadman, Harry G. Petroleum Firm Foreign Investment in Non-OPEC Developing Countries: A Theoretical Perspective. *Pachauri, R. K., ed.*, 1987, pp. 547–60. **[G: LDCs]**

Brown, Jonathan C. Domestic Politics and Foreign Investment: British Development of Mexican Petroleum, 1889–1911. *Bus. Hist. Rev.*, Autumn 1987, *61*(3), pp. 387–416. **[G: Mexico]**

Buckley, Peter J. and Artisien, Patrick. Policy Issues of Intra-EC Direct Investment: British, French and German Multinationals in Greece, Portugal and Spain, with Special Reference to Employment Effects. *J. Common Market Stud.*, December 1987, *26*(2), pp. 207–30. **[G: EEC]**

Burton, F. N. and Inoue, Hisashi. A Country Risk Appraisal Model of Foreign Asset Expropriation in Developing Countries. *Appl. Econ.*, August 1987, *19*(8), pp. 1009–48. **[G: LDCs]**

Buthelezi, Mangosuthu G. Discerning the Divestment Debate. *Sethi, S. P., ed.*, 1987, pp. 165–69. **[G: S. Africa]**

Campbell, Dennis. Joint Ventures between East and West. *Bull. Int. Fiscal Doc.*, July 1987, *41*(7), pp. 299–303. **[G: E. Europe; OECD]**

Cantwell, John. The Reorganization of European Industries After Integration: Selected Evidence on the Role of Multinational Enterprise Activities. *J. Common Market Stud.*, December 1987, *26*(2), pp. 127–51. **[G: EEC]**

Carrada-Bravo, Francisco. International Trade, Investment, Regional Security, and the Prospects of the Mexico–U.S. Relations. *Tremblay, R., ed.*, 1987, pp. 531–48. **[G: Mexico; U.S.]**

Casas Sánchez, Roberto. The Fiscal Residence of Companies: Mexico. *International Fiscal Association, ed. (I)*, 1987, pp. 403–12. **[G: Mexico]**

Casson, Mark and Pearce, Robert D. Multinational Enterprises in LDCs. *Gemmell, N., ed.*, 1987, pp. 90–132.

Casti, John. (M,R)-Systems as a Framework for Modeling Structural Change in a Global Industry. *Batten, D.; Casti, J. and Johansson, B., eds.*, 1987, pp. 313–34.

Castro, Emilio. Church Groups Lead the Battle against Apartheid: International Campaign. *Sethi, S. P., ed.*, 1987, pp. 271–78. **[G: S. Africa; U.S.]**

Chandler, Alfred D., Jr. A Framework for Analyzing the Modern Multinational Enterprise and Its Competitive Advantage. *Atack, J., ed.*, 1987, pp. 3–17. **[G: U.S.]**

Chandra, Subodh. The Fiscal Residence of Companies: India. *International Fiscal Association, ed. (I)*, 1987, pp. 345–52. **[G: India]**

Chapman, S. D. Investment Groups in India and South Africa [British-based Investment Groups

before 1914]. *Econ. Hist. Rev., 2nd Ser.*, May 1987, *40*(2), pp. 275–80. **[G: U.K.]**

Chen, Tain-Jy and Tang, De-Piao. Comparing Technical Efficiency between Import-Substitution-Oriented and Export-Oriented Foreign Firms in a Developing Economy. *J. Devel. Econ.*, August 1987, *26*(2), pp. 277–89. **[G: Taiwan]**

Chen, Tain-Jy and Tang, De-Piao. Offshore Assembly and Short-run Labor–Labor Substitution. *Weltwirtsch. Arch.*, 1987, *123*(1), pp. 140–48. **[G: Taiwan]**

Chevassus, Emmanuelle and Green, Raúl H. Les investissements croisés France–États-Unis dans l'agro-alimentaire. (U.S.–French Crossed Investment in Food Industry. With English summary.) *Écon. Soc.*, July 1987, *21*(7), pp. 57–90. **[G: U.S.; France]**

Cochran, Sherman. Losing Money Abroad: The Swedish Match Company in China during the 1930s. *Atack, J., ed.*, 1987, pp. 83–91. **[G: China]**

Colombo, Caterina. Exchange Rate and Prices: Firms' Behaviour in the Open Economy. *Giorn. Econ.*, Mar.-Apr. 1987, *46*(3–4), pp. 149–74.

Condor, Ioan. Taxation of Joint Ventures and Non-residents: Romania. *Bull. Int. Fiscal Doc.*, July 1987, *41*(7), pp. 337–42. **[G: Romania]**

Coons, Christopher. Divestment Steamroller Seeks to Bury Apartheid. *Sethi, S. P., ed.*, 1987, pp. 295–306. **[G: S. Africa]**

Cowell, Noel M. The Impact of Bauxite Mining on Peasant and Community Relations in Jamaica. *Soc. Econ. Stud.*, March 1987, *36*(1), pp. 171–216. **[G: Jamaica]**

Cowling, Keith and Sugden, Roger. Market Exchange and the Concept of a Transnational Corporation: Analysing the Nature of the Firm. *Brit. Rev. Econ. Issues*, Spring 1987, *9*(20), pp. 57–68. **[G: U.S.]**

Culem, Claudy G. Pourquoi les multinationales? Une revue de la littérature sur les motivations de la croissance multinationale des firmes. (With English summary.) *Cah. Écon. Bruxelles*, Third Trimester 1987, (115), pp. 3–33.

D'Avino, Carey R. The Fiscal Residence of Companies: United States. *International Fiscal Association, ed. (I)*, 1987, pp. 299–312. **[G: U.S.]**

Das, Sanghamitra. Externalities, and Technology Transfer through Multinational Corporations: A Theoretical Analysis. *J. Int. Econ.*, February 1987, *22*(1/2), pp. 171–82.

Desai, Padma. The Soviet Union and the Third World: A Faltering Partnership? *Desai, P.*, 1987, *1984*, pp. 256–73. **[G: U.S.S.R.; LDCs]**

Dibb, Douglas N. H. J. Heinz Success in Zimbabwe. *Challenge*, Jan./Feb. 1987, *29*(6), pp. 32–36. **[G: Zimbabwe]**

Dohse, Knuth. Innovations in Collective Bargaining through the Multinationalisation of Japanese Auto Companies, the Cases of Nummi

(USA) and Nissan (UK). *Trevor, M., ed.*, 1987, pp. 124–49. **[G: U.S.; U.K.; Japan]**

Dombois, Rainer. The New International Division of Labour, Labour Market and Automobile Production: The Case of Mexico. *Tolliday, S. and Zeitlin, J., eds.*, 1987, pp. 244–57. **[G: Mexico]**

Doz, Yves. International Industries: Fragmentation versus Globalization. *Guile, B. R. and Brooks, H., eds.*, 1987, pp. 96–118.

Drucker, Peter F. Japan's Choices. *Foreign Aff.*, Summer 1987, *65*(5), pp. 923–41. **[G: Japan]**

Dunning, John H. and Archer, Howard. The Eclectic Paradigm and the Growth of UK Multinational Enterprise 1870–1983. *Atack, J., ed.*, 1987, pp. 19–49. **[G: U.K.]**

Dunning, John H. and Norman, G. The Location Choice of Offices of International Companies. *Environ. Planning A*, May 1987, *19*(5), pp. 613–31. **[G: U.K.]**

Dunning, John H. and Robson, Peter. Multinational Corporate Integration and Regional Economic Integration. *J. Common Market Stud.*, December 1987, *26*(2), pp. 103–25. **[G: EEC]**

Edgar, Tim. The Corporate Interest Deduction and the Financing of Foreign Subsidiaries. *Australian Tax Forum*, 1987, *4*(4), pp. 491–528. **[G: Canada; Australia]**

Edwards, P. S. A. The Fiscal Residence of Companies: Hong Kong. *International Fiscal Association, ed. (I)*, 1987, pp. 333–43. **[G: Hong Kong]**

Enderwick, Peter. The Strategy and Structure of Service-Sector Multinationals: Implications for Potential Host Regions. *Reg. Stud.*, June 1987, *21*(3), pp. 215–23. **[G: OECD; Korea; Singapore]**

Etemad, Hamid and Dulude, Louise Séguin. The Development of Technology in MNEs: A Cross-Country and Industry Study. *Safarian, A. E. and Bertin, G. Y., eds.*, 1987, pp. 101–19. **[G: OECD]**

Evans, Keith R. Canada for Sale: The Investment Canada Act. *J. World Trade Law*, June 1987, *21*(3), pp. 85–97. **[G: Canada]**

Francis, A. A. Excess Capacity in Alumina: Some Implications for the Bauxite–Alumina Industry of Jamaica. *Soc. Econ. Stud.*, March 1987, *36*(1), pp. 269–87. **[G: Jamaica]**

French, Michael J. The Emergence of a U.S. Multinational Enterprise: The Goodyear Tire and Rubber Company, 1910–1939. *Econ. Hist. Rev., 2nd Ser.*, February 1987, *40*(1), pp. 64–79. **[G: U.S.]**

Fuss, Melvyn A. and Waverman, Leonard. The Japanese Productivity Advantage in Automobile Production: Can It Be Transferred to North America? *Safarian, A. E. and Bertin, G. Y., eds.*, 1987, pp. 191–206. **[G: Japan]**

Gabrielli, A. R. The Fiscal Residence of Companies: Argentina. *International Fiscal Association, ed. (I)*, 1987, pp. 177–99. **[G: Argentina]**

Galli, Giovanni B. The Fiscal Residence of Companies: Italy. *International Fiscal Association,* *ed. (I)*, 1987, pp. 369–87. **[G: Italy]**

Gassner, Wolfgang. Die steuerliche Ansässigkeit von Kapitalgesellschaften: Österreich. (The Fiscal Residence of Companies: Austria. With English summary.) *International Fiscal Association, ed. (I)*, 1987, pp. 217–29. **[G: Austria]**

Gaudard, Gaston. Foreign Investment and Transnational Corporations. *Dicke, D. C., ed.*, 1987, pp. 33–41.

George, Edward Y. Impact of the Maquilas on Manpower Development and Economic Growth on the U.S./Mexico Border. *Tremblay, R., ed.*, 1987, pp. 549–78. **[G: U.S.; Mexico]**

Gereffi, Gary and Evans, Peter. Transnational Corporations, Dependent Development, and State Policy in the Semiperiphery: A Comparison of Brazil and Mexico. *Dietz, J. L. and Street, J. H., eds.*, 1987, *1981*, pp. 159–90. **[G: Brazil; Mexico]**

Gershenberg, Irving. The Training and Spread of Managerial Know-How, a Comparative Analysis of Multinational and Other Firms in Kenya. *World Devel.*, July 1987, *15*(7), pp. 931–39. **[G: Kenya]**

Girvan, Norman P. Transnational Corporations and Non-fuel Primary Commodities in Developing Countries. *World Devel.*, May 1987, *15*(5), pp. 713–40. **[G: LDCs]**

Glade, William P. Multinationals and the Third World. *J. Econ. Issues*, December 1987, *21*(4), pp. 1889–1920.

Gomez-Samper, Henry and Villalba, Julian. A Venezuelan Paradox: The Prospects for Attracting (or Repatriating) Foreign Investment. *Salazar-Carrillo, J. and Tirado de Alonzo, I., eds.*, 1987, pp. 1–10. **[G: Venezuela]**

Gonçalves, Reinaldo. Competitividade internacional, vantagem comparativa e empresas multinancionais: o caso das exportações brasileiras de manufaturados. (With English summary.) *Pesquisa Planejamento Econ.*, August 1987, *17*(2), pp. 411–36. **[G: Brazil]**

Goodman, Louis W. Food Transnational Corporations and Developing Countries: The Case of the Improved Seed Industry in Mexico. *Ruttan, V. W. and Pray, C. E., eds.*, 1987, pp. 433–49. **[G: Mexico]**

Goto, Mitsuya. Nissan's International Strategy. *Trevor, M., ed.*, 1987, pp. 73–76. **[G: Japan]**

Grubaugh, Stephen G. The Process of Direct Foreign Investment. *Southern Econ. J.*, October 1987, *54*(2), pp. 351–60. **[G: U.S.]**

Halperin, Robert M. and Srinidhi, Bin. The Effects of the U.S. Income Tax Regulations' Transfer Pricing Rules on Allocative Efficiency. *Accounting Rev.*, October 1987, *62*(4), pp. 686–706. **[G: U.S.]**

Hammer, Richard M. and Rohrer, William D. U.S. Branch Taxation: A Venture into the Unknown. *Bull. Int. Fiscal Doc.*, January 1987, *41*(1), pp. 3–12. **[G: U.S.]**

Harley, Geoffrey John. The Fiscal Residence of Companies: New Zealand. *International Fiscal Association, ed. (I)*, 1987, pp. 423–37. **[G: New Zealand]**

Harvey, Charles and Taylor, Peter. Mineral

Wealth and Economic Development: Foreign Direct Investment in Spain, 1851–1913. *Econ. Hist. Rev., 2nd Ser.*, May 1987, *40*(2), pp. 185–207. **[G: Spain]**

Hausman, James S. and Tamaki, George T. The Fiscal Residence of Companies: Canada. *International Fiscal Association, ed. (I)*, 1987, pp. 263–72. **[G: Canada]**

Heise, H.-J. How to Eliminate Risk in Recruitment: Some Reflections on Executive Search and the Personnel Policies of Japanese Subsidiaries in Germany. *Trevor, M., ed.*, 1987, pp. 120–23. **[G: Japan; W. Germany]**

Helpman, Elhanan. A Simple Theory of International Trade with Multinational Corporations. *Bhagwati, J. N., ed.*, 1987, *1984*, pp. 477–97.

Hennart, Jean-Francois. Transaction Costs and the Multinational Enterprise: The Case of Tin. *Atack, J., ed.*, 1987, pp. 147–59. **[G: U.K.]**

Hernandez Berenguel, Luis, et al. The Fiscal Residence of Companies: Peru. *International Fiscal Association, ed. (I)*, 1987, pp. 459–74. **[G: Peru]**

Herr, Ellen M. Capital Expenditures by Majority-Owned Foreign Affiliates of U.S. Companies, 1987 and 1988. *Surv. Curr. Bus.*, September 1987, *67*(9), pp. 26–31. **[G: U.S.]**

Herr, Ellen M. Capital Expenditures by Majority-Owned Foreign Affiliates of U.S. Companies, 1987. *Surv. Curr. Bus.*, March 1987, *67*(3), pp. 26–31. **[G: U.S.]**

Herr, Ellen M. U.S. Business Enterprises Acquired or Established by Foreign Direct Investors in 1986. *Surv. Curr. Bus.*, May 1987, *67*(5), pp. 27–35. **[G: U.S.]**

Herrin, Alejandro N. and Pernia, Ernesto M. Factors Influencing the Choice of Location: Local and Foreign Firms in the Philippines. *Reg. Stud.*, December 1987, *21*(6), pp. 531–41. **[G: Philippines]**

Hill, Hal and Lindsey, C. W. Multinationals from Large and Small Countries: A Philippine Case Study. *Banca Naz. Lavoro Quart. Rev.*, March 1987, (160), pp. 77–92. **[G: Philippines]**

Hoechner, Kurt M. A Swiss Perspective on Conflicts of Jurisdiction. *Law Contemp. Probl.*, Summer 1987, *50*(3), pp. 271–82. **[G: Switzerland]**

Hofer, Erwin H. Der Wandel des Verhältnisses zwischen Staat und multinationaler Gesellschaft. (The Changing Relationship between State and Multinational Enterprise. With English summary.) *Aussenwirtschaft*, December 1987, *42*(4), pp. 403–19. **[G: OECD; LDCs]**

Holladay, J. Douglas. The Limits of American Influence. *Sethi, S. P., ed.*, 1987, pp. 63–71. **[G: S. Africa; U.S.]**

Hood, Neil and Young, Stephen. Inward Investment and the EC: UK Evidence on Corporate Integration Strategies. *J. Common Market Stud.*, December 1987, *26*(2), pp. 193–206. **[G: U.K.; EEC]**

Horstmann, Ignatius J. and Markusen, James R. Licensing versus Direct Investment: A Model of Internalization by the Multinational Enter-

prise. *Can. J. Econ.*, August 1987, *20*(3), pp. 464–81.

Horstmann, Ignatius J. and Markusen, James R. Strategic Investments and the Development of Multinationals. *Int. Econ. Rev.*, February 1987, *28*(1), pp. 109–21.

Howenstine, Ned G. U.S. Affiliates of Foreign Companies: Operations in 1985. *Surv. Curr. Bus.*, May 1987, *67*(5), pp. 36–51. **[G: U.S.]**

Hua, Zhou. Can an Individual Operator Be Qualified as a Principal in Doing Business with Foreign Countries? *Chinese Econ. Stud.*, Fall 1987, *21*(1), pp. 10–16. **[G: China]**

Itagaki, Takao. International Trade and Investment by Multinational Firms under Uncertainty. *Manchester Sch. Econ. Soc. Stud.*, December 1987, *55*(4), pp. 392–406.

Ivanov, Ivan D. Restructuring the Mechanism of Foreign Economic Relations in the USSR. *Soviet Econ.*, July-Sept. 1987, *3*(3), pp. 192–218. **[G: U.S.S.R.]**

Ivens, Michael. The Corporate Role in Fighting Apartheid: British Style. *Sethi, S. P., ed.*, 1987, pp. 319–31. **[G: S. Africa]**

Jagrén, Lars. Newly Established Fast Growing Nordic Companies. *Vartia, P., et al.*, 1987, pp. 209–35. **[G: Denmark; Finland; Sweden; Norway]**

Jain, Subhash C. Perspectives on International Strategic Alliances. *Cavusgil, S. T., ed.*, 1987, pp. 103–20.

Jeffcote, B. M. The Fiscal Residence of Companies: United Kingdom. *International Fiscal Association, ed. (I)*, 1987, pp. 503–22. **[G: U.K.]**

Jones, Geoffrey. The Imperial Bank of Iran and Iranian Economic Development, 1890–1952. *Atack, J., ed.*, 1987, pp. 69–80. **[G: Iran]**

Kaempfer, William H.; Lehman, James A. and Lowenberg, Anton D. Divestment, Investment Sanctions, and Disinvestment: An Evaluation of Anti-apartheid Policy Instruments. *Int. Organ.*, Summer 1987, *41*(3), pp. 457–73. **[G: S. Africa]**

Kajas, Ilkka. The Fiscal Residence of Companies: Finland. *International Fiscal Association, ed. (I)*, 1987, pp. 313–19. **[G: Finland]**

Kane, Edward J. Competitive Financial Reregulation: An International Perspective. *Portes, R. and Swoboda, A. K., eds.*, 1987, pp. 111–45. **[G: OECD]**

Kapoor, Ashok. International Business–Government Negotiations: A Study in India. *Zartman, I. W., ed. (I)*, 1987, pp. 430–51. **[G: India]**

Kassebaum, Nancy Landon. Caution Signs on the Road to Reform. *Sethi, S. P., ed.*, 1987, pp. 46–52. **[G: S. Africa]**

Knight, Arthur [Sir]. Courtaulds in Continental Europe in the 1950s and 1960s: Some Recollections and Reflections. *Atack, J., ed.*, 1987, pp. 213–26. **[G: U.K.]**

Kobrin, Stephen J. Testing the Bargaining Hypothesis in the Manufacturing Sector in Developing Countries. *Int. Organ.*, Autumn 1987, *41*(4), pp. 609–38. **[G: U.S.; LDCs]**

Kohli, Harinder S. and Sood, Anil. Fostering Enterprise Development. *Finance Develop.*, March 1987, *24*(1), pp. 34–36.

Kohona, Palitha T. B. Investment Protection Agreements: An Australian Perspective. *J. World Trade Law*, April 1987, *21*(2), pp. 79–103. **[G: Australia]**

Kozlow, Ralph. Errata: U.S. Direct Investment Abroad. *Surv. Curr. Bus.*, October 1987, *67*(10), pp. 22. **[G: U.S.]**

Kudo, Akira. From Commercial Controversy to Industrial and Technological Cooperation between Japan and the EC: The New Role of Japanese Direct Investment in the EC. *Trevor, M., ed.*, 1987, pp. 63–72. **[G: Japan; EEC]**

Kumar, B. and Steinmann, Horst. The Recruitment, Selection and Job Satisfaction of Expatriate Managers in Japanese and Geman Multinational Corporations. *Trevor, M., ed.*, 1987, pp. 177–97. **[G: Japan; W. Germany]**

Kumar, Nagesh. India's Economic and Technical Cooperation with the Co-developing Countries. *Agrawal, G. R., et al. (II)*, 1987, pp. 181–220. **[G: India]**

Kumar, Rajiv. Performance of Foreign and Domestic Firms in Export Processing Zones. *World Devel.*, Oct./Nov. 1987, *15*(10/11), pp. 1309–19. **[G: India]**

Lall, Sanjaya. Multinationals and Technology Development in Host LDCs. *Dunning, J. H. and Usui, M., eds.*, 1987, pp. 193–209. **[G: LDCs]**

Lapidoth, Arye. The Fiscal Residence of Companies: Israel. *International Fiscal Association, ed. (I)*, 1987, pp. 353–67. **[G: Israel]**

Laroche, Christian. Twists and Turns in the Tax Rules for Foreign Companies Owning Real Estate in France. *Bull. Int. Fiscal Doc.*, March 1987, *41*(3), pp. 120–36.

Lee, Chul Song and Kim, Woo Taik. The Fiscal Residence of Companies: Republic of Korea. *International Fiscal Association, ed. (I)*, 1987, pp. 497–501. **[G: S. Korea]**

Lemgruber, Rolando C. The Fiscal Residence of Companies: Brazil. *International Fiscal Association, ed. (I)*, 1987, pp. 245–61. **[G: Brazil]**

Licklider, Roy. The Arab Oil Weapon of 1973–74. *Leyton-Brown, D., ed.*, 1987, pp. 167–81. **[G: OPEC]**

Lipsey, Robert E. and Kravis, Irving B. The Competitiveness and Comparative Advantage of U.S. Multinationals 1957–1984. *Banca Naz. Lavoro Quart. Rev.*, June 1987, (161), pp. 147–65. **[G: U.S.]**

Little, Jane Sneddon. Intra-firm Trade: An Update. *New Eng. Econ. Rev.*, May/June 1987, pp. 46–51. **[G: U.S.]**

Llontop Chavarri, Carlos Enrique; Francesqui, Manuel Eduardo and Buckley, Tomas O. Branches of Foreign Companies—Income and Patrimony Tax Regimes: Peru. *Bull. Int. Fiscal Doc.*, January 1987, *41*(1), pp. 29–34. **[G: Peru]**

Lockett, Martin. Technical Innovation and Economic Reform in Socialist Economies with Special Reference to China. *Child, J. and Bate, P., eds.*, 1987, pp. 191–203. **[G: China]**

Luiselli Fernández, Cassio. Biotechnology and Food: The Scope for Cooperation. *Thorup, C. L., ed.*, 1987, pp. 167–85. **[G: Mexico; U.S.]**

MacCharles, D. C. Canadian Foreign Subsidiaries: Productivity and Trade Performance. *Tremblay, R., ed.*, 1987, pp. 331–50. **[G: Canada]**

MacCharles, D. C. International Knowledge Transfers and Competitiveness: Canada as a Case Study. *Safarian, A. E. and Bertin, G. Y., eds.*, 1987, pp. 53–69. **[G: Canada]**

Madian, Alan L. Technology and the Changing Industrial Balance. *Thorup, C. L., ed.*, 1987, pp. 41–66. **[G: Mexico; U.S.]**

Mainardi, Stefano. An Appraisal of Different Theoretical Approaches and Models of Foreign Direct Investment and International Trade. *Rivista Int. Sci. Econ. Com.*, May 1987, *34*(5), pp. 431–52.

Maizels, Alfred. Commodities in Crisis: An Overview of the Main Issues. *World Devel.*, May 1987, *15*(5), pp. 537–49. **[G: Global]**

Marin Arias, Manuel. La résidence fiscale des sociétés: Espagne. (The Fiscal Residence of Companies: Spain. With English summary.) *International Fiscal Association, ed. (I)*, 1987, pp. 287–97. **[G: Spain]**

Mason, Mark. Foreign Direct Investment and Japanese Economic Development, 1899–1931. *Atack, J., ed.*, 1987, pp. 93–107. **[G: Japan]**

Matsumura, Hideo. The Fiscal Residence of Companies: Japan. *International Fiscal Association, ed. (I)*, 1987, pp. 389–401. **[G: Japan]**

McBain, Helen. The Impact of the Bauxite–Alumina MNCs on Rural Jamaica: Constraints on Development of Small Farmers in Jamaica. *Soc. Econ. Stud.*, March 1987, *36*(1), pp. 137–70. **[G: Jamaica]**

McFetridge, D. G. The Timing, Mode and Terms of Technology Transfer: Some Recent Findings. *Safarian, A. E. and Bertin, G. Y., eds.*, 1987, pp. 135–50. **[G: Canada]**

Merz, Hans-Peter. The Internationalisation of the Japanese Economy: The Example of the Federal Republic of Germany. *Trevor, M., ed.*, 1987, pp. 36–49. **[G: Japan; W. Germany]**

Messerlin, Patrick A. International Investment, Protection and Technical Transfer: A Preliminary Examination of the Franco–Japanese Case. *Safarian, A. E. and Bertin, G. Y., eds.*, 1987, pp. 167–79. **[G: France; Japan]**

de Meza, David and van der Ploeg, Frederick. Production Flexibility as a Motive for Multinationality. *J. Ind. Econ.*, March 1987, *35*(3), pp. 343–51.

Michalet, Charles-Albert. Strategies of Multinational Companies in the Economic Crisis. *Dunning, J. H. and Usui, M., eds.*, 1987, pp. 211–25.

Mirus, Rolf and Yeung, Bernard. The Relevance of the Invoicing Currency in Intra-firm Trade Transactions. *J. Int. Money Finance*, December 1987, *6*(4), pp. 449–64. **[G: Canada]**

Miyajima, Ritsuko. The Comparative Values of British and Japanese Managers. *Trevor, M., ed.*, 1987, pp. 77–91. **[G: Japan; U.K.]**

Moore, Michael L.; Steece, Bert M. and Swenson, Charles W. An Analysis of the Impact of State Income Tax Rates and Bases on Foreign Investment. *Accounting Rev.*, October 1987, 62(4), pp. 671–85. **[G: U.S.]**

Morelle, H. Lévy. La résidence fiscale des sociétés: Belgique. (The Fiscal Residence of Companies: Belgium. With English summary.) *International Fiscal Association, ed. (I)*, 1987, pp. 231–43. **[G: Belgium]**

Mucchielli, Jean-Louis. Multinational Enterprises, International Investments and Transfers of Technology: The Elements of an Integrated Approach. *Safarian, A. E. and Bertin, G. Y., eds.*, 1987, pp. 11–33.

Murphy, D. G. Investment by Foreign Companies: Zimbabwe. *Bull. Int. Fiscal Doc.*, March 1987, 41(3), pp. 137–41.

Mytelka, Lynn Krieger and Delapierre, Michel. The Alliance Strategies of European Firms in the Information Technology Industry and the Role of ESPRIT. *J. Common Market Stud.*, December 1987, 26(2), pp. 231–53. **[G: EEC]**

Natke, Paul A. Foreign Ownership and Firm-Level Import Performance in Brazilian Manufacturing Industries. *Atlantic Econ. J.*, December 1987, 15(4), pp. 39–48. **[G: Brazil]**

Nauta, Klaas. The Fiscal Residence of Companies: Netherlands. *International Fiscal Association, ed. (I)*, 1987, pp. 439–58. **[G: Netherlands]**

Nicholas, Stephen. Empirical Tests of the Transaction Cost Model: The Evolution of the Pre-1939 British Manufacturing Multinational. *Atack, J., ed.*, 1987, pp. 133–45. **[G: U.K.]**

Nickel, Herman. Will Sanctions Harm the Oppressed or the Oppressor? *Sethi, S. P., ed.*, 1987, pp. 179–88. **[G: S. Africa]**

Nigh, Douglas and Schollhammer, Hans. Foreign Direct Investment, Political Conflict and Cooperation: The Asymmetric Response Hypothesis. *Managerial Dec. Econ.*, December 1987, 8(4), pp. 307–12. **[G: Japan]**

Noonberg, Eve. Extraterritorial Enforcement of Antitrust Laws against Foreign Firms. *Law Contemp. Probl.*, Summer 1987, 50(3), pp. 194–95. **[G: U.S.]**

November, Andràs. Telecommunications, Transfer of Technology and the Third World. *Hieronymi, O., ed.*, 1987, pp. 169–87. **[G: Global]**

O'Hearn, Denis. Estimates of New Foreign Manufacturing Employment in Ireland (1956–1972). *Econ. Soc. Rev.*, April 1987, 18(3), pp. 173–88. **[G: Ireland]**

Ohde, Bjorn. The Fiscal Residence of Companies: Sweden. *International Fiscal Association, ed. (I)*, 1987, pp. 535–42. **[G: Sweden]**

Ordover, Janusz A. Conflicts of Jurisdiction: Antitrust and Industrial Policy. *Law Contemp. Probl.*, Summer 1987, 50(3), pp. 165–77. **[G: U.S.]**

Paarlberg, Robert L. The 1980–81 U.S. Grain Embargo: Consequences for the Participants. *Leyton-Brown, D., ed.*, 1987, pp. 185–206. **[G: U.S.; U.S.S.R.]**

Park, Sung-Jo. The Investment Strategy of Korean Transnational Companies: Quantitative and Structural Aspects and a Typology of Korean Management Systems: Is Korea Following the Japanese Strategy? *Trevor, M., ed.*, 1987, pp. 28–35. **[G: S. Korea]**

Parsons, John E. Forms of GDR Economic Cooperation with the Nonsocialist World. *Comp. Econ. Stud.*, Summer 1987, 29(2), pp. 7–18. **[G: E. Germany]**

Paul, Karen. The Inadequacy of Sullivan Reporting. *Sethi, S. P., ed.*, 1987, pp. 403–12. **[G: U.S.; S. Africa]**

Pazos, Felipe. Foreign Investment Revisited. *Salazar-Carrillo, J. and Tirado de Alonzo, I., eds.*, 1987, pp. 1–20. **[G: Latin America]**

Petersmann, Ernst-Ulrich. Sovereignty, International Law and the United Nations Code of Conduct on Transnational Corporations. *Dicke, D. C., ed.*, 1987, pp. 310–36.

Phylatkis, K. International Lenders of Last Resort: Are Changes Required? Comment. *Res, Z. and Motamen, S., eds.*, 1987, pp. 164–66.

Plummer, James L. Energy and Environmental Technology Transfer from the United States to India. *Pachauri, R. K., ed.*, 1987, pp. 1193–1200. **[G: U.S.; India]**

Prindl, A. R. The Internationalisation of Japanese Financial Institutions. *Trevor, M., ed.*, 1987, pp. 111–19. **[G: Japan]**

Pyle, David H. Competitive Financial Reregulation: An International Perspective: Discussion. *Portes, R. and Swoboda, A. K., eds.*, 1987, pp. 145–49. **[G: OECD]**

Reilly, Bernard J. and DiAngelo, Joseph A., Jr. The Internationalized Environment of Business. *Bus. Econ.*, January 1987, 22(1), pp. 26–30. **[G: OECD]**

Richardson, G. V. C. The Fiscal Residence of Companies: South Africa. *International Fiscal Association, ed. (I)*, 1987, pp. 147–59. **[G: S. Africa]**

Rivier, Jean-Marc. The Fiscal Residence of Companies: General Report. *International Fiscal Association, ed. (I)*, 1987, pp. 47–143. **[G: Global]**

Rodrigues Pardal, Francisco. La résidence fiscale des sociétés: Portugal. (The Fiscal Residence of Companies: Portugal. With English summary.) *International Fiscal Association, ed. (I)*, 1987, pp. 475–96. **[G: Portugal]**

Rodrik, Dani. The Economics of Export-Performance Requirements. *Quart. J. Econ.*, August 1987, 102(3), pp. 633–50.

Rolt, Sidney C. and Burgum, Kathleen J. The Fiscal Residence of Companies: Singapore. *International Fiscal Association, ed. (I)*, 1987, pp. 523–33. **[G: Singapore]**

Ross, T. D. The Status and Strategies of the International Oil Corporations. *Rees, J. and Odell, P., eds.*, 1987, pp. 67–75. **[G: Global]**

Rugman, Alan M. Canadian Foreign Direct Investment. *Safarian, A. E. and Bertin, G. Y., eds.*, 1987, pp. 120–34. **[G: Canada; U.S.]**

Rugman, Alan M. Multinationals and Trade in Services: A Transaction Cost Approach. *Welt-*

wirtsch. Arch., 1987, *123*(4), pp. 651–67.
[G: Canada]
Rugman, Alan M. Strategies for International Competitiveness. *Tremblay, R., ed.*, 1987, pp. 315–25. [G: U.S.]
Runge, Berndt. Die steuerliche Ansässigkeit von Kapitalgesellschaften: Deutschland. (The Fiscal Residence of Companies: Germany. With English summary.) *International Fiscal Association, ed. (I)*, 1987, pp. 161–76.
[G: W. Germany]
Sacerdoti, Giorgio. Foreign and Foreign-Owned Corporations in International Economic Law. *Dicke, D. C., ed.*, 1987, pp. 289–309.
Sachak, Najma. The Impact of Land Acquisition by Bauxite–Alumina Transnational Corporations on Peasants in the Bauxite Land Economy. *Soc. Econ. Stud.*, March 1987, *36*(1), pp. 93–135. [G: Jamaica]
Saelens, F. H. Japanese Strategies for Serving Overseas Markets: The Case of Electronics. *Trevor, M., ed.*, 1987, pp. 50–62. [G: Japan]
Safarian, A. E. Nation States and Transnational Corporations: Introduction. *Dunning, J. H. and Usui, M., eds.*, 1987, pp. 177–92.
Sardinas, Joseph L., Jr. and Merrill, Susan. Regulation of International Data Communications and the Effect upon Multinational Corporations. *Most, Kenneth S., ed.*, 1987, pp. 305–15. [G: OECD]
Schatz, Sayre P. Assertive Pragmatism and the Multinational Enterprise. *Becker, D. G., et al.*, 1987, *1981*, pp. 107–29.
Sethi, S. Prakash. South Africa Beyond Apartheid Reformation of Institutions and Instruments of Change. *Sethi, S. P., ed.*, 1987, pp. 1–37.
[G: S. Africa]
Sklar, Richard L. Postimperialism: A Class Analysis of Multinational Corporate Expansion. *Becker, D. G., et al.*, 1987, *1976*, pp. 19–40.
Sleuwaegen, Leo. Multinationals, the European Community and Belgium: Recent Developments. *J. Common Market Stud.*, December 1987, *26*(2), pp. 255–72. [G: Belgium]
Small, David H. Managing Extraterritorial Jurisdiction Problems: The United States Government Approach. *Law Contemp. Probl.*, Summer 1987, *50*(3), pp. 283–302. [G: U.S.]
Smith, Alasdair. Strategic Investment, Multinational Corporations and Trade Policy. *Europ. Econ. Rev.*, Feb./Mar. 1987, *31*(1/2), pp. 89–96.
Smith, N. Craig. How the West Gains from Apartheid: The Case of the United Kingdom. *Sethi, S. P., ed.*, 1987, pp. 333–52. [G: U.K.; S. Africa]
Smith, Robert E. The Limited International Reach of U.S. Antitrust Policy. *Wills, R. L.; Caswell, J. A. and Culbertson, J. D., eds.*, 1987, pp. 148–65. [G: U.S.]
Soulié, Daniel. Technology Transfers in the Automotive Equipment Industry: The French Case. *Safarian, A. E. and Bertin, G. Y., eds.*, 1987, pp. 180–90. [G: France]
Stam, J. A. Japanese Direct Foreign Investment in the Netherlands: An Overview. *Trevor, M.,*

ed., 1987, pp. 198–202. [G: Japan; Netherlands]
Stam, J. A. The Internationalization of Japanese Business: European and Japanese Perspectives: Conclusion. *Trevor, M., ed.*, 1987, pp. 203–07. [G: Japan]
Stanislawski, Howard. The Impact of the Arab Boycott of Israel on the United States and Canada. *Leyton-Brown, D., ed.*, 1987, pp. 223–54. [G: U.S.; Canada]
Stoever, William A. Gradations of Legal Terms in Joint-Venture Agreements in Least-Developed Compared to More Advanced LDCs. *Can. J. Devel. Stud.*, 1987, *8*(1), pp. 27–47. [G: LDCs]
Storm-Nielsen, Truls. The Fiscal Residence of Companies: Norway. *International Fiscal Association, ed. (I)*, 1987, pp. 413–21. [G: Norway]
Streeten, Paul. "New" Directions for Private Resource Transfers. *Banca Naz. Lavoro Quart. Rev.*, March 1987, (160), pp. 61–76.
Sutcliffe, Michael O. Plenty of Propaganda to Prop Up Pretoria. *Sethi, S. P., ed.*, 1987, pp. 171–78. [G: S. Africa]
Suzman, Helen. The Folly of Economic Sanctions. *Sethi, S. P., ed.*, 1987, pp. 189–95.
[G: S. Africa]
Takahashi, Yoshiaki. The Theoretical Problems of the Transferability of Management Style. *Trevor, M., ed.*, 1987, pp. 156–76.
[G: Japan]
Tell, Björn. Scientific and Technical Information: Sweden and Malaysia. *Dedijer, S. and Jéquier, N., eds.*, 1987, pp. 128–38. [G: Sweden; Malaysia]
Thorup, Cathryn L. The United States and Mexico: Face to Face with New Technology. *Thorup, C. L., ed.*, 1987, pp. 1–24.
[G: U.S.; Mexico]
Tignor, Robert. British Textile Companies and the Egyptian Economy. *Atack, J., ed.*, 1987, pp. 53–67. [G: U.K.; Egypt]
Tirard, Jean-Marc. Taxation of Foreign Companies Doing Business in Algeria. *Bull. Int. Fiscal Doc.*, February 1987, *41*(2), pp. 51–55.
[G: Algeria]
Tonnel-Martinache, Mariette. Degré de développement des systèmes financiers et redéploiement géographique des banques. Une interprétation en termes d'avantages comparés de pays et de secteur. (The Current Development of Financial Systems and Geographical Trends in Banking: A Comparative Analysis of the Advantages by Country and by Sector. With English summary.) *Revue Écon.*, January 1987, *38*(1), pp. 117–47. [G: Global]
Tower, Edward and Willett, Thomas D. Enforceability and the Resolution of International Jurisdictional Conflicts: Comments. *Law Contemp. Probl.*, Summer 1987, *50*(3), pp. 189–93. [G: U.S.]
Trevor, Malcolm. Japanese Companies in the UK. *Trevor, M., ed.*, 1987, pp. 13–27.
[G: Japan; U.K.]
Trevor, Malcolm. What Is Internationalisation?

Trevor, M., ed., 1987, pp. 2–12. [G: Japan]

Tuan, Chyau. U.S. Influence on the Hong Kong Economy and Prospect. *Dutta, M., ed. (II),* 1987, pp. 199–221. [G: Hong Kong]

Turrell, Robert Vicat and Van-Helten, Jean Jacques. The Investment Group: The Missing Link in British Overseas Expansion before 1914? [British-based Investment Groups before 1914]. *Econ. Hist. Rev., 2nd Ser.,* May 1987, *40*(2), pp. 267–74. [G: U.K.]

Tutu, Desmond. A Plea for International Sanctions. *Sethi, S. P., ed.*, 1987, pp. 161–64. [G: S. Africa]

Vernon, Raymond. Codes on Transnationals: Ingredients for an Effective International Regime. *Dunning, J. H. and Usui, M., eds.*, 1987, pp. 227–40. [G: LDCs]

Vernon, Raymond. The Trading Company: Past and Future. *Visser, H. and Schoor, E., eds.,* 1987, pp. 283–89. [G: Japan]

Vitzthum, Wolfgang Graf. Technologietransfer und Technologieembargo im Völkerrecht. (Technology Transfer and Technology Embargo in International Law. With English summary.) *Lenel, H. O., et al., eds.*, 1987, pp. 233–63. [G: Global]

Wachtel, Michael H. The Fiscal Residence of Companies: Australia. *International Fiscal Association, ed. (I),* 1987, pp. 201–16. [G: Australia]

Warr, Peter G. Export Promotion via Industrial Enclaves: The Philippines' Bataan Export Processing Zone. *J. Devel. Stud.,* January 1987, *23*(2), pp. 220–41. [G: Philippines]

Weedon, D. Reid, Jr. The Evolution of Sullivan Principle Compliance. *Sethi, S. P., ed.,* 1987, pp. 393–402. [G: S. Africa; U.S.]

Whittemore, Frederick. The Internationalization of Investment Banking. *Patrick, H. T. and Tachi, R., eds.*, 1987, pp. 136–46. [G: Global]

Wilking, Lou H. Should U.S. Corporations Abandon South Africa? *Sethi, S. P., ed.*, 1987, pp. 383–91. [G: U.S.; S. Africa]

Williams, Walter E. How Business Transcends Politics. *Managerial Dec. Econ.,* March 1987, *8*(1), pp. 15–20.

Willmore, Larry N. Controle estrangeiro e concentração na indústria brasileira. (With English summary.) *Pesquisa Planejamento Econ.,* April 1987, *17*(1), pp. 161–89. [G: Brazil]

Wolf, Bernard M. Economic Impact on the United States of the Pipeline Sanctions. *Leyton-Brown, D., ed.*, 1987, pp. 207–20. [G: U.S.]

Wolf, Bernard M. The Reaction of U.S.-Based Multinational Enterprises to Free Trade between Canada and the United States: Impediments to Empirical Verification. *Tremblay, R., ed.*, 1987, pp. 351–66. [G: U.S.; Canada]

Wolpe, Howard. The Double Standard of American Foreign Policy. *Sethi, S. P., ed.*, 1987, pp. 53–61. [G: S. Africa; U.S.]

Womack, James P. Prospects for the U.S.–Mexican Relationship in the Motor Vehicle Sector. *Thorup, C. L., ed.*, 1987, pp. 101–25. [G: U.S.; Mexico]

Wonghanchao, Warin and Pongpissanupichit, Jeerasak. Contribution of Direct U.S. Investment to the Thai Economy. *Dutta, M., ed. (II),* 1987, pp. 225–52. [G: Thailand]

Wood, Diane P. Conflicts of Jurisdiction in Antitrust Law: A Comment. *Law Contemp. Probl.,* Summer 1987, *50*(3), pp. 179–88. [G: U.S.]

Wu, Rong-I. U.S. Direct Investment in Taiwan: An Economic Appraisal. *Dutta, M., ed. (II),* 1987, pp. 185–98. [G: Taiwan]

Yannopoulos, George N. European Community Tariff Preferences and Foreign Direct Investment. *Banca Naz. Lavoro Quart. Rev.,* March 1987, (160), pp. 93–109. [G: EEC]

Young, Stephen. Business Strategy and the Internationalization of Business: Recent Approaches. *Managerial Dec. Econ.,* March 1987, *8*(1), pp. 31–40.

Ziebart, David A. and Kim, David H. An Examination of the Market Reactions Associated with SFAS No. 8 and SFAS No. 52. *Accounting Rev.,* April 1987, *62*(2), pp. 343–57. [G: U.S.]

Zimmerman, Silvia. Die steuerliche Ansässigkeit von Kapitalgesellschaften: Schweiz. (The Fiscal Residence of Companies: Switzerland. With English summary.) *International Fiscal Association, ed. (I),* 1987, pp. 543–58. [G: Switzerland]

443 International Lending and Aid (public)

4430 International Lending and Aid (public)

Addison, Tony and Demery, Lionel. Alleviating Poverty under Structural Adjustment. *Finance Develop.,* December 1987, *24*(4), pp. 41–43.

Aghevli, Bijan B.; Kim, In-Su and Neiss, Hubert. Growth and Adjustment in South Asia. *Finance Develop.,* September 1987, *24*(3), pp. 12–16. [G: Bangladesh; India; Pakistan; Sri Lanka]

Akinrinade, Olusola. The Commonwealth and Development Efforts in Africa. *Akinrinade, O. and Barling, J. K., eds.*, 1987, pp. 149–73. [G: Africa]

Albornoz, Hugo E. Procesos de endeudamiento externo y ajuste de precios. (With English summary.) *Cuadernos Econ.,* December 1987, *24*(73), pp. 319–30.

Antrobus, Peggy. Funding for NGOs: Issues and Options. *World Devel.,* Supp. Autumn 1987, *15*, pp. 95–102. [G: Barbados]

Arriola, Salvador. Some Ideas on Financial and Monetary Co-operation among Developing Countries. *Dell, S., ed., Pt. 2,* 1987, pp. 639–64. [G: LDCs]

Avramovic, Dragoslav. Africa's Debts. *Agrawal, G. R., et al. (I),* 1987, pp. 77–86. [G: Africa]

Avramovic, Dragoslav. Problems of Low Income Countries: Role of Mutual Economic Cooperation. *Agrawal, G. R., et al. (I),* 1987, pp. 7–14. [G: LDCs]

Bacha, Edmar Lisboa. Balance of Payments Experience and Growth Prospects of Developing Countries: Terms of Reference for the Country Studies. *Dell, S., ed., Pt. 3,* 1987, pp. 1012–30.

Bacha, Edmar Lisboa. IMF Conditionality: Conceptual Problems and Policy Alternatives. *World Devel.*, December 1987, *15*(12), pp. 1457–67. **[G: LDCs]**

Bacha, Edmar Lisboa. O sistema de condicionalidades do FMI: uma proposta de reforma. (With English summary.) *Pesquisa Planejamento Econ.*, August 1987, *17*(2), pp. 333–42.

Balassa, Bela. Mexico's Debt Problem and Policies for the Future. *Tremblay, R., ed.*, 1987, pp. 11–29. **[G: Mexico]**

Bangura, Yusuf. IMF/World Bank Conditionality and Nigeria's Structural Adjustment Programme. *Havnevik, K. J., ed.*, 1987, pp. 95–116. **[G: Nigeria]**

Barling, J. Kurt. Aid and African Development. *Akinrinade, O. and Barling, J. K., eds.*, 1987, pp. 19–51. **[G: Africa]**

Baron, David P. Exim at Fifty: At a Crossroads? *Rodriguez, R. M., ed.*, 1987, pp. 107–32. **[G: U.S.]**

Bartlett, Will. The Problem of Indebtedness in Yugoslavia: Causes and Consequences. *Rivista Int. Sci. Econ. Com.*, Nov.-Dec. 1987, *34*(11–12), pp. 1179–95. **[G: Yugoslavia]**

Batchelor, Roy A. Country Risk: A Model for Predicting Debt Servicing Problems in Developing Countries: Comments. *Res, Z. and Motamen, S., eds.*, 1987, pp. 224–27. **[G: LDCs]**

Bazdresch P., Carlos. World Economic Outlook and Prospects for Latin America: Comment. *Martirena-Mantel, A. M., ed.*, 1987, pp. 51–55. **[G: Latin America]**

Bell, Michael W. and Sheehy, Robert L. Helping Structural Adjustment in Low-Income Countries. *Finance Develop.*, December 1987, *24*(4), pp. 6–9. **[G: LDCs]**

Berger, Thomas J. The U.S. Debt Initiative: A Status Report. *Tremblay, R., ed.*, 1987, pp. 51–54. **[G: U.S.; LDCs]**

Bergsten, C. Fred. The Second Debt Crisis is Coming. *Challenge*, Special Issue 1987, *30*(6), pp. 50–57. **[G: U.S.]**

Bernal, Richard L. Default as a Negotiating Tactic in Debt Rescheduling Strategies of Developing Countries: A Preliminary Note. *Salazar-Carrillo, J. and Tirado de Alonzo, I., eds.*, 1987, pp. 1–32. **[G: Ghana; Latin America]**

Bernal, Richard L. Resolving the Global Debt Crisis. *Econ. Int.*, May-Aug. 1987, *40*(2–3), pp. 155–71. **[G: U.S.]**

Berthélemy, Jean-Claude. Endettement international et théorie des transferts. (With English summary.) *Revue Écon. Polit.*, May-June 1987, *97*(3), pp. 253–81. **[G: LDCs]**

Bhaduri, Amit. Dependent and Self-reliant Growth with Foreign Borrowing. *Cambridge J. Econ.*, September 1987, *11*(3), pp. 269–73.

Bilquees, Faiz. The IMF Stabilization Package and Pakistan's Stabilization Experience. *Pakistan Devel. Rev.*, Winter 1987, *26*(4), pp. 767–74. **[G: Pakistan]**

Bird, Graham. Debt Conversion in Principle and Practice. *Banca Naz. Lavoro Quart. Rev.*, June 1987, (161), pp. 183–95. **[G: LDCs]**

Bird, Graham. Interest Rate Compensation and

Debt: Would a Cap Fit? *World Devel.*, September 1987, *15*(9), pp. 1237–42.

Boeri, Tito. Modelling Foreign Aid, Capital Inflows and Economic Development. *Rivista Int. Sci. Econ. Com.*, July 1987, *34*(7), pp. 623–47.

Borner, Silvio. International Financing for Development: Introduction. *Borner, S. and Taylor, A., eds.*, 1987, pp. 407–10.

Boucher, Carlston B. and Siebeck, Wolfgang E. UNCTAD VII: New Spirit in North–South Relations? *Finance Develop.*, December 1987, *24*(4), pp. 14–16. **[G: Global]**

Bowles, Paul. Foreign Aid and Domestic Savings in Less Developed Countries: Some Tests for Causality. *World Devel.*, June 1987, *15*(6), pp. 789–96. **[G: LDCs]**

Brainard, Lawrence J. Current Illusions about the International Debt Crisis. *Wilcox, J. A., ed.*, 1987, *1985*, pp. 321–29. **[G: Global]**

Brainard, Lawrence J. Managing the International Debt Crisis: The Future of the Baker Plan. *Contemp. Policy Issues*, July 1987, *5*(3), pp. 66–75. **[G: U.S.]**

Brainard, Lawrence J. and Shelton-Colby, Sally. Prospects for Cooperation between Commercial Banks and Multilateral Financial Institutions: The Future of the Baker Plan. *Myers, R. J., ed.*, 1987, pp. 159–67.

Brodhead, Tim. NGOs: In One Year, Out the Other? *World Devel.*, Supp. Autumn 1987, *15*, pp. 1–6. **[G: Global]**

Browne, Robert S. The IMF in Africa: A Case of Inappropriate Technology. *Myers, R. J., ed.*, 1987, pp. 65–80. **[G: Africa]**

Buira, Ariel. The Nature and Direction of International Monetary Reform. *Dell, S., ed., Pt. 3*, 1987, pp. 765–84.

Buira, Ariel. The Role of the IMF in the 1980s. *Dell, S., ed., Pt. 3*, 1987, pp. 713–21.

Bulmer-Thomas, Victor. The Balance-of-Payments Crisis and Adjustment Programmes in Central America. *Thorp, R. and Whitehead, L., eds.*, 1987, pp. 271–317. **[G: Central America]**

Burney, Nadeem A. Unilateral International Transfers and Their Effects on the Welfare of the Recipient and Donor Countries. *Pakistan Devel. Rev.*, Summer 1987, *26*(2), pp. 135–59.

Caballeros, Rómulo. External Debt in Central America. *CEPAL Rev.*, August 1987, (32), pp. 123–48. **[G: Central America]**

Cáceres Sandoval, Carlos. Garantía Oficial Implícita y Créditos Externos. (With English summary.) *Cuadernos Econ.*, August 1987, *24*(72), pp. 127–42. **[G: LDCs]**

Cardoso, Eliana A. Latin America's Debt: Which Way Now? *Challenge*, May/June 1987, *30*(2), pp. 11–17. **[G: Latin America]**

Carrada-Bravo, Francisco. International Trade, Investment, Regional Security, and the Prospects of the Mexico–U.S. Relations. *Tremblay, R., ed.*, 1987, pp. 531–48. **[G: Mexico; U.S.]**

Chae, Changhee. Hamiltonian Approaches to the

Analysis of External Debt. *Int. Econ. J.*, Winter 1987, *1*(4), pp. 19–33.

Chakravarty, Shanti P. The Latin American Debt. *Scot. J. Polit. Econ.*, May 1987, *34*(2), pp. 120–44.   [**G: Latin America**]

Chrystal, K. Alec. International Liquidity and the Position of Developing Countries in the 1980s. *Dell, S., ed., Pt. 2*, 1987, pp. 358–72.

Citron, Joel-Tomas and Nickelsburg, Gerald. Country Risk and Political Instability. *J. Devel. Econ.*, April 1987, *25*(2), pp. 385–92.
[**G: Latin America; Spain; Sweden**]

Cline, William R. International Financial Rescue: Viability and Modalities. *Dell, S., ed., Pt. 3*, 1987, pp. 875–905.   [**G: LDCs**]

Cohen, Benjamin J. Implications of the European Monetary System for Developing Nations. *Dell, S., ed., Pt. 1*, 1987, pp. 295–339.
[**G: W. Europe; LDCs**]

Cohen, Daniel. External and Domestic Debt Constraints of LDCs: A Theory with a Numerical Application to Brazil and Mexico. *Bryant, R. C. and Portes, R., eds.*, 1987, pp. 279–99.
[**G: Brazil; Mexico**]

Cohen, Daniel. The Management of Developing Country Debt. *[Marjolin, R.]*, 1987, pp. 49–63.   [**G: LDCs**]

Conway, Patrick. Baker Plan and International Indebtedness. *World Econ.*, June 1987, *10*(2), pp. 193–204.   [**G: LDCs**]

Corbo, Vittorio. Impact on Debtor Countries of World Economic Conditions: Comment. *Martirena-Mantel, A. M., ed.*, 1987, pp. 87–90.
[**G: Latin America**]

Cornelius, Peter. Zur Variation der Konditionalität bei IWF-unterstützten Anpassungsprogrammen. (On the Variation of Conditionality Associated with IMF-Supported Adjustment Programs. With English summary.) *Schweiz. Z. Volkswirtsch. Statist.*, June 1987, *123*(2), pp. 175–98.   [**G: Global**]

Dadzie, K. K. S. International Monetary and Financial Issues for the Developing Countries. *United Nations Conference on Trade and Development.*, 1987, pp. i–v.

Darby, Michael R. National Policies and the International Monetary System: Comment. *Officer, L. H., ed.*, 1987, pp. 271–74.
[**G: Global**]

Darity, William A., Jr. Debt, Finance, Production and Trade in a North–South Model: The Surplus Approach. *Cambridge J. Econ.*, September 1987, *11*(3), pp. 211–27.

Davis, Charles and Laberge, Marie-Paule. Professional Rewards in a Canada–Sénégal Cooperative Project in Engineering Education: The Case of the Projet de l'École Polytechnique de Thiès. *Can. J. Devel. Stud.*, 1987, *8*(2), pp. 283–97.   [**G: Canada; Senegal**]

Dell, Sidney. Proposal for the Establishment of a Medium-term Facility within the Framework of the International Monetary Fund. *Dell, S., ed., Pt. 1*, 1987, pp. 173–77.

Dell, Sidney, et al. Determination of Quotas and the Relative Position of Developing Countries in the International Monetary Fund: Structural

Adjustment Policies. *Dell, S., ed., Pt. 2*, 1987, pp. 541–56.   [**G: U.K.**]

Desai, Padma. The Soviet Union and Cancún. *Desai, P.*, 1987, *1982*, pp. 249–55.
[**G: U.S.S.R.**]

Devlin, Robert. Economic Restructuring in Latin America in the Face of the Foreign Debt and the External Transfer Problem. *CEPAL Rev.*, August 1987, (32), pp. 75–101.
[**G: Latin America**]

DeWitt, R. Peter. Policy Directions in International Lending, 1961–1984: The Case of the Inter-American Development Bank. *J. Devel. Areas*, April 1987, *21*(3), pp. 277–84.
[**G: Latin America**]

Dias Carneiro, Dionísio. Long-run Adjustment, the Debt Crisis and the Changing Role of Stabilisation Policies in the Recent Brazilian Experience. *Thorp, R. and Whitehead, L., eds.*, 1987, pp. 28–67.   [**G: Brazil**]

Díaz-Alejandro, Carlos F. International Financial and Goods Markets in 1982–3 and Beyond. *Borner, S. and Taylor, A., eds.*, 1987, pp. 429–43.

Díaz-Alejandro, Carlos F. Some Aspects of the Development Crisis in Latin America. *Thorp, R. and Whitehead, L., eds.*, 1987, pp. 9–27.
[**G: Latin America**]

Dietz, James L. Debt and Development: The Future of Latin America. *Dietz, J. L. and Street, J. H., eds.*, 1987, pp. 273–92.
[**G: Latin America**]

Dietz, James L. The Latin American Economies and Debt: Institutional and Structural Response to Crisis. *J. Econ. Issues*, June 1987, *21*(2), pp. 827–36.   [**G: Latin America**]

Dixon, Peter B. and Parmenter, Brian R. Foreign Debts, the Exchange Rate and Australia's Economic Prospects. *Australian Econ. Rev.*, Third Quarter 1987, (79), pp. 36–42. [**G: Australia**]

Dooley, Michael P. Market Valuation of External Debt. *Finance Develop.*, March 1987, *24*(1), pp. 6–9.   [**G: LDCs**]

Dornbusch, Rudiger. El problema de la deuda: Algunas soluciones. (The Debt Problem and Some Solutions. With English summary.) *Estud. Econ.*, July-December 1987, *2*(2), pp. 251–67.   [**G: LDCs**]

Dornbusch, Rudiger. Impact on Debtor Countries of World Economic Conditions. *Martirena-Mantel, A. M., ed.*, 1987, pp. 60–87.
[**G: Latin America**]

Dornbusch, Rudiger. North–South Interdependence: Overview. *Bryant, R. C. and Portes, R., eds.*, 1987, pp. 338–43.

Dornbusch, Rudiger and Fischer, Stanley. International Capital Flows and the World Debt Problem. *Razin, A. and Sadka, E., eds.*, 1987, pp. 211–54.   [**G: Global**]

Dornbusch, Rudiger and Fischer, Stanley. The World Debt Problem. *Dell, S., ed., Pt. 3*, 1987, pp. 907–59.   [**G: Selected LDCs**]

Drabek, Anne Gordon. Development Alternatives: The Challenge for NGOs—An Overview of the Issues. *World Devel.*, Supp. Autumn 1987, *15*, pp. ix–xv.   [**G: Global**]

Dung, Tran Huu. Commodity versus Capital Transfers. *J. Econ. Devel.*, December 1987, *12*(2), pp. 189–95.

Dunlevy, James A. and Seiver, Daniel A. Foreign Finance, Wealth Effects and Economic Development. *Appl. Econ.*, April 1987, *19*(4), pp. 467–81. **[G: LDCs]**

Eaton, Jonathan. External and Domestic Debt Constraints of LDCs: A Theory with a Numerical Application to Brazil and Mexico: Discussion. *Bryant, R. C. and Portes, R., eds.*, 1987, pp. 300–305. **[G: Brazil; Mexico]**

Eaton, Jonathan. Public Debt Guarantees and Private Capital Flight. *World Bank Econ. Rev.*, May 1987, *1*(3), pp. 377–95. **[G: LDCs]**

Echevarria, Oscar A. Beyond the Failure of Debt Restructuring. *[Marjolin, R.]*, 1987, pp. 65–83.

Eckstein, Zvi. Aspects of Capital Flows between Developing and Developed Countries: Comments. *Razin, A. and Sadka, E., eds.*, 1987, pp. 283–85. **[G: LDCs]**

Eggleston, Robert C. Determinants of the Levels and Distribution of PL 480 Food Aid: 1955–79. *World Devel.*, June 1987, *15*(6), pp. 797–808. **[G: U.S.]**

Eichengreen, Barry and Portes, Richard. The Anatomy of Financial Crises. *Portes, R. and Swoboda, A. K., eds.*, 1987, pp. 10–58. **[G: Global]**

Elliott, Charles. Some Aspects of Relations between the North and South in the NGO Sector. *World Devel.*, Supp. Autumn 1987, *15*, pp. 57–68. **[G: Global]**

Erb, Richard D. International Debt and Adjustment—Setting the Issues in a Global Perspective. *Tremblay, R., ed.*, 1987, pp. 1–3. **[G: Global]**

Faaland, Just. Economic Disarray and Dependence: The Case of the Sudan. *Havnevik, K. J., ed.*, 1987, pp. 117–26. **[G: Sudan]**

Feder, Gershon and Uy, Lily V. Policy Implications of International Creditworthiness in Trade-Gap and Savings-Gap Economies. *Salvatore, D., ed.*, 1987, pp. 526–50. **[G: LDCs]**

Feinberg, Richard E. Multilateral Lending and Latin America. *World Econ.*, June 1987, *10*(2), pp. 205–17. **[G: Latin America]**

Feinberg, Richard E. and Tucker, Stuart K. Export Credits in U.S. Trade, Development, and Industrial Policy. *Rodriguez, R. M., ed.*, 1987, pp. 133–43. **[G: U.S.]**

Fernandez, Aloysius P. NGOs in South Asia: People's Participation and Partnership. *World Devel.*, Supp. Autumn 1987, *15*, pp. 39–49. **[G: India; Bangladesh; Pakistan; Sri Lanka]**

Ferrer, A. Latin American Foreign Debt: Problems and Prospects. *Borner, S. and Taylor, A., eds.*, 1987, pp. 381–93. **[G: Argentina]**

Ffrench-Davis, Ricardo. Conversión de Pagarés de la Deuda Externa en Chile. (Conversion of Chilean Foreign Debt. With English summary.) *Colección Estud. CIEPLAN*, December 1987, (22), pp. 41–62. **[G: Chile]**

Findlay, Christopher. The Role of Aid and Private

Capital Inflows in Economic Development: Comment. *Holmes, F., ed.*, 1987, pp. 147–53. **[G: LDCs]**

Fischer, Stanley. Sharing the Burden of the International Debt Crisis. *Amer. Econ. Rev.*, May 1987, *77*(2), pp. 165–70. **[G: LDCs]**

Fishlow, Albert. Lições da década de 1890 para a de 1980. (With English summary.) *Pesquisa Planejamento Econ.*, December 1987, *17*(3), pp. 497–532. **[G: Argentina; Brazil]**

Fitzgerald, D. The Costs and Benefits of International Banking: Comments. *Res, Z. and Motamen, S., eds.*, 1987, pp. 136–38.

Fleisig, Heywood and Hill, Catharine. Some Issues Surrounding Government-Subsidized Export Credit. *Rodriguez, R. M., ed.*, 1987, pp. 145–55. **[G: U.S.]**

Fleming, Alexander and Smith, Mary Oakes. Raising Resources for IDA: The Eighth Replenishment. *Finance Develop.*, September 1987, *24*(3), pp. 23–26.

Forbes, Neil. London Banks, the German Standstill Agreements, and 'Economic Appeasement' in the 1930s. *Econ. Hist. Rev., 2nd Ser.*, November 1987, *40*(4), pp. 571–87. **[G: U.K.]**

Fox, Thomas H. NGOs from the United States. *World Devel.*, Supp. Autumn 1987, *15*, pp. 11–19. **[G: U.S.]**

Foxley, Alejandro. El problema de la deuda externa desde una perspectiva latinoamericana. (With English summary.) *Desarrollo Econ.*, July-Sept. 1987, *27*(106), pp. 223–43.

Foxley, Alejandro. Latin American Development After the Debt Crisis. *J. Devel. Econ.*, October 1987, *27*(1–2), pp. 201–25. **[G: Latin America]**

Foxley, Alejandro. Latin American Development After the Debt Crisis. *[Diaz-Alejandro, C. F.]*, 1987, pp. 201–25. **[G: Latin America]**

Frieden, Jeff. Third World Indebted Industrialization: International Finance and State Capitalism in Mexico, Brazil, Algeria, and South Korea. *Becker, D. G., et al.*, 1987, *1981*, pp. 131–59. **[G: Mexico; Brazil; Algeria; S. Korea]**

Friedman, Irving S. The International Monetary Fund: A Founder's Evaluation. *Myers, R. J., ed.*, 1987, pp. 13–32.

Fritsch, Winston. World Economic Outlook and Prospects for Latin America: Comment. *Martirena-Mantel, A. M., ed.*, 1987, pp. 55–59. **[G: Latin America]**

von Furstenberg, George M. The IMF as Market-Maker for Official Business between Nations. *Myers, R. J., ed.*, 1987, pp. 111–26.

Galbraith, James K. U.S. Macroeconomic Strategy and the Advanced Developing Countries. *Thorup, C. L., ed.*, 1987, pp. 83–99. **[G: U.S.; Mexico]**

Gardner, Charles S. Enhancing the Fund's Structural Adjustment Facility. *Finance Develop.*, September 1987, *24*(3), pp. 6–7.

Garilao, Ernesto D. Indigenous NGOs as Strategic Institutions: Managing the Relationship with Government and Resource Agencies.

World Devel., Supp. Autumn 1987, *15*, pp. 113–120. [G: Asia]

Gemmill, Robert F. The Anatomy of Financial Crises: Discussion. *Portes, R. and Swoboda, A. K., eds.*, 1987, pp. 58–61. [G: Global]

Gennotte, Gerard; Kharas, Homi J. and Sadeq, Sayeed. A Valuation Model of Developing-Country Debt with Endogenous Rescheduling. *World Bank Econ. Rev.*, January 1987, *1*(2), pp. 237–71. [G: LDCs]

Gollas, Manuel. Comments on the Mexican Economy in 1984. *Salazar-Carrillo, J. and Tirado de Alonzo, I., eds.*, 1987, pp. 1–5. [G: Mexico]

Goreux, Louis M. Responses by Representatives from the IMF and the World Bank. *Havnevik, K. J., ed.*, 1987, pp. 85–87.

Griffin, Keith. Doubts about Aid. *Griffin, K.*, 1987, *1986*, pp. 235–54. [G: LDCs]

Griffin, Keith. The Debt Crisis and the Poor. *Griffin, K.*, 1987, pp. 255–65.

Griffith-Jones, Stephany. Compensatory Financing Facility: A Review of Its Operation and Proposals for Improvement. *Dell, S., ed., Pt. 2*, 1987, pp. 691–712.

Griffith-Jones, Stephany and Lipton, Michael. International Lenders of Last Resort: Are Changes Required? *Res, Z. and Motamen, S., eds.*, 1987, pp. 141–63.

Guiliani Cury, Hugo. Economic Reform and Stabilization in Latin America: Preface. *Connolly, M. and González-Vega, C., eds.*, 1987, pp. xiii–xvii. [G: Dominican Republic]

Guitián, Manuel. External Debt Management and the International Monetary Fund. *Tremblay, R., ed.*, 1987, pp. 5–10.

Guitián, Manuel. The Fund's Role in Adjustment. *Finance Develop.*, June 1987, *24*(2), pp. 3–6.

Gulhati, Ravi. Responses by Representatives from the IMF and the World Bank. *Havnevik, K. J., ed.*, 1987, pp. 88–92.

Hajivassiliou, Vassilis A. The External Debt Repayments Problems of LDC's: An Econometric Model Based on Panel Data. *J. Econometrics*, Sept./Oct. 1987, *36*(1/2), pp. 205–30. [G: LDCs]

Haley, John C. Debt Crisis, Exchange Rates, the U.S. Deficit, and Electronic Reaction to the World Events. *Kaushik, S. K., ed.*, 1987, pp. 63–70.

Hardach, Gerd. The Marshall Plan in Germany, 1948–1952. *J. Europ. Econ. Hist.*, Winter 1987, *16*(3), pp. 433–85. [G: U.S.; W. Germany]

Hardy, Chandra. Debt Negotiations and the North–South Dialogue, 1974–1980. *Zartman, I. W., ed. (II)*, 1987, pp. 259–77. [G: LDCs]

Havnevik, Kjell J. The IMF and the World Bank in Africa: Introduction. *Havnevik, K. J., ed.*, 1987, pp. 9–23. [G: Africa]

Haxthausen, Ulrik. Nordic View on the IMF/World Bank: Discussion. *Havnevik, K. J., ed.*, 1987, pp. 173–74. [G: N. Europe]

Heffernan, Shelagh A. The Costs and Benefits of International Banking: Reply. *Res, Z. and Motamen, S., eds.*, 1987, pp. 139–40.

Heffernan, Shelagh A. The Costs and Benefits of International Banking. *Res, Z. and Motamen, S., eds.*, 1987, pp. 113–35.

van der Heijden, Hendrik. The Reconciliation of NGO Autonomy, Program Integrity and Operational Effectiveness with Accountability to Donors. *World Devel.*, Supp. Autumn 1987, *15*, pp. 103–12. [G: OECD]

Helleiner, Gerald K. Balance of Payments Experience and Growth Prospects of Developing Countries. *Dell, S., ed., Pt. 3*, 1987, pp. 961–1004. [G: LDCs]

Helleiner, Gerald K. Stabilization, Adjustment, and the Poor. *World Devel.*, December 1987, *15*(12), pp. 1499–1513. [G: Tanzania]

Helleiner, Gerald K. The Impact of the Exchange Rate System on the Developing Countries. *Dell, S., ed., Pt. 2*, 1987, pp. 407–510. [G: LDCs]

Helleiner, Gerald K. and Stewart, Frances. The International System and the Protection of the Vulnerable. *Cornia, G. A.; Jolly, R. and Stewart, F., eds.*, 1987, pp. 273–86.

Heller, H. Robert. The Debt Crisis and the Future of International Bank Lending. *Amer. Econ. Rev.*, May 1987, *77*(2), pp. 171–75. [G: LDCs]

Hellinger, Doug. NGOs and the Large Aid Donors: Changing the Terms of Engagement. *World Devel.*, Supp. Autumn 1987, *15*, pp. 135–143. [G: Global]

Hendra, John. Only "Fit to be Tied": A Comparison of the Canadian Tied Aid Policy with the Tied Aid Policies of Sweden, Norway and Denmark. *Can. J. Devel. Stud.*, 1987, *8*(2), pp. 261–81. [G: Canada; Sweden; Norway; Denmark]

Herbert-Copley, Brent. Canadian NGOs: Past Trends, Future Challenges. *World Devel.*, Supp. Autumn 1987, *15*, pp. 21–28. [G: Canada]

Herrhausen, Alfred. Internationale Investitionsfinanzierung in der Zukunft: Eine Herausforderung. (With English summary.) *Z. Betriebswirtshaft*, October 1987, *57*(10), pp. 966–77. [G: LDCs]

Heymann, Daniel. Impact on Debtor Countries of World Economic Conditions: Comment. *Martirena-Mantel, A. M., ed.*, 1987, pp. 90–94. [G: Latin America]

Heyndels, B. and Vuchelen, J. De valutasamenstelling van de Belgische Korte termijn buitenlandse schuld. (With English summary.) *Cah. Écon. Bruxelles*, Second Trimester 1987, (114), pp. 375–95. [G: Belgium]

van der Hoeven, Rolph and Richards, P. J. International Linkages. *International Labour Office.*, 1987, pp. 21–36. [G: OECD; LDCs]

Hojman, David E. Why the Latin American Countries Will Never Form a Debtors' Cartel. *Kyklos*, 1987, *40*(2), pp. 198–218. [G: Latin America]

Holzman, Franklyn D. Creditworthiness and Balance-of-Payments Adjustment Mechanisms of Centrally Planned Economies. *Holzman, F. D.*, 1987, *1981*, pp. 59–81. [G: E. Europe]

Hopkins, Raymond F. The Wheat Negotiations: Loss or Gain in North–South Relations? *Zartman, I. W., ed. (II)*, 1987, pp. 115–48.

Horowitz, Irving Louis. The "Rashomon Effect": Ideological Proclivities and Political Dilemmas of the IMF. *Myers, R. J., ed.*, 1987, pp. 93–109.

Huang, Yukon and Nicholas, Peter. The Social Costs of Adjustment. *Finance Develop.*, June 1987, *24*(2), pp. 22–24. **[G: LDCs]**

Hughes, Helen. The Role of Aid and Private Capital Inflows in Economic Development. *Holmes, F., ed.*, 1987, pp. 120–46.
[G: LDCs]

Iran Ministry Econ. Aff. and Finance. Trade Cooperation and Collective Self-reliance. *Agrawal, G. R., et al. (II)*, 1987, pp. 7–22.
[G: LDCs]

Jalal, Mahsoun. The Role of the Fund and the World Bank in Adjustment and Development: Comment. *El-Naggar, S., ed.*, 1987, pp. 88–91.

Johnson, D. Gale. Is Population Growth the Dominant Force in Development? [Population Growth, Economic Growth, and Foreign Aid]. *Cato J.*, Spring/Summer 1987, *7*(1), pp. 187–93. **[G: LDCs]**

Johnson, D. Gale. IMF Conditionality and Agriculture in the Developing Countries. *Myers, R. J., ed.*, 1987, pp. 127–40. **[G: LDCs]**

Johnston, Bruce F. Growth of Foreign Assistance and Its Impact on Agriculture: Commentary. *Mellor, J. W.; Delgado, C. L. and Blackie, M. J., eds.*, 1987, pp. 348–49. **[G: Africa]**

Jones, Michael. IMF Surveillance, Policy Coordination, and Time Consistency. *Int. Econ. Rev.*, February 1987, *28*(1), pp. 135–58.

Kadam, V. B. Implications for Developing Countries of Current Proposals for a Substitution Account. *Dell, S., ed., Pt. 1*, 1987, pp. 155–72.

Kajese, Kingston. An Agenda of Future Tasks for International and Indigenous NGOs: Views from the South. *World Devel.*, Supp. Autumn 1987, *15*, pp. 79–85. **[G: Global]**

Kaminarides, John. The International Debt Crisis—A Dynamite Issue. *Tremblay, R., ed.*, 1987, pp. 79–98. **[G: LDCs]**

Kanbur, S. M. Ravi. Structural Adjustment, Macroeconomic Adjustment and Poverty: A Methodology for Analysis. *World Devel.*, December 1987, *15*(12), pp. 1515–26.

Kemp, Murray C. and Kojima, Shoichi. More on the Welfare Economics of Foreign Aid. *J. Japanese Int. Economies*, March 1987, *1*(1), pp. 97–109.

Kenen, Peter B. Changing Views about the Role of the SDR and Implications for Its Attributes. *Dell, S., ed., Pt. 2*, 1987, pp. 373–85.

Kenen, Peter B. What Role for IMF Surveillance? *World Devel.*, December 1987, *15*(12), pp. 1445–56.

Khatkhate, Deena R. International Monetary System—Which Way? Editor's Perspective. *World Devel.*, December 1987, *15*(12), pp. vii–xvi. **[G: Global]**

Killick, Tony. Reflections on the IMF/World Bank Relationship. *Havnevik, K. J., ed.*, 1987, pp. 25–28. **[G: LDCs]**

Killick, Tony. Unsettled Questions about Adjustment with Growth. *United Nations Conference on Trade and Development.*, 1987, pp. 207–58. **[G: Latin America]**

Kim, Kwan S. Mexico's Debt Crisis and Adjustment Policies. *Tremblay, R., ed.*, 1987, pp. 55–70. **[G: Mexico]**

Kim, Youn-Suk. External Debt and Economic Development: The Case of Korea. *Dutta, M., ed. (II)*, 1987, pp. 151–61. **[G: S. Korea]**

Kindleberger, Charles P. An Excerpt from an Oral History, Truman Library. *Kindleberger, C. P.*, 1987, pp. 106–19. **[G: U.S.; W. Europe]**

Kindleberger, Charles P. Did Dollars Save the World? *Kindleberger, C. P.*, 1987, pp. 245–65. **[G: U.S.; Global]**

Kindleberger, Charles P. European Economic Integration. *Kindleberger, C. P.*, 1987, *1951*, pp. 46–63. **[G: W. Europe; U.S.]**

Kindleberger, Charles P. Excerpts from the Cleveland–Moore–Kindleberger Memorandum of 12 June 1947, on a European Recovery Program. *Kindleberger, C. P.*, 1987, pp. 1–24. **[G: U.S.; W. Europe]**

Kindleberger, Charles P. Germany and the Economic Recovery of Europe. *Kindleberger, C. P.*, 1987, *1949*, pp. 33–45. **[G: U.S.; W. Germany; W. Europe]**

Kindleberger, Charles P. Memorandum for the Files: Origins of the Marshall Plan. *Kindleberger, C. P.*, 1987, *1972*, pp. 25–32. **[G: U.S.; W. Europe]**

Kindleberger, Charles P. The American Origins of the Marshall Plan: A View from the State Department. *Kindleberger, C. P.*, 1987, *1984*, pp. 154–60. **[G: U.S.; W. Europe]**

Kindleberger, Charles P. The European Recovery Program. *Kindleberger, C. P.*, 1987, *1953*, pp. 64–91. **[G: U.S.; W. Europe]**

Kindleberger, Charles P. The Marshall Plan and the Cold War. *Kindleberger, C. P.*, 1987, *1968*, pp. 92–105. **[G: U.S.; W. Europe]**

Kindleberger, Charles P. Toward the Marshall Plan: A Memoir of Policy Development in Germany, 1945–47. *Kindleberger, C. P.*, 1987, pp. 161–208. **[G: U.S.; W. Europe]**

Kiwanuka, Richard N. The Thirteenth UN General Assembly Special Session: Lessons for Africa. *J. World Trade Law*, April 1987, *21*(2), pp. 65–78. **[G: Africa]**

Klein, Thomas M. Debt Relief for African Countries. *Finance Develop.*, December 1987, *24*(4), pp. 10–13. **[G: Africa]**

Klopstock, Fred H. Implications of a Substitution Account for the Eurocurrency Markets. *Dell, S., ed., Pt. 1*, 1987, pp. 205–20.

Koluri, Bharat R. and Giannaros, Demetrios S. Deficit and External Debt Effects on Money and Inflation in Brazil and Mexico: Some Evidence. *Eastern Econ. J.*, July-Sept. 1987, *13*(3), pp. 243–48. **[G: Brazil; Mexico]**

Konrad, Anton. Verschuldungskrise und Verschuldungsmodelle. (Debt Crisis and Debt Management Model. With English summary.) *Kredit Kapital*, 1987, 20(1), pp. 73–87.

Korpinen, Pekka. Nordic View on the IMF/World Bank: Discussion. *Havnevik, K. J., ed.*, 1987, pp. 167–69. **[G: N. Europe]**

Korten, David C. Third Generation NGO Strategies: A Key to People-Centered Development. *World Devel.*, Supp. Autumn 1987, 15, pp. 145–59. **[G: LDCs]**

Krueger, Anne O. Aspects of Capital Flows between Developing and Developed Countries. *Razin, A. and Sadka, E., eds.*, 1987, pp. 255–82. **[G: LDCs]**

Krueger, Anne O. Debt, Capital Flows, and LDC Growth. *Amer. Econ. Rev.*, May 1987, 77(2), pp. 159–64. **[G: LDCs]**

Krueger, Anne O. Origins of the Developing Countries' Debt Crisis 1970 to 1982. *J. Devel. Econ.*, October 1987, 27(1–2), pp. 165–87. **[G: LDCs]**

Krueger, Anne O. Origins of the Developing Countries' Debt Crisis 1970 to 1982. *[Diaz-Alejandro, C. F.]*, 1987, pp. 165–87. **[G: LDCs]**

Krugman, Paul R. Prospects for International Debt Reform. *United Nations Conference on Trade and Development.*, 1987, pp. 259–310. **[G: Latin America; Sub-Saharan Africa]**

Kuczynski, Pedro-Pablo. The IMF and the Debt Crisis. *Myers, R. J., ed.*, 1987, pp. 81–91.

Kuczynski, Pedro-Pablo. The Outlook for Latin American Debt. *Foreign Aff.*, Fall 1987, 66(1), pp. 129–49. **[G: Latin America]**

Kulatilaka, Nalin and Marcus, Alan J. A Model of Strategic Default of Sovereign Debt. *J. Econ. Dynam. Control*, December 1987, 11(4), pp. 483–98. **[G: LDCs]**

Kumar, Nagesh. India's Economic and Technical Cooperation with the Co-developing Countries. *Agrawal, G. R., et al. (II)*, 1987, pp. 181–220. **[G: India]**

Lächler, Ulrich and Nunnenkamp, Peter. The Effects of Debt versus Equity Inflows on Savings and Growth in Developing Economies. *Weltwirtsch. Arch.*, 1987, 123(4), pp. 631–50. **[G: LDCs]**

Lahera, Eugenio. The Conversion of Foreign Debt Viewed from Latin America. *CEPAL Rev.*, August 1987, (32), pp. 103–22. **[G: Latin America]**

Laird, Samuel and Yeats, Alexander J. On the Potential Contribution of Trade Policy Initiatives for Alleviating the International Debt Crisis. *J. Econ. Bus.*, August 1987, 39(3), pp. 209–24. **[G: OECD; LDCs]**

Landim, Leilah. Non-governmental Organizations in Latin America. *World Devel.*, Supp. Autumn 1987, 15, pp. 29–38. **[G: Latin America]**

Laney, Leroy O. The Secondary Market in Developing Country Debt: Some Observations and Policy Implications. *Fed. Res. Bank Dallas Econ. Rev.*, July 1987, pp. 1–12. **[G: LDCs]**

Langoni, Carlos Geraldo. The Lessons of the Crisis: A Developing Country View. *Res, Z. and* *Motamen, S., eds.*, 1987, 1983, pp. 41–55.

Lanyi, Anthony. Issues in Capital Flows to Developing Countries. *Finance Develop.*, September 1987, 24(3), pp. 27–30. **[G: LDCs]**

Lanyi, Anthony. World Economic Outlook and Prospects for Latin America. *Martirena-Mantel, A. M., ed.*, 1987, pp. 26–50. **[G: Latin America]**

de Larosière, J. Progress on the International Debt Strategy. *Finance Develop.*, March 1987, 24(1), pp. 10–11. **[G: LDCs]**

de Lattre, Anne. Growth of Foreign Assistance and Its Impact on Agriculture: Commentary. *Mellor, J. W.; Delgado, C. L. and Blackie, M. J., eds.*, 1987, pp. 346–48. **[G: Africa]**

Laussel, Didier and Soubeyran, Antoine. Le retour optimal à la solvabilité d'une économie endettée: Une introduction. (Optimal Adjustment Policies of a Small Open Indebted Economy: An Introduction. With English summary.) *Revue Écon.*, January 1987, 38(1), pp. 55–73.

Lavigne, Marie. External Finance as a Factor of Internal Regulation in Eastern European Economies. *Soviet E. Europ. Foreign Trade*, Summer 1987, 23(2), pp. 24–36. **[G: CMEA]**

Lecraw, Donald J. Big Bucks to the Philippines NOW. *Challenge*, Sept./Oct. 1987, 30(4), pp. 49–51. **[G: Philippines]**

Legarda, Benito. Issues Arising in Making the SDR the Principal International Reserve Asset. *Dell, S., ed., Pt. 2*, 1987, pp. 387–91.

Lele, Uma. Growth of Foreign Assistance and Its Impact on Agriculture. *Mellor, J. W.; Delgado, C. L. and Blackie, M. J., eds.*, 1987, pp. 321–42. **[G: Africa]**

Lemaresquier, Thierry. Prospects for Development Education: Some Strategic Issues Facing European NGOs. *World Devel.*, Supp. Autumn 1987, 15, pp. 189–200. **[G: W. Europe]**

Lemgruber, Antonio Carlos. New Directions in LDC Debt. *Bus. Econ.*, January 1987, 22(1), pp. 22–25. **[G: LDCs]**

Levy, Victor. Anticipated Development Assistance, Temporary Relief Aid, and Consumption Behaviour of Low-Income Countries. *Econ. J.*, June 1987, 97(386), pp. 446–58. **[G: Africa]**

Levy, Victor. Does Concessional Aid Lead to Higher Investment Rates in Low-Income Countries? *Rev. Econ. Statist.*, February 1987, 69(1), pp. 152–56. **[G: LDCs]**

Lim, David. Ability of the IMF-CFF to Stabilize Export Earnings. *J. World Trade Law*, October 1987, 21(5), pp. 91–95.

Lira, Paulo Pereira. The International Debt Crisis—A Growth-Oriented Management Approach. *Res, Z. and Motamen, S., eds.*, 1987, pp. 57–67. **[G: Brazil]**

Llach, Juan J. La naturaleza institucional e internacional de las hiperestabilizaciones. El caso de Alemania desde 1923 y algunas lecciones para la Argentina de 1985. (With English summary.) *Desarrollo Econ.*, Jan.-Mar. 1987, 26(104), pp. 527–60. **[G: Germany; Argentina]**

Looney, Robert E. Determinants of Third World Mineral-Oil Economies External Debt. *J. Econ. Devel.*, December 1987, *12*(2), pp. 39–56. **[G: LDCs]**

Looney, Robert E. Impact of Military Expenditures on Third World Debt. *Can. J. Devel. Stud.*, 1987, *8*(1), pp. 7–26. **[G: LDCs]**

Looney, Robert E. The Impact of Political Change, Debt Servicing and Fiscal Deficits on Argentinian Budgetary Priorities. *J. Econ. Stud.*, 1987, *14*(3), pp. 23–40.
[G: Argentina]

Loxley, John. Responses by Representatives from the IMF and the World Bank: Comment. *Havnevik, K. J., ed.*, 1987, pp. 92–94.

Loxley, John. The IMF, the World Bank, and Sub-Saharan Africa: Policies and Politics. *Havnevik, K. J., ed.*, 1987, pp. 47–63. **[G: Sub-Saharan Africa]**

Lundström, Hans. Nordic View on the IMF/World Bank: Discussion. *Havnevik, K. J., ed.*, 1987, pp. 170–72. **[G: N. Europe]**

Maenner, Ulrike. Verschuldung und aussenwirtschaftliche Anpassung von Entwicklungsländern—Erfolgsfall Indonesien? (Debt Problems and External Adjustment in Developing Countries: Indonesia, a Case of Success? With English summary.) *Konjunkturpolitik*, 1987, *33*(6), pp. 357–76. **[G: Indonesia]**

Mankiewicz, Zbigniew. It Is Easier to Restructure Debts Than the Economy. *Soviet E. Europ. Foreign Trade*, Fall 1987, *23*(3), pp. 97–102.
[G: Poland]

Marcano, Jorge. Adjustment, Indebtedness, and Economic Growth: Recent Experience: Comment. *Martirena-Mantel, A. M., ed.*, 1987, pp. 175–77. **[G: Latin America]**

Martin, Matthew. Crisis Management: Solving Africa's Debt Problem? *Akinrinade, O. and Barling, J. K., eds.*, 1987, pp. 218–38.
[G: Africa]

Martirena-Mantel, Ana María. External Debt, Savings, and Growth in Latin America: Introduction and Overview. *Martirena-Mantel, A. M., ed.*, 1987, pp. 1–25. **[G: Latin America]**

Mason, Will E. Happy-Face Economics versus the 'Dismal Science': Is the Borrowed Lunch Really Free? *[Marjolin, R.]*, 1987, pp. 137–51. **[G: U.S.]**

McGuire, Martin C. Foreign Assistance, Investment, and Defense: A Methodological Study with an Application to Israel, 1960–1979. *Econ. Develop. Cult. Change*, July 1987, *35*(4), pp. 847–73. **[G: Israel]**

McGuire, Martin C. U.S. Foreign Assistance, Israeli Resource Allocation and the Arms Race in the Middle East: An Analysis of Three Interdependent Resource Allocation Processes. *Schmidt, C., ed.*, 1987, pp. 197–238.
[G: U.S.; Israel; Middle East]

McLeod, Darryl L. and Salvatore, Dominick. The Employment Effects of Barriers to North–South Trade with and without Indexed Debt Service Payments. *Salvatore, D., ed.*, 1987, pp. 551–70. **[G: Global]**

McWilliams Tullberg, Rita. Military-Related

Debt in Non-oil Developing Countries, 1972–82. *Schmidt, C. and Blackaby, F., eds.*, 1987, pp. 302–16. **[G: LDCs]**

Meltzer, Allan H. International Debt Problems. *Contemp. Policy Issues*, January 1987, *5*(1), pp. 100–105. **[G: U.S.]**

Meltzer, Allan H. Notes on the Problem of International Debt. *Res, Z. and Motamen, S., eds.*, 1987, pp. 21–29. **[G: Latin America]**

Mensah, Moise C. Growth of Foreign Assistance and Its Impact on Agriculture: Commentary. *Mellor, J. W.; Delgado, C. L. and Blackie, M. J., eds.*, 1987, pp. 343–45. **[G: Africa]**

Michalopoulos, Constantine. World Bank Lending for Structural Adjustment. *Finance Develop.*, June 1987, *24*(2), pp. 7–10.

Milanović, Branko. On Grants and Lending. *Econ. Anal. Workers' Manage.*, 1987, *21*(3), pp. 299–312.

Mohammed, Azizali F. The Role of the Fund and the World Bank in Adjustment and Development. *El-Naggar, S., ed.*, 1987, pp. 73–87.

Morgan, John B. A Note on Eaton and Gersovitz's Model of Borrowing [LDC Participation in International Financial Markets] [Debt with Potential Repudiation: Theoretical and Empirical Analysis]. *J. Devel. Econ.*, February 1987, *25*(1), pp. 251–61. **[G: LDCs]**

Mosley, Paul; Hudson, John and Horrell, Sara. Aid, the Public Sector and the Market in Less Developed Countries. *Econ. J.*, September 1987, *97*(387), pp. 616–41. **[G: LDCs]**

Murphy, J. Carter. National Policies and the International Monetary System. *Officer, L. H., ed.*, 1987, pp. 203–70. **[G: Global]**

Narasimham, M. Debt Problem of the Low Income Countries. *Agrawal, G. R., et al. (I)*, 1987, pp. 59–76. **[G: LDCs]**

Narasimham, M. Shortcomings and Inequities of the Present International Monetary and Financial System. *Dell, S., ed., Pt. 3*, 1987, pp. 797–811.

Narasimham, M. Transfer of Resources to Developing Countries: Nature and Direction of Reform in the International Financial System. *Dell, S., ed., Pt. 3*, 1987, pp. 813–26.
[G: LDCs]

Neufeld, E. P. The International Debt Issue. *Tremblay, R., ed.*, 1987, pp. 43–49.

Nogueira Batista, Paulo, Jr. International Debt Rescheduling since Mid-1982: Rescue Operations and Their Implications for Commercial Banks and Debtor Countries. *Dell, S., ed., Pt. 3*, 1987, pp. 828–74. **[G: Latin America]**

Nunnenkamp, Peter. Die Rolle der Regierungen in Schuldner- und Gläubigerländern bei der Überwindung von Verschuldungsproblemen in der Dritten Welt. (The Role of Governments in Debtor and Creditor Countries in Overcoming the Debt Problems of the Third World. With English summary.) *Z. Wirtschaft. Sozialwissen.*, 1987, *107*(2), pp. 1210. **[G: LDCs]**

Nunnenkamp, Peter. Latin American Debt and Development: A Review. *Weltwirtsch. Arch.*, 1987, *123*(4), pp. 734–38.
[G: Latin America]

Nwankwo, G. O. Africa and the International

Monetary System. *Borner, S. and Taylor, A.*, *eds.*, 1987, pp. 337–57.   **[G: Africa]**

Nwankwo, G. O. Low-Income Countries and the International Monetary and Financial System. *Dell, S., ed., Pt. 3*, 1987, pp. 785–96.
[G: LDCs]

Ocampo, José Antonio. Crisis and Economic Policy in Colombia, 1980–5. *Thorp, R. and Whitehead, L., eds.*, 1987, pp. 239–70.
[G: Colombia]

Oppenheimer, Peter M. Impact of a Substitution Account on Euro-currency and Related Lending to Developing Countries. *Dell, S., ed., Pt. 1*, 1987, pp. 221–26.   **[G: LDCs]**

Ortega, Leonidas. Adjustment, Indebtedness, and Economic Growth: Recent Experience: Comment. *Martirena-Mantel, A. M., ed.*, 1987, pp. 177–79.   **[G: Latin America]**

Ortiz, Guillermo. Adjustment, Indebtedness, and Economic Growth: Recent Experience. *Martirena-Mantel, A. M., ed.*, 1987, pp. 154–75.
[G: Latin America]

Padron, Mario. Non-governmental Development Organizations: From Development Aid to Development Cooperation. *World Devel.*, Supp. Autumn 1987, *15*, pp. 69–77.
[G: Latin America]

Palmer, Ransford W. Debt and the Standard of Living in the Caribbean and Latin America. *Tremblay, R., ed.*, 1987, pp. 99–110.
[G: Latin America; Caribbean]

Panić, M. and Kumar, M. S. International Interdependence and the Debt Problem. *Borner, S. and Taylor, A., eds.*, 1987, pp. 359–80.
[G: LDCs]

Pastor, Manuel, Jr. The Effects of IMF Programs in the Third World: Debate and Evidence from Latin America. *World Devel.*, February 1987, *15*(2), pp. 249–62.   **[G: Latin America]**

Paul, Samuel. Community Participation in World Bank Projects. *Finance Develop.*, December 1987, *24*(4), pp. 20–23.   **[G: LDCs]**

Payer, Cheryl. The IMF and India. *Havnevik, K. J., ed.*, 1987, pp. 65–83.   **[G: India]**

Peet, Richard. Industrial Devolution, Underconsumption and the Third World Debt Crisis. *World Devel.*, June 1987, *15*(6), pp. 777–88.
[G: Global]

Phylatkis, K. International Lenders of Last Resort: Are Changes Required? Comment. *Res, Z. and Motamen, S., eds.*, 1987, pp. 164–66.

Pirie, Madsen and Young, Peter. Development with Aid: Public and Private Responsibilities in Privatization. *Hanke, S. H., ed.*, 1987, pp. 169–77.   **[G: LDCs]**

Quinn, Brian. A Central Banker's View about the International Debt Crisis. *Res, Z. and Motamen, S., eds.*, 1987, pp. 31–40.   **[G: Global]**

Rabushka, Alvin. From Austerity to Growth: A New Role for the IMF. *Myers, R. J., ed.*, 1987, pp. 141–58.

Rama, Martín. L'endettement extérieur dans un modèle de croissance en déséquilibre. (With English summary.) *Revue Écon.*, September 1987, *38*(5), pp. 933–48.

Rangarajan, C. and Hasib, A. Financial Problems

of Low Income and Least Developed Countries. *Agrawal, G. R., et al. (I)*, 1987, pp. 35–58.   **[G: LDCs]**

Ranis, Gustav. Latin American Debt and Adjustment. *J. Devel. Econ.*, October 1987, *27*(1–2), pp. 189–99.   **[G: Latin America]**

Ranis, Gustav. Latin American Debt and Adjustment. *[Diaz-Alejandro, C. F.]*, 1987, pp. 189–99.   **[G: Latin America]**

Res, Zannis and Motamen, Sima. International Debt and Central Banking in the 1980s: Introduction. *Res, Z. and Motamen, S., eds.*, 1987, pp. 1–17.   **[G: Global]**

Rieke, Wolfgang. Jahresversammlung von IWF und Weltbank 1987. (1987 IMF/World Bank Annual Meeting. With English Summary) *Kredit Kapital*, 1987, *20*(4), pp. 559–71.

Roberts, Paul Craig. Third World Debt: Legacy of Development Experts. *Cato J.*, Spring/Summer 1987, *7*(1), pp. 231–40.   **[G: LDCs]**

Roca, Santiago and Priale, Rodrigo. Devaluation, Inflationary Expectations and Stabilisation in Peru. *J. Econ. Stud.*, 1987, *14*(1), pp. 5–33.
[G: Peru]

Rodriguez, Rita M. Exim's Mission and Accomplishments: 1934–84. *Rodriguez, R. M., ed.*, 1987, pp. 1–33.   **[G: U.S.]**

Ros, Jaime. Mexico from the Oil Boom to the Debt Crisis: An Analysis of Policy Responses to External Shocks, 1978–85. *Thorp, R. and Whitehead, L., eds.*, 1987, pp. 68–116.
[G: Mexico]

Rybczynski, Tad M. The Anatomy of Financial Crises: Discussion. *Portes, R. and Swoboda, A. K., eds.*, 1987, pp. 61–66.   **[G: Global]**

Sachs, Jeffrey D. and Huizinga, Harry. U.S. Commercial Banks and the Developing-Country Debt Crisis. *Brookings Pap. Econ. Act.*, 1987, (2), pp. 555–601.   **[G: U.S.]**

Salmen, Lawrence F. Listening to the People. *Finance Develop.*, June 1987, *24*(2), pp. 36–39.

Schechter, Henry B. IMF Conditionality and the International Economy: A U.S. Labor Perspective. *Myers, R. J., ed.*, 1987, pp. 47–63.

Schedvin, C. B. The Australian Economy on the Hinge of History. *Australian Econ. Rev.*, First Quarter 1987, (77), pp. 20–30. **[G: Australia]**

Schick, Irvin C. and Tonak, E. Ahmet. The International Dimension: Trade, Aid, and Debt. *Schick, I. C. and Tonak, E. A., eds.*, 1987, pp. 333–63.   **[G: Turkey]**

Schwarz, J. Adam. Regulating the Loan Market for Developing Country Debt. *[Marjolin, R.]*, 1987, pp. 85–97.   **[G: LDCs]**

Selowsky, Marcelo. Adjustment in the 1980s: An Overview of Issues. *Finance Develop.*, June 1987, *24*(2), pp. 11–14.   **[G: LDCs]**

Serruya, Michel and Librowicz, Michel. Countertrade: A Partial Solution to Liquidity Crisis of Mexico. *Tremblay, R., ed.*, 1987, pp. 203–25.   **[G: Mexico; Canada]**

Sewell, John W. and Contee, Christine E. Foreign Aid and Gramm–Rudman. *Foreign Aff.*, Summer 1987, *65*(5), pp. 1015–36. **[G: U.S.]**

Shariff, Ismael. External Debt and Policy Issues

in the Developing Countries. *Indian Econ. J.*, Jan.-Mar. 1987, *34*(3), pp. 86–91. **[G: LDCs]**

Shields, Roger E. The Export–Import Bank: A Changing Mission? *Rodriguez, R. M., ed.*, 1987, pp. 157–65. **[G: U.S.]**

Shinn, Chang Min. Capital Imports in Economic Development: The Korean Case, 1962–85. *J. Econ. Devel.*, June 1987, *12*(1), pp. 49–63. **[G: Korea]**

Shoven, John B. U.S. Commercial Banks and the Developing-Country Debt Crisis: Comment. *Brookings Pap. Econ. Act.*, 1987, (2), pp. 602–04. **[G: U.S.]**

Siebert, Horst. Foreign Debt and Capital Accumulation. *Weltwirtsch. Arch.*, 1987, *123*(4), pp. 618–30.

Silva-Herzog F., Jesús. External Debt and Other Problems of Latin America. *[Wallich, H. C.]*, 1987, pp. 44–52. **[G: Latin America]**

Simon, Julian L. Population Growth, Economic Growth, and Foreign Aid. *Cato J.*, Spring/Summer 1987, *7*(1), pp. 159–86. **[G: LDCs]**

Simonsen, Mario Henrique. The Debt Crisis: Diagnosis and Prognosis. *Rodriguez, R. M., ed.*, 1987, pp. 77–85.

Smith, Brian H. An Agenda of Future Tasks for International and Indigenous NGOs: Views from the North. *World Devel.*, Supp. Autumn 1987, *15*, pp. 87–93. **[G: Global]**

Snowden, P. N. Chicago Schism on Banking Reforms and the Debt Crisis. *World Econ.*, June 1987, *10*(2), pp. 219–26. **[G: LDCs]**

Stevens, Christopher. The EC and Development Efforts in Africa. *Akinrinade, O. and Barling, J. K., eds.*, 1987, pp. 129–48. **[G: EEC; Africa]**

Stewart, Frances. Should Conditionality Change? *Havnevik, K. J., ed.*, 1987, pp. 29–45.

Stewart, Michael. A Survey of Some Recent Proposals for New International Facilities. *Dell, S., ed., Pt. 1*, 1987, pp. 179–98.

Stewart, Michael. An Elaboration of a Proposal for a Long-term Facility for Financing Purchases of Capital Goods by Developing Countries (Mexican Proposal). *Dell, S., ed., Pt. 1*, 1987, pp. 199–203. **[G: LDCs]**

Stowe, Robert C. United States Foreign Policy and the Conservation of Natural Resources: The Case of Tropical Deforestation. *Natural Res. J.*, Winter 1987, *27*(1), pp. 55–101. **[G: U.S.]**

Street, James H. Solutions for Mexico's External Debt Problem. *Tremblay, R., ed.*, 1987, pp. 31–41. **[G: Mexico]**

Street, James H. Values in Conflict: Developing Countries as Social Laboratories. *Dietz, J. L. and Street, J. H., eds.*, 1987, *1984*, pp. 261–69. **[G: Mexico; Argentina; Chile; Brazil; Uruguay]**

Streeten, Paul. Structural Adjustment: A Survey of the Issues and Options. *World Devel.*, December 1987, *15*(12), pp. 1469–82. **[G: LDCs]**

Stremlau, Carolyn. NGO Coordinating Bodies in Africa, Asia, and Latin America. *World Devel.*,

Supp. Autumn 1987, *15*, pp. 213–25. **[G: LDCs]**

Svendsen, Knud Erik. The Nordic Countries and the IMF/World Bank. *Havnevik, K. J., ed.*, 1987, pp. 161–65. **[G: N. Europe]**

Taffler, R. J. and Abassi, B. Country Risk: A Model for Predicting Debt Servicing Problems in Developing Countries. *Res, Z. and Motamen, S., eds.*, 1987, pp. 187–223. **[G: LDCs]**

Tanzi, Vito. Fiscal Policy, Growth, and Stabilization Programs. *Finance Develop.*, June 1987, *24*(2), pp. 15–17.

Tarshis, Lorie. Disarming the Debt Bomb. *Challenge*, May/June 1987, *30*(2), pp. 18–23. **[G: LDCs]**

Taylor, Lance. IMF Conditionality: Incomplete Theory, Policy Malpractice. *Myers, R. J., ed.*, 1987, pp. 33–45.

Thorp, Rosemary. Peruvian Adjustment Policies, 1978–85: The Effects of Prolonged Crisis. *Thorp, R. and Whitehead, L., eds.*, 1987, pp. 208–38. **[G: Peru]**

Thorp, Rosemary and Whitehead, Laurence. Latin American Debt and the Adjustment Crisis: Introduction. *Thorp, R. and Whitehead, L., eds.*, 1987, pp. 1–8. **[G: Latin America]**

Thorp, Rosemary and Whitehead, Laurence. Latin American Debt and the Adjustment Crisis: Review and Conclusions. *Thorp, R. and Whitehead, L., eds.*, 1987, pp. 318–54. **[G: Latin America]**

Toh, Kiertisak. Niger's External Debt: Legacy of Uranium-Led Growth Strategy. *Eastern Afr. Econ. Rev.*, June 1987, *3*(1), pp. 27–41. **[G: Niger]**

Tokman, Víctor E. and Wurgaft, J. The Recession and the Workers of Latin America. *International Labour Office.*, 1987, pp. 37–74. **[G: Latin America]**

Turits, Richard. Trade, Debt, and the Cuban Economy. *World Devel.*, January 1987, *15*(1), pp. 163–80. **[G: Cuba]**

Turits, Richard. Trade, Debt, and the Cuban Economy. *Zimbalist, A., ed.*, 1987, pp. 165–82. **[G: Cuba]**

Turner, Charlie G. Two Simple Measures of Dynamic Efficiency in the Global Economy. *Quart. Rev. Econ. Bus.*, Autumn 1987, *27*(3), pp. 40–55. **[G: Global]**

Twose, Nigel. European NGOs: Growth or Partnership? *World Devel.*, Supp. Autumn 1987, *15*, pp. 7–10. **[G: Europe]**

UNCTAD Secretariat. Determination of Quotas and the Relative Position of Developing Countries in the International Monetary Fund: Introduction. *Dell, S., ed., Pt. 2*, 1987, pp. 511–40.

Vaidya, Kalyan. Selected Measures of Financial Co-operation among Developing Countries. *Dell, S., ed., Pt. 2*, 1987, pp. 569–609. **[G: LDCs]**

Vines, David. Protectionism and the Debt Crisis: Discussion. *Bryant, R. C. and Portes, R., eds.*, 1987, pp. 331–36.

Volcker, Paul A. Statement to the U.S. Senate Subcommittee on International Finance and

Monetary Policy, Committee on Banking, Housing, and Urban Affairs, April 7, 1987. *Fed. Res. Bull.*, June 1987, *73*(6), pp. 425–30. [G: U.S.]

Voss, Jurgen. The Multilateral Investment Guarantee Agency: Status, Mandate, Concept, Features; Implications. *J. World Trade Law*, August 1987, *21*(4), pp. 5–23. [G: Global]

Walter, Ingo. Country Risk, Portfolio Decisions and Regulation in International Bank Lending. *Wilcox, J. A., ed.*, 1987, *1981*, pp. 342–56.

Wangwe, Samuel M. Impact of the IMF/World Bank Philosophy, the Case of Tanzania. *Havnevik, K. J., ed.*, 1987, pp. 149–60. [G: Tanzania]

Warren, Stanton A. and Romans, J. Thomas. The Debtor/Creditor Status of Latin American Countries and the Issue of Repudiation or Forgiveness of Debt. *Tremblay, R., ed.*, 1987, pp. 71–78. [G: Latin America]

Weaving, Rachel. Measuring Developing Countries' External Debt. *Finance Develop.*, March 1987, *24*(1), pp. 16–19. [G: LDCs]

Weck-Hannemann, Hannelore. Politisch-ökonomische Bestimmungsgründe der Vergabe von Entwicklungshilfe: Eine empirische Untersuchung für die Schweiz. (Politico-Economic Determinants of the Distribution of Foreign Aid: An Empirical Study for Switzerland. With English summary.) *Schweiz. Z. Volkswirtsch. Statist.*, December 1987, *123*(4), pp. 501–29. [G: Switzerland; LDCs]

Weck-Hannemann, Hannelore and Frey, Bruno S. Was erklärt die Entwicklungshilfe? (What Determines Development Aid? With English summary.) *Jahr. Nationalökon. Statist.*, March 1987, *203*(2), pp. 101–22. [G: LDCs]

Wellons, Philip A. Banks and the Export Credit Wars: Mixed Credits in the Sicartsa Financing. *Rodriguez, R. M., ed.*, 1987, pp. 167–203. [G: U.K.; Mexico]

Whitehead, Laurence. The Adjustment Process in Chile: A Comparative Perspective. *Thorp, R. and Whitehead, L., eds.*, 1987, pp. 117–61. [G: Chile]

Whiteman, Kaye. 'Francophonie,' Culture and Development: The Experience of the ACCT. *Akinrinade, O. and Barling, J. K., eds.*, 1987, pp. 174–98. [G: Africa; France]

Whitman, Marina von Neumann. The Impact of the Debt Problem on International Trade. *Rodriguez, R. M., ed.*, 1987, pp. 87–96. [G: LDCs]

van Wijnbergen, Sweder. Protectionism and the Debt Crisis. *Bryant, R. C. and Portes, R., eds.*, 1987, pp. 307–30.

Williamson, John. International Monetary Reform: A Survey of the Options. *Dell, S., ed., Pt. 1*, 1987, pp. 227–78. [G: LDCs]

Williamson, John. Reforming the IMF: Different or Better? *Myers, R. J., ed.*, 1987, pp. 1–12.

Williamson, John. Resource Transfer and the International Monetary System. *Williamson, J.*, 1987, pp. 157–77. [G: LDCs]

Williamson, John. The Why and How of Funding LDC Debt. *Williamson, J.*, 1987, *1982*, pp. 178–97. [G: LDCs]

Williamson, John. Valuation of the SDR: The Case for a Standard Five-Currency Logarithmic Basket. *Dell, S., ed., Pt. 2*, 1987, pp. 393–406.

Worswick, David. The IMF's World Economic Outlook: A Critique. *Dell, S., ed., Pt. 3*, 1987, pp. 723–41.

Xafa, Miranda. Export Credits and the Debt Crisis. *Finance Develop.*, March 1987, *24*(1), pp. 19–22. [G: LDCs]

Zombanakis, Minos. The International Debt Threat: A Way to Avoid a Crash. *Res, Z. and Motamen, S., eds.*, 1987, pp. 69–79. [G: Global]

500 Administration; Business Finance; Marketing; Accounting

510 ADMINISTRATION

511 Organization and Decision Theory

5110 Organization and Decision Theory

Allen, R. Douglas and Fry, Fred L. An Investigation of Sex as a Moderator of the Relationship between Occupational Stress and Perceived Organizational Effectiveness in Formal Groups. *J. Behav. Econ.*, Summer 1987, *16*(2), pp. 9–15.

Anderson, Lynn. Pillsbury's Improved Decision Making. *Shetty, Y. K. and Buehler, V. M., eds.*, 1987, pp. 247–52. [G: U.S.]

Argyris, Chris. Reasoning, Action Strategies, and Defensive Routines: The Case of OD Practitioners. *Woodman, R. W. and Pasmore, W. A., eds.*, 1987, pp. 89–128.

Ayres, Robert U. and Sandilya, Manalur S. Utility Maximization and Catastrophe Aversion: A Simulation Test. *J. Environ. Econ. Manage.*, December 1987, *14*(4), pp. 337–70.

Barba-Romero, Sergio. Panorámica actual de la decisión multicriterio discreta. (With English summary.) *Invest. Econ.*, May 1987, *11*(2), pp. 279–308.

Bate, Paul and Child, John. Paradigms and Understandings in Comparative Organizational Research. *Child, J. and Bate, P., eds.*, 1987, pp. 19–49.

Beckmann, Martin J. Managers as Principals and Agents. *Bamberg, G. and Spremann, K., eds.*, 1987, pp. 379–88.

Begin, James P. and Lee, Barbara A. NLRA Exclusion Criteria and Professional Work. *Ind. Relat.*, Winter 1987, *26*(1), pp. 83–95. [G: U.S.]

Beksiak, Janusz. Enterprise and Reform: The Polish Experience. *Europ. Econ. Rev.*, Feb./Mar. 1987, *31*(1/2), pp. 118–24. [G: Poland]

Benelli, Giuseppe; Loderer, Claudio and Lys, Thomas. Labor Participation in Corporate Policy-Making Decisions: West Germany's Experience with Codetermination. *J. Bus.*, October 1987, *60*(4), pp. 553–75. [G: W. Germany]

Benghozi, Pierre-Jean. L'harmonie des sphes: une réflexion sur l'éclatement des grandes organisations et l'émergence de rationalités contingentes irréductibles. (The Harmony of Spheres: Reflection on the Splitting of Large Organizations and the Emergence of Unyielding Contingent Rationalities. With English summary.) *Écon. Soc.*, June 1987, *21*(6), pp. 111–25.

Bernholz, Peter. Organizational Theory, Information Processing, and Short-run Dynamics: Theory and Empirical Tests: Comment. *J. Inst. Theoretical Econ.*, March 1987, *143*(1), pp. 225–28.   [G: U.S.]

Böcker, Franz and Gierl, Heribert. Determinanten der Diffusion neuer industrieller Produkte. (With English summary.) *Z. Betriebswirtshaft*, July 1987, *57*(7), pp. 684–98.
[G: W. Germany]

Boulding, Kenneth E. The Economy as an Ecosystem: Economics in the General System of the World. *Fox, K. A. and Miles, D. G., eds.*, 1987, pp. 3–18.

Brickley, James A. and Dark, Frederick H. The Choice of Organizational Form: The Case of Franchising. *J. Finan. Econ.*, June 1987, *18*(2), pp. 401–20.   [G: U.S.]

Brockett, Patrick L., et al. Cost–Volume–Utility Analysis with Partial Stochastic Information. *Quart. Rev. Econ. Bus.*, Autumn 1987, *27*(3), pp. 70–90.

Brockhoff, Klaus. Anforderungen an das Management in der Zukunft. (With English summary.) *Z. Betriebswirtshaft*, March 1987, *57*(3), pp. 239–50.

Bromiley, Philip and Marcus, Alfred A. Deadlines, Routines, and Change. *Policy Sci.*, 1987, *20*(2), pp. 85–103.

Brown, Clifton E. and Solomon, Ira. Effects of Outcome Information on Evaluations of Managerial Decisions. *Accounting Rev.*, July 1987, *62*(3), pp. 464–77.

Brown, L. David and Covey, Jane Gibson. Development Organizations and Organization Development: Toward an Expanded Paradigm for Organization Development. *Woodman, R. W. and Pasmore, W. A., eds.*, 1987, pp. 59–87.

Buitendam, Arend. The Horizontal Perspective of Organization Design and New Technology. *Pennings, J. M. and Buitendam, A., eds.*, 1987, pp. 59–86.

Bull, Clive and Ordover, Janusz A. Market Structure and Optimal Management Organizations. *Rand J. Econ.*, Winter 1987, *18*(4), pp. 480–91.

Bullock, R. J. and Tubbs, Mark E. The Case Meta-analysis Method for OD. *Woodman, R. W. and Pasmore, W. A., eds.*, 1987, pp. 171–228.

Child, John. Managerial Strategies, New Technology, and the Labor Process. *Pennings, J. M. and Buitendam, A., eds.*, 1987, pp. 141–77.

Child, John; Ganter, Hans-Dieter and Kieser, Alfred. Technological Innovation and Organizational Conservatism. *Pennings, J. M. and Buitendam, A., eds.*, 1987, pp. 87–115.
[G: U.K.; W. Germany]

Colorni, A. and Laniado, E. A Decision Support System for Choosing among Alternative Projects. *Merlo, M., et al., eds.*, 1987, pp. 39–51.

Cooperrider, David L. and Srivastva, Suresh. Appreciative Inquiry in Organizational Life. *Woodman, R. W. and Pasmore, W. A., eds.*, 1987, pp. 129–69.

Corfman, Kim P. and Lehmann, Donald R. Models of Cooperative Group Decision-Making and Relative Influence: An Experimental Investigation of Family Purchase Decisions. *J. Cons. Res.*, June 1987, *14*(1), pp. 1–13.   [G: U.S.]

Cummings, Thomas G. and Mohrman, Susan A. Self-designing Organizations: Towards Implementing Quality-of-Work-Life Innovations. *Woodman, R. W. and Pasmore, W. A., eds.*, 1987, pp. 275–310.

Dean, James W., Jr. Building the Future: The Justification Process for New Technology. *Pennings, J. M. and Buitendam, A., eds.*, 1987, pp. 35–58.

Declercq, D. Management in China. *Tijdschrift Econ. Manage.*, 1987, *32*(3), pp. 321–35.
[G: China]

Dégot, Vincent. L'argumentation des décisions économiquement non quantifiable (ou "argumentation môle"). (Argumentation of Soft Decisions—A Case Study. With English summary.) *Écon. Soc.*, June 1987, *21*(6), pp. 85–108.

Demski, Joel S. and Sappington, David E. M. Delegated Expertise. *J. Acc. Res.*, Spring 1987, *25*(1), pp. 68–89.

Dicle, I. Atilla. Japonya'da Insangücü Yönetimi ve Türkiye Açixindan Önemi. (With English summary.) *METU*, 1987, *14*(3), pp. 245–69.
[G: Japan; Turkey]

Dow, Gregory K. The Function of Authority in Transaction Cost Economics. *J. Econ. Behav. Organ.*, March 1987, *8*(1), pp. 13–38.

Drèze, Jacques H. Decision Criteria for Business Firms. *Drèze, J. H., 1987, 1982*, pp. 298–320.

Drèze, Jacques H. Decision Theory with Moral Hazard and State-Dependent Preferences. *Drèze, J. H.*, 1987, pp. 23–89.

Drèze, Jacques H. Econometrics and Decision Theory. *Drèze, J. H., 1987, 1972*, pp. 401–19.

Englander, Ernest J. The Inside Contract System of Production and Organization: A Neglected Aspect of the History of the Firm. *Labor Hist.*, Fall 1987, *28*(4), pp. 429–46.   [G: U.S.]

Ester, Jochen. A Fuzzy Concept of Efficiency. *Jahn, J. and Krabs, W., eds.*, 1987, pp. 257–64.

Ettlie, John E. and Bridges, William P. Technology Policy and Innovation in Organizations. *Pennings, J. M. and Buitendam, A., eds.*, 1987, pp. 117–37.   [G: U.S.]

Farquhar, Peter H. Applications of Utility Theory in Artificial Intelligence Research. *Sawaragi, Y.; Inoue, K. and Nakayama, H., eds.*, 1987, pp. 155–61.

Fiegenbaum, Avi; Sudharshan, D. and Thomas, Howard. The Concept of Stable Strategic Time Periods in Strategic Group Research. *Managerial Dec. Econ.*, June 1987, *8*(2), pp. 139–48.
[G: U.S.]

Firchau, Volker. Information Systems for Principal–Agent Problems. *Bamberg, G. and Spremann, K., eds.,* 1987, pp. 81–92.

Fishburn, Peter C. Reconsiderations in the Foundations of Decision under Uncertainty. *Econ. J.,* December 1987, 97(388), pp. 825–41.

FitzRoy, Felix R. and Kraft, Kornelius. Efficiency and Internal Organization: Works Councils in West German Firms. *Economica,* November 1987, 54(216), pp. 493–504. [G: W. Germany]

Foulds, L. R.; Giffin, J. W. and Evans, J. D. Toward a Decision Support System for Layout Managers. *Schultz, R. L., ed.,* 1987, pp. 93–129.

Fox, Karl A. Some Classic Examples of Systems Thinking in Several Sciences: Comments and Recommended Readings. *Fox, K. A. and Miles, D. G., eds.,* 1987, pp. 207–37.

Fox, Karl A. and Miles, Don G. Systems Economics: Summary and Overview. *Fox, K. A. and Miles, D. G., eds.,* 1987, pp. 180–93.

Gardner, Roy J. Systems Theory in Mathematical Economics. *Fox, K. A. and Miles, D. G., eds.,* 1987, pp. 50–66.

Gaulhofer, Manfred. Strategische Planung beim Controller?—Anmerkungen zu den Ausführungen von Pfohl und Zettlemeyer. (With English summary.) *Z. Betriebswirtshaft,* November 1987, 57(11), pp. 1121–27.

Gaynor, Martin and Kleindorfer, Paul R. Misperceptions, Equilibrium, and Incentives in Groups and Organizations. *Bamberg, G. and Spremann, K., eds.,* 1987, pp. 389–414.

Giordano, Yvonne. De la défaillance au redressement: le management omniprésent. (From Failure to Recovery: The Role of Management. With English summary.) *Écon. Soc.,* June 1987, 21(6), pp. 127–47.

Goldberg, Victor P. Organizational Theory, Information Processing, and Short-run Dynamics: Theory and Empirical Tests: Comment. *J. Inst. Theoretical Econ.,* March 1987, 143(1), pp. 222–24. [G: U.S.]

Gomez Pérez, José Patricio. Extensiones del método de los coeficientes variables en modelos no lineales: aplicación a un modelo de planificación estratégica. (With English summary.) *Invest. Econ.,* May 1987, 11(2), pp. 309–25.

Gougeon, Patrick. Assurance et diversification. (Insurance and Diversification. With English summary.) *L'Actual. Econ.,* June-September 1987, 63(2–3), pp. 187–99.

van Gunsteren, Lex A. Information Technology: A Managerial Perspective. *Pennings, J. M. and Buitendam, A., eds.,* 1987, pp. 277–89.

Guran, M. The Concept of Industrial Cybernetic System under the Impact Production Flexible Systems. *Econ. Computat. Cybern. Stud. Res.,* 1987, 22(3), pp. 89–95.

Hage, Jerald. Reflections on New Technology and Organizational Change. *Pennings, J. M. and Buitendam, A., eds.,* 1987, pp. 261–76. [G: Japan; U.S.]

Itoh, Hideshi. Information Processing Capacities of the Firm. *J. Japanese Int. Economies,* Sep-

tember 1987, 1(3), pp. 299–326. [G: Japan; U.S.]

Jarrell, Gregg A. and Poulsen, Annette B. Shark Repellents and Stock Prices: The Effects of Antitakeover Amendments since 1980. *J. Finan. Econ.,* September 1987, 19(1), pp. 127–68.

Jennergren, Lars Peter. Betriebswirtschaftslehre und Verfahrensforschung—Dreissig Jahre später. (With English summary.) *Z. Betriebswirtshaft,* February 1987, 57(2), pp. 189–94.

Johnson, Glenn L. Holistic Modeling of Multidisciplinary Subject Matter and Problem Domains. *Fox, K. A. and Miles, D. G., eds.,* 1987, pp. 85–109.

Jönsson, Sten. Limits of Information Technology for Facilitating Organizational Learning. *Pennings, J. M. and Buitendam, A., eds.,* 1987, pp. 217–34.

Jungermann, Helmut and Thüring, Manfred. The Use of Mental Models for Generating Scenarios. *Wright, G. and Ayton, P., eds.,* 1987, pp. 245–66.

Kaplan, Robert E.; Kofodimos, Joan R. and Drath, Wilfred H. Development at the Top: A Review and a Prospect. *Woodman, R. W. and Pasmore, W. A., eds.,* 1987, pp. 229–73.

Kasanen, Eero and Suomi, Reima. The Case Method in Information Systems Research. *Liiketaloudellinen Aikak.,* April 1987, 36(4), pp. 323–38.

Katzner, Donald W. The Efficiency of Organizational Forms. *Écon. Appl.,* 1987, 40(3), pp. 539–64.

Kay, N. M. and Diamantopoulos, Adamantios. Uncertainty and Synergy: Towards a Formal Model of Corporate Strategy. *Managerial Dec. Econ.,* June 1987, 8(2), pp. 121–30. [G: U.S.; U.K.; France; W. Germany]

Kersten, Gregory E. Two Aspects of Group Decision Support System Design. *Sawaragi, Y.; Inoue, K. and Nakayama, H., eds.,* 1987, pp. 373–82.

Kimberly, John R. Organizational and Contextual Influences on the Diffusion of Technological Innovation. *Pennings, J. M. and Buitendam, A., eds.,* 1987, pp. 237–59.

Kirby, Alison J. Discussion of Centralization versus Delegation and the Value of Communication. *J. Acc. Res.,* Supplement 1987, 25, pp. 19–21.

Kobayashi, Kiyoshi, et al. Multiactor Decision Analysis for Regional Investment Allocation. *Sawaragi, Y.; Inoue, K. and Nakayama, H., eds.,* 1987, pp. 422–31.

Koch, Helmut. Zur Theorie des Gewinnvorbehalts. (With English summary.) *Z. Betriebswirtshaft,* May/June 1987, 57(5/6), pp. 546–61.

Komiya, Ryutaro. Japanese Firms, Chinese Firms: Problems for Economic Reform in China: Part I. *J. Japanese Int. Economies,* March 1987, 1(1), pp. 31–61. [G: Japan; China]

Komiya, Ryutaro. Japanese Firms, Chinese Firms: Problems for Economic Reform in China: Part II. *J. Japanese Int. Economies,*

June 1987, *1*(2), pp. 229–47.   [G: Japan; China]

Kuhn, Klaus. Führungsstrukturen von Grossunternehmen. (With English summary.) *Z. Betriebswirtshaft*, May/June 1987, *57*(5/6), pp. 457–64.

Kurbel, Karl. EDV-orientierte Betriebswirtschafteslehre oder: an welchen Fronten kämpft die Betriebsinformatik? (With English summary.) *Z. Betriebswirtshaft*, May/June 1987, *57*(5/6), pp. 582–87.

Laaksonen, Oiva. Capitalist–Socialist Dialogue on Organizational Behaviour. *Child, J. and Bate, P., eds.*, 1987, pp. 1–15.

Lanen, William N. and Verrecchia, Robert E. Operating Decisions and the Disclosure of Management Accounting Information. *J. Acc. Res.*, Supplement 1987, *25*, pp. 165–89.

Lawlor, Michael S. Is the Economy a Closed System? General Equilibrium and General Systems Theory. *Fox, K. A. and Miles, D. G., eds.*, 1987, pp. 19–49.

Lawrence, David B. The Assessment of the Expected Value of Information in the Binary Decision Model. *Managerial Dec. Econ.*, December 1987, *8*(4), pp. 301–06.

Lewandowski, A.; Johnson, S. and Wierzbicki, A. A Prototype Selection Committee Decision Analysis and Support System, SCDAS: Theoretical Background and Computer Implementation. *Sawaragi, Y.; Inoue, K. and Nakayama, H., eds.*, 1987, pp. 358–65.

Lewin, David. Industrial Relations as a Strategic Variable. *Allen, S. G., et al.*, 1987, pp. 1–41. [G: U.S.]

Li, Duan and Haimes, Yacov Y. Risk Management in a Hierarchical Multiobjective Framework. *Sawaragi, Y.; Inoue, K. and Nakayama, H., eds.*, 1987, pp. 180–89.

MacLeod, W. Bentley. Behavior and the Organization of the Firm. *J. Compar. Econ.*, June 1987, *11*(2), pp. 207–20.

Macmillan, W. D. The Measurement of Efficiency in Multiunit Public Services. *Environ. Planning A*, November 1987, *19*(11), pp. 1511–24.

Magnan de Bornier, Jean. Propriété et contrôle dans la grande entreprise: une relecture de Berle et Means. (Ownership and Control in the Big Corporation: A Re-reading of Berle and Means. With English summary.) *Revue Écon.*, November 1987, *38*(6), pp. 1171–90.

Melumad, Nahum D. and Reichelstein, Stefan. Centralization versus Delegation and the Value of Communication. *J. Acc. Res.*, Supplement 1987, *25*, pp. 1–18.

Mentzer, John T. and Hunt, Kenneth A. The Use of Power: A Process Model of Marketing Channel Behavior. *Sheth, J. N., ed.*, 1987, pp. 211–36.

Michalowski, Wojtek. Multi-person Decision Support with Knowledge Base Systems. *Sawaragi, Y.; Inoue, K. and Nakayama, H., eds.*, 1987, pp. 383–92.

Miles, Don G. Systems Management, Repair, and Improvement: Systems Economics Applied to a Small, Constrained Poultry Farm. *Fox, K. A. and Miles, D. G., eds.*, 1987, pp. 110–17.

Miles, Don G. Wholistic Analysis, Problem Shifting Analysis, and Systems Economics. *Fox, K. A. and Miles, D. G., eds.*, 1987, pp. 195–206.

Moffet, Denis. Axiomes de rationalité en contexte d'incertitude. (Axioms of Rationality under Uncertainty. With English summary.) *L'Actual. Econ.*, June-September 1987, *63*(2–3), pp. 58–73.

Mohr, Lawrence B. Innovation Theory: As Assessment from the Vantage Point of the New Electronic Technology in Organizations. *Pennings, J. M. and Buitendam, A., eds.*, 1987, pp. 13–31.

Mori, Akio. Zum Stand der Betriebswirtschaftslehre in Japan. (With English summary.) *Z. Betriebswirtshaft*, September 1987, *57*(9), pp. 921–39.   [G: Japan]

Mura, Alberto. Verso una generalizzazione della teoria bayesiana delle decisioni. (Toward a Generalization of the Bayesian Decision Theory. With English summary.) *Econ. Scelte Pubbliche/J. Public Finance Public Choice*, Jan.-Apr. 1987, *5*(1), pp. 53–67.

Nakamori, Y. Interactive Modeling and Gaming-Simulation for Group Decision Making. *Sawaragi, Y.; Inoue, K. and Nakayama, H., eds.*, 1987, pp. 412–21.

Nishikawa, Y., et al. Design of a Decision-Support Workstation System for Hierarchical Multiobjective Inventory Control. *Sawaragi, Y.; Inoue, K. and Nakayama, H., eds.*, 1987, pp. 267–76.

Ozernoy, Vladimir M. A Framework for Choosing the Most Appropriate Discrete Alternative Multiple Criteria Decision-making Method in Decision Support Systems and Expert Systems. *Sawaragi, Y.; Inoue, K. and Nakayama, H., eds.*, 1987, pp. 56–64.

Patell, James M. Cost Accounting, Process Control, and Product Design: A Case Study of the Hewlett–Packard Personal Office Computer Division. *Accounting Rev.*, October 1987, *62*(4), pp. 808–39.   [G: U.S.]

Paul, Robert J.; Edabi, Yar M. and Dilts, David A. Commitment in Employee-Owned Firms: Involvement or Entrapment? *Quart. J. Bus. Econ.*, Autumn 1987, *26*(4), pp. 81–99.

Pennings, Johannes M. On the Nature of New Technology as Organizational Innovation. *Pennings, J. M. and Buitendam, A., eds.*, 1987, pp. 3–12.

Pfohl, Hans-Christian and Zettelmeyer, Bernd. Der Controller: Geringer oder anders qualifiziert als der Lineienmanager? Erwiderung zu den Anmerkungen von Mag. Dr. Manfred Gaulhofer. (With English summary.) *Z. Betriebswirtshaft*, November 1987, *57*(11), pp. 1128–35.

Pfohl, Hans-Christian and Zettelmeyer, Bernd. Stategisches Controlling? (With English summary.) *Z. Betriebswirtshaft*, February 1987, *57*(2), pp. 145–75.

Polishchuck, Leonid I. On Some Applications of Stochastic Dominance in Multiobjective Decision-Making. *Jahn, J. and Krabs, W., eds.*, 1987, pp. 208–21.

Porras, Jerry I. and Robertson, Peter J. Organization Development Theory: A Typology and Evaluation. *Woodman, R. W. and Pasmore, W. A., eds.*, 1987, pp. 1–57.

Predoi, A. Remote Diagnosis System. *Econ. Computat. Cybern. Stud. Res.*, 1987, 22(2), pp. 91–95.

Putterman, Louis. Corporate Governance, Risk-Bearing and Economic Power: A Comment on Recent Work by Oliver Williamson. *J. Inst. Theoretical Econ.*, September 1987, 143(3), pp. 422–34.

Rădăceanu, Ed. Implications of the Value Analysis of the Management Systems on the Information Systems Design. *Econ. Computat. Cybern. Stud. Res.*, 1987, 22(1), pp. 85–97.

Radner, Roy. Decentralization and Incentives. *[Hurwicz, L.]*, 1987, 1983, pp. 3–47.

Reiss, Michael. Aufbau- und ablauforientierte Heuristiken organisatorischer Gestaltung. (With English summary.) *Z. Betriebswirtshaft*, January 1987, 57(1), pp. 32–52.

Reponen, Tapio; Kasanen, Eero and Salonen, Tapani. Yritysjohto ja tietotekniikka. (Managers and Information Technology. With English summary.) *Liiketaloudellinen Aikak.*, 1987, 36(3), pp. 274–93.

Reutner, Friedrich. Determinanten des Unternehmenserfolges. (With English summary.) *Z. Betriebswirtshaft*, August 1987, 57(8), pp. 747–62.

Saaty, Thomas L. The General Case of Dependence in Hierarchic Decision Theory. *Sawaragi, Y.; Inoue, K. and Nakayama, H., eds.*, 1987, pp. 239–48.

Sabel, Hermann. Gegenwärtige Probleme des Managements in der chinesischen Wirtschaft. (With English summary.) *Z. Betriebswirtshaft*, February 1987, 57(2), pp. 124–44.
[G: W. Germany; China]

Sakawa, Masatoshi. An Interactive Fuzzy Satisficing Method for Multiobjective Linear Fractional Programming Problems with Fuzzy Parameters. *Sawaragi, Y.; Inoue, K. and Nakayama, H., eds.*, 1987, pp. 338–47.

Samson, Danny and Thomas, Howard. Linear Models as Decision Aids in Insurance Decision-making: The Case of Estimation of Automobile Insurance Claims. *Wright, G. and Ayton, P., eds.*, 1987, pp. 215–28.

Schanze, Erich. Contract, Agency, and the Delegation of Decision Making. *Bamberg, G. and Spremann, K., eds.*, 1987, pp. 461–71.

Schneeberger, H. A Generalized Problem of Optimum Allocation. *Jahr. Nationalökon. Statist.*, October 1987, 203(5–6), pp. 591–99.

Sengupta, Jati K. The Concept of Variety in Systems Behavior: Applications to Behavior Settings, Product-Differentiation, and Representative Firms. *Fox, K. A. and Miles, D. G., eds.*, 1987, pp. 67–81.

Seo, Fumiko. Socio-economic Interpretation of Multiple Agents Decision Making by Game Theory. *Sawaragi, Y.; Inoue, K. and Naka-*

yama, H., eds., 1987, pp. 393–402.

Siegel, Carole; Laska, Eugene and Lin, Shang. Decision Theory Models for Choosing Prospective Payment Schemes: A Negotiated Approach between Payers and Providers. *McGuire, T. G. and Scheffler, R. M., eds.*, 1987, pp. 143–55. [G: U.S.]

Simon, Herbert A. Rational Decision Making in Business Organizations. *Green, L. and Kagel, J. H., eds.*, 1987, 1978, pp. 18–47.

Stafford, Frank P. Organizational Theory and the Nature of Jobs. *J. Inst. Theoretical Econ.*, December 1987, 143(4), pp. 519–36.

Sterna-Karwat, Alicia. On the Existence of Cone-Efficient Points. *Jahn, J. and Krabs, W., eds.*, 1987, pp. 233–40.

Sydow, Jörg. Information Technology and Organizational Choice. *Child, J. and Bate, P., eds.*, 1987, pp. 85–100.

Tainio, Risto. Tiedon kasvun haasteet liikkeenjohtotutkimuksessa. (Growth of Knowledge in Management Studies. With English summary.) *Liiketaloudellinen Aikak.*, 1987, 36(1), pp. 95–102.

Tapiero, Charles S. A Systems Approach to Insurance Company Management. *Carraro, C. and Sartore, D., eds.*, 1987, pp. 279–304.

Tarng, Ming-Yueh and Chen, Miao-Sheng. On the Optimum Structure of the Hierarchy in an Organisation. *Math. Soc. Sci.*, December 1987, 14(3), pp. 239–50.

Ţigănescu, E. and Oprescu, G. Synthesis of an Integrated System of Cybernetic Models of the Economic Unit Management. *Econ. Computat. Cybern. Stud. Res.*, 1987, 22(4), pp. 13–27.

Ţigănescu, E.; Oprescu, G. and Goga, A. Cybernetic–Economic Analysis of the Scientific–Technical Progress Impact on the Economical Increase. *Econ. Computat. Cybern. Stud. Res.*, 1987, 22(3), pp. 5–21.

Tomer, John F. Developing Organizational Comparative Advantage via Industrial Policy. *J. Post Keynesian Econ.*, Spring 1987, 9(3), pp. 455–72.

Townsend, Robert M. Economic Organization with Limited Communication. *Amer. Econ. Rev.*, December 1987, 77(5), pp. 954–71.

Trueman, Brett. Discussion of Operating Decisions and the Disclosure of Management Accounting Information. *J. Acc. Res.*, Supplement 1987, 25, pp. 190–93.

Tylecote, Andrew. Time Horizons of Management Decisions: Causes and Effects. *J. Econ. Stud.*, 1987, 14(4), pp. 51–64. [G: U.S.; U.K.; Japan]

Vlačić, Lj.; Wierzbicki, A. and Matić, B. Aggregation Procedures for Hierarchically Grouped Decision Attributes with Application to Control System Performance Evaluation. *Jahn, J. and Krabs, W., eds.*, 1987, pp. 285–310.

Vodáček, Leo. Strategic Management of Innovation in Large Czechoslovak Firms. *Child, J. and Bate, P., eds.*, 1987, pp. 103–11.
[G: Czechoslovakia]

Wakker, Peter. Subjective Probabilities for State

Dependent Continuous Utility. *Math. Soc. Sci.*, December 1987, *14*(3), pp. 289–98.

Watada, J. and Tanaka, H. The Perspective of Possibilistic Models in Decision Making. *Sawaragi, Y.; Inoue, K. and Nakayama, H., eds.*, 1987, pp. 328–37.

Weber, M.; Eisenführ, F. and von Winterfeldt, Detlof. Bias in Assessment of Attribute Weights. *Sawaragi, Y.; Inoue, K. and Nakayama, H., eds.*, 1987, pp. 309–18.

Wiggins, Steven N. Organizational Theory, Information Processing, and Short-run Dynamics: Theory and Empirical Tests. *J. Inst. Theoretical Econ.*, March 1987, *143*(1), pp. 204–21. [G: U.S.]

Wildemann, Horst. Auftragsabwecklung in einer computergestützten Fertigung (CIM). (With English summary.) *Z. Betriebswirtshaft*, January 1987, *57*(1), pp. 6–31. [G: W. Germany]

Williamson, Oliver E. Transaction Cost Economics: The Comparative Contracting Perspective. *J. Econ. Behav. Organ.*, December 1987, *8*(4), pp. 617–25.

Wilson, David T. Qualitative Approaches to Organizational Buying Behavior Theory Development. *Woodside, A. G., ed.*, 1987, pp. 115–39.

Wolf, Johannes. Energiebeschaffung im Industrieunternehmen. (With English summary.) *Z. Betriebswirtshaft*, September 1987, *57*(9), pp. 901–20.

Ying, Mei-Qian. Scalarization, Optimality Conditions and Group Decision Making. *Sawaragi, Y.; Inoue, K. and Nakayama, H., eds.*, 1987, pp. 366–72.

Yu, P. L. and Chien, I. S. Foundation of Effective Goal Setting. *Jahn, J. and Krabs, W., eds.*, 1987, pp. 317–42.

Zamfir, Cătălin. Four Structural Problems of the Modern Enterprise: Similarities and Differences in Capitalist and Socialist Countries. *Child, J. and Bate, P., eds.*, 1987, pp. 73–83.

Zäpfel, Günther and Missbauer, Hubert. Produktionsplanung und -steuerung für die Fertigungsindustrie—ein Systemvergleich. (With English summary.) *Z. Betriebswirtshaft*, September 1987, *57*(9), pp. 882–900.

Zinam, Oleg. Functional and Dysfunctional Bureaucracy and Their Impact on Economic Development and Quality of Life. *Rivista Int. Sci. Econ. Com.*, March 1987, *34*(3), pp. 177–93.

512 Managerial Economics

5120 Managerial Economics

Abraham, H. and Gurzynski, Z. S. A. The Entrepreneur as a Non-factor. *S. Afr. J. Econ.*, June 1987, *55*(2), pp. 114–20.

Agrawal, Anup and Mandelker, Gershon N. Managerial Incentives and Corporate Investment and Financing Decisions. *J. Finance*, September 1987, *42*(4), pp. 823–37. [G: U.S.]

Alchian, Armen A. Some Perspectives on the Modern Theory of the Firm: A Conference in Honor of Armen A. Alchian: Concluding Remarks. *J. Inst. Theoretical Econ.*, March 1987, *143*(1), pp. 232–34.

Aoki, Masahiko. The Political Economy of Japan: The Japanese Firm in Transition. *Yamamura, K. and Yasuba, Y., eds.*, 1987, pp. 263–88. [G: Japan]

Bamberg, Günter. Risk Sharing and Subcontracting. *Bamberg, G. and Spremann, K., eds.*, 1987, pp. 61–79.

Barzel, Yoram. The Entrepreneur's Reward for Self-policing. *Econ. Inquiry*, January 1987, *25*(1), pp. 103–16.

Becker, Brian E. and Olson, Craig A. Labor Relations and Firm Performance. *Allen, S. G., et al.*, 1987, pp. 43–85.

Bernholz, Peter. Organizational Theory, Information Processing, and Short-run Dynamics: Theory and Empirical Tests: Comment. *J. Inst. Theoretical Econ.*, March 1987, *143*(1), pp. 225–28. [G: U.S.]

Block, Richard N., et al. Industrial Relations and the Performance of the Firm: An Overview. *Allen, S. G., et al.*, 1987, pp. 319–43.

Bogaschewsky, Ronald and Sierke, Bernt. Optimale Aggregatkombinationen bei zeitlich-intensitätsmässiger Anpassung und bei Kosten der Inbetriebnahme. (With English summary.) *Z. Betriebswirtshaft*, October 1987, *57*(10), pp. 978–1000.

Bonin, John P. and Fukuda, Wataru. Controlling a Risk-Averse, Effort-Selecting Manager in the Soviet Incentive Model. *J. Compar. Econ.*, June 1987, *11*(2), pp. 221–33. [G: U.S.S.R.]

Brickley, James A. and James, Christopher M. The Takeover Market, Corporate Board Composition, and Ownership Structure: The Case of Banking. *J. Law Econ.*, April 1987, *30*(1), pp. 161–80. [G: U.S.]

Brown, Clifton E. and Solomon, Ira. Effects of Outcome Information on Evaluations of Managerial Decisions. *Accounting Rev.*, July 1987, *62*(3), pp. 464–77.

Burch, E. Earl and Sumichrast, Robert T. Using Hierarchical Techniques to Schedule Machines with Simultaneous Production Capabilities. *Schultz, R. L., ed.*, 1987, pp. 61–92. [G: U.S.]

Campbell, Tim S. and Kracaw, William A. Optimal Managerial Incentive Contracts and the Value of Corporate Insurance. *J. Finan. Quant. Anal.*, September 1987, *22*(3), pp. 315–28.

Child, John. Managerial Strategies, New Technology, and the Labor Process. *Pennings, J. M. and Buitendam, A., eds.*, 1987, pp. 141–77.

Cornfield, Daniel B. Labor–Management Cooperation or Managerial Control? Emerging Patterns of Labor Relations in the United States. *Cornfield, D. B., ed.*, 1987, pp. 331–53. [G: U.S.]

Cosh, A. D. and Hughes, A. The Anatomy of Corporate Control: Directors, Shareholders and Executive Remuneration in Giant U.S. and U.K. Corporations. *Cambridge J. Econ.*, December 1987, *11*(4), pp. 285–313. [G: U.S.; U.K.]

Crook, J. N. and Allen, D. E. The Characteristics of Technically Orientated Firms: Evidence from the Unlisted Securities Market. *Managerial Dec. Econ.*, December 1987, *8*(4), pp. 271–84. **[G: U.K.]**

Darrough, Masako N. Managerial Incentives for Short-term Results: A Comment. *J. Finance*, September 1987, *42*(4), pp. 1097–1102.

Dave, Upendra. On Two Deterministic Inventory Models for Items with Decreasing Demand. *Econ. Computat. Cybern. Stud. Res.*, 1987, *22*(2), pp. 45–50.

Demski, Joel S. and Sappington, David E. M. Delegated Expertise. *J. Acc. Res.*, Spring 1987, *25*(1), pp. 68–89.

Dermine, Jean. Measuring the Market Value of a Bank, a Primer. *Finance*, December 1987, *8*(2), pp. 91–108.

Dichtl, Erwin, et al. Ulkomaille suuntautuminen vientimenestyksen edellytyksenä. (Foreign Orientation as a Precondition of Successful Export. With English summary.) *Liiketaloudellinen Aikak.*, 1987, *36*(3), pp. 260–73. **[G: Finland]**

Dolan, Robert J. Quantity Discounts: Managerial Issues and Research Opportunities: Reply. *Marketing Sci.*, Winter 1987, *6*(1), pp. 24.

Dolan, Robert J. Quantity Discounts: Managerial Issues and Research Opportunities. *Marketing Sci.*, Winter 1987, *6*(1), pp. 1–22.

Domozetov, Christo. Attitudes and Motivation of Production Managers in the Management of Technological Innovation. *Child, J. and Bate, P., eds.*, 1987, pp. 113–22. **[G: Bulgaria]**

Dussauge, Pierre. The Conversion of Military Activities: A Strategic Management of the Firm Perspective. *Schmidt, C. and Blackaby, F., eds.*, 1987, pp. 424–37. **[G: U.S.]**

Ehrenberg, Ronald G. and Milkovich, George T. Compensation and Firm Performance. *Allen, S. G., et al.*, 1987, pp. 87–122. **[G: U.S.]**

Emery, Gary W. An Optimal Financial Response to Variable Demand. *J. Finan. Quant. Anal.*, June 1987, *22*(2), pp. 209–25.

Etzioni, Amitai. Entrepreneurship, Adaptation and Legitimation: A Macro-behavioral Perspective. *J. Econ. Behav. Organ.*, June 1987, *8*(2), pp. 175–89.

Evans, Jonathan St. B. T. Beliefs and Expectations as Causes of Judgmental Bias. *Wright, G. and Ayton, P., eds.*, 1987, pp. 31–47.

Faerman, E. Iu. Coordinating Forecasts in Hierarchically Organized Units. *Matekon*, Spring 1987, *23*(3), pp. 28–49.

Farquhar, Peter H. Applications of Utility Theory in Artificial Intelligence Research. *Sawaragi, Y.; Inoue, K. and Nakayama, H., eds.*, 1987, pp. 155–61.

Fishelson, Gideon. Pricing Policies and Ownership of Shares as Substitutes for Vertical Integration. *J. Econ. Bus.*, February 1987, *39*(1), pp. 35–44.

Frey, John B. Quantity Discounts: Managerial Issues and Research Opportunities: Commen-

tary. *Marketing Sci.*, Winter 1987, *6*(1), pp. 23.

Gerstner, Eitan and Hess, James D. Why Do Hot Dogs Come in Packs of 10 and Buns in 8s or 12s? A Demand-Side Investigation. *J. Bus.*, October 1987, *60*(4), pp. 491–517. **[G: U.S.]**

Ghali, Moheb A. Seasonality, Aggregation and the Testing of the Production Smoothing Hypothesis. *Amer. Econ. Rev.*, June 1987, *77*(3), pp. 464–69. **[G: U.S.]**

Gliński, Bohdan. Variants of the Socialist Economic Management System in Eastern Europe. *Child, J. and Bate, P., eds.*, 1987, pp. 151–62. **[G: E. Europe]**

Goldberg, Victor P. Organizational Theory, Information Processing, and Short-run Dynamics: Theory and Empirical Tests: Comment. *J. Inst. Theoretical Econ.*, March 1987, *143*(1), pp. 222–24. **[G: U.S.]**

Gort, Michael and Singamsetti, Rao. Innovation and the Personality Profiles of Firms. *Int. J. Ind. Organ.*, March 1987, *5*(1), pp. 115–26. **[G: U.S.]**

Gougeon, Patrick. Assurance et diversification. (Insurance and Diversification. With English summary.) *L'Actual. Econ.*, June-September 1987, *63*(2–3), pp. 187–99.

Grout, Paul A. and Laisney, François. The Effects of the Dispersion of Shareholdings on Performance of Owner Controlled Firms. *Ann. Écon. Statist.*, Jan./Mar. 1987, (5), pp. 77–87.

Gui, Benedetto. Internal Pay Schedules and Labour Mobility: The Problem of Firm Survival. *Econ. Notes*, 1987, (2), pp. 89–101.

Hamilton, James L. and Philippart, Nancy L. On the Nonequivalence of Maximum Resale Price Maintenance and Vertical Integration. *Eastern Econ. J.*, October-December 1987, *13*(4), pp. 411–19. **[G: U.S.]**

Hanink, Dean M. and Cromley, R. G. A Risk-Return Model for Multiregion and Multiproduct Diversification of the Firm. *Environ. Planning A*, January 1987, *19*(1), pp. 81–92.

Harpaz, Giora and Thomadakis, Stavros B. Valuation under Imperfect Information: Bayesian Learning from the Performance of the Firm and the Market. *Managerial Dec. Econ.*, September 1987, *8*(3), pp. 229–34.

Harris, Frederick H. deB. Competing Theories of Firm Decision-Making under Risk. *Southern Econ. J.*, October 1987, *54*(2), pp. 271–86. **[G: U.S.]**

Haugen, Robert A. and Senbet, Lemma W. On the Resolution of Agency Problems by Complex Financial Instruments: A Reply. *J. Finance*, September 1987, *42*(4), pp. 1091–95.

Haugen, Robert A. and Taylor, William M. An Optimal-Incentive Contract for Managers with Exponential Utility. *Managerial Dec. Econ.*, June 1987, *8*(2), pp. 87–91.

Hayes, Beth. Competition and Two-Part Tariffs. *J. Bus.*, January 1987, *60*(1), pp. 41–54.

Hedderich, Rudolf and Hedderich, Barbara. Leistung und Kapazität im Handelsbetrieb. (With English summary.) *Z. Betriebswirtshaft,*

August 1987, 57(8), pp. 793–815.

Hergert, Michael. Integrating Forecasting Techniques into Corporate Financial Models. *Bus. Econ.*, July 1987, 22(3), pp. 38–42.

Highfield, Richard and Smiley, Robert. New Business Starts and Economic Activity: An Empirical Investigation. *Int. J. Ind. Organ.*, March 1987, 5(1), pp. 51–66. **[G: U.S.]**

Hilke, John C. and Nelson, Philip B. Caveat Innovator: Strategic and Structural Characteristics of New Product Introductions. *J. Econ. Behav. Organ.*, June 1987, 8(2), pp. 213–29.
[G: U.S.]

Hillman, Arye L.; Katz, Eliakim and Rosenberg, Jacob. Workers as Insurance: Anticipated Government Assistance and Factor Demand. *Oxford Econ. Pap.*, December 1987, 39(4), pp. 813–20.

Hollander, Abraham; Huarie, Alain and L'Ecuyer, Pierre. Ratchet Effects and the Cost of Incremental Incentive Schemes. *J. Econ. Dynam. Control*, September 1987, 11(3), pp. 373–89.

Jacobson, Robert. The Validity of ROI as a Measure of Business Performance. *Amer. Econ. Rev.*, June 1987, 77(3), pp. 470–78.
[G: U.S.]

Jobber, David and Hooley, Graham. Pricing Behaviour in UK Manufacturing and Service Industries. *Managerial Dec. Econ.*, June 1987, 8(2), pp. 167–71. **[G: U.K.]**

Johnston, Wesley J. and Spekman, Robert E. Industrial Buying Behavior: Where We Are and Where We Need to Go. *Sheth, J. N. and Hirschman, E., eds.*, 1987, pp. 83–111.

Kaulmann, Thomas. Managerialism versus the Property Rights Theory of the Firm. *Bamberg, G. and Spremann, K., eds.*, 1987, pp. 439–59. **[G: U.S.]**

Kawasaki, Seiichi and McMillan, John. The Design of Contracts: Evidence from Japanese Subcontracting. *J. Japanese Int. Economies*, September 1987, 1(3), pp. 327–49. **[G: Japan]**

Kim, H. Youn. Economies of Scale in Multi-product Firms: An Empirical Analysis. *Economica*, May 1987, 54(214), pp. 185–206. **[G: U.S.]**

Koch, Helmut. Zur Theorie des Gewinnvorbehalts. (With English summary.) *Z. Betriebswirtshaft*, May/June 1987, 57(5/6), pp. 546–61.

König, Heinz and Nerlove, Marc. Saisonale und konjunkturelle Komponenten in der Beziehung zwischen Erwartungen, Plänen und Realisationen in Konjunkturtests. (Seasonal and Cyclical Variations in Relationship among Expectations, Plans and Realizations in Business Test Surveys. With English summary.) *Ifo-Studien*, 1987, 33(3), pp. 161–93.
[G: W. Germany; France]

Kumar, K. Ravi. The Relationship between Mixed Strategies and Strategic Groups. *Managerial Dec. Econ.*, September 1987, 8(3), pp. 235–42.

La Manna, Manfredi M. A. The Simple Analytics of Agency Costs: A Pedagogical Comment. *Econ. Notes*, 1987, (2), pp. 145–56.

Laitinen, Erkki K. A Computer Model of the Failure Process of the Firm: Part II. *Liiketaloudellinen Aikak.*, April 1987, 36(4), pp. 339–65.
[G: Finland]

Laitinen, Erkki K. A Computer Model of the Failure Process of the Firm: Part I. *Liiketaloudellinen Aikak.*, 1987, 36(3), pp. 199–225.
[G: Finland]

Lanen, William N. and Verrecchia, Robert E. Operating Decisions and the Disclosure of Management Accounting Information. *J. Acc. Res.*, Supplement 1987, 25, pp. 165–89.

Leibenstein, Harvey. Entrepreneurship, Entrepreneurial Training, and X-Efficiency Theory. *J. Econ. Behav. Organ.*, June 1987, 8(2), pp. 191–205.

Li, Duan and Haimes, Yacov Y. Risk Management in a Hierarchical Multiobjective Framework. *Sawaragi, Y.; Inoue, K. and Nakayama, H., eds.*, 1987, pp. 180–89.

Lindberg, Thomas. An Intelligence Model for Managers. *Dedijer, S. and Jéquier, N., eds.*, 1987, pp. 197–210.

Link, Jörg. Schwachpunkte der kumulativen Abweichungsanalyse in der Erfolgskontrolle. (With English summary.) *Z. Betriebswirtshaft*, August 1987, 57(8), pp. 780–92.

Lock, Andy. Integrating Group Judgments in Subjective Forecasts. *Wright, G. and Ayton, P., eds.*, 1987, pp. 109–27.

Lowenthal, F. Learning Curves—An Axiomatic Approach. *Managerial Dec. Econ.*, September 1987, 8(3), pp. 195–200.

Marzen, Walter. Das Faktorsystem im Handel. (With English summary.) *Z. Betriebswirtshaft*, January 1987, 57(1), pp. 53–58.

McDermott, John H.; Bain, James A., Jr. and Miller, Jeffrey B. Price Control and Input Inventory: The Firm under Disequilibrium Trading. *J. Econ. Bus.*, August 1987, 39(3), pp. 239–50.

McDonald, Ian M. and Spindler, Karen J. An Empirical Investigation of Customer Market Analysis—A Microfoundation for Macroeconomics. *Appl. Econ.*, September 1987, 19(9), pp. 1149–74. **[G: U.S.; U.K.; Australia]**

McDonald, John. A New Model for Learning Curves, DARM: Reply. *J. Bus. Econ. Statist.*, July 1987, 5(3), pp. 338. **[G: U.S.]**

McDonald, John. A New Model for Learning Curves, DARM. *J. Bus. Econ. Statist.*, July 1987, 5(3), pp. 329–35. **[G: U.S.]**

McGee, John S. Compound Pricing. *Econ. Inquiry*, April 1987, 25(2), pp. 315–39.

McMillan, Henry. A Principal–Agent Analysis of Pension Policy. *Managerial Dec. Econ.*, December 1987, 8(4), pp. 313–19.

Miles, Don G. Systems Management, Repair, and Improvement: Systems Economics Applied to a Small, Constrained Poultry Farm. *Fox, K. A. and Miles, D. G., eds.*, 1987, pp. 110–17.

Moor, Roy E. Ethics for Businesses…and Their Economists. *Bus. Econ.*, October 1987, 22(4), pp. 11–14.

Müller-Manzke, Ulrich. Optimale Bestellmenge und Mengenrabatt. (With English summary.)

Z. *Betriebswirtshaft*, May/June 1987, 57(5/6), pp. 503–21. **[G: W. Germany]**

Munroe, Tapan. The Business Economist at Work: The Pacific Gas & Electric Company. *Bus. Econ.*, January 1987, 22(1), pp. 56–57. **[G: U.S.]**

Murali, R. Demand Uncertainty and Input Constraints. *Quart. Rev. Econ. Bus.*, Summer 1987, 27(2), pp. 22–41.

Narayanan, M. P. Managerial Incentives for Short-term Results: A Reply. *J. Finance*, September 1987, 42(4), pp. 1103–04.

Narayanan, M. P. On the Resolution of Agency Problems by Complex Financial Instruments: A Comment [Resolving the Agency Problems of External Capital through Stock Options]. *J. Finance*, September 1987, 42(4), pp. 1083–90.

Nguyen, Dung. Advertising, Random Sales Response, and Brand Competition: Some Theoretical and Econometric Implications. *J. Bus.*, April 1987, 60(2), pp. 259–79. **[G: U.S.]**

Nishikawa, Y., et al. Design of a Decision-Support Workstation System for Hierarchical Multiobjective Inventory Control. *Sawaragi, Y.; Inoue, K. and Nakayama, H., eds.*, 1987, pp. 267–76.

Osterman, Paul. Turnover, Employment Security, and the Performance of the Firm. *Allen, S. G., et al.*, 1987, pp. 275–317. **[G: U.S.]**

Ozernoy, Vladimir M. A Framework for Choosing the Most Appropriate Discrete Alternative Multiple Criteria Decision-making Method in Decision Support Systems and Expert Systems. *Sawaragi, Y.; Inoue, K. and Nakayama, H., eds.*, 1987, pp. 56–64.

Paché, Gilles and Paraponaris, Claude. Réorganisation du capital industriel et formes liées de la gestion de production. (Reorganization of Industrial Capital and Linked Forms to Management Production. With English summary.) *Écon. Soc.*, June 1987, 21(6), pp. 151–77.

Pearce, Frank T. Management Intelligence. *Dedijer, S. and Jéquier, N., eds.*, 1987, pp. 49–61.

Phillips, Lawrence D. On the Adequacy of Judgmental Forecasts. *Wright, G. and Ayton, P., eds.*, 1987, pp. 11–30.

Png, Ivan Paak Liang and Hirshleifer, D. Price Discrimination through Offers to Match Price. *J. Bus.*, July 1987, 60(3), pp. 365–83.

Polinsky, A. Mitchell. Fixed Price versus Spot Price Contracts: A Study in Risk Allocation. *J. Law, Econ., Organ.*, Spring 1987, 3(1), pp. 27–46. **[G: U.S.]**

Putterman, Louis. Corporate Governance, Risk-Bearing and Economic Power: A Comment on Recent Work by Oliver Williamson. *J. Inst. Theoretical Econ.*, September 1987, 143(3), pp. 422–34.

Raubitschek, Ruth S. A Model of Product Proliferation with Multiproduct Firms. *J. Ind. Econ.*, March 1987, 35(3), pp. 269–79.

Reid, Gavin C. Applying Field Research Techniques to the Business Enterprise. *Int. J. Soc. Econ.*, 1987, 14(11), pp. 3–25.

Ronen, Joshua. Comments [Entrepreneurship,

Adaption and Legitimation: A Macro-behavioral Perspective] [Entrepreneurship, Entrepreneurial Training, and X-Efficiency Theory]. *J. Econ. Behav. Organ.*, June 1987, 8(2), pp. 207–12.

Rong, Wenzuo. Establishing Socialist Joint Stock Companies: A Report of a Study on the Joint-Development Company of the China Tourism Souvenirs Enterprise. *Chinese Econ. Stud.*, Spring 1987, 20(3), pp. 46–62. **[G: China]**

Rothwell, Sheila. New Technology and New Supervisory Roles in U.K. Manufacturing Industry. *Child, J. and Bate, P., eds.*, 1987, pp. 123–35. **[G: U.K.]**

Saaty, Thomas L. The General Case of Dependence in Hierarchic Decision Theory. *Sawaragi, Y.; Inoue, K. and Nakayama, H., eds.*, 1987, pp. 239–48.

Sakawa, Masatoshi. An Interactive Fuzzy Satisficing Method for Multiobjective Linear Fractional Programming Problems with Fuzzy Parameters. *Sawaragi, Y.; Inoue, K. and Nakayama, H., eds.*, 1987, pp. 338–47.

Schapers, J. J. Success Factors for the Next Ten Years: An Approach to the Development of International Trading. *Visser, H. and Schoor, E., eds.*, 1987, pp. 291–99. **[G: Global]**

Schneeweiss, Christoph and Alscher, Jürgen. Zur Disposition von Mehrprodukt-Lägern unter Verwendung der klassischen Losgrössenformel. (With English summary.) *Z. Betriebswirtshaft*, May/June 1987, 57(5/6), pp. 483–502.

Schramm, Klaus. Über die Kapitalwertfunktion des klassischen Losgrössenmodells. (With English summary.) *Z. Betriebswirtshaft*, May/June 1987, 57(5/6), pp. 465–82.

Schwartz, Hugh H. Perception, Judgment, and Motivation in Manufacturing Enterprises: Findings and Preliminary Hypotheses from In-Depth Interviews. *J. Econ. Behav. Organ.*, December 1987, 8(4), pp. 543–65. **[G: U.S.; Mexico; Argentina]**

Sengupta, Jati K. Production Frontier Estimation to Measure Efficiency: A Critical Evaluation in Light of Data Envelopment Analysis. *Managerial Dec. Econ.*, June 1987, 8(2), pp. 93–99. **[G: U.S.]**

Sparkes, John R.; Buckley, Peter J. and Mirza, Hafiz. A Note on Japanese Pricing Policy. *Appl. Econ.*, June 1987, 19(6), pp. 729–32. **[G: Japan]**

Stabile, Donald R. The Du Pont Experiments in Scientific Management: Efficiency and Safety, 1911–1919. *Bus. Hist. Rev.*, Autumn 1987, 61(3), pp. 365–86. **[G: U.S.]**

Tapiero, Charles S. and Jacque, Laurent. The Expected Cost of Ruin and Insurance Premiums in Mutual Insurance. *J. Risk Ins.*, September 1987, 54(3), pp. 594–602.

Tarling, Roger and Wilkinson, Frank. The Level, Structure and Flexibility of Costs. *Tarling, R., ed.*, 1987, pp. 3–22.

Tehranian, Hassan; Travlos, Nickolaos G. and Waegelein, James F. The Effect of Long-term Performance Plans on Corporate Sell-Off–Induced Abnormal Returns. *J. Finance*, September 1987, *42*(4), pp. 933–42.   [G: U.S.]

Trueman, Brett. Discussion of Operating Decisions and the Disclosure of Management Accounting Information. *J. Acc. Res.*, Supplement 1987, *25*, pp. 190–93.

Tylecote, Andrew. Time Horizons of Management Decisions: Causes and Effects. *J. Econ. Stud.*, 1987, *14*(4), pp. 51–64.   [G: U.S.; U.K.; Japan]

Vicari, Paola. L'ipotesi di eterogeneità dei comportamenti di impresa. Un diverso modo di rapportarsi all'informazione. (The Hypothesis of the Heterogeneous Behaviour of Firms: A Different Way of Considering Information. With English summary.) *Econ. Lavoro*, Apr.-June 1987, *21*(2), pp. 31–45.   [G: Italy]

Vodáček, Leo. Strategic Management of Innovation in Large Czechoslovak Firms. *Child, J. and Bate, P., eds.*, 1987, pp. 103–11.   [G: Czechoslovakia]

Wäscher, Dieter. Gemeinkosten-Management im Material- und Logistik-Bereich. (With English summary.) *Z. Betriebswirtschaft*, March 1987, *57*(3), pp. 297–315.

Watada, J. and Tanaka, H. The Perspective of Possibilistic Models in Decision Making. *Sawaragi, Y.; Inoue, K. and Nakayama, H., eds.*, 1987, pp. 328–37.

Weber, M.; Eisenführ, F. and von Winterfeldt, Detlof. Bias in Assessment of Attribute Weights. *Sawaragi, Y.; Inoue, K. and Nakayama, H., eds.*, 1987, pp. 309–18.

Whitman, Marina von Neumann. New Directions for the Business Economist. *Bus. Econ.*, January 1987, *22*(1), pp. 51–55.

Wiggins, Steven N. Organizational Theory, Information Processing, and Short-run Dynamics: Theory and Empirical Tests. *J. Inst. Theoretical Econ.*, March 1987, *143*(1), pp. 204–21.   [G: U.S.]

Wilhelm, Jochen E. M. On Stakeholders' Unanimity. *Bamberg, G. and Spremann, K., eds.*, 1987, pp. 179–204.

Williamson, Oliver E. Assessing Contract. *Williamson, O.*, 1987, *1985*, pp. 161–89.

Williamson, Oliver E. Transaction Cost Economics: The Comparative Contracting Perspective. *J. Econ. Behav. Organ.*, December 1987, *8*(4), pp. 617–25.

Womer, Norman Keith and Patterson, J. Wayne. A New Model for Learning Curves, DARM: Comment. *J. Bus. Econ. Statist.*, July 1987, *5*(3), pp. 336–37.   [G: U.S.]

Yoo, Pil Hwa; Dolan, Robert J. and Rangan, V. Kasturi. Dynamic Pricing Strategy for New Consumer Durables. *Z. Betriebswirtschaft*, October 1987, *57*(10), pp. 1024–43.

Zäpfel, Günther and Missbauer, Hubert. Produktionsplanung und -steuerung für die Fertigungsindustrie—ein Systemvergleich. (With English summary.) *Z. Betriebswirtschaft*, September 1987, *57*(9), pp. 882–900.

Zhang, Shaojie and Zhang, Amei. The Present Management Environment in China's Industrial Enterprises. *Reynolds, B. L.*, 1987, pp. 47–58.   [G: China]

513 Business and Public Administration

5130 General

Amershi, Amin H. and Sunder, Shyam. Failure of Stock Prices to Discipline Managers in a Rational Expectations Economy. *J. Acc. Res.*, Autumn 1987, *25*(2), pp. 177–95.

Beatty, Richard W.; Schneier, Craig Eric and McEvoy, Glenn M. Executive Development and Management Succession. *Rowland, K. M. and Ferris, G. R., eds.*, 1987, pp. 289–322.

Bhagat, Sanjai; Brickley, James A. and Coles, Jeffrey L. Managerial Indemnification and Liability Insurance: The Effect on Shareholder Wealth. *J. Risk Ins.*, December 1987, *54*(4), pp. 721–36.   [G: U.S.]

Gebotys, Robert J.; Auerbach, Alan J. and Petrucci, Adriani. The Insurance Branch Manager: Correlates of Success. *J. Risk Ins.*, March 1987, *54*(1), pp. 157–61.   [G: Canada]

Gliński, Bohdan. Variants of the Socialist Economic Management System in Eastern Europe. *Child, J. and Bate, P., eds.*, 1987, pp. 151–62.   [G: E. Europe]

Gotsch, Carl H. Applications of Microcomputers in Third World Organizations. *Ruth, S. R. and Mann, C. K., eds.*, 1987, *1986*, pp. 39–48.   [G: LDCs]

Hanna, Nagy. Strategic Planning and the Management of Change. *Finance Develop.*, March 1987, *24*(1), pp. 30–33.   [G: U.S.; LDCs]

Hannaway, Jane. Supply Creates Demands: An Organizational Process View of Administrative Expansion. *J. Policy Anal. Manage.*, Fall 1987, *7*(1), pp. 118–34.   [G: U.S.]

Hattori, Tamio. Formation of the Korean Business Elite during the Era of Rapid Economic Growth. *Devel. Econ.*, December 1987, *25*(4), pp. 346–62.   [G: S. Korea]

Hattwick, Richard E. Kenneth Iverson of Nucor. *J. Behav. Econ.*, Fall 1987, *16*(3), pp. 99–104.   [G: U.S.]

Hattwick, Richard E. Tom Watson: Founder of IBM. *J. Behav. Econ.*, Spring 1987, *16*(1), pp. 109–26.

Haugen, Robert A. and Taylor, William M. An Optimal-Incentive Contract for Managers with Exponential Utility. *Managerial Dec. Econ.*, June 1987, *8*(2), pp. 87–91.

Healy, Paul M.; Kang, Sok-Hyon and Palepu, Krishna G. The Effect of Accounting Procedure Changes on CEOs' Cash Salary and Bonus Compensation. *J. Acc. Econ.*, April 1987, *9*(1), pp. 7–34.   [G: U.S.]

Hilton, Margaret and Straw, Ronnie. Cooperative Training in Telecommunications: Case Studies. *Mon. Lab. Rev.*, May 1987, *110*(5), pp. 32–36.   [G: U.S.]

Kaplan, Robert E.; Kofodimos, Joan R. and Drath, Wilfred H. Development at the Top: A Review and a Prospect. *Woodman, R. W. and Pasmore, W. A., eds.*, 1987, pp. 229–73.

Kliksberg, Bernardo. New Technological Frontiers of Management in Latin America. *CEPAL Rev.*, April 1987, (31), pp. 171–91.   [G: Latin America]

Larcker, David F. Short-term Compensation Contracts and Executive Expenditure Decisions: The Case of Commercial Banks. *J. Finan. Quant. Anal.*, March 1987, *22*(1), pp. 33–50. [G: U.S.]

Lewellen, Wilbur G.; Loderer, Claudio and Martin, Kenneth. Executive Compensation and Executive Incentive Problems: An Empirical Analysis. *J. Acc. Econ.*, December 1987, *9*(3), pp. 287–310. [G: U.S.]

Lupton, Tom. The Development of Education for Management in the United Kingdom. *Z. Betriebswirtshaft*, January 1987, *57*(1), pp. 86–99. [G: U.K.]

Michailin, Alexander. Aus- und Weiterbildung der Führungskräfte der Wirtschaft in der Sowjetunion. (With English summary.) *Z. Betriebswirtshaft*, January 1987, *57*(1), pp. 100–107. [G: U.S.S.R.]

Montgomery, John D. Probing Managerial Behavior: Image and Reality in Southern Africa. *World Devel.*, July 1987, *15*(7), pp. 911–29. [G: Africa]

Naisbitt, John. Re-inventing the Corporation. *Shetty, Y. K. and Buehler, V. M., eds.*, 1987, pp. 57–71. [G: U.S.]

Paul, Robert J. and Ebadi, Yar M. Employee Ownership and Organizational Slack—Some Thoughts toward a Model. *J. Behav. Econ.*, Fall 1987, *16*(3), pp. 23–34.

Sydow, Jörg. Information Technology and Organizational Choice. *Child, J. and Bate, P., eds.*, 1987, pp. 85–100.

Trewatha, Robert L. and Vaught, Bobby. The Role of Preferred Leader Behavior, Managerial Demographics, and Interpersonal Skills in Predicting Leadership Style. *J. Behav. Econ.*, Spring 1987, *16*(1), pp. 99–107.

Zamfir, Cătălin. Four Structural Problems of the Modern Enterprise: Similarities and Differences in Capitalist and Socialist Countries. *Child, J. and Bate, P., eds.*, 1987, pp. 73–83.

Zinam, Oleg. Functional and Dysfunctional Bureaucracy and Their Impact on Economic Development and Quality of Life. *Rivista Int. Sci. Econ. Com.*, March 1987, *34*(3), pp. 177–93.

5131 Business Administration

Agrawal, Anup and Mandelker, Gershon N. Managerial Incentives and Corporate Investment and Financing Decisions. *J. Finance*, September 1987, *42*(4), pp. 823–37. [G: U.S.]

Baker, George P. Discussion of an Analysis of the Use of Accounting and Market Measures of Performance in Executive Compensation Contracts. *J. Acc. Res.*, Supplement 1987, *25*, pp. 126–29.

Barrett, Diana and Campbell, Paul H. Walking Softly: The Role of Management in Altering Physician Practice Patterns in the Hospital Corporation of America. *Scheffler, R. M. and Rossiter, L. F., eds.*, 1987, pp. 157–78. [G: U.S.]

Barzel, Yoram. The Entrepreneur's Reward for

Self-policing. *Econ. Inquiry,* January 1987, *25*(1), pp. 103–16.

Beksiak, Janusz. Enterprise and Reform: The Polish Experience. *Europ. Econ. Rev.*, Feb./Mar. 1987, *31*(1/2), pp. 118–24. [G: Poland]

Campbell, Tim S. and Kracaw, William A. Optimal Managerial Incentive Contracts and the Value of Corporate Insurance. *J. Finan. Quant. Anal.*, September 1987, *22*(3), pp. 315–28.

Chhokar, Jagdeep S. Safety at the Workplace: A Behavioural Approach. *Int. Lab. Rev.*, Mar.-Apr. 1987, *126*(2), pp. 169–78.

Cosh, A. D. and Hughes, A. The Anatomy of Corporate Control: Directors, Shareholders and Executive Remuneration in Giant U.S. and U.K. Corporations. *Cambridge J. Econ.*, December 1987, *11*(4), pp. 285–313. [G: U.S.; U.K.]

Darrough, Masako N. Managerial Incentives for Short-term Results: A Comment. *J. Finance,* September 1987, *42*(4), pp. 1097–1102.

Darvish, Tikva and Kahana, Nava. The Ratchet Principle: A Diagrammatic Interpretation. *J. Compar. Econ.*, June 1987, *11*(2), pp. 245–49. [G: U.S.S.R.]

Domozetov, Christo. Attitudes and Motivation of Production Managers in the Management of Technological Innovation. *Child, J. and Bate, P., eds.*, 1987, pp. 113–22. [G: Bulgaria]

Estep, Tony. Manager Style and the Sources of Equity Returns. *J. Portfol. Manage.*, Winter 1987, *13*(2), pp. 4–10. [G: U.S.]

Feuer, M.; Glick, H. and Desai, Anand. Is Firm-Sponsored Education Viable? *J. Econ. Behav. Organ.*, March 1987, *8*(1), pp. 121–36. [G: U.S.]

Furtado, Eugene P. H. and Rozeff, Michael S. The Wealth Effects of Company Initiated Management Changes. *J. Finan. Econ.*, March 1987, *18*(1), pp. 147–60. [G: U.S.]

Gershenberg, Irving. The Training and Spread of Managerial Know-How, a Comparative Analysis of Multinational and Other Firms in Kenya. *World Devel.*, July 1987, *15*(7), pp. 931–39. [G: Kenya]

Giordano, Yvonne. De la défaillance au redressement: le management omniprésent. (From Failure to Recovery: The Role of Management. With English summary.) *Écon. Soc.*, June 1987, *21*(6), pp. 127–47.

Gray, Barbara and Allen, Robin G. Cognitive and Group Biases in Issues Management: What You Don't Know Can Hurt You. *Marcus, A. A.; Kaufman, A. M. and Beam, D. R., eds.*, 1987, pp. 195–208.

Grinblatt, Mark and Titman, Sheridan. How Clients Can Win the Gaming Game. *J. Portfol. Manage.*, Summer 1987, *13*(4), pp. 14–20.

Gupta, Nina; Schweizer, Timothy P. and Jenkins, G. Douglas, Jr. Pay-for-Knowledge Compensation Plans: Hypotheses and Survey Results. *Mon. Lab. Rev.*, October 1987, *110*(10), pp. 40–43. [G: U.S.]

Hall, Christopher D. Heterogeneous Firms: A Consumer's Report [Heterogeneous Firms and the Organization of Production]. *Econ. In-*

quiry, January 1987, *25*(1), pp. 175–80.

Heise, H.-J. How to Eliminate Risk in Recruitment: Some Reflections on Executive Search and the Personnel Policies of Japanese Subsidiaries in Germany. *Trevor, M., ed.*, 1987, pp. 120–23.　　　　　**[G: Japan; W. Germany]**

Jügens, Ulrich and Strömel, Hans-Peter. The Communication Structure between Management and Shop Floor: A Comparison of a Japanese and a German Plant. *Trevor, M., ed.*, 1987, pp. 92–110.　**[G: Japan; W. Germany]**

Kumar, B. and Steinmann, Horst. The Recruitment, Selection and Job Satisfaction of Expatriate Managers in Japanese and Geman Multinational Corporations. *Trevor, M., ed.*, 1987, pp. 177–97.　　　　　**[G: Japan; W. Germany]**

Laflamme, Gilles; Belanger, Laurent and Audet, Michel. Workers' Participation and Personnel Policies in Canada: Some Hopeful Signs. *Int. Lab. Rev.*, Mar.-Apr. 1987, *126*(2), pp. 219–28.　　　　　　　　　**[G: Canada]**

Lambert, Richard A. and Larcker, David F. An Analysis of the Use of Accounting and Market Measures of Performance in Executive Compensation Contracts. *J. Acc. Res.*, Supplement 1987, *25*, pp. 85–125.　　**[G: U.S.]**

McDonald, John. A New Model for Learning Curves, DARM. *J. Bus. Econ. Statist.*, July 1987, *5*(3), pp. 329–35.　　**[G: U.S.]**

McDonald, John. A New Model for Learning Curves, DARM: Reply. *J. Bus. Econ. Statist.*, July 1987, *5*(3), pp. 338.　　　　**[G: U.S.]**

Menon, Krishnagopal and Umapathy, Srinivasan. Control Systems for State-Owned Enterprises: A Conceptual Framework. *Ann. Pub. Co-op. Econ.*, July-Sept. 1987, *58*(3), pp. 287–303.

Miner, Craig. The New Wave, the Old Guard, and the Bank Committee: William J. Grede at J. I. Case Company, 1953–1961. *Bus. Hist. Rev.*, Summer 1987, *61*(2), pp. 243–90.　　　　　　　　　　　**[G: U.S.]**

Miyajima, Ritsuko. The Comparative Values of British and Japanese Managers. *Trevor, M., ed.*, 1987, pp. 77–91.　　**[G: Japan; U.K.]**

Narayanan, M. P. Managerial Incentives for Short-term Results: A Reply. *J. Finance*, September 1987, *42*(4), pp. 1103–04.

Oi, Walter Y. Heterogeneous Firms: Caveat Emptor [Heterogeneous Firms and the Organization of Production]. *Econ. Inquiry*, January 1987, *25*(1), pp. 181–84.

Oxenstierna, Susanne. Bonuses, Factor Demand, and Technical Efficiency in the Soviet Enterprise. *J. Compar. Econ.*, June 1987, *11*(2), pp. 234–44.　　　　　**[G: U.S.S.R.]**

Santos, Michael W. Laboring on the Periphery: Managers and Workers at the A. M. Byers Company, 1900–1956. *Bus. Hist. Rev.*, Spring 1987, *61*(1), pp. 113–33.

Shkurko, S. Collective Forms of Labor Organization and Work Incentives. *Prob. Econ.*, August 1987, *30*(4), pp. 63–78.　　**[G: U.S.S.R.]**

Starks, Laura T. Performance Incentive Fees: An Agency Theoretic Approach. *J. Finan. Quant. Anal.*, March 1987, *22*(1), pp. 17–32.

Steinmann, Horst; Fees, Werner and Gerum, Elmar. Wertsystem der Unternehmensführung und Mitbestimmung—Einige empirische Befunde. (With English summary.) *Z. Betriebswirtschaft*, April 1987, *57*(4), pp. 398–409.　　　　　　　　　**[G: W. Germany]**

Takahashi, Yoshiaki. The Theoretical Problems of the Transferability of Management Style. *Trevor, M., ed.*, 1987, pp. 156–76.　　　　　　　　　　　**[G: Japan]**

Tehranian, Hassan, et al. Management Compensation Contracts and Merger-Induced Abnormal Returns. *J. Acc. Res.*, Supplement 1987, *25*, pp. 51–76.　　**[G: U.S.]**

Tehranian, Hassan; Travlos, Nickolaos G. and Waegelein, James F. The Effect of Long-term Performance Plans on Corporate Sell-Off–Induced Abnormal Returns. *J. Finance*, September 1987, *42*(4), pp. 933–42.　**[G: U.S.]**

Treu, Tiziano and Negrelli, Serafino. Workers' Participation and Personnel Management Policies in Italy. *Int. Lab. Rev.*, Jan.-Feb. 1987, *126*(1), pp. 81–94.　　**[G: Italy]**

Womer, Norman Keith and Patterson, J. Wayne. A New Model for Learning Curves, DARM: Comment. *J. Bus. Econ. Statist.*, July 1987, *5*(3), pp. 336–37.　　　**[G: U.S.]**

5132 Public Administration

Antonio, James F. Setting Governmental Accounting and Financial Reporting Standards in a Multi-constituency Environment. *Chan, J. L., ed., Pt. B*, 1987, pp. 137–43.　**[G: U.S.]**

Arnold, David S. Management Policies in Local Government Finance: Purchasing and Risk Management. *Aronson, J. R. and Schwartz, E., eds.*, 1987, pp. 364–82.　**[G: U.S.]**

Arnold, R. Douglas. Political Control of Administrative Officials. *J. Law, Econ., Organ.*, Fall 1987, *3*(2), pp. 279–86.　　**[G: U.S.]**

Balachandran, Bala V. and Prince, Thomas R. An Information System for Administering Welfare Programs. *Chan, J. L., ed., Pt. A*, 1987, pp. 37–66.　　　　　**[G: U.S.]**

Banker, Rajiv D. and Patton, James M. Analytical Agency Theory and Municipal Accounting: An Introduction and an Application. *Chan, J. L., ed., Pt. B*, 1987, pp. 29–50.

Berry, Maureen. Financial Accountability in West German Government. *Most, Kenneth S., ed.*, 1987, pp. 39–84.　**[G: W. Germany]**

Brodman, Janice Z. Key Management Factors Determining the Impact of Microcomputers on Decision-making in the Governments of Developing Countries. *Ruth, S. R. and Mann, C. K., eds.*, 1987, pp. 117–42.　**[G: Kenya; Indonesia]**

Bromiley, Philip and Marcus, Alfred A. Deadlines, Routines, and Change. *Policy Sci.*, 1987, *20*(2), pp. 85–103.

Burris, Roland W. Improving Governmental Financial Reporting and Management: The Illinois Experience and a Proposal for the Federal Government. *Chan, J. L., ed., Pt. B*, 1987, pp. 145–63.　　　　　**[G: U.S.]**

Campbell, Nigel. Enterprise Autonomy in the Beijing Municipality. *Warner, M., ed.,* 1987, pp. 53–70. [G: China]

Castagnos, Jean-Claude. Performance et gestion publique: Un pari impossible? (Performance and Public Management: An Impossible Wager? With English summary.) *Écon. Soc.,* December 1987, *21*(12), pp. 141–73.

Child, John. Enterprise Reform in China—Progress and Problems. *Warner, M., ed.,* 1987, pp. 24–52. [G: China]

Derthick, Martha. The Plight of the Social Security Administration. *Berkowitz, E. D., ed.,* 1987, pp. 101–17. [G: U.S.]

Duncombe, Sydney and Kinney, Richard. Agency Budget Success: How It Is Defined by Budget Officials in Five Western States. *Public Budg. Finance,* Spring 1987, *7*(1), pp. 24–37. [G: U.S.]

Eavey, Cheryl L. Bureaucratic Competition and Agenda Control. *J. Conflict Resolution,* September 1987, *31*(3), pp. 503–24.

Ferejohn, John A. The Structure of Agency Decision Processes. *McCubbins, M. D. and Sullivan, T., eds.,* 1987, pp. 441–61. [G: U.S.]

Goldin, Harrison J. Improving New York City's Financial Reporting: A Ten Year Retrospective. *Chan, J. L., ed., Pt. B,* 1987, pp. 165–74. [G: U.S.]

Green, Cynthia B. The Use and Usefulness of Governmental Financial Reports: The Perspective of Citizen–Taxpayer Organizations. *Chan, J. L., ed., Pt. B,* 1987, pp. 189–213. [G: U.S.]

Herhold, Susan; Parry, Robert W., Jr. and Patton, James M. Behavioral Research in Municipal Accounting. *Chan, J. L., ed., Pt. B,* 1987, pp. 71–109.

Ingram, Robert W.; Raman, Krishnamurthy K. and Wilson, Earl R. Governmental Capital Markets Research in Accounting: A Review. *Chan, J. L., ed., Pt. B,* 1987, pp. 111–126.

Ives, Martin H. GASB Research on User Needs and Objectives of Governmental Financial Reporting: A Summary and Analysis. *Chan, J. L., ed., Pt. B,* 1987, pp. 227–35. [G: U.S.]

Jeffries, Ian and Melzer, Manfred. Command Planning and the Production Unit. *Jeffries, I. and Melzer, M., eds.,* 1987, pp. 12–25. [G: E. Germany]

Karvelis, Leon J., Jr. The Use and Usefulness of Governmental Financial Reports: The Perspective of Municipal Investors. *Chan, J. L., ed., Pt. B,* 1987, pp. 175–88. [G: U.S.]

Leonard, David K. The Political Realities of African Management. *World Devel.,* July 1987, *15*(7), pp. 899–910. [G: Africa]

Mackay, Robert J. The FTC Budget Process: Zero-Based Budgeting by Committee. *MacKay, R. J.; Miller, J. C., III and Yandle, B., eds.,* 1987, pp. 295–321. [G: U.S.]

McCubbins, Mathew D.; Noll, Roger G. and Weingast, Barry R. Administrative Procedures as Instruments of Political Control. *J. Law, Econ., Organ.,* Fall 1987, *3*(2), pp. 243–77. [G: U.S.]

Pinckney, Thomas C.; Cohen, John M. and Leonard, David K. Kenya's Introduction of Microcomputers to Improve Budgeting and Financial Management in the Ministry of Agriculture. *Ruth, S. R. and Mann, C. K., eds.,* 1987, pp. 67–93. [G: Kenya]

Ruchelman, Leonard I. The Finance Function in Local Government. *Aronson, J. R. and Schwartz, E., eds.,* 1987, pp. 3–29. [G: U.S.]

Schwartz, Eli. Management Policies in Local Government Finance: Inventory and Cash Management. *Aronson, J. R. and Schwartz, E., eds.,* 1987, pp. 342–63. [G: U.S.]

Wallace, Wanda A. Agency Theory and Governmental and Nonprofit Sector Research. *Chan, J. L., ed., Pt. B,* 1987, pp. 51–70.

Ward, James Gordon. The Use and Usefulness of Governmental Financial Reports: The Perspective of Public Sector Labor Unions. *Chan, J. L., ed., Pt. B,* 1987, pp. 215–26. [G: U.S.]

Wescott, Clay G. Microcomputers for Improved Government Budgeting: An Africa Experience. *Ruth, S. R. and Mann, C. K., eds.,* 1987, pp. 95–116. [G: Kenya]

Yandle, Bruce. Chairman Choice and Output Effects: The FTC Experience. *MacKay, R. J.; Miller, J. C., III and Yandle, B., eds.,* 1987, pp. 283–94. [G: U.S.]

514 Goals and Objectives of Firms

5140 Goals and Objectives of Firms

Abraham, H. and Gurzynski, Z. S. A. The Entrepreneur as a Non-factor. *S. Afr. J. Econ.,* June 1987, *55*(2), pp. 114–20.

Aoki, Masahiko. The Political Economy of Japan: The Japanese Firm in Transition. *Yamamura, K. and Yasuba, Y., eds.,* 1987, pp. 263–88. [G: Japan]

Barrett, Diana and Campbell, Paul H. Walking Softly: The Role of Management in Altering Physician Practice Patterns in the Hospital Corporation of America. *Scheffler, R. M. and Rossiter, L. F., eds.,* 1987, pp. 157–78. [G: U.S.]

Barzelay, Michael and Smith, Rogers M. The One Best System? A Political Analysis of Neoclassical Institutionalist Perspectives on the Modern Corporation. *Samuels, W. J. and Miller, A. S., eds.,* 1987, pp. 81–110. [G: U.S.]

Baysinger, Barry D.; Keim, Gerald D. and Zeithaml, Carl P. Constituency Building as a Political Strategy in the Petroleum Industry. *Marcus, A. A.; Kaufman, A. M. and Beam, D. R., eds.,* 1987, pp. 223–38. [G: U.S.]

Bearden, James and Mintz, Beth. The Structure of Class Cohesion: The Corporate Network and Its Dual. *Mizruchi, M. S. and Schwartz, M., eds.,* 1987, pp. 187–207. [G: U.S.]

Benjamin, Martin and Bronstein, Daniel A. Moral and Criminal Responsibility and Corporate Persons. *Samuels, W. J. and Miller, A. S., eds.,* 1987, pp. 277–82. [G: U.S.]

Cassidy, John C. and Halstead, J. Phillip. Management Systems for Enhancing the Productivity of Public Affairs at Clorox. *Marcus, A. A.; Kaufman, A. M. and Beam, D. R., eds.*, 1987, pp. 151–64. **[G: U.S.]**

Cochran, Philip L. and Nigh, Douglas. Illegal Corporate Behavior and the Question of Moral Agency: An Empirical Examination. *Frederick, W. C., ed.*, 1987, pp. 73–91. **[G: U.S.]**

Colodzin, Robert. Positioning the Company in Society: Implementing a Public Affairs Strategy at Champion International. *Marcus, A. A.; Kaufman, A. M. and Beam, D. R., eds.*, 1987, pp. 211–21. **[G: U.S.]**

Dégot, Vincent. L'argumentation des décisions économiquement non quantifiable (ou "argumentation môle"). (Argumentation of Soft Decisions—A Case Study. With English summary.) *Écon. Soc.*, June 1987, *21*(6), pp. 85–108.

Derry, Robbin. Moral Reasoning in Work-Related Conflicts. *Frederick, W. C., ed.*, 1987, pp. 25–49. **[G: U.S.]**

Eismeier, Theodore J. and Pollock, Philip H., III. The Retreat from Partisanship: Why the Dog Didn't Bark in the 1984 Election. *Marcus, A. A.; Kaufman, A. M. and Beam, D. R., eds.*, 1987, pp. 137–47. **[G: U.S.]**

Fleming, John E. A Survey and Critique of Business Ethics Research, 1986. *Frederick, W. C., ed.*, 1987, pp. 1–23. **[G: U.S.]**

Flynn, John J. The Jurisprudence of Corporate Personhood: The Misuse of a Legal Concept. *Samuels, W. J. and Miller, A. S., eds.*, 1987, pp. 131–59. **[G: U.S.]**

Frederick, William C. The Empirical Dimension of Business Ethics and Values. *Frederick, W. C., ed.*, 1987, pp. vii–xii.

Frederick, William C. and Weber, James. The Values of Corporate Managers and Their Critics: An Empirical Description and Normative Implications. *Frederick, W. C., ed.*, 1987, pp. 131–52. **[G: U.S.]**

Gale, Jeffrey and Buchholz, Rogene A. The Political Pursuit of Competitive Advantage: What Business Can Gain from Government. *Marcus, A. A.; Kaufman, A. M. and Beam, D. R., eds.*, 1987, pp. 31–41.

Gautschi, Frederick H., III and Jone, Thomas M. Illegal Corporate Behavior and Corporate Board Structure. *Frederick, W. C., ed.*, 1987, pp. 93–106. **[G: U.S.]**

Gray, Barbara and Allen, Robin G. Cognitive and Group Biases in Issues Management: What You Don't Know Can Hurt You. *Marcus, A. A.; Kaufman, A. M. and Beam, D. R., eds.*, 1987, pp. 195–208.

Haugen, Robert A. and Senbet, Lemma W. On the Resolution of Agency Problems by Complex Financial Instruments: A Reply. *J. Finance*, September 1987, *42*(4), pp. 1091–95.

Hennestad, Bjørn W. Organizations and the Computer Culture: The Mismanagement of Meaning? *Child, J. and Bate, P., eds.*, 1987, pp. 137–47.

Horwitz, Morton J. *Santa Clara* Revisited: The Development of Corporate Theory. *Samuels, W. J. and Miller, A. S., eds.*, 1987, pp. 13–63. **[G: U.S.]**

Kaufman, Allen M.; Karson, Marvin J. and Sohl, Jeffrey. Business Fragmentation and Solidarity: An Analysis of PAC Donations in the 1980 and 1982 Elections. *Marcus, A. A.; Kaufman, A. M. and Beam, D. R., eds.*, 1987, pp. 119–35. **[G: U.S.]**

Kaufman, Allen M.; Marcus, Alfred A. and Zacharias, Larry. How Business Manages Politics. *Marcus, A. A.; Kaufman, A. M. and Beam, D. R., eds.*, 1987, pp. 293–312. **[G: U.S.]**

Komiya, Ryutaro. Japanese Firms, Chinese Firms: Problems for Economic Reform in China: Part II. *J. Japanese Int. Economies*, June 1987, *1*(2), pp. 229–47. **[G: Japan; China]**

Littlejohn, Stephen E. Competition and Cooperation: New Trends in Issue Identification and Management at Monsanto and Gulf. *Marcus, A. A.; Kaufman, A. M. and Beam, D. R., eds.*, 1987, pp. 19–30. **[G: U.S.]**

Loescher, Samuel M. Toward More Competitive Diversity in a Market-Concentrated Economy. *Samuels, W. J. and Miller, A. S., eds.*, 1987, pp. 263–75. **[G: U.S.]**

Ma, Bin and Hong, Zhunyan. Enlivening Large State Enterprises: Where Is the Motive Force? *J. Compar. Econ.*, September 1987, *11*(3), pp. 503–08. **[G: China]**

Magnan de Bornier, Jean. Propriété et contrôle dans la grande entreprise: une relecture de Berle et Means. (Ownership and Control in the Big Corporation: A Re-reading of Berle and Means. With English summary.) *Revue Écon.*, November 1987, *38*(6), pp. 1171–90.

Maitland, Ian. Collective versus Individual Lobbying: How Business Ends Up the Loser. *Marcus, A. A.; Kaufman, A. M. and Beam, D. R., eds.*, 1987, pp. 95–104. **[G: U.S.]**

Marcus, Alfred A. and Irion, Mark S. The Continued Viability of the Corporate Public Affairs Function. *Marcus, A. A.; Kaufman, A. M. and Beam, D. R., eds.*, 1987, pp. 267–81. **[G: U.S.]**

Marcus, Alfred A.; Kaufman, Allen M. and Beam, David R. The Pursuit of Corporate Advantage and the Quest for Social Legitimacy. *Marcus, A. A.; Kaufman, A. M. and Beam, D. R., eds.*, 1987, pp. 1–16.

Martin, David Dale. The Corporation and Antitrust Law Policy: Double Standards. *Samuels, W. J. and Miller, A. S., eds.*, 1987, pp. 193–217. **[G: U.S.]**

Marx, Thomas G. Social Legitimacy and Strategic Issues Management at General Motors. *Marcus, A. A.; Kaufman, A. M. and Beam, D. R., eds.*, 1987, pp. 81–94. **[G: U.S.]**

Marzullo, Sal G. Corporations: Catalyst for Change. *Sethi, S. P., ed.*, 1987, pp. 371–80. **[G: S. Africa]**

Mathews, M. Cash. Codes of Ethics: Organizational Behavior and Misbehavior. *Frederick, W. C., ed.*, 1987, pp. 107–30. **[G: U.S.]**

Miller, Arthur S. Corporations and Our Two Constitutions. *Samuels, W. J. and Miller, A. S., eds.*, 1987, pp. 241–62. [G: U.S.]

Miner, Craig. The New Wave, the Old Guard, and the Bank Committee: William J. Grede at J. I. Case Company, 1953–1961. *Bus. Hist. Rev.*, Summer 1987, *61*(2), pp. 243–90. [G: U.S.]

Moor, Roy E. Ethics for Businesses...and Their Economists. *Bus. Econ.*, October 1987, *22*(4), pp. 11–14.

Narayanan, M. P. On the Resolution of Agency Problems by Complex Financial Instruments: A Comment [Resolving the Agency Problems of External Capital through Stock Options]. *J. Finance*, September 1987, *42*(4), pp. 1083–90.

Olian, Judy D. and Guthrie, James P. Cognitive Ability Tests in Employment: Ethical Perspectives of Employers and Society. *Frederick, W. C., ed.*, 1987, pp. 185–212. [G: U.S.]

Paul, Karen. The Inadequacy of Sullivan Reporting. *Sethi, S. P., ed.*, 1987, pp. 403–12. [G: U.S.; S. Africa]

Ravlin, Elizabeth C. and Meglino, Bruce M. Issues in Work Values Measurement. *Frederick, W. C., ed.*, 1987, pp. 153–83.

Roman, Paul M. and Blum, Terry C. The Relation of Employee Assistance Programs to Corporate Social Responsibility Attitudes: An Empirical Study. *Frederick, W. C., ed.*, 1987, pp. 213–35. [G: U.S.]

Samuels, Warren J. The Idea of the Corporation as a Person: On the Normative Significance of Judicial Language. *Samuels, W. J. and Miller, A. S., eds.*, 1987, pp. 113–29. [G: U.S.]

Samuels, Warren J. and Miller, Arthur S. Corporate America. *Samuels, W. J. and Miller, A. S., eds.*, 1987, pp. 1–9. [G: U.S.]

Sigman, Betsy Page and McDonald, Sarah-Kathryn. The Issues Manager as Public Opinion and Policy Analyst. *Marcus, A. A.; Kaufman, A. M. and Beam, D. R., eds.*, 1987, pp. 165–94.

Soifer, Aviam. The Paradox of Paternalism and Laissez-Faire Constitutionalism: The U.S. Supreme Court, 1888–1921. *Samuels, W. J. and Miller, A. S., eds.*, 1987, pp. 161–90. [G: U.S.]

Van Zyl, Johannes Christiaan. Business Offers a Bill of Rights for South Africa. *Sethi, S. P., ed.*, 1987, pp. 363–69. [G: S. Africa]

Velasquez, Manuel G. Ethics, Religion and the Modern Business Corporation. *Gannon, T. M., ed.*, 1987, pp. 55–75. [G: U.S.]

Victor, Bart and Cullen, John B. A Theory and Measure of Ethical Climate in Organizations. *Frederick, W. C., ed.*, 1987, pp. 51–71.

Weedon, D. Reid, Jr. The Evolution of Sullivan Principle Compliance. *Sethi, S. P., ed.*, 1987, pp. 393–402. [G: S. Africa; U.S.]

Wilking, Lou H. Should U.S. Corporations Abandon South Africa? *Sethi, S. P., ed.*, 1987, pp. 383–91. [G: U.S.; S. Africa]

520 BUSINESS FINANCE AND INVESTMENT

5200 Business Finance and Investment

Agrawal, Anup and Mandelker, Gershon N. Managerial Incentives and Corporate Investment and Financing Decisions. *J. Finance*, September 1987, *42*(4), pp. 823–37. [G: U.S.]

Barges, Alexander. The Marginal-Efficiency-of-Capital Function of the Firm. *Financial Rev.*, May 1987, *22*(2), pp. 321–38.

Hamada, Koichi and Horiuchi, Akiyoshi. The Political Economy of Japan: The Political Economy of the Financial Market. *Yamamura, K. and Yasuba, Y., eds.*, 1987, pp. 223–60. [G: Japan]

Hite, Gailen L.; Owers, James E. and Rogers, Ronald C. The Market for Interfirm Asset Sales: Partial Sell-offs and Total Liquidations. *J. Finan. Econ.*, June 1987, *18*(2), pp. 229–52. [G: U.S.]

Jose, Manuel L. and Stevens, Jerry L. Product Market Structure, Capital Intensity, and Systematic Risk: Empirical Results from the Theory of the Firm. *J. Finan. Res.*, Summer 1987, *10*(2), pp. 161–75. [G: U.S.]

Klammer, Thomas P. and Walker, Michael C. Capital Budgeting Questionnaires: A New Perspective. *Quart. J. Bus. Econ.*, Summer 1987, *26*(3), pp. 87–95. [G: U.S.]

Lustgarten, Steven and Thomadakis, Stavros B. Mobility Barriers and Tobin's q. *J. Bus.*, October 1987, *60*(4), pp. 519–37. [G: U.S.]

Taggart, Robert A., Jr. Allocating Capital among a Firm's Divisions: Hurdle Rates vs. Budgets. *J. Finan. Res.*, Fall 1987, *10*(3), pp. 177–89.

521 Business Finance

5210 Business Finance

Aarbakke, Magnus. Tax Problems of the Liquidation of Corporations: Norway. *International Fiscal Association, ed. (II)*, 1987, pp. 383–94. [G: Norway]

Adam, M. C. and Farber, A. Le financement de l'innovation technologique. Première partie: Les caractéristiques de l'investissement novateur. (With English summary.) *Cah. Écon. Bruxelles*, Fourth Trimester 1987, (116), pp. 3–23. [G: Belgium]

Aivazian, Varouj A. and Callen, Jeffrey L. Miller's Irrelevance Mechanism: A Note. *J. Finance*, March 1987, *42*(1), pp. 169–80.

Aivazian, Varouj A. and Turnbull, Stuart M. Taxation and Capital Structure: A Selected Review. *Mintz, J. M. and Purvis, D. D., eds.*, 1987, pp. 230–62.

Alderighi, Massimo. Tax Problems of the Liquidation of Corporations: Italy. *International Fiscal Association, ed. (II)*, 1987, pp. 321–35. [G: Italy]

Aldrich, Peter C. Active versus Passive: A New Look. *J. Portfol. Manage.*, Fall 1987, *14*(1), pp. 9–11. [G: U.S.]

Allen, D. E.; Carse, S. and Fujio, K. Trade Financing Procedures in Britain and Japan. *Appl. Econ.*, June 1987, *19*(6), pp. 711–28.
[G: U.K.; Japan]

Ambarish, Ramasastry; John, Kose and Williams, Joseph T. Efficient Signalling with Dividends and Investments. *J. Finance*, June 1987, *42*(2), pp. 321–43.

Aminoff, Philip. Bedömning av betalningsvillkors lönsamhet. (Evaluation of Profitability for Terms of Payment. With English summary.) *Liiketaloudellinen Aikak.*, 1987, *36*(2), pp. 180–93.
[G: Finland]

Antoniou, Andreas and Rowley, Robin. Finance and the Structural Adjustment of Canadian Corporations. *Écon. Appl.*, 1987, *40*(4), pp. 771–93.
[G: Canada]

Atiase, Rowland Kwame. Market Implications of Predisclosure Information: Size and Exchange Effects. *J. Acc. Res.*, Spring 1987, *25*(1), pp. 168–76.
[G: U.S.]

Auerbach, Alan J. and Poterba, James M. Why Have Corporate Tax Revenues Declined? *Summers, L. H., ed.*, 1987, pp. 1–28.
[G: U.S.]

Bagamery, Bruce D. On the Correspondence between the Baumol–Tobin and Miller–Orr Optimal Cash Balance Models. *Financial Rev.*, May 1987, *22*(2), pp. 313–19.

Baginski, Stephen P. Intraindustry Information Transfers Associated with Management Forecasts of Earnings. *J. Acc. Res.*, Autumn 1987, *25*(2), pp. 196–216.
[G: U.S.]

Bamber, Linda Smith. Unexpected Earnings, Firm Size, and Trading Volume around Quarterly Earnings Announcements. *Accounting Rev.*, July 1987, *62*(3), pp. 510–32.
[G: U.S.]

Bar-Yosef, Sasson; Callen, Jeffrey L. and Livnat, Joshua. Autoregressive Modeling of Earnings–Investment Causality. *J. Finance*, March 1987, *42*(1), pp. 11–28.
[G: U.S.]

Barclay, Michael J. Dividends, Taxes, and Common Stock Prices: The Ex-dividend Day Behavior of Common Stock Prices before the Income Tax. *J. Finan. Econ.*, September 1987, *19*(1), pp. 31–44.
[G: U.S.]

Barnea, Amir; Talmor, Eli and Haugen, Robert A. Debt and Taxes: A Multiperiod Investigation. *J. Banking Finance*, March 1987, *11*(1), pp. 79–97.

Baskin, Jonathan B. Corporate Liquidity in Games of Monopoly Power. *Rev. Econ. Statist.*, May 1987, *69*(2), pp. 312–19. **[G: U.S.]**

Becker, Brian E. Concession Bargaining: The Impact of Shareholders' Equity. *Ind. Lab. Relat. Rev.*, January 1987, *40*(2), pp. 268–79.
[G: U.S.]

Bernier, Gilles. Market Power and Systematic Risk: An Empirical Analysis Using Tobin's *q* Ratio. *J. Econ. Bus.*, May 1987, *39*(2), pp. 91–99.
[G: U.S.]

Bessis, Joël. Les déterminants réels du risque financier. (The Real Determinants of Financial Risk. With English summary.) *Finance*, June 1987, *8*(1), pp. 33–53. **[G: France]**

Bhagat, Sanjai; Brickley, James A. and Loewenstein, Uri. The Pricing Effects of Interfirm

Cash Tender Offers. *J. Finance*, September 1987, *42*(4), pp. 965–86.

Blazenko, George W. Managerial Preference, Asymmetric Information, and Financial Structure. *J. Finance*, September 1987, *42*(4), pp. 839–62.

Blitz, Rudolph C., et al. The Effect of Market Structure on the Cost of Borrowing. *Wills, R. L.; Caswell, J. A. and Culbertson, J. D., eds.*, 1987, pp. 333–44. **[G: U.S.]**

Bodie, Zvi, et al. Funding and Asset Allocation in Corporate Pension Plans: An Empirical Investigation. *Bodie, Z.; Shoven, J. B. and Wise, D. A., eds.*, 1987, pp. 15–44. **[G: U.S.]**

Booth, Laurence D. The Dividend Tax Credit and Canadian Ownership Objectives. *Can. J. Econ.*, May 1987, *20*(2), pp. 321–39.
[G: Canada]

Bosco, Bruno. Dividend Taxes and Corporate Dividend Policy: Further Econometric Results. *Rivista Int. Sci. Econ. Com.*, Nov.-Dec. 1987, *34*(11–12), pp. 1139–65. **[G: Italy]**

Boss, Edward H., Jr. Has the Growth in Corporate Debt Led to Increased Risk? *Bus. Econ.*, January 1987, *22*(1), pp. 46–50. **[G: U.S.]**

Botha, D.; Bosch, J. K. and van Zyl, G. J. J. The Effect of Dividend Policy on Changes in Shareholders' Wealth. *S. Afr. J. Econ.*, June 1987, *55*(2), pp. 101–13. **[G: S. Africa]**

Bowen, Robert M.; Burgstahler, David and Daley, Lane A. The Incremental Information Content of Accrual versus Cash Flows. *Accounting Rev.*, October 1987, *62*(4), pp. 723–47. **[G: U.S.]**

Bradford, William D. The Issue Decision of Manager–Owners under Information Asymmetry. *J. Finance*, December 1987, *42*(5), pp. 1245–60.

Branco da Silva, Rubens. Tax Problems of the Liquidation of Corporations: Brazil. *International Fiscal Association, ed. (II)*, 1987, pp. 221–27. **[G: Brazil]**

Bregman, Arie. Government Intervention in Industry: The Case of Israel. *J. Devel. Econ.*, April 1987, *25*(2), pp. 353–67. **[G: Israel]**

Brennan, Michael J. and Kraus, Alan. Efficient Financing under Asymmetric Information. *J. Finance*, December 1987, *42*(5), pp. 1225–43.

Brick, Ivan E. and Fisher, Lawrence. Effects of Classifying Equity or Debt on the Value of the Firm under Tax Asymmetry. *J. Finan. Quant. Anal.*, December 1987, *22*(4), pp. 383–99. **[G: U.S.]**

Brockhoff, Klaus. Budgetierungsstrategien für Forschung und Entwicklung. (With English summary.) *Z. Betriebswirtshaft*, September 1987, *57*(9), pp. 846–69.

Brown, Keith C. and Statman, Meir. The Benefits of Insured Stocks for Corporate Cash Management. *Fabozzi, F. J., ed.*, 1987, pp. 243–61.
[G: U.S.]

Brown, Lawrence D.; Richardson, Gordon D. and Schwager, Steven J. An Information Interpretation of Financial Analyst Superiority in Forecasting Earnings. *J. Acc. Res.*, Spring 1987, *25*(1), pp. 49–67. **[G: U.S.]**

Brown, Lawrence D., et al. Security Analyst Superiority Relative to Univariate Time-Series Models in Forecasting Quarterly Earnings. *J. Acc. Econ.*, April 1987, 9(1), pp. 61–87. [G: U.S.]

Browne, Lynn E. and Rosengren, Eric S. Are Hostile Takeovers Different? *Browne, L. E. and Rosengren, E. S., eds.*, 1987, pp. 199–229. [G: U.S.]

Buchenroth, Sherree and Jennings, Robert. A Descriptive Analysis of the Time Series Behavior of Financial Analysts' Earnings Forecasts. *Quart. J. Bus. Econ.*, Summer 1987, 26(3), pp. 22–41. [G: U.S.]

Bulow, Jeremy I.; Mørck, Randall and Summers, Lawrence H. How Does the Market Value Unfunded Pension Liabilities? *Bodie, Z.; Shoven, J. B. and Wise, D. A., eds.*, 1987, pp. 81–104. [G: U.S.]

Calvet, A. L. and Lefoll, J. Information Asymmetry and Wealth Effect of Canadian Corporate Acquisitions. *Financial Rev.*, November 1987, 22(4), pp. 415–31. [G: Canada]

Campbell, Tim S. and Kracaw, William A. Optimal Managerial Incentive Contracts and the Value of Corporate Insurance. *J. Finan. Quant. Anal.*, September 1987, 22(3), pp. 315–28.

Carlson, David Gray. Philosophy in Bankruptcy. *Mich. Law Rev.*, Apr.-May 1987, 85(5–6), pp. 1341–89.

Carrizosa, Mauricio and Urdinola, Antonio. Private Internal Debt in Colombia, 1970–1985. *CEPAL Rev.*, August 1987, (32), pp. 27–53. [G: Colombia]

de Carvalho, António Joaquim. Régime de liquidation des sociétés: Portugal. (Tax Problems of the Liquidation of Corporations: Portugal. With English summary.) *International Fiscal Association, ed. (II)*, 1987, pp. 435–43. [G: Portugal]

Castillo, Rosendo J. Financing Privatization. *Hanke, S. H., ed.*, 1987, pp. 119–26.

Cha, Jae-Neung. Tax Problems of the Liquidation of Corporations: Republic of Korea. *International Fiscal Association, ed. (II)*, 1987, pp. 445–54. [G: S. Korea]

Chan, K. Hung and Ho, Kwok. Forecasting of Seasonal and Cyclical Financial Variables: The Wiener–Kolmogorov Method vs. the Box–Jenkins Method. *Lee, C. F., ed.*, 1987, pp. 103–18. [G: U.S.]

Chapman, D. R. and Junor, C. W. Inflation, Firm Control-Type and Vulnerability to Takeover. *Oxford Econ. Pap.*, September 1987, 39(3), pp. 500–15. [G: Australia]

Cheung, Joseph K. Depreciation, Debt, and Equilibrium Tax Rates: A Reconsideration. *Quart. Rev. Econ. Bus.*, Spring 1987, 27(1), pp. 6–15.

Chirinko, Robert S. Tobin's Q and Financial Policy. *J. Monet. Econ.*, January 1987, 19(1), pp. 69–87. [G: U.S.]

Choi, Kwang. Tax Policy and Corporate Financial Structure in Korea. *Int. Econ. J.*, Winter 1987, 1(4), pp. 61–76. [G: S. Korea]

Ciocca, Pierluigi and Frasca, Francesco. I rap-

porti fra industria e finanza: problemi e prospettive. (With English summary.) *Polit. Econ.*, April 1987, 3(1), pp. 29–50. [G: Italy]

Clinch, Greg J. and Sinclair, Norman A. Intra-industry Information Releases: A Recursive Systems Approach. *J. Acc. Econ.*, April 1987, 9(1), pp. 89–106. [G: Australia]

Coffee, John C., Jr. Are Hostile Takeovers Different? Discussion. *Browne, L. E. and Rosengren, E. S., eds.*, 1987, pp. 230–42. [G: U.S.]

Comment, Robert and Jarrell, Gregg A. Two-Tier and Negotiated Tender Offers: the Imprisonment of the Free-Riding Shareholder. *J. Finan. Econ.*, December 1987, 19(2), pp. 283–310. [G: U.S.]

Corbett, Jenny. International Perspectives on Financing: Evidence from Japan. *Oxford Rev. Econ. Policy*, Winter 1987, 3(4), pp. 30–55. [G: Japan; U.K.]

Cosh, A. D. and Hughes, A. The Anatomy of Corporate Control: Directors, Shareholders and Executive Remuneration in Giant U.S. and U.K. Corporations. *Cambridge J. Econ.*, December 1987, 11(4), pp. 285–313. [G: U.S.; U.K.]

Courtenay, Stephen M. and Millar, James A. Accounting Earnings and Convertible Calls. *Tremblay, R., ed.*, 1987, pp. 579–93.

Daly, Michael J. and Jung, Jack. The Taxation of Corporate Investment Income in Canada: An Analysis of Marginal Effective Tax Rates. *Can. J. Econ.*, August 1987, 20(3), pp. 555–87. [G: Canada]

Darrough, Masako N. Managerial Incentives for Short-term Results: A Comment. *J. Finance*, September 1987, 42(4), pp. 1097–1102.

Dart, Robert J. and Minzberg, Samuel. Tax Problems of the Liquidation of Corporations: Canada. *International Fiscal Association, ed. (II)*, 1987, pp. 229–46. [G: Canada]

Davidson, Wallace N., III and McDonald, James L. Evidence of the Effect on Shareholder Wealth of Corporate Spinoffs: The Creation of Royalty Trusts. *J. Finan. Res.*, Winter 1987, 10(4), pp. 321–27. [G: U.S.]

De Alessi, Louis. Why Corporations Insure. *Econ. Inquiry*, July 1987, 25(3), pp. 429–38.

De Alessi, Louis and Fishe, Raymond P. H. Why Do Corporations Distribute Assets? An Analysis of Dividends and Capital Structure. *J. Inst. Theoretical Econ.*, March 1987, 143(1), pp. 34–51.

Defoort, Jos. Régime de liquidation des sociétés: Belgique. (Tax Problems of the Liquidation of Corporations: Belgium. With English summary.) *International Fiscal Association, ed. (II)*, 1987, pp. 201–20. [G: Belgium]

Dinkelbach, Werner. Zum internen Zinssatz bei Risiko. (With English summary.) *Z. Betriebswirtshaft*, April 1987, 57(4), pp. 384–94.

Dubois, Michel. Les déterminants du niveau d'endettement des entreprises: les théories à l'épreuve des faits. (Determinants of Financial Structure: Theories and Facts. With English summary.) *Écon. Soc.*, June 1987, *21*(6), pp. 5–29. **[G: France; U.S.; Canada; Mexico]**

Duménil, Gérard; Glick, Mark and Rangel, Jose. The Rate of Profit in the United States. *Cambridge J. Econ.*, December 1987, *11*(4), pp. 331–59. **[G: U.S.]**

Eaker, Mark R. and Grant, Dwight M. Crosshedging Foreign Currency Risk. *J. Int. Money Finance*, March 1987, *6*(1), pp. 85–105. **[G: Selected OECD; S. Africa]**

Edvardsson, Leif. Tax Problems of the Liquidation of Corporations: Sweden. *International Fiscal Association, ed. (II)*, 1987, pp. 475–89. **[G: Sweden]**

Edwards, Jeremy S. Recent Developments in the Theory of Corporate Finance. *Oxford Rev. Econ. Policy*, Winter 1987, *3*(4), pp. 1–12.

Eisenbeis, Robert A. Credit Granting: A Comparative Analysis of Classification Procedures: Discussion. *J. Finance*, July 1987, *42*(3), pp. 681–83.

Emery, Gary W. An Optimal Financial Response to Variable Demand. *J. Finan. Quant. Anal.*, June 1987, *22*(2), pp. 209–25.

Faivre, Michel. Régime de liquidation des sociétés: France. (Tax Problems of the Liquidation of Corporations: France. With English summary.) *International Fiscal Association, ed. (II)*, 1987, pp. 279–94. **[G: France]**

Fazzari, Steven M. and Athey, Michael J. Asymmetric Information, Financing Constraints, and Investment. *Rev. Econ. Statist.*, August 1987, *69*(3), pp. 481–87. **[G: U.S.]**

Fong, Nellie. Tax Problems of the Liquidation of Corporations: Hong Kong. *International Fiscal Association, ed. (II)*, 1987, pp. 295–303. **[G: Hong Kong]**

Fons, Jerome S. The Default Premium and Corporate Bond Experience. *J. Finance*, March 1987, *42*(1), pp. 81–97. **[G: U.S.]**

van Fraeyenhoven, Guy. Tax Problems of the Liquidation of Corporations: General Report. *International Fiscal Association, ed. (II)*, 1987, pp. 37–56.

Franke, Günter. Costless Signalling in Financial Markets. *J. Finance*, September 1987, *42*(4), pp. 809–22.

Franks, Julian R. and Hodges, Stewart D. Lease Valuation When Taxable Earnings Are a Scarce Resource. *J. Finance*, September 1987, *42*(4), pp. 987–1005. **[G: U.K.]**

Fraser, Peter M. Tax Problems of the Liquidation of Corporations: Australia. *International Fiscal Association, ed. (II)*, 1987, pp. 173–86. **[G: Australia]**

Freimüller, Hans-Ulrich and Burki, Nico H. Steuerliche Probleme der Liquidation von Körperschaften: Schweiz. (Tax Problems of the Liquidation of Corporations: Switzerland. With English summary.) *International Fiscal Association, ed. (II)*, 1987, pp. 491–513. **[G: Switzerland]**

Fricke, Friedrich. Asymmetric Information between Investors and Managers under the New German Accounting Legislation. *Bamberg, G.*

and Spremann, K., eds., 1987, pp. 311–26. **[G: W. Germany]**

Friend, Irwin and Tokutsu, Ichiro. The Cost of Capital to Corporations in Japan and the U.S.A. *J. Banking Finance*, June 1987, *11*(2), pp. 313–27. **[G: Japan; U.S.]**

Frydl, Edward J. The Free Cash Flow Theory of Takeovers: A Financial Perspective on Mergers and Acquisitions and the Economy: Discussion. *Browne, L. E. and Rosengren, E. S., eds.*, 1987, pp. 144–48. **[G: U.S.]**

Fullerton, Don. The Indexation of Interest, Depreciation, and Capital Gains and Tax Reform in the United States. *J. Public Econ.*, February 1987, *32*(1), pp. 25–51. **[G: U.S.]**

Fung, W. K. F. and Theobald, M. F. Taxes, Unequal Access, Public Debt and Corporate Financial Policy in the United Kingdom. *J. Banking Finance*, March 1987, *11*(1), pp. 65–78. **[G: U.K.]**

Gagnon, Jean-Marie; Suret, Jean-Marc and St-Pierre, Josée. Asymétrie de l'information, fiscalité et endettement au Canada. (Information Asymmetry, Taxes and Debt-Equity Ratios in Canada. With English summary.) *Finance*, June 1987, *8*(1), pp. 75–103. **[G: Canada]**

Gaier, Richard. Steuerliche Probleme der Liquidation von Körperschaften: Österreich. (Tax Problems of the Liquidation of Corporations: Austria. With English summary.) *International Fiscal Association, ed. (II)*, 1987, pp. 187–200. **[G: Austria]**

Gandhi, D. K. and Rashid, Muhammad. Costly Bankruptcy, Expected Growth and Market Valuation. *Tremblay, R., ed.*, 1987, pp. 603–16.

Gentry, James A. and Lee, Cheng F. Financial Forecasting and the X-11 Model: Preliminary Evidence. *Lee, C. F., ed.*, 1987, pp. 27–49. **[G: U.S.]**

Gerard, Marcel. Autour du débat fiscal belge: neutralité à l'égard des choix financiers et imposition effective des revenus de l'investissement. (With English summary.) *Cah. Écon. Bruxelles*, Fourth Trimester 1987, (116), pp. 25–63. **[G: Belgium]**

Gnes, Paolo. Banking and the Transformation of Italy's Productive Base: A Comment. *Rev. Econ. Cond. Italy*, Sept.-Dec. 1987, (3), pp. 479–84. **[G: Italy]**

Gomez de Parada, Rodolfo Garcia. Tax Problems of the Liquidation of Corporations: Mexico. *International Fiscal Association, ed. (II)*, 1987, pp. 369–82. **[G: Mexico]**

Gordon, Roger H. Taxation and Capital Structure: A Selected Review: Comment. *Mintz, J. M. and Purvis, D. D., eds.*, 1987, pp. 263–66.

Goudie, Andrew. Forecasting Corporate Failure: The Use of Discriminant Analysis within a Disaggregated Model of the Corporate Sector. *J. Roy. Statist. Soc.*, 1987, *150*(1), pp. 69–81. **[G: U.K.]**

Green, Richard C. and Jarrow, Robert A. Spanning and Completeness in Markets with Contingent Claims. *J. Econ. Theory*, February 1987, *41*(1), pp. 202–10.

Grieves, Robin and Singleton, J. Clay. Analytic Methods of the All-America Research Team. *J. Portfol. Manage.*, Fall 1987, *14*(1), pp. 4–8. [G: U.S.]

Grout, Paul A. Wider Share Ownership and Economic Performance. *Oxford Rev. Econ. Policy*, Winter 1987, *3*(4), pp. 13–29. [G: U.K.]

Grundfest, Joseph A. Why Are the Parts Worth More than the Sum? "Chop Shop," A Corporate Valuation Model: Discussion. *Browne, L. E. and Rosengren, E. S., eds.*, 1987, pp. 96–101.

Guntermann, Karl L. and Smith, Richard L. Derivation of Cost of Capital and Equity Rates from Market Data. *Amer. Real Estate Urban Econ. Assoc. J.*, Summer 1987, *15*(2), pp. 98–109. [G: U.S.]

Hall, Robert E. Tax Policy and Corporate Saving: Comment. *Brookings Pap. Econ. Act.*, 1987, (2), pp. 504–06. [G: U.S.]

Halpern, T. Lionel. Tax Problems of the Liquidation of Corporations: United Kingdom. *International Fiscal Association, ed. (II)*, 1987, pp. 455–74. [G: U.K.]

Ham, John C. and Melnik, Arie. Loan Demand: An Empirical Analysis Using Micro Data. *Rev. Econ. Statist.*, November 1987, *69*(4), pp. 704–09. [G: U.S.]

Hamada, Robert S. Differential Taxes and the Structure of Equilibrium Rates of Return: Managerial Implications and Remaining Conundrums. *Lee, C. F., ed.*, 1987, pp. 1–25.

Hansen, Robert G. A Theory for the Choice of Exchange Medium in Mergers and Acquisitions. *J. Bus.*, January 1987, *60*(1), pp. 75–95. [G: U.S.]

Harpaz, Giora and Thomadakis, Stavros B. Valuation under Imperfect Information: Bayesian Learning from the Performance of the Firm and the Market. *Managerial Dec. Econ.*, September 1987, *8*(3), pp. 229–34.

Harris, Frederick H. deB. Security and Penalty in Debt Contracts: Comment. *J. Inst. Theoretical Econ.*, March 1987, *143*(1), pp. 168–74.

Harris, Milton and Holmstrom, Bengt. On the Duration of Agreements. *Int. Econ. Rev.*, June 1987, *28*(2), pp. 389–406.

Hartmann-Wendels, Thomas. Dividend Policy under Asymmetric Information. *Bamberg, G. and Spremann, K., eds.*, 1987, pp. 229–53.

Haugen, Robert A. and Senbet, Lemma W. On the Resolution of Agency Problems by Complex Financial Instruments: A Reply. *J. Finance*, September 1987, *42*(4), pp. 1091–95.

Haydu, Frank W., III. Financial Innovation and Corporate Mergers: Discussion. *Browne, L. E. and Rosengren, E. S., eds.*, 1987, pp. 74–77. [G: U.S.]

Hergert, Michael. Integrating Forecasting Techniques into Corporate Financial Models. *Bus. Econ.*, July 1987, *22*(3), pp. 38–42.

Herrhausen, Alfred. Internationale Investitionsfinanzierung in der Zukunft: Eine Herausforderung. (With English summary.) *Z. Betriebswirtschaft*, October 1987, *57*(10), pp. 966–77. [G: LDCs]

Hess, James D. and Knoeber, Charles R. Security and Penalty in Debt Contracts. *J. Inst. Theoretical Econ.*, March 1987, *143*(1), pp. 149–67.

Houdayer, Robert. L'apport de la programmation lineaire a l'establissement de plans de financement. (Contribution of Linear Programming to the Setting up of Financing Projects. With English summary.) *Écon. Soc.*, December 1987, *21*(12), pp. 83–107.

Howe, Keith M. and Lapan, Harvey. Inflation and Asset Life: The Darby versus the Fisher Effect. *J. Finan. Quant. Anal.*, June 1987, *22*(2), pp. 249–58.

Hubbard, R. Glenn. Tax Policy and Corporate Saving: Comment. *Brookings Pap. Econ. Act.*, 1987, (2), pp. 504–13. [G: U.S.]

Jacobson, Robert. The Validity of ROI as a Measure of Business Performance. *Amer. Econ. Rev.*, June 1987, *77*(3), pp. 470–78. [G: U.S.]

Jahera, John S., Jr.; Lloyd, William P. and Page, Daniel E. Firm Diversification and Financial Performance. *Quart. Rev. Econ. Bus.*, Spring 1987, *27*(1), pp. 51–62. [G: U.S.]

Jarrell, Gregg A. Financial Innovation and Corporate Mergers. *Browne, L. E. and Rosengren, E. S., eds.*, 1987, pp. 52–73. [G: U.S.]

Jarrell, Gregg A. and Poulsen, Annette B. Shark Repellents and Stock Prices: The Effects of Antitakeover Amendments since 1980. *J. Finan. Econ.*, September 1987, *19*(1), pp. 127–68.

Jensen, Michael C. The Free Cash Flow Theory of Takeovers: A Financial Perspective on Mergers and Acquisitions and the Economy. *Browne, L. E. and Rosengren, E. S., eds.*, 1987, pp. 102–43. [G: U.S.]

John, Kose. Risk-Shifting Incentives and Signalling through Corporate Capital Structure. *J. Finance*, July 1987, *42*(3), pp. 623–41.

Johnson, Lewis D. Growth Prospects and Share Prices: A Systematic View. *J. Portfol. Manage.*, Winter 1987, *13*(2), pp. 58–60.

Kalay, Avner and Shimrat, Adam. Firm Value and Seasoned Equity Issues: Price Pressure, Wealth Redistribution, or Negative Information. *J. Finan. Econ.*, September 1987, *19*(1), pp. 109–26. [G: U.S.]

Kanatas, George. Commercial Paper, Bank Reserve Requirements, and the Informational Role of Loan Commitments. *J. Banking Finance*, September 1987, *11*(3), pp. 425–48.

Kapetanakis Sifakis, Catherine. L'influence de la taille sur l'endettement des entreprises industrielles grecques. (The Effect of Size on Financial Structure of Greek Industrial Companies. With English summary.) *L'Actual. Écon.*, December 1987, *63*(4), pp. 357–72. [G: Greece]

Kemp, Robert S., Jr. An Examination of the Relationship of Unfunded Vested Pension Liabilities and Selected Elements of Firm Value. *Schwartz, B. N., ed.*, 1987, pp. 59–71. [G: U.S.]

Kim, E. Han and Schatzberg, John D. Voluntary Corporate Liquidations. *J. Finan. Econ.*, December 1987, *19*(2), pp. 311–28.   [G: U.S.]

Klock, Mark S. On the Simultaneity of Real and Financial Policies. *J. Econ. Bus.*, February 1987, *39*(1), pp. 45–56.

Kormendi, Roger and Lipe, Robert. Earnings Innovations, Earnings Persistence, and Stock Returns. *J. Bus.*, July 1987, *60*(3), pp. 323–45.   [G: U.S.]

Krahnen, Jan P. and Meran, Georg. Why Leasing? An Introduction to Comparative Contractual Analysis. *Bamberg, G. and Spremann, K.*, eds., 1987, pp. 255–80.

Kuczynski, Pedro-Pablo. Marketing Divested State-Owned Enterprises in Developing Countries. *Hanke, S. H.*, ed., 1987, pp. 111–17.   [G: LDCs]

Laber, Gene. Effects of the Bell System Breakup on the Cost of Debt. *J. Econ. Bus.*, August 1987, *39*(3), pp. 185–97.   [G: U.S.]

Laitinen, Erkki K. A Computer Model of the Failure Process of the Firm: Part II. *Liiketaloudellinen Aikak.*, April 1987, *36*(4), pp. 339–65.   [G: Finland]

Lakonishok, Josef and Lev, Baruch. Stock Splits and Stock Dividends: Why, Who, and When. *J. Finance*, September 1987, *42*(4), pp. 913–32.   [G: U.S.]

Lau, Amy Hing-Ling. A Five-State Financial Distress Prediction Model. *J. Acc. Res.*, Spring 1987, *25*(1), pp. 127–38.

LeBaron, Dean and Speidell, Lawrence S. Why Are the Parts Worth More than the Sum? "Chop Shop," A Corporate Valuation Model. *Browne, L. E. and Rosengren, E. S.*, eds., 1987, pp. 78–95.   [G: U.S.]

Lee, Cheng F. and Kau, James B. Dividend Payment Behavior and Dividend Policy on REITs. *Quart. Rev. Econ. Bus.*, Summer 1987, *27*(2), pp. 6–21.   [G: U.S.]

Lee, Cheng F.; Wu, Chunchi and Djarraya, Mohamed. A Further Empirical Investigation of the Dividend Adjustment Process. *J. Econometrics*, July 1987, *35*(2/3), pp. 267–85.   [G: U.S.]

Levy, Mickey D. Corporate Profits and the U.S. Dollar Exchange Rate. *Bus. Econ.*, January 1987, *22*(1), pp. 31–36.   [G: U.S.]

Lewellen, Wilbur G. and Rosenfeld, Ahron. Optimal Bond Refunding Strategies. *Managerial Dec. Econ.*, September 1987, *8*(3), pp. 243–50.

Llerena, Patrick and Zuscovitch, Ehud. Valeur d'option et structure de marchés. Le cas du quasi-monopole. (Option Value and Market Structure: The Case of Quasi-monopoly. With English summary.) *Écon. Appl.*, 1987, *40*(1), pp. 97–113.

Lobez, Frédéric. Rédaction des contrats obligataires, théorie des mandats et asymétrie de l'information: étude des clauses limitant le crédit-bail. (Bond Contracting, Agency Theory and Information Asymmetry: A Study of Bond Covenants Which Limit Leasing Possibilities. With English summary.) *Écon. Soc.*, June 1987, *21*(6), pp. 31–49.

Loeys, Jan G. Interest Rate Swaps: A New Tool

for Managing Risk. *Wilcox, J. A.*, ed., 1987, *1985*, pp. 58–66.   [G: U.S.]

MacMinn, Richard D. Forward Markets, Stock Markets, and the Theory of the Firm. *J. Finance*, December 1987, *42*(5), pp. 1167–85.

MacMinn, Richard D. Insurance and Corporate Risk Management. *J. Risk Ins.*, December 1987, *54*(4), pp. 658–77.

Malinvaud, Edmond. The Legacy of European Stagflation. *Europ. Econ. Rev.*, Feb./Mar. 1987, *31*(1/2), pp. 53–65.   [G: W. Europe]

Marcus, Alan J. Corporate Pension Policy and the Value of PBGC Insurance. *Bodie, Z.; Shoven, J. B. and Wise, D. A.*, eds., 1987, pp. 49–76.   [G: U.S.]

Marcus, Richard D.; Swidler, Steve and Zivney, Terry L. An Explanation of Why Shareholders' Losses Are So Large after Drug Recalls. *Managerial Dec. Econ.*, December 1987, *8*(4), pp. 295–300.   [G: U.S.]

Marsh, Terry A. and Merton, Robert C. Dividend Behavior for the Aggregate Stock Market. *J. Bus.*, January 1987, *60*(1), pp. 1–40.   [G: U.S.]

Martin, John D. Alternative Net Present Value Models. *Lee, C. F.*, ed., 1987, pp. 51–66.

Mason, Colin. Venture Capital in the United Kingdom: A Geographical Perspective. *Nat. Westminster Bank Quart. Rev.*, May 1987, pp. 47–59.   [G: U.K.]

Masse, I.; Hanrahan, J. R. and Kushner, J. The Lease versus Borrow Decision from a Public Sector Perspective [Valuation of Financial Lease Contracts]. *Nat. Tax J.*, June 1987, *40*(2), pp. 271–74.

Mauer, David C. and Lewellen, Wilbur G. Debt Management under Corporate and Personal Taxation. *J. Finance*, December 1987, *42*(5), pp. 1275–91.

Mayer, Colin. The Assessment: Financial Systems and Corporate Investment. *Oxford Rev. Econ. Policy*, Winter 1987, *3*(4), pp. i–xvi.   [G: U.K.]

Mayers, David and Smith, Clifford W., Jr. Corporate Insurance and the Underinvestment Problem. *J. Risk Ins.*, March 1987, *54*(1), pp. 45–54.

Mayo, Wayne. Interest, Exempt Income and Inter-corporate Dividends. *Australian Tax Forum*, 1987, *4*(1), pp. 123–42.   [G: Australia]

McDermott, John E. and Sherman, William B. Tax Problems of the Liquidation of Corporations: United States. *International Fiscal Association, ed. (II)*, 1987, pp. 269–77.   [G: U.S.]

McLay, David. Tax Problems of the Liquidation of Corporations: New Zealand. *International Fiscal Association, ed. (II)*, 1987, pp. 395–402.   [G: New Zealand]

Michel, Allen and Shaked, Israel. Airline Deregulation and the Probability of Air Carrier Insolvency. *Financial Rev.*, February 1987, *22*(1), pp. 159–73.   [G: U.S.]

Miller, Merton H. The Informational Content of Dividends. *[Modigliani, F.]*, 1987, pp. 37–58.

Mitchell, Karlyn. Interest Rate Uncertainty and Corporate Debt Maturity. *J. Econ. Bus.*, May

1987, *39*(2), pp. 101–14.   **[G: U.S.]**
Mori, Akio and Albach, Horst. Das Finanzie-
rungsverhalten japanischer und deutscher
Unternehmen. (With English summary.) *Z.
Betriebswirtshaft*, March 1987, *57*(3), pp.
251–96.   **[G: Japan; W. Germany]**
Morris, Michael H. and Wittenbach, James L.
The First Year of Safe Harbor Leasing Activity:
A Look Back at Objectives and Results. *Jones,
S. M., ed.*, 1987, pp. 131–52.   **[G: U.S.]**
Möschel, Wernhard. Why Do Corporations Dis-
tribute Assets? An Analysis of Dividends and
Capital Structure: Comment. *J. Inst. Theoreti-
cal Econ.*, March 1987, *143*(1), pp. 58–61.
Mossetti, Giovanna. Loanable Funds and Output
in a Model of the Firm. *Giorn. Econ.*, Nov.-
Dec. 1987, *46*(11–12), pp. 617–38.
**Moyer, R. Charles; Marr, M. Wayne and Chat-
field, Robert E.** Nonconvertible Preferred
Stock Financing and Financial Distress: A
Note. *J. Econ. Bus.*, February 1987, *39*(1), pp.
81–89.   **[G: U.S.]**
Myers, Stewart C. The Informational Content of
Dividends: Comments. *[Modigliani, F.]*, 1987,
pp. 59–61.
Narayanan, M. P. Managerial Incentives for
Short-term Results: A Reply. *J. Finance*, Sep-
tember 1987, *42*(4), pp. 1103–04.
Narayanan, M. P. On the Resolution of Agency
Problems by Complex Financial Instruments:
A Comment [Resolving the Agency Problems
of External Capital through Stock Options]. *J.
Finance*, September 1987, *42*(4), pp. 1083–90.
Narayanaswamy, C. R. and Phillips, Herbert E.
CAPM, Valuation of Firms, and Financial Le-
verage. *Quart. J. Bus. Econ.*, Winter 1987,
26(1), pp. 86–93.
Newbury, Colin. Technology, Capital, and Con-
solidation: The Performance of De Beers Min-
ing Company Limited, 1880–1889. *Bus. Hist.
Rev.*, Spring 1987, *61*(1), pp. 1–42.
               [G: S. Africa]
Ngend-Ngend, Sam. Un outil de selection des
credits-clients: l'analyse en composantes prin-
cipales. (Accounts Receivable Policy Selection:
The Factor Analysis Method. With English
summary.) *Écon. Soc.*, December 1987,
21(12), pp. 57–82.
Nishina, Kazuhiko and Funaoka, Fumio. The
Role of the Market Price of Risk in the Invest-
ment Decision. *Econ. Rev. (Keizai Kenkyu)*,
April 1987, *38*(2), pp. 139–52.   **[G: Japan]**
**Noriega del Valle, Enrique; Carrión, Hugo Pa-
niague and Dueñas, César Rodríguez.** Tax
Problems of the Liquidation of Corporations:
Peru. *International Fiscal Association, ed. (II)*,
1987, pp. 423–34.   **[G: Peru]**
Ofer, Aharon R. and Natarajan, Ashok. Converti-
ble Call Policies: An Empirical Analysis of an
Information-signaling Hypothesis. *J. Finan.
Econ.*, September 1987, *19*(1), pp. 91–108.
               [G: U.S.]
Ofer, Aharon R. and Siegel, Daniel R. Corporate
Financial Policy, Information, and Market Ex-
pectations: An Empirical Investigation of Divi-

dends. *J. Finance*, September 1987, *42*(4), pp.
889–911.   **[G: U.S.]**
Ofer, Aharon R. and Thakor, Anjan V. A Theory
of Stock Price Responses to Alternative Corporate Cash Disbursement Methods: Stock Repurchases and Dividends. *J. Finance*, June
1987, *42*(2), pp. 365–94.
Outreville, J. François. The Transactions Demand for Cash Balances by Property and Lia-
bility Insurance Companies. *J. Risk Ins.*, September 1987, *54*(3), pp. 557–68. **[G: Canada]**
Pakes, Ariel. Mueller's *Profits in the Long Run.
Rand J. Econ.*, Summer 1987, *18*(2), pp. 319–
32.
Parmenter, Brian R. and Seyfort, Anthony. The
Imputation System of Company Tax: Context,
Characteristics, Critique. *Australian Econ.
Rev.*, First Quarter 1987, (77), pp. 3–8.
               [G: Australia]
Partch, M. Megan. The Creation of a Class of
Limited Voting Common Stock and Share-
holder Wealth. *J. Finan. Econ.*, June 1987,
18(2), pp. 313–39.   **[G: U.S.]**
Perold, André F. Funding and Asset Allocation
in Corporate Pension Plans: An Empirical In-
vestigation: Comment. *Bodie, Z.; Shoven, J.
B. and Wise, D. A., eds.*, 1987, pp. 44–47.
               [G: U.S.]
Perrakis, Stylianos. Option Bounds in Discrete
Time and the Pricing of Corporate Debt. *Fa-
bozzi, F. J., ed.*, 1987, pp. 179–207.
**Peterson, Pamela P.; Peterson, David R. and
Moore, Norman H.** The Adoption of New-Issue Dividend Reinvestment Plans and Share-
holder Wealth. *Financial Rev.*, May 1987,
22(2), pp. 221–32.   **[G: U.S.]**
Pitelis, Christos N. Corporate Retained Earnings
and the 'Kaldorian' Hypothesis of Saving. *Brit.
Rev. Econ. Issues*, Spring 1987, *9*(20), pp. 79–
95.   **[G: U.K.]**
Pitelis, Christos N. Corporate Retained Earnings
and Personal Sector Saving: A Test of the Life-
Cycle Hypothesis of Saving. *Appl. Econ.*, July
1987, *19*(7), pp. 907–13.   **[G: U.K.]**
Polinsky, A. Mitchell. Fixed Price versus Spot
Price Contracts: A Study in Risk Allocation.
J. Law, Econ., Organ., Spring 1987, *3*(1), pp.
27–46.   **[G: U.S.]**
Polonchek, John A. and Sushka, Marie E. The
Impact of Financial and Economic Conditions
on Aggregate Merger Activity. *Managerial
Dec. Econ.*, June 1987, *8*(2), pp. 113–19.
               [G: U.S.]
Poterba, James M. Tax Policy and Corporate Saving. *Brookings Pap. Econ. Act.*, 1987, (2), pp.
455–503.   **[G: U.S.]**
Poterba, James M. Taxation and Capital Structure: A Selected Review: Comment. *Mintz, J.
M. and Purvis, D. D., eds.*, 1987, pp. 267–
74.
Pound, John. The Effects of Antitakeover Amendments on Takeover Activity: Some Direct Evidence. *J. Law Econ.*, October 1987, *30*(2), pp.
353–67.   **[G: U.S.]**
Pozdena, Randall Johnston. Tax Policy and Corporate Capital Structure. *Fed. Res. Bank San*

Francisco Econ. Rev., Fall 1987, (4), pp. 37–51.   [G: U.S.]

Rafael, Amnon. Tax Problems of the Liquidation of Corporations: Israel. *International Fiscal Association, ed. (II)*, 1987, pp. 305–19.
[G: Israel]

Ramaswami, Murali. Stock Market Perception of Industrial Firm Bankruptcy. *Financial Rev.*, May 1987, 22(2), pp. 267–79.   [G: U.S.]

Rangazas, Peter and Abdullah, Dewan. Taxes and the Corporate Sector Debt Ratio: Some Time Series Evidence. *Rev. Econ. Statist.*, May 1987, 69(2), pp. 357–62.   [G: U.S.]

Ravid, S. Abraham. Safety First, Bankruptcy, and the Pricing and Investment Decisions of the Firm. *Econ. Inquiry*, October 1987, 25(4), pp. 695–706.

Resk, Carlos H. Tax Problems of the Liquidation of Corporations: Argentina. *International Fiscal Association, ed. (II)*, 1987, pp. 153–71.
[G: Argentina]

Rica, Narciso Amorós. Problemas fiscales de la liquidación de sociedades: Espagne. (Tax Problems of the Liquidation of Corporations: Spain. With English summary.) *International Fiscal Association, ed. (II)*, 1987, pp. 259–68.
[G: Spain]

Ricketts, Martin. Why Do Corporations Distribute Assets? An Analysis of Dividends and Capital Structure: Comment. *J. Inst. Theoretical Econ.*, March 1987, 143(1), pp. 52–57.

Ritter, Jay R. The Costs of Going Public. *J. Finan. Econ.*, December 1987, 19(2), pp. 269–81.
[G: U.S.]

Robison, Lindon J.; Barry, Peter J. and Burghardt, William G. Borrowing Behavior under Financial Stress by the Proprietary Firm: A Theoretical Analysis. *Western J. Agr. Econ.*, December 1987, 12(2), pp. 144–51.

Roe, Mark J. The Voting Prohibition in Bond Workouts. *Yale Law J.*, December 1987, 97(2), pp. 232–79.   [G: U.S.]

Ross, Stephen A. Arbitrage and Martingales with Taxation. *J. Polit. Econ.*, April 1987, 95(2), pp. 371–93.

Rubio Irigoyen, Gonzalo. El contenido informativo de los derechos de suscripcion e información asimétrica en los mercados primarios. (With English summary.) *Invest. Econ.*, May 1987, 11(2), pp. 219–42.   [G: Spain]

Schallheim, James S., et. al. The Determinants of Yields on Financial Leasing Contracts. *J. Finan. Econ.*, September 1987, 19(1), pp. 45–67.   [G: U.S.]

Scherr, Frederick C. A Multiperiod Mean-Variance Model of Optimal Capital Structure. *Financial Rev.*, February 1987, 22(1), pp. 1–31.

Scholes, Myron S. How Does the Market Value Unfunded Pension Liabilities? Comment. *Bodie, Z.; Shoven, J. B. and Wise, D. A., eds.*, 1987, pp. 104–09.   [G: U.S.]

Schumann, Jochen. Security and Penalty in Debt Contracts: Comment. *J. Inst. Theoretical Econ.*, March 1987, 143(1), pp. 175–79.

Scitovski, Rudolf. Ispodgodišnje ukamaćivanje. (On Determining Less-than-Annual Interest. With English summary.) *Econ. Anal. Workers' Manage.*, 1987, 21(2), pp. 243–57.
[G: Yugoslavia]

Shah, Salman and Thakor, Anjan V. Optimal Capital Structure and Project Financing. *J. Econ. Theory*, August 1987, 42(2), pp. 209–43.

Sharpe, William F. Corporate Pension Policy and the Value of PBGC Insurance: Comment. *Bodie, Z.; Shoven, J. B. and Wise, D. A., eds.*, 1987, pp. 77–79.   [G: U.S.]

Shevlin, Terry. Taxes and Off-Balance–Sheet Financing: Research and Development Limited Partnerships. *Accounting Rev.*, July 1987, 62(3), pp. 480–509.   [G: U.S.]

Shioda, Shigenori. Tax Problems of the Liquidation of Corporations: Japan. *International Fiscal Association, ed. (II)*, 1987, pp. 337–54.
[G: Japan]

Shoven, John B. The Tax Consequences of Share Repurchases and Other Non-dividend Cash Payments to Equity Owners. *Summers, L. H., ed.*, 1987, pp. 29–54.   [G: U.S.]

Sicherman, Neil W. and Pettway, Richard H. Acquisition of Divested Assets and Shareholders' Wealth. *J. Finance*, December 1987, 42(5), pp. 1261–73.   [G: U.S.]

Skantz, Terrance R. and Marchesini, Roberto. The Effect of Voluntary Corporate Liquidation on Shareholder Wealth. *J. Finan. Res.*, Spring 1987, 10(1), pp. 65–75.   [G: U.S.]

Skou, Jørgen and Ancher, Tom. Tax Problems of the Liquidation of Corporations: Denmark. *International Fiscal Association, ed. (II)*, 1987, pp. 247–58.   [G: Denmark]

Sloan, Frank A.; Morrisey, Michael A. and Valvona, Joseph. Capital Markets and the Growth of Multihospital Systems. *Scheffler, R. M. and Rossiter, L. F., eds.*, 1987, pp. 83–109.
[G: U.S.]

Smith, Janet Kiholm. Trade Credit and Informational Asymmetry. *J. Finance*, September 1987, 42(4), pp. 863–72.

Smith, Richard L. The Choice of Issuance Procedure and the Cost of Competitive and Negotiated Underwriting: An Examination of the Impact of Rule 50. *J. Finance*, July 1987, 42(3), pp. 703–20.   [G: U.S.]

Sobhan, Rehman and Ahsan, Ahmad. The Effect of Exchange Rate Depreciation on the Loan Repayment Performance of Private Enterprise in Bangladesh. *Bangladesh Devel. Stud.*, December 1987, 15(4), pp. 1–52.
[G: Bangladesh]

Soldatos, Gerasimos T. Electronic Banking Services and the Pattern of the Firm's Operations. *Greek Econ. Rev.*, 1987, 9(1), pp. 131–40.

Srinivasan, Venkat and Kim, Yong H. Credit Granting: A Comparative Analysis of Classification Procedures. *J. Finance*, July 1987, 42(3), pp. 665–81.

Stewart, Scott D. Biases in Performance Measurement during Contributions: A Note. *Financial Rev.*, May 1987, 22(2), pp. 339–43.

Strong, John S. and Meyer, John R. Asset Writedowns: Managerial Incentives and Security Returns. *J. Finance*, July 1987, *42*(3), pp. 643–61. **[G: U.S.]**

Sundararajan, V. The Debt–Equity Ratio of Firms and the Effectiveness of Interest Rate Policy: Analysis with a Dynamic Model of Saving, Investment, and Growth in Korea. *Int. Monet. Fund Staff Pap.*, June 1987, *34*(2), pp. 260–310. **[G: S. Korea]**

Sverdlik, Sh. B. The Enterprise and the Bank. *Prob. Econ.*, July 1987, *30*(3), pp. 85–98. **[G: U.S.S.R.]**

Swoboda, Peter. The Liquidation Decision as a Principal–Agent Problem. *Bamberg, G. and Spremann, K., eds.*, 1987, pp. 167–77.

Tehranian, Hassan; Travlos, Nickolaos G. and Waegelein, James F. The Effect of Long-term Performance Plans on Corporate Sell-Off–Induced Abnormal Returns. *J. Finance*, September 1987, *42*(4), pp. 933–42. **[G: U.S.]**

Thakor, Anjan V. Asset Writedowns: Managerial Incentives and Security Returns: Discussion. *J. Finance*, July 1987, *42*(3), pp. 661–63. **[G: U.S.]**

Thompson, Howard E. Determination of Benchmark Rates of Return. *Managerial Dec. Econ.*, December 1987, *8*(4), pp. 321–32. **[G: U.S.]**

Thompson, R. S. and Wright, M. Markets to Hierarchies and Back Again: The Implication of Management Buy-outs for Factory Supply. *J. Econ. Stud.*, 1987, *14*(3), pp. 5–22. **[G: U.K.]**

Thompson, Robert B., II; Olsen, Chris and Dietrich, J. Richard. Attributes of News about Firms: An Analysis of Firm-Specific News Reported in the *Wall Street Journal Index*. *J. Acc. Res.*, Autumn 1987, *25*(2), pp. 245–74. **[G: U.S.]**

Tidrick, Gene and Chen, Jiyuan. China's Industrial Reform: Characteristics of the Twenty Firms. *Tidrick, G. and Jiyuan, C., eds.*, 1987, pp. 11–38. **[G: China]**

Torabzadeh, Khalil M. and Bertin, William J. Leveraged Buyouts and Shareholder Returns. *J. Finan. Res.*, Winter 1987, *10*(4), pp. 313–19. **[G: U.S.]**

Travlos, Nickolaos G. Corporate Takeover Bids, Methods of Payment, and Bidding Firms' Stock Returns. *J. Finance*, September 1987, *42*(4), pp. 943–63. **[G: U.S.]**

VanDerhei, Jack L. The Effect of Voluntary Termination of Overfunded Pension Plans on Shareholder Wealth. *J. Risk Ins.*, March 1987, *54*(1), pp. 132–56. **[G: U.S.]**

Varaiya, Nikhil P. Determinants of Premiums in Acquisition Transactions. *Managerial Dec. Econ.*, September 1987, *8*(3), pp. 175–84. **[G: U.S.]**

Veenendaal, Augustus J., Jr. The Kansas City Southern Railway and the Dutch Connection. *Bus. Hist. Rev.*, Summer 1987, *61*(2), pp. 291–316. **[G: U.S.]**

Volt, Jürgen. Praktische Probleme des Zero-Base-Budgeting (Gemeinkostenwertanalyse). (With English summary.) *Z. Betriebswirtshaft*, September 1987, *57*(9), pp. 870–81.

Wansley, James W.; Lane, William R. and Yang,

Ho C. Gains to Bidder Firms in Cash and Securities Transactions. *Financial Rev.*, November 1987, *22*(4), pp. 403–14. **[G: U.S.]**

Wattel, Peter J. Tax Problems of the Liquidation of Corporations: Netherlands. *International Fiscal Association, ed. (II)*, 1987, pp. 403–21. **[G: Netherlands]**

Webb, David C. Conflict of Interest, Bond Rating and the Value Maximization Rule. *Economica*, November 1987, *54*(216), pp. 455–63.

Webb, David C. The Importance of Incomplete Information in Explaining the Existence of Costly Bankruptcy. *Economica*, August 1987, *54*(215), pp. 279–88.

Webb, Richard. Internal Debt and Financial Adjustment in Peru. *CEPAL Rev.*, August 1987, (32), pp. 55–74. **[G: Peru]**

Wellmann, Richard. Steuerliche Probleme der Liquidation von Körperschaften: Deutschland. (Tax Problems of the Liquidation of Corporations: Germany. With English summary.) *International Fiscal Association, ed. (II)*, 1987, pp. 133–51. **[G: W. Germany]**

Wilhelm, Jochen E. M. On Stakeholders' Unanimity. *Bamberg, G. and Spremann, K., eds.*, 1987, pp. 179–204.

Williams, Joseph T. Perquisites, Risk, and Capital Structure. *J. Finance*, March 1987, *42*(1), pp. 29–48.

Wilson, G. Peter. The Incremental Information Content of the Accrual and Funds Components of Earnings after Controlling for Earnings. *Accounting Rev.*, April 1987, *62*(2), pp. 293–322. **[G: U.S.]**

Xu, Jing'an. The Stock-Share System: A New Avenue for China's Economic Reform. *J. Compar. Econ.*, September 1987, *11*(3), pp. 509–14. **[G: China]**

Yagil, Joseph. An Exchange Ratio Determination Model for Mergers: A Note. *Financial Rev.*, February 1987, *22*(1), pp. 195–202.

Yen, Gili. Merger Proposals, Managerial Discretion, and Magnitude of Shareholders' Wealth Gains. *J. Econ. Bus.*, August 1987, *39*(3), pp. 251–66. **[G: U.S.]**

Zanetti, Giovanni. Structure and Financial Requirements in the Italian Business Sector. *Rev. Econ. Cond. Italy*, Sept.-Dec. 1987, (3), pp. 417–53. **[G: Italy]**

Zebda, Awni. The Choice of Management Accounting Normative Models: A Synthesis. *Schwartz, B. N., ed.*, 1987, pp. 73–98.

Ziebart, David A. The Effects of Annual Accounting Data on Stock Returns and Trading Activity: A Causal Model Study. *J. Amer. Statist. Assoc.*, September 1987, *82*(399), pp. 733–38. **[G: U.S.]**

522 Business Investment

5220 Business Investment

Albach, Horst. Investitionspolitik erfolgreicher Unternehmen. (With English summary.) *Z. Betriebswirtshaft*, July 1987, *57*(7), pp. 636–61. **[G: W. Germany]**

Albrecht, Peter. Die Versicherungsproduktion—eine Kuppelproduktion bei Risiko. (With English summary.) *Z. Betriebswirtshaft,* March 1987, *57*(3), pp. 316–28.

Aoki, Masahiko. The Political Economy of Japan: The Japanese Firm in Transition. *Yamamura, K. and Yasuba, Y., eds.,* 1987, pp. 263–88. **[G: Japan]**

Artana, Daniel. Incentivos fiscales a la inversión industrial. (Fiscal Incentives to the Industrial Investment. With English summary.) *Económica (La Plata),* January-June 1987, *33*(1), pp. 3–38. **[G: Argentina]**

Auerbach, Alan J. The Tax Reform Act of 1986 and the Cost of Capital. *J. Econ. Perspectives,* Summer 1987, *1*(1), pp. 73–86. **[G: U.S.]**

Auerbach, Alan J. The Theory and Measurement of Effective Tax Rates: Comment. *Mintz, J. M. and Purvis, D. D., eds.,* 1987, pp. 99–101.

Auerbach, Alan J. and Hines, James R., Jr. Anticipated Tax Changes and the Timing of Investment. *Feldstein, M., ed. (II),* 1987, pp. 85–87. **[G: U.S.]**

Auerbach, Alan J. and Poterba, James M. Tax-Loss Carryforwards and Corporate Tax Incentives. *Feldstein, M., ed. (II),* 1987, pp. 89–92. **[G: U.S.]**

Auerbach, Alan J. and Poterba, James M. Tax-Loss Carryforwards and Corporate Tax Incentives. *Feldstein, M., ed. (I),* 1987, pp. 305–38. **[G: U.S.]**

Ballentine, J. Gregory. The Impact of Fundamental Tax Reform on the Allocation of Resources: Comment. *Feldstein, M., ed. (I),* 1987, pp. 437–43. **[G: U.S.]**

Bar-Yosef, Sasson; Callen, Jeffrey L. and Livnat, Joshua. Autoregressive Modeling of Earnings–Investment Causality. *J. Finance,* March 1987, *42*(1), pp. 11–28. **[G: U.S.]**

Barry, Frank G. A Note on the Employment Effects of Investment Subsidies. *Econ. Soc. Rev.,* July 1987, *18*(4), pp. 307–14.

Barwise, T. Patrick; Marsh, Paul and Wensley, Robin. Strategic Investment Decisions. *Sheth, J. N., ed.,* 1987, pp. 1–57.

Begg, Hugh and McDowall, Stuart. The Effect of Regional Investment Incentives on Company Decisions. *Reg. Stud.,* October 1987, *21*(5), pp. 459–70. **[G: U.K.]**

Bennett, Robert J. A General Accounting Model of Intergovernmental Tax and Benefit Effects on Business. *Environ. Planning A,* November 1987, *19*(11), pp. 1495–1510. **[G: U.K.; W. Germany]**

Bessis, Joël. Les déteminants réels du risque financier. (The Real Determinants of Financial Risk. With English summary.) *Finance,* June 1987, *8*(1), pp. 33–53. **[G: France]**

Bischoff, Charles W. and Kokkelenberg, Edward C. Capacity Utilization and Depreciation-in-Use. *Appl. Econ.,* August 1987, *19*(8), pp. 995–1007. **[G: U.S.]**

Blazenko, George W. Managerial Preference, Asymmetric Information, and Financial Structure. *J. Finance,* September 1987, *42*(4), pp. 839–62.

Bluestone, Barry. Deindustrialization and Unemployment in America. *Staudohar, P. D. and Brown, H. E.,* 1987, *1984,* pp. 3–15. **[G: U.S.]**

Boadway, Robin W. The Theory and Measurement of Effective Tax Rates. *Mintz, J. M. and Purvis, D. D., eds.,* 1987, pp. 60–98.

Bradford, David F. Tax-Loss Carryforwards and Corporate Tax Incentives: Comment. *Feldstein, M., ed. (I),* 1987, pp. 339–42. **[G: U.S.]**

Bright, Geoff. Tax Changes and Machinery Investment. *J. Agr. Econ.,* January 1987, *38*(1), pp. 39–49. **[G: U.K.]**

Bromiley, Philip. A Comparison of Behavioral and Conventional Conceptions of Investment. *J. Behav. Econ.,* Spring 1987, *16*(1), pp. 1–20.

Carlson, C. E. Investeringars Lönsamhet. (The Profitability of Investments. With English summary.) *Ekon. Samfundets Tidskr.,* 1987, *40*(1), pp. 29–32.

Chan-Lee, James H. and Torres, Raymond. q de Tobin et taux d'accumulation en France. (Tobin's q and Investment in France. With English summary.) *Ann. Écon. Statist.,* Jan./Mar. 1987, (5), pp. 37–48. **[G: France]**

Chirinko, Robert S. The Ineffectiveness of Effective Tax Rates on Business Investment: A Critique of Feldstein's Fisher–Schultz Lecture. *J. Public Econ.,* April 1987, *32*(3), pp. 369–87. **[G: U.S.]**

Chirinko, Robert S. Tobin's Q and Financial Policy. *J. Monet. Econ.,* January 1987, *19*(1), pp. 69–87. **[G: U.S.]**

Dave, Upendra. On Two Deterministic Inventory Models for Items with Decreasing Demand. *Econ. Computat. Cybern. Stud. Res.,* 1987, *22*(2), pp. 45–50.

Devereux, Michael. Taxation and the Cost of Capital: The UK Experience. *Oxford Rev. Econ. Policy,* Winter 1987, *3*(4), pp. xvii–xxxii. **[G: U.K.]**

Duggal, Vijaya G. and Adams, F. Gerard. Corporate Tax Reform and Business Investment: Empirical Estimates for Structures and Equipment. *Empirical Econ.,* 1987, *12*(3), pp. 187–95. **[G: U.S.]**

Dyl, Edward A. and Hoffmeister, J. Ronald. Capital Budgeting Decisions: The Effect of Product Cannibalism and Competitive Product Markets. *Lee, C. F., ed.,* 1987, pp. 119–33.

Fazzari, Steven M. Tax Reform and Investment: How Big an Impact? *Fed. Res. Bank St. Louis Rev.,* January 1987, *69*(1), pp. 15–27. **[G: U.S.]**

Fazzari, Steven M. Tax Reform and Investment: Blessing or Curse? *Fed. Res. Bank St. Louis Rev.,* June/July 1987, *69*(6), pp. 23–33. **[G: U.S.]**

Fazzari, Steven M. and Athey, Michael J. Asymmetric Information, Financing Constraints, and Investment. *Rev. Econ. Statist.,* August 1987, *69*(3), pp. 481–87. **[G: U.S.]**

Fazzari, Steven M. and Mott, Tracy L. The Investment Theories of Kalecki and Keynes: An Empirical Study of Firm Data, 1970–1982. *J.*

Post Keynesian Econ., Winter 1986-87, *9*(2), pp. 171–87. **[G: U.S.]**

Feldstein, Martin S. Tax Rates and Business Investment: Reply [Inflation, Tax Rules and Investment: Some Econometric Evidence]. *J. Public Econ.*, April 1987, *32*(3), pp. 389–96. **[G: U.S.]**

Feldstein, Martin S. Tax Rules and Business Investment. *Feldstein, M., ed. (II)*, 1987, pp. 63–72. **[G: U.S.]**

Fischer, Klaus P.; Olson, David L. and Richard, Victor. Political Risk and the Trend of New Investment in the World Aluminum Industry. *J. Econ. Devel.*, June 1987, *12*(1), pp. 117–36. **[G: Global]**

Folmer, Henk and Nijkamp, Peter. Investment Premiums: Expensive but Hardly Effective. *Kyklos*, 1987, *40*(1), pp. 43–72. **[G: Netherlands]**

Freixas, Xavier. L'effet d'irréversibilité dans le choix de grands projets. (The Irreversibility Effect in the Choice among Large Projects. With English summary.) *Revue Écon.*, January 1987, *38*(1), pp. 149–55.

Fullerton, Don and Henderson, Yolanda Kodrzycki. The Impact of Fundamental Tax Reform on the Allocation of Resources. *Feldstein, M., ed. (I)*, 1987, pp. 401–37. **[G: U.S.]**

Galeotti, Marzio. On the Dual Relationship between Flexible Accelerator and *q* Theories of Investment. *Rivista Int. Sci. Econ. Com.*, August 1987, *34*(8), pp. 771–76.

Garofalo, Gasper A. and Malhotra, Devinder M. Regional Capital Formation in U.S. Manufacturing during the 1970s. *J. Reg. Sci.*, August 1987, *27*(3), pp. 391–401. **[G: U.S.]**

Gerard, Marcel. Autour du débat fiscal belge: neutralité à l'égard des choix financiers et imposition effective des revenus de l'investissement. (With English summary.) *Cah. Écon. Bruxelles*, Fourth Trimester 1987, (116), pp. 25–63. **[G: Belgium]**

Ghemawat, Pankaj. Investment in Lumpy Capacity. *J. Econ. Behav. Organ.*, June 1987, *8*(2), pp. 265–77.

Gilbert, Richard J. and Lieberman, Marvin B. Investment and Coordination in Oligopolistic Industries. *Rand J. Econ.*, Spring 1987, *18*(1), pp. 17–33. **[G: U.S.]**

Glass, Victor and Cahn, E. S. Energy Prices and Investment over the Business Cycle. *Energy Econ.*, October 1987, *9*(4), pp. 257–64.

Gopalakrishnan, S. Effect of Government Borrowing on Private Investment in India. *Indian Econ. J.*, Oct.-Dec. 1987, *35*(2), pp. 48–57. **[G: India]**

Gordon, Roger H.; Hines, James R., Jr. and Summers, Lawrence H. Notes on the Tax Treatment of Structures. *Feldstein, M., ed. (I)*, 1987, pp. 223–54. **[G: U.S.]**

Guth, Michael A. S. Functional Form in Finished Goods Inventory Investment: A Note. *J. Money, Credit, Banking*, August 1987, *19*(3), pp. 396–401. **[G: U.S.]**

Hall, Robert E. Tax Policy and Corporate Saving: Comment. *Brookings Pap. Econ. Act.*, 1987, (2), pp. 504–06. **[G: U.S.]**

Heaton, Hal. On the Bias of the Corporate Tax against High-Risk Projects. *J. Finan. Quant. Anal.*, September 1987, *22*(3), pp. 365–71.

Hedlund-Nyström, Torun; Jonung, Lars and Sandelin, Bo. Opublicerat manuskript av Knut Wicksell med en kapitalteoretisk modell. (An Unpublished Manuscript by Knut Wicksell on a Capital-Theoretical Model. With English summary.) *Ekon. Samfundets Tidskr.*, 1987, *40*(3), pp. 123–37.

Heim, Carol E. and Mirowski, Philip. Interest Rates and Crowding-Out during Britain's Industrial Revolution. *J. Econ. Hist.*, March 1987, *47*(1), pp. 117–39. **[G: U.K.]**

Herr, Ellen M. Capital Expenditures by Majority-Owned Foreign Affiliates of U.S. Companies, 1987 and 1988. *Surv. Curr. Bus.*, September 1987, *67*(9), pp. 26–31. **[G: U.S.]**

Herr, Ellen M. Capital Expenditures by Majority-Owned Foreign Affiliates of U.S. Companies, 1987. *Surv. Curr. Bus.*, March 1987, *67*(3), pp. 26–31. **[G: U.S.]**

Hines, James R., Jr. The Tax Treatment of Structures. *Feldstein, M., ed. (II)*, 1987, pp. 37–50. **[G: U.S.]**

Howe, Keith M. and Lapan, Harvey. Inflation and Asset Life: The Darby versus the Fisher Effect. *J. Finan. Quant. Anal.*, June 1987, *22*(2), pp. 249–58.

Hubbard, R. Glenn. Tax Policy and Corporate Saving: Comment. *Brookings Pap. Econ. Act.*, 1987, (2), pp. 504–13. **[G: U.S.]**

Jensen, Robert E. A Dynamic Analytic Hierarchy Process Analysis of Capital Budgeting under Stochastic Inflation Rates and Risk Premiums. *Lee, C. F., ed.*, 1987, pp. 269–302. **[G: U.S.]**

Klock, Mark S. On the Simultaneity of Real and Financial Policies. *J. Econ. Bus.*, February 1987, *39*(1), pp. 45–56.

Kohli, Ulrich and Ryan, Christopher J. Investment and Interest Rates: An Econometric Dissection. *J. Macroecon.*, Summer 1987, *9*(3), pp. 373–89. **[G: Australia]**

Kotlikoff, Laurence J. The Theory and Measurement of Effective Tax Rates: Comment. *Mintz, J. M. and Purvis, D. D., eds.*, 1987, pp. 102–04.

Levy, Victor. Does Concessionary Aid Lead to Higher Investment Rates in Low-Income Countries? *Rev. Econ. Statist.*, February 1987, *69*(1), pp. 152–56. **[G: LDCs]**

Lieberman, Marvin B. Excess Capacity as a Barrier to Entry: An Empirical Appraisal. *J. Ind. Econ.*, June 1987, *35*(4), pp. 607–27. **[G: U.S.]**

Lieberman, Marvin B. Postentry Investment and Market Structure in the Chemical Processing Industries. *Rand J. Econ.*, Winter 1987, *18*(4), pp. 533–49. **[G: U.S.]**

Majd, Saman and Myers, Stewart C. Tax Asymmetries and Corporate Income Tax Reform. *Feldstein, M., ed. (II)*, 1987, pp. 93–95. **[G: U.S.]**

Majd, Saman and Pindyck, Robert S. Time to Build, Option Value, and Investment Decisions. *J. Finan. Econ.*, March 1987, *18*(1), pp. 7–27.

Mayer, Colin. The Assessment: Financial Systems and Corporate Investment. *Oxford Rev. Econ. Policy*, Winter 1987, *3*(4), pp. i–xvi. [G: U.K.]

McMillin, W. Douglas and Laumas, G. S. Economic Policy and Consumption and Investment Expenditures: An Empirical Examination. *Appl. Econ.*, February 1987, *19*(2), pp. 167–77. [G: U.S.]

Morgan, Eleanor J. The UK Corporate Tax Reform and Business Investment Decisions. *Managerial Dec. Econ.*, June 1987, *8*(2), pp. 149–59. [G: U.K.]

Moussa, Hassouna. Tobin's *q*, the Demand for Investment and the Corporate Profit Taxation Policy in Canada (1950–1983). *Rech. Écon. Louvain*, 1987, *53*(1), pp. 27–50. [G: Canada]

Nishikawa, Y., et al. Design of a Decision-Support Workstation System for Hierarchical Multiobjective Inventory Control. *Sawaragi, Y.; Inoue, K. and Nakayama, H., eds.*, 1987, pp. 267–76.

Nishina, Kazuhiko and Funaoka, Fumio. The Role of the Market Price of Risk in the Investment Decision. *Econ. Rev. (Keizai Kenkyu)*, April 1987, *38*(2), pp. 139–52. [G: Japan]

Officer, Robert R. The Required Rate of Return and Tax Imputation: Estimating the Effect of the Imputation Tax on Investment Appraisal. *Australian Tax Forum*, 1987, *4*(3), pp. 405–17.

Papke, Leslie E. Subnational Taxation and Capital Mobility: Estimates of Tax–Price Elasticities. *Nat. Tax J.*, June 1987, *40*(2), pp. 191–203. [G: U.S.]

Poterba, James M. Tax Policy and Corporate Saving. *Brookings Pap. Econ. Act.*, 1987, (2), pp. 455–503. [G: U.S.]

Primeaux, Walter J., Jr. The Interdependence of the Life Cycle and Strategic Group Concepts: Theory and Evidence. *Lee, C. F., ed.*, 1987, pp. 67–85. [G: U.S.]

Ravid, S. Abraham. Safety First, Bankruptcy, and the Pricing and Investment Decisions of the Firm. *Econ. Inquiry*, October 1987, *25*(4), pp. 695–706.

Risager, Ole. The Effects of Currency Depreciation in a Model with Capital Formation. *Europ. Econ. Rev.*, Feb./Mar. 1987, *31*(1/2), pp. 399–406. [G: Denmark]

Romain, Robert F. J.; Penson, John B., Jr. and Lambert, Rémy E. Capacity Depreciation, Implicit Rental Price, and Investment Demand for Farm Tractors in Canada. *Can. J. Agr. Econ.*, July 1987, *35*(2), pp. 373–85. [G: Canada]

Roski, Reinhold. Planungsrelevante Aggregatskosten. (With English summary.) *Z. Betriebswirtschaft*, May/June 1987, *57*(5/6), pp. 527–45.

Rust, John. Optimal Replacement of GMC Bus Engines: An Empirical Model of Harold Zurcher. *Econometrica*, September 1987, *55*(5), pp. 999–1033. [G: U.S.]

Rutledge, Gary L. and Stergioulas, Nikolaos. Plant and Equipment Expenditures by Business for Pollution Abatement, 1986 and 1987. *Surv. Curr. Bus.*, October 1987, *67*(10), pp. 23–26. [G: U.S.]

Seskin, Eugene P. and Sullivan, David F. Plant and Equipment Expenditures, the Four Quarters of 1987. *Surv. Curr. Bus.*, June 1987, *67*(6), pp. 19–22. [G: U.S.]

Seskin, Eugene P. and Sullivan, David F. Plant and Equipment Expenditures, the Four Quarters of 1987. *Surv. Curr. Bus.*, September 1987, *67*(9), pp. 20–25. [G: U.S.]

Seskin, Eugene P. and Sullivan, David F. Plant and Equipment Expenditures. *Surv. Curr. Bus.*, December 1987, *67*(12), pp. 16–19. [G: U.S.]

Seskin, Eugene P. and Sullivan, David F. Plant and Equipment Expenditures, First and Second Quarters and Second Half of 1987. *Surv. Curr. Bus.*, April 1987, *67*(4), pp. 28–32. [G: U.S.]

Summers, Lawrence H. Corporate Capital Budgeting Practices and the Effects of Tax Policies on Investment. *Feldstein, M., ed. (II)*, 1987, pp. 27–36. [G: U.S.]

Summers, Lawrence H. Investment Incentives and the Discounting of Depreciation Allowances. *Feldstein, M., ed. (I)*, 1987, pp. 295–304. [G: U.S.]

Sundararajan, V. The Debt–Equity Ratio of Firms and the Effectiveness of Interest Rate Policy: Analysis with a Dynamic Model of Saving, Investment, and Growth in Korea. *Int. Monet. Fund Staff Pap.*, June 1987, *34*(2), pp. 260–310. [G: S. Korea]

Sunley, Emil M. Notes on the Tax Treatment of Structures: Comment. *Feldstein, M., ed. (I)*, 1987, pp. 254–57. [G: U.S.]

Thompson, R. S. and Wright, M. Markets to Hierarchies and Back Again: The Implication of Management Buy-outs for Factory Supply. *J. Econ. Stud.*, 1987, *14*(3), pp. 5–22. [G: U.K.]

Zeira, Joseph. Investment as a Process of Search. *J. Polit. Econ.*, February 1987, *95*(1), pp. 204–10.

Zhang, Shaojie, et al. Investment: Initial Changes in the Mechanism and Preliminary Ideas about Reform. *Reynolds, B. L.*, 1987, pp. 108–29. [G: China]

530 MARKETING AND ADVERTISING

531 Marketing and Advertising

5310 Marketing and Advertising

Abraham, Magid M. and Lodish, Leonard M. Promoter: An Automated Promotion Evaluation System. *Marketing Sci.*, Spring 1987, *6*(2), pp. 101–23. [G: U.S.]

Abraham, Magid M. and Lodish, Leonard M.

Promoter: An Automated Promotion Evaluation System: Reply. *Marketing Sci.*, Spring 1987, *6*(2), pp. 152–53.   [G: U.S.]

Alba, Joseph W. and Hutchinson, J. Wesley. Dimensions of Consumer Expertise. *J. Cons. Res.*, March 1987, *13*(4), pp. 411–54.

Alba, Joseph W. and Marmorstein, Howard. The Effects of Frequency Knowledge on Consumer Decision Making. *J. Cons. Res.*, June 1987, *14*(1), pp. 14–25.

Albion, Mark S. and Farris, Paul W. Manufacturer Advertising and Retail Gross Margins. *Bloom, P. N., ed.*, 1987, pp. 107–35.   [G: U.S.]

Amine, Lyn S. Toward a Conceptualization of Export Trading Companies in World Markets. *Cavusgil, S. T., ed.*, 1987, pp. 199–238.   [G: Japan; S. Korea; Brazil; U.S.]

Arshad, Fatimah Mohd and Gibbons, E. T. Investigating the Market Structure for Fish in Malaysia. *Young, R. H. and MacCormac, C. W., eds.*, 1987, pp. 121–42.   [G: Malaysia]

Barwise, T. Patrick and Ehrenberg, Andrew S. C. The Liking and Viewing of Regular TV Series. *J. Cons. Res.*, June 1987, *14*(1), pp. 63–70.   [G: U.S.]

Barwise, T. Patrick; Marsh, Paul and Wensley, Robin. Strategic Investment Decisions. *Sheth, J. N., ed.*, 1987, pp. 1–57.

Beatty, Sharon E. and Smith, Scott M. External Search Effort: An Investigation across Several Product Categories. *J. Cons. Res.*, June 1987, *14*(1), pp. 83–95.   [G: U.S.]

Belch, George E.; Belch, Michael A. and Villarreal, Angelina. Effects of Advertising Communications: Review of Research. *Sheth, J. N., ed.*, 1987, pp. 59–117.   [G: U.S.]

Belk, Russell W. Material Values in the Comics: A Content Analysis of Comic Books Featuring Themes of Wealth. *J. Cons. Res.*, June 1987, *14*(1), pp. 26–42.

Benton, Raymond, Jr. The Practical Domain of Marketing: The Notion of a 'Free' Enterprise Market Economy as a Guise for Institutionalized Marketing Power. *Amer. J. Econ. Soc.*, October 1987, *46*(4), pp. 415–30.

Bettman, James R. and Sujan, Mita. Effects of Framing on Evaluation of Comparable and Noncomparable Alternatives by Expert and Novice Consumers. *J. Cons. Res.*, September 1987, *14*(2), pp. 141–54.

Bilkey, Warren J. Toward a Theory of the Export Marketing Mix. *Cavusgil, S. T., ed.*, 1987, pp. 157–76.

Blair, Edward and Burton, Scot. Cognitive Processes Used by Survey Respondents to Answer Behavioral Frequency Questions. *J. Cons. Res.*, September 1987, *14*(2), pp. 280–88.   [G: U.S.]

Blattberg, Robert C. Modeling the Effectiveness and Profitability of Trade Promotions: Reply. *Marketing Sci.*, Spring 1987, *6*(2), pp. 154–55.   [G: U.S.]

Blattberg, Robert C. and Levin, Alan. Modeling the Effectiveness and Profitability of Trade Promotions. *Marketing Sci.*, Spring 1987, *6*(2), pp. 124–46.   [G: U.S.]

Blitzer, Herbert L. The Channel Design Decision: A Model and an Application: Commentary. *Marketing Sci.*, Spring 1987, *6*(2), pp. 175–76.

Böcker, Franz and Gierl, Heribert. Determinanten der Diffusion neuer industrieller Produkte. (With English summary.) *Z. Betriebswirtshaft*, July 1987, *57*(7), pp. 684–98.   [G: W. Germany]

Boyer, Marcel and Laffont, Jean-Jacques. Une analyse économique de l'usage de faux prix réguliers en publicité. (An Economic Analysis of the Use of False Regular Prices in Advertising. With English summary.) *L'Actual. Econ.*, June-September 1987, *63*(2–3), pp. 153–68.

Brown, Jacqueline Johnson and Reingen, Peter H. Social Ties and Word-of-Mouth Referral Behavior. *J. Cons. Res.*, December 1987, *14*(3), pp. 350–62.

Burroughs, W. Jeffrey and Feinberg, Richard A. Using Response Latency to Assess Spokesperson Effectiveness. *J. Cons. Res.*, September 1987, *14*(2), pp. 295–99.

Calder, Bobby J. and Tybout, Alice M. What Consumer Research Is . . . *J. Cons. Res.*, June 1987, *14*(1), pp. 136–40.

Cardino, Angelita G. Market Needs for Grain Drying in the Philippines. *Young, R. H. and MacCormac, C. W., eds.*, 1987, pp. 93–100.   [G: Philippines]

Carpenter, Gregory S. Modeling Competitive Marketing Strategies: The Impact of Marketing-Mix Relationships and Industry Structure. *Marketing Sci.*, Spring 1987, *6*(2), pp. 208–21.   [G: U.S.; Canada]

Cohen, Joel B. and Basu, Kunal. Alternative Models of Categorization: Toward a Contingent Processing Framework. *J. Cons. Res.*, March 1987, *13*(4), pp. 455–72.

Collins, William H. and Collins, Carol B. More on Advertising and Monopoly Power: The Case of the Electric Utility Industry. *Atlantic Econ. J.*, March 1987, *15*(1), pp. 71–76.   [G: U.S.]

Cooper, Lee G. Do We Need Critical Relativism? Comments [On Method in Consumer Research: A Critical Relativist Perspective]. *J. Cons. Res.*, June 1987, *14*(1), pp. 126–27.

Coppett, John I. and Voorhees, Roy Dale. Telemarketing. *Woodside, A. G., ed.*, 1987, pp. 1–15.   [G: U.S.]

Corfman, Kim P. and Lehmann, Donald R. Models of Cooperative Group Decision-Making and Relative Influence: An Experimental Investigation of Family Purchase Decisions. *J. Cons. Res.*, June 1987, *14*(1), pp. 1–13.   [G: U.S.]

Craig, C. Samuel; Douglas, Susan P. and Reddy, Srinivas K. Market Structure, Performance and Strategy: A Comparison of U.S. and European Markets. *Cavusgil, S. T., ed.*, 1987, pp. 1–21.   [G: U.S.; W. Europe]

Cude, Brenda J. Estimating the Returns to Informed Decision-Making. *J. Cons. Aff.*, Summer 1987, *21*(1), pp. 86–95.   [G: U.S.]

Curtis, Ranjana and Gunetileke, K. G. Market Needs for Vegetable Drying in Sri Lanka.

Young, R. H. and MacCormac, C. W., eds., 1987, pp. 78–92. **[G: Sri Lanka]**

Dannhaeuser, Norbert. From the Metropolis into the Up-country: The Stockist System in India's Developing Mass Consumer Market. *J. Devel. Areas,* April 1987, *21*(3), pp. 259–76. **[G: India]**

DeSarbo, Wayne S., et al. A Friction Model for Describing and Forecasting Price Changes. *Marketing Sci.,* Fall 1987, *6*(4), pp. 299–319. **[G: U.S.]**

Dholakia, Nikhilesh and Sherry, John F., Jr. Marketing and Development: A Resynthesis of Knowledge. *Sheth, J. N., ed.,* 1987, pp. 119–43.

Dietrich, Donald G. A Panel-Data Based Method for Merging Joint Space and Market Response Function Estimation: Commentary. *Marketing Sci.,* Winter 1987, *6*(1), pp. 43.

Dion, Paul A. Sales Objections as a Negotiation Tactic. *J. Behav. Econ.,* Spring 1987, *16*(1), pp. 33–47.

Dodson, Joe A. and Brodsky, John B. A Simulation Comparison of Methods for New Product Location: Commentary. *Marketing Sci.,* Spring 1987, *6*(2), pp. 202–03.

Dolan, Robert J. Quantity Discounts: Managerial Issues and Research Opportunities. *Marketing Sci.,* Winter 1987, *6*(1), pp. 1–22.

Dolan, Robert J. Quantity Discounts: Managerial Issues and Research Opportunities: Reply. *Marketing Sci.,* Winter 1987, *6*(1), pp. 24.

Duffy, Martyn H. Advertising and the Inter-product Distribution of Demand: A Rotterdam Model Approach. *Europ. Econ. Rev.,* July 1987, *31*(5), pp. 1051–70. **[G: U.K.]**

Eckard, E. Woodrow, Jr. Advertising, Competition, and Market Share Instability. *J. Bus.,* October 1987, *60*(4), pp. 539–52. **[G: U.S.]**

Edell, Julie A. and Burke, Marian Chapman. The Power of Feelings in Understanding Advertising Effects. *J. Cons. Res.,* December 1987, *14*(3), pp. 421–33.

Farley, John U. and Reddy, Srinivas K. Nutrition, Family Planning and "Social Marketing" of a Contraceptive and a Weaning Food in Sri Lanka. *Cavusgil, S. T., ed.,* 1987, pp. 47–63. **[G: Sri Lanka]**

Fase, Martin M. G. Modelling Multivariate Stochastic Time Series for Prediction: Another Look at the Lydia Pinkham Data. *Heijmans, R. and Neudecker, H., eds.,* 1987, pp. 205–22. **[G: U.S.]**

Folkes, Valerie S. The Role of Causal Inferences in Postpurchase Processes. *Sheth, J. N. and Hirschman, E., eds.,* 1987, pp. 137–60.

Folkes, Valerie S.; Koletsky, Susan and Graham, John L. A Field Study of Causal Inferences and Consumer Reaction: The View from the Airport. *J. Cons. Res.,* March 1987, *13*(4), pp. 534–39. **[G: U.S.]**

Ford, Gary T. and Smith, Ruth Ann. Inferential Beliefs in Consumer Evaluations: An Assessment of Alternative Processing Strategies. *J. Cons. Res.,* December 1987, *14*(3), pp. 363–71.

Frey, John B. Quantity Discounts: Managerial Issues and Research Opportunities: Commentary. *Marketing Sci.,* Winter 1987, *6*(1), pp. 23.

Friedman, Margaret L. and Churchill, Gilbert A., Jr. Using Consumer Perceptions and a Contingency Approach to Improve Health Care Delivery. *J. Cons. Res.,* March 1987, *13*(4), pp. 492–510.

Friedman, Monroe. Survey Data on Owner-Reported Car Problems: How Useful to Prospective Purchasers of Used Cars? *J. Cons. Res.,* December 1987, *14*(3), pp. 434–39. **[G: U.S.]**

Gaeth, Gary J. and Heath, Timothy B. The Cognitive Processing of Misleading Advertising in Young and Old Adults: Assessment and Training. *J. Cons. Res.,* June 1987, *14*(1), pp. 43–54. **[G: U.S.]**

Gardner, Meryl Paula. Effects of Mood States on Consumer Information Processing. *Sheth, J. N. and Hirschman, E., eds.,* 1987, pp. 113–35.

Gaski, John F. The Inverse Power Source Power Relationship: An Empirical Note on a Marketing Anomaly. *Sheth, J. N., ed.,* 1987, pp. 145–61.

Gensch, Dennis H. A Response to Malhotra's Comment on Testing the Homogeneity of Segments. *Marketing Sci.,* Winter 1987, *6*(1), pp. 100.

Gensch, Dennis H. A Two-Stage Disaggregate Attribute Choice Model. *Marketing Sci.,* Summer 1987, *6*(3), pp. 223–39. **[G: U.S.]**

Gensch, Dennis H. and Javalgi, Rajshekhar G. The Influence of Involvement on Disaggregate Attribute Choice Models. *J. Cons. Res.,* June 1987, *14*(1), pp. 71–82. **[G: U.S.]**

Gerstner, Eitan and Hess, James D. Why Do Hot Dogs Come in Packs of 10 and Buns in 8s or 12s? A Demand-Side Investigation. *J. Bus.,* October 1987, *60*(4), pp. 491–517. **[G: U.S.]**

Ginter, James L.; Young, Murray A. and Dickson, Peter R. A Market Efficiency Study of Used Car Reliability and Prices. *J. Cons. Aff.,* Winter 1987, *21*(2), pp. 258–76. **[G: U.S.]**

Goldberg, Marvin E. and Gorn, Gerald J. Happy and Sad TV Programs: How They Affect Reactions to Commercials. *J. Cons. Res.,* December 1987, *14*(3), pp. 387–403. **[G: U.S.]**

Graham, John L. and Lin, Chi-Yuan. A Comparison of Marketing Negotiations in the Republic of China (Taiwan) and the United States. *Cavusgil, S. T., ed.,* 1987, pp. 23–46. **[G: Taiwan; U.S.]**

Green, Paul E. and Krieger, Abba M. A Simple Heuristic for Selecting "Good" Products in Conjoint Analysis. *Schultz, R. L., ed.,* 1987, pp. 131–53.

Green, Robert T. and Srivastava, Rajendra K. Classification of Export Markets Based on Product Mix. *Cavusgil, S. T., ed.,* 1987, pp. 139–55.

Grønhaug, Kjell and Graham, John L. International Marketing Research Revisited. *Cavusgil, S. T., ed.,* 1987, pp. 121–37.

Grönroos, Christian. Konkurrenskraft i service-samhället. (Competitiveness in the Service Economy. With English summary.) *Ekon. Samfundets Tidskr.*, 1987, *40*(3), pp. 137–44.

Gwynn, Ronald M. A Survey Method of Obtaining Sales Data from Business-to-Business Advertising Inquiry Handling Systems. *Woodside, A. G., ed.*, 1987, pp. 17–54. **[G: U.S.]**

Hall, Graham. When Does Market-Share Matter? *J. Econ. Stud.*, 1987, *14*(3), pp. 41–54.

Hampton, Gerald M. and Buske, Erwin. The Global Marketing Perspective. *Cavusgil, S. T., ed.*, 1987, pp. 259–77. **[G: Global]**

Hawkins, M. H. and Higginson, N. Marketing Research in the Canadian Food Retail and Processing Industry, 1950–1986. *Can. J. Agr. Econ.*, May 1987, *34*, pp. 1–26. **[G: Canada]**

Helgeson, James G. and Beatty, Sharon E. Price Expectation and Price Recall Error: An Empirical Study. *J. Cons. Res.*, December 1987, *14*(3), pp. 379–86.

Henderson, Pamela W. and Rust, Roland T. An Integrative Physiological Model of Advertising Response. *Sheth, J. N., ed.*, 1987, pp. 185–210.

Hess, James D. and Gerstner, Eitan. Loss Leader Pricing and Rain Check Policy. *Marketing Sci.*, Fall 1987, *6*(4), pp. 358–74. **[G: U.S.]**

Higgins, Richard S. and McChesney, Fred S. Truth and Consequences: The Federal Trade Commission's Ad Substantiation Program. *MacKay, R. J.; Miller, J. C., III and Yandle, B., eds.*, 1987, pp. 181–204. **[G: U.S.]**

Hofmann, Hans-Joachim. Die Werbewirkung auf den Zigarettenkonsum in der Bundesrepublik Deutschland. (The Effect of Advertising on Cigarette Consumption in the Federal Republic of Germany. With English summary.) *Jahr. Nationalökon. Statist.*, May 1987, *203*(3), pp. 257–73. **[G: W. Germany]**

Holbrook, Morris B. What Is Consumer Research? *J. Cons. Res.*, June 1987, *14*(1), pp. 128–32.

Holbrook, Morris B. and Batra, Rajeev. Assessing the Role of Emotions as Mediators of Consumer Responses to Advertising. *J. Cons. Res.*, December 1987, *14*(3), pp. 404–20. **[G: U.S.]**

Horsky, Dan and Swyngedouw, Patrick. Does It Pay to Change Your Company's Name? A Stock Market Perspective. *Marketing Sci.*, Fall 1987, *6*(4), pp. 320–35.

Jain, Subhash C. Perspectives on International Strategic Alliances. *Cavusgil, S. T., ed.*, 1987, pp. 103–20.

Johansson, Johny K. and Nebenzahl, Israel D. Country-of-Origin, Social Norms and Behavioral Intentions. *Cavusgil, S. T., ed.*, 1987, pp. 65–79.

John, George; Weiss, Allen M. and Weitz, Barton. An Organizational Coordination Model of Salesforce Compensation Plans: Theoretical Analysis and Empirical Test. *J. Law, Econ., Organ.*, Fall 1987, *3*(2), pp. 373–95. **[G: U.S.]**

Johnson, James C. and Schneider, Kenneth C. Marketing Managers Discuss the Strengths and Weaknesses of Logistics Personnel. *Logist. Transp. Rev.*, August 1987, *23*(3), pp. 325–33. **[G: U.S.]**

Johnson, Michael D. and Fornell, Claes. The Nature and Methodological Implications of the Cognitive Representation of Products. *J. Cons. Res.*, September 1987, *14*(2), pp. 214–28.

Johnson, Richard M. A Simulation Comparison of Methods for New Product Location: Commentary. *Marketing Sci.*, Spring 1987, *6*(2), pp. 204–05.

Johnston, Wesley J. and Spekman, Robert E. Industrial Buying Behavior: Where We Are and Where We Need to Go. *Sheth, J. N. and Hirschman, E., eds.*, 1987, pp. 83–111.

Kahn, Barbara; Moore, William L. and Glazer, Rashi. Experiments in Constrained Choice. *J. Cons. Res.*, June 1987, *14*(1), pp. 96–113.

Keller, Kevin Lane. Memory Factors in Advertising: The Effect of Advertising Retrieval Cues on Brand Evaluations. *J. Cons. Res.*, December 1987, *14*(3), pp. 316–33. **[G: U.S.]**

Keller, Kevin Lane and Staelin, Richard. Effects of Quality and Quantity of Information on Decision Effectiveness. *J. Cons. Res.*, September 1987, *14*(2), pp. 200–213.

Kernan, Jerome B. Chasing the Holy Grail: Reflections on "What Is Consumer Research?" *J. Cons. Res.*, June 1987, *14*(1), pp. 133–35.

Kinnucan, Henry W. Effect of Canadian Advertising on Milk Demand: The Case of the Buffalo, New York Market. *Can. J. Agr. Econ.*, March 1987, *35*(1), pp. 181–96. **[G: Canada; U.S.]**

Klein, Noreen M. and Bither, Stewart W. An Investigation of Utility-Directed Cutoff Selection. *J. Cons. Res.*, September 1987, *14*(2), pp. 240–56.

Koon, Richard E. The Channel Design Decision: A Model and an Application: Commentary. *Marketing Sci.*, Spring 1987, *6*(2), pp. 177–78.

Krishnamurthi, Lakshman and Rangaswamy, Arvind. The Equity Estimator for Marketing Research. *Marketing Sci.*, Fall 1987, *6*(4), pp. 336–57.

Kruger, Michael W. Steps toward Mastering Trade Promotions: Commentary [Promoter: An Automated Promotion Evaluation System] [Modeling the Effectiveness and Profitability of Trade Promotions]. *Marketing Sci.*, Spring 1987, *6*(2), pp. 147–49. **[G: U.S.]**

LaBarbera, Priscilla A. Consumer Behavior and Born Again Christianity. *Sheth, J. N. and Hirschman, E., eds.*, 1987, pp. 193–222. **[G: U.S.]**

Lattin, James M. A Model of Balanced Choice Behavior. *Marketing Sci.*, Winter 1987, *6*(1), pp. 48–65. **[G: U.S.]**

Lawton, Joseph A. Kodak's Technet Center. *Shetty, Y. K. and Buehler, V. M., eds.*, 1987, pp. 253–63. **[G: U.S.]**

Link, Jörg. Schwachpunkte der kumulativen Abweichungsanalyse in der Erfolgskontrolle. (With English summary.) *Z. Betriebswirtshaft*, August 1987, *57*(8), pp. 780–92.

Livingstone, James M. The Marketing Concept in China—A Qualified Acceptance. *Warner, M., ed.*, 1987, pp. 86–98. **[G: China]**

MacInnis, Deborah J. and Price, Linda L. The Role of Imagery in Information Processing: Review and Extensions. *J. Cons. Res.*, March 1987, *13*(4), pp. 473–91.

Macklin, M. Carole. Preschoolers' Understanding of the Informational Function of Television Advertising. *J. Cons. Res.*, September 1987, *14*(2), pp. 229–39. **[G: U.S.]**

Madsen, Tage Koed. Empirical Export Performance Studies: A Review of Conceptualizations and Findings. *Cavusgil, S. T., ed.*, 1987, pp. 177–98.

Malhotra, Naresh K. Testing the Homogeneity of Segments for Estimating Disaggregate Choice Models: Comment. *Marketing Sci.*, Winter 1987, *6*(1), pp. 98–99.

Manilay, Alessandro A. Market Research for Grain Postharvest Systems. *Young, R. H. and MacCormac, C. W., eds.*, 1987, pp. 31–37.

Martin, S. K. and Zwart, A. C. Marketing Agencies and the Economics of Market Segmentation. *Australian J. Agr. Econ.*, December 1987, *31*(3), pp. 242–55. **[G: New Zealand]**

Mentzer, John T. and Hunt, Kenneth A. The Use of Power: A Process Model of Marketing Channel Behavior. *Sheth, J. N., ed.*, 1987, pp. 211–36.

Meyer, Robert J. The Learning of Multiattribute Judgment Policies. *J. Cons. Res.*, September 1987, *14*(2), pp. 155–73. **[G: U.S.]**

Middleton, Elliott. The Preference for Variety. *J. Behav. Econ.*, Spring 1987, *16*(1), pp. 49–54.

Moleeratanond, Wiboonkiet. Product Information to Improve Small-Scale Food Manufacture in Thailand. *Young, R. H. and MacCormac, C. W., eds.*, 1987, pp. 101–10. **[G: Thailand]**

Mongkolsmai, Dow. Supplementary Foods in Rural Thailand. *Young, R. H. and MacCormac, C. W., eds.*, 1987, pp. 57–68. **[G: Thailand]**

Moore, William L. and Winer, Russell S. A Panel-Data Based Method for Merging Joint Space and Market Response Function Estimation. *Marketing Sci.*, Winter 1987, *6*(1), pp. 25–42. **[G: U.S.]**

Moore, William L. and Winer, Russell S. A Panel-Data Based Method for Merging Joint Space and Market Response Function Estimation: Reply. *Marketing Sci.*, Winter 1987, *6*(1), pp. 46–47.

Moorthy, K. Sridhar. Managing Channel Profits: Comment. *Marketing Sci.*, Fall 1987, *6*(4), pp. 375–79.

Morello, G. The Consumer in World Trade. *Visser, H. and Schoor, E., eds.*, 1987, pp. 303–13. **[G: Global]**

Narula, Subhash C.; Lentnek, Barry and Harwitz, Mitchell. A Contextual Analysis of the Journey-to-Shop with Price Uncertainty. *J. Reg. Sci.*, August 1987, *27*(3), pp. 403–18.

Newman, Bruce I. and Sheth, Jagdish N. A Review of Political Marketing. *Sheth, J. N., ed.*, 1987, pp. 237–66. **[G: U.S.]**

Nguyen, Dung. Advertising, Random Sales Response, and Brand Competition: Some Theoretical and Econometric Implications. *J. Bus.*, April 1987, *60*(2), pp. 259–79. **[G: U.S.]**

Norton, Seth W. The Coase Theorem and Suboptimization in Marketing Channels. *Marketing Sci.*, Summer 1987, *6*(3), pp. 268–85.

Novak, Thomas P. and Stangor, Charles. Testing Competitive Market Structures: An Application of Weighted Least Squares Methodology to Brand Switching Data. *Marketing Sci.*, Winter 1987, *6*(1), pp. 82–97.

Ogawa, Kohsuke. An Approach to Simultaneous Estimation and Segmentation in Conjoint Analysis. *Marketing Sci.*, Winter 1987, *6*(1), pp. 66–81.

Outreville, J. François and Zins, Michel. Job-Related Responses of Insurance Agents: More Evidence. *J. Risk Ins.*, December 1987, *54*(4), pp. 800–803. **[G: U.S.]**

Pableo, Relli C. and Ignacio, Manuel C. Investigating the Marketing System for Groundnuts in the Philippines. *Young, R. H. and MacCormac, C. W., eds.*, 1987, pp. 111–20. **[G: Philippines]**

Parker, Richard and Funkhouser, G. Ray. The Consumer as a Performer of Marketing Functions. *Sheth, J. N. and Hirschman, E., eds.*, 1987, pp. 161–91.

Petroshius, Susan M. and Monroe, Kent B. Effect of Product-Line Pricing Characteristics on Product Evaluations. *J. Cons. Res.*, March 1987, *13*(4), pp. 511–19.

Piha, Kalevi. Marketing Audit as a Strategic Tool for Improving a Company's Decision Making. *Liiketaloudellinen Aikak.*, April 1987, *36*(4), pp. 366–75.

Pitelis, Christos N. The Causal Relationship between Advertising, Retained Profits and Aggregate Consumption: A Note. *Greek Econ. Rev.*, 1987, *9*(2), pp. 239–47. **[G: U.K.]**

Png, Ivan Paak Liang and Hirshleifer, D. Price Discrimination through Offers to Match Price. *J. Bus.*, July 1987, *60*(3), pp. 365–83.

Price, Linda L.; Feick, Lawrence F. and Higie, Robin A. Information Sensitive Consumers and Market Information. *J. Cons. Aff.*, Winter 1987, *21*(2), pp. 328–41.

Pushpamma, P. Supplementary Foods in Rural India. *Young, R. H. and MacCormac, C. W., eds.*, 1987, pp. 69–77. **[G: India]**

Puto, Christopher P. The Framing of Buying Decisions. *J. Cons. Res.*, December 1987, *14*(3), pp. 301–15.

Qualls, William J. Household Decision Behavior: The Impact of Husbands' and Wives' Sex Role Orientation. *J. Cons. Res.*, September 1987, *14*(2), pp. 264–79. **[G: U.S.]**

Rangan, V. Kasturi. The Channel Design Decision: A Model and an Application: Reply. *Marketing Sci.*, Spring 1987, *6*(2), pp. 179–81.

Rangan, V. Kasturi. The Channel Design Decision: A Model and an Application. *Marketing Sci.*, Spring 1987, *6*(2), pp. 156–74.

Ratneshwar, Srinivasan; Shocker, Allan D. and Stewart, David W. Toward Understanding the

Attraction Effect: The Implications of Product Stimulus Meaningfulness and Familiarity. *J. Cons. Res.*, March 1987, *13*(4), pp. 520–33. [G: U.S.]

Reichmann, Thomas and Kleinschnittger, Ulrich. Die Controllingfunktion in der Unternehmenspraxis. Empirische Untersuchung zur Funktionsbestimmung und -abgrenzung. (With English summary.) *Z. Betriebswirtshaft*, November 1987, *57*(11), pp. 1090–1120. [G: W. Germany]

Reilly, Michael D. and Wallendorf, Melanie. A Comparison of Group Differences in Food Consumption Using Household Refuse. *J. Cons. Res.*, September 1987, *14*(2), pp. 289–94. [G: U.S.]

Ries, Paul N. A Panel-Data Based Method for Merging Joint Space and Market Response Function Estimation: Commentary. *Marketing Sci.*, Winter 1987, *6*(1), pp. 44–45.

Robertson, Thomas S. and Gatignon, Hubert. The Diffusion of High Technology Innovations: A Marketing Perspective. *Pennings, J. M. and Buitendam, A., eds.*, 1987, pp. 179–96.

Rock, Steven M. and Hall, W. Clayton. Advertising and Monopoly Power: The Case of the Electric Utility Industry—Comment. *Atlantic Econ. J.*, March 1987, *15*(1), pp. 67–70. [G: U.S.]

Rogerson, William P. The Dissipation of Profits by Brand Name Investment and Entry when Price Guarantees Quality. *J. Polit. Econ.*, August 1987, *95*(4), pp. 797–809.

Rook, Dennis W. The Buying Impulse. *J. Cons. Res.*, September 1987, *14*(2), pp. 189–99.

Rosen, Dennis L. and Olshavsky, Richard W. A Protocol Analysis of Brand Choice Strategies Involving Recommendations. *J. Cons. Res.*, December 1987, *14*(3), pp. 440–44. [G: U.S.]

Rosenbaum, David I. Advertising and Entry: The Case of Light Beer. *Wills, R. L.; Caswell, J. A. and Culbertson, J. D., eds.*, 1987, pp. 223–34. [G: U.S.]

Roy, Raghu. Marketing Food and Technologies in Rural India. *Young, R. H. and MacCormac, C. W., eds.*, 1987, pp. 47–56. [G: India]

Rutman, Max and Bustamante, Waldo. Market Research for Nutrition Interventions. *Young, R. H. and MacCormac, C. W., eds.*, 1987, pp. 22–30. [G: LDCs]

Saghafi, Massoud M. Market Share Stability and Marketing Policy: An Axiomatic Approach. *Sheth, J. N., ed.*, 1987, pp. 267–84.

Samli, A. Coskun. An Alternative International Marketing Strategy: The "J" Model. *Cavusgil, S. T., ed.*, 1987, pp. 239–57.

Schroeter, John R.; Smith, Scott L. and Cox, Steven R. Advertising and Competition in Routine Legal Service Markets: An Empirical Investigation. *J. Ind. Econ.*, September 1987, *36*(1), pp. 49–60. [G: U.S.]

Schurr, Paul H. Evolutionary Approaches to Effective Selling. *Woodside, A. G., ed.*, 1987, pp. 55–80. [G: U.S.]

Seringhaus, F. H. Rolf. Do Experienced Export-ers Have Market Entry Problems? *Liiketaloudellinen Aikak.*, April 1987, *36*(4), pp. 376–88. [G: Canada]

Sexton, Richard J.; Johnson, Nancy Brown and Konakayama, Akira. Consumer Response to Continuous-Display Electricity-Use Monitors in a Time-of-Use Pricing Experiment. *J. Cons. Res.*, June 1987, *14*(1), pp. 55–62.

Sherry, John F., Jr. Heresy and the Useful Miracle: Rethinking Anthropology's Contributions to Marketing. *Sheth, J. N., ed.*, 1987, pp. 285–306.

Sherry, John F., Jr. and Camargo, Eduardo G. "May Your Life Be Marvelous:" English Language Labelling and the Semiotics of Japanese Promotion. *J. Cons. Res.*, September 1987, *14*(2), pp. 174–88. [G: Japan]

Steenkamp, Jan-Benedict E. M. Conjoint Measurement in Ham Quality Evaluation. *J. Agr. Econ.*, September 1987, *38*(3), pp. 473–80. [G: Netherlands]

Sternthal, Brian; Tybout, Alice M. and Calder, Bobby J. Confirmatory versus Comparative Approaches to Judging Theory Tests. *J. Cons. Res.*, June 1987, *14*(1), pp. 114–25.

Struse, Rudolph W., III. Approaches to Promotion Evaluation: A Practitioner's Viewpoint: Commentary [Promoter: An Automated Promotion Evaluation System] [Modeling the Effectiveness and Profitability of Trade Promotions]. *Marketing Sci.*, Spring 1987, *6*(2), pp. 150–51. [G: U.S.]

Stuart, Elnora W.; Shimp, Terence A. and Engle, Randall W. Classical Conditioning of Consumer Attitudes: Four Experiments in an Advertising Context. *J. Cons. Res.*, December 1987, *14*(3), pp. 334–49.

Sudharshan, D.; May, Jerrold H. and Shocker, Allan D. A Simulation Comparison of Methods for New Product Location. *Marketing Sci.*, Spring 1987, *6*(2), pp. 182–201.

Sudharshan, D.; May, Jerrold H. and Shocker, Allan D. A Simulation Comparison of Methods for New Product Location: Reply. *Marketing Sci.*, Spring 1987, *6*(2), pp. 206–07.

Sujan, Mita and Dekleva, Christine. Product Categorization and Inference Making: Some Implications for Comparative Advertising. *J. Cons. Res.*, December 1987, *14*(3), pp. 372–78.

Swan, John E. and Trawick, I. Fredrick, Jr. Building Customer Trust in the Industrial Salesperson: Process and Outcomes. *Woodside, A. G., ed.*, 1987, pp. 81–113. [G: U.S.]

Tan, Chin Tiong and Farley, John U. The Impact of Cultural Patterns on Cognition and Intention in Singapore. *J. Cons. Res.*, March 1987, *13*(4), pp. 540–44. [G: Singapore]

Tellis, Gerard J. and Wernerfelt, Birger. Competitive Price and Quality under Asymmetric Information. *Marketing Sci.*, Summer 1987, *6*(3), pp. 240–53. [G: U.S.]

Uri, Noel D. A Re-examination of the Advertising and Industrial Concentration Relationship. *Appl. Econ.*, April 1987, *19*(4), pp. 427–35. [G: U.S.]

Vanhonacker, Wilfried R. and Day, Diana. Cross-sectional Estimation in Marketing: Direct versus Reverse Regression. *Marketing Sci.*, Summer 1987, 6(3), pp. 254–67. [G: U.S.]

Weber, M.; Eisenführ, F. and von Winterfeldt, Detlof. Bias in Assessment of Attribute Weights. *Sawaragi, Y.; Inoue, K. and Nakayama, H., eds.*, 1987, pp. 309–18.

West, Michael J. Commercial Intelligence: A Priceless Commodity. *Dedijer, S. and Jéquier, N., eds.*, 1987, pp. 62–78. [G: LDCs]

West, Sandra J. and Earle, Mary D. Market Research in Development Projects. *Young, R. H. and MacCormac, C. W., eds.*, 1987, pp. 14–21. [G: LDCs]

Wilde, Louis L. Consumer Behavior under Imperfect Information: A Review of Psychological and Marketing Research as It Relates to Economic Theory. *Green, L. and Kagel, J. H., eds.*, 1987, pp. 219–48.

Wills, Robert L. Do Advertising-Induced Price Differences among Brands Explain Profit Differences among Products? *Wills, R. L.; Caswell, J. A. and Culbertson, J. D., eds.*, 1987, pp. 361–77.

Woodside, Arch G. Measuring Customer Awareness and Share-of-Requirements Awarded to Competing Industrial Distributors. *Woodside, A. G., ed.*, 1987, pp. 141–63. [G: U.S.]

Yammarino, Francis J. and Dubinsky, Alan J. On Job Satisfaction: It's the Relationships That Count! [Job Related Responses of Insurance Agents: A Multi-firm Investigation]. *J. Risk Ins.*, December 1987, 54(4), pp. 804–09. [G: U.S.]

Yoo, Pil Hwa; Dolan, Robert J. and Rangan, V. Kasturi. Dynamic Pricing Strategy for New Consumer Durables. *Z. Betriebswirtshaft*, October 1987, 57(10), pp. 1024–43.

Young, Gary G. Exhibit Marketing. *Woodside, A. G., ed.*, 1987, pp. 165–217.

Young, R. H. and MacCormac, C. W. Market Research and Food Technology in Developing Countries. *Young, R. H. and MacCormac, C. W., eds.*, 1987, pp. 3–13. [G: LDCs]

Zibrun, S. Michael. Converting Inquiries to Selling Opportunities through Telemarketing. *Woodside, A. G., ed.*, 1987, pp. 219–40. [G: U.S.]

540 ACCOUNTING

541 Accounting

5410 Accounting

Abdolmohammadi, Mohammad and Wright, Arnold. An Examination of the Effects of Experience and Task Complexity on Audit Judgments. *Accounting Rev.*, January 1987, 62(1), pp. 1–13. [G: U.S.]

Amershi, Amin H. and Sunder, Shyam. Failure of Stock Prices to Discipline Managers in a Rational Expectations Economy. *J. Acc. Res.*, Autumn 1987, 25(2), pp. 177–95.

Andel, Norbert. Determination of Company Profits. *Cnossen, S., ed.*, 1987, pp. 287–304. [G: EEC]

Antonio, James F. Setting Governmental Accounting and Financial Reporting Standards in a Multi-constituency Environment. *Chan, J. L., ed., Pt. B*, 1987, pp. 137–43. [G: U.S.]

Ashton, Robert H.; Willingham, John J. and Elliott, Robert K. An Empirical Analysis of Audit Delay. *J. Acc. Res.*, Autumn 1987, 25(2), pp. 275–92. [G: U.S.]

Atchison, Michael D. and Sanborn, Robert. Current Classification Criteria of New Financial Instruments. *Schwartz, B. N., ed.*, 1987, pp. 99–109. [G: U.S.]

Aukes, Robert. Double Counting Agricultural Income. *Can. J. Agr. Econ.*, July 1987, 35(2), pp. 463–79. [G: Canada]

Baber, William R.; Brooks, Eugene H. and Ricks, William E. An Empirical Investigation of the Market for Audit Services in the Public Sector. *J. Acc. Res.*, Autumn 1987, 25(2), pp. 293–305. [G: U.S.]

Baginski, Stephen P. Intraindustry Information Transfers Associated with Management Forecasts of Earnings. *J. Acc. Res.*, Autumn 1987, 25(2), pp. 196–216. [G: U.S.]

Baiman, Stanley; Evans, John H., III and Noel, James. Optimal Contracts with a Utility-Maximizing Auditor. *J. Acc. Res.*, Autumn 1987, 25(2), pp. 217–44.

Baker, George P. Discussion of an Analysis of the Use of Accounting and Market Measures of Performance in Executive Compensation Contracts. *J. Acc. Res.*, Supplement 1987, 25, pp. 126–29.

Balachandran, Bala V. and Prince, Thomas R. An Information System for Administering Welfare Programs. *Chan, J. L., ed., Pt. A*, 1987, pp. 37–66. [G: U.S.]

Balachandran, Bala V. and Ramakrishnan, Ram T. S. A Theory of Audit Partnerships: Audit Firm Size and Fees. *J. Acc. Res.*, Spring 1987, 25(1), pp. 111–26.

Ballwieser, Wolfgang. Auditing in an Agency Setting. *Bamberg, G. and Spremann, K., eds.*, 1987, pp. 327–46.

Banker, Rajiv D. and Patton, James M. Analytical Agency Theory and Municipal Accounting: An Introduction and an Application. *Chan, J. L., ed., Pt. B*, 1987, pp. 29–50.

Beaver, William H. The Properties of Sequential Regressions with Multiple Explanatory Variables. *Accounting Rev.*, January 1987, 62(1), pp. 137–44.

Beaver, William H.; Lambert, Richard A. and Ryan, Stephen G. The Information Content of Security Prices: A Second Look. *J. Acc. Econ.*, July 1987, 9(2), pp. 139–57. [G: U.S.]

Benston, George J. The Validity of Studies with Line of Business Data: Reply [The Validity of Profits-Structure Studies with Particular Reference to the FTC's Line of Business Data]. *Amer. Econ. Rev.*, March 1987, 77(1), pp. 218–23. [G: U.S.]

Bernard, Victor L. Cross-Sectional Dependence

and Problems in Inference in Market-Based Accounting Research. *J. Acc. Res.*, Spring 1987, 25(1), pp. 1–48. [G: U.S.]

Bernard, Victor L. and Ruland, Robert G. The Incremental Information Content of Historical Cost and Current Cost Income Numbers: Time-Series Analyses for 1962–1980. *Accounting Rev.*, October 1987, 62(4), pp. 707–22. [G: U.S.]

Berry, Leonard Eugene; Harwood, Gordon B. and Katz, Joseph L. Performance of Auditing Procedures by Governmental Auditors: Some Preliminary Evidence. *Accounting Rev.*, January 1987, 62(1), pp. 14–28. [G: U.S.]

Berry, Maureen. Financial Accountability in West German Government. *Most, Kenneth S., ed.*, 1987, pp. 39–84. [G: W. Germany]

Blocher, Edward. A General Bayesian Model of the Misstatement in an Accounting Population. *Schultz, R. L., ed.*, 1987, pp. 23–60.

Borthick, A. Faye. Artificial Intelligence in Auditing: Assumptions and Preliminary Development. *Schwartz, B. N., ed.*, 1987, pp. 179–204. [G: U.S.]

Bowen, Robert M.; Burgstahler, David and Daley, Lane A. The Incremental Information Content of Accrual versus Cash Flows. *Accounting Rev.*, October 1987, 62(4), pp. 723–47. [G: U.S.]

Bowsher, Charles A. Restructuring the Federal Budgeting and Accounting System. *Thai, K. V., ed.*, 1987, 1985, pp. 223–43. [G: U.S.]

Brinberg, David and Morris, Louis A. Advertising Prescription Drugs to Consumers. *Bloom, P. N., ed.*, 1987, pp. 1–40. [G: U.S.]

Brockett, Patrick L., et al. Cost–Volume–Utility Analysis with Partial Stochastic Information. *Quart. Rev. Econ. Bus.*, Autumn 1987, 27(3), pp. 70–90.

Brown, Lawrence D.; Richardson, Gordon D. and Schwager, Steven J. An Information Interpretation of Financial Analyst Superiority in Forecasting Earnings. *J. Acc. Res.*, Spring 1987, 25(1), pp. 49–67. [G: U.S.]

Brown, Lawrence D., et al. An Evaluation of Alternative Proxies for the Market's Assessment of Unexpected Earnings. *J. Acc. Econ.*, July 1987, 9(2), pp. 159–93. [G: U.S.]

Brown, Richard E. and Sprohge, Hans-Dieter. Governmental Managerial Accounting: What and Where Is It? *Public Budg. Finance*, Autumn 1987, 7(3), pp. 35–46.

Burris, Roland W. Improving Governmental Financial Reporting and Management: The Illinois Experience and a Proposal for the Federal Government. *Chan, J. L., ed., Pt. B*, 1987, pp. 145–63. [G: U.S.]

Chow, Chee W. and Wong-Boren, Adrian. Voluntary Financial Disclosure by Mexican Corporations. *Accounting Rev.*, July 1987, 62(3), pp. 533–41. [G: Mexico]

Christie, Andrew A. On Cross-Sectional Analysis in Accounting Research. *J. Acc. Econ.*, December 1987, 9(3), pp. 231–58. [G: U.S.]

Collins, Daniel W.; Kothari, S. P. and Rayburn, Judy Dawson. Firm Size and the Information Content of Prices with Respect to Earnings. *J. Acc. Econ.*, July 1987, 9(2), pp. 111–38. [G: U.S.]

Collins, Frank; Munter, Paul and Finn, Don W. The Budgeting Games People Play. *Accounting Rev.*, January 1987, 62(1), pp. 29–49.

Costley, Carolyn L. and Brucks, Merrie. The Roles of Product Knowledge and Age on Children's Responses to Deceptive Advertising. *Bloom, P. N., ed.*, 1987, pp. 41–63. [G: U.S.]

Courtenay, Stephen M. and Millar, James A. Accounting Earnings and Convertible Calls. *Tremblay, R., ed.*, 1987, pp. 579–93.

Cready, William M. and Shank, John K. Understanding Accounting Changes in an Efficient Market—A Comment, Replication, and Re-interpretation. *Accounting Rev.*, July 1987, 62(3), pp. 589–96. [G: U.S.]

Crook, J. N. and Allen, D. E. The Characteristics of Technically Orientated Firms: Evidence from the Unlisted Securities Market. *Managerial Dec. Econ.*, December 1987, 8(4), pp. 271–84. [G: U.K.]

Dellmann, Klaus. Kosten- oder Erfolgsanalyse als Basis der Wirtschaftlichkietskontrolle. (With English summary.) *Z. Betriebswirtshaft*, April 1987, 57(4), pp. 367–83.

Dirsmith, Mark and Ketz, J. Edward. A Fifty-Cent Test: An Approach to Teaching Integrity. *Schwartz, B. N., ed.*, 1987, pp. 129–41. [G: U.S.]

Donleavy, Gabriel D. Aspects of Hungarian Accounting. *Most, Kenneth S., ed.*, 1987, pp. 85–109. [G: Hungary]

Dopuch, Nicholas; Holthausen, Robert W. and Leftwich, Richard W. Predicting Audit Qualifications with Financial and Market Variables. *Accounting Rev.*, July 1987, 62(3), pp. 431–54. [G: U.S.]

Doupnik, Timothy S. The Brazilian System of Monetary Correction. *Most, Kenneth S., ed.*, 1987, pp. 111–35. [G: Brazil]

Elgers, Pieter; Callahan, Carolyn and Strock, Elizabeth. The Effect of Earnings Yields upon the Association between Unexpected Earnings and Security Returns: A Re-examination. *Accounting Rev.*, October 1987, 62(4), pp. 763–73. [G: U.S.]

Evans, John H., III and Patton, James M. Signaling and Monitoring in Public-Sector Accounting. *J. Acc. Res.*, Supplement 1987, 25, pp. 130–58.

Ewert, Ralf. The Financial Theory of Agency as a Tool for an Analysis of Problems in External Accounting. *Bamberg, G. and Spremann, K., eds.*, 1987, pp. 281–309.

Fekrat, M. Ali. Accounting for Forward Exchange Contracts: Theory and Implications for Practice. *Most, Kenneth S., ed.*, 1987, pp. 249–62. [G: U.S.]

Feroz, Ehsan H. Financial Accounting Standards Setting: A Social Science Perspective. *Schwartz, B. N., ed.*, 1987, pp. 3–14. [G: U.S.]

Filios, Vassilios P. The French Contribution to

the Theory of Accounting. *Most, Kenneth S., ed.*, 1987, pp. 137–51.   [G: France; EEC]

Finnerty, Joseph E. and Nunn, Kenneth P., Jr. Valuation and the Impact of Corporate Firm, Taxes, and Leverage on Multinational Net Income under FASB #8 and FASB #52. *Lee, C. F., ed.*, 1987, pp. 87–102.   [G: U.S.]

Fountain, James R. Governmental Accounting: Where Is It Heading. *Public Budg. Finance*, Winter 1987, 7(4), pp. 95–103.   [G: U.S.]

Francis, Jere R. and Simon, Daniel T. A Test of Audit Pricing in the Small-Client Segment of the U.S. Audit Market. *Accounting Rev.*, January 1987, 62(1), pp. 145–57.   [G: U.S.]

Freeman, Robert N. The Association between Accounting Earnings and Security Returns for Large and Small Firms. *J. Acc. Econ.*, July 1987, 9(2), pp. 195–228.   [G: U.S.]

Fricke, Friedrich. Asymmetric Information between Investors and Managers under the New German Accounting Legislation. *Bamberg, G. and Spremann, K., eds.*, 1987, pp. 311–26.   [G: W. Germany]

Gaumnitz, Bruce R. and Thompson, Joel E. Establishing the Common Stock Equivalence of Convertible Bonds. *Accounting Rev.*, July 1987, 62(3), pp. 601–22.

Gentry, James A. and Lee, Cheng F. Financial Forecasting and the X-11 Model: Preliminary Evidence. *Lee, C. F., ed.*, 1987, pp. 27–49.   [G: U.S.]

Goldin, Harrison J. Improving New York City's Financial Reporting: A Ten Year Retrospective. *Chan, J. L., ed., Pt. B*, 1987, pp. 165–74.   [G: U.S.]

Gordon, Irene M. and Mathews, M. R. The Attitudes of the Members of Three Canadian Accounting Organizations toward Continuing Education. *Most, Kenneth S., ed.*, 1987, pp. 357–82.   [G: Canada]

Green, Cynthia B. The Use and Usefulness of Governmental Financial Reports: The Perspective of Citizen–Taxpayer Organizations. *Chan, J. L., ed., Pt. B*, 1987, pp. 189–213.   [G: U.S.]

Grimlund, Richard A. and Felix, William L., Jr. Simulation Evidence and Analysis of Alternative Methods of Evaluating Dollar-Unit Samples. *Accounting Rev.*, July 1987, 62(3), pp. 455–79.

Halperin, Robert M. and Lanen, William N. The Effects of the *Thor Power Tool* Decision on the LIFO/FIFO Choice. *Accounting Rev.*, April 1987, 62(2), pp. 378–84.

Halperin, Robert M. and Srinidhi, Bin. The Effects of the U.S. Income Tax Regulations' Transfer Pricing Rules on Allocative Efficiency. *Accounting Rev.*, October 1987, 62(4), pp. 686–706.   [G: U.S.]

Haqiqi, Abdul Wassay and Pomeranz, Felix. Accounting Needs of Islamic Banking. *Most, Kenneth S., ed.*, 1987, pp. 153–68.   [G: Arab Countries]

Harper, Robert M., Jr.; Mister, William G. and Strawser, Jerry R. The Impact of New Pension Disclosure Rules on Perceptions of Debt. *J.*

Acc. Res., Autumn 1987, 25(2), pp. 327–30.

Harris, Trevor S. Discussion of Signaling and Monitoring in Public-Sector Accounting. *J. Acc. Res.*, Supplement 1987, 25, pp. 159–64.

Harris, Trevor S. and Ohlson, James A. Accounting Disclosures and the Market's Valuation of Oil and Gas Properties. *Accounting Rev.*, October 1987, 62(4), pp. 651–70.   [G: U.S.]

Haskins, Mark E. Client Control Environments: An Examination of Auditors' Perceptions. *Accounting Rev.*, July 1987, 62(3), pp. 542–63.   [G: U.S.]

Healy, Paul M.; Kang, Sok-Hyon and Palepu, Krishna G. The Effect of Accounting Procedure Changes on CEOs' Cash Salary and Bonus Compensation. *J. Acc. Econ.*, April 1987, 9(1), pp. 7–34.   [G: U.S.]

Heck, J. Louis and Huang, Jiunn C. Peer Assessment versus Citation Analysis of Contributions to the Accounting Literature. *Schwartz, B. N., ed.*, 1987, pp. 153–62.   [G: U.S.]

Herhold, Susan; Parry, Robert W., Jr. and Patton, James M. Behavioral Research in Municipal Accounting. *Chan, J. L., ed., Pt. B*, 1987, pp. 71–109.

Hirst, Mark K. The Effects of Setting Budget Goals and Task Uncertainty on Performance: A Theoretical Analysis. *Accounting Rev.*, October 1987, 62(4), pp. 774–84.

Hite, Peggy A. Qualifications for a Tax Specialist: Some Tax Partners' Views. *Jones, S. M., ed.*, 1987, pp. 183–98.   [G: U.S.]

Holder, William W. Management Policies in Local Government Finance: Financial Accounting, Reporting, and Auditing. *Aronson, J. R. and Schwartz, E., eds.*, 1987, pp. 158–75.   [G: U.S.]

Hoyt, Ronald E. and Legault, Michel. A Discriminant Analysis of Soviet Decision-Making Behavior in Selecting United States Suppliers of Goods and Services. *Most, Kenneth S., ed.*, 1987, pp. 263–85.   [G: U.S.S.R.; U.S.]

Hull, Rita P.; Everett, John O. and Hall, Steven D. Accounting Education: Practitioner's Views on the Value of a Five-Year Program. *Schwartz, B. N., ed.*, 1987, pp. 163–76.   [G: U.S.]

Ingram, Robert W. and Petersen, Russell J. An Evaluation of AICPA Tests for Predicting the Performance of Accounting Majors. *Accounting Rev.*, January 1987, 62(1), pp. 215–23.   [G: U.S.]

Ingram, Robert W.; Raman, Krishnamurthy K. and Wilson, Earl R. Governmental Capital Markets Research in Accounting: A Review. *Chan, J. L., ed., Pt. B*, 1987, pp. 111–126.

Ives, Martin H. GASB Research on User Needs and Objectives of Governmental Financial Reporting: A Summary and Analysis. *Chan, J. L., ed., Pt. B*, 1987, pp. 227–35.   [G: U.S.]

Jacobs, Fredric H. and Marshall, Ronald M. A Reciprocal Service Cost Approximation. *Accounting Rev.*, January 1987, 62(1), pp. 67–78.

Karlinsky, Stewart S.; Manegold, James G. and Cherry, Alan A. Accounting for Deferred Income Taxes: Preparers' Responses to Policy Proposals. *Schwartz, B. N., ed.*, 1987, pp. 15–38. **[G: U.S.]**

Karvelis, Leon J., Jr. The Use and Usefulness of Governmental Financial Reports: The Perspective of Municipal Investors. *Chan, J. L., ed., Pt. B*, 1987, pp. 175–88. **[G: U.S.]**

Kelley, Tim and Margheim, Loren. The Effect of Audit Billing Arrangement on Underreporting of Time and Audit Quality Reduction Acts. *Schwartz, B. N., ed.*, 1987, pp. 221–33. **[G: U.S.]**

Kettunen, Pertti. Kirjanpidon selittämisestä. (A New Approach to Accounting Theory. With English summary.) *Liiketaloudellinen Aikak.*, 1987, 36(1), pp. 37–67. **[G: Finland]**

Kirby, Alison J. Discussion of Centralization versus Delegation and the Value of Communication. *J. Acc. Res.*, Supplement 1987, 25, pp. 19–21.

Knapp, Michael C. An Empirical Study of Audit Committee Support for Auditors Involved in Technical Disputes with Client Management. *Accounting Rev.*, July 1987, 62(3), pp. 578–88. **[G: U.S.]**

Knechel, W. Robert and Snowball, Doug. Accounting Internships and Subsequent Academic Performance: An Empirical Study. *Accounting Rev.*, October 1987, 62(4), pp. 799–807. **[G: U.S.]**

Lambert, Richard A. and Larcker, David F. An Analysis of the Use of Accounting and Market Measures of Performance in Executive Compensation Contracts. *J. Acc. Res.*, Supplement 1987, 25, pp. 85–125. **[G: U.S.]**

Lanen, William N. and Verrecchia, Robert E. Operating Decisions and the Disclosure of Management Accounting Information. *J. Acc. Res.*, Supplement 1987, 25, pp. 165–89.

Lindsay, Daryl, et al. Independence of External Auditors: A Canadian Perspective. *Most, Kenneth S., ed.*, 1987, pp. 169–89. **[G: Canada]**

Lockhart, Julie A.; Long, Michael S. and Sefcik, Stephan E. Regulatory Accounting Principles, Forbearance, and the Perpetuation of the Savings and Loan Industry. *Housing Finance Rev.*, Spring 1987, 6(1), pp. 79–91. **[G: U.S.]**

Ludewig, Rainer. Möglichkeiten der verdeckten Bilanzpolitik für Kapitalgesellschaften auf der Grundlage des neuen Rechts. (With English summary.) *Z. Betriebswirtshaft*, April 1987, 57(4), pp. 426–33. **[G: W. Germany]**

Maher, John J. Pension Obligations and the Bond Credit Market: An Empirical Analysis of Accounting Numbers. *Accounting Rev.*, October 1987, 62(4), pp. 785–98. **[G: U.S.]**

McKeown, James C. Understanding Accounting Changes in an Efficient Market: Analysis of Variance Issues. *Accounting Rev.*, July 1987, 62(3), pp. 597–600. **[G: U.S.]**

Mear, Ross and Firth, Michael. Cue Usage and Self-insight of Financial Analysts. *Accounting Rev.*, January 1987, 62(1), pp. 176–82. **[G: New Zealand]**

Melumad, Nahum D. and Reichelstein, Stefan. Centralization versus Delegation and the Value

of Communication. *J. Acc. Res.*, Supplement 1987, 25, pp. 1–18.

Moses, O. Douglas. Income Smoothing and Incentives: Empirical Tests Using Accounting Changes. *Accounting Rev.*, April 1987, 62(2), pp. 358–77. **[G: U.S.]**

Nichols, Donald R. A Model of Auditors' Preliminary Evaluations of Internal Control from Audit Data. *Accounting Rev.*, January 1987, 62(1), pp. 183–90. **[G: U.S.]**

Nobes, Christopher W. Classification of Financial Reporting Practices. *Most, Kenneth S., ed.*, 1987, pp. 1–22. **[G: Global]**

Patell, James M. Cost Accounting, Process Control, and Product Design: A Case Study of the Hewlett–Packard Personal Office Computer Division. *Accounting Rev.*, October 1987, 62(4), pp. 808–39. **[G: U.S.]**

Petersen, Carol D.; Shear, William and Vehorn, Charles L. Cash Accounting Rules for Farmers: Differential Benefits and Federal Costs. *J. Econ. Issues*, June 1987, 21(2), pp. 639–47. **[G: U.S.]**

Pihlanto, Pekka. Power Paradigms and Accounting Research: A Complemented Subjectivist Notion of Power. *Liiketaloudellinen Aikak.*, 1987, 36(1), pp. 24–36.

Plaut, Hans Georg. Die Entwicklung der flexiblen Planostenrechnung zu einem Instrument der Unternehmensführung. (With English summary.) *Z. Betriebswirtshaft*, April 1987, 57(4), pp. 355–66. **[G: W. Germany]**

Reed, Sarah A. and Koch, Bruce S. The Race: A View from the "Pits" of Accounting. *Schwartz, B. N., ed.*, 1987, pp. 113–27. **[G: U.S.]**

Reinstein, Alan and Gabhart, David R. L. The Internal Auditor's Role in Public Sector Audit Committees. *Public Budg. Finance*, Summer 1987, 7(2), pp. 72–80. **[G: U.S.]**

Rivera, Juan M. Price-Adjusted Financial Information and Investment Returns in a Highly Inflationary Economy: An Evaluation. *Most, Kenneth S., ed.*, 1987, pp. 287–304. **[G: Mexico]**

Rubin, Marc A. A Theory of Demand for Municipal Audits and Audit Contracts. *Chan, J. L., ed., Pt. A*, 1987, pp. 3–33. **[G: U.S.]**

Rueschhoff, Norlin G. The Intrinsic Uniformity of International Accounting Standards. *Most, Kenneth S., ed.*, 1987, pp. 23–38. **[G: Global]**

Sami, Heibatollah and Trapnell, Jerry E. Inflation-Adjusted Data and Security Prices: Some Empirical Evidence. *Schwartz, B. N., ed.*, 1987, pp. 39–57. **[G: U.S.]**

Sarath, Bharat. Discussion of Collusion and Noncontrollable Cost Allocation. *J. Acc. Res.*, Supplement 1987, 25, pp. 47–50.

Scherer, F. M., et al. The Validity of Studies with Line of Business Data: Comment [The Validity of Profits-Structure Studies with Particular Reference to the FTC's Line of Business Data]. *Amer. Econ. Rev.*, March 1987, 77(1), pp. 205–17. **[G: U.S.]**

Schierenbeck, Henner. Modellanalytische Bilanzstrukturoptimierung. (Analytical Model to Optimize the Balance-Sheet Structure. With English Summary.) *Kredit Kapital*, 1987, *20*(4), pp. 496–521.

Schroeder, Richard G. and Verreault, Kathryn. An Empirical Analysis of Audit Withdrawal Decisions. *Schwartz, B. N., ed.*, 1987, pp. 205–20. [G: U.S.]

Shaw, Wayne H. Safe Harbor or Muddy Waters. *Accounting Rev.*, April 1987, *62*(2), pp. 385–400.

Shoulders, Craig D. Criteria for Identifying the Municipal Organizational Reporting Entity. *Chan, J. L., ed., Pt. A*, 1987, pp. 181–206. [G: U.S.]

Shriver, Keith A. An Empirical Examination of the Potential Measurement Error in Current Cost Data. *Accounting Rev.*, January 1987, *62*(1), pp. 79–96. [G: U.S.]

Smith, Ruth B.; Moschis, George P. and Moore, Roy L. Social Effects of Advertising and Personal Communication on the Elderly Consumer. *Bloom, P. N., ed.*, 1987, pp. 65–92. [G: U.S.]

Stanga, Keith G. Methods of Applying LIFO in Practice. *Schwartz, B. N., ed.*, 1987, pp. 143–52. [G: U.S.]

Steinbart, Paul J. The Construction of a Rule-Based Expert System as a Method for Studying Materiality Judgments. *Accounting Rev.*, January 1987, *62*(1), pp. 97–116. [G: U.S.]

Stevenson, Francis L. New Evidence on LIFO Adoptions: The Effects of More Precise Event Dates. *J. Acc. Res.*, Autumn 1987, *25*(2), pp. 306–16. [G: U.S.]

Stone, Mary S. A Financing Explanation for Overfunded Pension Plan Terminations. *J. Acc. Res.*, Autumn 1987, *25*(2), pp. 317–26. [G: U.S.]

Stone, Mary S.; Robbins, Walter A. and Phipps, David W. Disclosure Practices of Public Employee Retirement Systems: An Analysis of Incentives to Adopt Alternative Standards. *Chan, J. L., ed., Pt. A*, 1987, pp. 149–80. [G: U.S.]

Suh, Yoon S. Collusion and Noncontrollable Cost Allocation. *J. Acc. Res.*, Supplement 1987, *25*, pp. 22–46.

Swenson, Charles W. An Analysis of ACRS during Inflationary Periods. *Accounting Rev.*, January 1987, *62*(1), pp. 117–36. [G: U.S.]

Theunisse, Hilda. Accounting and Reporting in Belgium. *Most, Kenneth S., ed.*, 1987, pp. 191–248. [G: Belgium]

Thompson, Robert B., II; Olsen, Chris and Dietrich, J. Richard. Attributes of News about Firms: An Analysis of Firm-Specific News Reported in the *Wall Street Journal Index. J. Acc. Res.*, Autumn 1987, *25*(2), pp. 245–74. [G: U.S.]

Tipgos, Manuel A. A Comprehensive Model for Improving Accounting Education in Developing Countries. *Most, Kenneth S., ed.*, 1987, pp. 383–404. [G: LDCs]

Troberg, Pontus Henrik. Foreign Currency Translation: A Comparative Analysis of Approaches. *Most, Kenneth S., ed.*, 1987, pp. 317–56.

Trueman, Brett. Discussion of Operating Decisions and the Disclosure of Management Accounting Information. *J. Acc. Res.*, Supplement 1987, *25*, pp. 190–93.

Vruwink, David R. and Otto, Janon R. Evaluation of Teaching Techniques for Introductory Accounting Courses. *Accounting Rev.*, April 1987, *62*(2), pp. 402–08.

Waller, William S. and Felix, William L., Jr. Auditors' Covariation Judgments. *Accounting Rev.*, April 1987, *62*(2), pp. 275–92.

Ward, James Gordon. The Use and Usefulness of Governmental Financial Reports: The Perspective of Public Sector Labor Unions. *Chan, J. L., ed., Pt. B*, 1987, pp. 215–26. [G: U.S.]

Whittred, Greg. The Derived Demand for Consolidated Financial Reporting. *J. Acc. Econ.*, December 1987, *9*(3), pp. 259–85. [G: Australia]

Wild, John J. The Prediction Performance of a Structural Model of Accounting Numbers. *J. Acc. Res.*, Spring 1987, *25*(1), pp. 139–60. [G: U.S.]

Wilkerson, Jack E., Jr. Selecting Experimental and Comparison Samples for Use in Studies of Auditor Reporting Decisions. *J. Acc. Res.*, Spring 1987, *25*(1), pp. 161–67. [G: U.S.]

Wilson, G. Peter. The Incremental Information Content of the Accrual and Funds Components of Earnings after Controlling for Earnings. *Accounting Rev.*, April 1987, *62*(2), pp. 293–322. [G: U.S.]

Zebda, Awni. The Choice of Management Accounting Normative Models: A Synthesis. *Schwartz, B. N., ed.*, 1987, pp. 73–98.

Ziebart, David A. and Kim, David H. An Examination of the Market Reactions Associated with SFAS No. 8 and SFAS No. 52. *Accounting Rev.*, April 1987, *62*(2), pp. 343–57. [G: U.S.]

600 Industrial Organization; Technological Change; Industry Studies

610 INDUSTRIAL ORGANIZATION AND PUBLIC POLICY

611 Market Structure and Corporate Strategy

6110 Market Structure and Corporate Strategy

Abe, Y. Japanese Market Entry Strategy. The Case of Yamanouchi Pharmaceuticals in Western Europe. *Trevor, M., ed.*, 1987, pp. 150–55. [G: Japan; W. Europe]

Acs, Zoltan J. and Audretsch, David B. Innovation, Market Structure, and Firm Size. *Rev. Econ. Statist.*, November 1987, *69*(4), pp. 567–74. [G: U.S.]

Adam, M. C. and Farber, A. Le financement de l'innovation technologique. Première partie: Les caractéristiques de l'investissement novateur. (With English summary.) *Cah. Écon. Bruxelles*, Fourth Trimester 1987, (116), pp. 3–23. [G: Belgium]

Adams, Walter and Brock, James W. Bigness and Social Efficiency: A Case Study of the U.S. Auto Industry. *Samuels, W. J. and Miller, A. S., eds.*, 1987, pp. 219–37. [G: U.S.]

Adams, Walter and Brock, James W. Corporate Size and the Bailout Factor. *J. Econ. Issues*, March 1987, *21*(1), pp. 61–85. [G: U.S.]

Adams, Walter and Brock, James W. Global Competition and the Alleged Redundancy of Antitrust. *Wills, R. L.; Caswell, J. A. and Culbertson, J. D., eds.*, 1987, pp. 131–45. [G: U.S.]

Adams, William James. Should Merger Policy Be Changed? An Antitrust Perspective. *Browne, L. E. and Rosengren, E. S., eds.*, 1987, pp. 173–94. [G: U.S.]

Adkins, Roger L. Competitive Decline: Views of Two Disciplines. *J. Econ. Issues*, June 1987, *21*(2), pp. 869–76. [G: U.S.]

Aghion, Philippe and Bolton, Patrick. Contracts as a Barrier to Entry. *Amer. Econ. Rev.*, June 1987, *77*(3), pp. 388–401.

Agliardi, Elettra. Barriere all'entrata come beni pubblici in mercati oligopolistici. (Entry Barriers as Public Goods in Oligopolistic Markets. With English summary.) *Rivista Int. Sci. Econ. Com.*, June 1987, *34*(6), pp. 523–46.

Albach, Horst. Gewinn und gerechter Preis Überlegungen zur Preisbildung in der pharmazeutischen Industrie. (With English summary.) *Z. Betriebswirtshaft*, August 1987, *57*(8), pp. 816–24. [G: W. Germany]

Albach, Horst and Hunsdiek, Detlef. Die Bedeutung von Unternehmensgründungen für die Anpassung der Wirtschaft an veränderte Rahmenbedingungen. (With English summary.) *Z. Betriebswirtshaft*, May/June 1987, *57*(5/6), pp. 562–80. [G: W. Germany]

Alchian, Armen A. Some Perspectives on the Modern Theory of the Firm: A Conference in Honor of Armen A. Alchian: Concluding Remarks. *J. Inst. Theoretical Econ.*, March 1987, *143*(1), pp. 232–34.

Alchian, Armen A. and Woodward, Susan. Reflections on the Theory of the Firm. *J. Inst. Theoretical Econ.*, March 1987, *143*(1), pp. 110–36.

Allen, Paul R. and Sirmans, C. F. An Analysis of Gains to Acquiring Firm's Shareholders: The Special Case of REITs. *J. Finan. Econ.*, March 1987, *18*(1), pp. 175–84. [G: U.S.]

Allen, Ralph C. and Stone, Jack H. Amenities, Contestability and Economic Efficiency: A Note. *Southern Econ. J.*, July 1987, *54*(1), pp. 203–05.

Anderson, Richard K. and Enomoto, Carl E. Product Quality Regulation: A General Equilibrium Analysis. *Can. J. Econ.*, November 1987, *20*(4), pp. 735–49.

Anton, James J. and Yao, Dennis A. Second Sourcing and the Experience Curve: Price Competition in Defense Procurement. *Rand J. Econ.*, Spring 1987, *18*(1), pp. 57–76.

Antonelli, Cristiano. Dall'economia industriale all'organizzazione industriale. (From Industrial Economics to Industrial Organization. With English summary.) *Econ. Polít.*, August 1987, *4*(2), pp. 277–320.

Antoniou, Andreas and Rowley, Robin. Finance and the Structural Adjustment of Canadian Corporations. *Écon. Appl.*, 1987, *40*(4), pp. 771–93. [G: Canada]

Aoki, Masahiko. The Political Economy of Japan: The Japanese Firm in Transition. *Yamamura, K. and Yasuba, Y., eds.*, 1987, pp. 263–88. [G: Japan]

Appleby, Colin and Bessant, John. Adapting to Decline: Organizational Structures and Government Policy in the UK and West German Foundry Sectors. *Wilks, S. and Wright, M., eds.*, 1987, pp. 181–210. [G: U.K.; W. Germany]

Ashenfelter, Orley and Sullivan, Daniel. Nonparametric Tests of Market Structure: An Application to the Cigarette Industry. *J. Ind. Econ.*, June 1987, *35*(4), pp. 483–98. [G: U.S.]

Ashton, R. K. X-inefficiency and Market Power. *Managerial Dec. Econ.*, December 1987, *8*(4), pp. 333–38.

Attaran, Mohsen and Zwick, Martin. Entropy and Other Measures of Industrial Diversification. *Quart. J. Bus. Econ.*, Autumn 1987, *26*(4), pp. 17–34. [G: U.S.]

Azpiazu, Daniel. Los resultados de la política de promoción industrial al cabo de un decenio (1974–1983). (With English summary.) *Desarrollo Econ.*, Jan.-Mar. 1987, *26*(104), pp. 631–51. [G: Argentina]

Bae, Hyung. Market Structure, Competition, and Welfare Change Due to Technological Innovations. *Int. Econ. J.*, Spring 1987, *1*(1), pp. 67–74.

Baer, Werner; da Fonseca, Manuel A. R. and Guilhoto, Joaquim J. M. Structural Changes in Brazil's Industrial Economy, 1960–80. *World Devel.*, February 1987, *15*(2), pp. 275–86. [G: Brazil]

Bailly, Antoine S., et al. Services and Production: For a Reassessment of Economic Sectors. *Ann. Reg. Sci.*, July 1987, *21*(2), pp. 45–59. [G: Switzerland]

Baird, Douglas G. A World without Bankruptcy. *Law Contemp. Probl.*, Spring 1987, *50*(2), pp. 173–93.

Baker, James C. and Severiens, Jacobus T. Geographic Diversification and Concentration in U.S. Commercial Banking and Thrift Markets: A Regional Analysis. *Tremblay, R., ed.*, 1987, pp. 273–81. [G: U.S.]

Baldwin, John R. and Gorecki, Paul K. Plant Creation versus Plant Acquisition: The Entry Process in Canadian Manufacturing. *Int. J. Ind. Organ.*, March 1987, *5*(1), pp. 27–41. [G: Canada]

Ballwieser, Wolfgang. Transaction Cost Analysis of Structural Changes in the Distribution System: Reflections on Institutional Developments in the Federal Republic of Germany:

Comment. *J. Inst. Theoretical Econ.*, March 1987, *143*(1), pp. 86–90. **[G: W. Germany]**

Barron, John M.; Black, Dan A. and Loewenstein, Mark A. Employer Size: The Implications for Search, Training, Capital Investment, Starting Wages, and Wage Growth. *J. Lab. Econ.*, January 1987, *5*(1), pp. 76–89.
[G: U.S.]

Barth, James R.; Cordes, Joseph J. and Haber, Sheldon E. Employee Characteristics and Firm Size: Are There Systematic Empirical Relationships? *Appl. Econ.*, April 1987, *19*(4), pp. 555–67. **[G: U.S.]**

Barzelay, Michael and Smith, Rogers M. The One Best System? A Political Analysis of Neoclassical Institutionalist Perspectives on the Modern Corporation. *Samuels, W. J. and Miller, A. S., eds.*, 1987, pp. 81–110.
[G: U.S.]

Baskin, Jonathan B. Corporate Liquidity in Games of Monopoly Power. *Rev. Econ. Statist.*, May 1987, *69*(2), pp. 312–19. **[G: U.S.]**

Basu, Kaushik. Monopoly, Quality Uncertainty and 'Status' Goods. *Int. J. Ind. Organ.*, December 1987, *5*(4), pp. 435–46.

Baumol, William J. and Fischer, Dietrich. Peak Pricing, Congestion, and Fairness. *Feiwel, G. R., ed. (II)*, 1987, pp. 382–409.

Bearden, James and Mintz, Beth. The Structure of Class Cohesion: The Corporate Network and Its Dual. *Mizruchi, M. S. and Schwartz, M., eds.*, 1987, pp. 187–207. **[G: U.S.]**

Begun, James W., et al. Strategic Behavior Patterns of Small Multi-institutional Health Organizations. *Scheffler, R. M. and Rossiter, L. F., eds.*, 1987, pp. 195–214. **[G: U.S.]**

Belton, Terrence M. A Model of Duopoly and Meeting or Beating Competition. *Int. J. Ind. Organ.*, December 1987, *5*(4), pp. 399–417.

Benston, George J. The Validity of Studies with Line of Business Data: Reply [The Validity of Profits-Structure Studies with Particular Reference to the FTC's Line of Business Data]. *Amer. Econ. Rev.*, March 1987, *77*(1), pp. 218–23. **[G: U.S.]**

Benvignati, Anita M. Domestic Profit Advantages of Multinational Firms. *J. Bus.*, July 1987, *60*(3), pp. 449–61. **[G: U.S.]**

Berg, Hartmut. Internationaler Wettbewerb—Nationale Wettbewerbspolitik: Zielkonflikte unvermeidbar! (International Competitiveness—National Competition Policy: Conflicts Unavoidable! With English summary.) *Lenel, H. O., et al., eds.*, 1987, pp. 131–42.
[G: W. Germany]

Berman, Lawrence E. and Dunn, Donald A. Service Bundling and Strategic Equilibrium in the Information Services Industry. *J. Econ. Bus.*, May 1987, *39*(2), pp. 115–29.

Bernholz, Peter. Organizational Theory, Information Processing, and Short-run Dynamics: Theory and Empirical Tests: Comment. *J. Inst. Theoretical Econ.*, March 1987, *143*(1), pp. 225–28. **[G: U.S.]**

Bernier, Gilles. Market Power and Systematic Risk: An Empirical Analysis Using Tobin's *q* Ratio. *J. Econ. Bus.*, May 1987, *39*(2), pp. 91–99. **[G: U.S.]**

Besanko, David; Donnenfeld, Shabtai and White, Lawrence J. Monopoly and Quality Distortion: Effects and Remedies. *Quart. J. Econ.*, November 1987, *102*(4), pp. 743–67.

Bessis, Joël. Les déterminants réels du risque financier. (The Real Determinants of Financial Risk. With English summary.) *Finance*, June 1987, *8*(1), pp. 33–53. **[G: France]**

Bhatt, Swati. Strategic Product Choice in Differentiated Markets. *J. Ind. Econ.*, December 1987, *36*(2), pp. 207–16.

Blair, Roger D. and Fesmire, James M. Antitrust Treatment of Nonprofit and For-profit Hospital Mergers. *Scheffler, R. M. and Rossiter, L. F., eds.*, 1987, pp. 221–44. **[G: U.S.]**

Blanchflower, David G. and Oswald, Andrew J. Profit Sharing—Can It Work? *Sinclair, P.J.N., ed.*, 1987, pp. 1–19. **[G: U.K.]**

Blitz, Rudolph C., et al. The Effect of Market Structure on the Cost of Borrowing. *Wills, R. L.; Caswell, J. A. and Culbertson, J. D., eds.*, 1987, pp. 333–44. **[G: U.S.]**

Bohn, Henning. Monitoring Multiple Agents: The Role of Hierarchies. *J. Econ. Behav. Organ.*, June 1987, *8*(2), pp. 279–305.

Bonus, Holger. Property Rights and Transaction Costs: Theory and Evidence on Privately-Owned and Government-Owned Enterprises: Comment. *J. Inst. Theoretical Econ.*, March 1987, *143*(1), pp. 27–33. **[G: W. Germany]**

Booth, James R. and Smith, Richard L. An Examination of the Small-Firm Effect on the Basis of Skewness Preference. *J. Finan. Res.*, Spring 1987, *10*(1), pp. 77–86.

Borrie, Gordon [Sir]. Competition, Mergers and Price-Fixing. *Lloyds Bank Rev.*, April 1987, (164), pp. 1–15. **[G: U.K.]**

Boyd, Richard. Government–Industry Relations in Japan: Access, Communication, and Competitive Collaboration. *Wills, S. and Wright, M., eds.*, 1987, pp. 61–90. **[G: Japan]**

Brack, John. Price Adjustment within a Framework of Symmetric Oligopoly: An Analysis of Pricing in 380 U.S. Manufacturing Industries, 1958–71. *Int. J. Ind. Organ.*, September 1987, *5*(3), pp. 289–301. **[G: U.S.]**

Bradburd, Ralph M. and Caves, Richard E. Transaction-Cost Influences on the Adjustment of Industries' Prices and Outputs. *Rev. Econ. Statist.*, November 1987, *69*(4), pp. 575–83.
[G: U.S.]

Bradley, Michael. Effects of Mergers and Acquisitions on the Economy: An Industrial Organization Perspective: Discussion. *Browne, L. E. and Rosengren, E. S., eds.*, 1987, pp. 169–72. **[G: U.S.]**

Brannman, Lance; Klein, J. Douglass and Weiss, Leonard W. The Price Effects of Increased Competition in Auction Markets. *Rev. Econ. Statist.*, February 1987, *69*(1), pp. 24–32.
[G: U.S.]

Bregman, Arie. Government Intervention in Industry: The Case of Israel. *J. Devel. Econ.*, April 1987, *25*(2), pp. 353–67. **[G: Israel]**

Bresnahan, Timothy F. Competition and Collusion in the American Automobile Industry: The 1955 Price War. *J. Ind. Econ.*, June 1987, *35*(4), pp. 457–82. [G: U.S.]

Bresnahan, Timothy F. and Reiss, Peter C. Do Entry Conditions Vary across Markets? *Brookings Pap. Econ. Act.*, 1987, (3), pp. 833–71. [G: U.S.]

Bresnahan, Timothy F. and Schmalensee, Richard. The Empirical Renaissance in Industrial Economics: An Overview. *J. Ind. Econ.*, June 1987, *35*(4), pp. 371–78. [G: U.S.]

Brickley, James A. and Dark, Frederick H. The Choice of Organizational Form: The Case of Franchising. *J. Finan. Econ.*, June 1987, *18*(2), pp. 401–20. [G: U.S.]

Brickley, James A. and James, Christopher M. The Takeover Market, Corporate Board Composition, and Ownership Structure: The Case of Banking. *J. Law Econ.*, April 1987, *30*(1), pp. 161–80. [G: U.S.]

Brock, James W. Bigness Is the Problem, Not the Solution. *Challenge*, July/Aug. 1987, *30*(3), pp. 11–16. [G: U.S.]

Browne, Lynn E. and Rosengren, Eric S. Are Hostile Takeovers Different? *Browne, L. E. and Rosengren, E. S., eds.*, 1987, pp. 199–229. [G: U.S.]

Browne, Lynn E. and Rosengren, Eric S. The Merger Boom: An Overview. *Browne, L. E. and Rosengren, E. S., eds.*, 1987, pp. 1–16. [G: U.S.]

Browning, Edgar K. Comparing Monopoly and Competition: The Increasing-Cost Case. *Econ. Inquiry*, July 1987, *25*(3), pp. 535–42.

Bull, Clive and Ordover, Janusz A. Market Structure and Optimal Management Organizations. *Rand J. Econ.*, Winter 1987, *18*(4), pp. 480–91.

Bumpass, Donald L. The Trade-off between Market Power Increases and Efficiencies in Horizontal Mergers. *Atlantic Econ. J.*, December 1987, *15*(4), pp. 70–75. [G: U.S.]

Calvet, A. L. and Lefoll, J. Information Asymmetry and Wealth Effect of Canadian Corporate Acquisitions. *Financial Rev.*, November 1987, *22*(4), pp. 415–31. [G: Canada]

Carlson, David Gray. Successor Liability in Bankruptcy: Some Unifying Themes of Intertemporal Creditor Priorities Created by Running Covenants, Products Liability, and Toxic-Waste Cleanup. *Law Contemp. Probl.*, Spring 1987, *50*(2), pp. 119–71. [G: U.S.]

Carlsson, Bo. Reflections on 'Industrial Dynamics': The Challenges Ahead. *Int. J. Ind. Organ.*, June 1987, *5*(2), pp. 135–48.

Carpenter, Gregory S. Modeling Competitive Marketing Strategies: The Impact of Marketing-Mix Relationships and Industry Structure. *Marketing Sci.*, Spring 1987, *6*(2), pp. 208–21. [G: U.S.; Canada]

Caslin, Terry. Industrial and Market Structure in the UK. *Vane, H. and Caslin, T., eds.*, 1987, pp. 131–68. [G: U.K.]

Casti, John. (M,R)-Systems as a Framework for Modeling Structural Change in a Global Indus-

try. *Batten, D.; Casti, J. and Johansson, B., eds.*, 1987, pp. 313–34.

Caswell, Julie A. Aggregate Concentration: Significance, Trends, and Causes. *Wills, R. L.; Caswell, J. A. and Culbertson, J. D., eds.*, 1987, pp. 237–49. [G: U.S.]

Caves, Richard E. Effects of Mergers and Acquisitions on the Economy: An Industrial Organization Perspective. *Browne, L. E. and Rosengren, E. S., eds.*, 1987, pp. 149–68. [G: U.S.]

Chabot, Marc. La portée limitée des statistiques sur le nombre de faillites commerciales. (With English summary.) *Can. Public Policy*, June 1987, *13*(2), pp. 144–51.

Chalk, Andrew J. Property Rights and Transaction Costs: Theory and Evidence on Privately-Owned and Government-Owned Enterprises: Comment. *J. Inst. Theoretical Econ.*, March 1987, *143*(1), pp. 23–26.

Chandler, Alfred D., Jr. A Framework for Analyzing the Modern Multinational Enterprise and Its Competitive Advantage. *Atack, J., ed.*, 1987, pp. 3–17. [G: U.S.]

Chang, Philip C. Merger Waves and Stock Market Fluctuations: A Test of Causality. *Atlantic Econ. J.*, March 1987, *15*(1), pp. 122.

Chao, Hung-po and Wilson, Robert B. Priority Service: Pricing, Investment, and Market Organization. *Amer. Econ. Rev.*, December 1987, *77*(5), pp. 899–916.

Chapman, D. R. and Junor, C. W. Inflation, Firm Control-Type and Vulnerability to Takeover. *Oxford Econ. Pap.*, September 1987, *39*(3), pp. 500–15. [G: Australia]

Çinar, E. Miné; Kaytaz, Mehmet and Evcimen, Gümar. A Case Study on the Growth Potential of Small Scale Manufacturing Enterprises in Bursa, Turkey. *METU*, 1987, *14*(2), pp. 123–46. [G: Turkey]

Ciocca, Pierluigi and Frasca, Francesco. I rapporti fra industria e finanza: problemi e prospettive. (With English summary.) *Polit. Econ.*, April 1987, *3*(1), pp. 29–50. [G: Italy]

Clark, Jeffrey A. The Efficient Structure Hypothesis: More Evidence from Banking. *Quart. Rev. Econ. Bus.*, Autumn 1987, *27*(3), pp. 25–39. [G: U.S.]

Clements, Peter. The New City: Geared for the Wider World. *Brit. Rev. Econ. Issues*, Autumn 1987, *9*(21), pp. 51–64. [G: U.K.]

Clifford, Norman and Crawford, Vincent P. Short-term Contracting and Strategic Oil Reserves. *Rev. Econ. Stud.*, April 1987, *54*(2), pp. 311–23.

Coelho, Philip R. P. and McClure, James E. Barriers to Entry in the Market for Stud Services: Government and "Non-profit" Institutions in Collusion. *Econ. Inquiry*, October 1987, *25*(4), pp. 659–70. [G: U.S.]

Coffee, John C., Jr. Are Hostile Takeovers Different? Discussion. *Browne, L. E. and Rosengren, E. S., eds.*, 1987, pp. 230–42. [G: U.S.]

Cohen, Wesley M.; Levin, Richard C. and Mowery, David C. Firm Size and R&D Intensity:

A Re-examination. *J. Ind. Econ.*, June 1987, 35(4), pp. 543–65. [G: U.S.]

Collins, William H. and Collins, Carol B. More on Advertising and Monopoly Power: The Case of the Electric Utility Industry. *Atlantic Econ. J.*, March 1987, 15(1), pp. 71–76. [G: U.S.]

Comanor, William S. and Frech, H. E., III. The Competitive Effects of Vertical Agreements: Reply. *Amer. Econ. Rev.*, December 1987, 77(5), pp. 1069–72. [G: U.S.]

Comment, Robert and Jarrell, Gregg A. Two-Tier and Negotiated Tender Offers: the Imprisonment of the Free-Riding Shareholder. *J. Finan. Econ.*, December 1987, 19(2), pp. 283–310. [G: U.S.]

Conrad, Cecilia and Duchatelet, Martine. New Technology Adoption: Incumbent versus Entrant. *Int. J. Ind. Organ.*, September 1987, 5(3), pp. 315–21.

Conrad, Klaus. Quality and Reputation Policies of Duopolists under Asymmetric Information. *Carraro, C. and Sartore, D., eds.*, 1987, pp. 261–76.

Cosh, A. D. and Hughes, A. The Anatomy of Corporate Control: Directors, Shareholders and Executive Remuneration in Giant U.S. and U.K. Corporations. *Cambridge J. Econ.*, December 1987, 11(4), pp. 285–313. [G: U.S.; U.K.]

Cotterill, Ronald W. The Economic Efficiency of Alternative Forms of Business Enterprise. *Kilmer, R. L. and Armbruster, W. J., eds.*, 1987, pp. 107–29.

Cotterill, Ronald W. and Haller, Lawrence. Entry Patterns and Strategic Interaction in Food Retailing. *Wills, R. L.; Caswell, J. A. and Culbertson, J. D., eds.*, 1987, pp. 203–22. [G: U.S.]

Cowling, Keith. Merger Policy, Industrial Strategy and Democracy. *Brit. Rev. Econ. Issues*, Autumn 1987, 9(21), pp. 29–49.

Craig, C. Samuel; Douglas, Susan P. and Reddy, Srinivas K. Market Structure, Performance and Strategy: A Comparison of U.S. and European Markets. *Cavusgil, S. T., ed.*, 1987, pp. 1–21. [G: U.S.; W. Europe]

Crandall, Robert W. Should Merger Policy Be Changed? An Antitrust Perspective: Discussion. *Browne, L. E. and Rosengren, E. S., eds.*, 1987, pp. 195–98. [G: U.S.]

Cressy, Robert C. Equilibrium Costs and Prices in a Market with Imperfect Information and Technological Change. *Greek Econ. Rev.*, 1987, 9(2), pp. 162–82.

Cubbin, John S. and Geroski, Paul A. The Convergence of Profits in the Long Run: Inter-firm and Inter-industry Comparisons. *J. Ind. Econ.*, June 1987, 35(4), pp. 427–42. [G: U.K.]

Cubbin, John S. and Murfin, Andy. Regression Analysis versus Linear Programming in the Analysis of Price–Quality Relationships: An Application to the Determination of Market Shares. *Oxford Bull. Econ. Statist.*, November 1987, 49(4), pp. 385–99. [G: U.K.]

Culem, Claudy G. Pourquoi les multinationales? Une revue de la littérature sur les motivations de la croissance multinationale des firmes. (With English summary.) *Cah. Écon. Bruxelles*, Third Trimester 1987, (115), pp. 3–33.

Curien, Nicolas and Gensollen, Michel. De la théorie des structures industrielles à l'économie des réseaux de télécommunication. (From the Theory of Industry Structure to the Economics of Telecommunication Networks. With English summary.) *Revue Écon.*, March 1987, 38(2), pp. 521–78.

Dahremöller, Axel. Konzentration: Ein Messproblem. Ein Beitrag zur Konzentrationsdiskussion. (With English summary.) *Z. Betriebswirtshaft*, February 1987, 57(2), pp. 208–20. [G: W. Germany]

Daughety, Andrew F. and Forsythe, Robert. Industrywide Regulation and the Formation of Reputations: A Laboratory Analysis. *Bailey, E. E., ed.*, 1987, pp. 347–98.

Daughety, Andrew F. and Forsythe, Robert. The Effects of Industry-Wide Price Regulation on Industrial Organization. *J. Law, Econ., Organ.*, Fall 1987, 3(2), pp. 397–434.

Davidson, Wallace N., III; Garrison, Sharon Hatten and Henderson, Glenn V., Jr. Examining Merger Synergy with the Capital Asset Pricing Model. *Financial Rev.*, May 1987, 22(2), pp. 233–47. [G: U.S.]

Davies, David G. and Brucato, Peter F., Jr. Property Rights and Transaction Costs: Theory and Evidence on Privately-Owned and Government-Owned Enterprises. *J. Inst. Theoretical Econ.*, March 1987, 143(1), pp. 7–22. [G: Australia]

DeGraba, Patrick J. The Effects of Price Restrictions on Competition between National and Local Firms. *Rand J. Econ.*, Autumn 1987, 18(3), pp. 333–47.

Delbono, Flavio. Barriere multiple all'entrata. (Multiple Entry Deterrence. With English summary.) *Giorn. Econ.*, Jan.-Feb. 1987, 46(1–2), pp. 29–54.

Delfino, José A. Eficiencia, apertura de la economía y concentración industrial en Argentina. (Efficiency, Openness of the Economy and Industrial Concentration in Argentina. With English summary.) *Económica (La Plata)*, January-June 1987, 33(1), pp. 51–84. [G: Argentina]

Demski, Joel S.; Sappington, David E. M. and Spiller, Pablo T. Managing Supplier Switching. *Rand J. Econ.*, Spring 1987, 18(1), pp. 77–97.

Dewatripont, Mathias. Entry Deterrence under Trade Unions. *Europ. Econ. Rev.*, Feb./Mar. 1987, 31(1/2), pp. 149–56.

Diamantopoulos, Adamantios. Vertical Quasi-integration Revisited: The Role of Power. *Managerial Dec. Econ.*, September 1987, 8(3), pp. 185–94.

Dixit, Avinash K. Tariffs and Subsidies under Oligopoly: The Case of the U.S. Automobile Industry. *[Corden, W. M.]*, 1987, pp. 112–27. [G: U.S.]

Dobbs, Ian M.; Hill, M. B. and Waterson, Michael. Industrial Structure and the Employment Consequences of Technical Change. *Oxford Econ. Pap.*, September 1987, *39*(3), pp. 552–67.

Dobson, Allen. Mergers in Health Care: Implications for the Future. *Scheffler, R. M. and Rossiter, L. F., eds.*, 1987, pp. 271–77. **[G: U.S.]**

Domowitz, Ian; Hubbard, R. Glenn and Petersen, Bruce C. Oligopoly Supergames: Some Empirical Evidence on Prices and Margins. *J. Ind. Econ.*, June 1987, *35*(4), pp. 379–98. **[G: U.S.]**

Don, Yehuda and Paroush, Jacob. Cooperatives with Cost Saving. *Jones, D. C. and Svejnar, J., eds.*, 1987, pp. 183–99.

Dow, Gregory K. The Function of Authority in Transaction Cost Economics. *J. Econ. Behav. Organ.*, March 1987, *8*(1), pp. 13–38.

Dugger, William M. Corporate Hegemony and Market Mythology. *Challenge*, Jan./Feb. 1987, *29*(6), pp. 55–58. **[G: OECD]**

Dugger, William M. Power: An Institutional Framework of Analysis. *Albelda, R.; Gunn, C. and Waller, W., eds.*, 1987, *1980*, pp. 253–62.

Dunning, John H. and Archer, Howard. The Eclectic Paradigm and the Growth of UK Multinational Enterprise 1870–1983. *Atack, J., ed.*, 1987, pp. 19–49. **[G: U.K.]**

Dutt, Amitava Krishna. Competition, Monopoly Power and the Uniform Rate of Profit. *Rev. Radical Polit. Econ.*, Winter 1987, *19*(4), pp. 55–72.

Dyl, Edward A. and Hoffmeister, J. Ronald. Capital Budgeting Decisions: The Effect of Product Cannibalism and Competitive Product Markets. *Lee, C. F., ed.*, 1987, pp. 119–33.

Eaton, B. Curtis and Ware, Roger. A Theory of Market Structure with Sequential Entry. *Rand J. Econ.*, Spring 1987, *18*(1), pp. 1–16.

Eckard, E. Woodrow, Jr. Advertising, Competition, and Market Share Instability. *J. Bus.*, October 1987, *60*(4), pp. 539–52. **[G: U.S.]**

Eggerstedt, Harald. Wettbewerb und Regulierung auf Versicherungsmärkten. (Competition and Regulation in Insurance Markets. With English summary.) *Z. Wirtschaft. Sozialwissen.*, 1987, *107*(3), pp. 397–416. **[G: W. Germany]**

Eggertsson, Thráinn. Transaction Cost Analysis of Structural Changes in the Distribution System: Reflections on Institutional Developments in the Federal Republic of Germany: Comment. *J. Inst. Theoretical Econ.*, March 1987, *143*(1), pp. 82–85. **[G: W. Germany]**

Eichner, Alfred S. Prices and Pricing. *J. Econ. Issues*, December 1987, *21*(4), pp. 1555–84.

Eisenberg, Theodore. Bankruptcy in the Administrative State. *Law Contemp. Probl.*, Spring 1987, *50*(2), pp. 3–52. **[G: U.S.]**

Eliasson, Gunnar. Information Technology, Capital Structure and the Nature of Technical Change in the Firm. *Eliasson, G.*, 1987, pp. 51–78.

Ermann, Dan. Comments on Behavior and Performance. *Scheffler, R. M. and Rossiter, L.*

F., eds., 1987, pp. 215–17. **[G: U.S.]**

Ernst, Dieter. The Impact of Microelectronics on the Worldwide Restructuring of the Electronics Industry: Implications for the Third World. *Dunning, J. H. and Usui, M., eds.*, 1987, pp. 117–34. **[G: LDCs]**

Etzioni, Amitai. Entrepreneurship, Adaptation and Legitimation: A Macro-behavioral Perspective. *J. Econ. Behav. Organ.*, June 1987, *8*(2), pp. 175–89.

Evanoff, Douglas D. and Fortier, Diana. The Impact of Geographic Expansion in Banking: Some Axioms to Grind. *Wilcox, J. A., ed.*, 1987, *1986*, pp. 99–113. **[G: U.S.]**

Evans, David S. Tests of Alternative Theories of Firm Growth. *J. Polit. Econ.*, August 1987, *95*(4), pp. 657–74. **[G: U.S.]**

Evans, David S. The Relationship between Firm Growth, Size, and Age: Estimates for 100 Manufacturing Industries. *J. Ind. Econ.*, June 1987, *35*(4), pp. 567–81. **[G: U.S.]**

Ewell, C. Daniel. Rule 10b-5 and the Duty to Disclose Merger Negotiations in Corporate Statements. *Yale Law J.*, January 1987, *96*(3), pp. 547–68. **[G: U.S.]**

Falvey, Rodney E. and Kierzkowski, Henryk. Product Quality, Intra-industry Trade and (Im)perfect Competition. *[Corden, W. M.]*, 1987, pp. 143–61.

Farrell, Joseph. Cheap Talk, Coordination, and Entry. *Rand J. Econ.*, Spring 1987, *18*(1), pp. 34–39.

Feldenkirchen, Wilfried. Big Business in Interwar Germany: Organizational Innovation at Vereinigte Stahlwerke, IG Farben, and Siemens. *Bus. Hist. Rev.*, Autumn 1987, *61*(3), pp. 417–51.

Fershtman, Chaim and Judd, Kenneth L. Equilibrium Incentives in Oligopoly. *Amer. Econ. Rev.*, December 1987, *77*(5), pp. 927–40.

Fiegenbaum, Avi and Primeaux, Walter J., Jr. Strategic Groups and Mobility Barriers: The Level of Struggle in an Industry. *J. Behav. Econ.*, Fall 1987, *16*(3), pp. 67–92.

Fishelson, Gideon. Pricing Policies and Ownership of Shares as Substitutes for Vertical Integration. *J. Econ. Bus.*, February 1987, *39*(1), pp. 35–44.

Fisher, Franklin M. Horizontal Mergers: Triage and Treatment. *J. Econ. Perspectives*, Fall 1987, *1*(2), pp. 23–40. **[G: U.S.]**

Fisher, Franklin M. On the Misuse of the Profits–Sales Ratio to Infer Monopoly Power. *Rand J. Econ.*, Autumn 1987, *18*(3), pp. 384–96. **[G: U.S.]**

Fisher, Franklin M. Pan American to United: The *Pacific Division Transfer Case*. *Rand J. Econ.*, Winter 1987, *18*(4), pp. 492–508. **[G: U.S.]**

FitzRoy, Felix R. and Kraft, Kornelius. Cooperation, Productivity, and Profit Sharing. *Quart. J. Econ.*, February 1987, *102*(1), pp. 23–35. **[G: W. Germany]**

Flam, Harry. Reverse Dumping. *Europ. Econ. Rev.*, Feb./Mar. 1987, *31*(1/2), pp. 82–88.

Fort, Rodney and Hallagan, William. Who Bids the Most for Market Power? *Econ. Inquiry*,

October 1987, 25(4), pp. 671–80.

Franchon, B.; Rifkin, E. and Sengupta, Jati K. A Dynamic and Stochastic Model of Price Leadership. *Carraro, C. and Sartore, D., eds.,* 1987, pp. 239–60.

Franke, Günter. Reflections on the Theory of the Firm: Comment. *J. Inst. Theoretical Econ.,* March 1987, 143(1), pp. 143–48.

Frech, H. E., III. Comments on Antitrust Issues. *Scheffler, R. M. and Rossiter, L. F., eds.,* 1987, pp. 263–67. **[G: U.S.]**

Froeb, Luke and Geweke, John. Long Run Competition in the U.S. Aluminum Industry. *Int. J. Ind. Organ.,* March 1987, 5(1), pp. 67–78. **[G: U.S.]**

Frydl, Edward J. The Free Cash Flow Theory of Takeovers: A Financial Perspective on Mergers and Acquisitions and the Economy: Discussion. *Browne, L. E. and Rosengren, E. S., eds.,* 1987, pp. 144–48. **[G: U.S.]**

Fudenberg, Drew and Tirole, Jean. Understanding Rent Dissipation: On the Use of Game Theory in Industrial Organization. *Amer. Econ. Rev.,* May 1987, 77(2), pp. 176–83.

Fung, K. C. Industry Structure, Antitrust and Tariffs. *Int. J. Ind. Organ.,* December 1987, 5(4), pp. 447–56.

Furubotn, Eirik G. How Transaction Rights Are Shaped to Channel Innovativeness: Comment. *J. Inst. Theoretical Econ.,* March 1987, 143(1), pp. 196–200.

Gabel, H. Landis. Product Standardization and Competitive Strategy: Conclusion. *Gabel, H. L., ed.,* 1987, pp. 303–16.

Gábor, R. István and Horváth, D. Tamás. Failure and Retreat in the Hungarian Private Small-scale Industry (Data for a Revision of Government Policy towards the Small Industry in the Eighties). *Acta Oecon.,* 1987, 38(1–2), pp. 133–53. **[G: Hungary]**

Gagnon, Jean-Marie; Suret, Jean-Marc and St-Pierre, Josée. Asymétrie de l'information, fiscalité et endettement au Canada. (Information Asymmetry, Taxes and Debt-Equity Ratios in Canada. With English summary.) *Finance,* June 1987, 8(1), pp. 75–103. **[G: Canada]**

Gale, Jeffrey and Buchholz, Rogene A. The Political Pursuit of Competitive Advantage: What Business Can Gain from Government. *Marcus, A. A.; Kaufman, A. M. and Beam, D. R., eds.,* 1987, pp. 31–41.

Gautschi, Frederick H., III and Jone, Thomas M. Illegal Corporate Behavior and Corporate Board Structure. *Frederick, W. C., ed.,* 1987, pp. 93–106. **[G: U.S.]**

Geithman, Frederick E. Mergers: Does Empirical Evidence Support a Change in Public Policy? *Wills, R. L.; Caswell, J. A. and Culbertson, J. D., eds.,* 1987, pp. 251–75. **[G: U.S.]**

Gelfand, Matthew D. and Spiller, Pablo T. Entry Barriers and Multiproduct Oligopolies: Do They Forebear or Spoil? *Int. J. Ind. Organ.,* March 1987, 5(1), pp. 101–13. **[G: Uruguay]**

Gendron, Michel and Bernier, Gilles. Le marché de l'assurance responsabilité des municipalités québécoises est-il contestable? (On the Con-

testability of the Liability Insurance Market for Small Municipalities in the Province of Quebec. With English summary.) *L'Actual. Econ.,* March 1987, 63(1), pp. 43–52. **[G: Canada]**

Geroski, Paul A. and Masson, Robert T. Dynamic Market Models in Industrial Organization. *Int. J. Ind. Organ.,* March 1987, 5(1), pp. 1–13. **[G: U.S.]**

Geroski, Paul A.; Masson, Robert T. and Shaanan, Joseph. The Dynamics of Market Structure. *Int. J. Ind. Organ.,* March 1987, 5(1), pp. 93–100. **[G: U.S.]**

Geroski, Paul A.; Ulph, Alistair M. and Ulph, David T. A Model of the Crude Oil Market in Which Market Conduct Varies. *Econ. J.,* Supplement 1987, 97, pp. 77–86. **[G: Global]**

Gilbert, Richard J. and Lieberman, Marvin B. Investment and Coordination in Oligopolistic Industries. *Rand J. Econ.,* Spring 1987, 18(1), pp. 17–33. **[G: U.S.]**

Gnes, Paolo. Banking and the Transformation of Italy's Productive Base: A Comment. *Rev. Econ. Cond. Italy,* Sept.-Dec. 1987, (3), pp. 479–84. **[G: Italy]**

Goldberg, Victor P. Organizational Theory, Information Processing, and Short-run Dynamics: Theory and Empirical Tests: Comment. *J. Inst. Theoretical Econ.,* March 1987, 143(1), pp. 222–24. **[G: U.S.]**

Goldstein, Steven J.; McNulty, James E. and Verbrugge, James A. Scale Economies in the Savings and Loan Industry before Diversification. *J. Econ. Bus.,* August 1987, 39(3), pp. 199–207. **[G: U.S.]**

Golombek, Rolf and Hoel, Michael. The Relationship between the Price of Natural Gas and Crude Oil: Some Aspects of Efficient Contracts. *Golombek, R.; Hoel, M. and Vislie, J., eds.,* 1987, pp. 221–37.

Gorecki, Paul K. Barriers to Entry in the Canadian Pharmaceutical Industry: Comments, Clarification and Extensions. *J. Health Econ.,* March 1987, 6(1), pp. 59–72. **[G: Canada]**

Gort, Michael and Singamsetti, Rao. Innovation and the Personality Profiles of Firms. *Int. J. Ind. Organ.,* March 1987, 5(1), pp. 115–26. **[G: U.S.]**

Gottinger, Hans W. Economic Choice and Technology Diffusion in New Product Markets. *Weltwirtsch. Arch.,* 1987, 123(1), pp. 93–120. **[G: U.S.]**

Goudie, Andrew. Forecasting Corporate Failure: The Use of Discriminant Analysis within a Disaggregated Model of the Corporate Sector. *J. Roy. Statist. Soc.,* 1987, 150(1), pp. 69–81. **[G: U.K.]**

Green, Chris. Industrial Organization Paradigms, Empirical Evidence, and the Economic Case for Competition Policy. *Can. J. Econ.,* August 1987, 20(3), pp. 482–505. **[G: Canada]**

Green, Chris. Mergers in Canada and Canada's New Merger Law. *Antitrust Bull.,* Spring 1987, 32(1), pp. 253–73. **[G: Canada]**

Green, Milford B. Corporate-Merger–Defined Core–Periphery Relations for the United

States. *Growth Change*, Summer 1987, *18*(3), pp. 12–35. **[G: U.S.]**

Greenaway, David. The New Theories of Intra-industry Trade. *Bull. Econ. Res.*, April 1987, *39*(2), pp. 95–120.

Grossman, Sanford J. and Hart, Oliver. Vertical Integration and the Distribution of Property Rights. *Razin, A. and Sadka, E., eds.*, 1987, pp. 504–46.

Grundfest, Joseph A. Why Are the Parts Worth More than the Sum? "Chop Shop," A Corporate Valuation Model: Discussion. *Browne, L. E. and Rosengren, E. S., eds.*, 1987, pp. 96–101.

Guerin-Calvert, Margaret E.; McGuckin, Robert H. and Warren-Boulton, Frederick R. State and Federal Regulation in the Market for Corporate Control. *Antitrust Bull.*, Fall 1987, *32*(3), pp. 661–91. **[G: U.S.]**

Gul, Faruk. Noncooperative Collusion in Durable Goods Oligopoly. *Rand J. Econ.*, Summer 1987, *18*(2), pp. 248–54.

Haas-Wilson, Deborah. Tying Requirements in Markets with Many Sellers: The Contact Lens Industry. *Rev. Econ. Statist.*, February 1987, *69*(1), pp. 170–75. **[G: U.S.]**

Hall, Bronwyn H. The Relationship between Firm Size and Firm Growth in the U.S. Manufacturing Sector. *J. Ind. Econ.*, June 1987, *35*(4), pp. 583–606. **[G: U.S.]**

Hall, Christopher D. Heterogeneous Firms: A Consumer's Report [Heterogeneous Firms and the Organization of Production]. *Econ. Inquiry*, January 1987, *25*(1), pp. 175–80.

Hall, Graham. When Does Market-Share Matter? *J. Econ. Stud.*, 1987, *14*(3), pp. 41–54.

Hamilton, James L. and Philippart, Nancy L. On the Nonequivalence of Maximum Resale Price Maintenance and Vertical Integration. *Eastern Econ. J.*, October-December 1987, *13*(4), pp. 411–19. **[G: U.S.]**

Hannan, Timothy H. and Rhoades, Stephen A. Acquisition Targets and Motives: The Case of the Banking Industry. *Rev. Econ. Statist.*, February 1987, *69*(1), pp. 67–74. **[G: U.S.]**

Hansen, Robert G. A Theory for the Choice of Exchange Medium in Mergers and Acquisitions. *J. Bus.*, January 1987, *60*(1), pp. 75–95. **[G: U.S.]**

Hanson, Kenneth. On New Firm Entry and Macro Stability. *Eliasson, G., ed.*, 1987, pp. 63–72. **[G: Sweden]**

Harrington, Joseph E., Jr. Collusion in Multiproduct Oligopoly Games under a Finite Horizon. *Int. Econ. Rev.*, February 1987, *28*(1), pp. 1–14.

Harris, Frederick H. deB. Competing Theories of Firm Decision-Making under Risk. *Southern Econ. J.*, October 1987, *54*(2), pp. 271–86. **[G: U.S.]**

Harrison, Bennett. European and American Experience [Comparing European and American Experience with Plant Closing Laws]. *Staudohar, P. D. and Brown, H. E.*, 1987, *1984*, pp. 259–65. **[G: W. Europe]**

Harrison, Glenn W. Experimental Evaluation of

the Contestable Markets Hypothesis. *Bailey, E. E., ed.*, 1987, pp. 191–225.

Hart, P. E. Small Firms and Jobs. *Nat. Inst. Econ. Rev.*, August 1987, (121), pp. 60–63. **[G: U.K.]**

Hartman, Raymond S. Product Quality and Market Efficiency: The Effect of Product Recalls on Resale Prices and Firm Valuation. *Rev. Econ. Statist.*, May 1987, *69*(2), pp. 367–72. **[G: U.S.]**

Hattori, Tamio. Formation of the Korean Business Elite during the Era of Rapid Economic Growth. *Devel. Econ.*, December 1987, *25*(4), pp. 346–62. **[G: S. Korea]**

Hay, Donald A. Competition and Industrial Policies. *Oxford Rev. Econ. Policy*, Autumn 1987, *3*(3), pp. 27–40. **[G: U.K.]**

Haydu, Frank W., III. Financial Innovation and Corporate Mergers: Discussion. *Browne, L. E. and Rosengren, E. S., eds.*, 1987, pp. 74–77. **[G: U.S.]**

Heckathorn, Douglas D. and Maser, Steven M. Bargaining and the Sources of Transaction Costs: The Case of Government Regulation. *J. Law, Econ., Organ.*, Spring 1987, *3*(1), pp. 69–98. **[G: U.S.]**

Heitger, Bernhard. Corporatism, Technological Gaps and Growth in OECD Countries. *Weltwirtsch. Arch.*, 1987, *123*(3), pp. 463–73. **[G: OECD]**

Helfat, Constance E. and Teece, David J. Vertical Integration and Risk Reduction. *J. Law, Econ., Organ.*, Spring 1987, *3*(1), pp. 47–67. **[G: U.S.]**

Henderson, Robert P. The 1980s Merger Wave: An Industrial Organization Perspective: Discussion. *Browne, L. E. and Rosengren, E. S., eds.*, 1987, pp. 48–51. **[G: U.S.]**

Hendricks, Kenneth; Porter, Robert H. and Boudreau, Bryan. Information, Returns, and Bidding Behavior in OCS Auctions: 1954–1969. *J. Ind. Econ.*, June 1987, *35*(4), pp. 517–42. **[G: U.S.]**

Henley, Andrew. Labour's Shares and Profitability Crisis in the U.S.: Recent Experience and Post-war Trends. *Cambridge J. Econ.*, December 1987, *11*(4), pp. 315–30. **[G: U.S.]**

Henley, Andrew. Trades Unions, Market Concentration and Income Distribution in United States Manufacturing Industry. *Int. J. Ind. Organ.*, June 1987, *5*(2), pp. 193–210.

Hennart, Jean-Francois. Transaction Costs and the Multinational Enterprise: The Case of Tin. *Atack, J., ed.*, 1987, pp. 147–59. **[G: U.K.]**

Hexter, J. Lawrence. Measuring Relative Concentration [Relative Concentration of the Largest 500 Firms]. *Southern Econ. J.*, January 1987, *53*(3), pp. 777–78. **[G: U.S.]**

Heywood, John S. Wage Discrimination and Market Structure. *J. Post Keynesian Econ.*, Summer 1987, *9*(4), pp. 617–28. **[G: U.S.]**

Highfield, Richard and Smiley, Robert. New Business Starts and Economic Activity: An Empirical Investigation. *Int. J. Ind. Organ.*, March 1987, *5*(1), pp. 51–66. **[G: U.S.]**

Hill, Hal. Concentration in Indonesian Manufacturing. *Bull. Indonesian Econ. Stud.*, August 1987, *23*(2), pp. 71–100.   [G: Indonesia]

Hill, Hal and Lindsey, C. W. Multinationals from Large and Small Countries: A Philippine Case Study. *Banca Naz. Lavoro Quart. Rev.*, March 1987, (160), pp. 77–92.   [G: Philippines]

Hitchens, D. M. W. N. and O'Farrell, P. N. The Comparative Performance of Small Manufacturing Firms in Northern Ireland and South East England. *Reg. Stud.*, December 1987, *21*(6), pp. 543–53.   [G: U.K.]

Hite, Gailen L.; Owers, James E. and Rogers, Ronald C. The Market for Interfirm Asset Sales: Partial Sell-offs and Total Liquidations. *J. Finan. Econ.*, June 1987, *18*(2), pp. 229–52.   [G: U.S.]

Hoel, Michael and Strøm, Steinar. Supply Security and Import Diversification of Natural Gas. *Golombek, R.; Hoel, M. and Vislie, J., eds.*, 1987, pp. 151–72.   [G: W. Europe; Norway; U.S.S.R.]

Hollander, Abraham. On Price-Increasing Entry. *Economica*, August 1987, *54*(215), pp. 317–24.

Holt, Charles A. and Scheffman, David T. Facilitating Practices: The Effects of Advance Notice and Best-Price Policies. *Rand J. Econ.*, Summer 1987, *18*(2), pp. 187–97.

Horowitz, Ira. Market Structure Implications of Export-Price Uncertainty. *Managerial Dec. Econ.*, June 1987, *8*(2), pp. 131–37.

Horowitz, Ira. Regression-Estimated Market Demand and Quasi-Cournot Behavior. *Int. J. Ind. Organ.*, June 1987, *5*(2), pp. 247–53.

Hosier, Richard H. The Informal Sector in Kenya: Spatial Variation and Development Alternatives. *J. Devel. Areas*, July 1987, *21*(4), pp. 383–402.   [G: Kenya]

Howells, Jeremy. Developments in the Location, Technology and Industrial Organization of Computer Services: Some Trends and Research Issues. *Reg. Stud.*, December 1987, *21*(6), pp. 493–503.   [G: U.K.]

Huang, Yen-Sheng and Walkling, Ralph A. Target Abnormal Returns Associated with Acquisition Announcements: Payment, Acquisition Form, and Managerial Resistance. *J. Finan. Econ.*, December 1987, *19*(2), pp. 329–49.   [G: U.S.]

Huberman, Gur and Kandel, Shmuel. Value Line Rank and Firm Size. *J. Bus.*, October 1987, *60*(4), pp. 577–89.   [G: U.S.]

Iguchi, Tomio. Aggregate Concentration, Turnover, and Mobility among the Largest Manufacturing Firms in Japan. *Antitrust Bull.*, Winter 1987, *32*(4), pp. 939–65.   [G: Japan]

Jacobsen, Bjørn R. Some Experiences from Bargaining over Natural Gas. *Golombek, R.; Hoel, M. and Vislie, J., eds.*, 1987, pp. 181–92.   [G: Norway]

Jadlow, Joseph M.; Jadlow, Janice W. and Yu, Shirley S. Risk, Rivalry, and Innovation: The Case of Ethical Drugs. *Rivista Int. Sci. Econ. Com.*, July 1987, *34*(7), pp. 593–608.   [G: U.S.]

Jagrén, Lars. Concentration, Exit, Entry and Reconstruction of Swedish Manufacturing. *Elias-*

son, G., ed., 1987, pp. 39–50.   [G: Sweden]

Jahera, John S., Jr.; Lloyd, William P. and Page, Daniel E. The Relationship between Financial Performance and Stock Market Based Measures of Corporate Diversification. *Financial Rev.*, November 1987, *22*(4), pp. 379–89.   [G: U.S.]

Jarrell, Gregg A. Financial Innovation and Corporate Mergers. *Browne, L. E. and Rosengren, E. S., eds.*, 1987, pp. 52–73.   [G: U.S.]

Jarrell, Gregg A. and Poulsen, Annette B. Shark Repellents and Stock Prices: The Effects of Antitakeover Amendments since 1980. *J. Finan. Econ.*, September 1987, *19*(1), pp. 127–68.

Jensen, Michael C. The Free Cash Flow Theory of Takeovers: A Financial Perspective on Mergers and Acquisitions and the Economy. *Browne, L. E. and Rosengren, E. S., eds.*, 1987, pp. 102–43.   [G: U.S.]

Johnson, Richard L. and Smith, David D. Antitrust Division Merger Procedures and Policy, 1968–1984. *Antitrust Bull.*, Winter 1987, *32*(4), pp. 967–88.   [G: U.S.]

Johnson, Ronald N. and Parkman, Allen M. Spatial Competition and Vertical Integration; Cement and Concrete Revisited: Comment. *Amer. Econ. Rev.*, September 1987, *77*(4), pp. 750–53.   [G: U.S.]

Johnson, Ronald N. and Parkman, Allen M. The Role of Ideas in Antitrust Policy Toward Vertical Mergers: Evidence from the FTC Cement-Ready Mixed Concrete Cases. *Antitrust Bull.*, Winter 1987, *32*(4), pp. 841–83.   [G: U.S.]

Johnson, W. Bruce. Discussion of Management Compensation Contracts and Merger-Induced Abnormal Returns. *J. Acc. Res.*, Supplement 1987, *25*, pp. 77–84.   [G: U.S.]

Jones, S. R. H. Technology, Transaction Costs, and the Transition to Factory Production in the British Silk Industry, 1700–1870. *J. Econ. Hist.*, March 1987, *47*(1), pp. 71–96.   [G: U.K.]

Jorde, Thomas M. Coping with the Merger Guidelines and the Government's "Fix-It-First" Approach: A Modest Appeal for More Information. *Antitrust Bull.*, Fall 1987, *32*(3), pp. 579–608.   [G: U.S.]

Jorgenson, Dale W. Productivity and Changes in Ownership of Manufacturing Plants: Comments and Discussion. *Brookings Pap. Econ. Act.*, 1987, (3), pp. 674–78.   [G: U.S.]

Jose, Manuel L. and Stevens, Jerry L. Product Market Structure, Capital Intensity, and Systematic Risk: Empirical Results from the Theory of the Firm. *J. Finan. Res.*, Summer 1987, *10*(2), pp. 161–75.   [G: U.S.]

Joskow, Paul L. Contract Duration and Relationship-Specific Investments: Empirical Evidence from Coal Markets. *Amer. Econ. Rev.*, March 1987, *77*(1), pp. 168–85.   [G: U.S.]

Kania, John J. Profitability and Market Power in Industries with Regional–Local Markets. *Amer. Econ.*, Fall 1987, *31*(2), pp. 29–34.   [G: U.S.]

Kantarelis, D. and Veendorp, E. C. H. Buyer Concentration and Countervailing Power.

Quart. J. Bus. Econ., Summer 1987, *26*(3), pp. 42–56. **[G: U.S.]**

Kass, David I. State and Federal Regulation in the Market for Corporate Control: A Comment. *Antitrust Bull.*, Fall 1987, *32*(3), pp. 693–97. **[G: U.S.]**

Katzner, Donald W. The Efficiency of Organizational Forms. *Écon. Appl.*, 1987, *40*(3), pp. 539–64.

Kaufmann, Peter J. The Community Trademark; Its Role in Making the Internal Market Effective. *J. Common Market Stud.*, March 1987, *25*(3), pp. 223–35. **[G: EEC]**

Kaulmann, Thomas. Managerialism versus the Property Rights Theory of the Firm. *Bamberg, G. and Spremann, K., eds.*, 1987, pp. 439–59. **[G: U.S.]**

Kay, N. M. and Diamantopoulos, Adamantios. Uncertainty and Synergy: Towards a Formal Model of Corporate Strategy. *Managerial Dec. Econ.*, June 1987, *8*(2), pp. 121–30. **[G: U.S.; U.K.; France; W. Germany]**

Kelleher, Patricia. Familism in Irish Capitalism in the 1950s. *Econ. Soc. Rev.*, January 1987, *18*(2), pp. 75–94. **[G: Ireland]**

Kelton, Christina M. L. The Inflationary Contribution of Market Structure in Food and Tobacco Manufacturing. *Wills, R. L.; Caswell, J. A. and Culbertson, J. D., eds.*, 1987, pp. 345–59.

Kim, E. Han and Schatzberg, John D. Voluntary Corporate Liquidations. *J. Finan. Econ.*, December 1987, *19*(2), pp. 311–28. **[G: U.S.]**

Kim, H. Youn. Economies of Scale and Scope in Multiproduct Firms: Evidence from U.S. Railroads. *Appl. Econ.*, June 1987, *19*(6), pp. 733–41. **[G: U.S.]**

Kim, H. Youn. Economies of Scale in Multi-product Firms: An Empirical Analysis. *Economica*, May 1987, *54*(214), pp. 185–206. **[G: U.S.]**

Kirchner, Christian and Picot, Arnold. Transaction Cost Analysis of Structural Changes in the Distribution System: Reflections on Institutional Developments in the Federal Republic of Germany. *J. Inst. Theoretical Econ.*, March 1987, *143*(1), pp. 62–81. **[G: W. Germany]**

Klein, Bohuslav. Joint Enterprises in Czechoslovakia. *Czech. Econ. Digest.*, August 1987, (6), pp. 36–46. **[G: Czechoslovakia]**

Klein, Philip A. Power and Economic Performance: The Institutionalist View. *J. Econ. Issues*, September 1987, *21*(3), pp. 1341–77.

Klemperer, Paul. Entry Deterrence in Markets with Consumer Switching Costs. *Econ. J.*, Supplement 1987, *97*, pp. 99–117.

Klemperer, Paul. The Competitiveness of Markets with Switching Costs. *Rand J. Econ.*, Spring 1987, *18*(1), pp. 137–50.

Klevorick, Alvin K. and McGuire, Thomas G. Monopolistic Competition and Consumer Information: Pricing in the Market for Psychologists' Services. *McGuire, T. G. and Scheffler, R. M., eds.*, 1987, pp. 235–53. **[G: U.S.]**

Kreinin, Mordechai E.; Martin, Stephen and Sheehey, Edmund J. Differential Response of U.S. Import Prices and Quantities to Ex-

change-Rate Adjustments. *Weltwirtsch. Arch.*, 1987, *123*(3), pp. 449–62. **[G: U.S.]**

Kumar, K. Ravi. The Relationship between Mixed Strategies and Strategic Groups. *Managerial Dec. Econ.*, September 1987, *8*(3), pp. 235–42.

Kumar, Prem. Determinants of Corporate Growth: The Indian Experience. *Margin*, Apr.-June 1987, *19*(3), pp. 55–68. **[G: India]**

Laband, David N. and Sophocleus, John P. The Social Cost of Rent-Seeking: First Estimates. *Econ. Scelte Pubbliche/J. Public Finance Public Choice*, May-Aug. 1987, *5*(2), pp. 127–33. **[G: U.S.]**

Laitinen, Erkki K. A Computer Model of the Failure Process of the Firm: Part I. *Liiketaloudellinen Aikak.*, 1987, *36*(3), pp. 199–225. **[G: Finland]**

Laitinen, Erkki K. A Computer Model of the Failure Process of the Firm: Part II. *Liiketaloudellinen Aikak.*, April 1987, *36*(4), pp. 339–65. **[G: Finland]**

Lambson, Val Eugene. Is the Concentration–Profit Correlation Partly an Artifact of Lumpy Technology? *Amer. Econ. Rev.*, September 1987, *77*(4), pp. 731–33.

Lanning, Steven G. Costs of Maintaining a Cartel. *J. Ind. Econ.*, December 1987, *36*(2), pp. 147–74.

LeBaron, Dean and Speidell, Lawrence S. Why Are the Parts Worth More than the Sum? "Chop Shop," A Corporate Valuation Model. *Browne, L. E. and Rosengren, E. S., eds.*, 1987, pp. 78–95. **[G: U.S.]**

Lee, Li Way. The Coasian Firm. *J. Behav. Econ.*, Summer 1987, *16*(2), pp. 1–7.

Lee, Seung Hoon. The Price of Final Product after Vertical Integration. *Amer. Econ. Rev.*, December 1987, *77*(5), pp. 1013–16.

Leech, Dennis. Corporate Ownership and Control: A New Look at the Evidence of Berle and Means. *Oxford Econ. Pap.*, September 1987, *39*(3), pp. 534–51. **[G: U.S.]**

Leech, Dennis. Ownership Concentration and Control in Large U.S. Corporations in the 1930s: An Analysis of the TNEC Sample. *J. Ind. Econ.*, March 1987, *35*(3), pp. 333–42. **[G: U.S.]**

Leech, Dennis. Ownership Concentration and the Theory of the Firm: A Simple-Game-Theoretic Approach. *J. Ind. Econ.*, March 1987, *35*(3), pp. 225–40.

Legros, Patrick. Disadvantageous Syndicates and Stable Cartels: The Case of the Nucleolus. *J. Econ. Theory*, June 1987, *42*(1), pp. 30–49.

Lehnerd, Alvin P. Revitalizing the Manufacture and Design of Mature Global Products. *Guile, B. R. and Brooks, H., eds.*, 1987, pp. 49–64.

Leifer, Eric M. and White, Harrison C. A Structural Approach to Markets. *Mizruchi, M. S. and Schwartz, M., eds.*, 1987, pp. 85–108.

Lenel, Hans Otto. Ist zur Förderung der internationalen Wettbewerbsfähigkeit externes Unternehmenswachstum erstrebenswert? (Are Mergers Necessary to Secure International Competitiveness? With English summary.) *Le-*

nel, H. O., et al., eds., 1987, pp. 113–29.
[G: W. Germany]
Levin, Sharon G.; Levin, Stanford L. and Meisel, John B. A Dynamic Analysis of the Adoption of a New Technology: The Case of Optical Scanners. *Rev. Econ. Statist.,* February 1987, *69*(1), pp. 12–17. [G: U.S.]
Levine, Michael E. Airline Competition in Deregulated Markets: Theory, Firm Strategy, and Public Policy. *Yale J. Regul.,* Spring 1987, *4*(2), pp. 393–494. [G: U.S.]
Levy, Amnon and Bar-Niv, Ran. Macroeconomic Aspects of Firm Bankruptcy Analysis. *J. Macroecon.,* Summer 1987, *9*(3), pp. 407–15.
[G: U.S.]
Levy, David T. Testing the Specification of the Market Structure–Performance Relationship. *Rivista Int. Sci. Econ. Com.,* April 1987, *34*(4), pp. 337–52. [G: U.S.]
Levy, David T. The Speed of the Invisible Hand. *Int. J. Ind. Organ.,* March 1987, *5*(1), pp. 79–92. [G: U.S.]
Levy, David T. and Rodriguez, Alvaro. Does the Threat of Antitrust Policy Keep Prices Down? Or: Making Hay While the Sun Shines. *Int. J. Ind. Organ.,* September 1987, *5*(3), pp. 341–50.
Lichtenberg, Frank R. and Siegel, Donald. Productivity and Changes in Ownership of Manufacturing Plants. *Brookings Pap. Econ. Act.,* 1987, (3), pp. 643–73. [G: U.S.]
Lieberman, Marvin B. Excess Capacity as a Barrier to Entry: An Empirical Appraisal. *J. Ind. Econ.,* June 1987, *35*(4), pp. 607–27.
[G: U.S.]
Lieberman, Marvin B. Market Growth, Economies of Scale, and Plant Size in the Chemical Processing Industries. *J. Ind. Econ.,* December 1987, *36*(2), pp. 175–91. [G: U.S.]
Lieberman, Marvin B. Patents, Learning by Doing, and Market Structure in the Chemical Processing Industries. *Int. J. Ind. Organ.,* September 1987, *5*(3), pp. 257–76. [G: U.S.]
Lieberman, Marvin B. Postentry Investment and Market Structure in the Chemical Processing Industries. *Rand J. Econ.,* Winter 1987, *18*(4), pp. 533–49. [G: U.S.]
Little, Ian M. D. Small Manufacturing Enterprises in Developing Countries. *World Bank Econ. Rev.,* January 1987, *1*(2), pp. 203–35.
[G: Colombia; India]
Llerena, Patrick and Zuscovitch, Ehud. Valeur d'option et structure de marchés. Le cas du quasi-monopole. (Option Value and Market Structure: The Case of Quasi-monopoly. With English summary.) *Écon. Appl.,* 1987, *40*(1), pp. 97–113.
Loescher, Samuel M. Toward More Competitive Diversity in a Market-Concentrated Economy. *Samuels, W. J. and Miller, A. S., eds.,* 1987, pp. 263–75. [G: U.S.]
Lott, John R., Jr. Licensing and Nontransferable Rents. *Amer. Econ. Rev.,* June 1987, *77*(3), pp. 453–55.
Lustgarten, Steven and Thomadakis, Stavros B. Mobility Barriers and Tobin's q. *J. Bus.,* Octo-

ber 1987, *60*(4), pp. 519–37. [G: U.S.]
MacKie-Mason, Jeffrey K. and Pindyck, Robert S. Cartel Theory and Cartel Experience in International Minerals Markets. *[Adelman, M. A.],* 1987, pp. 187–214. [G: Global]
MacLeod, W. Bentley. Entry, Sunk Costs, and Market Structure. *Can. J. Econ.,* February 1987, *20*(1), pp. 140–51.
MacLeod, W. Bentley; Norman, G. and Thisse, Jacques-François. Competition, Tacit Collusion and Free Entry. *Econ. J.,* March 1987, *97*(385), pp. 189–98.
Macneil, Ian R. Relational Contract Theory as Sociology: A Reply. *J. Inst. Theoretical Econ.,* June 1987, *143*(2), pp. 272–90.
Maggi, Rico. Die Analyse der Wettbewerbsfähigkeit wirtschaftlicher Strukturen. (Competitive Structures. With English summary.) *Schweiz. Z. Volkswirtsch. Statist.,* September 1987, *123*(3), pp. 367–89. [G: Switzerland]
Mann, Arthur J. and Delons, Jacques R. The Buenos Aires Mini-Enterprise Sector. *Soc. Econ. Stud.,* June 1987, *36*(2), pp. 41–67.
[G: Argentina]
Mansfield, Edwin. Productivity and Changes in Ownership of Manufacturing Plants: Comments and Discussion. *Brookings Pap. Econ. Act.,* 1987, (3), pp. 678–81. [G: U.S.]
Marcus, Alfred A.; Kaufman, Allen M. and Beam, David R. The Pursuit of Corporate Advantage and the Quest for Social Legitimacy. *Marcus, A. A.; Kaufman, A. M. and Beam, D. R., eds.,* 1987, pp. 1–16.
Marion, Bruce W. Entry Barriers: Theory, Empirical Evidence, and the Food Industries. *Wills, R. L.; Caswell, J. A. and Culbertson, J. D., eds.,* 1987, pp. 187–202. [G: U.S.]
Marks, Stephen V. International Crude-Oil Resales: Theory and Recent History. *J. Energy Devel.,* Autumn 1987, *13*(1), pp. 87–100.
[G: OPEC]
Marlow, Michael L. and Wright, George E. Measuring Market Power as Competition over Time. *J. Econ. Bus.,* May 1987, *39*(2), pp. 171–83. [G: U.S.]
Martin, Robert E. Long-run Supply in Competitive Labor-Managed Industries. *Jones, D. C. and Svejnar, J., eds.,* 1987, pp. 113–28.
Masson, Robert T. and Shaanan, Joseph. Optimal Oligopoly Pricing and the Threat of Entry: Canadian Evidence. *Int. J. Ind. Organ.,* September 1987, *5*(3), pp. 323–39. [G: Canada]
Masulis, Ronald W. Changes in Ownership Structure: Conversions of Mutual Savings and Loans to Stock Charter. *J. Finan. Econ.,* March 1987, *18*(1), pp. 29–59. [G: U.S.]
Mathewson, G. Frank and Winter, Ralph A. The Competitive Effects of Vertical Agreements: Comment. *Amer. Econ. Rev.,* December 1987, *77*(5), pp. 1057–62. [G: U.S.]
Mathiesen, Lars; Roland, Kjell and Thonstad, Knut. The European Natural Gas Market: Degrees of Market Power on the Selling Side. *Golombek, R.; Hoel, M. and Vislie, J., eds.,* 1987, pp. 27–58. [G: W. Europe; Algeria; U.S.S.R.]

Matthews, Steven and Moore, John. Monopoly Provision of Quality and Warranties: An Exploration in the Theory of Multidimensional Screening. *Econometrica*, March 1987, 55(2), pp. 441–67.

Matutes, Carmen and Regibeau, Pierre. Standardization in Multi-component Industries. *Gabel, H. L., ed.*, 1987, pp. 23–28.

McBride, Mark E. Spatial Competition and Vertical Integration; Cement and Concrete Revisited: Reply. *Amer. Econ. Rev.*, September 1987, 77(4), pp. 754–56.   [G: U.S.]

McCombie, John S. L. Does the Aggregate Production Function Imply Anything about the Laws of Production? A Note. *Appl. Econ.*, August 1987, 19(8), pp. 1121–36.   [G: Australia]

McFadden, Daniel L. Technological Change, Sunk Costs, and Competition: Comments and Discussion. *Brookings Pap. Econ. Act.*, 1987, (3), pp. 938–41.

McGee, John S. Compound Pricing. *Econ. Inquiry*, April 1987, 25(2), pp. 315–39.

McKetta, Charles; Bobenrieth H., Eugenio and Avello A., Ricardo. Relación Insumo-Producto en los Mercados Forestales de Chile y sus Implicaciones. (With English summary.) *Cuadernos Econ.*, April 1987, 24(71), pp. 99–107.
    [G: Chile]

McMullen, B. Starr and Miklius, Walter. Measuring the Impact of Regulatory Reform on Firm Bankruptcies: The U.S. Motor Carrier Industry. *Int. J. Transport Econ.*, June 1987, 14(2), pp. 181–88.   [G: U.S.]

Meadowcroft, Shirley and Thompson, David. Partial Integration: A Loophole in Competition Law? *Fisc. Stud.*, February 1987, 8(1), pp. 24–47.   [G: U.K.]

Mendelson, Haim. Consolidation, Fragmentation, and Market Performance. *J. Finan. Quant. Anal.*, June 1987, 22(2), pp. 189–207.

Mentré, Paul. Regulation and Deregulation: An Economic Viewpoint. *van de Kar, H. M. and Wolfe, B. L., eds.*, 1987, pp. 293–305.

Mestelman, Stuart; Welland, Deborah and Welland, Douglas. Advance Production in Posted Offer Markets. *J. Econ. Behav. Organ.*, June 1987, 8(2), pp. 249–64.

Meyer, John R. and Oster, Clinton V., Jr. Market Structure, Public Policy, and the Future of Intercity Passenger Transportation. *Meyer, J. R. and Oster, C. V., Jr.*, 1987, pp. 205–24.
    [G: U.S.]

Meyer, John R. and Oster, Clinton V., Jr. The U.S. Experience with Airline Deregulation: Responses of the Old Guard. *Meyer, J. R. and Oster, C. V., Jr.*, 1987, pp. 55–81. [G: U.S.]

Meyer, John R. and Oster, Clinton V., Jr. The U.S. Experience with Airline Deregulation: The New Entrepreneurs. *Meyer, J. R. and Oster, C. V., Jr.*, 1987, pp. 39–53. [G: U.S.]

Milgrom, Paul R. and Roberts, John. Informational Asymmetries, Strategic Behavior, and Industrial Organization. *Amer. Econ. Rev.*, May 1987, 77(2), pp. 184–93.

Mizruchi, Mark S. and Schwartz, Michael. The Structural Analysis of Business: An Emerging Field. *Mizruchi, M. S. and Schwartz, M., eds.*, 1987, pp. 3–21.   [G: U.S.]

Mizzi, Philip J. Capital Adjustment Costs: A Nonrenewable Resource Industry. *Southern Econ. J.*, July 1987, 54(1), pp. 168–73.

Moore, Norman H. and Pruitt, Stephen W. The Market Pricing of Net Operating Loss Carryforwards: Implications of the Tax Motivations of Mergers. *J. Finan. Res.*, Summer 1987, 10(2), pp. 153–60.   [G: U.S.]

Moreno, Sergio Martín. La hipótesis de la estructura dual de la industria: el caso de la economía mexicana. (The Dual Industrial Structure Hypothesis: The Case of the Mexican Economy. With English summary.) *Estud. Econ.*, Jan.-June 1987, 2(1), pp. 81–112.   [G: Mexico]

Morrisey, Michael A. and Alexander, Jeffrey A. Hospital Participation in Multihospital Systems. *Scheffler, R. M. and Rossiter, L. F., eds.*, 1987, pp. 59–81.   [G: U.S.]

Morrison, Steven A. and Winston, Clifford. Empirical Implications and Tests of the Contestability Hypothesis. *J. Law Econ.*, April 1987, 30(1), pp. 53–66.   [G: U.S.]

Moulin, Hervé J. A Core Selection for Regulating a Single-Output Monopoly. *Rand J. Econ.*, Autumn 1987, 18(3), pp. 397–407.

Mulkey, David and Hagey, Ellen. Input/Market Linkages and Organizational Structure: An Empirical Study. *Rev. Reg. Stud.*, Winter 1987, 17(1), pp. 33–43.   [G: U.S.]

Müller-Hagedorn, Lothar. Handelskonzentration: Ein partielles Phänomen?—oder: Irreführende Handelsstatistiken. Weitere Anmerkungen. (With English summary.) *Z. Betriebswirtshaft*, February 1987, 57(2), pp. 200–207.   [G: W. Germany]

Mullner, Ross M. and Andersen, Ronald M. A Descriptive and Financial Ratio Analysis of Merged and Consolidated Hospitals: United States, 1980–1985. *Scheffler, R. M. and Rossiter, L. F., eds.*, 1987, pp. 41–58.   [G: U.S.]

Munkirs, John R. and Knoedler, Janet T. The Existence and Exercise of Corporate Power: An Opaque Fact. *J. Econ. Issues*, December 1987, 21(4), pp. 1679–1706.   [G: U.S.]

Muto, Shigeo. Possibility of Relicensing and Patent Protection. *Europ. Econ. Rev.*, June 1987, 31(4), pp. 927–45.

Mygind, Niels. Are Self-managed Firms Efficient? The Experience of Danish Fully and Partly Self-managed Firms. *Jones, D. C. and Svejnar, J., eds.*, 1987, pp. 243–323.   [G: Denmark]

Nadiri, M. Ishaq. Price Inertia and Inflation: Evidence and Theoretical Rationale. *Pasinetti, L. and Lloyd, P., eds.*, 1987, pp. 329–57.
    [G: U.S.]

Naisbitt, John. Re-inventing the Corporation. *Shetty, Y. K. and Buehler, V. M., eds.*, 1987, pp. 57–71.   [G: U.S.]

Nanjundan, S. Small and Medium Enterprises: Some Basic Development Issues. *Industry Devel.*, 1987, (20), pp. 1–50.   [G: LDCs]

Neumann, Manfred J. M. How Transaction Rights Are Shaped to Channel Innovativeness: Comment. *J. Inst. Theoretical Econ.*, March

1987, *143*(1), pp. 201–03.

Neven, Damien J. Endogenous Sequential Entry in a Spatial Model. *Int. J. Ind. Organ.*, December 1987, *5*(4), pp. 419–34.

Newbury, Colin. Technology, Capital, and Consolidation: The Performance of De Beers Mining Company Limited, 1880–1889. *Bus. Hist. Rev.*, Spring 1987, *61*(1), pp. 1–42.
[G: S. Africa]

Nicholas, Stephen. Empirical Tests of the Transaction Cost Model: The Evolution of the Pre-1939 British Manufacturing Multinational. *Atack, J., ed.*, 1987, pp. 133–45.   **[G: U.K.]**

Noreng, Øystein. Structure and Bargaining in the West European Gas Market. *Golombek, R.; Hoel, M. and Vislie, J., eds.*, 1987, pp. 7–26.
[G: W. Europe]

Nye, John Vincent. Firm Size and Economic Backwardness: A New Look at the French Industrialization Debate. *J. Econ. Hist.*, September 1987, *47*(3), pp. 649–69.   **[G: France]**

O'Farrell, P. N. and Crouchley, R. Manufacturing-Plant Closures: A Dynamic Survival Model. *Environ. Planning A*, March 1987, *19*(3), pp. 313–29.   **[G: Ireland]**

Ochoa, Eduardo M. On Differing Views of the Long Run: Reflections on *Monopoly or Competition in the U.S. Economy? Rev. Radical Polit. Econ.*, Fall 1987, *19*(3), pp. 69–74. **[G: U.S.]**

Odagiri, Hiroyuki and Yamashita, Takashi. Price Mark-Ups, Market Structure, and Business Fluctuation in Japanese Manufacturing Industries. *J. Ind. Econ.*, March 1987, *35*(3), pp. 317–31.   **[G: Japan]**

Ogliastri, Enrique and Dávila, Carlos. The Articulation of Power and Business Structures: A Study of Colombia. *Mizruchi, M. S. and Schwartz, M., eds.*, 1987, pp. 233–63.
[G: Colombia]

Oi, Walter Y. Heterogeneous Firms: Caveat Emptor [Heterogeneous Firms and the Organization of Production]. *Econ. Inquiry*, January 1987, *25*(1), pp. 181–84.

Okuguchi, Koji. Equilibrium Prices in the Bertrand and Cournot Oligopolies. *J. Econ. Theory*, June 1987, *42*(1), pp. 128–39.

Olasky, Marvin N. Anticompetitive Campaigns by Big Business in the Pre–World War II Period. *Marcus, A. A.; Kaufman, A. M. and Beam, D. R., eds.*, 1987, pp. 239–53.
[G: U.S.]

Ornstein, Stanley I. and Hanssens, Dominique M. Resale Price Maintenance: Output Increasing or Restricting? The Case of Distilled Spirits in the United States. *J. Ind. Econ.*, September 1987, *36*(1), pp. 1–18.   **[G: U.S.]**

Osborne, Martin J. and Pitchik, Carolyn. Cartels, Profits and Excess Capacity. *Int. Econ. Rev.*, June 1987, *28*(2), pp. 413–28.

Paché, Gilles and Paraponaris, Claude. Réorganisation du capital industriel et formes liées de la gestion de production. (Reorganization of Industrial Capital and Linked Forms to Management Production. With English summary.) *Écon. Soc.*, June 1987, *21*(6), pp. 151–77.

Pakes, Ariel. Mueller's *Profits in the Long Run.*

Rand J. Econ., Summer 1987, *18*(2), pp. 319–32.

Panzar, John C. and Rosse, James N. Testing for "Monopoly" Equilibrium. *J. Ind. Econ.*, June 1987, *35*(4), pp. 443–56.

Park, Young-Bum. Concentration and Wage Earnings in an Open Economy: A Case Study of Korea. *Int. Econ. J.*, Spring 1987, *1*(1), pp. 29–42.   **[G: S. Korea]**

Parker, Russell C. The Effects of Mergers and Entry on Concentration Change in SMA Grocery Retailing Markets. *Wills, R. L.; Caswell, J. A. and Culbertson, J. D., eds.*, 1987, pp. 293–313.   **[G: U.S.]**

Patrick, Hugh T. and Rohlen, Thomas P. The Political Economy of Japan: Small-Scale Family Enterprises. *Yamamura, K. and Yasuba, Y., eds.*, 1987, pp. 331–84.   **[G: Japan]**

Paulus, John D. and Gay, Robert S. U.S. Mergers Are Helping Productivity. *Challenge*, May/June 1987, *30*(2), pp. 54–57.   **[G: U.S.]**

Paulus, John D. and Waite, Stephen R. The 1980s Merger Wave: An Industrial Organization Perspective: Discussion. *Browne, L. E. and Rosengren, E. S., eds.*, 1987, pp. 38–47.
[G: U.S.]

Pauly, Mark V. Monopsony Power in Health Insurance: Thinking Straight while Standing on Your Head: Editorial. *J. Health Econ.*, March 1987, *6*(1), pp. 73–81.   **[G: U.S.]**

Peltzman, Sam. Technological Change, Sunk Costs, and Competition: Comments and Discussion. *Brookings Pap. Econ. Act.*, 1987, (3), pp. 941–46.

Pengilley, Warren. Trade Associations and Collective Boycotts in Australia and New Zealand: A Mistranslation of the Sherman Act Down Under. *Antitrust Bull.*, Winter 1987, *32*(4), pp. 1019–49.   **[G: Australia; New Zealand]**

Pfeffer, Jeffrey. A Resource Dependence Perspective on Intercorporate Relations. *Mizruchi, M. S. and Schwartz, M., eds.*, 1987, pp. 25–55.

Phillips, Almarin. The New Money and the Old Monopoly Problem. *Solomon, E. H., ed.*, 1987, pp. 193–209.   **[G: U.S.]**

Phillips, David M. Secured Credit and Bankruptcy: A Call for the Federalization of Personal Property Security Law. *Law Contemp. Probl.*, Spring 1987, *50*(2), pp. 53–88.
[G: U.S.]

Png, Ivan Paak Liang and Hirshleifer, D. Price Discrimination through Offers to Match Price. *J. Bus.*, July 1987, *60*(3), pp. 365–83.

Polach, Jay G. The Industry Structure and Pricing Policies in Oil International Transactions. *Pachauri, R. K., ed.*, 1987, pp. 35–57.
[G: Global]

Polonchek, John A. and Sushka, Marie E. The Impact of Financial and Economic Conditions on Aggregate Merger Activity. *Managerial Dec. Econ.*, June 1987, *8*(2), pp. 113–19.
[G: U.S.]

Porter, Philip K. and Scully, Gerald W. Economic Efficiency in Cooperatives. *J. Law*

Econ., October 1987, *30*(2), pp. 489–512. **[G: U.S.]**

Pound, John. The Effects of Antitakeover Amendments on Takeover Activity: Some Direct Evidence. *J. Law Econ.*, October 1987, *30*(2), pp. 353–67. **[G: U.S.]**

Powell, Irene. The Effect of Reductions in Concentration on Income Distribution. *Rev. Econ. Statist.*, February 1987, *69*(1), pp. 75–82.

Pozdena, Randall Johnston. Competition in the Semiconductor Industry. *Fed. Res. Bank San Francisco Econ. Rev.*, Spring 1987, (2), pp. 41–56. **[G: U.S.]**

Primeaux, Walter J., Jr. The Interdependence of the Life Cycle and Strategic Group Concepts: Theory and Evidence. *Lee, C. F., ed.*, 1987, pp. 67–85. **[G: U.S.]**

Putterman, Louis. Corporate Governance, Risk-Bearing and Economic Power: A Comment on Recent Work by Oliver Williamson. *J. Inst. Theoretical Econ.*, September 1987, *143*(3), pp. 422–34.

Ravenscraft, David J. The 1980s Merger Wave: An Industrial Organization Perspective. *Browne, L. E. and Rosengren, E. S., eds.*, 1987, pp. 17–37. **[G: U.S.]**

Ravenscraft, David J. and Scherer, F. M. Life after Takeover. *J. Ind. Econ.*, December 1987, *36*(2), pp. 147–56. **[G: U.S.]**

Ravid, S. Abraham. Safety First, Bankruptcy, and the Pricing and Investment Decisions of the Firm. *Econ. Inquiry*, October 1987, *25*(4), pp. 695–706.

Razin, E. and Shachar, A. Ownership of Industry and Plant Stability in Israel's Development Towns. *Urban Stud.*, August 1987, *24*(4), pp. 296–311. **[G: Israel]**

Reddy, N. Mohan. Technology, Standards, and Markets: A Market Institutionalization Perspective. *Gabel, H. L., ed.*, 1987, pp. 47–66.

Reed, Richard and Sharp, John A. Confirmation of the Specialization Ratio. *Appl. Econ.*, March 1987, *19*(3), pp. 393–405. **[G: U.K.]**

Reynolds, Stanley S. Capacity Investment, Preemption and Commitment in an Infinite Horizon Model. *Int. Econ. Rev.*, February 1987, *28*(1), pp. 69–88.

Rhoades, Stephen A. Determinants of Premiums Paid in Bank Acquisitions. *Atlantic Econ. J.*, March 1987, *15*(1), pp. 20–30. **[G: U.S.]**

Rhoades, Stephen A. The Effect of Nonbank Thrift Institutions on Commercial Bank Profit Performance in Local Markets. *Quart. Rev. Econ. Bus.*, Spring 1987, *27*(1), pp. 16–28. **[G: U.S.]**

Rhoades, Stephen A. The Operating Performance of Acquired Firms in Banking. *Wills, R. L.; Caswell, J. A. and Culbertson, J. D., eds.*, 1987, pp. 277–92. **[G: U.S.]**

Richardson, Peter. The Origins and Development of the Collins House Group, 1915–1951. *Australian Econ. Hist. Rev.*, March 1987, *27*(1), pp. 3–29. **[G: Australia]**

Riordan, Michael H. and Sappington, David E. M. Information, Incentives, and Organiza-

tional Mode. *Quart. J. Econ.*, May 1987, *102*(2), pp. 243–63.

Roberts, John. Battles for Market Share: Incomplete Information, Aggressive Strategic Pricing, and Competitive Dynamics. *Bewley, T. F., ed.*, 1987, pp. 157–95.

Robertson, Paul. The Strategic Development of Repco and National Consolidated Limited, 1945–1983. *Australian Econ. Hist. Rev.*, September 1987, *27*(2), pp. 3–36. **[G: Australia]**

Rock, Steven M. and Hall, W. Clayton. Advertising and Monopoly Power: The Case of the Electric Utility Industry—Comment. *Atlantic Econ. J.*, March 1987, *15*(1), pp. 67–70. **[G: U.S.]**

Roe, Mark J. The Voting Prohibition in Bond Workouts. *Yale Law J.*, December 1987, *97*(2), pp. 232–79. **[G: U.S.]**

Rogerson, William P. The Dissipation of Profits by Brand Name Investment and Entry when Price Guarantees Quality. *J. Polit. Econ.*, August 1987, *95*(4), pp. 797–809.

Romano, Richard E. A Note on Market Structure and Innovation When Inventors Can Enter. *J. Ind. Econ.*, March 1987, *35*(3), pp. 353–58.

Rongliang, Guo and Wei, He. Attach Importance to the Administration of Self-Employed Youth: An Investigative Report on Individually Owned Small Businesses in Wuxi City. *Chinese Econ. Stud.*, Fall 1987, *21*(1), pp. 26–36. **[G: China]**

Rose, John T. and Savage, Donald T. Interstate Banking and the Viability of Small, Independent Banks: Further Evidence on Market Share Accumulation by New Banks. *Antitrust Bull.*, Winter 1987, *32*(4), pp. 1007–18. **[G: U.S.]**

Rose, Peter S. The Impact of Mergers in Banking: Evidence from a Nationwide Sample of Federally Chartered Banks. *J. Econ. Bus.*, November 1987, *39*(4), pp. 289–312. **[G: U.S.]**

Rosenbaum, David I. Predatory Pricing and the Reconstituted Lemon Juice Industry. *J. Econ. Issues*, March 1987, *21*(1), pp. 237–58. **[G: U.S.]**

Rotemberg, Julio J. and Saloner, Garth. The Relative Rigidity of Monopoly Pricing. *Amer. Econ. Rev.*, December 1987, *77*(5), pp. 917–26.

Rothschild, R. The Theory of Monopolistic Competition: E. H. Chamberlin's Influence on Industrial Organisation Theory over Sixty Years. *J. Econ. Stud.*, 1987, *14*(1), pp. 34–54.

Rubinstein, Ariel and Wolinsky, Asher. Middlemen. *Quart. J. Econ.*, August 1987, *102*(3), pp. 581–93.

Russe, Catherine M. and Anderson, Gerard F. Hospital Reorganization: Examining the Effects on Medical Education. *Scheffler, R. M. and Rossiter, L. F., eds.*, 1987, pp. 141–56. **[G: U.S.]**

Saghafi, Massoud M. Market Share Stability and Marketing Policy: An Axiomatic Approach. *Sheth, J. N., ed.*, 1987, pp. 267–84.

Sah, Raaj Kumar and Stiglitz, Joseph E. The Invariance of Market Innovation to the Number of Firms. *Rand J. Econ.*, Spring 1987, *18*(1), pp. 98–108.

Saloner, Garth. Cournot Duopoly with Two Production Periods. *J. Econ. Theory*, June 1987, *42*(1), pp. 183–87.

Saloner, Garth. Predation, Mergers, and Incomplete Information. *Rand J. Econ.*, Summer 1987, *18*(2), pp. 165–86.

Salop, Steven C. Symposium on Mergers and Antitrust. *J. Econ. Perspectives*, Fall 1987, *1*(2), pp. 3–12. **[G: U.S.]**

Salop, Steven C. and Scheffman, David T. Cost-Raising Strategies. *J. Ind. Econ.*, September 1987, *36*(1), pp. 19–34.

Samuels, Warren J. and Miller, Arthur S. Corporate America. *Samuels, W. J. and Miller, A. S., eds.*, 1987, pp. 1–9. **[G: U.S.]**

Sawyer, Malcolm C. Mergers: A Case of Market Failure? *Brit. Rev. Econ. Issues*, Autumn 1987, *9*(21), pp. 1–28. **[G: U.K.]**

Scheffman, David T. and Spiller, Pablo T. Geographic Market Definition under the *U.S. Department of Justice Merger Guidelines. J. Law Econ.*, April 1987, *30*(1), pp. 123–47. **[G: U.S.]**

Scherer, F. M., et al. The Validity of Studies with Line of Business Data: Comment [The Validity of Profits-Structure Studies with Particular Reference to the FTC's Line of Business Data]. *Amer. Econ. Rev.*, March 1987, *77*(1), pp. 205–17. **[G: U.S.]**

Schipper, Katherine; Thompson, Rex and Weil, Roman L. Disentangling Interrelated Effects of Regulatory Changes on Shareholder Wealth: The Case of Motor Carrier Deregulation. *J. Law Econ.*, April 1987, *30*(1), pp. 67–100. **[G: U.S.]**

Schlesinger, Mark, et al. Multihospital Systems and Access to Health Care. *Scheffler, R. M. and Rossiter, L. F., eds.*, 1987, pp. 121–40. **[G: U.S.]**

Schmalensee, Richard. Collusion versus Differential Efficiency: Testing Alternative Hypotheses. *J. Ind. Econ.*, June 1987, *35*(4), pp. 399–425. **[G: U.S.]**

Schmalensee, Richard. Competitive Advantage and Collusive Optima. *Int. J. Ind. Organ.*, December 1987, *5*(4), pp. 351–67.

Schmalensee, Richard. Horizontal Merger Policy: Problems and Changes. *J. Econ. Perspectives*, Fall 1987, *1*(2), pp. 41–54. **[G: U.S.]**

Schrader, Lee F. The Economic Efficiency of Alternative Forms of Business Enterprise: A Discussion. *Kilmer, R. L. and Armbruster, W. J., eds.*, 1987, pp. 130–33.

Schroeter, John R. Competition and Value-of-Service Pricing in the Residential Real Estate Brokerage Market. *Quart. Rev. Econ. Bus.*, Spring 1987, *27*(1), pp. 29–40. **[G: U.S.]**

Schwalbach, Joachim. Entry by Diversified Firms into German Industries. *Int. J. Ind. Organ.*, March 1987, *5*(1), pp. 43–49. **[G: W. Germany]**

Schwartz, Hugh H. Perception, Judgment, and Motivation in Manufacturing Enterprises: Findings and Preliminary Hypotheses from In-Depth Interviews. *J. Econ. Behav. Organ.*, December 1987, *8*(4), pp. 543–65. **[G: U.S.; Mexico; Argentina]**

Schwartz, Marius. The Competitive Effects of Vertical Agreements: Comment. *Amer. Econ. Rev.*, December 1987, *77*(5), pp. 1063–68. **[G: U.S.]**

Scotchmer, Suzanne. Two-Tier Pricing of Shared Facilities in a Free-Entry Equilibrium: Erratum. *Rand J. Econ.*, Spring 1987, *18*(1), pp. 164.

Scott, John. Intercorporate Structures in Western Europe: A Comparative Historical Analysis. *Mizruchi, M. S. and Schwartz, M., eds.*, 1987, pp. 208–32. **[G: EEC]**

Scott, Kenneth E. Reflections on the Theory of the Firm: Comment. *J. Inst. Theoretical Econ.*, March 1987, *143*(1), pp. 137–42.

Scouller, John. The United Kingdom Merger Boom in Perspective. *Nat. Westminster Bank Quart. Rev.*, May 1987, pp. 14–30. **[G: U.K.]**

Sexton, Richard J. and Sexton, Terri A. Cooperatives as Entrants. *Rand J. Econ.*, Winter 1987, *18*(4), pp. 581–95.

Shackett, Joyce R. and Trapani, John M. Earnings Differentials and Market Structure. *J. Human Res.*, Fall 1987, *22*(4), pp. 518–31. **[G: U.S.]**

Shaffer, Sherrill. Two-Part Tariffs in a Contestable Natural Monopoly. *Economica*, August 1987, *54*(215), pp. 315–16.

Shaked, Avner and Sutton, John. Product Differentiation and Industrial Structure. *J. Ind. Econ.*, December 1987, *36*(2), pp. 131–46.

Shapiro, Daniel M. and Khemani, R. S. The Determinants of Entry and Exit Reconsidered. *Int. J. Ind. Organ.*, March 1987, *5*(1), pp. 15–26. **[G: Canada]**

Shepard, Andrea. Licensing to Enhance Demand for New Technologies. *Rand J. Econ.*, Autumn 1987, *18*(3), pp. 360–68.

Shutt, John and Whittington, Richard. Fragmentation Strategies and the Rise of Small Units: Cases from the North West. *Reg. Stud.*, February 1987, *21*(1), pp. 13–23. **[G: U.K.]**

Sicherman, Neil W. and Pettway, Richard H. Acquisition of Divested Assets and Shareholders' Wealth. *J. Finance*, December 1987, *42*(5), pp. 1261–73. **[G: U.S.]**

Silverberg, Gerald. Technical Progress, Capital Accumulation, and Effective Demand: A Self-organization Model. *Batten, D.; Casti, J. and Johansson, B., eds.*, 1987, pp. 116–44.

Sing, Merrile. Are Combination Gas and Electric Utilities Multiproduct Natural Monopolies? *Rev. Econ. Statist.*, August 1987, *69*(3), pp. 392–98. **[G: U.S.]**

Siu, Alan K. F. Applications of Influence Analysis. *Hong Kong Econ. Pap.*, 1987, (18), pp. 23–42. **[G: U.S.]**

Sklivas, Steven D. The Strategic Choice of Managerial Incentives. *Rand J. Econ.*, Autumn 1987, *18*(3), pp. 452–58.

Slade, Margaret E. Interfirm Rivalry in a Repeated Game: An Empirical Test of Tacit Collusion. *J. Ind. Econ.*, June 1987, *35*(4), pp. 499–516. **[G: Canada]**

Sloan, Frank A.; Morrisey, Michael A. and Valvona, Joseph. Capital Markets and the Growth of Multihospital Systems. *Scheffler, R. M. and Rossiter, L. F., eds.*, 1987, pp. 83–109. **[G: U.S.]**

Soref, Michael and Zeitlin, Maurice. Finance Capital and the Internal Structure of the Capitalist Class in the United States. *Mizruchi, M. S. and Schwartz, M., eds.*, 1987, pp. 56–84. **[G: U.S.]**

Sparkes, John R.; Buckley, Peter J. and Mirza, Hafiz. A Note on Japanese Pricing Policy. *Appl. Econ.*, June 1987, *19*(6), pp. 729–32. **[G: Japan]**

Starkweather, David B. and Carman, James M. Horizontal and Vertical Concentrations in the Evolution of Hospital Competition. *Scheffler, R. M. and Rossiter, L. F., eds.*, 1987, pp. 179–94. **[G: U.S.]**

Staten, Michael; Dunkelberg, William and Umbeck, John. Market Share and the Illusion of Power: Can Blue Cross Force Hospitals to Discount? *J. Health Econ.*, March 1987, *6*(1), pp. 43–58. **[G: U.S.]**

Steinmann, Horst; Fees, Werner and Gerum, Elmar. Wertsystem der Unternehmensführung und Mitbestimmung—Einige empirische Befunde. (With English summary.) *Z. Betriebswirtshaft*, April 1987, *57*(4), pp. 398–409. **[G: W. Germany]**

Stenbacka, Rune. Horizontal and Vertical Product Differentiation—A Comparison of the Consequences for International Trade. *Andersson, J. O., ed.*, 1987, pp. 171–84.

Stigler, George J. Do Entry Conditions Vary across Markets? Comments and Discussion. *Brookings Pap. Econ. Act.*, 1987, (3), pp. 876–79. **[G: U.S.]**

Stiglitz, Joseph E. Competition and the Number of Firms in a Market: Are Duopolies More Competitive than Atomistic Markets? *J. Polit. Econ.*, October 1987, *95*(5), pp. 1041–61.

Stiglitz, Joseph E. Technological Change, Sunk Costs, and Competition. *Brookings Pap. Econ. Act.*, 1987, (3), pp. 883–937.

Stopford, John M. and Baden-Fuller, Charles. Regional-level Competition in a Mature Industry: The Case of European Domestic Appliances. *J. Common Market Stud.*, December 1987, *26*(2), pp. 173–92. **[G: EEC]**

Storey, David J. and Johnson, Steven G. Regional Variations in Entrepreneurship in the U.K. *Scot. J. Polit. Econ.*, May 1987, *34*(2), pp. 161–73. **[G: U.K.]**

Storey, David J. and Jones, A. M. New Firm Formation—A Labour Market Approach to Industrial Entry. *Scot. J. Polit. Econ.*, February 1987, *34*(1), pp. 37–51. **[G: U.K.]**

Strand, Jon. Oligopolistic Fixed-Price Equilibria and the Number of Firms. *Scand. J. Econ.*, 1987, *89*(4), pp. 497–503.

Strand, Jon. The Relationship between Wages and Firm Size: An Information Theoretic Anal-

ysis. *Int. Econ. Rev.*, February 1987, *28*(1), pp. 51–68.

Strassmann, W. Paul. Home-Based Enterprises in Cities of Developing Countries. *Econ. Develop. Cult. Change*, October 1987, *36*(1), pp. 121–44. **[G: Peru; Sri Lanka; Zambia]**

Streeten, Paul. "New" Directions for Private Resource Transfers. *Banca Naz. Lavoro Quart. Rev.*, March 1987, (160), pp. 61–76.

Sullivan, Teresa A.; Warren, Elizabeth and Westbrook, Jay Lawrence. The Use of Empirical Data in Formulating Bankruptcy Policy. *Law Contemp. Probl.*, Spring 1987, *50*(2), pp. 195–235. **[G: U.S.]**

Sundberg, Matti. Har nordiskt stål en framtid? (Is There a Future for Nordic Steel? With English summary.) *Ekon. Samfundets Tidskr.*, 1987, *40*(3), pp. 115–22. **[G: Finland]**

Swann, G. M. P. Industry Standard Microprocessors and the Strategy of Second-Source Production. *Gabel, H. L., ed.*, 1987, pp. 239–62.

Szpiro, George G. Hirschman versus Herfindahl: Some Topological Properties for the Use of Concentration Indexes: Note. *Math. Soc. Sci.*, December 1987, *14*(3), pp. 299–302.

Taira, Koji and Wada, Teiichi. Business–Government Relations in Modern Japan: A Tōdai–Yakkai–Zaikai Complex? *Mizruchi, M. S. and Schwartz, M., eds.*, 1987, pp. 264–97. **[G: Japan]**

Tapvong, Churai. A Note on the Effect of Changes in Demand upon Price: A Durable-Goods Monopoly. *Singapore Econ. Rev.*, April 1987, *32*(1), pp. 62–70.

Tauman, Yair. Vertical Integration and the Distribution of Property Rights: Comments. *Razin, A. and Sadka, E., eds.*, 1987, pp. 547–48.

Teece, David J. Capturing Value from Technological Innovation: Integration, Strategic Partnering, and Licensing Decisions. *Guile, B. R. and Brooks, H., eds.*, 1987, pp. 65–95.

Tehranian, Hassan, et al. Management Compensation Contracts and Merger-Induced Abnormal Returns. *J. Acc. Res.*, Supplement 1987, *25*, pp. 51–76. **[G: U.S.]**

Thompson, R. S. and Wright, M. Markets to Hierarchies and Back Again: The Implication of Management Buy-outs for Factory Supply. *J. Econ. Stud.*, 1987, *14*(3), pp. 5–22. **[G: U.K.]**

Thordarson, Bodil. A Comparison of Worker-Owned Firms and Conventionally Owned Firms in Sweden. *Jones, D. C. and Svejnar, J., eds.*, 1987, pp. 225–42. **[G: Sweden]**

Tietz, Bruno. Zum Thema: Konzentration im Handel. (With English summary.) *Z. Betriebswirtshaft*, February 1987, *57*(2), pp. 196–99.

Torabzadeh, Khalil M. and Bertin, William J. Leveraged Buyouts and Shareholder Returns. *J. Finan. Res.*, Winter 1987, *10*(4), pp. 313–19. **[G: U.S.]**

Travlos, Nickolaos G. Corporate Takeover Bids, Methods of Payment, and Bidding Firms' Stock Returns. *J. Finance*, September 1987, *42*(4), pp. 943–63. **[G: U.S.]**

Tremblay, Victor J. Scale Economies, Technological Change, and Firm-Cost Asymmetries in the U.S. Brewing Industry. *Quart. Rev. Econ. Bus.*, Summer 1987, *27*(2), pp. 71–86.
[G: U.S.]

Trifts, Jack W. and Scanlon, Kevin P. Interstate Bank Mergers: The Early Evidence. *J. Finan. Res.*, Winter 1987, *10*(4), pp. 305–11.
[G: U.S.]

Uekusa, Masu. The Political Economy of Japan: Industrial Organization: The 1970s to the Present. *Yamamura, K. and Yasuba, Y., eds.*, 1987, pp. 469–515.
[G: Japan]

Uri, Noel D. A Re-examination of the Advertising and Industrial Concentration Relationship. *Appl. Econ.*, April 1987, *19*(4), pp. 427–35.
[G: U.S.]

Uri, Noel D. and Coate, Malcolm. The Search for a Critical Concentration Revisited. *Appl. Econ.*, August 1987, *19*(8), pp. 1049–57.
[G: U.S.]

Varaiya, Nikhil P. Determinants of Premiums in Acquisition Transactions. *Managerial Dec. Econ.*, September 1987, *8*(3), pp. 175–84.
[G: U.S.]

Vasconcellos e Sá, Jorge Alberto. A Typology of Industrial Products: Validity and Implications. *Economia (Portugal)*, October 1987, *11*(3), pp. 285–325.
[G: Portugal]

Vicari, Paola. L'ipotesi di eterogeneità dei comportamenti di impresa. Un diverso modo di rapportarsi all'informazione. (The Hypothesis of the Heterogeneous Behaviour of Firms: A Different Way of Considering Information. With English summary.) *Econ. Lavoro*, Apr.-June 1987, *21*(2), pp. 31–45.
[G: Italy]

Vince, Péter. Transformation of Industrial Organization—Without Genuine Changes. *Acta Oecon.*, 1987, *38*(1–2), pp. 117–31.
[G: Hungary]

Vorst, Karen S. A Note on Central Planning Core Banks and Correspondent Bank Balances [Centralized Private Sector Planning: An Institutionalist's Perspective on the Contemporary U.S. Economy]. *J. Econ. Issues*, March 1987, *21*(1), pp. 482–92.
[G: U.S.]

Wachter, Susan M. Residential Real Estate Brokerage: Rate Uniformity and Moral Hazard. *Jaffe, A. J., ed.*, 1987, pp. 189–210.
[G: U.S.]

Wagner, Joachim and Bellmann, Lutz. Produkt- und Prozessinnovationen als Unternehmensstrategien bei Importdruck. Eine ökonometrische Untersuchung für Industrien des Verarbeitenden Gewerbes in der Bundesrepublik Deutschland (1976–1983). (Product and Process Innovations: Strategies for Firms under Import Pressure. An Econometric Study for Manufacturing Industries in the Federal Republic of Germany [1976–1983]. With English summary.) *Ifo-Studien*, 1987, *33*(3), pp. 223–42.
[G: W. Germany]

Waldman, Michael. Noncooperative Entry Deterrence, Uncertainty, and the Free Rider Problem. *Rev. Econ. Stud.*, April 1987, *54*(2), pp. 301–10.

Wansley, James W.; Lane, William R. and Yang, Ho C. Gains to Bidder Firms in Cash and Securities Transactions. *Financial Rev.*, November 1987, *22*(4), pp. 403–14.
[G: U.S.]

Waterson, Michael. Recent Developments in the Theory of Natural Monopoly. *J. Econ. Surveys*, 1987, *1*(1), pp. 59–80.

Webb, David C. The Importance of Incomplete Information in Explaining the Existence of Costly Bankruptcy. *Economica*, August 1987, *54*(215), pp. 279–88.

Weidenbaum, Murray and Vogt, Stephen. The Pot versus the Kettle. *Challenge*, Sept./Oct. 1987, *30*(4), pp. 56–60.
[G: U.S.]

Weiss, Leonard W. Concentration and Price—A Progress Report. *Wills, R. L.; Caswell, J. A. and Culbertson, J. D., eds.*, 1987, pp. 317–32.

White, Lawrence J. Antitrust and Merger Policy: A Review and Critique. *J. Econ. Perspectives*, Fall 1987, *1*(2), pp. 13–22.
[G: U.S.]

Whittred, Greg. Taxation and the Evolution of Holding Company Form in Australia. *Australian Econ. Hist. Rev.*, September 1987, *27*(2), pp. 77–86.
[G: Australia]

Wiggins, Steven N. Organizational Theory, Information Processing, and Short-run Dynamics: Theory and Empirical Tests. *J. Inst. Theoretical Econ.*, March 1987, *143*(1), pp. 204–21.
[G: U.S.]

Wiggins, Steven N. and Libecap, Gary D. Firm Heterogeneities and Cartelization Efforts in Domestic Crude Oil. *J. Law, Econ., Organ.*, Spring 1987, *3*(1), pp. 1–25.
[G: U.S.]

Wilder, Ronald P. and Jacobs, Philip. Antitrust Considerations for Hospital Mergers: Market Definition and Market Concentration. *Scheffler, R. M. and Rossiter, L. F., eds.*, 1987, pp. 245–62.
[G: U.S.]

Wilks, Stephen and Wright, Maurice. Comparing Government–Industry Relations: States, Sectors, and Networks: Conclusion. *Wilks, S. and Wright, M., eds.*, 1987, pp. 274–313.

Williamson, Oliver E. Assessing Contract. *Williamson, O., 1987, 1985*, pp. 161–89.

Williamson, Oliver E. Kenneth Arrow and the New Institutional Economics. *Feiwel, G. R., ed. (II)*, 1987, pp. 584–99.

Williamson, Oliver E. The Vertical Integration of Production: Market Failure Considerations. *Williamson, O., 1987, 1971*, pp. 24–38.

Williamson, Oliver E. Transaction Cost Economics: The Comparative Contracting Perspective. *J. Econ. Behav. Organ.*, December 1987, *8*(4), pp. 617–25.

Willig, Robert. Do Entry Conditions Vary across Markets? Comments and Discussion. *Brookings Pap. Econ. Act.*, 1987, (3), pp. 872–76.
[G: U.S.]

Willmore, Larry N. Controle estrangeiro e concentração na indústria brasileira. (With English summary.) *Pesquisa Planejamento Econ.*, April 1987, *17*(1), pp. 161–89.
[G: Brazil]

Wills, Robert L. Do Advertising-Induced Price Differences among Brands Explain Profit Differences among Products? *Wills, R. L.; Caswell, J. A. and Culbertson, J. D., eds.*, 1987, pp. 361–77.

Windsperger, Josef. Zur Methode des Transaktionskostenansatzes. [Die Unhaltbarkeit des Transaktionskostenansatzes für die "Markt oder Unternehmung"—Diskussion.] (With English summary.) *Z. Betriebswirtschaft*, January 1987, 57(1), pp. 59–76.

Wintrobe, Ronald. The Market for Corporate Control and the Market for Political Control. *J. Law, Econ., Organ.*, Fall 1987, 3(2), pp. 435–48. [G: U.S.]

Witt, Ulrich. How Transaction Rights Are Shaped to Channel Innovativeness. *J. Inst. Theoretical Econ.*, March 1987, 143(1), pp. 180–95.

Wolinsky, Asher. Brand Names and Price Discrimination. *J. Ind. Econ.*, March 1987, 35(3), pp. 255–68.

Woodward, Allan. Comments on Ratio Analysis of Merged Hospitals. *Scheffler, R. M. and Rossiter, L. F., eds.*, 1987, pp. 115–17. [G: U.S.]

Wrigley, N. The Concentration of Capital in UK Grocery Retailing. *Environ. Planning A*, October 1987, 19(10), pp. 1283–88. [G: U.K.]

Xu, Lu. China's Industrial Reform: Industrial Corporations. *Tidrick, G. and Jiyuan, C., eds.*, 1987, pp. 281–96. [G: China]

Yagil, Joseph. An Exchange Ratio Determination Model for Mergers: A Note. *Financial Rev.*, February 1987, 22(1), pp. 195–202.

Yarbrough, Beth V. and Yarbrough, Robert M. Cooperation in the Liberalization of International Trade: After Hegemony, What? *Int. Organ.*, Winter 1987, 41(1), pp. 1–26. [G: Global]

Yen, Gili. Merger Proposals, Managerial Discretion, and Magnitude of Shareholders' Wealth Gains. *J. Econ. Bus.*, August 1987, 39(3), pp. 251–66. [G: U.S.]

Yoffie, David B. Corporate Strategies for Political Action: A Rational Model. *Marcus, A. A.; Kaufman, A. M. and Beam, D. R., eds.*, 1987, pp. 43–60. [G: U.S.]

Young, Stephen. Business Strategy and the Internationalization of Business: Recent Approaches. *Managerial Dec. Econ.*, March 1987, 8(1), pp. 31–40.

Yu, Shirley S. On Estimating an Individual Firm's Permanent Market Share. *Atlantic Econ. J.*, March 1987, 15(1), pp. 123.

Zaman, Raquibuz. Factors Determining the Survival of the Relatively Small Size U.S. Banks in the Late Eighties. *Tremblay, R., ed.*, 1987, pp. 283–97. [G: U.S.]

Zimmermann, Klaus F. Innovations, Market Structure, and Market Dynamics: Reply. *J. Inst. Theoretical Econ.*, September 1987, 143(3), pp. 505–08. [G: W. Germany]

Zimmermann, Klaus F. Trade and Dynamic Efficiency. *Kyklos*, 1987, 40(1), pp. 73–87. [G: W. Germany]

612 Public Policy Toward Monopoly and Competition

6120 Public Policy Toward Monopoly and Competition

Adams, Walter and Brock, James W. Bigness and Social Efficiency: A Case Study of the U.S. Auto Industry. *Samuels, W. J. and Miller, A. S., eds.*, 1987, pp. 219–37. [G: U.S.]

Adams, Walter and Brock, James W. Corporate Size and the Bailout Factor. *J. Econ. Issues*, March 1987, 21(1), pp. 61–85. [G: U.S.]

Adams, Walter and Brock, James W. Global Competition and the Alleged Redundancy of Antitrust. *Wills, R. L.; Caswell, J. A. and Culbertson, J. D., eds.*, 1987, pp. 131–45. [G: U.S.]

Adams, William James. Should Merger Policy Be Changed? An Antitrust Perspective. *Browne, L. E. and Rosengren, E. S., eds.*, 1987, pp. 173–94. [G: U.S.]

Albach, Horst. Gewinn und gerechter Preis Überlegungen zur Preisbildung in der pharmazeutischen Industrie. (With English summary.) *Z. Betriebswirtschaft*, August 1987, 57(8), pp. 816–24. [G: W. Germany]

Altrogge, Phyllis and Shughart, William F., II. The Regressive Nature of Civil Penalties. *MacKay, R. J.; Miller, J. C., III and Yandle, B., eds.*, 1987, 1984, pp. 240–54. [G: U.S.]

Amacher, Ryan C., et al. The Behavior of Regulatory Activity over the Business Cycle: An Empirical Test. *MacKay, R. J.; Miller, J. C., III and Yandle, B., eds.*, 1987, 1985, pp. 145–53. [G: U.S.]

Andersen, Poul Nyboe. Fra monopollov til konkurrencelov. (From Monopoly Act to Competition Act. With English summary.) *Nationaløkon. Tidsskr.*, 1987, 125(1), pp. 1–19. [G: Denmark]

Atwood, James R. Conflicts of Jurisdiction in the Antitrust Field: The Example of Export Cartels. *Law Contemp. Probl.*, Summer 1987, 50(3), pp. 153–64. [G: U.S.]

Bagby, John W.; Wartick, Steven L. and Stevens, John M. Cooperative Approaches to Business–Government Relations. *Marcus, A. A.; Kaufman, A. M. and Beam, D. R., eds.*, 1987, pp. 283–91. [G: U.S.]

Ballwieser, Wolfgang. Transaction Cost Analysis of Structural Changes in the Distribution System: Reflections on Institutional Developments in the Federal Republic of Germany: Comment. *J. Inst. Theoretical Econ.*, March 1987, 143(1), pp. 86–90. [G: W. Germany]

Benson, Bruce L.; Greenhut, M. L. and Holcombe, Randall G. Interest Groups and the Antitrust Paradox. *Cato J.*, Winter 1987, 6(3), pp. 801–17. [G: U.S.]

Berg, Hartmut. Internationaler Wettbewerb—Nationale Wettbewerbspolitik: Zielkonflikte unvermeidbar! (International Competitiveness—National Competition Policy: Conflicts Unavoidable! With English summary.) *Lenel,*

H. O., et al., eds., 1987, pp. 131–42.
[G: W. Germany]

Bittlingmayer, George. Chicago Credo. *J. Inst. Theoretical Econ.*, December 1987, *143*(4), pp. 658–67. [G: U.S.]

Bittlingmayer, George. The Application of the Sherman Act to the Smog Agreement. *Antitrust Bull.*, Winter 1987, *32*(4), pp. 885–915.
[G: U.S.]

Blackstone, Erwin A. and Bowman, Gary W. Antitrust Damages: The Loss from Delay. *Antitrust Bull.*, Spring 1987, *32*(1), pp. 93–100.
[G: U.S.]

Blair, Roger D. and Fesmire, James M. Antitrust Treatment of Nonprofit and For-profit Hospital Mergers. *Scheffler, R. M. and Rossiter, L. F., eds.*, 1987, pp. 221–44. [G: U.S.]

Blair, Roger D. and Schafer, Carolyn D. Evolutionary Models of Legal Change and the *Albrecht* Rule. *Antitrust Bull.*, Winter 1987, *32*(4), pp. 989–1006. [G: U.S.]

Blanchard, Margaret A. The Associated Press Antitrust Suit: A Philosophical Clash over Ownership of First Amendment Rights. *Bus. Hist. Rev.*, Spring 1987, *61*(1), pp. 43–85.

Bloom, Paul N. and Gerson, Walter. The Use of "Scrip" for Obtaining Consumer Redress in Antitrust Cases: Lessons from a Failed Application in the Real Estate Industry. *Bloom, P. N., ed.*, 1987, pp. 93–106. [G: U.S.]

Bond, Ronald S. and Mitler, James C., Jr. Voting Patterns of FTC Commissioners. *MacKay, R. J.; Miller, J. C., III and Yandle, B., eds.*, 1987, pp. 322–30. [G: U.S.]

Borrie, Gordon [Sir]. Competition, Mergers and Price-Fixing. *Lloyds Bank Rev.*, April 1987, (164), pp. 1–15. [G: U.K.]

Bouju, André. Direct Protection of Innovation: The "Critical" Chapters. *Kingston, W., ed.*, 1987, pp. 247–56. [G: OECD]

Brickley, James A. and James, Christopher M. The Takeover Market, Corporate Board Composition, and Ownership Structure: The Case of Banking. *J. Law Econ.*, April 1987, *30*(1), pp. 161–80. [G: U.S.]

Briggs, John DeQ. and Calkins, Stephen. Antitrust 1986–87: Power and Access (Part II). *Antitrust Bull.*, Fall 1987, *32*(3), pp. 699–740.
[G: U.S.]

Briggs, John DeQ. and Calkins, Stephen. Antitrust 1986–87: Power and Access (Part I). *Antitrust Bull.*, Summer 1987, *32*(2), pp. 275–333.
[G: U.S.]

Browne, Lynn E. and Rosengren, Eric S. Are Hostile Takeovers Different? *Browne, L. E. and Rosengren, E. S., eds.*, 1987, pp. 199–229. [G: U.S.]

Browne, Lynn E. and Rosengren, Eric S. Should States Restrict Takeovers? *New Eng. Econ. Rev.*, July/Aug. 1987, pp. 13–21. [G: U.S.]

Bulajic, Milan. International Protection of Intellectual Property and Foreign Investment. *Dicke, D. C., ed.*, 1987, pp. 42–67.
[G: Global]

Calvert, Randall L.; Moran, Mark J. and Wein-

gast, Barry R. Congressional Influence over Policy Making: The Case of the FTC. *McCubbins, M. D. and Sullivan, T., eds.*, 1987, pp. 493–522. [G: U.S.]

Carstensen, Peter C. Legal and Economic Analysis of Distribution Restraints: A Search for Reality or Myth-Making? *Wills, R. L.; Caswell, J. A. and Culbertson, J. D., eds.*, 1987, pp. 79–101. [G: U.S.]

Caslin, Terry. Industrial and Market Structure in the UK. *Vane, H. and Caslin, T., eds.*, 1987, pp. 131–68. [G: U.K.]

Ciscel, David H. and Chang, Cyril. The Potential for Structural Monopolization in Hospital Services. *J. Econ. Issues*, June 1987, *21*(2), pp. 847–57. [G: U.S.]

Clark, Nolan E. Bright Lines versus Case-by-Case Assessment in Antitrust Analysis—An Overview. *Antitrust Bull.*, Fall 1987, *32*(3), pp. 565–78. [G: U.S.]

Clodius, Robert L. A Personal View of the Contributions of Willard F. Mueller. *Wills, R. L.; Caswell, J. A. and Culbertson, J. D., eds.*, 1987, pp. 12–17. [G: U.S.]

Coffee, John C., Jr. Are Hostile Takeovers Different? Discussion. *Browne, L. E. and Rosengren, E. S., eds.*, 1987, pp. 230–42.
[G: U.S.]

Cohler, Charles B. The New Economics and Antitrust Policy. *Antitrust Bull.*, Summer 1987, *32*(2), pp. 401–14. [G: U.S.]

Colombatto, Enrico. Sulle deviazioni efficienti del prezzo dal costo marginale. (On Efficient Deviations of Price from Marginal Cost. With English summary.) *Econ. Scelte Pubbliche/J. Public Finance Public Choice*, May-Aug. 1987, *5*(2), pp. 105–25.

Corgel, John B. Occupational Boundary Setting and the Unauthorized Practice of Law by Real Estate Brokers. *Jaffe, A. J., ed.*, 1987, pp. 161–75. [G: U.S.]

Cotterill, Ronald W. and Haller, Lawrence. Entry Patterns and Strategic Interaction in Food Retailing. *Wills, R. L.; Caswell, J. A. and Culbertson, J. D., eds.*, 1987, pp. 203–22.
[G: U.S.]

Cox, James C. and Isaac, R. Mark. Mechanisms for Incentive Regulation: Theory and Experiment. *Rand J. Econ.*, Autumn 1987, *18*(3), pp. 348–59.

Crandall, Robert W. Should Merger Policy Be Changed? An Antitrust Perspective: Discussion. *Browne, L. E. and Rosengren, E. S., eds.*, 1987, pp. 195–98. [G: U.S.]

Culbertson, John D. Should Antitrust Use the Schumpeterian Model? The Case of the Food Industries. *Wills, R. L.; Caswell, J. A. and Culbertson, J. D., eds.*, 1987, pp. 103–12.
[G: U.S.]

Domberger, Simon and Sherr, Avrom. Competition in Conveyancing: An Analysis of Solicitors' Charges 1983–85. *Fisc. Stud.*, August 1987, *8*(3), pp. 17–28. [G: U.K.]

Eckel, Russel. Industrial Relations and High Technology: The Transformation of Telecommunications through Deregulation. *Child, J. and Bate, P.*, eds., 1987, pp. 173–89. [G: U.S.]

Eggertsson, Thráinn. Transaction Cost Analysis of Structural Changes in the Distribution System: Reflections on Institutional Developments in the Federal Republic of Germany: Comment. *J. Inst. Theoretical Econ.*, March 1987, *143*(1), pp. 82–85. [G: W. Germany]

Evenson, Robert E. and Putnam, Jonathan D. Institutional Change in Intellectual Property Rights. *Amer. J. Agr. Econ.*, May 1987, *69*(2), pp. 403–09. [G: Global]

Faith, Roger L.; Leavens, Donald R. and Tollison, Robert D. Antitrust Pork Barrel. *MacKay, R. J.; Miller, J. C., III and Yandle, B.*, eds., 1987, *1982*, pp. 15–29. [G: U.S.]

Fishel, Walter L. The Economics of Agricultural Biotechnology: Discussion. *Amer. J. Agr. Econ.*, May 1987, *69*(2), pp. 438–39.

Fisher, Alan A.; Johnson, Frederick I. and Lande, Robert H. Do the DOJ Vertical Restraints Guidelines Provide Guidance? *Antitrust Bull.*, Fall 1987, *32*(3), pp. 609–42. [G: U.S.]

Fisher, Franklin M. Horizontal Mergers: Triage and Treatment. *J. Econ. Perspectives*, Fall 1987, *1*(2), pp. 23–40. [G: U.S.]

Fisher, Franklin M. On Predation and Victimless Crime. *Antitrust Bull.*, Spring 1987, *32*(1), pp. 85–92. [G: U.S.]

Fisher, Franklin M. Pan American to United: The *Pacific Division Transfer Case. Rand J. Econ.*, Winter 1987, *18*(4), pp. 492–508. [G: U.S.]

Foreman-Peck, J. S. Natural Monopoly and Railway Policy in the Nineteenth Century. *Oxford Econ. Pap.*, December 1987, *39*(4), pp. 699–718. [G: U.K.]

Fourie, F. C. v. N. Issues and Problems in South African Competition Policy. *S. Afr. J. Econ.*, December 1987, *55*(4), pp. 333–54. [G: S. Africa]

Fourie, F. C. v. N. Mededingingsbeleid sedert 1984—'n nuwe wending? (Competition Policy since 1984—A New Turning? With English summary.) *S. Afr. J. Econ.*, September 1987, *55*(3), pp. 219–37. [G: S. Africa]

Frech, H. E., III. Comments on Antitrust Issues. *Scheffler, R. M. and Rossiter, L. F.*, eds., 1987, pp. 263–67. [G: U.S.]

Gale, Jeffrey and Buchholz, Rogene A. The Political Pursuit of Competitive Advantage: What Business Can Gain from Government. *Marcus, A. A.; Kaufman, A. M. and Beam, D. R.*, eds., 1987, pp. 31–41.

Garland, Merrick B. Antitrust and Federalism: A Response [Antitrust and State Action: Economic Efficiency and the Political Process]. *Yale Law J.*, May 1987, *96*(6), pp. 1291–95. [G: U.S.]

Garland, Merrick B. Antitrust and State Action: Economic Efficiency and the Political Process. *Yale Law J.*, January 1987, *96*(3), pp. 486–519. [G: U.S.]

Garoyan, Leon. Agricultural Cooperatives under EEC Antitrust Regulations. *Wills, R. L.; Cas-*

well, J. A. and Culbertson, J. D., eds., 1987, pp. 167–84. [G: EEC]

Geithman, Frederick E. Mergers: Does Empirical Evidence Support a Change in Public Policy? *Wills, R. L.; Caswell, J. A. and Culbertson, J. D.*, eds., 1987, pp. 251–75. [G: U.S.]

Gibbons, John J. Antitrust, Law and Economics, and Politics. *Law Contemp. Probl.*, Autumn 1987, *50*(4), pp. 217–24. [G: U.S.]

Gilbert, Richard J. Appropriating the Returns from Industrial Research and Development: Comments and Discussion. *Brookings Pap. Econ. Act.*, 1987, (3), pp. 821–24. [G: U.S.]

Glais, Michel. Les fondements micro-économiques de la jurisprudence concurrentielle (française et européenne). (The Microeconomic Foundations of French and EEC Antitrust Cases. With English summary.) *Revue Écon.*, January 1987, *38*(1), pp. 75–115. [G: France; EEC]

Gorecki, Paul K. Barriers to Entry in the Canadian Pharmaceutical Industry: Comments, Clarification and Extensions. *J. Health Econ.*, March 1987, *6*(1), pp. 59–72. [G: Canada]

Greco, Anthony J. State Fluid Milk Regulation: Antitrust and Price Controls. *Antitrust Bull.*, Spring 1987, *32*(1), pp. 165–88. [G: U.S.]

Green, Chris. Industrial Organization Paradigms, Empirical Evidence, and the Economic Case for Competition Policy. *Can. J. Econ.*, August 1987, *20*(3), pp. 482–505. [G: Canada]

Green, Chris. Mergers in Canada and Canada's New Merger Law. *Antitrust Bull.*, Spring 1987, *32*(1), pp. 253–73. [G: Canada]

Griliches, Zvi. Appropriating the Returns from Industrial Research and Development: Comments and Discussion. *Brookings Pap. Econ. Act.*, 1987, (3), pp. 824–29. [G: U.S.]

Grossman, Gene M. and Shapiro, Carl. Dynamic R&D Competition. *Econ. J.*, June 1987, *97*(386), pp. 372–87.

Guerin-Calvert, Margaret E.; McGuckin, Robert H. and Warren-Boulton, Frederick R. State and Federal Regulation in the Market for Corporate Control. *Antitrust Bull.*, Fall 1987, *32*(3), pp. 661–91. [G: U.S.]

Hamilton, James L. and Philippart, Nancy L. On the Nonequivalence of Maximum Resale Price Maintenance and Vertical Integration. *Eastern Econ. J.*, October-December 1987, *13*(4), pp. 411–19. [G: U.S.]

Hancher, Leigh and Ruete, Matthias. Legal Culture, Product Licensing, and the Drug Industry. *Wilks, S. and Wright, M.*, eds., 1987, pp. 148–80. [G: U.K.; W. Germany]

Hansen, Ole Mohon. Fra prisregulering til konkurrencefremme. (Price Controls and the Promotion of Competition. With English summary.) *Nationaløkon. Tidsskr.*, 1987, *125*(1), pp. 64–77. [G: Denmark]

Hexter, J. Lawrence. Measuring Relative Concentration [Relative Concentration of the Largest 500 Firms]. *Southern Econ. J.*, January 1987, *53*(3), pp. 777–78. [G: U.S.]

Higgins, Richard S.; Shughart, William F., II and Tollison, Robert D. Dual Enforcement of the Antitrust Laws. *MacKay, R. J.; Miller, J. C., III and Yandle, B., eds.*, 1987, pp. 154–80. **[G: U.S.]**

Hjorth-Andersen, Chr. Hvad skal vi med monopol/konkurrenceloven? (Do We Need Legislation on Competition Policy in Denmark? With English summary.) *Nationaløkon. Tidsskr.*, 1987, *125*(1), pp. 33–44. **[G: Denmark]**

Hoffman, A. C. Recollections of a Friend and Colleague. *Wills, R. L.; Caswell, J. A. and Culbertson, J. D., eds.*, 1987, pp. 18–22. **[G: U.S.]**

Holzman, Franklyn D. Countervailing Foreign Use of Monopoly Power: Commentary. *Holzman, F. D.*, 1987, *1979*, pp. 137–42. **[G: U.S.S.R.]**

Horwitz, Morton J. *Santa Clara* Revisited: The Development of Corporate Theory. *Samuels, W. J. and Miller, A. S., eds.*, 1987, pp. 13–63. **[G: U.S.]**

Johnson, Richard L. and Smith, David D. Antitrust Division Merger Procedures and Policy, 1968–1984. *Antitrust Bull.*, Winter 1987, *32*(4), pp. 967–88. **[G: U.S.]**

Johnson, Ronald N. and Parkman, Allen M. Spatial Competition and Vertical Integration; Cement and Concrete Revisited: Comment. *Amer. Econ. Rev.*, September 1987, *77*(4), pp. 750–53. **[G: U.S.]**

Johnson, Ronald N. and Parkman, Allen M. The Role of Ideas in Antitrust Policy Toward Vertical Mergers: Evidence from the FTC Cement-Ready Mixed Concrete Cases. *Antitrust Bull.*, Winter 1987, *32*(4), pp. 841–83. **[G: U.S.]**

de Jong, Henk Wouter. Direct Protection of Innovation: The "Critical" Chapters. *Kingston, W., ed.*, 1987, pp. 215–26.

Jordan, W. John and Jaffee, Bruce L. The Use of Exclusive Territories in the Distribution of Beer: Theoretical and Empirical Observations. *Antitrust Bull.*, Spring 1987, *32*(1), pp. 137–64. **[G: U.S.]**

Kaplow, Louis. Antitrust, Law and Economics, and the Courts. *Law Contemp. Probl.*, Autumn 1987, *50*(4), pp. 181–216. **[G: U.S.]**

Kass, David I. State and Federal Regulation in the Market for Corporate Control: A Comment. *Antitrust Bull.*, Fall 1987, *32*(3), pp. 693–97. **[G: U.S.]**

Kaufmann, Peter J. The Community Trademark; Its Role in Making the Internal Market Effective. *J. Common Market Stud.*, March 1987, *25*(3), pp. 223–35. **[G: EEC]**

Kay, John A. and Thompson, David. The Performance of the British Economy: Policy for Industry. *Dornbusch, R. and Layard, R., eds.*, 1987, pp. 180–210. **[G: U.K.]**

Kingston, William. Advantages of Protecting Innovation Directly. *Kingston, W., ed.*, 1987, pp. 87–123. **[G: W. Europe; N. America]**

Kingston, William. Direct Protection of Innovation: Response. *Kingston, W., ed.*, 1987, pp. 277–337.

Kingston, William. Kronz's "Innovation Patent." *Kingston, W., ed.*, 1987, pp. 35–58.

Kingston, William. The Innovation Warrant.

Kingston, W., ed., 1987, pp. 59–86.

Kingston, William. The Unexploited Potential of Patents. *Kingston, W., ed.*, 1987, pp. 1–34. **[G: W. Europe; N. America]**

Kirchner, Christian and Picot, Arnold. Transaction Cost Analysis of Structural Changes in the Distribution System: Reflections on Institutional Developments in the Federal Republic of Germany. *J. Inst. Theoretical Econ.*, March 1987, *143*(1), pp. 62–81. **[G: W. Germany]**

Kovacic, William E. The Federal Trade Commission and Congressional Oversight of Antitrust Enforcement: A Historical Perspective. *MacKay, R. J.; Miller, J. C., III and Yandle, B., eds.*, 1987, pp. 63–120. **[G: U.S.]**

Kramer, Victor H. The Road to *City of Berkeley*: The Antitrust Positions of Justice Thurgood Marshall. *Antitrust Bull.*, Summer 1987, *32*(2), pp. 335–71. **[G: U.S.]**

Krishna Rao, P. V. and Sastry, K. P. Unfair Trade Practices Policy in India. *Antitrust Bull.*, Winter 1987, *32*(4), pp. 1051–69. **[G: India]**

Kronz, Hermann. Response in Defence of the Innovation Patent Concept. *Kingston, W., ed.*, 1987, pp. 257–76.

Landes, William M. and Posner, Richard A. Trademark Law: An Economic Perspective. *J. Law Econ.*, October 1987, *30*(2), pp. 265–309. **[G: U.S.]**

Langenfeld, James. How Can Guidelines Reduce the Uncertainties of Antitrust Enforcement? *Antitrust Bull.*, Fall 1987, *32*(3), pp. 643–59. **[G: U.S.]**

Langenfeld, James and Rogowsky, Robert A. Settlement vs. Litigation in Antitrust Enforcement. *MacKay, R. J.; Miller, J. C., III and Yandle, B., eds.*, 1987, pp. 205–19. **[G: U.S.]**

Lanning, Steven G. Costs of Maintaining a Cartel. *J. Ind. Econ.*, December 1987, *36*(2), pp. 147–74.

Lenel, Hans Otto. Ist zur Förderung der internationalen Wettbewerbsfähigkeit externes Unternehmenswachstum erstrebenswert? (Are Mergers Necessary to Secure International Competitiveness? With English summary.) *Lenel, H. O., et al., eds.*, 1987, pp. 113–29. **[G: W. Germany]**

Levin, Richard C., et al. Appropriating the Returns from Industrial Research and Development. *Brookings Pap. Econ. Act.*, 1987, (3), pp. 783–820. **[G: U.S.]**

Levy, David T. and Rodriguez, Alvaro. Does the Threat of Antitrust Policy Keep Prices Down? Or: Making Hay While the Sun Shines. *Int. J. Ind. Organ.*, September 1987, *5*(3), pp. 341–50.

Lieberman, Marvin B. Excess Capacity as a Barrier to Entry: An Empirical Appraisal. *J. Ind. Econ.*, June 1987, *35*(4), pp. 607–27. **[G: U.S.]**

Lieberman, Marvin B. Patents, Learning by Doing, and Market Structure in the Chemical Processing Industries. *Int. J. Ind. Organ.*, September 1987, *5*(3), pp. 257–76. **[G: U.S.]**

Liebowitz, S. J. Some Puzzling Behavior by Owners of Intellectual Products: An Analysis. *Contemp. Policy Issues*, July 1987, *5*(3), pp. 44–53. **[G: U.S.]**

Loescher, Samuel M. Toward More Competitive Diversity in a Market-Concentrated Economy. *Samuels, W. J. and Miller, A. S., eds.*, 1987, pp. 263–75. **[G: U.S.]**

Lott, John R., Jr. Licensing and Nontransferable Rents. *Amer. Econ. Rev.*, June 1987, *77*(3), pp. 453–55.

Lovett, William A. Theory and Practice of Antitrust. *Wills, R. L.; Caswell, J. A. and Culbertson, J. D., eds.*, 1987, pp. 41–60. **[G: U.S.]**

Lunn, John. An Empirical Analysis of Firm Process and Product Patenting. *Appl. Econ.*, June 1987, *19*(6), pp. 743–51. **[G: U.S.]**

Lynk, William J. Antitrust Analysis and Hospital Certificate-of-Need Policy. *Antitrust Bull.*, Spring 1987, *32*(1), pp. 61–84. **[G: U.S.]**

Mackay, Robert J. The FTC Budget Process: Zero-Based Budgeting by Committee. *MacKay, R. J.; Miller, J. C., III and Yandle, B., eds.*, 1987, pp. 295–321. **[G: U.S.]**

Mackay, Robert J.; Miller, James C., III and Yandle, Bruce. Public Choice and Regulation: An Overview. *MacKay, R. J.; Miller, J. C., III and Yandle, B., eds.*, 1987, pp. 3–12. **[G: U.S.]**

Mandeville, Thomas and Macdonald, Stuart. Innovation Protection Viewed from an Information Perspective. *Kingston, W., ed.*, 1987, pp. 157–69.

Marion, Bruce W. Entry Barriers: Theory, Empirical Evidence, and the Food Industries. *Wills, R. L.; Caswell, J. A. and Culbertson, J. D., eds.*, 1987, pp. 187–202. **[G: U.S.]**

Martin, David Dale. The Corporation and Antitrust Law Policy: Double Standards. *Samuels, W. J. and Miller, A. S., eds.*, 1987, pp. 193–217. **[G: U.S.]**

Martin, David Dale. The Evolution of Industrial Policies: A World Perspective. *Wills, R. L.; Caswell, J. A. and Culbertson, J. D., eds.*, 1987, pp. 115–30. **[G: U.S.]**

McBride, Mark E. Spatial Competition and Vertical Integration; Cement and Concrete Revisited: Reply. *Amer. Econ. Rev.*, September 1987, *77*(4), pp. 754–56. **[G: U.S.]**

McCall, Charles W. Predatory Pricing: An Economic and Legal Analysis. *Antitrust Bull.*, Spring 1987, *32*(1), pp. 1–59. **[G: U.S.]**

McDonald, Bruce C. Abuse of Dominant Position: A New Monopoly Law for Canada. *Antitrust Bull.*, Fall 1987, *32*(3), pp. 795–827. **[G: Canada]**

McFarland, Henry. The Economics of Vertical Restraints and Relationships between Connecting Railroads. *Logist. Transp. Rev.*, June 1987, *23*(2), pp. 207–22. **[G: U.S.]**

McGee, John S. Compound Pricing. *Econ. Inquiry*, April 1987, *25*(2), pp. 315–39.

McKenzie, Richard B. and Sullivan, E. Thomas. Does the NCAA Exploit College Athletes? An Economics and Legal Reinterpretation. *Antitrust Bull.*, Summer 1987, *32*(2), pp. 373–99. **[G: U.S.]**

Meessen, Karl M. Intellectual Property Rights in International Trade. *J. World Trade Law*, February 1987, *21*(1), pp. 67–74. **[G: OECD]**

Miller, Arthur S. Corporations and Our Two Constitutions. *Samuels, W. J. and Miller, A. S., eds.*, 1987, pp. 241–62. **[G: U.S.]**

Moran, Theodore H. Managing an Oligopoly of Would-Be Sovereigns: The Dynamics of Joint Control and Self-Control in the International Oil Industry Past, Present, and Future. *Int. Organ.*, Autumn 1987, *41*(4), pp. 575–607. **[G: Global]**

Möschel, Wernhard. Use of Economic Evidence in Antitrust Litigation in the Federal Republic of Germany. *Antitrust Bull.*, Summer 1987, *32*(2), pp. 523–50. **[G: W. Germany]**

Mossin, Axel. Konkurrenceprocesser og konkurrencepolitik. (Competitive Processes and Competition Policy. With English summary.) *Nationaløkon. Tidsskr.*, 1987, *125*(1), pp. 45–63. **[G: Denmark]**

Moulin, Hervé J. A Core Selection for Regulating a Single-Output Monopoly. *Rand J. Econ.*, Autumn 1987, *18*(3), pp. 397–407.

Mueller, Willard F. Market Power and Its Control in the Food System. *Wills, R. L.; Caswell, J. A. and Culbertson, J. D., eds.*, 1987, 1983, pp. 23–37. **[G: U.S.]**

Muto, Shigeo. Possibility of Relicensing and Patent Protection. *Europ. Econ. Rev.*, June 1987, *31*(4), pp. 927–45.

Noonberg, Eve. Extraterritorial Enforcement of Antitrust Laws against Foreign Firms. *Law Contemp. Probl.*, Summer 1987, *50*(3), pp. 194–95. **[G: U.S.]**

Novos, Ian E. and Waldman, Michael. The Emergence of Copying Technologies: What Have We Learned? *Contemp. Policy Issues*, July 1987, *5*(3), pp. 34–43.

O'Connor, Kevin. Law and Economics: Collision or Synergy (The Case of Predation). *Wills, R. L.; Caswell, J. A. and Culbertson, J. D., eds.*, 1987, pp. 61–77. **[G: U.S.]**

Oberender, Peter and Rüter, Georg. Innovationsförderung: Einige grundsätzliche ordnungspolitische Bemerkungen. (Some Principal Remarks on Policies to Promote Innovation. With English summary.) *Lenel, H. O., et al., eds.*, 1987, pp. 143–54. **[G: W. Germany]**

Okada, Katsuya. U.S.–Japan Cooperative Efforts to Protect Intellectual Property Rights. *Finn, R. B., ed.*, 1987, pp. 59–74. **[G: U.S.; Japan]**

Oppermann, Thomas, et al. Rechtsgrundlagen von Technologiepolitik (Insbesondere nach Europarecht und Grundgesetz). (Legal Bases for a Technology Policy [with Particular Reference to European Community Law and German Constitutional Law (Grundgesetz)]. With English summary.) *Lenel, H. O., et al., eds.*, 1987, pp. 209–31. **[G: EEC]**

Ordover, Janusz A. Conflicts of Jurisdiction: Antitrust and Industrial Policy. *Law Contemp. Probl.*, Summer 1987, *50*(3), pp. 165–77. **[G: U.S.]**

Pedersen, H. Winding. Modernisering af monopolloven? (Is the Danish Restrictive Trade Practices Act in Need of Modernization? With English summary.) *Nationaløkon. Tidsskr.*, 1987, *125*(1), pp. 20–32. **[G: Denmark]**

Pengilley, Warren. Trade Associations and Collective Boycotts in Australia and New Zealand: A Mistranslation of the Sherman Act Down Under. *Antitrust Bull.*, Winter 1987, *32*(4), pp. 1019–49. **[G: Australia; New Zealand]**

Piatier, André. Innovation Patent, Invention Patent, or Both? Towards a Radical Reform of the Patent System. *Kingston, W., ed.*, 1987, pp. 125–55. **[G: OECD]**

Plott, Charles R. Dimensions of Parallelism: Some Policy Applications of Experimental Methods. *Roth, A. E., ed.*, 1987, pp. 193–219. **[G: U.S.]**

Rafiquzzaman, M. The Optimal Patent Term under Uncertainty. *Int. J. Ind. Organ.*, June 1987, *5*(2), pp. 233–46.

Riordan, Michael H. and Sappington, David E. M. Awarding Monopoly Franchises. *Amer. Econ. Rev.*, June 1987, *77*(3), pp. 375–87.

Rogowsky, Robert A. The Pyrrhic Victories of Section 7: A Political Economy Approach. *MacKay, R. J.; Miller, J. C., III and Yandle, B., eds.*, 1987, pp. 220–39. **[G: U.S.]**

Rose, John T. and Savage, Donald T. Interstate Banking and the Viability of Small, Independent Banks: Further Evidence on Market Share Accumulation by New Banks. *Antitrust Bull.*, Winter 1987, *32*(4), pp. 1007–18. **[G: U.S.]**

Rosenbaum, David I. Advertising and Entry: The Case of Light Beer. *Wills, R. L.; Caswell, J. A. and Culbertson, J. D., eds.*, 1987, pp. 223–34. **[G: U.S.]**

Rosenbaum, David I. Predatory Pricing and the Reconstituted Lemon Juice Industry. *J. Econ. Issues*, March 1987, *21*(1), pp. 237–58. **[G: U.S.]**

Rozek, Richard P. Protection of Intellectual Property Rights: Research and Development Decisions and Economic Growth. *Contemp. Policy Issues*, July 1987, *5*(3), pp. 54–65. **[G: LDCs]**

Salant, Stephen W. Treble Damage Awards in Private Lawsuits for Price Fixing. *J. Polit. Econ.*, December 1987, *95*(6), pp. 1326–36.

Salop, Steven C. Symposium on Mergers and Antitrust. *J. Econ. Perspectives*, Fall 1987, *1*(2), pp. 3–12. **[G: U.S.]**

Sanders, Elizabeth. The Regulatory Surge of the 1970s in Historical Perspective. *Bailey, E. E., ed.*, 1987, pp. 117–50. **[G: U.S.]**

Schäfers, Alfons. The Luxembourg Patent Convention, the Best Option for the Internal Market. *J. Common Market Stud.*, March 1987, *25*(3), pp. 193–207. **[G: EEC]**

Scheffman, David T. and Spiller, Pablo T. Geographic Market Definition under the *U.S. Department of Justice Merger Guidelines. J. Law Econ.*, April 1987, *30*(1), pp. 123–47. **[G: U.S.]**

Schmalensee, Richard. Horizontal Merger Policy: Problems and Changes. *J. Econ. Perspectives*,

Fall 1987, *1*(2), pp. 41–54. **[G: U.S.]**

Shughart, William F., II. Don't Revise the Clayton Act, Scrap It! *Cato J.*, Winter 1987, *6*(3), pp. 925–32. **[G: U.S.]**

Shughart, William F., II and Tollison, Robert D. Antitrust Recidivism in Federal Trade Commission Data: 1914–1982. *MacKay, R. J.; Miller, J. C., III and Yandle, B., eds.*, 1987, pp. 255–80. **[G: U.S.]**

Silberston, Aubrey. Direct Protection of Innovation: The "Critical" Chapters. *Kingston, W., ed.*, 1987, pp. 201–13.

Sing, Merrile. Are Combination Gas and Electric Utilities Multiproduct Natural Monopolies? *Rev. Econ. Statist.*, August 1987, *69*(3), pp. 392–98. **[G: U.S.]**

Sklar, Martin J. The Sherman Antitrust Act and the Corporate Reconstruction of American Capitalism, 1890–1914. *Samuels, W. J. and Miller, A. S., eds.*, 1987, pp. 65–80. **[G: U.S.]**

Smith, Robert E. The Limited International Reach of U.S. Antitrust Policy. *Wills, R. L.; Caswell, J. A. and Culbertson, J. D., eds.*, 1987, pp. 148–65. **[G: U.S.]**

Smith, W. James; Vaughan, Michael B. and Formby, John P. Cartels and Antitrust: The Role of Fines in Deterring Violations at the Margin. *Southern Econ. J.*, April 1987, *53*(4), pp. 985–96.

Soifer, Aviam. The Paradox of Paternalism and Laissez-Faire Constitutionalism: The U.S. Supreme Court, 1888–1921. *Samuels, W. J. and Miller, A. S., eds.*, 1987, pp. 161–90. **[G: U.S.]**

Squires, Dale. Public Regulation and the Structure of Production in Multiproduct Industries: An Application to the New England Otter Trawl Industry. *Rand J. Econ.*, Summer 1987, *18*(2), pp. 232–47. **[G: U.S.]**

Stallmann, Judith I. and Schmid, A. Allan. Property Rights in Plants: Implications for Biotechnology Research and Extension. *Amer. J. Agr. Econ.*, May 1987, *69*(2), pp. 432–37. **[G: U.S.]**

Starbatty, Joachim. Die ordnungspolitische Dimension der EG-Technologiepolitik. (EC-Technology Policy and the Economic Order. With English summary.) *Lenel, H. O., et al., eds.*, 1987, pp. 155–81. **[G: EEC]**

Taira, Koji and Wada, Teiichi. Business–Government Relations in Modern Japan: A Tōdai–Yakkai–Zaikai Complex? *Mizruchi, M. S. and Schwartz, M., eds.*, 1987, pp. 264–97. **[G: Japan]**

Tower, Edward and Willett, Thomas D. Enforceability and the Resolution of International Jurisdictional Conflicts: Comments. *Law Contemp. Probl.*, Summer 1987, *50*(3), pp. 189–93. **[G: U.S.]**

Tullock, Gordon. Concluding Thoughts on the Politics of Regulation. *MacKay, R. J.; Miller, J. C., III and Yandle, B., eds.*, 1987, pp. 333–43. **[G: U.S.]**

Tullock, Gordon. Intellectual Property. *Kingston, W., ed.*, 1987, pp. 171–99. **[G: U.S.]**

Tye, William B. The Voluntary Negotiations Approach to Rail Competitive Access in the Transition to Deregulation. *Antitrust Bull.*, Summer 1987, *32*(2), pp. 415–50. [G: U.S.]

Uekusa, Masu. The Political Economy of Japan: Industrial Organization: The 1970s to the Present. *Yamamura, K. and Yasuba, Y., eds.*, 1987, pp. 469–515. [G: Japan]

Vautier, Kerrin M. Competition Policy and Competition Law in New Zealand. *Bollard, A. and Buckle, R., eds.*, 1987, pp. 46–66. [G: New Zealand]

Venit, James S. Know-How Licensing under EEC Law: Where We Have Been, Where We Are, and Where We May Be Headed. *Antitrust Bull.*, Spring 1987, *32*(1), pp. 189–252. [G: EEC]

Wagner, Stanley P. Antitrust, the Korean Experience 1981–85. *Antitrust Bull.*, Summer 1987, *32*(2), pp. 471–522. [G: S. Korea]

Werden, Gregory J. and Simon, Marilyn J. Why Price Fixers Should Go to Prison. *Antitrust Bull.*, Winter 1987, *32*(4), pp. 917–37. [G: U.S.]

White, Lawrence J. Antitrust and Merger Policy: A Review and Critique. *J. Econ. Perspectives*, Fall 1987, *1*(2), pp. 13–22. [G: U.S.]

Wilder, Ronald P. and Jacobs, Philip. Antitrust Considerations for Hospital Mergers: Market Definition and Market Concentration. *Scheffler, R. M. and Rossiter, L. F., eds.*, 1987, pp. 245–62. [G: U.S.]

Wiley, John Shepard, Jr. Revision and Apology in Antitrust Federalism [Antitrust and State Action: Economic Efficiency and the Political Process]. *Yale Law J.*, May 1987, *96*(6), pp. 1277–90. [G: U.S.]

Williamson, Oliver E. Antitrust Enforcement and the Modern Corporation. *Williamson, O.*, 1987, *1972*, pp. 39–54. [G: U.S.]

Williamson, Oliver E. Antitrust Enforcement: Where It Has Been; Where It Is Going. *Williamson, O.*, 1987, *1983*, pp. 320–43. [G: U.S.]

Williamson, Oliver E. Assessing Contract. *Williamson, O.*, 1987, *1985*, pp. 161–89.

Williamson, Oliver E. Assessing Vertical Market Restrictions: Antitrust Ramifications of the Transaction Cost Approach. *Williamson, O.*, 1987, *1979*, pp. 123–60. [G: U.S.]

Williamson, Oliver E. Economies as an Antitrust Defense: The Welfare Trade-Offs. *Williamson, O.*, 1987, *1968*, pp. 3–23. [G: U.S.]

Williamson, Oliver E. Intellectual Foundations of Law and Economics: The Need for a Broader View. *Williamson, O.*, 1987, *1983*, pp. 311–19.

Williamson, Oliver E. Predatory Pricing: A Strategic and Welfare Analysis. *Williamson, O.*, 1987, *1978*, pp. 225–81.

Williamson, Oliver E. Pretrial Uses of Economists: On the Use of 'Incentive Logic' to Screen Predation. *Williamson, O.*, 1987, *1984*, pp. 282–300. [G: U.S.]

Williamson, Oliver E. The Economics of Antitrust: Transaction Cost Considerations. *Wil-*

liamson, O., 1987, *1974*, pp. 71–122.

Williamson, Oliver E. Vertical Merger Guidelines: Interpreting the 1982 Reforms. *Williamson, O.*, 1987, *1983*, pp. 55–68. [G: U.S.]

Williamson, Oliver E. Wage Rates as a Barrier to Entry: The Pennington Case in Perspective. *Williamson, O.*, 1987, *1968*, pp. 193–224. [G: U.S.]

Wills, Robert L. Do Advertising-Induced Price Differences among Brands Explain Profit Differences among Products? *Wills, R. L.; Caswell, J. A. and Culbertson, J. D., eds.*, 1987, pp. 361–77.

Wills, Robert L. Economists and Competition Policy: A Case Study. *Wills, R. L.; Caswell, J. A. and Culbertson, J. D., eds.*, 1987, pp. 3–8. [G: U.S.]

Wood, Diane P. Conflicts of Jurisdiction in Antitrust Law: A Comment. *Law Contemp. Probl.*, Summer 1987, *50*(3), pp. 179–88. [G: U.S.]

Wright, Brian D. On the Design of a System to Improve the Production of Innovations. *Kingston, W., ed.*, 1987, pp. 227–46.

Yandle, Bruce. Chairman Choice and Output Effects: The FTC Experience. *MacKay, R. J.; Miller, J. C., III and Yandle, B., eds.*, 1987, pp. 283–94. [G: U.S.]

Yandle, Bruce. Regulatory Reform in the Realm of the Rent Seekers. *MacKay, R. J.; Miller, J. C., III and Yandle, B., eds.*, 1987, pp. 121–42. [G: U.S.]

613 Regulation of Public Utilities

6130 Regulation of Public Utilities

Acton, Jan Paul and Besen, Stanley M. Assessing the Effects of Bulk Power Rate Regulation: Results from a Market Experiment. *Appl. Econ.*, May 1987, *19*(5), pp. 663–85. [G: U.S.]

Ault, Richard W. and Ekelund, Robert B., Jr. The Problem of Unnecessary Originality in Economics. *Southern Econ. J.*, January 1987, *53*(3), pp. 650–61.

Babilot, George; Frantz, Roger and Green, Louis. Natural Monopolies and Rent: A Georgist Remedy for X-Inefficiency among Publicly-Regulated Firms. *Amer. J. Econ. Soc.*, April 1987, *46*(2), pp. 205–17.

Baish, Richard O. The Role of the California Public Utilities Commission in Western Gas Markets. *Natural Res. J.*, Fall 1987, *27*(4), pp. 805–10. [G: U.S.]

Barnes, S. Arlene. How Far Will Electricity Deregulation Go? A Skeptical View from Wall Street. *Stewart, M. B., ed.*, 1987, pp. 95–98. [G: U.S.]

Batten, Dick and Schoonmaker, Sara. Deregulation, Technological Change, and Labor Relations in Telecommunications. *Cornfield, D. B., ed.*, 1987, pp. 311–27. [G: U.S.]

Bauer, Douglas C. Adapting to Competition: An Analysis of Alternative Proposals to Restructure the Electric Power Industry. *Stewart, M. B., ed.*, 1987, pp. 67–71. [G: U.S.]

Bernard, Jean-Thomas and Cairns, Robert D.

On Public Utility Pricing and Forgone Economic Benefits. *Can. J. Econ.*, February 1987, *20*(1), pp. 152–63. **[G: Canada]**

Berry, S. Keith. Rate-of-Return Regulation and Demand Uncertainty with a Symmetric Regulatory Constraint. *Amer. Econ.*, Fall 1987, *31*(2), pp. 8–12.

Berry, S. Keith. The Ratepayer and the Stockholder under Alternative Regulatory Policies: Comment. *Land Econ.*, May 1987, *63*(2), pp. 201–05. **[G: U.S.]**

Betancourt, Roger R. and Edwards, John H. Y. Economies of Scale and the Load Factor in Electricity Generation. *Rev. Econ. Statist.*, August 1987, *69*(3), pp. 551–56. **[G: U.S.]**

Bohman, Mats and Andersson, Roland. Pricing Cogenerated Electricity and Heat in Local Communities. *J. Public Econ.*, August 1987, *33*(3), pp. 333–56. **[G: Sweden]**

Brennan, Timothy J. Why Regulated Firms Should Be Kept Out of Unregulated Markets: Understanding the Divestiture in *United States v. AT&T. Antitrust Bull.*, Fall 1987, *32*(3), pp. 741–93. **[G: U.S.]**

Brewer, H. L. and Rahmatian, Morteza. Risk Adjusted Performance Measures for Diversified Public Utility Firms: Implications for Applied Regulatory Economics. *J. Energy Devel.*, Spring 1987, *12*(2), pp. 185–201. **[G: U.S.]**

Brown, Donald J. and Heal, Geoffrey M. Ramsey Pricing in Telecommunications Markets with Free Entry. *Crew, M. A., ed.*, 1987, pp. 77–83. **[G: U.S.]**

Caves, Douglas W.; Christensen, Laurits R. and Herriges, Joseph A. The Neoclassical Model of Consumer Demand with Identically Priced Commodities: An Application to Time-of-Use Electricity Pricing. *Rand J. Econ.*, Winter 1987, *18*(4), pp. 564–80.

Cawson, Alan; Holmes, Peter and Stevens, Anne. The Interaction between Firms and the State in France: The Telecommunications and Consumer Electronics Sectors. *Wilks, S. and Wright, M., eds.*, 1987, pp. 10–34. **[G: France]**

Crew, Michael A. Introduction to Regulating Utilities in an Era of Deregulation. *Crew, M. A., ed.*, 1987, pp. 1–5. **[G: U.S.]**

Crew, Michael A. and Kleindorfer, Paul R. Productivity Incentives and Rate-of-Return Regulation. *Crew, M. A., ed.*, 1987, pp. 7–23. **[G: U.S.]**

Crew, Michael A.; Kleindorfer, Paul R. and Schlenger, Donald L. Governance Costs of Regulation for Water Supply. *Crew, M. A., ed.*, 1987, pp. 43–62. **[G: U.S.]**

Curien, Nicolas. L'accès et l'usage téléphoniques: modélisation conjointe et tarification optimale. (Telephone Access and Usage: Joint Modelization and Optimal Pricing. With English summary.) *Revue Écon.*, March 1987, *38*(2), pp. 415–58.

Curien, Nicolas and Gensollen, Michel. De la théorie des structures industrielles à l'économie des réseaux de télécommunication. (From the Theory of Industry Structure to the Eco-

nomics of Telecommunication Networks. With English summary.) *Revue Écon.*, March 1987, *38*(2), pp. 521–78.

Eckel, Catherine C. Customer-Class Price Discrimination by Electric Utilities. *J. Econ. Bus.*, February 1987, *39*(1), pp. 19–33.

Einhorn, Michael A. Optimality and Sustainability: Regulation and Intermodal Competition in Telecommunications. *Rand J. Econ.*, Winter 1987, *18*(4), pp. 550–63.

Encaoua, David and Koebel, Philippe. Réglementation et déréglementation des télécommunications: Leçons anglo-saxonnes et perspectives d'évolution en France. (Regulation and Deregulation of the Telecommunication Industry: From the American and British Experiences to a Possible Evolution in France. With English summary.) *Revue Écon.*, March 1987, *38*(2), pp. 475–520. **[G: U.S.; U.K.]**

Encaoua, David and Moreaux, Michel. L'analyse théorique des problèmes de tarification et d'allocation des coûts dans les télécommunications. (The Theoretical Approach to Pricing and Cost Allocation for Telecommunication Services. With English summary.) *Revue Écon.*, March 1987, *38*(2), pp. 375–413.

Faruqui, Ahmad. Utility Planning and Industrial Structural Change. *Faruqui, A. and Broehl, J., eds.*, 1987, pp. 9–31. **[G: U.S.]**

Garbacz, Christopher. Residential Electricity Demand Modelling with Secret Data. *Crew, M. A., ed.*, 1987, pp. 137–54. **[G: U.S.]**

Gartman, John A. The "Bypass" Issue: What Effect Does Local Utility Bypass Have on Energy Prices and the Economy? *Stewart, M. B., ed.*, 1987, pp. 59–61. **[G: U.S.]**

German, Michael I. How Far Will Natural Gas Deregulation Go? What Effect Will Deregulation Have on Prices and the "Gas Bubble"? *Stewart, M. B., ed.*, 1987, pp. 27–32. **[G: U.S.]**

Glaister, Stephen. Regulation through Output Related Profits Tax. *J. Ind. Econ.*, March 1987, *35*(3), pp. 281–96.

Goldenberg, David H. Market Power and the Required Return to Electric Utilities. *Financial Rev.*, February 1987, *22*(1), pp. 175–93. **[G: U.S.]**

Grewlich, Klaus W. Telecommunications: A European Perspective. *Wilks, S. and Wright, M., eds.*, 1987, pp. 251–73. **[G: W. Europe]**

Griffin, James M. and Mayor, Thomas H. The Welfare Gain from Efficient Pricing of Local Telephone Services. *J. Law Econ.*, October 1987, *30*(2), pp. 465–87. **[G: U.S.]**

Guadagni, Alieto A. Decisiones energéticas para el futuro. (With English summary.) *Desarrollo Econ.*, Jan.-Mar. 1987, *26*(104), pp. 609–30. **[G: Argentina]**

Hanke, Steve H. The Economics of Canadian Municipal Water Supply: Applying the User-Pay Principle. *Kent, C. A., ed.*, 1987, pp. 177–94. **[G: Canada]**

Hayashi, Paul M.; Sevier, Melanie and Trapani, John M. An Analysis of Pricing and Production Efficiency of Electric Utilities by Mode of

Ownership. *Crew, M. A., ed.*, 1987, pp. 111–36. [G: U.S.]

Hayes, Kathy J. Cost Structure of the Water Utility Industry. *Appl. Econ.*, March 1987, *19*(3), pp. 417–25. [G: U.S.]

Helm, Dieter. Nuclear Power and the Privatisation of Electricity Generation. *Fisc. Stud.*, November 1987, *8*(4), pp. 69–73. [G: U.K.]

Henriet, Dominique and Volle, Michel. Services de télécommunication: intégration technique et différenciation économique. (Telecommunication Services: Technical Integration and Economic Differentiation. With English summary.) *Revue Écon.*, March 1987, *38*(2), pp. 459–74. [G: France]

Herod, J. Steven. Evolving Federal Policies on Electricity. *Stewart, M. B., ed.*, 1987, pp. 73–80. [G: U.S.]

Huettner, David A. The Effect of the Public Utility Regulatory Policy Act on the Electric Utility Industry. *Pachauri, R. K., ed.*, 1987, pp. 189–203. [G: U.S.]

Humphrey, Bruce G. Alternative Economic Growth Scenarios and Implications for Utility Strategic Planning. *Faruqui, A. and Broehl, J., eds.*, 1987, pp. 33–47. [G: U.S.]

Irwin, Manley R. Telecommunications and Government: The U.S. Experience. *Wilks, S. and Wright, M., eds.*, 1987, pp. 233–50. [G: U.S.]

Jenkins, Glenn P. Public Utility Finance and Pricing: A Reply. *Can. J. Econ.*, February 1987, *20*(1), pp. 172–76. [G: Canada]

Jha, Raghbendra and Murty, M. N. Distributional Equity and Optimal Prices for the Public Sector: The Flexible Coefficients Case. *Energy Econ.*, January 1987, *9*(1), pp. 46–54. [G: India]

Jorgenson, Dale W. and Slesnick, Daniel T. General Equilibrium Analysis of Natural Gas Price Regulation. *Bailey, E. E., ed.*, 1987, pp. 153–90. [G: U.S.]

Kellenyi, John. Which Utilities Gain or Lose from Deregulation? An Investor's Perspective. *Stewart, M. B., ed.*, 1987, pp. 89–93. [G: U.S.]

Makhija, Anil K. and Thompson, Howard E. The Ratepayer and the Stockholder under Alternative Regulatory Policies: Reply. *Land Econ.*, May 1987, *63*(2), pp. 206–08. [G: U.S.]

Malko, J. Robert and Edgar, George R. Energy Utility Diversification and Small Business: A Wisconsin Perspective. *J. Energy Devel.*, Autumn 1987, *13*(1), pp. 101–11. [G: U.S.]

Marino, Anthony M. and Sicilian, Joseph. Direct Investment in Conservation Measures by a Public Utility. *Energy J.*, April 1987, *8*(2), pp. 137–46.

Marlay, Robert C. Industrial Electricity Consumption and Changing Economic Conditions. *Faruqui, A. and Broehl, J., eds.*, 1987, pp. 77–114. [G: U.S.]

Melese, Francois and Kaserman, David L. Superconductors and the Future of Electric Utilities. *J. Policy Anal. Manage.*, Fall 1987, *7*(1), pp. 135–40.

Millward, Robert and Ward, Robert. The Costs of Public and Private Gas Enterprises in Late 19th Century Britain. *Oxford Econ. Pap.*, December 1987, *39*(4), pp. 719–37. [G: U.K.]

Munroe, Tapan. Electric Utility Competition: Lessons from Others. *J. Energy Devel.*, Spring 1987, *12*(2), pp. 203–14. [G: U.S.]

Neely, Walter P.; Brooking, Carl G. and Clary, Betsy Jane. Differences among Subsidiaries of Electric Utility Holding Companies: Recent Empirical Evidence. *Quart. Rev. Econ. Bus.*, Summer 1987, *27*(2), pp. 50–62. [G: U.S.]

Nelson, Jon P.; Roberts, Mark J. and Tromp, Emsley P. An Analysis of Ramsey Pricing in Electric Utilities. *Crew, M. A., ed.*, 1987, pp. 85–109. [G: U.S.]

Nelson, Randy A. and Primeaux, Walter J., Jr. An Examination of the Relationship between Technical Change and Regulatory Effectiveness. *Appl. Econ.*, June 1987, *19*(6), pp. 773–88. [G: U.S.]

Nelson, Randy A. and Wohar, Mark E. Regulation, Scale and Productivity: Reply. *Int. Econ. Rev.*, June 1987, *28*(2), pp. 535–39.

Neufeld, John L. Price Discrimination and the Adoption of the Electricity Demand Charge. *J. Econ. Hist.*, September 1987, *47*(3), pp. 693–709. [G: U.S.]

Newbery, David M. The Privatisation of British Gas and Possible Consequences for the European Gas Market. *Golombek, R.; Hoel, M. and Vislie, J., eds.*, 1987, pp. 59–93. [G: U.K.]

Ng, Yew-Kwang. Equity, Efficiency and Financial Viability: Public-Utility Pricing with Special Reference to Water Supply. *Australian Econ. Rev.*, Third Quarter 1987, (79), pp. 21–35.

Noll, Roger G. The Political Foundations of Regulatory Policy. *McCubbins, M. D. and Sullivan, T., eds.*, 1987, 1983, pp. 462–92.

Norton, Seth W. In Search of Regulatory Lag. *Quart. J. Bus. Econ.*, Autumn 1987, *26*(4), pp. 3–16. [G: U.S.]

Olasky, Marvin N. Anticompetitive Campaigns by Big Business in the Pre–World War II Period. *Marcus, A. A.; Kaufman, A. M. and Beam, D. R., eds.*, 1987, pp. 239–53. [G: U.S.]

Pasour, E. C., Jr. Marginal Cost Pricing: Implications for Public Utility Regulation. *Econ. Scelte Pubbliche/J. Public Finance Public Choice*, Jan.-Apr. 1987, *5*(1), pp. 45–51.

Paté-Cornell, M. E. Risk Analysis and Relevance of Uncertainties in Nuclear Safety Decisions. *Bailey, E. E., ed.*, 1987, pp. 227–53. [G: U.S.]

Patterson, Cleveland S. and Ursel, Nancy D. Public Utility Equity Financing Practices: A Test of Market Efficiency. *Crew, M. A., ed.*, 1987, pp. 63–76. [G: U.S.]

Peters, Lon L. and Seiden, Kenneth P. The Behaviour of Publicly Owned Utilities in Wholesale Electricity Markets: The Case of the Pacific Northwest. *Energy Econ.*, October 1987, *9*(4), pp. 241–50. [G: U.S.]

Pettway, Richard H. and Jordan, Bradford D. APT vs. CAPM Estimates of the Return-Generating Function Parameters for Regulated Public Utilities. *J. Finan. Res.*, Fall 1987, *10*(3), pp. 227–38. **[G: U.S.]**

Plourde, André. On the Role and Status of Canadian Natural Gas Carriers under Deregulation. *J. Energy Devel.*, Autumn 1987, *13*(1), pp. 1–25. **[G: Canada]**

Poole, Robert W., Jr. The Political Obstacles to Privatization. *Hanke, S. H., ed.*, 1987, pp. 33–45.

Pryke, Richard. Privatising Electricity Generation. *Fisc. Stud.*, August 1987, *8*(3), pp. 75–88. **[G: U.K.]**

Rahman, Abdul H.; Kryzanowski, Lawrence and Sim, Ah Boon. Systematic Risk in a Purely Random Market Model: Some Empirical Evidence for Individual Public Utilities. *J. Finan. Res.*, Summer 1987, *10*(2), pp. 143–52. **[G: U.S.]**

Ravid, S. Abraham. On Marginal Cost Pricing When Consumers Can Also Produce. *Energy J.*, October 1987, *8*(4), pp. 17–22.

Reece, William S. Consumer Welfare Implications of Changes in Interstate Telephone Pricing. *J. Cons. Aff.*, Summer 1987, *21*(1), pp. 141–54. **[G: U.S.]**

Roth, Gabriel. Roles of the Private Sector in the Supply of Public Services in Less Developed Countries. *Kent, C. A., ed.*, 1987, pp. 195–206. **[G: LDCs]**

Rothwell, Geoffrey S. and Eastman, Kelly A. A Note on Allowed and Realized Rates of Return of the U.S. Electric Utility Industry. *J. Ind. Econ.*, September 1987, *36*(1), pp. 105–10. **[G: U.S.]**

Schmidt, Ronald H. Deregulating Electric Utilities: Issues and Implications. *Fed. Res. Bank Dallas Econ. Rev.*, September 1987, pp. 13–26. **[G: U.S.]**

Schwarz, Peter M. and Taylor, Thomas N. Public Utility Pricing under Risk; the Case of Self-Rationing: Comment and Extension. *Amer. Econ. Rev.*, September 1987, *77*(4), pp. 734–39.

Shapiro, David L. Public Power Policy in the Pacific Northwest: The Legal Fall Out. *Quart. Rev. Econ. Bus.*, Winter 1987, *27*(4), pp. 18–37. **[G: U.S.]**

Sing, Merrile. Are Combination Gas and Electric Utilities Multiproduct Natural Monopolies? *Rev. Econ. Statist.*, August 1987, *69*(3), pp. 392–98. **[G: U.S.]**

Solo, Robert A. The Great Plains Gasification Project: The Problem of Juridical/Administrative Incompatibility. *Energy J.*, April 1987, *8*(2), pp. 153–68. **[G: U.S.]**

Spiro, Peter S. Public Utility Finance and the Cost of Capital: Comments. *Can. J. Econ.*, February 1987, *20*(1), pp. 164–71. **[G: Canada]**

Stewart, Marion B. Energy Deregulation and Economic Growth: Summary. *Stewart, M. B., ed.*, 1987, pp. 1–16. **[G: U.S.]**

Thompson, Howard E. Regulatory Policy under Uncertainty: How Should the Earned Rate of Return for a Public Utility Be Controlled?

Crew, M. A., ed., 1987, pp. 25–41.

Train, Kenneth E.; McFadden, Daniel L. and Goett, Andrew A. Consumer Attitudes and Voluntary Rate Schedules for Public Utilities. *Rev. Econ. Statist.*, August 1987, *69*(3), pp. 383–91. **[G: U.S.]**

Veall, Michael R. Bootstrapping the Probability Distribution of Peak Electricity Demand. *Int. Econ. Rev.*, February 1987, *28*(1), pp. 203–12. **[G: Canada]**

Volkonskii, Victor A. and Kuzovkin, A. I. Marginal Costs and Optimal Electricity Tariffs. *Matekon*, Fall 1987, *24*(1), pp. 43–69. **[G: U.S.S.R.]**

Vranitzky, Franz. Die Finanzierung der Gemeinwirtschaft in Österreich. (The Financing of Public Economy in Austria. With English summary.) *Ann. Pub. Co-op. Econ.*, Apr.-June 1987, *58*(2), pp. 141–50. **[G: Austria]**

Weingast, Barry R. and Moran, Mark J. Bureaucratic Discretion or Congressional Control? Regulatory Policymaking by the Federal Trade Commission. *MacKay, R. J.; Miller, J. C., III and Yandle, B., eds.*, 1987, *1983*, pp. 30–62. **[G: U.S.]**

Werbos, Paul J. Industrial Structural Shift: Causes and Consequences for Electricity Demand. *Faruqui, A. and Broehl, J., eds.*, 1987, pp. 115–26. **[G: U.S.]**

Zimmerman, Martin B. The Evolution of Civilian Nuclear Power. *[Adelman, M. A.]*, 1987, pp. 83–106. **[G: U.S.]**

Zweifel, Peter and Beck, Konstantin. Utilities and Cogeneration: Some Regulatory Problems. *Energy J.*, October 1987, *8*(4), pp. 1–15. **[G: U.S.]**

Cannon, Colin M. Peak-Pricing and Self-Rationing of Gas. *Energy Econ.*, April 1987, *9*(2), pp. 99–103. **[G: U.K.]**

614 Public Enterprises

6140 Public Enterprises

Adams, Carolyn Teich. The Politics of Privatization. *Turner, B.; Kemeny, J. and Lundqvist, L. J., eds.*, 1987, pp. 127–55. **[G: U.S.; W. Europe]**

Adie, Douglas K. Privatizing, Divesting, and Deregulating the Postal Service. *Kent, C. A., ed.*, 1987, pp. 123–34. **[G: U.S.]**

Atherton, Cliff and Windsor, Duane. Privatization of Urban Public Services. *Kent, C. A., ed.*, 1987, pp. 81–99.

Austin, James E. and Fox, Jonathan. State-Owned Enterprises: Food Policy Implementers. *Austin, J. E. and Esteva, G., eds.*, 1987, pp. 61–91. **[G: Mexico]**

Aylen, Jonathan. Privatization in Developing Countries. *Lloyds Bank Rev.*, January 1987, (163), pp. 15–30. **[G: LDCs]**

Ayub, Mahmood A. and Hegstad, Sven O. Determinants of Public Enterprise Performance. *Finance Develop.*, December 1987, *24*(4), pp. 26–29.

Ayub, Mahmood A. and Hegstad, Sven O. Management of Public Industrial Enterprises. *World Bank Res. Observer*, January 1987, 2(1), pp. 79–101. **[G: Selected Countries]**

Baim, Dean. Private Ownership Incentives in Professional Sports Facilities. *Kent, C. A., ed.*, 1987, pp. 109–21. **[G: U.S.]**

Baxter, Vern. Technological Change and Labor Relations in the United States Postal Service. *Cornfield, D. B., ed.*, 1987, pp. 91–110. **[G: U.S.]**

Berg, Elliot. The Role of Divestiture in Economic Growth. *Hanke, S. H., ed.*, 1987, pp. 23–31.

Bilgic, Mehmet. Privatization: The Case of Turkey. *Hanke, S. H., ed.*, 1987, pp. 195–203. **[G: Turkey]**

Blankart, Charles B. Eléments d'une théorie économique de la privatisation. (Elements of an Economic Theory of Privatization. With English summary.) *Schweiz. Z. Volkswirtsch. Statist.*, September 1987, 123(3), pp. 329–39.

Blankart, Charles B. Limits to Privatization. *Europ. Econ. Rev.*, Feb./Mar. 1987, 31(1/2), pp. 346–51.

Bonus, Holger. Property Rights and Transaction Costs: Theory and Evidence on Privately-Owned and Government-Owned Enterprises: Comment. *J. Inst. Theoretical Econ.*, March 1987, 143(1), pp. 27–33. **[G: W. Germany]**

Borge Gonzalez, Luis M.; Rojo Garcia, José Luis and Vicente Perdiz, Juan. Comportamiento tecnológico y productivo de la Empresa Pública española. (With English summary.) *Invest. Econ.*, May 1987, 11(2), pp. 261–78. **[G: Spain]**

Bös, Dieter. Privatization of Public Enterprises. *Europ. Econ. Rev.*, Feb./Mar. 1987, 31(1/2), pp. 352–60.

Bovbjerg, Randall R.; Held, Philip J. and Pauly, Mark V. Privatization and Bidding in the Health-Care Sector. *J. Policy Anal. Manage.*, Summer 1987, 6(4), pp. 648–66. **[G: U.S.]**

Burink, Franke. Privatization in Europe. *Kent, C. A., ed.*, 1987, pp. 162–76. **[G: U.K.; Netherlands]**

Burton, John. Privatization: The Thatcher Case. *Managerial Dec. Econ.*, March 1987, 8(1), pp. 21–29. **[G: U.K.]**

Castagnos, Jean-Claude. Performance et gestion publique: Un pari impossible? (Performance and Public Management: An Impossible Wager? With English summary.) *Écon. Soc.*, December 1987, 21(12), pp. 141–73.

Castillo, Rosendo J. Financing Privatization. *Hanke, S. H., ed.*, 1987, pp. 119–26.

Chalk, Andrew J. Property Rights and Transaction Costs: Theory and Evidence on Privately-Owned and Government-Owned Enterprises: Comment. *J. Inst. Theoretical Econ.*, March 1987, 143(1), pp. 23–26.

Chamberlin, John R. and Jackson, John E. Privatization as Institutional Choice. *J. Policy Anal. Manage.*, Summer 1987, 6(4), pp. 586–604.

Chen, Jiyuan. China's Industrial Reform: The Planning System. *Tidrick, G. and Jiyuan, C., eds.*, 1987, pp. 148–74. **[G: China]**

Cowan, L. Gray. A Global Overview of Privatization. *Hanke, S. H., ed.*, 1987, pp. 7–15. **[G: W. Europe; LDCs]**

Croissier, Luis C. Financing Policy for the Public Sector Companies in Spain. *Ann. Pub. Co-op. Econ.*, Apr.-June 1987, 58(2), pp. 165–73. **[G: Spain]**

Cubbin, John S.; Domberger, Simon and Meadowcroft, Shirley. Competitive Tendering and Refuse Collection: Identifying the Sources of Efficiency Gains. *Fisc. Stud.*, August 1987, 8(3), pp. 49–58. **[G: U.K.]**

Cuervo Garcia, Alvaro and Fernandez R. Casariego, Zulima. L'entreprise publique en Espagne. (Public Enterprises in Spain. With English summary.) *Ann. Pub. Co-op. Econ.*, Jan.-Mar. 1987, 58(1), pp. 3–22. **[G: Spain]**

Davies, David G. and Brucato, Peter F., Jr. Property Rights and Transaction Costs: Theory and Evidence on Privately-Owned and Government-Owned Enterprises. *J. Inst. Theoretical Econ.*, March 1987, 143(1), pp. 7–22. **[G: Australia]**

De Fraja, Giovanni and Flavio, Delboni. Oligopoly, Public Firm and Welfare Maximization: A Game-Theoretic Analysis. *Giorn. Econ.*, July-August 1987, 46(7–8), pp. 416–35.

Dodgson, John S. Privatization. *Vane, H. and Caslin, T., eds.*, 1987, pp. 220–39. **[G: U.K.]**

Dong, Fureng. China's Industrial Reform: Increasing the Vitality of Enterprises. *Tidrick, G. and Jiyuan, C., eds.*, 1987, pp. 44–59. **[G: China]**

Estrin, Saul and Pérotin, Virginie. The Regulation of British and French Nationalised Industries. *Europ. Econ. Rev.*, Feb./Mar. 1987, 31(1/2), pp. 361–67. **[G: U.K.; France]**

Fahning, Hans. Finanzierungsformen der regionalen und örtlichen öffentlichen Unternehmen in der B.R.D. (Forms of Financing of the Regional and Local Public Enterprises in Germany. With English summary.) *Ann. Pub. Co-op. Econ.*, Apr.-June 1987, 58(2), pp. 185–94. **[G: W. Germany]**

Ferner, Anthony. Industrial Relations and the Meso-politics of the Public Enterprise: The Transmission of State Objectives in the Spanish National Railways. *Brit. J. Ind. Relat.*, March 1987, 25(1), pp. 49–75. **[G: Spain]**

Garello, Jacques. Economic and Social Consequences of Socialist Policies in France. *Pejovich, S., ed.*, 1987, pp. 251–76. **[G: France]**

Georgakopoulos, Theodore A.; Prodromidis, K. and Loizides, J. Public Enterprises in Greece. *Ann. Pub. Co-op. Econ.*, Oct.-Dec. 1987, 58(4), pp. 351–67. **[G: Greece]**

Granick, David. The Industrial Environment in China and the CMEA Countries. *Tidrick, G. and Jiyuan, C., eds.*, 1987, pp. 103–31. **[G: China; CMEA]**

Grosh, Barbara. Performance of Agricultural Public Enterprises in Kenya: Lessons from the First Two Decades of Independence. *Eastern Afr. Econ. Rev.*, June 1987, 3(1), pp. 51–64. **[G: Kenya]**

Hanke, Steve H. Successful Privatization Strate-

gies. *Hanke, S. H., ed.*, 1987, pp. 77–86.
[G: U.S.]

Hanke, Steve H. The Necessity of Property Rights. *Hanke, S. H., ed.*, 1987, pp. 47–51.

Hanke, Steve H. Toward a People's Capitalism. *Hanke, S. H., ed.*, 1987, pp. 213–21.

Henley, John S. and Ereisha, Mohamed M. State Control and the Labor Productivity Crisis: The Egyptian Textile Industry at Work. *Econ. Develop. Cult. Change*, April 1987, *35*(3), pp. 491–521.

Howell, Thomas. Steel and the State in Romania. *Comp. Econ. Stud.*, Summer 1987, *29*(2), pp. 71–100. **[G: Romania]**

Ingberman, Daniel E. Privatization as Institutional Choice: Comment. *J. Policy Anal. Manage.*, Summer 1987, *6*(4), pp. 607–11.

James, Jeffrey. The Choice of Technology in Public Enterprise: A Comparative Study of Manufacturing Industry in Kenya and Tanzania. *Stewart, F., ed.*, 1987, pp. 219–47.
[G: Kenya; Tanzania]

Jennings, Stephen and Cameron, Rob. State-Owned Enterprise Reform in New Zealand. *Bollard, A. and Buckle, R., eds.*, 1987, pp. 121–52. **[G: New Zealand]**

Jiang, Sidong and Xu, Xiaopo. The Financial "Two-Track System": Strengthen Credit and Open Up the Nonbank Market. *Reynolds, B. L.*, 1987, pp. 188–207. **[G: China]**

Kay, John A. and Thompson, David. The Performance of the British Economy: Policy for Industry. *Dornbusch, R. and Layard, R., eds.*, 1987, pp. 180–210. **[G: U.K.]**

Kent, Calvin A. Privatization of Public Functions: Promises and Problems. *Kent, C. A., ed.*, 1987, pp. 3–22.

Kent, Calvin A. and Wooten, Sandra P. Privatization: The Entrepreneurial Response. *Kent, C. A., ed.*, 1987, pp. 145–57 **[G: U.S.]**

Kimberly, John R. Privatization and Bidding in the Health-Care Sector: Comment. *J. Policy Anal. Manage.*, Summer 1987, *6*(4), pp. 671–73. **[G: U.S.]**

Kornai, János. The Dual Dependence of the State-Owned Firm in Hungary. *Tidrick, G. and Jiyuan, C., eds.*, 1987, pp. 317–38.
[G: Hungary]

Kornai, János and Matits, Ágnes. The Softness of Budgetary Constraints—An Analysis of Enterprise Data. *Eastern Europ. Econ.*, Summer 1987, *25*(4), pp. 1–34. **[G: Hungary]**

Kuczynski, Pedro-Pablo. Marketing Divested State-Owned Enterprises in Developing Countries. *Hanke, S. H., ed.*, 1987, pp. 111–17.
[G: LDCs]

Laitinen, Erkki K. A Distributed Lag Model of a Public Enterprise. *Liiketaloudellinen Aikak.*, 1987, *36*(1), pp. 3–23. **[G: Finland]**

Levy, Brian. A Theory of Public Enterprise Behavior. *J. Econ. Behav. Organ.*, March 1987, *8*(1), pp. 75–96.

Liu, Guoguang. Problems in the Reform of Ownership Relations in China. *Warner, M., ed.*, 1987, pp. 165–75. **[G: China]**

Lovik, Lawrence W. Bureaucracy, Privatization, and the Supply of Public Goods. *Kent, C. A., ed.*, 1987, pp. 23–34.

Ma, Bin and Hong, Zhunyan. Enlivening Large State Enterprises: Where Is the Motive Force? *J. Compar. Econ.*, September 1987, *11*(3), pp. 503–08. **[G: China]**

Mahmood, Mir Annice and Sahibzada, Shamim A. The Performance of Public Sector Enterprises: 1981–1986. *Pakistan Devel. Rev.*, Winter 1987, *26*(4), pp. 793–801. **[G: Pakistan]**

Marceau, Ian. Privatization of Agriculture and Agribusiness. *Hanke, S. H., ed.*, 1987, pp. 141–48.

Marston, Lance. Preparing for Privatization: A Decision-maker's Checklist. *Hanke, S. H., ed.*, 1987, pp. 67–76.

McPherson, M. Peter. The Promise of Privatization. *Hanke, S. H., ed.*, 1987, pp. 17–20.

Menon, Krishnagopal and Umapathy, Srinivasan. Control Systems for State-Owned Enterprises: A Conceptual Framework. *Ann. Pub. Co-op. Econ.*, July-Sept. 1987, *58*(3), pp. 287–303.

Mickwitz, Gösta. Statsbolagens effektivitet i en marknadsekonomi. (The Efficiency of State Companies in a Market Economy. With English summary.) *Ekon. Samfundets Tidskr.*, 1987, *40*(4), pp. 185–90. **[G: Finland]**

Mills, Edwin S. Privatization of Public-Sector Services in Practice: Experience and Potential: Comment. *J. Policy Anal. Manage.*, Summer 1987, *6*(4), pp. 625–27. **[G: U.S.]**

Molyneux, Richard and Thompson, David. Nationalised Industry Performance: Still Third-Rate? *Fisc. Stud.*, February 1987, *8*(1), pp. 48–82. **[G: U.K.]**

Neves, Julio Henriques. Description et problemes actuels des entreprises publiques au Portugal. (Description and Current Problems of Public Enterprises in Portugal. With English summary.) *Ann. Pub. Co-op. Econ.*, Jan.-Mar. 1987, *58*(1), pp. 31–47. **[G: Portugal]**

Newbery, David M. The Privatisation of British Gas and Possible Consequences for the European Gas Market. *Golombek, R.; Hoel, M. and Vislie, J., eds.*, 1987, pp. 59–93. **[G: U.K.]**

Ng, Yew-Kwang. Equity, Efficiency and Financial Viability: Public-Utility Pricing with Special Reference to Water Supply. *Australian Econ. Rev.*, Third Quarter 1987, (79), pp. 21–35.

Ohashi, Ted M. Marketing State-Owned Enterprises. *Hanke, S. H., ed.*, 1987, pp. 101–10.

Ohashi, Ted M. Privatization: The Case of British Columbia. *Hanke, S. H., ed.*, 1987, pp. 189–94. **[G: Canada]**

Pack, Janet Rothenberg. Privatization of Public-Sector Services in Theory and Practice. *J. Policy Anal. Manage.*, Summer 1987, *6*(4), pp. 523–40. **[G: U.S.]**

Palm, Alexis. La performance technique de dix huit-services postaux. (Technical Efficiency in 18 Postal Services. With English summary.) *Ann. Pub. Co-op. Econ.*, July-Sept. 1987, *58*(3), pp. 305–19. **[G: OECD]**

Park, Young C. Evaluating the Performance of Korea's Government-Invested Enterprises. *Fi-*

nance Develop., June 1987, 24(2), pp. 25–27.
[G: S. Korea]

Pauwels, Jean-Pierre. Nouvelles techniques de financement des entreprises et services publics. (New Financing Techniques of the Public Enterprises and Services. With English summary.) Ann. Pub. Co-op. Econ., Apr.-June 1987, 58(2), pp. 175–84. [G: Belgium]

Pestieau, Pierre. Entreprise et propriété publiques. (Public Enterprise and Government Ownership. With English summary.) Revue Écon., November 1987, 38(6), pp. 1191–1201.

Peters, Lon L. and Seiden, Kenneth P. The Behaviour of Publicly Owned Utilities in Wholesale Electricity Markets: The Case of the Pacific Northwest. Energy Econ., October 1987, 9(4), pp. 241–50. [G: U.S.]

Phillips, Almarin. Privatization, Information and Incentives: Comment. J. Policy Anal. Manage., Summer 1987, 6(4), pp. 585.

Piacentino, Diego. Funzioni e finanziamento di una rete radiotelevisiva pubblica. Le conclusioni di un rapporto al governo britannico. (The Tasks and Financing of a Public Broadcasting Network: The Conclusions of a Report to the British Government. With English summary.) Econ. Scelte Pubbliche/J. Public Finance Public Choice, Sept.-Dec. 1987, 5(3), pp. 201–12.
[G: U.K.]

Pirie, Madsen and Young, Peter. Development with Aid: Public and Private Responsibilities in Privatization. Hanke, S. H., ed., 1987, pp. 169–77. [G: LDCs]

Poole, Robert W., Jr. The Political Obstacles to Privatization. Hanke, S. H., ed., 1987, pp. 33–45.

Poole, Robert W., Jr. and Fixler, Philip E., Jr. Privatization of Public-Sector Services in Practice: Experience and Potential. J. Policy Anal. Manage., Summer 1987, 6(4), pp. 612–25.
[G: U.S.]

Redwood, John. Privatization: The Case of Britain. Hanke, S. H., ed., 1987, pp. 181–88.
[G: U.K.]

Reinhardt, Uwe E. Privatization and Bidding in the Health-Care Sector: Comment. J. Policy Anal. Manage., Summer 1987, 6(4), pp. 666–71. [G: U.S.]

Rose-Ackerman, Susan. Privatization as Institutional Choice: Comment. J. Policy Anal. Manage., Summer 1987, 6(4), pp. 604–07.

Roth, Gabriel. Privatization of Public Services. Hanke, S. H., ed., 1987, pp. 129–39.
[G: LDCs]

Roy, Donald. Financial Structure, Investment Appraisal and Statutory Obligations in the Public Corporations—United Kingdom Experience and Prospects. Ann. Pub. Co-op. Econ., Apr.-June 1987, 58(2), pp. 213–18. [G: U.K.]

Sandri, Stefano. Financing the partecipazioni statali System in Italy. Ann. Pub. Co-op. Econ., Apr.-June 1987, 58(2), pp. 151–64. [G: Italy]

Sappington, David E. M. and Stiglitz, Joseph E. Privatization, Information and Incentives. J. Policy Anal. Manage., Summer 1987, 6(4), pp. 567–82.

Sarmad, Khwaja. The Performance of Public Sector Enterprises: 1981–1986: Comments. Pakistan Devel. Rev., Winter 1987, 26(4), pp. 802–03. [G: Pakistan]

Sarti, Armando. Le financement des entreprises publiques locales en Italie. (The Financing of Local Public Enterprises in Italy. With English summary.) Ann. Pub. Co-op. Econ., Apr.-June 1987, 58(2), pp. 195–212. [G: Italy]

Shaikh, Abdul Hafeez. Performance Evaluation of Public Enterprises: Lessons from the Pakistan Experience. Ann. Pub. Co-op. Econ., Oct.-Dec. 1987, 58(4), pp. 397–414.
[G: Pakistan]

Shay, Donald. Privatization: The Case of Grenada. Hanke, S. H., ed., 1987, pp. 205–09.
[G: Grenada]

Sundqvist, Ulf. Statsbolagens roll i det framtida Finland. (The Role of State Companies in Finland's Future. With English summary.) Ekon. Samfundets Tidskr., 1987, 40(4), pp. 175–84.
[G: Finland]

Tang, Zongkun. China's Industrial Reform: Supply and Marketing. Tidrick, G. and Jiyuan, C., eds., 1987, pp. 210–36. [G: China]

Tanoira, Manuel. Privatization as Politics. Hanke, S. H., ed., 1987, pp. 53–64. [G: Argentina]

Thomas, Peter. The Legal and Tax Considerations of Privatization. Hanke, S. H., ed., 1987, pp. 87–100.

Thompson, David. Privatisation in the U.K.: Deregulation and the Advantage of Incumbency. Europ. Econ. Rev., Feb./Mar. 1987, 31(1/2), pp. 368–74. [G: U.K.]

Tidrick, Gene. China's Industrial Reform: Planning and Supply. Tidrick, G. and Jiyuan, C., eds., 1987, pp. 175–209. [G: China]

Vranitzky, Franz. Die Finanzierung der Gemeinwirtschaft in Österreich. (The Financing of Public Economy in Austria. With English summary.) Ann. Pub. Co-op. Econ., Apr.-June 1987, 58(2), pp. 141–50. [G: Austria]

Walker, Jill and Moore, Roger. The Impact of Privatization on the United Kingdom Local Government Labour Market. Tarling, R., ed., 1987, pp. 197–223. [G: U.K.]

Waters, Alan Rufus. Privatization: A Viable Policy Option? Kent, C. A., ed., 1987, pp. 35–64.

White, Lawrence H. Privatization of Financial Sectors. Hanke, S. H., ed., 1987, pp. 149–60.

Wilks, Stephen and Wright, Maurice. Comparative Government–Industry Relations: Introduction. Wilks, S. and Wright, M., eds., 1987, pp. 1–9.

Wintrobe, Ronald. The Market for Corporate Control and the Market for Political Control. J. Law, Econ., Organ., Fall 1987, 3(2), pp. 435–48. [G: U.S.]

Xu, Jing'an. The Stock-Share System: A New Avenue for China's Economic Reform. J. Compar. Econ., September 1987, 11(3), pp. 509–14.
[G: China]

Xu, Lu. China's Industrial Reform: Industrial Corporations. Tidrick, G. and Jiyuan, C., eds., 1987, pp. 281–96. [G: China]

Yoo, Dennis A. Privatization, Information and Incentives: Comment. *J. Policy Anal. Manage.*, Summer 1987, *6*(4), pp. 582–84.

Zhang, Shaojie and Zhang, Amei. The Present Management Environment in China's Industrial Enterprises. *Reynolds, B. L.*, 1987, pp. 47–58. **[G: China]**

Zhang, Shaojie, et al. Investment: Initial Changes in the Mechanism and Preliminary Ideas about Reform. *Reynolds, B. L.*, 1987, pp. 108–29. **[G: China]**

Zhao, Yujiang. Management of Extrabudgetary Funds. *Reynolds, B. L.*, 1987, pp. 130–41. **[G: China]**

Zheng, Guangliang. China's Industrial Reform: The Leadership System. *Tidrick, G. and Jiyuan, C., eds.*, 1987, pp. 297–312. **[G: China]**

615 Economics of Transportation

6150 Economics of Transportation

Abouchar, Alan. How Do We Price America's Highways? *Challenge*, May/June 1987, *30*(2), pp. 52–54. **[G: U.S.]**

Adie, Douglas K. Privatizing, Divesting, and Deregulating the Postal Service. *Kent, C. A., ed.*, 1987, pp. 123–34. **[G: U.S.]**

Ambler, John. Factors Controlling Recent Performance on Soviet Railways. *Tismer, J. F.; Ambler, J. and Symons, L., eds.*, 1987, pp. 32–77. **[G: U.S.S.R.]**

Armstrong, Terence. Soviet Ideas for Pioneering Shipping in the Central Arctic Basin. *Tismer, J. F.; Ambler, J. and Symons, L., eds.*, 1987, pp. 175–84. **[G: U.S.S.R.]**

Auerbach, Alan J. Right of Way and Congestion Toll: Comments. *Razin, A. and Sadka, E., eds.*, 1987, pp. 370–71.

Bagchi, Prabir K.; Raghunathan, T. S. and Bardi, Edward J. The Implications of Just-in-Time Inventory Policies on Carrier Selection. *Logist. Transp. Rev.*, December 1987, *23*(4), pp. 373–84. **[G: U.S.]**

Barrett, W. Brian, et al. The Adjustment of Stock Prices to Completely Unanticipated Events. *Financial Rev.*, November 1987, *22*(4), pp. 345–54. **[G: U.S.]**

Bates, John J. Measuring Travel Time Values with a Discrete Choice Model: A Note. *Econ. J.*, June 1987, *97*(386), pp. 493–98.

Baumgartner, J. P. Looking Back at Transport Forecasts. *Int. J. Transport Econ.*, February 1987, *14*(1), pp. 45–56. **[G: Switzerland]**

Beilock, Richard and Freeman, James. The Effect on Rate Levels and Structures of Removing Entry and Rate Controls on Motor Carriers. *J. Transp. Econ. Policy*, May 1987, *21*(2), pp. 167–88. **[G: U.S.]**

Bej, Emil. Soviet Transportation Policies, 1922–1965: A Survey of Irregularities in Passenger Traffic. *Int. J. Transport Econ.*, February 1987, *14*(1), pp. 19–43. **[G: U.S.S.R.]**

Berechman, Joseph. Cost Structure and Production Technology in Transit: An Application to the Israeli Bus Transit Sector. *Reg. Sci. Urban Econ.*, November 1987, *17*(4), pp. 519–34. **[G: Israel]**

Berglas, Eitan; Fresko, David and Pines, David. Right of Way and Congestion Toll. *Razin, A. and Sadka, E., eds.*, 1987, pp. 343–69.

Berman, Zygmunt and Alvstam, Claes G. Investment Policy in the Polish Transport Sector—Assessments of the 1970s and Prospects for the 1990s. *Tismer, J. F.; Ambler, J. and Symons, L., eds.*, 1987, pp. 328–78. **[G: Poland]**

Bigras, Yvon and Nguyen, Sang V. Un modèle des flux interrégionaux de marchandises au Canada. (A Model of Interregional Freight Flows for Canada. With English summary.) *L'Actual. Econ.*, March 1987, *63*(1), pp. 26–42. **[G: Canada]**

Birks, K. Stuart and Buurman, Gary B. Rationing and Careless Days: Comment. *New Zealand Econ. Pap.*, 1987, *21*, pp. 117–20. **[G: New Zealand]**

Blair, Roger D.; Kaserman, David L. and McClave, James T. Competition on Trial: Florida Deregulates Trucking. *Challenge*, Sept./Oct. 1987, *30*(4), pp. 60–64. **[G: U.S.]**

Bolyard, Joan E. International Travel and Passenger Fares, 1986. *Surv. Curr. Bus.*, June 1987, *67*(6), pp. 23–25. **[G: U.S.]**

Boncher, William. The Current Soviet Campaign to Increase Freight Train Weight. *Tismer, J. F.; Ambler, J. and Symons, L., eds.*, 1987, pp. 78–115. **[G: U.S.S.R.]**

Bookbinder, James H. and Sereda, Noreen A. A DRP-Approach to the Management of Rail Car Inventories. *Logist. Transp. Rev.*, August 1987, *23*(3), pp. 265–80.

Boyer, Kenneth D. The Costs of Price Regulation: Lessons from Railroad Deregulation. *Rand J. Econ.*, Autumn 1987, *18*(3), pp. 408–16. **[G: U.S.]**

Bruning, Edward R. Legislative and Administrative Reforms in the Motor Carrier Industry and Returns to Stockholders. *J. Transp. Econ. Policy*, September 1987, *21*(3), pp. 289–305. **[G: U.S.]**

Cappelli, Peter. Collective Bargaining in American Industry: Airlines. *Lipsky, D. B. and Donn, C. B., eds.*, 1987, pp. 135–86. **[G: U.S.]**

Carey, David E. and Mahmassani, Hani S. Air Travel Considerations in Planning for Technology-Based Economic Development: A Case Study of Austin, Texas. *Reg. Sci. Persp.*, 1987, *17*(1), pp. 20–41. **[G: U.S.]**

Caves, Douglas W., et al. An Assessment of the Efficiency Effects of U.S. Airline Deregulation via an International Comparison. *Bailey, E. E., ed.*, 1987, pp. 285–320. **[G: U.S.]**

Chalk, Andrew J. Market Forces and Commercial Aircraft Safety. *J. Ind. Econ.*, September 1987, *36*(1), pp. 61–81. **[G: U.S.]**

Chance, Don M. and Ferris, Stephen P. The Effect of Aviation Disasters on the Air Transport Industry: A Financial Market Perspective. *J. Transp. Econ. Policy*, May 1987, *21*(2), pp. 151–65. **[G: Global]**

Chandra, Suresh and Saxena, P. K. Cost/Completion-Date Tradeoffs in Quadratic Fractional Transportation Problem. *Econ. Computat. Cybern. Stud. Res.*, 1987, 22(3), pp. 67–72.

Christensen, Laurits R. and Huston, John H. A Reexamination of the Cost Structure for Specialized Motor Carriers. *Logist. Transp. Rev.*, December 1987, 23(4), pp. 339–51. [G: U.S.]

Cohen, Yuval. Commuter Welfare under Peak-period Congestion Tolls: Who Gains and Who Loses? *Int. J. Transport Econ.*, October 1987, 14(3), pp. 239–66.

Crainic, Teodor Gabriel. Operations Research Models of Intercity Freight Transportation: The Current State and Future Research Issues. *Logist. Transp. Rev.*, June 1987, 23(2), pp. 189–206.

Cunningham, Lawrence F. and Eckard, E. Woodrow, Jr. U.S. Small Community Air Service Subsidies: Essential or Superfluous? *J. Transp. Econ. Policy*, September 1987, 21(3), pp. 255–77. [G: U.S.]

Davidson, Wallace N., III; Chandy, P. R. and Cross, Mark. Large Losses, Risk Management and Stock Returns in the Airline Industry. *J. Risk Ins.*, March 1987, 54(1), pp. 162–72. [G: U.S.]

Davis, Grant M.; Weintraub, Norman and Holley, William H., Jr. Employee Stock Ownership Programs and Their Use in Trucking: Capital Formation, Employee Participation, or Survival? *Logist. Transp. Rev.*, August 1987, 23(3), pp. 243–63. [G: U.S.]

Dawson, Andrew H. Transport and the Pattern of Settlement in Poland—The Impact of Postwar Policies. *Tismer, J. F.; Ambler, J. and Symons, L., eds.*, 1987, pp. 306–27. [G: Poland]

Dawson, D. A. and Parent, L. P. Positive Steps in Transport Deregulation—The Prairies. *Can. Public Policy*, March 1987, 13(1), pp. 86–96. [G: Canada]

Dick, H. W. Prahu Shipping Eastern Indonesia in the Interwar Period. *Bull. Indonesian Econ. Stud.*, April 1987, 23(1), pp. 104–21. [G: Indonesia]

Due, John F. Abandonment of Rail Lines and the Smaller Railroad Alternative. *Logist. Transp. Rev.*, March 1987, 23(1), pp. 109–34. [G: U.S.]

Dunkerley, Joy and Hoch, Irving. Energy for Transport in Developing Countries. *Energy J.*, July 1987, 8(3), pp. 57–72. [G: LDCs]

Ellison, Anthony P. Developments in Transport Policy: Canada. *J. Transp. Econ. Policy*, January 1987, 21(1), pp. 91–96.

Evans, Andrew. A Theoretical Comparison of Competition with Other Economic Regimes for Bus Services. *J. Transp. Econ. Policy*, January 1987, 21(1), pp. 7–36.

Fisher, Franklin M. Pan American to United: The *Pacific Division Transfer Case*. *Rand J. Econ.*, Winter 1987, 18(4), pp. 492–508. [G: U.S.]

Folkes, Valerie S.; Koletsky, Susan and Graham, John L. A Field Study of Causal Inferences and Consumer Reaction: The View from the Airport. *J. Cons. Res.*, March 1987, 13(4), pp. 534–39. [G: U.S.]

Foreman-Peck, J. S. Natural Monopoly and Railway Policy in the Nineteenth Century. *Oxford Econ. Pap.*, December 1987, 39(4), pp. 699–718. [G: U.K.]

Funck, Rolf H. and Kowalski, Jan S. Impact of Transportation Bottlenecks on Production— The Polish Case. *Tismer, J. F.; Ambler, J. and Symons, L., eds.*, 1987, pp. 292–305. [G: Poland]

Gallick, Edward C. and Sisk, David E. A Reconsideration of Taxi Regulation. *J. Law, Econ., Organ.*, Spring 1987, 3(1), pp. 117–28. [G: U.S.]

Garbacz, Christopher and Kelly, J. Gregory. Automobile Safety Inspection: New Econometric and Benefit/Cost Estimates. *Appl. Econ.*, June 1987, 19(6), pp. 763–71. [G: U.S.]

Garcia-Ferrer, Antonio and del Hoyo, Juan. Analysis of the Car Accident Indexes in Spain: A Multiple Time Series Approach. *J. Bus. Econ. Statist.*, January 1987, 5(1), pp. 27–38. [G: Spain]

Garrod, Peter V. and Miklius, Walter. "Captive Shippers" and the Success of Railroads in Capturing Monopoly Rent. *J. Law Econ.*, October 1987, 30(2), pp. 423–42. [G: U.S.]

Gómez-Ibáñez, José A. Deregulation and the Future of Intercity Travel: Costs of the Various Intercity Modes. *Meyer, J. R. and Oster, C. V., Jr.*, 1987, pp. 225–47. [G: U.S.]

Gorys, Julius M. L. The Intercity Carriage of Dangerous Goods in the Province of Ontario. *Logist. Transp. Rev.*, August 1987, 23(3), pp. 307–24. [G: Canada]

Guria, Jagadish C. Optimal Pricing in an Integrated Transport System. *Int. J. Transport Econ.*, October 1987, 14(3), pp. 267–82.

Guria, Jagadish C. Regulatory Change in the Transport Sector. *Bollard, A. and Buckle, R., eds.*, 1987, pp. 67–85. [G: New Zealand]

Haghani, Ali E. and Daskin, Mark S. A Combined Model of Train Routing, Makeup, and Empty Car Distribution. *Logist. Transp. Rev.*, June 1987, 23(2), pp. 173–87. [G: U.S.]

Haitovsky, Y.; Salomon, Ilan and Silman, L. A. The Economic Impact of Charter Flights on Tourism to Israel: An Econometric Approach. *J. Transp. Econ. Policy*, May 1987, 21(2), pp. 111–34. [G: Israel]

Hall, Derek R. Albania's Transport Cooperation with Her Neighbors. *Tismer, J. F.; Ambler, J. and Symons, L., eds.*, 1987, pp. 379–99. [G: Albania]

Harper, Donald V. and Johnson, James C. The Potential Consequences of Deregulation of Transportation Revisited. *Land Econ.*, May 1987, 63(2), pp. 137–46. [G: U.S.]

Hartman, Raymond S. Product Quality and Market Efficiency: The Effect of Product Recalls on Resale Prices and Firm Valuation. *Rev. Econ. Statist.*, May 1987, 69(2), pp. 367–72. [G: U.S.]

Hausman, William J. The English Coastal Coal Trade, 1691–1910: How Rapid Was Productivity Growth? [Total Factor Productivity in the English Shipping Industry: The North-east Coal Trade, 1700–1850]. *Econ. Hist. Rev., 2nd Ser.*, November 1987, *40*(4), pp. 588–96. **[G: U.K.]**

Hay, Donald A. Competition and Industrial Policies. *Oxford Rev. Econ. Policy*, Autumn 1987, *3*(3), pp. 27–40. **[G: U.K.]**

Hayashi, Paul M. and Trapani, John M. The Impact of Energy Costs on Domestic Airline Passenger Travel. *J. Transp. Econ. Policy*, January 1987, *21*(1), pp. 73–86.

Hazard, John L. The Institutionalization of Transportation Policy—Two Decades of DOT. *Logist. Transp. Rev.*, March 1987, *23*(1), pp. 33–56. **[G: U.S.]**

Hensher, David A. and Milthorpe, Frank W. An Empirical Comparison of Alternative Approaches to Modelling Vehicle Choice. *Int. J. Transport Econ.*, June 1987, *14*(2), pp. 139–80. **[G: Australia]**

Hill, Daniel H. Derived Demand Estimation with Survey Experiments: Commercial Electric Vehicles. *Rev. Econ. Statist.*, May 1987, *69*(2), pp. 277–85.

Hunter, Holland. Tracing the Effects of Sectoral Transport Demands on the Soviet Transport System. *Tismer, J. F.; Ambler, J. and Symons, L., eds.*, 1987, pp. 1–31. **[G: U.S.S.R.]**

Huth, William L. and Eriksen, Steven E. Airline Traffic Forecasting Using Deterministic and Stochastic Time Series Decomposition. *Logist. Transp. Rev.*, December 1987, *23*(4), pp. 401–09. **[G: U.S.]**

Hwang, Ming-Jeng and Mann, Patrick C. Deregulation and Efficiency in the Rail Industry. *Atlantic Econ. J.*, July 1987, *15*(2), pp. 47–52. **[G: U.S.]**

Intrator, Jacob and Weiss, Joseph. Exhaustive Iterations—An Improving Approach for Long Transportation Problems. *Econ. Computat. Cybern. Stud. Res.*, 1987, *22*(3), pp. 73–87.

James, George W. The Business Economist: Work in an Airline. *Bus. Econ.*, April 1987, *22*(2), pp. 54–56. **[G: U.S.]**

Jordan, W. John. The Theory of Optimal Highway Pricing and Investment: Reply. *Southern Econ. J.*, January 1987, *53*(3), pp. 783–85.

Kakumoto, Ryohei. Developments in Transport Policy: Japan. *J. Transp. Econ. Policy*, January 1987, *21*(1), pp. 97–98.

Kerr, Geoff and Cullen, Ross. Non-market Valuation in New Zealand: Comment. *New Zealand Econ. Pap.*, 1987, *21*, pp. 125–29. **[G: New Zealand]**

Kim, H. Youn. Economies of Scale and Scope in Multiproduct Firms: Evidence from U.S. Railroads. *Appl. Econ.*, June 1987, *19*(6), pp. 733–41. **[G: U.S.]**

Kim, Moshe. Multilateral Relative Efficiency Levels in Regional Canadian Trucking. *Logist. Transp. Rev.*, June 1987, *23*(2), pp. 155–72. **[G: Canada]**

Klein, A. and Verbeke, A. The Design of an Optimal Short Term Forecasting System for Sea Port Management: An Application to the Port

of Antwerp. *Int. J. Transport Econ.*, February 1987, *14*(1), pp. 57–70. **[G: Netherlands]**

Kondo, Katsunao and Kitamura, Ryuichi. Time–Space Constraints and the Formation of Trip Chains. *Reg. Sci. Urban Econ.*, February 1987, *17*(1), pp. 49–65. **[G: Japan]**

Kumbhakar, Subal C. Production Frontiers and Panel Data: An Application to U.S. Class 1 Railroads. *J. Bus. Econ. Statist.*, April 1987, *5*(2), pp. 249–55. **[G: U.S.]**

Levine, Michael E. Airline Competition in Deregulated Markets: Theory, Firm Strategy, and Public Policy. *Yale J. Regul.*, Spring 1987, *4*(2), pp. 393–494. **[G: U.S.]**

Lewis, Frank and MacKinnon, Mary. Government Loan Guarantees and the Failure of the Canadian Northern Railway. *J. Econ. Hist.*, March 1987, *47*(1), pp. 175–96. **[G: Canada]**

Loeb, Peter D. The Determinants of Automobile Fatalities, with Special Consideration to Policy Variables. *J. Transp. Econ. Policy*, September 1987, *21*(3), pp. 279–87. **[G: U.S.]**

Lydolph, Paul E. Soviet Maritime Transport in an Overcrowded Market. *Tismer, J. F.; Ambler, J. and Symons, L., eds.*, 1987, pp. 140–74. **[G: U.S.S.R.]**

MacDonald, James M. Competition and Rail Rates for the Shipment of Corn, Soybeans, and Wheat. *Rand J. Econ.*, Spring 1987, *18*(1), pp. 151–63. **[G: U.S.]**

Majumdar, Badiul A. Upstart or Flying Start? The Rise of Airbus Industrie. *World Econ.*, December 1987, *10*(4), pp. 497–518. **[G: U.S.; Europe]**

Mannering, Fred and Winston, Clifford. Recent Automobile Occupant Safety Proposals. *Winston, C., et al.*, 1987, pp. 68–88. **[G: U.S.]**

McCarthy, Patrick S. and Oesterle, William. The Deterrent Effects of Stiffer DUI Laws: An Empirical Study. *Logist. Transp. Rev.*, December 1987, *23*(4), pp. 353–71. **[G: U.S.]**

McFarland, Henry. Did Railroad Deregulation Lead to Monopoly Pricing? An Application of *q. J. Bus.*, July 1987, *60*(3), pp. 385–400. **[G: U.S.]**

McFarland, Henry. The Economics of Vertical Restraints and Relationships between Connecting Railroads. *Logist. Transp. Rev.*, June 1987, *23*(2), pp. 207–22. **[G: U.S.]**

McMullen, B. Starr. The Impact of Regulatory Reform on U.S. Motor Carrier Costs: A Preliminary Examination. *J. Transp. Econ. Policy*, September 1987, *21*(3), pp. 307–19. **[G: U.S.]**

McMullen, B. Starr and Miklius, Walter. Measuring the Impact of Regulatory Reform on Firm Bankruptcies: The U.S. Motor Carrier Industry. *Int. J. Transport Econ.*, June 1987, *14*(2), pp. 181–88. **[G: U.S.]**

McNeill, William H. The Eccentricity of Wheels, or Eurasian Transportation in Historical Perspective. *Amer. Hist. Rev.*, December 1987, *92*(5), pp. 1111–26.

Meyer, Hans-Reinhard. Die Schweizerischen Bundesbahnen—keine Unternehmung mehr. (The Swiss Federal Railway Company. With

English summary.) *Schweiz. Z. Volkswirtsch. Statist.*, December 1987, *123*(4), pp. 483–99. **[G: Switzerland]**

Meyer, John R. and Oster, Clinton V., Jr. A Turning Point in Transportation Policy. *Meyer, J. R. and Oster, C. V., Jr.*, 1987, pp. 1–5. **[G: U.S.]**

Meyer, John R. and Oster, Clinton V., Jr. Market Structure, Public Policy, and the Future of Intercity Passenger Transportation. *Meyer, J. R. and Oster, C. V., Jr.*, 1987, pp. 205–24. **[G: U.S.]**

Meyer, John R. and Oster, Clinton V., Jr. The U.S. Experience with Airline Deregulation: Antecedents and Consequences. *Meyer, J. R. and Oster, C. V., Jr.*, 1987, pp. 9–16. **[G: U.S.]**

Meyer, John R. and Oster, Clinton V., Jr. The U.S. Experience with Airline Deregulation: Productivity, Employment, and Labor Relations. *Meyer, J. R. and Oster, C. V., Jr.*, 1987, pp. 83–107. **[G: U.S.]**

Meyer, John R. and Oster, Clinton V., Jr. The U.S. Experience with Airline Deregulation: Responses of the Old Guard. *Meyer, J. R. and Oster, C. V., Jr.*, 1987, pp. 55–81. **[G: U.S.]**

Meyer, John R. and Oster, Clinton V., Jr. The U.S. Experience with Airline Deregulation: The New Entrepreneurs. *Meyer, J. R. and Oster, C. V., Jr.*, 1987, pp. 39–53. **[G: U.S.]**

Meyer, John R.; Oster, Clinton V., Jr. and Strong, John S. Airline Financial Performance since Deregulation. *Meyer, J. R. and Oster, C. V., Jr.*, 1987, pp. 17–38. **[G: U.S.]**

Meyer, John R.; Oster, Clinton V., Jr. and Strong, John S. The U.S. Experience with Airline Deregulation: The Effect on Travelers: Fares and Service. *Meyer, J. R. and Oster, C. V., Jr.*, 1987, pp. 109–24. **[G: U.S.]**

Meyer, John R., et al. The Economics of Competition in Intercity Passenger Travel: The Other Modes: Rail, Bus, and Auto. *Meyer, J. R. and Oster, C. V., Jr.*, 1987, pp. 161–82. **[G: U.S.]**

Meyer, John R., et al. The U.S. Experience with Airline Deregulation: Changes in Distribution Channels and the Travel Agency Business. *Meyer, J. R. and Oster, C. V., Jr.*, 1987, pp. 125–36. **[G: U.S.]**

Meyer, John R., et al. Toward an Equilibrium in Intercity Travel Choices. *Meyer, J. R. and Oster, C. V., Jr.*, 1987, pp. 183–203. **[G: U.S.]**

Meyers, Harry G. Displacement Effects of Federal Highway Grants. *Nat. Tax J.*, June 1987, *40*(2), pp. 221–35. **[G: U.S.]**

Michel, Allen and Shaked, Israel. Airline Deregulation and the Probability of Air Carrier Insolvency. *Financial Rev.*, February 1987, *22*(1), pp. 159–73. **[G: U.S.]**

Michel, Allen and Shaked, Israel. Trucking Deregulation and Motor-Carrier Performance: The Shareholders' Perspective. *Financial Rev.*, May 1987, *22*(2), pp. 295–311. **[G: U.S.]**

Miller, Rory. Transferring Techniques: Railway Building and Management on the West Coast

of South America. *Dewey, C., ed.*, 1987, pp. 155–91. **[G: Peru; Chile; Bolivia; Argentina]**

Mills, Gordon. Road User Fees and Road Funding in Australia. *J. Transp. Econ. Policy*, September 1987, *21*(3), pp. 327–29. **[G: Australia]**

Mogridge, M. J. H., et al. The Downs/Thomson Paradox and the Transportation Planning Process. *Int. J. Transport Econ.*, October 1987, *14*(3), pp. 283–311.

Mohring, Herbert; Schroeter, John R. and Wiboonchutikula, Paitoon. The Values of Waiting Time, Travel Time, and a Seat on a Bus. *Rand J. Econ.*, Spring 1987, *18*(1), pp. 40–56. **[G: Singapore]**

Mongula, Benedict S. and Ng'andwe, Chiselebwe. Limits to Development in Southern Africa: Energy, Transport and Communications in SADCC Countries. *Amin, S.; Chitala, D. and Mandaza, I., eds.*, 1987, pp. 85–108. **[G: Southern Africa]**

Morgan, Ivor P. The U.S. Experience with Airline Deregulation: International Consequences. *Meyer, J. R. and Oster, C. V., Jr.*, 1987, pp. 137–57. **[G: U.S.; Global]**

Morrison, Steven A. The Equity and Efficiency of Runway Pricing. *J. Public Econ.*, October 1987, *34*(1), pp. 45–60. **[G: U.S.]**

Morrison, Steven A. The Theory of Optimal Highway Pricing and Investment: Comment. *Southern Econ. J.*, January 1987, *53*(3), pp. 779–82.

Morrison, Steven A. and Winston, Clifford. Empirical Implications and Tests of the Contestability Hypothesis. *J. Law Econ.*, April 1987, *30*(1), pp. 53–66. **[G: U.S.]**

Mubayi, A. Economics of Transporting Solids by Pipe-line—Comparison of a Coal Slurry Pipeline and Movement by Rail. *Pachauri, R. K., ed.*, 1987, pp. 919–34.

Müller, A. L. The Economic Awakening of the Eastern Cape, 1795–1820. *S. Afr. J. Econ.*, March 1987, *55*(1), pp. 40–52. **[G: S. Africa]**

Murfin, Andy. Price Discrimination and Tax Differences in the European Motor Industry. *Cnossen, S., ed.*, 1987, pp. 171–94. **[G: EEC]**

Mwase, Ngila R. L. Railway Pricing in Developing Countries: A Comparative Analysis of the Tariffs and Unit Costs of the TAZARA and of Competing Routes in Southern Africa. *J. Transp. Econ. Policy*, May 1987, *21*(2), pp. 189–217. **[G: Africa]**

Mwase, Ngila R. L. Reflections on the Proposed Botswana–Namibia Trans-Kalahari Railway. *Eastern Afr. Econ. Rev.*, June 1987, *3*(1), pp. 65–75. **[G: Botswana; Namibia]**

Mwase, Ngila R. L. The Financing of Transport and Communications Sector in Developing Countries: Reflections on Independent Namibia. *Int. J. Transport Econ.*, June 1987, *14*(2), pp. 189–99. **[G: Namibia]**

Nelson, James C. Politics and Economics in Transport Regulation and Deregulation—A Century Perspective of the ICC's Role. *Logist. Transp. Rev.*, March 1987, *23*(1), pp. 5–32. **[G: U.S.]**

Nordvik, Helge W. The Bergen Shipping Industry in the 19th and 20th Centuries. *Scand. Econ. Hist. Rev.*, 1987, 35(1), pp. 130–34. [G: Norway]

North, Robert N. Current Developments in Transport and Traffic between the Soviet Union and Eastern Europe. *Tismer, J. F.; Ambler, J. and Symons, L.*, eds., 1987, pp. 270–91. [G: U.S.S.R.; E. Europe]

Orlando, Enrico. Recent Developments Concerning the Legal Regime and Insurance Problems Related to the Transportation of Hazardous Materials by Sea. *Kleindorfer, P. R. and Kunreuther, H. C.*, ed., 1987, pp. 454–57.

Owen, A. D. and Phillips, Garry D. A. The Characteristics of Railway Passenger Demand. *J. Transp. Econ. Policy*, September 1987, 21(3), pp. 231–53. [G: U.K.]

Pickrell, Don H. Deregulation and the Future of Intercity Travel: Models of Intercity Travel Demand. *Meyer, J. R. and Oster, C. V., Jr.*, 1987, pp. 249–60. [G: U.S.]

Plott, Charles R. Dimensions of Parallelism: Some Policy Applications of Experimental Methods. *Roth, A. E.*, ed., 1987, pp. 193–219. [G: U.S.]

Polo, Yolanda and Salas, Vicente. El automóvil en España. Determinantes socioeconomicos de su aceptación. (With English summary.) *Invest. Econ.*, September 1987, 11(3), pp. 463–82. [G: Spain]

Pustay, Michael W. Shifting the Burden of Proof. *Logist. Transp. Rev.*, December 1987, 23(4), pp. 411–25. [G: U.S.]

Putterill, Martin S. Information Systems for Road Maintenance Management: A Value for Money Approach. *Chan, J. L.*, ed., Pt. A, 1987, pp. 131–45. [G: U.S.]

Rhea, Marti J. and Shrock, David L. Measuring Distribution Effectiveness with Key Informant Reports. *Logist. Transp. Rev.*, August 1987, 23(3), pp. 295–306.

Richardson, David. The Costs of Survival: The Transport of Slaves in the Middle Passage and the Profitability of the 18th-Century British Slave Trade. *Exploration Econ. Hist.*, April 1987, 24(2), pp. 178–96. [G: U.K.]

Rimmer, P. J. The World Bank's Urban Transport Policy: Authorised Version, Revised Version and the Apocrypha. *Environ. Planning A*, December 1987, 19(12), pp. 1569–77. [G: LDCs]

Roberts, Merrill J. Residual Railroad Rate Control: The Unmet Challenge of Deregulation. *Logist. Transp. Rev.*, March 1987, 23(1), pp. 83–108. [G: U.S.]

Rose, Nancy L. Labor Rent Sharing and Regulation: Evidence from the Trucking Industry. *J. Polit. Econ.*, December 1987, 95(6), pp. 1146–78. [G: U.S.]

Roth, Gabriel. Roles of the Private Sector in the Supply of Public Services in Less Developed Countries. *Kent, C. A.*, ed., 1987, pp. 195–206. [G: LDCs]

Ruppenthal, Karl M. U.S. Airline Deregulation—Winners and Losers. *Logist. Transp. Rev.*, March 1987, 23(1), pp. 65–82. [G: U.S.]

Schipper, Katherine; Thompson, Rex and Weil, Roman L. Disentangling Interrelated Effects of Regulatory Changes on Shareholder Wealth: The Case of Motor Carrier Deregulation. *J. Law Econ.*, April 1987, 30(1), pp. 67–100. [G: U.S.]

Schöler, Klaus. Spatial Price Policy and the Demand for Transportation: A Note. *J. Reg. Sci.*, February 1987, 27(1), pp. 135–36.

Sheehan, Dennis and Winston, Clifford. Expectations and Automobile Policy. *Winston, C., et al.*, 1987, pp. 89–102. [G: U.S.]

Shostak, Arthur B. Technology, Air Traffic Control, and Labor–Management Relations. *Cornfield, D. B.*, ed., 1987, pp. 153–72. [G: U.S.]

Smith, Roger S. Motor Vehicle Tax Harmonization. *Cnossen, S.*, ed., 1987, pp. 141–70. [G: EEC]

St. Seidenfus, Hellmuth. European Ports in the Context of the World Economy and the European Economy: Changes in Sea Transport. *Int. J. Transport Econ.*, June 1987, 14(2), pp. 133–38. [G: W. Europe]

St. Seidenfus, Hellmuth. From the "Rhine–Main–Danube Canal" to the "Main–Danube Connection." *Tismer, J. F.; Ambler, J. and Symons, L.*, eds., 1987, pp. 429–48. [G: W. Germany; E. Europe]

Stadelbauer, Jörg. Transport and the Pattern of Settlement in Soviet Caucasia. *Tismer, J. F.; Ambler, J. and Symons, L.*, eds., 1987, pp. 218–69. [G: U.S.S.R.]

Symons, Leslie. The Rise and Fall of Soviet Influence on the Chinese Aircraft Industry and Air Transport. *Tismer, J. F.; Ambler, J. and Symons, L.*, eds., 1987, pp. 449–67. [G: China; U.S.S.R.]

Teal, Roger F. and Berglund, Mary. The Impact of Taxicab Deregulation in the USA. *J. Transp. Econ. Policy*, January 1987, 21(1), pp. 37–56. [G: U.S.]

Tismer, Johannes F.; Ambler, John and Symons, Leslie. Transport and Economic Development—Soviet Union and Eastern Europe: Preface. *Tismer, J. F.; Ambler, J. and Symons, L.*, eds., 1987, pp. xii–xxiii. [G: CMEA]

Tolofari, S. R. Open Registry Costs and Freight Rates: Are They Related? *Int. J. Transport Econ.*, February 1987, 14(1), pp. 85–103. [G: U.S.; Europe; Japan]

Tolofari, S. R.; Button, K. J. and Pitfield, D. E. An Econometric Analysis of the Cost Structure of the Tank Sector of the Shipping Industry. *Int. J. Transport Econ.*, February 1987, 14(1), pp. 71–84.

Truong, Truong P. and Hensher, David A. Measuring Travel Time Values with a Discrete Choice Model: A Reply. *Econ. J.*, June 1987, 97(386), pp. 499–501. [G: Australia]

Tucci, Ugo. Venetian Ship-Owners in the XVIth Century. *J. Europ. Econ. Hist.*, Fall 1987, 16(2), pp. 277–96. [G: Italy]

Turnbull, Gerard. Canals, Coal and Regional Growth during the Industrial Revolution.

Econ. Hist. Rev., 2nd Ser., November 1987, *40*(4), pp. 537–60. **[G: U.K.]**

Turnock, David. The Danube–Black Sea Canal and Its Impact on Southern Romania. *Tismer, J. F.; Ambler, J. and Symons, L., eds.*, 1987, pp. 400–428. **[G: Romania]**

Tye, William B. Pricing Rail Competitive Access in the Transition to Deregulation with the Revenue/Variable Cost Test. *Antitrust Bull.*, Spring 1987, *32*(1), pp. 101–35. **[G: U.S.]**

Tye, William B. The Voluntary Negotiations Approach to Rail Competitive Access in the Transition to Deregulation. *Antitrust Bull.*, Summer 1987, *32*(2), pp. 415–50. **[G: U.S.]**

Tyler, P. and Kitson, M. Geographical Variations in Transport Costs of Manufacturing Firms in Great Britain. *Urban Stud.*, February 1987, *24*(1), pp. 61–73. **[G: U.K.]**

Veenendaal, Augustus J., Jr. The Kansas City Southern Railway and the Dutch Connection. *Bus. Hist. Rev.*, Summer 1987, *61*(2), pp. 291–316. **[G: U.S.]**

Ville, Simon. Defending Productivity Growth in the English Coal Trade during the Eighteenth and Nineteenth Centuries. *Econ. Hist. Rev., 2nd Ser.*, November 1987, *40*(4), pp. 597–602. **[G: U.K.]**

Viscencio-Brambila, Hector and Fuller, Stephen. Estimated Effect of Deepened U.S. Gulf Ports on Export-Grain Flow Patterns and Logistics Costs. *Logist. Transp. Rev.*, June 1987, *23*(2), pp. 139–54. **[G: U.S.]**

Volmuller, J. Is Road Pricing a Real Contribution to Urban Transport Policy? *Int. J. Transport Econ.*, February 1987, *14*(1), pp. 7–18.

Walker, David J. Rationing and Careless Days: Reply. *New Zealand Econ. Pap.*, 1987, *21*, pp. 121–23. **[G: New Zealand]**

Walton, Gary M. River Transportation and the Old Northwest Territory. *Klingaman, D. C. and Vedder, R. K., eds.*, 1987, pp. 225–42. **[G: U.S.]**

Wang, Hsiao-Fan. Application of Iterative Scaling Method to Calibrate a Combined Trip Distribution and Mode Choice Model. *Logist. Transp. Rev.*, August 1987, *23*(3), pp. 281–94.

Waters, Alan Rufus. Privatization: A Viable Policy Option? *Kent, C. A., ed.*, 1987, pp. 35–64.

Waters, L. L. Federal and State Transport Policies Mostly about Motor Carriers. *Logist. Transp. Rev.*, March 1987, *23*(1), pp. 57–64. **[G: U.S.]**

Waters, W. G., II. Authors of Articles Related to Transportation in Major Economics Journals 1960–1983. *J. Transp. Econ. Policy*, January 1987, *21*(1), pp. 87–90.

Westwood, John. Soviet Inland Waterways' Prospects for Offering Relief to the Railways. *Tismer, J. F.; Ambler, J. and Symons, L., eds.*, 1987, pp. 116–39. **[G: U.S.S.R.]**

Whitelegg, John. Rural Railways and Disinvestment in Rural Areas. *Reg. Stud.*, February 1987, *21*(1), pp. 55–63. **[G: U.K.]**

Wilson, David. The Consumption of Automotive Oil Products in Soviet Road Transport. *Tismer,*

J. F.; Ambler, J. and Symons, L., eds., 1987, pp. 185–217. **[G: U.S.S.R.]**

Yochum, Gilbert R. and Agarwal, Vinod B. Economic Impact of a Port on a Regional Economy: Note. *Growth Change*, Summer 1987, *18*(3), pp. 74–87. **[G: U.S.]**

Zannetos, Zenon S. Oil Tanker Makets: Continuity amidst Change. *[Adelman, M. A.]*, 1987, pp. 235–57.

Zelenko, Breda. The Rational Division of Freight Traffic between Road and Rail. *J. Transp. Econ. Policy*, September 1987, *21*(3), pp. 321–26. **[G: Yugoslavia]**

Zlatoper, Thomas J. Factors Affecting Motor Vehicle Deaths in the USA: Some Cross-sectional Evidence. *Appl. Econ.*, June 1987, *19*(6), pp. 753–61. **[G: U.S.]**

Zlatoper, Thomas J. Testing for Functional Form and Autocorrelation in the Analysis of Motor Vehicle Deaths. *Quart. Rev. Econ. Bus.*, Winter 1987, *27*(4), pp. 6–17. **[G: U.S.]**

616 Industrial Policy

6160 Industrial Policy

Andreff, Wladimir. Some National Industrial Policies Examined: Comment. *Saunders, C. T., ed.*, 1987, pp. 250–53.

Apostolakis, Bobby E. Output and Input Subsidies as a Means of Industrial Decentralization: The Greek Case. *Devel. Econ.*, June 1987, *25*(2), pp. 171–87. **[G: Greece]**

Apostolakis, Bobby E. The Subsidy Incidence on Industrialization. *Rivista Int. Sci. Econ. Com.*, April 1987, *34*(4), pp. 291–307.

Appleby, Colin and Bessant, John. Adapting to Decline: Organizational Structures and Government Policy in the UK and West German Foundry Sectors. *Wilks, S. and Wright, M., eds.*, 1987, pp. 181–210. **[G: U.K.; W. Germany]**

Arndt, H. W. Industrial Policy in East Asia. *Industry Devel.*, 1987, (22), pp. 1–66. **[G: E. Asia]**

Atkinson, Michael M. and Powers, Richard A. Inside the Industrial Policy Garbage Can: Selective Subsidies to Business in Canada. *Can. Public Policy*, June 1987, *13*(2), pp. 208–17. **[G: Canada]**

Azpiazu, Daniel. Los resultados de la política de promoción industrial al cabo de un decenio (1974–1983). (With English summary.) *Desarrollo Econ.*, Jan.-Mar. 1987, *26*(104), pp. 631–51. **[G: Argentina]**

Bahl, Roy. Industrial Policy and the States. *Goldstein, H. A., ed.*, 1987, pp. 176–88. **[G: U.S.]**

Balassa, Bela. China's Economic Reforms in a Comparative Perspective. *J. Compar. Econ.*, September 1987, *11*(3), pp. 410–26. **[G: China]**

Barber, John and White, Geoff. Current Policy Practice and Problems from a UK Perspective. *Dasgupta, P. and Stoneman, P., eds.*, 1987, pp. 24–50. **[G: U.K.]**

Behrend, Hilde. Some Reflections on Industrial Policies Based on British Experience. *Gemper, B. B., ed.,* 1987, pp. 175–86.   [G: U.K.]

Bergman, Edward M. and Goldstein, Harvey A. Advocates, Institutional Arrangements, and Industrial Policy. *Goldstein, H. A., ed.,* 1987, pp. 114–30.   [G: U.S.]

Blakely, Edward J. and Shapira, Philip. Public Policies for Industry [Industrial Restructuring: Public Policies for Investment in Advanced Industrial Society]. *Staudohar, P. D. and Brown, H. E.,* 1987, *1984,* pp. 139–52.   [G: U.S.]

Bluestone, Barry. Deindustrialization and Unemployment in America. *Staudohar, P. D. and Brown, H. E.,* 1987, *1984,* pp. 3–15.   [G: U.S.]

Bluestone, Barry. In Support of the Deindustrialization Thesis [Is Deindustrialization a Myth? Capital Mobility versus Absorptive Capacity in the U.S. Economy]. *Staudohar, P. D. and Brown, H. E.,* 1987, *1984,* pp. 41–52.   [G: U.S.]

Bluestone, Barry; Harrison, Bennett and Gorham, Lucy. The State and Local Industrial Policy Question: Storm Clouds on the Horizon. *Goldstein, H. A., ed.,* 1987, pp. 16–33.   [G: U.S.]

Bognár, József. Some National Industrial Policies Examined: Comment. *Saunders, C. T., ed.,* 1987, pp. 261–66.

Bognár, József. Technological Policy in Industry: Comment. *Saunders, C. T., ed.,* 1987, pp. 153.

Boyd, Richard. Government–Industry Relations in Japan: Access, Communication, and Competitive Collaboration. *Wilks, S. and Wright, M., eds.,* 1987, pp. 61–90.   [G: Japan]

Brada, Josef C. and Dunn, Robin L. Industrial Policies in East and West Europe Compared. *Saunders, C. T., ed.,* 1987, pp. 57–77.   [G: Europe]

Bradshaw, Ted K. and Blakely, Edward J. Unanticipated Consequences of Government Programs on Rural Economic Development. *U.S.D.A., Econ. Res. Serv., Agr. and Rural Econ. Div.,* 1987, pp. 11.1–17.   [G: U.S.]

Brinkman, Richard L. Democratic Planning in a Market Economy and Social Values. *Gemper, B. B., ed.,* 1987, pp. 21–36.   [G: U.S.; W. Germany; Japan; U.K.]

Browder, John O. Brazil's Export Promotion Policy (1980–1984): Impacts on the Amazon's Industrial Wood Sector. *J. Devel. Areas,* April 1987, *21*(3), pp. 285–304.   [G: Brazil]

Brown, Kenneth M. Changes in Industrial Structure and Foreign Competition—The Policy Arguments. *Cagan, P., ed.,* 1987, pp. 97–128.   [G: U.S.]

Brundenius, Claes. Development and Prospects of Capital Goods Production in Revolutionary Cuba. *World Devel.,* January 1987, *15*(1), pp. 95–112.   [G: Cuba]

Brunel, Andre and Burke, Michael P. Promoting High-Technology Industry: Initiatives and Policies for State Governments: Pennsylvania. *Schmandt, J. and Wilson, R., eds.,* 1987, pp. 191–229.   [G: U.S.]

Bryson, Phillip J. GDR Economic Planning and Social Policy in the 1980s. *Comp. Econ. Stud.,* Summer 1987, *29*(2), pp. 19–38.   [G: E. Germany]

Buchanan, James M. What Is the State? *Buchanan, J. M. (I),* 1987, pp. 51–55.

Burke, Michael P. and Dowling, Michael. Promoting High-Technology Industry: Initiatives and Policies for State Governments: Introduction. *Schmandt, J. and Wilson, R., eds.,* 1987, pp. 1–10.   [G: U.S.]

Cannon, Tom. The Contribution of New Enterprise to Economic Growth and Employment: The Experience of the Scottish Enterprise Foundation. *Gemper, B. B., ed.,* 1987, pp. 131–43.   [G: U.K.]

Carriero, Libero. Technology and International Relations: Considerations on the Industrial Development of the OAPEC Countries. *Hieronymi, O., ed.,* 1987, pp. 141–56.   [G: OAPEC]

Caslin, Terry. De-industrialization in the UK. *Vane, H. and Caslin, T., eds.,* 1987, pp. 240–64.   [G: U.K.]

Caves, Richard E. Industrial Policy and Trade Policy: The Connections. *[Corden, W. M.],* 1987, pp. 68–85.

Cawson, Alan; Holmes, Peter and Stevens, Anne. The Interaction between Firms and the State in France: The Telecommunications and Consumer Electronics Sectors. *Wilks, S. and Wright, M., eds.,* 1987, pp. 10–34.   [G: France]

Chen, Tain-Jy and Tang, De-Piao. Comparing Technical Efficiency between Import-Substitution-Oriented and Export-Oriented Foreign Firms in a Developing Economy. *J. Devel. Econ.,* August 1987, *26*(2), pp. 277–89.   [G: Taiwan]

Cheng, Leonard K. Optimal Trade and Technology Policies: Dynamic Linkages. *Int. Econ. Rev.,* October 1987, *28*(3), pp. 757–76.

Cheval, Jean. New Trends in Industrial Performance and Industrial Policy in France. *Saunders, C. T., ed.,* 1987, pp. 167–82.   [G: France]

Chowdhury, A. and Kirkpatrick, Colin. Industrial Restructuring in a Newly Industrializing Country: The Identification of Priority Industries in Singapore. *Appl. Econ.,* July 1987, *19*(7), pp. 915–26.   [G: Singapore]

Chrisman, James J.; Carroll, Archie B. and Gatewood, Elizabeth J. The Case against Legislation [What's Wrong with Plant-Closing Legislation and Industrial Policy?]. *Staudohar, P. D. and Brown, H. E.,* 1987, *1985,* pp. 321–33.   [G: U.S.]

Cooper, Richard N. Industrial Policy and Trade Distortion. *Salvatore, D., ed.,* 1987, pp. 233–65.   [G: W. Europe; U.S.; Japan]

Cooper, Richard N. Industrial Policy and Trade Distortion: A Policy Perspective. *[Kitamura, H.],* 1987, pp. 37–69.   [G: U.S.; Japan; LDCs]

Csikos-Nagy, Béla. Export-Oriented Policies under Severe Import Regimes: A Case Study for

Hungary. *Saunders, C. T., ed.*, 1987, pp. 239–49. **[G: Hungary]**

Cypher, James M. Military Spending, Technical Change, and Economic Growth: A Disguised Form of Industrial Policy? *J. Econ. Issues*, March 1987, *21*(1), pp. 33–59. **[G: U.S.]**

Czepurko, Aleksander. Industrial Policies and Structural Change: Overall Assessments and Comparisons: Comment. *Saunders, C. T., ed.*, 1987, pp. 99–101.

De Bandt, Jacques. Des mesures combinées de politique commerciale et de politique industrielle: tendance ou non au protectionnisme? (Combined Trade and Industrial Policy Measures: More Protectionism or Not? With English summary.) *Écon. Soc.*, April 1987, *21*(4), pp. 47–71. **[G: Global]**

DeRosa, Dean A. and Nye, William W. Industrial Targeting and International Competitiveness in a Two Country Model of Monopolistic Competition. *Amer. Econ.*, Spring 1987, *31*(1), pp. 9–18.

Dewar, Margaret E. Development Analysis Confronts Politics. *Goldstein, H. A., ed.*, 1987, pp. 148–60. **[G: U.S.]**

Dholakia, Nikhilesh. Industrial Policy, Competitiveness, and the Restructuring of World Markets. *Bloom, P. N., ed.*, 1987, pp. 187–216.

Diebold, William. Western Industrial Policies and East–West Economic Relations. *Saunders, C. T., ed.*, 1987, pp. 21–44.

Duchêne, François. Managing Industrial Change in Western Europe: Policies for a Wider World. *Duchêne, F. and Shepherd, G., eds.*, 1987, pp. 210–41. **[G: W. Germany; U.K.; France; Italy]**

Duchêne, François and Shepherd, Geoffrey. Sources of Industrial Policy. *Duchêne, F. and Shepherd, G., eds.*, 1987, pp. 7–20.

Eads, George C. and Yamamura, Kozo. The Political Economy of Japan: The Future of Industrial Policy. *Yamamura, K. and Yasuba, Y., eds.*, 1987, pp. 423–68. **[G: Japan]**

Eaton, Jonathan and Grossman, Gene M. Optimal Trade and Industrial Policy under Oligopoly. *Bhagwati, J. N., ed.*, 1987, *1986*, pp. 161–82.

Eliasson, Gunnar. Industrial Targeting: Defensive or Offensive Strategies in a Neo-Schumpeterian Perspective. *Eliasson, G.*, 1987, pp. 21–48.

Eliasson, Gunnar. Industrial Targeting: Defensive or Offensive Strategies in a Neo-Schumpeterian Perspective. *Giersch, H., ed.*, 1987, pp. 333–60.

Etzioni, Amitai. U.S. Technological, Economic, and Social Development for the 21st Century. *Nagel, S. S., ed.*, 1987, pp. 241–70. **[G: U.S.]**

Evstigneev, Ruben. State Scientific and Technological Policy and Incentives for Enterprises. *Saunders, C. T., ed.*, 1987, pp. 119–28. **[G: U.S.S.R.]**

Faux, Jeff. Industrial Policy and Democratic Institutions. *Goldstein, H. A., ed.*, 1987, pp. 105–13. **[G: U.S.]**

Feinberg, Richard E. and Tucker, Stuart K. Export Credits in U.S. Trade, Development, and Industrial Policy. *Rodriguez, R. M., ed.*, 1987, pp. 133–43. **[G: U.S.]**

Fischer, Harald and Peck, Amy Miriam. Promoting High-Technology Industry: Initiatives and Policies for State Governments: New York. *Schmandt, J. and Wilson, R., eds.*, 1987, pp. 129–62. **[G: U.S.]**

Flaherty, M. Therese. Industrial Policy in Japan: Overview and Evaluation: Discussion. *Sato, R. and Wachtel, P., eds.*, 1987, pp. 83–85. **[G: Japan]**

Franzmeyer, Fritz. Concepts of Industrial Policy in the Industrial West: Are Mutual Trade Relations in Danger? Reply. *Saunders, C. T., ed.*, 1987, pp. 103–04.

Franzmeyer, Fritz. Concepts of Industrial Policy in the Industrial West: Are Mutual Trade Relations in Danger? *Saunders, C. T., ed.*, 1987, pp. 45–56.

Franzmeyer, Fritz. Some National Industrial Policies Examined: Comment. *Saunders, C. T., ed.*, 1987, pp. 256–58.

Freudenberg, Michael and Henderson, Tracy L. Promoting High-Technology Industry: Initiatives and Policies for State Governments: Florida. *Schmandt, J. and Wilson, R., eds.*, 1987, pp. 35–64. **[G: U.S.]**

Freyman, Jeffrey B. Industrial Policy: Patterns of Convergence and Divergence. *Waltman, J. L. and Studlar, D. T., eds.*, 1987, pp. 44–68. **[G: U.K.; U.S.]**

Friedman, Miles and Culbertson, Deborah. State–Local Economic Development Programs. *Lynch, J. E., ed.*, 1987, pp. 175–90. **[G: U.S.]**

Gemper, Bodo B. Industrial Policy in a Free Market Economy: A Matter of Conviction or Desperation? *Gemper, B. B., ed.*, 1987, pp. 11–20.

Glickman, Norman J. and Van Wagner, Marcia. Two Cheers for Industrial Policy: A Critical Look at Some Urban and Distributional Effects. *Goldstein, H. A., ed.*, 1987, pp. 34–53. **[G: U.S.]**

Goldstein, Harvey A. Why State and Local Industrial Policy? An Introduction to the Debate. *Goldstein, H. A., ed.*, 1987, pp. 1–10. **[G: U.S.]**

Graham, Edward M. World Trade Law and Government Subsidies to Industrial Innovation. *Hieronymi, O., ed.*, 1987, pp. 25–41. **[G: MDCs]**

Graham, Otis L., Jr. The State and Local Industrial Policy Question: Here We Go Again—Or Do We? *Goldstein, H. A., ed.*, 1987, pp. 11–15. **[G: U.S.]**

Grant, Wyn; Paterson, William and Whitston, Colin. Government–Industry Relations in the Chemical Industry: An Anglo–German Comparison. *Wilks, S. and Wright, M., eds.*, 1987, pp. 35–60. **[G: U.K.; W. Germany]**

Grewlich, Klaus W. Telecommunications: A European Perspective. *Wilks, S. and Wright, M., eds.*, 1987, pp. 251–73. **[G: W. Europe]**

Gunther, William D. and Leathers, Charles G. British Enterprise Zones: A Critical Assessment. *Rev. Reg. Stud.*, Winter 1987, *17*(1), pp. 1–12. **[G: U.K.]**

Hacker, Sidney Bailey and Sommerfeld, Robert D. Promoting High-Technology Industry: Initiatives and Policies for State Governments: Minnesota. *Schmandt, J. and Wilson, R., eds.*, 1987, pp. 97–127. **[G: U.S.]**

Herrin, Alejandro N. and Pernia, Ernesto M. Factors Influencing the Choice of Location: Local and Foreign Firms in the Philippines. *Reg. Stud.*, December 1987, *21*(6), pp. 531–41. **[G: Philippines]**

Hooks, Gregory. Comparison of the United States, Sweden, and France [The Policy Response to Factory Closings: A Comparison of the United States, Sweden, and France]. *Staudohar, P. D. and Brown, H. E.*, 1987, *1984*, pp. 245–58. **[G: U.S.; France; Sweden]**

Horn, Ernst-Jürgen. Germany: A Market-Led Process. *Duchêne, F. and Shepherd, G., eds.*, 1987, pp. 41–75. **[G: W. Germany]**

Howard, Mark and Kragie, Mary. Promoting High-Technology Industry: Initiatives and Policies for State Governments: North Carolina. *Schmandt, J. and Wilson, R., eds.*, 1987, pp. 163–90. **[G: U.S.]**

Jenkis, Helmut W. Stabilisation of the Social Structure versus Change of the Industrial Structure: The Case of the Ruhr District. *Gemper, B. B., ed.*, 1987, pp. 57–88. **[G: W. Germany]**

Johnes, Geraint. Regional Policy and Industrial Strategy in the Welsh Economy. *Reg. Stud.*, December 1987, *21*(6), pp. 555–64. **[G: U.K.]**

Karsten, Siegfried G. The Meaning and Validity of a U.S. Industrial Policy. *Gemper, B. B., ed.*, 1987, pp. 155–64. **[G: U.S.]**

Katz, Barbara Goody. Industrial Policy in Japan: Overview and Evaluation: Discussion. *Sato, R. and Wachtel, P., eds.*, 1987, pp. 79–83. **[G: Japan]**

Kay, John A. and Thompson, David. The Performance of the British Economy: Policy for Industry. *Dornbusch, R. and Layard, R., eds.*, 1987, pp. 180–210. **[G: U.K.]**

Kirby, M. W. The Policy Debate: Industrial Policy. *Glynn, S. and Booth, A., eds.*, 1987, pp. 125–39. **[G: U.K.]**

Kreinin, Mordechai E. Comparative Advantage and Possible Trade Restrictions in High-Technology Products. *Salvatore, D., ed.*, 1987, pp. 297–332. **[G: U.S.]**

Krejci, Herbert. A Market Economist's View on Industrial Policy. *Saunders, C. T., ed.*, 1987, pp. 155–62. **[G: Austria]**

Krugman, Paul R. Strategic Sectors and International Competition. *Stern, R. M., ed.*, 1987, pp. 207–32. **[G: U.S.]**

Krugman, Paul R. Targeted Industrial Policies: Theory and Evidence. *Salvatore, D., ed.*, 1987, pp. 266–96. **[G: Japan; U.S.]**

Lacina, Ferdinand. Industrial Policy in a Mixed Economy: The Austrian Case. *Saunders, C. T., ed.*, 1987, pp. 163–66. **[G: Austria]**

Lang, Rikard and Vojnić, Dragomir. Long-term Programme for Economic Stabilisation and the Industrial Structure of Yugoslavia. *Saunders, C. T., ed.*, 1987, pp. 205–14. **[G: Yugoslavia]**

Latsis, Otto R. Individual Labor in a Modern Socialist Economy. *Prob. Econ.*, August 1987, *30*(4), pp. 37–49. **[G: U.S.S.R.]**

Lawrence, Robert Z. Is Deindustrialization a Myth? [The Myth of U.S. Deindustrialization]. *Staudohar, P. D. and Brown, H. E.*, 1987, *1983*, pp. 25–40. **[G: U.S.; OECD]**

Lawrence, Robert Z. and Bosworth, Barry P. Adjusting to Slower Economic Growth: The External Sector. *Bosworth, B. P. and Rivlin, A. M., eds.*, 1987, pp. 55–96. **[G: Sweden]**

Little, Ian M. D. Small Manufacturing Enterprises in Developing Countries. *World Bank Econ. Rev.*, January 1987, *1*(2), pp. 203–35. **[G: Colombia; India]**

Luger, Michael I. The States and Industrial Development: Program Mix and Policy Effectiveness. *Quigley, J. M., ed.*, 1987, pp. 29–63. **[G: U.S.]**

Lukaszewicz, Aleksander. Industrial Policies and Structural Change: Overall Assessments and Comparisons: Comment. *Saunders, C. T., ed.*, 1987, pp. 102–03.

Lukaszewicz, Aleksander. Technological Policy in Industry: Comment. *Saunders, C. T., ed.*, 1987, pp. 152–53.

Lukaszewicz, Aleksander and Pajestka, Józef. Industrial Policy and Structural Change: The Polish Case. *Saunders, C. T., ed.*, 1987, pp. 227–37. **[G: Poland]**

MacMillan, Keith and Turner, Ian. The Cost-Containment Issue: A Study of Government–Industry Relations in the Pharmaceutical Sectors of the United Kingdom and West Germany. *Wilks, S. and Wright, M., eds.*, 1987, pp. 117–47. **[G: U.K.; W. Germany]**

Madian, Alan L. Technology and the Changing Industrial Balance. *Thorup, C. L., ed.*, 1987, pp. 41–66. **[G: Mexico; U.S.]**

de Maria y Campos, Mauricio. Mexico's New Industrial Development Strategy. *Thorup, C. L., ed.*, 1987, pp. 67–81. **[G: Mexico]**

Mayes, David G. European Industrial Policy. *Macmillen, M.; Mayes, D. G. and van Veen, P., eds.*, 1987, pp. 247–67. **[G: EEC]**

Mazier, Jacques. Politique sélective des importations et relance de l'investissement industriel: un essai d'évaluation. (Import Policy on Industrial Investment: An Evaluation Attempt. With English summary.) *Écon. Soc.*, April 1987, *21*(4), pp. 73–100. **[G: OECD]**

Mbelle, A. V. Y. Pathology of a Crisis in Industrial Development: Tanzania after 1974. *Eastern Afr. Econ. Rev.*, December 1987, *3*(2), pp. 95–103. **[G: Tanzania]**

McHone, W. Warren. Factors in the Adoption of Industrial Development Incentives by States. *Appl. Econ.*, January 1987, *19*(1), pp. 17–29. **[G: U.S.]**

Merrigan, Kathleen A. and Smith, Suzanne E. Promoting High-Technology Industry: Initiatives and Policies for State Governments: Massachusetts. *Schmandt, J. and Wilson, R., eds.,* 1987, pp. 65–96. [G: U.S.]

Messerlin, Patrick A. France: The Ambitious State. *Duchêne, F. and Shepherd, G., eds.,* 1987, pp. 76–110. [G: France]

Mieli, Renato. Some National Industrial Policies Examined: Comment. *Saunders, C. T., ed.,* 1987, pp. 259–61.

Mier, Robert; Moe, Kari J. and Sherr, Irene. Strategic Planning and the Pursuit of Reform, Economic Development, and Equity. *Goldstein, H. A., ed.,* 1987, pp. 161–75.
[G: U.S.]

Milbergs, Egils. Turning U.S. Competitive Position Around. *Shetty, Y. K. and Buehler, V. M., eds.,* 1987, pp. 33–43. [G: U.S.]

Milkove, Daniel L. and Sullivan, Patrick J. Financial Aid Programs as a Component of Economic Development Strategy. *U.S.D.A., Econ. Res. Serv., Agr. and Rural Econ. Div.,* 1987, pp. 14.1–22. [G: U.S.]

Molitor, Bernhard. Industrial Policy in a Free Market Economy: Slogan or Solution? *Gemper, B. B., ed.,* 1987, pp. 3–10.

Molyneux, Richard and Thompson, David. Nationalised Industry Performance: Still Third-Rate? *Fisc. Stud.,* February 1987, *8*(1), pp. 48–82. [G: U.K.]

Monke, Eric A.; Pearson, Scott R. and Silva-Carvalho, José-Paulo. Welfare Effects of a Processing Cartel: Flour Milling in Portugal. *Econ. Develop. Cult. Change,* January 1987, *35*(2), pp. 393–407. [G: Portugal]

Moynot, Jean-Louis. The Left, Industrial Policy and the *Filière Électronique. Ross, G.; Hoffmann, S. and Malzacher, S., eds.,* 1987, pp. 263–76. [G: France]

Naisbitt, John. Re-inventing the Corporation. *Shetty, Y. K. and Buehler, V. M., eds.,* 1987, pp. 57–71. [G: U.S.]

Nikić, Gorazd. Some National Industrial Policies Examined: Comment. *Saunders, C. T., ed.,* 1987, pp. 253–56.

Noyelle, Thierry J. Services, Urban Economic Development, and Industrial Policy: Some Critical Linkages. *Goldstein, H. A., ed.,* 1987, pp. 73–84. [G: U.S.]

Ordover, Janusz A. Conflicts of Jurisdiction: Antitrust and Industrial Policy. *Law Contemp. Probl.,* Summer 1987, *50*(3), pp. 165–77.
[G: U.S.]

Peterson, George E. Infrastructure Support for Industrial Policy. *Goldstein, H. A., ed.,* 1987, pp. 95–104. [G: U.S.]

Portes, Richard. Industrial Targeting: Defensive or Offensive Strategies in a Neo-Schumpeterian Perspective: Comment. *Giersch, H., ed.,* 1987, pp. 361–65.

Pugh, Cedric. Industry Policy and Structural Change in Australia. *Gemper, B. B., ed.,* 1987, pp. 107–30. [G: Australia]

Ranci, Pippo. Italy: The Weak State. *Duchêne, F. and Shepherd, G., eds.,* 1987, pp. 111–44.
[G: Italy]

Rees, John. The Diffusion of New Production

Technology: Implications for State and Local Industrial Policy. *Goldstein, H. A., ed.,* 1987, pp. 60–72. [G: U.S.]

Román, Zoltán and Bayer, Kurt. Structural Policy in Hungary and Austria. *Saunders, C. T., ed.,* 1987, pp. 79–99. [G: Hungary; Austria]

Rosenfeld, Stuart A. Education, Training, and Industrial Policy. *Goldstein, H. A., ed.,* 1987, pp. 86–94. [G: U.S.]

Salvatore, Dominick. The New Protectionist Threat to World Welfare: Introduction. *Salvatore, D., ed.,* 1987, pp. 1–27. [G: Global]

Sandri, Stefano. Financing the *partecipazioni statali* System in Italy. *Ann. Pub. Co-op. Econ.,* Apr.-June 1987, *58*(2), pp. 151–64. [G: Italy]

Saunders, Christopher. Industrial Policies and Structural Change: Introduction. *Saunders, C. T., ed.,* 1987, pp. 1–19.

Saxonhouse, Gary R. Strategic Sectors and International Competition: Comment. *Stern, R. M., ed.,* 1987, pp. 239–43. [G: U.S.]

Schatz, Klaus-Werner. The Contribution of Small and New Enterprise to Growth and Employment. *Gemper, B. B., ed.,* 1987, pp. 89–104.
[G: W. Europe]

Schenk, Winfried. Technological Policy in Industry: Comment. *Saunders, C. T., ed.,* 1987, pp. 151–52.

Schmenner, Roger W. Productivity in the Factory and Industrial Policy. *Goldstein, H. A., ed.,* 1987, pp. 54–59. [G: U.S.]

Schoneweg, Ergon. Views of Both Sides of Industry on an EEC Industrial Policy. *Gemper, B. B., ed.,* 1987, pp. 167–74. [G: EEC]

Sercovich, Francisco C. Política technológica y reestructuración industrial: los temas centrales. (With English summary.) *Desarrollo Econ.,* Jan.-Mar. 1987, *26*(104), pp. 561–78.
[G: LDCs]

Sharp, Margaret. Europe: Collaboration in the High Technology Sectors. *Oxford Rev. Econ. Policy,* Spring 1987, *3*(1), pp. 52–65.
[G: W. Europe; Japan; U.S.]

Shepherd, Geoffrey. United Kingdom: A Resistance to Change. *Duchêne, F. and Shepherd, G., eds.,* 1987, pp. 145–77. [G: U.K.]

Shepherd, Geoffrey and Duchêne, François. Managing Industrial Change in Western Europe: Introduction. *Duchêne, F. and Shepherd, G., eds.,* 1987, pp. 1–6.
[G: W. Germany; France; U.K.; Italy]

Shepherd, James. Industrial Support Policies. *Nat. Inst. Econ. Rev.,* November 1987, (122), pp. 59–71. [G: U.K.]

Shimizu, Hikaru. Long-run Economic Policy: A Positive Appraisal. *Finn, R. B., ed.,* 1987, pp. 31–43. [G: U.S.; Japan]

Silbert, Lance. Promoting High-Technology Industry: Initiatives and Policies for State Governments: California. *Schmandt, J. and Wilson, R., eds.,* 1987, pp. 11–33. [G: U.S.]

Silver, Hilary and Burton, Dudley. The Politics of State-Level Industrial Policy. *Goldstein, H. A., ed.,* 1987, pp. 131–47. [G: U.S.]

Sočan, Lojze. Federal Industrialisation Policies

in Yugoslavia. *Saunders, C. T., ed.*, 1987, pp. 215–26.   [G: Yugoslavia]

Sparks, Leigh. Retailing in Enterprise Zones: The Example of Swansea. *Reg. Stud.*, February 1987, *21*(1), pp. 37–42.   [G: U.K.]

Stoneman, Paul. Some Analytical Observations on Diffusion Policies. *Dasgupta, P. and Stoneman, P., eds.*, 1987, pp. 154–68.

Streit, Manfred E. Industrial Policies and Structural Change: Overall Assessments and Comparisons: Comment. *Saunders, C. T., ed.*, 1987, pp. 101–02.

Streit, Manfred E. Industrial Policies for Technological Change: The Case of West Germany. *Saunders, C. T., ed.*, 1987, pp. 129–42.
                              [G: W. Germany]

Streit, Manfred E. Industrial Policies for Technological Change: The Case of West Germany: Reply. *Saunders, C. T., ed.*, 1987, pp. 154.

Streit, Manfred E. Some National Industrial Policies Examined: Comment. *Saunders, C. T., ed.*, 1987, pp. 258–59.

Subbarao, A. V. Influence of Political Structure on Worker Participation in Developing Asian Countries. *Can. J. Devel. Stud.*, 1987, *8*(1), pp. 97–115. [G: India; Sri Lanka; Singapore]

Succar, Patricia. The Need for Industrial Policy in LDC's—A Re-statement of the Infant Industry Argument. *Int. Econ. Rev.*, June 1987, *28*(2), pp. 521–34.

Suzumura, Kotaro and Okuno-Fujiwara, Masahiro. Industrial Policy in Japan: Overview and Evaluation. *Sato, R. and Wachtel, P., eds.*, 1987, pp. 50–79.   [G: Japan]

Sydow, Peter. Growth, Technical Progress and International Division of Labour: A View from the GDR. *Saunders, C. T., ed.*, 1987, pp. 143–51.   [G: E. Germany]

Tabaczyński, Eugeniusz. Export-Oriented Changes in Polish Industry. *Eastern Europ. Econ.*, Spring 1987, *25*(3), pp. 86–92.
                                [G: Poland]

Teitel, Simón and Thoumi, Francisco E. De la sustitución de importaciones a las exportaciones: la experiencia de las exportaciones manufactureras de la Argentina y el Brasil. (With English summary.) *Desarrollo Econ.*, Apr.-June 1987, *27*(105), pp. 29–60.
                          [G: Argentina; Brazil]

Tekeli, Ilhan. Savaşmayan Ülkenin Savaş Ekonomisi: Üretimden Tüketime Pamuklu Dokuma. (With English summary.) *METU*, 1987, *14*(1), pp. 1–48.   [G: Turkey]

Thiel, Eberhard. Sectoral and Regional Elements of Industrial Policy. *Gemper, B. B., ed.*, 1987, pp. 47–55.   [G: W. Germany]

Thomas, Ian C. and Drudy, P. J. The Impact of Factory Development on 'Growth Town' Employment in Mid-Wales. *Urban Stud.*, October 1987, *24*(5), pp. 361–78.   [G: U.K.]

Thompson, Grahame. The Supply Side and Industrial Policy. *Thompson, G.; Brown, V. and Levačić, R., eds.*, 1987, pp. 254–92.
                        [G: U.S.; U.K.; W. Europe]

Tomer, John F. Developing Organizational Comparative Advantage via Industrial Policy. *J. Post*

Keynesian Econ., Spring 1987, *9*(3), pp. 455–72.

Toumanoff, Peter. The Use of Production Functions to Investigate Soviet Industrial Reform. *Comp. Econ. Stud.*, Fall 1987, *29*(3), pp. 94–111.   [G: U.S.S.R.]

Truett, Lila J. and Truett, Dale B. The Mexican Automobile Industry and International Trade, 1970–1983. *J. Econ. Devel.*, June 1987, *12*(1), pp. 65–85.   [G: Mexico]

Uekusa, Masu. The Political Economy of Japan: Industrial Organization: The 1970s to the Present. *Yamamura, K. and Yasuba, Y., eds.*, 1987, pp. 469–515.   [G: Japan]

Vincent, Peter; Chell, Elizabeth and Haworth, Jean. Regional Distribution of Consultancy Firms Servicing the MAPCON Scheme: A Preliminary Analysis. *Reg. Stud.*, December 1987, *21*(6), pp. 505–18.   [G: U.K.]

Vogel, David. Government–Industry Relations in the United States: An Overview. *Wilks, S. and Wright, M., eds.*, 1987, pp. 91–116.
                                 [G: U.S.]

Wakiyama, Takashi. The Implementation and Effectiveness of MITI's Administrative Guidance. *Wilks, S. and Wright, M., eds.*, 1987, pp. 211–32.   [G: Japan]

van der Walt, Nicolaas. The Envisaged Revised Industrial Development Strategy of South Africa. *Gemper, B. B., ed.*, 1987, pp. 145–54.
                              [G: S. Africa]

Warr, Peter G. Malaysia's Industrial Enclaves: Benefits and Costs. *Devel. Econ.*, March 1987, *25*(1), pp. 30–55.   [G: Malaysia]

Whitman, Marina von Neumann. Strategic Sectors and International Competition: Comment. *Stern, R. M., ed.*, 1987, pp. 233–38.
                                 [G: U.S.]

Wilks, Stephen and Wright, Maurice. Comparative Government–Industry Relations: Introduction. *Wilks, S. and Wright, M., eds.*, 1987, pp. 1–9.

Wilks, Stephen and Wright, Maurice. Comparing Government–Industry Relations: States, Sectors, and Networks: Conclusion. *Wilks, S. and Wright, M., eds.*, 1987, pp. 274–313.

Wood, Diane P. Conflicts of Jurisdiction in Antitrust Law: A Comment. *Law Contemp. Probl.*, Summer 1987, *50*(3), pp. 179–88. [G: U.S.]

Wünsche, Horst Friedrich. Does Industrial Policy Comply with Ludwig Erhard's Conception of the Social Market Economy? *Gemper, B. B., ed.*, 1987, pp. 37–43.

Zschau, Ed. Meeting the Global Competitive Challenge. *Shetty, Y. K. and Buehler, V. M., eds.*, 1987, pp. 45–56.   [G: U.S.]

619 Economics of Regulation

6190 Economics of Regulation

Abrams, Burton A. and Lewis, Kenneth A. A Median-Voter Model of Economic Regulation. *Public Choice*, 1987, *52*(2), pp. 125–42.

Acton, Jan Paul and Besen, Stanley M. Assessing the Effects of Bulk Power Rate Regulation: Results from a Market Experiment. *Appl. Econ.*, May 1987, *19*(5), pp. 663–85. [G: U.S.]

Adams, Walter and Brock, James W. Corporate Size and the Bailout Factor. *J. Econ. Issues*, March 1987, *21*(1), pp. 61–85. [G: U.S.]

Amacher, Ryan C., et al. The Behavior of Regulatory Activity over the Business Cycle: An Empirical Test. *MacKay, R. J.; Miller, J. C., III and Yandle, B., eds.*, 1987, *1985*, pp. 145–53. [G: U.S.]

Anderson, Richard K. and Enomoto, Carl E. Product Quality Regulation: A General Equilibrium Analysis. *Can. J. Econ.*, November 1987, *20*(4), pp. 735–49.

Appleby, Colin and Bessant, John. Adapting to Decline: Organizational Structures and Government Policy in the UK and West German Foundry Sectors. *Wilks, S. and Wright, M., eds.*, 1987, pp. 181–210. [G: U.K.; W. Germany]

Ashton, Peter K. Some Economic Effects of Standards—Comment [Some Economic Effects of Standards]. *Appl. Econ.*, November 1987, *19*(11), pp. 1515–19. [G: Canada]

Baca, Alvin. FERC & ERA: Issues in Natural Gas Regulation. *Natural Res. J.*, Fall 1987, *27*(4), pp. 815–22. [G: U.S.]

Bagby, John W.; Wartick, Steven L. and Stevens, John M. Cooperative Approaches to Business–Government Relations. *Marcus, A. A.; Kaufman, A. M. and Beam, D. R., eds.*, 1987, pp. 283–91. [G: U.S.]

Baish, Richard O. The Role of the California Public Utilities Commission in Western Gas Markets. *Natural Res. J.*, Fall 1987, *27*(4), pp. 805–10. [G: U.S.]

Baron, David P. and Besanko, David. Commitment and Fairness in a Dynamic Regulatory Relationship. *Rev. Econ. Stud.*, July 1987, *54*(3), pp. 413–36.

Bartel, Ann P. and Thomas, Lacy Glenn. Predation through Regulation: The Wage and Profit Effects of the Occupational Safety and Health Administration and the Environmental Protection Agency. *J. Law Econ.*, October 1987, *30*(2), pp. 239–64. [G: U.S.]

Beavis, Brian and Dobbs, Ian. Firm Behaviour under Regulatory Control of Stochastic Environmental Wastes by Probabilistic Constraints. *J. Environ. Econ. Manage.*, June 1987, *14*(2), pp. 112–27.

Beilock, Richard and Freeman, James. The Effect on Rate Levels and Structures of Removing Entry and Rate Controls on Motor Carriers. *J. Transp. Econ. Policy*, May 1987, *21*(2), pp. 167–88. [G: U.S.]

Benson, Bruce L.; Greenhut, M. L. and Holcombe, Randall G. Interest Groups and the Antitrust Paradox. *Cato J.*, Winter 1987, *6*(3), pp. 801–17. [G: U.S.]

Berg, Sanford V. Public Policy and Corporate Strategies in the AM Stereo Market. *Gabel, H. L., ed.*, 1987, pp. 149–70. [G: U.S.]

Berry, S. Keith. Rate-of-Return Regulation and Demand Uncertainty with a Symmetric Regu-

latory Constraint. *Amer. Econ.*, Fall 1987, *31*(2), pp. 8–12.

Berry, S. Keith. The Ratepayer and the Stockholder under Alternative Regulatory Policies: Comment. *Land Econ.*, May 1987, *63*(2), pp. 201–05. [G: U.S.]

Besanko, David. Performance versus Design Standards in the Regulation of Pollution. *J. Public Econ.*, October 1987, *34*(1), pp. 19–44.

Besanko, David; Donnenfeld, Shabtai and White, Lawrence J. Monopoly and Quality Distortion: Effects and Remedies. *Quart. J. Econ.*, November 1987, *102*(4), pp. 743–67.

Blair, Roger D.; Kaserman, David L. and McClave, James T. Competition on Trial: Florida Deregulates Trucking. *Challenge*, Sept./Oct. 1987, *30*(4), pp. 60–64. [G: U.S.]

Blankart, Charles B. Eléments d'une théorie économique de la privatisation. (Elements of an Economic Theory of Privatization. With English summary.) *Schweiz. Z. Volkswirtsch. Statist.*, September 1987, *123*(3), pp. 329–39.

Blankart, Charles B. Limits to Privatization. *Europ. Econ. Rev.*, Feb./Mar. 1987, *31*(1/2), pp. 346–51.

Blomley, N. K. Retail Regulation in England and Wales: The Results of a Survey. *Environ. Planning A*, October 1987, *19*(10), pp. 1399–1406. [G: U.K.]

Blume, Lawrence and Rubinfeld, Daniel L. Compensation for Takings: An Economic Analysis. *Jaffe, A. J., ed.*, 1987, pp. 53–103. [G: U.S.]

Bold, Frederick C. Responses to Energy Efficiency Regulations. *Energy J.*, April 1987, *8*(2), pp. 111–23.

Bollard, Alan. More Market: The Deregulation of Industry. *Bollard, A. and Buckle, R., eds.*, 1987, pp. 25–45. [G: New Zealand]

Bös, Dieter. Privatization of Public Enterprises. *Europ. Econ. Rev.*, Feb./Mar. 1987, *31*(1/2), pp. 352–60.

Boudreaux, Don and Ekelund, Robert B., Jr. Regulation as an Exogenous Response to Market Failure: A Neo-Schumpeterian Response. *J. Inst. Theoretical Econ.*, December 1987, *143*(4), pp. 537–54.

Boyer, Kenneth D. The Costs of Price Regulation: Lessons from Railroad Deregulation. *Rand J. Econ.*, Autumn 1987, *18*(3), pp. 408–16. [G: U.S.]

Bregman, Arie. Government Intervention in Industry: The Case of Israel. *J. Devel. Econ.*, April 1987, *25*(2), pp. 353–67. [G: Israel]

Brennan, Timothy J. Why Regulated Firms Should Be Kept Out of Unregulated Markets: Understanding the Divestiture in *United States v. AT&T*. *Antitrust Bull.*, Fall 1987, *32*(3), pp. 741–93. [G: U.S.]

Breyer, Stephen G. Judicial Review of Questions of Law and Policy. *Bailey, E. E., ed.*, 1987, pp. 45–72. [G: U.S.]

Campbell, Michael. The Implications of Gas Policy for the Western States: A Producer Perspective. *Natural Res. J.*, Fall 1987, *27*(4), pp. 823–28. [G: U.S.]

Carter, Stephen L. The Beast That Might Not Exist: Some Speculations on the Constitution and the Independent Regulatory Agencies. *Marshall, B., ed.*, 1987, pp. 76–102. [G: U.S.]

Cave, Jonathan and Salant, Stephen W. Cartels That Vote: Agricultural Marketing Boards and Induced Voting Behavior. *Bailey, E. E., ed.*, 1987, pp. 255–83. [G: U.S.]

Chabot, Marc. La portée limitée des statistiques sur le nombre de faillites commerciales. (With English summary.) *Can. Public Policy*, June 1987, *13*(2), pp. 144–51.

Coelho, Philip R. P. and McClure, James E. Barriers to Entry in the Market for Stud Services: Government and "Non-profit" Institutions in Collusion. *Econ. Inquiry*, October 1987, *25*(4), pp. 659–70. [G: U.S.]

Cohen, Mark A. Optimal Enforcement Strategy to Prevent Oil Spills: An Application of a Principal–Agent Model with Moral Hazard. *J. Law Econ.*, April 1987, *30*(1), pp. 23–51. [G: U.S.]

Cox, James C. and Isaac, R. Mark. Mechanisms for Incentive Regulation: Theory and Experiment. *Rand J. Econ.*, Autumn 1987, *18*(3), pp. 348–59.

Craig, Steven G. and Sailors, Joel W. Interstate Trade Barriers and the Constitution. *Cato J.*, Winter 1987, *6*(3), pp. 819–35. [G: U.S.]

Crandall, Robert W. and Keller, Theodore E. Public Policy and the Private Auto. *[Adelman, M. A.]*, 1987, pp. 137–60. [G: U.S.]

Crew, Michael A. and Kleindorfer, Paul R. Productivity Incentives and Rate-of-Return Regulation. *Crew, M. A., ed.*, 1987, pp. 7–23. [G: U.S.]

Cubbin, John S.; Domberger, Simon and Meadowcroft, Shirley. Competitive Tendering and Refuse Collection: Identifying the Sources of Efficiency Gains. *Fisc. Stud.*, August 1987, *8*(3), pp. 49–58. [G: U.K.]

Culy, John and Gale, Stephen. Regulatory Change in the Energy Sector. *Bollard, A. and Buckle, R., eds.*, 1987, pp. 153–80. [G: New Zealand]

Daughety, Andrew F. and Forsythe, Robert. Industrywide Regulation and the Formation of Reputations: A Laboratory Analysis. *Bailey, E. E., ed.*, 1987, pp. 347–98.

Daughety, Andrew F. and Forsythe, Robert. The Effects of Industry-Wide Price Regulation on Industrial Organization. *J. Law, Econ., Organ.*, Fall 1987, *3*(2), pp. 397–434.

David, Paul A. Some New Standards for the Economics of Standardization in the Information Age. *Dasgupta, P. and Stoneman, P., eds.*, 1987, pp. 206–39.

Dawson, D. A. and Parent, L. P. Positive Steps in Transport Deregulation—The Prairies. *Can. Public Policy*, March 1987, *13*(1), pp. 86–96. [G: Canada]

Demski, Joel S. and Sappington, David E. M. Hierarchical Regulatory Control. *Rand J. Econ.*, Autumn 1987, *18*(3), pp. 369–83.

Dower, Roger C. and Scodari, Paul F. Compen-sation for Natural Resource Injury: An Emerging Federal Framework. *Marine Resource Econ.*, 1987, *4*(3), pp. 155–74. [G: U.S.]

Eggerstedt, Harald. Wettbewerb und Regulierung auf Versicherungsmärkten. (Competition and Regulation in Insurance Markets. With English summary.) *Z. Wirtschaft. Sozialwissen.*, 1987, *107*(3), pp. 397–416. [G: W. Germany]

Eisenberg, Meyer. The Current Status of the Regulation of Financial Services and Products in the United States: Developments and Trends. *de Cecco, M., ed.*, 1987, pp. 28–76. [G: U.S.]

Eisenberg, Theodore. Bankruptcy in the Administrative State. *Law Contemp. Probl.*, Spring 1987, *50*(2), pp. 3–52. [G: U.S.]

Elliott, E. Donald. Regulating the Deficit after *Bowsher v. Synar*. *Yale J. Regul.*, Spring 1987, *4*(2), pp. 317–62. [G: U.S.]

Ellis, Joan T. State Regulation in a Deregulated Environment: A State-Level Regulator's Lament. *Natural Res. J.*, Fall 1987, *27*(4), pp. 799–803. [G: U.S.]

Ellison, Anthony P. Developments in Transport Policy: Canada. *J. Transp. Econ. Policy*, January 1987, *21*(1), pp. 91–96.

Encaoua, David and Koebel, Philippe. Réglementation et déréglementation des télécommunications: Leçons anglo-saxonnes et perspectives d'évolution en France. (Regulation and Deregulation of the Telecommunication Industry: From the American and British Experiences to a Possible Evolution in France. With English summary.) *Revue Écon.*, March 1987, *38*(2), pp. 475–520. [G: U.S.; U.K.]

Estrin, Saul and Pérotin, Virginie. The Regulation of British and French Nationalised Industries. *Europ. Econ. Rev.*, Feb./Mar. 1987, *31*(1/2), pp. 361–67. [G: U.K.; France]

Ewell, C. Daniel. Rule 10b-5 and the Duty to Disclose Merger Negotiations in Corporate Statements. *Yale Law J.*, January 1987, *96*(3), pp. 547–68. [G: U.S.]

Farny, Dieter. Über Regulierung und Deregulierung von Versicherungsmärkten. (With English summary.) *Z. Betriebswirtshaft*, October 1987, *57*(10), pp. 1001–23. [G: W. Germany]

Felder, Stefan and Finsinger, Jörg. Auswirkungen protektionistischer und preisstützender Submissionsvorschriften auf die Baubranche. (The Consequences of Non-competitive and Protectionist Government Purchasing Behavior. With English summary.) *Schweiz. Z. Volkswirtsch. Statist.*, June 1987, *123*(2), pp. 147–73. [G: Switzerland]

Fuchs, Edward Paul and Anderson, James. Institutionalizing Cost–Benefit Analysis in Regulatory Agencies. *Nagel, S. S., ed.*, 1987, pp. 187–211. [G: U.S.]

Gallick, Edward C. and Sisk, David E. A Reconsideration of Taxi Regulation. *J. Law, Econ., Organ.*, Spring 1987, *3*(1), pp. 117–28. [G: U.S.]

Garland, Merrick B. Antitrust and State Action:

Economic Efficiency and the Political Process. *Yale Law J.*, January 1987, *96*(3), pp. 486–519. [G: U.S.]

Gifford, Adam, Jr. Rent Seeking and Nonprice Competition. *Quart. Rev. Econ. Bus.*, Summer 1987, *27*(2), pp. 63–70.

Glaister, Stephen. Regulation through Output Related Profits Tax. *J. Ind. Econ.*, March 1987, *35*(3), pp. 281–96.

Goldberg, Victor P. and Erickson, John R. Quantity and Price Adjustment in Long-term Contracts: A Case Study of Petroleum Coke. *J. Law Econ.*, October 1987, *30*(2), pp. 369–98. [G: U.S.]

Gorton, Gary B. and Mullineaux, Donald J. The Joint Production of Confidence: Endogenous Regulation and Nineteenth Century Commercial-Bank Clearinghouses. *J. Money, Credit, Banking*, November 1987, *19*(4), pp. 457–68. [G: U.S.]

Grant, Robert M. The Effects of Product Standardization on Competition: Octane Grading of Petrol in the UK. *Gabel, H. L., ed.*, 1987, pp. 283–302. [G: U.K.]

Grant, Wyn; Paterson, William and Whitston, Colin. Government–Industry Relations in the Chemical Industry: An Anglo–German Comparison. *Wilks, S. and Wright, M., eds.*, 1987, pp. 35–60. [G: U.K.; W. Germany]

de Grauwe, Paul. Financial Deregulation in Developing Countries. *Tijdschrift Econ. Manage.*, 1987, *32*(4), pp. 381–401. [G: LDCs]

Gray, Wayne B. The Cost of Regulation: OSHA, EPA and the Productivity Slowdown. *Amer. Econ. Rev.*, December 1987, *77*(5), pp. 998–1006. [G: U.S.]

Greenbaum, Stuart I. and Thakor, Anjan V. Bank Funding Modes: Securitization versus Deposits. *J. Banking Finance*, September 1987, *11*(3), pp. 379–401.

Greenberg, Ward A. Liquor Price Affirmation Statutes and the Dormant Commerce Clause. *Mich. Law Rev.*, October 1987, *86*(1), pp. 186–211.

Griffin, Ronald C. Environmental Policy for Spatial and Persistent Pollutants. *J. Environ. Econ. Manage.*, March 1987, *14*(1), pp. 41–53.

Haddock, David D. and Macey, Jonathan R. Regulation on Demand: A Private Interest Model, with an Application to Insider Trading Regulation. *J. Law Econ.*, October 1987, *30*(2), pp. 311–52. [G: U.S.]

Hall, Maximilian J. B. Reform of the London Stock Exchange: The Prudential Issues. *Banca Naz. Lavoro Quart. Rev.*, June 1987, (161), pp. 167–81. [G: U.K.]

Harper, David A. and Karacaoglu, Girol. Financial Policy Reform in New Zealand. *Bollard, A. and Buckle, R., eds.*, 1987, pp. 206–35. [G: New Zealand]

Harper, Donald V. and Johnson, James C. The Potential Consequences of Deregulation of Transportation Revisited. *Land Econ.*, May 1987, *63*(2), pp. 137–46. [G: U.S.]

Harrington, Scott E. A Note on the Impact of

Auto Insurance Rate Regulation. *Rev. Econ. Statist.*, February 1987, *69*(1), pp. 166–70. [G: U.S.]

Hayashi, Paul M. and Trapani, John M. The Impact of Energy Costs on Domestic Airline Passenger Travel. *J. Transp. Econ. Policy*, January 1987, *21*(1), pp. 73–86.

Hazledine, Tim and Wigington, Ian. Canadian Auto Policy. *Can. Public Policy*, December 1987, *13*(4), pp. 490–501. [G: Canada]

Heckathorn, Douglas D. and Maser, Steven M. Bargaining and the Sources of Transaction Costs: The Case of Government Regulation. *J. Law, Econ., Organ.*, Spring 1987, *3*(1), pp. 69–98. [G: U.S.]

Higgins, Richard S.; Shughart, William F., II and Tollison, Robert D. Dual Enforcement of the Antitrust Laws. *MacKay, R. J.; Miller, J. C., III and Yandle, B., eds.*, 1987, pp. 154–80. [G: U.S.]

Hirshleifer, Jack. Toward a More General Theory of Regulation: Comment. *Hirshleifer, J.*, 1987, *1976*, pp. 164–68.

Houston, Douglas A. The Mixed Interest in Regulation and Deregulation [Rent Seeking and Profit Seeking]. *Land Econ.*, November 1987, *63*(4), pp. 403–05.

Hwang, Ming-Jeng and Mann, Patrick C. Deregulation and Efficiency in the Rail Industry. *Atlantic Econ. J.*, July 1987, *15*(2), pp. 47–52. [G: U.S.]

Jadlow, Joseph M.; Jadlow, Janice W. and Yu, Shirley S. Risk, Rivalry, and Innovation: The Case of Ethical Drugs. *Rivista Int. Sci. Econ. Com.*, July 1987, *34*(7), pp. 593–608. [G: U.S.]

Joffrion, Theresa and Rose, Peter S. Savings and Loans' Response to Deregulation: Evidence from Multivariate Models and a National Survey. *Housing Finance Rev.*, Spring 1987, *6*(1), pp. 17–38. [G: U.S.]

Kahn, Alfred E. and Shew, William B. Current Issues in Telecommunications Regulation: Pricing. *Yale J. Regul.*, Spring 1987, *4*(2), pp. 191–256. [G: U.S.]

Kakumoto, Ryohei. Developments in Transport Policy: Japan. *J. Transp. Econ. Policy*, January 1987, *21*(1), pp. 97–98.

Katz, Lawrence F. and Rosen, Kenneth T. The Interjurisdictional Effects of Growth Controls on Housing Prices. *J. Law Econ.*, April 1987, *30*(1), pp. 149–60. [G: U.S.]

Kay, John A. and Morris, C. N. The Economic Efficiency of Sunday Trading Restrictions. *J. Ind. Econ.*, December 1987, *36*(2), pp. 113–29. [G: U.K.]

Kay, John A. and Thompson, David. The Performance of the British Economy: Policy for Industry. *Dornbusch, R. and Layard, R., eds.*, 1987, pp. 180–210. [G: U.K.]

Kelly, Suedeen G. Regulatory Reform of the U.S. Natural Gas Industry: A Summing Up. *Natural Res. J.*, Fall 1987, *27*(4), pp. 841–63. [G: U.S.]

Kim, Moshe and Spiegel, Menahem. The Effects of Lump-Sum Subsidies on the Structure of

Production and Productivity in Regulated Industries. *J. Public Econ.*, October 1987, *34*(1), pp. 105–19. **[G: Israel]**

Laffont, Jean-Jacques and Maskin, Eric. Monopoly with Asymmetric Information about Quality: Behavior and Regulation. *Europ. Econ. Rev.*, Feb./Mar. 1987, *31*(1/2), pp. 483–89.

Laffont, Jean-Jacques and Tirole, Jean. Comparative Statics of the Optimal Dynamic Incentive Contract. *Europ. Econ. Rev.*, June 1987, *31*(4), pp. 901–26.

Langevoort, Donald C. Statutory Obsolescence and the Judicial Process: The Revisionist Role of the Courts in Federal Banking Regulation. *Mich. Law Rev.*, February 1987, *85*(4), pp. 672–733. **[G: U.S.]**

Lee, Wayne Y. and Thakor, Anjan V. Regulatory Pricing and Capital Investment under Asymmetric Information about Cost. *Southern Econ. J.*, January 1987, *53*(3), pp. 720–34.

Lesser, William and Madhavan, Ananth. Economic Impacts of a National Deposit Law: Cost Estimates and Policy Questions. *J. Cons. Aff.*, Summer 1987, *21*(1), pp. 122–40. **[G: U.S.]**

Levine, Michael E. Airline Competition in Deregulated Markets: Theory, Firm Strategy, and Public Policy. *Yale J. Regul.*, Spring 1987, *4*(2), pp. 393–494. **[G: U.S.]**

Llewellyn, David T. Competition and the Regulatory Mix. *Nat. Westminster Bank Quart. Rev.*, August 1987, pp. 4–13. **[G: U.K.]**

MacAvoy, Paul W. The Record of the Environmental Protection Agency in Controlling Industrial Air Pollution. *[Adelman, M. A.]*, 1987, pp. 107–36. **[G: U.S.]**

MacMillan, Keith and Turner, Ian. The Cost-Containment Issue: A Study of Government–Industry Relations in the Pharmaceutical Sectors of the United Kingdom and West Germany. *Wilks, S. and Wright, M.*, eds., 1987, pp. 117–47. **[G: U.K.; W. Germany]**

Makhija, Anil K. and Thompson, Howard E. The Ratepayer and the Stockholder under Alternative Regulatory Policies: Reply. *Land Econ.*, May 1987, *63*(2), pp. 206–08. **[G: U.S.]**

Mashaw, Jerry L. and Harfst, David L. Regulation and Legal Culture: The Case of Motor Vehicle Safety. *Yale J. Regul.*, Spring 1987, *4*(2), pp. 257–316. **[G: U.S.]**

McFarland, Henry. Did Railroad Deregulation Lead to Monopoly Pricing? An Application of *q. J. Bus.*, July 1987, *60*(3), pp. 385–400. **[G: U.S.]**

McFarland, Henry. The Economics of Vertical Restraints and Relationships between Connecting Railroads. *Logist. Transp. Rev.*, June 1987, *23*(2), pp. 207–22. **[G: U.S.]**

Mentré, Paul. Regulation and Deregulation: An Economic Viewpoint. *van de Kar, H. M. and Wolfe, B. L.*, eds., 1987, pp. 293–305.

Michel, Allen and Shaked, Israel. Airline Deregulation and the Probability of Air Carrier Insolvency. *Financial Rev.*, February 1987, *22*(1), pp. 159–73. **[G: U.S.]**

Michel, Allen and Shaked, Israel. Trucking Deregulation and Motor-Carrier Performance:

The Shareholders' Perspective. *Financial Rev.*, May 1987, *22*(2), pp. 295–311. **[G: U.S.]**

Mochizuki, Hiroshi and Murata, Satoshi. The Impact of Deregulation on Financial Markets in the United States and Japan: Is the Market Always Right? *Finn, R. B., ed.*, 1987, pp. 97–108. **[G: U.S.; Japan]**

Moorhouse, John C. and Elavia, Tony H. The Effects of Selective Decontrol in the NYC Rental Housing Market. *Atlantic Econ. J.*, July 1987, *15*(2), pp. 11–24. **[G: U.S.]**

Nefussi, J. Les facteurs macro-économiques de la croissance des industries agro-alimentaires depuis les années 50. (Macro-economic Factors of Growth of I.A.A. since the Fifties. With English summary.) *Écon. Soc.*, July 1987, *21*(7), pp. 91–109. **[G: France]**

Nelson, James C. Politics and Economics in Transport Regulation and Deregulation—A Century Perspective of the ICC's Role. *Logist. Transp. Rev.*, March 1987, *23*(1), pp. 5–32. **[G: U.S.]**

Noll, Roger G. Magat, Krupnick, and Harrington's *Rules in the Making: A Statistical Analysis of Regulatory Agency Behavior. Rand J. Econ.*, Autumn 1987, *18*(3), pp. 461–64.

Nyman, John A. Improving the Quality of Nursing Homes: Regulation or Competition? *J. Policy Anal. Manage.*, Winter 1987, *6*(2), pp. 247–51. **[G: U.S]**

Pelkmans, Jacques and Beuter, Rita. Standardization and Competitiveness: Private and Public Strategies in the EC Color TV Industry. *Gabel, H. L., ed.*, 1987, pp. 171–215. **[G: W. Europe]**

Peltzman, Sam. Regulation and Health: The Case of Mandatory Prescriptions and an Extension. *Managerial Dec. Econ.*, March 1987, *8*(1), pp. 41–46. **[G: Selected Countries]**

Pustay, Michael W. Shifting the Burden of Proof. *Logist. Transp. Rev.*, December 1987, *23*(4), pp. 411–25. **[G: U.S.]**

Robinson, Colin. A Liberalized Coal Market? *Lloyds Bank Rev.*, April 1987, (164), pp. 16–35. **[G: U.K.]**

Romer, Thomas and Rosenthal, Howard. Modern Political Economy and the Study of Regulation. *Bailey, E. E., ed.*, 1987, pp. 73–116. **[G: U.S.]**

Rose, Nancy L. Labor Rent Sharing and Regulation: Evidence from the Trucking Industry. *J. Polit. Econ.*, December 1987, *95*(6), pp. 1146–78. **[G: U.S.]**

Sanders, Elizabeth. The Regulatory Surge of the 1970s in Historical Perspective. *Bailey, E. E., ed.*, 1987, pp. 117–50. **[G: U.S.]**

Sappington, David E. M. and Stiglitz, Joseph E. Information and Regulation. *Bailey, E. E., ed.*, 1987, pp. 3–43.

Sardinas, Joseph L., Jr. and Merrill, Susan. Regulation of International Data Communications and the Effect upon Multinational Corporations. *Most, Kenneth S., ed.*, 1987, pp. 305–15. **[G: OECD]**

Schipper, Katherine; Thompson, Rex and Weil, Roman L. Disentangling Interrelated Effects

of Regulatory Changes on Shareholder Wealth: The Case of Motor Carrier Deregulation. *J. Law Econ.*, April 1987, *30*(1), pp. 67–100.
[G: U.S.]

Schorsch, Louis L. Can Big Steel Change Bad Habits? *Challenge*, July/Aug. 1987, *30*(3), pp. 32–40. [G: U.S.; W. Europe]

Sullivan, Arthur M. Policy Options for Toxics Disposal: Laissez-Faire, Subsidization, and Enforcement. *J. Environ. Econ. Manage.*, March 1987, *14*(1), pp. 58–71.

Sullivan, Teresa A.; Warren, Elizabeth and Westbrook, Jay Lawrence. The Use of Empirical Data in Formulating Bankruptcy Policy. *Law Contemp. Probl.*, Spring 1987, *50*(2), pp. 195–235. [G: U.S.]

Teal, Roger F. and Berglund, Mary. The Impact of Taxicab Deregulation in the USA. *J. Transp. Econ. Policy*, January 1987, *21*(1), pp. 37–56. [G: U.S.]

Thompson, David. Privatisation in the U.K.: Deregulation and the Advantage of Incumbency. *Europ. Econ. Rev.*, Feb./Mar. 1987, *31*(1/2), pp. 368–74. [G: U.K.]

Trebing, Harry M. Regulation of Industry: An Institutionalist Approach. *J. Econ. Issues*, December 1987, *21*(4), pp. 1707–37.

Tueting, William F. and King, Christopher Q. Funds Protections: An Overview of What Happens When a Commodity Broker Becomes Insolvent. *J. Futures Markets*, February 1987, *7*(1), pp. 93–101. [G: U.S.]

Tye, William B. Pricing Rail Competitive Access in the Transition to Deregulation with the Revenue/Variable Cost Test. *Antitrust Bull.*, Spring 1987, *32*(1), pp. 101–35. [G: U.S.]

Viscusi, W. Kip. Regulatory Economics in the Courts: An Analysis of Judge Scalia's NHTSA Bumper Decision. *Law Contemp. Probl.*, Autumn 1987, *50*(4), pp. 17–31. [G: U.S.]

Vogel, David. Government–Industry Relations in the United States: An Overview. *Wilks, S. and Wright, M., eds.*, 1987, pp. 91–116.
[G: U.S.]

Wall, Larry D. Has Bank Holding Companies' Diversification Affected Their Risk of Failure? *J. Econ. Bus.*, November 1987, *39*(4), pp. 313–26. [G: U.S.]

Wall, Larry D. and Peterson, David R. The Effect of Capital Adequacy Guidelines on Large Bank Holding Companies. *J. Banking Finance*, December 1987, *11*(4), pp. 581–600.
[G: U.S.]

Wellinghoff, Jon. What Do "436," "436-A," "451," "311," "7(c)," Mean to the Residential Gas Consumer. *Natural Res. J.*, Fall 1987, *27*(4), pp. 829–40. [G: U.S.]

White, Frederick L. Legal and Regulatory Developments: The Exchange-Trading Requirement of the Commodity Exchange Act. *J. Futures Markets*, February 1987, *7*(1), pp. 109–10.

White, William D. The Introduction of Professional Regulation and Labor Market Conditions—Occupational Licensure of Registered Nurses. *Policy Sci.*, April 1987, *20*(1), pp. 27–51. [G: U.S.]

Wilks, Stephen and Wright, Maurice. Comparative Government–Industry Relations: Introduction. *Wilks, S. and Wright, M., eds.*, 1987, pp. 1–9.

Wilks, Stephen and Wright, Maurice. Comparing Government–Industry Relations: States, Sectors, and Networks: Conclusion. *Wilks, S. and Wright, M., eds.*, 1987, pp. 274–313.

Zhan, Wu. Proper Attention Should Be Paid to the Supplementary Role of Microeconomic Regulation in Enterprises. *Chinese Econ. Stud.*, Winter 1986-87, *20*(2), pp. 83–89.
[G: China]

620 ECONOMICS OF TECHNOLOGICAL CHANGE

621 Technological Change; Innovation; Research and Development

6210 General

Albach, Horst and Hunsdiek, Detlef. Die Bedeutung von Unternehmensgründungen für die Anpassung der Wirtschaft an veränderte Rahmenbedingungen. (With English summary.) *Z. Betriebswirtschaft*, May/June 1987, *57*(5/6), pp. 562–80. [G: W. Germany]

Andersson, Åke. Creativity and Economic Dynamics Modelling. *Batten, D.; Casti, J. and Johansson, B., eds.*, 1987, pp. 27–45.

Audretsch, David B. An Empirical Test of the Industry Life Cycle. *Weltwirtsch. Arch.*, 1987, *123*(2), pp. 297–308. [G: U.S.]

Barjon, Michel. Integrating Economic Strategy with Science and Technology. *Hieronymi, O., ed.*, 1987, pp. 189–92.

Bartel, Ann P. and Lichtenberg, Frank R. The Skill Distribution and Competitive Trade Advantage of High-Technology Industries. *Lewin, D.; Lipsky, D. B. and Sockell, D., eds.*, 1987, pp. 161–76. [G: U.S.]

Bernholz, Peter. Organizational Theory, Information Processing, and Short-run Dynamics: Theory and Empirical Tests: Comment. *J. Inst. Theoretical Econ.*, March 1987, *143*(1), pp. 225–28. [G: U.S.]

Bognár, József. Technological Policy in Industry: Comment. *Saunders, C. T., ed.*, 1987, pp. 153.

Crook, J. N. and Allen, D. E. The Characteristics of Technically Orientated Firms: Evidence from the Unlisted Securities Market. *Managerial Dec. Econ.*, December 1987, *8*(4), pp. 271–84. [G: U.K.]

Csaba, László. Die Investitions- und Innovationspolitischen Befugnisse der Unternehmung in der DDR, der Sowjetunion und in Ungarn. (Freedom of Enterprises in Innovation and in Investment Decisions in the Post-Reform Period: Experiences of the GDR, the Soviet Union and Hungary. With English summary.) *Konjunkturpolitik*, 1987, *33*(3), pp. 167–84.
[G: U.S.S.R.; Hungary; E. Germany]

Dasgupta, Partha and David, Paul A. Information Disclosure and the Economics of Science and Technology. *Feiwel, G. R., ed. (I)*, 1987, pp. 519–42.

Dasgupta, Partha and Maskin, Eric. The Simple Economics of Research Portfolios. *Econ. J.*, September 1987, *97*(387), pp. 581–95.

De Gregori, Thomas R. Resources Are Not; They Become: An Institutional Theory. *J. Econ. Issues*, September 1987, *21*(3), pp. 1241–63. **[G: U.S.]**

Espenshade, Thomas J. and Stolnitz, George J. Technological Prospects and Population Trends: An Overview. *Espenshade, T. and Stolnitz, G. J., eds.*, 1987, pp. 1–10.

Field, Alexander J. Modern Business Enterprise as a Capital-Saving Innovation. *J. Econ. Hist.*, June 1987, *47*(2), pp. 473–85. **[G: U.S.]**

Funke, Michael. A Generated Goodwin Model Incorporating Technical Progress and Variable Prices. *Econ. Notes*, 1987, (2), pp. 36–47.

Galkin, A. and Timofeev, T. Socio-economic Aspects of the Technological Revolution. *Rivista Int. Sci. Econ. Com.*, October 1987, *34*(10), pp. 1025–40.

Glikman, Pawel. Assessing the Effectiveness of Scientific–Technological Ventures. *Eastern Europ. Econ.*, Fall 1987, *26*(1), pp. 88–104.

Goldberg, Victor P. Organizational Theory, Information Processing, and Short-run Dynamics: Theory and Empirical Tests: Comment. *J. Inst. Theoretical Econ.*, March 1987, *143*(1), pp. 222–24. **[G: U.S.]**

Gort, Michael and Singamsetti, Rao. Innovation and the Personality Profiles of Firms. *Int. J. Ind. Organ.*, March 1987, *5*(1), pp. 115–26. **[G: U.S.]**

Harris, Christopher and Vickers, John. Racing with Uncertainty. *Rev. Econ. Stud.*, January 1987, *54*(1), pp. 1–21.

Ježek, Jiří. Direct Relations in Economic and Scientific–Technological Cooperation. *Czech. Econ. Digest.*, June 1987, (5), pp. 8–20. **[G: CMEA]**

Lo Cascio, Martino. Technology and the Terms of Trade. *Hieronymi, O., ed.*, 1987, pp. 157–68.

Lower, Milton D. The Concept of Technology within the Institutionalist Perspective. *J. Econ. Issues*, September 1987, *21*(3), pp. 1147–76.

Lukaszewicz, Aleksander. Technological Policy in Industry: Comment. *Saunders, C. T., ed.*, 1987, pp. 152–53.

Mark, Jerome A. Technological Change and Employment: Some Results from BLS Research. *Mon. Lab. Rev.*, April 1987, *110*(4), pp. 26–29. **[G: U.S.]**

Mickwitz, Gösta. Investering i vetenskap. (Investment in Sciences. With English summary.) *Ekon. Samfundets Tidskr.*, 1987, *40*(2), pp. 59–61. **[G: Finland]**

Mikami, Yoshiki. Exchange of Ideas and People: Cooperation in Science and Technology between the United States and Japan. *Finn, R. B., ed.*, 1987, pp. 45–58. **[G: U.S.; Japan]**

Osunbor, Oserheimen A. Law and Policy on the Registration of Technology Transfer Transactions in Nigeria. *J. World Trade Law*, October 1987, *21*(5), pp. 13–30. **[G: Nigeria]**

Rostow, Walt W. India and the Fourth Industrial Revolution. *Rostow, W. W.*, 1987, pp. 134–50. **[G: India]**

Santarelli, Enrico. Generation and Diffusion of New Technologies. *Rivista Int. Sci. Econ. Com.*, September 1987, *34*(9), pp. 829–52. **[G: U.S.; U.K.]**

Sato, Ryuzo and Ramachandran, Rama V. Factor Price Variation and the Hicksian Hypothesis: A Microeconomic Model. *Oxford Econ. Pap.*, June 1987, *39*(2), pp. 343–56.

Savage, James. Federal R&D Budget Policy in the Reagan Administration. *Public Budg. Finance*, Summer 1987, *7*(2), pp. 37–51. **[G: U.S.]**

Schenk, Winfried. Technological Policy in Industry: Comment. *Saunders, C. T., ed.*, 1987, pp. 151–52.

Streit, Manfred E. Industrial Policies for Technological Change: The Case of West Germany: Reply. *Saunders, C. T., ed.*, 1987, pp. 154.

Streit, Manfred E. Industrial Policies for Technological Change: The Case of West Germany. *Saunders, C. T., ed.*, 1987, pp. 129–42. **[G: W. Germany]**

Sydow, Peter. Growth, Technical Progress and International Division of Labour: A View from the GDR. *Saunders, C. T., ed.*, 1987, pp. 143–51. **[G: E. Germany]**

Teitel, Simón. Science and Technology Indicators, Country Size and Economic Development: An International Comparison. *World Devel.*, September 1987, *15*(9), pp. 1225–35. **[G: Global]**

Țigănescu, E.; Oprescu, G. and Goga, A. Cybernetic–Economic Analysis of the Scientific–Technical Progress Impact on the Economical Increase. *Econ. Computat. Cybern. Stud. Res.*, 1987, *22*(3), pp. 5–21.

Venit, James S. Know-How Licensing under EEC Law: Where We Have Been, Where We Are, and Where We May Be Headed. *Antitrust Bull.*, Spring 1987, *32*(1), pp. 189–252. **[G: EEC]**

Vincent, Peter; Chell, Elizabeth and Haworth, Jean. Regional Distribution of Consultancy Firms Servicing the MAPCON Scheme: A Preliminary Analysis. *Reg. Stud.*, December 1987, *21*(6), pp. 505–18. **[G: U.K.]**

Waller, William T., Jr. Ceremonial Encapsulation and Corporate Cultural Hegemony. *J. Econ. Issues*, March 1987, *21*(1), pp. 321–28.

Watanabe, Susumu. Technological Capability and Industrialisation. Effects of Aid and Sanctions in the United Republic of Tanzania and Zimbabwe. *Int. Lab. Rev.*, Sept.-Oct. 1987, *126*(5), pp. 525–41. **[G: Zimbabwe; Tanzania]**

Wiggins, Steven N. Organizational Theory, Information Processing, and Short-run Dynamics: Theory and Empirical Tests. *J. Inst. Theoretical Econ.*, March 1987, *143*(1), pp. 204–21. **[G: U.S.]**

Wild, Wolfgang. High Tech in Bavaria. *Atlantic Econ. J.*, September 1987, *15*(3), pp. 22–29. **[G: W. Germany]**

Zimmermann, Klaus F. Trade and Dynamic Effi-

ciency. *Kyklos*, 1987, *40*(1), pp. 73–87.
[G: W. Germany]

6211 Technological Change and Innovation

Aach, David L. Designing Citibank's Computer Support System. *Shetty, Y. K. and Buehler, V. M., eds.*, 1987, pp. 197–206.   [G: U.S.]

Abalkin, Leonid I., et al. Reflections on Technology in Postwar Reconstruction. *Soviet Econ.*, October-December 1987, *3*(4), pp. 353–59.
[G: U.S.S.R.]

Ablin, Eduardo and Katz, Jorge M. From Infant Industry to Technology Exports: The Argentine Experience in the International Sale of Industrial Plants and Engineering Works. *Katz, J. M., ed.*, 1987, pp. 446–77.
[G: Argentina]

Acs, Zoltan J. and Audretsch, David B. Innovation, Market Structure, and Firm Size. *Rev. Econ. Statist.*, November 1987, *69*(4), pp. 567–74.   [G: U.S.]

Aganbegyan, Abel G. Some Characteristic Features of the Present Stage of the Scientific–Technological Revolution. *Rivista Int. Sci. Econ. Com.*, October 1987, *34*(10), pp. 937–56.   [G: U.S.S.R.]

Aganbegyan, Abel G. The Strategy of Scientific-Technological Progress. *Prob. Econ.*, December 1987, *30*(8), pp. 6–21.   [G: U.S.S.R.]

Ahlburg, Dennis A., et al. Technological Change, Market Decline, and Industrial Relations in the U.S. Steel Industry. *Cornfield, D. B., ed.*, 1987, pp. 229–45.   [G: U.S.]

Ahmed, Iftikhar. Technology, Production Linkages and Women's Employment in South Asia. *Int. Lab. Rev.*, Jan.-Feb. 1987, *126*(1), pp. 21–40.   [G: S. Asia]

Akinrinade, Olusola. The Commonwealth and Development Efforts in Africa. *Akinrinade, O. and Barling, J. K., eds.*, 1987, pp. 149–73.
[G: Africa]

de Albuquerque, Marcos Cintra C. Uma análise translog sobre mudança tecnológica e efeitos de escala: um caso de modernização ineficiente. (With English summary.) *Pesquisa Planejamento Econ.*, April 1987, *17*(1), pp. 191–220.
[G: Brazil]

Allen, Bruce T. Microelectronics, Employment and Labour in the United States Automobile Industry. *Watanabe, S., ed.*, 1987, pp. 79–106.
[G: U.S.]

Ancona, Deborah Gladstein and Caldwell, David F. Management Issues Facing New-Product Teams in High-Technology Companies. *Lewin, D.; Lipsky, D. B. and Sockell, D., eds.*, 1987, pp. 199–221.

Antonelli, Cristiano and Ghezzii, Luca. Un'analisi teorica dei processi di diffusion e dell'innovazione tecnologica in regime di monopolio temporaneo. (A Theoretical Analysis of Diffusion Processees of Innovation under Temporary Monopoly. With English summary.) *Giorn. Econ.*, Mar.-Apr. 1987, *46*(3–4), pp. 125–48.

Aukutsionek, S. P. On Theories of Cycles in Technical Progress. *Matekon*, Spring 1987, *23*(3), pp. 50–75.

Bacová, Viera. Scientific–Technological Development and Effectiveness in the Economy. *Eastern Europ. Econ.*, Fall 1987, *26*(1), pp. 5–19.
[G: Czechoslovakia]

Bae, Hyung. Market Structure, Competition, and Welfare Change Due to Technological Innovations. *Int. Econ. J.*, Spring 1987, *1*(1), pp. 67–74.

Bairam, Erkin I. Returns to Scale, Technical Progress and Output Growth in Branches of Industry: The Case of Soviet Republics, 1962–74. *Scot. J. Polit. Econ.*, August 1987, *34*(3), pp. 249–66.   [G: U.S.S.R.]

Bairam, Erkin I. Returns to Scale, Technical Progress and Output Growth in Branches of Industry: The Case of COMECON, 1961–75. *METU*, 1987, *14*(2), pp. 105–22. [G: CMEA]

Banta, H. David. Aging and New Health Care Technology. *Economic Council of Canada.*, 1987, pp. 115–22.   [G: Canada]

Banta, H. David and Gelijns, Annetine. Health Care Costs: Technology and Policy. *Schramm, C. J., ed.*, 1987, pp. 252–74.   [G: U.S]

Baran, Barbara. The Technological Transformation of White-Collar Work: A Case Study of the Insurance Industry. *Hartmann, H. I., ed.*, 1987, pp. 25–62.   [G: U.S.]

Baranson, Jack. Ideology versus Innovation in Soviet Industry. *World Econ.*, March 1987, *10*(1), pp. 85–95.   [G: U.S.S.R.]

Baranson, Jack. Trade Liberalization and the New Generation of Manufacturing Technologies: Implications for Canadian Industry in North American Markets. *Tremblay, R., ed.*, 1987, pp. 407–17.   [G: Canada; U.S.]

Barber, John and White, Geoff. Current Policy Practice and Problems from a UK Perspective. *Dasgupta, P. and Stoneman, P., eds.*, 1987, pp. 24–50.   [G: U.K.]

Barr, Trevor. International Information Issues: Whose Revolution? *Barr, T., ed.*, 1987, pp. 161–70.   [G: Global]

Barras, Richard. Technical Change and the Urban Development Cycle. *Urban Stud.*, February 1987, *24*(1), pp. 5–30.   [G: U.K.]

Bartoli, Henri. La matrise des cots humains du travail. Condition de la matrise des transformations technologiques dans les pays du Tiers Monde. (Mastering the Human Cost of Labour: An Essential Condition for Mastery of Technological Change in the third world. With English summary.) *Écon. Soc.*, November 1987, *21*(11), pp. 101–26.   [G: LDCs]

Batra, Raveendra N. and Lahiri, Sajal. Imported Technologies, Urban Unemployment and the North–South Dialogue. *J. Devel. Econ.*, February 1987, *25*(1), pp. 21–32.   [G: LDCs]

Batten, Dick and Schoonmaker, Sara. Deregulation, Technological Change, and Labor Relations in Telecommunications. *Cornfield, D. B., ed.*, 1987, pp. 311–27.   [G: U.S.]

Baxter, Vern. Technological Change and Labor Relations in the United States Postal Service. *Cornfield, D. B., ed.*, 1987, pp. 91–110.
[G: U.S.]

Beath, John; Katsoulacos, Yannis and Ulph, Da-

vid T. Sequential Product Innovation and Industry Evolution. *Econ. J.*, Supplement 1987, 97, pp. 32–43.

Belova, S. Accelerating the Modernization of Productive Fixed Capital. *Prob. Econ.*, April 1987, 29(12), pp. 54–72. [G: U.S.S.R.]

Bentham, Richard W. The International Legal Structure of Petroleum Exploration. *Rees, J. and Odell, P., eds.*, 1987, pp. 57–66.
[G: Global]

Bentley, Jeffery W. Portuguese Agriculture in Transition: Technical Change in a Northwest Parish. *Pearson, S. R., et al.*, 1987, pp. 167–86. [G: Portugal]

Bertin, Gilles Y. Multinational Enterprises: Transfer Partners and Transfer Policies. *Safarian, A. E. and Bertin, G. Y., eds.*, 1987, pp. 85–100. [G: OECD]

Betcherman, Gordon and Rebne, Douglas. Technology and Control of the Labor Process: Fifty Years of Longshoring on the U.S. West Coast. *Cornfield, D. B., ed.*, 1987, pp. 73–89.
[G: U.S.]

Bhatia, Ramesh. Economics of Ethanol Production in India: A Study in Social Benefit–Cost Analysis. *Pachauri, R. K., ed.*, 1987, pp. 143–88. [G: India]

Binswanger, Hans P. and Pingali, Prabhu L. The Evolution of Farming Systems and Agricultural Technology in Sub-Saharan Africa. *Ruttan, V. W. and Pray, C. E., eds.*, 1987, pp. 283–318.
[G: Sub-Saharan]

Blommestein, Hans and Nijkamp, Peter. Adoption and Diffusion of Innovations and the Evolution of Spatial Systems. *Batten, D.; Casti, J. and Johansson, B., eds.*, 1987, pp. 368–80.

Bluestone, Barry. Impact of Trade, Technology, and Management Factors on U.S. Manufacturing. *Faruqui, A. and Broehl, J., eds.*, 1987, pp. 165–77. [G: U.S.]

de Boissieu, Christian. Lessons from the French Experience as Compared with Some Other OECD Countries. *de Cecco, M., ed.*, 1987, pp. 212–28. [G: France; OECD]

Bond, Eric W. and Samuelson, Larry. Durable Goods, Market Structure and the Incentives to Innovate. *Economica*, February 1987, 54(213), pp. 57–67.

Bonin, Bernard. Contractual Agreements and International Technology Transfers: The Empirical Studies. *Safarian, A. E. and Bertin, G. Y., eds.*, 1987, pp. 73–84.

Bouju, André. Direct Protection of Innovation: The "Critical" Chapters. *Kingston, W., ed.*, 1987, pp. 247–56. [G: OECD]

Boussard, J.-M. Le progrès technique et l'équilibre agriculture–industrie dans les modèles calculables d'équilibre général. (The Consequences of Technical Progress for Agriculture/Industry Balance as Described by Computable General Equilibrium Models. With English summary.) *Écon. Soc.*, July 1987, 21(7), pp. 7–36.

Bowman, Mary Jean. Education, Population Trends, and Technological Change. *Espen-*

shade, T. and Stolnitz, G. J., eds., 1987, 1985, pp. 71–103. [G: Global]

Branscomb, Lewis M. National and Corporate Technology Strategies in an Interdependent World Economy. *Guile, B. R. and Brooks, H., eds.*, 1987, pp. 246–56.

Brodman, Janice Z. Key Management Factors Determining the Impact of Microcomputers on Decision-making in the Governments of Developing Countries. *Ruth, S. R. and Mann, C. K., eds.*, 1987, pp. 117–42. [G: Kenya; Indonesia]

Brooks, Harvey and Guile, Bruce R. Technology and Global Industry: Overview. *Guile, B. R. and Brooks, H., eds.*, 1987, pp. 1–15.

Brugger, Ernst A. and Stuckey, Barbara. Regional Economic Structure and Innovative Behaviour in Switzerland. *Reg. Stud.*, June 1987, 21(3), pp. 241–54. [G: Switzerland]

Bruton, Henry. Technology Choice and Factor Proportions Problems in LDCs. *Gemmell, N., ed.*, 1987, pp. 236–65.

Buchholz, H. E. Research Investments in New Products: Bioethanol and Industrial Use of Agricultural Products. *Kettunen, L., ed.*, 1987, pp. 249–69.

Buitendam, Arend. The Horizontal Perspective of Organization Design and New Technology. *Pennings, J. M. and Buitendam, A., eds.*, 1987, pp. 59–86.

Burke, John. The Impact of Technology on Community Information Processes. *Barr, T., ed.*, 1987, pp. 57–65. [G: Australia]

Burmeister, Larry L. The South Korean Green Revolution: Induced or Directed Innovation? *Econ. Develop. Cult. Change*, July 1987, 35(4), pp. 767–90. [G: S. Korea]

Canitrot, Adolfo. A Model for Evaluating the Incidence of Macroeconomic Variables in the Analysis of Technological Decisions. *Katz, J. M., ed.*, 1987, pp. 499–534.

Caranza, Cesare and Cottarelli, Carlo. Financial Innovation in Italy: A Lop-Sided Process. *de Cecco, M., ed.*, 1987, pp. 172–211. [G: Italy]

Carey, David E. and Mahmassani, Hani S. Air Travel Considerations in Planning for Technology-Based Economic Development: A Case Study of Austin, Texas. *Reg. Sci. Persp.*, 1987, 17(1), pp. 20–41. [G: U.S.]

Carlberg, Michael. Makroökonomik der technologischen Arbeitslosigkeit. (Macroeconomics of Technological Unemployment. With English summary.) *Jahr. Nationalökon. Statist.*, March 1987, 203(2), pp. 123–37.

Carter, Anne P. Can Technology Change Too Fast? *Pasinetti, L. and Lloyd, P., eds.*, 1987, pp. 13–26.

Čengić, Drago. The Social Frame of Innovation: The Example of Yugoslavia. *Child, J. and Bate, P., eds.*, 1987, pp. 163–71. [G: Yugoslavia]

Centeno, Máximo Vega. Nature and Determinants of Technical Change: The Peruvian Industrial Sector. *Katz, J. M., ed.*, 1987, pp. 431–45. [G: Peru]

Chan, M. W. Luke and Mountain, Dean C. Technological Change and Economies of Scale in

Canadian Financial Institutions: A Selection from Competing Hypotheses. *J. Econ. Bus.*, February 1987, 39(1), pp. 57–66. [G: Canada]

Chatterjee, Lata and Lakshmanan, T. R. The Role of Women in Technical Change. *Fischer, M. M. and Nijkamp, P., eds.*, 1987, pp. 345–66. [G: OECD]

Chaudhuri, T. Datta; Khan, M. Ali and Tang, Min. Technical Progress and Structural Change. *J. Inst. Theoretical Econ.*, June 1987, 143(2), pp. 310–23.

Child, John. Managerial Strategies, New Technology, and the Labor Process. *Pennings, J. M. and Buitendam, A., eds.*, 1987, pp. 141–77.

Child, John; Ganter, Hans-Dieter and Kieser, Alfred. Technological Innovation and Organizational Conservatism. *Pennings, J. M. and Buitendam, A., eds.*, 1987, pp. 87–115. [G: U.K.; W. Germany]

Choi, Jai-Young and Yu, Eden S. H. Technical Progress and Outputs under Variable Returns to Scale. *Economica*, May 1987, 54(214), pp. 249–53.

Chuah, Donald G. S. Dilemma in Solar Energy Development Works in a Developing Country—Malaysia. *Pachauri, R. K., ed.*, 1987, pp. 1187–92. [G: Malaysia]

Cohen, Avi J. Factor Substitution and Induced Innovation in North American Kraft Pulping: 1914–1940. *Exploration Econ. Hist.*, April 1987, 24(2), pp. 197–217. [G: U.S.; Canada]

Cole, William E. and Mogab, John W. The Transfer of Soft Technologies to Less-Developed Countries: Some Implications for the Technology/Ceremony Dichotomy. *J. Econ. Issues*, March 1987, 21(1), pp. 309–20. [G: U.S.; Mexico]

Collinson, Michael. Potential and Practice in Food Production Technology Development: Commentary. *Mellor, J. W.; Delgado, C. L. and Blackie, M. J., eds.*, 1987, pp. 167–70. [G: Africa]

Collinson, Michael. Potential and Practice in Food Production Technology Development: Eastern and Southern Africa. *Mellor, J. W.; Delgado, C. L. and Blackie, M. J., eds.*, pp. 78–96. [G: E. Africa; Southern Africa]

Conrad, Cecilia and Duchatelet, Martine. New Technology Adoption: Incumbent versus Entrant. *Int. J. Ind. Organ.*, September 1987, 5(3), pp. 315–21.

Cook, P. Lesley. Research and Development Networks and Markets in a Complex Industry: The Example of Offshore Oil Equipment. *Saunders, C. T., ed.*, 1987, pp. 105–17.

Cornfield, Daniel B. Women in the Automated Office: Computers, Work, and Prospects for Unionization. *Lewin, D.; Lipsky, D. B. and Sockell, D., eds.*, 1987, pp. 177–98. [G: U.S.]

Cornfield, Daniel B. Workers, Managers, and Technological Change. *Cornfield, D. B., ed.*, 1987, pp. 3–24. [G: U.S.]

Cornfield, Daniel B., et al. Office Automation, Clerical Workers, and Labor Relations in the Insurance Industry. *Cornfield, D. B., ed.*, 1987, pp. 111–34. [G: U.S.]

Couto, Richard A. Changing Technologies and Consequences for Labor in Coal Mining. *Cornfield, D. B., ed.*, 1987, pp. 175–202. [G: U.S.]

Crow, Michael M. Synthetic Fuel Technology Nondevelopment and the Hiatus Effect: The Implications of Inconsistent Public Policy. *Yanarella, E. J. and Green, W. C., eds.*, 1987, pp. 33–50. [G: U.S.]

Cypher, James M. Military Spending, Technical Change, and Economic Growth: A Disguised Form of Industrial Policy? *J. Econ. Issues*, March 1987, 21(1), pp. 33–59. [G: U.S.]

Dahlman, Carl J. and Fonseca, Fernando Valadares. From Technological Dependence to Technological Development: The Case of the USIMINAS Steel Plant in Brazil. *Katz, J. M., ed.*, 1987, pp. 154–82. [G: Brazil]

Dahlman, Carl J.; Ross-Larson, Bruce and Westphal, Larry E. Managing Technological Development: Lessons from the Newly Industrializing Countries. *World Devel.*, June 1987, 15(6), pp. 759–75. [G: LDCs]

Darbellay, C. What Technologies for Mountain Agriculture? The Example of Medicinal and Aromatic Plants. *Merlo, M., et al., eds.*, 1987, pp. 291–97. [G: Switzerland]

Das, Sanghamitra. Externalities, and Technology Transfer through Multinational Corporations: A Theoretical Analysis. *J. Int. Econ.*, February 1987, 22(1/2), pp. 171–82.

Dasgupta, Partha. The Economic Theory of Technology Policy: An Introduction. *Dasgupta, P. and Stoneman, P., eds.*, 1987, pp. 7–23.

David, Paul A. Some New Standards for the Economics of Standardization in the Information Age. *Dasgupta, P. and Stoneman, P., eds.*, 1987, pp. 206–39.

De Bresson, Chris. The Evolutionary Paradigm and the Economics of Technological Change. *J. Econ. Issues*, June 1987, 21(2), pp. 751–62.

De Gregori, Thomas R. Finite Resources or Finite Imaginations? A Reply [Technology and Negative Entropy]. *J. Econ. Issues*, March 1987, 21(1), pp. 477–82.

Dean, James W., Jr. Building the Future: The Justification Process for New Technology. *Pennings, J. M. and Buitendam, A., eds.*, 1987, pp. 35–58.

Deber, Raisa B. Advances in Medical Technology. *Economic Council of Canada.*, 1987, pp. 133–38. [G: Canada]

Deger, Saadet and Sen, S. Defence Industrialisation, Technology Transfer and Choice of Techniques in LDCs. *Borner, S. and Taylor, A., eds.*, 1987, pp. 233–54. [G: LDCs]

Dekker, W. High-Tech and the Changing Shape of World Trade. *Visser, H. and Schoor, E., eds.*, 1987, pp. 77–86. [G: Global]

Delfino, José A. Eficiencia, apertura de la economía y concentración industrial en Argentina. (Efficiency, Openness of the Economy and Industrial Concentration in Argentina. With English summary.) *Económica (La Plata)*, Janu-

ary-June 1987, *33*(1), pp. 51–84.
[G: Argentina]

Delforce, J. C. and MacAulay, T. G. Use of Tractors in South Sulawesi: A Case Study Approach. *Bull. Indonesian Econ. Stud.*, August 1987, *23*(2), pp. 101–17. [G: Indonesia]

Delgado, Christopher L.; Mellor, John W. and Blackie, Malcolm J. Strategic Issues in Food Production in Sub-Saharan Africa. *Mellor, J. W.; Delgado, C. L. and Blackie, M. J., eds.*, 1987, pp. 3–22. [G: Africa]

Delgado, Christopher L. and Ranade, Chandrashekhar G. Technological Change and Agricultural Labor Use. *Mellor, J. W.; Delgado, C. L. and Blackie, M. J., eds.*, 1987, pp. 118–34. [G: Africa]

Desai, Meghnad and Low, William. Measuring the Opportunity for Product Innovation. *de Cecco, M., ed.*, 1987, pp. 112–40. [G: U.S.]

Desai, Padma. The Production Function and Technical Change in Postwar Soviet Industry: A Reexamination. *Desai, P.*, 1987, *1976*, pp. 63–77. [G: U.S.S.R.]

Desai, Padma. The Soviet Union and the Third World: A Faltering Partnership? *Desai, P.*, 1987, *1984*, pp. 256–73. [G: U.S.S.R.; LDCs]

Deutsch, Steven. Successful Worker Training Programs Help Ease Impact of Technology. *Mon. Lab. Rev.*, November 1987, *110*(11), pp. 14–20. [G: U.S.]

Di Matteo, Massimo. Relative Prices and Technical Change: A Suggested Approach to Long Waves. *Vasko, T., ed.*, 1987, pp. 326–32.

Diewert, Walter Erwin. The Effects of an Innovation: A Trade Theory Approach. *Can. J. Econ.*, November 1987, *20*(4), pp. 694–714.

Dobbs, Ian M.; Hill, M. B. and Waterson, Michael. Industrial Structure and the Employment Consequences of Technical Change. *Oxford Econ. Pap.*, September 1987, *39*(3), pp. 552–67.

Domozetov, Christo. Attitudes and Motivation of Production Managers in the Management of Technological Innovation. *Child, J. and Bate, P., eds.*, 1987, pp. 113–22. [G: Bulgaria]

Downes, Andrew S. Production Function Analysis in the Manufacturing Sector of Barbados: An Econometric Approach. *J. Econ. Devel.*, December 1987, *12*(2), pp. 161–82.
[G: Barbados]

Dudler, Hermann-Josef. Financial Innovation in Germany. *de Cecco, M., ed.*, 1987, pp. 158–71. [G: W. Germany]

Duff, Bart. Changes in Small Farm Paddy Threshing Technology in Thailand and the Philippines. *Stewart, F., ed.*, 1987, pp. 95–139.
[G: Thailand; Philippines]

Duncan, Cynthia M. and Tickamyer, Ann R. Public Ambivalence about Synthetic Fuels and Other New Energy Development. *Yanarella, E. J. and Green, W. C., eds.*, 1987, pp. 127–44. [G: U.S.]

Duncan, Joseph W. Technology, Costs, and the New Economics of Statistics. *Alonso, W. and Starr, P., eds.*, 1987, pp. 395–413. [G: U.S.]

Eastman, H. C. The Protection of Intellectual Property: Pharmaceutical Products in Canada. *Safarian, A. E. and Bertin, G. Y., eds.*, 1987, pp. 153–66. [G: Canada]

Ebel, Karl-H. and Ulrich, Erhard. Some Workplace Effects of CAD and CAM. *Int. Lab. Rev.*, 1987, *126*(3), pp. 351–70. [G: OECD]

Eckel, Russel. Industrial Relations and High Technology: The Transformation of Telecommunications through Deregulation. *Child, J. and Bate, P., eds.*, 1987, pp. 173–89.
[G: U.S.]

Edquist, Charles and Jacobsson, Staffan. The Integrated Circuit Industries of India and the Republic of Korea in an International Technoeconomic Context. *Industry Devel.*, 1987, (21), pp. 1–62. [G: India; S. Korea]

Edwards, Averill. Library Resources in the Age of Information Technology. *Barr, T., ed.*, 1987, pp. 93–111. [G: Australia]

Eliasson, Gunnar. Dynamic Micro–Macro Co-ordination, Technical Change and Trade. *Eliasson, G.*, 1987, pp. 81–118. [G: Sweden]

Eliasson, Gunnar. Information Technology, Capital Structure and the Nature of Technical Change in the Firm. *Eliasson, G.*, 1987, pp. 51–78.

Eliasson, Gunnar. Technological Competition and Trade in the Experimentally Organized Economy—The Themes. *Eliasson, G.*, 1987, pp. 9–18.

Ergas, Henry. The Importance of Technology Policy. *Dasgupta, P. and Stoneman, P., eds.*, 1987, pp. 51–96. [G: OECD]

Ernst, Dieter. The Impact of Microelectronics on the Worldwide Restructuring of the Electronics Industry: Implications for the Third World. *Dunning, J. H. and Usui, M., eds.*, 1987, pp. 117–34. [G: LDCs]

Etemad, Hamid and Dulude, Louise Séguin. The Development of Technology in MNEs: A Cross-Country and Industry Study. *Safarian, A. E. and Bertin, G. Y., eds.*, 1987, pp. 101–19. [G: OECD]

Ettlie, John E. and Bridges, William P. Technology Policy and Innovation in Organizations. *Pennings, J. M. and Buitendam, A., eds.*, 1987, pp. 117–37. [G: U.S.]

Etzioni, Amitai. U.S. Technological, Economic, and Social Development for the 21st Century. *Nagel, S. S., ed.*, 1987, pp. 241–70.
[G: U.S.]

Evans, Roger W. Some Thoughts on Advances in Medical Technology. *Economic Council of Canada.*, 1987, pp. 122–33. [G: Canada]

Evenson, Robert E.; Evenson, Donald D. and Putnam, Jonathan D. Private Sector Agricultural Invention in Developing Countries. *Ruttan, V. W. and Pray, C. E., eds.*, 1987, pp. 469–511.

Fagerberg, Jan. Diffusion of Technology, Structural Change and Intra-industry Trade: The Case of the Nordic Countries 1961–1983. *Andersson, J. O., ed.*, 1987, pp. 73–102.
[G: N. Europe]

Falkinger, Josef. Technological Unemployment:

A Note. *J. Post Keynesian Econ.*, Fall 1987, *10*(1), pp. 37–43.

Farrell, Joseph and Saloner, Garth. Competition, Compatibility and Standards: The Economics of Horses, Penguins and Lemmings. *Gabel, H. L., ed.*, 1987, pp. 1–21.

Fernández Kelly, M. Patricia. Technology and Employment along the U.S.–Mexican Border. *Thorup, C. L., ed.*, 1987, pp. 149–66.
[G: U.S.; Mexico]

Ferraz, João Carlos. O desempenho tecnológico da indústria brasileira: padrão de maturação e seus determinantes. (With English summary.) *Pesquisa Planejamento Econ.*, August 1987, *17*(2), pp. 437–56. [G: Brazil]

Ferreira dos Santos, Robério. Processo de modernização da agricultura brasileira: Um teste da hipótese da inovação induzida. (With English summary.) *Pesquisa Planejamento Econ.*, December 1987, *17*(3), pp. 679–710.
[G: Brazil]

Fidel, Julio and Lucángeli, Jorge. Cost–Benefit of Different Technological Options in the Context of a Differentiated Oligopoly: The Case of the Argentine Cigarette Industry. *Katz, J. M., ed.*, 1987, pp. 283–317. [G: Argentina]

Finch, Henry. Technology Policy and the State in Uruguay, 1900–1935. *Dewey, C., ed.*, 1987, pp. 288–318. [G: Uruguay]

Fiorentini, Gianluca. Un modello di diffusione-generazione del mutamento tecnico. (A Diffusion-Generation Model of Technical Change. With English summary.) *Rivista Int. Sci. Econ. Com.*, June 1987, *34*(6), pp. 547–71.

Fischer, Robert A. Information Strategy at McDonnell Douglas. *Shetty, Y. K. and Buehler, V. M., eds.*, 1987, pp. 207–20. [G: U.S.]

Fishel, Walter L. The Economics of Agricultural Biotechnology: Discussion. *Amer. J. Agr. Econ.*, May 1987, *69*(2), pp. 438–39.

Florescu, Mihail. The Role of Science and Technology in Automation, Robotization, Electronization and Informatization Processes in the Economic and Social Development. *Econ. Computat. Cybern. Stud. Res.*, 1987, *22*(1), pp. 5–17. [G: Romania]

Fontela, Emilio. Technology as a Factor of Economic Leadership. *Hieronymi, O., ed.*, 1987, pp. 97–104.

Formica, Piero and Mandelli, Giancarlo. Premesse e implicazioni micro e macroeconomiche dell'atuomazione flessibile. (The Micro and Macro-Economic Promises and Implications of Flexible Automation. With English summary.) *Econ. Lavoro*, Oct.-Dec. 1987, *21*(4), pp. 29–44.

Forsyth, John H. Financial Innovation in Britain. *de Cecco, M., ed.*, 1987, pp. 141–57.
[G: U.K.]

Fox, Roger and Finan, Timothy J. Portuguese Agriculture in Transition: Patterns of Technical Change in the Northwest. *Pearson, S. R., et al.*, 1987, pp. 187–201. [G: Portugal]

Fox, Roger and Finan, Timothy J. Portuguese Agriculture in Transition: Future Technical and Structural Adjustments in Northwestern

Agriculture. *Pearson, S. R., et al.*, 1987, pp. 202–20. [G: Portugal]

Franco, Malerba. Apprendimento, innovazioni incrementali e tecnologia: un'analisi interindustriale. (Learning, Incremental Innovations and Technology: An Interindustry Analysis. With English summary.) *Giorn. Econ.*, May-June 1987, *46*(5–6), pp. 227–55.

Frankel, Allen B. and Marquardt, Jeffrey C. International Payments and EFT Links. *Solomon, E. H., ed.*, 1987, pp. 111–30.

Fraser, Bryna Shore. New Office and Business Technologies: The Structure of Education and (Re)Training Opportunities. *Hartmann, H. I., ed.*, 1987, pp. 343–72.

Freeman, Christopher. Information Technology and Change in Techno-economic Paradigm. *Freeman, C. and Soete, L., eds.*, 1987, pp. 49–69.

Freeman, Christopher. Technical Innovation, Diffusion, and Long Cycles of Economic Development. *Vasko, T., ed.*, 1987, pp. 295–309.

Freeman, Christopher and Soete, Luc. Factor Substitution and Technical Change. *Freeman, C. and Soete, L., eds.*, 1987, pp. 36–48.

Freeman, Christopher and Soete, Luc. Technical Change and Full Employment: Policy Conclusions. *Freeman, C. and Soete, L., eds.*, 1987, pp. 237–56. [G: U.K.]

Freeman, Christopher and Soete, Luc. Technical Change and Full Employment: Conclusions. *Freeman, C. and Soete, L., eds.*, 1987, pp. 257–64.

Fritsch, Bruno. Shaping the Future through the Use of Innovation: Some Observations on Innovation and Value Changes in Europe. *[Kitamura, H.]*, 1987, pp. 70–84.

Fujita, Natsuki and James, William E. Exports and Technological Changes in the Adjustment Process of the Japanese Economy in the 1970s. *Hitotsubashi J. Econ.*, December 1987, *28*(2), pp. 107–22. [G: Japan]

Gang, Ira N. and Gangopadhyay, Shubhashis. Employment, Output and the Choice of Techniques: The Trade-Off Revisited. *J. Devel. Econ.*, April 1987, *25*(2), pp. 321–27.
[G: LDCs]

Garnier, Jean-Pierre. Les nouvelles technologies de l'aliénation. (The New Technologies of Alienation. With English summary.) *Écon. Soc.*, August 1987, *21*(8), pp. 129–52.

Garvalova, Mariia. A Study of the Influence of Scientific–Technological Progress on Economic Growth. *Eastern Europ. Econ.*, Fall 1987, *26*(1), pp. 20–33. [G: Bulgaria]

Geller, Henry. Telecommunications Policy Issues: The New Money Delivery Modes. *Solomon, E. H., ed.*, 1987, pp. 63–78. [G: U.S.]

George, Kenneth D. and Mainwaring, Lynn. The Welsh Economy in the 1980s. *Day, G. and Rees, G., eds.*, 1987, pp. 7–37. [G: U.K.]

Ginzberg, Eli. Technology, Women, and Work: Policy Perspectives. *Hartmann, H. I., ed.*, 1987, pp. 3–22. [G: U.S.]

Goldin, Claudia. Women's Employment and Technological Change: A Historical Perspec-

tive. *Hartmann, H. I., ed.*, 1987, pp. 185–222.
[G: U.S.]

Goldsworthy, Ashley W. Expanding Economic Horizons. *Barr, T., ed.*, 1987, pp. 38–53.
[G: Australia]

Goodman, Louis W. Food Transnational Corporations and Developing Countries: The Case of the Improved Seed Industry in Mexico. *Ruttan, V. W. and Pray, C. E., eds.*, 1987, pp. 433–49. [G: Mexico]

Gordon, Gerald, et al. Computer-Based Automation and Labor Relations in the Construction Equipment Industry. *Cornfield, D. B., ed.*, 1987, pp. 247–62. [G: U.S.]

Gotsch, Carl H. Applications of Microcomputers in Third World Organizations. *Ruth, S. R. and Mann, C. K., eds.*, 1987, *1986*, pp. 39–48.
[G: LDCs]

Gottinger, Hans W. Economic Choice and Technology Diffusion in New Product Markets. *Weltwirtsch. Arch.*, 1987, *123*(1), pp. 93–120.
[G: U.S.]

Gowdy, John M. GAIA and Technological Utopianism: Comment [Technology and Negative Entropy]. *J. Econ. Issues*, March 1987, *21*(1), pp. 473–76.

Grabowski, Richard and Sanchez, Onesimo. Technological Change in Mexican Agriculture: 1950–1979. *Soc. Econ. Stud.*, June 1987, *36*(2), pp. 187–205. [G: Mexico]

Grafton, Carl. Public Policy for Dangerous Inventions. *Policy Sci.*, 1987, *20*(3), pp. 207–34.
[G: U.S.]

Graham, Edward M. World Trade Law and Government Subsidies to Industrial Innovation. *Hieronymi, O., ed.*, 1987, pp. 25–41.
[G: MDCs]

Griliches, Zvi; Pakes, Ariel and Hall, Bronwyn H. The Value of Patents as Indicators of Inventive Activity. *Dasgupta, P. and Stoneman, P., eds.*, 1987, pp. 97–124. [G: U.S.]

de Grolier, Eric. Government, the Information Industry and Social Intelligence. *Dedijer, S. and Jéquier, N., eds.*, 1987, pp. 79–92.

Guglielmotto, Enrica and Passatore, Giuseppe. The Private ECU Market: A Case of International Financial Innovation. *de Cecco, M., ed.*, 1987, pp. 260–319. [G: W. Europe]

van Gunsteren, Lex A. Information Technology: A Managerial Perspective. *Pennings, J. M. and Buitendam, A., eds.*, 1987, pp. 277–89.

Guralnik, Jack M. and Schneider, Edward L. Prospects and Implications of Extending Life Expectancy. *Espenshade, T. and Stolnitz, G. J., eds.*, 1987, pp. 125–45. [G: U.S.]

Gürlich, Josef. Original Creative Activity in the Process of Intensification of the Czechoslovak Economy. *Czech. Econ. Digest.*, June 1987, (4), pp. 80–96. [G: Czechoslovakia]

Haag, Günter; Weidlich, Wolfgang and Mensch, Gerhard O. The Schumpeter Clock. *Batten, D.; Casti, J. and Johansson, B., eds.*, 1987, pp. 187–226. [G: W. Germany]

Hage, Jerald. Reflections on New Technology and Organizational Change. *Pennings, J. M. and*

Buitendam, A., eds., 1987, pp. 261–76.
[G: Japan; U.S.]

Haggblade, Steve. Vertical Considerations in Choice-of-Technique Studies: Evidence from Africa's Indigenous Beer Industry. *Econ. Develop. Cult. Change*, July 1987, *35*(4), pp. 723–42. [G: Botswana]

Hamlett, Patrick W. Technological Policy Making in Congress: The Creation of the U.S. Synthetic Fuels Corporation. *Yanarella, E. J. and Green, W. C., eds.*, 1987, pp. 53–69.
[G: U.S.]

Hancher, Leigh and Ruete, Matthias. Legal Culture, Product Licensing, and the Drug Industry. *Wilks, S. and Wright, M., eds.*, 1987, pp. 148–80. [G: U.K.; W. Germany]

Hannan, Timothy H. and McDowell, John M. Rival Precedence and the Dynamics of Technology Adoption: An Empirical Analysis. *Economica*, May 1987, *54*(214), pp. 155–71.
[G: U.S.]

Harris, S. A. The Provision of Carbohydrates for the European Community's Biotechnology and Chemical Industries. *J. Agr. Econ.*, September 1987, *38*(3), pp. 423–34. [G: EEC]

Harwood, Richard R. Low Input Technologies for Sustainable Agricultural Systems. *Ruttan, V. W. and Pray, C. E., eds.*, 1987, pp. 319–31.

Haustein, Heinz-Dieter. The Pathway of Dynamic Efficiency: Economic Trajectory of a Technical Revolution. *Vasko, T., ed.*, 1987, pp. 198–215.

Havrilesky, Thomas M. Monetary Modeling in a World of Financial Innovation. *Solomon, E. H., ed.*, 1987, pp. 159–87. [G: U.S.]

Hayami, Yujiro and Ruttan, Vernon W. Population Growth and Agricultural Productivity. *Espenshade, T. and Stolnitz, G. J., eds.*, 1987, pp. 11–69.

Heitger, Bernhard. Corporatism, Technological Gaps and Growth in OECD Countries. *Weltwirtsch. Arch.*, 1987, *123*(3), pp. 463–73.
[G: OECD]

Henderson, Paul B., Jr. Modern Money. *Solomon, E. H., ed.*, 1987, pp. 17–37. [G: U.S.]

Hennestad, Bjørn W. Organizations and the Computer Culture: The Mismanagement of Meaning? *Child, J. and Bate, P., eds.*, 1987, pp. 137–47.

Henwood, Felicity and Wyatt, Sally. Managing Technological Change: Responses of Government, Employers, and Trade Unions in Western Europe and Canada. *Hartmann, H. I., ed.*, 1987, pp. 395–431. [G: OECD]

Hergert, Michael. Technical Standards and Competition in the Microcomputer Industry. *Gabel, H. L., ed.*, 1987, pp. 67–89.

Hester, Donald D. On the Empirical Detection of Financial Innovation. *de Cecco, M., ed.*, 1987, pp. 77–111. [G: U.S.]

Hieronymi, Otto. Reflections on Technology, International Order and Economic Growth. *Hieronymi, O., ed.*, 1987, pp. 69–95. [G: OECD]

Hieronymi, Otto. Technology and International

Relations: Introduction. *Hieronymi, O., ed.*, 1987, pp. 5–8.

Hilke, John C. and Nelson, Philip B. Caveat Innovator: Strategic and Structural Characteristics of New Product Introductions. *J. Econ. Behav. Organ.*, June 1987, *8*(2), pp. 213–29.
[G: U.S.]

Holzman, Franklyn D. and Portes, Richard. Trade, Technology, and Leverage: The Limits of Pressure. *Holzman, F. D.*, 1987, *1978*, pp. 113–20.

Honko, Jaakko. Kansainvälinen kilpailukyky ja tieteellinen tutkimus. (International Competitiveness and Scientific Research. With English summary.) *Liiketaloudellinen Aikak.*, 1987, *36*(2), pp. 107–15.
[G: Finland]

Hrbek, Rudolf and Erdmann, Vera. Integrationsschub durch Technologiepolitik? Zur Reichweite neuer Aktivitäten in der EG. (Technology Policy—Push towards More Integration? Considering the Scope of New Activities in the EC. With English summary.) *Lenel, H. O., et al., eds.*, 1987, pp. 183–207.
[G: EEC]

Humphrey, David B. Payments System Risk, Market Failure, and Public Policy. *Solomon, E. H., ed.*, 1987, pp. 83–109. [G: U.S.]

Hunt, H. Allan and Hunt, Timothy L. Recent Trends in Clerical Employment: The Impact of Technological Change. *Hartmann, H. I., ed.*, 1987, pp. 223–67. [G: U.S.]

Hyman, Eric L. The Strategy of Production and Distribution of Improved Charcoal Stoves in Kenya. *World Devel.*, March 1987, *15*(3), pp. 375–86. [G: Kenya]

Idachaba, Francis S. Agriculture and Central Physical Grid Infrastructure: Commentary. *Mellor, J. W.; Delgado, C. L. and Blackie, M. J., eds.*, 1987, pp. 232–38. [G: Africa]

Jadlow, Joseph M.; Jadlow, Janice W. and Yu, Shirley S. Risk, Rivalry, and Innovation: The Case of Ethical Drugs. *Rivista Int. Sci. Econ. Com.*, July 1987, *34*(7), pp. 593–608.
[G: U.S.]

James, Jeffrey. Population and Technical Change in the Manufacturing Sector of Developing Countries. *Johnson, D. G. and Lee, R. D., eds.*, 1987, pp. 225–56. [G: LDCs]

James, Jeffrey. The Choice of Technology in Public Enterprise: A Comparative Study of Manufacturing Industry in Kenya and Tanzania. *Stewart, F., ed.*, 1987, pp. 219–47.
[G: Kenya; Tanzania]

Java, R. L. Intergrating Biomass Energy Programmes. *Pachauri, R. K., ed.*, 1987, pp. 413–19. [G: India]

Johansson, Börje. Technological Vintages and Substitution Processes. *Batten, D.; Casti, J. and Johansson, B., eds.*, 1987, pp. 145–84.

Johansson, Börje; Batten, David F. and Casti, John. Economic Dynamics, Evolution and Structural Adjustment. *Batten, D.; Casti, J. and Johansson, B., eds.*, 1987, pp. 1–23.

Johansson, Börje and Karlsson, Charlie. Processes of Industrial Change: Scale, Location and Type of Job. *Fischer, M. M. and Nijkamp,*

P., eds., 1987, pp. 139–65.

Jones, Barry. Towards a National Information Policy. *Barr, T., ed.*, 1987, pp. 1–9.
[G: Australia]

de Jong, Henk Wouter. Direct Protection of Innovation: The "Critical" Chapters. *Kingston, W., ed.*, 1987, pp. 215–26.

Jönsson, Sten. Limits of Information Technology for Facilitating Organizational Learning. *Pennings, J. M. and Buitendam, A., eds.*, 1987, pp. 217–34.

Joshi, P. C. Technological Potentialities of Peasant Agriculture: East–West Parallels and Contrasts. *Joshi, P. C.*, 1987, pp. 159–89.
[G: Asia; W. Europe]

Joskow, Paul L. Productivity Growth and Technical Change in the Generation of Electricity. *Energy J.*, January 1987, *8*(1), pp. 17–38.
[G: U.S.]

Jovanovic, Boyan and Rob, Rafael. Demand-Driven Innovation and Spatial Competition over Time. *Rev. Econ. Stud.*, January 1987, *54*(1), pp. 63–72.

Jürgens, Ulrich; Dohse, Knuth and Malsch, Thomas. New Production Concepts in West German Car Plants. *Tolliday, S. and Zeitlin, J., eds.*, 1987, pp. 258–81. [G: W. Germany]

Kabir, M. and Mangla, I. Financial Innovations in Canada and Forecasting Money Stocks: An Econometric Analysis (1967–1985). *Tremblay, R., ed.*, 1987, pp. 299–314. [G: Canada]

Kahana, Nava. The Multifactor Illyrian Firm Revisited: Comment. *J. Compar. Econ.*, December 1987, *11*(4), pp. 611–12.

Kako, Toshiyuki. Development of the Farm Machinery Industry in Japan: A Case Study of the Walking Type Tractor. *Hitotsubashi J. Econ.*, December 1987, *28*(2), pp. 155–71.
[G: Japan]

Kalirajan, K. South–South Co-operation: Technology Transfer for Improving Productivity. *Indian Econ. J.*, Jan.-Mar. 1987, *34*(3), pp. 60–72. [G: LDCs]

Kalleberg, Arne L., et al. The Eclipse of Craft: The Changing Face of Labor in the Newspaper Industry. *Cornfield, D. B., ed.*, 1987, pp. 47–71. [G: U.S.]

Kalter, Robert J. and Tauer, Loren W. Potential Economic Impacts of Agricultural Biotechnology. *Amer. J. Agr. Econ.*, May 1987, *69*(2), pp. 420–25. [G: U.S.]

Kaplinsky, Raphael. Appropriate Technology in Sugar Manufacturing. *Stewart, F., ed.*, 1987, pp. 192–218. [G: India; Kenya]

Katz, Jorge M. Domestic Technological Innovations and Dynamic Comparative Advantages: Further Reflections on a Comparative Case Study Programme. *Dunning, J. H. and Usui, M., eds.*, 1987, pp. 135–55. [G: LDCs]

Katz, Jorge M. Domestic Technology Generation in LDCs: A Review of Research Findings. *Katz, J. M., ed.*, 1987, pp. 13–55.
[G: LDCs]

Katz, Jorge M. Productivity and Domestic Technological Search Efforts: The Growth Path of a Rayon Plant in Argentina. *Katz, J. M., ed.*,

1987, pp. 192–240.   [G: Argentina]

Kawamiya, Nobuo. Thermophysical Analysis of Resource Substitution, Technological Developments and the Environmental Problems in Their Interrelation. *Pillet, G. and Murota, T., eds.*, 1987, pp. 37–51.

Keir, Marie. Brave New Wired World. *Barr, T., ed.*, 1987, pp. 66–80.   [G: Australia]

Kemme, David M. The Failure of Effective Technological Transfer in Polish Industry. *Econ. Planning*, 1987, *21*(1), pp. 1–12. [G: Poland]

Khang, Chulsoon. Export-led Economic Growth: The Case of Technology Transfer. *Econ. Stud. Quart.*, June 1987, *38*(2), pp. 131–47.
[G: S. Korea; Hong Kong; Singapore; Taiwan]

Kimberly, John R. Organizational and Contextual Influences on the Diffusion of Technological Innovation. *Pennings, J. M. and Buitendam, A., eds.*, 1987, pp. 237–59.

King, Alexander. Science, Technology and International Relations: Some Comments and a Speculation. *Hieronymi, O., ed.*, 1987, pp. 9–24.

Kingston, William. Advantages of Protecting Innovation Directly. *Kingston, W., ed.*, 1987, pp. 87–123.   [G: W. Europe; N. America]

Kingston, William. Direct Protection of Innovation: Response. *Kingston, W., ed.*, 1987, pp. 277–337.

Kingston, William. Kronz's "Innovation Patent." *Kingston, W., ed.*, 1987, pp. 35–58.

Kingston, William. The Innovation Warrant. *Kingston, W., ed.*, 1987, pp. 59–86.

Kingston, William. The Unexploited Potential of Patents. *Kingston, W., ed.*, 1987, pp. 1–34.
[G: W. Europe; N. America]

Kirby, Michael G. New Technology and International Privacy Issues. *Barr, T., ed.*, 1987, pp. 146–58.   [G: Global]

Kiyokawa, Yukihiko and Ishikawa, Shigeru. The Significance of Standardization in the Development of the Machine-Tool Industry: The Cases of Japan and China (Part 1). *Hitotsubashi J. Econ.*, December 1987, *28*(2), pp. 123–54.
[G: China; Japan]

Kleinknecht, Alfred. Rates of Innovations and Profits in the Long Wave. *Vasko, T., ed.*, 1987, pp. 216–38.

Kreinin, Mordechai E. Comparative Advantage and Possible Trade Restrictions in High-Technology Products. *Salvatore, D., ed.*, 1987, pp. 297–332.   [G: U.S.]

Krelle, Wilhelm. Long-term Fluctuations of Technical Progress and Growth. *J. Inst. Theoretical Econ.*, September 1987, *143*(3), pp. 379–401.
[G: OECD; CMEA]

Krommenacker, Raymond. Services and Space Technology: The Emergence of Space Generated, Highly Integrated Goods and Services (IGS). *Giarini, O., ed.*, 1987, pp. 173–92.

Kronz, Hermann. Response in Defence of the Innovation Patent Concept. *Kingston, W., ed.*, 1987, pp. 257–76.

Krugman, Paul R. Market Access and Competition in High Technology Industries: A Simula-

tion Exercise. *[Corden, W. M.]*, 1987, pp. 128–42.

Kubík, Jaroslav. Improving the Management of Scientific–Technological Development in Branch Production Units. *Eastern Europ. Econ.*, Fall 1987, *26*(1), pp. 41–71.
[G: Czechoslovakia]

ter Kuile, Coenrad H. H. Potential and Practice in Food Production Technology Development: The Humid and Subhumid Tropics. *Mellor, J. W.; Delgado, C. L. and Blackie, M. J., eds.*, 1987, pp. 97–108.   [G: Africa]

Kumar, Nagesh. Technology Imports and Local Research and Development in Indian Manufacturing. *Devel. Econ.*, September 1987, *25*(3), pp. 220–33.   [G: India]

Kumar, Shubh K. Women's Role and Agricultural Technology. *Mellor, J. W.; Delgado, C. L. and Blackie, M. J., eds.*, 1987, pp. 135–47.
[G: Africa]

Lahiri, Sajal and Batra, Raveendra N. Imported Technologies, North–South Dialogue and the Optimal Subsidy Policy. *Indian Econ. J.*, Jan.-Mar. 1987, *34*(3), pp. 81–85.

Lall, Sanjaya. Multinationals and Technology Development in Host LDCs. *Dunning, J. H. and Usui, M., eds.*, 1987, pp. 193–209.
[G: LDCs]

Lamberton, Don. The Australian Information Economy: A Sectoral Analysis. *Barr, T., ed.*, 1987, pp. 13–29.   [G: Australia]

Langdale, John. Transborder Data Flows and National Sovereignty. *Barr, T., ed.*, 1987, pp. 137–45.

Lawrence, Colin and Spiller, Pablo T. International Technological Diffusion, Product Differentiation and Economies of Scale. *Dunning, J. H. and Usui, M., eds.*, 1987, pp. 95–115.
[G: LDCs]

Lawton, Joseph A. Kodak's Technet Center. *Shetty, Y. K. and Buehler, V. M., eds.*, 1987, pp. 253–63.   [G: U.S.]

Lefebvre, Louis-A. and Lefebvre, Élisabeth. L'entreprise innovatrice. Un regard vers deamain. (The Innovation Organization: A Look at the Future. With English summary.) *L'Actual. Econ.*, March 1987, *63*(1), pp. 53–76.
[G: Canada]

Leistritz, F. Larry and Murdock, Steve H. Socioeconomic Impacts of Large-Scale Development Projects in the Western United States: Implications for Synthetic Fuels Commercialization. *Yanarella, E. J. and Green, W. C., eds.*, 1987, pp. 145–70.   [G: U.S.]

Lemeshev, M. Ecological and Economic Evaluation of Scientific-Technological Progress. *Prob. Econ.*, September 1987, *30*(5), pp. 82–97.
[G: U.S.S.R.]

Levin, Sharon G.; Levin, Stanford L. and Meisel, John B. A Dynamic Analysis of the Adoption of a New Technology: The Case of Optical Scanners. *Rev. Econ. Statist.*, February 1987, *69*(1), pp. 12–17.   [G: U.S.]

Lichtman, Rob. Toward the Diffusion of Rural Energy Technologies: Some Lessons from the Indian Biogas Program. *World Devel.*, March

1987, *15*(3), pp. 347–74.   **[G: India]**

Link, Albert N. and Tassey, Gregory. The Impact of Standards on Technology-Based Industries: The Case of Numerically Controlled Machine Tools in Automated Batch Manufacturing. *Gabel, H. L., ed.*, 1987, pp. 217–37.   **[G: U.S.]**

Lintner, V. G., et al. Trade Unions and Technological Change in the U.K. Mechanical Engineering Industry. *Brit. J. Ind. Relat.*, March 1987, *25*(1), pp. 19–29.   **[G: U.K.]**

Lipton, Michael. Agriculture and Central Physical Grid Infrastructure. *Mellor, J. W.; Delgado, C. L. and Blackie, M. J., eds.*, 1987, pp. 210–26.   **[G: Africa]**

Lloyd-Jones, Roger. Innovation, Industrial Structure and the Long Wave: The British Economy c. 1873–1914. *J. Europ. Econ. Hist.*, Fall 1987, *16*(2), pp. 315–53.   **[G: U.K.]**

Lockett, Martin. Technical Innovation and Economic Reform in Socialist Economies with Special Reference to China. *Child, J. and Bate, P., eds.*, 1987, pp. 191–203.   **[G: China]**

Lockwood, R. C. Diffusion and Adoption of New Technology at the Farm Level. *Can. J. Agr. Econ.*, May 1987, *34*, pp. 147–50.

Long, Stewart L. Technological Change and Institutional Response: The Creation of American Broadcasting. *J. Econ. Issues*, June 1987, *21*(2), pp. 743–49.   **[G: U.S.]**

Longworth, John W. Biotechnology: Scientific Potential and Socio-economic Implications for Agriculture. *Rev. Marketing Agr. Econ.*, December 1987, *55*(3), pp. 187–99.

Lubrano, Linda L. The Attentive Public for Soviet Science and Technology. *Millar, J. R., ed.*, 1987, pp. 142–68.   **[G: U.S.S.R.]**

de Lucia, Russell J. and Poole, Alan D. Biomass Fuels for Industry: Implications for Fuel Cycle Economics. *Pachauri, R. K., ed.*, 1987, pp. 421–47.

Lusser, Markus. Policy and Financial Innovation: Will There Be a Switch from Deregulation to Reregulation? *Portes, R. and Swoboda, A. K., eds.*, 1987, pp. 257–62.

Lyons, Bruce. International Trade and Technology Policy. *Dasgupta, P. and Stoneman, P., eds.*, 1987, pp. 169–205.

Lyons, John S. Powerloom Profitability and Steam Power Costs: Britain in the 1830s. *Exploration Econ. Hist.*, October 1987, *24*(4), pp. 392–408.   **[G: U.K.]**

MacCharles, D. C. International Knowledge Transfers and Competitiveness: Canada as a Case Study. *Safarian, A. E. and Bertin, G. Y., eds.*, 1987, pp. 53–69.   **[G: Canada]**

Madeuf, Bernadette. Trends in Technological Competitiveness within the OECD, 1970–80. *Safarian, A. E. and Bertin, G. Y., eds.*, 1987, pp. 34–52.   **[G: OECD]**

Madian, Alan L. Technology and the Changing Industrial Balance. *Thorup, C. L., ed.*, 1987, pp. 41–66.   **[G: Mexico; U.S.]**

Maier, Harry. Basic Innovations and the Next Long Wave of Productivity Growth: Socioeconomic Implications and Consequences. *Vasko, T., ed.*, 1987, pp. 46–65.

Makarov, V. L. On Dynamic Models of the Economy and the Development of L. V. Kantorovich's Ideas. *Matekon*, Summer 1987, *23*(4), pp. 48–74.

Mandeville, Thomas. An International Comparison. *Barr, T., ed.*, 1987, pp. 30–37.   **[G: Global]**

Mandeville, Thomas and Macdonald, Stuart. Innovation Protection Viewed from an Information Perspective. *Kingston, W., ed.*, 1987, pp. 157–69.

Mann, Charles K. Beyond the Metaphor: Microcomputers in Public Policy and Human Capital Development. *Ruth, S. R. and Mann, C. K., eds.*, 1987, pp. 7–22.   **[G: Tunisia; Kenya]**

Mann, Charles K. Microcomputers in Development: Concluding Observations. *Ruth, S. R. and Mann, C. K., eds.*, 1987, pp. 159–61.   **[G: LDCs]**

Manton, Kenneth G. The Population Implications of Breakthroughs in Biomedical Technologies for Controlling Mortality and Fertility. *Espenshade, T. and Stolnitz, G. J., eds.*, 1987, pp. 147–93.

de Maria y Campos, Mauricio. Mexico's New Industrial Development Strategy. *Thorup, C. L., ed.*, 1987, pp. 67–81.   **[G: Mexico]**

Marsden, James R.; Salas-Fumas, Vicente and Whinston, Andrew. Technology Transfer: Measuring the Impact of Organisational and Managerial Structures on Production Efficiency. *Pasinetti, L. and Lloyd, P., eds.*, 1987, pp. 47–73.

Martellaro, Joseph A. and Chen, Jing-Yau. Some Aspects of Growth and Technical Progress in the People's Republic of China. *Econ. Int.*, November 1987, *40*(4), pp. 301–16.   **[G: China]**

Martinello, Felice. Substitution, Technical Change and Returns to Scale in British Columbian Wood Products Industries. *Appl. Econ.*, April 1987, *19*(4), pp. 483–96.   **[G: Canada]**

Matjka, Karel. The First Step...And the Next. *Czech. Econ. Digest.*, June 1987, (4), pp. 44–55.   **[G: CMEA]**

Matlon, Peter J. Potential and Practice in Food Production Technology Development: The West African Semiarid Tropics. *Mellor, J. W.; Delgado, C. L. and Blackie, M. J., eds.*, 1987, pp. 59–77.   **[G: W. Africa]**

Matthews, Derek. The Technical Transformation of the Late Nineteenth-Century Gas Industry. *J. Econ. Hist.*, December 1987, *47*(4), pp. 967–80.   **[G: U.K.]**

Maurer, Martin. Technological Pluralism: Why Do Technologies in Use Differ. A Closer Look at Some Case Studies. *Rivista Int. Sci. Econ. Com.*, Jan.-Feb. 1987, *34*(1–2), pp. 129–46.   **[G: Africa]**

Maxwell, Philip. Adequate Technological Strategy in an Imperfect Economic Context: A Case-Study of the Evolution of the Acindar Steel-plant in Rosario, Argentina. *Katz, J. M., ed.*, 1987, pp. 119–53.   **[G: Argentina]**

Maxwell, Philip. Technical Change and Appropriate Technology: A Review of Some Latin American Case Studies. *Stewart, F., ed.*, 1987, pp. 248–70. **[G: Latin America]**

McCurdy, Thomas H. Some Employment, Income, and Occupational Effects of Microelectronic-Based Technical Change: A Multisectoral Simulation for Canada. *J. Policy Modeling,* Summer 1987, *9*(2), pp. 337–65. **[G: Canada]**

McFetridge, D. G. The Timing, Mode and Terms of Technology Transfer: Some Recent Findings. *Safarian, A. E. and Bertin, G. Y., eds.,* 1987, pp. 135–50. **[G: Canada]**

McHugh, Richard and Lane, Julia. The Age of Capital, the Age of Utilized Capital, and Tests of the Embodiment Hypothesis. *Rev. Econ. Statist.,* May 1987, *69*(2), pp. 362–67. **[G: U.S.]**

McHugh, Richard and Lane, Julia. The Role of Embodied Technological Change in the Decline of Labor Productivity. *Southern Econ. J.,* April 1987, *53*(4), pp. 915–24. **[G: U.S.]**

McNicoll, Geoffrey. Agrarian and Industrial Futures: Comments [Population Growth and Agricultural Productivity] [Education, Population Trends, and Technological Change]. *Espenshade, T. and Stolnitz, G. J., eds.,* 1987, pp. 105–14.

Meacci, Sergio. Real Innovation and Implications for Customer Growth. Assessment of Credit and New Services. *Rev. Econ. Cond. Italy,* Sept.-Dec. 1987, (3), pp. 383–415. **[G: Italy]**

Meessen, Karl M. Intellectual Property Rights in International Trade. *J. World Trade Law,* February 1987, *21*(1), pp. 67–74. **[G: OECD]**

Mellor, John W.; Delgado, Christopher L. and Blackie, Malcolm J. Priorities for Accelerating Food Production Growth in Sub-Saharan Africa. *Mellor, J. W.; Delgado, C. L. and Blackie, M. J., eds.,* 1987, pp. 353–75. **[G: Africa]**

Messerlin, Patrick A. International Investment, Protection and Technical Transfer: A Preliminary Examination of the Franco–Japanese Case. *Safarian, A. E. and Bertin, G. Y., eds.,* 1987, pp. 167–79. **[G: France; Japan]**

Metcalfe, J. S. and Gibbons, Michael. On the Economics of Structural Change and the Evolution of Technology. *Pasinetti, L. and Lloyd, P., eds.,* 1987, pp. 91–102.

Miller, Rory. Transferring Techniques: Railway Building and Management on the West Coast of South America. *Dewey, C., ed.,* 1987, pp. 155–91. **[G: Peru; Chile; Bolivia; Argentina]**

Mishra, R. N. Technology Transfer in an Indian Underground Coal-Mine—A Case Study. *Pachauri, R. K., ed.,* 1987, pp. 811–19. **[G: India]**

Mitchell, John C. A State Government's Experience with the Synthetic Fuels Movement: The Case of Kentucky. *Yanarella, E. J. and Green, W. C., eds.,* 1987, pp. 89–98. **[G: U.S.]**

Mody, Ashoka and Wheeler, David. Prices, Costs, and Competition at the Technology Frontier: A Model for Semiconductor Memories. *J. Policy Modeling,* Summer 1987, *9*(2), pp. 367–82. **[G: U.S.]**

Mody, Ashoka and Wheeler, David. Towards a Vanishing Middle: Competition in the World Garment Industry. *World Devel.,* Oct./Nov. 1987, *15*(10/11), pp. 1269–84. **[G: LDCs]**

Mohr, Lawrence B. Innovation Theory: As Assessment from the Vantage Point of the New Electronic Technology in Organizations. *Pennings, J. M. and Buitendam, A., eds.,* 1987, pp. 13–31.

Monkiewicz, Jan. The Theory of the Dominant Economy and East–West Technology Transfer: A Pending Issue. *Konjunkturpolitik,* 1987, *33*(6), pp. 338–56. **[G: OECD; CMEA]**

Moore, Linda K. S. Payments and the Economic Transaction Chain. *Solomon, E. H., ed.,* 1987, pp. 39–62. **[G: U.S.]**

Morgan, Kevin. High Technology Industry and Regional Development: For Wales, See Greater Boston? *Day, G. and Rees, G., eds.,* 1987, pp. 39–51. **[G: U.K.]**

Mosekilde, Erik; Rasmussen, Steen and Zebrowski, Maciej. Technoeconomic Succession and the Economic Long Wave. *Vasko, T., ed.,* 1987, pp. 257–73.

Mudenda, Gilbert N. The Development of a Local Technological Capacity in the SADCC Region. *Amin, S.; Chitala, D. and Mandaza, I., eds.,* 1987, pp. 128–46. **[G: Southern Africa]**

Mullen, John K. and Williams, Martin. Technical Progress in Urban Manufacturing: North–South Comparisons. *J. Urban Econ.,* March 1987, *21*(2), pp. 194–208. **[G: U.S.]**

Mupawose, Robbie M. Potential and Practice in Food Production Technology Development: Commentary. *Mellor, J. W.; Delgado, C. L. and Blackie, M. J., eds.,* 1987, pp. 164–67. **[G: Africa]**

Murphree, Mary C. New Technology nd Office Trdition: The Not-So-Changing World of the Secretary. *Hartmann, H. I., ed.,* 1987, pp. 98–135.

Nakicenovic, Nebojsa. Technological Substitution and Long Waves in the USA. *Vasko, T., ed.,* 1987, pp. 76–103. **[G: U.S.]**

Nell, Edward J. The Rate of Profit and the Choice of Technique in Competitive Conditions. *[Marrama, V.], Vol. 1,* 1987, pp. 449–55.

Nelson, Randy A. Alternative Technological Indices and Factor Demands in the Electric Power Industry. *Energy J.,* July 1987, *8*(3), pp. 135–47. **[G: U.S.]**

Nelson, Randy A. and Wohar, Mark E. Regulation, Scale and Productivity: Reply. *Int. Econ. Rev.,* June 1987, *28*(2), pp. 535–39.

Nelson, Richard R. Innovation and Economic Development Theoretical Retrospect and Prospect. *Katz, J. M., ed.,* 1987, pp. 78–93.

Newton, Walter L. Refining Developments in the Non-OECD Area. *Pachauri, R. K., ed.,* 1987, pp. 291–313. **[G: Global]**

Nijkamp, Peter. New Technology and Regional Development. *Vasko, T., ed.,* 1987, pp. 274–84. **[G: Netherlands]**

November, Andràs. Telecommunications, Transfer of Technology and the Third World. *Hieronymi, O., ed.,* 1987, pp. 169–87. **[G: Global]**

Noyelle, Thierry J. The New Technology and the New Economy: Some Implications for Equal Employment Opportunity. *Hartmann, H. I., ed.*, 1987, pp. 373–94. [G: U.S.]

Offutt, Susan E.; Garcia, Philip and Pinar, Musa. The Distribution of Gains from Technological Advance when Input Quality Varies. *Amer. J. Agr. Econ.*, May 1987, 69(2), pp. 321–27. [G: U.S.]

Offutt, Susan E. and Kuchler, Fred. Issues and Developments in Biotechnology: What's an Economist to Do? *Agr. Econ. Res.*, Winter 1987, 39(1), pp. 25–33. [G: U.S.]

Okada, Katsuya. U.S.–Japan Cooperative Efforts to Protect Intellectual Property Rights. *Finn, R. B., ed.*, 1987, pp. 59–74. [G: U.S.; Japan]

Okimoto, Daniel I. and Saxonhouse, Gary R. The Political Economy of Japan: Technology and the Future of the Economy. *Yamamura, K. and Yasuba, Y., eds.*, 1987, pp. 385–419. [G: Japan]

Opocher, Arrigo. Technical Change in a Neo-Ricardian Model of the Small Open Economy. A Dual Approach. *Econ. Notes*, 1987, (3), pp. 20–36.

Oppermann, Thomas, et al. Rechtsgrundlagen von Technologiepolitik (Insbesondere nach Europarecht und Grundgesetz). (Legal Bases for a Technology Policy [with Particular Reference to European Community Law and German Constitutional Law (Grundgesetz)]. With English summary.) *Lenel, H. O., et al., eds.*, 1987, pp. 209–31. [G: EEC]

Ozawa, Terutomo. Can the Market Alone Manage Structural Upgrading? A Challenge Posed by Economic Interdependence. *Dunning, J. H. and Usui, M., eds.*, 1987, pp. 45–61.

Palladino, Grace. When Militancy Isn't Enough: The Impact of Automation on New York City Building Service Workers, 1934–1970. *Labor Hist.*, Spring 1987, 28(2), pp. 196–220. [G: U.S.]

Palmedo, Philip F. Energy Applications of Microcomputers in Developing Countries. *Ruth, S. R. and Mann, C. K., eds.*, 1987, pp. 49–65. [G: LDCs]

Patel, Pari and Pavitt, Keith. The Elements of British Technological Competitiveness. *Nat. Inst. Econ. Rev.*, November 1987, (122), pp. 72–83. [G: U.K.]

Patel, Pari and Soete, Luc. Technological Trends and Employment in the UK Manufacturing Sectors. *Freeman, C. and Soete, L., eds.*, 1987, pp. 122–68. [G: U.K.]

Pearson, Ruth. Transfer of Technology and Domestic Innovation in the Cement Industry. *Katz, J. M., ed.*, 1987, pp. 352–427. [G: Argentina]

Peck, Francis and Townsend, Alan. The Impact of Technological Change upon the Spatial Pattern of UK Employment within Major Corporations. *Reg. Stud.*, June 1987, 21(3), pp. 225–39. [G: U.K.]

Pelkmans, Jacques. The New Approach to Technical Harmonization and Standardization. *J.*

Common Market Stud., March 1987, 25(3), pp. 249–69. [G: EEC]

Penning de Vries, Frits W. T. and de Wit, Cornelis T. Potential and Practice in Food Production Technology Development: Identifying Technological Potentials. *Mellor, J. W.; Delgado, C. L. and Blackie, M. J., eds.*, 1987, pp. 109–17. [G: Africa]

Pennings, Johannes M. On the Nature of New Technology as Organizational Innovation. *Pennings, J. M. and Buitendam, A., eds.*, 1987, pp. 3–12.

Pennings, Johannes M. Technological Innovations in Manufacturing. *Pennings, J. M. and Buitendam, A., eds.*, 1987, pp. 197–216.

Pérez, Luis Alberto and Pérez y Peniche, José de Jesús. A Summary of the Principal Findings of the Case-Study on the Technological Behaviour of the Mexican Steel Firm Altos Hornos de Mexico. *Katz, J. M., ed.*, 1987, pp. 183–91. [G: Mexico]

Peterson, Kent D. Computerized Instruction, Information Systems, and School Teachers: Labor Relations in Education. *Cornfield, D. B., ed.*, 1987, pp. 135–51. [G: U.S.]

Phillips, Michael J. and Lu, Yao-chi. Impact of Emerging Technologies on Food and Agricultural Productive Capacity. *Amer. J. Agr. Econ.*, May 1987, 69(2), pp. 448–53. [G: U.S.]

Piatier, André. Innovation Patent, Invention Patent, or Both? Towards a Radical Reform of the Patent System. *Kingston, W., ed.*, 1987, pp. 125–55. [G: OECD]

Pietsch, Anna-Jutta; Vogel, Heinrich and Schroeder, Gertrude E. Displacement by Technological Progress in the USSR (Social and Educational Problems and Their Treatment). *Adam, J., ed.*, 1987, pp. 149–70. [G: U.S.S.R.]

Piganiol, Pierre. Intelligence in Science and Technology Policy. *Dedijer, S. and Jéquier, N., eds.*, 1987, pp. 183–96. [G: LDCs]

Pinckney, Thomas C.; Cohen, John M. and Leonard, David K. Kenya's Introduction of Microcomputers to Improve Budgeting and Financial Management in the Ministry of Agriculture. *Ruth, S. R. and Mann, C. K., eds.*, 1987, pp. 67–93. [G: Kenya]

van der Ploeg, Frederick. Growth Cycles, Induced Technical Change, and Perpetual Conflict over the Distribution of Income. *J. Macroecon.*, Winter 1987, 9(1), pp. 1–12.

Plummer, James L. Energy and Environmental Technology Transfer from the United States to India. *Pachauri, R. K., ed.*, 1987, pp. 1193–1200. [G: U.S.; India]

Pohl, Hans. Cooperation between Business and Science in the Third Reich: The Association for the Promotion of German Industry of 1942. *Pohl, H. and Rudolph, B., eds.*, 1987, pp. 65–91. [G: Germany]

Polo, Yolanda. Determinantes empresariales de la adopción de innovaciones: Terminales de teleproceso en el sector bancario español. (With English summary.) *Invest. Econ.*, May 1987, 11(2), pp. 243–60. [G: Spain]

Pushpamma, P. Supplementary Foods in Rural India. *Young, R. H. and MacCormac, C. W., eds.*, 1987, pp. 69–77. **[G: India]**

Quinn, James Brian. The Impacts of Technology in the Services Sector. *Guile, B. R. and Brooks, H., eds.*, 1987, pp. 119–59.

Rada, Juan F. Information Technology and Services. *Giarini, O., ed.*, 1987, pp. 127–71. **[G: U.S.; Canada; W. Europe]**

Rafiquzzaman, M. The Optimal Patent Term under Uncertainty. *Int. J. Ind. Organ.*, June 1987, *5*(2), pp. 233–46.

Rakitskaia, G. The Socioeconomic Nature of Scientific-Technological Progress. *Prob. Econ.*, October 1987, *30*(6), pp. 89–104.

Ramsay, William. Bio-energy and Development Issues. *Pachauri, R. K., ed.*, 1987, pp. 449–66.

Ramsay, William and Lipman-Blumen, Jean. Institutional Issues in Biomass Energy Policy: The No-Man's Land between Agricultural, Forestry, and Energy Policies in Developing Nations. *Pachauri, R. K., ed.*, 1987, pp. 205–15. **[G: LDCs]**

Ray, George F. On Long Cycles: Kondratiev and All That. *Hieronymi, O., ed.*, 1987, pp. 43–52.

Reddy, N. Mohan. Technology, Standards, and Markets: A Market Institutionalization Perspective. *Gabel, H. L., ed.*, 1987, pp. 47–66.

Rees, John. The Diffusion of New Production Technology: Implications for State and Local Industrial Policy. *Goldstein, H. A., ed.*, 1987, pp. 60–72. **[G: U.S.]**

Reimund, Donn and Petrulis, Mindy. Performance of the Agricultural Sector. *U.S.D.A., Econ. Res. Serv., Agr. and Rural Econ. Div.*, 1987, pp. 4.1–30. **[G: U.S.]**

Reinecke, Ian. Wealth and Poverty in the Information Society. *Barr, T., ed.*, 1987, pp. 81–92. **[G: Australia]**

Render, Barry K. and Ruth, Stephen R. The Dilemma of Acquiring Micro-based Software in Developing Countries. *Ruth, S. R. and Mann, C. K., eds.*, 1987, pp. 143–48. **[G: LDCs]**

Rettig, Richard A. Medical Technology in a Changing Health Care Environment. *Meyer, J. A. and Lewin, M. E., eds.*, 1987, pp. 98–117. **[G: U.S.]**

Rietveld, Piet and Nijkamp, Peter. Technological Development and Regional Labour Markets. *Fischer, M. M. and Nijkamp, P., eds.*, 1987, pp. 117–38.

Roberts, Richard. French Colonialism, Imported Technology, and the Handicraft Textile Industry in the Western Sudan, 1898–1918. *J. Econ. Hist.*, June 1987, *47*(2), pp. 461–72. **[G: Sudan]**

Robertson, Thomas S. and Gatignon, Hubert. The Diffusion of High Technology Innovations: A Marketing Perspective. *Pennings, J. M. and Buitendam, A., eds.*, 1987, pp. 179–96.

Rodriguez Romero, Luis. Elasticidad de sustitución entre inputs primarios en las grandes empresas industriales españolas. (With English

summary.) *Invest. Econ.*, September 1987, *11*(3), pp. 399–426. **[G: Spain]**

Rothwell, Roy, et al. Methodological Aspects of Innovation Research: Lessons from a Comparison of Project SAPPHO and FIP. *Teubal, M.*, 1987, pp. 51–75. **[G: Israel]**

Rothwell, Sheila. New Technology and New Supervisory Roles in U.K. Manufacturing Industry. *Child, J. and Bate, P., eds.*, 1987, pp. 123–35. **[G: U.K.]**

Roy, Raghu. Marketing Food and Technologies in Rural India. *Young, R. H. and MacCormac, C. W., eds.*, 1987, pp. 47–56. **[G: India]**

Rozenova, L. Price and the Quality of Machinery. *Prob. Econ.*, January 1987, *29*(9), pp. 79–95. **[G: U.S.S.R.]**

Rudolph, Joseph R., Jr. Synthetic Fuels Abroad: Energy Development in High Energy Dependency Areas. *Yanarella, E. J. and Green, W. C., eds.*, 1987, pp. 173–92. **[G: U.S.; W. Europe]**

Rudra, Ashok. Technology Choice in Agriculture in India over the Past Three Decades. *Stewart, F., ed.*, 1987, pp. 22–73. **[G: India]**

Rugman, Alan M. Strategies for International Competitiveness. *Tremblay, R., ed.*, 1987, pp. 315–25. **[G: U.S.]**

Rully, A. Donald. IBM View of Information Systems: Trends, Issues, and Technology. *Shetty, Y. K. and Buehler, V. M., eds.*, 1987, pp. 183–95. **[G: U.S.]**

Ruth, Stephen R. Technology Sharing Organizations: A Goal-Oriented Approach to More Efficient Solution of Smaller Scale Problems of Development. *Ruth, S. R. and Mann, C. K., eds.*, 1987, pp. 149–58. **[G: LDCs]**

Ruth, Stephen R. and Mann, Charles K. Microcomputers in Public Policy: Applications for Developing Countries: Introduction. *Ruth, S. R. and Mann, C. K., eds.*, 1987, pp. 1–5. **[G: LDCs]**

Sagasti, Francisco R. Techno-economic Intelligence for Development. *Dedijer, S. and Jéquier, N., eds.*, 1987, pp. 173–82. **[G: LDCs]**

Sanderson, Susan Walsh. Automated Manufacturing and Offshore Assembly in Mexico. *Thorup, C. L., ed.*, 1987, pp. 127–48. **[G: Mexico]**

Sanderson, Susan Walsh, et al. Impacts of Computer-Aided Manufacturing on Offshore Assembly and Future Manufacturing Locations. *Reg. Stud.*, April 1987, *21*(2), pp. 131–41. **[G: Mexico; Singapore; U.S.]**

Santarelli, Enrico. The Financial Determinants of Technological Change. An Expository Survey. *Econ. Notes*, 1987, (3), pp. 37–58.

Sava, Dan. Technological Progress—The Basic Factor in the Intensive Development of Industry. *Eastern Europ. Econ.*, Fall 1987, *26*(1), pp. 34–40. **[G: Romania]**

Schilizzi, Steven G. M. Physical Economics, Technology, and Agroecosystems. *Pillet, G. and Murota, T., eds.*, 1987, pp. 109–28. **[G: France; Vietnam]**

Schoenberger, Erica. Technological and Organizational Change in Automobile Production:

Spatial Implications. *Reg. Stud.*, June 1987, *21*(3), pp. 199–214. [G: France]

Schütz, Joachim and Frey, Martin. Zur Arbeitslosigkeit infolge technologischer Revolutionen. (On Unemployment by Technological Revolutions. With English summary.) *Konjunkturpolitik*, 1987, *33*(4), pp. 211–18. [G: OECD]

Schware, Robert and Trembour, Alice. Rethinking Microcomputer Technology Transfer to Third World Countries. *Ruth, S. R. and Mann, C. K., eds.*, 1987, *1985*, pp. 23–37. [G: Tunisia; Egypt]

Schwartz, Arthur R., et al. The Impact of Technological Change on Labor Relations in the Commercial Aircraft Industry. *Cornfield, D. B., ed.*, 1987, pp. 263–80. [G: U.S.]

Seering, Warren. Robotics, Numerical Control and the Computer. *Watanabe, S., ed.*, 1987, pp. 25–40.

Sercovich, Francisco C. Design Engineering and Endogenous Technical Change. *Katz, J. M., ed.*, 1987, pp. 241–80.

Sharma, H. R.; Sharma, S. K. and Singh, Kamlesh. Improved Technology and Returns to Scale—A Study of Marginal Farms. *Margin*, Jan.-Mar. 1987, *19*(2), pp. 83–87. [G: India]

Shepard, Andrea. Licensing to Enhance Demand for New Technologies. *Rand J. Econ.*, Autumn 1987, *18*(3), pp. 360–68.

Shetty, Y. K. and Buehler, Vernon M. Strategies for Gaining Competitive Advantage: An Introduction. *Shetty, Y. K. and Buehler, V. M., eds.*, 1987, pp. 3–9. [G: U.S.]

Shostak, Arthur B. Technology, Air Traffic Control, and Labor–Management Relations. *Cornfield, D. B., ed.*, 1987, pp. 153–72. [G: U.S.]

Silberston, Aubrey. Direct Protection of Innovation: The "Critical" Chapters. *Kingston, W., ed.*, 1987, pp. 201–13.

Silberston, Aubrey. Microelectronics, Automation and Employment in the Automobile Industry: Foreword. *Watanabe, S., ed.*, 1987, pp. xi–xiii.

Silva, Francesco; Ferri, Piero and Enrietti, Aldo. Robots, Employment and Industrial Relations in the Italian Automobile Industry. *Watanabe, S., ed.*, 1987, pp. 131–53. [G: Italy]

Silverberg, Gerald. Technical Progress, Capital Accumulation, and Effective Demand: A Self-organization Model. *Batten, D.; Casti, J. and Johansson, B., eds.*, 1987, pp. 116–44.

Simon, Denis F. Managing Technology in China—Is the Development and Application of Computers the Answer? *Warner, M., ed.*, 1987, pp. 198–216. [G: China]

Smith, Steve. Technical Progress and Economic Development. *Vane, H. and Caslin, T., eds.*, 1987, pp. 265–92. [G: U.K.]

Soete, Luc. Employment, Unemployment and Technical Change: A Review of the Economic Debate. *Freeman, C. and Soete, L., eds.*, 1987, pp. 22–35.

Solomon, Elinor Harris. Electronic Funds Transfers and Payments: The Public Policy Issues: Introduction. *Solomon, E. H., ed.*, 1987, pp. 1–11.

Solomon, Elinor Harris. EFT: A Consumer's View. *Solomon, E. H., ed.*, 1987, pp. 211–37. [G: U.S.]

Sosin, Kim and Fairchild, Loretta. Capital Intensity and Export Propensity in Some Latin American Countries. *Oxford Bull. Econ. Statist.*, May 1987, *49*(2), pp. 191–208. [G: Latin America]

Soulié, Daniel. Technology Transfers in the Automotive Equipment Industry: The French Case. *Safarian, A. E. and Bertin, G. Y., eds.*, 1987, pp. 180–90. [G: France]

Srinivasan, V. K. Development and Transfer of Technology, Oil Exploration, and Production—The Third-World Needs. *Pachauri, R. K., ed.*, 1987, pp. 1167–86. [G: LDCs]

Stageberg, Stephen P. The Impact of Technological Change in the Textile Industry. *Atlantic Econ. J.*, March 1987, *15*(1), pp. 124. [G: U.S.]

Stallmann, Judith I. and Schmid, A. Allan. Property Rights in Plants: Implications for Biotechnology Research and Extension. *Amer. J. Agr. Econ.*, May 1987, *69*(2), pp. 432–37. [G: U.S.]

Starbatty, Joachim. Die ordnungspolitische Dimension der EG-Technologiepolitik. (EC-Technology Policy and the Economic Order. With English summary.) *Lenel, H. O., et al., eds.*, 1987, pp. 155–81. [G: EEC]

Steedman, Hilary and Wagner, Karin. A Second Look at Productivity, Machinery and Skills in Britain and Germany. *Nat. Inst. Econ. Rev.*, November 1987, (122), pp. 84–95. [G: U.K.; W. Germany]

Stefanou, Spiro E. Technical Change, Uncertainty, and Investment. *Amer. J. Agr. Econ.*, February 1987, *69*(1), pp. 158–65.

Steinberg, Gerald M. Science and Politics: The Links between Israel and the European Community. *Greilsammer, I. and Weiler, J. H. H., eds.*, 1987, pp. 337–48. [G: EEC; Israel]

Stewart, Frances. Macro-policies for Appropriate Technology: An Introductory Classification. *Stewart, F., ed.*, 1987, pp. 1–21. [G: LDCs]

Stewart, Frances. Macro-policies for Appropriate Technology in Developing Countries: Overview and Conclusions. *Stewart, F., ed.*, 1987, pp. 271–99. [G: LDCs]

Stewart, Frances. Technical Change in the North: Some Implications for Southern Options. *Pasinetti, L. and Lloyd, P., eds.*, 1987, pp. 27–45. [G: LDCs]

Stewart, William L. Absolute and Relative Trends in U.S. Research and Development Investment. *Faruqui, A. and Broehl, J., eds.*, 1987, pp. 219–46. [G: U.S.]

Stiglitz, Joseph E. Learning to Learn, Localized Learning and Technological Progress. *Dasgupta, P. and Stoneman, P., eds.*, 1987, pp. 125–53.

Stiglitz, Joseph E. On the Microeconomics of Technical Progress. *Katz, J. M., ed.*, 1987, pp. 56–77.

Stolnitz, George J. Technological Prospects and Population Trends: Conclusions. *Espenshade,*

T. and Stolnitz, G. J., eds., 1987, pp. 195–211.

Stoneman, Paul. Some Analytical Observations on Diffusion Policies. *Dasgupta, P. and Stoneman, P., eds.*, 1987, pp. 154–68.

Street, James H. The Technological Frontier in Latin America: Creativity and Productivity. *Dietz, J. L. and Street, J. H., eds.*, 1987, pp. 200–216. **[G: Latin America]**

Strober, Myra H. and Arnold, Carolyn L. Integrated Circuits/Segregated Labor: Women in Computer-Related Occupations and High-Tech Industries. *Hartmann, H. I., ed.*, 1987, pp. 136–82. **[G: U.S.]**

Suarez-Villa, Luis. Entrepreneurship and the International Diffusion of Innovations in Manufacturing: A General Approach. *Rivista Int. Sci. Econ. Com.*, May 1987, *34*(5), pp. 369–91. **[G: Global]**

Succar, Patricia. International Technology Transfer: A Model of Endogenous Technological Assimilation. *J. Devel. Econ.*, August 1987, *26*(2), pp. 375–95. **[G: LDCs]**

Suzuki, Yoshio. Financial Innovation in Japan: Its Origins, Diffusion and Impacts. *de Cecco, M., ed.*, 1987, pp. 229–59. **[G: Japan]**

Sydow, Jörg. Information Technology and Organizational Choice. *Child, J. and Bate, P., eds.*, 1987, pp. 85–100.

Szegö, Giorgio P. Economic Factors Affecting the Development of Alternative Energy Sources. *Maillet, P.; Hague, D. and Rowland, C., eds.*, 1987, pp. 146–82.

Tauile, José Ricardo. Microelectronics and the Internationalization of the Brazilian Automobile Industry. *Watanabe, S., ed.*, 1987, pp. 155–80. **[G: Brazil]**

Taylor, T. Ajibola. Potential and Practice in Food Production Technology Development: Commentary. *Mellor, J. W.; Delgado, C. L. and Blackie, M. J., eds.*, 1987, pp. 161–64. **[G: Africa]**

Tchijov, Iouri and Sytchova, Irene. Technological Progress Analysis: Some Input–Output Approaches. *Tchijov, I. and Tomaszewicz, L., eds.*, 1987, pp. 59–65. **[G: Japan]**

Teece, David J. Capturing Value from Technological Innovation: Integration, Strategic Partnering, and Licensing Decisions. *Guile, B. R. and Brooks, H., eds.*, 1987, pp. 65–95.

Teitel, Simón. Towards an Understanding of Technical Change in Semi-industrialized Countries. *Katz, J. M., ed.*, 1987, pp. 94–115.

Teitel, Simón. Towards Conceptualisation of Technological Development as an Evolutionary Process. *Dunning, J. H. and Usui, M., eds.*, 1987, pp. 157–73. **[G: LDCs]**

Tell, Björn. Scientific and Technical Information: Sweden and Malaysia. *Dedijer, S. and Jéquier, N., eds.*, 1987, pp. 128–38. **[G: Sweden; Malaysia]**

Teubal, Morris. Innovation and Development: A Review of Some Work at the IDB/ECLA/UNDP Programme. *Katz, J. M., ed.*, 1987, pp. 481–98. **[G: Latin America]**

Teubal, Morris. On User Needs and Need Determination: Aspects of the Theory of Technological Innovation. *Teubal, M.*, 1987, pp. 76–96.

Teubal, Morris. The Accumulation of Intangibles by High-Technology Firms. *Teubal, M.*, 1987, pp. 153–72.

Teubal, Morris. The Engineering Sector in a Model of Economic Development. *Teubal, M.*, 1987, pp. 280–94.

Teubal, Morris. The Role of Technological Learning in the Exports of Manufactured Goods: The Case of Selected Capital Goods in Brazil. *Teubal, M.*, 1987, pp. 104–30. **[G: Brazil]**

Teubal, Morris; Arnon, Naftali and Trachtenberg, Manuel. Performance in Innovation in the Israeli Electronics Industry: A Case Study of Biomedical Electronics Instrumentation. *Teubal, M.*, 1987, pp. 10–31. **[G: Israel]**

Teubal, Morris and Steinmueller, Edward. Government Policy, Innovation, and Economic Growth: A Study of Satellite Communications. *Teubal, M.*, 1987, pp. 233–58. **[G: U.S.]**

Teubal, Morris and Steinmueller, Edward. The Introduction of a Major New Technology: Externalities and Government Policy. *Teubal, M.*, 1987, pp. 259–79.

Thompson, Grahame. Unemployment and Technology. *Thompson, G.; Brown, V. and Levačić, R., eds.*, 1987, pp. 134–60. **[G: U.K.]**

Thomson, Ross. Learning by Selling and Invention: The Case of the Sewing Machine. *J. Econ. Hist.*, June 1987, *47*(2), pp. 433–45. **[G: U.S.]**

Thorup, Cathryn L. The United States and Mexico: Face to Face with New Technology. *Thorup, C. L., ed.*, 1987, pp. 1–24. **[G: U.S.; Mexico]**

Tiffin, Scott; Adjebeng-Asem, Selina and Afolabi, Oladele. Technological Innovation and Technical Entrepreneurship for the Development of a Nigerian Agricultural Machinery Industry. *World Devel.*, March 1987, *15*(3), pp. 387–98. **[G: Nigeria]**

Tobin, James. Monetary Rules and Control in Brave New World. *Solomon, E. H., ed.*, 1987, pp. 137–57.

Tucci, Marco P. Flexible Functional Forms and the Simultanaeous Estimation of Embodied and Disembodied Technical Progress. *Econ. Notes*, 1987, (2), pp. 102–20.

Tullock, Gordon. Intellectual Property. *Kingston, W., ed.*, 1987, pp. 171–99. **[G: U.S.]**

Tuma, Elias H. Technology Transfer and Economic Development: Lessons of History. *J. Devel. Areas*, July 1987, *21*(4), pp. 403–27. **[G: Middle East]**

Tweeten, Luther and Welsh, Mike. The Economics of Agricultural Biotechnology: Discussion. *Amer. J. Agr. Econ.*, May 1987, *69*(2), pp. 440–42. **[G: U.S.]**

Tyner, Wallace E. A Comparative Evaluation of Selected Renewable Energy Technologies in China, India, West Africa and Brazil. *Pachauri, R. K., ed.*, 1987, pp. 217–26. **[G: China; India; W. Africa; Brazil]**

Uekusa, Masu. The Political Economy of Japan: Industrial Organization: The 1970s to the Present. *Yamamura, K. and Yasuba, Y., eds.*, 1987, pp. 469–515. **[G: Japan]**

Usui, Mikoto. Technological Development and Economic Interdependence: Introduction. *Dunning, J. H. and Usui, M., eds.*, 1987, pp. 83–94. **[G: LDCs]**

Utterback, James M. Innovation and Industrial Evolution in Manufacturing Industries. *Guile, B. R. and Brooks, H., eds.*, 1987, pp. 16–48.

Vakil, C. N. and Brahmananda, P. R. Technical Knowledge and Managerial Capacity as Limiting Factors on Industrial Expansion in Underdeveloped Countries. *Dupriez, L. H., ed.*, 1987, *1955*, pp. 153–72.

Valenta, František. Intensive Development of Socialist Economy. (The Evolution of Theoretical Approach) *Czech. Econ. Pap.*, 1987, (24), pp. 7–33. **[G: Czechoslovakia]**

Vallaeys, Guy, et al. Development and Extension of Agricultural Production Technology. *Mellor, J. W.; Delgado, C. L. and Blackie, M. J., eds.*, 1987, pp. 148–60. **[G: Africa]**

Vernon, Raymond. Coping with Technological Change: U.S. Problems and Prospects. *Guile, B. R. and Brooks, H., eds.*, 1987, pp. 160–90. **[G: U.S.]**

Vietor, Richard H. K. Business, Government, and Markets: Synthetic Fuels Policy in America. *Yanarella, E. J. and Green, W. C., eds.*, 1987, pp. 3–32. **[G: U.S.]**

Viniegra Gonzalez, Gustavo. Generating and Disseminating Technology. *Austin, J. E. and Esteva, G., eds.*, 1987, pp. 133–47.
[G: Mexico]

Vitelli, Guillermo. Technological Change, Market Structure and Employment in the Argentine Construction Industry. *Katz, J. M., ed.*, 1987, pp. 318–51. **[G: Argentina]**

Vitzthum, Wolfgang Graf. Technologietransfer und Technologieembargo im Völkerrecht. (Technology Transfer and Technology Embargo in International Law. With English summary.) *Lenel, H. O., et al., eds.*, 1987, pp. 233–63. **[G: Global]**

Vodáček, Leo. Strategic Management of Innovation in Large Czechoslovak Firms. *Child, J. and Bate, P., eds.*, 1987, pp. 103–11.
[G: Czechoslovakia]

Wagner, Joachim and Bellmann, Lutz. Produkt- und Prozessinnovationen als Unternehmensstrategien bei Importdruck. Eine ökonometrische Untersuchung für Industrien des Verarbeitenden Gewerbes in der Bundesrepublik Deutschland (1976–1983). (Product and Process Innovations: Strategies for Firms under Import Pressure. An Econometric Study for Manufacturing Industries in the Federal Republic of Germany [1976–1983]. With English summary.) *Ifo-Studien*, 1987, *33*(3), pp. 223–42. **[G: W. Germany]**

Wanmali, Sudhir. Agriculture and Central Physical Grid Infrastructure: Commentary. *Mellor, J. W.; Delgado, C. L. and Blackie, M. J., eds.*, 1987, pp. 227–32. **[G: Africa]**

Ward, Geoffrey Layzell. Information Technology

Policy in Western Australia. *Barr, T., ed.*, 1987, pp. 126–34. **[G: Australia]**

Watanabe, Susumu. Flexible Automation and Labour Productivity in the Japanese Automobile Industry. *Watanabe, S., ed.*, 1987, pp. 41–77. **[G: Japan]**

Watanabe, Susumu. Microelectronics and Rationalization of the French Automobile Industry. *Watanabe, S., ed.*, 1987, pp. 107–29.
[G: France]

Watanabe, Susumu. Microelectronics, Automation and Employment in the Automobile Industry: Introduction. *Watanabe, S., ed.*, 1987, pp. 1–24. **[G: Selected Countries]**

Watanabe, Susumu. Microelectronics, Automation and Employment in the Automobile Industry: A Synthesis of Findings. *Watanabe, S., ed.*, 1987, pp. 181–97.
[G: Selected Countries]

Webber, M. J. and Tonkin, S. Technical Changes and the Rate of Profit in the Canadian Food Industry. *Environ. Planning A*, December 1987, *19*(12), pp. 1579–96. **[G: Canada]**

Wescott, Clay G. Microcomputers for Improved Government Budgeting: An Africa Experience. *Ruth, S. R. and Mann, C. K., eds.*, 1987, pp. 95–116. **[G: Kenya]**

Westin, Alan F. Technological Change and the Constitution: Preserving the Framers' Balances in a Computer Age. *Marshall, B., ed.*, 1987, pp. 189–207. **[G: U.S.]**

Wilbanks, Thomas J. Prospects of Synthetic Fuels in the United States: Past Lessons and Future Requirements. *Yanarella, E. J. and Green, W. C., eds.*, 1987, pp. 193–211. **[G: U.S.]**

Willis, Sabrina. The Synthetic Fuels Corporation as an Organizational Failure in Policy Mobilization. *Yanarella, E. J. and Green, W. C., eds.*, 1987, pp. 71–87. **[G: U.S.]**

Wolek, Francis W. Support Structures for Technology Transfer in Agriculture. *Ruttan, V. W. and Pray, C. E., eds.*, 1987, pp. 451–67.
[G: U.S.]

Wozniak, Gregory D. Human Capital, Information, and the Early Adoption of New Technology. *J. Human Res.*, Winter 1987, *22*(1), pp. 101–12. **[G: U.S.]**

Wright, Brian D. On the Design of a System to Improve the Production of Innovations. *Kingston, W., ed.*, 1987, pp. 227–46.

Yakovets, Yu. V. Scientific and Technological Cycles: Program- and Aim-Oriented Planning. *Vasko, T., ed.*, 1987, pp. 285–94.

Yanarella, Ernest J. and Green, William C. The Unfulfilled Promise of Synthetic Fuels: Technological Failure, Policy Immobilism, or Commercial Illusion: Preface. *Yanarella, E. J. and Green, W. C., eds.*, 1987, pp. xiii–xxii.
[G: U.S.]

Yang, Mu. The New Technological Revolution and the Technological Progress in Industries. *Chinese Econ. Stud.*, Summer 1987, *20*(4), pp. 50–67. **[G: China]**

Ye, Yuansheng. The World Technological Revolution and China's Policy of Technological Innovation. *Chinese Econ. Stud.*, Summer 1987, *20*(4), pp. 68–80. [G: China]

Yu, Eden S. H. Inter-industrial Externalities, Technical Progress and Welfare. *Southern Econ. J.*, October 1987, *54*(2), pp. 412–21.

Zimmermann, Klaus F. Innovations, Market Structure, and Market Dynamics: Reply. *J. Inst. Theoretical Econ.*, September 1987, *143*(3), pp. 505–08. [G: W. Germany]

6212 Research and Development

Achi, Peter B.U. Developing Local Industry through Centres for Industrial Studies in Tertiary Institutions in Developing Countries. *Industry Devel.*, 1987, (21), pp. 99–109. [G: LDCs]

Adam, M. C. and Farber, A. Le financement de l'innovation technologique. Première partie: Les caractéristiques de l'investissement novateur. (With English summary.) *Cah. Écon. Bruxelles*, Fourth Trimester 1987, (116), pp. 3–23. [G: Belgium]

Albach, Horst. Die Führung eines forschenden Unternehmens Die Erfolgsstory der Schering AG. (With English summary.) *Z. Betriebswirtshaft*, November 1987, *57*(11), pp. 1069–89. [G: W. Germany; Japan]

Albrecht, Ulrich. The Current Warfare/Welfare Alternative and the Evidence from Technology. *Schmidt, C. and Blackaby, F., eds.*, 1987, pp. 233–49.

Alves, Eliseu. Mobilizing Political Support for the Brazilian Agricultural Research System. *Ruttan, V. W. and Pray, C. E., eds.*, 1987, pp. 363–76. [G: Brazil]

Antonelli, Cristiano. The Determinants of the Distribution of Innovative Activity in a Metropolitan Area: The Case of Turin. *Reg. Stud.*, April 1987, *21*(2), pp. 85–93. [G: Italy]

Ashton, Peter K. Some Economic Effects of Standards—Comment [Some Economic Effects of Standards]. *Appl. Econ.*, November 1987, *19*(11), pp. 1515–19. [G: Canada]

Autenne, J. Tax Incentives for Scientific Research Activities: Belgium. *Bull. Int. Fiscal Doc.*, Aug.-Sept. 1987, *41*(8–9), pp. 407–09. [G: Belgium]

Averch, Harvey A. Measuring the Cost-Efficiency Basic Research Investment: Input–Output Approaches. *J. Policy Anal. Manage.*, Spring 1987, *6*(3), pp. 342–61. [G: U.S.]

Barber, John and White, Geoff. Current Policy Practice and Problems from a UK Perspective. *Dasgupta, P. and Stoneman, P., eds.*, 1987, pp. 24–50. [G: U.K.]

Bartel, Ann P. and Lichtenberg, Frank R. The Comparative Advantage of Educated Workers in Implementing New Technology. *Rev. Econ. Statist.*, February 1987, *69*(1), pp. 1–11.

Blackaby, Frank and Ohlson, Thomas. Military Expenditure and the Arms Trade: Problems' of the Data. *Schmidt, C., ed.*, 1987, pp. 3–24. [G: Global]

Bonnen, James T. A Century of Science in Agriculture: Lessons for Science Policy. *Ruttan,*

V. W. and Pray, C. E., eds., 1987, pp. 105–37. [G: U.S.]

Brockhoff, Klaus. Budgetierungsstrategien für Forschung und Entwicklung. (With English summary.) *Z. Betriebswirtshaft*, September 1987, *57*(9), pp. 846–69.

Brockhoff, Klaus. Die Produktivität der Forschung und Entwicklung eines Industrieunternehmens: Eine Erwiderung. (With English summary.) *Z. Betriebswirtshaft*, January 1987, *57*(1), pp. 81–85. [G: W. Germany]

Brunel, Andre and Burke, Michael P. Promoting High-Technology Industry: Initiatives and Policies for State Governments: Pennsylvania. *Schmandt, J. and Wilson, R., eds.*, 1987, pp. 191–229. [G: U.S.]

Burke, Michael P. and Dowling, Michael. Promoting High-Technology Industry: Initiatives and Policies for State Governments: Introduction. *Schmandt, J. and Wilson, R., eds.*, 1987, pp. 1–10. [G: U.S.]

Čengić, Drago. The Social Frame of Innovation: The Example of Yugoslavia. *Child, J. and Bate, P., eds.*, 1987, pp. 163–71. [G: Yugoslavia]

Cheng, Leonard K. Optimal Trade and Technology Policies: Dynamic Linkages. *Int. Econ. Rev.*, October 1987, *28*(3), pp. 757–76.

Clark, Kim B.; Chew, W. Bruce and Fujimoto, Takahiro. Product Development in the World Auto Industry. *Brookings Pap. Econ. Act.*, 1987, (3), pp. 729–71. [G: Global]

Cohen, Wesley M.; Levin, Richard C. and Mowery, David C. Firm Size and R&D Intensity: A Re-examination. *J. Ind. Econ.*, June 1987, *35*(4), pp. 543–65. [G: U.S.]

Crosby, Edwin A. Private Sector Agricultural Research in the United States. *Ruttan, V. W. and Pray, C. E., eds.*, 1987, pp. 395–409. [G: U.S.]

Crow, Michael M. and Bozeman, Barry L. A New Typology for R&D Laboratories: Implications for Policy Analysts. *J. Policy Anal. Manage.*, Spring 1987, *6*(3), pp. 328–41. [G: U.S.]

Dasgupta, Partha. The Economic Theory of Technology Policy: An Introduction. *Dasgupta, P. and Stoneman, P., eds.*, 1987, pp. 7–23.

Dasgupta, Partha and Stoneman, Paul. Economic Policy and Technological Performance: Introduction. *Dasgupta, P. and Stoneman, P., eds.*, 1987, pp. 1–6.

Delbono, Flavio. Barriere multiple all'entrata. (Multiple Entry Deterrence. With English summary.) *Giorn. Econ.*, Jan.-Feb. 1987, *46*(1–2), pp. 29–54.

Deutsch, Edwin. Efficiency, Industry and Alternative Weapons Procurement Policies: Note. *Schmidt, C., ed.*, 1987, pp. 301–03. [G: U.S.; EEC]

Deutsch, Edwin and Schöpp, Wolfgang. Civil versus Military R&D Expenditures and Industrial Productivity. *Schmidt, C., ed.*, 1987, pp. 336–56. [G: OECD]

Dowling, Michael. Science and Technology Policy: Present Developments and Future Trends.

Schmandt, J. and Wilson, R., eds., 1987, pp. 259–69. **[G: U.S.]**

Doz, Yves. International Industries: Fragmentation versus Globalization. *Guile, B. R. and Brooks, H., eds.*, 1987, pp. 96–118.

Duncan, Joseph W. The Importance of Entrepreneurs and Small Business in the Economy of the United States. *Faruqui, A. and Broehl, J., eds.*, 1987, pp. 247–56. **[G: U.S.]**

Dzis', G.; Lysenkov, Iu. and Rymaruk, A. Consumer Goods Production and Scientific–Technological Progress. *Prob. Econ.*, June 1987, 30(2), pp. 71–83. **[G: U.S.S.R.]**

Eckel, Russel. Industrial Relations and High Technology: The Transformation of Telecommunications through Deregulation. *Child, J. and Bate, P., eds.*, 1987, pp. 173–89. **[G: U.S.]**

Elliott, Howard. The Use of Events Analysis in Evaluating National Research Systems. *Ruttan, V. W. and Pray, C. E., eds.*, 1987, pp. 377–87. **[G: Panama]**

Ergas, Henry. Does Technology Policy Matter? *Guile, B. R. and Brooks, H., eds.*, 1987, pp. 191–245. **[G: U.K.; U.S.; France; Japan]**

Ergas, Henry. The Importance of Technology Policy. *Dasgupta, P. and Stoneman, P., eds.*, 1987, pp. 51–96. **[G: OECD]**

Etzioni, Amitai. U.S. Technological, Economic, and Social Development for the 21st Century. *Nagel, S. S., ed.*, 1987, pp. 241–70. **[G: U.S.]**

Evenson, Robert E.; Evenson, Donald D. and Putnam, Jonathan D. Private Sector Agricultural Invention in Developing Countries. *Ruttan, V. W. and Pray, C. E., eds.*, 1987, pp. 469–511.

Evstigneev, Ruben. State Scientific and Technological Policy and Incentives for Enterprises. *Saunders, C. T., ed.*, 1987, pp. 119–28. **[G: U.S.S.R.]**

Fel'zenbaum, V. and Shapovalova, E. Material Incentives and the Economic Effect of New Technology. *Prob. Econ.*, August 1987, 30(4), pp. 79–94. **[G: U.S.S.R.]**

Feller, Irwin. Technology Transfer, Public Policy, and the Cooperative Extension Service. *Ruttan, V. W. and Pray, C. E., eds.*, 1987, pp. 175–210. **[G: U.S.]**

Fischer, Harald and Peck, Amy Miriam. Promoting High-Technology Industry: Initiatives and Policies for State Governments: New York. *Schmandt, J. and Wilson, R., eds.*, 1987, pp. 129–62. **[G: U.S.]**

Fischer, Karl-Heinz. Die produktivität der Forschung und Entwicklung eines Industrieunternehmens: Ein Kommentar. (With English summary.) *Z. Betriebswirtshaft*, January 1987, 57(1), pp. 77–80. **[G: W. Germany]**

Flam, Harry and Helpman, Elhanan. Industrial Policy under Monopolistic Competition. *J. Int. Econ.*, February 1987, 22(1/2), pp. 79–102.

Fontanel, Jacques. Military Expenditure and the Arms Trade: Problems of the Data: Note. *Schmidt, C., ed.*, 1987, pp. 25–28. **[G: Global]**

Fox, Glenn. Models of Resource Allocation in Public Agricultural Research: A Survey. *J. Agr. Econ.*, September 1987, 38(3), pp. 449–62.

Freudenberg, Michael and Henderson, Tracy L. Promoting High-Technology Industry: Initiatives and Policies for State Governments: Florida. *Schmandt, J. and Wilson, R., eds.*, 1987, pp. 35–64. **[G: U.S.]**

Ghiselin, Michael T. The Economics of Scientific Discovery. *Radnitzky, G. and Bernholz, P., eds.*, 1987, pp. 271–82.

Gilbert, Richard J. Appropriating the Returns from Industrial Research and Development: Comments and Discussion. *Brookings Pap. Econ. Act.*, 1987, (3), pp. 821–24. **[G: U.S.]**

Grabowski, Henry G. and Vernon, John M. Pioneers, Imitators, and Generics—A Simulation Model of Schumpeterian Competition. *Quart. J. Econ.*, August 1987, 102(3), pp. 491–525. **[G: U.S.]**

Griliches, Zvi. Appropriating the Returns from Industrial Research and Development: Comments and Discussion. *Brookings Pap. Econ. Act.*, 1987, (3), pp. 824–29. **[G: U.S.]**

Griliches, Zvi; Pakes, Ariel and Hall, Bronwyn H. The Value of Patents as Indicators of Inventive Activity. *Dasgupta, P. and Stoneman, P., eds.*, 1987, pp. 97–124. **[G: U.S.]**

Grossman, Gene M. and Shapiro, Carl. Dynamic R&D Competition. *Econ. J.*, June 1987, 97(386), pp. 372–87.

Hacker, Sidney Bailey and Sommerfeld, Robert D. Promoting High-Technology Industry: Initiatives and Policies for State Governments: Minnesota. *Schmandt, J. and Wilson, R., eds.*, 1987, pp. 97–127. **[G: U.S.]**

Hartley, Keith. Efficiency, Industry and Alternative Weapons Procurement Policies. *Schmidt, C., ed.*, 1987, pp. 283–300. **[G: U.S.; EEC]**

Heichel, Gary H. Anticipating Advances in Crop Technology. *Ruttan, V. W. and Pray, C. E., eds.*, 1987, pp. 235–44. **[G: U.S.]**

Heim, Carol E. R&D, Defense, and Spatial Divisions of Labor in Twentieth-Century Britain. *J. Econ. Hist.*, June 1987, 47(2), pp. 365–78. **[G: U.K.]**

Herdt, Robert W. and Anderson, Jock R. The Contribution of the CGIAR Centers to World Agricultural Research. *Ruttan, V. W. and Pray, C. E., eds.*, 1987, pp. 39–64. **[G: Global]**

Hicks, Donald A. Geo-Industrial Shifts in Advanced Metropolitan Economies. *Urban Stud.*, December 1987, 24(6), pp. 460–79. **[G: U.S.]**

Hirsch, Barry T. and Link, Albert N. Labor Union Effects on Innovative Activity. *J. Lab. Res.*, Fall 1987, 8(4), pp. 323–32. **[G: U.S.]**

Howard, Mark and Kragie, Mary. Promoting High-Technology Industry: Initiatives and Policies for State Governments: North Carolina. *Schmandt, J. and Wilson, R., eds.*, 1987, pp. 163–90. **[G: U.S.]**

Idachaba, Francis S. Agricultural Research in Nigeria: Organization and Policy. *Ruttan, V. W.*

and Pray, C. E., eds., 1987, pp. 333–62.
[G: Nigeria]

Jacquemin, Alexis. Comportements collusifs et accords en recherche-développement. (With English summary.) *Revue Écon. Polit.*, Jan.-Feb. 1987, 97(1), pp. 1–23.

James, Dilmus D. The Economics of Technological Progress: A Comparison of Non-institutionalist and Institutionalist Dissent from the Neoclassical Position. *J. Econ. Issues*, June 1987, 21(2), pp. 733–41.

Jensen, Elizabeth J. Research Expenditures and the Discovery of New Drugs. *J. Ind. Econ.*, September 1987, 36(1), pp. 83–95. [G: U.S.]

Jensen, Richard and Thursby, Marie C. A Decision Theoretic Model of Innovation, Technology Transfer, and Trade. *Rev. Econ. Stud.*, October 1987, 54(4), pp. 631–47.

Judd, M. Ann; Boyce, James K. and Evenson, Robert E. Investment in Agricultural Research and Extension. *Ruttan, V. W. and Pray, C. E., eds.*, 1987, pp. 7–38. [G: Global]

Justman, Moshe and Teubal, Morris. Innovation Policy in an Open Economy: A Normative Framework for Strategic and Tactical Issues. *Teubal, M.*, 1987, pp. 204–32.

Katz, Michael L. and Shapiro, Carl. R&D Rivalry with Licensing or Imitation. *Amer. Econ. Rev.*, June 1987, 77(3), pp. 402–20.

King, Alexander. Science, Technology and International Relations: Some Comments and a Speculation. *Hieronymi, O., ed.*, 1987, pp. 9–24.

Kleinknecht, Alfred. Measuring R&D in Small Firms: How Much Are We Missing? *J. Ind. Econ.*, December 1987, 36(2), pp. 253–56.
[G: OECD]

Krajewski, Stefan. Constraints on the Options for Technological Development Strategies of Economic Organizations: Strategies of Technological Progress of Economic Organizations. *Eastern Europ. Econ.*, Fall 1987, 26(1), pp. 72–87. [G: Poland]

Kumar, Nagesh. Technology Imports and Local Research and Development in Indian Manufacturing. *Devel. Econ.*, September 1987, 25(3), pp. 220–33. [G: India]

Le, Can D. The Role of R&D in High-Technology Trade: An Empirical Analysis. *Atlantic Econ. J.*, December 1987, 15(4), pp. 32–38.
[G: OECD]

Levin, Richard C., et al. Appropriating the Returns from Industrial Research and Development. *Brookings Pap. Econ. Act.*, 1987, (3), pp. 783–820. [G: U.S.]

Lichtenberg, Frank R. Changing Market Opportunities and the Structure of R&D Investment: The Case of Energy. *Energy Econ.*, July 1987, 9(3), pp. 154–58. [G: U.S.]

Lichtenberg, Frank R. The Effect of Government Funding on Private Industrial Research and Development: A Re-assessment. *J. Ind. Econ.*, September 1987, 36(1), pp. 97–104.
[G: U.S.]

Lieberman, Marvin B. Patents, Learning by Doing, and Market Structure in the Chemical Processing Industries. *Int. J. Ind. Organ.*, September 1987, 5(3), pp. 257–76. [G: U.S.]

Lipman-Blumen, Jean. Priority Setting in Agricultural Research. *Ruttan, V. W. and Pray, C. E., eds.*, 1987, pp. 139–73. [G: U.S.]

Lippman, Steven A. and McCardle, Kevin F. Dropout Behavior in R&D Races with Learning. *Rand J. Econ.*, Summer 1987, 18(2), pp. 287–95.

Lockett, Martin. Technical Innovation and Economic Reform in Socialist Economies with Special Reference to China. *Child, J. and Bate, P., eds.*, 1987, pp. 191–203. [G: China]

Luiselli Fernández, Cassio. Biotechnology and Food: The Scope for Cooperation. *Thorup, C. L., ed.*, 1987, pp. 167–85. [G: Mexico; U.S.]

Lunn, John. An Empirical Analysis of Firm Process and Product Patenting. *Appl. Econ.*, June 1987, 19(6), pp. 743–51. [G: U.S.]

Madeuf, Bernadette. Trends in Technological Competitiveness within the OECD, 1970–80. *Safarian, A. E. and Bertin, G. Y., eds.*, 1987, pp. 34–52. [G: OECD]

Maier, Harry. Basic Innovations and the Next Long Wave of Productivity Growth: Socioeconomic Implications and Consequences. *Vasko, T., ed.*, 1987, pp. 46–65.

Manilay, Alessandro A. Market Research for Grain Postharvest Systems. *Young, R. H. and MacCormac, C. W., eds.*, 1987, pp. 31–37.

McFadden, Daniel L. Technological Change, Sunk Costs, and Competition: Comments and Discussion. *Brookings Pap. Econ. Act.*, 1987, (3), pp. 938–41.

McMahon, Walter W. The Relation of Education and R&D to Productivity Growth in the Developing Countries of Africa. *Econ. Educ. Rev.*, 1987, 6(2), pp. 183–94. [G: Africa]

Meacci, Sergio. Real Innovation and Implications for Customer Growth. Assessment of Credit and New Services. *Rev. Econ. Cond. Italy*, Sept.-Dec. 1987, (3), pp. 383–415. [G: Italy]

Merrigan, Kathleen A. and Smith, Suzanne E. Promoting High-Technology Industry: Initiatives and Policies for State Governments: Massachusetts. *Schmandt, J. and Wilson, R., eds.*, 1987, pp. 65–96. [G: U.S.]

Meyer, John R. Product Development in the World Auto Industry: Comments and Discussion. *Brookings Pap. Econ. Act.*, 1987, (3), pp. 772–76.

Muller, Brian and Dowling, Michael. Promoting High-Technology Industry: Initiatives and Policies for State Governments: Texas. *Schmandt, J. and Wilson, R., eds.*, 1987, pp. 231–57.
[G: U.S.]

Muto, Shigeo. Possibility of Relicensing and Patent Protection. *Europ. Econ. Rev.*, June 1987, 31(4), pp. 927–45.

Nelson, Richard R. Roles of Government in a Mixed Economy. *J. Policy Anal. Manage.*, Summer 1987, 6(4), pp. 541–57.

Noyce, Robert N. Intel's Leader Looks at the Computer Evolution in the 21st Century. *Shetty, Y. K. and Buehler, V. M., eds.*, 1987, pp. 223–34. [G: U.S.]

Oberender, Peter and Rüter, Georg. Innovationsförderung: Einige grundsätzliche ordnungspolitische Bemerkungen. (Some Principal Remarks on Policies to Promote Innovation. With English summary.) *Lenel, H. O., et al., eds.*, 1987, pp. 143–54. **[G: W. Germany]**

Okimoto, Daniel I. and Saxonhouse, Gary R. The Political Economy of Japan: Technology and the Future of the Economy. *Yamamura, K. and Yasuba, Y., eds.*, 1987, pp. 385–419. **[G: Japan]**

Oppermann, Thomas, et al. Rechtsgrundlagen von Technologiepolitik (Insbesondere nach Europarecht und Grundgesetz). (Legal Bases for a Technology Policy [with Particular Reference to European Community Law and German Constitutional Law (Grundgesetz)]. With English summary.) *Lenel, H. O., et al., eds.*, 1987, pp. 209–31. **[G: EEC]**

Pavitt, Keith; Robson, Michael and Townsend, Joe. The Size Distribution of Innovating Firms in the UK: 1945–1983. *J. Ind. Econ.*, March 1987, 35(3), pp. 297–316. **[G: U.K.]**

Peltzman, Sam. Technological Change, Sunk Costs, and Competition: Comments and Discussion. *Brookings Pap. Econ. Act.*, 1987, (3), pp. 941–46.

Phillips, Almarin. Measuring the Cost-Efficiency Basic Research Investment: Input–Output Approaches: A Comment. *J. Policy Anal. Manage.*, Spring 1987, 6(3), pp. 362–64. **[G: U.S.]**

Piganiol, Pierre. Intelligence in Science and Technology Policy. *Dedijer, S. and Jéquier, N., eds.*, 1987, pp. 183–96. **[G: LDCs]**

Pohl, Hans. Cooperation between Business and Science in the Third Reich: The Association for the Promotion of German Industry of 1942. *Pohl, H. and Rudolph, B., eds.*, 1987, pp. 65–91. **[G: Germany]**

Pray, Carl E. Private Sector Agricultural Research in Asia. *Ruttan, V. W. and Pray, C. E., eds.*, 1987, pp. 411–31. **[G: Asia]**

Radnitzky, Gerard. Cost–Benefit Thinking in the Methodology of Research: The "Economic Approach" Applied to Key Problems of the Philosophy of Science. *Radnitzky, G. and Bernholz, P., eds.*, 1987, pp. 283–331.

Reich, Leonard S. Edison, Coolidge, and Langmuir: Evolving Approaches to American Industrial Research. *J. Econ. Hist.*, June 1987, 47(2), pp. 341–51. **[G: U.S.]**

Rogers, J. S. Some Long-term Impacts of $(US)15 Oil on Energy Policy and on Engineering R&D Policy: Results from the EMCAN Model. *Can. Public Policy*, March 1987, 13(1), pp. 41–48. **[G: Canada]**

Rothwell, Roy, et al. Methodological Aspects of Innovation Research: Lessons from a Comparison of Project SAPPHO and FIP. *Teubal, M.*, 1987, pp. 51–75. **[G: Israel]**

Rozek, Richard P. Protection of Intellectual Property Rights: Research and Development Decisions and Economic Growth. *Contemp. Policy Issues*, July 1987, 5(3), pp. 54–65. **[G: LDCs]**

Ruttan, Vernon W. Toward a Global Agricultural Research System. *Ruttan, V. W. and Pray, C. E., eds.*, 1987, pp. 65–97.

Sah, Raaj Kumar and Stiglitz, Joseph E. The Invariance of Market Innovation to the Number of Firms. *Rand J. Econ.*, Spring 1987, 18(1), pp. 98–108.

Sarnat, Marshall. On the Use of Risk Analysis for the Evaluation of Industrial R&D Expenditures. *Managerial Dec. Econ.*, September 1987, 8(3), pp. 255–58.

Sauer, Richard J. and Pray, Carl E. Mobilizing Support for Agricultural Research at the Minnesota Agricultural Experiment Station. *Ruttan, V. W. and Pray, C. E., eds.*, 1987, pp. 211–33. **[G: U.S.]**

Scanlon, Jack M. AT&T Projects the Fourth Era of Computing. *Shetty, Y. K. and Buehler, V. M., eds.*, 1987, pp. 235–44. **[G: U.S.]**

Scherer, F. M. Product Development in the World Auto Industry: Comments and Discussion. *Brookings Pap. Econ. Act.*, 1987, (3), pp. 776–79.

Schmidt, Christian. Alternative Approaches to the Arms Industry: Some Suggestions for a Research Programme. *Borner, S. and Taylor, A., eds.*, 1987, pp. 255–63.

Schwartz, Arthur R., et al. The Impact of Technological Change on Labor Relations in the Commercial Aircraft Industry. *Cornfield, D. B., ed.*, 1987, pp. 263–80. **[G: U.S.]**

Scott, John T. and Pascoe, George. Purposive Diversification of R&D in Manufacturing. *J. Ind. Econ.*, December 1987, 36(2), pp. 193–205. **[G: U.S.]**

Seldon, Barry J. A Nonresidual Estimation of Welfare Gains from Research: The Case of Public R&D in a Forest Product Industry. *Southern Econ. J.*, July 1987, 54(1), pp. 64–80. **[G: U.S.]**

Shevlin, Terry. Taxes and Off-Balance–Sheet Financing: Research and Development Limited Partnerships. *Accounting Rev.*, July 1987, 62(3), pp. 480–509. **[G: U.S.]**

Silbert, Lance. Promoting High-Technology Industry: Initiatives and Policies for State Governments: California. *Schmandt, J. and Wilson, R., eds.*, 1987, pp. 11–33. **[G: U.S.]**

Spiller, Pablo T. and Teubal, Morris. Analysis of R&D Failure. *Teubal, M.*, 1987, pp. 32–50. **[G: Israel]**

Starbatty, Joachim. Die ordnungspolitische Dimension der EG-Technologiepolitik. (EC-Technology Policy and the Economic Order. With English summary.) *Lenel, H. O., et al., eds.*, 1987, pp. 155–81. **[G: EEC]**

Steinberg, Gerald M. Science and Politics: The Links between Israel and the European Community. *Greilsammer, I. and Weiler, J. H. H., eds.*, 1987, pp. 337–48. **[G: EEC; Israel]**

Stensland, Gunnar and Nystad, Arild N. Optimal Choice of R&D Strategy for Enhanced Recovery from Petroleum Reservoirs. *Energy J.*, January 1987, 8(1), pp. 125–32.

Stewart, William L. Absolute and Relative Trends in U.S. Research and Development Investment. *Faruqui, A. and Broehl, J., eds.*, 1987, pp. 219–46. **[G: U.S.]**

Stiglitz, Joseph E. On the Microeconomics of Technical Progress. *Katz, J. M., ed.*, 1987, pp. 56–77.

Stiglitz, Joseph E. Technological Change, Sunk Costs, and Competition. *Brookings Pap. Econ. Act.*, 1987, (3), pp. 883–937.

Stoneman, Paul. Some Analytical Observations on Diffusion Policies. *Dasgupta, P. and Stoneman, P., eds.*, 1987, pp. 154–68.

Street, James H. The Technological Frontier in Latin America: Creativity and Productivity. *Dietz, J. L. and Street, J. H., eds.*, 1987, pp. 200–216. **[G: Latin America]**

Teitel, Simón. Towards an Understanding of Technical Change in Semi-industrialized Countries. *Katz, J. M., ed.*, 1987, pp. 94–115.

Teitel, Simón. Towards Conceptualisation of Technological Development as an Evolutionary Process. *Dunning, J. H. and Usui, M., eds.*, 1987, pp. 157–73. **[G: LDCs]**

Teubal, Morris. Neutrality in Science Policy: The Promotion of Sophisticated Industrial Technology in Israel. *Teubal, M.*, 1987, pp. 179–203. **[G: Israel]**

Teubal, Morris. On User Needs and Need Determination: Aspects of the Theory of Technological Innovation. *Teubal, M.*, 1987, pp. 76–96.

Teubal, Morris. The Accumulation of Intangibles by High-Technology Firms. *Teubal, M.*, 1987, pp. 153–72.

Teubal, Morris. The R&D Performance through Time of Young, High-Technology Firms: Methodology and an Illustration. *Teubal, M.*, 1987, pp. 131–52. **[G: Israel]**

Teubal, Morris. The Role of Technological Learning in the Exports of Manufactured Goods: The Case of Selected Capital Goods in Brazil. *Teubal, M.*, 1987, pp. 104–30. **[G: Brazil]**

Teubal, Morris; Arnon, Naftali and Trachtenberg, Manuel. Performance in Innovation in the Israeli Electronics Industry: A Case Study of Biomedical Electronics Instrumentation. *Teubal, M.*, 1987, pp. 10–31. **[G: Israel]**

Teubal, Morris and Steinmueller, Edward. Government Policy, Innovation, and Economic Growth: A Study of Satellite Communications. *Teubal, M.*, 1987, pp. 233–58. **[G: U.S.]**

Teubal, Morris and Steinmueller, Edward. The Introduction of a Major New Technology: Externalities and Government Policy. *Teubal, M.*, 1987, pp. 259–79.

Thompson, Fred. Managing Defense Expenditures. *Thai, K. V., ed.*, 1987, 1985, pp. 129–46. **[G: U.S.]**

Trigo, Eduardo J. Agricultural Research Organization in the Developing World: Diversity and Evolution. *Ruttan, V. W. and Pray, C. E., eds.*, 1987, pp. 251–81. **[G: LDCs]**

Trojer, Felix J. A Comparison of R&D Strategies in Europe and Japan. *Hieronymi, O., ed.*, 1987, pp. 105–21. **[G: W. Europe; Japan; U.S.]**

Uekusa, Masu. The Political Economy of Japan: Industrial Organization: The 1970s to the Pres-

ent. *Yamamura, K. and Yasuba, Y., eds.*, 1987, pp. 469–515. **[G: Japan]**

Van Cayseele, Patrick. Economies of Scope in Research and Development. *J. Econ. (Z. Nationalökon.)*, 1987, 47(3), pp. 273–85.

Wade, Nicholas. Agriculture: Research Planning Paralyzed by Pork-Barrel Politics. *Ruttan, V. W. and Pray, C. E., eds.*, 1987, 1973, pp. 515–26. **[G: U.S.]**

Whatley, Warren C. Southern Agrarian Labor Contracts as Impediments to Cotton Mechanization. *J. Econ. Hist.*, March 1987, 47(1), pp. 45–70. **[G: U.S.]**

630 INDUSTRY STUDIES

6300 General

Abdul Aziz, Abdul Rahman. Identification of Structural Constraints in Sectoral Development Using the Diamond–Laumas Key Sector Method: With West Malaysian Case Study. *Singapore Econ. Rev.*, October 1987, 32(2), pp. 75–91. **[G: Malaysia]**

Abdul Aziz, Abdul Rahman. Identification of Structural Constraints in Sectoral Development using the Diamond–Laumas Key Sector Method: With West Malaysian Case Study. *Singapore Econ. Rev.*, April 1987, 32(1), pp. 32–45. **[G: Malaysia]**

Aliouche, El-Hachemi. Heavy Industrialization: The Algerian Experience. *England, R. W., ed.*, 1987, pp. 257–90. **[G: Algeria]**

Andrikopoulos, Andreas A.; Brox, James A. and Carvalho, Emanuel. A Further Test of the Competitive Effect in Shift-Share Analysis. *Rev. Reg. Stud.*, Fall 1987, 17(3), pp. 23–30. **[G: Canada]**

Bailly, Antoine S., et al. Services and Production: For a Reassessment of Economic Sectors. *Ann. Reg. Sci.*, July 1987, 21(2), pp. 45–59. **[G: Switzerland]**

Baranson, Jack. Ideology versus Innovation in Soviet Industry. *World Econ.*, March 1987, 10(1), pp. 85–95. **[G: U.S.S.R.]**

Bedrossian, Arakel and Petoussis, Emmanuel. The Disaggregated Demand for Labour in Greek Industry. *Appl. Econ.*, June 1987, 19(6), pp. 809–17. **[G: Greece]**

Belova, S. Accelerating the Modernization of Productive Fixed Capital. *Prob. Econ.*, April 1987, 29(12), pp. 54–72. **[G: U.S.S.R.]**

Benston, George J. The Validity of Studies with Line of Business Data: Reply [The Validity of Profits-Structure Studies with Particular Reference to the FTC's Line of Business Data]. *Amer. Econ. Rev.*, March 1987, 77(1), pp. 218–23. **[G: U.S.]**

Boretsky, Michael. The Tenability of the CIA Estimates of Soviet Economic Growth. *J. Compar. Econ.*, December 1987, 11(4), pp. 517–42. **[G: U.S.S.R.; U.S.; W. Germany]**

Bornstein, Morris. Soviet Price Policies. *Soviet Econ.*, April-June 1987, 3(2), pp. 96–134. **[G: U.S.S.R.]**

Brooks, Harvey and Guile, Bruce R. Technology

and Global Industry: Overview. *Guile, B. R. and Brooks, H., eds.*, 1987, pp. 1–15.

Brüninghaus, Beate. A Review of the New Literature on Business History. *Pohl, H. and Rudolph, B., eds.*, 1987, pp. 117–39. **[G: W. Germany]**

Burton, John. Privatization: The Thatcher Case. *Managerial Dec. Econ.*, March 1987, *8*(1), pp. 21–29. **[G: U.K.]**

Byrd, William A. The Impact of the Two-Tier Plan/Market System in Chinese Industry. *J. Compar. Econ.*, September 1987, *11*(3), pp. 295–308. **[G: China]**

Casetti, Emilio and Pandit, Kavita. The Non Linear Dynamics of Sectoral Shifts. *Econ. Geogr.*, July 1987, *63*(3), pp. 241–58.

Cassetti, Mario. Gli effetti moltiplicativi degli investimenti per settore di destinazione sulla produzione, sulle importazioni e sull'occupazione in Italia, dal 1970 al 1982. Un'analisi intersettoriale. (The Effect of Investment Demands by Destination on Total Production, Imports and Employment in Italy, since 1970 to 1982. An Intersectoral Analysis. With English summary.) *Ricerche Econ.*, Apr.-June 1987, *41*(2), pp. 231–61. **[G: Italy]**

Chekhlov, N. I. Prices and Rates in Industry. *Prob. Econ.*, March 1987, *29*(11), pp. 62–77. **[G: U.S.S.R.]**

Chrystal, K. Alec and Chatterji, Monojit. Money and Disaggregate Supply in the United States, 1950–1982. *Europ. Econ. Rev.*, August 1987, *31*(6), pp. 1211–28. **[G: U.S.]**

Cipolletta, A. Heimler and Calcagnini, G. Restructuring and Adjustment in Italian Industry. *Rev. Econ. Cond. Italy*, Sept.-Dec. 1987, (3), pp. 341–81. **[G: Italy]**

Conti, Vittorio and Silvani, Marco. Foreign Trade and Industrial Structure in Italy: An Input–Output Multiplier Analysis. *Saunders, C. T., ed.*, 1987, pp. 183–203. **[G: Italy]**

Dixon, Peter B. On Using Applied General Equilibrium Models for Analysing Structural Change. *Pasinetti, L. and Lloyd, P., eds.*, 1987, pp. 149–58.

Ershov, E. B. and Sadykov, I. S. Aggregational Analysis of Production Possibility Frontiers for Industrial Branches in the USSR. *Matekon*, Summer 1987, *23*(4), pp. 28–47. **[G: U.S.S.R.]**

Fel'zenbaum, V. and Shapovalova, E. Material Incentives and the Economic Effect of New Technology. *Prob. Econ.*, August 1987, *30*(4), pp. 79–94. **[G: U.S.S.R.]**

Feldman, Stanley J.; McClain, David and Palmer, Karen. Sources of Structural Change in the United States, 1963–78: An Input–Output Perspective. *Rev. Econ. Statist.*, August 1987, *69*(3), pp. 503–10. **[G: U.S.]**

Filho, Ugo Fasano. Uma comparação entre o índice de vantagem comparativa de Bowen e o tradicional índice de vantagem comparativa revelada: o caso brasileiro—1964/81. (With English summary.) *Pesquisa Planejamento Econ.*, August 1987, *17*(2), pp. 457–69. **[G: Brazil]**

Fujita, Natsuki and James, William E. Exports

and Technological Changes in the Adjustment Process of the Japanese Economy in the 1970s. *Hitotsubashi J. Econ.*, December 1987, *28*(2), pp. 107–22. **[G: Japan]**

van Gemert, Henk G. Structural Change in Industrial Countries. *Macmillen, M.; Mayes, D. G. and van Veen, P., eds.*, 1987, pp. 89–118. **[G: U.S.; EEC]**

van Gemert, Henk G. Structural Change in OECD Countries: A Normal Pattern Analysis. *De Economist*, 1987, *135*(1), pp. 29–51. **[G: OECD]**

Gemmell, Norman. A Model of Unbalanced Growth: The Market versus the Non-market Sector of the Economy. *Oxford Econ. Pap.*, June 1987, *39*(2), pp. 253–67.

Glaser, Václav and Ungerman, Jaroslav. Some Aspects of a New Cycle of a Work on a Long-term Outlook. *Czech. Econ. Digest.*, January 1987, (2), pp. 20–33. **[G: Czechoslovakia]**

Goldstein, Harvey A. and Cruze, Alvin M. An Evaluation of State Projections of Industry, Occupational Employment. *Mon. Lab. Rev.*, October 1987, *110*(10), pp. 29–38. **[G: U.S.]**

Gramm, Cynthia L. New Measures of the Propensity to Strike during Contract Negotiations, 1971–1980. *Ind. Lab. Relat. Rev.*, April 1987, *40*(3), pp. 406–17. **[G: U.S.]**

Haber, Sheldon E.; Lamas, Enrique J. and Lichtenstein, Jules H. On Their Own: The Self-employed and Others in Private Business. *Mon. Lab. Rev.*, May 1987, *110*(5), pp. 17–23. **[G: U.S.]**

Haji, J. A. Key Sectors and the Structure of Production in Kuwait—An Input–Output Approach. *Appl. Econ.*, September 1987, *19*(9), pp. 1187–1200. **[G: Kuwait]**

Hall, Christopher D. Heterogeneous Firms: A Consumer's Report [Heterogeneous Firms and the Organization of Production]. *Econ. Inquiry*, January 1987, *25*(1), pp. 175–80.

Jungenfelt, Karl. Structural Adjustment in Industrially Advanced Countries: Discussion and Conclusions. *Pasinetti, L. and Lloyd, P., eds.*, 1987, pp. 177–85. **[G: MDCs]**

Kutscher, Ronald E. and Personick, Valerie A. Deindustrialization and the Shift to Services. *Econ. Lavoro*, Jan.-Mar. 1987, *21*(1), pp. 123–29. **[G: U.S.]**

Lang, Rikard and Vojnić, Dragomir. Long-term Programme for Economic Stabilisation and the Industrial Structure of Yugoslavia. *Saunders, C. T., ed.*, 1987, pp. 205–14. **[G: Yugoslavia]**

Leslie, Derek. Real Wage and Real Labour Cost Growth, 1948–81: A Disaggregated Study. *Appl. Econ.*, May 1987, *19*(5), pp. 635–50. **[G: U.K.]**

Lloyd, Peter J. Structural Change in a Selection of Countries: Discussion and Conclusions. *Pasinetti, L. and Lloyd, P., eds.*, 1987, pp. 263–66.

Lukaszewicz, Aleksander and Pajestka, Józef. Industrial Policy and Structural Change: The Polish Case. *Saunders, C. T., ed.*, 1987, pp. 227–37. **[G: Poland]**

Lyons, Thomas P. Interprovincial Trade and Development in China, 1957–1979. *Econ. Develop. Cult. Change*, January 1987, *35*(2), pp. 223–56.   [G: China]

Moreno, Sergio Martín. La hipótesis de la estructura dual de la industria: el caso de la economía mexicana. (The Dual Industrial Structure Hypothesis: The Case of the Mexican Economy. With English summary.) *Estud. Econ.*, Jan.-June 1987, *2*(1), pp. 81–112.   [G: Mexico]

Odedokun, Matthew O. Fungibility and Effectiveness of Selective Credit Policies: Evidence from Nigerian Data. *Devel. Econ.*, September 1987, *25*(3), pp. 234–48.   [G: Nigeria]

Oi, Walter Y. Heterogeneous Firms: Caveat Emptor [Heterogeneous Firms and the Organization of Production]. *Econ. Inquiry*, January 1987, *25*(1), pp. 181–84.

Patrick, Hugh T. and Rohlen, Thomas P. The Political Economy of Japan: Small-Scale Family Enterprises. *Yamamura, K. and Yasuba, Y., eds.*, 1987, pp. 331–84.   [G: Japan]

Peattie, Lisa. An Idea in Good Currency and How It Grew: The Informal Sector. *World Devel.*, July 1987, *15*(7), pp. 851–60.

Perkins, Joseph. Creating a Climate for Black Business. *Perkins, J., ed.*, 1987, pp. 63–74.   [G: U.S.]

Personick, Valerie A. Industry Output and Employment through the End of the Century. *Mon. Lab. Rev.*, September 1987, *110*(9), pp. 30–45.   [G: U.S.]

Rosti, Luisa. L'occupazione indipendente in Italia: stock e flussi. (Self-Employment in Italy: Stock and Flow. With English summary.) *Econ. Lavoro*, Oct.-Dec. 1987, *21*(4), pp. 15–27.   [G: Italy]

Rzheshevskii, V. Application of the New Methods of Management in 1986. *Prob. Econ.*, April 1987, *29*(12), pp. 73–86.   [G: U.S.S.R.]

Scherer, F. M., et al. The Validity of Studies with Line of Business Data: Comment [The Validity of Profits-Structure Studies with Particular Reference to the FTC's Line of Business Data]. *Amer. Econ. Rev.*, March 1987, *77*(1), pp. 205–17.   [G: U.S.]

Segura, Julio and Restoy, Fernando. Notas sobre el cambio en la estructura productiva de la economía española 1975–1980. (With English summary.) *Invest. Econ.*, September 1987, *11*(3), pp. 521–52.   [G: Spain]

Sercovich, Francisco C. Política technológica y reestructuración industrial: los temas centrales. (With English summary.) *Desarrollo Econ.*, Jan.-Mar. 1987, *26*(104), pp. 561–78.   [G: LDCs]

Seskin, Eugene P. and Sullivan, David F. Plant and Equipment Expenditures, the Four Quarters of 1987. *Surv. Curr. Bus.*, September 1987, *67*(9), pp. 20–25.   [G: U.S.]

Shupp, Franklin R. Disinflation and Sectoral Productivity Gains. *J. Econ. Dynam. Control*, June 1987, *11*(2), pp. 207–12.   [G: U.S.]

Smith, Alasdair. A Current Cost Accounting Measure of Britain's Stock of Equipment. *Nat. Inst. Econ. Rev.*, May 1987, (120), pp. 42–57.   [G: U.K.]

Taxell, Christoffer. Näringslivets roll i undervisningsoch forskningspolitiken. (The Role of Industries in Education and Research Policy. With English summary.) *Ekon. Samfundets Tidskr.*, 1987, *40*(4), pp. 191–99.   [G: Finland]

Toumanoff, Peter. The Use of Production Functions to Investigate Soviet Industrial Reform. *Comp. Econ. Stud.*, Fall 1987, *29*(3), pp. 94–111.   [G: U.S.S.R.]

Val'tukh, Konstantin K. and Lavrovskii, B. L. The Nation's Production Apparatus: Utilization and Reconstruction. *Prob. Econ.*, April 1987, *29*(12), pp. 35–53.   [G: U.S.S.R.]

Vasconcellos e Sá, Jorge Alberto. A Typology of Industrial Products: Validity and Implications. *Economia (Portugal)*, October 1987, *11*(3), pp. 285–325.   [G: Portugal]

van der Walt, Nicolaas and Swanepoel, J. J. Indicative Labour and Capital Programming: An Exercise on the Frontiers of Empirical Economics. *J. Stud. Econ. Econometrics*, July 1987, *11*(2), pp. 19–67.   [G: S. Africa]

Wu, Jinglian and Zhao, Renwei. The Dual Pricing System in China's Industry. *J. Compar. Econ.*, September 1987, *11*(3), pp. 309–18.   [G: China]

Yang, Mu. The New Technological Revolution and the Technological Progress in Industries. *Chinese Econ. Stud.*, Summer 1987, *20*(4), pp. 50–67.   [G: China]

Yokokura, Hiroyuki. Interindustry Analysis and Unit Structure in the Yugoslav Economy. *Econ. Anal. Workers' Manage.*, 1987, *21*(3), pp. 313–32.   [G: Yugoslavia]

Zanetti, Giovanni. Structure and Financial Requirements in the Italian Business Sector. *Rev. Econ. Cond. Italy*, Sept.-Dec. 1987, (3), pp. 417–53.   [G: Italy]

631 Industry Studies: Manufacturing

6310 General

Ady, Robert. Normal Industrial Plant Redevelopment Process. *Lynch, J. E., ed.*, 1987, pp. 137–54.   [G: U.S.]

Agthe, Donald E. and Billings, R. Bruce. Equity, Price Elasticity, and Household Income under Increasing Block Rates for Water. *Amer. J. Econ. Soc.*, July 1987, *46*(3), pp. 273–86.   [G: U.S.]

Ahmed, Shaghil. Wage Stickiness and the Nonneutrality of Money: A Cross-Industry Analysis. *J. Monet. Econ.*, July 1987, *20*(1), pp. 25–50.   [G: Canada]

Ali, Ifzal. India's Manufactured Exports: An Analysis of Supply Factors. *Devel. Econ.*, June 1987, *25*(2), pp. 152–70.   [G: India]

Altman, Morris. A Revision of Canadian Economic Growth: 1870–1910 (A Challenge to the Gradualist Interpretation). *Can. J. Econ.*, February 1987, *20*(1), pp. 86–113.   [G: Canada]

Anderson, Kym. The Australian Economy in the Long Run: Tariffs and the Manufacturing Sector. *Maddock, R. and McLean, I. W., eds.*, 1987, pp. 165–94.   [G: Australia]

Ansar, J., et al. A Vintage Model of Labour Demand by U.K. Manufacturing. *Rech. Écon. Louvain*, 1987, 53(1), pp. 3–26.   [G: U.K.]

Artus, Patrick. Les exportations industrielles sont-elles déterminées par l'offre ou par la demande. (With English summary.) *Revue Écon.*, September 1987, 38(5), pp. 995–1015.
[G: France]

Attaran, Mohsen and Zwick, Martin. Entropy and Other Measures of Industrial Diversification. *Quart. J. Bus. Econ.*, Autumn 1987, 26(4), pp. 17–34.   [G: U.S.]

Audretsch, David B. An Empirical Test of the Industry Life Cycle. *Weltwirtsch. Arch.*, 1987, 123(2), pp. 297–308.   [G: U.S.]

Azpiazu, Daniel. Los resultados de la política de promoción industrial al cabo de un decenio (1974–1983). (With English summary.) *Desarrollo Econ.*, Jan.-Mar. 1987, 26(104), pp. 631–51.   [G: Argentina]

Baer, Werner; da Fonseca, Manuel A. R. and Guilhoto, Joaquim J. M. Structural Changes in Brazil's Industrial Economy, 1960–80. *World Devel.*, February 1987, 15(2), pp. 275–86.   [G: Brazil]

Bairam, Erkin I. Orthodox Production Functions with Variable Returns to Scale: Some Analysis and Testing Using Soviet and Polish Regional Data. *Keio Econ. Stud.*, 1987, 24(1), pp. 63–83.   [G: U.S.S.R.; Poland]

Bairam, Erkin I. Returns to Scale, Technical Progress and Output Growth in Branches of Industry: The Case of Soviet Republics, 1962–74. *Scot. J. Polit. Econ.*, August 1987, 34(3), pp. 249–66.   [G: U.S.S.R.]

Bairam, Erkin I. Returns to Scale, Technical Progress and Output Growth in Branches of Industry: The Case of COMECON, 1961–75. *METU*, 1987, 14(2), pp. 105–22. [G: CMEA]

Bairam, Erkin I. Technical Change and Returns to Scale. The Jordanian Experience. *METU*, 1987, 14(4), pp. 397–402.

Bairam, Erkin I. Technical Change and Returns to Scale: The Jordanian Experience: A Rejoinder. *METU*, 1987, 14(4), pp. 405–07.

Bairam, Erkin I. The Verdoorn Law, Returns to Scale and Industrial Growth: A Review of the Literature. *Australian Econ. Pap.*, June 1987, 26(48), pp. 20–42.   [G: OECD]

Bajo, Oscar. Organización industrial y comportamiento exportador de los sectores industriales españoles ante la C.E.E. (With English summary.) *Invest. Econ.*, September 1987, 11(3), pp. 497–520.   [G: EEC; Spain]

Baldwin, John R. and Gorecki, Paul K. Plant Creation versus Plant Acquisition: The Entry Process in Canadian Manufacturing. *Int. J. Ind. Organ.*, March 1987, 5(1), pp. 27–41.
[G: Canada]

Baldwin, John R. and Gorecki, Paul K. The Impact of High Tariffs and Imperfect Market Structure on Plant Scale Inefficiency in Canadian Manufacturing Industries in the 1970's. *Rech. Écon. Louvain*, 1987, 53(1), pp. 51–73.
[G: Canada]

Bar-El, Raphael. Rural Industrialization in Israel: A Summary of Experiences. *Bar-El, R., ed.*, 1987, pp. 1–20.   [G: Israel]

Bar-El, Raphael; Erickson, Eugene and Nesher, Ariela. Rural Industrialization in Israel: Concluding Considerations. *Bar-El, R., ed.*, 1987, pp. 169–89.   [G: Israel]

Baranson, Jack. Trade Liberalization and the New Generation of Manufacturing Technologies: Implications for Canadian Industry in North American Markets. *Tremblay, R., ed.*, 1987, pp. 407–17.   [G: Canada; U.S.]

Battese, George E. and Malik, Sohail J. Estimation of Elasticities of Substitution for CES Production Functions Using Data on Selected Manufacturing Industries in Pakistan. *Pakistan Devel. Rev.*, Summer 1987, 26(2), pp. 161–77.   [G: Pakistan]

Beeson, Patricia. Total Factor Productivity Growth and Agglomeration Economies in Manufacturing, 1959–73. *J. Reg. Sci.*, May 1987, 27(2), pp. 183–99.   [G: U.S.]

Beladi, Hamid and Brunner, Lawrence P. Trade Unions and Money Wage Changes in U.S. Manufacturing Industries: Further Empirical Evidence. *Quart. J. Bus. Econ.*, Summer 1987, 26(3), pp. 79–86.   [G: U.S.]

Bell, Trevor. International Competition and Industrial Decentralization in South Africa. *World Devel.*, Oct./Nov. 1987, 15(10/11), pp. 1291–1307.   [G: S. Africa]

Bemmels, Brian. How Unions Affect Productivity in Manufacturing Plants. *Ind. Lab. Relat. Rev.*, January 1987, 40(2), pp. 241–53.   [G: U.S.]

Bentolila, David J. The Non-agricultural Village. *Bar-El, R., ed.*, 1987, pp. 105–42.
[G: Israel]

Berndt, Ernst R. and Wood, David O. Energy Price Shocks and Productivity Growth: A Survey. *[Adelman, M. A.]*, 1987, pp. 305–42.

Bhattacherjee, Debashish. Union-Type Effects on Bargaining Outcomes in Indian Manufacturing. *Brit. J. Ind. Relat.*, July 1987, 25(2), pp. 247–66.   [G: India]

Bils, Mark. The Cyclical Behavior of Marginal Cost and Price. *Amer. Econ. Rev.*, December 1987, 77(5), pp. 838–55.   [G: U.S.]

Bischoff, Charles W. and Kokkelenberg, Edward C. Capacity Utilization and Depreciation-in-Use. *Appl. Econ.*, August 1987, 19(8), pp. 995–1007.   [G: U.S.]

Bitros, George C. Foreign Direct Investment in Manufacturing: A Note. *Greek Econ. Rev.*, 1987, 9(1), pp. 108–12.

Bittlingmayer, George. The Application of the Sherman Act to the Smog Agreement. *Antitrust Bull.*, Winter 1987, 32(4), pp. 885–915.
[G: U.S.]

Bluestone, Barry. Impact of Trade, Technology, and Management Factors on U.S. Manufacturing. *Faruqui, A. and Broehl, J., eds.*, 1987, pp. 165–77.   [G: U.S.]

Boyd, Gale A., et al. Separating the Changing Composition of U.S. Manufacturing Production from Energy Efficiency Improvements: A

Divisia Index Approach. *Energy J.*, April 1987, 8(2), pp. 77–96.   **[G: U.S.; Sweden; U.K.; Mexico]**

Brack, John. Price Adjustment within a Framework of Symmetric Oligopoly: An Analysis of Pricing in 380 U.S. Manufacturing Industries, 1958–71. *Int. J. Ind. Organ.*, September 1987, 5(3), pp. 289–301.   **[G: U.S.]**

Bradburd, Ralph M. and Caves, Richard E. Transaction-Cost Influences on the Adjustment of Industries' Prices and Outputs. *Rev. Econ. Statist.*, November 1987, 69(4), pp. 575–83.   **[G: U.S.]**

Bradford, Colin I., Jr. Trade and Structural Change: NICs and Next Tier NICs as Transitional Economies. *World Devel.*, March 1987, 15(3), pp. 299–316.   **[G: LDCs]**

Brundenius, Claes. Development and Prospects of Capital Goods Production in Revolutionary Cuba. *World Devel.*, January 1987, 15(1), pp. 95–112.   **[G: Cuba]**

Bryne, Dennis M. and King, Randall H. Import Penetration and Strike Activity in Manufacturing, 1961–77. *Atlantic Econ. J.*, July 1987, 15(2), pp. 77–84.   **[G: U.S.]**

Chan, M. W. Luke and Okasanen, E. H. Regional Energy Input Prices in Canadian Manufacturing: An Index Number Approach. *Energy Econ.*, April 1987, 9(2), pp. 66–72.   **[G: Canada]**

Chawluk, Antoni. Is Soviet Capital Too Old? *Economica*, August 1987, 54(215), pp. 335–54.   **[G: U.S.S.R.]**

Chia, Siow-Yue. Industrial Restructuring in a Newly Industrialising Country: The Case of Singapore. *Pasinetti, L. and Lloyd, P., eds.,* 1987, pp. 213–32.   **[G: Singapore]**

Chow, Peter C. Y. Causality between Export Growth and Industrial Development: Empirical Evidence from the NICs. *J. Devel. Econ.*, June 1987, 26(1), pp. 55–63.   **[G: LDCs]**

Chowdhury, A. and Kirkpatrick, Colin. Industrial Restructuring in a Newly Industrializing Country: The Identification of Priority Industries in Singapore. *Appl. Econ.*, July 1987, 19(7), pp. 915–26.   **[G: Singapore]**

Chung, Jae Wan. On the Estimation of Factor Substitution in the Translog Model. *Rev. Econ. Statist.*, August 1987, 69(3), pp. 409–17.   **[G: U.S.]**

Chung, Ming Wong. Trends and Patterns of Singapore's Trade in Manufactures. *Bradford, C. I., Jr. and Branson, W. H., eds.,* 1987, pp. 379–432.   **[G: Singapore]**

Çinar, E. Miné; Kaytaz, Mehmet and Evcimen, Gümar. A Case Study on the Growth Potential of Small Scale Manufacturing Enterprises in Bursa, Turkey. *METU*, 1987, 14(2), pp. 123–46.   **[G: Turkey]**

Ciocca, Pierluigi and Frasca, Francesco. I rapporti fra industria e finanza: problemi e prospettive. (With English summary.) *Polit. Econ.*, April 1987, 3(1), pp. 29–50.   **[G: Italy]**

Coelen, Stephen P.; Nakosteen, Robert A. and Zimmer, Michael A. An Aggregate Model of Manufacturing Firm Migration. *Rev. Reg.*

Stud., Spring 1987, 17(2), pp. 57–66.   **[G: U.S.]**

Conrad, Klaus and Unger, Ralph. Ex post Tests for Short- and Long-run Optimization. *J. Econometrics*, November 1987, 36(3), pp. 339–58.   **[G: W. Germany]**

Cordes, Joseph J.; Watson, Harry S. and Hauger, J. Scott. Effects of Tax Reform on High Technology Firms. *Nat. Tax J.*, September 1987, 40(3), pp. 373–91.   **[G: U.S.]**

Culem, Claudy G. Foreign Trade Behavior in a Small Open Economy (Belgium 1970–1980). *Scand. J. Econ.*, 1987, 89(1), pp. 55–70.   **[G: Belgium]**

Czamanski, Daniel Z. and Meyer-Brodnitz, Michael B. Industrialization in Arab Villages in Israel. *Bar-El, R., ed.,* 1987, pp. 143–68.   **[G: Israel]**

Dabir-Alai, Parviz. Trends in Productivity Growth across Large Scale Manufacturing Industries of India: 1973/74 to 1978/79. *Indian Econ. Rev.*, July-Dec. 1987, 22(2), pp. 151–78.   **[G: India]**

DeGrasse, Robert W., Jr. Corporate Diversification and Conversion Experience. *Lynch, J. E., ed.,* 1987, pp. 91–120.   **[G: U.S.]**

Delfino, José A. Eficiencia, apertura de la economía y concentración industrial en Argentina. (Efficiency, Openness of the Economy and Industrial Concentration in Argentina. With English summary.) *Económica (La Plata)*, January-June 1987, 33(1), pp. 51–84.   **[G: Argentina]**

Desai, Padma. Total Factor Productivity in Postwar Soviet Industry and Its Branches. *Desai, P.,* 1987, 1985, pp. 78–98.   **[G: U.S.S.R.]**

Desai, Padma and Martin, Ricardo. Efficiency Loss from Resource Misallocation in Soviet Industry. *Desai, P., 1987, 1983,* pp. 117–29.   **[G: U.S.S.R.]**

Diewert, Walter Erwin and Wales, Terence J. Flexible Functional Forms and Global Curvature Conditions. *Econometrica*, January 1987, 55(1), pp. 43–68.   **[G: U.S.]**

Don, Yehuda and Leviatan, Uri. Kibbutz Industrialization. *Bar-El, R., ed.,* 1987, pp. 21–55.   **[G: Israel]**

Downes, Andrew S. Production Function Analysis in the Manufacturing Sector of Barbados: An Econometric Approach. *J. Econ. Devel.*, December 1987, 12(2), pp. 161–82.   **[G: Barbados]**

Duffy, Neal E. Returns to Scale Behavior and Manufacturing Agglomeration Economies in U.S. Urban Areas. *Reg. Sci. Persp.*, 1987, 17(1), pp. 42–54.   **[G: U.S.]**

Dunstan, Roger H. and Long, William T., III. Structure and Technology of Manufacturing in Texas and Louisiana. *Fed. Res. Bank Dallas Econ. Rev.*, January 1987, pp. 15–27.   **[G: U.S.]**

Eckard, E. Woodrow, Jr. Advertising, Competition, and Market Share Instability. *J. Bus.*, October 1987, 60(4), pp. 539–52.   **[G: U.S.]**

Elder, Harold W. An Economic Analysis of Factor Usage and Workplace Regulation: Reply.

Southern Econ. J., January 1987, 53(3), pp. 790. [G: U.S.]

Estrin, Saul; Jones, Derek C. and Svejnar, Jan. The Productivity Effects of Worker Participation: Producer Cooperatives in Western Economies. *J. Compar. Econ.*, March 1987, 11(1), pp. 40–61. [G: Spain; Italy; U.K.; France]

Evans, David S. Tests of Alternative Theories of Firm Growth. *J. Polit. Econ.*, August 1987, 95(4), pp. 657–74. [G: U.S.]

Fabella, Raul V. Rural Manufacturing Employment in the Philippines: Contribution and Determinants. *Islam, R., ed.*, 1987, pp. 135–70. [G: Philippines]

Feldman, Stanley J. Impact of Final Demand Changes on Interindustry Growth Prospects. *Faruqui, A. and Broehl, J., eds.*, 1987, pp. 143–59. [G: U.S.]

Flaherty, Sean. Strike Activity, Worker Militancy, and Productivity Change in Manufacturing, 1961–1981. *Ind. Lab. Relat. Rev.*, July 1987, 40(4), pp. 585–600. [G: U.S.]

Fluet, Claude and Lefebvre, Pierre. The Sharing of Total Factor Productivity Gains in Canadian Manufacturing: A Price Accounting Approach 1965–1980. *Appl. Econ.*, February 1987, 19(2), pp. 245–57. [G: Canada]

Fortune, J. Neill. Some Determinants of Labour Productivity. *Appl. Econ.*, June 1987, 19(6), pp. 839–43. [G: U.S.]

Franco, Malerba. Apprendimento, innovazioni incrementali e tecnologia: un'analisi interindustriale. (Learning, Incremental Innovations and Technology: An Interindustry Analysis. With English summary.) *Giorn. Econ.*, May-June 1987, 46(5–6), pp. 227–55.

Frantzen, Dirk J. Cost Shifting and the Falling Share of Profits in Manufacturing Industry: A Study for Belgium. *Rivista Int. Sci. Econ. Com.*, Jan.-Feb. 1987, 34(1–2), pp. 159–76. [G: Belgium]

Garofalo, Gasper A. and Malhotra, Devinder M. Regional Capital Formation in U.S. Manufacturing during the 1970s. *J. Reg. Sci.*, August 1987, 27(3), pp. 391–401. [G: U.S.]

Goudie, Andrew; Meeks, Geoffrey and Weale, Martin. The Cambridge Multisectoral Dynamic Model of the British Economy: The Company Sector. *Barker, T. and Peterson, W., eds.*, 1987, pp. 389–410. [G: U.S.]

Gourieroux, Christian and Peaucelle, I. Vérification empirique de la rationalité des anticipations de la demande par les entreprises. (With English summary.) *Rech. Écon. Louvain*, 1987, 53(3), pp. 223–46. [G: France]

Greenman, J. V. and Drollas, Leonidas P. The Price of Energy and Factor Substitution in the U.S. Economy. *Energy Econ.*, July 1987, 9(3), pp. 159–66. [G: U.S.]

Gregory, Mary; Lobban, Peter and Thomson, Andrew. Pay Settlements in Manufacturing Industry, 1979–84: A Micro-data Study of the Impact of Product and Labour Market Pressures. *Oxford Bull. Econ. Statist.*, February 1987, 49(1), pp. 129–50. [G: U.K.]

Griffin, Keith. Industrial Reforms in China. *Grif-*

fin, K., 1987, pp. 109–46. [G: China]

Gullickson, William and Harper, Michael J. Multifactor Productivity in U.S. Manufacturing, 1949–83. *Mon. Lab. Rev.*, October 1987, 110(10), pp. 18–28. [G: U.S.]

Guth, Michael A. S. Functional Form in Finished Goods Inventory Investment: A Note. *J. Money, Credit, Banking*, August 1987, 19(3), pp. 396–401. [G: U.S.]

Gyourko, Joseph. Effects of Local Tax Structures on the Factor Intensity Composition of Manufacturing Activity across Cities. *J. Urban Econ.*, September 1987, 22(2), pp. 151–64. [G: U.S.]

Hall, Bronwyn H. The Relationship between Firm Size and Firm Growth in the U.S. Manufacturing Sector. *J. Ind. Econ.*, June 1987, 35(4), pp. 583–606. [G: U.S.]

Hammad, Khalil. Technical Change and Returns to Scale: The Jordanian Experience: A Reply. *METU*, 1987, 14(4), pp. 403.

Hansen, Gary B. American Labor and International Trade: Adjustment Strategies to Assist Workers Displaced in Plant Closings and Permanent Layoffs. *Econ. Lavoro*, Jan.-Mar. 1987, 21(1), pp. 115–22. [G: U.S.]

Harris, R. I. D. The Role of Manufacturing in Regional Growth. *Reg. Stud.*, August 1987, 21(4), pp. 301–12. [G: U.K.]

Haynes, Kingsley E. and Machunda, Zachary B. Spatial Restructuring of Manufacturing and Employment Growth in the Rural Midwest: An Analysis for Indiana. *Econ. Geogr.*, October 1987, 63(4), pp. 319–33. [G: U.S.]

Heikkinen, Sakari and Hjerppe, Riitta. The Growth of Finnish Industry in 1860–1913. Causes and Linkages. *J. Europ. Econ. Hist.*, Fall 1987, 16(2), pp. 227–44. [G: Finland]

Henley, Andrew. Labour's Shares and Profitability Crisis in the U.S.: Recent Experience and Post-war Trends. *Cambridge J. Econ.*, December 1987, 11(4), pp. 315–30. [G: U.S.]

Henley, Andrew. Trades Unions, Market Concentration and Income Distribution in United States Manufacturing Industry. *Int. J. Ind. Organ.*, June 1987, 5(2), pp. 193–210.

Hicks, Donald A. Geo-Industrial Shifts in Advanced Metropolitan Economies. *Urban Stud.*, December 1987, 24(6), pp. 460–79. [G: U.S.]

Hill, Hal. Concentration in Indonesian Manufacturing. *Bull. Indonesian Econ. Stud.*, August 1987, 23(2), pp. 71–100. [G: Indonesia]

Hitchens, D. M. W. N. and O'Farrell, P. N. The Comparative Performance of Small Manufacturing Firms in Northern Ireland and South East England. *Reg. Stud.*, December 1987, 21(6), pp. 543–53. [G: U.K.]

Hoke, Donald. British and American Horology: Time to Test Factor-Substitution Models. *J. Econ. Hist.*, June 1987, 47(2), pp. 321–27. [G: U.S.; U.K.]

Hosier, Richard H. The Informal Sector in Kenya: Spatial Variation and Development Alternatives. *J. Devel. Areas*, July 1987, 21(4), pp. 383–402. [G: Kenya]

Human, L. and Greenacre, M. J. Labor Market Discrimination in the Manufacturing Sector: The Impact of Race, Gender, Education and Age on Income. *S. Afr. J. Econ.*, June 1987, 55(2), pp. 150–64. **[G: S. Africa]**

Iguchi, Tomio. Aggregate Concentration, Turnover, and Mobility among the Largest Manufacturing Firms in Japan. *Antitrust Bull.*, Winter 1987, 32(4), pp. 939–65. **[G: Japan]**

Jagrén, Lars. Concentration, Exit, Entry and Reconstruction of Swedish Manufacturing. *Eliasson, G., ed.*, 1987, pp. 39–50. **[G: Sweden]**

Jagrén, Lars. Newly Established Fast Growing Nordic Companies. *Vartia, P., et al.*, 1987, pp. 209–35. **[G: Denmark; Finland; Sweden; Norway]**

James, Jeffrey. Population and Technical Change in the Manufacturing Sector of Developing Countries. *Johnson, D. G. and Lee, R. D., eds.*, 1987, pp. 225–56. **[G: LDCs]**

Jansen, Jaap C. and Kuyvenhoven, Arie. Capital Utilisation in Indonesian Medium and Large Scale Manufacturing. *Bull. Indonesian Econ. Stud.*, April 1987, 23(1), pp. 70–103. **[G: Indonesia]**

Jaumandreu, Jordi. Producción, empleo, cambio técnico y costes relativos en la industria española, 1964–85. (With English summary.) *Invest. Econ.*, September 1987, 11(3), pp. 427–61. **[G: Spain]**

Jensen, Keith Christian; Kamath, Shyam J. and Bennett, Robert E. Money in the Production Function: An Alternative Test Procedure. *Eastern Econ. J.*, July-Sept. 1987, 13(3), pp. 259–69. **[G: U.S.]**

Jimeno, Juan F. La flexibilidad de los costes laborales nominales en la industria española (1978–1982). (With English summary.) *Invest. Econ.*, September 1987, 11(3), pp. 483–96. **[G: Spain]**

Jobber, David and Hooley, Graham. Pricing Behaviour in UK Manufacturing and Service Industries. *Managerial Dec. Econ.*, June 1987, 8(2), pp. 167–71. **[G: U.K.]**

de Jong, Piet. Rational Economic Data Revisions. *J. Bus. Econ. Statist.*, October 1987, 5(4), pp. 539–48. **[G: Canada]**

Jorgenson, Dale W. Productivity and Changes in Ownership of Manufacturing Plants: Comments and Discussion. *Brookings Pap. Econ. Act.*, 1987, (3), pp. 674–78. **[G: U.S.]**

Kaiser, Carl P. Layoffs, Average Hours, and Unemployment Insurance in U.S. Manufacturing Industries. *Quart. Rev. Econ. Bus.*, Winter 1987, 27(4), pp. 80–99. **[G: U.S.]**

Kantarelis, D. and Veendorp, E. C. H. Buyer Concentration and Countervailing Power. *Quart. J. Bus. Econ.*, Summer 1987, 26(3), pp. 42–56. **[G: U.S.]**

Karmel, T. S. and Jain, Malti. Comparison of Purposive and Random Sampling Schemes for Estimating Capital Expenditure. *J. Amer. Statist. Assoc.*, March 1987, 82(397), pp. 52–57. **[G: Australia]**

Kemme, David M. Productivity Growth in Polish Industry. *J. Compar. Econ.*, March 1987, 11(1), pp. 1–20. **[G: Poland]**

Kemme, David M. The Failure of Effective Technological Transfer in Polish Industry. *Econ. Planning*, 1987, 21(1), pp. 1–12. **[G: Poland]**

Klingaman, David C. The Nature of Midwest Manufacturing in 1890. *Klingaman, D. C. and Vedder, R. K., eds.*, 1987, pp. 275–98. **[G: U.S.]**

Kobrin, Stephen J. Testing the Bargaining Hypothesis in the Manufacturing Sector in Developing Countries. *Int. Organ.*, Autumn 1987, 41(4), pp. 609–38. **[G: U.S.; LDCs]**

Kohli, Ulrich and Ryan, Christopher J. Investment and Interest Rates: An Econometric Dissection. *J. Macroecon.*, Summer 1987, 9(3), pp. 373–89. **[G: Australia]**

Kol, Jacob. Exports from Developing Countries: Some Facts and Scope. *Europ. Econ. Rev.*, Feb./Mar. 1987, 31(1/2), pp. 466–74. **[G: LDCs; OECD]**

Kraft, Kornelius. Quasi-fixity of White-Collar and Blue-Collar Workers and of Their Houses of Work in West-German Manufacturing Industries. *J. Inst. Theoretical Econ.*, September 1987, 143(3), pp. 477–96. **[G: W. Germany]**

Kreinin, Mordechai E. Comparative Advantage and Possible Trade Restrictions in High-Technology Products. *Salvatore, D., ed.*, 1987, pp. 297–332. **[G: U.S.]**

Kreinin, Mordechai E.; Martin, Stephen and Sheehey, Edmund J. Differential Response of U.S. Import Prices and Quantities to Exchange-Rate Adjustments. *Weltwirtsch. Arch.*, 1987, 123(3), pp. 449–62. **[G: U.S.]**

Krugman, Paul R. Imports in Japan: Closed Markets or Minds? Comment. *Brookings Pap. Econ. Act.*, 1987, (2), pp. 549–52. **[G: Japan]**

Krugman, Paul R. and Hatsopoulos, George N. The Problem of U.S. Competitiveness in Manufacturing. *New Eng. Econ. Rev.*, Jan./Feb. 1987, pp. 18–29. **[G: U.S.]**

Kulatilaka, Nalin. The Specification of Partial Static Equilibrium Models. *Rev. Econ. Statist.*, May 1987, 69(2), pp. 327–35. **[G: U.S.]**

Kumar, Nagesh. Technology Imports and Local Research and Development in Indian Manufacturing. *Devel. Econ.*, September 1987, 25(3), pp. 220–33. **[G: India]**

Kyer, Ben L. Real Money Balances and the Productivity Growth Slowdown: The U.S. Manufacturing Sector, 1955–81. *Atlantic Econ. J.*, March 1987, 15(1), pp. 42–55. **[G: U.S.]**

Lall, Sanjaya; Khanna, Ashok and Alikhani, Iradj. Determinants of Manufactured Export Performance in Low-Income Africa: Kenya and Tanzania. *World Devel.*, September 1987, 15(9), pp. 1219–24. **[G: Kenya; Tanzania]**

Lawrence, Robert Z. Imports in Japan: Closed Markets or Minds? *Brookings Pap. Econ. Act.*, 1987, (2), pp. 517–48. **[G: Japan]**

Lawrence, Robert Z. Is Deindustrialization a Myth? [The Myth of U.S. Deindustrialization]. *Staudohar, P. D. and Brown, H. E.*, 1987, 1983, pp. 25–40. **[G: U.S.; OECD]**

Lawson, James. Civilian Market Opportunities for Defense Industry. *Lynch, J. E., ed.*, 1987, pp. 155–74. **[G: U.S.]**

Lawson, James. Industrial Plant Reuse and Conversion. *Lynch, J. E., ed.*, 1987, pp. 129–36. **[G: U.S.]**

Leamer, Edward E. Paths of Development in the Three-Factor, *n*-Good General Equilibrium Model. *J. Polit. Econ.*, October 1987, 95(5), pp. 961–99. **[G: Selected Countries]**

Lewis, J. R. and Williams, A. M. Productive Decentralization or Indigenous Growth? Small Manufacturing Enterprises and Regional Development in Central Portugal. *Reg. Stud.*, August 1987, 21(4), pp. 343–61. **[G: Portugal]**

Lichtenberg, Frank R. and Siegel, Donald. Productivity and Changes in Ownership of Manufacturing Plants. *Brookings Pap. Econ. Act.*, 1987, (3), pp. 643–73. **[G: U.S.]**

Little, Ian M. D. Small Manufacturing Enterprises in Developing Countries. *World Bank Econ. Rev.*, January 1987, 1(2), pp. 203–35. **[G: Colombia; India]**

Lloyd-Jones, Roger. Innovation, Industrial Structure and the Long Wave: The British Economy c. 1873–1914. *J. Europ. Econ. Hist.*, Fall 1987, 16(2), pp. 315–53. **[G: U.K.]**

Lynch, John E. Economic Adjustment and Conversion of Defense Industries: Introduction. *Lynch, J. E., ed.*, 1987, pp. 1–12. **[G: U.S.]**

Madian, Alan L. Technology and the Changing Industrial Balance. *Thorup, C. L., ed.*, 1987, pp. 41–66. **[G: Mexico; U.S.]**

Magnus, Jan R. and Woodland, Alan D. Interfuel Substitution in Dutch Manufacturing. *Appl. Econ.*, December 1987, 19(12), pp. 1639–64. **[G: Netherlands]**

Mair, Douglas. Prices and Income Distribution in Manufacturing Industry: Comment. *J. Post Keynesian Econ.*, Fall 1987, 10(1), pp. 154–60. **[G: Italy; U.S.]**

Malle, Silvana. Capacity Utilization and the Shift Coefficient in Soviet Planning. *Econ. Planning*, 1987, 21(2–3), pp. 63–86. **[G: U.S.S.R.]**

Mandelbaum, Thomas B. Is Eighth District Manufacturing Endangered? *Fed. Res. Bank St. Louis Rev.*, November 1987, 69(9), pp. 5–15. **[G: U.S.]**

Mansfield, Edwin. Productivity and Changes in Ownership of Manufacturing Plants: Comments and Discussion. *Brookings Pap. Econ. Act.*, 1987, (3), pp. 678–81. **[G: U.S.]**

de Maria y Campos, Mauricio. Mexico's New Industrial Development Strategy. *Thorup, C. L., ed.*, 1987, pp. 67–81. **[G: Mexico]**

Mayes, David G. Does Manufacturing Matter? *Nat. Inst. Econ. Rev.*, November 1987, (122), pp. 47–58. **[G: U.K.]**

Mbelle, A. V. Y. Pathology of a Crisis in Industrial Development: Tanzania after 1974. *Eastern Afr. Econ. Rev.*, December 1987, 3(2), pp. 95–103. **[G: Tanzania]**

McCombie, John S. L. Does the Aggregate Production Function Imply Anything about the Laws of Production? A Note. *Appl. Econ.*, August 1987, 19(8), pp. 1121–36. **[G: Australia]**

McElroy, Marjorie B. Additive General Error Models for Production, Cost, and Derived Demand or Share Systems. *J. Polit. Econ.*, August 1987, 95(4), pp. 737–57. **[G: U.S.]**

McHugh, Richard and Lane, Julia. The Age of Capital, the Age of Utilized Capital, and Tests of the Embodiment Hypothesis. *Rev. Econ. Statist.*, May 1987, 69(2), pp. 362–67. **[G: U.S.]**

McUsic, Molly. U.S. Manufacturing: Any Cause for Alarm? *New Eng. Econ. Rev.*, Jan./Feb. 1987, pp. 3–17. **[G: U.S.]**

Michl, Thomas R. Is There Evidence for a Marginalist Demand for Labour? *Cambridge J. Econ.*, December 1987, 11(4), pp. 361–73. **[G: U.S.]**

Montgomery, Edward and Wascher, William L. Race and Gender Wage Inequality in Services and Manufacturing. *Ind. Relat.*, Fall 1987, 26(3), pp. 284–90. **[G: U.S.]**

Moore, Michael L.; Steece, Bert M. and Swenson, Charles W. An Analysis of the Impact of State Income Tax Rates and Bases on Foreign Investment. *Accounting Rev.*, October 1987, 62(4), pp. 671–85. **[G: U.S.]**

Mullen, John K. and Williams, Martin. Technical Progress in Urban Manufacturing: North–South Comparisons. *J. Urban Econ.*, March 1987, 21(2), pp. 194–208. **[G: U.S.]**

Nakosteen, Robert A. and Zimmer, Michael A. Determinants of Regional Migration by Manufacturing Firms. *Econ. Inquiry*, April 1987, 25(2), pp. 351–62. **[G: U.S.]**

Natke, Paul A. Foreign Ownership and Firm-Level Import Performance in Brazilian Manufacturing Industries. *Atlantic Econ. J.*, December 1987, 15(4), pp. 39–48. **[G: Brazil]**

Ndlela, Daniel B. The Manufacturing Sector in the East and Southern African Subregion, with Emphasis on the SADCC. *Amin, S.; Chitala, D. and Mandaza, I., eds.*, 1987, pp. 37–61. **[G: E. Africa; Southern Africa]**

Neef, Arthur and Thomas, James. Trends in Manufacturing Productivity and Labor Costs in the U.S. and Abroad. *Mon. Lab. Rev.*, December 1987, 110(12), pp. 25–30. **[G: OECD]**

Nissan, Edward and Caveny, Regina. A Composite Manufacturing Growth Index: 1954–1978. *Rev. Reg. Stud.*, Winter 1987, 17(1), pp. 67–70. **[G: U.S.]**

Norwood, Janet L. The Labor Force of the Future. *Bus. Econ.*, July 1987, 22(3), pp. 9–14. **[G: U.S.]**

O'Farrell, P. N. and Crouchley, R. Manufacturing-Plant Closures: A Dynamic Survival Model. *Environ. Planning A*, March 1987, 19(3), pp. 313–29. **[G: Ireland]**

O'Neill, Dave M. We're Not Losing Our Industrial Base. *Challenge*, Sept./Oct. 1987, 30(4), pp. 19–25. **[G: U.S.]**

Odagiri, Hiroyuki and Yamashita, Takashi. Price Mark-Ups, Market Structure, and Business Fluctuation in Japanese Manufacturing Industries. *J. Ind. Econ.*, March 1987, 35(3), pp. 317–31. **[G: Japan]**

Ohno, Koichi and Imaoka, Hideki. The Experience of Dual-Industrial Growth: Korea and Taiwan. *Devel. Econ.*, December 1987, 25(4), pp. 310–24. **[G: S. Korea; Taiwan]**

Olson, Dennis O. and Shieh, Yeung-Nan. An Economic Analysis of Factor Usage and Workplace Regulation: Comment. *Southern Econ. J.*, January 1987, 53(3), pp. 786–89. **[G: U.S.]**

Osmani, S. R. The Impact of Economic Liberalisation on the Small-Scale and Rural Industries of Sri Lanka. *Islam, R., ed.*, 1987, pp. 171–209. **[G: Sri Lanka]**

Oulton, Nicholas. Plant Closures and the Productivity 'Miracle' in Manufacturing. *Nat. Inst. Econ. Rev.*, August 1987, (121), pp. 53–59. **[G: U.K.]**

Parker, William N. Native Origins of Modern Industry: Heavy Industrialization in the Old Northwest before 1900. *Klingaman, D. C. and Vedder, R. K., eds.*, 1987, pp. 243–74. **[G: U.S.]**

Parker, William N. New England's Early Industrialization: A Sketch. *Kilby, P., ed.*, 1987, pp. 17–46. **[G: U.S.]**

Patel, Pari and Soete, Luc. Technological Trends and Employment in the UK Manufacturing Sectors. *Freeman, C. and Soete, L., eds.*, 1987, pp. 122–68. **[G: U.K.]**

Paulus, John D. and Gay, Robert S. U.S. Mergers Are Helping Productivity. *Challenge*, May/June 1987, 30(2), pp. 54–57. **[G: U.S.]**

Pennings, Johannes M. Technological Innovations in Manufacturing. *Pennings, J. M. and Buitendam, A., eds.*, 1987, pp. 197–216.

Perna, Nicholas S. The Shift from Manufacturing to Services: A Concerned View. *New Eng. Econ. Rev.*, Jan./Feb. 1987, pp. 30–38.

Pigliaru, Francesco. The Performance of the Mezzogiorno's Indigenous Manufacturing Sector, 1951–70: A Discussion on Graziani's Effect and the Cumulative Causation Hypothesis. *Stud. Econ.*, 1987, 42(33), pp. 3–40. **[G: Italy]**

Pollak, Robert A. and Wales, Terence J. Specification and Estimation of Nonseparable Two-Stage Technologies: The Leontief CES and the Cobb–Douglas CES. *J. Polit. Econ.*, April 1987, 95(2), pp. 311–33. **[G: U.S.]**

Pousette, Tomas and Lindberg, Thomas. Services in Production and Production of Services in Swedish Manufacturing. *Eliasson, G., ed.*, 1987, pp. 51–62. **[G: Sweden]**

Powell, Irene. The Effect of Reductions in Concentration on Income Distribution. *Rev. Econ. Statist.*, February 1987, 69(1), pp. 75–82.

Ray, George F. Erratum [Labour Costs in Manufacturing]. *Nat. Inst. Econ. Rev.*, November 1987, (122), pp. 96. **[G: OECD]**

Ray, George F. Labour Costs in Manufacturing. *Nat. Inst. Econ. Rev.*, May 1987, (120), pp. 71–74. **[G: OECD]**

Rios, Sandra Maria C. Polônia. Exportações brasileiras de produtos manufaturados: uma avaliação econométrica para o período 1964/84. (With English summary.) *Pesquisa Planejamento Econ.*, August 1987, 17(2), pp. 299–332. **[G: Brazil]**

Robertson, Paul. The Strategic Development of Repco and National Consolidated Limited, 1945–1983. *Australian Econ. Hist. Rev.*, September 1987, 27(2), pp. 3–36. **[G: Australia]**

Rodriguez Romero, Luis. Elasticidad de sustitución entre inputs primarios en las grandes empresas industriales españolas. (With English summary.) *Invest. Econ.*, September 1987, 11(3), pp. 399–426. **[G: Spain]**

Roy, Dilip Kumar. Employment Linkages in Bangladesh Industries. *Industry Devel.*, 1987, (21), pp. 63–74. **[G: Bangladesh]**

Roy, Dilip Kumar. Exports and Labour Absorption: The Case of Bangladesh Manufactures. *Industry Devel.*, 1987, (22), pp. 67–92. **[G: Bangladesh]**

Rozenova, L. Price and the Quality of Machinery. *Prob. Econ.*, January 1987, 29(9), pp. 79–95. **[G: U.S.S.R.]**

Rutledge, Gary L. and Stergioulas, Nikolaos. Plant and Equipment Expenditures by Business for Pollution Abatement, 1986 and 1987. *Surv. Curr. Bus.*, October 1987, 67(10), pp. 23–26. **[G: U.S.]**

Saicheua, Supavud. Input Substitution in Thailand's Manufacturing Sector: Implications for Energy Policy. *Energy Econ.*, January 1987, 9(1), pp. 55–63. **[G: Thailand]**

Saith, Ashwani. Contrasting Experiences in Rural Industrialisation: Are the East Asian Successes Transferable? *Islam, R., ed.*, 1987, pp. 241–303. **[G: Japan; Taiwan; S. Korea]**

Salvary, Stanley C. W. An Empirical Test of the Dominant Industry Hypothesis: Some Preliminary Evidence. *Reg. Sci. Persp.*, 1987, 17(1), pp. 77–102. **[G: U.S.]**

Salvatore, Dominick. The New Protectionist Threat to World Welfare: Introduction. *Salvatore, D., ed.*, 1987, pp. 1–27. **[G: Global]**

Sanderson, Susan Walsh, et al. Impacts of Computer-Aided Manufacturing on Offshore Assembly and Future Manufacturing Locations. *Reg. Stud.*, April 1987, 21(2), pp. 131–41. **[G: Mexico; Singapore; U.S.]**

Schwalbach, Joachim. Entry by Diversified Firms into German Industries. *Int. J. Ind. Organ.*, March 1987, 5(1), pp. 43–49. **[G: W. Germany]**

Schwartz, Moshe, et al. Moshav-Based Industry. *Bar-El, R., ed.*, 1987, pp. 57–104. **[G: Israel]**

Scott, John T. and Pascoe, George. Purposive Diversification of R&D in Manufacturing. *J. Ind. Econ.*, December 1987, 36(2), pp. 193–205. **[G: U.S.]**

Sharp, Margaret. Europe: Collaboration in the High Technology Sectors. *Oxford Rev. Econ. Policy*, Spring 1987, 3(1), pp. 52–65. **[G: W. Europe; Japan; U.S.]**

Siddayao, Corazon Morales, et al. Estimates of Energy and Non-energy Elasticities in Selected Asian Manufacturing Sectors: Policy Implications. *Energy Econ.*, April 1987, 9(2), pp. 115–28. **[G: Bangladesh; Philippines; Thailand]**

Smith, Richard L. The Choice of Issuance Procedure and the Cost of Competitive and Negotiated Underwriting: An Examination of the Impact of Rule 50. *J. Finance*, July 1987, *42*(3), pp. 703–20. [G: U.S.]

Soares, Maria Isabel R. T. L'utilisation de l'énergie dans un contexte interindustriel: analyse du profil enérgétique de l'inudstrie portugaise des textiles et de l'habillement. (With English summary.) *Economia (Portugal)*, May 1987, *11*(2), pp. 157–70. [G: Portugal]

Sosin, Kim and Fairchild, Loretta. Capital Intensity and Export Propensity in Some Latin American Countries. *Oxford Bull. Econ. Statist.*, May 1987, *49*(2), pp. 191–208. [G: Latin America]

de Sousa, Maria da Conceição Sampaio. Avaliação econômica do Programa Nacional do Álcool (PROÁLCOOL): uma análise de equilíbrio geral. (With English summary.) *Pesquisa Planejamento Econ.*, August 1987, *17*(2), pp. 381–410. [G: Brazil]

Stavrinos, Vasilios G. The Intertemporal Stability of Kaldor's First and Second Growth Laws in the UK. *Appl. Econ.*, September 1987, *19*(9), pp. 1201–09. [G: U.K.]

Stirati, Antonella. Differenze retributive e segregazione occupazionale per sesso nell'industria manifatturiera. (Wage Differences and Occupational Segregation by Sex in the Manufacturing Industries. With English summary.) *Econ. Lavoro*, July-Sept. 1987, *21*(3), pp. 51–76. [G: Italy]

Struckmeyer, Charles S. The Putty-Clay Perspective on the Capital–Energy Complementarity Debate. *Rev. Econ. Statist.*, May 1987, *69*(2), pp. 320–26. [G: U.S.]

Sylos-Labini, Paolo. Reply [Prices and Income Distribution in Manufacturing Industry]. *J. Post Keynesian Econ.*, Fall 1987, *10*(1), pp. 161–62. [G: U.S.; Italy]

Teitel, Simón and Thoumi, Francisco E. De la sustitución de importaciones a las exportaciones: la experiencia de las exportaciones manufactureras de la Argentina y el Brasil. (With English summary.) *Desarrollo Econ.*, Apr.-June 1987, *27*(105), pp. 29–60. [G: Argentina; Brazil]

Terweduwe, D. The Newly and Semi-industrialized Countries: A Critical Appraisal of the Country Classifications. *Tijdschrift Econ. Manage.*, 1987, *32*(1), pp. 55–71. [G: Selected LDCs]

Teubal, Morris. Neutrality in Science Policy: The Promotion of Sophisticated Industrial Technology in Israel. *Teubal, M.*, 1987, pp. 179–203. [G: Israel]

Teubal, Morris. The Role of Technological Learning in the Exports of Manufactured Goods: The Case of Selected Capital Goods in Brazil. *Teubal, M.*, 1987, pp. 104–30. [G: Brazil]

Thompson, Wilbur R. and Thompson, Philip R. National Industries and Local Occupational Strengths: The Cross-Hairs of Targeting. *Urban Stud.*, December 1987, *24*(6), pp. 547–60. [G: U.S.]

Tidrick, Gene and Chen, Jiyuan. China's Industrial Reform: Characteristics of the Twenty Firms. *Tidrick, G. and Jiyuan, C., eds.*, 1987, pp. 11–38. [G: China]

Tyler, P. and Kitson, M. Geographical Variations in Transport Costs of Manufacturing Firms in Great Britain. *Urban Stud.*, February 1987, *24*(1), pp. 61–73. [G: U.K.]

Udis, Bernard. European Conversion Experience. *Lynch, J. E., ed.*, 1987, pp. 121–28. [G: W. Europe]

Utterback, James M. Innovation and Industrial Evolution in Manufacturing Industries. *Guile, B. R. and Brooks, H., eds.*, 1987, pp. 16–48.

Vernon, Raymond. Coping with Technological Change: U.S. Problems and Prospects. *Guile, B. R. and Brooks, H., eds.*, 1987, pp. 160–90. [G: U.S.]

Wagner, Joachim and Bellmann, Lutz. Importdruck, Anpassungsstrategien und Qualifikationsstruktur: Eineökonometrische Untersuchung für Industrien des Verarbeitenden Gewerbes in der Bundesrepublik Deutschland 1976–1983. (Import Pressure, Adjustment Strategies, and Structure of Employment—An Econometric Study for Manufacturing Industries in the Federal Republic of Germany, 1976–1983. With English summary.) *Z. Wirtschaft. Sozialwissen.*, 1987, *107*(4), pp. 513–35. [G: W. Germany]

Wagner, Joachim and Bellmann, Lutz. Produkt- und Prozessinnovationen als Unternehmensstrategien bei Importdruck. Eine ökonometrische Untersuchung für Industrien des Verarbeitenden Gewerbes in der Bundesrepublik Deutschland (1976–1983). (Product and Process Innovations: Strategies for Firms under Import Pressure. An Econometric Study for Manufacturing Industries in the Federal Republic of Germany [1976–1983]. With English summary.) *Ifo-Studien*, 1987, *33*(3), pp. 223–42. [G: W. Germany]

Watanabe, Susumu. Technological Capability and Industrialisation. Effects of Aid and Sanctions in the United Republic of Tanzania and Zimbabwe. *Int. Lab. Rev.*, Sept.-Oct. 1987, *126*(5), pp. 525–41. [G: Zimbabwe; Tanzania]

Whiteman, John L. Productivity and Growth in Australian Manufacturing Industry. *J. Post Keynesian Econ.*, Summer 1987, *9*(4), pp. 576–92. [G: Australia]

Winiecki, Jan. Überdimensionierung des industriellen Sektors bei zentraler Planung: Empirische Evidenz und Auswirkungen auf Allokation und Wachstum. (The Oversized Industrial Sector in Centrally Planned Economies: Empirical Evidence and Effects on Resource Allocation and Growth. With English summary.) *Ifo-Studien*, 1987, *33*(4), pp. 251–75. [G: E. Europe]

Yordon, Wesley J. Evidence against Diminishing Returns in Manufacturing and Comments on Short-run Models of Price–Output Behavior. *J. Post Keynesian Econ.*, Summer 1987, *9*(4), pp. 593–603. [G: U.S.]

Zimbalist, Andrew. Cuban Industrial Growth,

1965–84. *Zimbalist, A., ed.*, 1987, pp. 85–95.
[G: Cuba]
Zimbalist, Andrew. Cuban Industrial Growth, 1965–84. *World Devel.*, January 1987, *15*(1), pp. 83–93. [G: Cuba]
Zohar, Uri and Luski, Israel. A Note on the Measurement of the Slowdown in Total Factor Productivity. *Appl. Econ.*, September 1987, *19*(9), pp. 1211–19. [G: Canada]

6312 Metals (iron, steel, and other)

Adams, F. Gerard. Industrial Modeling with Input–Output: An Application to the Italian Metal Mechanical Industry. *Tchijov, I. and Tomaszewicz, L., eds.*, 1987, pp. 125–37.
[G: Italy]
Ahlburg, Dennis A., et al. Technological Change, Market Decline, and Industrial Relations in the U.S. Steel Industry. *Cornfield, D. B., ed.*, 1987, pp. 229–45. [G: U.S.]
Appleby, Colin and Bessant, John. Adapting to Decline: Organizational Structures and Government Policy in the UK and West German Foundry Sectors. *Wilks, S. and Wright, M., eds.*, 1987, pp. 181–210. [G: U.K.; W. Germany]
Brown, Martin and Nuwer, Michael. Strategic Jobs and Wage Structure in the Steel Industry: 1910–1930. *Ind. Relat.*, Fall 1987, *26*(3), pp. 253–66. [G: U.S.]
Collins, James F. Trends in the U.S. Steel Industry. *Faruqui, A. and Broehl, J., eds.*, 1987, pp. 271–85. [G: U.S.]
Crandall, Robert W. The Effects of U.S. Trade Protection for Autos and Steel. *Brookings Pap. Econ. Act.*, 1987, (1), pp. 271–88. [G: U.S.]
Dahlman, Carl J. and Fonseca, Fernando Valadares. From Technological Dependence to Technological Development: The Case of the USIMINAS Steel Plant in Brazil. *Katz, J. M., ed.*, 1987, pp. 154–82. [G: Brazil]
Dicke, Hugo and Glismann, Hans H. The Rise and Decline of West German Steel Industry: The Role of National and Supranational Agencies. *Aussenwirtschaft*, December 1987, *42*(4), pp. 421–41. [G: W. Germany]
Fischer, Klaus P.; Olson, David L. and Richard, Victor. Political Risk and the Trend of New Investment in the World Aluminum Industry. *J. Econ. Devel.*, June 1987, *12*(1), pp. 117–36. [G: Global]
FitzRoy, Felix R. and Kraft, Kornelius. Cooperation, Productivity, and Profit Sharing. *Quart. J. Econ.*, February 1987, *102*(1), pp. 23–35. [G: W. Germany]
Francis, A. A. Excess Capacity in Alumina: Some Implications for the Bauxite–Alumina Industry of Jamaica. *Soc. Econ. Stud.*, March 1987, *36*(1), pp. 269–87. [G: Jamaica]
Gajanan, S. N. Input Substitution in Indian Iron and Steel: A Regional Analysis. *Margin*, December 1987, *20*(1), pp. 30–41. [G: India]
Hattwick, Richard E. Kenneth Iverson of Nucor. *J. Behav. Econ.*, Fall 1987, *16*(3), pp. 99–104. [G: U.S.]

Hogan, William T. Protectionism in the Steel Industry: A Historical Perspective. *Salvatore, D., ed.*, 1987, pp. 352–64. [G: Global]
Howell, Thomas. Steel and the State in Romania. *Comp. Econ. Stud.*, Summer 1987, *29*(2), pp. 71–100. [G: Romania]
Inwood, Kris. Progress without Planning: The Economic History of Ontario from Confederation to the Second World War: The Iron and Steel Industry. *Drummond, I. M.*, 1987, pp. 185–207. [G: Canada]
Kenward, Lloyd R. The Decline of the U.S. Steel Industry. *Finance Develop.*, December 1987, *24*(4), pp. 30–33. [G: U.S.]
Krugman, Paul R. Targeted Industrial Policies: Theory and Evidence. *Salvatore, D., ed.*, 1987, pp. 266–96. [G: Japan; U.S.]
Link, Albert N. and Tassey, Gregory. The Impact of Standards on Technology-Based Industries: The Case of Numerically Controlled Machine Tools in Automated Batch Manufacturing. *Gabel, H. L., ed.*, 1987, pp. 217–37. [G: U.S.]
Maxwell, Philip. Adequate Technological Strategy in an Imperfect Economic Context: A Case-Study of the Evolution of the Acindar Steelplant in Rosario, Argentina. *Katz, J. M., ed.*, 1987, pp. 119–53. [G: Argentina]
McCaffray, Susan P. Origins of Labor Policy in the Russian Coal and Steel Industry, 1874–1900. *J. Econ. Hist.*, December 1987, *47*(4), pp. 951–65. [G: Russia]
Pérez, Luis Alberto and Pérez y Peniche, José de Jesús. A Summary of the Principal Findings of the Case-Study on the Technological Behaviour of the Mexican Steel Firm Altos Hornos de Mexico. *Katz, J. M., ed.*, 1987, pp. 183–91. [G: Mexico]
Pindyck, Robert S. and Rotemberg, Julio J. Are Imports to Blame? Attribution of Injury under the 1974 Trade Act. *J. Law Econ.*, April 1987, *30*(1), pp. 101–22. [G: U.S.]
Rogers, Robert P. Unobservable Transactions Price and the Measurement of a Supply and Demand Model for the American Steel Industry. *J. Bus. Econ. Statist.*, July 1987, *5*(3), pp. 407–15. [G: U.S.]
Sato, Mitsuaki. Costs and Benefits to the United States of the 1985 Steel Import Quota Program: Discussion. *Sato, R. and Wachtel, P., eds.*, 1987, pp. 181–83. [G: U.S.; Japan]
Schorsch, Louis L. Can Big Steel Change Bad Habits? *Challenge*, July/Aug. 1987, *30*(3), pp. 32–40. [G: U.S.; W. Europe]
Sherwood, Mark K. Performance of Multifactor Productivity in the Steel and Motor Vehicles Industries. *Mon. Lab. Rev.*, August 1987, *110*(8), pp. 22–31. [G: U.S.]
Sundberg, Matti. Har nordiskt stål en framtid? (Is There a Future for Nordic Steel? With English summary.) *Ekon. Samfundets Tidskr.*, 1987, *40*(3), pp. 115–22. [G: Finland]
Tarr, David G. Costs and Benefits to the United States of the 1985 Steel Import Quota Program. *Sato, R. and Wachtel, P., eds.*, 1987, pp. 159–77. [G: Japan; U.S.]
Tiffany, Paul. Opportunity Denied: The Abortive

Attempt to Internationalize the American Steel Industry, 1903–1929. *Atack, J., ed.,* 1987, pp. 229–47. **[G: U.S.]**

Villa, Paola. Systems of Flexible Working in the Italian Steel Industry. *Tarling, R., ed.,* 1987, pp. 307–45. **[G: Italy]**

Vollebergh, Ad. The European Steel Industry— A Model for European Co-operation? *Macmillen, M.; Mayes, D. G. and van Veen, P., eds.,* 1987, pp. 194–228. **[G: EEC]**

White, Lawrence J. Costs and Benefits to the United States of the 1985 Steel Import Quota Program: Discussion. *Sato, R. and Wachtel, P., eds.,* 1987, pp. 177–81. **[G: U.S.; Japan]**

6313 Machinery (tools, electrical equipment, computers, communication equipment, and appliances)

Alic, John A.; Harris, Martha Caldwell and Miller, Robert R. The U.S. Electronics Industry in the World Economy. *Faruqui, A. and Broehl, J., eds.,* 1987, pp. 329–47. **[G: U.S.]**

Anderson, Oskar. Zur Treffsicherheit der Antizipationen im Ifo-Konjunkturtest (KT) in Abhängigkeit von der Betriebsgrösse. (The Accuracy of Anticipations in the Ifo-Business-Test Dependent on the Firm Size. With English summary.) *Jahr. Nationalökon. Statist.,* October 1987, *203*(5–6), pp. 451–55. **[G: W. Germany]**

Blang, Hans-Georg and Schöler, Klaus. Informationsgrundlagen und Preiserwartungen. Eine empirische Untersuchung der Verkaufspreiserwartungen in der deutschen Industrie. (Information Sets and Price Expectations. An Empirical Investigation of the German Industrial Selling Price Expectations. With English summary.) *Ifo-Studien,* 1987, *33*(2), pp. 133–51. **[G: W. Germany]**

Brundenius, Claes. Development and Prospects of Capital Goods Production in Revolutionary Cuba. *Zimbalist, A., ed.,* 1987, pp. 97–114. **[G: Cuba]**

Burton, F. N. and Saelens, F. H. Trade Barriers and Japanese Foreign Direct Investment in the Colour Television Industry. *Managerial Dec. Econ.,* December 1987, *8*(4), pp. 285–93. **[G: Japan]**

Cawson, Alan; Holmes, Peter and Stevens, Anne. The Interaction between Firms and the State in France: The Telecommunications and Consumer Electronics Sectors. *Wilks, S. and Wright, M., eds.,* 1987, pp. 10–34. **[G: France]**

Chen, Tain-Jy and Tang, De-Piao. Comparing Technical Efficiency between Import-Substitution-Oriented and Export-Oriented Foreign Firms in a Developing Economy. *J. Devel. Econ.,* August 1987, *26*(2), pp. 277–89. **[G: Taiwan]**

Chen, Tain-Jy and Tang, De-Piao. Offshore Assembly and Short-run Labor–Labor Substitution. *Weltwirtsch. Arch.,* 1987, *123*(1), pp. 140–48. **[G: Taiwan]**

Edquist, Charles and Jacobsson, Staffan. The In-

tegrated Circuit Industries of India and the Republic of Korea in an International Technoeconomic Context. *Industry Devel.,* 1987, (21), pp. 1–62. **[G: India; S. Korea]**

Ernst, Dieter. The Impact of Microelectronics on the Worldwide Restructuring of the Electronics Industry: Implications for the Third World. *Dunning, J. H. and Usui, M., eds.,* 1987, pp. 117–34. **[G: LDCs]**

Gabel, H. Landis. Open Standards in the European Computer Industry: The Case of X/Open. *Gabel, H. L., ed.,* 1987, pp. 91–123.

Graham, George M., Jr. Total Quality at Texas Instruments. *Shetty, Y. K. and Buehler, V. M., eds.,* 1987, pp. 331–38. **[G: U.S.]**

Hartley, Keith. Public Procurement and Competitiveness: A Community Market for Military Hardware and Technology? *J. Common Market Stud.,* March 1987, *25*(3), pp. 237–47. **[G: EEC]**

Henderson, Jeffrey. Semiconductors, Scotland and the International Division of Labour. *Urban Stud.,* October 1987, *24*(5), pp. 389–408. **[G: Scotland]**

Hergert, Michael. Technical Standards and Competition in the Microcomputer Industry. *Gabel, H. L., ed.,* 1987, pp. 67–89.

Howells, Jeremy. Developments in the Location, Technology and Industrial Organization of Computer Services: Some Trends and Research Issues. *Reg. Stud.,* December 1987, *21*(6), pp. 493–503. **[G: U.K.]**

Hyman, Eric L. The Strategy of Production and Distribution of Improved Charcoal Stoves in Kenya. *World Devel.,* March 1987, *15*(3), pp. 375–86. **[G: Kenya]**

Jun, Yongwook. The Reverse Direct Investment: The Case of the Korean Consumer Electronics Industry. *Int. Econ. J.,* Autumn 1987, *1*(3), pp. 91–104. **[G: S. Korea]**

Kako, Toshiyuki. Development of the Farm Machinery Industry in Japan: A Case Study of the Walking Type Tractor. *Hitotsubashi J. Econ.,* December 1987, *28*(2), pp. 155–71. **[G: Japan]**

Kiyokawa, Yukihiko and Ishikawa, Shigeru. The Significance of Standardization in the Development of the Machine-Tool Industry: The Cases of Japan and China (Part 1). *Hitotsubashi J. Econ.,* December 1987, *28*(2), pp. 123–54. **[G: China; Japan]**

Kubát, Milan. We Know What We Must Do. *Czech. Econ. Digest.,* January 1987, (2), pp. 3–12. **[G: Czechoslovakia]**

Kuchler, Fred and Vroomen, Harry. Impacts of the PIK Program on the Farm Machinery Market. *J. Agr. Econ. Res.,* Summer 1987, *39*(3), pp. 2–11. **[G: U.S.]**

Lehnerd, Alvin P. Revitalizing the Manufacture and Design of Mature Global Products. *Guile, B. R. and Brooks, H., eds.,* 1987, pp. 49–64.

Lintner, V. G., et al. Trade Unions and Technological Change in the U.K. Mechanical Engineering Industry. *Brit. J. Ind. Relat.,* March 1987, *25*(1), pp. 19–29. **[G: U.K.]**

Martin, Fernand and Tremblay, Rodrigue. The

Canadian Industries of Telecommunication Equipments and Computers, and North American Trade Liberalization. *Tremblay, R., ed.,* 1987, pp. 377–405.   **[G: Canada; U.S.]**

Meir, Peter and Gadgil, Ashok. Use of Microcomputers in Energy Economics and Planning in LDCs. *Pachauri, R. K., ed.,* 1987, pp. 1237–47.   **[G: LDCs]**

Mody, Ashoka and Wheeler, David. Prices, Costs, and Competition at the Technology Frontier: A Model for Semiconductor Memories. *J. Policy Modeling,* Summer 1987, *9*(2), pp. 367–82.   **[G: U.S.]**

Mohnen, P. The Effects of U.S. Shocks on Canadian Total Factor Productivity Growth: The Case of the Electrical Products Industry. *Empirical Econ.,* 1987, *12*(4), pp. 221–47.

Moussa, Hassouna. Tobin's *q*, the Demand for Investment and the Corporate Profit Taxation Policy in Canada (1950–1983). *Rech. Écon. Louvain,* 1987, *53*(1), pp. 27–50.   **[G: Canada]**

Noyce, Robert N. Intel's Leader Looks at the Computer Evolution in the 21st Century. *Shetty, Y. K. and Buehler, V. M., eds.,* 1987, pp. 223–34.   **[G: U.S.]**

O'Neil, Barbara A. The Mining Machinery Industry: Labor Productivity Trends, 1972–84. *Mon. Lab. Rev.,* June 1987, *110*(6), pp. 31–36.   **[G: U.S.]**

Pelkmans, Jacques and Beuter, Rita. Standardization and Competitiveness: Private and Public Strategies in the EC Color TV Industry. *Gabel, H. L., ed.,* 1987, pp. 171–215.   **[G: W. Europe]**

Pozdena, Randall Johnston. Competition in the Semiconductor Industry. *Fed. Res. Bank San Francisco Econ. Rev.,* Spring 1987, (2), pp. 41–56.   **[G: U.S.]**

Pudup, Mary Beth. From Farm to Factory: Structuring and Location of the U.S. Farm Machinery Industry. *Econ. Geogr.,* July 1987, *63*(3), pp. 203–22.   **[G: U.S.]**

Pugel, Thomas A. Limits of Trade Policy toward High Technology Industries: The Case of Semiconductors. *Sato, R. and Wachtel, P., eds.,* 1987, pp. 184–223.   **[G: U.S.; Japan]**

Ramachandran, Rama V. Limits of Trade Policy toward High Technology Industries: The Case of Semiconductors: Discussion. *Sato, R. and Wachtel, P., eds.,* 1987, pp. 223–30.   **[G: U.S.; Japan]**

Raubitschek, Ruth S. Limits of Trade Policy toward High Technology Industries: The Case of Semiconductors: Discussion. *Sato, R. and Wachtel, P., eds.,* 1987, pp. 230–37.   **[G: Japan; U.S.]**

Rees, John. The Diffusion of New Production Technology: Implications for State and Local Industrial Policy. *Goldstein, H. A., ed.,* 1987, pp. 60–72.   **[G: U.S.]**

Rully, A. Donald. IBM View of Information Systems: Trends, Issues, and Technology. *Shetty, Y. K. and Buehler, V. M., eds.,* 1987, pp. 183–95.   **[G: U.S.]**

Saelens, F. H. Japanese Strategies for Serving

Overseas Markets: The Case of Electronics. *Trevor, M., ed.,* 1987, pp. 50–62. **[G: Japan]**

Sanderson, Susan Walsh. Automated Manufacturing and Offshore Assembly in Mexico. *Thorup, C. L., ed.,* 1987, pp. 127–48.   **[G: Mexico]**

Scanlon, Jack M. AT&T Projects the Fourth Era of Computing. *Shetty, Y. K. and Buehler, V. M., eds.,* 1987, pp. 235–44.   **[G: U.S.]**

Scott, A. J. The Semiconductor Industry in South-East Asia: Organization, Location and the International Division of Labour. *Reg. Stud.,* April 1987, *21*(2), pp. 143–59. **[G: S.E. Asia]**

Scott, A. J. and Angel, D. P. The U.S. Semiconductor Industry: A Locational Analysis. *Environ. Planning A,* July 1987, *19*(7), pp. 875–912.   **[G: U.S.]**

Seeber, Ronald L. Collective Bargaining in American Industry: Agricultural Machinery. *Lipsky, D. B. and Donn, C. B., eds.,* 1987, pp. 55–78.   **[G: U.S.]**

Silbert, Lance. Promoting High-Technology Industry: Initiatives and Policies for State Governments: California. *Schmandt, J. and Wilson, R., eds.,* 1987, pp. 11–33.   **[G: U.S.]**

Stopford, John M. and Baden-Fuller, Charles. Regional-level Competition in a Mature Industry: The Case of European Domestic Appliances. *J. Common Market Stud.,* December 1987, *26*(2), pp. 173–92.   **[G: EEC]**

Swann, G. M. P. Industry Standard Microprocessors and the Strategy of Second-Source Production. *Gabel, H. L., ed.,* 1987, pp. 239–62.

Swann, G. M. P. International Differences in Product Design and Their Economic Significance. *Appl. Econ.,* February 1987, *19*(2), pp. 201–13.   **[G: U.K.]**

Teece, David J. Capturing Value from Technological Innovation: Integration, Strategic Partnering, and Licensing Decisions. *Guile, B. R. and Brooks, H., eds.,* 1987, pp. 65–95.

Teubal, Morris. The Engineering Sector in a Model of Economic Development. *Teubal, M.,* 1987, pp. 280–94.

Teubal, Morris; Arnon, Naftali and Trachtenberg, Manuel. Performance in Innovation in the Israeli Electronics Industry: A Case Study of Biomedical Electronics Instrumentation. *Teubal, M.,* 1987, pp. 10–31.   **[G: Israel]**

Teubal, Morris and Steinmueller, Edward. Government Policy, Innovation, and Economic Growth: A Study of Satellite Communications. *Teubal, M.,* 1987, pp. 233–58.   **[G: U.S.]**

Thomson, Ross. Learning by Selling and Invention: The Case of the Sewing Machine. *J. Econ. Hist.,* June 1987, *47*(2), pp. 433–45.   **[G: U.S.]**

6314 Transportation Equipment

Adams, Walter and Brock, James W. Bigness and Social Efficiency: A Case Study of the U.S. Auto Industry. *Samuels, W. J. and Miller, A. S., eds.,* 1987, pp. 219–37.   **[G: U.S.]**

Aizcorbe, Ana; Winston, Clifford and Friedlaender, Ann. Cost Competitiveness of the U.S. Automobile Industry. *Winston, C., et al.,* 1987, pp. 6–35.   **[G: U.S.]**

Allen, Bruce T. Microelectronics, Employment and Labour in the United States Automobile Industry. *Watanabe, S., ed.*, 1987, pp. 79–106. [G: U.S.]

Bigazzi, Duccio. Management Strategies in the Italian Car Industry 1906–1945: Fiat and Alfa Romeo. *Tolliday, S. and Zeitlin, J., eds.*, 1987, pp. 76–96. [G: Italy]

Bresnahan, Timothy F. Competition and Collusion in the American Automobile Industry: The 1955 Price War. *J. Ind. Econ.*, June 1987, 35(4), pp. 457–82. [G: U.S.]

Brundenius, Claes. Development and Prospects of Capital Goods Production in Revolutionary Cuba. *Zimbalist, A., ed.*, 1987, pp. 97–114. [G: Cuba]

Cantwell, John. The Reorganization of European Industries After Integration: Selected Evidence on the Role of Multinational Enterprise Activities. *J. Common Market Stud.*, December 1987, 26(2), pp. 127–51. [G: EEC]

Chard, John S. European Competition Policy and the Pricing of Cars: An Economic Analysis of the Motor Vehicle Block Exemption Regulation. *Macmillen, M.; Mayes, D. G. and van Veen, P., eds.*, 1987, pp. 152–93. [G: EEC]

Clark, Kim B.; Chew, W. Bruce and Fujimoto, Takahiro. Product Development in the World Auto Industry. *Brookings Pap. Econ. Act.*, 1987, (3), pp. 729–71. [G: Global]

Cohen, Malcolm S. and Fulton, George A. Unions and Jobs: The U.S. Auto Industry—Comment. *J. Lab. Res.*, Summer 1987, 8(3), pp. 307–10. [G: U.S.]

Collyns, Charles and Dunaway, Steven. The Cost of Trade Restraints: The Case of Japanese Automobile Exports to the United States. *Int. Monet. Fund Staff Pap.*, March 1987, 34(1), pp. 150–75. [G: Japan; U.S.]

Contini, Giovanni. The Rise and Fall of Shop-Floor Bargaining at Fiat 1945–1980. *Tolliday, S. and Zeitlin, J., eds.*, 1987, pp. 144–67. [G: Italy]

Crandall, Robert W. The Effects of U.S. Trade Protection for Autos and Steel. *Brookings Pap. Econ. Act.*, 1987, (1), pp. 271–88. [G: U.S.]

Cubbin, John S. and Murfin, Andy. Regression Analysis versus Linear Programming in the Analysis of Price–Quality Relationships: An Application to the Determination of Market Shares. *Oxford Bull. Econ. Statist.*, November 1987, 49(4), pp. 385–99. [G: U.K.]

Deutsch, Edwin. Efficiency, Industry and Alternative Weapons Procurement Policies: Note. *Schmidt, C., ed.*, 1987, pp. 301–03. [G: U.S.; EEC]

Dixit, Avinash K. Tariffs and Subsidies under Oligopoly: The Case of the U.S. Automobile Industry. *[Corden, W. M.]*, 1987, pp. 112–27. [G: U.S.]

Dohse, Knuth. Innovations in Collective Bargaining through the Multinationalisation of Japanese Auto Companies, the Cases of Nummi (USA) and Nissan (UK). *Trevor, M., ed.*, 1987, pp. 124–49. [G: U.S.; U.K.; Japan]

Dombois, Rainer. The New International Divi-

sion of Labour, Labour Market and Automobile Production: The Case of Mexico. *Tolliday, S. and Zeitlin, J., eds.*, 1987, pp. 244–57. [G: Mexico]

Dunn, James A., Jr. Automobiles in International Trade: Regime Change or Persistence? *Int. Organ.*, Spring 1987, 41(2), pp. 225–52. [G: Global]

Eads, George C. Industrial Relations and Productivity in the U.S. Automobile Industry: Comments and Discussions. *Brookings Pap. Econ. Act.*, 1987, (3), pp. 720–25.

Ephlin, Donald F. UAW's View of Union's Role at Saturn Plant. *Shetty, Y. K. and Buehler, V. M., eds.*, 1987, pp. 149–61. [G: U.S.]

Feenstra, Robert C. Automobile Prices and Protection: The U.S.–Japan Trade Restraint. *Salvatore, D., ed.*, 1987, pp. 333–51. [G: U.S.; Japan]

Feenstra, Robert C. Voluntary Export Restraint in U.S. Autos, 1980–81: Quality, Employment, and Welfare Effects. *Bhagwati, J. N., ed.*, 1987, 1984, pp. 203–30. [G: U.S.; Japan]

Flaherty, Sean. Strike Activity & Productivity Change: The U.S. Auto Industry. *Ind. Relat.*, Spring 1987, 26(2), pp. 174–85. [G: U.S.]

Fuss, Melvyn A. and Waverman, Leonard. The Japanese Productivity Advantage in Automobile Production: Can It Be Transferred to North America? *Safarian, A. E. and Bertin, G. Y., eds.*, 1987, pp. 191–206. [G: Japan]

Ginter, James L.; Young, Murray A. and Dickson, Peter R. A Market Efficiency Study of Used Car Reliability and Prices. *J. Cons. Aff.*, Winter 1987, 21(2), pp. 258–76. [G: U.S.]

Glasmeier, Amy K. and McCluskey, Richard E. U.S. Auto Parts Production: An Analysis of the Organization and Location of a Changing Industry. *Econ. Geogr.*, April 1987, 63(2), pp. 142–59. [G: U.S.]

Gordon, Gerald, et al. Computer-Based Automation and Labor Relations in the Construction Equipment Industry. *Cornfield, D. B., ed.*, 1987, pp. 247–62. [G: U.S.]

Goto, Mitsuya. Nissan's International Strategy. *Trevor, M., ed.*, 1987, pp. 73–76. [G: Japan]

Gunderson, Morley and Melino, Angelo. Estimating Strike Effects in a General Model of Prices and Quantities. *J. Lab. Econ.*, January 1987, 5(1), pp. 1–19. [G: U.S.]

Harris, Harry G. Foreign Competition Stimulates Management Initiatives—A Look at the American Automobile Industry. *Tremblay, R., ed.*, 1987, pp. 595–601. [G: U.S.]

Hartley, Keith. Efficiency, Industry and Alternative Weapons Procurement Policies. *Schmidt, C., ed.*, 1987, pp. 283–300. [G: U.S.; EEC]

Hartley, Keith. Public Procurement and Competitiveness: A Community Market for Military Hardware and Technology? *J. Common Market Stud.*, March 1987, 25(3), pp. 237–47. [G: EEC]

Hartley, Keith. The Evaluation of Efficiency in the Arms Industry. *Borner, S. and Taylor, A., eds.*, 1987, pp. 181–201.

Hartman, Raymond S. Product Quality and Market Efficiency: The Effect of Product Recalls on Resale Prices and Firm Valuation. *Rev. Econ. Statist.*, May 1987, *69*(2), pp. 367–72. **[G: U.S.]**

Hazledine, Tim and Wigington, Ian. Canadian Auto Policy. *Can. Public Policy*, December 1987, *13*(4), pp. 490–501. **[G: Canada]**

Hensher, David A. Automobile Loss Rates and the Expected Capital Cost of Vehicles: An Empirical Note. *Econ. Rec.*, September 1987, *63*(182), pp. 247–54. **[G: Australia]**

Hoffer, George E.; Pruitt, Stephen W. and Reilly, Robert J. Automotive Recalls and Informational Efficiency. *Financial Rev.*, November 1987, *22*(4), pp. 433–42. **[G: U.S.]**

Indergaard, Michael and Cushion, Michael. Conflict, Cooperation, and the Global Auto Factory. *Cornfield, D. B., ed.*, 1987, pp. 203–28. **[G: U.S.]**

Jürgens, Ulrich; Dohse, Knuth and Malsch, Thomas. New Production Concepts in West German Car Plants. *Tolliday, S. and Zeitlin, J., eds.*, 1987, pp. 258–81. **[G: W. Germany]**

Jusela, Gary E., et al. Work Innovations at Ford Motor. *Shetty, Y. K. and Buehler, V. M., eds.*, 1987, pp. 123–45. **[G: U.S.]**

Karper, Mark D. Collective Bargaining in American Industry: Tires. *Lipsky, D. B. and Donn, C. B., eds.*, 1987, pp. 79–101. **[G: U.S.]**

Katz, Harry C. Collective Bargaining in American Industry: Automobiles. *Lipsky, D. B. and Donn, C. B., eds.*, 1987, pp. 13–53. **[G: U.S.]**

Katz, Harry C. Recent Developments in U.S. Auto Labour Relations. *Tolliday, S. and Zeitlin, J., eds.*, 1987, pp. 282–304. **[G: U.S.]**

Katz, Harry C.; Kochan, Thomas A. and Keefe, Jeffrey H. Industrial Relations and Productivity in the U.S. Automobile Industry. *Brookings Pap. Econ. Act.*, 1987, (3), pp. 685–715. **[G: U.S.]**

Kaufman, Robert S. and Kaufman, Roger T. Union Effects on Productivity, Personnel Practices, and Survival in the Automotive Parts Industry. *J. Lab. Res.*, Fall 1987, *8*(4), pp. 333–50. **[G: U.S.]**

Kolodziej, Edward A. Re-evaluating Economic and Technological Variables to Explain Global Arms Production and Sales. *Schmidt, C., ed.*, 1987, pp. 304–35. **[G: LDCs]**

Lazear, Edward P. Industrial Relations and Productivity in the U.S. Automobile Industry: Comments and Discussion. *Brookings Pap. Econ. Act.*, 1987, (3), pp. 716–20. **[G: U.S.]**

Lichtenstein, Nelson. Reutherism on the Shop Floor: Union Strategy and Shop-Floor Conflict in the USA 1946–70. *Tolliday, S. and Zeitlin, J., eds.*, 1987, pp. 121–43. **[G: U.S.]**

Lyons, Thomas P. Spatial Aspects of Development in China: The Motor Vehicle Industry, 1956–1985. *Int. Reg. Sci. Rev.*, 1987, *11*(1), pp. 75–96. **[G: China]**

Majumdar, Badiul A. Upstart or Flying Start? The Rise of Airbus Industrie. *World Econ.*,

December 1987, *10*(4), pp. 497–518. **[G: U.S.; Europe]**

Mannering, Fred and Winston, Clifford. Economic Effects of Voluntary Export Restrictions. *Winston, C., et al.*, 1987, pp. 61–67. **[G: U.S.]**

Mannering, Fred and Winston, Clifford. Recent Automobile Occupant Safety Proposals. *Winston, C., et al.*, 1987, pp. 68–88. **[G: U.S.]**

Mannering, Fred and Winston, Clifford. U.S. Automobile Market Demand. *Winston, C., et al.*, 1987, pp. 36–60. **[G: U.S.]**

Marx, Thomas G. Social Legitimacy and Strategic Issues Management at General Motors. *Marcus, A. A.; Kaufman, A. M. and Beam, D. R., eds.*, 1987, pp. 81–94. **[G: U.S.]**

Mashaw, Jerry L. and Harfst, David L. Regulation and Legal Culture: The Case of Motor Vehicle Safety. *Yale J. Regul.*, Spring 1987, *4*(2), pp. 257–316. **[G: U.S.]**

Meyer, John R. Product Development in the World Auto Industry: Comments and Discussion. *Brookings Pap. Econ. Act.*, 1987, (3), pp. 772–76.

Moran, Larry R. Motor Vehicles, Model Year 1987. *Surv. Curr. Bus.*, November 1987, *67*(11), pp. 19–23. **[G: U.S.]**

Oberhauser, Ann. Labour, Production and the State: Decentralization of the French Automobile Industry. *Reg. Stud.*, October 1987, *21*(5), pp. 445–58. **[G: France]**

Ohta, Makoto. Hedonic Price Indexes of Japanese Passenger Cars Over 1970–83: A Note. *Econ. Stud. Quart.*, September 1987, *38*(3), pp. 264–74. **[G: Japan]**

Okayama, Reiko. Industrial Relations in the Japanese Automobile Industry 1945–70: The Case of Toyota. *Tolliday, S. and Zeitlin, J., eds.*, 1987, pp. 168–89. **[G: Japan]**

Reynolds, Morgan O. Unions and Jobs: The U.S. Auto Industry—Reply. *J. Lab. Res.*, Summer 1987, *8*(3), pp. 311–15. **[G: U.S.]**

Ricard, Leonard J. GM's Just-in-Time Operating Philosophy. *Shetty, Y. K. and Buehler, V. M., eds.*, 1987, pp. 315–29. **[G: U.S.]**

Scherer, F. M. Product Development in the World Auto Industry: Comments and Discussion. *Brookings Pap. Econ. Act.*, 1987, (3), pp. 776–79.

Schoenberger, Erica. Technological and Organizational Change in Automobile Production: Spatial Implications. *Reg. Stud.*, June 1987, *21*(3), pp. 199–214. **[G: France]**

Schwartz, Arthur R., et al. The Impact of Technological Change on Labor Relations in the Commercial Aircraft Industry. *Cornfield, D. B., ed.*, 1987, pp. 263–80. **[G: U.S.]**

Seering, Warren. Robotics, Numerical Control and the Computer. *Watanabe, S., ed.*, 1987, pp. 25–40.

Sengenberger, Werner and Kohler, Ch. Policies of Workforce Reduction and Labour Market Structures in the American and German Automobile Industry. *Tarling, R., ed.*, 1987, pp. 245–69. **[G: W. Germany; U.S.]**

Sheehan, Dennis and Winston, Clifford. Expectations and Automobile Policy. *Winston, C., et al.*, 1987, pp. 89–102. [G: U.S.]

Sherwood, Mark K. Performance of Multifactor Productivity in the Steel and Motor Vehicles Industries. *Mon. Lab. Rev.*, August 1987, *110*(8), pp. 22–31. [G: U.S.]

Shimokawa, Koichi. Product and Labour Strategies in Japan. *Tolliday, S. and Zeitlin, J., eds.*, 1987, pp. 224–43. [G: Japan]

Silberston, Aubrey. Microelectronics, Automation and Employment in the Automobile Industry: Foreword. *Watanabe, S., ed.*, 1987, pp. xi–xiii.

Silva, Francesco; Ferri, Piero and Enrietti, Aldo. Robots, Employment and Industrial Relations in the Italian Automobile Industry. *Watanabe, S., ed.*, 1987, pp. 131–53. [G: Italy]

Sobey, Albert J. Trends in the U.S. Automotive Industry. *Faruqui, A. and Broehl, J., eds.*, 1987, pp. 257–67. [G: U.S.]

Soulié, Daniel. Technology Transfers in the Automotive Equipment Industry: The French Case. *Safarian, A. E. and Bertin, G. Y., eds.*, 1987, pp. 180–90. [G: France]

Symons, Leslie. The Rise and Fall of Soviet Influence on the Chinese Aircraft Industry and Air Transport. *Tismer, J. F.; Ambler, J. and Symons, L., eds.*, 1987, pp. 449–67. [G: China; U.S.S.R.]

Tauile, José Ricardo. Microelectronics and the Internationalization of the Brazilian Automobile Industry. *Watanabe, S., ed.*, 1987, pp. 155–80. [G: Brazil]

Thompson, R. S. New Entry and Hedonic Price Discounts: The Case of the Irish Car Market. *Oxford Bull. Econ. Statist.*, November 1987, *49*(4), pp. 373–84. [G: Ireland]

Tolliday, Steven. Management and Labour in Britain 1896–1939. *Tolliday, S. and Zeitlin, J., eds.*, 1987, pp. 29–56. [G: U.K.]

Tolliday, Steven and Zeitlin, Jonathan. Shop-Floor Bargaining, Contract Unionism and Job Control: An Anglo–American Comparison. *Tolliday, S. and Zeitlin, J., eds.*, 1987, pp. 99–120. [G: U.S.; U.K.]

Tolliday, Steven and Zeitlin, Jonathan. The Automobile Industry and Its Workers: Between Fordism and Flexibility: Introduction. *Tolliday, S. and Zeitlin, J., eds.*, 1987, pp. 1–25. [G: U.S.; Europe; Japan]

Traves, Tom. The Development of the Ontario Automobile Industry to 1939. *Drummond, I. M.*, 1987, pp. 208–23. [G: Canada]

Truett, Lila J. and Truett, Dale B. The Mexican Automobile Industry and International Trade, 1970–1983. *J. Econ. Devel.*, June 1987, *12*(1), pp. 65–85. [G: Mexico]

Van de Casteele-Schweitzer, Sylvie. Management and Labour in France 1914–39. *Tolliday, S. and Zeitlin, J., eds.*, 1987, pp. 57–75. [G: France]

Volpato, Giuseppe. The Automobile Industry in Transition: Product Market Changes and Firm Strategies in the 1970s and 1980s. *Tolliday, S. and Zeitlin, J., eds.*, 1987, pp. 193–223. [G: Global]

Watanabe, Susumu. Flexible Automation and Labour Productivity in the Japanese Automobile Industry. *Watanabe, S., ed.*, 1987, pp. 41–77. [G: Japan]

Watanabe, Susumu. Microelectronics and Rationalization of the French Automobile Industry. *Watanabe, S., ed.*, 1987, pp. 107–29. [G: France]

Watanabe, Susumu. Microelectronics, Automation and Employment in the Automobile Industry: Introduction. *Watanabe, S., ed.*, 1987, pp. 1–24. [G: Selected Countries]

Watanabe, Susumu. Microelectronics, Automation and Employment in the Automobile Industry: A Synthesis of Findings. *Watanabe, S., ed.*, 1987, pp. 181–97. [G: Selected Countries]

Wilking, Lou H. Should U.S. Corporations Abandon South Africa? *Sethi, S. P., ed.*, 1987, pp. 383–91. [G: U.S.; S. Africa]

Willman, Paul. Labour-Relations Strategy at BL Cars. *Tolliday, S. and Zeitlin, J., eds.*, 1987, pp. 305–27. [G: U.K.]

Winston, Clifford. Blind Intersection? Policy and the Automobile Industry: Introduction and Summary. *Winston, C., et al.*, 1987, pp. 1–5. [G: U.S.]

Winston, Clifford. Public Policy and Auto Industry Evolution. *Winston, C., et al.*, 1987, pp. 103–05. [G: U.S.]

Womack, James P. Prospects for the U.S.–Mexican Relationship in the Motor Vehicle Sector. *Thorup, C. L., ed.*, 1987, pp. 101–25. [G: U.S.; Mexico]

Wulf, Herbert. Arms Production in Third World Countries, Effects on Industrialisation. *Schmidt, C., ed.*, 1987, pp. 357–83. [G: LDCs]

Yoder, Dale and Staudohar, Paul D. Management and Public Policy [Management and Public Policy in Plant Closure]. *Staudohar, P. D. and Brown, H. E.*, 1987, 1985, pp. 183–200. [G: U.S.]

6315 Chemicals, Drugs, Plastics, Ceramics, Glass, Cement, and Rubber

Abe, Y. Japanese Market Entry Strategy. The Case of Yamanouchi Pharmaceuticals in Western Europe. *Trevor, M., ed.*, 1987, pp. 150–55. [G: Japan; W. Europe]

Albach, Horst. Gewinn und gerechter Preis Überlegungen zur Preisbildung in der pharmazeutischen Industrie. (With English summary.) *Z. Betriebswirtshaft*, August 1987, *57*(8), pp. 816–24. [G: W. Germany]

Baram, Michael S. Chemical Industry Hazards: Liability, Insurance, and the Role of Risk Analysis. *Kleindorfer, P. R. and Kunreuther, H. C., ed.*, 1987, pp. 415–42.

Bernholz, Peter. Organizational Theory, Information Processing, and Short-run Dynamics: Comment. *J. Inst. Theoretical Econ.*, March 1987, *143*(1), pp. 225–28. [G: U.S.]

Brinberg, David and Morris, Louis A. Advertising Prescription Drugs to Consumers. *Bloom, P. N., ed.*, 1987, pp. 1–40. **[G: U.S.]**

Brodovsky, Joan. The Mexican Pharmochemical and Pharmaceutical Industries. *Thorup, C. L., ed.*, 1987, pp. 187–213. **[G: Mexico]**

Cantwell, John. The Reorganization of European Industries After Integration: Selected Evidence on the Role of Multinational Enterprise Activities. *J. Common Market Stud.*, December 1987, *26*(2), pp. 127–51. **[G: EEC]**

Capone, Charles A., Jr. and Elzinga, Kenneth G. Technology and Energy Use before, during, and after OPEC: The U.S. Portland Cement Industry. *Energy J.*, July 1987, *8*(3), pp. 93–112. **[G: U.S.]**

Cassidy, John C. and Halstead, J. Phillip. Management Systems for Enhancing the Productivity of Public Affairs at Clorox. *Marcus, A. A.; Kaufman, A. M. and Beam, D. R., eds.*, 1987, pp. 151–64. **[G: U.S.]**

Cohen, Adrian V. Chemical Industry Hazards: Liability, Insurance, and the Role of Risk Analysis: Discussion. *Kleindorfer, P. R. and Kunreuther, H. C., ed.*, 1987, pp. 442–47.

Corley, T. A. B. Interactions between the British and American Patent Medicine Industries 1708–1914. *Atack, J., ed.*, 1987, pp. 111–29. **[G: U.S.; U.K.]**

Covello, Vincent T. and Merkhofer, Miley. The Inexact Science of Chemical Hazard Risk Assessment: A Description and Critical Evaluation of Available Methods. *Kleindorfer, P. R. and Kunreuther, H. C., ed.*, 1987, pp. 229–76.

Da Silva, Roberto and Dellva, Wilfred L. Evidence of the Size Effect on Stock Returns in the Chemical Industry. *Quart. J. Bus. Econ.*, Spring 1987, *26*(2), pp. 22–40. **[G: U.S.]**

Eastman, H. C. The Protection of Intellectual Property: Pharmaceutical Products in Canada. *Safarian, A. E. and Bertin, G. Y., eds.*, 1987, pp. 153–66. **[G: Canada]**

Fiegenbaum, Avi; Sudharshan, D. and Thomas, Howard. The Concept of Stable Strategic Time Periods in Strategic Group Research. *Managerial Dec. Econ.*, June 1987, *8*(2), pp. 139–48. **[G: U.S.]**

French, Michael J. The Emergence of a U.S. Multinational Enterprise: The Goodyear Tire and Rubber Company, 1910–1939. *Econ. Hist. Rev., 2nd Ser.*, February 1987, *40*(1), pp. 64–79. **[G: U.S.]**

Ghali, Moheb A. Seasonality, Aggregation and the Testing of the Production Smoothing Hypothesis. *Amer. Econ. Rev.*, June 1987, *77*(3), pp. 464–69. **[G: U.S.]**

Gilbert, Richard J. and Lieberman, Marvin B. Investment and Coordination in Oligopolistic Industries. *Rand J. Econ.*, Spring 1987, *18*(1), pp. 17–33. **[G: U.S.]**

Goldberg, Victor P. Organizational Theory, Information Processing, and Short-run Dynamics: Theory and Empirical Tests: Comment. *J. Inst. Theoretical Econ.*, March 1987, *143*(1), pp. 222–24. **[G: U.S.]**

Gorecki, Paul K. Barriers to Entry in the Cana-

dian Pharmaceutical Industry: Comments, Clarification and Extensions. *J. Health Econ.*, March 1987, *6*(1), pp. 59–72. **[G: Canada]**

Grabowski, Henry G. and Vernon, John M. Pioneers, Imitators, and Generics—A Simulation Model of Schumpeterian Competition. *Quart. J. Econ.*, August 1987, *102*(3), pp. 491–525. **[G: U.S.]**

Grant, Wyn; Paterson, William and Whitston, Colin. Government–Industry Relations in the Chemical Industry: An Anglo–German Comparison. *Wilks, S. and Wright, M., eds.*, 1987, pp. 35–60. **[G: U.K.; W. Germany]**

Hagan, P. J. and Henry, G. G. Family-Based Social Welfare Schemes: The Case of Pharmaceuticals. *Butler, J. R. G. and Doessel, D. P., eds.*, 1987, pp. 165–93. **[G: Australia]**

Hancher, Leigh and Ruete, Matthias. Legal Culture, Product Licensing, and the Drug Industry. *Wilks, S. and Wright, M., eds.*, 1987, pp. 148–80. **[G: U.K.; W. Germany]**

Harris, S. A. The Provision of Carbohydrates for the European Community's Biotechnology and Chemical Industries. *J. Agr. Econ.*, September 1987, *38*(3), pp. 423–34. **[G: EEC]**

Harvey, Roy. The Industries Assistance Commission's Report on Pharmaceutical Products: Discussion. *Butler, J. R. G. and Doessel, D. P., eds.*, 1987, pp. 160–64. **[G: Australia]**

Hayes, Peter. Carl Bosch and Carl Krauch: Chemistry and the Political Economy of Germany, 1925–1945. *J. Econ. Hist.*, June 1987, *47*(2), pp. 353–63. **[G: Germany]**

Hrivnák, Pavel. There Are Gaps to be Closed. *Czech. Econ. Digest.*, June 1987, (4), pp. 3–9. **[G: Czechoslovakia]**

Jadlow, Joseph M.; Jadlow, Janice W. and Yu, Shirley S. Risk, Rivalry, and Innovation: The Case of Ethical Drugs. *Rivista Int. Sci. Econ. Com.*, July 1987, *34*(7), pp. 593–608. **[G: U.S.]**

Jensen, Elizabeth J. Research Expenditures and the Discovery of New Drugs. *J. Ind. Econ.*, September 1987, *36*(1), pp. 83–95. **[G: U.S.]**

Johnson, Ronald N. and Parkman, Allen M. The Role of Ideas in Antitrust Policy Toward Vertical Mergers: Evidence from the FTC Cement-Ready Mixed Concrete Cases. *Antitrust Bull.*, Winter 1987, *32*(4), pp. 841–83. **[G: U.S.]**

Katz, Jorge M. Productivity and Domestic Technological Search Efforts: The Growth Path of a Rayon Plant in Argentina. *Katz, J. M., ed.*, 1987, pp. 192–240. **[G: Argentina]**

Kirim, Arman. Uluslararasi Ilaç Endüstrisinin Ekonomisi. (With English summary.) *METU*, 1987, *14*(2), pp. 147–77. **[G: Global]**

Knight, Arthur [Sir]. Courtaulds in Continental Europe in the 1950s and 1960s: Some Recollections and Reflections. *Atack, J., ed.*, 1987, pp. 213–26. **[G: U.K.]**

León, Carlos; D'Amato, Laura and Iturregui, María E. El mercado de plaguicidas en la Argentina. (With English summary.) *Desarrollo Econ.*, Apr.-June 1987, *27*(105), pp. 129–44. **[G: Argentina]**

Lieberman, Marvin B. Excess Capacity as a Bar-

rier to Entry: An Empirical Appraisal. *J. Ind. Econ.*, June 1987, *35*(4), pp. 607–27.
[G: U.S.]

Lieberman, Marvin B. Market Growth, Economies of Scale, and Plant Size in the Chemical Processing Industries. *J. Ind. Econ.*, December 1987, *36*(2), pp. 175–91. [G: U.S.]

Lieberman, Marvin B. Patents, Learning by Doing, and Market Structure in the Chemical Processing Industries. *Int. J. Ind. Organ.*, September 1987, *5*(3), pp. 257–76. [G: U.S.]

Lieberman, Marvin B. Postentry Investment and Market Structure in the Chemical Processing Industries. *Rand J. Econ.*, Winter 1987, *18*(4), pp. 533–49. [G: U.S.]

Littlejohn, Stephen E. Competition and Cooperation: New Trends in Issue Identification and Management at Monsanto and Gulf. *Marcus, A. A.; Kaufman, A. M. and Beam, D. R., eds.*, 1987, pp. 19–30. [G: U.S.]

Luiselli Fernández, Cassio. Biotechnology and Food: The Scope for Cooperation. *Thorup, C. L., ed.*, 1987, pp. 167–85. [G: Mexico; U.S.]

MacMillan, Keith and Turner, Ian. The Cost-Containment Issue: A Study of Government–Industry Relations in the Pharmaceutical Sectors of the United Kingdom and West Germany. *Wilks, S. and Wright, M., eds.*, 1987, pp. 117–47. [G: U.K.; W. Germany]

Mahon, John F. and Post, James E. The Evolution of Political Strategies during the 1980 Superfund Debate. *Marcus, A. A.; Kaufman, A. M. and Beam, D. R., eds.*, 1987, pp. 61–78. [G: U.S.]

Mendoza, Antonio Gómez. Oligopoly and Economic Efficiency: Portland Cement in Spain (1899–1935). *Rivista Storia Econ.*, S.S., Int. Issue, 1987, *4*, pp. 76–95. [G: Spain]

Nelson, Daniel. Mass Production and the U.S. Tire Industry. *J. Econ. Hist.*, June 1987, *47*(2), pp. 329–39. [G: U.S.]

Pearson, Ruth. Transfer of Technology and Domestic Innovation in the Cement Industry. *Katz, J. M., ed.*, 1987, pp. 352–427. [G: Argentina]

Penm, Jammie H. and Vincent, D. P. Some Estimates of the Price Elasticity of Demand for Phosphatic and Nitrogenous Fertilisers. *Australian J. Agr. Econ.*, April 1987, *31*(1), pp. 65–73. [G: Australia]

Sercovich, Francisco C. Design Engineering and Endogenous Technical Change. *Katz, J. M., ed.*, 1987, pp. 241–80.

Sheppard, William J. Trends in the U.S. Chemical Industry. *Faruqui, A. and Broehl, J., eds.*, 1987, pp. 293–311. [G: U.S.]

Tatchell, Michael. Family-Based Social Welfare Schemes: The Case of Pharmaceuticals: Discussion. *Butler, J. R. G. and Doessel, D. P., eds.*, 1987, pp. 194–96. [G: Australia]

Teeples, Ronald K. and Glyer, David. Estimating Demand by Self-Supplying Firms: Comments. *Water Resources Res.*, May 1987, *23*(5), pp. 968–70. [G: U.S.]

Wallace, Robert. The Industries Assistance Com-'s Report on Pharmaceutical Products.

Butler, J. R. G. and Doessel, D. P., eds., 1987, pp. 144–59. [G: Australia]

Wiggins, Steven N. Organizational Theory, Information Processing, and Short-run Dynamics: Theory and Empirical Tests. *J. Inst. Theoretical Econ.*, March 1987, *143*(1), pp. 204–21. [G: U.S.]

6316 Textiles, Leather, and Clothing

Cable, Vincent. Textiles and Clothing in a New Round of Trade Negotiations. *World Bank Econ. Rev.*, September 1987, *1*(4), pp. 619–46. [G: Global]

Chang, Eui Tae. Protective Effects of Discriminatory Quantitative Restrictions. *Int. Econ. J.*, Spring 1987, *1*(1), pp. 15–28. [G: U.S.]

Chmura, Christine. The Effect of Exchange Rate Variation on U.S. Textile and Apparel Imports. *Fed. Res. Bank Richmond Econ. Rev.*, May/June 1987, *73*(3), pp. 17–23. [G: U.S.]

Chorley, Patrick. The Cloth Exports of Flanders and Northern France during the Thirteenth Century: A Luxury Trade? *Econ. Hist. Rev.*, 2nd Ser., August 1987, *40*(3), pp. 349–79. [G: France; Flanders]

Clark, Gregory. Why Isn't the Whole World Developed? Lessons from the Cotton Mills. *J. Econ. Hist.*, March 1987, *47*(1), pp. 141–73.

Faroqhi, Suraiya. Notes on the Production of Cotton and Cotton Cloth in Sixteenth- and Seventeenth-Century Anatolia. *Islamoglu-Inan, H., ed.*, 1987, *1979*, pp. 262–70. [G: Ottoman Empire]

Field, Alfred J. An Estimate of the Textile and Clothing Sector Production Function for Selected Countries in the Early 1970s. *World Devel.*, Oct./Nov. 1987, *15*(10/11), pp. 1285–90. [G: Selected Countries]

Henley, John S. and Ereisha, Mohamed M. State Control and the Labor Productivity Crisis: The Egyptian Textile Industry at Work. *Econ. Develop. Cult. Change*, April 1987, *35*(3), pp. 491–521.

Jenkins, Glenn P. Costs and Consequences of the New Protectionism. The Case of Canada's Clothing Sector. *[Harberger, A.]*, 1987, pp. 217–53. [G: Canada]

Jones, S. R. H. Technology, Transaction Costs, and the Transition to Factory Production in the British Silk Industry, 1700–1870. *J. Econ. Hist.*, March 1987, *47*(1), pp. 71–96. [G: U.K.]

Kumar, Prem. Determinants of Corporate Growth: The Indian Experience. *Margin*, Apr.-June 1987, *19*(3), pp. 55–68. [G: India]

Laumas, Prem S. and Williams, Martin. Cotton Textiles—An Agro-industry. *World Devel.*, June 1987, *15*(6), pp. 841–45. [G: India]

Lazonick, William. Stubborn Mules: Some Comments [New Evidence of the Stubborn English Mule and the Cotton Industry, 1878–1920]. *Econ. Hist. Rev.*, 2nd Ser., February 1987, *40*(1), pp. 80–86. [G: U.K.]

Lyons, John S. Powerloom Profitability and Steam Power Costs: Britain in the 1830s. *Exploration*

Econ. Hist., October 1987, *24*(4), pp. 392–408.
[G: U.K.]

McKenzie, Richard B. and Smith, Stephen D. Loss of Textile and Apparel Jobs: Is Protectionism Warranted? *Cato J.*, Winter 1987, *6*(3), pp. 731–46. [G: U.S.]

Mody, Ashoka and Wheeler, David. Towards a Vanishing Middle: Competition in the World Garment Industry. *World Devel.*, Oct./Nov. 1987, *15*(10/11), pp. 1269–84. [G: LDCs]

Nye, John Vincent. Firm Size and Economic Backwardness: A New Look at the French Industrialization Debate. *J. Econ. Hist.*, September 1987, *47*(3), pp. 649–69. [G: France]

Primeaux, Walter J., Jr. The Interdependence of the Life Cycle and Strategic Group Concepts: Theory and Evidence. *Lee, C. F., ed.*, 1987, pp. 67–85. [G: U.S.]

Saxonhouse, Gary R. and Wright, Gavin. Stubborn Mules and Vertical Integration: The Disappearing Constraint? [New Evidence of the Stubborn English Mule and the Cotton Industry, 1878–1920]. *Econ. Hist. Rev.*, *2nd Ser.*, February 1987, *40*(1), pp. 87–94. [G: U.K.]

Solinas, Giovanni. Labour Market Segmentation and Workers' Careers: The Case of the Italian Knitwear Industry. *Tarling, R., ed.*, 1987, pp. 271–305. [G: Italy]

Spinanger, Dean. Will the Multi-fibre Arrangement Keep Bangladesh Humble? *World Econ.*, March 1987, *10*(1), pp. 75–84. [G: Bangladesh]

Stageberg, Stephen P. The Impact of Technological Change in the Textile Industry. *Atlantic Econ. J.*, March 1987, *15*(1), pp. 124. [G: U.S.]

Tekeli, Ilhan. Savaşmayan Ülkenin Savaş Ekonomisi: Uretimden Tüketime Pamuklu Dokuma. (With English summary.) *METU*, 1987, *14*(1), pp. 1–48. [G: Turkey]

Tignor, Robert. British Textile Companies and the Egyptian Economy. *Atack, J., ed.*, 1987, pp. 53–67. [G: U.K.; Egypt]

Verma, P. C. Domestic Demand for Jute Goods in India. *Margin*, Jan.-Mar. 1987, *19*(2), pp. 43–49. [G: India]

Wilkins, Mira. Efficiency and Management: A Comment on Gregory Clark's "Why Isn't the Whole World Developed?" *J. Econ. Hist.*, December 1987, *47*(4), pp. 981–88.

Yonekawa, Shin'ichi. Flotation Booms in the Cotton Spinning Industry, 1870–1890: A Comparative Study. *Bus. Hist. Rev.*, Winter 1987, *61*(4), pp. 551–81. [G: Japan; U.S.; U.K.; India]

6317 Forest Products, Lumber, Paper, and Printing and Publishing

Åström, Sven-Erik. Northeastern Europe's Timber Trade between the Napoleonic and Crimean Wars: A Preliminary Survey. *Scand. Econ. Hist. Rev.*, 1987, *35*(2), pp. 170–77. [G: Finland; U.S.S.R.]

Boyd, Roy G. and Krutilla, Kerry. The Welfare Impacts of U.S. Trade Restrictions against the Canadian Softwood Lumber Industry: A Spatial Equilibrium Analysis. *Can. J. Econ.*, February 1987, *20*(1), pp. 17–35. [G: Canada]

Brautzsch, Hans-Ulrich. The Input–Output Model of the GDR Forest Sector. *Tchijov, I. and Tomaszewicz, L., eds.*, 1987, pp. 153–62. [G: E. Germany]

Cohen, Avi J. Factor Substitution and Induced Innovation in North American Kraft Pulping: 1914–1940. *Exploration Econ. Hist.*, April 1987, *24*(2), pp. 197–217. [G: U.S.; Canada]

Colodzin, Robert. Positioning the Company in Society: Implementing a Public Affairs Strategy at Champion International. *Marcus, A. A.; Kaufman, A. M. and Beam, D. R., eds.*, 1987, pp. 211–21. [G: U.S.]

Johnson, Ronald N. and Parkman, Allen M. Spatial Competition and Vertical Integration; Cement and Concrete Revisited: Comment. *Amer. Econ. Rev.*, September 1987, *77*(4), pp. 750–53. [G: U.S.]

Kalleberg, Arne L., et al. The Eclipse of Craft: The Changing Face of Labor in the Newspaper Industry. *Cornfield, D. B., ed.*, 1987, pp. 47–71. [G: U.S.]

Lancey, Stanley. Energy Consumption by the Paper Industry. *Faruqui, A. and Broehl, J., eds.*, 1987, pp. 315–24. [G: U.S.]

Lee, Carie E. and Sugiyama, Samuel O. IN-DEPTH Case Study: Pulp and Paper Process Model. *Faruqui, A. and Broehl, J., eds.*, 1987, pp. 435–49. [G: U.S.]

Martinello, Felice. Substitution, Technical Change and Returns to Scale in British Columbian Wood Products Industries. *Appl. Econ.*, April 1987, *19*(4), pp. 483–96. [G: Canada]

McBride, Mark E. Spatial Competition and Vertical Integration; Cement and Concrete Revisited: Reply. *Amer. Econ. Rev.*, September 1987, *77*(4), pp. 754–56. [G: U.S.]

McChesney, Fred S. Sensationalism, Newspaper Profits and the Marginal Value of Watergate. *Econ. Inquiry*, January 1987, *25*(1), pp. 135–44. [G: U.S.]

Nyankori, James C. O. and Nodine, Stephen K. Implications of Restrictions on Imports of Canadian Softwood Lumber to the Southern Softwood Lumber Industry. *Rev. Reg. Stud.*, Winter 1987, *17*(1), pp. 45–52. [G: U.S.; Canada]

Smyshlayev, Anatoli. Supply Rigidities in Input–Output Modeling of the Wood and Paper Industry Development. *Tchijov, I. and Tomaszewicz, L., eds.*, 1987, pp. 139–52. [G: U.S.S.R.]

Steedman, Hilary and Wagner, Karin. A Second Look at Productivity, Machinery and Skills in Britain and Germany. *Nat. Inst. Econ. Rev.*, November 1987, (122), pp. 84–95. [G: U.K.; W. Germany]

Teeples, Ronald K. and Glyer, David. Estimating Demand by Self-Supplying Firms: Comments. *Water Resources Res.*, May 1987, *23*(5), pp. 968–70. [G: U.S.]

Westoby, Jack C. Forest Industries for Socio-economic Development. *Westoby, J.*, 1987, *1978*, pp. 241–54. [G: LDCs]

Westoby, Jack C. Prospects for Expanding Forest Products Exports from Developing Countries. *Westoby, J.*, 1987, *1964*, pp. 71–114.
[G: LDCs]

6318 Food Processing, Tobacco, and Beverages

Ahmed, Ziaul Z. and Sieling, Mark. Two Decades of Productivity Growth in Poultry Dressing and Processing. *Mon. Lab. Rev.*, April 1987, *110*(4), pp. 34–39. [G: U.S.]

Ashenfelter, Orley and Sullivan, Daniel. Nonparametric Tests of Market Structure: An Application to the Cigarette Industry. *J. Ind. Econ.*, June 1987, *35*(4), pp. 483–98.
[G: U.S.]

Chevassus, Emmanuelle and Green, Raúl H. Les investissements croisés France–États-Unis dans l'agro-alimentaire. (U.S.–French Crossed Investment in Food Industry. With English summary.) *Écon. Soc.*, July 1987, *21*(7), pp. 57–90. [G: U.S.; France]

Culbertson, John D. Should Antitrust Use the Schumpeterian Model? The Case of the Food Industries. *Wills, R. L.; Caswell, J. A. and Culbertson, J. D., eds.*, 1987, pp. 103–12.
[G: U.S.]

Feuer, Carl Henry. The Performance of the Cuban Sugar Industry, 1981–85. *Zimbalist, A., ed.*, 1987, pp. 69–83. [G: Cuba]

Fidel, Julio and Lucángeli, Jorge. Cost–Benefit of Different Technological Options in the Context of a Differentiated Oligopoly: The Case of the Argentine Cigarette Industry. *Katz, J. M., ed.*, 1987, pp. 283–317. [G: Argentina]

Haggblade, Steve. Vertical Considerations in Choice-of-Technique Studies: Evidence from Africa's Indigenous Beer Industry. *Econ. Develop. Cult. Change*, July 1987, *35*(4), pp. 723–42. [G: Botswana]

Harris, Jeffrey E. The 1983 Increase in the Federal Cigarette Excise Tax. *Summers, L. H., ed.*, 1987, pp. 87–111. [G: U.S.]

Hofmann, Hans-Joachim. Die Werbewirkung auf den Zigarettenkonsum in der Bundesrepublik Deutschland. (The Effect of Advertising on Cigarette Consumption in the Federal Republic of Germany. With English summary.) *Jahr. Nationalökon. Statist.*, May 1987, *203*(3), pp. 257–73. [G: W. Germany]

Jordan, W. John and Jaffee, Bruce L. The Use of Exclusive Territories in the Distribution of Beer: Theoretical and Empirical Observations. *Antitrust Bull.*, Spring 1987, *32*(1), pp. 137–64. [G: U.S.]

Kaplinsky, Raphael. Appropriate Technology in Sugar Manufacturing. *Stewart, F., ed.*, 1987, pp. 192–218. [G: India; Kenya]

Kelton, Christina M. L. The Inflationary Contribution of Market Structure in Food and Tobacco Manufacturing. *Wills, R. L.; Caswell, J. A. and Culbertson, J. D., eds.*, 1987, pp. 345–59.

Marion, Bruce W. Entry Barriers: Theory, Empirical Evidence, and the Food Industries. *Wills, R. L.; Caswell, J. A. and Culbertson,*

J. D., eds., 1987, pp. 187–202. [G: U.S.]

Mars, Gerald and Altman, Yochanan. Case Studies in Second Economy Production and Transportation in Soviet Georgia. *Alessandrini, S. and Dallago, B., eds.*, 1987, pp. 197–217.
[G: U.S.S.R.]

Moleeratanond, Wiboonkiet. Product Information to Improve Small-Scale Food Manufacture in Thailand. *Young, R. H. and MacCormac, C. W., eds.*, 1987, pp. 101–10. [G: Thailand]

Monke, Eric A.; Pearson, Scott R. and Silva-Carvalho, José-Paulo. Welfare Effects of a Processing Cartel: Flour Milling in Portugal. *Econ. Develop. Cult. Change*, January 1987, *35*(2), pp. 393–407. [G: Portugal]

Mueller, Willard F. Market Power and Its Control in the Food System. *Wills, R. L.; Caswell, J. A. and Culbertson, J. D., eds.*, 1987, *1983*, pp. 23–37. [G: U.S.]

Nefussi, J. Les facteurs macro-économiques de la croissance des industries agro-alimentaires depuis les années 50. (Macro-economic Factors of Growth of I.A.A. since the Fifties. With English summary.) *Écon. Soc.*, July 1987, *21*(7), pp. 91–109. [G: France]

Ornstein, Stanley I. and Hanssens, Dominique M. Resale Price Maintenance: Output Increasing or Restricting? The Case of Distilled Spirits in the United States. *J. Ind. Econ.*, September 1987, *36*(1), pp. 1–18. [G: U.S.]

Oyugi, L. A.; Mukhebi, A. W. and Mwangi, W. M. The Impact of Cash Cropping on Food Production: A Case Study of Tobacco and Maize in Migori Division, South Nyanza District of Kenya. *Eastern Afr. Econ. Rev.*, June 1987, *3*(1), pp. 43–50. [G: Kenya]

Pearson, Scott R. Prospects for Corn Sweeteners. *Timmer, C. P., ed.*, 1987, pp. 175–92.
[G: Indonesia]

Radell, Willard W., Jr. Comparative Performance of Large Cuban Sugar Factories in the 1984 "Zafra." *Mesa-Lago, C., ed.*, 1987, pp. 141–55. [G: Cuba]

Rosenbaum, David I. Advertising and Entry: The Case of Light Beer. *Wills, R. L.; Caswell, J. A. and Culbertson, J. D., eds.*, 1987, pp. 223–34. [G: U.S.]

Rosenbaum, David I. Predatory Pricing and the Reconstituted Lemon Juice Industry. *J. Econ. Issues*, March 1987, *21*(1), pp. 237–58.
[G: U.S.]

Slade, John. The Ways Cigarettes Contribute to GNP. *Eastern Econ. J.*, October-December 1987, *13*(4), pp. 353–59. [G: U.S.]

Sumner, Daniel A. and Alston, Julian M. Substitutability for Farm Commodities: The Demand for U.S. Tobacco in Cigarette Manufacturing. *Amer. J. Agr. Econ.*, May 1987, *69*(2), pp. 258–65. [G: U.S.]

Tremblay, Victor J. Scale Economies, Technological Change, and Firm-Cost Asymmetries in the U.S. Brewing Industry. *Quart. Rev. Econ. Bus.*, Summer 1987, *27*(2), pp. 71–86.
[G: U.S.]

Tribe, M. A. and Alpine, R. L. W. Sources of Scale Economies: Sugar Production in Less

Developed Countries. *Oxford Bull. Econ. Statist.*, May 1987, *49*(2), pp. 209–26.
[G: Kenya; Ghana; Bangladesh; India; Pakistan]
Vroman, Susan B. and Russell, Louise B. The Net Social Benefits of a Product Improvement: The Case of Freeze-Dried Coffee. *Appl. Econ.*, January 1987, *19*(1), pp. 127–42. **[G: U.S.]**
Webber, M. J. and Tonkin, S. Technical Changes and the Rate of Profit in the Canadian Food Industry. *Environ. Planning A*, December 1987, *19*(12), pp. 1579–96. **[G: Canada]**

632 Industry Studies: Extractive Industries

6320 General

Girvan, Norman P. Transnational Corporations and Non-fuel Primary Commodities in Developing Countries. *World Devel.*, May 1987, *15*(5), pp. 713–40. **[G: LDCs]**
MacKie-Mason, Jeffrey K. and Pindyck, Robert S. Cartel Theory and Cartel Experience in International Minerals Markets. *[Adelman, M. A.]*, 1987, pp. 187–214. **[G: Global]**
Ray, George F. The Decline of Primary Producer Power. *Nat. Inst. Econ. Rev.*, August 1987, (121), pp. 40–45. **[G: Global]**
Sassin, Wolfgang. Fossil Energy and Its Alternatives: A Problem beyond Costs and Prices. *Maillet, P.; Hague, D. and Rowland, C., eds.*, 1987, pp. 51–75.
Shelest, V. A. Alternative Sources of Energy in the National Economy of the Soviet Union. *Maillet, P.; Hague, D. and Rowland, C., eds.*, 1987, pp. 258–74. **[G: U.S.S.R.]**

6322 Mining (metal, coal, and other nonmetallic minerals)

Beckford, George L. The Social Economy of Bauxite in the Jamaican Man–Space. *Soc. Econ. Stud.*, March 1987, *36*(1), pp. 1–55.
[G: Jamaica]
Boadway, Robin W., et al. Marginal Effective Tax Rates for Capital in the Canadian Mining Industry. *Can. J. Econ.*, February 1987, *20*(1), pp. 1–16. **[G: Canada]**
Boyd, Gale A. Factor Intensity and Site Geology as Determinants of Returns to Scale in Coal Mining. *Rev. Econ. Statist.*, February 1987, *69*(1), pp. 18–23. **[G: U.S.]**
Bradley, Paul G. Cost and Output Analysis in Mineral and Petroleum Production. *[Adelman, M. A.]*, 1987, pp. 281–303.
Byrnes, Patricia and Färe, Rolf. Surface Mining of Coal: Efficiency of U.S. Interior Mines. *Appl. Econ.*, December 1987, *19*(12), pp. 1665–73. **[G: U.S.]**
Cappelli, Peter. Bargaining Structure and Wage Outcomes in the British Coal Industry. *Ind. Relat.*, Spring 1987, *26*(2), pp. 127–45.
[G: U.K.]
Coke, Lloyd B.; Weir, Colin C. and Hill, Vincent G. Environmental Impact of Bauxite Mining and Processing in Jamaica. *Soc. Econ. Stud.*,

March 1987, *36*(1), pp. 289–333.
[G: Jamaica]
Couto, Richard A. Changing Technologies and Consequences for Labor in Coal Mining. *Cornfield, D. B., ed.*, 1987, pp. 175–202.
[G: U.S.]
Cowell, Noel M. The Impact of Bauxite Mining on Peasant and Community Relations in Jamaica. *Soc. Econ. Stud.*, March 1987, *36*(1), pp. 171–216. **[G: Jamaica]**
Curry, Robert L., Jr. Botswana's Macroeconomic Management of Its Mineral-Based Growth: It Used Mining Revenues for Development and Services but Must Now Broaden the Beneficiaries. *Amer. J. Econ. Soc.*, October 1987, *46*(4), pp. 473–88. **[G: Botswana]**
Di Tella, Torcuato S. Las huelgas en la minería mexicana, 1826–1828. (With English summary.) *Desarrollo Econ.*, Jan.-Mar. 1987, *26*(104), pp. 579–608. **[G: Mexico]**
Dore, M. H. I. Mineral Taxation in Jamaica: An Oligopoly Confronts Taxes on Resource Rents—and Prevails. *Amer. J. Econ. Soc.*, April 1987, *46*(2), pp. 179–204. **[G: Jamaica]**
Francis, A. A. Excess Capacity in Alumina: Some Implications for the Bauxite–Alumina Industry of Jamaica. *Soc. Econ. Stud.*, March 1987, *36*(1), pp. 269–87. **[G: Jamaica]**
Froeb, Luke and Geweke, John. Long Run Competition in the U.S. Aluminum Industry. *Int. J. Ind. Organ.*, March 1987, *5*(1), pp. 67–78.
[G: U.S.]
George, Peter J. Ontario's Mining Industry, 1870–1940. *Drummond, I. M.*, 1987, pp. 52–76. **[G: Canada]**
Golabi, Kamal. Assessing the Uranium Resources of the United States. *Schultz, R. L., ed.*, 1987, pp. 197–235. **[G: U.S.]**
Gordon, Richard L. Coal Policy in Perspective. *[Adelman, M. A.]*, 1987, pp. 59–82.
[G: Global]
Gottlieb, Peter. Black Miners and the 1925–28 Bituminous Coal Strike: The Colored Committee of Non-Union Miners, Montour Mine No. 1, Pittsburgh Coal Company. *Labor Hist.*, Spring 1987, *28*(2), pp. 233–37. **[G: U.S.]**
Harvey, Charles and Taylor, Peter. Mineral Wealth and Economic Development: Foreign Direct Investment in Spain, 1851–1913. *Econ. Hist. Rev., 2nd Ser.*, May 1987, *40*(2), pp. 185–207. **[G: Spain]**
Hennart, Jean-Francois. Transaction Costs and the Multinational Enterprise: The Case of Tin. *Atack, J., ed.*, 1987, pp. 147–59. **[G: U.K.]**
Hirsch, Barry T. and Hausman, William J. Labouring: A Reply [Labour Productivity in the British and South Wales Coal Industry, 1874–1914]. *Economica*, November 1987, *54*(216), pp. 525. **[G: U.K.]**
Joskow, Paul L. Contract Duration and Relationship-Specific Investments: Empirical Evidence from Coal Markets. *Amer. Econ. Rev.*, March 1987, *77*(1), pp. 168–85. **[G: U.S.]**
Kaiser, Ronald A. and Fletcher, James E. State Policies and Practices in Coal Severance Taxa-

tion. *Natural Res. J.*, Summer 1987, 27(3), pp. 591–604. [G: U.S.]

Kalyala, Denny H. and Mudenda, Gilbert N. The Effects of the World Economic Recession on the Mining Sector in the SADCC Region. *Amin, S.; Chitala, D. and Mandaza, I., eds.*, 1987, pp. 109–27. [G: Southern Africa]

Kumar, Raj and Radetzki, Marian. Alternative Fiscal Regimes for Mining in Developing Countries. *World Devel.*, May 1987, 15(5), pp. 741–58. [G: LDCs]

Le Franc, Elsie. The Bauxite Labour Force in Jamaica: A High Wage Sector in a Dual Economy. *Soc. Econ. Stud.*, March 1987, 36(1), pp. 217–68. [G: Jamaica]

Liu, Jing-Tong. China's Energy and Economic Development. *Dutta, M., ed. (II)*, 1987, pp. 53–63. [G: China]

Lougheed, Alan. The Cyanide Process and God Extraction in Australia and New Zealand 1888–1913. *Australian Econ. Hist. Rev.*, March 1987, 27(1), pp. 44–60. [G: Australia; New Zealand]

Lowe, B. Thomas. Regulatory Enforcement of the Surface Mine Control and Reclamation Act of 1977, PL 95/87: A Comparison of State and Federal Compliance in Three Midwestern States. *Natural Res. J.*, Winter 1987, 27(1), pp. 201–11. [G: U.S.]

Lucas, Robert E. B. Emigration to South Africa's Mines. *Amer. Econ. Rev.*, June 1987, 77(3), pp. 313–30. [G: S. Africa; Botswana; Lesotho; Malawi; Mozambique]

McBain, Helen. The Impact of the Bauxite–Alumina MNCs on Rural Jamaica: Constraints on Development of Small Farmers in Jamaica. *Soc. Econ. Stud.*, March 1987, 36(1), pp. 137–70. [G: Jamaica]

McCaffray, Susan P. Origins of Labor Policy in the Russian Coal and Steel Industry, 1874–1900. *J. Econ. Hist.*, December 1987, 47(4), pp. 951–65. [G: Russia]

Mishra, R. N. Technology Transfer in an Indian Underground Coal-Mine—A Case Study. *Pachauri, R. K., ed.*, 1987, pp. 811–19. [G: India]

Mubayi, A. Economics of Transporting Solids by Pipe-line—Comparison of a Coal Slurry Pipeline and Movement by Rail. *Pachauri, R. K., ed.*, 1987, pp. 919–34.

Newbury, Colin. Technology, Capital, and Consolidation: The Performance of De Beers Mining Company Limited, 1880–1889. *Bus. Hist. Rev.*, Spring 1987, 61(1), pp. 1–42. [G: S. Africa]

Newcomb, Richard T. Substitution, Technical Change, and World Coal Demands. *Pachauri, R. K., ed.*, 1987, pp. 935–51. [G: Global]

Pariser, David B. and Khilji, Nasir M. Federal Coal Leasing and Capitalization of Economic Rents. *J. Energy Devel.*, Spring 1987, 12(2), pp. 269–85. [G: U.S.]

Polinsky, A. Mitchell. Fixed Price versus Spot Price Contracts: A Study in Risk Allocation. *J. Law, Econ., Organ.*, Spring 1987, 3(1), pp. 27–46. [G: U.S.]

Ratick, Samuel J. and Kuby, Michael J. Regional Assessment of Coal Utilization Technologies Using Mathematical Programming. *Schultz, R. L., ed.*, 1987, pp. 155–95. [G: U.S.]

Rittenberg, Libby and Manuel, Ernest H., Jr. Sources of Labor Productivity Variation in the U.S. Surface Coal Mining Industry, 1960–1976. *Energy J.*, January 1987, 8(1), pp. 87–100. [G: U.S.]

Robinson, Colin. A Liberalized Coal Market? *Lloyds Bank Rev.*, April 1987, (164), pp. 16–35. [G: U.K.]

Robinson, Colin. World Coal Demand: Bridging the Energy Future? *Stevens, P., ed.*, 1987, pp. 125–54. [G: Global]

Rose, Adam and Soelistijo, Ukar. The Potential of Coal in the Development of Oil-Rich LDCs: The Case of Indonesia. *Pachauri, R. K., ed.*, 1987, pp. 793–809. [G: Indonesia]

Rubin, Edward S. Environmental Control Costs for Coal Energy Technologies. *Maillet, P.; Hague, D. and Rowland, C., eds.*, 1987, pp. 434–60. [G: OECD]

Sachak, Najma. The Impact of Land Acquisition by Bauxite–Alumina Transnational Corporations on Peasants in the Bauxite Land Economy. *Soc. Econ. Stud.*, March 1987, 36(1), pp. 93–135. [G: Jamaica]

Salmon, Michael G. Land Utilization within Jamaica's Bauxite Land Economy. *Soc. Econ. Stud.*, March 1987, 36(1), pp. 57–92. [G: Jamaica]

Treble, John G. Sliding Scales and Conciliation Boards: Risk-Sharing in the Late 19th Century British Coal Industry. *Oxford Econ. Pap.*, December 1987, 39(4), pp. 679–98. [G: U.K.]

Turnbull, Gerard. Canals, Coal and Regional Growth during the Industrial Revolution. *Econ. Hist. Rev.*, 2nd Ser., November 1987, 40(4), pp. 537–60. [G: U.K.]

Ventura, Arnaldo K. Jamaica's Bauxite Battle. *Dedijer, S. and Jéquier, N., eds.*, 1987, pp. 110–27. [G: Jamaica]

de Vletter, Fion. Foreign Labour on the South African Gold Mines: New Insights on an Old Problem. *Int. Lab. Rev.*, Mar.-Apr. 1987, 126(2), pp. 199–218. [G: S. Africa]

Wardley, Peter. Labouring over Productivity Estimates: A Comment on Hirsch and Hausman's Model of Coal Miners' Productivity, 1874–1914 [Labour Productivity in the British and South Wales Coal Industry, 1874–1914]. *Economica*, November 1987, 54(216), pp. 521–24. [G: U.K.]

Yanarella, Ernest J. and Reid, Herbert G. Class-Based Environmentalism in a Small Town: ERDA's "Gasifiers in Industry" Program and the Georgetown, Kentucky, Controversy. *Yanarella, E. J. and Green, W. C., eds.*, 1987, pp. 99–125. [G: U.S.]

6323 Oil, Gas, and Other Fuels

Adelman, M. A. The Economics of the International Oil Industry. *Rees, J. and Odell, P., eds.*, 1987, pp. 27–56. [G: Global]

Aivazian, Varouj A., et al. Economies of Scale versus Technological Change in the Natural Gas Transmission Industry. *Rev. Econ. Statist.*, August 1987, *69*(3), pp. 556–61. [G: U.S.]

Al-Sahlawi, Mohammed A. and Boyd, Roy G. Energy Demand in Developing Countries and Third World Response to Changes in the International Oil Market. *J. Energy Devel.*, Spring 1987, *12*(2), pp. 225–43. [G: LDCs]

Amano, Akihiro. A Small Forecasting Model of the World Oil Market. *J. Policy Modeling*, Winter 1987, *9*(4), pp. 615–35.

Andrews, Donald R. An Export-Base Analysis of Louisiana's Petroleum Driven Economy. *Ann. Reg. Sci.*, March 1987, *21*(1), pp. 65–79. [G: U.S.]

Baca, Alvin. FERC & ERA: Issues in Natural Gas Regulation. *Natural Res. J.*, Fall 1987, *27*(4), pp. 815–22. [G: U.S.]

Bacon, Pamela S. Mines and Minerals—A Mineral Lessee's Rights and Obligations in New Mexico. *Natural Res. J.*, Fall 1987, *27*(4), pp. 899–912. [G: U.S.]

Baish, Richard O. The Role of the California Public Utilities Commission in Western Gas Markets. *Natural Res. J.*, Fall 1987, *27*(4), pp. 805–10. [G: U.S.]

Banks, Ferdinand F. The Reserve–Production Ratio. *Energy J.*, April 1987, *8*(2), pp. 147–51.

Baysinger, Barry D.; Keim, Gerald D. and Zeithaml, Carl P. Constituency Building as a Political Strategy in the Petroleum Industry. *Marcus, A. A.; Kaufman, A. M. and Beam, D. R., eds.*, 1987, pp. 223–38. [G: U.S.]

Bean, Charles R. The Performance of the British Economy: The Impact of North Sea Oil. *Dornbusch, R. and Layard, R., eds.*, 1987, pp. 64–96. [G: U.K.]

Bentham, Richard W. The International Legal Structure of Petroleum Exploration. *Rees, J. and Odell, P., eds.*, 1987, pp. 57–66. [G: Global]

Bird, Peter J. W. N. Continuity and Reversal in Oil Spot Price Movements. *Energy Econ.*, April 1987, *9*(2), pp. 73–81. [G: Global]

Bird, Peter J. W. N. Futures Trading and the European Oil Market. *Energy J.*, July 1987, *8*(3), pp. 149–55. [G: W. Europe]

Bohi, Douglas R. Evolution of the Oil Market and Energy Security Policy. *Contemp. Policy Issues*, July 1987, *5*(3), pp. 20–33. [G: U.S.]

Bohi, Douglas R. and Toman, Michael A. Futures Trading and Oil Market Conditions. *J. Futures Markets*, April 1987, *7*(2), pp. 203–21. [G: Global]

Bopp, Anthony E. and Sitzer, Scott. Are Petroleum Futures Prices Good Predictors of Cash Value? *J. Futures Markets*, December 1987, *7*(6), pp. 705–19. [G: U.S.]

Boucher, Jacqueline; Hefting, Tom and Smeers, Yves. Economic Analysis of Natural Gas Contracts. *Golombek, R.; Hoel, M. and Vislie, J., eds.*, 1987, pp. 193–220. [G: Norway]

Boucher, Jacqueline and Smeers, Yves. Economic Forces in the European Gas Market—A 1985 Prospective. *Energy Econ.*, January 1987, *9*(1), pp. 2–16. [G: Europe; Algeria]

Bowie, Paddy. Oil, Gas and Development in Malaysia. *Hills, P. and Bowie, P., 1987, pp. 85–148.* [G: Malaysia]

Broadman, Harry G. Competition in Natural Gas Pipeline Wellhead Supply Purchases. *Energy J.*, July 1987, *8*(3), pp. 113–34. [G: U.S.]

Broadman, Harry G. Corporate Strategies of Foreign Investment in Oil Exploration outside North America. *J. Energy Devel.*, Autumn 1987, *13*(1), pp. 27–44. [G: U.S.; Canada]

Brown, Jonathan C. Domestic Politics and Foreign Investment: British Development of Mexican Petroleum, 1889–1911. *Bus. Hist. Rev.*, Autumn 1987, *61*(3), pp. 387–416. [G: Mexico]

Campbell, Michael. The Implications of Gas Policy for the Western States: A Producer Perspective. *Natural Res. J.*, Fall 1987, *27*(4), pp. 823–28. [G: U.S.]

Carpenter, Paul R.; Jacoby, Henry D. and Wright, Arthur W. Adapting to Change in Natural Gas Markets. *[Adelman, M. A.]*, 1987, pp. 1–29. [G: U.S.]

Carrie, J. L. Long-term Balance on the World Oil Market. *Pachauri, R. K., ed.*, 1987, pp. 663–71. [G: Global]

Carriero, Libero. Technology and International Relations: Considerations on the Industrial Development of the OAPEC Countries. *Hieronymi, O., ed.*, 1987, pp. 141–56. [G: OAPEC]

Chen, K. C.; Sears, R. Stephen and Tzang, Dah-Nein. Oil Prices and Energy Futures. *J. Futures Markets*, October 1987, *7*(5), pp. 501–18. [G: U.S.]

Cicchetti, Charles J. Can Natural Gas Deregulation Be a Model for the Electric Power Industry? *Stewart, M. B., ed.*, 1987, pp. 81–87. [G: U.S.]

Cook, P. Lesley. Research and Development Networks and Markets in a Complex Industry: The Example of Offshore Oil Equipment. *Saunders, C. T., ed.*, 1987, pp. 105–17.

Danielsen, Albert L. and Cartwright, Phillip A. Inventory Theory in Cartelized Markets. *Energy Econ.*, July 1987, *9*(3), pp. 167–75. [G: U.S.]

Dayo, Felix B. and Adegbulugbe, Anthony O. Oil Demand Elasticities in Nigeria. *Energy J.*, April 1987, *8*(2), pp. 31–41. [G: Nigeria]

Deagle, Edwin A., Jr. The International Community and International Oil. *Rees, J. and Odell, P., eds.*, 1987, pp. 19–26. [G: Global]

Desai, Meghnad. The Political Economy of World Oil. *Rees, J. and Odell, P., eds.*, 1987, pp. 130–36.

Desprairies, Pierre. Oil Demand Prospects. *Stevens, P., ed.*, 1987, pp. 109–24. [G: U.S.; Global]

Dunkerley, Joy and Hoch, Irving. Energy for Transport in Developing Countries. *Energy J.*, July 1987, *8*(3), pp. 57–72. [G: LDCs]

Dyrstad, Jan Morten. Resource Boom, Wages

and Unemployment: Theory and Evidence from the Norwegian Petroleum Experience. *Scand. J. Econ.*, 1987, *89*(2), pp. 125–43. [G: Norway]

Ellis, Joan T. State Regulation in a Deregulated Environment: A State-Level Regulator's Lament. *Natural Res. J.*, Fall 1987, *27*(4), pp. 799–803. [G: U.S.]

Erikson, Edward W. World Oil Prices and the Emerging World Gas Market. *Pachauri, R. K., ed.*, 1987, pp. 673–81. [G: Global]

Fender, John and Nandakumar, Parameswar. Oil in an Intertemporal Macroeconomic Model. *Greek Econ. Rev.*, 1987, *9*(1), pp. 38–56.

Flåm, Sjur D. and Moxnes, Erling. Exploration for Petroleum and the Inventory of Proven Reserves. *Energy Econ.*, July 1987, *9*(3), pp. 190–94. [G: Norway]

Fobelli, Paolo. A Process for Decision-Making on Natural Gas: Fiscal Competitiveness in Reservoir Development. *Energy Econ.*, October 1987, *9*(4), pp. 265–73. [G: Global]

Fuller, J. David. The Impact of $(US)15 Oil Prices on Canadian Energy Markets. *Can. Public Policy*, March 1987, *13*(1), pp. 34–40. [G: Canada]

Garretty, Jeanette A. Financing the Energy Industry: An Economist's Perspective. *J. Energy Devel.*, Spring 1987, *12*(2), pp. 215–23. [G: U.S.]

Gartman, John A. The "Bypass" Issue: What Effect Does Local Utility Bypass Have on Energy Prices and the Economy? *Stewart, M. B., ed.*, 1987, pp. 59–61. [G: U.S.]

German, Michael I. How Far Will Natural Gas Deregulation Go? What Effect Will Deregulation Have on Prices and the "Gas Bubble"? *Stewart, M. B., ed.*, 1987, pp. 27–32. [G: U.S.]

Geroski, Paul A.; Ulph, Alistair M. and Ulph, David T. A Model of the Crude Oil Market in Which Market Conduct Varies. *Econ. J.*, Supplement 1987, *97*, pp. 77–86. [G: Global]

Gibbons, Elizabeth and Halpin, Gerald F. Import Price Declines in 1986 Reflected Reduced Oil Prices. *Mon. Lab. Rev.*, April 1987, *110*(4), pp. 3–17. [G: U.S.]

Goldberg, Victor P. and Erickson, John R. Quantity and Price Adjustment in Long-term Contracts: A Case Study of Petroleum Coke. *J. Law Econ.*, October 1987, *30*(2), pp. 369–98. [G: U.S.]

Golombek, Rolf and Hoel, Michael. The Relationship between the Price of Natural Gas and Crude Oil: Some Aspects of Efficient Contracts. *Golombek, R.; Hoel, M. and Vislie, J., eds.*, 1987, pp. 221–37.

Golombek, Rolf; Hoel, Michael and Vislie, Jon. Natural Gas Markets and Contracts: An Introduction. *Golombek, R.; Hoel, M. and Vislie, J., eds.*, 1987, pp. 1–6. [G: W. Europe]

Gould, Brian W. The Impacts of the Market Pricing of Canadian Energy Resources on the Alberta Oil Industry. *Western J. Agr. Econ.*, July 1987, *12*(1), pp. 65–77. [G: Canada]

Grant, Robert M. The Effects of Product Standardization on Competition: Octane Grading of Petrol in the UK. *Gabel, H. L., ed.*, 1987, pp. 283–302. [G: U.K.]

Gray, Dale. Framework for Projecting Petroleum Product Demand Including the Effect of Energy Prices. *Pachauri, R. K., ed.*, 1987, pp. 1009–34.

Guadagni, Alieto A. Decisiones energéticas para el futuro. (With English summary.) *Desarrollo Econ.*, Jan.-Mar. 1987, *26*(104), pp. 609–30. [G: Argentina]

Haar, Lawrence. The Role and Importance of Crude and Product Futures Markets. *Pachauri, R. K., ed.*, 1987, pp. 683–701.

Harris, Anthony H., et al. Incoming Industry and Structural Change: Oil and the Aberdeen Economy. *Scot. J. Polit. Econ.*, February 1987, *34*(1), pp. 69–90. [G: U.K.]

Harris, Trevor S. and Ohlson, James A. Accounting Disclosures and the Market's Valuation of Oil and Gas Properties. *Accounting Rev.*, October 1987, *62*(4), pp. 651–70. [G: U.S.]

Harvie, Charles. The Structural Effects of North Sea Oil upon the U.K. Economy: Alternative Viewpoints and Evidence. *J. Energy Devel.*, Autumn 1987, *13*(1), pp. 45–86. [G: U.K.]

Hawdon, David. Short and Long-run Crude Oil Price Expectations in 1986—Results of a Survey. *Stevens, P., ed.*, 1987, pp. 166–76. [G: Global]

Henderson, David R. The IEA Oil-sharing Plan: Who Shares with Whom? *Energy J.*, October 1987, *8*(4), pp. 23–31. [G: OECD]

Hendricks, Kenneth; Porter, Robert H. and Boudreau, Bryan. Information, Returns, and Bidding Behavior in OCS Auctions: 1954–1969. *J. Ind. Econ.*, June 1987, *35*(4), pp. 517–42. [G: U.S.]

Hertzmark, Donald I. Alternative Transport Fuels in an Era of Falling Energy Prices: The Case of Alcohol Fuel in the Philippines. *Pachauri, R. K., ed.*, 1987, pp. 467–79. [G: Philippines]

Hietarinta, Kai. Oljepriset och östhandelns utveckling. (The Price of Oil and the Development Trade with Eastern Europe. With English summary.) *Ekon. Samfundets Tidskr.*, 1987, *40*(1), pp. 7–10. [G: Finland; U.S.S.R.]

Hills, Peter. The Development of the Petroleum Industry in the People's Republic of China. *Hills, P. and Bowie, P.*, 1987, pp. 1–84. [G: China]

Hoel, Michael and Strøm, Steinar. Supply Security and Import Diversification of Natural Gas. *Golombek, R.; Hoel, M. and Vislie, J., eds.*, 1987, pp. 151–72. [G: W. Europe; Norway; U.S.S.R.]

Hognestad, Gunnar. The Role of the Norwegian Government When Selling Natural Gas. *Golombek, R.; Hoel, M. and Vislie, J., eds.*, 1987, pp. 173–80. [G: Norway]

Houthakker, Hendrik S. The Ups and Downs of Oil. *Cagan, P., ed.*, 1987, pp. 153–79. [G: U.S.]

Hubbard, R. Glenn and Weiner, Robert J. Natural Gas Contracting in Practice: Evidence from the United States. *Golombek, R.; Hoel, M. and Vislie, J., eds.*, 1987, pp. 279–313. [G: U.S.]

Isaac, R. Mark. Cooperative Institutions for Information Sharing in the Oil Industry. *J. Environ. Econ. Manage.*, September 1987, *14*(3), pp. 191–211. [G: U.S.]

Itteilag, Richard L. An Analysis of Actual and Forecasted Conservation in the Residential Gas Space Heating Market. *Pachauri, R. K., ed.*, 1987, pp. 737–50. [G: U.S.]

Jacobsen, Bjørn R. Some Experiences from Bargaining over Natural Gas. *Golombek, R.; Hoel, M. and Vislie, J., eds.*, 1987, pp. 181–92. [G: Norway]

James, Zan. Intrastate Pipelines in a Changing Marketplace. *Natural Res. J.*, Fall 1987, *27*(4), pp. 811–14. [G: U.S.]

Jenkins-Smith, Hank C. An Industry in Turmoil: The Remaking of the Natural Gas Industry. *Natural Res. J.*, Fall 1987, *27*(4), pp. 773–80. [G: U.S.]

Jenkins-Smith, Hank C. Natural Gas Regulation in the Western U.S.: Perspectives on Regulation in the Next Decade: Editor's Introduction. *Natural Res. J.*, Fall 1987, *27*(4), pp. 771–72. [G: U.S.]

Kelly, Suedeen G. Regulatory Reform of the U.S. Natural Gas Industry: A Summing Up. *Natural Res. J.*, Fall 1987, *27*(4), pp. 841–63. [G: U.S.]

Kirchgässner, Gebhard. Zur Anpassung der schweizerischen Mineralölpreise an die internationale Entwicklung. Empirische Tests einiger Hypothesen. (On the Adjustment of Swiss Oil Prices to the International Development. With English summary.) *Schweiz. Z. Volkswirtsch. Statist.*, June 1987, *123*(2), pp. 123–46. [G: Switzerland]

Krapels, Edward N. Implementing Efficient Petroleum Product Pricing Programs in Developing Countries. *Energy J.*, January 1987, *8*(1), pp. 39–52. [G: LDCs]

Krol, Robert and Svorny, Shirley V. A Time-Series Analysis of U.S. Petroleum Industry Inventory Behavior. *Energy J.*, October 1987, *8*(4), pp. 65–78. [G: U.S.]

Levinson, Marc. Alcohol Fuels Revisited: The Costs and Benefits of Energy Independence in Brazil. *J. Devel. Areas*, April 1987, *21*(3), pp. 243–57. [G: Brazil]

Livernois, John R. Empirical Evidence on the Characteristics of Extractive Technologies: The Case of Oil. *J. Environ. Econ. Manage.*, March 1987, *14*(1), pp. 72–86. [G: Canada]

Lucke, Robert and Toder, Eric. Assessing the U.S. Federal Tax Burden on Oil and Gas Extraction. *Energy J.*, October 1987, *8*(4), pp. 51–64. [G: U.S.]

Makarov, A. A. Extreme Strategies for the Longterm Development of the Energy Industry. *Matekon*, Fall 1987, *24*(1), pp. 21–42. [G: U.S.S.R.]

Marks, Stephen V. International Crude-Oil Resales: Theory and Recent History. *J. Energy*

Devel., Autumn 1987, *13*(1), pp. 87–100. [G: OPEC]

Martellaro, Joseph A. The Nineteenth Century Development of the Russian Petroleum Industry. *Rivista Int. Sci. Econ. Com.*, August 1987, *34*(8), pp. 777–92. [G: U.S.S.R.]

Mathiesen, Lars; Roland, Kjell and Thonstad, Knut. The European Natural Gas Market: Degrees of Market Power on the Selling Side. *Golombek, R.; Hoel, M. and Vislie, J., eds.*, 1987, pp. 27–58. [G: W. Europe; Algeria; U.S.S.R.]

Matthews, Derek. The Technical Transformation of the Late Nineteenth-Century Gas Industry. *J. Econ. Hist.*, December 1987, *47*(4), pp. 967–80. [G: U.K.]

Metwally, M. M. and Arab, A. T. Price Elasticity of Demand for Oil and the Terms of Trade of the OPEC Countries. *Energy J.*, January 1987, *8*(1), pp. 53–67. [G: OPEC]

Mikdashi, Z. Oil Funding and International Financial Markets. *Rees, J. and Odell, P., eds.*, 1987, pp. 88–106. [G: Global]

Mongula, Benedict S. and Ng'andwe, Chiselebwe. Limits to Development in Southern Africa: Energy, Transport and Communications in SADCC Countries. *Amin, S.; Chitala, D. and Mandaza, I., eds.*, 1987, pp. 85–108. [G: Southern Africa]

Moran, Theodore H. Managing an Oligopoly of Would-Be Sovereigns: The Dynamics of Joint Control and Self-Control in the International Oil Industry Past, Present, and Future. *Int. Organ.*, Autumn 1987, *41*(4), pp. 575–607. [G: Global]

da Motta, Ronaldo Serôa. The Social Viability of Ethanol Production in Brazil. *Energy Econ.*, July 1987, *9*(3), pp. 176–82. [G: Brazil]

Moxnes, Erling. The Dynamics of Interfuel Substitution in the OECD-Europe Industrial Sector. *Golombek, R.; Hoel, M. and Vislie, J., eds.*, 1987, pp. 95–120. [G: W. Europe]

Moxnes, Erling. Uncertainty in Future Oil Price Predictions. *Pachauri, R. K., ed.*, 1987, pp. 1105–21.

Muchlinski, P. T. Law and the Analysis of the International Oil Industry. *Rees, J. and Odell, P., eds.*, 1987, pp. 142–58.

Naeve, Michael. The Future of the Natural Gas Market: Regulation and Prices. *Natural Res. J.*, Fall 1987, *27*(4), pp. 781–88. [G: U.S.]

Newbery, David M. The Privatisation of British Gas and Possible Consequences for the European Gas Market. *Golombek, R.; Hoel, M. and Vislie, J., eds.*, 1987, pp. 59–93. [G: U.K.]

Newton, Walter L. Refining Developments in the Non-OECD Area. *Pachauri, R. K., ed.*, 1987, pp. 291–313. [G: Global]

Noreng, Øystein. Structure and Bargaining in the West European Gas Market. *Golombek, R.; Hoel, M. and Vislie, J., eds.*, 1987, pp. 7–26. [G: W. Europe]

Nystad, Arild N. Petroleum Taxes and Resource Management. *Pachauri, R. K., ed.*, 1987, pp. 19–34.

Nystad, Arild N. Rate Sensitivity and the Optimal

Choice of Production Capacity of Petroleum Reservoirs. *Energy Econ.*, January 1987, 9(1), pp. 37–45.

Odell, Peter R. Gas Demand Prospects. *Stevens, P., ed.*, 1987, pp. 71–81. **[G: Global]**

Odell, Peter R. The Prospect for Oil Prices and the Energy Market. *Lloyds Bank Rev.*, July 1987, (165), pp. 1–14. **[G: Global]**

Osaki, Kazumasa. End of an Era: OPEC's Temporary Retreat. *Finn, R. B., ed.*, 1987, pp. 119–34. **[G: OPEC; U.S.; Japan]**

Osten, James A. The Impact of $(US)15 Oil Prices on Canadian Energy Markets. *Can. Public Policy*, March 1987, 13(1), pp. 26–33. **[G: Canada]**

Overdahl, James A. The Use of Crude Oil Futures by the Governments of Oil-Producing States. *J. Futures Markets*, December 1987, 7(6), pp. 603–17. **[G: U.S.]**

Parhizgari, Ali M. Optimum Depletion of Oil Resources in a Developing Country. *Energy J.*, July 1987, 8(3), pp. 31–56. **[G: LDCs]**

Penrose, Edith. The Structure of the International Oil Industry: Multinationals, Governments and OPEC. *Rees, J. and Odell, P., eds.*, 1987, pp. 9–18. **[G: Global]**

Pérez-López, Jorge F. Cuban Oil Reexports: Significance and Prospects. *Energy J.*, January 1987, 8(1), pp. 1–16. **[G: Cuba]**

Philip, G. Government, Interests and World Oil. *Rees, J. and Odell, P., eds.*, 1987, pp. 136–42.

Pinto, Brian. Nigeria during and after the Oil Boom: A Policy Comparison with Indonesia. *World Bank Econ. Rev.*, May 1987, 1(3), pp. 419–45. **[G: Nigeria; Indonesia]**

Plourde, André. On the Role and Status of Canadian Natural Gas Carriers under Deregulation. *J. Energy Devel.*, Autumn 1987, 13(1), pp. 1–25. **[G: Canada]**

Plourde, André. The Impact of $(US)15 Oil on the Canadian Economy: Evidence from the MACE Model. *Can. Public Policy*, March 1987, 13(1), pp. 19–25. **[G: Canada]**

Polach, Jay G. The Industry Structure and Pricing Policies in Oil International Transactions. *Pachauri, R. K., ed.*, 1987, pp. 35–57. **[G: Global]**

Primeaux, Walter J., Jr. The Interdependence of the Life Cycle and Strategic Group Concepts: Theory and Evidence. *Lee, C. F., ed.*, 1987, pp. 67–85. **[G: U.S.]**

Rampa, Lorenzo. On Endogenous Oil Market Fluctuations. *Rivista Int. Sci. Econ. Com.*, August 1987, 34(8), pp. 761–69.

Randol, William L. World Oil Dynamics: The Political Dimension. *Stewart, M. B., ed.*, 1987, pp. 21–25. **[G: OPEC; Saudi Arabia]**

Rees, Judith and Odell, Peter R. International Oil Issues and Perspectives. *Rees, J. and Odell, P., eds.*, 1987, pp. 1–8. **[G: Global]**

Reid, R. G. A View of European Oil and Gas Issues. *Rees, J. and Odell, P., eds.*, 1987, pp. 76–87. **[G: Europe]**

Ros, Jaime. Mexico from the Oil Boom to the Debt Crisis: An Analysis of Policy Responses to External Shocks, 1978–85. *Thorp, R. and Whitehead, L., eds.*, 1987, pp. 68–116. **[G: Mexico]**

Ross, T. D. The Status and Strategies of the International Oil Corporations. *Rees, J. and Odell, P., eds.*, 1987, pp. 67–75. **[G: Global]**

Rowse, John. Canadian Natural Gas Exports, Domestic Gas Prices, and Future Gas Supply Costs. *Energy J.*, April 1987, 8(2), pp. 43–62. **[G: Canada]**

Rowse, John. The Economic Impact of Prolonged Low Oil Prices. *Can. Public Policy*, March 1987, 13(1), pp. 49–55. **[G: Canada]**

Samii, Massood V. The Organization of the Petroleum Exporting Countries and the Oil Market: Different Views. *J. Energy Devel.*, Spring 1987, 12(2), pp. 159–73. **[G: OPEC]**

Sanderson, Susan Walsh. Automated Manufacturing and Offshore Assembly in Mexico. *Thorup, C. L., ed.*, 1987, pp. 127–48. **[G: Mexico]**

Saunders, Michael. Oil Taxation: The Cross-Field Allowance. *Fisc. Stud.*, November 1987, 8(4), pp. 55–68. **[G: U.K.]**

Scheffman, David T. and Spiller, Pablo T. Geographic Market Definition under the *U.S. Department of Justice Merger Guidelines. J. Law Econ.*, April 1987, 30(1), pp. 123–47. **[G: U.S.]**

Siddayao, Corazon Morales. Capital Investment Requirements for Oil and Gas Development: Constraints in Developing Countries. *Pachauri, R. K., ed.*, 1987, pp. 751–73.

Stewart, Marion B. Energy Deregulation and Economic Growth: Summary. *Stewart, M. B., ed.*, 1987, pp. 1–16. **[G: U.S.]**

Strange, Susan. States, Markets and Oil: An International Relations Perspective. *Rees, J. and Odell, P., eds.*, 1987, pp. 163–67.

Tuck, Bradford H. Structural Change in Alaska: The Impact of the Petroleum Industry. *Lane, T., ed.*, 1987, pp. 233–49. **[G: U.S.]**

Van Vactor, Samuel A. and Tussing, Arlon R. Retrospective on Oil Prices. *Contemp. Policy Issues*, July 1987, 5(3), pp. 1–19. **[G: Global]**

Verleger, Philip K., Jr. The Evolution of Oil as a Commodity. *[Adelman, M. A.]*, 1987, pp. 161–86.

Vislie, Jon. Long-term Bilateral Contracts for Natural Gas. *Golombek, R.; Hoel, M. and Vislie, J., eds.*, 1987, pp. 267–77.

Wade, Doug. Assessing Future Energy and Oil Demand. *Stevens, P., ed.*, 1987, pp. 82–108. **[G: OECD; LDCs]**

Waldman, Andrea K. Natural Gas Imports: Federal Policy and Competition for U.S. Markets. *Natural Res. J.*, Fall 1987, 27(4), pp. 789–98. **[G: U.S.]**

Watkins, G. Campbell. Living under a Shadow: U.S. Oil Policies and Canadian Oil Pricing. *[Adelman, M. A.]*, 1987, pp. 31–57. **[G: U.S.; Canada]**

Wellinghoff, Jon. What Do "436," "436-A," "451," "311," "7(c)," Mean to the Residential Gas Consumer. *Natural Res. J.*, Fall 1987, 27(4), pp. 829–40. **[G: U.S.]**

Wiggins, Steven N. and Libecap, Gary D. Firm

Heterogeneities and Cartelization Efforts in Domestic Crude Oil. *J. Law, Econ., Organ.*, Spring 1987, *3*(1), pp. 1–25.   [G: U.S.]

Williams, Harold R. and Mount, Randall I. OPEC and the U.S. Demand for Motor Gasoline: Short-run and Long-run Price Elasticities. *Rivista Int. Sci. Econ. Com.*, Jan.-Feb. 1987, *34*(1–2), pp. 147–58.   [G: U.S.]

Wilson, David. The Consumption of Automotive Oil Products in Soviet Road Transport. *Tismer, J. F.; Ambler, J. and Symons, L.*, eds., 1987, pp. 185–217.   [G: U.S.S.R.]

Zakariya, Hasan S. The Third World Perspective on Petroleum: The Travails of the 'Haves' and the Plight of the 'Have-Nots.' *Rees, J. and Odell, P.*, eds., 1987, pp. 107–28. [G: LDCs]

Zandi, Mark. What Impact Will Energy Price Changes Have on Economic Growth in the United States? *Stewart, M. B.*, ed., 1987, pp. 41–54.   [G: U.S.]

633 Industry Studies: Distributive Trades

6330 General

Ballwieser, Wolfgang. Transaction Cost Analysis of Structural Changes in the Distribution System: Reflections on Institutional Developments in the Federal Republic of Germany: Comment. *J. Inst. Theoretical Econ.*, March 1987, *143*(1), pp. 86–90.   [G: W. Germany]

Cicchetti, Charles J. Can Natural Gas Deregulation Be a Model for the Electric Power Industry? *Stewart, M. B.*, ed., 1987, pp. 81–87.   [G: U.S.]

Eggertsson, Thráinn. Transaction Cost Analysis of Structural Changes in the Distribution System: Reflections on Institutional Developments in the Federal Republic of Germany: Comment. *J. Inst. Theoretical Econ.*, March 1987, *143*(1), pp. 82–85.   [G: W. Germany]

Hundert, Gershon David. The Role of the Jews in Commerce in Early Modern Poland–Lithuania. *J. Europ. Econ. Hist.*, Fall 1987, *16*(2), pp. 245–75.   [G: Poland; Lithuania]

Kirchner, Christian and Picot, Arnold. Transaction Cost Analysis of Structural Changes in the Distribution System: Reflections on Institutional Developments in the Federal Republic of Germany. *J. Inst. Theoretical Econ.*, March 1987, *143*(1), pp. 62–81.   [G: W. Germany]

McDonald, Ian M. and Spindler, Karen J. An Empirical Investigation of Customer Market Analysis—A Microfoundation for Macroeconomics. *Appl. Econ.*, September 1987, *19*(9), pp. 1149–74.   [G: U.S.; U.K.; Australia]

6333 Retail Trade

Albion, Mark S. and Farris, Paul W. Manufacturer Advertising and Retail Gross Margins. *Bloom, P. N.*, ed., 1987, pp. 107–35.   [G: U.S.]

Aronson, Nancy R.; Pulver, Glen C. and Buse, Rueben C. The Influence of Community Characteristics on the Level of Retail Trade. *Reg.*

Sci. Persp., 1987, *17*(1), pp. 3–19.   [G: U.S.]

Blomley, N. K. Retail Regulation in England and Wales: The Results of a Survey. *Environ. Planning A*, October 1987, *19*(10), pp. 1399–1406.   [G: U.K.]

Caron-Salmona, Hélène and Lesourne, Jacques. Dynamics of a Retail Market with Search Processes. *Europ. Econ. Rev.*, July 1987, *31*(5), pp. 995–1021.

Cotterill, Ronald W. and Haller, Lawrence. Entry Patterns and Strategic Interaction in Food Retailing. *Wills, R. L.; Caswell, J. A. and Culbertson, J. D.*, eds., 1987, pp. 203–22.   [G: U.S.]

Dahremöller, Axel. Konzentration: Ein Messproblem. Ein Beitrag zur Konzentrationsdiskussion. (With English summary.) *Z. Betriebswirtshaft*, February 1987, *57*(2), pp. 208–20.   [G: W. Germany]

Hattwick, Richard E. Mary Kay Ash. *J. Behav. Econ.*, Winter 1987, *16*(4), pp. 61–70.

Herman, Arthur S. and Henneberger, J. Edwin. Productivity Trends in the Furniture and Home Furnishings Stores Industry. *Mon. Lab. Rev.*, May 1987, *110*(5), pp. 24–29. [G: U.S.]

Hess, James D. and Gerstner, Eitan. Loss Leader Pricing and Rain Check Policy. *Marketing Sci.*, Fall 1987, *6*(4), pp. 358–74.   [G: U.S.]

Hundley, Jay. J. C. Penney Relies on People Power. *Shetty, Y. K. and Buehler, V. M.*, eds., 1987, pp. 81–92.   [G: U.S.]

Kay, John A. and Morris, C. N. The Economic Efficiency of Sunday Trading Restrictions. *J. Ind. Econ.*, December 1987, *36*(2), pp. 113–29.   [G: U.K.]

Levin, Sharon G.; Levin, Stanford L. and Meisel, John B. A Dynamic Analysis of the Adoption of a New Technology: The Case of Optical Scanners. *Rev. Econ. Statist.*, February 1987, *69*(1), pp. 12–17.   [G: U.S.]

Mars, Gerald and Altman, Yochanan. Case Studies in Second Economy Distribution in Soviet Georgia. *Alessandrini, S. and Dallago, B.*, eds., 1987, pp. 219–45.   [G: U.S.S.R.]

Müller-Hagedorn, Lothar. Handelskonzentration: Ein partielles Phänomen?—oder: Irreführende Handelsstatistiken. Weitere Anmerkungen. (With English summary.) *Z. Betriebswirtschaft*, February 1987, *57*(2), pp. 200–207.   [G: W. Germany]

Nattrass, Nicoli Jean. Street Trading in Transkei—A Struggle against Poverty, Persecution, and Prosecution. *World Devel.*, July 1987, *15*(7), pp. 861–75.   [G: S. Africa]

Parker, Russell C. The Effects of Mergers and Entry on Concentration Change in SMA Grocery Retailing Markets. *Wills, R. L.; Caswell, J. A. and Culbertson, J. D.*, eds., 1987, pp. 293–313.   [G: U.S.]

Sit, Victor F. S. Urban Fairs in China. *Econ. Geogr.*, October 1987, *63*(4), pp. 306–18.   [G: China]

Slade, Margaret E. Interfirm Rivalry in a Repeated Game: An Empirical Test of Tacit Collusion. *J. Ind. Econ.*, June 1987, *35*(4), pp. 499–516. **[G: Canada]**

Sparks, Leigh. Retailing in Enterprise Zones: The Example of Swansea. *Reg. Stud.*, February 1987, *21*(1), pp. 37–42. **[G: U.K.]**

Stein, Stanley R. McDonald's Growth through People. *Shetty, Y. K. and Buehler, V. M., eds.*, 1987, pp. 103–10. **[G: U.S.]**

Thomas, Colin J. and Bromley, Rosemary D. F. The Growth and Functioning of an Unplanned Retail Park: The Swansea Enterprise Zone. *Reg. Stud.*, August 1987, *21*(4), pp. 287–300. **[G: U.K.]**

Tietz, Bruno. Zum Thema: Konzentration im Handel. (With English summary.) *Z. Betriebswirtshaft*, February 1987, *57*(2), pp. 196–99.

Wrigley, N. The Concentration of Capital in UK Grocery Retailing. *Environ. Planning A*, October 1987, *19*(10), pp. 1283–88. **[G: U.K.]**

York, James D. Retail Liquor Stores Experience Flat Trend in Productivity. *Mon. Lab. Rev.*, February 1987, *110*(2), pp. 25–29. **[G: U.S.]**

634 Industry Studies: Construction

6340 Construction

Ablin, Eduardo and Katz, Jorge M. From Infant Industry to Technology Exports: The Argentine Experience in the International Sale of Industrial Plants and Engineering Works. *Katz, J. M., ed.*, 1987, pp. 446–77. **[G: Argentina]**

Allen, Steven G. Can Union Labor Ever Cost Less? *Quart. J. Econ.*, May 1987, *102*(2), pp. 347–73. **[G: U.S.]**

Barras, Richard and Ferguson, D. Dynamic Modelling of the Building Cycle: 1. Theoretical Framework. *Environ. Planning A*, March 1987, *19*(3), pp. 353–67.

Barras, Richard and Ferguson, D. Dynamic Modelling of the Building Cycle: 2: Empirical Results. *Environ. Planning A*, April 1987, *19*(4), pp. 493–520. **[G: U.K.]**

Bourassa, Steven C. Land Value Taxation and New Housing Development in Pittsburgh. *Growth Change*, Fall 1987, *18*(4), pp. 44–56. **[G: U.S.]**

Buyst, Erik. Investeringen in woongebouwen in België tijdens de grote depressie van de jaren dertig en gedurende de huidige economische crisis: Een verkennende vergelijking. (With English summary.) *Cah. Écon. Bruxelles*, Fourth Trimester 1987, (116), pp. 99–116. **[G: Belgium]**

Dixon, Peter B. The Effects on the Australian Economy of Shorter Standard Working Hours in Construction and Related Industries. *Australian Bull. Lab.*, September 1987, *13*(4), pp. 264–89. **[G: Australia]**

Fenoaltea, Stefano. Construction in Italy, 1861–1913. *Rivista Storia Econ.*, S.S., Int. Issue, 1987, *4*, pp. 21–53. **[G: Italy]**

Gabriel, Stuart A. Housing and Mortgage Markets: The Post-1982 Expansion. *Fed. Res. Bull.*, December 1987, *73*(12), pp. 893–903. **[G: U.S.]**

Goodman, John L., Jr. Housing and the Weather. *Amer. Real Estate Urban Econ. Assoc. J.*, Spring 1987, *15*(1), pp. 638–63. **[G: U.S.]**

Schulze, William D., et al. Benefits and Costs of Earthquake Resistant Buildings. *Southern Econ. J.*, April 1987, *53*(4), pp. 934–51. **[G: U.S.]**

Sklarz, Michael A.; Miller, Norman G. and Gersch, Will. Forecasting Using Long-Order Autoregressive Processes: An Example Using Housing Starts. *Amer. Real Estate Urban Econ. Assoc. J.*, Winter 1987, *15*(4), pp. 374–88. **[G: U.S.]**

Vitelli, Guillermo. Technological Change, Market Structure and Employment in the Argentine Construction Industry. *Katz, J. M., ed.*, 1987, pp. 318–51. **[G: Argentina]**

635 Industry Studies: Services and Related Industries

6350 General

Aanestad, James M. Measurement Problems of the Service Sector. *Bus. Econ.*, April 1987, *22*(2), pp. 32–37. **[G: U.S.]**

Akehurst, Gary. The Economics of Services: An Introduction. *Akehurst, G. and Gadrey, J., eds.*, 1987, pp. 1–11.

d'Alcantara, Gonzales. Reflections about Some Basic Concepts for Services Economics. *Akehurst, G. and Gadrey, J., eds.*, 1987, pp. 72–81.

Ascher, Bernard and Whichard, Obie G. Improving Services Trade Data. *Giarini, O., ed.*, 1987, pp. 255–81. **[G: U.S.]**

Bailly, Antoine S.; Maillat, D. and Coffey, W. J. Service Activities and Regional Development: Some European Examples. *Environ. Planning A*, May 1987, *19*(5), pp. 653–68. **[G: W. Europe]**

Bender, Lloyd D. The Role of Services in Rural Development Policies. *Land Econ.*, February 1987, *63*(1), pp. 62–71. **[G: U.S.]**

Bhagwati, Jagdish N. International Trade in Services and Its Relevance for Economic Development. *Giarini, O., ed.*, 1987, pp. 3–34.

Bhagwati, Jagdish N. Trade in Services and the Multilateral Trade Negotiations. *World Bank Econ. Rev.*, September 1987, *1*(4), pp. 549–69. **[G: LDCs; OECD]**

Blades, Derek. Goods and Services in OECD Countries. *OECD Econ. Stud.*, Spring 1987, (8), pp. 159–84. **[G: OECD]**

Carter, Michael G. The Australian Economy in the Long Run: The Service Sector. *Maddock, R. and McLean, I. W., eds.*, 1987, pp. 195–226. **[G: Australia]**

Coffey, W. J. and Polèse, M. Trade and Location of Producer Services: A Canadian Perspective. *Environ. Planning A*, May 1987, *19*(5), pp. 597–611. **[G: Canada]**

Cooper, C. Joseph, Jr. White-Collar Salaries Vary Widely in the Service Industries. *Mon. Lab. Rev.*, November 1987, *110*(11), pp. 21–23. **[G: U.S.]**

Coppieters, Piet. Development of the Service Sector: A Critical Survey of Macro-economic Models. *Akehurst, G. and Gadrey, J., eds.,* 1987, pp. 89–98.

Delmas, Bernard and Gadrey, Jean. On the Substitution of Goods and Services. *Akehurst, G. and Gadrey, J., eds.,* 1987, pp. 12–25.

van Dinteren, J. H. J. The Role of Business-Service Offices in the Economy of Medium-sized Cities. *Environ. Planning A,* May 1987, *19*(5), pp. 669–86. **[G: Netherlands]**

Driver, Ciaran and Naisbitt, Barry. Cyclical Variations in Service Industries' Employment in the UK. *Appl. Econ.,* April 1987, *19*(4), pp. 541–54. **[G: U.K.]**

Enderwick, Peter. The Strategy and Structure of Service-Sector Multinationals: Implications for Potential Host Regions. *Reg. Stud.,* June 1987, *21*(3), pp. 215–23. **[G: OECD; Korea; Singapore]**

Filip, Zdenk. Paid Services in the Period of the 7th Five-Year Plan. *Czech. Econ. Digest.,* June 1987, (4), pp. 97–109. **[G: Czechoslovakia]**

Gadrey, Jean. The Double Dynamics of Services. *Akehurst, G. and Gadrey, J., eds.,* 1987, pp. 125–38. **[G: France; U.S.]**

Gershuny, Jonathan I. The Future of Service Employment. *Giarini, O., ed.,* 1987, pp. 105–24. **[G: U.K.]**

Gershuny, Jonathan I. Time Use and the Dynamics of the Service Sector. *Akehurst, G. and Gadrey, J., eds.,* 1987, pp. 56–71. **[G: U.K.]**

Giarini, Orio and Roulet, Jean Rémy. From the Rigidity of Supply to the Service Economy. *Akehurst, G. and Gadrey, J., eds.,* 1987, pp. 110–24.

Gillespie, A. E. and Green, A. E. The Changing Geography of Producer Services Employment in Britain. *Reg. Stud.,* October 1987, *21*(5), pp. 397–411. **[G: U.K.]**

Gilmer, Robert William; Keil, Stanley R. and Mack, Richard S. Export Potential of Services in the Tennessee Valley. *Reg. Sci. Persp.,* 1987, *17*(2), pp. 18–33. **[G: U.S.]**

Grönroos, Christian. Konkurrenskraft i servicesamhället. (Competitiveness in the Service Economy. With English summary.) *Ekon. Samfundets Tidskr.,* 1987, *40*(3), pp. 137–44.

Grubel, Herbert G. All Traded Services Are Embodied in Materials or People. *World Econ.,* September 1987, *10*(3), pp. 319–30. **[G: OECD]**

Guy, Ken. The UK Tertiary Service Sector. *Freeman, C. and Soete, L., eds.,* 1987, pp. 169–88. **[G: U.K.]**

Hindley, Brian. International Trade in Services and Its Relevance for Economic Development: Comment. *Giarini, O., ed.,* 1987, pp. 35–39.

Hong, Hai. The Service Sector in China's Economic Reform Policy. *Singapore Econ. Rev.,* October 1987, *32*(2), pp. 16–27. **[G: China]**

Jobber, David and Hooley, Graham. Pricing Behaviour in UK Manufacturing and Service Industries. *Managerial Dec. Econ.,* June 1987, *8*(2), pp. 167–71. **[G: U.K.]**

Kendrick, John W. Service Sector Productivity.

Bus. Econ., April 1987, *22*(2), pp. 18–24. **[G: U.S.]**

Kierzkowski, Henryk. International Trade in Services and Its Relevance for Economic Development: Comment. *Giarini, O., ed.,* 1987, pp. 39–43.

Kirk, Robert. Are Business Services Immune to the Business Cycle? *Growth Change,* Spring 1987, *18*(2), pp. 15–23. **[G: U.S.]**

Koekkoek, Ad and de Leeuw, Jeroen. The Applicability of GATT to International Trade in Services: General Considerations and the Interest of Developing Countries. *Aussenwirtschaft,* April 1987, *42*(1), pp. 65–84. **[G: LDCs]**

Landefeld, J. Steven. International Trade in Services: Its Composition, Importance and Links to Merchandise Trade. *Bus. Econ.,* April 1987, *22*(2), pp. 25–31. **[G: U.S.]**

Ley, David and Hutton, Thomas. Vancouver's Corporate Complex and Producer Services Sector: Linkages and Divergence within a Provincial Staple Economy. *Reg. Stud.,* October 1987, *21*(5), pp. 413–24. **[G: Canada]**

Marshall, J. N.; Damesick, P. and Wood, P. Understanding the Location and Role of Producer Services in the United Kingdom. *Environ. Planning A,* May 1987, *19*(5), pp. 575–95. **[G: U.K.]**

Montgomery, Edward and Wascher, William L. Race and Gender Wage Inequality in Services and Manufacturing. *Ind. Relat.,* Fall 1987, *26*(3), pp. 284–90. **[G: U.S.]**

Moore, Goeffrey H. The Service Industries and the Business Cycle. *Bus. Econ.,* April 1987, *22*(2), pp. 12–17. **[G: U.S.]**

Norman, Victor D. and Strandenes, Siri P. International Trade in Services and Its Relevance for Economic Development: Comment. *Giarini, O., ed.,* 1987, pp. 44–49.

O'Connor, K. The Location of Services Involved with International Trade. *Environ. Planning A,* May 1987, *19*(5), pp. 687–700. **[G: U.S.; Australia]**

Ott, Mack. The Growing Share of Services in the U.S. Economy— Degeneration or Evolution? *Fed. Res. Bank St. Louis Rev.,* June/July 1987, *69*(6), pp. 5–22. **[G: U.S.]**

Patton, Spiro G. and Reilly, Bernard J. The Role of Private Services in the American Economy. *Bus. Econ.,* April 1987, *22*(2), pp. 7–11. **[G: U.S.]**

Pousette, Tomas and Lindberg, Thomas. Services in Production and Production of Services in Swedish Manufacturing. *Eliasson, G., ed.,* 1987, pp. 51–62. **[G: Sweden]**

Quinn, James Brian. The Impacts of Technology in the Services Sector. *Guile, B. R. and Brooks, H., eds.,* 1987, pp. 119–59.

Richardson, John B. A Sub-sectoral Approach to Services' Trade Theory. *Giarini, O., ed.,* 1987, pp. 59–82.

Riddle, Dorothy I. The Role of the Service Sector in Economic Development: Similarities and Differences by Development Category. *Giarini, O., ed.,* 1987, pp. 83–104. **[G: LDCs]**

Rugman, Alan M. Multinationals and Trade in

Services: A Transaction Cost Approach. *Welt-wirtsch. Arch.*, 1987, *123*(4), pp. 651–67.
[G: Canada]

Ruyssen, Olivier. The New Deal in Services—A Challenge for Europe. *Akehurst, G. and Gad-rey, J., eds.*, 1987, pp. 99–109.
[G: W. Germany; France; Italy; U.K.; U.S.]

Sapir, André. International Trade in Services and Its Relevance for Economic Development: Comment. *Giarini, O., ed.*, 1987, pp. 49–54.

Stern, Robert M. and Hoekman, Bernard M. Issues and Data Needs for GATT Negotiations on Services. *World Econ.*, March 1987, *10*(1), pp. 39–60.

Tordoir, Pieter. Services Markets and the Economics of Social Interaction. *Akehurst, G. and Gadrey, J., eds.*, 1987, pp. 82–88.

Waelbroeck, Jean. International Trade in Services and Its Relevance for Economic Development: Comment. *Giarini, O., ed.*, 1987, pp. 54–57.

Whichard, Obie G. U.S. Sales of Services to Foreigners. *Surv. Curr. Bus.*, January 1987, *67*(1), pp. 22–41.
[G: U.S.]

6352 Electrical, Gas, Communication, and Information Services

Acton, Jan Paul and Besen, Stanley M. Assessing the Effects of Bulk Power Rate Regulation: Results from a Market Experiment. *Appl. Econ.*, May 1987, *19*(5), pp. 663–85.
[G: U.S.]

Alleman, James H. and Gupta, Veena. Estimation and Linking of Economic and Financial Costs in Telecommunications. *Crew, M. A., ed.*, 1987, pp. 171–96.
[G: U.S.]

Andrews, Laurel M. INDEPTH Level I Results: Econometric Forecast Models for 20 Industries. *Faruqui, A. and Broehl, J., eds.*, 1987, pp. 395–409.
[G: U.S.]

Barnes, Douglas F. and Samanta, B. B. Rural Electrification and the Village Economy in India. *Pachauri, R. K., ed.*, 1987, pp. 1155–66.
[G: India]

Barnes, S. Arlene. How Far Will Electricity Deregulation Go? A Skeptical View from Wall Street. *Stewart, M. B., ed.*, 1987, pp. 95–98.
[G: U.S.]

Barr, Trevor. International Information Issues: Whose Revolution? *Barr, T., ed.*, 1987, pp. 161–70.
[G: Global]

Batten, Dick and Schoonmaker, Sara. Deregulation, Technological Change, and Labor Relations in Telecommunications. *Cornfield, D. B., ed.*, 1987, pp. 311–27.
[G: U.S.]

Bauer, Douglas C. Adapting to Competition: An Analysis of Alternative Proposals to Restructure the Electric Power Industry. *Stewart, M. B., ed.*, 1987, pp. 67–71.
[G: U.S.]

Berg, Sanford V. Public Policy and Corporate Strategies in the AM Stereo Market. *Gabel, H. L., ed.*, 1987, pp. 149–70.
[G: U.S.]

Bernard, Jean-Thomas and Veall, Michael R. The Probability Distribution of Future Demand: The Case of Hydro Quebec. *J. Bus. Econ. Statist.*, July 1987, *5*(3), pp. 417–24.
[G: Canada]

Berry, S. Keith and Loudenslager, Samuel. The Impact of Nuclear Power Plant Construction Activity on the Electric Utility Industry's Cost of Capital. *Energy J.*, April 1987, *8*(2), pp. 63–75.
[G: U.S.]

Betancourt, Roger R. and Edwards, John H. Y. Economies of Scale and the Load Factor in Electricity Generation. *Rev. Econ. Statist.*, August 1987, *69*(3), pp. 551–56.
[G: U.S.]

Blanchard, Margaret A. The Associated Press Antitrust Suit: A Philosophical Clash over Ownership of First Amendment Rights. *Bus. Hist. Rev.*, Spring 1987, *61*(1), pp. 43–85.

Bohman, Mats and Andersson, Roland. Pricing Cogenerated Electricity and Heat in Local Communities. *J. Public Econ.*, August 1987, *33*(3), pp. 333–56.
[G: Sweden]

Brewer, H. L. and Rahmatian, Morteza. Risk Adjusted Performance Measures for Diversified Public Utility Firms: Implications for Applied Regulatory Economics. *J. Energy Devel.*, Spring 1987, *12*(2), pp. 185–201.
[G: U.S.]

Broehl, John H. INDEPTH Level II Results. *Faruqui, A. and Broehl, J., eds.*, 1987, pp. 417–30.
[G: U.S.]

Brown, Donald J. and Heal, Geoffrey M. Ramsey Pricing in Telecommunications Markets with Free Entry. *Crew, M. A., ed.*, 1987, pp. 77–83.
[G: U.S.]

Cannon, Colin M. Peak-Pricing and Self-Rationing of Gas. *Energy Econ.*, April 1987, *9*(2), pp. 99–103.
[G: U.K.]

Caves, Douglas W., et al. A Bayesian Approach to Combining Conditional Demand and Engineering Models of Electricity Usage. *Rev. Econ. Statist.*, August 1987, *69*(3), pp. 438–48.
[G: U.S.]

Chan, K. Hung and Ho, Kwok. Forecasting of Seasonal and Cyclical Financial Variables: The Wiener–Kolmogorov Method vs. the Box–Jenkins Method. *Lee, C. F., ed.*, 1987, pp. 103–18.
[G: U.S.]

Cicchetti, Charles J. Can Natural Gas Deregulation Be a Model for the Electric Power Industry? *Stewart, M. B., ed.*, 1987, pp. 81–87.
[G: U.S.]

Claggett, E. Tylor, Jr. Cooperative Distributors of Electrical Power: Operations and Scale Economies. *Quart. J. Bus. Econ.*, Summer 1987, *26*(3), pp. 3–21.
[G: U.S.]

Clifford, Thomas E. and Mead, Walter J. The External Costs of Electric Power from Coal-Fired and Nuclear Power Plants. *Pachauri, R. K., ed.*, 1987, pp. 315–29.
[G: U.S.]

Collins, Hugh. Conflict and Co-operation in the Establishment of Telecommunications and Data Communications Standards in Europe. *Gabel, H. L., ed.*, 1987, pp. 125–48.
[G: W. Europe]

Collins, William H. and Collins, Carol B. More on Advertising and Monopoly Power: The Case of the Electric Utility Industry. *Atlantic Econ. J.*, March 1987, *15*(1), pp. 71–76.
[G: U.S.]

Cozanet, Eric and Gensollen, Michel. Les modèles de prévision de la demande téléphonique en France. (The Econometric Modeling of

Telephone Access in France. With English summary.) *Revue Écon.*, March 1987, *38*(2), pp. 257–305. **[G: France]**

Curien, Nicolas. L'accès et l'usage téléphoniques: modélisation conjointe et tarification optimale. (Telephone Access and Usage: Joint Modelization and Optimal Pricing. With English summary.) *Revue Écon.*, March 1987, *38*(2), pp. 415–58.

Curien, Nicolas and Gensollen, Michel. De la théorie des structures industrielles à l'économie des réseaux de télécommunication. (From the Theory of Industry Structure to the Economics of Telecommunication Networks. With English summary.) *Revue Écon.*, March 1987, *38*(2), pp. 521–78.

Curien, Nicolas and Gensollen, Michel. Les théories de la demande de raccordement téléphonique. (The Theory of Demand for Telephone Access. With English summary.) *Revue Écon.*, March 1987, *38*(2), pp. 203–55.

Curran, P. J. and Hobson, T. A. Landsat MSS Imagery to Estimate Residential Heat-Load Density. *Environ. Planning A*, December 1987, *19*(12), pp. 1597–1610. **[G: U.K.]**

David, Paul A. Some New Standards for the Economics of Standardization in the Information Age. *Dasgupta, P. and Stoneman, P., eds.*, 1987, pp. 206–39.

Dennerlein, Rudolf K.-H. Residential Demand for Electrical Appliances and Electricity in the Federal Republic of Germany. *Energy J.*, January 1987, *8*(1), pp. 69–86. **[G: W. Germany]**

Desai, V. V. A Strategy for Rural Electrification. *Pachauri, R. K., ed.*, 1987, pp. 1143–53.
[G: Asia]

Eckel, Russel. Industrial Relations and High Technology: The Transformation of Telecommunications through Deregulation. *Child, J. and Bate, P., eds.*, 1987, pp. 173–89.
[G: U.S.]

Edwards, Averill. Library Resources in the Age of Information Technology. *Barr, T., ed.*, 1987, pp. 93–111. **[G: Australia]**

Einhorn, Michael A. Optimality and Sustainability: Regulation and Intermodal Competition in Telecommunications. *Rand J. Econ.*, Winter 1987, *18*(4), pp. 550–63.

Encaoua, David and Koebel, Philippe. Réglementation et déréglementation des télécommunications: Leçons anglo-saxonnes et perspectives d'évolution en France. (Regulation and Deregulation of the Telecommunication Industry: From the American and British Experiences to a Possible Evolution in France. With English summary.) *Revue Écon.*, March 1987, *38*(2), pp. 475–520. **[G: U.S.; U.K.]**

Encaoua, David and Moreaux, Michel. L'analyse théorique des problèmes de tarification et d'allocation des coûts dans les télécommunications. (The Theoretical Approach to Pricing and Cost Allocation for Telecommunication Services. With English summary.) *Revue Écon.*, March 1987, *38*(2), pp. 375–413.

Engelbrecht, Hans-Jürgen. An Information Sector Perspective of Employment Expansion in the Republic of Korea, 1975–80. *Devel. Econ.*, March 1987, *25*(1), pp. 19–29. **[G: S. Korea]**

Faruqui, Ahmad. Utility Planning and Industrial Structural Change. *Faruqui, A. and Broehl, J., eds.*, 1987, pp. 9–31. **[G: U.S.]**

Feibig, Denzil G. and Bewley, Ronald. International Telecommunications Forecasting: An Investigation of Alternative Functional Forms. *Appl. Econ.*, July 1987, *19*(7), pp. 949–60.
[G: Australia]

Flavin, Christopher. Electrifying the Third World. *Brown, L. R., et al.*, 1987, pp. 81–100. **[G: LDCs]**

Fliess, Barbara A. The World Administrative Radio Conference 1979 Negotiations: Toward More Equitable Sharing of the Global Radio Resources. *Zartman, I. W., ed. (II)*, 1987, pp. 171–212. **[G: Global]**

Freeman, Christopher. Information Technology and Change in Techno-economic Paradigm. *Freeman, C. and Soete, L., eds.*, 1987, pp. 49–69.

Garber, Steven. The Economics and Political Economy of Broadcasting: Challenges in Developing an Analytic Foundation: A Comment. *Public Finance Quart.*, July 1987, *15*(3), pp. 189–98.

Garnier, Jean-Pierre. Les nouvelles technologies de l'aliénation. (The New Technologies of Alienation. With English summary.) *Écon. Soc.*, August 1987, *21*(8), pp. 129–52.

Garretty, Jeanette A. Financing the Energy Industry: An Economist's Perspective. *J. Energy Devel.*, Spring 1987, *12*(2), pp. 215–23.
[G: U.S.]

Goldenberg, David H. Market Power and the Required Return to Electric Utilities. *Financial Rev.*, February 1987, *22*(1), pp. 175–93.
[G: U.S.]

Goldsworthy, Ashley W. Expanding Economic Horizons. *Barr, T., ed.*, 1987, pp. 38–53.
[G: Australia]

Grewlich, Klaus W. Telecommunications: A European Perspective. *Wilks, S. and Wright, M., eds.*, 1987, pp. 251–73. **[G: W. Europe]**

Griffin, James M. and Mayor, Thomas H. The Welfare Gain from Efficient Pricing of Local Telephone Services. *J. Law Econ.*, October 1987, *30*(2), pp. 465–87. **[G: U.S.]**

Guadagni, Alieto A. Decisiones energéticas para el futuro. (With English summary.) *Desarrollo Econ.*, Jan.-Mar. 1987, *26*(104), pp. 609–30.
[G: Argentina]

Guéhenno, Jean-Marie. France and the Electronic Media: The Economics of Freedom. *Ross, G.; Hoffmann, S. and Malzacher, S., eds.*, 1987, pp. 277–90. **[G: France]**

Gupta, Pradeep C.; Faruqui, Ahmad and Wharton, Joseph B. Structural Change in U.S. Manufacturing and Future Electricity Demand. *Pachauri, R. K., ed.*, 1987, pp. 75–90.
[G: U.S.]

van Helden, G. Jan; Leeflang, Peter S. H. and Sterken, Elmer. Estimation of the Demand for Electricity. *Appl. Econ.*, January 1987, *19*(1), pp. 69–82. **[G: Netherlands]**

Helm, Dieter. Nuclear Power and the Privatisation of Electricity Generation. *Fisc. Stud.*, November 1987, *8*(4), pp. 69–73. [G: U.K.]

Hendricks, Wallace E. Collective Bargaining in American Industry: Telecommunications. *Lipsky, D. B. and Donn, C. B., eds.*, 1987, pp. 103–33. [G: U.S.]

Henriet, Dominique and Volle, Michel. Services de télécommunication: intégration technique et différenciation économique. (Telecommunication Services: Technical Integration and Economic Differentiation. With English summary.) *Revue Écon.*, March 1987, *38*(2), pp. 459–74. [G: France]

Herod, J. Steven. Evolving Federal Policies on Electricity. *Stewart, M. B., ed.*, 1987, pp. 73–80. [G: U.S.]

Herrera, Alejandra. Telecomunicaciones: reestructuración productiva y empleo en la República Argentina. (With English summary.) *Desarrollo Econ.*, Apr.-June 1987, *27*(105), pp. 107–28. [G: Argentina]

Hilton, Margaret and Straw, Ronnie. Cooperative Training in Telecommunications: Case Studies. *Mon. Lab. Rev.*, May 1987, *110*(5), pp. 32–36. [G: U.S.]

Hirst, Eric. Energy and Economic Effects of Utility Financial Incentive Programs: The BPA Residential Weatherization Program. *Energy J.*, April 1987, *8*(2), pp. 97–110. [G: U.S.]

Howard-Merriam, Kathleen. The Impact of Rural Electrification on Egyptian Farm Women's Lives. *Pachauri, R. K., ed.*, 1987, pp. 271–90. [G: Egypt]

Howells, Jeremy. Developments in the Location, Technology and Industrial Organization of Computer Services: Some Trends and Research Issues. *Reg. Stud.*, December 1987, *21*(6), pp. 493–503. [G: U.K.]

Humphrey, Bruce G. Alternative Economic Growth Scenarios and Implications for Utility Strategic Planning. *Faruqui, A. and Broehl, J., eds.*, 1987, pp. 33–47. [G: U.S.]

Irwin, Manley R. Telecommunications and Government: The U.S. Experience. *Wilks, S. and Wright, M., eds.*, 1987, pp. 233–50. [G: U.S.]

Itteilag, Richard L. and Swanson, Christina A. A Life-Cycle Study of Commercial Cogeneration/Cooling: A State-of-the-Art of Gas Technology. *Crew, M. A., ed.*, 1987, pp. 155–70. [G: U.S.]

Jéquier, Nicolas and Dedijer, Stevan. Intelligence for Economic Development: General Conclusions. *Dedijer, S. and Jéquier, N., eds.*, 1987, pp. 225–41.

Jha, Raghbendra and Murty, M. N. Distributional Equity and Optimal Prices for the Public Sector: The Flexible Coefficients Case. *Energy Econ.*, January 1987, *9*(1), pp. 46–54. [G: India]

Jones, Barry. Towards a National Information Policy. *Barr, T., ed.*, 1987, pp. 1–9. [G: Australia]

Joskow, Paul L. Productivity Growth and Technical Change in the Generation of Electricity. *Energy J.*, January 1987, *8*(1), pp. 17–38. [G: U.S.]

Joskow, Paul L. and Schmalensee, Richard. The Performance of Coal-Burning Electric Generating Units in the United States: 1960–1980. *J. Appl. Econometrics*, April 1987, *2*(2), pp. 85–109. [G: U.S.]

Kahn, Alfred E. and Shew, William B. Current Issues in Telecommunications Regulation: Pricing. *Yale J. Regul.*, Spring 1987, *4*(2), pp. 191–256. [G: U.S.]

Keir, Marie. Brave New Wired World. *Barr, T., ed.*, 1987, pp. 66–80. [G: Australia]

Kellenyi, John. Which Utilities Gain or Lose from Deregulation? An Investor's Perspective. *Stewart, M. B., ed.*, 1987, pp. 89–93. [G: U.S.]

Keng, C. W. Kenneth. Forecasting Canadian Nuclear Power Station Construction Costs. *Pachauri, R. K., ed.*, 1987, pp. 353–91. [G: Canada]

Kirby, Michael G. New Technology and International Privacy Issues. *Barr, T., ed.*, 1987, pp. 146–58. [G: Global]

Kiss, Ferenc and Lefebvre, Bernard. Econometric Models of Telecommunications Firms. *Revue Écon.*, March 1987, *38*(2), pp. 307–73. [G: Canada]

Krommenacker, Raymond. Services and Space Technology: The Emergence of Space Generated, Highly Integrated Goods and Services (IGS). *Giarini, O., ed.*, 1987, pp. 173–92.

Laber, Gene. Effects of the Bell System Breakup on the Cost of Debt. *J. Econ. Bus.*, August 1987, *39*(3), pp. 185–97. [G: U.S.]

Lamberton, Don. The Australian Information Economy: A Sectoral Analysis. *Barr, T., ed.*, 1987, pp. 13–29. [G: Australia]

Langdale, John. Transborder Data Flows and National Sovereignty. *Barr, T., ed.*, 1987, pp. 137–45.

Lee, Carie E. and Sugiyama, Samuel O. IN-DEPTH Case Study: Pulp and Paper Process Model. *Faruqui, A. and Broehl, J., eds.*, 1987, pp. 435–49. [G: U.S.]

Levin, Nissan and Zahavi, Jacob. Electricity Equilibrium Models with Stochastic Demands. *Energy Econ.*, October 1987, *9*(4), pp. 227–40.

Liebowitz, S. J. Some Puzzling Behavior by Owners of Intellectual Products: An Analysis. *Contemp. Policy Issues*, July 1987, *5*(3), pp. 44–53. [G: U.S.]

Long, Stewart L. Technological Change and Institutional Response: The Creation of American Broadcasting. *J. Econ. Issues*, June 1987, *21*(2), pp. 743–49. [G: U.S.]

Malko, J. Robert and Edgar, George R. Energy Utility Diversification and Small Business: A Wisconsin Perspective. *J. Energy Devel.*, Autumn 1987, *13*(1), pp. 101–11. [G: U.S.]

Mandeville, Thomas. An International Comparison. *Barr, T., ed.*, 1987, pp. 30–37. [G: Global]

Marlay, Robert C. Industrial Electricity Consumption and Changing Economic Conditions.

Faruqui, A. and Broehl, J., eds., 1987, pp. 77–114. **[G: U.S.]**

Moiseev, N. N. and Pavlovskii, Iu. N. Informatics as a Branch of the Economy: Its Special Features, Rates of Growth, and Trends. *Matekon*, Spring 1987, 23(3), pp. 76–83.

Mongula, Benedict S. and Ng'andwe, Chiselebwe. Limits to Development in Southern Africa: Energy, Transport and Communications in SADCC Countries. *Amin, S.; Chitala, D. and Mandaza, I., eds.*, 1987, pp. 85–108. **[G: Southern Africa]**

Moss, Mitchell L. Telecommunications, World Cities, and Urban Policy. *Urban Stud.*, December 1987, 24(6), pp. 534–46. **[G: Global]**

Munroe, Tapan. Electric Utility Competition: Lessons from Others. *J. Energy Devel.*, Spring 1987, 12(2), pp. 203–14. **[G: U.S.]**

Mytelka, Lynn Krieger and Delapierre, Michel. The Alliance Strategies of European Firms in the Information Technology Industry and the Role of ESPRIT. *J. Common Market Stud.*, December 1987, 26(2), pp. 231–53. **[G: EEC]**

Neely, Walter P.; Brooking, Carl G. and Clary, Betsy Jane. Differences among Subsidiaries of Electric Utility Holding Companies: Recent Empirical Evidence. *Quart. Rev. Econ. Bus.*, Summer 1987, 27(2), pp. 50–62. **[G: U.S.]**

Nelson, Jon P.; Roberts, Mark J. and Tromp, Emsley P. An Analysis of Ramsey Pricing in Electric Utilities. *Crew, M. A., ed.*, 1987, pp. 85–109. **[G: U.S.]**

Nelson, Randy A. Alternative Technological Indices and Factor Demands in the Electric Power Industry. *Energy J.*, July 1987, 8(3), pp. 135–47. **[G: U.S.]**

Nelson, Randy A. and Primeaux, Walter J., Jr. An Examination of the Relationship between Technical Change and Regulatory Effectiveness. *Appl. Econ.*, June 1987, 19(6), pp. 773–88. **[G: U.S.]**

Nelson, Randy A. and Wohar, Mark E. Regulation, Scale and Productivity: Reply. *Int. Econ. Rev.*, June 1987, 28(2), pp. 535–39.

Neufeld, John L. Price Discrimination and the Adoption of the Electricity Demand Charge. *J. Econ. Hist.*, September 1987, 47(3), pp. 693–709. **[G: U.S.]**

Noam, Eli M. A Public and Private-Choice Model of Broadcasting. *Public Choice*, September 1987, 55(1–2), pp. 163–87.

November, Andràs. Telecommunications, Transfer of Technology and the Third World. *Hieronymi, O., ed.*, 1987, pp. 169–87. **[G: Global]**

Oren, Shmuel S.; Smith, Stephen A. and Wilson, Robert B. Multi-product Pricing for Electric Power. *Energy Econ.*, April 1987, 9(2), pp. 104–14.

Peters, Lon L. and Seiden, Kenneth P. The Behaviour of Publicly Owned Utilities in Wholesale Electricity Markets: The Case of the Pacific Northwest. *Energy Econ.*, October 1987, 9(4), pp. 241–50. **[G: U.S.]**

Piacentino, Diego. Funzioni e finanziamento di una rete radiotelevisiva pubblica. Le conclu-

sioni di un rapporto al governo britannico. (The Tasks and Financing of a Public Broadcasting Network: The Conclusions of a Report to the British Government. With English summary.) *Econ. Scelte Pubbliche/J. Public Finance Public Choice*, Sept.-Dec. 1987, 5(3), pp. 201–12. **[G: U.K.]**

Pouris, A. On the Economics of Nuclear and Coal-Fired Electricity Generation. *S. Afr. J. Econ.*, December 1987, 55(4), pp. 407–24. **[G: S. Africa]**

Pryke, Richard. Privatising Electricity Generation. *Fisc. Stud.*, August 1987, 8(3), pp. 75–88. **[G: U.K.]**

Rada, Juan F. Information Technology and Services. *Giarini, O., ed.*, 1987, pp. 127–71. **[G: U.S.; Canada; W. Europe]**

Reece, William S. Consumer Welfare Implications of Changes in Interstate Telephone Pricing. *J. Cons. Aff.*, Summer 1987, 21(1), pp. 141–54. **[G: U.S.]**

Reinecke, Ian. Wealth and Poverty in the Information Society. *Barr, T., ed.*, 1987, pp. 81–92. **[G: Australia]**

Render, Barry K. and Ruth, Stephen R. The Dilemma of Acquiring Micro-based Software in Developing Countries. *Ruth, S. R. and Mann, C. K., eds.*, 1987, pp. 143–48. **[G: LDCs]**

Rhys, J. M. W. Electricity Trends and Outlook. *Stevens, P., ed.*, 1987, pp. 155–65. **[G: Global]**

Rock, Steven M. and Hall, W. Clayton. Advertising and Monopoly Power: The Case of the Electric Utility Industry—Comment. *Atlantic Econ. J.*, March 1987, 15(1), pp. 67–70. **[G: U.S.]**

Ruderman, Henry; Levine, Mark D. and McMahon, James E. The Behavior of the Market for Energy Efficiency in Residential Appliances Including Heating and Cooling Equipment. *Energy J.*, January 1987, 8(1), pp. 101–24. **[G: U.S.]**

Sardinas, Joseph L., Jr. and Merrill, Susan. Regulation of International Data Communications and the Effect upon Multinational Corporations. *Most, Kenneth S., ed.*, 1987, pp. 305–15. **[G: OECD]**

Schware, Robert. Software Industry Development in the Third World: Policy Guidelines, Institutional Options, and Constraints. *World Devel.*, Oct./Nov. 1987, 15(10/11), pp. 1249–67. **[G: LDCs]**

Searl, Milton F. The Relationship of Electricity to Aggregate Economic Activity in Industrial Economies—Some Empirical Observations. *Pachauri, R. K., ed.*, 1987, pp. 601–20. **[G: MDCs]**

Sen Gupta, D. P. and de Gromard, Christian. Rural Electrification: Alternatives to Grid Extension. *Pachauri, R. K., ed.*, 1987, pp. 1123–42. **[G: India]**

Shapiro, David L. Public Power Policy in the Pacific Northwest: The Legal Fall Out. *Quart. Rev. Econ. Bus.*, Winter 1987, 27(4), pp. 18–37. **[G: U.S.]**

Sing, Merrile. Are Combination Gas and Electric

Utilities Multiproduct Natural Monopolies? *Rev. Econ. Statist.*, August 1987, *69*(3), pp. 392–98. [G: U.S.]

Soete, Luc. The Newly Emerging Information Technology Sector. *Freeman, C. and Soete, L., eds.*, 1987, pp. 189–220. [G: U.K.]

Stanovnik, Tine. Appliance-Specific Electricity Consumption in Slovene Households. *Energy Econ.*, January 1987, *9*(1), pp. 31–36. [G: Yugoslavia]

Train, Kenneth E.; McFadden, Daniel L. and Ben-Akiva, Moshe. The Demand for Local Telephone Service: A Fully Discrete Model of Residential Calling Patterns and Service Choices. *Rand J. Econ.*, Spring 1987, *18*(1), pp. 109–23. [G: U.S.]

Train, Kenneth E.; McFadden, Daniel L. and Goett, Andrew A. Consumer Attitudes and Voluntary Rate Schedules for Public Utilities. *Rev. Econ. Statist.*, August 1987, *69*(3), pp. 383–91. [G: U.S.]

Veall, Michael R. Bootstrapping the Probability Distribution of Peak Electricity Demand. *Int. Econ. Rev.*, February 1987, *28*(1), pp. 203–12. [G: Canada]

Veljanovski, Cento. British Cable and Satellite Television Policies. *Nat. Westminster Bank Quart. Rev.*, November 1987, pp. 28–40. [G: U.K.]

Vincent, Peter; Chell, Elizabeth and Haworth, Jean. Regional Distribution of Consultancy Firms Servicing the MAPCON Scheme: A Preliminary Analysis. *Reg. Stud.*, December 1987, *21*(6), pp. 505–18. [G: U.K.]

Visintini, Alfredo and Bastos, Carlos. Hacia un nuevo plan eléctrico. (With English summary.) *Desarrollo Econ.*, Oct.-Dec. 1987, *27*(107), pp. 377–95. [G: Argentina]

Volkonskii, Victor A. and Kuzovkin, A. I. Marginal Costs and Optimal Electricity Tariffs. *Matekon*, Fall 1987, *24*(1), pp. 43–69. [G: U.S.S.R.]

Ward, Geoffrey Layzell. Information Technology Policy in Western Australia. *Barr, T., ed.*, 1987, pp. 126–34. [G: Australia]

Werbos, Paul J. Industrial Structural Shift: Causes and Consequences for Electricity Demand. *Faruqui, A. and Broehl, J., eds.*, 1987, pp. 115–26. [G: U.S.]

Woolf, Arthur G. The Residential Adoption of Electricity in Early Twentieth-Century America. *Energy J.*, April 1987, *8*(2), pp. 19–30.

6353 Personal Services

Kim, Yoon Hyung and Smith, Kirk R. Electric Power in Economic Development: The Northeast Asian Experience. *Pachauri, R. K., ed.*, 1987, pp. 621–42. [G: Japan; Taiwan; S. Korea]

6354 Business and Legal Services

Daub, M. An Institutional Approach to the Rationality of Expectations. *Appl. Econ.*, October 1987, *19*(10), pp. 1303–16. [G: Canada]

Meyer, John R., et al. The U.S. Experience with Airline Deregulation: Changes in Distribution Channels and the Travel Agency Business. *Meyer, J. R. and Oster, C. V., Jr.*, 1987, pp. 125–36. [G: U.S.]

Schroeter, John R.; Smith, Scott L. and Cox, Steven R. Advertising and Competition in Routine Legal Service Markets: An Empirical Investigation. *J. Ind. Econ.*, September 1987, *36*(1), pp. 49–60. [G: U.S.]

Tschetter, John. Producer Services Industries: Why Are They Growing So Rapidly? *Mon. Lab. Rev.*, December 1987, *110*(12), pp. 31–40. [G: U.S.]

6356 Insurance

Aiuppa, Thomas A. and Trieschmann, James S. An Empirical Analysis of the Magnitude and Accuracy of Incurred-but-Not-Reported Reserves. *J. Risk Ins.*, March 1987, *54*(1), pp. 100–118. [G: U.S.]

Albrecht, Peter. Die Versicherungsproduktion—eine Kuppelproduktion bei Risiko. (With English summary.) *Z. Betriebswirtshaft*, March 1987, *57*(3), pp. 316–28.

Anderson, Dan R. Financing Asbestos Claims: Coverage Issues, Manville's Bankruptcy and the Claims Facility. *J. Risk Ins.*, September 1987, *54*(3), pp. 429–51. [G: U.S.]

Ang, James S. and Lai, Tsong-Yue. Insurance Premium Pricing and Ratemaking in Competitive Insurance and Capital Asset Markets. *J. Risk Ins.*, December 1987, *54*(4), pp. 767–79.

Auerbach, Alan J. and Kotlikoff, Laurence J. Life Insurance of the Elderly: Adequacy and Determinants. *Burtless, G., ed.*, 1987, pp. 229–67. [G: U.S.]

Baker, Antony M. Liberalization of Trade in Services—The World Insurance Industry. *Giarini, O., ed.*, 1987, pp. 193–211. [G: Global]

Baram, Michael S. Chemical Industry Hazards: Liability, Insurance, and the Role of Risk Analysis. *Kleindorfer, P. R. and Kunreuther, H. C., ed.*, 1987, pp. 415–42.

Baran, Barbara. The Technological Transformation of White-Collar Work: A Case Study of the Insurance Industry. *Hartmann, H. I., ed.*, 1987, pp. 25–62. [G: U.S.]

Barham, Vicky; Poddar, S. N. and Whalley, John. The Tax Treatment of Insurance under a Consumption Type, Destination Basis VAT. *Nat. Tax J.*, June 1987, *40*(2), pp. 171–82.

Blume, Lawrence and Rubinfeld, Daniel L. Compensation for Takings: An Economic Analysis. *Jaffe, A. J., ed.*, 1987, pp. 53–103. [G: U.S.]

Boyer, Marcel and Dionne, Georges. Description and Analysis of the Quebec Automobile Insurance Plan. *Can. Public Policy*, June 1987, *13*(2), pp. 181–95. [G: Canada]

Briys, Eric. Demande d'assurance, décisions de consommation et de portefeuille: Une analyse en temps continu. (Insurance Demand, Consumption and Portfolio Decisions. With English summary.) *L'Actual. Econ.*, June-September 1987, *63*(2–3), pp. 200–212.

Cameron, Norman E. Inflation and Nominal Policy Yields on Participating Life Insurance. *J. Risk Ins.*, September 1987, *54*(3), pp. 542–56. **[G: U.S.]**

Cherin, Antony C. and Hutchins, Robert C. The Rate of Return on Universal Life Insurance. *J. Risk Ins.*, December 1987, *54*(4), pp. 691–711. **[G: U.S.]**

Cho, Yoon-Je. How the United States Broke into Korea's Insurance Market. *World Econ.*, December 1987, *10*(4), pp. 483–96. **[G: U.S.; S. Korea]**

Chung, Yosup and Skipper, Harold D., Jr. The Effect of Interest Rates on Surrender Values of Universal Life Policies. *J. Risk Ins.*, June 1987, *54*(2), pp. 341–47. **[G: U.S.]**

Cohen, Adrian V. Chemical Industry Hazards: Liability, Insurance, and the Role of Risk Analysis: Discussion. *Kleindorfer, P. R. and Kunreuther, H. C., ed.*, 1987, pp. 442–47.

Cooper, Russell and Hayes, Beth. Multi-period Insurance Contracts. *Int. J. Ind. Organ.*, June 1987, *5*(2), pp. 211–31.

Cornfield, Daniel B., et al. Office Automation, Clerical Workers, and Labor Relations in the Insurance Industry. *Cornfield, D. B., ed.*, 1987, pp. 111–34. **[G: U.S.]**

Cowell, John G. The Role of Insurance in Risk Spreading and Risk Bearing: Discussion. *Kleindorfer, P. R. and Kunreuther, H. C., ed.*, 1987, pp. 486–92.

Cresta, Jean-Paul and Laffont, Jean-Jacques. Incentive Compatibility of Insurance Contracts and the Value of Information. *J. Risk Ins.*, September 1987, *54*(3), pp. 520–40.

Cummins, J. David. Revitalizing Risk and Insurance Education and Research. *J. Risk Ins.*, March 1987, *54*(1), pp. 9–20.

Cummins, J. David and Outreville, J. François. An International Analysis of Underwriting Cycles in Property-Liability Insurance. *J. Risk Ins.*, June 1987, *54*(2), pp. 246–62. **[G: OECD]**

Curatola, Anthony P.; Dickens, Thomas L. and Fields, Kent T. Increased Salary as an Alternative to Group Term Life Insurance. *J. Risk Ins.*, March 1987, *54*(1), pp. 120–30. **[G: U.S.]**

D'Arcy, Stephen P. and Lee, Keun Chang. Universal/Variable Life Insurance versus Similar Unbundled Investment Strategies. *J. Risk Ins.*, September 1987, *54*(3), pp. 452–77. **[G: U.S.]**

Dahlby, B. G. Monopoly versus Competition in an Insurance Market with Adverse Selection. *J. Risk Ins.*, June 1987, *54*(2), pp. 325–31.

Danzon, Patricia M. Compensation for Occupational Disease: Evaluating the Options. *J. Risk Ins.*, June 1987, *54*(2), pp. 265–82.

De Alessi, Louis. Why Corporations Insure. *Econ. Inquiry,* July 1987, *25*(3), pp. 429–38.

Dionne, Georges and Lasserre, Pierre. Adverse Selection and Finite-Horizon Insurance Contracts. *Europ. Econ. Rev.*, June 1987, *31*(4), pp. 843–61.

Drèze, Jacques H. Inferring Risk Tolerance from Deductibles in Insurance Contracts. *Drèze, J. H.*, 1987, *1981*, pp. 113–16.

Eggerstedt, Harald. Wettbewerb and Regulierung auf Versicherungsmärkten. (Competition and Regulation in Insurance Markets. With English summary.) *Z. Wirtschaft. Sozialwissen.*, 1987, *107*(3), pp. 397–416. **[G: W. Germany]**

Farny, Dieter. Über Regulierung und Deregulierung von Versicherungsmärkten. (With English summary.) *Z. Betriebswirtshaft*, October 1987, *57*(10), pp. 1001–23. **[G: W. Germany]**

Feldman, Roger. Health Insurance in the United States: Is Market Failure Avoidable? *J. Risk Ins.*, June 1987, *54*(2), pp. 289–313. **[G: U.S.]**

Fields, Joseph A. and Venezian, Emilio C. Investment Income—Is There a Company Effect? *J. Risk Ins.*, March 1987, *54*(1), pp. 173–78. **[G: U.S.]**

Finsinger, Jörg and von der Schulenburg, J.-Matthias Graf. Nachfragerverhalten bei unvollständigen Preisinformationen—eine Marktanalyse am Beispiel der Kraftfahrzeugversicherung. (Consumer Behavior under Incomplete Price Information—Survey Results from the Automobile Insurance Market. With English summary.) *Jahr. Nationalökon. Statist.*, May 1987, *203*(3), pp. 244–56. **[G: W. Germany]**

Fitzgerald, John. The Effects of Social Security on Life Insurance Demand by Married Couples. *J. Risk Ins.*, March 1987, *54*(1), pp. 86–99. **[G: U.S.]**

Forbes, Stephen W. Life Insurance Financial Management Issues. *J. Risk Ins.*, September 1987, *54*(3), pp. 603–13.

Garcia-Ferrer, Antonio and del Hoyo, Juan. Analysis of the Car Accident Indexes in Spain: A Multiple Time Series Approach. *J. Bus. Econ. Statist.*, January 1987, *5*(1), pp. 27–38. **[G: Spain]**

Garven, James R. On the Application of Finance Theory to the Insurance Firm. *J. Finan. Services Res.*, September 1987, *1*(1), pp. 57–76. **[G: U.S.]**

Gebotys, Robert J.; Auerbach, Alan J. and Petrucci, Adriani. The Insurance Branch Manager: Correlates of Success. *J. Risk Ins.*, March 1987, *54*(1), pp. 157–61. **[G: Canada]**

Gendron, Michel and Bernier, Gilles. Le marché de l'assurance responsabilité des municipalités québécoises est-il contestable? (On the Contestability of the Liability Insurance Market for Small Municipalities in the Province of Quebec. With English summary.) *L'Actual. Econ.*, March 1987, *63*(1), pp. 43–52. **[G: Canada]**

Gerke, Wolfgang and Kayser, Ottmar. Bewertung eines Rückversicherungskonzepts für die Deckung von Kreditausfallrisiken der Kreditinstitute. (With English summary.) *Z. Betriebswirtshaft*, July 1987, *57*(7), pp. 662–83.

Gollier, Christian. The Design of Optimal Insurance Contracts without the Nonnegativity Constraint on Claims. *J. Risk Ins.*, June 1987, 54(2), pp. 314–24.

Hagan, P. J. and Henry, G. G. Family-Based Social Welfare Schemes: The Case of Pharmaceuticals. *Butler, J. R. G. and Doessel, D. P., eds.*, 1987, pp. 165–93. [G: Australia]

Harrington, Scott E. A Note on the Impact of Auto Insurance Rate Regulation. *Rev. Econ. Statist.*, February 1987, 69(1), pp. 166–70. [G: U.S.]

Henriet, Dominique and Rochet, Jean-Charles. Some Reflections on Insurance Pricing. *Europ. Econ. Rev.*, June 1987, 31(4), pp. 863–85. [G: France]

Hofflander, Alfred E. and Nye, Blaine F. An Analysis of Premium Tax Revenue and Rate in California: The Case of Structured Settlement Annuities. *J. Risk Ins.*, December 1987, 54(4), pp. 760–66. [G: U.S.]

Holder, Harold D. and Blose, James O. Mental Health Treatment and the Reduction of Health Care Costs: A Four-Year Study of U.S. Federal Employees Enrollment with the Aetna Life Insurance Company. *McGuire, T. G. and Scheffler, R. M., eds.*, 1987, pp. 157–74. [G: U.S.]

Jennison, Kathleen and Ellis, Randall P. A Comparison of Psychiatric Service Utilization in a Single Group Practice under Multiple Insurance Systems. *McGuire, T. G. and Scheffler, R. M., eds.*, 1987, pp. 175–94. [G: U.S.]

Klaus, Alfred. Practical Aspects of Environmental Impairment Liability. *Kleindorfer, P. R. and Kunreuther, H. C., ed.*, 1987, pp. 448–53.

Kleindorfer, Paul R. and Kunreuther, Howard. From Seveso to Bhopal and Beyond. *Kleindorfer, P. R. and Kunreuther, H. C., ed.*, 1987, pp. 499–507.

Kokubugata, Kenzo. Life Insurance Sales Systems: Japanese Wine in a U.S. Bottle. *Finn, R. B., ed.*, 1987, pp. 109–18. [G: U.S.; Japan]

Leatham, David J.; McCarl, Bruce A. and Richardson, James W. Implications of Crop Insurance for Farmers and Lenders. *Southern J. Agr. Econ.*, December 1987, 19(2), pp. 113–20.

Marquis, M. Susan and Phelps, Charles E. Price Elasticity and Adverse Selection in the Demand for Supplementary Health Insurance. *Econ. Inquiry*, April 1987, 25(2), pp. 299–313. [G: U.S.]

Mayers, David and Smith, Clifford W., Jr. Corporate Insurance and the Underinvestment Problem. *J. Risk Ins.*, March 1987, 54(1), pp. 45–54.

Nye, Blaine F. and Hofflander, Alfred E. Economics of Oligopoly: Medical Malpractice Insurance as a Classic Illustration. *J. Risk Ins.*, September 1987, 54(3), pp. 502–19. [G: U.S.]

O'Driscoll, Gerald P., Jr. The Liability Crisis: A Law and Economics Analysis. *Fed. Res. Bank Dallas Econ. Rev.*, November 1987, (11), pp. 1–13. [G: U.S.]

Orlando, Enrico. Recent Developments Concerning the Legal Regime and Insurance Problems Related to the Transportation of Hazardous Materials by Sea. *Kleindorfer, P. R. and Kunreuther, H. C., ed.*, 1987, pp. 454–57.

Outreville, J. François and Zins, Michel. Job-Related Responses of Insurance Agents: More Evidence. *J. Risk Ins.*, December 1987, 54(4), pp. 800–803. [G: U.S.]

Pauly, Mark V. Monopsony Power in Health Insurance: Thinking Straight while Standing on Your Head: Editorial. *J. Health Econ.*, March 1987, 6(1), pp. 73–81. [G: U.S.]

Pfennigstorf, Werner. The Role of Insurance in Risk Spreading and Risk Bearing. *Kleindorfer, P. R. and Kunreuther, H. C., ed.*, 1987, pp. 465–85.

Podgursky, Michael and Swaim, Paul. Health Insurance Loss: The Case of the Displaced Worker. *Mon. Lab. Rev.*, April 1987, 110(4), pp. 30–33. [G: U.S.]

Priest, George L. The Current Insurance Crisis and Modern Tort Law. *Yale Law J.*, June 1987, 96(7), pp. 1521–90. [G: U.S.]

Ransom, Roger L. and Sutch, Richard. Tontine Insurance and the Armstrong Investigation: A Case of Stifled Innovation, 1868–1905. *J. Econ. Hist.*, June 1987, 47(2), pp. 379–90. [G: U.S.]

Rejda, George E.; Schmidt, James R. and McNamara, Michael J. The Impact of Social Security Tax Contributions on Group Life Insurance Premiums. *J. Risk Ins.*, December 1987, 54(4), pp. 712–20. [G: U.S.]

Rokes, Willis Park. Remedies Afforded Private Parties against Insurers for Unfair Claims Practices. *J. Risk Ins.*, September 1987, 54(3), pp. 478–501. [G: U.S.]

Rubin, Jeffrey. Discrimination and Insurance Coverage of the Mentally Ill. *McGuire, T. G. and Scheffler, R. M., eds.*, 1987, pp. 195–209. [G: U.S.]

Samson, Danny and Thomas, Howard. Linear Models as Decision Aids in Insurance Decision-making: The Case of Estimation of Automobile Insurance Claims. *Wright, G. and Ayton, P., eds.*, 1987, pp. 215–28.

Schlesinger, Harris. Monopoly Profits for Contingent-Claims Contracts When Preferences Are State Dependent. *J. Risk Ins.*, March 1987, 54(1), pp. 179–84.

Schlesinger, Harris. Optimal Insurance Coverage: Comment. *J. Risk Ins.*, December 1987, 54(4), pp. 810–12.

Schlitz, M. T. A New Method of Assessment of the Insurance Service Production. *Rev. Income Wealth*, December 1987, 33(4), pp. 431–37.

Skipper, Harold D., Jr. Protectionism in the Provision of International Insurance Services. *J. Risk Ins.*, March 1987, 54(1), pp. 56–85.

Smith, Michael L. and Buser, Stephen A. Risk Aversion, Insurance Costs and Optimal Property-Liability Coverages. *J. Risk Ins.*, June 1987, 54(2), pp. 226–45.

Spühler, Jürgen. The Role of Insurance in Risk Spreading and Risk Bearing: Discussion. *Klein-*

dorfer, P. R. and Kunreuther, H. C., ed., 1987, pp. 492–98.

Staten, Michael; Dunkelberg, William and Umbeck, John. Market Share and the Illusion of Power: Can Blue Cross Force Hospitals to Discount? *J. Health Econ.,* March 1987, *6*(1), pp. 43–58.   **[G: U.S.]**

Szopo, Peter. Skalenerträge in der österreichischen Lebensversicherungswirtschaft. Ein Beitrag zur Interpretation des Versicherungsaufsichtsgesetzes. (With English summary.) *Empirica,* 1987, *14*(1), pp. 77–97.
                                            [G: Austria]

Szpiro, George G. Optimal Insurance Coverage: Reply. *J. Risk Ins.,* December 1987, *54*(4), pp. 813–15.

Tapiero, Charles S. A Systems Approach to Insurance Company Management. *Carraro, C. and Sartore, D., eds.,* 1987, pp. 279–304.

Tapiero, Charles S. and Jacque, Laurent. The Expected Cost of Ruin and Insurance Premiums in Mutual Insurance. *J. Risk Ins.,* September 1987, *54*(3), pp. 594–602.

Tatchell, Michael. Family-Based Social Welfare Schemes: The Case of Pharmaceuticals: Discussion. *Butler, J. R. G. and Doessel, D. P., eds.,* 1987, pp. 194–96.   **[G: Australia]**

Trieschmann, James S. and Leverett, E. J., Jr. A Sensitivity Analysis of Selected Variables in Agency Valuation. *J. Risk Ins.,* June 1987, *54*(2), pp. 357–63.

Tryfos, Peter. The Equity of Classification Systems in Automobile Insurance. *J. Risk Ins.,* September 1987, *54*(3), pp. 569–81.

Venezian, Emilio C. and Fields, Joseph A. Informational Asymmetries in Retroactive Insurance. *J. Risk Ins.,* December 1987, *54*(4), pp. 780–89.

Warshawsky, Mark. Sensitivity to Market Incentives: The Case of Policy Loans. *Rev. Econ. Statist.,* May 1987, *69*(2), pp. 286–95.
                                            [G: U.S.]

Weiss, Mary A. Macroeconomic Insurance Output Estimation. *J. Risk Ins.,* September 1987, *54*(3), pp. 582–93.   **[G: U.S.]**

Yammarino, Francis J. and Dubinsky, Alan J. On Job Satisfaction: It's the Relationships That Count! [Job Related Responses of Insurance Agents: A Multi-firm Investigation]. *J. Risk Ins.,* December 1987, *54*(4), pp. 804–09.
                                            [G: U.S.]

Zuckerman, Stephen. Commercial Insurers and All-Payer Regulation: Evidence on Hospitals' Responses to Financial Need. *J. Health Econ.,* September 1987, *6*(3), pp. 165–87.   **[G: U.S.]**

6357 Real Estate

Ang, James S.; Chiang, Raymond and Corgel, John B. Illustrations of Financing and Tax Transfers in Owner Financed Real Estate Sales. *J. Econ. Bus.,* November 1987, *39*(4), pp. 363–72.   **[G: U.S.]**

Bauman, Gus and Ethier, William H. Development Exactions and Impact Fees: A Survey of American Practices. *Law Contemp. Probl.,*

Winter 1987, *50*(1), pp. 51–68.   **[G: U.S.]**

Bloom, Paul N. and Gerson, Walter. The Use of "Scrip" for Obtaining Consumer Redress in Antitrust Cases: Lessons from a Failed Application in the Real Estate Industry. *Bloom, P. N., ed.,* 1987, pp. 93–106.   **[G: U.S.]**

Corcoran, Patrick J. Explaining the Commercial Real Estate Market. *J. Portfol. Manage.,* Spring 1987, *13*(3), pp. 15–21.   **[G: U.S.]**

Corgel, John B. Occupational Boundary Setting and the Unauthorized Practice of Law by Real Estate Brokers. *Jaffe, A. J., ed.,* 1987, pp. 161–75.   **[G: U.S.]**

Ellson, Richard W. and McDermott, John H. Zoning Uncertainty and the Urban Land Development Firm. *J. Urban Econ.,* September 1987, *22*(2), pp. 209–22.

Frew, James R. Multiple Listing Service Participation in the Real Estate Brokerage Industry: Cooperation or Competition? *J. Urban Econ.,* May 1987, *21*(3), pp. 272–86.   **[G: U.S.]**

Frew, James R. and Jud, G. Donald. Who Pays the Real Estate Broker's Commission? *Jaffe, A. J., ed.,* 1987, pp. 177–87.   **[G: U.S.]**

Froland, Charles. What Determines Cap Rates on Real Estate? *J. Portfol. Manage.,* Summer 1987, *13*(4), pp. 77–82.   **[G: U.S.]**

Gau, George W. Efficient Real Estate Markets: Paradox or Paradigm? *Amer. Real Estate Urban Econ. Assoc. J.,* Summer 1987, *15*(2), pp. 1–12.

Gladstone, Robert. Tax Reform and the U.S. Economy: Effects on Real Estate: Comments. *Pechman, J. A., ed.,* 1987, pp. 94–97.
                                            [G: U.S.]

Grissom, Terry V.; Hartzell, David J. and Liu, Crocker H. An Approach to Industrial Real Estate Market Segmentation and Valuation Using the Arbitrage Pricing Paradigm. *Amer. Real Estate Urban Econ. Assoc. J.,* Fall 1987, *15*(3), pp. 199–219.   **[G: U.S.]**

Grissom, Terry V.; Kuhle, James L. and Walther, Carl H. Diversification Works in Real Estate, Too. *J. Portfol. Manage.,* Winter 1987, *13*(2), pp. 66–71.   **[G: U.S.]**

Guntermann, Karl L. and Smith, Richard L. Efficiency of the Market for Residential Real Estate. *Land Econ.,* February 1987, *63*(1), pp. 34–45.   **[G: U.S.]**

Harris, Curtis C., Jr. and McConnell, Virginia D. Surpluses in Disequilibrium Urban Land Markets. *Amer. Real Estate Urban Econ. Assoc. J.,* Winter 1987, *15*(4), pp. 359–73.
                                            [G: U.S.]

Hartzell, David J.; Hekman, John S. and Miles, Mike E. Real Estate Returns and Inflation. *Amer. Real Estate Urban Econ. Assoc. J.,* Spring 1987, *15*(1), pp. 617–37.   **[G: U.S.]**

Hendershott, Patric H.; Follain, James R. and Ling, David C. Tax Reform and the U.S. Economy: Effects on Real Estate. *Pechman, J. A., ed.,* 1987, pp. 71–94.   **[G: U.S.]**

Johnson, Larry J. and Wofford, Larry E. On Contracts as Options: Some Evidence from Condominium Developments: Comment. *Amer. Real Estate Urban Econ. Assoc. J.,*

Spring 1987, *15*(1), pp. 739–41.   [G: U.S.]

Klemperer, W. David and O'Neil, Cherie J. Effects of an Inflation-Adjusted Basis on Asset Values after Capital Gains Taxes. *Land Econ.*, November 1987, *63*(4), pp. 386–95.

Kling, John L. and McCue, Thomas E. Office Building Investment and the Macoreconomy: Empirical Evidence, 1973–1985. *Amer. Real Estate Urban Econ. Assoc. J.*, Fall 1987, *15*(3), pp. 234–55.   [G: U.S.]

MacLaran, Andrew; MacLaran, Morag and Malone, Patrick. Property Cycles in Dublin: The Anatomy of Boom and Slump in the Industrial and Office Property Sectors. *Econ. Soc. Rev.*, July 1987, *18*(4), pp. 237–56.   [G: Ireland]

Marcus, Richard D. Transferable Tax Liabilities on Real Estate. *Land Econ.*, February 1987, *63*(1), pp. 102–06.   [G: U.S.]

Rayburn, William; Devaney, Michael and Evans, Richard. A Test of Weak-Form Efficiency in Residential Real Estate Returns. *Amer. Real Estate Urban Econ. Assoc. J.*, Fall 1987, *15*(3), pp. 220–33.   [G: U.S.]

Schaeffer, P. V. and Hopkins, L. D. Behavior of Land Developers: Planning and the Economics of Information. *Environ. Planning A*, September 1987, *19*(9), pp. 1221–32.

Schroeter, John R. Competition and Value-of-Service Pricing in the Residential Real Estate Brokerage Market. *Quart. Rev. Econ. Bus.*, Spring 1987, *27*(1), pp. 29–40.   [G: U.S.]

Shilling, James D.; Sirmans, C. F. and Benjamin, John D. On Option-Pricing Models in Real Estate: A Critique: Reply [Contracts as Options: Some Evidence from Condominium Developments]. *Amer. Real Estate Urban Econ. Assoc. J.*, Spring 1987, *15*(1), pp. 742–52.   [G: U.S.]

Shilling, James D.; Sirmans, C. F. and Corgel, John B. Price Adjustment Process for Rental Office Space. *J. Urban Econ.*, July 1987, *22*(1), pp. 90–100.   [G: U.S.]

Sirmans, G. Stacy and Sirmans, C. F. The Historical Perspective of Real Estate Returns. *J. Portfol. Manage.*, Spring 1987, *13*(3), pp. 22–31.

Wachter, Susan M. Residential Real Estate Brokerage: Rate Uniformity and Moral Hazard. *Jaffe, A. J., ed.*, 1987, pp. 189–210.   [G: U.S.]

Webb, James R. and Rubens, Jack H. How Much in Real Estate? A Surprising Answer. *J. Portfol. Manage.*, Spring 1987, *13*(3), pp. 10–14.   [G: U.S.]

Wheaton, William C. The Cyclical Behavior of the National Office Market. *Amer. Real Estate Urban Econ. Assoc. J.*, Winter 1987, *15*(4), pp. 281–99.   [G: U.S.]

Yinger, John. Tax Reform and the U.S. Economy: Effects on Real Estate: Comments. *Pechman, J. A., ed.*, 1987, pp. 97–102.   [G: U.S.]

6358 Entertainment, Recreation, Tourism

Aickin, R. Malcolm. Insuring Environmental Liabilities. *Kleindorfer, P. R. and Kunreuther, H. C., ed.*, 1987, pp. 458–63.

Asch, Peter and Quandt, Richard E. Efficiency and Profitability in Exotic Bets. *Economica*, August 1987, *54*(215), pp. 289–98.

Avery, Albert E. and Colonna, Carl M. The Market for Collectible Antique and Reproduction Firearms: An Economic and Financial Analysis. *J. Cult. Econ.*, December 1987, *11*(2), pp. 49–64.   [G: U.S.]

Baim, Dean. Private Ownership Incentives in Professional Sports Facilities. *Kent, C. A., ed.*, 1987, pp. 109–21.   [G: U.S.]

Barwise, T. Patrick and Ehrenberg, Andrew S. C. The Liking and Viewing of Regular TV Series. *J. Cons. Res.*, June 1987, *14*(1), pp. 63–70.   [G: U.S.]

Bird, Ron; McCrae, Michael and Beggs, John J. Are Gamblers Really Risk Takers? *Australian Econ. Pap.*, December 1987, *26*(49), pp. 237–53.   [G: Australia]

Borland, Jeff. The Demand for Australian Rules Football. *Econ. Rec.*, September 1987, *63*(182), pp. 220–30.   [G: Australia]

Cairns, John A. Evaluating Changes in League Structure: The Reorganization of the Scottish Football League. *Appl. Econ.*, February 1987, *19*(2), pp. 259–75.   [G: U.K.]

Cymrot, Donald J. and Dunlevy, James A. Are Free Agents Perspicacious Peregrinators? *Rev. Econ. Statist.*, February 1987, *69*(1), pp. 50–58.   [G: U.S.]

Dworkin, James B. Collective Bargaining in American Industry: Professional Sports. *Lipsky, D. B. and Donn, C. B., eds.*, 1987, pp. 187–223.   [G: U.S.]

Feketekuty, Geza. About Trade in Tourism Services. *Giarini, O., ed.*, 1987, pp. 245–51.   [G: Global]

Frey, Bruno S. and Pommerehne, Werner W. International Trade in Art: Attitudes and Behaviour. *Rivista Int. Sci. Econ. Com.*, June 1987, *34*(6), pp. 465–86.   [G: U.S.; Europe]

Fujii, Edwin T.; Khaled, Mohammed and Mak, James. An Empirical Comparison of Systems of Demand Equations for Tourist Expenditures in Resort Destinations. *Philippine Rev. Econ. Bus.*, Mar.-June 1987, *24*(1–2), pp. 79–102.   [G: U.S.]

Gibbons, Jean D. and Fish, Mary. World Tourism Forecasts and the Outlook for the U.S. Virgin Islands. *Soc. Econ. Stud.*, December 1987, *36*(4), pp. 193–207.   [G: U.S.]

Haitovsky, Y.; Salomon, Ilan and Silman, L. A. The Economic Impact of Charter Flights on Tourism to Israel: An Econometric Approach. *J. Transp. Econ. Policy*, May 1987, *21*(2), pp. 111–34.   [G: Israel]

Hendon, William S. Economic Incentives: Theater and Cultural Programming. *J. Cult. Econ.*, June 1987, *11*(1), pp. 76–93.   [G: U.S.]

van der Hoeven, W. H. M. and Thurik, A. R. Pricing in the Hotel and Catering Sector. *De Economist*, 1987, *135*(2), pp. 201–18.   [G: Netherlands]

Hull, Brooks B. The Effect of Foreign and Local Visitors on Granting Park Concessions. *New*

Zealand Econ. Pap., 1987, *21*, pp. 83–96.
[G: New Zealand]
Janssens, P. and Késenne, Stefan. Belgian Soccer Attendances. *Tijdschrift Econ. Manage.*, 1987, *32*(3), pp. 305–15. [G: Belgium]
Jones, J. C. H. and Walsh, W. D. The World Hockey Association and Player Exploitation in the National Hockey League. *Quart. Rev. Econ. Bus.*, Summer 1987, *27*(2), pp. 87–101.
[G: U.S.]
Kerr, Geoff and Cullen, Ross. Non-market Valuation in New Zealand: Comment. *New Zealand Econ. Pap.*, 1987, *21*, pp. 125–29.
[G: New Zealand]
Késenne, Stefan and Butzen, Paul. Subsidizing Sports Facilities: The Shadow Price-Elasticities of Sports. *Appl. Econ.*, January 1987, *19*(1), pp. 101–10. [G: Belgium]
Lavoie, Marc; Grenier, Gilles and Coulombe, Serge. Discrimination and Performance Differentials in the National Hockey League. *Can. Public Policy*, December 1987, *13*(4), pp. 407–22. [G: U.S.; Canada]
Marcinová, Elena and Spička, Jan. Selected Economic Aspects of the Development of Culture. *Czech. Econ. Digest.*, December 1987, (8), pp. 54–66. [G: Czechoslovakia]
McCain, Roger A. Scalping: Optimal Contingent Pricing of Performances in the Arts and Sports. *J. Cult. Econ.*, June 1987, *11*(1), pp. 1–21.
McConkey, C. William and Warren, William E. Psychographic and Demographic Profiles of State Lottery Ticket Purchasers. *J. Cons. Aff.*, Winter 1987, *21*(2), pp. 314–27. [G: U.S.]
McCormick, Robert E. and Tensley, Maurice. Athletics versus Academics? Evidence from SAT Scores. *J. Polit. Econ.*, October 1987, *95*(5), pp. 1103–16. [G: U.S.]
McKenzie, Richard B. and Sullivan, E. Thomas. Does the NCAA Exploit College Athletes? An Economics and Legal Reinterpretation. *Antitrust Bull.*, Summer 1987, *32*(2), pp. 373–99.
[G: U.S.]
Moulin, Claude. Éducation, tourisme, Tiers Monde. *Can. J. Devel. Stud.*, 1987, *8*(2), pp. 251–60. [G: LDCs]
Pescatrice, Donn R. A Parimutuel Principle. *Eastern Econ. J.*, Apr.-June 1987, *13*(2), pp. 143–48. [G: U.S.]
Richter, Christine. Tourism Services. *Giarini, O., ed.*, 1987, pp. 213–44. [G: Global]
Schuster, J. Mark Davidson. Making Compromises to Make Comparisons in Cross-National Arts Policy Research. *J. Cult. Econ.*, December 1987, *11*(2), pp. 1–36. [G: OECD]
Simmons, Susan A. and Sharp, Robert. State Lotteries' Effects on Thoroughbred Horse Racing. *J. Policy Anal. Manage.*, Spring 1987, *6*(3), pp. 446–48. [G: U.S.]
van Soest, Arthur and Kooreman, Peter. A Micro-econometric Analysis of Vacation Behaviour. *J. Appl. Econometrics*, July 1987, *2*(3), pp. 215–26. [G: Netherlands]
Špaček, Petr. Exchange Rates and the Effectiveness of Foreign Tourist Traffic in CMEA Member-Countries. *Soviet E. Europ. Foreign*

Trade, Winter 1987-1988, *23*(4), pp. 67–93.
[G: CMEA]
Srivastava, D. K. and Mittal, Ashok. On the Economics of Entertainment: Optimal Length of Movie Runs. *Indian Econ. J.*, July-Sept. 1987, *35*(1), pp. 66–82. [G: India]
Truett, Dale B. and Truett, Lila J. The Response of Tourism to International Economic Conditions: Greece, Mexico, and Spain. *J. Devel. Areas*, January 1987, *21*(2), pp. 177–89.
[G: Greece; Mexico; Spain]
Wagner, G. Oliver, V. College and Professional Football Scores: A Multiple Regression Analysis. *Amer. Econ.*, Spring 1987, *31*(1), pp. 33–37. [G: U.S.]

636 Nonprofit Industries: Theory and Studies

6360 Nonprofit Industries: Theory and Studies

Annis, Sheldon. Can Small-scale Development Be a Large-scale Policy? The Case of Latin America. *World Devel.*, Supp. Autumn 1987, *15*, pp. 129–134. [G: Latin America]
Antrobus, Peggy. Funding for NGOs: Issues and Options. *World Devel.*, Supp. Autumn 1987, *15*, pp. 95–102. [G: Barbados]
Barron, Fraser. A Mission Renewed: The Survival of the National Endowment for the Arts, 1981–1983. *J. Cult. Econ.*, June 1987, *11*(1), pp. 23–75. [G: U.S.]
Brodhead, Tim. NGOs: In One Year, Out the Other? *World Devel.*, Supp. Autumn 1987, *15*, pp. 1–6. [G: Global]
Brown, Eleanor. Tax Incentives and Charitable Giving: Evidence from New Survey Data. *Public Finance Quart.*, October 1987, *15*(4), pp. 386–96. [G: U.S.]
Carson, Emmett D. The Charitable Activities of Black Americans: A Portrait of Self-help? *Rev. Black Polit. Econ.*, Winter 1987, *15*(3), pp. 100–111. [G: U.S.]
Cooper, Mary Anderson. The Role of Religious and Nonprofit Organizations in Combating Homelessness. *Bingham, R. D.; Green, R. E. and White, S. B., eds.*, 1987, pp. 130–49.
[G: U.S.]
Drabek, Anne Gordon. Development Alternatives: The Challenge for NGOs—An Overview of the Issues. *World Devel.*, Supp. Autumn 1987, *15*, pp. ix–xv. [G: Global]
Elliott, Charles. Some Aspects of Relations between the North and South in the NGO Sector. *World Devel.*, Supp. Autumn 1987, *15*, pp. 57–68. [G: Global]
Feigenbaum, Susan. Competition and Performance in the Nonprofit Sector: The Case of U.S. Medical Research Charities. *J. Ind. Econ.*, March 1987, *35*(3), pp. 241–53.
[G: U.S.]
Fernandez, Aloysius P. NGOs in South Asia: People's Participation and Partnership. *World Devel.*, Supp. Autumn 1987, *15*, pp. 39–49.
[G: India; Bangladesh; Pakistan; Sri Lanka]
Fox, Thomas H. NGOs from the United States. *World Devel.*, Supp. Autumn 1987, *15*, pp. 11–19. [G: U.S.]

Frantz, Telmo Rudi. The Role of NGOs in the Strengthening of Civil Society. *World Devel.*, Supp. Autumn 1987, *15*, pp. 121–127.
[G: Brazil]

Garilao, Ernesto D. Indigenous NGOs as Strategic Institutions: Managing the Relationship with Government and Resource Agencies. *World Devel.*, Supp. Autumn 1987, *15*, pp. 113–120.
[G: Asia]

Green, Cynthia B. The Use and Usefulness of Governmental Financial Reports: The Perspective of Citizen–Taxpayer Organizations. *Chan, J. L., ed., Pt. B*, 1987, pp. 189–213.
[G: U.S.]

Gui, Benedetto. Productive Private Nonprofit Organizations: A Conceptual Framework. *Ann. Pub. Co-op. Econ.*, Oct.-Dec. 1987, *58*(4), pp. 415–34.

Hansmann, Henry. The Effect of Tax Exemption and Other Factors on the Market Share of Nonprofit versus For-Profit Firms. *Nat. Tax J.*, March 1987, *40*(1), pp. 71–82.
[G: U.S.]

van der Heijden, Hendrik. The Reconciliation of NGO Autonomy, Program Integrity and Operational Effectiveness with Accountability to Donors. *World Devel.*, Supp. Autumn 1987, *15*, pp. 103–12.
[G: OECD]

Hellinger, Doug. NGOs and the Large Aid Donors: Changing the Terms of Engagement. *World Devel.*, Supp. Autumn 1987, *15*, pp. 135–143.
[G: Global]

Hendon, William S. Economic Incentives: Theater and Cultural Programming. *J. Cult. Econ.*, June 1987, *11*(1), pp. 76–93.
[G: U.S.]

Herbert-Copley, Brent. Canadian NGOs: Past Trends, Future Challenges. *World Devel.*, Supp. Autumn 1987, *15*, pp. 21–28.
[G: Canada]

Heskin, Allan David. The Homeless in Contemporary Society: Los Angeles: Innovative Local Approaches. *Bingham, R. D.; Green, R. E. and White, S. B., eds.*, 1987, pp. 170–83.
[G: U.S.]

Jenkins, Stephen and Austen-Smith, David. Interdependent Decision-Making in Non-profit Industries: A Simultaneous Equation Analysis of English Provincial Theatre. *Int. J. Ind. Organ.*, June 1987, *5*(2), pp. 149–74. [G: U.K.]

Johnston, Denis and Rudney, Gabriel. Characteristics of Workers in Nonprofit Organizations. *Mon. Lab. Rev.*, July 1987, *110*(7), pp. 28–33.
[G: U.S.]

Kajese, Kingston. An Agenda of Future Tasks for International and Indigenous NGOs: Views from the South. *World Devel.*, Supp. Autumn 1987, *15*, pp. 79–85. [G: Global]

Korten, David C. Third Generation NGO Strategies: A Key to People-Centered Development. *World Devel.*, Supp. Autumn 1987, *15*, pp. 145–59. [G: LDCs]

Landim, Leilah. Non-governmental Organizations in Latin America. *World Devel.*, Supp. Autumn 1987, *15*, pp. 29–38.
[G: Latin America]

Lemaresquier, Thierry. Prospects for Development Education: Some Strategic Issues Facing

European NGOs. *World Devel.*, Supp. Autumn 1987, *15*, pp. 189–200.
[G: W. Europe]

van Meerhaeghe, Marcel, A. G. The Church and the Economy. *Econ. Scelte Pubbliche/J. Public Finance Public Choice*, May-Aug. 1987, *5*(2), pp. 97–104.

Menchik, Paul L. and Weisbrod, Burton A. Volunteer Labor Supply. *J. Public Econ.*, March 1987, *32*(2), pp. 159–83. [G: U.S.]

Minear, Larry. The Other Missions of NGOs: Education and Advocacy. *World Devel.*, Supp. Autumn 1987, *15*, pp. 201–11. [G: U.S.]

Nogueira, Roberto Martinez. Life Cycle and Learning in Grassroots Development Organizations. *World Devel.*, Supp. Autumn 1987, *15*, pp. 169–77.

Nyoni, Sithembiso. Indigenous NGOs: Liberation, Self-reliance, and Development. *World Devel.*, Supp. Autumn 1987, *15*, pp. 51–56.
[G: Zimbabwe]

Padron, Mario. Non-governmental Development Organizations: From Development Aid to Development Cooperation. *World Devel.*, Supp. Autumn 1987, *15*, pp. 69–77.
[G: Latin America]

Pauly, Mark V. Nonprofit Firms in Medical Markets. *Amer. Econ. Rev.*, May 1987, *77*(2), pp. 257–62. [G: U.S.]

Romero, Carol Jusenius. Retirement and Older Americans' Participation in Volunteer Activities. *Sandell, S. H., ed.*, 1987, pp. 218–27.
[G: U.S.]

Rose-Ackerman, Susan. Ideals versus Dollars: Donors, Charity Managers, and Government Grants. *J. Polit. Econ.*, August 1987, *95*(4), pp. 810–23.

Rubinstein, A. J. Issues of Price and Subsidy in the Arts in the U.S.S.R. *J. Cult. Econ.*, December 1987, *11*(2), pp. 65–83.
[G: U.S.S.R.]

Russe, Catherine M. and Anderson, Gerard F. Hospital Reorganization: Examining the Effects on Medical Education. *Scheffler, R. M. and Rossiter, L. F., eds.*, 1987, pp. 141–56.
[G: U.S.]

Schuster, J. Mark Davidson. Making Compromises to Make Comparisons in Cross-National Arts Policy Research. *J. Cult. Econ.*, December 1987, *11*(2), pp. 1–36. [G: OECD]

Sen, Biswajit. NGO Self-evaluation: Issues of Concern. *World Devel.*, Supp. Autumn 1987, *15*, pp. 161–67.

Smith, Brian H. An Agenda of Future Tasks for International and Indigenous NGOs: Views from the North. *World Devel.*, Supp. Autumn 1987, *15*, pp. 87–93. [G: Global]

Steinberg, Richard S. Voluntary Donations and Public Expenditures in a Federalist System. *Amer. Econ. Rev.*, March 1987, *77*(1), pp. 24–36.

Stremlau, Carolyn. NGO Coordinating Bodies in Africa, Asia, and Latin America. *World Devel.*, Supp. Autumn 1987, *15*, pp. 213–25.
[G: LDCs]

Twose, Nigel. European NGOs: Growth or Partnership? *World Devel.*, Supp. Autumn 1987, 15, pp. 7–10. **[G: Europe]**

Wallace, Wanda A. Agency Theory and Governmental and Nonprofit Sector Research. *Chan, J. L., ed., Pt. B*, 1987, pp. 51–70.

West, Edwin G. Nonprofit versus Profit Firms in the Performing Arts. *J. Cult. Econ.*, December 1987, 11(2), pp. 37–47.

Yudelman, Sally W. The Integration of Women into Development Projects: Observations on the NGO Experience in General and in Latin America in Particular. *World Devel.*, Supp. Autumn 1987, 15, pp. 179–87.

[G: Latin America]

640 ECONOMIC CAPACITY

641 Economic Capacity

6410 Economic Capacity

Belova, S. Accelerating the Modernization of Productive Fixed Capital. *Prob. Econ.*, April 1987, 29(12), pp. 54–72. **[G: U.S.S.R.]**

Bischoff, Charles W. and Kokkelenberg, Edward C. Capacity Utilization and Depreciation-in-Use. *Appl. Econ.*, August 1987, 19(8), pp. 995–1007. **[G: U.S.]**

Conrad, Klaus and Schröder, Michael. Die Effekte einer Rohölpreissenkung auf Produktionsauslastung und Wohlfahrt. Eine Anwendung der temporären Gleichgewichtsanalyse. (Effects of an Oil Price Decrease on Welfare and Capacity Utilization: An Applied Temporary Equilibrium Analysis. With English summary.) *Jahr. Nationalökon. Statist.*, July 1987, 203(4), pp. 390–407. **[G: W. Germany]**

Jansen, Jaap C. and Kuyvenhoven, Arie. Capital Utilisation in Indonesian Medium and Large Scale Manufacturing. *Bull. Indonesian Econ. Stud.*, April 1987, 23(1), pp. 70–103. **[G: Indonesia]**

Lipinski, Czeslaw. Changes of Output Capacity Utilization Caused by Structural Changes of Material Inputs. *Tchijov, I. and Tomaszewicz, L., eds.*, 1987, pp. 99–106. **[G: Poland]**

Reynolds, Stanley S. Capacity Investment, Preemption and Commitment in an Infinite Horizon Model. *Int. Econ. Rev.*, February 1987, 28(1), pp. 69–88.

Val'tukh, Konstantin K. and Lavrovskii, B. L. The Nation's Production Apparatus: Utilization and Reconstruction. *Prob. Econ.*, April 1987, 29(12), pp. 35–53. **[G: U.S.S.R.]**

700 Agriculture; Natural Resources

710 AGRICULTURE

7100 Agriculture

Albagli, Claude. Structures sociales, besoins et pouvoir: le verrou agricole. (Social Structures, Needs and Power: The Agricultural Deadlock. With English summary.) *Écon. Soc.*, July 1987, 21(7), pp. 149–68. **[G: Africa]**

Aukes, Robert. Double Counting Agricultural Income. *Can. J. Agr. Econ.*, July 1987, 35(2), pp. 463–79. **[G: Canada]**

Avramovic, Dragoslav. Problems of Low Income Countries: Role of Mutual Economic Cooperation. *Agrawal, G. R., et al. (I)*, 1987, pp. 7–14. **[G: LDCs]**

Bartoli, Pierre. L'agriculture dans le développement économique et les politiques communautaires en Méditerranée. (Agriculture in the Economic Development and E.E.C. Policies in the Mediterranean. With English summary.) *Écon. Soc.*, July 1987, 21(7), pp. 111–48.

[G: EEC]

Bateman, Lanny. Agricultural Economics: A Fork in the Road or a Crooked Trail? *Southern J. Agr. Econ.*, July 1987, 19(1), pp. 1–5.

[G: U.S.]

Beattie, Bruce R. and Watts, Myles J. The Proper Preeminent Role of Parent Disciplines and Learned Societies in Setting the Agenda at Land Grant Universities. *Western J. Agr. Econ.*, December 1987, 12(2), pp. 95–103.

[G: U.S.]

Bilsborrow, Richard E. Population Pressures and Agricultural Development in Developing Countries: A Conceptual Framework and Recent Evidence. *World Devel.*, February 1987, 15(2), pp. 183–203. **[G: LDCs]**

Burmeister, Larry L. The South Korean Green Revolution: Induced or Directed Innovation? *Econ. Develop. Cult. Change*, July 1987, 35(4), pp. 767–90. **[G: S. Korea]**

Caraveli-Ioannidis, Helen. Farm Income Disparity in Greece and Membership of the EC. *Europ. Rev. Agr. Econ.*, 1987, 14(2), pp. 239–49. **[G: Greece; EEC]**

Chan, M. W. Luke and Mountain, Dean C. Measuring Contributing Factors to Interregional Agricultural Labor Productivity Differentials: A Joint Profit Formulation. *J. Reg. Sci.*, May 1987, 27(2), pp. 269–81. **[G: Canada]**

Chendroyaperumal, Chendrayan. X-Inefficiency in Agriculture: A Note. *Indian Econ. J.*, Apr.-June 1987, 34(4), pp. 122–23.

Clark, Gregory. Productivity Growth without Technical Change in European Agriculture before 1850. *J. Econ. Hist.*, June 1987, 47(2), pp. 419–32. **[G: Europe; U.S.]**

Dahlgran, Roger A. Agricultural Economists in the Information Age: Awareness, Usage, and Attitudes toward Electronic Bibliographic Databases. *Amer. J. Agr. Econ.*, February 1987, 69(1), pp. 166–73.

Debertin, David L. and Bradford, Garnett L. Agricultural Economics Research and the Experiment Station System. *Southern J. Agr. Econ.*, December 1987, 19(2), pp. 195–201.

Dhakal, Dharmendra; Grabowski, Richard and Belbase, Krishna. The Effect of Education in Nepal's Traditional Agriculture. *Econ. Educ. Rev.*, 1987, 6(1), pp. 27–34. **[G: Nepal]**

Dobbs, Thomas L. Toward More Effective Involvement of Agricultural Economists in Multidisciplinary Research and Extension Programs. *Western J. Agr. Econ.*, July 1987, *12*(1), pp. 8–16. **[G: U.S.]**

Evenson, Robert E.; Evenson, Donald D. and Putnam, Jonathan D. Private Sector Agricultural Invention in Developing Countries. *Ruttan, V. W. and Pray, C. E., eds.*, 1987, pp. 469–511.

Ferreira dos Santos, Robério. Processo de modernização da agricultura brasileira: Um teste da hipótese da inovação induzida. (With English summary.) *Pesquisa Planejamento Econ.*, December 1987, *17*(3), pp. 679–710. **[G: Brazil]**

Fishel, Walter L. The Economics of Agricultural Biotechnology: Discussion. *Amer. J. Agr. Econ.*, May 1987, *69*(2), pp. 438–39.

Fontaine, Jean-Marc. Les projets de libéralisation des agricultures africaines. Un point de vue critique appuyé sur les cas kenyan et tanzanien. (On Economic Liberalism and African Agriculture. With English summary.) *Écon. Soc.*, July 1987, *21*(7), pp. 185–208. **[G: Kenya; Tanzania]**

Ghatak, Subrata. Agriculture and Economic Development. *Gemmell, N., ed.*, 1987, pp. 341–72.

Giles, A. K. No Fixed Address—Presidential Address. *J. Agr. Econ.*, September 1987, *38*(3), pp. 371–91. **[G: U.K.]**

Gios, Geremia and Miglierina, Claudio. Cost Structure and Integration in the Agro-food Sectors: A Comparative Study in EC Countries. *Europ. Rev. Agr. Econ.*, 1987, *14*(2), pp. 179–94. **[G: EEC]**

Goodell, Grace. The Peasant Betrayed: Agriculture and Land Reform in the Third World: The Philippines. *Powelson, J. P. and Stock, R.*, 1987, pp. 11–26. **[G: Philippines]**

Gowdy, John M.; Miller, Jack L. and Kherbachi, Hamid. Energy Use in U.S. Agriculture: Early Adjustment to the 1973–74 Price Shock. *Southern J. Agr. Econ.*, December 1987, *19*(2), pp. 33–41. **[G: U.S.]**

Griffin, Keith and Hay, Roger. Problems of Agricultural Development in Socialist Ethiopia. *Griffin, K.*, 1987, *1985*, pp. 203–34. **[G: Ethiopia]**

Habakkuk, H. J. The Agrarian History of England and Wales: Regional Farming Systems and Agrarian Change, 1640–1750. *Econ. Hist. Rev., 2nd Ser.*, May 1987, *40*(2), pp. 281–96. **[G: U.K.]**

Hady, Thomas F. Is There a Farm Crisis? *J. Econ. Educ.*, Fall 1987, *18*(4), pp. 409–20. **[G: U.S.]**

Harnos, Zsolt. Agricultural Models. *Braat, L. C. and van Lierop, W. F. J., eds.*, 1987, pp. 100–116.

Henry, E. W. The Impact of the Agriculture and Dependent Food Processing Sectors on the Irish Economy during 1982. *Irish J. Agr. Econ. Rural Soc.*, 1987, *12*, pp. 1–17. **[G: Ireland]**

Hite, James C. Agricultural Economics Undergraduate and Graduate Curricula: Are We Competitive? Discussion. *Southern J. Agr. Econ.*, July 1987, *19*(1), pp. 55–57. **[G: U.S.]**

Hobkhoo, Ahmad. Les industries agro-alimentaires ivoiriennes: évolution et prospective. (The Ivorian Food and Aricultural Industries: Evolution and Prospective. With English summary.) *Écon. Soc.*, July 1987, *21*(7), pp. 209–25. **[G: Ivory Coast]**

Ireson, W. Randall. Landholding, Agricultural Modernization, and Income Concentration: A Mexican Example. *Econ. Develop. Cult. Change*, January 1987, *35*(2), pp. 351–66. **[G: Mexico]**

Islam, Nurul. Tensions between Economics and Politics in Dealing with Agriculture: Comment. *Meier, G. M., ed.*, 1987, pp. 39–48.

Islam, Nurul. The World Food Situation and Prospects: Introduction. *Borner, S. and Taylor, A., eds.*, 1987, pp. 51–63.

Joshi, P. C. Agrarian Constraints Reconsidered. *Joshi, P. C.*, 1987, pp. 287–325. **[G: India]**

Joshi, P. C. Agrarian Debate since Independence: Between Landlord and Peasant Perspectives. *Joshi, P. C.*, 1987, *1978*, pp. 49–67.

Joshi, P. C. Agrarian Retrogression under British Rule: The Colonial Legacy. *Joshi, P. C.*, 1987, pp. 3–15. **[G: India]**

Joshi, P. C. Colonial Modernisation and Agricultural Stagnation: The Case of Bengal under Colonial Impact. *Joshi, P. C.*, 1987, pp. 16–27. **[G: India]**

Joshi, P. C. Conflicting Pulls of Productivity and Employment: Contemporary Choices in the Light of Historical Experience. *Joshi, P. C.*, 1987, pp. 135–58. **[G: India; Japan]**

Joshi, P. C. From Semi-feudalism to Structural Dualism: Towards an Institutional Approach to Agricultural Development. *Joshi, P. C.*, 1987, *1986*, pp. 252–86. **[G: India]**

Joshi, P. C. Perspectives of Agrarian Reconstruction: India in the Asian Context. *Joshi, P. C.*, 1987, *1986*, pp. 68–103. **[G: India]**

Joshi, P. C. Pre-independence Thinking on Agrarian Policy: Landlords versus Peasants as Agents of Agricultural Development. *Joshi, P. C.*, 1987, *1967*, pp. 28–45. **[G: India]**

Klein, K. K. Information, Communication, and Frustration: Publication of Interdisciplinary Research in Agriculture. *Can. J. Agr. Econ.*, May 1987, *34*, pp. 151–62.

Koopmans, Tom Th. An Application of an Agroeconomic Model to Environmental Issues in the EC: A Case Study. *Europ. Rev. Agr. Econ.*, 1987, *14*(2), pp. 147–59. **[G: EEC]**

Koppel, Bruce. Does Integrated Area Development Work? Insight from the Bicol River Basin Development Program. *World Devel.*, February 1987, *15*(2), pp. 205–20. **[G: Philippines]**

Larsson, Gunnar; Medin, Knut and Wilson, Bernt. A Farm Bookkeeping Survey as Part of Official Agricultural Statistics: The Case of Sweden. *Statist. J.*, May 1987, *4*(3), pp. 245–57. **[G: Sweden]**

Lee, George E. Teamwork on Interdisciplinary Programs. *Can. J. Agr. Econ.*, May 1987, *34*, pp. 144–46.

Lindner, Bob. Toward a Framework for Evaluating Agricultural Economics Research. *Austra-*

lian J. Agr. Econ., August 1987, *31*(2), pp. 95–111.

Longworth, John W. Biotechnology: Scientific Potential and Socio-economic Implications for Agriculture. *Rev. Marketing Agr. Econ.*, December 1987, *55*(3), pp. 187–99.

Lundahl, Mats. 'Efficient but Poor'—Schultz' Theory of Traditional Agriculture. *Scand. Econ. Hist. Rev.*, 1987, *35*(1), pp. 108–29.

Margulies, Ronnie and Yildizoğlu, Ergin. Agrarian Change: 1923–70. *Schick, I. C. and Tonak, E. A., eds.*, 1987, pp. 269–92. **[G: Turkey]**

Martin, James E. Land-Grant Organization to Meet the Future. *Southern J. Agr. Econ.*, July 1987, *19*(1), pp. 31–34. **[G: U.S.]**

Önal, Hayri. Effects of Income Distribution in Non-agriculture on Agricultural Prices and Income: The Turkish Case. *Europ. Rev. Agr. Econ.*, 1987, *14*(4), pp. 413–25. **[G: Turkey]**

Pearson, Scott R. and Monke, Eric A. Constraints on the Development of Portuguese Agriculture. *Pearson, S. R., et al.*, 1987, pp. 17–28. **[G: Portugal]**

Reinhardt, Nola. Modernizing Peasant Agriculture: Lessons from El Palmar, Colombia. *World Devel.*, February 1987, *15*(2), pp. 221–47. **[G: Colombia]**

Robinson, Warren C. and Schutjer, Wayne A. Reply to Djavad Salehi-Isfahani's Clarifications [Agricultural Development and Demographic Change: A Generalization of the Boserup Model]. *Econ. Develop. Cult. Change*, July 1987, *35*(4), pp. 883. **[G: LDCs]**

Salehi-Isfahani, Djavad. On the Generalization of the Boserup Model: Some Clarifications. *Econ. Develop. Cult. Change*, July 1987, *35*(4), pp. 875–81.

Schultz, Theodore W. Tensions between Economics and Politics in Dealing with Agriculture. *Meier, G. M., ed.*, 1987, pp. 17–38.

Sen, Amartya K. Goods and People. *Urquidi, V. L., ed.*, 1987, pp. 153–77.

Spircu, Liliana, et al. An Interactive System of Programmes for the Analysis and Processing of Statistical Data in Agriculture. *Econ. Computat. Cybern. Stud. Res.*, 1987, *22*(1), pp. 29–39.

Stallmann, Judith I. and Schmid, A. Allan. Property Rights in Plants: Implications for Biotechnology Research and Extension. *Amer. J. Agr. Econ.*, May 1987, *69*(2), pp. 432–37. **[G: U.S.]**

Theen, Rolf H. W. Hierarchical Reform: The Case of Agriculture. *Comp. Econ. Stud.*, Winter 1987, *29*(4), pp. 86–102. **[G: U.S.S.R.]**

Thomas, Barbara P. Development through Harambee: Who Wins and Who Loses? Rural Self-help Projects in Kenya. *World Devel.*, April 1987, *15*(4), pp. 463–81. **[G: Kenya]**

Thomas, John K. and Goodwin, H. L., Jr. Employment Compensation among Farm Workers in the Lower Rio Grande Valley. *Soc. Sci. Quart.*, September 1987, *68*(3), pp. 621–30. **[G: U.S.]**

Tiffin, Scott; Adjebeng-Asem, Selina and Afolabi, Oladele. Technological Innovation and Techni-

cal Entrepreneurship for the Development of a Nigerian Agricultural Machinery Industry. *World Devel.*, March 1987, *15*(3), pp. 387–98. **[G: Nigeria]**

Trigo, Eduardo J. Agricultural Research Organization in the Developing World: Diversity and Evolution. *Ruttan, V. W. and Pray, C. E., eds.*, 1987, pp. 251–81. **[G: LDCs]**

Valdés, Alberto. Food Security: A Stabilisation Problem for Developing Countries. *Borner, S. and Taylor, A., eds.*, 1987, pp. 105–24. **[G: LDCs]**

Vratusa, Anton. Role of South–South Cooperation: A Comment. *Agrawal, G. R., et al. (I)*, 1987, pp. 15–17. **[G: LDCs]**

Wade, Robert. The Management of Common Property Resources: Finding a Cooperative Solution. *World Bank Res. Observer*, July 1987, *2*(2), pp. 219–34. **[G: India]**

Whatley, Warren C. Southern Agrarian Labor Contracts as Impediments to Cotton Mechanization. *J. Econ. Hist.*, March 1987, *47*(1), pp. 45–70. **[G: U.S.]**

Williams, F. W. Agricultural Economics Undergraduate and Graduate Curricula: Are We Competitive? *Southern J. Agr. Econ.*, July 1987, *19*(1), pp. 49–54. **[G: U.S.]**

Yamaguchi, Mitoshi and Kennedy, George. A Comparison of Conventional and General Equilibrium Growth Accounting: The Case of Japanese Agriculture, 1880–1970. *Kobe Univ. Econ.*, 1987, *33*, pp. 49–69. **[G: Japan]**

711 Agricultural Supply and Demand Analysis

7110 Agricultural Supply and Demand Analysis

Aboyade, Ojetunji. Growth Strategy and the Agricultural Sector. *Mellor, J. W.; Delgado, C. L. and Blackie, M. J., eds.*, 1987, pp. 241–52. **[G: Africa]**

Adamowicz, M. and Kos, C. Some Aspects of Specialization and Integration of Agriculture and Forestry in Solving the Food Problem in Poland. *Merlo, M., et al., eds.*, 1987, pp. 553–61. **[G: Poland]**

Adams, Philip D. Agricultural Supply Response in ORANI. *Rev. Marketing Agr. Econ.*, December 1987, *55*(3), pp. 213–29. **[G: Australia]**

Ahmad, Bashir and Chaudhry, Ali Muhammad. Profitability of Pakistan's Agriculture. *Pakistan Devel. Rev.*, Winter 1987, *26*(4), pp. 457–67. **[G: Pakistan]**

Ahmad, Ehtisham; Stern, Nicholas H. and Leung, H.-M. The Demand for Wheat under Non-linear Pricing in Pakistan. *J. Econometrics*, Sept./Oct. 1987, *36*(1/2), pp. 55–65. **[G: Pakistan]**

Ahmad, Khan Masood. Uncertainty, Resource Use Efficiency, and Tenurial Arrangements in Indian Agriculture. *Indian J. Quant. Econ.*, 1987, *3*(1), pp. 52–66. **[G: India]**

Ahmad, Manzur. Intra-sectoral and Intersectoral Parity Issues in Pricing of Agricultural Crops: A Preliminary Analysis: Comments. *Pakistan*

Devel. Rev., Winter 1987, *26*(4), pp. 415–17. **[G: Pakistan]**

Ahmadi-Esfahani, Fredoun Z. and Carter, Colin A. A Dynamic Analysis of U.S. Export Wheat Pricing and Market Shares. *Australian J. Agr. Econ.*, December 1987, *31*(3), pp. 191–203. **[G: U.S.]**

Akiyama, T. and Trivedi, Pravin K. Vintage Production Approach to Perennial Crop Supply: An Application to Tea in Major Producing Countries. *J. Econometrics*, Sept./Oct. 1987, *36*(1/2), pp. 133–61. **[G: India; Sri Lanka; Kenya]**

de Albuquerque, Marcos Cintra C. Uma análise translog sobre mudança tecnológica e efeitos de escala: um caso de modernização ineficiente. (With English summary.) *Pesquisa Planejamento Econ.*, April 1987, *17*(1), pp. 191–220. **[G: Brazil]**

Alexeev, Michael. Microeconomic Modeling of Parallel Markets: The Case of Agricultural Goods in the USSR. *J. Compar. Econ.*, December 1987, *11*(4), pp. 543–57. **[G: U.S.S.R.]**

Ali, Ifzal. Rice in Indonesia: Price Policy and Comparative Advantage. *Bull. Indonesian Econ. Stud.*, December 1987, *23*(3), pp. 80–99. **[G: Indonesia]**

Alston, Julian M. and Chalfant, James A. Weak Separability and a Test for the Specification of Income in Demand Models with an Application to the Demand for Meat in Australia. *Australian J. Agr. Econ.*, April 1987, *31*(1), pp. 1–15. **[G: Australia]**

Alves, Eliseu. Mobilizing Political Support for the Brazilian Agricultural Research System. *Ruttan, V. W. and Pray, C. E., eds.*, 1987, pp. 363–76. **[G: Brazil]**

Anderson, Kym and Tyers, Rodney. Economic Growth and Market Liberalization in China: Implications for Agricultural Trade. *Devel. Econ.*, June 1987, *25*(2), pp. 124–51. **[G: China]**

Andrade, Armando and Blanc, Nicole. SAM's Cost and Impact on Production. *Austin, J. E. and Esteva, G., eds.*, 1987, pp. 215–48. **[G: Mexico]**

Andrikopoulos, Andreas A.; Brox, James A. and Georgakopoulos, Theodore A. Short-run Expenditure and Price Elasticities for Agricultural Commodities: The Case of Greece, 1951–1983. *Europ. Rev. Agr. Econ.*, 1987, *14*(3), pp. 335–46. **[G: Greece]**

Aradhyula, Satheesh V. Rational Expectations and Policy Modeling: The Case of Wheat in India. *J. Policy Modeling*, Winter 1987, *9*(4), pp. 667–70. **[G: India]**

Arif, Syed Muhammad. Past Production and Future Potential of Fruit Production in Baluchistan. *Pakistan Econ. Soc. Rev.*, Winter 1987, *25*(2), pp. 89–107. **[G: Pakistan]**

Atsain, Achi. Food Policy and the Choice of Trade Regime: Commentary. *Mellor, J. W.; Delgado, C. L. and Blackie, M. J., eds.*, 1987, pp. 274–75. **[G: Africa]**

Attwood, Donald W. Irrigation and Imperialism: The Causes and Consequences of a Shift from Subsistence to Cash Cropping. *J. Devel. Stud.*, April 1987, *23*(3), pp. 341–66. **[G: India]**

Austin, James E. and Fox, Jonathan. State-Owned Enterprises: Food Policy Implementers. *Austin, J. E. and Esteva, G., eds.*, 1987, pp. 61–91. **[G: Mexico]**

Avillez, Francisco and Langworthy, Mark. Intensive Agriculture in the Vale do Tejo. *Pearson, S. R., et al.*, 1987, pp. 107–23. **[G: Portugal]**

Azzam, Azzeddine and Yanagida, John F. A Cautionary Note on Polynomial Distributed Lag Formulations of Supply Response. *Western J. Agr. Econ.*, July 1987, *12*(1), pp. 60–64. **[G: U.S.]**

Babula, Ronald A. An Armington Model of U.S. Cotton Exports. *J. Agr. Econ. Res.*, Fall 1987, *39*(4), pp. 12–22. **[G: U.S.]**

Baffoe, J. K.; Stonehouse, D. Peter and Kay, B. D. A Methodology for Farm-Level Economic Analysis of Soil Erosion Effects under Alternative Crop Rotational Systems in Ontario. *Can. J. Agr. Econ.*, March 1987, *35*(1), pp. 55–73. **[G: Canada]**

Balintfy, Joseph L. and Taj, Shahram. A Utility Maximization-Based Decision Support System for USDA Family Food Plans. *Schultz, R. L., ed.*, 1987, pp. 1–22. **[G: U.S.]**

Baltagi, Badi H. and Goel, Rajeev K. Quasi-experimental Price Elasticities of Cigarette Demand and the Bootlegging Effect. *Amer. J. Agr. Econ.*, November 1987, *69*(4), pp. 750–54. **[G: U.S.]**

Baltas, Nicholas C. Supply Response for Greek Cereals. *Europ. Rev. Agr. Econ.*, 1987, *14*(2), pp. 195–220. **[G: Greece]**

Barkin, David. SAM and Seeds. *Austin, J. E. and Esteva, G., eds.*, 1987, pp. 111–32. **[G: Mexico]**

Bathaiah, D. and Reddy, K. Satyanrayana. Factor-Product in Growing Sugarcane—A Case Study of Cuddapah District of Andhra Pradesh. *Margin*, Jan.-Mar. 1987, *19*(2), pp. 74–82. **[G: India]**

Bayri, T. Y. and Furtan, William Hartley. An Economic Analysis of Technological Change in the Spring Wheat Region of Turkey. *METU*, 1987, *14*(4), pp. 291–313. **[G: Turkey]**

Belchamber, G. D. The Impact of Wages and Industrial Policy on the Performance of the Agricultural Sector from an ACTU Perspective. *Rev. Marketing Agr. Econ.*, April 1987, *55*(1), pp. 88–97. **[G: Australia]**

Bentley, Jeffery W. Portuguese Agriculture in Transition: Technical Change in a Northwest Parish. *Pearson, S. R., et al.*, 1987, pp. 167–86. **[G: Portugal]**

Bernegger, Urs. Experience with the Milk Quota System in Switzerland. *Kettunen, L., ed.*, 1987, pp. 19–28. **[G: Switzerland]**

Berthélemy, Jean-Claude and Gagey, F. The Agricultural Supply Price Elasticity in Africa: A Note on Peasants' Rationality in a Non-Walrasian Context. *Europ. Econ. Rev.*, December 1987, *31*(8), pp. 1493–1507. **[G: Cameroon]**

Berthélemy, Jean-Claude and Morrisson, C.

Manufactured Goods Supply and Cash Crops in Sub-Saharan Africa. *World Devel.*, Oct./Nov. 1987, *15*(10/11), pp. 1353–67. **[G: Africa]**

Bewley, Ronald. The Demand for Milk in Australia: Estimation of Price and Income Effects from the 1984 Household Expenditure Survey. *Australian J. Agr. Econ.*, December 1987, *31*(3), pp. 204–18. **[G: Australia]**

Bewley, Ronald; Young, Trevor and Colman, David. A System Approach to Modelling Supply Equations in Agriculture. *J. Agr. Econ.*, May 1987, *38*(2), pp. 151–66. **[G: U.K.]**

Bhati, U. N. Supply and Demand Responses for Poultry Meat in Australia. *Australian J. Agr. Econ.*, December 1987, *31*(3), pp. 256–65. **[G: Australia]**

Bhujangarao, C. Determinants of Foodgrain Prices in India: An Empirical Study, 1961–83. *Indian Econ. Rev.*, Jan.-June 1987, *22*(1), pp. 51–77. **[G: India]**

Binswanger, Hans P. and Pingali, Prabhu L. The Evolution of Farming Systems and Agricultural Technology in Sub-Saharan Africa. *Ruttan, V. W. and Pray, C. E., eds.*, 1987, pp. 283–318. **[G: Sub-Saharan]**

Binswanger, Hans P., et al. On the Determinants of Cross-country Aggregate Agricultural Supply. *J. Econometrics*, Sept./Oct. 1987, *36*(1/2), pp. 111–31. **[G: LDCs]**

Blanc, Michel. Family and Employment in Agriculture: Recent Changes in France. *J. Agr. Econ.*, May 1987, *38*(2), pp. 289–301. **[G: France]**

Blank, Steven C. Evaluating International Price Relationships Using Causal Models. *Europ. Rev. Agr. Econ.*, 1987, *14*(3), pp. 305–23. **[G: OECD]**

Bobst, Barry W. and Davis, Joe T. Beef Cow Numbers, Crop Acreage, and Crop Policy. *Amer. J. Agr. Econ.*, November 1987, *69*(4), pp. 771–76. **[G: U.S.]**

Bond, Marian E. An Econometric Study of Primary Commodity Exports from Developing Country Regions to the World. *Int. Monet. Fund Staff Pap.*, June 1987, *34*(2), pp. 191–227. **[G: Global]**

Boussard, J.-M. Le progrès technique et l'équilibre agriculture–industrie dans les modèles calculables d'équilibre général. (The Consequences of Technical Progress for Agriculture/Industry Balance as Described by Computable General Equilibrium Models. With English summary.) *Écon. Soc.*, July 1987, *21*(7), pp. 7–36.

Boyle, G. E. Measurement of the Total Factor Productivity of Irish Agriculture: 1960–1982. *Irish J. Agr. Econ. Rural Soc.*, 1987, *12*, pp. 29–49. **[G: Ireland]**

Brandt, Jon A., et al. Live Hog and Pork Imports: Past and Projected Consequences for the U.S. Pork Sector. *Southern J. Agr. Econ.*, December 1987, *19*(2), pp. 133–44. **[G: U.S.]**

Brandt, Loren. Farm Household Behavior, Factor Markets, and the Distributive Consequences of Commercialization in Early Twentieth-Century China. *J. Econ. Hist.*, September 1987, *47*(3), pp. 711–37. **[G: China]**

Braverman, Avishay; Hammer, Jeffrey S. and Gron, Anne. Multimarket Analysis of Agricultural Price Policies in an Operational Context: The Case of Cyprus. *World Bank Econ. Rev.*, January 1987, *1*(2), pp. 337–56. **[G: Cyprus]**

Brinkman, George L. The Competitive Position of Canadian Agriculture. *Can. J. Agr. Econ.*, July 1987, *35*(2), pp. 263–88. **[G: Canada]**

Brorsen, B. Wade; Chavas, Jean-Paul and Grant, Warren R. A Market Equilibrium Analysis of the Impact of Risk on the U.S. Rice Industry. *Amer. J. Agr. Econ.*, November 1987, *69*(4), pp. 733–39. **[G: U.S.]**

Brown, Lester R. Sustaining World Agriculture. *Brown, L. R., et al.*, 1987, pp. 122–38. **[G: Global]**

Buchholz, H. E. Research Investments in New Products: Bioethanol and Industrial Use of Agricultural Products. *Kettunen, L., ed.*, 1987, pp. 249–69.

Byerlee, Derek. The Political Economy of Third World Food Imports: The Case of Wheat. *Econ. Develop. Cult. Change*, January 1987, *35*(2), pp. 307–28. **[G: LDCs]**

Byers, J. D. and Peel, David A. Forecasting Livestock Slaughter: An Empirical Assessment of MLC Forecasts. *J. Agr. Econ.*, May 1987, *38*(2), pp. 235–41. **[G: U.K.]**

Carraro, Kenneth C. A Review of the Eighth District's Agricultural Economy in 1986. *Fed. Res. Bank St. Louis Rev.*, April 1987, *69*(4), pp. 5–15. **[G: U.S.]**

Chaudhary, Muhammad Ali; Majid, Syed Abdul and Saleem, Nighat. An Analysis of Price and Income Elasticities of Demand for Foodgrains. *Pakistan Econ. Soc. Rev.*, Summer 1987, *25*(1), pp. 21–38. **[G: Pakistan]**

Chaudhry, M. Ghaffar. Profitability of Pakistan's Agriculture: Comments. *Pakistan Devel. Rev.*, Winter 1987, *26*(4), pp. 468–69. **[G: Pakistan]**

Chesher, Andrew and Rees, Hedley. Income Elasticities of Demand for Foods in Great Britain. *J. Agr. Econ.*, September 1987, *38*(3), pp. 435–48. **[G: U.K.]**

Chowdhury, Nuimuddin. Seasonality of Foodgrain Price and Procurement Programme in Bangladesh since Liberation: An Exploratory Study. *Bangladesh Devel. Stud.*, March 1987, *15*(1), pp. 105–28. **[G: Bangladesh]**

Clegg, Martin. Notes for Address Concerning the EEC Milk Superlevy and Quota System. *Kettunen, L., ed.*, 1987, pp. 5–17. **[G: EEC]**

Collinson, Michael. Potential and Practice in Food Production Technology Development: Eastern and Southern Africa. *Mellor, J. W.; Delgado, C. L. and Blackie, M. J., eds.*, 1987, pp. 78–96. **[G: E. Africa; Southern Africa]**

Collinson, Michael. Potential and Practice in Food Production Technology Development: Commentary. *Mellor, J. W.; Delgado, C. L. and Blackie, M. J., eds.*, 1987, pp. 167–70. **[G: Africa]**

Contamin, B. La politique alimentaire de la Tanzanie: le jeu complexe de l'effet-prix. (Food Policy in Tanzania: Complex Play of Price–Effect. With English summary.) *Écon. Soc.*, July 1987, *21*(7), pp. 169–84. **[G: Tanzania]**

Conway, Roger K. An Examination of the 'Schuh Controversy': Is the Demand for U.S. Agricultural Exports Elastic? *Appl. Econ.*, July 1987, *19*(7), pp. 853–73. **[G: U.S.]**

Crabtree, J. R. Response of UK Milk Producers to the Imposition of Production Quotas. *Kettunen, L., ed.*, 1987, pp. 133–46. **[G: U.K.]**

Curtis, Ranjana and Gunetileke, K. G. Market Needs for Vegetable Drying in Sri Lanka. *Young, R. H. and MacCormac, C. W., eds.*, 1987, pp. 78–92. **[G: Sri Lanka]**

Dahlgran, Roger A. Complete Flexibility Systems and the Stationarity of U.S. Meat Demands. *Western J. Agr. Econ.*, December 1987, *12*(2), pp. 152–63. **[G: U.S.]**

Darbellay, C. What Technologies for Mountain Agriculture? The Example of Medicinal and Aromatic Plants. *Merlo, M., et al., eds.*, 1987, pp. 291–97. **[G: Switzerland]**

Davidovici, I. The Feedback and the Efficiency of the Agricultural Process. *Econ. Computat. Cybern. Stud. Res.*, 1987, *22*(4), pp. 39–43.

Dawson, P. J. and Hubbard, L. J. Management and Size Economies in the England and Wales Dairy Sector. *J. Agr. Econ.*, January 1987, *38*(1), pp. 27–37. **[G: U.K.]**

Dawson, P. J. and Lingard, J. Dummy Variable Estimators of Technical Efficiency: A Reply. *J. Agr. Econ.*, May 1987, *38*(2), pp. 339–41.

Delgado, Christopher L.; Mellor, John W. and Blackie, Malcolm J. Strategic Issues in Food Production in Sub-Saharan Africa. *Mellor, J. W.; Delgado, C. L. and Blackie, M. J., eds.*, 1987, pp. 3–22. **[G: Africa]**

Delgado, Christopher L. and Ranade, Chandrashekhar G. Technological Change and Agricultural Labor Use. *Mellor, J. W.; Delgado, C. L. and Blackie, M. J., eds.*, 1987, pp. 118–34. **[G: Africa]**

Desai, Padma. Rise in Variability of Weather-Adjusted Grain Yields under Brezhnev. *Desai, P.*, 1987, pp. 230–45. **[G: U.S.S.R.]**

Desai, Padma. Weather and Grain Yields in the Soviet Union. *Desai, P.*, 1987, pp. 192–230. **[G: U.S.S.R.]**

Devadoss, S. and Meyers, William H. Relative Prices and Money: Further Results for the United States. *Amer. J. Agr. Econ.*, November 1987, *69*(4), pp. 838–42. **[G: U.S.]**

Dhakal, Dharmendra; Grabowski, Richard and Belbase, Krishna. The Effect of Education in Nepal's Traditional Agriculture. *Econ. Educ. Rev.*, 1987, *6*(1), pp. 27–34. **[G: Nepal]**

Dietrich, Raymond A.; Amosson, Stephen H. and Crawford, Richard P. Bovine Brucellosis Programs: An Economic/Epidemiologic Analysis. *Can. J. Agr. Econ.*, March 1987, *35*(1), pp. 127–40. **[G: U.S.]**

van Dijk, G. and Veerman, C. P. Efficiency Considerations of Supply Management. *Kettunen, L., ed.*, 1987, pp. 311–21.

Dorosh, Paul A. International Trade in Corn. *Timmer, C. P., ed.*, 1987, pp. 235–50. **[G: Indonesia]**

Dorosh, Paul A., et al. Introduction to the Corn Economy of Indonesia. *Timmer, C. P., ed.*, 1987, pp. 19–37. **[G: Indonesia]**

Duffy, Patricia A.; Richardson, James W. and Wohlgenant, Michael K. Regional Cotton Acreage Response. *Southern J. Agr. Econ.*, July 1987, *19*(1), pp. 99–109. **[G: U.S.]**

Eastwood, David B.; Brooker, John R. and Orr, Robert H. Consumer Preferences for Local versus Out-of-state Grown Selected Fresh Produce: The Case of Knoxville, Tennessee. *Southern J. Agr. Econ.*, December 1987, *19*(2), pp. 183–94. **[G: U.S.]**

Eggleston, Robert C. Determinants of the Levels and Distribution of PL 480 Food Aid: 1955–79. *World Devel.*, June 1987, *15*(6), pp. 797–808. **[G: U.S.]**

Ekanayake, S. A. B. Location Specificity, Settler Type and Productive Efficiency: A Study of the Mahaweli Project in Sri Lanka. *J. Devel. Stud.*, July 1987, *23*(4), pp. 509–21. **[G: Sri Lanka]**

Elliott, Howard. The Use of Events Analysis in Evaluating National Research Systems. *Ruttan, V. W. and Pray, C. E., eds.*, 1987, pp. 377–87. **[G: Panama]**

Errington, Andrew. Labour Use and Labour Requirements in UK Agriculture. *J. Agr. Econ.*, May 1987, *38*(2), pp. 271–79. **[G: U.K.]**

Esfahani, Hadi Salehi. Growth, Employment and Income Distribution in Egyptian Agriculture, 1964–79. *World Devel.*, September 1987, *15*(9), pp. 1201–17. **[G: Egypt]**

Esfahani, Hadi Salehi. Technical Change, Employment, and Supply Response of Agriculture in the Nile Delta: A System-Wide Approach. *J. Devel. Econ.*, February 1987, *25*(1), pp. 167–96. **[G: Egypt]**

Esteva, Gustavo. Food Needs and Capacities: Four Centuries of Conflict. *Austin, J. E. and Esteva, G., eds.*, 1987, pp. 23–47. **[G: Mexico]**

Feder, Gershon. Land Ownership Security and Farm Productivity: Evidence from Thailand. *J. Devel. Stud.*, October 1987, *24*(1), pp. 16–30. **[G: Thailand]**

Feuer, Carl Henry. The Performance of the Cuban Sugar Industry, 1981–85. *Zimbalist, A., ed.*, 1987, pp. 69–83. **[G: Cuba]**

Feuer, Carl Henry. The Performance of the Cuban Sugar Industry, 1981–85. *World Devel.*, January 1987, *15*(1), pp. 67–81. **[G: Cuba]**

Finan, Timothy J. Portuguese Agriculture in Transition: Intensive Agriculture in the Northwest. *Pearson, S. R., et al.*, 1987, pp. 141–63. **[G: Portugal]**

Fontaine, Jean-Marc. Les projets de libéralisation des agricultures africaines. Un point de vue critique appuyé sur les cas kenyan et tanzanien. (On Economic Liberalism and African Agriculture. With English summary.) *Écon. Soc.*, July 1987, *21*(7), pp. 185–208. **[G: Kenya; Tanzania]**

Forster, Bruce A. Agricultural Impacts of Acid

Deposition: Some Issues to Consider. *Can. J. Agr. Econ.*, March 1987, *35*(1), pp. 241–47.
[G: Canada]

Fox, Glenn. An Economic Assessment of the Impact of Alachlor Deregistration on Corn and Soybean Producers in Ontario. *Can. J. Agr. Econ.*, July 1987, *35*(2), pp. 317–31.
[G: Canada]

Fox, Roger. Extensive Farming in the Alentejo. *Pearson, S. R., et al.*, 1987, pp. 85–106.
[G: Portugal]

Fox, Roger and Finan, Timothy J. Portuguese Agriculture in Transition: Future Technical and Structural Adjustments in Northwestern Agriculture. *Pearson, S. R., et al.*, 1987, pp. 202–20.
[G: Portugal]

Fox, Roger and Finan, Timothy J. Portuguese Agriculture in Transition: Patterns of Technical Change in the Northwest. *Pearson, S. R., et al.*, 1987, pp. 187–201.
[G: Portugal]

Franklin, David L.; Harrell, Marielouise W. and Leonard, Jerry B. Income Effects of Donated Commodities in Rural Panama. *Amer. J. Agr. Econ.*, February 1987, *69*(1), pp. 115–22.
[G: Panama]

Fraser, R. W. and Salerian, Soy Nia. Agricultural Exports and the Western Australian Economy. *Australian J. Agr. Econ.*, April 1987, *31*(1), pp. 74–82.
[G: Australia]

Freebairn, John W. Implications of Wages and Industrial Policies on the Competitiveness of Agricultural Export Industries. *Rev. Marketing Agr. Econ.*, April 1987, *55*(1), pp. 79–87.
[G: Australia]

Freebairn, John W. The Australian Economy in the Long Run: Natural Resource Industries. *Maddock, R. and McLean, I. W., eds.*, 1987, pp. 133–64.
[G: Australia]

French, Ben C. Farm Price Estimation When There is Bargaining: The Case of Processed Fruit and Vegetables. *Western J. Agr. Econ.*, July 1987, *12*(1), pp. 17–26.
[G: U.S.]

Gafar, John. The Supply Response for Sugar Cane in Trinidad and Tobago: Some Preliminary Results. *Appl. Econ.*, September 1987, *19*(9), pp. 1221–31.
[G: Trinidad and Tobago]

Gaiha, Raghav. Inequality, Earnings and Participation among the Poor in Rural India. *J. Devel. Stud.*, July 1987, *23*(4), pp. 491–508.
[G: India]

Galab, S. and Sarma, P. V. S. R. L. Returns to Irrigation in Indian Agriculture: A Case Study. *Margin*, July-Sept. 1987, *19*(4), pp. 55–61.
[G: India]

Gallagher, Paul. U.S. Soybean Yields: Estimation and Forecasting with Nonsymmetric Disturbances. *Amer. J. Agr. Econ.*, November 1987, *69*(4), pp. 796–803.
[G: U.S.]

Gamaledinn, Maknun. State Policy and Famine in the Awash Valley of Ethiopia: The Lessons for Conservation. *Anderson, D. and Grove, R., eds.*, 1987, pp. 327–44.
[G: Ethiopia]

Gardner, Bruce L. Efficiency in Commodity Storage. *Kilmer, R. L. and Armbruster, W. J., eds.*, 1987, pp. 274–85.
[G: U.S.]

George, Kenneth D. and Mainwaring, Lynn. The Welsh Economy in the 1980s. *Day, G. and Rees, G., eds.*, 1987, pp. 7–37.
[G: U.K.]

Ghosh, Dipak. A Theoretical Model of Behaviour of Marketed Surplus in a Partially Monetized Economy. *Indian Econ. J.*, Apr.-June 1987, *34*(4), pp. 39–54.
[G: India]

van der Giessen, L. B. and Post, J. H. Micro- and Macro-effects of the Super Levy in the Netherlands. *Kettunen, L., ed.*, 1987, pp. 105–20.
[G: Netherlands]

Gilmour, Brad and Fawcett, Peter. The Relationship between U.S. and Canadian Wheat Prices. *Can. J. Agr. Econ.*, November 1987, *35*(3), pp. 571–89.
[G: U.S.; Canada]

Gonzales, L. A. Rice Production and Regional Crop Diversification in the Philippines: Economic Issues. *Philippine Rev. Econ. Bus.*, Mar.-June 1987, *24*(1–2), pp. 125–48.
[G: Philippines]

Grabowski, Richard and Sanchez, Onesimo. Technological Change in Mexican Agriculture: 1950–1979. *Soc. Econ. Stud.*, June 1987, *36*(2), pp. 187–205.
[G: Mexico]

Ground, Richard L. Agricultural Development and Macroeconomic Balance in Latin America: An Overview of Some Basic Policy Issues. *CEPAL Rev.*, December 1987, (33), pp. 29–38.
[G: Latin America]

Gunawardana, P. J. and Quilkey, J. J. Issues in Smallholder Tropical Dairying: A Comment. *Bull. Indonesian Econ. Stud.*, April 1987, *23*(1), pp. 122–26.
[G: Indonesia]

Guzhvin, P. The Yield of Land and the Structure of Investment. *Prob. Econ.*, February 1987, *29*(10), pp. 38–54.
[G: U.S.S.R.]

Gyimah-Brempong, Kwabena. Scale Elasticities in Ghanaian Cocoa Production. *Appl. Econ.*, October 1987, *19*(10), pp. 1383–90.
[G: Ghana]

Gyimah-Brempong, Kwabena; Akaah, Ishael P. and Dadzie, Kofi Q. Cocoa Production Technology in Ghana: An Application of the Translog Production Function. *Eastern Afr. Econ. Rev.*, June 1987, *3*(1), pp. 15–20.
[G: Ghana]

Gyimah-Brempong, Kwabena and Apraku, Kofi Konadu. Structural Change in Supply Response of Ghanaian Cocoa Production: 1933–1983. *J. Devel. Areas*, October 1987, *22*(1), pp. 59–70.
[G: Ghana]

Hall, Nigel and Bardsley, Peter. Dummy Variable Estimators of Technical Efficiency: A Comment. *J. Agr. Econ.*, May 1987, *38*(2), pp. 335–39.

Harriss, Barbara. Regional Growth Linkages from Agriculture. *J. Devel. Stud.*, January 1987, *23*(2), pp. 275–89.
[G: LDCs]

Hartford, Kathleen. Socialist Countries in the World Food System: The Soviet Union, Hungary, and China. *Food Res. Inst. Stud.*, 1987, *20*(3), pp. 181–243. [G: U.S.S.R.; Hungary; China]

Harthoorn, R. and Wossink, G. A. A. Backward and Forward Effects of Dutch Agriculture. *Europ. Rev. Agr. Econ.*, 1987, *14*(3), pp. 325–33.
[G: Netherlands]

Hartley, Michael J.; Nerlove, Marc and Peters, R. Kyle, Jr. An Analysis of Rubber Supply in Sri Lanka. *Amer. J. Agr. Econ.*, November 1987, *69*(4), pp. 755–61. **[G: Sri Lanka]**

Hayami, Yujiro and Ruttan, Vernon W. Population Growth and Agricultural Productivity. *Espenshade, T. and Stolnitz, G. J., eds.*, 1987, pp. 11–69.

Hayami, Yujiro and Ruttan, Vernon W. Population Growth and Agricultural Productivity. *Johnson, D. G. and Lee, R. D., eds.*, 1987, pp. 57–101. **[G: Global]**

Hayes, Dermot J. and Schmitz, Andrew. Hog Cycles and Countercyclical Production Response. *Amer. J. Agr. Econ.*, November 1987, *69*(4), pp. 762–70. **[G: U.S.]**

Hazell, Peter and Slade, Roger H. Regional Growth Linkages from Agriculture: A Reply. *J. Devel. Stud.*, January 1987, *23*(2), pp. 290–94. **[G: LDCs]**

Hegrenes, Agnar and Norum, Leopold. Macromodel Calculations of Effects of Different Policy Instruments on Agricultural Output, Resource Use, and Farm Income. *Kettunen, L., ed.*, 1987, pp. 331–41. **[G: Norway]**

Heichel, Gary H. Anticipating Advances in Crop Technology. *Ruttan, V. W. and Pray, C. E., eds.*, 1987, pp. 235–44. **[G: U.S.]**

Hemmi, Kenzo. Agricultural Reform Efforts in Japan: Political Feasibility and Consequences for Trade with the United States and Third Countries. *Johnson, D. G., ed.*, 1987, pp. 24–46. **[G: Japan; U.S.]**

Herdt, Robert W. A Retrospective View of Technological and Other Changes in Philippine Rice Farming, 1965–1982. *Econ. Develop. Cult. Change*, January 1987, *35*(2), pp. 329–49. **[G: Philippines]**

Herdt, Robert W. and Anderson, Jock R. The Contribution of the CGIAR Centers to World Agricultural Research. *Ruttan, V. W. and Pray, C. E., eds.*, 1987, pp. 39–64. **[G: Global]**

Hertel, Thomas W. Estimating Substitution and Expansion Effects: Comment. *Amer. J. Agr. Econ.*, February 1987, *69*(1), pp. 188–92. **[G: Canada]**

Hertel, Thomas W. Inferring Long-run Elasticities from a Short-run Quadratic Profit Function. *Can. J. Agr. Econ.*, March 1987, *35*(1), pp. 169–80.

Hickson, A. B. and Carter, Colin A. An Analysis of Policy Changes in the Canadian Feed Grain Market. *Western J. Agr. Econ.*, December 1987, *12*(2), pp. 126–34. **[G: Canada]**

Hillman, Jimmye S. Domestic and Export Demand for U.S. Agricultural Products: Discussion. *Amer. J. Agr. Econ.*, May 1987, *69*(2), pp. 459–60. **[G: U.S.]**

Hodge, Ian. The Cap and the Soil: A Preliminary Analysis. *Merlo, M., et al., eds.*, 1987, pp. 523–33. **[G: U.K.]**

Hopkins, Raymond F. The Wheat Negotiations: Loss or Gain in North–South Relations? *Zartman, I. W., ed. (II)*, 1987, pp. 115–48.

Hossain, Mahabub. Agricultural Growth Link-

ages—The Bangladesh Case. *Bangladesh Devel. Stud.*, March 1987, *15*(1), pp. 1–30. **[G: Bangladesh]**

Huang, Wen-Yuan; Eswaramoorthy, K. and Johnson, Stanley R. Computing an Asymmetric Competitive Market Equilibrium. *J. Agr. Econ. Res.*, Summer 1987, *39*(3), pp. 20–29.

Hubbard, L. J. The Price of Dairy Quota in England and Wales. *Kettunen, L., ed.*, 1987, pp. 343–51. **[G: U.K.]**

Hurt, Verner G. Optional Uses for Excess Resources in U.S. Agriculture: Discussion. *Amer. J. Agr. Econ.*, May 1987, *69*(2), pp. 463–64. **[G: U.S.]**

Iakimets, V. Dynamics of an Agricultural Development under Many Objectives. *Merlo, M., et al., eds.*, 1987, pp. 19–38.

Idachaba, Francis S. Agriculture and Central Physical Grid Infrastructure: Commentary. *Mellor, J. W.; Delgado, C. L. and Blackie, M. J., eds.*, 1987, pp. 232–38. **[G: Africa]**

Ireson, W. Randall. Landholding, Agricultural Modernization, and Income Concentration: A Mexican Example. *Econ. Develop. Cult. Change*, January 1987, *35*(2), pp. 351–66. **[G: Mexico]**

Islam, Nurul. The World Food Situation and Prospects: Introduction. *Borner, S. and Taylor, A., eds.*, 1987, pp. 51–63.

Johnston, Bruce F. Growth of Foreign Assistance and Its Impact on Agriculture: Commentary. *Mellor, J. W.; Delgado, C. L. and Blackie, M. J., eds.*, 1987, pp. 348–49. **[G: Africa]**

Josling, Timothy and Tangermann, Stefan. Portuguese Agriculture in Transition: Commodity Policies. *Pearson, S. R., et al.*, 1987, pp. 41–61. **[G: Portugal]**

Judd, M. Ann; Boyce, James K. and Evenson, Robert E. Investment in Agricultural Research and Extension. *Ruttan, V. W. and Pray, C. E., eds.*, 1987, pp. 7–38. **[G: Global]**

Kainth, Gursharan Singh. Foodgrains Prices in India, 1971–85: Determinants and Developmental Implications. *Indian Econ. J.*, Oct.-Dec. 1987, *35*(2), pp. 115–25. **[G: India]**

Kalirajan, K. South–South Co-operation: Technology Transfer for Improving Productivity. *Indian Econ. J.*, Jan.-Mar. 1987, *34*(3), pp. 60–72. **[G: LDCs]**

Karim, Rezaul; Mondal, A. Hye and Seyfried, W. R. Estimation of Gross Upazila Crop Product—A Suggested Methodology. *Bangladesh Devel. Stud.*, December 1987, *15*(4), pp. 149–54. **[G: Bangladesh]**

Kashem, M. A. Small Farmers' Constraints in the Adoption of Modern Rice Technology. *Bangladesh Devel. Stud.*, December 1987, *15*(4), pp. 119–30. **[G: Bangladesh]**

Kazi, Shahnaz. Intersectoral Terms of Trade for Pakistan's Economy: 1970-71–1981-82. *Pakistan Devel. Rev.*, Spring 1987, *26*(1), pp. 81–105. **[G: Pakistan]**

Kerin, John. The Impact of Wages and Industrial Policies on the Performance of the Agricultural Export Industries: Official Opening Speech.

Rev. Marketing Agr. Econ., April 1987, 55(1), pp. 74–78. **[G: Australia]**

Kettunen, Lauri. Experiences in Controlling Milk Supply in Finland. *Kettunen, L., ed.*, 1987, pp. 147–57. **[G: Finland]**

Keyzer, M. A. Consequences of Increased Foodgrain Production on the Bangladesh Economy. *Talman, D. and van der Laan, G., eds.*, 1987, pp. 59–83. **[G: Bangladesh]**

Kim, C. S.; Bolling, Christine and Wainio, John. Import Demand for Feed Grains in Venezuela. *J. Agr. Econ. Res.*, Summer 1987, 39(3), 12–19. **[G: Venezuela; U.S.]**

Kim, C. S. and Schaible, Glenn. Monopsonistic Food Processing and Farm Prices: Comment [Monopsonistic Food Processing and Farm Prices: The Case of the West Alabama Catfish Industry]. *Southern J. Agr. Econ.*, December 1987, 19(2), pp. 223–24. **[G: U.S.]**

Kinnucan, Henry W. and Forker, Olan D. Asymmetry in Farm-Retail Price Transmission for Major Dairy Products. *Amer. J. Agr. Econ.*, May 1987, 69(2), pp. 285–92. **[G: U.S.]**

Kinnucan, Henry W. and Sullivan, Gregory. Monopsonistic Food Processing and Farm Prices: Reply [Monopsonistic Food Processing and Farm Prices: The Case of the West Alabama Catfish Industry]. *Southern J. Agr. Econ.*, December 1987, 19(2), pp. 225. **[G: U.S.]**

Knapp, Keith C. Dynamic Equilibrium in Markets for Perennial Crops. *Amer. J. Agr. Econ.*, February 1987, 69(1), pp. 97–105. **[G: U.S.]**

Kristensen, Thorkil. Landbrugets fremtid. (The Prospects for Danish Agriculture. With English summary.) *Nationaløkon. Tidsskr.*, 1987, 125(3), pp. 316–20. **[G: Denmark]**

Krueger, Anne O. Growth Strategy and the Agricultural Sector: Commentary. *Mellor, J. W.; Delgado, C. L. and Blackie, M. J., eds.*, 1987, pp. 253–56. **[G: Africa]**

ter Kuile, Coenrad H. H. Potential and Practice in Food Production Technology Development: The Humid and Subhumid Tropics. *Mellor, J. W.; Delgado, C. L. and Blackie, M. J., eds.*, 1987, pp. 97–108. **[G: Africa]**

Kumar, Shubh K. The Nutrition Situation and Its Food Policy Links. *Mellor, J. W.; Delgado, C. L. and Blackie, M. J., eds.*, 1987, pp. 39–52. **[G: Africa]**

Kumar, Shubh K. Women's Role and Agricultural Technology. *Mellor, J. W.; Delgado, C. L. and Blackie, M. J., eds.*, 1987, pp. 135–47. **[G: Africa]**

Kurmuş, Orhan. The Cotton Famine and Its Effects on the Ottoman Empire. *Islamoglu-Inan, H., ed.*, 1987, pp. 160–69. **[G: Ottoman Empire]**

Kuroda, Yoshimi. The Production Structure and Demand for Labor in Postwar Japanese Agriculture, 1952–82. *Amer. J. Agr. Econ.*, May 1987, 69(2), pp. 328–37. **[G: Japan]**

Langworthy, Mark. Dairying in the Azores. *Pearson, S. R., et al.*, 1987, pp. 124–40. **[G: Portugal]**

de Lattre, Anne. Growth of Foreign Assistance and Its Impact on Agriculture: Commentary. *Mellor, J. W.; Delgado, C. L. and Blackie, M. J., eds.*, 1987, pp. 346–48. **[G: Africa]**

Lee, Jonq-Ying. The Demand for Varied Diet with Econometric Models for Count Data. *Amer. J. Agr. Econ.*, August 1987, 69(3), pp. 687–92. **[G: U.S.]**

Lele, Uma. Growth of Foreign Assistance and Its Impact on Agriculture. *Mellor, J. W.; Delgado, C. L. and Blackie, M. J., eds.*, 1987, pp. 321–42. **[G: Africa]**

Lewis, Philip E. T. Short-run Substitution in the Sheep and Beef Industries. *Australian J. Agr. Econ.*, December 1987, 31(3), pp. 266–71. **[G: Australia]**

Lien, Da-Hsiang Donald. The Inventory Effect in Commodity Futures Markets: An Empirical Study. *J. Futures Markets*, December 1987, 7(6), pp. 637–52. **[G: U.S.]**

Lipman-Blumen, Jean. Priority Setting in Agricultural Research. *Ruttan, V. W. and Pray, C. E., eds.*, 1987, pp. 139–73. **[G: U.S.]**

Lipton, Michael. Agriculture and Central Physical Grid Infrastructure. *Mellor, J. W.; Delgado, C. L. and Blackie, M. J., eds.*, 1987, pp. 210–26. **[G: Africa]**

López Cordovez, Luis. Crisis, Adjustment Policies and Agriculture. *CEPAL Rev.*, December 1987, (33), pp. 7–28. **[G: Latin America]**

Lopez, Ramon E. Estimating Substitution and Expansion Effects: Reply. *Amer. J. Agr. Econ.*, February 1987, 69(1), pp. 193. **[G: Canada]**

Lowry, Mark, et al. Pricing and Storage of Field Crops: A Quarterly Model Applied to Soybeans. *Amer. J. Agr. Econ.*, November 1987, 69(4), pp. 740–49. **[G: U.S.]**

Lucas, Robert E. B. Emigration to South Africa's Mines. *Amer. Econ. Rev.*, June 1987, 77(3), pp. 313–30. **[G: S. Africa; Botswana; Lesotho; Malawi; Mozambique]**

Manilay, Alessandro A. Market Research for Grain Postharvest Systems. *Young, R. H. and MacCormac, C. W., eds.*, 1987, pp. 31–37.

Markkola, Usko and Mäkinen, Paavo. Finnish Quota System. *Kettunen, L., ed.*, 1987, pp. 55–61. **[G: Finland]**

Martin, S. K. and Zwart, A. C. Marketing Agencies and the Economics of Market Segmentation. *Australian J. Agr. Econ.*, December 1987, 31(3), pp. 242–55. **[G: New Zealand]**

Martínez, Astrid. Colombia: Effects of the Adjustment Policy on Agricultural Development. *CEPAL Rev.*, December 1987, (33), pp. 91–105. **[G: Colombia]**

Mate, Mavis. Pastoral Farming in South-east England in the Fifteenth Century. *Econ. Hist. Rev.*, 2nd Ser., November 1987, 40(4), pp. 523–36. **[G: U.K.]**

Matlon, Peter J. Potential and Practice in Food Production Technology Development: The West African Semiarid Tropics. *Mellor, J. W.; Delgado, C. L. and Blackie, M. J., eds.*, 1987, pp. 59–77. **[G: W. Africa]**

Matthews, Alan. Agricultural Income Distribution and Public Policy: A Dynamic Analysis.

Léon, Y. and Mahé, L., eds., 1987, pp. 463–76. **[G: Ireland]**

McClain, Emily A. and McLemore, Dan L. Optimal Organization of a Statewide Livestock Auction Market System: The Case of Tennessee. *Southern J. Agr. Econ.*, December 1987, *19*(2), pp. 121–31. **[G: U.S.]**

McCorriston, S. and Sheldon, Ian M. EC Integration and the Agricultural Supply Industries. *Macmillen, M.; Mayes, D. G. and van Veen, P.*, eds., 1987, pp. 119–51. **[G: EEC]**

McNicoll, Geoffrey. Agrarian and Industrial Futures: Comments [Population Growth and Agricultural Productivity] [Education, Population Trends, and Technological Change]. *Espenshade, T. and Stolnitz, G. J.*, eds., 1987, pp. 105–14.

McStocker, Robert. The Indonesian Coffee Industry. *Bull. Indonesian Econ. Stud.*, April 1987, *23*(1), pp. 40–69. **[G: Indonesia]**

Mensah, Moise C. Growth of Foreign Assistance and Its Impact on Agriculture: Commentary. *Mellor, J. W.; Delgado, C. L. and Blackie, M. J.*, eds., 1987, pp. 343–45. **[G: Africa]**

Merkel, Konrad. The East German Economy: Agriculture. *Jeffries, I. and Melzer, M.*, eds., 1987, pp. 202–34. **[G: E. Germany]**

Merriam, John G. Egyptian Agricultural Energy Incentives. *Pachauri, R. K.*, ed., 1987, pp. 255–70. **[G: Egypt]**

Mészáros, Sándor. Possibility of an Export Oriented Price Policy as a Tool of Supply Management. *Kettunen, L.*, ed., 1987, pp. 205–19. **[G: Hungary]**

Meyers, William H.; Devadoss, S. and Helmar, Michael D. Agricultural Trade Liberalization: Cross-Commodity and Cross-Country Impact Products. *J. Policy Modeling*, Fall 1987, *9*(3), pp. 455–82.

Mink, Stephen D. Corn in the Livestock Economy. *Timmer, C. P.*, ed., 1987, pp. 142–74. **[G: Indonesia]**

Mink, Stephen D. The Economics of Input Use. *Timmer, C. P.*, ed., 1987, pp. 88–104. **[G: Indonesia]**

Mink, Stephen D. and Dorosh, Paul A. An Overview of Corn Production. *Timmer, C. P.*, ed., 1987, pp. 41–61. **[G: Indonesia]**

Mink, Stephen D.; Dorosh, Paul A. and Perry, Douglas H. Corn Production Systems. *Timmer, C. P.*, ed., 1987, pp. 62–87. **[G: Indonesia]**

Mitra, Neelanjana. Supply Response in the Indian Tea Industry: 1960–80. *J. Quant. Econ.*, July 1987, *3*(2), pp. 313–34. **[G: India]**

Monke, Eric A.; Cory, Dennis C. and Heckerman, Donald G. Surplus Disposal in World Markets: An Application to Egyptian Cotton. *Amer. J. Agr. Econ.*, August 1987, *69*(3), pp. 570–79. **[G: Egypt]**

Monteverde, Richard T. and Mink, Stephen D. Household Corn Consumption. *Timmer, C. P.*, ed., 1987, pp. 111–41. **[G: Indonesia]**

Mudahar, Mohinder S. Measuring the Contribution of Fertilizer to Food Production. *Indian J. Quant. Econ.*, 1987, *3*(2), pp. 1–19. **[G: India]**

Mumbengegwi, Clever. Food and Agriculture Cooperation in the SADCC: Progress, Problems and Prospects. *Amin, S.; Chitala, D. and Mandaza, I.*, eds., 1987, pp. 62–84. **[G: Southern Africa]**

Mupawose, Robbie M. Potential and Practice in Food Production Technology Development: Commentary. *Mellor, J. W.; Delgado, C. L. and Blackie, M. J.*, eds., 1987, pp. 164–67. **[G: Africa]**

Murphy, J. A.; O'Connell, John J. and Quinn, S. Price Relationships for Beef in Smithfield Market. *J. Agr. Econ.*, September 1987, *38*(3), pp. 489–90. **[G: U.K.]**

Murshid, K. A. S. Micro-level Adjustments to Foodgrain Shortages in Bangladesh. *Bangladesh Devel. Stud.*, June 1987, *15*(2), pp. 25–63. **[G: Bangladesh]**

Murshid, K. A. S. Weather, New Technology and Instability in Foodgrain Production in Bangladesh. *Bangladesh Devel. Stud.*, March 1987, *15*(1), pp. 31–56. **[G: Bangladesh]**

Myers, Lester H.; Blaylock, James R. and White, T. Kelly. Domestic and Export Demand for U.S. Agricultural Products. *Amer. J. Agr. Econ.*, May 1987, *69*(2), pp. 443–47. **[G: U.S.]**

Nash, Peter. The Concept of Readaptation Applied to the Irish Dairy Industry. *Irish J. Agr. Econ. Rural Soc.*, 1987, *12*, pp. 79–93. **[G: Ireland]**

Nieuwoudt, W. L. and Frank, D. B. An Economic Evaluation of Alternative Maize Policies. *S. Afr. J. Econ.*, December 1987, *55*(4), pp. 355–69. **[G: S. Africa]**

Nyankori, James C. O.; Rosson, C. Parr and Rathwell, P. J. Estimates of the Effects of Canadian Tariff on Fresh Peach Imports from the United States. *Can. J. Agr. Econ.*, March 1987, *35*(1), pp. 75–87. **[G: Canada; U.S.]**

O'Mara, L. P. The Contribution of the Farm Sector to Annual Variations in Gross Domestic Product in Australia. *Econ. Rec.*, September 1987, *63*(182), pp. 255–69. **[G: Australia]**

Offutt, Susan E. and Kuchler, Fred. Issues and Developments in Biotechnology: What's an Economist to Do? *Agr. Econ. Res.*, Winter 1987, *39*(1), pp. 25–33. **[G: U.S.]**

Okuniewski, Jósef. The Use of Planning and of the Market to Achieve a Growth of Agricultural Production in Poland. *Kettunen, L.*, ed., 1987, pp. 169–81. **[G: Poland]**

Okyere, William A. and Johnson, Stanley R. Variability in Forecasts in a Nonlinear Model of the U.S. Beef Sector. *Appl. Econ.*, November 1987, *19*(11), pp. 1457–70. **[G: U.S.]**

Olmstead, Alan L. and Wooten, Donald B. Bee Pollination and Productivity Growth: The Case of Alfalfa. *Amer. J. Agr. Econ.*, February 1987, *69*(1), pp. 56–63. **[G: U.S.]**

Ortmann, G. F. Land Rents and Production Costs in the South African Sugar Industry. *S. Afr. J. Econ.*, September 1987, *55*(3), pp. 249–58. **[G: S. Africa]**

Ortner, K. M. An Outline of the Milk Quota Policy in Austria. *Kettunen, L., ed.*, 1987, pp. 69–75.   [G: Austria]

Oyejide, T. Ademola. Food Policy and the Choice of Trade Regime. *Mellor, J. W.; Delgado, C. L. and Blackie, M. J., eds.*, 1987, pp. 257–73.   [G: Africa]

Paul, Satya. A Cost Function Analysis of Wheat Production in India. *Europ. Rev. Agr. Econ.*, 1987, *14*(2), pp. 221–38.   [G: India]

Paulino, Leonardo A. The Evolving Food Situation. *Mellor, J. W.; Delgado, C. L. and Blackie, M. J., eds.*, 1987, pp. 23–38.   [G: Africa]

Pearson, Scott R. Prospects for Corn Sweeteners. *Timmer, C. P., ed.*, 1987, pp. 175–92.   [G: Indonesia]

Penm, Jammie H. and Vincent, D. P. Some Estimates of the Price Elasticity of Demand for Phosphatic and Nitrogenous Fertilisers. *Australian J. Agr. Econ.*, April 1987, *31*(1), pp. 65–73.   [G: Australia]

Penning de Vries, Frits W. T. and de Wit, Cornelis T. Potential and Practice in Food Production Technology Development: Identifying Technological Potentials. *Mellor, J. W.; Delgado, C. L. and Blackie, M. J., eds.*, 1987, pp. 109–17.   [G: Africa]

Piggott, R. R., et al. Short-run Costs and Throughput Variability for a NSW Abattoir. *Australian J. Agr. Econ.*, April 1987, *31*(1), pp. 56–64.   [G: Australia]

Pingali, Prabhu L. and Binswanger, Hans P. Population Density and Agricultural Intensification: A Study of the Evolution of Technologies in Tropical Agriculture. *Johnson, D. G. and Lee, R. D., eds.*, 1987, pp. 27–56.   [G: LDCs]

Prakash, Om. Opium Monopoly in India and Indonesia in the Eighteenth Century. *Indian Econ. Soc. Hist. Rev.*, Jan.-Mar. 1987, *24*(1), pp. 63–80.   [G: India; Indonesia]

Pray, Carl E. Private Sector Agricultural Research in Asia. *Ruttan, V. W. and Pray, C. E., eds.*, 1987, pp. 411–31.   [G: Asia]

Prescott, David M. and Stengos, Thanasis. Bootstrapping Confidence Intervals: An Application to Forecasting the Supply of Pork. *Amer. J. Agr. Econ.*, May 1987, *69*(2), pp. 266–73.   [G: U.S.]

Prior, M. J. A Method for Estimating the Demand for Agricultural Machinery in the UK. *J. Agr. Econ.*, May 1987, *38*(2), pp. 281–88.   [G: U.K.]

Purcell, Joseph C. Optional Uses for Excess Resources in U.S. Agriculture. *Amer. J. Agr. Econ.*, May 1987, *69*(2), pp. 454–58.   [G: U.S.]

Quaisser, Wolfgang. The New Agricultural Reform in China: From the People's Communes to Peasant Agriculture. *Gey, P.; Kosta, J. and Quaisser, W., eds.*, 1987, pp. 173–96.   [G: China]

Qureshi, Sarfraz Khan. Intra-sector and Intersectoral Parity Issues in Pricing of Agricultural Crops: A Preliminary Analysis. *Pakistan Devel.*

Rev., Winter 1987, *26*(4), pp. 401–14.   [G: Pakistan]

Rabinowicz, Ewa and Bolin, Olof. Price or Supply Management. *Kettunen, L., ed.*, 1987, pp. 301–09.   [G: Sweden]

Rahman, Atiq. Resource Use in Bangladesh Agriculture—An Empirical Analysis. *Bangladesh Devel. Stud.*, June 1987, *15*(2), pp. 1–23.   [G: Bangladesh]

Rahman, Sultan Hafeez. An Analysis of Seasonal Jute Price Behaviour. *Bangladesh Devel. Stud.*, September 1987, *15*(3), pp. 43–61.   [G: Bangladesh]

Ravallion, Martin. Trade and Stabilization: Another Look at British India's Controversial Foodgrain Exports. *Exploration Econ. Hist.*, October 1987, *24*(4), pp. 354–70.   [G: India]

Ray, S. K. Stabilization through Food Stock Operation. *J. Quant. Econ.*, January 1987, *3*(1), pp. 101–15.   [G: India]

Rehman, Tahir and Romero, Carlos. Multiple Criteria Decision Techniques and Multi Purpose Agriculture. *Merlo, M., et al., eds.*, 1987, pp. 7–18.

Reimund, Donn and Petrulis, Mindy. Performance of the Agricultural Sector. *U.S.D.A., Econ. Res. Serv., Agr. and Rural Econ. Div.*, 1987, pp. 4.1–30.   [G: U.S.]

Remenyi, J. V. Issues in Smallholder Tropical Dairying: A Reply. *Bull. Indonesian Econ. Stud.*, April 1987, *23*(1), pp. 127–30.   [G: Indonesia]

Remenyi, J. V. and Bodman, Phil. Meeting Policy Data Needs on Smallholder Agriculture. *Barker, P.; Bodman, P. and Remenyl, J., eds.*, 1987, pp. 1–3.   [G: Papua New Guinea]

Repetto, Robert. Economic Incentives for Sustainable Production. *Ann. Reg. Sci.*, November 1987, *21*(3), pp. 44–59.   [G: Africa]

Roarty, Michael J. The Impact of the Common Agricultural Policy on Agricultural Trade and Development. *Nat. Westminster Bank Quart. Rev.*, February 1987, pp. 12–28.   [G: EEC]

Rosa, F. Multiobjective Agriculture: Finding an Optimal Solution among Competing Agents. *Merlo, M., et al., eds.*, 1987, pp. 53–68.

Rosen, Sherwin. Dynamic Animal Economics. *Amer. J. Agr. Econ.*, August 1987, *69*(3), pp. 547–57.

Rudra, Ashok. Technology Choice in Agriculture in India over the Past Three Decades. *Stewart, F., ed.*, 1987, pp. 22–73.   [G: India]

Ruttan, Vernon W. Toward a Global Agricultural Research System. *Ruttan, V. W. and Pray, C. E., eds.*, 1987, pp. 65–97.

Sahn, David E. and von Braun, Joachim. The Relationship between Food Production and Consumption Variability: Policy Implications for Developing Countries. *J. Agr. Econ.*, May 1987, *38*(2), pp. 315–27.   [G: LDCs]

Salamon, Petra. An Evaluation of the Milk Quota Regime in the Federal Republic of Germany. *Kettunen, L., ed.*, 1987, pp. 29–54.   [G: W. Germany]

Sampson, John A. and Gerrard, Christopher D. Government Interventions and the Production of Wheat in Saskatchewan and North Dakota: An Empirical Analysis. *Can. J. Agr. Econ.,* March 1987, 35(1), pp. 1–20. [G: U.S.; Canada]

Sapsford, David and Varoufakis, Y. An ARIMA Analysis of Tea Prices. *J. Agr. Econ.,* May 1987, 38(2), pp. 329–34. [G: U.K.]

Sato, Takashi. Agricultural Reform Efforts in the United States and Japan: Remarks. *Johnson, D. G., ed.,* 1987, pp. 77–81. [G: U.S.; Japan]

Schatan W., Jacobo. SAM's Influence on Food Consumption and Nutrition. *Austin, J. E. and Esteva, G., eds.,* 1987, pp. 249–59. [G: Mexico]

Schuh, G. Edward. The Changing Context of Food and Agricultural Development Policy. *Gittinger, J. P.; Leslie, J. and Hoisington, C., eds.,* 1987, pp. 72–88. [G: Global]

Schweizer, Thomas. Agrarian Transformation? Rice Production in a Javanese Village. *Bull. Indonesian Econ. Stud.,* August 1987, 23(2), pp. 38–70. [G: Indonesia]

Seale, James L., Jr. and Shonkwiler, J. S. Rationality, Price Risk, and Response. *Southern J. Agr. Econ.,* July 1987, 19(1), pp. 111–18. [G: U.S.]

Sebestyén, Mária. The Management of Agricultural Supply in a Centrally Planned Country: The Case of Hungary. *Kettunen, L., ed.,* 1987, pp. 221–30. [G: Hungary]

Selmi, Giovanna Trevisan. Vitivinicoltura italiana e politica comunitaria delle strutture. (The Italian Viti-Vine-Growing and the E.E.C.'s Structures Policy. With English summary.) *Ricerche Econ.,* Jan.-Mar. 1987, 41(1), pp. 123–35. [G: Italy]

Shadlow, John. NSO Data Needs and Involvement in Smallholder Agricultural Statistics. *Barker, P.; Bodman, P. and Remenyl, J., eds.,* 1987, pp. 11–13. [G: Papua New Guinea]

Shahabuddin, Quazi. Interrelationships in the Public Foodgrain Distribution System in Bangladesh—An Econometric Analysis. *Bangladesh Devel. Stud.,* March 1987, 15(1), pp. 57–81. [G: Bangladesh]

Sharples, Jerry A. Efficiency in Commodity Storage: A Discussion. *Kilmer, R. L. and Armbruster, W. J., eds.,* 1987, pp. 286–89. [G: U.S.]

Shideed, Kamil H.; White, Fred C. and Brannen, Stephen J. The Responsiveness of U.S. Corn and Soybean Acreages to Conditional Price Expectations: An Application to the 1985 Farm Bill. *Southern J. Agr. Econ.,* December 1987, 19(2), pp. 153–61. [G: U.S.]

Shumway, C. Richard; Jegasothy, Kandiah and Alexander, William P. Production Interrelationships in Sri Lankan Peasant Agriculture. *Australian J. Agr. Econ.,* April 1987, 31(1), pp. 16–28. [G: Sri Lanka]

Sinclair, Peter W. The North and the North-west: Forestry and Agriculture. *Drummond, I. M.,* 1987, pp. 77–90. [G: Canada]

Sniekers, Peter and Wong, Gordon. The Causality between U.S.A. and Australian Wheat

Prices. *Rev. Marketing Agr. Econ.,* April 1987, 55(1), pp. 37–50. [G: U.S.; Australia]

Srinivasan, T. N. Population and Food. *Johnson, D. G. and Lee, R. D., eds.,* 1987, pp. 3–26. [G: Global]

Stolnitz, George J. Technological Prospects and Population Trends: Conclusions. *Espenshade, T. and Stolnitz, G. J., eds.,* 1987, pp. 195–211.

Stubbs, Jean. Gender Issues in Contemporary Cuban Tobacco Farming. *World Devel.,* January 1987, 15(1), pp. 41–65. [G: Cuba]

Taylor, T. Ajibola. Potential and Practice in Food Production Technology Development: Commentary. *Mellor, J. W.; Delgado, C. L. and Blackie, M. J., eds.,* 1987, pp. 161–64. [G: Africa]

Thomson, K. J. Supply Control in a Multi-national Context: Cereals Policy in the EEC. *Kettunen, L., ed.,* 1987, pp. 281–300. [G: EEC]

Thraen, Cameron S. and Hammond, Jerome W. Price Enhancement, Returns Variability, and Supply Response in the U.S. Dairy Sector. *Southern J. Agr. Econ.,* December 1987, 19(2), pp. 83–92. [G: U.S.]

Thurman, Walter N. The Poultry Market: Demand Stability and Industry Structure. *Amer. J. Agr. Econ.,* February 1987, 69(1), pp. 30–37. [G: U.S.]

Timmer, C. Peter. Corn Marketing. *Timmer, C. P., ed.,* 1987, pp. 201–34. [G: Indonesia]

Timmer, C. Peter. Price Policy and the Political Economy of Markets. *Gittinger, J. P.; Leslie, J. and Hoisington, C., eds.,* 1987, pp. 264–76.

Tobin, James. A Statistical Demand Function for Food in the U.S.A. *Tobin, J. (II),* 1987, 1950, pp. 399–439. [G: U.S.]

Tomich, Thomas P. and Gotsch, Carl H. Private Land Reclamation in Egypt: Development Policy and Project Design. *Food Res. Inst. Stud.,* 1987, 20(2), pp. 107–39. [G: Egypt]

Tømte, Eugen D. and Sand, Cato. The Norwegian Milk Quota System: A General Report. *Kettunen, L., ed.,* 1987, pp. 121–31. [G: Norway]

Tshibaka, Tshikala B. Food Policy and the Choice of Trade Regime: Commentary. *Mellor, J. W.; Delgado, C. L. and Blackie, M. J., eds.,* 1987, pp. 276–77. [G: Africa]

Ulrich, Alvin; Furtan, William Hartley and Schmitz, Andrew. The Cost of a Licensing System Regulation: An Example from Canadian Prairie Agriculture. *J. Polit. Econ.,* February 1987, 95(1), pp. 160–78. [G: Canada]

Vallaeys, Guy, et al. Development and Extension of Agricultural Production Technology. *Mellor, J. W.; Delgado, C. L. and Blackie, M. J., eds.,* 1987, pp. 148–60. [G: Africa]

Vamoer, Alexander P. Defining the Food and Nutrition Problem: Commentary. *Mellor, J. W.; Delgado, C. L. and Blackie, M. J., eds.,* 1987, pp. 53–56. [G: Africa]

Van Der Willigen, Tessa A. Cash Crop Production and the Balance of Trade in a Less Developed Economy: A Model of Temporary Equilibrium with Rationing. *Sinclair, P. J. N., ed.,* 1987, *1986,* pp. 452–70.

Veeman, Michele M. Hedonic Price Functions for Wheat in the World Market: Implications for Canadian Wheat Export Strategy. *Can. J. Agr. Econ.,* November 1987, *35*(3), pp. 535–52.

Verma, B. N. and Bromley, Daniel W. The Political Economy of Farm Size in India: The Elusive Quest. *Econ. Develop. Cult. Change,* July 1987, *35*(4), pp. 791–808.   **[G: India]**

Viniegra Gonzalez, Gustavo. Generating and Disseminating Technology. *Austin, J. E. and Esteva, G., eds.,* 1987, pp. 133–47.
                                          [G: Mexico]

Wagstaff, Howard. Implementing a Two-Tier Price System for Regulating Production and Incomes in Agriculture. *Kettunen, L., ed.,* 1987, pp. 353–62.   **[G: EEC]**

Waller, William T., Jr. Transfer Program Structure and Effectiveness. *J. Econ. Issues,* June 1987, *21*(2), pp. 775–83.   **[G: U.S.]**

Wanmali, Sudhir. Agriculture and Central Physical Grid Infrastructure: Commentary. *Mellor, J. W.; Delgado, C. L. and Blackie, M. J., eds.,* 1987, pp. 227–32.   **[G: Africa]**

Westcott, Paul C.; Stillman, Richard P. and Collins, Keith J. Quarterly Livestock Sector Adjustments to Changes in Feed Grain Prices. *Agr. Econ. Res.,* Winter 1987, *39*(1), pp. 13–24.   **[G: U.S.]**

Whatley, Warren C. Southern Agrarian Labor Contracts as Impediments to Cotton Mechanization. *J. Econ. Hist.,* March 1987, *47*(1), pp. 45–70.   **[G: U.S.]**

White, B. Forecasting Milk Output in England and Wales. *J. Agr. Econ.,* May 1987, *38*(2), pp. 223–34.   **[G: U.K.]**

Wohlgenant, Michael K. and Mullen, John D. Modeling the Farm–Retail Price Spread for Beef. *Western J. Agr. Econ.,* December 1987, *12*(2), pp. 119–25.   **[G: U.S.]**

Wolf, Edward C. Raising Agricultural Productivity. *Brown, L. R., et al.,* 1987, pp. 139–56.
                                          [G: Global]

Zanias, George P. Dynamic Interrelated Demand Functions for Factors of Production and the Aggregate Production Function in United Kingdom Agriculture. *J. Agr. Econ.,* May 1987, *38*(2), pp. 211–21.   **[G: U.K.]**

712 Agricultural Situation and Outlook

7120 Agricultural Situation and Outlook

Allen, Joyce E. The Role of Alternative Agricultural Enterprises in a Changing Agricultural Economy: Discussion. *Southern J. Agr. Econ.,* July 1987, *19*(1), pp. 17–20.   **[G: U.S.]**

Austin, James E. and Esteva, Gustavo. Food Policy in Mexico: The Search for Self-sufficiency: The Path of Exploration. *Austin, J. E. and Esteva, G., eds.,* 1987, pp. 13–19. **[G: Mexico]**

Babb, Emerson M. and Long, B. F. The Role of Alternative Agricultural Enterprises in a Changing Agricultural Economy. *Southern J.*

Agr. Econ., July 1987, *19*(1), pp. 7–15.
                                          [G: U.S.]

Baker, C. B. Changes in Financial Markets and Their Effects on Agriculture. *Fed. Res. Bank St. Louis Rev.,* October 1987, *69*(8), pp. 13–19.   **[G: U.S.]**

Binswanger, Hans P. and Pingali, Prabhu L. The Evolution of Farming Systems and Agricultural Technology in Sub-Saharan Africa. *Ruttan, V. W. and Pray, C. E., eds.,* 1987, pp. 283–318.   **[G: Sub-Saharan]**

Brown, Lester R. Sustaining World Agriculture. *Brown, L. R., et al.,* 1987, pp. 122–38.
                                          [G: Global]

Carraro, Kenneth C. A Review of the Eighth District's Agricultural Economy in 1986. *Fed. Res. Bank St. Louis Rev.,* April 1987, *69*(4), pp. 5–15.   **[G: U.S.]**

Cuccia, Luis R. and Navajas, Fernando H. Argentina: Crisis, Adjustment Policies and Agricultural Development, 1980–1985. *CEPAL Rev.,* December 1987, (33), pp. 77–82.
                                          [G: Argentina]

Dixon, John A. The Renewable Natural Resource Base. *Martin, L. G., ed.,* 1987, pp. 88–91.
                                          [G: ASEAN]

Dorosh, Paul A., et al. Introduction to the Corn Economy of Indonesia. *Timmer, C. P., ed.,* 1987, pp. 19–37.   **[G: Indonesia]**

Fakiolas, Tassos. Soviet Agriculture: The Problems and Their Causes. Prospects. *Rivista Int. Sci. Econ. Com.,* March 1987, *34*(3), pp. 249–68.   **[G: U.S.S.R.]**

Ferenczi, Tibor. Agricultural Development and the Hungarian Society. *[Marrama, V.], Vol.* 2, 1987, pp. 539–58.   **[G: Hungary]**

Gottfried, Robert R. Can Energy Cane Stem the Tide? *Soc. Econ. Stud.,* September 1987, *36*(3), pp. 177–202.   **[G: Puerto Rico]**

Graham, Douglas H.; Gauthier, Howard and Mendonça de Barros, José Roberto. Thirty Years of Agricultural Growth in Brazil: Crop Performance, Regional Profile, and Recent Policy Review. *Econ. Develop. Cult. Change,* October 1987, *36*(1), pp. 1–34.   **[G: Brazil]**

Griffin, Keith. World Hunger and the World Economy. *Griffin, K.,* 1987, pp. 1–24.
                                          [G: Global]

Ground, Richard L. Agricultural Development and Macroeconomic Balance in Latin America: An Overview of Some Basic Policy Issues. *CEPAL Rev.,* December 1987, (33), pp. 29–38.   **[G: Latin America]**

Hady, Thomas F. Is There a Farm Crisis? *J. Econ. Educ.,* Fall 1987, *18*(4), pp. 409–20.
                                          [G: U.S.]

Hartford, Kathleen. Socialist Countries in the World Food System: The Soviet Union, Hungary, and China. *Food Res. Inst. Stud.,* 1987, *20*(3), pp. 181–243. **[G: U.S.S.R.; Hungary; China]**

Harwood, Richard R. Low Input Technologies for Sustainable Agricultural Systems. *Ruttan, V. W. and Pray, C. E., eds.,* 1987, pp. 319–31.

Iguíñiz, Javier. Peru: Agriculture, Crisis and Macroeconomic Policy. *CEPAL Rev.*, December 1987, (33), pp. 157–70. **[G: Peru]**

Ivanova, Vera. Agroindustrial Complexes and Personal Holdings in Bulgaria—Does That Mean a "Mixed" Policy? *Saunders, C. T., ed.*, 1987, pp. 295–305. **[G: Bulgaria]**

Johnson, D. Gale. IMF Conditionality and Agriculture in the Developing Countries. *Myers, R. J., ed.*, 1987, pp. 127–40. **[G: LDCs]**

Johnson, D. Gale. World Agriculture in Disarray Revisited. *Australian J. Agr. Econ.*, August 1987, *31*(2), pp. 142–53.

Jones, William I. Agriculture's Changing Role in International Trade and Aid: Tastes and Techniques. *Hieronymi, O., ed.*, 1987, pp. 53–68.

Joshi, P. C. Agrarian Constraints Reconsidered. *Joshi, P. C.*, 1987, pp. 287–325. **[G: India]**

Kalter, Robert J. and Tauer, Loren W. Potential Economic Impacts of Agricultural Biotechnology. *Amer. J. Agr. Econ.*, May 1987, *69*(2), pp. 420–25. **[G: U.S.]**

Kerin, John. The Impact of Wages and Industrial Policies on the Performance of the Agricultural Export Industries: Official Opening Speech. *Rev. Marketing Agr. Econ.*, April 1987, 55(1), pp. 74–78. **[G: Australia]**

Kristensen, Thorkil. Landbrugets fremtid. (The Prospects for Danish Agriculture. With English summary.) *Nationaløkon. Tidsskr.*, 1987, *125*(3), pp. 316–20. **[G: Denmark]**

Larkin, Andrew. Institutional Adjustment in Norway's Rural Economy: An Instrumental Evaluation. *J. Econ. Issues*, June 1987, *21*(2), pp. 629–37. **[G: Norway]**

León, Carlos; D'Amato, Laura and Iturregui, María E. El mercado de plaguicidas en la Argentina. (With English summary.) *Desarrollo Econ.*, Apr.-June 1987, *27*(105), pp. 129–44. **[G: Argentina]**

Linnemann, Hans. World Food Prospects till 2000. *Borner, S. and Taylor, A., eds.*, 1987, pp. 87–103.

López Cordovez, Luis. Crisis, Adjustment Policies and Agriculture. *CEPAL Rev.*, December 1987, (33), pp. 7–28. **[G: Latin America]**

Loucks, Daniel P. Water Quality—Economic Modeling. *Braat, L. C. and van Lierop, W. F. J., eds.*, 1987, pp. 135–48.

Mellor, John W.; Delgado, Christopher L. and Blackie, Malcolm J. Priorities for Accelerating Food Production Growth in Sub-Saharan Africa. *Mellor, J. W.; Delgado, C. L. and Blackie, M. J., eds.*, 1987, pp. 353–75. **[G: Africa]**

de Melo, Fernando Homem. The External Crisis, Adjustment Policies and Agricultural Development in Brazil. *CEPAL Rev.*, December 1987, (33), pp. 83–90. **[G: Brazil]**

Murshid, K. A. S. Micro-level Adjustments to Foodgrain Shortages in Bangladesh. *Bangladesh Devel. Stud.*, June 1987, *15*(2), pp. 25–63. **[G: Bangladesh]**

Ølgaard, Anders. Dansk landbrugs fremtid. (The Future Problems of Danish Agriculture. With English summary.) *Nationaløkon. Tidsskr.*, 1987, *125*(2), pp. 171–84. **[G: Denmark; EEC]**

Oskam, Arie J. and van der Stelt-Scheele, D. D. Two Years of Experience with the EC Super Levy System: A Quantitative Analysis of Recent and Future Policy Alternatives. *Kettunen, L., ed.*, 1987, pp. 77–103. **[G: EEC]**

Owens, Raymond E. The Agricultural Outlook for 1987…Financial Turnaround Unlikely. *Fed. Res. Bank Richmond Econ. Rev.*, Jan./Feb. 1987, *73*(1), pp. 24–31. **[G: U.S.]**

Pearse, Peter H. and Walters, Carl J. Perspectives on the Application of Economic–Ecological Models. *Braat, L. C. and van Lierop, W. F. J., eds.*, 1987, pp. 269–81.

Pearson, Scott R. Portuguese Agricultural Strategies. *Pearson, S. R., et al.*, 1987, pp. 259–71. **[G: Portugal; EEC]**

Plath, Joel C.; Holland, David W. and Carvalho, Joe W. Labor Migration in Southern Africa and Agricultural Development: Some Lessons from Lesotho. *J. Devel. Areas*, January 1987, *21*(2), pp. 159–75. **[G: Lesotho]**

Pringle, W. A. South African Agriculture: A Need for Reform? *S. Afr. J. Econ.*, March 1987, 55(1), pp. 53–62. **[G: S. Africa]**

Raup, Philip M. Structural Change in Agriculture in the United States. *Saunders, C. T., ed.*, 1987, pp. 267–85. **[G: U.S.]**

Ray, George F. The Decline of Primary Producer Power. *Nat. Inst. Econ. Rev.*, August 1987, (121), pp. 40–45. **[G: Global]**

Reimund, Donn and Petrulis, Mindy. Performance of the Agricultural Sector. *U.S.D.A., Econ. Res. Serv., Agr. and Rural Econ. Div.*, 1987, pp. 4.1–30. **[G: U.S.]**

Ros, Jaime and Rodríguez, Gonzalo. Mexico: Study on the Financial Crisis, the Adjustment Policies and Agricultural Development. *CEPAL Rev.*, December 1987, (33), pp. 145–55. **[G: Mexico]**

Runge, Carlisle Ford and Halbach, Daniel W. Neopopulism and the New Agriculture. *Rev. Marketing Agr. Econ.*, August 1987, 55(2), pp. 155–61. **[G: U.S.]**

Salgado, Germánico. Ecuador: Crisis and Adjustment Policies. Their Effect on Agriculture. *CEPAL Rev.*, December 1987, (33), pp. 129–43. **[G: Ecuador]**

Schneider, Matthias. Structural Changes and Current Problems in Austrian Agriculture. *Saunders, C. T., ed.*, 1987, pp. 345–48. **[G: Austria]**

Schuh, G. Edward. The World Food Situation. *Borner, S. and Taylor, A., eds.*, 1987, pp. 65–85. **[G: Global]**

Sediari, Tommaso. Aspects of the Market for Tobacco EEC: Need of Planning. *Kettunen, L., ed.*, 1987, pp. 271–79. **[G: EEC]**

Smith, Matthew G. Entry, Exit, and the Age Distribution of Farm Operators, 1974–82. *J. Agr. Econ. Res.*, Fall 1987, *39*(4), pp. 2–11. **[G: U.S.]**

Tweeten, Luther and Welsh, Mike. The Economics of Agricultural Biotechnology: Discussion. *Amer. J. Agr. Econ.*, May 1987, *69*(2), pp. 440–42. **[G: U.S.]**

Valdés, Alberto. Food Security: A Stabilisation

Problem for Developing Countries. *Borner, S. and Taylor, A., eds.*, 1987, pp. 105–24. **[G: LDCs]**

Villasuso, Juan M. Costa Rica: Crisis, Adjustment Policies and Rural Development. *CEPAL Rev.*, December 1987, (33), pp. 107–13. **[G: Costa Rica]**

Woś, Augustyn. Polish Agriculture in Conditions of Economic Reform. *Kettunen, L., ed.*, 1987, pp. 159–68. **[G: Poland]**

713 Agricultural Policy, Domestic and International

7130 Agricultural Policy, Domestic and International

Abbott, Philip C.; Paarlberg, Philip L. and Sharples, Jerry A. Targeted Agricultural Export Subsidies and Social Welfare. *Amer. J. Agr. Econ.*, November 1987, 69(4), pp. 723–32. **[G: U.S.]**

Adamowicz, M. and Kos, C. Some Aspects of Specialization and Integration of Agriculture and Forestry in Solving the Food Problem in Poland. *Merlo, M., et al., eds.*, 1987, pp. 553–61. **[G: Poland]**

Ahmad, Manzur. Intra-sectoral and Intersectoral Parity Issues in Pricing of Agricultural Crops: A Preliminary Analysis: Comments. *Pakistan Devel. Rev.*, Winter 1987, 26(4), pp. 415–17. **[G: Pakistan]**

Ahmadi-Esfahani, Fredoun Z. and Carter, Colin A. A Dynamic Analysis of U.S. Export Wheat Pricing and Market Shares. *Australian J. Agr. Econ.*, December 1987, 31(3), pp. 191–203. **[G: U.S.]**

de Alcantara, Cynthia Hewitt. Feeding Mexico City. *Austin, J. E. and Esteva, G., eds.*, 1987, pp. 172–99. **[G: Mexico]**

Ali, Ifzal. Rice in Indonesia: Price Policy and Comparative Advantage. *Bull. Indonesian Econ. Stud.*, December 1987, 23(3), pp. 80–99. **[G: Indonesia]**

Alston, Julian M. and Scobie, Grant M. A Differentiated Goods Model of the Effects of European Policies in International Poultry Markets. *Southern J. Agr. Econ.*, July 1987, 19(1), pp. 19–68. **[G: EEC]**

Alvarez-Coque, J. M. G. and Barcelo, L. V. The Welfare Evaluation of the Spanish Price Policy: An Integrated Approach. *Europ. Rev. Agr. Econ.*, 1987, 14(1), pp. 117–34. **[G: Spain]**

Alves, Eliseu. Mobilizing Political Support for the Brazilian Agricultural Research System. *Ruttan, V. W. and Pray, C. E., eds.*, 1987, pp. 363–76. **[G: Brazil]**

Amstutz, Daniel G. Agricultural Reform Efforts in the United States and Japan: Remarks. *Johnson, D. G., ed.*, 1987, pp. 82–87. **[G: U.S.; Japan]**

Anderson, Kym and Tyers, Rodney. Japan's Agricultural Policy in International Perspective. *J. Japanese Int. Economies*, June 1987, 1(2), pp. 131–46. **[G: Japan]**

Anderson, Kym and Warr, Peter G. General

Equilibrium Effects of Agricultural Price Distortions: A Simple Model for Korea. *Food Res. Inst. Stud.*, 1987, 20(3), pp. 245–63. **[G: S. Korea]**

Andrade, Armando and Blanc, Nicole. SAM's Cost and Impact on Production. *Austin, J. E. and Esteva, G., eds.*, 1987, pp. 215–48. **[G: Mexico]**

Aradhyula, Satheesh V. Rational Expectations and Policy Modeling: The Case of Wheat in India. *J. Policy Modeling*, Winter 1987, 9(4), pp. 667–70. **[G: India]**

Atkinson, Roy. Farm Policy: The Good, the Bad and the Devastating. *Can. J. Agr. Econ.*, May 1987, 34, pp. 127–39. **[G: Canada]**

Atsain, Achi. Food Policy and the Choice of Trade Regime: Commentary. *Mellor, J. W.; Delgado, C. L. and Blackie, M. J., eds.*, 1987, pp. 274–75. **[G: Africa]**

Austin, James E. and Esteva, Gustavo. Food Policy in Mexico: The Search for Self-sufficiency: Final Reflections. *Austin, J. E. and Esteva, G., eds.*, 1987, pp. 353–73. **[G: Mexico]**

Austin, James E. and Esteva, Gustavo. Food Policy in Mexico: The Search for Self-sufficiency: The Path of Exploration. *Austin, J. E. and Esteva, G., eds.*, 1987, pp. 13–19. **[G: Mexico]**

Austin, James E. and Fox, Jonathan. State-Owned Enterprises: Food Policy Implementers. *Austin, J. E. and Esteva, G., eds.*, 1987, pp. 61–91. **[G: Mexico]**

Babb, Emerson M. The Science and Art of Efficiency Analysis: The Role of Other Performance Criteria: A Discussion. *Kilmer, R. L. and Armbruster, W. J., eds.*, 1987, pp. 88–90.

Balassa, Bela. China's Economic Reforms in a Comparative Perspective. *J. Compar. Econ.*, September 1987, 11(3), pp. 410–26. **[G: China]**

Balisacan, Arsenio M.; Lee, Chung H. and Roumasset, James A. National Food Policies of the Asia-Pacific Region and Their International Implications. *Dutta, M., ed. (I)*, 1987, pp. 221–41. **[G: Asia-Pacific]**

Balisacan, Arsenio M. and Roumasset, James A. Public Choice of Economic Policy: The Growth of Agricultural Protection. *Weltwirtsch. Arch.*, 1987, 123(2), pp. 232–48. **[G: Global]**

Barkin, David. SAM and Seeds. *Austin, J. E. and Esteva, G., eds.*, 1987, pp. 111–32. **[G: Mexico]**

Bartoli, Pierre. L'agriculture dans le développement économique et les politiques communautaires en Méditerranée. (Agriculture in the Economic Development and E.E.C. Policies in the Mediterranean. With English summary.) *Écon. Soc.*, July 1987, 21(7), pp. 111–48. **[G: EEC]**

Bates, Robert H. Pressure Groups, Public Policy, and Agricultural Development: A Study of Divergent Outcomes. *Bates, R. H., 1987, 1980*, pp. 61–91. **[G: Ghana; Kenya]**

Bates, Robert H. The Nature and Origins of Agricultural Policies in Africa. *Bates, R. H., 1987*, pp. 107–33. **[G: Africa]**

Bender, P. J. and Shute, J. C. M. Perceptions of Agricultural Extension in Santa Cruz, Bolivia: An Identity Crisis Revealed. *Can. J. Devel. Stud.*, 1987, 8(2), pp. 317–27.
[G: Bolivia]

Bernegger, Urs. Experience with the Milk Quota System in Switzerland. *Kettunen, L., ed.*, 1987, pp. 19–28. [G: Switzerland]

Bevan, D. L., et al. Peasant Supply Response in Rationed Economies. *World Devel.*, April 1987, 15(4), pp. 431–39. [G: LDCs]

Bhati, U. N. Supply and Demand Responses for Poultry Meat in Australia. *Australian J. Agr. Econ.*, December 1987, 31(3), pp. 256–65.
[G: Australia]

Bienen, Henry. Domestic Political Considerations for Food Policy. *Mellor, J. W.; Delgado, C. L. and Blackie, M. J., eds.*, 1987, pp. 296–308. [G: Africa]

Bigman, David. Targeted Subsidy Programs under Instability: A Simulation and an Illustration for Pakistan. *J. Policy Modeling*, Fall 1987, 9(3), pp. 483–501. [G: Pakistan]

Bigman, David. The Theory of Variable Levies. *Oxford Econ. Pap.*, June 1987, 39(2), pp. 357–77.

Bockstael, Nancy E. Economic Efficiency Issues of Grading and Minimum Quality Standards. *Kilmer, R. L. and Armbruster, W. J., eds.*, 1987, pp. 231–50. [G: U.S.]

Bogomolov, Oleg T. Agricultural Policies in European CMEA Countries and Their International Aspects. *Saunders, C. T., ed.*, 1987, pp. 287–94. [G: CMEA]

Bonnen, James T. A Century of Science in Agriculture: Lessons for Science Policy. *Ruttan, V. W. and Pray, C. E., eds.*, 1987, pp. 105–37. [G: U.S.]

Bornstein, Morris. Soviet Price Policies. *Soviet Econ.*, April-June 1987, 3(2), pp. 96–134.
[G: U.S.S.R.]

Braverman, Avishay; Hammer, Jeffrey S. and Gron, Anne. Multimarket Analysis of Agricultural Price Policies in an Operational Context: The Case of Cyprus. *World Bank Econ. Rev.*, January 1987, 1(2), pp. 337–56. [G: Cyprus]

Braverman, Avishay and Kanbur, S. M. Ravi. Urban Bias and the Political Economy of Agricultural Reform. *World Devel.*, September 1987, 15(9), pp. 1179–87. [G: LDCs]

Breimyer, Harold F. The Farmers' Split Personality on Trade. *Challenge*, July/Aug. 1987, 30(3), pp. 56–59. [G: U.S.]

Brown, David L. and Deavers, Kenneth L. Rural Change and the Rural Economic Policy Agenda for the 1980's. *U.S.D.A., Econ. Res. Serv., Agr. and Rural Econ. Div.*, 1987, pp. 1.1–31.
[G: U.S.]

Buchholz, H. E. Research Investments in New Products: Bioethanol and Industrial Use of Agricultural Products. *Kettunen, L., ed.*, 1987, pp. 249–69.

Burmeister, Larry L. The South Korean Green Revolution: Induced or Directed Innovation? *Econ. Develop. Cult. Change*, July 1987, 35(4), pp. 767–90. [G: S. Korea]

Burniaux, Jean Marc. Does the European Agricultural Lobby Retard Economic Recovery? A General Equilibrium Approach. *Econ. Notes*, 1987, (1), pp. 72–99. [G: EEC]

Burrell, Alison. EC Agricultural Surpluses and Budget Control. *J. Agr. Econ.*, January 1987, 38(1), pp. 1–14. [G: EEC]

Byerlee, Derek. The Political Economy of Third World Food Imports: The Case of Wheat. *Econ. Develop. Cult. Change*, January 1987, 35(2), pp. 307–28. [G: LDCs]

Carter, Colin A. and Mooney, W. Japanese Tariff Protection of Rapeseed and Soybean Processing. *Can. J. Agr. Econ.*, July 1987, 35(2), pp. 305–15. [G: Japan]

Carter, Michael R. Risk Sharing and Incentives in the Decollectivization of Agriculture. *Oxford Econ. Pap.*, September 1987, 39(3), pp. 577–95.

Centner, Terence J. and Wetzstein, Michael E. Reducing Moral Hazard Associated with Implied Warranties of Animal Health. *Amer. J. Agr. Econ.*, February 1987, 69(1), pp. 143–50. [G: U.S.]

Chaney, Elsa M. Women's Components in Integrated Rural Development Projects. *Deere, C. D. and León, M., eds.*, 1987, pp. 191–211.
[G: Jamaica; Dominican Republic]

Clegg, Martin. Notes for Address Concerning the EEC Milk Superlevy and Quota System. *Kettunen, L., ed.*, 1987, pp. 5–17. [G: EEC]

Cloke, P. J. and Little, J. K. Rural Policies in the Gloucestershire Structural Plan: 2. Implementation and the Country–District Relationship. *Environ. Planning A*, August 1987, 19(8), pp. 1027–50. [G: U.K.]

Coffin, H. Garth. The Internationalization of Canadian Agriculture. *Can. J. Agr. Econ.*, December 1987, 35(4), pp. 691–707.
[G: Canada]

Collier, P. The Effect on Agricultural Support Prices of Different Agrimonetary Systems: A Note. *Irish J. Agr. Econ. Rural Soc.*, 1987, 12, pp. 103–06. [G: Ireland]

Collinson, Michael. Potential and Practice in Food Production Technology Development: Commentary. *Mellor, J. W.; Delgado, C. L. and Blackie, M. J., eds.*, 1987, pp. 167–70.
[G: Africa]

Contamin, B. La politique alimentaire de la Tanzanie: le jeu complexe de l'effet-prix. (Food Policy in Tanzania: Complex Play of Price–Effect. With English summary.) *Écon. Soc.*, July 1987, 21(7), pp. 169–84. [G: Tanzania]

Cornelisse, Peter A. and Kuijpers, Bart. A Policy Model of the Wheat and Rice Economy of Pakistan. *Pakistan Devel. Rev.*, Winter 1987, 26(4), pp. 385–96. [G: Pakistan]

Cox, P. G. The Case for Tradeable Milk Production Quotas: A Note. *Irish J. Agr. Econ. Rural Soc.*, 1987, 12, pp. 95–102. [G: EEC]

Crabtree, J. R. Response of UK Milk Producers to the Imposition of Production Quotas. *Kettunen, L., ed.*, 1987, pp. 133–46. [G: U.K.]

Croci-Angelini, Elisabetta and Tarditi, Secondo. Social Costs and Benefits of Price Policies in

Integrated Economies: Impact on Land Use. *Merlo, M., et al., eds.*, 1987, pp. 81–98.
[G: EEC]

Delgado, Christopher L. and Mellor, John W. A Structural View of Policy Issues in African Agricultural Development: Reply. *Amer. J. Agr. Econ.*, May 1987, *69*(2), pp. 389–91.
[G: Africa]

Dietrich, Raymond A.; Amosson, Stephen H. and Crawford, Richard P. Bovine Brucellosis Programs: An Economic/Epidemiologic Analysis. *Can. J. Agr. Econ.*, March 1987, *35*(1), pp. 127–40.
[G: U.S.]

Dubgaard, A. Reconciliation of Agricultural Policy and Environmental Interests in Denmark (Regarding Controls on Nitrogen Fertilizer). *Merlo, M., et al., eds.*, 1987, pp. 535–44.
[G: Denmark]

Edwards, Geoff W. Agricultural Policy Debate: A Survey. *Econ. Rec.*, June 1987, *63*(181), pp. 129–43.
[G: Australia]

Edwards, Geoff W. U.S. Farm Policy: An Australian Perspective. *Fed. Res. Bank St. Louis Rev.*, October 1987, *69*(8), pp. 20–31.
[G: U.S.; Australia]

Eggleston, Robert C. Determinants of the Levels and Distribution of PL 480 Food Aid: 1955–79. *World Devel.*, June 1987, *15*(6), pp. 797–808.
[G: U.S.]

Eicher, Carl K. Food Price Policy and Equity: Commentary. *Mellor, J. W.; Delgado, C. L. and Blackie, M. J., eds.*, 1987, pp. 290–92.
[G: Africa]

Elliott, Howard. The Use of Events Analysis in Evaluating National Research Systems. *Ruttan, V. W. and Pray, C. E., eds.*, 1987, pp. 377–87.
[G: Panama]

Esfahani, Hadi Salehi. Technical Change, Employment, and Supply Response of Agriculture in the Nile Delta: A System-Wide Approach. *J. Devel. Econ.*, February 1987, *25*(1), pp. 167–96.
[G: Egypt]

Esteva, Gustavo. Food Needs and Capacities: Four Centuries of Conflict. *Austin, J. E. and Esteva, G., eds.*, 1987, pp. 23–47.
[G: Mexico]

Evans, Lewis. Farming in a Changing Economic Environment. *Bollard, A. and Buckle, R., eds.*, 1987, pp. 102–20.
[G: New Zealand]

Faminow, Merle D. and Hillman, Jimmye S. Embargoes and the Emergence of Brazil's Soyabean Industry. *World Econ.*, September 1987, *10*(3), pp. 351–66.
[G: Brazil]

Farrell, Kenneth R. Policy Issues and Options for Agriculture and Rural America. *Gannon, T. M., ed.*, 1987, pp. 128–37.
[G: U.S.]

Feder, Gershon; Lau, Lawrence J. and Slade, Roger H. Does Agricultural Extension Pay? The Training and Visit System in Northwest India. *Amer. J. Agr. Econ.*, August 1987, *69*(3), pp. 677–86.
[G: India]

Feller, Irwin. Technology Transfer, Public Policy, and the Cooperative Extension Service. *Ruttan, V. W. and Pray, C. E., eds.*, 1987, pp. 175–210.
[G: U.S.]

Feller, Irwin. Technology Transfer, Public Policy,

and the Cooperative Extension Service-OMB Imbroglio. *J. Policy Anal. Manage.*, Spring 1987, *6*(3), pp. 307–27.
[G: U.S.]

Fennell, Rosemary. Reform of the CAP: Shadow or Substance? *J. Common Market Stud.*, September 1987, *26*(1), pp. 61–77.
[G: EEC]

Fesl, J. The Austrian Dairy System. *Kettunen, L., ed.*, 1987, pp. 63–68.
[G: Austria]

Filius, A. M. Forestry Incentives in the Netherlands. *Merlo, M., et al., eds.*, 1987, pp. 433–43.
[G: Netherlands]

Finan, Timothy J. Portuguese Agriculture in Transition: Intensive Agriculture in the Northwest. *Pearson, S. R., et al.*, 1987, pp. 141–63.
[G: Portugal]

Fischer, Herbert and Sydow, Peter. Structural Policies for Agriculture: Comment. *Saunders, C. T., ed.*, 1987, pp. 343–44. [G: Bulgaria]

Fontaine, Jean-Marc. Les projets de libéralisation des agricultures africaines. Un point de vue critique appuyé sur les cas kenyan et tanzanien. (On Economic Liberalism and African Agriculture. With English summary.) *Écon. Soc.*, July 1987, *21*(7), pp. 185–208.
[G: Kenya; Tanzania]

Fox, Glenn. An Economic Assessment of the Impact of Alachlor Deregistration on Corn and Soybean Producers in Ontario. *Can. J. Agr. Econ.*, July 1987, *35*(2), pp. 317–31.
[G: Canada]

Fox, Glenn. Models of Resource Allocation in Public Agricultural Research: A Survey. *J. Agr. Econ.*, September 1987, *38*(3), pp. 449–62.

Franzmeyer, Fritz. Structural Policies for Agriculture: Comment. *Saunders, C. T., ed.*, 1987, pp. 342–43.

Freshwater, David. Farm Finance and the Public Sector: A Macroeconomic Perspective. *Can. J. Agr. Econ.*, December 1987, *35*(4), pp. 709–33.
[G: U.S.; Canada]

Fulton, Murray. Canadian Agricultural Policy. *Can. J. Agr. Econ.*, May 1987, *34*, pp. 109–26.
[G: Canada]

Furuseth, Owen J. Public Attitudes toward Local Farmland Protection Programs. *Growth Change*, Summer 1987, *18*(3), pp. 49–61.
[G: U.S.]

Gardner, Bruce L. Causes of U.S. Farm Commodity Programs. *J. Polit. Econ.*, April 1987, *95*(2), pp. 290–310.
[G: U.S.]

Gerritsen, Rolf and Murray, Anabel. Rural Policy Survey, 1986: The Battle for the Agenda. *Rev. Marketing Agr. Econ.*, April 1987, *55*(1), pp. 7–23.
[G: Australia]

Ghai, Dharam and Smith, Lawrence. Food Price Policy and Equity. *Mellor, J. W.; Delgado, C. L. and Blackie, M. J., eds.*, 1987, pp. 278–89.
[G: Africa]

Giaever, Harald. Attempts to Predict Farmers' Responses to Government Policy Measures through Linear Programming Models. *Kettunen, L., ed.*, 1987, pp. 323–30. [G: Norway]

Gibson, Bill; Lustig, Nora and Taylor, Lance. SAM's Impact on Income Distribution. *Austin, J. E. and Esteva, G., eds.*, 1987, pp. 298–311.
[G: Mexico]

van der Giessen, L. B. and Post, J. H. Micro- and Macro-effects of the Super Levy in the Netherlands. *Kettunen, L., ed.*, 1987, pp. 105–20. **[G: Netherlands]**

Gilbert, Christopher L. International Commodity Agreements: Design and Performance. *World Devel.*, May 1987, *15*(5), pp. 591–616. **[G: LDCs]**

Glover, David J. Increasing the Benefits to Small-holders from Contract Farming: Problems for Farmers' Organizations and Policy Makers. *World Devel.*, April 1987, *15*(4), pp. 441–48. **[G: LDCs]**

Goodman, Louis W. Food Transnational Corporations and Developing Countries: The Case of the Improved Seed Industry in Mexico. *Ruttan, V. W. and Pray, C. E., eds.*, 1987, pp. 433–49. **[G: Mexico]**

Gordon, Kathryn and Oriach, Philippe. Politique agricole américaine et macro-économie. (American Agricultural Policy and the Macro-economy. With English summary.) *Écon. Soc.*, July 1987, *21*(7), pp. 37–55. **[G: U.S.]**

de Gorter, Harry. Agricultural Policies and International Trade Negotiations: Research Issues. *Can. J. Agr. Econ.*, May 1987, *34*, pp. 280–94. **[G: Canada; U.S.; EEC]**

de Gorter, Harry and Meilke, Karl D. The EEC's Wheat Price Policies and International Trade in Differentiated Products. *Amer. J. Agr. Econ.*, May 1987, *69*(2), pp. 223–29. **[G: EEC]**

Gottfried, Robert R. Can Energy Cane Stem the Tide? *Soc. Econ. Stud.*, September 1987, *36*(3), pp. 177–202. **[G: Puerto Rico]**

Gould, Peter. Agricultural Issues in a Comprehensive Canada–U.S. Trade Agreement: A Canadian Perspective: A Response. *Can. J. Agr. Econ.*, May 1987, *34*, pp. 230–32. **[G: Canada]**

Graham, Douglas H.; Gauthier, Howard and Mendonça de Barros, José Roberto. Thirty Years of Agricultural Growth in Brazil: Crop Performance, Regional Profile, and Recent Policy Review. *Econ. Develop. Cult. Change*, October 1987, *36*(1), pp. 1–34. **[G: Brazil]**

Greco, Anthony J. State Fluid Milk Regulation: Antitrust and Price Controls. *Antitrust Bull.*, Spring 1987, *32*(1), pp. 165–88. **[G: U.S.]**

Greenwald, Joseph A. Dealing with the Agricultural Trade Crisis in the Uruguay Round Negotiations. *World Econ.*, June 1987, *10*(2), pp. 227–28. **[G: Global]**

Ground, Richard L. Agricultural Development and Macroeconomic Balance in Latin America: An Overview of Some Basic Policy Issues. *CEPAL Rev.*, December 1987, (33), pp. 29–38. **[G: Latin America]**

Hall, Anthony. Agrarian Crisis in Brazilian Amazonia: The Grande Carajás Programme. *J. Devel. Stud.*, July 1987, *23*(4), pp. 522–52. **[G: Brazil]**

Harker, Trevor. Agricultural Sector Policy and Macro-economic Planning. *CEPAL Rev.*, December 1987, (33), pp. 69–75. **[G: Caribbean]**

Harou, P. A. A Possible Methodology to Justify and Evaluate Production Incentives for Private Forests in the EEC. *Merlo, M., et al., eds.*, 1987, pp. 501–10. **[G: EEC]**

Harrington, David H. Agricultural Programs: Their Contribution to Rural Development and Economic Well-Being. *U.S.D.A., Econ. Res. Serv., Agr. and Rural Econ. Div.*, 1987, pp. 12.1–23. **[G: U.S.]**

Hartford, Kathleen. Socialist Countries in the World Food System: The Soviet Union, Hungary, and China. *Food Res. Inst. Stud.*, *20*(3), pp. 181–243. **[G: U.S.S.R.; Hungary; China]**

Hegrenes, Agnar and Norum, Leopold. Macro-model Calculations of Effects of Different Policy Instruments on Agricultural Output, Resource Use, and Farm Income. *Kettunen, L., ed.*, 1987, pp. 331–41. **[G: Norway]**

Heifner, Richard G. Comments on Economic Efficiency, Public Programs, and Private Strategies. *Kilmer, R. L. and Armbruster, W. J., eds.*, 1987, pp. 290–97.

Helles, F. Aspects of a Grant Scheme for Small Private Woodlands in Denmark. *Merlo, M., et al., eds.*, 1987, pp. 445–54. **[G: Denmark]**

Hellström, Mats. Den nya GATT-rundan: implikationer för protektionism och jordbruk. (The New GATT Round: Implications for Protectionism and Agriculture. With English summary.) *Ekon. Samfundets Tidskr.*, 1987, *40*(2), pp. 71–79. **[G: Global]**

Helms, Gary L.; Bailey, DeeVon and Glover, Terrence F. Government Programs and Adoption of Conservation Tillage Practices on Nonirrigated Wheat Farms. *Amer. J. Agr. Econ.*, November 1987, *69*(4), pp. 786–95. **[G: U.S.]**

Hemmi, Kenzo. Agricultural Reform Efforts in Japan: Political Feasibility and Consequences for Trade with the United States and Third Countries. *Johnson, D. G., ed.*, 1987, pp. 24–46. **[G: Japan; U.S.]**

Herr, Bettina. The Peasant Betrayed: Agriculture and Land Reform in the Third World: Algeria. *Powelson, J. P. and Stock, R.*, 1987, pp. 125–39. **[G: Algeria]**

Hickson, A. B. and Carter, Colin A. An Analysis of Policy Changes in the Canadian Feed Grain Market. *Western J. Agr. Econ.*, December 1987, *12*(2), pp. 126–34. **[G: Canada]**

Hogg, Richard. Settlement, Pastoralism and the Commons: The Ideology and Practice of Irrigation Development in Northern Kenya. *Anderson, D. and Grove, R., eds.*, 1987, pp. 293–306. **[G: Kenya]**

Hopcraft, Peter. Grain Marketing Policies and Institutions in Africa. *Finance Develop.*, March 1987, *24*(1), pp. 37–40. **[G: Africa]**

Hubbard, L. J. The Price of Dairy Quota in England and Wales. *Kettunen, L., ed.*, 1987, pp. 343–51. **[G: U.K.]**

Hueth, Darrell L. and Just, Richard E. Policy Implications of Agricultural Biotechnology. *Amer. J. Agr. Econ.*, May 1987, *69*(2), pp. 426–31. **[G: U.S.]**

Hussain, Zakir. Subsidizing Agricultural Production on Imperfect Markets: Comments. *Pakistan Devel. Rev.*, Winter 1987, *26*(4), pp. 456. [G: Pakistan]

Hybel, Jan. Policy Support to the Development of Production Services in the Individual Agriculture in Poland. *Kettunen, L., ed.*, 1987, pp. 183–94. [G: Poland]

Idachaba, Francis S. Agricultural Research in Nigeria: Organization and Policy. *Ruttan, V. W. and Pray, C. E., eds.*, 1987, pp. 333–62. [G: Nigeria]

Idachaba, Francis S. Agriculture and Central Physical Grid Infrastructure: Commentary. *Mellor, J. W.; Delgado, C. L. and Blackie, M. J., eds.*, 1987, pp. 232–38. [G: Africa]

Iguiñiz, Javier. Peru: Agriculture, Crisis and Macroeconomic Policy. *CEPAL Rev.*, December 1987, (33), pp. 157–70. [G: Peru]

Insley, H. Incentives for Private Forestry in Great Britain. *Merlo, M., et al., eds.*, 1987, pp. 455–63. [G: U.K.]

Ivanova, Vera. Agroindustrial Complexes and Personal Holdings in Bulgaria—Does That Mean a "Mixed" Policy? *Saunders, C. T., ed.*, 1987, pp. 295–305. [G: Bulgaria]

de Janvry, Alain and Sadoulet, Elisabeth. Agricultural Price Policy in General Equilibrium Models: Results and Comparisons. *Amer. J. Agr. Econ.*, May 1987, *69*(2), pp. 230–46. [G: Selected LDCs]

Jesse, Edward V. Economic Efficiency and Marketing Orders. *Kilmer, R. L. and Armbruster, W. J., eds.*, 1987, pp. 217–28. [G: U.S.]

Johnson, D. Gale. Agricultural Reform Efforts in the United States and Japan: Introduction. *Johnson, D. G., ed.*, 1987, pp. 1–4. [G: U.S.; Japan]

Johnson, D. Gale. Agricultural Reform Efforts in the United States and Japan: Concluding Comments. *Johnson, D. G., ed.*, 1987, pp. 88–90. [G: U.S.; Japan]

Johnson, D. Gale. World Agriculture in Disarray Revisited. *Australian J. Agr. Econ.*, August 1987, *31*(2), pp. 142–53.

Johnson, J. A. and Nicholls, D. C. The Value of Fiscal Measures to the Private Woodland Owner in Britain. *Merlo, M., et al., eds.*, 1987, pp. 475–86. [G: U.K.]

Jolly, Curtis M. and Diop, Oumar. The Negative Effects of Inappropriate Price Stimulation; the Case of Senegal: Rice Price Increases to Encourage Production May Harm Families of Non-responsive Subsistence Farmers. *Amer. J. Econ. Soc.*, July 1987, *46*(3), pp. 355–68. [G: Senegal]

Jones, William I. Agriculture's Changing Role in International Trade and Aid: Tastes and Techniques. *Hieronymi, O., ed.*, 1987, pp. 53–68.

Joshi, P. C. Institutional and Technological Factors in Agricultural Planning: Reflections on the Mahalanobis Approach. *Joshi, P. C.*, 1987, 1982, pp. 104–31. [G: India]

Josling, Timothy and Tangermann, Stefan. Portuguese Agriculture in Transition: Commodity Policies. *Pearson, S. R., et al.*, 1987, pp. 41–61. [G: Portugal]

Josling, Timothy and Tangermann, Stefan. Portuguese Agriculture in Transition: Future Commodity Policies. *Pearson, S. R., et al.*, 1987, pp. 223–38. [G: Portugal]

Judd, M. Ann; Boyce, James K. and Evenson, Robert E. Investment in Agricultural Research and Extension. *Ruttan, V. W. and Pray, C. E., eds.*, 1987, pp. 7–38. [G: Global]

Kaldor, Nicholas. The Role of Commodity Prices in Economic Recovery. *World Devel.*, May 1987, *15*(5), pp. 551–58. [G: EEC; U.S.]

Kaser, Michael. Structural Policies for Agriculture: Comment. *Saunders, C. T., ed.*, 1987, pp. 340–42.

Kenney, Mary C. Marketing Orders and Efficiency: A Discussion. *Kilmer, R. L. and Armbruster, W. J., eds.*, 1987, pp. 229–30. [G: U.S.]

Kettunen, Lauri. Experiences in Controlling Milk Supply in Finland. *Kettunen, L., ed.*, 1987, pp. 147–57. [G: Finland]

Kim, C. S.; Bolling, Christine and Wainio, John. Import Demand for Feed Grains in Venezuela. *J. Agr. Econ. Res.*, Summer 1987, *39*(3), pp. 12–19. [G: Venezuela; U.S.]

Kirke, A. W. and Moss, J. E. A Linear Programming Study of Family-Run Dairy Farms in Northern Ireland. *J. Agr. Econ.*, May 1987, *38*(2), pp. 257–69. [G: N. Ireland]

Klank, Leszek. Income Disparities among Farm Households and Agricultural Policy in Poland. *Léon, Y. and Mahé, L., eds.*, 1987, pp. 449–62. [G: Poland]

Klein, K. K. and Jetter, F. P. Economic Benefits from the Alberta Warble Control Program. *Can. J. Agr. Econ.*, July 1987, *35*(2), pp. 289–303. [G: Canada]

Knight, Thomas O.; Johnson, Stanley R. and Finley, Robert M. Extension Program Evaluation Using Normative Decision Models. *Amer. J. Agr. Econ.*, May 1987, *69*(2), pp. 338–48. [G: U.S.]

Knight, Thomas O. and Kubiak, Kathryn A. Extension Decision Aids for the Dairy Termination Program: A Comparative Analysis. *Amer. J. Agr. Econ.*, November 1987, *69*(4), pp. 777–85. [G: U.S.]

Koester, Ulrich. How to Open the Common Agricultural Market. *Giersch, H., ed.*, 1987, pp. 515–31. [G: EEC]

Kohl, David M.; Shabman, Leonard A. and Stoevener, Herbert H. Agricultural Transition: Its Implications for Agricultural Economics Extension in the Southeast. *Southern J. Agr. Econ.*, July 1987, *19*(1), pp. 35–43. [G: U.S.]

Kraus, Josef. Can Contract Prices Be Based on Regional Prices? *Soviet E. Europ. Foreign Trade*, Winter 1987-1988, *23*(4), pp. 5–21. [G: EEC]

Kula, Erhun. Prospects for Farmers to Improve Incomes by Switching Crops in N. Ireland: An Analysis to Improve Government Support Schemes. *Léon, Y. and Mahé, L., eds.*, 1987, pp. 297–307. [G: U.K.]

Kumar, Shubh K. The Nutrition Situation and Its Food Policy Links. *Mellor, J. W.; Delgado, C. L. and Blackie, M. J., eds.*, 1987, pp. 39–52. **[G: Africa]**

Landheer, J. D. The Ratio of Fat Value to Non-fat Value of Milk: An Econometric Model of Effects on Intervention Price Changes in the EC. *Europ. Rev. Agr. Econ.*, 1987, *14*(2), pp. 161–78. **[G: EEC]**

Lembit, M. and Bhati, U. N. Farm Cost Effects of Dairy Policies in New South Wales and Victoria. *Rev. Marketing Agr. Econ.*, December 1987, *55*(3), pp. 201–11. **[G: Australia]**

León, Magdalena. Colombian Agricultural Policies and the Debate on Policies toward Rural Women. *Deere, C. D. and León, M., eds.*, 1987, pp. 84–104. **[G: Colombia]**

Leu, Gwo-Jiun M.; Schmitz, Andrew and Knutson, Ronald D. Gains and Losses of Sugar Program Policy Options. *Amer. J. Agr. Econ.*, August 1987, *69*(3), pp. 591–602. **[G: U.S.]**

Lien, Da-Hsiang Donald and Bates, Robert H. Political Behavior in the Coffee Agreement. *Econ. Develop. Cult. Change*, April 1987, *35*(3), pp. 629–36. **[G: Selected Countries]**

Lin, Justin Yifu. The Household Responsibility System Reform in China: A Peasant's Institutional Choice. *Amer. J. Agr. Econ.*, May 1987, *69*(2), pp. 410–15. **[G: China]**

Lipman-Blumen, Jean. Priority Setting in Agricultural Research. *Ruttan, V. W. and Pray, C. E., eds.*, 1987, pp. 139–73. **[G: U.S.]**

Lipton, Michael. Agriculture and Central Physical Grid Infrastructure. *Mellor, J. W.; Delgado, C. L. and Blackie, M. J., eds.*, 1987, pp. 210–26. **[G: Africa]**

Lloyd, A. G. The Australia–New Zealand Farm Problem and the Appropriate Role of Government. *Australian Econ. Rev.*, Third Quarter 1987, (79), pp. 3–20. **[G: Australia; New Zealand]**

Longhurst, Richard. Policy Approaches towards Small Farmers. *Cornia, G. A.; Jolly, R. and Stewart, F., eds.*, 1987, pp. 183–96. **[G: LDCs]**

Lowenberg-DeBoer, J. and Turvey, Calum Greig. A Note on the Changing Tax Treatment of Farmland Capital Gains and Losses in Canada and the United States. *Can. J. Agr. Econ.*, November 1987, *35*(3), pp. 605–13. **[G: U.S.; Canada]**

MacBean, Alasdair and Nguyen, Duc Tin. International Commodity Agreements: Shadow and Substance. *World Devel.*, May 1987, *15*(5), pp. 575–90. **[G: LDCs]**

Mahé, Louis. The Common Agricultural Policy: A French Point of View. *Saunders, C. T., ed.*, 1987, pp. 323–40. **[G: France]**

Mahé, Louis and Moreddu, Catherine. An Illustrative Trade Model to Analyse CAP Changes: Unilateral Moves and Interaction with USA. *Econ. Notes*, 1987, (1), pp. 52–71. **[G: EEC; U.S.]**

Manegold, D. Aspects of Agricultural Policy in the European Community 1986/87. *Rev. Mar-*keting Agr. Econ., August 1987, *55*(2), pp. 117–39. **[G: EEC]**

Marceau, Ian. Privatization of Agriculture and Agribusiness. *Hanke, S. H., ed.*, 1987, pp. 141–48.

Marggraf, Rainer and Zingel, Wolfgang-Peter. Subsidizing Agricultural Production on Imperfect Markets. *Pakistan Devel. Rev.*, Winter 1987, *26*(4), pp. 447–55. **[G: Pakistan]**

Markkola, Usko and Mäkinen, Paavo. Finnish Quota System. *Kettunen, L., ed.*, 1987, pp. 55–61. **[G: Finland]**

Marsh, John S. A British View of the Common Agricultural Policy (CAP). *Saunders, C. T., ed.*, 1987, pp. 307–22. **[G: U.K.]**

Marsh, John S. Alternative Policies for Agriculture in Europe. *Europ. Rev. Agr. Econ.*, 1987, *14*(1), pp. 11–21. **[G: EEC]**

Maruyama, Magoroh. Japan's Agricultural Policy Failure. *Challenge*, Jan./Feb. 1987, *29*(6), pp. 50–52. **[G: Japan]**

Mathiesen, Lars. International Trade in Grains: Domestic Policies and Trade Impacts: Comment. *Scand. J. Econ.*, 1987, *89*(3), pp. 285–86. **[G: Global]**

McBain, Helen. The Impact of the Bauxite–Alumina MNCs on Rural Jamaica: Constraints on Development of Small Farmers in Jamaica. *Soc. Econ. Stud.*, March 1987, *36*(1), pp. 137–70. **[G: Jamaica]**

McMahon, Gary. Does a Small Developing Country Benefit from International Commodity Agreements? The Case of Coffee and Kenya. *Econ. Develop. Cult. Change*, January 1987, *35*(2), pp. 409–23. **[G: Kenya]**

Medellin E., Rodrigo A. The Peasant Initiative. *Austin, J. E. and Esteva, G., eds.*, 1987, pp. 148–71. **[G: Mexico]**

Meester, Gerrit. Budgetary Constraints and International Realities in the CAP. *Europ. Rev. Agr. Econ.*, 1987, *14*(1), pp. 37–47. **[G: EEC]**

Mellor, John W.; Delgado, Christopher L. and Blackie, Malcolm J. Priorities for Accelerating Food Production Growth in Sub-Saharan Africa. *Mellor, J. W.; Delgado, C. L. and Blackie, M. J., eds.*, 1987, pp. 353–75. **[G: Africa]**

de Melo, Fernando Homem. The External Crisis, Adjustment Policies and Agricultural Development in Brazil. *CEPAL Rev.*, December 1987, (33), pp. 83–90. **[G: Brazil]**

Merkel, Konrad. The East German Economy: Agriculture. *Jeffries, I. and Melzer, M., eds.*, 1987, pp. 202–34. **[G: E. Germany]**

Merriam, John G. Egyptian Agricultural Energy Incentives. *Pachauri, R. K., ed.*, 1987, pp. 255–70. **[G: Egypt]**

Mészáros, Sándor. Possibility of an Export Oriented Price Policy as a Tool of Supply Management. *Kettunen, L., ed.*, 1987, pp. 205–19. **[G: Hungary]**

Millington, Andrew C. Environmental Degradation, Soil Conservation and Agricultural Policies in Sierra Leone, 1895–1984. *Anderson, D. and Grove, R., eds.*, 1987, pp. 229–48. **[G: Sierra Leone]**

Milon, J. Walter. The Science and Art of Efficiency Analysis: The Role of Other Performance Criteria. *Kilmer, R. L. and Armbruster, W. J., eds.*, 1987, pp. 67–87.

Mohammad, Faiz. Agricultural Taxation in Pakistan Revisited. *Pakistan Devel. Rev.*, Winter 1987, *26*(4), pp. 419–29. **[G: Pakistan]**

Monke, Eric A. Portuguese Agriculture in Transition: Future Policies Influencing Agricultural Factor Markets. *Pearson, S. R., et al.*, 1987, pp. 239–58. **[G: Portugal]**

Monke, Eric A.; Cory, Dennis C. and Heckerman, Donald G. Surplus Disposal in World Markets: An Application to Egyptian Cotton. *Amer. J. Agr. Econ.*, August 1987, *69*(3), pp. 570–79. **[G: Egypt]**

Montanari, Mario. The Conception of SAM. *Austin, J. E. and Esteva, G., eds.*, 1987, pp. 48–58. **[G: Mexico]**

Moore, Thomas Gale. Farm Policy: Justifications, Failures and the Need for Reform. *Fed. Res. Bank St. Louis Rev.*, October 1987, *69*(8), pp. 5–12. **[G: U.S.]**

Moschini, Giancarlo. Least-Cost Subsidization Alternatives: Comment. *Amer. J. Agr. Econ.*, February 1987, *69*(1), pp. 187.

da Motta, Ronaldo Serôa. Um estudo de custo–benefício do PROÁLCOOL. (With English summary.) *Pesquisa Planejamento Econ.*, April 1987, *17*(1), pp. 65–92. **[G: Brazil]**

Muleya, Benson Kabeta. Domestic Political Considerations for Food Policy: Commentary. *Mellor, J. W.; Delgado, C. L. and Blackie, M. J., eds.*, 1987, pp. 309–10. **[G: Africa]**

Mumbengegwi, Clever. Food and Agriculture Cooperation in the SADCC: Progress, Problems and Prospects. *Amin, S.; Chitala, D. and Mandaza, I., eds.*, 1987, pp. 62–84. **[G: Southern Africa]**

Mupawose, Robbie M. Potential and Practice in Food Production Technology Development: Commentary. *Mellor, J. W.; Delgado, C. L. and Blackie, M. J., eds.*, 1987, pp. 164–67. **[G: Africa]**

Narayana, N. S. S.; Parikh, Kirit S. and Srinivasan, T. N. Indian Agricultural Policy: An Applied General Equilibrium Model. *J. Policy Modeling*, Winter 1987, *9*(4), pp. 527–58. **[G: India]**

Ndegwa, Philip. Domestic Political Considerations for Food Policy: Commentary. *Mellor, J. W.; Delgado, C. L. and Blackie, M. J., eds.*, 1987, pp. 310–13. **[G: Africa]**

Nelson, Carl H. and Loehman, Edna T. Further toward a Theory of Agricultural Insurance. *Amer. J. Agr. Econ.*, August 1987, *69*(3), pp. 523–31.

Nichols, John P. Economic Efficiency Issues of Grading and Minimum Quality Standards: A Discussion. *Kilmer, R. L. and Armbruster, W. J., eds.*, 1987, pp. 251–55. **[G: U.S.]**

Nieuwoudt, W. L. Allocation of Beef Permits and Quotas. *S. Afr. J. Econ.*, September 1987, *55*(3), pp. 278–85. **[G: S. Africa]**

Nieuwoudt, W. L. and Frank, D. B. An Economic Evaluation of Alternative Maize Poli-

cies. *S. Afr. J. Econ.*, December 1987, *55*(4), pp. 355–69. **[G: S. Africa]**

Norton, George W.; Ganoza, Victor G. and Pomareda, Carlos. Potential Benefits of Agricultural Research and Extension in Peru. *Amer. J. Agr. Econ.*, May 1987, *69*(2), pp. 247–57. **[G: Peru]**

Nyankori, James C. O.; Rosson, C. Parr and Rathwell, P. J. Estimates of the Effects of Canadian Tariff on Fresh Peach Imports from the United States. *Can. J. Agr. Econ.*, March 1987, *35*(1), pp. 75–87. **[G: Canada; U.S.]**

Ohkawa, Kazushi. Domestic Political Considerations for Food Policy: Commentary. *Mellor, J. W.; Delgado, C. L. and Blackie, M. J., eds.*, 1987, pp. 313–18. **[G: Africa]**

Okuniewski, Jósef. The Use of Planning and of the Market to Achieve a Growth of Agricultural Production in Poland. *Kettunen, L., ed.*, 1987, pp. 169–81. **[G: Poland]**

Oleson, Brian T. and Brooks, H. G. Canadian Wheat Board Proposal: Basis Change for Initial Payment Freight Deductions. *Can. J. Agr. Econ.*, May 1987, *34*, pp. 83–98. **[G: Canada]**

Ølgaard, Anders. Dansk landbrugs fremtid. (The Future Problems of Danish Agriculture. With English summary.) *Nationaløkon. Tidsskr.*, 1987, *125*(2), pp. 171–84. **[G: Denmark; EEC]**

Ortmann, G. F. and Nieuwoudt, W. L. An Evaluation of a Two-Tier Price Scheme and Possible Ethanol Production in the South African Sugar Industry. *S. Afr. J. Econ.*, June 1987, *55*(2), pp. 121–35. **[G: S. Africa]**

Ortmann, G. F. and Nieuwoudt, W. L. Estimating Social Costs of Alternative Sugar Policies in South Africa. *J. Agr. Econ.*, May 1987, *38*(2), pp. 303–13. **[G: S. Africa]**

Ortner, K. M. An Outline of the Milk Quota Policy in Austria. *Kettunen, L., ed.*, 1987, pp. 69–75. **[G: Austria]**

Oskam, Arie J. and van der Stelt-Scheele, D. D. Two Years of Experience with the EC Super Levy System: A Quantitative Analysis of Recent and Future Policy Alternatives. *Kettunen, L., ed.*, 1987, pp. 77–103. **[G: EEC]**

Østeras, Magne. The GATT International Dairy Arrangement. *Kettunen, L., ed.*, 1987, pp. 231–48.

Owens, Raymond E. An Overview of Agricultural Policy...Past, Present, and Future. *Fed. Res. Bank Richmond Econ. Rev.*, May/June 1987, *73*(3), pp. 39–50. **[G: U.S.]**

Oyejide, T. Ademola. Food Policy and the Choice of Trade Regime. *Mellor, J. W.; Delgado, C. L. and Blackie, M. J., eds.*, 1987, pp. 257–73. **[G: Africa]**

Padilla, Martha Luz; Murguialday, Clara and Criquillon, Ana. Impact of the Sandinista Agrarian Reform on Rural Women's Subordination. *Deere, C. D. and León, M., eds.*, 1987, pp. 124–41. **[G: Nicaragua]**

Pearson, Scott R. Portuguese Agricultural Strategies. *Pearson, S. R., et al.*, 1987, pp. 259–71. **[G: Portugal; EEC]**

Pearson, Scott R. Portuguese Agriculture in Transition: Methods of Analysis. *Pearson, S. R., et al.*, 1987, pp. 29–40. [G: Portugal]

Petrakov, Nikolay. Prospects for Change in the Systems of Price Formation, Finance and Credit in the USSR. *Soviet Econ.*, April-June 1987, *3*(2), pp. 135–44. [G: U.S.S.R.]

Phillips, Lynne. Women, Development, and the State in Rural Ecuador. *Deere, C. D. and León, M., eds.*, 1987, pp. 105–23. [G: Ecuador]

Pinckney, Thomas C.; Cohen, John M. and Leonard, David K. Kenya's Introduction of Microcomputers to Improve Budgeting and Financial Management in the Ministry of Agriculture. *Ruth, S. R. and Mann, C. K., eds.*, 1987, pp. 67–93. [G: Kenya]

Pinckney, Thomas C. and Gotsch, Carl H. Simulation and Optimization of Price Stabilization Policies: Maize in Kenya. *Food Res. Inst. Stud.*, 1987, *20*(3), pp. 265–98. [G: Kenya]

Pitts, E.; Haines, M. and Jenkins, T. N. Dairy Industry Structure and Milk Price Comparisons: A Comment. *J. Agr. Econ.*, September 1987, *38*(3), pp. 505–08. [G: U.K.]

Polopolus, Leo C. Agricultural Transition and Implications for Agricultural Economics Extension Programs: Discussion. *Southern J. Agr. Econ.*, July 1987, *19*(1), pp. 45–47. [G: U.S.]

Prentice, Barry E. Agricultural Issues in a Comprehensive Canada–U.S. Trade Agreement: A Canadian Perspective: A Discussion. *Can. J. Agr. Econ.*, May 1987, *34*, pp. 228–29. [G: Canada]

Puz, Valery. Management in USSR Agriculture: Some Recent Developments. *Kettunen, L., ed.*, 1987, pp. 195–204. [G: U.S.S.R.]

Quaisser, Wolfgang. The New Agricultural Reform in China: From the People's Communes to Peasant Agriculture. *Gey, P.; Kosta, J. and Quaisser, W., eds.*, 1987, pp. 173–96. [G: China]

Quasem, Md. Abul. Farmers' Participation in the Paddy Markets, Their Marketed Surplus and Factors Affecting It in Bangladesh. *Bangladesh Devel. Stud.*, March 1987, *15*(1), pp. 83–1044. [G: Bangladesh]

Qureshi, Sarfraz Khan. Agricultural Taxation in Pakistan Revisited: Comments. *Pakistan Devel. Rev.*, Winter 1987, *26*(4), pp. 430–32. [G: Pakistan]

Qureshi, Sarfraz Khan. Intra-sector and Intersectoral Parity Issues in Pricing of Agricultural Crops: A Preliminary Analysis. *Pakistan Devel. Rev.*, Winter 1987, *26*(4), pp. 401–14. [G: Pakistan]

Rabinowicz, Ewa and Bolin, Olof. Price or Supply Management. *Kettunen, L., ed.*, 1987, pp. 301–09. [G: Sweden]

Raup, Philip M. Structural Change in Agriculture in the United States. *Saunders, C. T., ed.*, 1987, pp. 267–85. [G: U.S.]

Ravallion, Martin. Towards a Theory of Famine Relief Policy. *J. Public Econ.*, June 1987, *33*(1), pp. 21–39. [G: Asia]

Recalde de Bernardi, María Luisa. Precio sostén o subsidio al fertilizante beneficios y costos.

(Price Support or Fertilizer Subsidy: Benefits and Costs. With English summary.) *Económica (La Plata)*, July-Dec. 1987, *33*(2), pp. 185–212. [G: Argentina]

Reeves, George W. World Agricultural Trade and the New GATT Round. *J. Agr. Econ.*, September 1987, *38*(3), pp. 393–405. [G: Global]

Reinhardt, Nola. Agro-exports and the Peasantry in the Agrarian Reforms of El Salvador and Nicaragua. *World Devel.*, July 1987, *15*(7), pp. 941–59. [G: El Salvador; Nicaragua]

Repetto, Robert. Economic Incentives for Sustainable Production. *Ann. Reg. Sci.*, November 1987, *21*(3), pp. 44–59. [G: Africa]

Roarty, Michael J. The Impact of the Common Agricultural Policy on Agricultural Trade and Development. *Nat. Westminster Bank Quart. Rev.*, February 1987, pp. 12–28. [G: EEC]

Robb, Andrew. Non-government Organisations: A Synopsis by the National Farmers' Federation. *Chisholm, A. and Dumsday, R., eds.*, 1987, pp. 268–70. [G: Australia]

Robson, Nigel; Gasson, Ruth and Hill, Berkeley. Part Time Farming—Implications for Farm Family Income. *J. Agr. Econ.*, May 1987, *38*(2), pp. 167–91. [G: U.K.]

Rodríguez, José Luiz. Agricultural Policy and Development in Cuba. *World Devel.*, January 1987, *15*(1), pp. 23–39. [G: Cuba]

Rodríguez, José Luiz. Agricultural Policy and Development in Cuba. *Zimbalist, A., ed.*, 1987, pp. 25–41. [G: Cuba]

Roger, C. L'évaluation de la protection d'une agriculture. (Protection Evaluation in Agriculture. With English summary.) *Écon. Soc.*, April 1987, *21*(4), pp. 127–66. [G: OECD]

Ros, Jaime and Rodríguez, Gonzalo. Mexico: Study on the Financial Crisis, the Adjustment Policies and Agricultural Development. *CEPAL Rev.*, December 1987, (33), pp. 145–55. [G: Mexico]

Rucker, Randal R. and Alston, Lee J. Farm Failures and Government Intervention: A Case Study of the 1930's. *Amer. Econ. Rev.*, September 1987, *77*(4), pp. 724–30. [G: U.S.]

Runge, Carlisle Ford and Halbach, Daniel W. Neopopulism and the New Agriculture. *Rev. Marketing Agr. Econ.*, August 1987, *55*(2), pp. 155–61. [G: U.S.]

Runge, Carlisle Ford and von Witzke, Harald. Institutional Change in the Common Agricultural Policy of the European Community. *Amer. J. Agr. Econ.*, May 1987, *69*(2), pp. 213–22. [G: EEC]

Ruttan, Vernon W. Toward a Global Agricultural Research System. *Ruttan, V. W. and Pray, C. E., eds.*, 1987, pp. 65–97.

Sahn, David E. and von Braun, Joachim. The Relationship between Food Production and Consumption Variability: Policy Implications for Developing Countries. *J. Agr. Econ.*, May 1987, *38*(2), pp. 315–27. [G: LDCs]

Salam, Abdul. A Policy Model of the Wheat and Rice Economy of Pakistan: Comments. *Pakistan Devel. Rev.*, Winter 1987, *26*(4), pp. 397–400. [G: Pakistan]

Salamon, Petra. An Evaluation of the Milk Quota Regime in the Federal Republic of Germany. *Kettunen, L., ed.,* 1987, pp. 29–54.
[G: W. Germany]

Sampson, John A. and Gerrard, Christopher D. Government Interventions and the Production of Wheat in Saskatchewan and North Dakota: An Empirical Analysis. *Can. J. Agr. Econ.,* March 1987, 35(1), pp. 1–20. [G: U.S.; Canada]

Sanderson, Fred H. United States–Japan Negotiating Issues and Opportunities in the GATT. *Johnson, D. G., ed.,* 1987, pp. 47–76.
[G: U.S.; Japan]

Sanfuentes, Andrés. Chile: Effects of the Adjustment Policies on the Agriculture and Forestry Sector. *CEPAL Rev.,* December 1987, (33), pp. 115–27. [G: Chile]

Santana, Carlos Augusto Mattos. Efeitos das Políticas Econômicas Brasileiras sobre o Setor Doméstico de soja em Grão. (With English summary.) *Pesquisa Planejamento Econ.,* December 1987, 17(3), pp. 633–78. [G: Brazil]

Sarris, Alexander H. Domestic Price Policies and International Distortions: The Cases of Wheat and Rice. *Econ. Notes,* 1987, (2), pp. 5–35.
[G: LDCs; MDCs]

Sathirathai, Surakiart and Siamwalla, Ammar. GATT Law, Agricultural Trade, and Developing Countries: Lessons from Two Case Studies. *World Bank Econ. Rev.,* September 1987, 1(4), pp. 595–618. [G: Thailand; U.S.; EEC]

Sato, Takashi. Agricultural Reform Efforts in the United States and Japan: Remarks. *Johnson, D. G., ed.,* 1987, pp. 77–81. [G: U.S.; Japan]

Sauer, Richard J. and Pray, Carl E. Mobilizing Support for Agricultural Research at the Minnesota Agricultural Experiment Station. *Ruttan, V. W. and Pray, C. E., eds.,* 1987, pp. 211–33. [G: U.S.]

Schatan W., Jacobo. SAM's Influence on Food Consumption and Nutrition. *Austin, J. E. and Esteva, G., eds.,* 1987, pp. 249–59.
[G: Mexico]

Schiff, Maurice. A Structural View of Policy Issues in African Agricultural Development: Comment. *Amer. J. Agr. Econ.,* May 1987, 69(2), pp. 384–88. [G: Africa]

Schnittker, John A. Agricultural Reform Efforts in the United States: Feasibility and Consequences for Japan and Third Countries. *Johnson, D. G., ed.,* 1987, pp. 5–23. [G: U.S.; Japan]

Schoney, Richard A. and Nicholson, R. C. The Effect of Tax Classification of Part-time Farming in Saskatchewan. *Can. J. Agr. Econ.,* July 1987, 35(2), pp. 421–39. [G: Canada]

Schuh, G. Edward. The Changing Context of Food and Agricultural Development Policy. *Gittinger, J. P.; Leslie, J. and Hoisington, C., eds.,* 1987, pp. 72–88. [G: Global]

Sebestyén, Mária. The Management of Agricultural Supply in a Centrally Planned Country: The Case of Hungary. *Kettunen, L., ed.,* 1987, pp. 221–30. [G: Hungary]

Sediari, Tommaso. Aspects of the Market for Tobacco EEC: Need of Planning. *Kettunen, L., ed.,* 1987, pp. 271–79. [G: EEC]

Selmi, Giovanna Trevisan. Vitivinicoltura italiana e politica comunitaria delle strutture. (The Italian Viti-Vine-Growing and the E.E.C.'s Structures Policy. With English summary.) *Ricerche Econ.,* Jan.-Mar. 1987, 41(1), pp. 123–35.
[G: Italy]

Sequeira, Carlos Guillermo. SAM and the Mexican Private Sector. *Austin, J. E. and Esteva, G., eds.,* 1987, pp. 200–212. [G: Mexico]

Shedd, M. S.; Farrell, D. L. and Kerr, William A. Capital Gains and Pension Incomes: Security and Equity Implications for Canadian Farmers. *Can. J. Agr. Econ.,* November 1987, 35(3), pp. 615–26. [G: Canada]

Shefer, Daniel. The Effect of Agricultural Price-Support Policies on Interregional and Rural-to-Urban Migration in Korea: 1976–1980. *Reg. Sci. Urban Econ.,* August 1987, 17(3), pp. 333–44. [G: Korea]

Shideed, Kamil H.; White, Fred C. and Brannen, Stephen J. The Responsiveness of U.S. Corn and Soybean Acreages to Conditional Price Expectations: An Application to the 1985 Farm Bill. *Southern J. Agr. Econ.,* December 1987, 19(2), pp. 153–61. [G: U.S.]

Spencer, Dunstan S. C. Food Price Policy and Equity: Commentary. *Mellor, J. W.; Delgado, C. L. and Blackie, M. J., eds.,* 1987, pp. 292–95. [G: Africa]

de Spoelberch, Guillaume and Shaw, Robert D'Arcy. A Model: The Aga Khan Rural Support Program. *Challenge,* Jan./Feb. 1987, 29(6), pp. 26–31. [G: Pakistan]

Squires, Dale and Tabor, Steven. Integration of Staple Food Commodity Markets in Java. *Singapore Econ. Rev.,* October 1987, 32(2), pp. 1–15. [G: Singapore]

Stiglitz, Joseph E. Some Theoretical Aspects of Agricultural Policies. *World Bank Res. Observer,* January 1987, 2(1), pp. 43–60.
[G: LDCs]

Stubbs, Jean and Alvarez, Mavis. Women on the Agenda: The Cooperative Movement in Rural Cuba. *Deere, C. D. and León, M., eds.,* 1987, pp. 142–61. [G: Cuba]

Tangermann, Stefan. How to Open the Common Agricultural Market: Comment. *Giersch, H., ed.,* 1987, pp. 532–38. [G: EEC]

Tangermann, Stefan; Josling, Timothy and Pearson, Scott R. Multilateral Negotiations on Farm-Support Levels. *World Econ.,* September 1987, 10(3), pp. 265–82.

Tarditi, Secondo. The 'Green Paper' in a Long-term Perspective. *Europ. Rev. Agr. Econ.,* 1987, 14(1), pp. 23–35. [G: EEC]

Tarditi, Secondo. The Common Agricultural Policy: The Implications for Italian Agriculture. *J. Agr. Econ.,* September 1987, 38(3), pp. 407–21. [G: Italy]

Tarditi, Secondo and Croci-Angelini, Elisabetta. Efficiency and Equity Components of Sector Policy Analysis and Evaluation. *Léon, Y. and Mahé, L., eds.,* 1987, pp. 43–80. [G: Italy]

Thiesenhusen, William C. Incomes on Some Agrarian Reform Asentamientos in Panama. *Econ. Develop. Cult. Change*, July 1987, *35*(4), pp. 809–31. [G: Panama]

Thompson, Robert L. U.S. Farm Policy: Implications for the Future. *Can. J. Agr. Econ.*, May 1987, *34*, pp. 101–08. [G: U.S.]

Thomson, K. J. A Model of the Common Agricultural Policy. *J. Agr. Econ.*, May 1987, *38*(2), pp. 193–210. [G: EEC]

Thomson, K. J. Supply Control in a Multi-national Context: Cereals Policy in the EEC. *Kettunen, L., ed.*, 1987, pp. 281–300. [G: EEC]

Thraen, Cameron S. and Hammond, Jerome W. Price Enhancement, Returns Variability, and Supply Response in the U.S. Dairy Sector. *Southern J. Agr. Econ.*, December 1987, *19*(2), pp. 83–92. [G: U.S.]

Timmer, C. Peter. Corn in Indonesia's Food Policy. *Timmer, C. P., ed.*, 1987, pp. 253–85. [G: Indonesia]

Timmer, C. Peter. Price Policy and the Political Economy of Markets. *Gittinger, J. P.; Leslie, J. and Hoisington, C., eds.*, 1987, pp. 264–76.

Timmer, C. Peter. SAM, Energy, and Structural Change in the Agricultural Sector. *Austin, J. E. and Esteva, G., eds.*, 1987, pp. 260–97. [G: Mexico]

Tømte, Eugen D. and Sand, Cato. The Norwegian Milk Quota System: A General Report. *Kettunen, L., ed.*, 1987, pp. 121–31. [G: Norway]

Tourinho, Octávio Augusto Fontes; Ferreira, Léo da Rocha and Pimentel, Ruderico Ferraz. Agricultura e produção de energia: um modelo de programação linear para avaliação econômica do PROÁLCOOL. (With English summary.) *Pesquisa Planejamento Econ.*, April 1987, *17*(1), pp. 19–63. [G: Brazil]

Trela, Irene; Whalley, John and Wigle, Randall. International Trade in Grains: Domestic Policies and Trade Impacts. *Scand. J. Econ.*, 1987, *89*(3), pp. 271–83. [G: Global]

Trigo, Eduardo J. Agricultural Research Organization in the Developing World: Diversity and Evolution. *Ruttan, V. W. and Pray, C. E., eds.*, 1987, pp. 251–81. [G: LDCs]

Tshibaka, Tshikala B. Food Policy and the Choice of Trade Regime: Commentary. *Mellor, J. W.; Delgado, C. L. and Blackie, M. J., eds.*, 1987, pp. 276–77. [G: Africa]

Ulrich, Alvin; Furtan, William Hartley and Schmitz, Andrew. The Cost of a Licensing System Regulation: An Example from Canadian Prairie Agriculture. *J. Polit. Econ.*, February 1987, *95*(1), pp. 160–78. [G: Canada]

Uusitalo, Matti. GATT-rundan och Finlands jordbruk. (The GATT Round and Finnish Agriculture. With English summary.) *Ekon. Samfundets Tidskr.*, 1987, *40*(2), pp. 81–83. [G: Finland]

Valdés, Alberto. Agriculture in the Uruguay Round: Interests of Developing Countries.

World Bank Econ. Rev., September 1987, *1*(4), pp. 571–93. [G: LDCs]

Valdés, Alberto and Zietz, Joachim. Export Subsidies and Minimum Access Guarantees in Agricultural Trade: A Developing Country Perspective. *World Devel.*, May 1987, *15*(5), pp. 673–83. [G: Global]

Valenzuela, Eduardo. Agricultural Planning in the Countries of the Caribbean Community (CARICOM). *CEPAL Rev.*, December 1987, (33), pp. 61–67. [G: Caribbean]

Vamoer, Alexander P. Defining the Food and Nutrition Problem: Commentary. *Mellor, J. W.; Delgado, C. L. and Blackie, M. J., eds.*, 1987, pp. 53–56. [G: Africa]

de Veer, Jan. Perspectives for the CAP. *Europ. Rev. Agr. Econ.*, 1987, *14*(1), pp. 1–10. [G: EEC]

Villasuso, Juan M. Costa Rica: Crisis, Adjustment Policies and Rural Development. *CEPAL Rev.*, December 1987, (33), pp. 107–13. [G: Costa Rica]

Wade, Nicholas. Agriculture: Research Planning Paralyzed by Pork-Barrel Politics. *Ruttan, V. W. and Pray, C. E., eds.*, 1987, *1973*, pp. 515–26. [G: U.S.]

Wagstaff, Howard. Implementing a Two-Tier Price System for Regulating Production and Incomes in Agriculture. *Kettunen, L., ed.*, 1987, pp. 353–62. [G: EEC]

Wanmali, Sudhir. Agriculture and Central Physical Grid Infrastructure: Commentary. *Mellor, J. W.; Delgado, C. L. and Blackie, M. J., eds.*, 1987, pp. 227–32. [G: Africa]

Warley, T. K. Issues Facing Agriculture in the GATT Negotiations. *Can. J. Agr. Econ.*, November 1987, *35*(3), pp. 515–34. [G: OECD]

Warley, T. K. and Barichello, R. R. Agricultural Issues in a Comprehensive Canada–U.S. Trade Agreement: A Canadian Perspective. *Can. J. Agr. Econ.*, May 1987, *34*, pp. 213–27. [G: Canada]

Weinschenck, Günther. The Economic or the Ecological Way? Basic Alternatives for the EC's Agricultural Policy. *Europ. Rev. Agr. Econ.*, 1987, *14*(1), pp. 49–60. [G: EEC]

Westlake, M. J. The Measurement of Agricultural Price Distortion in Developing Countries. *J. Devel. Stud.*, April 1987, *23*(3), pp. 367–81. [G: Kenya]

Wiens, Thomas B. Issues in the Structural Reform of Chinese Agriculture. *J. Compar. Econ.*, September 1987, *11*(3), pp. 372–84. [G: China]

Williams, Roland E. Dairy Industry Structure and Milk Price Comparisons: A Rejoinder. *J. Agr. Econ.*, September 1987, *38*(3), pp. 509–16. [G: U.K.]

Wills, Ian R. Resource Degradation on Agricultural Land: Information Problems, Market Failures and Government Intervention. *Australian J. Agr. Econ.*, April 1987, *31*(1), pp. 45–55. [G: Australia]

Winters, L. Alan. The Economic Consequences of Agricultural Support: A Survey. *OECD*

Econ. Stud., Autumn 1987, (9), pp. 7–54.

Winters, L. Alan. The Political Economy of the Agricultural Policy of Industrial Countries. *Europ. Rev. Agr. Econ.*, 1987, *14*(3), pp. 285–304.   [G: OECD]

Wolek, Francis W. Support Structures for Technology Transfer in Agriculture. *Ruttan, V. W. and Pray, C. E., eds.*, 1987, pp. 451–67.
[G: U.S.]

Woś, Augustyn. Polish Agriculture in Conditions of Economic Reform. *Kettunen, L., ed.*, 1987, pp. 159–68.   [G: Poland]

Yanagida, John F.; Azzam, Azzeddine and Linsenmeyer, Dean. Two Alternative Methods of Removing Price Supports: Implications to the U.S. Corn and Livestock Industries. *J. Policy Modeling*, Summer 1987, *9*(2), pp. 311–20.
[G: U.S.]

Yeats, Alexander J. A Note on the Functioning of International Commodity Price Stabilisation Agreements in Periods of Fluctuating Monetary Exchange Rates. *J. Devel. Stud.*, April 1987, *23*(3), pp. 382–401.

Zachariasse, Vinus. Income Disparities among Farm Households and Agricultural Policy: Concluding Comments. *Léon, Y. and Mahé, L., eds.*, 1987, pp. 499–505.

Zalkin, Michael. Food Policy and Class Transformation in Revolutionary Nicaragua, 1979–86. *World Devel.*, July 1987, *15*(7), pp. 961–84.
[G: Nicaragua]

714 Agricultural Finance

7140 Agricultural Finance

Angell, Wayne D. Statement to the U.S. House Committee on Banking, Finance and Urban Affairs, September 30, 1987. *Fed. Res. Bull.*, November 1987, *73*(11), pp. 857–59.
[G: U.S.]

Ashmead, Ralph. Emerging Roles in Financing Agriculture. *Can. J. Agr. Econ.*, May 1987, *34*, pp. 170–84.   [G: Canada]

Babb, Emerson M. Computer-Assisted Instruction for Financial Management. *Southern J. Agr. Econ.*, July 1987, *19*(1), pp. 119–22.

Barau, A. D. and Clark, J. H. Evaluating Alternative Mortgage Instruments for Low-Equity Ontario Dairy Farms. *Can. J. Agr. Econ.*, November 1987, *35*(3), pp. 553–69.   [G: Canada]

Belongia, Michael T. and Gilbert, R. Alton. Agricultural Banks: Causes of Failures and the Condition of Survivors. *Fed. Res. Bank St. Louis Rev.*, May 1987, *69*(5), pp. 30–37.   [G: U.S.]

Belongia, Michael T. and Gilbert, R. Alton. The Farm Economies of the Plains. *Rev. Reg. Stud.*, Fall 1987, *17*(3), pp. 47–57.   [G: U.S.]

Blackie, Malcolm J. Restructuring Marketing Systems for Smallholders: Cases in Zimbabwe. *Mellor, J. W.; Delgado, C. L. and Blackie, M. J., eds.*, 1987, pp. 187–98.
[G: Zimbabwe]

Boyette, Deborah K. and White, Fred C. Factors Affecting Demand and Supply of Agricultural

Real Estate Debt. *Western J. Agr. Econ.*, December 1987, *12*(2), pp. 174–81.   [G: U.S.]

Carraro, Kenneth C. A Review of the Eighth District's Agricultural Economy in 1986. *Fed. Res. Bank St. Louis Rev.*, April 1987, *69*(4), pp. 5–15.   [G: U.S.]

Centner, Terence J. and White, Fred C. FmHA's Efforts Against Delinquent Borrowers: Property Interests and Transaction Costs. *Western J. Agr. Econ.*, July 1987, *12*(1), pp. 35–41.
[G: U.S.]

Edwards, Geoff W. U.S. Farm Policy: An Australian Perspective. *Fed. Res. Bank St. Louis Rev.*, October 1987, *69*(8), pp. 20–31.
[G: U.S.; Australia]

Eichengreen, Barry. Agricultural Mortgages in the Populist Era: Reply. *J. Econ. Hist.*, September 1987, *47*(3), pp. 757–60.   [G: U.S.]

Estenson, Paul S. Farm Debt and Financial Instability. *J. Econ. Issues*, June 1987, *21*(2), pp. 616–27.   [G: U.S.]

Featherstone, Allen M. and Baker, Timothy G. An Examination of Farm Sector Real Asset Dynamics: 1910–85. *Amer. J. Agr. Econ.*, August 1987, *69*(3), pp. 532–46.   [G: U.S.]

Foweraker, Joe. What's Good for Citicorp... *Challenge*, Jan./Feb. 1987, *29*(6), pp. 47–50.
[G: U.S.]

Freshwater, David. Farm Finance and the Public Sector: A Macroeconomic Perspective. *Can. J. Agr. Econ.*, December 1987, *35*(4), pp. 709–33.   [G: U.S.; Canada]

Gangopadhyay, Shubhashis and Sengupta, Kunal. Small Farmers, Moneylenders and Trading Activity. *Oxford Econ. Pap.*, June 1987, *39*(2), pp. 333–42.

Gangopadhyay, Shubhashis and Sengupta, Kunal. Usury and Collateral Pricing: Towards an Alternative Explanation. *Cambridge J. Econ.*, March 1987, *11*(1), pp. 47–54.

Graham, Douglas H.; Gauthier, Howard and Mendonça de Barros, José Roberto. Thirty Years of Agricultural Growth in Brazil: Crop Performance, Regional Profile, and Recent Policy Review. *Econ. Develop. Cult. Change*, October 1987, *36*(1), pp. 1–34.   [G: Brazil]

Gupta, Manash Ranjan. A Nutrition-Based Theory of Interlinkage. *J. Quant. Econ.*, July 1987, *3*(2), pp. 189–202.

Hardy, William E., Jr., et al. An Analysis of Factors that Affect the Quality of Federal Land Bank Loans. *Southern J. Agr. Econ.*, December 1987, *19*(2), pp. 175–82.   [G: U.S.]

Hutchison, Gary and Winslade, Ralph S. After-Tax Costs of Capital Purchases. *Can. J. Agr. Econ.*, May 1987, *34*, pp. 40–61.

Ireson, W. Randall. Landholding, Agricultural Modernization, and Income Concentration: A Mexican Example. *Econ. Develop. Cult. Change*, January 1987, *35*(2), pp. 351–66.
[G: Mexico]

LeBlanc, Michael; Yanagida, John F. and Conway, Roger K. The Derived Demand for Real Cash Balances in Agricultural Production.

Western J. Agr. Econ., July 1987, *12*(1), pp. 78–85.   [G: U.S.]

Mappleback, L. Farm Management, Credit and Survival. *Can. J. Agr. Econ.*, May 1987, *34*, pp. 185–212.

Melichar, Emanuel. Turning the Corner on Troubled Farm Debt. *Fed. Res. Bull.*, July 1987, *73*(7), pp. 523–36.   [G: U.S.]

Meyers, William H. The Farm Economies of the Plains: Comment. *Rev. Reg. Stud.*, Fall 1987, *17*(3), pp. 58–59.   [G: U.S.]

Monke, Eric A. Portuguese Agriculture in Transition: Agricultural Factor Markets. *Pearson, S. R., et al.*, 1987, pp. 62–82.   [G: Portugal]

Mumey, G. A. Improving On-Farm Financial Management. *Can. J. Agr. Econ.*, December 1987, *35*(4), pp. 735–40.

Nelson, Carl H. and Loehman, Edna T. Further toward a Theory of Agricultural Insurance. *Amer. J. Agr. Econ.*, August 1987, *69*(3), pp. 523–31.

Owens, Raymond E. The Agricultural Outlook for 1987…Financial Turnaround Unlikely. *Fed. Res. Bank Richmond Econ. Rev.*, Jan./Feb. 1987, *73*(1), pp. 24–31.   [G: U.S.]

Patalinghug, Epictetus E. Rediscounting, Savings Mobilization, and the Rural Banking System. *Philippine Rev. Econ. Bus.*, Mar.-June 1987, *24*(1–2), pp. 103–23.   [G: Philippines]

Pessah, Raul. Channeling Credit to the Countryside. *Austin, J. E. and Esteva, G., eds.*, 1987, pp. 92–110.   [G: Mexico]

Platteau, Jean-Philippe and Abraham, Anita. An Inquiry into Quasi-credit Contracts: The Role of Reciprocal Credit and Interlinked Deals in Small-scale Fishing Communities. *J. Devel. Stud.*, July 1987, *23*(4), pp. 461–90.
                                             [G: LDCs]

Rao, J. Mohan. Productivity and Distribution under Cropsharing Tenancy. *World Devel.*, September 1987, *15*(9), pp. 1163–78.

Saleem, Samir Taha. On the Determination of Interest Rates in Rural Credit Markets: A Case Study from the Sudan. *Cambridge J. Econ.*, June 1987, *11*(2), pp. 165–72.   [G: Sudan]

Schnitkey, Gary D.; Barry, Peter J. and Ellinger, Paul N. A Microcomputer Analysis of Farm Financial Performance. *Southern J. Agr. Econ.*, December 1987, *19*(2), pp. 203–09.

Shrestha, Chandra M.; Debertin, David L. and Anschel, Kurt R. Stochastic Efficiency versus Mean–Variance Criteria as Predictors of Adoption of Reduced Tillage: Comment. *Amer. J. Agr. Econ.*, November 1987, *69*(4), pp. 857–60.   [G: U.S.]

Smith, Hilary H. Agricultural Lending: Bank Closures and Branch Banking. *Fed. Res. Bank Dallas Econ. Rev.*, September 1987, pp. 27–38.
                                             [G: U.S.]

Weisser, Michael R. Rural Crisis and Rural Credit in XVIIth-Century Castile. *J. Europ. Econ. Hist.*, Fall 1987, *16*(2), pp. 297–313.
                                             [G: Spain]

Zering, K. D.; McCorkle, C. O. and Moore, Charles V. The Utility of Multiple Peril Crop Insurance for Irrigated, Multiple-Crop Agricul-

ture. *Western J. Agr. Econ.*, July 1987, *12*(1), pp. 50–59.   [G: U.S.]

715 Agricultural Markets and Marketing; Cooperatives

7150 Agricultural Markets and Marketing; Cooperatives

Ahmadi-Esfahani, Fredoun Z. and Carter, Colin A. A Dynamic Analysis of U.S. Export Wheat Pricing and Market Shares. *Australian J. Agr. Econ.*, December 1987, *31*(3), pp. 191–203.
                                             [G: U.S.]

de Alcantara, Cynthia Hewitt. Feeding Mexico City. *Austin, J. E. and Esteva, G., eds.*, 1987, pp. 172–99.   [G: Mexico]

Ali, Ifzal. Rice in Indonesia: Price Policy and Comparative Advantage. *Bull. Indonesian Econ. Stud.*, December 1987, *23*(3), pp. 80–99.   [G: Indonesia]

Antonovitz, Frances and Roe, Terry. Economic Efficiency and Market Information. *Kilmer, R. L. and Armbruster, W. J., eds.*, 1987, pp. 181–204.   [G: U.S.]

Ardy, Brian. Instability in World Grain Markets: A Comment. *J. Agr. Econ.*, May 1987, *38*(2), pp. 343–45.   [G: Global]

Armbruster, Walter J. Economic Efficiency in Agricultural and Food Marketing. *Kilmer, R. L. and Armbruster, W. J., eds.*, 1987, pp. ix–xii.

Bates, Robert H. Pressure Groups, Public Policy, and Agricultural Development: A Study of Divergent Outcomes. *Bates, R. H.*, 1987, *1980*, pp. 61–91.   [G: Ghana; Kenya]

Berg, Ernst. A Sequential Decision Model to Determine Optimal Farm-Level Grain Marketing Policies. *Europ. Rev. Agr. Econ.*, 1987, *14*(1), pp. 91–116.   [G: W. Germany]

Bernegger, Urs. Experience with the Milk Quota System in Switzerland. *Kettunen, L., ed.*, 1987, pp. 19–28.   [G: Switzerland]

Bessler, David A. and Babula, Ronald A. Forecasting Wheat Exports: Do Exchange Rates Matter? *J. Bus. Econ. Statist.*, July 1987, *5*(3), pp. 397–406.   [G: U.S.]

Bhujangarao, C. Determinants of Foodgrain Prices in India: An Empirical Study, 1961–83. *Indian Econ. Rev.*, Jan.-June 1987, *22*(1), pp. 51–77.   [G: India]

Blackie, Malcolm J. Restructuring Marketing Systems for Smallholders: Cases in Zimbabwe. *Mellor, J. W.; Delgado, C. L. and Blackie, M. J., eds.*, 1987, pp. 187–98.
                                             [G: Zimbabwe]

Blanc, Gérard. The Grain Traders: Masters of the Intelligence Game. *Dedijer, S. and Jéquier, N., eds.*, 1987, pp. 139–57.

Bredahl, Maury E.; Schmitz, Andrew and Hillman, Jimmye S. Rent Seeking in International Trade: The Great Tomato War. *Amer. J. Agr. Econ.*, February 1987, *69*(1), pp. 1–10.
                                             [G: U.S.; Mexico]

Cardino, Angelita G. Market Needs for Grain Drying in the Philippines. *Young, R. H. and*

MacCormac, C. W., eds., 1987, pp. 93–100. [G: Philippines]

Cave, Jonathan and Salant, Stephen W. Cartels That Vote: Agricultural Marketing Boards and Induced Voting Behavior. *Bailey, E. E., ed.*, 1987, pp. 255–83. [G: U.S.]

Christy, Ralph D. The Role of Farmer Cooperatives in a Changing Agricultural Economy. *Southern J. Agr. Econ.*, July 1987, *19*(1), pp. 21–28. [G: U.S.]

Clegg, Martin. Notes for Address Concerning the EEC Milk Superlevy and Quota System. *Kettunen, L., ed.*, 1987, pp. 5–17. [G: EEC]

Coffey, Joseph D. The Role of Farmer Cooperatives in a Changing Agricultural Economy: Discussion. *Southern J. Agr. Econ.*, July 1987, *19*(1), pp. 29–30. [G: U.S.]

Coffin, H. Garth. The Internationalization of Canadian Agriculture. *Can. J. Agr. Econ.*, December 1987, *35*(4), pp. 691–707.
[G: Canada]

Cook, Edward C. Soviet Food Markets: Will the Situation Improve under Gorbachev? *Comp. Econ. Stud.*, Spring 1987, *29*(1), pp. 1–36. [G: U.S.S.R.]

Cox, P. G. The Case for Tradeable Milk Production Quotas: A Note. *Irish J. Agr. Econ. Rural Soc.*, 1987, *12*, pp. 95–102. [G: EEC]

Curtis, Ranjana and Gunetileke, K. G. Market Needs for Vegetable Drying in Sri Lanka. *Young, R. H. and MacCormac, C. W., eds.*, 1987, pp. 78–92. [G: Sri Lanka]

Desai, Gunvant M. Support Systems for Agricultural Development: Commentary. *Mellor, J. W.; Delgado, C. L. and Blackie, M. J., eds.*, 1987, pp. 199–202. [G: Africa]

Durham, Stephen E. and Lee, David R. An Evaluation of Alternative Approaches to Market Share Analysis with Application to the Kuwaiti Poultry Market. *J. Agr. Econ.*, January 1987, *38*(1), pp. 85–97. [G: Kuwait]

Dutton, John and Grennes, Thomas. Alternative Measures of Effective Exchange Rates for Agricultural Trade. *Europ. Rev. Agr. Econ.*, 1987, *14*(4), pp. 427–42. [G: U.S.]

Edwards, Clark. The Exchange Rate and U.S. Agricultural Exports. *Agr. Econ. Res.*, Winter 1987, *39*(1), pp. 1–12. [G: U.S.]

Falusi, Abiodun O. Support Systems for Agricultural Development: Commentary. *Mellor, J. W.; Delgado, C. L. and Blackie, M. J., eds.*, 1987, pp. 202–03. [G: Africa]

Faminow, Merle D. and Benson, Bruce L. Price Reporting in Experimental Markets. *Can. J. Agr. Econ.*, July 1987, *35*(2), pp. 357–71.

Ferris, Stephen P. and Chance, Don M. Trading Time Effects in Financial and Commodity Futures Markets. *Financial Rev.*, May 1987, *22*(2), pp. 281–94. [G: U.S.]

Fesl, J. The Austrian Dairy System. *Kettunen, L., ed.*, 1987, pp. 63–68. [G: Austria]

Feuer, Carl Henry. The Performance of the Cuban Sugar Industry, 1981–85. *World Devel.*, January 1987, *15*(1), pp. 67–81. [G: Cuba]

Frankel, Jeffrey A. Expectations and Commodity Price Dynamics: The Overshooting Model: Re-

ply. *Amer. J. Agr. Econ.*, November 1987, *69*(4), pp. 856.

French, Ben C. Farm Price Estimation When There is Bargaining: The Case of Processed Fruit and Vegetables. *Western J. Agr. Econ.*, July 1987, *12*(1), pp. 17–26. [G: U.S.]

Gapare, Robinson L. Support Systems for Agricultural Development: Commentary. *Mellor, J. W.; Delgado, C. L. and Blackie, M. J., eds.*, 1987, pp. 206–09. [G: Africa]

Gardner, Bruce L. Efficiency in Commodity Storage. *Kilmer, R. L. and Armbruster, W. J., eds.*, 1987, pp. 274–85. [G: U.S.]

Garoyan, Leon. Agricultural Cooperatives under EEC Antitrust Regulations. *Wills, R. L.; Caswell, J. A. and Culbertson, J. D., eds.*, 1987, pp. 167–84. [G: EEC]

van der Giessen, L. B. and Post, J. H. Micro- and Macro-effects of the Super Levy in the Netherlands. *Kettunen, L., ed.*, 1987, pp. 105–20. [G: Netherlands]

Glover, David J. Increasing the Benefits to Smallholders from Contract Farming: Problems for Farmers' Organizations and Policy Makers. *World Devel.*, April 1987, *15*(4), pp. 441–48. [G: LDCs]

Goddard, E. W. Imperfect Competition in World Beef Trade. *Can. J. Agr. Econ.*, May 1987, *34*, pp. 265–79. [G: Canada]

Gordon, J. Douglas. Expectations and Commodity Price Dynamics: The Overshooting Model: Comment. *Amer. J. Agr. Econ.*, November 1987, *69*(4), pp. 852–55.

Goss, Barry A. Wool Prices and Publicly Available Information. *Australian Econ. Pap.*, December 1987, *26*(49), pp. 225–36. [G: Australia]

Grosh, Barbara. Performance of Agricultural Public Enterprises in Kenya: Lessons from the First Two Decades of Independence. *Eastern Afr. Econ. Rev.*, June 1987, *3*(1), pp. 51–64. [G: Kenya]

Gunawardana, P. J. and Quilkey, J. J. Issues in Smallholder Tropical Dairying: A Comment. *Bull. Indonesian Econ. Stud.*, April 1987, *23*(1), pp. 122–26. [G: Indonesia]

Hastings, Trevor. Price Variations of Yearling Thoroughbreds at Australian Auctions. *Irish J. Agr. Econ. Rural Soc.*, 1987, *12*, pp. 19–28. [G: Australia]

Hauser, Robert J. and Andersen, Dane K. Hedging with Options under Variance Uncertainty: An Illustration of Pricing New-Crop Soybeans. *Amer. J. Agr. Econ.*, February 1987, *69*(1), pp. 38–45. [G: U.S.]

Hawkins, M. H. and Higginson, N. Marketing Research in the Canadian Food Retail and Processing Industry, 1950–1986. *Can. J. Agr. Econ.*, May 1987, *34*, pp. 1–26. [G: Canada]

Heifner, Richard G. Comments on Economic Efficiency, Public Programs, and Private Strategies. *Kilmer, R. L. and Armbruster, W. J., eds.*, 1987, pp. 290–97.

Henderson, Dennis R. Economic Efficiency and Market Information: A Discussion. *Kilmer, R. L. and Armbruster, W. J., eds.*, 1987, pp. 205–08.

Hopcraft, Peter. Grain Marketing Policies and Institutions in Africa. *Finance Develop.*, March 1987, *24*(1), pp. 37–40. **[G: Africa]**

Hudson, Michael A.; Leuthold, Raymond M. and Sarassoro, Gboroton F. Commodity Futures Price Changes: Recent Evidence for Wheat, Soybeans and Live Cattle. *J. Futures Markets,* June 1987, *7*(3), pp. 287–301.

Jabara, Cathy L. and Schwartz, Nancy E. Flexible Exchange Rates and Commodity Price Changes: The Case of Japan. *Amer. J. Agr. Econ.,* August 1987, *69*(3), pp. 580–90. **[G: Japan]**

Jesse, Edward V. Economic Efficiency and Marketing Orders. *Kilmer, R. L. and Armbruster, W. J., eds.,* 1987, pp. 217–28. **[G: U.S.]**

Johnson, D. Gale. Agricultural Reform Efforts in the United States and Japan: Introduction. *Johnson, D. G., ed.,* 1987, pp. 1–4. **[G: U.S.; Japan]**

Jordan, James V., et al. Transactions Data Tests of the Black Model for Soybean Futures Options. *J. Futures Markets,* October 1987, *7*(5), pp. 535–54. **[G: U.S.]**

Josling, Timothy and Tangermann, Stefan. Portuguese Agriculture in Transition: Commodity Policies. *Pearson, S. R., et al.,* 1987, pp. 41–61. **[G: Portugal]**

Kamara, Avraham and Siegel, Andrew F. Optimal Hedging in Futures Markets with Multiple Delivery Specifications. *J. Finance,* September 1987, *42*(4), pp. 1007–21. **[G: U.S.]**

Karp, Larry S. Methods for Selecting the Optimal Dynamic Hedge when Production Is Stochastic. *Amer. J. Agr. Econ.,* August 1987, *69*(3), pp. 647–57. **[G: U.S.]**

Kenney, Mary C. Marketing Orders and Efficiency: A Discussion. *Kilmer, R. L. and Armbruster, W. J., eds.,* 1987, pp. 229–30. **[G: U.S.]**

Kenyon, David, et al. Factors Affecting Agricultural Futures Price Variance. *J. Futures Markets,* February 1987, *7*(1), pp. 73–91. **[G: U.S.]**

Kettunen, Lauri. Experiences in Controlling Milk Supply in Finland. *Kettunen, L., ed.,* 1987, pp. 147–57. **[G: Finland]**

Kilmer, Richard L. and Armbruster, Walter J. Economic Efficiency and Future Research. *Kilmer, R. L. and Armbruster, W. J., eds.,* 1987, pp. 301–15.

Kinnucan, Henry W. Effect of Canadian Advertising on Milk Demand: The Case of the Buffalo, New York Market. *Can. J. Agr. Econ.,* March 1987, *35*(1), pp. 181–96. **[G: Canada; U.S.]**

Kuchler, Fred and Vroomen, Harry. Impacts of the PIK Program on the Farm Machinery Market. *J. Agr. Econ. Res.,* Summer 1987, *39*(3), pp. 2–11. **[G: U.S.]**

Ladd, George W. The Food Marketing System: The Relevance of Economic Efficiency Measures: A Discussion. *Kilmer, R. L. and Armbruster, W. J., eds.,* 1987, pp. 32–36.

Loyns, R. M. A., et al. Toward an Improved Model of Farm Management: The Case for In-cluding Marketing. *Can. J. Agr. Econ.,* May 1987, *34*, pp. 70–82. **[G: Canada]**

Maizels, Alfred. Commodities in Crisis: An Overview of the Main Issues. *World Devel.,* May 1987, *15*(5), pp. 537–49. **[G: Global]**

Malick, William M. and Ward, Ronald W. Stock Effects and Seasonality in the FCOJ Futures Basis. *J. Futures Markets,* April 1987, *7*(2), pp. 157–67. **[G: U.S.]**

Manegold, D. Aspects of Agricultural Policy in the European Community 1986/87. *Rev. Marketing Agr. Econ.,* August 1987, *55*(2), pp. 117–39. **[G: EEC]**

Martin, S. K. and Zwart, A. C. Marketing Agencies and the Economics of Market Segmentation. *Australian J. Agr. Econ.,* December 1987, *31*(3), pp. 242–55. **[G: New Zealand]**

Maruyama, Magoroh. Japan's Agricultural Policy Failure. *Challenge,* Jan./Feb. 1987, *29*(6), pp. 50–52. **[G: Japan]**

Mathiesen, Lars. International Trade in Grains: Domestic Policies and Trade Impacts: Comment. *Scand. J. Econ.,* 1987, *89*(3), pp. 285–86. **[G: Global]**

McClain, Emily A. and McLemore, Dan L. Optimal Organization of a Statewide Livestock Auction Market System: The Case of Tennessee. *Southern J. Agr. Econ.,* December 1987, *19*(2), pp. 121–31. **[G: U.S.]**

Milonas, Nikolaos T. The Effects of USDA Crop Announcements on Commodity Prices. *J. Futures Markets,* October 1987, *7*(5), pp. 571–89. **[G: U.S.]**

Mitchell, Donald O. and Duncan, Ronald C. Market Behavior of Grains Exporters. *World Bank Res. Observer,* January 1987, *2*(1), pp. 3–21. **[G: Selected Countries]**

Mongkolsmai, Dow. Supplementary Foods in Rural Thailand. *Young, R. H. and MacCormac, C. W., eds.,* 1987, pp. 57–68. **[G: Thailand]**

Mumbengegwi, Clever. Food and Agriculture Co-operation in the SADCC: Progress, Problems and Prospects. *Amin, S.; Chitala, D. and Mandaza, I., eds.,* 1987, pp. 62–84. **[G: Southern Africa]**

Murphy, J. Austin. The Seasonality of Risk and Return on Agricultural Futures Positions. *Amer. J. Agr. Econ.,* August 1987, *69*(3), pp. 639–46. **[G: U.S.]**

Olayide, S. O. and Idachaba, Francis S. Input and Output Marketing Systems: A Nigerian Case. *Mellor, J. W.; Delgado, C. L. and Blackie, M. J., eds.,* 1987, pp. 173–86. **[G: Nigeria]**

Oleson, Brian T. World Grain Trade: An Economic Perspective of the Current Price War. *Can. J. Agr. Econ.,* November 1987, *35*(3), pp. 501–14. **[G: Global]**

Oleson, Brian T. and Brooks, H. G. Canadian Wheat Board Proposal: Basis Change for Initial Payment Freight Deductions. *Can. J. Agr. Econ.,* May 1987, *34*, pp. 83–98. **[G: Canada]**

Ortner, K. M. An Outline of the Milk Quota Policy in Austria. *Kettunen, L., ed.,* 1987, pp. 69–75. **[G: Austria]**

Oskam, Arie J. and van der Stelt-Scheele, D. D. Two Years of Experience with the EC Super Levy System: A Quantitative Analysis of Recent and Future Policy Alternatives. *Kettunen, L., ed.*, 1987, pp. 77–103.   [G: EEC]

Pableo, Relli C. and Ignacio, Manuel C. Investigating the Marketing System for Groundnuts in the Philippines. *Young, R. H. and MacCormac, C. W., eds.*, 1987, pp. 111–20.
[G: Philippines]

Peck, Anne E. Futures Markets and Intertemporal Commodity Pricing. *Kilmer, R. L. and Armbruster, W. J., eds.*, 1987, pp. 256–69.
[G: U.S.]

Peck, Anne E. and Budge, Carlos C. The Effects of Extraordinary Speculative Margins in the 1947–48 Grain Futures Markets. *Food Res. Inst. Stud.*, 1987, *20*(2), pp. 165–80.
[G: U.S.]

Porter, Philip K. and Scully, Gerald W. Economic Efficiency in Cooperatives. *J. Law Econ.*, October 1987, *30*(2), pp. 489–512.
[G: U.S.]

Pushpamma, P. Supplementary Foods in Rural India. *Young, R. H. and MacCormac, C. W., eds.*, 1987, pp. 69–77.   [G: India]

Rahman, Abdul H. Memory in Commodity Futures Prices in Canada: Using Akaike Information Criterion under Heteroskedasticity. *Can. J. Agr. Econ.*, March 1987, *35*(1), pp. 229–40.

Rausser, Gordon C.; Perloff, Jeffrey M. and Zusman, Pinhas. The Food Marketing System: The Relevance of Economic Efficiency Measures. *Kilmer, R. L. and Armbruster, W. J., eds.*, 1987, pp. 3–31.

Ray, S. K. Stabilization through Food Stock Operation. *J. Quant. Econ.*, January 1987, *3*(1), pp. 101–15.   [G: India]

Remenyi, J. V. Issues in Smallholder Tropical Dairying: A Reply. *Bull. Indonesian Econ. Stud.*, April 1987, *23*(1), pp. 127–30.
[G: Indonesia]

Romero, Carlos; Amador, Francisco and Barco, Antonio. Multiple Objectives in Agricultural Planning: A Compromise Programming Application. *Amer. J. Agr. Econ.*, February 1987, *69*(1), pp. 78–86.   [G: Spain]

Roy, Raghu. Marketing Food and Technologies in Rural India. *Young, R. H. and MacCormac, C. W., eds.*, 1987, pp. 47–56.   [G: India]

Rutman, Max and Bustamante, Waldo. Market Research for Nutrition Interventions. *Young, R. H. and MacCormac, C. W., eds.*, 1987, pp. 22–30.   [G: LDCs]

Salamon, Petra. An Evaluation of the Milk Quota Regime in the Federal Republic of Germany. *Kettunen, L., ed.*, 1987, pp. 29–54.
[G: W. Germany]

Sathirathai, Surakiart and Siamwalla, Ammar. GATT Law, Agricultural Trade, and Developing Countries: Lessons from Two Case Studies. *World Bank Econ. Rev.*, September 1987, *1*(4), pp. 595–618.   [G: Thailand; U.S.; EEC]

Satish, S. Efficiencies in Agricultural Markets: A Quantitative Appraisal. *Indian J. Quant.*

Econ., 1987, *3*(2), pp. 43–56.   [G: India]

Schluter, Michael. Support Systems for Agricultural Development: Commentary. *Mellor, J. W.; Delgado, C. L. and Blackie, M. J., eds.*, 1987, pp. 203–06.   [G: Africa]

Sebestyén, Mária. The Management of Agricultural Supply in a Centrally Planned Country: The Case of Hungary. *Kettunen, L., ed.*, 1987, pp. 221–30.   [G: Hungary]

Sequeira, Carlos Guillermo. SAM and the Mexican Private Sector. *Austin, J. E. and Esteva, G., eds.*, 1987, pp. 200–212.   [G: Mexico]

Shahabuddin, Quazi. Interrelationships in the Public Foodgrain Distribution System in Bangladesh—An Econometric Analysis. *Bangladesh Devel. Stud.*, March 1987, *15*(1), pp. 57–81.   [G: Bangladesh]

Sharples, Jerry A. Efficiency in Commodity Storage: A Discussion. *Kilmer, R. L. and Armbruster, W. J., eds.*, 1987, pp. 286–89.   [G: U.S.]

Shaviro, Frieda W. An Analysis of Cash and Futures Prices in the Delivery Period of Maturing Contracts in the Coffee "C" Market, 1972–1981. *J. Futures Markets*, August 1987, *7*(4), pp. 413–41.   [G: U.S.]

Sheales, Terence C. and Tomek, William G. Hedging Australian Wheat Exports Using Futures Markets. *J. Futures Markets*, October 1987, *7*(5), pp. 519–33.   [G: Australia]

Sheldon, Ian M. Testing for Weak Form Efficiency in New Agricultural Futures Markets: Some UK Evidence. *J. Agr. Econ.*, January 1987, *38*(1), pp. 51–64.   [G: U.K.]

So, Jacky C. Commodity Futures Risk Premium and Unstable Systematic Risk. *J. Futures Markets*, June 1987, *7*(3), pp. 311–26.   [G: U.S.]

Squires, Dale and Tabor, Steven. Integration of Staple Food Commodity Markets in Java. *Singapore Econ. Rev.*, October 1987, *32*(2), pp. 1–15.   [G: Singapore]

St-Pierre, Normand R. and Scobie, Grant M. The Component Pricing of Milk Revisited. *Amer. J. Agr. Econ.*, August 1987, *69*(3), pp. 693–96.   [G: U.S.]

Taub, B. A Model of Medieval Grain Prices: Comment [Corn at Interest: The Extent and Cost of Grain Storage in Medieval England]. *Amer. Econ. Rev.*, December 1987, *77*(5), pp. 1048–53.   [G: U.K.]

Thompson, Sarahelen R. Futures Markets and Intertemporal Commodity Pricing: A Discussion. *Kilmer, R. L. and Armbruster, W. J., eds.*, 1987, pp. 270–73.   [G: U.S.]

Thompson, Sarahelen R. and Waller, Mark L. The Execution Cost of Trading in Commodity Futures Markets. *Food Res. Inst. Stud.*, 1987, *20*(2), pp. 141–63.   [G: U.S.]

Thompson, Stanley R. and Bond, Gary E. Offshore Commodity Hedging under Floating Exchange Rates. *Amer. J. Agr. Econ.*, February 1987, *69*(1), pp. 46–55.   [G: U.S.; Australia]

Timmer, C. Peter. Corn Marketing. *Timmer, C. P., ed.*, 1987, pp. 201–34.   [G: Indonesia]

Tømte, Eugen D. and Sand, Cato. The Norwegian Milk Quota System: A General Report.

Kettunen, L., ed., 1987, pp. 121–31.
[G: Norway]

Trela, Irene; Whalley, John and Wigle, Randall. International Trade in Grains: Domestic Policies and Trade Impacts. *Scand. J. Econ.*, 1987, 89(3), pp. 271–83. [G: Global]

Veeman, Michele M. Hedonic Price Functions for Wheat in the World Market: Implications for Canadian Wheat Export Strategy. *Can. J. Agr. Econ.*, November 1987, 35(3), pp. 535–52.

Veeman, Michele M. and Taylor, Ellen Moreau. Two Tests of Pricing Efficiency in the Rapeseed Futures Market. *Can. J. Agr. Econ.*, March 1987, 35(1), pp. 21–32.

Wagstaff, Howard. Implementing a Two-Tier Price System for Regulating Production and Incomes in Agriculture. *Kettunen, L., ed.*, 1987, pp. 353–62. [G: EEC]

Waller, William T., Jr. Transfer Program Structure and Effectiveness. *J. Econ. Issues*, June 1987, 21(2), pp. 775–83. [G: U.S.]

Ward, Ronald W. Comments on Concepts for Evaluating Economic Efficiency. *Kilmer, R. L. and Armbruster, W. J., eds.*, 1987, pp. 209–14.

West, Sandra J. and Earle, Mary D. Market Research in Development Projects. *Young, R. H. and MacCormac, C. W., eds.*, 1987, pp. 14–21. [G: LDCs]

Westlake, M. J. The Measurement of Agricultural Price Distortion in Developing Countries. *J. Devel. Stud.*, April 1987, 23(3), pp. 367–81. [G: Kenya]

White, B. Forecasting Milk Output in England and Wales. *J. Agr. Econ.*, May 1987, 38(2), pp. 223–34. [G: U.K.]

Wiens, Thomas B. Issues in the Structural Reform of Chinese Agriculture. *J. Compar. Econ.*, September 1987, 11(3), pp. 372–84. [G: China]

Wilson, William W., et al. Import Loyalty in International Wheat Markets. *Can. J. Agr. Econ.*, May 1987, 34, pp. 295–305. [G: Global]

Wohlgenant, Michael K. and Mullen, John D. Modeling the Farm–Retail Price Spread for Beef. *Western J. Agr. Econ.*, December 1987, 12(2), pp. 119–25. [G: U.S.]

Young, R. H. and MacCormac, C. W. Market Research and Food Technology in Developing Countries. *Young, R. H. and MacCormac, C. W., eds.*, 1987, pp. 3–13. [G: LDCs]

Zacharias, Thomas P., et al. A Producer-level Cross-hedge for Rough Rice Using Wheat Futures. *Southern J. Agr. Econ.*, December 1987, 19(2), pp. 75–82. [G: U.S.]

Zalkin, Michael. Food Policy and Class Transformation in Revolutionary Nicaragua, 1979–86. *World Devel.*, July 1987, 15(7), pp. 961–84. [G: Nicaragua]

Zanias, George P. Adjustment Costs and Rational Expectations: An Application to a Tobacco Export Model. *Amer. J. Agr. Econ.*, February 1987, 69(1), pp. 22–29. [G: Greece]

7151 Corporate Agriculture

Caswell, Julie A. Aggregate Concentration: Significance, Trends, and Causes. *Wills, R. L.; Caswell, J. A. and Culbertson, J. D., eds.*, 1987, pp. 237–49. [G: U.S.]

Caswell, Julie A. Dominant Forms of Corporate Control in the U.S. Agribusiness Sector. *Amer. J. Agr. Econ.*, February 1987, 69(1), pp. 11–21. [G: U.S.]

Costa, P. AGRIMODEST: A Model of the Interaction between Agribusiness and the Rest of the Italian Economy. *Merlo, M., et al., eds.*, 1987, pp. 147–61. [G: Italy]

Crosby, Edwin A. Private Sector Agricultural Research in the United States. *Ruttan, V. W. and Pray, C. E., eds.*, 1987, pp. 395–409. [G: U.S.]

Goodman, Louis W. Food Transnational Corporations and Developing Countries: The Case of the Improved Seed Industry in Mexico. *Ruttan, V. W. and Pray, C. E., eds.*, 1987, pp. 433–49. [G: Mexico]

Landheer, J. D. The Ratio of Fat Value to Nonfat Value of Milk: An Econometric Model of Effects on Intervention Price Changes in the EC. *Europ. Rev. Agr. Econ.*, 1987, 14(2), pp. 161–78. [G: EEC]

Laumas, Prem S. and Williams, Martin. Cotton Textiles—An Agro-industry. *World Devel.*, June 1987, 15(6), pp. 841–45. [G: India]

Ortmann, G. F. and Nieuwoudt, W. L. An Evaluation of a Two-Tier Price Scheme and Possible Ethanol Production in the South African Sugar Industry. *S. Afr. J. Econ.*, June 1987, 55(2), pp. 121–35. [G: S. Africa]

Pray, Carl E. Private Sector Agricultural Research in Asia. *Ruttan, V. W. and Pray, C. E., eds.*, 1987, pp. 411–31. [G: Asia]

Ward, Clement E. Productivity-Concentration Relationship in the U.S. Meatpacking Industry. *Southern J. Agr. Econ.*, December 1987, 19(2), pp. 217–22. [G: U.S.]

716 Farm Management

7160 Farm Management

Ahmad, Khan Masood. Uncertainty, Resource Use Efficiency, and Tenurial Arrangements in Indian Agriculture. *Indian J. Quant. Econ.*, 1987, 3(1), pp. 52–66. [G: India]

Allen, Joyce E. The Role of Alternative Agricultural Enterprises in a Changing Agricultural Economy: Discussion. *Southern J. Agr. Econ.*, July 1987, 19(1), pp. 17–20. [G: U.S.]

Aly, Hassan Y., et al. The Technical Efficiency of Illinois Grain Farms: An Application of a Ray-Homothetic Production Function. *Southern J. Agr. Econ.*, July 1987, 19(1), pp. 69–78. [G: U.S.]

Anderson, John and Fearon, Gervan. Risk Management Strategy: Effects on Efficiency and Costs. *Can. J. Agr. Econ.*, May 1987, 34, pp. 62–66.

Antle, John M. Econometric Estimation of Producers' Risk Attitudes. *Amer. J. Agr. Econ.*, August 1987, *69*(3), pp. 509–22.   **[G: India]**

Arsalanbod, Mohamadreza. Farm Size Structure and the Distribution of Income in the Rural Areas of Iran. *Léon, Y. and Mahé, L., eds.*, 1987, pp. 137–44.   **[G: Iran]**

Arun Kumar, K. S., et al. Income Inequality in Rural India 1965–1983. *Léon, Y. and Mahé, L., eds.*, 1987, pp. 129–36.   **[G: India]**

Atack, Jeremy and Bateman, Fred. Yankee Farming and Settlement in the Old Northwest: A Comparative Analysis. *Klingaman, D. C. and Vedder, R. K., eds.*, 1987, pp. 77–102.
   [G: U.S.]

Avillez, Francisco and Langworthy, Mark. Intensive Agriculture in the Vale do Tejo. *Pearson, S. R., et al.*, 1987, pp. 107–23. **[G: Portugal]**

Babb, Emerson M. and Long, B. F. The Role of Alternative Agricultural Enterprises in a Changing Agricultural Economy. *Southern J. Agr. Econ.*, July 1987, *19*(1), pp. 7–15.
   [G: U.S.]

Babcock, Bruce A.; Chalfant, James A. and Collender, Robert N. Simultaneous Input Demands and Land Allocation in Agricultural Production under Uncertainty. *Western J. Agr. Econ.*, December 1987, *12*(2), pp. 207–15.

Baffoe, J. K.; Stonehouse, D. Peter and Kay, B. D. A Methodology for Farm-Level Economic Analysis of Soil Erosion Effects under Alternative Crop Rotational Systems in Ontario. *Can. J. Agr. Econ.*, March 1987, *35*(1), pp. 55–73.   **[G: Canada]**

Ball, R. M. Agricultural Contractors: Some Survey Findings. *J. Agr. Econ.*, September 1987, *38*(3), pp. 481–87.   **[G: U.K.]**

Bardhan, Pranab and Singh, Nirvikar. On Moral Hazard and Cost Sharing under Sharecropping. *Amer. J. Agr. Econ.*, May 1987, *69*(2), pp. 382–83.

Bardsley, Peter and Harris, M. An Approach to the Econometric Estimation of Attitudes to Risk in Agriculture. *Australian J. Agr. Econ.*, August 1987, *31*(2), pp. 112–26.
   [G: Australia]

Bates, Robert H. Pressure Groups, Public Policy, and Agricultural Development: A Study of Divergent Outcomes. *Bates, R. H.*, 1987, *1980*, pp. 61–91.   **[G: Ghana; Kenya]**

Beck, A. C. and Dent, J. B. A Farm Growth Model for Policy Analysis in an Extensive Pastoral Production System. *Australian J. Agr. Econ.*, April 1987, *31*(1), pp. 29–44.
   [G: New Zealand]

Belaid, Abderrezak and Miller, Stanley F. Measuring Farmers' Risk Attitudes: A Case Study of the Eastern High Plateau Region of Algeria. *Western J. Agr. Econ.*, December 1987, *12*(2), pp. 198–206.   **[G: Algeria]**

Bentley, Jeffery W. Portuguese Agriculture in Transition: Technical Change in a Northwest Parish. *Pearson, S. R., et al.*, 1987, pp. 167–86.   **[G: Portugal]**

Berg, Ernst. A Sequential Decision Model to Determine Optimal Farm-Level Grain Marketing Policies. *Europ. Rev. Agr. Econ.*, 1987, *14*(1), pp. 91–116.   **[G: W. Germany]**

Berni, P. and Begalli, D. Path Analysis: A Methodological Approach to the Interpretation of Family Farms. *Merlo, M., et al., eds.*, 1987, pp. 131–46.   **[G: Italy]**

Berthélemy, Jean-Claude and Gagey, F. The Agricultural Supply Price Elasticity in Africa: A Note on Peasants' Rationality in a Non-Walrasian Context. *Europ. Econ. Rev.*, December 1987, *31*(8), pp. 1493–1507.   **[G: Cameroon]**

Bevan, D. L., et al. Peasant Supply Response in Rationed Economies. *World Devel.*, April 1987, *15*(4), pp. 431–39.   **[G: LDCs]**

Bishop, A. L.; Lodge, G. M. and Waterhouse, D. B. A Proposed Expert System for the Management of Lucerne—LATIS. *Rev. Marketing Agr. Econ.*, August 1987, *55*(2), pp. 174–77.
   [G: Australia]

Bosch, Darrell J. and Eidman, Vernon R. Valuing Information when Risk Preferences Are Nonneutral: An Application to Irrigation Scheduling. *Amer. J. Agr. Econ.*, August 1987, *69*(3), pp. 658–68.   **[G: U.S.]**

Bouzaher, Aziz and Mendoza, Guillermo A. Goal Programming: Potential and Limitations for Agricultural Economics. *Can. J. Agr. Econ.*, March 1987, *35*(1), pp. 89–107.

Boyd, Michael L. The Performance of Private and Cooperative Socialist Organization: Postwar Yugoslav Agriculture. *Rev. Econ. Statist.*, May 1987, *69*(2), pp. 205–14.   **[G: Yugoslavia]**

Bradford, Garnett L. An Opportunity Cost View of Fixed Asset Theory and the Overproduction Trap: Comment. *Amer. J. Agr. Econ.*, May 1987, *69*(2), pp. 392–94.

Brandt, Loren. Farm Household Behavior, Factor Markets, and the Distributive Consequences of Commercialization in Early Twentieth-Century China. *J. Econ. Hist.*, September 1987, *47*(3), pp. 711–37.   **[G: China]**

Bright, Geoff. Tax Changes and Machinery Investment. *J. Agr. Econ.*, January 1987, *38*(1), pp. 39–49.   **[G: U.K.]**

Briquel, Vincent and Baschet, Jean-François. Les disparités catégorielles de revenus: quelques facteurs d'évolution. (With English summary.) *Léon, Y. and Mahé, L., eds.*, 1987, pp. 145–56.   **[G: France]**

Brown, William J. A Risk Efficiency Analysis of Crop Rotations in Saskatchewan. *Can. J. Agr. Econ.*, July 1987, *35*(2), pp. 333–55.
   [G: Canada]

Brun, André. La pluriactivité des agriculteurs et des familles agricoles. Etude du cas français. (With English summary.) *Léon, Y. and Mahé, L., eds.*, 1987, pp. 395–413.   **[G: France]**

Buchholz, H. E. Research Investments in New Products: Bioethanol and Industrial Use of Agricultural Products. *Kettunen, L., ed.*, 1987, pp. 249–69.

Burt, Oscar R.; Frank, Michael D. and Beattie, Bruce R. Prior Information and Heuristic Ridge Regression for Production Function Estimation. *Western J. Agr. Econ.*, December 1987, *12*(2), pp. 135–43.   **[G: U.S.]**

Burton, Robert O., Jr., et al. Nearly Optimal Linear Programming Solutions: Some Conceptual Issues and a Farm Management Application. *Amer. J. Agr. Econ.*, November 1987, 69(4), pp. 813–18. **[G: U.S.]**

Butault, Jean-Pierre; Lerouvillois, Philippe and Rousselle, Jean-Marc. Les facteurs de dispersion des revenus agricoles (RICA—France 1979). (With English summary.) *Léon, Y. and Mahé, L., eds.*, 1987, pp. 157–75. **[G: France]**

Byrnes, Patricia, et al. Technical Efficiency and Size: The Case of Illinois Grain Farms. *Europ. Rev. Agr. Econ.*, 1987, 14(4), pp. 367–81. **[G: U.S.]**

Carter, Colin A., et al. Agricultural Labor Strikes and Farmers' Income. *Econ. Inquiry*, January 1987, 25(1), pp. 121–33. **[G: U.S.]**

Carter, Michael R. Risk Sharing and Incentives in the Decollectivization of Agriculture. *Oxford Econ. Pap.*, September 1987, 39(3), pp. 577–95.

Cecora, James. Agriculture—Its Effects on the Level-of-Living and Subsistence Technology of Farming Households. *Léon, Y. and Mahé, L., eds.*, 1987, pp. 7–24. **[G: W. Germany]**

Chambers, Robert G. and Lopez, Ramon E. Tax Policies and the Financially Constrained Farm Household. *Amer. J. Agr. Econ.*, May 1987, 69(2), pp. 369–77.

Christy, Ralph D. The Role of Farmer Cooperatives in a Changing Agricultural Economy. *Southern J. Agr. Econ.*, July 1987, 19(1), pp. 21–28. **[G: U.S.]**

Coffey, Joseph D. The Role of Farmer Cooperatives in a Changing Agricultural Economy: Discussion. *Southern J. Agr. Econ.*, July 1987, 19(1), pp. 29–30. **[G: U.S.]**

Colomb, Robert M. Knowledge-Based Decision Support Systems: A Background to Expert Systems. *Rev. Marketing Agr. Econ.*, August 1987, 55(2), pp. 162–66. **[G: Australia]**

Cordellier, Christian. Les revenus des familles d'agriculteurs en 1978: composition et disparités. (With English summary.) *Léon, Y. and Mahé, L., eds.*, 1987, pp. 217–36. **[G: France]**

Dawson, P. J. Farm-Specific Technical Efficiency in the England and Wales Dairy Sector. *Europ. Rev. Agr. Econ.*, 1987, 14(4), pp. 383–94. **[G: U.K.]**

Delforce, J. C. and MacAulay, T. G. Use of Tractors in South Sulawesi: A Case Study Approach. *Bull. Indonesian Econ. Stud.*, August 1987, 23(2), pp. 101–17. **[G: Indonesia]**

Deolalikar, Anil B. and Vijverberg, Wim P. M. A Test of Heterogeneity of Family and Hired Labour in Asian Agriculture. *Oxford Bull. Econ. Statist.*, August 1987, 49(3), pp. 291–305. **[G: India; Malaysia]**

van Dijk, G. and Veerman, C. P. Efficiency Considerations of Supply Management. *Kettunen, L., ed.*, 1987, pp. 311–21.

Dijkhuizen, A. A.; Stelwagen, J. and Renkema, J. A. An Economic Simulation Model to Support Management Decisions in Dairy Herds.

Europ. Rev. Agr. Econ., 1987, 14(4), pp. 395–412.

Driver, H. C. Technology and Managerial Skills: Cost Economies or Diseconomies? *Can. J. Agr. Econ.*, May 1987, 34, pp. 27–39. **[G: Canada]**

Duff, Bart. Changes in Small Farm Paddy Threshing Technology in Thailand and the Philippines. *Stewart, F., ed.*, 1987, pp. 95–139. **[G: Thailand; Philippines]**

Dumondel, Michel. Pluriactivité et disparités socio-économiques au niveau communal suisse. (With English summary.) *Léon, Y. and Mahé, L., eds.*, 1987, pp. 237–53. **[G: Switzerland]**

Eddleman, Bobby R. Impacts of Emerging Technologies on Food and Agricultural Productive Capacity: Discussion. *Amer. J. Agr. Econ.*, May 1987, 69(2), pp. 461–62. **[G: U.S.]**

Ekanayake, S. A. B. Location Specificity, Settler Type and Productive Efficiency: A Study of the Mahaweli Project in Sri Lanka. *J. Devel. Stud.*, July 1987, 23(4), pp. 509–21. **[G: Sri Lanka]**

Ekanayake, S. A. B. and Jayasuriya, Sisira K. Measurement of Firm-Specific Technical Efficiency: A Comparison of Methods. *J. Agr. Econ.*, January 1987, 38(1), pp. 115–22. **[G: Sri Lanka]**

Ethridge, Don E. and Neeper, Jarral T. Producer Returns from Cotton Strength and Uniformity: An Hedonic Price Approach. *Southern J. Agr. Econ.*, July 1987, 19(1), pp. 91–97. **[G: U.S.]**

Evans, David S. Empirical Analysis of the Size Distribution of Farms: Discussion. *Amer. J. Agr. Econ.*, May 1987, 69(2), pp. 484–85.

Falk, Constance L.; Tilley, Daniel S. and Schatzer, R. Joe. The Packing Simulation Model. *Southern J. Agr. Econ.*, December 1987, 19(2), pp. 211–15.

Feder, Gershon; Lau, Lawrence J. and Slade, Roger H. Does Agricultural Extension Pay? The Training and Visit System in Northwest India. *Amer. J. Agr. Econ.*, August 1987, 69(3), pp. 677–86. **[G: India]**

Feder, Gershon and Onchan, Tongroj. Land Ownership Security and Farm Investment in Thailand. *Amer. J. Agr. Econ.*, May 1987, 69(2), pp. 311–20. **[G: Thailand]**

Finan, Timothy J. Portuguese Agriculture in Transition: Intensive Agriculture in the Northwest. *Pearson, S. R., et al.*, 1987, pp. 141–63. **[G: Portugal]**

Fontaine, Jean-Marc. Les projets de libéralisation des agricultures africaines. Un point de vue critique appuyé sur les cas kenyan et tanzanien. (On Economic Liberalism and African Agriculture. With English summary.) *Écon. Soc.*, July 1987, 21(7), pp. 185–208. **[G: Kenya; Tanzania]**

Fox, Roger. Extensive Farming in the Alentejo. *Pearson, S. R., et al.*, 1987, pp. 85–106. **[G: Portugal]**

Fox, Roger and Finan, Timothy J. Portuguese Agriculture in Transition: Future Technical and Structural Adjustments in Northwestern

Agriculture. *Pearson, S. R., et al.*, 1987, pp. 202–20. [G: Portugal]

Fox, Roger and Finan, Timothy J. Portuguese Agriculture in Transition: Patterns of Technical Change in the Northwest. *Pearson, S. R., et al.*, 1987, pp. 187–201. [G: Portugal]

Garcia, Philip; Offutt, Susan E. and Sonka, Steven T. Size Distribution and Growth in a Sample of Illinois Cash Grain Farms. *Amer. J. Agr. Econ.*, May 1987, 69(2), pp. 471–76. [G: U.S.]

Garoian, L.; Conner, J. R. and Scifres, C. J. A Discrete Stochastic Programming Model to Estimate Optimal Burning Schedules on Rangeland. *Southern J. Agr. Econ.*, December 1987, 19(2), pp. 53–60. [G: U.S.]

Gebauer, Rolf H. Socio-economic Classification of Farm Households. *Léon, Y. and Mahé, L., eds.*, 1987, pp. 177–98. [G: W. Germany]

Gebauer, Rolf H. Socio-economic Classification of Farm Households—Conceptual, Methodological and Empirical Considerations. *Europ. Rev. Agr. Econ.*, 1987, 14(3), pp. 261–83. [G: W. Germany]

Giaever, Harald. Attempts to Predict Farmers' Responses to Government Policy Measures through Linear Programming Models. *Kettunen, L., ed.*, 1987, pp. 323–30. [G: Norway]

Gineo, Wayne M. A Graphic Interpretation of Risk Programming Models. *Can. J. Agr. Econ.*, March 1987, 35(1), pp. 155–67.

Glover, David J. Increasing the Benefits to Smallholders from Contract Farming: Problems for Farmers' Organizations and Policy Makers. *World Devel.*, April 1987, 15(4), pp. 441–48. [G: LDCs]

Gopalakrishnan, Chennat. Energy–Nonenergy Input Substitution in Western U.S. Agriculture: Some Findings. *Energy J.*, January 1987, 8(1), pp. 133–45. [G: U.S.]

Gordon, Kathryn and Oriach, Philippe. Politique agricole américaine et macro-économie. (American Agricultural Policy and the Macroeconomy. With English summary.) *Écon. Soc.*, July 1987, 21(7), pp. 37–55. [G: U.S.]

Griffin, Ronald C.; Montgomery, John M. and Rister, M. Edward. Selecting Functional Form in Production Function Analysis. *Western J. Agr. Econ.*, December 1987, 12(2), pp. 216–27.

Griffiths, William E.; Anderson, Jock R. and Hamal, K. B. Subjective Distributions as Econometric Response Data. *Australian J. Agr. Econ.*, August 1987, 31(2), pp. 127–41. [G: Nepal]

Grimm, Sadi S.; Paris, Quirino and Williams, William A. A von Liebig Model for Water and Nitrogen Crop Response. *Western J. Agr. Econ.*, December 1987, 12(2), pp. 182–92. [G: U.S.]

Gyimah-Brempong, Kwabena; Akaah, Ishael P. and Dadzie, Kofi Q. Cocoa Production Technology in Ghana: An Application of the Translog Production Function. *Eastern Afr. Econ. Rev.*, June 1987, 3(1), pp. 15–20. [G: Ghana]

Hall, Bronwyn H. Empirical Analysis of the Size Distribution of Farms: Discussion. *Amer. J. Agr. Econ.*, May 1987, 69(2), pp. 486–87.

Hanley, N. and Lingard, J. Controlling Straw Burning: Farm Management Modelling of the Policy Options Using Linear Programming. *J. Agr. Econ.*, January 1987, 38(1), pp. 15–25. [G: U.K.]

Hardesty, Sermin D.; Carman, Hoy F. and Moore, Charles V. Dynamic Analysis of Income Taxes on Farm Firms. *Amer. J. Agr. Econ.*, May 1987, 69(2), pp. 358–68. [G: U.S.]

Hearn, A. B. SIRATAC: A Decision Support System for Cotton Management. *Rev. Marketing Agr. Econ.*, August 1987, 55(2), pp. 170–73. [G: Australia]

Helms, Gary L.; Bailey, DeeVon and Glover, Terrence F. Government Programs and Adoption of Conservation Tillage Practices on Nonirrigated Wheat Farms. *Amer. J. Agr. Econ.*, November 1987, 69(4), pp. 786–95. [G: U.S.]

Herdt, Robert W. A Retrospective View of Technological and Other Changes in Philippine Rice Farming, 1965–1982. *Econ. Develop. Cult. Change*, January 1987, 35(2), pp. 329–49. [G: Philippines]

Hertel, Thomas W. Inferring Long-run Elasticities from a Short-run Quadratic Profit Function. *Can. J. Agr. Econ.*, March 1987, 35(1), pp. 169–80.

Higgins, James. The Distribution of Income on Irish Farms. *Léon, Y. and Mahé, L., eds.*, 1987, pp. 255–70. [G: Ireland]

Hill, Berkeley. Income Disparities in UK Agriculture: Information and Inference. *Léon, Y. and Mahé, L., eds.*, 1987, pp. 415–32. [G: U.K.]

Howard, Wayne H., et al. Information and Herd Health Management Practices in Texas Dairies. *Southern J. Agr. Econ.*, December 1987, 19(2), pp. 1–10. [G: U.S.]

Hubbard, L. J. and Dawson, P. J. Ex ante and Ex post Long-run Average Cost Functions. *Appl. Econ.*, October 1987, 19(10), pp. 1411–19. [G: U.K.]

Hung, Hsien-Ming and Fuller, Wayne A. Regression Estimation of Crop Acreages with Transformed Landsat Data as Auxiliary Variables. *J. Bus. Econ. Statist.*, October 1987, 5(4), pp. 475–82. [G: U.S.]

Hybel, Jan. Policy Support to the Development of Production Services in the Individual Agriculture in Poland. *Kettunen, L., ed.*, 1987, pp. 183–94. [G: Poland]

Johnson, Frank; Spreen, Thomas H. and Hewitt, Timothy. A Stochastic Dominance Analysis of Contract Grazing Feeder Cattle. *Southern J. Agr. Econ.*, December 1987, 19(2), pp. 11–19. [G: U.S.]

Jolly, Curtis M. and Diop, Oumar. The Negative Effects of Inappropriate Price Stimulation; the Case of Senegal: Rice Price Increases to Encourage Production May Harm Families of Non-responsive Subsistence Farmers. *Amer.*

J. Econ. Soc., July 1987, *46*(3), pp. 355–68.
[G: Senegal]

Jorgensen, Aage Walter. Measuring Income, Income Distribution and Economic Return in Danish Agriculture. *Léon, Y. and Mahé, L., eds.*, 1987, pp. 109–26. [G: Denmark]

Josephson, R. M. An Overview of Microelectronics in Agriculture. *Can. J. Agr. Econ.*, May 1987, *34*, pp. 233–48. [G: Canada]

Joshi, P. C. Technological Potentialities of Peasant Agriculture: East–West Parallels and Contrasts. *Joshi, P. C.*, 1987, pp. 159–89.
[G: Asia; W. Europe]

Josling, Timothy and Tangermann, Stefan. Portuguese Agriculture in Transition: Future Commodity Policies. *Pearson, S. R., et al.*, 1987, pp. 223–38. [G: Portugal]

Kako, Toshiyuki. Development of the Farm Machinery Industry in Japan: A Case Study of the Walking Type Tractor. *Hitotsubashi J. Econ.*, December 1987, *28*(2), pp. 155–71.
[G: Japan]

Kaylen, Michael S.; Preckel, Paul V. and Loehman, Edna T. Risk Modeling via Direct Utility Maximization Using Numerical Quadrature. *Amer. J. Agr. Econ.*, August 1987, *69*(3), pp. 701–06.

Kenyon, David and Clay, John. Analysis of Profit Margin Hedging Strategies for Hog Producers. *J. Futures Markets*, April 1987, *7*(2), pp. 183–202. [G: U.S.]

Kessler, Peter and Gantner, Urs. Disparités des revenus des familles d'agriculteurs en Suisse. (With English summary.) *Léon, Y. and Mahé, L., eds.*, 1987, pp. 433–47. [G: Switzerland]

Khandker, Shahidur R.; Mestelman, Stuart and Feeny, David. Allocative Efficiency, the Aggregation of Labour Inputs, and the Effects of Farm Size and Tenancy Status: Tests from Rural Bangladesh. *J. Devel. Stud.*, October 1987, *24*(1), pp. 31–42. [G: Bangladesh]

Kingma, Douwe and Oskam, Arie J. Measuring Income Disparities between (and within) Farm Households and Non-farm Households by Means of the Individual Welfare Function of Income. *Léon, Y. and Mahé, L., eds.*, 1987, pp. 25–42. [G: Netherlands]

Kirke, A. W. and Moss, J. E. A Linear Programming Study of Family-Run Dairy Farms in Northern Ireland. *J. Agr. Econ.*, May 1987, *38*(2), pp. 257–69. [G: N. Ireland]

Klank, Leszek. Income Disparities among Farm Households and Agricultural Policy in Poland. *Léon, Y. and Mahé, L., eds.*, 1987, pp. 449–62. [G: Poland]

Klein, K. K. and Tkatchyk, S. J. Impacts of Land Purchase on Financial Health of Saskatchewan Crop Farms: A Whole-Farm Simulation. *Can. J. Agr. Econ.*, November 1987, *35*(3), pp. 639–52. [G: Canada]

Knight, Thomas O. and Kubiak, Kathryn A. Extension Decision Aids for the Dairy Termination Program: A Comparative Analysis. *Amer. J. Agr. Econ.*, November 1987, *69*(4), pp. 777–85. [G: U.S.]

Kraft, Daryl F. Computers and Information Management in Agriculture. *Can. J. Agr. Econ.*, May 1987, *34*, pp. 249–57.

Kula, Erhun. Prospects for Farmers to Improve Incomes by Switching Crops in N. Ireland: An Analysis to Improve Government Support Schemes. *Léon, Y. and Mahé, L., eds.*, 1987, pp. 297–307. [G: U.K.]

Lamble, Wayne. Learning: Considerations for Farm Management Training. *Can. J. Agr. Econ.*, December 1987, *35*(4), pp. 741–54.

Langworthy, Mark. Dairying in the Azores. *Pearson, S. R., et al.*, 1987, pp. 124–40.
[G: Portugal]

Leatham, David J.; McCarl, Bruce A. and Richardson, James W. Implications of Crop Insurance for Farmers and Lenders. *Southern J. Agr. Econ.*, December 1987, *19*(2), pp. 113–20.

Lee, John G.; Ellis, John R. and Lacewell, Ronald D. Evaluation of Production and Financial Risk: A Stochastic Dominance Approach. *Can. J. Agr. Econ.*, March 1987, *35*(1), pp. 109–26. [G: U.S.]

Leuthold, Raymond M. and Peterson, Paul E. A Portfolio Approach to Optimal Hedging for a Commercial Cattle Feedlot. *J. Futures Markets*, April 1987, *7*(2), pp. 119–33. [G: U.S.]

Levy, Béatrice. Le patrimoine des agriculteurs en France. (With English summary.) *Léon, Y. and Mahé, L., eds.*, 1987, pp. 309–23.
[G: France]

Lichtenberg, Erik. Integrated versus Chemical Pest Management: The Case of Rice Field Mosquito Control. *J. Environ. Econ. Manage.*, September 1987, *14*(3), pp. 304–12.
[G: U.S.]

Lockheed, Marlaine E.; Jamison, Dean T. and Lau, Lawrence J. Farmer Education and Farm Efficiency: Reply. *Econ. Develop. Cult. Change*, April 1987, *35*(3), pp. 643–44.

Lockwood, R. C. Diffusion and Adoption of New Technology at the Farm Level. *Can. J. Agr. Econ.*, May 1987, *34*, pp. 147–50.

Loyns, R. M. A., et al. Toward an Improved Model of Farm Management: The Case for Including Marketing. *Can. J. Agr. Econ.*, May 1987, *34*, pp. 70–82. [G: Canada]

Marini, M. A Typology of Farm Families in Southern Italian Marginal Areas. *Merlo, M., et al., eds.*, 1987, pp. 261–76. [G: Italy]

Marra, Michele C. and Carlson, Gerald A. The Role of Farm Size and Resource Constraints in the Choice between Risky Technologies. *Western J. Agr. Econ.*, December 1987, *12*(2), pp. 109–18. [G: U.S.]

McCamley, Francis and Kliebenstein, James B. Describing and Identifying the Complete Set of Target MOTAD Solutions. *Amer. J. Agr. Econ.*, August 1987, *69*(3), pp. 669–76.

McCamley, Francis and Kliebenstein, James B. Identifying the Set of SSD-Efficient Mixtures of Risky Alternatives. *Western J. Agr. Econ.*, July 1987, *12*(1), pp. 86–94.

McCarl, Bruce A., et al. Stochastic Dominance over Potential Portfolios: Caution Regarding Covariance. *Amer. J. Agr. Econ.*, November

1987, *69*(4), pp. 804–12.

McSweeny, William T.; Kenyon, David and Kramer, Randall A. Toward an Appropriate Measure of Uncertainty in a Risk Programming Model. *Amer. J. Agr. Econ.*, February 1987, *69*(1), pp. 87–96. [G: U.S.]

Miles, Don G. Systems Management, Repair, and Improvement: Systems Economics Applied to a Small, Constrained Poultry Farm. *Fox, K. A. and Miles, D. G., eds.*, 1987, pp. 110–17.

Mink, Stephen D. The Economics of Input Use. *Timmer, C. P., ed.*, 1987, pp. 88–104. [G: Indonesia]

Mink, Stephen D.; Dorosh, Paul A. and Perry, Douglas H. Corn Production Systems. *Timmer, C. P., ed.*, 1987, pp. 62–87. [G: Indonesia]

Moffitt, L. Joe and Farnsworth, Richard L. Thresholds for Chemical Control of Agricultural Pests in a Dynamic Ecosystem. *Can. J. Agr. Econ.*, November 1987, *35*(3), pp. 627–37.

Monke, Eric A. Portuguese Agriculture in Transition: Future Policies Influencing Agricultural Factor Markets. *Pearson, S. R., et al.*, 1987, pp. 239–58. [G: Portugal]

Mudahar, Mohinder S. Measuring the Contribution of Fertilizer to Food Production. *Indian J. Quant. Econ.*, 1987, *3*(2), pp. 1–19. [G: India]

Mumey, G. A. Improving On-Farm Financial Management. *Can. J. Agr. Econ.*, December 1987, *35*(4), pp. 735–40.

Narayana, N. S. S. and Parikh, Kirit S. Estimation of Yield Functions for Major Cereals in India. *J. Quant. Econ.*, July 1987, *3*(2), pp. 287–312. [G: India]

Nehen, I. K. and Wills, Ian R. Efficiency and Distribution: The Case of Tractors in Sawah Land Preparation in West Java, Indonesia. *Bull. Indonesian Econ. Stud.*, December 1987, *23*(3), pp. 34–51. [G: Indonesia]

Niessler, Rudolf. Income Distribution in Austrian Agriculture (Empirical Findings, Theories and Strategies Concerning Income Policy). *Léon, Y. and Mahé, L., eds.*, 1987, pp. 325–38. [G: Austria]

Nitzan, Shmuel and Schnytzer, Adi. Diligence and Laziness in the Chinese Countryside Revisited. *J. Devel. Econ.*, August 1987, *26*(2), pp. 407–18. [G: China]

Nix, John. Appraisal of Curent and Future Challenges Facing the Farm Management Specialist. *Can. J. Agr. Econ.*, December 1987, *35*(4), pp. 675–90.

Norton, Geoff. Developments in Expert Systems for Pest Management at Imperial College, U.K. *Rev. Marketing Agr. Econ.*, August 1987, *55*(2), pp. 167–70. [G: U.K.]

Odhiambo, Mark Ollunga. An Application of Stochastic Econometric Production Risk Model: The Case of Egyptian Cotton Production. *Eastern Afr. Econ. Rev.*, December 1987, *3*(2), pp. 131–42. [G: Egypt]

Offutt, Susan E.; Garcia, Philip and Pinar, Musa. The Distribution of Gains from Technological Advance when Input Quality Varies. *Amer. J. Agr. Econ.*, May 1987, *69*(2), pp. 321–27. [G: U.S.]

Oyugi, L. A.; Mukhebi, A. W. and Mwangi, W. M. The Impact of Cash Cropping on Food Production: A Case Study of Tobacco and Maize in Migori Division, South Nyanza District of Kenya. *Eastern Afr. Econ. Rev.*, June 1987, *3*(1), pp. 43–50. [G: Kenya]

Park, William M. and Sawyer, David G. Cost Effectiveness of Alternative Subsidy Strategies for Soil Erosion Control. *Southern J. Agr. Econ.*, December 1987, *19*(2), pp. 21–32. [G: U.S.]

Peterson, Paul E. and Leuthold, Raymond M. A Portfolio Approach to Optimal Hedging for a Commercial Cattle Feedlot. *J. Futures Markets*, August 1987, *7*(4), pp. 443–57. [G: U.S.]

Phillip, Dayo O. A. and Abalu, George O. I. Price Expectations Formation and Revision in the Nerlovian Framework with Application to Nigerian Farmers. *J. Agr. Econ.*, September 1987, *38*(3), pp. 491–95. [G: Nigeria]

Phillips, Joseph M. A Comment on Farmer Education and Farm Efficiency: A Survey. *Econ. Develop. Cult. Change*, April 1987, *35*(3), pp. 637–41.

Phillips, Michael J. and Lu, Yao-chi. Impact of Emerging Technologies on Food and Agricultural Productive Capacity. *Amer. J. Agr. Econ.*, May 1987, *69*(2), pp. 448–53. [G: U.S.]

Pingali, Prabhu L. and Binswanger, Hans P. Population Density and Agricultural Intensification: A Study of the Evolution of Technologies in Tropical Agriculture. *Johnson, D. G. and Lee, R. D., eds.*, 1987, pp. 27–56. [G: LDCs]

Plankl, Reiner. Identification and Estimation of the Number of Low-income Farmers in Federal Republic of Germany by Means of a Sample of Bookkeeping Test Farmers. *Léon, Y. and Mahé, L., eds.*, 1987, pp. 339–60. [G: W. Germany]

Platteau, Jean-Philippe and Abraham, Anita. An Inquiry into Quasi-credit Contracts: The Role of Reciprocal Credit and Interlinked Deals in Small-scale Fishing Communities. *J. Devel. Stud.*, July 1987, *23*(4), pp. 461–90. [G: LDCs]

Poppe, Krijn J. and Zachariasse, Vinus. Income Disparities among Farm Households and Agricultural Policy Case: The Netherlands. *Léon, Y. and Mahé, L., eds.*, 1987, pp. 361–76. [G: Netherlands]

Preckel, Paul V.; Loehman, Edna T. and Kaylen, Michael S. The Value of Public Information for Microeconomic Production Decisions. *Western J. Agr. Econ.*, December 1987, *12*(2), pp. 193–97. [G: U.S.]

Pudup, Mary Beth. From Farm to Factory: Structuring and Location of the U.S. Farm Machinery Industry. *Econ. Geogr.*, July 1987, *63*(3), pp. 203–22. [G: U.S.]

Putterman, Louis. The Incentive Problem and

the Demise of Team Farming in China. *J. Devel. Econ.*, June 1987, *26*(1), pp. 103–27. **[G: China]**

Puz, Valery. Management in USSR Agriculture: Some Recent Developments. *Kettunen, L., ed.*, 1987, pp. 195–204. **[G: U.S.S.R.]**

Quaisser, Wolfgang. The New Agricultural Reform in China: From the People's Communes to Peasant Agriculture. *Gey, P.; Kosta, J. and Quaisser, W., eds.*, 1987, pp. 173–96. **[G: China]**

Quasem, Md. Abul. Farmers' Participation in the Paddy Markets, Their Marketed Surplus and Factors Affecting It in Bangladesh. *Bangladesh Devel. Stud.*, March 1987, *15*(1), pp. 83–1044. **[G: Bangladesh]**

Rao, J. Mohan. Productivity and Distribution under Cropsharing Tenancy. *World Devel.*, September 1987, *15*(9), pp. 1163–78.

Rawat, J. K., et al. A Pest and Timber Management Model: Jack Pine Budworm and Jack Pine. *Can. J. Agr. Econ.*, July 1987, *35*(2), pp. 441–61. **[G: Canada]**

Reddy, Y. V. R., et al. Dryland Farming: Constraints to Improved Technology. *Margin*, Apr.-June 1987, *19*(3), pp. 48–54. **[G: India]**

Rehman, Tahir and Romero, Carlos. Multiple Criteria Decision Techniques and Multi Purpose Agriculture. *Merlo, M., et al., eds.*, 1987, pp. 7–18.

Reid, Donald W. and Bradford, Garnett L. A Farm Firm Model of Machinery Investment Decisions. *Amer. J. Agr. Econ.*, February 1987, *69*(1), pp. 64–77.

Ribeiro da Costa, Manuel. Uma análise econométric das relações de substituição entre os factores de produção na agricultura portuguesa (1950–1980). (With English summary.) *Economia (Portugal)*, January 1987, *11*(1), pp. 15–49. **[G: Portugal]**

Rickson, Roy, et al. Social Bases of Farmers' Responses to Land Degradation. *Chisholm, A. and Dumsday, R., eds.*, 1987, pp. 187–200. **[G: Australia]**

Roberts, Roland K. and Garrod, Peter V. Demand for Plant Nutrients in Tennessee Disaggregated by Mixed Fertilizers and Direct Application Materials. *Southern J. Agr. Econ.*, December 1987, *19*(2), pp. 145–51. **[G: U.S.]**

Robson, Nigel; Gasson, Ruth and Hill, Berkeley. Part Time Farming—Implications for Farm Family Income. *J. Agr. Econ.*, May 1987, *38*(2), pp. 167–91. **[G: U.K.]**

Romain, Robert F. J.; Penson, John B., Jr. and Lambert, Rémy E. Capacity Depreciation, Implicit Rental Price, and Investment Demand for Farm Tractors in Canada. *Can. J. Agr. Econ.*, July 1987, *35*(2), pp. 373–85. **[G: Canada]**

Romero, Carlos; Amador, Francisco and Barco, Antonio. Multiple Objectives in Agricultural Planning: A Compromise Programming Application. *Amer. J. Agr. Econ.*, February 1987, *69*(1), pp. 78–86. **[G: Spain]**

Roszkowski, Wojciech. Large Estates and Small Farms in the Polish Agrarian Economy between the Wars (1918–1938). *J. Europ. Econ. Hist.*, Spring 1987, *16*(1), pp. 75–88. **[G: Poland]**

Roumasset, James A. and Uy, Marilou. Agency Costs and the Agricultural Firm. *Land Econ.*, August 1987, *63*(3), pp. 290–302. **[G: Philippines]**

Saith, Ashwani. Contrasting Experiences in Rural Industrialisation: Are the East Asian Successes Transferable? *Islam, R., ed.*, 1987, pp. 241–303. **[G: Japan; Taiwan; S. Korea]**

Salassi, Michael E.; Eddleman, Bobby R. and Hamill, James G. Economic Survivability of Mississippi Rice Farms: A Deterministic Simulation Approach. *Southern J. Agr. Econ.*, December 1987, *19*(2), pp. 163–73. **[G: U.S.]**

Santana, Carlos Augusto Mattos. Efeitos das Políticas Econômicas Brasileiras sobre o Setor Doméstico de soja em Grão. (With English summary.) *Pesquisa Planejamento Econ.*, December 1987, *17*(3), pp. 633–78. **[G: Brazil]**

Satish, S. Efficiencies in Agricultural Markets: A Quantitative Appraisal. *Indian J. Quant. Econ.*, 1987, *3*(2), pp. 43–56. **[G: India]**

Schilizzi, Steven G. M. Physical Economics, Technology, and Agroecosystems. *Pillet, G. and Murota, T., eds.*, 1987, pp. 109–28. **[G: France; Vietnam]**

Schnitkey, Gary D.; Barry, Peter J. and Ellinger, Paul N. A Microcomputer Analysis of Farm Financial Performance. *Southern J. Agr. Econ.*, December 1987, *19*(2), pp. 203–09.

Schoney, Richard A. New Developments in Farm Planning Models: The Top Management Model. *Can. J. Agr. Econ.*, May 1987, *34*, pp. 258–64.

Schoney, Richard A. and Nicholson, R. C. The Effect of Tax Classification of Part-time Farming in Saskatchewan. *Can. J. Agr. Econ.*, July 1987, *35*(2), pp. 421–39. **[G: Canada]**

Segarra, Eduardo and Taylor, Daniel B. Farm Level Dynamic Analysis of Soil Conservation: An Application to the Piedmont Area of Virginia. *Southern J. Agr. Econ.*, December 1987, *19*(2), pp. 61–73. **[G: U.S.]**

Shaban, Radwan Ali. Testing between Competing Models of Sharecropping. *J. Polit. Econ.*, October 1987, *95*(5), pp. 893–920. **[G: India]**

Shahabuddin, Quazi and Feeny, David. Efficiency, Share Tenancy, and Allocative Behavior in Peasant Farming: A Safety-First Approach. *J. Econ. Devel.*, June 1987, *12*(1), pp. 149–60.

Shapiro, Daniel M.; Bollman, Ray D. and Ehrensaft, Philip. Farm Size and Growth in Canada. *Amer. J. Agr. Econ.*, May 1987, *69*(2), pp. 477–83. **[G: Canada]**

Sharma, H. R.; Sharma, S. K. and Singh, Kamlesh. Improved Technology and Returns to Scale—A Study of Marginal Farms. *Margin*, Jan.-Mar. 1987, *19*(2), pp. 83–87. **[G: India]**

Shedd, M. S.; Farrell, D. L. and Kerr, William A. Capital Gains and Pension Incomes: Security and Equity Implications for Canadian

Farmers. *Can. J. Agr. Econ.*, November 1987, *35*(3), pp. 615–26. **[G: Canada]**

Shrestha, Chandra M.; Debertin, David L. and Anschel, Kurt R. Stochastic Efficiency versus Mean–Variance Criteria as Predictors of Adoption of Reduced Tillage: Comment. *Amer. J. Agr. Econ.*, November 1987, *69*(4), pp. 857–60. **[G: U.S.]**

Shumway, C. Richard; Jegasothy, Kandiah and Alexander, William P. Production Interrelationships in Sri Lankan Peasant Agriculture. *Australian J. Agr. Econ.*, April 1987, *31*(1), pp. 16–28. **[G: Sri Lanka]**

Smith, G. Scott; Wetzstein, Michael E. and Douce, G. Keith. Evaluation of Various Pest-Management Characteristics. *Southern J. Agr. Econ.*, December 1987, *19*(2), pp. 93–101. **[G: U.S.]**

Soares, Fernando B. Regional Disparities on Farm Income in Portugal: Will EEC Membership Be a Remedial or Aggravating Factor? *Léon, Y. and Mahé, L., eds.*, 1987, pp. 477–88. **[G: Portugal]**

Squires, Dale. Long-run Profit Functions for Multiproduct Firms. *Amer. J. Agr. Econ.*, August 1987, *69*(3), pp. 558–69. **[G: U.S.]**

SriRamaratnam, S., et al. Fertilization under Uncertainty: An Analysis Based on Producer Yield Expectations. *Amer. J. Agr. Econ.*, May 1987, *69*(2), pp. 349–57. **[G: U.S.]**

Stefanou, Spiro E. Technical Change, Uncertainty, and Investment. *Amer. J. Agr. Econ.*, February 1987, *69*(1), pp. 158–65.

Stonehouse, D. Peter; Baffoe, J. K. and Kay, B. D. The Impacts of Changes in Key Economic Variables on Crop Rotational Choices on Ontario Cash-Cropping. *Can. J. Agr. Econ.*, July 1987, *35*(2), pp. 403–20. **[G: Canada]**

Sumner, Daniel A. and Leiby, James D. An Econometric Analysis of the Effects of Human Capital on Size and Growth among Dairy Farms. *Amer. J. Agr. Econ.*, May 1987, *69*(2), pp. 465–70. **[G: U.S.]**

Taub, B. A Model of Medieval Grain Prices: Comment [Corn at Interest: The Extent and Cost of Grain Storage in Medieval England]. *Amer. Econ. Rev.*, December 1987, *77*(5), pp. 1048–53. **[G: U.K.]**

Tew, Bernard V. and Reid, Donald W. More Evidence on Expected Value-Variance Analysis versus Direct Utility Maximization. *J. Finan. Res.*, Fall 1987, *10*(3), pp. 249–57. **[G: U.S.]**

Thompson, Shelley J. and von Witzke, Harald. Income Inequality within Agriculture: Relevant Dimensions and Methods of Analysis. *Léon, Y. and Mahé, L., eds.*, 1987, pp. 81–94. **[G: W. Germany]**

Tillieut, Michel. Disparité des revenus en agriculture dans la Communauté Européenne. (With English summary.) *Léon, Y. and Mahé, L., eds.*, 1987, pp. 199–214. **[G: EEC]**

Turvey, Calum Greig and Driver, H. C. Systematic and Nonsystematic Risks in Agriculture. *Can. J. Agr. Econ.*, July 1987, *35*(2), pp. 387–401. **[G: U.S.]**

Ulrich, Alvin; Furtan, William Hartley and

Schmitz, Andrew. The Cost of a Licensing System Regulation: An Example from Canadian Prairie Agriculture. *J. Polit. Econ.*, February 1987, *95*(1), pp. 160–78. **[G: Canada]**

Upton, Martin and Haworth, Simon. The Growth of Farms. *Europ. Rev. Agr. Econ.*, 1987, *14*(4), pp. 351–66. **[G: U.K.]**

Verma, B. N. and Bromley, Daniel W. The Political Economy of Farm Size in India: The Elusive Quest. *Econ. Develop. Cult. Change*, July 1987, *35*(4), pp. 791–808. **[G: India]**

Vert, Eric. Les revenus des agriculteurs. Comparaison avec les autres catégories sociales et rôle des revenus non agricoles. (With English summary.) *Léon, Y. and Mahé, L., eds.*, 1987, pp. 377–91. **[G: France]**

Viallon, Jean Baptiste. Recherche d'indicateurs du revenu issu de l'agriculture à partir de comptabilités. (With English summary.) *Léon, Y. and Mahé, L., eds.*, 1987, pp. 95–108. **[G: France]**

Vincze, Maria. Statistical Procedure for a Comparative Analysis of a Rational Use of Production Resources. *Econ. Computat. Cybern. Stud. Res.*, 1987, *22*(1), pp. 61–65.

Winslade, Ralph S. The Accounting Study—An Insider's Report. *Can. J. Agr. Econ.*, May 1987, *34*, pp. 163–69.

Witt, Harvey J.; Schroeder, Ted C. and Hayenga, Marvin L. Comparison of Analytical Approaches for Estimating Hedge Ratios for Agricultural Commodities. *J. Futures Markets*, April 1987, *7*(2), pp. 135–46. **[G: U.S.]**

Zachariasse, Vinus. Income Disparities among Farm Households and Agricultural Policy: Concluding Comments. *Léon, Y. and Mahé, L., eds.*, 1987, pp. 499–505.

Zanias, George P. Adjustment Costs and Rational Expectations: An Application to a Tobacco Export Model. *Amer. J. Agr. Econ.*, February 1987, *69*(1), pp. 22–29. **[G: Greece]**

Zering, K. D.; McCorkle, C. O. and Moore, Charles V. The Utility of Multiple Peril Crop Insurance for Irrigated, Multiple-Crop Agriculture. *Western J. Agr. Econ.*, July 1987, *12*(1), pp. 50–59. **[G: U.S.]**

717 Land Reform and Land Use

7170 General

Ahmad, Bashir and Chaudhry, Ali Muhammad. Profitability of Pakistan's Agriculture. *Pakistan Devel. Rev.*, Winter 1987, *26*(4), pp. 457–67. **[G: Pakistan]**

Chaudhry, M. Ghaffar. Profitability of Pakistan's Agriculture: Comments. *Pakistan Devel. Rev.*, Winter 1987, *26*(4), pp. 468–69. **[G: Pakistan]**

Gunjal, Kisan; Lavoie, Gilbert and Raghaven, G. S. V. Economics of Soil Compaction Due to Machinery Traffic and Implications for Machinery Selection. *Can. J. Agr. Econ.*, November 1987, *35*(3), pp. 591–603. **[G: Canada]**

Kirby, Michael G. and Blyth, Michael J. Economic Aspects of Land Degradation in Australia. *Australian J. Agr. Econ.*, August 1987, *31*(2), pp. 154–74. **[G: Australia]**

Narayanan, Rangesan and Shane, Ronald L. Agricultural Productive and Consumptive Use Components of Rural Land Values in Texas: Comment. *Amer. J. Agr. Econ.*, February 1987, *69*(1), pp. 176–78. **[G: U.S.]**

Pope, C. Arden, III. Agricultural Productive and Consumptive Use Components of Rural Land Values in Texas: Reply. *Amer. J. Agr. Econ.*, February 1987, *69*(1), pp. 179–81. **[G: U.S.]**

Tomich, Thomas P. and Gotsch, Carl H. Private Land Reclamation in Egypt: Development Policy and Project Design. *Food Res. Inst. Stud.*, 1987, *20*(2), pp. 107–39. **[G: Egypt]**

7171 Land Ownership and Tenure; Land Reform

Ahmad, Khan Masood. Uncertainty, Resource Use Efficiency, and Tenurial Arrangements in Indian Agriculture. *Indian J. Quant. Econ.*, 1987, *3*(1), pp. 52–66. **[G: India]**

Alig, Ralph J. and Healy, Robert G. Urban and Built-Up Land Area Changes in the United States: An Empirical Investigation of Determinants. *Land Econ.*, August 1987, *63*(3), pp. 215–26. **[G: U.S.]**

Arizpe, Lourdes and Botey, Carlota. Mexican Agricultural Development Policy and Its Impact on Rural Women. *Deere, C. D. and León, M., eds.*, 1987, pp. 67–83. **[G: Mexico]**

Arsalanbod, Mohamadreza. Farm Size Structure and the Distribution of Income in the Rural Areas of Iran. *Léon, Y. and Mahé, L., eds.*, 1987, pp. 137–44. **[G: Iran]**

Bardhan, Pranab and Singh, Nirvikar. On Moral Hazard and Cost Sharing under Sharecropping. *Amer. J. Agr. Econ.*, May 1987, *69*(2), pp. 382–83.

Barker, Michael. Land Degradation: Legal Issues and Institutional Constraints: Commentary. *Chisholm, A. and Dumsday, R., eds.*, 1987, pp. 168–74. **[G: Australia]**

Bradsen, John and Fowler, Robert. Land Degradation: Legal Issues and Institutional Constraints. *Chisholm, A. and Dumsday, R., eds.*, 1987, pp. 129–67. **[G: Australia]**

Carrad, Bruce. Data Objectives and Needs for PNG's Smallholder Export Tree Crops Sector. *Barker, P.; Bodman, P. and Remenyl, J., eds.*, 1987, pp. 4–10. **[G: Papua New Guinea]**

Cobbett, M. The Land Question in South Africa: A Preliminary Assessment. *S. Afr. J. Econ.*, March 1987, *55*(1), pp. 63–77. **[G: S. Africa]**

Deere, Carmen Diana. The Latin American Agrarian Reform Experience. *Deere, C. D. and León, M., eds.*, 1987, pp. 165–90. **[G: Latin America]**

Esfahani, Hadi Salehi. Growth, Employment and Income Distribution in Egyptian Agriculture, 1964–79. *World Devel.*, September 1987, *15*(9), pp. 1201–17. **[G: Egypt]**

Evans, Lewis. Farming in a Changing Economic Environment. *Bollard, A. and Buckle, R., eds.*, 1987, pp. 102–20. **[G: New Zealand]**

Feder, Gershon. Land Ownership Security and

Farm Productivity: Evidence from Thailand. *J. Devel. Stud.*, October 1987, *24*(1), pp. 16–30. **[G: Thailand]**

Feder, Gershon and Noronha, Raymond. Land Rights Systems and Agricultural Development in Sub-Saharan Africa. *World Bank Res. Observer*, July 1987, *2*(2), pp. 143–69. **[G: Sub-Saharan Africa]**

Feder, Gershon and Onchan, Tongroj. Land Ownership Security and Farm Investment in Thailand. *Amer. J. Agr. Econ.*, May 1987, *69*(2), pp. 311–20. **[G: Thailand]**

Gaiha, Raghav. Impoverishment, Technology and Growth in Rural India. *Cambridge J. Econ.*, March 1987, *11*(1), pp. 23–46. **[G: India]**

Goodell, Grace. The Peasant Betrayed: Agriculture and Land Reform in the Third World: The Philippines. *Powelson, J. P. and Stock, R.*, 1987, pp. 11–26. **[G: Philippines]**

Griffin, Keith. Communal Land Tenure Systems and Their Role in Rural Development. *Griffin, K.*, 1987, *1986*, pp. 64–91. **[G: Global]**

Gunn, Susan. The Peasant Betrayed: Agriculture and Land Reform in the Third World: Somalia. *Powelson, J. P. and Stock, R.*, 1987, pp. 109–24. **[G: Somalia]**

Herdt, Robert W. A Retrospective View of Technological and Other Changes in Philippine Rice Farming, 1965–1982. *Econ. Develop. Cult. Change*, January 1987, *35*(2), pp. 329–49. **[G: Philippines]**

Herr, Bettina. The Peasant Betrayed: Agriculture and Land Reform in the Third World: Algeria. *Powelson, J. P. and Stock, R.*, 1987, pp. 125–39. **[G: Algeria]**

Howe, Charles W. The Peasant Betrayed: Agriculture and Land Reform in the Third World: Indonesia. *Powelson, J. P. and Stock, R.*, 1987, pp. 217–25. **[G: Indonesia]**

Ireson, W. Randall. Landholding, Agricultural Modernization, and Income Concentration: A Mexican Example. *Econ. Develop. Cult. Change*, January 1987, *35*(2), pp. 351–66. **[G: Mexico]**

Joshi, P. C. Agrarian Debate since Independence: Between Landlord and Peasant Perspectives. *Joshi, P. C., 1987, 1978*, pp. 49–67.

Joshi, P. C. Conflicting Pulls of Productivity and Employment: Contemporary Choices in the Light of Historical Experience. *Joshi, P. C.*, 1987, pp. 135–58. **[G: India; Japan]**

Joshi, P. C. Harmonising Self-reliance and Poverty Alleviation Objectives—Role of Land Reforms. *Joshi, P. C.*, 1987, pp. 216–28. **[G: India]**

Joshi, P. C. Land Reforms and the Indian Elite: Problems and Dilemmas of Land Policy in the Second Stage. *Joshi, P. C.*, 1987, pp. 193–215. **[G: India]**

Joshi, P. C. Poverty and Class Conflict in Rural India: Impact of New Technology in a Dualistic Structure. *Joshi, P. C., 1987, 1980*, pp. 229–51. **[G: India]**

Khan, Mahmood Hasan. Agrarian Transition in Sind: An Analysis of Interlinked Rural Factor Markets: Comments. *Pakistan Devel. Rev.*,

Winter 1987, *26*(4), pp. 445–46.
[G: Pakistan]

Khan, Saleem M. The Role of Agriculture in Asia-Pacific Economies: Comments [Negotiating Fishing Access Rights in the South Pacific: An Economic Framework] [Sharecropping in Dual Agrarian Economies: Implications for Land Reform]. *Dutta, M., ed. (I)*, 1987, pp. 283–85.
[G: Asia-Pacific; S. Pacific]

Khandker, Shahidur R.; Mestelman, Stuart and Feeny, David. Allocative Efficiency, the Aggregation of Labour Inputs, and the Effects of Farm Size and Tenancy Status: Tests from Rural Bangladesh. *J. Devel. Stud.*, October 1987, *24*(1), pp. 31–42.
[G: Bangladesh]

Kibreab, Gaim. Rural Refugee Land Settlements in Eastern Sudan: On the Road to Self-sufficiency? *Nobel, P., ed.*, 1987, pp. 63–71.
[G: Sudan]

Kula, Erhun. Prospects for Farmers to Improve Incomes by Switching Crops in N. Ireland: An Analysis to Improve Government Support Schemes. *Léon, Y. and Mahé, L., eds.*, 1987, pp. 297–307.
[G: U.K.]

Lianos, Theodore P. and Parliarou, Despina. Land Tenure in Greek Agriculture. *Land Econ.*, August 1987, *63*(3), pp. 237–48.
[G: Greece]

Majd, Mohammad G. Land Reform Policies in Iran. *Amer. J. Agr. Econ.*, November 1987, *69*(4), pp. 843–48.
[G: Iran]

Majid, Normaan and Nadvi, Khalid M. Agrarian Transition in Sind: An Analysis of Interlinking Rural Factor Markets. *Pakistan Devel. Rev.*, Winter 1987, *26*(4), pp. 433–44.
[G: Pakistan]

Mitra, Gautam Kumar. Poverty, Land and Household Size: A Study of Three Andhra Pradesh Districts. *Margin*, July-Sept. 1987, *19*(4), pp. 51–54.
[G: India]

Ortmann, G. F. Land Rents and Production Costs in the South African Sugar Industry. *S. Afr. J. Econ.*, September 1987, *55*(3), pp. 249–58.
[G: S. Africa]

Padilla, Martha Luz; Murguialday, Clara and Criquillon, Ana. Impact of the Sandinista Agrarian Reform on Rural Women's Subordination. *Deere, C. D. and León, M., eds.*, 1987, pp. 124–41.
[G: Nicaragua]

Quibria, M. G. Sharecropping in Dual Agrarian Economies: Implications for Land Reform. *Dutta, M., ed. (I)*, 1987, pp. 259–81.

Rao, J. Mohan. Productivity and Distribution under Cropsharing Tenancy. *World Devel.*, September 1987, *15*(9), pp. 1163–78.

Reddy, M. Atchi. Rich Lands and Poor Lords: Temple Lands and Tenancy in Nellore District, 1860–1986. *Indian Econ. Soc. Hist. Rev.*, Jan.-Mar. 1987, *24*(1), pp. 1–33. [G: India]

Reddy, Y. V. R., et al. Dryland Farming: Constraints to Improved Technology. *Margin*, Apr.-June 1987, *19*(3), pp. 48–54. [G: India]

Reid, Joseph D., Jr. The Theory of Sharecropping: Occam's Razor and Economic Analysis. *Hist. Polit. Econ.*, Winter 1987, *19*(4), pp. 551–69.

Reinhardt, Nola. Agro-exports and the Peasantry in the Agrarian Reforms of El Salvador and Nicaragua. *World Devel.*, July 1987, *15*(7), pp. 941–59. [G: El Salvador; Nicaragua]

Remenyi, J. V. and Bodman, Phil. Meeting Policy Data Needs on Smallholder Agriculture. *Barker, P.; Bodman, P. and Remenyl, J., eds.*, 1987, pp. 1–3. [G: Papua New Guinea]

Rodríguez, José Luiz. Agricultural Policy and Development in Cuba. *Zimbalist, A., ed.*, 1987, pp. 25–41. [G: Cuba]

Rodríguez, José Luiz. Agricultural Policy and Development in Cuba. *World Devel.*, January 1987, *15*(1), pp. 23–39. [G: Cuba]

Shaban, Radwan Ali. Testing between Competing Models of Sharecropping. *J. Polit. Econ.*, October 1987, *95*(5), pp. 893–920. [G: India]

Soltow, Lee C. Inequalities on the Eve of Mass Migration: Agricultural Holdings in Sweden and the United States in 1845–1850. *Scand. Econ. Hist. Rev.*, 1987, *35*(3), pp. 219–36.
[G: U.S.; Sweden]

Tanner, Christopher. Malnutrition and the Development of Rural Households in the Agreste of Paraiba State, North-East Brazil. *J. Devel. Stud.*, January 1987, *23*(2), pp. 242–64.
[G: Brazil]

Thiesenhusen, William C. Incomes on Some Agrarian Reform Asentamientos in Panama. *Econ. Develop. Cult. Change*, July 1987, *35*(4), pp. 809–31. [G: Panama]

Verma, B. N. and Bromley, Daniel W. The Political Economy of Farm Size in India: The Elusive Quest. *Econ. Develop. Cult. Change*, July 1987, *35*(4), pp. 791–808. [G: India]

Viaene, Jean-Marie. Factor Accumulation in a Minimum-Wage Economy. *Europ. Econ. Rev.*, August 1987, *31*(6), pp. 1313–28.
[G: Netherlands]

Whatley, Warren C. Southern Agrarian Labor Contracts as Impediments to Cotton Mechanization. *J. Econ. Hist.*, March 1987, *47*(1), pp. 45–70. [G: U.S.]

Winder, Samuel. *South Carolina v. Catawba:* A State's Statute of Limitations Found Applicable to an Eastern Tribe's Land Claim. *Natural Res. J.*, Fall 1987, *27*(4), pp. 913–30. [G: U.S.]

Young, Michael. Land Tenure: Plaything of Governments or an Effective Instrument? *Chisholm, A. and Dumsday, R., eds.*, 1987, pp. 175–86. [G: Australia]

Zalkin, Michael. Food Policy and Class Transformation in Revolutionary Nicaragua, 1979–86. *World Devel.*, July 1987, *15*(7), pp. 961–84.
[G: Nicaragua]

Zohir, Sajjad. Output Sharing as a Form of Wage Payment during Harvest. *Bangladesh Devel. Stud.*, June 1987, *15*(2), pp. 121–32.
[G: Bangladesh]

7172 Land Development; Land Use; Irrigation Policy

Abeels, P. F. The Insertion of Multiple Objectives in Rural Land Management. *Merlo, M., et al., eds.*, 1987, pp. 515–22. [G: Europe]

Ablasser, Gottfried. Issues in Settlement of New Lands. *Finance Develop.*, March 1987, *24*(1), pp. 45–48. [G: LDCs]

Adams, William M. Approaches to Water Resource Development, Sokoto Valley, Nigeria: The Problem of Sustainability. *Anderson, D. and Grove, R., eds.*, 1987, pp. 307–25. [G: Nigeria]

Agostini, D. and Franceschetti, G. Local Institutions and Land Policy: The Case of Cadore Mountain Communities. *Merlo, M., et al., eds.*, 1987, pp. 227–33. [G: Italy]

Alley, William M. and Schefter, John E. External Effects of Irrigators' Pumping Decisions, High Plains Aquifer. *Water Resources Res.*, July 1987, *23*(7), pp. 1123–30. [G: U.S.]

Attwood, Donald W. Irrigation and Imperialism: The Causes and Consequences of a Shift from Subsistence to Cash Cropping. *J. Devel. Stud.*, April 1987, *23*(3), pp. 341–66. [G: India]

Barker, Michael. Land Degradation: Legal Issues and Institutional Constraints: Commentary. *Chisholm, A. and Dumsday, R., eds.*, 1987, pp. 168–74. [G: Australia]

Barrocas, José Manuel. Risk Programming for an Irrigated Area in the South of Portugal. *Economia (Portugal)*, October 1987, *11*(3), pp. 363–97. [G: Portugal]

Bell, R. H. V. Conservation with a Human Face: Conflict and Reconciliation in African Land Use Planning. *Anderson, D. and Grove, R., eds.*, 1987, pp. 79–101. [G: Africa]

Bernardo, Daniel J., et al. An Irrigation Model for Management of Limited Water Supplies. *Western J. Agr. Econ.*, December 1987, *12*(2), pp. 164–73. [G: U.S.]

Biggs, Stephen and Griffith, Jon. Irrigation in Bangladesh. *Stewart, F., ed.*, 1987, pp. 74–94. [G: Bangladesh]

Bilsborrow, Richard E. Population Pressures and Agricultural Development in Developing Countries: A Conceptual Framework and Recent Evidence. *World Devel.*, February 1987, *15*(2), pp. 183–203. [G: LDCs]

Binswanger, Hans P. and Pingali, Prabhu L. The Evolution of Farming Systems and Agricultural Technology in Sub-Saharan Africa. *Ruttan, V. W. and Pray, C. E., eds.*, 1987, pp. 283–318. [G: Sub-Saharan]

Blyth, Michael J. and McCallum, Andrew. Onsite Costs of Land Degradation in Agriculture and Forestry. *Chisholm, A. and Dumsday, R., eds.*, 1987, pp. 79–98. [G: Australia]

Bosch, Darrell J. and Eidman, Vernon R. Valuing Information when Risk Preferences Are Nonneutral: An Application to Irrigation Scheduling. *Amer. J. Agr. Econ.*, August 1987, *69*(3), pp. 658–68. [G: U.S.]

Bradsen, John and Fowler, Robert. Land Degradation: Legal Issues and Institutional Constraints. *Chisholm, A. and Dumsday, R., eds.*, 1987, pp. 129–67. [G: Australia]

Bras, Rafael L. and Seo, Dong-Jun. Irrigation Control in the Presence of Salinity: Extended Linear Quadratic Approach. *Water Resources Res.*, July 1987, *23*(7), pp. 1153–61. [G: U.S.]

Brichese, F. and Povellato, A. A Proposed Regional Park: The Case Study of Caorle Lagoon. *Merlo, M., et al., eds.*, 1987, pp. 193–206. [G: Italy]

Burch, Gordon; Graetz, Dean and Noble, Ian. Biological and Physical Phenomena in Land Degradation. *Chisholm, A. and Dumsday, R., eds.*, 1987, pp. 27–48. [G: Australia]

Carter, Michael R. Risk Sharing and Incentives in the Decollectivization of Agriculture. *Oxford Econ. Pap.*, September 1987, *39*(3), pp. 577–95.

Clark, Gordon L. Adjudicating Jurisdictional Disputes in Chicago and Toronto: Legal Formalism and Urban Structure. *Feldman, E. J. and Goldberg, M. A., eds.*, 1987, pp. 225–46. [G: U.S.; Canada]

Coke, Lloyd B.; Weir, Colin C. and Hill, Vincent G. Environmental Impact of Bauxite Mining and Processing in Jamaica. *Soc. Econ. Stud.*, March 1987, *36*(1), pp. 289–333. [G: Jamaica]

Collinson, Michael. Potential and Practice in Food Production Technology Development: Eastern and Southern Africa. *Mellor, J. W.; Delgado, C. L. and Blackie, M. J., eds.*, 1987, pp. 78–96. [G: E. Africa; Southern Africa]

Corrado, G. and Sediari, Tommaso. Countryside Planning Experiences in Umbria (Central Italy). *Merlo, M., et al., eds.*, 1987, pp. 583–91. [G: Italy]

Croci-Angelini, Elisabetta and Tarditi, Secondo. Social Costs and Benefits of Price Policies in Integrated Economies: Impact on Land Use. *Merlo, M., et al., eds.*, 1987, pp. 81–98. [G: EEC]

Dalziel, Paul C. Optimal Water Storage and Pricing: The Effect of Monopoly. *New Zealand Econ. Pap.*, 1987, *21*, pp. 3–16. [G: New Zealand]

Daniels, Rudolph. The Nature of the Agrarian Land Question in the Republic of South Africa. *Amer. J. Econ. Soc.*, January 1987, *46*(1), pp. 1–16. [G: S. Africa]

Dhawan, B. D. Agricultural Productivity of Water in India. *Indian J. Quant. Econ.*, 1987, *3*(2), pp. 81–94. [G: India]

Downing, P. and Brandon, O. A Forestry Enterprise on Farms in an England Lowland Context. *Merlo, M., et al., eds.*, 1987, pp. 421–32. [G: U.K.]

Ekanayake, S. A. B. Location Specificity, Settler Type and Productive Efficiency: A Study of the Mahaweli Project in Sri Lanka. *J. Devel. Stud.*, July 1987, *23*(4), pp. 509–21. [G: Sri Lanka]

Esfahani, Hadi Salehi. Technical Change, Employment, and Supply Response of Agriculture in the Nile Delta: A System-Wide Approach. *J. Devel. Econ.*, February 1987, *25*(1), pp. 167–96. [G: Egypt]

Feldman, Elliot J. On the Fringe: Controlling Urban Sprawl in Canada and the United States.

Feldman, E. J. and Goldberg, M. A., eds., 1987, pp. 125–46.   **[G: Canada; U.S.]**

Feldman, Elliot J. and Goldberg, Michael A. General Lessons from Diverse Cases. *Feldman, E. J. and Goldberg, M. A., eds.*, 1987, pp. 271–82.   **[G: U.S.; Canada]**

Feldman, Elliot J. and Goldberg, Michael A. Land Rites and Wrongs: Introduction. *Feldman, E. J. and Goldberg, M. A., eds.*, 1987, pp. 1–19.   **[G: U.S.; Canada]**

Fox, Roger and Finan, Timothy J. Portuguese Agriculture in Transition: Future Technical and Structural Adjustments in Northwestern Agriculture. *Pearson, S. R., et al.*, 1987, pp. 202–20.   **[G: Portugal]**

Fox, Roger and Finan, Timothy J. Portuguese Agriculture in Transition: Patterns of Technical Change in the Northwest. *Pearson, S. R., et al.*, 1987, pp. 187–201.   **[G: Portugal]**

Furuseth, Owen J. Public Attitudes toward Local Farmland Protection Programs. *Growth Change*, Summer 1987, *18*(3), pp. 49–61.   **[G: U.S.]**

Galab, S. and Sarma, P. V. S. R. L. Returns to Irrigation in Indian Agriculture: A Case Study. *Margin*, July-Sept. 1987, *19*(4), pp. 55–61.   **[G: India]**

Galante, E. and Sala, C. A Survey of Less Favoured Mountain Areas in Italy. *Merlo, M., et al., eds.*, 1987, pp. 277–90.   **[G: Italy]**

Gios, Geremia; Pilati, L. and Ricci, G. Integration between Agroforestry and Tourism in Alpine Areas. *Merlo, M., et al., eds.*, 1987, pp. 235–44.   **[G: Italy]**

Goldberg, Michael A. Evaluating Urban Land Use and Development. *Feldman, E. J. and Goldberg, M. A., eds.*, 1987, pp. 39–72.   **[G: U.S.; Canada]**

Greig, Peter. Social Costs of Land Degradation: Commentary. *Chisholm, A. and Dumsday, R., eds.*, 1987, pp. 119–25.   **[G: Australia]**

Guha, Sumit. The Land Market in Upland Maharashtra c. 1820–1960—I. *Indian Econ. Soc. Hist. Rev.*, Apr.-June 1987, *24*(2), pp. 117–44.   **[G: India]**

Guha, Sumit. The Land Market in Upland Maharashtra c. 1820–1960—II. *Indian Econ. Soc. Hist. Rev.*, July-Sept. 1987, *24*(3), pp. 291–322.   **[G: India]**

Guzhvin, P. The Yield of Land and the Structure of Investment. *Prob. Econ.*, February 1987, *29*(10), pp. 38–54.   **[G: U.S.S.R.]**

Hall, Anthony. Agrarian Crisis in Brazilian Amazonia: The Grande Carajás Programme. *J. Devel. Stud.*, July 1987, *23*(4), pp. 522–52.   **[G: Brazil]**

Hartia, S. and Scutaru, Cornelia. Model for Simulating the Economic Efficiency of Land Improvement Work. *Econ. Computat. Cybern. Stud. Res.*, 1987, *22*(1), pp. 57–59.

Hodge, Ian. The Cap and the Soil: A Preliminary Analysis. *Merlo, M., et al., eds.*, 1987, pp. 523–33.   **[G: U.K.]**

Hodge, Ian. Uncertainty, Irreversibility and the Loss of Agricultural Land: A Reply. *J. Agr. Econ.*, January 1987, *38*(1), pp. 81–82.   **[G: Australia]**

Hung, Hsien-Ming and Fuller, Wayne A. Regression Estimation of Crop Acreages with Transformed Landsat Data as Auxiliary Variables. *J. Bus. Econ. Statist.*, October 1987, *5*(4), pp. 475–82.   **[G: U.S.]**

Hurt, Verner G. Optional Uses for Excess Resources in U.S. Agriculture: Discussion. *Amer. J. Agr. Econ.*, May 1987, *69*(2), pp. 463–64.   **[G: U.S.]**

Kennedy, John O. S. Uncertainty, Irreversibility and the Loss of Agricultural Land: A Rejoinder. *J. Agr. Econ.*, January 1987, *38*(1), pp. 83.   **[G: Australia]**

Kennedy, John O. S. Uncertainty, Irreversibility and the Loss of Agricultural Land: A Reconsideration. *J. Agr. Econ.*, January 1987, *38*(1), pp. 75–80.   **[G: Australia]**

Lee, John G.; Ellis, John R. and Lacewell, Ronald D. Evaluation of Production and Financial Risk: A Stochastic Dominance Approach. *Can. J. Agr. Econ.*, March 1987, *35*(1), pp. 109–26.   **[G: U.S.]**

Lee, John G., et al. Regional Impact of Urban Water Use on Irrigated Agriculture. *Southern J. Agr. Econ.*, December 1987, *19*(2), pp. 43–51.   **[G: U.S.]**

Leman, Christopher K. A Forest of Institutions: Patterns of Choice on North American Timberlands. *Feldman, E. J. and Goldberg, M. A., eds.*, 1987, pp. 149–200.   **[G: U.S.; Canada]**

Leman, Christopher K. The Concepts of Public and Private and Their Applicability to North American Lands. *Feldman, E. J. and Goldberg, M. A., eds.*, 1987, pp. 23–37.   **[G: U.S.; Canada]**

Luzar, E. Jane. Institutional Change at the Local Level: Pattern Model Analysis of Virginia's Farmland Retention Policy. *J. Econ. Issues*, June 1987, *21*(2), pp. 605–15.   **[G: U.S.]**

MacDonald, J. S.; Pianetti, F. and Zanetto, G. The Ecosystem Facing Economic Development: Conflict between Agriculture and Other Uses. *Merlo, M., et al., eds.*, 1987, pp. 207–14.   **[G: Italy]**

Mann, Roger; Sparling, Edward and Young, Robert A. Regional Economic Growth from Irrigation Development: Evidence from Northern High-Plains Ogallala Groundwater Resource. *Water Resources Res.*, September 1987, *23*(9), pp. 1711–16.   **[G: U.S.]**

McGuckin, J. Thomas, et al. Optimal Control of Irrigation Scheduling Using a Random Time Frame. *Amer. J. Agr. Econ.*, February 1987, *69*(1), pp. 123–33.   **[G: U.S.]**

McKelvey, Robert. Groundwater-Based Agriculture in the Arid America West: Modeling the Transition to a Steady-State Renewable Resource Economy. *Vincent, T. L., et al., eds.*, 1987, pp. 222–35.   **[G: U.S.]**

McNicoll, Iain H. and Davies, J. R. Measuring the Secondary Impact of the Left Bank Outfall Drain on the Economy of Sindh. *Pakistan J. Appl. Econ.*, Summer 1987, *6*(1), pp. 23–40.   **[G: Pakistan]**

Mulkey, David and Clouser, Rodney L. Market and Market–Institutional Perspectives on the Agricultural Land Preservation Issue. *Growth Change*, Winter 1987, *18*(1), pp. 72–81. [G: U.S.]

Neutze, Max. The Supply of Land for a Particular Use. *Urban Stud.*, October 1987, *24*(5), pp. 379–88.

Nola, L. Multipurpose Land Reclamation in Italy. *Merlo, M., et al., eds.*, 1987, pp. 573–81. [G: Italy]

Nougarede, O.; Larrere, R. and Poupardin, D. The Aigoual Forest: Theatre of Latent Conflicts of Interest and Competences. *Merlo, M., et al., eds.*, 1987, pp. 179–91. [G: France]

Nunan, Donald. Price Trends for Agricultural Land in Ireland 1901–1986. *Irish J. Agr. Econ. Rural Soc.*, 1987, *12*, pp. 51–77. [G: Ireland]

Paderanga, Cayetano, Jr. A Review of Land Settlements in the Philippines, 1900–1975. *Philippine Rev. Econ. Bus.*, Mar.-June 1987, *24*(1–2), pp. 1–54. [G: Philippines]

Palanisami, K. and Easter, K. William. Small-Scale Surface (Tank) Irrigation in Asia. *Water Resources Res.*, May 1987, *23*(5), pp. 774–80.

Purcell, Joseph C. Optional Uses for Excess Resources in U.S. Agriculture. *Amer. J. Agr. Econ.*, May 1987, *69*(2), pp. 454–58. [G: U.S.]

Rees, William E. Politics, Power, and Northern Land-Use Planning. *Lane, T., ed.*, 1987, *1985*, pp. 109–32. [G: Canada]

Ristoratore, Mario. Siting Toxic Waste Disposal Facilities: Best and Worst Cases in North America. *Feldman, E. J. and Goldberg, M. A., eds.*, 1987, pp. 201–21. [G: U.S.; Canada]

Robertson, Graeme. Towards More Effective Policies for Controlling Land Degradation: Contributions from the Physical and Biological Sciences. *Chisholm, A. and Dumsday, R., eds.*, 1987, pp. 305–14. [G: Australia]

Sachak, Najma. The Impact of Land Acquisition by Bauxite–Alumina Transnational Corporations on Peasants in the Bauxite Land Economy. *Soc. Econ. Stud.*, March 1987, *36*(1), pp. 93–135. [G: Jamaica]

Salmon, Michael G. Land Utilization within Jamaica's Bauxite Land Economy. *Soc. Econ. Stud.*, March 1987, *36*(1), pp. 57–92. [G: Jamaica]

Shahabuddin, Quazi. The Investment Analysis Model: An Application to Water Resources Planning in Bangladesh. *Bangladesh Devel. Stud.*, September 1987, *15*(3), pp. 63–94. [G: Bangladesh]

Shucksmith, M. Conflicting Land Uses in the English Lake District. *Merlo, M., et al., eds.*, 1987, pp. 545–52. [G: U.K.]

Sillani, S. Land Consolidation and Environment. *Merlo, M., et al., eds.*, 1987, pp. 299–306. [G: Italy]

Susmel, L. Multipurpose Management of Alpine Forests. *Merlo, M., et al., eds.*, 1987, pp. 221–25. [G: Italy]

Thomas, John. Onsite Costs of Land Degradation in Agriculture and Forestry: Comments. *Chisholm, A. and Dumsday, R., eds.*, 1987, pp. 363–64. [G: Australia]

Vink, N. and Kassier, W. E. The 'Tragedy of the Commons' and Livestock Farming in Southern Africa. *S. Afr. J. Econ.*, June 1987, *55*(2), pp. 165–82. [G: S. Africa]

Wade, Robert. The Management of Common Property Resources: Finding a Cooperative Solution. *World Bank Res. Observer*, July 1987, *2*(2), pp. 219–34. [G: India]

Webb, Adrian. Physical and Biological Aspects of Land Degradation: Commentary. *Chisholm, A. and Dumsday, R., eds.*, 1987, pp. 70–75. [G: Australia]

Whittlesey, Norman K. and Herrell, Jon P. Impacts of Energy Cost Increases on Irrigated Land Values. *Western J. Agr. Econ.*, July 1987, *12*(1), pp. 1–7. [G: U.S.]

Wills, Ian R. Resource Degradation on Agricultural Land: Information Problems, Market Failures and Government Intervention. *Australian J. Agr. Econ.*, April 1987, *31*(1), pp. 45–55. [G: Australia]

Woods, Lance. Degradation Pressures from Non-agricultural Land Uses. *Chisholm, A. and Dumsday, R., eds.*, 1987, pp. 108–18. [G: Australia]

Young, Michael. Land Tenure: Plaything of Governments or an Effective Instrument? *Chisholm, A. and Dumsday, R., eds.*, 1987, pp. 175–86. [G: Australia]

718 Rural Economics

7180 Rural Economics

Adelman, Irma and Sunding, David. Economic Policy and Income Distribution in China. *J. Compar. Econ.*, September 1987, *11*(3), pp. 444–61. [G: China]

Ahmed, Iftikhar. Technology, Production Linkages and Women's Employment in South Asia. *Int. Lab. Rev.*, Jan.-Feb. 1987, *126*(1), pp. 21–40. [G: S. Asia]

Ahmed, Rais Uddin. A Structural Perspective of Farm and Non-farm Households in Bangladesh. *Bangladesh Devel. Stud.*, June 1987, *15*(2), pp. 87–112. [G: Bangladesh]

Allen, Bryant J. A Review of Smallholder Data Sources in PNG Relevant to the Export Tree Crops Sector. *Barker, P.; Bodman, P. and Remenyl, J., eds.*, 1987, pp. 14–54. [G: Papua New Guinea]

d'Arc, Hélène Rivière and Prévôt-Schapira, Marie-France. La voie zapotèque du développement face à l'état mexicain modernisateur. (With English summary.) *Can. J. Devel. Stud.*, 1987, *8*(2), pp. 329–50. [G: Mexico]

Arizpe, Lourdes and Botey, Carlota. Mexican Agricultural Development Policy and Its Impact on Rural Women. *Deere, C. D. and León, M., eds.*, 1987, pp. 67–83. [G: Mexico]

Arun Kumar, K. S., et al. Income Inequality in Rural India 1965–1983. *León, Y. and Mahé,*

L., eds., 1987, pp. 129–36.   **[G: India]**

Attwood, Donald W. Irrigation and Imperialism: The Causes and Consequences of a Shift from Subsistence to Cash Cropping. *J. Devel. Stud.*, April 1987, *23*(3), pp. 341–66.   **[G: India]**

Bar-El, Raphael. Rural Industrialization in Israel: A Summary of Experiences. *Bar-El, R., ed.*, 1987, pp. 1–20.   **[G: Israel]**

Bar-El, Raphael; Erickson, Eugene and Nesher, Ariela. Rural Industrialization in Israel: Concluding Considerations. *Bar-El, R., ed.*, 1987, pp. 169–89.   **[G: Israel]**

Barnes, Douglas F. and Samanta, B. B. Rural Electrification and the Village Economy in India. *Pachauri, R. K., ed.*, 1987, pp. 1155–66.   **[G: India]**

Basu, Kaushik. Disneyland Monopoly, Interlinkage and Usurious Interest Rates. *J. Public Econ.*, October 1987, *34*(1), pp. 1–17.

Bates, Robert H. The Commercialization of Agriculture and the Rise of Rural Political Protest. *Bates, R. H.*, 1987, *1979*, pp. 92–104.   **[G: Africa]**

Bates, Robert H. The Preservation of Order in Stateless Societies: A Reinterpretation of Evans-Pritchard's *The Nuer. Bates, R. H.*, 1987, *1979*, pp. 7–20.   **[G: Africa]**

Beckford, George L. The Social Economy of Bauxite in the Jamaican Man–Space. *Soc. Econ. Stud.*, March 1987, *36*(1), pp. 1–55.   **[G: Jamaica]**

Belongia, Michael T. and Gilbert, R. Alton. The Farm Economies of the Plains. *Rev. Reg. Stud.*, Fall 1987, *17*(3), pp. 47–57. **[G: U.S.]**

Bender, Lloyd D. The Role of Services in Rural Development Policies. *Land Econ.*, February 1987, *63*(1), pp. 62–71.   **[G: U.S.]**

Bentolila, David J. The Non-agricultural Village. *Bar-El, R., ed.*, 1987, pp. 105–42.   **[G: Israel]**

Bevan, D. L., et al. Peasant Supply Response in Rationed Economies. *World Devel.*, April 1987, *15*(4), pp. 431–39.   **[G: LDCs]**

Binford, Leigh and Cook, Scott. Toward a Marxist Rethinking of Third World Rural Industrialization. *England, R. W., ed.*, 1987, pp. 61–85.   **[G: Mexico; LDCs]**

Binswanger, Hans P. and McIntire, John. Behavioral and Material Determinants of Production Relations in Land-Abundant Tropical Agriculture. *Econ. Develop. Cult. Change*, October 1987, *36*(1), pp. 73–99.

Bishop, Christine E. Swing Beds: Assessing Flexible Health Care in Rural Communities: Cost Issues: Comments. *Wiener, J. M., ed.*, 1987, pp. 59–63.   **[G: U.S.]**

Bloomquist, Leonard E. Performance of the Rural Manufacturing Sector. *U.S.D.A., Econ. Res. Serv., Agr. and Rural Econ. Div.*, 1987, pp. 3.1–33.   **[G: U.S.]**

Bradshaw, Ted K. and Blakely, Edward J. Unanticipated Consequences of Government Programs on Rural Economic Development. *U.S.D.A., Econ. Res. Serv., Agr. and Rural Econ. Div.*, 1987, pp. 11.1–17.   **[G: U.S.]**

Brandt, Loren. Farm Household Behavior, Factor Markets, and the Distributive Consequences of Commercialization in Early Twentieth-Century China. *J. Econ. Hist.*, September 1987, *47*(3), pp. 711–37.   **[G: China]**

Braverman, Avishay and Kanbur, S. M. Ravi. Urban Bias and the Political Economy of Agricultural Reform. *World Devel.*, September 1987, *15*(9), pp. 1179–87.   **[G: LDCs]**

Brignol Mendes, Raúl. The Rural Sector in the Socio-economic Context of Brazil. *CEPAL Rev.*, December 1987, (33), pp. 39–59.   **[G: Brazil]**

Brown, David L. and Deavers, Kenneth L. Rural Change and the Rural Economic Policy Agenda for the 1980's. *U.S.D.A., Econ. Res. Serv., Agr. and Rural Econ. Div.*, 1987, pp. 1.1–31.   **[G: U.S.]**

Brown, Deborah J. and Pheasant, James. Sources of Cyclical Employment Instability in Rural Counties. *Amer. J. Agr. Econ.*, November 1987, *69*(4), pp. 819–27.   **[G: U.S.]**

Cain, Stephen R. and Kerr, William A. China's Changing Development Strategy: The Case of Rural Electrification. *Can. J. Devel. Stud.*, 1987, *8*(1), pp. 81–96.   **[G: China]**

Carrad, Bruce. Data Objectives and Needs for PNG's Smallholder Export Tree Crops Sector. *Barker, P.; Bodman, P. and Remenyl, J., eds.*, 1987, pp. 4–10.   **[G: Papua New Guinea]**

Cecelski, Elizabeth. Energy and Rural Women's Work: Crisis, Response and Policy Alternatives. *Int. Lab. Rev.*, Jan.-Feb. 1987, *126*(1), pp. 41–64.   **[G: Selected LDCs]**

Chaney, Elsa M. Women's Components in Integrated Rural Development Projects. *Deere, C. D. and León, M., eds.*, 1987, pp. 191–211.   **[G: Jamaica; Dominican Republic]**

Chaudhry, M. Ghaffar and Khan, Zubeda. Female Labour Force Participation Rates in Rural Pakistan: Some Fundamental Explanations and Policy Implications. *Pakistan Devel. Rev.*, Winter 1987, *26*(4), pp. 687–96. **[G: Pakistan]**

Cloke, P. J. and Little, J. K. Rural Policies in the Gloucestershire Structure Plan: 1. A Study of Motives an Mechanisms. *Environ. Planning A*, July 1987, *19*(7), pp. 959–81.

Conn, Stephen. Rural Legal Process and Development in the North. *Lane, T., ed.*, 1987, pp. 199–229.   **[G: U.S.]**

Conway, Gordon. Rapid Rural Appraisal Strategies for Collecting and Analysing Data. *Barker, P.; Bodman, P. and Remenyl, J., eds.*, 1987, pp. 64–82.   **[G: Papua New Guinea]**

Coverdale, A. G. and Healey, J. M. Project Appraisal and Project Aid: A Decade of Experience in Rural Development. *J. Agr. Econ.*, January 1987, *38*(1), pp. 99–105.   **[G: Africa]**

Coward, Raymond. Swing Beds: Assessing Flexible Health Care in Rural Communities: Access and Case-Mix Patterns: Comments. *Wiener, J. M., ed.*, 1987, pp. 100–103.   **[G: U.S.]**

Cowell, Noel M. The Impact of Bauxite Mining on Peasant and Community Relations in Jamaica. *Soc. Econ. Stud.*, March 1987, *36*(1), pp. 171–216.   **[G: Jamaica]**

Cowper, Patricia A. and Kushman, John E. A Spatial Analysis of Primary Health Care Markets in Rural Areas. *Amer. J. Agr. Econ.*, August 1987, *69*(3), pp. 613–25.   [G: U.S.]

Crummett, María de los Angeles. Rural Women and Migration in Latin America. *Deere, C. D. and León, M., eds.*, 1987, pp. 239–60.
[G: Latin America]

Czamanski, Daniel Z. and Meyer-Brodnitz, Michael B. Industrialization in Arab Villages in Israel. *Bar-El, R., ed.*, 1987, pp. 143–68.
[G: Israel]

Das Gupta, Monica. Informal Security Mechanisms and Population Retention in Rural India. *Econ. Develop. Cult. Change*, October 1987, *36*(1), pp. 101–20.   [G: India]

Deavers, Kenneth L. Choosing a Rural Policy for the 1980's and '90's. *U.S.D.A., Econ. Res. Serv., Agr. and Rural Econ. Div.*, 1987, pp. 17.1–17.   [G: U.S.]

Deere, Carmen Diana. The Latin American Agrarian Reform Experience. *Deere, C. D. and León, M., eds.*, 1987, pp. 165–90.
[G: Latin America]

Deere, Carmen Diana and León, Magdalena. Rural Women and State Policy: Feminist Perspectives on Latin American Agricultural Development: Introduction. *Deere, C. D. and León, M., eds.*, 1987, pp. 1–17.
[G: Latin America]

Desai, V. V. A Strategy for Rural Electrification. *Pachauri, R. K., ed.*, 1987, pp. 1143–53.
[G: Asia]

Don, Yehuda and Leviatan, Uri. Kibbutz Industrialization. *Bar-El, R., ed.*, 1987, pp. 21–55.
[G: Israel]

Donaldson, Graham. Community Participation in Northern Pakistan. *Finance Develop.*, December 1987, *24*(4), pp. 23–25.   [G: Pakistan]

Eicher, Carl K. Food Price Policy and Equity: Commentary. *Mellor, J. W.; Delgado, C. L. and Blackie, M. J., eds.*, 1987, pp. 290–92.
[G: Africa]

Esfahani, Hadi Salehi. Growth, Employment and Income Distribution in Egyptian Agriculture, 1964–79. *World Devel.*, September 1987, *15*(9), pp. 1201–17.   [G: Egypt]

Fabella, Raul V. Rural Manufacturing Employment in the Philippines: Contribution and Determinants. *Islam, R., ed.*, 1987, pp. 135–70.
[G: Philippines]

Finkler, Steven A. Swing Beds: Assessing Flexible Health Care in Rural Communities: Cost Issues. *Wiener, J. M., ed.*, 1987, pp. 42–59.
[G: U.S.]

Flora, Cornelia Butler. Income Generation Projects for Rural Women. *Deere, C. D. and León, M., eds.*, 1987, pp. 212–38.
[G: Latin America]

Fox, William F. Public Infrastructure and Economic Development. *U.S.D.A., Econ. Res. Serv., Agr. and Rural Econ. Div.*, 1987, pp. 13.1–23.   [G: U.S.]

Gaiha, Raghav. Impoverishment, Technology and Growth in Rural India. *Cambridge J. Econ.*, March 1987, *11*(1), pp. 23–46.   [G: India]

Gaiha, Raghav. Inequality, Earnings and Participation among the Poor in Rural India. *J. Devel. Stud.*, July 1987, *23*(4), pp. 491–508.
[G: India]

Gangopadhyay, Shubhashis and Sengupta, Kunal. Small Farmers, Moneylenders and Trading Activity. *Oxford Econ. Pap.*, June 1987, *39*(2), pp. 333–42.

Gaude, J., et al. Rural Development and Labour-Intensive Schemes: Impact Studies of Some Pilot Programmes. *Int. Lab. Rev.*, July-Aug. 1987, *126*(4), pp. 423–46. [G: Burkina Faso; Burundi; Rwanda; Nepal; Tanzania]

Ghai, Dharam and Smith, Lawrence. Food Price Policy and Equity. *Mellor, J. W.; Delgado, C. L. and Blackie, M. J., eds.*, 1987, pp. 278–89.   [G: Africa]

Griffin, Keith. Communal Land Tenure Systems and Their Role in Rural Development. *Griffin, K.*, 1987, *1986*, pp. 64–91.   [G: Global]

Griffin, Keith. Rural Development in Arid Regions: The Case of Xinjiang. *Griffin, K.*, 1987, pp. 147–82.   [G: China]

Griffin, Keith. Rural Poverty in Asia: Analysis and Policy Alternatives. *Griffin, K.*, 1987, *1985*, pp. 25–63.

Gupta, Manash Ranjan. A Nutrition-Based Theory of Interlinkage. *J. Quant. Econ.*, July 1987, *3*(2), pp. 189–202.

Harrington, David H. Agricultural Programs: Their Contribution to Rural Development and Economic Well-Being. *U.S.D.A., Econ. Res. Serv., Agr. and Rural Econ. Div.*, 1987, pp. 12.1–23.   [G: U.S.]

Hawes, Catherine. Swing Beds: Assessing Flexible Health Care in Rural Communities: Quality of Care: Comments. *Wiener, J. M., ed.*, 1987, pp. 114–17.   [G: U.S.]

Holahan, John. Swing-Bed Reimbursement: Objectives and Options. *Wiener, J. M., ed.*, 1987, pp. 64–81.   [G: U.S.]

Hossain, Mahabub. Agricultural Growth Linkages—The Bangladesh Case. *Bangladesh Devel. Stud.*, March 1987, *15*(1), pp. 1–30.
[G: Bangladesh]

Hossain, Mahabub. Employment Generation through Cottage Industries—Potentials and Constraints: The Case of Bangladesh. *Islam, R., ed.*, 1987, pp. 19–57.   [G: Bangladesh]

Hossain, Shaikh I. Allocative and Technical Efficiency: A Study of Rural Enterprises in Bangladesh. *Devel. Econ.*, March 1987, *25*(1), pp. 56–72.   [G: Bangladesh]

Howard-Merriam, Kathleen. The Impact of Rural Electrification on Egyptian Farm Women's Lives. *Pachauri, R. K., ed.*, 1987, pp. 271–90.   [G: Egypt]

Islam, Rizwanul. Rural Industrialisation and Employment in Asia: Issues and Evidence. *Islam, R., ed.*, 1987, pp. 1–18.   [G: Asia]

Islam, Rizwanul and Shrestha, Ram Prasad. Employment Expansion through Cottage Industries in Nepal: Potentials and Constraints. *Islam, R., ed.*, 1987, pp. 107–33. [G: Nepal]

Islamoğlu-Inan, Huri. State and Peasants in the Ottoman Empire: A Study of Peasant Economy in North-central Anatolia during the Sixteenth Century. *Islamoglu-Inan, H., ed.*, 1987, pp. 101–59. **[G: Ottoman Empire]**

John, Jacqueline Ann. Swing Beds: Assessing Flexible Health Care in Rural Communities: Quality of Care: Comments. *Wiener, J. M., ed.*, 1987, pp. 117–19. **[G: U.S.]**

Johns, P. M. and Leat, P. M. K. The Application of Modified Grit Input–Output Procedures to Rural Development Analysis in Grampian Region. *J. Agr. Econ.*, May 1987, *38*(2), pp. 243–56. **[G: U.K.]**

Johnson, Marshall; Parish, William L. and Lin, Elizabeth. Chinese Women, Rural Society, and External Markets. *Econ. Develop. Cult. Change*, January 1987, *35*(2), pp. 257–77. **[G: China]**

Joshi, P. C. Poverty and Class Conflict in Rural India: Impact of New Technology in a Dualistic Structure. *Joshi, P. C.*, 1987, *1980*, pp. 229–51. **[G: India]**

Keller, Edmond J. Ethiopian Socialism, Decentralization, and the Political Economy of Rural Development. *Picard, L. A. and Zariski, R., eds.*, 1987, pp. 208–23. **[G: Ethiopia]**

Khalily, M. A. Baqui; Meyer, Richard L. and Hushak, Leroy J. Deposit Mobilization in Bangladesh: Implications for Rural Financial Institutions and Financial Policies. *Bangladesh Devel. Stud.*, December 1987, *15*(4), pp. 85–117. **[G: Bangladesh]**

Khan, Mahmood Hasan. Rural Poverty in Bangladesh, India and Pakistan: Profiles and Policies. *Pakistan Devel. Rev.*, Autumn 1987, *26*(3), pp. 309–36. **[G: Bangladesh; India; Pakistan]**

Khan, Shakeeb A. Peasants and Classes: A Critique. *Bangladesh Devel. Stud.*, December 1987, *15*(4), pp. 155–62. **[G: Bangladesh]**

Khandker, Shahidur R. Women's Role in Household Productive Activities and Fertility in Bangladesh. *J. Econ. Devel.*, June 1987, *12*(1), pp. 87–115. **[G: Bangladesh]**

Khandker, Shahidur R. Women's Time Allocation and Household Nonmarket Production in Rural Bangladesh. *J. Devel. Areas*, October 1987, *22*(1), pp. 85–101. **[G: Bangladesh]**

Khandker, Shahidur R. and Butterfield, David W. Consumption, Family Size, Schooling and Labor Supply Decisions: Estimates of a Linear Expenditure System for Bangladesh. *J. Econ. Devel.*, December 1987, *12*(2), pp. 89–113. **[G: Bangladesh]**

Khandker, Shahidur R.; Mestelman, Stuart and Feeny, David. Allocative Efficiency, the Aggregation of Labour Inputs, and the Effects of Farm Size and Tenancy Status: Tests from Rural Bangladesh. *J. Devel. Stud.*, October 1987, *24*(1), pp. 31–42. **[G: Bangladesh]**

Killian, Molly Sizer and Hady, Thomas F. The Economic Performance of Rural Labor Markets. *U.S.D.A., Econ. Res. Serv., Agr. and Rural Econ. Div.*, 1987, pp. 8.1–23. **[G: U.S.]**

Knickman, James R. Swing Beds: Assessing Flexible Health Care in Rural Communities: Access and Case-Mix Patterns: Comments. *Wiener,*

J. M., ed., 1987, pp. 103–04. **[G: U.S.]**

Koppel, Bruce. Does Integrated Area Development Work? Insight from the Bicol River Basin Development Program. *World Devel.*, February 1987, *15*(2), pp. 205–20. **[G: Philippines]**

Kovner, Anthony R. and Richardson, Hila. Swing Beds: Assessing Flexible Health Care in Rural Communities: The Robert Wood Johnson Demonstration Program. *Wiener, J. M., ed.*, 1987, pp. 24–41. **[G: U.S.]**

Kyereme, Stephen S. and Thorbecke, Erik. Food Poverty Profile and Decomposition Applied to Ghana. *World Devel.*, September 1987, *15*(9), pp. 1189–99. **[G: Ghana]**

Lago, María Soledad. Rural Women and the Neoliberal Model in Chile. *Deere, C. D. and León, M., eds.*, 1987, pp. 21–34. **[G: Chile]**

Lai, K. C. Project Impact Monitoring: A Misnomer. *J. Agr. Econ.*, January 1987, *38*(1), pp. 107–13.

León, Magdalena. Colombian Agricultural Policies and the Debate on Policies toward Rural Women. *Deere, C. D. and León, M., eds.*, 1987, pp. 84–104. **[G: Colombia]**

Lisk, Franklyn and Stevens, Yvette. Government Policy and Rural Women's Work in Sierre Leone. *Oppong, C., ed.*, 1987, pp. 182–202. **[G: Sierre Leone]**

Lloyd, A. G. The Australia–New Zealand Farm Problem and the Appropriate Role of Government. *Australian Econ. Rev.*, Third Quarter 1987, (79), pp. 3–20. **[G: Australia; New Zealand]**

Longhurst, Richard. Policy Approaches towards Small Farmers. *Cornia, G. A.; Jolly, R. and Stewart, F., eds.*, 1987, pp. 183–96. **[G: LDCs]**

Lu, Yingzhong. The Prospects of Rural Energy in the People's Republic of China (PRS). *Pachauri, R. K., ed.*, 1987, pp. 227–53. **[G: China]**

Mackenzie, Fiona and Taylor, D. R. F. District Focus as a Strategy for Rural Development in Kenya: The Case of Murang'a District, Central Province. *Can. J. Devel. Stud.*, 1987, *8*(2), pp. 299–316. **[G: Kenya]**

Malik, Sohail J. Rural Poverty in Bangladesh, India and Pakistan: Profiles and Policies: Comments. *Pakistan Devel. Rev.*, Autumn 1987, *26*(3), pp. 339–40. **[G: Bangladesh; India; Pakistan]**

Malley, James R. and Hady, Thomas F. The Impact of Macroeconomic Policies on Rural Employment. *U.S.D.A., Econ. Res. Serv., Agr. and Rural Econ. Div.*, 1987, pp. 10.1–19. **[G: U.S.]**

Manning, Chris. Rural Economic Change and Labour Mobility: A Case Study from West Java. *Bull. Indonesian Econ. Stud.*, December 1987, *23*(3), pp. 52–79. **[G: Indonesia]**

McBain, Helen. The Impact of the Bauxite–Alumina MNCs on Rural Jamaica: Constraints on Development of Small Farmers in Jamaica. *Soc. Econ. Stud.*, March 1987, *36*(1), pp. 137–70. **[G: Jamaica]**

McCracken, John. Conservation Priorities and

Rural Communities: Introduction. *Anderson, D. and Grove, R., eds.,* 1987, pp. 189–92.
[G: Africa]

McGranahan, David A. The Role of Rural Workers in the National Economy. *U.S.D.A., Econ. Res. Serv., Agr. and Rural Econ. Div.,* 1987, pp. 2.1–23. **[G: U.S.]**

Medellin E., Rodrigo A. The Peasant Initiative. *Austin, J. E. and Esteva, G., eds.,* 1987, pp. 148–71. **[G: Mexico]**

Melichar, Emanuel. Turning the Corner on Troubled Farm Debt. *Fed. Res. Bull.,* July 1987, 73(7), pp. 523–36. **[G: U.S.]**

Meyers, William H. The Farm Economies of the Plains: Comment. *Rev. Reg. Stud.,* Fall 1987, 17(3), pp. 58–59. **[G: U.S.]**

Milkove, Daniel L. and Sullivan, Patrick J. Financial Aid Programs as a Component of Economic Development Strategy. *U.S.D.A., Econ. Res. Serv., Agr. and Rural Econ. Div.,* 1987, pp. 14.1–22. **[G: U.S.]**

Miller, James P. and Bluestone, Herman. Prospects for Service Sector Employment Growth in Nonmetro America. *U.S.D.A., Econ. Res. Serv., Agr. and Rural Econ. Div.,* 1987, pp. 6.1–21. **[G: U.S.]**

Mitra, Gautam Kumar. Poverty, Land and Household Size: A Study of Three Andhra Pradesh Districts. *Margin,* July-Sept. 1987, 19(4), pp. 51–54. **[G: India]**

Mones, Belkis and Grant, Lydia. Agricultural Development, the Economic Crisis, and Rural Women in the Dominican Republic. *Deere, C. D. and León, M., eds.,* 1987, pp. 35–50. **[G: Dominican Republic]**

Moore, Kenneth. Swing-Bed Reimbursement: Objectives and Options: Comments. *Wiener, J. M., ed.,* 1987, pp. 84–85. **[G: U.S.]**

Muraleedharan, V. R. Rural Health Care in Madras Presidency: 1919–39. *Indian Econ. Soc. Hist. Rev.,* July-Sept. 1987, 24(3), pp. 323–34. **[G: India]**

Namasivayam, D.; Naidu, C. Gajendra and Mohanan, N. NREP in Tamil Nadu; Comparison of Growth and Equity by Taxanomic Method. *Margin,* December 1987, 20(1), pp. 56–73. **[G: India]**

Narayanan, Rangesan and Shane, Ronald L. Agricultural Productive and Consumptive Use Components of Rural Land Values in Texas: Comment. *Amer. J. Agr. Econ.,* February 1987, 69(1), pp. 176–78. **[G: U.S.]**

Nyoni, Sithembiso. Indigenous NGOs: Liberation, Self-reliance, and Development. *World Devel.,* Supp. Autumn 1987, 15, pp. 51–56. **[G: Zimbabwe]**

Osmani, S. R. The Impact of Economic Liberalisation on the Small-Scale and Rural Industries of Sri Lanka. *Islam, R., ed.,* 1987, pp. 171–209. **[G: Sri Lanka]**

Padilla, Martha Luz; Murguialday, Clara and Criquillon, Ana. Impact of the Sandinista Agrarian Reform on Rural Women's Subordination. *Deere, C. D. and León, M., eds.,* 1987, pp. 124–41. **[G: Nicaragua]**

Panda, Manoj Kumar. Poverty in Rural Orissa (1960–1983). *Margin,* December 1987, 20(1), pp. 42–55. **[G: India]**

Papola, T. S. Rural Industrialisation and Agricultural Growth: A Case Study on India. *Islam, R., ed.,* 1987, pp. 59–106. **[G: India]**

Peide, Yan. A Summary of the Discussion on Present Rural Business Operations with Hired Labor. *Chinese Econ. Stud.,* Fall 1987, 21(1), pp. 17–24. **[G: China]**

Pessah, Raul. Channeling Credit to the Countryside. *Austin, J. E. and Esteva, G., eds.,* 1987, pp. 92–110. **[G: Mexico]**

Petterson, John S. Subsistence Continuity and Economic Abundance in the North. *Lane, T., ed.,* 1987, pp. 91–106. **[G: U.S.]**

Phillips, Lynne. Women, Development, and the State in Rural Ecuador. *Deere, C. D. and León, M., eds.,* 1987, pp. 105–23. **[G: Ecuador]**

Platteau, Jean-Philippe and Abraham, Anita. An Inquiry into Quasi-credit Contracts: The Role of Reciprocal Credit and Interlinked Deals in Small-scale Fishing Communities. *J. Devel. Stud.,* July 1987, 23(4), pp. 461–90. **[G: LDCs]**

Pope, C. Arden, III. Agricultural Productive and Consumptive Use Components of Rural Land Values in Texas: Reply. *Amer. J. Agr. Econ.,* February 1987, 69(1), pp. 179–81. **[G: U.S.]**

Rahman, Atiq and Islam, Rizwanul. An Empirical Account of Hired Labour Market in Rural Bangladesh: Comment. *Bangladesh Devel. Stud.,* March 1987, 15(1), pp. 129–42. **[G: Bangladesh]**

Rahman, Atiur. Peasants and Classes: Reply. *Bangladesh Devel. Stud.,* December 1987, 15(4), pp. 163–69. **[G: Bangladesh]**

Rajaraman, Indira. Contractual Aspects of Daily Hire: Rural Labor in India. *J. Devel. Areas,* July 1987, 21(4), pp. 459–80. **[G: India]**

Ranis, Gustav and Stewart, Frances. Rural Linkages in the Philippines and Taiwan. *Stewart, F., ed.,* 1987, pp. 140–91. **[G: Taiwan; Philippines]**

Reid, J. Norman and Long, Richard W. Rural Policy Objectives: Defining Problems and Choosing Approaches. *U.S.D.A., Econ. Res. Serv., Agr. and Rural Econ. Div.,* 1987, pp. 9.1–16. **[G: U.S.]**

Reinhardt, Nola. Modernizing Peasant Agriculture: Lessons from El Palmar, Colombia. *World Devel.,* February 1987, 15(2), pp. 221–47. **[G: Colombia]**

Remenyi, J. V. and Bodman, Phil. Meeting Policy Data Needs on Smallholder Agriculture. *Barker, P.; Bodman, P. and Remenyl, J., eds.,* 1987, pp. 1–3. **[G: Papua New Guinea]**

Rodríguez, José Luiz. Agricultural Policy and Development in Cuba. *World Devel.,* January 1987, 15(1), pp. 23–39. **[G: Cuba]**

Romijn, Hendrika A. Employment Generation through Cottage Industries in Rural Thailand: Potentials and Constraints. *Islam, R., ed.,* 1987, pp. 211–40. **[G: Thailand]**

Ross, Peggy J. and Rosenfeld, Stuart A. Human Resource Policies and Economic Develop-

ment. *U.S.D.A., Econ. Res. Serv., Agr. and Rural Econ. Div.*, 1987, pp. 15.1–25.
[G: U.S.]

Roy, Sanjit. The Tilonia Model. A Successful Indian Grass Root Rural Development Strategy. *Can. J. Devel. Stud.*, 1987, *8*(2), pp. 355–74.
[G: India]

Ryan, Vernon D. The Significance of Community Development to Rural Economic Development Initiatives. *U.S.D.A., Econ. Res. Serv., Agr. and Rural Econ. Div.*, 1987, pp. 16.1–15.
[G: U.S.]

Sachak, Najma. The Impact of Land Acquisition by Bauxite–Alumina Transnational Corporations on Peasants in the Bauxite Land Economy. *Soc. Econ. Stud.*, March 1987, *36*(1), pp. 93–135.
[G: Jamaica]

Saith, Ashwani. Contrasting Experiences in Rural Industrialisation: Are the East Asian Successes Transferable? *Islam, R., ed.*, 1987, pp. 241–303.
[G: Japan; Taiwan; S. Korea]

Salmon, Michael G. Land Utilization within Jamaica's Bauxite Land Economy. *Soc. Econ. Stud.*, March 1987, *36*(1), pp. 57–92.
[G: Jamaica]

Schaefer, Donald F. A Model of Migration and Wealth Accumulation: Farmers at the Antebellum Southern Frontier. *Exploration Econ. Hist.*, April 1987, *24*(2), pp. 130–57.
[G: U.S.]

Schlenker, Robert. Swing-Bed Reimbursement: Objectives and Options: Comments. *Wiener, J. M., ed.*, 1987, pp. 81–84. [G: U.S.]

Schwartz, Moshe, et al. Moshav-Based Industry. *Bar-El, R., ed.*, 1987, pp. 57–104.
[G: Israel]

Schweizer, Thomas. Agrarian Transformation? Rice Production in a Javanese Village. *Bull. Indonesian Econ. Stud.*, August 1987, *23*(2), pp. 38–70. [G: Indonesia]

Sen Gupta, D. P. and de Gromard, Christian. Rural Electrification: Alternatives to Grid Extension. *Pachauri, R. K., ed.*, 1987, pp. 1123–42. [G: India]

Seroka, Jim. Variation in Rural County Administrative Agenda. *Reg. Sci. Persp.*, 1987, *17*(1), pp. 103–17. [G: U.S.]

Shadlow, John. NSO Data Needs and Involvement in Smallholder Agricultural Statistics. *Barker, P.; Bodman, P. and Remenyl, J., eds.*, 1987, pp. 11–13. [G: Papua New Guinea]

Shahabuddin, Quazi and Feeny, David. Efficiency, Share Tenancy, and Allocative Behavior in Peasant Farming: A Safety-First Approach. *J. Econ. Devel.*, June 1987, *12*(1), pp. 149–60.

Shand, R. T. Income Distribution in a Dynamic Rural Sector: Some Evidence from Malaysia. *Econ. Develop. Cult. Change*, October 1987, *36*(1), pp. 35–50. [G: Malaysia]

Shaughnessy, Peter W. Swing Beds: Assessing Flexible Health Care in Rural Communities: Access and Case-Mix Patterns. *Wiener, J. M., ed.*, 1987, pp. 86–100. [G: U.S.]

Spencer, Dunstan S. C. Food Price Policy and Equity: Commentary. *Mellor, J. W.; Delgado,*

C. L. and Blackie, M. J., eds., 1987, pp. 292–95. [G: Africa]

Spindel, Cheywa R. The Social Invisibility of Women's Work in Brazilian Agriculture. *Deere, C. D. and León, M., eds.*, 1987, pp. 51–66. [G: Brazil]

de Spoelberch, Guillaume and Shaw, Robert D'Arcy. A Model: The Aga Khan Rural Support Program. *Challenge*, Jan./Feb. 1987, *29*(6), pp. 26–31. [G: Pakistan]

Stabler, Jack C. Non-metropolitan Population Growth and the Evolution of Rural Service Centres in the Canadian Prairie Region. *Reg. Stud.*, February 1987, *21*(1), pp. 45–53.
[G: Canada]

Stanziani, Alessandro. L'impresa familiare nel pensiero di A. V. Čajanov. (With English summary.) *Stud. Econ.*, 1987, *42*(32), pp. 61–117.

Stellin, G. Agriculture and Rural Integrated Development in a Mountain Area. *Merlo, M., et al., eds.*, 1987, pp. 245–60. [G: Italy]

Stubbs, Jean and Alvarez, Mavis. Women on the Agenda: The Cooperative Movement in Rural Cuba. *Deere, C. D. and León, M., eds.*, 1987, pp. 142–61. [G: Cuba]

Swanson, Linda L. and Butler, Margaret A. Human Resource Base of Rural Economies. *U.S.D.A., Econ. Res. Serv., Agr. and Rural Econ. Div.*, 1987, pp. 7.1–23. [G: U.S.]

Tanner, Christopher. Malnutrition and the Development of Rural Households in the Agreste of Paraiba State, North-East Brazil. *J. Devel. Stud.*, January 1987, *23*(2), pp. 242–64.
[G: Brazil]

Taylor, J. Edward. Undocumented Mexico–U.S. Migration and the Returns to Households in Rural Mexico. *Amer. J. Agr. Econ.*, August 1987, *69*(3), pp. 626–38. [G: U.S.; Mexico]

Thakur, D. S. A Survey of Rural Unemployment in India: A Critique of Unidimensional Approach. *Indian Econ. J.*, July-Sept. 1987, *35*(1), pp. 120–35. [G: India]

Thomas, Barbara P. Development through Harambee: Who Wins and Who Loses? Rural Self-help Projects in Kenya. *World Devel.*, April 1987, *15*(4), pp. 463–81. [G: Kenya]

Villasuso, Juan M. Costa Rica: Crisis, Adjustment Policies and Rural Development. *CEPAL Rev.*, December 1987, (33), pp. 107–13.
[G: Costa Rica]

Vink, N. and Kassier, W. E. The 'Tragedy of the Commons' and Livestock Farming in Southern Africa. *S. Afr. J. Econ.*, June 1987, *55*(2), pp. 165–82. [G: S. Africa]

Wade, Robert. The Management of Common Property Resources: Finding a Cooperative Solution. *World Bank Res. Observer*, July 1987, *2*(2), pp. 219–34. [G: India]

Wade, Robert. The Management of Common Property Resources: Collective Action as an Alternative to Privatisation or State Regulation. *Cambridge J. Econ.*, June 1987, *11*(2), pp. 95–106.

Weisser, Michael R. Rural Crisis and Rural Credit in XVIIth-Century Castile. *J. Europ. Econ.*

Hist., Fall 1987, *16*(2), pp. 297–313.
[G: Spain]

Whitelegg, John. Rural Railways and Disinvestment in Rural Areas. *Reg. Stud.*, February 1987, *21*(1), pp. 55–63. [G: U.K.]

Wiener, Joshua M. Swing Beds: Assessing Flexible Health Care in Rural Communities: Policy Issues. *Wiener, J. M., ed.*, 1987, pp. 13–23. [G: U.S.]

Wiener, Joshua M. Swing Beds: Assessing Flexible Health Care in Rural Communities: Introduction and Summary. *Wiener, J. M., ed.*, 1987, pp. 1–12. [G: U.S.]

Wiens, Thomas B. Issues in the Structural Reform of Chinese Agriculture. *J. Compar. Econ.*, September 1987, *11*(3), pp. 372–84. [G: China]

Wilson, Donald A. Swing Beds: Assessing Flexible Health Care in Rural Communities: Cost Issues: Comments. *Wiener, J. M., ed.*, 1987, pp. 63.

Yotopoulos, Pan A. Rural Poverty in Bangladesh, India and Pakistan: Profiles and Policies: Comments. *Pakistan Devel. Rev.*, Autumn 1987, *26*(3), pp. 337–38. [G: Bangladesh; India; Pakistan]

Zweig, David. From Village to City: Reforming Urban–Rural Relations in China. *Int. Reg. Sci. Rev.*, 1987, *11*(1), pp. 43–58. [G: China]

720 NATURAL RESOURCES

721 Natural Resources

7210 General

Adamowicz, M. and Kos, C. Some Aspects of Specialization and Integration of Agriculture and Forestry in Solving the Food Problem in Poland. *Merlo, M., et al., eds.*, 1987, pp. 553–61. [G: Poland]

Adams, Charles M.; Prochaska, Fred J. and Spreen, Thomas H. Price Determination in the U.S. Shrimp Market. *Southern J. Agr. Econ.*, December 1987, *19*(2), pp. 103–11. [G: U.S.]

Adams, William M. Approaches to Water Resource Development, Sokoto Valley, Nigeria: The Problem of Sustainability. *Anderson, D. and Grove, R., eds.*, 1987, pp. 307–25. [G: Nigeria]

Ågren, Goran I. Models for Forestry. *Braat, L. C. and van Lierop, W. F. J., eds.*, 1987, pp. 87–99.

Alam, Manzoor. Supply and Demand of Fuel Wood in the Domestic Sector—The Case of Hyderabad City. *Pachauri, R. K., ed.*, 1987, pp. 529–46. [G: India]

Allen, Bryant J. A Review of Smallholder Data Sources in PNG Relevant to the Export Tree Crops Sector. *Barker, P.; Bodman, P. and Remenyl, J., eds.*, 1987, pp. 14–54. [G: Papua New Guinea]

Alley, William M. and Schefter, John E. External Effects of Irrigators' Pumping Decisions, High Plains Aquifer. *Water Resources Res.*, July

1987, *23*(7), pp. 1123–30. [G: U.S.]

Anderson, Curt L. The Production Process: Inputs and Wastes. *J. Environ. Econ. Manage.*, March 1987, *14*(1), pp. 1–12. [G: U.S.]

Anderson, David M. Managing the Forest: The Conservation History of Lembus, Kenya, 1904–63. *Anderson, D. and Grove, R., eds.*, 1987, pp. 249–68. [G: Kenya]

Anderson, Dennis. Economic Aspects of Afforestation and Soil Conservation Projects. *Ann. Reg. Sci.*, November 1987, *21*(3), pp. 100–110. [G: Nigeria; Niger; Chad; Cameroon]

Anderson, Lee G. A Management Agency Perspective of the Economics of Fisheries Regulation. *Marine Resource Econ.*, 1987, *4*(2), pp. 123–31.

Areola, Olusegun. The Political Reality of Conservation in Nigeria. *Anderson, D. and Grove, R., eds.*, 1987, pp. 277–92. [G: Nigeria]

Arshad, Fatimah Mohd and Gibbons, E. T. Investigating the Market Structure for Fish in Malaysia. *Young, R. H. and MacCormac, C. W., eds.*, 1987, pp. 121–42. [G: Malaysia]

Asheim, G. B. Erratum [Hartwick's Rule in Open Economies]. *Can. J. Econ.*, February 1987, *20*(1), pp. 177.

Atkinson, Karen J. The Alaska National Interest Lands Conservation Act: Striking the Balance in Favor of "Customary and Traditional" Subsistence Uses by Alaska Natives. *Natural Res. J.*, Spring 1987, *27*(2), pp. 421–40. [G: U.S.]

Bacon, Pamela S. Mines and Minerals—A Mineral Lessee's Rights and Obligations in New Mexico. *Natural Res. J.*, Fall 1987, *27*(4), pp. 899–912. [G: U.S.]

Baden, John and Blood, Tom. Ecology and Enterprise: Toward the Private Management of Wildlife Resources. *Kent, C. A., ed.*, 1987, pp. 67–79.

Bartholomew, R. B. and Densley, D. R. J. Data Needs, Output and Options: Smallholder Component—PNG Export Tree Crop Study. *Barker, P.; Bodman, P. and Remenyl, J., eds.*, 1987, pp. 55–63. [G: Papua New Guinea]

Beck, M. B. Water Quality Modeling: A Review of the Analysis of Uncertainty. *Water Resources Res.*, August 1987, *23*(8), pp. 1393–1442.

Beck, M. B. and Finney, B. A. Operational Water Quality Management: Problem Context and Evaluation of a Model for River Quality. *Water Resources Res.*, November 1987, *23*(11), pp. 2030–42. [G: U.K.]

Becker, H. The Impact of Agroforestry Systems on Smallholder Development in Sub-Saharan Agricultural Societies. *Merlo, M., et al., eds.*, 1987, pp. 333–43. [G: Sub-Saharan Africa]

Behrman, Jere R. Commodity Price Instability and Economic Goal Attainment in Developing Countries. *World Devel.*, May 1987, *15*(5), pp. 559–73. [G: Chile; Zambia; Brazil; Ivory Coast; El Salvador]

Bell, Frederick W. and Leeworthy, Vernon R. Economic Demand for Marinas and Projected Impact on Wetlands. *Land Econ.*, February 1987, *63*(1), pp. 79–91. [G: U.S.]

Bergstrom, John C. and Stoll, John R. A Test of Contingent Market Bid Elicitation Procedures for Piecewise Valuation. *Western J. Agr. Econ.*, December 1987, *12*(2), pp. 104–08. [G: U.S.]

Bernardo, Daniel J., et al. An Irrigation Model for Management of Limited Water Supplies. *Western J. Agr. Econ.*, December 1987, *12*(2), pp. 164–73. [G: U.S.]

Binkley, Clark S. When Is the Optimal Economic Rotation Longer Than the Rotation of Maximum Sustained Yield? *J. Environ. Econ. Manage.*, June 1987, *14*(2), pp. 152–58.

Bjørndal, Trond. Production Economics and Optimal Stock Size in a North Atlantic Fishery. *Scand. J. Econ.*, 1987, *89*(2), pp. 145–64. [G: Norway]

Bjørndal, Trond and Conrad, Jon M. Capital Dynamics in the North Sea Herring Fishery. *Marine Resource Econ.*, 1987, *4*(1), pp. 63–74. [G: Norway]

Bjørndal, Trond and Conrad, Jon M. The Dynamics of an Open Access Fishery. *Can. J. Econ.*, February 1987, *20*(1), pp. 74–85. [G: Norway]

Blackwell, Ann Lowes. Examination of Institutional Structures in Multiple Resource, Multiple Management Systems: A Control Theoretic Approach. *Vincent, T. L., et al., eds.*, 1987, pp. 287–302. [G: U.S.]

Blyth, Michael J. and McCallum, Andrew. Onsite Costs of Land Degradation in Agriculture and Forestry. *Chisholm, A. and Dumsday, R., eds.*, 1987, pp. 79–98. [G: Australia]

Boadway, Robin W., et al. Marginal Effective Tax Rates for Capital in the Canadian Mining Industry. *Can. J. Econ.*, February 1987, *20*(1), pp. 1–16. [G: Canada]

Bodvarsson, Örn B. Monitoring with No Moral Hazard: The Case of Small Vessel Commercial Fishing. *Eastern Econ. J.*, October-December 1987, *13*(4), pp. 421–34. [G: U.S.]

Bogardi, Istvan. Water Resources Models. *Braat, L. C. and van Lierop, W. F. J., eds.*, 1987, pp. 117–34.

Boskin, Michael J. and Robinson, Marc S. The Value of Federal Mineral Rights, Correction and Update: Erratum [Government Saving, Capital Formation and Wealth in the United States, 1947–1985]. *Amer. Econ. Rev.*, December 1987, *77*(5), pp. 1073–74. [G: U.S.]

Botsford, Louis W. Modeling for Biological Resource Management: Comment. *Vincent, T. L., et al., eds.*, 1987, pp. 40–41.

Bouldouyre, M. Fiscal and Social Actions to Promote Farmers Working in Woods Belonging to Others. *Merlo, M., et al., eds.*, 1987, pp. 487–90. [G: France]

Boyle, Kevin J. and Bishop, Richard C. Valuing Wildlife in Benefit–Cost Analyses: A Case Study Involving Endangered Species. *Water Resources Res.*, May 1987, *23*(5), pp. 943–50. [G: U.S.]

Braat, Leon C. and van Lierop, Wal F. J. Economic–Ecological Modeling: Evaluation. *Braat, L. C. and van Lierop, W. F. J., eds.*, 1987, pp. 282–85.

Braat, Leon C. and van Lierop, Wal F. J. Environment, Policy, and Modeling. *Braat, L. C. and van Lierop, W. F. J., eds.*, 1987, pp. 7–19.

Braat, Leon C. and van Lierop, Wal F. J. Integrated Economic–Ecological Modeling. *Braat, L. C. and van Lierop, W. F. J., eds.*, 1987, pp. 49–68.

Bradley, Paul G. Cost and Output Analysis in Mineral and Petroleum Production. *[Adelman, M. A.]*, 1987, pp. 281–303.

Brandl, H. Forestry Incentives in Baden-Württemberg. *Merlo, M., et al., eds.*, 1987, pp. 389–98. [G: W. Germany]

Bulfin, M. and Connolly, J. The Response of Irish Landowners to Forestry Incentives for Afforestation and Management. *Merlo, M., et al., eds.*, 1987, pp. 399–408. [G: Ireland]

Buttoud, G. and Normandin, D. Discussing Public Control over Private Forest Wealth Management: The French Experience. *Merlo, M., et al., eds.*, 1987, pp. 409–19. [G: France]

Cairns, Robert D. An Economic Assessment of the Resource Amendment. *Can. Public Policy*, December 1987, *13*(4), pp. 502–14. [G: Canada]

Caputo, María Graciela and Herzer, Hilda. Reflexiones sobre el manejo de las inundaciones y su incorporación a las políticas de desarrollo regional. (With English summary.) *Desarrollo Econ.*, July-Sept. 1987, *27*(106), pp. 245–60. [G: Argentina]

Carnegie, A. R. The Law of the Sea: Commonwealth Caribbean Perspectives. *Soc. Econ. Stud.*, September 1987, *36*(3), pp. 99–117. [G: Caribbean]

Carrad, Bruce. Data Objectives and Needs for PNG's Smallholder Export Tree Crops Sector. *Barker, P.; Bodman, P. and Remenyi, J., eds.*, 1987, pp. 4–10. [G: Papua New Guinea]

Cassing, James H.; Wells, Jerome C. and Zamalloa, Edgar L. On Resource Booms and Busts: Some Aspects of the Dutch Disease in Six Developing Economies. *Eastern Econ. J.*, October-December 1987, *13*(4), pp. 373–87. [G: LDCs]

Cave, Jonathan. Long-term Competition in a Dynamic Game: The Cold Fish War. *Rand J. Econ.*, Winter 1987, *18*(4), pp. 596–610.

Chapman, Duane. Computation Techniques for Intertemporal Allocation of Natural Resources. *Amer. J. Agr. Econ.*, February 1987, *69*(1), pp. 134–42.

Chassany, J. P. Agroforestry and Afforestation of Marginal Land. *Merlo, M., et al., eds.*, 1987, pp. 345–57. [G: France]

Clark, Colin W. Behavioral Modelling and Resource Management. *Vincent, T. L., et al., eds.*, 1987, pp. 11–19.

Clark, Colin W. Fisheries as Renewable Resources. *Braat, L. C. and van Lierop, W. F. J., eds.*, 1987, pp. 73–86.

Clarke, Harry R. and Shrestha, Ram M. Renewable Resource Management with a Backstop

Substitute and Nonautonomous Prices. *J. Environ. Econ. Manage.*, June 1987, *14*(2), pp. 159–82.

Clifford, Norman and Crawford, Vincent P. Short-term Contracting and Strategic Oil Reserves. *Rev. Econ. Stud.*, April 1987, *54*(2), pp. 311–23.

Cochrane, N. J. Identification of Water Demand Models from Noisy Data: Comment. *Water Resources Res.*, April 1987, *23*(4), pp. 744.
[G: U.S.]

Coggins, George Cameron and Harris, Anne Fleishel. The Greening of American Law? The Recent Evolution of Federal Law for Preserving Floral Diversity. *Natural Res. J.*, Spring 1987, *27*(2), pp. 247–307. [G: U.S.]

Cohen, Yosef. Approaches to Adaptive Policy Design for Harvest Management: Comment. *Vincent, T. L., et al., eds.*, 1987, pp. 123.

Cohen, Yosef. Identification and Control of Stochastic Linear Multispecies Ecosystem Models. *Vincent, T. L., et al., eds.*, 1987, pp. 66–79.

Cook, B. A. and Copes, Parzival. Optimal Levels for Canada's Pacific Halibut Catch. *Marine Resource Econ.*, 1987, *4*(1), pp. 45–61.
[G: Canada]

Crabbé, Philippe J. The Quasi-Option Value of Irreversible Investment: A Comment [The Quasi-Option Value of Irreversible Development]. *J. Environ. Econ. Manage.*, December 1987, *14*(4), pp. 384–85.

Crew, Michael A.; Kleindorfer, Paul R. and Schlenger, Donald L. Governance Costs of Regulation for Water Supply. *Crew, M. A., ed.*, 1987, pp. 43–62. [G: U.S.]

Crouter, Jan P. Hedonic Estimation Applied to a Water Rights Market. *Land Econ.*, August 1987, *63*(3), pp. 259–71. [G: U.S.]

Cumberland, John H. Need Economic Development Be Hazardous to the Health of the Chesapeake Bay? *Marine Resource Econ.*, 1987, *4*(2), pp. 81–93. [G: U.S.]

Dalziel, Paul C. Optimal Water Storage and Pricing: The Effect of Monopoly. *New Zealand Econ. Pap.*, 1987, *21*, pp. 3–16.
[G: New Zealand]

Dangler, Hugh W. *Sierra Club vs. Block*, Wilderness Water Rights Projected Where Not in Conflict with Purposes of National Forest in Colorado. *Natural Res. J.*, Spring 1987, *27*(2), pp. 441–56. [G: U.S.]

Davis, Lance E.; Gallman, Robert E. and Hutchins, Teresa D. Technology, Productivity, and Profits: British–American Whaling Competition in the North Atlantic, 1816–1842. *Oxford Econ. Pap.*, December 1987, *39*(4), pp. 738–59. [G: U.S.; U.K.]

De Gregori, Thomas R. Resources Are Not; They Become: An Institutional Theory. *J. Econ. Issues*, September 1987, *21*(3), pp. 1241–63.
[G: U.S.]

Dixon, John A. Managing Watershed Resources. *Ann. Reg. Sci.*, November 1987, *21*(3), pp. 111–23. [G: Philippines]

Dixon, John A. The Renewable Natural Resource

Base. *Martin, L. G., ed.*, 1987, pp. 88–91.
[G: ASEAN]

Dower, Roger C. and Scodari, Paul F. Compensation for Natural Resource Injury: An Emerging Federal Framework. *Marine Resource Econ.*, 1987, *4*(3), pp. 155–74. [G: U.S.]

Downing, P. and Brandon, O. A Forestry Enterprise on Farms in an England Lowland Context. *Merlo, M., et al., eds.*, 1987, pp. 421–32. [G: U.K.]

Eagan, Vince. The Optimal Depletion of the Theory of Exhaustible Resources. *J. Post Keynesian Econ.*, Summer 1987, *9*(4), pp. 565–71.

Eheart, J. Wayland, et al. Cost Efficiency of Time-Varying Discharge Permit Programs for Water Quality Management. *Water Resources Res.*, February 1987, *23*(2), pp. 245–51.
[G: U.S.]

Emel, Jacque L. Groundwater Rights: Definition and Transfer. *Natural Res. J.*, Summer 1987, *27*(3), pp. 653–73. [G: U.S.]

Emerson, M. Jarvin and Akhavipour, Hossein. The Impact on Metropolitan Areas of Hinterland Resource Depletion. *Reg. Sci. Persp.*, 1987, *17*(2), pp. 57–69. [G: U.S.]

Farber, Stephen C. The Value of Coastal Wetlands for Protection of Property against Hurricane Wind Damage. *J. Environ. Econ. Manage.*, June 1987, *14*(2), pp. 143–51. [G: U.S.]

Filius, A. M. Forestry Incentives in the Netherlands. *Merlo, M., et al., eds.*, 1987, pp. 433–43. [G: Netherlands]

Fisher, Anthony C. and Hanemann, W. Michael. Quasi-option Value: Some Misconceptions Dispelled. *J. Environ. Econ. Manage.*, June 1987, *14*(2), pp. 183–90.

Flåm, Sjur D. and Moxnes, Erling. Exploration for Petroleum and the Inventory of Proven Reserves. *Energy Econ.*, July 1987, *9*(3), pp. 190–94. [G: Norway]

Fletcher, Jerald J.; Howitt, Richard E. and Johnston, Warren E. Management of Multipurpose Heterogeneous Fishing Fleets under Uncertainty. *Marine Resource Econ.*, 1987, *4*(4), pp. 249–70. [G: U.S.]

Freebairn, John W. The Australian Economy in the Long Run: Natural Resource Industries. *Maddock, R. and McLean, I. W., eds.*, 1987, pp. 133–64. [G: Australia]

Friedheim, Robert L. The Third United Nations Conference on the Law of the Sea: North–South Bargaining on Ocean Issues. *Zartman, I. W., ed. (II)*, 1987, pp. 73–114.

Fujiwara, O.; Jenchaimahakoon, B. and Edirisinghe, N. C. P. A Modified Linear Programming Gradient Method for Optimal Design of Looped Water Distribution Networks. *Water Resources Res.*, June 1987, *23*(6), pp. 977–82.

Galante, E. and Sala, C. A Survey of Less Favoured Mountain Areas in Italy. *Merlo, M., et al., eds.*, 1987, pp. 277–90. [G: Italy]

Gamaledinn, Maknun. State Policy and Famine in the Awash Valley of Ethiopia: The Lessons for Conservation. *Anderson, D. and Grove, R., eds.*, 1987, pp. 327–44. [G: Ethiopia]

Geha, Susan. International Regulation of Whaling: The United States' Compromise. *Natural Res. J.*, Fall 1987, 27(4), pp. 931–40. [G: U.S.]

Geroski, Paul A.; Ulph, Alistair M. and Ulph, David T. A Model of the Crude Oil Market in Which Market Conduct Varies. *Econ. J.*, Supplement 1987, 97, pp. 77–86. [G: Global]

Getz, Wayne M. Modeling for Biological Resource Management. *Vincent, T. L., et al., eds.*, 1987, pp. 22–40.

Ghosh, A. Technical Costs of Environmental Protection and Its Redistribution in the Economy. *Econ. Planning*, 1987, 21(2–3), pp. 115–22.

Gillmor, Desmond A. The Irish Sea Fisheries: Development and Curtailment of a Renewable Resource Industry. *Amer. J. Econ. Soc.*, April 1987, 46(2), pp. 165–78. [G: Ireland]

Gios, Geremia; Pilati, L. and Ricci, G. Integration between Agroforestry and Tourism in Alpine Areas. *Merlo, M., et al., eds.*, 1987, pp. 235–44. [G: Italy]

Grundy, D. Multipurpose Agriculture and Forestry: An Overview and Some Remarks on the Seminar. *Merlo, M., et al., eds.*, 1987, pp. 619–22.

Guillard, J. Multipurpose Agriculture and Forestry: An Overview and Some Remarks on the Seminar. *Merlo, M., et al., eds.*, 1987, pp. 622–24.

Hanna, Susan S. Behavioral Modelling and Resource Management: Comment. *Vincent, T. L., et al., eds.*, 1987, pp. 20–21.

Hanna, Susan S. The Structure of Fishing Systems and the Implementation of Management Policy. *Vincent, T. L., et al., eds.*, 1987, pp. 264–73. [G: U.S.]

Harou, P. A. A Possible Methodology to Justify and Evaluate Production Incentives for Private Forests in the EEC. *Merlo, M., et al., eds.*, 1987, pp. 501–10. [G: EEC]

Harou, P. A. Multipurpose Agriculture and Forestry: An Overview and Some Remarks on the Seminar. *Merlo, M., et al., eds.*, 1987, pp. 624–29. [G: W. Europe]

Harris, Bruce. The Survival of Respect: Economic Power and the Persistence of Community. *Lane, T., ed.*, 1987, pp. 161–80. [G: U.S.]

Harris, Trevor S. and Ohlson, James A. Accounting Disclosures and the Market's Valuation of Oil and Gas Properties. *Accounting Rev.*, October 1987, 62(4), pp. 651–70. [G: U.S.]

Hayes, Kathy J. Cost Structure of the Water Utility Industry. *Appl. Econ.*, March 1987, 19(3), pp. 417–25. [G: U.S.]

Helles, F. Aspects of a Grant Scheme for Small Private Woodlands in Denmark. *Merlo, M., et al., eds.*, 1987, pp. 445–54. [G: Denmark]

Hogg, Richard. Settlement, Pastoralism and the Commons: The Ideology and Practice of Irrigation Development in Northern Kenya. *Anderson, D. and Grove, R., eds.*, 1987, pp. 293–306. [G: Kenya]

Howe, Charles W. On the Theory of Optimal Regional Development Based on an Exhaustible Resource. *Growth Change*, Spring 1987, 18(2), pp. 53–68.

Howe, Charles W. Project Benefits and Costs from National and Regional Viewpoints: Methodological Issues and Case Study of the Colorado–Big Thompson Project. *Natural Res. J.*, Winter 1987, 27(1), pp. 5–20. [G: U.S.]

Hudgins, Linda L. Negotiating Fishing Access Rights in the South Pacific: An Economic Framework. *Dutta, M., ed. (I)*, 1987, pp. 243–57. [G: S. Pacific]

Huffaker, Ray and Gardner, B. Delworth. Rancher Stewardship on Public Ranges: A Recent Court Decision. *Natural Res. J.*, Fall 1987, 27(4), pp. 887–98. [G: U.S.]

Hughes, Francine. Conflicting Uses for Forest Resources in the Lower Tana River Basin of Kenya. *Anderson, D. and Grove, R., eds.*, 1987, pp. 211–28. [G: Kenya]

Hyde, William F.; Boyd, Roy G. and Daniels, Barbara L. The Impacts of Public Interventions: An Examination of the Forestry Sector. *J. Policy Anal. Manage.*, Fall 1987, 7(1), pp. 40–61. [G: U.S.]

Ikeda, Saburo. Economic–Ecological Models in Regional Total Systems. *Braat, L. C. and van Lierop, W. F. J., eds.*, 1987, pp. 185–202.

Insley, H. Incentives for Private Forestry in Great Britain. *Merlo, M., et al., eds.*, 1987, pp. 455–63. [G: U.K.]

Isaac, R. Mark. The Value of Information in Resource Exploration: The Interaction of Strategic Plays and Institutional Rules. *J. Environ. Econ. Manage.*, December 1987, 14(4), pp. 313–22.

James, I. R. and Knuiman, M. W. An Application of Bayes Methodology to the Analysis of Diary Records from a Water Use Study. *J. Amer. Statist. Assoc.*, September 1987, 82(399), pp. 705–11. [G: Australia]

Jeffers, J. N. R. Ecological Modeling: Shortcomings and Perspectives. *Braat, L. C. and van Lierop, W. F. J., eds.*, 1987, pp. 36–48.

Johansson, Per-Olov and Löfgren, Karl-Gustaf. A Bargaining Approach to the Modeling of the Swedish Roundwood Market: Reply. *Land Econ.*, May 1987, 63(2), pp. 211–12.

Johnson, J. A. and Nicholls, D. C. The Value of Fiscal Measures to the Private Woodland Owner in Britain. *Merlo, M., et al., eds.*, 1987, pp. 475–86. [G: U.K.]

Kahn, James R. Measuring the Economic Damages Associated With Terrestrial Pollution of Marine Ecosystems. *Marine Resource Econ.*, 1987, 4(3), pp. 193–209.

Kaldor, Nicholas. The Role of Commodity Prices in Economic Recovery. *World Devel.*, May 1987, 15(5), pp. 551–58. [G: EEC; U.S.]

Karpoff, Jonathan M. Suboptimal Controls in Common Resource Management: The Case of the Fishery. *J. Polit. Econ.*, February 1987, 95(1), pp. 179–94.

Katzman, Martin T. Ecology, Natural Resources, and Economic Growth: Underdeveloping the Amazon: Review Article. *Econ. Develop. Cult. Change*, January 1987, 35(2), pp. 425–36. [G: Brazil]

Kennedy, John O. S. A Computable Game Theoretic Approach to Modelling Competitive Fishing. *Marine Resource Econ.*, 1987, *4*(1), pp. 1–14.

Khachaturov, T. S. Natural Resources and the Environment: Introduction. *Borner, S. and Taylor, A., eds.*, 1987, pp. 7–17.

Khan, Saleem M. The Role of Agriculture in Asia-Pacific Economies: Comments [Negotiating Fishing Access Rights in the South Pacific: An Economic Framework] [Sharecropping in Dual Agrarian Economies: Implications for Land Reform]. *Dutta, M., ed. (I)*, 1987, pp. 283–85. [G: Asia-Pacific; S. Pacific]

Kim, H. Youn and Clark, Robert M. Input Substitution and Demand in the Water Supply Production Process. *Water Resources Res.*, February 1987, *23*(2), pp. 239–44. [G: U.S.]

Kirby, Michael G. and Blyth, Michael J. An Economic Perspective on Government Intervention in Land Degradation. *Chisholm, A. and Dumsday, R., eds.*, 1987, pp. 213–22. [G: Australia]

Kirkwood, Geoff P. Approaches to Adaptive Policy Design for Harvest Management: Comment. *Vincent, T. L., et al., eds.*, 1987, pp. 124.

Kirkwood, Geoff P. Modeling for Biological Resource Management: Comment. *Vincent, T. L., et al., eds.*, 1987, pp. 41–42.

Kirkwood, Geoff P. Optimal Harvest Policies for Fisheries with Uncertain Stock Sizes. *Vincent, T. L., et al., eds.*, 1987, pp. 43–51.

Kirkwood, Geoff P. Optimal Harvest Policies for Fisheries with Uncertain Stock Sizes: Reply. *Vincent, T. L., et al., eds.*, 1987, pp. 52.

Kivell, P. T. Derelict Land in England: Policy Responses to a Continuing Problem. *Reg. Stud.*, June 1987, *21*(3), pp. 265–70. [G: U.K.]

Kokoski, Mary F. and Smith, V. Kerry. A General Equilibrium Analysis of Partial-Equilibrium Welfare Measures: The Case of Climate Change. *Amer. Econ. Rev.*, June 1987, *77*(3), pp. 331–41. [G: U.S.]

Kula, Erhun. Public Sector Forestry and Intergenerational Justice: A Cost–Benefit Analysis of Ulster Forestry with Modified Discounting. *Merlo, M., et al., eds.*, 1987, pp. 69–79. [G: U.K.]

Kula, Erhun. The Developing Framework for the Economic Evaluation of Forestry in the United Kingdom: A Reply. *J. Agr. Econ.*, September 1987, *38*(3), pp. 501–03. [G: U.K.]

Lamb, F. Bruce. The Role of Anthropology in Tropical Forest Ecosystem Resource Management and Development. *J. Devel. Areas*, July 1987, *21*(4), pp. 429–58.

Lane, Theodore. Developing America's Northern Frontier: Introduction. *Lane, T., ed.*, 1987, pp. xiii–xix. [G: U.S.; Canada]

Langdon, Stephen. Commercial Fisheries: Implications for Western Alaska Development. *Lane, T., ed.*, 1987, pp. 3–26. [G: U.S.]

Larrere, R. and de la Soudiere, M. We Won't Go to the Woods . . . Picking Is Regulated in

the Margeride. *Merlo, M., et al., eds.*, 1987, pp. 563–72. [G: France]

Laurent, C. The Maintenance of Biomass in Mountain Areas: A Public Service or State Aid to Farmers and Foresters? *Merlo, M., et al., eds.*, 1987, pp. 113–30. [G: France]

Leconte, Roberte; Hughes, Trevor C. and Narayanan, Rangesan. Economic Efficiency and Investment Timing for Dual Water Systems. *Water Resources Res.*, October 1987, *23*(10), pp. 1807–15.

Lee, John G., et al. Regional Impact of Urban Water Use on Irrigated Agriculture. *Southern J. Agr. Econ.*, December 1987, *19*(2), pp. 43–51. [G: U.S.]

Leman, Christopher K. A Forest of Institutions: Patterns of Choice on North American Timberlands. *Feldman, E. J. and Goldberg, M. A., eds.*, 1987, pp. 149–200. [G: U.S.; Canada]

Leman, Christopher K. The Concepts of Public and Private and Their Applicability to North American Lands. *Feldman, E. J. and Goldberg, M. A., eds.*, 1987, pp. 23–37. [G: U.S.; Canada]

Leslie, A. J. The Purpose of Forests: Follies of Development: Foreword. *Westoby, J.*, 1987, pp. vii–xiii.

Leveque, F. A Reappraisal of the Role of Timber Status in Agriculture and Prospects for Development. *Merlo, M., et al., eds.*, 1987, pp. 321–31. [G: France]

Lichtenberg, Erik and Zilberman, David. Regulation of Marine Contamination under Environmental Uncertainty: Shellfish Contamination in California. *Marine Resource Econ.*, 1987, *4*(3), pp. 211–25. [G: U.S.]

Lin, Biing-Hwan; Richards, Hugh S. and Terry, Joseph M. An Analysis of the Exvessel Demand for Pacific Halibut. *Marine Resource Econ.*, 1987, *4*(4), pp. 305–14. [G: U.S.; Canada]

Little, Peter D. and Brokensha, David W. Local Institutions, Tenure and Resource Management in East Africa. *Anderson, D. and Grove, R., eds.*, 1987, pp. 193–209. [G: E. Africa]

Livernois, John R. Empirical Evidence on the Characteristics of Extractive Technologies: The Case of Oil. *J. Environ. Econ. Manage.*, March 1987, *14*(1), pp. 72–86. [G: Canada]

Livernois, John R. and Uhler, Russell S. Extraction Costs and the Economics of Nonrenewable Resources. *J. Polit. Econ.*, February 1987, *95*(1), pp. 195–203.

Loomis, John B. Balancing Public Trust Resources of Mono Lake and Los Angeles' Water Right: An Economic Approach. *Water Resources Res.*, August 1987, *23*(8), pp. 1449–56. [G: U.S.]

Loomis, John B. Economic Efficiency Analysis, Bureaucrats, and Budgets: A Test of Hypotheses. *Western J. Agr. Econ.*, July 1987, *12*(1), pp. 27–34. [G: U.S.]

Loomis, John B. Expanding Contingent Value Sample Estimates to Aggregate Benefit Estimates: Current Practices and Proposed Solutions. *Land Econ.*, November 1987, *63*(4), pp. 396–402. [G: U.S.]

Lowe, B. Thomas. Regulatory Enforcement of the Surface Mine Control and Reclamation Act of 1977, PL 95/87: A Comparison of State and Federal Compliance in Three Midwestern States. *Natural Res. J.*, Winter 1987, 27(1), pp. 201–11. **[G: U.S.]**

Ludwig, Donald. Optimal Harvest Policies for Fisheries with Uncertain Stock Sizes: Comment. *Vincent, T. L., et al., eds.*, 1987, pp. 51–52.

MacKellar, F. Landis and Vining, Daniel R., Jr. Natural Resource Scarcity: A Global Survey. *Johnson, D. G. and Lee, R. D., eds.*, 1987, pp. 259–329. **[G: Global]**

Madariaga, Bruce and McConnell, Kenneth E. Exploring Existence Value. *Water Resources Res.*, May 1987, 23(5), pp. 936–42.

Mann, Roger; Sparling, Edward and Young, Robert A. Regional Economic Growth from Irrigation Development: Evidence from Northern High-Plains Ogallala Groundwater Resource. *Water Resources Res.*, September 1987, 23(9), pp. 1711–16. **[G: U.S.]**

Marsh, James Barney. Multinational Marine Resource Development in Disputed Boundary Areas: Southeast Asian Examples. *J. Energy Devel.*, Spring 1987, 12(2), pp. 245–68. **[G: Asia]**

Martin, Quentin W. Estimating Freshwater Inflow Needs for Texas Estuaries by Mathematical Programming. *Water Resources Res.*, February 1987, 23(2), pp. 230–38. **[G: U.S.]**

Mary, F. Economic and Ecological Functions of Farm Plantations: What Possible Alternative to Forests? *Merlo, M., et al., eds.*, 1987, pp. 359–70. **[G: Indonesia]**

McKelvey, Robert. Fur Seal and Blue Whale: The Bioeconomics of Extinction. *Cohen, Y., ed.*, 1987, pp. 57–82.

McKetta, Charles; Bobenrieth H., Eugenio and Avello A., Ricardo. Relación Insumo-Producto en los Mercados Forestales de Chile y sus Implicaciones. (With English summary.) *Cuadernos Econ.*, April 1987, 24(71), pp. 99–107. **[G: Chile]**

McNicoll, Iain H. and Davies, J. R. Measuring the Secondary Impact of the Left Bank Outfall Drain on the Economy of Sindh. *Pakistan J. Appl. Econ.*, Summer 1987, 6(1), pp. 23–40. **[G: Pakistan]**

Merlo, M. Multipurpose Agriculture and Forestry: An Overview and Some Remarks on the Seminar. *Merlo, M., et al., eds.*, 1987, pp. 629–32.

Miller, Jon R. The Political Economy of Western Water Finance: Cost Allocation and the Bonneville Unit of the Central Utah Project. *Amer. J. Agr. Econ.*, May 1987, 69(2), pp. 303–10. **[G: U.S.]**

Miller, Kathleen A. The Right to Use versus the Right to Sell: Spillover Effects and Constraints on the Water Rights of Irrigation Organization Members. *Water Resources Res.*, December 1987, 23(12), pp. 2166–74.

Millington, Andrew C. Environmental Degradation, Soil Conservation and Agricultural Poli-cies in Sierra Leone, 1895–1984. *Anderson, D. and Grove, R., eds.*, 1987, pp. 229–48. **[G: Sierra Leone]**

Miltz, David and White, David C. Sedimentation and the Economics of Selecting an Optimum Reservoir Size. *Water Resources Res.*, August 1987, 23(8), pp. 1443–48. **[G: U.S.]**

Mizzi, Philip J. Capital Adjustment Costs: A Nonrenewable Resource Industry. *Southern Econ. J.*, July 1987, 54(1), pp. 168–73.

Mohai, Paul. Public Participation and Natural Resource Decision-Making: The Case of the RARE II Decisions. *Natural Res. J.*, Winter 1987, 27(1), pp. 123–55. **[G: U.S.]**

Moncur, James E. T. Urban Water Pricing and Drought Management. *Water Resources Res.*, March 1987, 23(3), pp. 393–98. **[G: U.S.]**

Moreau, David H. and Snyder, Thomas P. Financial Burdens and Economic Costs in Expanding Urban Water Systems. *Water Resources Res.*, July 1987, 23(7), pp. 1139–44.

Mumbengegwi, Clever. Food and Agriculture Cooperation in the SADCC: Progress, Problems and Prospects. *Amin, S.; Chitala, D. and Mandaza, I., eds.*, 1987, pp. 62–84. **[G: Southern Africa]**

Muraoka, Dennis D. and Mead, Walter J. Diligence Requirements in Federal Natural Resource Sale and Leasing. *Natural Res. J.*, Fall 1987, 27(4), pp. 865–76. **[G: U.S.]**

Myers, Norman. The Environmental Basis of Sustainable Development. *Ann. Reg. Sci.*, November 1987, 21(3), pp. 33–43. **[G: LDCs]**

Nellor, David C. L. Sovereignty and Natural Resource Taxation in Developing Countries. *Econ. Develop. Cult. Change*, January 1987, 35(2), pp. 367–92. **[G: LDCs]**

Newcombe, Ken. An Economic Justification for Rural Afforestation: The Case of Ethiopia. *Ann. Reg. Sci.*, November 1987, 21(3), pp. 80–99. **[G: Ethiopia]**

Nijkamp, Peter. Economic Modeling: Shortcomings and Perspectives. *Braat, L. C. and van Lierop, W. F. J., eds.*, 1987, pp. 20–35.

Nystad, Arild N. Rate Sensitivity and the Optimal Choice of Production Capacity of Petroleum Reservoirs. *Energy Econ.*, January 1987, 9(1), pp. 37–45.

Odum, Howard T. Models for National, International, and Global Systems Policy. *Braat, L. C. and van Lierop, W. F. J., eds.*, 1987, pp. 203–51.

Ollikainen, Markku and Salonen, Hannu. A Bargaining Approach to the Modeling of the Swedish Roundwood Market: Comment. *Land Econ.*, May 1987, 63(2), pp. 209–10.

Østdahl, Torbjørn. Estimating the Distribution of Water Quality in Two Different Populations of Water Masses in a River Structure. *Statist. J.*, May 1987, 4(3), pp. 259–69. **[G: Norway]**

Parhizgari, Ali M. Optimum Depletion of Oil Resources in a Developing Country. *Energy J.*, July 1987, 8(3), pp. 31–56. **[G: LDCs]**

Parsons, George R. The Opportunity Costs of Residential Displacement Due to Coastal Land Use Restrictions: A Conceptual Framework.

Marine Resource Econ., 1987, *4*(2), pp. 111–22. **[G: U.S.]**

Pearce, David and Markandya, Anil. Marginal Opportunity Cost as a Planning Concept in Natural Resource Management. *Ann. Reg. Sci.*, November 1987, *21*(3), pp. 18–32. **[G: LDCs]**

Pearson, Charles and Hufschmidt, Maynard. Incorporating the Environment in Development Planning. *Borner, S. and Taylor, A., eds.,* 1987, pp. 19–34.

Pettenella, D. and Russo, G. Simbruini Mountains (Central Italy): Conflict in the Use of Forest Resources between Wood Production and Environmental Protection. *Merlo, M., et al., eds.,* 1987, pp. 611–17. **[G: Italy]**

Pharo, Helge. Conflict and Cooperation in the Indo–Norwegian Fisheries Project 1952–1972. *Dewey, C., ed.,* 1987, pp. 319–51. **[G: Norway; India]**

Pindyck, Robert S. On Monopoly Power in Extractive Resource Markets. *J. Environ. Econ. Manage.,* June 1987, *14*(2), pp. 128–42.

van der Ploeg, Frederick. Inefficiency of Credible Strategies in Oligopolistic Resource Markets with Uncertainty. *J. Econ. Dynam. Control,* March 1987, *11*(1), pp. 123–45.

Plummer, Mark L. Supply Uncertainty and Option Value: Reply. *Land Econ.,* November 1987, *63*(4), pp. 408.

Price, Colin. The Developing Framework for the Economic Evaluation of Forestry in the United Kingdom: A Comment. *J. Agr. Econ.,* September 1987, *38*(3), pp. 497–500. **[G: U.K.]**

Rafsnider, Giles T.; Skold, Melvin D. and Sampath, Rajan K. Range Survey Cost Sharing and the Efficiency of Rangeland Use. *Land Econ.,* February 1987, *63*(1), pp. 92–101. **[G: U.S.]**

Rajasenan, D. and Jessy, John C. Fish Production Models for Forecasting the Major Marine Species in Kerala Based on Seasonal Landing Patterns. *Indian J. Quant. Econ.,* 1987, *3*(2), pp. 35–42. **[G: India]**

Rauscher, Michael. Trade with an Exhaustible Resource When Demand Reactions Are Lagged. *Europ. Econ. Rev.,* December 1987, *31*(8), pp. 1597–1604.

Rawat, J. K., et al. A Pest and Timber Management Model: Jack Pine Budworm and Jack Pine. *Can. J. Agr. Econ.,* July 1987, *35*(2), pp. 441–61. **[G: Canada]**

Rehman, Tahir and Romero, Carlos. Multiple Criteria Decision Techniques and Multi Purpose Agriculture. *Merlo, M., et al., eds.,* 1987, pp. 7–18.

Resendiz-Carrillo, Daniel and Lave, Lester B. Optimizing Spillway Capacity with an Estimated Distribution of Floods. *Water Resources Res.,* November 1987, *23*(11), pp. 2043–49. **[G: U.S.]**

Ridler, N. and Kabir, M. A Cross-Sectional Analysis of Costs of Farming Atlantic Salmon (Salmo Salar). *Can. J. Agr. Econ.,* March 1987, *35*(1), pp. 141–54. **[G: Norway]**

Romero, Carlos and Rehman, Tahir. Natural Resource Management and the Use of Multiple Criteria Decision-Making Techniques: A Review. *Europ. Rev. Agr. Econ.,* 1987, *14*(1), pp. 61–89.

Romm, Jeff and Washburn, Courtland. Public Subsidy and Private Forestry Investment: Analyzing the Selectivity and Leverage of a Common Policy Form. *Land Econ.,* May 1987, *63*(2), pp. 153–67. **[G: U.S.]**

Rosenzweig, Michael L. Behavioral Modelling and Resource Management: Comment. *Vincent, T. L., et al., eds.,* 1987, pp. 19–20.

Rugman, Alan M. and Anderson, Andrew. A Fishy Business: The Abuse of American Trade Law in the Atlantic Groundfish Case of 1985–1986. *Can. Public Policy,* June 1987, *13*(2), pp. 152–64. **[G: U.S.; Canada]**

Ruiz Aviles, P. and Millan Campos, S. Demographic Consequences of Forestry Management Intervention in an Area of Low Mountains in Spain. *Merlo, M., et al., eds.,* 1987, pp. 593–610. **[G: Spain]**

Sachs, Ignacy. Ecodevelopment: The Concept, the Applications and the Stakes. *Sachs, I.,* 1987, pp. 25–32.

Sadan, Ezra and Ben-Zvi, Ruth. The Value of Institutional Change in Israel's Water Economy. *Water Resources Res.,* January 1987, *23*(1), pp. 1–8. **[G: Israel]**

Saliba, Bonnie Colby. Do Water Markets "Work"? Market Transfers and Trade-Offs in the Southwestern States. *Water Resources Res.,* July 1987, *23*(7), pp. 1113–22. **[G: U.S.]**

Saliba, Bonnie Colby, et al. Do Water Market Prices Appropriately Measure Water Values? *Natural Res. J.,* Summer 1987, *27*(3), pp. 617–51. **[G: U.S.]**

Salvatici, S. and Vieceli, A. Incentives for Private Forestry in Italy. *Merlo, M., et al., eds.,* 1987, pp. 491–99. **[G: Italy]**

Sanfuentes, Andrés. Chile: Effects of the Adjustment Policies on the Agriculture and Forestry Sector. *CEPAL Rev.,* December 1987, (33), pp. 115–27. **[G: Chile]**

Sapsford, David. The Determinants of the Demand for Internationally Traded Primary Commodities: An Empirical Analysis. *J. Econ. Stud.,* 1987, *14*(3), pp. 55–60.

Sathiendrakumar, R. and Tisdell, Clem A. Optimal Economic Fishery Effort in the Maldivian Tuna Fishery: An Appropriate Model. *Marine Resource Econ.,* 1987, *4*(1), pp. 15–44. **[G: Australia]**

Schefter, John E. Increasing Block Rate Tariffs as Faulty Transmitters of Marginal Willingness to Pay. *Land Econ.,* February 1987, *63*(1), pp. 21–33. **[G: U.S.]**

Scheraga, Joel D. Establishing Property Rights in Outer Space. *Cato J.,* Winter 1987, *6*(3), pp. 889–903. **[G: Global]**

Schoolmaster, F. Andrew. A Cartographic Analysis of Water Development Referenda in Texas, 1957–85. *Growth Change,* Fall 1987, *18*(4), pp. 20–43. **[G: U.S.]**

Segerson, Kathleen. Risk-Sharing and Liability in the Control of Stochastic Externalities. *Ma-*

rine Resource Econ., 1987, *4*(3), pp. 175–92. [G: U.S.]

Segerson, Kathleen. Supply Uncertainty and Option Value: Comment. *Land Econ.*, November 1987, *63*(4), pp. 406–07.

Seldon, Barry J. A Nonresidual Estimation of Welfare Gains from Research: The Case of Public R&D in a Forest Product Industry. *Southern Econ. J.*, July 1987, *54*(1), pp. 64–80. [G: U.S.]

Sewell, W. R. Derrick. The Politics of Hydromegaprojects: Damming with Faint Praise in Australia, New Zealand, and British Columbia. *Natural Res. J.*, Summer 1987, *27*(3), pp. 497–532. [G: Australia; New Zealand; Canada]

Shabman, Leonard A. and Batie, Sandra S. Mitigating Damages from Coastal Wetlands Development: Policy, Economics and Financing. *Marine Resource Econ.*, 1987, *4*(3), pp. 227–48. [G: U.S.]

Shahabuddin, Quazi. The Investment Analysis Model: An Application to Water Resources Planning in Bangladesh. *Bangladesh Devel. Stud.*, September 1987, *15*(3), pp. 63–94. [G: Bangladesh]

Shortle, James S. and Miranowski, John A. Intertemporal Soil Resource Use: Is It Socially Excessive? *J. Environ. Econ. Manage.*, June 1987, *14*(2), pp. 99–111.

Siebert, Horst. Neue Nutzungsrechte und internationale Rohstoffversorgung. (New Property Rights and International Resource Supply. With English summary.) *Ifo-Studien*, 1987, *33*(2), pp. 71–99. [G: W. Europe; U.S.]

Sillani, S. Land Consolidation and Environment. *Merlo, M., et al., eds.*, 1987, pp. 299–306. [G: Italy]

Simonovic, Slobodan. The Implicit Stochastic Model for Reservoir Yield Optimization. *Water Resources Res.*, December 1987, *23*(12), pp. 2159–65.

Sinclair, Peter W. The North and the North-west: Forestry and Agriculture. *Drummond, I. M.*, 1987, pp. 77–90. [G: Canada]

Slade, Margaret E. Natural Resources, Population Growth, and Economic Well-being. *Johnson, D. G. and Lee, R. D., eds.*, 1987, pp. 331–69.

Sluczanowski, Philip R. Examination of Institutional Structures in Multiple Resource, Multiple Management Systems: A Control Theoretic Approach: Comment. *Vincent, T. L., et al., eds.*, 1987, pp. 302. [G: U.S.]

Smith, James L. The Common Pool, Bargaining, and the Rule of Capture. *Econ. Inquiry*, October 1987, *25*(4), pp. 631–44.

Snoy, Th.; Reginster, Y. and Devillez, F. The Small Forest-Owner in Wallonia: Images of a Multiple-Faced Reality. *Merlo, M., et al., eds.*, 1987, pp. 465–74. [G: Belgium]

Southworth, F. and Chin, S.-M. Network Evacuation Modeling for Flooding as a Result of Dam Failure. *Environ. Planning A*, November 1987, *19*(11), pp. 1543–58.

Spangler, George R. The Structure of Fishing Systems and the Implementation of Management Policy: Comment. *Vincent, T. L., et al., eds.*, 1987, pp. 274–75. [G: U.S.]

Squires, Dale. Fishing Effort: Its Testing, Specification, and Internal Structure in Fisheries Economics and Management. *J. Environ. Econ. Manage.*, September 1987, *14*(3), pp. 268–82. [G: U.S.]

Squires, Dale. Long-run Profit Functions for Multiproduct Firms. *Amer. J. Agr. Econ.*, August 1987, *69*(3), pp. 558–69. [G: U.S.]

Squires, Dale. Public Regulation and the Structure of Production in Multiproduct Industries: An Application to the New England Otter Trawl Industry. *Rand J. Econ.*, Summer 1987, *18*(2), pp. 232–47. [G: U.S.]

Staley, Michael. The Practice of Resource Modeling. *Braat, L. C. and van Lierop, W. F. J., eds.*, 1987, pp. 257–68.

Staniford, Andrew. The Effects of the Pot Reduction in the South Australian Southern Zone Rock Lobster Fishery. *Marine Resource Econ.*, 1987, *4*(4), pp. 271–88. [G: Australia]

Ştefănescu, V. A Method for Evaluating the Average Content of Useful Mineral Substance in a Deposit. *Econ. Computat. Cybern. Stud. Res.*, 1987, *22*(4), pp. 61–75.

Stensland, Gunnar and Nystad, Arild N. Optimal Choice of R&D Strategy for Enhanced Recovery from Petroleum Reservoirs. *Energy J.*, January 1987, *8*(1), pp. 125–32.

Stollery, Kenneth R. Cooperatives as an Alternative to Regulation in Commercial Fisheries. *Marine Resource Econ.*, 1987, *4*(4), pp. 289–304. [G: Canada]

Stollery, Kenneth R. Mineral Processing in an Open Economy. *Land Econ.*, May 1987, *63*(2), pp. 128–36.

Stowe, Robert C. United States Foreign Policy and the Conservation of Natural Resources: The Case of Tropical Deforestation. *Natural Res. J.*, Winter 1987, *27*(1), pp. 55–101. [G: U.S.]

Strong, Maurice. The Changing Role of Natural Resources. *Natural Res. J.*, Winter 1987, *27*(1), pp. 1–4.

Strycharczyk, Jerzy B. and Stedinger, Jery R. Evaluation of a "Reliability Programming" Reservoir Model. *Water Resources Res.*, February 1987, *23*(2), pp. 225–29.

Susmel, L. Multipurpose Management of Alpine Forests. *Merlo, M., et al., eds.*, 1987, pp. 221–25. [G: Italy]

Tait, E. J. Research Policy and Review 14. Environmental Issues and the Social Sciences. *Environ. Planning A*, April 1987, *19*(4), pp. 437–45. [G: U.K.]

Talib, Abu and Bienstock, Daniel. Wood: An Ancient Fuel with New Potential for Developing Countries. *Pachauri, R. K., ed.*, 1987, pp. 393–411. [G: LDCs]

Taurand, Francis and Hung, Nguyen Manh. Pitfalls in a Received Idea: Ricardian Decreasing Returns at the Extensive Margin of a Natural Resource. *Can. J. Econ.*, February 1987, *20*(1), pp. 61–73.

Teeples, Ronald K. and Glyer, David. Cost of

Water Delivery Systems: Specification and Ownership Effects. *Rev. Econ. Statist.*, August 1987, *69*(3), pp. 399–408. **[G: U.S.]**

Teeples, Ronald K. and Glyer, David. Estimating Demand by Self-Supplying Firms: Comments. *Water Resources Res.*, May 1987, *23*(5), pp. 968–70. **[G: U.S.]**

Teeples, Ronald K. and Glyer, David. Production Functions for Water Delivery Systems: Analysis and Estimation Using Dual Cost Function and Implicit Price Specifications. *Water Resources Res.*, May 1987, *23*(5), pp. 765–73. **[G: U.S.]**

Thomas, John. Onsite Costs of Land Degradation in Agriculture and Forestry: Comments. *Chisholm, A. and Dumsday, R., eds.*, 1987, pp. 363–64. **[G: Australia]**

Tóth, Ferenc L. Analyzing Productivity of Multiple Resource Systems. *Braat, L. C. and van Lierop, W. F. J., eds.*, 1987, pp. 166–84. **[G: U.S.]**

Trezos, Thanos and Yeh, William W.-G. Use of Stochastic Dynamic Programming for Reservoir Management. *Water Resources Res.*, June 1987, *23*(6), pp. 983–96. **[G: U.S.]**

Uri, Noel D. Helium Conservation: Supply and Demand Projections in the USA Reconsidered. *Energy Econ.*, April 1987, *9*(2), pp. 93–98.

Vencill, Betsy. The Federal Power Act and Western Water Law—Can States Maintain Their Own Water Use Priorities? Comment. *Natural Res. J.*, Winter 1987, *27*(1), pp. 213–34.

Vislie, Jon. On the Optimal Management of Transboundary Renewable Resources: A Comment. *Can. J. Econ.*, November 1987, *20*(4), pp. 870–75.

Wacker, Holger. Über die ökonomische Nutzung der antarktischen Bartenwale. (On the Economic Utilization of Antarctic Baleen Whales. With English summary.) *Z. Wirtschaft. Sozialwissen.*, 1987, *107*(2), pp. 243–59.

Wagner, Brian J. and Gorelick, Steven M. Optimal Groundwater Quality Management under Parameter Uncertainty. *Water Resources Res.*, July 1987, *23*(7), pp. 1162–74.

Walker, Warren E. and Veen, Meinaard A. Screening Tactics in a Water Management Policy Analysis for the Netherlands. *Water Resources Res.*, July 1987, *23*(7), pp. 1145–51. **[G: Netherlands]**

Walters, Carl J. Approaches to Adaptive Policy Design for Harvest Management. *Vincent, T. L., et al., eds.*, 1987, pp. 114–22.

Warford, Jeremy J. Natural Resources and Economic Policy in Developing Countries. *Ann. Reg. Sci.*, November 1987, *21*(3), pp. 3–17. **[G: LDCs]**

Weber, Bruce A.; Castle, Emery N. and Shriver, Ann L. The Performance of Natural Resource Industries. *U.S.D.A., Econ. Res. Serv., Agr. and Rural Econ. Div.*, 1987, pp. 5.1–37. **[G: U.S.]**

Westoby, Jack C. 'Making Green the Motherland': Forestry in China. *Westoby, J.*, 1987, *1975*, pp. 270–87. **[G: China]**

Westoby, Jack C. Forest Industries for Socio-eco-

nomic Development. *Westoby, J.*, 1987, *1978*, pp. 241–54. **[G: LDCs]**

Westoby, Jack C. Foresters and Politics. *Westoby, J.*, 1987, *1985*, pp. 319–32.

Westoby, Jack C. Forestry and Underdevelopment Revisited. *Westoby, J.*, 1987, *1985*, pp. 304–18. **[G: LDCs]**

Westoby, Jack C. Forestry Education: To Whom and for What? *Westoby, J.*, 1987, *1971*, pp. 193–205.

Westoby, Jack C. Forestry, Foresters and Society. *Westoby, J.*, 1987, *1978*, pp. 288–303. **[G: New Zealand]**

Westoby, Jack C. Making Trees Serve People. *Westoby, J.*, 1987, *1975*, pp. 257–69.

Westoby, Jack C. On Behalf of the Uninvited Guests. *Westoby, J.*, 1987, *1974*, pp. 217–30. **[G: Australia]**

Westoby, Jack C. One-World Forestry: New Zealand's Role. *Westoby, J.*, 1987, *1970*, pp. 160–75. **[G: New Zealand]**

Westoby, Jack C. Prospects for Expanding Forest Products Exports from Developing Countries. *Westoby, J.*, 1987, *1964*, pp. 71–114. **[G: LDCs]**

Westoby, Jack C. Quo Vadis? A Note for Discussion. *Westoby, J.*, 1987, pp. 206–16.

Westoby, Jack C. The Forester as Agent of Change. *Westoby, J.*, 1987, *1968*, pp. 115–42.

Westoby, Jack C. The Purpose of Forests: Follies of Development: Responsibility. *Westoby, J.*, 1987, *1974*, pp. 231–40. **[G: Australia]**

Westoby, Jack C. World Forest Development: Markets, Men and Methods. *Westoby, J.*, 1987, *1965*, pp. 143–59. **[G: Canada; LDCs]**

Willems, A. Agroforestry in the Netherlands: An Option for EEC Agricultural Policy? *Merlo, M., et al., eds.*, 1987, pp. 311–20. **[G: Netherlands]**

Wirl, Franz. Joint Production of Substitutable, Exhaustible Resources, Or: Is Flaring Gas Rational? *J. Econ. Dynam. Control*, December 1987, *11*(4), pp. 499–511.

7211 Recreational Aspects of Natural Resources

Abala, Daniel O. A Theoretical and Empirical Investigation of the Willingness to Pay for Recreational Services: A Case Study of Nairobi National Park. *Eastern Afr. Econ. Rev.*, December 1987, *3*(2), pp. 111–19. **[G: Kenya]**

Areola, Olusegun. The Political Reality of Conservation in Nigeria. *Anderson, D. and Grove, R., eds.*, 1987, pp. 277–92. **[G: Nigeria]**

Bockstael, Nancy E.; Hanemann, W. Michael and Kling, Catherine L. Estimating the Value of Water Quality Improvements in a Recreational Demand Framework. *Water Resources Res.*, May 1987, *23*(5), pp. 951–60. **[G: U.S.]**

Bockstael, Nancy E. and Strand, Ivar E., Jr. The Effect of Common Sources of Regression Error on Benefit Estimates. *Land Econ.*, February 1987, *63*(1), pp. 11–20.

Bockstael, Nancy E.; Strand, Ivar E., Jr. and Hannemann, W. Michael. Time and the Recreational Demand Model. *Amer. J. Agr. Econ.*,

May 1987, *69*(2), pp. 293–302.   [G: U.S.]

Brichese, F. and Povellato, A. A Proposed Regional Park: The Case Study of Caorle Lagoon. *Merlo, M., et al., eds.*, 1987, pp. 193–206.
[G: Italy]

Brookshire, David S. and Smith, V. Kerry. Measuring Recreation Benefits: Conceptual and Empirical Issues. *Water Resources Res.*, May 1987, *23*(5), pp. 931–35.

Cameron, Trudy Ann and James, Michelle D. Efficient Estimation Methods for "Closed-ended" Contingent Valuation Surveys. *Rev. Econ. Statist.*, May 1987, *69*(2), pp. 269–76.
[G: Canada]

Cory, Dennis C. and Saliba, Bonnie Colby. Requiem for Option Value. *Land Econ.*, February 1987, *63*(1), pp. 1–10.

Desvousges, William H.; Smith, V. Kerry and Fisher, Ann. Option Price Estimates for Water Quality Improvements: A Contingent Valuation Study for the Monongahela River. *J. Environ. Econ. Manage.*, September 1987, *14*(3), pp. 248–67.   [G: U.S.]

Gios, Geremia; Pilati, L. and Ricci, G. Integration between Agroforestry and Tourism in Alpine Areas. *Merlo, M., et al., eds.*, 1987, pp. 235–44.   [G: Italy]

Hanemann, W. Michael. Welfare Evaluations in Contingent Valuation Experiments with Discrete Responses: Reply. *Amer. J. Agr. Econ.*, February 1987, *69*(1), pp. 185–86.   [G: U.S.]

Hull, Brooks B. The Effect of Foreign and Local Visitors on Granting Park Concessions. *New Zealand Econ. Pap.*, 1987, *21*, pp. 83–96.
[G: New Zealand]

Kerr, Geoff and Cullen, Ross. Non-market Valuation in New Zealand: Comment. *New Zealand Econ. Pap.*, 1987, *21*, pp. 125–29.
[G: New Zealand]

Kling, Catherine L. A Simulation Approach to Comparing Multiple Site Recreation Demand Models Using Chesapeake Bay Survey Data. *Marine Resource Econ.*, 1987, *4*(2), pp. 95–109.   [G: U.S.]

Kushman, John E. Welfare Evaluation in Contingent Valuation Experiments with Discrete Responses: Comment. *Amer. J. Agr. Econ.*, February 1987, *69*(1), pp. 182–84.   [G: U.S.]

Lindsay, W. Keith. Integrating Parks and Pastoralists: Some Lessons from Amboseli. *Anderson, D. and Grove, R., eds.*, 1987, pp. 149–67.   [G: Kenya]

Long, Roger B. Effects of Recession, Inflation and High Interest Rates on Growth in a Recreation Region. *Ann. Reg. Sci.*, July 1987, *21*(2), pp. 86–107.   [G: U.S.]

Marinelli, A. and Romano, D. An Evaluation of Recreation Benefits for Multipurpose Forestry Management. *Merlo, M., et al., eds.*, 1987, pp. 99–112.   [G: Italy]

Matulich, Scott C.; Workman, William G. and Jubenville, Alan. Recreation Economics: Taking Stock [Problems and Solutions in Estimating the Demand for and Value of Rural Outdoor Recreation]. *Land Econ.*, August 1987, *63*(3), pp. 310–16.   [G: U.S.]

Mendelsohn, Robert. Modeling the Demand for Outdoor Recreation. *Water Resources Res.*, May 1987, *23*(5), pp. 961–67.

Nougarede, O.; Larrere, R. and Poupardin, D. The Aigoual Forest: Theatre of Latent Conflicts of Interest and Competences. *Merlo, M., et al., eds.*, 1987, pp. 179–91.   [G: France]

van der Ploeg, S. W. Floris. Models for Outdoor Recreation. *Braat, L. C. and van Lierop, W. F. J., eds.*, 1987, pp. 149–65.

Rosenthal, Donald H. The Necessity for Substitute Prices in Recreation Demand Analyses. *Amer. J. Agr. Econ.*, November 1987, *69*(4), pp. 828–37.   [G: U.S.]

Smith, V. Kerry and Kaoru, Yoshiaki. The Hedonic Travel Cost Model: A View from the Trenches. *Land Econ.*, May 1987, *63*(2), pp. 179–92.   [G: U.S.]

Turton, David. The Mursi and National Park Development in the Lower Omo Valley. *Anderson, D. and Grove, R., eds.*, 1987, pp. 169–86.   [G: Ethiopia]

Wilman, Elizabeth A. A Simple Repackaging Model of Recreational Choices. *Amer. J. Agr. Econ.*, August 1987, *69*(3), pp. 603–12.
[G: U.S.]

Wilman, Elizabeth A. and Pauls, Richard J. Sensitivity of Consumers' Surplus Estimates to Variation in the Parameters of the Travel Cost Model. *Can. J. Agr. Econ.*, March 1987, *35*(1), pp. 197–212.   [G: Canada]

722 Conservation and Pollution

7220 Conservation and Pollution

Adams, William M. Approaches to Water Resource Development, Sokoto Valley, Nigeria: The Problem of Sustainability. *Anderson, D. and Grove, R., eds.*, 1987, pp. 307–25.
[G: Nigeria]

Adedeji, Adebayo. An Ecology for Economic Change. *Challenge*, Jan./Feb. 1987, *29*(6), pp. 4–8.   [G: Africa]

Agostini, D. and Franceschetti, G. Local Institutions and Land Policy: The Case of Cadore Mountain Communities. *Merlo, M., et al., eds.*, 1987, pp. 227–33.   [G: Italy]

Ahn, Byong-hun; Nesbitt, Dale M. and Phillips, Robert L. Integrated Analysis for Energy Policies—Oil Consumption Reduction Programmes in Korea. *Pachauri, R. K., ed.*, 1987, pp. 331–52.   [G: S. Korea]

Aickin, R. Malcolm. Insuring Environmental Liabilities. *Kleindorfer, P. R. and Kunreuther, H. C., ed.*, 1987, pp. 458–63.

Alfsen, Knut H. and Glomsrød, Solveig. Future Emissions to Air in Norway: Forecasts Based on the Macroeconomic Model MSG-4E. *Statist. J.*, May 1987, *4*(3), pp. 219–36.
[G: Norway]

Amir, Shmuel. Energy Pricing, Biomass Accumulation, and Project Appraisal: A Thermodynamic Approach to the Economics of Ecosystem Management. *Pillet, G. and Murota, T., eds.*, 1987, pp. 53–108.

Anandalingam, G. The Economics of Industrial Energy Conservation in the Developing Countries. *Pachauri, R. K., ed.,* 1987, pp. 643–61.
[G: LDCs]

Anderson, Curt L. The Production Process: Inputs and Wastes. *J. Environ. Econ. Manage.,* March 1987, *14*(1), pp. 1–12. [G: U.S.]

Anderson, David M. Managing the Forest: The Conservation History of Lembus, Kenya, 1904–63. *Anderson, D. and Grove, R., eds.,* 1987, pp. 249–68. [G: Kenya]

Anderson, David M. and Grove, Richard. The Scramble for Eden: Past, Present and Future in African Conservation. *Anderson, D. and Grove, R., eds.,* 1987, pp. 1–12. [G: Africa]

Anderson, M. A. A War of Words: Public Inquiry into the Designation of the North Pennines as an Area of Outstanding Natural Beauty. *Merlo, M., et al., eds.,* 1987, pp. 167–77.
[G: U.K.]

Areola, Olusegun. The Political Reality of Conservation in Nigeria. *Anderson, D. and Grove, R., eds.,* 1987, pp. 277–92. [G: Nigeria]

Ashworth, John; Papps, Ivy and Storey, David J. Assessing the Impact upon the British Chlor-Alkali Industry of the EEC Directive on Discharges of Mercury into Waterways. *Land Econ.,* February 1987, *63*(1), pp. 72–78.
[G: EEC]

Atkinson, Scott E. and Tietenberg, T. H. Economic Implications of Emissions Trading Rules for Local and Regional Pollutants. *Can. J. Econ.,* May 1987, *20*(2), pp. 370–86.
[G: U.S.]

Baba, Norio. Microcomputer-Based Games for the Purposes of Environmental Protection and Managemental Training. *Sawaragi, Y.; Inoue, K. and Nakayama, H., eds.,* 1987, pp. 403–11.

Baffoe, J. K.; Stonehouse, D. Peter and Kay, B. D. A Methodology for Farm-Level Economic Analysis of Soil Erosion Effects under Alternative Crop Rotational Systems in Ontario. *Can. J. Agr. Econ.,* March 1987, *35*(1), pp. 55–73. [G: Canada]

Ballard, John. Pressure Groups and Policy Formulation. *Chisholm, A. and Dumsday, R., eds.,* 1987, pp. 263–67. [G: Australia]

Baram, Michael S. Chemical Industry Hazards: Liability, Insurance, and the Role of Risk Analysis. *Kleindorfer, P. R. and Kunreuther, H. C., ed.,* 1987, pp. 415–42.

Barker, Michael. Land Degradation: Legal Issues and Institutional Constraints: Commentary. *Chisholm, A. and Dumsday, R., eds.,* 1987, pp. 168–74. [G: Australia]

Barskii, L. A., et al. Techniques for Ecological and Economic Appraisal of the Development of Waste-Free Factories. *Matekon,* Fall 1987, *24*(1), pp. 70–85. [G: U.S.S.R.]

Bartel, Ann P. and Thomas, Lacy Glenn. Predation through Regulation: The Wage and Profit Effects of the Occupational Safety and Health Administration and the Environmental Protection Agency. *J. Law Econ.,* October 1987, *30*(2), pp. 239–64. [G: U.S.]

Bartelmus, Peter. Beyond GDP—New Approaches to Applied Statistics. *Rev. Income Wealth,* December 1987, *33*(4), pp. 347–58.

Bartlett, Robert V. and Baber, Walter F. Matrix Organization Theory and Environmental Impact Analysis: A Fertile Union? *Natural Res. J.,* Summer 1987, *27*(3), pp. 605–15.
[G: U.S.]

Beavis, Brian and Dobbs, Ian. Firm Behaviour under Regulatory Control of Stochastic Environmental Wastes by Probabilistic Constraints. *J. Environ. Econ. Manage.,* June 1987, *14*(2), pp. 112–27.

Beinart, William. Conservation Ideologies in Africa: Introduction. *Anderson, D. and Grove, R., eds.,* 1987, pp. 15–19. [G: Africa]

Bell, R. H. V. Conservation with a Human Face: Conflict and Reconciliation in African Land Use Planning. *Anderson, D. and Grove, R., eds.,* 1987, pp. 79–101. [G: Africa]

Bertolini, Gérard. Économie de la collecte des résidus ménagers: les articulations entre récupération et élimination. (With English summary.) *Revue Écon. Polit.,* Sept.-Oct. 1987, *97*(5), pp. 631–48.

Besanko, David. Performance versus Design Standards in the Regulation of Pollution. *J. Public Econ.,* October 1987, *34*(1), pp. 19–44.

Bingham, Taylor H.; Anderson, Donald W. and Cooley, Philip C. Distribution of the Generation of Air Pollution. *J. Environ. Econ. Manage.,* March 1987, *14*(1), pp. 30–40.
[G: U.S.]

Bird, Peter J. W. N. The Transferability and Depletability of Externalities. *J. Environ. Econ. Manage.,* March 1987, *14*(1), pp. 54–57.

Bittlingmayer, George. The Application of the Sherman Act to the Smog Agreement. *Antitrust Bull.,* Winter 1987, *32*(4), pp. 885–915.
[G: U.S.]

Blackwell, Ann Lowes. Uncertain Dynamical Systems: An Application to River Pollution Control: Comment. *Vincent, T. L., et al., eds.,* 1987, pp. 184–85.

Blyth, Michael J. and McCallum, Andrew. Onsite Costs of Land Degradation in Agriculture and Forestry. *Chisholm, A. and Dumsday, R., eds.,* 1987, pp. 79–98. [G: Australia]

Boyle, Kevin J. and Bishop, Richard C. Valuing Wildlife in Benefit–Cost Analyses: A Case Study Involving Endangered Species. *Water Resources Res.,* May 1987, *23*(5), pp. 943–50.
[G: U.S.]

Braat, Leon C. and van Lierop, Wal F. J. Environment, Policy, and Modeling. *Braat, L. C. and van Lierop, W. F. J., eds.,* 1987, pp. 7–19.

Braden, John B., et al. A Displacement Model of Regulatory Compliance and Costs. *Land Econ.,* November 1987, *63*(4), pp. 323–36.
[G: U.S.]

Bradsen, John and Fowler, Robert. Land Degradation: Legal Issues and Institutional Constraints. *Chisholm, A. and Dumsday, R., eds.,* 1987, pp. 129–67. [G: Australia]

Brichese, F. and Povellato, A. A Proposed Regional Park: The Case Study of Caorle Lagoon. *Merlo, M., et al., eds.*, 1987, pp. 193–206. **[G: Italy]**

Bromiley, Philip and Marcus, Alfred A. Deadlines, Routines, and Change. *Policy Sci.*, 1987, *20*(2), pp. 85–103.

Brooks, Michael A. and Heijdra, Ben J. Rent-Seeking and Pollution Taxation: An Extension. *Southern Econ. J.*, October 1987, *54*(2), pp. 335–42.

Brown, Lester R. and Postel, Sandra. Thresholds of Change. *Brown, L. R., et al.*, 1987, pp. 3–19. **[G: Global]**

Brown, Lester R. and Wolf, Edward C. Charting a Sustainable Course. *Brown, L. R., et al.*, 1987, pp. 196–213. **[G: Global]**

Burch, Gordon; Graetz, Dean and Noble, Ian. Biological and Physical Phenomena in Land Degradation. *Chisholm, A. and Dumsday, R., eds.*, 1987, pp. 27–48. **[G: Australia]**

Caputo, María Graciela and Herzer, Hilda. Reflexiones sobre el manejo de las inundaciones y su incorporación a las políticas de desarrollo regional. (With English summary.) *Desarrollo Econ.*, July-Sept. 1987, *27*(106), pp. 245–60. **[G: Argentina]**

Carlson, David Gray. Successor Liability in Bankruptcy: Some Unifying Themes of Intertemporal Creditor Priorities Created by Running Covenants, Products Liability, and Toxic-Waste Cleanup. *Law Contemp. Probl.*, Spring 1987, *50*(2), pp. 119–71. **[G: U.S.]**

Carlson, J. Lon and Bausell, Charles W., Jr. Financing Superfund: An Evaluation of Alternative Tax Mechanisms. *Natural Res. J.*, Winter 1987, *27*(1), pp. 103–22. **[G: U.S.]**

Chandler, William U. Designing Sustainable Economies. *Brown, L. R., et al.*, 1987, pp. 177–95. **[G: Global]**

Chapman, Duane. A Social Tariff: Global Wage and Pollution Standards. *Pachauri, R. K., ed.*, 1987, pp. 911–18. **[G: Global]**

Chartres, Colin. Australia's Land Resources at Risk. *Chisholm, A. and Dumsday, R., eds.*, 1987, pp. 7–26. **[G: Australia]**

Chisholm, Anthony. Abatement of Land Degradation: Regulations versus Economic Incentives. *Chisholm, A. and Dumsday, R., eds.*, 1987, pp. 223–47. **[G: Australia]**

Chisholm, Anthony. Rational Approaches to Environmental Issues. *Chisholm, A. and Dumsday, R., eds.*, 1987, pp. 341–56. **[G: Australia]**

Clifford, Thomas E. and Mead, Walter J. The External Costs of Electric Power from Coal-Fired and Nuclear Power Plants. *Pachauri, R. K., ed.*, 1987, pp. 315–29. **[G: U.S.]**

Coggins, George Cameron and Harris, Anne Fleishel. The Greening of American Law? The Recent Evolution of Federal Law for Preserving Floral Diversity. *Natural Res. J.*, Spring 1987, *27*(2), pp. 247–307. **[G: U.S.]**

Cohen, Adrian V. Chemical Industry Hazards: Liability, Insurance, and the Role of Risk Analysis: Discussion. *Kleindorfer, P. R. and Kunreuther, H. C., ed.*, 1987, pp. 442–47.

Cohen, Mark A. Optimal Enforcement Strategy

to Prevent Oil Spills: An Application of a Principal–Agent Model with Moral Hazard. *J. Law Econ.*, April 1987, *30*(1), pp. 23–51. **[G: U.S.]**

Coke, Lloyd B.; Weir, Colin C. and Hill, Vincent G. Environmental Impact of Bauxite Mining and Processing in Jamaica. *Soc. Econ. Stud.*, March 1987, *36*(1), pp. 289–333. **[G: Jamaica]**

Collett, David. Pastoralists and Wildlife: Image and Reality in Kenya Maasailand. *Anderson, D. and Grove, R., eds.*, 1987, pp. 129–48. **[G: Kenya]**

Colorni, A. and Laniado, E. A Decision Support System for Choosing among Alternative Projects. *Merlo, M., et al., eds.*, 1987, pp. 39–51.

Conrad, Klaus. An Incentive Scheme for Optimal Pricing and Environmental Protection. *J. Inst. Theoretical Econ.*, September 1987, *143*(3), pp. 402–21.

Corrado, G. and Sediari, Tommaso. Countryside Planning Experiences in Umbria (Central Italy). *Merlo, M., et al., eds.*, 1987, pp. 583–91. **[G: Italy]**

Costantini, G. B. Multipurpose Forest Policies for the Development of Mountain Areas in the Veneto Region. *Merlo, M., et al., eds.*, 1987, pp. 215–19. **[G: Italy]**

Covello, Vincent T. and Merkhofer, Miley. The Inexact Science of Chemical Hazard Risk Assessment: A Description and Critical Evaluation of Available Methods. *Kleindorfer, P. R. and Kunreuther, H. C., ed.*, 1987, pp. 229–76.

Cowell, John G. The Role of Insurance in Risk Spreading and Risk Bearing: Discussion. *Kleindorfer, P. R. and Kunreuther, H. C., ed.*, 1987, pp. 486–92.

Crabbé, Philippe J. The Quasi-Option Value of Irreversible Investment: A Comment [The Quasi-Option Value of Irreversible Development]. *J. Environ. Econ. Manage.*, December 1987, *14*(4), pp. 384–85.

Crandall, Robert W. and Keller, Theodore E. Public Policy and the Private Auto. *[Adelman, M. A.]*, 1987, pp. 137–60. **[G: U.S.]**

Cullander, Nicholas. *New York v. Shore Realty* 759 F.2d 1032 (2d Cir. 1985). *Natural Res. J.*, Spring 1987, *27*(2), pp. 409–20. **[G: U.S.]**

Cumberland, John H. Need Economic Development Be Hazardous to the Health of the Chesapeake Bay? *Marine Resource Econ.*, 1987, *4*(2), pp. 81–93. **[G: U.S.]**

Daly, Herman E. Filters against Folly in Environmental Economics: The Impossible, the Undesirable, and the Uneconomic. *Pillet, G. and Murota, T., eds.*, 1987, pp. 1–10.

Davidson, Bruce. Comments [Australia's Land Resources at Risk] [Biological and Physical Causes of Land Degradation]. *Chisholm, A. and Dumsday, R., eds.*, 1987, pp. 357–62. **[G: Australia]**

Davis, Bruce. Towards More Effective Policies for Controlling Land Degradation: The Practicalities of Policy Solutions. *Chisholm, A. and*

Dumsday, R., eds., 1987, pp. 335–40.
[G: Australia]

Deprimoz, J. Compensation for Exceptional Environmental Damage Caused by Industrial Activities: Discussion. *Kleindorfer, P. R. and Kunreuther, H. C., ed.*, 1987, pp. 138–41.

Dobozi, Istvan. The 'Invisible' Source of Alternative Energy: A Comparison of Energy Conservation Performance in East and West. *Maillet, P.; Hague, D. and Rowland, C., eds.*, 1987, pp. 183–207. [G: OECD; CMEA]

Dower, Roger C. and Scodari, Paul F. Compensation for Natural Resource Injury: An Emerging Federal Framework. *Marine Resource Econ.*, 1987, *4*(3), pp. 155–74. [G: U.S.]

Dubgaard, A. Reconciliation of Agricultural Policy and Environmental Interests in Denmark (Regarding Controls on Nitrogen Fertilizer). *Merlo, M., et al., eds.*, 1987, pp. 535–44. [G: Denmark]

Dumsday, Robert. Towards More Effective Policies for Controlling Land Degradation: Contributions from the Social Sciences. *Chisholm, A. and Dumsday, R., eds.*, 1987, pp. 315–34. [G: Australia]

Edwards, Geoff W. Land Degradation: Problems and Policies: Commentary. *Chisholm, A. and Dumsday, R., eds.*, 1987, pp. 248–59. [G: Australia]

Edwards, Steven F. and Anderson, Glen D. Overlooked Biases in Contingent Valuation Surveys: Some Considerations. *Land Econ.*, May 1987, *63*(2), pp. 168–78. [G: U.S.]

Endres, Alfred. On the Efficacy of Public Finance Instruments in Protecting the Environment. *van de Kar, H. M. and Wolfe, B. L., eds.*, 1987, pp. 181–92.

England, Richard W. Ecology, Social Class, and Political Conflict. *England, R. W., ed.*, 1987, pp. 118–53. [G: U.S.; Global]

Farber, Kit D. and Rutledge, Gary L. Pollution Abatement and Control Expenditures, 1982–85. *Surv. Curr. Bus.*, May 1987, *67*(5), pp. 21–26. [G: U.S.]

Feldman, David Lewis. The Defeat of the Blue Ridge Pump–Storage Project as Microcosm of Environmental Policy Change. *Policy Sci.*, 1987, *20*(3), pp. 235–58. [G: U.S.]

Fisher, Anthony C. and Hanemann, W. Michael. Quasi-option Value: Some Misconceptions Dispelled. *J. Environ. Econ. Manage.*, June 1987, *14*(2), pp. 183–90.

Flavin, Christopher. Reassessing Nuclear Power. *Brown, L. R., et al.*, 1987, pp. 57–80. [G: Global]

Forster, Bruce A. Agricultural Impacts of Acid Deposition: Some Issues to Consider. *Can. J. Agr. Econ.*, March 1987, *35*(1), pp. 241–47. [G: Canada]

Frankel, Marvin. Taxes, Pollution, and Optimal Abatement in an Urban Economy. *J. Urban Econ.*, September 1987, *22*(2), pp. 117–35.

Frey, René L. Wirtschaftswachstum und Umweltqualität: Auf der Suche nach einer neuen Wachstumspolitik. (Economic Growth and Environmental Quality: In Search of a New Growth Policy. With English summary.) *Schweiz. Z. Volkswirtsch. Statist.*, September 1987, *123*(3), pp. 289–315.

Fuller, Dan A. Compliance, Avoidance, and Evasion: Emissions Control under Imperfect Enforcement in Steam-Electric Generation. *Rand J. Econ.*, Spring 1987, *18*(1), pp. 124–37.

Furuseth, Owen J. Public Attitudes toward Local Farmland Protection Programs. *Growth Change*, Summer 1987, *18*(3), pp. 49–61. [G: U.S.]

Gamaledinn, Maknun. State Policy and Famine in the Awash Valley of Ethiopia: The Lessons for Conservation. *Anderson, D. and Grove, R., eds.*, 1987, pp. 327–44. [G: Ethiopia]

Gaudard, Gaston. Regional Economic Development and the Future of Environment. *Pillet, G. and Murota, T., eds.*, 1987, pp. 155–67.

Ghosh, A. Technical Costs of Environmental Protection and Its Redistribution in the Economy. *Econ. Planning*, 1987, *21*(2–3), pp. 115–22.

Gowdy, John M. Bio-economics: Social Economy versus the Chicago School. *Int. J. Soc. Econ.*, 1987, *14*(1), pp. 32–42.

Gray, Wayne B. The Cost of Regulation: OSHA, EPA and the Productivity Slowdown. *Amer. Econ. Rev.*, December 1987, *77*(5), pp. 998–1006. [G: U.S.]

Gregory, Robin and McDaniels, Tim. Valuing Environmental Losses: What Promise Does the Right Measure Hold? *Policy Sci.*, April 1987, *20*(1), pp. 11–26.

Greig, Peter. Social Costs of Land Degradation: Commentary. *Chisholm, A. and Dumsday, R., eds.*, 1987, pp. 119–25. [G: Australia]

Griffin, Ronald C. Environmental Policy for Spatial and Persistent Pollutants. *J. Environ. Econ. Manage.*, March 1987, *14*(1), pp. 41–53.

Grove, Richard. Early Themes in African Conservation: The Cape in the Nineteenth Century. *Anderson, D. and Grove, R., eds.*, 1987, pp. 21–39. [G: Africa]

Grundy, D. Multipurpose Agriculture and Forestry: An Overview and Some Remarks on the Seminar. *Merlo, M., et al., eds.*, 1987, pp. 619–22.

Guillard, J. Multipurpose Agriculture and Forestry: An Overview and Some Remarks on the Seminar. *Merlo, M., et al., eds.*, 1987, pp. 622–24.

Hahn, Robert W. Jobs and Environmental Quality: Some Implications for Instrument Choice. *Policy Sci.*, 1987, *20*(4), pp. 289–306. [G: U.S.]

Hanley, N. and Lingard, J. Controlling Straw Burning: Farm Management Modelling of the Policy Options Using Linear Programming. *J. Agr. Econ.*, January 1987, *38*(1), pp. 15–25. [G: U.K.]

Hanna, Susan S. The Structure of Fishing Systems and the Implementation of Management Policy. *Vincent, T. L., et al., eds.*, 1987, pp. 264–73. [G: U.S.]

Hannon, Bruce. The Discounting of Concern: A Basis for the Study of Conflict. *Pillet, G. and*

Murota, T., eds., 1987, pp. 227–41.

Harford, Jon D. Self-Reporting of Pollution and the Firm's Behavior under Imperfectly Enforceable Regulations. *J. Environ. Econ. Manage.*, September 1987, *14*(3), pp. 293–303.

Harford, Jon D. Violation-Minimizing Fine Schedules. *Atlantic Econ. J.*, December 1987, *15*(4), pp. 49–56.

Harou, P. A. Multipurpose Agriculture and Forestry: An Overview and Some Remarks on the Seminar. *Merlo, M., et al., eds.*, 1987, pp. 624–29. **[G: W. Europe]**

Hodge, Ian. The Cap and the Soil: A Preliminary Analysis. *Merlo, M., et al., eds.*, 1987, pp. 523–33. **[G: U.K.]**

Hogg, Richard. Settlement, Pastoralism and the Commons: The Ideology and Practice of Irrigation Development in Northern Kenya. *Anderson, D. and Grove, R., eds.*, 1987, pp. 293–306. **[G: Kenya]**

Homewood, Katherine and Rodgers, William A. Pastoralism, Conservation and the Overgrazing Controversy. *Anderson, D. and Grove, R., eds.*, 1987, pp. 111–28. **[G: Africa]**

Howell, Paul. Wildlife, Parks and Pastoralists: Introduction. *Anderson, D. and Grove, R., eds.*, 1987, pp. 105–09. **[G: Africa]**

Huffaker, Ray and Gardner, B. Delworth. Rancher Stewardship on Public Ranges: A Recent Court Decision. *Natural Res. J.*, Fall 1987, *27*(4), pp. 887–98. **[G: U.S.]**

Hughes, Francine. Conflicting Uses for Forest Resources in the Lower Tana River Basin of Kenya. *Anderson, D. and Grove, R., eds.*, 1987, pp. 211–28. **[G: Kenya]**

Ikeda, Saburo. Economic–Ecological Models in Regional Total Systems. *Braat, L. C. and van Lierop, W. F. J., eds.*, 1987, pp. 185–202.

Jirát, Josef. Protection of the Human Environment in the Czech Socialist Republic in the 7th Five-Year Plan Period. *Czech. Econ. Digest.*, June 1987, (4), pp. 110–24. **[G: Czechoslovakia]**

Jones, T. Jeffrey and Swanson, Steven M. Regulating Environmental Risks: A Comparative Perspective: Discussion. *Kleindorfer, P. R. and Kunreuther, H. C., ed.*, 1987, pp. 411–14.

Junor, Robert and Watkins, Warwick. Policy Agents: Their Interaction and Effectiveness. *Chisholm, A. and Dumsday, R., eds.*, 1987, pp. 275–94. **[G: Australia]**

Kahn, James R. Measuring the Economic Damages Associated With Terrestrial Pollution of Marine Ecosystems. *Marine Resource Econ.*, 1987, *4*(3), pp. 193–209.

Kasperson, Roger E. Rethinking the Siting of Hazardous Waste Facilities. *Kleindorfer, P. R. and Kunreuther, H. C., ed.*, 1987, pp. 203–25.

Katzman, Martin T. Ecology, Natural Resources, and Economic Growth: Underdeveloping the Amazon: Review Article. *Econ. Develop. Cult. Change*, January 1987, *35*(2), pp. 425–36. **[G: Brazil]**

Katzman, Martin T. Environmental Risk Manage-

ment through Insurance. *Cato J.*, Winter 1987, *6*(3), pp. 775–99. **[G: U.S.]**

Katzman, Martin T. Multiattribute Utility Elicitation Techniques and Public Policy: A Meta-analysis of Empirical Applications. *Schultz, R. L., ed.*, 1987, pp. 237–303. **[G: U.S.]**

Kawamiya, Nobuo. Thermophysical Analysis of Resource Substitution, Technological Developments and the Environmental Problems in Their Interrelation. *Pillet, G. and Murota, T., eds.*, 1987, pp. 37–51.

Kerin, John. Land Degradation and Government. *Chisholm, A. and Dumsday, R., eds.*, 1987, pp. 1–4. **[G: Australia]**

Khachaturov, T. S. Natural Resources and the Environment: Introduction. *Borner, S. and Taylor, A., eds.*, 1987, pp. 7–17.

Kirby, Michael G. and Blyth, Michael J. An Economic Perspective on Government Intervention in Land Degradation. *Chisholm, A. and Dumsday, R., eds.*, 1987, pp. 213–22. **[G: Australia]**

Kirby, Michael G. and Blyth, Michael J. Economic Aspects of Land Degradation in Australia. *Australian J. Agr. Econ.*, August 1987, *31*(2), pp. 154–74. **[G: Australia]**

Kirkwood, Geoff P. Great Lakes Fisheries: Are Explicit Controls Necessary? Comment. *Vincent, T. L., et al., eds.*, 1987, pp. 245. **[G: U.S.]**

Kirsch, Guy. Solidarity between Generations: Intergenerational Distributional Problems in Environmental and Resource Policy. *Pillet, G. and Murota, T., eds.*, 1987, pp. 201–25.

Klaus, Alfred. Practical Aspects of Environmental Impairment Liability. *Kleindorfer, P. R. and Kunreuther, H. C., ed.*, 1987, pp. 448–53.

Kleindorfer, Paul R. and Kunreuther, Howard. From Seveso to Bhopal and Beyond. *Kleindorfer, P. R. and Kunreuther, H. C., ed.*, 1987, pp. 499–507.

Kleindorfer, Paul R. and Kunreuther, Howard. Insurance and Compensation as Policy Instruments for Hazardous Waste Management. *Kleindorfer, P. R. and Kunreuther, H. C., ed.*, 1987, pp. 145–72.

Kohn, Robert E. The Technology of Pollution Avoidance by Firms. *Public Finance*, 1987, *42*(3), pp. 384–94.

Kolstad, Charles D. Uniformity versus Differentiation in Regulating Externalities. *J. Environ. Econ. Manage.*, December 1987, *14*(4), pp. 386–99.

Koopmans, Tom Th. An Application of an Agroeconomic Model to Environmental Issues in the EC: A Case Study. *Europ. Rev. Agr. Econ.*, 1987, *14*(2), pp. 147–59. **[G: EEC]**

Kozloff, Keith. Overcoming Barriers to Improved Energy Efficiency: U.S. Experiences and Relevance to Developing Countries. *Pachauri, R. K., ed.*, 1987, pp. 967–93. **[G: U.S.; LDCs]**

Kunreuther, Howard, et al. A Compensation Mechanism for Siting Noxious Facilities: Theory and Experimental Design. *J. Environ. Econ. Manage.*, December 1987, *14*(4), pp. 371–83.

Lamb, F. Bruce. The Role of Anthropology in Tropical Forest Ecosystem Resource Management and Development. *J. Devel. Areas*, July 1987, *21*(4), pp. 429–58.

Langdon, Stephen. Commercial Fisheries: Implications for Western Alaska Development. *Lane, T., ed.*, 1987, pp. 3–26. [G: U.S.]

Larrere, R. and de la Soudiere, M. We Won't Go to the Woods . . . Picking Is Regulated in the Margeride. *Merlo, M., et al., eds.*, 1987, pp. 563–72. [G: France]

Laurent, C. The Maintenance of Biomass in Mountain Areas: A Public Service or State Aid to Farmers and Foresters? *Merlo, M., et al., eds.*, 1987, pp. 113–30. [G: France]

Lee, Cho Seng and Leitmann, George. Uncertain Dynamical Systems: An Application to River Pollution Control. *Vincent, T. L., et al., eds.*, 1987, pp. 167–84.

Leimgruber, Roland. Migros Switzerland: A Pioneer in Alimentation, Handling, and Environmental Protection. *Pillet, G. and Murota, T., eds.*, 1987, pp. 249–56. [G: Switzerland]

Lemeshev, M. Ecological and Economic Evaluation of Scientific-Technological Progress. *Prob. Econ.*, September 1987, *30*(5), pp. 82–97. [G: U.S.S.R.]

Lesser, William and Madhavan, Ananth. Economic Impacts of a National Deposit Law: Cost Estimates and Policy Questions. *J. Cons. Aff.*, Summer 1987, *21*(1), pp. 122–40. [G: U.S.]

Lichtenberg, Erik. Integrated versus Chemical Pest Management: The Case of Rice Field Mosquito Control. *J. Environ. Econ. Manage.*, September 1987, *14*(3), pp. 304–12. [G: U.S.]

Lichtenberg, Erik and Zilberman, David. Regulation of Marine Contamination under Environmental Uncertainty: Shellfish Contamination in California. *Marine Resource Econ.*, 1987, *4*(3), pp. 211–25. [G: U.S.]

Lindsay, W. Keith. Integrating Parks and Pastoralists: Some Lessons from Amboseli. *Anderson, D. and Grove, R., eds.*, 1987, pp. 149–67. [G: Kenya]

Little, Peter D. and Brokensha, David W. Local Institutions, Tenure and Resource Management in East Africa. *Anderson, D. and Grove, R., eds.*, 1987, pp. 193–209. [G: E. Africa]

Littlejohn, Stephen E. Competition and Cooperation: New Trends in Issue Identification and Management at Monsanto and Gulf. *Marcus, A. A.; Kaufman, A. M. and Beam, D. R., eds.*, 1987, pp. 19–30. [G: U.S.]

Livingston, Marie Leigh. Evaluating the Performance of Environmental Policy: Contributions of Neoclassical, Public Choice, and Institutional Models. *J. Econ. Issues*, March 1987, *21*(1), pp. 281–94.

Lonsdale, John M. Consequences for Conservation and Development: Introduction. *Anderson, D. and Grove, R., eds.*, 1987, pp. 271–75. [G: Africa]

de Lucia, Russell J. and Poole, Alan D. Biomass Fuels for Industry: Implications for Fuel Cycle

Economics. *Pachauri, R. K., ed.*, 1987, pp. 421–47.

Lukaszewicz, Aleksander. Natural Resources and Socio-economic Effects of Recycling. *Borner, S. and Taylor, A., eds.*, 1987, pp. 35–47.

MacAvoy, Paul W. The Record of the Environmental Protection Agency in Controlling Industrial Air Pollution. *[Adelman, M. A.]*, 1987, pp. 107–36. [G: U.S.]

MacIntyre, Angus A. Why Pesticides Received Extensive Use in America: A Political Economy of Agricultural Pest Management to 1970. *Natural Res. J.*, Summer 1987, *27*(3), pp. 533–78. [G: U.S.]

MacKellar, F. Landis and Vining, Daniel R., Jr. Natural Resource Scarcity: A Global Survey. *Johnson, D. G. and Lee, R. D., eds.*, 1987, pp. 259–329. [G: Global]

MacKenzie, John M. Chivalry, Social Darwinism and Ritualised Killing: The Hunting Ethos in Central Africa up to 1914. *Anderson, D. and Grove, R., eds.*, 1987, pp. 41–61. [G: Africa]

Maes, Denise. Transboundary Waste Dumping: The United States and Mexico Take a Stand. *Natural Res. J.*, Fall 1987, *27*(4), pp. 941–48. [G: U.S.; Mexico]

Mahon, John F. and Post, James E. The Evolution of Political Strategies during the 1980 Superfund Debate. *Marcus, A. A.; Kaufman, A. M. and Beam, D. R., eds.*, 1987, pp. 61–78. [G: U.S.]

Mäler, Karl-Göran. Energy Options and Environmental Considerations: The Case of Sweden. *Maillet, P.; Hague, D. and Rowland, C., eds.*, 1987, pp. 407–33. [G: Sweden]

March, Frederic and Shrivastava, Vinod. Rational Policies for Inducement of Energy Conservation in Developing Countries. *Pachauri, R. K., ed.*, 1987, pp. 995–1007. [G: LDCs]

McCracken, John. Colonialism, Capitalism and the Ecological Crisis in Malawi: A Reassessment. *Anderson, D. and Grove, R., eds.*, 1987, pp. 63–77. [G: Malawi]

McCracken, John. Conservation Priorities and Rural Communities: Introduction. *Anderson, D. and Grove, R., eds.*, 1987, pp. 189–92. [G: Africa]

McKelvey, Robert. Great Lakes Fisheries: Are Explicit Controls Necessary? Comment. *Vincent, T. L., et al., eds.*, 1987, pp. 245–46. [G: U.S.]

McKelvey, Robert. Groundwater-Based Agriculture in the Arid America West: Modeling the Transition to a Steady-State Renewable Resource Economy. *Vincent, T. L., et al., eds.*, 1987, pp. 222–35. [G: U.S.]

Meran, Georg and Schwalbe, Ulrich. Pollution Control and Collective Penalties. *J. Inst. Theoretical Econ.*, December 1987, *143*(4), pp. 616–29.

Merlo, M. Multipurpose Agriculture and Forestry: An Overview and Some Remarks on the Seminar. *Merlo, M., et al., eds.*, 1987, pp. 629–32.

Meyer, Richard and Yandle, Bruce. The Political

Economy of Acid Rain. *Cato J.*, Fall 1987, 7(2), pp. 527–45. [G: U.S.]

Mezzalira, G. An Attempt to Evaluate the Multiple Functions of Shelterbelts. *Merlo, M., et al., eds.*, 1987, pp. 371–83. [G: Italy]

Miller, C. Efficiency, Equity and Pollution: The Case of Radioactive Waste. *Environ. Planning A*, July 1987, 19(7), pp. 913–24. [G: U.K.]

Millington, Andrew C. Environmental Degradation, Soil Conservation and Agricultural Policies in Sierra Leone, 1895–1984. *Anderson, D. and Grove, R., eds.*, 1987, pp. 229–48. [G: Sierra Leone]

Montange, Charles H. Federal Nuclear Waste Disposal Policy. *Natural Res. J.*, Spring 1987, 27(2), pp. 309–408. [G: U.S.]

Moore, Walter B. and McCarl, Bruce A. Off-Site Costs of Soil Erosion: A Case Study in the Willamette Valley. *Western J. Agr. Econ.*, July 1987, 12(1), pp. 42–49. [G: U.S.]

Mosley, Geoff. Non-government Organisations: A Synopsis by the Australian Conservation Foundation. *Chisholm, A. and Dumsday, R., eds.*, 1987, pp. 271–74. [G: Australia]

Murali, R. Demand Uncertainty and Input Constraints. *Quart. Rev. Econ. Bus.*, Summer 1987, 27(2), pp. 22–41.

Murota, Takeshi. Environmental Economics of the Water Planet Earth. *Pillet, G. and Murota, T., eds.*, 1987, pp. 185–99.

Nichols, Joanne. Insurance and Compensation as Policy Instruments for Hazardous Waste Management: Discussion. *Kleindorfer, P. R. and Kunreuther, H. C., ed.*, 1987, pp. 173–77.

Nola, L. Multipurpose Land Reclamation in Italy. *Merlo, M., et al., eds.*, 1987, pp. 573–81. [G: Italy]

Norris, Patricia E. and Batie, Sandra S. Virginia Farmers' Soil Conservation Decisions: An Application of Tobit Analysis. *Southern J. Agr. Econ.*, July 1987, 19(1), pp. 79–90. [G: U.S.]

Nougarede, O.; Larrere, R. and Poupardin, D. The Aigoual Forest: Theatre of Latent Conflicts of Interest and Competences. *Merlo, M., et al., eds.*, 1987, pp. 179–91. [G: France]

O'Riordan, Timothy and Wynne, Brian. Regulating Environmental Risks: A Comparative Perspective. *Kleindorfer, P. R. and Kunreuther, H. C., ed.*, 1987, pp. 389–410.

Ohline, Beverly A. Clean Air Act—Transboundary Acid Rain Pollution Abatement—Administrative Discretion Citizen Suit. *Natural Res. J.*, Summer 1987, 27(3), pp. 707–22. [G: U.S.]

Orlando, Enrico. Recent Developments Concerning the Legal Regime and Insurance Problems Related to the Transportation of Hazardous Materials by Sea. *Kleindorfer, P. R. and Kunreuther, H. C., ed.*, 1987, pp. 454–57.

Ostro, Bart D. Air Pollution and Morbidity Revisited: A Specification Test. *J. Environ. Econ. Manage.*, March 1987, 14(1), pp. 87–98. [G: U.S.]

Otway, Harry. Value Tree Analysis: An Introduction and an Application to Offshore Oil Drilling: Discussion. *Kleindorfer, P. R. and Kun-*

reuther, H. C., ed., 1987, pp. 377–83.

Park, William M. and Sawyer, David G. Cost Effectiveness of Alternative Subsidy Strategies for Soil Erosion Control. *Southern J. Agr. Econ.*, December 1987, 19(2), pp. 21–32. [G: U.S.]

Paruelo, Jose M., et al. Energy Use and Economic Output for Argentina. *Pillet, G. and Murota, T., eds.*, 1987, pp. 169–84. [G: Argentina]

Paté-Cornell, M. E. Risk Analysis and Relevance of Uncertainties in Nuclear Safety Decisions. *Bailey, E. E., ed.*, 1987, pp. 227–53. [G: U.S.]

Paterson, John. Policy Agents: Their Interaction and Effectiveness: Commentary. *Chisholm, A. and Dumsday, R., eds.*, 1987, pp. 295–301. [G: Australia]

Payne, B. A.; Olshansky, S. Jay and Segel, T. E. The Effects on Property Values of Proximity to a Site Contaminated with Radioactive Waste. *Natural Res. J.*, Summer 1987, 27(3), pp. 579–90. [G: U.S.]

Pearse, Peter H. and Walters, Carl J. Perspectives on the Application of Economic–Ecological Models. *Braat, L. C. and van Lierop, W. F. J., eds.*, 1987, pp. 269–81.

Pearson, Charles and Hufschmidt, Maynard. Incorporating the Environment in Development Planning. *Borner, S. and Taylor, A., eds.*, 1987, pp. 19–34.

Peck, Stephen C. and Richels, Richard G. The Value of Information to the Acidic Deposition Debates. *J. Bus. Econ. Statist.*, April 1987, 5(2), pp. 205–17.

Pettenella, D. and Russo, G. Simbruini Mountains (Central Italy): Conflict in the Use of Forest Resources between Wood Production and Environmental Protection. *Merlo, M., et al., eds.*, 1987, pp. 611–17. [G: Italy]

Pfennigstorf, Werner. The Role of Insurance in Risk Spreading and Risk Bearing. *Kleindorfer, P. R. and Kunreuther, H. C., ed.*, 1987, pp. 465–85.

Pillet, Gonzague. Exergy, Emergy, and Entropy. *Pillet, G. and Murota, T., eds.*, 1987, pp. 277–302.

Pillet, Gonzague. Externalities in Environmental Macroeconomics. *Pillet, G. and Murota, T., eds.*, 1987, pp. 129–53.

Pinto, Frank J. P. The Economics of, and Potential for, Energy Conservation and Substitution. *Pachauri, R. K., ed.*, 1987, pp. 703–36.

Pollock, Cynthia. Realizing Recycling's Potential. *Brown, L. R., et al.*, 1987, pp. 101–21. [G: Global]

Pope, Catherine E. Environmental Law—Federal Indian Law—Recent Developments— *State of Washington, Department of Ecology v. United States Environmental Protection Agency*, 752 F.2d 1465 (9th Cir. 1985). *Natural Res. J.*, Summer 1987, 27(3), pp. 739–55. [G: U.S.]

Posner, Michael V. Problems Concerning the Implementation of Energy Policies. *Maillet, P.;*

Hague, D. and Rowland, C., eds., 1987, pp. 76–92.

Postel, Sandra. Stabilizing Chemical Cycles. *Brown, L. R., et al.*, 1987, pp. 157–76. [G: Global]

Prato, Tony. Allocation of Federal Assistance to Soil Conservation. *Land Econ.*, May 1987, 63(2), pp. 193–200. [G: U.S.]

Quiggin, John. Land Degradation: Behavioural Causes. *Chisholm, A. and Dumsday, R., eds.*, 1987, pp. 203–12. [G: Australia]

Rabinowitz, Joseph. The Impact of Noise on Man and His Environment. *Pillet, G. and Murota, T., eds.*, 1987, pp. 243–47.

Rafsnider, Giles T.; Skold, Melvin D. and Sampath, Rajan K. Range Survey Cost Sharing and the Efficiency of Rangeland Use. *Land Econ.*, February 1987, 63(1), pp. 92–101. [G: U.S.]

Ramsay, William and Lipman-Blumen, Jean. Institutional Issues in Biomass Energy Policy: The No-Man's Land between Agricultural, Forestry, and Energy Policies in Developing Nations. *Pachauri, R. K., ed.*, 1987, pp. 205–15. [G: LDCs]

Rao, K. R. Energy Conservation Strategies for Large Commercial and Office Buildings in Developing Countries. *Pachauri, R. K., ed.*, 1987, pp. 953–65. [G: LDCs]

Rawat, J. K., et al. A Pest and Timber Management Model: Jack Pine Budworm and Jack Pine. *Can. J. Agr. Econ.*, July 1987, 35(2), pp. 441–61. [G: Canada]

Reilly, J. M., et al. Uncertainty Analysis of the IEA/ORAU CO823 Emissions Model. *Energy J.*, July 1987, 8(3), pp. 1–29. [G: OECD]

Repetto, Robert. The Policy Implications of Nonconvex Environmental Damages: A Smog Control Case Study. *J. Environ. Econ. Manage.*, March 1987, 14(1), pp. 13–29. [G: U.S.]

Rickson, Roy, et al. Social Bases of Farmers' Responses to Land Degradation. *Chisholm, A. and Dumsday, R., eds.*, 1987, pp. 187–200. [G: Australia]

Ristoratore, Mario. Siting Toxic Waste Disposal Facilities: Best and Worst Cases in North America. *Feldman, E. J. and Goldberg, M. A., eds.*, 1987, pp. 201–21. [G: U.S.; Canada]

Ritschel, Dennis. Search and Seizure—Aerial Surveillance—Administrative Inspections—*Dow Chemical v. United States*, __U.S.__, 106 S.Ct. 1819 (1986). *Natural Res. J.*, Summer 1987, 27(3), pp. 693–706. [G: U.S.]

Robb, Andrew. Non-government Organisations: A Synopsis by the National Farmers' Federation. *Chisholm, A. and Dumsday, R., eds.*, 1987, pp. 268–70. [G: Australia]

Robertson, Graeme. Towards More Effective Policies for Controlling Land Degradation: Contributions from the Physical and Biological Sciences. *Chisholm, A. and Dumsday, R., eds.*, 1987, pp. 305–14. [G: Australia]

Rosa, F. Multiobjective Agriculture: Finding an Optimal Solution among Competing Agents. *Merlo, M., et al., eds.*, 1987, pp. 53–68.

Rosenthal, Isadore. Value Tree Analysis: An In-

troduction and an Application to Offshore Oil Drilling: Discussion. *Kleindorfer, P. R. and Kunreuther, H. C., ed.*, 1987, pp. 383–85.

Rubin, Edward S. Environmental Control Costs for Coal Energy Technologies. *Maillet, P.; Hague, D. and Rowland, C., eds.*, 1987, pp. 434–60. [G: OECD]

Rugge, Dale R. Judicial Review of Environmental Protection Agency Rule Promulgation—Clean Air Act State Implementation Plan Requirement—*New Mexico EID v. Thomas*, 789 F.2D 825 (10th Cir. 1986). *Natural Res. J.*, Summer 1987, 27(3), pp. 723–37. [G: U.S.]

Runge, Carlisle Ford. Induced Agricultural Innovation and Environmental Quality: The Case of Groundwater Regulation. *Land Econ.*, August 1987, 63(3), pp. 249–58. [G: U.S.]

Rutledge, Gary L. and Stergioulas, Nikolaos. Plant and Equipment Expenditures by Business for Pollution Abatement, 1986 and 1987. *Surv. Curr. Bus.*, October 1987, 67(10), pp. 23–26. [G: U.S.]

Sachs, Carolyn; Blair, Dorothy and Richter, Carolyn. Consumer Pesticide Concerns: A 1965 and 1984 Comparison. *J. Cons. Aff.*, Summer 1987, 21(1), pp. 96–107. [G: U.S.]

Schilizzi, Steven G. M. Physical Economics, Technology, and Agroecosystems. *Pillet, G. and Murota, T., eds.*, 1987, pp. 109–28. [G: France; Vietnam]

Schneider, Hans-Karl and Schulz, Walter. The Implementation of Energy Policy Goals. *Maillet, P.; Hague, D. and Rowland, C., eds.*, 1987, pp. 93–111.

Schulze, William D., et al. Benefits and Costs of Earthquake Resistant Buildings. *Southern Econ. J.*, April 1987, 53(4), pp. 934–51. [G: U.S.]

Scienceman, David M. Energy and Emergy. *Pillet, G. and Murota, T., eds.*, 1987, pp. 257–76.

Segarra, Eduardo and Taylor, Daniel B. Farm Level Dynamic Analysis of Soil Conservation: An Application to the Piedmont Area of Virginia. *Southern J. Agr. Econ.*, December 1987, 19(2), pp. 61–73. [G: U.S.]

Segerson, Kathleen. Risk-Sharing and Liability in the Control of Stochastic Externalities. *Marine Resource Econ.*, 1987, 4(3), pp. 175–92. [G: U.S.]

Shabman, Leonard A. and Batie, Sandra S. Mitigating Damages from Coastal Wetlands Development: Policy, Economics and Financing. *Marine Resource Econ.*, 1987, 4(3), pp. 227–48.

Shaw, Bill; Winslett, Brenda J. and Cross, Frank B. The Global Environment: A Proposal to Eliminate Marine Oil Pollution. *Natural Res. J.*, Winter 1987, 27(1), pp. 157–85.

Shortle, James S. and Willett, Keith D. A Computable Market Equilibrium Model with Markets for Transferable Discharge Permits. *Managerial Dec. Econ.*, December 1987, 8(4), pp. 263–70.

Shucksmith, M. Conflicting Land Uses in the English Lake District. *Merlo, M., et al., eds.,* 1987, pp. 545–52. **[G: U.K.]**

Sims, John H. and Baumann, Duane D. The Adoption of Residential Flood Mitigation Measures: What Price Success? *Econ. Geogr.,* July 1987, *63*(3), pp. 259–72. **[G: U.S.]**

Slade, Margaret E. Natural Resources, Population Growth, and Economic Well-being. *Johnson, D. G. and Lee, R. D., eds.,* 1987, pp. 331–69.

Smets, Henri. Compensation for Exceptional Environmental Damage Caused by Industrial Activities. *Kleindorfer, P. R. and Kunreuther, H. C., ed.,* 1987, pp. 79–138. **[G: Global]**

Smith, G. Scott; Wetzstein, Michael E. and Douce, G. Keith. Evaluation of Various Pest-Management Characteristics. *Southern J. Agr. Econ.,* December 1987, *19*(2), pp. 93–101. **[G: U.S.]**

Smith, V. Kerry. Nonuse Values in Benefit Cost Analysis. *Southern Econ. J.,* July 1987, *54*(1), pp. 19–26.

Smith, V. Kerry and Desvousges, William H. An Empirical Analysis of the Economic Value of Risk Changes. *J. Polit. Econ.,* February 1987, *95*(1), pp. 89–114. **[G: U.S.]**

Söderbaum, Peter W. O. Environmental Management: A Non-traditional Approach. *J. Econ. Issues,* March 1987, *21*(1), pp. 139–65.

Southworth, F. and Chin, S.-M. Network Evacuation Modeling for Flooding as a Result of Dam Failure. *Environ. Planning A,* November 1987, *19*(11), pp. 1543–58.

Spangler, George R. Great Lakes Fisheries: Are Explicit Controls Necessary? *Vincent, T. L., et al., eds.,* 1987, pp. 236–45. **[G: U.S.]**

Spangler, George R. The Structure of Fishing Systems and the Implementation of Management Policy: Comment. *Vincent, T. L., et al., eds.,* 1987, pp. 274–75. **[G: U.S.]**

Spühler, Jürgen. The Role of Insurance in Risk Spreading and Risk Bearing: Discussion. *Kleindorfer, P. R. and Kunreuther, H. C., ed.,* 1987, pp. 492–98.

Staley, Michael. The Practice of Resource Modeling. *Braat, L. C. and van Lierop, W. F. J., eds.,* 1987, pp. 257–68.

Stowe, Robert C. United States Foreign Policy and the Conservation of Natural Resources: The Case of Tropical Deforestation. *Natural Res. J.,* Winter 1987, *27*(1), pp. 55–101. **[G: U.S.]**

Sullivan, Arthur M. Policy Options for Toxics Disposal: Laissez-Faire, Subsidization, and Enforcement. *J. Environ. Econ. Manage.,* March 1987, *14*(1), pp. 58–71.

Susmel, L. Multipurpose Management of Alpine Forests. *Merlo, M., et al., eds.,* 1987, pp. 221–25. **[G: Italy]**

Swaney, James A. Building Instrumental Environmental Control Institutions. *J. Econ. Issues,* March 1987, *21*(1), pp. 295–308. **[G: U.S.]**

Swaney, James A. Elements of a Neoinstitutional Environmental Economics. *J. Econ. Issues,* December 1987, *21*(4), pp. 1739–79.

Swaney, James A. Response-Ability of Environmental Controls. *J. Econ. Issues,* June 1987, *21*(2), pp. 911–19. **[G: U.S.]**

Tait, E. J. Research Policy and Review 14. Environmental Issues and the Social Sciences. *Environ. Planning A,* April 1987, *19*(4), pp. 437–45. **[G: U.K.]**

Teclaff, Ludwik A. and Teclaff, Eileen. International Control of Cross-media Pollution—An Ecosystem Approach. *Natural Res. J.,* Winter 1987, *27*(1), pp. 21–53.

Thomas, John. Onsite Costs of Land Degradation in Agriculture and Forestry: Comments. *Chisholm, A. and Dumsday, R., eds.,* 1987, pp. 363–64. **[G: Australia]**

Thompson, James L. Citizen Suits and Civil Penalties under the Clean Water Act. *Mich. Law Rev.,* June 1987, *85*(7), pp. 1656–80. **[G: U.S.]**

Tsuchida, Atsushi and Murota, Takeshi. Fundamentals in the Entropy Theory of Ecocycle and Human Economy. *Pillet, G. and Murota, T., eds.,* 1987, pp. 11–35.

Tuck, Bradford H. Structural Change in Alaska: The Impact of the Petroleum Industry. *Lane, T., ed.,* 1987, pp. 233–49. **[G: U.S.]**

Turton, David. The Mursi and National Park Development in the Lower Omo Valley. *Anderson, D. and Grove, R., eds.,* 1987, pp. 169–86. **[G: Ethiopia]**

von Ungern-Sternberg, Thomas. Environmental Protection with Several Pollutants: On the Division of Labor between Natural Scientists and Economists. *J. Inst. Theoretical Econ.,* December 1987, *143*(4), pp. 555–67.

Upstill, Garrett and Yapp, Timothy. Offsite Costs of Land Degradation. *Chisholm, A. and Dumsday, R., eds.,* 1987, pp. 99–107. **[G: Australia]**

Van Kooten, G. C. and Furtan, William Hartley. A Review of Issues Pertaining to Soil Deterioration in Canada. *Can. J. Agr. Econ.,* March 1987, *35*(1), pp. 33–54. **[G: Canada; U.S.]**

Wacker, Holger. Die optimale Allokation von Arbeit in Abfallbehandlungsaktivitäten. (The Optimal Allocation of Labour into Waste Activities. With English summary.) *Schweiz. Z. Volkswirtsch. Statist.,* December 1987, *123*(4), pp. 467–81.

Wasson, Robert. Detection and Measurement of Land Degradation Processes. *Chisholm, A. and Dumsday, R., eds.,* 1987, pp. 49–69. **[G: Australia]**

Webb, Adrian. Physical and Biological Aspects of Land Degradation: Commentary. *Chisholm, A. and Dumsday, R., eds.,* 1987, pp. 70–75. **[G: Australia]**

Weirick, William N. Amenities, Factor Mobility, and Market Prices. *Land Econ.,* August 1987, *63*(3), pp. 272–83.

Westoby, Jack C. 'Making Green the Motherland': Forestry in China. *Westoby, J.,* 1987, *1975,* pp. 270–87. **[G: China]**

Westoby, Jack C. Making Trees Serve People. *Westoby, J.,* 1987, *1975,* pp. 257–69.

Westoby, Jack C. On Behalf of the Uninvited

Guests. *Westoby, J.*, 1987, *1974*, pp. 217–30.
[G: Australia]

Westoby, Jack C. One-World Forestry: New Zealand's Role. *Westoby, J.*, 1987, *1970*, pp. 160–75. [G: New Zealand]

Westoby, Jack C. Quo Vadis? A Note for Discussion. *Westoby, J.*, 1987, pp. 206–16.

Westoby, Jack C. The Changing Objectives of Forest Management. *Westoby, J.*, 1987, *1968*, pp. 179–92.

Westoby, Jack C. The Forester as Agent of Change. *Westoby, J.*, 1987, *1968*, pp. 115–42.

Westoby, Jack C. World Forest Development: Markets, Men and Methods. *Westoby, J.*, 1987, *1965*, pp. 143–59. [G: Canada; LDCs]

White, Thomas U. Section 119 of the Clean Air Act and Phelps Dodge Reduction Works: A Case Study of EPA Inaction. *Natural Res. J.*, Spring 1987, *27*(2), pp. 457–67. [G: U.S.]

von Winterfeldt, Detlof. Value Tree Analysis: An Introduction and an Application to Offshore Oil Drilling. *Kleindorfer, P. R. and Kunreuther, H. C., ed.*, 1987, pp. 349–77.

Woodbury, Stephen E. Aesthetic Nuisance: The Time Has Come to Recognize It. *Natural Res. J.*, Fall 1987, *27*(4), pp. 877–86. [G: U.S.]

Woods, Lance. Degradation Pressures from Non-agricultural Land Uses. *Chisholm, A. and Dumsday, R., eds.*, 1987, pp. 108–18.
[G: Australia]

Yanarella, Ernest J. and Reid, Herbert G. Class-Based Environmentalism in a Small Town: ERDA's "Gasifiers in Industry" Program and the Georgetown, Kentucky, Controversy. *Yanarella, E. J. and Green, W. C., eds.*, 1987, pp. 99–125. [G: U.S.]

Young, Michael. Land Tenure: Plaything of Governments or an Effective Instrument? *Chisholm, A. and Dumsday, R., eds.*, 1987, pp. 175–86. [G: Australia]

723 Energy

7230 Energy

Adelman, M. A. The Economics of the International Oil Industry. *Rees, J. and Odell, P., eds.*, 1987, pp. 27–56. [G: Global]

Ahn, Byong-hun; Nesbitt, Dale M. and Phillips, Robert L. Integrated Analysis for Energy Policies—Oil Consumption Reduction Programmes in Korea. *Pachauri, R. K., ed.*, 1987, pp. 331–52. [G: S. Korea]

Akacem, Mohammed. The Future of the Organization of the Petroleum Exporting Countries. *J. Energy Devel.*, Autumn 1987, *13*(1), pp. 123–39. [G: OPEC]

Al-Sahlawi, Mohammed A. and Boyd, Roy G. Energy Demand in Developing Countries and Third World Response to Changes in the International Oil Market. *J. Energy Devel.*, Spring 1987, *12*(2), pp. 225–43. [G: LDCs]

Alam, Manzoor. Supply and Demand of Fuel Wood in the Domestic Sector—The Case of Hyderabad City. *Pachauri, R. K., ed.*, 1987, pp. 529–46. [G: India]

Amano, Akihiro. A Small Forecasting Model of the World Oil Market. *J. Policy Modeling*, Winter 1987, *9*(4), pp. 615–35.

Amaya, N. Policy Choices in Developed Countries: Two Japanese Views (A). *Maillet, P.; Hague, D. and Rowland, C., eds.*, 1987, pp. 283–86. [G: Japan]

Anand, Sudhir and Nalebuff, Barry. Issues in the Application of Cost–Benefit Analysis to Energy Projects in Developing Countries. *Oxford Econ. Pap.*, March 1987, *39*(1), pp. 190–222. [G: LDCs]

Anand, Sudhir and Nalebuff, Barry. Issues in the Application of Cost–Benefit Analysis to Energy Projects in Developing Countries. *Sinclair, P. J. N., ed.*, 1987, pp. 190–222. [G: LDCs]

Anandalingam, G. The Economics of Industrial Energy Conservation in the Developing Countries. *Pachauri, R. K., ed.*, 1987, pp. 643–61. [G: LDCs]

Andrews, Laurel M. INDEPTH Level I Results: Econometric Forecast Models for 20 Industries. *Faruqui, A. and Broehl, J., eds.*, 1987, pp. 395–409. [G: U.S.]

Ang, B. W. A Cross-Sectional Analysis of Energy–Output Correlation. *Energy Econ.*, October 1987, *9*(4), pp. 274–86. [G: Global]

Antille, Gabrielle and Laplanche, Bernadette. Impact of Constraints in Energy Imports and Energy Production of Final Domestic Demand. *Tchijov, I. and Tomaszewicz, L., eds.*, 1987, pp. 169–83. [G: Switzerland]

Asplund, Rita. Residential Demand for Electric Space Heating in Finland. *Europ. Econ. Rev.*, July 1987, *31*(5), pp. 981–93. [G: Finland]

Attiga, Ali A. The Price of Oil and the Energy Market. *Pachauri, R. K., ed.*, 1987, pp. 9–18.

Baca, Alvin. FERC & ERA: Issues in Natural Gas Regulation. *Natural Res. J.*, Fall 1987, *27*(4), pp. 815–22. [G: U.S.]

Bailey, Richard. Energy Policy after Chernobyl. *Nat. Westminster Bank Quart. Rev.*, November 1987, pp. 2–14. [G: U.K.]

Baillard-Haurie, D., et al. What Does $(US)15 versus $(US)23 Oil Mean for Long-range Energy Choices in the Province of Quebec? *Can. Public Policy*, March 1987, *13*(1), pp. 56–61. [G: Canada]

Baish, Richard O. The Role of the California Public Utilities Commission in Western Gas Markets. *Natural Res. J.*, Fall 1987, *27*(4), pp. 805–10. [G: U.S.]

Banks, Ferdinand E. The Reserve–Production Ratio. *Energy J.*, April 1987, *8*(2), pp. 147–51.

Barnes, Douglas F. and Samanta, B. B. Rural Electrification and the Village Economy in India. *Pachauri, R. K., ed.*, 1987, pp. 1155–66. [G: India]

Barth, Bjorn. Global Energy Interactions: A Presentation. *Pachauri, R. K., ed.*, 1987, pp. 1229–36.

Baumgartner, Thomas and Midttun, Atle. Energy Forecasting and Political Structure: Some Comparative Notes. *Baumgartner, T. and*

Midttun, A., eds., 1987, pp. 267–89.
[G: OECD]

Baumgartner, Thomas and Midttun, Atle. Energy Forecasting: Science, Art, and Politics. *Baumgartner, T. and Midttun, A., eds.*, 1987, pp. 3–10.

Baumgartner, Thomas and Midttun, Atle. Modelling and Forecasting in Self-reactive Policy Contexts: Some Meta-methodological Comments. *Baumgartner, T. and Midttun, A., eds.*, 1987, pp. 290–308.

Baumgartner, Thomas and Midttun, Atle. The Socio-political Context of Energy Forecasting. *Baumgartner, T. and Midttun, A., eds.*, 1987, pp. 11–29.

Bean, Charles R. The Performance of the British Economy: The Impact of North Sea Oil. *Dornbusch, R. and Layard, R., eds.*, 1987, pp. 64–96. [G: U.K.]

Benjamin, Nancy C.; Devarajan, Shantayanan and Weiner, Robert J. Oil Revenues, Capital Expenditure, and the "Dutch Disease": The Case of Cameroon. *Pachauri, R. K., ed.*, 1987, pp. 59–74. [G: Cameroon]

Bentham, Richard W. The International Legal Structure of Petroleum Exploration. *Rees, J. and Odell, P., eds.*, 1987, pp. 57–66.
[G: Global]

Bergman, Lars. Oil Price Increases and Macroeconomic Instability: General Equilibrium Calculations on the Basis of Swedish Data. *Maillet, P.; Hague, D. and Rowland, C., eds.*, 1987, pp. 208–25. [G: Sweden]

Berkowitz, Michael K. and Haines, George H., Jr. A Disaggregate Model of Residential Heating Mode Choice: A Multinomial Probit Modelling Approach. *Appl. Econ.*, May 1987, *19*(5), pp. 581–96. [G: Canada]

Bernard, Jean-Thomas and Cauchon, Pierre. Thermal and Economic Measures of Energy Use: Differences and Implications. *Energy J.*, April 1987, *8*(2), pp. 125–35. [G: Canada]

Bernard, Jean-Thomas; Lemieux, Michel and Thivierge, Simon. Residential Energy Demand: An Integrated Two-Level Approach. *Energy Econ.*, July 1987, *9*(3), pp. 139–44. [G: Canada]

Bernard, Jean-Thomas and Veall, Michael R. The Probability Distribution of Future Demand: The Case of Hydro Quebec. *J. Bus. Econ. Statist.*, July 1987, *5*(3), pp. 417–24. [G: Canada]

Berndt, Ernst R. and Wood, David O. Energy Price Shocks and Productivity Growth: A Survey. *[Adelman, M. A.]*, 1987, pp. 305–42.

Berry, S. Keith and Loudenslager, Samuel. The Impact of Nuclear Power Plant Construction Activity on the Electric Utility Industry's Cost of Capital. *Energy J.*, April 1987, *8*(2), pp. 63–75. [G: U.S.]

Berthélemy, Jean-Claude and Devezeaux de Lavergne, Jean-Guy. L'impact des chocs pétroliers. Une simulation rétrospective: 1973–1982. (Oil Shocks Effects: A Retrospective Simulation: 1973–1982. With English summary.)

Revue Écon., July 1987, *38*(4), pp. 877–96.
[G: France]

Berthélemy, Jean-Claude and Devezeaux de Lavergne, Jean-Guy. Le modèle mélodie: un modèle énergétique de long terme pour l'écomomie française. (With English summary.) *Revue Écon. Polit.*, Sept.-Oct. 1987, *97*(5), pp. 649–72. [G: France]

Bethkenhagen, Jochen. The Energy Situation in the Soviet Union and Eastern Europe. *Marer, P. and van Veen, P., eds.*, 1987, pp. 35–41.
[G: E. Europe]

Bhatia, Ramesh. Economics of Ethanol Production in India: A Study in Social Benefit–Cost Analysis. *Pachauri, R. K., ed.*, 1987, pp. 143–88. [G: India]

Binmore, Ken. Bargaining Models. *Golombek, R.; Hoel, M. and Vislie, J., eds.*, 1987, pp. 239–52.

Birks, K. Stuart and Buurman, Gary B. Rationing and Careless Days: Comment. *New Zealand Econ. Pap.*, 1987, *21*, pp. 117–20.
[G: New Zealand]

Bohi, Douglas R. Evolution of the Oil Market and Energy Security Policy. *Contemp. Policy Issues*, July 1987, *5*(3), pp. 20–33. [G: U.S.]

Bold, Frederick C. Responses to Energy Efficiency Regulations. *Energy J.*, April 1987, *8*(2), pp. 111–23.

Bolle, Friedel. Zum Problem der Verbrauchsabhängigen Heizkostenabrechnung. Eine theoretische Bestimmung der effizienten Aufteilung. (The Efficient Distribution of Heating Costs—A Theoretical Analysis. With English summary.) *Ifo-Studien*, 1987, *33*(1), pp. 27–42.

Boucher, Jacqueline; Hefting, Tom and Smeers, Yves. Economic Analysis of Natural Gas Contracts. *Golombek, R.; Hoel, M. and Vislie, J., eds.*, 1987, pp. 193–220. [G: Norway]

Boucher, Jacqueline and Smeers, Yves. Economic Forces in the European Gas Market—A 1985 Prospective. *Energy Econ.*, January 1987, *9*(1), pp. 2–16. [G: Europe; Algeria]

Bowie, Paddy. Oil, Gas and Development in Malaysia. *Hills, P. and Bowie, P.*, 1987, pp. 85–148. [G: Malaysia]

Boyd, Gale A., et al. Separating the Changing Composition of U.S. Manufacturing Production from Energy Efficiency Improvements: A Divisia Index Approach. *Energy J.*, April 1987, *8*(2), pp. 77–96. [G: U.S.; Sweden; U.K.; Mexico]

Bradley, Paul G. Cost and Output Analysis in Mineral and Petroleum Production. *[Adelman, M. A.]*, 1987, pp. 281–303.

Broadman, Harry G. Competition in Natural Gas Pipeline Wellhead Supply Purchases. *Energy J.*, July 1987, *8*(3), pp. 113–34. [G: U.S.]

Broadman, Harry G. Petroleum Firm Foreign Investment in Non-OPEC Developing Countries: A Theoretical Perspective. *Pachauri, R. K., ed.*, 1987, pp. 547–60. [G: LDCs]

Broehl, John H. INDEPTH Level II Results. *Faruqui, A. and Broehl, J., eds.*, 1987, pp. 417–30. [G: U.S.]

Buffie, Edward F. Input Price Shocks in the Small Open Economy. *Sinclair, P. J. N., ed.*, 1987, *1986*, pp. 233–47.

Cain, Stephen R. and Kerr, William A. China's Changing Development Strategy: The Case of Rural Electrification. *Can. J. Devel. Stud.*, 1987, *8*(1), pp. 81–96. **[G: China]**

Campbell, Michael. The Implications of Gas Policy for the Western States: A Producer Perspective. *Natural Res. J.*, Fall 1987, *27*(4), pp. 823–28. **[G: U.S.]**

Cannon, Colin M. Peak-Pricing and Self-Rationing of Gas. *Energy Econ.*, April 1987, *9*(2), pp. 99–103. **[G: U.K.]**

Capone, Charles A., Jr. and Elzinga, Kenneth G. Technology and Energy Use before, during, and after OPEC: The U.S. Portland Cement Industry. *Energy J.*, July 1987, *8*(3), pp. 93–112. **[G: U.S.]**

Carlevaro, Fabrizio; Chaze, Jean-Paul and Spierer, Charles. Le déterminants de l'évolution annuelle de la consommation d'énergie en Suisse. (The Determinants of the Evolution of the Annual Energy Consumption in Switzerland. With English summary.) *Schweiz. Z. Volkswirtsch. Statist.*, March 1987, *123*(1), pp. 1–22. **[G: Switzerland]**

Carlevaro, Fabrizio and Spierer, Charles. Dynamic Energy Demand Models with Latest Equipment. *Pachauri, R. K., ed.*, 1987, *1983*, pp. 91–118. **[G: Switzerland]**

Carpenter, Paul R.; Jacoby, Henry D. and Wright, Arthur W. Adapting to Change in Natural Gas Markets. *[Adelman, M. A.]*, 1987, pp. 1–29. **[G: U.S.]**

Carrie, J. L. Long-term Balance on the World Oil Market. *Pachauri, R. K., ed.*, 1987, pp. 663–71. **[G: Global]**

de Castro, Antonio Barros. Brazilian Energy Policy at a Cross-road. *Maillet, P.; Hague, D. and Rowland, C., eds.*, 1987, pp. 307–23. **[G: Brazil]**

Caves, Douglas W., et al. A Bayesian Approach to Combining Conditional Demand and Engineering Models of Electricity Usage. *Rev. Econ. Statist.*, August 1987, *69*(3), pp. 438–48. **[G: U.S.]**

Cecelski, Elizabeth. Energy and Rural Women's Work: Crisis, Response and Policy Alternatives. *Int. Lab. Rev.*, Jan.-Feb. 1987, *126*(1), pp. 41–64. **[G: Selected LDCs]**

Chan, M. W. Luke and Okasanen, E. H. Regional Energy Input Prices in Canadian Manufacturing: An Index Number Approach. *Energy Econ.*, April 1987, *9*(2), pp. 66–72. **[G: Canada]**

Chandler, William U. Designing Sustainable Economies. *Brown, L. R., et al.*, 1987, pp. 177–95. **[G: Global]**

Chen, K. C.; Sears, R. Stephen and Tzang, Dah-Nein. Oil Prices and Energy Futures. *J. Futures Markets*, October 1987, *7*(5), pp. 501–18. **[G: U.S.]**

Chern, Wen S. An Econometric Analysis of Sectoral Energy Demand in Taiwan. *Pachauri, R. K., ed.*, 1987, pp. 119–41. **[G: Taiwan]**

Chuah, Donald G. S. Dilemma in Solar Energy Development Works in a Developing Country—Malaysia. *Pachauri, R. K., ed.*, 1987, pp. 1187–92. **[G: Malaysia]**

Claggett, E. Tylor, Jr. Cooperative Distributors of Electrical Power: Operations and Scale Economies. *Quart. J. Bus. Econ.*, Summer 1987, *26*(3), pp. 3–21. **[G: U.S.]**

Clifford, Norman and Crawford, Vincent P. Short-term Contracting and Strategic Oil Reserves. *Rev. Econ. Stud.*, April 1987, *54*(2), pp. 311–23.

Clifford, Thomas E. and Mead, Walter J. The External Costs of Electric Power from Coal-Fired and Nuclear Power Plants. *Pachauri, R. K., ed.*, 1987, pp. 315–29. **[G: U.S.]**

Conrad, Klaus and Schröder, Michael. Die Effekte einer Rohölpreissenkung auf Produktionsauslastung und Wohlfahrt. Eine Anwendung der temporären Gleichgewichtsanalyse. (Effects of an Oil Price Decrease on Welfare and Capacity Utilization: An Applied Temporary Equilibrium Analysis. With English summary.) *Jahr. Nationalökon. Statist.*, July 1987, *203*(4), pp. 390–407. **[G: W. Germany]**

Cooper, Benjamin S. Energy Legislation in the 98th Congress. *Pachauri, R. K., ed.*, 1987, pp. 847–56. **[G: U.S.]**

Crampton, Colin. The Potential Development of Northern Canadian Physical and Biological Resources. *Lane, T., ed.*, 1987, pp. 27–44. **[G: Canada]**

Crandall, Robert W. and Keller, Theodore E. Public Policy and the Private Auto. *[Adelman, M. A.]*, 1987, pp. 137–60. **[G: U.S.]**

Crow, Michael M. Synthetic Fuel Technology Nondevelopment and the Hiatus Effect: The Implications of Inconsistent Public Policy. *Yanarella, E. J. and Green, W. C., eds.*, 1987, pp. 33–50. **[G: U.S.]**

Culy, John and Gale, Stephen. Regulatory Change in the Energy Sector. *Bollard, A. and Buckle, R., eds.*, 1987, pp. 153–80. **[G: New Zealand]**

Curran, P. J. and Hobson, T. A. Landsat MSS Imagery to Estimate Residential Heat-Load Density. *Environ. Planning A*, December 1987, *19*(12), pp. 1597–1610. **[G: U.K.]**

Dagsvik, John K., et al. Residential Demand for Natural Gas: A Dynamic Discrete-Continuous Choice Approach. *Golombek, R.; Hoel, M. and Vislie, J., eds.*, 1987, pp. 121–50. **[G: W. Europe]**

Danielsen, Albert L. Issues in the Indexation of Crude Oil and Natural Gas Prices. *Pachauri, R. K., ed.*, 1987, pp. 1049–61.

Dayo, Felix B. and Adegbulugbe, Anthony O. Oil Demand Elasticities in Nigeria. *Energy J.*, April 1987, *8*(2), pp. 31–41. **[G: Nigeria]**

De Saram, P. S. P. S.; Anandalingam, G. and Mubayi, V. Demand Elasticities for Petroleum Products in Sri Lanka. *Pachauri, R. K., ed.*, 1987, pp. 585–99. **[G: Sri Lanka]**

Deagle, Edwin A., Jr. The International Community and International Oil. *Rees, J. and Odell, P., eds.*, 1987, pp. 19–26. **[G: Global]**

Dennerlein, Rudolf K.-H. Residential Demand for Electrical Appliances and Electricity in the Federal Republic of Germany. *Energy J.*, January 1987, *8*(1), pp. 69–86. [G: W. Germany]

Dennerlein, Rudolf K.-H. Stromverbrauch der privaten Haushalte 1960 bis 1985 Ergebnisse eines makroökonomischen Ansatzes. (The Stock of Electrical Appliances and Electricity Consumption of Private Households from 1960–1985. With English summary.) *Ifo-Studien*, 1987, *33*(4), pp. 277–302. [G: W. Germany]

Dennerlein, Rudolf K.-H. Stromverbrauch in Ausgewählten Privaten Haushalten: Ergebnisse eines Mikroanalytischen Ansatzes. (The Effects of Income and Prices on the Residential Stock of Electrical Appliances and Electricity Consumption: Some Results from a Microanayltic Approach. With English summary.) *Ifo-Studien*, 1987, *33*(1), pp. 43–62. [G: W. Germany]

Desai, Meghnad. The Political Economy of World Oil. *Rees, J. and Odell, P., eds.*, 1987, pp. 130–36.

Desai, V. V. A Strategy for Rural Electrification. *Pachauri, R. K., ed.*, 1987, pp. 1143–53. [G: Asia]

Desprairies, Pierre. Oil Demand Prospects. *Stevens, P., ed.*, 1987, pp. 109–24. [G: U.S.; Global]

Diefenbacher, Hans and Johnson, Jeffrey. Energy Forecasting in West Germany: Confrontation and Convergence. *Baumgartner, T. and Midttun, A., eds.*, 1987, pp. 61–84. [G: W. Germany]

Dilnot, Andrew and Helm, Dieter. Energy Policy, Merit Goods and Social Security. *Fisc. Stud.*, August 1987, *8*(3), pp. 29–48. [G: U.K.]

Dobozi, Istvan. The 'Invisible' Source of Alternative Energy: A Comparison of Energy Conservation Performance in East and West. *Maillet, P.; Hague, D. and Rowland, C., eds.*, 1987, pp. 183–207. [G: OECD; CMEA]

Dobozi, Istvan. The Special Source of Alternative Energy: Comparing Energy Conservation Performance of the East and West. *Pasinetti, L. and Lloyd, P., eds.*, 1987, pp. 503–21. [G: OECD; CMEA]

Drollas, Leonidas P. Wabe's Cross-Section Analysis of the Demand for Gasoline—A Reply. *Energy Econ.*, October 1987, *9*(4), pp. 289–91. [G: U.S.; W. Europe]

Duncan, Cynthia M. and Tickamyer, Ann R. Public Ambivalence about Synthetic Fuels and Other New Energy Development. *Yanarella, E. J. and Green, W. C., eds.*, 1987, pp. 127–44. [G: U.S.]

Dunkerley, Joy and Hoch, Irving. Energy for Transport in Developing Countries. *Energy J.*, July 1987, *8*(3), pp. 57–72. [G: LDCs]

Eckbo, Paul Leo. Worldwide Petroleum Taxation: The Pressure for Revision. *[Adelman, M. A.]*, 1987, pp. 215–33. [G: Global]

Einhorn, Michael A. Appliance Depreciation and the Demand for Energy. *Energy J.*, January 1987, *8*(1), pp. 147–49.

Ellis, Joan T. State Regulation in a Deregulated Environment: A State-Level Regulator's Lament. *Natural Res. J.*, Fall 1987, *27*(4), pp. 799–803. [G: U.S.]

Enis, Charles R.; Stuart, William T. and Hourihan, John J. Local Revenue Policy in Less Developed Countries: The Case for Energy Consumption Taxation. *Jones, S. M., ed.*, 1987, pp. 85–107. [G: Philippines]

Erdösi, P. Special Input–Output Model for Analyzing the Effectiveness of the Energy Supply Systems. *Tchijov, I. and Tomaszewicz, L., eds.*, 1987, pp. 185–94. [G: Hungary]

Erikson, Edward W. World Oil Prices and the Emerging World Gas Market. *Pachauri, R. K., ed.*, 1987, pp. 673–81. [G: Global]

Erol, Umit and Yu, Eden S. H. On the Causal Relationship between Energy and Income for Industrialized Countries. *J. Energy Devel.*, Autumn 1987, *13*(1), pp. 113–22. [G: Europe; Canada; U.K.; Japan]

Faruqui, Ahmad. Utility Planning and Industrial Structural Change. *Faruqui, A. and Broehl, J., eds.*, 1987, pp. 9–31. [G: U.S.]

Fiebig, Denzil G.; Seale, James L., Jr. and Theil, Henri. The Demand for Energy: Evidence from a Cross-Country Demand System. *Energy Econ.*, July 1987, *9*(3), pp. 149–53. [G: Selected Countries]

Fišer, Miroslav and Rain, Vladimír. Changes in the Fuels and Energy Balance of Czechoslovakia and Its Expected Development up to the Year 1990. *Czech. Econ. Digest.*, January 1987, (2), pp. 34–48. [G: Czechoslovakia]

Flåm, Sjur D. and Moxnes, Erling. Exploration for Petroleum and the Inventory of Proven Reserves. *Energy Econ.*, July 1987, *9*(3), pp. 190–94. [G: Norway]

Flavin, Christopher. Electrifying the Third World. *Brown, L. R., et al.*, 1987, pp. 81–100. [G: LDCs]

Flavin, Christopher. Reassessing Nuclear Power. *Brown, L. R., et al.*, 1987, pp. 57–80. [G: Global]

Fobelli, Paolo. A Process for Decision-Making on Natural Gas: Fiscal Competitiveness in Reservoir Development. *Energy Econ.*, October 1987, *9*(4), pp. 265–73. [G: Global]

Fuller, J. David. The Impact of $(US)15 Oil Prices on Canadian Energy Markets. *Can. Public Policy*, March 1987, *13*(1), pp. 34–40. [G: Canada]

Garretty, Jeanette A. Financing the Energy Industry: An Economist's Perspective. *J. Energy Devel.*, Spring 1987, *12*(2), pp. 215–23. [G: U.S.]

Gartman, John A. The "Bypass" Issue: What Effect Does Local Utility Bypass Have on Energy Prices and the Economy? *Stewart, M. B., ed.*, 1987, pp. 59–61. [G: U.S.]

German, Michael I. How Far Will Natural Gas Deregulation Go? What Effect Will Deregulation Have on Prices and the "Gas Bubble"? *Stewart, M. B., ed.*, 1987, pp. 27–32. [G: U.S.]

Glass, Victor and Cahn, E. S. Energy Prices and Investment over the Business Cycle. *Energy Econ.*, October 1987, *9*(4), pp. 257–64.

Golabi, Kamal. Assessing the Uranium Resources of the United States. *Schultz, R. L., ed.*, 1987, pp. 197–235. [G: U.S.]

Golombek, Rolf and Hoel, Michael. The Relationship between the Price of Natural Gas and Crude Oil: Some Aspects of Efficient Contracts. *Golombek, R.; Hoel, M. and Vislie, J., eds.*, 1987, pp. 221–37.

Golombek, Rolf; Hoel, Michael and Vislie, Jon. Natural Gas Markets and Contracts: An Introduction. *Golombek, R.; Hoel, M. and Vislie, J., eds.*, 1987, pp. 1–6. [G: W. Europe]

Gopalakrishnan, Chennat. Energy–Nonenergy Input Substitution in Western U.S. Agriculture: Some Findings. *Energy J.*, January 1987, *8*(1), pp. 133–45. [G: U.S.]

Gordon, Richard L. Coal Policy in Perspective. *[Adelman, M. A.]*, 1987, pp. 59–82. [G: Global]

Gordon, Richard L.; Jacoby, Henry D. and Zimmerman, Martin B. Energy: Markets and Regulation: Essays in Honor of M. A. Adelman: Foreword. *[Adelman, M. A.]*, 1987, pp. xiii–xxi. [G: U.S.]

Gould, Brian W. The Impacts of the Market Pricing of Canadian Energy Resources on the Alberta Oil Industry. *Western J. Agr. Econ.*, July 1987, *12*(1), pp. 65–77. [G: Canada]

Gouni, Lucien. Reflections on Energy Planning in France. *Maillet, P.; Hague, D. and Rowland, C., eds.*, 1987, pp. 235–57. [G: France]

Govind, Har. Tax Approaches to Energy Management: India. *Bull. Int. Fiscal Doc.*, February 1987, *41*(2), pp. 80–88. [G: India]

Gowdy, John M. and Miller, Jack L. Technological and Demand Change in Energy Use: An Input–Output Analysis. *Environ. Planning A*, October 1987, *19*(10), pp. 1387–98. [G: U.S.]

Gowdy, John M.; Miller, Jack L. and Kherbachi, Hamid. Energy Use in U.S. Agriculture: Early Adjustment to the 1973–74 Price Shock. *Southern J. Agr. Econ.*, December 1987, *19*(2), pp. 33–41. [G: U.S.]

Grais, W. M. Coping with a Decline in World Energy Prices: Macroeconomic and Income Distribution Effects in Thailand. *J. Devel. Econ.*, August 1987, *26*(2), pp. 235–55. [G: Thailand]

Gray, Dale. Framework for Projecting Petroleum Product Demand Including the Effect of Energy Prices. *Pachauri, R. K., ed.*, 1987, pp. 1009–34.

Green, Rodney D. Regional Variations in U.S. Consumer Response to Price Changes in Home Heating Fuels: The Northeast and the South. *Appl. Econ.*, September 1987, *19*(9), pp. 1261–68. [G: U.S.]

Greenberger, Martin and Hogan, William W. Energy-Policy Modelling in the U.S.: Competing Societal Alternatives. *Baumgartner, T. and Midttun, A., eds.*, 1987, pp. 241–63. [G: U.S.]

Greenman, J. V. and Drollas, Leonidas P. The Price of Energy and Factor Substitution in the U.S. Economy. *Energy Econ.*, July 1987, *9*(3), pp. 159–66. [G: U.S.]

Grohnheit, Poul Erik and Laut, Peter. Nuclear Power and Coal-Fired CHP. *Energy Econ.*, April 1987, *9*(2), pp. 82–92. [G: Denmark]

Guadagni, Alieto A. Decisiones energéticas para el futuro. (With English summary.) *Desarrollo Econ.*, Jan.-Mar. 1987, *26*(104), pp. 609–30. [G: Argentina]

Guanglin, Zheng. The Rural Energy Situation in China Today and Its Future Development. *Maillet, P.; Hague, D. and Rowland, C., eds.*, 1987, pp. 386–96. [G: China]

Gupta, Pradeep C.; Faruqui, Ahmad and Wharton, Joseph B. Structural Change in U.S. Manufacturing and Future Electricity Demand. *Pachauri, R. K., ed.*, 1987, pp. 75–90. [G: U.S.]

Hagen, Ronald E. Oil Demand in Several Nations East of Suez. *Pachauri, R. K., ed.*, 1987, pp. 881–94. [G: Asia; Africa; Oceana]

Haldeman, Virginia A.; Peters, Jeanne M. and Tripple, Patricia A. Measuring a Consumer Energy Conservation Ethic: An Analysis of Components. *J. Cons. Aff.*, Summer 1987, *21*(1), pp. 70–85. [G: U.S.]

Hamlett, Patrick W. Technological Policy Making in Congress: The Creation of the U.S. Synthetic Fuels Corporation. *Yanarella, E. J. and Green, W. C., eds.*, 1987, pp. 53–69. [G: U.S.]

Havel, Stanislav. The Czechoslovak Nuclear Energy Industry and Its Prospects. *Czech. Econ. Digest.*, August 1987, (6), pp. 47–53.

Hawdon, David. Short and Long-run Crude Oil Price Expectations in 1986—Results of a Survey. *Stevens, P., ed.*, 1987, pp. 166–76. [G: Global]

Hayashi, Paul M. and Trapani, John M. The Impact of Energy Costs on Domestic Airline Passenger Travel. *J. Transp. Econ. Policy*, January 1987, *21*(1), pp. 73–86.

Hayes, Kathy J. and Porter-Hudak, Susan. Regional Welfare Loss Measures of the 1973 Oil Embargo: A Numerical Methods Approach. *Appl. Econ.*, October 1987, *19*(10), pp. 1317–27. [G: U.S.]

Helliwell, John F., et al. Supply Oriented Macroeconomics: The MACE Model of Canada. *Econ. Modelling*, July 1987, *4*(3), pp. 318–40. [G: Canada]

Helm, Dieter. Nuclear Power and the Privatisation of Electricity Generation. *Fisc. Stud.*, November 1987, *8*(4), pp. 69–73. [G: U.K.]

Henderson, David R. The IEA Oil-sharing Plan: Who Shares with Whom? *Energy J.*, October 1987, *8*(4), pp. 23–31. [G: OECD]

Herbert, John H. Demand for Natural Gas by Households at the State Level: Twenty Years of Effort. *Rev. Reg. Stud.*, Fall 1987, *17*(3), pp. 79–87. [G: U.S.]

Hertzmark, Donald I. Alternative Transport Fu-

els in an Era of Falling Energy Prices: The Case of Alcohol Fuel in the Philippines. *Pachauri, R. K., ed.*, 1987, pp. 467–79.
[G: Philippines]

Hickman, Bert G. Macroeconomic Impacts of Energy Shocks and Policy Responses: A Structural Comparison of Fourteen Models. *Hickman, B. G.; Huntington, H. G. and Sweeney, J. L., eds.*, 1987, pp. 125–98. [G: U.S.]

Hickman, Bert G. and Huntington, Hillard G. EMF 7 Study Design. *Hickman, B. G.; Huntington, H. G. and Sweeney, J. L., eds.*, 1987, pp. 237–67. [G: U.S.]

Hietarinta, Kai. Oljepriset och östhandelns utveckling. (The Price of Oil and the Development Trade with Eastern Europe. With English summary.) *Ekon. Samfundets Tidskr.*, 1987, *40*(1), pp. 7–10. [G: Finland; U.S.S.R.]

Hills, Peter. The Development of the Petroleum Industry in the People's Republic of China. *Hills, P. and Bowie, P.*, 1987, pp. 1–84.
[G: China]

Hirst, Eric. Energy and Economic Effects of Utility Financial Incentive Programs: The BPA Residential Weatherization Program. *Energy J.*, April 1987, *8*(2), pp. 97–110. [G: U.S.]

Hoel, Michael and Strøm, Steinar. Supply Security and Import Diversification of Natural Gas. *Golombek, R.; Hoel, M. and Vislie, J., eds.*, 1987, pp. 151–72. [G: W. Europe; Norway; U.S.S.R.]

Hoel, Michael and Vislie, Jon. Bargaining, Bilateral Monopoly and Exhaustible Resources. *Golombek, R.; Hoel, M. and Vislie, J., eds.*, 1987, pp. 253–65.

Hoffman, Kenneth C. and de Terra, Niels. Energy Planning and Long-term Strategies for Developing Countries. *Pachauri, R. K., ed.*, 1987, pp. 1063–85. [G: LDCs]

Hognestad, Gunnar. The Role of the Norwegian Government When Selling Natural Gas. *Golombek, R.; Hoel, M. and Vislie, J., eds.*, 1987, pp. 173–80. [G: Norway]

Hope, C. W. and Rowley, I. T. Towards Planning under Uncertainty. *Pachauri, R. K., ed.*, 1987, pp. 1087–1103.

Houthakker, Hendrik S. The Ups and Downs of Oil. *Cagan, P., ed.*, 1987, pp. 153–79.
[G: U.S.]

Howard-Merriam, Kathleen. The Impact of Rural Electrification on Egyptian Farm Women's Lives. *Pachauri, R. K., ed.*, 1987, pp. 271–90. [G: Egypt]

Howell, Craig; Burns, Roger and Clem, Andrew G. Sharp Drop in Energy Prices Holds Inflation in Check during 1986. *Mon. Lab. Rev.*, May 1987, *110*(5), pp. 3–9. [G: U.S.]

Hubbard, R. Glenn and Weiner, Robert J. Natural Gas Contracting in Practice: Evidence from the United States. *Golombek, R.; Hoel, M. and Vislie, J., eds.*, 1987, pp. 279–313. [G: U.S.]

Hüber, Gerhard. Lignite—A Domestic Resource in the GDR's Energy Policy: Macroeconomic Problems. *Maillet, P.; Hague, D. and Rowland, C., eds.*, 1987, pp. 275–82.
[G: E. Germany]

Humphrey, Bruce G. Alternative Economic Growth Scenarios and Implications for Utility Strategic Planning. *Faruqui, A. and Broehl, J., eds.*, 1987, pp. 33–47. [G: U.S.]

Hunt, Gary L. The Impact of Oil Price Fluctuations on the Economies of Energy Producing States. *Rev. Reg. Stud.*, Fall 1987, *17*(3), pp. 60–76. [G: U.S.]

Huntington, Hillard G. and Eschbach, Joseph E. Macroeconomic Models and Energy Policy Issues. *Hickman, B. G.; Huntington, H. G. and Sweeney, J. L., eds.*, 1987, pp. 199–236.
[G: U.S.]

Huntington, Hillard G. and Myers, John G. Sectoral Shift and Industrial Energy Demand: What Have We Learned? *Faruqui, A. and Broehl, J., eds.*, 1987, pp. 353–88. [G: U.S.]

Hyman, Eric L. The Strategy of Production and Distribution of Improved Charcoal Stoves in Kenya. *World Devel.*, March 1987, *15*(3), pp. 375–86. [G: Kenya]

Ikuta, Toyoaki. Policy Choices in Developed Countries: Two Japanese Views (B). *Maillet, P.; Hague, D. and Rowland, C., eds.*, 1987, pp. 287–98. [G: Japan]

Isserman, Andrew M. and Merrifield, John D. Quasi-experimental Control Group Methods for Regional Analysis: An Application to an Energy Boomtown and Growth Pole Theory. *Econ. Geogr.*, January 1987, *63*(1), pp. 3–19.
[G: U.S.]

Itteilag, Richard L. An Analysis of Actual and Forecasted Conservation in the Residential Gas Space Heating Market. *Pachauri, R. K., ed.*, 1987, pp. 737–50. [G: U.S.]

Itteilag, Richard L. and Swanson, Christina A. A Life-Cycle Study of Commercial Cogeneration/Cooling: A State-of-the-Art of Gas Technology. *Crew, M. A., ed.*, 1987, pp. 155–70.
[G: U.S.]

Jacobsen, Bjørn R. Some Experiences from Bargaining over Natural Gas. *Golombek, R.; Hoel, M. and Vislie, J., eds.*, 1987, pp. 181–92.
[G: Norway]

James, Zan. Intrastate Pipelines in a Changing Marketplace. *Natural Res. J.*, Fall 1987, *27*(4), pp. 811–14. [G: U.S.]

Java, R. L. Intergrating Biomass Energy Programmes. *Pachauri, R. K., ed.*, 1987, pp. 413–19. [G: India]

Jenkins-Smith, Hank C. An Industry in Turmoil: The Remaking of the Natural Gas Industry. *Natural Res. J.*, Fall 1987, *27*(4), pp. 773–80.
[G: U.S.]

Jenkins-Smith, Hank C. Natural Gas Regulation in the Western U.S.: Perspectives on Regulation in the Next Decade: Editor's Introduction. *Natural Res. J.*, Fall 1987, *27*(4), pp. 771–72.
[G: U.S.]

Jones, David. Energy Demand Prospects in the IEA Countries. *Stevens, P., ed.*, 1987, pp. 6–27. [G: OECD]

Joskow, Paul L. Productivity Growth and Technical Change in the Generation of Electricity. *Energy J.*, January 1987, *8*(1), pp. 17–38.
[G: U.S.]

Joskow, Paul L. and Schmalensee, Richard. The Performance of Coal-Burning Electric Generating Units in the United States: 1960–1980. *J. Appl. Econometrics*, April 1987, *2*(2), pp. 85–109. [G: U.S.]

Kadekodi, Gopal. A Welfare Approach to Energy Pricing: A Case Study from India. *Pachauri, R. K., ed.*, 1987, pp. 1035–47.

Kahn, Edward and Goldman, Charles A. Impact of Tax Reform on Renewable Energy and Cogeneration Projects. *Energy Econ.*, October 1987, *9*(4), pp. 215–26. [G: U.S.]

Karl, Kurt. Long-term U.S. Economic Outlook. *Faruqui, A. and Broehl, J., eds.*, 1987, pp. 127–37. [G: U.S.]

Katzman, Martin T. Multiattribute Utility Elicitation Techniques and Public Policy: A Meta-analysis of Empirical Applications. *Schultz, R. L., ed.*, 1987, pp. 237–303. [G: U.S.]

Kaufman, Gordon M. Oil and Gas Resource and Supply Assessment. *[Adelman, M. A.]*, 1987, pp. 259–80.

Kaushik, S. K. The Changing Nature of International Financing. *Pachauri, R. K., ed.*, 1987, pp. 821–34. [G: Global]

Keepin, Bill and Wynne, Brian. The Roles of Models—What Can We Expect from Science? A Study of the IIASA World Energy Model. *Baumgartner, T. and Midttun, A., eds.*, 1987, pp. 33–57.

Kelly, Suedeen G. Regulatory Reform of the U.S. Natural Gas Industry: A Summing Up. *Natural Res. J.*, Fall 1987, *27*(4), pp. 841–63. [G: U.S.]

Keng, C. W. Kenneth. Forecasting Canadian Nuclear Power Station Construction Costs. *Pachauri, R. K., ed.*, 1987, pp. 353–91. [G: Canada]

Kessler, Richard J. Multilateral Attempts at Managing Energy Resources: The Responses from the North and the South. *Pachauri, R. K., ed.*, 1987, pp. 857–80.

Khazzoom, J. Daniel. Energy Saving Resulting from the Adoption of More Efficient Appliances. *Energy J.*, October 1987, *8*(4), pp. 85–89.

Khazzoom, J. Daniel. The Demand for Insulation—A Study in the Household Demand for Conservation. *Energy J.*, July 1987, *8*(3), pp. 73–92. [G: U.S.]

Kher, Lov Kumar; Sioshansi, Fereidoon P. and Sorooshian, Soroosh. Energy Demand Modeling with Noisy Input–Output Variables. *Energy J.*, October 1987, *8*(4), pp. 33–50. [G: U.S.]

Kim, Yoon Hyung and Smith, Kirk R. Electric Power in Economic Development: The Northeast Asian Experience. *Pachauri, R. K., ed.*, 1987, pp. 621–42. [G: Japan; Taiwan; S. Korea]

Kirchgässner, Gebhard. Zur Anpassung der schweizerischen Mineralölpreise an die internationale Entwicklung. Empirische Tests einiger Hypothesen. (On the Adjustment of Swiss Oil Prices to the International Development. With English summary.) *Schweiz. Z. Volks-*

wirtsch. Statist., June 1987, *123*(2), pp. 123–46. [G: Switzerland]

Kleinpeter, M. French Energy Policy Planning: A New Approach. *Pachauri, R. K., ed.*, 1987, pp. 895–910. [G: France]

Kozloff, Keith. Overcoming Barriers to Improved Energy Efficiency: U.S. Experiences and Relevance to Developing Countries. *Pachauri, R. K., ed.*, 1987, pp. 967–93. [G: U.S.; LDCs]

Krapels, Edward N. Implementing Efficient Petroleum Product Pricing Programs in Developing Countries. *Energy J.*, January 1987, *8*(1), pp. 39–52. [G: LDCs]

Lau, Knud Lindholm. Electricity Forecasting in Denmark: Conflicts between Ministries and Utilities. *Baumgartner, T. and Midttun, A., eds.*, 1987, pp. 155–79. [G: Denmark]

Lee, Lung-Fei and Pitt, Mark M. Microeconometric Models of Rationing, Imperfect Markets, and Non-negativity Constraints. *J. Econometrics*, Sept./Oct. 1987, *36*(1/2), pp. 89–110. [G: Indonesia]

Leistritz, F. Larry and Murdock, Steve H. Socioeconomic Impacts of Large-Scale Development Projects in the Western United States: Implications for Synthetic Fuels Commercialization. *Yanarella, E. J. and Green, W. C., eds.*, 1987, pp. 145–70. [G: U.S.]

Lesbirel, S. Hayden. The Political Economy of Project Delay. *Policy Sci.*, 1987, *20*(2), pp. 153–71. [G: Japan]

Levin, Nissan and Zahavi, Jacob. Electricity Equilibrium Models with Stochastic Demands. *Energy Econ.*, October 1987, *9*(4), pp. 227–40.

Levinson, Marc. Alcohol Fuels Revisited: The Costs and Benefits of Energy Independence in Brazil. *J. Devel. Areas*, April 1987, *21*(3), pp. 243–57. [G: Brazil]

Lichtenberg, Frank R. Changing Market Opportunities and the Structure of R&D Investment: The Case of Energy. *Energy Econ.*, July 1987, *9*(3), pp. 154–58. [G: U.S.]

Lichtman, Rob. Toward the Diffusion of Rural Energy Technologies: Some Lessons from the Indian Biogas Program. *World Devel.*, March 1987, *15*(3), pp. 347–74. [G: India]

Liesen, Klaus. The Response of the Energy Industry to Structural Transformation. *Pohl, H. and Rudolph, B., eds.*, 1987, pp. 1–11. [G: W. Germany]

Lipton, Milton. Financial and Economic Implications of the Energy Markets. *Kaushik, S. K., ed.*, 1987, pp. 23–29.

Liu, Jing-Tong. China's Energy and Economic Development. *Dutta, M., ed. (II)*, 1987, pp. 53–63. [G: China]

Lu, Yingzhong. The Prospects of Rural Energy in the People's Republic of China (PRS). *Pachauri, R. K., ed.*, 1987, pp. 227–53. [G: China]

de Lucia, Russell J. and Poole, Alan D. Biomass Fuels for Industry: Implications for Fuel Cycle Economics. *Pachauri, R. K., ed.*, 1987, pp. 421–47.

Lunde, Tormod and Midttun, Atle. Electricity

Forecasting in Norway: Administrative Centralism. *Baumgartner, T. and Midttun, A., eds.*, 1987, pp. 137–54. **[G: Norway]**

Magnus, Jan R. and Woodland, Alan D. Inter-fuel Substitution in Dutch Manufacturing. *Appl. Econ.*, December 1987, *19*(12), pp. 1639–64. **[G: Netherlands]**

Mahajan, V. S. Economic Development in Third World Countries: The Role of Existing Sources of Energy and Alternative Choices. *Pasinetti, L. and Lloyd, P., eds.*, 1987, pp. 537–51. **[G: LDCs]**

Mahajan, V. S. Planning for Alternative Energy Sources—Experience of Developing Economy of India and Possible Lessons. *Maillet, P.; Hague, D. and Rowland, C., eds.*, 1987, pp. 360–72. **[G: India]**

Maillet, Pierre. Economic Aspects of Alternative Energy Sources: Discussion and Conclusions. *Pasinetti, L. and Lloyd, P., eds.*, 1987, pp. 553–57.

Maillet, Pierre. Economic Aspects of Alternative Energy Sources: An Introduction. *Pasinetti, L. and Lloyd, P., eds.*, 1987, pp. 487–89.

Maillet, Pierre. Energy Options: Interface Connections between the Energy Sphere and the Rest of the Economy. *Maillet, P.; Hague, D. and Rowland, C., eds.*, 1987, pp. 19–44.

Maillet, Pierre. Main Economic Aspects of Energy Choices and Policies. *Pasinetti, L. and Lloyd, P., eds.*, 1987, pp. 491–501.

Maillet, Pierre. The Economics of Choice between Energy Sources: Presentation of the Conference. *Maillet, P.; Hague, D. and Rowland, C., eds.*, 1987, pp. 1–16.

Makarov, A. A. Extreme Strategies for the Long-term Development of the Energy Industry. *Matekon*, Fall 1987, *24*(1), pp. 21–42. **[G: U.S.S.R.]**

Mäler, Karl-Göran. Energy Options and Environmental Considerations: The Case of Sweden. *Maillet, P.; Hague, D. and Rowland, C., eds.*, 1987, pp. 407–33. **[G: Sweden]**

Malko, J. Robert and Edgar, George R. Energy Utility Diversification and Small Business: A Wisconsin Perspective. *J. Energy Devel.*, Autumn 1987, *13*(1), pp. 101–11. **[G: U.S.]**

de Man, Reinier. The Dutch Energy Scenario Game: Corporatist Search for Consensus. *Baumgartner, T. and Midttun, A., eds.*, 1987, pp. 85–109. **[G: Netherlands]**

de Man, Reinier. United Kingdom Energy Policy and Forecasting: Technocratic Conflict Resolution. *Baumgartner, T. and Midttun, A., eds.*, 1987, pp. 110–34. **[G: U.K.]**

March, Frederic and Shrivastava, Vinod. Rational Policies for Inducement of Energy Conservation in Developing Countries. *Pachauri, R. K., ed.*, 1987, pp. 995–1007. **[G: LDCs]**

Marino, Anthony M. and Sicilian, Joseph. Direct Investment in Conservation Measures by a Public Utility. *Energy J.*, April 1987, *8*(2), pp. 137–46.

Marks, Stephen V. International Crude-Oil Resales: Theory and Recent History. *J. Energy Devel.*, Autumn 1987, *13*(1), pp. 87–100. **[G: OPEC]**

Mathiesen, Lars; Roland, Kjell and Thonstad, Knut. The European Natural Gas Market: Degrees of Market Power on the Selling Side. *Golombek, R.; Hoel, M. and Vislie, J., eds.*, 1987, pp. 27–58. **[G: W. Europe; Algeria; U.S.S.R.]**

McCants, Blaine E. Projecting Soviet Energy Requirements Using a Vintage Capital Model. *J. Compar. Econ.*, December 1987, *11*(4), pp. 572–83. **[G: U.S.S.R.]**

Meir, Peter and Gadgil, Ashok. Use of Micro-computers in Energy Economics and Planning in LDCs. *Pachauri, R. K., ed.*, 1987, pp. 1237–47. **[G: LDCs]**

Melese, Francois and Kaserman, David L. Superconductors and the Future of Electric Utilities. *J. Policy Anal. Manage.*, Fall 1987, *7*(1), pp. 135–40.

Merriam, John G. Egyptian Agricultural Energy Incentives. *Pachauri, R. K., ed.*, 1987, pp. 255–70. **[G: Egypt]**

Mesquita e Cunha, António Gabriel. On the Problematic Use of Cost–Benefit Analysis to Evaluate Alternative Nuclear Energy Programs. *Economia (Portugal)*, October 1987, *11*(3), pp. 327–61. **[G: U.S.]**

Metwally, M. M. and Arab, A. T. Price Elasticity of Demand for Oil and the Terms of Trade of the OPEC Countries. *Energy J.*, January 1987, *8*(1), pp. 53–67. **[G: OPEC]**

Mikdashi, Z. Oil Funding and International Financial Markets. *Rees, J. and Odell, P., eds.*, 1987, pp. 88–106. **[G: Global]**

Mishra, R. N. Technology Transfer in an Indian Underground Coal-Mine—A Case Study. *Pachauri, R. K., ed.*, 1987, pp. 811–19. **[G: India]**

Mitchell, John C. A State Government's Experience with the Synthetic Fuels Movement: The Case of Kentucky. *Yanarella, E. J. and Green, W. C., eds.*, 1987, pp. 89–98. **[G: U.S.]**

Mongula, Benedict S. and Ng'andwe, Chiselebwe. Limits to Development in Southern Africa: Energy, Transport and Communications in SADCC Countries. *Amin, S.; Chitala, D. and Mandaza, I., eds.*, 1987, pp. 85–108. **[G: Southern Africa]**

Moran, Theodore H. Managing an Oligopoly of Would-Be Sovereigns: The Dynamics of Joint Control and Self-Control in the International Oil Industry Past, Present, and Future. *Int. Organ.*, Autumn 1987, *41*(4), pp. 575–607. **[G: Global]**

Mork, Knut Anton. Some General-Equilibrium Considerations for the Analysis of Oil Import Restrictions. *Energy J.*, October 1987, *8*(4), pp. 79–84.

Morris, A. J. A Dynamic Framework for Petroleum Legislation in Developing Countries: Interaction between Economic and Legal Issues. *Pachauri, R. K., ed.*, 1987, pp. 835–46. **[G: LDCs]**

da Motta, Ronaldo Serôa. The Social Viability of Ethanol Production in Brazil. *Energy Econ.*,

July 1987, *9*(3), pp. 176–82.   [G: Brazil]

da Motta, Ronaldo Serôa. Um estudo de custo–benefício do PROÁLCOOL. (With English summary.) *Pesquisa Planejamento Econ.*, April 1987, *17*(1), pp. 65–92.   [G: Brazil]

Moxnes, Erling. The Dynamics of Interfuel Substitution in the OECD-Europe Industrial Sector. *Golombek, R.; Hoel, M. and Vislie, J.,* eds., 1987, pp. 95–120.   [G: W. Europe]

Moxnes, Erling. Uncertainty in Future Oil Price Predictions. *Pachauri, R. K., ed.*, 1987, pp. 1105–21.

Mubayi, A. Economics of Transporting Solids by Pipe-line—Comparison of a Coal Slurry Pipeline and Movement by Rail. *Pachauri, R. K., ed.*, 1987, pp. 919–34.

Munasinghe, Mohan. Developing Country Energy Issues and Prospects. *Pachauri, R. K., ed.*, 1987, pp. 775–91.   [G: LDCs]

Muraoka, Dennis D. and Mead, Walter J. Economic Issues in Federal Geothermal Leasing Procedures. *Natural Res. J.*, Summer 1987, *27*(3), pp. 675–92.   [G: U.S.]

Naeve, Michael. The Future of the Natural Gas Market: Regulation and Prices. *Natural Res. J.*, Fall 1987, *27*(4), pp. 781–88.   [G: U.S.]

Nagle, George. How Do Energy Price Changes Affect the Relative Attractiveness of Mid-Atlantic States to New Business? *Stewart, M. B., ed.*, 1987, pp. 55–58.   [G: U.S.]

Newbery, David M. The Privatisation of British Gas and Possible Consequences for the European Gas Market. *Golombek, R.; Hoel, M. and Vislie, J., eds.*, 1987, pp. 59–93.   [G: U.K.]

Newcomb, Richard T. Substitution, Technical Change, and World Coal Demands. *Pachauri, R. K., ed.*, 1987, pp. 935–51.   [G: Global]

Newcombe, Ken. An Economic Justification for Rural Afforestation: The Case of Ethiopia. *Ann. Reg. Sci.*, November 1987, *21*(3), pp. 80–99.   [G: Ethiopia]

Newton, Walter L. Refining Developments in the Non-OECD Area. *Pachauri, R. K., ed.*, 1987, pp. 291–313.   [G: Global]

Nguyen, Hong V. Energy Elasticities under Divisia and Btu Aggregation. *Energy Econ.*, October 1987, *9*(4), pp. 210–14.   [G: U.S.]

Nystad, Arild N. Petroleum Taxes and Resource Management. *Pachauri, R. K., ed.*, 1987, pp. 19–34.

Odell, Peter R. Gas Demand Prospects. *Stevens, P., ed.*, 1987, pp. 71–81.   [G: Global]

Odell, Peter R. The Prospect for Oil Prices and the Energy Market. *Lloyds Bank Rev.*, July 1987, (165), pp. 1–14.   [G: Global]

Ohta, Makoto. Gasoline Cost and Hedonic Price Indexes of U.S. Used Cars for 1970–1983. *J. Bus. Econ. Statist.*, October 1987, *5*(4), pp. 521–28.   [G: U.S.]

Ortmann, G. F. and Nieuwoudt, W. L. An Evaluation of a Two-Tier Price Scheme and Possible Ethanol Production in the South African Sugar Industry. *S. Afr. J. Econ.*, June 1987, *55*(2), pp. 121–35.   [G: S. Africa]

Osaki, Kazumasa. End of an Era: OPEC's Temporary Retreat. *Finn, R. B., ed.*, 1987, pp. 119–34.   [G: OPEC; U.S.; Japan]

Osten, James A. The Impact of $(US)15 Oil Prices on Canadian Energy Markets. *Can. Public Policy*, March 1987, *13*(1), pp. 26–33.   [G: Canada]

Overdahl, James A. The Use of Crude Oil Futures by the Governments of Oil-Producing States. *J. Futures Markets*, December 1987, *7*(6), pp. 603–17.   [G: U.S.]

Palmedo, Philip F. Energy Applications of Microcomputers in Developing Countries. *Ruth, S. R. and Mann, C. K., eds.*, 1987, pp. 49–65.   [G: LDCs]

Pant, K. C. Global Energy Interactions: Inaugural Address. *Pachauri, R. K., ed.*, 1987, pp. 1–7.

Paruelo, Jose M., et al. Energy Use and Economic Output for Argentina. *Pillet, G. and Murota, T., eds.*, 1987, pp. 169–84.   [G: Argentina]

Paté-Cornell, M. E. Risk Analysis and Relevance of Uncertainties in Nuclear Safety Decisions. *Bailey, E. E., ed.*, 1987, pp. 227–53.   [G: U.S.]

Pavlátová, Dana. Prospects of Nuclear Energy in the CMEA Countries. *Czech. Econ. Digest.*, December 1987, (8), pp. 24–28.   [G: CMEA]

Pearson, Peter J. G. Energy Demand in the Third World. *Stevens, P., ed.*, 1987, pp. 28–47.   [G: LDCs]

Pearson, Peter J. G. and Stevens, P. J. Integrated Energy Policies in Less Developed Countries: The Relations between Traditional and Commercial Energy Sources. *Pachauri, R. K., ed.*, 1987, pp. 1249–72.   [G: LDCs]

Penrose, Edith. The Structure of the International Oil Industry: Multinationals, Governments and OPEC. *Rees, J. and Odell, P., eds.*, 1987, pp. 9–18.   [G: Global]

Pérez-López, Jorge F. Cuban Oil Reexports: Significance and Prospects. *Energy J.*, January 1987, *8*(1), pp. 1–16.   [G: Cuba]

Perryman, M. Ray. The Impact of Oil Price Fluctuations on the Economies of Energy Producing States: Comment. *Rev. Reg. Stud.*, Fall 1987, *17*(3), pp. 77–78.   [G: U.S.]

Peterson, William. The Cambridge Multisectoral Dynamic Model of the British Economy: The Demand for Energy. *Barker, T. and Peterson, W., eds.*, 1987, pp. 275–91.   [G: U.K.]

Philip, G. Government, Interests and World Oil. *Rees, J. and Odell, P., eds.*, 1987, pp. 136–42.

Pillet, Gonzague. Exergy, Emergy, and Entropy. *Pillet, G. and Murota, T., eds.*, 1987, pp. 277–302.

Pillet, Gonzague. Externalities in Environmental Macroeconomics. *Pillet, G. and Murota, T., eds.*, 1987, pp. 129–53.

Pinto, Frank J. P. The Economics of, and Potential for, Energy Conservation and Substitution. *Pachauri, R. K., ed.*, 1987, pp. 703–36.

Pintz, Peter and Havinga, Ivo C. An Energy Input–Output Table of Pakistan for 1979–80 and Some Applications. *Pakistan Devel. Rev.*, Winter 1987, *26*(4), pp. 593–606.   [G: Pakistan]

Plourde, André. On the Role and Status of Canadian Natural Gas Carriers under Deregulation. *J. Energy Devel.*, Autumn 1987, *13*(1), pp. 1–25. **[G: Canada]**

Plourde, André. The Impact of $(US)15 Oil on the Canadian Economy: Evidence from the MACE Model. *Can. Public Policy*, March 1987, *13*(1), pp. 19–25. **[G: Canada]**

Plummer, James L. Energy and Environmental Technology Transfer from the United States to India. *Pachauri, R. K., ed.*, 1987, pp. 1193–1200. **[G: U.S.; India]**

Polach, Jay G. The Industry Structure and Pricing Policies in Oil International Transactions. *Pachauri, R. K., ed.*, 1987, pp. 35–57. **[G: Global]**

Pollio, Gerald. Financing Energy Development: Trends and Prospects. *J. Energy Devel.*, Spring 1987, *12*(2), pp. 175–84. **[G: LDCs]**

Posner, Michael V. Governments in Energy Markets. *Pasinetti, L. and Lloyd, P., eds.*, 1987, pp. 523–35. **[G: OECD]**

Posner, Michael V. Problems Concerning the Implementation of Energy Policies. *Maillet, P.; Hague, D. and Rowland, C., eds.*, 1987, pp. 76–92.

Pouris, A. On the Economics of Nuclear and Coal-Fired Electricity Generation. *S. Afr. J. Econ.*, December 1987, *55*(4), pp. 407–24. **[G: S. Africa]**

Pouris, A. The Price Elasticity of Electricity Demand in South Africa. *Appl. Econ.*, September 1987, *19*(9), pp. 1269–77. **[G: S. Africa]**

Prasad, Kamta and Ramesh, S. Energy Development Choices for India. *Maillet, P.; Hague, D. and Rowland, C., eds.*, 1987, pp. 347–59. **[G: India]**

Puiseux, Louis. The Ups and Downs of Electricity Forecasting in France: Technocratic Elitism. *Baumgartner, T. and Midttun, A., eds.*, 1987, pp. 180–207. **[G: France]**

Qurashi, M. M. An Energy Input–Output Table of Pakistan for 1979–80 and Some Applications: Comments. *Pakistan Devel. Rev.*, Winter 1987, *26*(4), pp. 607–08. **[G: Pakistan]**

Rahman, Sultan Hafeez. A Macro-econometric Energy Policy Model for Oil Importing Developing Countries. *Pachauri, R. K., ed.*, 1987, pp. 1201–11. **[G: Selected LDCs]**

Rampa, Lorenzo. On Endogenous Oil Market Fluctuations. *Rivista Int. Sci. Econ. Com.*, August 1987, *34*(8), pp. 761–69.

Ramsay, William. Bio-energy and Development Issues. *Pachauri, R. K., ed.*, 1987, pp. 449–66.

Ramsay, William and Lipman-Blumen, Jean. Institutional Issues in Biomass Energy Policy: The No-Man's Land between Agricultural, Forestry, and Energy Policies in Developing Nations. *Pachauri, R. K., ed.*, 1987, pp. 205–15. **[G: LDCs]**

Randol, William L. World Oil Dynamics: The Political Dimension. *Stewart, M. B., ed.*, 1987, pp. 21–25. **[G: OPEC; Saudi Arabia]**

Rees, Judith. Spatial Interrelationships, Distributions and Geopolitics. *Rees, J. and Odell, P.,*

eds., 1987, pp. 158–62.

Rees, Judith and Odell, Peter R. International Oil Issues and Perspectives. *Rees, J. and Odell, P., eds.*, 1987, pp. 1–8. **[G: Global]**

Reid, R. G. A View of European Oil and Gas Issues. *Rees, J. and Odell, P., eds.*, 1987, pp. 76–87. **[G: Europe]**

Reister, David B. Validating Allocation Functions in Energy Models: A Comment. *Energy J.*, January 1987, *8*(1), pp. 151–52.

Reitler, W.; Rudolph, M. and Schaefer, H. Analysis of the Factors Influencing Energy Consumption in Industry: A Revised Method. *Energy Econ.*, July 1987, *9*(3), pp. 145–48.

Revesz, T. Input–Output Model for Analyzing National Economics of Varying Energy Intensities. *Tchijov, I. and Tomaszewicz, L., eds.*, 1987, pp. 163–67. **[G: Hungary]**

Rhys, J. M. W. Electricity Trends and Outlook. *Stevens, P., ed.*, 1987, pp. 155–65. **[G: Global]**

Riaz, T. Energy and Economic Growth: A Case Study of Pakistan. *Energy Econ.*, July 1987, *9*(3), pp. 195–204. **[G: Pakistan]**

Roberds, William and Todd, Richard M. Forecasting and Modeling the U.S. Economy in 1986–88. *Fed. Res. Bank Minn. Rev.*, Winter 1987, *11*(1), pp. 7–20. **[G: U.S.]**

Robinson, Colin. World Coal Demand: Bridging the Energy Future? *Stevens, P., ed.*, 1987, pp. 125–54. **[G: Global]**

Robinson, John B. and Hooker, Clifford A. Future Imperfect: Energy Policy and Modelling in Canada Institutional Mandates and Constitutional Conflict. *Baumgartner, T. and Midttun, A., eds.*, 1987, pp. 211–40. **[G: Canada]**

Rogers, J. S. Some Long-term Impacts of $(US)15 Oil on Energy Policy and on Engineering R&D Policy: Results from the EMCAN Model. *Can. Public Policy*, March 1987, *13*(1), pp. 41–48. **[G: Canada]**

Rose, Adam and Soelistijo, Ukar. The Potential of Coal in the Development of Oil-Rich LDCs: The Case of Indonesia. *Pachauri, R. K., ed.*, 1987, pp. 793–809. **[G: Indonesia]**

Ross, T. D. The Status and Strategies of the International Oil Corporations. *Rees, J. and Odell, P., eds.*, 1987, pp. 67–75. **[G: Global]**

Rowse, John. The Economic Impact of Prolonged Low Oil Prices. *Can. Public Policy*, March 1987, *13*(1), pp. 49–55. **[G: Canada]**

Ruderman, Henry; Levine, Mark D. and McMahon, James E. The Behavior of the Market for Energy Efficiency in Residential Appliances Including Heating and Cooling Equipment. *Energy J.*, January 1987, *8*(1), pp. 101–24. **[G: U.S.]**

Rudolph, Joseph R., Jr. Energy Policy in the United States and Britain. *Waltman, J. L. and Studlar, D. T., eds.*, 1987, pp. 120–49. **[G: U.K.; U.S.]**

Rudolph, Joseph R., Jr. Synthetic Fuels Abroad: Energy Development in High Energy Dependency Areas. *Yanarella, E. J. and Green, W. C., eds.*, 1987, pp. 173–92. **[G: U.S.; W. Europe]**

Sadli, Mahammad. Alternative Energy Options in Indonesia. *Maillet, P.; Hague, D. and Rowland, C., eds.,* 1987, pp. 373–85.
[G: Indonesia]

Saicheua, Supavud. Input Substitution in Thailand's Manufacturing Sector: Implications for Energy Policy. *Energy Econ.,* January 1987, 9(1), pp. 55–63. [G: Thailand]

Salinas, Jose A. and Weyant, John P. A Comparison of Macroeconomic Model Structures. *Hickman, B. G.; Huntington, H. G. and Sweeney, J. L., eds.,* 1987, pp. 269–331. [G: U.S.]

Samii, Massood V. The Organization of the Petroleum Exporting Countries and the Oil Market: Different Views. *J. Energy Devel.,* Spring 1987, 12(2), pp. 159–73. [G: OPEC]

Sassin, Wolfgang. Energy Options: Interface Connections between the Energy Sphere and the Rest of the Economy: Comment. *Maillet, P.; Hague, D. and Rowland, C., eds.,* 1987, pp. 45–50.

Sassin, Wolfgang. Fossil Energy and Its Alternatives: A Problem beyond Costs and Prices. *Maillet, P.; Hague, D. and Rowland, C., eds.,* 1987, pp. 51–75.

Sathaye, J., et al. Energy Demand and Energy Efficiency in the Developing Countries. *Pachauri, R. K., ed.,* 1987, pp. 561–71.
[G: LDCs]

Sav, G. Thomas. Tax Incentives for Innovative Energy Sources: Extensions of E–K Complementarity. *Public Finance Quart.,* October 1987, 15(4), pp. 417–27. [G: U.S.]

Schneider, Hans-Karl and Schulz, Walter. The Implementation of Energy Policy Goals. *Maillet, P.; Hague, D. and Rowland, C., eds.,* 1987, pp. 93–111.

Schramm, Gunter. Managing Urban/Industrial Wood Fuel Supply and Demand in Africa. *Ann. Reg. Sci.,* November 1987, 21(3), pp. 60–79. [G: Africa]

Schuler, G. Henry M. The International Oil Negotiations. *Zartman, I. W., ed. (I),* 1987, pp. 124–207. [G: OPEC]

Scienceman, David M. Energy and Emergy. *Pillet, G. and Murota, T., eds.,* 1987, pp. 257–76.

Searl, Milton F. The Relationship of Electricity to Aggregate Economic Activity in Industrial Economies—Some Empirical Observations. *Pachauri, R. K., ed.,* 1987, pp. 601–20.
[G: MDCs]

Sen Gupta, D. P. and de Gromard, Christian. Rural Electrification: Alternatives to Grid Extension. *Pachauri, R. K., ed.,* 1987, pp. 1123–42. [G: India]

Sewell, W. R. Derrick. The Politics of Hydromegaprojects: Damming with Faint Praise in Australia, New Zealand, and British Columbia. *Natural Res. J.,* Summer 1987, 27(3), pp. 497–532. [G: Australia; New Zealand; Canada]

Shapiro, David L. Public Power Policy in the Pacific Northwest: The Legal Fall Out. *Quart. Rev. Econ. Bus.,* Winter 1987, 27(4), pp. 18–37. [G: U.S.]

Shelest, V. A. Alternative Sources of Energy in

the National Economy of the Soviet Union. *Maillet, P.; Hague, D. and Rowland, C., eds.,* 1987, pp. 258–74. [G: U.S.S.R.]

Siddayao, Corazon Morales. Capital Investment Requirements for Oil and Gas Development: Constraints in Developing Countries. *Pachauri, R. K., ed.,* 1987, pp. 751–73.

Siddayao, Corazon Morales, et al. Estimates of Energy and Non-energy Elasticities in Selected Asian Manufacturing Sectors: Policy Implications. *Energy Econ.,* April 1987, 9(2), pp. 115–28. [G: Bangladesh; Philippines; Thailand]

Skea, Jim. A Simulation Model of Interfuel Substitution in the Industrial Boiler Market. *Energy Econ.,* January 1987, 9(1), pp. 17–30.
[G: U.K.]

Slesser, Malcolm and Hounam, Ian. Thermodynamic Implications of Energy Scarcity. *Pachauri, R. K., ed.,* 1987, pp. 1213–27.

Smith, V. Kerry and Hill, Lawrence J. On Straw Men, Free Parameters, and Validating Allocation Functions: A Reply [Validating Allocation Functions in Energy Models: An Experimental Methodology]. *Energy J.,* January 1987, 8(1), pp. 153–56.

Soares, Maria Isabel R. T. L'utilisation de l'énergie dans un contexte interindustriel: analyse du profil enérgétique de l'inudstrie portugaise des textiles et de l'habillement. (With English summary.) *Economia (Portugal),* May 1987, 11(2), pp. 157–70. [G: Portugal]

Solo, Robert A. The Great Plains Gasification Project: The Problem of Juridical/Administrative Incompatibility. *Energy J.,* April 1987, 8(2), pp. 153–68. [G: U.S.]

Solomon, Barry D. and Georgianna, Thomas D. Optimal Subsidies to New Energy Sources. *Energy Econ.,* July 1987, 9(3), pp. 183–89.

Solow, John L. The Capital–Energy Complementarity Debate Revisited. *Amer. Econ. Rev.,* September 1987, 77(4), pp. 605–14.

Srinivasan, V. K. Development and Transfer of Technology, Oil Exploration, and Production—The Third-World Needs. *Pachauri, R. K., ed.,* 1987, pp. 1167–86. [G: LDCs]

Stanislaw, Joe. The Need for All Available Sources of Energy. *Maillet, P.; Hague, D. and Rowland, C., eds.,* 1987, pp. 119–45.
[G: OECD; LDCs]

Stewart, Marion B. Energy Deregulation and Economic Growth: Summary. *Stewart, M. B., ed.,* 1987, pp. 1–16. [G: U.S.]

Stewart, Marion B. The Economics of Oil Prices: How Long Will World Supply Exceed Demand? *Stewart, M. B., ed.,* 1987, pp. 17–20.
[G: OPEC]

Struckmeyer, Charles S. The Putty-Clay Perspective on the Capital–Energy Complementarity Debate. *Rev. Econ. Statist.,* May 1987, 69(2), pp. 320–26. [G: U.S.]

Sweeney, James L. Price Asymmetries in the Demand for Energy. *Stevens, P., ed.,* 1987, pp. 48–70.

Sweeney, James L. The Response of Energy Demand to Higher Prices: What Have We

Learned? *Pachauri, R. K., ed.*, 1987, pp. 573–84.

Szegö, Giorgio P. Economic Factors Affecting the Development of Alternative Energy Sources. *Maillet, P.; Hague, D. and Rowland, C., eds.*, 1987, pp. 146–82.

Talib, Abu and Bienstock, Daniel. Wood: An Ancient Fuel with New Potential for Developing Countries. *Pachauri, R. K., ed.*, 1987, pp. 393–411. [G: LDCs]

Tatom, John A. The Macroeconomic Effects of the Recent Fall in Oil Prices. *Fed. Res. Bank St. Louis Rev.*, June/July 1987, 69(6), pp. 34–45. [G: OECD]

Timmer, C. Peter. SAM, Energy, and Structural Change in the Agricultural Sector. *Austin, J. E. and Esteva, G., eds.*, 1987, pp. 260–97. [G: Mexico]

Tobin, James. Does the Energy Crisis Endanger the American Life-Style? *Tobin, J. (III)*, 1987, *1974*, pp. 454–61. [G: U.S.]

Tobin, James. Energy Strategy and Macroeconomic Policies. *Tobin, J. (III)*, 1987, *1981*, pp. 462–72. [G: U.S.]

Tourinho, Octávio Augusto Fontes; Ferreira, Léo da Rocha and Pimentel, Ruderico Ferraz. Agricultura e produção de energia: um modelo de programação linear para avaliação econômica do PROÁLCOOL. (With English summary.) *Pesquisa Planejamento Econ.*, April 1987, 17(1), pp. 19–63. [G: Brazil]

Toyoda, Toshihisa; Ohtani, Kazuhiro and Katayama, Sei-ichi. Structural Change in Oil Consumption in Japan: An Econometric Analysis of Effects of the Two Oil Crises. *Kobe Univ. Econ.*, 1987, 33, pp. 33–47. [G: Japan]

Train, Kenneth E. and Strebel, Judi E. Energy Conservation and Rebates in Commercial Food Enterprises. *Amer. J. Agr. Econ.*, February 1987, 69(1), pp. 106–14. [G: U.S.]

Tuck, Bradford H. Structural Change in Alaska: The Impact of the Petroleum Industry. *Lane, T., ed.*, 1987, pp. 233–49. [G: U.S.]

Tyner, Wallace E. A Comparative Evaluation of Selected Renewable Energy Technologies in China, India, West Africa and Brazil. *Pachauri, R. K., ed.*, 1987, pp. 217–26. [G: China; India; W. Africa; Brazil]

Tzeng, Gwo-Hshiung. A Study on the Characteristics and Demand Model for Household Energy Consumption in Taiwan. *Pachauri, R. K., ed.*, 1987, pp. 481–528. [G: Taiwan]

Uzcategui, José Miguel. The Economics of Alternative Sources of Energy: A View from Venezuela. *Maillet, P.; Hague, D. and Rowland, C., eds.*, 1987, pp. 324–33. [G: Venezuela]

Van Vactor, Samuel A. and Tussing, Arlon R. Retrospective on Oil Prices. *Contemp. Policy Issues*, July 1987, 5(3), pp. 1–19. [G: Global]

Verleger, Philip K., Jr. The Evolution of Oil as a Commodity. *[Adelman, M. A.]*, 1987, pp. 161–86.

Vietor, Richard H. K. Business, Government, and Markets: Synthetic Fuels Policy in America. *Yanarella, E. J. and Green, W. C., eds.*, 1987, pp. 3–32. [G: U.S.]

Visintini, Alfredo and Bastos, Carlos. Hacia un nuevo plan eléctrico. (With English summary.) *Desarrollo Econ.*, Oct.-Dec. 1987, 27(107), pp. 377–95. [G: Argentina]

Vlachou, Andriana and Field, Barry C. Regional Energy Substitution: Results from a Dynamic Input Demand Model. *Southern Econ. J.*, April 1987, 53(4), pp. 952–66. [G: U.S.]

Vlek, Charles and Otten, Wilma. Judgmental Handling of Energy Scenarios: A Psychological Analysis and Experiment. *Wright, G. and Ayton, P., eds.*, 1987, pp. 267–89.

Wabe, J. Stuart. The Demand for Gasoline: A Comment on the Cross-Section Analysis by Drollas. *Energy Econ.*, October 1987, 9(4), pp. 287–89. [G: U.S.; W. Europe]

Wade, Doug. Assessing Future Energy and Oil Demand. *Stevens, P., ed.*, 1987, pp. 82–108. [G: OECD; LDCs]

Waldman, Andrea K. Natural Gas Imports: Federal Policy and Competition for U.S. Markets. *Natural Res. J.*, Fall 1987, 27(4), pp. 789–98. [G: U.S.]

Walker, David J. Rationing and Careless Days: Reply. *New Zealand Econ. Pap.*, 1987, 21, pp. 121–23. [G: New Zealand]

Watkins, G. Campbell. Living under a Shadow: U.S. Oil Policies and Canadian Oil Pricing. *[Adelman, M. A.]*, 1987, pp. 31–57. [G: U.S.; Canada]

Waverman, Leonard. The Impact of $(US)15 Oil: Good News and/or Bad News? *Can. Public Policy*, March 1987, 13(1), pp. 1–18. [G: Canada]

Wellinghoff, Jon. What Do "436," "436-A," "451," "311," "7(c)," Mean to the Residential Gas Consumer. *Natural Res. J.*, Fall 1987, 27(4), pp. 829–40. [G: U.S.]

Werbos, Paul J. Industrial Structural Shift: Causes and Consequences for Electricity Demand. *Faruqui, A. and Broehl, J., eds.*, 1987, pp. 115–26. [G: U.S.]

Wilbanks, Thomas J. Prospects of Synthetic Fuels in the United States: Past Lessons and Future Requirements. *Yanarella, E. J. and Green, W. C., eds.*, 1987, pp. 193–211. [G: U.S.]

Willett, Keith D. and Naghshpour, Shahdad. Residential Demand for Energy Commodities: A Household Production Function Approach. *Energy Econ.*, October 1987, 9(4), pp. 251–56.

Williams, Harold R. and Mount, Randall I. OECD Gasoline Demand Elasticities: An Analysis of Consumer Behavior with Implications for U.S. Energy Policy. *J. Behav. Econ.*, Spring 1987, 16(1), pp. 69–79. [G: OECD]

Williams, Harold R. and Mount, Randall I. OPEC and the U.S. Demand for Motor Gasoline: Short-run and Long-run Price Elasticities. *Rivista Int. Sci. Econ. Com.*, Jan.-Feb. 1987, 34(1–2), pp. 147–58. [G: U.S.]

Willis, Sabrina. The Synthetic Fuels Corporation as an Organizational Failure in Policy Mobilization. *Yanarella, E. J. and Green, W. C., eds.*, 1987, pp. 71–87. [G: U.S.]

Wilson, Ernest J., III. World Politics and International Energy Markets. *Int. Organ.*, Winter 1987, *41*(1), pp. 125–49. **[G: Global]**

Wionczek, Miguel S. Energy Planning and Oil in Mexico: The Outstanding Issues in Historical Perspective. *Maillet, P.; Hague, D. and Rowland, C., eds.*, 1987, pp. 334–43.
[G: Mexico]

Xu, Shubo and Liu, Bao. The New Dynamic Priorities Model and an Analysis of China's Energy Strategy for the Future. *Sawaragi, Y.; Inoue, K. and Nakayama, H., eds.*, 1987, pp. 249–56. **[G: China]**

Yanarella, Ernest J. and Green, William C. The Unfulfilled Promise of Synthetic Fuels: Technological Failure, Policy Immobilism, or Commercial Illusion: Preface. *Yanarella, E. J. and Green, W. C., eds.*, 1987, pp. xiii–xxii.
[G: U.S.]

Yanarella, Ernest J. and Reid, Herbert G. Class-Based Environmentalism in a Small Town: ERDA's "Gasifiers in Industry" Program and the Georgetown, Kentucky, Controversy. *Yanarella, E. J. and Green, W. C., eds.*, 1987, pp. 99–125. **[G: U.S.]**

Zakariya, Hasan S. The Third World Perspective on Petroleum: The Travails of the 'Haves' and the Plight of the 'Have-Nots.' *Rees, J. and Odell, P., eds.*, 1987, pp. 107–28. **[G: LDCs]**

Zandi, Mark. What Impact Will Energy Price Changes Have on Economic Growth in the United States? *Stewart, M. B., ed.*, 1987, pp. 41–54. **[G: U.S.]**

Zannetos, Zenon S. Oil Tanker Makets: Continuity amidst Change. *[Adelman, M. A.]*, 1987, pp. 235–57.

Zimmerman, Martin B. The Evolution of Civilian Nuclear Power. *[Adelman, M. A.]*, 1987, pp. 83–106. **[G: U.S.]**

730 ECONOMIC GEOGRAPHY

731 Economic Geography

7310 Economic Geography

Baxter, M. J. Testing for Misspecification in Models of Spatial Flows. *Environ. Planning A*, September 1987, *19*(9), pp. 1153–60.

Breheny, M. J. The Context for Methods: The Constraints of the Policy Process on the Use of Quantitative Methods. *Environ. Planning A*, November 1987, *19*(11), pp. 1449–62.

Clark, William A. V. Urban Restructuring from a Demographic Perspective. *Econ. Geogr.*, April 1987, *63*(2), pp. 103–25. **[G: U.S.]**

Clarke, M. and Openshaw, S. The AGW Spatial Interaction Workstation. *Environ. Planning A*, September 1987, *19*(9), pp. 1261–68.

Clarke, M. and Wilson, A. G. Towards an Applicable Human Geography: Some Developments and Observations. *Environ. Planning A*, November 1987, *19*(11), pp. 1525–41.

Cloke, P. J. and Little, J. K. Rural Policies in the Gloucestershire Structure Plan: 1. A Study of Motives an Mechanisms. *Environ. Planning A*, July 1987, *19*(7), pp. 959–81.

Dunn, Richard; Forrest, Ray and Murie, Alan.

The Geography of Council House Sales in England—1979–85. *Urban Stud.*, February 1987, *24*(1), pp. 47–59. **[G: U.K.]**

Ettlinger, N. and Archer, J. C. City-Size Distributions and the World Urban Sytem in the Twentieth Century. *Environ. Planning A*, September 1987, *19*(9), pp. 1161–74.
[G: Global]

Gilbert, A. Research Policy and Review 15. From Little Englanders into Big Englanders: Thoughts on the Relevance of Relevant Research. *Environ. Planning A*, February 1987, *19*(2), pp. 143–51.

Haining, Robert. Small Area Aggregate Income Models: Theory and Methods with an Application to Urban and Rural Income Data for Pennsylvania. *Reg. Stud.*, December 1987, *21*(6), pp. 519–29. **[G: U.S.]**

Ishikawa, Y. An Empirical Study of the Competing Destinations Model Using Japanese Interaction Data. *Environ. Planning A*, October 1987, *19*(10), pp. 1359–73. **[G: Japan]**

Isserman, Andrew M. and Merrifield, John D. Quasi-experimental Control Group Methods for Regional Analysis: An Application to an Energy Boomtown and Growth Pole Theory. *Econ. Geogr.*, January 1987, *63*(1), pp. 3–19.
[G: U.S.]

Lentnek, Barry; Harwitz, Mitchell and Narula, Subhash C. A Contextual Theory of Demand: Beyond Spatial Analysis in Economic Geography. *Econ. Geogr.*, October 1987, *63*(4), pp. 334–48.

Munt, I. Economic Restructuring, Culture, and Gentrification: A Case Study in Battersea, London. *Environ. Planning A*, September 1987, *19*(9), pp. 1175–97. **[G: U.K.]**

O'Brien, L. G. User Control versus Randomisation in Geographical Probability Sampling: A Compromise Solution Using Controlled Sampling. *Environ. Planning A*, July 1987, *19*(7), pp. 949–58. **[G: U.K.]**

O'Connor, K. The Location of Services Involved with International Trade. *Environ. Planning A*, May 1987, *19*(5), pp. 687–700. **[G: U.S.; Australia]**

Openshaw, S. and Goddard, John. Some Implications of the Commodification of Information and the Emerging Information Economy for Applied Geographical Analysis of the United Kingdom. *Environ. Planning A*, November 1987, *19*(11), pp. 1423–39. **[G: U.K.]**

Palmer, Donald A. and Friedland, Roger. Corporation, Class and City System. *Mizruchi, M. S. and Schwartz, M., eds.*, 1987, pp. 145–84.
[G: U.S.]

Papageorgiou, Y. Y. Spatial Public Goods. 1: Theory. *Environ. Planning A*, March 1987, *19*(3), pp. 331–52.

Papageorgiou, Y. Y. Spatial Public Goods: 2. Applications. *Environ. Planning A*, April 1987, *19*(4), pp. 471–92.

Rees, Judith. Spatial Interrelationships, Distributions and Geopolitics. *Rees, J. and Odell, P., eds.*, 1987, pp. 158–62.

Schmenner, Roger W.; Huber, Joel C. and Cook, Randall L. Geographic Differences and the Location of New Manufacturing Facilities. *J. Urban Econ.*, January 1987, *21*(1), pp. 83–104. [G: U.S.]

Scott, A. J. The Semiconductor Industry in South-East Asia: Organization, Location and the International Division of Labour. *Reg. Stud.*, April 1987, *21*(2), pp. 143–59. [G: S.E. Asia]

Scott, A. J. and Angel, D. P. The U.S. Semiconductor Industry: A Locational Analysis. *Environ. Planning A*, July 1987, *19*(7), pp. 875–912. [G: U.S.]

Smith, Neil and Dennis, Ward. The Restructuring of Geographical Scale: Coalescence and Fragmentation of the Northern Core Region. *Econ. Geogr.*, April 1987, *63*(2), pp. 160–82. [G: U.S.]

Thomas, Colin J. and Bromley, Rosemary D. F. The Growth and Functioning of an Unplanned Retail Park: The Swansea Enterprise Zone. *Reg. Stud.*, August 1987, *21*(4), pp. 287–300. [G: U.K.]

Tyler, P. and Kitson, M. Geographical Variations in Transport Costs of Manufacturing Firms in Great Britain. *Urban Stud.*, February 1987, *24*(1), pp. 61–73. [G: U.K.]

Vincent, Peter; Chell, Elizabeth and Haworth, Jean. Regional Distribution of Consultancy Firms Servicing the MAPCON Scheme: A Preliminary Analysis. *Reg. Stud.*, December 1987, *21*(6), pp. 505–18. [G: U.K.]

Webber, M. J. Quantitative Measurement of Some Marxist Categories. *Environ. Planning A*, October 1987, *19*(10), pp. 1303–21.

Winter, Nils H. Den ekonomiska geografin och dess utmaningar. (Economic Geography and Its Challenges. With English summary.) *Ekon. Samfundets Tidskr.*, 1987, *40*(3), pp. 145–47.

Randol, William L. World Oil Dynamics: The Political Dimension. *Stewart, M. B., ed.*, 1987, pp. 21–25. [G: OPEC; Saudi Arabia]

800 Manpower; Labor; Population

8000 General

Maupain, Francis. Federalism and International Labour Conventions. Some Reflections Prompted by Two Anniversaries. *Int. Lab. Rev.*, Nov.-Dec. 1987, *126*(6), pp. 625–51.

Piore, Michael J. American Labor and the Industrial Crisis. *Challenge*, Special Issue 1987, *30*(6), pp. 24–30. [G: U.S.]

810 Manpower Training and Development; Labor Force and Supply

811 Manpower Training and Development

8110 Manpower Training and Development

Adams, Arvil V.; Mangum, Stephen L. and Wirtz, Philip W. Postschool Education and Training: Accessible to All? *Rev. Black Polit. Econ.*, Winter 1987, *15*(3), pp. 68–86. [G: U.S.]

Alagh, Yoginder K. Employment and Structural

Change in the Indian Economy. *Amjad, R., ed.*, 1987, pp. 285–303. [G: India]

Amjad, Rashid. Human Resource Development: The Asian Experience in Employment and Manpower Planning—An Overview. *Amjad, R., ed.*, 1987, pp. 1–37. [G: Asia]

Ashenfelter, Orley. The Case for Evaluating Training Programs with Randomized Trials. *Econ. Educ. Rev.*, 1987, *6*(4), pp. 333–38. [G: U.S.]

Barnow, Burt S. The Impact of CETA Programs on Earnings: A Review of the Literature. *J. Human Res.*, Spring 1987, *22*(2), pp. 157–93. [G: U.S.]

Bassi, Laurie J. Estimating the Effect of Job Training Programs, Using Longitudinal Data: Ashenfelter's Findings Reconsidered: A Comment. *J. Human Res.*, Spring 1987, *22*(2), pp. 300–303. [G: U.S.]

Blau, David M. and Robins, Philip K. Training Programs and Wages: A General Equilibrium Analysis of the Effects of Program Size. *J. Human Res.*, Winter 1987, *22*(1), pp. 113–25. [G: U.S.]

Briggs, Vernon M., Jr. *Youth Employment and Training Programs:* A Review. *Ind. Lab. Relat. Rev.*, October 1987, *41*(1), pp. 137–40. [G: U.S.]

Briggs, Vernon M., Jr. Human Resource Development and the Formulation of National Economic Policy. *J. Econ. Issues*, September 1987, *21*(3), pp. 1207–40. [G: U.S.]

Brunel, Andre and Burke, Michael P. Promoting High-Technology Industry: Initiatives and Policies for State Governments: Pennsylvania. *Schmandt, J. and Wilson, R., eds.*, 1987, pp. 191–229. [G: U.S.]

Cohn, Andrew and McElroy, Kathleen. The Dane County, Wisconsin Dislocated Worker Project. *Cook, R. F., ed.*, 1987, pp. 173–92. [G: U.S.]

Cook, Robert F. Worker Dislocation: Case Studies of Causes and Cures: Findings and Conclusions. *Cook, R. F., ed.*, 1987, pp. 193–210. [G: U.S.]

Cook, Robert F. Worker Dislocation: Case Studies of Causes and Cures: Introduction. *Cook, R. F., ed.*, 1987, pp. 1–14. [G: U.S.]

Deutsch, Steven. Successful Worker Training Programs Help Ease Impact of Technology. *Mon. Lab. Rev.*, November 1987, *110*(11), pp. 14–20. [G: U.S.]

Dickinson, Katherine P.; Johnson, Terry R. and West, Richard W. The Impact of CETA Programs on Components of Participants' Earnings. *Ind. Lab. Relat. Rev.*, April 1987, *40*(3), pp. 430–41. [G: U.S.]

Dolphyne, Florence Abena. The Ghana National Council on Women and Development: An Example of Concerted Action. *Oppong, C., ed.*, 1987, pp. 213–18. [G: Ghana]

Dommel, Paul R. The Cleveland, Ohio United Labor Agency Dislocated Worker Project. *Cook, R. F., ed.*, 1987, pp. 111–27. [G: U.S.]

Dutton, Patricia. Policies for the Youth Labour Market: YTS: Training or a Placebo? *Junankar,*

P. N., ed., 1987, pp. 217–37. **[G: U.K.]**

Elmore, Richard F. Youth Employment in the United States: Problem, Structure, Policy. *Pedersen, P. J. and Lund, R.*, eds., 1987, pp. 241–57. **[G: U.S.]**

Fapohunda, Eleanor R. Urban Women's Roles and Nigerian Government Development Strategies. *Oppong, C.*, ed., 1987, pp. 203–12. **[G: Nigeria]**

Fraker, Thomas and Maynard, Rebecca. The Adequacy of Comparison Group Designs for Evaluations of Employment-Related Programs. *J. Human Res.*, Spring 1987, *22*(2), pp. 194–227. **[G: U.S.]**

Greenhalgh, Christine and Stewart, Mark B. The Effects and Determinants of Training. *Oxford Bull. Econ. Statist.*, May 1987, *49*(2), pp. 171–90. **[G: U.K.]**

Hollister, Robinson G., Jr. Youth Employment and Training Programs: Reply. *Ind. Lab. Relat. Rev.*, October 1987, *41*(1), pp. 141–45. **[G: U.S.]**

Hougland, James G., Jr. Criteria for Client Evaluation of Public Programs: A Comparison of Objective and Perceptual Measures. *Soc. Sci. Quart.*, June 1987, *68*(2), pp. 386–94. **[G: U.S.]**

Howard, Mark and Kragie, Mary. Promoting High-Technology Industry: Initiatives and Policies for State Governments: North Carolina. *Schmandt, J. and Wilson, R.*, eds., 1987, pp. 163–90. **[G: U.S.]**

Islam, Iyanatul. Manpower and Educational Planning in Singapore. *Amjad, R.*, ed., 1987, pp. 114–50. **[G: Singapore]**

Jantzen, Robert H. Adult CETA Training in Boston: Impact on Earnings, Hours Worked, and Wages. *J. Econ. Bus.*, February 1987, *39*(1), pp. 1–17. **[G: U.S.]**

Jimenez, Emmanuel and Kugler, Bernardo. The Earnings Impact of Training Duration in a Developing Country: An Ordered Probit Selection Model of Colombia's *Servicio Nacional de Aprendizaje* (SENA). *J. Human Res.*, Spring 1987, *22*(2), pp. 228–47. **[G: Colombia]**

Kemal, A. R. Pakistan's Experience in Employment and Manpower Planning. *Amjad, R.*, ed., 1987, pp. 234–56. **[G: Pakistan]**

Khan, M. R. Employment, Manpower and Educational Development in Bangladesh. *Amjad, R.*, ed., 1987, pp. 304–17. **[G: Bangladesh]**

Kim, Yoo Bae. Evaluation of Manpower Policies in the Republic of Korea. *Amjad, R.*, ed., 1987, pp. 198–220. **[G: S. Korea]**

Knowles, David R. The ASARCO Copper Smelter Project. *Cook, R. F.*, ed., 1987, pp. 151–72. **[G: U.S.]**

Koike, Kazuo. Skill Formation Systems: A Thai–Japan Comparison. *J. Japanese Int. Economies*, December 1987, *1*(4), pp. 408–40. **[G: Japan; Thailand]**

Koike, Kazuo. The Political Economy of Japan: Human Resource Development and Labor–Management Relations. *Yamamura, K. and Yasuba, Y.*, eds., 1987, pp. 289–330. **[G: Japan]**

Kotliar, A. Labor Resources and the Current Economic Development of the USSR. *Prob. Econ.*, April 1987, *29*(12), pp. 5–22. **[G: U.S.S.R.]**

MacManus, Susan A. The Houston Community College–Texas Employment Commission Dislocated Worker Project. *Cook, R. F.*, ed., 1987, pp. 129–50. **[G: U.S.]**

Mangum, Stephen L. and Adams, Arvil V. The Labor Market Impacts of Post-school Occupational Training for Young Men. *Growth Change*, Fall 1987, *18*(4), pp. 57–73. **[G: U.S.]**

Mehmet, Ozay. The Malaysian Experience in Manpower Planning and Labour Market Policies. *Amjad, R.*, ed., 1987, pp. 84–113. **[G: Malaysia]**

Miller, David and Davenport, E. Closing the Skills Gap. *Reg. Stud.*, December 1987, *21*(6), pp. 564–67. **[G: U.K.]**

Moffitt, Robert. Symposium on the Econometric Evaluation of Manpower Training Programs: Introduction. *J. Human Res.*, Spring 1987, *22*(2), pp. 149–56. **[G: U.S.]**

Ng, Sek-Hong. Training Problems and Challenges in a Newly Industrialising Economy: The Case of Hong Kong. *Int. Lab. Rev.*, July-Aug. 1987, *126*(4), pp. 467–78. **[G: Hong Kong]**

Oechslin, Jean-Jacques. Training and the Business World: The French Experience. *Int. Lab. Rev.*, Nov.-Dec. 1987, *126*(6), pp. 653–67. **[G: France]**

Pitayanon, Sumalee. Thailand's Experience in Manpower Planning and Labour Market Policies. *Amjad, R.*, ed., 1987, pp. 38–83. **[G: Thailand]**

Raffe, David. Small Expectations: The First Year of the Youth Training Scheme. *Junankar, P. N.*, ed., 1987, pp. 238–62. **[G: U.K.]**

Rajan, Amin. The Young Workers' Scheme: A Preliminary Assessment. *Junankar, P. N.*, ed., 1987, pp. 263–84. **[G: U.K.]**

Robertson, David B. Labor Market Surgery, Labor Market Abandonment: The Thatcher and Reagan Unemployment Remedies. *Waltman, J. L. and Studlar, D. T.*, eds., 1987, pp. 69–97. **[G: U.K.; U.S.]**

Rodrigo, Chandra; Korale, R. B. M. and Aturupana, D. H. C. Employment and Manpower Planning in Sri Lanka. *Amjad, R.*, ed., 1987, pp. 257–84. **[G: Sri Lanka]**

Rosenfeld, Stuart A. Education, Training, and Industrial Policy. *Goldstein, H. A.*, ed., 1987, pp. 86–94. **[G: U.S.]**

Ross, Peggy J. and Rosenfeld, Stuart A. Human Resource Policies and Economic Development. *U.S.D.A.*, Econ. Res. Serv., Agr. and Rural Econ. Div., 1987, pp. 15.1–25. **[G: U.S.]**

Rupp, Kalman, et al. Government Employment and Training Programs, and Older Americans. *Sandell, S. H.*, ed., 1987, pp. 121–42. **[G: U.S.]**

Schutte, P. C. Investeringseise van menslike kapitaal in 'n veranderende Suid-Afrika. (The Demand for Investment in Human Capital in a Changing South Africa. With English summary.) *S. Afr. J. Econ.*, December 1987, 55(4), pp. 370–80. **[G: S. Africa]**

Sorensen, Duane L. The Cummins Engine Company Dislocated Worker Project. *Cook, R. F., ed.*, 1987, pp. 15–30. **[G: U.S.]**

Spring, William J. Youth Unemployment and the Transition from School to Work: Programs in Boston, Frankfurt, and London. *New Eng. Econ. Rev.*, Mar./Apr. 1987, pp. 3–16. **[G: U.S.; U.K.; W. Germany]**

Steedman, Hilary. Vocational Training in France and Britain: Office Work. *Nat. Inst. Econ. Rev.*, May 1987, (120), pp. 58–70. **[G: France; U.K.]**

Steinberg, Danny and Monforte, Frank A. Estimating the Effects of Job Search Assistance and Training Programs on the Unemployment Durations of Displaced Workers. *Lang, K. and Leonard, J. S., eds.*, 1987, pp. 186–206. **[G: U.S.]**

Suroto and Tjiptoherijanto, Prijono. Employment, Manpower and Educational Planning in Indonesia. *Amjad, R., ed.*, 1987, pp. 181–97. **[G: Indonesia]**

Tan, Edita A. and Alonzo, Ruperto P. The Philippine Experience in Manpower Planning and Labour Market Policies. *Amjad, R., ed.*, 1987, pp. 151–80. **[G: Philippines]**

Tannen, Michael B. Is the Army College Fund Meeting Its Objectives? *Ind. Lab. Relat. Rev.*, October 1987, 41(1), pp. 50–62. **[G: U.S.]**

Tomey, E. Allan. The Missouri Dislocated Worker Program: Job Search Assistance, Inc. *Cook, R. F., ed.*, 1987, pp. 71–91. **[G: U.S.]**

Turnage, Wayne M. The Hillsborough, North Carolina Dislocated Worker Project. *Cook, R. F., ed.*, 1987, pp. 93–109. **[G: U.S.]**

Warner, Malcolm. China's Managerial Training Revolution. *Warner, M., ed.*, 1987, pp. 73–85. **[G: China]**

Winter, Søren. Implementation of Danish Youth Employment Policy. *Pedersen, P. J. and Lund, R., eds.*, 1987, pp. 259–84. **[G: Denmark]**

Wohl, Lawrence A. The Minnesota Iron Range Dislocated Worker Project. *Cook, R. F., ed.*, 1987, pp. 47–70. **[G: U.S.]**

Zhijian, Zhang. Labour Force Planning in the People's Republic of China. *Amjad, R., ed.*, 1987, pp. 221–33. **[G: China]**

Ziderman, Adrian. Initial vs Recurrent Training for Skilled Trades in Israel—Results of a 7-Year Follow-up Study. *Econ. Educ. Rev.*, 1987, 6(2), pp. 91–98. **[G: Israel]**

812 Occupation

8120 Occupation

Anderson, Kathryn H.; Hill, M. Anne and Butler, John S. Age at Marriage in Malaysia: A Hazard Model of Marriage Timing. *J. Devel. Econ.*, August 1987, 26(2), pp. 223–34. **[G: Malaysia]**

Appelbaum, Eileen. Restructuring Work: Temporary, Part-time, and At-Home Employment. *Hartmann, H. I., ed.*, 1987, pp. 268–310. **[G: U.S.]**

Bai, Nanfeng. Young People's Attitudes and Aspirations: Will They Welcome Reform? *Reynolds, B. L.*, 1987, pp. 161–87. **[G: China]**

Baran, Barbara. The Technological Transformation of White-Collar Work: A Case Study of the Insurance Industry. *Hartmann, H. I., ed.*, 1987, pp. 25–62. **[G: U.S.]**

Bartel, Ann P. and Lichtenberg, Frank R. The Skill Distribution and Competitive Trade Advantage of High-Technology Industries. *Lewin, D.; Lipsky, D. B. and Sockell, D., eds.*, 1987, pp. 161–76. **[G: U.S.]**

Bedrossian, Arakel and Petoussis, Emmanuel. The Disaggregated Demand for Labour in Greek Industry. *Appl. Econ.*, June 1987, 19(6), pp. 809–17. **[G: Greece]**

Bentolila, David J. The Non-agricultural Village. *Bar-El, R., ed.*, 1987, pp. 105–42. **[G: Israel]**

Bergmann, Barbara R. Pay Equity—Surprising Answers to Hard Questions. *Challenge*, May/June 1987, 30(2), pp. 45–51. **[G: U.S.]**

Bianchi, Suzanne M. and Rytina, Nancy. Comment on Das Gupta's Comment [The Decline in Occupational Sex Segregation during the 1970s: Census and CPS Comparisons]. *Demography*, May 1987, 24(2), pp. 297. **[G: U.S.]**

Blau, Francine D. and Ferber, Marianne A. Occupations and Earnings of Women Workers. *Koziara, K. S.; Moskow, M. H. and Tanner, L. D., eds.*, 1987, pp. 37–68. **[G: U.S.]**

Blossfeld, Hans-Peter. Entry into the Labor Market and Occupational Career in the Federal Republic: A Comparison with American Studies. *Teckenberg, W., ed.*, 1987, pp. 86–115. **[G: W. Germany]**

Burkhauser, Richard V. Occupational Effects on the Health and Work Capacity of Older Men: Comment. *Burtless, G., ed.*, 1987, pp. 142–50. **[G: U.S.]**

Burtless, Gary. Occupational Effects on the Health and Work Capacity of Older Men. *Burtless, G., ed.*, 1987, pp. 103–42. **[G: U.S.]**

Chapman, Bruce J. Labour Turnover and Wage Determination. *Australian Econ. Pap.*, June 1987, 26(48), pp. 119–29. **[G: Australia]**

Chillemi, Ottorino. Qualche considerazione su retribuzioni universitarie e processi di autoselezione. (Some Notes on University Remunerations and the Auto-selection Process. With English summary.) *Econ. Lavoro*, Apr.-June 1987, 21(2), pp. 59–66.

Corcoran, Mary E. and Courant, Paul N. Sex-Role Socialization and Occupational Segregation: An Exploratory Investigation. *J. Post Keynesian Econ.*, Spring 1987, 9(3), pp. 330–46. **[G: U.S.]**

Cornfield, Daniel B., et al. Office Automation, Clerical Workers, and Labor Relations in the Insurance Industry. *Cornfield, D. B., ed.*, 1987, pp. 111–34. **[G: U.S.]**

Cross, Gary and Shergold, Peter R. "We Think We Are of the Oppressed": Gender, White Collar Work, and Grievances of Late Nineteenth-Century Women. *Labor Hist.*, Winter 1987, 28(1), pp. 23–53. **[G: U.S.]**

Daniels, Rudolph. The Structure of the South African Labor Market, 1970–83. *Rev. Black Polit. Econ.*, Spring 1987, *15*(4), pp. 63–78.
[G: S. Africa]

Das Gupta, Prithwis. The Decline in Occupational Sex Segregation during the 1970s: Census and CPS Comparisons: Comment. *Demography*, May 1987, *24*(2), pp. 291–95.
[G: U.S.]

Dionne, Georges; Langlois, Alain and Lemire, Nicole. More on the Geographical Distribution of Physicians. *J. Health Econ.*, December 1987, *6*(4), pp. 365–74.

Dutton, Patricia. Policies for the Youth Labour Market: YTS: Training or a Placebo? *Junankar, P. N., ed.*, 1987, pp. 217–37. [G: U.K.]

Eberts, Randall W. Union-Negotiated Employment Rules and Teacher Quits. *Econ. Educ. Rev.*, 1987, *6*(1), pp. 15–25. [G: U.S.]

Elias, P. and Blanchflower, David G. Local Labour-Market Influences on Early Occupational Attainment. *Gordon, I., ed.*, 1987, pp. 158–71. [G: U.K.]

Emmi, P. C. Structural Determinants of Occupational Mobility in a Regional Labor Market. *Environ. Planning A*, July 1987, *19*(7), pp. 925–48. [G: U.S.]

Fosu, Augustin Kwasi. Explaining Post-1964 Earnings Gains by Black Women: Race or Sex? *Rev. Black Polit. Econ.*, Winter 1987, *15*(3), pp. 41–55. [G: U.S.]

Freeman, Christopher and Soete, Luc. Technical Change and Full Employment: Policy Conclusions. *Freeman, C. and Soete, L., eds.*, 1987, pp. 237–56. [G: U.K.]

Ginzberg, Eli. Technology, Women, and Work: Policy Perspectives. *Hartmann, H. I., ed.*, 1987, pp. 3–22. [G: U.S.]

Goldstein, Harvey A. and Cruze, Alvin M. An Evaluation of State Projections of Industry, Occupational Employment. *Mon. Lab. Rev.*, October 1987, *110*(10), pp. 29–38. [G: U.S.]

Greenhalgh, Christine and Stewart, Mark B. The Effects and Determinants of Training. *Oxford Bull. Econ. Statist.*, May 1987, *49*(2), pp. 171–90. [G: U.K.]

Hartmann, Heidi I. Internal Labor Markets and Gender: A Case Study of Promotion. *Brown, C. and Pechman, J. A., eds.*, 1987, pp. 59–92. [G: U.S.]

Headen, Alvin E., Jr. Price Discrimination in Physician Services Markets Based on Race: New Test of an Old Implicit Hypothesis. *Rev. Black Polit. Econ.*, Spring 1987, *15*(4), pp. 5–20. [G: U.S.]

Hibbs, Douglas A., Jr. Economic Outcomes and Political Support for British Governments among the Occupational Classes: A Dynamic Analysis. *Hibbs, D. A., Jr.*, 1987, *1982*, pp. 258–89. [G: U.K.]

Hoffman, Emily P. Determinants of Youths' Educational and Occupational Goals: Sex and Race Differences. *Econ. Educ. Rev.*, 1987, *6*(1), pp. 41–48. [G: U.S.]

Holden, Karen C. and Hansen, W. Lee. Part-time Work, Full-time Work, and Occupational

Segregation. *Brown, C. and Pechman, J. A., eds.*, 1987, pp. 217–40. [G: U.S.]

Hunt, H. Allan and Hunt, Timothy L. Recent Trends in Clerical Employment: The Impact of Technological Change. *Hartmann, H. I., ed.*, 1987, pp. 223–67. [G: U.S.]

Iams, Howard M. Jobs of Persons Working after Receiving Retired-Worker Benefits. *Soc. Sec. Bull.*, November 1987, *50*(11), pp. 4–18.
[G: U.S.]

Islam, Iyanatul. Manpower and Educational Planning in Singapore. *Amjad, R., ed.*, 1987, pp. 114–50. [G: Singapore]

Jacobs, Jerry A. The Sex Typing of Aspirations and Occupations: Instability during the Careers of Young Women. *Soc. Sci. Quart.*, March 1987, *68*(1), pp. 122–37. [G: U.S.]

James, Robert G. and Morlock, Mark J. The Determinants of Intra-occupational Wage Dispersion. *Appl. Econ.*, July 1987, *19*(7), pp. 969–81. [G: U.S.]

Jensen, Peter and Westergård-Nielsen, Niels C. A Search Model Applied to the Transition from Education to Work. *Rev. Econ. Stud.*, July 1987, *54*(3), pp. 461–72. [G: Denmark]

Jorrat, Jorge Ral. Exploraciones sobre movilidad ocupacional intergeneracional masculina en el Gran Buenos Aires. (With English summary.) *Desarrollo Econ.*, July-Sept. 1987, *27*(106), pp. 261–78. [G: Argentina]

Kappelhoff, Peter and Teckenberg, Wolfgang. Intergenerational and Career Mobility in the Federal Republic and the United States. *Teckenberg, W., ed.*, 1987, pp. 3–49.
[G: W. Germany; U.S.]

Kelley, Maryellen R. Internal Labor Markets and Gender: A Case Study of Promotion: Comments. *Brown, C. and Pechman, J. A., eds.*, 1987, pp. 97–105. [G: U.S.]

Kemna, Harrie J. M. I. Working Conditions and the Relationship between Schooling and Health. *J. Health Econ.*, September 1987, *6*(3), pp. 189–210. [G: U.S.]

Kim, Yoo Bae. Evaluation of Manpower Policies in the Republic of Korea. *Amjad, R., ed.*, 1987, pp. 198–220. [G: S. Korea]

König, Wolfgang. Employment and Career Mobility of Women in France and the Federal Republic. *Teckenberg, W., ed.*, 1987, pp. 53–85. [G: France; W. Germany]

Kritz, Mary M. Socio-economic Issues Arising from Immigration in Receiving Countries. *Borner, S. and Taylor, A., eds.*, 1987, pp. 141–58.

Lasser, Carol. The Domestic Balance of Power: Relations between Mistress and Maid in Nineteenth-Century New England. *Labor Hist.*, Winter 1987, *28*(1), pp. 5–22. [G: U.S.]

Lehrer, Evelyn L. and White, William D. Hospital Market Structure and the Return to Nursing Education: Comment [Hospital Market Structure and the Return to Nursing Education]. *J. Human Res.*, Fall 1987, *22*(4), pp. 607–08.
[G: U.S.]

Leigh, J. Paul. Gender, Firm Size, Industry, and Estimations of the Value-of-Life. *J. Health*

Econ., September 1987, *6*(3), pp. 255–73.

Lewis, Donald E. and Mangan, John. Wage Inflexibility and Quality Adjustment in Australian Academic Labour Markets: A Constrained Case. *Appl. Econ.*, October 1987, *19*(10), pp. 1279–90. **[G: Australia]**

Maxwell, Nan L. Occupational Differences in the Determination of U.S. Workers' Earnings: Both the Human Capital and the Structured Labor Market Hypotheses Are Useful in Analysis. *Amer. J. Econ. Soc.*, October 1987, *46*(4), pp. 431–43. **[G: U.S.]**

McKinney, Frederick W. The Economic Survival of Black Physicians: Swimming in Turbulent Waters. *Rev. Black Polit. Econ.*, Spring 1987, *15*(4), pp. 35–46. **[G: U.S.]**

Mehmet, Ozay. The Malaysian Experience in Manpower Planning and Labour Market Policies. *Amjad, R., ed.*, 1987, pp. 84–113. **[G: Malaysia]**

Murnane, Richard J.; Singer, Judith D. and Willett, John B. Changes in Teacher Salaries during the 1970s: The Role of School District Demographics. *Econ. Educ. Rev.*, 1987, *6*(4), pp. 379–88. **[G: U.S.]**

Murphree, Mary C. New Technology nd Office Trdition: The Not-So-Changing World of the Secretary. *Hartmann, H. I., ed.*, 1987, pp. 98–135.

Ohsfeldt, Robert L.; Culler, Steven D. and Becker, Edmund R. Sex Differences in the Economic Advantages of Physician Board Certification. *Southern Econ. J.*, October 1987, *54*(2), pp. 343–50. **[G: U.S.]**

Olson, Josephine E.; Frieze, Irene Hanson and Good, Deborah Cain. The Effects of Job Type and Industry on the Income of Male and Female MBAs. *J. Human Res.*, Fall 1987, *22*(4), pp. 532–41. **[G: U.S.]**

Osterman, Paul. Internal Labor Markets and Gender: A Case Study of Promotion: Comments. *Brown, C. and Pechman, J. A., eds.*, 1987, pp. 92–97. **[G: U.S.]**

Pfeffer, Jeffrey and O'Reilly, Charles A., III. Hospital Demography and Turnover among Nurses. *Ind. Relat.*, Spring 1987, *26*(2), pp. 158–73. **[G: U.S.]**

Pitayanon, Sumalee. Thailand's Experience in Manpower Planning and Labour Market Policies. *Amjad, R., ed.*, 1987, pp. 38–83. **[G: Thailand]**

Presser, Harriet B. Work Shifts of Full-Time Dual-Earner Couples: Patterns and Contrasts by Sex of Spouse. *Demography*, February 1987, *24*(1), pp. 99–112.

Rayack, Wendy. Sources and Centers of Cyclical Movement in Real Wages: Evidence from Panel Data. *J. Post Keynesian Econ.*, Fall 1987, *10*(1), pp. 3–21. **[G: U.S.]**

Riach, Peter A. and Rich, Judith. Testing for Sexual Discrimination in the Labour Market. *Australian Econ. Pap.*, December 1987, *26*(49), pp. 165–78. **[G: Australia]**

Rotella, Elyce J. The Dynamics of Occupational Segregation among Bank Tellers: Comments.

Brown, C. and Pechman, J. A., eds., 1987, pp. 149–54. **[G: U.S.]**

Rumberger, Russell W. The Impact of Salary Differentials on Teacher Shortages and Turnover: The Case of Mathematics and Science Teachers. *Econ. Educ. Rev.*, 1987, *6*(4), pp. 389–99. **[G: U.S.]**

Ruyssen, Olivier. The New Deal in Services—A Challenge for Europe. *Akehurst, G. and Gadrey, J., eds.*, 1987, pp. 99–109. **[G: W. Germany; France; Italy; U.K.; U.S.]**

Sanderson, J. Defining Functional Occupational Groupings. *Environ. Planning A*, September 1987, *19*(9), pp. 1199–1220. **[G: U.K.]**

Sauvy, Alfred. Occupational Migration and Training as Conditions and Consequences of Progress. *Dupriez, L. H., ed.*, 1987, pp. 277–90. **[G: France]**

Shapiro, David and Sandell, Steven H. The Reduced Pay of Older Job Losers: Age Discrimination and Other Explanations. *Sandell, S. H., ed.*, 1987, pp. 37–51. **[G: U.S.]**

Shaw, Kathryn L. Occupation Change, Employer Change, and the Tranferability of Skills. *Southern Econ. J.*, January 1987, *53*(3), pp. 702–19. **[G: U.S.]**

Silvestri, George T. and Lukasiewicz, John M. A Look at Occupational Employment Trends to the Year 2000. *Mon. Lab. Rev.*, September 1987, *110*(9), pp. 46–63. **[G: U.S.]**

Spurr, Stephen J. How the Market Solves an Assignment Problem: The Matching of Lawyers with Legal Claims. *J. Lab. Econ.*, Part 1, Oct. 1987, *5*(4), pp. 502–32. **[G: U.S.]**

Stanback, Thomas M., Jr. Development under Adversity: The Importance of Services, Technology, and Labor. *McKee, D. L. and Bennett, R. E., eds.*, 1987, pp. 85–108. **[G: U.S.]**

Stano, Miron. A Further Analysis of the Physician Inducement Controversy. *J. Health Econ.*, September 1987, *6*(3), pp. 227–38.

Steedman, Hilary. Vocational Training in France and Britain: Office Work. *Nat. Inst. Econ. Rev.*, May 1987, (120), pp. 58–70. **[G: France; U.K.]**

Stern, David. Part-time Work, Full-time Work, and Occupational Segregation: Comments. *Brown, C. and Pechman, J. A., eds.*, 1987, pp. 240–46. **[G: U.S.]**

Stewart, Charles T., Jr. Structural Change and Intergenerational Occupational Mobility. *J. Devel. Areas*, January 1987, *21*(2), pp. 141–57. **[G: Korea; Kuwait; Japan; Taiwan]**

Stirati, Antonella. Differenze retributive e segregazione occupazionale per sesso nell'industria manifatturiera. (Wage Differences and Occupational Segregation by Sex in the Manufacturing Industries. With English summary.) *Econ. Lavoro*, July-Sept. 1987, *21*(3), pp. 51–76. **[G: Italy]**

Stone, Charles F. and Sawhill, Isabel V. Trade's Impact on U.S. Jobs. *Challenge*, Sept./Oct. 1987, *30*(4), pp. 12–18. **[G: U.S.]**

Straub, LaVonne A. and Lane, Julia. Response [Hospital Market Structure and the Return to

Nursing Education]. *J. Human Res.*, Fall 1987, 22(4), pp. 609–10. [G: U.S.]

Strober, Myra H. and Arnold, Carolyn L. Integrated Circuits/Segregated Labor: Women in Computer-Related Occupations and High-Tech Industries. *Hartmann, H. I., ed.*, 1987, pp. 136–82. [G: U.S.]

Strober, Myra H. and Arnold, Carolyn L. The Dynamics of Occupational Segregation among Bank Tellers. *Brown, C. and Pechman, J. A., eds.*, 1987, pp. 107–48. [G: U.S.]

Strom, Sharon Hartman. "Machines Instead of Clerks": Technology and the Feminization of Bookkeeping, 1910–1950. *Hartmann, H. I., ed.*, 1987, pp. 63–97. [G: U.S.]

Svorny, Shirley V. Physician Licensure: A New Approach to Examining the Role of Professional Interests. *Econ. Inquiry*, July 1987, 25(3), pp. 497–509. [G: U.S.]

Swafford, Michael. Perceptions of Social Status in the USSR. *Millar, J. R., ed.*, 1987, pp. 279–300. [G: U.S.S.R.]

Taube, Paul M. A Cross-Sectional Analysis of the Job Market for Economists. *J. Behav. Econ.*, Winter 1987, 16(4), pp. 33–39. [G: U.S.]

Teckenberg, Wolfgang. Comparative Studies of Social Structure: Recent Research on France, the United States, and the Federal Republic of Germany: Summary and Discussion. *Teckenberg, W., ed.*, 1987, pp. 191–94.
[G: W. Germany]

Tucker, Irvin B., III. The Impact of Consumer Credentialism on Employee and Entrepreneur Returns to Higher Education. *Econ. Educ. Rev.*, 1987, 6(1), pp. 35–40. [G: U.S.]

Ulman, Lloyd. The Dynamics of Occupational Segregation among Bank Tellers: Comments. *Brown, C. and Pechman, J. A., eds.*, 1987, pp. 154–57. [G: U.S.]

Westin, Alan F. Employer Policies to Enhance the Application of Office System Technology to Clerical Work. *Hartmann, H. I., ed.*, 1987, pp. 313–42. [G: U.S.]

White, William D. The Introduction of Professional Regulation and Labor Market Conditions—Occupational Licensure of Registered Nurses. *Policy Sci.*, April 1987, 20(1), pp. 27–51. [G: U.S.]

Wilson, Robert A. Rates of Return to Entering the Legal Profession: Some Further Evidence. *Scot. J. Polit. Econ.*, May 1987, 34(2), pp. 174–91. [G: U.K.]

Wilson, Robert A. Returns to Entering the Medical Profession in the U.K. *J. Health Econ.*, December 1987, 6(4), pp. 339–63. [G: U.K.]

Wilson, Robert A. The Determinants of the Earnings of Professional Engineers in Great Britain in 1981. *Appl. Econ.*, July 1987, 19(7), pp. 983–94. [G: U.K.]

Yang, Guansan, et al. Enterprise Cadres and Reform. *Reynolds, B. L.*, 1987, pp. 74–85.
[G: China]

Zimmerman, William. Mobilized Participation and the Nature of the Soviet Dictatorship. *Millar, J. R., ed.*, 1987, pp. 332–53.
[G: U.S.S.R.]

813 Labor Force

8130 General

Aben, Jacques and Smith, Ron P. Defence and Employment in the UK and France: A Comparative Study of the Existing Results. *Schmidt, C. and Blackaby, F., eds.*, 1987, pp. 384–98. [G: France; U.K.]

Alogoskoufis, George S. On Intertemporal Substitution and Aggregate Labor Supply. *J. Polit. Econ.*, October 1987, 95(5), pp. 938–60.
[G: U.S.]

Altmann, Franz-Lothar. Employment Policies in Czechoslovakia. *Adam, J., ed.*, 1987, pp. 78–102. [G: Czechoslovakia]

Amjad, Rashid. Human Resource Development: The Asian Experience in Employment and Manpower Planning—An Overview. *Amjad, R., ed.*, 1987, pp. 1–37. [G: Asia]

Anker, Richard; Khan, M. E. and Gupta, R. B. Biases in Measuring the Labor Force. Results of a Methods Test Survey in Uttar Pradesh, India. *Int. Lab. Rev.*, Mar.-Apr. 1987, 126(2), pp. 151–67. [G: India]

Bedrossian, Arakel and Petoussis, Emmanuel. The Disaggregated Demand for Labour in Greek Industry. *Appl. Econ.*, June 1987, 19(6), pp. 809–17. [G: Greece]

Blau, David M. A Time-Series Analysis of Self-employment in the United State. *J. Polit. Econ.*, June 1987, 95(3), pp. 445–67.
[G: U.S.]

Bloom, David E. and Freeman, Richard B. Population Growth, Labor Supply, and Employment in Developing Countries. *Johnson, D. G. and Lee, R. D., eds.*, 1987, pp. 105–47.
[G: LDCs]

Breev, B. Evaluating the Utilization of Labor Resources. *Prob. Econ.*, January 1987, 29(9), pp. 5–19. [G: U.S.S.R.]

Burtless, Gary. Taxes, Transfers, and Swedish Labor Supply. *Bosworth, B. P. and Rivlin, A. M., eds.*, 1987, pp. 185–249. [G: Sweden]

Butenko, A. How to Intensify the Reproduction of Skilled Labor Power. *Prob. Econ.*, January 1987, 29(9), pp. 32–42. [G: U.S.S.R.]

Czamanski, Daniel Z. and Meyer-Brodnitz, Michael B. Industrialization in Arab Villages in Israel. *Bar-El, R., ed.*, 1987, pp. 143–68.
[G: Israel]

Dutoya, C. and Gauvin, Annie. Assignment of Women Workers to Jobs and Company Strategies in France. *Tarling, R., ed.*, 1987, pp. 127–44. [G: France]

von Ende, Eleanor and Weiss, Thomas. Labor Force Changes in the Old Northwest. *Klingaman, D. C. and Vedder, R. K., eds.*, 1987, pp. 103–30. [G: U.S.]

Fallenbuchl, Zbigniew M. Employment Policies in Poland. *Adam, J., ed.*, 1987, pp. 27–54.
[G: Poland]

Flaim, Paul O. and Sehgal, Ellen. Reemployment and Earnings [Displaced Workers of 1979–83: How Well Have They Fared?]. *Staudohar, P. D. and Brown, H. E.*, 1987, 1985, pp. 101–30. [G: U.S.]

Freeman, Richard B. and Leonard, Jonathan S. Union Maids: Unions and the Female Work Force. *Brown, C. and Pechman, J. A., eds.*, 1987, pp. 189–212. **[G: U.S.]**

Fullerton, Howard N., Jr. Labor Force Projections: 1986 to 2000. *Mon. Lab. Rev.*, September 1987, *110*(9), pp. 19–29. **[G: U.S.]**

Ginzberg, Eli. Technology, Women, and Work: Policy Perspectives. *Hartmann, H. I., ed.*, 1987, pp. 3–22. **[G: U.S.]**

Goldin, Claudia. Women's Employment and Technological Change: A Historical Perspective. *Hartmann, H. I., ed.*, 1987, pp. 185–222. **[G: U.S.]**

Gramatzki, Hans-Erich. Regional Employment Policies in East European Countries. *Adam, J., ed.*, 1987, pp. 171–95.
[G: Czechoslovakia; Poland; Hungary; E. Germany]

Greenwood, Michael J. and Ladman, Jerry R. Intertemporal and Intersectoral Aspects of Income and Distribution in Mexico. *Rev. Soc. Econ.*, April 1987, *45*(1), pp. 48–63.
[G: Mexico]

Gregory, Paul R. Productivity, Slack, and Time Theft in the Soviet Economy. *Millar, J. R., ed.*, 1987, pp. 241–75. **[G: U.S.S.R.]**

Guy, Ken. The UK Tertiary Service Sector. *Freeman, C. and Soete, L., eds.*, 1987, pp. 169–88. **[G: U.K.]**

Haber, Sheldon E.; Lamas, Enrique J. and Lichtenstein, Jules H. On Their Own: The Self-employed and Others in Private Business. *Mon. Lab. Rev.*, May 1987, *110*(5), pp. 17–23. **[G: U.S.]**

Hall, Peter. The Anatomy of Job Creation: Nations, Regions and Cities in the 1960s and 1970s. *Reg. Stud.*, April 1987, *21*(2), pp. 95–106. **[G: U.S.; U.K.; W. Germany; Japan]**

Haller, Max. Positional and Sectoral Differences in Income: The Federal Republic, France, and the United States. *Teckenberg, W., ed.*, 1987, pp. 172–90. **[G: W. Germany; France; U.S.]**

Hausman, Jerry A. and Paquette, Lynn. Involuntary Early Retirement and Consumption. *Burtless, G., ed.*, 1987, pp. 151–75. **[G: U.S.]**

Hayghe, Howard V. and Haugen, Steven E. A Profile of Husbands in Today's Labor Market. *Mon. Lab. Rev.*, October 1987, *110*(10), pp. 12–17. **[G: U.S.]**

Holly, Sean and Smith, Peter N. A Two-Sector Analysis of the UK Labour Market. *Oxford Bull. Econ. Statist.*, February 1987, *49*(1), pp. 79–102. **[G: U.K.]**

Iuzbekov, Z. Intensification in a Labor-Surplus Region. *Prob. Econ.*, January 1987, *29*(9), pp. 20–31. **[G: U.S.S.R.]**

Johnston, Denis and Rudney, Gabriel. Characteristics of Workers in Nonprofit Organizations. *Mon. Lab. Rev.*, July 1987, *110*(7), pp. 28–33. **[G: U.S.]**

Joshi, Heather E. and Owen, Susan J. How Long Is a Piece of Elastic? The Measurement of Female Activity Rates in British Censuses, 1951–1981. *Cambridge J. Econ.*, March 1987, *11*(1), pp. 55–74. **[G: U.K.]**

Kappelhoff, Peter and Teckenberg, Wolfgang. Intergenerational and Career Mobility in the Federal Republic and the United States. *Teckenberg, W., ed.*, 1987, pp. 3–49.
[G: W. Germany; U.S.]

Khandker, Shahidur R. Labor Market Participation of Married Women in Bangladesh. *Rev. Econ. Statist.*, August 1987, *69*(3), pp. 536–41. **[G: Bangladesh]**

Kosta, Jiří. Manpower Problems in the GDR. *Adam, J., ed.*, 1987, pp. 55–77.
[G: E. Germany]

Kostakov, Vladimir G. Employment: Scarcity or Surplus? *Prob. Econ.*, July 1987, *30*(3), pp. 5–21. **[G: U.S.S.R.]**

Kotliar, A. Labor Resources and the Current Economic Development of the USSR. *Prob. Econ.*, April 1987, *29*(12), pp. 5–22. **[G: U.S.S.R.]**

Kutscher, Ronald E. Overview and Implications of the Projections to 2000. *Mon. Lab. Rev.*, September 1987, *110*(9), pp. 3–9. **[G: U.S.]**

Kutscher, Ronald E. and Personick, Valerie A. Deindustrialization and the Shift to Services. *Econ. Lavoro*, Jan.-Mar. 1987, *21*(1), pp. 123–29. **[G: U.S.]**

Laedlein, Valyrie K. Revisions of State and Local Area Labor Force Statistics. *Mon. Lab. Rev.*, July 1987, *110*(7), pp. 38–41. **[G: U.S.]**

Lazear, Edward P. Involuntary Early Retirement and Consumption: Comment. *Burtless, G., ed.*, 1987, pp. 175–81. **[G: U.S.]**

Lonner, Thomas D. Transient Work Forces as Casualties in Northern Frontier Development. *Lane, T., ed.*, 1987, pp. 181–97. **[G: U.S.; Canada]**

Lorence, Jon. Subjective Labor Force Commitment of U.S. Men and Women, 1973–1985. *Soc. Sci. Quart.*, December 1987, *68*(4), pp. 745–60. **[G: U.S.]**

Maloney, Timothy J. Employment Constraints and the Labor Supply of Married Women: A Reexamination of the Added Worker Effect. *J. Human Res.*, Winter 1987, *22*(1), pp. 51–61. **[G: U.S.]**

Mann, Arthur J. and Delons, Jacques R. The Buenos Aires Mini-Enterprise Sector. *Soc. Econ. Stud.*, June 1987, *36*(2), pp. 41–67.
[G: Argentina]

Martellato, Dino and van der Borg, Jan. The Economy of the Italian Labour Catching Areas. *Ricerche Econ.*, Jan.-Mar. 1987, *41*(1), pp. 96–122. **[G: Italy]**

McGranahan, David A. The Role of Rural Workers in the National Economy. *U.S.D.A., Econ. Res. Serv., Agr. and Rural Econ. Div.*, 1987, pp. 2.1–23. **[G: U.S.]**

Mittar, Vishwa. Wage-Structure in the Informal Sector: The Case of a Class 1 City in Punjab. *Margin*, July-Sept. 1987, *19*(4), pp. 41–50.
[G: India]

Moen, Jon. The Labor of Older Men: A Comment. *J. Econ. Hist.*, September 1987, *47*(3), pp. 761–67. **[G: U.S.]**

Moffitt, Robert. Life-Cycle Labor Supply and Social Security: A Time-Series Analysis. *Burtless, G., ed.*, 1987, pp. 183–220. **[G: U.S.]**

Murphy, Kevin M. and Topel, Robert H. Unemployment, Risk, and Earnings: Testing for Equalizing Wage Differences in the Labor Market. *Lang, K. and Leonard, J. S., eds.*, 1987, pp. 103–40. [G: U.S.]

Nardone, Thomas. Decline in Youth Population Does Not Lead to Lower Jobless Rates. *Mon. Lab. Rev.*, June 1987, *110*(6), pp. 37–41. [G: U.S.]

Nohara, H. and Silvestre, Jean-Jacques. Industrial Structures, Employment Trends and the Economic Crisis: The Case of France and Japan in the 1970s. *Tarling, R., ed.*, 1987, pp. 147–76. [G: France; Japan]

Norwood, Janet L. The Labor Force of the Future. *Bus. Econ.*, July 1987, *22*(3), pp. 9–14. [G: U.S.]

Noyelle, Thierry J. The New Technology and the New Economy: Some Implications for Equal Employment Opportunity. *Hartmann, H. I., ed.*, 1987, pp. 373–94. [G: U.S.]

Ong, Paul M. Immigrant Wives' Labor Force Participation. *Ind. Relat.*, Fall 1987, *26*(3), pp. 296–303. [G: U.S.]

Owen, Susan J. and Joshi, Heather E. Does Elastic Retract: The Effect of Recession on Women's Labour Force Participation. *Brit. J. Ind. Relat.*, March 1987, *25*(1), pp. 125–43. [G: U.K.]

Personick, Valerie A. Industry Output and Employment through the End of the Century. *Mon. Lab. Rev.*, September 1987, *110*(9), pp. 30–45. [G: U.S.]

Pietsch, Anna-Jutta; Vogel, Heinrich and Schroeder, Gertrude E. Displacement by Technological Progress in the USSR (Social and Educational Problems and Their Treatment). *Adam, J., ed.*, 1987, pp. 149–70. [G: U.S.S.R.]

Power, Marilyn. From Home Production to Wage Labor: Women as a Reserve Army of Labor. *England, R. W., ed.*, 1987, pp. 157–77. [G: U.S.]

Quinn, Joseph F. Life-Cycle Labor Supply and Social Security: A Time-Series Analysis: Comment. *Burtless, G., ed.*, 1987, pp. 220–28. [G: U.S.]

Rajaraman, Indira. Labour Supply Functions with Incomplete Information. *Indian Econ. J.*, Apr.-June 1987, *34*(4), pp. 112–21. [G: India]

Ransom, Michael R. An Empirical Model of Discrete and Continuous Choice in Family Labor Supply. *Rev. Econ. Statist.*, August 1987, *69*(3), pp. 465–72. [G: U.S.]

Ransom, Michael R. The Labor Supply of Married Men: A Switching Regressions Model. *J. Lab. Econ.*, January 1987, *5*(1), pp. 63–75. [G: U.S.]

Rau, William C. and Roncek, Dennis W. Labor Force Transformations among Seven Major Industrial Nations, 1920–1970. *Soc. Sci. Quart.*, June 1987, *68*(2), pp. 326–39. [G: OECD]

Ritter, A. R. M. The Labour Force, Employment and Unemployment in Kenya. *Can. J. Devel. Stud.*, 1987, *8*(2), pp. 203–26. [G: Kenya]

Saunders, Norman C. Economic Projections to the Year 2000. *Mon. Lab. Rev.*, September 1987, *110*(9), pp. 10–18. [G: U.S.]

Schroeder, Esther C. Testing Local Level Labor Force and Unemployment Projections. *Demography*, November 1987, *24*(4), pp. 649–61. [G: U.S.]

Schroeder, Gertrude E. Managing Labour Shortages in the Soviet Union. *Adam, J., ed.*, 1987, pp. 3–26. [G: U.S.S.R.]

Schultz, T. Paul. The Value and Allocation of Time in High-Income Countries: Implications for Fertility. *Davis, K.; Bernstam, M. S. and Ricardo-Campbell, R., eds.*, 1987, 1986, pp. 87–108. [G: U.S.]

Semenza, Renata. Riduzione dell'occupazione industriale e mobilità del lavoro. (The Reduction of Industrial Employment and Work Mobility. With English summary.) *Econ. Lavoro*, July-Sept. 1987, *21*(3), pp. 85–93. [G: Italy]

Shack-Marquez, Janice and Wascher, William L. Some Direct Evidence on the Importance of Borrowing Constraints to the Labor Force Participation of Married Women [The Labor Force Participation Behavior of Married Women Under Conditions of Constraints on Borrowing]. *J. Human Res.*, Fall 1987, *22*(4), pp. 593–602. [G: U.S.]

Siesto, Vincenzo. Situazione e prospettive del lavoro nel mezzogiorno. (Actual Situation and Future Prospects for the Labour Market in the Mezzogiorno Area. With English summary.) *Econ. Lavoro*, Jan.-Mar. 1987, *21*(1), pp. 77–95. [G: Italy]

Smith, Shirley J. Work Experience of the Labor Force during 1985. *Mon. Lab. Rev.*, April 1987, *110*(4), pp. 40–44. [G: U.S.]

Sorensen, Elaine. Union Maids: Unions and the Female Work Force: Comments. *Brown, C. and Pechman, J. A., eds.*, 1987, pp. 213–16. [G: U.S.]

Stewart, Charles T., Jr. Structural Change and Intergenerational Occupational Mobility. *J. Devel. Areas*, January 1987, *21*(2), pp. 141–57. [G: Korea; Kuwait; Japan; Taiwan]

Stollar, Andrew J. and Thompson, G. Rodney. Sectoral Employment Shares: A Comparative Systems Context. *J. Compar. Econ.*, March 1987, *11*(1), pp. 62–80.

Swanson, Linda L. and Butler, Margaret A. Human Resource Base of Rural Economies. *U.S.D.A., Econ. Res. Serv., Agr. and Rural Econ. Div.*, 1987, pp. 7.1–23. [G: U.S.]

Tan, Edita A. and Alonzo, Ruperto P. The Philippine Experience in Manpower Planning and Labour Market Policies. *Amjad, R., ed.*, 1987, pp. 151–80. [G: Philippines]

Terwey, Michael. Class Position and Income Inequality: Comparing Results for the Federal Republic with Current U.S. Research. *Teckenberg, W., ed.*, 1987, pp. 119–71. [G: W. Germany; U.S.]

Timár, János. Employment Policy in Hungary. *Adam, J., ed.*, 1987, pp. 103–24. [G: Hungary]

Wainerman, Catalina H. and Moreno, Martín. Incorporando las trabajadoras agrícolas a los censos de población. (With English summary.) *Desarrollo Econ.*, Oct.-Dec. 1987, *27*(107), pp. 347–76. **[G: Argentina; Paraguay]**

Weber, Bruce A.; Castle, Emery N. and Shriver, Ann L. The Performance of Natural Resource Industries. *U.S.D.A., Econ. Res. Serv., Agr. and Rural Econ. Div.*, 1987, pp. 5.1–37. **[G: U.S.]**

Wong, Yue-chim. The Role of Husband's and Wife's Economic Activity Status in the Demand for Children. *J. Devel. Econ.*, April 1987, *25*(2), pp. 329–52. **[G: Hong Kong]**

Woodland, Alan D. Determinants of the Labour Force Status of the Aged. *Econ. Rec.*, June 1987, *63*(181), pp. 97–114. **[G: Australia]**

Yamada, Tadashi and Yamada, Tetsuji. Labor Employment of Married Women in Japan: Part-time Work vs. Full-time Work. *Eastern Econ. J.*, Jan.-Mar. 1987, *13*(1), pp. 41–48. **[G: Japan]**

Yamada, Tadashi; Yamada, Tetsuji and Chaloupka, Frank. Using Aggregate Data to Estimate the Part-Time and Full-Time Work Behavior of Japanese Women [An Analysis of Trends in Female Labor Force Participation in Japan]. *J. Human Res.*, Fall 1987, *22*(4), pp. 574–83. **[G: Japan]**

8131 Agriculture

Blanc, Michel. Family and Employment in Agriculture: Recent Changes in France. *J. Agr. Econ.*, May 1987, *38*(2), pp. 289–301. **[G: France]**

Bouldouyre, M. Fiscal and Social Actions to Promote Farmers Working in Woods Belonging to Others. *Merlo, M., et al., eds.*, 1987, pp. 487–90. **[G: France]**

Delgado, Christopher L. and Ranade, Chandrashekhar G. Technological Change and Agricultural Labor Use. *Mellor, J. W.; Delgado, C. L. and Blackie, M. J., eds.*, 1987, pp. 118–34. **[G: Africa]**

Deolalikar, Anil B. and Vijverberg, Wim P. M. A Test of Heterogeneity of Family and Hired Labour in Asian Agriculture. *Oxford Bull. Econ. Statist.*, August 1987, *49*(3), pp. 291–305. **[G: India; Malaysia]**

Errington, Andrew. Labour Use and Labour Requirements in UK Agriculture. *J. Agr. Econ.*, May 1987, *38*(2), pp. 271–79. **[G: U.K.]**

Gebauer, Rolf H. Socio-economic Classification of Farm Households. *Léon, Y. and Mahé, L., eds.*, 1987, pp. 177–98. **[G: W. Germany]**

Monke, Eric A. Portuguese Agriculture in Transition: Agricultural Factor Markets. *Pearson, S. R., et al.*, 1987, pp. 62–82. **[G: Portugal]**

Philpott, John C. and Tyler, Godfrey J. Interpersonal Variation in Farm Workers' Earnings: Analysis of Wages and Employment Enquiry Data. *J. Agr. Econ.*, September 1987, *38*(3), pp. 463–72. **[G: U.K.]**

Smith, Matthew G. Entry, Exit, and the Age Distribution of Farm Operators, 1974–82. *J. Agr. Econ. Res.*, Fall 1987, *39*(4), pp. 2–11. **[G: U.S.]**

Thakur, D. S. A Survey of Rural Unemployment in India: A Critique of Unidimensional Approach. *Indian Econ. J.*, July-Sept. 1987, *35*(1), pp. 120–35. **[G: India]**

Thomas, John K. and Goodwin, H. L., Jr. Employment Compensation among Farm Workers in the Lower Rio Grande Valley. *Soc. Sci. Quart.*, September 1987, *68*(3), pp. 621–30. **[G: U.S.]**

Thomas, Robert J. Microchips and Macroharvests: Labor–Management Relations in Agriculture. *Cornfield, D. B., ed.*, 1987, pp. 27–45. **[G: U.S.]**

Vaupel, Suzanne and Martin, Philip L. Evaluating Employer Sanctions: Farm Labor Contractor Experience. *Ind. Relat.*, Fall 1987, *26*(3), pp. 304–13. **[G: U.S.]**

Wendenhof, Jon. People Innovation at Eaton. *Shetty, Y. K. and Buehler, V. M., eds.*, 1987, pp. 93–101. **[G: U.S.]**

8132 Manufacturing

Allen, Bruce T. Microelectronics, Employment and Labour in the United States Automobile Industry. *Watanabe, S., ed.*, 1987, pp. 79–106. **[G: U.S.]**

Clark, John A.; Patel, Pari and Soete, Luc. Future Employment Trends in UK Manufacturing Using a Capital–Vintage Simulation Model. *Freeman, C. and Soete, L., eds.*, 1987, pp. 99–118. **[G: U.K.]**

David, Paul A. Industrial Labor Market Adjustments in a Region of Recent Settlement: Chicago, 1848–1868. *Kilby, P., ed.*, 1987, pp. 47–97. **[G: U.S.]**

Dickens, William T. and Lang, Kevin. Where Have All the Good Jobs Gone? Deindustrialization and Labor Market Segmentation. *Lang, K. and Leonard, J. S., eds.*, 1987, pp. 90–102. **[G: U.S.]**

Jessen, J., et al. The Informal Work of Industrial Workers: Present Situation, Trend Prognosis and Policy Implications. *Alessandrini, S. and Dallago, B., eds.*, 1987, pp. 271–82.

Moorhouse, H. F. The 'Work' Ethic and 'Leisure' Activity: The Hot Rod in Post-war America. *Joyce, P., ed.*, 1987, pp. 237–57. **[G: U.S.]**

Patel, Pari and Soete, Luc. Technological Trends and Employment in the UK Manufacturing Sectors. *Freeman, C. and Soete, L., eds.*, 1987, pp. 122–68. **[G: U.K.]**

Roy, Dilip Kumar. Exports and Labour Absorption: The Case of Bangladesh Manufactures. *Industry Devel.*, 1987, (22), pp. 67–92. **[G: Bangladesh]**

Solinas, Giovanni. Labour Market Segmentation and Workers' Careers: The Case of the Italian Knitwear Industry. *Tarling, R., ed.*, 1987, pp. 271–305. **[G: Italy]**

Villa, Paola. Systems of Flexible Working in the Italian Steel Industry. *Tarling, R., ed.*, 1987, pp. 307–45. **[G: Italy]**

8133 Service

Alam, M. Shahid and Azhar, Rauf. Determinants of Employment Expansion in the Services Sec-

tor: A Cross-Country Study of LDCs. *J. Devel. Areas*, October 1987, *22*(1), pp. 25–40.
[G: LDCs]

Baran, Barbara. The Technological Transformation of White-Collar Work: A Case Study of the Insurance Industry. *Hartmann, H. I., ed.*, 1987, pp. 25–62. [G: U.S.]

Carter, Michael G. The Australian Economy in the Long Run: The Service Sector. *Maddock, R. and McLean, I. W., eds.*, 1987, pp. 195–226. [G: Australia]

Driver, Ciaran and Naisbitt, Barry. Cyclical Variations in Service Industries' Employment in the UK. *Appl. Econ.*, April 1987, *19*(4), pp. 541–54. [G: U.K.]

Gershuny, Jonathan I. The Future of Service Employment. *Giarini, O., ed.*, 1987, pp. 105–24.
[G: U.K.]

Miller, James P. and Bluestone, Herman. Prospects for Service Sector Employment Growth in Nonmetro America. *U.S.D.A., Econ. Res. Serv., Agr. and Rural Econ. Div.*, 1987, pp. 6.1–21. [G: U.S.]

Moore, Goeffrey H. The Service Industries and the Business Cycle. *Bus. Econ.*, April 1987, *22*(2), pp. 12–17. [G: U.S.]

Rotella, Elyce J. The Dynamics of Occupational Segregation among Bank Tellers: Comments. *Brown, C. and Pechman, J. A., eds.*, 1987, pp. 149–54. [G: U.S.]

Ruyssen, Olivier. The New Deal in Services—A Challenge for Europe. *Akehurst, G. and Gadrey, J., eds.*, 1987, pp. 99–109.
[G: W. Germany; France; Italy; U.K.; U.S.]

Strober, Myra H. and Arnold, Carolyn L. The Dynamics of Occupational Segregation among Bank Tellers. *Brown, C. and Pechman, J. A., eds.*, 1987, pp. 107–48. [G: U.S.]

Thrift, Nigel. The Growth of Service Class Labour Markets: The Case of Great Britain. *Fischer, M. M. and Nijkamp, P., eds.*, 1987, pp. 313–44. [G: U.K.]

Ulman, Lloyd. The Dynamics of Occupational Segregation among Bank Tellers: Comments. *Brown, C. and Pechman, J. A., eds.*, 1987, pp. 154–57. [G: U.S.]

8134 Professional

Agarwal, Vinod B. and Yochum, Gilbert R. The Eilberg Act, New Seed Immigration, and Professional Labor Markets. *Econ. Educ. Rev.*, 1987, *6*(3), pp. 275–83. [G: U.S.]

Andrisani, Paul and Daymont, Thomas. Age Changes in Productivity and Earnings among Managers and Professionals. *Sandell, S. H., ed.*, 1987, pp. 52–70. [G: U.S.]

Barbezat, Debra A. Salary Differentials by Sex in the Academic Labor Market. *J. Human Res.*, Summer 1987, *22*(3), pp. 422–28. [G: U.S.]

Bezold, Clement. Health Trends and Scenarios: Implications for the Health Care Professions. *Meyer, J. A. and Lewin, M. E., eds.*, 1987, pp. 77–97. [G: U.S.]

Bognanno, Mario F. Women in Professions: Academic Women. *Koziara, K. S.; Moskow, M.*

H. and Tanner, L. D., eds., 1987, pp. 245–64. [G: U.S.]

Brunel, Andre and Burke, Michael P. Promoting High-Technology Industry: Initiatives and Policies for State Governments: Pennsylvania. *Schmandt, J. and Wilson, R., eds.*, 1987, pp. 191–229. [G: U.S.]

Burke, Michael P. and Dowling, Michael. Promoting High-Technology Industry: Initiatives and Policies for State Governments: Introduction. *Schmandt, J. and Wilson, R., eds.*, 1987, pp. 1–10. [G: U.S.]

Davis, Michael. The Use of Professions. *Bus. Econ.*, October 1987, *22*(4), pp. 5–10.
[G: U.S.]

Ebert, Robert. The Changing Role of the Physician. *Schramm, C. J., ed.*, 1987, pp. 145–84.
[G: U.S.]

Eberts, Randall W. and Stone, Joe A. Teacher Unions and the Productivity of Public Schools. *Ind. Lab. Relat. Rev.*, April 1987, *40*(3), pp. 354–63. [G: U.S.]

Fischer, Harald and Peck, Amy Miriam. Promoting High-Technology Industry: Initiatives and Policies for State Governments: New York. *Schmandt, J. and Wilson, R., eds.*, 1987, pp. 129–62. [G: U.S.]

Freudenberg, Michael and Henderson, Tracy L. Promoting High-Technology Industry: Initiatives and Policies for State Governments: Florida. *Schmandt, J. and Wilson, R., eds.*, 1987, pp. 35–64. [G: U.S.]

Ginsburg, Paul B. Reforming Physician Reimbursement in Medicare. *Meyer, J. A. and Lewin, M. E., eds.*, 1987, pp. 35–50.
[G: U.S.]

Hacker, Sidney Bailey and Sommerfeld, Robert D. Promoting High-Technology Industry: Initiatives and Policies for State Governments: Minnesota. *Schmandt, J. and Wilson, R., eds.*, 1987, pp. 97–127. [G: U.S.]

Howard, Mark and Kragie, Mary. Promoting High-Technology Industry: Initiatives and Policies for State Governments: North Carolina. *Schmandt, J. and Wilson, R., eds.*, 1987, pp. 163–90. [G: U.S.]

Kindig, David A., et al. Trends in Physician Availability in 10 Urban Areas from 1963 to 1980. *Inquiry*, Summer 1987, *24*(2), pp. 136–46.
[G: U.S.]

Klevorick, Alvin K. and McGuire, Thomas G. Monopolistic Competition and Consumer Information: Pricing in the Market for Psychologists' Services. *McGuire, T. G. and Scheffler, R. M., eds.*, 1987, pp. 235–53. [G: U.S.]

Lee, Barbara A. and Parker, Joan. Supervisory Participation in Professional Associations: Implications of *North Shore University Hospital*. *Ind. Lab. Relat. Rev.*, April 1987, *40*(3), pp. 364–81.

Lehrer, Evelyn L. and White, William D. Hospital Market Structure and the Return to Nursing Education: Comment [Hospital Market Structure and the Return to Nursing Education]. *J. Human Res.*, Fall 1987, *22*(4), pp. 607–08.
[G: U.S.]

Merrigan, Kathleen A. and Smith, Suzanne E.

Promoting High-Technology Industry: Initiatives and Policies for State Governments: Massachusetts. *Schmandt, J. and Wilson, R., eds.*, 1987, pp. 65–96. [G: U.S.]

Morton, John D. BLS Prepares to Broaden Scope of Its White-Collar Pay Survey. *Mon. Lab. Rev.*, March 1987, *110*(3), pp. 3–7. [G: U.S.]

Muller, Brian and Dowling, Michael. Promoting High-Technology Industry: Initiatives and Policies for State Governments: Texas. *Schmandt, J. and Wilson, R., eds.*, 1987, pp. 231–57. [G: U.S.]

Shostak, Arthur B. Technology, Air Traffic Control, and Labor–Management Relations. *Cornfield, D. B., ed.*, 1987, pp. 153–72. [G: U.S.]

Silbert, Lance. Promoting High-Technology Industry: Initiatives and Policies for State Governments: California. *Schmandt, J. and Wilson, R., eds.*, 1987, pp. 11–33. [G: U.S.]

Spurr, Stephen J. How the Market Solves an Assignment Problem: The Matching of Lawyers with Legal Claims. *J. Lab. Econ.*, Part 1, Oct. 1987, *5*(4), pp. 502–32. [G: U.S.]

Straub, LaVonne A. and Lane, Julia. Response [Hospital Market Structure and the Return to Nursing Education]. *J. Human Res.*, Fall 1987, *22*(4), pp. 609–10. [G: U.S.]

Weiler, William C. Economic Issues in Faculty Retirement Plans in American Higher Education Institutions. *Econ. Educ. Rev.*, 1987, *6*(3), pp. 207–26. [G: U.S.]

Zahid, Khan H. An Analysis of the Institutional Affiliation of Recent Ph.D.s in Economics in the Top 18 Graduate Programs, by Fields of Specialization. *Amer. Econ.*, Fall 1987, *31*(2), pp. 64–68. [G: U.S.]

8135 Government Employees

Ali, Supian Haji. The Growing Sector: Malaysia. *Edgren, G., ed.*, 1987, pp. 99–146. [G: Malaysia]

Canlas, Dante B. The Growing Sector: Philippines. *Edgren, G., ed.*, 1987, pp. 147–72. [G: Philippines]

Crane, Jon R. and Wise, David A. Military Service and Civilian Earnings of Youths. *Wise, D. A., ed.*, 1987, pp. 119–37. [G: U.S.]

Desai, Ashok and Desai, Ena. The Growing Sector: India. *Edgren, G., ed.*, 1987, pp. 67–97. [G: India]

Edgren, Gus. The Growth of Public Sector Employment in Asia. *Edgren, G., ed.*, 1987, pp. 1–28. [G: Asia]

Ehrenberg, Ronald G. and Smith, Robert S. Comparable Worth in the Public Sector. *Wise, D. A., ed.*, 1987, pp. 243–88. [G: U.S.]

Ellwood, David T. and Wise, David A. Military Hiring and Youth Employment. *Wise, D. A., ed.*, 1987, pp. 79–95. [G: U.S.]

Ellwood, David T. and Wise, David A. Uncle Sam Wants You—Sometimes: Military Enlistments and the Youth Labor Market. *Wise, D. A., ed.*, 1987, pp. 97–118. [G: U.S.]

Frant, Howard L. and Leonard, Herman B. Promise Them Anything: The Incentive Structures of Local Public Pension Plans. *Wise, D. A., ed.*, 1987, pp. 215–37. [G: U.S.]

Freeman, Richard B. How Do Public Sector Wages and Employment Respond to Economic Conditions? *Wise, D. A., ed.*, 1987, pp. 183–207. [G: U.S.]

Hongladarom, Chira, et al. The Growing Sector: Thailand. *Edgren, G., ed.*, 1987, pp. 173–223. [G: Thailand]

Horn, Robert N. and Tomkiewicz, Joseph M. State Strategies of Control in the Public Sector. *England, R. W., ed.*, 1987, pp. 245–53. [G: U.S.]

Ingham, Michael D. Local Government Pay Drift: The Search for Causality. *Appl. Econ.*, January 1987, *19*(1), pp. 83–100. [G: U.K.]

Ippolito, Richard A. Why Federal Workers Don't Quit. *J. Human Res.*, Spring 1987, *22*(2), pp. 281–99. [G: U.S.]

Leonard, Herman B. Academic Ability, Earnings, and the Decision to Become a Teacher: Evidence from the National Longitudinal Study of the High School Class of 1972: Comment. *Wise, D. A., ed.*, 1987, pp. 312–16. [G: U.S.]

Leonard, Herman B. Investing in the Defense Work Force: The Debt and Structure of Military Pensions. *Wise, D. A., ed.*, 1987, pp. 47–73. [G: U.S.]

Lewin, David. Technological Change in the Public Sector: The Case of Sanitation Service. *Cornfield, D. B., ed.*, 1987, pp. 281–309. [G: U.S.]

Manski, Charles F. Academic Ability, Earnings, and the Decision to Become a Teacher: Evidence from the National Longitudinal Study of the High School Class of 1972. *Wise, D. A., ed.*, 1987, pp. 291–312. [G: U.S.]

Medoff, James L. Comparable Worth in the Public Sector: Comment. *Wise, D. A., ed.*, 1987, pp. 288–89. [G: U.S.]

Murshid, K. A. S. and Sobhan, Rehman. The Growing Sector: Bangladesh. *Edgren, G., ed.*, 1987, pp. 29–65. [G: Bangladesh]

Obermann, Gabriel. Capital Intensity and the Federal Sector: Some Further Evidence. *Public Choice*, 1987, *52*(2), pp. 193–99. [G: U.S.]

Ozaki, M. Labour Relations in the Public Service: 1. Methods of Determining Employment Conditions. *Int. Lab. Rev.*, 1987, *126*(3), pp. 277–99. [G: OECD]

Peltzman, Sam. How Do Public Sector Wages and Employment Respond to Economic Conditions? Comment. *Wise, D. A., ed.*, 1987, pp. 207–13. [G: U.S.]

Petersen, John E. Public Pension Fund Administration. *Aronson, J. R. and Schwartz, E., eds.*, 1987, pp. 318–41. [G: U.S.]

Phillips, Douglas W. and Wise, David A. Military versus Civilian Pay: A Descriptive Discussion. *Wise, D. A., ed.*, 1987, pp. 19–46. [G: U.S.]

Rosen, Harvey S. Comment [Military versus Civilian Pay: A Descriptive Discussion] [Investing in the Defense Work Force: The Debt and

Structure of Military Pensions]. *Wise, D. A., ed.*, 1987, pp. 73–77.   [G: U.S.]

Schumann, Richard E. State and Local Government Pay Increases Outpace Five-Year Rise in Private Industry. *Mon. Lab. Rev.*, February 1987, *110*(2), pp. 18–20.   [G: U.S.]

Smith, Sharon P. Wages in the Federal and Private Sectors: Comment. *Wise, D. A., ed.*, 1987, pp. 177–82.   [G: U.S.]

Thornton, Robert J. Unions, Wages, and Local Government Finance. *Aronson, J. R. and Schwartz, E., eds.*, 1987, pp. 383–99.
                                    [G: U.S.]

Venti, Steven F. Wages in the Federal and Private Sectors. *Wise, D. A., ed.*, 1987, pp. 147–77.
                                    [G: U.S.]

Wise, David A. Public Sector Payrolls: Overview. *Wise, D. A., ed.*, 1987, pp. 1–18.   [G: U.S.]

8136 Construction

Perloff, Jeffrey M. and Sickles, Robin C. Union Wage, Hours, and Earnings Differentials in the Construction Industry. *J. Lab. Econ.*, April 1987, *5*(2), pp. 174–210.   [G: U.S.]

8139 Other Sectors

Betcherman, Gordon and Rebne, Douglas. Technology and Control of the Labor Process: Fifty Years of Longshoring on the U.S. West Coast. *Cornfield, D. B., ed.*, 1987, pp. 73–89.
                                    [G: U.S.]

820 LABOR MARKETS; PUBLIC POLICY

821 Labor Economics

8210 Labor Economics: Theory and Empirical Studies Illustrating Theory

Abowd, John M. and Card, David. Intertemporal Labor Supply and Long-term Employment Contracts. *Amer. Econ. Rev.*, March 1987, *77*(1), pp. 50–68.   [G: U.S.]

Adams, James D. Intertemporal Wage Variation, Employment, and Unemployment. *J. Lab. Econ.*, January 1987, *5*(1), pp. 106–29.
                                    [G: U.S.]

Adnett, N. J. State Employment Agencies and Labour Market Efficiency. *Cambridge J. Econ.*, September 1987, *11*(3), pp. 183–96.
                                    [G: U.K.]

Albrecht, James W. Hare Today, Gone Tomorrow . . . Divorce, Unemployment, and Other Sorry States. *Lang, K. and Leonard, J. S., eds.*, 1987, pp. 207–11.   [G: U.S.]

Alogoskoufis, George S. Aggregate Employment and Intertemporal Substitution in the UK. *Econ. J.*, June 1987, *97*(386), pp. 403–15.
                                    [G: U.K.]

Alogoskoufis, George S. On Intertemporal Substitution and Aggregate Labor Supply. *J. Polit. Econ.*, October 1987, *95*(5), pp. 938–60.
                                    [G: U.S.]

Andersen, Torben M. Short- and Long-run Consequences of Shorter Working Hours. *Pedersen, P. J. and Lund, R., eds.*, 1987, pp. 147–65.

Anderson, Kathryn H.; Butler, John S. and Sloan, Frank A. Labor Market Segmentation: A Cluster Analysis of Job Groupings and Barriers to Entry. *Southern Econ. J.*, January 1987, *53*(3), pp. 571–90.   [G: U.S.]

Andrews, Martyn J. The Aggregate Labour Market: An Empirical Investigation into Market-Clearing for the UK. *Econ. J.*, March 1987, *97*(385), pp. 157–76.   [G: U.K.]

Andrews, Martyn J. and Nickell, Stephen J. A Disaggregated Disequilibrium Model of the Labour Market. *Sinclair, P. J. N., ed.*, 1987, *1986*, pp. 414–30.   [G: U.K.]

Appolito, Richard A. The Implicit Pension Contract *Developments and New Directions*. *J. Human Res.*, Summer 1987, *22*(3), pp. 441–67.

Aron, Debra J. Worker Reputation and Productivity Incentives. *J. Lab. Econ.*, Part 2, Oct. 1987, *5*(4), pp. S87–106.

Artus, Jacques R. Real Wages, Real Wage Aspirations, and Unemployment in Europe: Comment. *Lawrence, R. Z. and Schultze, C. L., eds.*, 1987, pp. 292–95.   [G: W. Europe]

Ashenfelter, Orley. The Work Response to a Guaranteed Income: A Survey of Experimental Evidence: Discussion. *Munnell, A. H., ed.*, 1987, pp. 53–55.   [G: U.S.]

Aspromourgos, Tony. Unemployment, Economic Theory and Labour–Market Deregulation. *Australian Econ. Pap.*, June 1987, *26*(48), pp. 130–44.   [G: Australia]

Balducci, Renato. Strategie sindacali e occupazione. (With English summary.) *Stud. Econ.*, 1987, *42*(31), pp. 7–34.

Ball, Laurence Markham. Externalities from Contract Length. *Amer. Econ. Rev.*, September 1987, *77*(4), pp. 615–29.

Bamberg, Günter. Beschäftigungseffekte ertragsabhängiger Entlohnungsschemata. (The Demand for Labor in a Share Economy. With English summary.) *Jahr. Nationalökon. Statist.*, October 1987, *203*(5–6), pp. 467–75.

Bandyopadhyay, Pradeep. Value and Post-Sraffa Marxian Analysis. *Albelda, R.; Gunn, C. and Waller, W., eds.*, 1987, *1984*, pp. 186–94.

Barro, Robert J. and Romer, Paul M. Ski-Lift Pricing, with Applications to Labor and Other Markets. *Amer. Econ. Rev.*, December 1987, *77*(5), pp. 875–90.

Barron, John M.; Fuess, Scott M., Jr. and Loewenstein, Mark A. Further Analysis of the Effect of Unions on Training [Union Wages, Temporary Layoffs, and Seniority]. *J. Polit. Econ.*, June 1987, *95*(3), pp. 632–40.

Baslé, Maurice. Les salaires et le cycle: fondements micro-économiques et analyse macro-économique des flexibilités. (Wages and the Cycle: Micro-economics' Foundations and Macro-economic Analysis of Flexibilities. With English summary.) *Écon. Soc.*, November 1987, *21*(11), pp. 57–81.   [G: OECD]

Basu, Kaushik. Disneyland Monopoly, Interlinkage and Usurious Interest Rates. *J. Public Econ.*, October 1987, *34*(1), pp. 1–17.

Batra, Raveendra N. and Lahiri, Sajal. Imported Technologies, Urban Unemployment and the

North–South Dialogue. *J. Devel. Econ.*, February 1987, *25*(1), pp. 21–32.   **[G: LDCs]**

Bean, Charles R. Real Wages, Real Wage Aspirations, and Unemployment in Europe: Comment. *Lawrence, R. Z. and Schultze, C. L., eds.*, 1987, pp. 295–99.   **[G: W. Europe]**

Beckmann, Martin J. On the Persistence of Fluctuations in Career Opportunities. *[Marrama, V.], Vol. 2*, 1987, pp. 769–76.

Beenstock, Michael. Budget Lines and Labour Supply Incentives. *Beenstock, M., et al.*, 1987, pp. 1–24.   **[G: U.K.]**

Beenstock, Michael. Work, Welfare and Taxation: Conclusions and Overview. *Beenstock, M., et al.*, 1987, pp. 261–67.   **[G: U.K.]**

Beenstock, Michael and Dalziel, Alan. Econometric Analysis of Labour Supply and Work Incentives. *Beenstock, M., et al.*, 1987, pp. 166–84.   **[G: U.K.]**

Beenstock, Michael and Minford, Patrick. Curing Unemployment through Labour-Market Competition. *Begg, D. K. H., et al.*, 1987, pp. 129–49.   **[G: U.S.; U.K.]**

Beladi, Hamid and Naqvi, Nadeem. The Theory of Interindustry Wage Differentials: An Intertemporal Analysis. *Can. J. Econ.*, May 1987, *20*(2), pp. 245–56.

Bell, Linda and Freeman, Richard B. Flexible Wage Structures and Employment. *Gunderson, M.; Meltz, N. M. and Ostry, S., eds.*, 1987, pp. 119–28.   **[G: U.S.]**

Ben-Horim, Moshe and Zuckerman, Dror. The Effect of Unemployment Insurance on Unemployment Duration. *J. Lab. Econ.*, July 1987, *5*(3), pp. 386–90.

Berry, Albert. The Labour Market and Human Capital in LDCs. *Gemmell, N., ed.*, 1987, pp. 205–35.

Bethune, John J. An Expansion of the Contemporary Theoretical Exposition Concerning the Work Disincentive Effects of Government Income Maintenance Programs. *Amer. Econ.*, Fall 1987, *31*(2), pp. 22–28.

Black, Dan A. The Social Security System, the Provision of Human Capital, and the Structure of Compensation. *J. Lab. Econ.*, April 1987, *5*(2), pp. 242–54.

Blanchard, Olivier Jean and Summers, Lawrence H. Fiscal Increasing Returns, Hysteresis, Real Wages and Unemployment. *Europ. Econ. Rev.*, April 1987, *31*(3), pp. 543–66.   **[G: OECD]**

Blanchard, Olivier Jean and Summers, Lawrence H. Hysteresis in Unemployment. *Europ. Econ. Rev.*, Feb./Mar. 1987, *31*(1/2), pp. 288–95.

Blomquist, N. Sören. Can Shorter Working Time Reduce Unemployment? Comment. *Siven, C.-H., ed.*, 1987, pp. 149–53.

Blundell, Richard. Econometric Approaches to the Specification of Life-Cycle Labour Supply and Commodity Demand Behaviour. *Econometric Rev.*, 1987, *6*(1), pp. 103–65.

Bodvarsson, Örn B. Monitoring with No Moral Hazard: The Case of Small Vessel Commercial Fishing. *Eastern Econ. J.*, October-December 1987, *13*(4), pp. 421–34.   **[G: U.S.]**

Booth, Alison L. and Schiantarelli, Fabio. The Employment Effects of a Shorter Working Week. *Economica*, May 1987, *54*(214), pp. 237–48.

Booth, Laurence D.; Finkelstein, John M. and Lee, Wayne Y. A Note on the Demand for Labor by Firms and the Phillips Curve Phenomenon. *J. Econ. Bus.*, November 1987, *39*(4), pp. 349–56.

Bosworth, Derek and Westaway, Tony. The Demand for Hours of Work. *Scot. J. Polit. Econ.*, November 1987, *34*(4), pp. 368–87.   **[G: U.K.]**

Boyd, D. A. C. The Historical Materialist–Symbolist Theory of Race Discrimination. *Soc. Econ. Stud.*, June 1987, *36*(2), pp. 123–43.

Bradbury, Katharine L. Non–Labor-Supply Responses to the Income Maintenance Experiments: Discussion. *Munnell, A. H., ed.*, 1987, pp. 122–26.   **[G: U.S.]**

Brown, James N. and Rosen, Harvey S. Taxation, Wage Variation, and Job Choice. *J. Lab. Econ.*, Part 1, Oct. 1987, *5*(4), pp. 430–51.   **[G: U.S.]**

Brown, Vivienne. Demand-Deficient Unemployment. *Thompson, G.; Brown, V. and Levačić, R., eds.*, 1987, pp. 105–33.   **[G: U.K.]**

Browning, Martin. Co-operatives, Closures, or Wage Cuts: The Choices Facing Workers in an Ailing Firm. *Can. J. Econ.*, February 1987, *20*(1), pp. 114–22.

Brüniche-Olsen, Paul. Unemployment, the Labour Queue and Positive Feedback in the Labour Market. *Pedersen, P. J. and Lund, R., eds.*, 1987, pp. 187–204.

Buchanan, James M. Equal Treatment and Reverse Discrimination. *Buchanan, J. M. (II)*, 1987, *1981*, pp. 276–88.

Buffie, Edward F. Labor Market Distortions, the Structure of Protection and Direct Foreign Investment. *J. Devel. Econ.*, October 1987, *27*(1–2), pp. 149–63.

Buffie, Edward F. Labor Market Distortions, the Structure of Protection and Direct Foreign Investment. *[Diaz-Alejandro, C. F.]*, 1987, pp. 149–63.

Bull, Clive. The Existence of Self-Enforcing Implicit Contracts. *Quart. J. Econ.*, February 1987, *102*(1), pp. 147–59.

Bull, Clive; Ornati, Oscar and Tedeschi, Piero. Search, Hiring Strategies, and Labor Market Intermediaries. *J. Lab. Econ.*, Part 2, Oct. 1987, *5*(4), pp. S1–17.

Burtless, Gary. Jobless Pay and High European Unemployment. *Lawrence, R. Z. and Schultze, C. L., eds.*, 1987, pp. 105–62.   **[G: U.S.; W. Europe]**

Burtless, Gary. The Work Response to a Guaranteed Income: A Survey of Experimental Evidence. *Munnell, A. H., ed.*, 1987, pp. 22–52.   **[G: U.S.]**

Burtless, Gary and Haveman, Robert H. Taxes, Transfers, and Labor Supply: The Evolving Views of U.S. Economists. *van de Kar, H. M.*

and Wolfe, B. L., eds., 1987, pp. 127–45.
[G: U.S.]

Calmfors, Lars. High Unemployment in Europe: Diagnosis and Policy Implications: Comment. *Siven, C.-H., ed.*, 1987, pp. 39–43.
[G: W. Europe]

Calvo, Guillermo A. The Economics of Supervision. *Nalbantian, H. R., ed.*, 1987, pp. 87–103.

Candela, Guido and Fabbri, Paolo. La distribuzione ottimale delle ferie: una nuova favola per l'efficienza. (The Optimal Timing of Workers' Holidays: A New Fable for Growth. With English summary.) *Econ. Lavoro*, Oct.-Dec. 1987, *21*(4), pp. 3–13.

Cantor, Richard. Long-term Contracts, Consumption Smoothing and Wage–Profit Dynamics. *J. Macroecon.*, Winter 1987, *9*(1), pp. 59–70.

Capparucci, Marina. Lavoro femminile tra marginalismo e marginalità. (Female Employment between Marginalism and Marginality. With English summary.) *Econ. Lavoro*, Jan.-Mar. 1987, *21*(1), pp. 47–63. [G: Italy]

Carruth, Alan A. and Oswald, Andrew J. On Union Preferences and Labour Market Models: Insiders and Outsiders. *Econ. J.*, June 1987, *97*(386), pp. 431–45.

Chan, Kenneth S. The Production Effect of Discrimination: A Conceptual Investigation. *J. Econ. Behav. Organ.*, June 1987, *8*(2), pp. 307–14.

Charette, Michael F. and Kaufmann, Barry. Short-run Variation in the Natural Rate of Unemployment. *J. Macroecon.*, Summer 1987, *9*(3), pp. 417–27. [G: Canada]

Chillemi, Ottorino. Qualche considerazione su retribuzioni universitarie e processi di autoselezione. (Some Notes on University Remunerations and the Auto-selection Process. With English summary.) *Econ. Lavoro*, Apr.-June 1987, *21*(2), pp. 59–66.

Chilosi, Alberto. Il principio di assunzione obbligatoria come strumento per eliminare la disoccupazione involontaria in un'economia di mercatato: un'analisi teorica e una proposta operativa. (The Principle of Obligatory Hirings as an Instrument for Eliminating Involuntary Unemployment in a Free Market Economy: A Theoretical Analysis and a Working Proposal. With English summary.) *Econ. Lavoro*, July-Sept. 1987, *21*(3), pp. 39–50. [G: Italy]

Chuma, Hiroyuki. Pensions, Wage Profiles, and Retirement Rules: Specific Human Capital Approach. *J. Econ. Dynam. Control*, March 1987, *11*(1), pp. 29–64. [G: Japan]

Clark, Gordon L. Job Search Theory and Indeterminate Information. *Fischer, M. M. and Nijkamp, P., eds.*, 1987, pp. 169–88.

Claycombe, Richard J. The Wife's Wage and the Division of Work at Home. *Amer. Econ.*, Fall 1987, *31*(2), pp. 13–21. [G: U.S.]

Clemenz, Gerhard. Adverse Selection and Imperfect Monitoring in a Labour Market: Some Game-Theoretic Remarks. *Empirica*, 1987, *14*(2), pp. 213–26.

Coen, Robert M. and Hickman, Bert G. Keynesian and Classical Unemployment in Four Countries. *Brookings Pap. Econ. Act.*, 1987, (1), pp. 123–93. [G: U.S.; U.K.; W. Germany; Austria]

Cross, Rod B. Hysteresis and Instability in the Natural Rate of Unemployment. *Scand. J. Econ.*, 1987, *89*(1), pp. 71–89.

Dahrendorf, Ralf. Slow Growth in Europe: Conceptual Issues: Comment. *Lawrence, R. Z. and Schultze, C. L., eds.*, 1987, pp. 76–79.
[G: W. Europe]

Das-Gupta, Arindam and Gang, Ira N. A Framework for Analyzing Economies with Wage Differentials. *Rivista Int. Sci. Econ. Com.*, September 1987, *34*(9), pp. 869–86.

Dasgupta, Partha and Ray, Debraj. Inequality as a Determinant of Malnutrition and Unemployment: Policy. *Econ. J.*, March 1987, *97*(385), pp. 177–88.

Davidson, Carl; Martin, Lawrence W. and Matusz, Steven J. Search, Unemployment, and the Production of Jobs. *Econ. J.*, December 1987, *97*(388), pp. 857–76.

Davidson, Paul. The Simple Macroeconomics of a Nonergodic Monetary Economy versus a Share Economy: Is Weitzman's Macroeconomics Too Simple? *J. Post Keynesian Econ.*, Winter 1986-87, *9*(2), pp. 212–25.

Deere, Donald R. Labor Turnover, Job-Specific Skills, and Efficiency in a Search Model. *Quart. J. Econ.*, November 1987, *102*(4), pp. 815–33.

Dickens, William T. and Katz, Lawrence F. Inter-industry Wage Differences and Industry Characteristics. *Lang, K. and Leonard, J. S., eds.*, 1987, pp. 48–89. [G: U.S.]

Dickens, William T. and Lang, Kevin. Where Have All the Good Jobs Gone? Deindustrialization and Labor Market Segmentation. *Lang, K. and Leonard, J. S., eds.*, 1987, pp. 90–102.
[G: U.S.]

Dionne, Georges and Eeckhoudt, Louis. Proportional Risk Aversion, Taxation and Labor Supply under Uncertainty. *J. Econ. (Z. Nationalökon.)*, 1987, *47*(4), pp. 353–66.

Djajić, Slobodan. Illegal Aliens, Unemployment and Immigration Policy. *J. Devel. Econ.*, February 1987, *25*(1), pp. 235–49. [G: U.S.]

Djajić, Slobodan and Purvis, Douglas D. Intersectoral Adjustment and the Dynamics of Wages and Employment Opportunities. *Weltwirtsch. Arch.*, 1987, *123*(2), pp. 216–31.

Drazen, Allan. Reciprocal Externality Models of Low Employment. *Europ. Econ. Rev.*, Feb./Mar. 1987, *31*(1/2), pp. 436–43.

Drèze, Jacques H. Human Capital and Risk-Bearing. *Drèze, J. H.*, 1987, *1979*, pp. 347–65.

Drèze, Jacques H. Slow Growth in Europe: Conceptual Issues: Comment. *Lawrence, R. Z. and Schultze, C. L., eds.*, 1987, pp. 79–93.
[G: W. Europe]

Drèze, Jacques H. Some Theory of Labour Management and Participation. *Drèze, J. H.*, 1987, *1976*, pp. 366–82.

Drèze, Jacques H. Underemployment Equilibrium: From Theory to Econometrics and Policy. *Europ. Econ. Rev.*, Feb./Mar. 1987, *31*(1/2), pp. 9–34. **[G: W. Europe]**

Dutt, Amitava Krishna. Wage Rigidity and Unemployment: The Simple Diagrammatics of Two Views. *J. Post Keynesian Econ.*, Winter 1986-87, *9*(2), pp. 279–90.

Dynarski, Mark and Sheffrin, Steven M. New Evidence on the Cyclical Behavior of Unemployment Durations. *Lang, K. and Leonard, J. S., eds.*, 1987, pp. 164–85. **[G: U.S.]**

Egginton, Don M. A Historical Analysis of Labour Supply Incentives. *Beenstock, M., et al.*, 1987, pp. 76–123. **[G: U.K.]**

Egginton, Don M. An Informal Empirical Analysis of Labour Supply Decisions in the UK. *Beenstock, M., et al.*, 1987, pp. 124–65. **[G: U.K.]**

Egginton, Don M. Case Studies of Labour Supply Incentives and Budget Lines. *Beenstock, M., et al.*, 1987, pp. 25–75. **[G: U.K.]**

Ellis, Christopher J. and Fender, John. Bargaining and Wage Resistance in an Open Macroeconomic Model. *Econ. J.*, March 1987, *97*(385), pp. 106–20.

Emerson, Michael. Labour Market Flexibility and Jobs: A Survey of Evidence from OECD Countries with Special Reference to Europe: Comments. *Layard, R. and Calmfors, L., eds.*, 1987, pp. 77–84. **[G: OECD]**

Erlich, S.; Ginsburgh, Victor and Van der Heyden, Ludo. Where Do Real Wage Policies Lead Belgium? A General Equilibrium Analysis. *Europ. Econ. Rev.*, October 1987, *31*(7), pp. 1369–83. **[G: Belgium]**

Falkinger, Josef. Lieber begehrt und im Überfluss als überflüssig und in Not: Ein Beispiel. (With English summary.) *Kyklos*, 1987, *40*(3), pp. 393–98.

Feinberg, Robert M. An Empirical Investigation of Owner–Manager Labor-Supply Behavior. *Managerial Dec. Econ.*, September 1987, *8*(3), pp. 213–16. **[G: U.S.]**

Felli, Leonardo. Do Firms Insure Workers, or Workers Insure Firms? *Econ. Lavoro*, Oct.-Dec. 1987, *21*(4), pp. 69–72.

Fethke, Gary and Policano, Andrew. Monetary Policy and the Timing of Wage Negotiations. *J. Monet. Econ.*, January 1987, *19*(1), pp. 89–105.

Findlay, Ronald and Lundahl, Mats. Racial Discrimination, Dualistic Labor Markets and Foreign Investment. *[Diaz-Alejandro, C. F.]*, 1987, pp. 139–48. **[G: S. Africa]**

Findlay, Ronald and Lundahl, Mats. Racial Discrimination, Dualistic Labor Markets and Foreign Investment. *J. Devel. Econ.*, October 1987, *27*(1–2), pp. 139–48. **[G: S. Africa]**

Fischer, Manfred M. and Nijkamp, Peter. Labour Market Theories: Perspectives, Problems and Policy Implications. *Fischer, M. M. and Nijkamp, P., eds.*, 1987, pp. 37–52.

Fischer, Manfred M. and Nijkamp, Peter. Regional Labour Market Analysis: Retrospect and Prospect. *Fischer, M. M. and Nijkamp, P., eds.*, 1987, pp. 485–88.

Fischer, Manfred M. and Nijkamp, Peter. Spatial Labour Market Analysis: Relevance and Scope. *Fischer, M. M. and Nijkamp, P., eds.*, 1987, pp. 1–33.

Flam, Harry. Equal Pay for Unequal Work. *Scand. J. Econ.*, 1987, *89*(4), pp. 435–50. **[G: Sweden]**

Flemming, John S. Wage Flexibility and Employment Stability. *Oxford Econ. Pap.*, March 1987, *39*(1), pp. 161–74.

Flemming, John S. Wage Flexibility and Employment Stability. *Sinclair, P. J. N., ed.*, 1987, pp. 161–74.

Flückiger, Yves. Effets de l'assurance-chômage sur la mobilité interrégionale du travail. (With English summary.) *Revue Écon.*, September 1987, *38*(5), pp. 1017–28.

Folbre, Nancy R. A Patriarchal Mode of Production. *Albelda, R.; Gunn, C. and Waller, W., eds.*, 1987, pp. 323–38.

Frank, Jeff. A Signalling Approach to Wage Rigidity and Layoffs. *Europ. Econ. Rev.*, October 1987, *31*(7), pp. 1385–1405.

Franz, Wolfgang. Hysteresis, Persistence, and the NAIRU: An Empirical Analysis for the Federal Republic of Germany. *Layard, R. and Calmfors, L., eds.*, 1987, pp. 91–122. **[G: W. Germany]**

Franz, Wolfgang. The End of Expansion in Employment in Germany: Beginnings of an Attempt at Evaluation of Structural Unemployment as a Partial Component of Joblessness. *Pedersen, P. J. and Lund, R., eds.*, 1987, pp. 81–103. **[G: W. Germany]**

Gallaway, Lowell and Vedder, Richard K. Wages, Prices, and Employment: Von Mises and the Progressives. *Rothbard, M. N., ed.*, 1987, pp. 33–80. **[G: U.S.; U.K.]**

Gang, Ira N. and Gangopadhyay, Shubhashis. Employment, Output and the Choice of Techniques: The Trade-Off Revisited. *J. Devel. Econ.*, April 1987, *25*(2), pp. 321–27. **[G: LDCs]**

Gang, Ira N. and Gangopadhyay, Shubhashis. Optimal Policies in a Dual Economy with Open Unemployment and Surplus Labour. *Oxford Econ. Pap.*, June 1987, *39*(2), pp. 378–87.

Gang, Ira N. and Gangopadhyay, Shubhashis. Welfare Aspects of a Harris–Todaro Economy with Underemployment and Variable Prices. *Devel. Econ.*, September 1987, *25*(3), pp. 203–19.

de Gaudemar, J.-P. Mobilization Networks and Strategies in the Labour Market. *Tarling, R., ed.*, 1987, pp. 105–26.

Giannelli, Gianna C. Implicit Contracts, Asymmetric Information and the Business Cycle. *Econ. Lavoro*, Jan.-Mar. 1987, *21*(1), pp. 35–45.

Gibbons, Robert. Piece-Rate Incentive Schemes. *J. Lab. Econ.*, Part 1, Oct. 1987, *5*(4), pp. 413–29.

Gintis, Herbert. The Nature of Labor Exchange and the Theory of Capitalist Production. *Albelda, R.; Gunn, C. and Waller, W., eds.*, 1987, *1976*, pp. 68–88.

Gintis, Herbert and Ishikawa, Tsuneo. Wages, Work Intensity, and Unemployment. *J. Japanese Int. Economies*, June 1987, *1*(2), pp. 195–228.

Glewwe, Paul. Unemployment in Developing Countries: Economist's Models in Light of Evidence from Sri Lanka. *Int. Econ. J.*, Winter 1987, *1*(4), pp. 1–17.   **[G: Sri Lanka]**

Golden, John M.; Orescovich, Robert and Ostafin, David. Optimality on the Short-run Phillips Curve: A "Misery Index" Criterion, a Note. *Amer. Econ.*, Fall 1987, *31*(2), pp. 72.

Goldfeld, Stephen M. Keynesian and Classical Unemployment in Four Countries: Comments. *Brookings Pap. Econ. Act.*, 1987, (1), pp. 194–97.   **[G: U.S.; U.K.; W. Germany; Austria]**

Gottfries, Nils and Horn, Henrik. Wage Formation and the Persistence of Unemployment. *Econ. J.*, December 1987, *97*(388), pp. 877–84.

Gramm, Warren S. Labor, Work, and Leisure: Human Well-Being and the Optimal Allocation of Time. *J. Econ. Issues*, March 1987, *21*(1), pp. 167–88.

Graves, Philip E.; Lee, Dwight R. and Sexton, Robert L. A Note on Interfirm Implications of Wages and Status. *J. Lab. Res.*, Spring 1987, *8*(2), pp. 209–12.   **[G: U.S.]**

Greenwald, Bruce C. and Stiglitz, Joseph E. Imperfect Information, Credit Markets and Unemployment. *Europ. Econ. Rev.*, Feb./Mar. 1987, *31*(1/2), pp. 444–56.

Greenwood, Jeremy and Huffman, Gregory W. A Dynamic Equilibrium Model of Inflation and Unemployment. *J. Monet. Econ.*, March 1987, *19*(2), pp. 203–28.

Guasch, J. Luis and Weiss, Andrew. Existence of an Optimal Random Monitor: The Labor Market Case. *Invest. Ecón.*, January 1987, *11*(1), pp. 95–99.

Gui, Benedetto. Internal Pay Schedules and Labour Mobility: The Problem of Firm Survival. *Econ. Notes*, 1987, (2), pp. 89–101.

Guido, Vincio. La teoria dei contratti impliciti: una rassegna critica. (The Theory of Implicit Contracts: A Critical Review. With English summary.) *Econ. Polít.*, April 1987, *4*(1), pp. 123–61.

Gupta, Manash Ranjan. Rural–Urban Migration and Urban Unemployment: A Note. *Scot. J. Polit. Econ.*, August 1987, *34*(3), pp. 295–305.

Gupta, Manash Ranjan. The Shadow Wage: A Note. *Math. Soc. Sci.*, June 1987, *13*(3), pp. 289–95.

Gustafson, Thomas A. The Incentive Effects of Private Pension Plans: Comment. *Bodie, Z.; Shoven, J. B. and Wise, D. A., eds.*, 1987, pp. 337–39.   **[G: U.S.]**

Gutowski, Armin. Slow Growth in Europe: Conceptual Issues: Comment. *Lawrence, R. Z. and Schultze, C. L., eds.*, 1987, pp. 93–98.
[G: W. Europe]

Hahn, Frank H. On Involuntary Unemployment. *Econ. J.*, Supplement 1987, 97, pp. 1–16.

Hall, Robert E. The Work Response to a Guaranteed Income: A Survey of Experimental Evidence: Discussion. *Munnell, A. H., ed.*, 1987, pp. 56–59.   **[G: U.S.]**

Haltiwanger, John and Plant, Mark. Alternative Measures of Slackness in the Labor Market and Their Relationship to Wage and Price Inflation. *Lang, K. and Leonard, J. S., eds.*, 1987, pp. 212–33.   **[G: U.S.]**

Hamermesh, Daniel S. The Costs of Worker Displacement. *Quart. J. Econ.*, February 1987, *102*(1), pp. 51–75.   **[G: U.S.]**

Hamilton, F. E. Ian. Industrial Organisation and Regional Labour Markets. *Fischer, M. M. and Nijkamp, P., eds.*, 1987, pp. 289–312.

Handa, Jagdish. Labor Characteristics and the Return to General and Specific Skills. *Eastern Econ. J.*, Apr.-June 1987, *13*(2), pp. 99–106.

Hansen, Per Vejrup. Turnover and Employment among Youth: Causes of the Particular Problems of Youth Employment. *Pedersen, P. J. and Lund, R., eds.*, 1987, pp. 129–45.
[G: Denmark]

Hanushek, Eric A. Non–Labor-Supply Responses to the Income Maintenance Experiments. *Munnell, A. H., ed.*, 1987, pp. 106–21.
[G: U.S.]

Harrigan, Frank J., et al. Bargaining Models of Regional Earnings Determination: Theory and Scottish Evidence. *Gordon, I., ed.*, 1987, pp. 44–66.   **[G: U.K.]**

Hart, Myra K. Specification Tests of the Lucas–Rapping Model. *Amer. Econ. Rev.*, June 1987, *77*(3), pp. 442–45.   **[G: U.S.]**

Hartmann, Heidi I. Internal Labor Markets and Gender: A Case Study of Promotion. *Brown, C. and Pechman, J. A., eds.*, 1987, pp. 59–92.   **[G: U.S.]**

Hazari, Bharat R. and Sgro, Pasquale M. Disguised, Urban Unemployment and Welfare in a General Equilibrium Model with Segmented Labor Markets. *J. Reg. Sci.*, August 1987, *27*(3), pp. 461–75.

Heady, Christopher. Alternative Theories of Wages in Less Developed Countries: An Empirical Test. *J. Devel. Stud.*, October 1987, *24*(1), pp. 5–15.   **[G: Colombia]**

Heckman, James and Scheinkman, Jose. The Importance of Bundling in a Gorman–Lancaster Model of Earnings. *Rev. Econ. Stud.*, April 1987, *54*(2), pp. 243–55.   **[G: U.S.]**

Hendricks, Wallace E. and Kahn, Lawrence M. Contract Length, Wage Indexation, and *Ex Ante* Variability of Real Wages. *J. Lab. Res.*, Summer 1987, *8*(3), pp. 221–36.   **[G: U.S.]**

Hersoug, Tor; Kjaer, Knut N. and Rødseth, Asbjorn. Wages, Taxes and the Utility-Maximizing Trade Union: A Confrontation with Norwegian Data. *Sinclair, P. J. N., ed.*, 1987, *1986*, pp. 431–51.   **[G: Norway]**

Hibbs, Douglas A., Jr. Industrial Conflict in Advanced Industrial Societies. *Hibbs, D. A., Jr.*, 1987, *1976*, pp. 17–51.   **[G: U.S.; W. Europe; Japan]**

Hibbs, Douglas A., Jr. Political Parties and Macroeconomic Policy. *Hibbs, D. A., Jr.*, 1987, *1977*, pp. 290–321.   **[G: U.K.; U.S.]**

Hibbs, Douglas A., Jr. Trade Union Power, Wage

Inflation, and Labor Militancy: A Comparative Analysis. *Hibbs, D. A., Jr.*, 1987, 1977, pp. 77–114. **[G: Italy; France; U.K.; U.S.]**

Hoel, Michael. Can Shorter Working Time Reduce Unemployment? *Siven, C.-H., ed.*, 1987, pp. 129–48.

Holly, Sean and Smith, Peter N. A Two-Sector Analysis of the UK Labour Market. *Oxford Bull. Econ. Statist.*, February 1987, 49(1), pp. 79–102. **[G: U.K.]**

Holmlund, Bertil. Unemployment and the Real Wage: Comment. *Siven, C.-H., ed.*, 1987, pp. 69–70.

Howitt, Peter and McAfee, R. Preston. Costly Search and Recruiting. *Int. Econ. Rev.*, February 1987, 28(1), pp. 89–107.

Hutchens, Robert M. A Test of Lazear's Theory of Delayed Payment Contracts. *J. Lab. Econ.*, Part 2, Oct. 1987, 5(4), pp. S153–70. **[G: U.S.]**

Ickes, Barry W. and Samuelson, Larry. Job Transfers and Incentives in Complex Organizations: Thwarting the Ratchet Effect. *Rand J. Econ.*, Summer 1987, 18(2), pp. 275–86.

Ioannides, Yannis M. and Sato, Ryuzo. On the Distribution of Wealth and Intergenerational Transfers. *J. Lab. Econ.*, July 1987, 5(3), pp. 366–85.

Jacobsen, Hans Jørgen and Schultz, Christian. A General Equilibrium View of Unemployment. *Pedersen, P. J. and Lund, R., eds.*, 1987, pp. 17–46.

Jenkins, Stephen. Snapshots versus Movies: 'Life-cycle Biases' and the Estimation of Intergenerational Earnings Inheritance. *Europ. Econ. Rev.*, July 1987, 31(5), pp. 1149–58. **[G: U.K.]**

Jensen, Peter. Transitions between Labour-Market States—An Empirical Analysis Using Danish Data. *Pedersen, P. J. and Lund, R., eds.*, 1987, pp. 67–80. **[G: Denmark]**

Jensen, Peter and Westergård-Nielsen, Niels C. A Search Model Applied to the Transition from Education to Work. *Rev. Econ. Stud.*, July 1987, 54(3), pp. 461–72. **[G: Denmark]**

Johansson, Börje and Karlsson, Charlie. Processes of Industrial Change: Scale, Location and Type of Job. *Fischer, M. M. and Nijkamp, P., eds.*, 1987, pp. 139–65.

Johansson, Per-Olov and Löfgren, Karl-Gustaf. Tariff Policy and Real Wage Adjustments in a Small Open Economy. *Siven, C.-H., ed.*, 1987, pp. 155–78.

John, George; Weiss, Allen M. and Weitz, Barton. An Organizational Coordination Model of Salesforce Compensation Plans: Theoretical Analysis and Empirical Test. *J. Law, Econ., Organ.*, Fall 1987, 3(2), pp. 373–95. **[G: U.S.]**

Jones, Stephen R. G. Minimum Wage Legislation in a Dual Labor Market. *Europ. Econ. Rev.*, August 1987, 31(6), pp. 1229–46.

Jovanovic, Boyan. Work, Rest, and Search: Unemployment, Turnover, and the Cycle. *J. Lab. Econ.*, April 1987, 5(2), pp. 131–48.

Junankar, P. N. and Neale, Adrian J. Relative Wages and the Youth Labour Market: A Rejoinder. *Junankar, P. N., ed.*, 1987, pp. 116–18. **[G: OECD]**

Junankar, P. N. and Neale, Adrian J. Relative Wages and the Youth Labour Market. *Junankar, P. N., ed.*, 1987, pp. 79–107. **[G: OECD]**

Kahn, Lawrence M. Unemployment Insurance, Job Queues, and Systematic Job Search: An Equilibrium Approach. *Southern Econ. J.*, October 1987, 54(2), pp. 397–411.

Kaufman, Bruce E. and Martinez-Vazquez, Jorge. The Ross–Dunlop Debate and Union Wage Concessions: A Median Voter Analysis. *J. Lab. Res.*, Summer 1987, 8(3), pp. 291–305.

Kelley, Maryellen R. Internal Labor Markets and Gender: A Case Study of Promotion: Comments. *Brown, C. and Pechman, J. A., eds.*, 1987, pp. 97–105. **[G: U.S.]**

Kelly, William A., Jr. and Miles, James A. A Fisherian Analysis of Individual Retirement Accounts. *Atlantic Econ. J.*, July 1987, 15(2), pp. 1–10.

Kemp, Murray C.; Léonard, Daniel and Long, Ngo Van. Trades Unions, Seniority and Unemployment. *Europ. Econ. Rev.*, July 1987, 31(5), pp. 1093–1112.

Kemp, Murray C. and Long, Ngo Van. Union Power in the Long Run. *Scand. J. Econ.*, 1987, 89(1), pp. 103–13.

Kempf, Hubert. Irregular Staggered Contracts and Monetary Policy. *Europ. Econ. Rev.*, August 1987, 31(6), pp. 1247–66.

Kidd, David P. and Oswald, Andrew J. A Dynamic Model of Trade Union Behaviour. *Economica*, August 1987, 54(215), pp. 355–65.

Kiefer, Nicholas M. A Proposition and an Example in the Theory of Job Search with Hours Constraints. *J. Lab. Econ.*, April 1987, 5(2), pp. 211–20.

Killingsworth, Mark R. Heterogeneous Preferences, Compensating Wage Differentials, and Comparable Worth. *Quart. J. Econ.*, November 1987, 102(4), pp. 727–42.

Kinoshita, Tomio. Working Hours and Hedonic Wages in the Market Equilibrium. *J. Polit. Econ.*, December 1987, 95(6), pp. 1262–77.

Klevmarken, N. Anders. Market and Nonmarket Service Production in Swedish Households. *Eliasson, G., ed.*, 1987, pp. 27–38. **[G: Sweden]**

Kniesner, Thomas J. and Goldsmith, Arthur H. A Survey of Alternative Models of the Aggregate U.S. Labor Market. *J. Econ. Lit.*, September 1987, 25(3), pp. 1241–80. **[G: U.S.]**

Knoester, Anthonie and van der Windt, Nico. Real Wages and Taxation in Ten OECD Countries. *Oxford Bull. Econ. Statist.*, February 1987, 49(1), pp. 151–69. **[G: OECD]**

Kooreman, Peter and Kapteyn, Arie. A Disaggregated Analysis of the Allocation of Time within the Household. *J. Polit. Econ.*, April 1987, 95(2), pp. 223–49. **[G: U.S.]**

Korkman, Sixten. Devaluation Policy and Employment. *Siven, C.-H., ed.*, 1987, pp. 195–200.

Koskela, Erkki. Changes in Tax Progression and Labour Supply under Wage Rate Uncertainty. *Public Finance*, 1987, *42*(2), pp. 214–26.

Kosters, Marvin H. and Ross, Murray N. The Influence of Employment Shifts and New Job Opportunities on the Growth and Distribution of Real Wages. *Cagan, P., ed.*, 1987, pp. 209–42. **[G: U.S.]**

Kotlikoff, Laurence J. and Wise, David A. The Incentive Effects of Private Pension Plans. *Bodie, Z.; Shoven, J. B. and Wise, D. A., eds.*, 1987, pp. 283–336. **[G: U.S.]**

Kouri, Pentti J. K. Real Wage, World Demand, and Unemployment in a Customer Market Model of a Small Open Economy. *Siven, C.-H., ed.*, 1987, pp. 183–94.

Kregel, Jan A. The Effective Demand Approach to Employment and Inflation Analysis. *J. Post Keynesian Econ.*, Fall 1987, *10*(1), pp. 133–45.

Krueger, Alan B. and Summers, Lawrence H. Reflections on the Inter-industry Wage Structure. *Lang, K. and Leonard, J. S., eds.*, 1987, pp. 17–47. **[G: Global]**

Krugman, Paul R. Slow Growth in Europe: Conceptual Issues. *Lawrence, R. Z. and Schultze, C. L., eds.*, 1987, pp. 48–76.
[G: W. Europe]

Kurz, Heinz D. and Salvadori, Neri. Burmeister on Sraffa and the Labor Theory of Value: A Comment [Sraffa, Labor Theories of Value, and the Economics of Real Wage Rate Determination]. *J. Polit. Econ.*, August 1987, *95*(4), pp. 870–81.

Lacroix, Robert and Robert, Jacques. Money-Wage Rigidities and the Effects of Wage Controls: An Analysis of Canadian Experience. *Steinherr, A. and Weiserbs, D., eds.*, 1987, pp. 185–212. **[G: Canada]**

Lancaster, Tony; Imbens, Guido and Dolton, Peter J. Job Separations and Job Matching. *Heijmans, R. and Neudecker, H., eds.*, 1987, pp. 31–43. **[G: U.K.]**

Lang, Kevin. Pareto Improving Minimum Wage Laws. *Econ. Inquiry*, January 1987, *25*(1), pp. 145–58.

Lang, Kevin; Leonard, Jonathan S. and Lilien, David M. Labor Market Structure, Wages and Unemployment. *Lang, K. and Leonard, J. S., eds.*, 1987, pp. 1–16.

Lawler, Edward E., III. Pay for Performance: A Motivational Analysis. *Nalbantian, H. R., ed.*, 1987, pp. 69–86. **[G: U.S.]**

Lawson, Tony. The Cambridge Multisectoral Dynamic Model of the British Economy: Incomes Policy and Earnings. *Barker, T. and Peterson, W., eds.*, 1987, pp. 341–72. **[G: U.K.]**

Layard, Richard and Nickell, Stephen J. The Performance of the British Economy: The Labour Market. *Dornbusch, R. and Layard, R., eds.*, 1987, pp. 131–79. **[G: U.K.]**

Lee, Jisoon. The Intertemporal Substitution Hypothesis: A Quantitative Reassessment. *Int. Econ. J.*, Winter 1987, *1*(4), pp. 77–99.
[G: U.S.]

Lee, Ronald D. The Value and Allocation of Time

in High-Income Countries: Implications for Fertility: Comment. *Davis, K.; Bernstam, M. S. and Ricardo-Campbell, R., eds.*, 1987, *1986*, pp. 108–10.

Leeds, Michael A. Bargaining as Search Behavior under Mutual Uncertainty. *Southern Econ. J.*, January 1987, *53*(3), pp. 677–84.

Leonard, Jonathan S. In the Wrong Place at the Wrong Time: The Extent of Frictional and Structural Unemployment. *Lang, K. and Leonard, J. S., eds.*, 1987, pp. 141–63.
[G: U.S.]

Leslie, Derek. Motivating Wage Structures. *Europ. Econ. Rev.*, August 1987, *31*(6), pp. 1267–83.

Leslie, Derek. Real Wage and Real Labour Cost Growth, 1948–81: A Disaggregated Study. *Appl. Econ.*, May 1987, *19*(5), pp. 635–50.
[G: U.K.]

Levačic, Rosalind. Inflation and Unemployment. *Thompson, G.; Brown, V. and Levaćić, R., eds.*, 1987, pp. 161–95.

Levačic, Rosalind. The Determinants of the Natural Rate of Unemployment. *Thompson, G.; Brown, V. and Levaćić, R., eds.*, 1987, pp. 77–104. **[G: U.K.]**

Lindbeck, Assar and Snower, Dennis J. Efficiency Wages versus Insiders and Outsiders. *Europ. Econ. Rev.*, Feb./Mar. 1987, *31*(1/2), pp. 407–16.

Lindbeck, Assar and Snower, Dennis J. Strike and Lock-Out Threats and Fiscal Policy. *Oxford Econ. Pap.*, December 1987, *39*(4), pp. 760–84.

Lindbeck, Assar and Snower, Dennis J. Union Activity, Unemployment Persistence and Wage–Employment Ratchets. *Europ. Econ. Rev.*, Feb./Mar. 1987, *31*(1/2), pp. 157–67.

Lommerud, Kjell Erik. Persistent Discrimination with Social Ability as a Productive Factor. *J. Inst. Theoretical Econ.*, June 1987, *143*(2), pp. 261–71.

Lord, William A. Welfare Effects of Capital Income Taxation under Variable and Fixed Labor Supply. *Southern Econ. J.*, July 1987, *54*(1), pp. 48–54.

Low, Stuart A. and Vilegas, Daniel J. An Alternative Approach to the Analysis of Wage Differentials. *Southern Econ. J.*, October 1987, *54*(2), pp. 449–62. **[G: U.S.]**

MacLeod, W. Bentley and Malcomson, James M. Involuntary Unemployment in Dynamic Contract Equilibria. *Europ. Econ. Rev.*, Feb./Mar. 1987, *31*(1/2), pp. 427–35.

Madan, Dilip B. Optimal Duration and Speed in the Long Run. *Rev. Econ. Stud.*, October 1987, *54*(4), pp. 695–700.

Maddala, G. S. Limited Dependent Variable Models Using Panel Data. *J. Human Res.*, Summer 1987, *22*(3), pp. 307–38.

Maier, Gunther. Job Search and Migration. *Fischer, M. M. and Nijkamp, P., eds.*, 1987, pp. 189–204.

Malcomson, James M. Trade Union Labour Contracts: An Introduction. *Europ. Econ. Rev.*, Feb./Mar. 1987, *31*(1/2), pp. 139–48.

Malinvaud, Edmond. Investment and the Inflation–Unemployment Tradeoff in a Macroeconomic Rationing Model with Monopolistic Competition: Comments. *Europ. Econ. Rev.*, April 1987, *31*(3), pp. 808–11.

Manning, Alan. An Integration of Trade Union Models in a Sequential Bargaining Framework. *Econ. J.*, March 1987, *97*(385), pp. 121–39.

Manning, Alan. Collective Bargaining Institutions and Efficiency: An Application of a Sequential Bargaining Model. *Europ. Econ. Rev.*, Feb./ Mar. 1987, *31*(1/2), pp. 168–76.

Maruyama, Shigeru. The Choice of Working Hours. *J. Econ. (Z. Nationalökon.)*, 1987, *47*(1), pp. 1–14.

Mavromaras, Kostas Gr. Reservation Wages and Occupational Security: An Empirical Study. *Appl. Econ.*, February 1987, *19*(2), pp. 155–66. [G: U.K.]

Mavromaras, Kostas Gr. Unemployment Benefits and Unemployment Rates Revisited: A General Equilibrium Job Search Model. *J. Public Econ.*, February 1987, *32*(1), pp. 101–18.

McCain, Roger A. Acceptable Contracts, Opportunism, and Rigid Hourly Wages. *Eastern Econ. J.*, July-Sept. 1987, *13*(3), pp. 205–13.

McCall, B. P. and McCall, J. J. A Sequential Study of Migration and Job Search. *J. Lab. Econ.*, Part 1, Oct. 1987, *5*(4), pp. 452–76.

McDermott, John H. Employment in a Controlled, Open Economy. *Connolly, M. and González-Vega, C., eds.*, 1987, pp. 325–39.

McDonald, Ian M. Customer Markets, Trade Unions and Stagflation. *Economica*, May 1987, *54*(214), pp. 139–53.

McKenna, Christopher J. Labour Market Participation in Matching Equilibrium. *Economica*, August 1987, *54*(215), pp. 325–33.

McKenna, Christopher J. Models of Search Market Equilibrium. *Hey, J. D. and Lambert, P. J., eds.*, 1987, pp. 110–23.

McNabb, Robert. Testing for Labour Market Segmentation in Britain. *Manchester Sch. Econ. Soc. Stud.*, September 1987, *55*(3), pp. 257–73. [G: U.K.]

Menchik, Paul L. and Weisbrod, Burton A. Volunteer Labor Supply. *J. Public Econ.*, March 1987, *32*(2), pp. 159–83. [G: U.S.]

de Menil, Georges and Gordon, Robert J. 10th International Seminar on Macroeconomics: Introduction. *Europ. Econ. Rev.*, April 1987, *31*(3), pp. 537–42.

Metcalf, David. Labour Market Flexibility and Jobs: A Survey of Evidence from OECD Countries with Special Reference to Europe. *Layard, R. and Calmfors, L., eds.*, 1987, pp. 48–76. [G: OECD]

Meyer, Margaret A. Labor Contracts under Asymmetric Information when Workers Are Free to Quit. *Quart. J. Econ.*, August 1987, *102*(3), pp. 527–51.

Michael, Robert T. Non–Labor-Supply Responses to the Income Maintenance Experiments: Discussion. *Munnell, A. H., ed.*, 1987, pp. 127–30. [G: U.S.]

Michl, Thomas R. Is There Evidence for a Mar-

ginalist Demand for Labour? *Cambridge J. Econ.*, December 1987, *11*(4), pp. 361–73. [G: U.S.]

Michon, François. Segmentation, Employment Structures and Productive Structures. *Tarling, R., ed.*, 1987, pp. 23–55.

Milgrom, Paul R. and Oster, Sharon. Job Discrimination, Market Forces, and the Invisibility Hypothesis. *Quart. J. Econ.*, August 1987, *102*(3), pp. 453–76.

Minford, Patrick. The Performance of the British Economy: The Labour Market: Comment. *Dornbusch, R. and Layard, R., eds.*, 1987, pp. 260–62. [G: U.K.]

Mistri, Maurizio. Comportamenti innovativi di impresa con aspettative inflazionistiche dualistiche e struttura del mercato del lavoro. (Innovative Behaviours with Dualistic Inflationary Expectations and Labour Market Structure. With English summary.) *Rivista Int. Sci. Econ. Com.*, July 1987, *34*(7), pp. 609–21.

Moene, Karl O. Keynesian Unemployment and Overmanning. *Econ. J.*, September 1987, *97*(387), pp. 740–45.

Moffitt, Robert. Life-Cycle Labor Supply and Social Security: A Time-Series Analysis. *Burtless, G., ed.*, 1987, pp. 183–220. [G: U.S.]

Munnell, Alicia H. Lessons from the Income Maintenance Experiments: An Overview. *Munnell, A. H., ed.*, 1987, pp. 1–21. [G: U.S.]

Murat, Marina and Paba, Sergio. Coalizioni e segmentazione nel mercato del lavoro in presenza di domanda variabile: il caso dei porti. (With English summary.) *Polit. Econ.*, April 1987, *3*(1), pp. 51–80.

Murphy, A. and Thom, D. Rodney. Labour Supply and Commodity Demands: An Application to Irish Data. *Econ. Soc. Rev.*, April 1987, *18*(3), pp 149–58 [G: Ireland]

Murphy, Kevin M. and Topel, Robert H. Unemployment, Risk, and Earnings: Testing for Equalizing Wage Differences in the Labor Market. *Lang, K. and Leonard, J. S., eds.*, 1987, pp. 103–40. [G: U.S.]

Muysken, Joan and van Zon, A. H. Employment and Unemployment in the Netherlands, 1960–1984: A Putty–Clay Approach. *Rech. Écon. Louvain*, 1987, *53*(2), pp. 101–33. [G: Netherlands]

Nalbantian, Haig R. Incentive Compensation in Perspective. *Nalbantian, H. R., ed.*, 1987, pp. 3–43.

Nalebuff, Barry and Scharfstein, David. Testing in Models of Asymmetric Information. *Rev. Econ. Stud.*, April 1987, *54*(2), pp. 265–77.

Newbery, David M. and Stiglitz, Joseph E. Wage Rigidity, Implicit Contracts, Unemployment and Economic Efficiency. *Econ. J.*, June 1987, *97*(386), pp. 416–30.

Newell, A. and Symons, J. S. V. Corporatism, Laissez-faire, and the Rise in Unemployment. *Europ. Econ. Rev.*, April 1987, *31*(3), pp. 567–601. [G: OECD]

Nickell, Stephen J. A Historical Perspective on Unemployment: A Review Article. *J. Polit.*

Econ., August 1987, *95*(4), pp. 857–69.

Nickell, Stephen J. Jobless Pay and High European Unemployment: Comment. *Lawrence, R. Z. and Schultze, C. L.*, eds., 1987, pp. 162–68. **[G: W. Europe]**

Nickell, Stephen J. Unemployment and the Real Wage. *Siven, C.-H.*, ed., 1987, pp. 45–68.

Nickell, Stephen J. Why Is Wage Inflation in Britain So High? *Oxford Bull. Econ. Statist.*, February 1987, *49*(1), pp. 103–28. **[G: U.K.]**

Ohashi, Isao. Cyclical Variations in Wage Differentials and Unemployment. *J. Lab. Econ.*, April 1987, *5*(2), pp. 278–300.

Ohyama, Michihiro. Unemployment and Inflation: Natural Wage Rate Hypothesis. *Keio Econ. Stud.*, 1987, *24*(2), pp. 11–26.

Okuno-Fujiwara, Masahiro. Monitoring Cost, Agency Relationships, and Equilibrium Modes of Labor Contracts. *J. Japanese Int. Economies*, June 1987, *1*(2), pp. 147–67. **[G: Japan]**

Ondrich, Jan. Job Search in a Cyclical Economy. *Southern Econ. J.*, July 1987, *54*(1), pp. 81–94.

Ondrich, Jan. Job Search: The Choice of Intensity: A Comment. *J. Polit. Econ.*, October 1987, *95*(5), pp. 1098–1102.

van Ophem, Hans. An Empirical Test of the Segmented Labour Market Theory for the Netherlands. *Appl. Econ.*, November 1987, *19*(11), pp. 1497–1514. **[G: Netherlands]**

Orsi, Renzo. A Spillover Model of Male and Female Labour Markets. *Giorn. Econ.*, Nov.-Dec. 1987, *46*(11–12), pp. 590–616. **[G: Italy]**

Osano, Hiroshi. Social Security and Lifetime Employment Contract. *Econ. Stud. Quart.*, June 1987, *38*(2), pp. 107–23.

Osberg, Lars; Apostle, Richard and Clairmont, Don. Segmented Labour Markets and the Estimation of Wage Functions. *Appl. Econ.*, December 1987, *19*(12), pp. 1603–24. **[G: Canada]**

Osterman, Paul. Choice of Employment Systems in Internal Labor Markets. *Ind. Relat.*, Winter 1987, *26*(1), pp. 46–67.

Osterman, Paul. Internal Labor Markets and Gender: A Case Study of Promotion: Comments. *Brown, C. and Pechman, J. A.*, eds., 1987, pp. 92–97. **[G: U.S.]**

Oswald, Andrew J. New Research on the Economics of Trade Unions and Labor Contracts. *Ind. Relat.*, Winter 1987, *26*(1), pp. 30–45.

Pedersen, Peder J. and Westergård-Nielsen, Niels C. Multiple Spells of Unemployment— The Danish Experience. *Pedersen, P. J. and Lund, R.*, eds., 1987, pp. 105–28. **[G: Denmark]**

Peterson, William. The Cambridge Multisectoral Dynamic Model of the British Economy: Employment. *Barker, T. and Peterson, W.*, eds., 1987, pp. 247–74. **[G: U.K.]**

Phaneuf, Louis. Propriétés dynamiques des modèles du cycle à contrats échelonnés. (The Dynamic Properties of Staggered Contracts Models. With English summary.) *Can. J. Econ.*, February 1987, *20*(1), pp. 123–39.

Pinch, S. P. Labour-Market Theory, Quantification, and Policy. *Environ. Planning A*, November 1987, *19*(11), pp. 1477–94.

Pissarides, Christopher A. A Critical Assessment of Some Recent Approaches to the Theory of Unemployment. *Pedersen, P. J. and Lund, R.*, eds., 1987, pp. 3–16.

Pissarides, Christopher A. Mass Unemployment: A Review Essay. *J. Monet. Econ.*, July 1987, *20*(1), pp. 183–88. **[G: E. Europe; U.S.]**

Pissarides, Christopher A. Search, Wage Bargains and Cycles. *Rev. Econ. Stud.*, July 1987, *54*(3), pp. 473–83.

Pissarides, Christopher A. Wages and Employment: A Framework for Analysis with Application to Three Policy Issues. *Econ. Rec.*, December 1987, *63*(183), pp. 301–12.

van der Ploeg, Frederick. Trade Unions, Investment, and Employment: A Non-cooperative Approach. *Europ. Econ. Rev.*, October 1987, *31*(7), pp. 1465–92.

Pohjola, Matti. Profit-Sharing, Collective Bargaining and Employment. *J. Inst. Theoretical Econ.*, June 1987, *143*(2), pp. 334–42.

Portes, Richard. Investment and the Inflation–Unemployment Tradeoff in a Macroeconomic Rationing Model with Monopolistic Competition: Comments. *Europ. Econ. Rev.*, April 1987, *31*(3), pp. 812–15.

Prachowny, Martin F. J. Conflict in the Labor Market: Seniority Rules and Unemployment. *J. Macroecon.*, Fall 1987, *9*(4), pp. 527–34. **[G: U.S.]**

Quah, Euston. Household Production and the GNP: A Model for Use in Valuation. *Econ. Int.*, November 1987, *40*(4), pp. 345–61.

Quandt, Richard E. and Rosen, Harvey S. Unemployment, Disequilibrium and the Short-run Phillips Curve: Correction and Extension. *J. Appl. Econometrics*, July 1987, *2*(3), pp. 247–49. **[G: U.S.]**

Quinn, Joseph F. Life-Cycle Labor Supply and Social Security: A Time-Series Analysis: Comment. *Burtless, G.*, ed., 1987, pp. 220–28. **[G: U.S.]**

Ransom, Michael R. An Empirical Model of Discrete and Continuous Choice in Family Labor Supply. *Rev. Econ. Statist.*, August 1987, *69*(3), pp. 465–72. **[G: U.S.]**

Ransom, Michael R. The Labor Supply of Married Men: A Switching Regressions Model. *J. Lab. Econ.*, January 1987, *5*(1), pp. 63–75. **[G: U.S.]**

Rebeyrol, Antoine. Gravitation et marché du travail. Un essai d'interprétation. (Gravitation and Labour Market: Essay of Interpretation. With English summary.) *Écon. Soc.*, March 1987, *21*(3), pp. 53–84.

Reder, Melvin W. Specialization, Search Costs, and the Degree of Resource Utilization. *Feiwel, G. R.*, ed. (*I*), 1987, pp. 498–518.

Rietveld, Piet and Nijkamp, Peter. Technological Development and Regional Labour Markets. *Fischer, M. M. and Nijkamp, P.*, eds., 1987, pp. 117–38.

Roberts, John. An Equilibrium Model with Involuntary Unemployment at Flexible, Competitive Prices and Wages. *Amer. Econ. Rev.*, December 1987, *77*(5), pp. 856–74.

Rodrigues, Maria João. Le système d'emploi comme alternative aux approches du marché du travail. (The Employment System as an Alternative to Labor Market Approaches. With English summary.) *Écon. Soc.*, November 1987, *21*(11), pp. 3–39.

Rogerson, Peter A. Competition among Applicants for Job Openings. *Fischer, M. M. and Nijkamp, P., eds.*, 1987, pp. 229–45.

Rogerson, Richard. An Equilibrium Model of Sectoral Reallocation. *J. Polit. Econ.*, August 1987, *95*(4), pp. 824–34.

Rothschild, Kurt W. Is There a Weitzman Miracle? *J. Post Keynesian Econ.*, Winter 1986-87, *9*(2), pp. 198–211.

Rouwendal, Jan and Nijkamp, Peter. Regional Economic Research on Labour Markets. *Fischer, M. M. and Nijkamp, P., eds.*, 1987, pp. 95–115.

Rowlatt, Penelope A. A Model of Wage Bargaining. *Oxford Bull. Econ. Statist.*, November 1987, *49*(4), pp. 347–72. **[G: U.K.]**

Ruggeri, Fedele. Unofficial Economy and the Meaning of Labour: Toward a Theoretical Hypothesis. *Alessandrini, S. and Dallago, B., eds.*, 1987, pp. 107–24.

Sachs, Jeffrey D. High Unemployment in Europe: Diagnosis and Policy Implications. *Siven, C.-H., ed.*, 1987, pp. 7–38. **[G: W. Europe]**

Sampson, Anthony A. A Note on Adverse Selection. *Bull. Econ. Res.*, October 1987, *39*(4), pp. 297–301.

Santiago, Carlos E. Rehiring, Seniority, and Labor Force Adjustment. *J. Lab. Econ.*, Part 2, Oct. 1987, *5*(4), pp. S18–35. **[G: U.S.]**

Schaeffer, P. V. A Dynamic Model of Labor-Market Change in International Labor Migrations when Demand for Labor Is Exogenous. *Environ. Planning A*, August 1987, *19*(8), pp. 1051–57.

Schmidt-Sørensen, Jan Beyer. Rekrutterings- og fastholdelses-problemer i den offentlige sektor. (The Problems of Recruiting and Keeping Employees in the Public Sector. With English summary.) *Nationaløkon. Tidsskr.*, 1987, *125*(3), pp. 355–75. **[G: Denmark]**

Schubert, Uwe, et al. Regional Labour Market Modelling: A State of the Art Review. *Fischer, M. M. and Nijkamp, P., eds.*, 1987, pp. 53–94.

Schultz, T. Paul. The Value and Allocation of Time in High-Income Countries: Implications for Fertility. *Davis, K.; Bernstam, M. S. and Ricardo-Campbell, R., eds.*, 1987, *1986*, pp. 87–108. **[G: U.S.]**

Schultze, Charles L. Real Wages, Real Wage Aspirations, and Unemployment in Europe. *Lawrence, R. Z. and Schultze, C. L., eds.*, 1987, pp. 230–91. **[G: W. Europe]**

Schwartz, Abba. The Effects of Labour Unions on Investment in Training: A Dynamic Model: Comments. *Razin, A. and Sadka, E., eds.*, 1987, pp. 479–94.

Sertel, Murat R. On Conquering Stagflation. *Econ. Anal. Workers' Manage.*, 1987, *21*(4), pp. 433–41.

Shields, Jon. Curing Unemployment through Labour-Market Competition: Commentary. *Begg, D. K. H., et al.*, 1987, pp. 150–54. **[G: U.K.]**

Silver, Hilary. Only So Many Hours in a Day: Time Constraints, Labour Pools and Demand for Consumer Services. *Akehurst, G. and Gadrey, J., eds.*, 1987, pp. 26–45. **[G: U.S.]**

Singh, Ram D. and Morey, Mathew J. The Value of Work-at-Home and Contributions of Wives' Household Service in Polygynous Families: Evidence from an African LDC. *Econ. Develop. Cult. Change*, July 1987, *35*(4), pp. 743–65. **[G: Burkina Faso]**

Sneessens, Henri R. Investment and the Inflation–Unemployment Tradeoff in a Macroeconomic Rationing Model with Monopolistic Competition. *Europ. Econ. Rev.*, April 1987, *31*(3), pp. 781–808.

Soete, Luc. Employment, Unemployment and Technical Change: A Review of the Economic Debate. *Freeman, C. and Soete, L., eds.*, 1987, pp. 22–35.

Sokolovskii, L. E. On Individual and Collective Forms of Labor Organization and Incentives. *Matekon*, Summer 1987, *23*(4), pp. 3–27. **[G: U.S.S.R.]**

Solimano, Andrés. Emprego e salários reais: Uma análise macroeconômica de desequilíbrio para o Chile e o Brasil. (With English summary.) *Pesquisa Planejamento Econ.*, December 1987, *17*(3), pp. 605–31. **[G: Chile; Brazil]**

Sørensen, Aage B. Employment Relations and Employment Processes. *Pedersen, P. J. and Lund, R., eds.*, 1987, pp. 47–65.

Spahn, H.-Peter. Sind "effiziente" Löhne zu hoch für die Vollbeschäftigung? Zur Erklärung von unfreiwilliger Arbeitslosigkeit in der Effizienzlohntheorie. (Are "Efficient" Wages Too High for Full Employment? With English summary.) *Jahr. Nationalökon. Statist.*, May 1987, *203*(3), pp. 225–43.

Spinelli, Franco. Labor Market Rigidities and Protectionism. *Salvatore, D., ed.*, 1987, pp. 181–200.

Stafford, Frank P. Organizational Theory and the Nature of Jobs. *J. Inst. Theoretical Econ.*, December 1987, *143*(4), pp. 519–36.

Steinherr, Alfred and Weiserbs, Daniel. Unemployment Policies under Constrained Growth. *Steinherr, A. and Weiserbs, D., eds.*, 1987, pp. 283–310. **[G: Belgium]**

Stern, Steven. Promotion and Optimal Retirement. *J. Lab. Econ.*, Part 2, Oct. 1987, *5*(4), pp. S107–23.

Stewart, Geoff. Managerial Discretion in the Labor-Managed Firm. *Jones, D. C. and Svejnar, J., eds.*, 1987, pp. 143–63.

Stiglitz, Joseph E. The Causes and Consequences of the Dependence of Quality on Price. *J. Econ. Lit.*, March 1987, *25*(1), pp. 1–48.

Stiglitz, Joseph E. The Design of Labor Contracts: The Economics of Incentives and Risk Sharing.

Nalbantian, H. R., ed., 1987, pp. 47–68.

Stiglitz, Joseph E. The Wage–Productivity Hypothesis: Its Economic Consequences and Policy Implications. *[Harberger, A.]*, 1987, pp. 130–65.

Strand, Jon. The Relationship between Wages and Firm Size: An Information Theoretic Analysis. *Int. Econ. Rev.*, February 1987, *28*(1), pp. 51–68.

Strand, Jon. Unemployment as a Discipline Device with Heterogeneous Labor [Equilibrium Unemployment as a Worker Discipline Device]. *Amer. Econ. Rev.*, June 1987, *77*(3), pp. 489–93.

Summers, Lawrence H. Corporatism, Laissez-faire, and the Rise in Unemployment: Comments. *Europ. Econ. Rev.*, April 1987, *31*(3), pp. 606–14. **[G: OECD]**

Sylos-Labini, Paolo. The Theory of Unemployment, Too, Is Historically Conditioned. *Banca Naz. Lavoro Quart. Rev.*, December 1987, (163), pp. 379–435. **[G: OECD]**

Tauman, Yair and Weiss, Yoram. Labor Unions and the Adoption of New Technology. *J. Lab. Econ.*, Part 1, Oct. 1987, *5*(4), pp. 477–501.

Taylor, John B. Externalities Associated with Nominal Price and Wage Rigidities. *Barnett, W. A. and Singleton, K. J., eds.*, 1987, pp. 350–67.

Taylor, Mark P. Further Developments in the Theory of Implicit Labour Contracts. *Hey, J. D. and Lambert, P. J., eds.*, 1987, pp. 151–72.

Taylor, Mark P. The Simple Analytics of Implicit Labour Contracts. *Hey, J. D. and Lambert, P. J., eds.*, 1987, pp. 124–50.

Taylor, Mark P. The Simple Analytics of Implicit Labour Contracts. *Bull. Econ. Res.*, January 1987, *39*(1), pp. 1–27.

Theeuwes, Jules. Jobless Pay and High European Unemployment: Comment. *Lawrence, R. Z. and Schultze, C. L., eds.*, 1987, pp. 168–72. **[G: W. Europe; U.S.]**

Thompson, Grahame. Unemployment and Technology. *Thompson, G.; Brown, V. and Levačić, R., eds.*, 1987, pp. 134–60. **[G: U.K.]**

Thornton, John. Inflation and Output Growth: A Note on Some Time Series Evidence. *S. Afr. J. Econ.*, December 1987, *55*(4), pp. 425–27.

Tobin, James. A Note on the Money Wage Problem. *Tobin, J. (I)*, 1987, *1941*, pp. 4–11.

Tobin, James. After Disinflation, Then What? *Tobin, J. (III)*, 1987, *1984*, pp. 348–67. **[G: U.S.]**

Tobin, James. Inflation and Unemployment. *Tobin, J. (II)*, 1987, *1972*, pp. 33–59.

Tobin, James. Keynesian and Classical Unemployment in Four Countries: Comments. *Brookings Pap. Econ. Act.*, 1987, (1), pp. 198–205. **[G: U.S.; U.K.; W. Germany; Austria]**

Tobin, James. Money Wage Rates and Employment. *Tobin, J. (I)*, 1987, *1947*, pp. 12–26.

Tobin, James. Phillips Curve Algebra. *Tobin, J. (II)*, 1987, pp. 11–15.

Tobin, James. The Cruel Dilemma. *Tobin, J. (II)*, 1987, *1967*, pp. 3–10. **[G: U.S.]**

Tobin, James. The Wage–Price Mechanism. *Tobin, J. (II)*, 1987, *1973*, pp. 17–32.

Tokman, Víctor E. Unequal Development and the Absorption of Labor. *Dietz, J. L. and Street, J. H., eds.*, 1987, pp. 228–40. **[G: Latin America]**

Tracy, Joseph S. An Empirical Test of an Asymmetric Information Model of Strikes. *J. Lab. Econ.*, April 1987, *5*(2), pp. 149–73. **[G: U.S.]**

Van Rompuy, Paul. Hysteresis, Persistence, and the NAIRU: An Empirical Analysis for the Federal Republic of Germany: Comments. *Layard, R. and Calmfors, L., eds.*, 1987, pp. 132–38. **[G: W. Germany]**

Vane, Howard. Supply-Side Economics. *Vane, H. and Caslin, T., eds.*, 1987, pp. 62–77. **[G: U.K.]**

Vinod, H. D. New Techniques for Estimation of Rational Expectation Models and Volcker Deflation. *Empirical Econ.*, 1987, *12*(3), pp. 157–74. **[G: U.S.]**

Vroman, Susan B. Behavior of the Firm in a Market for Heterogeneous Labor. *J. Econ. Dynam. Control*, September 1987, *11*(3), pp. 313–29.

Wadensjö, Eskil. Tariff Policy and Real Wage Adjustments in a Small Open Economy: Comment. *Siven, C.-H., ed.*, 1987, pp. 179–81.

Wadhwani, Sushil B. Profit-Sharing and Meade's Discriminating Labour–Capital Partnerships: A Review Article. *Oxford Econ. Pap.*, September 1987, *39*(3), pp. 421–42.

Wadhwani, Sushil B. The Effects of Inflation and Real Wages on Employment. *Economica*, February 1987, *54*(213), pp. 21–40. **[G: U.K.]**

Waelbroeck, Jean. Corporatism, Laissez-faire, and the Rise in Unemployment: Comments. *Europ. Econ. Rev.*, April 1987, *31*(3), pp. 602–05. **[G: OECD]**

Wagner, Helmut. Arbeitsangebot, Freizeitarbeit und Folgen einer Rationierung. Kritik und Erweiterung der traditionellen neoklassischen Arbeitsangebotstheorie. (Labor Supply and the Effects of Rationing. With English summary.) *Jahr. Nationalökon. Statist.*, March 1987, *203*(2), pp. 138–51.

Wan, Henry, Jr. Arrow and the Theory of Discrimination. *Feiwel, G. R., ed. (I)*, 1987, pp. 484–97.

Warburton, Peter. Labour Supply Incentives for the Retired. *Beenstock, M., et al.*, 1987, pp. 185–234. **[G: U.K.]**

Weiss, Yoram. The Effect of Labour Unions on Investment in Training: A Dynamic Model. *Razin, A. and Sadka, E., eds.*, 1987, pp. 435–67.

Weitzman, Martin L. Macroeconomic Aspects of Profit Sharing. *Nalbantian, H. R., ed.*, 1987, pp. 202–12. **[G: U.S.]**

Weitzman, Martin L. Steady State Unemployment under Profit Sharing. *Econ. J.*, March 1987, *97*(385), pp. 86–105.

Wells, William. Relative Wages and the Youth

Labour Market: A Reply. *Junankar, P. N., ed.,* 1987, pp. 108–15. **[G: OECD]**

Williams, Rhonda M. Capital, Competition, and Discrimination: A Reconsideration of Racial Earnings Inequality. *Rev. Radical Polit. Econ.,* Summer 1987, *19*(2), pp. 1–15.

Williamson, Oliver E. Wage Rates as a Barrier to Entry: The Pennington Case in Perspective. *Williamson, O.,* 1987, *1968,* pp. 193–224. **[G: U.S.]**

Wilson, Charles. The Effect of Labour Unions on Investment in Training: A Dynamic Model: Comments. *Razin, A. and Sadka, E., eds.,* 1987, pp. 468–78.

Wohlers, Eckhardt. Labour Market Flexibility and Jobs: A Survey of Evidence from OECD Countries with Special Reference to Europe: Comments. *Layard, R. and Calmfors, L., eds.,* 1987, pp. 85–90. **[G: OECD]**

Wolpin, Kenneth I. Estimating a Structural Search Model: The Transition from School to Work. *Econometrica,* July 1987, *55*(4), pp. 801–17. **[G: U.S.]**

Woodbury, Stephen A. Power in the Labor Market: Institutionalist Approaches to Labor Problems. *J. Econ. Issues,* December 1987, *21*(4), pp. 1781–1807.

Wright, Gavin. Labor History and Labor Economics. *Field, A. J., ed.,* 1987, pp. 313–48.

Wright, Randall D. Search, Layoffs, and Reservation Wages. *J. Lab. Econ.,* July 1987, *5*(3), pp. 354–65.

Wright, Randall D. and Loberg, Janine. Unemployment Insurance, Taxes, and Unemployment. *Can. J. Econ.,* February 1987, *20*(1), pp. 36–54.

Wulwick, Nancy J. The Phillips Curve: Which? Whose? To Do What? How? *Southern Econ. J.,* April 1987, *53*(4), pp. 834–57.

Wyplosz, Charles. Hysteresis, Persistence, and the NAIRU: An Empirical Analysis for the Federal Republic of Germany: Comments. *Layard, R. and Calmfors, L., eds.,* 1987, pp. 123–31. **[G: W. Germany]**

Yaniv, Gideon. Absenteeism, Overtime, and the Compressed Work Week. *J. Behav. Econ.,* Summer 1987, *16*(2), pp. 47–54.

Young, Leslie and Miyagiwa, Kaz F. Unemployment and the Formation of Duty-Free Zones. *J. Devel. Econ.,* August 1987, *26*(2), pp. 397–405. **[G: LDCs]**

822 Public Policy; Role of Government

8220 General

Aboud, Antone and Schram, Sanford F. Overview of Legislation [An Overview of Plant Closing Legislation and Issues]. *Staudohar, P. D. and Brown, H. E.,* 1987, *1984,* pp. 279–91. **[G: U.S.]**

Amjad, Rashid. Human Resource Development: The Asian Experience in Employment and Manpower Planning—An Overview. *Amjad, R., ed.,* 1987, pp. 1–37. **[G: Asia]**

Briggs, Vernon M., Jr. Human Resource Devel-

opment and the Formulation of National Economic Policy. *J. Econ. Issues,* September 1987, *21*(3), pp. 1207–40. **[G: U.S.]**

Brittan, Samuel. Innovative Supply-Side Policies to Reduce Unemployment: Commentary. *Begg, D. K. H., et al.,* 1987, pp. 122–27. **[G: U.K.]**

Brodsky, Melvin. OECD Meeting Calls for Job Growth, Flexibility, and Readjustment. *Mon. Lab. Rev.,* June 1987, *110*(6), pp. 53–54. **[G: OECD]**

Chan-Lee, James H.; Coe, David T. and Prywes, Menahem. Microeconomic Changes and Macroeconomic Wage Disinflation in the 1980s. *OECD Econ. Stud.,* Spring 1987, (8), pp. 121–57.

Charnovitz, Steve. The Influence of International Labour Standards on the World Trading Regime. A Historical Overview. *Int. Lab. Rev.,* Sept.-Oct. 1987, *126*(5), pp. 565–84.

Chrisman, James J.; Carroll, Archie B. and Gatewood, Elizabeth J. The Case against Legislation [What's Wrong with Plant-Closing Legislation and Industrial Policy?]. *Staudohar, P. D. and Brown, H. E.,* 1987, *1985,* pp. 321–33. **[G: U.S.]**

Fluet, Claude. Fraude fiscale et offre de travail au noir. (Tax Evasion and the Supply of Unofficial Labour. With English summary.) *L'Actual. Econ.,* June-September 1987, *63*(2–3), pp. 225–42.

Folbre, Nancy R.; Leighton, Julia L. and Roderick, Melissa R. Legislation in Maine [Plant Closings and Their Regulation in Maine, 1971–1982]. *Staudohar, P. D. and Brown, H. E.,* 1987, *1984,* pp. 293–306. **[G: U.S.]**

Ford, William D. Federal Legislation [Coping with Plant Closings]. *Staudohar, P. D. and Brown, H. E.,* 1987, *1985,* pp. 307–11. **[G: U.S.]**

Gray, Robert. The Languages of Factory Reform in Britain, *c.* 1830–1860. *Joyce, P., ed.,* 1987, pp. 143–79. **[G: U.K.]**

Hooks, Gregory. Comparison of the United States, Sweden, and France [The Policy Response to Factory Closings: A Comparison of the United States, Sweden, and France]. *Staudohar, P. D. and Brown, H. E.,* 1987, *1984,* pp. 245–58. **[G: U.S.; France; Sweden]**

Horn, Robert N. and Tomkiewicz, Joseph M. State Strategies of Control in the Public Sector. *England, R. W., ed.,* 1987, pp. 245–53. **[G: U.S.]**

Islam, Iyanatul. Manpower and Educational Planning in Singapore. *Amjad, R., ed.,* 1987, pp. 114–50. **[G: Singapore]**

Jackman, Richard and Layard, Richard. Innovative Supply-Side Policies to Reduce Unemployment. *Begg, D. K. H., et al.,* 1987, pp. 93–117. **[G: U.K.]**

Kemal, A. R. Pakistan's Experience in Employment and Manpower Planning. *Amjad, R., ed.,* 1987, pp. 234–56. **[G: Pakistan]**

Khan, M. R. Employment, Manpower and Educational Development in Bangladesh. *Amjad, R., ed.,* 1987, pp. 304–17. **[G: Bangladesh]**

Kim, Yoo Bae. Evaluation of Manpower Policies in the Republic of Korea. *Amjad, R., ed.,* 1987, pp. 198–220. **[G: S. Korea]**

Koziara, Karen Shallcross. Women and Work: The Evolving Policy. *Koziara, K. S.; Moskow, M. H. and Tanner, L. D., eds.,* 1987, pp. 374–408. **[G: U.S.]**

Landau, C. E. The Influence of ILO Standards on Australian Labour Law and Practice. *Int. Lab. Rev.,* Nov.-Dec. 1987, *126*(6), pp. 669–90.

Mehmet, Ozay. The Malaysian Experience in Manpower Planning and Labour Market Policies. *Amjad, R., ed.,* 1987, pp. 84–113. **[G: Malaysia]**

Moriani, Claudio. Il sistema informativo del lavoro nazionale: uno sguardo d'insieme. (The National Information System for Labour: An Overview. With English summary.) *Econ. Lavoro,* July-Sept. 1987, *21*(3), pp. 77–83. **[G: Italy]**

Nelson, Richard R. State Labor Legislation Enacted in 1986. *Mon. Lab. Rev.,* January 1987, *110*(1), pp. 49–66. **[G: U.S.]**

Nolan, Peter and O'Donnell, Kathy. Taming the Market Economy? A Critical Assessment of the GLC's Experiment in Restructuring for Labour: Review Article. *Cambridge J. Econ.,* September 1987, *11*(3), pp. 251–63. **[G: U.K.]**

Peel, David A. Innovative Supply-Side Policies to Reduce Unemployment: Commentary. *Begg, D. K. H., et al.,* 1987, pp. 118–21. **[G: U.K.]**

Pitayanon, Sumalee. Thailand's Experience in Manpower Planning and Labour Market Policies. *Amjad, R., ed.,* 1987, pp. 38–83. **[G: Thailand]**

Reid, Joseph D., Jr. and Faith, Roger L. Right-to-Work and Union Compensation Structure. *J. Lab. Res.,* Spring 1987, *8*(2), pp. 111–30. **[G: U.S.]**

Rodrigo, Chandra; Korale, R. B. M. and Aturupana, D. H. C. Employment and Manpower Planning in Sri Lanka. *Amjad, R., ed.,* 1987, pp. 257–84. **[G: Sri Lanka]**

Suroto and Tjiptoherijanto, Prijono. Employment, Manpower and Educational Planning in Indonesia. *Amjad, R., ed.,* 1987, pp. 181–97. **[G: Indonesia]**

Tan, Edita A. and Alonzo, Ruperto P. The Philippine Experience in Manpower Planning and Labour Market Policies. *Amjad, R., ed.,* 1987, pp. 151–80. **[G: Philippines]**

Tripp, Joseph F. Law and Social Control: Historians' Views of Progressive-Era Labor Legislation. *Labor Hist.,* Fall 1987, *28*(4), pp. 447–83. **[G: U.S.]**

Zhijian, Zhang. Labour Force Planning in the People's Republic of China. *Amjad, R., ed.,* 1987, pp. 221–33. **[G: China]**

8221 Wages and Hours

Allen, Stephen P. Taxes, Redistribution, and the Minimum Wage: A Theoretical Analysis. *Quart. J. Econ.,* August 1987, *102*(3), pp. 477–89.

Booth, Alison L. and Schiantarelli, Fabio. The Employment Effects of a Shorter Working Week. *Economica,* May 1987, *54*(214), pp. 237–48.

Donges, Juergen B. Chronic Unemployment in Europe Forever? Challenges for Policy Reform. *Siven, C.-H., ed.,* 1987, pp. 103–23. **[G: W. Europe]**

Ehrenberg, Ronald G. and Smith, Robert S. Comparable-Worth Wage Adjustments and Female Employment in the State and Local Sector. *J. Lab. Econ.,* January 1987, *5*(1), pp. 43–62. **[G: U.S.]**

Flanagan, Thomas. Equal Pay for Work of Equal Value: Some Theoretical Criticisms. *Can. Public Policy,* December 1987, *13*(4), pp. 435–44. **[G: Canada]**

van Ginnekin, Wouter. Wage Policies in Industrialized Market Economies from 1971 to 1986. Between Controls and Free Bargaining. *Int. Lab. Rev.,* July-Aug. 1987, *126*(4), pp. 379–404. **[G: OECD]**

Guesnerie, Roger and Roberts, Kevin. Minimum Wage Legislation as a Second Best Policy. *Europ. Econ. Rev.,* Feb./Mar. 1987, *31*(1/2), pp. 490–98.

Hashimoto, Masanori. The Minimum Wage Law and Youth Crimes: Time-series Evidence. *J. Law Econ.,* October 1987, *30*(2), pp. 443–64. **[G: U.S.]**

Herin, Jan. Chronic Unemployment in Europe Forever? Challenges for Policy Reform: Comment. *Siven, C.-H., ed.,* 1987, pp. 124–27. **[G: W. Europe]**

Jones, Stephen R. G. Minimum Wage Legislation in a Dual Labor Market. *Europ. Econ. Rev.,* August 1987, *31*(6), pp. 1229–46.

Kirkby, Diane. "The Wage-Earning Woman and the State": The National Women's Trade Union League and Protective Labor Legislation, 1903–1923. *Labor Hist.,* Winter 1987, *28*(1), pp. 54–74. **[G: U.S.]**

Lang, Kevin. Pareto Improving Minimum Wage Laws. *Econ. Inquiry,* January 1987, *25*(1), pp. 145–58.

Lee, Dwight R. and McKenzie, Richard B. Minimum Wage: A Weaker Case Both For and Against. *Challenge,* Sept./Oct. 1987, *30*(4), pp. 55–56.

McDermott, John H. Employment in a Controlled, Open Economy. *Connolly, M. and González-Vega, C., eds.,* 1987, pp. 325–39.

Mellor, Earl F. Workers at the Minimum Wage or Less: Who They Are and the Jobs They Hold. *Mon. Lab. Rev.,* July 1987, *110*(7), pp. 34–38. **[G: U.S.]**

Meyer, Dirk. Ein Recht auf Arbeit durch Einführung der 35-Std. Woche? (The Right to Work by Introducing the 35-Hour Week?. With English summary.) *Z. Wirtschaft. Sozialwissen.,* 1987, *107*(4), pp. 537–52. **[G: W. Germany]**

Robb, Roberta Edgecombe. Equal Pay for Work of Equal Value: Issues and Policies. *Can. Pub-*

lic Policy, December 1987, *13*(4), pp. 445–61.
[G: Canada; U.S.; Australia]
Rojas R., Patricio and Riveros, Luis A. Salarios mínimos y medios: Un análisis empirico de causalidad. Los casos de Argentina, Brasil y Chile. (With English summary.) *Cuadernos Econ.*, December 1987, *24*(73), pp. 289–318.
[G: Argentinand--ddT1-; Brazil; Chile]
Smith, Ralph E. and Vavrichek, Bruce. The Minimum Wage: Its Relation to Incomes and Poverty. *Mon. Lab. Rev.*, June 1987, *110*(6), pp. 24–30. [G: U.S.]
Smith, Russell E. Política salarial, mercado de trabajo y salarios industriales en San Pablo, 1960–1976: análisis sugn tamaño de las empresas y su condición de nacionales o extranjeras. (With English summary.) *Desarrollo Econ.*, Oct.-Dec. 1987, *27*(107), pp. 399–421.
[G: Brazil]
Sorensen, Elaine. Effect of Comparable Worth Policies on Earnings. *Ind. Relat.*, Fall 1987, *26*(3), pp. 227–39. [G: U.S.]
Tinsley, LaVerne C. Workers' Compensation: 1986 State Enactments. *Mon. Lab. Rev.*, January 1987, *110*(1), pp. 67–71. [G: U.S.]

8222 Workmen's Compensation and Vocational Rehabilitation

Aarts, Leo. Disability in the United Kingdom: Incidence, Social Security Benefits and Labour Market Effects: Comment. *Emanuel, H.; de Gier, E. H. and Konijn, P. A. B. K., eds.*, 1987, pp. 215–17. [G: U.K.]
Aarts, Leo. Work Capacity of the Disabled. *Emanuel, H.; de Gier, E. H. and Konijn, P. A. B. K., eds.*, 1987, pp. 113–36.
[G: Netherlands]
Boden, Leslie I. and Jones, Carol Adaire. Occupational Disease Remedies: The Asbestos Experience. *Bailey, E. E., ed.*, 1987, pp. 321–46. [G: U.S.]
Borba, Philip S. and Appel, David. The Propensity of Permanently Disabled Workers to Hire Lawyers. *Ind. Lab. Relat. Rev.*, April 1987, *40*(3), pp. 418–29. [G: U.S.]
Bronstein, Arturo S. The Protection of Workers' Claims in the Event of the Insolvency of Their Employer. From Civil Law to Social Security. *Int. Lab. Rev.*, Nov.-Dec. 1987, *126*(6), pp. 715–31.
Bruinsma, Hilbrand. Decision Criteria and the Question of Equity and Incentives: Comment. *Emanuel, H.; de Gier, E. H. and Konijn, P. A. B. K., eds.*, 1987, pp. 179–82.
[G: Netherlands]
Carroll, John J. Work Capacity of the Disabled: Comment. *Emanuel, H.; de Gier, E. H. and Konijn, P. A. B. K., eds.*, 1987, pp. 137–41.
[G: Netherlands]
Chelius, James R. and Smith, Robert S. Firm Size and Regulatory Compliance Costs: The Case of Workers' Compensation Insurance. *J. Policy Anal. Manage.*, Winter 1987, *6*(2), pp. 193–206. [G: U.S.]
Danzon, Patricia M. Compensation for Occupa-

tional Disease: Evaluating the Options. *J. Risk Ins.*, June 1987, *54*(2), pp. 265–82.
Elder, Harold W. An Economic Analysis of Factor Usage and Workplace Regulation: Reply. *Southern Econ. J.*, January 1987, *53*(3), pp. 790. [G: U.S.]
Emanuel, Han. The Dutch Research Program on Factors Determining Social Disability Benefit Recipiency: A Background Paper. *Emanuel, H.; de Gier, E. H. and Konijn, P. A. B. K., eds.*, 1987, pp. 7–50. [G: Netherlands]
Eriksen, Tor. Decision Criteria and the Question of Equity and Incentives: Comment. *Emanuel, H.; de Gier, E. H. and Konijn, P. A. B. K., eds.*, 1987, pp. 177–78. [G: Netherlands]
Fenn, Paul. Work Capacity and the Probability of Entry into the Dutch Disability Insurance Program: Comment. *Emanuel, H.; de Gier, E. H. and Konijn, P. A. B. K., eds.*, 1987, pp. 101–04. [G: Netherlands]
Fenn, Paul and Harris, Donald. Disability in the United Kingdom: Incidence, Social Security Benefits and Labour Market Effects. *Emanuel, H.; de Gier, E. H. and Konijn, P. A. B. K., eds.*, 1987, pp. 191–210. [G: U.K.]
de Graaf, Louw. Disablement for Work: The Interaction between Research and Policy. *Emanuel, H.; de Gier, E. H. and Konijn, P. A. B. K., eds.*, 1987, pp. 1–6. [G: Netherlands]
Harris, Donald. Disability Benefits: Factors Determining Applications and Awards: Reflections on the Meeting. *Emanuel, H.; de Gier, E. H. and Konijn, P. A. B. K., eds.*, 1987, pp. 261–64.
Haveman, Robert H. On the Determinants of Growth in Disability Income Support: A Conference Overview. *Emanuel, H.; de Gier, E. H. and Konijn, P. A. B. K., eds.*, 1987, pp. 265–75. [G: Netherlands; U.K.; U.S.]
Johnson, William G. Work Capacity and the Probability of Entry into the Dutch Disability Insurance Program: Comment. *Emanuel, H.; de Gier, E. H. and Konijn, P. A. B. K., eds.*, 1987, pp. 91–100. [G: Netherlands]
de Jong, Philip. Work Capacity and the Probability of Entry into the Dutch Disability Insurance Program: Reply. *Emanuel, H.; de Gier, E. H. and Konijn, P. A. B. K., eds.*, 1987, pp. 111–12. [G: Netherlands]
de Jong, Philip. Work Capacity and the Probability of Entry into the Dutch Disability Insurance Program. *Emanuel, H.; de Gier, E. H. and Konijn, P. A. B. K., eds.*, 1987, pp. 51–90.
[G: Netherlands]
Nagi, Saad Z. Decision Criteria and the Question of Equity and Incentives. *Emanuel, H.; de Gier, E. H. and Konijn, P. A. B. K., eds.*, 1987, pp. 157–76. [G: Netherlands]
Nagi, Saad Z. Decision Criteria and the Question of Equity and Incentives: Reply. *Emanuel, H.; de Gier, E. H. and Konijn, P. A. B. K., eds.*, 1987, pp. 183–84. [G: Netherlands]
Nagi, Saad Z. Work Capacity and the Probability of Entry into the Dutch Disability Insurance Program: Comment. *Emanuel, H.; de Gier,*

E. H. and Konijn, P. A. B. K., eds., 1987, pp. 105–08. **[G: Netherlands]**

Olson, Dennis O. and Shieh, Yeung-Nan. An Economic Analysis of Factor Usage and Workplace Regulation: Comment. *Southern Econ. J.*, January 1987, *53*(3), pp. 786–89. **[G: U.S.]**

Pfaff, Anita B. Work Capacity of the Disabled: Comment. *Emanuel, H.; de Gier, E. H. and Konijn, P. A. B. K., eds.*, 1987, pp. 143–49. **[G: Netherlands]**

Pfaff, Martin. The Demand for Disability Transfers: Recent Research and Research Needs: Comment. *Emanuel, H.; de Gier, E. H. and Konijn, P. A. B. K., eds.*, 1987, pp. 249–54. **[G: U.S.; Netherlands]**

Schäfer, Dieter. Disability in the United Kingdom: Incidence, Social Security Benefits and Labour Market Effects: Comment. *Emanuel, H.; de Gier, E. H. and Konijn, P. A. B. K., eds.*, 1987, pp. 211–14. **[G: U.K.]**

Schmit, Joan T. Lump-Sum Awards in Workers' Compensation. *J. Risk Ins.*, June 1987, *54*(2), pp. 332–40. **[G: U.S.]**

Stace, Sheila. Vocational Rehabilitation for Women with Disabilities. *Int. Lab. Rev.*, 1987, *126*(3), pp. 301–16. **[G: Global]**

Sundakov, Alex. Accident Compensation Law: An Economic View. *New Zealand Econ. Pap.*, 1987, *21*, pp. 57–73. **[G: New Zealand]**

Viscusi, W. Kip and Moore, Michael J. Workers' Compensation: Wage Effects, Benefit Inadequacies, and the Value of Health Losses. *Rev. Econ. Statist.*, May 1987, *69*(2), pp. 249–61. **[G: U.S.]**

Walls, Richard T. and Dowler, Denetta L. Benefits vs. Earnings for Vocational Rehabilitation Clients: The Anchoring Effect. *J. Behav. Econ.*, Spring 1987, *16*(1), pp. 55–67. **[G: U.S.]**

Wolfe, Barbara L. The Demand for Disability Transfers: Recent Research and Research Needs. *Emanuel, H.; de Gier, E. H. and Konijn, P. A. B. K., eds.*, 1987, pp. 223–48. **[G: U.S.; Netherlands]**

Zeitzer, Ilene R. and Beedon, Laurel E. Longterm Disability Programs in Selected Countries. *Soc. Sec. Bull.*, September 1987, *50*(9), pp. 8–21. **[G: OECD]**

8223 Factory Act and Safety Legislation

Bartel, Ann P. and Thomas, Lacy Glenn. Predation through Regulation: The Wage and Profit Effects of the Occupational Safety and Health Administration and the Environmental Protection Agency. *J. Law Econ.*, October 1987, *30*(2), pp. 239–64. **[G: U.S.]**

Boden, Leslie I. and Jones, Carol Adaire. Occupational Disease Remedies: The Asbestos Experience. *Bailey, E. E., ed.*, 1987, pp. 321–46. **[G: U.S.]**

Chhokar, Jagdeep S. Safety at the Workplace: A Behavioural Approach. *Int. Lab. Rev.*, Mar.-Apr. 1987, *126*(2), pp. 169–78.

Elder, Harold W. An Economic Analysis of Factor Usage and Workplace Regulation: Reply.

Southern Econ. J., January 1987, *53*(3), pp. 790. **[G: U.S.]**

Gray, Wayne B. The Cost of Regulation: OSHA, EPA and the Productivity Slowdown. *Amer. Econ. Rev.*, December 1987, *77*(5), pp. 998–1006. **[G: U.S.]**

Kahn, Shulamit. Occupational Safety and Workers Preferences: Is There a Marginal Worker? *Rev. Econ. Statist.*, May 1987, *69*(2), pp. 262–68. **[G: U.S.]**

Kirkby, Diane. "The Wage-Earning Woman and the State": The National Women's Trade Union League and Protective Labor Legislation, 1903–1923. *Labor Hist.*, Winter 1987, *28*(1), pp. 54–74. **[G: U.S.]**

Olson, Dennis O. and Shieh, Yeung-Nan. An Economic Analysis of Factor Usage and Workplace Regulation: Comment. *Southern Econ. J.*, January 1987, *53*(3), pp. 786–89. **[G: U.S.]**

Willim, Horst. Trade Unions and Occupational Safety in the German Democratic Republic. *Int. Lab. Rev.*, 1987, *126*(3), pp. 329–36. **[G: E. Germany]**

8224 Unemployment Insurance

Ben-Horim, Moshe and Zuckerman, Dror. The Effect of Unemployment Insurance on Unemployment Duration. *J. Lab. Econ.*, July 1987, *5*(3), pp. 386–90.

Booth, Alan. Unemployment and Interwar Politics. *Glynn, S. and Booth, A., eds.*, 1987, pp. 43–56. **[G: U.K.]**

Burtless, Gary. Jobless Pay and High European Unemployment. *Lawrence, R. Z. and Schultze, C. L., eds.*, 1987, pp. 105–62. **[G: U.S.; W. Europe]**

Cohn, Elchanan and Capen, Margaret M. A Note on the Adequacy of UI Benefits. *Ind. Relat.*, Winter 1987, *26*(1), pp. 106–11. **[G: U.S.]**

Deacon, Alan. Systems of Interwar Unemployment Relief. *Glynn, S. and Booth, A., eds.*, 1987, pp. 31–42. **[G: U.K.]**

Egginton, Don M. A Historical Analysis of Labour Supply Incentives. *Beenstock, M., et al.*, 1987, pp. 76–123. **[G: U.K.]**

Flanagan, Robert J. Labor Market Behavior and European Economic Growth. *Lawrence, R. Z. and Schultze, C. L., eds.*, 1987, pp. 175–211. **[G: W. Europe; U.S.]**

Flückiger, Yves. Effets de l'assurance-chômage sur la mobilité interrégionale du travail. (With English summary.) *Revue Écon.*, September 1987, *38*(5), pp. 1017–28.

Giuseppi, Russo. Disoccupazione e incertezza. Una applicazione della teoria dell'utilità attesa. (Unemployment and Uncertainty. An Application the the Expected Utility Theory. With English summary.) *Giorn. Econ.*, May-June 1987, *46*(5–6), pp. 317–46.

Glynn, Sean. The Road to Full Employment: The Scale and Nature of the Problem. *Glynn, S. and Booth, A., eds.*, 1987, pp. 3–16. **[G: U.K.]**

Ham, John C. and Rea, Samuel A., Jr. Unemployment Insurance and Male Unemployment

Duration in Canada. *J. Lab. Econ.*, July 1987, 5(3), pp. 325–53. **[G: Canada]**

Holmlund, Bertil. Labor Market Behavior and European Economic Growth: Comment. *Lawrence, R. Z. and Schultze, C. L., eds.*, 1987, pp. 211–17. **[G: W. Europe; U.S.]**

Homburg, Heidrun. From Unemployment Insurance to Compulsory Labour: The Transformation of the Benefit System in Germany 1927–33. *Evans, R. J. and Geary, D., eds.*, 1987, pp. 73–107. **[G: Germany]**

Kahn, Lawrence M. Unemployment Insurance, Job Queues, and Systematic Job Search: An Equilibrium Approach. *Southern Econ. J.*, October 1987, 54(2), pp. 397–411.

Kaiser, Carl P. Layoffs, Average Hours, and Unemployment Insurance in U.S. Manufacturing Industries. *Quart. Rev. Econ. Bus.*, Winter 1987, 27(4), pp. 80–99. **[G: U.S.]**

Lipford, Jody and Yandle, Bruce. Political Dominance and State Unemployment Benefits. *Public Choice*, 1987, 53(2), pp. 175–80. **[G: U.S.]**

Lovell, Malcolm R., Jr. More Options for the Displaced Worker. *Barfield, C. E. and Makin, J. H., eds.*, 1987, pp. 97–99. **[G: U.S.]**

Martin, John P. Labor Market Behavior and European Economic Growth: Comment. *Lawrence, R. Z. and Schultze, C. L., eds.*, 1987, pp. 217–26. **[G: W. Europe; U.S.]**

Mirkin, Barry Alan. Early Retirement as a Labor Force Policy: An International Overview. *Mon. Lab. Rev.*, March 1987, 110(3), pp. 19–33. **[G: OECD]**

Nickell, Stephen J. Jobless Pay and High European Unemployment: Comment. *Lawrence, R. Z. and Schultze, C. L., eds.*, 1987, pp. 162–68. **[G: W. Europe]**

Niehuss, Merith. From Welfare Provision to Social Insurance: The Unemployment in Augsburg 1918–27. *Evans, R. J. and Geary, D., eds.*, 1987, pp. 44–72. **[G: Germany]**

Nolan, Brian. More on Actual versus Hypothetical Replacement Ratios in Ireland. *Econ. Soc. Rev.*, April 1987, 18(3), pp. 159–72. **[G: Ireland]**

Ohtake, Fumio. Unemployment and the Employment Insurance System (In Japanese. With English summary.) *Econ. Stud. Quart.*, September 1987, 38(3), pp. 245–57.

Rockefeller, Jay. The Urgency of Assistance to Displaced Workers. *Barfield, C. E. and Makin, J. H., eds.*, 1987, pp. 100–103. **[G: U.S.]**

Runner, Diana. Changes in Unemployment Insurance Legislation during 1986. *Mon. Lab. Rev.*, February 1987, 110(2), pp. 21–24. **[G: U.S.]**

Samuel, Howard D. Myths Surrounding Displaced Workers. *Barfield, C. E. and Makin, J. H., eds.*, 1987, pp. 104–06. **[G: U.S.]**

Theeuwes, Jules. Jobless Pay and High European Unemployment: Comment. *Lawrence, R. Z. and Schultze, C. L., eds.*, 1987, pp. 168–72. **[G: W. Europe; U.S.]**

Woodbury, Stephen A. and Spiegelman, Robert G. Bonuses to Workers and Employers to Reduce Unemployment: Randomized Trials in Illinois. *Amer. Econ. Rev.*, September 1987, 77(4), pp. 513–30. **[G: U.S.]**

Wright, Randall D. and Loberg, Janine. Unemployment Insurance, Taxes, and Unemployment. *Can. J. Econ.*, February 1987, 20(1), pp. 36–54.

8225 Government Employment Policies (including employment services)

Adam, Jan. Similarities and Differences in the Treatment of Labour Shortages. *Adam, J., ed.*, 1987, pp. 127–48. **[G: U.S.S.R.; Poland; Czechoslovakia; Hungary]**

Adnett, N. J. State Employment Agencies and Labour Market Efficiency. *Cambridge J. Econ.*, September 1987, 11(3), pp. 183–96. **[G: U.K.]**

Altmann, Franz-Lothar. Employment Policies in Czechoslovakia. *Adam, J., ed.*, 1987, pp. 78–102. **[G: Czechoslovakia]**

Barrett, Nancy S. Sex-Based Employment Quotas in Sweden: Comments. *Brown, C. and Pechman, J. A., eds.*, 1987, pp. 299–301. **[G: Sweden]**

Bendick, Marc, Jr. and Egan, Mary Lou. Transfer Payment Diversion for Small Business Development: British and French Experience. *Ind. Lab. Relat. Rev.*, July 1987, 40(4), pp. 528–42. **[G: U.K.; France]**

Booth, Alan. Unemployment and Interwar Politics. *Glynn, S. and Booth, A., eds.*, 1987, pp. 43–56. **[G: U.K.]**

Breen, William J. Administrative Politics and Labor Policy in the First World War: The U.S. Employment Service and the Seattle Labor Market Experiment. *Bus. Hist. Rev.*, Winter 1987, 61(4), pp. 582–605. **[G: U.S.]**

Brown, Charles C. and Wilcher, Shirley J. Sex-Based Employment Quotas in Sweden. *Brown, C. and Pechman, J. A., eds.*, 1987, pp. 271–98. **[G: Sweden]**

Fallenbuchl, Zbigniew M. Employment Policies in Poland. *Adam, J., ed.*, 1987, pp. 27–54. **[G: Poland]**

Faradzhev, F. A. Solving Employment Problems in a Labour-Surplus Region of the USSR: The Case of Azerbaijan. *Int. Lab. Rev.*, 1987, 126(3), pp. 337–50. **[G: U.S.S.R.]**

Gera, Surendra. An Evaluation of the Canadian Employment Tax Credit Program. *Can. Public Policy*, June 1987, 13(2), pp. 196–207. **[G: Canada]**

Ginsburg, Helen. Sex-Based Employment Quotas in Sweden: Comments. *Brown, C. and Pechman, J. A., eds.*, 1987, pp. 301–08. **[G: Sweden]**

Gollub, James O. Increasing Employment Opportunities for Older Workers: Emerging State and Local Initiatives. *Sandell, S. H., ed.*, 1987, pp. 143–64. **[G: U.S.]**

Hansen, Gary B. American Labor and International Trade: Adjustment Strategies to Assist Workers Displaced in Plant Closings and Permanent Layoffs. *Econ. Lavoro*, Jan.-Mar. 1987, 21(1), pp. 115–22. **[G: U.S.]**

Haulman, Clyde A.; Raffa, Frederick A. and Rungeling, Brian. Assessing the Labor Market Intermediary Role of the Job Service: Note. *Growth Change*, Winter 1987, *18*(1), pp. 66–71. **[G: U.S.]**

Hillman, Arye L.; Katz, Eliakim and Rosenberg, Jacob. Workers as Insurance: Anticipated Government Assistance and Factor Demand. *Oxford Econ. Pap.*, December 1987, *39*(4), pp. 813–20.

Homburg, Heidrun. From Unemployment Insurance to Compulsory Labour: The Transformation of the Benefit System in Germany 1927–33. *Evans, R. J. and Geary, D., eds.*, 1987, pp. 73–107. **[G: Germany]**

Kulik, Jane and Fairchild, Charles. Worker Assistance and Placement Experience. *Lynch, J. E., ed.*, 1987, pp. 191–218. **[G: U.S.]**

Long, David A. Analyzing Social Program Production: An Assessment of Supported Work for Youths. *J. Human Res.*, Fall 1987, *22*(4), pp. 551–62. **[G: U.S.]**

Mann, Arthur J. and Smith, Robert. Public Transfers, Family Socioeconomic Traits, and the Job Search Behavior of the Unemployment: Evidence from Puerto Rico. *World Devel.*, June 1987, *15*(6), pp. 831–40.
[G: Puerto Rico]

Middleton, Roger. Treasury Policy on Unemployment. *Glynn, S. and Booth, A., eds.*, 1987, pp. 109–24. **[G: U.K.]**

Ohlsson, Henry. Cost–Benefit Rules in a Regionalized Disequilibrium Model. *Scand. J. Econ.*, 1987, *89*(2), pp. 165–82.

Richards, J. The Industrial Distribution of the Temporary Short-time Working Compensation Scheme. *Appl. Econ.*, January 1987, *19*(1), pp. 111–25. **[G: U.K.]**

Rupp, Kalman, et al. Government Employment and Training Programs, and Older Americans. *Sandell, S. H., ed.*, 1987, pp. 121–42.
[G: U.S.]

Sandell, Steven H. Labor Market Problems and Employment Policies Affecting Older Americans. *Sandell, S. H., ed.*, 1987, pp. 15–33.
[G: U.S.]

Sandell, Steven H. The Problem Isn't Age: Conclusions and Implications. *Sandell, S. H., ed.*, 1987, pp. 231–45. **[G: U.S.]**

Schneider, Ursula. Self Aid or State Aid for Alternative Projects? *Ann. Pub. Co-op. Econ.*, Jan.-Mar. 1987, *58*(1), pp. 83–101. **[G: Austria]**

Steinberg, Danny and Monforte, Frank A. Estimating the Effects of Job Search Assistance and Training Programs on the Unemployment Durations of Displaced Workers. *Lang, K. and Leonard, J. S., eds.*, 1987, pp. 186–206.
[G: U.S.]

Steinherr, Alfred and Weiserbs, Daniel. Unemployment Policies under Constrained Growth. *Steinherr, A. and Weiserbs, D., eds.*, 1987, pp. 283–310. **[G: Belgium]**

Stewart, Frances. Supporting Productive Employment among Vulnerable Groups. *Cornia, G. A.; Jolly, R. and Stewart, F., eds.*, 1987, pp. 197–217. **[G: LDCs]**

Timár, János. Employment Policy in Hungary. *Adam, J., ed.*, 1987, pp. 103–24.
[G: Hungary]

Wulff, Birgit. The Third Reich and the Unemployed: National Socialist Work-Creation Schemes in Hamburg 1933–4. *Evans, R. J. and Geary, D., eds.*, 1987, pp. 281–302.
[G: Germany]

Zuidema, Thijs. Cost–Benefit Analysis in a Situation of Unemployment: Calculating the Decline in Unemployment as a Result of the Realization of a Government Project. *Public Finance Quart.*, January 1987, *15*(1), pp. 105–15.

8226 Employment in the Public Sector

Ali, Supian Haji. The Growing Sector: Malaysia. *Edgren, G., ed.*, 1987, pp. 99–146.
[G: Malaysia]

Canlas, Dante B. The Growing Sector: Philippines. *Edgren, G., ed.*, 1987, pp. 147–72.
[G: Philippines]

Desai, Ashok and Desai, Ena. The Growing Sector: India. *Edgren, G., ed.*, 1987, pp. 67–97.
[G: India]

Edgren, Gus. The Growth of Public Sector Employment in Asia. *Edgren, G., ed.*, 1987, pp. 1–28. **[G: Asia]**

Ehrenberg, Ronald G. and Smith, Robert S. Comparable Worth in the Public Sector. *Wise, D. A., ed.*, 1987, pp. 243–88. **[G: U.S.]**

Frant, Howard L. and Leonard, Herman B. Promise Them Anything: The Incentive Structures of Local Public Pension Plans. *Wise, D. A., ed.*, 1987, pp. 215–37. **[G: U.S.]**

Freeman, Richard B. How Do Public Sector Wages and Employment Respond to Economic Conditions? *Wise, D. A., ed.*, 1987, pp. 183–207. **[G: U.S.]**

Hongladarom, Chira, et al. The Growing Sector: Thailand. *Edgren, G., ed.*, 1987, pp. 173–223.
[G: Thailand]

Ingham, Michael D. Local Government Demand for Labour in England and Wales. *Scot. J. Polit. Econ.*, August 1987, *34*(3), pp. 267–84.
[G: U.K.]

Johnson, Terry R.; Dickinson, Katherine P. and West, Richard W. Older Workers, Job Displacement, and the Employment Service. *Sandell, S. H., ed.*, 1987, pp. 100–117.
[G: U.S.]

Lazear, Edward P. Promise Them Anything: The Incentive Structures of Local Public Pension Plans: Comment. *Wise, D. A., ed.*, 1987, pp. 237–42. **[G: U.S.]**

Leonard, Herman B. Investing in the Defense Work Force: The Debt and Structure of Military Pensions. *Wise, D. A., ed.*, 1987, pp. 47–73. **[G: U.S.]**

Medoff, James L. Comparable Worth in the Public Sector: Comment. *Wise, D. A., ed.*, 1987, pp. 288–89. **[G: U.S.]**

Murshid, K. A. S. and Sobhan, Rehman. The Growing Sector: Bangladesh. *Edgren, G., ed.*, 1987, pp. 29–65. **[G: Bangladesh]**

Peltzman, Sam. How Do Public Sector Wages and Employment Respond to Economic Conditions? Comment. *Wise, D. A., ed.*, 1987, pp. 207–13. **[G: U.S.]**

Rosen, Harvey S. Comment [Military versus Civilian Pay: A Descriptive Discussion] [Investing in the Defense Work Force: The Debt and Structure of Military Pensions]. *Wise, D. A., ed.*, 1987, pp. 73–77. **[G: U.S.]**

Sargent, J. R. Public Service Pay: Comment. *Levitt, M. S., ed.*, 1987, pp. 85–90. **[G: U.K.]**

Schmidt-Sørensen, Jan Beyer. Rekrutterings- og fastholdelses-problemer i den offentlige sektor. (The Problems of Recruiting and Keeping Employees in the Public Sector. With English summary.) *Nationaløkon. Tidsskr.*, 1987, 125(3), pp. 355–75. **[G: Denmark]**

Schumann, Richard E. State and Local Government Pay Increases Outpace Five-Year Rise in Private Industry. *Mon. Lab. Rev.*, February 1987, 110(2), pp. 18–20. **[G: U.S.]**

Smith, Sharon P. Wages in the Federal and Private Sectors: Comment. *Wise, D. A., ed.*, 1987, pp. 177–82. **[G: U.S.]**

Trinder, Chris. Public Service Pay. *Levitt, M. S., ed.*, 1987, pp. 72–84. **[G: U.K.]**

Venti, Steven F. Wages in the Federal and Private Sectors. *Wise, D. A., ed.*, 1987, pp. 147–77. **[G: U.S.]**

Wise, David A. Public Sector Payrolls: Overview. *Wise, D. A., ed.*, 1987, pp. 1–18. **[G: U.S.]**

823 Labor Mobility; National and International Migration

8230 Labor Mobility; National and International Migration

Abella, Manolo I. Asian Labour Mobility: New Dimensions and Implications for Development. *Pakistan Devel. Rev.*, Autumn 1987, 26(3), pp. 363–77. **[G: Asia]**

Agarwal, Vinod B. and Yochum, Gilbert R. The Eilberg Act, New Seed Immigration, and Professional Labor Markets. *Econ. Educ. Rev.*, 1987, 6(3), pp. 275–83. **[G: U.S.]**

Ahmad, Meekal Aziz. Workers' Remittances from the Middle East and Their Effect on Pakistan's Economy: Comments. *Pakistan Devel. Rev.*, Winter 1987, 26(4), pp. 762–73. **[G: Pakistan]**

Baily, Martin Neil. Housing Markets, Unemployment and Labour Market Flexibility in the UK: Comments. *Europ. Econ. Rev.*, April 1987, 31(3), pp. 641–43. **[G: U.K.]**

Bates, John J. and Bracken, I. Migration Age Profiles for Local Authority Areas in England, 1971–1981. *Environ. Planning A*, April 1987, 19(4), pp. 521–35. **[G: U.K.]**

Bean, Frank D.; Telles, Edward E. and Lowell, B. Lindsay. Undocumented Migration to the United States: Perceptions and Evidence. *Population Devel. Rev.*, December 1987, 13(4), pp. 671–90. **[G: U.S.]**

Berger, Mark C. and Webb, Michael A. Commercial Policy and the Brain Drain. *Appl. Econ.*, February 1987, 19(2), pp. 143–53. **[G: U.S.]**

Berninghaus, Siegfried and Seifert-Vogt, Hans Günther. International Migration under Incomplete Information. *Schweiz. Z. Volkswirtsch. Statist.*, June 1987, 123(2), pp. 199–218.

Bilsborrow, Richard E., et al. The Impact of Origin Community Characteristics on Rural–Urban Out-Migration in a Developing Country. *Demography*, May 1987, 24(2), pp. 191–210. **[G: Ecuador]**

Binswanger, Hans P. and McIntire, John. Behavioral and Material Determinants of Production Relations in Land-Abundant Tropical Agriculture. *Econ. Develop. Cult. Change*, October 1987, 36(1), pp. 73–99.

Bond, Eric W. and Chen, Tain-Jy. The Welfare Effects of Illegal Immigration. *J. Int. Econ.*, November 1987, 23(3/4), pp. 315–28.

Borjas, George J. Immigrants, Minorities, and Labor Market Competition. *Ind. Lab. Relat. Rev.*, April 1987, 40(3), pp. 382–92. **[G: U.S.]**

Borjas, George J. Self-Selection and the Earnings of Immigrants. *Amer. Econ. Rev.*, September 1987, 77(4), pp. 531–53. **[G: U.S.]**

Bourne, L. S. Urbanization, Migration and Urban Research in Comparative Context: An Urban Systems Perspective. *Can. J. Devel. Stud.*, 1987, 8(1), pp. 69–80.

Brosnan, Peter and Poot, Jacques. Modelling the Determinants of Trans-Tasman Migration after World War II. *Econ. Rec.*, December 1987, 63(183), pp. 313–29. **[G: Australia; New Zealand]**

Bulcha, Mekuria. Historical, Political and Social Causes of Mass Flight from Ethiopia. *Nobel, P., ed.*, 1987, pp. 19–36. **[G: Africa; Ethiopia]**

Bulcha, Mekuria. Sociological and Economic Factors in Refugee Integration: The Case of Ethiopian Exiles in the Sudan. *Nobel, P., ed.*, 1987, pp. 73–90. **[G: Sudan]**

Bulcha, Mekuria; Kibreab, Gaim and Nobel, Peter. Sociology, Economy and Law: Views in Common. *Nobel, P., ed.*, 1987, pp. 93–103. **[G: Africa]**

Burney, Nadeem A. Asian Labour Mobility: New Dimensions and Implications for Development: Comments. *Pakistan Devel. Rev.*, Autumn 1987, 26(3), pp. 380–81. **[G: Asia]**

Burney, Nadeem A. Workers' Remittances from the Middle East and Their Effect on Pakistan's Economy. *Pakistan Devel. Rev.*, Winter 1987, 26(4), pp. 745–61. **[G: Pakistan]**

Casetti, Emilio and Pandit, Kavita. The Non Linear Dynamics of Sectoral Shifts. *Econ. Geogr.*, July 1987, 63(3), pp. 241–58.

Chitala, Derrick. The Political Economy of the SADCC and Imperialism's Response. *Amin, S.; Chitala, D. and Mandaza, I., eds.*, 1987, pp. 13–36. **[G: Southern Africa; S. Africa]**

Cloud, Patricia and Galenson, David W. Chinese Immigration and Contract Labor in the Late Nineteenth Century. *Exploration Econ. Hist.*,

January 1987, *24*(1), pp. 22–42.   [G: U.S.]

Cremer, Helmuth and Gathon, Henry-Jean. Les déterminants de la mobilité résidentielle: Une analyse probit. (With English summary.) *Cah. Écon. Bruxelles,* Third Trimester 1987, (115), pp. 53–75.   [G: Belgium]

Crew, Spencer R. The Great Migration of Afro-Americans, 1915–40. *Mon. Lab. Rev.,* March 1987, *110*(3), pp. 34–36.   [G: U.S.]

Crummett, María de los Angeles. Rural Women and Migration in Latin America. *Deere, C. D. and León, M., eds.,* 1987, pp. 239–60.
    [G: Latin America]

Cushing, Brian J. A Note on Specification of Climate Variables in Models of Population Migration. *J. Reg. Sci.,* November 1987, *27*(4), pp. 241–49.   [G: U.S.]

Cushing, Brian J. Location-Specific Amenities, Topography, and Population Migration. *Ann. Reg. Sci.,* July 1987, *21*(2), pp. 74–85.
    [G: U.S.]

Cymrot, Donald J. and Dunlevy, James A. Are Free Agents Perspicacious Peregrinators? *Rev. Econ. Statist.,* February 1987, *69*(1), pp. 50–58.   [G: U.S.]

Day, Richard H., et al. Instability in Rural–Urban Migration. *Econ. J.,* December 1987, *97*(388), pp. 940–50.

Dean, K. G. The Disaggregation of Migration Flows: The Case of Brittany, 1975–1982. *Reg. Stud.,* August 1987, *21*(4), pp. 313–25.
    [G: U.K.]

Desbarats, Jacqueline. Population Redistribution in the Socialist Republic of Vietnam. *Population Devel. Rev.,* March 1987, *13*(1), pp. 43–76.   [G: Vietnam]

Djajić, Slobodan. Illegal Aliens, Unemployment and Immigration Policy. *J. Devel. Econ.,* February 1987, *25*(1), pp. 235–49.   [G: U.S.]

Donges, Juergen B. International Migration and the International Division of Labor. *Alonso, W., ed.,* 1987, pp. 129–48.

Emmi, P. C. Structural Determinants of Occupational Mobility in a Regional Labor Market. *Environ. Planning A,* July 1987, *19*(7), pp. 925–48.   [G: U.S.]

Ervin, Delbert J. The Ecological Theory of Migration: Reconceptualizing Indigenous Labor Force. *Soc. Sci. Quart.,* December 1987, *68*(4), pp. 866–75.   [G: U.S.]

Evers-Koelman, Inge; Fischer, Manfred M. and Nijkamp, Peter. Results of Cross-National Comparisons of Regional Labour Markets in 15 Countries. *Fischer, M. M. and Nijkamp, P., eds.,* 1987, pp. 369–483.   [G: OECD; E. Europe]

Falaris, Evangelos M. A Nested Logit Migration Model with Selectivity. *Int. Econ. Rev.,* June 1987, *28*(2), pp. 429–43.   [G: Venezuela]

Findley, Sally E. An Interactive Contextual Model of Migration in Ilocos Norte, the Philippines. *Demography,* May 1987, *24*(2), pp. 163–90.   [G: Philippines]

Flückiger, Yves. Effets de l'assurance-chômage sur la mobilité interrégionale du travail. (With English summary.) *Revue Écon.,* September

1987, *38*(5), pp. 1017–28.

Gabriel, Stuart A.; Justman, Moshe and Levy, Amnon. A Simultaneous-Equations Analysis of Urban Development: Migration and Industrial Growth in Israel's New Towns. *J. Urban Econ.,* May 1987, *21*(3), pp. 364–77.   [G: Israel]

Gabriel, Stuart A.; Justman, Moshe and Levy, Amnon. Place-to-Place Migration in Israel: Estimates of a Logistic Model. *Reg. Sci. Urban Econ.,* November 1987, *17*(4), pp. 595–606.
    [G: Israel]

Gang, Ira N. and Gangopadhyay, Shubhashis. Optimal Policies in a Dual Economy with Open Unemployment and Surplus Labour. *Oxford Econ. Pap.,* June 1987, *39*(2), pp. 378–87.

George, Edward Y. Impact of the Maquilas on Manpower Development and Economic Growth on the U.S./Mexico Border. *Tremblay, R., ed.,* 1987, pp. 549–78. [G: U.S.; Mexico]

Goss, Ernst P. and Paul, Chris. Age, Skill Level, and Mobility. *Atlantic Econ. J.,* July 1987, *15*(2), pp. 90–91.

Gottschang, Thomas R. Economic Change, Disasters, and Migration: The Historical Case of Manchuria. *Econ. Develop. Cult. Change,* April 1987, *35*(3), pp. 461–90.   [G: China]

Grenier, Gilles. Earnings by Language Group in Quebec in 1980 and Emigration from Quebec between 1976 and 1981. *Can. J. Econ.,* November 1987, *20*(4), pp. 774–91.
    [G: Canada]

Grubb, Farley. Colonial Labor Markets and the Length of Indenture: Further Evidence. *Exploration Econ. Hist.,* January 1987, *24*(1), pp. 101–06.

Gupta, Manash Ranjan. Harris–Todaro Migration-Mechanism and the Optimum Development of the Urban Sector. *Indian Econ. Rev.,* July-Dec. 1987, *22*(2), pp. 179–94.
    [G: LDCs]

Gupta, Manash Ranjan. Rural–Urban Migration and Urban Unemployment: A Note. *Scot. J. Polit. Econ.,* August 1987, *34*(3), pp. 295–305.

Gupta, Manash Ranjan. The Shadow Wage: A Note. *Math. Soc. Sci.,* June 1987, *13*(3), pp. 289–95.

Heady, Christopher. Designing Taxes with Migration. *Econ. J.,* Supplement 1987, 97, pp. 87–98.   [G: LDCs]

Hill, John K. Immigrant Decisions Concerning Duration of Stay and Migratory Frequency. *J. Devel. Econ.,* February 1987, *25*(1), pp. 221–34.   [G: U.S.]

Hill, John K. and Pearce, James E. Enforcing Sanctions against Employers of Illegal Aliens. *Fed. Res. Bank Dallas Econ. Rev.,* May 1987, pp. 1–15.   [G: U.S.]

Hoffmann-Nowotny, Hans-Joachim. Social Integration and Cultural Pluralism: Structural and Cultural Problems of Immigration in European Industrial Countries. *Alonso, W., ed.,* 1987, pp. 149–72.   [G: W. Europe]

Huang, Wi-Chiao. A Pooled Cross-Section and Time-Series Study of Professional Indirect Immigration to the United States. *Southern Econ. J.,* July 1987, *54*(1), pp. 95–109.   [G: U.S.]

Hughes, Gordon A. and McCormick, Barry. Housing Markets, Unemployment and Labour Market Flexibility in the UK. *Europ. Econ. Rev.*, April 1987, *31*(3), pp. 615–41. [G: U.K.]

Inoki, Takenori. Housing Markets, Unemployment and Labour Market Flexibility in the UK: Comments. *Europ. Econ. Rev.*, April 1987, *31*(3), pp. 644–45. [G: U.K.]

Irfan, M. Asian Labour Mobility: New Dimensions and Implications for Development: Comments. *Pakistan Devel. Rev.*, Autumn 1987, *26*(3), pp. 378–79. [G: Asia]

Kappelhoff, Peter and Teckenberg, Wolfgang. Intergenerational and Career Mobility in the Federal Republic and the United States. *Teckenberg, W., ed.*, 1987, pp. 3–49. [G: W. Germany; U.S.]

Katz, Eliakim and Stark, Oded. International Migration under Asymmetric Information. *Econ. J.*, September 1987, *97*(387), pp. 718–26.

Katz, Eliakim and Stark, Oded. Migration, Information and the Costs and Benefits of Signalling. *Reg. Sci. Urban Econ.*, August 1987, *17*(3), pp. 323–31.

Kazi, Shahnaz. International Labour Migration—Theoretical Considerations and Evidence from the Experience of the Mediterranean Sending Countries: Comments. *Pakistan Devel. Rev.*, Winter 1987, *26*(4), pp. 733–34. [G: Oceania; N. America; W. Europe]

Kiani, M. Framurz. Migration and Fertility in Pakistan. *Pakistan Devel. Rev.*, Winter 1987, *26*(4), pp. 587–89. [G: Pakistan]

Kibreab, Gaim. Rural Eritrean Refugees in the Sudan: A Study of the Dynamics of Flight. *Nobel, P., ed.*, 1987, pp. 37–44. [G: Sudan]

Kibreab, Gaim. Rural Refugee Land Settlements in Eastern Sudan: On the Road to Self-sufficiency? *Nobel, P., ed.*, 1987, pp. 63–71. [G: Sudan]

Kjurčiev, T. Alexander. Contribution of Workers' Remittances to Development. *Borner, S. and Taylor, A., eds.*, 1987, pp. 159–72.

Koch, James V. The Incomes of Recent Immigrants: A Look at Ethnic Differences. *Soc. Sci. Quart.*, June 1987, *68*(2), pp. 294–310. [G: U.S.]

Körner, Heiko. International Labour Migration—Theoretical Considerations and Evidence from the Experience of the Mediterranean Sending Countries. *Pakistan Devel. Rev.*, Winter 1987, *26*(4), pp. 723–32. [G: W. Europe; N. America; Oceania]

Kritz, Mary M. Socio-economic Issues Arising from Immigration in Receiving Countries. *Borner, S. and Taylor, A., eds.*, 1987, pp. 141–58.

Lever, William F. New Trends in the Supply and Demand Patterns of Labour in Western Economies. *Fischer, M. M. and Nijkamp, P., eds.*, 1987, pp. 249–67. [G: W. Europe]

Liaw, Kao-Lee and Ledent, Jacques. Nested Logit Model and Maximum Quasi-likelihood Method: A Flexible Methodology for Analyzing Interregional Migration Patterns. *Reg. Sci. Ur-*

ban Econ., February 1987, *17*(1), pp. 67–88. [G: Canada]

Lien, Da-Hsiang Donald. Economic Analysis of Brain Drain. *J. Devel. Econ.*, February 1987, *25*(1), pp. 33–43.

Lucas, Robert E. B. Emigration to South Africa's Mines. *Amer. Econ. Rev.*, June 1987, *77*(3), pp. 313–30. [G: S. Africa; Botswana; Lesotho; Malawi; Mozambique]

Maier, Gunther. Job Search and Migration. *Fischer, M. M. and Nijkamp, P., eds.*, 1987, pp. 189–204.

Manning, Chris. Rural Economic Change and Labour Mobility: A Case Study from West Java. *Bull. Indonesian Econ. Stud.*, December 1987, *23*(3), pp. 52–79. [G: Indonesia]

McCall, B. P. and McCall, J. J. A Sequential Study of Migration and Job Search. *J. Lab. Econ.*, Part 1, Oct. 1987, *5*(4), pp. 452–76.

McNeill, William H. Migration in Premodern Times. *Alonso, W., ed.*, 1987, pp. 15–35.

Mears, R. R. Die rol van die owerheid in die verstedeliking van die bevolking van Suid-Afrika. (With English summary.) *J. Stud. Econ. Econometrics*, November 1987, *11*(3), pp. 51–81. [G: S. Africa]

Meng, Ronald. The Earnings of Canadian Immigrant and Native-Born Males. *Appl. Econ.*, August 1987, *19*(8), pp. 1107–19. [G: Canada]

de Meza, David. The Migration Multiplier. *Bull. Econ. Res.*, July 1987, *39*(3), pp. 243–48.

Milanovic, Branko. Remittances and Income Distribution. *J. Econ. Stud.*, 1987, *14*(5), pp. 24–37. [G: Yugoslavia]

Molho, Ian J. The Migration Decisions of Young Men in Great Britain. *Appl. Econ.*, February 1987, *19*(2), pp. 221–43. [G: U.K.]

Mwabu, Germano M. A Comment on Kenyan Migration Movements. *Eastern Afr. Econ. Rev.*, December 1987, *3*(2), pp. 143–45. [G: Kenya]

Nicholas, Stephen and Shergold, Peter R. Human Capital and the Pre-famine Irish Emigration to England. *Exploration Econ. Hist.*, April 1987, *24*(2), pp. 158–77. [G: U.K.; Ireland]

Nicholas, Stephen and Shergold, Peter R. Intercounty Labour Mobility during the Industrial Revolution: Evidence from Australian Transportation Records. *Oxford Econ. Pap.*, December 1987, *39*(4), pp. 624–40. [G: Australia]

Ong, Paul M. Immigrant Wives' Labor Force Participation. *Ind. Relat.*, Fall 1987, *26*(3), pp. 296–303. [G: U.S.]

Pasha, Hafiz A. and Altaf, Mir Anjum. Return Migration in a Life-Cycle Setting: An Exploratory Study of Pakistani Migrants in Saudi Arabia. *Pakistan J. Appl. Econ.*, Summer 1987, *6*(1), pp. 1–21. [G: Pakistan; Saudi Arabia]

Patterson, Orlando. The Emerging West Atlantic System: Migration, Culture, and Underdevelopment in the United States and the Circum-Caribbean Region. *Alonso, W., ed.*, 1987, pp. 227–60. [G: U.S.; Caribbean]

Percy, Michael B. and Woroby, Tamara. American Homesteaders and the Canadian Prairies, 1899 and 1909. *Exploration Econ. Hist.*, January 1987, *24*(1), pp. 77–100.   [G: U.S.]

Plath, Joel C.; Holland, David W. and Carvalho, Joe W. Labor Migration in Southern Africa and Agricultural Development: Some Lessons from Lesotho. *J. Devel. Areas*, January 1987, *21*(2), pp. 159–75.   [G: Lesotho]

Portes, Alejandro. Illegal Immigration and the International System, Lessons from Recent Legal Mexican Immigrants to the United States. *Menard, S. W. and Moen, E. W., eds.*, 1987, *1979*, pp. 300–311.   [G: Mexico; U.S.]

Rahman, Md. Mizanur. An Improvement of the National Growth Rate Method for Estimation of Internal Migration. *Bangladesh Devel. Stud.*, June 1987, *15*(2), pp. 113–19.   [G: Bangladesh]

Rees, P. H. and Ram, S. Projections of the Residential Distribution of an Ethnic Group: Indians in Bradford. *Environ. Planning A*, October 1987, *19*(10), pp. 1323–58.   [G: U.K.]

Roback, Jennifer. Determinants of the Local Unemployment Rate. *Southern Econ. J.*, January 1987, *53*(3), pp. 735–50.   [G: Colombia]

Rosenberg, Sam. Economic Contractions and Racial Differentials in Male Job Mobility. *Ind. Relat.*, Fall 1987, *26*(3), pp. 291–95.   [G: U.S.]

Ruhm, Christopher J. Job Loss and Job Change: Comment. *Ind. Lab. Relat. Rev.*, October 1987, *41*(1), pp. 47–49.   [G: U.S.]

Ruhm, Christopher J. The Economic Consequences of Labor Mobility. *Ind. Lab. Relat. Rev.*, October 1987, *41*(1), pp. 30–42.   [G: U.S.]

Saunders, Mark N. K. and Flowerdew, Robin. Spatial Aspects of the Provision of Job Information. *Fischer, M. M. and Nijkamp, P., eds.*, 1987, pp. 205–28.   [G: U.K.]

Schaefer, Donald F. A Model of Migration and Wealth Accumulation: Farmers at the Antebellum Southern Frontier. *Exploration Econ. Hist.*, April 1987, *24*(2), pp. 130–57.   [G: U.S.]

Schaeffer, P. V. A Dynamic Model of Labor-Market Change in International Labor Migrations when Demand for Labor Is Exogenous. *Environ. Planning A*, August 1987, *19*(8), pp. 1051–57.

Schubert, Renate. Interne Migration in Entwicklungsländern. Zur Rationalität von Land-Stadt-Wanderungen. (Internal Migration in Developing Countries—Rationality of Rural–Urban Migration. With English summary.) *Z. Wirtschaft. Sozialwissen.*, 1987, *107*(2), pp. 207–23.

Schweizer, Thomas. Agrarian Transformation? Rice Production in a Javanese Village. *Bull. Indonesian Econ. Stud.*, August 1987, *23*(2), pp. 38–70.   [G: Indonesia]

Semenza, Renata. Riduzione dell'occupazione industriale e mobilità del lavoro. (The Reduction of Industrial Employment and Work Mobility. With English summary.) *Econ. Lavoro*, July-Sept. 1987, *21*(3), pp. 85–93.   [G: Italy]

Shefer, Daniel. The Effect of Agricultural Price-Support Policies on Interregional and Rural-

to-Urban Migration in Korea: 1976–1980. *Reg. Sci. Urban Econ.*, August 1987, *17*(3), pp. 333–44.   [G: Korea]

Shrestha, Nanda R. Institutional Policies and Migration Behavior: A Selective Review. *World Devel.*, March 1987, *15*(3), pp. 329–45.   [G: LDCs]

Slottje, D. J. and Hayes, Kathy J. Income Inequality and Urban/Rural Migration. *Rev. Reg. Stud.*, Spring 1987, *17*(2), pp. 53–56.   [G: U.S.]

Stauth, Georg. Remigration and Social Change— Prospects for the Migrant Worker Sending Countries of the Middle East. *Pakistan Devel. Rev.*, Winter 1987, *26*(4), pp. 735–44.   [G: Middle East]

Straubhaar, Thomas. International Migration under Incomplete Information: A Comment. *Schweiz. Z. Volkswirtsch. Statist.*, June 1987, *123*(2), pp. 219–26.

Sutton, Francis X. Refugees and Mass Exoduses: The Search for a Humane, Effective Policy. *Alonso, W., ed.*, 1987, pp. 201–26.

Tabbarah, R. Economic Aspects of International Migration: Introduction. *Borner, S. and Taylor, A., eds.*, 1987, pp. 127–40.   [G: LDCs]

Taylor, J. Edward. Undocumented Mexico–U.S. Migration and the Returns to Households in Rural Mexico. *Amer. J. Agr. Econ.*, August 1987, *69*(3), pp. 626–38.   [G: U.S.; Mexico]

Todaro, Michael P. and Maruszko, Lydia. Illegal Migration and U.S. Immigration Reform: A Conceptual Framework. *Population Devel. Rev.*, March 1987, *13*(1), pp. 101–14.   [G: U.S.]

Ulph, David T. Tax Harmonisation and Labour Mobility. *Cnossen, S., ed.*, 1987, pp. 305–17.   [G: EEC]

Vasegh-Daneshvary, Nasser; Schlottmann, Alan M. and Herzog, Henry W., Jr. Immigration of Engineers, Scientists, and Physicians and the U.S. High Technology Renaissance. *Soc. Sci. Quart.*, June 1987, *68*(2), pp. 311–25.   [G: U.S.]

Vaupel, Suzanne and Martin, Philip L. Evaluating Employer Sanctions: Farm Labor Contractor Experience. *Ind. Relat.*, Fall 1987, *26*(3), pp. 304–13.   [G: U.S.]

de Vletter, Fion. Foreign Labour on the South African Gold Mines: New Insights on an Old Problem. *Int. Lab. Rev.*, Mar.-Apr. 1987, *126*(2), pp. 199–218.   [G: S. Africa]

Weiner, Myron. International Emigration and the Third World. *Alonso, W., ed.*, 1987, pp. 173–200.   [G: LDCs]

White-Means, Shelley I. Migrant Farmworker Earnings: A Human Capital Approach. *Rev. Black Polit. Econ.*, Spring 1987, *15*(4), pp. 21–33.   [G: U.S.]

White, Stephen E. Return Migration to Eastern Kentucky and the Stem Family Concept. *Growth Change*, Spring 1987, *18*(2), pp. 38–52.   [G: U.S.]

Wiesshuhn, Gernot. Mobility Patterns and Income Dynamics of Employees in the Federal Republic of Germany from 1974 until the Beginning of 1980: An Empirical Study Based on a Longitudianl Sample of German Employees. *Jahr. Nationalökon. Statist.*, July 1987, *203*(4), pp. 333–71. **[G: W. Germany]**

Withers, Glenn. The Australian Economy in the Long Run: Labour. *Maddock, R. and McLean, I. W., eds.*, 1987, pp. 248–88. **[G: Australia]**

Yousefi, Mahmood and Rives, Janet M. Migration Behavior of College Graduates: An Empirical Analysis. *J. Behav. Econ.*, Fall 1987, *16*(3), pp. 35–49. **[G: U.S.]**

Zamanian, Zaman. Government Policy and the Brain Drain. *Atlantic Econ. J.*, December 1987, *15*(4), pp. 65–69.

Zolberg, Aristide R. Wanted But Not Welcome: Alien Labor in Western Development. *Alonso, W., ed.*, 1987, pp. 36–73. **[G: Europe; N. America]**

Zweig, David. From Village to City: Reforming Urban–Rural Relations in China. *Int. Reg. Sci. Rev.*, 1987, *11*(1), pp. 43–58. **[G: China]**

824 Labor Market Studies, Wages, Employment

8240 General

Altmann, Franz-Lothar. Employment Policies in Czechoslovakia. *Adam, J., ed.*, 1987, pp. 78–102. **[G: Czechoslovakia]**

Anderson, Patrick Y. Informal Sector or Secondary Labour Market? Towards a Synthesis. *Soc. Econ. Stud.*, September 1987, *36*(3), pp. 149–76. **[G: Jamaica]**

Andrews, Martyn J. The Aggregate Labour Market: An Empirical Investigation into Market-Clearing for the UK. *Econ. J.*, March 1987, *97*(385), pp. 157–76. **[G: U.K.]**

Andrews, Martyn J. and Nickell, Stephen J. A Disaggregated Disequilibrium Model of the Labour Market. *Sinclair, P. J. N., ed.*, 1987, *1986*, pp. 414–30. **[G: U.K.]**

Artus, Patrick. Salaire réel et emploi. (Real Wages and Employment. With English summary.) *Revue Écon.*, May 1987, *38*(3), pp. 625–59. **[G: France]**

Bean, Charles R. Salaires, demande et chômage: une perspective internationale. (Wages, Demand and Unemployment: An International Comparison. With English summary.) *Revue Écon.*, May 1987, *38*(3), pp. 601–23. **[G: OECD]**

Bednarzik, Robert W. and Sabelhaus, John E. Job Creation and Losses in the U.S., 1973–1984: Low or High Wage Industries? *Econ. Lavoro*, Apr.-June 1987, *21*(2), pp. 125–33. **[G: U.S.]**

Blakemore, Arthur E.; Low, Stuart A. and Ormiston, Michael B. Employment Bonuses and Labor Turnover. *J. Lab. Econ.*, Part 2, Oct. 1987, *5*(4), pp. S124–35. **[G: U.S.]**

Claycombe, Richard J. Time Horizons and Turnover of Young Craftsmen. *J. Behav. Econ.*, Winter 1987, *16*(4), pp. 19–31. **[G: U.S.]**

D'Amico, Thomas F. The Conceit of Labor Mar-

ket Discrimination. *Amer. Econ. Rev.*, May 1987, *77*(2), pp. 310–15.

Deiaco, Enrico. Labor Market Flexibility in a Nordic Perspective. *Vartia, P., et al.*, 1987, pp. 303–28. **[G: Denmark; Sweden; Norway; Finland]**

Dore, Ronald. Citizenship and Employment in an Age of High Technology. *Brit. J. Ind. Relat.*, July 1987, *25*(2), pp. 201–25. **[G: U.K.; Japan]**

Dyrstad, Jan Morten. Resource Boom, Wages and Unemployment: Theory and Evidence from the Norwegian Petroleum Experience. *Scand. J. Econ.*, 1987, *89*(2), pp. 125–43. **[G: Norway]**

Easton, Brian. The Labour Market and Economic Liberalisation. *Bollard, A. and Buckle, R., eds.*, 1987, pp. 181–205. **[G: New Zealand]**

Fallenbuchl, Zbigniew M. Employment Policies in Poland. *Adam, J., ed.*, 1987, pp. 27–54. **[G: Poland]**

Flanagan, Robert J. Efficiency and Equality in Swedish Labor Markets. *Bosworth, B. P. and Rivlin, A. M., eds.*, 1987, pp. 125–84. **[G: Sweden]**

George, Edward Y. Impact of the Maquilas on Manpower Development and Economic Growth on the U.S./Mexico Border. *Tremblay, R., ed.*, 1987, pp. 549–78. **[G: U.S.; Mexico]**

Hall, S. G., et al. The UK Labour Market: Equilibrium or Disequilibrium? *Lloyds Bank Rev.*, July 1987, (165), pp. 27–39. **[G: U.K.]**

Haulman, Clyde A.; Raffa, Frederick A. and Rungeling, Brian. Assessing the Labor Market Intermediary Role of the Job Service: Note. *Growth Change*, Winter 1987, *18*(1), pp. 66–71. **[G: U.S.]**

Iams, Howard M. Jobs of Persons Working after Receiving Retired-Worker Benefits. *Soc. Sec. Bull.*, November 1987, *50*(11), pp. 4–18. **[G: U.S.]**

Karakitsos, Elias. Exchange Rate Dynamics and the Labour Market. *Chrystal, K. A. and Sedgwick, R., eds.*, 1987, pp. 164–98.

Killian, Molly Sizer and Hady, Thomas F. The Economic Performance of Rural Labor Markets. *U.S.D.A., Econ. Res. Serv., Agr. and Rural Econ. Div.*, 1987, pp. 8.1–23. **[G: U.S.]**

Kniesner, Thomas J. and Goldsmith, Arthur H. A Survey of Alternative Models of the Aggregate U.S. Labor Market. *J. Econ. Lit.*, September 1987, *25*(3), pp. 1241–80. **[G: U.S.]**

Lang, Kevin; Leonard, Jonathan S. and Lilien, David M. Labor Market Structure, Wages and Unemployment. *Lang, K. and Leonard, J. S., eds.*, 1987, pp. 1–16.

Le Franc, Elsie. The Bauxite Labour Force in Jamaica: A High Wage Sector in a Dual Economy. *Soc. Econ. Stud.*, March 1987, *36*(1), pp. 217–68. **[G: Jamaica]**

Pissarides, Christopher A. Wages and Employment: A Framework for Analysis with Application to Three Policy Issues. *Econ. Rec.*, December 1987, *63*(183), pp. 301–12.

Schroeder, Gertrude E. Managing Labour Shortages in the Soviet Union. *Adam, J., ed.*, 1987, pp. 3–26. **[G: U.S.S.R.]**

Sloan, Judith and Wooden, Mark. The Australian Labour Market, December 1987. *Australian Bull. Lab.*, December 1987, *14*(1), pp. 295–320. **[G: Australia]**

Spurr, Stephen J. How the Market Solves an Assignment Problem: The Matching of Lawyers with Legal Claims. *J. Lab. Econ.*, Part 1, Oct. 1987, *5*(4), pp. 502–32. **[G: U.S.]**

Tzannatos, Zafiris. The Greek Labour Market: Current Perspectives and Future Prospects. *Greek Econ. Rev.*, 1987, *9*(2), pp. 224–38. **[G: Greece]**

Wiesshuhn, Gernot. Mobility Patterns and Income Dynamics of Employees in the Federal Republic of Germany from 1974 until the Beginning of 1980: An Empirical Study Based on a Longitudianl Sample of German Employees. *Jahr. Nationalökon. Statist.*, July 1987, *203*(4), pp. 333–71. **[G: W. Germany]**

Withers, Glenn. The Australian Economy in the Long Run: Labour. *Maddock, R. and McLean, I. W., eds.*, 1987, pp. 248–88. **[G: Australia]**

Woodbury, Stephen A. Power in the Labor Market: Institutionalist Approaches to Labor Problems. *J. Econ. Issues*, December 1987, *21*(4), pp. 1781–1807.

Wooden, Mark and Dawkins, Peter. The Australian Labour Market, March 1987. *Australian Bull. Lab.*, March 1987, *13*(2), pp. 70–93. **[G: Australia]**

8241 Geographic Labor Market Studies

Browne, Lynn E. Too Much of a Good Thing? Higher Wages in New England. *New Eng. Econ. Rev.*, Jan./Feb. 1987, pp. 39–53. **[G: U.S.]**

Brunel, Andre and Burke, Michael P. Promoting High-Technology Industry: Initiatives and Policies for State Governments: Pennsylvania. *Schmandt, J. and Wilson, R., eds.*, 1987, pp. 191–229. **[G: U.S.]**

Fischer, Harald and Peck, Amy Miriam. Promoting High-Technology Industry: Initiatives and Policies for State Governments: New York. *Schmandt, J. and Wilson, R., eds.*, 1987, pp. 129–62. **[G: U.S.]**

Freudenberg, Michael and Henderson, Tracy L. Promoting High-Technology Industry: Initiatives and Policies for State Governments: Florida. *Schmandt, J. and Wilson, R., eds.*, 1987, pp. 35–64. **[G: U.S.]**

Gramatzki, Hans-Erich. Regional Employment Policies in East European Countries. *Adam, J., ed.*, 1987, pp. 171–95.
[G: Czechoslovakia; Poland; Hungary; E. Germany]

Hacker, Sidney Bailey and Sommerfeld, Robert D. Promoting High-Technology Industry: Initiatives and Policies for State Governments: Minnesota. *Schmandt, J. and Wilson, R., eds.*, 1987, pp. 97–127. **[G: U.S.]**

Howard, Mark and Kragie, Mary. Promoting High-Technology Industry: Initiatives and Pol-

icies for State Governments: North Carolina. *Schmandt, J. and Wilson, R., eds.*, 1987, pp. 163–90. **[G: U.S.]**

Hyclak, Thomas and Johnes, Geraint. On the Determinants of Full Employment Unemployment Rates in Local Labour Markets. *Appl. Econ.*, February 1987, *19*(2), pp. 191–200. **[G: U.S.]**

Lane, Theodore and Thomas, Cheryl K. The Labor Force Status of Alaska's Native Population. *Lane, T., ed.*, 1987, pp. 63–89. **[G: U.S.]**

Mandelbaum, Thomas B. Is Eighth District Manufacturing Endangered? *Fed. Res. Bank St. Louis Rev.*, November 1987, *69*(9), pp. 5–15. **[G: U.S.]**

Margo, Robert A. and Villaflor, Georgia C. The Growth of Wages in Antebellum America: New Evidence. *J. Econ. Hist.*, December 1987, *47*(4), pp. 873–95. **[G: U.S.]**

Merrigan, Kathleen A. and Smith, Suzanne E. Promoting High-Technology Industry: Initiatives and Policies for State Governments: Massachusetts. *Schmandt, J. and Wilson, R., eds.*, 1987, pp. 65–96. **[G: U.S.]**

Muller, Brian and Dowling, Michael. Promoting High-Technology Industry: Initiatives and Policies for State Governments: Texas. *Schmandt, J. and Wilson, R., eds.*, 1987, pp. 231–57. **[G: U.S.]**

Rahman, Atiq and Islam, Rizwanul. An Empirical Account of Hired Labour Market in Rural Bangladesh: Comment. *Bangladesh Devel. Stud.*, March 1987, *15*(1), pp. 129–42. **[G: Bangladesh]**

Schroeder, Esther C. Testing Local Level Labor Force and Unemployment Projections. *Demography*, November 1987, *24*(4), pp. 649–61. **[G: U.S.]**

Silbert, Lance. Promoting High-Technology Industry: Initiatives and Policies for State Governments: California. *Schmandt, J. and Wilson, R., eds.*, 1987, pp. 11–33. **[G: U.S.]**

Sloan, Judith and Tulsi, Narmon. The Australian Labour Market, September 1987. *Australian Bull. Lab.*, September 1987, *13*(4), pp. 199–224. **[G: Australia; OECD]**

Wright, Gavin. Postbellum Southern Labor Markets. *Kilby, P., ed.*, 1987, pp. 98–134. **[G: U.S.]**

8242 Wage, Hours, and Fringe Benefit Studies

Abowd, John M. and Card, David. Intertemporal Labor Supply and Long-term Employment Contracts. *Amer. Econ. Rev.*, March 1987, *77*(1), pp. 50–68. **[G: U.S.]**

Abraham, Katharine G. and Farber, Henry S. Job Duration, Seniority, and Earnings. *Amer. Econ. Rev.*, June 1987, *77*(3), pp. 278–97. **[G: U.S.]**

Adams, James D. Intertemporal Wage Variation, Employment, and Unemployment. *J. Lab. Econ.*, January 1987, *5*(1), pp. 106–29. **[G: U.S.]**

Akkermans, Timie and Hövels, Ben. Young Workers and Trade Unions. A Comparison with Women and Workers in General. *Econ. Lavoro*, Apr.-June 1987, *21*(2), pp. 119–23. [G: Netherlands]

Allen, Steven G. Relative Wage Variability in the United States, 1860–1983. *Rev. Econ. Statist.*, November 1987, *69*(4), pp. 617–26. [G: U.S.]

Allen, Steven G. and Clark, Robert L. Pensions and Firm Performance. *Allen, S. G., et al.*, 1987, pp. 195–242. [G: U.S.]

Alpert, William T. An Analysis of Fringe Benefits Using Time-Series Data. *Appl. Econ.*, January 1987, *19*(1), pp. 1–16. [G: U.S.]

Alston, Julian M. and Chalfant, James A. A Note on Causality between Money, Wages and Prices in Australia. *Econ. Rec.*, June 1987, *63*(181), pp. 115–19. [G: Australia]

Altonji, Joseph G. and Shakotko, Robert A. Do Wages Rise with Job Seniority? *Rev. Econ. Stud.*, July 1987, *54*(3), pp. 437–59. [G: U.S.]

Andersen, Torben M. Short- and Long-run Consequences of Shorter Working Hours. *Pedersen, P. J. and Lund, R., eds.*, 1987, pp. 147–65.

Anderson, Joseph M.; Kennell, David L. and Sheils, John F. Health Plan Costs, Medicare, and Employment of Older Workers. *Sandell, S. H., ed.*, 1987, pp. 206–17. [G: U.S.]

Anderson, Kathryn H.; Butler, John S. and Sloan, Frank A. Labor Market Segmentation: A Cluster Analysis of Job Groupings and Barriers to Entry. *Southern Econ. J.*, January 1987, *53*(3), pp. 571–90. [G: U.S.]

Andrews, Emily S. Changing Pension Policy and the Aging of America. *Contemp. Policy Issues*, April 1987, *5*(2), pp. 84–97. [G: U.S.]

Andrisani, Paul and Daymont, Thomas. Age Changes in Productivity and Earnings among Managers and Professionals. *Sandell, S. H., ed.*, 1987, pp. 52–70. [G: U.S.]

Antler, Jacob and Kahane, Yehuda. The Gross and Net Replacement Ratios in Designing Pension Schemes and in Financial Planning: The Israeli Experience. *J. Risk Ins.*, June 1987, *54*(2), pp. 283–97. [G: Israel]

Appelbaum, Eileen. Restructuring Work: Temporary, Part-time, and At-Home Employment. *Hartmann, H. I., ed.*, 1987, pp. 268–310. [G: U.S.]

Appolito, Richard A. The Implicit Pension Contract *Developments and New Directions. J. Human Res.*, Summer 1987, *22*(3), pp. 441–67.

Armstrong, Sarah J. Incentive Compensation: Incentive Design and Management Implications. *Nalbantian, H. R., ed.*, 1987, pp. 165–75. [G: U.S.]

Artoni, Roberto. La riforma del sistema pensionistico. (With English summary.) *Polit. Econ.*, April 1987, *3*(1), pp. 3–15. [G: Italy]

Artus, Jacques R. Real Wages, Real Wage Aspirations, and Unemployment in Europe: Comment. *Lawrence, R. Z. and Schultze, C. L., eds.*, 1987, pp. 292–95. [G: W. Europe]

Ashenfelter, Orley. The Work Response to a Guaranteed Income: A Survey of Experimental Evidence: Discussion. *Munnell, A. H., ed.*, 1987, pp. 53–55. [G: U.S.]

Auerbach, Alan J. and Kotlikoff, Laurence J. Life Insurance of the Elderly: Adequacy and Determinants. *Burtless, G., ed.*, 1987, pp. 229–67. [G: U.S.]

Barbezat, Debra A. Salary Differentials by Sex in the Academic Labor Market. *J. Human Res.*, Summer 1987, *22*(3), pp. 422–28. [G: U.S.]

Barnow, Burt S. The Impact of CETA Programs on Earnings: A Review of the Literature. *J. Human Res.*, Spring 1987, *22*(2), pp. 157–93. [G: U.S.]

Barron, John M.; Black, Dan A. and Loewenstein, Mark A. Employer Size: The Implications for Search, Training, Capital Investment, Starting Wages, and Wage Growth. *J. Lab. Econ.*, January 1987, *5*(1), pp. 76–89. [G: U.S.]

Bartel, Ann P. and Thomas, Lacy Glenn. Predation through Regulation: The Wage and Profit Effects of the Occupational Safety and Health Administration and the Environmental Protection Agency. *J. Law Econ.*, October 1987, *30*(2), pp. 239–64. [G: U.S.]

Bartoli, Henri. La matrise des cots humains du travail. Condition de la matrise des transformations technologiques dans les pays du Tiers Monde. (Mastering the Human Cost of Labour: An Essential Condition for Mastery of Technological Change in the third world. With English summary.) *Écon. Soc.*, November 1987, *21*(11), pp. 101–26. [G: LDCs]

Bassi, Laurie J. Estimating the Effect of Job Training Programs, Using Longitudinal Data: Ashenfelter's Findings Reconsidered: A Comment. *J. Human Res.*, Spring 1987, *22*(2), pp. 300–303. [G: U.S.]

Bean, Charles R. Real Wages, Real Wage Aspirations, and Unemployment in Europe: Comment. *Lawrence, R. Z. and Schultze, C. L., eds.*, 1987, pp. 295–99. [G: W. Europe]

Becker, William E. and Alter, George C. The Probabilities of Life and Work Force Status in the Calculation of Expected Earnings. *J. Risk Ins.*, June 1987, *54*(2), pp. 364–75.

Beenstock, Michael. Pensions and Labour Market Structure. *Oxford Econ. Pap.*, September 1987, *39*(3), pp. 568–76. [G: U.K.]

Beenstock, Michael. Real Wages and Unemployment in the 1930s: A Reply [Wages and Unemployment in Interwar Britain]. *Nat. Inst. Econ. Rev.*, February 1987, (119), pp. 76–78. [G: U.K.]

Behrens, Ruth A. Health Promotion in the Workplace. *Meyer, J. A. and Lewin, M. E., eds.*, 1987, pp. 133–48. [G: U.S.]

Beladi, Hamid and Brunner, Lawrence P. Trade Unions and Money Wage Changes in U.S. Manufacturing Industries: Further Empirical Evidence. *Quart. J. Bus. Econ.*, Summer 1987, *26*(3), pp. 79–86. [G: U.S.]

Bell, Linda and Freeman, Richard B. Flexible Wage Structures and Employment. *Gunderson, M.; Meltz, N. M. and Ostry, S., eds.*, 1987, pp. 119–28. [G: U.S.]

Benham, Harry C. Union–Nonunion Wage Differentials Revisited. *J. Lab. Res.*, Fall 1987, 8(4), pp. 569–83. [G: U.S.]

Bergmann, Barbara R. Pay Equity—Surprising Answers to Hard Questions. *Challenge*, May/June 1987, 30(2), pp. 45–51. [G: U.S.]

Bishop, John. The Recognition and Reward of Employee Performance. *J. Lab. Econ.*, Part 2, Oct. 1987, 5(4), pp. S36–56. [G: U.S.]

Björklund, Anders. Assessing the Decline of Wage Dispersion in Sweden. *Eliasson, G., ed.*, 1987, pp. 101–11. [G: Sweden]

Björklund, Anders. The Wage Structure and the Functioning of the Labor Market: Comment. *Siven, C.-H., ed.*, 1987, pp. 98–102. [G: Sweden]

Björklund, Anders and Moffitt, Robert. The Estimation of Wage Gains and Welfare Gains in Self-selection Models. *Rev. Econ. Statist.*, February 1987, 69(1), pp. 42–49. [G: Sweden]

Blackaby, D. H. and Manning, D. N. Regional Earnings Revisited. *Manchester Sch. Econ. Soc. Stud.*, June 1987, 55(2), pp. 158–83. [G: U.K.]

Blanchard, Olivier Jean. Aggregate and Individual Price Adjustment. *Brookings Pap. Econ. Act.*, 1987, (1), pp. 57–109. [G: U.S.]

Blau, Francine D. and Ferber, Marianne A. Occupations and Earnings of Women Workers. *Koziara, K. S.; Moskow, M. H. and Tanner, L. D., eds.*, 1987, pp. 37–68. [G: U.S.]

Blaug, Mark. An Economic Analysis of Personal Earnings in Thailand. *Blaug, M.*, 1987, 1974, pp. 301–31. [G: Thailand]

Blomquist, N. Sören. Can Shorter Working Time Reduce Unemployment? Comment. *Siven, C.-H., ed.*, 1987, pp. 149–53.

Blostin, Allan P. Mental Health Benefits Financed by Employers. *Mon. Lab. Rev.*, July 1987, 110(7), pp. 23–27. [G: U.S.]

Blundell, Richard and Meghir, Costas. Bivariate Alternatives to the Tobit Model. *J. Econometrics*, Jan./Feb. 1987, 34(1/2), pp. 179–200. [G: U.K.]

Bodie, Zvi; Shoven, John B. and Wise, David A. Issues in Pension Economics: Introduction. *Bodie, Z.; Shoven, J. B. and Wise, D. A., eds.*, 1987, pp. 1–11. [G: U.S.]

Bodie, Zvi, et al. Funding and Asset Allocation in Corporate Pension Plans: An Empirical Investigation. *Bodie, Z.; Shoven, J. B. and Wise, D. A., eds.*, 1987, pp. 15–44. [G: U.S.]

Boot, Pieter. Incentive Systems and Unemployment: The East European Experience. *Comp. Econ. Stud.*, Spring 1987, 29(1), pp. 37–61. [G: E. Europe]

Booth, Alison L. Extra-statutory Redundancy Payments in Britain. *Brit. J. Ind. Relat.*, November 1987, 25(3), pp. 401–18. [G: U.K.]

Borjas, George J. Immigrants, Minorities, and Labor Market Competition. *Ind. Lab. Relat. Rev.*, April 1987, 40(3), pp. 382–92. [G: U.S.]

Borjas, George J. Self-Selection and the Earnings of Immigrants. *Amer. Econ. Rev.*, September 1987, 77(4), pp. 531–53. [G: U.S.]

Boskin, Michael J. and Shoven, John B. Concepts and Measures of Earnings Replacement during Retirement. *Bodie, Z.; Shoven, J. B. and Wise, D. A., eds.*, 1987, pp. 113–41. [G: U.S.]

Botham, F. W. and Hunt, E. H. Wages in Britain during the Industrial Revolution. *Econ. Hist. Rev., 2nd Ser.*, August 1987, 40(3), pp. 380–99. [G: U.K.]

Branson, William H. Productivity, Wages, and Prices inside and outside Manufacturing in the U.S., Japan, and Europe: Comments. *Europ. Econ. Rev.*, April 1987, 31(3), pp. 733–36. [G: U.S.; Japan; Europe]

Bronstein, Arturo S. The Protection of Workers' Claims in the Event of the Insolvency of Their Employer. From Civil Law to Social Security. *Int. Lab. Rev.*, Nov.-Dec. 1987, 126(6), pp. 715–31.

Brown, Charles C. Comment [Military Hiring and Youth Employment] [Uncle Sam Wants You—Sometimes: Military Enlistments and the Youth Labor Market] [Military Service and Civilian Earnings of Youths]. *Wise, D. A., ed.*, 1987, pp. 140–45. [G: U.S.]

Brown, James N. and Rosen, Harvey S. Taxation, Wage Variation, and Job Choice. *J. Lab. Econ.*, Part 1, Oct. 1987, 5(4), pp. 430–51. [G: U.S.]

Brown, Martin and Nuwer, Michael. Strategic Jobs and Wage Structure in the Steel Industry: 1910–1930. *Ind. Relat.*, Fall 1987, 26(3), pp. 253–66. [G: U.S.]

Browne, Lynn E. Too Much of a Good Thing? Higher Wages in New England. *New Eng. Econ. Rev.*, Jan./Feb. 1987, pp. 39–53. [G: U.S.]

Bull, Clive. Business Cycle and Wage Determination in the United States. *Nalbantian, H. R., ed.*, 1987, pp. 213–28. [G: U.S.]

Bulow, Jeremy I. Pension Plan Integration as Insurance against Social Security Risk: Comment. *Bodie, Z.; Shoven, J. B. and Wise, D. A., eds.*, 1987, pp. 169–72. [G: U.S.]

Bulow, Jeremy I.; Mørck, Randall and Summers, Lawrence H. How Does the Market Value Unfunded Pension Liabilities? *Bodie, Z.; Shoven, J. B. and Wise, D. A., eds.*, 1987, pp. 81–104. [G: U.S.]

Burtless, Gary. The Work Response to a Guaranteed Income: A Survey of Experimental Evidence. *Munnell, A. H., ed.*, 1987, pp. 22–52. [G: U.S.]

Calmfors, Lars. Work Sharing: Why? How? How Not . . . : Comments. *Layard, R. and Calmfors, L., eds.*, 1987, pp. 198–204. [G: OECD]

Calvo, Guillermo A. The Economics of Supervision. *Nalbantian, H. R., ed.*, 1987, pp. 87–103.

Capie, Forrest H. Unemployment and Real Wages. *Glynn, S. and Booth, A., eds.*, 1987, pp. 57–69. [G: U.K.]

Cappelli, Peter. Bargaining Structure and Wage Outcomes in the British Coal Industry. *Ind.*

Relat., Spring 1987, *26*(2), pp. 127–45.
[G: U.K.]

Carruth, Alan A. and Oswald, Andrew J. Wage Inflexibility in Britain. *Oxford Bull. Econ. Statist.*, February 1987, *49*(1), pp. 59–78.
[G: U.K.]

Carter, Michael G. and Maddock, Rodney. Leisure and Australian Wellbeing 1911–81. *Australian Econ. Hist. Rev.*, March 1987, *27*(1), pp. 30–43.
[G: Australia]

Cecchetti, Stephen G. Indexation and Incomes Policy: A Study of Wage Adjustment in Unionized Manufacturing. *J. Lab. Econ.*, July 1987, *5*(3), pp. 391–412.
[G: U.S.]

Chan-Lee, James H.; Coe, David T. and Prywes, Menahem. Microeconomic Changes and Macroeconomic Wage Disinflation in the 1980s. *OECD Econ. Stud.*, Spring 1987, (8), pp. 121–57.

Chapman, Bruce J. Labour Turnover and Wage Determination. *Australian Econ. Pap.*, June 1987, *26*(48), pp. 119–29.
[G: Australia]

Christofides, Louis N. Wage Adjustment in Contracts Containing Cost-of-Living Allowance Clauses. *Rev. Econ. Statist.*, August 1987, *69*(3), pp. 531–36.
[G: Canada; U.S.]

Clark, Robert L. Aging and Relative Earnings. *Sandell, S. H., ed.*, 1987, pp. 71–83.
[G: U.S.]

Codina Jiménez, Alexis. Worker Incentives in Cuba. *Zimbalist, A., ed.*, 1987, pp. 129–40.
[G: Cuba]

Cohen, Malcolm S. and Fulton, George A. Unions and Jobs: The U.S. Auto Industry—Comment. *J. Lab. Res.*, Summer 1987, *8*(3), pp. 307–10.
[G: U.S.]

Collins, David J. Taxation of Fringe Benefits—An Economist's Perspective. *Australian Tax Forum*, 1987, *4*(1), pp. 95–121.
[G: Australia]

Cooper, C. Joseph, Jr. White-Collar Salaries Vary Widely in the Service Industries. *Mon. Lab. Rev.*, November 1987, *110*(11), pp. 21–23.
[G: U.S.]

Crane, Jon R. and Wise, David A. Military Service and Civilian Earnings of Youths. *Wise, D. A., ed.*, 1987, pp. 119–37.
[G: U.S.]

Creedy, John. Variations in Earnings and Responsibility. *J. Roy. Statist. Soc.*, 1987, *150*(1), pp. 57–68.
[G: U.K.]

Cymrot, Donald J. and Dunlevy, James A. Are Free Agents Perspicacious Peregrinators? *Rev. Econ. Statist.*, February 1987, *69*(1), pp. 50–58.
[G: U.S.]

Dalto, Guy C. Economic Segmentation, Human Capital, and Tax-Favored Fringe Benefits. *Soc. Sci. Quart.*, September 1987, *68*(3), pp. 583–97.
[G: U.S.]

Daniels, Rudolph. The Structure of the South African Labor Market, 1970–83. *Rev. Black Polit. Econ.*, Spring 1987, *15*(4), pp. 63–78.
[G: S. Africa]

Del Boca, Daniela. Wage Discrimination: Empirical Findings from Direct and Reverse Regres-

sion. *Ricerche Econ.*, Jan.-Mar. 1987, *41*(1), pp. 82–95.
[G: W. Germany; Italy; U.S.; U.K.]

Demetriades, Euripides L. and Psacharopoulos, George. Educational Expansion and the Returns to Education: Evidence from Cyprus. *Int. Lab. Rev.*, Sept.-Oct. 1987, *126*(5), pp. 597–602.
[G: Cyprus]

Dickens, William T. and Katz, Lawrence F. Inter-industry Wage Differences and Industry Characteristics. *Lang, K. and Leonard, J. S., eds.*, 1987, pp. 48–89.
[G: U.S.]

Dickie, Mark and Gerking, Shelby. Interregional Wage Differentials: An Equilibrium Perspective. *J. Reg. Sci.*, November 1987, *27*(4), pp. 571–85.
[G: U.S.]

Dickinson, Katherine P.; Johnson, Terry R. and West, Richard W. The Impact of CETA Programs on Components of Participants' Earnings. *Ind. Lab. Relat. Rev.*, April 1987, *40*(3), pp. 430–41.
[G: U.S.]

Dillon, Patricia and Gang, Ira N. Earnings Effects of Labor Organizations in 1890. *Ind. Lab. Relat. Rev.*, July 1987, *40*(4), pp. 516–27.
[G: U.S.]

Disney, Richard. Statutory Sick Pay: An Appraisal. *Fisc. Stud.*, May 1987, *8*(2), pp. 58–76.
[G: U.K.]

Dolton, Peter J. and Makepeace, Gerald H. Marital Status, Child Rearing and Earnings Differentials in the Graduate Labour Market. *Econ. J.*, December 1987, *97*(388), pp. 897–922.
[G: U.K.]

Dombois, Rainer and Osterland, M. New Forms of Flexible Utilization of Labour: Part-time and Contract Work. *Tarling, R., ed.*, 1987, pp. 225–43.
[G: W. Germany]

Donges, Juergen B. Chronic Unemployment in Europe Forever? Challenges for Policy Reform. *Siven, C.-H., ed.*, 1987, pp. 103–23.
[G: W. Europe]

Dorsey, Stuart. The Economic Functions of Private Pensions: An Empirical Analysis. *J. Lab. Econ.*, Part 2, Oct. 1987, *5*(4), pp. S171–89.
[G: U.S.]

Drewes, Torben. Regional Wage Spillover in Canada. *Rev. Econ. Statist.*, May 1987, *69*(2), pp. 224–31.
[G: Canada]

Drèze, Jacques H. Work Sharing: Why? How? How Not . . . *Layard, R. and Calmfors, L., eds.*, 1987, pp. 139–92.
[G: OECD]

Dutton, Patricia. Policies for the Youth Labour Market: YTS: Training or a Placebo? *Junankar, P. N., ed.*, 1987, pp. 217–37.
[G: U.K.]

Egginton, Don M. A Historical Analysis of Labour Supply Incentives. *Beenstock, M., et al.*, 1987, pp. 76–123.
[G: U.K.]

Egginton, Don M. An Informal Empirical Analysis of Labour Supply Decisions in the UK. *Beenstock, M., et al.*, 1987, pp. 124–65.
[G: U.K.]

Ehrenberg, Ronald G. and Milkovich, George T. Compensation and Firm Performance. *Allen, S. G., et al.*, 1987, pp. 87–122.
[G: U.S.]

Ehrenberg, Ronald G. and Smith, Robert S.

Comparable Worth in the Public Sector. *Wise, D. A., ed.*, 1987, pp. 243–88.   [G: U.S.]

Ehrenberg, Ronald G. and Smith, Robert S. Comparable-Worth Wage Adjustments and Female Employment in the State and Local Sector. *J. Lab. Econ.*, January 1987, *5*(1), pp. 43–62.   [G: U.S.]

Eichengreen, Barry. The Impact of Late Nineteenth-Century Unions on Labor Earnings and Hours: Iowa in 1894. *Ind. Lab. Relat. Rev.*, July 1987, *40*(4), pp. 501–15.   [G: U.S.]

Elliott, R. F. and Murphy, P. D. The Relative Pay of Public and Private Sector Employees, 1970–1984. *Cambridge J. Econ.*, June 1987, *11*(2), pp. 107–32.   [G: U.K.]

Ellis, I. A.; Pearson, J. M. and Periton, P. D. Trade Unions and Wage Inflation in the United Kingdom: A Re-estimation of Hines' Model. *Appl. Econ.*, May 1987, *19*(5), pp. 597–608.   [G: U.K.]

Falus-Szikra, Katalin. Hungarian Wage Relations: An International Comparison. *Acta Oecon.*, 1987, *38*(1–2), pp. 61–77.   [G: Hungary]

Farber, Stephen C. and Newman, Robert J. Accounting for South/Non-South Real Wage Differentials and for Changes in Those Differentials over Time. *Rev. Econ. Statist.*, May 1987, *69*(2), pp. 215–23.   [G: U.S.]

Fecher, Fabienne. Politique d'austérité et récession économique. Incidence sur la distribution du revenu des belges de 1980 à 1984. (With English summary.) *Cah. Écon. Bruxelles*, Second Trimester 1987, (114), pp. 397–420.   [G: Belgium]

Figart, Deborah M. Gender, Unions, and Internal Labor Markets: Evidence from the Public Sector in Two States. *Amer. Econ. Rev.*, May 1987, *77*(2), pp. 252–56.   [G: U.S.]

Filer, Randall K. Joint Estimates of the Supply of Labor Hours and the Intensity of Work Effort. *J. Behav. Econ.*, Fall 1987, *16*(3), pp. 1–12.   [G: U.S.]

Flaim, Paul O. and Sehgal, Ellen. Reemployment and Earnings [Displaced Workers of 1979–83: How Well Have They Fared?]. *Staudohar, P. D. and Brown, H. E.*, 1987, *1985*, pp. 101–30.   [G: U.S.]

Flanagan, Robert J. Labor Market Behavior and European Economic Growth. *Lawrence, R. Z. and Schultze, C. L., eds.*, 1987, pp. 175–211.   [G: W. Europe; U.S.]

Fosu, Augustin Kwasi. Explaining Post-1964 Earnings Gains by Black Women: Race or Sex? *Rev. Black Polit. Econ.*, Winter 1987, *15*(3), pp. 41–55.   [G: U.S.]

Fraker, Thomas and Maynard, Rebecca. The Adequacy of Comparison Group Designs for Evaluations of Employment-Related Programs. *J. Human Res.*, Spring 1987, *22*(2), pp. 194–227.   [G: U.S.]

Frank, Richard G., et al. Economic Rents Derived from Hospital Privileges in the Market for Podiatric Services. *J. Health Econ.*, December 1987, *6*(4), pp. 319–37.   [G: U.S.]

Frant, Howard L. and Leonard, Herman B. Promise Them Anything: The Incentive Structures of Local Public Pension Plans. *Wise, D. A., ed.*, 1987, pp. 215–37.   [G: U.S.]

Freeman, Richard B. How Do Public Sector Wages and Employment Respond to Economic Conditions? *Wise, D. A., ed.*, 1987, pp. 183–207.   [G: U.S.]

Freeman, Richard B. and Leonard, Jonathan S. Union Maids: Unions and the Female Work Force. *Brown, C. and Pechman, J. A., eds.*, 1987, pp. 189–212.   [G: U.S.]

Freeman, Richard B. and Weitzman, Martin L. Bonuses and Employment in Japan. *J. Japanese Int. Economies*, June 1987, *1*(2), pp. 168–94.   [G: Japan]

Gabriel, Paul E. and Schmitz, Susanne. The Relative Earnings of Native and Immigrant Males in the United States. *Quart. Rev. Econ. Bus.*, Autumn 1987, *27*(3), pp. 91–101.   [G: U.S.]

Garnsey, Elizabeth. Working Hours and Workforce Divisions. *Tarling, R., ed.*, 1987, pp. 85–103.

Garofalo, Gasper A. and Fogarty, Michael S. The Role of Labor Costs in Regional Capital Formation. *Rev. Econ. Statist.*, November 1987, *69*(4), pp. 593–99.   [G: U.S.]

Garside, W. R. The Real Wage Debate and British Interwar Unemployment. *Glynn, S. and Booth, A., eds.*, 1987, pp. 70–81.   [G: U.K.]

Gerhart, Barry A. and Jarley, Paul. Comment [A Tale of Employment Decline in Two Cities: How Bad Was the Worst of Times?]. *Ind. Lab. Relat. Rev.*, January 1987, *40*(2), pp. 280–84.   [G: U.S.]

Gerlach, Knut. A Note on Male–Female Wage Differences in West Germany. *J. Human Res.*, Fall 1987, *22*(4), pp. 584–92.   [G: W. Germany]

Goldin, Claudia. The Gender Gap in Historical Perspective. *Kilby, P., ed.*, 1987, pp. 135–70.   [G: U.S.]

Goldin, Claudia and Polachek, Solomon W. Residual Differences by Sex: Perspectives on the Gender Gap in Earnings. *Amer. Econ. Rev.*, May 1987, *77*(2), pp. 143–51.   [G: U.S.]

Gordon, Robert J. Aggregate and Individual Price Adjustment: Comments. *Brookings Pap. Econ. Act.*, 1987, (1), pp. 110–17.   [G: U.S.]

Gordon, Robert J. Productivity, Wages, and Prices inside and outside of Manufacturing in the U.S., Japan, and Europe. *Europ. Econ. Rev.*, April 1987, *31*(3), pp. 685–733.   [G: U.S.; Japan; Europe]

Gordon, Robert J. The Wage and Price Adjustment Process in Six Large OECD Countries. *Aliber, R. Z., ed.*, 1987, pp. 70–91.   [G: OECD]

Grant, E. Kenneth; Swidinsky, Robert and Vanderkamp, John. Canadian Union–Nonunion Wage Differentials. *Ind. Lab. Relat. Rev.*, October 1987, *41*(1), pp. 93–107.   [G: Canada]

Graves, Philip E.; Lee, Dwight R. and Sexton, Robert L. A Note on Interfirm Implications of Wages and Status. *J. Lab. Res.*, Spring 1987, *8*(2), pp. 209–12.   [G: U.S.]

Greenhalgh, Christine and Stewart, Mark B. The Effects and Determinants of Training. *Oxford*

Bull. Econ. Statist., May 1987, *49*(2), pp. 171–90. [G: U.K.]

Gregory, Mary; Lobban, Peter and Thomson, Andrew. Pay Settlements in Manufacturing Industry, 1979–84: A Micro-data Study of the Impact of Product and Labour Market Pressures. *Oxford Bull. Econ. Statist.*, February 1987, *49*(1), pp. 129–50. [G: U.K.]

Grenier, Gilles. Earnings by Language Group in Quebec in 1980 and Emigration from Quebec between 1976 and 1981. *Can. J. Econ.*, November 1987, *20*(4), pp. 774–91. [G: Canada]

Grubb, David. Wage Behaviour and Macroeconomic Policy. *Gunderson, M.; Meltz, N. M. and Ostry, S., eds.*, 1987, pp. 103–07. [G: U.S.; W. Europe; Canada]

Gunderson, Morley; Meltz, Noah M. and Ostry, Sylvia. Unemployment: International Perspectives: Introduction: A Summary of the Issues. *Gunderson, M.; Meltz, N. M. and Ostry, S., eds.*, 1987, pp. 1–10.

Gustafson, Thomas A. The Incentive Effects of Private Pension Plans: Comment. *Bodie, Z.; Shoven, J. B. and Wise, D. A., eds.*, 1987, pp. 337–39. [G: U.S.]

Gustman, Alan L. Concepts and Measures of Earnings Replacement during Retirement: Comment. *Bodie, Z.; Shoven, J. B. and Wise, D. A., eds.*, 1987, pp. 141–46. [G: U.S.]

Guzzo, Richard A. and Katzell, Raymond A. Effects of Economic Incentives on Productivity: A Psychological View. *Nalbantian, H. R., ed.*, 1987, pp. 107–19.

Hall, Robert E. The Work Response to a Guaranteed Income: A Survey of Experimental Evidence: Discussion. *Munnell, A. H., ed.*, 1987, pp. 56–59. [G: U.S.]

Hall, S. G. and Henry, Samuel G. Brian. Wage Models. *Nat. Inst. Econ. Rev.*, February 1987, (119), pp. 70–75. [G: U.K.]

Haller, Max. Positional and Sectoral Differences in Income: The Federal Republic, France, and the United States. *Teckenberg, W., ed.*, 1987, pp. 172–90. [G: W. Germany; France; U.S.]

Hamermesh, Daniel S. Unemployment: United States: Comment. *Gunderson, M.; Meltz, N. M. and Ostry, S., eds.*, 1987, pp. 129–32. [G: U.S.]

Hammerman, Herbert. Five Case Studies [Five Case Studies of Displaced Workers]. *Staudohar, P. D. and Brown, H. E.*, 1987, *1964*, pp. 75–88. [G: U.S.]

Harper, Robert M., Jr.; Mister, William G. and Strawser, Jerry R. The Impact of New Pension Disclosure Rules on Perceptions of Debt. *J. Acc. Res.*, Autumn 1987, *25*(2), pp. 327–30.

Harrigan, Frank J., et al. Bargaining Models of Regional Earnings Determination: Theory and Scottish Evidence. *Gordon, I., ed.*, 1987, pp. 44–66. [G: U.K.]

Harris, R. I. D. and Wass, V. J. The Effect of Collective Bargaining on Earnings in Northern Ireland in 1973. *Econ. Soc. Rev.*, October 1987, *19*(1), pp. 1–14. [G: U.K.]

Harrison, Bennett. Cold Bath or Restructuring? An Expansion of the Weisskopf–Bowles–Gordon Framework. *Sci. Soc.*, Spring 1987, *51*(1), pp. 72–82. [G: U.S.]

Havinga, Ivo C. Skill Formation, Employment and Earnings in the Urban Informal Sector: Comments. *Pakistan Devel. Rev.*, Winter 1987, *26*(4), pp. 718–19. [G: Pakistan]

Heady, Christopher. Alternative Theories of Wages in Less Developed Countries: An Empirical Test. *J. Devel. Stud.*, October 1987, *24*(1), pp. 5–15. [G: Colombia]

Hegrenes, Agnar and Norum, Leopold. Macromodel Calculations of Effects of Different Policy Instruments on Agricultural Output, Resource Use, and Farm Income. *Kettunen, L., ed.*, 1987, pp. 331–41. [G: Norway]

Henley, John S. and Nyaw, Mee-Kau. The Development of Work Incentives in Chinese Industrial Enterprises—Material versus Non-material Incentives. *Warner, M., ed.*, 1987, pp. 127–48. [G: China]

Herin, Jan. Chronic Unemployment in Europe Forever? Challenges for Policy Reform: Comment. *Siven, C.-H., ed.*, 1987, pp. 124–27. [G: W. Europe]

Hersoug, Tor; Kjaer, Knut N. and Rødseth, Asbjorn. Wages, Taxes and the Utility-Maximizing Trade Union: A Confrontation with Norwegian Data. *Sinclair, P. J. N., ed.*, 1987, *1986*, pp. 431–51. [G: Norway]

Heywood, John S. Wage Discrimination and Market Structure. *J. Post Keynesian Econ.*, Summer 1987, *9*(4), pp. 617–28. [G: U.S.]

Hill, Diane B. Employer-Sponsored Long-term Disability Insurance. *Mon. Lab. Rev.*, July 1987, *110*(7), pp. 16–22. [G: U.S.]

Hill, Stephen. Working Time Changes and Employment Growth. *Lloyds Bank Rev.*, January 1987, (163), pp. 31–46. [G: U.K.]

Hirsch, Barry T. and Neufeld, John L. Nominal and Real Union Wage Differentials and the Effects of Industry and SMSA Density: 1973–83. *J. Human Res.*, Winter 1987, *22*(1), pp. 138–48. [G: U.S.]

Hoel, Michael. Can Shorter Working Time Reduce Unemployment? *Siven, C.-H., ed.*, 1987, pp. 129–48.

Holden, Karen C. and Hansen, W. Lee. Part-time Work, Full-time Work, and Occupational Segregation. *Brown, C. and Pechman, J. A., eds.*, 1987, pp. 217–40. [G: U.S.]

Holly, Sean and Smith, Peter N. A Two-Sector Analysis of the UK Labour Market. *Oxford Bull. Econ. Statist.*, February 1987, *49*(1), pp. 79–102. [G: U.K.]

Holmlund, Bertil. Labor Market Behavior and European Economic Growth: Comment. *Lawrence, R. Z. and Schultze, C. L., eds.*, 1987, pp. 211–17. [G: W. Europe; U.S.]

Holmstrom, Bengt. Incentive Compensation: Practical Design from a Theory Point of View. *Nalbantian, H. R., ed.*, 1987, pp. 176–85.

Horlick, Max. The Relationships between Public and Private Pension Schemes: An Introductory Overview. *Soc. Sec. Bull.*, July 1987, *50*(7), pp. 15–24. [G: W. Europe]

House, William J. Labor Market Differentiation in a Developing Economy: An Example from Urban Juba, Southern Sudan. *World Devel.*, July 1987, *15*(7), pp. 877–97. [G: Sudan]

Huang, Cliff J.; Sloan, Frank A. and Adamache, Killard W. Estimation of Seemingly Unrelated Tobit Regressions via the EM Algorithm. *J. Bus. Econ. Statist.*, July 1987, *5*(3), pp. 425–30. [G: U.S.]

Hubbard, R. Glenn. Uncertain Lifetimes, Pensions, and Individual Saving. *Bodie, Z.; Shoven, J. B. and Wise, D. A., eds.*, 1987, pp. 175–206. [G: U.S.]

Human, L. and Greenacre, M. J. Labor Market Discrimination in the Manufacturing Sector: The Impact of Race, Gender, Education and Age on Income. *S. Afr. J. Econ.*, June 1987, *55*(2), pp. 150–64. [G: S. Africa]

Hundley, Greg. The Threat of Unionism and Wage-Coverage Effects. *J. Lab. Res.*, Summer 1987, *8*(3), pp. 237–51. [G: U.S.]

Hunt, Janet C.; Kiker, B. F. and Williams, C. Glyn. The Effect of Type of Union on Member–Nonmember Wage Differentials. *J. Lab. Res.*, Winter 1987, *8*(1), pp. 59–65. [G: U.S.]

Hutchens, Robert M. A Test of Lazear's Theory of Delayed Payment Contracts. *J. Lab. Econ.*, Part 2, Oct. 1987, *5*(4), pp. S153–70. [G: U.S.]

Ingham, Michael D. Local Government Pay Drift: The Search for Causality. *Appl. Econ.*, January 1987, *19*(1), pp. 83–100. [G: U.K.]

Işikli, Alpaslan. Wage Labor and Unionization. *Schick, I. C. and Tonak, E. A., eds.*, 1987, pp. 309–32. [G: Turkey]

Izraeli, Oded. The Effect of Environmental Attributes on Earnings and Housing Values across SMSAs. *J. Urban Econ.*, November 1987, *22*(3), pp. 361–76. [G: U.S.]

Jackson, R. V. The Structure of Pay in Nineteenth-century Britain. *Econ. Hist. Rev.*, 2nd Ser., November 1987, *40*(4), pp. 561–70. [G: U.K.]

Jacobson, Louis. Reply [A Tale of Employment Decline in Two Cities: How Bad Was the Worst of Times?]. *Ind. Lab. Relat. Rev.*, January 1987, *40*(2), pp. 284–87. [G: U.S.]

Jahnke, Wilfried. Arbeitsmarkt und Lohnentwicklung in der deutschen Wirtschaft. (The Labour Market and Wages in the German Economy. With English summary.) *Jahr. Nationalökon. Statist.*, March 1987, *203*(2), pp. 152–66. [G: W. Germany]

James, Robert G. and Morlock, Mark J. The Determinants of Intra-occupational Wage Dispersion. *Appl. Econ.*, July 1987, *19*(7), pp. 969–81. [G: U.S.]

Jamison, Dean T. and van der Gaag, Jacques. Education and Earnings in the People's Republic of China. *Econ. Educ. Rev.*, 1987, *6*(2), pp. 161–66. [G: China]

Jantzen, Robert H. Adult CETA Training in Boston: Impact on Earnings, Hours Worked, and Wages. *J. Econ. Bus.*, February 1987, *39*(1), pp. 1–17. [G: U.S.]

Jimenez, Emmanuel and Kugler, Bernardo. The

Earnings Impact of Training Duration in a Developing Country: An Ordered Probit Selection Model of Colombia's *Servicio Nacional de Aprendizaje* (SENA). *J. Human Res.*, Spring 1987, *22*(2), pp. 228–47. [G: Colombia]

Jimeno, Juan F. La flexibilidad de los costes laborales nominales en la industria española (1978–1982). (With English summary.) *Invest. Econ.*, September 1987, *11*(3), pp. 483–96. [G: Spain]

Jondrow, Jim; Brechling, Frank and Marcus, Alan J. Older Workers in the Market for Part-time Employment. *Sandell, S. H., ed.*, 1987, pp. 84–99. [G: U.S.]

Jones, J. C. H. and Walsh, W. D. The World Hockey Association and Player Exploitation in the National Hockey League. *Quart. Rev. Econ. Bus.*, Summer 1987, *27*(2), pp. 87–101. [G: U.S.]

Jorgensen, Aage Walter. Measuring Income, Income Distribution and Economic Return in Danish Agriculture. *Léon, Y. and Mahé, L., eds.*, 1987, pp. 109–26. [G: Denmark]

Junankar, P. N. The Labour Market for Young People. *Junankar, P. N., ed.*, 1987, pp. 1–12. [G: OECD]

Junankar, P. N. and Neale, Adrian J. Relative Wages and the Youth Labour Market. *Junankar, P. N., ed.*, 1987, pp. 79–107. [G: OECD]

Junankar, P. N. and Neale, Adrian J. Relative Wages and the Youth Labour Market: A Rejoinder. *Junankar, P. N., ed.*, 1987, pp. 116–18. [G: OECD]

Kahn, Lawrence M. and Curme, Michael. Unions and Nonunion Wage Dispersion. *Rev. Econ. Statist.*, November 1987, *69*(4), pp. 600–607. [G: U.S.]

Karier, Thomas. A Note on Wage Rates in Defense Industries. *Ind. Relat.*, Spring 1987, *26*(2), pp. 195–200. [G: U.S.]

Kasimovskii, E. Social Justice and the Improvement of Distribution Relations in the USSR. *Prob. Econ.*, September 1987, *30*(5), pp. 61–81. [G: U.S.S.R.]

Kaufman, Bruce E. and Stephan, Paula E. Determinants of Interindustry Wage Growth in the Seventies. *Ind. Relat.*, Spring 1987, *26*(2), pp. 186–94. [G: U.S.]

Kazi, Shahnaz. Skill Formation, Employment and Earnings in the Urban Informal Sector. *Pakistan Devel. Rev.*, Winter 1987, *26*(4), pp. 711–17. [G: Pakistan]

Kemp, Robert S., Jr. An Examination of the Relationship of Unfunded Vested Pension Liabilities and Selected Elements of Firm Value. *Schwartz, B. N., ed.*, 1987, pp. 59–71. [G: U.S.]

Kendrick, John W. Group Financial Incentives: An Evaluation. *Nalbantian, H. R., ed.*, 1987, pp. 120–36. [G: U.S.]

Kertesi, Gábor and Cukor, Eszter. Interfirm Wage Differentials in Hungary: Causes and Consequences. *Acta Oecon.*, 1987, *38*(1–2), pp. 79–115. [G: Hungary]

Kertesi, Gábor and Sziraczki, Gyorgy. The Institutional System, Labour Market and Segmentation in Hungary. *Tarling, R., ed.*, 1987, pp. 177–96. **[G: Hungary]**

Kiker, B. F. and Rhine, Sherrie L. W. Fringe Benefits and the Earnings Equation: A Test of the Consistency Hypothesis. *J. Human Res.*, Winter 1987, *22*(1), pp. 126–37. **[G: U.S.]**

Kingma, Douwe and Oskam, Arie J. Measuring Income Disparities between (and within) Farm Households and Non-farm Households by Means of the Individual Welfare Function of Income. *Léon, Y. and Mahé, L., eds.*, 1987, pp. 25–42. **[G: Netherlands]**

Knight, J. B. and Mayhew, K. Wage Determination and Labour Market Inflexibility: Introduction. *Oxford Bull. Econ. Statist.*, February 1987, *49*(1), pp. 1–8.

Knight, J. B. and Sabot, Richard H. Educational Expansion, Government Policy and Wage Compression. *J. Devel. Econ.*, August 1987, *26*(2), pp. 201–21. **[G: Kenya; Tanzania]**

Knight, J. B. and Sabot, Richard H. The Rate of Return on Educational Expansion. *Econ. Educ. Rev.*, 1987, *6*(3), pp. 255–62. **[G: Kenya; Tanzania]**

Knoester, Anthonie and van der Windt, Nico. Real Wages and Taxation in Ten OECD Countries. *Oxford Bull. Econ. Statist.*, February 1987, *49*(1), pp. 151–69. **[G: OECD]**

Koch, James V. The Incomes of Recent Immigrants: A Look at Ethnic Differences. *Soc. Sci. Quart.*, June 1987, *68*(2), pp. 294–310. **[G: U.S.]**

Kochan, Thomas A. Unemployment: United States: Comment. *Gunderson, M.; Meltz, N. M. and Ostry, S., eds.*, 1987, pp. 133–37. **[G: U.S.]**

Kokoski, Mary F. Employment and Wage Changes of Families from CE Survey Data. *Mon. Lab. Rev.*, February 1987, *110*(2), pp. 31–33. **[G: U.S.]**

König, Heinz. Productivity, Wages, and Prices inside and outside of Manufacturing in the U.S., Japan, and Europe: Comments. *Europ. Econ. Rev.*, April 1987, *31*(3), pp. 736–39.

Kosters, Marvin H. and Ross, Murray N. The Influence of Employment Shifts and New Job Opportunities on the Growth and Distribution of Real Wages. *Cagan, P., ed.*, 1987, pp. 209–42. **[G: U.S.]**

Kotlikoff, Laurence J. and Wise, David A. The Incentive Effects of Private Pension Plans. *Bodie, Z.; Shoven, J. B. and Wise, D. A., eds.*, 1987, pp. 283–336. **[G: U.S.]**

Krashinsky, Michael. The Returns to University Schooling in Canada: A Comment. *Can. Public Policy*, June 1987, *13*(2), pp. 218–21. **[G: Canada]**

Krueger, Alan B. and Summers, Lawrence H. Reflections on the Inter-industry Wage Structure. *Lang, K. and Leonard, J. S., eds.*, 1987, pp. 17–47. **[G: Global]**

Krumm, Ronald J. Regional Wage Differentials and Race: 1973–1978. *J. Reg. Sci.*, February 1987, *27*(1), pp. 119–28. **[G: U.S.]**

Kuhn, Peter J. Sex Discrimination in Labor Mar-

kets: The Role of Statistical Evidence. *Amer. Econ. Rev.*, September 1987, *77*(4), pp. 567–83. **[G: U.S.; Canada]**

Kuzmin, Franc. Razčlenitev razlik v realnih osebnih dohodkih med Slovenijo in Jugoslovijo po posameznih komponentah. (Determining Factors of Wage Differentials between Slovenia and Yugoslavia as a Whole. With English summary.) *Econ. Anal. Workers' Manage.*, 1987, *21*(1), pp. 27–48. **[G: Yugoslavia]**

Lawler, Edward E., III. Pay for Performance: A Motivational Analysis. *Nalbantian, H. R., ed.*, 1987, pp. 69–86. **[G: U.S.]**

Layard, Richard and Nickell, Stephen J. The Performance of the British Economy: The Labour Market. *Dornbusch, R. and Layard, R., eds.*, 1987, pp. 131–79. **[G: U.K.]**

Lazear, Edward P. Promise Them Anything: The Incentive Structures of Local Public Pension Plans: Comment. *Wise, D. A., ed.*, 1987, pp. 237–42. **[G: U.S.]**

Lazear, Edward P. and Rosen, Sherwin. Pension Inequality. *Bodie, Z.; Shoven, J. B. and Wise, D. A., eds.*, 1987, pp. 341–59. **[G: U.S.]**

Lehrer, Evelyn L. and White, William D. Hospital Market Structure and the Return to Nursing Education: Comment [Hospital Market Structure and the Return to Nursing Education]. *J. Human Res.*, Fall 1987, *22*(4), pp. 607–08. **[G: U.S.]**

Leonard, Herman B. Academic Ability, Earnings, and the Decision to Become a Teacher: Evidence from the National Longitudinal Study of the High School Class of 1972: Comment. *Wise, D. A., ed.*, 1987, pp. 312–16. **[G: U.S.]**

Leonard, Herman B. Investing in the Defense Work Force: The Debt and Structure of Military Pensions. *Wise, D. A., ed.*, 1987, pp. 47–73. **[G: U.S.]**

Leonard, Jonathan S. Carrots and Sticks: Pay, Supervision, and Turnover. *J. Lab. Econ.*, Part 2, Oct. 1987, *5*(4), pp. S136–52. **[G: U.S.]**

Leslie, Derek. Real Wage and Real Labour Cost Growth, 1948–81: A Disaggregated Study. *Appl. Econ.*, May 1987, *19*(5), pp. 635–50. **[G: U.K.]**

Lewis, Donald E. and Mangan, John. Wage Inflexibility and Quality Adjustment in Australian Academic Labour Markets: A Constrained Case. *Appl. Econ.*, October 1987, *19*(10), pp. 1279–90. **[G: Australia]**

Lewis, Philip E. T. and Kirby, Michael G. The Impact of Incomes Policy on Aggregate Wage Determination in Australia. *Econ. Rec.*, June 1987, *63*(181), pp. 156–61. **[G: Australia]**

van Loggerenberg, Bazil J. A Deterministic Analysis of Change in International Unit Labor Costs: Import Implications for U.S. Industry. *Managerial Dec. Econ.*, December 1987, *8*(4), pp. 339–42. **[G: U.S.]**

Lovett, William A. Profit Sharing and ESOPs: Improved Incentives and Equity. *Samuels, W. J. and Miller, A. S., eds.*, 1987, pp. 283–312. **[G: U.S.]**

Low, Stuart A. and Vilegas, Daniel J. An Alternative Approach to the Analysis of Wage Differentials. *Southern Econ. J.*, October 1987, *54*(2), pp. 449–62. **[G: U.S.]**

Lynch, Lisa M. Individual Differences in the Youth Labour Market: A Cross-Section Analysis of London Youths. *Junankar, P. N., ed.*, 1987, pp. 185–214. **[G: U.K.]**

Maani, Sholeh A. Maximizing and Satisficing Job Search Behavior in the U.S. and Chile. *J. Behav. Econ.*, Summer 1987, *16*(2), pp. 17–32. **[G: U.S.; Chile]**

MacPherson, David A. and Stewart, James B. Unionism and the Dispersion of Wages among Blue-Collar Women. *J. Lab. Res.*, Fall 1987, *8*(4), pp. 395–405. **[G: U.S.]**

Madden, Janice Fanning. Gender Differences in the Cost of Displacement: An Empirical Test of Discrimination in the Labor Market. *Amer. Econ. Rev.*, May 1987, *77*(2), pp. 246–51. **[G: U.S.]**

Main, Brian G. M. Earnings, Expected Earnings, and Unemployment amongst School Leavers. *Junankar, P. N., ed.*, 1987, pp. 145–84. **[G: U.K.]**

Maital, Shlomo. Reducing Unemployment. *Gunderson, M.; Meltz, N. M. and Ostry, S., eds.*, 1987, pp. 215–24. **[G: U.S.; Canada]**

Malcomson, James M. and Sartor, Nicola. Tax Push Inflation in a Unionized Labour Market. *Europ. Econ. Rev.*, December 1987, *31*(8), pp. 1581–96. **[G: Italy]**

Maloney, Timothy J. Employment Constraints and the Labor Supply of Married Women: A Reexamination of the Added Worker Effect. *J. Human Res.*, Winter 1987, *22*(1), pp. 51–61. **[G: U.S.]**

Manski, Charles F. Academic Ability, Earnings, and the Decision to Become a Teacher: Evidence from the National Longitudinal Study of the High School Class of 1972. *Wise, D. A., ed.*, 1987, pp. 291–312. **[G: U.S.]**

Marcus, Alan J. Corporate Pension Policy and the Value of PBGC Insurance. *Bodie, Z.; Shoven, J. B. and Wise, D. A., eds.*, 1987, pp. 49–76. **[G: U.S.]**

Margo, Robert A. and Villaflor, Georgia C. The Growth of Wages in Antebellum America: New Evidence. *J. Econ. Hist.*, December 1987, *47*(4), pp. 873–95. **[G: U.S.]**

Marris, Robin. Does Britain Really Have a Wages Problem? *Lloyds Bank Rev.*, April 1987, (164), pp. 36–55. **[G: U.K.]**

Marsden, David. Collective Bargaining and Industrial Adjustment in Britain, France, Italy and West Germany. *Duchêne, F. and Shepherd, G., eds.*, 1987, pp. 178–209. **[G: U.K.; France; Italy; W. Germany]**

Marsden, David. Youth Pay in Some OECD Countries since 1966. *Junankar, P. N., ed.*, 1987, pp. 15–50. **[G: OECD]**

Marshall, Ray and Paulin, Beth. Employment and Earnings of Women: Historical Perspective. *Koziara, K. S.; Moskow, M. H. and Tanner, L. D., eds.*, 1987, pp. 1–36. **[G: U.S.]**

Marshall, Robert C. and Zarkin, Gary A. The Effect of Job Tenure on Wage Offers. *J. Lab.*

Econ., July 1987, *5*(3), pp. 301–24. **[G: U.S.]**

Martin, John P. Labor Market Behavior and European Economic Growth: Comment. *Lawrence, R. Z. and Schultze, C. L., eds.*, 1987, pp. 217–26. **[G: W. Europe; U.S.]**

Mavromaras, Kostas Gr. Reservation Wages and Occupational Security: An Empirical Study. *Appl. Econ.*, February 1987, *19*(2), pp. 155–66. **[G: U.K.]**

Maxwell, Nan L. Occupational Differences in the Determination of U.S. Workers' Earnings: Both the Human Capital and the Structured Labor Market Hypotheses Are Useful in Analysis. *Amer. J. Econ. Soc.*, October 1987, *46*(4), pp. 431–43. **[G: U.S.]**

McNabb, Robert. Testing for Labour Market Segmentation in Britain. *Manchester Sch. Econ. Soc. Stud.*, September 1987, *55*(3), pp. 257–73. **[G: U.K.]**

Medoff, James L. Comparable Worth in the Public Sector: Comment. *Wise, D. A., ed.*, 1987, pp. 288–89. **[G: U.S.]**

Mellor, Earl F. Weekly Earnings in 1986: A Look at More Than 200 Occupations. *Mon. Lab. Rev.*, June 1987, *110*(6), pp. 41–46. **[G: U.S.]**

Mellor, Earl F. Workers at the Minimum Wage or Less: Who They Are and the Jobs They Hold. *Mon. Lab. Rev.*, July 1987, *110*(7), pp. 34–38. **[G: U.S.]**

Meng, Ronald. The Earnings of Canadian Immigrant and Native-Born Males. *Appl. Econ.*, August 1987, *19*(8), pp. 1107–19. **[G: Canada]**

Merton, Robert C.; Bodie, Zvi and Marcus, Alan J. Pension Plan Integration as Insurance against Social Security Risk. *Bodie, Z.; Shoven, J. B. and Wise, D. A., eds.*, 1987, pp. 147–69. **[G: U.S.]**

Miller, Paul W. Gender Differences in Observed and Offered Wages in Canada, 1980. *Can. J. Econ.*, May 1987, *20*(2), pp. 225–44. **[G: Canada]**

Miller, Paul W. The Wage Effect of the Occupational Segregation of Women in Britain. *Econ. J.*, December 1987, *97*(388), pp. 885–96. **[G: U.K.]**

Miller, Paul W. and Volker, Paul. The Youth Labour Market In Australia. *Econ. Rec.*, September 1987, *63*(182), pp. 203–19. **[G: Australia]**

Minford, Patrick. The Performance of the British Economy: The Labour Market: Comment. *Dornbusch, R. and Layard, R., eds.*, 1987, pp. 260–62. **[G: U.K.]**

Mitchell, Olivia S. Uncertain Lifetimes, Pensions, and Individual Saving: Comment. *Bodie, Z.; Shoven, J. B. and Wise, D. A., eds.*, 1987, pp. 206–10. **[G: U.S.]**

Mittar, Vishwa. Wage-Structure in the Informal Sector: The Case of a Class 1 City in Punjab. *Margin*, July-Sept. 1987, *19*(4), pp. 41–50. **[G: India]**

Monke, Eric A. Portuguese Agriculture in Transition: Agricultural Factor Markets. *Pearson, S. R., et al.*, 1987, pp. 62–82. **[G: Portugal]**

Montgomery, Edward and Wascher, William L.

Race and Gender Wage Inequality in Services and Manufacturing. *Ind. Relat.*, Fall 1987, 26(3), pp. 284–90. **[G: U.S.]**

Moore, Robert L. Are Male/Female Earnings Differentials Related to Life-Expectancy-Caused Pension Cost Differences? *Econ. Inquiry*, July 1987, 25(3), pp. 389–401. **[G: U.S.]**

Moore, William J. and Raisian, John. Union–Nonunion Wage Differentials in the Public Administration, Educational, and Private Sectors: 1970–1983. *Rev. Econ. Statist.*, November 1987, 69(4), pp. 608–16. **[G: U.S.]**

Morton, John D. BLS Prepares to Broaden Scope of Its White-Collar Pay Survey. *Mon. Lab. Rev.*, March 1987, 110(3), pp. 3–7. **[G: U.S.]**

Mroz, Thomas A. The Sensitivity of an Empirical Model of Married Women's Hours of Work to Economic and Statistical Assumptions. *Econometrica*, July 1987, 55(4), pp. 765–99. **[G: U.S.]**

Mulert, Jürgen. Wealth Sharing and Capital Formation for Employees of the Robert Bosch Company between 1886 and 1945. *Pohl, H. and Rudolph, B., eds.*, 1987, pp. 41–64. **[G: Germany]**

Munnell, Alicia H. Pension Contributions and the Stock Market. *New Eng. Econ. Rev.*, Nov./Dec. 1987, pp. 3–14. **[G: U.S.]**

Murnane, Richard J.; Singer, Judith D. and Willett, John B. Changes in Teacher Salaries during the 1970s: The Role of School District Demographics. *Econ. Educ. Rev.*, 1987, 6(4), pp. 379–88. **[G: U.S.]**

Murphy, Kevin M. and Topel, Robert H. Unemployment, Risk, and Earnings: Testing for Equalizing Wage Differences in the Labor Market. *Lang, K. and Leonard, J. S., eds.*, 1987, pp. 103–40. **[G: U.S.]**

Myers, Daniel A.; Burkhauser, Richard V. and Holden, Karen C. The Transition from Wife to Widow: The Importance of Survivor Benefits to Widows. *J. Risk Ins.*, December 1987, 54(4), pp. 752–59.

Nakosteen, Robert A. and Zimmer, Michael A. Marital Status and Earnings of Young Men: A Model with Endogenous Selection. *J. Human Res.*, Spring 1987, 22(2), pp. 248–68. **[G: U.S.]**

Nathan, Felicia. Analyzing Employers' Costs for Wages, Salaries, and Benefits. *Mon. Lab. Rev.*, October 1987, 110(10), pp. 3–11. **[G: U.S.]**

von Natzmer, W. Social Security Contributions, Economic Activity, and Distribution. *Empirical Econ.*, 1987, 12(1), pp. 29–49. **[G: W. Germany]**

Neef, Arthur and Thomas, James. Trends in Manufacturing Productivity and Labor Costs in the U.S. and Abroad. *Mon. Lab. Rev.*, December 1987, 110(12), pp. 25–30. **[G: OECD]**

Nickell, Stephen J. Why Is Wage Inflation in Britain So High? *Oxford Bull. Econ. Statist.*, February 1987, 49(1), pp. 103–28. **[G: U.K.]**

Nohara, H. and Silvestre, Jean-Jacques. Industrial Structures, Employment Trends and the Economic Crisis: The Case of France and Japan in the 1970s. *Tarling, R., ed.*, 1987, pp. 147–76. **[G: France; Japan]**

Nord, Stephen. An Analysis of the Effects of College on the Inequality in Male and Female Wages in the United States: A Human Capital Approach. *Rivista Int. Sci. Econ. Com.*, Jan.-Feb. 1987, 34(1–2), pp. 109–28. **[G: U.S.]**

Nord, Stephen. Productivity and the Role of College in Narrowing the Male–Female Wage Differential in the USA in 1980. *Appl. Econ.*, January 1987, 19(1), pp. 51–67. **[G: U.S.]**

Nord, Stephen. Schooling and Changes in the Inequality in Male and Female Earnings in the United States over the 1970s. *Appl. Econ.*, August 1987, 19(8), pp. 1083–1105. **[G: U.S.]**

Nyland, Chris. Worktime in the 1920s. *Australian Econ. Hist. Rev.*, September 1987, 27(2), pp. 37–55. **[G: U.S.]**

Olson, Josephine E.; Frieze, Irene Hanson and Good, Deborah Cain. The Effects of Job Type and Industry on the Income of Male and Female MBAs. *J. Human Res.*, Fall 1987, 22(4), pp. 532–41. **[G: U.S.]**

Ono, Akira. Two Competing Hypotheses for the Nenko Wage System—Skill or Living Cost Compensation? *Hitotsubashi J. Econ.*, June 1987, 28(1), pp. 1–25. **[G: Japan]**

Osberg, Lars; Apostle, Richard and Clairmont, Don. Segmented Labour Markets and the Estimation of Wage Functions. *Appl. Econ.*, December 1987, 19(12), pp. 1603–24. **[G: Canada]**

Osipenko, O. Unearned Income and Forms of Its Manifestation. *Prob. Econ.*, August 1987, 30(4), pp. 50–62. **[G: U.S.S.R.]**

Packard, Michael D. Income of New Disabled-Worker Beneficiaries and Their Families: Findings from the New Beneficiary Survey. *Soc. Sec. Bull.*, March 1987, 50(3), pp. 5–23. **[G: U.S.]**

Park, Young-Bum. Concentration and Wage Earnings in an Open Economy: A Case Study of Korea. *Int. Econ. J.*, Spring 1987, 1(1), pp. 29–42. **[G: S. Korea]**

Peltzman, Sam. How Do Public Sector Wages and Employment Respond to Economic Conditions? Comment. *Wise, D. A., ed.*, 1987, pp. 207–13. **[G: U.S.]**

Perloff, Jeffrey M. and Sickles, Robin C. Union Wage, Hours, and Earnings Differentials in the Construction Industry. *J. Lab. Econ.*, April 1987, 5(2), pp. 174–210. **[G: U.S.]**

Perold, André F. Funding and Asset Allocation in Corporate Pension Plans: An Empirical Investigation: Comment. *Bodie, Z.; Shoven, J. B. and Wise, D. A., eds.*, 1987, pp. 44–47. **[G: U.S.]**

Pesando, James E. Discontinuities in Pension Benefit Formulas and the Spot Model of the Labor Market: Implications for Financial Economists. *Econ. Inquiry*, April 1987, 25(2), pp. 215–38. **[G: U.S.]**

Petersen, John E. Public Pension Fund Administration. *Aronson, J. R. and Schwartz, E., eds.*, 1987, pp. 318–41. **[G: U.S.]**

Pfeffermann, Guy. Economic Crisis and the Poor

in Some Latin American Countries. *Finance Develop.*, June 1987, *24*(2), pp. 32–35.

Phillips, Douglas W. and Wise, David A. Military versus Civilian Pay: A Descriptive Discussion. *Wise, D. A., ed.,* 1987, pp. 19–46. **[G: U.S.]**

Pierenkemper, Toni. The Standard of Living and Employment in Germany, 1850–1980: An Overview. *J. Europ. Econ. Hist.*, Spring 1987, *16*(1), pp. 51–73. **[G: Germany]**

Pissarides, Christopher A. Work Sharing: Why? How? How Not . . . : Comments. *Layard, R. and Calmfors, L., eds.,* 1987, pp. 193–97. **[G: OECD]**

Podgursky, Michael and Swaim, Paul. Job Displacement and Earnings Loss: Evidence from the Displaced Worker Survey. *Ind. Lab. Relat. Rev.*, October 1987, *41*(1), pp. 17–29. **[G: U.S.]**

Podgursky, Michael and Swaim, Paul. Job Loss and Job Change: Comment. *Ind. Lab. Relat. Rev.*, October 1987, *41*(1), pp. 45–46. **[G: U.S.]**

Podgursky, Michael and Swaim, Paul. Labor Market Equilibrium and Sun-belt–Frostbelt Earnings Gaps. *Eastern Econ. J.*, Apr.-June 1987, *13*(2), pp. 107–13. **[G: U.S.]**

Polachek, Solomon W.; Wunnava, Phanindra V. and Hutchins, Michael T. Panel Estimates of Union Effects on Wages and Wage Growth. *Rev. Econ. Statist.*, August 1987, *69*(3), pp. 527–31. **[G: U.S.]**

Polachek, Solomon W. and Yoon, Bong Joon. A Two-tiered Earnings Frontier Estimation of Employer and Employee Information in the Labor Market. *Rev. Econ. Statist.*, May 1987, *69*(2), pp. 296–302. **[G: U.S.]**

Powell, David E. Manpower Constraints and the Use of Pensioners in the Soviet Economy. *Adam, J., ed.,* 1987, pp. 196–215. **[G: U.S.S.R.]**

Presser, Harriet B. Work Shifts of Full-Time Dual-Earner Couples: Patterns and Contrasts by Sex of Spouse. *Demography*, February 1987, *24*(1), pp. 99–112.

Rabeau, Yves. L'expérience de déflation au Canada et le comportement des salaires. (With English summary.) *Revue Écon. Polit.*, Sept.-Oct. 1987, *97*(5), pp. 556–74.

Raff, Daniel M. G. and Summers, Lawrence H. Did Henry Ford Pay Efficiency Wages? *J. Lab. Econ.*, Part 2, Oct. 1987, *5*(4), pp. S57–86. **[G: U.S.]**

Rajaraman, Indira. Contractual Aspects of Daily Hire: Rural Labor in India. *J. Devel. Areas*, July 1987, *21*(4), pp. 459–80. **[G: India]**

Ray, George F. Erratum [Labour Costs in Manufacturing]. *Nat. Inst. Econ. Rev.*, November 1987, (122), pp. 96. **[G: OECD]**

Ray, George F. Labour Costs in Manufacturing. *Nat. Inst. Econ. Rev.*, May 1987, (120), pp. 71–74. **[G: OECD]**

Rayack, Wendy. Sources and Centers of Cyclical Movement in Real Wages: Evidence from Panel Data. *J. Post Keynesian Econ.*, Fall 1987, *10*(1), pp. 3–21. **[G: U.S.]**

Reid, Frank. Work-Time Reduction. *Gunderson,*

M.; Meltz, N. M. and Ostry, S., eds., 1987, pp. 210–14. **[G: Canada; U.S.]**

Reid, Joseph D., Jr. and Faith, Roger L. Right-to-Work and Union Compensation Structure. *J. Lab. Res.*, Spring 1987, *8*(2), pp. 111–30. **[G: U.S.]**

Reilly, Barry. Wages, Sex Discrimination and the Irish Labour Market for Young Workers. *Econ. Soc. Rev.*, July 1987, *18*(4), pp. 271–305. **[G: Ireland]**

Reynolds, Morgan O. Unions and Jobs: The U.S. Auto Industry—Reply. *J. Lab. Res.*, Summer 1987, *8*(3), pp. 311–15. **[G: U.S.]**

Reynolds, Peter J. Wage Rises and Income Distribution—A Note. *Manchester Sch. Econ. Soc. Stud.*, March 1987, *55*(1), pp. 77–87. **[G: U.K.]**

Rhine, Sherrie L. W. The Determinants of Fringe Benefits: Additional Evidence. *J. Risk Ins.*, December 1987, *54*(4), pp. 790–99. **[G: U.S.]**

Rich, Jude T. and Larson, John A. Why Some Long-term Incentives Fail. *Nalbantian, H. R., ed.,* 1987, *1984*, pp. 151–62. **[G: U.S.]**

Robb, Roberta Edgecombe. Equal Pay for Work of Equal Value: Issues and Policies. *Can. Public Policy*, December 1987, *13*(4), pp. 445–61. **[G: Canada; U.S.; Australia]**

Robinson, Derek. How Inflexible Are Negotiated Wages in Britain? *Oxford Bull. Econ. Statist.*, February 1987, *49*(1), pp. 37–57. **[G: U.K.]**

Robson, Peter. A View from the Unions. *Stegman, T., et al.,* 1987, pp. 53–63. **[G: Australia]**

Roche, William K. Leisure, Insecurity and Union Policy in Britain: A Critical Extension of Bienefeld's Theory of Hours Rounds. *Brit. J. Ind. Relat.*, March 1987, *25*(1), pp. 1–17. **[G: U.K.]**

Rojas R., Patricio and Riveros, Luis A. Salarios mínimos y medios: Un análisis empírico de causalidad. Los casos de Argentina, Brasil y Chile. (With English summary.) *Cuadernos Econ.*, December 1987, *24*(73), pp. 289–318. **[G: Argentinand- -ddT1-; Brazil; Chile]**

Roman, Paul M. and Blum, Terry C. The Relation of Employee Assistance Programs to Corporate Social Responsibility Attitudes: An Empirical Study. *Frederick, W. C., ed.,* 1987, pp. 213–35. **[G: U.S.]**

Rose, Nancy L. Labor Rent Sharing and Regulation: Evidence from the Trucking Industry. *J. Polit. Econ.*, December 1987, *95*(6), pp. 1146–78. **[G: U.S.]**

Rosen, Harvey S. Comment [Military versus Civilian Pay: A Descriptive Discussion] [Investing in the Defense Work Force: The Debt and Structure of Military Pensions]. *Wise, D. A., ed.,* 1987, pp. 73–77. **[G: U.S.]**

Rosen, Sherwin. Some Economics of Teaching. *J. Lab. Econ.*, Part 1, Oct. 1987, *5*(4), pp. 561–75. **[G: U.S.]**

Rosholt, A. M. The South African Private Sector: Agent for Change or Government Stooge? *Sethi, S. P., ed.,* 1987, pp. 355–61. **[G: S. Africa]**

Ross, Russell T. Disaggregate Labour Supply

Functions for Married Women in New Zealand. *New Zealand Econ. Pap.*, 1987, 21, pp. 41–55. **[G: New Zealand]**

Rowlatt, Penelope A. A Model of Wage Bargaining. *Oxford Bull. Econ. Statist.*, November 1987, 49(4), pp. 347–72. **[G: U.K.]**

Ruhm, Christopher J. Job Loss and Job Change: Comment. *Ind. Lab. Relat. Rev.*, October 1987, 41(1), pp. 47–49. **[G: U.S.]**

Ruhm, Christopher J. The Economic Consequences of Labor Mobility. *Ind. Lab. Relat. Rev.*, October 1987, 41(1), pp. 30–42. **[G: U.S.]**

Rumberger, Russell W. The Impact of Surplus Schooling on Productivity and Earnings. *J. Human Res.*, Winter 1987, 22(1), pp. 24–50. **[G: U.S.]**

Rutgaizer, V. M. and Sheviakhov, Iu. E. Distribution According to One's Labor. *Prob. Econ.*, November 1987, 30(7), pp. 31–46. **[G: CMEA]**

Ryan, Paul. Trade Unionism and the Pay of Young Workers. *Junankar, P. N., ed.*, 1987, pp. 119–42. **[G: OECD]**

Schieber, Sylvester J. Pension Inequality: Comment. *Bodie, Z.; Shoven, J. B. and Wise, D. A., eds.*, 1987, pp. 359–63. **[G: U.S.]**

Scholes, Myron S. How Does the Market Value Unfunded Pension Liabilities? Comment. *Bodie, Z.; Shoven, J. B. and Wise, D. A., eds.*, 1987, pp. 104–09. **[G: U.S.]**

Schott, Kerry. Lessons for Australia. *Stegman, T., et al.*, 1987, pp. 25–52. **[G: Australia; W. Europe; U.K.; Japan]**

Schultze, Charles L. Real Wages, Real Wage Aspirations, and Unemployment in Europe. *Lawrence, R. Z. and Schultze, C. L., eds.*, 1987, pp. 230–91. **[G: W. Europe]**

Schumann, Richard E. State and Local Government Pay Increases Outpace Five-Year Rise in Private Industry. *Mon. Lab. Rev.*, February 1987, 110(2), pp. 18–20. **[G: U.S.]**

Sengenberger, Werner and Kohler, Ch. Policies of Workforce Reduction and Labour Market Structures in the American and German Automobile Industry. *Tarling, R., ed.*, 1987, pp. 245–69. **[G: W. Germany; U.S.]**

Shackett, Joyce R. and Trapani, John M. Earnings Differentials and Market Structure. *J. Human Res.*, Fall 1987, 22(4), pp. 518–31. **[G: U.S.]**

Shapiro, Daniel M. and Stelcner, Morton. Earnings Disparities among Linguistic Groups in Quebec, 1970–1980. *Can. Public Policy*, March 1987, 13(1), pp. 97–104. **[G: Canada]**

Shapiro, Daniel M. and Stelcner, Morton. The Persistence of the Male–Female Earnings Gap in Canada, 1970–1980: The Impact of Equal Pay Laws and Language Policies. *Can. Public Policy*, December 1987, 13(4), pp. 462–76. **[G: Canada]**

Shapiro, David and Sandell, Steven H. The Reduced Pay of Older Job Losers: Age Discrimination and Other Explanations. *Sandell, S. H., ed.*, 1987, pp. 37–51. **[G: U.S.]**

Sharpe, William F. Corporate Pension Policy and the Value of PBGC Insurance: Comment. *Bodie, Z.; Shoven, J. B. and Wise, D. A., eds.*, 1987, pp. 77–79. **[G: U.S.]**

Shcherbakov, V. I. The Wholesale Restructuring of Wages. *Prob. Econ.*, October 1987, 30(6), pp. 72–88. **[G: U.S.S.R.]**

Siebert, W. S. Black Trade Unions and the Wage Gap in South Africa. *Managerial Dec. Econ.*, March 1987, 8(1), pp. 55–65. **[G: S. Africa]**

Silver, Hilary. Only So Many Hours in a Day: Time Constraints, Labour Pools and Demand for Consumer Services. *Akehurst, G. and Gadrey, J., eds.*, 1987, pp. 26–45. **[G: U.S.]**

Simes, R. M. and Richardson, C. J. Wage Determination in Australia. *Econ. Rec.*, June 1987, 63(181), pp. 144–55. **[G: Australia]**

Sims, Christopher A. Aggregate and Individual Price Adjustment: Comments. *Brookings Pap. Econ. Act.*, 1987, (1), pp. 117–20. **[G: U.S.]**

Siven, Claes-Henric. The Wage Structure and the Functioning of the Labor Market. *Siven, C.-H., ed.*, 1987, pp. 71–97. **[G: Sweden]**

Sloan, Judith. The Australian Labour Market, June 1987. *Australian Bull. Lab.*, June 1987, 13(3), pp. 130–42. **[G: Australia]**

Smith, D. Alton. Military Service and Civilian Earnings of Youths: Comment. *Wise, D. A., ed.*, 1987, pp. 138–40. **[G: U.S.]**

Smith, Sharon P. Wages in the Federal and Private Sectors: Comment. *Wise, D. A., ed.*, 1987, pp. 177–82. **[G: U.S.]**

Sneessens, Henri R. and Drèze, Jacques H. A Discussion of Belgian Unemployment, Combining Traditional Concepts and Disequilibrium Econometrics. *Steinherr, A. and Weiserbs, D., eds.*, 1987, pp. 239–82. **[G: Belgium]**

Soon, Lee-Ying. Self-Employment vs Wage Employment: Estimation of Earnings Functions in LDCs. *Econ. Educ. Rev.*, 1987, 6(2), pp. 81–89. **[G: Malaysia]**

Sorensen, Elaine. Effect of Comparable Worth Policies on Earnings. *Ind. Relat.*, Fall 1987, 26(3), pp. 227–39. **[G: U.S.]**

Sorensen, Elaine. Union Maids: Unions and the Female Work Force: Comments. *Brown, C. and Pechman, J. A., eds.*, 1987, pp. 213–16. **[G: U.S.]**

Soroka, Lewis A. Male/Female Income Distributions, City Size and Urban Characteristics: Canada, 1970–1980. *Urban Stud.*, October 1987, 24(5), pp. 417–26. **[G: Canada]**

Spencer, Marilyn K. Reservation Wages of Mexican Americans: The Pessimists Are Pleasantly Surprised. *Rev. Soc. Econ.*, October 1987, 45(2), pp. 163–77. **[G: U.S.]**

Stern, David. Part-time Work, Full-time Work, and Occupational Segregation: Comments. *Brown, C. and Pechman, J. A., eds.*, 1987, pp. 240–46. **[G: U.S.]**

Stewart, Mark B. Collective Bargaining Arrangements, Closed Shops and Relative Pay. *Econ. J.*, March 1987, 97(385), pp. 140–56. **[G: U.K.]**

Stirati, Antonella. Differenze retributive e segregazione occupazionale per sesso nell'industria

manifatturiera. (Wage Differences and Occupational Segregation by Sex in the Manufacturing Industries. With English summary.) *Econ. Lavoro*, July-Sept. 1987, *21*(3), pp. 51–76.
[G: Italy]

Stone, Mary S.; Robbins, Walter A. and Phipps, David W. Disclosure Practices of Public Employee Retirement Systems: An Analysis of Incentives to Adopt Alternative Standards. *Chan, J. L., ed., Pt. A*, 1987, pp. 149–80. **[G: U.S.]**

Straub, LaVonne A. and Lane, Julia. Response [Hospital Market Structure and the Return to Nursing Education]. *J. Human Res.*, Fall 1987, *22*(4), pp. 609–10. **[G: U.S.]**

Tachibanaki, Toshiaki. The Determination of the Promotion Process in Organizations and of Earnings Differentials. *J. Econ. Behav. Organ.*, December 1987, *8*(4), pp. 603–16.
[G: Japan]

Taylor, John B. The Role of Contracts in Macroeconomic Performance. *Nalbantian, H. R., ed.*, 1987, pp. 189–201. **[G: U.S.]**

Terwey, Michael. Class Position and Income Inequality: Comparing Results for the Federal Republic with Current U.S. Research. *Teckenberg, W., ed.*, 1987, pp. 119–71.
[G: W. Germany; U.S.]

Thomas, John K. and Goodwin, H. L., Jr. Employment Compensation among Farm Workers in the Lower Rio Grande Valley. *Soc. Sci. Quart.*, September 1987, *68*(3), pp. 621–30.
[G: U.S.]

Thornton, Robert J. Unions, Wages, and Local Government Finance. *Aronson, J. R. and Schwartz, E., eds.*, 1987, pp. 383–99.
[G: U.S.]

Tonak, E. Ahmet. The U.S. Welfare State and the Working Class, 1952–1980. *Rev. Radical Polit. Econ.*, Spring 1987, *19*(1), pp. 47–72.
[G: U.S.]

Turner, Robert W. Are Taxes Responsible for the Growth in Fringe Benefits? *Nat. Tax J.*, June 1987, *40*(2), pp. 205–20. **[G: U.S.]**

Turner, Robert W. Taxes and the Number of Fringe Benefits Received. *J. Public Econ.*, June 1987, *33*(1), pp. 41–57. **[G: U.S.]**

Tzannatos, Zafiris. Union *versus* Non-union Wages, Arithmetic *versus* Geometric Means and Grouped Data Revisited. *Bull. Econ. Res.*, January 1987, *39*(1), pp. 91–94.

Vaillancourt, François; Carpentier, Josee and Henriques, Irene. The Returns to University Schooling in Canada: A Rejoinder. *Can. Public Policy*, September 1987, *13*(3), pp. 389–90.
[G: Canada]

Van Poeck, A. Labour Market Characteristics, Stabilization Policy and Real Wage Rigidity. *Tijdschrift Econ. Manage.*, 1987, *32*(2), pp. 189–213. **[G: OECD]**

Venti, Steven F. Wages in the Federal and Private Sectors. *Wise, D. A., ed.*, 1987, pp. 147–77.
[G: U.S.]

Verma, Anil. Union and Nonunion Wages at the Firm Level: A Combined Institutional and Econometric Analysis. *J. Lab. Res.*, Winter 1987, *8*(1), pp. 67–83. **[G: U.S.]**

Viallon, Jean Baptiste. Recherche d'indicateurs du revenu issu de l'agriculture à partir de comptabilités. (With English summary.) *Léon, Y. and Mahé, L., eds.*, 1987, pp. 95–108.
[G: France]

Villa, Paola. Systems of Flexible Working in the Italian Steel Industry. *Tarling, R., ed.*, 1987, pp. 307–45. **[G: Italy]**

Vinokur, Aaron and Ofer, Gur. Inequality of Earnings, Household Income, and Wealth in the Soviet Union in the 1970s. *Millar, J. R., ed.*, 1987, pp. 171–202. **[G: U.S.S.R.]**

Viscusi, W. Kip and Moore, Michael J. Workers' Compensation: Wage Effects, Benefit Inadequacies, and the Value of Health Losses. *Rev. Econ. Statist.*, May 1987, *69*(2), pp. 249–61.
[G: U.S.]

Weiermair, Klaus. Unemployment: Western Europe: Comment. *Gunderson, M.; Meltz, N. M. and Ostry, S., eds.*, 1987, pp. 108–10.
[G: W. Europe]

Weiss, Andrew. Incentives and Worker Behavior: Some Evidence. *Nalbantian, H. R., ed.*, 1987, pp. 137–50. **[G: U.S.]**

Weitzman, Martin L. Macroeconomic Aspects of Profit Sharing. *Nalbantian, H. R., ed.*, 1987, pp. 202–12. **[G: U.S.]**

Wells, William. Relative Wages and the Youth Labour Market: A Reply. *Junankar, P. N., ed.*, 1987, pp. 108–15. **[G: OECD]**

Wells, William. The Relative Pay and Employment of Young People. *Junankar, P. N., ed.*, 1987, pp. 51–78. **[G: OECD]**

White-Means, Shelley I. Migrant Farmworker Earnings: A Human Capital Approach. *Rev. Black Polit. Econ.*, Spring 1987, *15*(4), pp. 21–33. **[G: U.S.]**

Whiteford, Peter. Unemployment and Families. *Australian Bull. Lab.*, December 1987, *14*(1), pp. 338–57. **[G: Australia]**

Wilkinson, Frank. Deregulation, Structured Labour Markets and Unemployment. *Pedersen, P. J. and Lund, R., eds.*, 1987, pp. 167–85.
[G: W. Europe]

Wilson, Robert A. Returns to Entering the Medical Profession in the U.K. *J. Health Econ.*, December 1987, *6*(4), pp. 339–63. **[G: U.K.]**

Wilson, Robert A. The Determinants of the Earnings of Professional Engineers in Great Britain in 1981. *Appl. Econ.*, July 1987, *19*(7), pp. 983–94. **[G: U.K.]**

Wise, David A. Public Sector Payrolls: Overview. *Wise, D. A., ed.*, 1987, pp. 1–18. **[G: U.S.]**

Wolff, Edward N. The Effects of Pensions and Social Security on the Distribution of Wealth in the U.S. *Wolff, E. N., ed.*, 1987, pp. 208–47. **[G: U.S.]**

Ziderman, Adrian. Initial vs Recurrent Training for Skilled Trades in Israel—Results of a 7-Year Follow-up Study. *Econ. Educ. Rev.*, 1987, *6*(2), pp. 91–98. **[G: Israel]**

Zohir, Sajjad. Output Sharing as a Form of Wage Payment during Harvest. *Bangladesh Devel. Stud.*, June 1987, *15*(2), pp. 121–32.
[G: Bangladesh]

8243 Employment Studies; Unemployment and Vacancies; Retirements and Quits

Aben, Jacques and Smith, Ron P. Defence and Employment in the UK and France: A Comparative Study of the Existing Results. *Schmidt, C. and Blackaby, F., eds.*, 1987, pp. 384–98. **[G: France; U.K.]**

Aboagye, A.; Gozo, K. and Ahmed, Iftikhar. World Recession and Global Interdependence: Sub-Saharan Africa. *International Labour Office.*, 1987, pp. 75–98. **[G: Sub-Saharan Africa]**

Aboud, Antone and Schram, Sanford F. Overview of Legislation [An Overview of Plant Closing Legislation and Issues]. *Staudohar, P. D. and Brown, H. E.*, 1987, *1984*, pp. 279–91. **[G: U.S.]**

Abraham, Katharine G. Help-Wanted Advertising, Job Vacancies, and Unemployment. *Brookings Pap. Econ. Act.*, 1987, (1), pp. 207–43. **[G: U.S.]**

Abraham, Katharine G. and Farber, Henry S. Job Duration, Seniority, and Earnings. *Amer. Econ. Rev.*, June 1987, 77(3), pp. 278–97. **[G: U.S.]**

Adams, Gordon. Conversion: A Dead-end Strategy? *Lynch, J. E., ed.*, 1987, pp. 219–32. **[G: U.S.]**

Addison, John T. and Castro, Alberto C. The Importance of Lifetime Jobs: Differences between Union and Nonunion Workers. *Ind. Lab. Relat. Rev.*, April 1987, 40(3), pp. 393–405. **[G: U.S.]**

Addison, John T. and Portugal, Pedro. Job Loss and Job Change: Comment. *Ind. Lab. Relat. Rev.*, October 1987, 41(1), pp. 43–45. **[G: U.S.]**

Addison, John T. and Portugal, Pedro. On the Distributional Shape of Unemployment Duration. *Rev. Econ. Statist.*, August 1987, 69(3), pp. 521–26. **[G: U.S.]**

Addison, John T. and Portugal, Pedro. The Effect of Advance Notification of Plant Closings on Unemployment. *Ind. Lab. Relat. Rev.*, October 1987, 41(1), pp. 3–16. **[G: U.S.]**

Aitkin, M. and Healey, R. Statistical Modelling of the EEC Labour Force Survey: A Project History. *Hand, D. J. and Everitt, B. S., eds.*, 1987, pp. 171–79. **[G: EEC]**

Alagh, Yoginder K. Employment and Structural Change in the Indian Economy. *Amjad, R., ed.*, 1987, pp. 285–303. **[G: India]**

Alam, M. Shahid and Azhar, Rauf. Determinants of Employment Expansion in the Services Sector: A Cross-Country Study of LDCs. *J. Devel. Areas*, October 1987, 22(1), pp. 25–40. **[G: LDCs]**

Alaouze, Chris M. Empirical Evidence on the Sign of the Slope of the Hazard Rate from Unemployment from a Fixed Effects Model. *J. Appl. Econometrics*, April 1987, 2(2), pp. 159–68. **[G: U.S.]**

Albrecht, James W. Hare Today, Gone Tomorrow . . . Divorce, Unemployment, and Other Sorry States. *Lang, K. and Leonard, J. S., eds.*, 1987, pp. 207–11. **[G: U.S.]**

Alogoskoufis, George S. Aggregate Employment and Intertemporal Substitution in the UK. *Econ. J.*, June 1987, 97(386), pp. 403–15. **[G: U.K.]**

Alogoskoufis, George S. On Intertemporal Substitution and Aggregate Labor Supply. *J. Polit. Econ.*, October 1987, 95(5), pp. 938–60. **[G: U.S.]**

Anderson, Kathryn H.; Butler, John S. and Sloan, Frank A. Labor Market Segmentation: A Cluster Analysis of Job Groupings and Barriers to Entry. *Southern Econ. J.*, January 1987, 53(3), pp. 571–90. **[G: U.S.]**

Ansar, J., et al. A Vintage Model of Labour Demand by U.K. Manufacturing. *Rech. Écon. Louvain*, 1987, 53(1), pp. 3–26. **[G: U.K.]**

Appelbaum, Eileen. Restructuring Work: Temporary, Part-time, and At-Home Employment. *Hartmann, H. I., ed.*, 1987, pp. 268–310. **[G: U.S.]**

Armstrong, T. E. Unemployment: Industrial Relations: Comment. *Gunderson, M.; Meltz, N. M. and Ostry, S., eds.*, 1987, pp. 196–99. **[G: Canada]**

Arndt, Helmut H. Arten und Ursachen der Arbeitslosigkeit in ihrer Bedeutung für die Beschäftigungspolitik. (Unemployment: Varieties and Their Causes. With English summary.) *Z. Wirtschaft. Sozialwissen.*, 1987, 107(4), pp. 505–12.

Artus, Jacques R. Real Wages, Real Wage Aspirations, and Unemployment in Europe: Comment. *Lawrence, R. Z. and Schultze, C. L., eds.*, 1987, pp. 292–95. **[G: W. Europe]**

Baily, Martin Neil. Aging and the Ability to Work: Policy Issues and Recent Trends. *Burtless, G., ed., 1987*, pp. 59–97. **[G: U.S.]**

Baily, Martin Neil. Rising Unemployment in the United States. *Gunderson, M.; Meltz, N. M. and Ostry, S., eds.*, 1987, pp. 63–73. **[G: U.S.]**

Baran, Barbara. The Technological Transformation of White-Collar Work: A Case Study of the Insurance Industry. *Hartmann, H. I., ed.*, 1987, pp. 25–62. **[G: U.S.]**

Barrett, Nancy S. Sex-Based Employment Quotas in Sweden: Comments. *Brown, C. and Pechman, J. A., eds.*, 1987, pp. 299–301. **[G: Sweden]**

Bartel, Ann P. and Lichtenberg, Frank R. The Comparative Advantage of Educated Workers in Implementing New Technology. *Rev. Econ. Statist.*, February 1987, 69(1), pp. 1–11.

Barth, James R.; Cordes, Joseph J. and Haber, Sheldon E. Employee Characteristics and Firm Size: Are There Systematic Empirical Relationships? *Appl. Econ.*, April 1987, 19(4), pp. 555–67. **[G: U.S.]**

Bates, Timothy. Self-employed Minorities: Traits and Trends. *Soc. Sci. Quart.*, September 1987, 68(3), pp. 539–51. **[G: U.S.]**

Beach, Charles M. and Kaliski, Stefan F. The Distribution of Unemployment Spells: Canada,

1978–82. *Ind. Lab. Relat. Rev.*, January 1987, *40*(2), pp. 254–67. **[G: Canada]**

Bean, Charles R. Real Wages, Real Wage Aspirations, and Unemployment in Europe: Comment. *Lawrence, R. Z. and Schultze, C. L., eds.*, 1987, pp. 295–99. **[G: W. Europe]**

Beenstock, Michael. Real Wages and Unemployment in the 1930s: A Reply [Wages and Unemployment in Interwar Britain]. *Nat. Inst. Econ. Rev.*, February 1987, (119), pp. 76–78. **[G: U.K.]**

Beenstock, Michael. Work, Welfare and Taxation: Conclusions and Overview. *Beenstock, M., et al.*, 1987, pp. 261–67. **[G: U.K.]**

Beenstock, Michael and Dalziel, Alan. Econometric Analysis of Labour Supply and Work Incentives. *Beenstock, M., et al.*, 1987, pp. 166–84. **[G: U.K.]**

Beenstock, Michael and Minford, Patrick. Curing Unemployment through Labour-Market Competition. *Begg, D. K. H., et al.*, 1987, pp. 129–49. **[G: U.S.; U.K.]**

Begg, David K. H. Long-run Implications of the Increase in Taxation and Public Debt for Employment and Economic Growth in Europe: Comments. *Europ. Econ. Rev.*, April 1987, *31*(3), pp. 775–77. **[G: W. Europe]**

Bell, Donald and Marclay, William. Trends in Retirement Eligibility and Pension Benefits, 1974–83. *Mon. Lab. Rev.*, April 1987, *110*(4), pp. 18–25. **[G: U.S.]**

Bell, Linda and Freeman, Richard B. Flexible Wage Structures and Employment. *Gunderson, M.; Meltz, N. M. and Ostry, S., eds.*, 1987, pp. 119–28. **[G: U.S.]**

Bendick, Marc, Jr. and Egan, Mary Lou. Transfer Payment Diversion for Small Business Development: British and French Experience. *Ind. Lab. Relat. Rev.*, July 1987, *40*(4), pp. 528–42. **[G: U.K.; France]**

Bessel, Richard. Unemployment and Demobilisation in Germany after the First World War. *Evans, R. J. and Geary, D., eds.*, 1987, pp. 23–43. **[G: Germany]**

Bierens, Herman J. ARMAX Model Specification Testing, with an Application to Unemployment in the Netherlands. *J. Econometrics*, May 1987, *35*(1), pp. 161–90. **[G: Netherlands]**

Björklund, Anders. The Wage Structure and the Functioning of the Labor Market: Comment. *Siven, C.-H., ed.*, 1987, pp. 98–102. **[G: Sweden]**

Blades, Derek. Goods and Services in OECD Countries. *OECD Econ. Stud.*, Spring 1987, (8), pp. 159–84. **[G: OECD]**

Blanc, Michel. Family and Employment in Agriculture: Recent Changes in France. *J. Agr. Econ.*, May 1987, *38*(2), pp. 289–301. **[G: France]**

Blau, David M. A Time-Series Analysis of Self-employment in the United State. *J. Polit. Econ.*, June 1987, *95*(3), pp. 445–67. **[G: U.S.]**

Blaug, Mark. Educated Unemployment in Asia: A Contrast between India and the Philippines.

Blaug, M., 1987, *1972*, pp. 276–300. **[G: Philippines; India]**

Bloch, Charlotte. Female Unemployment and Knowledge of Self. *Pedersen, P. J. and Lund, R., eds.*, 1987, pp. 339–53. **[G: Denmark]**

Blomqvist, H. C. The Causes of Unemployment in Finland, 1970–82: Some Empirical Evidence. *Appl. Econ.*, May 1987, *19*(5), pp. 687–93. **[G: Finland]**

Blomqvits, H. C. Sysselsättningsforskningskommissionens betänkande. En kommentar. (The Report by the Commission of Employment Research. A Comment. With English summary.) *Ekon. Samfundets Tidskr.*, 1987, *40*(3), pp. 149–57. **[G: Finland]**

Bloom, David E. and Freeman, Richard B. Population Growth, Labor Supply, and Employment in Developing Countries. *Johnson, D. G. and Lee, R. D., eds.*, 1987, pp. 105–47. **[G: LDCs]**

Blossfeld, Hans-Peter. Entry into the Labor Market and Occupational Career in the Federal Republic: A Comparison with American Studies. *Teckenberg, W., ed.*, 1987, pp. 86–115. **[G: W. Germany]**

Bluestone, Barry. Deindustrialization and Unemployment in America. *Staudohar, P. D. and Brown, H. E.*, 1987, *1984*, pp. 3–15. **[G: U.S.]**

Bluestone, Barry. Impact of Trade, Technology, and Management Factors on U.S. Manufacturing. *Faruqui, A. and Broehl, J., eds.*, 1987, pp. 165–77. **[G: U.S.]**

Bluestone, Barry. In Support of the Deindustrialization Thesis [Is Deindustrialization a Myth? Capital Mobility versus Absorptive Capacity in the U.S. Economy]. *Staudohar, P. D. and Brown, H. E.*, 1987, *1984*, pp. 41–52. **[G: U.S.]**

Bluestone, Barry; Harrison, Bennett and Gorham, Lucy. The State and Local Industrial Policy Question: Storm Clouds on the Horizon. *Goldstein, H. A., ed.*, 1987, pp. 16–33. **[G: U.S.]**

Blundell, Richard; Ham, John C. and Meghir, Costas. Unemployment and Female Labour Supply. *Econ. J.*, Supplement 1987, *97*, pp. 44–64. **[G: U.K.]**

Boaz, Rachel Floersheim. Labor Market Behavior of Older Workers Approaching Retirement: A Summary of the Evidence from the 1970s. *Meyer, C. W., ed.*, 1987, pp. 103–26. **[G: U.S.]**

Boccella, Nicola and Pugliese, Enrico. Disoccupazione, Mezzogiorno e paradossi. (Unemployment, the "Mezzogiorno" and Paradoxes. With English summary.) *Econ. Lavoro*, July-Sept. 1987, *21*(3), pp. 95–103. **[G: Italy]**

Boddy, Martin. Bristol: Sunbelt City? *Hausner, V. A., et al.*, 1987, pp. 44–98. **[G: U.K.]**

Bonnell, Sheila M. The Effect of Equal Pay for Females on the Composition of Employment in Australia. *Econ. Rec.*, December 1987, *63*(183), pp. 340–51. **[G: Australia]**

Boot, Pieter. Incentive Systems and Unemployment: The East European Experience. *Comp.*

Econ. Stud., Spring 1987, *29*(1), pp. 37–61. [G: E. Europe]

Booth, Alan. Unemployment and Interwar Politics. *Glynn, S. and Booth, A., eds.*, 1987, pp. 43–56. [G: U.K.]

Bosworth, Derek and Westaway, Tony. Labour Hoarding, Discouraged Workers and Recorded Unemployment: An International Comparison. *Australian Bull. Lab.*, June 1987, *13*(3), pp. 143–61. [G: Australia; Japan; U.S.; U.K.]

Bosworth, Derek and Westaway, Tony. The Demand for Hours of Work. *Scot. J. Polit. Econ.*, November 1987, *34*(4), pp. 368–87. [G: U.K.]

Braun, Bertram and Lynch, John E. Economic Adjustment and Conversion of Defense Industries: Annotated Bibliography. *Lynch, J. E., ed.*, 1987, pp. 245–304.

Brinkman, Christian. Unemployment in the Federal Republic of Germany: Recent Empirical Evidence. *Pedersen, P. J. and Lund, R., eds.*, 1987, pp. 285–304. [G: W. Germany]

Brittan, Samuel. Innovative Supply-Side Policies to Reduce Unemployment: Commentary. *Begg, D. K. H., et al.*, 1987, pp. 122–27. [G: U.K.]

Bronars, Stephen G. and Jansen, Dennis W. The Geographic Distribution of Unemployment Rates in the U.S.: A Spatial–Time Series Analysis. *J. Econometrics*, November 1987, *36*(3), pp. 251–79. [G: U.S.]

Brown, Charles C. and Wilcher, Shirley J. Sex-Based Employment Quotas in Sweden. *Brown, C. and Pechman, J. A., eds.*, 1987, pp. 271–98. [G: Sweden]

Brown, Deborah J. and Pheasant, James. Sources of Cyclical Employment Instability in Rural Counties. *Amer. J. Agr. Econ.*, November 1987, *69*(4), pp. 819–27. [G: U.S.]

Brown, Sharon P. How Often Do Workers Receive Advance Notice of Layoffs? *Mon. Lab. Rev.*, June 1987, *110*(6), pp. 13–17. [G: U.S.]

Brown, Vivienne. Demand-Deficient Unemployment. *Thompson, G.; Brown, V. and Levačić, R., eds.*, 1987, pp. 105–33. [G: U.K.]

Brüniche-Olsen, Paul. Mobiliteten på det danske arbejdsmarked. (Mobility in the Danish Labour Market. With English summary.) *Nationaløkon. Tidsskr.*, 1987, *125*(3), pp. 321–36. [G: Denmark]

Brüniche-Olsen, Paul. Unemployment, the Labour Queue and Positive Feedback in the Labour Market. *Pedersen, P. J. and Lund, R., eds.*, 1987, pp. 187–204.

Bruno, Michael. Stagflation in the Industrial Countries: An Updated Overview. *Hitotsubashi J. Econ.*, October 1987, 27, pp. 57–74. [G: OECD]

Buck, Nick; Gordon, Ian R. and Young, Ken. London: Employment Problems and Prospects. *Hausner, V. A., et al.*, 1987, pp. 99–131. [G: U.K.]

Buckley, Peter J. and Artisien, Patrick. Policy Issues of Intra-EC Direct Investment: British, French and German Multinationals in Greece,

Portugal and Spain, with Special Reference to Employment Effects. *J. Common Market Stud.*, December 1987, *26*(2), pp. 207–30. [G: EEC]

Budd, Alan; Levine, Paul and Smith, Peter N. Long-term Unemployment and the Shifting U–V Curve: A Multi-country Study. *Europ. Econ. Rev.*, Feb./Mar. 1987, *31*(1/2), pp. 296–305. [G: U.K.; W. Germany; Netherlands; U.S.]

Burkhauser, Richard V. Occupational Effects on the Health and Work Capacity of Older Men: Comment. *Burtless, G., ed.*, 1987, pp. 142–50. [G: U.S.]

Burtless, Gary. Jobless Pay and High European Unemployment. *Lawrence, R. Z. and Schultze, C. L., eds.*, 1987, pp. 105–62. [G: U.S.; W. Europe]

Burtless, Gary. Occupational Effects on the Health and Work Capacity of Older Men. *Burtless, G., ed.*, 1987, pp. 103–42. [G: U.S.]

Byrd, William A. and Tidrick, Gene. China's Industrial Reform: Factor Allocation and Enterprise Incentives. *Tidrick, G. and Jiyuan, C., eds.*, 1987, pp. 60–102. [G: China]

Calmfors, Lars. European Unemployment—An Introduction. *Layard, R. and Calmfors, L., eds.*, 1987, pp. 1–10. [G: W. Europe]

Calmfors, Lars. High Unemployment in Europe: Diagnosis and Policy Implications: Comment. *Siven, C.-H., ed.*, 1987, pp. 39–43. [G: W. Europe]

Calmfors, Lars. Work Sharing: Why? How? How Not . . . : Comments. *Layard, R. and Calmfors, L., eds.*, 1987, pp. 198–204. [G: OECD]

Cannon, Tom. The Contribution of New Enterprise to Economic Growth and Employment. The Experience of the Scottish Enterprise Foundation. *Gemper, B. B., ed.*, 1987, pp. 131–43. [G: U.K.]

Canton, Richard and Wenninger, John. Current Labor Market Trends and Inflation. *Fed. Res. Bank New York Quart. Rev.*, Autumn 1987, *12*(3), pp. 36–48. [G: U.S.]

Capie, Forrest H. Unemployment and Real Wages. *Glynn, S. and Booth, A., eds.*, 1987, pp. 57–69. [G: U.K.]

Card, David and Farber, Henry S. Semiparametric Estimation of Employment Duration Models: Comments. *Econometric Rev.*, 1987, *6*(1), pp. 41–54.

Carroll, Archie B. Management's Social Responsibilities [When Business Closes Down: Social Responsibilities and Management Actions]. *Staudohar, P. D. and Brown, H. E.*, 1987, *1984*, pp. 167–81. [G: U.S.]

Cartwright, Joseph V. and Trott, Edward A., Jr. Defense-Related Employment for Selected Weapon Systems. *Lynch, J. E., ed.*, 1987, pp. 51–58. [G: U.S.]

Caselli, Gian Paolo and Pastrello, Gabriele. Un suggerimento hobsoniano su terziario e occupazione: USA 1960–1983. La specificità americana e la debolezza europea. (With English summary.) *Polit. Econ.*, April 1987, *3*(1), pp. 105–29. **[G: U.S.; EEC]**

Challier, Marie-Christine. Inactivité et chômage caché. (Non-participation and Hidden Unemployment. With English summary.) *Écon. Soc.*, November 1987, *21*(11), pp. 83–100. **[G: France]**

Charette, Michael F. and Kaufmann, Barry. Short-run Variation in the Natural Rate of Unemployment. *J. Macroecon.*, Summer 1987, *9*(3), pp. 417–27. **[G: Canada]**

Chesher, Andrew and Irish, Margaret. Residual Analysis in the Grouped and Censored Normal Linear Model. *J. Econometrics*, Jan./Feb. 1987, *34*(1/2), pp. 33–61. **[G: U.K.]**

Chotigeat, Tosporn. Measurement of Industrial Employment Volatility in an Open Economy. *Soc. Econ. Stud.*, December 1987, *36*(4), pp. 113–25. **[G: Puerto Rico]**

Chrisman, James J.; Carroll, Archie B. and Gatewood, Elizabeth J. The Case against Legislation [What's Wrong with Plant-Closing Legislation and Industrial Policy?]. *Staudohar, P. D. and Brown, H. E.*, 1987, *1985*, pp. 321–33. **[G: U.S.]**

Christ, Carl. Unemployment and Macroeconomics. *Gannon, T. M.*, ed., 1987, pp. 116–27. **[G: U.S.]**

Chua, Tin Chiu and Fuller, Wayne A. A Model for Multinomial Response Error Applied to Labor Flows. *J. Amer. Statist. Assoc.*, March 1987, *82*(397), pp. 46–51. **[G: U.S.]**

Clark, Gordon L. Job Search Theory and Indeterminate Information. *Fischer, M. M. and Nijkamp, P.*, eds., 1987, pp. 169–88.

Clark, John A. and Freeman, Christopher. Quantitative Analysis of the Future of UK Employment. *Freeman, C. and Soete, L.*, eds., 1987, pp. 223–36. **[G: U.K.]**

Clark, John A.; Patel, Pari and Soete, Luc. Future Employment Trends in UK Manufacturing Using a Capital–Vintage Simulation Model. *Freeman, C. and Soete, L.*, eds., 1987, pp. 99–118. **[G: U.K.]**

Clements, Benedict J. and Kim, Kwan S. The Distributional and Employment Consequences of Export Promotion and Import Substitution in Brazil. *Eastern Econ. J.*, October-December 1987, *13*(4), pp. 435–46. **[G: Brazil]**

Coen, Robert M. and Hickman, Bert G. Keynesian and Classical Unemployment in Four Countries. *Brookings Pap. Econ. Act.*, 1987, (1), pp. 123–93. **[G: U.S.; U.K.; W. Germany; Austria]**

Cohany, Sharon R. Labor Force Status of Vietnam-Era Veterans. *Mon. Lab. Rev.*, February 1987, *110*(2), pp. 11–17. **[G: U.S.]**

Cohen, Daniel and Michel, Philippe. Théorie et pratique du chômage en France. (Theory and Practice of French Unemployment. With English summary.) *Revue Écon.*, May 1987, *38*(3), pp. 661–75. **[G: France]**

Cohn, Andrew and McElroy, Kathleen. The Dane County, Wisconsin Dislocated Worker Project. *Cook, R. F.*, ed., 1987, pp. 173–92. **[G: U.S.]**

Cook, Robert F. Worker Dislocation: Case Studies of Causes and Cures: Introduction. *Cook, R. F.*, ed., 1987, pp. 1–14. **[G: U.S.]**

Cook, Robert F. Worker Dislocation: Case Studies of Causes and Cures: Findings and Conclusions. *Cook, R. F.*, ed., 1987, pp. 193–210. **[G: U.S.]**

Cornfield, Daniel B. Women in the Automated Office: Computers, Work, and Prospects for Unionization. *Lewin, D.; Lipsky, D. B. and Sockell, D.*, eds., 1987, pp. 177–98. **[G: U.S.]**

Crafts, N. F. R. Long-term Unemployment in Britain in the 1930s. *Econ. Hist. Rev.*, 2nd Ser., August 1987, *40*(3), pp. 418–32. **[G: U.K.]**

Crispo, John. Unemployment: Industrial Relations: Comment. *Gunderson, M.; Meltz, N. M. and Ostry, S.*, eds., 1987, pp. 193–96. **[G: Canada]**

Curry, Robert L., Jr. Poverty and Mass Unemployment in Mineral-Rich Botswana. *Amer. J. Econ. Soc.*, January 1987, *46*(1), pp. 71–87. **[G: Botswana]**

Dahrendorf, Ralf. Slow Growth in Europe: Conceptual Issues: Comment. *Lawrence, R. Z. and Schultze, C. L.*, eds., 1987, pp. 76–79. **[G: W. Europe]**

Daniels, Rudolph. The Structure of the South African Labor Market, 1970–83. *Rev. Black Polit. Econ.*, Spring 1987, *15*(4), pp. 63–78. **[G: S. Africa]**

Davis, Douglas D. Maximal Quality Selection and Discrimination in Employment. *J. Econ. Behav. Organ.*, March 1987, *8*(1), pp. 97–112. **[G: U.S.]**

Davis, Steven J. Fluctuations in the Pace of Labor Reallocations. *Carnegie–Rochester Conf. Ser. Public Policy*, Autumn 1987, 27, pp. 335–402. **[G: U.S.]**

Deacon, Alan. Systems of Interwar Unemployment Relief. *Glynn, S. and Booth, A.*, eds., 1987, pp. 31–42. **[G: U.K.]**

Devens, Richard M., Jr. Industrial Structure Has Little Impact on Jobless Rate of Experienced Workers. *Mon. Lab. Rev.*, May 1987, *110*(5), pp. 30–32. **[G: U.S.]**

Dickens, William T. The Evolution of Unemployment in the United States: 1968–1985: Comment. *Fischer, S.*, ed., 1987, pp. 58–63. **[G: U.S.]**

Dickens, William T. and Lang, Kevin. Where Have All the Good Jobs Gone? Deindustrialization and Labor Market Segmentation. *Lang, K. and Leonard, J. S.*, eds., 1987, pp. 90–102. **[G: U.S.]**

Dilnot, Andrew and Kell, Michael. Male Unemployment and Women's Work. *Fisc. Stud.*, August 1987, *8*(3), pp. 1–16. **[G: U.K.]**

Dixon, Peter B. The Effects on the Australian Economy of Shorter Standard Working Hours in Construction and Related Industries. *Australian Bull. Lab.*, September 1987, *13*(4), pp. 264–89. **[G: Australia]**

Dombois, Rainer and Osterland, M. New Forms of Flexible Utilization of Labour: Part-time and

Contract Work. *Tarling, R., ed.*, 1987, pp. 225–43. **[G: W. Germany]**

Dommel, Paul R. The Cleveland, Ohio United Labor Agency Dislocated Worker Project. *Cook, R. F., ed.*, 1987, pp. 111–27. **[G: U.S.]**

Donges, Juergen B. Chronic Unemployment in Europe Forever? Challenges for Policy Reform. *Siven, C.-H., ed.*, 1987, pp. 103–23. **[G: W. Europe]**

Drèze, Jacques H. Slow Growth in Europe: Conceptual Issues: Comment. *Lawrence, R. Z. and Schultze, C. L., eds.*, 1987, pp. 79–93. **[G: W. Europe]**

Drèze, Jacques H. Work Sharing: Why? How? How Not . . . *Layard, R. and Calmfors, L., eds.*, 1987, pp. 139–92. **[G: OECD]**

Driver, Ciaran and Naisbitt, Barry. Cyclical Variations in Service Industries' Employment in the UK. *Appl. Econ.*, April 1987, *19*(4), pp. 541–54. **[G: U.K.]**

Dunlop, John T. Industrial Relations and Unemployment. *Gunderson, M.; Meltz, N. M. and Ostry, S., eds.*, 1987, pp. 184–92. **[G: U.S.]**

Dunn, Richard. Analysing Spatial Time Series of Local Unemployment: A Graphical Approach Using Principal Components Analysis and Seasonal Adjustment Procedures. *Environ. Planning A*, February 1987, *19*(2), pp. 225–46. **[G: U.K.]**

Dutkowsky, Donald H. Unanticipated Money Growth, Interest Rate Volatility, and Unemployment in the United States. *Rev. Econ. Statist.*, February 1987, *69*(1), pp. 144–48. **[G: U.S.]**

Dutoya, C. and Gauvin, Annie. Assignment of Women Workers to Jobs and Company Strategies in France. *Tarling, R., ed.*, 1987, pp. 127–44. **[G: France]**

Dutton, Patricia. Policies for the Youth Labour Market: YTS: Training or a Placebo? *Junankar, P. N., ed.*, 1987, pp. 217–37. **[G: U.K.]**

Dymond, W. R. Unemployment: International Perspectives: Prospects. *Gunderson, M.; Meltz, N. M. and Ostry, S., eds.*, 1987, pp. 41–46. **[G: Global]**

Dynarski, Mark and Sheffrin, Steven M. Consumption and Unemployment. *Quart. J. Econ.*, May 1987, *102*(2), pp. 411–28. **[G: U.S.]**

Dynarski, Mark and Sheffrin, Steven M. New Evidence on the Cyclical Behavior of Unemployment Durations. *Lang, K. and Leonard, J. S., eds.*, 1987, pp. 164–85. **[G: U.S.]**

de Edwards, Alejandra Cox. Mercado Laboral Chileno Durante la Década de 1974–1983: Problemas de Ajuste. (With English summary.) *Cuadernos Econ.*, August 1987, *24*(72), pp. 165–95. **[G: Chile]**

Edwards, Richard. Youth Labor and the Changing Industrial Relations System: Towards a Research Agenda. *Econ. Lavoro*, Jan.-Mar. 1987, *21*(1), pp. 65–75. **[G: U.S.]**

Ehrenberg, Ronald G. and Sherman, Daniel R. Employment while in College, Academic Achievement, and Postcollege Outcomes: A

Summary of Results. *J. Human Res.*, Winter 1987, *22*(1), pp. 1–23. **[G: U.S.]**

Ehrenberg, Ronald G. and Smith, Robert S. Comparable-Worth Wage Adjustments and Female Employment in the State and Local Sector. *J. Lab. Econ.*, January 1987, *5*(1), pp. 43–62. **[G: U.S.]**

Eichengreen, Barry. Unemployment in Interwar Britain: Dole or Doldrums? *Oxford Econ. Pap.*, December 1987, *39*(4), pp. 597–623. **[G: U.K.]**

Ellman, Michael. Unemployment: International Perspectives: Eurosclerosis? *Gunderson, M.; Meltz, N. M. and Ostry, S., eds.*, 1987, 47–62. **[G: U.S.; W. Europe]**

Ellwood, David T. and Wise, David A. Military Hiring and Youth Employment. *Wise, D. A., ed.*, 1987, pp. 79–95. **[G: U.S.]**

Ellwood, David T. and Wise, David A. Uncle Sam Wants You—Sometimes: Military Enlistments and the Youth Labor Market. *Wise, D. A., ed.*, 1987, pp. 97–118. **[G: U.S.]**

Elmore, Richard F. Youth Employment in the United States: Problem, Structure, Policy. *Pedersen, P. J. and Lund, R., eds.*, 1987, pp. 241–57. **[G: U.S.]**

Emerson, Michael. Labour Market Flexibility and Jobs: A Survey of Evidence from OECD Countries with Special Reference to Europe: Comments. *Layard, R. and Calmfors, L., eds.*, 1987, pp. 77–84. **[G: OECD]**

Engelbrecht, Hans-Jürgen. An Information Sector Perspective of Employment Expansion in the Republic of Korea, 1975–80. *Devel. Econ.*, March 1987, *25*(1), pp. 19–29. **[G: S. Korea]**

Eriksson, Tor. Arbetslöshetsskillnaderna i ljuset av flödesdata. (The Differences in Unemployment in the Light of Flow Data. With English summary.) *Ekon. Samfundets Tidskr.*, 1987, *40*(4), pp. 201–14. **[G: Finland]**

Erlich, S.; Ginsburgh, Victor and Van der Heyden, Ludo. Where Do Real Wage Policies Lead Belgium? A General Equilibrium Analysis. *Europ. Econ. Rev.*, October 1987, *31*(7), pp. 1369–83. **[G: Belgium]**

Errington, Andrew. Labour Use and Labour Requirements in UK Agriculture. *J. Agr. Econ.*, May 1987, *38*(2), pp. 271–79. **[G: U.K.]**

Espenshade, Thomas J. Aging and the Ability to Work: Policy Issues and Recent Trends: Comment. *Burtless, G., ed.*, 1987, pp. 97–102. **[G: U.S.]**

Evans, Richard J. The Experience of Unemployment in the Weimar Republic. *Evans, R. J. and Geary, D., eds.*, 1987, pp. 1–22. **[G: Germany]**

Evans, Richard J. and Geary, Dick. The German Unemployed: Experiences and Consequences of Mass Unemployment from the Weimar Republic to the Third Reich: Preface. *Evans, R. J. and Geary, D., eds.*, 1987, pp. xiii–xviii. **[G: Germany]**

Evers-Koelman, Inge; Fischer, Manfred M. and Nijkamp, Peter. Results of Cross-National Comparisons of Regional Labour Markets in 15 Countries. *Fischer, M. M. and Nijkamp,*

P., *eds.*, 1987, pp. 369–483.   [G: OECD; E. Europe]

Fabella, Raul V. Rural Manufacturing Employment in the Philippines: Contribution and Determinants. *Islam, R., ed.*, 1987, pp. 135–70.   [G: Philippines]

Faradzhev, F. A. Solving Employment Problems in a Labour-Surplus Region of the USSR: The Case of Azerbaijan. *Int. Lab. Rev.*, 1987, *126*(3), pp. 337–50.   [G: U.S.S.R.]

Farley, John E. Disproportionate Black and Hispanic Unemployment in U.S. Metropolitan Areas: The Roles of Racial Inequality, Segregation and Discrimination in Male Joblessness. *Amer. J. Econ. Soc.*, April 1987, *46*(2), pp. 129–50.   [G: U.S.]

Feldstein, Martin S. Long-run Implications of the Increase in Taxation and Public Debt for Employment and Economic Growth in Europe: Comments. *Europ. Econ. Rev.*, April 1987, *31*(3), pp. 778–80.   [G: W. Europe]

Fernández Kelly, M. Patricia. Technology and Employment along the U.S.–Mexican Border. *Thorup, C. L., ed.*, 1987, pp. 149–66.   [G: U.S.; Mexico]

Fields, Gary S. and Mitchell, Olivia S. Restructuring Social Security: How Will Retirement Ages Respond? *Sandell, S. H., ed.*, 1987, pp. 192–205.   [G: U.S.]

Fischer, Manfred M. and Nijkamp, Peter. Current Trends in Regional Labour Markets. *Gordon, I., ed.*, 1987, pp. 15–43.   [G: E. Europe; W. Europe; N. America; Australia]

Fischer, Manfred M. and Nijkamp, Peter. Spatial Labour Market Analysis: Relevance and Scope. *Fischer, M. M. and Nijkamp, P., eds.*, 1987, pp. 1–33.

Flaim, Paul O. and Sehgal, Ellen. Reemployment and Earnings [Displaced Workers of 1979–83: How Well Have They Fared?]. *Staudohar, P. D. and Brown, H. E.*, 1987, *1985*, pp. 101–30.   [G: U.S.]

Flanagan, Robert J. Labor Market Behavior and European Economic Growth. *Lawrence, R. Z. and Schultze, C. L., eds.*, 1987, pp. 175–211.   [G: W. Europe; U.S.]

Folbre, Nancy R.; Leighton, Julia L. and Roderick, Melissa R. Legislation in Maine [Plant Closings and Their Regulation in Maine, 1971–1982]. *Staudohar, P. D. and Brown, H. E.*, 1987, *1984*, pp. 293–306.   [G: U.S.]

Foot, David K. and Li, Jeanne C. Demographic Determinants of Unemployment. *Gunderson, M.; Meltz, N. M. and Ostry, S., eds.*, 1987, pp. 140–51.   [G: Canada]

Ford, William D. Federal Legislation [Coping with Plant Closings]. *Staudohar, P. D. and Brown, H. E.*, 1987, *1985*, pp. 307–11.   [G: U.S.]

Formica, Piero and Mandelli, Giancarlo. Premesse e implicazioni micro e macroeconomiche dell'atuomazione flessibile. (The Micro and Macro-Economic Promises and Implications of Flexible Automation. With English summary.)

Econ. Lavoro, Oct.-Dec. 1987, *21*(4), pp. 29–44.

Fortin, Pierre. Unemployment in Canada: Macroeconomic Disease, Macroeconomic Cure. *Gunderson, M.; Meltz, N. M. and Ostry, S., eds.*, 1987, pp. 74–83.   [G: Canada]

Franz, Wolfgang. Hysteresis, Persistence, and the NAIRU: An Empirical Analysis for the Federal Republic of Germany. *Layard, R. and Calmfors, L., eds.*, 1987, pp. 91–122.   [G: W. Germany]

Franz, Wolfgang. The End of Expansion in Employment in Germany: Beginnings of an Attempt at Evaluation of Structural Unemployment as a Partial Component of Joblessness. *Pedersen, P. J. and Lund, R., eds.*, 1987, pp. 81–103.   [G: W. Germany]

Freeman, Christopher and Luc, Soete. Technical Change and Full Employment: Introduction. *Freeman, C. and Soete, L., eds.*, 1987, pp. 1–6.   [G: U.K.]

Freeman, Christopher and Soete, Luc. Technical Change and Full Employment: Conclusions. *Freeman, C. and Soete, L., eds.*, 1987, pp. 257–64.

Freeman, Christopher and Soete, Luc. Technical Change and Full Employment: Policy Conclusions. *Freeman, C. and Soete, L., eds.*, 1987, pp. 237–56.   [G: U.K.]

Freeman, Richard B. The Relation of Criminal Activity to Black Youth Employment. *Rev. Black Polit. Econ.*, Summer-Fall 1987, *16*(1–2), pp. 99–107.   [G: U.S.]

Freeman, Richard B. and Weitzman, Martin L. Bonuses and Employment in Japan. *J. Japanese Int. Economies*, June 1987, *1*(2), pp. 168–94.   [G: Japan]

Fryer, John. Unemployment: Industrial Relations: Comment. *Gunderson, M.; Meltz, N. M. and Ostry, S., eds.*, 1987, pp. 201–06.   [G: Canada]

Gallaway, Lowell and Vedder, Richard K. Wages, Prices, and Employment: Von Mises and the Progressives. *Rothbard, M. N., ed.*, 1987, pp. 33–80.   [G: U.S.; U.K.]

Garside, W. R. The Real Wage Debate and British Interwar Unemployment. *Glynn, S. and Booth, A., eds.*, 1987, pp. 70–81.   [G: U.K.]

Gastwirth, Joseph L. and Greenhouse, Samuel W. Estimating a Common Relative Risk: Application in Equal Employment. *J. Amer. Statist. Assoc.*, March 1987, *82*(397), pp. 38–45.   [G: U.S.]

Geary, Dick. Unemployment and Working-Class Solidarity: The Germany Experience 1929–33. *Evans, R. J. and Geary, D., eds.*, 1987, pp. 261–80.   [G: Germany]

Gera, Surendra. An Evaluation of the Canadian Employment Tax Credit Program. *Can. Public Policy*, June 1987, *13*(2), pp. 196–207.   [G: Canada]

Gerhart, Barry A. and Jarley, Paul. Comment [A Tale of Employment Decline in Two Cities: How Bad Was the Worst of Times?]. *Ind. Lab. Relat. Rev.*, January 1987, *40*(2), pp. 280–84.   [G: U.S.]

Giannini, Mirella. Donne e lavoro nel contesto meridionale. (Women and Work in the Mezzogiorno. With English summary.) *Econ. Lavoro*, Apr.-June 1987, *21*(2), pp. 67–85.   **[G: Italy]**

Gillespie, A. E. and Green, A. E. The Changing Geography of Producer Services Employment in Britain. *Reg. Stud.*, October 1987, *21*(5), pp. 397–411.   **[G: U.K.]**

Ginsburg, Helen. Sex-Based Employment Quotas in Sweden: Comments. *Brown, C. and Pechman, J. A., eds.*, 1987, pp. 301–08.
   [G: Sweden]

Glade, William P. The Employment Question and Development Policies in Latin America. *Dietz, J. L. and Street, J. H., eds.*, 1987, pp. 219–27.   **[G: Latin America]**

Gleave, David. Dynamics in Spatial Variations in Unemployment. *Fischer, M. M. and Nijkamp, P., eds.*, 1987, pp. 269–88.
   [G: U.K.]

Glewwe, Paul. Unemployment in Developing Countries: Economist's Models in Light of Evidence from Sri Lanka. *Int. Econ. J.*, Winter 1987, *1*(4), pp. 1–17.   **[G: Sri Lanka]**

Glynn, Sean. The Road to Full Employment: The Scale and Nature of the Problem. *Glynn, S. and Booth, A., eds.*, 1987, pp. 3–16.
   [G: U.K.]

Goldberg, Matthew S. and Warner, John T. Military Experience, Civilian Experience, and the Earnings of Veterans. *J. Human Res.*, Winter 1987, *22*(1), pp. 62–81.   **[G: U.S.]**

Goldfeld, Stephen M. Keynesian and Classical Unemployment in Four Countries: Comments. *Brookings Pap. Econ. Act.*, 1987, (1), pp. 194–97.   **[G: U.S.; U.K.; W. Germany; Austria]**

Goldstein, Harvey A. and Cruze, Alvin M. An Evaluation of State Projections of Industry, Occupational Employment. *Mon. Lab. Rev.*, October 1987, *110*(10), pp. 29–38.   **[G: U.S.]**

Good, David H. and Pirog-Good, Maureen A. A Simultaneous Probit Model of Crime and Employment for Black and White Teenage Males. *Rev. Black Polit. Econ.*, Summer-Fall 1987, *16*(1–2), pp. 109–27.   **[G: U.S.]**

Good, David H. and Pirog-Good, Maureen A. Employment, Crime, and Race. *Contemp. Policy Issues*, October 1987, *5*(4), pp. 91–104.
   [G: U.S.]

Gordon, Ian R. The Structural Element in Regional Unemployment. *Gordon, I., ed.*, 1987, pp. 67–88.   **[G: U.K.]**

Grancelli, Bruno. Political Trade-Offs, Collective Bargaining, Individual Tradings: Some Remarks on Industrial Relations in Italy. *Alessandrini, S. and Dallago, B., eds.*, 1987, pp. 257–70.   **[G: Italy]**

Gregerman, Alan and Penne, R. Leo. Community Economic Adjustment to Defense Industrial Cutbacks. *Lynch, J. E., ed.*, 1987, pp. 59–80.   **[G: U.S.]**

Gregory, R. G. Unemployment: International Perspectives: An Overview: Comment. *Gunderson, M.; Meltz, N. M. and Ostry, S., eds.*, 1987, pp. 84–86.

Grimes, Paul W. Right-to-Work Legislation and the Economic Position of Black Workers. *Rev. Black Polit. Econ.*, Spring 1987, *15*(4), pp. 79–88.   **[G: U.S.]**

de Grip, Andries. Causes of Labour Supply and Demand Mismatches in the Dutch Building Trades. *De Economist*, 1987, *135*(2), pp. 182–200.   **[G: Netherlands]**

Gunderson, Morley and Meltz, Noah M. Labour-Market Rigidities and Unemployment. *Gunderson, M.; Meltz, N. M. and Ostry, S., eds.*, 1987, pp. 164–75.   **[G: Canada]**

Gunderson, Morley; Meltz, Noah M. and Ostry, Sylvia. Unemployment: International Perspectives: Introduction: A Summary of the Issues. *Gunderson, M.; Meltz, N. M. and Ostry, S., eds.*, 1987, pp. 1–10.

Gustafson, Thomas A. The Incentive Effects of Private Pension Plans: Comment. *Bodie, Z.; Shoven, J. B. and Wise, D. A., eds.*, 1987, pp. 337–39.   **[G: U.S.]**

Gutowski, Armin. Slow Growth in Europe: Conceptual Issues: Comment. *Lawrence, R. Z. and Schultze, C. L., eds.*, 1987, pp. 93–98.
   [G: W. Europe]

Guy, Ken. The UK Tertiary Service Sector. *Freeman, C. and Soete, L., eds.*, 1987, pp. 169–88.   **[G: U.K.]**

Haltiwanger, John and Plant, Mark. Alternative Measures of Slackness in the Labor Market and Their Relationship to Wage and Price Inflation. *Lang, K. and Leonard, J. S., eds.*, 1987, pp. 212–33.   **[G: U.S.]**

Ham, John C. and Rea, Samuel A., Jr. Unemployment Insurance and Male Unemployment Duration in Canada. *J. Lab. Econ.*, July 1987, *5*(3), pp. 325–53.   **[G: Canada]**

Hamermesh, Daniel S. The Costs of Worker Displacement. *Quart. J. Econ.*, February 1987, *102*(1), pp. 51–75.   **[G: U.S.]**

Hamermesh, Daniel S. Unemployment: United States: Comment. *Gunderson, M.; Meltz, N. M. and Ostry, S., eds.*, 1987, pp. 129–32.
   [G: U.S.]

Hammerman, Herbert. Five Case Studies [Five Case Studies of Displaced Workers]. *Staudohar, P. D. and Brown, H. E., 1987, 1964*, pp. 75–88.   **[G: U.S.]**

Hansen, Gary B. American Labor and International Trade: Adjustment Strategies to Assist Workers Displaced in Plant Closings and Permanent Layoffs. *Econ. Lavoro*, Jan.-Mar. 1987, *21*(1), pp. 115–22.   **[G: U.S.]**

Hansen, Per Vejrup. Turnover and Employment among Youth: Causes of the Particular Problems of Youth Employment. *Pedersen, P. J. and Lund, R., eds.*, 1987, pp. 129–45.
   [G: Denmark]

Harris, Candee S. Magnitude of Job Loss [The Magnitude of Job Loss from Plant Closings and the Generation of Replacement Jobs: Some Recent Evidence]. *Staudohar, P. D. and Brown, H. E., 1987, 1984*, pp. 89–100.   **[G: U.S.]**

Harrison, Bennett. European and American Experience [Comparing European and American Experience with Plant Closing Laws]. *Staudo-*

har, P. D. and Brown, H. E., 1987, *1984*, pp. 259–65. **[G: W. Europe]**

Hart, P. E. Small Firms and Jobs. *Nat. Inst. Econ. Rev.*, August 1987, (121), pp. 60–63. **[G: U.K.]**

Harvey, Elizabeth. Youth Unemployment and the State: Public Policies towards Unemployed Youth in Hamburg during the World Economic Crisis. *Evans, R. J. and Geary, D., eds.*, 1987, pp. 142–71. **[G: Germany]**

Hausman, Jerry A. and Paquette, Lynn. Involuntary Early Retirement and Consumption. *Burtless, G., ed.*, 1987, pp. 151–75. **[G: U.S.]**

Hausner, Victor A. Economic Change and Urban Policy. *Hausner, V. A., et al.*, 1987, pp. 1–43. **[G: U.K.]**

Henry, David K. and Oliver, Richard P. The Defense Buildup, 1977–85: Effects on Production and Employment. *Mon. Lab. Rev.*, August 1987, *110*(8), pp. 3–11. **[G: U.S.]**

Herin, Jan. Chronic Unemployment in Europe Forever? Challenges for Policy Reform: Comment. *Siven, C.-H., ed.*, 1987, pp. 124–27. **[G: W. Europe]**

Herrera, Alejandra. Telecomunicaciones: reestructuración productiva y empleo en la República Argentina. (With English summary.) *Desarrollo Econ.*, Apr.-June 1987, *27*(105), pp. 107–28. **[G: Argentina]**

Hibbs, Douglas A., Jr. The Mass Public and Macroeconomic Performance: Dynamics of Public Opinion toward Unemployment and Inflation. *Hibbs, D. A., Jr.*, 1987, *1979*, pp. 117–42. **[G: U.S.]**

Hickman, Bert G. Real Wages, Aggregate Demand, and Unemployment. *Europ. Econ. Rev.*, December 1987, *31*(8), pp. 1531–60. **[G: U.S.]**

Hill, Edward W. What Is the Effect of Random Variation in State Unemployment Rates? *Mon. Lab. Rev.*, December 1987, *110*(12), pp. 41–46. **[G: U.S.]**

Hill, Stephen. Working Time Changes and Employment Growth. *Lloyds Bank Rev.*, January 1987, (163), pp. 31–46. **[G: U.K.]**

Holly, Sean and Smith, Peter N. A Two-Sector Analysis of the UK Labour Market. *Oxford Bull. Econ. Statist.*, February 1987, *49*(1), pp. 79–102. **[G: U.K.]**

Holmlund, Bertil. Labor Market Behavior and European Economic Growth: Comment. *Lawrence, R. Z. and Schultze, C. L., eds.*, 1987, pp. 211–17. **[G: W. Europe; U.S.]**

Holzer, Harry J. Hiring Procedures in the Firm: Their Economic Determinants and Outcomes. *Allen, S. G., et al.*, 1987, pp. 243–74. **[G: U.S.]**

Holzer, Harry J. Informal Job Search and Black Youth Unemployment. *Amer. Econ. Rev.*, June 1987, *77*(3), pp. 446–52. **[G: U.S.]**

Holzer, Harry J. Job Search by Employed and Unemployed Youth. *Ind. Lab. Relat. Rev.*, July 1987, *40*(4), pp. 601–11. **[G: U.S.]**

Homburg, Heidrun. From Unemployment Insurance to Compulsory Labour: The Transformation of the Benefit System in Germany 1927–

33. *Evans, R. J. and Geary, D., eds.*, 1987, pp. 73–107. **[G: Germany]**

Honig, Marjorie and Reimers, Cordelia. Retirement, Re-entry, and Part-time Work. *Eastern Econ. J.*, October-December 1987, *13*(4), pp. 361–71. **[G: U.S.]**

Hooks, Gregory. Comparison of the United States, Sweden, and France [The Policy Response to Factory Closings: A Comparison of the United States, Sweden, and France]. *Staudohar, P. D. and Brown, H. E.*, 1987, *1984*, pp. 245–58. **[G: U.S.; France; Sweden]**

Horowitz, Joel L. and Neumann, George R. Semiparametric Estimation of Employment Duration Models. *Econometric Rev.*, 1987, *6*(1), pp. 5–40. **[G: U.S.]**

Horowitz, Joel L. and Neumann, George R. Semiparametric Estimation of Employment Duration Models: Reply. *Econometric Rev.*, 1987, *6*(1), pp. 79–81. **[G: U.S.]**

Horridge, Mark; Parmenter, Brian R. and Warr, Peter G. Buying Australian. *Econ. Rec.*, September 1987, *63*(182), pp. 231–46. **[G: Australia]**

Horrigan, Michael W. Time Spent Unemployed: A New Look at Data from the CPS. *Mon. Lab. Rev.*, July 1987, *110*(7), pp. 3–15. **[G: U.S.]**

Horvath, Francis W. The Pulse of Economic Change: Displaced Workers of 1981–85. *Mon. Lab. Rev.*, June 1987, *110*(6), pp. 3–12. **[G: U.S.]**

Hossain, Mahabub. Employment Generation through Cottage Industries—Potentials and Constraints: The Case of Bangladesh. *Islam, R., ed.*, 1987, pp. 19–57. **[G: Bangladesh]**

House, William J. Labor Market Differentiation in a Developing Economy: An Example from Urban Juba, Southern Sudan. *World Devel.*, July 1987, *15*(7), pp. 877–97. **[G: Sudan]**

Howe, Wayne J. Strong Employment Growth Highlights First Half of 1987. *Mon. Lab. Rev.*, September 1987, *110*(9), pp. 64–69. **[G: U.S.]**

Hunt, H. Allan. The GM–UAW Metropolitan Pontiac Retraining and Employment Program (PREP). *Cook, R. F., ed.*, 1987, pp. 31–46. **[G: U.S.]**

Hunt, H. Allan and Hunt, Timothy L. Recent Trends in Clerical Employment: The Impact of Technological Change. *Hartmann, H. I., ed.*, 1987, pp. 223–67. **[G: U.S.]**

Huskey, Lee. Import Substitution in Frontier Regions. *Lane, T., ed.*, 1987, *1985*, pp. 47–61. **[G: U.S.]**

Hyclak, Thomas and Johnes, Geraint. On the Determinants of Full Employment Unemployment Rates in Local Labour Markets. *Appl. Econ.*, February 1987, *19*(2), pp. 191–200. **[G: U.S.]**

Hyman, Richard. Unemployment and Trade Unions in Britain: The Politics of Industrial Relations in the Crisis. *Pedersen, P. J. and Lund, R., eds.*, 1987, pp. 207–23. **[G: U.K.]**

Ippolito, Richard A. Why Federal Workers Don't Quit. *J. Human Res.*, Spring 1987, *22*(2), pp. 281–99. **[G: U.S.]**

Islam, Rizwanul. Rural Industrialisation and Employment in Asia: Issues and Evidence. *Islam, R., ed.*, 1987, pp. 1–18. **[G: Asia]**

Islam, Rizwanul and Shrestha, Ram Prasad. Employment Expansion through Cottage Industries in Nepal: Potentials and Constraints. *Islam, R., ed.*, 1987, pp. 107–33. **[G: Nepal]**

Iversen, Lars. Some Health Effects of the Closure of a Danish Shipyard a Three-Year Follow-Up Study. *Pedersen, P. J. and Lund, R., eds.*, 1987, pp. 305–20. **[G: Denmark]**

Jackman, Richard and Layard, Richard. Innovative Supply-Side Policies to Reduce Unemployment. *Begg, D. K. H., et al.*, 1987, pp. 93–117. **[G: U.K.]**

Jackman, Richard and Roper, S. Structural Unemployment. *Oxford Bull. Econ. Statist.*, February 1987, *49*(1), pp. 9–36. **[G: U.K.]**

Jacobson, Louis. Reply [A Tale of Employment Decline in Two Cities: How Bad Was the Worst of Times?]. *Ind. Lab. Relat. Rev.*, January 1987, *40*(2), pp. 284–87. **[G: U.S.]**

Jahoda, Marie. Unemployment: Facts, Experience and Social Consequences. *Freeman, C. and Soete, L., eds.*, 1987, pp. 9–21. **[G: OECD]**

Jaumandreu, Jordi. Producción, empleo, cambio técnico y costes relativos en la industria española, 1964–85. (With English summary.) *Invest. Econ.*, September 1987, *11*(3), pp. 427–61. **[G: Spain]**

Jenkinson, Tim. The Natural Rate of Unemployment: Does It Exist? *Oxford Rev. Econ. Policy*, Autumn 1987, *3*(3), pp. 20–26. **[G: U.K.]**

Jensen, Peter. Arbejdsløshed og beskæftigelseæen empirisk analyse af individuel arbejdsmarkedsadfærd. (Unemployment and Employment Empirical Analysis of Individual Labour Market Behaviour. With English summary.) *Nationaløkon. Tidsskr.*, 1987, *125*(3), pp. 337–54. **[G: Denmark]**

Jensen, Peter. Transitions between Labour-Market States—An Empirical Analysis Using Danish Data. *Pedersen, P. J. and Lund, R., eds.*, 1987, pp. 67–80. **[G: Denmark]**

Jensen, Peter and Westergård-Nielsen, Niels C. A Search Model Applied to the Transition from Education to Work. *Rev. Econ. Stud.*, July 1987, *54*(3), pp. 461–72. **[G: Denmark]**

Jian, Chen. An Effective Way to Increase Employment: A Report on Beijing's Self-Employed Sector. *Chinese Econ. Stud.*, Fall 1987, *21*(1), pp. 43–71. **[G: China]**

Johnes, Geraint; Taylor, Jim and Ferguson, Glenys. The Employability of New Graduates: A Study of Differences between UK Universities. *Appl. Econ.*, May 1987, *19*(5), pp. 695–710. **[G: U.K.]**

Johnson, Terry R.; Dickinson, Katherine P. and West, Richard W. Older Workers, Job Displacement, and the Employment Service. *Sandell, S. H., ed.*, 1987, pp. 100–117. **[G: U.S.]**

Jørgensen, Birte Bech. Unemployment and the Cultures of Young Women. *Pedersen, P. J. and Lund, R., eds.*, 1987, pp. 321–37. **[G: Denmark]**

Junankar, P. N. The Labour Market for Young People. *Junankar, P. N., ed.*, 1987, pp. 1–12. **[G: OECD]**

Kaiser, Carl P. Layoffs, Average Hours, and Unemployment Insurance in U.S. Manufacturing Industries. *Quart. Rev. Econ. Bus.*, Winter 1987, *27*(4), pp. 80–99. **[G: U.S.]**

Kaliski, Stefan F. Accounting for Unemployment—A Labour Market Perspective. *Can. J. Econ.*, November 1987, *20*(4), pp. 665–93. **[G: Canada]**

Kaliski, Stefan F. Unemployment: Canada: Comment. *Gunderson, M.; Meltz, N. M. and Ostry, S., eds.*, 1987, pp. 176–79. **[G: Canada]**

Kappelhoff, Peter and Teckenberg, Wolfgang. Intergenerational and Career Mobility in the Federal Republic and the United States. *Teckenberg, W., ed.*, 1987, pp. 3–49. **[G: W. Germany; U.S.]**

Kennedy, Bruce. Youth Employment in Canada: A Comment. *Can. Public Policy*, September 1987, *13*(3), pp. 384–88. **[G: Canada]**

Kim, Won Bae. Urban Unemployment and Labor Force Participation in Korea. *Ann. Reg. Sci.*, March 1987, *21*(1), pp. 44–55. **[G: S. Korea]**

Kirk, Robert. Are Business Services Immune to the Business Cycle? *Growth Change*, Spring 1987, *18*(2), pp. 15–23. **[G: U.S.]**

Knight, J. B. and Mayhew, K. Wage Determination and Labour Market Inflexibility: Introduction. *Oxford Bull. Econ. Statist.*, February 1987, *49*(1), pp. 1–8.

Knight, J. B. and Sabot, Richard H. Educational Expansion, Government Policy and Wage Compression. *J. Devel. Econ.*, August 1987, *26*(2), pp. 201–21. **[G: Kenya; Tanzania]**

Knowles, David R. The ASARCO Copper Smelter Project. *Cook, R. F., ed.*, 1987, pp. 151–72. **[G: U.S.]**

Kochan, Thomas A. Unemployment: United States: Comment. *Gunderson, M.; Meltz, N. M. and Ostry, S., eds.*, 1987, pp. 133–37. **[G: U.S.]**

Koken, Bernd K. Unemployment: Industrial Relations: Comment. *Gunderson, M.; Meltz, N. M. and Ostry, S., eds.*, 1987, pp. 199–201. **[G: Canada]**

Kokoski, Mary F. Employment and Wage Changes of Families from CE Survey Data. *Mon. Lab. Rev.*, February 1987, *110*(2), pp. 31–33. **[G: U.S.]**

König, Wolfgang. Employment and Career Mobility of Women in France and the Federal Republic. *Teckenberg, W., ed.*, 1987, pp. 53–85. **[G: France; W. Germany]**

Kosta, Jiří. Manpower Problems in the GDR. *Adam, J., ed.*, 1987, pp. 55–77. **[G: E. Germany]**

Kosters, Marvin H. and Ross, Murray N. The Influence of Employment Shifts and New Job Opportunities on the Growth and Distribution of Real Wages. *Cagan, P., ed.*, 1987, pp. 209–42. **[G: U.S.]**

Kotlikoff, Laurence J. and Wise, David A. The

Incentive Effects of Private Pension Plans. *Bodie, Z.; Shoven, J. B. and Wise, D. A.*, eds., 1987, pp. 283–336. **[G: U.S.]**

Kowalski, Jan S. Unemployment within Enterprises in Centrally Planned Economies: A Regionalised View. *Gordon, I.*, ed., 1987, pp. 89–98. **[G: Poland]**

Kraft, Kornelius. Quasi-fixity of White-Collar and Blue-Collar Workers and of Their Houses of Work in West-German Manufacturing Industries. *J. Inst. Theoretical Econ.*, September 1987, *143*(3), pp. 477–96. **[G: W. Germany]**

Krugman, Paul R. Slow Growth in Europe: Conceptual Issues. *Lawrence, R. Z. and Schultze, C. L.*, eds., 1987, pp. 48–76. **[G: W. Europe]**

Kulik, Jane and Fairchild, Charles. Worker Assistance and Placement Experience. *Lynch, J. E.*, ed., 1987, pp. 191–218. **[G: U.S.]**

Landon, Stuart. Unanticipated Policy Shocks, Regime Changes and Unemployment in Canada, 1967–83. *Appl. Econ.*, August 1987, *19*(8), pp. 1065–81. **[G: Canada]**

Larsson, Rune; Lund, Reinhard and Møller, Jørgen. Trade Union Stratey towards Unemployment at the Local Level. *Pedersen, P. J. and Lund, R.*, eds., 1987, pp. 225–39. **[G: Denmark]**

Lawrence, Anne T. Union Responses to Plant Closure. *Staudohar, P. D. and Brown, H. E.*, 1987, pp. 201–15. **[G: U.S.]**

Lawrence, Robert Z. Is Deindustrialization a Myth? [The Myth of U.S. Deindustrialization]. *Staudohar, P. D. and Brown, H. E.*, 1987, *1983*, pp. 25–40. **[G: U.S.; OECD]**

Lawrence, Robert Z. and Schultze, Charles L. Barriers to European Growth: Overview. *Lawrence, R. Z. and Schultze, C. L.*, eds., 1987, pp. 1–47. **[G: W. Europe]**

Layard, Richard. Labour Market Flexibility in Japan in Comparison with Europe and the U.S.: Comments. *Europ. Econ. Rev.*, April 1987, *31*(3), pp. 678–81. **[G: Japan; OECD]**

Layard, Richard and Nickell, Stephen J. The Performance of the British Economy: The Labour Market. *Dornbusch, R. and Layard, R.*, eds., 1987, pp. 131–79. **[G: U.K.]**

Lazear, Edward P. Involuntary Early Retirement and Consumption: Comment. *Burtless, G.*, ed., 1987, pp. 175–81. **[G: U.S.]**

Lecaillon, Jacques and Grangeas, Geneviève. Salaires, répartition et cycles. (With English summary.) *Revue Écon. Polit.*, July-Aug. 1987, *97*(4), pp. 363–80. **[G: France]**

Lee, E. World Recession and Developing Economies in Asia. *International Labour Office.*, 1987, pp. 99–132. **[G: Asia]**

Leonard, Jonathan S. In the Wrong Place at the Wrong Time: The Extent of Frictional and Structural Unemployment. *Lang, K. and Leonard, J. S.*, eds., 1987, pp. 141–63. **[G: U.S.]**

Leonard, Jonathan S. The Interaction of Residential Segregation and Employment Discrimination. *J. Urban Econ.*, May 1987, *21*(3), pp. 323–46. **[G: U.S.]**

Lesage, James P. and Magura, Michael. A Leading Indicator Model for Ohio SMSA Employment. *Growth Change*, Summer 1987, *18*(3), pp. 36–48. **[G: U.S.]**

Lever, William F. New Trends in the Supply and Demand Patterns of Labour in Western Economies. *Fischer, M. M. and Nijkamp, P.*, eds., 1987, pp. 249–67. **[G: W. Europe]**

Lever, William F. The Inner Cities Research Programme: The Clydeside Case-Study. *Hausner, V. A., et al.*, 1987, pp. 182–217. **[G: U.K.]**

Levin, M. and Horn, G. S. Phillips Curves for Selected South African Labour Markets, 1969–1985. *J. Stud. Econ. Econometrics*, November 1987, *11*(3), pp. 25–50. **[G: S. Africa]**

Lewis, Donald E. and Mangan, John. Wage Inflexibility and Quality Adjustment in Australian Academic Labour Markets: A Constrained Case. *Appl. Econ.*, October 1987, *19*(10), pp. 1279–90. **[G: Australia]**

Lilien, David M. The Evolution of Unemployment in the United States: 1968–1985: Comment. *Fischer, S.*, ed., 1987, pp. 63–67. **[G: U.S.]**

Lindner, W.-D. and Heinzemann, B. Comment [Labour Flexibility and Older Worker Marginalisation: The Need for a New Strategy]. *Int. Lab. Rev.*, 1987, *126*(3), pp. 371–72. **[G: EEC]**

Lipsey, Richard G. Unemployment: International Perspectives: Overview: Comment. *Gunderson, M.; Meltz, N. M. and Ostry, S.*, eds., 1987, pp. 86–92.

Lovell, Malcolm R., Jr. More Options for the Displaced Worker. *Barfield, C. E. and Makin, J. H.*, eds., 1987, pp. 97–99. **[G: U.S.]**

Lynch, John E. Adjustment and Conversion Policy Issues. *Lynch, J. E.*, ed., 1987, pp. 29–50. **[G: U.S.]**

Lynch, John E. Economic Adjustment and Conversion of Defense Industries: Conclusion: Dealing with Major Plant Closures. *Lynch, J. E.*, ed., 1987, pp. 233–44. **[G: U.S.]**

Lynch, Lisa M. Individual Differences in the Youth Labour Market: A Cross-Section Analysis of London Youths. *Junankar, P. N.*, ed., 1987, pp. 185–214. **[G: U.K.]**

Maani, Sholeh A. Maximizing and Satisficing Job Search Behavior in the U.S. and Chile. *J. Behav. Econ.*, Summer 1987, *16*(2), pp. 17–32. **[G: U.S.; Chile]**

MacManus, Susan A. The Houston Community College–Texas Employment Commission Dislocated Worker Project. *Cook, R. F.*, ed., 1987, pp. 129–50.

Magura, Michael and Shapiro, Edward. The Black Dropout Rate and the Black Youth Unemployment Rate: A Granger-Causal Analysis. *Rev. Black Polit. Econ.*, Winter 1987, *15*(3), pp. 56–67. **[G: U.S.]**

Main, Brian G. M. Earnings, Expected Earnings, and Unemployment amongst School Leavers. *Junankar, P. N.*, ed., 1987, pp. 145–84. **[G: U.K.]**

Main, Brian G. M. The Wage Expectations and Unemployment Experience of School Leavers.

Scot. J. Polit. Econ., November 1987, *34*(4), pp. 349–67. **[G: Scotland]**

Mairesse, Jacques. Labour Market Flexibility in Japan in Comparison with Europe and the U.S.: Comments. *Europ. Econ. Rev.*, April 1987, *31*(3), pp. 681–84. **[G: Japan; OECD]**

Maital, Shlomo. Reducing Unemployment. *Gunderson, M.; Meltz, N. M. and Ostry, S., eds.*, 1987, pp. 215–24. **[G: U.S.; Canada]**

Malley, James R. and Hady, Thomas F. The Impact of Macroeconomic Policies on Rural Employment. *U.S.D.A., Econ. Res. Serv., Agr. and Rural Econ. Div.*, 1987, pp. 10.1–19. **[G: U.S.]**

Mann, Arthur J. and Delons, Jacques R. The Buenos Aires Mini-Enterprise Sector. *Soc. Econ. Stud.*, June 1987, *36*(2), pp. 41–67. **[G: Argentina]**

Mann, Arthur J. and Smith, Robert. Public Transfers, Family Socioeconomic Traits, and the Job Search Behavior of the Unemployment: Evidence from Puerto Rico. *World Devel.*, June 1987, *15*(6), pp. 831–40. **[G: Puerto Rico]**

Manning, Chris. Rural Economic Change and Labour Mobility: A Case Study from West Java. *Bull. Indonesian Econ. Stud.*, December 1987, *23*(3), pp. 52–79. **[G: Indonesia]**

Manski, Charles F. Semiparametric Estimation of Employment Duration Models: Comment. *Econometric Rev.*, 1987, *6*(1), pp. 59–64.

Marcel, Mario. Empleo agregado en Chile 1974–85. Una aproximación econométrica. (Aggregate Employment in Chile, 1974–85. An Econometric Approach. With English summary.) *Colección Estud. CIEPLAN*, June 1987, (21), pp. 77–115. **[G: Chile]**

Mark, Jerome A. Technological Change and Employment: Some Results from BLS Research. *Mon. Lab. Rev.*, April 1987, *110*(4), pp. 26–29. **[G: U.S.]**

Marsden, David. Youth Pay in Some OECD Countries since 1966. *Junankar, P. N., ed.*, 1987, pp. 15–50. **[G: OECD]**

Martin, John P. Labor Market Behavior and European Economic Growth: Comment. *Lawrence, R. Z. and Schultze, C. L., eds.*, 1987, pp. 217–26. **[G: W. Europe; U.S.]**

Matthews, Kent G. P. Unemployment in Interwar Britain: An Equilibrium Approach. *Bull. Econ. Res.*, April 1987, *39*(2), pp. 151–69. **[G: U.K.]**

McCallum, John. Unemployment in Canada and the United States. *Can. J. Econ.*, November 1987, *20*(4), pp. 802–22. **[G: Canada; U.S.]**

McCurdy, Thomas H. Some Employment, Income, and Occupational Effects of Microelectronic-Based Technical Change: A Multisectoral Simulation for Canada. *J. Policy Modeling*, Summer 1987, *9*(2), pp. 337–65. **[G: Canada]**

McDonald, James B. and Butler, Richard J. Some Generalized Mixture Distributions with an Application to Unemployment Duration. *Rev. Econ. Statist.*, May 1987, *69*(2), pp. 232–40. **[G: U.S.]**

McDonald, John F. The Identification of Urban Employment Subcenters. *J. Urban Econ.*, March 1987, *21*(2), pp. 242–58. **[G: U.S.]**

McElligott, Anthony. Mobilising the Unemployed: The KPD and the Unemployed Workers' Movement in Hamburg-Altona during the Weimar Republic. *Evans, R. J. and Geary, D., eds.*, 1987, pp. 228–60. **[G: Germany]**

McGahey, Richard. Crime and Employment Research: A Continuing Deadlock? *Rev. Black Polit. Econ.*, Summer-Fall 1987, *16*(1–2), pp. 223–30. **[G: U.S.]**

McKenzie, Richard B. and Smith, Stephen D. Loss of Textile and Apparel Jobs: Is Protectionism Warranted? *Cato J.*, Winter 1987, *6*(3), pp. 731–46. **[G: U.S.]**

McUsic, Molly. U.S. Manufacturing: Any Cause for Alarm? *New Eng. Econ. Rev.*, Jan./Feb. 1987, pp. 3–17. **[G: U.S.]**

Mertens, L. and Richards, P. J. Recession and Employment in Mexico. *Int. Lab. Rev.*, Mar.-Apr. 1987, *126*(2), pp. 229–43. **[G: Mexico]**

Metcalf, David. Labour Market Flexibility and Jobs: A Survey of Evidence from OECD Countries with Special Reference to Europe. *Layard, R. and Calmfors, L., eds.*, 1987, pp. 48–76. **[G: OECD]**

Mettelin, Pierre. Les activités informelles en Afrique noire: les réalités urbaines. (With English summary.) *Can. J. Devel. Stud.*, 1987, *8*(1), pp. 49–68. **[G: Africa]**

Meyer, John R. and Oster, Clinton V., Jr. The U.S. Experience with Airline Deregulation: Productivity, Employment, and Labor Relations. *Meyer, J. R. and Oster, C. V., Jr.*, 1987, pp. 83–107. **[G: U.S.]**

Mickwitz, Gösta. Strukturomvandling och arbetslöshet. (Structural Change and Unemployment. With English summary.) *Ekon. Samfundets Tidskr.*, 1987, *40*(2), pp. 85–102. **[G: Finland]**

Miller, Paul W. and Volker, Paul. The Youth Labour Market In Australia. *Econ. Rec.*, September 1987, *63*(182), pp. 203–19. **[G: Australia]**

Minford, Patrick. The Performance of the British Economy: The Labour Market: Comment. *Dornbusch, R. and Layard, R., eds.*, 1987, pp. 260–62. **[G: U.K.]**

Mirkin, Barry Alan. Early Retirement as a Labor Force Policy: An International Overview. *Mon. Lab. Rev.*, March 1987, *110*(3), pp. 19–33. **[G: OECD]**

Mitchell, William F. The Nairu, Structural Imbalance and the Macroequilibrium Unemployment Rate. *Australian Econ. Pap.*, June 1987, *26*(48), pp. 101–18. **[G: Australia]**

Mitchell, William F. What Is the Full Employment Unemployment Rate? Some Empirical Evidence of Structural Unemployment in Australia, 1966 to 1986. *Australian Bull. Lab.*, December 1987, *14*(1), pp. 321–37. **[G: Australia]**

Mittar, Vishwa. Wage-Structure in the Informal Sector: The Case of a Class 1 City in Punjab.

Margin, July-Sept. 1987, *19*(4), pp. 41–50.
[G: India]

Modigliani, Franco, et al. Reducing Unemployment in Europe: The Role of Capital Formation. *Layard, R. and Calmfors, L., eds.,* 1987, pp. 11–47. [G: W. Europe]

Molho, Ian J. Decentralisation in the London Region: Some Policy Simulations. *Gordon, I., ed.,* 1987, pp. 116–38. [G: U.K.]

Montgomery, Mark R. The Impacts of Urban Population Growth on Urban Labor Markets and the Costs of Urban Service Delivery: A Review. *Johnson, D. G. and Lee, R. D., eds.,* 1987, pp. 149–88. [G: LDCs]

Moore, Gary A. Analytical Perspectives on Employment Discrimination under Title VII: Economic, Legal, and Statistical Approaches. *Amer. Econ.,* Fall 1987, *31*(2), pp. 53–63.
[G: U.S.]

Moore, Goeffrey H. The Service Industries and the Business Cycle. *Bus. Econ.,* April 1987, *22*(2), pp. 12–17. [G: U.S.]

Munnell, Alicia H. Lessons from the Income Maintenance Experiments: An Overview. *New Eng. Econ. Rev.,* May/June 1987, pp. 32–44.
[G: U.S.]

Murphy, Kevin M. and Topel, Robert H. The Evolution of Unemployment in the United States: 1968–1985. *Fischer, S., ed.,* 1987, pp. 11–58. [G: U.S.]

Murphy, Kevin M. and Topel, Robert H. Unemployment, Risk, and Earnings: Testing for Equalizing Wage Differences in the Labor Market. *Lang, K. and Leonard, J. S., eds.,* 1987, pp. 103–40. [G: U.S.]

Muysken, Joan and van Zon, A. H. Employment and Unemployment in the Netherlands, 1960–1984: A Putty–Clay Approach. *Rech. Écon. Louvain,* 1987, *53*(2), pp. 101–33.
[G: Netherlands]

Myers, Robert J. Forecasting the Number of Social Security Retirees: Improving Forecasts for Better Policy Making: Comment. *J. Policy Anal. Manage.,* Fall 1987, *7*(1), pp. 70–73.
[G: U.S.]

Myers, Samuel L., Jr. and Sabol, William J. Unemployment and Racial Differences in Imprisonment. *Rev. Black Polit. Econ.,* Summer-Fall 1987, *16*(1–2), pp. 189–209. [G: U.S.]

Naples, Michele I. An Analysis of Defensive Strikes. *Ind. Relat.,* Winter 1987, *26*(1), pp. 96–105. [G: U.S.]

Neelin, Janet. Sectoral Shifts and Canadian Unemployment. *Rev. Econ. Statist.,* November 1987, *69*(4), pp. 718–23. [G: Canada]

Newell, A. and Symons, J. S. V. Corporatism, Laissez-faire, and the Rise in Unemployment. *Europ. Econ. Rev.,* April 1987, *31*(3), pp. 567–601. [G: OECD]

Newton, Keith. Unemployment: Canada: Comment. *Gunderson, M.; Meltz, N. M. and Ostry, S., eds.,* 1987, pp. 179–81. [G: Canada]

Nickell, Stephen J. Jobless Pay and High European Unemployment: Comment. *Lawrence, R. Z. and Schultze, C. L., eds.,* 1987, pp. 162–68. [G: W. Europe]

Niehuss, Merith. From Welfare Provision to Social Insurance: The Unemployment in Augsburg 1918–27. *Evans, R. J. and Geary, D., eds.,* 1987, pp. 44–72. [G: Germany]

Noyelle, Thierry J. Services, Urban Economic Development, and Industrial Policy: Some Critical Linkages. *Goldstein, H. A., ed.,* 1987, pp. 73–84. [G: U.S.]

Noyelle, Thierry J. The New Technology and the New Economy: Some Implications for Equal Employment Opportunity. *Hartmann, H. I., ed.,* 1987, pp. 373–94. [G: U.S.]

Nuti, Domenico Mario. Profit-Sharing and Employment: Claims and Overclaims. *Ind. Relat.,* Winter 1987, *26*(1), pp. 18–29.

O'Hearn, Denis. Estimates of New Foreign Manufacturing Employment in Ireland (1956–1972). *Econ. Soc. Rev.,* April 1987, *18*(3), pp. 173–88. [G: Ireland]

Oberhauser, Ann. Labour, Production and the State: Decentralization of the French Automobile Industry. *Reg. Stud.,* October 1987, *21*(5), pp. 445–58. [G: France]

Oi, Walter Y. Comment on the Relation between Unemployment and Sectoral Shifts [Fluctuations in the Pace of Labor Reallocations]. *Carnegie–Rochester Conf. Ser. Public Policy,* Autumn 1987, *27,* pp. 403–20. [G: U.S.]

Olian, Judy D. and Guthrie, James P. Cognitive Ability Tests in Employment: Ethical Perspectives of Employers and Society. *Frederick, W. C., ed.,* 1987, pp. 185–212. [G: U.S.]

Osterman, Paul. Choice of Employment Systems in Internal Labor Markets. *Ind. Relat.,* Winter 1987, *26*(1), pp. 46–67.

Osterman, Paul. Turnover, Employment Security, and the Performance of the Firm. *Allen, S. G., et al.,* 1987, pp. 275–317. [G: U.S.]

Owen, Susan J. and Joshi, Heather E. Does Elastic Retract: The Effect of Recession on Women's Labour Force Participation. *Brit. J. Ind. Relat.,* March 1987, *25*(1), pp. 125–43.
[G: U.K.]

Palazzi, Paolo. Occupazione e orario di apertura dei negozi. (Employment and Shop Opening Hours. With English summary.) *Econ. Lavoro,* Jan.-Mar. 1987, *21*(1), pp. 19–33. [G: Italy]

Paldam, Martin. How Much Does One Percent of Growth Change the Unemployment Rate? A Study of 17 OECD Countries, 1948–1985. *Europ. Econ. Rev.,* Feb./Mar. 1987, *31*(1/2), pp. 306–13. [G: OECD]

Patel, Pari and Soete, Luc. Technological Trends and Employment in the UK Manufacturing Sectors. *Freeman, C. and Soete, L., eds.,* 1987, pp. 122–68. [G: U.K.]

Patton, Spiro G. and Reilly, Bernard J. The Role of Private Services in the American Economy. *Bus. Econ.,* April 1987, *22*(2), pp. 7–11.
[G: U.S.]

Peck, Francis and Townsend, Alan. The Impact of Technological Change upon the Spatial Pattern of UK Employment within Major Corporations. *Reg. Stud.,* June 1987, *21*(3), pp. 225–39. [G: U.K.]

Pedersen, Peder J. and Westergård-Nielsen,

Niels C. Multiple Spells of Unemployment—
The Danish Experience. *Pedersen, P. J. and
Lund, R., eds.*, 1987, pp. 105–28.
[G: Denmark]

Pedullà, Giovanna. Concetti e metodi utilizzati
in contabilità nazionale per la stima delle unità
di lavoro. (Concepts and Methods Utilized in
National Accounting for Estimating Work.
With English summary.) *Econ. Lavoro*, July-
Sept. 1987, *21*(3), pp. 23–37.   [G: Italy]

Peel, David A. Innovative Supply-Side Policies
to Reduce Unemployment: Commentary.
Begg, D. K. H., et al., 1987, pp. 118–21.
[G: U.K.]

Personick, Valerie A. Industry Output and Employment through the End of the Century.
Mon. Lab. Rev., September 1987, *110*(9), pp.
30–45.   [G: U.S.]

Peterson, William. The Cambridge Multisectoral
Dynamic Model of the British Economy: Employment. *Barker, T. and Peterson, W., eds.*,
1987, pp. 247–74.   [G: U.K.]

Peukert, Detlev. The Lost Generation: Youth Unemployment at the End of the Weimar Republic. *Evans, R. J. and Geary, D., eds.*, 1987,
pp. 172–93.   [G: Germany]

Pfeffer, Jeffrey and O'Reilly, Charles A., III.
Hospital Demography and Turnover among
Nurses. *Ind. Relat.*, Spring 1987, *26*(2), pp.
158–73.   [G: U.S.]

Pfeffermann, Guy. Economic Crisis and the Poor
in Some Latin American Countries. *Finance
Develop.*, June 1987, *24*(2), pp. 32–35.

Phillips, Llad and Votey, Harold L., Jr. The
Choice between Legitimate and Illegitimate
Work: Micro Study of Individual Behavior.
Contemp. Policy Issues, October 1987, *5*(4),
pp. 59–72.   [G: U.S.]

Philpott, John C. and Tyler, Godfrey J. Interpersonal Variation in Farm Workers' Earnings:
Analysis of Wages and Employment Enquiry
Data. *J. Agr. Econ.*, September 1987, *38*(3),
pp. 463–72.   [G: U.K.]

Piachaud, David. The Distribution of Income and
Work. *Oxford Rev. Econ. Policy*, Autumn
1987, *3*(3), pp. 41–61.   [G: U.K.]

Pierenkemper, Toni. The Standard of Living and
Employment in Germany, 1850–1980: An
Overview. *J. Europ. Econ. Hist.*, Spring 1987,
16(1), pp. 51–73.   [G: Germany]

Pietsch, Anna-Jutta; Vogel, Heinrich and Schroeder, Gertrude E. Displacement by Technological Progress in the USSR (Social and Educational Problems and Their Treatment). *Adam,
J., ed.*, 1987, pp. 149–70.   [G: U.S.S.R.]

Piore, Michael J. Historical Perspectives and the
Interpretation of Unemployment. *J. Econ.
Lit.*, December 1987, *25*(4), pp. 1834–50.
[G: U.S.; Europe]

Pissarides, Christopher A. Mass Unemployment:
A Review Essay. *J. Monet. Econ.*, July 1987,
20(1), pp. 183–88.   [G: E. Europe; U.S.]

Pissarides, Christopher A. Work Sharing: Why?
How? How Not . . . : Comments. *Layard, R.
and Calmfors, L., eds.*, 1987, pp. 193–97.
[G: OECD]

Podgursky, Michael and Swaim, Paul. Duration
of Joblessness Following Displacement. *Ind.
Relat.*, Fall 1987, *26*(3), pp. 213–26.
[G: U.S.]

Podgursky, Michael and Swaim, Paul. Job Displacement and Earnings Loss: Evidence from
the Displaced Worker Survey. *Ind. Lab. Relat.
Rev.*, October 1987, *41*(1), pp. 17–29.
[G: U.S.]

Podgursky, Michael and Swaim, Paul. Job Loss
and Job Change: Comment. *Ind. Lab. Relat.
Rev.*, October 1987, *41*(1), pp. 45–46.
[G: U.S.]

Powell, David E. Manpower Constraints and the
Use of Pensioners in the Soviet Economy.
Adam, J., ed., 1987, pp. 196–215.
[G: U.S.S.R.]

Powell, James L. Semiparametric Estimation of
Employment Duration Models: Comment.
Econometric Rev., 1987, *6*(1), pp. 65–78.
[G: U.S.]

Primorac, E. and Charette, Michael F. Regional
Aspects of Youth Unemployment in Yugoslavia. *Econ. Anal. Workers' Manage.*, 1987,
21(2), pp. 193–219.   [G: Yugoslavia]

Protti, Ray. Unemployment: Industrial Relations:
Comment. *Gunderson, M.; Meltz, N. M. and
Ostry, S., eds.*, 1987, pp. 206–08.
[G: Canada]

Pugh, Robert E. Forecasting the Number of So-
cial Security Retirees: Improving Forecasts for
Better Policy Making. *J. Policy Anal. Manage.*,
Fall 1987, *7*(1), pp. 62–69.   [G: U.S.]

Raffe, David. Small Expectations: The First Year
of the Youth Training Scheme. *Junankar, P.
N., ed.*, 1987, pp. 238–62.   [G: U.K.]

Rajan, Amin. The Young Workers' Scheme: A
Preliminary Assessment. *Junankar, P. N., ed.*,
1987, pp. 263–84.   [G: U.K.]

Rayack, Wendy. Sources and Centers of Cyclical
Movement in Real Wages: Evidence from
Panel Data. *J. Post Keynesian Econ.*, Fall 1987,
10(1), pp. 3–21.   [G: U.S.]

Rebitzer, James B. Unemployment, Long-term
Employment Relations, and Productivity
Growth. *Rev. Econ. Statist.*, November 1987,
69(4), pp. 627–35.   [G: U.S.]

Reichlin, Lucrezia. Broken Trends and Random
Walks: The Case of Italian Unemployment. *Ricerche Econ.*, Jan.-Mar. 1987, *41*(1), pp. 41–
61.   [G: Italy]

Reynolds, Bruce L. Trade, Employment, and In-
equality in Postreform China. *J. Compar.
Econ.*, September 1987, *11*(3), pp. 479–89.
[G: China]

Richards, J. The Industrial Distribution of the
Temporary Short-time Working Compensation
Scheme. *Appl. Econ.*, January 1987, *19*(1), pp.
111–25.   [G: U.K.]

Riddell, W. Craig. Reducing Unemployment:
Medium- and Long-term Considerations. *Gunderson, M.; Meltz, N. M. and Ostry, S., eds.*,
1987, pp. 152–63.   [G: Canada]

Ritter, A. R. M. The Labour Force, Employment
and Unemployment in Kenya. *Can. J. Devel.
Stud.*, 1987, *8*(2), pp. 203–26.   [G: Kenya]

Rives, Janet M. and Turner, Keith K. Women's Occupations as a Factor in Their Unemployment Rate Volatility. *Quart. Rev. Econ. Bus.*, Winter 1987, 27(4), pp. 55–64. **[G: U.S.]**

Roback, Jennifer. Determinants of the Local Unemployment Rate. *Southern Econ. J.*, January 1987, 53(3), pp. 735–50. **[G: Colombia]**

Robertson, David B. Labor Market Surgery, Labor Market Abandonment: The Thatcher and Reagan Unemployment Remedies. *Waltman, J. L. and Studlar, D. T., eds.*, 1987, pp. 69–97. **[G: U.K.; U.S.]**

Rockefeller, Jay. The Urgency of Assistance to Displaced Workers. *Barfield, C. E. and Makin, J. H., eds.*, 1987, pp. 100–103. **[G: U.S.]**

Rojas R., Patricio. Un Análisis Empírico de la demanda por Trabajo en Chile 1977–1985. (With English summary.) *Cuadernos Econ.*, April 1987, 24(71), pp. 77–97. **[G: Chile]**

Romijn, Hendrika A. Employment Generation through Cottage Industries in Rural Thailand: Potentials and Constraints. *Islam, R., ed.*, 1987, pp. 211–40. **[G: Thailand]**

Root, Lawrence S. Britain's Redundancy Payments for Displaced Workers. *Mon. Lab. Rev.*, June 1987, 110(6), pp. 18–23. **[G: U.K.]**

Rosenhaft, Eve. The Unemployed in the Neighbourhood: Social Dislocation and Political Mobilisation in Germany 1929–33. *Evans, R. J. and Geary, D., eds.*, 1987, pp. 194–227. **[G: Germany]**

Rosti, Luisa. L'occupazione indipendente in Italia: stock e flussi. (Self-Employment in Italy: Stock and Flow. With English summary.) *Econ. Lavoro*, Oct.-Dec. 1987, 21(4), pp. 15–27. **[G: Italy]**

Rotella, Elyce J. The Dynamics of Occupational Segregation among Bank Tellers: Comments. *Brown, C. and Pechman, J. A., eds.*, 1987, pp. 149–54. **[G: U.S.]**

Roy, Dilip Kumar. Employment Linkages in Bangladesh Industries. *Industry Devel.*, 1987, (21), pp. 63–74. **[G: Bangladesh]**

Ruhm, Christopher J. Job Tenure and Cyclical Changes in the Labor Market [Demographic Differences in Cyclical Employment Variations]. *Rev. Econ. Statist.*, May 1987, 69(2), pp. 372–78. **[G: U.S.]**

Rumberger, Russell W. The Impact of Salary Differentials on Teacher Shortages and Turnover: The Case of Mathematics and Science Teachers. *Econ. Educ. Rev.*, 1987, 6(4), pp. 389–99. **[G: U.S.]**

Sachs, Jeffrey D. High Unemployment in Europe: Diagnosis and Policy Implications. *Siven, C.-H., ed.*, 1987, pp. 7–38. **[G: W. Europe]**

Sammartino, Frank J. The Effect of Health on Retirement. *Soc. Sec. Bull.*, February 1987, 50(2), pp. 31–47.

Samuel, Howard D. Myths Surrounding Displaced Workers. *Barfield, C. E. and Makin, J. H., eds.*, 1987, pp. 104–06. **[G: U.S.]**

Sandell, Steven H. Labor Market Problems and Employment Policies Affecting Older Americans. *Sandell, S. H., ed.*, 1987, pp. 15–33. **[G: U.S.]**

Sandell, Steven H. Prospects for Older Workers: The Demographic and Economic Context. *Sandell, S. H., ed.*, 1987, pp. 3–14. **[G: U.S.]**

Santiago, Carlos E. Rehiring, Seniority, and Labor Force Adjustment. *J. Lab. Econ.*, Part 2, Oct. 1987, 5(4), pp. S18–35. **[G: U.S.]**

Santiago, Carlos E. The Impact of Foreign Direct Investment on Export Structure and Employment Generation. *World Devel.*, March 1987, 15(3), pp. 317–28. **[G: Puerto Rico]**

Saunders, Mark N. K. and Flowerdew, Robin. Spatial Aspects of the Provision of Job Information. *Fischer, M. M. and Nijkamp, P., eds.*, 1987, pp. 205–28. **[G: U.K.]**

Schatz, Klaus-Werner. The Contribution of Small and New Enterprise to Growth and Employment. *Gemper, B. B., ed.*, 1987, pp. 89–104. **[G: W. Europe]**

Schoer, Karl. Part-time Employment: Britain and West Germany. *Cambridge J. Econ.*, March 1987, 11(1), pp. 83–94. **[G: U.K.; W. Germany]**

Schott, Kerry. Lessons for Australia. *Stegman, T., et al.*, 1987, pp. 25–52. **[G: Australia; W. Europe; U.K.; Japan]**

Schultze, Charles L. Real Wages, Real Wage Aspirations, and Unemployment in Europe. *Lawrence, R. Z. and Schultze, C. L., eds.*, 1987, pp. 230–91. **[G: W. Europe]**

Schütz, Joachim and Frey, Martin. Zur Arbeitslosigkeit infolge technologischer Revolutionen. (On Unemployment by Technological Revolutions. With English summary.) *Konjunkturpolitik*, 1987, 33(4), pp. 211–18. **[G: OECD]**

Schwab, Donald P.; Rynes, Sara L. and Aldag, Ramon J. Theories and Research on Job Search and Choice. *Rowland, K. M. and Ferris, G. R., eds.*, 1987, pp. 129–66. **[G: U.S.]**

Seeborg, Michael and DeBoer, Larry. The Narrowing Male–Female Unemployment Differential. *Growth Change*, Spring 1987, 18(2), pp. 24–37. **[G: U.S.]**

Sengenberger, Werner and Kohler, Ch. Policies of Workforce Reduction and Labour Market Structures in the American and German Automobile Industry. *Tarling, R., ed.*, 1987, pp. 245–69. **[G: W. Germany; U.S.]**

Shank, Susan E. and Haugen, Steven E. The Employment Situation during 1986: Job Gains Continue, Unemployment Dips. *Mon. Lab. Rev.*, February 1987, 110(2), pp. 3–10. **[G: U.S.]**

Shaw, Kathryn L. The Quit Propensity of Married Men. *J. Lab. Econ.*, Part 1, Oct. 1987, 5(4), pp. 533–60. **[G: U.S.]**

Shields, Jon. Curing Unemployment through Labour-Market Competition: Commentary. *Begg, D. K. H., et al.*, 1987, pp. 150–54. **[G: U.K.]**

Shulman, Steven. Discrimination, Human Capital, and Black–White Unemployment: Evidence from Cities. *J. Human Res.*, Summer 1987, 22(3), pp. 361–76. **[G: U.S.]**

Siegel, Lewis B. BLS Surveys Mass Layoffs and Plant Closings in 1986. *Mon. Lab. Rev.*, October 1987, *110*(10), pp. 39–40.   [G: U.S.]

Siesto, Vincenzo. Situazione e prospettive del lavoro nel mezzogiorno. (Actual Situation and Future Prospects for the Labour Market in the Mezzogiorno Area. With English summary.) *Econ. Lavoro,* Jan.-Mar. 1987, *21*(1), pp. 77–95.   [G: Italy]

Simon, Curtis J. Industrial Diversity, Vacancy Dispersion, and Unemployment. *Ann. Reg. Sci.,* July 1987, *21*(2), pp. 60–73.   [G: U.S.]

Siven, Claes-Henric. The Wage Structure and the Functioning of the Labor Market. *Siven, C.-H., ed.,* 1987, pp. 71–97.   [G: Sweden]

Slade, Frederic P. Retirement Status and State Dependence: A Longitudinal Study of Older Men. *J. Lab. Econ.,* January 1987, *5*(1), pp. 90–105.   [G: U.S.]

Sloan, Judith. The Australian Labour Market, June 1987. *Australian Bull. Lab.,* June 1987, *13*(3), pp. 130–42.   [G: Australia]

Sloan, Judith and Tulsi, Narmon. The Australian Labour Market, September 1987. *Australian Bull. Lab.,* September 1987, *13*(4), pp. 199–224.   [G: Australia; OECD]

Sneessens, Henri R. and Drèze, Jacques H. A Discussion of Belgian Unemployment, Combining Traditional Concepts and Disequilibrium Econometrics. *Steinherr, A. and Weiserbs, D., eds.,* 1987, pp. 239–82.
     [G: Belgium]

Sørensen, Aage B. Employment Relations and Employment Processes. *Pedersen, P. J. and Lund, R., eds.,* 1987, pp. 47–65.

Sorensen, Duane L. The Cummins Engine Company Dislocated Worker Project. *Cook, R. F., ed.,* 1987, pp. 15–30.   [G: U.S.]

Sorrentino, Constance. Japanese Unemployment: BLS Updates Its Analysis. *Mon. Lab. Rev.,* June 1987, *110*(6), pp. 47–53.   [G: Japan]

Spencer, Ken. The West Midlands: An Economy in Crisis. *Hausner, V. A., et al.,* 1987, pp. 218–53.   [G: U.K.]

Spring, William J. Youth Unemployment and the Transition from School to Work: Programs in Boston, Frankfurt, and London. *New Eng. Econ. Rev.,* Mar./Apr. 1987, pp. 3–16.
     [G: U.S.; U.K.; W. Germany]

Staiger, Robert W.; Deardorff, Alan V. and Stern, Robert M. Employment Effects of Japanese and American Protectionism. *Salvatore, D., ed.,* 1987, pp. 164–80.   [G: U.S.; Japan]

Standing, Guy. Reply [Labour Flexibility and Older Worker Marginalisation: The Need for a New Strategy]. *Int. Lab. Rev.,* 1987, *126*(3), pp. 372–74.   [G: EEC]

Steinberg, Danny and Monforte, Frank A. Estimating the Effects of Job Search Assistance and Training Programs on the Unemployment Durations of Displaced Workers. *Lang, K. and Leonard, J. S., eds.,* 1987, pp. 186–206.
     [G: U.S.]

Stewart, Frances. Supporting Productive Employment among Vulnerable Groups. *Cornia, G. A.; Jolly, R. and Stewart, F., eds.,* 1987, pp. 197–217.   [G: LDCs]

Stinson, John F., Jr. Moonlighting: A Key to Dif-

ferences in Measuring Employment Growth. *Mon. Lab. Rev.,* February 1987, *110*(2), pp. 30–31.   [G: U.S.]

Stone, Charles F. and Sawhill, Isabel V. Trade's Impact on U.S. Jobs. *Challenge,* Sept./Oct. 1987, *30*(4), pp. 12–18.   [G: U.S.]

Strober, Myra H. and Arnold, Carolyn L. The Dynamics of Occupational Segregation among Bank Tellers. *Brown, C. and Pechman, J. A., eds.,* 1987, pp. 107–48.   [G: U.S.]

Strom, Sharon Hartman. "Machines Instead of Clerks": Technology and the Feminization of Bookkeeping, 1910–1950. *Hartmann, H. I., ed.,* 1987, pp. 63–97.   [G: U.S.]

Summers, Lawrence H. Corporatism, Laissez-faire, and the Rise in Unemployment: Comments. *Europ. Econ. Rev.,* April 1987, *31*(3), pp. 606–14.   [G: OECD]

Sylos-Labini, Paolo. The Theory of Unemployment, Too, Is Historically Conditioned. *Banca Naz. Lavoro Quart. Rev.,* December 1987, (163), pp. 379–435.   [G: OECD]

Tachibanaki, Toshiaki. Labour Market Flexibility in Japan in Comparison with Europe and the U.S. *Europ. Econ. Rev.,* April 1987, *31*(3), pp. 647–78.   [G: Japan; OECD]

Tarantelli, Ezio. Monetary Policy and the Regulation of Inflation and Unemployment. *Gunderson, M.; Meltz, N. M. and Ostry, S., eds.,* 1987, pp. 94–102.   [G: W. Europe]

Thakur, D. S. A Survey of Rural Unemployment in India: A Critique of Unidimensional Approach. *Indian Econ. J.,* July-Sept. 1987, *35*(1), pp. 120–35.   [G: India]

Theeuwes, Jules. Jobless Pay and High European Unemployment: Comment. *Lawrence, R. Z. and Schultze, C. L., eds.,* 1987, pp. 168–72.
     [G: W. Europe; U.S.]

Thomas, Ian C. and Drudy, P. J. The Impact of Factory Development on 'Growth Town' Employment in Mid-Wales. *Urban Stud.,* October 1987, *24*(5), pp. 361–78.   [G: U.K.]

Thompson, Grahame. Unemployment and Technology. *Thompson, G.; Brown, V. and Levačić, R., eds.,* 1987, pp. 134–60.   [G: U.K.]

Thrift, Nigel. The Growth of Service Class Labour Markets: The Case of Great Britain. *Fischer, M. M. and Nijkamp, P., eds.,* 1987, pp. 313–44.   [G: U.K.]

Timár, János. Employment Policy in Hungary. *Adam, J., ed.,* 1987, pp. 103–24.
     [G: Hungary]

Tobin, James. Keynesian and Classical Unemployment in Four Countries: Comments. *Brookings Pap. Econ. Act.,* 1987, (1), pp. 198–205. [G: U.S.; U.K.; W. Germany; Austria]

Tobin, James. Macroeconomic Diagnosis and Prescription. *Gunderson, M.; Meltz, N. M. and Ostry, S., eds.,* 1987, pp. 12–40. [G: OECD]

Tobin, James. Running the Economy with Less Unemployment and Poverty (Comments on the Bishops' Pastoral Letter on Catholic Social Teaching and the Economy). *Tobin, J. (III),* 1987, *1985,* pp. 488–94.   [G: U.S.]

Tobin, James. Unemployment in the 1980s: Macroeconomic Diagnosis and Prescription. *Tobin,*

J. (III), 1987, *1984*, pp. 386–414.   [G: U.S.; OECD]

Tokman, Víctor E. Unequal Development and the Absorption of Labor. *Dietz, J. L. and Street, J. H., eds.*, 1987, pp. 228–40.
[G: Latin America]

Tokman, Víctor E. and Wurgaft, J. The Recession and the Workers of Latin America. *International Labour Office.*, 1987, pp. 37–74.
[G: Latin America]

Tomey, E. Allan. The Missouri Dislocated Worker Program: Job Search Assistance, Inc. *Cook, R. F., ed.*, 1987, pp. 71–91. [G: U.S.]

Trivedi, Pravin K. and Hui, W. T. An Empirical Study of Long-term Unemployment in Australia. *J. Lab. Econ.*, January 1987, *5*(1), pp. 20–42.   [G: Australia]

Tullio, Giuseppe. Long-run Implications of the Increase in Taxation and Public Debt for Employment and Economic Growth in Europe. *Europ. Econ. Rev.*, April 1987, *31*(3), pp. 741–74.   [G: W. Europe]

Turnage, Wayne M. The Hillsborough, North Carolina Dislocated Worker Project. *Cook, R. F., ed.*, 1987, pp. 93–109.   [G: U.S.]

Turner, David S.; Wallis, Kenneth F. and Whitley, John D. Evaluating Special Employment Measures with Macroeconometric Models. *Oxford Rev. Econ. Policy*, Autumn 1987, *3*(3), pp. xxv–xxxvi.   [G: U.K.]

Ulman, Lloyd. The Dynamics of Occupational Segregation among Bank Tellers: Comments. *Brown, C. and Pechman, J. A., eds.*, 1987, pp. 154–57.   [G: U.S.]

Van Rompuy, Paul. Hysteresis, Persistence, and the NAIRU: An Empirical Analysis for the Federal Republic of Germany: Comments. *Layard, R. and Calmfors, L., eds.*, 1987, pp. 132–38.
[G: W. Germany]

Vane, Howard. Unemployment: Causes of, Cures for, and Costs of. *Vane, H. and Caslin, T., eds.*, 1987, pp. 103–30.   [G: U.K.]

Vijverberg, Wim P. M. Decomposing the Earnings Differentials in Peninsular Malaysia. *Singapore Econ. Rev.*, April 1987, *32*(1), pp. 24–36.

Vipond, Joan; Bradbury, Bruce and Encel, Diana. Unemployment and Poverty: Measures of Association. *Australian Bull. Lab.*, June 1987, *13*(3), pp. 179–92.   [G: Australia]

Wachter, Michael. Keynesian and Classical Unemployment in Four Countries: Comments. *Brookings Pap. Econ. Act.*, 1987, (1), pp. 244–47.   [G: U.S.]

Wadhwani, Sushil B. The Effects of Inflation and Real Wages on Employment. *Economica*, February 1987, *54*(213), pp. 21–40.   [G: U.K.]

Waelbroeck, Jean. Corporatism, Laissez-faire, and the Rise in Unemployment: Comments. *Europ. Econ. Rev.*, April 1987, *31*(3), pp. 602–05.   [G: OECD]

Wallis, John Joseph. Employment, Politics, and Economic Recovery during the Great Depression. *Rev. Econ. Statist.*, August 1987, *69*(3), pp. 516–20.   [G: U.S.]

Warburton, Peter. Labour Supply Incentives for

the Retired. *Beenstock, M., et al.*, 1987, pp. 185–234.   [G: U.K.]

Weber, Arnold R. and Taylor, David P. Problems of Advance Notice [Procedures for Employee Displacement: Advance Notice of Plant Shutdown]. *Staudohar, P. D. and Brown, H. E.*, 1987, *1963*, pp. 135–38.   [G: U.S.]

Weber, Bruce A.; Castle, Emery N. and Shriver, Ann L. The Performance of Natural Resource Industries. *U.S.D.A., Econ. Res. Serv., Agr. and Rural Econ. Div.*, 1987, pp. 5.1–37.
[G: U.S.]

Weiler, William C. Economic Issues in Faculty Retirement Plans in American Higher Education Institutions. *Econ. Educ. Rev.*, 1987, *6*(3), pp. 207–26.   [G: U.S.]

Weller, Barry R. and Kurre, James A. Applicability of the Transfer Function Approach to Forecasting Employment Levels in Small Regions. *Ann. Reg. Sci.*, March 1987, *21*(1), pp. 34–43.   [G: U.S.]

Wells, William. The Relative Pay and Employment of Young People. *Junankar, P. N., ed.*, 1987, pp. 51–78.   [G: OECD]

Westerhoff, Horst-Dieter. Probleme der Arbeitslosenstatistik. (Problems of Unemployment Statistics. With English summary.) *Ifo-Studien*, 1987, *33*(2), pp. 101–32.
[G: W. Germany]

White, Gordon. Labour Market Reform in Chinese Industry. *Warner, M., ed.*, 1987, pp. 113–26.   [G: China]

Whiteford, Peter. Unemployment and Families. *Australian Bull. Lab.*, December 1987, *14*(1), pp. 338–57.   [G: Australia]

Whiteside, Noel. The Social Consequences of Interwar Unemployment. *Glynn, S. and Booth, A., eds.*, 1987, pp. 17–30.   [G: U.K.]

Wielgosz, John B. and Carpenter, Susan. The Effectiveness of Alternative Methods of Searching for Jobs and Finding Them: An Exploratory Analysis of the Data Bearing upon the Ways of Coping with Joblessness. *Amer. J. Econ. Soc.*, April 1987, *46*(2), pp. 151–64.
[G: U.S.]

Wilkinson, Frank. Deregulation, Structured Labour Markets and Unemployment. *Pedersen, P. J. and Lund, R., eds.*, 1987, pp. 167–85.
[G: W. Europe]

Winter, Søren. Implementation of Danish Youth Employment Policy. *Pedersen, P. J. and Lund, R., eds.*, 1987, pp. 259–84.   [G: Denmark]

Wohl, Lawrence A. The Minnesota Iron Range Dislocated Worker Project. *Cook, R. F., ed.*, 1987, pp. 47–70.   [G: U.S.]

Wohlers, Eckhardt. Labour Market Flexibility and Jobs: A Survey of Evidence from OECD Countries with Special Reference to Europe: Comments. *Layard, R. and Calmfors, L., eds.*, 1987, pp. 85–90.   [G: OECD]

Wolpin, Kenneth I. Estimating a Structural Search Model: The Transition from School to Work. *Econometrica*, July 1987, *55*(4), pp. 801–17.   [G: U.S.]

Woodbury, Stephen A. and Spiegelman, Robert G. Bonuses to Workers and Employers to Reduce Unemployment: Randomized Trials in Illinois. *Amer. Econ. Rev.*, September 1987, 77(4), pp. 513–30. [G: U.S.]

Wooden, Mark and Sloan, Judith. Plant Shutdown: A Case Study in Managed Change. *Australian Bull. Lab.*, December 1987, 14(1), pp. 358–81. [G: Australia]

Worrall, Leslie. Information Systems for Urban Labour-Market Planning and Analysis. *Gordon, I., ed.*, 1987, pp. 139–57. [G: U.K.]

Wulff, Birgit. The Third Reich and the Unemployed: National Socialist Work-Creation Schemes in Hamburg 1933–4. *Evans, R. J. and Geary, D., eds.*, 1987, pp. 281–302. [G: Germany]

Wyplosz, Charles. Hysteresis, Persistence, and the NAIRU: An Empirical Analysis for the Federal Republic of Germany: Comments. *Layard, R. and Calmfors, L., eds.*, 1987, pp. 123–31. [G: W. Germany]

Yamada, Tadashi and Yamada, Tetsuji. Labor Employment of Married Women in Japan: Part-time Work vs. Full-time Work. *Eastern Econ. J.*, Jan.-Mar. 1987, 13(1), pp. 41–48. [G: Japan]

Yamada, Tadashi and Yamada, Tetsuji. Part-time Work of Married Women in Urban Japan. *Quart. Rev. Econ. Bus.*, Spring 1987, 27(1), pp. 41–50. [G: Japan]

Yamada, Tadashi; Yamada, Tetsuji and Chaloupka, Frank. Using Aggregate Data to Estimate the Part-Time and Full-Time Work Behavior of Japanese Women [An Analysis of Trends in Female Labor Force Participation in Japan]. *J. Human Res.*, Fall 1987, 22(4), pp. 574–83. [G: Japan]

Yoder, Dale and Staudohar, Paul D. Management and Public Policy [Management and Public Policy in Plant Closure]. *Staudohar, P. D. and Brown, H. E.*, 1987, 1985, pp. 183–200. [G: U.S.]

825 Productivity Studies: Labor, Capital, and Total Factor

8250 Productivity Studies: Labor, Capital, and Total Factor

Adams, Charles; Fenton, Paul R. and Larsen, Flemming. Potential Output in Major Industrial Countries. *International Monetary Fund Research Department.*, 1987, pp. 1–38. [G: OECD]

Ahmed, Ziaul Z. and Sieling, Mark. Two Decades of Productivity Growth in Poultry Dressing and Processing. *Mon. Lab. Rev.*, April 1987, 110(4), pp. 34–39. [G: U.S.]

Altman, Morris. A Revision of Canadian Economic Growth: 1870–1910 (A Challenge to the Gradualist Interpretation). *Can. J. Econ.*, February 1987, 20(1), pp. 86–113. [G: Canada]

Andrisani, Paul and Daymont, Thomas. Age Changes in Productivity and Earnings among Managers and Professionals. *Sandell, S. H., ed.*, 1987, pp. 52–70. [G: U.S.]

Auer, Ludwig. Canadian Hospital Costs and Productivity. *Economic Council of Canada.*, 1987, pp. 179–85. [G: Canada]

d'Autume, Antoine and Michel, Philippe. Repères sur la substitution capital-travail. (Notes on Capital Labor Substitution. With English summary.) *Revue Écon.*, May 1987, 38(3), pp. 703–23. [G: France]

Baily, Martin Neil. Crazy Explanations for the Productivity Slowdown: Comment. *Fischer, S., ed.*, 1987, pp. 205–08.

Bairam, Erkin I. Returns to Scale, Technical Progress and Output Growth in Branches of Industry: The Case of Soviet Republics, 1962–74. *Scot. J. Polit. Econ.*, August 1987, 34(3), pp. 249–66. [G: U.S.S.R.]

Bairam, Erkin I. The Verdoorn Law, Returns to Scale and Industrial Growth: A Review of the Literature. *Australian Econ. Pap.*, June 1987, 26(48), pp. 20–42. [G: OECD]

Bartel, Ann P. and Lichtenberg, Frank R. The Skill Distribution and Competitive Trade Advantage of High-Technology Industries. *Lewin, D.; Lipsky, D. B. and Sockell, D., eds.*, 1987, pp. 161–76. [G: U.S.]

Beeson, Patricia. Total Factor Productivity Growth and Agglomeration Economies in Manufacturing, 1959–73. *J. Reg. Sci.*, May 1987, 27(2), pp. 183–99. [G: U.S.]

Bemmels, Brian. How Unions Affect Productivity in Manufacturing Plants. *Ind. Lab. Relat. Rev.*, January 1987, 40(2), pp. 241–53. [G: U.S.]

Bergson, Abram. Comparative Productivity: The USSR, Eastern Europe, and the West. *Amer. Econ. Rev.*, June 1987, 77(3), pp. 342–57. [G: OECD; CMEA]

Bernanke, Ben S. Crazy Explanations for the Productivity Slowdown: Comment. *Fischer, S., ed.*, 1987, pp. 202–05.

Berndt, Ernst R. and Wood, David O. Energy Price Shocks and Productivity Growth: A Survey. *[Adelman, M. A.]*, 1987, pp. 305–42.

Bishop, John. The Recognition and Reward of Employee Performance. *J. Lab. Econ.*, Part 2, Oct. 1987, 5(4), pp. S36–56. [G: U.S.]

Björklund, Anders. The Wage Structure and the Functioning of the Labor Market: Comment. *Siven, C.-H., ed.*, 1987, pp. 98–102. [G: Sweden]

Blades, Derek. Goods and Services in OECD Countries. *OECD Econ. Stud.*, Spring 1987, (8), pp. 159–84. [G: OECD]

Branson, William H. Productivity, Wages, and Prices inside and outside Manufacturing in the U.S., Japan, and Europe: Comments. *Europ. Econ. Rev.*, April 1987, 31(3), pp. 733–36. [G: U.S.; Japan; Europe]

Breev, B. Evaluating the Utilization of Labor Resources. *Prob. Econ.*, January 1987, 29(9), pp. 5–19. [G: U.S.S.R.]

Brockhoff, Klaus. Die Produktivität der Forschung und Entwicklung eines Industrieunternehmens: Eine Erwiderung. (With English summary.) *Z. Betriebswirtshaft*, January 1987, 57(1), pp. 81–85. [G: W. Germany]

Byrnes, Patricia and Färe, Rolf. Surface Mining of Coal: Efficiency of U.S. Interior Mines.

Appl. Econ., December 1987, *19*(12), pp. 1665–73. **[G: U.S.]**

Carter, Michael G. The Australian Economy in the Long Run: The Service Sector. *Maddock, R. and McLean, I. W., eds.*, 1987, pp. 195–226. **[G: Australia]**

Caves, Douglas W., et al. An Assessment of the Efficiency Effects of U.S. Airline Deregulation via an International Comparison. *Bailey, E. E., ed.*, 1987, pp. 285–320. **[G: U.S.]**

Chan, M. W. Luke and Mountain, Dean C. Measuring Contributing Factors to Interregional Agricultural Labor Productivity Differentials: A Joint Profit Formulation. *J. Reg. Sci.*, May 1987, *27*(2), pp. 269–81. **[G: Canada]**

Chen, Tain-Jy and Tang, De-Piao. Offshore Assembly and Short-run Labor–Labor Substitution. *Weltwirtsch. Arch.*, 1987, *123*(1), pp. 140–48. **[G: Taiwan]**

Clark, Gregory. Productivity Growth without Technical Change in European Agriculture before 1850. *J. Econ. Hist.*, June 1987, *47*(2), pp. 419–32. **[G: Europe; U.S.]**

Clark, John A. A Vintage–Capital Simulation Model. *Freeman, C. and Soete, L., eds.*, 1987, pp. 86–98.

Clark, John A.; Patel, Pari and Soete, Luc. Future Employment Trends in UK Manufacturing Using a Capital–Vintage Simulation Model. *Freeman, C. and Soete, L., eds.*, 1987, pp. 99–118. **[G: U.K.]**

Crafts, N. F. R. British Economic Growth, 1700–1850; Some Difficulties of Interpretation. *Exploration Econ. Hist.*, July 1987, *24*(3), pp. 245–68. **[G: U.K.]**

Crew, Michael A. and Kleindorfer, Paul R. Productivity Incentives and Rate-of-Return Regulation. *Crew, M. A., ed.*, 1987, pp. 7–23. **[G: U.S.]**

Crosby, Philip B. A Journey for Quality Improvement. *Shetty, Y. K. and Buehler, V. M., eds.*, 1987, pp. 285–99. **[G: U.S.]**

Dabir-Alai, Parviz. Trends in Productivity Growth across Large Scale Manufacturing Industries of India: 1973/74 to 1978/79. *Indian Econ. Rev.*, July-Dec. 1987, *22*(2), pp. 151–78. **[G: India]**

Desai, Padma. Total Factor Productivity in Postwar Soviet Industry and Its Branches. *Desai, P.*, 1987, *1985*, pp. 78–98. **[G: U.S.S.R.]**

Desai, Padma and Martin, Ricardo. Efficiency Loss from Resource Misallocation in Soviet Industry. *Desai, P.*, 1987, *1983*, pp. 117–29. **[G: U.S.S.R.]**

Deutsch, Edwin and Schöpp, Wolfgang. Civil versus Military R&D Expenditures and Industrial Productivity. *Schmidt, C., ed.*, 1987, pp. 336–56. **[G: OECD]**

Eads, George C. Industrial Relations and Productivity in the U.S. Automobile Industry: Comments and Discussions. *Brookings Pap. Econ. Act.*, 1987, (3), pp. 720–25.

Eberts, Randall W. and Stone, Joe A. Teacher Unions and the Productivity of Public Schools. *Ind. Lab. Relat. Rev.*, April 1987, *40*(3), pp. 354–63. **[G: U.S.]**

Eden, Benjamin. Trading Uncertainty, Markups, and Productivity: A Comment [Productivity and the Business Cycle]. *Carnegie–Rochester Conf. Ser. Public Policy*, Autumn 1987, *27*, pp. 445–52. **[G: U.S.]**

Edmondson, Harold E. Manufacturing Excellence at HP in an Autonomous Environment. *Shetty, Y. K. and Buehler, V. M., eds.*, 1987, pp. 363–71. **[G: U.S.]**

Estrin, Saul; Jones, Derek C. and Svejnar, Jan. The Productivity Effects of Worker Participation: Producer Cooperatives in Western Economies. *J. Compar. Econ.*, March 1987, *11*(1), pp. 40–61. **[G: Spain; Italy; U.K.; France]**

Everitt, Leo H., Jr. FMC's Manufacturing Strategy Makes It Happen. *Shetty, Y. K. and Buehler, V. M., eds.*, 1987, pp. 373–81. **[G: U.S.]**

Fel'zenbaum, V. and Shapovalova, E. Material Incentives and the Economic Effect of New Technology. *Prob. Econ.*, August 1987, *30*(4), pp. 79–94. **[G: U.S.S.R.]**

Ferleger, Lou and Mandle, Jay R. Democracy and Productivity in the Future American Economy. *Rev. Radical Polit. Econ.*, Winter 1987, *19*(4), pp. 1–15. **[G: U.S.]**

Feuer, Carl Henry. The Performance of the Cuban Sugar Industry, 1981–85. *Zimbalist, A., ed.*, 1987, pp. 69–83. **[G: Cuba]**

Fischer, Karl-Heinz. Die produktivität der Forschung und Entwicklung eines Industrieunternehmens: Ein Kommentar. (With English summary.) *Z. Betriebswirtshaft*, January 1987, *57*(1), pp. 77–80. **[G: W. Germany]**

FitzRoy, Felix R. and Kraft, Kornelius. Cooperation, Productivity, and Profit Sharing. *Quart. J. Econ.*, February 1987, *102*(1), pp. 23–35. **[G: W. Germany]**

Flaherty, Sean. Strike Activity & Productivity Change: The U.S. Auto Industry. *Ind. Relat.*, Spring 1987, *26*(2), pp. 174–85. **[G: U.S.]**

Flaherty, Sean. Strike Activity, Worker Militancy, and Productivity Change in Manufacturing, 1961–1981. *Ind. Lab. Relat. Rev.*, July 1987, *40*(4), pp. 585–600. **[G: U.S.]**

Fluet, Claude and Lefebvre, Pierre. The Sharing of Total Factor Productivity Gains in Canadian Manufacturing: A Price Accounting Approach 1965–1980. *Appl. Econ.*, February 1987, *19*(2), pp. 245–57. **[G: Canada]**

Fortune, J. Neill. Some Determinants of Labour Productivity. *Appl. Econ.*, June 1987, *19*(6), pp. 839–43. **[G: U.S.]**

Fuss, Melvyn A. and Waverman, Leonard. The Japanese Productivity Advantage in Automobile Production: Can It Be Transferred to North America? *Safarian, A. E. and Bertin, G. Y., eds.*, 1987, pp. 191–206. **[G: Japan]**

George, Edward Y. Impact of the Maquilas on Manpower Development and Economic Growth on the U.S./Mexico Border. *Tremblay, R., ed.*, 1987, pp. 549–78. **[G: U.S.; Mexico]**

Godden, David. (Thinly) Disguised Politics? *Rev. Marketing Agr. Econ.*, August 1987, *55*(2), pp. 115–16. **[G: Australia]**

Gordon, Robert J. Productivity, Wages, and Prices inside and outside of Manufacturing in

the U.S., Japan, and Europe. *Europ. Econ. Rev.*, April 1987, *31*(3), pp. 685–733.
[G: U.S.; Japan; Europe]

Goudriaan, René; De Groot, Hans and van Tulder, Frank. Public Sector Productivity: Recent Empirical Findings and Policy Applications. *van de Kar, H. M. and Wolfe, B. L., eds.*, 1987, pp. 193–209. [G: U.S.; Netherlands]

Graham, George M., Jr. Total Quality at Texas Instruments. *Shetty, Y. K. and Buehler, V. M., eds.*, 1987, pp. 331–38. [G: U.S.]

Graves, Philip E.; Lee, Dwight R. and Sexton, Robert L. A Note on Interfirm Implications of Wages and Status. *J. Lab. Res.*, Spring 1987, *8*(2), pp. 209–12. [G: U.S.]

Gray, Wayne B. The Cost of Regulation: OSHA, EPA and the Productivity Slowdown. *Amer. Econ. Rev.*, December 1987, *77*(5), pp. 998–1006. [G: U.S.]

Gregory, Paul R. Productivity, Slack, and Time Theft in the Soviet Economy. *Millar, J. R., ed.*, 1987, pp. 241–75. [G: U.S.S.R.]

Gullickson, William and Harper, Michael J. Multifactor Productivity in U.S. Manufacturing, 1949–83. *Mon. Lab. Rev.*, October 1987, *110*(10), pp. 18–28. [G: U.S.]

Guzzo, Richard A. and Katzell, Raymond A. Effects of Economic Incentives on Productivity: A Psychological View. *Nalbantian, H. R., ed.*, 1987, pp. 107–19.

Gyimah-Brempong, Kwabena. Elasticity of Factor Substitution in Police Agencies: Evidence from Florida. *J. Bus. Econ. Statist.*, April 1987, *5*(2), pp. 257–65. [G: U.S.]

Hall, Robert E. Productivity and the Business Cycle. *Carnegie–Rochester Conf. Ser. Public Policy*, Autumn 1987, 27, pp. 421–44. [G: U.S.]

Harris, Harry G. Foreign Competition Stimulates Management Initiatives—A Look at the American Automobile Industry. *Tremblay, R., ed.*, 1987, pp. 595–601. [G: U.S.]

Harrison, Bennett. Cold Bath or Restructuring? An Expansion of the Weisskopf–Bowles–Gordon Framework. *Sci. Soc.*, Spring 1987, *51*(1), pp. 72–82. [G: U.S.]

Hartley, Keith. The Evaluation of Efficiency in the Arms Industry. *Borner, S. and Taylor, A., eds.*, 1987, pp. 181–201.

Hausman, William J. The English Coastal Coal Trade, 1691–1910: How Rapid Was Productivity Growth? [Total Factor Productivity in the English Shipping Industry: The North-east Coal Trade, 1700–1850]. *Econ. Hist. Rev., 2nd Ser.*, November 1987, *40*(4), pp. 588–96. [G: U.K.]

Hayami, Yujiro and Ruttan, Vernon W. Population Growth and Agricultural Productivity. *Johnson, D. G. and Lee, R. D., eds.*, 1987, pp. 57–101. [G: Global]

Heichel, Gary H. Anticipating Advances in Crop Technology. *Ruttan, V. W. and Pray, C. E., eds.*, 1987, pp. 235–44. [G: U.S.]

Henley, John S. and Ereisha, Mohamed M. State Control and the Labor Productivity Crisis: The Egyptian Textile Industry at Work. *Econ. Develop. Cult. Change*, April 1987, *35*(3), pp. 491–521.

Herman, Arthur S. Productivity Gains Continued in Many Industries during 1985. *Mon. Lab. Rev.*, April 1987, *110*(4), pp. 48–52. [G: U.S.]

Herman, Arthur S. and Henneberger, J. Edwin. Productivity Trends in the Furniture and Home Furnishings Stores Industry. *Mon. Lab. Rev.*, May 1987, *110*(5), pp. 24–29. [G: U.S.]

Hirsch, Barry T. and Hausman, William J. Labouring: A Reply [Labour Productivity in the British and South Wales Coal Industry, 1874–1914]. *Economica*, November 1987, *54*(216), pp. 525. [G: U.K.]

Hoke, Donald. British and American Horology: Time to Test Factor-Substitution Models. *J. Econ. Hist.*, June 1987, *47*(2), pp. 321–27. [G: U.S.; U.K.]

Hossain, Mahabub. Employment Generation through Cottage Industries—Potentials and Constraints: The Case of Bangladesh. *Islam, R., ed.*, 1987, pp. 19–57. [G: Bangladesh]

Hossain, Shaikh I. Allocative and Technical Efficiency: A Study of Rural Enterprises in Bangladesh. *Devel. Econ.*, March 1987, *25*(1), pp. 56–72. [G: Bangladesh]

Inoue, Tadashi. A Comparison of the Labor Productivities between Japan and the United States. *Dutta, M., ed. (II)*, 1987, pp. 29–40. [G: Japan; U.S.]

Islam, Rizwanul and Shrestha, Ram Prasad. Employment Expansion through Cottage Industries in Nepal: Potentials and Constraints. *Islam, R., ed.*, 1987, pp. 107–33. [G: Nepal]

Jimeno, Juan F. La flexibilidad de los costes laborales nominales en la industria española (1978–1982). (With English summary.) *Invest. Econ.*, September 1987, *11*(3), pp. 483–96. [G: Spain]

Jones, Derek C. The Productivity Effects of Worker Directors and Financial Participation by Employees in the Firm: The Case of British Retail Cooperatives. *Ind. Lab. Relat. Rev.*, October 1987, *41*(1), pp. 79–92. [G: U.K.]

Jones, Graham. Contemporary Industrial Relations: Dilemmas and Prospects. *Australian Bull. Lab.*, June 1987, *13*(3), pp. 162–78. [G: Australia]

Jorgenson, Dale W. Productivity and Changes in Ownership of Manufacturing Plants: Comments and Discussion. *Brookings Pap. Econ. Act.*, 1987, (3), pp. 674–78. [G: U.S.]

Jorgenson, Dale W.; Kuroda, Masahiro and Nishimizu, Mieko. Japan–U.S. Industry-Level Productivity Comparisons, 1960–1979. *J. Japanese Int. Economies*, March 1987, *1*(1), pp. 1–30. [G: U.S.; Japan]

Joskow, Paul L. Productivity Growth and Technical Change in the Generation of Electricity. *Energy J.*, January 1987, *8*(1), pp. 17–38. [G: U.S.]

Juran, Joseph M. Upper Management and Quality. *Shetty, Y. K. and Buehler, V. M., eds.*, 1987, pp. 275–83. [G: U.S.]

Jürgens, Ulrich; Dohse, Knuth and Malsch, Thomas. New Production Concepts in West German Car Plants. *Tolliday, S. and Zeitlin, J., eds.,* 1987, pp. 258–81.
[G: W. Germany]

Juyal, R. K. Contribution of Health to Productivity in a Developing Area: An Economic Analysis. *Margin,* Apr.-June 1987, *19*(3), pp. 80–89.
[G: LDCs]

Kasimovskii, E. Social Justice and the Improvement of Distribution Relations in the USSR. *Prob. Econ.,* September 1987, *30*(5), pp. 61–81.
[G: U.S.S.R.]

Katz, Harry C.; Kochan, Thomas A. and Keefe, Jeffrey H. Industrial Relations and Productivity in the U.S. Automobile Industry. *Brookings Pap. Econ. Act.,* 1987, (3), pp. 685–715.
[G: U.S.]

Kaufman, Robert S. and Kaufman, Roger T. Union Effects on Productivity, Personnel Practices, and Survival in the Automotive Parts Industry. *J. Lab. Res.,* Fall 1987, *8*(4), pp. 333–50.
[G: U.S.]

Kemme, David M. Productivity Growth in Polish Industry. *J. Compar. Econ.,* March 1987, *11*(1), pp. 1–20.
[G: Poland]

Kendrick, John W. Group Financial Incentives: An Evaluation. *Nalbantian, H. R., ed.,* 1987, pp. 120–36.
[G: U.S.]

Kendrick, John W. Happiness Is Personal Productivity Growth. *Challenge,* May/June 1987, *30*(2), pp. 37–44.

Kendrick, John W. Service Sector Productivity. *Bus. Econ.,* April 1987, *22*(2), pp. 18–24.
[G: U.S.]

Kim, Moshe and Spiegel, Menahem. The Effects of Lump-Sum Subsidies on the Structure of Production and Productivity in Regulated Industries. *J. Public Econ.,* October 1987, *34*(1), pp. 105–19.
[G: Israel]

King, Kenneth L. How 3M Melds Deming's, Juran's, and Crosby's Techniques. *Shetty, Y. K. and Buehler, V. M., eds.,* 1987, pp. 303–13.
[G: U.S.]

Knight, J. B. and Sabot, Richard H. Educational Policy and Labour Productivity: An Output Accounting Exercise. *Econ. J.,* March 1987, *97*(385), pp. 199–214. [G: Kenya; Tanzania]

Koike, Kazuo. Skill Formation Systems: A Thai–Japan Comparison. *J. Japanese Int. Economies,* December 1987, *1*(4), pp. 408–40.
[G: Japan; Thailand]

König, Heinz. Productivity, Wages, and Prices inside and outside of Manufacturing in the U.S., Japan, and Europe: Comments. *Europ. Econ. Rev.,* April 1987, *31*(3), pp. 736–39.

Krelle, Wilhelm. Long-term Fluctuations of Technical Progress and Growth. *J. Inst. Theoretical Econ.,* September 1987, *143*(3), pp. 379–401.
[G: OECD; CMEA]

Kunst, Robert and Marin, Dalia. The Export-Productivity Relationship: A Time Series Representation for Austria. *Empirica,* 1987, *14*(1), pp. 55–75.
[G: Austria]

Kyer, Ben L. Real Money Balances and the Productivity Growth Slowdown: The U.S. Manu-

facturing Sector, 1955–81. *Atlantic Econ. J.,* March 1987, *15*(1), pp. 42–55.
[G: U.S.]

Lazear, Edward P. Industrial Relations and Productivity in the U.S. Automobile Industry: Comments and Discussion. *Brookings Pap. Econ. Act.,* 1987, (3), pp. 716–20. [G: U.S.]

Lemeshev, M. Ecological and Economic Evaluation of Scientific-Technological Progress. *Prob. Econ.,* September 1987, *30*(5), pp. 82–97.
[G: U.S.S.R.]

Leslie, Derek. Real Wage and Real Labour Cost Growth, 1948–81: A Disaggregated Study. *Appl. Econ.,* May 1987, *19*(5), pp. 635–50.
[G: U.K.]

Lichtenberg, Frank R. and Siegel, Donald. Productivity and Changes in Ownership of Manufacturing Plants. *Brookings Pap. Econ. Act.,* 1987, (3), pp. 643–73. [G: U.S.]

van Loggerenberg, Bazil J. A Deterministic Analysis of Change in International Unit Labor Costs: Import Implications for U.S. Industry. *Managerial Dec. Econ.,* December 1987, *8*(4), pp. 339–42. [G: U.S.]

Maddison, Angus. Growth and Slowdown in Advanced Capitalist Economies: Techniques of Quantitative Assessment. *J. Econ. Lit.,* June 1987, *25*(2), pp. 649–98. [G: OECD]

Mansfield, Edwin. Productivity and Changes in Ownership of Manufacturing Plants: Comments and Discussion. *Brookings Pap. Econ. Act.,* 1987, (3), pp. 678–81. [G: U.S.]

Marris, Robin. Does Britain Really Have a Wages Problem? *Lloyds Bank Rev.,* April 1987, (164), pp. 36–55. [G: U.K.]

Mathur, Ashok. 'Why Growth Rates Differ' within India: An Alternative Approach. *J. Devel. Stud.,* January 1987, *23*(2), pp. 167–99.
[G: India]

McHugh, Richard and Lane, Julia. The Role of Embodied Technological Change in the Decline of Labor Productivity. *Southern Econ. J.,* April 1987, *53*(4), pp. 915–24. [G: U.S.]

McUsic, Molly. U.S. Manufacturing: Any Cause for Alarm? *New Eng. Econ. Rev.,* Jan./Feb. 1987, pp. 3–17. [G: U.S.]

Meyer, John R. and Oster, Clinton V., Jr. The U.S. Experience with Airline Deregulation: Productivity, Employment, and Labor Relations. *Meyer, J. R. and Oster, C. V., Jr.,* 1987, pp. 83–107. [G: U.S.]

Michon, François. Segmentation, Employment Structures and Productive Structures. *Tarling, R., ed.,* 1987, pp. 23–55.

Milholland, Dick E. Johnson Wax Regains a Competitive Edge through Manufacturing. *Shetty, Y. K. and Buehler, V. M., eds.,* 1987, pp. 383–91. [G: U.S.]

Mohnen, P. The Effects of U.S. Shocks on Canadian Total Factor Productivity Growth: The Case of the Electrical Products Industry. *Empirical Econ.,* 1987, *12*(4), pp. 221–47.

Mokyr, Joel. Has the Industrial Revolution Been Crowded Out? Some Reflections on Crafts and Williamson. *Exploration Econ. Hist.,* July 1987, *24*(3), pp. 293–325.

Molyneux, Richard and Thompson, David. Nationalised Industry Performance: Still Third-Rate? *Fisc. Stud.*, February 1987, *8*(1), pp. 48–82. **[G: U.K.]**

Mygind, Niels. Are Self-managed Firms Efficient? The Experience of Danish Fully and Partly Self-managed Firms. *Jones, D. C. and Svejnar, J., eds.*, 1987, pp. 243–323. **[G: Denmark]**

Nagel, Stuart S. The New Productivity. *Nagel, S. S., ed.*, 1987, pp. 271–84. **[G: U.S.]**

Neef, Arthur and Thomas, James. Trends in Manufacturing Productivity and Labor Costs in the U.S. and Abroad. *Mon. Lab. Rev.*, December 1987, *110*(12), pp. 25–30. **[G: OECD]**

Norwood, Janet L. The Labor Force of the Future. *Bus. Econ.*, July 1987, *22*(3), pp. 9–14. **[G: U.S.]**

O'Neil, Barbara A. The Mining Machinery Industry: Labor Productivity Trends, 1972–84. *Mon. Lab. Rev.*, June 1987, *110*(6), pp. 31–36. **[G: U.S.]**

Obermann, Gabriel. Capital Intensity and the Federal Sector: Some Further Evidence. *Public Choice*, 1987, *52*(2), pp. 193–99. **[G: U.S.]**

Oulton, Nicholas. Plant Closures and the Productivity 'Miracle' in Manufacturing. *Nat. Inst. Econ. Rev.*, August 1987, (121), pp. 53–59. **[G: U.K.]**

Papola, T. S. Rural Industrialisation and Agricultural Growth: A Case Study on India. *Islam, R., ed.*, 1987, pp. 59–106. **[G: India]**

Paulus, John D. and Gay, Robert S. U.S. Mergers Are Helping Productivity. *Challenge*, May/June 1987, *30*(2), pp. 54–57. **[G: U.S.]**

Perna, Nicholas S. The Shift from Manufacturing to Services: A Concerned View. *New Eng. Econ. Rev.*, Jan./Feb. 1987, pp. 30–38.

Prais, S. J. Educating for Productivity: Comparisons of Japanese and English Schooling and Vocational Preparation. *Nat. Inst. Econ. Rev.*, February 1987, (119), pp. 40–56. **[G: U.K.; Japan]**

Radell, Willard W., Jr. Comparative Performance of Large Cuban Sugar Factories in the 1984 "Zafra." *Mesa-Lago, C., ed.*, 1987, pp. 141–55. **[G: Cuba]**

Ray, George F. Erratum [Labour Costs in Manufacturing]. *Nat. Inst. Econ. Rev.*, November 1987, (122), pp. 96. **[G: OECD]**

Ray, George F. Labour Costs in Manufacturing. *Nat. Inst. Econ. Rev.*, May 1987, (120), pp. 71–74. **[G: OECD]**

Rebitzer, James B. Unemployment, Long-term Employment Relations, and Productivity Growth. *Rev. Econ. Statist.*, November 1987, *69*(4), pp. 627–35. **[G: U.S.]**

Ricard, Leonard J. GM's Just-in-Time Operating Philosophy. *Shetty, Y. K. and Buehler, V. M., eds.*, 1987, pp. 315–29. **[G: U.S.]**

Rich, Jude T. and Larson, John A. Why Some Long-term Incentives Fail. *Nalbantian, H. R., ed.*, 1987, *1984*, pp. 151–62. **[G: U.S.]**

Rittenberg, Libby and Manuel, Ernest H., Jr. Sources of Labor Productivity Variation in the U.S. Surface Coal Mining Industry, 1960–

1976. *Energy J.*, January 1987, *8*(1), pp. 87–100. **[G: U.S.]**

Romer, Paul M. Crazy Explanations for the Productivity Slowdown. *Fischer, S., ed.*, 1987, pp. 163–202.

Schilizzi, Steven G. M. Physical Economics, Technology, and Agroecosystems. *Pillet, G. and Murota, T., eds.*, 1987, pp. 109–28. **[G: France; Vietnam]**

Schmenner, Roger W. Productivity in the Factory and Industrial Policy. *Goldstein, H. A., ed.*, 1987, pp. 54–59. **[G: U.S.]**

Scott, Gordon. A View from the Employers. *Stegman, T., et al.*, 1987, pp. 64–75. **[G: Australia]**

Shapiro, Matthew D. Are Cyclical Fluctuation in Productivity Due More to Supply Shocks or Demand Shocks? *Amer. Econ. Rev.*, May 1987, *77*(2), pp. 118–24. **[G: U.S.]**

Sherwood, Mark K. Performance of Multifactor Productivity in the Steel and Motor Vehicles Industries. *Mon. Lab. Rev.*, August 1987, *110*(8), pp. 22–31. **[G: U.S.]**

Shetty, Y. K. and Buehler, Vernon M. Lessons for Managerial Strategy. *Shetty, Y. K. and Buehler, V. M., eds.*, 1987, pp. 395–98. **[G: U.S.]**

Shetty, Y. K. and Buehler, Vernon M. Strategies for Gaining Competitive Advantage: An Introduction. *Shetty, Y. K. and Buehler, V. M., eds.*, 1987, pp. 3–9. **[G: U.S.]**

Shimokawa, Koichi. Product and Labour Strategies in Japan. *Tolliday, S. and Zeitlin, J., eds.*, 1987, pp. 224–43. **[G: Japan]**

Shupp, Franklin R. Disinflation and Sectoral Productivity Gains. *J. Econ. Dynam. Control*, June 1987, *11*(2), pp. 207–12. **[G: U.S.]**

Siven, Claes Henric. The Wage Structure and the Functioning of the Labor Market. *Siven, C.-H., ed.*, 1987, pp. 71–97. **[G: Sweden]**

Steedman, Hilary and Wagner, Karin. A Second Look at Productivity, Machinery and Skills in Britain and Germany. *Nat. Inst. Econ. Rev.*, November 1987, (122), pp. 84–95. **[G: U.K.; W. Germany]**

Stewart, Frances. Supporting Productive Employment among Vulnerable Groups. *Cornia, G. A.; Jolly, R. and Stewart, F., eds.*, 1987, pp. 197–217. **[G: LDCs]**

Stiglitz, Joseph E. The Wage–Productivity Hypothesis: Its Economic Consequences and Policy Implications. *[Harberger, A.]*, 1987, pp. 130–65.

Syrquin, Moshe. Growth Accounting with Intermediate Inputs and the Transmission of Technical Change. *J. Devel. Econ.*, June 1987, *26*(1), pp. 17–23.

Tarling, Roger and Wilkinson, Frank. The Level, Structure and Flexibility of Costs. *Tarling, R., ed.*, 1987, pp. 3–22.

Thurow, Lester C. Can America Compete in the World Economy? *Shetty, Y. K. and Buehler, V. M., eds.*, 1987, pp. 11–32. **[G: U.S.]**

Thurow, Lester C. Economic Paradigms and Slow American Productivity Growth. *Eastern Econ.*

J., October-December 1987, *13*(4), pp. 333–43. [G: U.S.]

Tomer, John F. Productivity through Intra-firm Cooperation: A Behavioral Economic Analysis. *J. Behav. Econ.*, Spring 1987, *16*(1), pp. 83–95.

Toumanoff, Peter. The Use of Production Functions to Investigate Soviet Industrial Reform. *Comp. Econ. Stud.*, Fall 1987, *29*(3), pp. 94–111. [G: U.S.S.R.]

Tsang, Mun Chiu. The Impact of Underutilization of Education on Productivity: A Case Study of the U.S. Bell Companies. *Econ. Educ. Rev.*, 1987, *6*(3), pp. 239–54. [G: U.S.]

Ville, Simon. Defending Productivity Growth in the English Coal Trade during the Eighteenth and Nineteenth Centuries. *Econ. Hist. Rev.*, 2nd Ser., November 1987, *40*(4), pp. 597–602. [G: U.K.]

Volpato, Giuseppe. The Automobile Industry in Transition: Product Market Changes and Firm Strategies in the 1970s and 1980s. *Tolliday, S. and Zeitlin, J., eds.*, 1987, pp. 193–223. [G: Global]

Wardley, Peter. Labouring over Productivity Estimates: A Comment on Hirsch and Hausman's Model of Coal Miners' Productivity, 1874–1914 [Labour Productivity in the British and South Wales Coal Industry, 1874–1914]. *Economica*, November 1987, *54*(216), pp. 521–24. [G: U.K.]

Watanabe, Susumu. Flexible Automation and Labour Productivity in the Japanese Automobile Industry. *Watanabe, S., ed.*, 1987, pp. 41–77. [G: Japan]

Watanabe, Susumu. Microelectronics, Automation and Employment in the Automobile Industry: A Synthesis of Findings. *Watanabe, S., ed.*, 1987, pp. 181–97. [G: Selected Countries]

Weiss, Andrew. Incentives and Worker Behavior: Some Evidence. *Nalbantian, H. R., ed.*, 1987, pp. 137–50. [G: U.S.]

Wheelwright, Steven C. Building Excellence in Manufacturing. *Shetty, Y. K. and Buehler, V. M., eds.*, 1987, pp. 341–62. [G: U.S.]

Whipp, Richard. 'A Time to Every Purpose': An Essay on Time and Work. *Joyce, P., ed.*, 1987, pp. 210–36. [G: U.K.]

White, Gordon. Labour Market Reform in Chinese Industry. *Warner, M., ed.*, 1987, pp. 113–26. [G: China]

Whiteman, John L. Productivity and Growth in Australian Manufacturing Industry. *J. Post Keynesian Econ.*, Summer 1987, *9*(4), pp. 576–92. [G: Australia]

Williamson, Jeffrey G. Debating the British Industrial Revolution. *Exploration Econ. Hist.*, July 1987, *24*(3), pp. 269–92. [G: U.S.]

Williamson, Oliver E. Wage Rates as a Barrier to Entry: The Pennington Case in Perspective. *Williamson, O.*, 1987, *1968*, pp. 193–224. [G: U.S.]

Willman, Paul. Labour-Relations Strategy at BL Cars. *Tolliday, S. and Zeitlin, J., eds.*, 1987, pp. 305–27. [G: U.K.]

Wolf, Edward C. Raising Agricultural Productivity. *Brown, L. R., et al.*, 1987, pp. 139–56. [G: Global]

Wooden, Mark and Dawkins, Peter. The Australian Labour Market, March 1987. *Australian Bull. Lab.*, March 1987, *13*(2), pp. 70–93. [G: Australia]

York, James D. Retail Liquor Stores Experience Flat Trend in Productivity. *Mon. Lab. Rev.*, February 1987, *110*(2), pp. 25–29. [G: U.S.]

Zohar, Uri and Luski, Israel. A Note on the Measurement of the Slowdown in Total Factor Productivity. *Appl. Econ.*, September 1987, *19*(9), pp. 1211–19. [G: Canada]

826 Labor Markets: Demographic Characteristics

8260 Labor Markets: Demographic Characteristics

Abella, Manolo I. Female Labour Force Participation Rates in Rural Pakistan: Some Fundamental Explanations and Policy Implications: Comments. *Pakistan Devel. Rev.*, Winter 1987, *26*(4), pp. 697. [G: Pakistan]

Afzal, Mohammad and Nasir, Zafar Moeen. Is Female Labour Force Participation Really Low and Declining in Pakistan? A Look at Alternative Data Sources. *Pakistan Devel. Rev.*, Winter 1987, *26*(4), pp. 699–707. [G: Pakistan]

Ahmed, Iftikhar. Technology, Production Linkages and Women's Employment in South Asia. *Int. Lab. Rev.*, Jan.-Feb. 1987, *126*(1), pp. 21–40. [G: S. Asia]

Albrecht, James W. Hare Today, Gone Tomorrow . . . Divorce, Unemployment, and Other Sorry States. *Lang, K. and Leonard, J. S., eds.*, 1987, pp. 207–11. [G: U.S.]

Altmann, Franz-Lothar. Employment Policies in Czechoslovakia. *Adam, J., ed.*, 1987, pp. 78–102. [G: Czechoslovakia]

Amsden, Alice H. Gender and the Dynamics of Subcontracting in Mexico City: Comments. *Brown, C. and Pechman, J. A., eds.*, 1987, pp. 183–85. [G: Mexico]

Anderson, Joseph M.; Kennell, David L. and Sheils, John F. Health Plan Costs, Medicare, and Employment of Older Workers. *Sandell, S. H., ed.*, 1987, pp. 206–17. [G: U.S.]

Andrisani, Paul and Daymont, Thomas. Age Changes in Productivity and Earnings among Managers and Professionals. *Sandell, S. H., ed.*, 1987, pp. 52–70. [G: U.S.]

Appelbaum, Eileen. Restructuring Work: Temporary, Part-time, and At-Home Employment. *Hartmann, H. I., ed.*, 1987, pp. 268–310. [G: U.S.]

Arizpe, Lourdes and Botey, Carlota. Mexican Agricultural Development Policy and Its Impact on Rural Women. *Deere, C. D. and León, M., eds.*, 1987, pp. 67–83. [G: Mexico]

Bai, Nanfeng. Young People's Attitudes and Aspirations: Will They Welcome Reform? *Reynolds, B. L.*, 1987, pp. 161–87. [G: China]

Benería, Lourdes. Gender and the Dynamics of

Subcontracting in Mexico City. *Brown, C. and Pechman, J. A., eds.*, 1987, pp. 159–82.
[G: Mexico]

Berg, Maxine. Women's Work, Mechanisation and the Early Phases of Industrialisation in England. *Joyce, P., ed.*, 1987, pp. 64–98.
[G: U.K.]

Bergmann, Barbara R. Women's Roles in the Economy: Teaching the Issues. *J. Econ. Educ.*, Fall 1987, 18(4), pp. 393–407.

Bergmann, Barbara R. and Roberts, Mark D. Income for the Single Parent: Child Support, Work, and Welfare. *Brown, C. and Pechman, J. A., eds.*, 1987, pp. 247–63.
[G: U.S.]

Blau, Francine D. and Ferber, Marianne A. Occupations and Earnings of Women Workers. *Koziara, K. S.; Moskow, M. H. and Tanner, L. D., eds.*, 1987, pp. 37–68.
[G: U.S.]

Bloch, Charlotte. Female Unemployment and Knowledge of Self. *Pedersen, P. J. and Lund, R., eds.*, 1987, pp. 339–53.
[G: Denmark]

Blundell, Richard; Ham, John C. and Meghir, Costas. Unemployment and Female Labour Supply. *Econ. J.*, Supplement 1987, 97, pp. 44–64.
[G: U.K.]

Boaz, Rachel Floersheim. Labor Market Behavior of Older Workers Approaching Retirement: A Summary of the Evidence from the 1970s. *Meyer, C. W., ed.*, 1987, pp. 103–26.
[G: U.S.]

Bognanno, Mario F. Women in Professions: Academic Women. *Koziara, K. S.; Moskow, M. H. and Tanner, L. D., eds.*, 1987, pp. 245–64.
[G: U.S.]

Breslaw, Jon A. and Stelcner, Morton. The Effect of Health on the Labor Force Behavior of Elderly Men in Canada. *J. Human Res.*, Fall 1987, 22(4), pp. 490–517.
[G: Canada]

Brown, Clair. Consumption Norms, Work Roles, and Economic Growth, 1918–80. *Brown, C. and Pechman, J. A., eds.*, 1987, pp. 13–49.
[G: U.S.]

Brown, Clair and Pechman, Joseph A. Gender in the Workplace: Introduction. *Brown, C. and Pechman, J. A., eds.*, 1987, pp. 1–11.
[G: U.S.]

Brüniche-Olsen, Paul. Unemployment, the Labour Queue and Positive Feedback in the Labour Market. *Pedersen, P. J. and Lund, R., eds.*, 1987, pp. 187–204.

Burtless, Gary. Income for the Single Parent: Child Support, Work, and Welfare: Comments. *Brown, C. and Pechman, J. A., eds.*, 1987, pp. 263–67.
[G: U.S.]

Capparucci, Marina. Lavoro femminile tra marginalismo e marginalità. (Female Employment between Marginalism and Marginality. With English summary.) *Econ. Lavoro*, Jan.-Mar. 1987, 21(1), pp. 47–63.
[G: Italy]

Carter, Susan B. Consumption Norms, Work Roles, and Economic Growth, 1918–80: Comments. *Brown, C. and Pechman, J. A., eds.*, 1987, pp. 49–54.
[G: U.S.]

Challier, Marie-Christine. Inactivité et chômage caché. (Non-participation and Hidden Unemployment. With English summary.) *Écon.*

Soc., November 1987, 21(11), pp. 83–100.
[G: France]

Chatterjee, Lata and Lakshmanan, T. R. The Role of Women in Technical Change. *Fischer, M. M. and Nijkamp, P., eds.*, 1987, pp. 345–66.
[G: OECD]

Chaudhry, M. Ghaffar and Khan, Zubeda. Female Labour Force Participation Rates in Rural Pakistan: Some Fundamental Explanations and Policy Implications. *Pakistan Devel. Rev.*, Winter 1987, 26(4), pp. 687–96.
[G: Pakistan]

Clark, Robert L. Aging and Relative Earnings. *Sandell, S. H., ed.*, 1987, pp. 71–83.
[G: U.S.]

Colwill, Nina L. Men and Women in Organizations: Roles and Status, Stereotypes and Power. *Koziara, K. S.; Moskow, M. H. and Tanner, L. D., eds.*, 1987, pp. 97–117.
[G: U.S.]

Cook, Alice H. International Comparisons: Problems and Research in the Industrialized World. *Koziara, K. S.; Moskow, M. H. and Tanner, L. D., eds.*, 1987, pp. 332–73.
[G: Global]

Corcoran, Mary E. and Courant, Paul N. Sex-Role Socialization and Occupational Segregation: An Exploratory Investigation. *J. Post Keynesian Econ.*, Spring 1987, 9(3), pp. 330–46.
[G: U.S.]

Cornfield, Daniel B. Women in the Automated Office: Computers, Work, and Prospects for Unionization. *Lewin, D.; Lipsky, D. B. and Sockell, D., eds.*, 1987, pp. 177–98.
[G: U.S.]

Crane, Jon R. and Wise, David A. Military Service and Civilian Earnings of Youths. *Wise, D. A., ed.*, 1987, pp. 119–37.
[G: U.S.]

Di Domenico, Catherine; de Cola, Lee and Leishman, Jennifer. Urban Yoruba Mothers: At Home and at Work. *Oppong, C., ed.*, 1987, pp. 118–32.
[G: Nigeria]

Dipboye, Robert L. Problems and Progress of Women in Management. *Koziara, K. S.; Moskow, M. H. and Tanner, L. D., eds.*, 1987, pp. 118–53.
[G: U.S.]

Doeringer, Peter B. Gender and the Dynamics of Subcontracting in Mexico City: Comments. *Brown, C. and Pechman, J. A., eds.*, 1987, pp. 185–88.
[G: Mexico]

Dolphyne, Florence Abena. The Ghana National Council on Women and Development: An Example of Concerted Action. *Oppong, C., ed.*, 1987, pp. 213–18.
[G: Ghana]

Dutoya, C. and Gauvin, Annie. Assignment of Women Workers to Jobs and Company Strategies in France. *Tarling, R., ed.*, 1987, pp. 127–44.
[G: France]

Dutton, Patricia. Policies for the Youth Labour Market: YTS: Training or a Placebo? *Junankar, P. N., ed.*, 1987, pp. 217–37.
[G: U.K.]

Easterlin, Richard A. The New Age Structure of Poverty in America: Permanent or Transient? *Population Devel. Rev.*, June 1987, 13(2), pp. 195–208.
[G: U.S.]

Edwards, Richard. Youth Labor and the Changing Industrial Relations System: Towards a Research Agenda. *Econ. Lavoro*, Jan.-Mar. 1987, 21(1), pp. 65–75.   [G: U.S.]

Egginton, Don M. An Informal Empirical Analysis of Labour Supply Decisions in the UK. *Beenstock, M., et al.*, 1987, pp. 124–65.
[G: U.K.]

Egginton, Don M. Case Studies of Labour Supply Incentives and Budget Lines. *Beenstock, M., et al.*, 1987, pp. 25–75.   [G: U.K.]

Ellwood, David T. and Wise, David A. Military Hiring and Youth Employment. *Wise, D. A., ed.*, 1987, pp. 79–95.   [G: U.S.]

Ellwood, David T. and Wise, David A. Uncle Sam Wants You—Sometimes: Military Enlistments and the Youth Labor Market. *Wise, D. A., ed.*, 1987, pp. 97–118.   [G: U.S.]

Elmore, Richard F. Youth Employment in the United States: Problem, Structure, Policy. *Pedersen, P. J. and Lund, R., eds.*, 1987, pp. 241–57.   [G: U.S.]

Even, William E. Career Interruptions Following Childbirth. *J. Lab. Econ.*, April 1987, 5(2), pp. 255–77.   [G: U.S.]

Fallenbuchl, Zbigniew M. Employment Policies in Poland. *Adam, J., ed.*, 1987, pp. 27–54.
[G: Poland]

Farooqui, M. N. I. Is Female Labour Force Participation Really Low and Declining in Pakistan? A Look at Alternative Data Sources: Comments. *Pakistan Devel. Rev.*, Winter 1987, 26(4), pp. 708–09.   [G: Pakistan]

Flaim, Paul O. and Sehgal, Ellen. Reemployment and Earnings [Displaced Workers of 1979–83: How Well Have They Fared?]. *Staudohar, P. D. and Brown, H. E.*, 1987, 1985, pp. 101–30.   [G: U.S.]

Foner, Philip S. Women and the American Labor Movement: A Historical Perspective. *Koziara, K. S.; Moskow, M. H. and Tanner, L. D., eds.*, 1987, pp. 154–86.   [G: U.S.]

Foot, David K. and Li, Jeanne C. Demographic Determinants of Unemployment. *Gunderson, M.; Meltz, N. M. and Ostry, S., eds.*, 1987, pp. 140–51.   [G: Canada]

Freeman, Richard B. and Leonard, Jonathan S. Union Maids: Unions and the Female Work Force. *Brown, C. and Pechman, J. A., eds.*, 1987, pp. 189–212.   [G: U.S.]

Fullerton, Howard N., Jr. Labor Force Projections: 1986 to 2000. *Mon. Lab. Rev.*, September 1987, 110(9), pp. 19–29.   [G: U.S.]

Ginzberg, Eli. Technology, Women, and Work: Policy Perspectives. *Hartmann, H. I., ed.*, 1987, pp. 3–22.   [G: U.S.]

Goldin, Claudia. The Gender Gap in Historical Perspective. *Kilby, P., ed.*, 1987, pp. 135–70.
[G: U.S.]

Goldin, Claudia. Women's Employment and Technological Change: A Historical Perspective. *Hartmann, H. I., ed.*, 1987, pp. 185–222.
[G: U.S.]

Gollub, James O. Increasing Employment Opportunities for Older Workers: Emerging State and Local Initiatives. *Sandell, S. H., ed.*, 1987, pp. 143–64.   [G: U.S.]

Good, David H. and Pirog-Good, Maureen A.

Employment, Crime, and Race. *Contemp. Policy Issues*, October 1987, 5(4), pp. 91–104.
[G: U.S.]

Gottfried, Heidi. Assembling Gendered Subjects at Work: A Review Essay. *Rev. Radical Polit. Econ.*, Fall 1987, 19(3), pp. 75–79.

Gramatzki, Hans-Erich. Regional Employment Policies in East European Countries. *Adam, J., ed.*, 1987, pp. 171–95.
[G: Czechoslovakia; Poland; Hungary; E. Germany]

Gray, Lois S. Professional Careers for Women in Industrial Relations. *Koziara, K. S.; Moskow, M. H. and Tanner, L. D., eds.*, 1987, pp. 225–44.   [G: U.S.]

Hammerman, Herbert. Five Case Studies [Five Case Studies of Displaced Workers]. *Staudohar, P. D. and Brown, H. E.*, 1987, 1964, pp. 75–88.   [G: U.S.]

Hansen, Per Vejrup. Turnover and Employment among Youth: Causes of the Particular Problems of Youth Employment. *Pedersen, P. J. and Lund, R., eds.*, 1987, pp. 129–45.
[G: Denmark]

Hartmann, Heidi I. Internal Labor Markets and Gender: A Case Study of Promotion. *Brown, C. and Pechman, J. A., eds.*, 1987, pp. 59–92.   [G: U.S.]

Harvey, Elizabeth. Youth Unemployment and the State: Public Policies towards Unemployed Youth in Hamburg during the World Economic Crisis. *Evans, R. J. and Geary, D., eds.*, 1987, pp. 142–71.   [G: Germany]

Hayghe, Howard V. and Haugen, Steven E. A Profile of Husbands in Today's Labor Market. *Mon. Lab. Rev.*, October 1987, 110(10), pp. 12–17.   [G: U.S.]

Henwood, Felicity and Wyatt, Sally. Managing Technological Change: Responses of Government, Employers, and Trade Unions in Western Europe and Canada. *Hartmann, H. I., ed.*, 1987, pp. 395–431.   [G: OECD]

Holden, Karen C. and Hansen, W. Lee. Part-time Work, Full-time Work, and Occupational Segregation. *Brown, C. and Pechman, J. A., eds.*, 1987, pp. 217–40.   [G: U.S.]

Holzer, Harry J. Informal Job Search and Black Youth Unemployment. *Amer. Econ. Rev.*, June 1987, 77(3), pp. 446–52.   [G: U.S.]

Holzer, Harry J. Job Search by Employed and Unemployed Youth. *Ind. Lab. Relat. Rev.*, July 1987, 40(4), pp. 601–11.   [G: U.S.]

House, William J. Labor Market Differentiation in a Developing Economy: An Example from Urban Juba, Southern Sudan. *World Devel.*, July 1987, 15(7), pp. 877–97.   [G: Sudan]

Human, L. and Greenacre, M. J. Labor Market Discrimination in the Manufacturing Sector: The Impact of Race, Gender, Education and Age on Income. *S. Afr. J. Econ.*, June 1987, 55(2), pp. 150–64.   [G: S. Africa]

Humphries, Jane. "...The Most Free From Objection..." The Sexual Division of Labor and Women's Work in Nineteenth-Century England. *J. Econ. Hist.*, December 1987, 47(4), pp. 929–49.   [G: U.K.]

Jensen, Peter. Transitions between Labour-Market States—An Empirical Analysis Using Danish Data. *Pedersen, P. J. and Lund, R., eds.,* 1987, pp. 67–80. **[G: Denmark]**

Johnson, Terry R.; Dickinson, Katherine P. and West, Richard W. Older Workers, Job Displacement, and the Employment Service. *Sandell, S. H., ed.,* 1987, pp. 100–117.
[G: U.S.]

Johnston, Denis and Rudney, Gabriel. Characteristics of Workers in Nonprofit Organizations. *Mon. Lab. Rev.,* July 1987, *110*(7), pp. 28–33. **[G: U.S.]**

Jondrow, Jim; Brechling, Frank and Marcus, Alan J. Older Workers in the Market for Part-time Employment. *Sandell, S. H., ed.,* 1987, pp. 84–99. **[G: U.S.]**

Jones, F. L. Occupational Statistics Revisited: The Female Labour Force in Early British and Australian Censuses. *Australian Econ. Hist. Rev.,* September 1987, *27*(2), pp. 56–76. **[G: U.K.; Australia]**

Jørgensen, Birte Bech. Unemployment and the Cultures of Young Women. *Pedersen, P. J. and Lund, R., eds.,* 1987, pp. 321–37.
[G: Denmark]

Jorrat, Jorge Ral. Exploraciones sobre movilidad ocupacional intergeneracional masculina en el Gran Buenos Aires. (With English summary.) *Desarrollo Econ.,* July-Sept. 1987, *27*(106), pp. 261–78. **[G: Argentina]**

Joshi, Heather E. and Owen, Susan J. How Long Is a Piece of Elastic? The Measurement of Female Activity Rates in British Censuses, 1951–1981. *Cambridge J. Econ.,* March 1987, *11*(1), pp. 55–74. **[G: U.K.]**

Junankar, P. N. The Labour Market for Young People. *Junankar, P. N., ed.,* 1987, pp. 1–12.
[G: OECD]

Junankar, P. N. and Neale, Adrian J. Relative Wages and the Youth Labour Market: A Rejoinder. *Junankar, P. N., ed.,* 1987, pp. 116–18. **[G: OECD]**

Junankar, P. N. and Neale, Adrian J. Relative Wages and the Youth Labour Market. *Junankar, P. N., ed.,* 1987, pp. 79–107.
[G: OECD]

Kelley, Maryellen R. Internal Labor Markets and Gender: A Case Study of Promotion: Comments. *Brown, C. and Pechman, J. A., eds.,* 1987, pp. 97–105. **[G: U.S.]**

Khandker, Shahidur R. Labor Market Participation of Married Women in Bangladesh. *Rev. Econ. Statist.,* August 1987, *69*(3), pp. 536–41. **[G: Bangladesh]**

Killian, Molly Sizer and Hady, Thomas F. The Economic Performance of Rural Labor Markets. *U.S.D.A., Econ. Res. Serv., Agr. and Rural Econ. Div.,* 1987, pp. 8.1–23.
[G: U.S.]

Klevmarken, N. Anders. Market and Nonmarket Service Production in Swedish Households. *Eliasson, G., ed.,* 1987, pp. 27–38.
[G: Sweden]

König, Wolfgang. Employment and Career Mobility of Women in France and the Federal Republic. *Teckenberg, W., ed.,* 1987, pp. 53–85. **[G: France; W. Germany]**

Koziara, Karen Shallcross. Women and Work: The Evolving Policy. *Koziara, K. S.; Moskow, M. H. and Tanner, L. D., eds.,* 1987, pp. 374–408. **[G: U.S.]**

Koziara, Karen Shallcross; Moskow, Michael H. and Tanner, Lucretia Dewey. Working Women—A Summary of Research Knowledge and Research Needs. *Koziara, K. S.; Moskow, M. H. and Tanner, L. D., eds.,* 1987, pp. vii–xxii.

Kramer, Helgard. Frankfurt's Working Women: Scapegoats or Winners of the Great Depression? *Evans, R. J. and Geary, D., eds.,* 1987, pp. 108–41. **[G: Germany]**

Kumar, Shubh K. Women's Role and Agricultural Technology. *Mellor, J. W.; Delgado, C. L. and Blackie, M. J., eds.,* 1987, pp. 135–47.
[G: Africa]

Ladipo, Patricia. Women in a Maize Storage Cooperative in Nigeria: Family Planning, Credit and Technological Change. *Oppong, C., ed.,* 1987, pp. 101–17. **[G: Nigeria]**

Lebergott, Stanley. Consumption Norms, Work Roles, and Economic Growth, 1918–80: Comments. *Brown, C. and Pechman, J. A., eds.,* 1987, pp. 54–58. **[G: U.S.]**

Leigh, Duane E. and Hills, Stephen M. Male–Female Differences in the Potential for Union Growth Outside Traditionally Unionized Industries. *J. Lab. Res.,* Spring 1987, *8*(2), pp. 131–42. **[G: U.S.]**

León, Magdalena. Colombian Agricultural Policies and the Debate on Policies toward Rural Women. *Deere, C. D. and León, M., eds.,* 1987, pp. 84–104. **[G: Colombia]**

Lewis, Donald E. and Shorten, Brett. Female Participation in the Australian Labour Force. *Australian Bull. Lab.,* September 1987, *13*(4), pp. 237–63. **[G: Australia]**

Lichter, Daniel T. and Costanzo, Janice A. How Do Demographic Changes Affect Labor Force Participation of Women? *Mon. Lab. Rev.,* November 1987, *110*(11), pp. 23–25. **[G: U.S.]**

Lindner, W.-D. and Heinzemann, B. Comment [Labour Flexibility and Older Worker Marginalisation: The Need for a New Strategy]. *Int. Lab. Rev.,* 1987, *126*(3), pp. 371–72.
[G: EEC]

Lisk, Franklyn and Stevens, Yvette. Government Policy and Rural Women's Work in Sierre Leone. *Oppong, C., ed.,* 1987, pp. 182–202.
[G: Sierre Leone]

Lordoğlu, Kuvvet. Yüksek Eğitim Gören Kadin işgücü Adaylari ve Çalişma eğilimleri. (With English summary.) *METU,* 1987, *14*(3), pp. 215–43. **[G: Turkey]**

Lynch, Lisa M. Individual Differences in the Youth Labour Market: A Cross-Section Analysis of London Youths. *Junankar, P. N., ed.,* 1987, pp. 185–214. **[G: U.K.]**

MacPherson, David A. and Stewart, James B. Unionism and the Dispersion of Wages among Blue-Collar Women. *J. Lab. Res.,* Fall 1987, *8*(4), pp. 395–405. **[G: U.S.]**

Magura, Michael and Shapiro, Edward. The Black Dropout Rate and the Black Youth Unemployment Rate: A Granger-Causal Analysis. *Rev. Black Polit. Econ.*, Winter 1987, *15*(3), pp. 56–67. **[G: U.S.]**

Main, Brian G. M. Earnings, Expected Earnings, and Unemployment amongst School Leavers. *Junankar, P. N., ed.*, 1987, pp. 145–84. **[G: U.K.]**

Main, Brian G. M. The Wage Expectations and Unemployment Experience of School Leavers. *Scot. J. Polit. Econ.*, November 1987, *34*(4), pp. 349–67. **[G: Scotland]**

Maloney, Timothy J. Employment Constraints and the Labor Supply of Married Women: A Reexamination of the Added Worker Effect. *J. Human Res.*, Winter 1987, *22*(1), pp. 51–61. **[G: U.S.]**

Malveaux, Julianne and Wallace, Phyllis. Minority Women in the Workplace. *Koziara, K. S.; Moskow, M. H. and Tanner, L. D., eds.*, 1987, pp. 265–98. **[G: U.S.]**

Marsden, David. Youth Pay in Some OECD Countries since 1966. *Junankar, P. N., ed.*, 1987, pp. 15–50. **[G: OECD]**

Marshall, Ray and Paulin, Beth. Employment and Earnings of Women: Historical Perspective. *Koziara, K. S.; Moskow, M. H. and Tanner, L. D., eds.*, 1987, pp. 1–36. **[G: U.S.]**

Miller, Paul W. and Volker, Paul. The Youth Labour Market In Australia. *Econ. Rec.*, September 1987, *63*(182), pp. 203–19. **[G: Australia]**

Mirkin, Barry Alan. Early Retirement as a Labor Force Policy: An International Overview. *Mon. Lab. Rev.*, March 1987, *110*(3), pp. 19–33. **[G: OECD]**

Mitchell, William F. What Is the Full Employment Unemployment Rate? Some Empirical Evidence of Structural Unemployment in Australia, 1966 to 1986. *Australian Bull. Lab.*, December 1987, *14*(1), pp. 321–37. **[G: Australia]**

Mones, Belkis and Grant, Lydia. Agricultural Development, the Economic Crisis, and Rural Women in the Dominican Republic. *Deere, C. D. and León, M., eds.*, 1987, pp. 35–50. **[G: Dominican Republic]**

Mroz, Thomas A. The Sensitivity of an Empirical Model of Married Women's Hours of Work to Economic and Statistical Assumptions. *Econometrica*, July 1987, *55*(4), pp. 765–99. **[G: U.S.]**

Nakosteen, Robert A. and Zimmer, Michael A. Marital Status and Earnings of Young Men: A Model with Endogenous Selection. *J. Human Res.*, Spring 1987, *22*(2), pp. 248–68. **[G: U.S.]**

Needleman, Ruth and Tanner, Lucretia Dewey. Women in Unions: Current Issues. *Koziara, K. S.; Moskow, M. H. and Tanner, L. D., eds.*, 1987, pp. 187–224. **[G: U.S.]**

Newey, Whitney K. Specification Tests for Distributional Assumptions in the Tobit Model. *J. Econometrics*, Jan./Feb. 1987, *34*(1/2), pp. 125–45. **[G: U.K.]**

Nohara, H. and Silvestre, Jean-Jacques. Industrial Structures, Employment Trends and the Economic Crisis: The Case of France and Japan in the 1970s. *Tarling, R., ed.*, 1987, pp. 147–76. **[G: France; Japan]**

Norwood, Janet L. The Labor Force of the Future. *Bus. Econ.*, July 1987, *22*(3), pp. 9–14. **[G: U.S.]**

Oechslin, Jean-Jacques. Training and the Business World: The French Experience. *Int. Lab. Rev.*, Nov.-Dec. 1987, *126*(6), pp. 653–67. **[G: France]**

Oppong, Christine. Sex Roles, Population and Development in West Africa: Introduction. *Oppong, C., ed.*, 1987, pp. 1–17. **[G: W. Africa]**

Orsi, Renzo. A Spillover Model of Male and Female Labour Markets. *Giorn. Econ.*, Nov.-Dec. 1987, *46*(11–12), pp. 590–616. **[G: Italy]**

Osterman, Paul. Internal Labor Markets and Gender: A Case Study of Promotion: Comments. *Brown, C. and Pechman, J. A., eds.*, 1987, pp. 92–97. **[G: U.S.]**

Owen, Susan J. and Joshi, Heather E. Does Elastic Retract: The Effect of Recession on Women's Labour Force Participation. *Brit. J. Ind. Relat.*, March 1987, *25*(1), pp. 125–43. **[G: U.K.]**

Paul, Carolyn. Work Alternatives for Older Americans: A Management Perspective. *Sandell, S. H., ed.*, 1987, pp. 165–76. **[G: U.S.]**

Peukert, Detlev. The Lost Generation: Youth Unemployment at the End of the Weimar Republic. *Evans, R. J. and Geary, D., eds.*, 1987, pp. 172–93. **[G: Germany]**

Phillips, Llad and Votey, Harold L., Jr. The Choice between Legitimate and Illegitimate Work: Micro Study of Individual Behavior. *Contemp. Policy Issues*, October 1987, *5*(4), pp. 59–72. **[G: U.S.]**

Pittin, Renée. Documentation of Women's Work in Nigeria: Problems and Solutions. *Oppong, C., ed.*, 1987, pp. 25–44. **[G: Nigeria]**

Powell, David E. Manpower Constraints and the Use of Pensioners in the Soviet Economy. *Adam, J., ed.*, 1987, pp. 196–215. **[G: U.S.S.R.]**

Prieto, Yolanda. Cuban Women in the U.S. Labor Force: Perspectives on the Nature of Change. *Mesa-Lago, C., ed.*, 1987, pp. 73–91. **[G: Cuba]**

Primorac, E. and Charette, Michael F. Regional Aspects of Youth Unemployment in Yugoslavia. *Econ. Anal. Workers' Manage.*, 1987, *21*(2), pp. 193–219. **[G: Yugoslavia]**

Raffe, David. Small Expectations: The First Year of the Youth Training Scheme. *Junankar, P. N., ed.*, 1987, pp. 238–62. **[G: U.K.]**

Rajan, Amin. The Young Workers' Scheme: A Preliminary Assessment. *Junankar, P. N., ed.*, 1987, pp. 263–84. **[G: U.K.]**

Rives, Janet M. and Turner, Keith K. Women's Occupations as a Factor in Their Unemployment Rate Volatility. *Quart. Rev. Econ. Bus.*, Winter 1987, *27*(4), pp. 55–64. **[G: U.S.]**

Rongliang, Guo and Wei, He. Attach Importance to the Administration of Self-Employed Youth: An Investigative Report on Individually Owned Small Businesses in Wuxi City. *Chinese Econ. Stud.*, Fall 1987, *21*(1), pp. 26–36.
[G: China]

Root, Lawrence S. and Zarrugh, Laura H. Private-Sector Employment Practices for Older Workers. *Sandell, S. H., ed.*, 1987, pp. 177–91.
[G: U.S.]

Rosenberg, Sam. Economic Contractions and Racial Differentials in Male Job Mobility. *Ind. Relat.*, Fall 1987, *26*(3), pp. 291–95.
[G: U.S.]

Ross, Russell T. Disaggregate Labour Supply Functions for Married Women in New Zealand. *New Zealand Econ. Pap.*, 1987, *21*, pp. 41–55.
[G: New Zealand]

Rotella, Elyce J. The Dynamics of Occupational Segregation among Bank Tellers: Comments. *Brown, C. and Pechman, J. A., eds.*, 1987, pp. 149–54.
[G: U.S.]

Ruhm, Christopher J. Job Tenure and Cyclical Changes in the Labor Market [Demographic Differences in Cyclical Employment Variations]. *Rev. Econ. Statist.*, May 1987, *69*(2), pp. 372–78.
[G: U.S.]

Rupp, Kalman, et al. Government Employment and Training Programs, and Older Americans. *Sandell, S. H., ed.*, 1987, pp. 121–42.
[G: U.S.]

Ryan, Paul. Trade Unionism and the Pay of Young Workers. *Junankar, P. N., ed.*, 1987, pp. 119–42.
[G: OECD]

Sandell, Steven H. Labor Market Problems and Employment Policies Affecting Older Americans. *Sandell, S. H., ed.*, 1987, pp. 15–33.
[G: U.S.]

Sandell, Steven H. Prospects for Older Workers: The Demographic and Economic Context. *Sandell, S. H., ed.*, 1987, pp. 3–14.
[G: U.S.]

Sandell, Steven H. The Problem Isn't Age: Conclusions and Implications. *Sandell, S. H., ed.*, 1987, pp. 231–45.
[G: U.S.]

Sawhill, Isabel V. Income for the Single Parent: Child Support, Work, and Welfare: Comments. *Brown, C. and Pechman, J. A., eds.*, 1987, pp. 268–70.
[G: U.S.]

Schroeder, Esther C. Testing Local Level Labor Force and Unemployment Projections. *Demography*, November 1987, *24*(4), pp. 649–61.
[G: U.S.]

Scott, Joan W. 'L'ouvrière! Mot impie, sordide . . .': Women Workers in the Discourse of French Political Economy, 1840–1860. *Joyce, P., ed.*, 1987, pp. 119–42.
[G: France]

Seeborg, Michael and DeBoer, Larry. The Narrowing Male–Female Unemployment Differential. *Growth Change*, Spring 1987, *18*(2), pp. 24–37.
[G: U.S.]

Shack-Marquez, Janice and Wascher, William L. Some Direct Evidence on the Importance of Borrowing Constraints to the Labor Force Participation of Married Women [The Labor Force Participation Behavior of Married Women Under Conditions of Constraints on Borrowing]. *J. Human Res.*, Fall 1987, *22*(4), pp. 593–602.
[G: U.S.]

Shank, Susan E. and Haugen, Steven E. The Employment Situation during 1986: Job Gains Continue, Unemployment Dips. *Mon. Lab. Rev.*, February 1987, *110*(2), pp. 3–10.
[G: U.S.]

Shapiro, David and Sandell, Steven H. The Reduced Pay of Older Job Losers: Age Discrimination and Other Explanations. *Sandell, S. H., ed.*, 1987, pp. 37–51.
[G: U.S.]

Shaw, Lois B. and Shapiro, David. Women's Work Plans: Contrasting Expectations and Actual Work Experience. *Mon. Lab. Rev.*, November 1987, *110*(11), pp. 7–13.
[G: U.S.]

Shaw, Lois B. and Shaw, Rachel. From Midlife to Retirement: The Middle-Aged Women Worker. *Koziara, K. S.; Moskow, M. H. and Tanner, L. D., eds.*, 1987, pp. 299–331.
[G: U.S.]

Smith, Richard J. Testing for Exogeneity in Limited Dependent Variable Models Using a Simplified Likelihood Ratio Statistic. *J. Appl. Econometrics*, July 1987, *2*(3), pp. 237–45.

Sorensen, Elaine. Union Maids: Unions and the Female Work Force: Comments. *Brown, C. and Pechman, J. A., eds.*, 1987, pp. 213–16.
[G: U.S.]

Spindel, Cheywa R. The Social Invisibility of Women's Work in Brazilian Agriculture. *Deere, C. D. and León, M., eds.*, 1987, pp. 51–66.
[G: Brazil]

Spring, William J. Youth Unemployment and the Transition from School to Work: Programs in Boston, Frankfurt, and London. *New Eng. Econ. Rev.*, Mar./Apr. 1987, pp. 3–16.
[G: U.S.; U.K.; W. Germany]

Standing, Guy. Reply [Labour Flexibility and Older Worker Marginalisation: The Need for a New Strategy]. *Int. Lab. Rev.*, 1987, *126*(3), pp. 372–74.
[G: EEC]

Stern, David. Part-time Work, Full-time Work, and Occupational Segregation: Comments. *Brown, C. and Pechman, J. A., eds.*, 1987, pp. 240–46.
[G: U.S.]

Stirati, Antonella. Differenze retributive e segregazione occupazionale per sesso nell'industria manifatturiera. (Wage Differences and Occupational Segregation by Sex in the Manufacturing Industries. With English summary.) *Econ. Lavoro*, July-Sept. 1987, *21*(3), pp. 51–76.
[G: Italy]

Strober, Myra H. and Arnold, Carolyn L. Integrated Circuits/Segregated Labor: Women in Computer-Related Occupations and High-Tech Industries. *Hartmann, H. I., ed.*, 1987, pp. 136–82.
[G: U.S.]

Strober, Myra H. and Arnold, Carolyn L. The Dynamics of Occupational Segregation among Bank Tellers. *Brown, C. and Pechman, J. A., eds.*, 1987, pp. 107–48.
[G: U.S.]

Strom, Sharon Hartman. "Machines Instead of Clerks": Technology and the Feminization of Bookkeeping, 1910–1950. *Hartmann, H. I., ed.*, 1987, pp. 63–97.
[G: U.S.]

Terwey, Michael. Class Position and Income Inequality: Comparing Results for the Federal Republic with Current U.S. Research. *Teckenberg, W., ed.*, 1987, pp. 119–71.
[G: W. Germany; U.S.]

Timár, János. Employment Policy in Hungary. *Adam, J., ed.*, 1987, pp. 103–24.
[G: Hungary]

Tzannatos, Zafiris. The Greek Labour Market: Current Perspectives and Future Prospects. *Greek Econ. Rev.*, 1987, 9(2), pp. 224–38.
[G: Greece]

Ulman, Lloyd. The Dynamics of Occupational Segregation among Bank Tellers: Comments. *Brown, C. and Pechman, J. A., eds.*, 1987, pp. 154–57. [G: U.S.]

de Vletter, Fion. Foreign Labour on the South African Gold Mines: New Insights on an Old Problem. *Int. Lab. Rev.*, Mar.-Apr. 1987, 126(2), pp. 199–218. [G: S. Africa]

Voydanoff, Patricia. Women's Work, Family, and Health. *Koziara, K. S.; Moskow, M. H. and Tanner, L. D., eds.*, 1987, pp. 69–96.
[G: U.S.]

Wadensjö, Eskil. The Youth Labor Market in Sweden: Changes in the 1980's. *Econ. Lavoro*, Jan.-Mar. 1987, 21(1), pp. 97–104.
[G: Sweden]

Weiss, Thomas. Demographic Aspects of the Urban Population, 1800–1840. *Kilby, P., ed.*, 1987, pp. 171–213. [G: U.S.]

Wells, William. Relative Wages and the Youth Labour Market: A Reply. *Junankar, P. N., ed.*, 1987, pp. 108–15. [G: OECD]

Wells, William. The Relative Pay and Employment of Young People. *Junankar, P. N., ed.*, 1987, pp. 51–78. [G: OECD]

Wéry, René. Women in Bamako: Activities and Relations. *Oppong, C., ed.*, 1987, pp. 45–62.
[G: Mali]

Westin, Alan F. Employer Policies to Enhance the Application of Office System Technology to Clerical Work. *Hartmann, H. I., ed.*, 1987, pp. 313–42. [G: U.S.]

Wial, Howard. Youth Entry into Internal Labor Markets in the United States: The Case of Ethnic Neighborhood Labor Markets. *Econ. Lavoro*, Jan.-Mar. 1987, 21(1), pp. 105–13.
[G: U.S.]

Wielgosz, John B. and Carpenter, Susan. The Effectiveness of Alternative Methods of Searching for Jobs and Finding Them: An Exploratory Analysis of the Data Bearing upon the Ways of Coping with Joblessness. *Amer. J. Econ. Soc.*, April 1987, 46(2), pp. 151–64.
[G: U.S.]

Winckler, Victoria. Women and Work in Contemporary Wales. *Day, G. and Rees, G., eds.*, 1987, pp. 53–71. [G: U.K.]

Winegarden, C. R. Women's Labour Force Participation and the Distribution of Household Incomes: Evidence from Cross-national Data. *Economica*, May 1987, 54(214), pp. 223–36.
[G: U.S.; U.K.]

Winter, Søren. Implementation of Danish Youth Employment Policy. *Pedersen, P. J. and Lund,*

R., *eds.*, 1987, pp. 259–84. [G: Denmark]

Wong, Yue-chim. Women's Work and the Demand for Children in Hong Kong. *Devel. Econ.*, June 1987, 25(2), pp. 188–200.
[G: Hong Kong]

Yamada, Tadashi and Yamada, Tetsuji. Labor Employment of Married Women in Japan: Part-time Work vs. Full-time Work. *Eastern Econ. J.*, Jan.-Mar. 1987, 13(1), pp. 41–48.
[G: Japan]

Yamada, Tadashi and Yamada, Tetsuji. Part-time Work of Married Women in Urban Japan. *Quart. Rev. Econ. Bus.*, Spring 1987, 27(1), pp. 41–50. [G: Japan]

830 TRADE UNIONS; COLLECTIVE BARGAINING; LABOR–MANAGEMENT RELATIONS

8300 General

Bloom, David E. and Bloom, Steven M. Institutional Change and Labour-Market Adjustment. *Gunderson, M.; Meltz, N. M. and Ostry, S., eds.*, 1987, pp. 112–18. [G: U.S.]

Cornfield, Daniel B. Workers, Managers, and Technological Change. *Cornfield, D. B., ed.*, 1987, pp. 3–24. [G: U.S.]

Flanagan, Robert J. Efficiency and Equality in Swedish Labor Markets. *Bosworth, B. P. and Rivlin, A. M., eds.*, 1987, pp. 125–84.
[G: Sweden]

Heery, Edmund. Chronicle: Industrial Relations in the United Kingdom April–July 1987. *Brit. J. Ind. Relat.*, November 1987, 25(3), pp. 437–50. [G: U.K.]

Joyce, Patrick. The Historical Meanings of Work. *Joyce, P., ed.*, 1987, pp. 1–30. [G: U.K.]

Layard, Richard and Nickell, Stephen J. The Performance of the British Economy: The Labour Market. *Dornbusch, R. and Layard, R., eds.*, 1987, pp. 131–79. [G: U.K.]

Meyer, Dirk. Rationalisierungsschutz. Soziale Beherrschung des technischen Fortschritts durch tarifliche Investitionslenkung? (The Right to Work by Introducing the 35-Hour Week? With English summary.) *Z. Wirtschaft. Sozialwissen.*, 1987, 107(3), pp. 431–40.

Minford, Patrick. The Performance of the British Economy: The Labour Market: Comment. *Dornbusch, R. and Layard, R., eds.*, 1987, pp. 260–62. [G: U.K.]

Reynolds, Morgan O. Labor Relations at the Shop Floor Level. *Managerial Dec. Econ.*, March 1987, 8(1), pp. 47–53.

Saltzman, Gregory M. Congressional Voting on Labor Issues: The Role of PACs. *Ind. Lab. Relat. Rev.*, January 1987, 40(2), pp. 163–79.
[G: U.S.]

831 Trade Unions

8310 Trade Unions

Abboushi, Suhail. Union Leaders' Willingness to Negotiate Concessions. *J. Lab. Res.*, Winter 1987, 8(1), pp. 47–58. [G: U.S.]

Addison, John T. and Castro, Alberto C. The Importance of Lifetime Jobs: Differences between Union and Nonunion Workers. *Ind. Lab. Relat. Rev.*, April 1987, *40*(3), pp. 393–405.   [G: U.S.]

Akkermans, Timie and Hövels, Ben. Young Workers and Trade Unions. A Comparison with Women and Workers in General. *Econ. Lavoro*, Apr.-June 1987, *21*(2), pp. 119–23.   [G: Netherlands]

Alexander, Kenneth O. The Worker, the Union and the Democratic Workplace. *Amer. J. Econ. Soc.*, October 1987, *46*(4), pp. 385–97.   [G: U.S.]

Allen, Steven G. Can Union Labor Ever Cost Less? *Quart. J. Econ.*, May 1987, *102*(2), pp. 347–73.   [G: U.S.]

Arnesen, Eric. To Rule or Ruin: New Orleans Dock Workers' Struggle for Control 1902–1903. *Labor Hist.*, Spring 1987, *28*(2), pp. 139–66.   [G: U.S.]

Ashenfelter, Orley. Arbitrator Behavior. *Amer. Econ. Rev.*, May 1987, *77*(2), pp. 342–46.   [G: U.S.]

Balducci, Renato. Strategie sindacali e occupazione. (With English summary.) *Stud. Econ.*, 1987, *42*(31), pp. 7–34.

Barron, John M.; Fuess, Scott M., Jr. and Loewenstein, Mark A. Further Analysis of the Effect of Unions on Training [Union Wages, Temporary Layoffs, and Seniority]. *J. Polit. Econ.*, June 1987, *95*(3), pp. 632–40.

Bassett, Philip. Consultation and the Right to Manage, 1980–1984. *Brit. J. Ind. Relat.*, July 1987, *25*(2), pp. 283–86.   [G: U.K.]

Beaumont, P. B. Individual Union Success in Obtaining Recognition: Some British Evidence. *Brit. J. Ind. Relat.*, November 1987, *25*(3), pp. 323–34.   [G: U.K.]

Becker, Brian E. and Olson, Craig A. Labor Relations and Firm Performance. *Allen, S. G., et al.*, 1987, pp. 43–85.

Beggs, John J. and Chapman, Bruce J. An Empirical Analysis of Australian Strike Activity: Estimating the Industrial Relations Effect of the First Three Years of the Prices and Incomes Accord. *Econ. Rec.*, March 1987, *63*(180), pp. 46–60.

Beladi, Hamid and Brunner, Lawrence P. Trade Unions and Money Wage Changes in U.S. Manufacturing Industries: Further Empirical Evidence. *Quart. J. Bus. Econ.*, Summer 1987, *26*(3), pp. 79–86.   [G: U.S.]

Bemmels, Brian. How Unions Affect Productivity in Manufacturing Plants. *Ind. Lab. Relat. Rev.*, January 1987, *40*(2), pp. 241–53.   [G: U.S.]

Benham, Harry C. Union–Nonunion Wage Differentials Revisited. *J. Lab. Res.*, Fall 1987, *8*(4), pp. 569–83.   [G: U.S.]

Bennett, James T. and DiLorenzo, Thomas J. Tax-Funded Unionism II: The Facade of Culture and Democracy. *J. Lab. Res.*, Winter 1987, *8*(1), pp. 31–46.   [G: U.S.]

Bennett, James T. and DiLorenzo, Thomas J. Tax-Funded Unionism III: Front Organiza-

tions. *J. Lab. Res.*, Spring 1987, *8*(2), pp. 179–89.   [G: U.S.]

Betcherman, Gordon and Rebne, Douglas. Technology and Control of the Labor Process: Fifty Years of Longshoring on the U.S. West Coast. *Cornfield, D. B., ed.*, 1987, pp. 73–89.   [G: U.S.]

Bhattacherjee, Debashish. Union-Type Effects on Bargaining Outcomes in Indian Manufacturing. *Brit. J. Ind. Relat.*, July 1987, *25*(2), pp. 247–66.   [G: India]

Block, Richard N., et al. Industrial Relations and the Performance of the Firm: An Overview. *Allen, S. G., et al.*, 1987, pp. 319–43.

Blum, Albert A. and Pataranapich, Somsong. Productivity and the Path to House Unionism: Structural Change in the Singapore Labour Movement. *Brit. J. Ind. Relat.*, November 1987, *25*(3), pp. 389–400.   [G: Singapore]

Boulle, Laurence and Julyan, Jacky. The Legal Structure of the Apartheid State. *Sethi, S. P., ed.*, 1987, pp. 127–48.   [G: S. Africa]

Brody, David. Elements of Paradox in U.S. Labor History. *Mon. Lab. Rev.*, August 1987, *110*(8), pp. 48–50.   [G: U.S.]

Bull, Clive. Business Cycle and Wage Determination in the United States. *Nalbantian, H. R., ed.*, 1987, pp. 213–28.   [G: U.S.]

Carruth, Alan A. and Oswald, Andrew J. On Union Preferences and Labour Market Models: Insiders and Outsiders. *Econ. J.*, June 1987, *97*(386), pp. 431–45.

Cecchetti, Stephen G. Indexation and Incomes Policy: A Study of Wage Adjustment in Unionized Manufacturing. *J. Lab. Econ.*, July 1987, *5*(3), pp. 391–412.   [G: U.S.]

Chaison, Gary N. and Andiappan, P. Profiles of Local Union Officers: Females v. Males. *Ind. Relat.*, Fall 1987, *26*(3), pp. 281–83.   [G: Canada]

Chamot, Dennis. Unions Need to Confront the Results of New Technology. *Mon. Lab. Rev.*, August 1987, *110*(8), pp. 45.   [G: U.S.]

Clark, Gordon L. and Johnston, K. The Geography of U.S. Union Elections 2: Performance of the United Auto Workers Union and the International Brotherhood of Electrical Workers Union, 1970–82. *Environ. Planning A*, February 1987, *19*(2), pp. 153–72. [G: U.S.]

Clark, Gordon L. and Johnston, K. The Geography of U.S. Union Elections 3: The Context and Structure of Union Electoral Performance (the International Brotherhood of Electrical Workers Union and the United Auto Workers Union, 1970–82). *Environ. Planning A*, March 1987, *19*(3), pp. 289–311.   [G: U.S.]

Clark, Gordon L. and Johnston, K. The Geography of U.S. Union Elections 4: Patterns of Close Elections and Determinants of the Margins of Victory and Loss (The International Brotherhood of Electrical Workers Union and the United Auto Workers Union, 1970–82). *Environ. Planning A*, April 1987, *19*(4), pp. 447–69.   [G: U.S.]

Clark, Gordon L. and Johnston, K. The Geography of U.S. Union Elections 5: Reconceptualizing the Theory of Industrial Unionism. *Environ. Planning A*, June 1987, *19*(6), pp. 719–34. [G: U.S.]

Clark, Gordon L. and Johnston, K. The Geography of U.S. Union Elections 1: The Crisis of U.S. Unions and a Critical Review of the Literature. *Environ. Planning A*, January 1987, *19*(1), pp. 33–57. [G: U.S.]

Cohen, Malcolm S. and Fulton, George A. Unions and Jobs: The U.S. Auto Industry—Comment. *J. Lab. Res.*, Summer 1987, *8*(3), pp. 307–10. [G: U.S.]

Contini, Giovanni. The Rise and Fall of Shop-Floor Bargaining at Fiat 1945–1980. *Tolliday, S. and Zeitlin, J., eds.*, 1987, pp. 144–67. [G: Italy]

Cornfield, Daniel B. Labor–Management Cooperation or Managerial Control? Emerging Patterns of Labor Relations in the United States. *Cornfield, D. B., ed.*, 1987, pp. 331–53. [G: U.S.]

Cornfield, Daniel B. Women in the Automated Office: Computers, Work, and Prospects for Unionization. *Lewin, D.; Lipsky, D. B. and Sockell, D., eds.*, 1987, pp. 177–98. [G: U.S.]

Costello, Cynthia B. Technological Change and Unionization in the Service Sector. *Mon. Lab. Rev.*, August 1987, *110*(8), pp. 45–46. [G: U.S.]

Denison, Ray. Protecting Workers in the Marketplace: New Union Benefit Privileges. *Mon. Lab. Rev.*, August 1987, *110*(8), pp. 39–40. [G: U.S.]

Dewatripont, Mathias. Entry Deterrence under Trade Unions. *Europ. Econ. Rev.*, Feb./Mar. 1987, *31*(1/2), pp. 149–56.

Di Tella, Torcuato S. Las huelgas en la minería mexicana, 1826–1828. (With English summary.) *Desarrollo Econ.*, Jan.-Mar. 1987, *26*(104), pp. 579–608. [G: Mexico]

Dickens, William T.; Wholey, Douglas R. and Robinson, James C. Correlates of Union Support in NLRB Elections. *Ind. Relat.*, Fall 1987, *26*(3), pp. 240–52. [G: U.S.]

DiGiacomo, Gordon. Trade Unions and the Reform of the Quality of Work Life: Ergonomic and Other QWL Reforms Have Limited Goals and Are Held No Substitute for Labor Involvement. *Amer. J. Econ. Soc.*, October 1987, *46*(4), pp. 399–414.

Dillon, Patricia and Gang, Ira N. Earnings Effects of Labor Organizations in 1890. *Ind. Lab. Relat. Rev.*, July 1987, *40*(4), pp. 516–27. [G: U.S.]

Dommel, Paul R. The Cleveland, Ohio United Labor Agency Dislocated Worker Project. *Cook, R. F., ed.*, 1987, pp. 111–27. [G: U.S.]

Donahue, Thomas R. and Oswald, Rudolph A. Labor Views the Pastoral Letter on the Economy. *Gannon, T. M., ed.*, 1987, pp. 228–45. [G: U.S.]

Dubofsky, Melvyn. The Extension of Solidarity Conflicts with the Spirit of Individualism. *Mon.*

Lab. Rev., August 1987, *110*(8), pp. 36–37. [G: U.S.]

Eberts, Randall W. Union-Negotiated Employment Rules and Teacher Quits. *Econ. Educ. Rev.*, 1987, *6*(1), pp. 15–25. [G: U.S.]

Eberts, Randall W. and Stone, Joe A. Teacher Unions and the Productivity of Public Schools. *Ind. Lab. Relat. Rev.*, April 1987, *40*(3), pp. 354–63. [G: U.S.]

Eichengreen, Barry. The Impact of Late Nineteenth-Century Unions on Labor Earnings and Hours: Iowa in 1894. *Ind. Lab. Relat. Rev.*, July 1987, *40*(4), pp. 501–15. [G: U.S.]

Ellis, I. A.; Pearson, J. M. and Periton, P. D. Trade Unions and Wage Inflation in the United Kingdom: A Re-estimation of Hines' Model. *Appl. Econ.*, May 1987, *19*(5), pp. 597–608. [G: U.K.]

Ellwood, David T. and Fine, Glenn. The Impact of Right-to-Work Laws on Union Organizing. *J. Polit. Econ.*, April 1987, *95*(2), pp. 250–73. [G: U.S.]

Ephlin, Donald F. UAW's View of Union's Role at Saturn Plant. *Shetty, Y. K. and Buehler, V. M., eds.*, 1987, pp. 149–61. [G: U.S.]

Faith, Roger L. and Reid, Joseph D., Jr. An Agency Theory of Unionism. *J. Econ. Behav. Organ.*, March 1987, *8*(1), pp. 39–60.

Faley, Robert H. and Froggatt, Kirk L. A Longitudinal Examination of the Membership Patterns of Minorities and Women in Referral Unions. *J. Lab. Res.*, Winter 1987, *8*(1), pp. 93–101. [G: U.S.]

Fields, Mitchell W.; Masters, Marick F. and Thacker, James W. Union Commitment and Membership Support for Political Action: An Exploratory Analysis. *J. Lab. Res.*, Spring 1987, *8*(2), pp. 143–57. [G: U.S.]

Figart, Deborah M. Gender, Unions, and Internal Labor Markets: Evidence from the Public Sector in Two States. *Amer. Econ. Rev.*, May 1987, *77*(2), pp. 252–56. [G: U.S.]

Fiorito, Jack. Political Instrumentality Perceptions and Desires for Union Representation. *J. Lab. Res.*, Summer 1987, *8*(3), pp. 271–89. [G: U.S.]

Fiorito, Jack and Hendricks, Wallace E. The Characteristics of National Unions. *Lewin, D.; Lipsky, D. B. and Sockell, D., eds.*, 1987, pp. 1–42. [G: U.S.]

Fiorito, Jack and Hendricks, Wallace E. Union Characteristics and Bargaining Outcomes. *Ind. Lab. Relat. Rev.*, July 1987, *40*(4), pp. 569–84. [G: U.S.]

Fiorito, Jack; Lowman, Christopher and Nelson, Forrest D. The Impact of Human Resource Policies on Union Organizing. *Ind. Relat.*, Spring 1987, *26*(2), pp. 113–26. [G: U.S.]

Fiorito, Jack and Maranto, Cheryl L. The Contemporary Decline of Union Strength. *Contemp. Policy Issues*, October 1987, *5*(4), pp. 12–27. [G: U.S.]

Flam, Harry. Equal Pay for Unequal Work. *Scand. J. Econ.*, 1987, *89*(4), pp. 435–50. [G: Sweden]

Florkowski, Gary and Schuster, Michael. Predicting the Decisions to Vote and Support Unions in Certification Elections: An Integrated Perspective. *J. Lab. Res.*, Spring 1987, *8*(2), pp. 191–207. **[G: U.S.]**

Foner, Philip S. Women and the American Labor Movement: A Historical Perspective. *Koziara, K. S.; Moskow, M. H. and Tanner, L. D., eds.*, 1987, pp. 154–86. **[G: U.S.]**

Fullagar, Clive and Barling, Julian. Toward a Model of Union Commitment. *Lewin, D.; Lipsky, D. B. and Sockell, D., eds.*, 1987, pp. 43–78.

Gottfries, Nils and Horn, Henrik. Wage Formation and the Persistence of Unemployment. *Econ. J.*, December 1987, *97*(388), pp. 877–84.

Gottlieb, Peter. Black Miners and the 1925–28 Bituminous Coal Strike: The Colored Committee of Non-Union Miners, Montour Mine No. 1, Pittsburgh Coal Company. *Labor Hist.*, Spring 1987, *28*(2), pp. 233–37. **[G: U.S.]**

Grancelli, Bruno. Political Trade-Offs, Collective Bargaining, Individual Tradings: Some Remarks on Industrial Relations in Italy. *Alessandrini, S. and Dallago, B., eds.*, 1987, pp. 257–70. **[G: Italy]**

Grant, E. Kenneth; Swidinsky, Robert and Vanderkamp, John. Canadian Union–Nonunion Wage Differentials. *Ind. Lab. Relat. Rev.*, October 1987, *41*(1), pp. 93–107. **[G: Canada]**

Grant, Wyn; Paterson, William and Whitston, Colin. Government–Industry Relations in the Chemical Industry: An Anglo–German Comparison. *Wilks, S. and Wright, M., eds.*, 1987, pp. 35–60. **[G: U.K.; W. Germany]**

Gray, Robert. The Languages of Factory Reform in Britain, *c.* 1830–1860. *Joyce, P., ed.*, 1987, pp. 143–79. **[G: U.K.]**

Gregory, Mary; Lobban, Peter and Thomson, Andrew. Pay Settlements in Manufacturing Industry, 1979–84: A Micro-data Study of the Impact of Product and Labour Market Pressures. *Oxford Bull. Econ. Statist.*, February 1987, *49*(1), pp. 129–50. **[G: U.K.]**

Grimes, John A. Are the Media Shortchanging Organized Labor? *Mon. Lab. Rev.*, August 1987, *110*(8), pp. 53–54. **[G: U.S.]**

Grimes, Paul W. Right-to-Work Legislation and the Economic Position of Black Workers. *Rev. Black Polit. Econ.*, Spring 1987, *15*(4), pp. 79–88. **[G: U.S.]**

Hanson, Charles G. Economic Significance of British Labor Law Reform. *Cato J.*, Winter 1987, *6*(3), pp. 851–68. **[G: U.K.]**

Harris, William H. The Black Labor Movement and the Fight for Social Advance. *Mon. Lab. Rev.*, August 1987, *110*(8), pp. 37–38. **[G: U.S.]**

Hartmann, Heinz and Horstmann, Jörg. A Trade Union Information Strategy–The Case of the German Metal Workers Union. *Brit. J. Ind. Relat.*, November 1987, *25*(3), pp. 371–88. **[G: W. Germany]**

Henley, Andrew. Trades Unions, Market Concentration and Income Distribution in United States Manufacturing Industry. *Int. J. Ind. Or-*

gan., June 1987, *5*(2), pp. 193–210.

Henwood, Felicity and Wyatt, Sally. Managing Technological Change: Responses of Government, Employers, and Trade Unions in Western Europe and Canada. *Hartmann, H. I., ed.*, 1987, pp. 395–431. **[G: OECD]**

Hersoug, Tor; Kjaer, Knut N. and Rødseth, Asbjorn. Wages, Taxes and the Utility-Maximizing Trade Union: A Confrontation with Norwegian Data. *Sinclair, P. J. N., ed.*, 1987, *1986*, pp. 431–51. **[G: Norway]**

Hibbs, Douglas A., Jr. Trade Union Power, Wage Inflation, and Labor Militancy: A Comparative Analysis. *Hibbs, D. A., Jr.*, 1987, *1977*, pp. 77–114. **[G: Italy; France; U.K.; U.S.]**

Hill, Norman. Forging a Partnership between Blacks and Unions. *Mon. Lab. Rev.*, August 1987, *110*(8), pp. 38–39. **[G: U.S.]**

Hirsch, Barry T. and Connolly, Robert A. Do Unions Capture Monopoly Profits? *Ind. Lab. Relat. Rev.*, October 1987, *41*(1), pp. 118–36. **[G: U.S.]**

Hirsch, Barry T. and Link, Albert N. Labor Union Effects on Innovative Activity. *J. Lab. Res.*, Fall 1987, *8*(4), pp. 323–32. **[G: U.S.]**

Hirsch, Barry T. and Neufeld, John L. Nominal and Real Union Wage Differentials and the Effects of Industry and SMSA Density: 1973–83. *J. Human Res.*, Winter 1987, *22*(1), pp. 138–48. **[G: U.S.]**

Hoyman, Michele M. and Stallworth, Lamont. Participation in Local Unions: A Comparison of Black and White Members. *Ind. Lab. Relat. Rev.*, April 1987, *40*(3), pp. 323–35. **[G: U.S.]**

Hundley, Greg. The Threat of Unionism and Wage-Coverage Effects. *J. Lab. Res.*, Summer 1987, *8*(3), pp. 237–51. **[G: U.S.]**

Hunt, Janet C.; Kiker, B. F. and Williams, C. Glyn. The Effect of Type of Union on Member–Nonmember Wage Differentials. *J. Lab. Res.*, Winter 1987, *8*(1), pp. 59–65. **[G: U.S.]**

Hyman, Richard. Unemployment and Trade Unions in Britain: The Politics of Industrial Relations in the Crisis. *Pedersen, P. J. and Lund, R., eds.*, 1987, pp. 207–23. **[G: U.K.]**

Işikli, Alpaslan. Wage Labor and Unionization. *Schick, I. C. and Tonak, E. A., eds.*, 1987, pp. 309–32. **[G: Turkey]**

Jacobs, David C. The UAW and the Committee for National Health Insurance: The Contours of Social Unionism. *Lewin, D.; Lipsky, D. B. and Sockell, D., eds.*, 1987, pp. 119–40. **[G: U.S.]**

Janick, Herbert. Yale Blue: Unionization at Yale University, 1931–1985. *Labor Hist.*, Summer 1987, *28*(3), pp. 349–69. **[G: U.S.]**

Kahn, Lawrence M. and Curme, Michael. Unions and Nonunion Wage Dispersion. *Rev. Econ. Statist.*, November 1987, *69*(4), pp. 600–607. **[G: U.S.]**

Kalleberg, Arne L., et al. The Eclipse of Craft: The Changing Face of Labor in the Newspaper Industry. *Cornfield, D. B., ed.*, 1987, pp. 47–71. **[G: U.S.]**

Katz, Harry C. Recent Developments in U.S.

Auto Labour Relations. *Tolliday, S. and Zeitlin, J., eds.*, 1987, pp. 282–304.   [G: U.S.]

Kaufman, Bruce E. and Martinez-Vazquez, Jorge. The Ross–Dunlop Debate and Union Wage Concessions: A Median Voter Analysis. *J. Lab. Res.*, Summer 1987, *8*(3), pp. 291–305.

Kaufman, Robert S. and Kaufman, Roger T. Union Effects on Productivity, Personnel Practices, and Survival in the Automotive Parts Industry. *J. Lab. Res.*, Fall 1987, *8*(4), pp. 333–50.   [G: U.S.]

Keegan, Carol. How Union Members and Nonmembers View the Role of Unions. *Mon. Lab. Rev.*, August 1987, *110*(8), pp. 50–51.
[G: U.S.]

Kelly, John. Trade Unions through the Recession, 1980–1984. *Brit. J. Ind. Relat.*, July 1987, *25*(2), pp. 275–82.

Kemp, Murray C.; Léonard, Daniel and Long, Ngo Van. Trades Unions, Seniority and Unemployment. *Europ. Econ. Rev.*, July 1987, *31*(5), pp. 1093–1112.

Kemp, Murray C. and Long, Ngo Van. Union Power in the Long Run. *Scand. J. Econ.*, 1987, *89*(1), pp. 103–13.

Kessler-Harris, Alice. Trade Unions Mirror Society in Conflict between Collectivism and Individualism. *Mon. Lab. Rev.*, August 1987, *110*(8), pp. 32–36.   [G: U.S.]

Kidd, David P. and Oswald, Andrew J. A Dynamic Model of Trade Union Behaviour. *Economica*, August 1987, *54*(215), pp. 355–65.

Klay, William Earle. How Are Japanese Unions Responding to Microelectronics-Based Automation? *Mon. Lab. Rev.*, March 1987, *110*(3), pp. 39–40.   [G: Japan]

Knight, Thomas R. Tactical Use on the Union's Duty of Fair Representation: An Empirical Analysis. *Ind. Lab. Relat. Rev.*, January 1987, *40*(2), pp. 180–94.   [G: Canada]

Kurth, Michael M. Teachers' Unions and Excellence in Education: An Analysis of the Decline in SAT Scores. *J. Lab. Res.*, Fall 1987, *8*(4), pp. 351–67.   [G: U.S.]

Larsson, Rune; Lund, Reinhard and Møller, Jørgen. Trade Union Stratey towards Unemployment at the Local Level. *Pedersen, P. J. and Lund, R., eds.*, 1987, pp. 225–39.
[G: Denmark]

Lawrence, Anne T. Union Responses to Plant Closure. *Staudohar, P. D. and Brown, H. E.*, 1987, pp. 201–15.   [G: U.S.]

Leigh, Duane E. and Hills, Stephen M. Male–Female Differences in the Potential for Union Growth Outside Traditionally Unionized Industries. *J. Lab. Res.*, Spring 1987, *8*(2), pp. 131–42.   [G: U.S.]

Lewin, David. Industrial Relations as a Strategic Variable. *Allen, S. G., et al.*, 1987, pp. 1–41.
[G: U.S.]

Lichtenstein, Nelson. Reutherism on the Shop Floor: Union Strategy and Shop-Floor Conflict in the USA 1946–70. *Tolliday, S. and Zeitlin, J., eds.*, 1987, pp. 121–43.   [G: U.S.]

Lindbeck, Assar and Snower, Dennis J. Strike and Lock-Out Threats and Fiscal Policy. *Oxford Econ. Pap.*, December 1987, *39*(4), pp. 760–84.

Lindbeck, Assar and Snower, Dennis J. Union Activity, Unemployment Persistence and Wage–Employment Ratchets. *Europ. Econ. Rev.*, Feb./Mar. 1987, *31*(1/2), pp. 157–67.

Lintner, V. G., et al. Trade Unions and Technological Change in the U.K. Mechanical Engineering Industry. *Brit. J. Ind. Relat.*, March 1987, *25*(1), pp. 19–29.   [G: U.K.]

Lynch, Lisa M. and Sandver, Marcus H. Determinants of the Decertification Process: Evidence from Employer-Initiated Elections. *J. Lab. Res.*, Winter 1987, *8*(1), pp. 85–91.
[G: U.S.]

MacPherson, David A. and Stewart, James B. Unionism and the Dispersion of Wages among Blue-Collar Women. *J. Lab. Res.*, Fall 1987, *8*(4), pp. 395–405.   [G: U.S.]

Maki, Dennis R. and Meredith, Lindsay N. A Note on Unionization and the Elasticity of Substitution. *Can. J. Econ.*, November 1987, *20*(4), pp. 792–801.   [G: Canada]

Malcomson, James M. Trade Union Labour Contracts: An Introduction. *Europ. Econ. Rev.*, Feb./Mar. 1987, *31*(1/2), pp. 139–48.

Malcomson, James M. and Sartor, Nicola. Tax Push Inflation in a Unionized Labour Market. *Europ. Econ. Rev.*, December 1987, *31*(8), pp. 1581–96.   [G: Italy]

Manning, Alan. An Integration of Trade Union Models in a Sequential Bargaining Framework. *Econ. J.*, March 1987, *97*(385), pp. 121–39.

Maranto, Cheryl L. and Fiorito, Jack. The Effect of Union Characteristics on the Outcome of NLRB Certification Elections. *Ind. Lab. Relat. Rev.*, January 1987, *40*(2), pp. 225–40.
[G: U.S.]

Marchington, Mick. A Review and Critique of Research on Developments in Joint Consultation. *Brit. J. Ind. Relat.*, November 1987, *25*(3), pp. 339–52.   [G: U.K.]

Masters, Marick F. and Delaney, John Thomas. Union Legislative Records during President Reagan's First Term. *J. Lab. Res.*, Winter 1987, *8*(1), pp. 1–18.   [G: U.S.]

Masters, Marick F. and Delaney, John Thomas. Union Political Activities: A Review of the Empirical Literature. *Ind. Lab. Relat. Rev.*, April 1987, *40*(3), pp. 336–53.

Masters, Marick F. and Zardkoohi, Asghar. Labor Unions and the U.S. Congress: PAC Allocations and Legislative Voting. *Lewin, D.; Lipsky, D. B. and Sockell, D., eds.*, 1987, pp. 79–117.   [G: U.S.]

McCallum, Ronald C. Civil Liberties and Industrial Relations; *Hein v. Jaques Ltd. Australian Bull. Lab.*, September 1987, *13*(4), pp. 225–36.   [G: Australia]

McClelland, Keith. Time to Work, Time to Live: Some Aspects of Work and the Re-formation of Class in Britain, 1850–1880. *Joyce, P., ed.*, 1987, pp. 180–209.   [G: U.K.]

Mickwitz, Gösta. Fackföreningarna och individerna. (Trade Unions and Individuals. With

English summary.) *Ekon. Samfundets Tidskr.*, 1987, *40*(1), pp. 3–4.

Mills, Herb and Wellman, David. Contractually Sanctioned Job Action and Workers' Control: The Case of San Francisco Longshoremen. *Labor Hist.*, Spring 1987, *28*(2), pp. 167–95.
[G: U.S.]

Mitchell, Daniel J. B. The Share Economy and Industrial Relations. *Ind. Relat.*, Winter 1987, *26*(1), pp. 1–17. [G: U.S.]

Moore, William J. and Raisian, John. Union–Nonunion Wage Differentials in the Public Administration, Educational, and Private Sectors: 1970–1983. *Rev. Econ. Statist.*, November 1987, *69*(4), pp. 608–16. [G: U.S.]

Needleman, Ruth and Tanner, Lucretia Dewey. Women in Unions: Current Issues. *Koziara, K. S.; Moskow, M. H. and Tanner, L. D., eds.*, 1987, pp. 187–224. [G: U.S.]

Nelson, Daniel. Unions' Struggle to Survive Goes Beyond Modern Technology. *Mon. Lab. Rev.*, August 1987, *110*(8), pp. 41–45. [G: U.S.]

Ng, Sek-Hong and Lansbury, Russell D. The Workers' Congress in Chinese Enterprises. *Warner, M., ed.*, 1987, pp. 149–61.
[G: China]

Okayama, Reiko. Industrial Relations in the Japanese Automobile Industry 1945–70: The Case of Toyota. *Tolliday, S. and Zeitlin, J., eds.*, 1987, pp. 168–89. [G: Japan]

Oswald, Andrew J. New Research on the Economics of Trade Unions and Labor Contracts. *Ind. Relat.*, Winter 1987, *26*(1), pp. 30–45.

Pearce, Thomas G. and Peterson, Richard B. Regionality in NLRB Decertification Cases. *J. Lab. Res.*, Summer 1987, *8*(3), pp. 253–69.
[G: U.S.]

Perloff, Jeffrey M. and Sickles, Robin C. Union Wage, Hours, and Earnings Differentials in the Construction Industry. *J. Lab. Econ.*, April 1987, *5*(2), pp. 174–210. [G: U.S.]

Peterson, Richard B. and Peterson, Mark R. Toward a Systematic Understanding of the Labor Mediation Process. *Lewin, D.; Lipsky, D. B. and Sockell, D., eds.*, 1987, pp. 141–60.
[G: U.S.]

Pissarides, Christopher A. A Critical Assessment of Some Recent Approaches to the Theory of Unemployment. *Pedersen, P. J. and Lund, R., eds.*, 1987, pp. 3–16.

Polachek, Solomon W.; Wunnava, Phanindra V. and Hutchins, Michael T. Panel Estimates of Union Effects on Wages and Wage Growth. *Rev. Econ. Statist.*, August 1987, *69*(3), pp. 527–31. [G: U.S.]

Price, Jamie and Yandle, Bruce. Labor Markets and Sunday Closing Laws. *J. Lab. Res.*, Fall 1987, *8*(4), pp. 407–14. [G: U.S.]

Reid, Joseph D., Jr. and Faith, Roger L. Right-to-Work and Union Compensation Structure. *J. Lab. Res.*, Spring 1987, *8*(2), pp. 111–30.
[G: U.S.]

Reynolds, Morgan O. Unions and Jobs: The U.S. Auto Industry—Reply. *J. Lab. Res.*, Summer 1987, *8*(3), pp. 311–15. [G: U.S.]

Rico, Leonard. The New Industrial Relations:

British Electricians' New-Style Agreements. *Ind. Lab. Relat. Rev.*, October 1987, *41*(1), pp. 63–78. [G: U.K.]

Robson, Peter. A View from the Unions. *Stegman, T., et al.*, 1987, pp. 53–63. [G: Australia]

Roche, William K. Leisure, Insecurity and Union Policy in Britain: A Critical Extension of Bienefeld's Theory of Hours Rounds. *Brit. J. Ind. Relat.*, March 1987, *25*(1), pp. 1–17.
[G: U.K.]

Rose, Nancy L. Labor Rent Sharing and Regulation: Evidence from the Trucking Industry. *J. Polit. Econ.*, December 1987, *95*(6), pp. 1146–78. [G: U.S.]

Rosenzweig, Roy. American Labor History: A Conspiracy of Silence? *Mon. Lab. Rev.*, August 1987, *110*(8), pp. 51–53. [G: U.S.]

Rosholt, A. M. The South African Private Sector: Agent for Change or Government Stooge? *Sethi, S. P., ed.*, 1987, pp. 355–61.
[G: S. Africa]

Ross, George. From One Left to Another: *Le Social* in Mitterrand's France. *Ross, G.; Hoffmann, S. and Malzacher, S., eds.*, 1987, pp. 199–216. [G: France]

Rubery, Jill. Flexibility of Labour Costs in Nonunion Firms. *Tarling, R., ed.*, 1987, pp. 59–83.

Rule, John. The Property of Skill in the Period of Manufacture. *Joyce, P., ed.*, 1987, pp. 99–118. [G: U.K.]

Ryan, Paul. Trade Unionism and the Pay of Young Workers. *Junankar, P. N., ed.*, 1987, pp. 119–42. [G: OECD]

Samuel, Howard D. AFL-CIO Favors Enlisting Workers in Search of Quality. *Shetty, Y. K. and Buehler, V. M., eds.*, 1987, pp. 163–71.
[G: U.S.]

Schwartz, Abba. The Effects of Labour Unions on Investment in Training: A Dynamic Model: Comments. *Razin, A. and Sadka, E., eds.*, 1987, pp. 479–94.

Schwochau, Susan. Union Effects on Job Attitudes. *Ind. Lab. Relat. Rev.*, January 1987, *40*(2), pp. 209–24. [G: U.S.]

Shaiken, Harley. Globalization and the Worldwide Division of Labor. *Mon. Lab. Rev.*, August 1987, *110*(8), pp. 47. [G: U.S.]

Shostak, Arthur B. Technology, Air Traffic Control, and Labor–Management Relations. *Cornfield, D. B., ed.*, 1987, pp. 153–72. [G: U.S.]

Siebert, W. S. Black Trade Unions and the Wage Gap in South Africa. *Managerial Dec. Econ.*, March 1987, *8*(1), pp. 55–65. [G: S. Africa]

Sockell, Donna and Delany, John Thomas. Union Organizing and the Reagan NLRB. *Contemp. Policy Issues*, October 1987, *5*(4), pp. 28–45.
[G: U.S.]

Sonenscher, Michael. Mythical Work: Workshop Production and the *Compagnonnages* of Eighteenth-Century France. *Joyce, P., ed.*, 1987, pp. 31–63. [G: France]

Spilsbury, M., et al. A Note on the Trade Union Membership Patterns of Young Adults. *Brit. J. Ind. Relat.*, July 1987, *25*(2), pp. 267–74.
[G: U.K.]

Sproull, Alan and MacInnes, John. Patterns of Union Recognition in Scottish Electronics. *Brit. J. Ind. Relat.*, November 1987, *25*(3), pp. 335–38. **[G: U.K.]**

Stewart, Mark B. Collective Bargaining Arrangements, Closed Shops and Relative Pay. *Econ. J.*, March 1987, *97*(385), pp. 140–56. **[G: U.K.]**

Tauman, Yair and Weiss, Yoram. Labor Unions and the Adoption of New Technology. *J. Lab. Econ.*, Part 1, Oct. 1987, *5*(4), pp. 477–501.

Taylor, John B. The Role of Contracts in Macroeconomic Performance. *Nalbantian, H. R., ed.*, 1987, pp. 189–201. **[G: U.S.]**

Thomas, Robert J. Microchips and Macroharvests: Labor–Management Relations in Agriculture. *Cornfield, D. B., ed.*, 1987, pp. 27–45. **[G: U.S.]**

Thornton, Robert J. Unions, Wages, and Local Government Finance. *Aronson, J. R. and Schwartz, E., eds.*, 1987, pp. 383–99. **[G: U.S.]**

Tolliday, Steven. Management and Labour in Britain 1896–1939. *Tolliday, S. and Zeitlin, J., eds.*, 1987, pp. 29–56. **[G: U.K.]**

Tolliday, Steven and Zeitlin, Jonathan. Shop-Floor Bargaining, Contract Unionism and Job Control: An Anglo–American Comparison. *Tolliday, S. and Zeitlin, J., eds.*, 1987, pp. 99–120. **[G: U.S.; U.K.]**

Tomlins, Christopher L. Criminal Conspiracy and Early Labor Combinations: Massachusetts, 1824–1840. *Labor Hist.*, Summer 1987, *28*(3), pp. 370–85. **[G: U.S.]**

Townley, Barbara. Union Recognition: A Comparative Analysis of the Pros and Cons of a Legal Procedure. *Brit. J. Ind. Relat.*, July 1987, *25*(2), pp. 177–99. **[G: U.S.; U.K.]**

Turner, Stephen. The Swedish Model: What Went Wrong? *Eliasson, G., ed.*, 1987, pp. 73–84. **[G: Sweden]**

Tzannatos, Zafiris. Union *versus* Non-union Wages, Arithmetic *versus* Geometric Means and Grouped Data Revisited. *Bull. Econ. Res.*, January 1987, *39*(1), pp. 91–94.

Van Heerden, J. H. P. and Van Tonder, J. J. Ekonomiese oorsake van vakbondgroei in Suid-Afrika. (With English summary.) *S. Afr. J. Econ.*, March 1987, *55*(1), pp. 34–39. **[G: S. Africa]**

Verma, Anil. Union and Nonunion Wages at the Firm Level: A Combined Institutional and Econometric Analysis. *J. Lab. Res.*, Winter 1987, *8*(1), pp. 67–83. **[G: U.S.]**

Verma, Anil and McKersie, Robert B. Employee Involvement: The Implications of Noninvolvement by Unions. *Ind. Lab. Relat. Rev.*, July 1987, *40*(4), pp. 556–68. **[G: U.S.]**

Villa, Paola. Systems of Flexible Working in the Italian Steel Industry. *Tarling, R., ed.*, 1987, pp. 307–45. **[G: Italy]**

Voos, Paula B. Union Organizing Expenditures: Determinants and Their Implications for Union Growth. *J. Lab. Res.*, Winter 1987, *8*(1), pp. 19–30. **[G: U.S.]**

Weiss, Yoram. The Effect of Labour Unions on Investment in Training: A Dynamic Model. *Razin, A. and Sadka, E., eds.*, 1987, pp. 435–67.

Willim, Horst. Trade Unions and Occupational Safety in the German Democratic Republic. *Int. Lab. Rev.*, 1987, *126*(3), pp. 329–36. **[G: E. Germany]**

Wilson, Charles. The Effect of Labour Unions on Investment in Training: A Dynamic Model: Comments. *Razin, A. and Sadka, E., eds.*, 1987, pp. 468–78.

Winckler, Victoria. Women and Work in Contemporary Wales. *Day, G. and Rees, G., eds.*, 1987, pp. 53–71. **[G: U.K.]**

Withers, Glenn. The Australian Economy in the Long Run: Labour. *Maddock, R. and McLean, I. W., eds.*, 1987, pp. 248–88. **[G: Australia]**

Yanaev, G. I. Soviet Restructuring: The Position and Role of the Trade Unions. *Int. Lab. Rev.*, Nov.-Dec. 1987, *126*(6), pp. 703–13.

Zeleza, Paul Tiyambe. Trade Union Imperialism: American Labour, the ICFTU and the Kenyan Labour Movement. *Soc. Econ. Stud.*, June 1987, *36*(2), pp. 145–70. **[G: Kenya]**

832 Collective Bargaining

8320 General

Armstrong, T. E. Unemployment: Industrial Relations: Comment. *Gunderson, M.; Meltz, N. M. and Ostry, S., eds.*, 1987, pp. 196–99. **[G: Canada]**

Becker, Brian E. and Olson, Craig A. Labor Relations and Firm Performance. *Allen, S. G., et al.*, 1987, pp. 43–85.

Beggs, John J. and Chapman, Bruce J. An Empirical Analysis of Australian Strike Activity: Estimating the Industrial Relations Effect of the First Three Years of the Prices and Incomes Accord. *Econ. Rec.*, March 1987, *63*(180), pp. 46–60.

Begin, James P. and Lee, Barbara A. NLRA Exclusion Criteria and Professional Work. *Ind. Relat.*, Winter 1987, *26*(1), pp. 83–95. **[G: U.S.]**

Block, Richard N., et al. Industrial Relations and the Performance of the Firm: An Overview. *Allen, S. G., et al.*, 1987, pp. 319–43.

Ciudad Reynaud, Adolfo. Labour Relations in Peru: The Outlook for Change. *Int. Lab. Rev.*, July-Aug. 1987, *126*(4), pp. 457–66. **[G: Peru]**

Crispo, John. Unemployment: Industrial Relations: Comment. *Gunderson, M.; Meltz, N. M. and Ostry, S., eds.*, 1987, pp. 193–96. **[G: Canada]**

De Alessi, Louis. Specific Human Capital and Collective Codetermination Rights: Comment. *Pethig, R. and Schlieper, U., eds.*, 1987, pp. 149–51.

Dickens, William T.; Wholey, Douglas R. and Robinson, James C. Correlates of Union Support in NLRB Elections. *Ind. Relat.*, Fall 1987, *26*(3), pp. 240–52. **[G: U.S.]**

DuBose, Philip B. and Bigoness, William J. A

Test of Wheeler's Closed-Offer Arbitration System: An Experimental Study. *J. Lab. Res.*, Fall 1987, *8*(4), pp. 385–93.   [G: U.S.]

Dunlop, John T. Industrial Relations and Unemployment. *Gunderson, M.; Meltz, N. M. and Ostry, S.*, eds., 1987, pp. 184–92.   [G: U.S.]

Fryer, John. Unemployment: Industrial Relations: Comment. *Gunderson, M.; Meltz, N. M. and Ostry, S.*, eds., 1987, pp. 201–06.
[G: Canada]

Geary, Dick. Unemployment and Working-Class Solidarity: The Germany Experience 1929–33. *Evans, R. J. and Geary, D.*, eds., 1987, pp. 261–80.   [G: Germany]

Gunderson, Morley and Melino, Angelo. Estimating Strike Effects in a General Model of Prices and Quantities. *J. Lab. Econ.*, January 1987, *5*(1), pp. 1–19.   [G: U.S.]

Hancock, Keith. Regulation and Deregulation in the Australian Labour Market. *Australian Bull. Lab.*, March 1987, *13*(2), pp. 94–107.
[G: Australia]

Hanson, Charles G. Economic Significance of British Labor Law Reform. *Cato J.*, Winter 1987, *6*(3), pp. 851–68.   [G: U.K.]

Hendricks, Wallace E. and Kahn, Lawrence M. Contract Length, Wage Indexation, and *Ex Ante* Variability of Real Wages. *J. Lab. Res.*, Summer 1987, *8*(3), pp. 221–36.   [G: U.S.]

Hibbs, Douglas A., Jr. Industrial Conflict in Advanced Industrial Societies. *Hibbs, D. A., Jr.*, 1987, *1976*, pp. 17–51.   [G: U.S.; W. Europe; Japan]

Hibbs, Douglas A., Jr. On the Political Economy of Long-run Trends in Strike Activity. *Hibbs, D. A., Jr.*, 1987, *1978*, pp. 52–76.
[G: W. Europe; Canada; U.S.]

Hibbs, Douglas A., Jr. The Political Economy of Industrial Democracies: Introduction. *Hibbs, D. A., Jr.*, 1987, pp. 1–13.

Hiltrop, Jean M. Reply [Dispute Settlement and Mediation]. *Ind. Relat.*, Fall 1987, *26*(3), pp. 317.   [G: U.K.]

Hodges-Aeberhard, Jane and Odero de Dios, Alberto. Principles of the Committee on Freedom of Association Concerning Strikes. *Int. Lab. Rev.*, Sept.-Oct. 1987, *126*(5), pp. 543–63.   [G: Global]

Hundley, Greg and Koreisha, Sergio. The Specification of Econometric Strike Models: A VARMA Approach. *Appl. Econ.*, April 1987, *19*(4), pp. 511–30.   [G: U.S.]

Jacoby, Sanford M. The Development of Cost-of-Living Escalators in the United States. *Labor Hist.*, Fall 1987, *28*(4), pp. 515–33.
[G: U.S.]

Kaufman, Bruce E. and Martinez-Vazquez, Jorge. The Ross–Dunlop Debate and Union Wage Concessions: A Median Voter Analysis. *J. Lab. Res.*, Summer 1987, *8*(3), pp. 291–305.

Koken, Bernd K. Unemployment: Industrial Relations: Comment. *Gunderson, M.; Meltz, N. M. and Ostry, S.*, eds., 1987, pp. 199–201.
[G: Canada]

Leeds, Michael A. Bargaining as Search Behavior under Mutual Uncertainty. *Southern Econ. J.*,

January 1987, *53*(3), pp. 677–84.

Lewin, David. Industrial Relations as a Strategic Variable. *Allen, S. G., et al.*, 1987, pp. 1–41.
[G: U.S.]

Manning, Alan. Collective Bargaining Institutions and Efficiency: An Application of a Sequential Bargaining Model. *Europ. Econ. Rev.*, Feb./Mar. 1987, *31*(1/2), pp. 168–76.

Marsden, David. Collective Bargaining and Industrial Adjustment in Britain, France, Italy and West Germany. *Duchêne, F. and Shepherd, G.*, eds., 1987, pp. 178–209. [G: U.K.; France; Italy; W. Germany]

Monissen, Hans G. and Wenger, Ekkehard. Specific Human Capital and Collective Codetermination Rights. *Pethig, R. and Schlieper, U.*, eds., 1987, pp. 127–48.   [G: W. Germany]

Pearce, Thomas G. and Peterson, Richard B. Regionality in NLRB Decertification Cases. *J. Lab. Res.*, Summer 1987, *8*(3), pp. 253–69.
[G: U.S.]

Peterson, Richard B. and Peterson, Mark R. Toward a Systematic Understanding of the Labor Mediation Process. *Lewin, D.; Lipsky, D. B. and Sockell, D.*, eds., 1987, pp. 141–60.
[G: U.S.]

Petith, Howard C. Strike Costs, Ability to Win and the Determination of Wage Settlements. *Rech. Écon. Louvain*, 1987, *53*(4), pp. 345–55.

Pissarides, Christopher A. A Critical Assessment of Some Recent Approaches to the Theory of Unemployment. *Pedersen, P. J. and Lund, R.*, eds., 1987, pp. 3–16.

van der Ploeg, Frederick. Trade Unions, Investment, and Employment: A Non-cooperative Approach. *Europ. Econ. Rev.*, October 1987, *31*(7), pp. 1465–92.

Pohjola, Matti. Profit-Sharing, Collective Bargaining and Employment. *J. Inst. Theoretical Econ.*, June 1987, *143*(2), pp. 334–42.

Protti, Ray. Unemployment: Industrial Relations: Comment. *Gunderson, M.; Meltz, N. M. and Ostry, S.*, eds., 1987, pp. 206–08.
[G: Canada]

Singh, Ramsumair. Dispute Settlement and Mediation. *Ind. Relat.*, Fall 1987, *26*(3), pp. 314–16.   [G: U.K.]

Tobin, James. After Disinflation, Then What? *Tobin, J. (III)*, 1987, *1984*, pp. 348–67.
[G: U.S.]

Tracy, Joseph S. An Empirical Test of an Asymmetric Information Model of Strikes. *J. Lab. Econ.*, April 1987, *5*(2), pp. 149–73.
[G: U.S.]

Ulman, Lloyd. Who Wanted Collective Bargaining in the First Place? *Contemp. Policy Issues*, October 1987, *5*(4), pp. 1–11.   [G: U.S.; W. Europe]

8321 Collective Bargaining in the Private Sector

Abboushi, Suhail. Union Leaders' Willingness to Negotiate Concessions. *J. Lab. Res.*, Winter 1987, *8*(1), pp. 47–58.   [G: U.S.]

Ahlburg, Dennis A., et al. Technological Change,

Market Decline, and Industrial Relations in the U.S. Steel Industry. *Cornfield, D. B., ed.*, 1987, pp. 229–45.   [G: U.S.]

Ashenfelter, Orley. Arbitrator Behavior. *Amer. Econ. Rev.*, May 1987, 77(2), pp. 342–46.
          [G: U.S.]

Bacharach, Samuel B.; Schmidle, Timothy P. and Bauer, Scott C. Collective Bargaining in American Industry: Higher Education. *Lipsky, D. B. and Donn, C. B., eds.*, 1987, pp. 225–64.
          [G: U.S.]

Baxter, Vern. Technological Change and Labor Relations in the United States Postal Service. *Cornfield, D. B., ed.*, 1987, pp. 91–110.
          [G: U.S.]

Becker, Brian E. Concession Bargaining: The Impact of Shareholders' Equity. *Ind. Lab. Relat. Rev.*, January 1987, 40(2), pp. 268–79.
          [G: U.S.]

Beggs, John J. and Chapman, Bruce J. Declining Strike Activity in Australia 1983–85: An International Phenomenon? *Econ. Rec.*, December 1987, 63(183), pp. 330–39.   [G: Australia]

Bernard, Jean-Paul. Internationalisation des firmes et conflictualité: le cas des entreprises situées en Picardie (1982–85). (Internationalizing Firms Facing Industrial Conflict. Set Up Plans in Picardy: The Case (1982–85). With English summary.) *Écon. Soc.*, June 1987, 21(6), pp. 53–83.   [G: France]

Betcherman, Gordon and Rebne, Douglas. Technology and Control of the Labor Process: Fifty Years of Longshoring on the U.S. West Coast. *Cornfield, D. B., ed.*, 1987, pp. 73–89.
          [G: U.S.]

Bhattacherjee, Debashish. Union-Type Effects on Bargaining Outcomes in Indian Manufacturing. *Brit. J. Ind. Relat.*, July 1987, 25(2), pp. 247–66.   [G: India]

Block, Richard N. and Stieber, Jack. The Impact of Attorneys and Arbitrators on Arbitration Awards. *Ind. Lab. Relat. Rev.*, July 1987, 40(4), pp. 543–55.   [G: U.S.]

Bloom, David E. and Cavanagh, Christopher L. Negotiator Behavior under Arbitration. *Amer. Econ. Rev.*, May 1987, 77(2), pp. 353–58.
          [G: U.S.]

Borum, Joan; Conley, James and Wasilewski, Edward. Collective Bargaining in 1987: Local, Regional Issues to Set Tone. *Mon. Lab. Rev.*, January 1987, 110(1), pp. 23–36.   [G: U.S.]

Bryne, Dennis M. and King, Randall H. Import Penetration and Strike Activity in Manufacturing, 1961–77. *Atlantic Econ. J.*, July 1987, 15(2), pp. 77–84.   [G: U.S.]

Cappelli, Peter. Bargaining Structure and Wage Outcomes in the British Coal Industry. *Ind. Relat.*, Spring 1987, 26(2), pp. 127–45.
          [G: U.K.]

Cappelli, Peter. Collective Bargaining in American Industry: Airlines. *Lipsky, D. B. and Donn, C. B., eds.*, 1987, pp. 135–86.
          [G: U.S.]

Carruth, Alan A. and Oswald, Andrew J. Wage Inflexibility in Britain. *Oxford Bull. Econ. Sta-*

tist., February 1987, 49(1), pp. 59–78.
          [G: U.K.]

Carter, Colin A., et al. Agricultural Labor Strikes and Farmers' Income. *Econ. Inquiry,* January 1987, 25(1), pp. 121–33.   [G: U.S.]

Cecchetti, Stephen G. Indexation and Incomes Policy: A Study of Wage Adjustment in Unionized Manufacturing. *J. Lab. Econ.*, July 1987, 5(3), pp. 391–412.   [G: U.S.]

Chan-Lee, James H.; Coe, David T. and Prywes, Menahem. Microeconomic Changes and Macroeconomic Wage Disinflation in the 1980s. *OECD Econ. Stud.*, Spring 1987, (8), pp. 121–57.

Contini, Giovanni. The Rise and Fall of Shop-Floor Bargaining at Fiat 1945–1980. *Tolliday, S. and Zeitlin, J., eds.*, 1987, pp. 144–67.
          [G: Italy]

Couto, Richard A. Changing Technologies and Consequences for Labor in Coal Mining. *Cornfield, D. B., ed.*, 1987, pp. 175–202.
          [G: U.S.]

Dohse, Knuth. Innovations in Collective Bargaining through the Multinationalisation of Japanese Auto Companies, the Cases of Nummi (USA) and Nissan (UK). *Trevor, M., ed.*, 1987, pp. 124–49.   [G: U.S.; U.K.; Japan]

Donn, Clifford B. and Lipsky, David B. Collective Bargaining in American Industry: A Synthesis. *Lipsky, D. B. and Donn, C. B., eds.*, 1987, pp. 307–32.   [G: U.S.]

Dworkin, James B. Collective Bargaining in American Industry: Professional Sports. *Lipsky, D. B. and Donn, C. B., eds.*, 1987, pp. 187–223.   [G: U.S.]

Eckel, Russel. Industrial Relations and High Technology: The Transformation of Telecommunications through Deregulation. *Child, J. and Bate, P., eds.*, 1987, pp. 173–89.
          [G: U.S.]

Evans, Stephen. The Use of Injunctions in Industrial Disputes, May 1984–April 1987. *Brit. J. Ind. Relat.*, November 1987, 25(3), pp. 419–35.   [G: U.K.]

Farber, Henry S. and Bazerman, Max H. Why Is There Disagreement in Bargaining? *Amer. Econ. Rev.*, May 1987, 77(2), pp. 347–52.

Flaherty, Sean. Strike Activity, Worker Militancy, and Productivity Change in Manufacturing, 1961–1981. *Ind. Lab. Relat. Rev.*, July 1987, 40(4), pp. 585–600.   [G: U.S.]

Gordon, Gerald, et al. Computer-Based Automation and Labor Relations in the Construction Equipment Industry. *Cornfield, D. B., ed.*, 1987, pp. 247–62.   [G: U.S.]

Gramm, Cynthia L. New Measures of the Propensity to Strike during Contract Negotiations, 1971–1980. *Ind. Lab. Relat. Rev.*, April 1987, 40(3), pp. 406–17.   [G: U.S.]

Gregory, Mary; Lobban, Peter and Thomson, Andrew. Pay Settlements in Manufacturing Industry, 1979–84: A Micro-data Study of the Impact of Product and Labour Market Pressures. *Oxford Bull. Econ. Statist.*, February 1987, 49(1), pp. 129–50.   [G: U.K.]

Hamermesh, Daniel S. Who "Wins" in Wage Bargaining? *Zartman, I. W., ed. (I)*, 1987, *1973*, pp. 510–15. **[G: U.S.]**

Harris, R. I. D. and Wass, V. J. The Effect of Collective Bargaining on Earnings in Northern Ireland in 1973. *Econ. Soc. Rev.*, October 1987, *19*(1), pp. 1–14. **[G: U.K.]**

Hendricks, Wallace E. Collective Bargaining in American Industry: Telecommunications. *Lipsky, D. B. and Donn, C. B., eds.*, 1987, pp. 103–33. **[G: U.S.]**

Ichniowski, Casey and Lewin, David. Grievance Procedures and Firm Performance. *Allen, S. G., et al.*, 1987, pp. 159–93. **[G: U.S.]**

Indergaard, Michael and Cushion, Michael. Conflict, Cooperation, and the Global Auto Factory. *Cornfield, D. B., ed.*, 1987, pp. 203–28. **[G: U.S.]**

James, Wilmot G. Grounds for a Strike: South African Gold Mining in the 1940s. *African Econ. Hist.*, 1987, (16), pp. 1–22. **[G: S. Africa]**

Karper, Mark D. Collective Bargaining in American Industry: Tires. *Lipsky, D. B. and Donn, C. B., eds.*, 1987, pp. 79–101. **[G: U.S.]**

Katz, Harry C. Collective Bargaining in American Industry: Automobiles. *Lipsky, D. B. and Donn, C. B., eds.*, 1987, pp. 13–53. **[G: U.S.]**

Katz, Harry C. Recent Developments in U.S. Auto Labour Relations. *Tolliday, S. and Zeitlin, J., eds.*, 1987, pp. 282–304. **[G: U.S.]**

Knoester, Anthonie and van der Windt, Nico. Real Wages and Taxation in Ten OECD Countries. *Oxford Bull. Econ. Statist.*, February 1987, *49*(1), pp. 151–69. **[G: OECD]**

Koch, Marianne; Lewin, David and Sockell, Donna. The Determinants of Bargaining Structure: A Case Study of AT&T. *Lewin, D.; Lipsky, D. B. and Sockell, D., eds.*, 1987, pp. 223–51. **[G: U.S.]**

Lacombe, John and Borum, Joan. Major Labor Contracts in 1986 Provided Record Low Wage Adjustments. *Mon. Lab. Rev.*, May 1987, *110*(5), pp. 10–16. **[G: U.S.]**

Lee, Barbara A. and Parker, Joan. Supervisory Participation in Professional Associations: Implications of *North Shore University Hospital*. *Ind. Lab. Relat. Rev.*, April 1987, *40*(3), pp. 364–81.

Lichtenstein, Nelson. Reutherism on the Shop Floor: Union Strategy and Shop-Floor Conflict in the USA 1946–70. *Tolliday, S. and Zeitlin, J., eds.*, 1987, pp. 121–43. **[G: U.S.]**

Lipsky, David B. and Donn, Clifford B. Collective Bargaining in American Industry: Introduction. *Lipsky, D. B. and Donn, C. B., eds.*, 1987, pp. 1–12. **[G: U.S.]**

Naples, Michele I. An Analysis of Defensive Strikes. *Ind. Relat.*, Winter 1987, *26*(1), pp. 96–105. **[G: U.S.]**

Neal, Alan C. Co-determination in the Federal Republic of Germany: An External Perspective from the United Kingdom. *Brit. J. Ind. Relat.*, July 1987, *25*(2), pp. 227–45. **[G: W. Germany; U.K.]**

Newell, A. and Symons, J. S. V. Corporatism, Laissez-faire, and the Rise in Unemployment. *Europ. Econ. Rev.*, April 1987, *31*(3), pp. 567–601. **[G: OECD]**

Okayama, Reiko. Industrial Relations in the Japanese Automobile Industry 1945–70: The Case of Toyota. *Tolliday, S. and Zeitlin, J., eds.*, 1987, pp. 168–89. **[G: Japan]**

Peterson, Richard B. Swedish Collective Bargaining—A Changing Scene. *Brit. J. Ind. Relat.*, March 1987, *25*(1), pp. 31–48. **[G: Sweden]**

Quataert, Donald. A Provisional Report Concerning the Impact of European Capital on Ottoman Port Workers, 1880–1909. *Islamoglu-Inan, H., ed.*, 1987, *1983*, pp. 300–308. **[G: Ottoman Empire]**

Raskin, A. H. The Newspaper Strike: A Step-by-Step Account. *Zartman, I. W., ed. (I)*, 1987, *1963*, pp. 452–80. **[G: U.S.]**

Robinson, Derek. How Inflexible Are Negotiated Wages in Britain? *Oxford Bull. Econ. Statist.*, February 1987, *49*(1), pp. 37–57. **[G: U.K.]**

Ruben, George. Labor–Management Scene in 1986 Reflects Continuing Difficulties. *Mon. Lab. Rev.*, January 1987, *110*(1), pp. 37–48. **[G: U.S.]**

Schnell, John F. An Ordered Choice Model of Promotion Rules. *J. Lab. Res.*, Spring 1987, *8*(2), pp. 159–78. **[G: U.S.]**

Schnell, John F. and Gramm, Cynthia L. Learning by Striking: Estimates of the Teetotaler Effect. *J. Lab. Econ.*, April 1987, *5*(2), pp. 221–41. **[G: U.S.]**

Schor, Juliet B. and Bowles, Samuel. Employment Rents and the Incidence of Strikes. *Rev. Econ. Statist.*, November 1987, *69*(4), pp. 584–92. **[G: U.S.]**

Schwartz, Arthur R., et al. The Impact of Technological Change on Labor Relations in the Commercial Aircraft Industry. *Cornfield, D. B., ed.*, 1987, pp. 263–80. **[G: U.S.]**

Screpanti, Ernesto. Long Cycles in Strike Activity: An Empirical Investigation. *Brit. J. Ind. Relat.*, March 1987, *25*(1), pp. 99–124. **[G: France; Italy; U.K.; U.S.; W. Germany]**

Seeber, Ronald L. Collective Bargaining in American Industry: Agricultural Machinery. *Lipsky, D. B. and Donn, C. B., eds.*, 1987, pp. 55–78. **[G: U.S.]**

Shostak, Arthur B. Technology, Air Traffic Control, and Labor–Management Relations. *Cornfield, D. B., ed.*, 1987, pp. 153–72. **[G: U.S.]**

Stewart, Mark B. Collective Bargaining Arrangements, Closed Shops and Relative Pay. *Econ. J.*, March 1987, *97*(385), pp. 140–56. **[G: U.K.]**

Summers, Lawrence H. Corporatism, Laissez-faire, and the Rise in Unemployment: Comments. *Europ. Econ. Rev.*, April 1987, *31*(3), pp. 606–14. **[G: OECD]**

Tolliday, Steven and Zeitlin, Jonathan. Shop-Floor Bargaining, Contract Unionism and Job Control: An Anglo–American Comparison. *Tolliday, S. and Zeitlin, J., eds.*, 1987, pp. 99–120. **[G: U.S.; U.K.]**

Treble, John G. Sliding Scales and Conciliation Boards: Risk-Sharing in the Late 19th Century

British Coal Industry. *Oxford Econ. Pap.*, December 1987, *39*(4), pp. 679–98.   [G: U.K.]

Waelbroeck, Jean. Corporatism, Laissez-faire, and the Rise in Unemployment: Comments. *Europ. Econ. Rev.*, April 1987, *31*(3), pp. 602–05.   [G: OECD]

Willman, Paul. Labour-Relations Strategy at BL Cars. *Tolliday, S. and Zeitlin, J.*, eds., 1987, pp. 305–27.   [G: U.K.]

8322 Collective Bargaining in the Public Sector

Bacharach, Samuel B.; Schmidle, Timothy P. and Bauer, Scott C. Collective Bargaining in American Industry: Higher Education. *Lipsky, D. B. and Donn, C. B.*, eds., 1987, pp. 225–64.   [G: U.S.]

Borum, Joan; Conley, James and Wasilewski, Edward. Collective Bargaining in 1987: Local, Regional Issues to Set Tone. *Mon. Lab. Rev.*, January 1987, *110*(1), pp. 23–36.   [G: U.S.]

Delaney, John Thomas and Feuille, Peter. Collective Bargaining in American Industry: Police. *Lipsky, D. B. and Donn, C. B.*, eds., 1987, pp. 265–306.   [G: U.S.]

Eberts, Randall W. Union-Negotiated Employment Rules and Teacher Quits. *Econ. Educ. Rev.*, 1987, *6*(1), pp. 15–25.   [G: U.S.]

Ferner, Anthony. Industrial Relations and the Meso-politics of the Public Enterprise: The Transmission of State Objectives in the Spanish National Railways. *Brit. J. Ind. Relat.*, March 1987, *25*(1), pp. 49–75.   [G: Spain]

Horn, Robert N. and Tomkiewicz, Joseph M. State Strategies of Control in the Public Sector. *England, R. W.*, ed., 1987, pp. 245–53.   [G: U.S.]

Lewin, David. Technological Change in the Public Sector: The Case of Sanitation Service. *Cornfield, D. B.*, ed., 1987, pp. 281–309.   [G: U.S.]

Ozaki, M. Labour Relations in the Public Service: 2. Labour Disputes and Their Settlement. *Int. Lab. Rev.*, July-Aug. 1987, *126*(4), pp. 405–22.   [G: Global]

Thornton, Robert J. Unions, Wages, and Local Government Finance. *Aronson, J. R. and Schwartz, E.*, eds., 1987, pp. 383–99.   [G: U.S.]

Walker, Jill and Moore, Roger. The Impact of Privatization on the United Kingdom Local Government Labour Market. *Tarling, R.*, ed., 1987, pp. 197–223.   [G: U.K.]

833 Labor–Management Relations

8330 General

Allen, R. Douglas and Fry, Fred L. An Investigation of Sex as a Moderator of the Relationship between Occupational Stress and Perceived Organizational Effectiveness in Formal Groups. *J. Behav. Econ.*, Summer 1987, *16*(2), pp. 9–15.

Armstrong, Sarah J. Incentive Compensation: Incentive Design and Management Implications. *Nalbantian, H. R.*, ed., 1987, pp. 165–75.   [G: U.S.]

Armstrong, T. E. Unemployment: Industrial Relations: Comment. *Gunderson, M.; Meltz, N. M. and Ostry, S.*, eds., 1987, pp. 196–99.   [G: Canada]

Backhaus, Jürgen. The Emergence of Worker Participation: Evolution and Legislation Compared. *J. Econ. Issues*, June 1987, *21*(2), pp. 895–910.   [G: U.S.; EEC]

Bartlett, Will. Enterprise Investment and Public Consumption in a Self-managed Economy. *Jones, D. C. and Svejnar, J.*, eds., 1987, pp. 165–81.   [G: Yugoslavia]

Beggs, John J. and Chapman, Bruce J. An Empirical Analysis of Australian Strike Activity: Estimating the Industrial Relations Effect of the First Three Years of the Prices and Incomes Accord. *Econ. Rec.*, March 1987, *63*(180), pp. 46–60.

Behrens, Ruth A. Health Promotion in the Workplace. *Meyer, J. A. and Lewin, M. E.*, eds., 1987, pp. 133–48.   [G: U.S.]

Blanchflower, David G. and Oswald, Andrew J. Profit Sharing—Can It Work? *Sinclair, P. J. N.*, ed., 1987, pp. 1–19.   [G: U.K.]

Blanchflower, David G. and Oswald, Andrew J. Profit Sharing—Can It Work? *Oxford Econ. Pap.*, March 1987, *39*(1), pp. 1–19.   [G: U.K.]

Blyton, Paul. The Working Time Debate in Western Europe. *Ind. Relat.*, Spring 1987, *26*(2), pp. 201–07.   [G: W. Europe]

Bradley, Keith and Gelb, Alan. Cooperative Labour Relations: Mondragon's Response to Recession. *Brit. J. Ind. Relat.*, March 1987, *25*(1), pp. 77–97.   [G: Spain]

Cable, John. Some Tests of Employee Participation Indices. *Jones, D. C. and Svejnar, J.*, eds., 1987, pp. 79–90.

Calmfors, Lars. Work Sharing: Why? How? How Not . . . : Comments. *Layard, R. and Calmfors, L.*, eds., 1987, pp. 198–204.   [G: OECD]

Carmody, G. F. Alternative Wages and Industrial Relations Policies: Pressures for Change. *Rev. Marketing Agr. Econ.*, April 1987, *55*(1), pp. 98–109.   [G: Australia]

Child, John. Managerial Strategies, New Technology, and the Labor Process. *Pennings, J. M. and Buitendam, A.*, eds., 1987, pp. 141–77.

Chuma, Hiroyuki. Pensions, Wage Profiles, and Retirement Rules: Specific Human Capital Approach. *J. Econ. Dynam. Control*, March 1987, *11*(1), pp. 29–64.   [G: Japan]

Clarke, Shaun G. Rethinking the Adversarial Model in Labor Relations: An Argument for Repeal of Section 8(a)(2) *Yale Law J.*, July 1987, *96*(8), pp. 2021–50.   [G: U.S.]

Codina Jiménez, Alexis. Workers Incentives in Cuba. *World Devel.*, January 1987, *15*(1), pp. 127–38.   [G: Cuba]

Cornfield, Daniel B. Labor–Management Cooperation or Managerial Control? Emerging Patterns of Labor Relations in the United States.

Cornfield, D. B., ed., 1987, pp. 331–53.
[G: U.S.]

Crispo, John. Unemployment: Industrial Relations: Comment. *Gunderson, M.; Meltz, N. M. and Ostry, S., eds.*, 1987, pp. 193–96.
[G: Canada]

Dalton, Amy H. and Marcis, John G. Gender Differences in Job Satisfaction among Young Adults. *J. Behav. Econ.*, Spring 1987, *16*(1), pp. 21–32.
[G: U.S.]

DiGiacomo, Gordon. Trade Unions and the Reform of the Quality of Work Life: Ergonomic and Other QWL Reforms Have Limited Goals and Are Held No Substitute for Labor Involvement. *Amer. J. Econ. Soc.*, October 1987, *46*(4), pp. 399–414.

Drèze, Jacques H. Some Theory of Labour Management and Participation. *Drèze, J. H.*, 1987, *1976*, pp. 366–82.

Drèze, Jacques H. Work Sharing: Why? How? How Not . . . *Layard, R. and Calmfors, L., eds.*, 1987, pp. 139–92.
[G: OECD]

Dugger, William M. Democratic Economic Planning and Worker Ownership. *J. Econ. Issues*, March 1987, *21*(1), pp. 87–99.
[G: U.S.]

Dunlop, John T. Economists in Labor–Management–Government Proceedings. *Bus. Econ.*, October 1987, *22*(4), pp. 21–26.

Dunlop, John T. Industrial Relations and Unemployment. *Gunderson, M.; Meltz, N. M. and Ostry, S., eds.*, 1987, pp. 184–92. [G: U.S.]

Fryer, John. Unemployment: Industrial Relations: Comment. *Gunderson, M.; Meltz, N. M. and Ostry, S., eds.*, 1987, pp. 201–06.
[G: Canada]

Fullagar, Clive and Barling, Julian. Toward a Model of Union Commitment. *Lewin, D.; Lipsky, D. B. and Sockell, D., eds.*, 1987, pp. 43–78.

Fuller, Linda. Power at the Workplace: The Resolution of Worker–Management Conflict in Cuba. *World Devel.*, January 1987, *15*(1), pp. 139–52. [G: Cuba]

Fürstenberg, Friedrich. Das Entwicklungspotential industrieller Arbeitsbeziehungen im gesellschaftlichen Strukturwandel. (Potentials for Future Development of Industrial Relations in a Changing Society. With English summary.) *Z. Wirtschaft. Sozialwissen.*, 1987, *107*(1), pp. 85–97.

Gray, Lois S. Professional Careers for Women in Industrial Relations. *Koziara, K. S.; Moskow, M. H. and Tanner, L. D., eds.*, 1987, pp. 225–44. [G: U.S.]

Grout, Paul A. The Wider Share Ownership Programme. *Fisc. Stud.*, August 1987, *8*(3), pp. 59–74. [G: U.K.]

van Gunsteren, Lex A. Information Technology: A Managerial Perspective. *Pennings, J. M. and Buitendam, A., eds.*, 1987, pp. 277–89.

Hage, Jerald. Reflections on New Technology and Organizational Change. *Pennings, J. M. and Buitendam, A., eds.*, 1987, pp. 261–76.
[G: Japan; U.S.]

Hancock, Keith. Regulation and Deregulation in the Australian Labour Market. *Australian Bull.*

Lab., March 1987, *13*(2), pp. 94–107.
[G: Australia]

Heery, Edmund. Chronicle: Industrial Relations in the United Kingdom December 1986–March 1987. *Brit. J. Ind. Relat.*, July 1987, *25*(2), pp. 295–305. [G: U.K.]

Henwood, Felicity and Wyatt, Sally. Managing Technological Change: Responses of Government, Employers, and Trade Unions in Western Europe and Canada. *Hartmann, H. I., ed.*, 1987, pp. 395–431. [G: OECD]

Hodgson, Geoffrey M. Economic Pluralism and Self-management. *Jones, D. C. and Svejnar, J., eds.*, 1987, pp. 129–42.

Hurd, Richard W. Scientific Management, Human Relations, and the Class Struggle: The Evolution of the Labor Process in the United States. *England, R. W., ed.*, 1987, pp. 226–44. [G: U.S.]

Hyman, Richard. Unemployment and Trade Unions in Britain: The Politics of Industrial Relations in the Crisis. *Pedersen, P. J. and Lund, R., eds.*, 1987, pp. 207–23. [G: U.K.]

Ireland, Norman J. The Economic Analysis of Labour-Managed Firms. *Bull. Econ. Res.*, October 1987, *39*(4), pp. 249–72.

Jones, Stephen G. The Economics of Worksharing in Western Europe: Some Policy Considerations. *Brit. Rev. Econ. Issues*, Autumn 1987, *9*(21), pp. 91–117. [G: EEC]

Jönsson, Sten. Limits of Information Technology for Facilitating Organizational Learning. *Pennings, J. M. and Buitendam, A., eds.*, 1987, pp. 217–34.

Kelly, John. Trade Unions through the Recession, 1980–1984. *Brit. J. Ind. Relat.*, July 1987, *25*(2), pp. 275–82.

Klein, Howard J.; Snell, Scott A. and Wexley, Kenneth N. Systems Model of the Performance Appraisal Interview Process. *Ind. Relat.*, Fall 1987, *26*(3), pp. 267–80.

Koike, Kazuo. The Political Economy of Japan: Human Resource Development and Labor–Management Relations. *Yamamura, K. and Yasuba, Y., eds.*, 1987, pp. 289–330.
[G: Japan]

Koken, Bernd K. Unemployment: Industrial Relations: Comment. *Gunderson, M.; Meltz, N. M. and Ostry, S., eds.*, 1987, pp. 199–201.
[G: Canada]

Kolb, Deborah M. Corporate Ombudsman and Organization Conflict Resolution. *J. Conflict Resolution*, December 1987, *31*(4), pp. 673–91.

Krislov, Joseph and Mead, John. Changes in IR Programs since the Mid-Sixties. *Ind. Relat.*, Spring 1987, *26*(2), pp. 208–12. [G: U.S.]

Lewin, David. Dispute Resolution in the Nonunion Firm: A Theoretical and Empirical Analysis. *J. Conflict Resolution*, September 1987, *31*(3), pp. 465–502. [G: U.S.]

Lewin, David. Industrial Relations as a Strategic Variable. *Allen, S. G., et al.*, 1987, pp. 1–41.
[G: U.S.]

Lipsky, David B. and Donn, Clifford B. Collective Bargaining in American Industry: Introduction. *Lipsky, D. B. and Donn, C. B., eds.,* 1987, pp. 1–12. **[G: U.S.]**

Lowe, Rodney. The Policy Debate: Labour Policy. *Glynn, S. and Booth, A., eds.,* 1987, pp. 140–53. **[G: U.K.]**

Maier, Charles S. Society as Factory. *Maier, C. S.,* 1987, pp. 19–69. **[G: U.S.; Germany; Italy]**

Michon, François. Segmentation, Employment Structures and Productive Structures. *Tarling, R., ed.,* 1987, pp. 23–55.

Mitchell, Daniel J. B. The Share Economy and Industrial Relations. *Ind. Relat.,* Winter 1987, *26*(1), pp. 1–17. **[G: U.S.]**

Mukhopadhyay, Arun K. and Chamard, John. Government Incentives for a Profit Sharing System: A Case for Subsidy through Pay Insurance. *Can. Public Policy,* December 1987, *13*(4), pp. 529–33.

Nebenhaus, Daniel. La participation aux décisions dans une PME. Etude de cas. (Participation to Decision Process in SMB. A Case Study. With English summary.) *Écon. Soc.,* December 1987, *21*(12), pp. 111–37.

Nelson, Daniel. Mass Production and the U.S. Tire Industry. *J. Econ. Hist.,* June 1987, *47*(2), pp. 329–39. **[G: U.S.]**

Nuti, Domenico Mario. Profit-Sharing and Employment: Claims and Overclaims. *Ind. Relat.,* Winter 1987, *26*(1), pp. 18–29.

Paul, Carolyn. Work Alternatives for Older Americans: A Management Perspective. *Sandell, S. H., ed.,* 1987, pp. 165–76. **[G: U.S.]**

Paul, Robert J.; Edabi, Yar M. and Dilts, David A. Commitment in Employee-Owned Firms: Involvement or Entrapment? *Quart. J. Bus. Econ.,* Autumn 1987, *26*(4), pp. 81–99.

Pejovich, Svetozar. The Case of Self-management in Yugoslavia. *Pejovich, S., ed.,* 1987, pp. 239–49. **[G: Yugoslavia]**

Pissarides, Christopher A. Work Sharing: Why? How? How Not . . . : Comments. *Layard, R. and Calmfors, L., eds.,* 1987, pp. 193–97. **[G: OECD]**

Protti, Ray. Unemployment: Industrial Relations: Comment. *Gunderson, M.; Meltz, N. M. and Ostry, S., eds.,* 1987, pp. 206–08. **[G: Canada]**

Reid, Frank. Work-Time Reduction. *Gunderson, M.; Meltz, N. M. and Ostry, S., eds.,* 1987, pp. 210–14. **[G: Canada; U.S.]**

Rothwell, Sheila. New Technology and New Supervisory Roles in U.K. Manufacturing Industry. *Child, J. and Bate, P., eds.,* 1987, pp. 123–35. **[G: U.K.]**

Ruggeri, Fedele. Unofficial Economy and the Meaning of Labour: Toward a Theoretical Hypothesis. *Alessandrini, S. and Dallago, B., eds.,* 1987, pp. 107–24.

Schmidt, Herbert. Labororiented Management-policy in Industry within a Social Market Economy. *Gemper, B. B., ed.,* 1987, pp. 187–200. **[G: W. Germany]**

Shea, Gregory P. and Guzzo, Richard A. Groups as Human Resources. *Rowland, K. M. and Ferris, G. R., eds.,* 1987, pp. 323–56.

Stark, Oded. Cooperating Adversaries. *Kyklos,* 1987, *40*(4), pp. 515–28.

Szul, Roman and Kirejczyk, Edward. Dilemmas of Economic Reform and Self-management in Poland. *Econ. Anal. Workers' Manage.,* 1987, *21*(3), pp. 373–91. **[G: Poland]**

Veretennikov, V. G. The Economic Mechanism and Self-management. *Prob. Econ.,* October 1987, *30*(6), pp. 19–33. **[G: U.S.S.R.]**

Wadhwani, Sushil B. Profit-Sharing and Meade's Discriminating Labour–Capital Partnerships: A Review Article. *Oxford Econ. Pap.,* September 1987, *39*(3), pp. 421–42.

Walker, Jill and Moore, Roger. The Impact of Privatization on the United Kingdom Local Government Labour Market. *Tarling, R., ed.,* 1987, pp. 197–223. **[G: U.K.]**

Watrin, Christian. The Case of Codetermination in West Germany. *Pejovich, S., ed.,* 1987, pp. 277–314. **[G: W. Germany]**

Westin, Alan F. Employer Policies to Enhance the Application of Office System Technology to Clerical Work. *Hartmann, H. I., ed.,* 1987, pp. 313–42. **[G: U.S.]**

Whyte, William Foote. From Human Relations to Organizational Behavior: Reflections on the Changing Scene. *Ind. Lab. Relat. Rev.,* July 1987, *40*(4), pp. 487–500. **[G: U.S.]**

Wooden, Mark and Dawkins, Peter. The Australian Labour Market, March 1987. *Australian Bull. Lab.,* March 1987, *13*(2), pp. 70–93. **[G: Australia]**

Wrege, Charles D.; Greenwood, Ronald G. and Hata, Sakae. The International Management Institute and Political Opposition to Its Efforts in Europe, 1925–1934. *Atack, J., ed.,* 1987, pp. 249–65. **[G: Europe; U.S.]**

8331 Labor–Management Relations in Private Sector

Addison, John T. and Castro, Alberto C. The Importance of Lifetime Jobs: Differences between Union and Nonunion Workers. *Ind. Lab. Relat. Rev.,* April 1987, *40*(3), pp. 393–405. **[G: U.S.]**

Alexander, Kenneth O. The Worker, the Union and the Democratic Workplace. *Amer. J. Econ. Soc.,* October 1987, *46*(4), pp. 385–97. **[G: U.S.]**

Allen, Steven G. and Clark, Robert L. Pensions and Firm Performance. *Allen, S. G., et al.,* 1987, pp. 195–242. **[G: U.S.]**

Ancona, Deborah Gladstein and Caldwell, David F. Management Issues Facing New-Product Teams in High-Technology Companies. *Lewin, D.; Lipsky, D. B. and Sockell, D., eds.,* 1987, pp. 199–221.

Bacharach, Samuel B.; Schmidle, Timothy P. and Bauer, Scott C. Collective Bargaining in American Industry: Higher Education. *Lipsky, D. B. and Donn, C. B., eds.,* 1987, pp. 225–64. **[G: U.S.]**

Baird, Charles W. Labor Law and Labor–Management Cooperation: Two Incompatible Views. *Cato J.,* Winter 1987, *6*(3), pp. 933–50. **[G: U.S.]**

Barrère-Maurisson, Marie-Agnès. Gestion de la main-d'oeuvre et paternalisme: tradition et modernité dans les stratégies des entreprises. (Workforce Management and Paternalism: Tradition and Modernity in Company Strategy. With English summary.) *Écon. Soc.*, November 1987, *21*(11), pp. 41–56.

Bassett, Philip. Consultation and the Right to Manage, 1980–1984. *Brit. J. Ind. Relat.*, July 1987, *25*(2), pp. 283–86. **[G: U.K.]**

Batten, Dick and Schoonmaker, Sara. Deregulation, Technological Change, and Labor Relations in Telecommunications. *Cornfield, D. B., ed.*, 1987, pp. 311–27. **[G: U.S.]**

Becker, Brian E. and Olson, Craig A. Labor Relations and Firm Performance. *Allen, S. G., et al.*, 1987, pp. 43–85.

Bemmels, Brian. How Unions Affect Productivity in Manufacturing Plants. *Ind. Lab. Relat. Rev.*, January 1987, *40*(2), pp. 241–53. **[G: U.S.]**

Benelli, Giuseppe; Loderer, Claudio and Lys, Thomas. Labor Participation in Corporate Policy-Making Decisions: West Germany's Experience with Codetermination. *J. Bus.*, October 1987, *60*(4), pp. 553–75. **[G: W. Germany]**

Bernard, Jean-Paul. Internationalisation des firmes en conflictualité: le cas des entreprises situées en Picardie (1982–85). (Internationalizing Firms Facing Industrial Conflict. Set Up Plans in Picardy: The Case (1982–85). With English summary.) *Écon. Soc.*, June 1987, *21*(6), pp. 53–83. **[G: France]**

Bigazzi, Duccio. Management Strategies in the Italian Car Industry 1906–1945: Fiat and Alfa Romeo. *Tolliday, S. and Zeitlin, J., eds.*, 1987, pp. 76–96. **[G: Italy]**

Blain, Nicholas; Goodman, John and Loewenberg, Joseph. Mediation, Conciliation and Arbitration. An International Comparison of Australia, Great Britain and the United States. *Int. Lab. Rev.*, Mar.-Apr. 1987, *126*(2), pp. 179–98. **[G: Australia; U.K.; U.S.]**

Block, Richard N., et al. Industrial Relations and the Performance of the Firm: An Overview. *Allen, S. G., et al.*, 1987, pp. 319–43.

Bodvarsson, Örn B. Monitoring with No Moral Hazard: The Case of Small Vessel Commercial Fishing. *Eastern Econ. J.*, October-December 1987, *13*(4), pp. 421–34. **[G: U.S.]**

Booth, Alison L. Extra-statutory Redundancy Payments in Britain. *Brit. J. Ind. Relat.*, November 1987, *25*(3), pp. 401–18. **[G: U.K.]**

Bradley, Keith and Hill, Stephen. Quality Circles and Managerial Interests. *Ind. Relat.*, Winter 1987, *26*(1), pp. 68–82. **[G: U.K.; U.S.]**

Bradley, Michael D. and Smith, Stephen C. Some Microeconomic Analysis of Income-Sharing Firms. *Jones, D. C. and Svejnar, J., eds.*, 1987, pp. 91–111.

Breen, William J. Administrative Politics and Labor Policy in the First World War: The U.S. Employment Service and the Seattle Labor Market Experiment. *Bus. Hist. Rev.*, Winter 1987, *61*(4), pp. 582–605. **[G: U.S.]**

Brown, William. Pay Determination: British Workplace Industrial Relations 1980–84, Chap-

ter 9. *Brit. J. Ind. Relat.*, July 1987, *25*(2), pp. 291–94. **[G: U.K.]**

Cappelli, Peter. Collective Bargaining in American Industry: Airlines. *Lipsky, D. B. and Donn, C. B., eds.*, 1987, pp. 135–86. **[G: U.S.]**

Carroll, Archie B. Management's Social Responsibilities [When Business Closes Down: Social Responsibilities and Management Actions]. *Staudohar, P. D. and Brown, H. E.*, 1987, *1984*, pp. 167–81. **[G: U.S.]**

Chhokar, Jagdeep S. Safety at the Workplace: A Behavioural Approach. *Int. Lab. Rev.*, Mar.-Apr. 1987, *126*(2), pp. 169–78.

Contini, Giovanni. The Rise and Fall of Shop-Floor Bargaining at Fiat 1945–1980. *Tolliday, S. and Zeitlin, J., eds.*, 1987, pp. 144–67. **[G: Italy]**

Cornfield, Daniel B., et al. Office Automation, Clerical Workers, and Labor Relations in the Insurance Industry. *Cornfield, D. B., ed.*, 1987, pp. 111–34. **[G: U.S.]**

Couto, Richard A. Changing Technologies and Consequences for Labor in Coal Mining. *Cornfield, D. B., ed.*, 1987, pp. 175–202. **[G: U.S.]**

Crosby, Philip B. A Journey for Quality Improvement. *Shetty, Y. K. and Buehler, V. M., eds.*, 1987, pp. 285–99. **[G: U.S.]**

Deutsch, Steven. Successful Worker Training Programs Help Ease Impact of Technology. *Mon. Lab. Rev.*, November 1987, *110*(11), pp. 14–20. **[G: U.S.]**

Dohse, Knuth. Innovations in Collective Bargaining through the Multinationalisation of Japanese Auto Companies, the Cases of Nummi (USA) and Nissan (UK). *Trevor, M., ed.*, 1987, pp. 124–49. **[G: U.S.; U.K.; Japan]**

Donn, Clifford B. and Lipsky, David B. Collective Bargaining in American Industry: A Synthesis. *Lipsky, D. B. and Donn, C. B., eds.*, 1987, pp. 307–32. **[G: U.S.]**

Dworkin, James B. Collective Bargaining in American Industry: Professional Sports. *Lipsky, D. B. and Donn, C. B., eds.*, 1987, pp. 187–223. **[G: U.S.]**

Eads, George C. Industrial Relations and Productivity in the U.S. Automobile Industry: Comments and Discussions. *Brookings Pap. Econ. Act.*, 1987, (3), pp. 720–25.

Ebel, Karl-H. and Ulrich, Erhard. Some Workplace Effects of CAD and CAM. *Int. Lab. Rev.*, 1987, *126*(3), pp. 351–70. **[G: OECD]**

Eckel, Russel. Industrial Relations and High Technology: The Transformation of Telecommunications through Deregulation. *Child, J. and Bate, P., eds.*, 1987, pp. 173–89. **[G: U.S.]**

Edwards, Paul K. Industrial Action 1980–1984. *Brit. J. Ind. Relat.*, July 1987, *25*(2), pp. 287–90. **[G: U.K.]**

Ehrenberg, Ronald G. and Milkovich, George T. Compensation and Firm Performance. *Allen, S. G., et al.*, 1987, pp. 87–122. **[G: U.S.]**

Ephlin, Donald F. UAW's View of Union's Role

at Saturn Plant. *Shetty, Y. K. and Buehler, V. M., eds.*, 1987, pp. 149–61. [G: U.S.]

Estrin, Saul; Jones, Derek C. and Svejnar, Jan. The Productivity Effects of Worker Participation: Producer Cooperatives in Western Economies. *J. Compar. Econ.*, March 1987, *11*(1), pp. 40–61. [G: Spain; Italy; U.K.; France]

Evans, Stephen. The Use of Injunctions in Industrial Disputes, May 1984–April 1987. *Brit. J. Ind. Relat.*, November 1987, *25*(3), pp. 419–35. [G: U.K.]

Fischer, Robert A. Information Strategy at McDonnell Douglas. *Shetty, Y. K. and Buehler, V. M., eds.*, 1987, pp. 207–20. [G: U.S.]

FitzRoy, Felix R. and Kraft, Kornelius. Efficiency and Internal Organization: Works Councils in West German Firms. *Economica*, November 1987, *54*(216), pp. 493–504. [G: W. Germany]

Flaherty, Sean. Strike Activity & Productivity Change: The U.S. Auto Industry. *Ind. Relat.*, Spring 1987, *26*(2), pp. 174–85. [G: U.S.]

Ford, William D. Federal Legislation [Coping with Plant Closings]. *Staudohar, P. D. and Brown, H. E.*, 1987, *1985*, pp. 307–11. [G: U.S.]

Fraser, Bryna Shore. New Office and Business Technologies: The Structure of Education and (Re)Training Opportunities. *Hartmann, H. I., ed.*, 1987, pp. 343–72.

Friedman, Andrew. Specialist Labour in Japan: Computer Skilled Staff and the Subcontracting System. *Brit. J. Ind. Relat.*, November 1987, *25*(3), pp. 353–69. [G: Japan]

de Gaudemar, J.-P. Mobilization Networks and Strategies in the Labour Market. *Tarling, R., ed.*, 1987, pp. 105–26.

Gershenfeld, Walter J. Employee Participation in Firm Decisions. *Allen, S. G., et al.*, 1987, pp. 123–58. [G: U.S.]

Grancelli, Bruno. Political Trade-Offs, Collective Bargaining, Individual Tradings: Some Remarks on Industrial Relations in Italy. *Alessandrini, S. and Dallago, B., eds.*, 1987, pp. 257–70. [G: Italy]

Greenblum, Joseph and Bye, Barry. Work Values of Disabled Beneficiaries. *Soc. Sec. Bull.*, April 1987, *50*(4), pp. 67–74. [G: U.S.]

Gupta, Nina; Schweizer, Timothy P. and Jenkins, G. Douglas, Jr. Pay-for-Knowledge Compensation Plans: Hypotheses and Survey Results. *Mon. Lab. Rev.*, October 1987, *110*(10), pp. 40–43. [G: U.S.]

Hagan, Maury and Warders, Dave. Human Resources: Key to Excellence at Dana. *Shetty, Y. K. and Buehler, V. M., eds.*, 1987, pp. 111–20. [G: U.S.]

Hattwick, Richard E. Democratizing the Workplace: The Case of Irl C. Martin and the Woodward Governor Company. *J. Behav. Econ.*, Summer 1987, *16*(2), pp. 69–77.

Hendricks, Wallace E. Collective Bargaining in American Industry: Telecommunications. *Lipsky, D. B. and Donn, C. B., eds.*, 1987, pp. 103–33. [G: U.S.]

Hilton, Margaret and Straw, Ronnie. Coopera-

tive Training in Telecommunications: Case Studies. *Mon. Lab. Rev.*, May 1987, *110*(5), pp. 32–36. [G: U.S.]

Hundley, Jay. J. C. Penney Relies on People Power. *Shetty, Y. K. and Buehler, V. M., eds.*, 1987, pp. 81–92. [G: U.S.]

Ichniowski, Casey and Lewin, David. Grievance Procedures and Firm Performance. *Allen, S. G., et al.*, 1987, pp. 159–93. [G: U.S.]

Jones, Derek C. The Productivity Effects of Worker Directors and Financial Participation by Employees in the Firm: The Case of British Retail Cooperatives. *Ind. Lab. Relat. Rev.*, October 1987, *41*(1), pp. 79–92. [G: U.K.]

Jones, Graham. Contemporary Industrial Relations: Dilemmas and Prospects. *Australian Bull. Lab.*, June 1987, *13*(3), pp. 162–78. [G: Australia]

Jügens, Ulrich and Strömel, Hans-Peter. The Communication Structure between Management and Shop Floor: A Comparison of a Japanese and a German Plant. *Trevor, M., ed.*, 1987, pp. 92–110. [G: Japan; W. Germany]

Juran, Joseph M. Upper Management and Quality. *Shetty, Y. K. and Buehler, V. M., eds.*, 1987, pp. 275–83. [G: U.S.]

Jürgens, Ulrich; Dohse, Knuth and Malsch, Thomas. New Production Concepts in West German Car Plants. *Tolliday, S. and Zeitlin, J., eds.*, 1987, pp. 258–81. [G: W. Germany]

Jusela, Gary E., et al. Work Innovations at Ford Motor. *Shetty, Y. K. and Buehler, V. M., eds.*, 1987, pp. 123–45. [G: U.S.]

Kalleberg, Arne L., et al. The Eclipse of Craft: The Changing Face of Labor in the Newspaper Industry. *Cornfield, D. B., ed.*, 1987, pp. 47–71. [G: U.S.]

Karper, Mark D. Collective Bargaining in American Industry: Tires. *Lipsky, D. B. and Donn, C. B., eds.*, 1987, pp. 79–101. [G: U.S.]

Katz, Harry C. Collective Bargaining in American Industry: Automobiles. *Lipsky, D. B. and Donn, C. B., eds.*, 1987, pp. 13–53. [G: U.S.]

Katz, Harry C. Recent Developments in U.S. Auto Labour Relations. *Tolliday, S. and Zeitlin, J., eds.*, 1987, pp. 282–304. [G: U.S.]

Katz, Harry C.; Kochan, Thomas A. and Keefe, Jeffrey H. Industrial Relations and Productivity in the U.S. Automobile Industry. *Brookings Pap. Econ. Act.*, 1987, (3), pp. 685–715. [G: U.S.]

Keil, Thomas J. "Democracy" in Worker-Owned Enterprises: The U.S. Experience. *Child, J. and Bate, P., eds.*, 1987, pp. 221–36. [G: U.S.]

Kendrick, John W. Happiness Is Personal Productivity Growth. *Challenge*, May/June 1987, *30*(2), pp. 37–44.

King, Kenneth L. How 3M Melds Deming's, Juran's, and Crosby's Techniques. *Shetty, Y. K. and Buehler, V. M., eds.*, 1987, pp. 303–13. [G: U.S.]

Klay, William Earle. How Are Japanese Unions Responding to Microelectronics-Based Automation? *Mon. Lab. Rev.*, March 1987, *110*(3), pp. 39–40. **[G: Japan]**

Laflamme, Gilles; Belanger, Laurent and Audet, Michel. Workers' Participation and Personnel Policies in Canada: Some Hopeful Signs. *Int. Lab. Rev.*, Mar.-Apr. 1987, *126*(2), pp. 219–28. **[G: Canada]**

Lazear, Edward P. Industrial Relations and Productivity in the U.S. Automobile Industry: Comments and Discussion. *Brookings Pap. Econ. Act.*, 1987, (3), pp. 716–20. **[G: U.S.]**

Lichtenstein, Nelson. Reutherism on the Shop Floor: Union Strategy and Shop-Floor Conflict in the USA 1946–70. *Tolliday, S. and Zeitlin, J., eds.*, 1987, pp. 121–43. **[G: U.S.]**

Lovett, William A. Profit Sharing and ESOPs: Improved Incentives and Equity. *Samuels, W. J. and Miller, A. S., eds.*, 1987, pp. 283–312. **[G: U.S.]**

Marchington, Mick. A Review and Critique of Research on Developments in Joint Consultation. *Brit. J. Ind. Relat.*, November 1987, *25*(3), pp. 339–52. **[G: U.K.]**

Martin, Robert E. Long-run Supply in Competitive Labor-Managed Industries. *Jones, D. C. and Svejnar, J., eds.*, 1987, pp. 113–28.

Masters, Marick F. Corporations, Human Resources Management, and Political Action. *Rowland, K. M. and Ferris, G. R., eds.*, 1987, pp. 357–93.

McCaffray, Susan P. Origins of Labor Policy in the Russian Coal and Steel Industry, 1874–1900. *J. Econ. Hist.*, December 1987, *47*(4), pp. 951–65. **[G: Russia]**

McCallum, Ronald C. Civil Liberties and Industrial Relations; Hein v. Jaques Ltd. *Australian Bull. Lab.*, September 1987, *13*(4), pp. 225–36. **[G: Australia]**

McShane, Steven L. and McPhillips, David C. Predicting Reasonable Notice in Canadian Wrongful Dismissal Cases. *Ind. Lab. Relat. Rev.*, October 1987, *41*(1), pp. 108–17. **[G: Canada]**

Meyer, John R. and Oster, Clinton V., Jr. The U.S. Experience with Airline Deregulation: Productivity, Employment, and Labor Relations. *Meyer, J. R. and Oster, C. V., Jr.*, 1987, pp. 83–107. **[G: U.S.]**

Mygind, Niels. Are Self-managed Firms Efficient? The Experience of Danish Fully and Partly Self-managed Firms. *Jones, D. C. and Svejnar, J., eds.*, 1987, pp. 243–323. **[G: Denmark]**

Neal, Alan C. Co-determination in the Federal Republic of Germany: An External Perspective from the United Kingdom. *Brit. J. Ind. Relat.*, July 1987, *25*(2), pp. 227–45. **[G: W. Germany; U.K.]**

Okayama, Reiko. Industrial Relations in the Japanese Automobile Industry 1945–70: The Case of Toyota. *Tolliday, S. and Zeitlin, J., eds.*, 1987, pp. 168–89. **[G: Japan]**

Osterman, Paul. Turnover, Employment Security, and the Performance of the Firm. *Allen, S. G., et al.*, 1987, pp. 275–317. **[G: U.S.]**

Paul, Robert J. and Ebadi, Yar M. Employee Ownership and Organizational Slack—Some

Thoughts toward a Model. *J. Behav. Econ.*, Fall 1987, *16*(3), pp. 23–34.

Peet, Richard. Industrial Devolution, Underconsumption and the Third World Debt Crisis. *World Devel.*, June 1987, *15*(6), pp. 777–88. **[G: Global]**

Pérotin, Virginie. Conditions of Survival and Closure of French Worker Cooperatives: Some Preliminary Findings. *Jones, D. C. and Svejnar, J., eds.*, 1987, pp. 201–24. **[G: France]**

Peterson, Kent D. Computerized Instruction, Information Systems, and School Teachers: Labor Relations in Education. *Cornfield, D. B., ed.*, 1987, pp. 135–51. **[G: U.S.]**

Raucher, Alan. Employee Relations at General Motors: The "My Job Contest," 1947. *Labor Hist.*, Spring 1987, *28*(2), pp. 221–32. **[G: U.S.]**

Rico, Leonard. The New Industrial Relations: British Electricians' New-Style Agreements. *Ind. Lab. Relat. Rev.*, October 1987, *41*(1), pp. 63–78. **[G: U.K.]**

Rubery, Jill. Flexibility of Labour Costs in Nonunion Firms. *Tarling, R., ed.*, 1987, pp. 59–83.

Samuel, Howard D. AFL-CIO Favors Enlisting Workers in Search of Quality. *Shetty, Y. K. and Buehler, V. M., eds.*, 1987, pp. 163–71. **[G: U.S.]**

Santos, Michael W. Laboring on the Periphery: Managers and Workers at the A. M. Byers Company, 1900–1956. *Bus. Hist. Rev.*, Spring 1987, *61*(1), pp. 113–33.

Schnell, John F. An Ordered Choice Model of Promotion Rules. *J. Lab. Res.*, Spring 1987, *8*(2), pp. 159–78. **[G: U.S.]**

Schor, Juliet B. and Bowles, Samuel. Employment Rents and the Incidence of Strikes. *Rev. Econ. Statist.*, November 1987, *69*(4), pp. 584–92. **[G: U.S.]**

Schregle, J. Workers' Participation in the Federal Republic of Germany in an International Perspective. *Int. Lab. Rev.*, 1987, *126*(3), pp. 317–27. **[G: W. Germany]**

Schwochau, Susan. Union Effects on Job Attitudes. *Ind. Lab. Relat. Rev.*, January 1987, *40*(2), pp. 209–24. **[G: U.S.]**

Scott, Gordon. A View from the Employers. *Stegman, T., et al.*, 1987, pp. 64–75. **[G: Australia]**

Seeber, Ronald L. Collective Bargaining in American Industry: Agricultural Machinery. *Lipsky, D. B. and Donn, C. B., eds.*, 1987, pp. 55–78. **[G: U.S.]**

Shapira, Zur. Preference for Job Attributes: Tradeoffs from Present Position. *Ind. Relat.*, Spring 1987, *26*(2), pp. 46–57. **[G: Israel]**

Shimokawa, Koichi. Product and Labour Strategies in Japan. *Tolliday, S. and Zeitlin, J., eds.*, 1987, pp. 224–43. **[G: Japan]**

Silva, Francesco; Ferri, Piero and Enrietti, Aldo. Robots, Employment and Industrial Relations in the Italian Automobile Industry. *Watanabe, S., ed.*, 1987, pp. 131–53. **[G: Italy]**

Solinas, Giovanni. Labour Market Segmentation

and Workers' Careers: The Case of the Italian Knitwear Industry. *Tarling, R., ed.,* 1987, pp. 271–305. **[G: Italy]**

Stabile, Donald R. The Du Pont Experiments in Scientific Management: Efficiency and Safety, 1911–1919. *Bus. Hist. Rev.,* Autumn 1987, *61*(3), pp. 365–86. **[G: U.S.]**

Stein, Stanley R. McDonald's Growth through People. *Shetty, Y. K. and Buehler, V. M., eds.,* 1987, pp. 103–10. **[G: U.S.]**

Stewart, Geoff. Managerial Discretion in the Labor-Managed Firm. *Jones, D. C. and Svejnar, J., eds.,* 1987, pp. 143–63.

Subbarao, A. V. Influence of Political Structure on Worker Participation in Developing Asian Countries. *Can. J. Devel. Stud.,* 1987, *8*(1), pp. 97–115. **[G: India; Sri Lanka; Singapore]**

Thomas, Robert J. Microchips and Macroharvests: Labor–Management Relations in Agriculture. *Cornfield, D. B., ed.,* 1987, pp. 27–45. **[G: U.S.]**

Thordarson, Bodil. A Comparison of Worker-Owned Firms and Conventionally Owned Firms in Sweden. *Jones, D. C. and Svejnar, J., eds.,* 1987, pp. 225–42. **[G: Sweden]**

Tolliday, Steven. Management and Labour in Britain 1896–1939. *Tolliday, S. and Zeitlin, J., eds.,* 1987, pp. 29–56. **[G: U.K.]**

Tolliday, Steven and Zeitlin, Jonathan. Shop-Floor Bargaining, Contract Unionism and Job Control: An Anglo–American Comparison. *Tolliday, S. and Zeitlin, J., eds.,* 1987, pp. 99–120. **[G: U.S.; U.K.]**

Tolliday, Steven and Zeitlin, Jonathan. The Automobile Industry and Its Workers: Between Fordism and Flexibility: Introduction. *Tolliday, S. and Zeitlin, J., eds.,* 1987, pp. 1–25. **[G: U.S.; Europe; Japan]**

Treu, Tiziano. Italian Labor Relations: A System in Transition. *Mon. Lab. Rev.,* March 1987, *110*(3), pp. 37–39. **[G: Italy]**

Treu, Tiziano and Negrelli, Serafino. Workers' Participation and Personnel Management Policies in Italy. *Int. Lab. Rev.,* Jan.-Feb. 1987, *126*(1), pp. 81–94. **[G: Italy]**

Turner, Stephen. The Swedish Model: What Went Wrong? *Eliasson, G., ed.,* 1987, pp. 73–84. **[G: Sweden]**

Van de Casteele-Schweitzer, Sylvie. Management and Labour in France 1914–39. *Tolliday, S. and Zeitlin, J., eds.,* 1987, pp. 57–75. **[G: France]**

Vanek, Jaroslav. Toward a Just, Efficient, and Fully Democratic Society. *Jones, D. C. and Svejnar, J., eds.,* 1987, pp. 13–78.

Vanek, Jaroslav. Workers' Profit Participation, Unemployment, and the Keynesian Equilibrium. *Jones, D. C. and Svejnar, J., eds.,* 1987, pp. 5–11.

Verma, Anil and McKersie, Robert B. Employee Involvement: The Implications of Noninvolvement by Unions. *Ind. Lab. Relat. Rev.,* July 1987, *40*(4), pp. 556–68. **[G: U.S.]**

Villa, Paola. Systems of Flexible Working in the Italian Steel Industry. *Tarling, R., ed.,* 1987, pp. 307–45. **[G: Italy]**

Voos, Paula B. Managerial Perceptions of the Economic Impact of Labor Relations Programs. *Ind. Lab. Relat. Rev.,* January 1987, *40*(2), pp. 195–208. **[G: U.S.]**

Weber, Arnold R. and Taylor, David P. Problems of Advance Notice [Procedures for Employee Displacement: Advance Notice of Plant Shutdown]. *Staudohar, P. D. and Brown, H. E.,* 1987, *1963,* pp. 135–38. **[G: U.S.]**

Weedon, D. Reid, Jr. The Evolution of Sullivan Principle Compliance. *Sethi, S. P., ed.,* 1987, pp. 393–402. **[G: S. Africa; U.S.]**

Whyte, William Foote. The Employee Ownership Alternative [Employee Ownership: Lessons Learned]. *Staudohar, P. D. and Brown, H. E.,* 1987, *1985,* pp. 217–26. **[G: U.S.]**

Willman, Paul. Labour-Relations Strategy at BL Cars. *Tolliday, S. and Zeitlin, J., eds.,* 1987, pp. 305–27. **[G: U.K.]**

Wood, Stephen. Towards Socialist–Capitalist Comparisons of the Organizational Problem. *Child, J. and Bate, P., eds.,* 1987, pp. 51–71.

Wooden, Mark and Sloan, Judith. Plant Shutdown: A Case Study in Managed Change. *Australian Bull. Lab.,* December 1987, *14*(1), pp. 358–81. **[G: Australia]**

Yoder, Dale and Staudohar, Paul D. Management and Public Policy [Management and Public Policy in Plant Closure]. *Staudohar, P. D. and Brown, H. E.,* 1987, *1985,* pp. 183–200. **[G: U.S.]**

Zeitlin, Jonathan. From Labour History to the History of Industrial Relations. *Econ. Hist. Rev., 2nd Ser.,* May 1987, *40*(2), pp. 159–84. **[G: U.K.]**

8332 Labor–Management Relations in Public Sector

Bacharach, Samuel B.; Schmidle, Timothy P. and Bauer, Scott C. Collective Bargaining in American Industry: Higher Education. *Lipsky, D. B. and Donn, C. B., eds.,* 1987, pp. 225–64. **[G: U.S.]**

Bank, John. Teaching the Chinese about Quality Circles—A Personal Account. *Warner, M., ed.,* 1987, pp. 99–110. **[G: China]**

Baranenkova, T. Ways of Strengthening Labor Discipline. *Prob. Econ.,* February 1987, *29*(10), pp. 55–69. **[G: U.S.S.R.]**

Child, John. Enterprise Reform in China—Progress and Problems. *Warner, M., ed.,* 1987, pp. 24–52. **[G: China]**

Codina Jiménez, Alexis. Worker Incentives in Cuba. *Zimbalist, A., ed.,* 1987, pp. 129–40. **[G: Cuba]**

Delaney, John Thomas and Feuille, Peter. Collective Bargaining in American Industry: Police. *Lipsky, D. B. and Donn, C. B., eds.,* 1987, pp. 265–306. **[G: U.S.]**

Ferner, Anthony. Industrial Relations and the Meso-politics of the Public Enterprise: The Transmission of State Objectives in the Spanish National Railways. *Brit. J. Ind. Relat.,* March 1987, *25*(1), pp. 49–75. **[G: Spain]**

FitzRoy, Felix R. and Kraft, Kornelius. Cooperation, Productivity, and Profit Sharing. *Quart. J. Econ.*, February 1987, *102*(1), pp. 23–35. [G: W. Germany]

Fuller, Linda. Power at the Workplace: The Resolution of Worker–Management Conflict in Cuba. *Zimbalist, A., ed.*, 1987, pp. 141–54. [G: Cuba]

Grancelli, Bruno. Managerial Practices and Patterns of Employee Behaviour in the Soviet Enterprise. *Child, J. and Bate, P., eds.*, 1987, pp. 205–20. [G: U.S.S.R.]

Gregory, Paul R. Productivity, Slack, and Time Theft in the Soviet Economy. *Millar, J. R., ed.*, 1987, pp. 241–75. [G: U.S.S.R.]

Henley, John S. and Ereisha, Mohamed M. State Control and the Labor Productivity Crisis: The Egyptian Textile Industry at Work. *Econ. Develop. Cult. Change*, April 1987, *35*(3), pp. 491–521.

Hyclak, Thomas. Worker Self-management and Economic Reform in Poland. *Int. J. Soc. Econ.*, 1987, *14*(7/8/9), pp. 127–35. [G: Poland]

Kuznetsova, T. Cooperative Relations in a Socialist Economy. *Prob. Econ.*, September 1987, *30*(5), pp. 6–23. [G: U.S.S.R.]

Laky, Teréz. The Economic Work Teams as Enterprises and the Enterprises' Interests. *Eastern Europ. Econ.*, Summer 1987, *25*(4), pp. 62–92. [G: Hungary]

Lockett, Martin. The Economic Environment of Management. *Warner, M., ed.*, 1987, pp. 8–23. [G: China]

Ng, Sek-Hong and Lansbury, Russell D. The Workers' Congress in Chinese Enterprises. *Warner, M., ed.*, 1987, pp. 149–61. [G: China]

Ozaki, M. Labour Relations in the Public Service: 1. Methods of Determining Employment Conditions. *Int. Lab. Rev.*, 1987, *126*(3), pp. 277–99. [G: OECD]

Schrenk, Martin. The Self-managed Firm in Yugoslavia. *Tidrick, G. and Jiyuan, C., eds.*, 1987, pp. 339–69. [G: Yugoslavia; China]

Shkurko, S. Collective Forms of Labor Organization and Work Incentives. *Prob. Econ.*, August 1987, *30*(4), pp. 63–78. [G: U.S.S.R.]

Silva, Francesco; Ferri, Piero and Enrietti, Aldo. Robots, Employment and Industrial Relations in the Italian Automobile Industry. *Watanabe, S., ed.*, 1987, pp. 131–53. [G: Italy]

Sokolovskii, L. E. On Individual and Collective Forms of Labor Organization and Incentives. *Matekon*, Summer 1987, *23*(4), pp. 3–27. [G: U.S.S.R.]

Szita, Éva. New Types of Entrepreneurial and Organizational Forms in the Hungarian Economy. *Alessandrini, S. and Dallago, B., eds.*, 1987, pp. 181–93. [G: Hungary]

Szmicsek, Sándor. The Economic Work Teams in Enterprises—After Two Years. *Eastern Europ. Econ.*, Summer 1987, *25*(4), pp. 35–61. [G: Hungary]

Ward, James Gordon. The Use and Usefulness of Governmental Financial Reports: The Perspective of Public Sector Labor Unions. *Chan, J. L., ed., Pt. B*, 1987, pp. 215–26. [G: U.S.]

Warner, Malcolm. Management Reforms in China: Introduction. *Warner, M., ed.*, 1987, pp. 3–7. [G: China]

Wood, Stephen. Towards Socialist–Capitalist Comparisons of the Organizational Problem. *Child, J. and Bate, P., eds.*, 1987, pp. 51–71.

Yang, Guansan, et al. Enterprise Cadres and Reform. *Reynolds, B. L.*, 1987, pp. 74–85. [G: China]

840 DEMOGRAPHIC ECONOMICS

841 Demographic Economics

8410 Demographic Economics

Adeokun, Lawrence A. Creole and Yoruba Households and Family Size. *Oppong, C., ed.*, 1987, pp. 91–100. [G: Nigeria]

Afsar, Rita. Women's Roles: The Achievement versus Ascription Dialectic. *Bangladesh Devel. Stud.*, June 1987, *15*(2), pp. 65–85. [G: Bangladesh]

Afzal, Mohammad. Intercensal Change and the Indirect Estimation of Mortality: The Case of Pakistan: Comments. *Pakistan Devel. Rev.*, Winter 1987, *26*(4), pp. 583–85. [G: Pakistan]

Agresta, Anthony. The Migration Turnaround: End of a Phenomenon? *Menard, S. W. and Moen, E. W., eds.*, 1987, *1985*, pp. 336–38. [G: U.S.]

Ahlburg, Dennis A. The Impact of Population Growth on Economic Growth in Developing Nations: The Evidence from Macroeconomic–Demographic Models. *Johnson, D. G. and Lee, R. D., eds.*, 1987, pp. 479–521. [G: LDCs]

Ahmed, Bashir. Determinants of Contraceptive Use in Rural Bangladesh: The Demand for Children, Supply of Children, and Costs of Fertility Regulation. *Demography*, August 1987, *24*(3), pp. 361–73. [G: Bangladesh]

Ahmed, Rais Uddin. A Structural Perspective of Farm and Non-farm Households in Bangladesh. *Bangladesh Devel. Stud.*, June 1987, *15*(2), pp. 87–112. [G: Bangladesh]

Akhter, Halida Hanum. Predictors of Contraceptive Continuation among Urban Family Planning Acceptors of Bangladesh. *Bangladesh Devel. Stud.*, September 1987, *15*(3), pp. 101–19. [G: Bangladesh]

Akuffo, Felix Odei. Teenage Pregnancies and School Drop-outs: The Relevance of Family Life Education and Vocational Training to Girls' Employment Opportunities. *Oppong, C., ed.*, 1987, pp. 154–64. [G: Ghana]

Albagli, Claude. Structures sociales, besoins et pouvoir: le verrou agricole. (Social Structures, Needs and Power: The Agricultural Deadlock. With English summary.) *Écon. Soc.*, July 1987, *21*(7), pp. 149–68. [G: Africa]

Alonso, William. Identity and Population. *Alonso, W., ed.*, 1987, pp. 95–125. [G: Japan; U.S.; U.K.; W. Europe]

Alonso, William. Population North and South. *Alonso, W., ed.*, 1987, pp. 1–11.

Amin, Ruhul; Mariam, A. G. and Faruqee, Rashid. Trends and Differentials in Knowledge, Ever Use, Current Use, and Future Intended Use of Contraceptives in Rural Bangladesh: Evidence from Three Surveys. *Pakistan Devel. Rev.*, Summer 1987, *26*(2), pp. 201–14. **[G: Bangladesh]**

Anderson, Annelise. U.S. Social Security under Low Fertility: Comment. *Davis, K.; Bernstam, M. S. and Ricardo-Campbell, R., eds.*, 1987, *1986*, pp. 313–17. **[G: U.S.]**

Anderson, Barbara A. The Life Course of Soviet Women Born 1905–1960. *Millar, J. R., ed.*, 1987, pp. 203–40. **[G: U.S.S.R.]**

Anderson, Kathryn H.; Hill, M. Anne and Butler, John S. Age at Marriage in Malaysia: A Hazard Model of Marriage Timing. *J. Devel. Econ.*, August 1987, *26*(2), pp. 223–34. **[G: Malaysia]**

Anderton, Douglas L., et al. Intergenerational Transmission of Relative Fertility and Life Course Patterns. *Demography*, November 1987, *24*(4), pp. 467–80. **[G: U.S.]**

Armitage, Jane and Sabot, Richard H. Socioeconomic Background and the Returns to Schooling in Two Low-income Economies. *Economica*, February 1987, *54*(213), pp. 103–08. **[G: U.K.; Kenya; Tanzania]**

Azia, Naheed. Sex Differentials in Mortality: A Corollary of Son Preference? Comments. *Pakistan Devel. Rev.*, Winter 1987, *26*(4), pp. 566–68. **[G: Pakistan]**

Bachrach, Christine A. Cohabitation and Reproductive Behavior in the U.S. *Demography*, November 1987, *24*(4), pp. 623–37. **[G: U.S.]**

Bahry, Donna. Politics, Generations, and Change in the USSR. *Millar, J. R., ed.*, 1987, pp. 61–99. **[G: U.S.S.R.]**

Bailey, Mohamed and Weller, Robert H. Fertility Differentials in Rural Sierra Leone: A Path Analysis. *J. Devel. Areas*, January 1987, *21*(2), pp. 191–207. **[G: Sierra Leone]**

Bailey, Wilma R.; Lee, Amy and Wynter, Hugh H. Distance and Continuation Rates in a Family Planning Clinic: A Case Study from Jamaica. *Soc. Econ. Stud.*, September 1987, *36*(3), pp. 203–17. **[G: Jamaica]**

Balakrishnan, T. R., et al. A Hazard Model Analysis of the Covariates of Marriage Dissolution in Canada. *Demography*, August 1987, *24*(3), pp. 395–406. **[G: Canada]**

Bates, John J. and Bracken, I. Migration Age Profiles for Local Authority Areas in England, 1971–1981. *Environ. Planning A*, April 1987, *19*(4), pp. 521–35. **[G: U.K.]**

Batina, Raymond G. The Consumption Tax in the Presence of Altruistic Cash and Human Capital Bequests with Endogenous Fertility Decisions. *J. Public Econ.*, December 1987, *34*(3), pp. 329–54.

Bean, Frank D.; Telles, Edward E. and Lowell, B. Lindsay. Undocumented Migration to the United States: Perceptions and Evidence. *Population Devel. Rev.*, December 1987, *13*(4), pp. 671–90. **[G: U.S.]**

Beaumont, Paul M. and Isserman, Andrew M.

Tests of Forecast Accuracy and Bias for County Population Projections: Comment. *J. Amer. Statist. Assoc.*, December 1987, *82*(400), pp. 1004–09. **[G: U.S.]**

Becker, Gary S. and Barro, Robert J. Altruism and the Economic Theory of Fertility. *Davis, K.; Bernstam, M. S. and Ricardo-Campbell, R., eds.*, 1987, *1986*, pp. 69–76.

Behar, Cem L. Malthus and the Development of Demographic Analysis. *Population Stud.*, July 1987, *41*(2), pp. 269–81.

Behrman, Jere R. Is Child Schooling a Poor Proxy for Child Quality? *Demography*, August 1987, *24*(3), pp. 341–59.

Behrman, Jere R. and Wolfe, Barbara L. How Does Mother's Schooling Affect Family Health, Nutrition, Medical Care Usage, and Household Sanitation? *J. Econometrics*, Sept./Oct. 1987, *36*(1/2), pp. 185–204. **[G: Nicaragua]**

Behrman, Jere R. and Wolfe, Barbara L. Investments in Schooling in Two Generations in Prerevolutionary Nicaragua: The Roles of Family Background and School Supply. *J. Devel. Econ.*, October 1987, *27*(1–2), pp. 395–419. **[G: Nicaragua]**

Behrman, Jere R. and Wolfe, Barbara L. Investments in Schooling in Two Generations in Prerevolutionary Nicaragua: The Roles of Family Background and School Supply. *[Diaz-Alejandro, C. F.]*, 1987, pp. 395–419. **[G: Nicaragua]**

Berninghaus, Siegfried and Seifert-Vogt, Hans Günther. International Migration under Incomplete Information. *Schweiz. Z. Volkswirtsch. Statist.*, June 1987, *123*(2), pp. 199–218.

Bernstam, Mikhail S. Competitive Human Markets, Interfamily Transfers, and Below-Replacement Fertility. *Davis, K.; Bernstam, M. S. and Ricardo-Campbell, R., eds.*, 1987, *1986*, pp. 111–36. **[G: U.S.; U.S.S.R.]**

Berthold, Norbert. Umschichtung des Lebenseinkommens als verteilungspolitische Aufgabe der Familienpolitik. (Intertemporal Allocation of Life Income as a Distributional Task of Family Policy. With English summary.) *Jahr. Nationalökon. Statist.*, January 1987, *203*(1), pp. 12–25. **[G: W. Germany]**

Bilsborrow, Richard E. Population Pressures and Agricultural Development in Developing Countries: A Conceptual Framework and Recent Evidence. *World Devel.*, February 1987, *15*(2), pp. 183–203. **[G: LDCs]**

Bilsborrow, Richard E., et al. The Impact of Origin Community Characteristics on Rural–Urban Out-Migration in a Developing Country. *Demography*, May 1987, *24*(2), pp. 191–210. **[G: Ecuador]**

Bleek, Wolf. Family and Family Planning in Southern Ghana. *Oppong, C., ed.*, 1987, pp. 138–53. **[G: Ghana]**

Bloom, David E. and Freeman, Richard B. Population Growth, Labor Supply, and Employment in Developing Countries. *Johnson, D. G. and Lee, R. D., eds.*, 1987, pp. 105–47. **[G: LDCs]**

Bongaarts, John. Does Family Planning Reduce Infant Mortality Rates? *Population Devel. Rev.*, June 1987, *13*(2), pp. 323–34.
[G: LDCs]

Bongaarts, John. The Proximate Determinants of Exceptionally High Fertility. *Population Devel. Rev.*, March 1987, *13*(1), pp. 133–39.
[G: Yemen; Zimbabwe; Kenya; Syria; Jordan]

Bonitsis, Theologos Homer and Geithman, David T. Does Income Affect Fertility or Does Fertility Affect Income? *Eastern Econ. J.*, October-December 1987, *13*(4), pp. 447–51.
[G: Latin America]

Boserup, Ester. Economic Growth with Below-Replacement Fertility: Comment. *Davis, K.; Bernstam, M. S. and Ricardo-Campbell, R.*, eds., 1987, *1986*, pp. 238–43. [G: U.S.]

Boserup, Ester. Population and Technology in Preindustrial Europe. *Population Devel. Rev.*, December 1987, *13*(4), pp. 691–701.
[G: Europe]

Boskin, Michael J. Intergenerational Aspects of Government Policy under Changing Demographic and Economic Conditions. *Bus. Econ.*, July 1987, *22*(3), pp. 18–24. [G: U.S.]

Boulle, Laurence and Julyan, Jacky. The Legal Structure of the Apartheid State. *Sethi, S. P.*, ed., 1987, pp. 127–48. [G: S. Africa]

Bourgeois-Pichat, Jean. The Unprecedented Shortage of Births in Europe. *Davis, K.; Bernstam, M. S. and Ricardo-Campbell, R.*, eds., 1987, *1986*, pp. 3–25. [G: Europe]

Bowman, Mary Jean. Education, Population Trends, and Technological Change. *Espenshade, T. and Stolnitz, G. J.*, eds., 1987, *1985*, pp. 71–103. [G: Global]

Bowman, Mary Jean. The Importance of Examining Cohort Uniqueness in the Formulation of Human Investment Policies. *Econ. Educ. Rev.*, 1987, *6*(2), pp. 67–79.

Bremer, Stuart A. The GLOBUS Model: Computer Simulation of Worldwide Political and Economic Development: Demographic Processes. *Bremer, S. A.*, ed., 1987, pp. 283–324.
[G: Global]

Bretz, M.; Esposito, I. and Fleischer, H. The Precision of Statistics of International Migrations—A Study of Flows between Italy and the Federal Republic of Germany. *Statist. J.*, December 1987, *5*(1), pp. 1–12. [G: Italy; W. Germany]

Broome, John. The Economic Value of Life: A Reply. *Economica*, August 1987, *54*(215), pp. 0240.

Brown, Lawrence A. and Goetz, Andrew R. Development-Related Contextual Effects and Individual Attributes in Third World Migration Processes: A Venezuelan Example. *Demography*, November 1987, *24*(4), pp. 497–516.
[G: Venezuela]

Brown, Lester R. Analyzing the Demographic Trap. *Brown, L. R., et al.*, 1987, pp. 20–37.
[G: Global]

Bull, Hedley. Population and the Present World Structure. *Alonso, W.*, ed., 1987, pp. 74–94.
[G: Global]

Bumpass, Larry L. The Risk of an Unwanted Birth: The Changing Context of Contraceptive Sterilization in the U.S. *Population Stud.*, November 1987, *41*(3), pp. 347–63. [G: U.S.]

Burch, Thomas K. and Matthews, Beverly J. Household Formation in Developed Societies. *Population Devel. Rev.*, September 1987, *13*(3), pp. 495–511.

Butt, Abdul Rauf. Impact of Population Planning on the Size Distribution of Income: A Theoretical and Methodological Framework. *Pakistan Econ. Soc. Rev.*, Winter 1987, *25*(2), pp. 59–72. [G: Pakistan]

Cain, Glen G. The Income Maintenance Experiments and the Issues of Marital Stability and Family Composition. *Munnell, A. H.*, ed., 1987, pp. 60–93. [G: U.S.]

Caldwell, John C. and Caldwell, Pat. The Cultural Context of High Fertility in Sub-Saharan Africa. *Population Devel. Rev.*, September 1987, *13*(3), pp. 409–37. [G: Africa]

Carmichael, Gordon A. Bust after Boom: First Marriage Trends in Australia. *Demography*, May 1987, *24*(2), pp. 245–64. [G: Australia]

Cerone, Pietro. On Stable Population Theory with Immigration. *Demography*, August 1987, *24*(3), pp. 431–38. [G: U.S.]

Cerquone, Joseph. Southeast Asian Refugees: Back to the Future. *U.S. Committee for Refugees.*, 1987, pp. 34–35. [G: U.S.]

Chaudhary, Mohammad Ashraf. Social and Demographic Determinants of Rise in Female Age at Marriage in Taiwan 1961–76. *Pakistan Econ. Soc. Rev.*, Winter 1987, *25*(2), pp. 73–87.
[G: Taiwan]

Chen, Jain-Shing A., et al. The "Synthesis Framework" and Determinants of Fertility in Syria. *Econ. Develop. Cult. Change*, October 1987, *36*(1), pp. 145–59. [G: Syria]

Cheung, H. Y.-F. and Liaw, Kao-Lee. Metropolitan Out-Migration of Elderly Females in Canada: Characterization and Explanation. *Environ. Planning A*, December 1987, *19*(12), pp. 1659–71. [G: Canada]

Chiswick, Barry R. Immigration as a Counter to Below-Replacement Fertility in the United States: Comment. *Davis, K.; Bernstam, M. S. and Ricardo-Campbell, R.*, eds., 1987, *1986*, pp. 269–70. [G: U.S.]

Chiswick, Carmel U. Economic Growth with Below-Replacement Fertility: Comment. *Davis, K.; Bernstam, M. S. and Ricardo-Campbell, R.*, eds., 1987, *1986*, pp. 244–47. [G: U.S.]

Chu, C. Y. Cyrus. The Dynamics of Population Growth, Differential Fertility, and Inequality: Note. *Amer. Econ. Rev.*, December 1987, *77*(5), pp. 1054–56. [G: Brazil]

Clark, William A. V. Urban Restructuring from a Demographic Perspective. *Econ. Geogr.*, April 1987, *63*(2), pp. 103–25. [G: U.S.]

Cleland, John and Wilson, Christopher. Demand Theories of the Fertility Transition: An Iconoclastic View. *Population Stud.*, March 1987, *41*(1), pp. 5–30. [G: W. Europe; LDCs]

Coale, Ansley J. Demographic Effects of Below-Replacement Fertility and Their Social Implications. *Davis, K.; Bernstam, M. S. and Ricardo-Campbell, R., eds.*, 1987, *1986*, pp. 203–16. [G: U.S.]

Coale, Ansley J. How a Population Ages or Grows Younger. *Menard, S. W. and Moen, E. W., eds.*, 1987, *1964*, pp. 365–71.

Cohn, Raymond L. The Determinants of Individual Immigrant Mortality on Sailing Ships, 1836–1853. *Exploration Econ. Hist.*, October 1987, *24*(4), pp. 371–91. [G: U.S.]

Conk, Margo A. The 1980 Census in Historical Perspective. *Alonso, W. and Starr, P., eds.*, 1987, pp. 155–86. [G: U.S.]

Constantinides, Marietta A. Optimum Population, Overlapping Generations and Social Security in a Model Mximizing $u(c^1, c^2, X)$. *J. Econ. (Z. Nationalökon.)*, 1987, *47*(1), pp. 69–75.

de Cooman, Eric; Ermisch, John and Joshi, Heather E. The Next Birth and the Labour Market: A Dynamic Model of Births in England and Wales. *Population Stud.*, July 1987, *41*(2), pp. 237–68. [G: U.K.]

Corman, Hope; Joyce, Theodore J. and Grossman, Michael. Birth Outcome Production Function in the United States. *J. Human Res.*, Summer 1987, *22*(3), pp. 339–60. [G: U.S.]

Cornia, Giovanni Andrea. Economic Decline and Human Welfare in the First Half of the 1980s. *Cornia, G. A.; Jolly, R. and Stewart, F., eds.*, 1987, pp. 11–47. [G: Global]

Cramer, James C. Social Factors and Infant Mortality: Identifying High-Risk Groups and Proximate Causes. *Demography*, August 1987, *24*(3), pp. 299–322. [G: U.S.]

Cremer, Helmuth; Kessler, Denis and Pestieau, Pierre. Fertility Differentials and the Regressive Effect of Public Debt. *Economica*, February 1987, *54*(213), pp. 79–87.

Cressie, Noel. Census Undercount Adjustment and the Quality of Geographic Population Distributions: Comment. *J. Amer. Statist. Assoc.*, December 1987, *82*(400), pp. 980–83. [G: U.S.]

Crew, Spencer R. The Great Migration of Afro-Americans, 1915–40. *Mon. Lab. Rev.*, March 1987, *110*(3), pp. 34–36. [G: U.S.]

Cushing, Brian J. A Note on Specification of Climate Variables in Models of Population Migration. *J. Reg. Sci.*, November 1987, *27*(4), pp. 241–49. [G: U.S.]

Cushing, Brian J. Location-Specific Amenities, Topography, and Population Migration. *Ann. Reg. Sci.*, July 1987, *21*(2), pp. 74–85. [G: U.S.]

Das Gupta, Monica. Selective Discrimination against Female Children in Rural Punjab, India. *Population Devel. Rev.*, March 1987, *13*(1), pp. 77–100. [G: India]

Das, Narayan. Sex Preference and Fertility Behavior: A Study of Recent Indian Data. *Demography*, November 1987, *24*(4), pp. 517–30. [G: India]

Dasgupta, Partha. The Ethical Foundations of Population Policies. *Johnson, D. G. and Lee, R. D., eds.*, 1987, pp. 631–59.

David, Paul A. Altruism and the Economic Theory of Fertility: Comment. *Davis, K.; Bernstam, M. S. and Ricardo-Campbell, R., eds.*, 1987, *1986*, pp. 77–86.

David, Paul A. and Sanderson, Warren C. The Emergence of a Two-Child Norm among American Birth-Controllers. *Population Devel. Rev.*, March 1987, *13*(1), pp. 1–41. [G: U.S.]

Davis, Kingsley. Low Fertility in Evolutionary Perspective. *Davis, K.; Bernstam, M. S. and Ricardo-Campbell, R., eds.*, 1987, *1986*, pp. 48–65. [G: OECD]

Davis, Kingsley. The Theory of Change and Response in Modern Demographic History. *Menard, S. W. and Moen, E. W., eds.*, 1987, *1963*, pp. 37–41. [G: Japan]

Davis, Kingsley. The Urbanization of the Human Population. *Menard, S. W. and Moen, E. W., eds.*, 1987, *1965*, pp. 322–30.

Day, Alice Taylor and Day, Lincoln H. Cross-National Comparison of Population Density. *Menard, S. W. and Moen, E. W., eds.*, 1987, *1973*, pp. 342–52. [G: W. Europe; U.S.]

Day, John. Crises and Trends in the Late Middle Ages. *Day, J.*, 1987, pp. 185–224. [G: Europe]

Day, Richard H., et al. Instability in Rural–Urban Migration. *Econ. J.*, December 1987, *97*(388), pp. 940–50.

De Gregori, Thomas R. and Darity, William A., Jr. Surplus People and Expendable Children: The Structure of Apartheid and the Mortality Crisis in South Africa. *Rev. Black Polit. Econ.*, Spring 1987, *15*(4), pp. 47–62. [G: S. Africa]

De Vos, Susan. Latin American Households in Comparative Perspective. *Population Stud.*, November 1987, *41*(3), pp. 501–17. [G: Latin America]

Dean, K. G. The Disaggregation of Migration Flows: The Case of Brittany, 1975–1982. *Reg. Stud.*, August 1987, *21*(4), pp. 313–25. [G: U.K.]

Deardorff, Alan V. Trade and Capital Mobility in a World of Diverging Populations. *Johnson, D. G. and Lee, R. D., eds.*, 1987, pp. 561–88. [G: LDCs; MDCs]

Demeny, Paul. Pronatalist Policies in Low-Fertility Countries: Patterns, Performance, and Prospects. *Davis, K.; Bernstam, M. S. and Ricardo-Campbell, R., eds.*, 1987, *1986*, pp. 335–58. [G: U.S.]

Demeny, Paul. Re-linking Fertility Behavior and Economic Security in Old Age: A Pronatalist Reform. *Population Devel. Rev.*, March 1987, *13*(1), pp. 128–32.

Desbarats, Jacqueline. Population Redistribution in the Socialist Republic of Vietnam. *Population Devel. Rev.*, March 1987, *13*(1), pp. 43–76. [G: Vietnam]

Di Domenico, Catherine; de Cola, Lee and Leishman, Jennifer. Urban Yoruba Mothers: At Home and at Work. *Oppong, C., ed.*, 1987, pp. 118–32. [G: Nigeria]

Din, Shams-ud. Demographic Changes and Nationality Problems in Soviet Central Asia, Kazakhstan and Azerbaijan. *Gidadhubli, R. G., ed.*, 1987, pp. 85–100.　　　　**[G: U.S.S.R.]**

Dolton, Peter J. and Makepeace, Gerald H. Marital Status, Child Rearing and Earnings Differentials in the Graduate Labour Market. *Econ. J.*, December 1987, *97*(388), pp. 897–922.　　　　　　　　　　**[G: U.K.]**

Domínguez, Virginia R. Sex, Gender, and Revolution: The Problem of Construction and the Construction of a Problem. *Mesa-Lago, C., ed.*, 1987, pp. 7–23.　　　　**[G: Cuba]**

Easterlin, Richard A. The New Age Structure of Poverty in America: Permanent or Transient? *Population Devel. Rev.*, June 1987, *13*(2), pp. 195–208.　　　　**[G: U.S.]**

Ellwood, David T. The Income Maintenance Experiments and the Issues of Marital Stability and Family Composition: Discussion. *Munnell, A. H., ed.*, 1987, pp. 94–98.　　**[G: U.S.]**

Espenshade, Thomas J. Population Dynamics with Immigration and Low Fertility. *Davis, K.; Bernstam, M. S. and Ricardo-Campbell, R., eds.*, 1987, *1986*, pp. 248–61.　**[G: U.S.]**

Espenshade, Thomas J. and Minarik, Joseph J. Demographic Implications of the 1986 U.S. Tax Reform. *Population Devel. Rev.*, March 1987, *13*(1), pp. 115–27.　　　　**[G: U.S.]**

Espenshade, Thomas J. and Stolnitz, George J. Technological Prospects and Population Trends: An Overview. *Espenshade, T. and Stolnitz, G. J., eds.*, 1987, pp. 1–10.

Even, William E. Career Interruptions Following Childbirth. *J. Lab. Econ.*, April 1987, *5*(2), pp. 255–77.　　　　　　　**[G: U.S.]**

Faerman, E. Iu. and Portianskii, I. A. Systems Forecasting of Urban Settlement. *Matekon*, Winter 1987-88, *24*(2), pp. 69–87.
　　　　　　　　　　　　[G: U.S.S.R.]

Falaris, Evangelos M. A Nested Logit Migration Model with Selectivity. *Int. Econ. Rev.*, June 1987, *28*(2), pp. 429–43.　　**[G: Venezuela]**

Falaris, Evangelos M. An Empirical Study of the Timing and Spacing of Childbearing. *Southern Econ. J.*, October 1987, *54*(2), pp. 287–300.
　　　　　　　　　　　　[G: U.S.]

Fapohunda, Eleanor R. Urban Women's Roles and Nigerian Government Development Strategies. *Oppong, C., ed.*, 1987, pp. 203–12.　　　　　　　　　**[G: Nigeria]**

Farooq, Ghazi M.; Ekanem, Ita I. and Ojelade, Sina. Family Size Preferences and Fertility in South-western Nigeria. *Oppong, C., ed.*, 1987, pp. 75–85.　　　　　**[G: Nigeria]**

Feeney, Griffith and Yu, Jingyuan. Period Parity Progression Measures of Fertility in China. *Population Stud.*, March 1987, *41*(1), pp. 77–102.　　　　　　　　　　**[G: China]**

Findley, Sally E. An Interactive Contextual Model of Migration in Ilocos Norte, the Philippines. *Demography*, May 1987, *24*(2), pp. 163–90.　　　　　　　　**[G: Philippines]**

Fong, Chan-Onn. Population-Development Program Implementation: The Malaysian Experience. *Econ. Develop. Cult. Change*, April 1987, *35*(3), pp. 539–60.　**[G: Malaysia]**

Ford, Kathleen and Kim, Young. Distributions

of Postpartum Amenorrhea: Some New Evidence. *Demography*, August 1987, *24*(3), pp. 413–30.　　　　　　　　　　**[G: U.S.]**

Frank, Odile and McNicoll, Geoffrey. An Interpretation of Fertility and Population Policy in Kenya. *Population Devel. Rev.*, June 1987, *13*(2), pp. 209–43.　　　　**[G: Kenya]**

Gabriel, Stuart A.; Justman, Moshe and Levy, Amnon. Place-to-Place Migration in Israel: Estimates of a Logistic Model. *Reg. Sci. Urban Econ.*, November 1987, *17*(4), pp. 595–606.
　　　　　　　　　　　　[G: Israel]

Gedik, Ayşe. Savaş Sonrasinda Japonya'da Nüfusun Mekansal Dağilimi (1945–89) ve Gelişmekte Olan Ülkeler İçin Anlami. (The Spatial Distribution of Population in Postwar Japan [1945–80]. Implications for the Developing Countries. With English summary.) *METU*, 1987, *14*(4), pp. 339–72.　　**[G: Japan]**

Geronimus, Arline T. On Teenage Childbearing and Neonatal Mortality in the United States. *Population Devel. Rev.*, June 1987, *13*(2), pp. 245–79.　　　　　　　　　**[G: U.S.]**

Getman, Thomas R. and Flory, David. South Africa's Refugees. *U.S. Committee for Refugees.*, 1987, pp. 13–18.　　**[G: S. Africa]**

Giannini, Mirella. Donne e lavoro nel contesto meridionale. (Women and Work in the Mezzogiorno. With English summary.) *Econ. Lavoro*, Apr.-June 1987, *21*(2), pp. 67–85.　**[G: Italy]**

Gibson, Campbell. The Population in Large Urban Concentrations in the United States, 1790–1980: A Delineation Using Highly Urbanized Counties. *Demography*, November 1987, *24*(4), pp. 601–14.　　　　　　**[G: U.S.]**

Gidadhubli, R. G. Socio-economic Transformation of Soviet Central Asia: Introduction. *Gidadhubli, R. G., ed.*, 1987, pp. ix–xx.
　　　　　　　　　　　　[G: U.S.S.R.]

Goldman, Noreen and Lord, Graham. On "A New Look at Entropy and the Life Table": Reply. *Demography*, August 1987, *24*(3), pp. 441–42.

Goldman, Noreen; Westoff, Charles F. and Paul, Lois E. Variations in Natural Fertility: The Effect of Lactation and Other Determinants. *Population Stud.*, March 1987, *41*(1), pp. 127–46.
　　　　　　　　　　　　[G: LDCs]

Goodman, Allen C. Using Lorenz Curves to Characterise Urban Elderly Populations. *Urban Stud.*, February 1987, *24*(1), pp. 77–80.
　　　　　　　　　　　　[G: U.S.]

Gottschang, Thomas R. Economic Change, Disasters, and Migration: The Historical Case of Manchuria. *Econ. Develop. Cult. Change*, April 1987, *35*(3), pp. 461–90.　**[G: China]**

Gove, Walter R. Sex, Marital Status, and Mortality. *Menard, S. W. and Moen, E. W., eds.*, 1987, *1973*, pp. 138–52.　　　**[G: U.S.]**

Gray, Alan. Intermarriage: Opportunity and Preference. *Population Stud.*, November 1987, *41*(3), pp. 365–79.

Greene, Margaret E. Intercensal Change and the Indirect Estimation of Mortality: The Case of Pakistan. *Pakistan Devel. Rev.*, Winter 1987, *26*(4), pp. 569–82.　　　**[G: Pakistan]**

Guralnik, Jack M. and Schneider, Edward L. Prospects and Implications of Extending Life Expectancy. *Espenshade, T. and Stolnitz, G. J., eds.,* 1987, pp. 125–45. [G: U.S.]

Haines, Michael R. Economic History and Historical Demography: Past, Present, and Future. *Field, A. J., ed.,* 1987, pp. 185–253.

Hakkert, Ralph. Life Table Transformations and Inequality Measures: Some Noteworthy Formal Relationships. *Demography,* November 1987, *24*(4), pp. 615–22.

Halter, William A. and Hemming, Richard. The Impact of Demographic Change on Social Security Financing. *Int. Monet. Fund Staff Pap.,* September 1987, *34*(3), pp. 471–502.
[G: W. Germany; Japan; U.K.; U.S.]

Hamermesh, Daniel S. and Menchik, Paul L. Planned and Unplanned Bequests. *Econ. Inquiry,* January 1987, *25*(1), pp. 55–66.
[G: U.S.]

Hammer, Jeffrey S. The Demographic Transition and Aggregate Savings in Less Developed Countries. *J. Econ. Devel.,* December 1987, *12*(2), pp. 21–37. [G: LDCs]

Hamnett, C. A Tale of Two Cities: Sociotenurial Polarisation in London and the South East, 1966–1981. *Environ. Planning A,* April 1987, *19*(4), pp. 537–56. [G: U.K.]

Hardin, Garrett. The Tragedy of the Commons. *Menard, S. W. and Moen, E. W., eds.,* 1987, *1968,* pp. 106–12.

Harter, Carl L. The "Good Times" Cohort of the 1930s: Sometimes Less Means More (and More Means Less). *Menard, S. W. and Moen, E. W., eds.,* 1987, *1971,* pp. 372–76. [G: U.S.]

Hartford, Robert B. The Case of the Elusive Infant Mortality Rate. *Menard, S. W. and Moen, E. W., eds.,* 1987, *1984,* pp. 153–55.
[G: U.S.]

Haub, Carl. Sun Belt Growth: Not What It Seems? *Menard, S. W. and Moen, E. W., eds.,* 1987, *1984,* pp. 339–41. [G: U.S.]

Hauser, Philip M. The U.S. Census Undercount. *Menard, S. W. and Moen, E. W., eds.,* 1987, *1981,* pp. 434–40. [G: U.S.]

Hayami, Yujiro and Ruttan, Vernon W. Population Growth and Agricultural Productivity. *Johnson, D. G. and Lee, R. D., eds.,* 1987, pp. 57–101. [G: Global]

Hayami, Yujiro and Ruttan, Vernon W. Population Growth and Agricultural Productivity. *Espenshade, T. and Stolnitz, G. J., eds.,* 1987, pp. 11–69.

Hayes, Kathy J. and Slottje, D. J. Measures of Publicness Based on Demographic Scaling. *Rev. Econ. Statist.,* November 1987, *69*(4), pp. 713–18. [G: U.S.]

Hecht, Jacqueline. Johann Peter Süssmilch: A German Prophet in Foreign Countries. *Population Stud.,* March 1987, *41*(1), pp. 31–58.
[G: W. Europe]

Heer, David M. Immigration as a Counter to Below-Replacement Fertility in the United States. *Davis, K.; Bernstam, M. S. and Ricardo-Campbell, R., eds.,* 1987, *1986,* pp. 262–69. [G: U.S.]

Heldal, J.; Swensen, A. Rygh and Thomsen, I.

Census Statistics through Combined Use of Surveys and Registers? *Statist. J.,* December 1987, *5*(1), pp. 43–51. [G: Norway]

Hensher, David A. and Beesley, M. E. Identification of Segmentation Criteria for the Improvement of Population Forecasts. *Environ. Planning A,* June 1987, *19*(6), pp. 807–18.
[G: Australia]

Hohemberg, Paul M. Urbanization and Population Dynamics in History: Review Article. *J. Europ. Econ. Hist.,* Spring 1987, *16*(1), pp. 171–77.

Huang, Wi-Chiao. A Pooled Cross-Section and Time-Series Study of Professional Indirect Immigration to the United States. *Southern Econ. J.,* July 1987, *54*(1), pp. 95–109. [G: U.S.]

Huffman, Sandra L., et al. Nutrition and Fertility in Bangladesh: Breastfeeding and Post Partum Amenorrhoea. *Population Stud.,* November 1987, *41*(3), pp. 447–62. [G: Bangladesh]

Hull, Terence H. and Larson, Ann. Dynamic Disequilibrium: Demographic Policies and Trends in Asia. *Asian-Pacific Econ. Lit.,* May 1987, *1*(1), pp. 25–59. [G: Asia]

Hwang, Sean-Shong and Albrecht, Don E. Constraints to the Fulfillment of Residential Preferences among Texas Homebuyers. *Demography,* February 1987, *24*(1), pp. 61–76.
[G: U.S.]

James, Jeffrey. Population and Technical Change in the Manufacturing Sector of Developing Countries. *Johnson, D. G. and Lee, R. D., eds.,* 1987, pp. 225–56. [G: LDCs]

Jenkins, Stephen. Snapshots versus Movies: 'Lifecycle Biases' and the Estimation of Intergenerational Earnings Inheritance. *Europ. Econ. Rev.,* July 1987, *31*(5), pp. 1149–58.
[G: U.K.]

Jenkins, Stephen. The Implications of 'Stochastic' Demographic Assumptions for Models of the Distribution of Inherited Wealth: Correction. *Bull. Econ. Res.,* April 1987, *39*(2), pp. 185.

Johansson, S. Ryan. Status Anxiety and Demographic Contraction of Privileged Populations. *Population Devel. Rev.,* September 1987, *13*(3), pp. 439–70. [G: W. Europe]

Johansson, S. Ryan and Mosk, Carl. Exposure, Resistance and Life Expectancy: Disease and Death during the Economic Development of Japan, 1900–1960. *Population Stud.,* July 1987, *41*(2), pp. 207–35. [G: Japan; Italy; U.K.]

John, A. Meredith; Menken, Jane A. and Chowdhury, A. K. M. Alauddin. The Effects of Breastfeeding and Nutrition on Fecundability in Rural Bangladesh: A Hazards-Model Analysis. *Population Stud.,* November 1987, *41*(3), pp. 433–46. [G: Bangladesh]

Johnson, D. Gale. Is Population Growth the Dominant Force in Development? [Population Growth, Economic Growth, and Foreign Aid]. *Cato J.,* Spring/Summer 1987, *7*(1), pp. 187–93. [G: LDCs]

Jones-Lee, M. W. The Economic Value of Life: A Comment. *Economica,* August 1987, *54*(215), pp. 397–400.

Joyce, Theodore J. The Impact of Induced Abortion on Black and White Birth Outcomes in the United States. *Demography*, May 1987, 24(2), pp. 229–44. [G: U.S.]

Kalmuss, Debra S. The Use of Infertility Services among Fertility-Impaired Couples. *Demography*, November 1987, 24(4), pp. 575–85. [G: U.S.]

Katz, Eliakim and Stark, Oded. International Migration under Asymmetric Information. *Econ. J.*, September 1987, 97(387), pp. 718–26.

Kaushik, Devendra. Soviet Nationalities Policy in Central Asia: A Survey and Appraisal. *Gidadhubli, R. G., ed.*, 1987, pp. 1–20. [G: U.S.S.R.]

Keeley, Michael C. The Effects of Experimental Negative Income Tax Programs on Marital Dissolution: Evidence from the Seattle and Denver Income Maintenance Experiments. *Int. Econ. Rev.*, February 1987, 28(1), pp. 241–57. [G: U.S.]

Kelman, Steven. The Political Foundations of American Statistical Policy. *Alonso, W. and Starr, P., eds.*, 1987, pp. 275–302. [G: U.S.]

Ketkar, Kusum W. and Ketkar, Suhas L. Population Dynamics and Consumer Demand. *Appl. Econ.*, November 1987, 19(11), pp. 1483–95. [G: U.S.]

Keyfitz, Nathan. The Family That Does Not Reproduce Itself. *Davis, K.; Bernstam, M. S. and Ricardo-Campbell, R., eds.*, 1987, 1986, pp. 139–54. [G: OECD]

Keyfitz, Nathan. The Social and Political Context of Population Forecasting. *Alonso, W. and Starr, P., eds.*, 1987, pp. 235–58. [G: U.S.]

Khandker, Shahidur R. Women's Role in Household Productive Activities and Fertility in Bangladesh. *J. Econ. Devel.*, June 1987, 12(1), pp. 87–115. [G: Bangladesh]

Khandker, Shahidur R. Women's Time Allocation and Household Nonmarket Production in Rural Bangladesh. *J. Devel. Areas*, October 1987, 22(1), pp. 85–101. [G: Bangladesh]

Khandker, Shahidur R. and Butterfield, David W. Consumption, Family Size, Schooling and Labor Supply Decisions: Estimates of a Linear Expenditure System for Bangladesh. *J. Econ. Devel.*, December 1987, 12(2), pp. 89–113. [G: Bangladesh]

Kiani, M. Framurz. Migration and Fertility in Pakistan. *Pakistan Devel. Rev.*, Winter 1987, 26(4), pp. 587–89. [G: Pakistan]

Kidane, Asmerom. Determinants of Saving in Ethiopia with Reference to the Role of Demographic Variables. *Eastern Afr. Econ. Rev.*, December 1987, 3(2), pp. 121–29. [G: Ethiopia]

Kim, Kyung-Hwan and McDonald, John F. Sufficient Conditions for Negative Exponential Densities: A Further Analysis. *J. Reg. Sci.*, May 1987, 27(2), pp. 295–98.

King, Elizabeth M. The Effect of Family Size on Family Welfare: What Do We Know? *Johnson, D. G. and Lee, R. D., eds.*, 1987, pp. 373–411. [G: LDCs]

Kirby, Andrew and Lynch, A. Karen. A Ghost in the Growth Machine: The Aftermath of Rapid Population Growth in Houston. *Urban*

Stud., December 1987, 24(6), pp. 587–96. [G: U.S.]

Knodel, John. Starting, Stopping and Spacing during the Early Stages of Fertility Transition: The Experience of German Village Populations in the 18th and 19th Centuries. *Demography*, May 1987, 24(2), pp. 143–62. [G: W. Germany]

Koch, James V. The Incomes of Recent Immigrants: A Look at Ethnic Differences. *Soc. Sci. Quart.*, June 1987, 68(2), pp. 294–310. [G: U.S.]

Kono, Shigemi. Perspective on Nuptiality and Fertility: Comment. *Davis, K.; Bernstam, M. S. and Ricardo-Campbell, R., eds.*, 1987, 1986, pp. 171–75. [G: OECD]

Kooreman, Peter and Kapteyn, Arie. A Disaggregated Analysis of the Allocation of Time within the Household. *J. Polit. Econ.*, April 1987, 95(2), pp. 223–49. [G: U.S.]

Krashinsky, Michael. The Cooke Report on Child Care: A Critique. *Can. Public Policy*, September 1987, 13(3), pp. 294–303. [G: Canada]

Krug, Barbara and Frey, Bruno S. Ökonomik der Familie: Patriarchalismus in China. (Economics of the Family. Patriarchalism in China. With English summary.) *Z. Wirtschaft. Sozialwissen.*, 1987, 107(1), pp. 67–84. [G: China]

Kunitz, Stephen J. Explanations and Ideologies of Mortality Patterns. *Population Devel. Rev.*, September 1987, 13(3), pp. 379–408. [G: U.S.]

Kux, Jaroslav. International Comparisons of Economic Activity of the Population. *Czech. Econ. Digest.*, June 1987, (4), pp. 61–79. [G: Europe]

Kuznets, Simon. Population, Income and Capital. *Dupriez, L. H., ed.*, 1987, 1955, pp. 3–20. [G: Global]

Lam, David. Distribution Issues in the Relationship between Population Growth and Economic Development. *Johnson, D. G. and Lee, R. D., eds.*, 1987, pp. 589–627. [G: Selected Countries]

Landers, J. Mortality and Metropolis: The Case of London 1675–1825. *Population Stud.*, March 1987, 41(1), pp. 59–76. [G: U.K.]

Ledent, Jacques and Rogers, A. Spatial Dynamics of Populations with Changing Birth, Death, and Migration Rates: A Generalization of Multiregional Stable Population Theory. *Environ. Planning A*, June 1987, 19(6), pp. 819–28.

Lee, Everett S., et al. Population Research: Trends and Prospects. *Menard, S. W. and Moen, E. W., eds.*, 1987, 1982, pp. 441–45. [G: U.S.]

Lee, Maw Lin and Loschky, David. Malthusian Population Oscillations. *Econ. J.*, September 1987, 97(387), pp. 727–39. [G: U.S.]

Lee, Ronald D. Population Dynamics of Humans and Other Animals. *Demography*, November 1987, 24(4), pp. 443–65. [G: OECD]

Lee, Ronald D. The Value and Allocation of Time in High-Income Countries: Implications for Fertility: Comment. *Davis, K.; Bernstam, M.*

S. and Ricardo-Campbell, R., eds., 1987, 1986, pp. 108–10.

Leete, Richard. The Post-demographic Transition in East and South East Asia: Similarities and Contrasts with Europe. *Population Stud.*, July 1987, 41(2), pp. 187–206. [G: Asia; Sweden; U.K.]

Lempert, David. A Demographic–Economic Explanation of Political Stabilty: Mauritius as a Microcosm. *Eastern Afr. Econ. Rev.*, June 1987, 3(1), pp. 77–90. [G: Mauritus]

Leneman, Leah and Mitchison, Rosalind. Scottish Illegitimacy Ratios in the Early Modern Period. *Econ. Hist. Rev.*, 2nd Ser., February 1987, 40(1), pp. 41–63. [G: Scotland]

Leppel, Karen. Household Formation and Unrelated Housemates. *Amer. Econ.*, Spring 1987, 31(1), pp. 38–47. [G: U.S.]

Levine, Nancy E. Differential Child Care in Three Tibetan Communities: Beyond Son Preference. *Population Devel. Rev.*, June 1987, 13(2), pp. 281–304. [G: Nepal]

Lewis, Maureen A. Cost Recovery in Family Planning. *Econ. Develop. Cult. Change*, October 1987, 36(1), pp. 161–82. [G: LDCs]

Liaw, Kao-Lee and Ledent, Jacques. Nested Logit Model and Maximum Quasi-likelihood Method: A Flexible Methodology for Analyzing Interregional Migration Patterns. *Reg. Sci. Urban Econ.*, February 1987, 17(1), pp. 67–88. [G: Canada]

Loslier, Luc. Disparités socio-spatiales de mortalité à Porto-Rico. (With English summary.) *Can. J. Devel. Stud.*, 1987, 8(1), pp. 117–32. [G: Puerto Rico]

Lucas, Robert E. B. Emigration to South Africa's Mines. *Amer. Econ. Rev.*, June 1987, 77(3), pp. 313–30. [G: S. Africa; Botswana; Lesotho; Malawi; Mozambique]

Lutz, Wolfgang. Factors Associated with the Finnish Fertility Decline since 1776. *Population Stud.*, November 1987, 41(3), pp. 463–82. [G: Finland]

Maharatna, Arup. Optimum Family Size, Surplus Labour, and the Rationality of Poor Peasants. *Indian Econ. J.*, Apr.-June 1987, 34(4), pp. 25–38. [G: LDCs]

Maksudov, S. Some Causes of Rising Mortality in the U.S.S.R. *Menard, S. W. and Moen, E. W., eds.*, 1987, pp. 156–73. [G: U.S.S.R.]

Malthus, Thomas Robert. An Essay on the Principle of Population. *Menard, S. W. and Moen, E. W., eds.*, 1987, 1798, pp. 97–103.

Mănescu, Manea. The Population—The Most Valuable Wealth of the Nation. *Econ. Computat. Cybern. Stud. Res.*, 1987, 22(4), pp. 5–11.

Manton, Kenneth G. The Interaction of Population Aging and Health Transitions at Later Ages: New Evidence and Insights. *Schramm, C. J., ed.*, 1987, pp. 185–221. [G: U.S.]

Manton, Kenneth G. The Population Implications of Breakthroughs in Biomedical Technologies for Controlling Mortality and Fertility. *Espenshade, T. and Stolnitz, G. J., eds.*, 1987, pp. 147–93.

Mason, Andrew. National Saving Rates and Population Growth: A New Model and New Evidence. *Johnson, D. G. and Lee, R. D., eds.*, 1987, pp. 523–60.

Mason, Karen Oppenheim and Cope, Lisa G. Sources of Age and Date-of-Birth Misreporting in the 1900 U.S. Census. *Demography*, November 1987, 24(4), pp. 563–73. [G: U.S.]

Mason, Karen Oppenheim and Taj, Anju Malhotra. Differences between Women's and Men's Reproductive Goals in Developing Countries. *Population Devel. Rev.*, December 1987, 13(4), pp. 611–38. [G: LDCs]

Mason, Karen Oppenheim; Weinstein, Maxine and Laslett, Barbara. The Decline of Fertility in Los Angeles, California, 1880–1900. *Population Stud.*, November 1987, 41(3), pp. 483–99. [G: U.S.]

Maxwell, Nan L. Influencing on the Timing of First Childbearing. *Contemp. Policy Issues*, April 1987, 5(2), pp. 113–22. [G: U.S.]

McCarthy, James and Oni, Gbolahan A. Desired Family Size and Its Determinants among Urban Nigerian Women: A Two-Stage Analysis. *Demography*, May 1987, 24(2), pp. 279–90. [G: Nigeria]

McCrate, Elaine. Trade, Merger and Employment: Economic Theory on Marriage. *Rev. Radical Polit. Econ.*, Spring 1987, 19(1), pp. 73–89. [G: U.S.]

McDaniel, Susan A. Demographic Aging as a Guiding Paradigm in Canada's Welfare State. *Can. Public Policy*, September 1987, 13(3), pp. 330–36. [G: Canada]

McFalls, Joseph A., Jr. Frustrated Fertility: A Population Paradox. *Menard, S. W. and Moen, E. W., eds.*, 1987, 1979, pp. 191–97.

McIntosh, C. Alison. Recent Pronatalist Policies in Western Europe. *Davis, K.; Bernstam, M. S. and Ricardo-Campbell, R., eds.*, 1987, 1986, pp. 318–34. [G: W. Europe]

McNeill, William H. Migration in Premodern Times. *Alonso, W., ed.*, 1987, pp. 15–35.

McNicoll, Geoffrey. Agrarian and Industrial Futures: Comments [Population Growth and Agricultural Productivity] [Education, Population Trends, and Technological Change]. *Espenshade, T. and Stolnitz, G. J., eds.*, 1987, pp. 105–14.

McNicoll, Geoffrey. Economic Growth with Below-Replacement Fertility. *Davis, K.; Bernstam, M. S. and Ricardo-Campbell, R., eds.*, 1987, 1986, pp. 217–38. [G: U.S.]

Menard, Scott. Regional Variations in Population Histories. *Menard, S. W. and Moen, E. W., eds.*, 1987, pp. 10–15.

Menard, Scott and Moen, Elizabeth W. The Relative Importance of Family Planning and Development for Fertility Reduction: Critique of Research and Development of Theory. *Menard, S. W. and Moen, E. W., eds.*, 1987, 1982, pp. 229–41.

Menendez, Eduardo L. Estratificación social y condiciones de morbimortalidad. Algunas reflexiones sobre la crisis y recuperación teórica de esta relación. (With English summary.) *De-*

sarrollo Econ., Apr.-June 1987, *27*(105), pp. 87–106.

de Meza, David. The Migration Multiplier. *Bull. Econ. Res.*, July 1987, *39*(3), pp. 243–48.

Micheli, Giuseppi A. Cicli post-transizionali e modelli di volterra. (Post-transitional Fluctuations and Lotka–Volterra Models. With English summary.) *Giorn. Econ.*, Sept.-Oct. 1987, *46*(9–10), pp. 509–24.

Mitchelson, Ronald L. and Fisher, James S. Long-Distance Commuting and Population Change in Georgia, 1960–80. *Growth Change*, Winter 1987, *18*(1), pp. 44–65. [G: U.S.]

Mitra, S. About the Effect of Changes in Age-Specific Mortality on Life Expectancy. *Population Stud.*, March 1987, *41*(1), pp. 161–62. [G: Sweden; Selected Countries]

Mitra, S. On "A New Look at Entropy and the Life Table." *Demography*, August 1987, *24*(3), pp. 439.

Modak, Ashok. Soviet Muslim Policy. *Gidadhubli, R. G., ed.*, 1987, pp. 50–84. [G: U.S.S.R.]

Moen, Elizabeth W. Voodoo Forecasting: Technical, Political, and Ethical Issues Regarding the Projection of Local Population Growth. *Menard, S. W. and Moen, E. W., eds.*, 1987, *1984*, pp. 446–60. [G: U.S.]

Moen, Elizabeth W. What Does "Control over Our Bodies" Really Mean? *Menard, S. W. and Moen, E. W., eds.*, 1987, *1979*, pp. 277–87.

Mohan, V. Nationalities Question of the USSR: The Muslim Dimension. *Gidadhubli, R. G., ed.*, 1987, pp. 21–49. [G: U.S.S.R.]

Montgomery, Mark R. A New Look at the Easterlin "Synthesis" Framework. *Demography*, November 1987, *24*(4), pp. 481–96. [G: Sri Lanka; Colombia]

Montgomery, Mark R. The Impacts of Urban Population Growth on Urban Labor Markets and the Costs of Urban Service Delivery: A Review. *Johnson, D. G. and Lee, R. D., eds.*, 1987, pp. 149–88. [G: LDCs]

Moore, Thomas Gale. Economic Growth with Below-Replacement Fertility: Comment. *Davis, K.; Bernstam, M. S. and Ricardo-Campbell, R., eds.*, 1987, *1986*, pp. 243–44. [G: U.S.]

Moore, Thomas Gale. Social Security in Aging Societies: Comment. *Davis, K.; Bernstam, M. S. and Ricardo-Campbell, R., eds.*, 1987, *1986*, pp. 295.

Moreno-Navarro, Lorenzo. Fertility Change in Five Latin American Countries: A Covariance Analysis of Birth Intervals. *Demography*, February 1987, *24*(1), pp. 23–41. [G: Colombia; Costa Rica; Mexico; Peru; Panama]

Morrison, Peter A. Changing Demographics: What to Watch For. *Bus. Econ.*, July 1987, *22*(3), pp. 5–8. [G: U.S.]

Munnell, Alicia H. Lessons from the Income Maintenance Experiments: An Overview. *Munnell, A. H., ed.*, 1987, pp. 1–21. [G: U.S.]

Mwabu, Germano M. A Comment on Kenyan Migration Movements. *Eastern Afr. Econ.*

Rev., December 1987, *3*(2), pp. 143–45. [G: Kenya]

Myers, Daniel A.; Burkhauser, Richard V. and Holden, Karen C. The Transition from Wife to Widow: The Importance of Survivor Benefits to Widows. *J. Risk Ins.*, December 1987, *54*(4), pp. 752–59.

Nakosteen, Robert A. and Zimmer, Michael A. Marital Status and Earnings of Young Men: A Model with Endogenous Selection. *J. Human Res.*, Spring 1987, *22*(2), pp. 248–68. [G: U.S.]

Nathan, Richard P. The Politics of Printouts: The Use of Official Numbers to Allocate Federal Grants-in-Aid. *Alonso, W. and Starr, P., eds.*, 1987, pp. 331–42. [G: U.S.]

de Neufville, Judith Innes. Federal Statistics in Local Governments. *Alonso, W. and Starr, P., eds.*, 1987, pp. 343–62.

Newhouse, Joseph P. Public Policy Implications of Declining Old-Age Mortality: Comment. *Burtless, G., ed.*, 1987, pp. 51–58. [G: U.S.]

Newland, Kathleen. Refugees: The New International Politics of Displacement. *Menard, S. W. and Moen, E. W., eds.*, 1987, *1981*, pp. 314–21. [G: Global]

Ní Bhrolcháin, Máire. Period Parity Progression Ratios and Birth Intervals in England and Wales, 1941–1971: A Synthetic Life Table Analysis. *Population Stud.*, March 1987, *41*(1), pp. 103–25. [G: U.K.]

Okabe, Atsuyuki. A Theoretical Relationship between the Rank-Size Rule and Clark's Law of Urban Population Distribution: Duality in the Rank-Size Rule. *Reg. Sci. Urban Econ.*, May 1987, *17*(2), pp. 307–19.

Oppong, Christine. Responsible Fatherhood and Birth Planning. *Oppong, C., ed.*, 1987, pp. 165–78. [G: Ghana]

Oppong, Christine. Sex Roles, Population and Development in West Africa: Introduction. *Oppong, C., ed.*, 1987, pp. 1–17. [G: W. Africa]

Orubuloye, Oyetunji. Values and Costs of Daughters and Sons to Yoruba Mothers and Fathers. *Oppong, C., ed.*, 1987, pp. 86–90. [G: Nigeria]

Patterson, Orlando. The Emerging West Atlantic System: Migration, Culture, and Underdevelopment in the United States and the Circum-Caribbean Region. *Alonso, W., ed.*, 1987, pp. 227–60. [G: U.S.; Caribbean]

Paulino, Leonardo A. The Evolving Food Situation. *Mellor, J. W.; Delgado, C. L. and Blackie, M. J., eds.*, 1987, pp. 23–38. [G: Africa]

Pebley, Anne R. and Stupp, Paul W. Reproductive Patterns and Child Mortality in Guatemala. *Demography*, February 1987, *24*(1), pp. 43–60. [G: Guatemala]

Pérez-Stable, Marifeli. Cuban Women and the Struggle for "Conciencia." *Mesa-Lago, C., ed.*, 1987, pp. 51–72. [G: Cuba]

Petersen, William. Politics and the Measurement of Ethnicity. *Alonso, W. and Starr, P., eds.*, 1987, pp. 187–233. [G: U.S.]

Phillips, Carla Rahn. Time and Duration: A Model for the Economy of Early Modern Spain. *Amer. Hist. Rev.*, June 1987, *92*(3), pp. 531–62. [G: Spain]

Pingali, Prabhu L. and Binswanger, Hans P. Population Density and Agricultural Intensification: A Study of the Evolution of Technologies in Tropical Agriculture. *Johnson, D. G. and Lee, R. D., eds.*, 1987, pp. 27–56. [G: LDCs]

Plath, Joel C.; Holland, David W. and Carvalho, Joe W. Labor Migration in Southern Africa and Agricultural Development: Some Lessons from Lesotho. *J. Devel. Areas*, January 1987, *21*(2), pp. 159–75. [G: Lesotho]

Pope, David. Population and Australian Economic Development 1900–1930. *Maddock, R. and McLean, I. W., eds.*, 1987, pp. 33–60. [G: Australia]

Portes, Alejandro. Illegal Immigration and the International System, Lessons from Recent Legal Mexican Immigrants to the United States. *Menard, S. W. and Moen, E. W., eds.*, 1987, *1979*, pp. 300–311. [G: Mexico; U.S.]

Poston, Dudley L., Jr. and Gu, Boachang. Socioeconomic Development, Family Planning, and Fertility in China. *Demography*, November 1987, *24*(4), pp. 531–51. [G: China]

Poston, Dudley L., Jr. and Shu, Jing. The Demographic and Socioeconomic Composition of China's Ethnic Minorities. *Population Devel. Rev.*, December 1987, *13*(4), pp. 703–22. [G: China]

Poterba, James M. and Summers, Lawrence H. Public Policy Implications of Declining Old-Age Mortality. *Burtless, G., ed.*, 1987, pp. 19–51. [G: U.S.]

Powell-Griner, Eve and Trent, Katherine. Sociodemographic Determinants of Abortion in the United States. *Demography*, November 1987, *24*(4), pp. 553–61. [G: U.S.]

Presser, Harriet B. Changing Values and Falling Birth Rates: Comment. *Davis, K.; Bernstam, M. S. and Ricardo-Campbell, R., eds.*, 1987, *1986*, pp. 196–200. [G: OECD]

Presser, Harriet B. Work Shifts of Full-Time Dual-Earner Couples: Patterns and Contrasts by Sex of Spouse. *Demography*, February 1987, *24*(1), pp. 99–112.

Preston, Samuel H. Changing Values and Falling Birth Rates. *Davis, K.; Bernstam, M. S. and Ricardo-Campbell, R., eds.*, 1987, *1986*, pp. 176–95. [G: OECD]

Preston, Samuel H. Children and the Elderly: Divergent Paths for America's Dependents. *Menard, S. W. and Moen, E. W., eds.*, 1987, *1984*, pp. 377–94. [G: U.S.]

Preston, Samuel H. The Decline of Fertility in Non-European Industrialized Countries. *Davis, K.; Bernstam, M. S. and Ricardo-Campbell, R., eds.*, 1987, *1986*, pp. 26–47. [G: Australia; Canada; Japan; New Zealand; U.S.]

Prewitt, Kenneth. Public Statistics and Democratic Politics. *Alonso, W. and Starr, P., eds.*, 1987, pp. 261–74. [G: U.S.]

Priest, Gordon E. Considerations for the Definitions and Classification of Households and Families and Related Variables for the 1990 Round of Censuses. *Statist. J.*, May 1987, *4*(3), pp. 271–303.

Prieto, Yolanda. Cuban Women in the U.S. Labor Force: Perspectives on the Nature of Change. *Mesa-Lago, C., ed.*, 1987, pp. 73–91. [G: Cuba]

Pullum, Thomas W.; Casterline, John B. and Shah, Iqbal H. Adapting Fertility Exposure Analysis to the Study of Fertility Change. *Population Stud.*, November 1987, *41*(3), pp. 381–99. [G: Pakistan]

Quah, Euston. Valuing Family Household Production: A Contingent Evaluation Approach. *Appl. Econ.*, July 1987, *19*(7), pp. 875–89.

Rainford, P. and Masser, Ian. Population Forecasting and Urban Planning Practice: A Case Study. *Environ. Planning A*, November 1987, *19*(11), pp. 1463–75. [G: U.K.]

Rajan, S. Irudaya. Family Planning Programme in India: An Economic Evaluation. *Indian Econ. J.*, Apr.-June 1987, *34*(4), pp. 79–86. [G: India]

Ravallion, Martin. Towards a Theory of Famine Relief Policy. *J. Public Econ.*, June 1987, *33*(1), pp. 21–39. [G: Asia]

Rees, P. H. and Ram, S. Projections of the Residential Distribution of an Ethnic Group: Indians in Bradford. *Environ. Planning A*, October 1987, *19*(10), pp. 1323–58. [G: U.K.]

Rele, J. R. Fertility Levels and Trends in India, 1951–81. *Population Devel. Rev.*, September 1987, *13*(3), pp. 513–30. [G: India]

Ricardo-Campbell, Rita. U.S. Social Security under Low Fertility. *Davis, K.; Bernstam, M. S. and Ricardo-Campbell, R., eds.*, 1987, *1986*, pp. 296–312.

Richards, Toni; White, Michael J. and Tsui, Amy Ong. Changing Living Arrangements: A Hazard Model of Transitions among Household Types. *Demography*, February 1987, *24*(1), pp. 77–97. [G: U.S.]

Rindfuss, Ronald R.; Bumpass, Larry L. and Palmore, James A. Analyzing Fertility Histories: Do Restrictions Bias Results? *Demography*, February 1987, *24*(1), pp. 113–22. [G: S. Korea]

Robinson, Warren C. The "New Beginning" in Pakistan's Family Planning Programme. *Pakistan Devel. Rev.*, Spring 1987, *26*(1), pp. 107–18. [G: Pakistan]

Robinson, Warren C. The Time Cost of Children and Other Household Production. *Population Stud.*, July 1987, *41*(2), pp. 313–23. [G: U.S.]

Robinson, Warren C. and Schutjer, Wayne A. Reply to Djavad Salehi-Isfahani's Clarifications [Agricultural Development and Demographic Change: A Generalization of the Boserup Model]. *Econ. Develop. Cult. Change*, July 1987, *35*(4), pp. 883. [G: LDCs]

Rosenzweig, Mark R. and Schultz, T. Paul. Fertility and Investments in Human Capital: Estimates of the Consequence of Imperfect Fertil-

ity Control in Malaysia. *J. Econometrics*, Sept./ Oct. 1987, *36*(1/2), pp. 163–84.
[G: Malaysia]

Rubin, Robert. The Empowerment of the Refugee Community. *U.S. Committee for Refugees.*, 1987, pp. 19–23. [G: U.S.]

Rudge, Philip. World Refugee Survey: Fortress Europe. *U.S. Committee for Refugees.*, 1987, pp. 5–12. [G: Europe]

Ruiz Alvarez, José Luis and Carrasco Garcia, Nicolás. Desarrollo económico y niveles de salud en España. (With English summary.) *Invest. Econ.*, January 1987, *11*(1), pp. 133–50.
[G: Spain]

Ruiz Aviles, P. and Millan Campos, S. Demographic Consequences of Forestry Management Intervention in an Area of Low Mountains in Spain. *Merlo, M., et al., eds.*, 1987, pp. 593–610. [G: Spain]

Sandell, Steven H. Prospects for Older Workers: The Demographic and Economic Context. *Sandell, S. H., ed.*, 1987, pp. 3–14.
[G: U.S.]

Sanderson, Warren C. Below-Replacement Fertility in Nineteenth Century America. *Population Devel. Rev.*, June 1987, *13*(2), pp. 305–13. [G: U.S.]

Santow, Gigi. Reassessing the Contraceptive Effect of Breastfeeding. *Population Stud.*, March 1987, *41*(1), pp. 147–60. [G: Indonesia]

Sathar, Zeba A. Seeking Explanations for High Levels of Infant Mortality in Pakistan. *Pakistan Devel. Rev.*, Spring 1987, *26*(1), pp. 55–70.
[G: Pakistan]

Sathar, Zeba A. Sex Differentials in Mortality: A Corollary of Son Preference? *Pakistan Devel. Rev.*, Winter 1987, *26*(4), pp. 555–65.
[G: Pakistan]

Schirm, Allen L. and Preston, Samuel H. Census Undercount Adjustment and the Quality of Geographic Population Distributions. *J. Amer. Statist. Assoc.*, December 1987, 82(400), pp. 965–78. [G: U.S.]

Schirm, Allen L. and Preston, Samuel H. Census Undercount Adjustment and the Quality of Geographic Population Distributions: Rejoinder. *J. Amer. Statist. Assoc.*, December 1987, 82(400), pp. 986–90.

Schubert, Renate. Interne Migration in Entwicklungsländern. Zur Rationalität von Land-Stadt-Wanderungen. (Internal Migration in Developing Countries—Rationality of Rural–Urban Migration. With English summary.) *Z. Wirtschaft. Sozialwissen.*, 1987, *107*(2), pp. 207–23.

Schultz, T. Paul. School Expenditures and Enrollments, 1960–80: The Effects of Income, Prices, and Population Growth. *Johnson, D. G. and Lee, R. D., eds.*, 1987, pp. 413–76.
[G: Global]

Schultz, T. Paul. The Value and Allocation of Time in High-Income Countries: Implications for Fertility. *Davis, K.; Bernstam, M. S. and Ricardo-Campbell, R., eds.*, 1987, 1986, pp. 87–108. [G: U.S.]

Schwartz, Moshe, et al. Moshav-Based Industry.

Bar-El, R., ed., 1987, pp. 57–104.
[G: Israel]

Serow, William J.; Sly, David F. and Micklin, Michael. Structural Change within the Older Population: Economic Implications. *Contemp. Policy Issues*, April 1987, *5*(2), pp. 73–83.
[G: U.S.]

Sharma, R. R. Class and Social–Agrarian Transformation in Soviet Central Asia: A Historical–Cultural Context. *Gidadhubli, R. G., ed.*, 1987, pp. 116–36. [G: U.S.S.R.]

Shefer, Daniel. The Effect of Agricultural Price-Support Policies on Interregional and Rural-to-Urban Migration in Korea: 1976–1980. *Reg. Sci. Urban Econ.*, August 1987, *17*(3), pp. 333–44. [G: Korea]

Shlomowitz, Ralph. Fertility and Fiji's Indian Migrants, 1879–1919. *Indian Econ. Soc. Hist. Rev.*, Apr.-June 1987, *24*(2), pp. 205–17.
[G: India]

Shrestha, Nanda R. Institutional Policies and Migration Behavior: A Selective Review. *World Devel.*, March 1987, *15*(3), pp. 329–45.
[G: LDCs]

Siegers, Jacques J. An Economic Analysis of Fertility. *De Economist*, 1987, *135*(1), pp. 94–111.
[G: Netherlands]

Simon, Julian L. Population Growth, Economic Growth, and Foreign Aid. *Cato J.*, Spring/ Summer 1987, *7*(1), pp. 159–86. [G: LDCs]

Singh, Ram D. and Morey, Mathew J. The Value of Work-at-Home and Contributions of Wives' Household Service in Polygynous Families: Evidence from an African LDC. *Econ. Develop. Cult. Change*, July 1987, *35*(4), pp. 743–65. [G: Burkina Faso]

Sinnett, M. W. Method versus Methodology: A Note on *The Ultimate Resource*. *Rothbard, M. N., ed.*, 1987, pp. 207–23.

Slade, Margaret E. Natural Resources, Population Growth, and Economic Well-being. *Johnson, D. G. and Lee, R. D., eds.*, 1987, pp. 331–69.

Smeeding, Timothy; Torrey, Barbara Boyle and Rein, Martin. Comparative Well-being of Children and Elderly. *Contemp. Policy Issues*, April 1987, *5*(2), pp. 57–72. [G: U.S.]

Smith, Peter C. Micro-level Aspects of Demographic Change. *Martin, L. G., ed.*, 1987, pp. 37–39. [G: ASEAN]

Smith, Stanley K. Tests of Forecast Accuracy and Bias for County Population Projections. *J. Amer. Statist. Assoc.*, December 1987, 82(400), pp. 991–1003. [G: U.S.]

Smith, Stanley K. Tests of Forecast Accuracy and Bias for County Population Projections: Rejoinder. *J. Amer. Statist. Assoc.*, December 1987, 82(400), pp. 1009–12. [G: U.S.]

South, Scott J. Metropolitan Migration and Social Problems. *Soc. Sci. Quart.*, March 1987, *68*(1), pp. 3–18. [G: U.S.]

Spencer, Bruce D. Census Undercount Adjustment and the Quality of Geographic Population Distributions: Comment. *J. Amer. Statist. Assoc.*, December 1987, 82(400), pp. 984–86.
[G: U.S.]

Srinivasan, K. and Muthiah, A. C. Fertility Estimation from Retrospective Surveys: Biases Attributable to Pregnancy-Related Movement of Mothers. *Demography*, May 1987, 24(2), pp. 271–78.   [G: India; Nepal; Bangladesh]

Srinivasan, T. N. Population and Food. *Johnson, D. G. and Lee, R. D., eds.*, 1987, pp. 3–26.
[G: Global]

Stabler, Jack C. Non-metropolitan Population Growth and the Evolution of Rural Service Centres in the Canadian Prairie Region. *Reg. Stud.*, February 1987, 21(1), pp. 45–53.
[G: Canada]

Stafford, Frank P. Women's Work, Sibling Competition, and Children's School Performance. *Amer. Econ. Rev.*, December 1987, 77(5), pp. 972–80.   [G: U.S.]

Starr, Paul and Corson, Ross. Who Will Have the Numbers? The Rise of the Statistical Services Industry and the Politics of Public Data. *Alonso, W. and Starr, P., eds.*, 1987, pp. 415–47.   [G: U.S.]

Stern, Gary H. The Federal Budget's Effects on Intergenerational Equity: Undone or Not Undone? *Fed. Res. Bank Minn. Rev.*, Winter 1987, 11(1), pp. 2–6.   [G: U.S.]

Stolnitz, George J. Technological Prospects and Population Trends: Conclusions. *Espenshade, T. and Stolnitz, G. J., eds.*, 1987, pp. 195–211.

Straubhaar, Thomas. International Migration under Incomplete Information: A Comment. *Schweiz. Z. Volkswirtsch. Statist.*, June 1987, 123(2), pp. 219–26.

Suh, Seoung Hwan. The Long Run Effect of Green Belt Amenities upon the Population Growth: The Case of Almost Linear Demand Function. *Int. Econ. J.*, Summer 1987, 1(2), pp. 71–78.

Sullivan, Patricia A. and Damrosch, Shirley P. Homeless Women and Children. *Bingham, R. D.; Green, R. E. and White, S. B., eds.*, 1987, pp. 82–98.   [G: U.S.]

Swanson, Linda L. and Butler, Margaret A. Human Resource Base of Rural Economies. *U.S.D.A., Econ. Res. Serv., Agr. and Rural Econ. Div.*, 1987, pp. 7.1–23.   [G: U.S.]

Swepston, Lee. Indigenous and Tribal Populations: A Return to Centre Stage. *Int. Lab. Rev.*, July-Aug. 1987, 126(4), pp. 447–55.
[G: Latin America]

Teitelbaum, Michael S. Relevance of Demographic Transition Theory for Developing Countries. *Menard, S. W. and Moen, E. W., eds.*, 1987, 1976, pp. 29–36.   [G: LDCs]

Thernstrom, Abigail. Statistics and the Politics of Minority Representation: The Evolution of the Voting Rights Act since 1965. *Alonso, W. and Starr, P., eds.*, 1987, pp. 303–27.

Thisen, Jean K. A Theory of Love in the Contemporary World. *Int. J. Soc. Econ.*, 1987, 14(12), pp. 31–53.

Thornton, Arland and Camburn, Donald. The Influence of the Family on Premarital Sexual Attitudes and Behavior. *Demography*, August 1987, 24(3), pp. 323–40.   [G: U.S.]

Thornton, Arland and Rodgers, Willard L. The Influence of Individual and Historical Time on Marital Dissolution. *Demography*, February 1987, 24(1), pp. 1–22.   [G: U.S.]

Tikhomirov, N. P. Measuring the Accuracy of Population Forecasts. *Matekon*, Winter 1987-88, 24(2), pp. 49–68.   [G: U.S.S.R.]

Todaro, Michael P. and Maruszko, Lydia. Illegal Migration and U.S. Immigration Reform: A Conceptual Framework. *Population Devel. Rev.*, March 1987, 13(1), pp. 101–14.
[G: U.S.]

Tucker, C. Jack and Urton, William L. Frequency of Geographic Mobility: Findings from the National Health Interview Survey. *Demography*, May 1987, 24(2), pp. 265–70.
[G: U.S.]

Tuma, Nancy Brandon. The Income Maintenance Experiments and the Issues of Marital Stability and Family Composition: Discussion. *Munnell, A. H., ed.*, 1987, pp. 99–105.   [G: U.S.]

Twomey, J. Local Authority Fiscal Stance and the Pattern of Residential Migration in the North West of England. *Appl. Econ.*, October 1987, 19(10), pp. 1391–1401.   [G: U.K.]

Umarov, Khodji. Development and Socio-cultural Transformation: The Rule of Education in Tajekistan. *Gidadhubli, R. G., ed.*, 1987, pp. 101–15.   [G: U.S.S.R.]

Vasegh-Daneshvary, Nasser; Schlottmann, Alan M. and Herzog, Henry W., Jr. Immigration of Engineers, Scientists, and Physicians and the U.S. High Technology Renaissance. *Soc. Sci. Quart.*, June 1987, 68(2), pp. 311–25.
[G: U.S.]

Vaupel, James W. A Rejoinder [How Change in Age-Specific Mortality Affects Life Expectancy]. *Population Stud.*, March 1987, 41(1), pp. 163.   [G: Selected Countries; Sweden]

Vaupel, James W. and Goodwin, Dianne G. The Concentration of Reproduction among U.S. Women, 1917–80. *Population Devel. Rev.*, December 1987, 13(4), pp. 723–30.   [G: U.S.]

Vaupel, James W. and Yashin, Anatoli I. Repeated Resuscitation: How Lifesaving Alters Life Tables. *Demography*, February 1987, 24(1), pp. 123–35.   [G: U.S.]

Venkatacharya, K. and Teklu, Tesfay. On Some Robust Estimates of Birth Rate under Nonstable Conditions. *Demography*, November 1987, 24(4), pp. 639–48.   [G: Africa]

Vinokur, Aaron and Ofer, Gur. Inequality of Earnings, Household Income, and Wealth in the Soviet Union in the 1970s. *Millar, J. R., ed.*, 1987, pp. 171–202.   [G: U.S.S.R.]

Vishnevskii, A. The Human Factor in Demographic Measurement. *Prob. Econ.*, June 1987, 30(2), pp. 5–21.   [G: U.S.S.R.]

Wainerman, Catalina H. and Moreno, Martín. Incorporando las trabajadoras agrícolas a los censos de población. (With English summary.) *Desarrollo Econ.*, Oct.-Dec. 1987, 27(107), pp. 347–76.   [G: Argentina; Paraguay]

Wang, Gungwu. Ethnicity and Religion in Social Development. *Martin, L. G., ed.*, 1987, pp. 40–43.   [G: ASEAN]

Warren, Robert and Passel, Jeffrey S. A Count of the Uncountable: Estimates of Undocumented Aliens Counted in the 1980 United States Census. *Demography*, August 1987, *24*(3), pp. 375–93. **[G: U.S.]**

Wasserstrom, Jeffrey. Resistance to the One-Child Family. *Menard, S. W. and Moen, E. W., eds.*, 1987, *1984*, pp. 269–76. **[G: China]**

Weaver, Carolyn L. Social Security in Aging Societies. *Davis, K.; Bernstam, M. S. and Ricardo-Campbell, R., eds.*, 1987, *1986*, pp. 273–94. **[G: OECD]**

Weidlich, Wolfgang and Haag, Günter. A Dynamic Phase Transition Model for Spatial Agglomeration Processes. *J. Reg. Sci.*, November 1987, *27*(4), pp. 529–69.

Weiss, Thomas. Demographic Aspects of the Urban Population, 1800–1840. *Kilby, P., ed.*, 1987, pp. 171–213. **[G: U.S.]**

Weller, Robert H.; Eberstein, Isaac W. and Bailey, Mohamed. Pregnancy Wantedness and Maternal Behavior during Pregnancy. *Demography*, August 1987, *24*(3), pp. 407–12. **[G: U.S.]**

Westoff, Charles F. Perspective on Nuptiality and Fertility. *Davis, K.; Bernstam, M. S. and Ricardo-Campbell, R., eds.*, 1987, *1986*, pp. 155–70. **[G: OECD]**

White, Stephen E. Return Migration to Eastern Kentucky and the Stem Family Concept. *Growth Change*, Spring 1987, *18*(2), pp. 38–52. **[G: U.S.]**

Whyte, Martin King and Gu, S. Z. Popular Response to China's Fertility Transition. *Population Devel. Rev.*, September 1987, *13*(3), pp. 471–93. **[G: China]**

Willis, Robert J. Externalities and Population. *Johnson, D. G. and Lee, R. D., eds.*, 1987, pp. 661–702.

Willis, Robert J. What Have We Learned from the Economics of the Family? *Amer. Econ. Rev.*, May 1987, *77*(2), pp. 68–81.

Wilson, Franklin D. Metropolitan and Nonmetropolitan Migration Streams: 1935–1980. *Demography*, May 1987, *24*(2), pp. 211–28. **[G: U.S.]**

Winter, Roger P. World Refugee Survey: The Year in Review. *U.S. Committee for Refugees.*, 1987, pp. 2–4.

Wolter, Kirk M. Census Undercount Adjustment and the Quality of Geographic Population Distributions: Comment. *J. Amer. Statist. Assoc.*, December 1987, *82*(400), pp. 978–80. **[G: U.S.]**

Wong, Aline K. and Cheung, Paul P. L. Demographic and Social Development: Taking Stock for the Morrow. *Martin, L. G., ed.*, 1987, pp. 17–36. **[G: ASEAN]**

Wong, Yue-chim. The Role of Husband's and Wife's Economic Activity Status in the Demand for Children. *J. Devel. Econ.*, April 1987, *25*(2), pp. 329–52. **[G: Hong Kong]**

Wong, Yue-chim. Women's Work and the Demand for Children in Hong Kong. *Devel. Econ.*, June 1987, *25*(2), pp. 188–200. **[G: Hong Kong]**

Woods, R. I. Approaches to the Fertility Transition in Victorian England. *Population Stud.*, July 1987, *41*(2), pp. 283–311. **[G: U.K.]**

Xizhe, Peng. Demographic Consequences of the Great Leap Forward in China's Provinces. *Population Devel. Rev.*, December 1987, *13*(4), pp. 639–70. **[G: China]**

Zajonc, R. B. Family Configuration and Intelligence. *Menard, S. W. and Moen, E. W., eds.*, 1987, *1976*, pp. 408–23. **[G: U.S.]**

Zamanian, Zaman. Government Policy and the Brain Drain. *Atlantic Econ. J.*, December 1987, *15*(4), pp. 65–69.

Zarkovich, S. S. An Epilogue to the World Fertility Survey. *Jahr. Nationalökon. Statist.*, October 1987, *203*(5–6), pp. 656–59. **[G: Global]**

850 HUMAN CAPITAL; VALUE OF HUMAN LIFE

851 Human Capital; Value of Human Life

8510 Human Capital; Value of Human Life

Adams, Arvil V.; Mangum, Stephen L. and Wirtz, Philip W. Postschool Education and Training: Accessible to All? *Rev. Black Polit. Econ.*, Winter 1987, *15*(3), pp. 68–86. **[G: U.S.]**

Akuffo, Felix Odei. Teenage Pregnancies and School Drop-outs: The Relevance of Family Life Education and Vocational Training to Girls' Employment Opportunities. *Oppong, C., ed.*, 1987, pp. 154–64. **[G: Ghana]**

Armitage, Jane and Sabot, Richard H. Socioeconomic Background and the Returns to Schooling in Two Low-income Economies. *Economica*, February 1987, *54*(213), pp. 103–08. **[G: U.K.; Kenya; Tanzania]**

Barnow, Burt S. The Impact of CETA Programs on Earnings: A Review of the Literature. *J. Human Res.*, Spring 1987, *22*(2), pp. 157–93. **[G: U.S.]**

Bartel, Ann P. and Lichtenberg, Frank R. The Comparative Advantage of Educated Workers in Implementing New Technology. *Rev. Econ. Statist.*, February 1987, *69*(1), pp. 1–11.

Becker, William E. and Alter, George C. The Probabilities of Life and Work Force Status in the Calculation of Expected Earnings. *J. Risk Ins.*, June 1987, *54*(2), pp. 364–75.

Behrman, Jere R. Schooling and Other Human Capital Investments: Can the Effects Be Identified? *Econ. Educ. Rev.*, 1987, *6*(3), pp. 301–05.

Behrman, Jere R. Schooling in Developing Countries: Which Countries are the Over- and Underachievers and What Is the Schooling Impact? *Econ. Educ. Rev.*, 1987, *6*(2), pp. 111–27. **[G: LDCs]**

Behrman, Jere R. and Birdsall, Nancy. Returns to Education: A Further International Update and Implications: Comment. *J. Human Res.*, Fall 1987, *22*(4), pp. 603–06. **[G: Selected Countries]**

Behrman, Jere R. and Wolfe, Barbara L. Investments in Schooling in Two Generations in Pre-

revolutionary Nicaragua: The Roles of Family Background and School Supply. *[Diaz-Alejandro, C. F.]*, 1987, pp. 395–419.
[G: Nicaragua]

Behrman, Jere R. and Wolfe, Barbara L. Investments in Schooling in Two Generations in Prerevolutionary Nicaragua: The Roles of Family Background and School Supply. *J. Devel. Econ.*, October 1987, 27(1–2), pp. 395–419.
[G: Nicaragua]

Berry, Albert. The Labour Market and Human Capital in LDCs. *Gemmell, N., ed.*, 1987, pp. 205–35.

Black, Dan A. The Social Security System, the Provision of Human Capital, and the Structure of Compensation. *J. Lab. Econ.*, April 1987, 5(2), pp. 242–54.

Blaug, Mark. An Economic Analysis of Personal Earnings in Thailand. *Blaug, M.*, 1987, *1974*, pp. 301–31. [G: Thailand]

Blaug, Mark. Approaches to Educational Planning. *Blaug, M.*, 1987, *1967*, pp. 50–75.

Blaug, Mark. Educated Unemployment in Asia: A Contrast between India and the Philippines. *Blaug, M.*, 1987, *1972*, pp. 276–300.
[G: Philippines; India]

Blaug, Mark. Education, Economic Situation and Prospects of India, 1971. *Blaug, M.*, 1987, *1971*, pp. 265–75. [G: India]

Blaug, Mark. The Correlation between Education and Earnings: What Does It Signify? *Blaug, M.*, 1987, *1972*, pp. 76–99.

Blaug, Mark. The Empirical Status of Human Capital Theory: A Slightly Jaundiced Survey. *Blaug, M.*, 1987, *1976*, pp. 100–128.

Blaug, Mark. The Rate of Return on Investment in Education in Great Britain. *Blaug, M.*, 1987, *1965*, pp. 3–49. [G: U.K.]

Blaug, Mark. The Rate of Return on Investment in Education in Thailand. *Blaug, M.*, 1987, *1976*, pp. 332–45. [G: Thailand]

Blaug, Mark. Where Are We Now in the Economics of Education? *Blaug, M.*, 1987, *1985*, pp. 129–40.

Borsook, Ian. Earnings, Ability and International Trade. *J. Int. Econ.*, May 1987, 22(3/4), pp. 281–95.

Bowman, Mary Jean. Education, Population Trends, and Technological Change. *Espenshade, T. and Stolnitz, G. J., eds.*, 1987, *1985*, pp. 71–103. [G: Global]

Bowman, Mary Jean. The Importance of Examining Cohort Uniqueness in the Formulation of Human Investment Policies. *Econ. Educ. Rev.*, 1987, 6(2), pp. 67–79.

Briggs, Vernon M., Jr. Human Resource Development and the Formulation of National Economic Policy. *J. Econ. Issues*, September 1987, 21(3), pp. 1207–40. [G: U.S.]

Broome, John. The Economic Value of Life: A Reply. *Economica*, August 1987, 54(215), pp. 0240.

Buhofer, Heinz and Frey, Bruno S. Lösegeld für Gefangene. (Ransom for Prisoners. With English summary.) *Konjunkturpolitik*, 1987, 33(1), pp. 27–46. [G: Europe]

Catsiapis, George. A Model of Educational Investment Decisions. *Rev. Econ. Statist.*, February 1987, 69(1), pp. 33–41. [G: U.S.]

Chapman, Bruce J. Labour Turnover and Wage Determination. *Australian Econ. Pap.*, June 1987, 26(48), pp. 119–29. [G: Australia]

Chillemi, Ottorino. Produzione di capitale umano e incertezza. (Product of Human Capital and Uncertainty. With English summary.) *Rivista Int. Sci. Econ. Com.*, April 1987, 34(4), pp. 353–60.

Chuma, Hiroyuki. Pensions, Wage Profiles, and Retirement Rules: Specific Human Capital Approach. *J. Econ. Dynam. Control*, March 1987, 11(1), pp. 29–64. [G: Japan]

Conlisk, John. Notes on Mincer's Log-Earnings Model. *Econ. Inquiry*, January 1987, 25(1), pp. 165–74.

Dalto, Guy C. Economic Segmentation, Human Capital, and Tax-Favored Fringe Benefits. *Soc. Sci. Quart.*, September 1987, 68(3), pp. 583–97. [G: U.S.]

De Alessi, Louis. Specific Human Capital and Collective Codetermination Rights: Comment. *Pethig, R. and Schlieper, U., eds.*, 1987, pp. 149–51.

Demetriades, Euripides L. and Psacharopoulos, George. Educational Expansion and the Returns to Education: Evidence from Cyprus. *Int. Lab. Rev.*, Sept.-Oct. 1987, 126(5), pp. 597–602. [G: Cyprus]

Dhakal, Dharmendra; Grabowski, Richard and Belbase, Krishna. The Effect of Education in Nepal's Traditional Agriculture. *Econ. Educ. Rev.*, 1987, 6(1), pp. 27–34. [G: Nepal]

Drèze, Jacques H. Human Capital and Risk-Bearing. *Drèze, J. H.*, 1987, *1979*, pp. 347–65.

Ehrenberg, Ronald G. and Sherman, Daniel R. Employment while in College, Academic Achievement, and Postcollege Outcomes: A Summary of Results. *J. Human Res.*, Winter 1987, 22(1), pp. 1–23. [G: U.S.]

Ehrlich, Isaac and Chuma, Hiroyuki. The Demand for Life: Theory and Applications. *Radnitzky, G. and Bernholz, P., eds.*, 1987, pp. 243–68.

England, Richard W. Capital Accumulation, Class Struggle, and School Finance Reform. *England, R. W., ed.*, 1987, pp. 203–25.
[G: U.S.]

Feuer, M.; Glick, H. and Desai, Anand. Is Firm-Sponsored Education Viable? *J. Econ. Behav. Organ.*, March 1987, 8(1), pp. 121–36.
[G: U.S.]

Fischer, Charles C. Forensic Economics and the Wrongful Death of a Household Producer: Current Practices, Methodological Biases and Alternative Solutions of Losses. *Amer. J. Econ. Soc.*, April 1987, 46(2), pp. 219–28.

Fraser, Bryna Shore. New Office and Business Technologies: The Structure of Education and (Re)Training Opportunities. *Hartmann, H. I., ed.*, 1987, pp. 343–72.

Gabriel, Paul E. and Schmitz, Susanne. The Relative Earnings of Native and Immigrant Males in the United States. *Quart. Rev. Econ. Bus.*,

Autumn 1987, 27(3), pp. 91–101. [G: U.S.]

Ghosh, B. N. Stocks and Flows of Knowledge: A Critique of Machlup. *Indian Econ. J.*, Apr.-June 1987, 34(4), pp. 9–17.

Grubb, Farley. Colonial Immigrant Literacy: An Economic Analysis of Pennsylvania—German Evidence, 1727–1775. *Exploration Econ. Hist.*, January 1987, 24(1), pp. 63–76.
[G: U.S.]

Hamermesh, Daniel S. The Costs of Worker Displacement. *Quart. J. Econ.*, February 1987, 102(1), pp. 51–75. [G: U.S.]

Handa, Jagdish. Labor Characteristics and the Return to General and Specific Skills. *Eastern Econ. J.*, Apr.-June 1987, 13(2), pp. 99–106.

Hungerford, Thomas and Solon, Gary. Sheepskin Effects in the Returns to Education. *Rev. Econ. Statist.*, February 1987, 69(1), pp. 175–77.
[G: U.S.]

Hunt, H. Allan. The GM–UAW Metropolitan Pontiac Retraining and Employment Program (PREP). *Cook, R. F., ed.*, 1987, pp. 31–46.
[G: U.S.]

Inman, Robert P. The Economic Consequences of Debilitating Illness: The Case of Multiple Sclerosis. *Rev. Econ. Statist.*, November 1987, 69(4), pp. 651–60. [G: U.S.]

Islam, Iyanatul. Manpower and Educational Planning in Singapore. *Amjad, R., ed.*, 1987, pp. 114–50. [G: Singapore]

James, Estelle and Benjamin, Gail. Educational Distribution and Income Redistribution through Education in Japan. *J. Human Res.*, Fall 1987, 22(4), pp. 469–89. [G: Japan; U.S.]

Jamison, Dean T. and van der Gaag, Jacques. Education and Earnings in the People's Republic of China. *Econ. Educ. Rev.*, 1987, 6(2), pp. 161–66. [G: China]

Jenkins, Stephen. Snapshots versus Movies: 'Lifecycle Biases' and the Estimation of Intergenerational Earnings Inheritance. *Europ. Econ. Rev.*, July 1987, 31(5), pp. 1149–58.
[G: U.K.]

Johnson, William R. Income Redistribution as Human Capital Insurance. *J. Human Res.*, Spring 1987, 22(2), pp. 269–80. [G: U.S.]

Jones-Lee, M. W. The Economic Value of Life: A Comment. *Economica*, August 1987, 54(215), pp. 397–400.

Kemna, Harrie J. M. I. Working Conditions and the Relationship between Schooling and Health. *J. Health Econ.*, September 1987, 6(3), pp. 189–210. [G: U.S.]

Kleiman, Ephraim. Opportunity Cost, Human Capital, and Some Related Economic Concepts in Talmudic Literature. *Hist. Polit. Econ.*, Summer 1987, 19(2), pp. 261–87.

Knight, J. B. and Sabot, Richard H. Educational Expansion, Government Policy and Wage Compression. *J. Devel. Econ.*, August 1987, 26(2), pp. 201–21. [G: Kenya; Tanzania]

Knight, J. B. and Sabot, Richard H. Educational Policy and Labour Productivity: An Output Accounting Exercise. *Econ. J.*, March 1987, 97(385), pp. 199–214. [G: Kenya; Tanzania]

Knight, J. B. and Sabot, Richard H. The Rate of Return on Educational Expansion. *Econ. Educ. Rev.*, 1987, 6(3), pp. 255–62.
[G: Kenya; Tanzania]

Koike, Kazuo. The Political Economy of Japan: Human Resource Development and Labor–Management Relations. *Yamamura, K. and Yasuba, Y., eds.*, 1987, pp. 289–330.
[G: Japan]

Krashinsky, Michael. The Returns to University Schooling in Canada: A Comment. *Can. Public Policy*, June 1987, 13(2), pp. 218–21.
[G: Canada]

Lehrer, Evelyn L. and White, William D. Hospital Market Structure and the Return to Nursing Education: Comment [Hospital Market Structure and the Return to Nursing Education]. *J. Human Res.*, Fall 1987, 22(4), pp. 607–08.
[G: U.S.]

Leigh, J. Paul. Gender, Firm Size, Industry, and Estimations of the Value-of-Life. *J. Health Econ.*, September 1987, 6(3), pp. 255–73.

Levin, Henry M. and Tsang, Mun Chiu. The Economics of Student Time. *Econ. Educ. Rev.*, 1987, 6(4), pp. 357–64.

Li, Ze-Gao. China's Modernization and Manpower Base: Forecasts of Experts and Professionals in the Year 2000 in China—A Technical Note. *Dutta, M., ed. (II)*, 1987, pp. 45–52.
[G: China]

Main, Brian G. M. The Wage Expectations and Unemployment Experience of School Leavers. *Scot. J. Polit. Econ.*, November 1987, 34(4), pp. 349–67. [G: Scotland]

Mangum, Stephen L. and Adams, Arvil V. The Labor Market Impacts of Post-school Occupational Training for Young Men. *Growth Change*, Fall 1987, 18(4), pp. 57–73.
[G: U.S.]

Mann, Charles K. Beyond the Metaphor: Microcomputers in Public Policy and Human Capital Development. *Ruth, S. R. and Mann, C. K., eds.*, 1987, pp. 7–22. [G: Tunisia; Kenya]

Martellaro, Joseph A. Investment in Human Resources: The Experience of Five Third World Nations. *Rivista Int. Sci. Econ. Com.*, April 1987, 34(4), pp. 273–90. [G: Egypt; Ethiopia; Mongolia; Pakistan; Paraguay]

Martin, Linda G. Human Resources and Economic Development. *Martin, L. G., ed.*, 1987, pp. 92–96. [G: ASEAN]

McMahon, Walter W. The Relation of Education and R&D to Productivity Growth in the Developing Countries of Africa. *Econ. Educ. Rev.*, 1987, 6(2), pp. 183–94. [G: Africa]

McNicoll, Geoffrey. Agrarian and Industrial Futures: Comments [Population Growth and Agricultural Productivity] [Education, Population Trends, and Technological Change]. *Espenshade, T. and Stolnitz, G. J., eds.*, 1987, pp. 105–14.

Mehmet, Ozay. The Malaysian Experience in Manpower Planning and Labour Market Policies. *Amjad, R., ed.*, 1987, pp. 84–113.
[G: Malaysia]

Moffitt, Robert. Life-Cycle Labor Supply and Social Security: A Time-Series Analysis. *Burtless, G., ed.*, 1987, pp. 183–220.   [G: U.S.]

Monissen, Hans G. and Wenger, Ekkehard. Specific Human Capital and Collective Codetermination Rights. *Pethig, R. and Schlieper, U., eds.*, 1987, pp. 127–48.   [G: W. Germany]

Nakata, Yoshi-fumi and Mosk, Carl. The Demand for College Education in Postwar Japan. *J. Human Res.*, Summer 1987, 22(3), pp. 377–404.   [G: Japan; Selected OECD]

Nord, Stephen. An Analysis of the Effects of College on the Inequality in Male and Female Wages in the United States: A Human Capital Approach. *Rivista Int. Sci. Econ. Com.*, Jan.-Feb. 1987, 34(1–2), pp. 109–28.   [G: U.S.]

Nord, Stephen. Schooling and Changes in the Inequality in Male and Female Earnings in the United States over the 1970s. *Appl. Econ.*, August 1987, 19(8), pp. 1083–1105.   [G: U.S.]

Ohrenstein, Roman A. and Gordon, Barry. Some Aspects of Human Capital in Talmudic Literature. *Int. J. Soc. Econ.*, 1987, 14(3/4/5), pp. 185–90.

Orazem, Peter F. Black–White Differences in Schooling Investment and Human Capital Production in Segregated Schools. *Amer. Econ. Rev.*, September 1987, 77(4), pp. 714–23.   [G: U.S.]

Pitayanon, Sumalee. Thailand's Experience in Manpower Planning and Labour Market Policies. *Amjad, R., ed.*, 1987, pp. 38–83.   [G: Thailand]

Prais, S. J. Educating for Productivity: Comparisons of Japanese and English Schooling and Vocational Preparation. *Nat. Inst. Econ. Rev.*, February 1987, (119), pp. 40–56.   [G: U.K.; Japan]

Prescott, Edward C. and Boyd, John H. Dynamic Coalitions, Growth, and the Firm. *Prescott, E. C. and Wallace, N., eds.*, 1987, pp. 146–60.

Quinn, Joseph F. Life-Cycle Labor Supply and Social Security: A Time-Series Analysis: Comment. *Burtless, G., ed.*, 1987, pp. 220–28.   [G: U.S.]

Ritzen, J. M. M. Human Capital and Economic Cycles. *Econ. Educ. Rev.*, 1987, 6(2), pp. 151–60.   [G: Netherlands]

Rogerson, Peter A. Competition among Applicants for Job Openings. *Fischer, M. M. and Nijkamp, P., eds.*, 1987, pp. 229–45.

Rosenfeld, Stuart A. Education, Training, and Industrial Policy. *Goldstein, H. A., ed.*, 1987, pp. 86–94.   [G: U.S.]

Rosenzweig, Mark R. and Schultz, T. Paul. Fertility and Investments in Human Capital: Estimates of the Consequence of Imperfect Fertility Control in Malaysia. *J. Econometrics*, Sept./Oct. 1987, 36(1/2), pp. 163–84.   [G: Malaysia]

Rubery, Jill. Flexibility of Labour Costs in Nonunion Firms. *Tarling, R., ed.*, 1987, pp. 59–83.

Rumberger, Russell W. The Impact of Surplus Schooling on Productivity and Earnings. *J. Human Res.*, Winter 1987, 22(1), pp. 24–50.   [G: U.S.]

Schutte, P. C. Investeringseise van menslike kapitaal in 'n veranderende Suid-Afrika. (The Demand for Investment in Human Capital in a Changing South Africa. With English summary.) *S. Afr. J. Econ.*, December 1987, 55(4), pp. 370–80.   [G: S. Africa]

Schwartz, Abba. The Effects of Labour Unions on Investment in Training: A Dynamic Model: Comments. *Razin, A. and Sadka, E., eds.*, 1987, pp. 479–94.

Shackett, Joyce R. and Slottje, D. J. Labor Supply Decisions, Human Capital Attributes, and Inequality in the Size Distribution of Earnings in the U.S., 1952–81. *J. Human Res.*, Winter 1987, 22(1), pp. 82–100.   [G: U.S.]

Shaw, Kathryn L. Occupation Change, Employer Change, and the Tranferability of Skills. *Southern Econ. J.*, January 1987, 53(3), pp. 702–19.   [G: U.S.]

Shulman, Steven. Discrimination, Human Capital, and Black–White Unemployment: Evidence from Cities. *J. Human Res.*, Summer 1987, 22(3), pp. 361–76.   [G: U.S.]

Soon, Lee-Ying. Self-Employment vs Wage Employment: Estimation of Earnings Functions in LDCs. *Econ. Educ. Rev.*, 1987, 6(2), pp. 81–89.   [G: Malaysia]

Stafford, Frank P. Women's Work, Sibling Competition, and Children's School Performance. *Amer. Econ. Rev.*, December 1987, 77(5), pp. 972–80.   [G: U.S.]

Steedman, Hilary. Vocational Training in France and Britain: Office Work. *Nat. Inst. Econ. Rev.*, May 1987, (120), pp. 58–70.   [G: France; U.K.]

Stolnitz, George J. Technological Prospects and Population Trends: Conclusions. *Espenshade, T. and Stolnitz, G. J., eds.*, 1987, pp. 195–211.

Straub, LaVonne A. and Lane, Julia. Response [Hospital Market Structure and the Return to Nursing Education]. *J. Human Res.*, Fall 1987, 22(4), pp. 609–10.   [G: U.S.]

Sumner, Daniel A. and Leiby, James D. An Econometric Analysis of the Effects of Human Capital on Size and Growth among Dairy Farms. *Amer. J. Agr. Econ.*, May 1987, 69(2), pp. 465–70.   [G: U.S.]

Tan, Edita A. and Alonzo, Ruperto P. The Philippine Experience in Manpower Planning and Labour Market Policies. *Amjad, R., ed.*, 1987, pp. 151–80.   [G: Philippines]

Texler, Jiří. Education as a Factor of Development. *Czech. Econ. Pap.*, 1987, (24), pp. 83–97.   [G: Czechoslovakia]

Tsang, Mun Chiu. The Impact of Underutilization of Education on Productivity: A Case Study of the U.S. Bell Companies. *Econ. Educ. Rev.*, 1987, 6(3), pp. 239–54.   [G: U.S.]

Tucker, Irvin B., III. The Impact of Consumer Credentialism on Employee and Entrepreneur Returns to Higher Education. *Econ. Educ. Rev.*, 1987, 6(1), pp. 35–40.   [G: U.S.]

Vaillancourt, François; Carpentier, Josee and

Henriques, Irene. The Returns to University Schooling in Canada: A Rejoinder. *Can. Public Policy*, September 1987, *13*(3), pp. 389–90.
[G: Canada]

Vélez, Eduardo and Psacharopoulos, George. The External Efficiency of Diversified Secondary Schools in Colombia. *Econ. Educ. Rev.*, 1987, *6*(2), pp. 99–110. [G: Colombia]

Weiss, Yoram. The Effect of Labour Unions on Investment in Training: A Dynamic Model. *Razin, A. and Sadka, E., eds.*, 1987, pp. 435–67.

Wilson, Charles. The Effect of Labour Unions on Investment in Training: A Dynamic Model: Comments. *Razin, A. and Sadka, E., eds.*, 1987, pp. 468–78.

Wilson, Robert A. Rates of Return to Entering the Legal Profession: Some Further Evidence. *Scot. J. Polit. Econ.*, May 1987, *34*(2), pp. 174–91. [G: U.K.]

Wozniak, Gregory D. Human Capital, Information, and the Early Adoption of New Technology. *J. Human Res.*, Winter 1987, *22*(1), pp. 101–12. [G: U.S.]

900 Welfare Programs; Consumer Economics; Urban and Regional Economics

910 WELFARE; HEALTH; EDUCATION

9100 General

Atkinson, Anthony B.; Hills, John and Le Grand, Julian. The Performance of the British Economy: The Welfare State. *Dornbusch, R. and Layard, R., eds.*, 1987, pp. 211–52.
[G: U.K.]

Bethune, John J. An Expansion of the Contemporary Theoretical Exposition Concerning the Work Disincentive Effects of Government Income Maintenance Programs. *Amer. Econ.*, Fall 1987, *31*(2), pp. 22–28.

Bixby, Ann Kallman. Public Social Welfare Expenditures, Fiscal Year 1984. *Soc. Sec. Bull.*, June 1987, *50*(6), pp. 21–32. [G: U.S.]

Bradshaw, Ted K. and Blakely, Edward J. Unanticipated Consequences of Government Programs on Rural Economic Development. *U.S.D.A., Econ. Res. Serv., Agr. and Rural Econ. Div.*, 1987, pp. 11.1–17. [G: U.S.]

Bryson, Phillip J. GDR Economic Planning and Social Policy in the 1980s. *Comp. Econ. Stud.*, Summer 1987, *29*(2), pp. 19–38.
[G: E. Germany]

Burtless, Gary and Haveman, Robert H. Taxes and Transfers: How Much Economic Loss? *Challenge*, Mar./Apr. 1987, *30*(1), pp. 45–51.
[G: U.S.]

Caslin, Terry. Welfare Policy. *Vane, H. and Caslin, T., eds.*, 1987, pp. 195–219. [G: U.K.]

Chamlin, Mitchell B. General Assistance among Cities: An Examination of the Need, Economic Threat, and Benign Neglect Hypotheses. *Soc.*

Sci. Quart., December 1987, *68*(4), pp. 834–46. [G: U.S.]

Cornia, Giovanni Andrea; Jolly, Richard and Stewart, Frances. Adjustment with a Human Face: Protecting the Vulnerable and Promoting Growth: Summary and Conclusions. *Cornia, G. A.; Jolly, R. and Stewart, F., eds.*, 1987, pp. 287–97.

Coyle, Dennis J. and Wildavsky, Aaron. Requisites of Radical Reform: Income Maintenance versus Tax Preferences. *J. Policy Anal. Manage.*, Fall 1987, *7*(1), pp. 1–16. [G: U.S.]

Crosnier, Marie-Agnès. La protection sociale en Union Soviétique. (Welfare Benefits in the Soviet Union. With English summary.) *Écon. Soc.*, February 1987, *21*(2), pp. 29–75.
[G: U.S.S.R.]

Dixon, William J. Progress in the Provision of Basic Human Needs: Latin America, 1960–1980. *J. Devel. Areas*, January 1987, *21*(2), pp. 129–39. [G: Latin America]

Duchêne, Gérard. Les transferts sociaux dans les économies centralement planifiées. (Welfare Benefits in the Centrally Planned Economies. With English summary.) *Écon. Soc.*, February 1987, *21*(2), pp. 5–27. [G: E. Europe]

Egginton, Don M. A Historical Analysis of Labour Supply Incentives. *Beenstock, M., et al.*, 1987, pp. 76–123. [G: U.K.]

Ferge, Zsuzsa. The Crisis and the 'Welfare State' in Eastern Europe with a Focus on Hungary. *Europ. Econ. Rev.*, Feb./Mar. 1987, *31*(1/2), pp. 212–19. [G: Hungary]

Glanz, Milton P.; Kerns, Wilmer L. and Schmulowitz, Jack. Private Social Welfare Expenditures, 1972–84. *Soc. Sec. Bull.*, May 1987, *50*(5), pp. 59–67. [G: U.S.]

Goodin, Robert E. and Dryzck, John. Risk-Sharing and Social Justice: The Motivational Foundations of the Post-war Welfare State. *Goodin, R. E. and Le Grand, J.*, 1987, pp. 37–73.
[G: U.K.]

Goudriaan, René; De Groot, Hans and van Tulder, Frank. Public Sector Productivity: Recent Empirical Findings and Policy Applications. *van de Kar, H. M. and Wolfe, B. L., eds.*, 1987, pp. 193–209. [G: U.S.; Netherlands]

Gramlich, Edward M. Cooperation and Competition in Public Welfare Policies. *J. Policy Anal. Manage.*, Spring 1987, *6*(3), pp. 417–31.
[G: U.S.]

Hammond, Claire Holton. Some Methodological Developments in the Measurement of the Benefit of an In-Kind Transfer. *Amer. Econ.*, Fall 1987, *31*(2), pp. 44–52.

Le Grand, Julian. The Middle-Class Use of the British Social Services. *Goodin, R. E. and Le Grand, J.*, 1987, pp. 91–107. [G: U.K.]

Le Grand, Julian and Winter, David. The Middle Classes and the Defence of the British Welfare State. *Goodin, R. E. and Le Grand, J.*, 1987, pp. 147–68. [G: U.K.]

Lee, Dwight R. The Tradeoff between Equality and Efficiency: Short-run Politics and Long-run

Realities. *Public Choice*, 1987, *53*(2), pp. 149–65.

Levitan, Sar A. and Shapiro, Isaac. What's Missing in Welfare Reform? *Challenge*, July/Aug. 1987, *30*(3), pp. 41–48. [G: U.S.]

Lindbeck, Assar. Is the Welfare State in Trouble? *Eastern Econ. J.*, October-December 1987, *13*(4), pp. 345–51.

Ravallion, Martin. Towards a Theory of Famine Relief Policy. *J. Public Econ.*, June 1987, *33*(1), pp. 21–39. [G: Asia]

Redslob, Alain. De l'incantation à l'initiative ou la métamorphose de la politique sociale. (With English summary.) *Revue Écon. Polit.*, July-Aug. 1987, *97*(4), pp. 381–96. [G: France]

Richet, Xavier. Transferts sociaux et socialisme de marché: le cas hongrois. (Welfare Benefits and Market Socialism: The Case of Hungary. With English summary.) *Écon. Soc.*, February 1987, *21*(2), pp. 77–105. [G: Hungary]

Solano, Paul L. and Brams, Marvin R. Management Policies in Local Government Finance: Budgeting. *Aronson, J. R. and Schwartz, E., eds.*, 1987, pp. 118–57. [G: U.S.]

Stephens, Robert J. Social Policy Reform: In Retrospect and Prospect. *Bollard, A. and Buckle, R., eds.*, 1987, pp. 299–329. [G: New Zealand]

Studlar, Donley T. Policy Convergence? Political Economy in the United States and Britain. *Waltman, J. L. and Studlar, D. T., eds.*, 1987, pp. 3–15. [G: U.S.; U.K.]

Szymkiewicz, Krystyna. Les transferts sociaux dans une économie socialiste en crise: le cas polonais. (Welfare Benefits in a Crisis Context: The Case of Poland. With English summary.) *Écon. Soc.*, February 1987, *21*(2), pp. 107–55. [G: Poland]

Tonak, E. Ahmet. The U.S. Welfare State and the Working Class, 1952–1980. *Rev. Radical Polit. Econ.*, Spring 1987, *19*(1), pp. 47–72. [G: U.S.]

Waltman, Jerold L. The Strength of Policy Inheritance. *Waltman, J. L. and Studlar, D. T., eds.*, 1987, pp. 259–69. [G: U.K.; U.S.]

Wolfson, Dirk J. Controlling the Welfare State: A Case Study of Retrenchment in the Netherlands. *Public Finance*, 1987, *42*(2), pp. 165–80. [G: Netherlands]

911 General Welfare Programs

9110 General Welfare Programs

Adams, Carolyn Teich. The Politics of Privatization. *Turner, B.; Kemeny, J. and Lundqvist, L. J., eds.*, 1987, pp. 127–55. [G: U.S.; W. Europe]

Ashenfelter, Orley. The Work Response to a Guaranteed Income: A Survey of Experimental Evidence: Discussion. *Munnell, A. H., ed.*, 1987, pp. 53–55. [G: U.S.]

Balachandran, Bala V. and Prince, Thomas R. An Information System for Administering Welfare Programs. *Chan, J. L., ed., Pt. A*, 1987, pp. 37–66. [G: U.S.]

Basiotis, P. Peter, et al. Food Stamps, Food Costs, Nutrient Availability, and Nutrient Intake. *J. Policy Modeling*, Fall 1987, *9*(3), pp. 383–404. [G: U.S.]

Bergmann, Barbara R. A Fresh Start on Welfare Reform. *Challenge*, Nov./Dec. 1987, *30*(5), pp. 44–50. [G: U.S.]

Bergmann, Barbara R. and Roberts, Mark D. Income for the Single Parent: Child Support, Work, and Welfare. *Brown, C. and Pechman, J. A., eds.*, 1987, pp. 247–63. [G: U.S.]

Bigman, David. Targeted Subsidy Programs under Instability: A Simulation and an Illustration for Pakistan. *J. Policy Modeling*, Fall 1987, *9*(3), pp. 483–501. [G: Pakistan]

Blaylock, James R. Evaluating Food Plans and Poverty Thresholds. *Appl. Econ.*, October 1987, *19*(10), pp. 1341–52. [G: U.S.]

Block, Fred. Social Policy and Accumulation: A Critique of the New Consensus. *Rein, M.; Esping-Andersen, G. and Rainwater, L., eds.*, 1987, pp. 13–31. [G: U.S.]

Blum, Barbara B. Lessons from the Income Maintenance Experiments: Views of a Policymaker and Public Administrator. *Munnell, A. H., ed.*, 1987, pp. 227–41. [G: U.S.]

Bradbury, Katharine L. Non–Labor-Supply Responses to the Income Maintenance Experiments: Discussion. *Munnell, A. H., ed.*, 1987, pp. 122–26. [G: U.S.]

Burtless, Gary. Income for the Single Parent: Child Support, Work, and Welfare: Comments. *Brown, C. and Pechman, J. A., eds.*, 1987, pp. 263–67. [G: U.S.]

Burtless, Gary. Taxes, Transfers, and Swedish Labor Supply. *Bosworth, B. P. and Rivlin, A. M., eds.*, 1987, pp. 185–249. [G: Sweden]

Burtless, Gary. The Work Response to a Guaranteed Income: A Survey of Experimental Evidence. *Munnell, A. H., ed.*, 1987, pp. 22–52. [G: U.S.]

Burtless, Gary and Haveman, Robert H. Taxes, Transfers, and Labor Supply: The Evolving Views of U.S. Economists. *van de Kar, H. M. and Wolfe, B. L., eds.*, 1987, pp. 127–45. [G: U.S.]

Cain, Glen G. The Income Maintenance Experiments and the Issues of Marital Stability and Family Composition. *Munnell, A. H., ed.*, 1987, pp. 60–93. [G: U.S.]

Cohen, Wilbur J. Lessons from the Income Maintenance Experiments: Views of a Policymaker and Public Administrator: Discussion. *Munnell, A. H., ed.*, 1987, pp. 242–44. [G: U.S.]

Coyle, Dennis J. and Wildavsky, Aaron. Social Experimentation in the Face of Formidable Fables. *Munnell, A. H., ed.*, 1987, pp. 167–84. [G: U.S.]

Cuomo, Mario M. The State Role: New York State's Approach to Homelessness. *Bingham, R. D.; Green, R. E. and White, S. B., eds.*, 1987, pp. 199–215. [G: U.S.]

Dumont, J.-P. The Evolution of Social Security during the Recession. *Int. Lab. Rev.*, Jan.-Feb. 1987, *126*(1), pp. 1–19. [G: Selected Countries]

Ellwood, David T. The Income Maintenance Experiments and the Issues of Marital Stability and Family Composition: Discussion. *Munnell, A. H., ed.*, 1987, pp. 94–98.   [G: U.S.]

Elmore, Richard F. A Political Scientist's View of the Income Maintenance Experiments. *Munnell, A. H., ed.*, 1987, pp. 206–13.
[G: U.S.]

Esping-Andersen, Gøsta. Citizenship and Socialism: De-commodification and Solidarity in the Welfare State. *Rein, M.; Esping-Andersen, G. and Rainwater, L., eds.*, 1987, pp. 78–101.
[G: W. Europe]

Esping-Andersen, Gøsta. The Comparison of Policy Regimes: An Introduction. *Rein, M.; Esping-Andersen, G. and Rainwater, L., eds.*, 1987, pp. 3–12.

Euzéby, Chantal. A Minimum Guaranteed Income: Experiments and Proposals. *Int. Lab. Rev.*, 1987, *126*(3), pp. 253–76.   [G: OECD]

Feaster, Dan; Gottschalk, Peter and Jakubson, George. Impact of 1981 AFDC Reforms on Months Worked and Welfare Duration. *J. Human Res.*, Fall 1987, *22*(4), pp. 542–50.
[G: U.S.]

Garello, Jacques. Economic and Social Consequences of Socialist Policies in France. *Pejovich, S., ed.*, 1987, pp. 251–76.   [G: France]

Goodin, Robert E. and Le Grand, Julian. Creeping Universalism in the Australian Welfare State. *Goodin, R. E. and Le Grand, J.*, 1987, pp. 108–26.   [G: Australia]

Goodin, Robert E. and Le Grand, Julian. Not Only the Poor: Conclusion. *Goodin, R. E. and Le Grand, J.*, 1987, pp. 203–27.   [G: U.S.; U.K.]

Goodin, Robert E. and Le Grand, Julian. Not Only the Poor: The Middle Classes and the Welfare State: Introduction. *Goodin, R. E. and Le Grand, J.*, 1987, pp. 3–16.   [G: U.K.]

Gramlich, Edward M. An Economist's View of the Income Maintenance Experiments: Discussion. *Munnell, A. H., ed.*, 1987, pp. 223–26.
[G: U.S.]

Hall, Robert E. The Work Response to a Guaranteed Income: A Survey of Experimental Evidence: Discussion. *Munnell, A. H., ed.*, 1987, pp. 56–59.   [G: U.S.]

Hanson, Russell L. The Expansion and Contraction of the American Welfare State. *Goodin, R. E. and Le Grand, J.*, 1987, pp. 169–99.
[G: U.S.]

Hanushek, Eric A. Non–Labor-Supply Responses to the Income Maintenance Experiments. *Munnell, A. H., ed.*, 1987, pp. 106–21.
[G: U.S.]

Hausman, Jerry A. Evaluating the Methodology of Social Experiments: Discussion. *Munnell, A. H., ed.*, 1987, pp. 158–61.   [G: U.S.]

Haveman, Robert H. U.S. Anti-poverty Policy and the Non-poor: Some Estimates and Their Implications. *Goodin, R. E. and Le Grand, J.*, 1987, pp. 77–90.   [G: U.S.]

Heclo, Hugh. Social Experimentation in the Face of Formidable Fables: Discussion. *Munnell, A. H., ed.*, 1987, pp. 185–88.   [G: U.S.]

Kahn, Arthur L. Program and Demographic Characteristics of Supplemental Security Income Recipients, December 1985. *Soc. Sec. Bull.*, May 1987, *50*(5), pp. 23–57.   [G: U.S.]

Keeley, Michael C. The Effects of Experimental Negative Income Tax Programs on Marital Dissolution: Evidence from the Seattle and Denver Income Maintenance Experiments. *Int. Econ. Rev.*, February 1987, *28*(1), pp. 241–57.   [G: U.S.]

Koch, June Q. The Federal Role in Aiding the Homeless. *Bingham, R. D.; Green, R. E. and White, S. B., eds.*, 1987, pp. 216–30.
[G: U.S.]

Krashinsky, Michael. The Cooke Report on Child Care: A Critique. *Can. Public Policy*, September 1987, *13*(3), pp. 294–303.   [G: Canada]

Lawrance, Emily C. Transfers to the Poor and Long Run Savings. *Econ. Inquiry*, July 1987, *25*(3), pp. 459–78.   [G: U.S.]

Mead, Lawrence M. Social Experimentation in the Face of Formidable Fables: Discussion. *Munnell, A. H., ed.*, 1987, pp. 189–93.
[G: U.S.]

Metcalf, Charles E. Evaluating the Methodology of Social Experiments: Discussion. *Munnell, A. H., ed.*, 1987, pp. 162–66.   [G: U.S.]

Michael, Robert T. Non–Labor-Supply Responses to the Income Maintenance Experiments: Discussion. *Munnell, A. H., ed.*, 1987, pp. 127–30.   [G: U.S.]

Misiolek, Walter S. and Elder, Harold W. Cost-Effective Redistribution: Implications of a Basic Needs Approach to Public Assistance. *Public Finance Quart.*, January 1987, *15*(1), pp. 76–97.

Moffitt, Robert. Historical Growth in Participation in Aid to Families with Dependent Children: Was There a Structural Shift? *J. Post Keynesian Econ.*, Spring 1987, *9*(3), pp. 347–63.   [G: U.S.]

Moffitt, Robert and Rothschild, Michael. Variable Earnings and Nonlinear Taxation. *J. Human Res.*, Summer 1987, *22*(3), pp. 405–21.
[G: U.S.]

Munnell, Alicia H. Lessons from the Income Maintenance Experiments: An Overview. *New Eng. Econ. Rev.*, May/June 1987, pp. 32–44.
[G: U.S.]

Munnell, Alicia H. Lessons from the Income Maintenance Experiments: An Overview. *Munnell, A. H., ed.*, 1987, pp. 1–21.
[G: U.S.]

Munnell, Alicia H. The Current Status of Our Social Welfare System. *New Eng. Econ. Rev.*, July/Aug. 1987, pp. 3–12.   [G: U.S.]

Murray, Charles. A Sociologist's View of the Income Maintenance Experiments: Discussion. *Munnell, A. H., ed.*, 1987, pp. 202–05.
[G: U.S.]

Nathan, Richard P. Lessons for Future Public Policy and Research. *Munnell, A. H., ed.*, 1987, pp. 245–55.   [G: U.S.]

Niehuss, Merith. From Welfare Provision to Social Insurance: The Unemployment in Augsburg 1918–27. *Evans, R. J. and Geary, D.,* *eds.,* 1987, pp. 44–72. [G: Germany]

O'Neill, June A.; Bassi, Laurie J. and Wolf, Douglas A. The Duration of Welfare Spells. *Rev. Econ. Statist.,* May 1987, 69(2), pp. 241–48. [G: U.S.]

Pinstrup-Andersen, Per. Adjustment with a Human Face: Protecting the Vulnerable and Promoting Growth: Nutrition Interventions. *Cornia, G. A.; Jolly, R. and Stewart, F., eds.,* 1987, pp. 241–56. [G: LDCs]

Rainwater, Lee. A Sociologist's View of the Income Maintenance Experiments. *Munnell, A. H., ed.,* 1987, pp. 194–201. [G: U.S.]

Ranney, Christine K. and Kushman, John E. Cash Equivalence, Welfare Stigma, and Food Stamps. *Southern Econ. J.,* April 1987, 53(4), pp. 1011–27. [G: U.S.]

Rein, Martin and Rainwater, Lee. From Welfare State to Welfare Society. *Rein, M.; Esping-Andersen, G. and Rainwater, L., eds.,* 1987, pp. 143–59. [G: OECD]

Reischauer, Robert D. A Political Scientist's View of the Income Maintenance Experiments: Discussion. *Munnell, A. H., ed.,* 1987, pp. 214–17. [G: U.S.]

Rimlinger, G. V. Social Policy under German Fascism. *Rein, M.; Esping-Andersen, G. and Rainwater, L., eds.,* 1987, pp. 59–77. [G: Germany]

Ross, Peggy J. and Rosenfeld, Stuart A. Human Resource Policies and Economic Development. *U.S.D.A., Econ. Res. Serv., Agr. and Rural Econ. Div.,* 1987, pp. 15.1–25. [G: U.S.]

Ruggles, Patricia and O'Higgins, Michael. Retrenchment and the New Right: A Comparative Analysis of the Impacts of the Thatcher and Reagan Administrations. *Rein, M.; Esping-Andersen, G. and Rainwater, L., eds.,* 1987, pp. 160–90. [G: U.S.; U.K.]

Sawhill, Isabel V. Income for the Single Parent: Child Support, Work, and Welfare: Comments. *Brown, C. and Pechman, J. A., eds.,* 1987, pp. 268–70. [G: U.S.]

Seidl, Vladimir and Pruŝs, Ladislav. La sécurité sociale en Tchécoslovaquie: Évolution 1970–1985. (Social Security in Czechoslovakia, 1970–1985. With English summary.) *Écon. Soc.,* February 1987, 21(2), pp. 157–71. [G: Czechoslovakia]

Skocpol, Theda. America's Incomplete Welfare State: The Limits of New Deal Reforms and the Origins of the Present Crisis. *Rein, M.; Esping-Andersen, G. and Rainwater, L., eds.,* 1987, pp. 35–58. [G: U.S.]

Solow, Robert M. An Economist's View of the Income Maintenance Experiments. *Munnell, A. H., ed.,* 1987, pp. 218–22. [G: U.S.]

Szelenyi, Ivan and Manchin, Robert. Social Policy under State Socialism: Market Redistribution and Social Inequalities in East European Socialist Societies. *Rein, M.; Esping-Andersen, G. and Rainwater, L., eds.,* 1987, pp. 102–39. [G: E. Europe]

Torgersen, Ulf. Housing: The Wobbly Pillar under the Welfare State. *Turner, B.; Kemeny, J. and Lundqvist, L. J., eds.,* 1987, pp. 116–26. [G: U.K.; Norway; Sweden]

Tuma, Nancy Brandon. The Income Maintenance Experiments and the Issues of Marital Stability and Family Composition: Discussion. *Munnell, A. H., ed.,* 1987, pp. 99–105. [G: U.S.]

Weaver, Carolyn L. Support of the Elderly before the Depression: Individual and Collective Arrangements. *Cato J.,* Fall 1987, 7(2), pp. 503–25. [G: U.S.]

Weinberg, Daniel H. Filling the "Poverty Gap," 1979–84. *J. Human Res.,* Fall 1987, 22(4), pp. 563–73. [G: U.S.]

Williams, Flora L. Effect of Policy Change upon Reallocation of Resources: The Case of the Food Stamp Program. *Rev. Soc. Econ.,* October 1987, 45(2), pp. 200–208. [G: U.S.]

Wixon, Bernard; Bridges, Benjamin, Jr. and Pattison, David. Policy Analysis through Microsimulation: The STATS Model. *Soc. Sec. Bull.,* December 1987, 50(12), pp. 4–12. [G: U.S.]

Woodward, Alison E. Public Housing Communes: A Swedish Response to Postmaterial Demands. *van Vliet—, W., et al., eds.,* 1987, pp. 215–38. [G: Sweden]

Ysander, Bengt-Christer. Public Policy Evaluation in Sweden. *Eliasson, G., ed.,* 1987, pp. 147–58. [G: Sweden]

Zellner, Arnold and Rossi, Peter E. Evaluating the Methodology of Social Experiments. *Munnell, A. H., ed.,* 1987, pp. 131–57. [G: U.S.]

Zellner, James A. and Traub, Larry G. In-Kind Food Assistance and Consumer Food Choice. *J. Cons. Aff.,* Winter 1987, 21(2), pp. 221–37. [G: U.S.]

912 Economics of Education

9120 Economics of Education

Andersson, Roland and Samartin, Avelino. Evaluation of School Plans. *J. Urban Econ.,* January 1987, 21(1), pp. 45–58. [G: Sweden]

Arnott, Richard J. and Rowse, John. Peer Group Effects and Educational Attainment. *J. Public Econ.,* April 1987, 32(3), pp. 287–305.

Bacharach, Samuel B.; Schmidle, Timothy P. and Bauer, Scott C. Collective Bargaining in American Industry: Higher Education. *Lipsky, D. B. and Donn, C. B., eds.,* 1987, pp. 225–64. [G: U.S.]

Baril, Robert; Robidoux, Benoît and Lemelin, Clément. La Demande d'éducation des jeunes québécois. (The Demand for Education in Quebec. With English summary.) *L'Actual. Econ.,* March 1987, 63(1), pp. 5–25. [G: Canada]

Behrman, Jere R. Is Child Schooling a Poor Proxy for Child Quality? *Demography,* August 1987, 24(3), pp. 341–59.

Behrman, Jere R. Schooling in Developing Countries: Which Countries are the Over- and Underachievers and What Is the Schooling Impact? *Econ. Educ. Rev.,* 1987, 6(2), pp. 111–27. [G: LDCs]

Behrman, Jere R. and Birdsall, Nancy. Returns to Education: A Further International Update and Implications: Comment. *J. Human Res.*, Fall 1987, *22*(4), pp. 603–06.
[G: Selected Countries]

Behrman, Jere R. and Wolfe, Barbara L. Investments in Schooling in Two Generations in Prerevolutionary Nicaragua: The Roles of Family Background and School Supply. *J. Devel. Econ.*, October 1987, *27*(1–2), pp. 395–419.
[G: Nicaragua]

Behrman, Jere R. and Wolfe, Barbara L. Investments in Schooling in Two Generations in Prerevolutionary Nicaragua: The Roles of Family Background and School Supply. *[Diaz-Alejandro, C. F.]*, 1987, pp. 395–419.
[G: Nicaragua]

Blaug, Mark. Approaches to Educational Planning. *Blaug, M.*, 1987, *1967*, pp. 50–75.

Blaug, Mark. Can Independent Education Be Suppressed? *Blaug, M.*, 1987, *1981*, pp. 197–203.
[G: U.K.]

Blaug, Mark. Declining Subsidies to Higher Education: An Economic Analysis. *Blaug, M.*, 1987, *1983*, pp. 227–43.
[G: OECD]

Blaug, Mark. Economics of Education in Developing Countries: Current Trends and New Properties. *Blaug, M.*, 1987, *1979*, pp. 346–56.
[G: LDCs]

Blaug, Mark. Educated Unemployment in Asia: A Contrast between India and the Philippines. *Blaug, M.*, 1987, *1972*, pp. 276–300.
[G: Philippines; India]

Blaug, Mark. Education Vouchers—It All Depends on What You Mean. *Blaug, M.*, 1987, *1985*, pp. 244–61.

Blaug, Mark. Education, Economic Situation and Prospects of India, 1971. *Blaug, M.*, 1987, *1971*, pp. 265–75.
[G: India]

Blaug, Mark. The Distributional Effects of Higher Education Subsidies. *Blaug, M.*, 1987, *1982*, pp. 204–26.
[G: U.S.]

Blaug, Mark. The Economics of Education and the Education of an Economist: Introduction. *Blaug, M.*, 1987, pp. vii–x.

Blaug, Mark. The Rate of Return on Investment in Education in Thailand. *Blaug, M.*, 1987, *1976*, pp. 332–45.
[G: Thailand]

Blaug, Mark. Where Are We Now in the Economics of Education? *Blaug, M.*, 1987, *1985*, pp. 129–40.

Blaug, Mark and Mace, John. Recurrent Education—The New Jerusalem. *Blaug, M.*, 1987, *1977*, pp. 143–65.
[G: OECD]

Blaug, Mark and Woodhall, Maureen. Patterns of Subsidies to Higher Education in Europe. *Blaug, M.*, 1987, *1979*, pp. 166–96.
[G: W. Europe]

Blum, Albert A. Countertrading Textiles for Tuitions: A Way to Secure More Foreign Students. *Econ. Educ. Rev.*, 1987, *6*(3), pp. 307–09.
[G: U.S.]

Brazer, Harvey E. and McCarty, Therese A. Interaction between Demand for Education and for Municipal Services. *Nat. Tax J.*, December 1987, *40*(4), pp. 555–66.
[G: U.S.]

Brown, Byron W. and Saks, Daniel H. The Microeconomics of the Allocation of Teachers' Time and Student Learning. *Econ. Educ. Rev.*, 1987, *6*(4), pp. 319–32.
[G: U.S.]

Bunting, Brendan; Saris, Willem E. and McCormack, Joe. A Second-Order Factor Analysis of the Reliability and Validity of the 11 Plus Examination in Northern Ireland. *Econ. Soc. Rev.*, April 1987, *18*(3), pp. 137–47.
[G: Ireland]

Catsiapis, George. A Model of Educational Investment Decisions. *Rev. Econ. Statist.*, February 1987, *69*(1), pp. 33–41.
[G: U.S.]

Cavin, Edward S.; Murnane, Richard J. and Brown, Randall S. How Enrollment Declines Affect per Pupil Expenditure Levels in Public School Districts. *Quigley, J. M., ed.*, 1987, pp. 159–96.
[G: U.S.]

Cheremnykh, S. V. and Poliak, Iu. E. The Computerization of Education—Problems of Mass Learning. *Prob. Econ.*, April 1987, *29*(12), pp. 23–34.
[G: U.S.S.R.]

Cohn, Elchanan. Federal and State Grants to Education: Are They Stimulative or Substitutive? *Econ. Educ. Rev.*, 1987, *6*(4), pp. 339–44.
[G: U.S.]

Cohn, Elchanan. Revenue and Formula Effects of School Finance Reform on Wealth Neutrality. *Appl. Econ.*, December 1987, *19*(12), pp. 1685–95.
[G: U.S.]

Correa, Hector and Gruver, Gene W. Teacher–Student Interaction: A Game Theoretic Extension of the Economic Theory of Education. *Math. Soc. Sci.*, February 1987, *13*(1), pp. 19–47.

Crockett, Geoff. Socio-economic Background of Students in Tertiary Education in Australia: Some Additional Evidence. *Australian Bull. Lab.*, March 1987, *13*(2), pp. 120–25.
[G: Australia]

Davis, Charles and Laberge, Marie-Paule. Professional Rewards in a Canada–Sénégal Cooperative Project in Engineering Education: The Case of the Projet de l'École Polytechnique de Thiès. *Can. J. Devel. Stud.*, 1987, *8*(2), pp. 283–97.
[G: Canada; Senegal]

Dhakal, Dharmendra; Grabowski, Richard and Belbase, Krishna. The Effect of Education in Nepal's Traditional Agriculture. *Econ. Educ. Rev.*, 1987, *6*(1), pp. 27–34.
[G: Nepal]

Dolan, Robert C. and Schmidt, Robert M. Assessing the Impact of Expenditure on Achievement: Some Methodological and Policy Considerations. *Econ. Educ. Rev.*, 1987, *6*(3), pp. 285–99.
[G: U.S.]

Dynarski, Mark. The Scholastic Aptitude Test: Participation and Performance. *Econ. Educ. Rev.*, 1987, *6*(3), pp. 263–73.
[G: U.S.]

Eberts, Randall W. Union-Negotiated Employment Rules and Teacher Quits. *Econ. Educ. Rev.*, 1987, *6*(1), pp. 15–25.
[G: U.S.]

Eberts, Randall W. and Stone, Joe A. Teacher Unions and the Productivity of Public Schools. *Ind. Lab. Relat. Rev.*, April 1987, *40*(3), pp. 354–63.
[G: U.S.]

Ehrenberg, Ronald G. and Sherman, Daniel R.

Employment while in College, Academic Achievement, and Postcollege Outcomes: A Summary of Results. *J. Human Res.*, Winter 1987, *22*(1), pp. 1–23.   [G: U.S.]

England, Richard W. Capital Accumulation, Class Struggle, and School Finance Reform. *England, R. W., ed.*, 1987, pp. 203–25.
[G: U.S.]

Frantz, Telmo Rudi. The Role of NGOs in the Strengthening of Civil Society. *World Devel.*, Supp. Autumn 1987, *15*, pp. 121–127.
[G: Brazil]

Freudenberg, Michael and Henderson, Tracy L. Promoting High-Technology Industry: Initiatives and Policies for State Governments: Florida. *Schmandt, J. and Wilson, R., eds.*, 1987, pp. 35–64.   [G: U.S.]

Garbers, Johan G. Black Education in South Africa: Parameters, Scenarios, Needs. *Sethi, S. P., ed.*, 1987, pp. 245–52.   [G: S. Africa]

Gardner, Eileen M. Back to Basics for Black Education. *Perkins, J., ed.*, 1987, pp. 37–47.
[G: U.S.]

Heath, Julia A. and Tuckman, Howard P. The Effects of Tuition Level and Financial Aid on the Demand for Undergraduate and Advanced Terminal Degrees. *Econ. Educ. Rev.*, 1987, *6*(3), pp. 227–38.   [G: U.S.]

Hoenack, Stephen A. and Davidson, Colleen T. University Marginal Instructional Costs: Implications for Charges to Overseas Students. *Econ. Educ. Rev.*, 1987, *6*(4), pp. 345–55.
[G: U.S.]

Hoffman, Emily P. Determinants of Youths' Educational and Occupational Goals: Sex and Race Differences. *Econ. Educ. Rev.*, 1987, *6*(1), pp. 41–48.   [G: U.S.]

Hull, Rita P.; Everett, John O. and Hall, Steven D. Accounting Education: Practitioner's Views on the Value of a Five-Year Program. *Schwartz, B. N., ed.*, 1987, pp. 163–76.
[G: U.S.]

Islam, Iyanatul. Manpower and Educational Planning in Singapore. *Amjad, R., ed.*, 1987, pp. 114–50.   [G: Singapore]

James, Estelle. The Public/Private Division of Responsibility for Education: An International Comparison. *Econ. Educ. Rev.*, 1987, *6*(1), pp. 1–14.   [G: U.S.; Japan; Holland; India]

James, Estelle and Benjamin, Gail. Educational Distribution and Income Redistribution through Education in Japan. *J. Human Res.*, Fall 1987, *22*(4), pp. 469–89.   [G: Japan; U.S.]

Jamison, Dean T. and Lockheed, Marlaine E. Participation in Schooling: Determinants and Learning Outcomes in Nepal. *Econ. Develop. Cult. Change*, January 1987, *35*(2), pp. 279–306.   [G: Nepal]

Jimenez, Emmanuel and Tan, Jee-Peng. Selecting the Brightest for Post Secondary Education in Colombia: The Impact on Equity. *Econ. Educ. Rev.*, 1987, *6*(2), pp. 129–35.
[G: Colombia]

Johnes, Geraint; Taylor, Jim and Ferguson, Glenys. The Employability of New Graduates: A Study of Differences between UK Universities. *Appl. Econ.*, May 1987, *19*(5), pp. 695–710.
[G: U.K.]

Jolly, Richard. Adjustment with a Human Face: Protecting the Vulnerable and Promoting Growth: Education. *Cornia, G. A.; Jolly, R. and Stewart, F., eds.*, 1987, pp. 232–40.
[G: LDCs]

Khan, M. R. Employment, Manpower and Educational Development in Bangladesh. *Amjad, R., ed.*, 1987, pp. 304–17.   [G: Bangladesh]

Khan, Shahrukh Rafi; Siddiqui, Rehana and Hussain, Fazal. An Analysis of School Level Drop-Out Rates and Output in Pakistan. *Pakistan Econ. Soc. Rev.*, Summer 1987, *25*(1), pp. 1–19.   [G: Pakistan]

King, Elizabeth M. and Lillard, Lee A. Education Policy and Schooling Attainment in Malaysia and the Philippines. *Econ. Educ. Rev.*, 1987, *6*(2), pp. 167–81.   [G: Malaysia; Philippines]

Kurth, Michael M. Teachers' Unions and Excellence in Education: An Analysis of the Decline in SAT Scores. *J. Lab. Res.*, Fall 1987, *8*(4), pp. 351–67.   [G: U.S.]

Lee, Ronald D. The Value and Allocation of Time in High-Income Countries: Implications for Fertility: Comment. *Davis, K.; Bernstam, M. S. and Ricardo-Campbell, R., eds.*, 1987, *1986*, pp. 108–10.

Leonard, Herman B. Academic Ability, Earnings, and the Decision to Become a Teacher: Evidence from the National Longitudinal Study of the High School Class of 1972: Comment. *Wise, D. A., ed.*, 1987, pp. 312–16.
[G: U.S.]

Levin, Henry M. Education as a Public and Private Good. *J. Policy Anal. Manage.*, Summer 1987, *6*(4), pp. 628–41.

Levin, Henry M. and Tsang, Mun Chiu. The Economics of Student Time. *Econ. Educ. Rev.*, 1987, *6*(4), pp. 357–64.

Lockheed, Marlaine E.; Jamison, Dean T. and Lau, Lawrence J. Farmer Education and Farm Efficiency: Reply. *Econ. Develop. Cult. Change*, April 1987, *35*(3), pp. 643–44.

Lott, John R., Jr. The Institutional Arrangement of Public Education: The Puzzle of Exclusive Territories. *Public Choice*, 1987, *54*(1), pp. 89–96.

Lott, John R., Jr. Why Is Education Publicly Provided? A Critical Survey. *Cato J.*, Fall 1987, *7*(2), pp. 475–501.

Magura, Michael and Shapiro, Edward. The Black Dropout Rate and the Black Youth Unemployment Rate: A Granger-Causal Analysis. *Rev. Black Polit. Econ.*, Winter 1987, *15*(3), pp. 56–67.   [G: U.S.]

Manski, Charles F. Academic Ability, Earnings, and the Decision to Become a Teacher: Evidence from the National Longitudinal Study of the High School Class of 1972. *Wise, D. A., ed.*, 1987, pp. 291–312.   [G: U.S.]

Margo, Robert A. Accounting for Racial Differences in School Attendance in the American South, 1900: The Role of Separate-but-Equal.

Rev. Econ. Statist., November 1987, *69*(4), pp. 661–66. **[G: U.S.]**

Matos-Díaz, Horacio. University Education as a Homogenizing Process: An Exploratory Study. *Econ. Educ. Rev.*, 1987, *6*(1), pp. 49–54. **[G: Puerto Rico]**

McCarney, Bernard J. Substitution and Complementarity in Education: An Approach to Educational Reform [The School Reform Debate]. *J. Econ. Educ.*, Winter 1987, *18*(1), pp. 68–70.

McCormick, Robert E. and Tensley, Maurice. Athletics versus Academics? Evidence from SAT Scores. *J. Polit. Econ.*, October 1987, *95*(5), pp. 1103–16. **[G: U.S.]**

Monk, David H. School District Enrollment and Inequality in the Supply of Classes. *Econ. Educ. Rev.*, 1987, *6*(4), pp. 365–77. **[G: U.S.]**

Monk, David H. Secondary School Size and Curriculum Comprehensiveness. *Econ. Educ. Rev.*, 1987, *6*(2), pp. 137–50. **[G: U.S.]**

de Moura Castro, Cláudio. Is Vocational Education Really That Bad? *Int. Lab. Rev.*, Sept.-Oct. 1987, *126*(5), pp. 603–10. **[G: LDCs]**

Murnane, Richard J.; Singer, Judith D. and Willett, John B. Changes in Teacher Salaries during the 1970s: The Role of School District Demographics. *Econ. Educ. Rev.*, 1987, *6*(4), pp. 379–88. **[G: U.S.]**

Murphy, Joseph. The Apartheid Debate on American Campuses. *Sethi, S. P., ed.*, 1987, pp. 285–93. **[G: U.S.; S. Africa]**

Nakata, Yoshi-fumi and Mosk, Carl. The Demand for College Education in Postwar Japan. *J. Human Res.*, Summer 1987, *22*(3), pp. 377–404. **[G: Japan; Selected OECD]**

Orazem, Peter F. Black–White Differences in Schooling Investment and Human Capital Production in Segregated Schools. *Amer. Econ. Rev.*, September 1987, *77*(4), pp. 714–23. **[G: U.S.]**

Paton-Saltzberg, R. and Lindsay, R. O. Free Lunches in Higher Education? [The Behaviour of a Resource Reducing Bureaucracy. A Case Study of an English Polytechnic]. *Appl. Econ.*, October 1987, *19*(10), pp. 1337–39. **[G: U.K.]**

Pelissero, John P. and Morgan, David R. State Aid to Public Schools: An Analysis of State Responsiveness to School District Needs. *Soc. Sci. Quart.*, September 1987, *68*(3), pp. 466–77. **[G: U.S.]**

Peterson, Kent D. Computerized Instruction, Information Systems, and School Teachers: Labor Relations in Education. *Cornfield, D. B., ed.*, 1987, pp. 135–51. **[G: U.S.]**

Phillips, Joseph M. A Comment on Farmer Education and Farm Efficiency: A Survey. *Econ. Develop. Cult. Change*, April 1987, *35*(3), pp. 637–41.

Power, Colin and Robertson, Frances. Participation and Equity in Higher Education: Socioeconomic Profiles of Higher Education Students Revisited. *Australian Bull. Lab.*, March 1987, *13*(2), pp. 108–19. **[G: Australia]**

Prost, Antoine. The Educational Maelstrom. *Ross, G.; Hoffmann, S. and Malzacher, S., eds.*, 1987, pp. 229–36. **[G: France]**

Quan, Nguyen T. and Beck, John H. Public Education Expenditures and State Economic Growth: Northeast and Sunbelt Regions. *Southern Econ. J.*, October 1987, *54*(2), pp. 361–76. **[G: U.S.]**

Rice, Patricia G. The Demand for Post-compulsory Education in the UK and the Effects of Educational Maintenance Allowances. *Economica*, November 1987, *54*(216), pp. 465–75. **[G: U.K.]**

Rosen, Sherwin. Some Economics of Teaching. *J. Lab. Econ.*, Part 1, Oct. 1987, *5*(4), pp. 561–75. **[G: U.S.]**

Ross, Peggy J. and Rosenfeld, Stuart A. Human Resource Policies and Economic Development. *U.S.D.A., Econ. Res. Serv., Agr. and Rural Econ. Div.*, 1987, pp. 15.1–25. **[G: U.S.]**

Roth, Gabriel. Roles of the Private Sector in the Supply of Public Services in Less Developed Countries. *Kent, C. A., ed.*, 1987, pp. 195–206. **[G: LDCs]**

Rubinfeld, Daniel L.; Shapiro, Perry and Roberts, Judith. Tiebout Bias and the Demand for Local Public Schooling. *Rev. Econ. Statist.*, August 1987, *69*(3), pp. 426–37. **[G: U.S.]**

Rubinstein, W. D. Education and the Social Origins of British Elites, 1880–1970. *Rubinstein, W. D.*, 1987, *1986*, pp. 172–221. **[G: U.K.]**

Rudd, Ernest. The Educational Qualifications and Social Class of the Parents of Undergraduates Entering British Universities in 1984. *J. Roy. Statist. Soc.*, 1987, *150*(4), pp. 346–372. **[G: U.K.]**

Rudd, Joel and Buttolph, Vicki L. Consumer Curriculum Materials: The First Content Analysis. *J. Cons. Aff.*, Summer 1987, *21*(1), pp. 108–21. **[G: U.S.]**

Rumberger, Russell W. The Impact of Salary Differentials on Teacher Shortages and Turnover: The Case of Mathematics and Science Teachers. *Econ. Educ. Rev.*, 1987, *6*(4), pp. 389–99. **[G: U.S.]**

Russe, Catherine M. and Anderson, Gerard F. Hospital Reorganization: Examining the Effects on Medical Education. *Scheffler, R. M. and Rossiter, L. F., eds.*, 1987, pp. 141–56. **[G: U.S.]**

Sav, G. Thomas. Institutional Structure, Finance, and Race in Higher Education: Public–Private Sectoral Differences. *Public Choice*, October 1987, *55*(3), pp. 257–64. **[G: U.S.]**

Schultz, T. Paul. School Expenditures and Enrollments, 1960–80: The Effects of Income, Prices, and Population Growth. *Johnson, D. G. and Lee, R. D., eds.*, 1987, pp. 413–76. **[G: Global]**

Schultz, T. Paul. The Value and Allocation of Time in High-Income Countries: Implications for Fertility. *Davis, K.; Bernstam, M. S. and Ricardo-Campbell, R., eds.*, 1987, *1986*, pp. 87–108. **[G: U.S.]**

Shanker, Albert. A Comment on Restructuring

Schooling [The School Reform Debate]. *J. Econ. Educ.*, Winter 1987, *18*(1), pp. 66–67.

Shanker, Albert. Education as a Public and Private Good: Comment. *J. Policy Anal. Manage.*, Summer 1987, *6*(4), pp. 643–47.

Silbert, Lance. Promoting High-Technology Industry: Initiatives and Policies for State Governments: California. *Schmandt, J. and Wilson, R., eds.*, 1987, pp. 11–33. **[G: U.S.]**

Snellings, Eleanor C. Classrooms as Commons. *Atlantic Econ. J.*, September 1987, *15*(3), pp. 76.

Steedman, Hilary. Vocational Training in France and Britain: Office Work. *Nat. Inst. Econ. Rev.*, May 1987, (120), pp. 58–70.
[G: France; U.K.]

Stevens, Edward W., Jr. Structural and Ideological Dimensions of Literacy and Education in the Old Northwest. *Klingaman, D. C. and Vedder, R. K., eds.*, 1987, pp. 157–85. **[G: U.S.]**

Street, James H. The Reality of Power and the Poverty of Economic Doctrine. *Dietz, J. L. and Street, J. H., eds.*, 1987, *1983*, pp. 16–32. **[G: Chile; Argentina; Paraguay; Uruguay]**

Street, James H. The Technological Frontier in Latin America: Creativity and Productivity. *Dietz, J. L. and Street, J. H., eds.*, 1987, pp. 200–216. **[G: Latin America]**

Summers, Anita A. Education as a Public and Private Good: Comment. *J. Policy Anal. Manage.*, Summer 1987, *6*(4), pp. 641–43.

Suroto and Tjiptoherijanto, Prijono. Employment, Manpower and Educational Planning in Indonesia. *Amjad, R., ed.*, 1987, pp. 181–97.
[G: Indonesia]

Swanson, Linda L. and Butler, Margaret A. Human Resource Base of Rural Economies. *U.S.D.A., Econ. Res. Serv., Agr. and Rural Econ. Div.*, 1987, pp. 7.1–23. **[G: U.S.]**

Tan, Edita A. and Alonzo, Ruperto P. The Philippine Experience in Manpower Planning and Labour Market Policies. *Amjad, R., ed.*, 1987, pp. 151–80. **[G: Philippines]**

Taxell, Christoffer. Näringslivets roll i undervisningsoch forskningspolitiken. (The Role of Industries in Education and Research. Policy. With English summary.) *Ekon. Samfundets Tidskr.*, 1987, *40*(4), pp. 191–99.
[G: Finland]

Texler, Jiří. Education as a Factor of Development. *Czech. Econ. Pap.*, 1987, (24), pp. 83–97. **[G: Czechoslovakia]**

Thembela, Alexander Jabulan. The State of Education for Blacks in South Africa. *Sethi, S. P., ed.*, 1987, pp. 231–44. **[G: S. Africa]**

Tilak, Jandhyala B. G. Costs of Education in Two Clusters in Haryana. *Margin*, December 1987, *20*(1), pp. 74–96. **[G: India]**

Toma, Eugenia F. and Long, James E. Public Employees' Consumption of Government Goods: The Case of Education. *Public Choice*, 1987, *53*(3), pp. 289–96. **[G: U.S.]**

Turnbull, Geoffrey K. Alternative Local Public Education Expenditure Functions: An Econometric Evaluation. *Public Finance Quart.*, January 1987, *15*(1), pp. 45–60. **[G: U.S.]**

Umarov, Khodji. Development and Socio-cultural Transformation: The Rule of Education in Tajekistan. *Gidadhubli, R. G., ed.*, 1987, pp. 101–15. **[G: U.S.S.R.]**

Van Niekerk Viljoen, Gerrit. Education for Black People in South Africa: Challenges and Progress. *Sethi, S. P., ed.*, 1987, pp. 221–29.
[G: S. Africa]

Vélez, Eduardo and Psacharopoulos, George. The External Efficiency of Diversified Secondary Schools in Colombia. *Econ. Educ. Rev.*, 1987, *6*(2), pp. 99–110. **[G: Colombia]**

Watts, Michael. Student Gender and School District Differences Affecting the Stock and Flow of Economic Knowledge. *Rev. Econ. Statist.*, August 1987, *69*(3), pp. 561–66. **[G: U.S.]**

Weiler, William C. Economic Issues in Faculty Retirement Plans in American Higher Education Institutions. *Econ. Educ. Rev.*, 1987, *6*(3), pp. 207–26. **[G: U.S.]**

Weiss, Janet A. and Gruber, Judith E. The Managed Irrelevance of Federal Education Statistics. *Alonso, W. and Starr, P., eds.*, 1987, pp. 363–91. **[G: U.S.]**

Westoby, Jack C. Forestry Education: To Whom and for What? *Westoby, J.*, 1987, *1971*, pp. 193–205.

Woodhall, Maureen. Financing Student Flows: The Effects of Recent Policy Trends. *Econ. Educ. Rev.*, 1987, *6*(2), pp. 195–204.
[G: Global]

913 Economics of Health (including medical subsidy programs)

9130 Economics of Health (including medical subsidy programs)

Abel-Smith, Brian. Funding Health for All—Is Insurance the Answer? Reply. *World Health Organization.*, 1987, *1986*, pp. 82–83.
[G: Global]

Abel-Smith, Brian. Funding Health for All—Is Insurance the Answer? *World Health Organization.*, 1987, *1986*, pp. 55–63. **[G: Global]**

Abel-Smith, Brian. Health Care Costs Out of Control: The Experience of Switzerland: Discussion. *World Health Organization.*, 1987, *1985*, pp. 112–14. **[G: LDCs]**

Abel-Smith, Brian. Improving Cost-Effectiveness in Health Care. *World Health Organization.*, 1987, *1984*, pp. 6–8.

Abelson, Peter W. The Use of Regional Allocation Formulae for the Allocation of Health Funds to Regions: With Special Reference to New South Wales. *Butler, J. R. G. and Doessel, D. P., eds.*, 1987, pp. 227–50. **[G: Australia]**

Abernethy, Margaret A. and Stoelwinder, Johannes U. Goal Orientations and the Use of Budgeting Information: A Comparison between Physicians and Non-physicians in Public Teaching Hospitals. *Butler, J. R. G. and Doessel, D. P., eds.*, 1987, pp. 67–92.
[G: Australia]

Aday, Lu Ann. Ambulatory Care and Insurance Coverage in an Era of Constraint: Actual Access to Care. *Andersen, R. M., et al.*, 1987, pp. 97–110. [G: U.S.]

Aday, Lu Ann and Andersen, Ronald M. Ambulatory Care and Insurance Coverage in an Era of Constraint: Summary and Implications. *Andersen, R. M., et al.*, 1987, pp. 179–93. [G: U.S.]

Aday, Lu Ann; Cornelius, Llewellyn J. and Andersen, Ronald M. Organizational and Financial Dimensions of Health Policy. *Andersen, R. M., et al.*, 1987, pp. 1–17. [G: U.S.]

Akin, John and Birdsall, Nancy. Financing of Health Services in LDCs. *Finance Develop.*, June 1987, *24*(2), pp. 40–43. [G: U.S.]

Andersen, Ronald M. Ambulatory Care and Insurance Coverage in an Era of Constraint: Analytic Plan. *Andersen, R. M., et al.*, 1987, pp. 41–47. [G: U.S.]

Andersen, Ronald M. and Lyttle, Christopher S. Ambulatory Care and Insurance Coverage in an Era of Constraint: Care and Coverage Lessons from the Special Samples. *Andersen, R. M., et al.*, 1987, pp. 147–78. [G: U.S.]

Andersen, Ronald M.; Lyttle, Christopher S. and Cornelius, Llewellyn J. Sources and Financing of Medical Care. *Andersen, R. M., et al.*, 1987, pp. 49–73. [G: U.S.]

Anderson, Gerard F.; Erickson, Jane and Feigenbaum, Susan. Examining the Relationship between Capital Investment and Hospital Operating Expenditures. *Rev. Econ. Statist.*, November 1987, *69*(4), pp. 709–13. [G: U.S.]

Anderson, Joseph M.; Kennell, David L. and Sheils, John F. Health Plan Costs, Medicare, and Employment of Older Workers. *Sandell, S. H., ed.*, 1987, pp. 206–17. [G: U.S.]

Auer, Ludwig. Aging with Limited Health Resources: Some Statistical Background Material. *Economic Council of Canada.*, 1987, pp. 187–99. [G: Canada]

Auer, Ludwig. Canadian Hospital Costs and Productivity. *Economic Council of Canada.*, 1987, pp. 179–85. [G: Canada]

Aznar, Antonio. Contenido informativo y selección de modelos econométricos. (With English summary.) *Invest. Econ.*, January 1987, *11*(1), pp. 25–39. [G: Spain]

Baily, Martin Neil. Aging and the Ability to Work: Policy Issues and Recent Trends. *Burtless, G., ed.*, 1987, pp. 59–97. [G: U.S.]

Banerji, D. Funding Health for All—Is Insurance the Answer? Discussion. *World Health Organization.*, 1987, *1986*, pp. 64–66. [G: Global]

Banta, H. David. Aging and New Health Care Technology. *Economic Council of Canada.*, 1987, pp. 115–22. [G: Canada]

Banta, H. David and Gelijns, Annetine. Health Care Costs: Technology and Policy. *Schramm, C. J., ed.*, 1987, pp. 252–74. [G: U.S]

Barrett, Diana and Campbell, Paul H. Walking Softly: The Role of Management in Altering Physician Practice Patterns in the Hospital Corporation of America. *Scheffler, R. M. and Rossiter, L. F., eds.*, 1987, pp. 157–78. [G: U.S.]

Basiotis, P. Peter, et al. Food Stamps, Food

Costs, Nutrient Availability, and Nutrient Intake. *J. Policy Modeling*, Fall 1987, *9*(3), pp. 383–404. [G: U.S.]

Begun, James W., et al. Strategic Behavior Patterns of Small Multi-institutional Health Organizations. *Scheffler, R. M. and Rossiter, L. F., eds.*, 1987, pp. 195–214. [G: U.S.]

Behrens, Ruth A. Health Promotion in the Workplace. *Meyer, J. A. and Lewin, M. E., eds.*, 1987, pp. 133–48. [G: U.S.]

Behrman, Jere R. and Deolalikar, Anil B. Will Developing Country Nutrition Improve with Income? A Case Study for Rural South India. *J. Polit. Econ.*, June 1987, *95*(3), pp. 492–507. [G: India]

Behrman, Jere R. and Wolfe, Barbara L. How Does Mother's Schooling Affect Family Health, Nutrition, Medical Care Usage, and Household Sanitation? *J. Econometrics*, Sept./Oct. 1987, *36*(1/2), pp. 185–204. [G: Nicaragua]

Bekele, G. and Holtmann, A. G. A Cost Function for Nursing Homes: Toward a System of Diagnostic Reimbursement Groupings. *Eastern Econ. J.*, Apr.-June 1987, *13*(2), pp. 115–22. [G: U.S.]

Berger, Mark C., et al. Valuing Changes in Health Risks: A Comparison of Alternative Measures. *Southern Econ. J.*, April 1987, *53*(4), pp. 967–84. [G: U.S.]

Bezold, Clement. Health Trends and Scenarios: Implications for the Health Care Professions. *Meyer, J. A. and Lewin, M. E., eds.*, 1987, pp. 77–97. [G: U.S.]

Birch, Stephen and Donaldson, Cam. Applications of Cost–Benefit Analysis to Health Care: Departures from Welfare Economic Theory. *J. Health Econ.*, September 1987, *6*(3), pp. 211–25.

Bishop, Christine E. Swing Beds: Assessing Flexible Health Care in Rural Communities: Cost Issues: Comments. *Wiener, J. M., ed.*, 1987, pp. 59–63. [G: U.S.]

Blair, Roger D. and Fesmire, James M. Antitrust Treatment of Nonprofit and For-profit Hospital Mergers. *Scheffler, R. M. and Rossiter, L. F., eds.*, 1987, pp. 221–44. [G: U.S.]

Blanchet, Madeleine. Advances in Preventive Medicine. *Economic Council of Canada.*, 1987, pp. 79–92. [G: Canada]

Blank, Susan. Health, Health Care, and Economic Self-sufficiency. *Meyer, J. A. and Lewin, M. E., eds.*, 1987, pp. 160–86. [G: U.S.]

Blanpain, Jan E. Health Care Costs Out of Control: The Experience of Switzerland: Discussion. *World Health Organization.*, 1987, *1985*, pp. 114. [G: Switzerland]

Blendon, Robert J. and Altman, Drew E. Public Opinion and Health Care Costs. *Schramm, C. J., ed.*, 1987, pp. 49–63. [G: U.S.]

Blostin, Allan P. Mental Health Benefits Financed by Employers. *Mon. Lab. Rev.*, July 1987, *110*(7), pp. 23–27. [G: U.S.]

Bovbjerg, Randall R.; Held, Philip J. and Pauly, Mark V. Privatization and Bidding in the Health-Care Sector. *J. Policy Anal. Manage.*, Summer 1987, *6*(4), pp. 648–66. [G: U.S.]

Bradbury, Robert C. A Community Approach to Health Care Competition. *Inquiry*, Fall 1987, *24*(3), pp. 253–65. **[G: U.S.]**

Branch, E. Raphael. Comparing Medical Care Expenditures of Two Diverse U.S. Data Sources. *Mon. Lab. Rev.*, March 1987, *110*(3), pp. 15–18. **[G: U.S.]**

Breslaw, Jon A. and Stelcner, Morton. The Effect of Health on the Labor Force Behavior of Elderly Men in Canada. *J. Human Res.*, Fall 1987, *22*(4), pp. 490–517. **[G: Canada]**

Breyer, Friedrich. The Specification of a Hospital Cost Function: A Comment on the Recent Literature. *J. Health Econ.*, June 1987, *6*(2), pp. 147–57.

Breyer, Friedrich and von der Schulenburg, J.-Matthias Graf. Family Structure and Intergenerational Transfers in Social Health Insurance: A Public Choice Model. *Pethig, R. and Schlieper, U., eds.*, 1987, pp. 63–80.

Brinberg, David and Morris, Louis A. Advertising Prescription Drugs to Consumers. *Bloom, P. N., ed.*, 1987, pp. 1–40. **[G: U.S.]**

Brooks, R. G. The Economics of Health: Review Article. *J. Econ. Stud.*, 1987, *14*(5), pp. 63–72. **[G: U.K.]**

Broome, John. The Economic Value of Life: A Reply. *Economica*, August 1987, *54*(215), pp. 0240.

Brunet, Jacques. The Impact of an Aging Population on Health Services. *Economic Council of Canada.*, 1987, pp. 162–68. **[G: Canada]**

Buck, Carol. How Direct Is the Path toward Lengthening the Life Span and Improving the Quality of Life? *Economic Council of Canada.*, 1987, pp. 101–04. **[G: Canada]**

Burkhauser, Richard V. Occupational Effects on the Health and Work Capacity of Older Men: Comment. *Burtless, G., ed.*, 1987, pp. 142–50. **[G: U.S.]**

Burtless, Gary. Occupational Effects on the Health and Work Capacity of Older Men. *Burtless, G., ed.*, 1987, pp. 103–42. **[G: U.S.]**

Butler, J. R. G. The Economics and Financing of Hospitals in Australia: Discussion. *Butler, J. R. G. and Doessel, D. P., eds.*, 1987, pp. 22–24. **[G: Australia]**

Butler, John S., et al. Measurement Error in Self-reported Health Variables. *Rev. Econ. Statist.*, November 1987, *69*(4), pp. 644–50. **[G: U.S.]**

Butt, Shaheen A. and Mahmood, Tallat. Food and Nutrition in Pakistan (A Cross-regional Study). *Pakistan Devel. Rev.*, Winter 1987, *26*(4), pp. 485–96. **[G: Pakistan]**

Bye, Barry; Riley, Gerald and Lubitz, James. Medicare Utilization by Disabled-Worker Beneficiaries: A Longitudinal Analysis. *Soc. Sec. Bull.*, December 1987, *50*(12), pp. 13–28. **[G: U.S.]**

Carter, Carol and Cromwell, Jerry. Variations in Hospital Malpractice Costs, 1983–1985. *Inquiry*, Winter 1987, *24*(4), pp. 392–404. **[G: U.S.]**

Cauley, Stephen Day. The Time Price of Medical

Care. *Rev. Econ. Statist.*, February 1987, *69*(1), pp. 59–66. **[G: U.S.]**

Chen, Meei-Shia and Cornelius, Llewellyn J. Health Care Needs. *Andersen, R. M., et al.*, 1987, pp. 75–95. **[G: U.S.]**

Chen, Meei-Shia and Lyttle, Christopher S. Ambulatory Care and Insurance Coverage in an Era of Constraint: Multivariate Analysis of Access to Care. *Andersen, R. M., et al.*, 1987, pp. 111–45. **[G: U.S.]**

Chernick, Howard A.; Holmer, Martin R. and Weinberg, Daniel H. Tax Policy toward Health Insurance and the Demand for Medical Services. *J. Health Econ.*, March 1987, *6*(1), pp. 1–25. **[G: U.S.]**

Christianson, Jon B. Comments on Diversification of Health Care Services. *Scheffler, R. M. and Rossiter, L. F., eds.*, 1987, pp. 111–14. **[G: U.S.]**

Ciscel, David H. and Chang, Cyril. The Potential for Structural Monopolization in Hospital Services. *J. Econ. Issues*, June 1987, *21*(2), pp. 847–57. **[G: U.S.]**

Coffey, Rosanna M. Payment Systems and Hospital Resource Use: A Comparative Analysis of Psychiatric, Medical and Obstetric Services: Comments. *McGuire, T. G. and Scheffler, R. M., eds.*, 1987, pp. 97–101. **[G: U.S.]**

Cohodes, Donald R. The Loss of Innocence: Health Care under Siege. *Schramm, C. J., ed.*, 1987, pp. 64–104. **[G: U.S.]**

Corman, Hope; Joyce, Theodore J. and Grossman, Michael. Birth Outcome Production Function in the United States. *J. Human Res.*, Summer 1987, *22*(3), pp. 339–60. **[G: U.S.]**

Cornelius, Llewellyn J. and Aday, Lu Ann. Empirical and Methodological Studies of Care and Coverage. *Andersen, R. M., et al.*, 1987, pp. 19–28. **[G: U.S.]**

Cotter, Diane M. and Macon, Janet A. Deaths in Industry, 1985: BLS Survey Findings. *Mon. Lab. Rev.*, April 1987, *110*(4), pp. 45–47. **[G: U.S.]**

Coward, Raymond. Swing Beds: Assessing Flexible Health Care in Rural Communities: Access and Case-Mix Patterns: Comments. *Wiener, J. M., ed.*, 1987, pp. 100–103. **[G: U.S.]**

Cowper, Patricia A. and Kushman, John E. A Spatial Analysis of Primary Health Care Markets in Rural Areas. *Amer. J. Agr. Econ.*, August 1987, *69*(3), pp. 613–25. **[G: U.S.]**

Coyte, Peter C. Alternative Methods of Reimbursing Hospitals and the Impact of Certificate-of-Need and Rate Regulation for the Hospital Sector. *Southern Econ. J.*, April 1987, *53*(4), pp. 858–73.

Danzon, Patricia M. Compensation for Occupational Disease: Evaluating the Options. *J. Risk Ins.*, June 1987, *54*(2), pp. 265–82.

Dardanoni, Valentino and Wagstaff, Adam. Uncertainty, Inequalities in Health and the Demand for Health. *J. Health Econ.*, December 1987, *6*(4), pp. 283–90.

Dasgupta, Partha and Ray, Debraj. Inequality as a Determinant of Malnutrition and Unemployment: Policy. *Econ. J.*, March 1987, 97(385), pp. 177–88.

Davis, Karen. Medicare Financing and Beneficiary Income: Symposium Report. *Inquiry*, Winter 1987, 24(4), pp. 309–23. **[G: U.S.]**

Deber, Raisa B. Advances in Medical Technology. *Economic Council of Canada.*, 1987, pp. 133–38. **[G: Canada]**

DesHarnais, Susan, et al. The Early Effects of the Prospective Payment System on Inpatient Utilization and the Quality of Care. *Inquiry*, Spring 1987, 24(1), pp. 7–16. **[G: U.S.]**

Dionne, Georges; Langlois, Alain and Lemire, Nicole. More on the Geographical Distribution of Physicians. *J. Health Econ.*, December 1987, 6(4), pp. 365–74.

Dobson, Allen. Mergers in Health Care: Implications for the Future. *Scheffler, R. M. and Rossiter, L. F., eds.*, 1987, pp. 271–77. **[G: U.S.]**

Doessel, D. P. The Cost-Effectiveness of the City mission Hospice Program, Melbourne: Discussion. *Butler, J. R. G. and Doessel, D. P., eds.*, 1987, pp. 131–35. **[G: Australia]**

Domberger, Simon; Meadowcroft, Shirley and Thompson, David. The Impact of Competitive Tendering on the Costs of Hospital Domestic Services. *Fisc. Stud.*, November 1987, 8(4), pp. 39–54. **[G: U.K.]**

Dor, Avi; Gertler, Paul and van der Gaag, Jacques. Non-price Rationing and the Choice of Medical Care Providers in Rural Cote d'Ivoire. *J. Health Econ.*, December 1987, 6(4), pp. 291–304. **[G: Ivory Coast]**

Dorwart, Robert A. Shrinking Costs vs. Costing Shrinks: A Clinician's Perspective. *McGuire, T. G. and Scheffler, R. M., eds.*, 1987, pp. 127–31. **[G: U.S.]**

Dowd, Bryan E. and Feldman, Roger. Voluntary Reduction in Health Insurance Coverage: A Theoretical Analysis. *Eastern Econ. J.*, July-Sept. 1987, 13(3), pp. 215–32.

Dranove, David. Rate-Setting by Diagnosis Related Groups and Hospital Specialization. *Rand J. Econ.*, Autumn 1987, 18(3), pp. 417–27. **[G: U.S.]**

Dranove, David and White, William D. Agency and the Organization of Health Care Delivery. *Inquiry*, Winter 1987, 24(4), pp. 405–15. **[G: U.S.]**

Duckett, S. J. The Use of Regional Allocation Formulae for the Allocation of Health Funds to Regions: With Special Reference to New South Wales: Discussion. *Butler, J. R. G. and Doessel, D. P., eds.*, 1987, pp. 251–53. **[G: Australia]**

Dunt, David R.; Cantwell, Annie M. and Temple-Smith, Meredith J. The Cost-Effectiveness of the Citymission Hospice Program, Melbourne. *Butler, J. R. G. and Doessel, D. P., eds.*, 1987, pp. 116–30. **[G: Australia]**

Ebert, Robert. The Changing Role of the Physician. *Schramm, C. J., ed.*, 1987, pp. 145–84. **[G: U.S.]**

Eeckhoudt, Louis; Bauwens, Luc and Lebrun, Thérèse. Théorie de l'information et diagnostic

médical: Une analyse coût-efficacité. (Information Theory and Medical Diagnosis: A Cost-Efficiency Analysis. With English summary.) *L'Actual. Econ.*, June-September 1987, 63(2–3), pp. 243–55.

Ellis, Randall P. Payment System Alternatives for Addressing Systematic Risk in a Prospective Payment System. *McGuire, T. G. and Scheffler, R. M., eds.*, 1987, pp. 49–69. **[G: U.S.]**

Ermann, Dan. Comments on Behavior and Performance. *Scheffler, R. M. and Rossiter, L. F., eds.*, 1987, pp. 215–17. **[G: U.S.]**

Espenshade, Thomas J. Aging and the Ability to Work: Policy Issues and Recent Trends: Comment. *Burtless, G., ed.*, 1987, pp. 97–102. **[G: U.S.]**

Essock, Susan M. The Influence of Medical Co-morbidities and Other Patient Characteristics on Resource Consumption on Psychiatric Wards. *McGuire, T. G. and Scheffler, R. M., eds.*, 1987, pp. 133–42. **[G: U.S.]**

Evans, David B. Problems and Progress in Health Economics in Thailand: Discussion. *Butler, J. R. G. and Doessel, D. P., eds.*, 1987, pp. 142–43. **[G: Thailand]**

Evans, Robert G. Hang Together, or Hang Separately: The Viability of a Universal Health Care System in an Aging Society. *Can. Public Policy*, June 1987, 13(2), pp. 165–80. **[G: U.S.; Canada]**

Evans, Roger W. Some Thoughts on Advances in Medical Technology. *Economic Council of Canada.*, 1987, pp. 122–33. **[G: Canada]**

Feigenbaum, Susan. Risk Bearing in Health Care Finance. *Schramm, C. J., ed.*, 1987, pp. 105–44. **[G: U.S.]**

Feldman, Roger. Health Insurance in the United States: Is Market Failure Avoidable? *J. Risk Ins.*, June 1987, 54(2), pp. 289–313. **[G: U.S.]**

Ferguson, Brian S. The Case for Universal Bulk Billing: Discussion. *Butler, J. R. G. and Doessel, D. P., eds.*, 1987, pp. 224–26. **[G: Australia]**

Ferguson, Brian S. and Crawford, Allan. Testing a Disequilibrium Model of Supplier-Induced Demand. *Butler, J. R. G. and Doessel, D. P., eds.*, 1987, pp. 25–40. **[G: Canada]**

de Ferranti, David. Paying for Health Services in Developing Countries: A Call for Realism. *World Health Organization.*, 1987, 1985, pp. 37–43. **[G: LDCs]**

Ferris, James M. and Graddy, Elizabeth. What Governs the Decision to Contract Out for Local Hospital Services? *Inquiry*, Fall 1987, 24(3), pp. 285–94. **[G: U.S.]**

Finkler, Steven A. Swing Beds: Assessing Flexible Health Care in Rural Communities: Cost Issues. *Wiener, J. M., ed.*, 1987, pp. 42–59. **[G: U.S.]**

Forget, Claude E. The Canadian Health Insurance System: Is Good the Enemy of Better? *Economic Council of Canada.*, 1987, pp. 155–62. **[G: Canada]**

Frank, Richard G., et al. Economic Rents Derived from Hospital Privileges in the Market for Podiatric Services. *J. Health Econ.*, December 1987, *6*(4), pp. 319–37.

Frank, Richard G., et al. The Impact of Medicare's Prospective Payment System on Psychiatric Patients Treated in Scatterbeds. *McGuire, T. G. and Scheffler, R. M., eds.,* 1987, pp. 1–21.   [G: U.S.]

Frech, H. E., III. Comments on Antitrust Issues. *Scheffler, R. M. and Rossiter, L. F., eds.,* 1987, pp. 263–67.   [G: U.S.]

Freiman, Marc P.; Mitchell, Janet B. and Rosenbach, Margo L. Modifications of the Prospective Payment System and Payments for Medicare Psychiatric Admissions. *McGuire, T. G. and Scheffler, R. M., eds.,* 1987, pp. 23–47.   [G: U.S.]

Friedman, Margaret L. and Churchill, Gilbert A., Jr. Using Consumer Perceptions and a Contingency Approach to Improve Health Care Delivery. *J. Cons. Res.*, March 1987, *13*(4), pp. 492–510.

Fuchs, Beth C. Health Policy in a Period of Resource Limits and Conservative Politics. *Waltman, J. L. and Studlar, D. T., eds.,* 1987, pp. 207–32.   [G: U.K.; U.S.]

Fuchs, Victor R. Arrow's Contributions to Health Economics. *Feiwel, G. R., ed. (II),* 1987, pp. 680–81.

Fuchs, Victor R. and Zeckhauser, Richard J. Valuing Health—A "Priceless" Commodity. *Amer. Econ. Rev.*, May 1987, *77*(2), pp. 263–68.

Gafni, Amiram and Feder, Aya. Willingness to Pay in an Equitable Society: The Case of the Kibbutz. *Int. J. Soc. Econ.*, 1987, *14*(1), pp. 16–21.   [G: Israel]

Gallagher, Jack. Economic Limits and Bioethics. *Economic Council of Canada.*, 1987, pp. 141–44.   [G: Canada]

Gertler, Paul; Locay, Luis and Sanderson, Warren C. Are User Fees Regressive? The Welfare Implications of Health Care Financing Proposals in Peru. *J. Econometrics*, Sept./Oct. 1987, *36*(1/2), pp. 67–88.   [G: Peru]

Gilliand, Pierre. Health Care Costs Out of Control: The Experience of Switzerland: Discussion. *World Health Organization.*, 1987, *1985*, pp. 115–16.   [G: Switzerland]

Ginsburg, Paul B. Reforming Physician Reimbursement in Medicare. *Meyer, J. A. and Lewin, M. E., eds.,* 1987, pp. 35–50.
                    [G: U.S.]

Glaser, William A. Canadian Health Care Problems and Foreign Solutions. *Economic Council of Canada.*, 1987, pp. 5–15.   [G: Canada]

Goldfarb, Marsha G. and Coffey, Rosanna M. Case-Mix Differences between Teaching and Nonteaching Hospitals. *Inquiry*, Spring 1987, *24*(1), pp. 68–84.   [G: U.S.]

Goldman, Howard H.; Scheffler, Richard M. and Cheadle, Allen. Demand for Psychiatric Services: A Clinical Episode Model for Specifying "The Product." *McGuire, T. G. and Scheffler, R. M., eds.,* 1987, pp. 255–73.   [G: U.S.]

Gomaa, Ramsis A. Funding Health for All—Is Insurance the Answer? Discussion. *World Health Organization.*, 1987, *1986*, pp. 66–68.
                    [G: Global]

Goodin, Robert E.; Le Grand, Julian and Gibson, D. M. Distributional Biases in Social Service Delivery Systems. *Goodin, R. E. and Le Grand, J.,* 1987, pp. 127–43.   [G: Australia]

Goodman, John C. Privatizing Medicare. *Kent, C. A., ed.,* 1987, pp. 101–08.

de Graaf, Louw. Disablement for Work: The Interaction between Research and Policy. *Emanuel, H.; de Gier, E. H. and Konijn, P. A. B. K., eds.,* 1987, pp. 1–6.   [G: Netherlands]

Grazier, Kyle L. and McGuire, Thomas G. Payment Systems and Hospital Resource Use: A Comparative Analysis of Psychiatric, Medical and Obstetric Services. *McGuire, T. G. and Scheffler, R. M., eds.,* 1987, pp. 75–95.
                    [G: U.S.]

Greaney, Thomas L. and Sindelar, Jody L. An Assessment of the Anticompetitive Effects of Preferred Provider Organizations. *Inquiry*, Winter 1987, *24*(4), pp. 384–91.   [G: U.S.]

Green, F. Terri. The Costs of Long-Stay Hospital Care of the Dependent Elderly. *Butler, J. R. G. and Doessel, D. P., eds.,* 1987, pp. 95–112.
                    [G: New Zealand]

Grosse, Robert N. and Plessas, Demetrius J. Counting the Cost of Primary Health Care. *World Health Organization.*, 1987, *1984*, pp. 86–90.   [G: LDCs]

Grosskopf, Shawna and Valdmanis, V. Measuring Hospital Performance: A Non-parametric Approach. *J. Health Econ.*, June 1987, *6*(2), pp. 89–107.   [G: U.S.]

Guralnik, Jack M. and Schneider, Edward L. Prospects and Implications of Extending Life Expectancy. *Espenshade, T. and Stolnitz, G. J., eds.,* 1987, pp. 125–45.   [G: U.S.]

Haas-Wilson, Deborah. Markov and Other Models of Episodes of Mental Health Treatment: Comments. *McGuire, T. G. and Scheffler, R. M., eds.,* 1987, pp. 299–302.   [G: U.S.]

Haas-Wilson, Deborah. Tying Requirements in Markets with Many Sellers: The Contact Lens Industry. *Rev. Econ. Statist.*, February 1987, *69*(1), pp. 170–75.   [G: U.S.]

Hacker, George A. Taxing Booze for Health and Wealth. *J. Policy Anal. Manage.*, Summer 1987, *6*(4), pp. 701–08.   [G: U.S.]

Hagan, P. J. and Henry, G. G. Family-Based Social Welfare Schemes: The Case of Pharmaceuticals. *Butler, J. R. G. and Doessel, D. P., eds.,* 1987, pp. 165–93.   [G: Australia]

Harrington, Charlene and Swan, James H. The Impact of State Medicaid Nursing Home Policies on Utilization and Expenditures. *Inquiry*, Summer 1987, *24*(2), pp. 157–71.   [G: U.S.]

Harrington, Winston and Portney, Paul R. Valuing the Benefits of Health and Safety Regulation. *J. Urban Econ.*, July 1987, *22*(1), pp. 101–12.

Harris, Donald. Disability Benefits: Factors Determining Applications and Awards: Reflections on the Meeting. *Emanuel, H.; de Gier, E. H. and Konijn, P. A. B. K., eds.,* 1987, pp. 261–64.

Harvey, Roy. The Industries Assistance Commission's Report on Pharmaceutical Products: Discussion. *Butler, J. R. G. and Doessel, D. P.*, *eds.*, 1987, pp. 160–64. **[G: Australia]**

Havens, Betty. Intra and Inter National Proposals. *Economic Council of Canada.*, 1987, pp. 18–22. **[G: Canada]**

Hawes, Catherine. Swing Beds: Assessing Flexible Health Care in Rural Communities: Quality of Care: Comments. *Wiener, J. M., ed.*, 1987, pp. 114–17. **[G: U.S.]**

Hay, Joel W.; Leu, Robert and Rohrer, Paul. Ordinary Least Squares and Sample-Selection Models of Health-Care Demand. *J. Bus. Econ. Statist.*, October 1987, *5*(4), pp. 499–506. **[G: Switzerland]**

Headen, Alvin E., Jr. Price Discrimination in Physician Services Markets Based on Race: New Test of an Old Implicit Hypothesis. *Rev. Black Polit. Econ.*, Spring 1987, *15*(4), pp. 5–20. **[G: U.S.]**

Heiber, S. and Deber, R. Banning Extra-billing in Canada: Just What the Doctor Didn't Order. *Can. Public Policy*, March 1987, *13*(1), pp. 62–74. **[G: Canada]**

Herz, Barbara K. and Measham, Anthony R. Maternal Health and Development. *Finance Develop.*, June 1987, *24*(2), pp. 44–45.

Hickson, W. J. Nominal and Real Growth in Expenditures in New South Wales Public Hospitals: 1980–81 to 1985–86. *Butler, J. R. G. and Doessel, D. P., eds.*, 1987, pp. 45–66. **[G: Australia]**

Hill, Diane B. Employer-Sponsored Long-term Disability Insurance. *Mon. Lab. Rev.*, July 1987, *110*(7), pp. 16–22. **[G: U.S.]**

Hirshleifer, Jack. Disaster and Recovery: The Black Death in Western Europe. *Hirshleifer, J.*, 1987, 1966, pp. 95–115. **[G: W. Europe]**

Hodne, Fritz and Basberg, Bjørn. Public Infrastructure, Its Indispensability for Economic Growth: The Case of Norwegian Public Health Measures 1850–1940. *Scand. Econ. Hist. Rev.*, 1987, *35*(2), pp. 145–69. **[G: Norway]**

Holahan, John. Swing-Bed Reimbursement: Objectives and Options. *Wiener, J. M., ed.*, 1987, pp. 64–81. **[G: U.S.]**

Holder, Harold D. and Blose, James O. Mental Health Treatment and the Reduction of Health Care Costs: A Four-Year Study of U.S. Federal Employees Enrollment with the Aetna Life Insurance Company. *McGuire, T. G. and Scheffler, R. M., eds.*, 1987, pp. 157–74. **[G: U.S.]**

Horgan, Constance and Salkever, David. The Demand for Outpatient Mental Health Care from Nonspecialty Providers. *McGuire, T. G. and Scheffler, R. M., eds.*, 1987, pp. 211–33. **[G: U.S.]**

Horne, John M. Beyond "De-institutionalizing" the Elderly: Financial Savings from a More Radical Approach to Alternative Health Care Delivery Methods by the Year 2021. *Economic Council of Canada.*, 1987, pp. 72–77. **[G: Canada]**

Howard, Lee M. What Are the Financial Re-

sources for "Health 2000"? *World Health Organization.*, 1987, *1981*, pp. 30–36. **[G: Global]**

Hsiao, William C. The Resource-Based Relative Value Scale: An Option for Physician Payment: Symposium Report. *Inquiry*, Winter 1987, *24*(4), pp. 360–61. **[G: U.S.]**

Hsiao, William C. and Dunn, Daniel L. The Impact of DRG Payment on New Jersey Hospitals. *Inquiry*, Fall 1987, *24*(3), pp. 212–20. **[G: U.S.]**

Hutter, Michael. Family Structure and Intergenerational Transfers in Social Health Insurance: A Public Choice Model: Comment. *Pethig, R. and Schlieper, U., eds.*, 1987, pp. 81–82.

Inman, Robert P. The Economic Consequences of Debilitating Illness: The Case of Multiple Sclerosis. *Rev. Econ. Statist.*, November 1987, *69*(4), pp. 651–60. **[G: U.S.]**

d'Intignano, Béatrice Majnoni. Funding Health for All—Is Insurance the Answer? Discussion. *World Health Organization.*, 1987, *1986*, pp. 68–70. **[G: Global]**

Iversen, Lars. Some Health Effects of the Closure of a Danish Shipyard a Three-Year Follow-Up Study. *Pedersen, P. J. and Lund, R., eds.*, 1987, pp. 305–20. **[G: Denmark]**

Jacobs, David C. The UAW and the Committee for National Health Insurance: The Contours of Social Unionism. *Lewin, D.; Lipsky, D. B. and Sockell, D., eds.*, 1987, pp. 119–40. **[G: U.S.]**

Jajoo, U. N.; Gupta, O. P. and Jain, A. P. Rural Health Services: Towards a New Strategy? *World Health Organization.*, 1987, *1985*, pp. 99–101. **[G: India]**

Jancloes, M., et al. Primary Health Care in a Senegalese Town: How the Local People Took Part. *World Health Organization.*, 1987, *1982*, pp. 102–05. **[G: Senegal]**

Jennison, Kathleen and Ellis, Randall P. A Comparison of Psychiatric Service Utilization in a Single Group Practice under Multiple Insurance Systems. *McGuire, T. G. and Scheffler, R. M., eds.*, 1987, pp. 175–94. **[G: U.S.]**

Jérôme-Forget, Monique. Health Care Cost Control: The Need to Articulate Measurable Objectives. *Economic Council of Canada.*, 1987, pp. 107–13. **[G: Canada]**

Joglekar, Prafulla N. Cost–Benefit Studies of Health Care Programs: Choosing Methods for Desired Results. *Cordray, D. S. and Lipsey, M. W., eds.*, 1987, *1984*, pp. 343–61.

John, Jacqueline Ann. Swing Beds: Assessing Flexible Health Care in Rural Communities: Quality of Care: Comments. *Wiener, J. M., ed.*, 1987, pp. 117–19. **[G: U.S.]**

Johns, Lucy. Selective Contracting for Health Services in California. *Meyer, J. A. and Lewin, M. E., eds.*, 1987, pp. 51–73. **[G: U.S.]**

Jones-Lee, M. W. The Economic Value of Life: A Comment. *Economica*, August 1987, *54*(215), pp. 397–400.

Jones, Stanley B.; DuVal, Merlin K. and Lesparre, Michael. Competition or Conscience? Mixed-Mission Dilemmas of the Voluntary

Hospital. *Inquiry*, Summer 1987, *24*(2), pp. 110–18. [G: U.S.]

Jönsson, Bengt. Health Care Costs Out of Control: The Experience of Switzerland: Discussion. *World Health Organization.*, 1987, 1985, pp. 117–18. [G: Sweden]

Juyal, R. K. Contribution of Health to Productivity in a Developing Area: An Economic Analysis. *Margin*, Apr.-June 1987, *19*(3), pp. 80–89. [G: LDCs]

Kane, Robert L. An American's View of the Canadian Health Care System: The Not So Innocents Abroad. *Economic Council of Canada.*, 1987, pp. 15–18. [G: Canada]

Kaplan, Mark S. Implications of Individualism in Public Health Policy. *J. Econ. Issues*, March 1987, *21*(1), pp. 349–56. [G: U.S.]

Karim, Rezaul and Ahmad, Khan Masood. An Economic Approach to Nutritional Surveillance. *Bangladesh Devel. Stud.*, September 1987, *15*(3), pp. 121–25.

Kass, David I. Economies of Scale and Scope in the Provision of Home Health Services. *J. Health Econ.*, June 1987, *6*(2), pp. 129–46. [G: U.S.]

Keeler, Emmett B. and Cretin, Shan. Uses of Cost–Benefit Analysis: Editorial. *J. Health Econ.*, September 1987, *6*(3), pp. 275–78.

Keeler, Emmett B.; Wells, Kenneth B. and Manning, Willard G. Markov and Other Models of Episodes of Mental Health Treatment. *McGuire, T. G. and Scheffler, R. M., eds.*, 1987, pp. 279–98. [G: U.S.]

Kemna, Harrie J. M. I. Working Conditions and the Relationship between Schooling and Health. *J. Health Econ.*, September 1987, *6*(3), pp. 189–210. [G: U.S.]

Kenny, Nuala. The Ethics of Restraint. *Economic Council of Canada.*, 1987, pp. 151–53.

Kimberly, John R. Privatization and Bidding in the Health-Care Sector: Comment. *J. Policy Anal. Manage.*, Summer 1987, *6*(4), pp. 671–73. [G: U.S.]

Kindig, David A., et al. Trends in Physician Availability in 10 Urban Areas from 1963 to 1980. *Inquiry*, Summer 1987, *24*(2), pp. 136–46. [G: U.S.]

Klees, Barbara and Warfield, Carter. Actuarial Status of the HI and SMI Trust Funds. *Soc. Sec. Bull.*, June 1987, *50*(6), pp. 11–20. [G: U.S.]

Klevorick, Alvin K. and McGuire, Thomas G. Monopolistic Competition and Consumer Information: Pricing in the Market for Psychologists' Services. *McGuire, T. G. and Scheffler, R. M., eds.*, 1987, pp. 235–53. [G: U.S.]

Knickman, James R. Swing Beds: Assessing Flexible Health Care in Rural Communities: Access and Case-Mix Patterns: Comments. *Wiener, J. M., ed.*, 1987, pp. 103–04. [G: U.S.]

Komlos, John. The Height and Weight of West Point Cadets: Dietary Change in Antebellum America. *J. Econ. Hist.*, December 1987, *47*(4), pp. 897–927. [G: U.S.]

Kovner, Anthony R. and Richardson, Hila. Swing Beds: Assessing Flexible Health Care in Rural

Communities: The Robert Wood Johnson Demonstration Program. *Wiener, J. M., ed.*, 1987, pp. 24–41. [G: U.S.]

Kumar, Shubh K. The Nutrition Situation and Its Food Policy Links. *Mellor, J. W.; Delgado, C. L. and Blackie, M. J., eds.*, 1987, pp. 39–52. [G: Africa]

Lairson, David R. and Herd, J. Alan. The Role of Health Practices, Health Status, and Prior Health Care Claims in HMO Selection Bias. *Inquiry*, Fall 1987, *24*(3), pp. 276–84. [G: U.S.]

Lapsley, Helen M. Goal Orientations and the Use of Budgeting Information: A Comparison between Physicians and Non-physicians in Public Teaching Hospitals: Discussion. *Butler, J. R. G. and Doessel, D. P., eds.*, 1987, pp. 93–94. [G: Australia]

Le Grand, Julian. Inequalities in Health: Some International Comparisons. *Europ. Econ. Rev.*, Feb./Mar. 1987, *31*(1/2), pp. 182–91. [G: Global]

Lee, Barbara A. and Parker, Joan. Supervisory Participation in Professional Associations: Implications of *North Shore University Hospital*. *Ind. Lab. Relat. Rev.*, April 1987, *40*(3), pp. 364–81.

Lehrer, Evelyn L. and White, William D. Hospital Market Structure and the Return to Nursing Education: Comment [Hospital Market Structure and the Return to Nursing Education]. *J. Human Res.*, Fall 1987, *22*(4), pp. 607–08. [G: U.S.]

Lingle, Earle W., Jr.; Kirk, Kenneth W. and Kelly, William R. The Impact of Outpatient Drug Benefits on the Use and Costs of Health Care Services for the Elderly. *Inquiry*, Fall 1987, *24*(3), pp. 203–11. [G: U.S.]

de Lissovoy, Gregory, et al. Preferred Provider Organizations One Year Later. *Inquiry*, Summer 1987, *24*(2), pp. 127–35. [G: U.S.]

Loslier, Luc. Disparités socio-spatiales de mortalité à Porto-Rico. (With English summary.) *Can. J. Devel. Stud.*, 1987, *8*(1), pp. 117–32. [G: Puerto Rico]

Lubitz, James. Health Status Adjustments for Medicare Capitation. *Inquiry*, Winter 1987, *24*(4), pp. 362–75. [G: U.S.]

Ludlow, Stephen E. Food and Nutrition in Pakistan (A Cross-regional Study): Comments. *Pakistan Devel. Rev.*, Winter 1987, *26*(4), pp. 497–98. [G: Pakistan]

Lynk, William J. Antitrust Analysis and Hospital Certificate-of-Need Policy. *Antitrust Bull.*, Spring 1987, *32*(1), pp. 61–84. [G: U.S.]

Lynk, William J. and Morrisey, Michael A. The Economic Basis of *Hyde*: Are Market Power and Hospital Exclusive Contracts Related? *J. Law Econ.*, October 1987, *30*(2), pp. 399–421. [G: U.S.]

Lyttle, Christopher S. Ambulatory Care and Insurance Coverage in an Era of Constraint: Description of Variables. *Andersen, R. M., et al.*, 1987, pp. 195–215. [G: U.S.]

Lyttle, Christopher S. Ambulatory Care and Insurance Coverage in an Era of Constraint: Standard Errors of Estimates. *Andersen, R. M., et al.*, 1987, pp. 217–27.   [G: U.S.]

Lyttle, Christopher S. and Aday, Lu Ann. Ambulatory Care and Insurance Coverage in an Era of Constraint: Description of Data Sets. *Andersen, R. M., et al.*, 1987, pp. 29–40.
     [G: U.S.]

Manning, Willard G., et al. Health Insurance and the Demand for Medical Care: Evidence from a Randomized Experiment. *Amer. Econ. Rev.*, June 1987, 77(3), pp. 251–77.   [G: U.S.]

Manton, Kenneth G. The Interaction of Population Aging and Health Transitions at Later Ages: New Evidence and Insights. *Schramm, C. J., ed.*, 1987, pp. 185–221.   [G: U.S.]

Manton, Kenneth G. The Linkage of Morbidity and Mortality: Implications of Increasing Life Expectancy at Later Ages for Health Service Demand. *Economic Council of Canada.*, 1987, pp. 39–50.   [G: Canada]

Manton, Kenneth G. The Population Implications of Breakthroughs in Biomedical Technologies for Controlling Mortality and Fertility. *Espenshade, T. and Stolnitz, G. J., eds.*, 1987, pp. 147–93.

Marquis, M. Susan and Phelps, Charles E. Price Elasticity and Adverse Selection in the Demand for Supplementary Health Insurance. *Econ. Inquiry*, April 1987, 25(2), pp. 299–313.
     [G: U.S.]

Maxwell, James H. and Sapolsky, Harvey M. The First DRG: Lessons from the End Stage Renal Disease Program for the Prospective Payment System. *Inquiry*, Spring 1987, 24(1), pp. 57–67.   [G: U.S.]

Maxwell, Judith. Aging with Limited Health Resources: Closing Remarks. *Economic Council of Canada.*, 1987, pp. 175–76.   [G: Canada]

Maxwell, Judith. Aging with Limited Health Resources: Introduction. *Economic Council of Canada.*, 1987, pp. 1–3.   [G: Canada]

McKinney, Frederick W. The Economic Survival of Black Physicians: Swimming in Turbulent Waters. *Rev. Black Polit. Econ.*, Spring 1987, 15(4), pp. 35–46.   [G: U.S.]

McMenamin, Peter. Medicare Part B: Rising Assignment Rates, Rising Costs: Symposium Report. *Inquiry*, Winter 1987, 24(4), pp. 344–59.   [G: U.S.]

Mercenier, P. and Van Balen, H. Primary Health Care for Less Than a Dollar a Year. *World Health Organization.*, 1987, 1984, pp. 91–95.
     [G: Zaire]

Merrill, Jeffrey C. and Cohen, Alan B. The Emperor's New Clothes: Unraveling the Myths about Rationing. *Inquiry*, Summer 1987, 24(2), pp. 105–09.   [G: U.S.]

Meyer, Jack A. and Lewin, Marion Ein. Charting the Future of Health Care: Introduction. *Meyer, J. A. and Lewin, M. E., eds.*, 1987, pp. 1–9.   [G: U.S.]

Midgley, James. Funding Health for All—Is Insurance the Answer? Discussion. *World Health Organization.*, 1987, 1986, pp. 70–73.
     [G: Global]

Miller, Irwin. Interpreneurship: A Community

Coalition Approach to Health Care Reform. *Inquiry*, Fall 1987, 24(3), pp. 266–75.
     [G: U.S.]

Miranda Gutiérrez, Guido. Funding Health for All—Is Insurance the Answer? Discussion. *World Health Organization.*, 1987, 1986, pp. 73–75.   [G: Global]

Mitchell, Janet B., et. al. Packaging Physician Services: Alternative Approaches to Medicare Part B Reimbursement: Symposium Report. *Inquiry*, Winter 1987, 24(4), pp. 324–43.
     [G: U.S.]

Mitchell, Jean M. Demand for Psychiatric Services: A Clinical Episode Model for Specifying "The Product": Comments. *McGuire, T. G. and Scheffler, R. M., eds.*, 1987, pp. 275–78.
     [G: U.S.]

Moore, Kenneth. Swing-Bed Reimbursement: Objectives and Options: Comments. *Wiener, J. M., ed.*, 1987, pp. 84–85.   [G: U.S.]

Morrisey, Michael A. and Alexander, Jeffrey A. Hospital Participation in Multihospital Systems. *Scheffler, R. M. and Rossiter, L. F., eds.*, 1987, pp. 59–81.   [G: U.S.]

Mosley, W. Henry and Jolly, Richard. Health Policy and Programme Options: Compensating for the Negative Effects of Economic Adjustment. *Cornia, G. A.; Jolly, R. and Stewart, F., eds.*, 1987, pp. 218–31.   [G: LDCs]

Muhr, Gerd. Funding Health for All—Is Insurance the Answer? Discussion. *World Health Organization.*, 1987, 1986, pp. 75–78.
     [G: W. Germany]

Mullner, Ross M. and Andersen, Ronald M. A Descriptive and Financial Ratio Analysis of Merged and Consolidated Hospitals: United States, 1980–1985. *Scheffler, R. M. and Rossiter, L. F., eds.*, 1987, pp. 41–58.   [G: U.S.]

Muraleedharan, V. R. Rural Health Care in Madras Presidency: 1919–39. *Indian Econ. Soc. Hist. Rev.*, July-Sept. 1987, 24(3), pp. 323–34.   [G: India]

Murphy, Mary Zimmerman. The Importance of Sample Selection Bias in the Estimation of Medical Care Demand Equations. *Eastern Econ. J.*, Jan.-Mar. 1987, 13(1), pp. 19–29.
     [G: U.S.]

Mustard, Fraser. Canada's Future Health Care Program: Options for Change. *Economic Council of Canada.*, 1987, pp. 168–73.
     [G: Canada]

Newhouse, Joseph P. Cross National Differences in Health Spending: What Do They Mean? Editorial. *J. Health Econ.*, June 1987, 6(2), pp. 159–62.   [G: U.S.]

Newhouse, Joseph P. Health Economics and Econometrics. *Amer. Econ. Rev.*, May 1987, 77(2), pp. 269–74.   [G: U.S.]

Nye, Blaine F. and Hofflander, Alfred E. Economics of Oligopoly: Medical Malpractice Insurance as a Classic Illustration. *J. Risk Ins.*, September 1987, 54(3), pp. 502–19.
     [G: U.S.]

Nyman, John A. Improving the Quality of Nursing Homes: Regulation or Competition? *J. Policy*

Anal. Manage., Winter 1987, *6*(2), pp. 247–51. [G: U.S.]

Ohsfeldt, Robert L.; Culler, Steven D. and Becker, Edmund R. Sex Differences in the Economic Advantages of Physician Board Certification. *Southern Econ. J.*, October 1987, *54*(2), pp. 343–50. [G: U.S.]

Owen, Jack W. The Meaning of the Swing-Bed Experience: Comments. *Wiener, J. M., ed.*, 1987, pp. 135–37. [G: U.S.]

Palmer, George R. The Economics and Financing of Hospitals in Australia. *Butler, J. R. G. and Doessel, D. P., eds.*, 1987, pp. 1–21. [G: Australia]

Parkin, David; McGuire, Alistair and Yule, Brian. Aggregate Health Care Expenditures and National Income: Is Health Care a Luxury Good? *J. Health Econ.*, June 1987, *6*(2), pp. 109–27. [G: OECD]

Pauly, Mark V. Monopsony Power in Health Insurance: Thinking Straight while Standing on Your Head: Editorial. *J. Health Econ.*, March 1987, *6*(1), pp. 73–81. [G: U.S.]

Pauly, Mark V. Nonprofit Firms in Medical Markets. *Amer. Econ. Rev.*, May 1987, *77*(2), pp. 257–62. [G: U.S.]

Peltzman, Sam. Regulation and Health: The Case of Mandatory Prescriptions and an Extension. *Managerial Dec. Econ.*, March 1987, *8*(1), pp. 41–46. [G: Selected Countries]

Peltzman, Sam. The Health Effects of Mandatory Prescriptions. *J. Law Econ.*, October 1987, *30*(2), pp. 207–38. [G: U.S.]

Pfeffer, Jeffrey and O'Reilly, Charles A., III. Hospital Demography and Turnover among Nurses. *Ind. Relat.*, Spring 1987, *26*(2), pp. 158–73. [G: U.S.]

Philips, T. J. The Costs of Long-Stay Hospital Care of the Dependent Elderly: Discussion. *Butler, J. R. G. and Doessel, D. P., eds.*, 1987, pp. 113–15. [G: New Zealand]

Pinstrup-Andersen, Per. Adjustment with a Human Face: Protecting the Vulnerable and Promoting Growth: Nutrition Interventions. *Cornia, G. A.; Jolly, R. and Stewart, F., eds.*, 1987, pp. 241–56. [G: LDCs]

Podgursky, Michael and Swaim, Paul. Health Insurance Loss: The Case of the Displaced Worker. *Mon. Lab. Rev.*, April 1987, *110*(4), pp. 30–33. [G: U.S.]

Press, Stephen. The Meaning of the Swing-Bed Experience: Comments. *Wiener, J. M., ed.*, 1987, pp. 132–35.

Rappaport, Anna M. and Kalman, Robert W. The Future of Employer-Sponsored Retiree Medical Plans. *Inquiry*, Spring 1987, *24*(1), pp. 26–35. [G: U.S.]

Register, Charles Alan and Bruning, Edward R. Profit Incentives and Technical Efficiency in the Production of Hospital Care. *Southern Econ. J.*, April 1987, *53*(4), pp. 899–914. [G: U.S.]

Regula, Ralph. National Policy and the Medically Uninsured. *Inquiry*, Spring 1987, *24*(1), pp. 48–56. [G: U.S.]

Reinhardt, Hsiao Lien; Reinhardt, Hsiao Nio and

Reinhardt, Uwe E. Lessons for Hospital Payment for Ornithology. *J. Policy Anal. Manage.*, Spring 1987, *6*(3), pp. 449–50.

Reinhardt, Uwe E. A Clarification of Theories and Evidence on Supplier-Induced Demand for Physicians' Services: Comment [The Theory of Physician-Induced Demand After a Decade]. *J. Human Res.*, Fall 1987, *22*(4), pp. 621–23. [G: U.S.]

Reinhardt, Uwe E. Privatization and Bidding in the Health-Care Sector: Comment. *J. Policy Anal. Manage.*, Summer 1987, *6*(4), pp. 666–71. [G: U.S.]

Renn, Steven C. The Structure and Financing of the Health Care Delivery System of the 1980s. *Schramm, C. J., ed.*, 1987, pp. 8–48. [G: U.S.]

Rettig, Richard A. Medical Technology in a Changing Health Care Environment. *Meyer, J. A. and Lewin, M. E., eds.*, 1987, pp. 98–117. [G: U.S.]

Rice, Thomas. Induced Demand—Can We Ever Know Its Extent? Comment. *J. Health Econ.*, December 1987, *6*(4), pp. 375–76.

Rice, Thomas. Payment System Alternatives for Addressing Systematic Risk in a Prospective Payment System: Comments. *McGuire, T. G. and Scheffler, R. M., eds.*, 1987, pp. 71–73. [G: U.S.]

Richardson, Jeff. Testing a Disequilibrium Model of Supplier-Induced Demand: Discussion. *Butler, J. R. G. and Doessel, D. P., eds.*, 1987, pp. 41–44. [G: Canada]

Richardson, Jeff. The Case for Universal Bulk Billing. *Butler, J. R. G. and Doessel, D. P., eds.*, 1987, pp. 197–223. [G: Australia]

Riley, Gerald, et al. The Use and Costs of Medicare Services by Cause of Death. *Inquiry*, Fall 1987, *24*(3), pp. 233–44. [G: U.S.]

Robertson, Duncan. Alternative Methods of Health Care Delivery for Canada's Aging Population. *Economic Council of Canada.*, 1987, pp. 59–68. [G: Canada]

Roemer, Milton I. Funding Health for All—Is Insurance the Answer? Discussion. *World Health Organization.*, 1987, *1986*, pp. 78–80. [G: Latin America]

Roos, Noralou P.; Shapiro, Evelyn and Havens, Betty. Aging with Limited Resources: What Should We Really Be Worried About? *Economic Council of Canada.*, 1987, pp. 50–56. [G: Canada]

Rossiter, Louis F. and Wilensky, Gail R. Health Economist-Induced Demand for Theories of Physician-Induced Demand. *J. Human Res.*, Fall 1987, *22*(4), pp. 624–27. [G: U.S.]

Roth, Gabriel. Roles of the Private Sector in the Supply of Public Services in Less Developed Countries. *Kent, C. A., ed.*, 1987, pp. 195–206. [G: LDCs]

Rowland, Diane. Meeting the Long-term Care Needs of an Aging Population. *Schramm, C. J., ed.*, 1987, pp. 222–51. [G: U.S.]

Rowntree, J. A. Some Recent Developments in Health Service Information in England: The Korner Review and Performance Indicators.

Statist. J., December 1987, 5(1), pp. 13–41.
[G: U.K.]

Rubin, Jeffrey. Discrimination and Insurance Coverage of the Mentally Ill. *McGuire, T. G. and Scheffler, R. M., eds.*, 1987, pp. 195–209.
[G: U.S.]

Ruiz Alvarez, José Luis and Carrasco Garcia, Nicolás. Desarrollo económico y niveles de salud en España. (With English summary.) *Invest. Econ.*, January 1987, 11(1), pp. 133–50.
[G: Spain]

Russe, Catherine M. and Anderson, Gerard F. Hospital Reorganization: Examining the Effects on Medical Education. *Scheffler, R. M. and Rossiter, L. F., eds.*, 1987, pp. 141–56.
[G: U.S.]

Russell, Louise B. Cost-Effectiveness Analysis in Setting Priorities for Prevention: Promises and Problems. *Meyer, J. A. and Lewin, M. E., eds.*, 1987, pp. 121–32.
[G: U.S.]

Rutten, Frans F. H. Health Care Costs Out of Control: The Experience of Switzerland: Discussion. *World Health Organization.*, 1987, 1985, pp. 118–20.
[G: Switzerland]

Sammartino, Frank J. The Effect of Health on Retirement. *Soc. Sec. Bull.*, February 1987, 50(2), pp. 31–47.

Santana, Sarah M. The Cuban Health Care System: Responsiveness to Changing Needs and Demands. *Zimbalist, A., ed.*, 1987, pp. 115–27.
[G: Cuba]

Santana, Sarah M. The Cuban Health Care System: Responsiveness to Changing Population Needs and Demands. *World Devel.*, January 1987, 15(1), pp. 113–25.
[G: Cuba]

Sathar, Zeba A. Health for All by the Year 2000: Can Pakistan Meet the Target? Comments. *Pakistan Devel. Rev.*, Winter 1987, 26(4), pp. 482–84.
[G: Pakistan]

Schick, Allen. Controlling the "Uncontrollables": Budgeting for Health Care in an Age of Megadeficits. *Meyer, J. A. and Lewin, M. E., eds.*, 1987, pp. 13–34.
[G: U.S.]

Schieber, George J. Recent Trends in Health Care Expenditure and Utilization in OECD Countries. *Atlantic Econ. J.*, September 1987, 15(3), pp. 9–21.
[G: OECD]

Schlenker, Robert. Swing-Bed Reimbursement: Objectives and Options: Comments. *Wiener, J. M., ed.*, 1987, pp. 81–84.
[G: U.S.]

Schlesinger, Mark, et al. Multihospital Systems and Access to Health Care. *Scheffler, R. M. and Rossiter, L. F., eds.*, 1987, pp. 121–40.
[G: U.S.]

Schwefel, Detlef. Health Care Costs Out of Control: The Experience of Switzerland: Discussion. *World Health Organization.*, 1987, 1985, pp. 120–22.
[G: W. Germany]

Seidl, Vladimir and Pruss, Ladislav. La sécurité sociale en Tchécoslovaquie: Évolution 1970–1985. (Social Security in Czechoslovakia, 1970–1985. With English summary.) *Écon. Soc.*, February 1987, 21(2), pp. 157–71.
[G: Czechoslovakia]

Shaughnessy, Peter W. Swing Beds: Assessing Flexible Health Care in Rural Communities:

Access and Case-Mix Patterns. *Wiener, J. M., ed.*, 1987, pp. 86–100.
[G: U.S.]

Short, Tobin and Goldfarb, Marsha G. Redistribution of Revenues under a Prototypical Prospective Payment System: Characteristics of Winners and Losers. *J. Policy Anal. Manage.*, Spring 1987, 6(3), pp. 385–401.
[G: U.S.]

Shortell, Stephen M., et al. Diversification of Health Care Services: The Effects of Ownership, Environment, and Strategy. *Scheffler, R. M. and Rossiter, L. F., eds.*, 1987, pp. 3–40.
[G: U.S.]

Showstack, Jonathan A., et. al. Episode-of-Care Physician Payment: A Study of Coronary Artery Bypass Graft Surgery. *Inquiry*, Winter 1987, 24(4), pp. 376–83.
[G: U.S.]

Siegel, Carole; Laska, Eugene and Lin, Shang. Decision Theory Models for Choosing Prospective Payment Schemes: A Negotiated Approach between Payers and Providers. *McGuire, T. G. and Scheffler, R. M., eds.*, 1987, pp. 143–55.
[G: U.S.]

Silverman, Mervyn F. AIDS—Past, Present, and Future Issues. *Meyer, J. A. and Lewin, M. E., eds.*, 1987, pp. 149–59.
[G: U.S.]

Simanis, Joseph G. Health Care Expenditures: International Comparisons, 1970–80. *Soc. Sec. Bull.*, October 1987, 50(10), pp. 19–24.
[G: OECD]

Sisk, Jane E., et al. An Analysis of Methods to Reform Medicare Payment for Physician Services. *Inquiry*, Spring 1987, 24(1), pp. 36–47.
[G: U.S.]

Slade, John. The Ways Cigarettes Contribute to GNP. *Eastern Econ. J.*, October-December 1987, 13(4), pp. 353–59.
[G: U.S.]

Sloan, Frank A.; Morrisey, Michael A. and Valvona, Joseph. Capital Markets and the Growth of Multihospital Systems. *Scheffler, R. M. and Rossiter, L. F., eds.*, 1987, pp. 83–109.
[G: U.S.]

Smits, Helen L. Swing Beds: Assessing Flexible Health Care in Rural Communities: Quality of Care. *Wiener, J. M., ed.*, 1987, pp. 105–14.
[G: U.S.]

Somerville, Margaret A. Structuring the Decision Making in the Allocation of Scarce Medical Resources. *Economic Council of Canada.*, 1987, pp. 144–51.
[G: Canada]

Sommer, Jürg H. Health Care Costs Out of Control: The Experience of Switzerland. *World Health Organization.*, 1987, pp. 106–12.
[G: Switzerland]

Stano, Miron. A Clarification of Theories and Evidence on Supplier-Induced Demand for Physicians' Services [The Theory of Physician-Initiated Demand]. *J. Human Res.*, Fall 1987, 22(4), pp. 611–20.
[G: U.S.]

Stano, Miron. A Further Analysis of the Physician Inducement Controversy. *J. Health Econ.*, September 1987, 6(3), pp. 227–38.

Starkweather, David B. and Carman, James M. Horizontal and Vertical Concentrations in the Evolution of Hospital Competition. *Scheffler, R. M. and Rossiter, L. F., eds.*, 1987, pp. 179–94.
[G: U.S.]

Staten, Michael; Dunkelberg, William and Umbeck, John. Market Share and the Illusion of Power: Can Blue Cross Force Hospitals to Discount? *J. Health Econ.*, March 1987, *6*(1), pp. 43–58. [G: U.S.]

Stavrinos, Vasilios G. The Effects of an Anti-smoking Campaign on Cigarette Consumption: Empirical Evidence from Greece. *Appl. Econ.*, March 1987, *19*(3), pp. 323–29. [G: Greece]

Stoddart, Greg L. Alternative Methods of Health Care Delivery for Canada's Aging Population: Commentary. *Economic Council of Canada.*, 1987, pp. 68–71. [G: Canada]

Straub, LaVonne A. and Lane, Julia. Response [Hospital Market Structure and the Return to Nursing Education]. *J. Human Res.*, Fall 1987, *22*(4), pp. 609–10. [G: U.S.]

Strauss, Anselm, et al. The Hospital and Its Negotiated Order. *Zartman, I. W., ed. (I)*, 1987, *1963*, pp. 98–117.

Streett, Craig A. State Programs and Supplemental Security Income for the Aged, Blind, and Disabled, April 1987. *Soc. Sec. Bull.*, May 1987, *50*(5), pp. 67–70. [G: U.S.]

Svorny, Shirley V. Physician Licensure: A New Approach to Examining the Role of Professional Interests. *Econ. Inquiry*, July 1987, *25*(3), pp. 497–509. [G: U.S.]

Tanner, Christopher. Malnutrition and the Development of Rural Households in the Agreste of Paraiba State, North-East Brazil. *J. Devel. Stud.*, January 1987, *23*(2), pp. 242–64. [G: Brazil]

Tarimo, E. Good Intentions Are Not Enough. *World Health Organization.*, 1987, *1984*, pp. 24–29. [G: Africa]

Tatchell, Michael. Family-Based Social Welfare Schemes: The Case of Pharmaceuticals: Discussion. *Butler, J. R. G. and Doessel, D. P., eds.*, 1987, pp. 194–96. [G: Australia]

Tell, Eileen J.; Cohen, Marc A. and Wallack, Stanley S. Life Care at Home: A New Model for Financing and Delivering Long-term Care. *Inquiry*, Fall 1987, *24*(3), pp. 245–52. [G: U.S.]

Thorpe, Kenneth E. The Distributional Implications of Using Relative Prices in DRG Payment Systems. *Inquiry*, Spring 1987, *24*(1), pp. 85–95. [G: U.S.]

Tolley, H. Dennis; Manton, Kenneth G. and Vertrees, James. An Evaluation of Three Payment Strategies for Capitation for Medicare. *J. Risk Ins.*, December 1987, *54*(4), pp. 678–90. [G: U.S.]

Vamoer, Alexander P. Defining the Food and Nutrition Problem: Commentary. *Mellor, J. W.; Delgado, C. L. and Blackie, M. J., eds.*, 1987, pp. 53–56. [G: Africa]

Viscusi, W. Kip; Magat, Wesley A. and Huber, Joel C. An Investigation of the Rationality of Consumer Valuations of Multiple Health Risks. *Rand J. Econ.*, Winter 1987, *18*(4), pp. 465–79. [G: U.S.]

Vitaliano, Donald F. On the Estimation of Hospital Cost Functions. *J. Health Econ.*, December 1987, *6*(4), pp. 305–18. [G: U.S.]

Vladeck, Bruce C. The Meaning of the Swing-Bed Experience. *Wiener, J. M., ed.*, 1987, pp. 120–32. [G: U.S.]

van Vliet, René C. J. A. and van Praag, Bernard M. S. Health Status Estimation on the Basis of Mimic-Health Care Models. *J. Health Econ.*, March 1987, *6*(1), pp. 27–42. [G: Netherlands]

Vongvipanond, Pairoj. Problems and Progress in Health Economics in Thailand. *Butler, J. R. G. and Doessel, D. P., eds.*, 1987, pp. 136–41.

Wadhawan, Sahdev K. Health Insurance in India: The Case for Reform. *Int. Lab. Rev.*, July-Aug. 1987, *126*(4), pp. 479–94. [G: India]

Walker, Alan. Meeting the Needs of Canada's Elderly with Limited Health Resources: Some Observations Based on British Experience. *Economic Council of Canada.*, 1987, pp. 27–39. [G: Canada]

Wallace, Robert. The Industries Assistance Commission's Report on Pharmaceutical Products. *Butler, J. R. G. and Doessel, D. P., eds.*, 1987, pp. 144–59. [G: Australia]

Wallen, Jacqueline. Resource Use by Psychiatric Patients in Community Hospitals: The Influence of Illness Severity, Physician Specialty, and Presence of a Psychiatric Unit. *McGuire, T. G. and Scheffler, R. M., eds.*, 1987, pp. 103–26. [G: U.S.]

Weisbrod, Burton A. Research Issues in Economics and Mental Health. *McGuire, T. G. and Scheffler, R. M., eds.*, 1987, pp. 303–05.

Welch, W. P. Do All Teaching Hospitals Deserve an Add-on Payment under the Prospective Payment System? *Inquiry*, Fall 1987, *24*(3), pp. 221–32. [G: U.S.]

Weller, Robert H.; Eberstein, Isaac W. and Bailey, Mohamed. Pregnancy Wantedness and Maternal Behavior during Pregnancy. *Demography*, August 1987, *24*(3), pp. 407–12. [G: U.S.]

White-Means, Shelley I. Migrant Farmworker Earnings: A Human Capital Approach. *Rev. Black Polit. Econ.*, Spring 1987, *15*(4), pp. 21–33. [G: U.S.]

White, William D. The Introduction of Professional Regulation and Labor Market Conditions—Occupational Licensure of Registered Nurses. *Policy Sci.*, April 1987, *20*(1), pp. 27–51. [G: U.S.]

Whiteside, Noel. Counting the Cost: Sickness and Disability among Working People in an Era of Industrial Recession, 1920–39. *Econ. Hist. Rev., 2nd Ser.*, May 1987, *40*(2), pp. 228–46. [G: U.S.]

Wiemer, Calla. Optimal Disease Control through Combined Use of Preventive and Curative Measures. *J. Devel. Econ.*, April 1987, *25*(2), pp. 301–19. [G: China]

Wiener, Joshua M. Swing Beds: Assessing Flexible Health Care in Rural Communities: Policy Issues. *Wiener, J. M., ed.*, 1987, pp. 13–23. [G: U.S.]

Wiener, Joshua M. Swing Beds: Assessing Flexible Health Care in Rural Communities: Introduction and Summary. *Wiener, J. M., ed.*, 1987, pp. 1–12. **[G: U.S.]**

Wigle, Donald T. Health Objectives for Canada. *Economic Council of Canada.*, 1987, pp. 92–101. **[G: Canada]**

Wilder, Ronald P. and Jacobs, Philip. Antitrust Considerations for Hospital Mergers: Market Definition and Market Concentration. *Scheffler, R. M. and Rossiter, L. F., eds.*, 1987, pp. 245–62. **[G: U.S.]**

Willim, Horst. Trade Unions and Occupational Safety in the German Democratic Republic. *Int. Lab. Rev.*, 1987, *126*(3), pp. 329–36. **[G: E. Germany]**

Wilson, Donald A. Swing Beds: Assessing Flexible Health Care in Rural Communities: Cost Issues: Comments. *Wiener, J. M., ed.*, 1987, pp. 63.

Wilson, Robert A. Returns to Entering the Medical Profession in the U.K. *J. Health Econ.*, December 1987, *6*(4), pp. 339–63. **[G: U.K.]**

Włodarczyk, W. Cezary. Funding Health for All—Is Insurance the Answer? Discussion. *World Health Organization.*, 1987, *1986*, pp. 80–82. **[G: Global]**

Wolfe, Barbara L. and Behrman, Jere R. Women's Schooling and Children's Health: Are the Effects Robust with Adult Sibling Control for the Women's Childhood Background? *J. Health Econ.*, September 1987, *6*(3), pp. 239–54. **[G: Nicaragua]**

Woodward, Allan. Comments on Ratio Analysis of Merged Hospitals. *Scheffler, R. M. and Rossiter, L. F., eds.*, 1987, pp. 115–17. **[G: U.S.]**

Worrall, John D.; Appel, David and Butler, Richard J. Sex, Marital Status, and Medical Utilization by Injured Workers. *J. Risk Ins.*, March 1987, *54*(1), pp. 27–44. **[G: U.S.]**

Wright, James D. The National Health Care for the Homeless Program. *Bingham, R. D.; Green, R. E. and White, S. B., eds.*, 1987, pp. 150–69. **[G: U.S.]**

Wyszewianski, Leon; Thomas, J. William and Friedman, Bruce A. Case-Based Payment and the Control of Quality and Efficiency in Hospitals. *Inquiry*, Spring 1987, *24*(1), pp. 17–25. **[G: U.S.]**

Ycas, Martynas A. Recent Trends in Health near the Age of Retirement: New Findings from the Health Interview Survey. *Soc. Sec. Bull.*, February 1987, *50*(2), pp. 5–30. **[G: U.S.]**

Zaidi, S. Akbar. Health for All by the Year 2000: Can Pakistan Meet the Target? *Pakistan Devel. Rev.*, Winter 1987, *26*(4), pp. 473–81. **[G: Pakistan]**

Zanias, George P. The Demand for Cigarettes: Habit Formation and Health Scare. *Greek Econ. Rev.*, 1987, *9*(2), pp. 248–62. **[G: Greece]**

Zuckerman, Stephen. Commercial Insurers and All-Payer Regulation: Evidence on Hospitals' Responses to Financial Need. *J. Health Econ.*, September 1987, *6*(3), pp. 165–87. **[G: U.S.]**

9140 Economics of Poverty

Aboagye, A.; Gozo, K. and Ahmed, Iftikhar. World Recession and Global Interdependence: Sub-Saharan Africa. *International Labour Office.*, 1987, pp. 75–98. **[G: Sub-Saharan Africa]**

Addison, Tony and Demery, Lionel. Alleviating Poverty under Structural Adjustment. *Finance Develop.*, December 1987, *24*(4), pp. 41–43.

Anderson, Gary Michael. Welfare Programs in the Rent-Seeking Society. *Southern Econ. J.*, October 1987, *54*(2), pp. 377–86. **[G: U.S.]**

Atkinson, Anthony B. On the Measurement of Poverty. *Econometrica*, July 1987, *55*(4), pp. 749–64. **[G: U.S.]**

Bergmann, Barbara R. A Fresh Start on Welfare Reform. *Challenge*, Nov./Dec. 1987, *30*(5), pp. 44–50. **[G: U.S.]**

Bigsten, Arne. Poverty, Inequality and Development. *Gemmell, N., ed.*, 1987, pp. 135–71. **[G: LDCs]**

Bird, Richard M. A New Look at Indirect Taxation in Developing Countries. *World Devel.*, September 1987, *15*(9), pp. 1151–61. **[G: LDCs]**

Blaylock, James R. Evaluating Food Plans and Poverty Thresholds. *Appl. Econ.*, October 1987, *19*(10), pp. 1341–52. **[G: U.S.]**

Bradbury, Bruce; Rossiter, Chris and Vipond, Joan. Housing and Poverty in Australia. *Urban Stud.*, April 1987, *24*(2), pp. 95–102. **[G: Australia]**

Brown, Charles C. and Oates, Wallace E. Assistance to the Poor in a Federal System. *J. Public Econ.*, April 1987, *32*(3), pp. 307–30. **[G: U.S.; U.K.]**

Burns, Leland S. Third World Solutions to the Homelessness Problem. *Bingham, R. D.; Green, R. E. and White, S. B., eds.*, 1987, pp. 231–48.

Carliner, Michael S. Homelessness: A Housing Problem? *Bingham, R. D.; Green, R. E. and White, S. B., eds.*, 1987, pp. 119–28. **[G: U.S.]**

Carson, Emmett D. The Charitable Activities of Black Americans: A Portrait of Self-help? *Rev. Black Polit. Econ.*, Winter 1987, *15*(3), pp. 100–111. **[G: U.S.]**

Cooper, Mary Anderson. The Role of Religious and Nonprofit Organizations in Combating Homelessness. *Bingham, R. D.; Green, R. E. and White, S. B., eds.*, 1987, pp. 130–49. **[G: U.S.]**

Cornelisse, Peter A. A 'World' Distribution of Income and of Real Poverty and Affluence: Comments. *Pakistan Devel. Rev.*, Autumn 1987, *26*(3), pp. 300–302. **[G: Global]**

Cornia, Giovanni Andrea. Adjustment at the Household Level: Potentials and Limitations of Survival Strategies. *Cornia, G. A.; Jolly, R. and Stewart, F., eds.*, 1987, pp. 90–104. **[G: LDCs]**

Cornia, Giovanni Andrea. Adjustment Policies

1980–1985: Effects on Child Welfare. *Cornia, G. A.; Jolly, R. and Stewart, F., eds.*, 1987, pp. 48–72. **[G: LDCs]**

Cornia, Giovanni Andrea. Economic Decline and Human Welfare in the First Half of the 1980s. *Cornia, G. A.; Jolly, R. and Stewart, F., eds.*, 1987, pp. 11–47. **[G: Global]**

Cornia, Giovanni Andrea. Social Policy-making: Restructuring, Targeting Efficiency. *Cornia, G. A.; Jolly, R. and Stewart, F., eds.*, 1987, pp. 165–82.

Cornia, Giovanni Andrea; Jolly, Richard and Stewart, Frances. Adjustment with a Human Face: Protecting the Vulnerable and Promoting Growth: An Overview of the Alternative Approach. *Cornia, G. A.; Jolly, R. and Stewart, F., eds.*, 1987, pp. 131–46.

Cornia, Giovanni Andrea; Jolly, Richard and Stewart, Frances. Adjustment with a Human Face: Protecting the Vulnerable and Promoting Growth: Summary and Conclusions. *Cornia, G. A.; Jolly, R. and Stewart, F., eds.*, 1987, pp. 287–97.

Cornia, Giovanni Andrea; Jolly, Richard and Stewart, Frances. Adjustment with a Human Face: Protecting the Vulnerable and Promoting Growth: Introduction. *Cornia, G. A.; Jolly, R. and Stewart, F., eds.*, 1987, pp. 1–8.

Cornia, Giovanni Andrea and Stewart, Frances. Country Experience with Adjustment. *Cornia, G. A.; Jolly, R. and Stewart, F., eds.*, 1987, pp. 105–27. **[G: LDCs]**

Cuomo, Mario M. The State Role: New York State's Approach to Homelessness. *Bingham, R. D.; Green, R. E. and White, S. B., eds.*, 1987, pp. 199–215. **[G: U.S.]**

Curry, Robert L., Jr. Poverty and Mass Unemployment in Mineral-Rich Botswana. *Amer. J. Econ. Soc.*, January 1987, 46(1), pp. 71–87. **[G: Botswana]**

Danziger, Sheldon and Gottschalk, Peter. Earnings Inequality, the Spatial Concentration of Poverty, and the Underclass. *Amer. Econ. Rev.*, May 1987, 77(2), pp. 211–15. **[G: U.S.]**

Darity, William A., Jr. and Myers, Samuel L., Jr. Do Transfer Payments Keep the Poor in Poverty? *Amer. Econ. Rev.*, May 1987, 77(2), pp. 216–22. **[G: U.S.]**

Das Gupta, Monica. Informal Security Mechanisms and Population Retention in Rural India. *Econ. Develop. Cult. Change*, October 1987, 36(1), pp. 101–20. **[G: India]**

Demery, Lionel and Addison, Tony. Stabilization Policy and Income Distribution in Developing Countries. *World Devel.*, December 1987, 15(12), pp. 1483–98. **[G: LDCs]**

Donnison, David. Poverty, Power and Stigma: The Case of the Single Homeless. *Turner, B.; Kemeny, J. and Lundqvist, L. J., eds.*, 1987, pp. 107–15. **[G: U.K.]**

Easterlin, Richard A. The New Age Structure of Poverty in America: Permanent or Transient? *Population Devel. Rev.*, June 1987, 13(2), pp. 195–208. **[G: U.S.]**

Euzéby, Chantal. A Minimum Guaranteed Income: Experiments and Proposals. *Int. Lab. Rev.*, 1987, 126(3), pp. 253–76. **[G: OECD]**

Griffin, Keith. Rural Poverty in Asia: Analysis and Policy Alternatives. *Griffin, K.*, 1987, 1985, pp. 25–63.

Griffin, Keith. The Economic Crisis in Ethiopia. *Griffin, K.*, 1987, pp. 183–202. **[G: Ethiopia]**

Griffin, Keith. World Hunger and the World Economy. *Griffin, K.*, 1987, pp. 1–24. **[G: Global]**

Gupta, Vinod K. Removal of Poverty and Commodity Taxation: A Suggested Approach. *Indian Econ. J.*, July-Sept. 1987, 35(1), pp. 83–96. **[G: India]**

Gutman, Pablo. Pobreza urbana: explorando algunas microsoluciones para macroproblemas. (With English summary.) *Desarrollo Econ.*, July-Sept. 1987, 27(106), pp. 279–89. **[G: Argentina]**

Hagenaars, Aldi J. M. A Class of Poverty Indices. *Int. Econ. Rev.*, October 1987, 28(3), pp. 583–607.

Haveman, Robert H. U.S. Anti-poverty Policy and the Non-poor: Some Estimates and Their Implications. *Goodin, R. E. and Le Grand, J.*, 1987, pp. 77–90. **[G: U.S.]**

Helleiner, Gerald K. Stabilization, Adjustment, and the Poor. *World Devel.*, December 1987, 15(12), pp. 1499–1513. **[G: Tanzania]**

Helleiner, Gerald K. and Stewart, Frances. The International System and the Protection of the Vulnerable. *Cornia, G. A.; Jolly, R. and Stewart, F., eds.*, 1987, pp. 273–86.

Hemenway, David. Fire Fatalities and Poverty. *Atlantic Econ. J.*, March 1987, 15(1), pp. 125. **[G: U.S.]**

Hennock, E. P. The Measurement of Urban Poverty: From the Metropolis to the Nation, 1880–1920. *Econ. Hist. Rev., 2nd Ser.*, May 1987, 40(2), pp. 208–27. **[G: U.K.]**

Heskin, Allan David. The Homeless in Contemporary Society: Los Angeles: Innovative Local Approaches. *Bingham, R. D.; Green, R. E. and White, S. B., eds.*, 1987, pp. 170–83. **[G: U.S.]**

Hoch, Charles. A Brief History of the Homeless Problem in the United States. *Bingham, R. D.; Green, R. E. and White, S. B., eds.*, 1987, pp. 16–32. **[G: U.S.]**

House, William J. Labor Market Differentiation in a Developing Economy: An Example from Urban Juba, Southern Sudan. *World Devel.*, July 1987, 15(7), pp. 877–97. **[G: Sudan]**

Huang, Yukon and Nicholas, Peter. The Social Costs of Adjustment. *Finance Develop.*, June 1987, 24(2), pp. 22–24. **[G: LDCs]**

Jahiel, Rene I. The Situation of Homelessness. *Bingham, R. D.; Green, R. E. and White, S. B., eds.*, 1987, pp. 99–118. **[G: U.S.]**

Jamal, Haroon and Malik, Salman. Working with Statistics of Quality of Life: Pakistan, 1960 to 1983. *Devel. Econ.*, September 1987, 25(3), pp. 270–80. **[G: Pakistan]**

Johnson, David. The Calculation and Use of Poverty Lines in Australia. *Australian Econ. Rev.*,

Fourth Quarter 1987, (80), pp. 45–55.
[G: Australia]
Jones, John Paul, III. Work, Welfare, and Poverty among Black Female-Headed Families. *Econ. Geogr.*, January 1987, *63*(1), pp. 20–34.
[G: U.S.]
Joshi, P. C. Harmonising Self-reliance and Poverty Alleviation Objectives—Role of Land Reforms. *Joshi, P. C.*, 1987, pp. 216–28.
[G: India]
Kanbur, S. M. Ravi. Measurement and Alleviation of Poverty: With an Application to the Effects of Macroeconomic Adjustment. *Int. Monet. Fund Staff Pap.*, March 1987, *34*(1), pp. 60–85.
Kanbur, S. M. Ravi. Structural Adjustment, Macroeconomic Adjustment and Poverty: A Methodology for Analysis. *World Devel.*, December 1987, *15*(12), pp. 1515–26.
van Kempen, Eva. High-Rise Estates and the Concentration of Poverty. *van Vliet—, W., et al., eds.*, 1987, pp. 191–212.
[G: Netherlands]
Keyserling, Leon H. Will It Be Progress or Poverty? *Challenge*, May/June 1987, *30*(2), pp. 30–36.
[G: U.S.]
Khan, Mahmood Hasan. A 'World' Distribution of Income and of Real Poverty and Affluence: Comments. *Pakistan Devel. Rev.*, Autumn 1987, *26*(3), pp. 303–04.
[G: Global]
Khan, Mahmood Hasan. Rural Poverty in Bangladesh, India and Pakistan: Profiles and Policies. *Pakistan Devel. Rev.*, Autumn 1987, *26*(3), pp. 309–36.
[G: Bangladesh; India; Pakistan]
Khare, Diwakar. A General Class of Poverty Measures. *Eastern Afr. Econ. Rev.*, June 1987, *3*(1), pp. 1–5.
Khare, Diwakar and Sethi, V. K. Construction of New Measures of Poverty. *Margin*, Apr.-June 1987, *19*(3), pp. 69–79.
Kidd, Alan J. Historians or Polemicists? How the Webbs Wrote Their History of the English Poor Laws. *Econ. Hist. Rev., 2nd Ser.*, August 1987, *40*(3), pp. 400–417.
[G: U.K.]
Knight, Rudolph H. Homelessness: An American Problem? *Bingham, R. D.; Green, R. E. and White, S. B., eds.*, 1987, pp. 249–72.
[G: U.S.]
Koch, June Q. The Federal Role in Aiding the Homeless. *Bingham, R. D.; Green, R. E. and White, S. B., eds.*, 1987, pp. 216–30.
[G: U.S.]
Krug, Walter. An International Statistical System for Reporting on Poverty. *Jahr. Nationalökon. Statist.*, October 1987, *203*(5–6), pp. 547–53.
[G: W. Germany; Denmark; U.K.]
Kumar, Shubh K. The Nutrition Situation and Its Food Policy Links. *Mellor, J. W.; Delgado, C. L. and Blackie, M. J., eds.*, 1987, pp. 39–52.
[G: Africa]
Kyereme, Stephen S. and Thorbecke, Erik. Food Poverty Profile and Decomposition Applied to Ghana. *World Devel.*, September 1987, *15*(9), pp. 1189–99.
[G: Ghana]
Levitan, Sar A. and Shapiro, Isaac. What's Missing in Welfare Reform? *Challenge*, July/Aug.

1987, *30*(3), pp. 41–48.
[G: U.S.]
Lustig, Nora. Crisis económica y niveles de vida en México: 1982–1985. (Economic Crisis and Living Standards in Mexico. With English summary.) *Estud. Econ.*, July-December 1987, *2*(2), pp. 227–49.
[G: Mexico]
Luttgens, A.; Perelman, S. and Pestieau, Pierre. La pauvreté en Belgique: interprétation d'une enquê. (With English summary.) *Cah. Écon. Bruxelles*, Third Trimester 1987, (115), pp. 35–52.
[G: Belgium]
MacKinnon, Mary. English Poor Law Policy and the Crusade against Outrelief. *J. Econ. Hist.*, September 1987, *47*(3), pp. 603–25.
Malik, Muhammad Hussain. A 'World' Distribution of Income and of Real Poverty and Affluence: Comments. *Pakistan Devel. Rev.*, Autumn 1987, *26*(3), pp. 305–06.
Malik, Sohail J. Rural Poverty in Bangladesh, India and Pakistan: Profiles and Policies: Comments. *Pakistan Devel. Rev.*, Autumn 1987, *26*(3), pp. 339–40.
[G: Bangladesh; India; Pakistan]
Minhas, B. S., et al. On the Choice of Appropriate Consumer Price Indices and Data Sets for Estimating the Incidence of Poverty in India. *Indian Econ. Rev.*, Jan.-June 1987, *22*(1), pp. 19–49.
[G: India]
Mitra, Gautam Kumar. Poverty, Land and Household Size: A Study of Three Andhra Pradesh Districts. *Margin*, July-Sept. 1987, *19*(4), pp. 51–54.
[G: India]
Neenan, William B. Poverty: Measurement, Trends and Causes. *Gannon, T. M., ed.*, 1987, pp. 107–15.
[G: U.S.]
Peroff, Kathleen. Who Are the Homeless and How Many Are There? *Bingham, R. D.; Green, R. E. and White, S. B., eds.*, 1987, pp. 33–45.
[G: U.S.]
Peterson, Janice. The Feminization of Poverty. *J. Econ. Issues*, March 1987, *21*(1), pp. 329–37.
[G: U.S.]
Pfeffermann, Guy. Economic Crisis and the Poor in Some Latin American Countries. *Finance Develop.*, June 1987, *24*(2), pp. 32–35.
Pinstrup-Andersen, Per; Jaramillo, Maurice and Stewart, Frances. Adjustment with a Human Face: Protecting the Vulnerable and Promoting Growth: The Impact on Government Expenditure. *Cornia, G. A.; Jolly, R. and Stewart, F., eds.*, 1987, pp. 73–89.
[G: LDCs]
Pyatt, Graham. Measuring Welfare, Poverty and Inequality. *Econ. J.*, June 1987, *97*(386), pp. 459–67.
Radner, Daniel B. Money Incomes of Aged and Nonaged Family Units, 1967–84. *Soc. Sec. Bull.*, August 1987, *50*(8), pp. 9–28.
[G: U.S.]
Ranney, Christine K. and Kushman, John E. Cash Equivalence, Welfare Stigma, and Food Stamps. *Southern Econ. J.*, April 1987, *53*(4), pp. 1011–27.
[G: U.S.]
Ritzdorf, Marsha and Sharpe, Sumner M. The Homeless in Contemporary Society: Portland, Oregon: A Comprehensive Approach. *Bingham, R. D.; Green, R. E. and White, S. B.,*

eds., 1987, pp. 184–98.   [G: U.S.]

Robertson, Marjorie J. Homeless Veterans: An Emerging Problem? *Bingham, R. D.; Green, R. E. and White, S. B., eds.*, 1987, pp. 64–81.   [G: U.S.]

Ross, Christine M.; Danziger, Sheldon and Smolensky, Eugene. The Level and Trend of Poverty in the United States, 1939–1979. *Demography*, November 1987, *24*(4), pp. 587–600.   [G: U.S.]

Sahn, David E. Changes in the Living Standards of the Poor in Sri Lanka during a Period of Macroeconomic Restructuring. *World Devel.*, June 1987, *15*(6), pp. 809–30.
[G: Sri Lanka]

Skok, Charles D. Key Theological Positions Underlying the Bishops' Pastoral Letter on Catholic Social Teaching and the U.S. Economy. *Int. J. Soc. Econ.*, 1987, *14*(1), pp. 3–15.
[G: U.S.]

Smeeding, Timothy; Torrey, Barbara Boyle and Rein, Martin. Comparative Well-being of Children and Elderly. *Contemp. Policy Issues*, April 1987, *5*(2), pp. 57–72.   [G: U.S.]

Smith, James P. and Welch, Finis. Race and Poverty: A Forty-Year Record. *Amer. Econ. Rev.*, May 1987, *77*(2), pp. 152–58.

Smith, Ralph E. and Vavrichek, Bruce. The Minimum Wage: Its Relation to Incomes and Poverty. *Mon. Lab. Rev.*, June 1987, *110*(6), pp. 24–30.   [G: U.S.]

Stefl, Mary E. The New Homeless: A National Perspective. *Bingham, R. D.; Green, R. E. and White, S. B., eds.*, 1987, pp. 46–63.
[G: U.S.]

Stewart, Frances. Adjustment with a Human Face: Protecting the Vulnerable and Promoting Growth: Alternative Macro Policies, Meso Policies, and Vulnerable Groups. *Cornia, G. A.; Jolly, R. and Stewart, F., eds.*, 1987, pp. 147–64.   [G: LDCs]

Stewart, Frances. Monitoring and Statistics for Adjustment with a Human Face. *Cornia, G. A.; Jolly, R. and Stewart, F., eds.*, 1987, pp. 257–72.

Stewart, Frances. Supporting Productive Employment among Vulnerable Groups. *Cornia, G. A.; Jolly, R. and Stewart, F., eds.*, 1987, pp. 197–217.   [G: LDCs]

Sullivan, Patricia A. and Damrosch, Shirley P. Homeless Women and Children. *Bingham, R. D.; Green, R. E. and White, S. B., eds.*, 1987, pp. 82–98.   [G: U.S.]

Swinton, David H. Economic Theory and Working Class Poverty towards a Reformulation. *Amer. Econ. Rev.*, May 1987, *77*(2), pp. 223–28.

Thomas, Vinod. Differences in Income and Poverty with in Brazil. *World Devel.*, February 1987, *15*(2), pp. 263–73.   [G: Brazil]

Vaughan, R. N. Welfare Approaches to the Measurement of Poverty. *Econ. J.*, Supplement 1987, *97*, pp. 160–70.

Vipond, Joan; Bradbury, Bruce and Encel, Diana. Unemployment and Poverty: Measures of Association. *Australian Bull. Lab.*, June

1987, *13*(3), pp. 179–92.   [G: Australia]

Weicher, John C. Mismeasuring Poverty and Progress. *Cato J.*, Winter 1987, *6*(3), pp. 715–30.   [G: U.S.]

Weinberg, Daniel H. Filling the "Poverty Gap," 1979–84. *J. Human Res.*, Fall 1987, *22*(4), pp. 563–73.   [G: U.S.]

Weinberg, Daniel H. Poverty Spending and the Poverty Gap. *J. Policy Anal. Manage.*, Winter 1987, *6*(2), pp. 230–41.   [G: U.S.]

Woodson, Robert L. Empowering Poor Neighborhoods. *Perkins, J., ed.*, 1987, pp. 49–61.
[G: U.S.]

Wright, James D. The National Health Care for the Homeless Program. *Bingham, R. D.; Green, R. E. and White, S. B., eds.*, 1987, pp. 150–69.   [G: U.S.]

Yotopoulos, Pan A. A 'World' Distribution of Income and of Real Poverty and Affluence. *Pakistan Devel. Rev.*, Autumn 1987, *26*(3), pp. 275–99.   [G: Global]

Yotopoulos, Pan A. Rural Poverty in Bangladesh, India and Pakistan: Profiles and Policies: Comments. *Pakistan Devel. Rev.*, Autumn 1987, *26*(3), pp. 337–38.   [G: Bangladesh; India; Pakistan]

Wren, Colin. The Relative Effects of Local Authority Financial Assistance Policies. *Urban Stud.*, August 1987, *24*(4), pp. 268–78.
[G: U.K.]

915 Social Security

9150 Social Security

Aaron, Henry J. Social Security: Problems of Maturity. *van de Kar, H. M. and Wolfe, B. L., eds.*, 1987, pp. 83–95.   [G: OECD]

Aaron, Henry J. and Thompson, Lawrence H. Social Security and the Economists. *Berkowitz, E. D., ed.*, 1987, pp. 79–99.   [G: U.S.]

Aarts, Leo. Disability in the United Kingdom: Incidence, Social Security Benefits and Labour Market Effects: Comment. *Emanuel, H.; de Gier, E. H. and Konijn, P. A. B. K., eds.*, 1987, pp. 215–17.   [G: U.K.]

Abel, Andrew B. Aggregate Savings in the Presence of Private and Social Insurance. *[Modigliani, F.]*, 1987, pp. 131–57.

Achenbaum, W. Andrew. Social Security: A Source of Support for All Ages. *Berkowitz, E. D., ed.*, 1987, pp. 119–39.   [G: U.S.]

Anderson, Annelise. U.S. Social Security under Low Fertility: Comment. *Davis, K.; Bernstam, M. S. and Ricardo-Campbell, R., eds.*, 1987, 1986, pp. 313–17.   [G: U.S.]

Andrews, Emily S. Changing Pension Policy and the Aging of America. *Contemp. Policy Issues*, April 1987, *5*(2), pp. 84–97.   [G: U.S.]

Antler, Jacob and Kahane, Yehuda. The Gross and Net Replacement Ratios in Designing Pension Schemes and in Financial Planning: The Israeli Experience. *J. Risk Ins.*, June 1987, *54*(2), pp. 283–97.   [G: Israel]

Appolito, Richard A. The Implicit Pension Contract *Developments and New Directions. J. Hu-*

man Res., Summer 1987, 22(3), pp. 441–67.

Artoni, Roberto. La riforma del sistema pensionistico. (With English summary.) *Polit. Econ.*, April 1987, 3(1), pp. 3–15. **[G: Italy]**

Ballantyne, Harry C. Actuarial Status of the OASI and DI Trust Funds. *Soc. Sec. Bull.*, June 1987, 50(6), pp. 5–9. **[G: U.S.]**

Beenstock, Michael. Work, Welfare and Taxation: Conclusions and Overview. *Beenstock, M., et al.*, 1987, pp. 261–67. **[G: U.K.]**

Beenstock, Michael and Parker, Michael. The New Social Security System. *Beenstock, M., et al.*, 1987, pp. 235–60. **[G: U.K.]**

Berkowitz, Edward D. Social Security Celebrates an Anniversary. *Berkowitz, E. D., ed.*, 1987, pp. 3–28. **[G: U.S.]**

Berkowitz, Edward D. The First Advisory Council and the 1939 Amendments. *Berkowitz, E. D., ed.*, 1987, pp. 55–78. **[G: U.S.]**

Bernheim, B. Douglas. The Economic Effects of Social Security: Toward a Reconciliation of Theory and Measurement. *J. Public Econ.*, August 1987, 33(3), pp. 273–304. **[G: U.S.]**

Berthold, Norbert. Umschichtung des Lebenseinkommens als verteilungspolitische Aufgabe der Familienpolitik. (Intertemporal Allocation of Life Income as a Distributional Task of Family Policy. With English summary.) *Jahr. Nationalökon. Statist.*, January 1987, 203(1), pp. 12–25. **[G: W. Germany]**

Black, Dan A. The Social Security System, the Provision of Human Capital, and the Structure of Compensation. *J. Lab. Econ.*, April 1987, 5(2), pp. 242–54.

Boaz, Rachel Floersheim. Labor Market Behavior of Older Workers Approaching Retirement: A Summary of the Evidence from the 1970s. *Meyer, C. W., ed.*, 1987, pp. 103–26. **[G: U.S.]**

Boskin, Michael J. Intergenerational Aspects of Government Policy under Changing Demographic and Economic Conditions. *Bus. Econ.*, July 1987, 22(3), pp. 18–24. **[G: U.S.]**

Boskin, Michael J. and Puffert, Douglas J. Social Security and the American Family. *Summers, L. H., ed.*, 1987, pp. 139–59. **[G: U.S.]**

Boskin, Michael J. and Shoven, John B. Concepts and Measures of Earnings Replacement during Retirement. *Bodie, Z.; Shoven, J. B. and Wise, D. A., eds.*, 1987, pp. 113–41. **[G: U.S.]**

Boskin, Michael J., et al. Social Security: A Financial Appraisal across and within Generations. *Nat. Tax J.*, March 1987, 40(1), pp. 19–34. **[G: U.S.]**

Breyer, Friedrich and von der Schulenburg, J.-Matthias Graf. Voting on Social Security: The Family as Decision-Making Unit. *Kyklos*, 1987, 40(4), pp. 529–47.

Buchanan, James M. The Public Choice Perspective. *Buchanan, J. M. (I)*, 1987, 1983, pp. 253–60. **[G: U.S.]**

Bulow, Jeremy I. Pension Plan Integration as Insurance against Social Security Risk: Comment. *Bodie, Z.; Shoven, J. B. and Wise, D. A., eds.*, 1987, pp. 169–72. **[G: U.S.]**

Burtless, Gary. Taxes, Transfers, and Swedish Labor Supply. *Bosworth, B. P. and Rivlin, A. M., eds.*, 1987, pp. 185–249. **[G: Sweden]**

Chau, L. C. Central Provident Fund: Symposium. *Hong Kong Econ. Pap.*, 1987, (18), pp. 59–64. **[G: Hong Kong]**

Chu, C. Y. Cyrus. The Effect of Social Security on the Steady State Distribution of Consumption. *J. Public Econ.*, November 1987, 34(2), pp. 189–210.

Cohen, Wilbur J. Social Security in 1995: The Future as a Reflection of the Past. *Berkowitz, E. D., ed.*, 1987, pp. 141–52. **[G: U.S.]**

Constantinides, Marietta A. Optimum Population, Overlapping Generations and Social Security in a Model Mximizing $u(c^1, c^2, X)$. *J. Econ. (Z. Nationalökon.)*, 1987, 47(1), pp. 69–75.

Dejardin, Jérôme. The International Social Security Association at 60. *Int. Lab. Rev.*, Sept.-Oct. 1987, 126(5), pp. 585–95. **[G: Global]**

Derthick, Martha. The Plight of the Social Security Administration. *Berkowitz, E. D., ed.*, 1987, pp. 101–17. **[G: U.S.]**

Dilnot, Andrew; Stark, Graham and Webb, Steven J. The Targeting of Benefits: Two Approaches. *Fisc. Stud.*, February 1987, 8(1), pp. 83–93. **[G: U.K.]**

Dinkel, Reiner H. Die "lautlose Rentenform": Konsolidierung oder Aktualisierung der allgemeinen Bemessungsgrundlage der Gesetzlichen Rentenversicherung. (The "Silent" Pension Reform in Germany: How and Why Actualization of the Replacement Formula Works as a Major Consolidation Step. With English summary.) *Konjunkturpolitik*, 1987, 33(2), pp. 116–25. **[G: W. Germany]**

Disney, Richard. Statutory Sick Pay: An Appraisal. *Fisc. Stud.*, May 1987, 8(2), pp. 58–76. **[G: U.K.]**

Dumont, J.-P. The Evolution of Social Security during the Recession. *Int. Lab. Rev.*, Jan.-Feb. 1987, 126(1), pp. 1–19. **[G: Selected Countries]**

Egginton, Don M. Case Studies of Labour Supply Incentives and Budget Lines. *Beenstock, M., et al.*, 1987, pp. 25–75. **[G: U.K.]**

Emanuel, Han. The Dutch Research Program on Factors Determining Social Disability Benefit Recipiency: A Background Paper. *Emanuel, H.; de Gier, E. H. and Konijn, P. A. B. K., eds.*, 1987, pp. 7–50. **[G: Netherlands]**

Feldstein, Martin S. Should Social Security Benefits Be Means Tested? *J. Polit. Econ.*, June 1987, 95(3), pp. 468–84. **[G: U.S.]**

Feldstein, Martin S. The Welfare Cost of Social Security's Impact on Private Saving. *[Harberger, A.]*, 1987, pp. 1–13.

Fenn, Paul and Harris, Donald. Disability in the United Kingdom: Incidence, Social Security Benefits and Labour Market Effects. *Emanuel, H.; de Gier, E. H. and Konijn, P. A. B. K., eds.*, 1987, pp. 191–210. **[G: U.K.]**

Fields, Gary S. and Mitchell, Olivia S. Restructuring Social Security: How Will Retirement Ages Respond? *Sandell, S. H., ed.*, 1987, pp. 192–205. **[G: U.S.]**

Fitzgerald, John. The Effects of Social Security on Life Insurance Demand by Married Couples. *J. Risk Ins.*, March 1987, *54*(1), pp. 86–99.   [G: U.S.]

Freeman, Gary P. Do Policy Issues Determine Politics? State Pensions Policy. *Waltman, J. L. and Studlar, D. T., eds.*, 1987, pp. 182–206.   [G: U.K.; U.S.]

Fry, Vanessa and Stark, Graham. The Take-Up of Supplementary Benefit: Gaps in the 'Safety Net'? *Fisc. Stud.*, November 1987, *8*(4), pp. 1–14.   [G: U.K.]

Greenblum, Joseph and Bye, Barry. Work Values of Disabled Beneficiaries. *Soc. Sec. Bull.*, April 1987, *50*(4), pp. 67–74.   [G: U.S.]

Greenwood, John G. Central Provident Fund: Symposium. *Hong Kong Econ. Pap.*, 1987, (18), pp. 67–69.   [G: Hong Kong]

Gustman, Alan L. Concepts and Measures of Earnings Replacement during Retirement: Comment. *Bodie, Z.; Shoven, J. B. and Wise, D. A., eds.*, 1987, pp. 141–46.   [G: U.S.]

Haanes-Olsen, Leif. Social Security Reform in Denmark. *Soc. Sec. Bull.*, November 1987, *50*(11), pp. 20–26.   [G: Denmark]

Halter, William A. and Hemming, Richard. The Impact of Demographic Change on Social Security Financing. *Int. Monet. Fund Staff Pap.*, September 1987, *34*(3), pp. 471–502.
          [G: W. Germany; Japan; U.K.; U.S.]

Hambor, John C. Economic Policy, Intergenerational Equity, and the Social Security Trust Fund Buildup. *Soc. Sec. Bull.*, October 1987, *50*(10), pp. 13–18.   [G: U.S.]

Hardy, Dorcas R. Remarks by the Commissioner. *Soc. Sec. Bull.*, September 1987, *50*(9), pp. 3–7.   [G: U.S.]

Hardy, Dorcas R. The Future of Social Security. *Soc. Sec. Bull.*, August 1987, *50*(8), pp. 5–7.
                                      [G: U.S.]

Hauser, Richard. Comparing the Influence of Social Security Systems on the Relative Economic Positions of Selected Groups in Six Major Industrialized Countries: The Case of One-Parent Families. *Europ. Econ. Rev.*, Feb./Mar. 1987, *31*(1/2), pp. 192–201. [G: N. America; U.K.; Sweden; Israel; W. Germany]

Ho, Lok Sang. Central Provident Fund: Symposium. *Hong Kong Econ. Pap.*, 1987, (18), pp. 65–66.   [G: Hong Kong]

Hoon, Hian Teck. The Effects of a CPF Cut: A Note. *Singapore Econ. Rev.*, October 1987, *32*(2), pp. 66–74.   [G: Singapore]

Horlick, Max. The Relationships between Public and Private Pension Schemes: An Introductory Overview. *Soc. Sec. Bull.*, July 1987, *50*(7), pp. 15–24.   [G: W. Europe]

Hu, Sheng Cheng. Uncertain Inflation and Social Security Indexation. *J. Econ. Dynam. Control*, September 1987, *11*(3), pp. 359–72.

Huang, Xiaojing and Yang, Xiao. From Iron Rice-bowls to Labor Markets: Reforming the Social Security System. *Reynolds, B. L.*, 1987, pp. 147–60.   [G: China]

Hubbard, R. Glenn. Uncertain Lifetimes, Pensions, and Individual Saving. *Bodie, Z.; Sho-

ven, J. B. and Wise, D. A., eds.*, 1987, pp. 175–206.   [G: U.S.]

Hubbard, R. Glenn and Judd, Kenneth L. Social Security and Individual Welfare: Precautionary Saving, Borrowing Constraints, and the Payroll Tax. *Amer. Econ. Rev.*, September 1987, *77*(4), pp. 630–46.   [G: U.S.]

Iams, Howard M. Jobs of Persons Working after Receiving Retired-Worker Benefits. *Soc. Sec. Bull.*, November 1987, *50*(11), pp. 4–18.
                                      [G: U.S.]

Inman, Robert P. Justifying Public Provision of Social Security: Comment. *J. Policy Anal. Manage.*, Summer 1987, *6*(4), pp. 689–92.
                                      [G: U.S.]

Kahn, Arthur L. Program and Demographic Characteristics of Supplemental Security Income Recipients, December 1985. *Soc. Sec. Bull.*, May 1987, *50*(5), pp. 23–57. [G: U.S.]

Klees, Barbara and Warfield, Carter. Actuarial Status of the HI and SMI Trust Funds. *Soc. Sec. Bull.*, June 1987, *50*(6), pp. 11–20.
                                      [G: U.S.]

Kotlikoff, Laurence J. Justifying Public Provision of Social Security. *J. Policy Anal. Manage.*, Summer 1987, *6*(4), pp. 674–89.   [G: U.S.]

Leff, Mark H. Historical Perspectives on Old-Age Insurance: The State of the Art on the Art of the State. *Berkowitz, E. D., ed.*, 1987, pp. 29–53.   [G: U.S.]

Lesnoy, Selig D. and Leimer, Dean R. Social Security and Private Saving: Theory and Historical Evidence. *Meyer, C. W., ed.*, 1987, *1985*, pp. 69–101.   [G: U.S.]

Leung, Edward H. K. Central Provident Fund: Symposium. *Hong Kong Econ. Pap.*, 1987, (18), pp. 57–58.   [G: Hong Kong]

Lipka, Roland. Effects of Taxation of Social Security Benefits on Portfolio Revisions. *J. Risk Ins.*, December 1987, *54*(4), pp. 737–51.
                                      [G: U.S.]

Lopez, Eduard A. Constitutional Background to the Social Security Act of 1935. *Soc. Sec. Bull.*, January 1987, *50*(1), pp. 5–11.   [G: U.S.]

McIntosh, C. Alison. Recent Pronatalist Policies in Western Europe. *Davis, K.; Bernstam, M. S. and Ricardo-Campbell, R., eds.*, 1987, *1986*, pp. 318–34.   [G: W. Europe]

Merton, Robert C.; Bodie, Zvi and Marcus, Alan J. Pension Plan Integration as Insurance against Social Security Risk. *Bodie, Z.; Shoven, J. B. and Wise, D. A., eds.*, 1987, pp. 147–69.   [G: U.S.]

Meyer, Charles W. Social Security: Past, Present, and Future. *Meyer, C. W., ed.*, 1987, pp. 1–34.   [G: U.S.]

Meyer, Charles W. The Economic and Political Implications of a Phase-Out: A Summing Up. *Meyer, C. W., ed.*, 1987, pp. 127–48.
                                      [G: U.S.]

Meyer, Charles W. and Wolff, Nancy L. Intercohort and Intracohort Redistribution under Old Age Insurance: The 1962–1972 Retirement Cohorts. *Public Finance Quart.*, July 1987, *15*(3), pp. 259–81.   [G: U.S.]

Meyer, Charles W. and Wolff, Nancy L. Intercohort and Intracohort Redistribution under Social Security. *Meyer, C. W., ed.,* 1987, pp. 49–68. **[G: U.S.]**

Mitchell, Olivia S. Uncertain Lifetimes, Pensions, and Individual Saving: Comment. *Bodie, Z.; Shoven, J. B. and Wise, D. A., eds.,* 1987, pp. 206–10. **[G: U.S.]**

Moffitt, Robert. Life-Cycle Labor Supply and Social Security: A Time-Series Analysis. *Burtless, G., ed.,* 1987, pp. 183–220. **[G: U.S.]**

Moore, Thomas Gale. Social Security in Aging Societies: Comment. *Davis, K.; Bernstam, M. S. and Ricardo-Campbell, R., eds.,* 1987, *1986,* pp. 295.

Munnell, Alicia H. Justifying Public Provision of Social Security: Comment. *J. Policy Anal. Manage.,* Summer 1987, *6*(4), pp. 692–96. **[G: U.S.]**

Munnell, Alicia H. The Current Status of Our Social Welfare System. *New Eng. Econ. Rev.,* July/Aug. 1987, pp. 3–12. **[G: U.S.]**

Myers, Robert J. Forecasting the Number of Social Security Retirees: Improving Forecasts for Better Policy Making: Comment. *J. Policy Anal. Manage.,* Fall 1987, *7*(1), pp. 70–73. **[G: U.S.]**

Myers, Robert J. Social Security in 1995: The Future as a Reflection of the Past: A Reply. *Berkowitz, E. D., ed.,* 1987, pp. 153–57. **[G: U.S.]**

von Natzmer, W. Social Security Contributions, Economic Activity, and Distribution. *Empirical Econ.,* 1987, *12*(1), pp. 29–49. **[G: W. Germany]**

Nelissen, Jan. The Redistributive Impact of the General Old Age Pensions Act on Lifetime Income in the Netherlands. *Europ. Econ. Rev.,* October 1987, *31*(7), pp. 1419–41. **[G: Netherlands]**

Osano, Hiroshi. Social Security and Lifetime Employment Contract. *Econ. Stud. Quart.,* June 1987, *38*(2), pp. 107–23.

Packard, Michael D. Income of New Disabled-Worker Beneficiaries and Their Families: Findings from the New Beneficiary Survey. *Soc. Sec. Bull.,* March 1987, *50*(3), pp. 5–23. **[G: U.S.]**

Patel, D. K. Central Provident Fund: Symposium. *Hong Kong Econ. Pap.,* 1987, (18), pp. 71–73. **[G: Hong Kong]**

Pfaff, Martin. The Demand for Disability Transfers: Recent Research and Research Needs: Comment. *Emanuel, H.; de Gier, E. H. and Konijn, P. A. B. K., eds.,* 1987, pp. 249–54. **[G: U.S.; Netherlands]**

Pollard, William B. and Speer, Charles C. An Analysis of the Impact of Recent Social Security Legislation on Marginal Tax Rates. *Public Budg. Finance,* Spring 1987, *7*(1), pp. 104–10. **[G: U.S.]**

Pugh, Robert E. Forecasting the Number of Social Security Retirees: Improving Forecasts for Better Policy Making. *J. Policy Anal. Manage.,* Fall 1987, *7*(1), pp. 62–69. **[G: U.S.]**

Quinn, Joseph F. Life-Cycle Labor Supply and Social Security: A Time-Series Analysis: Com-

ment. *Burtless, G., ed.,* 1987, pp. 220–28. **[G: U.S.]**

Rejda, George E.; Schmidt, James R. and McNamara, Michael J. The Impact of Social Security Tax Contributions on Group Life Insurance Premiums. *J. Risk Ins.,* December 1987, *54*(4), pp. 712–20. **[G: U.S.]**

Ricardo-Campbell, Rita. U.S. Social Security under Low Fertility. *Davis, K.; Bernstam, M. S. and Ricardo-Campbell, R., eds.,* 1987, *1986,* pp. 296–312.

Rocklin, Sarah G. and Mattson, David R. The Employment Opportunities for Disabled Americans Act: Legislative History and Summary of Provisions. *Soc. Sec. Bull.,* March 1987, *50*(3), pp. 25–35. **[G: U.S.]**

Ross, Jane L. Research and Social Security Policy in the United States. *Soc. Sec. Bull.,* October 1987, *50*(10), pp. 4–12. **[G: U.S.]**

Sammartino, Frank J. The Effect of Health on Retirement. *Soc. Sec. Bull.,* February 1987, *50*(2), pp. 31–47.

Schäfer, Dieter. Disability in the United Kingdom: Incidence, Social Security Benefits and Labour Market Effects: Comment. *Emanuel, H.; de Gier, E. H. and Konijn, P. A. B. K., eds.,* 1987, pp. 211–14. **[G: U.K.]**

Seidl, Vladimir and Pruš, Ladislav. La sécurité sociale en Tchécoslovaquie: Évolution 1970–1985. (Social Security in Czechoslovakia, 1970–1985. With English summary.) *Écon. Soc.,* February 1987, *21*(2), pp. 157–71. **[G: Czechoslovakia]**

Sharpe, Don. The Cambridge Multisectoral Dynamic Model of the British Economy: Social Security Benefits and Personal Income Tax. *Barker, T. and Peterson, W., eds.,* 1987, pp. 373–87. **[G: U.K.]**

Skocpol, Theda. America's Incomplete Welfare State: The Limits of New Deal Reforms and the Origins of the Present Crisis. *Rein, M.; Esping-Andersen, G. and Rainwater, L., eds.,* 1987, pp. 35–58. **[G: U.S.]**

Stein, Bruno. Phasing Out Social Security: A Critique of Ferrara's Proposal. *Meyer, C. W., ed.,* 1987, pp. 35–48. **[G: U.S.]**

Streett, Craig A. State Programs and Supplemental Security Income for the Aged, Blind, and Disabled, April 1987. *Soc. Sec. Bull.,* May 1987, *50*(5), pp. 67–70. **[G: U.S.]**

Tang, Shu-Hung, et al. Central Provident Fund: Symposium. *Hong Kong Econ. Pap.,* 1987, (18), pp. 75–80. **[G: Hong Kong]**

Van Imhoff, Evert. On the Independence of Financing Methods and Redistributive Aspects of Public Pensions: A Comment. *Public Finance,* 1987, *42*(3), pp. 448–53.

Verbon, H. A. A. On the Independence of Financing Methods and Redistributive Aspects of Pension Schemes: A Reply. *Public Finance,* 1987, *42*(3), pp. 454–56.

Verbon, H. A. A. The Rise and Evolution of Public Pension Systems. *Public Choice,* 1987, *52*(1), pp. 75–100. **[G: Netherlands]**

Warburton, Peter. Labour Supply Incentives for

the Retired. *Beenstock, M., et al.*, 1987, pp. 185–234. **[G: U.K.]**

Weaver, Carolyn L. Social Security in Aging Societies. *Davis, K.; Bernstam, M. S. and Ricardo-Campbell, R., eds.*, 1987, *1986*, pp. 273–94. **[G: OECD]**

Weinberg, Daniel H. Poverty Spending and the Poverty Gap. *J. Policy Anal. Manage.*, Winter 1987, *6*(2), pp. 230–41. **[G: U.S.]**

Wixon, Bernard; Bridges, Benjamin, Jr. and Pattison, David. Policy Analysis through Microsimulation: The STATS Model. *Soc. Sec. Bull.*, December 1987, *50*(12), pp. 4–12. **[G: U.S.]**

Wolfe, Barbara L. The Demand for Disability Transfers: Recent Research and Research Needs. *Emanuel, H.; de Gier, E. H. and Konijn, P. A. B. K., eds.*, 1987, pp. 223–48. **[G: U.S.; Netherlands]**

Wolff, Edward N. The Effects of Pensions and Social Security on the Distribution of Wealth in the U.S. *Wolff, E. N., ed.*, 1987, pp. 208–47. **[G: U.S.]**

Wolfson, Michael C. Lifetime Coverage: The Adequacy of Canada's Retirement Income System. *Wolff, E. N., ed.*, 1987, pp. 179–207. **[G: Canada]**

Wong, Richard Yue-Chim. Central Provident Fund: Symposium. *Hong Kong Econ. Pap.*, 1987, (18), pp. 81–85. **[G: Hong Kong]**

Ycas, Martynas A. Recent Trends in Health near the Age of Retirement: New Findings from the Health Interview Survey. *Soc. Sec. Bull.*, February 1987, *50*(2), pp. 5–30. **[G: U.S.]**

Ycas, Martynas A. and Grad, Susan. Income of Retirement-Aged Persons in the United States. *Soc. Sec. Bull.*, July 1987, *50*(7), pp. 5–14. **[G: U.S.]**

Zeitzer, Ilene R. and Beedon, Laurel E. Long-term Disability Programs in Selected Countries. *Soc. Sec. Bull.*, September 1987, *50*(9), pp. 8–21. **[G: OECD]**

916 Economics of Law; Economics of Crime

9160 Economics of Law; Economics of Crime

Abbott, Kenneth W. Collective Goods, Mobile Resources, and Extraterritorial Trade Controls. *Law Contemp. Probl.*, Summer 1987, *50*(3), pp. 117–52. **[G: U.S.]**

Altrogge, Phyllis and Shughart, William F., II. The Regressive Nature of Civil Penalties. *MacKay, R. J.; Miller, J. C., III and Yandle, B., eds.*, 1987, *1984*, pp. 240–54. **[G: U.S.]**

An, Tang. The Law Applicable to a Transnational Economic Development Contract. *J. World Trade Law*, August 1987, *21*(4), pp. 95–146. **[G: Global]**

Anderson, Dan R. Financing Asbestos Claims: Coverage Issues, Manville's Bankruptcy and the Claims Facility. *J. Risk Ins.*, September 1987, *54*(3), pp. 429–51. **[G: U.S.]**

Arlacchi, Pino. Effects of the New Anti-Mafia Law on the Proceeds of Crime and on the Italian Economy. *Alessandrini, S. and Dallago, B., eds.*, 1987, pp. 247–55. **[G: Italy]**

Asch, Peter and Levy, David T. Does the Minimum Drinking Age Affect Traffic Fatalities? *J. Policy Anal. Manage.*, Winter 1987, *6*(2), pp. 180–92. **[G: U.S.]**

Ashenfelter, Orley and Oaxaca, Ronald. The Economics of Discrimination: Economists Enter the Courtroom. *Amer. Econ. Rev.*, May 1987, *77*(2), pp. 321–25.

Atkinson, Scott E.; Sandler, Todd and Tschirhart, John. Terrorism in a Bargaining Framework. *J. Law Econ.*, April 1987, *30*(1), pp. 1–21. **[G: Global]**

Atwood, James R. Conflicts of Jurisdiction in the Antitrust Field: The Example of Export Cartels. *Law Contemp. Probl.*, Summer 1987, *50*(3), pp. 153–64. **[G: U.S.]**

Austin, Robert P. Regulatory Principles and the Internationalization of Securities Markets. *Law Contemp. Probl.*, Summer 1987, *50*(3), pp. 221–50. **[G: U.S.]**

Avio, Kenneth L. The Quality of Mercy: Exercise of the Royal Prerogative in Canada. *Can. Public Policy*, September 1987, *13*(3), pp. 366–79. **[G: Canada]**

Baird, Douglas G. A World without Bankruptcy. *Law Contemp. Probl.*, Spring 1987, *50*(2), pp. 173–93.

Barker, Michael. Land Degradation: Legal Issues and Institutional Constraints: Commentary. *Chisholm, A. and Dumsday, R., eds.*, 1987, pp. 168–74. **[G: Australia]**

Behney, Thomas Amos, Jr. Extraterritoriality of Economic Legislation: Bibliography. *Law Contemp. Probl.*, Summer 1987, *50*(3), pp. 303–47.

Benjamin, Martin and Bronstein, Daniel A. Moral and Criminal Responsibility and Corporate Persons. *Samuels, W. J. and Miller, A. S., eds.*, 1987, pp. 277–82. **[G: U.S.]**

Bentham, Richard W. Questions of Hardship in Transnational Agreements. *Dicke, D. C., ed.*, 1987, pp. 163–76.

Bićanić, Ivo. The Inequality Impact of the Unofficial Economy in Yugoslavia. *Alessandrini, S. and Dallago, B., eds.*, 1987, pp. 323–36. **[G: Yugoslavia]**

Blair, Roger D. and Schafer, Carolyn D. Evolutionary Models of Legal Change and the *Albrecht* Rule. *Antitrust Bull.*, Winter 1987, *32*(4), pp. 989–1006. **[G: U.S.]**

Block, Walter. Trading Money for Silence. *Radnitzky, G. and Bernholz, P., eds.*, 1987, pp. 157–217.

Blume, Lawrence and Rubinfeld, Daniel L. Compensation for Takings: An Economic Analysis. *Jaffe, A. J., ed.*, 1987, pp. 53–103. **[G: U.S.]**

Bowles, Roger. Settlement Range and Cost Allocation Rules: A Comment on Avery Katz's *Measuring the Demand for Litigation: Is the English Rule Really Cheaper?*. *J. Law, Econ., Organ.*, Fall 1987, *3*(2), pp. 177–84.

Boynton, Charles E., IV and Robison, Jack. Factors Empirically Associated with Federal Tax Trial Case Loads. *Jones, S. M., ed.*, 1987, pp. 169–82. **[G: U.S.]**

Bradsen, John and Fowler, Robert. Land Degradation: Legal Issues and Institutional Constraints. *Chisholm, A. and Dumsday, R., eds.,* 1987, pp. 129–67. [G: Australia]

Breyer, Stephen G. Economics and Judging: An Afterword on Cooter and Wald. *Law Contemp. Probl.,* Autumn 1987, *50*(4), pp. 245–52. [G: U.S.]

Breyer, Stephen G. Judicial Review of Questions of Law and Policy. *Bailey, E. E., ed.,* 1987, pp. 45–72. [G: U.S.]

Brigham, John. The "Giving Issue": A View of Land, Property Rights and Industrial Development in Maine and Nova Scotia. *Feldman, E. J. and Goldberg, M. A., eds.,* 1987, pp. 247–68. [G: U.S.; Canada]

Brilmayer, Lea. The Extraterritorial Application of American Law: A Methodological and Constitutional Appraisal. *Law Contemp. Probl.,* Summer 1987, *50*(3), pp. 11–38. [G: U.S.]

Bromfield, David H. Women and the Law of Property in Early America. *Mich. Law Rev.,* Apr.-May 1987, *85*(5–6), pp. 1109–16.

Buchanan, James M. Equal Treatment and Reverse Discrimination. *Buchanan, J. M. (II),* 1987, *1981*, pp. 276–88.

Bulcha, Mekuria; Kibreab, Gaim and Nobel, Peter. Sociology, Economy and Law: Views in Common. *Nobel, P., ed.,* 1987, pp. 93–103. [G: Africa]

Cadot, Olivier. Corruption as a Gamble. *J. Public Econ.,* July 1987, *33*(2), pp. 223–44.

Cameron, Samuel. A Disaggregated Study of Police Clear-Up Rates for England and Wales. *J. Behav. Econ.,* Winter 1987, *16*(4), pp. 1–18. [G: U.K.]

Cameron, Samuel. Hidden Costs of Unemployment: The Case of Excess Fire Service Expenditures. *Appl. Econ.,* November 1987, *19*(11), pp. 1421–31. [G: U.K.]

Cameron, Samuel. Substitution between Offence Categories in the Supply of Property Crime: Some New Evidence. *Int. J. Soc. Econ.,* 1987, *14*(11), pp. 48–60. [G: U.K.]

Carlson, David Gray. Successor Liability in Bankruptcy: Some Unifying Themes of Intertemporal Creditor Priorities Created by Running Covenants, Products Liability, and Toxic-Waste Cleanup. *Law Contemp. Probl.,* Spring 1987, *50*(2), pp. 119–71. [G: U.S.]

Carter, Stephen L. The Beast That Might Not Exist: Some Speculations on the Constitution and the Independent Regulatory Agencies. *Marshall, B., ed.,* 1987, pp. 76–102. [G: U.S.]

Cassel, Dieter and Cichy, Ulrich. The Shadow Economy and Economic Policy in East and West: A Comparative System Approach. *Alessandrini, S. and Dallago, B., eds.,* 1987, pp. 127–46.

Centner, Terence J. and Wetzstein, Michael E. Reducing Moral Hazard Associated with Implied Warranties of Animal Health. *Amer. J. Agr. Econ.,* February 1987, *69*(1), pp. 143–50. [G: U.S.]

Chowdhury, Subrata Roy. Reasonable Expecta-

tions of the Foreign Investor and the Host State. *Dicke, D. C., ed.,* 1987, pp. 259–67.

Clark, Gordon L. Adjudicating Jurisdictional Disputes in Chicago and Toronto: Legal Formalism and Urban Structure. *Feldman, E. J. and Goldberg, M. A., eds.,* 1987, pp. 225–46. [G: U.S.; Canada]

Cloninger, Dale O. Capital Punishment and Deterrence: A Revision. *J. Behav. Econ.,* Winter 1987, *16*(4), pp. 55–57. [G: U.S.]

Cochran, Philip L. and Nigh, Douglas. Illegal Corporate Behavior and the Question of Moral Agency: An Empirical Examination. *Frederick, W. C., ed.,* 1987, pp. 73–91. [G: U.S.]

Coggins, George Cameron and Harris, Anne Fleishel. The Greening of American Law? The Recent Evolution of Federal Law for Preserving Floral Diversity. *Natural Res. J.,* Spring 1987, *27*(2), pp. 247–307. [G: U.S.]

Colijn, Leendert. Some Proposed Methodologies to Quantify the Influence of Macroeconomic Disequilibrium on the Size of the Second Economy in Poland. *Alessandrini, S. and Dallago, B., eds.,* 1987, pp. 337–45. [G: Poland]

Conn, Stephen. Rural Legal Process and Development in the North. *Lane, T., ed.,* 1987, pp. 199–229. [G: U.S.]

Cooter, Robert D. Liberty, Efficiency, and Law. *Law Contemp. Probl.,* Autumn 1987, *50*(4), pp. 141–63.

Cooter, Robert D. Why Litigants Disagree: A Comment on George Priest's "Measuring Legal Change." *J. Law, Econ., Organ.,* Fall 1987, *3*(2), pp. 227–34. [G: U.S.]

Corgel, John B. Occupational Boundary Setting and the Unauthorized Practice of Law by Real Estate Brokers. *Jaffe, A. J., ed.,* 1987, pp. 161–75. [G: U.S.]

Corman, Hope; Joyce, Theodore J. and Lovitch, Norman. Crime, Deterrence and the Business Cycle in New York City: A VAR Approach. *Rev. Econ. Statist.,* November 1987, *69*(4), pp. 695–700. [G: U.S.]

Cowell, Frank A. The Economic Analysis of Tax Evasion. *Hey, J. D. and Lambert, P. J., eds.,* 1987, *1985*, pp. 173–203.

Craig, Steven G. The Deterrent Impact of Police: An Examination of a Locally Provided Public Service. *J. Urban Econ.,* May 1987, *21*(3), pp. 298–311. [G: U.S.]

Craig, Steven G. and Sailors, Joel W. Interstate Trade Barriers and the Constitution. *Cato J.,* Winter 1987, *6*(3), pp. 819–35. [G: U.S.]

Culp, Jerome M. Economists on the Bench: Foreword. *Law Contemp. Probl.,* Autumn 1987, *50*(4), pp. 1–16.

Culp, Jerome M. Judex Economicus. *Law Contemp. Probl.,* Autumn 1987, *50*(4), pp. 95–140. [G: U.S.]

Dale-Johnson, David; Dietrich, J. Kimball and Langetieg, Terence C. A Legal and Economic Analysis of the Due-on-Sale Clause: A Retrospective Examination. *Jaffe, A. J., ed.,* 1987, pp. 105–27. [G: U.S.]

Dallago, Bruno. The Underground Economy in the West and the East: A Comparative Approach. *Alessandrini, S. and Dallago, B., eds.,* 1987, pp. 147–63.

Deutsch, Joseph; Hakim, Simon and Weinblatt, J. A Micro Model of the Criminal's Location Choice. *J. Urban Econ.,* September 1987, 22(2), pp. 198–208.

Dicke, Detlev Chr. Unjust Enrichment and Compensation. *Dicke, D. C., ed.,* 1987, pp. 268–80.

Dieng, Adama. Background to and Growth of the Right to Development: The Role of Law and Lawyers in Development. *Nobel, P., ed.,* 1987, pp. 55–60. [G: Senegal]

Djajić, Slobodan. Illegal Aliens, Unemployment and Immigration Policy. *J. Devel. Econ.,* February 1987, 25(1), pp. 235–49. [G: U.S.]

Dobosiewicz, Zbigniew. The Role of Unofficial Economy in North African Countries. *Alessandrini, S. and Dallago, B., eds.,* 1987, pp. 165–74. [G: N. Africa]

Du Bois, W. E. B. The Negro Criminal. *Rev. Black Polit. Econ.,* Summer-Fall 1987, 16(1–2), pp. 17–31. [G: U.S.]

Ehrlich, Isaac and Brower, George D. On the Issue of Causality in the Economic Model of Crime and Law Enforcement: Some Theoretical Considerations and Experimental Evidence. *Amer. Econ. Rev.,* May 1987, 77(2), pp. 99–106. [G: U.S.]

Eisenberg, Theodore. Bankruptcy in the Administrative State. *Law Contemp. Probl.,* Spring 1987, 50(2), pp. 3–52. [G: U.S.]

Feige, Edgar L. Sweden's "Underground Economy." *Eliasson, G., ed.,* 1987, pp. 113–28. [G: Sweden]

Feige, Edgar L. The Anatomy of the Underground Economy. *Alessandrini, S. and Dallago, B., eds.,* 1987, pp. 83–106. [G: U.S.]

Finlayson, Grant E. Rethinking the Overlapping Jurisdictions of Section 337 and the U.S. Courts. *J. World Trade Law,* April 1987, 21(2), pp. 41–63. [G: U.S.]

Fischer, Charles C. Forensic Economics and the Wrongful Death of a Household Producer: Current Practices, Methodological Biases and Alternative Solutions of Losses. *Amer. J. Econ. Soc.,* April 1987, 46(2), pp. 219–28.

Fisher, Franklin M. Pan American to United: The *Pacific Division Transfer Case. Rand J. Econ.,* Winter 1987, 18(4), pp. 492–508. [G: U.S.]

Fisher, Sethard. Economic Development and Crime: Two May Be Associated as an Adaptation to Industrialism in Social Revolution. *Amer. J. Econ. Soc.,* January 1987, 46(1), pp. 17–34.

Flynn, John J. The Jurisprudence of Corporate Personhood: The Misuse of a Legal Concept. *Samuels, W. J. and Miller, A. S., eds.,* 1987, pp. 131–59. [G: U.S.]

Fox, Eleanor M. Chairman Miller, the Federal Trade Commission, Economics, and *Rashomon. Law Contemp. Probl.,* Autumn 1987, 50(4), pp. 33–55. [G: U.S.]

Freeman, Richard B. The Relation of Criminal Activity to Black Youth Employment. *Rev. Black Polit. Econ.,* Summer-Fall 1987, 16(1–2), pp. 99–107. [G: U.S.]

Friedman, Joseph; Hakim, Simon and Spiegel, Uriel. The Effects of Community Size on the Mix of Private and Public Use of Security Services. *J. Urban Econ.,* September 1987, 22(2), pp. 230–41. [G: U.S.]

Furlong, William J. A General Equilibrium Model of Crime Commission and Prevention. *J. Public Econ.,* October 1987, 34(1), pp. 87–103.

Galanter, Marc. Conceptualizing Legal Change and Its Effects: A Comment on George Priest's "Measuring Legal Change." *J. Law, Econ., Organ.,* Fall 1987, 3(2), pp. 235–41.

Gann, Pamela B. Issues in Extraterritoriality. *Law Contemp. Probl.,* Summer 1987, 50(3), pp. 1–10. [G: U.S.]

Garland, Merrick B. Antitrust and State Action: Economic Efficiency and the Political Process. *Yale Law J.,* January 1987, 96(3), pp. 486–519. [G: U.S.]

Gautschi, Frederick H., III and Jone, Thomas M. Illegal Corporate Behavior and Corporate Board Structure. *Frederick, W. C., ed.,* 1987, pp. 93–106. [G: U.S.]

Gibbons, John J. Antitrust, Law and Economics, and Politics. *Law Contemp. Probl.,* Autumn 1987, 50(4), pp. 217–24. [G: U.S.]

Goetz, Charles J. Public Choice and the Law: The Paradox of Tullock. *[Tullock, G.],* 1987, pp. 171–80.

Good, David H. and Pirog-Good, Maureen A. A Simultaneous Probit Model of Crime and Employment for Black and White Teenage Males. *Rev. Black Polit. Econ.,* Summer-Fall 1987, 16(1–2), pp. 109–27. [G: U.S.]

Good, David H. and Pirog-Good, Maureen A. Employment, Crime, and Race. *Contemp. Policy Issues,* October 1987, 5(4), pp. 91–104. [G: U.S.]

Greenberg, Ward A. Liquor Price Affirmation Statutes and the Dormant Commerce Clause. *Mich. Law Rev.,* October 1987, 86(1), pp. 186–211.

Gyimah-Brempong, Kwabena. Economies of Scale in Municipal Police Departments: The Case of Florida. *Rev. Econ. Statist.,* May 1987, 69(2), pp. 352–56. [G: U.S.]

Gyimah-Brempong, Kwabena. Elasticity of Factor Substitution in Police Agencies: Evidence from Florida. *J. Bus. Econ. Statist.,* April 1987, 5(2), pp. 257–65. [G: U.S.]

Haddock, David D. and Macey, Jonathan R. Regulation on Demand: A Private Interest Model, with an Application to Insider Trading Regulation. *J. Law Econ.,* October 1987, 30(2), pp. 311–52. [G: U.S.]

Harris, Frederick H. deB. Security and Penalty in Debt Contracts: Comment. *J. Inst. Theoretical Econ.,* March 1987, 143(1), pp. 168–74.

Hartman, Raymond S. and Doane, Michael J. The Use of Hedonic Analysis for Certification and Damage Calculations in Class Action Complaints. *J. Law, Econ., Organ.,* Fall 1987, 3(2), pp. 351–72. [G: U.S.]

Hashimoto, Masanori. The Minimum Wage Law and Youth Crimes: Time-series Evidence. *J. Law Econ.*, October 1987, *30*(2), pp. 443–64.
[G: U.S.]

Hauch, Jeanne M. Insider Trading by Intermediaries: A Contract Remedy for Acquirers' Increased Costs of Takeovers. *Yale Law J.*, November 1987, *97*(1), pp. 115–34. [G: U.S.]

Heertje, Arnold. Some Observations on the Welfare Economic Aspects of the Unofficial Economy. *Alessandrini, S. and Dallago, B., eds.*, 1987, pp. 303–10.

Hess, James D. and Knoeber, Charles R. Security and Penalty in Debt Contracts. *J. Inst. Theoretical Econ.*, March 1987, *143*(1), pp. 149–67.

Higgins, Richard S.; Shughart, William F., II and Tollison, Robert D. Dual Enforcement of the Antitrust Laws. *MacKay, R. J.; Miller, J. C., III and Yandle, B., eds.*, 1987, pp. 154–80. [G: U.S.]

Higgs, Robert and Twight, Charlotte. National Emergency and the Erosion of Private Property Rights. *Cato J.*, Winter 1987, *6*(3), pp. 747–73. [G: U.S.]

Hill, John K. Immigrant Decisions Concerning Duration of Stay and Migratory Frequency. *J. Devel. Econ.*, February 1987, *25*(1), pp. 221–34. [G: U.S.]

Hill, John K. and Pearce, James E. Enforcing Sanctions against Employers of Illegal Aliens. *Fed. Res. Bank Dallas Econ. Rev.*, May 1987, pp. 1–15. [G: U.S.]

Hirsch, Werner Z. Landlord–Tenant Laws and Indigent Black Tenants. *Jaffe, A. J., ed.*, 1987, pp. 129–41. [G: U.S.]

Hirshleifer, Jack. Evolutionary Models in Economics and Law: Cooperation versus Conflict Strategies. *Hirshleifer, J.*, 1987, *1982*, pp. 211–72.

Hirshleifer, Jack. Privacy: Its Origin, Function, and Future. *Hirshleifer, J.*, 1987, *1980*, pp. 194–210.

Hoechner, Kurt M. A Swiss Perspective on Conflicts of Jurisdiction. *Law Contemp. Probl.*, Summer 1987, *50*(3), pp. 271–82.
[G: Switzerland]

Horwitz, Morton J. *Santa Clara* Revisited: The Development of Corporate Theory. *Samuels, W. J. and Miller, A. S., eds.*, 1987, pp. 13–63. [G: U.S.]

Horwitz, Morton J. History and Theory. *Yale Law J.*, July 1987, *96*(8), pp. 1825–35. [G: U.S.]

Hourihan, Kevin. Local Community Involvement and Participation in Neighbourhood Watch: A Case-study in Cork, Ireland. *Urban Stud.*, April 1987, *24*(2), pp. 129–36. [G: Ireland]

Howsen, Roy M. and Jarrell, Stephen B. Some Determinants of Property Crime: Economic Factors Influence Criminal Behavior but Cannot Completely Explain the Syndrome. *Amer. J. Econ. Soc.*, October 1987, *46*(4), pp. 445–57. [G: U.S.]

Im, Eric Iksoon; Cauley, Jon and Sandler, Todd. Cycles and Substitutions in Terrorist Activities:

A Spectral Approach. *Kyklos*, 1987, *40*(2), pp. 238–55. [G: Global]

Jaenicke, Günther. Consequences of a Breach of an Investment Agreement Governed by International Law, by General Principles of Law, or by Domestic Law of the Host State. *Dicke, D. C., ed.*, 1987, pp. 177–93.

Jegouzo, Guenhaël. Les sources non agricoles des revenus de ménage chez les petits paysans et les autres agriculteurs français. (With English summary.) *Léon, Y. and Mahé, L., eds.*, 1987, pp. 271–96. [G: France]

Johnson, Manuel H., Jr. Statement to the U.S. House Subcommittee on Financial Institutions Supervision, Regulation and Insurance of the Committee on Banking, Finance and Urban Affairs, June 9, 1987. *Fed. Res. Bull.*, August 1987, *73*(8), pp. 649–54. [G: U.S.]

Jordan, J. Phillip and Leiner, Frederick C. American Jurisdiction over Foreign Corporations in Product Liability Lawsuits: The ASAHI Decision and Beyond. *J. World Trade Law*, October 1987, *21*(5), pp. 31–44. [G: U.S.]

Juenger, Friedrich K. Constitutional Control of Extraterritoriality? A Comment. *Law Contemp. Probl.*, Summer 1987, *50*(3), pp. 39–46. [G: U.S.]

Kadane, Joseph B. Corrigenda [Is Victimization Chronic? A Bayesian Analysis of Multinomial Missing Data]. *J. Econometrics*, July 1987, *35*(2/3), pp. 393. [G: U.S.]

Kalscheur, Gregory A. Dormant Commerce Clause Claims under 42 U.S.C. § 1983: Protecting the Right to Be Free of Protectionist State Action. *Mich. Law Rev.*, October 1987, *86*(1), pp. 157–85.

Kalscheur, Gregory A. The Wrong Side of the Tracks: A Revolutionary Rediscovery of the Common Law Tradition of Fairness in the Struggle against Inequality. *Mich. Law Rev.*, Apr.-May 1987, *85*(5–6), pp. 1124–29.

Kaplow, Louis. Antitrust, Law and Economics, and the Courts. *Law Contemp. Probl.*, Autumn 1987, *50*(4), pp. 181–216. [G: U.S.]

Katz, Avery. Measuring the Demand for Litigation: Is the English Rule Really Cheaper? *J. Law, Econ., Organ.*, Fall 1987, *3*(2), pp. 143–76.

Katzenbach, Nicholas deB. The Constitution and Foreign Policy. *Marshall, B., ed.*, 1987, pp. 59–75. [G: U.S.]

Kirby, Michael G. New Technology and International Privacy Issues. *Barr, T., ed.*, 1987, pp. 146–58. [G: Global]

Lambooy, Jan G. and Renooy, P. H. Informal Economy and the Labour Market: Relations with the Economic Order. *Gordon, I., ed.*, 1987, pp. 172–91. [G: Netherlands]

Landau, Zbigniew. Selected Problems of Unofficial Economy in Poland. *Alessandrini, S. and Dallago, B., eds.*, 1987, pp. 175–79.
[G: Poland]

Landes, William M. and Posner, Richard A. Trademark Law: An Economic Perspective. *J. Law Econ.*, October 1987, *30*(2), pp. 265–309.
[G: U.S.]

Lang, Kevin and Bell, Duran. An Economic Model of the Intake Disposition of Juvenile Offenders. *J. Public Econ.*, February 1987, 32(1), pp. 79–99. [G: U.S.]

Langenfeld, James and Rogowsky, Robert A. Settlement vs. Litigation in Antitrust Enforcement. *MacKay, R. J.; Miller, J. C., III and Yandle, B., eds.*, 1987, pp. 205–19. [G: U.S.]

Latin, Howard. Legal and Economic Considerations in the Decisions of Judge Breyer. *Law Contemp. Probl.*, Autumn 1987, 50(4), pp. 57–86. [G: U.S.]

Leonard, Herman B. and Zeckhauser, Richard J. Amnesty, Enforcement, and Tax Policy. *Summers, L. H., ed.*, 1987, pp. 55–85. [G: U.S.]

Leyton-Brown, David. Extraterritoriality in United States Trade Sanctions. *Leyton-Brown, D., ed.*, 1987, pp. 255–67. [G: U.S.]

Leyton-Brown, David. The Utility of International Economic Sanctions: Introduction. *Leyton-Brown, D., ed.*, 1987, pp. 1–4.

Liebhafsky, Herbert H. Law and Economics from Different Perspectives. *J. Econ. Issues*, December 1987, 21(4), pp. 1809–36.

Lillich, Richard B. Lump Sum Agreements: Standards Therein and Impact Thereof. *Dicke, D. C., ed.*, 1987, pp. 239–58. [G: U.S.; Global]

Logan, John R. and Messner, Steven F. Racial Residential Segregation and Suburban Violent Crime. *Soc. Sci. Quart.*, September 1987, 68(3), pp. 510–27. [G: U.S.]

Lott, John R., Jr. Should the Wealthy Be Able to "Buy Justice"? *J. Polit. Econ.*, December 1987, 95(6), pp. 1307–16.

Lowe, B. Thomas. Regulatory Enforcement of the Surface Mine Control and Reclamation Act of 1977, PL 95/87: A Comparison of State and Federal Compliance in Three Midwestern States. *Natural Res. J.*, Winter 1987, 27(1), pp. 201–11. [G: U.S.]

Macneil, Ian R. Relational Contract Theory as Sociology: A Reply. *J. Inst. Theoretical Econ.*, June 1987, 143(2), pp. 272–90.

Madeo, Silvia A.; Schepanski, Albert and Uecker, Wilfred C. Modeling Judgments of Taxpayer Compliance. *Accounting Rev.*, April 1987, 62(2), pp. 323–42. [G: U.S.]

Magat, Wesley A. Howard Latin's Analysis of the Legal and Economic Considerations in the Decisions of Judge Breyer. *Law Contemp. Probl.*, Autumn 1987, 50(4), pp. 87–93. [G: U.S.]

Manne, Henry G. Intellectual Styles and the Evolution of American Corporation Law. *Radnitzky, G. and Bernholz, P., eds.*, 1987, pp. 219–41. [G: U.S.]

Marrelli, M. The Economic Analysis of Tax Evasion: Empirical Aspects. *Hey, J. D. and Lambert, P. J., eds.*, 1987, pp. 204–28. [G: U.S.; W. Europe]

Mars, Gerald and Altman, Yochanan. Case Studies in Second Economy Distribution in Soviet Georgia. *Alessandrini, S. and Dallago, B., eds.*, 1987, pp. 219–45. [G: U.S.S.R.]

Mars, Gerald and Altman, Yochanan. Case Studies in Second Economy Production and Transportation in Soviet Georgia. *Alessandrini, S. and Dallago, B., eds.*, 1987, pp. 197–217. [G: U.S.S.R.]

Mathews, M. Cash. Codes of Ethics: Organizational Behavior and Misbehavior. *Frederick, W. C., ed.*, 1987, pp. 107–30. [G: U.S.]

McCarthy, Patrick S. and Oesterle, William. The Deterrent Effects of Stiffer DUI Laws: An Empirical Study. *Logist. Transp. Rev.*, December 1987, 23(4), pp. 353–71. [G: U.S.]

McGahey, Richard. Crime and Employment Research: A Continuing Deadlock? *Rev. Black Polit. Econ.*, Summer-Fall 1987, 16(1–2), pp. 223–30. [G: U.S.]

McKenzie, Richard B. and Sullivan, E. Thomas. Does the NCAA Exploit College Athletes? An Economics and Legal Reinterpretation. *Antitrust Bull.*, Summer 1987, 32(2), pp. 373–99. [G: U.S.]

Meessen, Karl M. Conflicts of Jurisdiction under the New Restatement. *Law Contemp. Probl.*, Summer 1987, 50(3), pp. 47–69. [G: U.S.]

Meessen, Karl M. Intellectual Property Rights in International Trade. *J. World Trade Law*, February 1987, 21(1), pp. 67–74. [G: OECD]

Melossi, Dario. Political Business Cycles and Imprisonment Rates in Italy: Report on a Work in Progress. *Rev. Black Polit. Econ.*, Summer-Fall 1987, 16(1–2), pp. 211–18. [G: Italy]

Miller, Arthur S. Corporations and Our Two Constitutions. *Samuels, W. J. and Miller, A. S., eds.*, 1987, pp. 241–62. [G: U.S.]

Mills, Geofrey and Rockoff, Hugh. Compliance with Price Controls in the United States and the United Kingdom during World War II. *J. Econ. Hist.*, March 1987, 47(1), pp. 197–213. [G: U.S.; U.K.]

Morris, A. J. A Dynamic Framework for Petroleum Legislation in Developing Countries: Interaction between Economic and Legal Issues. *Pachauri, R. K., ed.*, 1987, pp. 835–46. [G: LDCs]

Muchlinski, P. T. Law and the Analysis of the International Oil Industry. *Rees, J. and Odell, P., eds.*, 1987, pp. 142–58.

Mulherin, J. Harold and Muller, Walter J., III. Volatile Interest Rates and the Divergence of Incentives in Mortgage Contracts. *J. Law, Econ., Organ.*, Spring 1987, 3(1), pp. 99–115.

Myers, Samuel L., Jr. Special Issue on Race and Crime: Introduction. *Rev. Black Polit. Econ.*, Summer-Fall 1987, 16(1–2), pp. 5–15. [G: U.S.]

Myers, Samuel L., Jr. and Sabol, William J. Business Cycles and Racial Disparities in Punishment. *Contemp. Policy Issues*, October 1987, 5(4), pp. 46–58. [G: U.S.]

Myers, Samuel L., Jr. and Sabol, William J. Unemployment and Racial Differences in Imprisonment. *Rev. Black Polit. Econ.*, Summer-Fall 1987, 16(1–2), pp. 189–209. [G: U.S.]

Myrdal, Gunnar. Inequality of Justice. *Rev. Black Polit. Econ.*, Summer-Fall 1987, 16(1–2), pp. 81–98. [G: U.S.]

Nalebuff, Barry. Credible Pretrial Negotiation. *Rand J. Econ.*, Summer 1987, *18*(2), pp. 198–210.

Nimmer, Raymond T. Consumer Bankruptcy Abuse. *Law Contemp. Probl.*, Spring 1987, *50*(2), pp. 89–118. **[G: U.S.]**

Noonberg, Eve. Extraterritorial Enforcement of Antitrust Laws against Foreign Firms. *Law Contemp. Probl.*, Summer 1987, *50*(3), pp. 194–95. **[G: U.S.]**

Nossal, Kim Richard. Economic Sanctions in the League of Nations and the United Nations. *Leyton-Brown, D., ed.*, 1987, pp. 7–21.

Novos, Ian E. and Waldman, Michael. The Emergence of Copying Technologies: What Have We Learned? *Contemp. Policy Issues*, July 1987, *5*(3), pp. 34–43.

O'Driscoll, Gerald P., Jr. The Liability Crisis: A Law and Economics Analysis. *Fed. Res. Bank Dallas Econ. Rev.*, November 1987, (11), pp. 1–13. **[G: U.S.]**

Oppermann, Thomas, et al. Rechtsgrundlagen von Technologiepolitik (Insbesondere nach Europarecht und Grundgesetz). (Legal Bases for a Technology Policy [with Particular Reference to European Community Law and German Constitutional Law (Grundgesetz)]. With English summary.) *Lenel, H. O., et al., eds.*, 1987, pp. 209–31. **[G: EEC]**

Ordover, Janusz A. Conflicts of Jurisdiction: Antitrust and Industrial Policy. *Law Contemp. Probl.*, Summer 1987, *50*(3), pp. 165–77. **[G: U.S.]**

Osunbor, Oserheimen A. Law and Policy on the Registration of Technology Transfer Transactions in Nigeria. *J. World Trade Law*, October 1987, *21*(5), pp. 13–30. **[G: Nigeria]**

Page, Joseph A. Asbestos and the Dalkon Shield: Corporate America on Trial. *Mich. Law Rev.*, Apr.-May 1987, *85*(5–6), pp. 1324–40.

Perry, Clifton. Tort Reform and the Market-Share Rule. *Cato J.*, Fall 1987, *7*(2), pp. 449–60. **[G: U.S.]**

Petersmann, Ernst-Ulrich. Sovereignty, International Law and the United Nations Code of Conduct on Transnational Corporations. *Dicke, D. C., ed.*, 1987, pp. 310–36.

Phillips, David M. Secured Credit and Bankruptcy: A Call for the Federalization of Personal Property Security Law. *Law Contemp. Probl.*, Spring 1987, *50*(2), pp. 53–88. **[G: U.S.]**

Phillips, Llad. Race and Crime: Comments. *Rev. Black Polit. Econ.*, Summer-Fall 1987, *16*(1–2), pp. 219–21.

Phillips, Llad and Votey, Harold L., Jr. Crimes by Youth: Deterrence and Moral Compliance with the Law. *Contemp. Policy Issues*, October 1987, *5*(4), pp. 73–90. **[G: U.S.]**

Phillips, Llad and Votey, Harold L., Jr. Rational Choice Models of Crimes by Youth. *Rev. Black Polit. Econ.*, Summer-Fall 1987, *16*(1–2), pp. 129–87. **[G: U.S.]**

Phillips, Llad and Votey, Harold L., Jr. Women's Changing Involvement with Crime: A Labor Force Participation Perspective. *Eastern Econ.*

J., July-Sept. 1987, *13*(3), pp. 233–42. **[G: U.S.]**

Plott, Charles R. Legal Fees: A Comparison of the American and English Rules. *J. Law, Econ., Organ.*, Fall 1987, *3*(2), pp. 185–92.

Png, Ivan Paak Liang. Litigation, Liability, and Incentives for Care. *J. Public Econ.*, October 1987, *34*(1), pp. 61–85.

Popenoe, David. Suburbanization, Privatization, and Juvenile Delinquency: Some Possible Relationships. *van Vliet—, W., et al., eds.*, 1987, pp. 119–37.

Posner, Richard A. The Law and Economics Movement. *Amer. Econ. Rev.*, May 1987, *77*(2), pp. 1–13.

Priest, George L. Measuring Legal Change. *J. Law, Econ., Organ.*, Fall 1987, *3*(2), pp. 193–225. **[G: U.S.]**

Richter, Rudolf. The Efficiency of the Common Law: A New Institutional Economics Perspective: Comment. *Pethig, R. and Schlieper, U., eds.*, 1987, pp. 123–25. **[G: U.S.]**

Rizzo, Mario J. and Arnold, Frank S. An Economic Framework for Statutory Interpretation. *Law Contemp. Probl.*, Autumn 1987, *50*(4), pp. 165–80.

Rogowsky, Robert A. The Pyrrhic Victories of Section 7: A Political Economy Approach. *MacKay, R. J.; Miller, J. C., III and Yandle, B., eds.*, 1987, pp. 220–39. **[G: U.S.]**

Rokes, Willis Park. Remedies Afforded Private Parties against Insurers for Unfair Claims Practices. *J. Risk Ins.*, September 1987, *54*(3), pp. 478–501. **[G: U.S.]**

Rose-Ackerman, Susan. Tullock and the Inefficiency of the Common Law. *[Tullock, G.]*, 1987, pp. 181–85. **[G: U.S.]**

Rowley, Charles K. and Brough, Wayne. The Efficiency of the Common Law: A New Institutional Economics Perspective. *Pethig, R. and Schlieper, U., eds.*, 1987, pp. 103–21. **[G: U.S.]**

Rubinfeld, Daniel L. and Sappington, David E. M. Efficient Awards and Standards of Proof in Judicial Proceedings. *Rand J. Econ.*, Summer 1987, *18*(2), pp. 308–15.

Rubinstein, W. D. The End of 'Old Corruption' in Britain, 1780–1860. *Rubinstein, W. D.*, 1987, *1983*, pp. 265–303. **[G: U.K.]**

Russell, A. M. and Rickard, J. A. A Model of Tax Evasion Incorporating Income Variation and Retroactive Penalities. *Australian Econ. Pap.*, December 1987, *26*(49), pp. 254–64.

Sacerdoti, Giorgio. Foreign and Foreign-Owned Corporations in International Economic Law. *Dicke, D. C., ed.*, 1987, pp. 289–309.

Sachs, Ignacy. The Crisis, Technological Progress and the Hidden Economy. *Sachs, I.*, 1987, pp. 95–104.

Sadanand, Asha. Lost Profits, Market Damages, and Specific Performance: An Economic Analysis of Buyer's Breach. *Can. J. Econ.*, November 1987, *20*(4), pp. 750–73.

Saffer, Henry and Grossman, Michael. Drinking Age Laws and Highway Mortality Rates: Cause and Effect. *Econ. Inquiry*, July 1987, *25*(3), pp. 403–17.   [G: U.S.]

Samuels, Warren J. The Idea of the Corporation as a Person: On the Normative Significance of Judicial Language. *Samuels, W. J. and Miller, A. S., eds.*, 1987, pp. 113–29.
[G: U.S.]

Schumann, Jochen. Security and Penalty in Debt Contracts: Comment. *J. Inst. Theoretical Econ.*, March 1987, *143*(1), pp. 175–79.

Schwartz, Pedro. The Market and the Meta-market: A Review of the Contributions of the Economic Theory of Property Rights. *Pejovich, S., ed.*, 1987, pp. 11–32.

Schwartz, Warren F. The Logic of the Law Revisited. *[Tullock, G.]*, 1987, pp. 186–88.

Scully, Gerald W. The Choice of Law and the Extent of Liberty. *J. Inst. Theoretical Econ.*, December 1987, *143*(4), pp. 595–615.

Seaquist, Gwen. An Inquiry into the Enforceability of the Insider Trading Sanctions Act (ITSA) of 1984: The Record of Prosecution Thus Far and the Prospects for the Future. *Tremblay, R., ed.*, 1987, pp. 617–29.   [G: U.S.]

Seger, Martha R. Statement to the U.S. House Subcommittee on Financial Institutions Supervision, Regulation and Insurance of the Committee on Banking, Finance and Urban Affairs, May 6, 1987. *Fed. Res. Bull.*, July 1987, *73*(7), pp. 560–63.   [G: U.S.]

Seidl-Hohenveldern, Ignaz. Semantics of Wealth Deprivation and Their Legal Significance. *Dicke, D. C., ed.*, 1987, pp. 218–38.

Seidman, Louis Michael. Public Principle and Private Choice: The Uneasy Case for a Boundary Maintenance Theory of Constitutional Law. *Yale Law J.*, April 1987, *96*(5), pp. 1006–59.
[G: U.S.]

Sellin, Thorsten. The Negro and the Problem of Law Observance and Administration in the Light of Social Research. *Rev. Black Polit. Econ.*, Summer-Fall 1987, *16*(1–2), pp. 71–80.
[G: U.S.]

Shavell, Steven. A Model of Optimal Incapacitation. *Amer. Econ. Rev.*, May 1987, *77*(2), pp. 107–10.

Shavell, Steven. The Optimal Use of Nonmonetary Sanctions as a Deterrent. *Amer. Econ. Rev.*, September 1987, *77*(4), pp. 584–92.

Shiers, Alden F. and Williamson, Daniel P. Nonbusiness Bankruptcies and the Law: Some Empirical Results. *J. Cons. Aff.*, Winter 1987, *21*(2), pp. 277–92.   [G: U.S.]

Siliciano, John A. Corporate Behavior and the Social Efficiency of Tort Law. *Mich. Law Rev.*, August 1987, *85*(8), pp. 1820–64.   [G: U.S.]

Sinder, Janet. Economists as Judges: A Selective, Annotated Bibliography. *Law Contemp. Probl.*, Autumn 1987, *50*(4), pp. 279–86.

Skolka, Jiri. A Few Facts about the Hidden Economy. *Alessandrini, S. and Dallago, B., eds.*, 1987, pp. 35–59.   [G: U.S.]

Small, David H. Managing Extraterritorial Jurisdiction Problems: The United States Government Approach. *Law Contemp. Probl.*, Summer 1987, *50*(3), pp. 283–302.   [G: U.S.]

Soifer, Aviam. The Paradox of Paternalism and Laissez-Faire Constitutionalism: The U.S. Supreme Court, 1888–1921. *Samuels, W. J. and Miller, A. S., eds.*, 1987, pp. 161–90.
[G: U.S.]

Sullivan, Teresa A.; Warren, Elizabeth and Westbrook, Jay Lawrence. The Use of Empirical Data in Formulating Bankruptcy Policy. *Law Contemp. Probl.*, Spring 1987, *50*(2), pp. 195–235.   [G: U.S.]

Sundakov, Alex. Accident Compensation Law: An Economic View. *New Zealand Econ. Pap.*, 1987, *21*, pp. 57–73.   [G: New Zealand]

Thomas, Peter. The Legal and Tax Considerations of Privatization. *Hanke, S. H., ed.*, 1987, pp. 87–100.

Thompson, Larry D. Dealing with Black-on-Black Crime. *Perkins, J., ed.*, 1987, pp. 27–35.
[G: U.S.]

Tower, Edward and Willett, Thomas D. Enforceability and the Resolution of International Jurisdictional Conflicts: Comments. *Law Contemp. Probl.*, Summer 1987, *50*(3), pp. 189–93.   [G: U.S.]

Trooboff, Peter D. The Revised Restatement of the Foreign Relations Law of the United States: Reaffirmation of Established International Legal Principles Governing State Responsibility toward Foreign-Owned Investment. *Dicke, D. C., ed.*, 1987, pp. 201–17.   [G: U.S.]

Vaupel, Suzanne and Martin, Philip L. Evaluating Employer Sanctions: Farm Labor Contractor Experience. *Ind. Relat.*, Fall 1987, *26*(3), pp. 304–13.   [G: U.S.]

Viscusi, W. Kip. Regulatory Economics in the Courts: An Analysis of Judge Scalia's NHTSA Bumper Decision. *Law Contemp. Probl.*, Autumn 1987, *50*(4), pp. 17–31.   [G: U.S.]

Vitzthum, Wolfgang Graf. Technologietransfer und Technologieembargo im Völkerrecht. (Technology Transfer and Technology Embargo in International Law. With English summary.) *Lenel, H. O., et al., eds.*, 1987, pp. 233–63.   [G: Global]

Voeller, Joachim. A Note on Fair Equality of Rules. *Bamberg, G. and Spremann, K., eds.*, 1987, pp. 473–80.   [G: W. Germany]

de Waart, Paul J. I. M. ICSID and Other Forms of Arbitration and Conciliation: Institutionalization of Dispute Settlement in the Context of the Right of Development. *Dicke, D. C., ed.*, 1987, pp. 116–36.

Wald, Patricia M. Limits on the Use of Economic Analysis in Judicial Decisionmaking. *Law Contemp. Probl.*, Autumn 1987, *50*(4), pp. 225–44.   [G: U.S.]

Waters, Robert Craig. Judicial Immunity vs. Due Process: When Should a Judge Be Subject to Suit? *Cato J.*, Fall 1987, *7*(2), pp. 461–74.

Werden, Gregory J. and Simon, Marilyn J. Why Price Fixers Should Go to Prison. *Antitrust Bull.*, Winter 1987, *32*(4), pp. 917–37.
[G: U.S.]

Westin, Alan F. Technological Change and the Constitution: Preserving the Framers' Balances in a Computer Age. *Marshall, B., ed.*, 1987, pp. 189–207. **[G: U.S.]**

Whichard, Willis P. A Common Law Judge's View of the Appropriate Use of Economics in Common Law Adjudication. *Law Contemp. Probl.*, Autumn 1987, *50*(4), pp. 253–63.

Wiles, Peter. The Second Economy, Its Definitional Problems. *Alessandrini, S. and Dallago, B., eds.*, 1987, pp. 21–33.

Wilkinson, Charles F. The Law of the American West: A Critical Bibliography of the Nonlegal Sources. *Mich. Law Rev.*, Apr.-May 1987, *85*(5–6), pp. 953–1011.

Wilkinson, James T. Reducing Drunken Driving: Which Polices Are Most Effective? *Southern Econ. J.*, October 1987, *54*(2), pp. 322–34. **[G: U.S.]**

Willcox, Walter F. Negro Criminality. *Rev. Black Polit. Econ.*, Summer-Fall 1987, *16*(1–2), pp. 33–45. **[G: U.S.]**

Williamson, Oliver E. Assessing Contract. *Williamson, O.*, 1987, *1985*, pp. 161–89.

Williamson, Oliver E. Intellectual Foundations of Law and Economics: The Need for a Broader View. *Williamson, O.*, 1987, *1983*, pp. 311–19.

Williamson, Oliver E. Pretrial Uses of Economists: On the Use of 'Incentive Logic' to Screen Predation. *Williamson, O.*, 1987, *1984*, pp. 282–300. **[G: U.S.]**

Witte, Ann D. The Nature and Extent of Unrecorded Activity: A Survey Concentrating on Recent U.S. Research. *Alessandrini, S. and Dallago, B., eds.*, 1987, pp. 61–81. **[G: U.S.]**

Wonnell, Christopher T. Problems in the Application of Political Philosophy to Law. *Mich. Law Rev.*, October 1987, *86*(1), pp. 123–55.

Wood, Diane P. Conflicts of Jurisdiction in Antitrust Law: A Comment. *Law Contemp. Probl.*, Summer 1987, *50*(3), pp. 179–88. **[G: U.S.]**

Woodbury, Stephen E. Aesthetic Nuisance: The Time Has Come to Recognize It. *Natural Res. J.*, Fall 1987, *27*(4), pp. 877–86. **[G: U.S.]**

Work, Monroe N. Negro Criminality in the South. *Rev. Black Polit. Econ.*, Summer-Fall 1987, *16*(1–2), pp. 63–69. **[G: U.S.]**

Yablon, Charles M. Arguing about Rights. *Mich. Law Rev.*, Apr.-May 1987, *85*(5–6), pp. 871–94.

917 Economics of Minorities; Economics of Discrimination

9170 Economics of Minorities; Economics of Discrimination

Adams, Arvil V.; Mangum, Stephen L. and Wirtz, Philip W. Postschool Education and Training: Accessible to All? *Rev. Black Polit. Econ.*, Winter 1987, *15*(3), pp. 68–86. **[G: U.S.]**

Akkermans, Timie and Hövels, Ben. Young Workers and Trade Unions. A Comparison with Women and Workers in General. *Econ. Lavoro*, Apr.-June 1987, *21*(2), pp. 119–23. **[G: Netherlands]**

Alonso, William. Identity and Population. *Alonso, W., ed.*, 1987, pp. 95–125. **[G: Japan; U.S.; U.K.; W. Europe]**

Amin, Samir. SADCC Prospects for Disengagement and Development in Southern Africa: Preface. *Amin, S.; Chitala, D. and Mandaza, I., eds.*, 1987, pp. 1–7. **[G: S. Africa]**

Amsden, Alice H. Gender and the Dynamics of Subcontracting in Mexico City: Comments. *Brown, C. and Pechman, J. A., eds.*, 1987, pp. 183–85. **[G: Mexico]**

Anders, Gary C. and Anders, Kathleen. Incompatible Goals in Unconventional Organizations: The Politics of Alaska Native Corporations. *Lane, T., ed.*, 1987, pp. 133–57. **[G: U.S.]**

Anderson, Barbara A. The Life Course of Soviet Women Born 1905–1960. *Millar, J. R., ed.*, 1987, pp. 203–40. **[G: U.S.S.R.]**

Arizpe, Lourdes and Botey, Carlota. Mexican Agricultural Development Policy and Its Impact on Rural Women. *Deere, C. D. and León, M., eds.*, 1987, pp. 67–83. **[G: Mexico]**

Ashenfelter, Orley and Oaxaca, Ronald. The Economics of Discrimination: Economists Enter the Courtroom. *Amer. Econ. Rev.*, May 1987, *77*(2), pp. 321–25.

Azia, Naheed. Sex Differentials in Mortality: A Corollary of Son Preference? Comments. *Pakistan Devel. Rev.*, Winter 1987, *26*(4), pp. 566–68. **[G: Pakistan]**

Barbezat, Debra A. Salary Differentials by Sex in the Academic Labor Market. *J. Human Res.*, Summer 1987, *22*(3), pp. 422–28. **[G: U.S.]**

Barratt, C. John A. Can External Leverage Pressure South Africa? *Sethi, S. P., ed.*, 1987, pp. 205–17. **[G: S. Africa]**

Barrett, Nancy S. Sex-Based Employment Quotas in Sweden: Comments. *Brown, C. and Pechman, J. A., eds.*, 1987, pp. 299–301. **[G: Sweden]**

Bates, Timothy. Self-employed Minorities: Traits and Trends. *Soc. Sci. Quart.*, September 1987, *68*(3), pp. 539–51. **[G: U.S.]**

Benería, Lourdes. Gender and the Dynamics of Subcontracting in Mexico City. *Brown, C. and Pechman, J. A., eds.*, 1987, pp. 159–82. **[G: Mexico]**

Berg, Maxine. Women's Work, Mechanisation and the Early Phases of Industrialisation in England. *Joyce, P., ed.*, 1987, pp. 64–98. **[G: U.K.]**

Bergmann, Barbara R. Pay Equity—Surprising Answers to Hard Questions. *Challenge*, May/June 1987, *30*(2), pp. 45–51. **[G: U.S.]**

Bergmann, Barbara R. Women's Roles in the Economy: Teaching the Issues. *J. Econ. Educ.*, Fall 1987, *18*(4), pp. 393–407.

Bergmann, Barbara R. and Roberts, Mark D. Income for the Single Parent: Child Support, Work, and Welfare. *Brown, C. and Pechman, J. A., eds.*, 1987, pp. 247–63. **[G: U.S.]**

Bianchi, Suzanne M. and Rytina, Nancy. Comment on Das Gupta's Comment [The Decline in Occupational Sex Segregation during the 1970s: Census and CPS Comparisons]. *Demography*, May 1987, *24*(2), pp. 297. **[G: U.S.]**

Black, Harold A. and Schweitzer, Robert L. The Effect of Common Bond on Credit Union Performance: The Case of Black-Controlled Credit Unions. *Rev. Black Polit. Econ.*, Spring 1987, *15*(4), pp. 89–98. **[G: U.S.]**

Blau, Francine D. and Ferber, Marianne A. Discrimination: Empirical Evidence from the United States. *Amer. Econ. Rev.*, May 1987, *77*(2), pp. 316–20. **[G: U.S.]**

Bloch, Charlotte. Female Unemployment and Knowledge of Self. *Pedersen, P. J. and Lund, R., eds.*, 1987, pp. 339–53. **[G: Denmark]**

Boehm, Thomas P. and Hofler, Richard A. A Frontier Approach to Measuring the Effect of Market Discrimination: A Housing Illustration. *Southern Econ. J.*, October 1987, *54*(2), pp. 301–15. **[G: U.S.]**

Bognanno, Mario F. Women in Professions: Academic Women. *Koziara, K. S.; Moskow, M. H. and Tanner, L. D., eds.*, 1987, pp. 245–64. **[G: U.S.]**

Bonnell, Sheila M. The Effect of Equal Pay for Females on the Composition of Employment in Australia. *Econ. Rec.*, December 1987, *63*(183), pp. 340–51. **[G: Australia]**

Borjas, George J. Immigrants, Minorities, and Labor Market Competition. *Ind. Lab. Relat. Rev.*, April 1987, *40*(3), pp. 382–92. **[G: U.S.]**

Boulle, Laurence and Julyan, Jacky. The Legal Structure of the Apartheid State. *Sethi, S. P., ed.*, 1987, pp. 127–48. **[G: S. Africa]**

Boyd, D. A. C. The Historical Materialist–Symbolist Theory of Race Discrimination. *Soc. Econ. Stud.*, June 1987, *36*(2), pp. 123–43.

Brand, Simon S. How Economic Sanctions Could Cripple Reform. *Sethi, S. P., ed.*, 1987, pp. 197–203. **[G: S. Africa]**

Bromfield, David H. Women and the Law of Property in Early America. *Mich. Law Rev.*, Apr.-May 1987, *85*(5–6), pp. 1109–16.

Brown, Charles C. and Wilcher, Shirley J. Sex-Based Employment Quotas in Sweden. *Brown, C. and Pechman, J. A., eds.*, 1987, pp. 271–98. **[G: Sweden]**

Brown, Clair. Consumption Norms, Work Roles, and Economic Growth, 1918–80. *Brown, C. and Pechman, J. A., eds.*, 1987, pp. 13–49. **[G: U.S.]**

Brown, Clair and Pechman, Joseph A. Gender in the Workplace: Introduction. *Brown, C. and Pechman, J. A., eds.*, 1987, pp. 1–11. **[G: U.S.]**

Buchanan, James M. Equal Treatment and Reverse Discrimination. *Buchanan, J. M. (II)*, 1987, *1981*, pp. 276–88.

Burtless, Gary. Income for the Single Parent: Child Support, Work, and Welfare: Comments. *Brown, C. and Pechman, J. A., eds.*, 1987, pp. 263–67. **[G: U.S.]**

Buthelezi, Mangosuthu G. Discerning the Divestment Debate. *Sethi, S. P., ed.*, 1987, pp. 165–69. **[G: S. Africa]**

Butler, Richard J. and McDonald, James B. Interdistributional Income Inequality. *J. Bus.*

Econ. Statist., January 1987, *5*(1), pp. 13–18. **[G: U.S.]**

Carrington, Selwyn H. H. The American Revolution and the British West Indies' Economy. *Solow, B. L. and Engerman, S. L., eds.*, 1987, pp. 135–61. **[G: Caribbean; U.K.]**

Carson, Emmett D. The Charitable Activities of Black Americans: A Portrait of Self-help? *Rev. Black Polit. Econ.*, Winter 1987, *15*(3), pp. 100–111. **[G: U.S.]**

Carter, Gregg Lee. Local Police Force Size and the Severity of the 1960s Black Rioting. *J. Conflict Resolution*, December 1987, *31*(4), pp. 601–14. **[G: U.S.]**

Carter, Susan B. Consumption Norms, Work Roles, and Economic Growth, 1918–80: Comments. *Brown, C. and Pechman, J. A., eds.*, 1987, pp. 49–54. **[G: U.S.]**

Castro, Emilio. Church Groups Lead the Battle against Apartheid: International Campaign. *Sethi, S. P., ed.*, 1987, pp. 271–78. **[G: S. Africa; U.S.]**

Chan, Kenneth S. The Production Effect of Discrimination: A Conceptual Investigation. *J. Econ. Behav. Organ.*, June 1987, *8*(2), pp. 307–14.

Chandhoke, Neera. The Apartheid State: Crisis of Legitimacy. *Ali, S. S. and Gupta, A., eds.*, 1987, pp. 146–63. **[G: S. Africa]**

Chaney, Elsa M. Women's Components in Integrated Rural Development Projects. *Deere, C. D. and León, M., eds.*, 1987, pp. 191–211. **[G: Jamaica; Dominican Republic]**

Chapman, Bruce J. Labour Turnover and Wage Determination. *Australian Econ. Pap.*, June 1987, *26*(48), pp. 119–29. **[G: Australia]**

Chatterjee, Lata and Lakshmanan, T. R. The Role of Women in Technical Change. *Fischer, M. M. and Nijkamp, P., eds.*, 1987, pp. 345–66. **[G: OECD]**

Clark, Robert L. Aging and Relative Earnings. *Sandell, S. H., ed.*, 1987, pp. 71–83. **[G: U.S.]**

Clarke, S. E.; Kirby, Andrew and McNown, Robert F. Research Policy and Review 18. *Losing Ground*—or Losing Credibility? An Examination of a Recent Policy Debate in the United States. *Environ. Planning A*, August 1987, *19*(8), pp. 1015–25. **[G: U.S.]**

Cloutier, Norman R. Who Gains from Racism? The Impact of Racial Inequality on White Income Distribution. *Rev. Soc. Econ.*, October 1987, *45*(2), pp. 152–62. **[G: U.S.]**

Cobbett, M. The Land Question in South Africa: A Preliminary Assessment. *S. Afr. J. Econ.*, March 1987, *55*(1), pp. 63–77. **[G: S. Africa]**

Colwill, Nina L. Men and Women in Organizations: Roles and Status, Stereotypes and Power. *Koziara, K. S.; Moskow, M. H. and Tanner, L. D., eds.*, 1987, pp. 97–117. **[G: U.S.]**

Cook, Alice H. International Comparisons: Problems and Research in the Industrialized World. *Koziara, K. S.; Moskow, M. H. and Tanner, L. D., eds.*, 1987, pp. 332–73. **[G: Global]**

Coons, Christopher. Divestment Steamroller

Seeks to Bury Apartheid. *Sethi, S. P., ed.*, 1987, pp. 295–306.　　　　**[G: S. Africa]**

Corcoran, Mary E. and Courant, Paul N. Sex-Role Socialization and Occupational Segregation: An Exploratory Investigation. *J. Post Keynesian Econ.*, Spring 1987, *9*(3), pp. 330–46.　　　　**[G: U.S.]**

Craton, Michael. What and Who to Whom and What: The Significance of Slave Resistance. *Solow, B. L. and Engerman, S. L., eds.*, 1987, pp. 259–82.　　　　**[G: Caribbean]**

Cross, Gary and Shergold, Peter R. "We Think We Are of the Oppressed": Gender, White Collar Work, and Grievances of Late Nineteenth-Century Women. *Labor Hist.*, Winter 1987, *28*(1), pp. 23–53.　　**[G: U.S.]**

Crummett, María de los Angeles. Rural Women and Migration in Latin America. *Deere, C. D. and León, M., eds.*, 1987, pp. 239–60.　　　　**[G: Latin America]**

D'Amico, Thomas F. The Conceit of Labor Market Discrimination. *Amer. Econ. Rev.*, May 1987, *77*(2), pp. 310–15.

Dagum, Camilo. Measuring the Economic Affluence between Populations of Income Receivers. *J. Bus. Econ. Statist.*, January 1987, *5*(1), pp. 5–12.　　　　**[G: U.S.]**

Damodaran, A. K. The Anti-apartheid Struggle: Indians and India. *Ali, S. S. and Gupta, A., eds.*, 1987, pp. 215–25.　　**[G: S. Africa]**

Daniels, Rudolph. The Nature of the Agrarian Land Question in the Republic of South Africa. *Amer. J. Econ. Soc.*, January 1987, *46*(1), pp. 1–16.　　　　**[G: S. Africa]**

Daniels, Rudolph. The Structure of the South African Labor Market, 1970–83. *Rev. Black Polit. Econ.*, Spring 1987, *15*(4), pp. 63–78.　　　　**[G: S. Africa]**

Danziger, Sheldon and Gottschalk, Peter. Earnings Inequality, the Spatial Concentration of Poverty, and the Underclass. *Amer. Econ. Rev.*, May 1987, *77*(2), pp. 211–15.　　　　**[G: U.S.]**

Darity, William A., Jr. Abram Harris: An Odyssey from Howard to Chicago. *Rev. Black Polit. Econ.*, Winter 1987, *15*(3), pp. 4–40.

Das Gupta, Monica. Selective Discrimination against Female Children in Rural Punjab, India. *Population Devel. Rev.*, March 1987, *13*(1), pp. 77–100.　　**[G: India]**

Das Gupta, Prithwis. The Decline in Occupational Sex Segregation during the 1970s: Census and CPS Comparisons: Comment. *Demography*, May 1987, *24*(2), pp. 291–95.　　　　**[G: U.S.]**

Davis, David Brion. Capitalism, Abolitionism, and Hegemony. *Solow, B. L. and Engerman, S. L., eds.*, 1987, pp. 209–27.

Davis, Douglas D. Maximal Quality Selection and Discrimination in Employment. *J. Econ. Behav. Organ.*, March 1987, *8*(1), pp. 97–112.　　　　**[G: U.S.]**

De Gregori, Thomas R. and Darity, William A., Jr. Surplus People and Expendable Children: The Structure of Apartheid and the Mortality Crisis in South Africa. *Rev. Black Polit. Econ.*,

Spring 1987, *15*(4), pp. 47–62. **[G: S. Africa]**

Deere, Carmen Diana. The Latin American Agrarian Reform Experience. *Deere, C. D. and León, M., eds.*, 1987, pp. 165–90.　　　　**[G: Latin America]**

Deere, Carmen Diana and León, Magdalena. Rural Women and State Policy: Feminist Perspectives on Latin American Agricultural Development: Conclusion. *Deere, C. D. and León, M., eds.*, 1987, pp. 261–64.

Deere, Carmen Diana and León, Magdalena. Rural Women and State Policy: Feminist Perspectives on Latin American Agricultural Development: Introduction. *Deere, C. D. and León, M., eds.*, 1987, pp. 1–17.　　　　**[G: Latin America]**

Del Boca, Daniela. Wage Discrimination: Empirical Findings from Direct and Reverse Regression. *Ricerche Econ.*, Jan.-Mar. 1987, *41*(1), pp. 82–95.　　**[G: W. Germany; Italy; U.S.; U.K.]**

Dipboye, Robert L. Problems and Progress of Women in Management. *Koziara, K. S.; Moskow, M. H. and Tanner, L. D., eds.*, 1987, pp. 118–53.　　　　**[G: U.S.]**

Doeringer, Peter B. Gender and the Dynamics of Subcontracting in Mexico City: Comments. *Brown, C. and Pechman, J. A., eds.*, 1987, pp. 185–88.　　　　**[G: Mexico]**

Dolphyne, Florence Abena. The Ghana National Council on Women and Development: An Example of Concerted Action. *Oppong, C., ed.*, 1987, pp. 213–18.　　**[G: Ghana]**

Dolton, Peter J. and Makepeace, Gerald H. Marital Status, Child Rearing and Earnings Differentials in the Graduate Labour Market. *Econ. J.*, December 1987, *97*(388), pp. 897–922.　　　　**[G: U.K.]**

Drescher, Seymour. Paradigms Tossed: Capitalism and the Political Sources of Abolition. *Solow, B. L. and Engerman, S. L., eds.*, 1987, pp. 191–208.

Du Bois, W. E. B. The Negro Criminal. *Rev. Black Polit. Econ.*, Summer-Fall 1987, *16*(1–2), pp. 17–31.　　　　**[G: U.S.]**

Dunn, Richard S. "Dreadful Idlers" in the Cane Fields: The Slave Labor Pattern on a Jamaican Sugar Estate, 1762–1831. *Solow, B. L. and Engerman, S. L., eds.*, 1987, pp. 163–90.　　　　**[G: Jamaica]**

Dutoya, C. and Gauvin, Annie. Assignment of Women Workers to Jobs and Company Strategies in France. *Tarling, R., ed.*, 1987, pp. 127–44.　　　　**[G: France]**

Ehrenberg, Ronald G. and Smith, Robert S. Comparable Worth in the Public Sector. *Wise, D. A., ed.*, 1987, pp. 243–88.　　**[G: U.S.]**

Ehrenberg, Ronald G. and Smith, Robert S. Comparable-Worth Wage Adjustments and Female Employment in the State and Local Sector. *J. Lab. Econ.*, January 1987, *5*(1), pp. 43–62.　　　　**[G: U.S.]**

Ervin, Delbert J. The Ecological Theory of Migration: Reconceptualizing Indigenous Labor Force. *Soc. Sci. Quart.*, December 1987, *68*(4), pp. 866–75.　　　　**[G: U.S.]**

Faley, Robert H. and Froggatt, Kirk L. A Longitudinal Examination of the Membership Patterns of Minorities and Women in Referral Unions. *J. Lab. Res.*, Winter 1987, *8*(1), pp. 93–101.   **[G: U.S.]**

Fapohunda, Eleanor R. Urban Women's Roles and Nigerian Government Development Strategies. *Oppong, C., ed.*, 1987, pp. 203–12.
                    [G: Nigeria]

Farley, John E. Disproportionate Black and Hispanic Unemployment in U.S. Metropolitan Areas: The Roles of Racial Inequality, Segregation and Discrimination in Male Joblessness. *Amer. J. Econ. Soc.*, April 1987, *46*(2), pp. 129–50.
                    [G: U.S.]

Fava, Sylvia F. Diversity in New Communities: A Case Study of Reston, Virginia, at Age 20. *van Vliet—, W., et al., eds.*, 1987, pp. 139–54.   **[G: U.S.]**

Feiner, Susan F. and Morgan, Barbara A. Women and Minorities in Introductory Economics Textbooks: 1974 to 1984. *J. Econ. Educ.*, Fall 1987, *18*(4), pp. 376–92.

Figart, Deborah M. Gender, Unions, and Internal Labor Markets: Evidence from the Public Sector in Two States. *Amer. Econ. Rev.*, May 1987, *77*(2), pp. 252–56.   **[G: U.S.]**

Findlay, Ronald and Lundahl, Mats. Racial Discrimination, Dualistic Labor Markets and Foreign Investment. *J. Devel. Econ.*, October 1987, *27*(1–2), pp. 139–48.   **[G: S. Africa]**

Findlay, Ronald and Lundahl, Mats. Racial Discrimination, Dualistic Labor Markets and Foreign Investment. *[Diaz-Alejandro, C. F.]*, 1987, pp. 139–48.   **[G: S. Africa]**

Fischer, Charles C. Toward a More Complete Understanding of Occupational Sex Discrimination. *J. Econ. Issues*, March 1987, *21*(1), pp. 113–38.   **[G: U.S.]**

Flora, Cornelia Butler. Income Generation Projects for Rural Women. *Deere, C. D. and León, M., eds.*, 1987, pp. 212–38.
                    [G: Latin America]

Folbre, Nancy R. A Patriarchal Mode of Production. *Albelda, R.; Gunn, C. and Waller, W., eds.*, 1987, pp. 323–38.

Fosu, Augustin Kwasi. Explaining Post-1964 Earnings Gains by Black Women: Race or Sex? *Rev. Black Polit. Econ.*, Winter 1987, *15*(3), pp. 41–55.   **[G: U.S.]**

Freeman, Richard B. The Relation of Criminal Activity to Black Youth Employment. *Rev. Black Polit. Econ.*, Summer-Fall 1987, *16*(1–2), pp. 99–107.   **[G: U.S.]**

Freeman, Richard B. and Leonard, Jonathan S. Union Maids: Unions and the Female Work Force. *Brown, C. and Pechman, J. A., eds.*, 1987, pp. 189–212.   **[G: U.S.]**

Gabriel, Paul E. and Schmitz, Susanne. The Relative Earnings of Native and Immigrant Males in the United States. *Quart. Rev. Econ. Bus.*, Autumn 1987, *27*(3), pp. 91–101.   **[G: U.S.]**

Gabriel, Stuart A. Economic Effects of Racial Integration: An Analysis of Hedonic Housing Prices and the Willingness to Pay. *Amer. Real Estate Urban Econ. Assoc. J.*, Fall 1987, *15*(3), pp. 268–79.   **[G: U.S.]**

Galster, George C. Residential Segregation and Interracial Economic Disparities: A Simultaneous-Equations Approach. *J. Urban Econ.*, January 1987, *21*(1), pp. 22–44.   **[G: U.S.]**

Garbers, Johan G. Black Education in South Africa: Parameters, Scenarios, Needs. *Sethi, S. P., ed.*, 1987, pp. 245–52.   **[G: S. Africa]**

Gardner, Eileen M. Back to Basics for Black Education. *Perkins, J., ed.*, 1987, pp. 37–47.
                    [G: U.S.]

Gastwirth, Joseph L. and Greenhouse, Samuel W. Estimating a Common Relative Risk: Application in Equal Employment. *J. Amer. Statist. Assoc.*, March 1987, *82*(397), pp. 38–45.
                    [G: U.S.]

Geiger, Susan. Women and Class in Africa: A Review. *African Econ. Hist.*, 1987, (16), pp. 115–22.   **[G: Africa]**

Gerlach, Knut. A Note on Male–Female Wage Differences in West Germany. *J. Human Res.*, Fall 1987, *22*(4), pp. 584–92.
                    [G: W. Germany]

Getman, Thomas R. and Flory, David. South Africa's Refugees. *U.S. Committee for Refugees.*, 1987, pp. 13–18.   **[G: S. Africa]**

Giannini, Mirella. Donne e lavoro nel contesto meridionale. (Women and Work in the Mezzogiorno. With English summary.) *Econ. Lavoro*, Apr.-June 1987, *21*(2), pp. 67–85.   **[G: Italy]**

Ginsburg, Helen. Sex-Based Employment Quotas in Sweden: Comments. *Brown, C. and Pechman, J. A., eds.*, 1987, pp. 301–08.
                    [G: Sweden]

Goldin, Claudia. The Gender Gap in Historical Perspective. *Kilby, P., ed.*, 1987, pp. 135–70.
                    [G: U.S.]

Goldin, Claudia and Polachek, Solomon W. Residual Differences by Sex: Perspectives on the Gender Gap in Earnings. *Amer. Econ. Rev.*, May 1987, *77*(2), pp. 143–51.   **[G: U.S.]**

Good, David H. and Pirog-Good, Maureen A. A Simultaneous Probit Model of Crime and Employment for Black and White Teenage Males. *Rev. Black Polit. Econ.*, Summer-Fall 1987, *16*(1–2), pp. 109–27.   **[G: U.S.]**

Good, David H. and Pirog-Good, Maureen A. Employment, Crime, and Race. *Contemp. Policy Issues*, October 1987, *5*(4), pp. 91–104.
                    [G: U.S.]

Gray, Lois S. Professional Careers for Women in Industrial Relations. *Koziara, K. S.; Moskow, M. H. and Tanner, L. D., eds.*, 1987, pp. 225–44.   **[G: U.S.]**

Green, William A. Race and Slavery: Considerations on the Williams Thesis. *Solow, B. L. and Engerman, S. L., eds.*, 1987, pp. 25–49.
                    [G: Caribbean; U.S.]

Grenier, Gilles. Earnings by Language Group in Quebec in 1980 and Emigration from Quebec between 1976 and 1981. *Can. J. Econ.*, November 1987, *20*(4), pp. 774–91.
                    [G: Canada]

Griffin, Mary C. Making the Army Safe for Diversity: A Title VII Remedy for Discrimination in the Military. *Yale Law J.*, July 1987, *96*(8), pp. 2082–2109. [G: U.S.]

Grimes, Paul W. Right-to-Work Legislation and the Economic Position of Black Workers. *Rev. Black Polit. Econ.*, Spring 1987, *15*(4), pp. 79–88. [G: U.S.]

Gupta, Vijay. Dialectics of Southern African Crisis: Basic Contradictions. *Ali, S. S. and Gupta, A., eds.*, 1987, pp. 164–81.
[G: Southern Africa]

Harris, Robert L., Jr. The Flowering of Afro-American History: Review Article. *Amer. Hist. Rev.*, December 1987, *92*(5), pp. 1150–61.
[G: U.S.]

Hartmann, Heidi I. Internal Labor Markets and Gender: A Case Study of Promotion. *Brown, C. and Pechman, J. A., eds.*, 1987, pp. 59–92. [G: U.S.]

Headen, Alvin E., Jr. Price Discrimination in Physician Services Markets Based on Race: New Test of an Old Implicit Hypothesis. *Rev. Black Polit. Econ.*, Spring 1987, *15*(4), pp. 5–20. [G: U.S.]

Henderson, Alexa Benson. Herman E. Perry and Black Enterprise in Atlanta, 1908–1925. *Bus. Hist. Rev.*, Summer 1987, *61*(2), pp. 216–42.
[G: U.S.]

Heywood, John S. Wage Discrimination and Market Structure. *J. Post Keynesian Econ.*, Summer 1987, *9*(4), pp. 617–28. [G: U.S.]

Hirsch, Werner Z. Landlord–Tenant Laws and Indigent Black Tenants. *Jaffe, A. J., ed.*, 1987, pp. 129–41. [G: U.S.]

Hoffman, Emily P. Determinants of Youths' Educational and Occupational Goals: Sex and Race Differences. *Econ. Educ. Rev.*, 1987, *6*(1), pp. 41–48. [G: U.S.]

Holden, Karen C. and Hansen, W. Lee. Part-time Work, Full-time Work, and Occupational Segregation. *Brown, C. and Pechman, J. A., eds.*, 1987, pp. 217–40. [G: U.S.]

Holzer, Harry J. Informal Job Search and Black Youth Unemployment. *Amer. Econ. Rev.*, June 1987, *77*(3), pp. 446–52. [G: U.S.]

Howard-Merriam, Kathleen. The Impact of Rural Electrification on Egyptian Farm Women's Lives. *Pachauri, R. K., ed.*, 1987, pp. 271–90. [G: Egypt]

Hoyman, Michele M. and Stallworth, Lamont. Participation in Local Unions: A Comparison of Black and White Members. *Ind. Lab. Relat. Rev.*, April 1987, *40*(3), pp. 323–35.
[G: U.S.]

Hughes, Mark Alan. Moving Up and Moving Out: Confusing Ends and Means about Ghetto Dispersal. *Urban Stud.*, December 1987, *24*(6), pp. 503–17. [G: U.S.]

Human, L. and Greenacre, M. J. Labor Market Discrimination in the Manufacturing Sector: The Impact of Race, Gender, Education and Age on Income. *S. Afr. J. Econ.*, June 1987, *55*(2), pp. 150–64. [G: S. Africa]

Humphries, Jane. "...The Most Free From Objection..." The Sexual Division of Labor and Women's Work in Nineteenth-Century En-

gland. *J. Econ. Hist.*, December 1987, *47*(4), pp. 929–49. [G: U.K.]

Inikori, Joseph E. Slavery and the Development of Industrial Capitalism in England. *Solow, B. L. and Engerman, S. L., eds.*, 1987, pp. 79–101. [G: U.K.]

Ivens, Michael. The Corporate Role in Fighting Apartheid: British Style. *Sethi, S. P., ed.*, 1987, pp. 319–31. [G: S. Africa]

Jacobs, Jerry A. The Sex Typing of Aspirations and Occupations: Instability during the Careers of Young Women. *Soc. Sci. Quart.*, March 1987, *68*(1), pp. 122–37. [G: U.S.]

James, Franklin J. and Clark, Thomas A. Minority Business in Urban Economies. *Urban Stud.*, December 1987, *24*(6), pp. 489–502.
[G: U.S.]

Johnson, Marshall; Parish, William L. and Lin, Elizabeth. Chinese Women, Rural Society, and External Markets. *Econ. Develop. Cult. Change*, January 1987, *35*(2), pp. 257–77.
[G: China]

Jondrow, Jim; Brechling, Frank and Marcus, Alan J. Older Workers in the Market for Part-time Employment. *Sandell, S. H., ed.*, 1987, pp. 84–99. [G: U.S.]

Jones, John Paul, III. Work, Welfare, and Poverty among Black Female-Headed Families. *Econ. Geogr.*, January 1987, *63*(1), pp. 20–34.
[G: U.S.]

Jørgensen, Birte Bech. Unemployment and the Cultures of Young Women. *Pedersen, P. J. and Lund, R., eds.*, 1987, pp. 321–37.
[G: Denmark]

Kaempfer, William H.; Lehman, James A. and Lowenberg, Anton D. The Economics of the Call for Anti-apartheid Investment Sanctions. *Soc. Sci. Quart.*, September 1987, *68*(3), pp. 528–38. [G: S. Africa]

Karklins, Rasma. Nationality Policy and Ethnic Relations in the USSR. *Millar, J. R., ed.*, 1987, pp. 301–31. [G: U.S.S.R.]

Kassebaum, Nancy Landon. Caution Signs on the Road to Reform. *Sethi, S. P., ed.*, 1987, pp. 46–52. [G: S. Africa]

Kelley, Maryellen R. Internal Labor Markets and Gender: A Case Study of Promotion: Comments. *Brown, C. and Pechman, J. A., eds.*, 1987, pp. 97–105. [G: U.S.]

Kennedy, Bruce. Youth Employment in Canada: A Comment. *Can. Public Policy*, September 1987, *13*(3), pp. 384–88. [G: Canada]

Khandker, Shahidur R. Women's Role in Household Productive Activities and Fertility in Bangladesh. *J. Econ. Devel.*, June 1987, *12*(1), pp. 87–115. [G: Bangladesh]

Killingsworth, Mark R. Heterogeneous Preferences, Compensating Wage Differentials, and Comparable Worth. *Quart. J. Econ.*, November 1987, *102*(4), pp. 727–42.

Kirkby, Diane. "The Wage-Earning Woman and the State": The National Women's Trade Union League and Protective Labor Legislation, 1903–1923. *Labor Hist.*, Winter 1987, *28*(1), pp. 54–74. [G: U.S.]

König, Wolfgang. Employment and Career Mobility of Women in France and the Federal Republic. *Teckenberg, W., ed.*, 1987, pp. 53–85. **[G: France; W. Germany]**

Koziara, Karen Shallcross. Women and Work: The Evolving Policy. *Koziara, K. S.; Moskow, M. H. and Tanner, L. D., eds.*, 1987, pp. 374–408. **[G: U.S.]**

Koziara, Karen Shallcross; Moskow, Michael H. and Tanner, Lucretia Dewey. Working Women—A Summary of Research Knowledge and Research Needs. *Koziara, K. S.; Moskow, M. H. and Tanner, L. D., eds.*, 1987, pp. vii–xxii.

Kozlowski, Gregory C. Muslim Women and the Control of Property in North India. *Indian Econ. Soc. Hist. Rev.*, Apr.-June 1987, *24*(2), pp. 163–81. **[G: India]**

Kramer, Helgard. Frankfurt's Working Women: Scapegoats or Winners of the Great Depression? *Evans, R. J. and Geary, D., eds.*, 1987, pp. 108–41. **[G: Germany]**

Krumm, Ronald J. Regional Wage Differentials and Race: 1973–1978. *J. Reg. Sci.*, February 1987, *27*(1), pp. 119–28. **[G: U.S.]**

Krynski, Kathy J. Women and Work: A Survey of Textbooks. *J. Econ. Educ.*, Fall 1987, *18*(4), pp. 437–44. **[G: U.S.]**

Kuhn, Peter J. Sex Discrimination in Labor Markets: The Role of Statistical Evidence. *Amer. Econ. Rev.*, September 1987, *77*(4), pp. 567–83. **[G: U.S.; Canada]**

Kumar, Shubh K. Women's Role and Agricultural Technology. *Mellor, J. W.; Delgado, C. L. and Blackie, M. J., eds.*, 1987, pp. 135–47. **[G: Africa]**

Laband, David N. A Qualitative Test of Journal Discrimination against Women. *Eastern Econ. J.*, Apr.-June 1987, *13*(2), pp. 149–53. **[G: U.S.]**

Lago, María Soledad. Rural Women and the Neoliberal Model in Chile. *Deere, C. D. and León, M., eds.*, 1987, pp. 21–34. **[G: Chile]**

Lebergott, Stanley. Consumption Norms, Work Roles, and Economic Growth, 1918–80: Comments. *Brown, C. and Pechman, J. A., eds.*, 1987, pp. 54–58. **[G: U.S.]**

León, Magdalena. Colombian Agricultural Policies and the Debate on Policies toward Rural Women. *Deere, C. D. and León, M., eds.*, 1987, pp. 84–104. **[G: Colombia]**

Leonard, Jonathan S. The Interaction of Residential Segregation and Employment Discrimination. *J. Urban Econ.*, May 1987, *21*(3), pp. 323–46. **[G: U.S.]**

Levin, M. and Horn, G. S. Phillips Curves for Selected South African Labour Markets, 1969–1985. *J. Stud. Econ. Econometrics*, November 1987, *11*(3), pp. 25–50. **[G: S. Africa]**

Lewis, Donald E. and Shorten, Brett. Female Participation in the Australian Labour Force. *Australian Bull. Lab.*, September 1987, *13*(4), pp. 237–63. **[G: Australia]**

Logan, John R. and Messner, Steven F. Racial Residential Segregation and Suburban Violent Crime. *Soc. Sci. Quart.*, September 1987, *68*(3), pp. 510–27. **[G: U.S.]**

Lommerud, Kjell Erik. Persistent Discrimination with Social Ability as a Productive Factor. *J. Inst. Theoretical Econ.*, June 1987, *143*(2), pp. 261–71.

Lordoğlu, Kuvvet. Yüksek Eğitim Gören Kadin işgücü Adaylari ve Çalişma eğilimleri. (With English summary.) *METU*, 1987, *14*(3), pp. 215–43. **[G: Turkey]**

Loury, Glenn C. A Call to Arms for Black Conservatives. *Perkins, J., ed.*, 1987, pp. 9–17. **[G: U.S.]**

Loutfi, Martha F. Development with Women: Action, Not Alibis. *Int. Lab. Rev.*, Jan.-Feb. 1987, *126*(1), pp. 111–24.

Low, Stuart A. and Vilegas, Daniel J. An Alternative Approach to the Analysis of Wage Differentials. *Southern Econ. J.*, October 1987, *54*(2), pp. 449–62. **[G: U.S.]**

Madden, Janice Fanning. Gender Differences in the Cost of Displacement: An Empirical Test of Discrimination in the Labor Market. *Amer. Econ. Rev.*, May 1987, *77*(2), pp. 246–51. **[G: U.S.]**

Magura, Michael and Shapiro, Edward. The Black Dropout Rate and the Black Youth Unemployment Rate: A Granger-Causal Analysis. *Rev. Black Polit. Econ.*, Winter 1987, *15*(3), pp. 56–67. **[G: U.S.]**

Malveaux, Julianne and Wallace, Phyllis. Minority Women in the Workplace. *Koziara, K. S.; Moskow, M. H. and Tanner, L. D., eds.*, 1987, pp. 265–98. **[G: U.S.]**

Marcuse, Peter. The Other Side of Housing: Oppression and Liberation. *Turner, B.; Kemeny, J. and Lundqvist, L. J., eds.*, 1987, pp. 232–70.

Margo, Robert A. Accounting for Racial Differences in School Attendance in the American South, 1900: The Role of Separate-but-Equal. *Rev. Econ. Statist.*, November 1987, *69*(4), pp. 661–66. **[G: U.S.]**

Marlin, Alice Tepper. Social Investing: Potent Force for Political Change. *Sethi, S. P., ed.*, 1987, pp. 307–16. **[G: U.S.; S. Africa]**

Marshall, Ray and Paulin, Beth. Employment and Earnings of Women: Historical Perspective. *Koziara, K. S.; Moskow, M. H. and Tanner, L. D., eds.*, 1987, pp. 1–36. **[G: U.S.]**

Marzullo, Sal G. Corporations: Catalyst for Change. *Sethi, S. P., ed.*, 1987, pp. 371–80. **[G: S. Africa]**

McCrate, Elaine. Trade, Merger and Employment: Economic Theory on Marriage. *Rev. Radical Polit. Econ.*, Spring 1987, *19*(1), pp. 73–89. **[G: U.S.]**

McKinney, Frederick W. The Economic Survival of Black Physicians: Swimming in Turbulent Waters. *Rev. Black Polit. Econ.*, Spring 1987, *15*(4), pp. 35–46. **[G: U.S.]**

Medoff, James L. Comparable Worth in the Public Sector: Comment. *Wise, D. A., ed.*, 1987, pp. 288–89. **[G: U.S.]**

Milgrom, Paul R. and Oster, Sharon. Job Discrimination, Market Forces, and the Invisibility Hypothesis. *Quart. J. Econ.*, August 1987, *102*(3), pp. 453–76.

Miller, Paul W. Gender Differences in Observed and Offered Wages in Canada, 1980. *Can. J. Econ.*, May 1987, *20*(2), pp. 225–44.
[G: Canada]

Miller, Paul W. The Wage Effect of the Occupational Segregation of Women in Britain. *Econ. J.*, December 1987, *97*(388), pp. 885–96.
[G: U.K.]

Milley, Donald J. Consumer Demand by Black Americans. *Rev. Black Polit. Econ.*, Winter 1987, *15*(3), pp. 87–99. [G: U.S.]

Moen, Elizabeth W. What Does "Control over Our Bodies" Really Mean? *Menard, S. W. and Moen, E. W., eds.*, 1987, *1979*, pp. 277–87.

van Moeseke, Paul. Allocative Cost of Weighted Discrimination. *Math. Soc. Sci.*, August 1987, *14*(1), pp. 51–57.

Mones, Belkis and Grant, Lydia. Agricultural Development, the Economic Crisis, and Rural Women in the Dominican Republic. *Deere, C. D. and León, M., eds.*, 1987, pp. 35–50.
[G: Dominican Republic]

Montgomery, Edward and Wascher, William L. Race and Gender Wage Inequality in Services and Manufacturing. *Ind. Relat.*, Fall 1987, *26*(3), pp. 284–90. [G: U.S.]

Moore, Gary A. Analytical Perspectives on Employment Discrimination under Title VII: Economic, Legal, and Statistical Approaches. *Amer. Econ.*, Fall 1987, *31*(2), pp. 53–63.
[G: U.S.]

Moore, Robert L. Are Male/Female Earnings Differentials Related to Life-Expectancy-Caused Pension Cost Differences? *Econ. Inquiry*, July 1987, *25*(3), pp. 389–401. [G: U.S.]

Murphy, Joseph. The Apartheid Debate on American Campuses. *Sethi, S. P., ed.*, 1987, pp. 285–93. [G: U.S.; S. Africa]

Myers, Samuel L., Jr. Special Issue on Race and Crime: Introduction. *Rev. Black Polit. Econ.*, Summer-Fall 1987, *16*(1–2), pp. 5–15.
[G: U.S.]

Myers, Samuel L., Jr. and Sabol, William J. Business Cycles and Racial Disparities in Punishment. *Contemp. Policy Issues*, October 1987, *5*(4), pp. 46–58. [G: U.S.]

Myers, Samuel L., Jr. and Sabol, William J. Unemployment and Racial Differences in Imprisonment. *Rev. Black Polit. Econ.*, Summer-Fall 1987, *16*(1–2), pp. 189–209. [G: U.S.]

Myrdal, Gunnar. Inequality of Justice. *Rev. Black Polit. Econ.*, Summer-Fall 1987, *16*(1–2), pp. 81–98. [G: U.S.]

Needleman, Ruth and Tanner, Lucretia Dewey. Women in Unions: Current Issues. *Koziara, K. S.; Moskow, M. H. and Tanner, L. D., eds.*, 1987, pp. 187–224. [G: U.S.]

Nickel, Herman. Will Sanctions Harm the Oppressed or the Oppressor? *Sethi, S. P., ed.*, 1987, pp. 179–88. [G: S. Africa]

Nord, Stephen. Productivity and the Role of College in Narrowing the Male–Female Wage Differential in the USA in 1980. *Appl. Econ.*, January 1987, *19*(1), pp. 51–67. [G: U.S.]

Nord, Stephen. Schooling and Changes in the Inequality in Male and Female Earnings in the United States over the 1970s. *Appl. Econ.*, August 1987, *19*(8), pp. 1083–1105. [G: U.S.]

Noyelle, Thierry J. The New Technology and the New Economy: Some Implications for Equal Employment Opportunity. *Hartmann, H. I., ed.*, 1987, pp. 373–94. [G: U.S.]

Oc, Taner. Ethnic Minorities, Scarce Housing Resources, and Urban Renewal in Britain. *van Vliet—, W., et al., eds.*, 1987, pp. 91–104.
[G: U.K.]

Ohsfeldt, Robert L.; Culler, Steven D. and Becker, Edmund R. Sex Differences in the Economic Advantages of Physician Board Certification. *Southern Econ. J.*, October 1987, *54*(2), pp. 343–50. [G: U.S.]

van Ophem, Hans. An Empirical Test of the Segmented Labour Market Theory for the Netherlands. *Appl. Econ.*, November 1987, *19*(11), pp. 1497–1514. [G: Netherlands]

Orazem, Peter F. Black–White Differences in Schooling Investment and Human Capital Production in Segregated Schools. *Amer. Econ. Rev.*, September 1987, *77*(4), pp. 714–23.
[G: U.S.]

Orsi, Renzo. A Spillover Model of Male and Female Labour Markets. *Giorn. Econ.*, Nov.-Dec. 1987, *46*(11–12), pp. 590–616.
[G: Italy]

Osterman, Paul. Internal Labor Markets and Gender: A Case Study of Promotion: Comments. *Brown, C. and Pechman, J. A., eds.*, 1987, pp. 92–97. [G: U.S.]

Padilla, Martha Luz; Murguialday, Clara and Criquillon, Ana. Impact of the Sandinista Agrarian Reform on Rural Women's Subordination. *Deere, C. D. and León, M., eds.*, 1987, pp. 124–41. [G: Nicaragua]

Paul, Karen. The Inadequacy of Sullivan Reporting. *Sethi, S. P., ed.*, 1987, pp. 403–12.
[G: U.S.; S. Africa]

Pérez-Stable, Marifeli. Cuban Women and the Struggle for "Conciencia." *Mesa-Lago, C., ed.*, 1987, pp. 51–72. [G: Cuba]

Perkins, Joseph. An Agenda for Black America. *Perkins, J., ed.*, 1987, pp. 75–80. [G: U.S.]

Perkins, Joseph. Creating a Climate for Black Business. *Perkins, J., ed.*, 1987, pp. 63–74.
[G: U.S.]

Perkins, Joseph. Critical Issues: A Conservative Agenda for Black Americans: Introduction. *Perkins, J., ed.*, 1987, pp. 1–7. [G: U.S.]

Petersen, William. Politics and the Measurement of Ethnicity. *Alonso, W. and Starr, P., eds.*, 1987, pp. 187–233. [G: U.S.]

Phillips, Llad and Votey, Harold L., Jr. Rational Choice Models of Crimes by Youth. *Rev. Black Polit. Econ.*, Summer-Fall 1987, *16*(1–2), pp. 129–87. [G: U.S.]

Phillips, Llad and Votey, Harold L., Jr. Women's Changing Involvement with Crime: A Labor Force Participation Perspective. *Eastern Econ. J.*, July-Sept. 1987, *13*(3), pp. 233–42.
[G: U.S.]

Phillips, Lynne. Women, Development, and the State in Rural Ecuador. *Deere, C. D. and León, M., eds.*, 1987, pp. 105–23. [G: Ecuador]

Pittin, Renée. Documentation of Women's Work in Nigeria: Problems and Solutions. *Oppong, C., ed.*, 1987, pp. 25–44. **[G: Nigeria]**

Power, Marilyn. From Home Production to Wage Labor: Women as a Reserve Army of Labor. *England, R. W., ed.*, 1987, pp. 157–77. **[G: U.S.]**

Power, Marilyn. Unity and Division among Women: Feminist Theories of Gender and Class in Capitalist Society. *England, R. W., ed.*, 1987, *1984*, pp. 178–99. **[G: U.S.]**

Randall, Vicky and Smyth, Ailbhe. Bishops and Bailiwicks: Obstacles to Women's Political Participation in Ireland. *Econ. Soc. Rev.*, April 1987, *18*(3), pp. 189–214. **[G: Ireland]**

Rea, Samuel A., Jr. The Market Response to the Elimination of Sex-Based Annuities. *Southern Econ. J.*, July 1987, *54*(1), pp. 55–63.

Reid, Nelson and Lowe, Gary. Ethnic Utopianism and Market Reality in South Africa. *Cato J.*, Winter 1987, *6*(3), pp. 869–88.
[G: S. Africa]

Reilly, Barry. Wages, Sex Discrimination and the Irish Labour Market for Young Workers. *Econ. Soc. Rev.*, July 1987, *18*(4), pp. 271–305.
[G: Ireland]

Riach, Peter A. and Rich, Judith. Testing for Sexual Discrimination in the Labour Market. *Australian Econ. Pap.*, December 1987, *26*(49), pp. 165–78. **[G: Australia]**

Richardson, David. The Slave Trade, Sugar, and British Economic Growth, 1748–1776. *Solow, B. L. and Engerman, S. L., eds.*, 1987, pp. 103–33. **[G: U.K.; Caribbean]**

Root, Lawrence S. and Zarrugh, Laura H. Private-Sector Employment Practices for Older Workers. *Sandell, S. H., ed.*, 1987, pp. 177–91. **[G: U.S.]**

Rosholt, A. M. The South African Private Sector: Agent for Change or Government Stooge? *Sethi, S. P., ed.*, 1987, pp. 355–61.
[G: S. Africa]

Ross, Russell T. Disaggregate Labour Supply Functions for Married Women in New Zealand. *New Zealand Econ. Pap.*, 1987, *21*, pp. 41–55. **[G: New Zealand]**

Rotella, Elyce J. The Dynamics of Occupational Segregation among Bank Tellers: Comments. *Brown, C. and Pechman, J. A., eds.*, 1987, pp. 149–54. **[G: U.S.]**

Rothchild, Donald. Racial Stratification and Bargaining: The Kenya Experience. *Zartman, I. W., ed. (I)*, 1987, *1973*, pp. 235–54.
[G: Kenya]

Rubin, Jeffrey. Discrimination and Insurance Coverage of the Mentally Ill. *McGuire, T. G. and Scheffler, R. M., eds.*, 1987, pp. 195–209.
[G: U.S.]

Rubin, Robert. The Empowerment of the Refugee Community. *U.S. Committee for Refugees.*, 1987, pp. 19–23. **[G: U.S.]**

Sandell, Steven H. Labor Market Problems and Employment Policies Affecting Older Americans. *Sandell, S. H., ed.*, 1987, pp. 15–33.
[G: U.S.]

Sathar, Zeba A. Sex Differentials in Mortality: A

Corollary of Son Preference? *Pakistan Devel. Rev.*, Winter 1987, *26*(4), pp. 555–65.
[G: Pakistan]

Sav, G. Thomas. Institutional Structure, Finance, and Race in Higher Education: Public–Private Sectoral Differences. *Public Choice*, October 1987, *55*(3), pp. 257–64. **[G: U.S.]**

Sawhill, Isabel V. Income for the Single Parent: Child Support, Work, and Welfare: Comments. *Brown, C. and Pechman, J. A., eds.*, 1987, pp. 268–70. **[G: U.S.]**

Schafer, Daniel W. Measurement-Error Diagnostics and the Sex Discrimination Problem. *J. Bus. Econ. Statist.*, October 1987, *5*(4), pp. 529–37. **[G: U.S.]**

Schwartz, Herman. The 1986 and 1987 Affirmative Action Cases: It's All Over but the Shouting. *Mich. Law Rev.*, December 1987, *86*(3), pp. 524–76. **[G: U.S.]**

Scott, Joan W. 'L'ouvrière! Mot impie, sordide . . .': Women Workers in the Discourse of French Political Economy, 1840–1860. *Joyce, P., ed.*, 1987, pp. 119–42. **[G: France]**

Sellin, Thorsten. The Negro and the Problem of Law Observance and Administration in the Light of Social Research. *Rev. Black Polit. Econ.*, Summer-Fall 1987, *16*(1–2), pp. 71–80.
[G: U.S.]

Sethi, S. Prakash. South Africa Beyond Apartheid Reformation of Institutions and Instruments of Change. *Sethi, S. P., ed.*, 1987, pp. 1–37.
[G: S. Africa]

Shank, Susan E. and Haugen, Steven E. The Employment Situation during 1986: Job Gains Continue, Unemployment Dips. *Mon. Lab. Rev.*, February 1987, *110*(2), pp. 3–10.
[G: U.S.]

Shapiro, Daniel M. and Stelcner, Morton. Earnings Disparities among Linguistic Groups in Quebec, 1970–1980. *Can. Public Policy*, March 1987, *13*(1), pp. 97–104. **[G: Canada]**

Shapiro, Daniel M. and Stelcner, Morton. The Persistence of the Male–Female Earnings Gap in Canada, 1970–1980: The Impact of Equal Pay Laws and Language Policies. *Can. Public Policy*, December 1987, *13*(4), pp. 462–76.
[G: Canada]

Shapiro, David and Sandell, Steven H. The Reduced Pay of Older Job Losers: Age Discrimination and Other Explanations. *Sandell, S. H., ed.*, 1987, pp. 37–51. **[G: U.S.]**

Shaw, Lois B. and Shapiro, David. Women's Work Plans: Contrasting Expectations and Actual Work Experience. *Mon. Lab. Rev.*, November 1987, *110*(11), pp. 7–13. **[G: U.S.]**

Shaw, Lois B. and Shaw, Rachel. From Midlife to Retirement: The Middle-Aged Women Worker. *Koziara, K. S.; Moskow, M. H. and Tanner, L. D., eds.*, 1987, pp. 299–331.
[G: U.S.]

Shulman, Steven. Discrimination, Human Capital, and Black–White Unemployment: Evidence from Cities. *J. Human Res.*, Summer 1987, *22*(3), pp. 361–76. **[G: U.S.]**

Siebert, W. S. Black Trade Unions and the Wage Gap in South Africa. *Managerial Dec. Econ.*,

March 1987, *8*(1), pp. 55–65. **[G: S. Africa]**

Singh, Ram D. and Morey, Mathew J. The Value of Work-at-Home and Contributions of Wives' Household Service in Polygynous Families: Evidence from an African LDC. *Econ. Develop. Cult. Change*, July 1987, *35*(4), pp. 743–65. **[G: Burkina Faso]**

Smith, James P. and Welch, Finis. Race and Poverty: A Forty-Year Record. *Amer. Econ. Rev.*, May 1987, *77*(2), pp. 152–58.

Smith, N. Craig. How the West Gains from Apartheid: The Case of the United Kingdom. *Sethi, S. P., ed.*, 1987, pp. 333–52. **[G: U.K.; S. Africa]**

Smith, Rebecca L. and Thomson, C. Lee. Restricted Housing Markets for Female-Headed Households in U.S. Metropolitan Areas. *van Vliet—, W., et al., eds.*, 1987, pp. 279–90. **[G: U.S.]**

Solow, Barbara L. Capitalism and Slavery in the Exceedingly Long Run. *Solow, B. L. and Engerman, S. L., eds.*, 1987, pp. 51–77.

Solow, Barbara L. and Engerman, Stanley L. British Capitalism and Caribbean Slavery: The Legacy of Eric Williams: An Introduction. *Solow, B. L. and Engerman, S. L., eds.*, 1987, pp. 1–23. **[G: Caribbean]**

Sorensen, Elaine. Union Maids: Unions and the Female Work Force: Comments. *Brown, C. and Pechman, J. A., eds.*, 1987, pp. 213–16. **[G: U.S.]**

Soroka, Lewis A. Male/Female Income Distributions, City Size and Urban Characteristics: Canada, 1970–1980. *Urban Stud.*, October 1987, *24*(5), pp. 417–26. **[G: Canada]**

Spindel, Cheywa R. The Social Invisibility of Women's Work in Brazilian Agriculture. *Deere, C. D. and León, M., eds.*, 1987, pp. 51–66. **[G: Brazil]**

Spring, William J. Youth Unemployment and the Transition from School to Work: Programs in Boston, Frankfurt, and London. *New Eng. Econ. Rev.*, Mar./Apr. 1987, pp. 3–16. **[G: U.S.; U.K.; W. Germany]**

Stace, Sheila. Vocational Rehabilitation for Women with Disabilities. *Int. Lab. Rev.*, 1987, *126*(3), pp. 301–16. **[G: Global]**

Stern, David. Part-time Work, Full-time Work, and Occupational Segregation: Comments. *Brown, C. and Pechman, J. A., eds.*, 1987, pp. 240–46. **[G: U.S.]**

Stirati, Antonella. Differenze retributive e segregazione occupazionale per sesso nell'industria manifatturiera. (Wage Differences and Occupational Segregation by Sex in the Manufacturing Industries. With English summary.) *Econ. Lavoro*, July-Sept. 1987, *21*(3), pp. 51–76. **[G: Italy]**

Strober, Myra H. and Arnold, Carolyn L. Integrated Circuits/Segregated Labor: Women in Computer-Related Occupations and High-Tech Industries. *Hartmann, H. I., ed.*, 1987, pp. 136–82. **[G: U.S.]**

Strober, Myra H. and Arnold, Carolyn L. The Dynamics of Occupational Segregation among Bank Tellers. *Brown, C. and Pechman, J. A.,*

eds., 1987, pp. 107–48. **[G: U.S.]**

Strom, Sharon Hartman. "Machines Instead of Clerks": Technology and the Feminization of Bookkeeping, 1910–1950. *Hartmann, H. I., ed.*, 1987, pp. 63–97. **[G: U.S.]**

Stubbs, Jean. Gender Issues in Contemporary Cuban Tobacco Farming. *World Devel.*, January 1987, *15*(1), pp. 41–65. **[G: Cuba]**

Stubbs, Jean and Alvarez, Mavis. Women on the Agenda: The Cooperative Movement in Rural Cuba. *Deere, C. D. and León, M., eds.*, 1987, pp. 142–61. **[G: Cuba]**

Sullivan, Patricia A. and Damrosch, Shirley P. Homeless Women and Children. *Bingham, R. D.; Green, R. E. and White, S. B., eds.*, 1987, pp. 82–98. **[G: U.S.]**

Sutcliffe, Michael O. Plenty of Propaganda to Prop Up Pretoria. *Sethi, S. P., ed.*, 1987, pp. 171–78. **[G: S. Africa]**

Suzman, Helen. The Folly of Economic Sanctions. *Sethi, S. P., ed.*, 1987, pp. 189–95. **[G: S. Africa]**

Swinton, David H. Economic Theory and Working Class Poverty towards a Reformulation. *Amer. Econ. Rev.*, May 1987, *77*(2), pp. 223–28.

Taylor, Dalmas A. and Moriarty, Beatrice F. In-group Bias as a Function of Competition and Race. *J. Conflict Resolution*, March 1987, *31*(1), pp. 192–99.

Temperley, Howard. Eric Williams and Abolition: The Birth of a New Orthodoxy. *Solow, B. L. and Engerman, S. L., eds.*, 1987, pp. 229–57.

Thembela, Alexander Jabulan. The State of Education for Blacks in South Africa. *Sethi, S. P., ed.*, 1987, pp. 231–44. **[G: S. Africa]**

Thernstrom, Abigail. Statistics and the Politics of Minority Representation: The Evolution of the Voting Rights Act since 1965. *Alonso, W. and Starr, P., eds.*, 1987, pp. 303–27.

Thompson, James L. Discrimination, Jobs, and Politics: The Struggle for Equal Employment Opportunity in the United States since the New Deal. *Mich. Law Rev.*, Apr.-May 1987, *85*(5–6), pp. 1025–30.

Thompson, Larry D. Dealing with Black-on-Black Crime. *Perkins, J., ed.*, 1987, pp. 27–35. **[G: U.S.]**

Tutu, Desmond. A Plea for International Sanctions. *Sethi, S. P., ed.*, 1987, pp. 161–64. **[G: S. Africa]**

Tzannatos, Zafiris. A General Equilibrium Model of Discrimination and Its Effects on Incomes. *Scot. J. Polit. Econ.*, February 1987, *34*(1), pp. 19–36. **[G: U.K.]**

Tzannatos, Zafiris. The Greek Labour Market: Current Perspectives and Future Prospects. *Greek Econ. Rev.*, 1987, *9*(2), pp. 224–38. **[G: Greece]**

Ulman, Lloyd. The Dynamics of Occupational Segregation among Bank Tellers: Comments. *Brown, C. and Pechman, J. A., eds.*, 1987, pp. 154–57. **[G: U.S.]**

Van Niekerk Viljoen, Gerrit. Education for Black People in South Africa: Challenges and Prog-

ress. *Sethi, S. P., ed.*, 1987, pp. 221–29.
[G: S. Africa]
Van Zyl, Johannes Christiaan. Business Offers a Bill of Rights for South Africa. *Sethi, S. P., ed.*, 1987, pp. 363–69. [G: S. Africa]
Wan, Henry, Jr. Arrow and the Theory of Discrimination. *Feiwel, G. R., ed. (I)*, 1987, pp. 484–97.
Weedon, D. Reid, Jr. The Evolution of Sullivan Principle Compliance. *Sethi, S. P., ed.*, 1987, pp. 393–402. [G: S. Africa; U.S.]
Wéry, René. Women in Bamako: Activities and Relations. *Oppong, C., ed.*, 1987, pp. 45–62.
[G: Mali]
Wilking, Lou H. Should U.S. Corporations Abandon South Africa? *Sethi, S. P., ed.*, 1987, pp. 383–91. [G: U.S.; S. Africa]
Willcox, Walter F. Negro Criminality. *Rev. Black Polit. Econ.*, Summer-Fall 1987, *16*(1–2), pp. 33–45. [G: U.S.]
Williams, Rhonda M. Capital, Competition, and Discrimination: A Reconsideration of Racial Earnings Inequality. *Rev. Radical Polit. Econ.*, Summer 1987, *19*(2), pp. 1–15.
Williams, Walter E. How Business Transcends Politics. *Managerial Dec. Econ.*, March 1987, *8*(1), pp. 15–20.
Winckler, Victoria. Women and Work in Contemporary Wales. *Day, G. and Rees, G., eds.*, 1987, pp. 53–71. [G: U.K.]
Wolpe, Howard. The Double Standard of American Foreign Policy. *Sethi, S. P., ed.*, 1987, pp. 53–61. [G: S. Africa; U.S.]
Woodson, Robert L. Empowering Poor Neighborhoods. *Perkins, J., ed.*, 1987, pp. 49–61.
[G: U.S.]
Work, Monroe N. Negro Criminality in the South. *Rev. Black Polit. Econ.*, Summer-Fall 1987, *16*(1–2), pp. 63–69. [G: U.S.]
Wright, Elizabeth. Needed: A Moral Revival. *Perkins, J., ed.*, 1987, pp. 19–25. [G: U.S.]
Wright, Gavin. Capitalism and Slavery on the Islands: A Lesson from the Mainland. *Solow, B. L. and Engerman, S. L., eds.*, 1987, pp. 283–302. [G: Caribbean; U.S.]
Wuertz, Karen and van der Pennen, Ton. Participation by Ethnic Minorities in Urban Renewal in the Netherlands. *van Vliet—, W., et al., eds.*, 1987, pp. 105–16. [G: Netherlands]
Yamada, Tadashi; Yamada, Tetsuji and Chaloupka, Frank. Using Aggregate Data to Estimate the Part-Time and Full-Time Work Behavior of Japanese Women [An Analysis of Trends in Female Labor Force Participation in Japan]. *J. Human Res.*, Fall 1987, *22*(4), pp. 574–83. [G: Japan]
Yudelman, Sally W. The Integration of Women into Development Projects: Observations on the NGO Experience in General and in Latin America in Particular. *World Devel.*, Supp. Autumn 1987, *15*, pp. 179–87.
[G: Latin America]
Zarenda, H. Divergent Approaches to Discrimination and Apartheid (Review Note). *S. Afr. J. Econ.*, March 1987, *55*(1), pp. 78–82.
[G: S. Africa]

918 Economics of Aging

9180 Economics of Aging

Anderson, Joseph M.; Kennell, David L. and Sheils, John F. Health Plan Costs, Medicare, and Employment of Older Workers. *Sandell, S. H., ed.*, 1987, pp. 206–17. [G: U.S.]
Andrisani, Paul and Daymont, Thomas. Age Changes in Productivity and Earnings among Managers and Professionals. *Sandell, S. H., ed.*, 1987, pp. 52–70. [G: U.S.]
Auerbach, Alan J. and Kotlikoff, Laurence J. Life Insurance of the Elderly: Adequacy and Determinants. *Burtless, G., ed.*, 1987, pp. 229–67.
[G: U.S.]
Baily, Martin Neil. Aging and the Ability to Work: Policy Issues and Recent Trends. *Burtless, G., ed.*, 1987, pp. 59–97. [G: U.S.]
Banta, H. David. Aging and New Health Care Technology. *Economic Council of Canada.*, 1987, pp. 115–22. [G: Canada]
Bernheim, B. Douglas. Dissaving after Retirement: Testing the Pure Life Cycle Hypothesis. *Bodie, Z.; Shoven, J. B. and Wise, D. A., eds.*, 1987, pp. 237–74. [G: U.S.]
Blanchet, Madeleine. Advances in Preventive Medicine. *Economic Council of Canada.*, 1987, pp. 79–92. [G: Canada]
Boaz, Rachel Floersheim. Labor Market Behavior of Older Workers Approaching Retirement: A Summary of the Evidence from the 1970s. *Meyer, C. W., ed.*, 1987, pp. 103–26.
[G: U.S.]
Boskin, Michael J. and Shoven, John B. Concepts and Measures of Earnings Replacement during Retirement. *Bodie, Z.; Shoven, J. B. and Wise, D. A., eds.*, 1987, pp. 113–41. [G: U.S.]
Brunet, Jacques. The Impact of an Aging Population on Health Services. *Economic Council of Canada.*, 1987, pp. 162–68. [G: Canada]
Buck, Carol. How Direct Is the Path toward Lengthening the Life Span and Improving the Quality of Life? *Economic Council of Canada.*, 1987, pp. 101–04. [G: Canada]
Burkhauser, Richard V. Occupational Effects on the Health and Work Capacity of Older Men: Comment. *Burtless, G., ed.*, 1987, pp. 142–50. [G: U.S.]
Burtless, Gary. Occupational Effects on the Health and Work Capacity of Older Men. *Burtless, G., ed.*, 1987, pp. 103–42. [G: U.S.]
Burtless, Gary. Work, Health, and Income among the Elderly: Introduction and Summary. *Burtless, G., ed.*, 1987, pp. 1–18.
Clark, Robert L. Aging and Relative Earnings. *Sandell, S. H., ed.*, 1987, pp. 71–83.
[G: U.S.]
Deber, Raisa B. Advances in Medical Technology. *Economic Council of Canada.*, 1987, pp. 133–38. [G: Canada]
Espenshade, Thomas J. Aging and the Ability to Work: Policy Issues and Recent Trends: Comment. *Burtless, G., ed.*, 1987, pp. 97–102.
[G: U.S.]
Evans, Robert G. Hang Together, or Hang Sepa-

rately: The Viability of a Universal Health Care System in an Aging Society. *Can. Public Policy,* June 1987, *13*(2), pp. 165–80. [G: U.S.; Canada]

Evans, Roger W. Some Thoughts on Advances in Medical Technology. *Economic Council of Canada.,* 1987, pp. 122–33. [G: Canada]

Fields, Gary S. and Mitchell, Olivia S. Restructuring Social Security: How Will Retirement Ages Respond? *Sandell, S. H., ed.,* 1987, pp. 192–205. [G: U.S.]

Gallagher, Jack. Economic Limits and Bioethics. *Economic Council of Canada.,* 1987, pp. 141–44. [G: Canada]

Ginsberg, Yona. The Elderly in Central Tel Aviv. *van Vliet—, W., et al., eds.,* 1987, pp. 291–301. [G: Israel]

Gollub, James O. Increasing Employment Opportunities for Older Workers: Emerging State and Local Initiatives. *Sandell, S. H., ed.,* 1987, pp. 143–64. [G: U.S.]

Goodman, Allen C. Using Lorenz Curves to Characterise Urban Elderly Populations. *Urban Stud.,* February 1987, *24*(1), pp. 77–80. [G: U.S.]

Green, F. Terri. The Costs of Long-Stay Hospital Care of the Dependent Elderly. *Butler, J. R. G. and Doessel, D. P., eds.,* 1987, pp. 95–112. [G: New Zealand]

Gustman, Alan L. Concepts and Measures of Earnings Replacement during Retirement: Comment. *Bodie, Z.; Shoven, J. B. and Wise, D. A., eds.,* 1987, pp. 141–46. [G: U.S.]

Hausman, Jerry A. and Paquette, Lynn. Involuntary Early Retirement and Consumption. *Burtless, G., ed.,* 1987, pp. 151–75. [G: U.S.]

Havens, Betty. Intra and Inter National Proposals. *Economic Council of Canada.,* 1987, pp. 18–22. [G: Canada]

Horne, John M. Beyond "De-institutionalizing" the Elderly: Financial Savings from a More Radical Approach to Alternative Health Care Delivery Methods by the Year 2021. *Economic Council of Canada.,* 1987, pp. 72–77. [G: Canada]

Hu, Sheng Cheng. Uncertain Inflation and Social Security Indexation. *J. Econ. Dynam. Control,* September 1987, *11*(3), pp. 359–72.

Hurd, Michael D. Dissaving after Retirement: Testing the Pure Life Cycle Hypothesis: Comment. *Bodie, Z.; Shoven, J. B. and Wise, D. A., eds.,* 1987, pp. 275–79. [G: U.S.]

Johnson, Terry R.; Dickinson, Katherine P. and West, Richard W. Older Workers, Job Displacement, and the Employment Service. *Sandell, S. H., ed.,* 1987, pp. 100–117. [G: U.S.]

Jondrow, Jim; Brechling, Frank and Marcus, Alan J. Older Workers in the Market for Part-time Employment. *Sandell, S. H., ed.,* 1987, pp. 84–99. [G: U.S.]

Lazear, Edward P. Involuntary Early Retirement and Consumption: Comment. *Burtless, G., ed.,* 1987, pp. 175–81. [G: U.S.]

Lazear, Edward P. and Rosen, Sherwin. Pension Inequality. *Bodie, Z.; Shoven, J. B. and Wise,*

D. A., eds., 1987, pp. 341–59. [G: U.S.]

Lindner, W.-D. and Heinzemann, B. Comment [Labour Flexibility and Older Worker Marginalisation: The Need for a New Strategy]. *Int. Lab. Rev.,* 1987, *126*(3), pp. 371–72. [G: EEC]

Manton, Kenneth G. The Interaction of Population Aging and Health Transitions at Later Ages: New Evidence and Insights. *Schramm, C. J., ed.,* 1987, pp. 185–221. [G: U.S.]

Manton, Kenneth G. The Linkage of Morbidity and Mortality: Implications of Increasing Life Expectancy at Later Ages for Health Service Demand. *Economic Council of Canada.,* 1987, pp. 39–50. [G: Canada]

Maxwell, Judith. Aging with Limited Health Resources: Closing Remarks. *Economic Council of Canada.,* 1987, pp. 175–76. [G: Canada]

Maxwell, Judith. Aging with Limited Health Resources: Introduction. *Economic Council of Canada.,* 1987, pp. 1–3. [G: Canada]

McDaniel, Susan A. Demographic Aging as a Guiding Paradigm in Canada's Welfare State. *Can. Public Policy,* September 1987, *13*(3), pp. 330–36. [G: Canada]

Moen, Jon. The Labor of Older Men: A Comment. *J. Econ. Hist.,* September 1987, *47*(3), pp. 761–67. [G: U.S.]

Moffitt, Robert. Life-Cycle Labor Supply and Social Security: A Time-Series Analysis. *Burtless, G., ed.,* 1987, pp. 183–220. [G: U.S.]

Moore, Thomas Gale. Social Security in Aging Societies: Comment. *Davis, K.; Bernstam, M. S. and Ricardo-Campbell, R., eds.,* 1987, *1986,* pp. 295.

Mustard, Fraser. Canada's Future Health Care Program: Options for Change. *Economic Council of Canada.,* 1987, pp. 168–73. [G: Canada]

Newhouse, Joseph P. Public Policy Implications of Declining Old-Age Mortality: Comment. *Burtless, G., ed.,* 1987, pp. 51–58. [G: U.S.]

Newman, Sandra J. and Reschovsky, James D. Federal Policy and the Mobility of Older Homeowners. *J. Policy Anal. Manage.,* Spring 1987, *6*(3), pp. 402–16. [G: U.S.]

Owen, Jack W. The Meaning of the Swing-Bed Experience: Comments. *Wiener, J. M., ed.,* 1987, pp. 135–37. [G: U.S.]

Paul, Carolyn. Work Alternatives for Older Americans: A Management Perspective. *Sandell, S. H., ed.,* 1987, pp. 165–76. [G: U.S.]

Philips, T. J. The Costs of Long-Stay Hospital Care of the Dependent Elderly: Discussion. *Butler, J. R. G. and Doessel, D. P., eds.,* 1987, pp. 113–15. [G: New Zealand]

Poterba, James M. and Summers, Lawrence H. Public Policy Implications of Declining Old-Age Mortality. *Burtless, G., ed.,* 1987, pp. 19–51. [G: U.S.]

Powell, David E. Manpower Constraints and the Use of Pensioners in the Soviet Economy. *Adam, J., ed.,* 1987, pp. 196–215. [G: U.S.S.R.]

Press, Stephen. The Meaning of the Swing-Bed

Experience: Comments. *Wiener, J. M., ed.,* 1987, pp. 132–35.

Preston, Samuel H. Children and the Elderly: Divergent Paths for America's Dependents. *Menard, S. W. and Moen, E. W., eds.,* 1987, *1984,* pp. 377–94. **[G: U.S.]**

Quinn, Joseph F. Life-Cycle Labor Supply and Social Security: A Time-Series Analysis: Comment. *Burtless, G., ed.,* 1987, pp. 220–28. **[G: U.S.]**

Quinn, Joseph F. The Economic Status of the Elderly: Beware of the Mean. *Rev. Income Wealth,* March 1987, *33*(1), pp. 63–82.

Radner, Daniel B. Money Incomes of Aged and Nonaged Family Units, 1967–84. *Soc. Sec. Bull.,* August 1987, *50*(8), pp. 9–28. **[G: U.S.]**

Radner, Daniel B. and Vaughan, Denton R. Wealth, Income, and the Economic Status of Aged Households. *Wolff, E. N., ed.,* 1987, pp. 93–120. **[G: U.S.]**

Rappaport, Anna M. and Kalman, Robert W. The Future of Employer-Sponsored Retiree Medical Plans. *Inquiry,* Spring 1987, *24*(1), pp. 26–35. **[G: U.S.]**

Robertson, Duncan. Alternative Methods of Health Care Delivery for Canada's Aging Population. *Economic Council of Canada.,* 1987, pp. 59–68. **[G: Canada]**

Romero, Carol Jusenius. Retirement and Older Americans' Participation in Volunteer Activities. *Sandell, S. H., ed.,* 1987, pp. 218–27. **[G: U.S.]**

Roos, Noralou P.; Shapiro, Evelyn and Havens, Betty. Aging with Limited Resources: What Should We Really Be Worried About? *Economic Council of Canada.,* 1987, pp. 50–56. **[G: Canada]**

Root, Lawrence S. and Zarrugh, Laura H. Private-Sector Employment Practices for Older Workers. *Sandell, S. H., ed.,* 1987, pp. 177–91. **[G: U.S.]**

Ross, Christine M.; Danziger, Sheldon and Smolensky, Eugene. Interpreting Changes in the Economic Status of the Elderly, 1949–1979. *Contemp. Policy Issues,* April 1987, *5*(2), pp. 98–112. **[G: U.S.]**

Rowland, Diane. Meeting the Long-term Care Needs of an Aging Population. *Schramm, C. J., ed.,* 1987, pp. 222–51. **[G: U.S.]**

Rupp, Kalman, et al. Government Employment and Training Programs, and Older Americans. *Sandell, S. H., ed.,* 1987, pp. 121–42. **[G: U.S.]**

Sandell, Steven H. Labor Market Problems and Employment Policies Affecting Older Americans. *Sandell, S. H., ed.,* 1987, pp. 15–33. **[G: U.S.]**

Sandell, Steven H. Prospects for Older Workers: The Demographic and Economic Context. *Sandell, S. H., ed.,* 1987, pp. 3–14. **[G: U.S.]**

Sandell, Steven H. The Problem Isn't Age: Conclusions and Implications. *Sandell, S. H., ed.,* 1987, pp. 231–45. **[G: U.S.]**

Schieber, Sylvester J. Pension Inequality: Com-

ment. *Bodie, Z.; Shoven, J. B. and Wise, D. A., eds.,* 1987, pp. 359–63. **[G: U.S.]**

Smith, Ruth B.; Moschis, George P. and Moore, Roy L. Social Effects of Advertising and Personal Communication on the Elderly Consumer. *Bloom, P. N., ed.,* 1987, pp. 65–92. **[G: U.S.]**

Smits, Helen L. Swing Beds: Assessing Flexible Health Care in Rural Communities: Quality of Care. *Wiener, J. M., ed.,* 1987, pp. 105–14. **[G: U.S.]**

Somerville, Margaret A. Structuring the Decision Making in the Allocation of Scarce Medical Resources. *Economic Council of Canada.,* 1987, pp. 144–51. **[G: Canada]**

Standing, Guy. Reply [Labour Flexibility and Older Worker Marginalisation: The Need for a New Strategy]. *Int. Lab. Rev.,* 1987, *126*(3), pp. 372–74. **[G: EEC]**

Stoddart, Greg L. Alternative Methods of Health Care Delivery for Canada's Aging Population: Commentary. *Economic Council of Canada.,* 1987, pp. 68–71. **[G: Canada]**

Struyk, Raymond J. The Economic Behavior of the Elderly in Housing Markets. *Turner, B.; Kemeny, J. and Lundqvist, L. J., eds.,* 1987, pp. 71–101. **[G: U.S.]**

Vladeck, Bruce C. The Meaning of the Swing-Bed Experience. *Wiener, J. M., ed.,* 1987, pp. 120–32. **[G: U.S.]**

Walker, Alan. Meeting the Needs of Canada's Elderly with Limited Health Resources: Some Observations Based on British Experience. *Economic Council of Canada.,* 1987, pp. 27–39. **[G: Canada]**

Weaver, Carolyn L. Social Security in Aging Societies. *Davis, K.; Bernstam, M. S. and Ricardo-Campbell, R., eds.,* 1987, *1986,* pp. 273–94. **[G: OECD]**

Wigle, Donald T. Health Objectives for Canada. *Economic Council of Canada.,* 1987, pp. 92–101. **[G: Canada]**

Ycas, Martynas A. and Grad, Susan. Income of Retirement-Aged Persons in the United States. *Soc. Sec. Bull.,* July 1987, *50*(7), pp. 5–14. **[G: U.S.]**

920 CONSUMER ECONOMICS

921 Consumer Economics; Levels and Standards of Living

9210 General

Aizcorbe, Ana; Winston, Clifford and Friedlaender, Ann. Cost Competitiveness of the U.S. Automobile Industry. *Winston, C., et al.,* 1987, pp. 6–35. **[G: U.S.]**

Alba, Joseph W. and Marmorstein, Howard. The Effects of Frequency Knowledge on Consumer Decision Making. *J. Cons. Res.,* June 1987, *14*(1), pp. 14–25.

Anglin, Paul M. and Baye, Michael R. Information, Multiprice Search, and Cost-of-Living Index Theory. *J. Polit. Econ.,* December 1987, *95*(6), pp. 1179–95.

Archambault, Edith. The Family and the Dynamics of Personal Services. *Akehurst, G. and Gadrey, J., eds.,* 1987, pp. 46–55.

Avery, Robert B., et al. Changes in the Use of Transaction Accounts and Cash from 1984 to 1986. *Fed. Res. Bull.,* March 1987, *73*(3), pp. 179–96. **[G: U.S.]**

Barwise, T. Patrick and Ehrenberg, Andrew S. C. The Liking and Viewing of Regular TV Series. *J. Cons. Res.,* June 1987, *14*(1), pp. 63–70. **[G: U.S.]**

Battalio, Raymond C.; Kagel, John H. and Phillips, Owen R. Optimal Prices and Animal Consumers in Congested Markets: A Reply. *Econ. Inquiry,* October 1987, *25*(4), pp. 721–22.

Berthold, Norbert. Umschichtung des Lebenseinkommens als verteilungspolitische Aufgabe der Familienpolitik. (Intertemporal Allocation of Life Income as a Distributional Task of Family Policy. With English summary.) *Jahr. Nationalökon. Statist.,* January 1987, *203*(1), pp. 12–25. **[G: W. Germany]**

Blundell, Richard. Econometric Approaches to the Specification of Life-Cycle Labour Supply and Commodity Demand Behaviour. *Econometric Rev.,* 1987, *6*(1), pp. 103–65.

Bobst, Barry W., et al. Data Sources for Demand Analyses. *Raunikar, R. and Huang, C.-L., eds.,* 1987, pp. 33–53. **[G: U.S.]**

Brooks, Michael A. and Earl, Peter E. On the Implications of Jointness in a Normative Model of Behavior Based on an Activity Hierarchy. *J. Cons. Res.,* December 1987, *14*(3), pp. 445–48.

Calder, Bobby J. and Tybout, Alice M. What Consumer Research Is . . . *J. Cons. Res.,* June 1987, *14*(1), pp. 136–40.

Chavas, Jean-Paul and Segerson, Kathleen. Stochastic Specification and Estimation of Share Equation Systems. *J. Econometrics,* July 1987, *35*(2/3), pp. 337–58.

Cooper, Lee G. Do We Need Critical Relativism? Comments [On Method in Consumer Research: A Critical Relativist Perspective]. *J. Cons. Res.,* June 1987, *14*(1), pp. 126–27.

Corfman, Kim P. and Lehmann, Donald R. Models of Cooperative Group Decision-Making and Relative Influence: An Experimental Investigation of Family Purchase Decisions. *J. Cons. Res.,* June 1987, *14*(1), pp. 1–13. **[G: U.S.]**

Cox, Donald. Motives for Private Income Transfers. *J. Polit. Econ.,* June 1987, *95*(3), pp. 508–46. **[G: U.S.]**

Dzis', G.; Lysenkov, Iu. and Rymaruk, A. Consumer Goods Production and Scientific–Technological Progress. *Prob. Econ.,* June 1987, *30*(2), pp. 71–83. **[G: U.S.S.R.]**

Her, Jaewan. An Empirical Study on Regional Welfare Inequalities and National Expenditure Priorities. *Rev. Reg. Stud.,* Winter 1987, *17*(1), pp. 21–32. **[G: U.S.]**

Holbrook, Morris B. What Is Consumer Research? *J. Cons. Res.,* June 1987, *14*(1), pp. 128–32.

Johnson, William R. Income Redistribution as Human Capital Insurance. *J. Human Res.,*

Spring 1987, *22*(2), pp. 269–80. **[G: U.S.]**

Kernan, Jerome B. Chasing the Holy Grail: Reflections on "What Is Consumer Research?" *J. Cons. Res.,* June 1987, *14*(1), pp. 133–35.

Klein, Noreen M. and Bither, Stewart W. An Investigation of Utility-Directed Cutoff Selection. *J. Cons. Res.,* September 1987, *14*(2), pp. 240–56.

Kooreman, Peter and Kapteyn, Arie. A Disaggregated Analysis of the Allocation of Time within the Household. *J. Polit. Econ.,* April 1987, *95*(2), pp. 223–49. **[G: U.S.]**

Lastovicka, John L., et al. A Lifestyle Typology to Model Young Male Drinking and Driving. *J. Cons. Res.,* September 1987, *14*(2), pp. 257–63. **[G: U.S.]**

Leppel, Karen. Household Formation and Unrelated Housemates. *Amer. Econ.,* Spring 1987, *31*(1), pp. 38–47. **[G: U.S.]**

Lerman, Donald L. Perspectives on Household Portfolios, 1977–83. *Eastern Econ. J.,* October–December 1987, *13*(4), pp. 399–410. **[G: U.S.]**

Manski, Charles F. and Salomon, Ilan. The Demand for Teleshopping: An Application of Discrete Choice Models. *Reg. Sci. Urban Econ.,* February 1987, *17*(1), pp. 109–21.

McConnell, Kenneth E. and Phipps, T. T. Identification of Preference Parameters in Hedonic Models: Consumer Demands with Nonlinear Budgets. *J. Urban Econ.,* July 1987, *22*(1), pp. 35–52.

Megdal, Sharon Bernstein. The Econometrics of Piecewise–Linear Budget Constraints: A Monte Carlo Study. *J. Bus. Econ. Statist.,* April 1987, *5*(2), pp. 243–48.

Middleton, Elliott. The Preference for Variety. *J. Behav. Econ.,* Spring 1987, *16*(1), pp. 49–54.

Montmarquette, Claude and Monty, Luc. An Empirical Model of a Household's Choice of Activities. *J. Appl. Econometrics,* April 1987, *2*(2), pp. 145–58. **[G: Canada]**

Morello, G. The Consumer in World Trade. *Visser, H. and Schoor, E., eds.,* 1987, pp. 303–13. **[G: Global]**

Narula, Subhash C.; Lentnek, Barry and Harwitz, Mitchell. A Contextual Analysis of the Journey-to-Shop with Price Uncertainty. *J. Reg. Sci.,* August 1987, *27*(3), pp. 403–18.

Qualls, William J. Household Decision Behavior: The Impact of Husbands' and Wives' Sex Role Orientation. *J. Cons. Res.,* September 1987, *14*(2), pp. 264–79. **[G: U.S.]**

Rubin, Rose M.; Riney, Bobye J. and Johansen, Todd. Tax Effects on the Net Income of Wives in Dual-Earner Households, 1980–1983. *Public Finance Quart.,* October 1987, *15*(4), pp. 441–59. **[G: U.S.]**

Sachs, Ignacy. Lifestyles and Planning. *Sachs, I.,* 1987, pp. 33–51.

Sandler, Todd. On Optimal Prices and Animal Consumers in Congested Markets. *Econ. Inquiry,* October 1987, *25*(4), pp. 715–20.

Sau, Ranjit. Household Debt and National Income: A Simple Short-run Model. *J. Macro-*

econ., Winter 1987, *9*(1), pp. 127–37.
[G: U.S.]

Schefter, John E. Increasing Block Rate Tariffs as Faulty Transmitters of Marginal Willingness to Pay. *Land Econ.*, February 1987, *63*(1), pp. 21–33. [G: U.S.]

Sternthal, Brian; Tybout, Alice M. and Calder, Bobby J. Confirmatory versus Comparative Approaches to Judging Theory Tests. *J. Cons. Res.*, June 1987, *14*(1), pp. 114–25.

Taylor, Grant A. and Johnson, Lester W. The Frisch Conjecture and Demand Systems. *Quart. J. Bus. Econ.*, Winter 1987, *26*(1), pp. 63–77. [G: Australia; Sweden]

Warshawsky, Mark. Sensitivity to Market Incentives: The Case of Policy Loans. *Rev. Econ. Statist.*, May 1987, *69*(2), pp. 286–95.
[G: U.S.]

Yang, Guansan; Yang, Xiaodong and Xuan, Mingdong. The Public Response to Price Reform. *Reynolds, B. L.*, 1987, pp. 59–73. [G: China]

9211 Living Standards, Composition of Overall Expenditures, and Empirical Consumption and Savings Studies

Abadia, Antonio. Indice de precios de consumo, coste de vida y distribución del bienestar: 1976–1985. (With English summary.) *Invest. Econ.*, January 1987, *11*(1), pp. 179–90.
[G: Spain]

Abel, Andrew B. Operative Gift and Bequest Motives. *Amer. Econ. Rev.*, December 1987, *77*(5), pp. 1037–47.

Ahmad, Ehtisham and Ludlow, Stephen E. Aggregate and Regional Demand Response Patterns in Pakistan. *Pakistan Devel. Rev.*, Winter 1987, *26*(4), pp. 645–55. [G: Pakistan]

Alba, Joseph W. and Hutchinson, J. Wesley. Dimensions of Consumer Expertise. *J. Cons. Res.*, March 1987, *13*(4), pp. 411–54.

Aleksandrova, E. and Zelenoborskaia, L. The Rationalization of Personal Consumption (The Organizational Factor). *Prob. Econ.*, June 1987, *30*(2), pp. 84–97. [G: U.S.S.R.]

Algahtani, Ibrahim M. and Alhiyari, Mohd. Real Balance Effect and the Consumption Function in LDC: A Comment [The Effect of Liquid Assets on the Consumption Function of a Less Developed Economy: A Note]. *Amer. Econ.*, Spring 1987, *31*(1), pp. 62–63. [G: Iran]

Altonji, Joseph G. and Siow, Aloysius. Testing the Response of Consumption to Income Changes with (Noisy) Panel Data. *Quart. J. Econ.*, May 1987, *102*(2), pp. 293–328.
[G: U.S.]

Ando, Albert and Kennickell, Arthur B. How Much (or Little) Life Cycle Is There in Micro Data? The Cases of the United States and Japan. *[Modigliani, F.]*, 1987, pp. 159–223.
[G: U.S.; Japan]

Arestis, Philip and Driver, Ciaran. The Effects of Income Distribution on Consumer Imports. *J. Macroecon.*, Winter 1987, *9*(1), pp. 83–94.
[G: U.K.]

Atkinson, Anthony B. On the Measurement of

Poverty. *Econometrica*, July 1987, *55*(4), pp. 749–64. [G: U.S.]

Auerbach, Alan J. and Kotlikoff, Laurence J. Life Insurance of the Elderly: Adequacy and Determinants. *Burtless, G., ed.*, 1987, pp. 229–67.
[G: U.S.]

Balintfy, Joseph L. and Taj, Shahram. A Utility Maximization-Based Decision Support System for USDA Family Food Plans. *Schultz, R. L., ed.*, 1987, pp. 1–22. [G: U.S.]

Ballard, Charles L. Tax Policy and Consumer Foresight: A General Equilibrium Simulation Study. *Econ. Inquiry*, April 1987, *25*(2), pp. 267–84. [G: U.S.]

Bartik, Timothy J. Estimating Hedonic Demand Parameters with Single Market Data: The Problems Caused by Unobserved Tastes. *Rev. Econ. Statist.*, February 1987, *69*(1), pp. 178–80.

Bartik, Timothy J. The Estimation of Demand Parameters in Hedonic Price Models. *J. Polit. Econ.*, February 1987, *95*(1), pp. 81–88.
[G: U.S.]

Baseman, R. L. and Slottje, D. J. The Sensitivity of the True Cost of Living to Price-Induced and Income-Induced Changes in Aggregate Consumers' Tastes. *J. Bus. Econ. Statist.*, October 1987, *5*(4), pp. 483–98. [G: U.S.]

Batey, P. W. J.; Madden, M. and Weeks, M. J. Household Income and Expenditure in Extended Input–Output Models: A Comparative Theoretical and Empirical Analysis. *J. Reg. Sci.*, August 1987, *27*(3), pp. 341–56.
[G: U.S.]

Bawa, R. S. and Kainth, Gursharan Singh. Income Inequalities in Urban Areas: Measurement and Determinant. *Margin*, Jan.-Mar. 1987, *19*(2), pp. 60–73. [G: India]

Bernard, Victor L. and Frecka, Thomas J. Commodity Contracts and Common Stocks as Hedges against Relative Consumer Price Risk. *J. Finan. Quant. Anal.*, June 1987, *22*(2), pp. 169–88. [G: U.S.]

Bernheim, B. Douglas. Dissaving after Retirement: Testing the Pure Life Cycle Hypothesis. *Bodie, Z.; Shoven, J. B. and Wise, D. A., eds.*, 1987, pp. 237–74. [G: U.S.]

Bernheim, B. Douglas. The Economic Effects of Social Security: Toward a Reconciliation of Theory and Measurement. *J. Public Econ.*, August 1987, *33*(3), pp. 273–304. [G: U.S.]

Bhatia, Kul B. Real Estate Assets and Consumer Spending. *Quart. J. Econ.*, May 1987, *102*(2), pp. 437–44. [G: U.S.]

Bird, Richard M. A New Look at Indirect Taxation in Developing Countries. *World Devel.*, September 1987, *15*(9), pp. 1151–61.
[G: LDCs]

Blinder, Alan S. Why Is U.S. National Saving So Low? Comments. *Brookings Pap. Econ. Act.*, 1987, (2), pp. 636–38. [G: U.S.]

Blundell, Richard and Meghir, Costas. Bivariate Alternatives to the Tobit Model. *J. Econometrics*, Jan./Feb. 1987, *34*(1/2), pp. 179–200.
[G: U.K.]

Bondyová, Jana and Petrásková, Vera. The Stan-

dard of Living in Czechoslovakia. *Czech. Econ. Digest.*, June 1987, (4), pp. 23–43.
[G: Czechoslovakia]

Borooah, Vani. The Cambridge Multisectoral Dynamic Model of the British Economy: Consumers' Expenditure. *Barker, T. and Peterson, W., eds.*, 1987, pp. 125–49. [G: U.K.]

Boskin, Michael J. and Shoven, John B. Concepts and Measures of Earnings Replacement during Retirement. *Bodie, Z.; Shoven, J. B. and Wise, D. A., eds.*, 1987, pp. 113–41. [G: U.S.]

Botham, F. W. and Hunt, E. H. Wages in Britain during the Industrial Revolution. *Econ. Hist. Rev., 2nd Ser.*, August 1987, *40*(3), pp. 380–99. [G: U.K.]

Bowles, Paul. Foreign Aid and Domestic Savings in Less Developed Countries: Some Tests for Causality. *World Devel.*, June 1987, *15*(6), pp. 789–96. [G: LDCs]

Bronfenbrenner, Martin and Yasuba, Yasukichi. The Political Economy of Japan: Economic Welfare. *Yamamura, K. and Yasuba, Y., eds.*, 1987, pp. 93–136. [G: Japan]

Brown, Clair. Consumption Norms, Work Roles, and Economic Growth, 1918–80. *Brown, C. and Pechman, J. A., eds.*, 1987, pp. 13–49.
[G: U.S.]

Campbell, John Y. Does Saving Anticipate Declining Labor Income? An Alternative Test of the Permanent Income Hypothesis. *Econometrica*, November 1987, *55*(6), pp. 1249–73.
[G: U.S.]

Canner, Glenn B. and Fergus, James T. The Economic Effects of Proposed Ceilings on Credit Card Interest Rates. *Fed. Res. Bull.*, January 1987, *73*(1), pp. 1–13. [G: U.S.]

Carroll, Chris and Summers, Lawrence H. Why Have Private Savings Rates in the United States and Canada Diverged? *J. Monet. Econ.*, September 1987, *20*(2), pp. 249–79.
[G: U.S.; Canada]

Carter, Michael G. and Maddock, Rodney. Leisure and Australian Wellbeing 1911–81. *Australian Econ. Hist. Rev.*, March 1987, *27*(1), pp. 30–43. [G: Australia]

Carter, Susan B. Consumption Norms, Work Roles, and Economic Growth, 1918–80: Comments. *Brown, C. and Pechman, J. A., eds.*, 1987, pp. 49–54. [G: U.S.]

Cecora, James. Agriculture—Its Effects on the Level-of-Living and Subsistence Technology of Farming Households. *Léon, Y. and Mahé, L., eds.*, 1987, pp. 7–24. [G: W. Germany]

Chowdhury, Nuimuddin. Household Savings Behaviour in Bangladesh: Issues and Evidence. *Bangladesh Devel. Stud.*, September 1987, *15*(3), pp. 1–41. [G: Bangladesh]

Chowdhury, Nuimuddin. Urban Rationing in Bangladesh in Mid-1980s: The Distribution of Its Benefits. *Bangladesh Devel. Stud.*, December 1987, *15*(4), pp. 53–84. [G: Bangladesh]

Christelow, Dorothy B. Converging Household Debt Ratios of Four Industrial Countries. *Fed. Res. Bank New York Quart. Rev.*, Winter 1987-88, *12*(4), pp. 35–47. [G: U.S.; Japan; Germany; U.K.]

Christiano, Lawrence J. Is Consumption Insufficiently Sensitive to Innovations in Income? *Amer. Econ. Rev.*, May 1987, *77*(2), pp. 337–41. [G: U.S.]

Christiano, Lawrence J. Why is Consumption Less Volatile than Income? *Fed. Res. Bank Minn. Rev.*, Fall 1987, *11*(4), pp. 2–20.
[G: U.S.]

Cobb, Stephen A. Interarea Cost of Living Measurement with Nonmarket Goods: A Demand Systems Approach. *J. Urban Econ.*, September 1987, *22*(2), pp. 174–89. [G: U.S.]

Cohen, Joel B. and Basu, Kunal. Alternative Models of Categorization: Toward a Contingent Processing Framework. *J. Cons. Res.*, March 1987, *13*(4), pp. 455–72.

Coondoo, Dipankar and Majumder, Amita. A System of Demand Equations Based on Price Independent Generalized Linearity. *Int. Econ. Rev.*, February 1987, *28*(1), pp. 213–28.
[G: India]

Cornia, Giovanni Andrea. Adjustment at the Household Level: Potentials and Limitations of Survival Strategies. *Cornia, G. A.; Jolly, R. and Stewart, F., eds.*, 1987, pp. 90–104.
[G: LDCs]

Coursey, Don L. and Mason, Charles. Investigations Concerning the Dynamics of Consumer Behavior in Uncertain Environments. *Econ. Inquiry*, October 1987, *25*(4), pp. 549–64.

Craven, John A. and Haidacher, Richard C. Comparison of Estimates from Three Linear Expenditure Systems. *Raunikar, R. and Huang, C.-L., eds.*, 1987, pp. 91–113.
[G: U.S.]

Cude, Brenda J. Estimating the Returns to Informed Decision-Making. *J. Cons. Aff.*, Summer 1987, *21*(1), pp. 86–95. [G: U.S.]

Deaton, Angus. IRAs and Saving: Comment. *Feldstein, M., ed. (I)*, 1987, pp. 48–51.
[G: U.S.]

Deutsch, Antal and Zowall, Hanna. Inequalities in the Tax Impact of Compulsory Retirement Savings in Singapore. *Singapore Econ. Rev.*, October 1987, *32*(2), pp. 28–42.
[G: Singapore]

Deville, Jean-Claude. Sur la durée d'observation dans les enquêtes à carnets de compte. (On the Observation Periods in Surveys of Household Spending Records. With English summary.) *Ann. Écon. Statist.*, Jan./Mar. 1987, (5), pp. 183–95.

Divila, Emil and Goulli, Rochdi. The Relationship of Personal and Social Consumption of the Population—Prerequisites for Rationalization. *Czech. Econ. Pap.*, 1987, (24), pp. 119–39. [G: Czechoslovakia]

Dor, E.; Thurston, T. and Weiserbs, Daniel. On Testing the Permanent Income Hypothesis and Rational Expectations. *Empirical Econ.*, 1987, *12*(3), pp. 137–56. [G: U.S.]

Engle, Robert F. and Granger, Clive W. J. Co-integration and Error Correction: Representation, Estimation, and Testing. *Econometrica*, March 1987, *55*(2), pp. 251–76. [G: U.S.]

Erol, Umit and Yu, Eden S. H. On the Causal

Relationship between Energy and Income for Industrialized Countries. *J. Energy Devel.*, Autumn 1987, *13*(1), pp. 113–22.
[G: Europe; Canada; U.K.; Japan]

Ferson, Wayne E. and Merrick, John J., Jr. Non-stationarity and Stage-of-the-Business-Cycle Effects in Consumption-Based Asset Pricing Relations. *J. Finan. Econ.*, March 1987, *18*(1), pp. 127–46.
[G: U.S.]

Franklin, David L.; Harrell, Marielouise W. and Leonard, Jerry B. Income Effects of Donated Commodities in Rural Panama. *Amer. J. Agr. Econ.*, February 1987, *69*(1), pp. 115–22.
[G: Panama]

Friedman, Margaret L. and Churchill, Gilbert A., Jr. Using Consumer Perceptions and a Contingency Approach to Improve Health Care Delivery. *J. Cons. Res.*, March 1987, *13*(4), pp. 492–510.

Gadrey, Jean. The Double Dynamics of Services. *Akehurst, G. and Gadrey, J., eds.*, 1987, pp. 125–38.
[G: France; U.S.]

Giannaros, Demetrios S. and Lee, Jae Hyung. Private Savings Behavior and Estimation of Structural Change: The Case of Korea. *J. Econ. Devel.*, December 1987, *12*(2), pp. 57–71.
[G: S. Korea]

Giles, David E. A. and Hampton, Peter. A Regional Consumer Demand Model for New Zealand. *J. Reg. Sci.*, February 1987, *27*(1), pp. 103–18.
[G: New Zealand]

Gillingham, Robert and Greenlees, John S. The Impact of Direct Taxes on the Cost of Living. *J. Polit. Econ.*, August 1987, *95*(4), pp. 775–96.
[G: U.S.]

Glewwe, Paul and Bhalla, Surjit S. A Response to Comment [The Distribution of Income in Sri Lanka in 1969–70 and 1980–81: Sri Lankan Experience]. *World Bank Econ. Rev.*, May 1987, *1*(3), pp. 533–36.
[G: Sri Lanka; LDCs]

Goldman, Howard H.; Scheffler, Richard M. and Cheadle, Allen. Demand for Psychiatric Services: A Clinical Episode Model for Specifying "The Product." *McGuire, T. G. and Scheffler, R. M., eds.*, 1987, pp. 255–73.
[G: U.S.]

Graham, John W. International Differences in Saving Rates and the Life Cycle Hypothesis. *Europ. Econ. Rev.*, December 1987, *31*(8), pp. 1509–29.
[G: OECD]

Green, Richard; Hahn, William and Rocke, David. Standard Errors for Elasticities: A Comparison of Bootstrap and Asymptotic Standard Errors. *J. Bus. Econ. Statist.*, January 1987, *5*(1), pp. 145–49.
[G: Canada]

Green, Richard; Hassan, Zuhair and Johnson, Stanley R. Persistence in Consumption Patterns: Alternative Approaches and an Application of the Linear Expenditure System. *Raunikar, R. and Huang, C.-L., eds.*, 1987, pp. 114–27.
[G: Canada]

Gupta, Kanhaya L. Aggregate Savings, Financial Intermediation, and Interest Rate. *Rev. Econ. Statist.*, May 1987, *69*(2), pp. 303–11.
[G: Latin America; Asia]

Gupta, Kanhaya L. Inflation and Consumer Expenditures in India and South Korea. *Indian Econ. J.*, Oct.-Dec. 1987, *35*(2), pp. 152–56.
[G: India; S. Korea]

Gustman, Alan L. Concepts and Measures of Earnings Replacement during Retirement: Comment. *Bodie, Z.; Shoven, J. B. and Wise, D. A., eds.*, 1987, pp. 141–46.
[G: U.S.]

Hall, Robert E. Tax Policy and Corporate Saving: Comment. *Brookings Pap. Econ. Act.*, 1987, (2), pp. 504–06.
[G: U.S.]

Hamermesh, Daniel S. and Menchik, Paul L. Planned and Unplanned Bequests. *Econ. Inquiry*, January 1987, *25*(1), pp. 55–66.
[G: U.S.]

Hammer, Jeffrey S. The Demographic Transition and Aggregate Savings in Less Developed Countries. *J. Econ. Devel.*, December 1987, *12*(2), pp. 21–37.
[G: LDCs]

Hart, Keith. Commoditisation and the Standard of Living. *Sen, A. K., et al.*, 1987, pp. 70–93.
[G: W. Africa; U.K.]

Hasan, M. Aynul. Aggregate and Regional Demand Response Patterns in Pakistan: Comments. *Pakistan Devel. Rev.*, Winter 1987, *26*(4), pp. 656–57.
[G: Pakistan]

Hauser, Richard. Comparing the Influence of Social Security Systems on the Relative Economic Positions of Selected Groups in Six Major Industrialized Countries: The Case of One-Parent Families. *Europ. Econ. Rev.*, Feb./Mar. 1987, *31*(1/2), pp. 192–201.
[G: N. America; U.K.; Sweden; Israel; W. Germany]

Hawthorn, Geoffrey. The Standard of Living: Introduction. *Sen, A. K., et al.*, 1987, pp. vii–xiv.

Horowitz, Joel L. Identification and Stochastic Specification in Rosen's Hedonic Price Model. *J. Urban Econ.*, September 1987, *22*(2), pp. 165–73.

Hubbard, R. Glenn. Tax Policy and Corporate Saving: Comment. *Brookings Pap. Econ. Act.*, 1987, (2), pp. 504–13.
[G: U.S.]

Hubbard, R. Glenn. Uncertain Lifetimes, Pensions, and Individual Saving. *Bodie, Z.; Shoven, J. B. and Wise, D. A., eds.*, 1987, pp. 175–206.
[G: U.S.]

Hubbard, R. Glenn and Judd, Kenneth L. Social Security and Individual Welfare: Precautionary Saving, Borrowing Constraints, and the Payroll Tax. *Amer. Econ. Rev.*, September 1987, *77*(4), pp. 630–46.
[G: U.S.]

Hurd, Michael D. Dissaving after Retirement: Testing the Pure Life Cycle Hypothesis: Comment. *Bodie, Z.; Shoven, J. B. and Wise, D. A., eds.*, 1987, pp. 275–79.
[G: U.S.]

Hurd, Michael D. Savings of the Elderly and Desired Bequests. *Amer. Econ. Rev.*, June 1987, *77*(3), pp. 298–312.
[G: U.S.]

Isenman, Paul. Growth and Equity in Developing Countries: A Reinterpretation of the Sri Lankan Experience: A Comment. *World Bank Econ. Rev.*, May 1987, *1*(3), pp. 521–31.
[G: Sri Lanka; LDCs]

Jarque, Carlos M. Patrones de gasto en los hogares de la ciudad de México. (Household Expenditure Patterns in Mexico City. With English summary.) *Estud. Econ.*, Jan.-June 1987, *2*(1), pp. 37–64. **[G: Mexico]**

Jarque, Carlos M. Sample Splitting and Applied Econometric Modeling. *J. Bus. Econ. Statist.*, April 1987, *5*(2), pp. 267–74. **[G: Mexico]**

Jencks, Christopher. The Politics of Income Measurement. *Alonso, W. and Starr, P., eds.*, 1987, pp. 83–131. **[G: U.S.]**

Jones, Jonathan D. Are Future Taxes Anticipated by Consumers? More Evidence for the U.S., 1946–1985. *Econ. Notes*, 1987, (2), pp. 141–44. **[G: U.S.]**

Jorgenson, Dale W. and Slesnick, Daniel T. Aggregate Consumer Behavior and Household Equivalence Scales. *J. Bus. Econ. Statist.*, April 1987, *5*(2), pp. 219–32. **[G: U.S.]**

Kanbur, S. M. Ravi. The Standard of Living: Uncertainty, Inequality and Opportunity. *Sen, A. K., et al.*, 1987, pp. 59–69.

Kelly, William A., Jr. and Miles, James A. A Fisherian Analysis of Individual Retirement Accounts. *Atlantic Econ. J.*, July 1987, *15*(2), pp. 1–10.

Khan, Ashfaque H. Aggregate Consumption Function and Income Distribution Effect: Some Evidence from Developing Countries. *World Devel.*, Oct./Nov. 1987, *15*(10/11), pp. 1369–74. **[G: LDCs]**

Kidane, Asmerom. Determinants of Saving in Ethiopia with Reference to the Role of Demographic Variables. *Eastern Afr. Econ. Rev.*, December 1987, *3*(2), pp. 121–29. **[G: Ethiopia]**

King, Elizabeth M. The Effect of Family Size on Family Welfare: What Do We Know? *Johnson, D. G. and Lee, R. D., eds.*, 1987, pp. 373–411. **[G: LDCs]**

Kokoski, Mary F. Indices of Household Welfare and the Value of Leisure Time. *Rev. Econ. Statist.*, February 1987, *69*(1), pp. 83–89. **[G: U.S.]**

Kokoski, Mary F. Problems in the Measurement of Consumer Cost-of-Living Indexes. *J. Bus. Econ. Statist.*, January 1987, *5*(1), pp. 39–46. **[G: U.S.]**

Kosicki, George. A Test of the Relative Income Hypothesis. *Southern Econ. J.*, October 1987, *54*(2), pp. 422–34. **[G: U.S.]**

Kosicki, George. The Relative Income Hypothesis: A Review of the Cross Section Evidence. *Quart. J. Bus. Econ.*, Autumn 1987, *26*(4), pp. 65–80. **[G: U.S.]**

Kosta, Jiří. The Chinese Economic Reform: Approaches, Results and Prospects. *Gey, P.; Kosta, J. and Quaisser, W., eds.*, 1987, pp. 145–71. **[G: China]**

Krishnamurty, K.; Krishnaswamy, K. S. and Sharma, P. D. Determinants of Saving Rates in India. *J. Quant. Econ.*, July 1987, *3*(2), pp. 335–57. **[G: India]**

Kurz, Mordecai. The Life-Cycle Hypothesis as a Tool of Theory and Policy. *Feiwel, G. R., ed. (II)*, 1987, pp. 447–90. **[G: U.S.]**

LaBarbera, Priscilla A. Consumer Behavior and Born Again Christianity. *Sheth, J. N. and*

Hirschman, E., eds., 1987, pp. 193–222. **[G: U.S.]**

Lächler, Ulrich and Nunnenkamp, Peter. The Effects of Debt versus Equity Inflows on Savings and Growth in Developing Economies. *Weltwirtsch. Arch.*, 1987, *123*(4), pp. 631–50. **[G: LDCs]**

Lawrance, Emily C. Transfers to the Poor and Long Run Savings. *Econ. Inquiry*, July 1987, *25*(3), pp. 459–78. **[G: U.S.]**

Lebergott, Stanley. Consumption Norms, Work Roles, and Economic Growth, 1918–80: Comments. *Brown, C. and Pechman, J. A., eds.*, 1987, pp. 54–58. **[G: U.S.]**

Leff, Nathaniel H. and Sato, Kazuo. The Prospects for Higher Domestic Savings Rates in Latin America. *J. Policy Modeling*, Winter 1987, *9*(4), pp. 559–76. **[G: Latin America]**

Lesnoy, Selig D. and Leimer, Dean R. Social Security and Private Saving: Theory and Historical Evidence. *Meyer, C. W., ed.*, 1987, *1985*, pp. 69–101. **[G: U.S.]**

Levy, Frank and Michel, Richard C. Living Standards since OPEC: Unraveling a Paradox. *Bus. Econ.*, July 1987, *22*(3), pp. 15–17. **[G: U.S.]**

Lewbel, Arthur. Bliss Levels That Aren't [Stochastic Implications of the Life Cycle–Permanent Income Hypothesis: Theory and Evidence]. *J. Polit. Econ.*, February 1987, *95*(1), pp. 211–15. **[G: U.S.]**

Lustig, Nora. Crisis económica y niveles de vida en México: 1982–1985. (Economic Crisis and Living Standards in Mexico. With English summary.) *Estud. Econ.*, July-December 1987, *2*(2), pp. 227–49. **[G: Mexico]**

MacDonald, Ronald and Peel, David A. Consumer Expenditure, the Demand for Money, and the Hall Hypothesis. *Empirical Econ.*, 1987, *12*(1), pp. 3–17. **[G: OECD]**

Mankiw, N. Gregory. Consumer Spending and the After-Tax Real Interest Rate. *Feldstein, M., ed. (II)*, 1987, pp. 97–99. **[G: U.S.]**

Mariger, Randall P. A Life-cycle Consumption Model with Liquidity Constraints: Theory and Empirical Results. *Econometrica*, May 1987, *55*(3), pp. 533–57. **[G: U.S.]**

Mason, Andrew. National Saving Rates and Population Growth: A New Model and New Evidence. *Johnson, D. G. and Lee, R. D., eds.*, 1987, pp. 523–60.

McLean, Ian W. The Australian Economy in the Long Run: Economic Wellbeing. *Maddock, R. and McLean, I. W., eds.*, 1987, pp. 319–43. **[G: Australia]**

McMillin, W. Douglas and Laumas, G. S. Economic Policy and Consumption and Investment Expenditures: An Empirical Examination. *Appl. Econ.*, February 1987, *19*(2), pp. 167–77. **[G: U.S.]**

Mehdizadeh, Mostafa. Real Balance Effect and Consumption Function in Less Developed Countries: A Reply [The Effect of Liquid Assets on the Consumption Function of a Less Developed Economy: A Note]. *Amer. Econ.*, Spring 1987, *31*(1), pp. 64–65. **[G: Iran]**

Michel, Richard C., et al. Are We Better Off in

1984? *Challenge*, Special Issue 1987, *30*(6), pp. 37–44. [G: U.S.]

Millar, James R. and Clayton, Elizabeth. Politics, Work, and Daily Life in the USSR: Quality of Life: Subjective Measures of Relative Satisfaction. *Millar, J. R., ed.*, 1987, pp. 31–57. [G: U.S.S.R.]

Mitchell, Jean M. Demand for Psychiatric Services: A Clinical Episode Model for Specifying "The Product": Comments. *McGuire, T. G. and Scheffler, R. M., eds.*, 1987, pp. 275–78. [G: U.S.]

Mitchell, Olivia S. Uncertain Lifetimes, Pensions, and Individual Saving: Comment. *Bodie, Z.; Shoven, J. B. and Wise, D. A., eds.*, 1987, pp. 206–10. [G: U.S.]

Modigliani, Franco. Life Cycle, Individual Thrift, and the Wealth of Nations. *[Modigliani, F.]*, 1987, pp. 1–28.

Modigliani, Franco. The Key to Saving Is Growth, Not Thrift. *Challenge*, May/June 1987, *30*(2), pp. 24–29.

Modigliani, Franco and Jappelli, Tullio. Fiscal Policy and Saving in Italy since 1860. *Boskin, M. J.; Fleming, J. S. and Gorini, S., eds.*, 1987, pp. 126–70. [G: Italy]

Moffitt, Robert. Life-Cycle Labor Supply and Social Security: A Time-Series Analysis. *Burtless, G., ed.*, 1987, pp. 183–220. [G: U.S.]

Moore, Michael J. The Irish Consumption Function and Ricardian Equivalence. *Econ. Soc. Rev.*, October 1987, *19*(1), pp. 43–60. [G: Ireland]

Motley, Brian. Ricardo or Keynes: Does the Government Debt Affect Consumption? *Fed. Res. Bank San Francisco Econ. Rev.*, Winter 1987, (1), pp. 47–62.

Muellbauer, John. Estimating the Intertemporal Elasticity of Substitution for Consumption from Household Budget Data. *Heijmans, R. and Neudecker, H., eds.*, 1987, pp. 45–57. [G: U.K.]

Muellbauer, John. Professor Sen on the Standard of Living. *Sen, A. K., et al.*, 1987, pp. 39–58.

Mukhopadhyay, Rabindranath. A Study of Regional Patterns of Consumer Expenditure in Rural India. *J. Quant. Econ.*, January 1987, *3*(1), pp. 117–36. [G: India]

Musgrove, Philip. Ingreso y Consumo Permanente y su Relación, en Cuatro Ciudades Colombianas. (With English summary.) *Cuadernos Econ.*, April 1987, *24*(71), pp. 29–43. [G: Columbia]

Nakhaeizadeh, Gholamreza. The Causality Direction in Consumption—Income Process and Sensitivity to Lag Structure. *Appl. Econ.*, June 1987, *19*(6), pp. 829–38. [G: W. Germany]

Naughton, Barry. Macroeconomic Policy and Response in the Chinese Economy: The Impact of the Reform Process. *J. Compar. Econ.*, September 1987, *11*(3), pp. 334–53. [G: China]

Nelissen, Jan. The Redistributive Impact of the General Old Age Pensions Act on Lifetime Income in the Netherlands. *Europ. Econ. Rev.*, October 1987, *31*(7), pp. 1419–41. [G: Netherlands]

Nelson, Charles R. A Reappraisal of Recent Tests of the Permanent Income Hypothesis [Stochastic Implications of the Life Cycle–Permanent Income Hypothesis: Theory and Evidence]. *J. Polit. Econ.*, June 1987, *95*(3), pp. 641–46. [G: U.S.]

Nicol, C. J. The Implications of a Third-Order Translog Demand System and Some Empirical Results. *Empirical Econ.*, 1987, *12*(3), pp. 197–202. [G: U.S.]

Palmer, Ransford W. Debt and the Standard of Living in the Caribbean and Latin America. *Tremblay, R., ed.*, 1987, pp. 99–110. [G: Latin America; Caribbean]

Peek, Joe. The Distorting Effects of the Inflation Premium on Personal Income and Expenditures. *New Eng. Econ. Rev.*, Sept./Oct. 1987, pp. 10–24. [G: U.S.]

Peterson, William. The Cambridge Multisectoral Dynamic Model of the British Economy: The Demand for Energy. *Barker, T. and Peterson, W., eds.*, 1987, pp. 275–91. [G: U.K.]

Pierenkemper, Toni. The Standard of Living and Employment in Germany, 1850–1980: An Overview. *J. Europ. Econ. Hist.*, Spring 1987, *16*(1), pp. 51–73. [G: Germany]

Piggott, John. The Nation's Private Wealth—Some New Calculations for Australia. *Econ. Rec.*, March 1987, *63*(180), pp. 61–79. [G: Australia]

Pitelis, Christos N. Corporate Retained Earnings and Personal Sector Saving: A Test of the Life-Cycle Hypothesis of Saving. *Appl. Econ.*, July 1987, *19*(7), pp. 907–13. [G: U.K.]

Pitelis, Christos N. The Causal Relationship between Advertising, Retained Profits and Aggregate Consumption: A Note. *Greek Econ. Rev.*, 1987, *9*(2), pp. 239–47. [G: U.K.]

Pollak, Robert A. and Wales, Terence J. Pooling International Consumption Data. *Rev. Econ. Statist.*, February 1987, *69*(1), pp. 90–99. [G: Belgium; U.S.; U.K.]

Portes, Richard and Santorum, Anita. Money and the Consumption Goods Market in China. *J. Compar. Econ.*, September 1987, *11*(3), pp. 354–71. [G: China]

Poterba, James M. Tax Policy and Corporate Saving. *Brookings Pap. Econ. Act.*, 1987, (2), pp. 455–503. [G: U.S.]

Poterba, James M. and Summers, Lawrence H. Finite Lifetimes and the Effects of Budget Deficits on National Saving. *J. Monet. Econ.*, September 1987, *20*(2), pp. 369–91. [G: U.S.]

Pozdena, Randall Johnston. Inflation, Age, and Wealth. *Fed. Res. Bank San Francisco Econ. Rev.*, Winter 1987, (1), pp. 17–30. [G: U.S.]

Pyatt, Graham. Growth and Equity in Developing Countries: A Reinterpretation of the Sri Lankan Experience: A Comment. *World Bank Econ. Rev.*, May 1987, *1*(3), pp. 515–20. [G: Sri Lanka; LDCs]

Quinn, Joseph F. Life-Cycle Labor Supply and Social Security: A Time-Series Analysis: Comment. *Burtless, G., ed.*, 1987, pp. 220–28. [G: U.S.]

Quinn, Joseph F. The Economic Status of the Elderly: Beware of the Mean. *Rev. Income Wealth*, March 1987, *33*(1), pp. 63–82.

Raj, Baldev. Did the Cost of Living in Canada Increase Faster for the Rich during the Period 1950–1980? *Empirical Econ.*, 1987, *12*(1), pp. 19–28. **[G: Canada]**

Richter, Wolfram F. Taxation as Insurance and the Case of Rate Differentiation According to Consanguinity under Inheritance Taxation. *J. Public Econ.*, August 1987, *33*(3), pp. 363–76. **[G: W. Germany]**

Sahn, David E. Changes in the Living Standards of the Poor in Sri Lanka during a Period of Macroeconomic Restructuring. *World Devel.*, June 1987, *15*(6), pp. 809–30. **[G: Sri Lanka]**

Sapounas, George S. Allocation of Goods and Services in VAT: The Case of Greece. *Europ. Econ. Rev.*, August 1987, *31*(6), pp. 1285–98. **[G: Greece]**

Sato, Kazuo. The Political Economy of Japan: Saving and Investment. *Yamamura, K. and Yasuba, Y., eds.*, 1987, pp. 137–85. **[G: Japan]**

Sen, Amartya K. The Standard of Living: Lecture II, Lives and Capabilities. *Sen, A. K., et al.*, 1987, pp. 20–38.

Sen, Amartya K. The Standard of Living: Lecture I, Concepts and Critiques. *Sen, A. K., et al.*, 1987, pp. 1–19.

Sen, Amartya K. The Standard of Living: Reply. *Sen, A. K., et al.*, 1987, pp. 103–12.

Shahid, M. Alam. Savings and Industrialization: Some Hypotheses Suggested by Lewis and Others. *Singapore Econ. Rev.*, October 1987, *32*(2), pp. 56–65. **[G: LDCs]**

Smolensky, Eugene, et al. An Application of a Dynamic Cost-of-Living Index to the Evaluation of Changes in Social Welfare. *J. Post Keynesian Econ.*, Spring 1987, *9*(3), pp. 364–80. **[G: U.S.]**

Solow, Robert M. How Much (or Little) Life Cycle Is There in Micro Data? The Cases of the United States and Japan: Comments. *[Modigliani, F.]*, 1987, pp. 224–28. **[G: U.S.; Japan]**

Starck, Christian C. Intertemporal Substitution in Consumption: Some Empirical Evidence from Finnish Data. *Liiketaloudellinen Aikak.*, 1987, *36*(2), pp. 128–43. **[G: Finland]**

Steel, Mark F. J. Testing for Exogeneity: An Application to Consumption Behaviour. *Europ. Econ. Rev.*, October 1987, *31*(7), pp. 1443–63. **[G: Belgium]**

Summers, Lawrence H. and Carroll, Chris. Why Is U.S. National Saving So Low? *Brookings Pap. Econ. Act.*, 1987, (2), pp. 607–35. **[G: U.S.]**

Swofford, James L. and Whitney, Gerald A. Nonparametric Tests of Utility Maximization and Weak Separability for Consumption, Leisure and Money. *Rev. Econ. Statist.*, August 1987, *69*(3), pp. 458–64. **[G: U.S.]**

Tan, Chin Tiong and Farley, John U. The Impact of Cultural Patterns on Cognition and Intention in Singapore. *J. Cons. Res.*, March 1987, *13*(4), pp. 540–44. **[G: Singapore]**

Tellis, Gerard J. and Wernerfelt, Birger. Competitive Price and Quality under Asymmetric Information. *Marketing Sci.*, Summer 1987, *6*(3), pp. 240–53. **[G: U.S.]**

Thomas, Vinod. Differences in Income and Poverty with in Brazil. *World Devel.*, February 1987, *15*(2), pp. 263–73. **[G: Brazil]**

Tobin, James. A Statistical Demand Function for Food in the U.S.A. *Tobin, J. (II)*, 1987, *1950*, pp. 399–439. **[G: U.S.]**

Tobin, James. Consumer Debt and Spending: Some Evidence from Analysis of a Survey. *Tobin, J. (II)*, 1987, pp. 217–45. **[G: U.S.]**

Tobin, James. Multiple Probit Regression of Dichotomous Economic Variables. *Tobin, J. (II)*, 1987, pp. 447–66. **[G: U.S.]**

Tobin, James. On the Predictive Value of Consumer Intentions and Attitudes. *Tobin, J. (II)*, 1987, *1959*, pp. 299–318.

Unger, Laszlo. Changing Social Values and Lifestyles: From a Consumer towards a Conserver Society? *Hieronymi, O., ed.*, 1987, pp. 123–39. **[G: U.S.]**

Van Dyke, Daniel T. Will Debt Overwhelm the Consumer? *Bus. Econ.*, January 1987, *22*(1), pp. 41–45. **[G: U.S.]**

Venieris, Y. P. and Stewart, D. B. Sociopolitical Instability, Inequality and Consumption Behavior. *J. Econ. Devel.*, December 1987, *12*(2), pp. 7–20. **[G: Selected Countries]**

Venti, Steven F. and Wise, David A. IRAs and Saving. *Feldstein, M., ed. (I)*, 1987, pp. 7–48. **[G: U.S.]**

Watts, Harold W. and Tobin, James. Consumer Expenditures and the Capital Account. *Tobin, J. (II)*, 1987, *1960*, pp. 247–90. **[G: U.S.]**

Whiteford, Peter. Unemployment and Families. *Australian Bull. Lab.*, December 1987, *14*(1), pp. 338–57. **[G: Australia]**

Wilkinson, Frank. Deregulation, Structured Labour Markets and Unemployment. *Pedersen, P. J. and Lund, R., eds.*, 1987, pp. 167–85. **[G: W. Europe]**

Williams, Bernard. The Standard of Living: Interests and Capabilities. *Sen, A. K., et al.*, 1987, pp. 94–102.

Wise, David A. Individual Retirement Accounts and Saving. *Feldstein, M., ed. (II)*, 1987, pp. 3–15. **[G: U.S.]**

Xia, Xiaosun and Li, Jun. Consumption Expansion: A Grave Challenge to Reform and Development. *Reynolds, B. L.*, 1987, pp. 89–107. **[G: China]**

Yoo, Jong G. and Kwon, Jene K. Welfare Inequality among Urban Households in South Korea: 1965–83. *Appl. Econ.*, April 1987, *19*(4), pp. 497–510.

Zick, Cathleen D. and Gerner, Jennifer L. Family Composition and Investment in Household Capital: Contrasts in the Behavior of the Husband–Wife and Female-Headed Households. *J. Cons. Aff.*, Summer 1987, *21*(1), pp. 21–39. **[G: U.S.]**

9212 Expenditure Patterns and Consumption of Specific Items

Adrian, Manuella and Ferguson, Brian S. Demand for Domestic and Imported Alcohol in Canada. *Appl. Econ.*, April 1987, *19*(4), pp. 531–40. [G: Canada]

Agthe, Donald E. and Billings, R. Bruce. Equity, Price Elasticity, and Household Income under Increasing Block Rates for Water. *Amer. J. Econ. Soc.*, July 1987, *46*(3), pp. 273–86. [G: U.S.]

Alderman, Harold. Allocation of Goods through Non-price Mechanisms: Evidence on Distribution by Willingness to Wait. *J. Devel. Econ.*, February 1987, *25*(1), pp. 105–24. [G: Egypt]

Alexeev, Michael. Microeconomic Modeling of Parallel Markets: The Case of Agricultural Goods in the USSR. *J. Compar. Econ.*, December 1987, *11*(4), pp. 543–57. [G: U.S.S.R.]

Alper, Neil O.; Archibald, Robert B. and Jensen, Eric. At What Price Vanity? An Econometric Model of the Demand for Personalized License Plates. *Nat. Tax J.*, March 1987, *40*(1), pp. 103–09. [G: U.S.]

Alston, Julian M. and Chalfant, James A. Weak Separability and a Test for the Specification of Income in Demand Models with an Application to the Demand for Meat in Australia. *Australian J. Agr. Econ.*, April 1987, *31*(1), pp. 1–15. [G: Australia]

Anderson, Joan Gray and Kushman, John E. A Model of Household Heating Demand: Home Production with Satiety and an Endowment. *J. Cons. Aff.*, Summer 1987, *21*(1), pp. 1–20. [G: U.S.]

Andrikopoulos, Andreas A.; Brox, James A. and Georgakopoulos, Theodore A. Short-run Expenditure and Price Elasticities for Agricultural Commodities: The Case of Greece, 1951–1983. *Europ. Rev. Agr. Econ.*, 1987, *14*(3), pp. 335–46. [G: Greece]

Asplund, Rita. Residential Demand for Electric Space Heating in Finland. *Europ. Econ. Rev.*, July 1987, *31*(5), pp. 981–93. [G: Finland]

Ault, D. E. and Rutman, G. L. The Effect of Increases in Real Goldmining Wages on the Expenditure Patterns of Rural African Mineworkers. *S. Afr. J. Econ.*, December 1987, *55*(4), pp. 381–94. [G: S. Africa]

Behrman, Jere R. and Deolalikar, Anil B. Will Developing Country Nutrition Improve with Income? A Case Study for Rural South India. *J. Polit. Econ.*, June 1987, *95*(3), pp. 492–507. [G: India]

Belk, Russell W. Material Values in the Comics: A Content Analysis of Comic Books Featuring Themes of Wealth. *J. Cons. Res.*, June 1987, *14*(1), pp. 26–42.

Berkowitz, Michael K. and Haines, George H., Jr. A Disaggregate Model of Residential Heating Mode Choice: A Multinomial Probit Modelling Approach. *Appl. Econ.*, May 1987, *19*(5),

pp. 581–96. [G: Canada]

Bernard, Jean-Thomas; Lemieux, Michel and Thivierge, Simon. Residential Energy Demand: An Integrated Two-Level Approach. *Energy Econ.*, July 1987, *9*(3), pp. 139–44. [G: Canada]

Bernard, Jean-Thomas and Veall, Michael R. The Probability Distribution of Future Demand: The Case of Hydro Quebec. *J. Bus. Econ. Statist.*, July 1987, *5*(3), pp. 417–24. [G: Canada]

Bewley, Ronald. The Demand for Milk in Australia: Estimation of Price and Income Effects from the 1984 Household Expenditure Survey. *Australian J. Agr. Econ.*, December 1987, *31*(3), pp. 204–18. [G: Australia]

Bewley, Ronald and Young, Trevor. Applying Thiel's Multinomial Extension of the Linear Logit Model to Meat Expenditure Data. *Amer. J. Agr. Econ.*, February 1987, *69*(1), pp. 151–57. [G: U.K.]

Blaylock, James R. and Smallwood, David M. Intrahousehold Time Allocation: The Case of Grocery Shopping. *J. Cons. Aff.*, Winter 1987, *21*(2), pp. 183–201. [G: U.S.]

Blundell, Richard and Meghir, Costas. Engel Curve Estimation with Individual Data. *Heijmans, R. and Neudecker, H., eds.*, 1987, pp. 3–14. [G: U.K.]

Bobst, Barry W.; Huang, Chung L. and Tilley, Daniel S. Partial Systems of Demand Equations with a Commodity Emphasis. *Raunikar, R. and Huang, C.-L., eds.*, 1987, pp. 171–85. [G: U.S.]

Borland, Jeff. The Demand for Australian Rules Football. *Econ. Rec.*, September 1987, *63*(182), pp. 220–30. [G: Australia]

Borpujari, Jitendra G. Consumption and Productivity Patterns and Their Implications for the Production Structure. *Pasinetti, L. and Lloyd, P., eds.*, 1987, pp. 75–90. [G: Global]

Brookshire, David S.; Coursey, Don L. and Schulze, William D. The External Validity of Experimental Economics Techniques: Analysis of Demand Behavior. *Econ. Inquiry*, April 1987, *25*(2), pp. 239–50. [G: U.S.]

Browning, Martin. Eating, Drinking, Smoking, and Testing the Lifecycle Hypothesis. *Quart. J. Econ.*, May 1987, *102*(2), pp. 329–45. [G: U.K.]

Cairns, John A. Evaluating Changes in League Structure: The Reorganization of the Scottish Football League. *Appl. Econ.*, February 1987, *19*(2), pp. 259–75. [G: U.K.]

Capps, Oral, Jr. and Havlicek, Joseph, Jr. Analysis of Household Demand for Meat, Poultry, and Seafood Using the S_1-Branch System. *Raunikar, R. and Huang, C.-L., eds.*, 1987, pp. 128–42. [G: U.S.]

Chalfant, James A. A Globally Flexible, Almost Ideal Demand System. *J. Bus. Econ. Statist.*, April 1987, *5*(2), pp. 233–42. [G: U.S.]

Chatterjee, Srikanta and Ray, Ranjan. Net Import Content of Consumption in Rural and Urban India. *Indian Econ. J.*, Jan.-Mar. 1987, *34*(3), pp. 109–15. [G: India]

Chaudhary, Muhammad Ali; Majid, Syed Abdul and Saleem, Nighat. An Analysis of Price and Income Elasticities of Demand for Foodgrains. *Pakistan Econ. Soc. Rev.*, Summer 1987, 25(1), pp. 21–38. [G: Pakistan]

Chesher, Andrew and Rees, Hedley. Income Elasticities of Demand for Foods in Great Britain. *J. Agr. Econ.*, September 1987, 38(3), pp. 435–48. [G: U.K.]

Çinar, E. Miné. The Sensitivity of Extended Linear Expenditure System Household Scales to Income Declaration Errors. *J. Econometrics*, March 1987, 34(3), pp. 361–72. [G: U.S.; Turkey]

Cook, Edward C. Soviet Food Markets: Will the Situation Improve under Gorbachev? *Comp. Econ. Stud.*, Spring 1987, 29(1), pp. 1–36. [G: U.S.S.R.]

Dagsvik, John K., et al. Residential Demand for Natural Gas: A Dynamic Discrete-Continuous Choice Approach. *Golombek, R.; Hoel, M. and Vislie, J., eds.*, 1987, pp. 121–50. [G: W. Europe]

Dahlgran, Roger A. Complete Flexibility Systems and the Stationarity of U.S. Meat Demands. *Western J. Agr. Econ.*, December 1987, 12(2), pp. 152–63. [G: U.S.]

Dax, Peter. Estimation of Income Elasticities from Cross-Section Data. *Appl. Econ.*, November 1987, 19(11), pp. 1471–82. [G: U.K.]

De Saram, P. S. P. S.; Anandalingam, G. and Mubayi, V. Demand Elasticities for Petroleum Products in Sri Lanka. *Pachauri, R. K., ed.*, 1987, pp. 585–99. [G: Sri Lanka]

Deaton, Angus. Estimation of Own- and Cross-price Elasticities from Household Survey Data. *J. Econometrics*, Sept./Oct. 1987, 36(1/2), pp. 7–30. [G: Ivory Coast]

Dennerlein, Rudolf K.-H. Residential Demand for Electrical Appliances and Electricity in the Federal Republic of Germany. *Energy J.*, January 1987, 8(1), pp. 69–86. [G: W. Germany]

Dennerlein, Rudolf K.-H. Stromverbrauch der privaten Haushalte 1960 bis 1985 Ergebnisse eines makroökonomischen Ansatzes. (The Stock of Electrical Appliances and Electricity Consumption of Private Households from 1960–1985. With English summary.) *Ifo-Studien*, 1987, 33(4), pp. 277–302. [G: W. Germany]

Dennerlein, Rudolf K.-H. Stromverbrauch in Ausgewählten Privaten Haushalten: Ergebnisse eines Mikroanalytischen Ansatzes. (The Effects of Income and Prices on the Residential Stock of Electrical Appliances and Electricity Consumption: Some Results from a Microanayltic Approach. With English summary.) *Ifo-Studien*, 1987, 33(1), pp. 43–62. [G: W. Germany]

Dickie, Mark; Fisher, Ann and Gerking, Shelby. Market Transactions and Hypothetical Demand Data: A Comparative Study. *J. Amer. Statist. Assoc.*, March 1987, 82(397), pp. 69–75. [G: U.S.]

Dilnot, Andrew and Helm, Dieter. Energy Policy, Merit Goods and Social Security. *Fisc. Stud.*, August 1987, 8(3), pp. 29–48. [G: U.K.]

Dor, Avi; Gertler, Paul and van der Gaag, Jacques. Non-price Rationing and the Choice of Medical Care Providers in Rural Cote d'Ivoire. *J. Health Econ.*, December 1987, 6(4), pp. 291–304. [G: Ivory Coast]

Drollas, Leonidas P. Wabe's Cross-Section Analysis of the Demand for Gasoline—A Reply. *Energy Econ.*, October 1987, 9(4), pp. 289–91. [G: U.S.; W. Europe]

Duffy, Martyn H. Advertising and the Inter-product Distribution of Demand: A Rotterdam Model Approach. *Europ. Econ. Rev.*, July 1987, 31(5), pp. 1051–70. [G: U.K.]

Dunkerley, Joy and Hoch, Irving. Energy for Transport in Developing Countries. *Energy J.*, July 1987, 8(3), pp. 57–72. [G: LDCs]

Dynarski, Mark and Sheffrin, Steven M. Consumption and Unemployment. *Quart. J. Econ.*, May 1987, 102(2), pp. 411–28. [G: U.S.]

Eastwood, David B.; Brooker, John R. and Orr, Robert H. Consumer Preferences for Local versus Out-of-state Grown Selected Fresh Produce: The Case of Knoxville, Tennessee. *Southern J. Agr. Econ.*, December 1987, 19(2), pp. 183–94. [G: U.S.]

Eastwood, David B. and Sun, Theresa Y. Complete Demand Systems and Policy Analysis. *Raunikar, R. and Huang, C.-L., eds.*, 1987, pp. 154–67. [G: U.S.]

Faminow, Merle D. and Benson, Bruce L. On the Implications of Reporting Retail Food Prices over Extended Periods. *J. Cons. Aff.*, Summer 1987, 21(1), pp. 40–69. [G: U.S.]

Fiehig, Denzil G.; Seale, James L., Jr. and Theil, Henri. The Demand for Energy: Evidence from a Cross-Country Demand System. *Energy Econ.*, July 1987, 9(3), pp. 149–53. [G: Selected Countries]

Finsinger, Jörg and von der Schulenburg, J.-Matthias Graf. Nachfragerverhalten bei unvollständigen Preisinformationen—eine Marktanalyse am Beispiel der Kraftfahrzeugversicherung. (Consumer Behavior under Incomplete Price Information—Survey Results from the Automobile Insurance Market. With English summary.) *Jahr. Nationalökon. Statist.*, May 1987, 203(3), pp. 244–56. [G: W. Germany]

Folkes, Valerie S.; Koletsky, Susan and Graham, John L. A Field Study of Causal Inferences and Consumer Reaction: The View from the Airport. *J. Cons. Res.*, March 1987, 13(4), pp. 534–39. [G: U.S.]

Frech, H. E., III and Lee, William C. The Welfare Cost of Rationing-by-Queuing across Markets: Theory and Estimates from the U.S. Gasoline Crises. *Quart. J. Econ.*, February 1987, 102(1), pp. 97–108. [G: U.S.]

Friedman, Monroe. Survey Data on Owner-Reported Car Problems: How Useful to Prospective Purchasers of Used Cars? *J. Cons. Res.*,

December 1987, *14*(3), pp. 434–39.
[G: U.S.]

Garbacz, Christopher. Residential Electricity Demand Modelling with Secret Data. *Crew, M. A., ed.*, 1987, pp. 137–54.   [G: U.S.]

Georgantelis, S.; Phillips, Garry D. A. and Zhang, W. Estimating and Testing an Almost Ideal Demand System. *Heijmans, R. and Neudecker, H., eds.*, 1987, pp. 15–29. [G: U.K.]

Gershuny, Jonathan I. Time Use and the Dynamics of the Service Sector. *Akehurst, G. and Gadrey, J., eds.*, 1987, pp. 56–71. [G: U.K.]

Gerstner, Eitan and Hess, James D. Why Do Hot Dogs Come in Packs of 10 and Buns in 8s or 12s? A Demand-Side Investigation. *J. Bus.*, October 1987, *60*(4), pp. 491–517.
[G: U.S.]

Gieseman, Raymond. The Consumer Expenditure Survey: Quality Control by Comparative Analysis. *Mon. Lab. Rev.*, March 1987, *110*(3), pp. 8–14.   [G: U.S.]

Green, Rodney D. Regional Variations in U.S. Consumer Response to Price Changes in Home Heating Fuels: The Northeast and the South. *Appl. Econ.*, September 1987, *19*(9), pp. 1261–68.   [G: U.S.]

Gupta, Pradeep C.; Faruqui, Ahmad and Wharton, Joseph B. Structural Change in U.S. Manufacturing and Future Electricity Demand. *Pachauri, R. K., ed.*, 1987, pp. 75–90.
[G: U.S.]

Hagan, P. J. and Henry, G. G. Family-Based Social Welfare Schemes: The Case of Pharmaceuticals. *Butler, J. R. G. and Doessel, D. P., eds.*, 1987, pp. 165–93.   [G: Australia]

Hausman, Jerry A. and Paquette, Lynn. Involuntary Early Retirement and Consumption. *Burtless, G., ed.*, 1987, pp. 151–75.   [G: U.S.]

Hayes, Kathy J. and Porter-Hudak, Susan. Deadweight Loss: Theoretical Size Relationships and the Precision of Measurement. *J. Bus. Econ. Statist.*, January 1987, *5*(1), pp. 47–52.
[G: U.S.]

van Helden, G. Jan; Leeflang, Peter S. H. and Sterken, Elmer. Estimation of the Demand for Electricity. *Appl. Econ.*, January 1987, *19*(1), pp. 69–82.   [G: Netherlands]

Hensher, David A. and Milthorpe, Frank W. An Empirical Comparison of Alternative Approaches to Modelling Vehicle Choice. *Int. J. Transport Econ.*, June 1987, *14*(2), pp. 139–80.   [G: Australia]

Hensher, David A. and Milthorpe, Frank W. Selectivity Correction in Discrete-Continuous Choice Analysis: With Empirical Evidence for Vehicle Choice and Use. *Reg. Sci. Urban Econ.*, February 1987, *17*(1), pp. 123–50.
[G: U.S.]

Herbert, John H. Demand for Natural Gas by Households at the State Level: Twenty Years of Effort. *Rev. Reg. Stud.*, Fall 1987, *17*(3), pp. 79–87.   [G: U.S.]

Hill, Daniel H. Derived Demand Estimation with Survey Experiments: Commercial Electric Vehicles. *Rev. Econ. Statist.*, May 1987, *69*(2), pp. 277–85.

Hofmann, Hans-Joachim. Die Werbewirkung auf den Zigarettenkonsum in der Bundesrepublik Deutschland. (The Effect of Advertising on Cigarette Consumption in the Federal Republic of Germany. With English summary.) *Jahr. Nationalökon. Statist.*, May 1987, *203*(3), pp. 257–73.   [G: W. Germany]

Huntington, Hillard G. and Myers, John G. Sectoral Shift and Industrial Energy Demand: What Have We Learned? *Faruqui, A. and Broehl, J., eds.*, 1987, pp. 353–88. [G: U.S.]

Hyman, Eric L. The Strategy of Production and Distribution of Improved Charcoal Stoves in Kenya. *World Devel.*, March 1987, *15*(3), pp. 375–86.   [G: Kenya]

Itteilag, Richard L. An Analysis of Actual and Forecasted Conservation in the Residential Gas Space Heating Market. *Pachauri, R. K., ed.*, 1987, pp. 737–50.   [G: U.S.]

James, I. R. and Knuiman, M. W. An Application of Bayes Methodology to the Analysis of Diary Records from a Water Use Study. *J. Amer. Statist. Assoc.*, September 1987, *82*(399), pp. 705–11.   [G: Australia]

Jarque, Carlos M. An Application of LDV Models to Household Expenditure Analysis in Mexico. *J. Econometrics*, Sept./Oct. 1987, *36*(1/2), pp. 31–53.   [G: Mexico]

Kahn, Barbara; Moore, William L. and Glazer, Rashi. Experiments in Constrained Choice. *J. Cons. Res.*, June 1987, *14*(1), pp. 96–113.

Kasimovskii, E. Social Justice and the Improvement of Distribution Relations in the USSR. *Prob. Econ.*, September 1987, *30*(5), pp. 61–81.   [G: U.S.S.R.]

Katsaitis, Odysseus. On the Substitutability between Private Consumer Expenditure and Government Spending in Canada. *Can. J. Econ.*, August 1987, *20*(3), pp. 533–43.
[G: Canada]

Késenne, Stefan and Butzen, Paul. Subsidizing Sports Facilities: The Shadow Price-Elasticities of Sports. *Appl. Econ.*, January 1987, *19*(1), pp. 101–10.   [G: Belgium]

Ketkar, Kusum W. and Ketkar, Suhas L. Population Dynamics and Consumer Demand. *Appl. Econ.*, November 1987, *19*(11), pp. 1483–95.
[G: U.S.]

Ketkar, Kusum W. and Ketkar, Suhas L. Socio-Demographic Dynamics and Household Demand. *Eastern Econ. J.*, Jan.-Mar. 1987, *13*(1), pp. 55–62.   [G: U.S.]

Khandker, Shahidur R. and Butterfield, David W. Consumption, Family Size, Schooling and Labor Supply Decisions: Estimates of a Linear Expenditure System for Bangladesh. *J. Econ. Devel.*, December 1987, *12*(2), pp. 89–113.
[G: Bangladesh]

Khazzoom, J. Daniel. The Demand for Insulation—A Study in the Household Demand for Conservation. *Energy J.*, July 1987, *8*(3), pp. 73–92.   [G: U.S.]

Kinnucan, Henry W. Effect of Canadian Advertising on Milk Demand: The Case of the Buffalo, New York Market. *Can. J. Agr. Econ.*, March

1987, 35(1), pp. 181–96.   [G: Canada; U.S.]

Kodde, David A. and Palm, Franz C. A Parametric Test of the Negativity of the Substitution Matrix. *J. Appl. Econometrics*, July 1987, 2(3), pp. 227–35.   [G: W. Germany]

Lattin, James M. A Model of Balanced Choice Behavior. *Marketing Sci.*, Winter 1987, 6(1), pp. 48–65.   [G: U.S.]

Lazear, Edward P. Involuntary Early Retirement and Consumption: Comment. *Burtless, G., ed.*, 1987, pp. 175–81.   [G: U.S.]

Lee, Jonq-Ying. The Demand for Varied Diet with Econometric Models for Count Data. *Amer. J. Agr. Econ.*, August 1987, 69(3), pp. 687–92.   [G: U.S.]

Lewbel, Arthur. Fractional Demand Systems. *J. Econometrics*, November 1987, 36(3), pp. 311–37.

Majumder, Amita. Use of Pooled Data—An Empirical Note on Demand Analysis. *Indian Econ. Rev.*, Jan.-June 1987, 22(1), pp. 79–93.   [G: India]

Malik, Sohail J.; Abbas, Kalbe and Ghani, Ejaz. Rural–Urban Differences and the Stability of Consumption Behaviour: An Inter-temporal Analysis of the Household Income and Expenditure Survey Data for the Period 1963–64 to 1984–85. *Pakistan Devel. Rev.*, Winter 1987, 26(4), pp. 673–82.   [G: Pakistan]

Marlay, Robert C. Industrial Electricity Consumption and Changing Economic Conditions. *Faruqui, A. and Broehl, J., eds.*, 1987, pp. 77–114.   [G: U.S.]

Mason, Charles and Butler, Clifford. Errata [New Basket of Goods and Services Being Priced in Revised CPI]. *Mon. Lab. Rev.*, February 1987, 110(2), pp. 17.

Mason, Charles and Butler, Clifford. New Basket of Goods and Services Being Priced in Revised CPI. *Mon. Lab. Rev.*, January 1987, 110(1), pp. 3–22.   [G: U.S.]

McCracken, Vicki A. and Brandt, Jon A. Household Consumption of Food-Away-from-Home: Total Expenditure and by Type of Food Facility. *Amer. J. Agr. Econ.*, May 1987, 69(2), pp. 274–84.   [G: U.S.]

Milley, Donald J. Consumer Demand by Black Americans. *Rev. Black Polit. Econ.*, Winter 1987, 15(3), pp. 87–99.   [G: U.S.]

Moncur, James E. T. Urban Water Pricing and Drought Management. *Water Resources Res.*, March 1987, 23(3), pp. 393–98.   [G: U.S.]

Monteverde, Richard T. and Mink, Stephen D. Household Corn Consumption. *Timmer, C. P., ed.*, 1987, pp. 111–41.   [G: Indonesia]

Moreau, David H. and Snyder, Thomas P. Financial Burdens and Economic Costs in Expanding Urban Water Systems. *Water Resources Res.*, July 1987, 23(7), pp. 1139–44.

Morell, Mats. Eli F. Heckscher, the 'Food Budgets' and Swedish Food Consumption from the 16th to the 19th Century: The Summing Up and Conclusions of a Long Debate. *Scand. Econ. Hist. Rev.*, 1987, 35(1), pp. 67–107.   [G: Sweden]

Morgan, Karen J. Consumer Demand for Nutrients in Food. *Raunikar, R. and Huang, C.-L., eds.*, 1987, pp. 219–35.   [G: U.S.]

Murphy, A. and Thom, D. Rodney. Labour Supply and Commodity Demands: An Application to Irish Data. *Econ. Soc. Rev.*, April 1987, 18(3), pp. 149–58.   [G: Ireland]

Nguyen, Duc Tin and Rose, M. Demand for Tea in the UK 1874–1938: An Econometric Study. *J. Devel. Stud.*, October 1987, 24(1), pp. 43–59.   [G: U.K.]

Niazi, Mohammad Khan. Rural–Urban Differences and the Stability of Consumption Behaviour: An Inter-temporal Analysis of the Household Income and Expenditure Survey Data for the Period 1963–64 to 1984–85: Comments. *Pakistan Devel. Rev.*, Winter 1987, 26(4), pp. 683–84.   [G: Pakistan]

Nyankori, James C. O.; Rosson, C. Parr and Rathwell, P. J. Estimates of the Effects of Canadian Tariff on Fresh Peach Imports from the United States. *Can. J. Agr. Econ.*, March 1987, 35(1), pp. 75–87.   [G: Canada; U.S.]

Ogawa, Kohsuke. An Approach to Simultaneous Estimation and Segmentation in Conjoint Analysis. *Marketing Sci.*, Winter 1987, 6(1), pp. 66–81.

Osten, James A. The Impact of $(US)15 Oil Prices on Canadian Energy Markets. *Can. Public Policy*, March 1987, 13(1), pp. 26–33.   [G: Canada]

Owen, A. D. and Phillips, Garry D. A. The Characteristics of Railway Passenger Demand. *J. Transp. Econ. Policy*, September 1987, 21(3), pp. 231–53.   [G: U.K.]

Pickrell, Don H. Deregulation and the Future of Intercity Travel: Models of Intercity Travel Demand. *Meyer, J. R. and Oster, C. V., Jr.*, 1987, pp. 249–60.   [G: U.S.]

Polo, Yolanda and Salas, Vicente. El automóvil en España. Determinantes socioeconomicos de su aceptación. (With English summary.) *Invest. Econ.*, September 1987, 11(3), pp. 463–82.   [G: Spain]

Poterba, James M. and Rotemberg, Julio J. Money in the Utility Function: An Empirical Implementation. *Barnett, W. A. and Singleton, K. J., eds.*, 1987, pp. 219–40.   [G: U.S.]

Pouris, A. The Price Elasticity of Electricity Demand in South Africa. *Appl. Econ.*, September 1987, 19(9), pp. 1269–77.   [G: S. Africa]

Radecki, Lawrence J. and Garver, Cecily C. The Household Demand for Money: Estimates from Cross-sectional Data. *Fed. Res. Bank New York Quart. Rev.*, Spring 1987, 12(1), pp. 29–34.   [G: U.S.]

Raj, Baldev. An Economic Analysis of Consumers' Expenditure Shares in Canada 1950–1980. *Can. J. Agr. Econ.*, March 1987, 35(1), pp. 213–20.   [G: Canada]

Ranney, Christine K. and Kushman, John E. Cash Equivalence, Welfare Stigma, and Food Stamps. *Southern Econ. J.*, April 1987, 53(4), pp. 1011–27.   [G: U.S.]

Ransom, Michael R. A Comment on Consumer Demand Systems with Binding Non-negativity

Constraints. *J. Econometrics*, March 1987, 34(3), pp. 355–59.

Ravallion, Martin. Trade and Stabilization: Another Look at British India's Controversial Foodgrain Exports. *Exploration Econ. Hist.*, October 1987, 24(4), pp. 354–70. **[G: India]**

Razzolini, Laura. L'analisi della domanda dei servizi pubblici locali: Una stima dell'efficacia. (With English summary.) *Stud. Econ.*, 1987, 42(33), pp. 41–65. **[G: Italy]**

Reilly, Michael D. and Wallendorf, Melanie. A Comparison of Group Differences in Food Consumption Using Household Refuse. *J. Cons. Res.*, September 1987, 14(2), pp. 289–94. **[G: U.S.]**

Reinhardt, Uwe E. A Clarification of Theories and Evidence on Supplier-Induced Demand for Physicians' Services: Comment [The Theory of Physician-Induced Demand After a Decade]. *J. Human Res.*, Fall 1987, 22(4), pp. 621–23. **[G: U.S.]**

Rosenthal, Donald H. The Necessity for Substitute Prices in Recreation Demand Analyses. *Amer. J. Agr. Econ.*, November 1987, 69(4), pp. 828–37. **[G: U.S.]**

Rossi, Nicola. An Intertemporally Quasi Separable Demand System. *Rev. Econ. Statist.*, August 1987, 69(3), pp. 449–57. **[G: U.K.]**

Rossiter, Louis F. and Wilensky, Gail R. Health Economist-Induced Demand for Theories of Physician-Induced Demand. *J. Human Res.*, Fall 1987, 22(4), pp. 624–27. **[G: U.S.]**

Ruderman, Henry; Levine, Mark D. and McMahon, James E. The Behavior of the Market for Energy Efficiency in Residential Appliances Including Heating and Cooling Equipment. *Energy J.*, January 1987, 8(1), pp. 101–24. **[G: U.S.]**

Sexton, Richard J.; Johnson, Nancy Brown and Konakayama, Akira. Consumer Response to Continuous-Display Electricity-Use Monitors in a Time-of-Use Pricing Experiment. *J. Cons. Res.*, June 1987, 14(1), pp. 55–62.

Sexton, Richard J. and Sexton, Terri A. Theoretical and Methodological Perspectives on Consumer Response to Electricity Information. *J. Cons. Aff.*, Winter 1987, 21(2), pp. 238–57. **[G: U.S.]**

Shonkwiler, J. S.; Lee, Jonq-Ying and Taylor, Timothy G. An Empirical Model of the Demand for a Varied Diet. *Appl. Econ.*, October 1987, 19(10), pp. 1403–10. **[G: U.S.]**

Smith, V. Kerry and Kaoru, Yoshiaki. The Hedonic Travel Cost Model: A View from the Trenches. *Land Econ.*, May 1987, 63(2), pp. 179–92. **[G: U.S.]**

van Soest, Arthur and Kooreman, Peter. A Micro-econometric Analysis of Vacation Behaviour. *J. Appl. Econometrics*, July 1987, 2(3), pp. 215–26. **[G: Netherlands]**

Stano, Miron. A Clarification of Theories and Evidence on Supplier-Induced Demand for Physicians' Services [The Theory of Physician-Initiated Demand]. *J. Human Res.*, Fall 1987, 22(4), pp. 611–20. **[G: U.S.]**

Stanovnik, Tine. Appliance-Specific Electricity Consumption in Slovene Households. *Energy Econ.*, January 1987, 9(1), pp. 31–36. **[G: Yugoslavia]**

Stavrinos, Vasilios G. The Effects of an Anti-smoking Campaign on Cigarette Consumption: Empirical Evidence from Greece. *Appl. Econ.*, March 1987, 19(3), pp. 323–29. **[G: Greece]**

Tatchell, Michael. Family-Based Social Welfare Schemes: The Case of Pharmaceuticals: Discussion. *Butler, J. R. G. and Doessel, D. P.*, eds., 1987, pp. 194–96. **[G: Australia]**

Theil, Henri. Associated with an Income Distribution and a Demand System Is a Multidimensional Expenditure Distribution. *Heijmans, R. and Neudecker, H.*, eds., 1987, pp. 59–63.

Thompson, R. S. New Entry and Hedonic Price Discounts: The Case of the Irish Car Market. *Oxford Bull. Econ. Statist.*, November 1987, 49(4), pp. 373–84. **[G: Ireland]**

Townsend, Joy L. Cigarette Tax, Economic Welfare and Social Class Patterns of Smoking. *Appl. Econ.*, March 1987, 19(3), pp. 355–65. **[G: U.K.]**

Toyoda, Toshihisa; Ohtani, Kazuhiro and Katayama, Sei-ichi. Structural Change in Oil Consumption in Japan: An Econometric Analysis of Effects of the Two Oil Crises. *Kobe Univ. Econ.*, 1987, 33, pp. 33–47. **[G: Japan]**

Train, Kenneth E.; McFadden, Daniel L. and Ben-Akiva, Moshe. The Demand for Local Telephone Service: A Fully Discrete Model of Residential Calling Patterns and Service Choices. *Rand J. Econ.*, Spring 1987, 18(1), pp. 109–23. **[G: U.S.]**

Train, Kenneth E.; McFadden, Daniel L. and Goett, Andrew A. Consumer Attitudes and Voluntary Rate Schedules for Public Utilities. *Rev. Econ. Statist.*, August 1987, 69(3), pp. 383–91. **[G: U.S.]**

Tyrrell, Timothy J. and Mount, Timothy D. Analysis of Food and Other Expenditures Using a Linear Logit Model. *Raunikar, R. and Huang, C.-L.*, eds., 1987, pp. 143–53. **[G: U.S.]**

Tzeng, Gwo-Hshiung. A Study on the Characteristics and Demand Model for Household Energy Consumption in Taiwan. *Pachauri, R. K.*, ed., 1987, pp. 481–528. **[G: Taiwan]**

Verma, P. C. Domestic Demand for Jute Goods in India. *Margin*, Jan.-Mar. 1987, 19(2), pp. 43–49. **[G: India]**

Vroman, Susan B. and Russell, Louise B. The Net Social Benefits of a Product Improvement: The Case of Freeze-Dried Coffee. *Appl. Econ.*, January 1987, 19(1), pp. 127–42. **[G: U.S.]**

Wabe, J. Stuart. The Demand for Gasoline: A Comment on the Cross-Section Analysis by Drollas. *Energy Econ.*, October 1987, 9(4), pp. 287–89. **[G: U.S.; W. Europe]**

Werbos, Paul J. Industrial Structural Shift: Causes and Consequences for Electricity Demand. *Faruqui, A. and Broehl, J.*, eds., 1987, pp. 115–26. **[G: U.S.]**

Willett, Keith D. and Naghshpour, Shahdad. Residential Demand for Energy Commodities: A Household Production Function Approach.

Energy Econ., October 1987, *9*(4), pp. 251–56.

Williams, Harold R. and Mount, Randall I. OECD Gasoline Demand Elasticities: An Analysis of Consumer Behavior with Implications for U.S. Energy Policy. *J. Behav. Econ.*, Spring 1987, *16*(1), pp. 69–79. **[G: OECD]**

Williams, Harold R. and Mount, Randall I. OPEC and the U.S. Demand for Motor Gasoline: Short-run and Long-run Price Elasticities. *Rivista Int. Sci. Econ. Com.*, Jan.-Feb. 1987, *34*(1–2), pp. 147–58. **[G: U.S.]**

Wilman, Elizabeth A. and Pauls, Richard J. Sensitivity of Consumers' Surplus Estimates to Variation in the Parameters of the Travel Cost Model. *Can. J. Agr. Econ.*, March 1987, *35*(1), pp. 197–212. **[G: Canada]**

Woodside, Arch G. Measuring Customer Awareness and Share-of-Requirements Awarded to Competing Industrial Distributors. *Woodside, A. G., ed.*, 1987, pp. 141–63. **[G: U.S.]**

Zanias, George P. The Demand for Cigarettes: Habit Formation and Health Scare. *Greek Econ. Rev.*, 1987, *9*(2), pp. 248–62. **[G: Greece]**

Zellner, James A. and Traub, Larry G. In-Kind Food Assistance and Consumer Food Choice. *J. Cons. Aff.*, Winter 1987, *21*(2), pp. 221–37. **[G: U.S.]**

9213 Consumer Protection

Altrogge, Phyllis and Shughart, William F., II. The Regressive Nature of Civil Penalties. *MacKay, R. J.; Miller, J. C., III and Yandle, B., eds.*, 1987, *1984*, pp. 240–54. **[G: U.S.]**

Angell, Wayne D. Statement to the U.S. Senate Subcommitee on Consumer Affairs of the Committee on Banking, Housing, and Urban Affairs, February 5, 1987. *Fed. Res. Bull.*, April 1987, *73*(4), pp. 279–82. **[G: U.S.]**

Barnett, Kerry. Equitable Trusts: An Effective Remedy in Consumer Class Actions. *Yale Law J.*, June 1987, *96*(7), pp. 1591–1614. **[G: U.S.]**

Bloom, Paul N. and Gerson, Walter. The Use of "Scrip" for Obtaining Consumer Redress in Antitrust Cases: Lessons from a Failed Application in the Real Estate Industry. *Bloom, P. N., ed.*, 1987, pp. 93–106. **[G: U.S.]**

Bockstael, Nancy E. Economic Efficiency Issues of Grading and Minimum Quality Standards. *Kilmer, R. L. and Armbruster, W. J., eds.*, 1987, pp. 231–50. **[G: OECD]**

Boden, Leslie I. and Jones, Carol Adaire. Occupational Disease Remedies: The Asbestos Experience. *Bailey, E. E., ed.*, 1987, pp. 321–46. **[G: U.S.]**

Canner, Glenn B. and Maland, Ellen. Basic Banking. *Fed. Res. Bull.*, April 1987, *73*(4), pp. 255–69. **[G: U.S.]**

Costley, Carolyn L. and Brucks, Merrie. The Roles of Product Knowledge and Age on Children's Responses to Deceptive Advertising. *Bloom, P. N., ed.*, 1987, pp. 41–63. **[G: U.S.]**

Crandall, Robert W. and Keller, Theodore E. Public Policy and the Private Auto. *[Adelman, M. A.]*, 1987, pp. 137–60. **[G: U.S.]**

Dardis, Rachel and Lefkowitz, Camille. Motorcycle Helmet Laws: A Case Study of Consumer Protection. *J. Cons. Aff.*, Winter 1987, *21*(2), pp. 202–20. **[G: U.S.]**

Flickinger, Richard S. Consumer Policy: Qualified Convergence. *Waltman, J. L. and Studlar, D. T., eds.*, 1987, pp. 150–81. **[G: U.K.; U.S.]**

Folkes, Valerie S. The Role of Causal Inferences in Postpurchase Processes. *Sheth, J. N. and Hirschman, E., eds.*, 1987, pp. 137–60.

Garbacz, Christopher and Kelly, J. Gregory. Automobile Safety Inspection: New Econometric and Benefit/Cost Estimates. *Appl. Econ.*, June 1987, *19*(6), pp. 763–71. **[G: U.S.]**

Gilly, Mary C. Postcomplaint Processes: From Organizational Response to Repurchase Behavior. *J. Cons. Aff.*, Winter 1987, *21*(2), pp. 293–313. **[G: U.S.]**

Grant, Robert M. The Effects of Product Standardization on Competition: Octane Grading of Petrol in the UK. *Gabel, H. L., ed.*, 1987, pp. 283–302. **[G: U.K.]**

Hancher, Leigh and Ruete, Matthias. Legal Culture, Product Licensing, and the Drug Industry. *Wilks, S. and Wright, M., eds.*, 1987, pp. 148–80. **[G: U.K.; W. Germany]**

Higgins, Richard S. and McChesney, Fred S. Truth and Consequences: The Federal Trade Commission's Ad Substantiation Program. *MacKay, R. J.; Miller, J. C., III and Yandle, B., eds.*, 1987, pp. 181–204. **[G: U.S.]**

Irwin, Alan. Technical Expertise and Risk Conflict: An Institutional Study of the British Compulsory Seat Belt Debate. *Policy Sci.*, 1987, *20*(4), pp. 339–64. **[G: U.K.]**

Jordan, J. Phillip and Leiner, Frederick C. American Jurisdiction over Foreign Corporations in Product Liability Lawsuits: The ASAHI Decision and Beyond. *J. World Trade Law*, October 1987, *21*(5), pp. 31–44. **[G: U.S.]**

Loeb, Peter D. The Determinants of Automobile Fatalities, with Special Consideration to Policy Variables. *J. Transp. Econ. Policy*, September 1987, *21*(3), pp. 279–87. **[G: U.S.]**

Mannering, Fred and Winston, Clifford. Recent Automobile Occupant Safety Proposals. *Winston, C., et al.*, 1987, pp. 68–88. **[G: U.S.]**

Meyer, John R.; Oster, Clinton V., Jr. and Strong, John S. The U.S. Experience with Airline Deregulation: The Effect on Travelers: Fares and Service. *Meyer, J. R. and Oster, C. V., Jr.*, 1987, pp. 109–24. **[G: U.S.]**

Morgan, Karen J. Consumer Demand for Nutrients in Food. *Raunikar, R. and Huang, C.-L., eds.*, 1987, pp. 219–35. **[G: U.S.]**

Nichols, John P. Economic Efficiency Issues of Grading and Minimum Quality Standards: A Discussion. *Kilmer, R. L. and Armbruster, W. J., eds.*, 1987, pp. 251–55. **[G: U.S.]**

Nimmer, Raymond T. Consumer Bankruptcy Abuse. *Law Contemp. Probl.*, Spring 1987, *50*(2), pp. 89–118. **[G: U.S.]**

Phelps, Charles E. Risk and Perceived Risk of Drunk Driving among Young Drivers. *J. Policy Anal. Manage.*, Summer 1987, *6*(4), pp. 708–14. [G: U.S.]

Sachs, Carolyn; Blair, Dorothy and Richter, Carolyn. Consumer Pesticide Concerns: A 1965 and 1984 Comparison. *J. Cons. Aff.*, Summer 1987, *21*(1), pp. 96–107. [G: U.S.]

Saffer, Henry and Grossman, Michael. Drinking Age Laws and Highway Mortality Rates: Cause and Effect. *Econ. Inquiry*, July 1987, *25*(3), pp. 403–17. [G: U.S.]

Seger, Martha R. Statement to the U.S. Senate Subcommittee on Consumer Affairs of the Committee on Banking, Housing, and Urban Affairs, April 21, 1987. *Fed. Res. Bull.*, June 1987, *73*(6), pp. 430–35. [G: U.S.]

Sheehan, Dennis and Winston, Clifford. Expectations and Automobile Policy. *Winston, C., et al.*, 1987, pp. 89–102. [G: U.S.]

Siliciano, John A. Corporate Behavior and the Social Efficiency of Tort Law. *Mich. Law Rev.*, August 1987, *85*(8), pp. 1820–64. [G: U.S.]

Smith, V. Kerry and Desvousges, William H. An Empirical Analysis of the Economic Value of Risk Changes. *J. Polit. Econ.*, February 1987, *95*(1), pp. 89–114. [G: U.S.]

Solomon, Elinor Harris. EFT: A Consumer's View. *Solomon, E. H., ed.*, 1987, pp. 211–37. [G: U.S.]

Wilkinson, James T. Reducing Drunken Driving: Which Polices Are Most Effective? *Southern Econ. J.*, October 1987, *54*(2), pp. 322–34. [G: U.S.]

Zlatoper, Thomas J. Factors Affecting Motor Vehicle Deaths in the USA: Some Cross-sectional Evidence. *Appl. Econ.*, June 1987, *19*(6), pp. 753–61. [G: U.S.]

930 URBAN ECONOMICS

9300 General

d'Autume, Antoine and Michel, Philippe. Repères sur la substitution capital-travail. (Notes on Capital Labor Substitution. With English summary.) *Revue Écon.*, May 1987, *38*(3), pp. 703–23. [G: France]

931 Urban Economics and Public Policy

9310 Urban Economics and Public Policy

Alig, Ralph J. and Healy, Robert G. Urban and Built-Up Land Area Changes in the United States: An Empirical Investigation of Determinants. *Land Econ.*, August 1987, *63*(3), pp. 215–26. [G: U.S.]

Amos, Orley M., Jr. The Influence of Urban Areas on Regional Development. *Rev. Reg. Stud.*, Fall 1987, *17*(3), pp. 37–46. [G: U.S.]

Andersson, Roland and Samartin, Avelino. Evaluation of School Plans. *J. Urban Econ.*, January 1987, *21*(1), pp. 45–58. [G: Sweden]

Andrade, Thompson A. and dos Santos, Renato A. Z. Villela. Eficácia da institucionalização de regiões metropolitanas no Brasil: análise da evolução dos serviços de saneamento urbano. (With English summary.) *Pesquisa Planejamento Econ.*, April 1987, *17*(1), pp. 93–120. [G: Brazil]

Atherton, Cliff and Windsor, Duane. Privatization of Urban Public Services. *Kent, C. A., ed.*, 1987, pp. 81–99.

Barras, Richard. Technical Change and the Urban Development Cycle. *Urban Stud.*, February 1987, *24*(1), pp. 5–30. [G: U.K.]

Bawa, R. S. and Kainth, Gursharan Singh. Income Inequalities in Urban Areas: Measurement and Determinant. *Margin*, Jan.-Mar. 1987, *19*(2), pp. 60–73. [G: India]

Becker, Charles M. Urban Sector Income Distribution and Economic Development. *J. Urban Econ.*, March 1987, *21*(2), pp. 127–45. [G: LDCs]

Bennett, Robert J. Local Business Taxes: Theory and Practice. *Oxford Rev. Econ. Policy*, Summer 1987, *3*(2), pp. 60–80. [G: U.K.; W. Germany]

Berger, Mark C.; Blomquist, Glenn C. and Waldner, Werner. A Revealed-Preference Ranking of Quality of Life for Metropolitan Areas. *Soc. Sci. Quart.*, December 1987, *68*(4), pp. 761–78. [G: U.S.]

Bilsborrow, Richard E., et al. The Impact of Origin Community Characteristics on Rural–Urban Out-Migration in a Developing Country. *Demography*, May 1987, *24*(2), pp. 191–210. [G: Ecuador]

Blackley, Dixie M. and Follain, James R. Tests of Locational Equilibrium in the Standard Urban Model. *Land Econ.*, February 1987, *63*(1), pp. 46–61. [G: U.S.]

Blecha, Betty J. The Crowding Parameter and Samuelsonian Publicness [Micro Estimates of Public Spending Demand Functions and Tests of the Tiebout and Median-Voter Hypotheses]. *J. Polit. Econ.*, June 1987, *95*(3), pp. 622–31. [G: U.S.]

Bluestone, Barry. Postindustrial Prospects for the Industrial Midwest: Can Ohio Compete? *McKee, D. L. and Bennett, R. E., eds.*, 1987, pp. 115–21. [G: U.S.]

Boddy, Martin. Bristol: Sunbelt City? *Hausner, V. A., et al.*, 1987, pp. 44–98. [G: U.K.]

Booth, Douglas E. Regional Long Waves and Urban Policy. *Urban Stud.*, December 1987, *24*(6), pp. 447–59. [G: U.S.]

Bourne, L. S. Urbanization, Migration and Urban Research in Comparative Context: An Urban Systems Perspective. *Can. J. Devel. Stud.*, 1987, *8*(1), pp. 69–80.

Bradbury, Katharine L. and Ladd, Helen F. City Property Taxes: The Effects of Economic Change and Competitive Pressures. *New Eng. Econ. Rev.*, July/Aug. 1987, pp. 22–36. [G: U.S.]

Brown, Lester R. and Jacobson, Jodi. Assessing the Future of Urbanization. *Brown, L. R., et al.*, 1987, pp. 38–56. [G: Global]

Buck, Nick; Gordon, Ian R. and Young, Ken. London: Employment Problems and Prospects. *Hausner, V. A., et al.*, 1987, pp. 99–131. **[G: U.K.]**

Buhr, Walter. Empirical Analysis of Allocation. On the State of the Art in Urban Development Modeling. *Z. Wirtschaft. Sozialwissen.*, 1987, *107*(2), pp. 169–99.

Carlino, Gerald A. Comparisons of Agglomeration: Or What Chinitz Really Said: A Reply. *Urban Stud.*, February 1987, *24*(1), pp. 75–76. **[G: U.S.]**

Carter, Gregg Lee. Local Police Force Size and the Severity of the 1960s Black Rioting. *J. Conflict Resolution*, December 1987, *31*(4), pp. 601–14. **[G: U.S.]**

Clark, Gordon L. Adjudicating Jurisdictional Disputes in Chicago and Toronto: Legal Formalism and Urban Structure. *Feldman, E. J. and Goldberg, M. A., eds.*, 1987, pp. 225–46. **[G: U.S.; Canada]**

Clark, William A. V. Urban Restructuring from a Demographic Perspective. *Econ. Geogr.*, April 1987, *63*(2), pp. 103–25. **[G: U.S.]**

Clarke, M. and Openshaw, S. The AGW Spatial Interaction Workstation. *Environ. Planning A*, September 1987, *19*(9), pp. 1261–68.

Cobb, Stephen A. Interarea Cost of Living Measurement with Nonmarket Goods: A Demand Systems Approach. *J. Urban Econ.*, September 1987, *22*(2), pp. 174–89. **[G: U.S.]**

Coffey, W. J. and Polèse, M. Trade and Location of Producer Services: A Canadian Perspective. *Environ. Planning A*, May 1987, *19*(5), pp. 597–611. **[G: Canada]**

Colcord, Frank C., Jr. Saving the Center City. *Feldman, E. J. and Goldberg, M. A., eds.*, 1987, pp. 75–124. **[G: U.S.; Canada]**

Craig, Steven G. The Deterrent Impact of Police: An Examination of a Locally Provided Public Service. *J. Urban Econ.*, May 1987, *21*(3), pp. 298–311. **[G: U.S.]**

Crouchley, R. An Examination of the Equivalence of Three Alternative Mechanisms for Establishing the Equilibrium Solutions of the Production-Constrained Spatial Interaction Model. *Environ. Planning A*, July 1987, *19*(7), pp. 621–74.

Curran, P. J. and Hobson, T. A. Landsat MSS Imagery to Estimate Residential Heat-Load Density. *Environ. Planning A*, December 1987, *19*(12), pp. 1597–1610. **[G: U.K.]**

Dangschat, Jens and Blasius, Jörg. Social and Spatial Disparities in Warsaw in 1978: An Application of Correspondence Analysis to a 'Socialist' City. *Urban Stud.*, June 1987, *24*(3), pp. 173–91. **[G: Poland]**

Davis, Kingsley. The Urbanization of the Human Population. *Menard, S. W. and Moen, E. W., eds.*, 1987, *1965*, pp. 322–30.

Deutsch, Joseph; Hakim, Simon and Weinblatt, J. A Micro Model of the Criminal's Location Choice. *J. Urban Econ.*, September 1987, *22*(2), pp. 198–208.

DiMasi, Joseph A. The Effects of Site Value Taxation in an Urban Area: A General Equilibrium Computational Approach. *Nat. Tax J.*, December 1987, *40*(4), pp. 577–90. **[G: U.S.]**

van Dinteren, J. H. J. The Role of Business-Service Offices in the Economy of Medium-sized Cities. *Environ. Planning A*, May 1987, *19*(5), pp. 669–86. **[G: Netherlands]**

Duffy, Neal E. Returns to Scale Behavior and Manufacturing Agglomeration Economies in U.S. Urban Areas. *Reg. Sci. Persp.*, 1987, *17*(1), pp. 42–54. **[G: U.S.]**

Ellson, Richard W. and McDermott, John H. Zoning Uncertainty and the Urban Land Development Firm. *J. Urban Econ.*, September 1987, *22*(2), pp. 209–22.

Emerson, M. Jarvin and Akhavipour, Hossein. The Impact on Metropolitan Areas of Hinterland Resource Depletion. *Reg. Sci. Persp.*, 1987, *17*(2), pp. 57–69. **[G: U.S.]**

Eppink, Th. W. A. Lognormal and Pareto Estimates of City-Size Distributions: A Critique. *Environ. Planning A*, June 1987, *19*(6), pp. 829–33.

Erickson, Rodney A. and Wollover, David R. Local Tax Burdens and the Supply of Business Sites in Suburban Municipalities. *J. Reg. Sci.*, February 1987, *27*(1), pp. 25–37. **[G: U.S.]**

Ermisch, John. A Partial Equilibrium Model of the Location of Economic Activity in a Metropolitan Area. *Urban Stud.*, April 1987, *24*(2), pp. 103–08.

Ettlinger, N. and Archer, J. C. City-Size Distributions and the World Urban Sytem in the Twentieth Century. *Environ. Planning A*, September 1987, *19*(9), pp. 1161–74. **[G: Global]**

Faerman, E. Iu. and Portianskii, I. A. Systems Forecasting of Urban Settlement. *Matekon*, Winter 1987-88, *24*(2), pp. 69–87. **[G: U.S.S.R.]**

Feiock, Richard. Urban Economic Development: Local Government Strategies and Their Effects. *Nagel, S. S., ed.*, 1987, pp. 215–40. **[G: U.S.]**

Feldman, Elliot J. On the Fringe: Controlling Urban Sprawl in Canada and the United States. *Feldman, E. J. and Goldberg, M. A., eds.*, 1987, pp. 125–46. **[G: Canada; U.S.]**

Frankel, Marvin. Taxes, Pollution, and Optimal Abatement in an Urban Economy. *J. Urban Econ.*, September 1987, *22*(2), pp. 117–35.

Friedman, Joseph; Hakim, Simon and Spiegel, Uriel. The Effects of Community Size on the Mix of Private and Public Use of Security Services. *J. Urban Econ.*, September 1987, *22*(2), pp. 230–41. **[G: U.S.]**

Funkhouser, Richard and Lorenz, Edward. Fiscal and Employment Impacts of Enterprise Zones. *Atlantic Econ. J.*, July 1987, *15*(2), pp. 62–76. **[G: U.S.]**

Gabriel, Stuart A.; Justman, Moshe and Levy, Amnon. A Simultaneous-Equations Analysis of Urban Development: Migration and Industrial Growth in Israel's New Towns. *J. Urban Econ.*, May 1987, *21*(3), pp. 364–77. **[G: Israel]**

Galster, George C. Residential Segregation and Interracial Economic Disparities: A Simultaneous-Equations Approach. *J. Urban Econ.*, January 1987, *21*(1), pp. 22–44. **[G: U.S.]**

Gerber, Robert I. and Hewitt, Daniel P. Tax Competition and Redistribution Policy of Local Governments Competing for Business Capital. *J. Urban Econ.*, January 1987, *21*(1), pp. 69–82.

Gibson, Campbell. The Population in Large Urban Concentrations in the United States, 1790–1980: A Delineation Using Highly Urbanized Countries. *Demography*, November 1987, *24*(4), pp. 601–14. **[G: U.S.]**

Glickman, Norman J. and Van Wagner, Marcia. Two Cheers for Industrial Policy: A Critical Look at Some Urban and Distributional Effects. *Goldstein, H. A., ed.*, 1987, pp. 34–53. **[G: U.S.]**

Goddard, John; Robinson, Fred and Wren, Colin. Urban and Regional Policies and the Economic Development of the Newcastle Metropolitan Region. *Hausner, V. A., et al.*, 1987, pp. 132–81. **[G: U.K.]**

Goodman, Allen C. Using Lorenz Curves to Characterise Urban Elderly Populations. *Urban Stud.*, February 1987, *24*(1), pp. 77–80. **[G: U.S.]**

Grimaud, André. Substitution espace-travail dans une ville monocentrique. (With English summary.) *Revue Écon. Polit.*, Mar.-Apr. 1987, *97*(2), pp. 183–212.

Gunther, William D. and Leathers, Charles G. British Enterprise Zones: Implications for U.S. Urban Policy. *J. Econ. Issues*, June 1987, *21*(2), pp. 885–93. **[G: U.S.; U.K.]**

Gupta, Manash Ranjan. Harris–Todaro Migration-Mechanism and the Optimum Development of the Urban Sector. *Indian Econ. Rev.*, July-Dec. 1987, *22*(2), pp. 179–94. **[G: LDCs]**

Gutman, Pablo. Pobreza urbana: explorando algunas microsoluciones para macroproblemas. (With English summary.) *Desarrollo Econ.*, July-Sept. 1987, *27*(106), pp. 279–89. **[G: Argentina]**

Guy, C. M. Recent Advances in Spatial Interaction Modelling: An Application to the Forecasting of Shopping Travel. *Environ. Planning A*, February 1987, *19*(2), pp. 173–86. **[G: U.K.]**

Gyourko, Joseph. Effects of Local Tax Structures on the Factor Intensity Composition of Manufacturing Activity across Cities. *J. Urban Econ.*, September 1987, *22*(2), pp. 151–64. **[G: U.S.]**

Hagishima, S.; Mitsuyoshi, K. and Kurose, S. Estimation of Pedestrian Shopping Trips in a Neighborhood by Using a Spatial Interaction Model. *Environ. Planning A*, September 1987, *19*(9), pp. 1139–52. **[G: Japan]**

Hamnett, C. A Tale of Two Cities: Sociotenurial Polarisation in London and the South East, 1966–1981. *Environ. Planning A*, April 1987, *19*(4), pp. 537–56. **[G: U.K.]**

Hanjoul, Pierre and Peeters, Dominique. A Facility Location Problem with Clients' Preference Orderings. *Reg. Sci. Urban Econ.*, August 1987, *17*(3), pp. 451–73.

Harriss, C. L. Use of Income from Urban Land: Thoughts from U.S. Experience. *Econ. Scelte*

Pubbliche/J. Public Finance Public Choice, Sept.-Dec. 1987, *5*(3), pp. 213–17. **[G: U.S.]**

Hausner, Victor A. Economic Change and Urban Policy. *Hausner, V. A., et al.*, 1987, pp. 1–43. **[G: U.K.]**

Havinga, Ivo C. Skill Formation, Employment and Earnings in the Urban Informal Sector: Comments. *Pakistan Devel. Rev.*, Winter 1987, *26*(4), pp. 718–19. **[G: Pakistan]**

Hazari, Bharat R. and Sgro, Pasquale M. Disguised, Urban Unemployment and Welfare in a General Equilibrium Model with Segmented Labor Markets. *J. Reg. Sci.*, August 1987, *27*(3), pp. 461–75.

Henderson, J. Vernon. Industrialization and Urbanization: International Experience. *Johnson, D. G. and Lee, R. D., eds.*, 1987, pp. 189–224. **[G: Global]**

Hicks, Donald A. Geo-Industrial Shifts in Advanced Metropolitan Economies. *Urban Stud.*, December 1987, *24*(6), pp. 460–79. **[G: U.S.]**

Hicks, Donald A. Urban Policy in the U.S.: Introduction. *Urban Stud.*, December 1987, *24*(6), pp. 439–46. **[G: U.S.]**

Hirsch, Barry T. and Neufeld, John L. Nominal and Real Union Wage Differentials and the Effects of Industry and SMSA Density: 1973–83. *J. Human Res.*, Winter 1987, *22*(1), pp. 138–48. **[G: U.S.]**

Hobson, Paul A. R. Optimum Product Variety in Urban Areas. *J. Urban Econ.*, September 1987, *22*(2), pp. 190–97.

Hoch, Irving. City Size and U.S. Urban Policy. *Urban Stud.*, December 1987, *24*(6), pp. 570–86. **[G: U.S.]**

Hohemberg, Paul M. Urbanization and Population Dynamics in History: Review Article. *J. Europ. Econ. Hist.*, Spring 1987, *16*(1), pp. 171–77.

Hosier, Richard H. The Informal Sector in Kenya: Spatial Variation and Development Alternatives. *J. Devel. Areas*, July 1987, *21*(4), pp. 383–402. **[G: Kenya]**

Hourihan, Kevin. Local Community Involvement and Participation in Neighbourhood Watch: A Case-study in Cork, Ireland. *Urban Stud.*, April 1987, *24*(2), pp. 129–36. **[G: Ireland]**

Huffman, Forrest E. and Warner, Arthur E. Toward the Development of an Urban Growth Model That Recognizes the Importance of the Basic Nature of Services. *Amer. Real Estate Urban Econ. Assoc. J.*, Winter 1987, *15*(4), pp. 341–58. **[G: U.S.]**

Hughes, Mark Alan. Moving Up and Moving Out: Confusing Ends and Means about Ghetto Dispersal. *Urban Stud.*, December 1987, *24*(6), pp. 503–17. **[G: U.S.]**

Hutton, Thomas and Ley, David. Location, Linkages, and Labor: The Downtown Complex of Corporate Activities in a Medium Size City, Vancouver, British Columbia. *Econ. Geogr.*, April 1987, *63*(2), pp. 126–41. **[G: Canada]**

Hwang, Sean-Shong and Albrecht, Don E. Constraints to the Fulfillment of Residential Prefer-

ences among Texas Homebuyers. *Demography*, February 1987, *24*(1), pp. 61–76.
[G: U.S.]

James, Franklin J. and Clark, Thomas A. Minority Business in Urban Economies. *Urban Stud.*, December 1987, *24*(6), pp. 489–502.
[G: U.S.]

Johnson, Michael S. and Ragas, Wade R. CBD Land Values and Multiple Externalities. *Land Econ.*, November 1987, *63*(4), pp. 337–47.
[G: U.S.]

Kaufmann, Daniel and Quigley, John M. The Consumption Benefits of Investment in Infrastructure: The Evaluation of Sites-and-Services Programs in Underdeveloped Countries. *J. Devel. Econ.*, April 1987, *25*(2), pp. 263–84.
[G: El Salvador]

Kazi, Shahnaz. Skill Formation, Employment and Earnings in the Urban Informal Sector. *Pakistan Devel. Rev.*, Winter 1987, *26*(4), pp. 711–17. [G: Pakistan]

Kim, Kyung-Hwan and McDonald, John F. Sufficient Conditions for Negative Exponential Densities: A Further Analysis. *J. Reg. Sci.*, May 1987, *27*(2), pp. 295–98.

Kim, Won Bae. Urban Unemployment and Labor Force Participation in Korea. *Ann. Reg. Sci.*, March 1987, *21*(1), pp. 44–55. [G: S. Korea]

Kirby, Andrew and Lynch, A. Karen. A Ghost in the Growth Machine: The Aftermath of Rapid Population Growth in Houston. *Urban Stud.*, December 1987, *24*(6), pp. 587–96.
[G: U.S.]

Kirwan, Richard M. Fiscal Policy and the Price of Land and Housing in Japan. *Urban Stud.*, October 1987, *24*(5), pp. 345–60. [G: Japan]

Klaassen, Leo H. The Future of the Larger European Towns. *Urban Stud.*, August 1987, *24*(4), pp. 251–57. [G: W. Europe]

Klaassen, Leo H. and Van der Meer, J. Urban Change and Public Transport. *Int. J. Transport Econ.*, June 1987, *14*(2), pp. 123–32.
[G: W. Europe]

Krakover, S. Cluster of Cities versus City Region in Regional Planning. *Environ. Planning A*, October 1987, *19*(10), pp. 1375–86. [G: U.S.]

Landers, J. Mortality and Metropolis: The Case of London 1675–1825. *Population Stud.*, March 1987, *41*(1), pp. 59–76. [G: U.K.]

Landis, John D. An Empirical Basis for National Urban Policy. *Urban Stud.*, December 1987, *24*(6), pp. 518–33. [G: U.S.]

Lee, Haeduck and Wasylenko, Michael. A Comment on the Appropriate Estimation of Intrametropolitan Firm Location Models. *Land Econ.*, August 1987, *63*(3), pp. 306–09.
[G: U.S.]

Lesage, James P. and Magura, Michael. A Leading Indicator Model for Ohio SMSA Employment. *Growth Change*, Summer 1987, *18*(3), pp. 36–48. [G: U.S.]

Lesse, P. F. and Roy, J. R. Optimal Replacement and Maintenance of Urban Infrastructure. *Environ. Planning A*, August 1987, *19*(8), pp. 1115–21.

Lever, William F. The Inner Cities Research Programme: The Clydeside Case-Study. *Hausner, V. A., et al.*, 1987, pp. 182–217. [G: U.K.]

Levy, John M. The Limits of Local Economic Development Programs. *McKee, D. L. and Bennett, R. E., eds.*, 1987, pp. 122–36.
[G: U.S.]

Margolis, Julius. The Fiscal Problems of the Fragmented Metropolis. *Aronson, J. R. and Schwartz, E., eds.*, 1987, pp. 30–50.
[G: U.S.]

Masser, Ian and Foley, Paul. Delphi Revisited: Expert Opinion in Urban Analysis. *Urban Stud.*, June 1987, *24*(3), pp. 217–25.
[G: U.K.]

McDonald, John F. The Identification of Urban Employment Subcenters. *J. Urban Econ.*, March 1987, *21*(2), pp. 242–58. [G: U.S.]

McGuire, Therese J. The Effect of New Firm Locations on Local Property Taxes. *J. Urban Econ.*, September 1987, *22*(2), pp. 223–29.
[G: U.S.]

McKean, B. and Coulson, A. Enterprise Boards and Some Issues Raised by Taking Equity and Loan Stock in Major Companies. *Reg. Stud.*, August 1987, *21*(4), pp. 373–84. [G: U.K.]

McKee, David L. and Bennett, Richard E. Akron–Canton: A Twin Cities Solution to Structural Changes in Metropolitan Economies. *McKee, D. L. and Bennett, R. E., eds.*, 1987, pp. 25–40. [G: U.S.]

Melchert, David and Naroff, Joel L. Central City Revitalization: A Predictive Model. *Amer. Real Estate Urban Econ. Assoc. J.*, Spring 1987, *15*(1), pp. 664–83. [G: U.S.]

Menke, Terri. Economic Welfare and Urban Amenities across Race–Sex Groups. *Urban Stud.*, April 1987, *24*(2), pp. 151–61.
[G: U.S.]

Mettelin, Pierre. Les activités informelles en Afrique noire: les réalités urbaines. (With English summary.) *Can. J. Devel. Stud.*, 1987, *8*(1), pp. 49–68. [G: Africa]

Mier, Robert; Moe, Kari J. and Sherr, Irene. Strategic Planning and the Pursuit of Reform, Economic Development, and Equity. *Goldstein, H. A., ed.*, 1987, pp. 161–75. [G: U.S.]

Miller, David and Davenport, E. Closing the Skills Gap. *Reg. Stud.*, December 1987, *21*(6), pp. 564–67. [G: U.K.]

Mills, Edwin S. Non-urban Policies as Urban Policies. *Urban Stud.*, December 1987, *24*(6), pp. 561–69. [G: U.S.]

Mitchelson, Ronald L. and Fisher, James S. Long Distance Commuting and Income Change in the Towns of Upstate New York. *Econ. Geogr.*, January 1987, *63*(1), pp. 48–65. [G: U.S.]

Miyao, T. Long-run Urban Growth with Agglomeration Economies. *Environ. Planning A*, August 1987, *19*(8), pp. 1083–92.

Mohtadi, Hamid. Industrialization and Urban Inequality in LDCs: A Theoretical Analysis with Evidence from Prerevolutionary Iran. *J. Devel. Areas*, October 1987, *22*(1), pp. 41–57.
[G: Iran]

Monkkonen, Eric H. As Cities Become History. *Urban Stud.*, February 1987, *24*(1), pp. 1–3.

Montgomery, Mark R. The Impacts of Urban Population Growth on Urban Labor Markets and the Costs of Urban Service Delivery: A Review. *Johnson, D. G. and Lee, R. D., eds.*, 1987, pp. 149–88. **[G: LDCs]**

Moss, Mitchell L. Telecommunications, World Cities, and Urban Policy. *Urban Stud.*, December 1987, *24*(6), pp. 534–46. **[G: Global]**

Mullen, John K. and Williams, Martin. Technical Progress in Urban Manufacturing: North–South Comparisons. *J. Urban Econ.*, March 1987, *21*(2), pp. 194–208. **[G: U.S.]**

Munt, I. Economic Restructuring, Culture, and Gentrification: A Case Study in Battersea, London. *Environ. Planning A*, September 1987, *19*(9), pp. 1175–97. **[G: U.K.]**

de Neufville, Judith Innes and Barton, Stephen E. Myths and the Definition of Policy Problems: An Exploration of Home Ownership and Public–Private Partnerships. *Policy Sci.*, 1987, *20*(3), pp. 181–206. **[G: U.S.]**

Neutze, Max. The Supply of Land for a Particular Use. *Urban Stud.*, October 1987, *24*(5), pp. 379–88.

Norton, R. D. Ohio in the Regional Life Cycle: A Synthesis. *McKee, D. L. and Bennett, R. E., eds.*, 1987, pp. 229–39. **[G: U.S.]**

Norton, R. D. The Once and Present Urban Crisis. *Urban Stud.*, December 1987, *24*(6), pp. 480–88. **[G: U.S.]**

Noyelle, Thierry J. Services, Urban Economic Development, and Industrial Policy: Some Critical Linkages. *Goldstein, H. A., ed.*, 1987, pp. 73–84. **[G: U.S.]**

Okabe, Atsuyuki. A Theoretical Relationship between the Rank-Size Rule and Clark's Law of Urban Population Distribution: Duality in the Rank-Size Rule. *Reg. Sci. Urban Econ.*, May 1987, *17*(2), pp. 307–19.

Okabe, Atsuyuki and Suzuki, A. Stability of Spatial Competition for a Large Number of Firms on a Bounded Two-Dimensional Space. *Environ. Planning A*, August 1987, *19*(8), pp. 1067–82.

Okpala, Don C. I. Received Concepts and Theories in African Urbanisation Studies and Urban Management Strategies: A Critique. *Urban Stud.*, April 1987, *24*(2), pp. 137–50. **[G: Africa]**

Palmer, Donald A. and Friedland, Roger. Corporation, Class and City System. *Mizruchi, M. S. and Schwartz, M., eds.*, 1987, pp. 145–84. **[G: U.S.]**

Palumbo, George M. and Hutton, Patricia. On the Causality of Intraurban Location. *J. Urban Econ.*, July 1987, *22*(1), pp. 1–13. **[G: U.S.]**

Papageorgiou, Y. Y. Spatial Public Goods. 1: Theory. *Environ. Planning A*, March 1987, *19*(3), pp. 331–52.

Papageorgiou, Y. Y. Spatial Public Goods: 2. Applications. *Environ. Planning A*, April 1987, *19*(4), pp. 471–92.

Parr, John B. Interaction in an Urban System: Aspects of Trade and Commuting. *Econ. Geogr.*, July 1987, *63*(3), pp. 223–40.

Parr, John B. The Tinbergen Analysis of an Urban System and Alternative Approaches. *Environ. Planning A*, February 1987, *19*(2), pp. 187–204.

Pascal, Anthony. The Vanishing City. *Urban Stud.*, December 1987, *24*(6), pp. 597–603. **[G: W. Europe; U.S.; Japan]**

Pasha, Hafiz A. Housing for Temporary Residents: A Study of Pilgrims to Makkah. *Urban Stud.*, August 1987, *24*(4), pp. 312–23. **[G: Saudi Arabia]**

Peddle, Michael T. The Appropriate Estimation of Intrametropolitan Firm Location Models: An Empirical Note. *Land Econ.*, August 1987, *63*(3), pp. 303–05.

Peiser, Richard B. The Determinants of Nonresidential Urban Land Values. *J. Urban Econ.*, November 1987, *22*(3), pp. 340–60. **[G: U.S.]**

Phadke, V. S. Urbanisation in Soviet Central Asia. *Gidadhubli, R. G., ed.*, 1987, pp. 199–218. **[G: U.S.S.R.]**

Rainford, P. and Masser, Ian. Population Forecasting and Urban Planning Practice: A Case Study. *Environ. Planning A*, November 1987, *19*(11), pp. 1463–75. **[G: U.K.]**

Raymond, Richard and Pascarella, Thomas A. Local Economic Development Programs and Small City Growth in Northeastern Ohio, 1970–80. *McKee, D. L. and Bennett, R. E., eds.*, 1987, pp. 137–54. **[G: U.S.]**

Richardson, Harry W. The Costs of Urbanization: A Four-Country Comparison. *Econ. Develop. Cult. Change*, April 1987, *35*(3), pp. 561–80. **[G: Bangladesh; Egypt; Pakistan; Indonesia]**

Richardson, Harry W. Whither National Urban Policy in Developing Countries? *Urban Stud.*, June 1987, *24*(3), pp. 227–44. **[G: LDCs]**

Rolleston, Barbara Sherman. Determinants of Restrictive Suburban Zoning: An Empirical Analysis. *J. Urban Econ.*, January 1987, *21*(1), pp. 1–21. **[G: U.S.]**

Rosenfield, George H.; Fitzpatrick-Lins, Katherine and Johnson, Thomas L. Stratification of a Cityscape Using Census and Land Use Variables for Inventory of Building Materials. *Ann. Reg. Sci.*, March 1987, *21*(1), pp. 22–33. **[G: U.S.]**

Roy, J. R. An Alternative Information Theory Approach for Modelling Spatial Interaction. *Environ. Planning A*, March 1987, *19*(3), pp. 385–94.

Rubin, Marc A. A Theory of Demand for Municipal Audits and Audit Contracts. *Chan, J. L., ed., Pt. A*, 1987, pp. 3–33. **[G: U.S.]**

Ruchelman, Leonard I. The Finance Function in Local Government. *Aronson, J. R. and Schwartz, E., eds.*, 1987, pp. 3–29. **[G: U.S.]**

Sasaki, Komei. A Comparative Static Analysis of Urban Structure in the Setting of Endogenous Income. *J. Urban Econ.*, July 1987, *22*(1), pp. 53–72.

Shilling, James D.; Sirmans, C. F. and Corgel, John B. Price Adjustment Process for Rental

Office Space. *J. Urban Econ.*, July 1987, *22*(1), pp. 90–100. **[G: U.S.]**

Sigov, I. The Present and Future of Large Cities. *Prob. Econ.*, January 1987, *29*(9), pp. 43–55. **[G: U.S.S.R.]**

Simon, Curtis J. Industrial Diversity, Vacancy Dispersion, and Unemployment. *Ann. Reg. Sci.*, July 1987, *21*(2), pp. 60–73. **[G: U.S.]**

Simpson, Wayne. Workplace Location, Residential Location, and Urban Commuting. *Urban Stud.*, April 1987, *24*(2), pp. 119–28. **[G: Canada]**

Sit, Victor F. S. Urban Fairs in China. *Econ. Geogr.*, October 1987, *63*(4), pp. 306–18. **[G: China]**

Smith, Tony E. Poisson Gravity Models of Spatial Flows. *J. Reg. Sci.*, August 1987, *27*(3), pp. 315–40.

Soroka, Lewis A. Male/Female Income Distributions, City Size and Urban Characteristics: Canada, 1970–1980. *Urban Stud.*, October 1987, *24*(5), pp. 417–26. **[G: Canada]**

Spencer, Ken. The West Midlands: An Economy in Crisis. *Hausner, V. A., et al.*, 1987, pp. 218–53. **[G: U.K.]**

Squires, Gregory D., et al. Is Growth Working for Chicago? *Challenge*, Sept./Oct. 1987, *30*(4), pp. 42–48. **[G: U.S.]**

Stanback, Thomas M., Jr. Development under Adversity: The Importance of Services, Technology, and Labor. *McKee, D. L. and Bennett, R. E., eds.*, 1987, pp. 85–108. **[G: U.S.]**

Steen, Robert C. Effects of the Property Tax in Urban Areas. *J. Urban Econ.*, March 1987, *21*(2), pp. 146–65.

Steen, Robert C. Effects of Governmental Structure in Urban Areas. *J. Urban Econ.*, March 1987, *21*(2), pp. 166–79. **[G: U.S.]**

Stewart, Michael. Regional Economic Development Incentives: Applications for Youngstown, Ohio. *McKee, D. L. and Bennett, R. E., eds.*, 1987, pp. 41–57. **[G: U.S.]**

Stolnitz, George J. Technological Prospects and Population Trends: Conclusions. *Espenshade, T. and Stolnitz, G. J., eds.*, 1987, pp. 195–211.

Strassmann, W. Paul. Home-Based Enterprises in Cities of Developing Countries. *Econ. Develop. Cult. Change*, October 1987, *36*(1), pp. 121–44. **[G: Peru; Sri Lanka; Zambia]**

Suarez-Villa, Luis. Evolução metropolitana, mudança econômica setorial e distribuição de tamanhos de cidades. (With English summary.) *Pesquisa Planejamento Econ.*, April 1987, *17*(1), pp. 121–59.

Suh, Seoung Hwan. On the Size Distribution of Cities: An Economic Interpretation of the Pareto Coefficient. *Environ. Planning A*, June 1987, *19*(6), pp. 749–62.

Sullivan, Arthur M. The Spatial Effects of a General Capital Tax: Property Taxes and Urban Labor Markets. *Reg. Sci. Urban Econ.*, May 1987, *17*(2), pp. 209–22.

Thompson, Wilbur R. and Thompson, Philip R. Alternative Paths to Local Economic Development: Insights into Strategies for Northeastern

Ohio. *McKee, D. L. and Bennett, R. E., eds.*, 1987, pp. 58–84. **[G: U.S.]**

Tong, Dalin and Song, Yanming. Horizontal Economic Integration Is a Beachhead to Launch Urban Reform. *Chinese Econ. Stud.*, Winter 1986-87, *20*(2), pp. 26–35. **[G: China]**

Wang, Xiaoqiang and Zhang, Gang. An Overview of the CESRRI Survey. *Reynolds, B. L.*, 1987, pp. xxv–xxxii. **[G: China]**

Weiss, Dieter. Der informelle Sektor in den Metropolen der Entiwicklungsländer—Kunzeptionelle Ansätze zu einerr Neuorientierung von Regelungspolitiken. (On the Informal Sector in Developing Countries' Cities. With English summary.) *Konjunkturpolitik*, 1987, *33*(2), pp. 99–115. **[G: LDCs]**

Weiss, Thomas. Demographic Aspects of the Urban Population, 1800–1840. *Kilby, P., ed.*, 1987, pp. 171–213. **[G: U.S.]**

Werczberger, Elia. A Dynamic Model of Urban Land Use with Externalities. *Reg. Sci. Urban Econ.*, August 1987, *17*(3), pp. 391–410.

Whalen, Charles J. Consensus Mechanisms and Community Economic Development: The Buffalo Experience. *J. Econ. Issues*, June 1987, *21*(2), pp. 763–74. **[G: U.S.]**

Wheaton, William C. The Cyclical Behavior of the National Office Market. *Amer. Real Estate Urban Econ. Assoc. J.*, Winter 1987, *15*(4), pp. 281–99. **[G: U.S.]**

Wieand, Kenneth F. An Extension of the Monocentric Urban Spatial Equilibrium Model to a Multicenter Setting: The Case of the Two-Center City. *J. Urban Econ.*, May 1987, *21*(3), pp. 259–71.

Wilson, David. Urban Revitalization on the Upper West Side of Manhattan: An Urban Managerialist Assessment. *Econ. Geogr.*, January 1987, *63*(1), pp. 35–47. **[G: U.S.]**

Wilson, Franklin D. Metropolitan and Nonmetropolitan Migration Streams: 1935–1980. *Demography*, May 1987, *24*(2), pp. 211–28. **[G: U.S.]**

Worrall, Leslie. Information Systems for Urban Labour-Market Planning and Analysis. *Gordon, I., ed.*, 1987, pp. 139–57. **[G: U.K.]**

Wray, I. The Merseyside Development Corporation: Progress versus Objectives. *Reg. Stud.*, April 1987, *21*(2), pp. 163–67. **[G: U.K.]**

Yoo, Jong G. and Kwon, Jene K. Welfare Inequality among Urban Households in South Korea: 1965–83. *Appl. Econ.*, April 1987, *19*(4), pp. 497–510.

Zweig, David. From Village to City: Reforming Urban–Rural Relations in China. *Int. Reg. Sci. Rev.*, 1987, *11*(1), pp. 43–58. **[G: China]**

932 Housing Economics

9320 Housing Economics (including nonurban housing)

Adams, Carolyn Teich. The Politics of Privatization. *Turner, B.; Kemeny, J. and Lundqvist, L. J., eds.*, 1987, pp. 127–55. **[G: U.S.; W. Europe]**

Adler, Moshe. The Location of Owners and Renters in the City. *J. Urban Econ.*, May 1987, *21*(3), pp. 347–63. **[G: U.S.]**

Aitken, S. C. Households Moving within the Rental Sector: Mental Schemata and Search Spaces. *Environ. Planning A*, March 1987, *19*(3), pp. 369–83. **[G: U.K.]**

Allen, Paul R.; Shilling, James D. and Sirmans, C. F. Contracting, Contingencies and Single-Family House Prices. *Econ. Inquiry*, January 1987, *25*(1), pp. 159–64. **[G: U.S.]**

Arnott, Richard J. Rent Control: The International Experience. *Arnott, R. J. and Mintz, J. M., eds.*, 1987, pp. 3–14. **[G: Global]**

Asabere, Paul K. and McGowan, Carl. Some Factors Explaining Variations in Rents of Downtown Apartments for 49 Cities of the World. *Urban Stud.*, August 1987, *24*(4), pp. 279–84. **[G: Global]**

Atkinson, Scott E. and Crocker, Thomas D. A Bayesian Approach to Assessing the Robustness of Hedonic Property Value Studies. *J. Appl. Econometrics*, January 1987, *2*(1), pp. 27–45. **[G: U.S.]**

Baar, Kenneth K. Peacetime Municipal Rent Control Laws in the United States: Local Design Issues and Ideological Policy Debates. *van Vliet—, W., et al., eds.*, 1987, pp. 257–76. **[G: U.S.]**

Baily, Martin Neil. Housing Markets, Unemployment and Labour Market Flexibility in the UK: Comments. *Europ. Econ. Rev.*, April 1987, *31*(3), pp. 641–43. **[G: U.K.]**

Ball, M. A Critical Note on Ball's Reformulation of the Role of Urban Land Rent: Rent and Social Relations: A Reply. *Environ. Planning A*, February 1987, *19*(2), pp. 269–72.

Bauman, Gus and Ethier, William H. Development Exactions and Impact Fees: A Survey of American Practices. *Law Contemp. Probl.*, Winter 1987, *50*(1), pp. 51–68. **[G: U.S.]**

Benjamin, John D. and Sirmans, C. F. Who Benefits from Mortgage Revenue Bonds? *Nat. Tax J.*, March 1987, *40*(1), pp. 115–20. **[G: U.S.]**

Blackley, Dixie M. and Follain, James R. Tests of Locational Equilibrium in the Standard Urban Model. *Land Econ.*, February 1987, *63*(1), pp. 46–61. **[G: U.S.]**

Boehm, Thomas P. and Hofler, Richard A. A Frontier Approach to Measuring the Effect of Market Discrimination: A Housing Illustration. *Southern Econ. J.*, October 1987, *54*(2), pp. 301–15. **[G: U.S.]**

Bolle, Friedel. Zum Problem der Verbrauchsabhängigen Heizkostenabrechnung. Eine theoretische Bestimmung der effizienten Aufteilung. (The Efficient Distribution of Heating Costs—A Theoretical Analysis. With English summary.) *Ifo-Studien*, 1987, *33*(1), pp. 27–42.

Bourassa, Steven C. Land Value Taxation and New Housing Development in Pittsburgh. *Growth Change*, Fall 1987, *18*(4), pp. 44–56. **[G: U.S.]**

Bradbury, Bruce; Rossiter, Chris and Vipond, Joan. Housing and Poverty in Australia. *Urban Stud.*, April 1987, *24*(2), pp. 95–102. **[G: Australia]**

Brigham, John. The "Giving Issue": A View of Land, Property Rights and Industrial Development in Maine and Nova Scotia. *Feldman, E. J. and Goldberg, M. A., eds.*, 1987, pp. 247–68. **[G: U.S.; Canada]**

Broadberry, Stephen N. Cheap Money and the Housing Boom in Interwar Britain: An Econometric Appraisal. *Manchester Sch. Econ. Soc. Stud.*, December 1987, *55*(4), pp. 378–91. **[G: U.K.]**

Bunting, Trudi E. Changing Patterns in Inner-City Housing: A Canadian Example. *van Vliet—, W., et al., eds.*, 1987, pp. 73–89. **[G: Canada]**

Burman, Leonard E.; Neubig, Thomas S. and Wilson, D. Gordon. The Use and Abuse of Rental Project Models. *U.S. Treasury, Office of Tax Analysis.*, 1987, pp. 307–49. **[G: U.S.]**

Burns, Leland S. Third World Solutions to the Homelessness Problem. *Bingham, R. D.; Green, R. E. and White, S. B., eds.*, 1987, pp. 231–48.

Carliner, Michael S. Homelessness: A Housing Problem? *Bingham, R. D.; Green, R. E. and White, S. B., eds.*, 1987, pp. 119–28. **[G: U.S.]**

Carmon, Naomi and Gavarieli, Tamar. Improving Housing by Conventional versus Self-help Methods: Evidence from Israel. *Urban Stud.*, August 1987, *24*(4), pp. 324–32. **[G: Israel]**

Case, Karl E. and Shiller, Robert J. Prices of Single-Family Homes since 1970: New Indexes for Four Cities. *New Eng. Econ. Rev.*, Sept./Oct. 1987, pp. 45–56. **[G: U.S.]**

Clark, E. A Critical Note on Ball's Reformulation of the Role of Urban Land Rent. *Environ. Planning A*, February 1987, *19*(2), pp. 263–67.

Clark, E. On Ball's Reformulation—A Rejoinder. *Environ. Planning A*, August 1987, *19*(8), pp. 1123–24.

Clark, Gordon L. Adjudicating Jurisdictional Disputes in Chicago and Toronto: Legal Formalism and Urban Structure. *Feldman, E. J. and Goldberg, M. A., eds.*, 1987, pp. 225–46. **[G: U.S.; Canada]**

Clark, William A. V. Theory and Practice in Housing Market Research. *Turner, B.; Kemeny, J. and Lundqvist, L. J., eds.*, 1987, pp. 11–25. **[G: U.S.]**

Colcord, Frank C., Jr. Saving the Center City. *Feldman, E. J. and Goldberg, M. A., eds.*, 1987, pp. 75–124. **[G: U.S.; Canada]**

Coleman, David. Rent Control: The British Experience and Policy Response. *Arnott, R. J. and Mintz, J. M., eds.*, 1987, pp. 77–98. **[G: U.K.]**

Cooley, Thomas F. and Salyer, Kevin D. The Effects of Inflation-Induced Tax Increases on Stock and Housing Prices. *Scand. J. Econ.*, 1987, *89*(4), pp. 421–34. **[G: U.S.]**

Cooper, Mary Anderson. The Role of Religious and Nonprofit Organizations in Combating Homelessness. *Bingham, R. D.; Green, R. E.*

and White, S. B., eds., 1987, pp. 130–49. [G: U.S.]

Coulson, N. Edward and Engle, Robert F. Transportation Costs and the Rent Gradient. *J. Urban Econ.*, May 1987, *21*(3), pp. 287–97. [G: U.S.]

Cremer, Helmuth and Gathon, Henry-Jean. Les déterminants de la mobilité résidentielle: Une analyse probit. (With English summary.) *Cah. Écon. Bruxelles*, Third Trimester 1987, (115), pp. 53–75. [G: Belgium]

Cuomo, Mario M. The State Role: New York State's Approach to Homelessness. *Bingham, R. D.; Green, R. E. and White, S. B.*, eds., 1987, pp. 199–215. [G: U.S.]

Curwen, Peter. Comment [Local Taxation and Housing Finance: A Proposal for Reform]. *Lloyds Bank Rev.*, January 1987, (163), pp. 47. [G: U.K.]

Dangschat, Jens and Blasius, Jörg. Social and Spatial Disparities in Warsaw in 1978: An Application of Correspondence Analysis to a 'Socialist' City. *Urban Stud.*, June 1987, *24*(3), pp. 173–91. [G: Poland]

Dániel, Zsuzsa and Semjén, András. Housing Shortage and Rents: The Hungarian Experience. *Econ. Planning*, 1987, *21*(1), pp. 13–29. [G: Hungary]

De Borger, Bruno. Alternative Housing Concepts and the Benefits of Public Housing Programs. *J. Urban Econ.*, July 1987, *22*(1), pp. 73–89.

De Borger, Bruno. Composite Commodities, Housing Characteristics and the Hicksian Surplus Measures of Welfare Change. *Reg. Sci. Urban Econ.*, November 1987, *17*(4), pp. 475–94.

Deurloo, M. C.; Dieleman, F. M. and Clark, William A. V. Tenure Choice in the Dutch Housing Market. *Environ. Planning A*, June 1987, *19*(6), pp. 763–81. [G: Netherlands]

Donnison, David. Poverty, Power and Stigma: The Case of the Single Homeless. *Turner, B.; Kemeny, J. and Lundqvist, L. J.*, eds., 1987, pp. 107–15. [G: U.K.]

Dubin, Robin A. and Sung, Chein-Hsing. Spatial Variation in the Price of Housing: Rent Gradients in Non-monocentric Cities. *Urban Stud.*, June 1987, *24*(3), pp. 193–204. [G: U.S.]

Dunn, Richard; Forrest, Ray and Murie, Alan. The Geography of Council House Sales in England—1979–85. *Urban Stud.*, February 1987, *24*(1), pp. 47–59. [G: U.K.]

Dunn, Richard; Longley, P. and Wrigley, N. Graphical Procedures for Identifying Functional Form in Binary Discrete Choice Models: A Case Study of Revealed Tenure Choice. *Reg. Sci. Urban Econ.*, February 1987, *17*(1), pp. 151–71. [G: U.K.]

Fallis, George. Rent Control: The Citizen, the Market and the State. *Arnott, R. J. and Mintz, J. M.*, eds., 1987, pp. 163–74.

Fava, Sylvia F. Diversity in New Communities: A Case Study of Reston, Virginia, at Age 20. *van Vliet—, W., et al.*, eds., 1987, pp. 139–54. [G: U.S.]

Feldman, Elliot J. On the Fringe: Controlling Urban Sprawl in Canada and the United States. *Feldman, E. J. and Goldberg, M. A.*, eds., 1987, pp. 125–46. [G: Canada; U.S.]

Fender, John. Reply [Local Taxation and Housing Finance: A Proposal for Reform]. *Lloyds Bank Rev.*, January 1987, (163), pp. 47–48. [G: U.K.]

Folin, Marino. Housing Policies in West European Countries: The Beginning. *Turner, B.; Kemeny, J. and Lundqvist, L. J.*, eds., 1987, pp. 214–31. [G: W. Europe]

Forrest, Ray. Spatial Mobility, Tenure Mobility, and Emerging Social Divisions in the UK Housing Market. *Environ. Planning A*, December 1987, *19*(12), pp. 1611–30. [G: U.K.]

Francescato, Guido; Weidemann, Sue and Anderson, James R. Residential Satisfaction: Its Uses and Limitations in Housing Research. *van Vliet—, W., et al.*, eds., 1987, pp. 43–57.

Franck, Karen A. Shared Spaces, Small Spaces, and Spaces That Change: Examples of Housing Innovation in the United States. *van Vliet—, W., et al.*, eds., 1987, pp. 157–72. [G: U.S.]

Frew, James R. Multiple Listing Service Participation in the Real Estate Brokerage Industry: Cooperation or Competition? *J. Urban Econ.*, May 1987, *21*(3), pp. 272–86. [G: U.S.]

Frew, James R. and Jud, G. Donald. Who Pays the Real Estate Broker's Commission? *Jaffe, A. J.*, ed., 1987, pp. 177–87. [G: U.S.]

Friedman, David. Cold Houses in Warm Climates and Vice Versa: A Paradox of Rational Heating. *J. Polit. Econ.*, October 1987, *95*(5), pp. 1089–97.

Fujita, Masahisa and Smith, Tony E. Existence of Continuous Residential Land-Use Equilibria. *Reg. Sci. Urban Econ.*, November 1987, *17*(4), pp. 549–94.

Gabriel, Stuart A. Economic Effects of Racial Integration: An Analysis of Hedonic Housing Prices and the Willingness to Pay. *Amer. Real Estate Urban Econ. Assoc. J.*, Fall 1987, *15*(3), pp. 268–79. [G: U.S.]

Gabriel, Stuart A. Housing and Mortgage Markets: The Post-1982 Expansion. *Fed. Res. Bull.*, December 1987, *73*(12), pp. 893–903. [G: U.S.]

Galster, George C. Residential Segregation and Interracial Economic Disparities: A Simultaneous-Equations Approach. *J. Urban Econ.*, January 1987, *21*(1), pp. 22–44. [G: U.S.]

Ginsberg, Yona. The Elderly in Central Tel Aviv. *van Vliet—, W., et al.*, eds., 1987, pp. 291–301. [G: Israel]

Goldberg, Michael A. Evaluating Urban Land Use and Development. *Feldman, E. J. and Goldberg, M. A.*, eds., 1987, pp. 39–72. [G: U.S.; Canada]

Goldberg, Michael A. and Horwood, Peter J. The Costs of Buying and Selling Houses: Some Canadian Evidence. *Jaffe, A. J.*, ed., 1987, pp. 143–59. [G: Canada]

Goodman, John L., Jr. Housing and the Weather. *Amer. Real Estate Urban Econ. Assoc. J.*, Spring 1987, *15*(1), pp. 638–63. [G: U.S.]

Guasch, J. Luis and Marshall, Robert C. A Theoretical and Empirical Analysis of the Length of Residency Discount in the Rental Housing Market. *J. Urban Econ.*, November 1987, 22(3), pp. 291–311.   [G: U.S.]

Guntermann, Karl L. and Norrbin, Stefan. Explaining the Variability of Apartment Rents. *Amer. Real Estate Urban Econ. Assoc. J.*, Winter 1987, 15(4), pp. 321–40.   [G: U.S.]

Guntermann, Karl L. and Smith, Richard L. Efficiency of the Market for Residential Real Estate. *Land Econ.*, February 1987, 63(1), pp. 34–45.   [G: U.S.]

Haldeman, Virginia A.; Peters, Jeanne M. and Tripple, Patricia A. Measuring a Consumer Energy Conservation Ethic: An Analysis of Components. *J. Cons. Aff.*, Summer 1987, 21(1), pp. 70–85.   [G: U.S.]

Harloe, Michael and Martens, Maartje. Innovation in Housing Markets and Policies. *Turner, B.; Kemeny, J. and Lundqvist, L. J., eds.*, 1987, pp. 190–213.   [G: W. Europe]

Harris, Curtis C., Jr. and McConnell, Virginia D. Surpluses in Disequilibrium Urban Land Markets. *Amer. Real Estate Urban Econ. Assoc. J.*, Winter 1987, 15(4), pp. 359–73.   [G: U.S.]

Haurin, Donald R. and Gill, H. Leroy. Effects of Income Variability on the Demand for Owner-Occupied Housing. *J. Urban Econ.*, September 1987, 22(2), pp. 136–50.   [G: U.S.]

Henderson, J. Vernon and Ioannides, Yannis M. Owner Occupancy: Investment vs Consumption Demand. *J. Urban Econ.*, March 1987, 21(2), pp. 228–41.   [G: U.S.]

Heskin, Allan David. The Homeless in Contemporary Society: Los Angeles: Innovative Local Approaches. *Bingham, R. D.; Green, R. E. and White, S. B., eds.*, 1987, pp. 170–83.   [G: U.S.]

Hirsch, Werner Z. Landlord–Tenant Laws and Indigent Black Tenants. *Jaffe, A. J., ed.*, 1987, pp. 129–41.   [G: U.S.]

Hoch, Charles. A Brief History of the Homeless Problem in the United States. *Bingham, R. D.; Green, R. E. and White, S. B., eds.*, 1987, pp. 16–32.   [G: U.S.]

Horowitz, Joel L. Identification and Stochastic Specification in Rosen's Hedonic Price Model. *J. Urban Econ.*, September 1987, 22(2), pp. 165–73.

Howell, J. F. and Peristiani, S. The Estimation of a Hedonic Asking and Offer Rent Equation Model: An EM Algorithm Approach. *Empirical Econ.*, 1987, 12(4), pp. 203–20.   [G: U.S.]

Hughes, Gordon A. and McCormick, Barry. Housing Markets, Unemployment and Labour Market Flexibility in the UK. *Europ. Econ. Rev.*, April 1987, 31(3), pp. 615–41.   [G: U.K.]

Ihlanfeldt, Keith R. and Boehm, Thomas P. Government Intervention in the Housing Market: An Empirical Test of the Externalities Rationale. *J. Urban Econ.*, November 1987, 22(3), pp. 276–90.   [G: U.S.]

Inoki, Takenori. Housing Markets, Unemployment and Labour Market Flexibility in the UK: Comments. *Europ. Econ. Rev.*, April 1987, 31(3), pp. 644–45.   [G: U.K.]

Ioannides, Yannis M. Residential Mobility and Housing Tenure Choice. *Reg. Sci. Urban Econ.*, May 1987, 17(2), pp. 265–87.   [G: U.S.]

Izraeli, Oded. The Effect of Environmental Attributes on Earnings and Housing Values across SMSAs. *J. Urban Econ.*, November 1987, 22(3), pp. 361–76.   [G: U.S.]

Jahiel, Rene I. The Situation of Homelessness. *Bingham, R. D.; Green, R. E. and White, S. B., eds.*, 1987, pp. 99–118.   [G: U.S.]

Jones, Colin and Maclennan, Duncan. Building Societies and Credit Rationing: An Empirical Examination of Redlining. *Urban Stud.*, June 1987, 24(3), pp. 205–16.   [G: Scotland]

Kamara, Sheku G. Effect of Local Variations in Public Services on Housing Production at the Fringe of a Growth-Controlled Multi-country Metropolitan Area. *Urban Stud.*, April 1987, 24(2), pp. 109–17.   [G: U.S.; Canada]

Kanemoto, Yoshitsugu; Hayashi, Fumio and Wago, Hajime. An Econometric Analysis of a Capital Gains Tax on Land. *Econ. Stud. Quart.*, June 1987, 38(2), pp. 159–71.   [G: Japan]

Katz, Lawrence F. and Rosen, Kenneth T. The Interjurisdictional Effects of Growth Controls on Housing Prices. *J. Law Econ.*, April 1987, 30(1), pp. 149–60.   [G: U.S.]

Kau, James B. and Rubin, Paul H. The Political Economy of Urban Land Use. *Jaffe, A. J., ed.*, 1987, pp. 5–26.   [G: U.S.]

Kaufmann, Daniel and Quigley, John M. The Consumption Benefits of Investment in Infrastructure: The Evaluation of Sites-and-Services Programs in Underdeveloped Countries. *J. Devel. Econ.*, April 1987, 25(2), pp. 263–84.   [G: El Salvador]

van Kempen, Eva. High-Rise Estates and the Concentration of Poverty. *van Vliet—, W., et al., eds.*, 1987, pp. 191–212.   [G: Netherlands]

Kim, Sangphill and Chai, John J. Progressive Tax-Based Tenure Choice: A Study of Korean Housing Rentals. *Int. Econ. J.*, Summer 1987, 1(2), pp. 61–69.   [G: S. Korea]

Kirwan, Richard M. Fiscal Policy and the Price of Land and Housing in Japan. *Urban Stud.*, October 1987, 24(5), pp. 345–60.   [G: Japan]

Kleinman, Mark and Whitehead, Christine. Local Variations in the Sale of Council Houses in England, 1979–1984. *Reg. Stud.*, February 1987, 21(1), pp. 1–11.   [G: U.K.]

Knight, Rudolph H. Homelessness: An American Problem? *Bingham, R. D.; Green, R. E. and White, S. B., eds.*, 1987, pp. 249–72.   [G: U.S.]

Koch, June Q. The Federal Role in Aiding the Homeless. *Bingham, R. D.; Green, R. E. and White, S. B., eds.*, 1987, pp. 216–30.   [G: U.S.]

Krashinsky, Michael and Milne, William J. Housing Prices in Metropolitan Toronto: An Empirical Analysis. *Reg. Sci. Urban Econ.*, May 1987, *17*(2), pp. 289–305. **[G: Canada]**

Krumm, Ronald J. Intertemporal Tenure Choices. *J. Urban Econ.*, November 1987, *22*(3), pp. 263–75. **[G: U.S.]**

Leonard, Jonathan S. The Interaction of Residential Segregation and Employment Discrimination. *J. Urban Econ.*, May 1987, *21*(3), pp. 323–46. **[G: U.S.]**

Lerman, Donald L. and Reeder, William J. The Affordability of Adequate Housing. *Amer. Real Estate Urban Econ. Assoc. J.*, Winter 1987, *15*(4), pp. 389–404. **[G: U.S.]**

Lichtenstein, Larry and Kern, Clifford R. The Cost of Quality in Existing Housing: Estimates from an Implicit Markets Model. *J. Urban Econ.*, November 1987, *22*(3), pp. 324–39. **[G: U.S.]**

Linneman, Peter. The Effect of Rent Control on the Distribution of Income among New York City Renters. *J. Urban Econ.*, July 1987, *22*(1), pp. 14–34. **[G: U.S.]**

Logan, John R. and Messner, Steven F. Racial Residential Segregation and Suburban Violent Crime. *Soc. Sci. Quart.*, September 1987, *68*(3), pp. 510–27. **[G: U.S.]**

MacDonald, Don N.; Murdoch, James C. and White, Harry L. Uncertain Hazards, Insurance, and Consumer Choice: Evidence from Housing Markets. *Land Econ.*, November 1987, *63*(4), pp. 361–71. **[G: U.S.]**

Machielse, E. C. M. The Multiformity of Neighborhood Revitalization in the Netherlands. *van Vliet—, W., et al., eds.*, 1987, pp. 61–72. **[G: Netherlands]**

Maclennan, Duncan. Housing Choices and the Structure of Housing Markets. *Turner, B.; Kemeny, J. and Lundqvist, L. J., eds.*, 1987, pp. 26–52. **[G: U.K.]**

Malpezzi, Stephen and Mayo, Stephen K. The Demand for Housing in Developing Countries: Empirical Estimates from Household Data. *Econ. Develop. Cult. Change*, July 1987, *35*(4), pp. 687–721. **[G: Selected LDCs]**

Malpezzi, Stephen and Mayo, Stephen K. User Cost and Housing Tenure in Developing Countries. *J. Devel. Econ.*, February 1987, *25*(1), pp. 197–220. **[G: Selected LDCs]**

Malpezzi, Stephen; Ozanne, Larry and Thibodeau, Thomas G. Microeconomic Estimates of Housing Depreciation. *Land Econ.*, November 1987, *63*(4), pp. 372–85. **[G: U.S.]**

Manchester, Joyce. Inflation and Housing Demand: A New Perspective. *J. Urban Econ.*, January 1987, *21*(1), pp. 105–25. **[G: U.S.]**

Marcuse, Peter. The Other Side of Housing: Oppression and Liberation. *Turner, B.; Kemeny, J. and Lundqvist, L. J., eds.*, 1987, pp. 232–70.

Marshall, Robert C. and Zarkin, Gary A. Price-Tenure Regressions with Censored Data. *Oxford Bull. Econ. Statist.*, August 1987, *49*(3), pp. 335–41. **[G: U.S.]**

Martinez-Vazquez, Jorge and Ihlanfeldt, Keith R. Why Property Tax Capitalization Rates Differ: A Critical Analysis. *Quigley, J. M., ed.*, 1987, pp. 127–56. **[G: U.S.]**

Mattsson, L.-G. Urban Welfare Maximization and Housing Market Equilibrium in a Random Utility Setting. *Environ. Planning A*, February 1987, *19*(2), pp. 247–61.

Mayo, Stephen K. and Gross, David J. Sites and Services—and Subsidies: The Economics of Low-Cost Housing in Developing Countries. *World Bank Econ. Rev.*, January 1987, *1*(2), pp. 301–35. **[G: LDCs]**

Melchert, David and Naroff, Joel L. Central City Revitalization: A Predictive Model. *Amer. Real Estate Urban Econ. Assoc. J.*, Spring 1987, *15*(1), pp. 664–83. **[G: U.S.]**

Michelson, William. Congruence: The Evolution of a Contextual Concept. *van Vliet—, W., et al., eds.*, 1987, pp. 19–28.

Mills, Edwin S. Has the United States Overinvested in Housing? *Amer. Real Estate Urban Econ. Assoc. J.*, Spring 1987, *15*(1), pp. 601–16. **[G: U.S.]**

Molho, Ian J. Decentralisation in the London Region: Some Policy Simulations. *Gordon, I., ed.*, 1987, pp. 116–38. **[G: U.K.]**

Moore, James S. An Investigation of the Major Influences of Residential Liquidity: A Multivariate Approach. *Amer. Real Estate Urban Econ. Assoc. J.*, Spring 1987, *15*(1), pp. 684–703. **[G: U.S.]**

Moorhouse, John C. Long-term Rent Control and Tenant Subsidies. *Quart. Rev. Econ. Bus.*, Autumn 1987, *27*(3), pp. 6–24. **[G: U.S.]**

Moorhouse, John C. and Elavia, Tony H. The Effects of Selective Decontrol in the NYC Rental Housing Market. *Atlantic Econ. J.*, July 1987, *15*(2), pp. 11–24. **[G: U.S.]**

Moulton, Brent R. Diagnostics for Group Effects in Regression Analysis. *J. Bus. Econ. Statist.*, April 1987, *5*(2), pp. 275–82. **[G: U.S.]**

Murray, Michael P., et al. Analyzing Rent Control: The Case of Los Angeles. *Arnott, R. J. and Mintz, J. M., eds.*, 1987, pp. 17–53. **[G: U.S.]**

de Neufville, Judith Innes and Barton, Stephen E. Myths and the Definition of Policy Problems: An Exploration of Home Ownership and Public–Private Partnerships. *Policy Sci.*, 1987, *20*(3), pp. 181–206. **[G: U.S.]**

Nevile, J. W., et al. A Simple Model of Recent Changes in the Residential Property Market. *Econ. Rec.*, September 1987, *63*(182), pp. 270–80. **[G: Australia]**

Newman, Sandra J. and Reschovsky, James D. An Evaluation of the One-Time Capital Gains Exclusion for Older Homeowners. *Amer. Real Estate Urban Econ. Assoc. J.*, Spring 1987, *15*(1), pp. 704–24. **[G: U.S.]**

Newman, Sandra J. and Reschovsky, James D. Federal Policy and the Mobility of Older Homeowners. *J. Policy Anal. Manage.*, Spring 1987, *6*(3), pp. 402–16. **[G: U.S.]**

Oc, Taner. Ethnic Minorities, Scarce Housing Resources, and Urban Renewal in Britain. *van Vliet—, W., et al., eds.*, 1987, pp. 91–104. **[G: U.K.]**

Olsen, Edgar O. What Do Economists Know about the Effect of Rent Control on Housing Maintenance? *Arnott, R. J. and Mintz, J. M., eds.*, 1987, pp. 143–58.

Parsons, George R. The Opportunity Costs of Residential Displacement Due to Coastal Land Use Restrictions: A Conceptual Framework. *Marine Resource Econ.*, 1987, *4*(2), pp. 111–22. **[G: U.S.]**

Pasha, Hafiz A. Housing for Temporary Residents: A Study of Pilgrims to Makkah. *Urban Stud.*, August 1987, *24*(4), pp. 312–23. **[G: Saudi Arabia]**

Payne, B. A.; Olshansky, S. Jay and Segel, T. E. The Effects on Property Values of Proximity to a Site Contaminated with Radioactive Waste. *Natural Res. J.*, Summer 1987, *27*(3), pp. 579–90. **[G: U.S.]**

Peroff, Kathleen. Who Are the Homeless and How Many Are There? *Bingham, R. D.; Green, R. E. and White, S. B., eds.*, 1987, pp. 33–45. **[G: U.S.]**

Phipps, A. G. Households' Utilities and Hedonic Prices for Inner-City Homes. *Environ. Planning A*, January 1987, *19*(1), pp. 59–80. **[G: Canada]**

Plaut, Steven E. The Timing of Housing Tenure Transition. *J. Urban Econ.*, May 1987, *21*(3), pp. 312–22.

Popenoe, David. Suburbanization, Privatization, and Juvenile Delinquency: Some Possible Relationships. *van Vliet—, W., et al., eds.*, 1987, pp. 119–37.

Quigley, John M. Housing Market Information and the Benefits of Housing Programs. *Turner, B.; Kemeny, J. and Lundqvist, L. J., eds.*, 1987, pp. 53–70.

Quigley, John M. Interest Rate Variations, Mortgage Prepayments and Household Mobility. *Rev. Econ. Statist.*, November 1987, *69*(4), pp. 636–43. **[G: U.S.]**

Rätzer, Ernst. Mieterschutz und Wohnungsmarkt. Die Mietpreisbeschränkung im schweizerischen Missbrauchsbeschluss. (Tenant Protection and the Rental Housing Market. The Regulation of the Prices of Rental Housing in the Swiss Legislation against Abuses. With English summary.) *Schweiz. Z. Volkswirtsch. Statist.*, March 1987, *123*(1), pp. 23–45. **[G: Switzerland]**

Ritzdorf, Marsha and Sharpe, Sumner M. The Homeless in Contemporary Society: Portland, Oregon: A Comprehensive Approach. *Bingham, R. D.; Green, R. E. and White, S. B., eds.*, 1987, pp. 184–98. **[G: U.S.]**

Robertson, Marjorie J. Homeless Veterans: An Emerging Problem? *Bingham, R. D.; Green, R. E. and White, S. B., eds.*, 1987, pp. 64–81. **[G: U.S.]**

Rowntree, John T. and Rolph, Earl R. Efficient Community Management: A Profit-Maximizing Approach. *Quigley, J. M., ed.*, 1987, pp. 87–109. **[G: U.S.]**

Rudel, Thomas K. Housing Price Inflation, Family Growth, and the Move from Rented to

Owner Occupied Housing. *Urban Stud.*, August 1987, *24*(4), pp. 258–67. **[G: U.S.]**

Sa-Aadu, Jarjisu. Participation Behavior and Distributional Consequences under a Multiple Constrained Housing Program. *J. Urban Econ.*, November 1987, *22*(3), pp. 243–62. **[G: U.S.]**

Sanyal, Biswapriya. Problems of Cost-Recovery in Development Projects: Experience of the Lusaka Squatter Upgrading and Site/Service Project. *Urban Stud.*, August 1987, *24*(4), pp. 285–95. **[G: Zambia]**

Schaeffer, P. V. and Hopkins, L. D. Behavior of Land Developers: Planning and the Economics of Information. *Environ. Planning A*, September 1987, *19*(9), pp. 1221–32.

Schwartz, Nathan H. Housing Policy: Converging Trends, Divergent Futures. *Waltman, J. L. and Studlar, D. T., eds.*, 1987, pp. 233–58. **[G: U.K.; U.S.]**

Schwartz, Nathan H. The Relation of Politics to the Instruments of Housing Policy. *Turner, B.; Kemeny, J. and Lundqvist, L. J., eds.*, 1987, pp. 156–85. **[G: U.S.; U.K.]**

Simon, Joan C. and Wekerle, Gerda R. Planning with Scarce Resources: The Miniaturization of an Urban Neighborhood. *van Vliet—, W., et al., eds.*, 1987, pp. 173–89. **[G: Canada]**

Simpson, Wayne. Workplace Location, Residential Location, and Urban Commuting. *Urban Stud.*, April 1987, *24*(2), pp. 119–28. **[G: Canada]**

Sirmans, G. Stacy; Sirmans, C. F. and Smith, Stanley D. Creative Financing, House Prices, and Property Tax Inequities. *Urban Stud.*, October 1987, *24*(5), pp. 409–15. **[G: U.S.]**

Sklarz, Michael A.; Miller, Norman G. and Gersch, Will. Forecasting Using Long-Order Autoregressive Processes: An Example Using Housing Starts. *Amer. Real Estate Urban Econ. Assoc. J.*, Winter 1987, *15*(4), pp. 374–88. **[G: U.S.]**

Smith, Lawrence B. An Economic Assessment of Rent Controls: The Ontario Experience. *Arnott, R. J. and Mintz, J. M., eds.*, 1987, pp. 57–72. **[G: Canada]**

Smith, Rebecca L. and Thomson, C. Lee. Restricted Housing Markets for Female-Headed Households in U.S. Metropolitan Areas. *van Vliet—, W., et al., eds.*, 1987, pp. 279–90. **[G: U.S.]**

Smith, Ron P. and Merrett, S. Empty Dwellings: The Use of Rating Records in Identifying and Monitoring Vacant Private Housing in Britain. *Environ. Planning A*, June 1987, *19*(6), pp. 783–91. **[G: U.K.]**

Soltow, Lee C. The Distribution of Income in the United States in 1798: Estimates Based on the Federal Housing Inventory. *Rev. Econ. Statist.*, February 1987, *69*(1), pp. 181–85. **[G: U.S.]**

Stefl, Mary E. The New Homeless: A National Perspective. *Bingham, R. D.; Green, R. E. and White, S. B., eds.*, 1987, pp. 46–63. **[G: U.S.]**

Stover, Mark Edward. The Role of Infrastructure

in the Supply of Housing. *J. Reg. Sci.*, May 1987, *27*(2), pp. 254–67.　　　　**[G: U.S.]**

Struyk, Raymond J. The Economic Behavior of the Elderly in Housing Markets. *Turner, B.; Kemeny, J. and Lundqvist, L. J.*, eds., 1987, pp. 71–101.　　　　**[G: U.S.]**

Struyk, Raymond J. and Turner, Margery Austin. Simulating Housing Quality Changes in Developing Countries: A Tool for Policy Analysis. *World Devel.*, Oct./Nov. 1987, *15*(10/11), pp. 1375–87.　　　　**[G: Sri Lanka]**

Studer, Raymond G. Prospects for Realizing Congruent Housing Environments. *van Vliet—, W., et al.*, eds., 1987, pp. 29–41.

Sullivan, Arthur M. Efficient Taxation in an Isolated City: Variable-Rate Taxes on Property and Income. *Quigley, J. M.*, ed., 1987, pp. 111–25.　　　　**[G: U.S.]**

Sullivan, Patricia A. and Damrosch, Shirley P. Homeless Women and Children. *Bingham, R. D.; Green, R. E. and White, S. B.*, eds., 1987, pp. 82–98.　　　　**[G: U.S.]**

Tanzer, Ellen P. Effects of the Property Tax on Operating and Investment Decisions of Rental Property Owners: An Empirical Test. *Reg. Sci. Urban Econ.*, November 1987, *17*(4), pp. 535–47.　　　　**[G: U.S.]**

Tanzer, Ellen P. Housing Quality and the Structure Tax: Evidence from Microdata. *Amer. Real Estate Urban Econ. Assoc. J.*, Summer 1987, *15*(2), pp. 32–45.　　　　**[G: U.S.]**

Thalmann, Philippe. Explication empirique des loyers lausannois. (A Hedonic Approach to Explaining Rents in the Community of Lausanne. With English summary.) *Schweiz. Z. Volkswirtsch. Statist.*, March 1987, *123*(1), pp. 47–70.　　　　**[G: Switzerland]**

Thomas, John Clayton. Restructuring the Periphery: The Quasi-governmental Neighborhood in Cincinnati *Picard, L. A. and Zariski, R.*, eds., 1987, pp. 140–51.　　　　**[G: U.S.]**

Torgersen, Ulf. Housing: The Wobbly Pillar under the Welfare State. *Turner, B.; Kemeny, J. and Lundqvist, L. J.*, eds., 1987, pp. 116–26.　　**[G: U.K.; Norway; Sweden]**

Tosics, Iván. Dilemmas of Reducing Direct State Control: Recent Tendencies in Hungarian Housing Policy. *Turner, B.; Kemeny, J. and Lundqvist, L. J.*, eds., 1987, pp. 271–91.　　　　**[G: Hungary]**

Turner, Bengt. Economic and Political Aspects of Negotiated Rents in the Swedish Housing Market. *Arnott, R. J. and Mintz, J. M.*, eds., 1987, pp. 101–20.　　　　**[G: Sweden]**

Vaghari, Jila. Has Removal of the Mortgage Ceiling Rates Helped the Home-Buyers? *Indian Econ. J.*, Oct.-Dec. 1987, *35*(2), pp. 126–31.　　　　**[G: U.S.]**

van Vliet—, Willem. Housing and Neighborhoods: Introduction: Some Comments on Recent and Current Research. *van Vliet—, W., et al.*, eds., 1987, pp. 1–15.　**[G: U.K.; U.S.; W. Germany; France]**

Vorst, A. C. F. Optimal Housing Maintenance under Uncertainty. *J. Urban Econ.*, March 1987, *21*(2), pp. 209–27.

Wachter, Susan M. Residential Real Estate Brokerage: Rate Uniformity and Moral Hazard. *Jaffe, A. J.*, ed., 1987, pp. 189–210.　　　　**[G: U.S.]**

Walden, Michael L. Effects of Housing Codes on Local Housing Markets. *Amer. Real Estate Urban Econ. Assoc. J.*, Summer 1987, *15*(2), pp. 13–31.　　　　**[G: U.S.]**

Wallace, Nancy E. The Consistency Doctrine and the Market Effects of Zoning Undeveloped Land. *Jaffe, A. J.*, ed., 1987, pp. 27–52.　　　　**[G: U.S.]**

Weber, Shlomo and Wiesmeth, Hans. Contract Equilibria in a Regulated Rental Housing Market. *J. Urban Econ.*, January 1987, *21*(1), pp. 59–68.

van Weesep, Jan. Coping with Condominiums in the Netherlands. *van Vliet—, W., et al.*, eds., 1987, pp. 239–56.　　**[G: Netherlands]**

Weinrobe, Maurice. An Analysis of Home Equity Conversion in the RAM Program. *Amer. Real Estate Urban Econ. Assoc. J.*, Summer 1987, *15*(2), pp. 65–78.　　　　**[G: U.S.]**

Werczberger, Elia. Rent Control in Israel. *Arnott, R. J. and Mintz, J. M.*, eds., 1987, pp. 123–39.　　　　**[G: Israel]**

Williams, Ross A. Dwelling Commencements in Australia: Lags and Autocorrelation. *[Cochrane, D.]*, 1987, pp. 289–301. **[G: Australia]**

Woodson, Robert L. Empowering Poor Neighborhoods. *Perkins, J.*, ed., 1987, pp. 49–61.　　　　**[G: U.S.]**

Woodward, Alison E. Public Housing Communes: A Swedish Response to Postmaterial Demands. *van Vliet—, W., et al.*, eds., 1987, pp. 215–38.　　　　**[G: Sweden]**

Wright, James D. The National Health Care for the Homeless Program. *Bingham, R. D.; Green, R. E. and White, S. B.*, eds., 1987, pp. 150–69.　　　　**[G: U.S.]**

Wuertz, Karen and van der Pennen, Ton. Participation by Ethnic Minorities in Urban Renewal in the Netherlands. *van Vliet—, W., et al.*, eds., 1987, pp. 105–16.　　**[G: Netherlands]**

Zuehlke, Thomas W. Duration Dependence in the Housing Market. *Rev. Econ. Statist.*, November 1987, *69*(4), pp. 701–04.　　**[G: U.S.]**

933 Urban Transportation Economics

9330 Urban Transportation Economics

Auerbach, Alan J. Right of Way and Congestion Toll: Comments. *Razin, A. and Sadka, E.*, eds., 1987, pp. 370–71.

Berglas, Eitan; Fresko, David and Pines, David. Right of Way and Congestion Toll. *Razin, A. and Sadka, E.*, eds., 1987, pp. 343–69.

Coulson, N. Edward and Engle, Robert F. Transportation Costs and the Rent Gradient. *J. Urban Econ.*, May 1987, *21*(3), pp. 287–97.　　　　**[G: U.S.]**

Cummings, Thomas G. and Mohrman, Susan A. Self-designing Organizations: Towards Implementing Quality-of-Work-Life Innovations. *Woodman, R. W. and Pasmore, W. A.*, eds., 1987, pp. 275–310.

Dodgson, John S. and Topham, N. Benefit–Cost Rules for Urban Transit Subsidies. An Integration of Allocation, Distributional and Public Finance Issues. *J. Transp. Econ. Policy*, January 1987, *21*(1), pp. 57–71.

Evans, Andrew. A Theoretical Comparison of Competition with Other Economic Regimes for Bus Services. *J. Transp. Econ. Policy*, January 1987, *21*(1), pp. 7–36.

Frankena, Mark W. Capital-Biased Subsidies, Bureaucratic Monitoring, and Bus Scrapping. *J. Urban Econ.*, March 1987, *21*(2), pp. 180–93. **[G: Canada]**

Grimaud, André. Substitution espace-travail dans une ville monocentrique. (With English summary.) *Revue Écon. Polit.*, Mar.-Apr. 1987, *97*(2), pp. 183–212.

Hagishima, S.; Mitsuyoshi, K. and Kurose, S. Estimation of Pedestrian Shopping Trips in a Neighborhood by Using a Spatial Interaction Model. *Environ. Planning A*, September 1987, *19*(9), pp. 1139–52. **[G: Japan]**

Hanson, S. and Schwab, M. Accessibility and Intraurban Travel. *Environ. Planning A*, June 1987, *19*(6), pp. 735–48. **[G: Sweden]**

Kim, Moshe and Spiegel, Menahem. The Effects of Lump-Sum Subsidies on the Structure of Production and Productivity in Regulated Industries. *J. Public Econ.*, October 1987, *34*(1), pp. 105–19. **[G: Israel]**

Klaassen, Leo H. and Van der Meer, J. Urban Change and Public Transport. *Int. J. Transport Econ.*, June 1987, *14*(2), pp. 123–32. **[G: W. Europe]**

Kondo, Katsunao and Kitamura, Ryuichi. Time-Space Constraints and the Formation of Trip Chains. *Reg. Sci. Urban Econ.*, February 1987, *17*(1), pp. 49–65. **[G: Japan]**

Madan, Dilip B. and Groenhout, R. Modelling Travel Mode Choices for the Sydney Work Trip. *J. Transp. Econ. Policy*, May 1987, *21*(2), pp. 135–49. **[G: Australia]**

Niedercorn, John H. and Ammari, Nabil S. New Evidence on the Specification and Performance of Neoclassical Gravity Models in the Study of Urban Transportation. *Ann. Reg. Sci.*, March 1987, *21*(1), pp. 56–64. **[G: U.S.]**

de Rus Mendoza, Ginés. Discriminación de precios y subvenciones cruzadas en transporte público. (With English summary.) *Invest. Econ.*, May 1987, *11*(2), pp. 201–18. **[G: Spain]**

Serta, Ronaldo. Forecasting the Demand of a Subway Which Is to Provide Free Rides. *Logist. Transp. Rev.*, June 1987, *23*(2), pp. 223–35. **[G: Brazil]**

Teal, Roger F. and Berglund, Mary. The Impact of Taxicab Deregulation in the USA. *J. Transp. Econ. Policy*, January 1987, *21*(1), pp. 37–56. **[G: U.S.]**

Thiry, Bernard and Lawarree, J. Productivité, coût et caractéristiques technoligiques des sociétés belges de transports urbains. (Productivity, Cost and Technological Characteristics of Belgian Urban Transportation Firms. With English summary.) *Ann. Pub. Co-op. Econ.*, Oct.-Dec. 1987, *58*(4), pp. 369–96. **[G: Belgium]**

Volmuller, J. Is Road Pricing a Real Contribution to Urban Transport Policy? *Int. J. Transport Econ.*, February 1987, *14*(1), pp. 7–18.

White, P. R. and Turner, R. P. Development of Intensive Urban Minibus Services in Britain. *Logist. Transp. Rev.*, December 1987, *23*(4), pp. 385–400. **[G: U.K.]**

940 REGIONAL ECONOMICS

941 Regional Economics

9410 General

Abelson, Peter W. The Use of Regional Allocation Formulae for the Allocation of Health Funds to Regions: With Special Reference to New South Wales. *Butler, J. R. G. and Doessel, D. P., eds.*, 1987, pp. 227–50. **[G: Australia]**

Bolton, Roger. Regional Aspects of the Chinese Economic Reforms: Introduction to the Special Issue. *Int. Reg. Sci. Rev.*, 1987, *11*(1), pp. 1–3. **[G: China]**

Clark, William A. V. Urban Restructuring from a Demographic Perspective. *Econ. Geogr.*, April 1987, *63*(2), pp. 103–25. **[G: U.S.]**

Duckett, S. J. The Use of Regional Allocation Formulae for the Allocation of Health Funds to Regions: With Special Reference to New South Wales: Discussion. *Butler, J. R. G. and Doessel, D. P., eds.*, 1987, pp. 251–53. **[G: Australia]**

Gordon, Ian R. Unemployment, the Regions and Labour Markets: Reactions to Recession: Introduction: Space, Segmentation, and Labour-Market Processes. *Gordon, I., ed.*, 1987, pp. 1–11.

Hansen, Niles M. The Evolution of the French Regional Economy and French Regional Theory. *Rev. Reg. Stud.*, Fall 1987, *17*(3), pp. 3–13. **[G: France]**

Hjerppe, Reino T.; Niitamo, Olavi E. and Suur-Kujala, Markku. Regional Policy-Making and Regional Data Bases. *Rev. Income Wealth*, December 1987, *33*(4), pp. 387–400.

Krieger, M. H. Where Do Centers Come From? *Environ. Planning A*, September 1987, *19*(9), pp. 1251–60.

Mencinger, Jože. The Crisis and the Reform of the Yugoslav Economic System in the Eighties. *Gey, P.; Kosta, J. and Quaisser, W., eds.*, 1987, pp. 99–119. **[G: Yugoslavia]**

Salvary, Stanley C. W. An Empirical Test of the Dominant Industry Hypothesis: Some Preliminary Evidence. *Reg. Sci. Persp.*, 1987, *17*(1), pp. 77–102. **[G: U.S.]**

Thiel, Eberhard. Sectoral and Regional Elements of Industrial Policy. *Gemper, B. B., ed.*, 1987, pp. 47–55. **[G: W. Germany]**

Weirick, William N. Amenities, Factor Mobility, and Market Prices. *Land Econ.*, August 1987, *63*(3), pp. 272–83.

9411 Theory of Regional Economics

Anderson, Simon. Spatial Competition and Price Leadership. *Int. J. Ind. Organ.*, December 1987, *5*(4), pp. 369–98.

Apostolakis, Bobby E. Output and Input Subsidies as a Means of Industrial Decentralization: The Greek Case. *Devel. Econ.*, June 1987, 25(2), pp. 171–87. **[G: Greece]**

Baum, Donald N. The Economic Effects of State and Local Business Incentives. *Land Econ.*, November 1987, 63(4), pp. 348–60.

Beckmann, Martin J. Continuous Models of Spatial Dynamics. *Batten, D.; Casti, J. and Johansson, B., eds.*, 1987, pp. 337–48.

Benson, Bruce L. and Feinberg, Robert M. Chamberlin's Solution in a Spatial Model. *Rev. Reg. Stud.*, Spring 1987, 17(2), pp. 47–52.

Benson, Bruce L. and Hartigan, James C. Tariffs and Location Specific Income Redistribution. *Reg. Sci. Urban Econ.*, May 1987, 17(2), pp. 223–43.

Blommestein, Hans and Nijkamp, Peter. Adoption and Diffusion of Innovations and the Evolution of Spatial Systems. *Batten, D.; Casti, J. and Johansson, B., eds.*, 1987, pp. 368–80.

Bonanno, Giacomo. Location Choice, Product Proliferation and Entry Deterrence. *Rev. Econ. Stud.*, January 1987, 54(1), pp. 37–45.

Clark, Gordon L. Job Search Theory and Indeterminate Information. *Fischer, M. M. and Nijkamp, P., eds.*, 1987, pp. 169–88.

Coffey, W. J. and Polèse, M. Trade and Location of Producer Services: A Canadian Perspective. *Environ. Planning A*, May 1987, 19(5), pp. 597–611. **[G: Canada]**

Crouchley, R. An Examination of the Equivalence of Three Alternative Mechanisms for Establishing the Equilibrium Solutions of the Production-Constrained Spatial Interaction Model. *Environ. Planning A*, July 1987, 19(7), pp. 621–74.

Czamanski, Daniel Z. The Effect of Location Subsidies on Corporate Decisions. *Reg. Sci. Urban Econ.*, August 1987, 17(3), pp. 411–21.

Dafermos, Stella and Nagurney, Anna. Oligopolistic and Competitive Behavior of Spatially Separated Markets. *Reg. Sci. Urban Econ.*, May 1987, 17(2), pp. 245–54.

Dow, Sheila C. The Treatment of Money in Regional Economics. *J. Reg. Sci.*, February 1987, 27(1), pp. 13–24.

Erickson, Rodney A. and Wollover, David R. Local Tax Burdens and the Supply of Business Sites in Suburban Municipalities. *J. Reg. Sci.*, February 1987, 27(1), pp. 25–37. **[G: U.S.]**

Fischer, Manfred M. and Nijkamp, Peter. From Static Towards Dynamic Discrete Choice Modelling: A State of the Art Review. *Reg. Sci. Urban Econ.*, February 1987, 17(1), pp. 3–27.

Fischer, Manfred M. and Nijkamp, Peter. Regional Labour Market Analysis: Retrospect and Prospect. *Fischer, M. M. and Nijkamp, P., eds.*, 1987, pp. 485–88.

Fischer, Manfred M. and Nijkamp, Peter. Spatial Labour Market Analysis: Relevance and Scope. *Fischer, M. M. and Nijkamp, P., eds.*, 1987, pp. 1–33.

Friesz, Terry L. and Luque, Javier. Optimal Regional Growth Models: Multiple Objectives,

Singular Controls, and Sufficiency Conditions. *J. Reg. Sci.*, May 1987, 27(2), pp. 201–24.

Gabszewicz, Jean Jaskold and Garella, Paolo G. Price Search and Spatial Competition. *Europ. Econ. Rev.*, June 1987, 31(4), pp. 827–42.

Gaudard, Gaston. Regional Economic Development and the Future of Environment. *Pillet, G. and Murota, T., eds.*, 1987, pp. 155–67.

Gerber, Robert I. and Hewitt, Daniel P. Decentralized Tax Competition for Business Capital and National Economic Efficiency. *J. Reg. Sci.*, August 1987, 27(3), pp. 451–60.

Hamilton, F. E. Ian. Industrial Organisation and Regional Labour Markets. *Fischer, M. M. and Nijkamp, P., eds.*, 1987, pp. 289–312.

Hanink, Dean M. and Cromley, R. G. A Risk-Return Model for Multiregion and Multiproduct Diversification of the Firm. *Environ. Planning A*, January 1987, 19(1), pp. 81–92.

Hanjoul, Pierre and Thill, Jean-Claude. Elements of Planar Analysis in Spatial Competition. *Reg. Sci. Urban Econ.*, August 1987, 17(3), pp. 423–39.

Henderson, J. Vernon. Industrialization and Urbanization: International Experience. *Johnson, D. G. and Lee, R. D., eds.*, 1987, pp. 189–224. **[G: Global]**

Holden, D. R.; Swales, J. K. and Nairn, A. G. M. The Repeated Application of Shift-Share: A Structural Explanation of Regional Growth? *Environ. Planning A*, September 1987, 19(9), pp. 1233–50.

Howe, Charles W. On the Theory of Optimal Regional Development Based on an Exhaustible Resource. *Growth Change*, Spring 1987, 18(2), pp. 53–68.

Hwang, Hong and Mai, Chao-Cheng. Business Taxation and Industrial Location. *Rivista Int. Sci. Econ. Com.*, March 1987, 34(3), pp. 241–48.

Hwang, Hong and Mai, Chao-Cheng. Industrial Location and Rising Energy Prices: A Case of Bilateral Monopoly. *Reg. Sci. Urban Econ.*, May 1987, 17(2), pp. 255–64.

Johansson, Börje and Karlsson, Charlie. Processes of Industrial Change: Scale, Location and Type of Job. *Fischer, M. M. and Nijkamp, P., eds.*, 1987, pp. 139–65.

Jones, Donald W. and Krummel, John R. The Location Theory of the Plantation. *J. Reg. Sci.*, May 1987, 27(2), pp. 157–82.

Jovanovic, Boyan and Rob, Rafael. Demand-Driven Innovation and Spatial Competition over Time. *Rev. Econ. Stud.*, January 1987, 54(1), pp. 63–72.

Lambooy, Jan G. and Renooy, P. H. Informal Economy and the Labour Market: Relations with the Economic Order. *Gordon, I., ed.*, 1987, pp. 172–91. **[G: Netherlands]**

Lentnek, Barry; Harwitz, Mitchell and Narula, Subhash C. A Contextual Theory of Demand: Beyond Spatial Analysis in Economic Geography. *Econ. Geogr.*, October 1987, 63(4), pp. 334–48.

Mai, Chao-Cheng. Demand Function and Location Theory of the Firm under Price Uncertainty: A Reply. *Urban Stud.*, April 1987, *24*(2), pp. 162.

Marchand, Maurice and Pestieau, Pierre. Public Production and Employment Policies in a Two-Region Economy with Unemployment. *Reg. Sci. Urban Econ.*, August 1987, *17*(3), pp. 345–55.

Marchand, Maurice and Pestieau, Pierre. Should Employment Policy Making Be Entrusted to Regions? *Reg. Sci. Urban Econ.*, August 1987, *17*(3), pp. 357–65.

Martinich, Joseph S. and Hurter, Arthur P., Jr. A Note on Income Taxes and Degree One Production Homogeneity. *J. Reg. Sci.*, August 1987, *27*(3), pp. 477–82.

Merrifield, John D. A Neoclassical Anatomy of the Economic Base Multiplier. *J. Reg. Sci.*, May 1987, *27*(2), pp. 283–94.

Nagurney, Anna. Competitive Equilibrium Problems, Variational Inequalities and Regional Science. *J. Reg. Sci.*, November 1987, *27*(4), pp. 503–17.

Nagurney, Anna. Computational Comparisons of Spatial Price Equilibrium Methods. *J. Reg. Sci.*, February 1987, *27*(1), pp. 55–76.

Narula, Subhash C.; Lentnek, Barry and Harwitz, Mitchell. A Contextual Analysis of the Journey-to-Shop with Price Uncertainty. *J. Reg. Sci.*, August 1987, *27*(3), pp. 403–18.

Neven, Damien J. Endogenous Sequential Entry in a Spatial Model. *Int. J. Ind. Organ.*, December 1987, *5*(4), pp. 419–34.

Nijkamp, Peter and Poot, Jacques. Dynamics of Generalised Spatial Interaction Models. *Reg. Sci. Urban Econ.*, August 1987, *17*(3), pp. 367–90.

Ohlsson, Henry. Cost–Benefit Rules in a Regionalized Disequilibrium Model. *Scand. J. Econ.*, 1987, *89*(2), pp. 165–82.

Okabe, Atsuyuki and Suzuki, A. Stability of Spatial Competition for a Large Number of Firms on a Bounded Two-Dimensional Space. *Environ. Planning A*, August 1987, *19*(8), pp. 1067–82.

Osborne, Martin J. and Pitchik, Carolyn. Equilibrium in Hotelling's Model of Spatial Competition. *Econometrica*, July 1987, *55*(4), pp. 911–22.

de Palma, André; Ginsburgh, Victor and Thisse, Jacques-François. On Existence of Location Equilibria in the 3-Firm Hotelling Problem. *J. Ind. Econ.*, December 1987, *36*(2), pp. 245–52.

de Palma, André; Pontes, Jose Pedro and Thisse, Jacques-François. Spatial Competition under Uniform Delivered Pricing. *Reg. Sci. Urban Econ.*, August 1987, *17*(3), pp. 441–49.

Parr, John B. The Development of Spatial Structure and Regional Economic Growth. *Land Econ.*, May 1987, *63*(2), pp. 113–27. [G: U.S.]

Rietveld, Piet and Nijkamp, Peter. Technological Development and Regional Labour Markets. *Fischer, M. M. and Nijkamp, P., eds.*, 1987, pp. 117–38.

Rouwendal, Jan and Nijkamp, Peter. Regional Economic Research on Labour Markets. *Fischer, M. M. and Nijkamp, P., eds.*, 1987, pp. 95–115.

Ruane, Frances P. Spatial Bias and the Location of Footloose Industry: A Simple Regional Model. *Can. J. Econ.*, August 1987, *20*(3), pp. 506–18.

Sakashita, Noboru. Optimum Location of Public Facilities under the Influence of the Land Market. *J. Reg. Sci.*, February 1987, *27*(1), pp. 1–12.

Schöler, Klaus. Spatial Price Policy and the Demand for Transportation: A Note. *J. Reg. Sci.*, February 1987, *27*(1), pp. 135–36.

Shieh, Yeung-Nan. Increasing Returns to Scale and Location Theory of the Firm under Price Uncertainty [Demand Function and Location Theory of the Firm under Price Uncertainty]. *Urban Stud.*, April 1987, *24*(2), pp. 163–66.

Smith, Tony E. A Threshold Theory of Discretionary Interaction Behavior. *Reg. Sci. Urban Econ.*, November 1987, *17*(4), pp. 495–517.

Smith, Tony E. Poisson Gravity Models of Spatial Flows. *J. Reg. Sci.*, August 1987, *27*(3), pp. 315–40.

Suarez-Villa, Luis. Evolução metropolitana, mudança econômica setorial e distribuição de tamanhos de cidades. (With English summary.) *Pesquisa Planejamento Econ.*, April 1987, *17*(1), pp. 121–59.

Thisse, Jacques-François. Location Theory, Regional Science, and Economics. *J. Reg. Sci.*, November 1987, *27*(4), pp. 519–28.

Thompson, Wilbur R. and Thompson, Philip R. National Industries and Local Occupational Strengths: The Cross-Hairs of Targeting. *Urban Stud.*, December 1987, *24*(6), pp. 547–60. [G: U.S.]

Tobin, Roger L. Sensitivity Analysis for General Spatial Price Equilibria. *J. Reg. Sci.*, February 1987, *27*(1), pp. 77–102.

Weber, James. Elasticities of Constrained Gravity Models. *J. Reg. Sci.*, November 1987, *27*(4), pp. 621–40.

Weidlich, Wolfgang and Haag, Günter. A Dynamic Phase Transition Model for Spatial Agglomeration Processes. *J. Reg. Sci.*, November 1987, *27*(4), pp. 529–69.

Wilson, John Douglas. Trade in a Tiebout Economy. *Amer. Econ. Rev.*, June 1987, *77*(3), pp. 431–41.

Wilson, John Douglas. Trade, Capital Mobility, and Tax Competition. *J. Polit. Econ.*, August 1987, *95*(4), pp. 835–56.

9412 Regional Economic Studies

Abella, Manolo I. Female Labour Force Participation Rates in Rural Pakistan: Some Fundamental Explanations and Policy Implications: Comments. *Pakistan Devel. Rev.*, Winter 1987, *26*(4), pp. 697. [G: Pakistan]

Ahmad, Ehtisham and Ludlow, Stephen E. Aggregate and Regional Demand Response Patterns in Pakistan. *Pakistan Devel. Rev.*, Winter 1987, *26*(4), pp. 645–55. [G: Pakistan]

Ahsan, Syed M. and Sahni, Balbir S. La relation entre les dépenses et les recettes publiques dans un économie régionale: le Québec, 1955–82. (Relationship between Public Expenditure and Income in a Regional Economy: Quebec 1955–82. With English summary.) *L'Actual. Econ.*, December 1987, *63*(4), pp. 295–310. [G: Canada]

Alperovich, Gershon; Freeman, Daniel and Weksler, Itzhak. An Evaluation System for Regional–Regional and Regional–National Growth Impact. *Appl. Econ.*, October 1987, *19*(10), pp. 1367–82. [G: Israel]

Amos, Orley M., Jr. The Influence of Urban Areas on Regional Development. *Rev. Reg. Stud.*, Fall 1987, *17*(3), pp. 37–46. [G: U.S.]

Anders, Gary C. and Anders, Kathleen. Incompatible Goals in Unconventional Organizations: The Politics of Alaska Native Corporations. *Lane, T., ed.*, 1987, pp. 133–57. [G: U.S.]

Andrade, Thompson A. and dos Santos, Renato A. Z. Villela. Eficácia da institucionalização de regiões metropolitanas no Brasil: análise da evolução dos serviços de saneamento urbano. (With English summary.) *Pesquisa Planejamento Econ.*, April 1987, *17*(1), pp. 93–120. [G: Brazil]

Andrews, Donald R. An Export-Base Analysis of Louisiana's Petroleum Driven Economy. *Ann. Reg. Sci.*, March 1987, *21*(1), pp. 65–79. [G: U.S.]

Andrikopoulos, Andreas A.; Brox, James A. and Carvalho, Emanuel. A Further Test of the Competitive Effect in Shift-Share Analysis. *Rev. Reg. Stud.*, Fall 1987, *17*(3), pp. 23–30. [G: Canada]

Antonelli, Cristiano. The Determinants of the Distribution of Innovative Activity in a Metropolitan Area: The Case of Turin. *Reg. Stud.*, April 1987, *21*(2), pp. 85–93. [G: Italy]

Aronson, Nancy R.; Pulver, Glen C. and Buse, Rueben C. The Influence of Community Characteristics on the Level of Retail Trade. *Reg. Sci. Persp.*, 1987, *17*(1), pp. 3–19. [G: U.S.]

Attaran, Mohsen and Zwick, Martin. The Effect of Industrial Diversification on Employment and Income: A Case Study. *Quart. Rev. Econ. Bus.*, Winter 1987, *27*(4), pp. 38–54. [G: U.S.]

Bahl, Roy; Weist, Dana and Schulman, Wanda. The Fiscal Implications of Industrial Restructuring: The Case of Northeastern Ohio. *McKee, D. L. and Bennett, R. E., eds.*, 1987, pp. 155–202. [G: U.S.]

Baillard-Haurie, D., et al. What Does $(US)15 versus $(US)23 Oil Mean for Long-range Energy Choices in the Province of Quebec? *Can. Public Policy*, March 1987, *13*(1), pp. 56–61. [G: Canada]

Bairam, Erkin I. Orthodox Production Functions with Variable Returns to Scale: Some Analysis and Testing Using Soviet and Polish Regional Data. *Keio Econ. Stud.*, 1987, *24*(1), pp. 63–83. [G: U.S.S.R.; Poland]

Barrett, Thomas H. The Need for International

Competitiveness in Ohio. *McKee, D. L. and Bennett, R. E., eds.*, 1987, pp. 219–25. [G: U.S.]

Bates, John J. and Bracken, I. Migration Age Profiles for Local Authority Areas in England, 1971–1981. *Environ. Planning A*, April 1987, *19*(4), pp. 521–35. [G: U.K.]

Beaumont, J. R. Quantitative Methods in the Real World: A Consultant's View of Practice. *Environ. Planning A*, November 1987, *19*(11), pp. 1441–48. [G: U.K.]

Beck, Roger J. and Medsker, Larry R. Entity–Relationship Approach to Regional Economic Data Analysis. *Rev. Reg. Stud.*, Winter 1987, *17*(1), pp. 13–20. [G: U.S.]

Beeson, Patricia. Total Factor Productivity Growth and Agglomeration Economies in Manufacturing, 1959–73. *J. Reg. Sci.*, May 1987, *27*(2), pp. 183–99. [G: U.S.]

Begg, Hugh and McDowall, Stuart. The Effect of Regional Investment Incentives on Company Decisions. *Reg. Stud.*, October 1987, *21*(5), pp. 459–70. [G: U.K.]

Bell, Trevor. International Competition and Industrial Decentralization in South Africa. *World Devel.*, Oct./Nov. 1987, *15*(10/11), pp. 1291–1307. [G: S. Africa]

Belongia, Michael T. and Gilbert, R. Alton. The Farm Economies of the Plains. *Rev. Reg. Stud.*, Fall 1987, *17*(3), pp. 47–57. [G: U.S.]

Bentolila, David J. The Non-agricultural Village. *Bar-El, R., ed.*, 1987, pp. 105–42. [G: Israel]

Bianchi, Giuliano; Casini-Benvenuti, Stefano and Maltinti, Giovanni. Long Waves and Regional Take-Offs in Italy and Great Britain: Preliminary Investigations into Multiregional Disparities of Development. *Vasko, T., ed.*, 1987, pp. 187–97. [G: Italy; U.K.]

Bird, Richard M. Federalism and Regional Disparities: A Review Essay. *Can. Public Policy*, September 1987, *13*(3), pp. 380–83. [G: Canada]

Blackaby, D. H. and Manning, D. N. Regional Earnings Revisited. *Manchester Sch. Econ. Soc. Stud.*, June 1987, *55*(2), pp. 158–83. [G: U.K.]

Bluestone, Barry. Postindustrial Prospects for the Industrial Midwest: Can Ohio Compete? *McKee, D. L. and Bennett, R. E., eds.*, 1987, pp. 115–21. [G: U.S.]

Booth, Douglas E. Regional Long Waves and Urban Policy. *Urban Stud.*, December 1987, *24*(6), pp. 447–59. [G: U.S.]

Bronars, Stephen G. and Jansen, Dennis W. The Geographic Distribution of Unemployment Rates in the U.S.: A Spatial–Time Series Analysis. *J. Econometrics*, November 1987, *36*(3), pp. 251–79. [G: U.S.]

Brown, Stephen P. A. New Directions for Economic Growth: Redesigning Fiscal Policies in Louisiana, New Mexico, and Texas. *Fed. Res. Bank Dallas Econ. Rev.*, July 1987, pp. 13–20. [G: U.S.]

Brugger, Ernst A. and Stuckey, Barbara. Regional Economic Structure and Innovative Behaviour in Switzerland. *Reg. Stud.*, June 1987, *21*(3), pp. 241–54. **[G: Switzerland]**

Burns, Leland S. Regional Economic Intergration and National Economic Growth. *Reg. Stud.*, August 1987, *21*(4), pp. 327–42. **[G: U.S.]**

Campbell, Jim and Barnes, I. The Contribution of the European Investment Bank (EIB) to UK Regional Development. *Reg. Stud.*, April 1987, *21*(2), pp. 161–63. **[G: U.K.]**

Cannon, Tom. The Contribution of New Enterprise to Economic Growth and Employment: The Experience of the Scottish Enterprise Foundation. *Gemper, B. B., ed.*, 1987, pp. 131–43. **[G: U.K.]**

Canto, Victor A. and Webb, Robert I. The Effect of State Fiscal Policy on State Relative Economic Performance. *Southern Econ. J.*, July 1987, *54*(1), pp. 186–202. **[G: U.S.]**

Carey, David E. and Mahmassani, Hani S. Air Travel Considerations in Planning for Technology-Based Economic Development: A Case Study of Austin, Texas. *Reg. Sci. Persp.*, 1987, *17*(1), pp. 20–41. **[G: U.S.]**

Carlino, Gerald A. and Mills, Edwin S. The Determinants of County Growth. *J. Reg. Sci.*, February 1987, *27*(1), pp. 39–54. **[G: U.S.]**

Chan, M. W. Luke and Mountain, Dean C. Measuring Contributing Factors to Interregional Agricultural Labor Productivity Differentials: A Joint Profit Formulation. *J. Reg. Sci.*, May 1987, *27*(2), pp. 269–81. **[G: Canada]**

Chan, M. W. Luke and Okasanen, E. H. Regional Energy Input Prices in Canadian Manufacturing: An Index Number Approach. *Energy Econ.*, April 1987, *9*(2), pp. 66–72. **[G: Canada]**

Cobb, Stephen A. Interarea Cost of Living Measurement with Nonmarket Goods: A Demand Systems Approach. *J. Urban Econ.*, September 1987, *22*(2), pp. 174–89. **[G: U.S.]**

Coelen, Stephen P.; Nakosteen, Robert A. and Zimmer, Michael A. An Aggregate Model of Manufacturing Firm Migration. *Rev. Reg. Stud.*, Spring 1987, *17*(2), pp. 57–66. **[G: U.S.]**

Conn, Stephen. Rural Legal Process and Development in the North. *Lane, T., ed.*, 1987, pp. 199–229. **[G: U.S.]**

Connaughton, John E. and Madsen, Ronald A. Measuring Cyclical Sensitivity in State Performance: 1969–1984. *Reg. Sci. Persp.*, 1987, *17*(2), pp. 34–40. **[G: U.S.]**

Cooke, P. Research Policy and Review 19. Britain's New Spatial Paradigm: Technology, Locality and Society in Transition. *Environ. Planning A*, October 1987, *19*(10), pp. 1289–1301. **[G: U.K.]**

Corrado, G. and Sediari, Tommaso. Countryside Planning Experiences in Umbria (Central Italy). *Merlo, M., et al., eds.*, 1987, pp. 583–91. **[G: Italy]**

Coughlin, Cletus C. and Cartwright, Phillip A. An Examination of State Foreign Export Promotion and Manufacturing Exports. *J. Reg. Sci.*, August 1987, *27*(3), pp. 439–49. **[G: U.S.]**

Crampton, Colin. The Potential Development of Northern Canadian Physical and Biological Resources. *Lane, T., ed.*, 1987, pp. 27–44. **[G: Canada]**

Cushing, Brian J. Location-Specific Amenities, Topography, and Population Migration. *Ann. Reg. Sci.*, July 1987, *21*(2), pp. 74–85. **[G: U.S.]**

Dawson, Andrew H. Transport and the Pattern of Settlement in Poland—The Impact of Postwar Policies. *Tismer, J. F.; Ambler, J. and Symons, L., eds.*, 1987, pp. 306–27. **[G: Poland]**

Day, Frederick A. Changing Regional Inequalities in North Carolina, 1928–82. *Growth Change*, Winter 1987, *18*(1), pp. 13–31. **[G: U.S.]**

Day, Graham. The Reconstruction of Wales and Appalachia: Development and Regional Identity. *Day, G. and Rees, G., eds.*, 1987, pp. 73–89. **[G: U.K.; U.S.]**

Day, Graham and Rees, Gareth. Images of Contemporary Wales: Researching Social and Economic Change. *Day, G. and Rees, G., eds.*, 1987, pp. 1–6. **[G: U.K.]**

Dean, K. G. The Disaggregation of Migration Flows: The Case of Brittany, 1975–1982. *Reg. Stud.*, August 1987, *21*(4), pp. 313–25. **[G: U.K.]**

DePass, Rudolph E. State Personal Income, First Quarter 1987. *Surv. Curr. Bus.*, July 1987, *67*(7), pp. 129–34. **[G: U.S.]**

Dickie, Mark and Gerking, Shelby. Interregional Wage Differentials: An Equilibrium Perspective. *J. Reg. Sci.*, November 1987, *27*(4), pp. 571–85. **[G: U.S.]**

Dieperink, Han and Nijkamp, Peter. Multiple Criteria Location Model for Innovative Firms in a Communication Network. *Econ. Geogr.*, January 1987, *63*(1), pp. 66–73. **[G: Netherlands]**

Din, Shams-ud. Demographic Changes and Nationality Problems in Soviet Central Asia, Kazakhstan and Azerbaijan. *Gidadhubli, R. G., ed.*, 1987, pp. 85–100. **[G: U.S.S.R.]**

Drewes, Torben. Regional Wage Spillover in Canada. *Rev. Econ. Statist.*, May 1987, *69*(2), pp. 224–31. **[G: Canada]**

Dunn, Richard. Analysing Spatial Time Series of Local Unemployment: A Graphical Approach Using Principal Components Analysis and Seasonal Adjustment Procedures. *Environ. Planning A*, February 1987, *19*(2), pp. 225–46. **[G: U.K.]**

Dunstan, Roger H. and Long, William T., III. Structure and Technology of Manufacturing in Texas and Louisiana. *Fed. Res. Bank Dallas Econ. Rev.*, January 1987, pp. 15–27. **[G: U.S.]**

Ehrenberg, Ronald G. and Smith, Robert S. Comparable-Worth Wage Adjustments and Female Employment in the State and Local Sector. *J. Lab. Econ.*, January 1987, *5*(1), pp. 43–62. **[G: U.S.]**

Eichengreen, Barry. Agricultural Mortgages in

the Populist Era: Reply. *J. Econ. Hist.*, September 1987, *47*(3), pp. 757–60.   **[G: U.S.]**

Elis-Williams, D. G. The Effect of Spatial Population Distribution on the Cost of Delivering Local Services. *J. Roy. Statist. Soc.*, 1987, *150*(2), pp. 152–66.   **[G: U.S.]**

Emmi, P. C. Structural Determinants of Occupational Mobility in a Regional Labor Market. *Environ. Planning A*, July 1987, *19*(7), pp. 925–48.   **[G: U.S.]**

Enderwick, Peter. The Strategy and Structure of Service-Sector Multinationals: Implications for Potential Host Regions. *Reg. Stud.*, June 1987, *21*(3), pp. 215–23.   **[G: OECD; Korea; Singapore]**

Faini, Riccardo and Schiantarelli, Fabio. Incentives and Investment Decisions: The Effectiveness of Regional Policy. *Oxford Econ. Pap.*, September 1987, *39*(3), pp. 516–33.   **[G: U.K.]**

Faradzhev, F. A. Solving Employment Problems in a Labour-Surplus Region of the USSR: The Case of Azerbaijan. *Int. Lab. Rev.*, 1987, *126*(3), pp. 337–50.   **[G: U.S.S.R.]**

Farber, Stephen C. and Newman, Robert J. Accounting for South/Non-South Real Wage Differentials and for Changes in Those Differentials over Time. *Rev. Econ. Statist.*, May 1987, *69*(2), pp. 215–23.   **[G: U.S.]**

Farrell, Claude and Hall, William W., Jr. Tracking and Forecasting Local Economic Activity. *Rev. Reg. Stud.*, Fall 1987, *17*(3), pp. 31–36.   **[G: U.S.]**

Friendenberg, Howard L. Regional Nonfarm Personal Income in the Current Economic Expansion. *Surv. Curr. Bus.*, October 1987, *67*(10), pp. 27–41.   **[G: U.S.]**

Garofalo, Gasper A. and Fogarty, Michael S. The Role of Labor Costs in Regional Capital Formation. *Rev. Econ. Statist.*, November 1987, *69*(4), pp. 593–99.   **[G: U.S.]**

Garofalo, Gasper A. and Malhotra, Devinder M. Regional Capital Formation in U.S. Manufacturing during the 1970s. *J. Reg. Sci.*, August 1987, *27*(3), pp. 391–401.   **[G: U.S.]**

Garofoli, Gioacchino. Regional Inequalities and Development in the Mezzogiorno. *Econ. Notes*, 1987, (2), pp. 121–40.   **[G: Italy]**

George, Kenneth D. and Mainwaring, Lynn. The Welsh Economy in the 1980s. *Day, G. and Rees, G., eds.*, 1987, pp. 7–37.   **[G: U.K.]**

Gidadhubli, R. G. Process and Problems of Industrial Development in Soviet Central Asia. *Gidadhubli, R. G., ed.*, 1987, pp. 164–81.   **[G: U.S.S.R.]**

Gidadhubli, R. G. Socio-economic Transformation of Soviet Central Asia: Introduction. *Gidadhubli, R. G., ed.*, 1987, pp. ix–xx.   **[G: U.S.S.R.]**

Giles, David E. A. and Hampton, Peter. A Regional Consumer Demand Model for New Zealand. *J. Reg. Sci.*, February 1987, *27*(1), pp. 103–18.   **[G: New Zealand]**

Gillespie, A. E. and Green, A. E. The Changing Geography of Producer Services Employment

in Britain. *Reg. Stud.*, October 1987, *21*(5), pp. 397–411.   **[G: U.K.]**

Gilmer, Robert William; Keil, Stanley R. and Mack, Richard S. Export Potential of Services in the Tennessee Valley. *Reg. Sci. Persp.*, 1987, *17*(2), pp. 18–33.   **[G: U.S.]**

Glasmeier, Amy K. and McCluskey, Richard E. U.S. Auto Parts Production: An Analysis of the Organization and Location of a Changing Industry. *Econ. Geogr.*, April 1987, *63*(2), pp. 142–59.   **[G: U.S.]**

Gleave, David. Dynamics in Spatial Variations in Unemployment. *Fischer, M. M. and Nijkamp, P., eds.*, 1987, pp. 269–88.   **[G: U.K.]**

Goddard, John; Robinson, Fred and Wren, Colin. Urban and Regional Policies and the Economic Development of the Newcastle Metropolitan Region. *Hausner, V. A., et al.*, 1987, pp. 132–81.   **[G: U.K.]**

Gordon, Ian R. The Structural Element in Regional Unemployment. *Gordon, I., ed.*, 1987, pp. 67–88.   **[G: U.K.]**

Gramatzki, Hans-Erich. Regional Employment Policies in East European Countries. *Adam, J., ed.*, 1987, pp. 171–95.   **[G: Czechoslovakia; Poland; Hungary; E. Germany]**

Green, Milford B. Corporate-Merger–Defined Core–Periphery Relations for the United States. *Growth Change*, Summer 1987, *18*(3), pp. 12–35.   **[G: U.S.]**

Green, Rodney D. Regional Variations in U.S. Consumer Response to Price Changes in Home Heating Fuels: The Northeast and the South. *Appl. Econ.*, September 1987, *19*(9), pp. 1261–68.   **[G: U.S.]**

Greenwood, Michael J.; Hunt, Gary L. and Pfalzgraff, Ellen L. The Economic Effects of Space Science Activities on Colorado and the Western United States. *Ann. Reg. Sci.*, July 1987, *21*(2), pp. 21–44.   **[G: U.S.]**

Griffin, Keith. Rural Development in Arid Regions: The Case of Xinjiang. *Griffin, K.*, 1987, pp. 147–82.   **[G: China]**

Gripaios, P. and Herbert, C. The Role of New Firms in Economic Growth: Some Evidence from South West England. *Reg. Stud.*, June 1987, *21*(3), pp. 270–73.   **[G: U.K.]**

Gunther, William D. A New Approach to Positive Economics. *McKee, D. L. and Bennett, R. E., eds.*, 1987, pp. 109–12.   **[G: U.S.]**

Gunther, William D. and Leathers, Charles G. British Enterprise Zones: A Critical Assessment. *Rev. Reg. Stud.*, Winter 1987, *17*(1), pp. 1–12.   **[G: U.K.]**

Guy, C. M. Recent Advances in Spatial Interaction Modelling: An Application to the Forecasting of Shopping Travel. *Environ. Planning A*, February 1987, *19*(2), pp. 173–86.   **[G: U.K.]**

Gyourko, Joseph. Effects of Local Tax Structures on the Factor Intensity Composition of Manufacturing Activity across Cities. *J. Urban Econ.*, September 1987, *22*(2), pp. 151–64.   **[G: U.S.]**

Hall, Peter. The Anatomy of Job Creation: Nations, Regions and Cities in the 1960s and 1970s. *Reg. Stud.*, April 1987, *21*(2), pp. 95–106. [G: U.S.; U.K.; W. Germany; Japan]

Hansen, Eric R. Industrial Location Choice in Sao Paulo, Brazil: A Nested Logit Model. *Reg. Sci. Urban Econ.*, February 1987, *17*(1), pp. 89–108. [G: Brazil]

Hansen, Niles M. Urban and Regional Adaptability to Structural Economic Change. *McKee, D. L. and Bennett, R. E., eds.*, 1987, pp. 7–22. [G: U.S.]

Harris, Anthony H., et al. Incoming Industry and Structural Change: Oil and the Aberdeen Economy. *Scot. J. Polit. Econ.*, February 1987, *34*(1), pp. 69–90. [G: U.K.]

Harris, Bruce. The Survival of Respect: Economic Power and the Persistence of Community. *Lane, T., ed.*, 1987, pp. 161–80. [G: U.S.]

Harris, R. I. D. The Role of Manufacturing in Regional Growth. *Reg. Stud.*, August 1987, *21*(4), pp. 301–12. [G: U.K.]

Harriss, Barbara. Regional Growth Linkages from Agriculture. *J. Devel. Stud.*, January 1987, *23*(2), pp. 275–89. [G: LDCs]

Hasan, M. Aynul. Aggregate and Regional Demand Response Patterns in Pakistan: Comments. *Pakistan Devel. Rev.*, Winter 1987, *26*(4), pp. 656–57. [G: Pakistan]

Hayes, Kathy J. and Porter-Hudak, Susan. Regional Welfare Loss Measures of the 1973 Oil Embargo: A Numerical Methods Approach. *Appl. Econ.*, October 1987, *19*(10), pp. 1317–27. [G: U.S.]

Haynes, Kingsley E. and Machunda, Zachary B. Spatial Restructuring of Manufacturing and Employment Growth in the Rural Midwest: An Analysis for Indiana. *Econ. Geogr.*, October 1987, *63*(4), pp. 319–33. [G: U.S.]

Hazell, Peter and Slade, Roger H. Regional Growth Linkages from Agriculture: A Reply. *J. Devel. Stud.*, January 1987, *23*(2), pp. 290–94. [G: LDCs]

Heim, Carol E. R&D, Defense, and Spatial Divisions of Labor in Twentieth-Century Britain. *J. Econ. Hist.*, June 1987, *47*(2), pp. 365–78. [G: U.K.]

Henderson, Jeffrey. Semiconductors, Scotland and the International Division of Labour. *Urban Stud.*, October 1987, *24*(5), pp. 389–408. [G: Scotland]

Hepworth, M. E.; Green, A. E. and Gillespie, A. E. The Spatial Division of Information Labour in Great Britain. *Environ. Planning A*, June 1987, *19*(6), pp. 793–806. [G: U.K.]

Her, Jaewan. An Empirical Study on Regional Welfare Inequalities and National Expenditure Priorities. *Rev. Reg. Stud.*, Winter 1987, *17*(1), pp. 21–32. [G: U.S.]

Herbert, John H. Demand for Natural Gas by Households at the State Level: Twenty Years of Effort. *Rev. Reg. Stud.*, Fall 1987, *17*(3), pp. 79–87. [G: U.S.]

Herrin, Alejandro N. and Pernia, Ernesto M. Factors Influencing the Choice of Location: Local and Foreign Firms in the Philippines. *Reg.*

Stud., December 1987, *21*(6), pp. 531–41. [G: Philippines]

Higgins, Benjamin and Savoie, Donald J. Canadian Regional Development at Home and Abroad: A Comparative Perspective. *Can. J. Devel. Stud.*, 1987, *8*(2), pp. 227–50. [G: Canada]

Hill, Edward W. What Is the Effect of Random Variation in State Unemployment Rates? *Mon. Lab. Rev.*, December 1987, *110*(12), pp. 41–46. [G: U.S.]

Hill, Hal. Concentration in Indonesian Manufacturing. *Bull. Indonesian Econ. Stud.*, August 1987, *23*(2), pp. 71–100. [G: Indonesia]

Hitchens, D. M. W. N. and O'Farrell, P. N. The Comparative Performance of Small Manufacturing Firms in Northern Ireland and South East England. *Reg. Stud.*, December 1987, *21*(6), pp. 543–53. [G: U.K.]

Horn, Karen N. Emerging Technology and Its Impact on Regional Growth Prospects. *McKee, D. L. and Bennett, R. E., eds.*, 1987, pp. 211–18. [G: U.S.]

Howells, Jeremy. Developments in the Location, Technology and Industrial Organization of Computer Services: Some Trends and Research Issues. *Reg. Stud.*, December 1987, *21*(6), pp. 493–503. [G: U.K.]

Hunt, Gary L. The Impact of Oil Price Fluctuations on the Economies of Energy Producing States. *Rev. Reg. Stud.*, Fall 1987, *17*(3), pp. 60–76. [G: U.S.]

Hur, Jaewan. An Indirect Approach to Measure Governmental Perceptions of Regional Welfare Inequalities. *J. Econ. Devel.*, June 1987, *12*(1), pp. 195–209. [G: U.S.]

Huskey, Lee. Import Substitution in Frontier Regions. *Lane, T., ed.*, 1987, *1985*, pp. 47–61. [G: U.S.]

Ikemoto, Yukio and Limskul, Kitti. Income Inequality and Regional Disparity in Thailand, 1962–81. *Devel. Econ.*, September 1987, *25*(3), pp. 249–69. [G: Thailand]

Inwood, Kris. Progress without Planning: The Economic History of Ontario from Confederation to the Second World War: The Iron and Steel Industry. *Drummond, I. M.*, 1987, pp. 185–207. [G: Canada]

Ishikawa, Y. An Empirical Study of the Competing Destinations Model Using Japanese Interaction Data. *Environ. Planning A*, October 1987, *19*(10), pp. 1359–73. [G: Japan]

Isserman, Andrew M. and Merrifield, John D. Quasi-experimental Control Group Methods for Regional Analysis: An Application to an Energy Boomtown and Growth Pole Theory. *Econ. Geogr.*, January 1987, *63*(1), pp. 3–19. [G: U.S.]

Iuzbekov, Z. Intensification in a Labor-Surplus Region. *Prob. Econ.*, January 1987, *29*(9), pp. 20–31. [G: U.S.S.R.]

Jackman, Richard and Roper, S. Structural Unemployment. *Oxford Bull. Econ. Statist.*, February 1987, *49*(1), pp. 9–36. [G: U.K.]

Jacobson, Louis. Reply [A Tale of Employment Decline in Two Cities: How Bad Was the

Worst of Times?]. *Ind. Lab. Relat. Rev.*, January 1987, *40*(2), pp. 284–87. **[G: U.S.]**

Jenkis, Helmut W. Stabilisation of the Social Structure versus Change of the Industrial Structure: The Case of the Ruhr District. *Gemper, B. B., ed.*, 1987, pp. 57–88. **[G: W. Germany]**

Johnes, Geraint. Regional Policy and Industrial Strategy in the Welsh Economy. *Reg. Stud.*, December 1987, *21*(6), pp. 555–64. **[G: U.K.]**

Kania, John J. Profitability and Market Power in Industries with Regional–Local Markets. *Amer. Econ.*, Fall 1987, *31*(2), pp. 29–34. **[G: U.S.]**

Kannan, R. Banking Development and Regional Disparities. *Indian Econ. J.*, Oct.-Dec. 1987, *35*(2), pp. 58–76. **[G: India]**

Kaushik, Devendra. Soviet Nationalities Policy in Central Asia: A Survey and Appraisal. *Gidadhubli, R. G., ed.*, 1987, pp. 1–20. **[G: U.S.S.R.]**

Knox, Hugh W. The Nonmetropolitan South in the 1990s: Convergence or Stagnation? *Rev. Reg. Stud.*, Fall 1987, *17*(3), pp. 1–4.

Koppel, Bruce. Does Integrated Area Development Work? Insight from the Bicol River Basin Development Program. *World Devel.*, February 1987, *15*(2), pp. 205–20. **[G: Philippines]**

Kowalski, Jan S. Unemployment within Enterprises in Centrally Planned Economies: A Regionalised View. *Gordon, I., ed.*, 1987, pp. 89–98. **[G: Poland]**

Kozlowski, Paul J. Regional Cyclical Volatility: Tests of a Growth-Buffer Hypothesis. *Reg. Sci. Persp.*, 1987, *17*(2), pp. 41–56. **[G: U.S.]**

Krakover, S. Cluster of Cities versus City Region in Regional Planning. *Environ. Planning A*, October 1987, *19*(10), pp. 1375–86. **[G: U.S.]**

Krumm, Ronald J. Regional Wage Differentials and Race: 1973–1978. *J. Reg. Sci.*, February 1987, *27*(1), pp. 119–28. **[G: U.S.]**

Lakshmanan, T. R. and Hua, Chang-i. Regional Disparities in China. *Int. Reg. Sci. Rev.*, January 1987, *11*(1), pp. 97–104. **[G: China]**

Lane, Theodore. Developing America's Northern Frontier: Introduction. *Lane, T., ed.*, 1987, pp. xiii–xix. **[G: U.S.; Canada]**

Lane, Theodore and Thomas, Cheryl K. The Labor Force Status of Alaska's Native Population. *Lane, T., ed.*, 1987, pp. 63–89. **[G: U.S.]**

Langdon, Stephen. Commercial Fisheries: Implications for Western Alaska Development. *Lane, T., ed.*, 1987, pp. 3–26. **[G: U.S.]**

Lee, John G., et al. Regional Impact of Urban Water Use on Irrigated Agriculture. *Southern J. Agr. Econ.*, December 1987, *19*(2), pp. 43–51. **[G: U.S.]**

Leistritz, F. Larry and Murdock, Steve H. Socioeconomic Impacts of Large-Scale Development Projects in the Western United States: Implications for Synthetic Fuels Commercialization. *Yanarella, E. J. and Green, W. C., eds.*, 1987, pp. 145–70. **[G: U.S.]**

Lever, William F. New Trends in the Supply and Demand Patterns of Labour in Western Economies. *Fischer, M. M. and Nijkamp, P., eds.*, 1987, pp. 249–67. **[G: W. Europe]**

Levy, John M. The Limits of Local Economic Development Programs. *McKee, D. L. and Bennett, R. E., eds.*, 1987, pp. 122–36. **[G: U.S.]**

Lewis, J. R. and Williams, A. M. Productive Decentralization or Indigenous Growth? Small Manufacturing Enterprises and Regional Development in Central Portugal. *Reg. Stud.*, August 1987, *21*(4), pp. 343–61. **[G: Portugal]**

Ley, David and Hutton, Thomas. Vancouver's Corporate Complex and Producer Services Sector: Linkages and Divergence within a Provincial Staple Economy. *Reg. Stud.*, October 1987, *21*(5), pp. 413–24. **[G: Canada]**

Liaw, Kao-Lee and Ledent, Jacques. Nested Logit Model and Maximum Quasi-likelihood Method: A Flexible Methodology for Analyzing Interregional Migration Patterns. *Reg. Sci. Urban Econ.*, February 1987, *17*(1), pp. 67–88. **[G: Canada]**

Long, Roger B. Effects of Recession, Inflation and High Interest Rates on Growth in a Recreation Region. *Ann. Reg. Sci.*, July 1987, *21*(2), pp. 86–107. **[G: U.S.]**

Lonner, Thomas D. Transient Work Forces as Casualties in Northern Frontier Development. *Lane, T., ed.*, 1987, pp. 181–97. **[G: U.S.; Canada]**

Loslier, Luc. Disparités socio-spatiales de mortalité à Porto-Rico. (With English summary.) *Can. J. Devel. Stud.*, 1987, *8*(1), pp. 117–32. **[G: Puerto Rico]**

Lyons, Thomas P. Interprovincial Trade and Development in China, 1957–1979. *Econ. Develop. Cult. Change*, January 1987, *35*(2), pp. 223–56. **[G: China]**

Lyons, Thomas P. Spatial Aspects of Development in China: The Motor Vehicle Industry, 1956–1985. *Int. Reg. Sci. Rev.*, 1987, *11*(1), pp. 75–96. **[G: China]**

Malamud, Bernard. Regional Economic Growth and Decline: The Supply-Side Contribution. *Ann. Reg. Sci.*, July 1987, *21*(2), pp. 1–20. **[G: U.S.]**

Malik, Sohail J.; Abbas, Kalbe and Ghani, Ejaz. Rural–Urban Differences and the Stability of Consumption Behaviour: An Inter-temporal Analysis of the Household Income and Expenditure Survey Data for the Period 1963–64 to 1984–85. *Pakistan Devel. Rev.*, Winter 1987, *26*(4), pp. 673–82. **[G: Pakistan]**

Mandelbaum, Thomas B. A Review of the Eighth District's Business Economy in 1986. *Fed. Res. Bank St. Louis Rev.*, April 1987, *69*(4), pp. 22–31. **[G: U.S.]**

Mandelbaum, Thomas B. Is Eighth District Manufacturing Endangered? *Fed. Res. Bank St. Louis Rev.*, November 1987, *69*(9), pp. 5–15. **[G: U.S.]**

Mann, Roger; Sparling, Edward and Young, Robert A. Regional Economic Growth from Irrigation Development: Evidence from Northern High-Plains Ogallala Groundwater Resource. *Water Resources Res.*, September 1987, *23*(9), pp. 1711–16.   [G: U.S.]

Manrique, Gabriel G. Foreign Export Orientation and Regional Growth in the U.S. *Growth Change*, Winter 1987, *18*(1), pp. 1–12.
[G: U.S.]

Markley, Deborah Morentz. Impacts of Banking Deregulation on Rural Capital Markets: Evidence from Virginia and Tennessee. *Rev. Reg. Stud.*, Fall 1987, *17*(3), pp. 14–22. [G: U.S.]

Marshall, J. N. and Bachtler, J. Services and Regional Policy. *Reg. Stud.*, October 1987, *21*(5), pp. 471–75.   [G: W. Europe]

Marshall, J. N.; Damesick, P. and Wood, P. Understanding the Location and Role of Producer Services in the United Kingdom. *Environ. Planning A*, May 1987, *19*(5), pp. 575–95.
[G: U.K.]

Martellato, Dino and van der Borg, Jan. The Economy of the Italian Labour Catching Areas. *Ricerche Econ.*, Jan.-Mar. 1987, *41*(1), pp. 96–122.   [G: Italy]

Mathur, Ashok. 'Why Growth Rates Differ' within India: An Alternative Approach. *J. Devel. Stud.*, January 1987, *23*(2), pp. 167–99.
[G: India]

McKean, B. and Coulson, A. Enterprise Boards and Some Issues Raised by Taking Equity and Loan Stock in Major Companies. *Reg. Stud.*, August 1987, *21*(4), pp. 373–84.   [G: U.K.]

Mears, R. R. Die rol van die owerheid in die verstedeliking van die bevolking van Suid-Afrika. (With English summary.) *J. Stud. Econ. Econometrics*, November 1987, *11*(3), pp. 51–81.   [G: S. Africa]

Mehta, Vinod. Development Experience of Soviet Central Asia and the Countries of the Third World. *Gidadhubli, R. G., ed.*, 1987, pp. 219–38.   [G: U.S.S.R.; LDCs]

Melvin, James R. Regional Inequalities in Canada: Underlying Causes and Policy Implications. *Can. Public Policy*, September 1987, *13*(3), pp. 304–17.   [G: Canada]

Meyers, William H. The Farm Economies of the Plains: Comment. *Rev. Reg. Stud.*, Fall 1987, *17*(3), pp. 58–59.   [G: U.S.]

Milanovic, Branko. Patterns of Regional Growth in Yugoslavia, 1952–83. *J. Devel. Econ.*, February 1987, *25*(1), pp. 1–19. [G: Yugoslavia]

Mitchelson, Ronald L. and Fisher, James S. Long-Distance Commuting and Population Change in Georgia, 1960–80. *Growth Change*, Winter 1987, *18*(1), pp. 44–65.   [G: U.S.]

Molho, Ian J. The Migration Decisions of Young Men in Great Britain. *Appl. Econ.*, February 1987, *19*(2), pp. 221–43.   [G: U.K.]

Moore, Thomas W. Structural Change and Regional Growth. *Faruqui, A. and Broehl, J., eds.*, 1987, pp. 455–64.   [G: U.S.]

Morgan, Kevin. High Technology Industry and Regional Development: For Wales, See Greater Boston? *Day, G. and Rees, G., eds.*, 1987, pp. 39–51.   [G: U.K.]

Morris, J. L. Industrial Restructuring, Foreign Direct Investment, and Uneven Development:

The Case of Wales. *Environ. Planning A*, February 1987, *19*(2), pp. 205–24.   [G: U.K.]

Mubyarto. Economic Development in the Regions: A Conference Report. *Bull. Indonesian Econ. Stud.*, April 1987, *23*(1), pp. 131–37.
[G: Indonesia]

Mukhopadhyay, Rabindranath. A Study of Regional Patterns of Consumer Expenditure in Rural India. *J. Quant. Econ.*, January 1987, *3*(1), pp. 117–36.   [G: India]

Mullen, John K. and Williams, Martin. Technical Progress in Urban Manufacturing: North–South Comparisons. *J. Urban Econ.*, March 1987, *21*(2), pp. 194–208.   [G: U.S.]

Mulligan, Gordon F. Employment Multipliers and Functional Types of Communities: Effects of Public Transfer Payments. *Growth Change*, Summer 1987, *18*(3), pp. 1–11.   [G: U.S.]

Nachane, D. M. Regional Planning in the USSR: A Case Study of Soviet Central Asia. *Gidadhubli, R. G., ed.*, 1987, pp. 137–63.
[G: U.S.S.R.]

Nagle, George. How Do Energy Price Changes Affect the Relative Attractiveness of Mid-Atlantic States to New Business? *Stewart, M. B., ed.*, 1987, pp. 55–58.   [G: U.S.]

Nairn, A. G. M. and Swales, J. K. Area Policy Impacts: A Multiplier Analysis of GEAR. *Urban Stud.*, February 1987, *24*(1), pp. 31–45.
[G: U.K.]

Nakosteen, Robert A. and Zimmer, Michael A. Determinants of Regional Migration by Manufacturing Firms. *Econ. Inquiry*, April 1987, *25*(2), pp. 351–62.   [G: U.S.]

Niazi, Mohammad Khan. Rural–Urban Differences and the Stability of Consumption Behaviour: An Inter-temporal Analysis of the Household Income and Expenditure Survey Data for the Period 1963–64 to 1984–85: Comments. *Pakistan Devel. Rev.*, Winter 1987, *26*(4), pp. 683–84.   [G: Pakistan]

Nijkamp, Peter. New Technology and Regional Development. *Vasko, T., ed.*, 1987, pp. 274–84.   [G: Netherlands]

Nissan, Edward and Caveny, Regina. A Composite Manufacturing Growth Index: 1954–1978. *Rev. Reg. Stud.*, Winter 1987, *17*(1), pp. 67–70.   [G: U.S.]

Norton, R. D. Ohio in the Regional Life Cycle: A Synthesis. *McKee, D. L. and Bennett, R. E., eds.*, 1987, pp. 229–39.   [G: U.S.]

Nyankori, James C. O. and Nodine, Stephen K. Implications of Restrictions on Imports of Canadian Softwood Lumber to the Southern Softwood Lumber Industry. *Rev. Reg. Stud.*, Winter 1987, *17*(1), pp. 45–52.   [G: U.S.; Canada]

Ó Cinnéide, M. S. The Role of Development Agencies in Peripheral Areas with Special Reference to *údarás na Gaeltachta*. *Reg. Stud.*, February 1987, *21*(1), pp. 65–69.
[G: Ireland]

Oberhauser, Ann. Labour, Production and the State: Decentralization of the French Automobile Industry. *Reg. Stud.*, October 1987, *21*(5), pp. 445–58.   [G: France]

Parr, John B. The Development of Spatial Structure and Regional Economic Growth. *Land Econ.*, May 1987, *63*(2), pp. 113–27.
[G: U.S.]

Peck, Francis and Townsend, Alan. The Impact of Technological Change upon the Spatial Pattern of UK Employment within Major Corporations. *Reg. Stud.*, June 1987, *21*(3), pp. 225–39.
[G: U.K.]

Peddle, Michael T. The Appropriate Estimation of Intrametropolitan Firm Location Models: An Empirical Note. *Land Econ.*, August 1987, *63*(3), pp. 303–05.

Perryman, M. Ray. The Impact of Oil Price Fluctuations on the Economies of Energy Producing States: Comment. *Rev. Reg. Stud.*, Fall 1987, *17*(3), pp. 77–78.
[G: U.S.]

Petterson, John S. Subsistence Continuity and Economic Abundance in the North. *Lane, T., ed.*, 1987, pp. 91–106.
[G: U.S.]

Phadke, V. S. Urbanisation in Soviet Central Asia. *Gidadhubli, R. G., ed.*, 1987, pp. 199–218.
[G: U.S.S.R.]

Pigliaru, Francesco. The Performance of the Mezzogiorno's Indigenous Manufacturing Sector, 1951–70: A Discussion on Graziani's Effect and the Cumulative Causation Hypothesis. *Stud. Econ.*, 1987, *42*(33), pp. 3–40.
[G: Italy]

Podgursky, Michael and Swaim, Paul. Labor Market Equilibrium and Sun-belt–Frostbelt Earnings Gaps. *Eastern Econ. J.*, Apr.-June 1987, *13*(2), pp. 107–13.
[G: U.S.]

Popov, Sofija. Raspodela ličnih dohodaka po republikama i pokrajinama kao faktor nejedinstva jugoslovenskog tržišta. (Distribution of Personal Income among Republics and Provinces as a Factor of Disunity of the Yugoslav Market. With English summary.) *Econ. Anal. Workers' Manage.*, 1987, *21*(3), pp. 333–51.
[G: Yugoslavia]

Primorac, E. and Charette, Michael F. Regional Aspects of Youth Unemployment in Yugoslavia. *Econ. Anal. Workers' Manage.*, 1987, *21*(2), pp. 193–219.
[G: Yugoslavia]

Pudup, Mary Beth. From Farm to Factory: Structuring and Location of the U.S. Farm Machinery Industry. *Econ. Geogr.*, July 1987, *63*(3), pp. 203–22.
[G: U.S.]

Quan, Nguyen T. and Beck, John H. Public Education Expenditures and State Economic Growth: Northeast and Sunbelt Regions. *Southern Econ. J.*, October 1987, *54*(2), pp. 361–76.
[G: U.S.]

Rajalakshmi, K. Composition of State Domestic Products of India (An Indepth Analysis for the Period between 1971 to 1982). *Indian Econ. J.*, Apr.-June 1987, *34*(4), pp. 60–78.
[G: India]

Razin, E. and Shachar, A. Ownership of Industry and Plant Stability in Israel's Development Towns. *Urban Stud.*, August 1987, *24*(4), pp. 296–311.
[G: Israel]

Rees, John. The Diffusion of New Production Technology: Implications for State and Local Industrial Policy. *Goldstein, H. A., ed.*, 1987, pp. 60–72.
[G: U.S.]

Rees, William E. Politics, Power, and Northern Land-Use Planning. *Lane, T., ed.*, 1987, *1985*, pp. 109–32.
[G: Canada]

Reynolds, Bruce L. Trade, Employment, and Inequality in Postreform China. *J. Compar. Econ.*, September 1987, *11*(3), pp. 479–89.
[G: China]

Roback, Jennifer. Determinants of the Local Unemployment Rate. *Southern Econ. J.*, January 1987, *53*(3), pp. 735–50.
[G: Colombia]

Roberts, P. W. and Noon, D. The Role of Industrial Promotion and Inward Investment in the Process of Regional Development. *Reg. Stud.*, April 1987, *21*(2), pp. 167–73.
[G: U.K.]

Rothenberg, Jerome. Space, Interregional Economic Relations, and Structural Reform in China. *Int. Reg. Sci. Rev.*, 1987, *11*(1), pp. 5–22.
[G: China]

Saidmuradov, Kh. M. Industrialisation of the Formerly Backward Regions of the USSR—From the Experience of the Tadjek SSR. *Gidadhubli, R. G., ed.*, 1987, pp. 182–98.
[G: U.S.S.R.]

Saraceno, Pasquale. La questione meridionale nel 1987. (The "Southern Question" Today. With English summary.) *Ricerche Econ.*, Apr.-June 1987, *41*(2), pp. 163–73.
[G: Italy]

Saunders, Mark N. K. and Flowerdew, Robin. Spatial Aspects of the Provision of Job Information. *Fischer, M. M. and Nijkamp, P., eds.*, 1987, pp. 205–28.
[G: U.K.]

Schirm, Allen L. and Preston, Samuel H. Census Undercount Adjustment and the Quality of Geographic Population Distributions. *J. Amer. Statist. Assoc.*, December 1987, *82*(400), pp. 965–78.
[G: U.S.]

Schmenner, Roger W.; Huber, Joel C. and Cook, Randall L. Geographic Differences and the Location of New Manufacturing Facilities. *J. Urban Econ.*, January 1987, *21*(1), pp. 83–104.
[G: U.S.]

Schoenberger, Erica. Technological and Organizational Change in Automobile Production: Spatial Implications. *Reg. Stud.*, June 1987, *21*(3), pp. 199–214.
[G: France]

Scott, A. J. The Semiconductor Industry in South-East Asia: Organization, Location and the International Division of Labour. *Reg. Stud.*, April 1987, *21*(2), pp. 143–59. [G: S.E. Asia]

Scott, A. J. and Angel, D. P. The U.S. Semiconductor Industry: A Locational Analysis. *Environ. Planning A*, July 1987, *19*(7), pp. 875–912.
[G: U.S.]

Sharma, R. R. Class and Social–Agrarian Transformation in Soviet Central Asia: A Historical–Cultural Context. *Gidadhubli, R. G., ed.*, 1987, pp. 116–36.
[G: U.S.S.R.]

Shaul, Marnie S. Economic Development in Ohio. *McKee, D. L. and Bennett, R. E., eds.*, 1987, pp. 203–07.
[G: U.S.]

Shefer, Daniel. The Effect of Agricultural Price-Support Policies on Interregional and Rural-to-Urban Migration in Korea: 1976–1980. *Reg. Sci. Urban Econ.*, August 1987, *17*(3), pp. 333–44.
[G: Korea]

Shutt, John and Whittington, Richard. Fragmentation Strategies and the Rise of Small Units:

Cases from the North West. *Reg. Stud.*, February 1987, *21*(1), pp. 13–23. [G: U.K.]

da Silva Costa, Jose; Ellson, Richard W. and Martin, Randolph C. Public Capital, Regional Output, and Development: Some Empirical Evidence. *J. Reg. Sci.*, August 1987, *27*(3), pp. 419–37. [G: U.S.]

Simon, David. Spanning Muddy Waters: The Humber Bridge and Regional Development. *Reg. Stud.*, February 1987, *21*(1), pp. 25–36. [G: U.K.]

Sinclair, Peter W. The North and the North-west: Forestry and Agriculture. *Drummond, I. M.*, 1987, pp. 77–90. [G: Canada]

Slottje, D. J. and Hayes, Kathy J. Income Inequality and Urban/Rural Migration. *Rev. Reg. Stud.*, Spring 1987, *17*(2), pp. 53–56. [G: U.S.]

Smith, Neil and Dennis, Ward. The Restructuring of Geographical Scale: Coalescence and Fragmentation of the Northern Core Region. *Econ. Geogr.*, April 1987, *63*(2), pp. 160–82. [G: U.S.]

Smith, Peter C. Micro-level Aspects of Demographic Change. *Martin, L. G., ed.*, 1987, pp. 37–39. [G: ASEAN]

Snowden, Kenneth A. Mortgage Rates and American Capital Market Development in the Late Nineteenth Century. *J. Econ. Hist.*, September 1987, *47*(3), pp. 771–91. [G: U.S.]

Solinger, Dorothy J. Uncertain Paternalism: Tensions in Recent Regional Restructuring in China. *Int. Reg. Sci. Rev.*, 1987, *11*(1), pp. 23–42. [G: China]

Sparks, Leigh. Retailing in Enterprise Zones: The Example of Swansea. *Reg. Stud.*, February 1987, *21*(1), pp. 37–42. [G: U.K.]

Spencer, Ken. The West Midlands: An Economy in Crisis. *Hausner, V. A., et al.*, 1987, pp. 218–53. [G: U.K.]

Stabler, Jack C. Trade Center Evolution in the Great Plains. *J. Reg. Sci.*, May 1987, *27*(2), pp. 225–44. [G: Canada]

Stadelbauer, Jörg. Transport and the Pattern of Settlement in Soviet Caucasia. *Tismer, J. F.; Ambler, J. and Symons, L., eds.*, 1987, pp. 218–69. [G: U.S.S.R.]

Storey, David J. and Johnson, Steven G. Regional Variations in Entrepreneurship in the U.K. *Scot. J. Polit. Econ.*, May 1987, *34*(2), pp. 161–73. [G: U.K.]

Swallow, Brent M. and Johnson, Thomas G. A Fiscal Impact Model for Virginia Counties. *Rev. Reg. Stud.*, Spring 1987, *17*(2), pp. 67–74. [G: U.S.]

Syrett, S. J. The International Trading of Policies: The Portuguese Experience of Local Employment Initiatives. *Reg. Stud.*, October 1987, *21*(5), pp. 475–79. [G: Portugal]

Tam, Mo-Yin; Persky, Joseph and Schlaf, Eric. A Social Welfare Approach to Regional Convergence. *Rev. Reg. Stud.*, Winter 1987, *17*(1), pp. 53–66. [G: U.S.]

Tannewald, Robert. State Response in New England to Federal Tax Reform. *New Eng. Econ. Rev.*, Sept./Oct. 1987, pp. 25–44. [G: U.S.]

Thomas, Colin J. and Bromley, Rosemary D. F. The Growth and Functioning of an Unplanned Retail Park: The Swansea Enterprise Zone. *Reg. Stud.*, August 1987, *21*(4), pp. 287–300. [G: U.K.]

Thomas, Ian C. and Drudy, P. J. The Impact of Factory Development on 'Growth Town' Employment in Mid-Wales. *Urban Stud.*, October 1987, *24*(5), pp. 361–78. [G: U.K.]

Thomas, Vinod. Differences in Income and Poverty with in Brazil. *World Devel.*, February 1987, *15*(2), pp. 263–73. [G: Brazil]

Thrift, Nigel. The Growth of Service Class Labour Markets: The Case of Great Britain. *Fischer, M. M. and Nijkamp, P., eds.*, 1987, pp. 313–44. [G: U.K.]

Traves, Tom. The Development of the Ontario Automobile Industry to 1939. *Drummond, I. M.*, 1987, pp. 208–23. [G: Canada]

Tuppen, J. N. and Bateman, M. The Relaxation of Office Development Controls in Paris: An Assessment of the Consequences. *Reg. Stud.*, February 1987, *21*(1), pp. 69–74. [G: France]

Turnbull, Gerard. Canals, Coal and Regional Growth during the Industrial Revolution. *Econ. Hist. Rev., 2nd Ser.*, November 1987, *40*(4), pp. 537–60. [G: U.K.]

Tyler, P. and Kitson, M. Geographical Variations in Transport Costs of Manufacturing Firms in Great Britain. *Urban Stud.*, February 1987, *24*(1), pp. 61–73. [G: U.K.]

Vandenbroeke, Christian. The Regional Economy of Flanders and Industrial Modernization in the Eighteenth Century: A Discussion. *J. Europ. Econ. Hist.*, Spring 1987, *16*(1), pp. 149–70. [G: Flanders]

Vedder, Richard K. and Gallaway, Lowell. Economic Growth and Decline in the Old Northwest. *Klingaman, D. C. and Vedder, R. K., eds.*, 1987, pp. 299–318. [G: U.S.]

Vickerman, R. W. The Channel Tunnel: Consequences for Regional Growth and Development. *Reg. Stud.*, June 1987, *21*(3), pp. 187–97. [G: EEC]

Walters, R. J. A Framework for Regional Accounts: An Australian Perspective. *Rev. Income Wealth*, December 1987, *33*(4), pp. 401–15. [G: Australia]

Weiman, David F. Farmers and the Market in Antebellum America: A View from the Georgia Upcountry. *J. Econ. Hist.*, September 1987, *47*(3), pp. 627–47. [G: U.S.]

Wells, P. The Military Scientific Infrastructure and Regional Development. *Environ. Planning A*, December 1987, *19*(12), pp. 1631–58. [G: U.K.]

Wild, Wolfgang. High Tech in Bavaria. *Atlantic Econ. J.*, September 1987, *15*(3), pp. 22–29. [G: W. Germany]

Willis, K. G. Spatially Disaggregated Input–Output Tables: An Evaluation and Comparison of Survey and Non-survey Results. *Indian J. Quant. Econ.*, 1987, *3*(1), pp. 34–51. [G: U.K.]

Winckler, Victoria. Women and Work in Contemporary Wales. *Day, G. and Rees, G., eds.*, 1987, pp. 53–71.   [G: U.K.]

Wong, Christine P. W. Between Plan and Market: The Role of the Local Sector in Post-Mao China. *J. Compar. Econ.*, September 1987, *11*(3), pp. 385–98.   [G: China]

Wren, Colin. The Relative Effects of Local Authority Financial Assistance Policies. *Urban Stud.*, August 1987, *24*(4), pp. 268–78.
[G: U.K.]

Wright, Gavin. The Economic Revolution in the American South. *J. Econ. Perspectives*, Summer 1987, *1*(1), pp. 161–78.   [G: U.S.]

Yochum, Gilbert R. and Agarwal, Vinod B. Economic Impact of a Port on a Regional Economy: Note. *Growth Change*, Summer 1987, *18*(3), pp. 74–87.   [G: U.S.]

9413 Regional Economic Models and Forecasts

Batey, P. W. J.; Madden, M. and Weeks, M. J. Household Income and Expenditure in Extended Input–Output Models: A Comparative Theoretical and Empirical Analysis. *J. Reg. Sci.*, August 1987, *27*(3), pp. 341–56.
[G: U.S.]

Baxter, M. J. Testing for Misspecification in Models of Spatial Flows. *Environ. Planning A*, September 1987, *19*(9), pp. 1153–60.

Beckmann, Martin J. Continuous Models of Spatial Dynamics. *Batten, D.; Casti, J. and Johansson, B., eds.*, 1987, pp. 337–48.

Bigras, Yvon and Nguyen, Sang V. Un modèle des flux interrégionaux de marchandises au Canada. (A Model of Interregional Freight Flows for Canada. With English summary.) *L'Actual. Econ.*, March 1987, *63*(1), pp. 26–42.   [G: Canada]

Borgers, Aloys and Timmermans, Harry. Choice Model Specification, Substitution and Spatial Structure Effects: A Simulation Experiment. *Reg. Sci. Urban Econ.*, February 1987, *17*(1), pp. 29–47.

Bourque, Philip J. Synthetic I–O Models: A Comment [Regional Input–Output Analyis: A Comparison of Five "Ready-Made" Model Systems]. *Rev. Reg. Stud.*, Spring 1987, *17*(2), pp. 28–29.

Brucker, Sharon M.; Hastings, Steven E. and Latham, William R., III. Regional Input–Output Analysis: A Comparison of Five "Ready-Made" Model Systems. *Rev. Reg. Stud.*, Spring 1987, *17*(2), pp. 1–16.   [G: U.S.]

Clarke, M. and Openshaw, S. The AGW Spatial Interaction Workstation. *Environ. Planning A*, September 1987, *19*(9), pp. 1261–68.

Curry, L. Areal Heterogeneity and Labour Returns. *Gordon, I., ed.*, 1987, pp. 101–15.

Dendrinos, Dimitrios S. and Sonis, Michael. The Onset of Turbulence in Discrete Relative Multiple Spatial Dynamics. *Batten, D.; Casti, J. and Johansson, B., eds.*, 1987, pp. 349–64.

Domazlicky, Bruce R. A Comparison of Monthly Forecasting Methods for a Small Region. *Reg. Sci. Persp.*, 1987, *17*(2), pp. 3–17.   [G: U.S.]

Folmer, Henk and Nijkamp, Peter. Investment

Premiums: Expensive but Hardly Effective. *Kyklos*, 1987, *40*(1), pp. 43–72.
[G: Netherlands]

Garhart, Robert E. and Giarratani, Frank. Nonsurvey Input–Output Estimation Techniques: Evidence on the Structure of Errors. *J. Reg. Sci.*, May 1987, *27*(2), pp. 245–53. [G: U.S.]

Goldsmith, Oliver Scott; Berman, Matthew and Huskey, Lee. An Interactive Multiregional Model of a Frontier Economy: Anchorage and the State of Alaska. *Reg. Sci. Persp.*, 1987, *17*(1), pp. 55–76.   [G: U.S.]

Haining, Robert. Small Area Aggregate Income Models: Theory and Methods with an Application to Urban and Rural Income Data for Pennsylvania. *Reg. Stud.*, December 1987, *21*(6), pp. 519–29.   [G: U.S.]

Halvorson, Alan L. Alternative Approaches to the Estimation of Economic Impacts Resulting from Supply Constraints: Comment and Elaboration. *Ann. Reg. Sci.*, March 1987, *21*(1), pp. 80–83.

Harker, Patrick T. The Core of a Spatial Price Equilibrium Game. *J. Reg. Sci.*, August 1987, *27*(3), pp. 369–89.   [G: U.S.]

Harrigan, Frank J. and McGregor, Peter G. Interregional Arbitrage and the Supply of Loanable Funds: A Model of Intermediate Financial Capital Mobility. *J. Reg. Sci.*, August 1987, *27*(3), pp. 357–67.

Hoehn, John P.; Berger, Mark C. and Blomquist, Glenn C. A Hedonic Model of Interregional Wages, Rents, and Amenity Values. *J. Reg. Sci.*, November 1987, *27*(4), pp. 605–20.
[G: U.S.]

Jensen, R. C. On the Concept of Ready-Made Regional Input–Output Models. *Rev. Reg. Stud.*, Spring 1987, *17*(2), pp. 20–25.

Katz, Joseph L. and Burford, Roger L. Shortcut Multiplier Formulas for Interregional Input Output Models. *Rev. Reg. Stud.*, Spring 1987, *17*(2), pp. 31–45.   [G: Netherlands]

Khan, Mohsin S. and Treyz, George I. A Community Economic Forecasting and Simulation System: Description of a Satellite Model. *Growth Change*, Spring 1987, *18*(2), pp. 1–14.
[G: U.S.]

Knox, Hugh W. I–O to Go: A Comment on Ready-Made Multipliers. *Rev. Reg. Stud.*, Spring 1987, *17*(2), pp. 25–26.

Kobayashi, Kiyoshi, et al. Multiactor Decision Analysis for Regional Investment Allocation. *Sawaragi, Y.; Inoue, K. and Nakayama, H., eds.*, 1987, pp. 422–31.

Kozlowski, Paul J. Regional Indexes of Leading Indicators: An Evaluation of Forecasting Performance. *Growth Change*, Summer 1987, *18*(3), pp. 62–73.   [G: U.S.]

McNicoll, Iain H. and Davies, J. R. Measuring the Secondary Impact of the Left Bank Outfall Drain on the Economy of Sindh. *Pakistan J. Appl. Econ.*, Summer 1987, *6*(1), pp. 23–40.
[G: Pakistan]

Merrifield, John D. A Note on the General Mathematical Equivalency of Economic Base and Aggregate Input–Output Multipliers: Fact or

Fiction. *J. Reg. Sci.*, November 1987, *27*(4), pp. 651–54.

Miernyk, William H. Regional Input–Output Analysis: A Comparison of Five "Ready-Made" Model Systems: Comment. *Rev. Reg. Stud.*, Spring 1987, *17*(2), pp. 17.

Möhr, Malte; Crown, William H. and Polenske, Karen R. A Linear Programming Approach to Solving Infeasible RAS Problems. *J. Reg. Sci.*, November 1987, *27*(4), pp. 587–603.

Molle, Willem; Boeckhout, Sjaak and Vollering, Ans. The RESPONS Model: An Operational Two-level Regional Economic Model for The Netherlands. *Reg. Stud.*, April 1987, *21*(2), pp. 107–19. **[G: Netherlands]**

Nairn, A. G. M. and Swales, J. K. Area Policy Impacts: A Multiplier Analysis of GEAR. *Urban Stud.*, February 1987, *24*(1), pp. 31–45. **[G: U.K.]**

Ngo, T. W.; Jazayeri, A. and Richardson, Harry W. Regional Policy Simulations with an Interregional Input–Output Model of the Philippines. *Reg. Stud.*, April 1987, *21*(2), pp. 121–29. **[G: Philippines]**

Puu, Tönu. Complex Dynamics in Continuous Models of the Business Cycle. *Batten, D.; Casti, J. and Johansson, B.*, eds., 1987, pp. 227–59.

Ratick, Samuel J. and Kuby, Michael J. Regional Assessment of Coal Utilization Technologies Using Mathematical Programming. *Schultz, R. L.*, ed., 1987, pp. 155–95. **[G: U.S.]**

Round, Jeffery I. A Note on "Ready-Made" Regional Input–Output Models. *Rev. Reg. Stud.*, Spring 1987, *17*(2), pp. 26–27.

Sasaki, Komei; Shinmei, M. and Kunihisa, S. Multiregional Model with Endogenous Price System for Evaluating Road Construction Projects. *Environ. Planning A*, August 1987, *19*(8), pp. 1093–1114. **[G: U.S.]**

Schubert, Uwe, et al. Regional Labour Market Modelling: A State of the Art Review. *Fischer, M. M. and Nijkamp, P.*, eds., 1987, pp. 53–94.

Schulze, Peter M. Once Again: Testing for Regional Homogeneity. *J. Reg. Sci.*, February 1987, *27*(1), pp. 129–33. **[G: W. Germany]**

Scott, M. J. and Goldsmith, Oliver Scott. Assessing Regional Econometric Models: A Discussion and Application. *Ann. Reg. Sci.*, March 1987, *21*(1), pp. 1–21. **[G: U.S.]**

Stevens, Benjamin H. "Ready-Made" Regional Input–Output Model Systems: Model Accuracy and the Value of Limited Surveys: Comments. *Rev. Reg. Stud.*, Spring 1987, *17*(2), pp. 17–20.

Tóth, Ferenc L. Analyzing Productivity of Multiple Resource Systems. *Braat, L. C. and van Lierop, W. F. J.*, eds., 1987, pp. 166–84. **[G: U.S.]**

Vlachou, Andriana and Field, Barry C. Regional Energy Substitution: Results from a Dynamic Input Demand Model. *Southern Econ. J.*, April 1987, *53*(4), pp. 952–66. **[G: U.S.]**

Weller, Barry R. and Kurre, James A. Applicability of the Transfer Function Approach to Forecasting Employment Levels in Small Regions. *Ann. Reg. Sci.*, March 1987, *21*(1), pp. 34–43. **[G: U.S.]**

Willis, K. G. Spatially Disaggregated Input–Output Tables: An Evaluation and Comparison of Survey and Non-survey Results. *Indian J. Quant. Econ.*, 1987, *3*(1), pp. 34–51. **[G: U.K.]**

Willis, K. G. Spatially Disaggregated Input–Output Tables: An Evaluation and Comparison of Survey and Nonsurvey Results. *Environ. Planning A*, January 1987, *19*(1), pp. 107–16.

Yoshikawa, Kazuhiro; Kobayashi, Kiyoshi and Mun, Seil. A Land Use Model for Spatial Policy Analysis and Multi-criteria Evaluation of Regional Development Planning. *Sawaragi, Y.; Inoue, K. and Nakayama, H.*, eds., 1987, pp. 190–99. **[G: Japan]**

Topical Guide
To Classification Schedule

TOPICAL GUIDE TO CLASSIFICATION SCHEDULE

This index refers to the subject index *group, category,* or *subcategory* in which the listed topic may be found. The subject index classifications include, in most cases, related topics as well. The term *category* generally indicates that the topic may be found in all of the *subcategories* of the 3-digit code; the term *group,* indicates that the topics may be found in all of the *subcategories* in the 2-digit code. The classification schedule (p. xxxvi) serves to refer the user to cross references.

ABSENTEEISM: 8240

ACCELERATOR: 0233

ACCOUNTING: firm, 5410; national income, 2210, 2212; social, 2250

ADMINISTERED PRICES: theory, 0226; empirical studies, 6110; industry, 6354

ADMINISTRATION: 513 category; business, 5131; and planning, programming, and budgeting: national, 5132, 3226, state and local, 3241; public, 5132

ADVERTISING: industry, 6354; and marketing, 5310

AFFLUENT SOCIETY: 0510, 0110

AGENT THEORY, 0228

AGING: economics of, 9180

AGGREGATION: 2118; in input-output analysis, 2220; from micro to macro, 0220, 0230

AGREEMENTS: collective, 832 category; commodity, 4220, 7130; international trade, 4220

AGRIBUSINESS: *see* CORPORATE AGRICULTURE

AGRICULTURAL: commodity exchanges, 3132, 7150; cooperatives, 7150; credit, 7140; research and innovation, 621 category; employment, 8131; marketing, 7150; outlook, 7120; productivity, 7110, 7160; situation, 7120; supply and demand analysis, 7110; surpluses, 7130

AGRICULTURE: 710 group; government programs and policy, 7130; and development, 7100, 1120

AIR TRANSPORTATION: 6150

AIRPORT: 6150, 9410

AIRCRAFT MANUFACTURING: 6314

ALLOCATION: welfare aspects, 0242; and general equilibrium, 0210

ALUMINUM INDUSTRY: 6312

ANCIENT ECONOMIC HISTORY: 043 category

ANCIENT ECONOMIC THOUGHT: 0311; individuals, 0322

ANTITRUST POLICY: 6120

APPLIANCE INDUSTRY: 6313

APPRENTICESHIP: 8110

ARBITRATION: labor, 832 category

ASSISTANCE: foreign, 4430

ATOMIC ENERGY: conservation and pollution, 7220; industries, 6352, 7230

AUCTION MARKETS: theory, 0227

AUSTRIAN SCHOOL: 0315; individuals, 0322

AUTOMATION: employment: empirical studies, 8243, theory, 8210

AUTOMOBILE MANUFACTURING: 6314

BALANCE OF PAYMENTS: 431 category; accounting, 4310; empirical studies, 4313; theory, 4312

BANK FOR INTERNATIONAL SETTLEMENTS: 4320

BANKS: central, 3116; commercial, 3120; investment, 3140; other, 3140; portfolios, 3120; savings and loan, 3140; savings, 3140; supervision and regulation of, 3120, 3140, 3116

BARGAINING: collective, 832 category; theory, 0262

BAYESIAN ANALYSIS: 2115

BENEFIT–COST ANALYSIS: theory 0242; applied, see individual fields

BEQUESTS: empirical, 9211; theoretical, 0243

BEVERAGE INDUSTRIES: 6318

BIBLIOGRAPHY: 0110; see also the GENERAL heading under each subject

BIOGRAPHY: businessmen, 040 group; history of thought, 0322

BOND MARKET: 3132

BOOK PUBLISHING: 6352

BOYCOTTS, LABOR: 833 category; 832 category

BRAIN DRAIN: 8230, 8410

BRAND PREFERENCE: 5310; and consumers, 9212

BREAK-EVEN ANALYSIS: 5120

BRETTON WOODS AGREEMENT: 4320

BUDGETS: consumers, 9211; governments: theory, 3212, national studies, 3226, state and local studies, 3241

BUILDING: construction industry, 6340; materials industry, 6317

BUILDING SOCIETIES: 3152 and 3140
BUREAUCRACY, theory of, 0252
BUSINESS: credit, 3153; finance, 5210
BUSINESS CYCLE: and growth, 1312; empirical studies, 1313; policy, 1331; theory of, 1312; unemployment, 1312, 8210
BUSINESS SERVICES: 6354

CAPACITY OF INDUSTRY: 6410
CAPITAL: expenditure by firm, 5220; gains tax, 3230; human, 8510; international movements of: short term, 431 category; long term, 441 category; and personal savings, 9211
CAPITAL ASSET PRICING: 3131
CAPITAL BUDGETING: 5200
CAPITAL MARKETS: 313 category; efficiency of, 3131; studies and regulation, 3132; theory, 3131
CAPITAL-OUTPUT RATIOS: and growth, 111 category; empirical, 2212
CAPITAL THEORY: distributive shares: aggregate, 0235, factor, 0224; firm, 0223; and growth, 111 category; and technological progress, 6211
CAPITALIST SYSTEM: 0510
CARTELS: 6110; international, 4220
CATHOLIC ECONOMICS: 0321; individuals, 0322
CATTLE INDUSTRY: 7110
CEMENT INDUSTRY: 6315
CENSUS: population, 8410; regional, 2280
CENTRAL BANKS: 3116
CENTRALLY PLANNED ECONOMIES: country studies, 124 category; planning, 113 category; systems, 0520; theory, 027 category
CERAMICS INDUSTRY: 6315
CEREALS: supply and demand, 7110; marketing, 7150; processing, 6318, 7151
CHECK-OFF SYSTEM: 832 category
CHEMICAL INDUSTRY: 6315
CHILD LABOR LEGISLATION: 8221
CHOICE: consumer, 0222; social, 025 category
CHRISTIAN SOCIALISM: 0317; individuals, 0322
CIVIL SERVICE employment: 8135, legislation, 8226
CLASSICAL SCHOOL: 0314; individuals, 0322
CLOSED SHOP: 8310; 832 category
CLOTHING INDUSTRY: 6316
CLUBS, THEORY OF: 0252
COAL MINING: 6322, 7230
CODETERMINATION: 0510
COLLECTIVE BARGAINING: 832 category
COLLECTIVE DECISION: studies, 0252; theory, 0251
COLLECTIVE FARM: 7130; socialist, 0520; Kibbutz, 0510
COLLUSION, GOVERNMENT POLICY TOWARD: 6120
COMECON: 4230, 4233
COMMERCIAL BANKS: 3120

COMMERCIAL POLICY: *see* INTERNATIONAL TRADE CONTROLS
COMMITTEES: theory of, 0252
COMMODITY AGREEMENTS: 4220, agricultural, 7130
COMMODITY MARKETS, 3132
COMMUNICATION EQUIPMENT INDUSTRY: 6313
COMMUNICATION INDUSTRIES: 6352; regulation of, 6130
COMMUNIST SCHOOL: 0317; individuals, 0322
COMMUNIST SYSTEM: 0520
COMMUNITY RELATIONS OF THE FIRM: 5140
COMPANY UNIONS: 8310
COMPARATIVE COST THEORY: 4112
COMPARATIVE ECONOMIC HISTORY: 0412
COMPARATIVE ECONOMIC SYSTEMS: 0530
COMPETITION: 0225; government policy toward, 6120; imperfect, 0226; and innovation, 0225, 0226; non-price, 0226; spatial, 9411
COMPUTATIONAL TECHNIQUES: 2134; and computer programs, 2140
COMPUTER INDUSTRY: hardware, 6313; software, 6352
COMPUTER PROGRAMS: 2140
CONCENTRATION OF INDUSTRY: 6110; government policy toward, 6120
CONSERVATION: 7220
CONSTRUCTION INDUSTRY: 6340; labor force, 8136
CONSUMER DEMAND: theory, 0222
CONSUMER: economics, 921 category; expenditure on specific items, 9212; motivation, 9210; overall expenditure, 9211; protection, 9213; savings, 9211
CONSUMER FINANCE: 3151
CONSUMER PRICE INDEX: 2270; method, 2118
CONSUMER'S SURPLUS: 0222, 0240
CONSUMPTION: empirical studies, 9211; function, 0232
CONTROL THEORY: applications, 1331 and 2120; technical use, 2132
CONVERTIBILITY OF CURRENCIES: 4320
COOPERATIVES: 0510; agricultural marketing, 7150; housing, 9320
COPPER: manufacturing, 6312; mining, 6322
CORPORATE AGRICULTURE: 7151
COST: 0223
COST OF LIVING: index, 2270; index construction methods, 2118; studies, 9211
COTTON: crop, 7110; manufacturing, 6316; marketing, 7150
COUNTERVAILING POWER: 0510, 0110
COUNTRY STUDIES: centrally planned economies, 124 category; comparative, 1230; developed, 122 category; developing, 121 category
CREDIT: business, 3153; consumer, 3151; farm, 7140; housing, 3152

CREDITOR NATION: 4430
CRIME, ECONOMICS OF: 9160
CRUDE OIL INDUSTRY: 6323, 7230
CUSTOMS UNIONS: 423 category
CYCLE: *see* BUSINESS CYCLE

DAIRY PRODUCTS: 7110; marketing, 7150; processing, 7151
DAMS: 7210
DEBT: consumer, 3151; international, 4430; public: national, 3228, state and local, 3243
DEBTOR NATION: 4430
DECISION THEORY: 5110
DEFENSE CONTRACTS: 1140
DEFENSE ECONOMICS: 1140
DEFLATION: *see* INFLATION
DEINDUSTRIALIZATION: 6160
DEMAND: aggregate consumption, 0232; aggregate investment, 0233; factor, 0223; individual and household, 0222
DEMOGRAPHY: 8410; and cycles, 8410, 1313; and development, 1120; and growth, 111 category
DEPOSIT INSURANCE: 3120, 3140
DEPRECIATION: accounting, 5410; and taxation, 3230
DEPRESSED AREAS: 941 category; and poverty: rural, 7180, urban, 9310
DEVALUATION: 4314
DEVELOPING COUNTRIES: *see* COUNTRY STUDIES
DEVELOPMENT: agricultural, 7100, 1120; aid, 4430; and growth, 1120; in particular countries, 120 group; and research, 6212; and trade, 4114
DIFFERENTIATION OF PRODUCT: and advertising, 5310; theory, 0226
DIFFUSION: economic geography, 7310; spatial, 941 category; technological, 6211
DIRECT CONTROLS: 1332
DISARMAMENT: 1140
DISABILITY: fringe benefits, 8242; insurance, 6356, 9130; workmen's compensation, 8222
DISCRIMINATION: age, race, and sex, 9170; in education, 9120; in employment, 9170; in housing, 9320; price: empirical studies, 6110, theory, 0226; spatial, 9411
DISCRIMINANT ANALYSIS: 2114
DISEQUILIBRIUM THEORY: 021 category
DISGUISED UNEMPLOYMENT: 8210; and development, 8131, 1120
DISMISSAL COMPENSATION: 8242
DISSONANCE ANALYSIS: 5310
DISTRIBUTED LAGS: 2113
DISTRIBUTION: aggregate theory, 0235; empirical studies of income, 2213; empirical studies of wealth, 2240; factor theory, 0224
DIVIDENDS: 5210

DRAFT: 1140
DRAWING RIGHTS: 4320
DRUG INDUSTRY: 6315
DUOPOLY: 0226
DUMPING: 4220

ECONOMETRIC METHODS: 211 category; construction, analysis, and use of models, 2120
ECONOMETRIC MODELS: 132 category
ECONOMIC: current conditions and outlook, 120 group, 1330; imperialism, 4420
ECONOMIC DATA: 220 group
ECONOMIC FLUCTUATIONS: *see* BUSINESS CYCLES
ECONOMIC HISTORY: 040 group; development of the discipline, 0411
ECONOMIC PLANNING: 113 category
ECONOMIC SYSTEMS: 050 group
ECONOMIC THEORY: 020 group
ECONOMIC THOUGHT: history of, 030 group
ECONOMICS: relation to other disciplines, 0113; social values, 0114, 050 group; teaching, 0111
ECONOMIES OF SCALE: 0223; determinants of market structure, 6110
ECONOMIST: role of, 0112
EDUCATION: economics of, 9120; investment in, 8510; manpower training, 8110
ELASTICITY: of demand, 0222; of supply, 0223
ELECTRICAL EQUIPMENT INDUSTRY: 6313
ELECTRIC ENERGY: conservation, 7220; pollution, 7220; resource, 7230; utilities: industry studies, 6352, regulation of, 6130
EMPIRICAL METHOD: 0360, 0115
EMPLOYEE PARTICIPATION IN MANAGEMENT: in market economies, 0510; in socialist economies, 0520
EMPLOYMENT: data and levels, 8240, 8243; geographic, 8241; by industry, 813 category; services (private), 6354 (public policy), 8225; studies (general), 8243, studies (public sector), 8226; subsidies, 8240
EMPLOYMENT POLICY: 8225
ENERGY: conservation, 7220; industries, 632 group, 6352; sources, 7230
ENTERTAINMENT INDUSTRY: 6358
ENTREPRENEURSHIP: and development, 1120; in firms, 5140; in market economies, 0510; and profit, 0224
ENVIRONMENT: 7220
EQUILIBRIUM: general, 0210; in macroeconomics, 0230; partial, 0225, 0226
ESTATE TAX: 3230
EUROCURRENCIES: 4320
EUROPEAN ECONOMIC COMMUNITY: 4233
EUROPEAN FREE TRADE ASSOCIATION: 4233
EXCESS PROFITS TAX: 3230

EXCHANGE RATES: *see* FOREIGN EXCHANGE
EXCISE TAX: 3230
EXECUTIVES: 5130
EXPENDITURE, GOVERNMENT: national, 3221; state and local, 3241; theory, 3212; and welfare, 0243
EXPENDITURE, PERSONAL: 921 category
EXPERIMENTAL ECONOMIC METHODS: 215 category
EXPORTS: policies, 4220; restrictions, 4220; role in development, 4114; trade patterns, 4210
EXTERNALITIES: theory, 0244; for applications *see* individual fields
EXTRACTIVE INDUSTRIES: 632 category

FACTOR ANALYSIS: 2114
FACTOR PROPORTIONS: 0223; and growth, 111 category
FACTORS OF PRODUCTION AND DISTRIBUTIVE SHARES: *see* DISTRIBUTION
FAIR TRADE: 6120
FAMILY ALLOWANCES: 9110
FAMILY, ECONOMICS OF: *see* HOUSEHOLD, ECONOMICS OF
FARM: finance, 7140; management, 7160
FARM MACHINERY INDUSTRY: 6313
FARM MECHANIZATION: 7160
FARMERS' COOPERATIVES: 7150
FEDERAL RESERVE BOARD AND SYSTEM: 3116
FEDERAL-STATE FINANCIAL RELATIONS: 3250
FEED PROCESSING INDUSTRY: 7151
FERTILITY: 8410
FERTILIZER: industry, 6315; use, 7160
FEUDALISM: 0430
FIBER CROPS: 7110; manufacturing, 6316; marketing, 7150
FINANCIAL ACCOUNTS: 2230
FINANCIAL INTERMEDIARIES: 3140
FINANCIAL INTERMEDIATION: 3130
FINANCIAL STATISTICS: 2230
FIRM: financial structure, 5210; goals and objectives, 5140; investment, 5220; administrative organization, 5130; organization theory, 5110; regulation, 613 category; theory of, 0223
FISCAL POLICY: 3216; and fiscal theory, 3210
FISCAL THEORY: 3212
FISHERIES: 7210
FLOOD CONTROL: 7220
FLOW OF FUNDS ACCOUNTS: 2230
FLUCTUATIONS: *see* BUSINESS CYCLES
FOOD: consumption, 9212; and nutrition standards, 9130; and population, 8410; processing industry, 6318, 7151
FOOD-STAMP PLAN: 9110, 9140

FORECASTING: 132 category; for a country, 1322; methods and theory, 1324, 2120; for a region, 9413; for a specific sector, 1323
FOREIGN ASSISTANCE: 4430
FOREIGN DEBT: 4430
FOREIGN EXCHANGE: control, 4220; markets, 4314; rates, 4314
FOREIGN INVESTMENT: studies, 4412; theory, 4411
FOREIGN TRADE: *see* INTERNATIONAL TRADE
FOREST PRODUCTS INDUSTRIES: 6317
FORESTS: 7210; conservation, 7220
FOUNDATIONS: non-profit organizations, 6360
FRINGE BENEFITS: 8242
FRUITS: 7110; marketing of, 7150
FULL-COST PRICING: 0226, 5140
FURNITURE INDUSTRY: 6317
FUTURES MARKETS: 3132
FUTURISTS: 2260

GAME THEORY: 0262; game theoretic decision theory, 5110; and general equilibrium, 0210; in oligopoly, 0226; in social choice, 0251
GAS: conservation, 7220; pollution, 7220; resources, 7230; utilities: industry studies, 6352, regulation of, 6130
GENERAL AGREEMENT ON TARIFFS AND TRADE (GATT): 4220, 7130
GENERAL ECONOMICS: 010 group
GENERAL EQUILIBRIUM THEORY: 0210
GIFT TAX: 3230
GLASS MANUFACTURING: 6315
GOALS AND OBJECTIVES OF FIRMS: 5140
GOLD MINING: 6322
GOLD STANDARD: 4320
GOVERNMENT BONDS: market, 3132; national, 3228; state and local, 3243
GOVERNMENT employees: 8135
GOVERNMENT EXPENDITURES: *see* EXPENDITURES, GOVERNMENT
GRANTS-IN-AID: 3250
GRIEVANCE PROCEDURES: 832 category; 833 category
GROUP OF TWENTY: 4320
GROWTH: 111 category and 2260; country studies: LDCs, 121 category, MDCs, 122 category; centrally planned economies, 124 category; of firm, 0223; indicators, 2260; LDCs, 1120; MDCs, 2260; and technological change, 6211; theoretical models: one and two sector, 1112, monetary, 1114, multisector, 1113; socialist, 027 category or 1132

HARBORS: *see* PORTS
HEALTH, ECONOMICS OF: 9130
HEALTH INSURANCE: 9130, 6356; by the firm, 8242; medicaid, 9130; medicare, 9130

HIGHWAYS: 6150
HISTORICAL SCHOOL: 0318; individuals, 0322
HISTORICISM: 0360
HISTORY: *see* ECONOMIC HISTORY
HISTORY OF ECONOMIC THOUGHT: 030 group
HOLDING COMPANIES: 6110; public utility, 6130
HOURS OF LABOR: regulation, 8221; studies, 824 category
HOUSEHOLD, ECONOMICS OF: and consumer economics, 921 category; and employment and leisure, 8210; household formation, 8410; consumption theory, 0222
HOUSING: 9320; mortgage credit, 3152; statistics, 2240, 2250
HUMAN CAPITAL: 8510

IMPERFECT COMPETITION: 0226
IMPERIALISM: 4420; and capitalism, 0510
IMPORT-SUBSTITUTION: empirical studies, 4220; theory, 4114
IMPORTS: restrictions, 4220; trade patterns, 4210
INCENTIVES: in socialist systems, 0520, 0271; wage, 8242
INCOME: and employment theory, 0230; national accounting, 2212; personal distribution, 2213
INCOME TAX: national, 3230; state and local, 3242; theory, 3212
INCOMES POLICY: 1332
INDEX NUMBERS THEORY: 2118
INDEXATION: 1342
INDICATORS: of business conditions, 1330; of productivity, 2260
INDIFFERENCE ANALYSIS: 0222
INDUSTRIAL: capacity, 6410; location, 9411
INDUSTRIAL AND MARKET STRUCTURES: 6110
INDUSTRIAL POLICY: 6160
INDUSTRIAL RELATIONS: 833 category; legislation, 822 category, 833 category
INDUSTRIALIZATION: and development, 1120; historical studies, 040 group
INDUSTRY STUDIES: 630 group
INEQUALITY: age, race, and sex, 9170; income distribution, 2213; regional, 9412; welfare aspects: studies, 9110, 9140; theory, 0243
INFLATION AND DEFLATION: 134 category; theory, 1342; and wages, 1342, 8210
INFORMATION: and imperfect competition, 0226; and labor market theory, 8210; and marketing, 5310; statistical theory, 2114; theory, 0261
INFORMATION SERVICES: industry, 6352
INHERITANCE: redistributive aspects, theory 0243; savings and asset studies, 9211; tax, 3230
INNOVATION: 6211
INPUT–OUTPUT: mathematical structure, 0210; mod-

els and empirical studies, 2220; regional, 9413
INSTITUTIONALISM: 0360
INSTITUTIONALIST SCHOOL: 0318; individuals, 0322
INSURANCE: industry, 6356; social security, 9150
INTEGRATION, INTERNATIONAL ECONOMIC: policies and studies, 4233; theory, 4232
INTEREST: and capital, 0224, 0235; empirical studies and policy, 3116; monetary theories, 3112
INTERGOVERNMENTAL FINANCIAL RELATIONS: 3250
INTERNAL ORGANIZATION OF FIRM: 5130
INTERNAL TRANSFER PRICING: 5120
INTERNATIONAL: adjustment mechanisms, 431 category; capital movements: long term, 441 category, short term and speculative, 4312, 4313; economics, 400 group; lending, private, 4330; lending, public, 4430; liquidity, 4320; movement of factors theory, 4112 specialization, 4112; trade controls, 4220; trade patterns, 4210; trade theory, 4112
INTERNATIONAL BANK FOR RECONSTRUCTION AND DEVELOPMENT: 4430
INTERNATIONAL MONETARY ARRANGEMENTS: 4320
INTERNATIONAL MONETARY FUND (IMF): 4320
INTERNATIONAL TRADE ORGANIZATION (ITO): 4220
INTERTEMPORAL CHOICE: macroeconomics of, 0239; microeconomics of, 0229
INVENTORY: and business cycles, 131 category; policies of the firm, 5120; theory, 0223, 0233, 5220
INVESTMENT: by individual firm and/or industry, 5220; component of national income, 2212; function, 0233; and rate of return, 5220; relation to savings, 0233; in socialist system, 027 category; theory, 0223, 0233
INVESTMENT BANK: 3140

JOB SEARCH: theory, 8210

KEYNESIAN ECONOMICS: 023 category

LABOR: demand studies, 8243; demand theory, 8210; in economic development, 1120, 8210; supply of, *see* LABOR FORCE; theory of, 8210, 0223
LABOR DISPUTES: 832 category
LABOR ECONOMICS: 800 group
LABOR FORCE: 8130; agricultural, 8131; construction, 8136; government, 8135; manufacturing, 8132; professional, 8134; recruiting and training, 8110; services, 8133
LABOR LEGISLATION: 822 category
LABOR MARKET: demographic characteristics, 8260; studies, 824 category; theory, 8210
LABOR PRODUCTIVITY: 8250
LABOR-MANAGEMENT RELATIONS: 833 category

LABOR TURNOVER: 8243
LABOR UNIONS: *see* TRADE UNIONS
LAND: development and use, 7172; ownership and tenure, 7171; reform, 7171; taxes, 3242
LAUSANNE SCHOOL: 0316; individuals, 0322
LAW AND CRIME, ECONOMICS OF: 9160
LEASE–PURCHASE DECISIONS: 5210
LEATHER MANUFACTURING: 6316
LEISURE: and living standards, 9210; theory of, 8210; and utility, 0222
LENDING: international (public), 4430; (private) 4330
LESS DEVELOPED COUNTRIES: *see* COUNTRY STUDIES
LICENSING: 6120
LIFE-CYCLE THEORY: 0232
LINEAR AND NONLINEAR PROGRAMMING: 2135
LIQUIDITY PREFERENCE: 3112
LIVESTOCK: 7110; marketing of, 7150
LIVING STANDARDS: studies, 9211; rural, 7180
LOANABLE FUNDS THEORY OF INTEREST: 3112
LOCATION ECONOMICS: 9411, 7310
LUMBER INDUSTRY: 6317

MACHINE TOOLS MANUFACTURING: 6313
MACHINERY MANUFACTURING: 6313
MANAGEMENT: of farm, 7160; of firm, 5120; of personnel, 5130
MANAGERIAL ECONOMICS: 5120
MANPOWER TRAINING: 8110
MANUFACTURING INDUSTRIES: 631 category
MARGINAL: cost, 0223; efficiency of capital, 0224; productivity, 0224
MARGINALISM: 0315, 0360
MARKET: equilibrium, 0225; 0226; research, 5310; structure, 6110
MARKETING: 5310
MARKOV CHAIN: 2114
MARSHALLIAN SCHOOL: 0315; individuals, 0322
MARXIST SCHOOL: 0317; for individuals belonging to this group, 0322
MASS TRANSIT: 6150; urban, 9330
MATHEMATICAL PROGRAMMING: 2135
MATHEMATICAL METHODS AND MODELS: 213 category, 0115
MEDICAL CARE: *see* HEALTH, ECONOMICS OF
MEDICAL SUBSIDY PROGRAMS: 9130
MEDIEVAL: economic thought, 0311; individuals, 0322; economic history, 043 category
MERCANTILISTS: 0313; for individuals belonging to this group, 0322
MERCHANT MARINE: 6150
MERGERS: 6110; government policy toward, 6120
METAL MANUFACTURING: 6312
METHODS: 0115; experimental economic methods, 215 category

METHODOLOGY OF ECONOMICS: 0360
METROPOLITAN PLANNING STUDIES: *see* REGIONAL PLANNING
METROPOLITANIZATION: 9310
MICRODATA: 2290
MIGRATION: of labor, 8230; of population, 8410
MILITARY PROCUREMENT: 1140
MINERALS: 7210; energy producing minerals, 7230
MINING INDUSTRIES: 632 category, 7210; energy producing mining, 7320
MINORITIES: 9170
MOBILITY: *see* MIGRATION
MONETARY: growth theory, 1114; policy, 3116; theories of cycles, 3112, 1310; theory, 3112
MONEY: demand for, 3112; markets, 3130, 3132; supply of, 3112
MONOPOLISTIC COMPETITION: 0226
MONOPOLY: 0226; control of, 6120
MONOPSONY: 0226
MONTE CARLO METHOD: 2112
MORBIDITY RATES: 8410
MORTALITY RATES: 8410
MORTGAGE MARKET: 3152, 9320
MOTIVATION: consumer, 0222; and marketing, 5310; profit maximization, 0223, 5140
MOTION PICTURE INDUSTRY: 6358
MULTINATIONAL CORPORATION: 4420
MULTIPLIER: 0232; balanced budget, 3212; foreign trade, 4112; investment, 0233
MULTICOLLINEARITY: 2113
MULTIVARIATE ANALYSIS: 2114

NATALITY RATES: 8410
NATIONAL INCOME: accounting, 2212; distribution of, 2213; international comparisons of, 1230; theory and procedures, 2210
NATIONAL WEALTH: 2240
NATIONALIZATION OF INDUSTRY: domestic, 6140; foreign, 4420
NATURAL GAS: conservation, 7230; industry, 6323, 7230; resources, 7230; utilities, 6130, 7230
NATURAL RESOURCES: 7210; conservation, 7220; and population, 8410; recreational aspects, 7211; energy producing resources, 7230
NEGATIVE INCOME TAX: studies, 3230, 9140, 9110; theory, 3212
NEOCLASSICAL SCHOOL: 0315; individuals, 0322
NEW INTERNATIONAL ECONOMIC ORDER: 400 group
NEWSPAPER PUBLISHING: 6317
NON-MARXIST SOCIALISM: 0317, 0321
NON-PROFIT ORGANIZATIONS: 6360
NUTRITION: 9130

OCCUPATION: classification, 8120; safety, 8223; wage differentials, 8120, 8210, 8242

OLD AGE: assistance, 9110; and health, 9130; and poverty, 9140; retirement incidence, 8243; social security, 9150

OLDER WORKERS: 9180; discrimination, 9170; as part of labor force, 8260; retirement and pensions, 8242; social security, 9150

OLIGOPOLY: 0226

OLIGOPSONY: 0226

OPEN ECONOMY MACROECONOMICS: 430 group

OPEN MARKET OPERATIONS: 3116

OPERATIONS RESEARCH: 5110, 5120

OPTIMIZATION TECHNIQUES: 2132

ORGANIZATION: theory, 5110

OVERPRODUCTION THEORY OF CYCLES: 1312

OVERTIME PAY: 8242

PARITY PRICES AND INCOMES, AGRICULTURE: 7130

PARKING, URBAN: 9330

PAPER INDUSTRY: 6317

PATENTS: 6120; technology aspects, 6210

PEAK LOAD PRICING: 6131

PENSIONS, PRIVATE: 8242; investment of, 3140

PERIODICALS, ECONOMIC: 0110

PERMANENT INCOME HYPOTHESIS: studies, 9211; theory, 0232

PERSONAL SERVICES INDUSTRY: 6353

PERSONNEL MANAGEMENT: 5130

PHILANTHROPY: and welfare, 0243

PHILLIPS CURVE: 8210; and inflation, 1342

PHYSIOCRATS: 0312; individuals, 0322

PLANNING: 1130; policy, 1136; regional, 9412; regional models, 9413; theory, 1132; urban, 9310

PLASTICS MANUFACTURING: 6315

POLITICAL ARITHMETICIANS: 0312; for individuals belonging to this group, 0322

POLLUTION: 7220; energy industries, 7230

POPULATION: 8410; and development, 1120; and growth, 111 category; limits to growth, 2260; and pollution, 7220

PORTFOLIO SELECTION: 3131

PORTS: regional, 9410; shipping aspect, 6150; urban, 9310

POSITIVE ECONOMICS: 0360

POST OFFICE: 6140

POULTRY: 7110; marketing of, 7150

POVERTY: 9140; rural, 7180; urban, 9140

PRE-CLASSICAL SCHOOLS: 0312; individuals, 0322

PRICE AND INCOMES POLICY: 1332

PRICE CONTROL: 1332

PRICE LEVELS AND INDEXES: 2270; hedonic, 0222; method, 2118

PRINTING INDUSTRY: 6317

PRODUCERS' COOPERATIVES: agricultural, 7150; market economies, 0510; socialist economies, 0520, 6110

PRODUCTION: agricultural, 7110; factors of, 0223; function and income distribution, 0224, 0235; functions: aggregate, 0234, firm and industry, 0223; theory: aggregate (supply), 0234, firm, 0223

PRODUCTION INDEX: 2260; method of, 2118

PRODUCTIVITY: agricultural, 7110; and growth, 2260; labor, capital, and total factor, 8250; measurement of, 2260

PROFESSIONAL LICENSING: 6120 and 8134

PROFIT-SHARING: 0510

PROFITS: and distribution of income, 0235, 2213; and factor share, 0224; maximization, 5140; 0223; tax on: empirical studies, 3230, theory, 3212

PROGRAMMING MODELS: mathematical, 2135

PROPERTY RIGHTS: 0510; and welfare aspects, 0244

PROPERTY TAX: studies, 3242; theory, 3212

PROTECTION: commercial policy, 4220; consumer, 9213; and development, 4114; non-tariff barriers, 4220; theory, 4113

PUBLIC ENTERPRISE: 6140; administration of, 5131

PUBLIC EXPENDITURE: *see* EXPENDITURES

PUBLIC FINANCE: 320 group

PUBLIC GOODS: 0240, 3212

PUBLIC HOUSING: 9320

PUBLIC INVESTMENT: theory, 3212; and welfare aspects, 024 category

PUBLIC REVENUE: *see* REVENUE

PUBLIC SECTOR: 0240, 3212; centralization, 3200; growth, 3200

PUBLIC UTILITIES: 6130; energy related, 7230

PUBLIC WORKS: expenditure: national, 3221, state and local, 3241; and stabilization policy, 1331, 3212

PUBLISHING INDUSTRY: 6317

QUALITY OF LIFE: environmental, 7220; individual, 9211; and social indicators, 2250; in the workplace, 833 category

QUANTITATIVE MODELS: *see* ECONOMETRIC MODELS, INPUT–OUTPUT MODELS, AND PROGRAMMING MODELS

QUANTITY THEORY OF MONEY: 3112

QUEUING THEORY: 2114

QUIT RATES: 8243

QUOTAS: *see* COMMERCIAL POLICY

RACIAL GROUPS: and discrimination, 9170; in the labor force, 8260; in population, 8410

RADIO: broadcasting industry, 6352; equipment manufacturing, 6313

RAILROAD INDUSTRY: 6150

RAILWAYS, URBAN: 9330
RATE BASE: public utilities, 6130; railroads, 6150
RATE OF RETURN: on capital, 5220; on human capital, 8510; on international capital, 4412; of public utilities, 6130; of railroads, 6150; on securities, 3132
RATIONAL EXPECTATIONS: 0230, 3112; and inflation, 1342
REAL ESTATE SERVICES: 6357
RECLAMATION, LAND: 7172
RECREATION: 9210; and natural resources, 7211
REDEVELOPMENT: housing, 9330; urban, 9310
REDISTRIBUTION: and taxes, 3212; and welfare, 0243
REDISCOUNT POLICY: 3116; and effect on commercial banks, 3120
REGIONAL ECONOMICS: general, 9410; models, 9413; planning, 9412; studies, 9412; theory, 9411
REGIONAL TRADE ASSOCIATIONS: 4233
REGIONAL MONETARY ARRANGEMENTS: 4320
REGULATION: economics of, 6190; effects on industry, 6190; and public utilities, 6130
RELATIVE INCOME HYPOTHESIS: 0232
RENT: consumers' expenditure for, 9212; control, 1332; theory, 0224
RENT SEEKING: theory of, 0252
REPAIR SERVICES: 6355
RESEARCH AND DEVELOPMENT: 6212; and innovation, 6210; and taxes, 3230; and technological change, 6210
RESERVE REQUIREMENTS: 3116, 3120
RESTRICTIVE AGREEMENTS: 6120
RETAIL PRICE INDEX: 2270
RETAIL TRADE: 6333
RETIREMENT DECISION: 8243
RETIREMENT PENSIONS: *see* PENSIONS
RETRAINING: 8110
REVALUATION OF CURRENCY: 4314
REVEALED PREFERENCE: 0222
RUBBER MANUFACTURING: 6315
RURAL ECONOMICS: 7180

SAFETY OF WORKERS: 8223
SALES TAX: incidence, 3212; national, 3230; state and local, 3242
SAMPLING METHODS AND ERRORS: 2117
SAVINGS: corporate, 5210; empirical studies, 9211; function, 0232; personal, 9211; relation to investment, 0233, 5220; share of national income, 2212
SAVINGS AND LOAN ASSOCIATIONS: 3140
SECURITY MARKETS: 3132
SELECTIVE CONTROLS, MONETARY: 3116; and stabilization, 1331; theory, 3112
SERVICE INDUSTRIES: 635 category
SHIFTING OF TAXES, THEORY: 3212

SHIPBUILDING: 6314
SHIPPING: 6150
SHOPPING CENTERS: 6333, 9410
SICK BENEFITS: 8242
SILVER MINING: 6322
SILVER STANDARDS: 4320
SINGLE TIME SERIES ANALYSIS: 2116
SLAVE LABOR: *see* COUNTRY AND HISTORICAL STUDIES
SOCIAL CHOICE: 025 category
SOCIAL EXPERIMENTS: design of, 2119; experimental economic methods, 215 category
SOCIAL INDICATORS: 2250
SOCIAL SECURITY: 9150
SOCIAL WELFARE: 0240; function, 0240, 0251
SOCIALIST SCHOOL: 0317; individuals, 0322
SOCIALIST ECONOMICS: country studies, 124 category; planning, 113 category; systems, 0520; theory, 027 category
SOIL IMPROVEMENT: 7172
SPACE PROGRAM: 3221, 6212
SPATIAL COMPETITION: 9410
SPECTRAL ANALYSIS: *see* TIME SERIES
STABILITY CONDITIONS IN DYNAMIC SYSTEMS: 2133
STABILIZATION: theory and policies, 1331; agricultural, 7130; fiscal, 3210; and inflation, 1340; monetary, 3110
STAGFLATION: 1331, 1342
STANDARD OF LIVING: 9211; and social indicators, 2250
STATE AND LOCAL FINANCE: borrowing, 3243; expenditures and budgets, 3241; general, 3240; taxation, 3242
STATE TRADING IN INTERNATIONAL MARKETS: 4220
STATISTICAL: data, 220 category and individual subject areas; methods, 211 category
STERLING AREA: 4320
STOCK MARKETS: 3132
STRIKES: collective bargaining, 832 category; and trade unions, 8310
STRUCTURAL UNEMPLOYMENT: 8210
SUBSIDIES: 3230, 3242; agricultural, 7130; export, 4220; and fiscal theory, 3212; food stamps, 9110; and housing, 9320
SUBSTITUTION OF FACTORS OF PRODUCTION: 0223
SUPPLY: aggregate, 0234; factor, 0223; firm and industry, 0223; money, 3112
SURPLUS: agricultural products, 7130
SURVEY METHODS: 2117
SWEDISH SCHOOL: 0321; for individuals belonging to this group, 0322

TARIFF: policy, 4220; studies, 4220; theory, 4113
TAXES: and income distribution, 2213, 3212; na-

tional, 3230; state and local, 3242; theory, 3212; and welfare, 0243

TEACHING OF ECONOMICS: 0112

TECHNICAL ASSISTANCE, INTERNATIONAL: *see* ASSISTANCE, FOREIGN

TECHNOLOGICAL CHANGE: 6211; and competition, 0225, 0226; and development, 1120; effect on employment: theory, 8210, empirical studies, 8243; and growth, 111 category; and market structure, 6110

TELEVISION: equipment manufacturing, 6314; transmission industry, 6352

TENURE: land, 7171

TERMS OF TRADE: 4210

TEXTILE MANUFACTURING: 6316

TIME: and household economics, 0222; and human capital, 8510; and work choice, 8210

TIME SERIES: 2116

TIN MANUFACTURING: 6312

TOBACCO, MANUFACTURING: 6318

TOURISM: industry, 6358; effect on balance of payments, 4313

TRADE AGREEMENTS: agricultural, 7130; international, 4220

TRADE BARRIERS: *see* PROTECTION

TRADE UNIONS: 8310; and collective bargaining, 832 category

TRANSFER PAYMENTS: and fiscal policy, 3212; intergovernmental, 3250; national government, 3230; redistributive effects: studies, 2213; theory, 0243; state and local government, 3242

TRANSFER PRICING: 5210; multinational, 4420, 5210

TRANSFER PROBLEM, INTERNATIONAL: capital, 4411; labor, 8230; technology, 6210, 4420

TRANSPORTATION: 6150; and congestion, 7220, 0244; urban, 9320

TRANSPORTATION EQUIPMENT MANUFACTURING: 6314

TRUSTS, INDUSTRIAL: 6110; government policy toward, 6120

TURNOVER TAX: effect on international trade, 4220; studies, 3230; theory, 3212

UNCERTAINTY: theory, 0261

UNDERCONSUMPTION THEORY: 1312

UNDEREMPLOYMENT: 0230

UNDERGROUND ECONOMY: and GNP, 2212; and crime, 9160

UNEMPLOYMENT: 8243; insurance, 8224

UNION-MANAGEMENT RELATIONS: *see* INDUSTRIAL RELATIONS

UNIONS: *see* TRADE UNIONS

URBAN: general, 9310; transportation, 9330

UTILITY THEORY: 0222

VALUATION: of the firm, 5220; and portfolio theory, 3131

VACANCIES: *see* UNEMPLOYMENT

VALUE OF HUMAN LIFE: and human capital, 8510; and life insurance, 6356; and medical costs, 9130

VEGETABLES: 7110; marketing of, 7150

VELOCITY OF MONEY: 3112

VETERANS: benefits, 3230, 9110; reconversion to civilian life, 1140

VITAL STATISTICS: 8410

VOCATIONAL EDUCATION: 8110

VOLUNTEER ARMY: 1140

VOTING: 0252

WAGES: controls, 1332; differentials, 8210; factor payments, 0224; fringe benefits, 8242; guaranteed annual, 8242; levels, 8242; as part of macro models, 0230; regulation, 8221; and stabilization policy, 1331; theory, 8210

WAR ECONOMICS: 1140

WATER: irrigation, 7172; resources, 7210; transportation, 6150; utilities, 6130

WEALTH: national and individual distribution, 2240; saving and asset studies, 9211; theories of wealth distribution, 0243

WELFARE ECONOMICS: theory of, 024 category; and international trade theory, 4113

WELFARE PROGRAMS: 9110

WHOLESALE PRICE INDEX: 2270

WHOLESALE TRADE: 6332

WOMEN: as demographic component in labor force, 8260; discrimination, 9170; labor force participation, 8130; as a minority, 9170; *see* also HOUSEHOLD, ECONOMICS OF

WOOL: manufacturing, 6316

WORK-LEISURE CHOICE: 8210

WORKMEN'S COMPENSATION: 8222

WORLD GROWTH MODELS: 2260

YOUTH LABOR: as demographic component, 8260